NEW INTERNATIONAL VERSION

NIV WORSHIP TOGETHER BIBLE

Notes by John J. Thompson

ZONDERVAN®

Published by Zondervan
Grand Rapids, Michigan 49530, USA

www.zondervan.com

Library of Congress Catalog Card Number 2013932203

Printed in the United States of America N100511

13 14 15 16 17 18 19 20 /DCI/ 15 14 13 12 11 10 9 8 7 6 5 4 3 2 1

A portion of the purchase price of your NIV® Bible is provided to Biblica so together we support the mission of *Transforming lives through God's Word.*

Biblica provides God's Word to people through translation, publishing and Bible engagement in Africa, Asia Pacific, Europe, Latin America, Middle East, and North America. Through its worldwide reach, Biblica engages people with God's Word so that their lives are transformed through a relationship with Jesus Christ.

TABLE OF CONTENTS

THE OLD TESTAMENT

THE NEW TESTAMENT

FOREWORD

by Matt Maher

"This Book (the BIBLE) had to be written by one of three people: good men, bad men or G-D.

It couldn't have been written by good men because they said it was inspired by the revelation of G-D. Good men don't lie and deceive. It couldn't have been written by bad men because bad men would not write something that would condemn themselves. It leaves only one conclusion. It was given by divine inspiration of G-D." — John Wesley

"He who sings well prays twice."

— St. Augustine

"... the Bible can be read aloud in 70 hours — though you might want to take a nap between the Old and New Testaments. Nine out of every ten Americans own at least one Bible — what's up with the other guy?"

— Bob Dylan, *Theme Time Radio Hour,* Episode 19: "The Bible," 6 September 2006

Every week, around the world, churches gather to bear witness to, praise, exalt and worship the God revealed in the scriptures and traditions of the Church — the God of Abraham, Isaac and Jacob — he who is known as "I AM", revealed as a trinity of Father, Son and Holy Spirit.

We gather to remember and celebrate all he is, all he has done and all he is doing. We gather to hear the plight of our sinful hearts. Despite all differences in denomination, doctrine and directive, we all share many commonly held truths — most of them originating from the Word of God.

THE word. The "logos." He who existed before creation, who used words to speak all into existence. *THAT* word.

In a word? *Jesus.*

The grandest, greatest mystery revealed. God intersecting with man. Word creating flesh; flesh betraying word; word then becoming flesh and redeeming it; and so, like that great rescue that happened, it's still happening.

The Word still becomes flesh inside of us — through grace, through the scriptures and the story of salvation. These are the stories that we reference when we (this latest generation of songwriters) combine the Word of God with other images and phrases in a marriage of melody, rhythm and tempo. We walk in a long line of singers, all the way back to the songs of Moses and Miriam; the psalms of King David; the Lamentations of those in captivity, in grief; the songs of the prophets, desperately proclaiming a return to God; the songs Jesus learned in the synagogue, singing the Torah; the songs Paul talks of in speaking of how we should greet each other, how we should function as a community. Over two thousand years of cultures and peoples hearing this Word, then reading this Word, and being inspired to let, as Psalm 150 says, "everything that has breath praise the LORD."

The great hymn writers Wesley, Bridges, Luther, Newton, Beethoven, Bach, Mozart — they carried the great story of the scriptures in their hearts and were so inspired by it as to write songs and melodies the whole world knows. All of those songs — we carry those in our hearts and in our voices. When we sing new songs it all goes back to this deep well — the well of the scriptures. This is what I've tried to carry in my heart as I've accepted the task of going to the same well, to draw of the same life giving water and craft something that the people of God can all hang their hearts on in a moment of prayer.

I pray that as you read this, God may move your heart to worship and to sing a "new song" unto the Lord. The song of your life, right here, right now, unto the Lord. The song of your life, right here, right now.

HOW TO USE THIS BIBLE

Throughout my life I have been a student of the Bible, a worshipper and, for the last twenty-five years or so, a worship leader, a teacher, a small group leader and a youth leader. In these capacities I have frequently found myself in the following situations:

- Wondering which worship songs might tie-in with a particular teaching topic or Bible verse
- Wondering about the Scriptural inspiration behind certain hymns or modern worship songs
- Looking for ways to integrate hymns and worship songs into my own personal devotion time
- Considering the text and stories behind worship songs and hymns as possible discussion topics for classes, devotions, Bible studies or sermons

Those are some of the needs I attempted to address as I wrote the reflections and studies in this Bible. By exploring the stories behind these songs and connecting them to the verses that inspired them, I hope you may find an increasing connection between the songs you enjoy and the Word of God. Mostly I hope that your love of great worship music draws you deeper into God's Word in one way or another.

There are several ways you can use this Bible:

- Read through each devotional insert during your own personal devotional times.
- Reference the index in the back to help you find a particular song for a particular purpose.
- Read the studies aloud as a family devotion or Bible study.
- Use the included article about the meaning and history of worship for your own edification or to enhance your community's approach to worship, music and the Word.
- Use the included chord charts to sing some of these songs by yourself or with a group.

Who knows, maybe you will be inspired to write some of your own worship music in response to God's Word. However you choose to experience *The Worship Together Bible*, I hope and pray that these studies deepen your times of worship and add melody to your times of reading.

John J. Thompson
Creative Director, Capitol CMG Publishing
www.CapitolCMGPublishing.com
www.JohnJThompson.com

PREFACE

The goal of the New International Version (NIV) is to enable English-speaking people from around the world to read and hear God's eternal Word in their own language. Our work as translators is motivated by our conviction that the Bible is God's Word in written form. We believe that the Bible contains the divine answer to the deepest needs of humanity, sheds unique light on our path in a dark world and sets forth the way to our eternal well-being. Out of these deep convictions, we have sought to recreate as far as possible the experience of the original audience — blending transparency to the original text with accessibility for the millions of English speakers around the world. We have prioritized accuracy, clarity and literary quality with the goal of creating a translation suitable for public and private reading, evangelism, teaching, preaching, memorizing and liturgical use. We have also sought to preserve a measure of continuity with the long tradition of translating the Scriptures into English.

The complete NIV Bible was first published in 1978. It was a completely new translation made by over a hundred scholars working directly from the best available Hebrew, Aramaic and Greek texts. The translators came from the United States, Great Britain, Canada, Australia and New Zealand, giving the translation an international scope. They were from many denominations and churches — including Anglican, Assemblies of God, Baptist, Brethren, Christian Reformed, Church of Christ, Evangelical Covenant, Evangelical Free, Lutheran, Mennonite, Methodist, Nazarene, Presbyterian, Wesleyan and others. This breadth of denominational and theological perspective helped to safeguard the translation from sectarian bias. For these reasons, and by the grace of God, the NIV has gained a wide readership in all parts of the English-speaking world.

The work of translating the Bible is never finished. As good as they are, English translations must be regularly updated so that they will continue to communicate accurately the meaning of God's Word. Updates are needed in order to reflect the latest developments in our understanding of the biblical world and its languages and to keep pace with changes in English usage. Recognizing, then, that the NIV would retain its ability to communicate God's Word accurately only if it were regularly updated, the original translators established The Committee on Bible Translation (CBT). The committee is a self-perpetuating group of biblical scholars charged with keeping abreast of advances in biblical scholarship and changes in English and issuing periodic updates to the NIV. CBT is an independent, self-governing body and has sole responsibility for the NIV text. The committee mirrors the original group of translators in its diverse international and denominational makeup and in its unifying commitment to the Bible as God's inspired Word.

In obedience to its mandate, the committee has issued periodic updates to the NIV. An initial revision was released in 1984. A more thorough revision process was completed in 2005, resulting in the separately published Today's New International Version (TNIV). The updated NIV you now have in your hands builds on both the original NIV and the TNIV and represents the latest effort of the committee to articulate

God's unchanging Word in the way the original authors might have said it had they been speaking in English to the global English-speaking audience today.

The first concern of the translators has continued to be the accuracy of the translation and its faithfulness to the intended meaning of the biblical writers. This has moved the translators to go beyond a formal word-for-word rendering of the original texts. Because thought patterns and syntax differ from language to language, accurate communication of the meaning of the biblical authors demands constant regard for varied contextual uses of words and idioms and for frequent modifications in sentence structures.

As an aid to the reader, sectional headings have been inserted. They are not to be regarded as part of the biblical text and are not intended for oral reading. It is the committee's hope that these headings may prove more helpful to the reader than the traditional chapter divisions, which were introduced long after the Bible was written.

For the Old Testament the standard Hebrew text, the Masoretic Text as published in the latest edition of *Biblia Hebraica,* has been used throughout. The Masoretic Text tradition contains marginal notations that offer variant readings. These have sometimes been followed instead of the text itself. Because such instances involve variants within the Masoretic tradition, they have not been indicated in the textual notes. In a few cases, words in the basic consonantal text have been divided differently than in the Masoretic Text. Such cases are usually indicated in the textual footnotes. The Dead Sea Scrolls contain biblical texts that represent an earlier stage of the transmission of the Hebrew text. They have been consulted, as have been the Samaritan Pentateuch and the ancient scribal traditions concerning deliberate textual changes. The translators also consulted the more important early versions — the Greek Septuagint, Aquila, Symmachus and Theodotion, the Latin Vulgate, the Syriac Peshitta, the Aramaic Targums and, for the Psalms, the *Juxta Hebraica* of Jerome. Readings from these versions, the Dead Sea Scrolls and the scribal traditions were occasionally followed where the Masoretic Text seemed doubtful and where accepted principles of textual criticism showed that one or more of these textual witnesses appeared to provide the correct reading. In rare cases, the committee has emended the Hebrew text where it appears to have become corrupted at an even earlier stage of its transmission. These departures from the Masoretic Text are also indicated in the textual footnotes. Sometimes the vowel indicators (which are later additions to the basic consonantal text) found in the Masoretic Text did not, in the judgment of the committee, represent the correct vowels for the original text. Accordingly, some words have been read with a different set of vowels. These instances are usually not indicated in the footnotes.

The Greek text used in translating the New Testament is an eclectic one, based on the latest editions of the Nestle-Aland/United Bible Societies' Greek New Testament. The committee has made its choices among the variant readings in accordance with widely accepted principles of New Testament textual criticism. Footnotes call attention to places where uncertainty remains.

The New Testament authors, writing in Greek, often quote the Old Testament from its ancient Greek version, the Septuagint. This is one reason why some of the Old Testament quotations in the NIV New Testament are not identical to the corresponding passages in the NIV Old Testament. Such quotations in the New Testament are indicated with the footnote "(see Septuagint)."

Other footnotes in this version are of several kinds, most of which need no explanation. Those giving alternative translations begin with "Or" and generally introduce the alternative with the last word preceding it in the text, except when it is a single-word alternative. When poetry is quoted in a footnote, a slash mark indicates a line division.

It should be noted that references to diseases, minerals, flora and fauna, architectural details, clothing, jewelry, musical instruments and other articles cannot always be identified with precision. Also, linear measurements and measures of capacity can only be approximated (see the Table of Weights and Measures). Although *Selah,* used mainly in the Psalms, is probably a musical term, its meaning is uncertain. Since it may interrupt reading and distract the reader, this word has not been kept in the English text, but every occurrence has been signaled by a footnote.

One of the main reasons the task of Bible translation is never finished is the change in our own language, English. Although a basic core of the language remains relatively stable, many diverse and complex linguistic factors continue to bring about subtle shifts in the meanings and/or connotations of even old, well-established words and phrases. One of the shifts that creates particular challenges to writers and translators alike is the manner in which gender is presented. The original NIV (1978) was published in a time when "a man" would naturally be understood, in many contexts, to be referring to a person, whether male or female. But most English speakers today tend to hear a distinctly male connotation in this word. In recognition of this change in English, this edition of the NIV, along with almost all other recent English translations, substitutes other expressions when the original text intends to refer generically to men and women equally. Thus, for instance, the NIV (1984) rendering of 1 Corinthians 8:3, "But the man who loves God is known by God" becomes in this edition "But whoever loves God is known by God." On the other hand, "man" and "mankind," as ways of denoting the human race, are still widely used. This edition of the NIV therefore continues to use these words, along with other expressions, in this way.

A related shift in English creates a greater challenge for modern translations: the move away from using the third-person masculine singular pronouns — "he/him/his" — to refer to men and women equally. This usage does persist at a low level in some forms of English, and this revision therefore occasionally uses these pronouns in a generic sense. But the tendency, recognized in day-to-day usage and confirmed by extensive research, is away from the generic use of "he," "him" and "his." In recognition of this shift in language and in an effort to translate into the "common" English that people are actually using, this revision of the NIV generally uses other constructions when the biblical text is plainly addressed to men and women equally. The reader will frequently encounter a "they," "them" or "their" to express a generic singular idea. Thus, for instance, Mark 8:36 reads: "What good is it for someone to gain the whole world, yet forfeit their soul?" This generic use of the "indefinite" or "singular" "they/them/their" has a venerable place in English idiom and has quickly become established as standard English, spoken and written, all over the world. Where an individual emphasis is deemed to be present, "anyone" or "everyone" or some other equivalent is generally used as the antecedent of such pronouns.

Sometimes the chapter and/or verse numbering in English translations of the Old Testament differs from that found in published Hebrew texts. This is particularly the case in the Psalms, where the traditional titles are often included in the Hebrew verse numbering. Such differences are indicated in the footnotes at the bottom of the page. In the New Testament, verse numbers that marked off portions of the traditional English text not supported by the best Greek manuscripts now appear in brackets, with a footnote indicating the text that has been omitted (see, for example, Matthew 17:[21]).

Mark 16:9 – 20 and John 7:53 – 8:11, although long accorded virtually equal status with the rest of the Gospels in which they stand, have a very questionable — and confused — standing in the textual history of the New Testament, as noted in the bracketed annotations with which they are set off. A different typeface has been chosen for these passages to indicate even more clearly their uncertain status.

Basic formatting of the text, such as lining the poetry, paragraphing (both prose and poetry), setting up of (administrative-like) lists, indenting letters and lengthy prayers within narratives and the insertion of sectional headings, has been the work of the committee. However, the choice between single-column and double-column formats has been left to the publishers. Also the issuing of "red-letter" editions is a publisher's choice — one the committee does not endorse.

The committee has again been reminded that every human effort is flawed — including this revision of the NIV. We trust, however, that many will find in it an improved representation of the Word of God, through which they hear his call to faith in our Lord Jesus Christ and to service in his kingdom. We offer this version of the Bible to him in whose name and for whose glory it has been made.

The Committee on Bible Translation
September 2010

THE OLD TESTAMENT

GENESIS

The Beginning

1 In the beginning God created the
heavens and the earth. 2Now the earth
was formless and empty, darkness was
over the surface of the deep, and the
Spirit of God was hovering over the wa-
ters.

3And God said, "Let there be light," and
there was light. 4God saw that the light
was good, and he separated the light
from the darkness. 5God called the
light "day," and the darkness he called
"night." And there was evening, and
there was morning—the first day.

6And God said, "Let there be a vault be-
tween the waters to separate water
from water." 7So God made the vault
and separated the water under the
vault from the water above it. And it
was so. 8God called the vault "sky."
And there was evening, and there was
morning—the second day.

9And God said, "Let the water under the
sky be gathered to one place, and let dry
ground appear." And it was so. 10God
called the dry ground "land," and the
gathered waters he called "seas." And
God saw that it was good.

11Then God said, "Let the land pro-
duce vegetation: seed-bearing plants
and trees on the land that bear fruit
with seed in it, according to their var-
ious kinds." And it was so. 12The land
produced vegetation: plants bearing
seed according to their kinds and trees
bearing fruit with seed in it according
to their kinds. And God saw that it was
good. 13And there was evening, and
there was morning—the third day.

14And God said, "Let there be lights in the
vault of the sky to separate the day from
the night, and let them serve as signs to
mark sacred times, and days and years,
15and let them be lights in the vault of
the sky to give light on the earth." And it
was so. 16God made two great lights—
the greater light to govern the day and
the lesser light to govern the night. He
also made the stars. 17God set them
in the vault of the sky to give light on
the earth, 18to govern the day and the
night, and to separate light from dark-
ness. And God saw that it was good.
19And there was evening, and there was
morning—the fourth day.

20And God said, "Let the water teem with
living creatures, and let birds fly above
the earth across the vault of the sky."
21So God created the great creatures
of the sea and every living thing with
which the water teems and that moves
about in it, according to their kinds,
and every winged bird according to
its kind. And God saw that it was good.
22God blessed them and said, "Be fruit-
ful and increase in number and fill the
water in the seas, and let the birds in-
crease on the earth." 23And there was
evening, and there was morning—the
fifth day.

24And God said, "Let the land produce liv-
ing creatures according to their kinds:
the livestock, the creatures that move
along the ground, and the wild ani-
mals, each according to its kind." And
it was so. 25God made the wild animals
according to their kinds, the livestock
according to their kinds, and all the
creatures that move along the ground
according to their kinds. And God saw
that it was good.

26Then God said, "Let us make man-
kind in our image, in our likeness, so
that they may rule over the fish in the
sea and the birds in the sky, over the
livestock and all the wild animals,[a] and
over all the creatures that move along
the ground."

[a] *26* Probable reading of the original Hebrew text (see Syriac); Masoretic Text *the earth*

27 So God created mankind in his own
  image,
 in the image of God he created them;
 male and female he created them.

28 God blessed them and said to them, "Be fruitful and increase in number; fill the earth and subdue it. Rule over the fish in the sea and the birds in the sky and over every living creature that moves on the ground."

29 Then God said, "I give you every seed-bearing plant on the face of the whole earth and every tree that has fruit with seed in it. They will be yours for food. 30 And to all the beasts of the earth and all the birds in the sky and all the creatures that move along the ground—everything that has the breath of life in it—I give every green plant for food." And it was so.

31 God saw all that he had made, and it was very good. And there was evening, and there was morning—the sixth day.

2 Thus the heavens and the earth were completed in all their vast array.

2 By the seventh day God had finished the work he had been doing; so on the seventh day he rested from all his work. 3 Then God blessed the seventh day and made it holy, because on it he rested from all the work of creating that he had done.

Adam and Eve

4 This is the account of the heavens and the earth when they were created, when the LORD God made the earth and the heavens.

5 Now no shrub had yet appeared on the earth[a] and no plant had yet sprung up, for the LORD God had not sent rain on the earth and there was no one to work the ground, 6 but streams[b] came up from the earth and watered the whole surface of the ground. 7 Then the LORD God formed a man[c] from the dust of the ground and breathed into his nostrils the breath of life, and the man became a living being.

8 Now the LORD God had planted a garden in the east, in Eden; and there he put the man he had formed. 9 The LORD God made all kinds of trees grow out of the ground—trees that were pleasing to the eye and good for food. In the middle of the garden were the tree of life and the tree of the knowledge of good and evil.

10 A river watering the garden flowed from Eden; from there it was separated into four headwaters. 11 The name of the first is the Pishon; it winds through the entire land of Havilah, where there is gold. 12 (The gold of that land is good; aromatic resin[d] and onyx are also there.) 13 The name of the second river is the Gihon; it winds through the entire land of Cush.[e] 14 The name of the third river is the Tigris; it runs along the east side of Ashur. And the fourth river is the Euphrates.

15 The LORD God took the man and put him in the Garden of Eden to work it and take care of it. 16 And the LORD God commanded the man, "You are free to eat from any tree in the garden; 17 but you must not eat from the tree of the knowledge of good and evil, for when you eat from it you will certainly die."

18 The LORD God said, "It is not good for the man to be alone. I will make a helper suitable for him."

19 Now the LORD God had formed out of the ground all the wild animals and all the birds in the sky. He brought them to the man to see what he would name them; and whatever the man called each living creature, that was its name. 20 So the man gave names to all the livestock, the birds in the sky and all the wild animals.

But for Adam[f] no suitable helper was found. 21 So the LORD God caused the man to fall into a deep sleep; and while he was sleeping, he took one of the man's ribs[g] and then closed up the place with flesh. 22 Then the LORD God made a woman from the rib[h] he had taken out of the man, and he brought her to the man.

23 The man said,

"This is now bone of my bones
 and flesh of my flesh;
she shall be called 'woman,'
 for she was taken out of man."

[a] 5 Or *land*; also in verse 6 [b] 6 Or *mist* [c] 7 The Hebrew for *man (adam)* sounds like and may be related to the Hebrew for *ground (adamah)*; it is also the name *Adam* (see verse 20). [d] 12 Or *good; pearls* [e] 13 Possibly southeast Mesopotamia [f] 20 Or *the man* [g] 21 Or *took part of the man's side* [h] 22 Or *part*

24 That is why a man leaves his father and mother and is united to his wife, and they become one flesh.

25 Adam and his wife were both naked, and they felt no shame.

The Fall

3 Now the serpent was more crafty than any of the wild animals the LORD God had made. He said to the woman, "Did God really say, 'You must not eat from any tree in the garden'?"

2 The woman said to the serpent, "We may eat fruit from the trees in the garden, 3 but God did say, 'You must not eat fruit from the tree that is in the middle of the garden, and you must not touch it, or you will die.' "

4 "You will not certainly die," the serpent said to the woman. 5 "For God knows that when you eat from it your eyes will be opened, and you will be like God, knowing good and evil."

6 When the woman saw that the fruit of the tree was good for food and pleasing to the eye, and also desirable for gaining wisdom, she took some and ate it. She also gave some to her husband, who was with her, and he ate it. 7 Then the eyes of both of them were opened, and they realized they were naked; so they sewed fig leaves together and made coverings for themselves.

8 Then the man and his wife heard the sound of the LORD God as he was walking in the garden in the cool of the day, and they hid from the LORD God among the trees of the garden. 9 But the LORD God called to the man, "Where are you?"

10 He answered, "I heard you in the garden, and I was afraid because I was naked; so I hid."

11 And he said, "Who told you that you were naked? Have you eaten from the tree that I commanded you not to eat from?"

12 The man said, "The woman you put here with me—she gave me some fruit from the tree, and I ate it."

13 Then the LORD God said to the woman, "What is this you have done?"

The woman said, "The serpent deceived me, and I ate."

14 So the LORD God said to the serpent, "Because you have done this,

"Cursed are you above all livestock
    and all wild animals!
You will crawl on your belly
    and you will eat dust
    all the days of your life.
15 And I will put enmity
    between you and the woman,
    and between your offspring[a] and hers;
he will crush[b] your head,
    and you will strike his heel."

16 To the woman he said,

"I will make your pains in childbearing
        very severe;
    with painful labor you will give birth
        to children.
Your desire will be for your husband,
    and he will rule over you."

17 To Adam he said, "Because you listened to your wife and ate fruit from the tree about which I commanded you, 'You must not eat from it,'

"Cursed is the ground because of you;
    through painful toil you will eat food
        from it
    all the days of your life.
18 It will produce thorns and thistles for you,
    and you will eat the plants of the field.
19 By the sweat of your brow
    you will eat your food
until you return to the ground,
    since from it you were taken;
for dust you are
    and to dust you will return."

20 Adam[c] named his wife Eve,[d] because she would become the mother of all the living.

21 The LORD God made garments of skin for Adam and his wife and clothed them. 22 And the LORD God said, "The man has now become like one of us, knowing good and evil. He must not be allowed to reach out his hand and take also from the tree of life and eat, and live forever." 23 So the LORD God banished him from the Garden of Eden to work the ground from which he had been taken. 24 After he drove the man out, he placed on the east side[e] of the Garden of Eden cherubim and a flaming sword flashing back and forth to guard the way to the tree of life.

[a] 15 Or *seed* [b] 15 Or *strike* [c] 20 Or *The man* [d] 20 *Eve* probably means *living.* [e] 24 Or *placed in front*

HOW GREAT IS OUR GOD

Chris Tomlin, Jesse Reeves, Ed Cash

The splendor of the King
Clothed in majesty
Let all the earth rejoice
All the earth rejoice
He wraps himself in light
And darkness tries to hide
And trembles at his voice
And trembles at his voice

How great is our God
Sing with me
How great is our God
And all will see how great
How great is our God

And age to age he stands
And time is in his hands
Beginning and the End
Beginning and the End
The Godhead three in one
Father Spirit Son
The Lion and the Lamb
The Lion and the Lamb

Name above all names
Worthy of all praise
My heart will sing
How great is our God

THE INSPIRATION

Such knowledge is too wonderful for me, too lofty for me to attain.

—Psalm 139:6

Read also: Genesis 14:20; Job 1:13–21; Psalm 9:1–2

BEHIND THE SONG

When songwriter Chris Tomlin was contemplating the greatness of God, the English language came up short for him. He found himself apologizing to God as he wrote "How Great Is Our God."

"I thought, 'Lord, this is so simple, but these are the only words I know right now. Our English language only goes so far in saying how great you are,'" Tomlin said.

Tomlin's inability to articulate just how overwhelmed he was is certainly no new experience for Christian songwriters and worship leaders. Throughout Psalm 139, King David wonders aloud about the majesty, splendor and goodness of God, admitting that it was far too excellent for him to comprehend. "Such knowledge is too wonderful for me, too lofty for me to attain" (verse 6). There is something very powerful and freeing about confessing that God is too big to be contained by our human understanding.

Tomlin and the rest of the Passion community have traveled the globe and heard "How Great Is Our God" sung by believers everywhere. In 2011 Tomlin re-recorded a "World Edition" of the song that features the song being sung in 20 different languages. "It's the most special thing I've ever recorded," Tomlin insists. "I don't think I'll ever record anything like it again in my life. It gives you a sense that this is the whole world worshiping God."

Selah

Reflecting on the times you have been caught off guard by the greatness of God can be extremely helpful during the low times you are sure to experience throughout life. The thoughts and words you write down today may speak back into your life in the future.

- Have there been times in your life when you have felt overwhelmed by the goodness of God? What were those times?
- Which aspects of God's character do you tend to return to when you consider his greatness? Chris references "heavenly storehouses laden with snow." Are there visual pictures that come to you as you think about God?

Cain and Abel

4 Adam[a] made love to his wife Eve, and she became pregnant and gave birth to Cain.[b] She said, "With the help of the LORD I have brought forth[c] a man." 2Later she gave birth to his brother Abel.

Now Abel kept flocks, and Cain worked the soil. 3In the course of time Cain brought some of the fruits of the soil as an offering to the LORD. 4And Abel also brought an offering—fat portions from some of the firstborn of his flock. The LORD looked with favor on Abel and his offering, 5but on Cain and his offering he did not look with favor. So Cain was very angry, and his face was downcast.

6Then the LORD said to Cain, "Why are you angry? Why is your face downcast? 7If you do what is right, will you not be accepted? But if you do not do what is right, sin is crouching at your door; it desires to have you, but you must rule over it."

8Now Cain said to his brother Abel, "Let's go out to the field."[d] While they were in the field, Cain attacked his brother Abel and killed him.

9Then the LORD said to Cain, "Where is your brother Abel?"

"I don't know," he replied. "Am I my brother's keeper?"

10The LORD said, "What have you done? Listen! Your brother's blood cries out to me from the ground. 11Now you are under a curse and driven from the ground, which opened its mouth to receive your brother's blood from your hand. 12When you work the ground, it will no longer yield its crops for you. You will be a restless wanderer on the earth."

13Cain said to the LORD, "My punishment is more than I can bear. 14Today you are driving me from the land, and I will be hidden from your presence; I will be a restless wanderer on the earth, and whoever finds me will kill me."

15But the LORD said to him, "Not so[e]; anyone who kills Cain will suffer vengeance seven times over." Then the LORD put a mark on Cain so that no one who found him would kill him. 16So Cain went out from the LORD's presence and lived in the land of Nod,[f] east of Eden.

17Cain made love to his wife, and she became pregnant and gave birth to Enoch. Cain was then building a city, and he named it after his son Enoch. 18To Enoch was born Irad, and Irad was the father of Mehujael, and Mehujael was the father of Methushael, and Methushael was the father of Lamech.

19Lamech married two women, one named Adah and the other Zillah. 20Adah gave birth to Jabal; he was the father of those who live in tents and raise livestock. 21His brother's name was Jubal; he was the father of all who play stringed instruments and pipes. 22Zillah also had a son, Tubal-Cain, who forged all kinds of tools out of[g] bronze and iron. Tubal-Cain's sister was Naamah.

23Lamech said to his wives,

"Adah and Zillah, listen to me;
  wives of Lamech, hear my words.
I have killed a man for wounding me,
  a young man for injuring me.
24If Cain is avenged seven times,
  then Lamech seventy-seven times."

25Adam made love to his wife again, and she gave birth to a son and named him Seth,[h] saying, "God has granted me another child in place of Abel, since Cain killed him." 26Seth also had a son, and he named him Enosh.

At that time people began to call on[i] the name of the LORD.

From Adam to Noah

5 This is the written account of Adam's family line.

When God created mankind, he made them in the likeness of God. 2He created them male and female and blessed them. And he named them "Mankind"[j] when they were created.

3When Adam had lived 130 years, he had a son in his own likeness, in his own image; and he named him Seth. 4After Seth was born, Adam lived 800 years and had other sons and daughters. 5Altogether, Adam lived a total of 930 years, and then he died.

[a] *1* Or *The man* [b] *1* *Cain* sounds like the Hebrew for *brought forth* or *acquired.* [c] *1* Or *have acquired*
[d] *8* Samaritan Pentateuch, Septuagint, Vulgate and Syriac; Masoretic Text does not have *"Let's go out to the field."* [e] *15* Septuagint, Vulgate and Syriac; Hebrew *Very well* [f] *16* *Nod* means *wandering* (see verses 12 and 14). [g] *22* Or *who instructed all who work in* [h] *25* *Seth* probably means *granted.*
[i] *26* Or *to proclaim* [j] *2* Hebrew *adam*

[6]When Seth had lived 105 years, he became the father[a] of Enosh. [7]After he became the father of Enosh, Seth lived 807 years and had other sons and daughters. [8]Altogether, Seth lived a total of 912 years, and then he died.

[9]When Enosh had lived 90 years, he became the father of Kenan. [10]After he became the father of Kenan, Enosh lived 815 years and had other sons and daughters. [11]Altogether, Enosh lived a total of 905 years, and then he died.

[12]When Kenan had lived 70 years, he became the father of Mahalalel. [13]After he became the father of Mahalalel, Kenan lived 840 years and had other sons and daughters. [14]Altogether, Kenan lived a total of 910 years, and then he died.

[15]When Mahalalel had lived 65 years, he became the father of Jared. [16]After he became the father of Jared, Mahalalel lived 830 years and had other sons and daughters. [17]Altogether, Mahalalel lived a total of 895 years, and then he died.

[18]When Jared had lived 162 years, he became the father of Enoch. [19]After he became the father of Enoch, Jared lived 800 years and had other sons and daughters. [20]Altogether, Jared lived a total of 962 years, and then he died.

[21]When Enoch had lived 65 years, he became the father of Methuselah. [22]After he became the father of Methuselah, Enoch walked faithfully with God 300 years and had other sons and daughters. [23]Altogether, Enoch lived a total of 365 years. [24]Enoch walked faithfully with God; then he was no more, because God took him away.

[25]When Methuselah had lived 187 years, he became the father of Lamech. [26]After he became the father of Lamech, Methuselah lived 782 years and had other sons and daughters. [27]Altogether, Methuselah lived a total of 969 years, and then he died.

[28]When Lamech had lived 182 years, he had a son. [29]He named him Noah[b] and said, "He will comfort us in the labor and painful toil of our hands caused by the ground the LORD has cursed." [30]After Noah was born, Lamech lived 595 years and had other sons and daughters. [31]Altogether, Lamech lived a total of 777 years, and then he died.

[32]After Noah was 500 years old, he became the father of Shem, Ham and Japheth.

Wickedness in the World

6 When human beings began to increase in number on the earth and daughters were born to them, [2]the sons of God saw that the daughters of humans were beautiful, and they married any of them they chose. [3]Then the LORD said, "My Spirit will not contend with[c] humans forever, for they are mortal[d]; their days will be a hundred and twenty years."

[4]The Nephilim were on the earth in those days — and also afterward — when the sons of God went to the daughters of humans and had children by them. They were the heroes of old, men of renown.

[5]The LORD saw how great the wickedness of the human race had become on the earth, and that every inclination of the thoughts of the human heart was only evil all the time. [6]The LORD regretted that he had made human beings on the earth, and his heart was deeply troubled. [7]So the LORD said, "I will wipe from the face of the earth the human race I have created — and with them the animals, the birds and the creatures that move along the ground — for I regret that I have made them." [8]But Noah found favor in the eyes of the LORD.

Noah and the Flood

[9]This is the account of Noah and his family.

Noah was a righteous man, blameless among the people of his time, and he walked faithfully with God. [10]Noah had three sons: Shem, Ham and Japheth.

[11]Now the earth was corrupt in God's sight and was full of violence. [12]God saw how corrupt the earth had become, for all the people on earth had corrupted their ways. [13]So God said to Noah, "I am going to put an end to all people, for the earth is filled with violence because of them. I am surely going to destroy both them and the earth. [14]So make yourself an ark of cypress[e] wood; make rooms in it and coat it with pitch inside and out. [15]This is how you are to build it: The ark is to be three hundred cubits long, fifty

[a] 6 *Father* may mean *ancestor*; also in verses 7-26. [b] 29 *Noah* sounds like the Hebrew for *comfort.* [c] 3 Or *My spirit will not remain in* [d] 3 Or *corrupt* [e] 14 The meaning of the Hebrew for this word is uncertain.

cubits wide and thirty cubits high.[a] 16 Make a
roof for it, leaving below the roof an opening
one cubit[b] high all around.[c] Put a door in the
side of the ark and make lower, middle and
upper decks. 17 I am going to bring floodwa-
ters on the earth to destroy all life under the
heavens, every creature that has the breath
of life in it. Everything on earth will perish.
18 But I will establish my covenant with you,
and you will enter the ark — you and your
sons and your wife and your sons' wives
with you. 19 You are to bring into the ark two
of all living creatures, male and female, to
keep them alive with you. 20 Two of every
kind of bird, of every kind of animal and of
every kind of creature that moves along the
ground will come to you to be kept alive.
21 You are to take every kind of food that is to
be eaten and store it away as food for you and
for them."

22 Noah did everything just as God com-
manded him.

7 The LORD then said to Noah, "Go into
the ark, you and your whole family, be-
cause I have found you righteous in this gen-
eration. 2 Take with you seven pairs of every
kind of clean animal, a male and its mate,
and one pair of every kind of unclean an-
imal, a male and its mate, 3 and also seven
pairs of every kind of bird, male and female,
to keep their various kinds alive throughout
the earth. 4 Seven days from now I will send
rain on the earth for forty days and forty
nights, and I will wipe from the face of the
earth every living creature I have made."

5 And Noah did all that the LORD com-
manded him.

6 Noah was six hundred years old when
the floodwaters came on the earth. 7 And
Noah and his sons and his wife and his sons'
wives entered the ark to escape the waters of
the flood. 8 Pairs of clean and unclean ani-
mals, of birds and of all creatures that move
along the ground, 9 male and female, came to
Noah and entered the ark, as God had com-
manded Noah. 10 And after the seven days
the floodwaters came on the earth.

11 In the six hundredth year of Noah's
life, on the seventeenth day of the second
month — on that day all the springs of the
great deep burst forth, and the floodgates of
the heavens were opened. 12 And rain fell on
the earth forty days and forty nights.

13 On that very day Noah and his sons,
Shem, Ham and Japheth, together with his
wife and the wives of his three sons, entered
the ark. 14 They had with them every wild
animal according to its kind, all livestock
according to their kinds, every creature that
moves along the ground according to its
kind and every bird according to its kind, ev-
erything with wings. 15 Pairs of all creatures
that have the breath of life in them came to
Noah and entered the ark. 16 The animals go-
ing in were male and female of every living
thing, as God had commanded Noah. Then
the LORD shut him in.

17 For forty days the flood kept coming on
the earth, and as the waters increased they
lifted the ark high above the earth. 18 The
waters rose and increased greatly on the
earth, and the ark floated on the surface of
the water. 19 They rose greatly on the earth,
and all the high mountains under the en-
tire heavens were covered. 20 The waters
rose and covered the mountains to a depth
of more than fifteen cubits.[d,e] 21 Every living
thing that moved on land perished — birds,
livestock, wild animals, all the creatures
that swarm over the earth, and all mankind.
22 Everything on dry land that had the breath
of life in its nostrils died. 23 Every living thing
on the face of the earth was wiped out; peo-
ple and animals and the creatures that move
along the ground and the birds were wiped
from the earth. Only Noah was left, and
those with him in the ark.

24 The waters flooded the earth for a hun-
dred and fifty days.

8 But God remembered Noah and all the
wild animals and the livestock that were
with him in the ark, and he sent a wind over
the earth, and the waters receded. 2 Now the
springs of the deep and the floodgates of the
heavens had been closed, and the rain had
stopped falling from the sky. 3 The water re-
ceded steadily from the earth. At the end of
the hundred and fifty days the water had
gone down, 4 and on the seventeenth day of
the seventh month the ark came to rest on

[a] *15* That is, about 450 feet long, 75 feet wide and 45 feet high or about 135 meters long, 23 meters wide and 14 meters high [b] *16* That is, about 18 inches or about 45 centimeters [c] *16* The meaning of the Hebrew for this clause is uncertain. [d] *20* That is, about 23 feet or about 6.8 meters [e] *20* Or *rose more than fifteen cubits, and the mountains were covered*

the mountains of Ararat. 5 The waters continued to recede until the tenth month, and on the first day of the tenth month the tops of the mountains became visible.

6 After forty days Noah opened a window he had made in the ark 7 and sent out a raven, and it kept flying back and forth until the water had dried up from the earth. 8 Then he sent out a dove to see if the water had receded from the surface of the ground. 9 But the dove could find nowhere to perch because there was water over all the surface of the earth; so it returned to Noah in the ark. He reached out his hand and took the dove and brought it back to himself in the ark. 10 He waited seven more days and again sent out the dove from the ark. 11 When the dove returned to him in the evening, there in its beak was a freshly plucked olive leaf! Then Noah knew that the water had receded from the earth. 12 He waited seven more days and sent the dove out again, but this time it did not return to him.

13 By the first day of the first month of Noah's six hundred and first year, the water had dried up from the earth. Noah then removed the covering from the ark and saw that the surface of the ground was dry. 14 By the twenty-seventh day of the second month the earth was completely dry.

15 Then God said to Noah, 16 "Come out of the ark, you and your wife and your sons and their wives. 17 Bring out every kind of living creature that is with you — the birds, the animals, and all the creatures that move along the ground — so they can multiply on the earth and be fruitful and increase in number on it."

18 So Noah came out, together with his sons and his wife and his sons' wives. 19 All the animals and all the creatures that move along the ground and all the birds — everything that moves on land — came out of the ark, one kind after another.

20 Then Noah built an altar to the LORD and, taking some of all the clean animals and clean birds, he sacrificed burnt offerings on it. 21 The LORD smelled the pleasing aroma and said in his heart: "Never again will I curse the ground because of humans, even though[a] every inclination of the human heart is evil from childhood. And never again will I destroy all living creatures, as I have done.

22 "As long as the earth endures,
seedtime and harvest,
cold and heat,
summer and winter,
day and night
will never cease."

God's Covenant With Noah

9 Then God blessed Noah and his sons, saying to them, "Be fruitful and increase in number and fill the earth. 2 The fear and dread of you will fall on all the beasts of the earth, and on all the birds in the sky, on every creature that moves along the ground, and on all the fish in the sea; they are given into your hands. 3 Everything that lives and moves about will be food for you. Just as I gave you the green plants, I now give you everything.

4 "But you must not eat meat that has its lifeblood still in it. 5 And for your lifeblood I will surely demand an accounting. I will demand an accounting from every animal. And from each human being, too, I will demand an accounting for the life of another human being.

6 "Whoever sheds human blood,
by humans shall their blood be shed;
for in the image of God
has God made mankind.

7 As for you, be fruitful and increase in number; multiply on the earth and increase upon it."

8 Then God said to Noah and to his sons with him: 9 "I now establish my covenant with you and with your descendants after you 10 and with every living creature that was with you — the birds, the livestock and all the wild animals, all those that came out of the ark with you — every living creature on earth. 11 I establish my covenant with you: Never again will all life be destroyed by the waters of a flood; never again will there be a flood to destroy the earth."

12 And God said, "This is the sign of the covenant I am making between me and you and every living creature with you, a covenant for all generations to come: 13 I have set my rainbow in the clouds, and it will be

[a] 21 Or *humans, for*

the sign of the covenant between me and the
earth. 14 Whenever I bring clouds over the
earth and the rainbow appears in the clouds,
15 I will remember my covenant between me
and you and all living creatures of every
kind. Never again will the waters become a
flood to destroy all life. 16 Whenever the rain-
bow appears in the clouds, I will see it and
remember the everlasting covenant between
God and all living creatures of every kind on
the earth."
17 So God said to Noah, "This is the sign of
the covenant I have established between me
and all life on the earth."

The Sons of Noah

18 The sons of Noah who came out of the
ark were Shem, Ham and Japheth. (Ham was
the father of Canaan.) 19 These were the three
sons of Noah, and from them came the peo-
ple who were scattered over the whole earth.
20 Noah, a man of the soil, proceeded[a] to
plant a vineyard. 21 When he drank some of
its wine, he became drunk and lay uncov-
ered inside his tent. 22 Ham, the father of
Canaan, saw his father naked and told his
two brothers outside. 23 But Shem and Ja-
pheth took a garment and laid it across their
shoulders; then they walked in backward
and covered their father's naked body. Their
faces were turned the other way so that they
would not see their father naked.
24 When Noah awoke from his wine and
found out what his youngest son had done to
him, 25 he said,

"Cursed be Canaan!
The lowest of slaves
will he be to his brothers."

26 He also said,

"Praise be to the LORD, the God of Shem!
May Canaan be the slave of Shem.
27 May God extend Japheth's[b] territory;
may Japheth live in the tents of Shem,
and may Canaan be the slave of
Japheth."

28 After the flood Noah lived 350 years.
29 Noah lived a total of 950 years, and then he
died.

The Table of Nations

10 This is the account of Shem, Ham
and Japheth, Noah's sons, who them-
selves had sons after the flood.

The Japhethites

2 The sons[c] of Japheth:
Gomer, Magog, Madai, Javan, Tubal,
Meshek and Tiras.
3 The sons of Gomer:
Ashkenaz, Riphath and Togarmah.
4 The sons of Javan:
Elishah, Tarshish, the Kittites and the
Rodanites.[d] 5 (From these the mar-
itime peoples spread out into their
territories by their clans within their
nations, each with its own language.)

The Hamites

6 The sons of Ham:
Cush, Egypt, Put and Canaan.
7 The sons of Cush:
Seba, Havilah, Sabtah, Raamah and
Sabteka.
The sons of Raamah:
Sheba and Dedan.

8 Cush was the father[e] of Nimrod, who be-
came a mighty warrior on the earth. 9 He was
a mighty hunter before the LORD; that is why
it is said, "Like Nimrod, a mighty hunter be-
fore the LORD." 10 The first centers of his king-
dom were Babylon, Uruk, Akkad and Kalneh,
in[f] Shinar.[g] 11 From that land he went to As-
syria, where he built Nineveh, Rehoboth Ir,[h]
Calah 12 and Resen, which is between Nine-
veh and Calah—which is the great city.

13 Egypt was the father of
the Ludites, Anamites, Lehabites,
Naphtuhites, 14 Pathrusites, Kaslu-
hites (from whom the Philistines
came) and Caphtorites.
15 Canaan was the father of
Sidon his firstborn,[i] and of the Hit-
tites, 16 Jebusites, Amorites, Girga-

[a] 20 Or *soil, was the first* [b] 27 *Japheth* sounds like the Hebrew for *extend.* [c] 2 *Sons* may mean *descendants* or *successors* or *nations*; also in verses 3, 4, 6, 7, 20-23, 29 and 31. [d] 4 Some manuscripts of the Masoretic Text and Samaritan Pentateuch (see also Septuagint and 1 Chron. 1:7); most manuscripts of the Masoretic Text *Dodanites* [e] 8 *Father* may mean *ancestor* or *predecessor* or *founder*; also in verses 13, 15, 24 and 26. [f] 10 Or *Uruk and Akkad—all of them in* [g] 10 That is, Babylonia [h] 11 Or *Nineveh with its city squares* [i] 15 Or *of the Sidonians, the foremost*

shites, [17]Hivites, Arkites, Sinites,
[18]Arvadites, Zemarites and Hamath-
ites.

Later the Canaanite clans scattered [19]and
the borders of Canaan reached from Sidon
toward Gerar as far as Gaza, and then to-
ward Sodom, Gomorrah, Admah and Ze-
boyim, as far as Lasha.
[20]These are the sons of Ham by their clans
and languages, in their territories and na-
tions.

The Semites

[21]Sons were also born to Shem, whose
older brother was[a] Japheth; Shem was the
ancestor of all the sons of Eber.

[22]The sons of Shem:
Elam, Ashur, Arphaxad, Lud and
Aram.
[23]The sons of Aram:
Uz, Hul, Gether and Meshek.[b]
[24]Arphaxad was the father of[c] Shelah,
and Shelah the father of Eber.
[25]Two sons were born to Eber:
One was named Peleg,[d] because in
his time the earth was divided; his
brother was named Joktan.
[26]Joktan was the father of
Almodad, Sheleph, Hazarmaveth,
Jerah, [27]Hadoram, Uzal, Diklah,
[28]Obal, Abimael, Sheba, [29]Ophir,
Havilah and Jobab. All these were
sons of Joktan.
[30]The region where they lived stretched
from Mesha toward Sephar, in the eastern
hill country.
[31]These are the sons of Shem by their
clans and languages, in their territories and
nations.

[32]These are the clans of Noah's sons, ac-
cording to their lines of descent, within their
nations. From these the nations spread out
over the earth after the flood.

The Tower of Babel

11 Now the whole world had one lan-
guage and a common speech. [2]As
people moved eastward,[e] they found a plain
in Shinar[f] and settled there.
[3]They said to each other, "Come, let's
make bricks and bake them thoroughly."
They used brick instead of stone, and tar for
mortar. [4]Then they said, "Come, let us build
ourselves a city, with a tower that reaches to
the heavens, so that we may make a name
for ourselves; otherwise we will be scattered
over the face of the whole earth."
[5]But the LORD came down to see the city
and the tower the people were building.
[6]The LORD said, "If as one people speaking
the same language they have begun to do
this, then nothing they plan to do will be im-
possible for them. [7]Come, let us go down and
confuse their language so they will not un-
derstand each other."
[8]So the LORD scattered them from there
over all the earth, and they stopped build-
ing the city. [9]That is why it was called Ba-
bel[g]—because there the LORD confused
the language of the whole world. From there
the LORD scattered them over the face of the
whole earth.

From Shem to Abram

[10]This is the account of Shem's family line.

Two years after the flood, when Shem was
100 years old, he became the father[h] of Ar-
phaxad. [11]And after he became the father
of Arphaxad, Shem lived 500 years and had
other sons and daughters.
[12]When Arphaxad had lived 35 years, he
became the father of Shelah. [13]And after
he became the father of Shelah, Arphax-
ad lived 403 years and had other sons and
daughters.[i]
[14]When Shelah had lived 30 years, he be-
came the father of Eber. [15]And after he be-
came the father of Eber, Shelah lived 403
years and had other sons and daughters.

[a] 21 Or *Shem, the older brother of* [b] 23 See Septuagint and 1 Chron. 1:17; Hebrew *Mash.*
[c] 24 Hebrew; Septuagint *father of Cainan, and Cainan was the father of* [d] 25 *Peleg* means *division.*
[e] 2 Or *from the east*; or *in the east* [f] 2 That is, Babylonia [g] 9 That is, Babylon; *Babel* sounds like the Hebrew for *confused.* [h] 10 *Father* may mean *ancestor*; also in verses 11-25. [i] 12,13 Hebrew; Septuagint (see also Luke 3:35, 36 and note at Gen. 10:24) *35 years, he became the father of Cainan.* [13]*And after he became the father of Cainan, Arphaxad lived 430 years and had other sons and daughters, and then he died. When Cainan had lived 130 years, he became the father of Shelah. And after he became the father of Shelah, Cainan lived 330 years and had other sons and daughters*

[16]When Eber had lived 34 years, he became the father of Peleg. [17]And after he became the father of Peleg, Eber lived 430 years and had other sons and daughters.

[18]When Peleg had lived 30 years, he became the father of Reu. [19]And after he became the father of Reu, Peleg lived 209 years and had other sons and daughters.

[20]When Reu had lived 32 years, he became the father of Serug. [21]And after he became the father of Serug, Reu lived 207 years and had other sons and daughters.

[22]When Serug had lived 30 years, he became the father of Nahor. [23]And after he became the father of Nahor, Serug lived 200 years and had other sons and daughters.

[24]When Nahor had lived 29 years, he became the father of Terah. [25]And after he became the father of Terah, Nahor lived 119 years and had other sons and daughters.

[26]After Terah had lived 70 years, he became the father of Abram, Nahor and Haran.

Abram's Family

[27]This is the account of Terah's family line.

Terah became the father of Abram, Nahor and Haran. And Haran became the father of Lot. [28]While his father Terah was still alive, Haran died in Ur of the Chaldeans, in the land of his birth. [29]Abram and Nahor both married. The name of Abram's wife was Sarai, and the name of Nahor's wife was Milkah; she was the daughter of Haran, the father of both Milkah and Iskah. [30]Now Sarai was childless because she was not able to conceive.

[31]Terah took his son Abram, his grandson Lot son of Haran, and his daughter-in-law Sarai, the wife of his son Abram, and together they set out from Ur of the Chaldeans to go to Canaan. But when they came to Harran, they settled there.

[32]Terah lived 205 years, and he died in Harran.

The Call of Abram

12 The LORD had said to Abram, "Go from your country, your people and your father's household to the land I will show you.

[2]"I will make you into a great nation,
and I will bless you;
I will make your name great,
and you will be a blessing.[a]
[3]I will bless those who bless you,
and whoever curses you I will curse;
and all peoples on earth
will be blessed through you."[b]

[4]So Abram went, as the LORD had told him; and Lot went with him. Abram was seventy-five years old when he set out from Harran. [5]He took his wife Sarai, his nephew Lot, all the possessions they had accumulated and the people they had acquired in Harran, and they set out for the land of Canaan, and they arrived there.

[6]Abram traveled through the land as far as the site of the great tree of Moreh at Shechem. At that time the Canaanites were in the land. [7]The LORD appeared to Abram and said, "To your offspring[c] I will give this land." So he built an altar there to the LORD, who had appeared to him.

[8]From there he went on toward the hills east of Bethel and pitched his tent, with Bethel on the west and Ai on the east. There he built an altar to the LORD and called on the name of the LORD.

[9]Then Abram set out and continued toward the Negev.

Abram in Egypt

[10]Now there was a famine in the land, and Abram went down to Egypt to live there for a while because the famine was severe. [11]As he was about to enter Egypt, he said to his wife Sarai, "I know what a beautiful woman you are. [12]When the Egyptians see you, they will say, 'This is his wife.' Then they will kill me but will let you live. [13]Say you are my sister, so that I will be treated well for your sake and my life will be spared because of you."

[14]When Abram came to Egypt, the Egyptians saw that Sarai was a very beautiful woman. [15]And when Pharaoh's officials saw her, they praised her to Pharaoh, and she was taken into his palace. [16]He treated Abram well for her sake, and Abram acquired sheep and cattle, male and female donkeys, male and female servants, and camels.

[17]But the LORD inflicted serious diseases on Pharaoh and his household because of Abram's wife Sarai. [18]So Pharaoh summoned Abram. "What have you done to me?"

[a] 2 Or *be seen as blessed* [b] 3 Or *earth / will use your name in blessings* (see 48:20) [c] 7 Or *seed*

he said. "Why didn't you tell me she was your wife? [19]Why did you say, 'She is my sister,' so that I took her to be my wife? Now then, here is your wife. Take her and go!" [20]Then Pharaoh gave orders about Abram to his men, and they sent him on his way, with his wife and everything he had.

Abram and Lot Separate

13 So Abram went up from Egypt to the Negev, with his wife and everything he had, and Lot went with him. [2]Abram had become very wealthy in livestock and in silver and gold.

[3]From the Negev he went from place to place until he came to Bethel, to the place between Bethel and Ai where his tent had been earlier [4]and where he had first built an altar. There Abram called on the name of the LORD.

[5]Now Lot, who was moving about with Abram, also had flocks and herds and tents. [6]But the land could not support them while they stayed together, for their possessions were so great that they were not able to stay together. [7]And quarreling arose between Abram's herders and Lot's. The Canaanites and Perizzites were also living in the land at that time.

[8]So Abram said to Lot, "Let's not have any quarreling between you and me, or between your herders and mine, for we are close relatives. [9]Is not the whole land before you? Let's part company. If you go to the left, I'll go to the right; if you go to the right, I'll go to the left."

[10]Lot looked around and saw that the whole plain of the Jordan toward Zoar was well watered, like the garden of the LORD, like the land of Egypt. (This was before the LORD destroyed Sodom and Gomorrah.) [11]So Lot chose for himself the whole plain of the Jordan and set out toward the east. The two men parted company: [12]Abram lived in the land of Canaan, while Lot lived among the cities of the plain and pitched his tents near Sodom. [13]Now the people of Sodom were wicked and were sinning greatly against the LORD.

[14]The LORD said to Abram after Lot had parted from him, "Look around from where you are, to the north and south, to the east and west. [15]All the land that you see I will give to you and your offspring[a] forever. [16]I will make your offspring like the dust of the earth, so that if anyone could count the dust, then your offspring could be counted. [17]Go, walk through the length and breadth of the land, for I am giving it to you."

[18]So Abram went to live near the great trees of Mamre at Hebron, where he pitched his tents. There he built an altar to the LORD.

Abram Rescues Lot

14 At the time when Amraphel was king of Shinar,[b] Arioch king of Ellasar, Kedorlaomer king of Elam and Tidal king of Goyim, [2]these kings went to war against Bera king of Sodom, Birsha king of Gomorrah, Shinab king of Admah, Shemeber king of Zeboyim, and the king of Bela (that is, Zoar). [3]All these latter kings joined forces in the Valley of Siddim (that is, the Dead Sea Valley). [4]For twelve years they had been subject to Kedorlaomer, but in the thirteenth year they rebelled.

[5]In the fourteenth year, Kedorlaomer and the kings allied with him went out and defeated the Rephaites in Ashteroth Karnaim, the Zuzites in Ham, the Emites in Shaveh Kiriathaim [6]and the Horites in the hill country of Seir, as far as El Paran near the desert. [7]Then they turned back and went to En Mishpat (that is, Kadesh), and they conquered the whole territory of the Amalekites, as well as the Amorites who were living in Hazezon Tamar.

[8]Then the king of Sodom, the king of Gomorrah, the king of Admah, the king of Zeboyim and the king of Bela (that is, Zoar) marched out and drew up their battle lines in the Valley of Siddim [9]against Kedorlaomer king of Elam, Tidal king of Goyim, Amraphel king of Shinar and Arioch king of Ellasar — four kings against five. [10]Now the Valley of Siddim was full of tar pits, and when the kings of Sodom and Gomorrah fled, some of the men fell into them and the rest fled to the hills. [11]The four kings seized all the goods of Sodom and Gomorrah and all their food; then they went away. [12]They also carried off Abram's nephew Lot and his possessions, since he was living in Sodom.

[13]A man who had escaped came and reported this to Abram the Hebrew. Now

[a] *15* Or *seed;* also in verse 16 [b] *1* That is, Babylonia; also in verse 9

Abram was living near the great trees of Mamre the Amorite, a brother[a] of Eshkol and Aner, all of whom were allied with Abram. 14 When Abram heard that his relative had been taken captive, he called out the 318 trained men born in his household and went in pursuit as far as Dan. 15 During the night Abram divided his men to attack them and he routed them, pursuing them as far as Hobah, north of Damascus. 16 He recovered all the goods and brought back his relative Lot and his possessions, together with the women and the other people.

17 After Abram returned from defeating Kedorlaomer and the kings allied with him, the king of Sodom came out to meet him in the Valley of Shaveh (that is, the King's Valley).

18 Then Melchizedek king of Salem brought out bread and wine. He was priest of God Most High, 19 and he blessed Abram, saying,

"Blessed be Abram by God Most High,
  Creator of heaven and earth.
20 And praise be to God Most High,
  who delivered your enemies into your
    hand."

Then Abram gave him a tenth of everything.

21 The king of Sodom said to Abram, "Give me the people and keep the goods for yourself."

22 But Abram said to the king of Sodom, "With raised hand I have sworn an oath to the LORD, God Most High, Creator of heaven and earth, 23 that I will accept nothing belonging to you, not even a thread or the strap of a sandal, so that you will never be able to say, 'I made Abram rich.' 24 I will accept nothing but what my men have eaten and the share that belongs to the men who went with me — to Aner, Eshkol and Mamre. Let them have their share."

The LORD's Covenant With Abram

15 After this, the word of the LORD came to Abram in a vision:

"Do not be afraid, Abram.
  I am your shield,[b]
  your very great reward.[c]"

2 But Abram said, "Sovereign LORD, what can you give me since I remain childless and the one who will inherit[d] my estate is Eliezer of Damascus?" 3 And Abram said, "You have given me no children; so a servant in my household will be my heir."

4 Then the word of the LORD came to him: "This man will not be your heir, but a son who is your own flesh and blood will be your heir." 5 He took him outside and said, "Look up at the sky and count the stars — if indeed you can count them." Then he said to him, "So shall your offspring[e] be."

6 Abram believed the LORD, and he credited it to him as righteousness.

7 He also said to him, "I am the LORD, who brought you out of Ur of the Chaldeans to give you this land to take possession of it."

8 But Abram said, "Sovereign LORD, how can I know that I will gain possession of it?"

9 So the LORD said to him, "Bring me a heifer, a goat and a ram, each three years old, along with a dove and a young pigeon."

10 Abram brought all these to him, cut them in two and arranged the halves opposite each other; the birds, however, he did not cut in half. 11 Then birds of prey came down on the carcasses, but Abram drove them away.

12 As the sun was setting, Abram fell into a deep sleep, and a thick and dreadful darkness came over him. 13 Then the LORD said to him, "Know for certain that for four hundred years your descendants will be strangers in a country not their own and that they will be enslaved and mistreated there. 14 But I will punish the nation they serve as slaves, and afterward they will come out with great possessions. 15 You, however, will go to your ancestors in peace and be buried at a good old age. 16 In the fourth generation your descendants will come back here, for the sin of the Amorites has not yet reached its full measure."

17 When the sun had set and darkness had fallen, a smoking firepot with a blazing torch appeared and passed between the pieces. 18 On that day the LORD made a covenant with Abram and said, "To your descendants I give this land, from the Wadi[f] of Egypt to the great river, the Euphrates — 19 the land of the Kenites, Kenizzites, Kadmonites, 20 Hittites, Perizzites, Rephaites, 21 Amorites, Canaanites, Girgashites and Jebusites."

[a] 13 Or *a relative;* or *an ally* [b] 1 Or *sovereign* [c] 1 Or *shield; / your reward will be very great*
[d] 2 The meaning of the Hebrew for this phrase is uncertain. [e] 5 Or *seed* [f] 18 Or *river*

Hagar and Ishmael

16 Now Sarai, Abram's wife, had borne him no children. But she had an Egyptian slave named Hagar; [2]so she said to Abram, "The LORD has kept me from having children. Go, sleep with my slave; perhaps I can build a family through her."

Abram agreed to what Sarai said. [3]So after Abram had been living in Canaan ten years, Sarai his wife took her Egyptian slave Hagar and gave her to her husband to be his wife. [4]He slept with Hagar, and she conceived.

When she knew she was pregnant, she began to despise her mistress. [5]Then Sarai said to Abram, "You are responsible for the wrong I am suffering. I put my slave in your arms, and now that she knows she is pregnant, she despises me. May the LORD judge between you and me."

[6]"Your slave is in your hands," Abram said. "Do with her whatever you think best." Then Sarai mistreated Hagar; so she fled from her.

[7]The angel of the LORD found Hagar near a spring in the desert; it was the spring that is beside the road to Shur. [8]And he said, "Hagar, slave of Sarai, where have you come from, and where are you going?"

"I'm running away from my mistress Sarai," she answered.

[9]Then the angel of the LORD told her, "Go back to your mistress and submit to her." [10]The angel added, "I will increase your descendants so much that they will be too numerous to count."

[11]The angel of the LORD also said to her:

"You are now pregnant
and you will give birth to a son.
You shall name him Ishmael,[a]
for the LORD has heard of your misery.
[12]He will be a wild donkey of a man;
his hand will be against everyone
and everyone's hand against him,
and he will live in hostility
toward[b] all his brothers."

[13]She gave this name to the LORD who spoke to her: "You are the God who sees me," for she said, "I have now seen[c] the One who sees me." [14]That is why the well was called Beer Lahai Roi[d]; it is still there, between Kadesh and Bered.

[15]So Hagar bore Abram a son, and Abram gave the name Ishmael to the son she had borne. [16]Abram was eighty-six years old when Hagar bore him Ishmael.

The Covenant of Circumcision

17 When Abram was ninety-nine years old, the LORD appeared to him and said, "I am God Almighty[e]; walk before me faithfully and be blameless. [2]Then I will make my covenant between me and you and will greatly increase your numbers."

[3]Abram fell facedown, and God said to him, [4]"As for me, this is my covenant with you: You will be the father of many nations. [5]No longer will you be called Abram[f]; your name will be Abraham,[g] for I have made you a father of many nations. [6]I will make you very fruitful; I will make nations of you, and kings will come from you. [7]I will establish my covenant as an everlasting covenant between me and you and your descendants after you for the generations to come, to be your God and the God of your descendants after you. [8]The whole land of Canaan, where you now reside as a foreigner, I will give as an everlasting possession to you and your descendants after you; and I will be their God."

[9]Then God said to Abraham, "As for you, you must keep my covenant, you and your descendants after you for the generations to come. [10]This is my covenant with you and your descendants after you, the covenant you are to keep: Every male among you shall be circumcised. [11]You are to undergo circumcision, and it will be the sign of the covenant between me and you. [12]For the generations to come every male among you who is eight days old must be circumcised, including those born in your household or bought with money from a foreigner—those who are not your offspring. [13]Whether born in your household or bought with your money, they must be circumcised. My covenant in your flesh is to be an everlasting covenant. [14]Any uncircumcised male, who has not been circumcised in the flesh, will be cut

[a] *11 Ishmael* means *God hears.* [b] *12* Or *live to the east / of* [c] *13* Or *seen the back of* [d] *14 Beer Lahai Roi* means *well of the Living One who sees me.* [e] *1* Hebrew *El-Shaddai* [f] *5 Abram* means *exalted father.* [g] *5 Abraham* probably means *father of many.*

off from his people; he has broken my covenant."

[15]God also said to Abraham, "As for Sarai your wife, you are no longer to call her Sarai; her name will be Sarah. [16]I will bless her and will surely give you a son by her. I will bless her so that she will be the mother of nations; kings of peoples will come from her."

[17]Abraham fell facedown; he laughed and said to himself, "Will a son be born to a man a hundred years old? Will Sarah bear a child at the age of ninety?" [18]And Abraham said to God, "If only Ishmael might live under your blessing!"

[19]Then God said, "Yes, but your wife Sarah will bear you a son, and you will call him Isaac.[a] I will establish my covenant with him as an everlasting covenant for his descendants after him. [20]And as for Ishmael, I have heard you: I will surely bless him; I will make him fruitful and will greatly increase his numbers. He will be the father of twelve rulers, and I will make him into a great nation. [21]But my covenant I will establish with Isaac, whom Sarah will bear to you by this time next year." [22]When he had finished speaking with Abraham, God went up from him.

[23]On that very day Abraham took his son Ishmael and all those born in his household or bought with his money, every male in his household, and circumcised them, as God told him. [24]Abraham was ninety-nine years old when he was circumcised, [25]and his son Ishmael was thirteen; [26]Abraham and his son Ishmael were both circumcised on that very day. [27]And every male in Abraham's household, including those born in his household or bought from a foreigner, was circumcised with him.

The Three Visitors

18 The LORD appeared to Abraham near the great trees of Mamre while he was sitting at the entrance to his tent in the heat of the day. [2]Abraham looked up and saw three men standing nearby. When he saw them, he hurried from the entrance of his tent to meet them and bowed low to the ground.

[3]He said, "If I have found favor in your eyes, my lord,[b] do not pass your servant by. [4]Let a little water be brought, and then you may all wash your feet and rest under this tree. [5]Let me get you something to eat, so you can be refreshed and then go on your way—now that you have come to your servant."

"Very well," they answered, "do as you say."

[6]So Abraham hurried into the tent to Sarah. "Quick," he said, "get three seahs[c] of the finest flour and knead it and bake some bread."

[7]Then he ran to the herd and selected a choice, tender calf and gave it to a servant, who hurried to prepare it. [8]He then brought some curds and milk and the calf that had been prepared, and set these before them. While they ate, he stood near them under a tree.

[9]"Where is your wife Sarah?" they asked him.

"There, in the tent," he said.

[10]Then one of them said, "I will surely return to you about this time next year, and Sarah your wife will have a son."

Now Sarah was listening at the entrance to the tent, which was behind him. [11]Abraham and Sarah were already very old, and Sarah was past the age of childbearing. [12]So Sarah laughed to herself as she thought, "After I am worn out and my lord is old, will I now have this pleasure?"

[13]Then the LORD said to Abraham, "Why did Sarah laugh and say, 'Will I really have a child, now that I am old?' [14]Is anything too hard for the LORD? I will return to you at the appointed time next year, and Sarah will have a son."

[15]Sarah was afraid, so she lied and said, "I did not laugh."

But he said, "Yes, you did laugh."

Abraham Pleads for Sodom

[16]When the men got up to leave, they looked down toward Sodom, and Abraham walked along with them to see them on their way. [17]Then the LORD said, "Shall I hide from Abraham what I am about to do? [18]Abraham will surely become a great and powerful nation, and all nations on earth will be blessed through him.[d] [19]For I have chosen him, so that he will direct his children and his household after him to keep the way of the LORD by doing what is right and just, so that

[a] 19 *Isaac* means *he laughs.* [b] 3 Or *eyes, Lord* [c] 6 That is, probably about 36 pounds or about 16 kilograms [d] 18 Or *will use his name in blessings* (see 48:20)

the LORD will bring about for Abraham what
he has promised him."
20 Then the LORD said, "The outcry against
Sodom and Gomorrah is so great and their
sin so grievous 21 that I will go down and see
if what they have done is as bad as the outcry
that has reached me. If not, I will know."
22 The men turned away and went toward
Sodom, but Abraham remained standing
before the LORD.[a] 23 Then Abraham ap-
proached him and said: "Will you sweep
away the righteous with the wicked? 24 What
if there are fifty righteous people in the city?
Will you really sweep it away and not spare[b]
the place for the sake of the fifty righteous
people in it? 25 Far be it from you to do such a
thing — to kill the righteous with the wicked,
treating the righteous and the wicked alike.
Far be it from you! Will not the Judge of all
the earth do right?"
26 The LORD said, "If I find fifty righteous
people in the city of Sodom, I will spare the
whole place for their sake."
27 Then Abraham spoke up again: "Now
that I have been so bold as to speak to the
Lord, though I am nothing but dust and ash-
es, 28 what if the number of the righteous
is five less than fifty? Will you destroy the
whole city for lack of five people?"
"If I find forty-five there," he said, "I will
not destroy it."
29 Once again he spoke to him, "What if
only forty are found there?"
He said, "For the sake of forty, I will not
do it."
30 Then he said, "May the Lord not be an-
gry, but let me speak. What if only thirty can
be found there?"
He answered, "I will not do it if I find thir-
ty there."
31 Abraham said, "Now that I have been
so bold as to speak to the Lord, what if only
twenty can be found there?"
He said, "For the sake of twenty, I will not
destroy it."
32 Then he said, "May the Lord not be an-
gry, but let me speak just once more. What if
only ten can be found there?"
He answered, "For the sake of ten, I will
not destroy it."
33 When the LORD had finished speaking
with Abraham, he left, and Abraham re-
turned home.

Sodom and Gomorrah Destroyed

19 The two angels arrived at Sodom in
the evening, and Lot was sitting in
the gateway of the city. When he saw them,
he got up to meet them and bowed down
with his face to the ground. 2 "My lords," he
said, "please turn aside to your servant's
house. You can wash your feet and spend the
night and then go on your way early in the
morning."
"No," they answered, "we will spend the
night in the square."
3 But he insisted so strongly that they did
go with him and entered his house. He pre-
pared a meal for them, baking bread without
yeast, and they ate. 4 Before they had gone to
bed, all the men from every part of the city of
Sodom — both young and old — surrounded
the house. 5 They called to Lot, "Where are the
men who came to you tonight? Bring them
out to us so that we can have sex with them."
6 Lot went outside to meet them and shut
the door behind him 7 and said, "No, my
friends. Don't do this wicked thing. 8 Look,
I have two daughters who have never slept
with a man. Let me bring them out to you,
and you can do what you like with them.
But don't do anything to these men, for they
have come under the protection of my roof."
9 "Get out of our way," they replied. "This
fellow came here as a foreigner, and now he
wants to play the judge! We'll treat you worse
than them." They kept bringing pressure on
Lot and moved forward to break down the
door.
10 But the men inside reached out and
pulled Lot back into the house and shut the
door. 11 Then they struck the men who were
at the door of the house, young and old, with
blindness so that they could not find the door.
12 The two men said to Lot, "Do you have
anyone else here — sons-in-law, sons or
daughters, or anyone else in the city who be-
longs to you? Get them out of here, 13 because
we are going to destroy this place. The out-
cry to the LORD against its people is so great
that he has sent us to destroy it."
14 So Lot went out and spoke to his sons-in-
law, who were pledged to marry[c] his daugh-
ters. He said, "Hurry and get out of this place,
because the LORD is about to destroy the city!"
But his sons-in-law thought he was joking.

[a] *22* Masoretic Text; an ancient Hebrew scribal tradition *but the LORD remained standing before Abraham*
[b] *24* Or *forgive*; also in verse 26 [c] *14* Or *were married to*

15 With the coming of dawn, the angels
urged Lot, saying, "Hurry! Take your wife and
your two daughters who are here, or you will
be swept away when the city is punished."

16 When he hesitated, the men grasped his
hand and the hands of his wife and of his two
daughters and led them safely out of the city,
for the LORD was merciful to them. 17 As soon
as they had brought them out, one of them
said, "Flee for your lives! Don't look back,
and don't stop anywhere in the plain! Flee to
the mountains or you will be swept away!"

18 But Lot said to them, "No, my lords,[a]
please! 19 Your[b] servant has found favor in
your[b] eyes, and you[b] have shown great kind-
ness to me in sparing my life. But I can't flee
to the mountains; this disaster will overtake
me, and I'll die. 20 Look, here is a town near
enough to run to, and it is small. Let me flee
to it — it is very small, isn't it? Then my life
will be spared."

21 He said to him, "Very well, I will grant
this request too; I will not overthrow the
town you speak of. 22 But flee there quick-
ly, because I cannot do anything until you
reach it." (That is why the town was called
Zoar.[c])

23 By the time Lot reached Zoar, the sun
had risen over the land. 24 Then the LORD
rained down burning sulfur on Sodom and
Gomorrah — from the LORD out of the heav-
ens. 25 Thus he overthrew those cities and
the entire plain, destroying all those living
in the cities — and also the vegetation in the
land. 26 But Lot's wife looked back, and she
became a pillar of salt.

27 Early the next morning Abraham got up
and returned to the place where he had stood
before the LORD. 28 He looked down toward
Sodom and Gomorrah, toward all the land
of the plain, and he saw dense smoke rising
from the land, like smoke from a furnace.

29 So when God destroyed the cities of the
plain, he remembered Abraham, and he
brought Lot out of the catastrophe that over-
threw the cities where Lot had lived.

Lot and His Daughters

30 Lot and his two daughters left Zoar and
settled in the mountains, for he was afraid to
stay in Zoar. He and his two daughters lived
in a cave. 31 One day the older daughter said
to the younger, "Our father is old, and there
is no man around here to give us children —
as is the custom all over the earth. 32 Let's get
our father to drink wine and then sleep with
him and preserve our family line through
our father."

33 That night they got their father to drink
wine, and the older daughter went in and
slept with him. He was not aware of it when
she lay down or when she got up.

34 The next day the older daughter said to
the younger, "Last night I slept with my fa-
ther. Let's get him to drink wine again to-
night, and you go in and sleep with him so
we can preserve our family line through our
father." 35 So they got their father to drink
wine that night also, and the younger daugh-
ter went in and slept with him. Again he was
not aware of it when she lay down or when
she got up.

36 So both of Lot's daughters became preg-
nant by their father. 37 The older daughter
had a son, and she named him Moab[d]; he
is the father of the Moabites of today. 38 The
younger daughter also had a son, and she
named him Ben-Ammi[e]; he is the father of
the Ammonites[f] of today.

Abraham and Abimelek

20 Now Abraham moved on from there
into the region of the Negev and lived
between Kadesh and Shur. For a while he
stayed in Gerar, 2 and there Abraham said
of his wife Sarah, "She is my sister." Then
Abimelek king of Gerar sent for Sarah and
took her.

3 But God came to Abimelek in a dream
one night and said to him, "You are as good
as dead because of the woman you have tak-
en; she is a married woman."

4 Now Abimelek had not gone near her, so
he said, "Lord, will you destroy an innocent
nation? 5 Did he not say to me, 'She is my sis-
ter,' and didn't she also say, 'He is my broth-
er'? I have done this with a clear conscience
and clean hands."

6 Then God said to him in the dream, "Yes,
I know you did this with a clear conscience,
and so I have kept you from sinning against
me. That is why I did not let you touch her.

[a] 18 Or *No, Lord;* or *No, my lord* [b] 19 The Hebrew is singular. [c] 22 *Zoar* means *small.* [d] 37 *Moab* sounds like the Hebrew for *from father.* [e] 38 *Ben-Ammi* means *son of my father's people.* [f] 38 Hebrew *Bene-Ammon*

7 Now return the man's wife, for he is a prophet, and he will pray for you and you will live. But if you do not return her, you may be sure that you and all who belong to you will die."

8 Early the next morning Abimelek summoned all his officials, and when he told them all that had happened, they were very much afraid. 9 Then Abimelek called Abraham in and said, "What have you done to us? How have I wronged you that you have brought such great guilt upon me and my kingdom? You have done things to me that should never be done." 10 And Abimelek asked Abraham, "What was your reason for doing this?"

11 Abraham replied, "I said to myself, 'There is surely no fear of God in this place, and they will kill me because of my wife.' 12 Besides, she really is my sister, the daughter of my father though not of my mother; and she became my wife. 13 And when God had me wander from my father's household, I said to her, 'This is how you can show your love to me: Everywhere we go, say of me, "He is my brother." ' "

14 Then Abimelek brought sheep and cattle and male and female slaves and gave them to Abraham, and he returned Sarah his wife to him. 15 And Abimelek said, "My land is before you; live wherever you like."

16 To Sarah he said, "I am giving your brother a thousand shekels[a] of silver. This is to cover the offense against you before all who are with you; you are completely vindicated."

17 Then Abraham prayed to God, and God healed Abimelek, his wife and his female slaves so they could have children again, 18 for the LORD had kept all the women in Abimelek's household from conceiving because of Abraham's wife Sarah.

The Birth of Isaac

21 Now the LORD was gracious to Sarah as he had said, and the LORD did for Sarah what he had promised. 2 Sarah became pregnant and bore a son to Abraham in his old age, at the very time God had promised him. 3 Abraham gave the name Isaac[b] to the son Sarah bore him. 4 When his son Isaac was eight days old, Abraham circumcised him, as God commanded him. 5 Abraham was a hundred years old when his son Isaac was born to him.

6 Sarah said, "God has brought me laughter, and everyone who hears about this will laugh with me." 7 And she added, "Who would have said to Abraham that Sarah would nurse children? Yet I have borne him a son in his old age."

Hagar and Ishmael Sent Away

8 The child grew and was weaned, and on the day Isaac was weaned Abraham held a great feast. 9 But Sarah saw that the son whom Hagar the Egyptian had borne to Abraham was mocking, 10 and she said to Abraham, "Get rid of that slave woman and her son, for that woman's son will never share in the inheritance with my son Isaac."

11 The matter distressed Abraham greatly because it concerned his son. 12 But God said to him, "Do not be so distressed about the boy and your slave woman. Listen to whatever Sarah tells you, because it is through Isaac that your offspring[c] will be reckoned. 13 I will make the son of the slave into a nation also, because he is your offspring."

14 Early the next morning Abraham took some food and a skin of water and gave them to Hagar. He set them on her shoulders and then sent her off with the boy. She went on her way and wandered in the Desert of Beersheba.

15 When the water in the skin was gone, she put the boy under one of the bushes. 16 Then she went off and sat down about a bowshot away, for she thought, "I cannot watch the boy die." And as she sat there, she[d] began to sob.

17 God heard the boy crying, and the angel of God called to Hagar from heaven and said to her, "What is the matter, Hagar? Do not be afraid; God has heard the boy crying as he lies there. 18 Lift the boy up and take him by the hand, for I will make him into a great nation."

19 Then God opened her eyes and she saw a well of water. So she went and filled the skin with water and gave the boy a drink.

20 God was with the boy as he grew up. He lived in the desert and became an archer. 21 While he was living in the Desert of Paran, his mother got a wife for him from Egypt.

[a] *16* That is, about 25 pounds or about 12 kilograms [b] *3* *Isaac* means *he laughs.* [c] *12* Or *seed*
[d] *16* Hebrew; Septuagint *the child*

The Treaty at Beersheba

22 At that time Abimelek and Phicol the commander of his forces said to Abraham, "God is with you in everything you do. 23 Now swear to me here before God that you will not deal falsely with me or my children or my descendants. Show to me and the country where you now reside as a foreigner the same kindness I have shown to you."

24 Abraham said, "I swear it."

25 Then Abraham complained to Abimelek about a well of water that Abimelek's servants had seized. 26 But Abimelek said, "I don't know who has done this. You did not tell me, and I heard about it only today."

27 So Abraham brought sheep and cattle and gave them to Abimelek, and the two men made a treaty. 28 Abraham set apart seven ewe lambs from the flock, 29 and Abimelek asked Abraham, "What is the meaning of these seven ewe lambs you have set apart by themselves?"

30 He replied, "Accept these seven lambs from my hand as a witness that I dug this well."

31 So that place was called Beersheba,[a] because the two men swore an oath there.

32 After the treaty had been made at Beersheba, Abimelek and Phicol the commander of his forces returned to the land of the Philistines. 33 Abraham planted a tamarisk tree in Beersheba, and there he called on the name of the LORD, the Eternal God. 34 And Abraham stayed in the land of the Philistines for a long time.

Abraham Tested

22 Some time later God tested Abraham. He said to him, "Abraham!"

"Here I am," he replied.

2 Then God said, "Take your son, your only son, whom you love—Isaac—and go to the region of Moriah. Sacrifice him there as a burnt offering on a mountain I will show you."

3 Early the next morning Abraham got up and loaded his donkey. He took with him two of his servants and his son Isaac. When he had cut enough wood for the burnt offering, he set out for the place God had told him about. 4 On the third day Abraham looked up and saw the place in the distance. 5 He said to his servants, "Stay here with the donkey while I and the boy go over there. We will worship and then we will come back to you."

6 Abraham took the wood for the burnt offering and placed it on his son Isaac, and he himself carried the fire and the knife. As the two of them went on together, 7 Isaac spoke up and said to his father Abraham, "Father?"

"Yes, my son?" Abraham replied.

"The fire and wood are here," Isaac said, "but where is the lamb for the burnt offering?"

8 Abraham answered, "God himself will provide the lamb for the burnt offering, my son." And the two of them went on together.

9 When they reached the place God had told him about, Abraham built an altar there and arranged the wood on it. He bound his son Isaac and laid him on the altar, on top of the wood. 10 Then he reached out his hand and took the knife to slay his son. 11 But the angel of the LORD called out to him from heaven, "Abraham! Abraham!"

"Here I am," he replied.

12 "Do not lay a hand on the boy," he said. "Do not do anything to him. Now I know that you fear God, because you have not withheld from me your son, your only son."

13 Abraham looked up and there in a thicket he saw a ram[b] caught by its horns. He went over and took the ram and sacrificed it as a burnt offering instead of his son. 14 So Abraham called that place The LORD Will Provide. And to this day it is said, "On the mountain of the LORD it will be provided."

15 The angel of the LORD called to Abraham from heaven a second time 16 and said, "I swear by myself, declares the LORD, that because you have done this and have not withheld your son, your only son, 17 I will surely bless you and make your descendants as numerous as the stars in the sky and as the sand on the seashore. Your descendants will take possession of the cities of their enemies, 18 and through your offspring[c] all nations on earth will be blessed,[d] because you have obeyed me."

19 Then Abraham returned to his servants, and they set off together for Beersheba. And Abraham stayed in Beersheba.

[a] *31 Beersheba* can mean *well of seven* and *well of the oath.* [b] *13* Many manuscripts of the Masoretic Text, Samaritan Pentateuch, Septuagint and Syriac; most manuscripts of the Masoretic Text *a ram behind him* [c] *18* Or *seed* [d] *18* Or *and all nations on earth will use the name of your offspring in blessings* (see 48:20)

Nahor's Sons

20 Some time later Abraham was told, "Milkah is also a mother; she has borne sons to your brother Nahor: 21 Uz the firstborn, Buz his brother, Kemuel (the father of Aram), 22 Kesed, Hazo, Pildash, Jidlaph and Bethuel." 23 Bethuel became the father of Rebekah. Milkah bore these eight sons to Abraham's brother Nahor. 24 His concubine, whose name was Reumah, also had sons: Tebah, Gaham, Tahash and Maakah.

The Death of Sarah

23 Sarah lived to be a hundred and twenty-seven years old. 2 She died at Kiriath Arba (that is, Hebron) in the land of Canaan, and Abraham went to mourn for Sarah and to weep over her.

3 Then Abraham rose from beside his dead wife and spoke to the Hittites.[a] He said, 4 "I am a foreigner and stranger among you. Sell me some property for a burial site here so I can bury my dead."

5 The Hittites replied to Abraham, 6 "Sir, listen to us. You are a mighty prince among us. Bury your dead in the choicest of our tombs. None of us will refuse you his tomb for burying your dead."

7 Then Abraham rose and bowed down before the people of the land, the Hittites. 8 He said to them, "If you are willing to let me bury my dead, then listen to me and intercede with Ephron son of Zohar on my behalf 9 so he will sell me the cave of Machpelah, which belongs to him and is at the end of his field. Ask him to sell it to me for the full price as a burial site among you."

10 Ephron the Hittite was sitting among his people and he replied to Abraham in the hearing of all the Hittites who had come to the gate of his city. 11 "No, my lord," he said. "Listen to me; I give[b] you the field, and I give[b] you the cave that is in it. I give[b] it to you in the presence of my people. Bury your dead."

12 Again Abraham bowed down before the people of the land 13 and he said to Ephron in their hearing, "Listen to me, if you will. I will pay the price of the field. Accept it from me so I can bury my dead there."

14 Ephron answered Abraham, 15 "Listen to me, my lord; the land is worth four hundred shekels[c] of silver, but what is that between you and me? Bury your dead."

16 Abraham agreed to Ephron's terms and weighed out for him the price he had named in the hearing of the Hittites: four hundred shekels of silver, according to the weight current among the merchants.

17 So Ephron's field in Machpelah near Mamre—both the field and the cave in it, and all the trees within the borders of the field—was deeded 18 to Abraham as his property in the presence of all the Hittites who had come to the gate of the city. 19 Afterward Abraham buried his wife Sarah in the cave in the field of Machpelah near Mamre (which is at Hebron) in the land of Canaan. 20 So the field and the cave in it were deeded to Abraham by the Hittites as a burial site.

Isaac and Rebekah

24 Abraham was now very old, and the LORD had blessed him in every way. 2 He said to the senior servant in his household, the one in charge of all that he had, "Put your hand under my thigh. 3 I want you to swear by the LORD, the God of heaven and the God of earth, that you will not get a wife for my son from the daughters of the Canaanites, among whom I am living, 4 but will go to my country and my own relatives and get a wife for my son Isaac."

5 The servant asked him, "What if the woman is unwilling to come back with me to this land? Shall I then take your son back to the country you came from?"

6 "Make sure that you do not take my son back there," Abraham said. 7 "The LORD, the God of heaven, who brought me out of my father's household and my native land and who spoke to me and promised me on oath, saying, 'To your offspring[d] I will give this land'—he will send his angel before you so that you can get a wife for my son from there. 8 If the woman is unwilling to come back with you, then you will be released from this oath of mine. Only do not take my son back there." 9 So the servant put his hand under the thigh of his master Abraham and swore an oath to him concerning this matter.

10 Then the servant left, taking with him ten of his master's camels loaded with all kinds of good things from his master. He set

[a] *3* Or *the descendants of Heth*; also in verses 5, 7, 10, 16, 18 and 20 [b] *11* Or *sell* [c] *15* That is, about 10 pounds or about 4.6 kilograms [d] *7* Or *seed*

out for Aram Naharaim[a] and made his way to the town of Nahor. 11 He had the camels kneel down near the well outside the town; it was toward evening, the time the women go out to draw water.

12 Then he prayed, "LORD, God of my master Abraham, make me successful today, and show kindness to my master Abraham. 13 See, I am standing beside this spring, and the daughters of the townspeople are coming out to draw water. 14 May it be that when I say to a young woman, 'Please let down your jar that I may have a drink,' and she says, 'Drink, and I'll water your camels too'—let her be the one you have chosen for your servant Isaac. By this I will know that you have shown kindness to my master."

15 Before he had finished praying, Rebekah came out with her jar on her shoulder. She was the daughter of Bethuel son of Milkah, who was the wife of Abraham's brother Nahor. 16 The woman was very beautiful, a virgin; no man had ever slept with her. She went down to the spring, filled her jar and came up again.

17 The servant hurried to meet her and said, "Please give me a little water from your jar."

18 "Drink, my lord," she said, and quickly lowered the jar to her hands and gave him a drink.

19 After she had given him a drink, she said, "I'll draw water for your camels too, until they have had enough to drink." 20 So she quickly emptied her jar into the trough, ran back to the well to draw more water, and drew enough for all his camels. 21 Without saying a word, the man watched her closely to learn whether or not the LORD had made his journey successful.

22 When the camels had finished drinking, the man took out a gold nose ring weighing a beka[b] and two gold bracelets weighing ten shekels.[c] 23 Then he asked, "Whose daughter are you? Please tell me, is there room in your father's house for us to spend the night?"

24 She answered him, "I am the daughter of Bethuel, the son that Milkah bore to Nahor." 25 And she added, "We have plenty of straw and fodder, as well as room for you to spend the night."

26 Then the man bowed down and worshiped the LORD, 27 saying, "Praise be to the LORD, the God of my master Abraham, who has not abandoned his kindness and faithfulness to my master. As for me, the LORD has led me on the journey to the house of my master's relatives."

28 The young woman ran and told her mother's household about these things. 29 Now Rebekah had a brother named Laban, and he hurried out to the man at the spring. 30 As soon as he had seen the nose ring, and the bracelets on his sister's arms, and had heard Rebekah tell what the man said to her, he went out to the man and found him standing by the camels near the spring. 31 "Come, you who are blessed by the LORD," he said. "Why are you standing out here? I have prepared the house and a place for the camels."

32 So the man went to the house, and the camels were unloaded. Straw and fodder were brought for the camels, and water for him and his men to wash their feet. 33 Then food was set before him, but he said, "I will not eat until I have told you what I have to say."

"Then tell us," Laban said.

34 So he said, "I am Abraham's servant. 35 The LORD has blessed my master abundantly, and he has become wealthy. He has given him sheep and cattle, silver and gold, male and female servants, and camels and donkeys. 36 My master's wife Sarah has borne him a son in her old age, and he has given him everything he owns. 37 And my master made me swear an oath, and said, 'You must not get a wife for my son from the daughters of the Canaanites, in whose land I live, 38 but go to my father's family and to my own clan, and get a wife for my son.'

39 "Then I asked my master, 'What if the woman will not come back with me?'

40 "He replied, 'The LORD, before whom I have walked faithfully, will send his angel with you and make your journey a success, so that you can get a wife for my son from my own clan and from my father's family. 41 You will be released from my oath if, when you go to my clan, they refuse to give her to you—then you will be released from my oath.'

42 "When I came to the spring today, I said, 'LORD, God of my master Abraham, if you will, please grant success to the journey on which I have come. 43 See, I am standing beside this spring. If a young woman comes

[a] *10* That is, Northwest Mesopotamia [b] *22* That is, about 1/5 ounce or about 5.7 grams [c] *22* That is, about 4 ounces or about 115 grams

out to draw water and I say to her, “Please let
me drink a little water from your jar,” 44 and
if she says to me, “Drink, and I’ll draw water
for your camels too,” let her be the one the
LORD has chosen for my master’s son.’

45 “Before I finished praying in my heart,
Rebekah came out, with her jar on her shoul-
der. She went down to the spring and drew
water, and I said to her, ‘Please give me a
drink.’

46 “She quickly lowered her jar from her
shoulder and said, ‘Drink, and I’ll water your
camels too.’ So I drank, and she watered the
camels also.

47 “I asked her, ‘Whose daughter are you?’

“She said, ‘The daughter of Bethuel son of
Nahor, whom Milkah bore to him.’

“Then I put the ring in her nose and the
bracelets on her arms, 48 and I bowed down
and worshiped the LORD. I praised the LORD,
the God of my master Abraham, who had led
me on the right road to get the granddaugh-
ter of my master’s brother for his son. 49 Now
if you will show kindness and faithfulness
to my master, tell me; and if not, tell me, so I
may know which way to turn.”

50 Laban and Bethuel answered, “This is
from the LORD; we can say nothing to you
one way or the other. 51 Here is Rebekah; take
her and go, and let her become the wife of
your master’s son, as the LORD has directed.”

52 When Abraham’s servant heard what
they said, he bowed down to the ground be-
fore the LORD. 53 Then the servant brought out
gold and silver jewelry and articles of cloth-
ing and gave them to Rebekah; he also gave
costly gifts to her brother and to her mother.
54 Then he and the men who were with him
ate and drank and spent the night there.

When they got up the next morning, he
said, “Send me on my way to my master.”

55 But her brother and her mother replied,
“Let the young woman remain with us ten
days or so; then you[a] may go.”

56 But he said to them, “Do not detain me,
now that the LORD has granted success to my
journey. Send me on my way so I may go to
my master.”

57 Then they said, “Let’s call the young
woman and ask her about it.” 58 So they
called Rebekah and asked her, “Will you go
with this man?”

“I will go,” she said.

59 So they sent their sister Rebekah on her
way, along with her nurse and Abraham’s
servant and his men. 60 And they blessed Re-
bekah and said to her,

“Our sister, may you increase
  to thousands upon thousands;
may your offspring possess
  the cities of their enemies.”

61 Then Rebekah and her attendants got
ready and mounted the camels and went
back with the man. So the servant took Re-
bekah and left.

62 Now Isaac had come from Beer Lahai
Roi, for he was living in the Negev. 63 He went
out to the field one evening to meditate,[b] and
as he looked up, he saw camels approaching.
64 Rebekah also looked up and saw Isaac. She
got down from her camel 65 and asked the
servant, “Who is that man in the field com-
ing to meet us?”

“He is my master,” the servant answered.
So she took her veil and covered herself.

66 Then the servant told Isaac all he had
done. 67 Isaac brought her into the tent of
his mother Sarah, and he married Rebekah.
So she became his wife, and he loved her;
and Isaac was comforted after his mother’s
death.

The Death of Abraham

25 Abraham had taken another wife,
whose name was Keturah. 2 She bore
him Zimran, Jokshan, Medan, Midian, Ish-
bak and Shuah. 3 Jokshan was the father of
Sheba and Dedan; the descendants of De-
dan were the Ashurites, the Letushites and
the Leummites. 4 The sons of Midian were
Ephah, Epher, Hanok, Abida and Eldaah. All
these were descendants of Keturah.

5 Abraham left everything he owned to
Isaac. 6 But while he was still living, he gave
gifts to the sons of his concubines and sent
them away from his son Isaac to the land of
the east.

7 Abraham lived a hundred and seventy-
five years. 8 Then Abraham breathed his last
and died at a good old age, an old man and
full of years; and he was gathered to his peo-
ple. 9 His sons Isaac and Ishmael buried him
in the cave of Machpelah near Mamre, in the

[a] *55* Or *she* [b] *63* The meaning of the Hebrew for this word is uncertain.

field of Ephron son of Zohar the Hittite, [10]the
field Abraham had bought from the Hit-
tites.[a] There Abraham was buried with his
wife Sarah. [11]After Abraham's death, God
blessed his son Isaac, who then lived near
Beer Lahai Roi.

Ishmael's Sons

[12]This is the account of the family line of
Abraham's son Ishmael, whom Sarah's slave,
Hagar the Egyptian, bore to Abraham.

[13]These are the names of the sons of Ish-
mael, listed in the order of their birth: Neba-
ioth the firstborn of Ishmael, Kedar, Adbeel,
Mibsam, [14]Mishma, Dumah, Massa, [15]Ha-
dad, Tema, Jetur, Naphish and Kedemah.
[16]These were the sons of Ishmael, and these
are the names of the twelve tribal rulers ac-
cording to their settlements and camps.
[17]Ishmael lived a hundred and thirty-seven
years. He breathed his last and died, and he
was gathered to his people. [18]His descen-
dants settled in the area from Havilah to
Shur, near the eastern border of Egypt, as
you go toward Ashur. And they lived in hos-
tility toward[b] all the tribes related to them.

Jacob and Esau

[19]This is the account of the family line of
Abraham's son Isaac.

Abraham became the father of Isaac,
[20]and Isaac was forty years old when he
married Rebekah daughter of Bethuel the
Aramean from Paddan Aram[c] and sister of
Laban the Aramean.

[21]Isaac prayed to the LORD on behalf of his
wife, because she was childless. The LORD
answered his prayer, and his wife Rebekah
became pregnant. [22]The babies jostled each
other within her, and she said, "Why is this
happening to me?" So she went to inquire of
the LORD.

[23]The LORD said to her,

"Two nations are in your womb,
and two peoples from within you will
be separated;
one people will be stronger than the
other,
and the older will serve the younger."

[24]When the time came for her to give birth,
there were twin boys in her womb. [25]The first
to come out was red, and his whole body was
like a hairy garment; so they named him
Esau.[d] [26]After this, his brother came out,
with his hand grasping Esau's heel; so he was
named Jacob.[e] Isaac was sixty years old when
Rebekah gave birth to them.

[27]The boys grew up, and Esau became
a skillful hunter, a man of the open coun-
try, while Jacob was content to stay at home
among the tents. [28]Isaac, who had a taste for
wild game, loved Esau, but Rebekah loved
Jacob.

[29]Once when Jacob was cooking some
stew, Esau came in from the open country,
famished. [30]He said to Jacob, "Quick, let me
have some of that red stew! I'm famished!"
(That is why he was also called Edom.[f])

[31]Jacob replied, "First sell me your birth-
right."

[32]"Look, I am about to die," Esau said.
"What good is the birthright to me?"

[33]But Jacob said, "Swear to me first." So he
swore an oath to him, selling his birthright
to Jacob.

[34]Then Jacob gave Esau some bread and
some lentil stew. He ate and drank, and then
got up and left.

So Esau despised his birthright.

Isaac and Abimelek

26 Now there was a famine in the land—
besides the previous famine in Abra-
ham's time—and Isaac went to Abimelek
king of the Philistines in Gerar. [2]The LORD
appeared to Isaac and said, "Do not go down
to Egypt; live in the land where I tell you to
live. [3]Stay in this land for a while, and I will
be with you and will bless you. For to you
and your descendants I will give all these
lands and will confirm the oath I swore to
your father Abraham. [4]I will make your de-
scendants as numerous as the stars in the
sky and will give them all these lands, and
through your offspring[g] all nations on earth
will be blessed,[h] [5]because Abraham obeyed
me and did everything I required of him,
keeping my commands, my decrees and my
instructions." [6]So Isaac stayed in Gerar.

[a] *10* Or *the descendants of Heth* [b] *18* Or *lived to the east of* [c] *20* That is, Northwest Mesopotamia
[d] *25* *Esau* may mean *hairy.* [e] *26* *Jacob* means *he grasps the heel,* a Hebrew idiom for *he deceives.*
[f] *30* *Edom* means *red.* [g] *4* Or *seed* [h] *4* Or *and all nations on earth will use the name of your offspring in blessings* (see 48:20)

7 When the men of that place asked him
about his wife, he said, "She is my sister," be-
cause he was afraid to say, "She is my wife."
He thought, "The men of this place might
kill me on account of Rebekah, because she
is beautiful."

8 When Isaac had been there a long time,
Abimelek king of the Philistines looked
down from a window and saw Isaac caress-
ing his wife Rebekah. 9 So Abimelek sum-
moned Isaac and said, "She is really your
wife! Why did you say, 'She is my sister'?"

Isaac answered him, "Because I thought I
might lose my life on account of her."

10 Then Abimelek said, "What is this you
have done to us? One of the men might well
have slept with your wife, and you would
have brought guilt upon us."

11 So Abimelek gave orders to all the peo-
ple: "Anyone who harms this man or his wife
shall surely be put to death."

12 Isaac planted crops in that land and the
same year reaped a hundredfold, because
the LORD blessed him. 13 The man became
rich, and his wealth continued to grow until
he became very wealthy. 14 He had so many
flocks and herds and servants that the Phi-
listines envied him. 15 So all the wells that his
father's servants had dug in the time of his
father Abraham, the Philistines stopped up,
filling them with earth.

16 Then Abimelek said to Isaac, "Move
away from us; you have become too power-
ful for us."

17 So Isaac moved away from there and
encamped in the Valley of Gerar, where he
settled. 18 Isaac reopened the wells that had
been dug in the time of his father Abraham,
which the Philistines had stopped up after
Abraham died, and he gave them the same
names his father had given them.

19 Isaac's servants dug in the valley and
discovered a well of fresh water there. 20 But
the herders of Gerar quarreled with those
of Isaac and said, "The water is ours!" So he
named the well Esek,[a] because they disput-
ed with him. 21 Then they dug another well,
but they quarreled over that one also; so he
named it Sitnah.[b] 22 He moved on from there
and dug another well, and no one quarreled
over it. He named it Rehoboth,[c] saying, "Now
the LORD has given us room and we will
flourish in the land."

23 From there he went up to Beersheba.
24 That night the LORD appeared to him and
said, "I am the God of your father Abraham.
Do not be afraid, for I am with you; I will
bless you and will increase the number of
your descendants for the sake of my servant
Abraham."

25 Isaac built an altar there and called on
the name of the LORD. There he pitched his
tent, and there his servants dug a well.

26 Meanwhile, Abimelek had come to him
from Gerar, with Ahuzzath his personal ad-
viser and Phicol the commander of his forc-
es. 27 Isaac asked them, "Why have you come
to me, since you were hostile to me and sent
me away?"

28 They answered, "We saw clearly that the
LORD was with you; so we said, 'There ought
to be a sworn agreement between us' — be-
tween us and you. Let us make a treaty with
you 29 that you will do us no harm, just as we
did not harm you but always treated you well
and sent you away peacefully. And now you
are blessed by the LORD."

30 Isaac then made a feast for them, and
they ate and drank. 31 Early the next morning
the men swore an oath to each other. Then
Isaac sent them on their way, and they went
away peacefully.

32 That day Isaac's servants came and told
him about the well they had dug. They said,
"We've found water!" 33 He called it Shibah,[d]
and to this day the name of the town has
been Beersheba.[e]

Jacob Takes Esau's Blessing

34 When Esau was forty years old, he mar-
ried Judith daughter of Beeri the Hittite, and
also Basemath daughter of Elon the Hittite.
35 They were a source of grief to Isaac and Re-
bekah.

27 When Isaac was old and his eyes
were so weak that he could no longer
see, he called for Esau his older son and said
to him, "My son."

"Here I am," he answered.

2 Isaac said, "I am now an old man and
don't know the day of my death. 3 Now then,
get your equipment — your quiver and bow —

[a] 20 *Esek* means *dispute.* [b] 21 *Sitnah* means *opposition.* [c] 22 *Rehoboth* means *room.* [d] 33 *Shibah* can mean *oath* or *seven.* [e] 33 *Beersheba* can mean *well of the oath* and *well of seven.*

and go out to the open country to hunt some wild game for me. [4]Prepare me the kind of tasty food I like and bring it to me to eat, so that I may give you my blessing before I die."

[5]Now Rebekah was listening as Isaac spoke to his son Esau. When Esau left for the open country to hunt game and bring it back, [6]Rebekah said to her son Jacob, "Look, I overheard your father say to your brother Esau, [7]'Bring me some game and prepare me some tasty food to eat, so that I may give you my blessing in the presence of the LORD before I die.' [8]Now, my son, listen carefully and do what I tell you: [9]Go out to the flock and bring me two choice young goats, so I can prepare some tasty food for your father, just the way he likes it. [10]Then take it to your father to eat, so that he may give you his blessing before he dies."

[11]Jacob said to Rebekah his mother, "But my brother Esau is a hairy man while I have smooth skin. [12]What if my father touches me? I would appear to be tricking him and would bring down a curse on myself rather than a blessing."

[13]His mother said to him, "My son, let the curse fall on me. Just do what I say; go and get them for me."

[14]So he went and got them and brought them to his mother, and she prepared some tasty food, just the way his father liked it. [15]Then Rebekah took the best clothes of Esau her older son, which she had in the house, and put them on her younger son Jacob. [16]She also covered his hands and the smooth part of his neck with the goatskins. [17]Then she handed to her son Jacob the tasty food and the bread she had made.

[18]He went to his father and said, "My father."

"Yes, my son," he answered. "Who is it?"

[19]Jacob said to his father, "I am Esau your firstborn. I have done as you told me. Please sit up and eat some of my game, so that you may give me your blessing."

[20]Isaac asked his son, "How did you find it so quickly, my son?"

"The LORD your God gave me success," he replied.

[21]Then Isaac said to Jacob, "Come near so I can touch you, my son, to know whether you really are my son Esau or not."

[22]Jacob went close to his father Isaac, who touched him and said, "The voice is the voice of Jacob, but the hands are the hands of Esau." [23]He did not recognize him, for his hands were hairy like those of his brother Esau; so he proceeded to bless him. [24]"Are you really my son Esau?" he asked.

"I am," he replied.

[25]Then he said, "My son, bring me some of your game to eat, so that I may give you my blessing."

Jacob brought it to him and he ate; and he brought some wine and he drank. [26]Then his father Isaac said to him, "Come here, my son, and kiss me."

[27]So he went to him and kissed him. When Isaac caught the smell of his clothes, he blessed him and said,

"Ah, the smell of my son
  is like the smell of a field
  that the LORD has blessed.
[28]May God give you heaven's dew
  and earth's richness —
  an abundance of grain and new wine.
[29]May nations serve you
  and peoples bow down to you.
Be lord over your brothers,
  and may the sons of your mother bow
    down to you.
May those who curse you be cursed
  and those who bless you be blessed."

[30]After Isaac finished blessing him, and Jacob had scarcely left his father's presence, his brother Esau came in from hunting. [31]He too prepared some tasty food and brought it to his father. Then he said to him, "My father, please sit up and eat some of my game, so that you may give me your blessing."

[32]His father Isaac asked him, "Who are you?"

"I am your son," he answered, "your firstborn, Esau."

[33]Isaac trembled violently and said, "Who was it, then, that hunted game and brought it to me? I ate it just before you came and I blessed him — and indeed he will be blessed!"

[34]When Esau heard his father's words, he burst out with a loud and bitter cry and said to his father, "Bless me — me too, my father!"

[35]But he said, "Your brother came deceitfully and took your blessing."

[36]Esau said, "Isn't he rightly named Jacob[a]? This is the second time he has taken

[a] 36 *Jacob* means *he grasps the heel*, a Hebrew idiom for *he takes advantage of* or *he deceives.*

advantage of me: He took my birthright, and
now he's taken my blessing!" Then he asked,
"Haven't you reserved any blessing for me?"
37 Isaac answered Esau, "I have made him
lord over you and have made all his relatives
his servants, and I have sustained him with
grain and new wine. So what can I possibly
do for you, my son?"
38 Esau said to his father, "Do you have
only one blessing, my father? Bless me too,
my father!" Then Esau wept aloud.
39 His father Isaac answered him,

"Your dwelling will be
 away from the earth's richness,
 away from the dew of heaven above.
40 You will live by the sword
 and you will serve your brother.
But when you grow restless,
 you will throw his yoke
 from off your neck."

41 Esau held a grudge against Jacob be-
cause of the blessing his father had given
him. He said to himself, "The days of mourn-
ing for my father are near; then I will kill my
brother Jacob."
42 When Rebekah was told what her older
son Esau had said, she sent for her younger
son Jacob and said to him, "Your brother
Esau is planning to avenge himself by kill-
ing you. 43 Now then, my son, do what I say:
Flee at once to my brother Laban in Harran.
44 Stay with him for a while until your broth-
er's fury subsides. 45 When your brother is no
longer angry with you and forgets what you
did to him, I'll send word for you to come
back from there. Why should I lose both of
you in one day?"
46 Then Rebekah said to Isaac, "I'm dis-
gusted with living because of these Hittite
women. If Jacob takes a wife from among the
women of this land, from Hittite women like
these, my life will not be worth living."

28 So Isaac called for Jacob and blessed
him. Then he commanded him: "Do
not marry a Canaanite woman. 2 Go at once
to Paddan Aram,[a] to the house of your moth-
er's father Bethuel. Take a wife for yourself
there, from among the daughters of Laban,
your mother's brother. 3 May God Almighty[b]
bless you and make you fruitful and increase
your numbers until you become a commu-
nity of peoples. 4 May he give you and your
descendants the blessing given to Abraham,
so that you may take possession of the land
where you now reside as a foreigner, the land
God gave to Abraham." 5 Then Isaac sent
Jacob on his way, and he went to Paddan
Aram, to Laban son of Bethuel the Aramean,
the brother of Rebekah, who was the mother
of Jacob and Esau.
6 Now Esau learned that Isaac had blessed
Jacob and had sent him to Paddan Aram to
take a wife from there, and that when he
blessed him he commanded him, "Do not
marry a Canaanite woman," 7 and that Jacob
had obeyed his father and mother and had
gone to Paddan Aram. 8 Esau then realized
how displeasing the Canaanite women were
to his father Isaac; 9 so he went to Ishmael
and married Mahalath, the sister of Neba-
ioth and daughter of Ishmael son of Abra-
ham, in addition to the wives he already had.

Jacob's Dream at Bethel

10 Jacob left Beersheba and set out for Har-
ran. 11 When he reached a certain place, he
stopped for the night because the sun had set.
Taking one of the stones there, he put it un-
der his head and lay down to sleep. 12 He had
a dream in which he saw a stairway resting
on the earth, with its top reaching to heaven,
and the angels of God were ascending and
descending on it. 13 There above it[c] stood the
LORD, and he said: "I am the LORD, the God of
your father Abraham and the God of Isaac. I
will give you and your descendants the land
on which you are lying. 14 Your descendants
will be like the dust of the earth, and you will
spread out to the west and to the east, to the
north and to the south. All peoples on earth
will be blessed through you and your off-
spring.[d] 15 I am with you and will watch over
you wherever you go, and I will bring you
back to this land. I will not leave you until I
have done what I have promised you."
16 When Jacob awoke from his sleep, he
thought, "Surely the LORD is in this place,
and I was not aware of it." 17 He was afraid
and said, "How awesome is this place! This
is none other than the house of God; this is
the gate of heaven."

[a] 2 That is, Northwest Mesopotamia; also in verses 5, 6 and 7 [b] 3 Hebrew *El-Shaddai* [c] 13 Or *There beside him* [d] 14 Or *will use your name and the name of your offspring in blessings* (see 48:20)

18 Early the next morning Jacob took the stone he had placed under his head and set it up as a pillar and poured oil on top of it. 19 He called that place Bethel,[a] though the city used to be called Luz.

20 Then Jacob made a vow, saying, "If God will be with me and will watch over me on this journey I am taking and will give me food to eat and clothes to wear 21 so that I return safely to my father's household, then the LORD[b] will be my God 22 and[c] this stone that I have set up as a pillar will be God's house, and of all that you give me I will give you a tenth."

Jacob Arrives in Paddan Aram

29 Then Jacob continued on his journey and came to the land of the eastern peoples. 2 There he saw a well in the open country, with three flocks of sheep lying near it because the flocks were watered from that well. The stone over the mouth of the well was large. 3 When all the flocks were gathered there, the shepherds would roll the stone away from the well's mouth and water the sheep. Then they would return the stone to its place over the mouth of the well.

4 Jacob asked the shepherds, "My brothers, where are you from?"

"We're from Harran," they replied.

5 He said to them, "Do you know Laban, Nahor's grandson?"

"Yes, we know him," they answered.

6 Then Jacob asked them, "Is he well?"

"Yes, he is," they said, "and here comes his daughter Rachel with the sheep."

7 "Look," he said, "the sun is still high; it is not time for the flocks to be gathered. Water the sheep and take them back to pasture."

8 "We can't," they replied, "until all the flocks are gathered and the stone has been rolled away from the mouth of the well. Then we will water the sheep."

9 While he was still talking with them, Rachel came with her father's sheep, for she was a shepherd. 10 When Jacob saw Rachel daughter of his uncle Laban, and Laban's sheep, he went over and rolled the stone away from the mouth of the well and watered his uncle's sheep. 11 Then Jacob kissed Rachel and began to weep aloud. 12 He had told Rachel that he was a relative of her father and a son of Rebekah. So she ran and told her father.

13 As soon as Laban heard the news about Jacob, his sister's son, he hurried to meet him. He embraced him and kissed him and brought him to his home, and there Jacob told him all these things. 14 Then Laban said to him, "You are my own flesh and blood."

Jacob Marries Leah and Rachel

After Jacob had stayed with him for a whole month, 15 Laban said to him, "Just because you are a relative of mine, should you work for me for nothing? Tell me what your wages should be."

16 Now Laban had two daughters; the name of the older was Leah, and the name of the younger was Rachel. 17 Leah had weak[d] eyes, but Rachel had a lovely figure and was beautiful. 18 Jacob was in love with Rachel and said, "I'll work for you seven years in return for your younger daughter Rachel."

19 Laban said, "It's better that I give her to you than to some other man. Stay here with me." 20 So Jacob served seven years to get Rachel, but they seemed like only a few days to him because of his love for her.

21 Then Jacob said to Laban, "Give me my wife. My time is completed, and I want to make love to her."

22 So Laban brought together all the people of the place and gave a feast. 23 But when evening came, he took his daughter Leah and brought her to Jacob, and Jacob made love to her. 24 And Laban gave his servant Zilpah to his daughter as her attendant.

25 When morning came, there was Leah! So Jacob said to Laban, "What is this you have done to me? I served you for Rachel, didn't I? Why have you deceived me?"

26 Laban replied, "It is not our custom here to give the younger daughter in marriage before the older one. 27 Finish this daughter's bridal week; then we will give you the younger one also, in return for another seven years of work."

28 And Jacob did so. He finished the week with Leah, and then Laban gave him his daughter Rachel to be his wife. 29 Laban gave his servant Bilhah to his daughter Rachel as her attendant. 30 Jacob made love to Rachel also, and his love for Rachel was greater than

[a] 19 *Bethel* means *house of God.* [b] 20,21 Or *Since God . . . father's household, the* LORD
[c] 21,22 Or *household, and the* LORD *will be my God,* [22]*then* [d] 17 Or *delicate*

his love for Leah. And he worked for Laban another seven years.

Jacob's Children

31 When the LORD saw that Leah was not loved, he enabled her to conceive, but Rachel remained childless. 32 Leah became pregnant and gave birth to a son. She named him Reuben,[a] for she said, "It is because the LORD has seen my misery. Surely my husband will love me now."

33 She conceived again, and when she gave birth to a son she said, "Because the LORD heard that I am not loved, he gave me this one too." So she named him Simeon.[b]

34 Again she conceived, and when she gave birth to a son she said, "Now at last my husband will become attached to me, because I have borne him three sons." So he was named Levi.[c]

35 She conceived again, and when she gave birth to a son she said, "This time I will praise the LORD." So she named him Judah.[d] Then she stopped having children.

30 When Rachel saw that she was not bearing Jacob any children, she became jealous of her sister. So she said to Jacob, "Give me children, or I'll die!"

2 Jacob became angry with her and said, "Am I in the place of God, who has kept you from having children?"

3 Then she said, "Here is Bilhah, my servant. Sleep with her so that she can bear children for me and I too can build a family through her."

4 So she gave him her servant Bilhah as a wife. Jacob slept with her, 5 and she became pregnant and bore him a son. 6 Then Rachel said, "God has vindicated me; he has listened to my plea and given me a son." Because of this she named him Dan.[e]

7 Rachel's servant Bilhah conceived again and bore Jacob a second son. 8 Then Rachel said, "I have had a great struggle with my sister, and I have won." So she named him Naphtali.[f]

9 When Leah saw that she had stopped having children, she took her servant Zilpah and gave her to Jacob as a wife. 10 Leah's servant Zilpah bore Jacob a son. 11 Then Leah said, "What good fortune!"[g] So she named him Gad.[h]

12 Leah's servant Zilpah bore Jacob a second son. 13 Then Leah said, "How happy I am! The women will call me happy." So she named him Asher.[i]

14 During wheat harvest, Reuben went out into the fields and found some mandrake plants, which he brought to his mother Leah. Rachel said to Leah, "Please give me some of your son's mandrakes."

15 But she said to her, "Wasn't it enough that you took away my husband? Will you take my son's mandrakes too?"

"Very well," Rachel said, "he can sleep with you tonight in return for your son's mandrakes."

16 So when Jacob came in from the fields that evening, Leah went out to meet him. "You must sleep with me," she said. "I have hired you with my son's mandrakes." So he slept with her that night.

17 God listened to Leah, and she became pregnant and bore Jacob a fifth son. 18 Then Leah said, "God has rewarded me for giving my servant to my husband." So she named him Issachar.[j]

19 Leah conceived again and bore Jacob a sixth son. 20 Then Leah said, "God has presented me with a precious gift. This time my husband will treat me with honor, because I have borne him six sons." So she named him Zebulun.[k]

21 Some time later she gave birth to a daughter and named her Dinah.

22 Then God remembered Rachel; he listened to her and enabled her to conceive. 23 She became pregnant and gave birth to a son and said, "God has taken away my disgrace." 24 She named him Joseph,[l] and said, "May the LORD add to me another son."

Jacob's Flocks Increase

25 After Rachel gave birth to Joseph, Jacob said to Laban, "Send me on my way so I can go back to my own homeland. 26 Give me my

[a] 32 *Reuben* sounds like the Hebrew for *he has seen my misery*; the name means *see, a son.* [b] 33 *Simeon* probably means *one who hears.* [c] 34 *Levi* sounds like and may be derived from the Hebrew for *attached.* [d] 35 *Judah* sounds like and may be derived from the Hebrew for *praise.* [e] 6 *Dan* here means *he has vindicated.* [f] 8 *Naphtali* means *my struggle.* [g] 11 Or *"A troop is coming!"* [h] 11 *Gad* can mean *good fortune* or *a troop.* [i] 13 *Asher* means *happy.* [j] 18 *Issachar* sounds like the Hebrew for *reward.* [k] 20 *Zebulun* probably means *honor.* [l] 24 *Joseph* means *may he add.*

MIGHTY TO SAVE

Ben Fielding, Morgan Reuben

Everyone needs compassion
Love that's never failing
Let mercy fall on me
Everyone needs forgiveness
The kindness of a Savior
The hope of nations

Savior
He can move the mountains
My God is mighty to save
He is mighty to save
Forever
Author of salvation
He rose and conquered the grave
Jesus conquered the grave

So take me as you find me
All my fears and failures
Fill my life again
I give my life to follow
Everything I believe in
Now I surrender

Shine your light
And let the whole world see
We're singing for the glory
Of the risen King Jesus

THE INSPIRATION

The LORD your God is with you, the Mighty Warrior who saves. He will take great delight in you; in his love he will no longer rebuke you, but will rejoice over you with singing. —Zephaniah 3:17

Read also: Ezekiel 38:20; Hebrews 2:10

BEHIND THE SONG

In addition to understanding one's sinfulness and desperate need for salvation, it's important for people to realize that Jesus is absolutely qualified and empowered to save them. As that truth becomes known not only to the mind but also to the heart, it should rightly lead them to a place of worship. A person who doesn't marvel at the saving power of God may not be fully aware of the desperate condition they are in. Likewise, a person who doesn't fully understand the perfection and power of Christ may lack faith in his power to save them.

Sometimes we must get to the end of our own efforts before God will step in and put wind in our sails. Ben Fielding and Reuben Morgan, both worship leaders and songwriters from Hillsong Church in Australia, were sitting in Ben's kitchen working on a song idea that just wasn't coming together when they crafted "Mighty to Save."

"We had hit a dead end with it," Ben recalls. Suddenly a melody came to them and they sang it, along with the words adapted from Zephaniah 3. Morgan remembers them singing the phrase "mighty to save" over and over again. "I just wanted to repeat it again and again," he adds.

Selah

Have you studied the nature of Jesus and all of the ways God perfected him so that he could accomplish our salvation? If not, the book of Hebrews is an excellent place to start. Recall some of the aspects of Jesus' character or some of his accomplishments that cause you to feel at peace in his hands. Write these thoughts on this page or in your journal.

Fielding then stepped in and insisted they write more lyrics. The result was a simple song with profound meaning.

"Mighty to Save" first outlines every human's need for salvation, then details how perfectly qualified Jesus is to offer that salvation. Surely the God who can move mountains and conquer death, and who holds the very keys of justice and hope in his hands can handle whatever challenges might face us in this life and deliver us safely into the next.

In his very short book, the prophet Zephaniah first detailed wayward Israel's desperate condition. The people had turned their backs on God and would experience great suffering as a result. The end of this dire letter, however, promises that the Lord wants to save them and is definitely up to the task.

Centuries later the writer of Hebrews explained exactly how Jesus fit into the story of God and the rescuing of his people. Hebrews 2 begins with a warning to pay close attention to what is being said. The book then moves into several chapters relating to the sacrifice of Christ and his absolute power to provide the salvation he promises (see Hebrews 3 - 8).

wives and children, for whom I have served you, and I will be on my way. You know how much work I've done for you."

[27]But Laban said to him, "If I have found favor in your eyes, please stay. I have learned by divination that the LORD has blessed me because of you." [28]He added, "Name your wages, and I will pay them."

[29]Jacob said to him, "You know how I have worked for you and how your livestock has fared under my care. [30]The little you had before I came has increased greatly, and the LORD has blessed you wherever I have been. But now, when may I do something for my own household?"

[31]"What shall I give you?" he asked.

"Don't give me anything," Jacob replied. "But if you will do this one thing for me, I will go on tending your flocks and watching over them: [32]Let me go through all your flocks today and remove from them every speckled or spotted sheep, every dark-colored lamb and every spotted or speckled goat. They will be my wages. [33]And my honesty will testify for me in the future, whenever you check on the wages you have paid me. Any goat in my possession that is not speckled or spotted, or any lamb that is not dark-colored, will be considered stolen."

[34]"Agreed," said Laban. "Let it be as you have said." [35]That same day he removed all the male goats that were streaked or spotted, and all the speckled or spotted female goats (all that had white on them) and all the dark-colored lambs, and he placed them in the care of his sons. [36]Then he put a three-day journey between himself and Jacob, while Jacob continued to tend the rest of Laban's flocks.

[37]Jacob, however, took fresh-cut branches from poplar, almond and plane trees and made white stripes on them by peeling the bark and exposing the white inner wood of the branches. [38]Then he placed the peeled branches in all the watering troughs, so that they would be directly in front of the flocks when they came to drink. When the flocks were in heat and came to drink, [39]they mated in front of the branches. And they bore young that were streaked or speckled or spotted. [40]Jacob set apart the young of the flock by themselves, but made the rest face the streaked and dark-colored animals that belonged to Laban. Thus he made separate flocks for himself and did not put them with Laban's animals. [41]Whenever the stronger females were in heat, Jacob would place the branches in the troughs in front of the animals so they would mate near the branches, [42]but if the animals were weak, he would not place them there. So the weak animals went to Laban and the strong ones to Jacob. [43]In this way the man grew exceedingly prosperous and came to own large flocks, and female and male servants, and camels and donkeys.

Jacob Flees From Laban

31 Jacob heard that Laban's sons were saying, "Jacob has taken everything our father owned and has gained all this wealth from what belonged to our father." [2]And Jacob noticed that Laban's attitude toward him was not what it had been.

[3]Then the LORD said to Jacob, "Go back to the land of your fathers and to your relatives, and I will be with you."

[4]So Jacob sent word to Rachel and Leah to come out to the fields where his flocks were. [5]He said to them, "I see that your father's attitude toward me is not what it was before, but the God of my father has been with me. [6]You know that I've worked for your father with all my strength, [7]yet your father has cheated me by changing my wages ten times. However, God has not allowed him to harm me. [8]If he said, 'The speckled ones will be your wages,' then all the flocks gave birth to speckled young; and if he said, 'The streaked ones will be your wages,' then all the flocks bore streaked young. [9]So God has taken away your father's livestock and has given them to me.

[10]"In breeding season I once had a dream in which I looked up and saw that the male goats mating with the flock were streaked, speckled or spotted. [11]The angel of God said to me in the dream, 'Jacob.' I answered, 'Here I am.' [12]And he said, 'Look up and see that all the male goats mating with the flock are streaked, speckled or spotted, for I have seen all that Laban has been doing to you. [13]I am the God of Bethel, where you anointed a pillar and where you made a vow to me. Now leave this land at once and go back to your native land.' "

[14]Then Rachel and Leah replied, "Do we still have any share in the inheritance of our

father's estate? [15]Does he not regard us as foreigners? Not only has he sold us, but he has used up what was paid for us. [16]Surely all the wealth that God took away from our father belongs to us and our children. So do whatever God has told you."

[17]Then Jacob put his children and his wives on camels, [18]and he drove all his livestock ahead of him, along with all the goods he had accumulated in Paddan Aram,[a] to go to his father Isaac in the land of Canaan.

[19]When Laban had gone to shear his sheep, Rachel stole her father's household gods. [20]Moreover, Jacob deceived Laban the Aramean by not telling him he was running away. [21]So he fled with all he had, crossed the Euphrates River, and headed for the hill country of Gilead.

Laban Pursues Jacob

[22]On the third day Laban was told that Jacob had fled. [23]Taking his relatives with him, he pursued Jacob for seven days and caught up with him in the hill country of Gilead. [24]Then God came to Laban the Aramean in a dream at night and said to him, "Be careful not to say anything to Jacob, either good or bad."

[25]Jacob had pitched his tent in the hill country of Gilead when Laban overtook him, and Laban and his relatives camped there too. [26]Then Laban said to Jacob, "What have you done? You've deceived me, and you've carried off my daughters like captives in war. [27]Why did you run off secretly and deceive me? Why didn't you tell me, so I could send you away with joy and singing to the music of timbrels and harps? [28]You didn't even let me kiss my grandchildren and my daughters goodbye. You have done a foolish thing. [29]I have the power to harm you; but last night the God of your father said to me, 'Be careful not to say anything to Jacob, either good or bad.' [30]Now you have gone off because you longed to return to your father's household. But why did you steal my gods?"

[31]Jacob answered Laban, "I was afraid, because I thought you would take your daughters away from me by force. [32]But if you find anyone who has your gods, that person shall not live. In the presence of our relatives, see for yourself whether there is anything of yours here with me; and if so, take it." Now Jacob did not know that Rachel had stolen the gods.

[33]So Laban went into Jacob's tent and into Leah's tent and into the tent of the two female servants, but he found nothing. After he came out of Leah's tent, he entered Rachel's tent. [34]Now Rachel had taken the household gods and put them inside her camel's saddle and was sitting on them. Laban searched through everything in the tent but found nothing.

[35]Rachel said to her father, "Don't be angry, my lord, that I cannot stand up in your presence; I'm having my period." So he searched but could not find the household gods.

[36]Jacob was angry and took Laban to task. "What is my crime?" he asked Laban. "How have I wronged you that you hunt me down? [37]Now that you have searched through all my goods, what have you found that belongs to your household? Put it here in front of your relatives and mine, and let them judge between the two of us.

[38]"I have been with you for twenty years now. Your sheep and goats have not miscarried, nor have I eaten rams from your flocks. [39]I did not bring you animals torn by wild beasts; I bore the loss myself. And you demanded payment from me for whatever was stolen by day or night. [40]This was my situation: The heat consumed me in the daytime and the cold at night, and sleep fled from my eyes. [41]It was like this for the twenty years I was in your household. I worked for you fourteen years for your two daughters and six years for your flocks, and you changed my wages ten times. [42]If the God of my father, the God of Abraham and the Fear of Isaac, had not been with me, you would surely have sent me away empty-handed. But God has seen my hardship and the toil of my hands, and last night he rebuked you."

[43]Laban answered Jacob, "The women are my daughters, the children are my children, and the flocks are my flocks. All you see is mine. Yet what can I do today about these daughters of mine, or about the children they have borne? [44]Come now, let's make a covenant, you and I, and let it serve as a witness between us."

[a] *18* That is, Northwest Mesopotamia

45 So Jacob took a stone and set it up as a
pillar. 46 He said to his relatives, "Gather
some stones." So they took stones and piled
them in a heap, and they ate there by the
heap. 47 Laban called it Jegar Sahadutha, and
Jacob called it Galeed.[a]

48 Laban said, "This heap is a witness be-
tween you and me today." That is why it was
called Galeed. 49 It was also called Mizpah,[b]
because he said, "May the LORD keep watch
between you and me when we are away from
each other. 50 If you mistreat my daughters or
if you take any wives besides my daughters,
even though no one is with us, remember
that God is a witness between you and me."

51 Laban also said to Jacob, "Here is this
heap, and here is this pillar I have set up be-
tween you and me. 52 This heap is a witness,
and this pillar is a witness, that I will not go
past this heap to your side to harm you and
that you will not go past this heap and pil-
lar to my side to harm me. 53 May the God of
Abraham and the God of Nahor, the God of
their father, judge between us."

So Jacob took an oath in the name of the
Fear of his father Isaac. 54 He offered a sacri-
fice there in the hill country and invited his
relatives to a meal. After they had eaten, they
spent the night there.

55 Early the next morning Laban kissed
his grandchildren and his daughters and
blessed them. Then he left and returned
home.[c]

Jacob Prepares to Meet Esau

32[d] Jacob also went on his way, and the
angels of God met him. 2 When Ja-
cob saw them, he said, "This is the camp of
God!" So he named that place Mahanaim.[e]

3 Jacob sent messengers ahead of him to
his brother Esau in the land of Seir, the coun-
try of Edom. 4 He instructed them: "This is
what you are to say to my lord Esau: 'Your
servant Jacob says, I have been staying with
Laban and have remained there till now. 5 I
have cattle and donkeys, sheep and goats,
male and female servants. Now I am send-
ing this message to my lord, that I may find
favor in your eyes.' "

6 When the messengers returned to Jacob,
they said, "We went to your brother Esau,
and now he is coming to meet you, and four
hundred men are with him."

7 In great fear and distress Jacob divid-
ed the people who were with him into two
groups,[f] and the flocks and herds and cam-
els as well. 8 He thought, "If Esau comes and
attacks one group,[g] the group[g] that is left
may escape."

9 Then Jacob prayed, "O God of my father
Abraham, God of my father Isaac, LORD, you
who said to me, 'Go back to your country
and your relatives, and I will make you pros-
per,' 10 I am unworthy of all the kindness and
faithfulness you have shown your servant. I
had only my staff when I crossed this Jordan,
but now I have become two camps. 11 Save
me, I pray, from the hand of my brother Esau,
for I am afraid he will come and attack me,
and also the mothers with their children.
12 But you have said, 'I will surely make you
prosper and will make your descendants
like the sand of the sea, which cannot be
counted.' "

13 He spent the night there, and from what
he had with him he selected a gift for his
brother Esau: 14 two hundred female goats
and twenty male goats, two hundred ewes
and twenty rams, 15 thirty female camels
with their young, forty cows and ten bulls,
and twenty female donkeys and ten male
donkeys. 16 He put them in the care of his
servants, each herd by itself, and said to his
servants, "Go ahead of me, and keep some
space between the herds."

17 He instructed the one in the lead: "When
my brother Esau meets you and asks, 'Who
do you belong to, and where are you going,
and who owns all these animals in front of
you?' 18 then you are to say, 'They belong to
your servant Jacob. They are a gift sent to my
lord Esau, and he is coming behind us.' "

19 He also instructed the second, the third
and all the others who followed the herds:
"You are to say the same thing to Esau when
you meet him. 20 And be sure to say, 'Your
servant Jacob is coming behind us.' " For he
thought, "I will pacify him with these gifts I
am sending on ahead; later, when I see him,
perhaps he will receive me." 21 So Jacob's
gifts went on ahead of him, but he himself
spent the night in the camp.

[a] 47 The Aramaic *Jegar Sahadutha* and the Hebrew *Galeed* both mean *witness heap.* [b] 49 *Mizpah* means *watchtower.* [c] 55 In Hebrew texts this verse (31:55) is numbered 32:1. [d] In Hebrew texts 32:1-32 is numbered 32:2-33. [e] 2 *Mahanaim* means *two camps.* [f] 7 Or *camps* [g] 8 Or *camp*

Jacob Wrestles With God

22 That night Jacob got up and took his two
wives, his two female servants and his elev-
en sons and crossed the ford of the Jabbok.
23 After he had sent them across the stream,
he sent over all his possessions. 24 So Jacob
was left alone, and a man wrestled with
him till daybreak. 25 When the man saw that
he could not overpower him, he touched
the socket of Jacob's hip so that his hip was
wrenched as he wrestled with the man.
26 Then the man said, "Let me go, for it is day-
break."

But Jacob replied, "I will not let you go un-
less you bless me."

27 The man asked him, "What is your
name?"

"Jacob," he answered.

28 Then the man said, "Your name will
no longer be Jacob, but Israel,[a] because you
have struggled with God and with humans
and have overcome."

29 Jacob said, "Please tell me your name."

But he replied, "Why do you ask my
name?" Then he blessed him there.

30 So Jacob called the place Peniel,[b] say-
ing, "It is because I saw God face to face, and
yet my life was spared."

31 The sun rose above him as he passed Pe-
niel,[c] and he was limping because of his hip.
32 Therefore to this day the Israelites do not
eat the tendon attached to the socket of the
hip, because the socket of Jacob's hip was
touched near the tendon.

Jacob Meets Esau

33 Jacob looked up and there was Esau,
coming with his four hundred men;
so he divided the children among Leah,
Rachel and the two female servants. 2 He
put the female servants and their children
in front, Leah and her children next, and
Rachel and Joseph in the rear. 3 He him-
self went on ahead and bowed down to the
ground seven times as he approached his
brother.

4 But Esau ran to meet Jacob and em-
braced him; he threw his arms around his
neck and kissed him. And they wept. 5 Then
Esau looked up and saw the women and
children. "Who are these with you?" he
asked.

Jacob answered, "They are the children
God has graciously given your servant."

6 Then the female servants and their chil-
dren approached and bowed down. 7 Next,
Leah and her children came and bowed
down. Last of all came Joseph and Rachel,
and they too bowed down.

8 Esau asked, "What's the meaning of all
these flocks and herds I met?"

"To find favor in your eyes, my lord," he
said.

9 But Esau said, "I already have plenty, my
brother. Keep what you have for yourself."

10 "No, please!" said Jacob. "If I have found
favor in your eyes, accept this gift from me.
For to see your face is like seeing the face of
God, now that you have received me favor-
ably. 11 Please accept the present that was
brought to you, for God has been gracious to
me and I have all I need." And because Jacob
insisted, Esau accepted it.

12 Then Esau said, "Let us be on our way;
I'll accompany you."

13 But Jacob said to him, "My lord knows
that the children are tender and that I must
care for the ewes and cows that are nurs-
ing their young. If they are driven hard just
one day, all the animals will die. 14 So let
my lord go on ahead of his servant, while I
move along slowly at the pace of the flocks
and herds before me and the pace of the chil-
dren, until I come to my lord in Seir."

15 Esau said, "Then let me leave some of
my men with you."

"But why do that?" Jacob asked. "Just let
me find favor in the eyes of my lord."

16 So that day Esau started on his way back
to Seir. 17 Jacob, however, went to Sukkoth,
where he built a place for himself and made
shelters for his livestock. That is why the
place is called Sukkoth.[d]

18 After Jacob came from Paddan Aram,[e]
he arrived safely at the city of Shechem in
Canaan and camped within sight of the city.
19 For a hundred pieces of silver,[f] he bought
from the sons of Hamor, the father of She-
chem, the plot of ground where he pitched
his tent. 20 There he set up an altar and called
it El Elohe Israel.[g]

[a] 28 *Israel* probably means *he struggles with God.* [b] 30 *Peniel* means *face of God.* [c] 31 Hebrew *Penuel,* a variant of *Peniel* [d] 17 *Sukkoth* means *shelters.* [e] 18 That is, Northwest Mesopotamia [f] 19 Hebrew *hundred kesitahs;* a kesitah was a unit of money of unknown weight and value. [g] 20 *El Elohe Israel* can mean *El is the God of Israel* or *mighty is the God of Israel.*

Dinah and the Shechemites

34 Now Dinah, the daughter Leah had borne to Jacob, went out to visit the women of the land. 2When Shechem son of Hamor the Hivite, the ruler of that area, saw her, he took her and raped her. 3His heart was drawn to Dinah daughter of Jacob; he loved the young woman and spoke tenderly to her. 4And Shechem said to his father Hamor, "Get me this girl as my wife."

5When Jacob heard that his daughter Dinah had been defiled, his sons were in the fields with his livestock; so he did nothing about it until they came home.

6Then Shechem's father Hamor went out to talk with Jacob. 7Meanwhile, Jacob's sons had come in from the fields as soon as they heard what had happened. They were shocked and furious, because Shechem had done an outrageous thing in[a] Israel by sleeping with Jacob's daughter—a thing that should not be done.

8But Hamor said to them, "My son Shechem has his heart set on your daughter. Please give her to him as his wife. 9Intermarry with us; give us your daughters and take our daughters for yourselves. 10You can settle among us; the land is open to you. Live in it, trade[b] in it, and acquire property in it."

11Then Shechem said to Dinah's father and brothers, "Let me find favor in your eyes, and I will give you whatever you ask. 12Make the price for the bride and the gift I am to bring as great as you like, and I'll pay whatever you ask me. Only give me the young woman as my wife."

13Because their sister Dinah had been defiled, Jacob's sons replied deceitfully as they spoke to Shechem and his father Hamor. 14They said to them, "We can't do such a thing; we can't give our sister to a man who is not circumcised. That would be a disgrace to us. 15We will enter into an agreement with you on one condition only: that you become like us by circumcising all your males. 16Then we will give you our daughters and take your daughters for ourselves. We'll settle among you and become one people with you. 17But if you will not agree to be circumcised, we'll take our sister and go."

18Their proposal seemed good to Hamor and his son Shechem. 19The young man, who was the most honored of all his father's family, lost no time in doing what they said, because he was delighted with Jacob's daughter. 20So Hamor and his son Shechem went to the gate of their city to speak to the men of their city. 21"These men are friendly toward us," they said. "Let them live in our land and trade in it; the land has plenty of room for them. We can marry their daughters and they can marry ours. 22But the men will agree to live with us as one people only on the condition that our males be circumcised, as they themselves are. 23Won't their livestock, their property and all their other animals become ours? So let us agree to their terms, and they will settle among us."

24All the men who went out of the city gate agreed with Hamor and his son Shechem, and every male in the city was circumcised.

25Three days later, while all of them were still in pain, two of Jacob's sons, Simeon and Levi, Dinah's brothers, took their swords and attacked the unsuspecting city, killing every male. 26They put Hamor and his son Shechem to the sword and took Dinah from Shechem's house and left. 27The sons of Jacob came upon the dead bodies and looted the city where[c] their sister had been defiled. 28They seized their flocks and herds and donkeys and everything else of theirs in the city and out in the fields. 29They carried off all their wealth and all their women and children, taking as plunder everything in the houses.

30Then Jacob said to Simeon and Levi, "You have brought trouble on me by making me obnoxious to the Canaanites and Perizzites, the people living in this land. We are few in number, and if they join forces against me and attack me, I and my household will be destroyed."

31But they replied, "Should he have treated our sister like a prostitute?"

Jacob Returns to Bethel

35 Then God said to Jacob, "Go up to Bethel and settle there, and build an altar there to God, who appeared to you when you were fleeing from your brother Esau."

2So Jacob said to his household and to all who were with him, "Get rid of the foreign

Or *against* [b] 10 Or *move about freely*; also in verse 21 [c] 27 Or *because*

gods you have with you, and purify your-
selves and change your clothes. 3Then come,
let us go up to Bethel, where I will build an
altar to God, who answered me in the day of
my distress and who has been with me wher-
ever I have gone." 4So they gave Jacob all the
foreign gods they had and the rings in their
ears, and Jacob buried them under the oak at
Shechem. 5Then they set out, and the terror
of God fell on the towns all around them so
that no one pursued them.

6Jacob and all the people with him came
to Luz (that is, Bethel) in the land of Canaan.
7There he built an altar, and he called the
place El Bethel,[a] because it was there that
God revealed himself to him when he was
fleeing from his brother.

8Now Deborah, Rebekah's nurse, died
and was buried under the oak outside Beth-
el. So it was named Allon Bakuth.[b]

9After Jacob returned from Paddan
Aram,[c] God appeared to him again and
blessed him. 10God said to him, "Your name
is Jacob,[d] but you will no longer be called Ja-
cob; your name will be Israel.[e]" So he named
him Israel.

11And God said to him, "I am God Al-
mighty[f]; be fruitful and increase in number.
A nation and a community of nations will
come from you, and kings will be among
your descendants. 12The land I gave to Abra-
ham and Isaac I also give to you, and I will
give this land to your descendants after
you." 13Then God went up from him at the
place where he had talked with him.

14Jacob set up a stone pillar at the place
where God had talked with him, and he
poured out a drink offering on it; he also
poured oil on it. 15Jacob called the place
where God had talked with him Bethel.[g]

The Deaths of Rachel and Isaac

16Then they moved on from Bethel. While
they were still some distance from Ephrath,
Rachel began to give birth and had great dif-
ficulty. 17And as she was having great diffi-
culty in childbirth, the midwife said to her,
"Don't despair, for you have another son."
18As she breathed her last — for she was dy-
ing — she named her son Ben-Oni.[h] But his
father named him Benjamin.[i]

19So Rachel died and was buried on the
way to Ephrath (that is, Bethlehem). 20Over
her tomb Jacob set up a pillar, and to this day
that pillar marks Rachel's tomb.

21Israel moved on again and pitched his
tent beyond Migdal Eder. 22While Israel was
living in that region, Reuben went in and
slept with his father's concubine Bilhah, and
Israel heard of it.

Jacob had twelve sons:

23The sons of Leah:
  Reuben the firstborn of Jacob,
  Simeon, Levi, Judah, Issachar and Zebulun.
24The sons of Rachel:
  Joseph and Benjamin.
25The sons of Rachel's servant Bilhah:
  Dan and Naphtali.
26The sons of Leah's servant Zilpah:
  Gad and Asher.

These were the sons of Jacob, who were
born to him in Paddan Aram.

27Jacob came home to his father Isaac
in Mamre, near Kiriath Arba (that is, He-
bron), where Abraham and Isaac had stayed.
28Isaac lived a hundred and eighty years.
29Then he breathed his last and died and was
gathered to his people, old and full of years.
And his sons Esau and Jacob buried him.

Esau's Descendants

36 This is the account of the family line of Esau (that is, Edom).

2Esau took his wives from the wom-
en of Canaan: Adah daughter of Elon
the Hittite, and Oholibamah daughter
of Anah and granddaughter of Zibeon
the Hivite — 3also Basemath daughter
of Ishmael and sister of Nebaioth.

4Adah bore Eliphaz to Esau, Base-
math bore Reuel, 5and Oholibamah
bore Jeush, Jalam and Korah. These
were the sons of Esau, who were born to
him in Canaan.

6Esau took his wives and sons and
daughters and all the members of his
household, as well as his livestock and
all his other animals and all the goods
he had acquired in Canaan, and moved

[a] 7 *El Bethel* means *God of Bethel.* [b] 8 *Allon Bakuth* means *oak of weeping.* [c] 9 That is, Northwest Mesopotamia; also in verse 26 [d] 10 *Jacob* means *he grasps the heel,* a Hebrew idiom for *he deceives.* [e] 10 *Israel* probably means *he struggles with God.* [f] 11 Hebrew *El-Shaddai* [g] 15 *Bethel* means *house of God.* [h] 18 *Ben-Oni* means *son of my trouble.* [i] 18 *Benjamin* means *son of my right hand.*

to a land some distance from his broth-
er Jacob. 7 Their possessions were too
great for them to remain together; the
land where they were staying could
not support them both because of their
livestock. 8 So Esau (that is, Edom) set-
tled in the hill country of Seir.

9 This is the account of the family line of
Esau the father of the Edomites in the hill
country of Seir.

10 These are the names of Esau's sons:
Eliphaz, the son of Esau's wife Adah,
and Reuel, the son of Esau's wife Bas-
emath.
11 The sons of Eliphaz:
Teman, Omar, Zepho, Gatam and
Kenaz.
12 Esau's son Eliphaz also had a concu-
bine named Timna, who bore him
Amalek. These were grandsons of
Esau's wife Adah.
13 The sons of Reuel:
Nahath, Zerah, Shammah and Miz-
zah. These were grandsons of Esau's
wife Basemath.
14 The sons of Esau's wife Oholibamah
daughter of Anah and granddaughter
of Zibeon, whom she bore to Esau:
Jeush, Jalam and Korah.

15 These were the chiefs among Esau's de-
scendants:
The sons of Eliphaz the firstborn of
Esau:
Chiefs Teman, Omar, Zepho, Kenaz,
16 Korah,[a] Gatam and Amalek. These
were the chiefs descended from Eli-
phaz in Edom; they were grandsons
of Adah.
17 The sons of Esau's son Reuel:
Chiefs Nahath, Zerah, Shammah
and Mizzah. These were the chiefs
descended from Reuel in Edom; they
were grandsons of Esau's wife Base-
math.
18 The sons of Esau's wife Oholibamah:
Chiefs Jeush, Jalam and Korah. These
were the chiefs descended from
Esau's wife Oholibamah daughter of
Anah.

19 These were the sons of Esau (that is,
Edom), and these were their chiefs.

20 These were the sons of Seir the Horite,
who were living in the region:
Lotan, Shobal, Zibeon, Anah, 21 Di-
shon, Ezer and Dishan. These sons
of Seir in Edom were Horite chiefs.
22 The sons of Lotan:
Hori and Homam.[b] Timna was Lo-
tan's sister.
23 The sons of Shobal:
Alvan, Manahath, Ebal, Shepho and
Onam.
24 The sons of Zibeon:
Aiah and Anah. This is the Anah
who discovered the hot springs[c] in
the desert while he was grazing the
donkeys of his father Zibeon.
25 The children of Anah:
Dishon and Oholibamah daughter of
Anah.
26 The sons of Dishon[d]:
Hemdan, Eshban, Ithran and Keran.
27 The sons of Ezer:
Bilhan, Zaavan and Akan.
28 The sons of Dishan:
Uz and Aran.
29 These were the Horite chiefs:
Lotan, Shobal, Zibeon, Anah, 30 Di-
shon, Ezer and Dishan. These were
the Horite chiefs, according to their
divisions, in the land of Seir.

The Rulers of Edom

31 These were the kings who reigned in
Edom before any Israelite king reigned:
32 Bela son of Beor became king of Edom.
His city was named Dinhabah.
33 When Bela died, Jobab son of Zerah
from Bozrah succeeded him as king.
34 When Jobab died, Husham from the
land of the Temanites succeeded
him as king.
35 When Husham died, Hadad son of Be-
dad, who defeated Midian in the
country of Moab, succeeded him as
king. His city was named Avith.
36 When Hadad died, Samlah from Mas-
rekah succeeded him as king.
37 When Samlah died, Shaul from Reho-

[a] *16* Masoretic Text; Samaritan Pentateuch (also verse 11 and 1 Chron. 1:36) does not have *Korah.*
[b] *22* Hebrew *Hemam,* a variant of *Homam* (see 1 Chron. 1:39) [c] *24* Vulgate; Syriac *discovered water;* the meaning of the Hebrew for this word is uncertain. [d] *26* Hebrew *Dishan,* a variant of *Dishon*

both on the river succeeded him as king.
38 When Shaul died, Baal-Hanan son of Akbor succeeded him as king.
39 When Baal-Hanan son of Akbor died, Hadad[a] succeeded him as king. His city was named Pau, and his wife's name was Mehetabel daughter of Matred, the daughter of Me-Zahab.

40 These were the chiefs descended from Esau, by name, according to their clans and regions:
Timna, Alvah, Jetheth, 41 Oholibamah, Elah, Pinon, 42 Kenaz, Teman, Mibzar, 43 Magdiel and Iram. These were the chiefs of Edom, according to their settlements in the land they occupied.

This is the family line of Esau, the father of the Edomites.

Joseph's Dreams

37 Jacob lived in the land where his father had stayed, the land of Canaan.

2 This is the account of Jacob's family line.

Joseph, a young man of seventeen, was tending the flocks with his brothers, the sons of Bilhah and the sons of Zilpah, his father's wives, and he brought their father a bad report about them.

3 Now Israel loved Joseph more than any of his other sons, because he had been born to him in his old age; and he made an ornate[b] robe for him. 4 When his brothers saw that their father loved him more than any of them, they hated him and could not speak a kind word to him.

5 Joseph had a dream, and when he told it to his brothers, they hated him all the more.
6 He said to them, "Listen to this dream I had: 7 We were binding sheaves of grain out in the field when suddenly my sheaf rose and stood upright, while your sheaves gathered around mine and bowed down to it."

8 His brothers said to him, "Do you intend to reign over us? Will you actually rule us?" And they hated him all the more because of his dream and what he had said.

9 Then he had another dream, and he told it to his brothers. "Listen," he said, "I had another dream, and this time the sun and moon and eleven stars were bowing down to me."

10 When he told his father as well as his brothers, his father rebuked him and said, "What is this dream you had? Will your mother and I and your brothers actually come and bow down to the ground before you?" 11 His brothers were jealous of him, but his father kept the matter in mind.

Joseph Sold by His Brothers

12 Now his brothers had gone to graze their father's flocks near Shechem, 13 and Israel said to Joseph, "As you know, your brothers are grazing the flocks near Shechem. Come, I am going to send you to them."

"Very well," he replied.

14 So he said to him, "Go and see if all is well with your brothers and with the flocks, and bring word back to me." Then he sent him off from the Valley of Hebron.

When Joseph arrived at Shechem, 15 a man found him wandering around in the fields and asked him, "What are you looking for?"

16 He replied, "I'm looking for my brothers. Can you tell me where they are grazing their flocks?"

17 "They have moved on from here," the man answered. "I heard them say, 'Let's go to Dothan.'"

So Joseph went after his brothers and found them near Dothan. 18 But they saw him in the distance, and before he reached them, they plotted to kill him.

19 "Here comes that dreamer!" they said to each other. 20 "Come now, let's kill him and throw him into one of these cisterns and say that a ferocious animal devoured him. Then we'll see what comes of his dreams."

21 When Reuben heard this, he tried to rescue him from their hands. "Let's not take his life," he said. 22 "Don't shed any blood. Throw him into this cistern here in the wilderness, but don't lay a hand on him." Reuben said this to rescue him from them and take him back to his father.

23 So when Joseph came to his brothers, they stripped him of his robe — the ornate robe he was wearing — 24 and they took him

[a] 39 Many manuscripts of the Masoretic Text, Samaritan Pentateuch and Syriac (see also 1 Chron. 1:50); most manuscripts of the Masoretic Text *Hadar* [b] 3 The meaning of the Hebrew for this word is uncertain; also in verses 23 and 32.

and threw him into the cistern. The cistern
was empty; there was no water in it.
25 As they sat down to eat their meal, they
looked up and saw a caravan of Ishmael-
ites coming from Gilead. Their camels were
loaded with spices, balm and myrrh, and
they were on their way to take them down to
Egypt.
26 Judah said to his brothers, "What will
we gain if we kill our brother and cover up
his blood? 27 Come, let's sell him to the Ish-
maelites and not lay our hands on him; af-
ter all, he is our brother, our own flesh and
blood." His brothers agreed.
28 So when the Midianite merchants came
by, his brothers pulled Joseph up out of the
cistern and sold him for twenty shekels[a] of
silver to the Ishmaelites, who took him to
Egypt.
29 When Reuben returned to the cistern
and saw that Joseph was not there, he tore
his clothes. 30 He went back to his brothers
and said, "The boy isn't there! Where can I
turn now?"
31 Then they got Joseph's robe, slaughtered
a goat and dipped the robe in the blood.
32 They took the ornate robe back to their fa-
ther and said, "We found this. Examine it to
see whether it is your son's robe."
33 He recognized it and said, "It is my son's
robe! Some ferocious animal has devoured
him. Joseph has surely been torn to pieces."
34 Then Jacob tore his clothes, put on sack-
cloth and mourned for his son many days.
35 All his sons and daughters came to com-
fort him, but he refused to be comforted.
"No," he said, "I will continue to mourn until
I join my son in the grave." So his father wept
for him.
36 Meanwhile, the Midianites[b] sold Joseph
in Egypt to Potiphar, one of Pharaoh's offi-
cials, the captain of the guard.

Judah and Tamar

38 At that time, Judah left his brothers
and went down to stay with a man of
Adullam named Hirah. 2 There Judah met
the daughter of a Canaanite man named
Shua. He married her and made love to her;
3 she became pregnant and gave birth to
a son, who was named Er. 4 She conceived
again and gave birth to a son and named
him Onan. 5 She gave birth to still another
son and named him Shelah. It was at Kezib
that she gave birth to him.
6 Judah got a wife for Er, his firstborn, and
her name was Tamar. 7 But Er, Judah's first-
born, was wicked in the LORD's sight; so the
LORD put him to death.
8 Then Judah said to Onan, "Sleep with
your brother's wife and fulfill your duty to
her as a brother-in-law to raise up offspring
for your brother." 9 But Onan knew that the
child would not be his; so whenever he slept
with his brother's wife, he spilled his se-
men on the ground to keep from providing
offspring for his brother. 10 What he did was
wicked in the LORD's sight; so the LORD put
him to death also.
11 Judah then said to his daughter-in-law
Tamar, "Live as a widow in your father's
household until my son Shelah grows up."
For he thought, "He may die too, just like his
brothers." So Tamar went to live in her fa-
ther's household.
12 After a long time Judah's wife, the
daughter of Shua, died. When Judah had
recovered from his grief, he went up to
Timnah, to the men who were shearing his
sheep, and his friend Hirah the Adullamite
went with him.
13 When Tamar was told, "Your father-
in-law is on his way to Timnah to shear his
sheep," 14 she took off her widow's clothes,
covered herself with a veil to disguise her-
self, and then sat down at the entrance to
Enaim, which is on the road to Timnah. For
she saw that, though Shelah had now grown
up, she had not been given to him as his wife.
15 When Judah saw her, he thought she was
a prostitute, for she had covered her face.
16 Not realizing that she was his daughter-in-
law, he went over to her by the roadside and
said, "Come now, let me sleep with you."
"And what will you give me to sleep with
you?" she asked.
17 "I'll send you a young goat from my
flock," he said.
"Will you give me something as a pledge
until you send it?" she asked.
18 He said, "What pledge should I give
you?"
"Your seal and its cord, and the staff in
your hand," she answered. So he gave them

[a] 28 That is, about 8 ounces or about 230 grams [b] 36 Samaritan Pentateuch, Septuagint, Vulgate and
Syriac (see also verse 28); Masoretic Text *Medanites*

to her and slept with her, and she became pregnant by him. 19 After she left, she took off her veil and put on her widow's clothes again.

20 Meanwhile Judah sent the young goat by his friend the Adullamite in order to get his pledge back from the woman, but he did not find her. 21 He asked the men who lived there, "Where is the shrine prostitute who was beside the road at Enaim?"

"There hasn't been any shrine prostitute here," they said.

22 So he went back to Judah and said, "I didn't find her. Besides, the men who lived there said, 'There hasn't been any shrine prostitute here.' "

23 Then Judah said, "Let her keep what she has, or we will become a laughingstock. After all, I did send her this young goat, but you didn't find her."

24 About three months later Judah was told, "Your daughter-in-law Tamar is guilty of prostitution, and as a result she is now pregnant."

Judah said, "Bring her out and have her burned to death!"

25 As she was being brought out, she sent a message to her father-in-law. "I am pregnant by the man who owns these," she said. And she added, "See if you recognize whose seal and cord and staff these are."

26 Judah recognized them and said, "She is more righteous than I, since I wouldn't give her to my son Shelah." And he did not sleep with her again.

27 When the time came for her to give birth, there were twin boys in her womb. 28 As she was giving birth, one of them put out his hand; so the midwife took a scarlet thread and tied it on his wrist and said, "This one came out first." 29 But when he drew back his hand, his brother came out, and she said, "So this is how you have broken out!" And he was named Perez.[a] 30 Then his brother, who had the scarlet thread on his wrist, came out. And he was named Zerah.[b]

Joseph and Potiphar's Wife

39 Now Joseph had been taken down to Egypt. Potiphar, an Egyptian who was one of Pharaoh's officials, the captain of the guard, bought him from the Ishmaelites who had taken him there.

2 The LORD was with Joseph so that he prospered, and he lived in the house of his Egyptian master. 3 When his master saw that the LORD was with him and that the LORD gave him success in everything he did, 4 Joseph found favor in his eyes and became his attendant. Potiphar put him in charge of his household, and he entrusted to his care everything he owned. 5 From the time he put him in charge of his household and of all that he owned, the LORD blessed the household of the Egyptian because of Joseph. The blessing of the LORD was on everything Potiphar had, both in the house and in the field. 6 So Potiphar left everything he had in Joseph's care; with Joseph in charge, he did not concern himself with anything except the food he ate.

Now Joseph was well-built and handsome, 7 and after a while his master's wife took notice of Joseph and said, "Come to bed with me!"

8 But he refused. "With me in charge," he told her, "my master does not concern himself with anything in the house; everything he owns he has entrusted to my care. 9 No one is greater in this house than I am. My master has withheld nothing from me except you, because you are his wife. How then could I do such a wicked thing and sin against God?" 10 And though she spoke to Joseph day after day, he refused to go to bed with her or even be with her.

11 One day he went into the house to attend to his duties, and none of the household servants was inside. 12 She caught him by his cloak and said, "Come to bed with me!" But he left his cloak in her hand and ran out of the house.

13 When she saw that he had left his cloak in her hand and had run out of the house, 14 she called her household servants. "Look," she said to them, "this Hebrew has been brought to us to make sport of us! He came in here to sleep with me, but I screamed. 15 When he heard me scream for help, he left his cloak beside me and ran out of the house."

16 She kept his cloak beside her until his master came home. 17 Then she told him this story: "That Hebrew slave you brought us came to me to make sport of me. 18 But as

[a] 29 *Perez* means *breaking out.* [b] 30 *Zerah* can mean *scarlet* or *brightness.*

soon as I screamed for help, he left his cloak
beside me and ran out of the house."
[19]When his master heard the story his
wife told him, saying, "This is how your
slave treated me," he burned with anger.
[20]Joseph's master took him and put him in
prison, the place where the king's prisoners
were confined.
But while Joseph was there in the pris-
on, [21]the LORD was with him; he showed
him kindness and granted him favor in the
eyes of the prison warden. [22]So the warden
put Joseph in charge of all those held in the
prison, and he was made responsible for all
that was done there. [23]The warden paid no
attention to anything under Joseph's care,
because the LORD was with Joseph and gave
him success in whatever he did.

The Cupbearer and the Baker

40 Some time later, the cupbearer and
the baker of the king of Egypt offend-
ed their master, the king of Egypt. [2]Pharaoh
was angry with his two officials, the chief
cupbearer and the chief baker, [3]and put
them in custody in the house of the cap-
tain of the guard, in the same prison where
Joseph was confined. [4]The captain of the
guard assigned them to Joseph, and he at-
tended them.
After they had been in custody for some
time, [5]each of the two men — the cupbearer
and the baker of the king of Egypt, who were
being held in prison — had a dream the same
night, and each dream had a meaning of its
own.
[6]When Joseph came to them the next
morning, he saw that they were dejected.
[7]So he asked Pharaoh's officials who were
in custody with him in his master's house,
"Why do you look so sad today?"
[8]"We both had dreams," they answered,
"but there is no one to interpret them."
Then Joseph said to them, "Do not in-
terpretations belong to God? Tell me your
dreams."
[9]So the chief cupbearer told Joseph his
dream. He said to him, "In my dream I saw
a vine in front of me, [10]and on the vine were
three branches. As soon as it budded, it blos-
somed, and its clusters ripened into grapes.
[11]Pharaoh's cup was in my hand, and I took
the grapes, squeezed them into Pharaoh's
cup and put the cup in his hand."
[12]"This is what it means," Joseph said to
him. "The three branches are three days.
[13]Within three days Pharaoh will lift up your
head and restore you to your position, and
you will put Pharaoh's cup in his hand, just as
you used to do when you were his cupbearer.
[14]But when all goes well with you, remem-
ber me and show me kindness; mention me
to Pharaoh and get me out of this prison. [15]I
was forcibly carried off from the land of the
Hebrews, and even here I have done nothing
to deserve being put in a dungeon."
[16]When the chief baker saw that Joseph
had given a favorable interpretation, he
said to Joseph, "I too had a dream: On my
head were three baskets of bread.[a] [17]In the
top basket were all kinds of baked goods for
Pharaoh, but the birds were eating them out
of the basket on my head."
[18]"This is what it means," Joseph said.
"The three baskets are three days. [19]With-
in three days Pharaoh will lift off your head
and impale your body on a pole. And the
birds will eat away your flesh."
[20]Now the third day was Pharaoh's birth-
day, and he gave a feast for all his officials.
He lifted up the heads of the chief cupbear-
er and the chief baker in the presence of his
officials: [21]He restored the chief cupbearer
to his position, so that he once again put the
cup into Pharaoh's hand — [22]but he impaled
the chief baker, just as Joseph had said to
them in his interpretation.
[23]The chief cupbearer, however, did not
remember Joseph; he forgot him.

Pharaoh's Dreams

41 When two full years had passed,
Pharaoh had a dream: He was stand-
ing by the Nile, [2]when out of the river there
came up seven cows, sleek and fat, and they
grazed among the reeds. [3]After them, seven
other cows, ugly and gaunt, came up out of
the Nile and stood beside those on the riv-
erbank. [4]And the cows that were ugly and
gaunt ate up the seven sleek, fat cows. Then
Pharaoh woke up.
[5]He fell asleep again and had a second
dream: Seven heads of grain, healthy and
good, were growing on a single stalk. [6]After
them, seven other heads of grain sprouted —

[a] 16 Or *three wicker baskets*

thin and scorched by the east wind. 7The
thin heads of grain swallowed up the seven
healthy, full heads. Then Pharaoh woke up;
it had been a dream.

8In the morning his mind was troubled, so
he sent for all the magicians and wise men of
Egypt. Pharaoh told them his dreams, but no
one could interpret them for him.

9Then the chief cupbearer said to Phar-
aoh, "Today I am reminded of my short-
comings. 10Pharaoh was once angry with
his servants, and he imprisoned me and
the chief baker in the house of the captain
of the guard. 11Each of us had a dream the
same night, and each dream had a meaning
of its own. 12Now a young Hebrew was there
with us, a servant of the captain of the guard.
We told him our dreams, and he interpreted
them for us, giving each man the interpre-
tation of his dream. 13And things turned out
exactly as he interpreted them to us: I was
restored to my position, and the other man
was impaled."

14So Pharaoh sent for Joseph, and he was
quickly brought from the dungeon. When
he had shaved and changed his clothes, he
came before Pharaoh.

15Pharaoh said to Joseph, "I had a dream,
and no one can interpret it. But I have heard
it said of you that when you hear a dream you
can interpret it."

16"I cannot do it," Joseph replied to Phar-
aoh, "but God will give Pharaoh the answer
he desires."

17Then Pharaoh said to Joseph, "In my
dream I was standing on the bank of the
Nile, 18when out of the river there came up
seven cows, fat and sleek, and they grazed
among the reeds. 19After them, seven oth-
er cows came up — scrawny and very ugly
and lean. I had never seen such ugly cows in
all the land of Egypt. 20The lean, ugly cows
ate up the seven fat cows that came up first.
21But even after they ate them, no one could
tell that they had done so; they looked just as
ugly as before. Then I woke up.

22"In my dream I saw seven heads of grain,
full and good, growing on a single stalk. 23Af-
ter them, seven other heads sprouted — with-
ered and thin and scorched by the east wind.
24The thin heads of grain swallowed up the
seven good heads. I told this to the magicians,
but none of them could explain it to me."

25Then Joseph said to Pharaoh, "The
dreams of Pharaoh are one and the same.
God has revealed to Pharaoh what he is
about to do. 26The seven good cows are seven
years, and the seven good heads of grain are
seven years; it is one and the same dream.
27The seven lean, ugly cows that came up af-
terward are seven years, and so are the sev-
en worthless heads of grain scorched by the
east wind: They are seven years of famine.

28"It is just as I said to Pharaoh: God has
shown Pharaoh what he is about to do.
29Seven years of great abundance are com-
ing throughout the land of Egypt, 30but sev-
en years of famine will follow them. Then all
the abundance in Egypt will be forgotten,
and the famine will ravage the land. 31The
abundance in the land will not be remem-
bered, because the famine that follows it
will be so severe. 32The reason the dream
was given to Pharaoh in two forms is that the
matter has been firmly decided by God, and
God will do it soon.

33"And now let Pharaoh look for a discern-
ing and wise man and put him in charge of
the land of Egypt. 34Let Pharaoh appoint
commissioners over the land to take a fifth of
the harvest of Egypt during the seven years
of abundance. 35They should collect all the
food of these good years that are coming
and store up the grain under the authority
of Pharaoh, to be kept in the cities for food.
36This food should be held in reserve for the
country, to be used during the seven years of
famine that will come upon Egypt, so that the
country may not be ruined by the famine."

37The plan seemed good to Pharaoh and
to all his officials. 38So Pharaoh asked them,
"Can we find anyone like this man, one in
whom is the spirit of God[a]?"

39Then Pharaoh said to Joseph, "Since
God has made all this known to you, there is
no one so discerning and wise as you. 40You
shall be in charge of my palace, and all my
people are to submit to your orders. Only
with respect to the throne will I be greater
than you."

Joseph in Charge of Egypt

41So Pharaoh said to Joseph, "I here-
by put you in charge of the whole land of
Egypt." 42Then Pharaoh took his signet ring
from his finger and put it on Joseph's finger.

[a] *38* Or *of the gods*

He dressed him in robes of fine linen and put a gold chain around his neck. [43]He had him ride in a chariot as his second-in-command,[a] and people shouted before him, "Make way[b]!" Thus he put him in charge of the whole land of Egypt.

[44]Then Pharaoh said to Joseph, "I am Pharaoh, but without your word no one will lift hand or foot in all Egypt." [45]Pharaoh gave Joseph the name Zaphenath-Paneah and gave him Asenath daughter of Potiphera, priest of On,[c] to be his wife. And Joseph went throughout the land of Egypt.

[46]Joseph was thirty years old when he entered the service of Pharaoh king of Egypt. And Joseph went out from Pharaoh's presence and traveled throughout Egypt. [47]During the seven years of abundance the land produced plentifully. [48]Joseph collected all the food produced in those seven years of abundance in Egypt and stored it in the cities. In each city he put the food grown in the fields surrounding it. [49]Joseph stored up huge quantities of grain, like the sand of the sea; it was so much that he stopped keeping records because it was beyond measure.

[50]Before the years of famine came, two sons were born to Joseph by Asenath daughter of Potiphera, priest of On. [51]Joseph named his firstborn Manasseh[d] and said, "It is because God has made me forget all my trouble and all my father's household." [52]The second son he named Ephraim[e] and said, "It is because God has made me fruitful in the land of my suffering."

[53]The seven years of abundance in Egypt came to an end, [54]and the seven years of famine began, just as Joseph had said. There was famine in all the other lands, but in the whole land of Egypt there was food. [55]When all Egypt began to feel the famine, the people cried to Pharaoh for food. Then Pharaoh told all the Egyptians, "Go to Joseph and do what he tells you."

[56]When the famine had spread over the whole country, Joseph opened all the storehouses and sold grain to the Egyptians, for the famine was severe throughout Egypt. [57]And all the world came to Egypt to buy grain from Joseph, because the famine was severe everywhere.

Joseph's Brothers Go to Egypt

42 When Jacob learned that there was grain in Egypt, he said to his sons, "Why do you just keep looking at each other?" [2]He continued, "I have heard that there is grain in Egypt. Go down there and buy some for us, so that we may live and not die."

[3]Then ten of Joseph's brothers went down to buy grain from Egypt. [4]But Jacob did not send Benjamin, Joseph's brother, with the others, because he was afraid that harm might come to him. [5]So Israel's sons were among those who went to buy grain, for there was famine in the land of Canaan also.

[6]Now Joseph was the governor of the land, the person who sold grain to all its people. So when Joseph's brothers arrived, they bowed down to him with their faces to the ground. [7]As soon as Joseph saw his brothers, he recognized them, but he pretended to be a stranger and spoke harshly to them. "Where do you come from?" he asked.

"From the land of Canaan," they replied, "to buy food."

[8]Although Joseph recognized his brothers, they did not recognize him. [9]Then he remembered his dreams about them and said to them, "You are spies! You have come to see where our land is unprotected."

[10]"No, my lord," they answered. "Your servants have come to buy food. [11]We are all the sons of one man. Your servants are honest men, not spies."

[12]"No!" he said to them. "You have come to see where our land is unprotected."

[13]But they replied, "Your servants were twelve brothers, the sons of one man, who lives in the land of Canaan. The youngest is now with our father, and one is no more."

[14]Joseph said to them, "It is just as I told you: You are spies! [15]And this is how you will be tested: As surely as Pharaoh lives, you will not leave this place unless your youngest brother comes here. [16]Send one of your number to get your brother; the rest of you will be kept in prison, so that your words may be tested to see if you are telling the truth. If you are not, then as surely as Pharaoh lives, you are spies!" [17]And he put them all in custody for three days.

[18]On the third day, Joseph said to them,

[a] 43 Or *in the chariot of his second-in-command*; or *in his second chariot* [b] 43 Or *Bow down*
[c] 45 That is, Heliopolis; also in verse 50 [d] 51 *Manasseh* sounds like and may be derived from the Hebrew for *forget.* [e] 52 *Ephraim* sounds like the Hebrew for *twice fruitful.*

"Do this and you will live, for I fear God: [19]If you are honest men, let one of your brothers stay here in prison, while the rest of you go and take grain back for your starving households. [20]But you must bring your youngest brother to me, so that your words may be verified and that you may not die." This they proceeded to do.

[21]They said to one another, "Surely we are being punished because of our brother. We saw how distressed he was when he pleaded with us for his life, but we would not listen; that's why this distress has come on us."

[22]Reuben replied, "Didn't I tell you not to sin against the boy? But you wouldn't listen! Now we must give an accounting for his blood." [23]They did not realize that Joseph could understand them, since he was using an interpreter.

[24]He turned away from them and began to weep, but then came back and spoke to them again. He had Simeon taken from them and bound before their eyes.

[25]Joseph gave orders to fill their bags with grain, to put each man's silver back in his sack, and to give them provisions for their journey. After this was done for them, [26]they loaded their grain on their donkeys and left.

[27]At the place where they stopped for the night one of them opened his sack to get feed for his donkey, and he saw his silver in the mouth of his sack. [28]"My silver has been returned," he said to his brothers. "Here it is in my sack."

Their hearts sank and they turned to each other trembling and said, "What is this that God has done to us?"

[29]When they came to their father Jacob in the land of Canaan, they told him all that had happened to them. They said, [30]"The man who is lord over the land spoke harshly to us and treated us as though we were spying on the land. [31]But we said to him, 'We are honest men; we are not spies. [32]We were twelve brothers, sons of one father. One is no more, and the youngest is now with our father in Canaan.'

[33]"Then the man who is lord over the land said to us, 'This is how I will know whether you are honest men: Leave one of your brothers here with me, and take food for your starving households and go. [34]But bring your youngest brother to me so I will know that you are not spies but honest men. Then I will give your brother back to you, and you can trade[a] in the land.' "

[35]As they were emptying their sacks, there in each man's sack was his pouch of silver! When they and their father saw the money pouches, they were frightened. [36]Their father Jacob said to them, "You have deprived me of my children. Joseph is no more and Simeon is no more, and now you want to take Benjamin. Everything is against me!"

[37]Then Reuben said to his father, "You may put both of my sons to death if I do not bring him back to you. Entrust him to my care, and I will bring him back."

[38]But Jacob said, "My son will not go down there with you; his brother is dead and he is the only one left. If harm comes to him on the journey you are taking, you will bring my gray head down to the grave in sorrow."

The Second Journey to Egypt

43 Now the famine was still severe in the land. [2]So when they had eaten all the grain they had brought from Egypt, their father said to them, "Go back and buy us a little more food."

[3]But Judah said to him, "The man warned us solemnly, 'You will not see my face again unless your brother is with you.' [4]If you will send our brother along with us, we will go down and buy food for you. [5]But if you will not send him, we will not go down, because the man said to us, 'You will not see my face again unless your brother is with you.' "

[6]Israel asked, "Why did you bring this trouble on me by telling the man you had another brother?"

[7]They replied, "The man questioned us closely about ourselves and our family. 'Is your father still living?' he asked us. 'Do you have another brother?' We simply answered his questions. How were we to know he would say, 'Bring your brother down here'?"

[8]Then Judah said to Israel his father, "Send the boy along with me and we will go at once, so that we and you and our children may live and not die. [9]I myself will guarantee his safety; you can hold me personally responsible for him. If I do not bring him back to you and set him here before you, I will bear the blame before you all my life. [10]As it

[a] 34 Or *move about freely*

is, if we had not delayed, we could have gone
and returned twice."

11 Then their father Israel said to them,
"If it must be, then do this: Put some of the
best products of the land in your bags and
take them down to the man as a gift — a lit-
tle balm and a little honey, some spices and
myrrh, some pistachio nuts and almonds.
12 Take double the amount of silver with
you, for you must return the silver that was
put back into the mouths of your sacks. Per-
haps it was a mistake. 13 Take your brother
also and go back to the man at once. 14 And
may God Almighty[a] grant you mercy before
the man so that he will let your other broth-
er and Benjamin come back with you. As for
me, if I am bereaved, I am bereaved."

15 So the men took the gifts and double the
amount of silver, and Benjamin also. They
hurried down to Egypt and presented them-
selves to Joseph. 16 When Joseph saw Benja-
min with them, he said to the steward of his
house, "Take these men to my house, slaugh-
ter an animal and prepare a meal; they are to
eat with me at noon."

17 The man did as Joseph told him and took
the men to Joseph's house. 18 Now the men
were frightened when they were taken to his
house. They thought, "We were brought here
because of the silver that was put back into
our sacks the first time. He wants to attack us
and overpower us and seize us as slaves and
take our donkeys."

19 So they went up to Joseph's steward and
spoke to him at the entrance to the house.
20 "We beg your pardon, our lord," they said,
"we came down here the first time to buy
food. 21 But at the place where we stopped for
the night we opened our sacks and each of us
found his silver — the exact weight — in the
mouth of his sack. So we have brought it back
with us. 22 We have also brought additional
silver with us to buy food. We don't know
who put our silver in our sacks."

23 "It's all right," he said. "Don't be afraid.
Your God, the God of your father, has given
you treasure in your sacks; I received your
silver." Then he brought Simeon out to them.

24 The steward took the men into Jo-
seph's house, gave them water to wash their
feet and provided fodder for their donkeys.
25 They prepared their gifts for Joseph's ar-
rival at noon, because they had heard that
they were to eat there.

26 When Joseph came home, they present-
ed to him the gifts they had brought into the
house, and they bowed down before him to
the ground. 27 He asked them how they were,
and then he said, "How is your aged father
you told me about? Is he still living?"

28 They replied, "Your servant our father is
still alive and well." And they bowed down,
prostrating themselves before him.

29 As he looked about and saw his brother
Benjamin, his own mother's son, he asked,
"Is this your youngest brother, the one you
told me about?" And he said, "God be gra-
cious to you, my son." 30 Deeply moved at the
sight of his brother, Joseph hurried out and
looked for a place to weep. He went into his
private room and wept there.

31 After he had washed his face, he came
out and, controlling himself, said, "Serve the
food."

32 They served him by himself, the broth-
ers by themselves, and the Egyptians who
ate with him by themselves, because Egyp-
tians could not eat with Hebrews, for that
is detestable to Egyptians. 33 The men had
been seated before him in the order of their
ages, from the firstborn to the youngest; and
they looked at each other in astonishment.
34 When portions were served to them from
Joseph's table, Benjamin's portion was five
times as much as anyone else's. So they
feasted and drank freely with him.

A Silver Cup in a Sack

44 Now Joseph gave these instructions
to the steward of his house: "Fill the
men's sacks with as much food as they can
carry, and put each man's silver in the mouth
of his sack. 2 Then put my cup, the silver one,
in the mouth of the youngest one's sack,
along with the silver for his grain." And he
did as Joseph said.

3 As morning dawned, the men were sent
on their way with their donkeys. 4 They had
not gone far from the city when Joseph said
to his steward, "Go after those men at once,
and when you catch up with them, say to
them, 'Why have you repaid good with evil?
5 Isn't this the cup my master drinks from
and also uses for divination? This is a wick-
ed thing you have done.' "

[a] *14* Hebrew *El-Shaddai*

6When he caught up with them, he re-
peated these words to them. 7But they said
to him, "Why does my lord say such things?
Far be it from your servants to do anything
like that! 8We even brought back to you from
the land of Canaan the silver we found inside
the mouths of our sacks. So why would we
steal silver or gold from your master's house?
9If any of your servants is found to have it, he
will die; and the rest of us will become my
lord's slaves."
10"Very well, then," he said, "let it be as
you say. Whoever is found to have it will be-
come my slave; the rest of you will be free
from blame."
11Each of them quickly lowered his sack to
the ground and opened it. 12Then the stew-
ard proceeded to search, beginning with
the oldest and ending with the youngest.
And the cup was found in Benjamin's sack.
13At this, they tore their clothes. Then they
all loaded their donkeys and returned to the
city.
14Joseph was still in the house when Ju-
dah and his brothers came in, and they
threw themselves to the ground before him.
15Joseph said to them, "What is this you have
done? Don't you know that a man like me
can find things out by divination?"
16"What can we say to my lord?" Judah
replied. "What can we say? How can we
prove our innocence? God has uncovered
your servants' guilt. We are now my lord's
slaves — we ourselves and the one who was
found to have the cup."
17But Joseph said, "Far be it from me to do
such a thing! Only the man who was found to
have the cup will become my slave. The rest
of you, go back to your father in peace."
18Then Judah went up to him and said:
"Pardon your servant, my lord, let me speak
a word to my lord. Do not be angry with your
servant, though you are equal to Pharaoh
himself. 19My lord asked his servants, 'Do
you have a father or a brother?' 20And we an-
swered, 'We have an aged father, and there
is a young son born to him in his old age. His
brother is dead, and he is the only one of his
mother's sons left, and his father loves him.'
21"Then you said to your servants, 'Bring
him down to me so I can see him for myself.'
22And we said to my lord, 'The boy cannot
leave his father; if he leaves him, his father
will die.' 23But you told your servants, 'Un-
less your youngest brother comes down with
you, you will not see my face again.' 24When
we went back to your servant my father, we
told him what my lord had said.
25"Then our father said, 'Go back and buy
a little more food.' 26But we said, 'We can-
not go down. Only if our youngest brother is
with us will we go. We cannot see the man's
face unless our youngest brother is with us.'
27"Your servant my father said to us, 'You
know that my wife bore me two sons. 28One
of them went away from me, and I said, "He
has surely been torn to pieces." And I have
not seen him since. 29If you take this one
from me too and harm comes to him, you
will bring my gray head down to the grave
in misery.'
30"So now, if the boy is not with us when I
go back to your servant my father, and if my
father, whose life is closely bound up with
the boy's life, 31sees that the boy isn't there,
he will die. Your servants will bring the gray
head of our father down to the grave in sor-
row. 32Your servant guaranteed the boy's
safety to my father. I said, 'If I do not bring
him back to you, I will bear the blame before
you, my father, all my life!'
33"Now then, please let your servant re-
main here as my lord's slave in place of the
boy, and let the boy return with his brothers.
34How can I go back to my father if the boy is
not with me? No! Do not let me see the mis-
ery that would come on my father."

Joseph Makes Himself Known

45 Then Joseph could no longer con-
trol himself before all his attendants,
and he cried out, "Have everyone leave my
presence!" So there was no one with Joseph
when he made himself known to his broth-
ers. 2And he wept so loudly that the Egyp-
tians heard him, and Pharaoh's household
heard about it.
3Joseph said to his brothers, "I am Joseph!
Is my father still living?" But his brothers
were not able to answer him, because they
were terrified at his presence.
4Then Joseph said to his brothers, "Come
close to me." When they had done so, he
said, "I am your brother Joseph, the one you
sold into Egypt! 5And now, do not be dis-
tressed and do not be angry with yourselves
for selling me here, because it was to save
lives that God sent me ahead of you. 6For

two years now there has been famine in the
land, and for the next five years there will be
no plowing and reaping. 7But God sent me
ahead of you to preserve for you a remnant
on earth and to save your lives by a great de-
liverance.[a]

8"So then, it was not you who sent me
here, but God. He made me father to Phar-
aoh, lord of his entire household and ruler
of all Egypt. 9Now hurry back to my father
and say to him, 'This is what your son Joseph
says: God has made me lord of all Egypt.
Come down to me; don't delay. 10You shall
live in the region of Goshen and be near
me — you, your children and grandchildren,
your flocks and herds, and all you have. 11I
will provide for you there, because five years
of famine are still to come. Otherwise you
and your household and all who belong to
you will become destitute.'

12"You can see for yourselves, and so can
my brother Benjamin, that it is really I who
am speaking to you. 13Tell my father about
all the honor accorded me in Egypt and
about everything you have seen. And bring
my father down here quickly."

14Then he threw his arms around his
brother Benjamin and wept, and Benjamin
embraced him, weeping. 15And he kissed all
his brothers and wept over them. Afterward
his brothers talked with him.

16When the news reached Pharaoh's
palace that Joseph's brothers had come,
Pharaoh and all his officials were pleased.
17Pharaoh said to Joseph, "Tell your broth-
ers, 'Do this: Load your animals and return
to the land of Canaan, 18and bring your fa-
ther and your families back to me. I will give
you the best of the land of Egypt and you can
enjoy the fat of the land.'

19"You are also directed to tell them, 'Do
this: Take some carts from Egypt for your
children and your wives, and get your father
and come. 20Never mind about your belong-
ings, because the best of all Egypt will be
yours.' "

21So the sons of Israel did this. Joseph
gave them carts, as Pharaoh had com-
manded, and he also gave them provisions
for their journey. 22To each of them he gave
new clothing, but to Benjamin he gave three
hundred shekels[b] of silver and five sets of
clothes. 23And this is what he sent to his fa-
ther: ten donkeys loaded with the best things
of Egypt, and ten female donkeys loaded
with grain and bread and other provisions
for his journey. 24Then he sent his brothers
away, and as they were leaving he said to
them, "Don't quarrel on the way!"

25So they went up out of Egypt and came
to their father Jacob in the land of Canaan.
26They told him, "Joseph is still alive! In fact,
he is ruler of all Egypt." Jacob was stunned;
he did not believe them. 27But when they
told him everything Joseph had said to
them, and when he saw the carts Joseph had
sent to carry him back, the spirit of their fa-
ther Jacob revived. 28And Israel said, "I'm
convinced! My son Joseph is still alive. I will
go and see him before I die."

Jacob Goes to Egypt

46 So Israel set out with all that was his,
and when he reached Beersheba,
he offered sacrifices to the God of his father
Isaac.

2And God spoke to Israel in a vision at
night and said, "Jacob! Jacob!"

"Here I am," he replied.

3"I am God, the God of your father," he
said. "Do not be afraid to go down to Egypt,
for I will make you into a great nation there.
4I will go down to Egypt with you, and I will
surely bring you back again. And Joseph's
own hand will close your eyes."

5Then Jacob left Beersheba, and Israel's
sons took their father Jacob and their chil-
dren and their wives in the carts that Phar-
aoh had sent to transport him. 6So Jacob
and all his offspring went to Egypt, taking
with them their livestock and the posses-
sions they had acquired in Canaan. 7Jacob
brought with him to Egypt his sons and
grandsons and his daughters and grand-
daughters — all his offspring.

8These are the names of the sons of Isra-
el (Jacob and his descendants) who went to
Egypt:

Reuben the firstborn of Jacob.
9The sons of Reuben:
Hanok, Pallu, Hezron and Karmi.
10The sons of Simeon:
Jemuel, Jamin, Ohad, Jakin, Zohar

[a] 7 Or *save you as a great band of survivors* [b] 22 That is, about 7 1/2 pounds or about 3.5 kilograms

and Shaul the son of a Canaanite
woman.
[11]The sons of Levi:
Gershon, Kohath and Merari.
[12]The sons of Judah:
Er, Onan, Shelah, Perez and Zerah
(but Er and Onan had died in the
land of Canaan).
The sons of Perez:
Hezron and Hamul.
[13]The sons of Issachar:
Tola, Puah,[a] Jashub[b] and Shimron.
[14]The sons of Zebulun:
Sered, Elon and Jahleel.
[15]These were the sons Leah bore to Jacob
in Paddan Aram,[c] besides his daughter Di-
nah. These sons and daughters of his were
thirty-three in all.

[16]The sons of Gad:
Zephon,[d] Haggi, Shuni, Ezbon, Eri,
Arodi and Areli.
[17]The sons of Asher:
Imnah, Ishvah, Ishvi and Beriah.
Their sister was Serah.
The sons of Beriah:
Heber and Malkiel.
[18]These were the children born to Jacob
by Zilpah, whom Laban had given to his
daughter Leah — sixteen in all.

[19]The sons of Jacob's wife Rachel:
Joseph and Benjamin. [20]In Egypt,
Manasseh and Ephraim were born
to Joseph by Asenath daughter of Po-
tiphera, priest of On.[e]
[21]The sons of Benjamin:
Bela, Beker, Ashbel, Gera, Naaman,
Ehi, Rosh, Muppim, Huppim and
Ard.
[22]These were the sons of Rachel who were
born to Jacob — fourteen in all.

[23]The son of Dan:
Hushim.
[24]The sons of Naphtali:
Jahziel, Guni, Jezer and Shillem.
[25]These were the sons born to Jacob by
Bilhah, whom Laban had given to his daugh-
ter Rachel — seven in all.

[26]All those who went to Egypt with Ja-
cob — those who were his direct descen-
dants, not counting his sons' wives — num-
bered sixty-six persons. [27]With the two sons[f]
who had been born to Joseph in Egypt, the
members of Jacob's family, which went to
Egypt, were seventy[g] in all.

[28]Now Jacob sent Judah ahead of him to
Joseph to get directions to Goshen. When
they arrived in the region of Goshen, [29]Jo-
seph had his chariot made ready and went
to Goshen to meet his father Israel. As soon
as Joseph appeared before him, he threw his
arms around his father[h] and wept for a long
time.
[30]Israel said to Joseph, "Now I am ready to
die, since I have seen for myself that you are
still alive."
[31]Then Joseph said to his brothers and
to his father's household, "I will go up and
speak to Pharaoh and will say to him, 'My
brothers and my father's household, who
were living in the land of Canaan, have
come to me. [32]The men are shepherds; they
tend livestock, and they have brought along
their flocks and herds and everything they
own.' [33]When Pharaoh calls you in and asks,
'What is your occupation?' [34]you should an-
swer, 'Your servants have tended livestock
from our boyhood on, just as our fathers did.'
Then you will be allowed to settle in the re-
gion of Goshen, for all shepherds are detest-
able to the Egyptians."

47 Joseph went and told Pharaoh, "My
father and brothers, with their flocks
and herds and everything they own, have
come from the land of Canaan and are now
in Goshen." [2]He chose five of his brothers
and presented them before Pharaoh.
[3]Pharaoh asked the brothers, "What is
your occupation?"
"Your servants are shepherds," they re-
plied to Pharaoh, "just as our fathers were."
[4]They also said to him, "We have come to
live here for a while, because the famine is
severe in Canaan and your servants' flocks
have no pasture. So now, please let your ser-
vants settle in Goshen."

[a] *13* Samaritan Pentateuch and Syriac (see also 1 Chron. 7:1); Masoretic Text *Puvah* [b] *13* Samaritan Pentateuch and some Septuagint manuscripts (see also Num. 26:24 and 1 Chron. 7:1); Masoretic Text *Iob* [c] *15* That is, Northwest Mesopotamia [d] *16* Samaritan Pentateuch and Septuagint (see also Num. 26:15); Masoretic Text *Ziphion* [e] *20* That is, Heliopolis [f] *27* Hebrew; Septuagint *the nine children* [g] *27* Hebrew (see also Exodus 1:5 and note); Septuagint (see also Acts 7:14) *seventy-five* [h] *29* Hebrew *around him*

5 Pharaoh said to Joseph, "Your father and your brothers have come to you, 6 and the land of Egypt is before you; settle your father and your brothers in the best part of the land. Let them live in Goshen. And if you know of any among them with special ability, put them in charge of my own livestock."

7 Then Joseph brought his father Jacob in and presented him before Pharaoh. After Jacob blessed[a] Pharaoh, 8 Pharaoh asked him, "How old are you?"

9 And Jacob said to Pharaoh, "The years of my pilgrimage are a hundred and thirty. My years have been few and difficult, and they do not equal the years of the pilgrimage of my fathers." 10 Then Jacob blessed[b] Pharaoh and went out from his presence.

11 So Joseph settled his father and his brothers in Egypt and gave them property in the best part of the land, the district of Rameses, as Pharaoh directed. 12 Joseph also provided his father and his brothers and all his father's household with food, according to the number of their children.

Joseph and the Famine

13 There was no food, however, in the whole region because the famine was severe; both Egypt and Canaan wasted away because of the famine. 14 Joseph collected all the money that was to be found in Egypt and Canaan in payment for the grain they were buying, and he brought it to Pharaoh's palace. 15 When the money of the people of Egypt and Canaan was gone, all Egypt came to Joseph and said, "Give us food. Why should we die before your eyes? Our money is all gone."

16 "Then bring your livestock," said Joseph. "I will sell you food in exchange for your livestock, since your money is gone." 17 So they brought their livestock to Joseph, and he gave them food in exchange for their horses, their sheep and goats, their cattle and donkeys. And he brought them through that year with food in exchange for all their livestock.

18 When that year was over, they came to him the following year and said, "We cannot hide from our lord the fact that since our money is gone and our livestock belongs to you, there is nothing left for our lord except our bodies and our land. 19 Why should we perish before your eyes — we and our land as well? Buy us and our land in exchange for food, and we with our land will be in bondage to Pharaoh. Give us seed so that we may live and not die, and that the land may not become desolate."

20 So Joseph bought all the land in Egypt for Pharaoh. The Egyptians, one and all, sold their fields, because the famine was too severe for them. The land became Pharaoh's, 21 and Joseph reduced the people to servitude,[c] from one end of Egypt to the other. 22 However, he did not buy the land of the priests, because they received a regular allotment from Pharaoh and had food enough from the allotment Pharaoh gave them. That is why they did not sell their land.

23 Joseph said to the people, "Now that I have bought you and your land today for Pharaoh, here is seed for you so you can plant the ground. 24 But when the crop comes in, give a fifth of it to Pharaoh. The other four-fifths you may keep as seed for the fields and as food for yourselves and your households and your children."

25 "You have saved our lives," they said. "May we find favor in the eyes of our lord; we will be in bondage to Pharaoh."

26 So Joseph established it as a law concerning land in Egypt — still in force today — that a fifth of the produce belongs to Pharaoh. It was only the land of the priests that did not become Pharaoh's.

27 Now the Israelites settled in Egypt in the region of Goshen. They acquired property there and were fruitful and increased greatly in number.

28 Jacob lived in Egypt seventeen years, and the years of his life were a hundred and forty-seven. 29 When the time drew near for Israel to die, he called for his son Joseph and said to him, "If I have found favor in your eyes, put your hand under my thigh and promise that you will show me kindness and faithfulness. Do not bury me in Egypt, 30 but when I rest with my fathers, carry me out of Egypt and bury me where they are buried."

"I will do as you say," he said.

31 "Swear to me," he said. Then Joseph swore to him, and Israel worshiped as he leaned on the top of his staff.[d]

[a] 7 Or *greeted* [b] 10 Or *said farewell to* [c] 21 Samaritan Pentateuch and Septuagint (see also Vulgate); Masoretic Text *and he moved the people into the cities* [d] 31 Or *Israel bowed down at the head of his bed*

Manasseh and Ephraim

48 Some time later Joseph was told,
"Your father is ill." So he took his
two sons Manasseh and Ephraim along
with him. 2 When Jacob was told, "Your son
Joseph has come to you," Israel rallied his
strength and sat up on the bed.
3 Jacob said to Joseph, "God Almighty[a] ap-
peared to me at Luz in the land of Canaan,
and there he blessed me 4 and said to me, 'I
am going to make you fruitful and increase
your numbers. I will make you a communi-
ty of peoples, and I will give this land as an
everlasting possession to your descendants
after you.'
5 "Now then, your two sons born to you in
Egypt before I came to you here will be reck-
oned as mine; Ephraim and Manasseh will be
mine, just as Reuben and Simeon are mine.
6 Any children born to you after them will be
yours; in the territory they inherit they will be
reckoned under the names of their brothers.
7 As I was returning from Paddan,[b] to my sor-
row Rachel died in the land of Canaan while
we were still on the way, a little distance from
Ephrath. So I buried her there beside the road
to Ephrath" (that is, Bethlehem).
8 When Israel saw the sons of Joseph, he
asked, "Who are these?"
9 "They are the sons God has given me
here," Joseph said to his father.

Then Israel said, "Bring them to me so I
may bless them."
10 Now Israel's eyes were failing because of
old age, and he could hardly see. So Joseph
brought his sons close to him, and his father
kissed them and embraced them.
11 Israel said to Joseph, "I never expected
to see your face again, and now God has al-
lowed me to see your children too."
12 Then Joseph removed them from Isra-
el's knees and bowed down with his face to
the ground. 13 And Joseph took both of them,
Ephraim on his right toward Israel's left
hand and Manasseh on his left toward Is-
rael's right hand, and brought them close to
him. 14 But Israel reached out his right hand
and put it on Ephraim's head, though he
was the younger, and crossing his arms, he
put his left hand on Manasseh's head, even
though Manasseh was the firstborn.
15 Then he blessed Joseph and said,

"May the God before whom my fathers
Abraham and Isaac walked faithfully,
the God who has been my shepherd
all my life to this day,
16 the Angel who has delivered me from all
harm
— may he bless these boys.
May they be called by my name
and the names of my fathers Abraham
and Isaac,
and may they increase greatly
on the earth."

17 When Joseph saw his father placing his
right hand on Ephraim's head he was dis-
pleased; so he took hold of his father's hand
to move it from Ephraim's head to Manas-
seh's head. 18 Joseph said to him, "No, my fa-
ther, this one is the firstborn; put your right
hand on his head."
19 But his father refused and said, "I know,
my son, I know. He too will become a people,
and he too will become great. Nevertheless,
his younger brother will be greater than he,
and his descendants will become a group
of nations." 20 He blessed them that day and
said,

"In your[c] name will Israel pronounce this
blessing:
'May God make you like Ephraim and
Manasseh.'"

So he put Ephraim ahead of Manasseh.
21 Then Israel said to Joseph, "I am about
to die, but God will be with you[d] and take
you[d] back to the land of your[d] fathers. 22 And
to you I give one more ridge of land[e] than to
your brothers, the ridge I took from the Am-
orites with my sword and my bow."

Jacob Blesses His Sons

49 Then Jacob called for his sons and
said: "Gather around so I can tell you
what will happen to you in days to come.

2 "Assemble and listen, sons of Jacob;
listen to your father Israel.

3 "Reuben, you are my firstborn,
my might, the first sign of my strength,
excelling in honor, excelling in power.

[a] 3 Hebrew *El-Shaddai* [b] 7 That is, Northwest Mesopotamia [c] 20 The Hebrew is singular.
[d] 21 The Hebrew is plural. [e] 22 The Hebrew for *ridge of land* is identical with the place name Shechem.

[4]Turbulent as the waters, you will no
longer excel,
for you went up onto your father's bed,
onto my couch and defiled it.

[5]"Simeon and Levi are brothers—
their swords[a] are weapons of violence.
[6]Let me not enter their council,
let me not join their assembly,
for they have killed men in their anger
and hamstrung oxen as they pleased.
[7]Cursed be their anger, so fierce,
and their fury, so cruel!
I will scatter them in Jacob
and disperse them in Israel.

[8]"Judah,[b] your brothers will praise you;
your hand will be on the neck of your
enemies;
your father's sons will bow down to you.
[9]You are a lion's cub, Judah;
you return from the prey, my son.
Like a lion he crouches and lies down,
like a lioness—who dares to rouse him?
[10]The scepter will not depart from Judah,
nor the ruler's staff from between his
feet,[c]
until he to whom it belongs[d] shall come
and the obedience of the nations shall
be his.
[11]He will tether his donkey to a vine,
his colt to the choicest branch;
he will wash his garments in wine,
his robes in the blood of grapes.
[12]His eyes will be darker than wine,
his teeth whiter than milk.[e]

[13]"Zebulun will live by the seashore
and become a haven for ships;
his border will extend toward Sidon.

[14]"Issachar is a rawboned[f] donkey
lying down among the sheep pens.[g]
[15]When he sees how good is his resting
place
and how pleasant is his land,
he will bend his shoulder to the burden
and submit to forced labor.

[16]"Dan[h] will provide justice for his people
as one of the tribes of Israel.
[17]Dan will be a snake by the roadside,
a viper along the path,
that bites the horse's heels
so that its rider tumbles backward.

[18]"I look for your deliverance, LORD.

[19]"Gad[i] will be attacked by a band of
raiders,
but he will attack them at their heels.

[20]"Asher's food will be rich;
he will provide delicacies fit for a king.

[21]"Naphtali is a doe set free
that bears beautiful fawns.[j]

[22]"Joseph is a fruitful vine,
a fruitful vine near a spring,
whose branches climb over a wall.[k]
[23]With bitterness archers attacked him;
they shot at him with hostility.
[24]But his bow remained steady,
his strong arms stayed[l] limber,
because of the hand of the Mighty One of
Jacob,
because of the Shepherd, the Rock of
Israel,
[25]because of your father's God, who helps
you,
because of the Almighty,[m] who blesses
you
with blessings of the skies above,
blessings of the deep springs below,
blessings of the breast and womb.
[26]Your father's blessings are greater
than the blessings of the ancient
mountains,
than[n] the bounty of the age-old hills.
Let all these rest on the head of Joseph,
on the brow of the prince among[o] his
brothers.

[27]"Benjamin is a ravenous wolf;
in the morning he devours the prey,
in the evening he divides the
plunder."

[a] 5 The meaning of the Hebrew for this word is uncertain. [b] 8 *Judah* sounds like and may be derived from the Hebrew for *praise.* [c] *10* Or *from his descendants* [d] *10* Or *to whom tribute belongs*; the meaning of the Hebrew for this phrase is uncertain. [e] *12* Or *will be dull from wine, / his teeth white from milk* [f] *14* Or *strong* [g] *14* Or *the campfires*; or *the saddlebags* [h] *16* *Dan* here means *he provides justice.* [i] *19* *Gad* sounds like the Hebrew for *attack* and also for *band of raiders.* [j] *21* Or *free; / he utters beautiful words* [k] *22* Or *Joseph is a wild colt, / a wild colt near a spring, / a wild donkey on a terraced hill* [l] *23,24* Or *archers will attack . . . will shoot . . . will remain . . . will stay* [m] *25* Hebrew *Shaddai* [n] *26* Or *of my progenitors, / as great as* [o] *26* Or *of the one separated from*

[28]All these are the twelve tribes of Israel, and this is what their father said to them when he blessed them, giving each the blessing appropriate to him.

The Death of Jacob

[29]Then he gave them these instructions: "I am about to be gathered to my people. Bury me with my fathers in the cave in the field of Ephron the Hittite, [30]the cave in the field of Machpelah, near Mamre in Canaan, which Abraham bought along with the field as a burial place from Ephron the Hittite. [31]There Abraham and his wife Sarah were buried, there Isaac and his wife Rebekah were buried, and there I buried Leah. [32]The field and the cave in it were bought from the Hittites.[a]"

[33]When Jacob had finished giving instructions to his sons, he drew his feet up into the bed, breathed his last and was gathered to his people.

50 Joseph threw himself on his father and wept over him and kissed him. [2]Then Joseph directed the physicians in his service to embalm his father Israel. So the physicians embalmed him, [3]taking a full forty days, for that was the time required for embalming. And the Egyptians mourned for him seventy days.

[4]When the days of mourning had passed, Joseph said to Pharaoh's court, "If I have found favor in your eyes, speak to Pharaoh for me. Tell him, [5]'My father made me swear an oath and said, "I am about to die; bury me in the tomb I dug for myself in the land of Canaan." Now let me go up and bury my father; then I will return.' "

[6]Pharaoh said, "Go up and bury your father, as he made you swear to do."

[7]So Joseph went up to bury his father. All Pharaoh's officials accompanied him—the dignitaries of his court and all the dignitaries of Egypt— [8]besides all the members of Joseph's household and his brothers and those belonging to his father's household. Only their children and their flocks and herds were left in Goshen. [9]Chariots and horsemen[b] also went up with him. It was a very large company.

[10]When they reached the threshing floor of Atad, near the Jordan, they lamented loudly and bitterly; and there Joseph observed a seven-day period of mourning for his father. [11]When the Canaanites who lived there saw the mourning at the threshing floor of Atad, they said, "The Egyptians are holding a solemn ceremony of mourning." That is why that place near the Jordan is called Abel Mizraim.[c]

[12]So Jacob's sons did as he had commanded them: [13]They carried him to the land of Canaan and buried him in the cave in the field of Machpelah, near Mamre, which Abraham had bought along with the field as a burial place from Ephron the Hittite. [14]After burying his father, Joseph returned to Egypt, together with his brothers and all the others who had gone with him to bury his father.

Joseph Reassures His Brothers

[15]When Joseph's brothers saw that their father was dead, they said, "What if Joseph holds a grudge against us and pays us back for all the wrongs we did to him?" [16]So they sent word to Joseph, saying, "Your father left these instructions before he died: [17]'This is what you are to say to Joseph: I ask you to forgive your brothers the sins and the wrongs they committed in treating you so badly.' Now please forgive the sins of the servants of the God of your father." When their message came to him, Joseph wept.

[18]His brothers then came and threw themselves down before him. "We are your slaves," they said.

[19]But Joseph said to them, "Don't be afraid. Am I in the place of God? [20]You intended to harm me, but God intended it for good to accomplish what is now being done, the saving of many lives. [21]So then, don't be afraid. I will provide for you and your children." And he reassured them and spoke kindly to them.

The Death of Joseph

[22]Joseph stayed in Egypt, along with all his father's family. He lived a hundred and ten years [23]and saw the third generation of Ephraim's children. Also the children of Makir son of Manasseh were placed at birth on Joseph's knees.[d]

[24]Then Joseph said to his brothers, "I am

[a] 32 Or *the descendants of Heth* [b] 9 Or *charioteers* [c] 11 *Abel Mizraim* means *mourning of the Egyptians.* [d] 23 That is, were counted as his

about to die. But God will surely come to your aid and take you up out of this land to the land he promised on oath to Abraham, Isaac and Jacob."
[25]And Joseph made the Israelites swear an oath and said, "God will surely come to your aid, and then you must carry my bones up from this place."
[26]So Joseph died at the age of a hundred and ten. And after they embalmed him, he was placed in a coffin in Egypt.

EXODUS

The Israelites Oppressed

1 These are the names of the sons of Israel who went to Egypt with Jacob, each with his family: 2Reuben, Simeon, Levi and Judah; 3Issachar, Zebulun and Benjamin; 4Dan and Naphtali; Gad and Asher. 5The descendants of Jacob numbered seventy[a] in all; Joseph was already in Egypt.

6Now Joseph and all his brothers and all that generation died, 7but the Israelites were exceedingly fruitful; they multiplied greatly, increased in numbers and became so numerous that the land was filled with them.

8Then a new king, to whom Joseph meant nothing, came to power in Egypt. 9"Look," he said to his people, "the Israelites have become far too numerous for us. 10Come, we must deal shrewdly with them or they will become even more numerous and, if war breaks out, will join our enemies, fight against us and leave the country."

11So they put slave masters over them to oppress them with forced labor, and they built Pithom and Rameses as store cities for Pharaoh. 12But the more they were oppressed, the more they multiplied and spread; so the Egyptians came to dread the Israelites 13and worked them ruthlessly. 14They made their lives bitter with harsh labor in brick and mortar and with all kinds of work in the fields; in all their harsh labor the Egyptians worked them ruthlessly.

15The king of Egypt said to the Hebrew midwives, whose names were Shiphrah and Puah, 16"When you are helping the Hebrew women during childbirth on the delivery stool, if you see that the baby is a boy, kill him; but if it is a girl, let her live." 17The midwives, however, feared God and did not do what the king of Egypt had told them to do; they let the boys live. 18Then the king of Egypt summoned the midwives and asked them, "Why have you done this? Why have you let the boys live?"

19The midwives answered Pharaoh, "Hebrew women are not like Egyptian women; they are vigorous and give birth before the midwives arrive."

20So God was kind to the midwives and the people increased and became even more numerous. 21And because the midwives feared God, he gave them families of their own.

22Then Pharaoh gave this order to all his people: "Every Hebrew boy that is born you must throw into the Nile, but let every girl live."

The Birth of Moses

2 Now a man of the tribe of Levi married a Levite woman, 2and she became pregnant and gave birth to a son. When she saw that he was a fine child, she hid him for three months. 3But when she could hide him no longer, she got a papyrus basket[b] for him and coated it with tar and pitch. Then she placed the child in it and put it among the reeds along the bank of the Nile. 4His sister stood at a distance to see what would happen to him.

5Then Pharaoh's daughter went down to the Nile to bathe, and her attendants were walking along the riverbank. She saw the basket among the reeds and sent her female slave to get it. 6She opened it and saw the baby. He was crying, and she felt sorry for him. "This is one of the Hebrew babies," she said.

7Then his sister asked Pharaoh's daughter, "Shall I go and get one of the Hebrew women to nurse the baby for you?"

8"Yes, go," she answered. So the girl went and got the baby's mother. 9Pharaoh's daughter said to her, "Take this baby and nurse him for me, and I will pay you." So the woman took the baby and nursed him. 10When the child grew older, she took him to Pharaoh's daughter and he became her son.

[a] 5 Masoretic Text (see also Gen. 46:27); Dead Sea Scrolls and Septuagint (see also Acts 7:14 and note at Gen. 46:27) *seventy-five* [b] 3 The Hebrew can also mean *ark*, as in Gen. 6:14.

She named him Moses,[a] saying, "I drew him out of the water."

Moses Flees to Midian

11One day, after Moses had grown up, he went out to where his own people were and watched them at their hard labor. He saw an Egyptian beating a Hebrew, one of his own people. 12Looking this way and that and seeing no one, he killed the Egyptian and hid him in the sand. 13The next day he went out and saw two Hebrews fighting. He asked the one in the wrong, "Why are you hitting your fellow Hebrew?"

14The man said, "Who made you ruler and judge over us? Are you thinking of killing me as you killed the Egyptian?" Then Moses was afraid and thought, "What I did must have become known."

15When Pharaoh heard of this, he tried to kill Moses, but Moses fled from Pharaoh and went to live in Midian, where he sat down by a well. 16Now a priest of Midian had seven daughters, and they came to draw water and fill the troughs to water their father's flock. 17Some shepherds came along and drove them away, but Moses got up and came to their rescue and watered their flock.

18When the girls returned to Reuel their father, he asked them, "Why have you returned so early today?"

19They answered, "An Egyptian rescued us from the shepherds. He even drew water for us and watered the flock."

20"And where is he?" Reuel asked his daughters. "Why did you leave him? Invite him to have something to eat."

21Moses agreed to stay with the man, who gave his daughter Zipporah to Moses in marriage. 22Zipporah gave birth to a son, and Moses named him Gershom,[b] saying, "I have become a foreigner in a foreign land."

23During that long period, the king of Egypt died. The Israelites groaned in their slavery and cried out, and their cry for help because of their slavery went up to God. 24God heard their groaning and he remembered his covenant with Abraham, with Isaac and with Jacob. 25So God looked on the Israelites and was concerned about them.

Moses and the Burning Bush

3 Now Moses was tending the flock of Jethro his father-in-law, the priest of Midian, and he led the flock to the far side of the wilderness and came to Horeb, the mountain of God. 2There the angel of the LORD appeared to him in flames of fire from within a bush. Moses saw that though the bush was on fire it did not burn up. 3So Moses thought, "I will go over and see this strange sight—why the bush does not burn up."

4When the LORD saw that he had gone over to look, God called to him from within the bush, "Moses! Moses!"

And Moses said, "Here I am."

5"Do not come any closer," God said. "Take off your sandals, for the place where you are standing is holy ground." 6Then he said, "I am the God of your father,[c] the God of Abraham, the God of Isaac and the God of Jacob." At this, Moses hid his face, because he was afraid to look at God.

7The LORD said, "I have indeed seen the misery of my people in Egypt. I have heard them crying out because of their slave drivers, and I am concerned about their suffering. 8So I have come down to rescue them from the hand of the Egyptians and to bring them up out of that land into a good and spacious land, a land flowing with milk and honey—the home of the Canaanites, Hittites, Amorites, Perizzites, Hivites and Jebusites. 9And now the cry of the Israelites has reached me, and I have seen the way the Egyptians are oppressing them. 10So now, go. I am sending you to Pharaoh to bring my people the Israelites out of Egypt."

11But Moses said to God, "Who am I that I should go to Pharaoh and bring the Israelites out of Egypt?"

12And God said, "I will be with you. And this will be the sign to you that it is I who have sent you: When you have brought the people out of Egypt, you[d] will worship God on this mountain."

13Moses said to God, "Suppose I go to the Israelites and say to them, 'The God of your fathers has sent me to you,' and they ask me, 'What is his name?' Then what shall I tell them?"

14God said to Moses, "I AM WHO I AM.[e] This

[a] *10 Moses* sounds like the Hebrew for *draw out.* [b] *22 Gershom* sounds like the Hebrew for *a foreigner there.* [c] *6* Masoretic Text; Samaritan Pentateuch (see Acts 7:32) *fathers* [d] *12* The Hebrew is plural.
[e] *14* Or *I WILL BE WHAT I WILL BE*

is what you are to say to the Israelites: 'I AM
has sent me to you.'"
15 God also said to Moses, "Say to the Isra-
elites, 'The LORD,[a] the God of your fathers—
the God of Abraham, the God of Isaac and
the God of Jacob—has sent me to you.'

"This is my name forever,
the name you shall call me
from generation to generation.

16 "Go, assemble the elders of Israel and
say to them, 'The LORD, the God of your fa-
thers—the God of Abraham, Isaac and
Jacob—appeared to me and said: I have
watched over you and have seen what has
been done to you in Egypt. 17 And I have
promised to bring you up out of your misery
in Egypt into the land of the Canaanites, Hit-
tites, Amorites, Perizzites, Hivites and Jebu-
sites—a land flowing with milk and honey.'
18 "The elders of Israel will listen to you.
Then you and the elders are to go to the king
of Egypt and say to him, 'The LORD, the God
of the Hebrews, has met with us. Let us take
a three-day journey into the wilderness to
offer sacrifices to the LORD our God.' 19 But
I know that the king of Egypt will not let you
go unless a mighty hand compels him. 20 So I
will stretch out my hand and strike the Egyp-
tians with all the wonders that I will perform
among them. After that, he will let you go.
21 "And I will make the Egyptians favor-
ably disposed toward this people, so that
when you leave you will not go empty-hand-
ed. 22 Every woman is to ask her neighbor and
any woman living in her house for articles of
silver and gold and for clothing, which you
will put on your sons and daughters. And so
you will plunder the Egyptians."

Signs for Moses

4 Moses answered, "What if they do not
believe me or listen to me and say, 'The
LORD did not appear to you'?"
2 Then the LORD said to him, "What is that
in your hand?"
"A staff," he replied.
3 The LORD said, "Throw it on the ground."
Moses threw it on the ground and it be-
came a snake, and he ran from it. 4 Then the
LORD said to him, "Reach out your hand and
take it by the tail." So Moses reached out and
took hold of the snake and it turned back into
a staff in his hand. 5 "This," said the LORD, "is
so that they may believe that the LORD, the
God of their fathers—the God of Abraham,
the God of Isaac and the God of Jacob—has
appeared to you."
6 Then the LORD said, "Put your hand in-
side your cloak." So Moses put his hand into
his cloak, and when he took it out, the skin
was leprous[b]—it had become as white as
snow.
7 "Now put it back into your cloak," he said.
So Moses put his hand back into his cloak,
and when he took it out, it was restored, like
the rest of his flesh.
8 Then the LORD said, "If they do not be-
lieve you or pay attention to the first sign,
they may believe the second. 9 But if they do
not believe these two signs or listen to you,
take some water from the Nile and pour it on
the dry ground. The water you take from the
river will become blood on the ground."
10 Moses said to the LORD, "Pardon your
servant, Lord. I have never been eloquent, nei-
ther in the past nor since you have spoken to
your servant. I am slow of speech and tongue."
11 The LORD said to him, "Who gave hu-
man beings their mouths? Who makes them
deaf or mute? Who gives them sight or makes
them blind? Is it not I, the LORD? 12 Now go; I
will help you speak and will teach you what
to say."
13 But Moses said, "Pardon your servant,
Lord. Please send someone else."
14 Then the LORD's anger burned against
Moses and he said, "What about your broth-
er, Aaron the Levite? I know he can speak
well. He is already on his way to meet you,
and he will be glad to see you. 15 You shall
speak to him and put words in his mouth;
I will help both of you speak and will teach
you what to do. 16 He will speak to the peo-
ple for you, and it will be as if he were your
mouth and as if you were God to him. 17 But
take this staff in your hand so you can per-
form the signs with it."

Moses Returns to Egypt

18 Then Moses went back to Jethro his fa-
ther-in-law and said to him, "Let me return
to my own people in Egypt to see if any of
them are still alive."

[a] 15 The Hebrew for *LORD* sounds like and may be related to the Hebrew for *I AM* in verse 14.
[b] 6 The Hebrew word for *leprous* was used for various diseases affecting the skin.

Jethro said, "Go, and I wish you well."
19Now the LORD had said to Moses in
Midian, "Go back to Egypt, for all those who
wanted to kill you are dead." 20So Moses took
his wife and sons, put them on a donkey and
started back to Egypt. And he took the staff
of God in his hand.
21The LORD said to Moses, "When you re-
turn to Egypt, see that you perform before
Pharaoh all the wonders I have given you
the power to do. But I will harden his heart
so that he will not let the people go. 22Then
say to Pharaoh, 'This is what the LORD says:
Israel is my firstborn son, 23and I told you,
"Let my son go, so he may worship me." But
you refused to let him go; so I will kill your
firstborn son.' "
24At a lodging place on the way, the LORD
met Moses[a] and was about to kill him. 25But
Zipporah took a flint knife, cut off her son's
foreskin and touched Moses' feet with it.[b]
"Surely you are a bridegroom of blood to
me," she said. 26So the LORD let him alone.
(At that time she said "bridegroom of blood,"
referring to circumcision.)
27The LORD said to Aaron, "Go into the
wilderness to meet Moses." So he met Mo-
ses at the mountain of God and kissed him.
28Then Moses told Aaron everything the
LORD had sent him to say, and also about all
the signs he had commanded him to per-
form.
29Moses and Aaron brought together all
the elders of the Israelites, 30and Aaron told
them everything the LORD had said to Mo-
ses. He also performed the signs before the
people, 31and they believed. And when they
heard that the LORD was concerned about
them and had seen their misery, they bowed
down and worshiped.

Bricks Without Straw

5 Afterward Moses and Aaron went to
Pharaoh and said, "This is what the
LORD, the God of Israel, says: 'Let my people
go, so that they may hold a festival to me in
the wilderness.' "
2Pharaoh said, "Who is the LORD, that I
should obey him and let Israel go? I do not
know the LORD and I will not let Israel go."
3Then they said, "The God of the Hebrews
has met with us. Now let us take a three-day
journey into the wilderness to offer sacrific-
es to the LORD our God, or he may strike us
with plagues or with the sword."
4But the king of Egypt said, "Moses and
Aaron, why are you taking the people away
from their labor? Get back to your work!"
5Then Pharaoh said, "Look, the people of the
land are now numerous, and you are stop-
ping them from working."
6That same day Pharaoh gave this order
to the slave drivers and overseers in charge
of the people: 7"You are no longer to supply
the people with straw for making bricks; let
them go and gather their own straw. 8But
require them to make the same number
of bricks as before; don't reduce the quota.
They are lazy; that is why they are crying out,
'Let us go and sacrifice to our God.' 9Make
the work harder for the people so that they
keep working and pay no attention to lies."
10Then the slave drivers and the overseers
went out and said to the people, "This is what
Pharaoh says: 'I will not give you any more
straw. 11Go and get your own straw wherev-
er you can find it, but your work will not be
reduced at all.' " 12So the people scattered all
over Egypt to gather stubble to use for straw.
13The slave drivers kept pressing them, say-
ing, "Complete the work required of you for
each day, just as when you had straw." 14And
Pharaoh's slave drivers beat the Israelite
overseers they had appointed, demanding,
"Why haven't you met your quota of bricks
yesterday or today, as before?"
15Then the Israelite overseers went and
appealed to Pharaoh: "Why have you treated
your servants this way? 16Your servants are
given no straw, yet we are told, 'Make bricks!'
Your servants are being beaten, but the fault
is with your own people."
17Pharaoh said, "Lazy, that's what you
are—lazy! That is why you keep saying, 'Let
us go and sacrifice to the LORD.' 18Now get
to work. You will not be given any straw, yet
you must produce your full quota of bricks."
19The Israelite overseers realized they
were in trouble when they were told, "You
are not to reduce the number of bricks re-
quired of you for each day." 20When they left
Pharaoh, they found Moses and Aaron wait-
ing to meet them, 21and they said, "May the
LORD look on you and judge you! You have

[a] 24 Hebrew *him* [b] 25 The meaning of the Hebrew for this clause is uncertain.

made us obnoxious to Pharaoh and his officials and have put a sword in their hand to kill us."

God Promises Deliverance

[22]Moses returned to the LORD and said,
"Why, Lord, why have you brought trouble on this people? Is this why you sent me?
[23]Ever since I went to Pharaoh to speak in
your name, he has brought trouble on this people, and you have not rescued your people at all."

6 Then the LORD said to Moses, "Now you will see what I will do to Pharaoh: Because of my mighty hand he will let them go; because of my mighty hand he will drive them out of his country."

[2]God also said to Moses, "I am the LORD.
[3]I appeared to Abraham, to Isaac and to Jacob as God Almighty,[a] but by my name the LORD[b] I did not make myself fully known to
them. [4]I also established my covenant with
them to give them the land of Canaan, where they resided as foreigners. [5]Moreover, I have
heard the groaning of the Israelites, whom the Egyptians are enslaving, and I have remembered my covenant.

[6]"Therefore, say to the Israelites: 'I am
the LORD, and I will bring you out from under the yoke of the Egyptians. I will free you from being slaves to them, and I will redeem you with an outstretched arm and with mighty acts of judgment. [7]I will take
you as my own people, and I will be your God. Then you will know that I am the LORD your God, who brought you out from under the yoke of the Egyptians. [8]And I will bring
you to the land I swore with uplifted hand to give to Abraham, to Isaac and to Jacob. I will give it to you as a possession. I am the LORD.'"

[9]Moses reported this to the Israelites, but
they did not listen to him because of their discouragement and harsh labor.

[10]Then the LORD said to Moses, [11]"Go, tell
Pharaoh king of Egypt to let the Israelites go out of his country."

[12]But Moses said to the LORD, "If the Israelites will not listen to me, why would Pharaoh listen to me, since I speak with faltering lips[c]?"

Family Record of Moses and Aaron

[13]Now the LORD spoke to Moses and Aaron about the Israelites and Pharaoh king of Egypt, and he commanded them to bring the Israelites out of Egypt.

[14]These were the heads of their families[d]:

The sons of Reuben the firstborn son of Israel were Hanok and Pallu, Hezron and Karmi. These were the clans of Reuben.

[15]The sons of Simeon were Jemuel,
Jamin, Ohad, Jakin, Zohar and Shaul the son of a Canaanite woman. These were the clans of Simeon.

[16]These were the names of the sons
of Levi according to their records: Gershon, Kohath and Merari. Levi lived 137 years.

[17]The sons of Gershon, by clans,
were Libni and Shimei.

[18]The sons of Kohath were Amram,
Izhar, Hebron and Uzziel. Kohath lived 133 years.

[19]The sons of Merari were Mahli and
Mushi.

These were the clans of Levi according to their records.

[20]Amram married his father's sister Jochebed, who bore him Aaron and Moses. Amram lived 137 years.

[21]The sons of Izhar were Korah, Nepheg and Zikri.

[22]The sons of Uzziel were Mishael,
Elzaphan and Sithri.

[23]Aaron married Elisheba, daughter
of Amminadab and sister of Nahshon, and she bore him Nadab and Abihu, Eleazar and Ithamar.

[24]The sons of Korah were Assir, Elkanah and Abiasaph. These were the Korahite clans.

[25]Eleazar son of Aaron married one
of the daughters of Putiel, and she bore him Phinehas.

These were the heads of the Levite families, clan by clan.

[26]It was this Aaron and Moses to whom
the LORD said, "Bring the Israelites out of

[a] *3* Hebrew *El-Shaddai* [b] *3* See note at 3:15. [c] *12* Hebrew *I am uncircumcised of lips*; also in verse 30
[d] *14* The Hebrew for *families* here and in verse 25 refers to units larger than clans.

Egypt by their divisions." 27 They were the ones who spoke to Pharaoh king of Egypt about bringing the Israelites out of Egypt—this same Moses and Aaron.

Aaron to Speak for Moses

28 Now when the LORD spoke to Moses in Egypt, 29 he said to him, "I am the LORD. Tell Pharaoh king of Egypt everything I tell you."

30 But Moses said to the LORD, "Since I speak with faltering lips, why would Pharaoh listen to me?"

7 Then the LORD said to Moses, "See, I have made you like God to Pharaoh, and your brother Aaron will be your prophet. 2 You are to say everything I command you, and your brother Aaron is to tell Pharaoh to let the Israelites go out of his country. 3 But I will harden Pharaoh's heart, and though I multiply my signs and wonders in Egypt, 4 he will not listen to you. Then I will lay my hand on Egypt and with mighty acts of judgment I will bring out my divisions, my people the Israelites. 5 And the Egyptians will know that I am the LORD when I stretch out my hand against Egypt and bring the Israelites out of it."

6 Moses and Aaron did just as the LORD commanded them. 7 Moses was eighty years old and Aaron eighty-three when they spoke to Pharaoh.

Aaron's Staff Becomes a Snake

8 The LORD said to Moses and Aaron, 9 "When Pharaoh says to you, 'Perform a miracle,' then say to Aaron, 'Take your staff and throw it down before Pharaoh,' and it will become a snake."

10 So Moses and Aaron went to Pharaoh and did just as the LORD commanded. Aaron threw his staff down in front of Pharaoh and his officials, and it became a snake. 11 Pharaoh then summoned wise men and sorcerers, and the Egyptian magicians also did the same things by their secret arts: 12 Each one threw down his staff and it became a snake. But Aaron's staff swallowed up their staffs. 13 Yet Pharaoh's heart became hard and he would not listen to them, just as the LORD had said.

The Plague of Blood

14 Then the LORD said to Moses, "Pharaoh's heart is unyielding; he refuses to let the people go. 15 Go to Pharaoh in the morning as he goes out to the river. Confront him on the bank of the Nile, and take in your hand the staff that was changed into a snake. 16 Then say to him, 'The LORD, the God of the Hebrews, has sent me to say to you: Let my people go, so that they may worship me in the wilderness. But until now you have not listened. 17 This is what the LORD says: By this you will know that I am the LORD: With the staff that is in my hand I will strike the water of the Nile, and it will be changed into blood. 18 The fish in the Nile will die, and the river will stink; the Egyptians will not be able to drink its water.' "

19 The LORD said to Moses, "Tell Aaron, 'Take your staff and stretch out your hand over the waters of Egypt—over the streams and canals, over the ponds and all the reservoirs—and they will turn to blood.' Blood will be everywhere in Egypt, even in vessels[a] of wood and stone."

20 Moses and Aaron did just as the LORD had commanded. He raised his staff in the presence of Pharaoh and his officials and struck the water of the Nile, and all the water was changed into blood. 21 The fish in the Nile died, and the river smelled so bad that the Egyptians could not drink its water. Blood was everywhere in Egypt.

22 But the Egyptian magicians did the same things by their secret arts, and Pharaoh's heart became hard; he would not listen to Moses and Aaron, just as the LORD had said. 23 Instead, he turned and went into his palace, and did not take even this to heart. 24 And all the Egyptians dug along the Nile to get drinking water, because they could not drink the water of the river.

The Plague of Frogs

25 Seven days passed after the LORD struck

8[b] the Nile. 1 Then the LORD said to Moses, "Go to Pharaoh and say to him, 'This is what the LORD says: Let my people go, so that they may worship me. 2 If you refuse to let them go, I will send a plague of frogs on your whole country. 3 The Nile will teem with frogs. They will come up into your palace and your bedroom and onto your bed, into the houses of your officials and on your people, and into your ovens and kneading

[a] 19 Or *even on their idols* [b] In Hebrew texts 8:1-4 is numbered 7:26-29, and 8:5-32 is numbered 8:1-28.

troughs. 4 The frogs will come up on you and your people and all your officials.' "

5 Then the LORD said to Moses, "Tell Aaron, 'Stretch out your hand with your staff over the streams and canals and ponds, and make frogs come up on the land of Egypt.' "

6 So Aaron stretched out his hand over the waters of Egypt, and the frogs came up and covered the land. 7 But the magicians did the same things by their secret arts; they also made frogs come up on the land of Egypt.

8 Pharaoh summoned Moses and Aaron and said, "Pray to the LORD to take the frogs away from me and my people, and I will let your people go to offer sacrifices to the LORD."

9 Moses said to Pharaoh, "I leave to you the honor of setting the time for me to pray for you and your officials and your people that you and your houses may be rid of the frogs, except for those that remain in the Nile."

10 "Tomorrow," Pharaoh said.

Moses replied, "It will be as you say, so that you may know there is no one like the LORD our God. 11 The frogs will leave you and your houses, your officials and your people; they will remain only in the Nile."

12 After Moses and Aaron left Pharaoh, Moses cried out to the LORD about the frogs he had brought on Pharaoh. 13 And the LORD did what Moses asked. The frogs died in the houses, in the courtyards and in the fields. 14 They were piled into heaps, and the land reeked of them. 15 But when Pharaoh saw that there was relief, he hardened his heart and would not listen to Moses and Aaron, just as the LORD had said.

The Plague of Gnats

16 Then the LORD said to Moses, "Tell Aaron, 'Stretch out your staff and strike the dust of the ground,' and throughout the land of Egypt the dust will become gnats." 17 They did this, and when Aaron stretched out his hand with the staff and struck the dust of the ground, gnats came on people and animals. All the dust throughout the land of Egypt became gnats. 18 But when the magicians tried to produce gnats by their secret arts, they could not.

Since the gnats were on people and animals everywhere, 19 the magicians said to Pharaoh, "This is the finger of God." But Pharaoh's heart was hard and he would not listen, just as the LORD had said.

The Plague of Flies

20 Then the LORD said to Moses, "Get up early in the morning and confront Pharaoh as he goes to the river and say to him, 'This is what the LORD says: Let my people go, so that they may worship me. 21 If you do not let my people go, I will send swarms of flies on you and your officials, on your people and into your houses. The houses of the Egyptians will be full of flies; even the ground will be covered with them.

22 " 'But on that day I will deal differently with the land of Goshen, where my people live; no swarms of flies will be there, so that you will know that I, the LORD, am in this land. 23 I will make a distinction[a] between my people and your people. This sign will occur tomorrow.' "

24 And the LORD did this. Dense swarms of flies poured into Pharaoh's palace and into the houses of his officials; throughout Egypt the land was ruined by the flies.

25 Then Pharaoh summoned Moses and Aaron and said, "Go, sacrifice to your God here in the land."

26 But Moses said, "That would not be right. The sacrifices we offer the LORD our God would be detestable to the Egyptians. And if we offer sacrifices that are detestable in their eyes, will they not stone us? 27 We must take a three-day journey into the wilderness to offer sacrifices to the LORD our God, as he commands us."

28 Pharaoh said, "I will let you go to offer sacrifices to the LORD your God in the wilderness, but you must not go very far. Now pray for me."

29 Moses answered, "As soon as I leave you, I will pray to the LORD, and tomorrow the flies will leave Pharaoh and his officials and his people. Only let Pharaoh be sure that he does not act deceitfully again by not letting the people go to offer sacrifices to the LORD."

30 Then Moses left Pharaoh and prayed to the LORD, 31 and the LORD did what Moses asked. The flies left Pharaoh and his officials and his people; not a fly remained. 32 But this

[a] 23 Septuagint and Vulgate; Hebrew *will put a deliverance*

OUR GOD

Matt Redman, Chris Tomlin, Jonas Myrin, Jesse Reeves

Water you turned into wine
Opened the eyes of the blind
There's no one like you
None like you

Into the darkness you shine
Out of the ashes we rise
There's no one like you
None like you

Our God is greater
Our God is stronger
God, you are higher than any other
Our God is Healer
Awesome in power
Our God
Our God

And if our God is for us
Then who could ever stop us
And if our God is with us
Then what could stand against

THE INSPIRATION

I know that the LORD is great, that our Lord is greater than all gods.

—Psalm 135:5

Read also: Romans 8:31

BEHIND THE SONG

"Our God," one of the standout songs of the 2010 Passion conference, has made its way into the hearts and repertoire of the church faster than any other song in recent memory. Written as a team effort by Matt Redman, Chris Tomlin, Jonas Myrin and Jesse Reeves, this triumphant chorus perfectly captures the energy of the conference, a gathering of more than 22,000 college students.

Redman brought a partial song idea that he had been working on with Myrin to a gathering of worship leaders preparing for the Passion event. When Tomlin heard it, he knew Matt was on to something special.

"When [Redman] started playing it on his acoustic guitar, I heard that chorus and it was so singable. Then he got to the bridge and I thought it was the best bridge I had heard in years. I could totally hear people just shouting that out," Tomlin recalls. He and his bass player Jesse Reeves then got to work alongside Redman to dial in the verses. "We played it for everyone, and they all thought it was a good song," Tomlin adds, "but none of us had any idea what it would become."

Selah

It's powerful to hear your own voice say things that you know are true regardless of your circumstances. Spend some time speaking out loud about the power and greatness of God. Do the words of Romans 8:31 ring true for you? Do you believe that when God is for you no one can stand against you? Think about what it means that God is for us? Does it mean that God agrees with all of our ideas and desires? Does it mean that we will never face trouble or danger?

time also Pharaoh hardened his heart and
would not let the people go.

The Plague on Livestock

9 Then the LORD said to Moses, "Go to
Pharaoh and say to him, 'This is what
the LORD, the God of the Hebrews, says: "Let
my people go, so that they may worship me."
2 If you refuse to let them go and continue
to hold them back, 3 the hand of the LORD
will bring a terrible plague on your live-
stock in the field — on your horses, donkeys
and camels and on your cattle, sheep and
goats. 4 But the LORD will make a distinction
between the livestock of Israel and that of
Egypt, so that no animal belonging to the Is-
raelites will die.' "

5 The LORD set a time and said, "Tomorrow
the LORD will do this in the land." 6 And the
next day the LORD did it: All the livestock of
the Egyptians died, but not one animal be-
longing to the Israelites died. 7 Pharaoh in-
vestigated and found that not even one of
the animals of the Israelites had died. Yet his
heart was unyielding and he would not let
the people go.

The Plague of Boils

8 Then the LORD said to Moses and Aaron,
"Take handfuls of soot from a furnace and
have Moses toss it into the air in the pres-
ence of Pharaoh. 9 It will become fine dust
over the whole land of Egypt, and festering
boils will break out on people and animals
throughout the land."

10 So they took soot from a furnace and
stood before Pharaoh. Moses tossed it into
the air, and festering boils broke out on peo-
ple and animals. 11 The magicians could not
stand before Moses because of the boils that
were on them and on all the Egyptians. 12 But
the LORD hardened Pharaoh's heart and he
would not listen to Moses and Aaron, just as
the LORD had said to Moses.

The Plague of Hail

13 Then the LORD said to Moses, "Get up
early in the morning, confront Pharaoh and
say to him, 'This is what the LORD, the God
of the Hebrews, says: Let my people go, so
that they may worship me, 14 or this time I
will send the full force of my plagues against
you and against your officials and your peo-
ple, so you may know that there is no one like
me in all the earth. 15 For by now I could have
stretched out my hand and struck you and
your people with a plague that would have
wiped you off the earth. 16 But I have raised
you up[a] for this very purpose, that I might
show you my power and that my name might
be proclaimed in all the earth. 17 You still set
yourself against my people and will not let
them go. 18 Therefore, at this time tomorrow
I will send the worst hailstorm that has ever
fallen on Egypt, from the day it was founded
till now. 19 Give an order now to bring your
livestock and everything you have in the
field to a place of shelter, because the hail
will fall on every person and animal that
has not been brought in and is still out in the
field, and they will die.' "

20 Those officials of Pharaoh who feared
the word of the LORD hurried to bring their
slaves and their livestock inside. 21 But those
who ignored the word of the LORD left their
slaves and livestock in the field.

22 Then the LORD said to Moses, "Stretch
out your hand toward the sky so that hail will
fall all over Egypt — on people and animals
and on everything growing in the fields of
Egypt." 23 When Moses stretched out his
staff toward the sky, the LORD sent thunder
and hail, and lightning flashed down to the
ground. So the LORD rained hail on the land
of Egypt; 24 hail fell and lightning flashed
back and forth. It was the worst storm in
all the land of Egypt since it had become a
nation. 25 Throughout Egypt hail struck ev-
erything in the fields — both people and an-
imals; it beat down everything growing in
the fields and stripped every tree. 26 The only
place it did not hail was the land of Goshen,
where the Israelites were.

27 Then Pharaoh summoned Moses and
Aaron. "This time I have sinned," he said to
them. "The LORD is in the right, and I and my
people are in the wrong. 28 Pray to the LORD,
for we have had enough thunder and hail.
I will let you go; you don't have to stay any
longer."

29 Moses replied, "When I have gone out of
the city, I will spread out my hands in prayer
to the LORD. The thunder will stop and there
will be no more hail, so you may know that

[a] 16 Or *have spared you*

the earth is the LORD's. 30 But I know that you and your officials still do not fear the LORD God."

31 (The flax and barley were destroyed, since the barley had headed and the flax was in bloom. 32 The wheat and spelt, however, were not destroyed, because they ripen later.)

33 Then Moses left Pharaoh and went out of the city. He spread out his hands toward the LORD; the thunder and hail stopped, and the rain no longer poured down on the land. 34 When Pharaoh saw that the rain and hail and thunder had stopped, he sinned again: He and his officials hardened their hearts. 35 So Pharaoh's heart was hard and he would not let the Israelites go, just as the LORD had said through Moses.

The Plague of Locusts

10 Then the LORD said to Moses, "Go to Pharaoh, for I have hardened his heart and the hearts of his officials so that I may perform these signs of mine among them 2 that you may tell your children and grandchildren how I dealt harshly with the Egyptians and how I performed my signs among them, and that you may know that I am the LORD."

3 So Moses and Aaron went to Pharaoh and said to him, "This is what the LORD, the God of the Hebrews, says: 'How long will you refuse to humble yourself before me? Let my people go, so that they may worship me. 4 If you refuse to let them go, I will bring locusts into your country tomorrow. 5 They will cover the face of the ground so that it cannot be seen. They will devour what little you have left after the hail, including every tree that is growing in your fields. 6 They will fill your houses and those of all your officials and all the Egyptians — something neither your parents nor your ancestors have ever seen from the day they settled in this land till now.' " Then Moses turned and left Pharaoh.

7 Pharaoh's officials said to him, "How long will this man be a snare to us? Let the people go, so that they may worship the LORD their God. Do you not yet realize that Egypt is ruined?"

8 Then Moses and Aaron were brought back to Pharaoh. "Go, worship the LORD your God," he said. "But tell me who will be going."

9 Moses answered, "We will go with our young and our old, with our sons and our daughters, and with our flocks and herds, because we are to celebrate a festival to the LORD."

10 Pharaoh said, "The LORD be with you — if I let you go, along with your women and children! Clearly you are bent on evil.[a] 11 No! Have only the men go and worship the LORD, since that's what you have been asking for." Then Moses and Aaron were driven out of Pharaoh's presence.

12 And the LORD said to Moses, "Stretch out your hand over Egypt so that locusts swarm over the land and devour everything growing in the fields, everything left by the hail."

13 So Moses stretched out his staff over Egypt, and the LORD made an east wind blow across the land all that day and all that night. By morning the wind had brought the locusts; 14 they invaded all Egypt and settled down in every area of the country in great numbers. Never before had there been such a plague of locusts, nor will there ever be again. 15 They covered all the ground until it was black. They devoured all that was left after the hail — everything growing in the fields and the fruit on the trees. Nothing green remained on tree or plant in all the land of Egypt.

16 Pharaoh quickly summoned Moses and Aaron and said, "I have sinned against the LORD your God and against you. 17 Now forgive my sin once more and pray to the LORD your God to take this deadly plague away from me."

18 Moses then left Pharaoh and prayed to the LORD. 19 And the LORD changed the wind to a very strong west wind, which caught up the locusts and carried them into the Red Sea.[b] Not a locust was left anywhere in Egypt. 20 But the LORD hardened Pharaoh's heart, and he would not let the Israelites go.

The Plague of Darkness

21 Then the LORD said to Moses, "Stretch out your hand toward the sky so that darkness spreads over Egypt — darkness that can be felt." 22 So Moses stretched out his hand toward the sky, and total darkness covered all Egypt for three days. 23 No one could see

[a] 10 Or *Be careful, trouble is in store for you!* [b] 19 Or *the Sea of Reeds*

anyone else or move about for three days. Yet all the Israelites had light in the places where they lived.

[24]Then Pharaoh summoned Moses and said, "Go, worship the LORD. Even your women and children may go with you; only leave your flocks and herds behind."

[25]But Moses said, "You must allow us to have sacrifices and burnt offerings to present to the LORD our God. [26]Our livestock too must go with us; not a hoof is to be left behind. We have to use some of them in worshiping the LORD our God, and until we get there we will not know what we are to use to worship the LORD."

[27]But the LORD hardened Pharaoh's heart, and he was not willing to let them go. [28]Pharaoh said to Moses, "Get out of my sight! Make sure you do not appear before me again! The day you see my face you will die."

[29]"Just as you say," Moses replied. "I will never appear before you again."

The Plague on the Firstborn

11 Now the LORD had said to Moses, "I will bring one more plague on Pharaoh and on Egypt. After that, he will let you go from here, and when he does, he will drive you out completely. [2]Tell the people that men and women alike are to ask their neighbors for articles of silver and gold." [3](The LORD made the Egyptians favorably disposed toward the people, and Moses himself was highly regarded in Egypt by Pharaoh's officials and by the people.)

[4]So Moses said, "This is what the LORD says: 'About midnight I will go throughout Egypt. [5]Every firstborn son in Egypt will die, from the firstborn son of Pharaoh, who sits on the throne, to the firstborn son of the female slave, who is at her hand mill, and all the firstborn of the cattle as well. [6]There will be loud wailing throughout Egypt—worse than there has ever been or ever will be again. [7]But among the Israelites not a dog will bark at any person or animal.' Then you will know that the LORD makes a distinction between Egypt and Israel. [8]All these officials of yours will come to me, bowing down before me and saying, 'Go, you and all the people who follow you!' After that I will leave." Then Moses, hot with anger, left Pharaoh.

[9]The LORD had said to Moses, "Pharaoh will refuse to listen to you—so that my wonders may be multiplied in Egypt." [10]Moses and Aaron performed all these wonders before Pharaoh, but the LORD hardened Pharaoh's heart, and he would not let the Israelites go out of his country.

The Passover and the Festival of Unleavened Bread

12 The LORD said to Moses and Aaron in Egypt, [2]"This month is to be for you the first month, the first month of your year. [3]Tell the whole community of Israel that on the tenth day of this month each man is to take a lamb[a] for his family, one for each household. [4]If any household is too small for a whole lamb, they must share one with their nearest neighbor, having taken into account the number of people there are. You are to determine the amount of lamb needed in accordance with what each person will eat. [5]The animals you choose must be year-old males without defect, and you may take them from the sheep or the goats. [6]Take care of them until the fourteenth day of the month, when all the members of the community of Israel must slaughter them at twilight. [7]Then they are to take some of the blood and put it on the sides and tops of the doorframes of the houses where they eat the lambs. [8]That same night they are to eat the meat roasted over the fire, along with bitter herbs, and bread made without yeast. [9]Do not eat the meat raw or boiled in water, but roast it over a fire—with the head, legs and internal organs. [10]Do not leave any of it till morning; if some is left till morning, you must burn it. [11]This is how you are to eat it: with your cloak tucked into your belt, your sandals on your feet and your staff in your hand. Eat it in haste; it is the LORD's Passover.

[12]"On that same night I will pass through Egypt and strike down every firstborn of both people and animals, and I will bring judgment on all the gods of Egypt. I am the LORD. [13]The blood will be a sign for you on the houses where you are, and when I see the blood, I will pass over you. No destructive plague will touch you when I strike Egypt.

[14]"This is a day you are to commemorate; for the generations to come you shall cele-

[a] 3 The Hebrew word can mean *lamb* or *kid*; also in verse 4.

brate it as a festival to the LORD—a lasting ordinance. [15]For seven days you are to eat bread made without yeast. On the first day remove the yeast from your houses, for whoever eats anything with yeast in it from the first day through the seventh must be cut off from Israel. [16]On the first day hold a sacred assembly, and another one on the seventh day. Do no work at all on these days, except to prepare food for everyone to eat; that is all you may do.

[17]"Celebrate the Festival of Unleavened Bread, because it was on this very day that I brought your divisions out of Egypt. Celebrate this day as a lasting ordinance for the generations to come. [18]In the first month you are to eat bread made without yeast, from the evening of the fourteenth day until the evening of the twenty-first day. [19]For seven days no yeast is to be found in your houses. And anyone, whether foreigner or native-born, who eats anything with yeast in it must be cut off from the community of Israel. [20]Eat nothing made with yeast. Wherever you live, you must eat unleavened bread."

[21]Then Moses summoned all the elders of Israel and said to them, "Go at once and select the animals for your families and slaughter the Passover lamb. [22]Take a bunch of hyssop, dip it into the blood in the basin and put some of the blood on the top and on both sides of the doorframe. None of you shall go out of the door of your house until morning. [23]When the LORD goes through the land to strike down the Egyptians, he will see the blood on the top and sides of the doorframe and will pass over that doorway, and he will not permit the destroyer to enter your houses and strike you down.

[24]"Obey these instructions as a lasting ordinance for you and your descendants. [25]When you enter the land that the LORD will give you as he promised, observe this ceremony. [26]And when your children ask you, 'What does this ceremony mean to you?' [27]then tell them, 'It is the Passover sacrifice to the LORD, who passed over the houses of the Israelites in Egypt and spared our homes when he struck down the Egyptians.'" Then the people bowed down and worshiped. [28]The Israelites did just what the LORD commanded Moses and Aaron.

[29]At midnight the LORD struck down all the firstborn in Egypt, from the firstborn of Pharaoh, who sat on the throne, to the firstborn of the prisoner, who was in the dungeon, and the firstborn of all the livestock as well. [30]Pharaoh and all his officials and all the Egyptians got up during the night, and there was loud wailing in Egypt, for there was not a house without someone dead.

The Exodus

[31]During the night Pharaoh summoned Moses and Aaron and said, "Up! Leave my people, you and the Israelites! Go, worship the LORD as you have requested. [32]Take your flocks and herds, as you have said, and go. And also bless me."

[33]The Egyptians urged the people to hurry and leave the country. "For otherwise," they said, "we will all die!" [34]So the people took their dough before the yeast was added, and carried it on their shoulders in kneading troughs wrapped in clothing. [35]The Israelites did as Moses instructed and asked the Egyptians for articles of silver and gold and for clothing. [36]The LORD had made the Egyptians favorably disposed toward the people, and they gave them what they asked for; so they plundered the Egyptians.

[37]The Israelites journeyed from Rameses to Sukkoth. There were about six hundred thousand men on foot, besides women and children. [38]Many other people went up with them, and also large droves of livestock, both flocks and herds. [39]With the dough the Israelites had brought from Egypt, they baked loaves of unleavened bread. The dough was without yeast because they had been driven out of Egypt and did not have time to prepare food for themselves.

[40]Now the length of time the Israelite people lived in Egypt[a] was 430 years. [41]At the end of the 430 years, to the very day, all the LORD's divisions left Egypt. [42]Because the LORD kept vigil that night to bring them out of Egypt, on this night all the Israelites are to keep vigil to honor the LORD for the generations to come.

Passover Restrictions

[43]The LORD said to Moses and Aaron, "These are the regulations for the Passover meal:

[a] 40 Masoretic Text; Samaritan Pentateuch and Septuagint *Egypt and Canaan*

"No foreigner may eat it. 44Any slave you
have bought may eat it after you have cir-
cumcised him, 45but a temporary resident or
a hired worker may not eat it.

46"It must be eaten inside the house; take
none of the meat outside the house. Do not
break any of the bones. 47The whole commu-
nity of Israel must celebrate it.

48"A foreigner residing among you who
wants to celebrate the LORD's Passover must
have all the males in his household circum-
cised; then he may take part like one born in
the land. No uncircumcised male may eat it.
49The same law applies both to the native-
born and to the foreigner residing among
you."

50All the Israelites did just what the LORD
had commanded Moses and Aaron. 51And
on that very day the LORD brought the Isra-
elites out of Egypt by their divisions.

Consecration of the Firstborn

13 The LORD said to Moses, 2"Conse-
crate to me every firstborn male. The
first offspring of every womb among the Is-
raelites belongs to me, whether human or
animal."

3Then Moses said to the people, "Com-
memorate this day, the day you came out
of Egypt, out of the land of slavery, because
the LORD brought you out of it with a mighty
hand. Eat nothing containing yeast. 4Today,
in the month of Aviv, you are leaving. 5When
the LORD brings you into the land of the Ca-
naanites, Hittites, Amorites, Hivites and Jeb-
usites — the land he swore to your ancestors
to give you, a land flowing with milk and
honey — you are to observe this ceremony in
this month: 6For seven days eat bread made
without yeast and on the seventh day hold a
festival to the LORD. 7Eat unleavened bread
during those seven days; nothing with yeast
in it is to be seen among you, nor shall any
yeast be seen anywhere within your borders.
8On that day tell your son, 'I do this because
of what the LORD did for me when I came out
of Egypt.' 9This observance will be for you
like a sign on your hand and a reminder on
your forehead that this law of the LORD is to
be on your lips. For the LORD brought you out
of Egypt with his mighty hand. 10You must
keep this ordinance at the appointed time
year after year.

11"After the LORD brings you into the land
of the Canaanites and gives it to you, as he
promised on oath to you and your ancestors,
12you are to give over to the LORD the first off-
spring of every womb. All the firstborn males
of your livestock belong to the LORD. 13Re-
deem with a lamb every firstborn donkey,
but if you do not redeem it, break its neck.
Redeem every firstborn among your sons.

14"In days to come, when your son asks
you, 'What does this mean?' say to him,
'With a mighty hand the LORD brought
us out of Egypt, out of the land of slavery.
15When Pharaoh stubbornly refused to let
us go, the LORD killed the firstborn of both
people and animals in Egypt. This is why I
sacrifice to the LORD the first male offspring
of every womb and redeem each of my first-
born sons.' 16And it will be like a sign on your
hand and a symbol on your forehead that
the LORD brought us out of Egypt with his
mighty hand."

Crossing the Sea

17When Pharaoh let the people go, God
did not lead them on the road through the
Philistine country, though that was shorter.
For God said, "If they face war, they might
change their minds and return to Egypt."
18So God led the people around by the des-
ert road toward the Red Sea.[a] The Israelites
went up out of Egypt ready for battle.

19Moses took the bones of Joseph with
him because Joseph had made the Israelites
swear an oath. He had said, "God will surely
come to your aid, and then you must carry
my bones up with you from this place."[b]

20After leaving Sukkoth they camped at
Etham on the edge of the desert. 21By day the
LORD went ahead of them in a pillar of cloud
to guide them on their way and by night in a
pillar of fire to give them light, so that they
could travel by day or night. 22Neither the
pillar of cloud by day nor the pillar of fire by
night left its place in front of the people.

14 Then the LORD said to Moses, 2"Tell
the Israelites to turn back and en-
camp near Pi Hahiroth, between Migdol and
the sea. They are to encamp by the sea, di-
rectly opposite Baal Zephon. 3Pharaoh will
think, 'The Israelites are wandering around
the land in confusion, hemmed in by the

[a] 18 Or *the Sea of Reeds* [b] 19 See Gen. 50:25.

desert.' [4]And I will harden Pharaoh's heart, and he will pursue them. But I will gain glory for myself through Pharaoh and all his army, and the Egyptians will know that I am the LORD." So the Israelites did this.

[5]When the king of Egypt was told that the people had fled, Pharaoh and his officials changed their minds about them and said, "What have we done? We have let the Israelites go and have lost their services!" [6]So he had his chariot made ready and took his army with him. [7]He took six hundred of the best chariots, along with all the other chariots of Egypt, with officers over all of them. [8]The LORD hardened the heart of Pharaoh king of Egypt, so that he pursued the Israelites, who were marching out boldly. [9]The Egyptians — all Pharaoh's horses and chariots, horsemen[a] and troops — pursued the Israelites and overtook them as they camped by the sea near Pi Hahiroth, opposite Baal Zephon.

[10]As Pharaoh approached, the Israelites looked up, and there were the Egyptians, marching after them. They were terrified and cried out to the LORD. [11]They said to Moses, "Was it because there were no graves in Egypt that you brought us to the desert to die? What have you done to us by bringing us out of Egypt? [12]Didn't we say to you in Egypt, 'Leave us alone; let us serve the Egyptians'? It would have been better for us to serve the Egyptians than to die in the desert!"

[13]Moses answered the people, "Do not be afraid. Stand firm and you will see the deliverance the LORD will bring you today. The Egyptians you see today you will never see again. [14]The LORD will fight for you; you need only to be still."

[15]Then the LORD said to Moses, "Why are you crying out to me? Tell the Israelites to move on. [16]Raise your staff and stretch out your hand over the sea to divide the water so that the Israelites can go through the sea on dry ground. [17]I will harden the hearts of the Egyptians so that they will go in after them. And I will gain glory through Pharaoh and all his army, through his chariots and his horsemen. [18]The Egyptians will know that I am the LORD when I gain glory through Pharaoh, his chariots and his horsemen."

[19]Then the angel of God, who had been traveling in front of Israel's army, withdrew and went behind them. The pillar of cloud also moved from in front and stood behind them, [20]coming between the armies of Egypt and Israel. Throughout the night the cloud brought darkness to the one side and light to the other side; so neither went near the other all night long.

[21]Then Moses stretched out his hand over the sea, and all that night the LORD drove the sea back with a strong east wind and turned it into dry land. The waters were divided, [22]and the Israelites went through the sea on dry ground, with a wall of water on their right and on their left.

[23]The Egyptians pursued them, and all Pharaoh's horses and chariots and horsemen followed them into the sea. [24]During the last watch of the night the LORD looked down from the pillar of fire and cloud at the Egyptian army and threw it into confusion. [25]He jammed[b] the wheels of their chariots so that they had difficulty driving. And the Egyptians said, "Let's get away from the Israelites! The LORD is fighting for them against Egypt."

[26]Then the LORD said to Moses, "Stretch out your hand over the sea so that the waters may flow back over the Egyptians and their chariots and horsemen." [27]Moses stretched out his hand over the sea, and at daybreak the sea went back to its place. The Egyptians were fleeing toward[c] it, and the LORD swept them into the sea. [28]The water flowed back and covered the chariots and horsemen — the entire army of Pharaoh that had followed the Israelites into the sea. Not one of them survived.

[29]But the Israelites went through the sea on dry ground, with a wall of water on their right and on their left. [30]That day the LORD saved Israel from the hands of the Egyptians, and Israel saw the Egyptians lying dead on the shore. [31]And when the Israelites saw the mighty hand of the LORD displayed against the Egyptians, the people feared the LORD and put their trust in him and in Moses his servant.

The Song of Moses and Miriam

15 Then Moses and the Israelites sang this song to the LORD:

"I will sing to the LORD,
for he is highly exalted.

[a] 9 Or *charioteers*; also in verses 17, 18, 23, 26 and 28 [b] 25 See Samaritan Pentateuch, Septuagint and Syriac; Masoretic Text *removed* [c] 27 Or *from*

Both horse and driver
he has hurled into the sea.

2 "The LORD is my strength and my defense[a];
he has become my salvation.
He is my God, and I will praise him,
my father's God, and I will exalt him.
3 The LORD is a warrior;
the LORD is his name.
4 Pharaoh's chariots and his army
he has hurled into the sea.
The best of Pharaoh's officers
are drowned in the Red Sea.[b]
5 The deep waters have covered them;
they sank to the depths like a stone.
6 Your right hand, LORD,
was majestic in power.
Your right hand, LORD,
shattered the enemy.

7 "In the greatness of your majesty
you threw down those who opposed you.
You unleashed your burning anger;
it consumed them like stubble.
8 By the blast of your nostrils
the waters piled up.
The surging waters stood up like a wall;
the deep waters congealed in the heart of the sea.
9 The enemy boasted,
'I will pursue, I will overtake them.
I will divide the spoils;
I will gorge myself on them.
I will draw my sword
and my hand will destroy them.'
10 But you blew with your breath,
and the sea covered them.
They sank like lead
in the mighty waters.
11 Who among the gods
is like you, LORD?
Who is like you—
majestic in holiness,
awesome in glory,
working wonders?

12 "You stretch out your right hand,
and the earth swallows your enemies.
13 In your unfailing love you will lead
the people you have redeemed.
In your strength you will guide them
to your holy dwelling.
14 The nations will hear and tremble;
anguish will grip the people of Philistia.
15 The chiefs of Edom will be terrified,
the leaders of Moab will be seized with trembling,
the people[c] of Canaan will melt away;
16 terror and dread will fall on them.
By the power of your arm
they will be as still as a stone—
until your people pass by, LORD,
until the people you bought[d] pass by.
17 You will bring them in and plant them
on the mountain of your inheritance—
the place, LORD, you made for your dwelling,
the sanctuary, Lord, your hands established.

18 "The LORD reigns
for ever and ever."

19 When Pharaoh's horses, chariots and
horsemen[e] went into the sea, the LORD
brought the waters of the sea back over them,
but the Israelites walked through the sea on
dry ground. 20 Then Miriam the prophet,
Aaron's sister, took a timbrel in her hand,
and all the women followed her, with tim-
brels and dancing. 21 Miriam sang to them:

"Sing to the LORD,
for he is highly exalted.
Both horse and driver
he has hurled into the sea."

The Waters of Marah and Elim

22 Then Moses led Israel from the Red Sea
and they went into the Desert of Shur. For
three days they traveled in the desert with-
out finding water. 23 When they came to Ma-
rah, they could not drink its water because
it was bitter. (That is why the place is called
Marah.[f]) 24 So the people grumbled against
Moses, saying, "What are we to drink?"
25 Then Moses cried out to the LORD, and
the LORD showed him a piece of wood. He
threw it into the water, and the water be-
came fit to drink.

There the LORD issued a ruling and in-
struction for them and put them to the test.
26 He said, "If you listen carefully to the LORD

[a] 2 Or *song* [b] 4 Or *the Sea of Reeds*; also in verse 22 [c] 15 Or *rulers* [d] 16 Or *created*
[e] 19 Or *charioteers* [f] 23 *Marah* means *bitter*.

your God and do what is right in his eyes, if you pay attention to his commands and keep all his decrees, I will not bring on you any of the diseases I brought on the Egyptians, for I am the LORD, who heals you."

[27]Then they came to Elim, where there were twelve springs and seventy palm trees, and they camped there near the water.

Manna and Quail

16 The whole Israelite community set out from Elim and came to the Desert of Sin, which is between Elim and Sinai, on the fifteenth day of the second month after they had come out of Egypt. [2]In the desert the whole community grumbled against Moses and Aaron. [3]The Israelites said to them, "If only we had died by the LORD's hand in Egypt! There we sat around pots of meat and ate all the food we wanted, but you have brought us out into this desert to starve this entire assembly to death."

[4]Then the LORD said to Moses, "I will rain down bread from heaven for you. The people are to go out each day and gather enough for that day. In this way I will test them and see whether they will follow my instructions. [5]On the sixth day they are to prepare what they bring in, and that is to be twice as much as they gather on the other days."

[6]So Moses and Aaron said to all the Israelites, "In the evening you will know that it was the LORD who brought you out of Egypt, [7]and in the morning you will see the glory of the LORD, because he has heard your grumbling against him. Who are we, that you should grumble against us?" [8]Moses also said, "You will know that it was the LORD when he gives you meat to eat in the evening and all the bread you want in the morning, because he has heard your grumbling against him. Who are we? You are not grumbling against us, but against the LORD."

[9]Then Moses told Aaron, "Say to the entire Israelite community, 'Come before the LORD, for he has heard your grumbling.' "

[10]While Aaron was speaking to the whole Israelite community, they looked toward the desert, and there was the glory of the LORD appearing in the cloud.

[11]The LORD said to Moses, [12]"I have heard the grumbling of the Israelites. Tell them, 'At twilight you will eat meat, and in the morning you will be filled with bread. Then you will know that I am the LORD your God.' "

[13]That evening quail came and covered the camp, and in the morning there was a layer of dew around the camp. [14]When the dew was gone, thin flakes like frost on the ground appeared on the desert floor. [15]When the Israelites saw it, they said to each other, "What is it?" For they did not know what it was.

Moses said to them, "It is the bread the LORD has given you to eat. [16]This is what the LORD has commanded: 'Everyone is to gather as much as they need. Take an omer[a] for each person you have in your tent.' "

[17]The Israelites did as they were told; some gathered much, some little. [18]And when they measured it by the omer, the one who gathered much did not have too much, and the one who gathered little did not have too little. Everyone had gathered just as much as they needed.

[19]Then Moses said to them, "No one is to keep any of it until morning."

[20]However, some of them paid no attention to Moses; they kept part of it until morning, but it was full of maggots and began to smell. So Moses was angry with them.

[21]Each morning everyone gathered as much as they needed, and when the sun grew hot, it melted away. [22]On the sixth day, they gathered twice as much — two omers[b] for each person — and the leaders of the community came and reported this to Moses. [23]He said to them, "This is what the LORD commanded: 'Tomorrow is to be a day of sabbath rest, a holy sabbath to the LORD. So bake what you want to bake and boil what you want to boil. Save whatever is left and keep it until morning.' "

[24]So they saved it until morning, as Moses commanded, and it did not stink or get maggots in it. [25]"Eat it today," Moses said, "because today is a sabbath to the LORD. You will not find any of it on the ground today. [26]Six days you are to gather it, but on the seventh day, the Sabbath, there will not be any."

[27]Nevertheless, some of the people went out on the seventh day to gather it, but they found none. [28]Then the LORD said to Moses, "How long will you[c] refuse to keep my

[a] *16* That is, possibly about 3 pounds or about 1.4 kilograms; also in verses 18, 32, 33 and 36 [b] *22* That is, possibly about 6 pounds or about 2.8 kilograms [c] *28* The Hebrew is plural.

commands and my instructions? 29 Bear in
mind that the LORD has given you the Sab-
bath; that is why on the sixth day he gives
you bread for two days. Everyone is to stay
where they are on the seventh day; no one is
to go out." 30 So the people rested on the sev-
enth day.

31 The people of Israel called the bread
manna.[a] It was white like coriander seed
and tasted like wafers made with honey.
32 Moses said, "This is what the LORD has
commanded: 'Take an omer of manna and
keep it for the generations to come, so they
can see the bread I gave you to eat in the wil-
derness when I brought you out of Egypt.' "

33 So Moses said to Aaron, "Take a jar and
put an omer of manna in it. Then place it be-
fore the LORD to be kept for the generations
to come."

34 As the LORD commanded Moses, Aar-
on put the manna with the tablets of the
covenant law, so that it might be preserved.
35 The Israelites ate manna forty years, un-
til they came to a land that was settled; they
ate manna until they reached the border of
Canaan.

36 (An omer is one-tenth of an ephah.)

Water From the Rock

17 The whole Israelite community set
out from the Desert of Sin, traveling
from place to place as the LORD command-
ed. They camped at Rephidim, but there was
no water for the people to drink. 2 So they
quarreled with Moses and said, "Give us wa-
ter to drink."

Moses replied, "Why do you quarrel with
me? Why do you put the LORD to the test?"

3 But the people were thirsty for water
there, and they grumbled against Moses.
They said, "Why did you bring us up out of
Egypt to make us and our children and live-
stock die of thirst?"

4 Then Moses cried out to the LORD, "What
am I to do with these people? They are al-
most ready to stone me."

5 The LORD answered Moses, "Go out in
front of the people. Take with you some of
the elders of Israel and take in your hand the
staff with which you struck the Nile, and go.
6 I will stand there before you by the rock at
Horeb. Strike the rock, and water will come
out of it for the people to drink." So Moses
did this in the sight of the elders of Israel.
7 And he called the place Massah[b] and Mer-
ibah[c] because the Israelites quarreled and
because they tested the LORD saying, "Is the
LORD among us or not?"

The Amalekites Defeated

8 The Amalekites came and attacked the
Israelites at Rephidim. 9 Moses said to Josh-
ua, "Choose some of our men and go out to
fight the Amalekites. Tomorrow I will stand
on top of the hill with the staff of God in my
hands."

10 So Joshua fought the Amalekites as Mo-
ses had ordered, and Moses, Aaron and Hur
went to the top of the hill. 11 As long as Moses
held up his hands, the Israelites were win-
ning, but whenever he lowered his hands,
the Amalekites were winning. 12 When Mo-
ses' hands grew tired, they took a stone and
put it under him and he sat on it. Aaron and
Hur held his hands up—one on one side, one
on the other—so that his hands remained
steady till sunset. 13 So Joshua overcame the
Amalekite army with the sword.

14 Then the LORD said to Moses, "Write
this on a scroll as something to be remem-
bered and make sure that Joshua hears it,
because I will completely blot out the name
of Amalek from under heaven."

15 Moses built an altar and called it The
LORD is my Banner. 16 He said, "Because
hands were lifted up against[d] the throne of
the LORD,[e] the LORD will be at war against
the Amalekites from generation to genera-
tion."

Jethro Visits Moses

18 Now Jethro, the priest of Midian and
father-in-law of Moses, heard of ev-
erything God had done for Moses and for
his people Israel, and how the LORD had
brought Israel out of Egypt.

2 After Moses had sent away his wife Zip-
porah, his father-in-law Jethro received her
3 and her two sons. One son was named Ger-
shom,[f] for Moses said, "I have become a for-
eigner in a foreign land"; 4 and the other was
named Eliezer,[g] for he said, "My father's God

[a] 31 *Manna* sounds like the Hebrew for *What is it?* (see verse 15). [b] 7 *Massah* means *testing.*
[c] 7 *Meribah* means *quarreling.* [d] 16 Or *to* [e] 16 The meaning of the Hebrew for this clause is uncertain.
[f] 3 *Gershom* sounds like the Hebrew for *a foreigner there.* [g] 4 *Eliezer* means *my God is helper.*

was my helper; he saved me from the sword
of Pharaoh."
5 Jethro, Moses' father-in-law, together
with Moses' sons and wife, came to him in
the wilderness, where he was camped near
the mountain of God. 6 Jethro had sent word
to him, "I, your father-in-law Jethro, am
coming to you with your wife and her two
sons."
7 So Moses went out to meet his father-in-
law and bowed down and kissed him. They
greeted each other and then went into the
tent. 8 Moses told his father-in-law about ev-
erything the LORD had done to Pharaoh and
the Egyptians for Israel's sake and about all
the hardships they had met along the way
and how the LORD had saved them.
9 Jethro was delighted to hear about all the
good things the LORD had done for Israel in
rescuing them from the hand of the Egyp-
tians. 10 He said, "Praise be to the LORD, who
rescued you from the hand of the Egyptians
and of Pharaoh, and who rescued the peo-
ple from the hand of the Egyptians. 11 Now I
know that the LORD is greater than all other
gods, for he did this to those who had treat-
ed Israel arrogantly." 12 Then Jethro, Moses'
father-in-law, brought a burnt offering and
other sacrifices to God, and Aaron came
with all the elders of Israel to eat a meal with
Moses' father-in-law in the presence of God.
13 The next day Moses took his seat to
serve as judge for the people, and they stood
around him from morning till evening.
14 When his father-in-law saw all that Moses
was doing for the people, he said, "What is
this you are doing for the people? Why do
you alone sit as judge, while all these peo-
ple stand around you from morning till eve-
ning?"
15 Moses answered him, "Because the peo-
ple come to me to seek God's will. 16 When-
ever they have a dispute, it is brought to me,
and I decide between the parties and inform
them of God's decrees and instructions."
17 Moses' father-in-law replied, "What you
are doing is not good. 18 You and these people
who come to you will only wear yourselves
out. The work is too heavy for you; you can-
not handle it alone. 19 Listen now to me and I
will give you some advice, and may God be
with you. You must be the people's represen-
tative before God and bring their disputes to
him. 20 Teach them his decrees and instruc-
tions, and show them the way they are to live
and how they are to behave. 21 But select ca-
pable men from all the people—men who
fear God, trustworthy men who hate dis-
honest gain—and appoint them as officials
over thousands, hundreds, fifties and tens.
22 Have them serve as judges for the people
at all times, but have them bring every dif-
ficult case to you; the simple cases they can
decide themselves. That will make your load
lighter, because they will share it with you.
23 If you do this and God so commands, you
will be able to stand the strain, and all these
people will go home satisfied."
24 Moses listened to his father-in-law and
did everything he said. 25 He chose capable
men from all Israel and made them lead-
ers of the people, officials over thousands,
hundreds, fifties and tens. 26 They served as
judges for the people at all times. The dif-
ficult cases they brought to Moses, but the
simple ones they decided themselves.
27 Then Moses sent his father-in-law on his
way, and Jethro returned to his own country.

At Mount Sinai

19 On the first day of the third month af-
ter the Israelites left Egypt—on that
very day—they came to the Desert of Sinai.
2 After they set out from Rephidim, they en-
tered the Desert of Sinai, and Israel camped
there in the desert in front of the mountain.
3 Then Moses went up to God, and the
LORD called to him from the mountain and
said, "This is what you are to say to the de-
scendants of Jacob and what you are to tell
the people of Israel: 4 'You yourselves have
seen what I did to Egypt, and how I carried
you on eagles' wings and brought you to my-
self. 5 Now if you obey me fully and keep my
covenant, then out of all nations you will be
my treasured possession. Although the whole
earth is mine, 6 you[a] will be for me a kingdom
of priests and a holy nation.' These are the
words you are to speak to the Israelites."
7 So Moses went back and summoned the
elders of the people and set before them all
the words the LORD had commanded him to
speak. 8 The people all responded together,
"We will do everything the LORD has said."

[a] 5,6 Or *possession, for the whole earth is mine.* 6 *You*

So Moses brought their answer back to the LORD.

9 The LORD said to Moses, "I am going to come to you in a dense cloud, so that the people will hear me speaking with you and will always put their trust in you." Then Moses told the LORD what the people had said.

10 And the LORD said to Moses, "Go to the people and consecrate them today and tomorrow. Have them wash their clothes 11 and be ready by the third day, because on that day the LORD will come down on Mount Sinai in the sight of all the people. 12 Put limits for the people around the mountain and tell them, 'Be careful that you do not approach the mountain or touch the foot of it. Whoever touches the mountain is to be put to death. 13 They are to be stoned or shot with arrows; not a hand is to be laid on them. No person or animal shall be permitted to live.' Only when the ram's horn sounds a long blast may they approach the mountain."

14 After Moses had gone down the mountain to the people, he consecrated them, and they washed their clothes. 15 Then he said to the people, "Prepare yourselves for the third day. Abstain from sexual relations."

16 On the morning of the third day there was thunder and lightning, with a thick cloud over the mountain, and a very loud trumpet blast. Everyone in the camp trembled. 17 Then Moses led the people out of the camp to meet with God, and they stood at the foot of the mountain. 18 Mount Sinai was covered with smoke, because the LORD descended on it in fire. The smoke billowed up from it like smoke from a furnace, and the whole mountain[a] trembled violently. 19 As the sound of the trumpet grew louder and louder, Moses spoke and the voice of God answered him.[b]

20 The LORD descended to the top of Mount Sinai and called Moses to the top of the mountain. So Moses went up 21 and the LORD said to him, "Go down and warn the people so they do not force their way through to see the LORD and many of them perish. 22 Even the priests, who approach the LORD, must consecrate themselves, or the LORD will break out against them."

23 Moses said to the LORD, "The people cannot come up Mount Sinai, because you yourself warned us, 'Put limits around the mountain and set it apart as holy.' "

24 The LORD replied, "Go down and bring Aaron up with you. But the priests and the people must not force their way through to come up to the LORD, or he will break out against them."

25 So Moses went down to the people and told them.

The Ten Commandments

20 And God spoke all these words:

2 "I am the LORD your God, who brought you out of Egypt, out of the land of slavery.

3 "You shall have no other gods before[c] me.

4 "You shall not make for yourself an image in the form of anything in heaven above or on the earth beneath or in the waters below. 5 You shall not bow down to them or worship them; for I, the LORD your God, am a jealous God, punishing the children for the sin of the parents to the third and fourth generation of those who hate me, 6 but showing love to a thousand generations of those who love me and keep my commandments.

7 "You shall not misuse the name of the LORD your God, for the LORD will not hold anyone guiltless who misuses his name.

8 "Remember the Sabbath day by keeping it holy. 9 Six days you shall labor and do all your work, 10 but the seventh day is a sabbath to the LORD your God. On it you shall not do any work, neither you, nor your son or daughter, nor your male or female servant, nor your animals, nor any foreigner residing in your towns. 11 For in six days the LORD made the heavens and the earth, the sea, and all that is in them, but he rested on the seventh day. Therefore the LORD blessed the Sabbath day and made it holy.

[a] *18* Most Hebrew manuscripts; a few Hebrew manuscripts and Septuagint *and all the people*
[b] *19* Or *and God answered him with thunder*
[c] *3* Or *besides*

12 "Honor your father and your mother, so
that you may live long in the land
the LORD your God is giving you.
13 "You shall not murder.
14 "You shall not commit adultery.
15 "You shall not steal.
16 "You shall not give false testimony
against your neighbor.
17 "You shall not covet your neighbor's
house. You shall not covet your
neighbor's wife, or his male or
female servant, his ox or donkey,
or anything that belongs to your
neighbor."

18 When the people saw the thunder and
lightning and heard the trumpet and saw
the mountain in smoke, they trembled with
fear. They stayed at a distance 19 and said to
Moses, "Speak to us yourself and we will lis-
ten. But do not have God speak to us or we
will die."

20 Moses said to the people, "Do not be
afraid. God has come to test you, so that the
fear of God will be with you to keep you from
sinning."

21 The people remained at a distance,
while Moses approached the thick darkness
where God was.

Idols and Altars

22 Then the LORD said to Moses, "Tell the
Israelites this: 'You have seen for yourselves
that I have spoken to you from heaven: 23 Do
not make any gods to be alongside me; do
not make for yourselves gods of silver or gods
of gold.

24 " 'Make an altar of earth for me and sacri-
fice on it your burnt offerings and fellowship
offerings, your sheep and goats and your cat-
tle. Wherever I cause my name to be honored,
I will come to you and bless you. 25 If you make
an altar of stones for me, do not build it with
dressed stones, for you will defile it if you use
a tool on it. 26 And do not go up to my altar on
steps, or your private parts may be exposed.'

21 "These are the laws you are to set be-
fore them:

Hebrew Servants

2 "If you buy a Hebrew servant, he is to
serve you for six years. But in the seventh
year, he shall go free, without paying any-
thing. 3 If he comes alone, he is to go free
alone; but if he has a wife when he comes,
she is to go with him. 4 If his master gives him
a wife and she bears him sons or daughters,
the woman and her children shall belong to
her master, and only the man shall go free.

5 "But if the servant declares, 'I love my
master and my wife and children and do not
want to go free,' 6 then his master must take
him before the judges.[a] He shall take him to
the door or the doorpost and pierce his ear
with an awl. Then he will be his servant for
life.

7 "If a man sells his daughter as a servant,
she is not to go free as male servants do. 8 If
she does not please the master who has se-
lected her for himself,[b] he must let her be
redeemed. He has no right to sell her to for-
eigners, because he has broken faith with
her. 9 If he selects her for his son, he must
grant her the rights of a daughter. 10 If he
marries another woman, he must not de-
prive the first one of her food, clothing and
marital rights. 11 If he does not provide her
with these three things, she is to go free,
without any payment of money.

Personal Injuries

12 "Anyone who strikes a person with a
fatal blow is to be put to death. 13 However,
if it is not done intentionally, but God lets it
happen, they are to flee to a place I will des-
ignate. 14 But if anyone schemes and kills
someone deliberately, that person is to be
taken from my altar and put to death.

15 "Anyone who attacks[c] their father or
mother is to be put to death.

16 "Anyone who kidnaps someone is to be
put to death, whether the victim has been
sold or is still in the kidnapper's possession.

17 "Anyone who curses their father or
mother is to be put to death.

18 "If people quarrel and one person hits
another with a stone or with their fist[d] and
the victim does not die but is confined to
bed, 19 the one who struck the blow will not
be held liable if the other can get up and
walk around outside with a staff; however,
the guilty party must pay the injured person
for any loss of time and see that the victim is
completely healed.

[a] 6 Or *before God* [b] 8 Or *master so that he does not choose her* [c] 15 Or *kills* [d] 18 Or *with a tool*

20“Anyone who beats their male or female slave with a rod must be punished if the slave dies as a direct result, 21but they are not to be punished if the slave recovers after a day or two, since the slave is their property.

22“If people are fighting and hit a pregnant woman and she gives birth prematurely[a] but there is no serious injury, the offender must be fined whatever the woman’s husband demands and the court allows. 23But if there is serious injury, you are to take life for life, 24eye for eye, tooth for tooth, hand for hand, foot for foot, 25burn for burn, wound for wound, bruise for bruise.

26“An owner who hits a male or female slave in the eye and destroys it must let the slave go free to compensate for the eye. 27And an owner who knocks out the tooth of a male or female slave must let the slave go free to compensate for the tooth.

28“If a bull gores a man or woman to death, the bull is to be stoned to death, and its meat must not be eaten. But the owner of the bull will not be held responsible. 29If, however, the bull has had the habit of goring and the owner has been warned but has not kept it penned up and it kills a man or woman, the bull is to be stoned and its owner also is to be put to death. 30However, if payment is demanded, the owner may redeem his life by the payment of whatever is demanded. 31This law also applies if the bull gores a son or daughter. 32If the bull gores a male or female slave, the owner must pay thirty shekels[b] of silver to the master of the slave, and the bull is to be stoned to death.

33“If anyone uncovers a pit or digs one and fails to cover it and an ox or a donkey falls into it, 34the one who opened the pit must pay the owner for the loss and take the dead animal in exchange.

35“If anyone’s bull injures someone else’s bull and it dies, the two parties are to sell the live one and divide both the money and the dead animal equally. 36However, if it was known that the bull had the habit of goring, yet the owner did not keep it penned up, the owner must pay, animal for animal, and take the dead animal in exchange.

Protection of Property

22[c] “Whoever steals an ox or a sheep and slaughters it or sells it must pay back five head of cattle for the ox and four sheep for the sheep.

2“If a thief is caught breaking in at night and is struck a fatal blow, the defender is not guilty of bloodshed; 3but if it happens after sunrise, the defender is guilty of bloodshed.

“Anyone who steals must certainly make restitution, but if they have nothing, they must be sold to pay for their theft. 4If the stolen animal is found alive in their possession — whether ox or donkey or sheep — they must pay back double.

5“If anyone grazes their livestock in a field or vineyard and lets them stray and they graze in someone else’s field, the offender must make restitution from the best of their own field or vineyard.

6“If a fire breaks out and spreads into thornbushes so that it burns shocks of grain or standing grain or the whole field, the one who started the fire must make restitution.

7“If anyone gives a neighbor silver or goods for safekeeping and they are stolen from the neighbor’s house, the thief, if caught, must pay back double. 8But if the thief is not found, the owner of the house must appear before the judges, and they must[d] determine whether the owner of the house has laid hands on the other person’s property. 9In all cases of illegal possession of an ox, a donkey, a sheep, a garment, or any other lost property about which somebody says, ‘This is mine,’ both parties are to bring their cases before the judges.[e] The one whom the judges declare[f] guilty must pay back double to the other.

10“If anyone gives a donkey, an ox, a sheep or any other animal to their neighbor for safekeeping and it dies or is injured or is taken away while no one is looking, 11the issue between them will be settled by the taking of an oath before the LORD that the neighbor did not lay hands on the other person’s property. The owner is to accept this, and no restitution is required. 12But if the animal was stolen from the neighbor, restitution must be made to the owner. 13If it was torn to pieces

[a] 22 Or *she has a miscarriage* [b] 32 That is, about 12 ounces or about 345 grams [c] In Hebrew texts 22:1 is numbered 21:37, and 22:2-31 is numbered 22:1-30. [d] 8 Or *before God, and he will* [e] 9 Or *before God* [f] 9 Or *whom God declares*

by a wild animal, the neighbor shall bring in
the remains as evidence and shall not be re-
quired to pay for the torn animal.
14“If anyone borrows an animal from their
neighbor and it is injured or dies while the
owner is not present, they must make resti-
tution. 15But if the owner is with the animal,
the borrower will not have to pay. If the an-
imal was hired, the money paid for the hire
covers the loss.

Social Responsibility

16“If a man seduces a virgin who is not
pledged to be married and sleeps with her,
he must pay the bride-price, and she shall
be his wife. 17If her father absolutely refus-
es to give her to him, he must still pay the
bride-price for virgins.
18“Do not allow a sorceress to live.
19“Anyone who has sexual relations with
an animal is to be put to death.
20“Whoever sacrifices to any god other
than the LORD must be destroyed.[a]
21“Do not mistreat or oppress a foreigner,
for you were foreigners in Egypt.
22“Do not take advantage of the widow or
the fatherless. 23If you do and they cry out to
me, I will certainly hear their cry. 24My anger
will be aroused, and I will kill you with the
sword; your wives will become widows and
your children fatherless.
25“If you lend money to one of my people
among you who is needy, do not treat it like
a business deal; charge no interest. 26If you
take your neighbor's cloak as a pledge, re-
turn it by sunset, 27because that cloak is the
only covering your neighbor has. What else
can they sleep in? When they cry out to me, I
will hear, for I am compassionate.
28“Do not blaspheme God[b] or curse the
ruler of your people.
29“Do not hold back offerings from your
granaries or your vats.[c]
“You must give me the firstborn of your
sons. 30Do the same with your cattle and
your sheep. Let them stay with their moth-
ers for seven days, but give them to me on the
eighth day.
31“You are to be my holy people. So do
not eat the meat of an animal torn by wild
beasts; throw it to the dogs.

Laws of Justice and Mercy

23 “Do not spread false reports. Do not
help a guilty person by being a mali-
cious witness.
2“Do not follow the crowd in doing wrong.
When you give testimony in a lawsuit, do
not pervert justice by siding with the crowd,
3and do not show favoritism to a poor person
in a lawsuit.
4“If you come across your enemy's ox or
donkey wandering off, be sure to return it.
5If you see the donkey of someone who hates
you fallen down under its load, do not leave it
there; be sure you help them with it.
6“Do not deny justice to your poor people
in their lawsuits. 7Have nothing to do with a
false charge and do not put an innocent or
honest person to death, for I will not acquit
the guilty.
8“Do not accept a bribe, for a bribe blinds
those who see and twists the words of the in-
nocent.
9“Do not oppress a foreigner; you your-
selves know how it feels to be foreigners, be-
cause you were foreigners in Egypt.

Sabbath Laws

10“For six years you are to sow your fields
and harvest the crops, 11but during the sev-
enth year let the land lie unplowed and un-
used. Then the poor among your people may
get food from it, and the wild animals may
eat what is left. Do the same with your vine-
yard and your olive grove.
12“Six days do your work, but on the sev-
enth day do not work, so that your ox and
your donkey may rest, and so that the slave
born in your household and the foreigner
living among you may be refreshed.
13“Be careful to do everything I have said
to you. Do not invoke the names of other
gods; do not let them be heard on your lips.

The Three Annual Festivals

14“Three times a year you are to celebrate
a festival to me.
15“Celebrate the Festival of Unleavened
Bread; for seven days eat bread made with-
out yeast, as I commanded you. Do this at
the appointed time in the month of Aviv, for
in that month you came out of Egypt.

[a] *20* The Hebrew term refers to the irrevocable giving over of things or persons to the LORD, often by totally destroying them. [b] *28* Or *Do not revile the judges* [c] *29* The meaning of the Hebrew for this phrase is uncertain.

"No one is to appear before me empty-handed.

16 "Celebrate the Festival of Harvest with the firstfruits of the crops you sow in your field.

"Celebrate the Festival of Ingathering at the end of the year, when you gather in your crops from the field.

17 "Three times a year all the men are to appear before the Sovereign LORD.

18 "Do not offer the blood of a sacrifice to me along with anything containing yeast.

"The fat of my festival offerings must not be kept until morning.

19 "Bring the best of the firstfruits of your soil to the house of the LORD your God.

"Do not cook a young goat in its mother's milk.

God's Angel to Prepare the Way

20 "See, I am sending an angel ahead of you to guard you along the way and to bring you to the place I have prepared. 21 Pay attention to him and listen to what he says. Do not rebel against him; he will not forgive your rebellion, since my Name is in him. 22 If you listen carefully to what he says and do all that I say, I will be an enemy to your enemies and will oppose those who oppose you. 23 My angel will go ahead of you and bring you into the land of the Amorites, Hittites, Perizzites, Canaanites, Hivites and Jebusites, and I will wipe them out. 24 Do not bow down before their gods or worship them or follow their practices. You must demolish them and break their sacred stones to pieces. 25 Worship the LORD your God, and his blessing will be on your food and water. I will take away sickness from among you, 26 and none will miscarry or be barren in your land. I will give you a full life span.

27 "I will send my terror ahead of you and throw into confusion every nation you encounter. I will make all your enemies turn their backs and run. 28 I will send the hornet ahead of you to drive the Hivites, Canaanites and Hittites out of your way. 29 But I will not drive them out in a single year, because the land would become desolate and the wild animals too numerous for you. 30 Little by little I will drive them out before you, until you have increased enough to take possession of the land.

31 "I will establish your borders from the Red Sea[a] to the Mediterranean Sea,[b] and from the desert to the Euphrates River. I will give into your hands the people who live in the land, and you will drive them out before you. 32 Do not make a covenant with them or with their gods. 33 Do not let them live in your land or they will cause you to sin against me, because the worship of their gods will certainly be a snare to you."

The Covenant Confirmed

24 Then the LORD said to Moses, "Come up to the LORD, you and Aaron, Nadab and Abihu, and seventy of the elders of Israel. You are to worship at a distance, 2 but Moses alone is to approach the LORD; the others must not come near. And the people may not come up with him."

3 When Moses went and told the people all the LORD's words and laws, they responded with one voice, "Everything the LORD has said we will do." 4 Moses then wrote down everything the LORD had said.

He got up early the next morning and built an altar at the foot of the mountain and set up twelve stone pillars representing the twelve tribes of Israel. 5 Then he sent young Israelite men, and they offered burnt offerings and sacrificed young bulls as fellowship offerings to the LORD. 6 Moses took half of the blood and put it in bowls, and the other half he splashed against the altar. 7 Then he took the Book of the Covenant and read it to the people. They responded, "We will do everything the LORD has said; we will obey."

8 Moses then took the blood, sprinkled it on the people and said, "This is the blood of the covenant that the LORD has made with you in accordance with all these words."

9 Moses and Aaron, Nadab and Abihu, and the seventy elders of Israel went up 10 and saw the God of Israel. Under his feet was something like a pavement made of lapis lazuli, as bright blue as the sky. 11 But God did not raise his hand against these leaders of the Israelites; they saw God, and they ate and drank.

12 The LORD said to Moses, "Come up to me on the mountain and stay here, and I will give you the tablets of stone with the law and commandments I have written for their instruction."

[a] 31 Or *the Sea of Reeds* [b] 31 Hebrew *to the Sea of the Philistines*

13 Then Moses set out with Joshua his aide,
and Moses went up on the mountain of God.
14 He said to the elders, "Wait here for us un-
til we come back to you. Aaron and Hur are
with you, and anyone involved in a dispute
can go to them."
15 When Moses went up on the mountain,
the cloud covered it, 16 and the glory of the
LORD settled on Mount Sinai. For six days
the cloud covered the mountain, and on the
seventh day the LORD called to Moses from
within the cloud. 17 To the Israelites the glory
of the LORD looked like a consuming fire on
top of the mountain. 18 Then Moses entered
the cloud as he went on up the mountain.
And he stayed on the mountain forty days
and forty nights.

Offerings for the Tabernacle

25 The LORD said to Moses, 2 "Tell the
Israelites to bring me an offering.
You are to receive the offering for me from
everyone whose heart prompts them to give.
3 These are the offerings you are to receive
from them: gold, silver and bronze; 4 blue,
purple and scarlet yarn and fine linen; goat
hair; 5 ram skins dyed red and another type
of durable leather[a]; acacia wood; 6 olive oil
for the light; spices for the anointing oil and
for the fragrant incense; 7 and onyx stones
and other gems to be mounted on the ephod
and breastpiece.
8 "Then have them make a sanctuary for
me, and I will dwell among them. 9 Make
this tabernacle and all its furnishings exact-
ly like the pattern I will show you.

The Ark

10 "Have them make an ark[b] of acacia
wood — two and a half cubits long, a cubit
and a half wide, and a cubit and a half high.[c]
11 Overlay it with pure gold, both inside and
out, and make a gold molding around it.
12 Cast four gold rings for it and fasten them
to its four feet, with two rings on one side and
two rings on the other. 13 Then make poles of
acacia wood and overlay them with gold.
14 Insert the poles into the rings on the sides
of the ark to carry it. 15 The poles are to re-
main in the rings of this ark; they are not to
be removed. 16 Then put in the ark the tablets
of the covenant law, which I will give you.
17 "Make an atonement cover of pure
gold — two and a half cubits long and a cu-
bit and a half wide. 18 And make two cheru-
bim out of hammered gold at the ends of the
cover. 19 Make one cherub on one end and
the second cherub on the other; make the
cherubim of one piece with the cover, at the
two ends. 20 The cherubim are to have their
wings spread upward, overshadowing the
cover with them. The cherubim are to face
each other, looking toward the cover. 21 Place
the cover on top of the ark and put in the ark
the tablets of the covenant law that I will
give you. 22 There, above the cover between
the two cherubim that are over the ark of the
covenant law, I will meet with you and give
you all my commands for the Israelites.

The Table

23 "Make a table of acacia wood — two cu-
bits long, a cubit wide and a cubit and a half
high.[d] 24 Overlay it with pure gold and make a
gold molding around it. 25 Also make around
it a rim a handbreadth[e] wide and put a gold
molding on the rim. 26 Make four gold rings
for the table and fasten them to the four cor-
ners, where the four legs are. 27 The rings are
to be close to the rim to hold the poles used in
carrying the table. 28 Make the poles of acacia
wood, overlay them with gold and carry the
table with them. 29 And make its plates and
dishes of pure gold, as well as its pitchers and
bowls for the pouring out of offerings. 30 Put
the bread of the Presence on this table to be
before me at all times.

The Lampstand

31 "Make a lampstand of pure gold. Ham-
mer out its base and shaft, and make its
flowerlike cups, buds and blossoms of one
piece with them. 32 Six branches are to ex-
tend from the sides of the lampstand — three
on one side and three on the other. 33 Three
cups shaped like almond flowers with buds
and blossoms are to be on one branch, three
on the next branch, and the same for all six
branches extending from the lampstand.
34 And on the lampstand there are to be four

[a] *5* Possibly the hides of large aquatic mammals [b] *10* That is, a chest [c] *10* That is, about 3 3/4 feet long and 2 1/4 feet wide and high or about 1.1 meters long and 68 centimeters wide and high; similarly in verse 17 [d] *23* That is, about 3 feet long, 1 1/2 feet wide and 2 1/4 feet high or about 90 centimeters long, 45 centimeters wide and 68 centimeters high [e] *25* That is, about 3 inches or about 7.5 centimeters

cups shaped like almond flowers with buds and blossoms. 35 One bud shall be under the first pair of branches extending from the lampstand, a second bud under the second pair, and a third bud under the third pair — six branches in all. 36 The buds and branches shall all be of one piece with the lampstand, hammered out of pure gold.

37 "Then make its seven lamps and set them up on it so that they light the space in front of it. 38 Its wick trimmers and trays are to be of pure gold. 39 A talent[a] of pure gold is to be used for the lampstand and all these accessories. 40 See that you make them according to the pattern shown you on the mountain.

The Tabernacle

26 "Make the tabernacle with ten curtains of finely twisted linen and blue, purple and scarlet yarn, with cherubim woven into them by a skilled worker. 2 All the curtains are to be the same size — twenty-eight cubits long and four cubits wide.[b] 3 Join five of the curtains together, and do the same with the other five. 4 Make loops of blue material along the edge of the end curtain in one set, and do the same with the end curtain in the other set. 5 Make fifty loops on one curtain and fifty loops on the end curtain of the other set, with the loops opposite each other. 6 Then make fifty gold clasps and use them to fasten the curtains together so that the tabernacle is a unit.

7 "Make curtains of goat hair for the tent over the tabernacle — eleven altogether. 8 All eleven curtains are to be the same size — thirty cubits long and four cubits wide.[c] 9 Join five of the curtains together into one set and the other six into another set. Fold the sixth curtain double at the front of the tent. 10 Make fifty loops along the edge of the end curtain in one set and also along the edge of the end curtain in the other set. 11 Then make fifty bronze clasps and put them in the loops to fasten the tent together as a unit. 12 As for the additional length of the tent curtains, the half curtain that is left over is to hang down at the rear of the tabernacle. 13 The tent curtains will be a cubit[d] longer on both sides; what is left will hang over the sides of the tabernacle so as to cover it. 14 Make for the tent a covering of ram skins dyed red, and over that a covering of the other durable leather.[e]

15 "Make upright frames of acacia wood for the tabernacle. 16 Each frame is to be ten cubits long and a cubit and a half wide,[f] 17 with two projections set parallel to each other. Make all the frames of the tabernacle in this way. 18 Make twenty frames for the south side of the tabernacle 19 and make forty silver bases to go under them — two bases for each frame, one under each projection. 20 For the other side, the north side of the tabernacle, make twenty frames 21 and forty silver bases — two under each frame. 22 Make six frames for the far end, that is, the west end of the tabernacle, 23 and make two frames for the corners at the far end. 24 At these two corners they must be double from the bottom all the way to the top and fitted into a single ring; both shall be like that. 25 So there will be eight frames and sixteen silver bases — two under each frame.

26 "Also make crossbars of acacia wood: five for the frames on one side of the tabernacle, 27 five for those on the other side, and five for the frames on the west, at the far end of the tabernacle. 28 The center crossbar is to extend from end to end at the middle of the frames. 29 Overlay the frames with gold and make gold rings to hold the crossbars. Also overlay the crossbars with gold.

30 "Set up the tabernacle according to the plan shown you on the mountain.

31 "Make a curtain of blue, purple and scarlet yarn and finely twisted linen, with cherubim woven into it by a skilled worker. 32 Hang it with gold hooks on four posts of acacia wood overlaid with gold and standing on four silver bases. 33 Hang the curtain from the clasps and place the ark of the covenant law behind the curtain. The curtain will separate the Holy Place from the Most Holy Place. 34 Put the atonement cover on the ark of the covenant law in the Most Holy Place. 35 Place the table outside the curtain

[a] *39* That is, about 75 pounds or about 34 kilograms [b] *2* That is, about 42 feet long and 6 feet wide or about 13 meters long and 1.8 meters wide [c] *8* That is, about 45 feet long and 6 feet wide or about 13.5 meters long and 1.8 meters wide [d] *13* That is, about 18 inches or about 45 centimeters [e] *14* Possibly the hides of large aquatic mammals (see 25:5) [f] *16* That is, about 15 feet long and 2 1/4 feet wide or about 4.5 meters long and 68 centimeters wide

on the north side of the tabernacle and put the lampstand opposite it on the south side.

36 “For the entrance to the tent make a curtain of blue, purple and scarlet yarn and finely twisted linen — the work of an embroiderer. 37 Make gold hooks for this curtain and five posts of acacia wood overlaid with gold. And cast five bronze bases for them.

The Altar of Burnt Offering

27 “Build an altar of acacia wood, three cubits[a] high; it is to be square, five cubits long and five cubits wide.[b] 2 Make a horn at each of the four corners, so that the horns and the altar are of one piece, and overlay the altar with bronze. 3 Make all its utensils of bronze — its pots to remove the ashes, and its shovels, sprinkling bowls, meat forks and firepans. 4 Make a grating for it, a bronze network, and make a bronze ring at each of the four corners of the network. 5 Put it under the ledge of the altar so that it is halfway up the altar. 6 Make poles of acacia wood for the altar and overlay them with bronze. 7 The poles are to be inserted into the rings so they will be on two sides of the altar when it is carried. 8 Make the altar hollow, out of boards. It is to be made just as you were shown on the mountain.

The Courtyard

9 “Make a courtyard for the tabernacle. The south side shall be a hundred cubits[c] long and is to have curtains of finely twisted linen, 10 with twenty posts and twenty bronze bases and with silver hooks and bands on the posts. 11 The north side shall also be a hundred cubits long and is to have curtains, with twenty posts and twenty bronze bases and with silver hooks and bands on the posts.

12 “The west end of the courtyard shall be fifty cubits[d] wide and have curtains, with ten posts and ten bases. 13 On the east end, toward the sunrise, the courtyard shall also be fifty cubits wide. 14 Curtains fifteen cubits[e] long are to be on one side of the entrance, with three posts and three bases, 15 and curtains fifteen cubits long are to be on the other side, with three posts and three bases.

16 “For the entrance to the courtyard, provide a curtain twenty cubits[f] long, of blue, purple and scarlet yarn and finely twisted linen — the work of an embroiderer — with four posts and four bases. 17 All the posts around the courtyard are to have silver bands and hooks, and bronze bases. 18 The courtyard shall be a hundred cubits long and fifty cubits wide,[g] with curtains of finely twisted linen five cubits[h] high, and with bronze bases. 19 All the other articles used in the service of the tabernacle, whatever their function, including all the tent pegs for it and those for the courtyard, are to be of bronze.

Oil for the Lampstand

20 “Command the Israelites to bring you clear oil of pressed olives for the light so that the lamps may be kept burning. 21 In the tent of meeting, outside the curtain that shields the ark of the covenant law, Aaron and his sons are to keep the lamps burning before the LORD from evening till morning. This is to be a lasting ordinance among the Israelites for the generations to come.

The Priestly Garments

28 “Have Aaron your brother brought to you from among the Israelites, along with his sons Nadab and Abihu, Eleazar and Ithamar, so they may serve me as priests. 2 Make sacred garments for your brother Aaron to give him dignity and honor. 3 Tell all the skilled workers to whom I have given wisdom in such matters that they are to make garments for Aaron, for his consecration, so he may serve me as priest. 4 These are the garments they are to make: a breastpiece, an ephod, a robe, a woven tunic, a turban and a sash. They are to make these sacred garments for your brother Aaron and his sons, so they may serve me as priests. 5 Have them use gold, and blue, purple and scarlet yarn, and fine linen.

The Ephod

6 “Make the ephod of gold, and of blue, purple and scarlet yarn, and of finely twisted linen — the work of skilled hands. 7 It is to

[a] *1* That is, about 4 1/2 feet or about 1.4 meters [b] *1* That is, about 7 1/2 feet or about 2.3 meters long and wide [c] *9* That is, about 150 feet or about 45 meters; also in verse 11 [d] *12* That is, about 75 feet or about 23 meters; also in verse 13 [e] *14* That is, about 23 feet or about 6.8 meters; also in verse 15 [f] *16* That is, about 30 feet or about 9 meters [g] *18* That is, about 150 feet long and 75 feet wide or about 45 meters long and 23 meters wide [h] *18* That is, about 7 1/2 feet or about 2.3 meters

have two shoulder pieces attached to two of
its corners, so it can be fastened. 8 Its skillful-
ly woven waistband is to be like it — of one
piece with the ephod and made with gold,
and with blue, purple and scarlet yarn, and
with finely twisted linen.

9 "Take two onyx stones and engrave on
them the names of the sons of Israel 10 in the
order of their birth — six names on one stone
and the remaining six on the other. 11 En-
grave the names of the sons of Israel on the
two stones the way a gem cutter engraves a
seal. Then mount the stones in gold filigree
settings 12 and fasten them on the shoulder
pieces of the ephod as memorial stones for
the sons of Israel. Aaron is to bear the names
on his shoulders as a memorial before the
LORD. 13 Make gold filigree settings 14 and
two braided chains of pure gold, like a rope,
and attach the chains to the settings.

The Breastpiece

15 "Fashion a breastpiece for making de-
cisions — the work of skilled hands. Make it
like the ephod: of gold, and of blue, purple
and scarlet yarn, and of finely twisted linen.
16 It is to be square — a span[a] long and a span
wide — and folded double. 17 Then mount
four rows of precious stones on it. The first
row shall be carnelian, chrysolite and ber-
yl; 18 the second row shall be turquoise, lapis
lazuli and emerald; 19 the third row shall be
jacinth, agate and amethyst; 20 the fourth
row shall be topaz, onyx and jasper.[b] Mount
them in gold filigree settings. 21 There are to
be twelve stones, one for each of the names
of the sons of Israel, each engraved like a seal
with the name of one of the twelve tribes.

22 "For the breastpiece make braided
chains of pure gold, like a rope. 23 Make two
gold rings for it and fasten them to two cor-
ners of the breastpiece. 24 Fasten the two
gold chains to the rings at the corners of
the breastpiece, 25 and the other ends of the
chains to the two settings, attaching them to
the shoulder pieces of the ephod at the front.
26 Make two gold rings and attach them to the
other two corners of the breastpiece on the
inside edge next to the ephod. 27 Make two
more gold rings and attach them to the bot-
tom of the shoulder pieces on the front of the
ephod, close to the seam just above the waist-
band of the ephod. 28 The rings of the breast-
piece are to be tied to the rings of the ephod
with blue cord, connecting it to the waist-
band, so that the breastpiece will not swing
out from the ephod.

29 "Whenever Aaron enters the Holy Place,
he will bear the names of the sons of Israel
over his heart on the breastpiece of decision
as a continuing memorial before the LORD.
30 Also put the Urim and the Thummim in
the breastpiece, so they may be over Aar-
on's heart whenever he enters the presence
of the LORD. Thus Aaron will always bear the
means of making decisions for the Israelites
over his heart before the LORD.

Other Priestly Garments

31 "Make the robe of the ephod entirely of
blue cloth, 32 with an opening for the head in
its center. There shall be a woven edge like
a collar[c] around this opening, so that it will
not tear. 33 Make pomegranates of blue, pur-
ple and scarlet yarn around the hem of the
robe, with gold bells between them. 34 The
gold bells and the pomegranates are to al-
ternate around the hem of the robe. 35 Aaron
must wear it when he ministers. The sound
of the bells will be heard when he enters the
Holy Place before the LORD and when he
comes out, so that he will not die.

36 "Make a plate of pure gold and engrave
on it as on a seal: HOLY TO THE LORD. 37 Fas-
ten a blue cord to it to attach it to the turban;
it is to be on the front of the turban. 38 It will
be on Aaron's forehead, and he will bear the
guilt involved in the sacred gifts the Israel-
ites consecrate, whatever their gifts may be.
It will be on Aaron's forehead continually so
that they will be acceptable to the LORD.

39 "Weave the tunic of fine linen and
make the turban of fine linen. The sash is
to be the work of an embroiderer. 40 Make
tunics, sashes and caps for Aaron's sons to
give them dignity and honor. 41 After you put
these clothes on your brother Aaron and his
sons, anoint and ordain them. Consecrate
them so they may serve me as priests.

42 "Make linen undergarments as a cover-
ing for the body, reaching from the waist to
the thigh. 43 Aaron and his sons must wear
them whenever they enter the tent of meet-
ing or approach the altar to minister in the

[a] *16* That is, about 9 inches or about 23 centimeters [b] *20* The precise identification of some of these precious stones is uncertain. [c] *32* The meaning of the Hebrew for this word is uncertain.

Holy Place, so that they will not incur guilt
and die.
"This is to be a lasting ordinance for Aar-
on and his descendants.

Consecration of the Priests

29 "This is what you are to do to con-
secrate them, so they may serve me
as priests: Take a young bull and two rams
without defect. 2And from the finest wheat
flour make round loaves without yeast,
thick loaves without yeast and with olive oil
mixed in, and thin loaves without yeast and
brushed with olive oil. 3Put them in a bas-
ket and present them along with the bull and
the two rams. 4Then bring Aaron and his
sons to the entrance to the tent of meeting
and wash them with water. 5Take the gar-
ments and dress Aaron with the tunic, the
robe of the ephod, the ephod itself and the
breastpiece. Fasten the ephod on him by its
skillfully woven waistband. 6Put the turban
on his head and attach the sacred emblem
to the turban. 7Take the anointing oil and
anoint him by pouring it on his head. 8Bring
his sons and dress them in tunics 9and fas-
ten caps on them. Then tie sashes on Aaron
and his sons.[a] The priesthood is theirs by a
lasting ordinance.
"Then you shall ordain Aaron and his
sons.
10"Bring the bull to the front of the tent of
meeting, and Aaron and his sons shall lay
their hands on its head. 11Slaughter it in the
LORD's presence at the entrance to the tent
of meeting. 12Take some of the bull's blood
and put it on the horns of the altar with your
finger, and pour out the rest of it at the base
of the altar. 13Then take all the fat on the in-
ternal organs, the long lobe of the liver, and
both kidneys with the fat on them, and burn
them on the altar. 14But burn the bull's flesh
and its hide and its intestines outside the
camp. It is a sin offering.[b]
15"Take one of the rams, and Aaron and
his sons shall lay their hands on its head.
16Slaughter it and take the blood and splash
it against the sides of the altar. 17Cut the ram
into pieces and wash the internal organs and
the legs, putting them with the head and the
other pieces. 18Then burn the entire ram on
the altar. It is a burnt offering to the LORD, a
pleasing aroma, a food offering presented to
the LORD.
19"Take the other ram, and Aaron and
his sons shall lay their hands on its head.
20Slaughter it, take some of its blood and put
it on the lobes of the right ears of Aaron and
his sons, on the thumbs of their right hands,
and on the big toes of their right feet. Then
splash blood against the sides of the altar.
21And take some blood from the altar and
some of the anointing oil and sprinkle it on
Aaron and his garments and on his sons and
their garments. Then he and his sons and
their garments will be consecrated.
22"Take from this ram the fat, the fat tail,
the fat on the internal organs, the long lobe
of the liver, both kidneys with the fat on
them, and the right thigh. (This is the ram
for the ordination.) 23From the basket of
bread made without yeast, which is before
the LORD, take one round loaf, one thick loaf
with olive oil mixed in, and one thin loaf.
24Put all these in the hands of Aaron and his
sons and have them wave them before the
LORD as a wave offering. 25Then take them
from their hands and burn them on the altar
along with the burnt offering for a pleasing
aroma to the LORD, a food offering present-
ed to the LORD. 26After you take the breast of
the ram for Aaron's ordination, wave it be-
fore the LORD as a wave offering, and it will
be your share.
27"Consecrate those parts of the ordina-
tion ram that belong to Aaron and his sons:
the breast that was waved and the thigh that
was presented. 28This is always to be the
perpetual share from the Israelites for Aar-
on and his sons. It is the contribution the Is-
raelites are to make to the LORD from their
fellowship offerings.
29"Aaron's sacred garments will belong to
his descendants so that they can be anoint-
ed and ordained in them. 30The son who
succeeds him as priest and comes to the tent
of meeting to minister in the Holy Place is to
wear them seven days.
31"Take the ram for the ordination and
cook the meat in a sacred place. 32At the
entrance to the tent of meeting, Aaron and
his sons are to eat the meat of the ram and
the bread that is in the basket. 33They are to
eat these offerings by which atonement was

[a] 9 Hebrew; Septuagint *on them* [b] 14 Or *purification offering*; also in verse 36

made for their ordination and consecration. But no one else may eat them, because they are sacred. 34 And if any of the meat of the ordination ram or any bread is left over till morning, burn it up. It must not be eaten, because it is sacred.

35 “Do for Aaron and his sons everything I have commanded you, taking seven days to ordain them. 36 Sacrifice a bull each day as a sin offering to make atonement. Purify the altar by making atonement for it, and anoint it to consecrate it. 37 For seven days make atonement for the altar and consecrate it. Then the altar will be most holy, and whatever touches it will be holy.

38 “This is what you are to offer on the altar regularly each day: two lambs a year old. 39 Offer one in the morning and the other at twilight. 40 With the first lamb offer a tenth of an ephah[a] of the finest flour mixed with a quarter of a hin[b] of oil from pressed olives, and a quarter of a hin of wine as a drink offering. 41 Sacrifice the other lamb at twilight with the same grain offering and its drink offering as in the morning — a pleasing aroma, a food offering presented to the LORD.

42 “For the generations to come this burnt offering is to be made regularly at the entrance to the tent of meeting, before the LORD. There I will meet you and speak to you; 43 there also I will meet with the Israelites, and the place will be consecrated by my glory.

44 “So I will consecrate the tent of meeting and the altar and will consecrate Aaron and his sons to serve me as priests. 45 Then I will dwell among the Israelites and be their God. 46 They will know that I am the LORD their God, who brought them out of Egypt so that I might dwell among them. I am the LORD their God.

The Altar of Incense

30 “Make an altar of acacia wood for burning incense. 2 It is to be square, a cubit long and a cubit wide, and two cubits high[c] — its horns of one piece with it. 3 Overlay the top and all the sides and the horns with pure gold, and make a gold molding around it. 4 Make two gold rings for the altar below the molding — two on each of the opposite sides — to hold the poles used to carry it. 5 Make the poles of acacia wood and overlay them with gold. 6 Put the altar in front of the curtain that shields the ark of the covenant law — before the atonement cover that is over the tablets of the covenant law — where I will meet with you.

7 “Aaron must burn fragrant incense on the altar every morning when he tends the lamps. 8 He must burn incense again when he lights the lamps at twilight so incense will burn regularly before the LORD for the generations to come. 9 Do not offer on this altar any other incense or any burnt offering or grain offering, and do not pour a drink offering on it. 10 Once a year Aaron shall make atonement on its horns. This annual atonement must be made with the blood of the atoning sin offering[d] for the generations to come. It is most holy to the LORD.”

Atonement Money

11 Then the LORD said to Moses, 12 “When you take a census of the Israelites to count them, each one must pay the LORD a ransom for his life at the time he is counted. Then no plague will come on them when you number them. 13 Each one who crosses over to those already counted is to give a half shekel,[e] according to the sanctuary shekel, which weighs twenty gerahs. This half shekel is an offering to the LORD. 14 All who cross over, those twenty years old or more, are to give an offering to the LORD. 15 The rich are not to give more than a half shekel and the poor are not to give less when you make the offering to the LORD to atone for your lives. 16 Receive the atonement money from the Israelites and use it for the service of the tent of meeting. It will be a memorial for the Israelites before the LORD, making atonement for your lives.”

Basin for Washing

17 Then the LORD said to Moses, 18 “Make a bronze basin, with its bronze stand, for washing. Place it between the tent of meeting and the altar, and put water in it. 19 Aaron and his sons are to wash their hands and feet with

[a] *40* That is, probably about 3 1/2 pounds or about 1.6 kilograms [b] *40* That is, probably about 1 quart or about 1 liter [c] *2* That is, about 1 1/2 feet long and wide and 3 feet high or about 45 centimeters long and wide and 90 centimeters high [d] *10* Or *purification offering* [e] *13* That is, about 1/5 ounce or about 5.8 grams; also in verse 15

water from it. [20]Whenever they enter the tent of meeting, they shall wash with water so that they will not die. Also, when they approach the altar to minister by presenting a food offering to the LORD, [21]they shall wash their hands and feet so that they will not die. This is to be a lasting ordinance for Aaron and his descendants for the generations to come."

Anointing Oil

[22]Then the LORD said to Moses, [23]"Take the following fine spices: 500 shekels[a] of liquid myrrh, half as much (that is, 250 shekels) of fragrant cinnamon, 250 shekels[b] of fragrant calamus, [24]500 shekels of cassia — all according to the sanctuary shekel — and a hin[c] of olive oil. [25]Make these into a sacred anointing oil, a fragrant blend, the work of a perfumer. It will be the sacred anointing oil. [26]Then use it to anoint the tent of meeting, the ark of the covenant law, [27]the table and all its articles, the lampstand and its accessories, the altar of incense, [28]the altar of burnt offering and all its utensils, and the basin with its stand. [29]You shall consecrate them so they will be most holy, and whatever touches them will be holy.

[30]"Anoint Aaron and his sons and consecrate them so they may serve me as priests. [31]Say to the Israelites, 'This is to be my sacred anointing oil for the generations to come. [32]Do not pour it on anyone else's body and do not make any other oil using the same formula. It is sacred, and you are to consider it sacred. [33]Whoever makes perfume like it and puts it on anyone other than a priest must be cut off from their people.' "

Incense

[34]Then the LORD said to Moses, "Take fragrant spices — gum resin, onycha and galbanum — and pure frankincense, all in equal amounts, [35]and make a fragrant blend of incense, the work of a perfumer. It is to be salted and pure and sacred. [36]Grind some of it to powder and place it in front of the ark of the covenant law in the tent of meeting, where I will meet with you. It shall be most holy to you. [37]Do not make any incense with this formula for yourselves; consider it holy to the LORD. [38]Whoever makes incense like it to enjoy its fragrance must be cut off from their people."

Bezalel and Oholiab

31 Then the LORD said to Moses, [2]"See, I have chosen Bezalel son of Uri, the son of Hur, of the tribe of Judah, [3]and I have filled him with the Spirit of God, with wisdom, with understanding, with knowledge and with all kinds of skills — [4]to make artistic designs for work in gold, silver and bronze, [5]to cut and set stones, to work in wood, and to engage in all kinds of crafts. [6]Moreover, I have appointed Oholiab son of Ahisamak, of the tribe of Dan, to help him. Also I have given ability to all the skilled workers to make everything I have commanded you: [7]the tent of meeting, the ark of the covenant law with the atonement cover on it, and all the other furnishings of the tent — [8]the table and its articles, the pure gold lampstand and all its accessories, the altar of incense, [9]the altar of burnt offering and all its utensils, the basin with its stand — [10]and also the woven garments, both the sacred garments for Aaron the priest and the garments for his sons when they serve as priests, [11]and the anointing oil and fragrant incense for the Holy Place. They are to make them just as I commanded you."

The Sabbath

[12]Then the LORD said to Moses, [13]"Say to the Israelites, 'You must observe my Sabbaths. This will be a sign between me and you for the generations to come, so you may know that I am the LORD, who makes you holy.

[14]" 'Observe the Sabbath, because it is holy to you. Anyone who desecrates it is to be put to death; those who do any work on that day must be cut off from their people. [15]For six days work is to be done, but the seventh day is a day of sabbath rest, holy to the LORD. Whoever does any work on the Sabbath day is to be put to death. [16]The Israelites are to observe the Sabbath, celebrating it for the generations to come as a lasting covenant. [17]It will be a sign between me and the Israelites forever, for in six days the LORD made the heavens and the earth, and on the seventh day he rested and was refreshed.' "

[18]When the LORD finished speaking to Moses on Mount Sinai, he gave him the two tablets of the covenant law, the tablets of stone inscribed by the finger of God.

[a] *23* That is, about 12 1/2 pounds or about 5.8 kilograms; also in verse 24 [b] *23* That is, about 6 1/4 pounds or about 2.9 kilograms [c] *24* That is, probably about 1 gallon or about 3.8 liters

The Golden Calf

32 When the people saw that Moses was so long in coming down from the mountain, they gathered around Aaron and said, "Come, make us gods[a] who will go before us. As for this fellow Moses who brought us up out of Egypt, we don't know what has happened to him."

2 Aaron answered them, "Take off the gold earrings that your wives, your sons and your daughters are wearing, and bring them to me." 3 So all the people took off their earrings and brought them to Aaron. 4 He took what they handed him and made it into an idol cast in the shape of a calf, fashioning it with a tool. Then they said, "These are your gods,[b] Israel, who brought you up out of Egypt."

5 When Aaron saw this, he built an altar in front of the calf and announced, "Tomorrow there will be a festival to the LORD." 6 So the next day the people rose early and sacrificed burnt offerings and presented fellowship offerings. Afterward they sat down to eat and drink and got up to indulge in revelry.

7 Then the LORD said to Moses, "Go down, because your people, whom you brought up out of Egypt, have become corrupt. 8 They have been quick to turn away from what I commanded them and have made themselves an idol cast in the shape of a calf. They have bowed down to it and sacrificed to it and have said, 'These are your gods, Israel, who brought you up out of Egypt.'

9 "I have seen these people," the LORD said to Moses, "and they are a stiff-necked people. 10 Now leave me alone so that my anger may burn against them and that I may destroy them. Then I will make you into a great nation."

11 But Moses sought the favor of the LORD his God. "LORD," he said, "why should your anger burn against your people, whom you brought out of Egypt with great power and a mighty hand? 12 Why should the Egyptians say, 'It was with evil intent that he brought them out, to kill them in the mountains and to wipe them off the face of the earth'? Turn from your fierce anger; relent and do not bring disaster on your people. 13 Remember your servants Abraham, Isaac and Israel, to whom you swore by your own self: 'I will make your descendants as numerous as the stars in the sky and I will give your descendants all this land I promised them, and it will be their inheritance forever.' " 14 Then the LORD relented and did not bring on his people the disaster he had threatened.

15 Moses turned and went down the mountain with the two tablets of the covenant law in his hands. They were inscribed on both sides, front and back. 16 The tablets were the work of God; the writing was the writing of God, engraved on the tablets.

17 When Joshua heard the noise of the people shouting, he said to Moses, "There is the sound of war in the camp."

18 Moses replied:

"It is not the sound of victory,
  it is not the sound of defeat;
  it is the sound of singing that I hear."

19 When Moses approached the camp and saw the calf and the dancing, his anger burned and he threw the tablets out of his hands, breaking them to pieces at the foot of the mountain. 20 And he took the calf the people had made and burned it in the fire; then he ground it to powder, scattered it on the water and made the Israelites drink it.

21 He said to Aaron, "What did these people do to you, that you led them into such great sin?"

22 "Do not be angry, my lord," Aaron answered. "You know how prone these people are to evil. 23 They said to me, 'Make us gods who will go before us. As for this fellow Moses who brought us up out of Egypt, we don't know what has happened to him.' 24 So I told them, 'Whoever has any gold jewelry, take it off.' Then they gave me the gold, and I threw it into the fire, and out came this calf!"

25 Moses saw that the people were running wild and that Aaron had let them get out of control and so become a laughingstock to their enemies. 26 So he stood at the entrance to the camp and said, "Whoever is for the LORD, come to me." And all the Levites rallied to him.

27 Then he said to them, "This is what the LORD, the God of Israel, says: 'Each man strap a sword to his side. Go back and forth through the camp from one end to the other, each killing his brother and friend and neighbor.' " 28 The Levites did as Moses com-

[a] *1* Or *a god*; also in verses 23 and 31 [b] *4* Or *This is your god*; also in verse 8

manded, and that day about three thousand of the people died. 29Then Moses said, "You have been set apart to the LORD today, for you were against your own sons and brothers, and he has blessed you this day."

30The next day Moses said to the people, "You have committed a great sin. But now I will go up to the LORD; perhaps I can make atonement for your sin."

31So Moses went back to the LORD and said, "Oh, what a great sin these people have committed! They have made themselves gods of gold. 32But now, please forgive their sin—but if not, then blot me out of the book you have written."

33The LORD replied to Moses, "Whoever has sinned against me I will blot out of my book. 34Now go, lead the people to the place I spoke of, and my angel will go before you. However, when the time comes for me to punish, I will punish them for their sin."

35And the LORD struck the people with a plague because of what they did with the calf Aaron had made.

33 Then the LORD said to Moses, "Leave this place, you and the people you brought up out of Egypt, and go up to the land I promised on oath to Abraham, Isaac and Jacob, saying, 'I will give it to your descendants.' 2I will send an angel before you and drive out the Canaanites, Amorites, Hittites, Perizzites, Hivites and Jebusites. 3Go up to the land flowing with milk and honey. But I will not go with you, because you are a stiff-necked people and I might destroy you on the way."

4When the people heard these distressing words, they began to mourn and no one put on any ornaments. 5For the LORD had said to Moses, "Tell the Israelites, 'You are a stiff-necked people. If I were to go with you even for a moment, I might destroy you. Now take off your ornaments and I will decide what to do with you.'" 6So the Israelites stripped off their ornaments at Mount Horeb.

The Tent of Meeting

7Now Moses used to take a tent and pitch it outside the camp some distance away, calling it the "tent of meeting." Anyone inquiring of the LORD would go to the tent of meeting outside the camp. 8And whenever Moses went out to the tent, all the people rose and stood at the entrances to their tents, watching Moses until he entered the tent. 9As Moses went into the tent, the pillar of cloud would come down and stay at the entrance, while the LORD spoke with Moses. 10Whenever the people saw the pillar of cloud standing at the entrance to the tent, they all stood and worshiped, each at the entrance to their tent. 11The LORD would speak to Moses face to face, as one speaks to a friend. Then Moses would return to the camp, but his young aide Joshua son of Nun did not leave the tent.

Moses and the Glory of the LORD

12Moses said to the LORD, "You have been telling me, 'Lead these people,' but you have not let me know whom you will send with me. You have said, 'I know you by name and you have found favor with me.' 13If you are pleased with me, teach me your ways so I may know you and continue to find favor with you. Remember that this nation is your people."

14The LORD replied, "My Presence will go with you, and I will give you rest."

15Then Moses said to him, "If your Presence does not go with us, do not send us up from here. 16How will anyone know that you are pleased with me and with your people unless you go with us? What else will distinguish me and your people from all the other people on the face of the earth?"

17And the LORD said to Moses, "I will do the very thing you have asked, because I am pleased with you and I know you by name."

18Then Moses said, "Now show me your glory."

19And the LORD said, "I will cause all my goodness to pass in front of you, and I will proclaim my name, the LORD, in your presence. I will have mercy on whom I will have mercy, and I will have compassion on whom I will have compassion. 20But," he said, "you cannot see my face, for no one may see me and live."

21Then the LORD said, "There is a place near me where you may stand on a rock. 22When my glory passes by, I will put you in a cleft in the rock and cover you with my hand until I have passed by. 23Then I will remove my hand and you will see my back; but my face must not be seen."

The New Stone Tablets

34 The LORD said to Moses, "Chisel out two stone tablets like the first ones,

BLESSED BE YOUR NAME

Matt Redman, Beth Redman

Blessed be your name
In the land that is plentiful
Where your streams of abundance flow
Blessed be your name
Blessed be your name
When I'm found in the desert place
Though I walk through the wilderness
Blessed be your name

Every blessing you pour out
I'll turn back to praise
When the darkness closes in
Lord still I will say

Blessed be the name of the Lord
Blessed be your name
Blessed be the name of the Lord
Blessed be your glorious name

Blessed be your name
When the sun's shining down on me
When the world's all as it should be
Blessed be your name
Blessed be your name
On the road marked with suffering
Though there's pain in the offering
Blessed be your name

You give and take away
You give and take away
My heart will choose to say
Lord blessed be your name

THE INSPIRATION

"Naked I came from my mother's womb, and naked I will depart. The Lord gave and the Lord has taken away; may the name of the Lord be praised." —Job 1:21

Read also: Psalm 93:1; 104:1–3

BEHIND THE SONG

When Matt Redman composed "Blessed Be Your Name," it didn't have the feel of a "normal" worship song. "All over the Bible," he explains, "there are stories of people making choices to worship God in hard times."

Redman's mind went quickly to one of the most extreme instances of someone praising God during difficult circumstances — Job. "All of us live through hard things in life," he says. "The wonderful thing is when you can stand up in those times and still worship God and still trust him as an act of worship, still recognize his worth and say, 'Yet I will praise you.' "

Redman's vulnerable take on worship struck a chord with millions of Christians around the world. One of the primary jobs of a worship leader is to inspire people who may not be in the mood to worship. Hurting people may be reluctant to sing God's praises, but by doing so they may soon gain his perspective on their suffering. Redman has written many powerful songs for the church, but "Blessed Be Your Name" continues to minister to people.

"To be honest," he adds, "I've probably had more testimonies sent back from that song than from any other song because there is so much pain in the world — and so much pain in the church."

Selah

Are there times when your emotions do not line up with your worship? Have you experienced pain or suffering that has made it difficult to worship God? Do you fear that he has forgotten you? You're in good company. The Bible is full of people who felt that way. The good news is that God hadn't forgotten any of them, and he hasn't forgotten you.

and I will write on them the words that were on the first tablets, which you broke. [2]Be ready in the morning, and then come up on Mount Sinai. Present yourself to me there on top of the mountain. [3]No one is to come with you or be seen anywhere on the mountain; not even the flocks and herds may graze in front of the mountain."

[4]So Moses chiseled out two stone tablets like the first ones and went up Mount Sinai early in the morning, as the LORD had commanded him; and he carried the two stone tablets in his hands. [5]Then the LORD came down in the cloud and stood there with him and proclaimed his name, the LORD. [6]And he passed in front of Moses, proclaiming, "The LORD, the LORD, the compassionate and gracious God, slow to anger, abounding in love and faithfulness, [7]maintaining love to thousands, and forgiving wickedness, rebellion and sin. Yet he does not leave the guilty unpunished; he punishes the children and their children for the sin of the parents to the third and fourth generation."

[8]Moses bowed to the ground at once and worshiped. [9]"Lord," he said, "if I have found favor in your eyes, then let the Lord go with us. Although this is a stiff-necked people, forgive our wickedness and our sin, and take us as your inheritance."

[10]Then the LORD said: "I am making a covenant with you. Before all your people I will do wonders never before done in any nation in all the world. The people you live among will see how awesome is the work that I, the LORD, will do for you. [11]Obey what I command you today. I will drive out before you the Amorites, Canaanites, Hittites, Perizzites, Hivites and Jebusites. [12]Be careful not to make a treaty with those who live in the land where you are going, or they will be a snare among you. [13]Break down their altars, smash their sacred stones and cut down their Asherah poles.[a] [14]Do not worship any other god, for the LORD, whose name is Jealous, is a jealous God.

[15]"Be careful not to make a treaty with those who live in the land; for when they prostitute themselves to their gods and sacrifice to them, they will invite you and you will eat their sacrifices. [16]And when you choose some of their daughters as wives for your sons and those daughters prostitute themselves to their gods, they will lead your sons to do the same.

[17]"Do not make any idols.

[18]"Celebrate the Festival of Unleavened Bread. For seven days eat bread made without yeast, as I commanded you. Do this at the appointed time in the month of Aviv, for in that month you came out of Egypt.

[19]"The first offspring of every womb belongs to me, including all the firstborn males of your livestock, whether from herd or flock. [20]Redeem the firstborn donkey with a lamb, but if you do not redeem it, break its neck. Redeem all your firstborn sons.

"No one is to appear before me empty-handed.

[21]"Six days you shall labor, but on the seventh day you shall rest; even during the plowing season and harvest you must rest.

[22]"Celebrate the Festival of Weeks with the firstfruits of the wheat harvest, and the Festival of Ingathering at the turn of the year.[b] [23]Three times a year all your men are to appear before the Sovereign LORD, the God of Israel. [24]I will drive out nations before you and enlarge your territory, and no one will covet your land when you go up three times each year to appear before the LORD your God.

[25]"Do not offer the blood of a sacrifice to me along with anything containing yeast, and do not let any of the sacrifice from the Passover Festival remain until morning.

[26]"Bring the best of the firstfruits of your soil to the house of the LORD your God.

"Do not cook a young goat in its mother's milk."

[27]Then the LORD said to Moses, "Write down these words, for in accordance with these words I have made a covenant with you and with Israel." [28]Moses was there with the LORD forty days and forty nights without eating bread or drinking water. And he wrote on the tablets the words of the covenant — the Ten Commandments.

The Radiant Face of Moses

[29]When Moses came down from Mount Sinai with the two tablets of the covenant law in his hands, he was not aware that his face was radiant because he had spoken

[a] *13* That is, wooden symbols of the goddess Asherah

[b] *22* That is, in the autumn

with the LORD. 30When Aaron and all the Is-
raelites saw Moses, his face was radiant, and
they were afraid to come near him. 31But
Moses called to them; so Aaron and all the
leaders of the community came back to him,
and he spoke to them. 32Afterward all the Is-
raelites came near him, and he gave them all
the commands the LORD had given him on
Mount Sinai.

33When Moses finished speaking to them,
he put a veil over his face. 34But whenever he
entered the LORD's presence to speak with
him, he removed the veil until he came out.
And when he came out and told the Israelites
what he had been commanded, 35they saw
that his face was radiant. Then Moses would
put the veil back over his face until he went
in to speak with the LORD.

Sabbath Regulations

35 Moses assembled the whole Israelite
community and said to them, "These
are the things the LORD has commanded you
to do: 2For six days, work is to be done, but
the seventh day shall be your holy day, a day
of sabbath rest to the LORD. Whoever does
any work on it is to be put to death. 3Do not
light a fire in any of your dwellings on the
Sabbath day."

Materials for the Tabernacle

4Moses said to the whole Israelite com-
munity, "This is what the LORD has com-
manded: 5From what you have, take an of-
fering for the LORD. Everyone who is willing
is to bring to the LORD an offering of gold,
silver and bronze; 6blue, purple and scarlet
yarn and fine linen; goat hair; 7ram skins
dyed red and another type of durable leath-
er[a]; acacia wood; 8olive oil for the light; spic-
es for the anointing oil and for the fragrant
incense; 9and onyx stones and other gems to
be mounted on the ephod and breastpiece.

10"All who are skilled among you are to
come and make everything the LORD has
commanded: 11the tabernacle with its tent
and its covering, clasps, frames, crossbars,
posts and bases; 12the ark with its poles and
the atonement cover and the curtain that
shields it; 13the table with its poles and all
its articles and the bread of the Presence;
14the lampstand that is for light with its ac-
cessories, lamps and oil for the light; 15the
altar of incense with its poles, the anointing
oil and the fragrant incense; the curtain for
the doorway at the entrance to the taber-
nacle; 16the altar of burnt offering with its
bronze grating, its poles and all its uten-
sils; the bronze basin with its stand; 17the
curtains of the courtyard with its posts and
bases, and the curtain for the entrance to
the courtyard; 18the tent pegs for the taber-
nacle and for the courtyard, and their ropes;
19the woven garments worn for ministering
in the sanctuary — both the sacred garments
for Aaron the priest and the garments for his
sons when they serve as priests."

20Then the whole Israelite community
withdrew from Moses' presence, 21and ev-
eryone who was willing and whose heart
moved them came and brought an offering
to the LORD for the work on the tent of meet-
ing, for all its service, and for the sacred
garments. 22All who were willing, men and
women alike, came and brought gold jew-
elry of all kinds: brooches, earrings, rings
and ornaments. They all presented their
gold as a wave offering to the LORD. 23Every-
one who had blue, purple or scarlet yarn or
fine linen, or goat hair, ram skins dyed red
or the other durable leather brought them.
24Those presenting an offering of silver or
bronze brought it as an offering to the LORD,
and everyone who had acacia wood for any
part of the work brought it. 25Every skilled
woman spun with her hands and brought
what she had spun — blue, purple or scar-
let yarn or fine linen. 26And all the women
who were willing and had the skill spun the
goat hair. 27The leaders brought onyx stones
and other gems to be mounted on the ephod
and breastpiece. 28They also brought spices
and olive oil for the light and for the anoint-
ing oil and for the fragrant incense. 29All the
Israelite men and women who were willing
brought to the LORD freewill offerings for all
the work the LORD through Moses had com-
manded them to do.

Bezalel and Oholiab

30Then Moses said to the Israelites, "See,
the LORD has chosen Bezalel son of Uri, the
son of Hur, of the tribe of Judah, 31and he has
filled him with the Spirit of God, with wis-

[a] 7 Possibly the hides of large aquatic mammals; also in verse 23

dom, with understanding, with knowledge and with all kinds of skills— [32]to make artistic designs for work in gold, silver and bronze, [33]to cut and set stones, to work in wood and to engage in all kinds of artistic crafts. [34]And he has given both him and Oholiab son of Ahisamak, of the tribe of Dan, the ability to teach others. [35]He has filled them with skill to do all kinds of work as engravers, designers, embroiderers in blue, purple and scarlet yarn and fine linen, and weavers—all of them skilled workers and designers.

36 [1]So Bezalel, Oholiab and every skilled person to whom the LORD has given skill and ability to know how to carry out all the work of constructing the sanctuary are to do the work just as the LORD has commanded."

[2]Then Moses summoned Bezalel and Oholiab and every skilled person to whom the LORD had given ability and who was willing to come and do the work. [3]They received from Moses all the offerings the Israelites had brought to carry out the work of constructing the sanctuary. And the people continued to bring freewill offerings morning after morning. [4]So all the skilled workers who were doing all the work on the sanctuary left what they were doing [5]and said to Moses, "The people are bringing more than enough for doing the work the LORD commanded to be done."

[6]Then Moses gave an order and they sent this word throughout the camp: "No man or woman is to make anything else as an offering for the sanctuary." And so the people were restrained from bringing more, [7]because what they already had was more than enough to do all the work.

The Tabernacle

[8]All those who were skilled among the workers made the tabernacle with ten curtains of finely twisted linen and blue, purple and scarlet yarn, with cherubim woven into them by expert hands. [9]All the curtains were the same size—twenty-eight cubits long and four cubits wide.[a] [10]They joined five of the curtains together and did the same with the other five. [11]Then they made loops of blue material along the edge of the end curtain in one set, and the same was done with the end curtain in the other set. [12]They also made fifty loops on one curtain and fifty loops on the end curtain of the other set, with the loops opposite each other. [13]Then they made fifty gold clasps and used them to fasten the two sets of curtains together so that the tabernacle was a unit.

[14]They made curtains of goat hair for the tent over the tabernacle—eleven altogether. [15]All eleven curtains were the same size—thirty cubits long and four cubits wide.[b] [16]They joined five of the curtains into one set and the other six into another set. [17]Then they made fifty loops along the edge of the end curtain in one set and also along the edge of the end curtain in the other set. [18]They made fifty bronze clasps to fasten the tent together as a unit. [19]Then they made for the tent a covering of ram skins dyed red, and over that a covering of the other durable leather.[c]

[20]They made upright frames of acacia wood for the tabernacle. [21]Each frame was ten cubits long and a cubit and a half wide,[d] [22]with two projections set parallel to each other. They made all the frames of the tabernacle in this way. [23]They made twenty frames for the south side of the tabernacle [24]and made forty silver bases to go under them—two bases for each frame, one under each projection. [25]For the other side, the north side of the tabernacle, they made twenty frames [26]and forty silver bases—two under each frame. [27]They made six frames for the far end, that is, the west end of the tabernacle, [28]and two frames were made for the corners of the tabernacle at the far end. [29]At these two corners the frames were double from the bottom all the way to the top and fitted into a single ring; both were made alike. [30]So there were eight frames and sixteen silver bases—two under each frame.

[31]They also made crossbars of acacia wood: five for the frames on one side of the tabernacle, [32]five for those on the other side, and five for the frames on the west, at the far end of the tabernacle. [33]They made the center crossbar so that it extended from end to end at the middle of the frames. [34]They

[a] *9* That is, about 42 feet long and 6 feet wide or about 13 meters long and 1.8 meters wide [b] *15* That is, about 45 feet long and 6 feet wide or about 14 meters long and 1.8 meters wide [c] *19* Possibly the hides of large aquatic mammals (see 35:7) [d] *21* That is, about 15 feet long and 2 1/4 feet wide or about 4.5 meters long and 68 centimeters wide

overlaid the frames with gold and made gold
rings to hold the crossbars. They also over-
laid the crossbars with gold.
35They made the curtain of blue, pur-
ple and scarlet yarn and finely twisted lin-
en, with cherubim woven into it by a skilled
worker. 36They made four posts of acacia
wood for it and overlaid them with gold.
They made gold hooks for them and cast
their four silver bases. 37For the entrance to
the tent they made a curtain of blue, purple
and scarlet yarn and finely twisted linen —
the work of an embroiderer; 38and they made
five posts with hooks for them. They overlaid
the tops of the posts and their bands with
gold and made their five bases of bronze.

The Ark

37 Bezalel made the ark of acacia
wood — two and a half cubits long,
a cubit and a half wide, and a cubit and a
half high.[a] 2He overlaid it with pure gold,
both inside and out, and made a gold mold-
ing around it. 3He cast four gold rings for it
and fastened them to its four feet, with two
rings on one side and two rings on the oth-
er. 4Then he made poles of acacia wood and
overlaid them with gold. 5And he inserted
the poles into the rings on the sides of the
ark to carry it.
6He made the atonement cover of pure
gold — two and a half cubits long and a cubit
and a half wide. 7Then he made two cher-
ubim out of hammered gold at the ends of
the cover. 8He made one cherub on one end
and the second cherub on the other; at the
two ends he made them of one piece with
the cover. 9The cherubim had their wings
spread upward, overshadowing the cover
with them. The cherubim faced each other,
looking toward the cover.

The Table

10They[b] made the table of acacia wood —
two cubits long, a cubit wide and a cubit and
a half high.[c] 11Then they overlaid it with
pure gold and made a gold molding around
it. 12They also made around it a rim a hand-
breadth[d] wide and put a gold molding on the
rim. 13They cast four gold rings for the table
and fastened them to the four corners, where
the four legs were. 14The rings were put close
to the rim to hold the poles used in carrying
the table. 15The poles for carrying the table
were made of acacia wood and were over-
laid with gold. 16And they made from pure
gold the articles for the table — its plates and
dishes and bowls and its pitchers for the
pouring out of drink offerings.

The Lampstand

17They made the lampstand of pure gold.
They hammered out its base and shaft, and
made its flowerlike cups, buds and blossoms
of one piece with them. 18Six branches ex-
tended from the sides of the lampstand —
three on one side and three on the other.
19Three cups shaped like almond flowers
with buds and blossoms were on one branch,
three on the next branch and the same for all
six branches extending from the lampstand.
20And on the lampstand were four cups
shaped like almond flowers with buds and
blossoms. 21One bud was under the first pair
of branches extending from the lampstand,
a second bud under the second pair, and a
third bud under the third pair — six branch-
es in all. 22The buds and the branches were
all of one piece with the lampstand, ham-
mered out of pure gold.
23They made its seven lamps, as well as
its wick trimmers and trays, of pure gold.
24They made the lampstand and all its ac-
cessories from one talent[e] of pure gold.

The Altar of Incense

25They made the altar of incense out of
acacia wood. It was square, a cubit long and a
cubit wide and two cubits high[f] — its horns of
one piece with it. 26They overlaid the top and
all the sides and the horns with pure gold, and
made a gold molding around it. 27They made
two gold rings below the molding — two on
each of the opposite sides — to hold the poles
used to carry it. 28They made the poles of aca-
cia wood and overlaid them with gold.

[a] *1* That is, about 3 3/4 feet long and 2 1/4 feet wide and high or about 1.1 meters long and 68 centimeters wide and high; similarly in verse 6 [b] *10* Or *He;* also in verses 11-29 [c] *10* That is, about 3 feet long, 1 1/2 feet wide and 2 1/4 feet high or about 90 centimeters long, 45 centimeters wide and 68 centimeters high [d] *12* That is, about 3 inches or about 7.5 centimeters [e] *24* That is, about 75 pounds or about 34 kilograms [f] *25* That is, about 1 1/2 feet long and wide and 3 feet high or about 45 centimeters long and wide and 90 centimeters high

29 They also made the sacred anointing oil and the pure, fragrant incense — the work of a perfumer.

The Altar of Burnt Offering

38 They[a] built the altar of burnt offering of acacia wood, three cubits[b] high; it was square, five cubits long and five cubits wide.[c] 2 They made a horn at each of the four corners, so that the horns and the altar were of one piece, and they overlaid the altar with bronze. 3 They made all its utensils of bronze — its pots, shovels, sprinkling bowls, meat forks and firepans. 4 They made a grating for the altar, a bronze network, to be under its ledge, halfway up the altar. 5 They cast bronze rings to hold the poles for the four corners of the bronze grating. 6 They made the poles of acacia wood and overlaid them with bronze. 7 They inserted the poles into the rings so they would be on the sides of the altar for carrying it. They made it hollow, out of boards.

The Basin for Washing

8 They made the bronze basin and its bronze stand from the mirrors of the women who served at the entrance to the tent of meeting.

The Courtyard

9 Next they made the courtyard. The south side was a hundred cubits[d] long and had curtains of finely twisted linen, 10 with twenty posts and twenty bronze bases, and with silver hooks and bands on the posts. 11 The north side was also a hundred cubits long and had twenty posts and twenty bronze bases, with silver hooks and bands on the posts.

12 The west end was fifty cubits[e] wide and had curtains, with ten posts and ten bases, with silver hooks and bands on the posts. 13 The east end, toward the sunrise, was also fifty cubits wide. 14 Curtains fifteen cubits[f] long were on one side of the entrance, with three posts and three bases, 15 and curtains fifteen cubits long were on the other side of the entrance to the courtyard, with three posts and three bases. 16 All the curtains around the courtyard were of finely twisted linen. 17 The bases for the posts were bronze. The hooks and bands on the posts were silver, and their tops were overlaid with silver; so all the posts of the courtyard had silver bands.

18 The curtain for the entrance to the courtyard was made of blue, purple and scarlet yarn and finely twisted linen — the work of an embroiderer. It was twenty cubits[g] long and, like the curtains of the courtyard, five cubits[h] high, 19 with four posts and four bronze bases. Their hooks and bands were silver, and their tops were overlaid with silver. 20 All the tent pegs of the tabernacle and of the surrounding courtyard were bronze.

The Materials Used

21 These are the amounts of the materials used for the tabernacle, the tabernacle of the covenant law, which were recorded at Moses' command by the Levites under the direction of Ithamar son of Aaron, the priest. 22 (Bezalel son of Uri, the son of Hur, of the tribe of Judah, made everything the LORD commanded Moses; 23 with him was Oholiab son of Ahisamak, of the tribe of Dan — an engraver and designer, and an embroiderer in blue, purple and scarlet yarn and fine linen.) 24 The total amount of the gold from the wave offering used for all the work on the sanctuary was 29 talents and 730 shekels,[i] according to the sanctuary shekel.

25 The silver obtained from those of the community who were counted in the census was 100 talents[j] and 1,775 shekels,[k] according to the sanctuary shekel — 26 one beka per person, that is, half a shekel,[l] according to the sanctuary shekel, from everyone who had crossed over to those counted, twenty years old or more, a total of 603,550 men. 27 The 100 talents of silver were used to cast the bases for the sanctuary and for the curtain — 100 bases from the 100 talents, one

[a] *1* Or *He*; also in verses 2-9 [b] *1* That is, about 4 1/2 feet or about 1.4 meters [c] *1* That is, about 7 1/2 feet or about 2.3 meters long and wide [d] *9* That is, about 150 feet or about 45 meters [e] *12* That is, about 75 feet or about 23 meters [f] *14* That is, about 22 feet or about 6.8 meters [g] *18* That is, about 30 feet or about 9 meters [h] *18* That is, about 7 1/2 feet or about 2.3 meters [i] *24* The weight of the gold was a little over a ton or about 1 metric ton. [j] *25* That is, about 3 3/4 tons or about 3.4 metric tons; also in verse 27 [k] *25* That is, about 44 pounds or about 20 kilograms; also in verse 28 [l] *26* That is, about 1/5 ounce or about 5.7 grams

talent for each base. 28They used the 1,775 shekels to make the hooks for the posts, to overlay the tops of the posts, and to make their bands.

29The bronze from the wave offering was 70 talents and 2,400 shekels.[a] 30They used it to make the bases for the entrance to the tent of meeting, the bronze altar with its bronze grating and all its utensils, 31the bases for the surrounding courtyard and those for its entrance and all the tent pegs for the tabernacle and those for the surrounding courtyard.

The Priestly Garments

39 From the blue, purple and scarlet yarn they made woven garments for ministering in the sanctuary. They also made sacred garments for Aaron, as the LORD commanded Moses.

The Ephod

2They[b] made the ephod of gold, and of blue, purple and scarlet yarn, and of finely twisted linen. 3They hammered out thin sheets of gold and cut strands to be worked into the blue, purple and scarlet yarn and fine linen — the work of skilled hands. 4They made shoulder pieces for the ephod, which were attached to two of its corners, so it could be fastened. 5Its skillfully woven waistband was like it — of one piece with the ephod and made with gold, and with blue, purple and scarlet yarn, and with finely twisted linen, as the LORD commanded Moses.

6They mounted the onyx stones in gold filigree settings and engraved them like a seal with the names of the sons of Israel. 7Then they fastened them on the shoulder pieces of the ephod as memorial stones for the sons of Israel, as the LORD commanded Moses.

The Breastpiece

8They fashioned the breastpiece — the work of a skilled craftsman. They made it like the ephod: of gold, and of blue, purple and scarlet yarn, and of finely twisted linen. 9It was square — a span[c] long and a span wide — and folded double. 10Then they mounted four rows of precious stones on it. The first row was carnelian, chrysolite and beryl; 11the second row was turquoise, lapis lazuli and emerald; 12the third row was jacinth, agate and amethyst; 13the fourth row was topaz, onyx and jasper.[d] They were mounted in gold filigree settings. 14There were twelve stones, one for each of the names of the sons of Israel, each engraved like a seal with the name of one of the twelve tribes.

15For the breastpiece they made braided chains of pure gold, like a rope. 16They made two gold filigree settings and two gold rings, and fastened the rings to two of the corners of the breastpiece. 17They fastened the two gold chains to the rings at the corners of the breastpiece, 18and the other ends of the chains to the two settings, attaching them to the shoulder pieces of the ephod at the front. 19They made two gold rings and attached them to the other two corners of the breastpiece on the inside edge next to the ephod. 20Then they made two more gold rings and attached them to the bottom of the shoulder pieces on the front of the ephod, close to the seam just above the waistband of the ephod. 21They tied the rings of the breastpiece to the rings of the ephod with blue cord, connecting it to the waistband so that the breastpiece would not swing out from the ephod — as the LORD commanded Moses.

Other Priestly Garments

22They made the robe of the ephod entirely of blue cloth — the work of a weaver — 23with an opening in the center of the robe like the opening of a collar,[e] and a band around this opening, so that it would not tear. 24They made pomegranates of blue, purple and scarlet yarn and finely twisted linen around the hem of the robe. 25And they made bells of pure gold and attached them around the hem between the pomegranates. 26The bells and pomegranates alternated around the hem of the robe to be worn for ministering, as the LORD commanded Moses.

27For Aaron and his sons, they made tunics of fine linen — the work of a weaver — 28and the turban of fine linen, the linen caps and the undergarments of finely twisted linen. 29The sash was made of finely twisted linen and blue, purple and scarlet yarn — the work of an embroiderer — as the LORD commanded Moses.

[a] *29* The weight of the bronze was about 2 1/2 tons or about 2.4 metric tons. [b] *2* Or *He*; also in verses 7, 8 and 22 [c] *9* That is, about 9 inches or about 23 centimeters [d] *13* The precise identification of some of these precious stones is uncertain. [e] *23* The meaning of the Hebrew for this word is uncertain.

30 They made the plate, the sacred em-
blem, out of pure gold and engraved on it,
like an inscription on a seal: HOLY TO THE
LORD. 31 Then they fastened a blue cord to it
to attach it to the turban, as the LORD com-
manded Moses.

Moses Inspects the Tabernacle

32 So all the work on the tabernacle, the
tent of meeting, was completed. The Isra-
elites did everything just as the LORD com-
manded Moses. 33 Then they brought the
tabernacle to Moses: the tent and all its
furnishings, its clasps, frames, crossbars,
posts and bases; 34 the covering of ram skins
dyed red and the covering of another dura-
ble leather[a] and the shielding curtain; 35 the
ark of the covenant law with its poles and the
atonement cover; 36 the table with all its ar-
ticles and the bread of the Presence; 37 the
pure gold lampstand with its row of lamps
and all its accessories, and the olive oil for
the light; 38 the gold altar, the anointing oil,
the fragrant incense, and the curtain for
the entrance to the tent; 39 the bronze altar
with its bronze grating, its poles and all its
utensils; the basin with its stand; 40 the cur-
tains of the courtyard with its posts and bas-
es, and the curtain for the entrance to the
courtyard; the ropes and tent pegs for the
courtyard; all the furnishings for the taber-
nacle, the tent of meeting; 41 and the woven
garments worn for ministering in the sanc-
tuary, both the sacred garments for Aar-
on the priest and the garments for his sons
when serving as priests.

42 The Israelites had done all the work just
as the LORD had commanded Moses. 43 Mo-
ses inspected the work and saw that they had
done it just as the LORD had commanded. So
Moses blessed them.

Setting Up the Tabernacle

40 Then the LORD said to Moses: 2 "Set
up the tabernacle, the tent of meet-
ing, on the first day of the first month. 3 Place
the ark of the covenant law in it and shield
the ark with the curtain. 4 Bring in the table
and set out what belongs on it. Then bring in
the lampstand and set up its lamps. 5 Place
the gold altar of incense in front of the ark of
the covenant law and put the curtain at the
entrance to the tabernacle.

6 "Place the altar of burnt offering in front
of the entrance to the tabernacle, the tent of
meeting; 7 place the basin between the tent
of meeting and the altar and put water in it.
8 Set up the courtyard around it and put the
curtain at the entrance to the courtyard.

9 "Take the anointing oil and anoint the
tabernacle and everything in it; consecrate
it and all its furnishings, and it will be holy.
10 Then anoint the altar of burnt offering and
all its utensils; consecrate the altar, and it
will be most holy. 11 Anoint the basin and its
stand and consecrate them.

12 "Bring Aaron and his sons to the en-
trance to the tent of meeting and wash them
with water. 13 Then dress Aaron in the sacred
garments, anoint him and consecrate him so
he may serve me as priest. 14 Bring his sons
and dress them in tunics. 15 Anoint them just
as you anointed their father, so they may
serve me as priests. Their anointing will be
to a priesthood that will continue through-
out their generations." 16 Moses did every-
thing just as the LORD commanded him.

17 So the tabernacle was set up on the first
day of the first month in the second year.
18 When Moses set up the tabernacle, he put
the bases in place, erected the frames, in-
serted the crossbars and set up the posts.
19 Then he spread the tent over the taberna-
cle and put the covering over the tent, as the
LORD commanded him.

20 He took the tablets of the covenant law
and placed them in the ark, attached the
poles to the ark and put the atonement cov-
er over it. 21 Then he brought the ark into the
tabernacle and hung the shielding curtain
and shielded the ark of the covenant law, as
the LORD commanded him.

22 Moses placed the table in the tent of
meeting on the north side of the tabernacle
outside the curtain 23 and set out the bread
on it before the LORD, as the LORD com-
manded him.

24 He placed the lampstand in the tent of
meeting opposite the table on the south side
of the tabernacle 25 and set up the lamps be-
fore the LORD, as the LORD commanded him.

26 Moses placed the gold altar in the tent of
meeting in front of the curtain 27 and burned
fragrant incense on it, as the LORD com-
manded him.

28 Then he put up the curtain at the en-

[a] *34* Possibly the hides of large aquatic mammals

trance to the tabernacle. [29]He set the altar of
burnt offering near the entrance to the tab-
ernacle, the tent of meeting, and offered on
it burnt offerings and grain offerings, as the
LORD commanded him.

[30]He placed the basin between the tent
of meeting and the altar and put water in it
for washing, [31]and Moses and Aaron and his
sons used it to wash their hands and feet.
[32]They washed whenever they entered the
tent of meeting or approached the altar, as
the LORD commanded Moses.

[33]Then Moses set up the courtyard around
the tabernacle and altar and put up the cur-
tain at the entrance to the courtyard. And so
Moses finished the work.

The Glory of the LORD

[34]Then the cloud covered the tent of
meeting, and the glory of the LORD filled the
tabernacle. [35]Moses could not enter the tent
of meeting because the cloud had settled on
it, and the glory of the LORD filled the tab-
ernacle.

[36]In all the travels of the Israelites, when-
ever the cloud lifted from above the taberna-
cle, they would set out; [37]but if the cloud did
not lift, they did not set out—until the day
it lifted. [38]So the cloud of the LORD was over
the tabernacle by day, and fire was in the
cloud by night, in the sight of all the Israel-
ites during all their travels.

LEVITICUS

The Burnt Offering

1 The LORD called to Moses and spoke to
him from the tent of meeting. He said,
2 "Speak to the Israelites and say to them:
'When anyone among you brings an offering
to the LORD, bring as your offering an animal
from either the herd or the flock.

3 " 'If the offering is a burnt offering from
the herd, you are to offer a male without de-
fect. You must present it at the entrance to
the tent of meeting so that it will be accept-
able to the LORD. 4 You are to lay your hand
on the head of the burnt offering, and it will
be accepted on your behalf to make atone-
ment for you. 5 You are to slaughter the young
bull before the LORD, and then Aaron's sons
the priests shall bring the blood and splash it
against the sides of the altar at the entrance
to the tent of meeting. 6 You are to skin the
burnt offering and cut it into pieces. 7 The
sons of Aaron the priest are to put fire on the
altar and arrange wood on the fire. 8 Then
Aaron's sons the priests shall arrange the
pieces, including the head and the fat, on the
wood that is burning on the altar. 9 You are to
wash the internal organs and the legs with
water, and the priest is to burn all of it on the
altar. It is a burnt offering, a food offering, an
aroma pleasing to the LORD.

10 " 'If the offering is a burnt offering from
the flock, from either the sheep or the goats,
you are to offer a male without defect. 11 You
are to slaughter it at the north side of the al-
tar before the LORD, and Aaron's sons the
priests shall splash its blood against the
sides of the altar. 12 You are to cut it into piec-
es, and the priest shall arrange them, includ-
ing the head and the fat, on the wood that is
burning on the altar. 13 You are to wash the
internal organs and the legs with water, and
the priest is to bring all of them and burn
them on the altar. It is a burnt offering, a food
offering, an aroma pleasing to the LORD.

14 " 'If the offering to the LORD is a burnt
offering of birds, you are to offer a dove or a
young pigeon. 15 The priest shall bring it to
the altar, wring off the head and burn it on
the altar; its blood shall be drained out on
the side of the altar. 16 He is to remove the
crop and the feathers[a] and throw them down
east of the altar where the ashes are. 17 He
shall tear it open by the wings, not dividing
it completely, and then the priest shall burn
it on the wood that is burning on the altar. It
is a burnt offering, a food offering, an aroma
pleasing to the LORD.

The Grain Offering

2 " 'When anyone brings a grain offering
to the LORD, their offering is to be of the
finest flour. They are to pour olive oil on it,
put incense on it 2 and take it to Aaron's sons
the priests. The priest shall take a handful
of the flour and oil, together with all the in-
cense, and burn this as a memorial[b] portion
on the altar, a food offering, an aroma pleas-
ing to the LORD. 3 The rest of the grain offer-
ing belongs to Aaron and his sons; it is a most
holy part of the food offerings presented to
the LORD.

4 " 'If you bring a grain offering baked in
an oven, it is to consist of the finest flour:
either thick loaves made without yeast and
with olive oil mixed in or thin loaves made
without yeast and brushed with olive oil. 5 If
your grain offering is prepared on a griddle,
it is to be made of the finest flour mixed with
oil, and without yeast. 6 Crumble it and pour
oil on it; it is a grain offering. 7 If your grain
offering is cooked in a pan, it is to be made
of the finest flour and some olive oil. 8 Bring
the grain offering made of these things to the
LORD; present it to the priest, who shall take
it to the altar. 9 He shall take out the memo-
rial portion from the grain offering and burn
it on the altar as a food offering, an aroma
pleasing to the LORD. 10 The rest of the grain
offering belongs to Aaron and his sons; it is a

[a] *16* Or *crop with its contents*; the meaning of the Hebrew for this word is uncertain.
[b] *2* Or *representative*; also in verses 9 and 16

most holy part of the food offerings present-
ed to the LORD.
11“ ‘Every grain offering you bring to the
LORD must be made without yeast, for you
are not to burn any yeast or honey in a food
offering presented to the LORD. 12You may
bring them to the LORD as an offering of the
firstfruits, but they are not to be offered on
the altar as a pleasing aroma. 13Season all
your grain offerings with salt. Do not leave
the salt of the covenant of your God out of
your grain offerings; add salt to all your of-
ferings.
14“ ‘If you bring a grain offering of first-
fruits to the LORD, offer crushed heads of
new grain roasted in the fire. 15Put oil and
incense on it; it is a grain offering. 16The
priest shall burn the memorial portion of
the crushed grain and the oil, together with
all the incense, as a food offering presented
to the LORD.

The Fellowship Offering

3 “ ‘If your offering is a fellowship offer-
ing, and you offer an animal from the
herd, whether male or female, you are to pre-
sent before the LORD an animal without de-
fect. 2You are to lay your hand on the head of
your offering and slaughter it at the entrance
to the tent of meeting. Then Aaron’s sons the
priests shall splash the blood against the
sides of the altar. 3From the fellowship of-
fering you are to bring a food offering to the
LORD: the internal organs and all the fat that
is connected to them, 4both kidneys with the
fat on them near the loins, and the long lobe
of the liver, which you will remove with the
kidneys. 5Then Aaron’s sons are to burn it on
the altar on top of the burnt offering that is
lying on the burning wood; it is a food offer-
ing, an aroma pleasing to the LORD.
6“ ‘If you offer an animal from the flock
as a fellowship offering to the LORD, you are
to offer a male or female without defect. 7If
you offer a lamb, you are to present it be-
fore the LORD, 8lay your hand on its head
and slaughter it in front of the tent of meet-
ing. Then Aaron’s sons shall splash its blood
against the sides of the altar. 9From the fel-
lowship offering you are to bring a food of-
fering to the LORD: its fat, the entire fat tail
cut off close to the backbone, the internal
organs and all the fat that is connected to
them, 10both kidneys with the fat on them
near the loins, and the long lobe of the liv-
er, which you will remove with the kidneys.
11The priest shall burn them on the altar as a
food offering presented to the LORD.
12“ ‘If your offering is a goat, you are to pre-
sent it before the LORD, 13lay your hand on its
head and slaughter it in front of the tent of
meeting. Then Aaron’s sons shall splash its
blood against the sides of the altar. 14From
what you offer you are to present this food
offering to the LORD: the internal organs and
all the fat that is connected to them, 15both
kidneys with the fat on them near the loins,
and the long lobe of the liver, which you will
remove with the kidneys. 16The priest shall
burn them on the altar as a food offering, a
pleasing aroma. All the fat is the LORD’s.
17“ ‘This is a lasting ordinance for the gen-
erations to come, wherever you live: You
must not eat any fat or any blood.’ ”

The Sin Offering

4 The LORD said to Moses, 2“Say to the
Israelites: ‘When anyone sins uninten-
tionally and does what is forbidden in any of
the LORD’s commands—
3“ ‘If the anointed priest sins, bringing
guilt on the people, he must bring to the
LORD a young bull without defect as a sin
offering[a] for the sin he has committed. 4He
is to present the bull at the entrance to the
tent of meeting before the LORD. He is to lay
his hand on its head and slaughter it there
before the LORD. 5Then the anointed priest
shall take some of the bull’s blood and carry
it into the tent of meeting. 6He is to dip his
finger into the blood and sprinkle some of it
seven times before the LORD, in front of the
curtain of the sanctuary. 7The priest shall
then put some of the blood on the horns of
the altar of fragrant incense that is before the
LORD in the tent of meeting. The rest of the
bull’s blood he shall pour out at the base of
the altar of burnt offering at the entrance to
the tent of meeting. 8He shall remove all the
fat from the bull of the sin offering—all the
fat that is connected to the internal organs,
9both kidneys with the fat on them near the
loins, and the long lobe of the liver, which
he will remove with the kidneys— 10just as

[a] 3 Or *purification offering*; here and throughout this chapter

the fat is removed from the ox[a] sacrificed as a fellowship offering. Then the priest shall burn them on the altar of burnt offering. 11 But the hide of the bull and all its flesh, as well as the head and legs, the internal organs and the intestines— 12 that is, all the rest of the bull—he must take outside the camp to a place ceremonially clean, where the ashes are thrown, and burn it there in a wood fire on the ash heap.

13 " 'If the whole Israelite community sins unintentionally and does what is forbidden in any of the LORD's commands, even though the community is unaware of the matter, when they realize their guilt 14 and the sin they committed becomes known, the assembly must bring a young bull as a sin offering and present it before the tent of meeting. 15 The elders of the community are to lay their hands on the bull's head before the LORD, and the bull shall be slaughtered before the LORD. 16 Then the anointed priest is to take some of the bull's blood into the tent of meeting. 17 He shall dip his finger into the blood and sprinkle it before the LORD seven times in front of the curtain. 18 He is to put some of the blood on the horns of the altar that is before the LORD in the tent of meeting. The rest of the blood he shall pour out at the base of the altar of burnt offering at the entrance to the tent of meeting. 19 He shall remove all the fat from it and burn it on the altar, 20 and do with this bull just as he did with the bull for the sin offering. In this way the priest will make atonement for the community, and they will be forgiven. 21 Then he shall take the bull outside the camp and burn it as he burned the first bull. This is the sin offering for the community.

22 " 'When a leader sins unintentionally and does what is forbidden in any of the commands of the LORD his God, when he realizes his guilt 23 and the sin he has committed becomes known, he must bring as his offering a male goat without defect. 24 He is to lay his hand on the goat's head and slaughter it at the place where the burnt offering is slaughtered before the LORD. It is a sin offering. 25 Then the priest shall take some of the blood of the sin offering with his finger and put it on the horns of the altar of burnt offering and pour out the rest of the blood at the base of the altar. 26 He shall burn all the fat on the altar as he burned the fat of the fellowship offering. In this way the priest will make atonement for the leader's sin, and he will be forgiven.

27 " 'If any member of the community sins unintentionally and does what is forbidden in any of the LORD's commands, when they realize their guilt 28 and the sin they have committed becomes known, they must bring as their offering for the sin they committed a female goat without defect. 29 They are to lay their hand on the head of the sin offering and slaughter it at the place of the burnt offering. 30 Then the priest is to take some of the blood with his finger and put it on the horns of the altar of burnt offering and pour out the rest of the blood at the base of the altar. 31 They shall remove all the fat, just as the fat is removed from the fellowship offering, and the priest shall burn it on the altar as an aroma pleasing to the LORD. In this way the priest will make atonement for them, and they will be forgiven.

32 " 'If someone brings a lamb as their sin offering, they are to bring a female without defect. 33 They are to lay their hand on its head and slaughter it for a sin offering at the place where the burnt offering is slaughtered. 34 Then the priest shall take some of the blood of the sin offering with his finger and put it on the horns of the altar of burnt offering and pour out the rest of the blood at the base of the altar. 35 They shall remove all the fat, just as the fat is removed from the lamb of the fellowship offering, and the priest shall burn it on the altar on top of the food offerings presented to the LORD. In this way the priest will make atonement for them for the sin they have committed, and they will be forgiven.

5 " 'If anyone sins because they do not speak up when they hear a public charge to testify regarding something they have seen or learned about, they will be held responsible.

2 " 'If anyone becomes aware that they are guilty—if they unwittingly touch anything ceremonially unclean (whether the carcass of an unclean animal, wild or domestic, or of

[a] *10* The Hebrew word can refer to either male or female.

any unclean creature that moves along the ground) and they are unaware that they have become unclean, but then they come to realize their guilt; 3or if they touch human uncleanness (anything that would make them unclean) even though they are unaware of it, but then they learn of it and realize their guilt; 4or if anyone thoughtlessly takes an oath to do anything, whether good or evil (in any matter one might carelessly swear about) even though they are unaware of it, but then they learn of it and realize their guilt— 5when anyone becomes aware that they are guilty in any of these matters, they must confess in what way they have sinned. 6As a penalty for the sin they have committed, they must bring to the LORD a female lamb or goat from the flock as a sin offering[a]; and the priest shall make atonement for them for their sin.

7"'Anyone who cannot afford a lamb is to bring two doves or two young pigeons to the LORD as a penalty for their sin — one for a sin offering and the other for a burnt offering. 8They are to bring them to the priest, who shall first offer the one for the sin offering. He is to wring its head from its neck, not dividing it completely, 9and is to splash some of the blood of the sin offering against the side of the altar; the rest of the blood must be drained out at the base of the altar. It is a sin offering. 10The priest shall then offer the other as a burnt offering in the prescribed way and make atonement for them for the sin they have committed, and they will be forgiven.

11"'If, however, they cannot afford two doves or two young pigeons, they are to bring as an offering for their sin a tenth of an ephah[b] of the finest flour for a sin offering. They must not put olive oil or incense on it, because it is a sin offering. 12They are to bring it to the priest, who shall take a handful of it as a memorial[c] portion and burn it on the altar on top of the food offerings presented to the LORD. It is a sin offering. 13In this way the priest will make atonement for them for any of these sins they have committed, and they will be forgiven. The rest of the offering will belong to the priest, as in the case of the grain offering.'"

The Guilt Offering

14The LORD said to Moses: 15"When anyone is unfaithful to the LORD by sinning unintentionally in regard to any of the LORD's holy things, they are to bring to the LORD as a penalty a ram from the flock, one without defect and of the proper value in silver, according to the sanctuary shekel.[d] It is a guilt offering. 16They must make restitution for what they have failed to do in regard to the holy things, pay an additional penalty of a fifth of its value and give it all to the priest. The priest will make atonement for them with the ram as a guilt offering, and they will be forgiven.

17"If anyone sins and does what is forbidden in any of the LORD's commands, even though they do not know it, they are guilty and will be held responsible. 18They are to bring to the priest as a guilt offering a ram from the flock, one without defect and of the proper value. In this way the priest will make atonement for them for the wrong they have committed unintentionally, and they will be forgiven. 19It is a guilt offering; they have been guilty of[e] wrongdoing against the LORD."

6 [f]The LORD said to Moses: 2"If anyone sins and is unfaithful to the LORD by deceiving a neighbor about something entrusted to them or left in their care or about something stolen, or if they cheat their neighbor, 3or if they find lost property and lie about it, or if they swear falsely about any such sin that people may commit— 4when they sin in any of these ways and realize their guilt, they must return what they have stolen or taken by extortion, or what was entrusted to them, or the lost property they found, 5or whatever it was they swore falsely about. They must make restitution in full, add a fifth of the value to it and give it all to the owner on the day they present their guilt offering. 6And as a penalty they must bring to the priest, that is, to the LORD, their guilt offering, a ram from the flock, one without defect and of the proper value. 7In this way the priest will make atonement for them before the LORD, and they will be forgiven for any of the things they did that made them guilty."

[a] 6 Or *purification offering*; here and throughout this chapter [b] *11* That is, probably about 3 1/2 pounds or about 1.6 kilograms [c] *12* Or *representative* [d] *15* That is, about 2/5 ounce or about 12 grams [e] *19* Or *offering; atonement has been made for their* [f] In Hebrew texts 6:1-7 is numbered 5:20-26, and 6:8-30 is numbered 6:1-23.

The Burnt Offering

8The LORD said to Moses: 9"Give Aaron
and his sons this command: 'These are the
regulations for the burnt offering: The burnt
offering is to remain on the altar hearth
throughout the night, till morning, and the
fire must be kept burning on the altar. 10The
priest shall then put on his linen clothes,
with linen undergarments next to his body,
and shall remove the ashes of the burnt of-
fering that the fire has consumed on the al-
tar and place them beside the altar. 11Then
he is to take off these clothes and put on oth-
ers, and carry the ashes outside the camp to
a place that is ceremonially clean. 12The fire
on the altar must be kept burning; it must
not go out. Every morning the priest is to add
firewood and arrange the burnt offering on
the fire and burn the fat of the fellowship of-
ferings on it. 13The fire must be kept burning
on the altar continuously; it must not go out.

The Grain Offering

14" 'These are the regulations for the grain
offering: Aaron's sons are to bring it before
the LORD, in front of the altar. 15The priest is
to take a handful of the finest flour and some
olive oil, together with all the incense on
the grain offering, and burn the memorial[a]
portion on the altar as an aroma pleasing to
the LORD. 16Aaron and his sons shall eat the
rest of it, but it is to be eaten without yeast in
the sanctuary area; they are to eat it in the
courtyard of the tent of meeting. 17It must
not be baked with yeast; I have given it as
their share of the food offerings presented to
me. Like the sin offering[b] and the guilt offer-
ing, it is most holy. 18Any male descendant of
Aaron may eat it. For all generations to come
it is his perpetual share of the food offerings
presented to the LORD. Whatever touches
them will become holy.[c]' "

19The LORD also said to Moses, 20"This is
the offering Aaron and his sons are to bring
to the LORD on the day he[d] is anointed: a
tenth of an ephah[e] of the finest flour as a reg-
ular grain offering, half of it in the morning
and half in the evening. 21It must be pre-
pared with oil on a griddle; bring it well-
mixed and present the grain offering broken[f]
in pieces as an aroma pleasing to the LORD.
22The son who is to succeed him as anoint-
ed priest shall prepare it. It is the LORD's per-
petual share and is to be burned complete-
ly. 23Every grain offering of a priest shall be
burned completely; it must not be eaten."

The Sin Offering

24The LORD said to Moses, 25"Say to Aar-
on and his sons: 'These are the regulations
for the sin offering: The sin offering is to be
slaughtered before the LORD in the place the
burnt offering is slaughtered; it is most holy.
26The priest who offers it shall eat it; it is to be
eaten in the sanctuary area, in the courtyard
of the tent of meeting. 27Whatever touches
any of the flesh will become holy, and if any
of the blood is spattered on a garment, you
must wash it in the sanctuary area. 28The
clay pot the meat is cooked in must be bro-
ken; but if it is cooked in a bronze pot, the
pot is to be scoured and rinsed with water.
29Any male in a priest's family may eat it; it
is most holy. 30But any sin offering whose
blood is brought into the tent of meeting to
make atonement in the Holy Place must not
be eaten; it must be burned up.

The Guilt Offering

7 " 'These are the regulations for the guilt
offering, which is most holy: 2The guilt
offering is to be slaughtered in the place
where the burnt offering is slaughtered, and
its blood is to be splashed against the sides
of the altar. 3All its fat shall be offered: the
fat tail and the fat that covers the internal
organs, 4both kidneys with the fat on them
near the loins, and the long lobe of the liv-
er, which is to be removed with the kidneys.
5The priest shall burn them on the altar as
a food offering presented to the LORD. It is a
guilt offering. 6Any male in a priest's family
may eat it, but it must be eaten in the sanctu-
ary area; it is most holy.

7" 'The same law applies to both the sin of-
fering[g] and the guilt offering: They belong to
the priest who makes atonement with them.
8The priest who offers a burnt offering for

[a] 15 Or *representative* [b] 17 Or *purification offering;* also in verses 25 and 30 [c] 18 Or *Whoever touches them must be holy;* similarly in verse 27 [d] 20 Or *each* [e] 20 That is, probably about 3 1/2 pounds or about 1.6 kilograms [f] 21 The meaning of the Hebrew for this word is uncertain. [g] 7 Or *purification offering;* also in verse 37

anyone may keep its hide for himself. 9 Every grain offering baked in an oven or cooked in a pan or on a griddle belongs to the priest who offers it, 10 and every grain offering, whether mixed with olive oil or dry, belongs equally to all the sons of Aaron.

The Fellowship Offering

11 " 'These are the regulations for the fellowship offering anyone may present to the LORD:

12 " 'If they offer it as an expression of thankfulness, then along with this thank offering they are to offer thick loaves made without yeast and with olive oil mixed in, thin loaves made without yeast and brushed with oil, and thick loaves of the finest flour well-kneaded and with oil mixed in. 13 Along with their fellowship offering of thanksgiving they are to present an offering with thick loaves of bread made with yeast. 14 They are to bring one of each kind as an offering, a contribution to the LORD; it belongs to the priest who splashes the blood of the fellowship offering against the altar. 15 The meat of their fellowship offering of thanksgiving must be eaten on the day it is offered; they must leave none of it till morning.

16 " 'If, however, their offering is the result of a vow or is a freewill offering, the sacrifice shall be eaten on the day they offer it, but anything left over may be eaten on the next day. 17 Any meat of the sacrifice left over till the third day must be burned up. 18 If any meat of the fellowship offering is eaten on the third day, the one who offered it will not be accepted. It will not be reckoned to their credit, for it has become impure; the person who eats any of it will be held responsible.

19 " 'Meat that touches anything ceremonially unclean must not be eaten; it must be burned up. As for other meat, anyone ceremonially clean may eat it. 20 But if anyone who is unclean eats any meat of the fellowship offering belonging to the LORD, they must be cut off from their people. 21 Anyone who touches something unclean—whether human uncleanness or an unclean animal or any unclean creature that moves along the ground[a]—and then eats any of the meat of the fellowship offering belonging to the LORD must be cut off from their people.' "

Eating Fat and Blood Forbidden

22 The LORD said to Moses, 23 "Say to the Israelites: 'Do not eat any of the fat of cattle, sheep or goats. 24 The fat of an animal found dead or torn by wild animals may be used for any other purpose, but you must not eat it. 25 Anyone who eats the fat of an animal from which a food offering may be[b] presented to the LORD must be cut off from their people. 26 And wherever you live, you must not eat the blood of any bird or animal. 27 Anyone who eats blood must be cut off from their people.' "

The Priests' Share

28 The LORD said to Moses, 29 "Say to the Israelites: 'Anyone who brings a fellowship offering to the LORD is to bring part of it as their sacrifice to the LORD. 30 With their own hands they are to present the food offering to the LORD; they are to bring the fat, together with the breast, and wave the breast before the LORD as a wave offering. 31 The priest shall burn the fat on the altar, but the breast belongs to Aaron and his sons. 32 You are to give the right thigh of your fellowship offerings to the priest as a contribution. 33 The son of Aaron who offers the blood and the fat of the fellowship offering shall have the right thigh as his share. 34 From the fellowship offerings of the Israelites, I have taken the breast that is waved and the thigh that is presented and have given them to Aaron the priest and his sons as their perpetual share from the Israelites.' "

35 This is the portion of the food offerings presented to the LORD that were allotted to Aaron and his sons on the day they were presented to serve the LORD as priests. 36 On the day they were anointed, the LORD commanded that the Israelites give this to them as their perpetual share for the generations to come.

37 These, then, are the regulations for the burnt offering, the grain offering, the sin offering, the guilt offering, the ordination offering and the fellowship offering, 38 which the LORD gave Moses at Mount Sinai in the Desert of Sinai on the day he commanded the Israelites to bring their offerings to the LORD.

[a] *21* A few Hebrew manuscripts, Samaritan Pentateuch, Syriac and Targum (see 5:2); most Hebrew manuscripts *any unclean, detestable thing* [b] *25* Or *offering is*

The Ordination of Aaron and His Sons

8 The LORD said to Moses, 2“Bring Aaron and his sons, their garments, the anointing oil, the bull for the sin offering,[a] the two rams and the basket containing bread made without yeast, 3and gather the entire assembly at the entrance to the tent of meeting.” 4Moses did as the LORD commanded him, and the assembly gathered at the entrance to the tent of meeting.

5Moses said to the assembly, “This is what the LORD has commanded to be done.” 6Then Moses brought Aaron and his sons forward and washed them with water. 7He put the tunic on Aaron, tied the sash around him, clothed him with the robe and put the ephod on him. He also fastened the ephod with a decorative waistband, which he tied around him. 8He placed the breastpiece on him and put the Urim and Thummim in the breastpiece. 9Then he placed the turban on Aaron’s head and set the gold plate, the sacred emblem, on the front of it, as the LORD commanded Moses.

10Then Moses took the anointing oil and anointed the tabernacle and everything in it, and so consecrated them. 11He sprinkled some of the oil on the altar seven times, anointing the altar and all its utensils and the basin with its stand, to consecrate them. 12He poured some of the anointing oil on Aaron’s head and anointed him to consecrate him. 13Then he brought Aaron’s sons forward, put tunics on them, tied sashes around them and fastened caps on them, as the LORD commanded Moses.

14He then presented the bull for the sin offering, and Aaron and his sons laid their hands on its head. 15Moses slaughtered the bull and took some of the blood, and with his finger he put it on all the horns of the altar to purify the altar. He poured out the rest of the blood at the base of the altar. So he consecrated it to make atonement for it. 16Moses also took all the fat around the internal organs, the long lobe of the liver, and both kidneys and their fat, and burned it on the altar. 17But the bull with its hide and its flesh and its intestines he burned up outside the camp, as the LORD commanded Moses.

18He then presented the ram for the burnt offering, and Aaron and his sons laid their hands on its head. 19Then Moses slaughtered the ram and splashed the blood against the sides of the altar. 20He cut the ram into pieces and burned the head, the pieces and the fat. 21He washed the internal organs and the legs with water and burned the whole ram on the altar. It was a burnt offering, a pleasing aroma, a food offering presented to the LORD, as the LORD commanded Moses.

22He then presented the other ram, the ram for the ordination, and Aaron and his sons laid their hands on its head. 23Moses slaughtered the ram and took some of its blood and put it on the lobe of Aaron’s right ear, on the thumb of his right hand and on the big toe of his right foot. 24Moses also brought Aaron’s sons forward and put some of the blood on the lobes of their right ears, on the thumbs of their right hands and on the big toes of their right feet. Then he splashed blood against the sides of the altar. 25After that, he took the fat, the fat tail, all the fat around the internal organs, the long lobe of the liver, both kidneys and their fat and the right thigh. 26And from the basket of bread made without yeast, which was before the LORD, he took one thick loaf, one thick loaf with olive oil mixed in, and one thin loaf, and he put these on the fat portions and on the right thigh. 27He put all these in the hands of Aaron and his sons, and they waved them before the LORD as a wave offering. 28Then Moses took them from their hands and burned them on the altar on top of the burnt offering as an ordination offering, a pleasing aroma, a food offering presented to the LORD. 29Moses also took the breast, which was his share of the ordination ram, and waved it before the LORD as a wave offering, as the LORD commanded Moses.

30Then Moses took some of the anointing oil and some of the blood from the altar and sprinkled them on Aaron and his garments and on his sons and their garments. So he consecrated Aaron and his garments and his sons and their garments.

31Moses then said to Aaron and his sons, “Cook the meat at the entrance to the tent of meeting and eat it there with the bread from the basket of ordination offerings, as I was commanded: ‘Aaron and his sons are to eat it.’ 32Then burn up the rest of the meat and the bread. 33Do not leave the entrance to the

[a] 2 Or *purification offering*; also in verse 14

tent of meeting for seven days, until the days of your ordination are completed, for your ordination will last seven days. [34]What has been done today was commanded by the LORD to make atonement for you. [35]You must stay at the entrance to the tent of meeting day and night for seven days and do what the LORD requires, so you will not die; for that is what I have been commanded."

[36]So Aaron and his sons did everything the LORD commanded through Moses.

The Priests Begin Their Ministry

9 On the eighth day Moses summoned Aaron and his sons and the elders of Israel. [2]He said to Aaron, "Take a bull calf for your sin offering[a] and a ram for your burnt offering, both without defect, and present them before the LORD. [3]Then say to the Israelites: 'Take a male goat for a sin offering, a calf and a lamb—both a year old and without defect—for a burnt offering, [4]and an ox[b] and a ram for a fellowship offering to sacrifice before the LORD, together with a grain offering mixed with olive oil. For today the LORD will appear to you.'"

[5]They took the things Moses commanded to the front of the tent of meeting, and the entire assembly came near and stood before the LORD. [6]Then Moses said, "This is what the LORD has commanded you to do, so that the glory of the LORD may appear to you."

[7]Moses said to Aaron, "Come to the altar and sacrifice your sin offering and your burnt offering and make atonement for yourself and the people; sacrifice the offering that is for the people and make atonement for them, as the LORD has commanded."

[8]So Aaron came to the altar and slaughtered the calf as a sin offering for himself. [9]His sons brought the blood to him, and he dipped his finger into the blood and put it on the horns of the altar; the rest of the blood he poured out at the base of the altar. [10]On the altar he burned the fat, the kidneys and the long lobe of the liver from the sin offering, as the LORD commanded Moses; [11]the flesh and the hide he burned up outside the camp.

[12]Then he slaughtered the burnt offering. His sons handed him the blood, and he splashed it against the sides of the altar. [13]They handed him the burnt offering piece by piece, including the head, and he burned them on the altar. [14]He washed the internal organs and the legs and burned them on top of the burnt offering on the altar.

[15]Aaron then brought the offering that was for the people. He took the goat for the people's sin offering and slaughtered it and offered it for a sin offering as he did with the first one.

[16]He brought the burnt offering and offered it in the prescribed way. [17]He also brought the grain offering, took a handful of it and burned it on the altar in addition to the morning's burnt offering.

[18]He slaughtered the ox and the ram as the fellowship offering for the people. His sons handed him the blood, and he splashed it against the sides of the altar. [19]But the fat portions of the ox and the ram—the fat tail, the layer of fat, the kidneys and the long lobe of the liver— [20]these they laid on the breasts, and then Aaron burned the fat on the altar. [21]Aaron waved the breasts and the right thigh before the LORD as a wave offering, as Moses commanded.

[22]Then Aaron lifted his hands toward the people and blessed them. And having sacrificed the sin offering, the burnt offering and the fellowship offering, he stepped down.

[23]Moses and Aaron then went into the tent of meeting. When they came out, they blessed the people; and the glory of the LORD appeared to all the people. [24]Fire came out from the presence of the LORD and consumed the burnt offering and the fat portions on the altar. And when all the people saw it, they shouted for joy and fell facedown.

The Death of Nadab and Abihu

10 Aaron's sons Nadab and Abihu took their censers, put fire in them and added incense; and they offered unauthorized fire before the LORD, contrary to his command. [2]So fire came out from the presence of the LORD and consumed them, and they died before the LORD. [3]Moses then said to Aaron, "This is what the LORD spoke of when he said:

"'Among those who approach me
I will be proved holy;
in the sight of all the people
I will be honored.'"

Aaron remained silent.

[a] *2* Or *purification offering*; here and throughout this chapter [b] *4* The Hebrew word can refer to either male or female; also in verses 18 and 19.

4Moses summoned Mishael and Elzaphan, sons of Aaron's uncle Uzziel, and said to them, "Come here; carry your cousins outside the camp, away from the front of the sanctuary." 5So they came and carried them, still in their tunics, outside the camp, as Moses ordered.

6Then Moses said to Aaron and his sons Eleazar and Ithamar, "Do not let your hair become unkempt[a] and do not tear your clothes, or you will die and the LORD will be angry with the whole community. But your relatives, all the Israelites, may mourn for those the LORD has destroyed by fire. 7Do not leave the entrance to the tent of meeting or you will die, because the LORD's anointing oil is on you." So they did as Moses said.

8Then the LORD said to Aaron, 9"You and your sons are not to drink wine or other fermented drink whenever you go into the tent of meeting, or you will die. This is a lasting ordinance for the generations to come, 10so that you can distinguish between the holy and the common, between the unclean and the clean, 11and so you can teach the Israelites all the decrees the LORD has given them through Moses."

12Moses said to Aaron and his remaining sons, Eleazar and Ithamar, "Take the grain offering left over from the food offerings prepared without yeast and presented to the LORD and eat it beside the altar, for it is most holy. 13Eat it in the sanctuary area, because it is your share and your sons' share of the food offerings presented to the LORD; for so I have been commanded. 14But you and your sons and your daughters may eat the breast that was waved and the thigh that was presented. Eat them in a ceremonially clean place; they have been given to you and your children as your share of the Israelites' fellowship offerings. 15The thigh that was presented and the breast that was waved must be brought with the fat portions of the food offerings, to be waved before the LORD as a wave offering. This will be the perpetual share for you and your children, as the LORD has commanded."

16When Moses inquired about the goat of the sin offering[b] and found that it had been burned up, he was angry with Eleazar and Ithamar, Aaron's remaining sons, and asked, 17"Why didn't you eat the sin offering in the sanctuary area? It is most holy; it was given to you to take away the guilt of the community by making atonement for them before the LORD. 18Since its blood was not taken into the Holy Place, you should have eaten the goat in the sanctuary area, as I commanded."

19Aaron replied to Moses, "Today they sacrificed their sin offering and their burnt offering before the LORD, but such things as this have happened to me. Would the LORD have been pleased if I had eaten the sin offering today?" 20When Moses heard this, he was satisfied.

Clean and Unclean Food

11 The LORD said to Moses and Aaron, 2"Say to the Israelites: 'Of all the animals that live on land, these are the ones you may eat: 3You may eat any animal that has a divided hoof and that chews the cud.

4" 'There are some that only chew the cud or only have a divided hoof, but you must not eat them. The camel, though it chews the cud, does not have a divided hoof; it is ceremonially unclean for you. 5The hyrax, though it chews the cud, does not have a divided hoof; it is unclean for you. 6The rabbit, though it chews the cud, does not have a divided hoof; it is unclean for you. 7And the pig, though it has a divided hoof, does not chew the cud; it is unclean for you. 8You must not eat their meat or touch their carcasses; they are unclean for you.

9" 'Of all the creatures living in the water of the seas and the streams you may eat any that have fins and scales. 10But all creatures in the seas or streams that do not have fins and scales—whether among all the swarming things or among all the other living creatures in the water—you are to regard as unclean. 11And since you are to regard them as unclean, you must not eat their meat; you must regard their carcasses as unclean. 12Anything living in the water that does not have fins and scales is to be regarded as unclean by you.

13" 'These are the birds you are to regard as unclean and not eat because they are unclean: the eagle,[c] the vulture, the black vulture, 14the red kite, any kind of black kite, 15any kind of raven, 16the horned owl,

[a] 6 Or *Do not uncover your heads* [b] 16 Or *purification offering*; also in verses 17 and 19 [c] 13 The precise identification of some of the birds, insects and animals in this chapter is uncertain.

the screech owl, the gull, any kind of hawk,
17 the little owl, the cormorant, the great owl,
18 the white owl, the desert owl, the osprey,
19 the stork, any kind of heron, the hoopoe
and the bat.

20 " 'All flying insects that walk on all fours
are to be regarded as unclean by you. 21 There
are, however, some flying insects that walk
on all fours that you may eat: those that have
jointed legs for hopping on the ground. 22 Of
these you may eat any kind of locust, katy-
did, cricket or grasshopper. 23 But all other
flying insects that have four legs you are to
regard as unclean.

24 " 'You will make yourselves unclean by
these; whoever touches their carcasses will
be unclean till evening. 25 Whoever picks
up one of their carcasses must wash their
clothes, and they will be unclean till evening.

26 " 'Every animal that does not have a di-
vided hoof or that does not chew the cud is
unclean for you; whoever touches the car-
cass of any of them will be unclean. 27 Of all
the animals that walk on all fours, those that
walk on their paws are unclean for you; who-
ever touches their carcasses will be unclean
till evening. 28 Anyone who picks up their
carcasses must wash their clothes, and they
will be unclean till evening. These animals
are unclean for you.

29 " 'Of the animals that move along the
ground, these are unclean for you: the wea-
sel, the rat, any kind of great lizard, 30 the
gecko, the monitor lizard, the wall lizard,
the skink and the chameleon. 31 Of all those
that move along the ground, these are un-
clean for you. Whoever touches them when
they are dead will be unclean till evening.
32 When one of them dies and falls on some-
thing, that article, whatever its use, will be
unclean, whether it is made of wood, cloth,
hide or sackcloth. Put it in water; it will be
unclean till evening, and then it will be
clean. 33 If one of them falls into a clay pot,
everything in it will be unclean, and you
must break the pot. 34 Any food you are al-
lowed to eat that has come into contact with
water from any such pot is unclean, and
any liquid that is drunk from such a pot is
unclean. 35 Anything that one of their car-
casses falls on becomes unclean; an oven
or cooking pot must be broken up. They are
unclean, and you are to regard them as un-
clean. 36 A spring, however, or a cistern for
collecting water remains clean, but anyone
who touches one of these carcasses is un-
clean. 37 If a carcass falls on any seeds that
are to be planted, they remain clean. 38 But if
water has been put on the seed and a carcass
falls on it, it is unclean for you.

39 " 'If an animal that you are allowed to
eat dies, anyone who touches its carcass will
be unclean till evening. 40 Anyone who eats
some of its carcass must wash their clothes,
and they will be unclean till evening. Any-
one who picks up the carcass must wash
their clothes, and they will be unclean till
evening.

41 " 'Every creature that moves along the
ground is to be regarded as unclean; it is not
to be eaten. 42 You are not to eat any crea-
ture that moves along the ground, whether
it moves on its belly or walks on all fours or
on many feet; it is unclean. 43 Do not defile
yourselves by any of these creatures. Do
not make yourselves unclean by means of
them or be made unclean by them. 44 I am
the LORD your God; consecrate yourselves
and be holy, because I am holy. Do not make
yourselves unclean by any creature that
moves along the ground. 45 I am the LORD,
who brought you up out of Egypt to be your
God; therefore be holy, because I am holy.

46 " 'These are the regulations concerning
animals, birds, every living thing that moves
about in the water and every creature that
moves along the ground. 47 You must distin-
guish between the unclean and the clean,
between living creatures that may be eaten
and those that may not be eaten.' "

Purification After Childbirth

12 The LORD said to Moses, 2 "Say to the
Israelites: 'A woman who becomes
pregnant and gives birth to a son will be cer-
emonially unclean for seven days, just as she
is unclean during her monthly period. 3 On
the eighth day the boy is to be circumcised.
4 Then the woman must wait thirty-three
days to be purified from her bleeding. She
must not touch anything sacred or go to the
sanctuary until the days of her purification
are over. 5 If she gives birth to a daughter, for
two weeks the woman will be unclean, as
during her period. Then she must wait six-
ty-six days to be purified from her bleeding.

6 " 'When the days of her purification for
a son or daughter are over, she is to bring

to the priest at the entrance to the tent of meeting a year-old lamb for a burnt offering and a young pigeon or a dove for a sin offering.[a] 7 He shall offer them before the LORD to make atonement for her, and then she will be ceremonially clean from her flow of blood.

" 'These are the regulations for the woman who gives birth to a boy or a girl. 8 But if she cannot afford a lamb, she is to bring two doves or two young pigeons, one for a burnt offering and the other for a sin offering. In this way the priest will make atonement for her, and she will be clean.' "

Regulations About Defiling Skin Diseases

13 The LORD said to Moses and Aaron, 2 "When anyone has a swelling or a rash or a shiny spot on their skin that may be a defiling skin disease,[b] they must be brought to Aaron the priest or to one of his sons[c] who is a priest. 3 The priest is to examine the sore on the skin, and if the hair in the sore has turned white and the sore appears to be more than skin deep, it is a defiling skin disease. When the priest examines that person, he shall pronounce them ceremonially unclean. 4 If the shiny spot on the skin is white but does not appear to be more than skin deep and the hair in it has not turned white, the priest is to isolate the affected person for seven days. 5 On the seventh day the priest is to examine them, and if he sees that the sore is unchanged and has not spread in the skin, he is to isolate them for another seven days. 6 On the seventh day the priest is to examine them again, and if the sore has faded and has not spread in the skin, the priest shall pronounce them clean; it is only a rash. They must wash their clothes, and they will be clean. 7 But if the rash does spread in their skin after they have shown themselves to the priest to be pronounced clean, they must appear before the priest again. 8 The priest is to examine that person, and if the rash has spread in the skin, he shall pronounce them unclean; it is a defiling skin disease.

9 "When anyone has a defiling skin disease, they must be brought to the priest. 10 The priest is to examine them, and if there is a white swelling in the skin that has turned the hair white and if there is raw flesh in the swelling, 11 it is a chronic skin disease and the priest shall pronounce them unclean. He is not to isolate them, because they are already unclean.

12 "If the disease breaks out all over their skin and, so far as the priest can see, it covers all the skin of the affected person from head to foot, 13 the priest is to examine them, and if the disease has covered their whole body, he shall pronounce them clean. Since it has all turned white, they are clean. 14 But whenever raw flesh appears on them, they will be unclean. 15 When the priest sees the raw flesh, he shall pronounce them unclean. The raw flesh is unclean; they have a defiling disease. 16 If the raw flesh changes and turns white, they must go to the priest. 17 The priest is to examine them, and if the sores have turned white, the priest shall pronounce the affected person clean; then they will be clean.

18 "When someone has a boil on their skin and it heals, 19 and in the place where the boil was, a white swelling or reddish-white spot appears, they must present themselves to the priest. 20 The priest is to examine it, and if it appears to be more than skin deep and the hair in it has turned white, the priest shall pronounce that person unclean. It is a defiling skin disease that has broken out where the boil was. 21 But if, when the priest examines it, there is no white hair in it and it is not more than skin deep and has faded, then the priest is to isolate them for seven days. 22 If it is spreading in the skin, the priest shall pronounce them unclean; it is a defiling disease. 23 But if the spot is unchanged and has not spread, it is only a scar from the boil, and the priest shall pronounce them clean.

24 "When someone has a burn on their skin and a reddish-white or white spot appears in the raw flesh of the burn, 25 the priest is to examine the spot, and if the hair in it has turned white, and it appears to be more than skin deep, it is a defiling disease that has broken out in the burn. The priest shall pronounce them unclean; it is a defiling skin disease. 26 But if the priest examines it and there is no white hair in the spot and if it is not more than skin deep and has faded, then the priest is to isolate them for

[a] 6 Or *purification offering*; also in verse 8 [b] 2 The Hebrew word for *defiling skin disease*, traditionally translated "leprosy," was used for various diseases affecting the skin; here and throughout verses 3-46. [c] 2 Or *descendants*

seven days. 27 On the seventh day the priest is to examine that person, and if it is spreading in the skin, the priest shall pronounce them unclean; it is a defiling skin disease. 28 If, however, the spot is unchanged and has not spread in the skin but has faded, it is a swelling from the burn, and the priest shall pronounce them clean; it is only a scar from the burn.

29 "If a man or woman has a sore on their head or chin, 30 the priest is to examine the sore, and if it appears to be more than skin deep and the hair in it is yellow and thin, the priest shall pronounce them unclean; it is a defiling skin disease on the head or chin. 31 But if, when the priest examines the sore, it does not seem to be more than skin deep and there is no black hair in it, then the priest is to isolate the affected person for seven days. 32 On the seventh day the priest is to examine the sore, and if it has not spread and there is no yellow hair in it and it does not appear to be more than skin deep, 33 then the man or woman must shave themselves, except for the affected area, and the priest is to keep them isolated another seven days. 34 On the seventh day the priest is to examine the sore, and if it has not spread in the skin and appears to be no more than skin deep, the priest shall pronounce them clean. They must wash their clothes, and they will be clean. 35 But if the sore does spread in the skin after they are pronounced clean, 36 the priest is to examine them, and if he finds that the sore has spread in the skin, he does not need to look for yellow hair; they are unclean. 37 If, however, the sore is unchanged so far as the priest can see, and if black hair has grown in it, the affected person is healed. They are clean, and the priest shall pronounce them clean.

38 "When a man or woman has white spots on the skin, 39 the priest is to examine them, and if the spots are dull white, it is a harmless rash that has broken out on the skin; they are clean.

40 "A man who has lost his hair and is bald is clean. 41 If he has lost his hair from the front of his scalp and has a bald forehead, he is clean. 42 But if he has a reddish-white sore on his bald head or forehead, it is a defiling disease breaking out on his head or forehead. 43 The priest is to examine him, and if the swollen sore on his head or forehead is reddish-white like a defiling skin disease, 44 the man is diseased and is unclean. The priest shall pronounce him unclean because of the sore on his head.

45 "Anyone with such a defiling disease must wear torn clothes, let their hair be unkempt,[a] cover the lower part of their face and cry out, 'Unclean! Unclean!' 46 As long as they have the disease they remain unclean. They must live alone; they must live outside the camp.

Regulations About Defiling Molds

47 "As for any fabric that is spoiled with a defiling mold — any woolen or linen clothing, 48 any woven or knitted material of linen or wool, any leather or anything made of leather — 49 if the affected area in the fabric, the leather, the woven or knitted material, or any leather article, is greenish or reddish, it is a defiling mold and must be shown to the priest. 50 The priest is to examine the affected area and isolate the article for seven days. 51 On the seventh day he is to examine it, and if the mold has spread in the fabric, the woven or knitted material, or the leather, whatever its use, it is a persistent defiling mold; the article is unclean. 52 He must burn the fabric, the woven or knitted material of wool or linen, or any leather article that has been spoiled; because the defiling mold is persistent, the article must be burned.

53 "But if, when the priest examines it, the mold has not spread in the fabric, the woven or knitted material, or the leather article, 54 he shall order that the spoiled article be washed. Then he is to isolate it for another seven days. 55 After the article has been washed, the priest is to examine it again, and if the mold has not changed its appearance, even though it has not spread, it is unclean. Burn it, no matter which side of the fabric has been spoiled. 56 If, when the priest examines it, the mold has faded after the article has been washed, he is to tear the spoiled part out of the fabric, the leather, or the woven or knitted material. 57 But if it reappears in the fabric, in the woven or knitted material, or in the leather article, it is a spreading mold; whatever has the mold must be burned. 58 Any fabric, woven or knitted material, or any leather article that has

[a] 45 Or *clothes, uncover their head*

been washed and is rid of the mold, must be washed again. Then it will be clean."

[59]These are the regulations concerning defiling molds in woolen or linen clothing, woven or knitted material, or any leather article, for pronouncing them clean or unclean.

Cleansing From Defiling Skin Diseases

14 The LORD said to Moses, [2]"These are the regulations for any diseased person at the time of their ceremonial cleansing, when they are brought to the priest: [3]The priest is to go outside the camp and examine them. If they have been healed of their defiling skin disease,[a] [4]the priest shall order that two live clean birds and some cedar wood, scarlet yarn and hyssop be brought for the person to be cleansed. [5]Then the priest shall order that one of the birds be killed over fresh water in a clay pot. [6]He is then to take the live bird and dip it, together with the cedar wood, the scarlet yarn and the hyssop, into the blood of the bird that was killed over the fresh water. [7]Seven times he shall sprinkle the one to be cleansed of the defiling disease, and then pronounce them clean. After that, he is to release the live bird in the open fields.

[8]"The person to be cleansed must wash their clothes, shave off all their hair and bathe with water; then they will be ceremonially clean. After this they may come into the camp, but they must stay outside their tent for seven days. [9]On the seventh day they must shave off all their hair; they must shave their head, their beard, their eyebrows and the rest of their hair. They must wash their clothes and bathe themselves with water, and they will be clean.

[10]"On the eighth day they must bring two male lambs and one ewe lamb a year old, each without defect, along with three-tenths of an ephah[b] of the finest flour mixed with olive oil for a grain offering, and one log[c] of oil. [11]The priest who pronounces them clean shall present both the one to be cleansed and their offerings before the LORD at the entrance to the tent of meeting.

[12]"Then the priest is to take one of the male lambs and offer it as a guilt offering, along with the log of oil; he shall wave them before the LORD as a wave offering. [13]He is to slaughter the lamb in the sanctuary area where the sin offering[d] and the burnt offering are slaughtered. Like the sin offering, the guilt offering belongs to the priest; it is most holy. [14]The priest is to take some of the blood of the guilt offering and put it on the lobe of the right ear of the one to be cleansed, on the thumb of their right hand and on the big toe of their right foot. [15]The priest shall then take some of the log of oil, pour it in the palm of his own left hand, [16]dip his right forefinger into the oil in his palm, and with his finger sprinkle some of it before the LORD seven times. [17]The priest is to put some of the oil remaining in his palm on the lobe of the right ear of the one to be cleansed, on the thumb of their right hand and on the big toe of their right foot, on top of the blood of the guilt offering. [18]The rest of the oil in his palm the priest shall put on the head of the one to be cleansed and make atonement for them before the LORD.

[19]"Then the priest is to sacrifice the sin offering and make atonement for the one to be cleansed from their uncleanness. After that, the priest shall slaughter the burnt offering [20]and offer it on the altar, together with the grain offering, and make atonement for them, and they will be clean.

[21]"If, however, they are poor and cannot afford these, they must take one male lamb as a guilt offering to be waved to make atonement for them, together with a tenth of an ephah[e] of the finest flour mixed with olive oil for a grain offering, a log of oil, [22]and two doves or two young pigeons, such as they can afford, one for a sin offering and the other for a burnt offering.

[23]"On the eighth day they must bring them for their cleansing to the priest at the entrance to the tent of meeting, before the LORD. [24]The priest is to take the lamb for the guilt offering, together with the log of oil, and wave them before the LORD as a wave offering. [25]He shall slaughter the lamb for

[a] *3* The Hebrew word for *defiling skin disease*, traditionally translated "leprosy," was used for various diseases affecting the skin; also in verses 7, 32, 54 and 57. [b] *10* That is, probably about 11 pounds or about 5 kilograms [c] *10* That is, about 1/3 quart or about 0.3 liter; also in verses 12, 15, 21 and 24 [d] *13* Or *purification offering*; also in verses 19, 22 and 31 [e] *21* That is, probably about 3 1/2 pounds or about 1.6 kilograms

the guilt offering and take some of its blood and put it on the lobe of the right ear of the one to be cleansed, on the thumb of their right hand and on the big toe of their right foot. 26 The priest is to pour some of the oil into the palm of his own left hand, 27 and with his right forefinger sprinkle some of the oil from his palm seven times before the LORD. 28 Some of the oil in his palm he is to put on the same places he put the blood of the guilt offering — on the lobe of the right ear of the one to be cleansed, on the thumb of their right hand and on the big toe of their right foot. 29 The rest of the oil in his palm the priest shall put on the head of the one to be cleansed, to make atonement for them before the LORD. 30 Then he shall sacrifice the doves or the young pigeons, such as the person can afford, 31 one as a sin offering and the other as a burnt offering, together with the grain offering. In this way the priest will make atonement before the LORD on behalf of the one to be cleansed."

32 These are the regulations for anyone who has a defiling skin disease and who cannot afford the regular offerings for their cleansing.

Cleansing From Defiling Molds

33 The LORD said to Moses and Aaron, 34 "When you enter the land of Canaan, which I am giving you as your possession, and I put a spreading mold in a house in that land, 35 the owner of the house must go and tell the priest, 'I have seen something that looks like a defiling mold in my house.' 36 The priest is to order the house to be emptied before he goes in to examine the mold, so that nothing in the house will be pronounced unclean. After this the priest is to go in and inspect the house. 37 He is to examine the mold on the walls, and if it has greenish or reddish depressions that appear to be deeper than the surface of the wall, 38 the priest shall go out the doorway of the house and close it up for seven days. 39 On the seventh day the priest shall return to inspect the house. If the mold has spread on the walls, 40 he is to order that the contaminated stones be torn out and thrown into an unclean place outside the town. 41 He must have all the inside walls of the house scraped and the material that is scraped off dumped into an unclean place outside the town. 42 Then they are to take other stones to replace these and take new clay and plaster the house.

43 "If the defiling mold reappears in the house after the stones have been torn out and the house scraped and plastered, 44 the priest is to go and examine it and, if the mold has spread in the house, it is a persistent defiling mold; the house is unclean. 45 It must be torn down — its stones, timbers and all the plaster — and taken out of the town to an unclean place.

46 "Anyone who goes into the house while it is closed up will be unclean till evening. 47 Anyone who sleeps or eats in the house must wash their clothes.

48 "But if the priest comes to examine it and the mold has not spread after the house has been plastered, he shall pronounce the house clean, because the defiling mold is gone. 49 To purify the house he is to take two birds and some cedar wood, scarlet yarn and hyssop. 50 He shall kill one of the birds over fresh water in a clay pot. 51 Then he is to take the cedar wood, the hyssop, the scarlet yarn and the live bird, dip them into the blood of the dead bird and the fresh water, and sprinkle the house seven times. 52 He shall purify the house with the bird's blood, the fresh water, the live bird, the cedar wood, the hyssop and the scarlet yarn. 53 Then he is to release the live bird in the open fields outside the town. In this way he will make atonement for the house, and it will be clean."

54 These are the regulations for any defiling skin disease, for a sore, 55 for defiling molds in fabric or in a house, 56 and for a swelling, a rash or a shiny spot, 57 to determine when something is clean or unclean.

These are the regulations for defiling skin diseases and defiling molds.

Discharges Causing Uncleanness

15 The LORD said to Moses and Aaron, 2 "Speak to the Israelites and say to them: 'When any man has an unusual bodily discharge, such a discharge is unclean. 3 Whether it continues flowing from his body or is blocked, it will make him unclean. This is how his discharge will bring about uncleanness:

4 " 'Any bed the man with a discharge lies on will be unclean, and anything he sits on will be unclean. 5 Anyone who touches his bed must wash their clothes and bathe with

water, and they will be unclean till evening. 6 Whoever sits on anything that the man with a discharge sat on must wash their clothes and bathe with water, and they will be unclean till evening.

7 " 'Whoever touches the man who has a discharge must wash their clothes and bathe with water, and they will be unclean till evening.

8 " 'If the man with the discharge spits on anyone who is clean, they must wash their clothes and bathe with water, and they will be unclean till evening.

9 " 'Everything the man sits on when riding will be unclean, 10 and whoever touches any of the things that were under him will be unclean till evening; whoever picks up those things must wash their clothes and bathe with water, and they will be unclean till evening.

11 " 'Anyone the man with a discharge touches without rinsing his hands with water must wash their clothes and bathe with water, and they will be unclean till evening.

12 " 'A clay pot that the man touches must be broken, and any wooden article is to be rinsed with water.

13 " 'When a man is cleansed from his discharge, he is to count off seven days for his ceremonial cleansing; he must wash his clothes and bathe himself with fresh water, and he will be clean. 14 On the eighth day he must take two doves or two young pigeons and come before the LORD to the entrance to the tent of meeting and give them to the priest. 15 The priest is to sacrifice them, the one for a sin offering[a] and the other for a burnt offering. In this way he will make atonement before the LORD for the man because of his discharge.

16 " 'When a man has an emission of semen, he must bathe his whole body with water, and he will be unclean till evening. 17 Any clothing or leather that has semen on it must be washed with water, and it will be unclean till evening. 18 When a man has sexual relations with a woman and there is an emission of semen, both of them must bathe with water, and they will be unclean till evening.

19 " 'When a woman has her regular flow of blood, the impurity of her monthly period will last seven days, and anyone who touches her will be unclean till evening.

20 " 'Anything she lies on during her period will be unclean, and anything she sits on will be unclean. 21 Anyone who touches her bed will be unclean; they must wash their clothes and bathe with water, and they will be unclean till evening. 22 Anyone who touches anything she sits on will be unclean; they must wash their clothes and bathe with water, and they will be unclean till evening. 23 Whether it is the bed or anything she was sitting on, when anyone touches it, they will be unclean till evening.

24 " 'If a man has sexual relations with her and her monthly flow touches him, he will be unclean for seven days; any bed he lies on will be unclean.

25 " 'When a woman has a discharge of blood for many days at a time other than her monthly period or has a discharge that continues beyond her period, she will be unclean as long as she has the discharge, just as in the days of her period. 26 Any bed she lies on while her discharge continues will be unclean, as is her bed during her monthly period, and anything she sits on will be unclean, as during her period. 27 Anyone who touches them will be unclean; they must wash their clothes and bathe with water, and they will be unclean till evening.

28 " 'When she is cleansed from her discharge, she must count off seven days, and after that she will be ceremonially clean. 29 On the eighth day she must take two doves or two young pigeons and bring them to the priest at the entrance to the tent of meeting. 30 The priest is to sacrifice one for a sin offering and the other for a burnt offering. In this way he will make atonement for her before the LORD for the uncleanness of her discharge.

31 " 'You must keep the Israelites separate from things that make them unclean, so they will not die in their uncleanness for defiling my dwelling place,[b] which is among them.' "

32 These are the regulations for a man with a discharge, for anyone made unclean by an emission of semen, 33 for a woman in her monthly period, for a man or a woman with a discharge, and for a man who has sexual relations with a woman who is ceremonially unclean.

[a] *15* Or *purification offering*; also in verse 30 [b] *31* Or *my tabernacle*

The Day of Atonement

16 The LORD spoke to Moses after the death of the two sons of Aaron who died when they approached the LORD. 2 The LORD said to Moses: "Tell your brother Aaron that he is not to come whenever he chooses into the Most Holy Place behind the curtain in front of the atonement cover on the ark, or else he will die. For I will appear in the cloud over the atonement cover.

3 "This is how Aaron is to enter the Most Holy Place: He must first bring a young bull for a sin offering[a] and a ram for a burnt offering. 4 He is to put on the sacred linen tunic, with linen undergarments next to his body; he is to tie the linen sash around him and put on the linen turban. These are sacred garments; so he must bathe himself with water before he puts them on. 5 From the Israelite community he is to take two male goats for a sin offering and a ram for a burnt offering.

6 "Aaron is to offer the bull for his own sin offering to make atonement for himself and his household. 7 Then he is to take the two goats and present them before the LORD at the entrance to the tent of meeting. 8 He is to cast lots for the two goats — one lot for the LORD and the other for the scapegoat.[b] 9 Aaron shall bring the goat whose lot falls to the LORD and sacrifice it for a sin offering. 10 But the goat chosen by lot as the scapegoat shall be presented alive before the LORD to be used for making atonement by sending it into the wilderness as a scapegoat.

11 "Aaron shall bring the bull for his own sin offering to make atonement for himself and his household, and he is to slaughter the bull for his own sin offering. 12 He is to take a censer full of burning coals from the altar before the LORD and two handfuls of finely ground fragrant incense and take them behind the curtain. 13 He is to put the incense on the fire before the LORD, and the smoke of the incense will conceal the atonement cover above the tablets of the covenant law, so that he will not die. 14 He is to take some of the bull's blood and with his finger sprinkle it on the front of the atonement cover; then he shall sprinkle some of it with his finger seven times before the atonement cover.

15 "He shall then slaughter the goat for the sin offering for the people and take its blood behind the curtain and do with it as he did with the bull's blood: He shall sprinkle it on the atonement cover and in front of it. 16 In this way he will make atonement for the Most Holy Place because of the uncleanness and rebellion of the Israelites, whatever their sins have been. He is to do the same for the tent of meeting, which is among them in the midst of their uncleanness. 17 No one is to be in the tent of meeting from the time Aaron goes in to make atonement in the Most Holy Place until he comes out, having made atonement for himself, his household and the whole community of Israel.

18 "Then he shall come out to the altar that is before the LORD and make atonement for it. He shall take some of the bull's blood and some of the goat's blood and put it on all the horns of the altar. 19 He shall sprinkle some of the blood on it with his finger seven times to cleanse it and to consecrate it from the uncleanness of the Israelites.

20 "When Aaron has finished making atonement for the Most Holy Place, the tent of meeting and the altar, he shall bring forward the live goat. 21 He is to lay both hands on the head of the live goat and confess over it all the wickedness and rebellion of the Israelites — all their sins — and put them on the goat's head. He shall send the goat away into the wilderness in the care of someone appointed for the task. 22 The goat will carry on itself all their sins to a remote place; and the man shall release it in the wilderness.

23 "Then Aaron is to go into the tent of meeting and take off the linen garments he put on before he entered the Most Holy Place, and he is to leave them there. 24 He shall bathe himself with water in the sanctuary area and put on his regular garments. Then he shall come out and sacrifice the burnt offering for himself and the burnt offering for the people, to make atonement for himself and for the people. 25 He shall also burn the fat of the sin offering on the altar.

26 "The man who releases the goat as a scapegoat must wash his clothes and bathe himself with water; afterward he may come into the camp. 27 The bull and the goat for the sin offerings, whose blood was brought into the Most Holy Place to make atonement, must be taken outside the camp; their hides,

[a] *3* Or *purification offering*; here and throughout this chapter [b] *8* The meaning of the Hebrew for this word is uncertain; also in verses 10 and 26.

HERE I AM TO WORSHIP

Tim Hughes

Light of the World, you stepped down into darkness
Opened my eyes, let me see
Beauty that made this heart adore you
Hope of a life spent with you.

Here I am to worship, here I am to bow down
Here I am to say that you're my God
You're altogether lovely, altogether worthy
Altogether wonderful to me

King of all days, oh so highly exalted
Glorious in heaven above
Humbly you came to the Earth you created
All for love's sake became poor

And I'll never know how much it cost
To see my sin upon that cross
I'll never know how much it cost
To see my sin upon that cross
I'll never know how much it cost
To see my sin upon that cross
I'll never know how much it cost
To see my sin upon that cross

THE INSPIRATION

Being found in appearance as a man, he humbled himself by becoming obedient to death — even death on a cross!

— Philippians 2:8

Read also: John 8:12; Philippians 2:1 – 11; Hebrews 2:7 – 8

BEHIND THE SONG

Seemingly simple in lyric and melody, "Here I Am to Worship" was an exercise in patience and reflection for writer Tim Hughes.

"During that time I had been thinking about and meditating on the cross," he says. "I began to concentrate on Philippians 2, about Christ's humility and how he became obedient to the point of death on a cross. I was challenged with the wonder of his sacrifice for us."

The verses came fairly easily to Hughes, but the chorus was another story entirely. "The original one was embarrassingly bad," he admits. It took another six months before he felt prepared to write the final chorus. "I began to ask, 'How are we going to respond to Christ's great sacrifice on the cross?' Do we bow down? Do we scream out? Sometimes we don't know how to respond, even though we desperately want to."

Selah

The second chapter of Paul's letter to the Philippians starts with a bold and eloquently written challenge to Christians about how they should interact with each other: "Make my joy complete by being like-minded, having the same love, being one in spirit and of one mind" (verse 2). The way we relate to others should sharply contrast with how people in the world around us interact. Hopefully it is obvious to the people watching our lives that something is different about us and our priorities. Ultimately, it comes down to humility.

Humility does not come naturally to people, but the realization of God's awesome glory and the incredible weight of Christ's sacrifice can move our hearts back into alignment with the heart of God.

Can you recall a time when your heart needed to change and worship helped that to happen? Spend some time thinking about the character and ministry of Jesus and see how it changes your perspective on relating to his people.

flesh and intestines are to be burned up. 28 The man who burns them must wash his clothes and bathe himself with water; afterward he may come into the camp.

29 "This is to be a lasting ordinance for you: On the tenth day of the seventh month you must deny yourselves[a] and not do any work—whether native-born or a foreigner residing among you— 30 because on this day atonement will be made for you, to cleanse you. Then, before the LORD, you will be clean from all your sins. 31 It is a day of sabbath rest, and you must deny yourselves; it is a lasting ordinance. 32 The priest who is anointed and ordained to succeed his father as high priest is to make atonement. He is to put on the sacred linen garments 33 and make atonement for the Most Holy Place, for the tent of meeting and the altar, and for the priests and all the members of the community.

34 "This is to be a lasting ordinance for you: Atonement is to be made once a year for all the sins of the Israelites."

And it was done, as the LORD commanded Moses.

Eating Blood Forbidden

17 The LORD said to Moses, 2 "Speak to Aaron and his sons and to all the Israelites and say to them: 'This is what the LORD has commanded: 3 Any Israelite who sacrifices an ox,[b] a lamb or a goat in the camp or outside of it 4 instead of bringing it to the entrance to the tent of meeting to present it as an offering to the LORD in front of the tabernacle of the LORD—that person shall be considered guilty of bloodshed; they have shed blood and must be cut off from their people. 5 This is so the Israelites will bring to the LORD the sacrifices they are now making in the open fields. They must bring them to the priest, that is, to the LORD, at the entrance to the tent of meeting and sacrifice them as fellowship offerings. 6 The priest is to splash the blood against the altar of the LORD at the entrance to the tent of meeting and burn the fat as an aroma pleasing to the LORD. 7 They must no longer offer any of their sacrifices to the goat idols[c] to whom they prostitute themselves. This is to be a lasting ordinance for them and for the generations to come.'

8 "Say to them: 'Any Israelite or any foreigner residing among them who offers a burnt offering or sacrifice 9 and does not bring it to the entrance to the tent of meeting to sacrifice it to the LORD must be cut off from the people of Israel.

10 " 'I will set my face against any Israelite or any foreigner residing among them who eats blood, and I will cut them off from the people. 11 For the life of a creature is in the blood, and I have given it to you to make atonement for yourselves on the altar; it is the blood that makes atonement for one's life.[d] 12 Therefore I say to the Israelites, "None of you may eat blood, nor may any foreigner residing among you eat blood."

13 " 'Any Israelite or any foreigner residing among you who hunts any animal or bird that may be eaten must drain out the blood and cover it with earth, 14 because the life of every creature is its blood. That is why I have said to the Israelites, "You must not eat the blood of any creature, because the life of every creature is its blood; anyone who eats it must be cut off."

15 " 'Anyone, whether native-born or foreigner, who eats anything found dead or torn by wild animals must wash their clothes and bathe with water, and they will be ceremonially unclean till evening; then they will be clean. 16 But if they do not wash their clothes and bathe themselves, they will be held responsible.' "

Unlawful Sexual Relations

18 The LORD said to Moses, 2 "Speak to the Israelites and say to them: 'I am the LORD your God. 3 You must not do as they do in Egypt, where you used to live, and you must not do as they do in the land of Canaan, where I am bringing you. Do not follow their practices. 4 You must obey my laws and be careful to follow my decrees. I am the LORD your God. 5 Keep my decrees and laws, for the person who obeys them will live by them. I am the LORD.

6 " 'No one is to approach any close relative to have sexual relations. I am the LORD.

7 " 'Do not dishonor your father by having sexual relations with your mother. She is your mother; do not have relations with her.

[a] 29 Or *must fast*; also in verse 31 [b] 3 The Hebrew word can refer to either male or female. [c] 7 Or *the demons* [d] 11 Or *atonement by the life in the blood*

8 “ ‘Do not have sexual relations with your father’s wife; that would dishonor your father.

9 “ ‘Do not have sexual relations with your sister, either your father’s daughter or your mother’s daughter, whether she was born in the same home or elsewhere.

10 “ ‘Do not have sexual relations with your son’s daughter or your daughter’s daughter; that would dishonor you.

11 “ ‘Do not have sexual relations with the daughter of your father’s wife, born to your father; she is your sister.

12 “ ‘Do not have sexual relations with your father’s sister; she is your father’s close relative.

13 “ ‘Do not have sexual relations with your mother’s sister, because she is your mother’s close relative.

14 “ ‘Do not dishonor your father’s brother by approaching his wife to have sexual relations; she is your aunt.

15 “ ‘Do not have sexual relations with your daughter-in-law. She is your son’s wife; do not have relations with her.

16 “ ‘Do not have sexual relations with your brother’s wife; that would dishonor your brother.

17 “ ‘Do not have sexual relations with both a woman and her daughter. Do not have sexual relations with either her son’s daughter or her daughter’s daughter; they are her close relatives. That is wickedness.

18 “ ‘Do not take your wife’s sister as a rival wife and have sexual relations with her while your wife is living.

19 “ ‘Do not approach a woman to have sexual relations during the uncleanness of her monthly period.

20 “ ‘Do not have sexual relations with your neighbor’s wife and defile yourself with her.

21 “ ‘Do not give any of your children to be sacrificed to Molek, for you must not profane the name of your God. I am the LORD.

22 “ ‘Do not have sexual relations with a man as one does with a woman; that is detestable.

23 “ ‘Do not have sexual relations with an animal and defile yourself with it. A woman must not present herself to an animal to have sexual relations with it; that is a perversion.

24 “ ‘Do not defile yourselves in any of these ways, because this is how the nations that I am going to drive out before you became defiled. 25 Even the land was defiled; so I punished it for its sin, and the land vomited out its inhabitants. 26 But you must keep my decrees and my laws. The native-born and the foreigners residing among you must not do any of these detestable things, 27 for all these things were done by the people who lived in the land before you, and the land became defiled. 28 And if you defile the land, it will vomit you out as it vomited out the nations that were before you.

29 “ ‘Everyone who does any of these detestable things — such persons must be cut off from their people. 30 Keep my requirements and do not follow any of the detestable customs that were practiced before you came and do not defile yourselves with them. I am the LORD your God.’ ”

Various Laws

19 The LORD said to Moses, 2 “Speak to the entire assembly of Israel and say to them: ‘Be holy because I, the LORD your God, am holy.

3 “ ‘Each of you must respect your mother and father, and you must observe my Sabbaths. I am the LORD your God.

4 “ ‘Do not turn to idols or make metal gods for yourselves. I am the LORD your God.

5 “ ‘When you sacrifice a fellowship offering to the LORD, sacrifice it in such a way that it will be accepted on your behalf. 6 It shall be eaten on the day you sacrifice it or on the next day; anything left over until the third day must be burned up. 7 If any of it is eaten on the third day, it is impure and will not be accepted. 8 Whoever eats it will be held responsible because they have desecrated what is holy to the LORD; they must be cut off from their people.

9 “ ‘When you reap the harvest of your land, do not reap to the very edges of your field or gather the gleanings of your harvest. 10 Do not go over your vineyard a second time or pick up the grapes that have fallen. Leave them for the poor and the foreigner. I am the LORD your God.

11 “ ‘Do not steal.

“ ‘Do not lie.

“ ‘Do not deceive one another.

12 “ ‘Do not swear falsely by my name and so profane the name of your God. I am the LORD.

13 “ ‘Do not defraud or rob your neighbor.

“‘Do not hold back the wages of a hired worker overnight.

14 “‘Do not curse the deaf or put a stumbling block in front of the blind, but fear your God. I am the LORD.

15 “‘Do not pervert justice; do not show partiality to the poor or favoritism to the great, but judge your neighbor fairly.

16 “‘Do not go about spreading slander among your people.

“‘Do not do anything that endangers your neighbor’s life. I am the LORD.

17 “‘Do not hate a fellow Israelite in your heart. Rebuke your neighbor frankly so you will not share in their guilt.

18 “‘Do not seek revenge or bear a grudge against anyone among your people, but love your neighbor as yourself. I am the LORD.

19 “‘Keep my decrees.

“‘Do not mate different kinds of animals.

“‘Do not plant your field with two kinds of seed.

“‘Do not wear clothing woven of two kinds of material.

20 “‘If a man sleeps with a female slave who is promised to another man but who has not been ransomed or given her freedom, there must be due punishment.[a] Yet they are not to be put to death, because she had not been freed. 21 The man, however, must bring a ram to the entrance to the tent of meeting for a guilt offering to the LORD. 22 With the ram of the guilt offering the priest is to make atonement for him before the LORD for the sin he has committed, and his sin will be forgiven.

23 “‘When you enter the land and plant any kind of fruit tree, regard its fruit as forbidden.[b] For three years you are to consider it forbidden[b]; it must not be eaten. 24 In the fourth year all its fruit will be holy, an offering of praise to the LORD. 25 But in the fifth year you may eat its fruit. In this way your harvest will be increased. I am the LORD your God.

26 “‘Do not eat any meat with the blood still in it.

“‘Do not practice divination or seek omens.

27 “‘Do not cut the hair at the sides of your head or clip off the edges of your beard.

28 “‘Do not cut your bodies for the dead or put tattoo marks on yourselves. I am the LORD.

29 “‘Do not degrade your daughter by making her a prostitute, or the land will turn to prostitution and be filled with wickedness.

30 “‘Observe my Sabbaths and have reverence for my sanctuary. I am the LORD.

31 “‘Do not turn to mediums or seek out spiritists, for you will be defiled by them. I am the LORD your God.

32 “‘Stand up in the presence of the aged, show respect for the elderly and revere your God. I am the LORD.

33 “‘When a foreigner resides among you in your land, do not mistreat them. 34 The foreigner residing among you must be treated as your native-born. Love them as yourself, for you were foreigners in Egypt. I am the LORD your God.

35 “‘Do not use dishonest standards when measuring length, weight or quantity. 36 Use honest scales and honest weights, an honest ephah[c] and an honest hin.[d] I am the LORD your God, who brought you out of Egypt.

37 “‘Keep all my decrees and all my laws and follow them. I am the LORD.’ ”

Punishments for Sin

20 The LORD said to Moses, 2 “Say to the Israelites: ‘Any Israelite or any foreigner residing in Israel who sacrifices any of his children to Molek is to be put to death. The members of the community are to stone him. 3 I myself will set my face against him and will cut him off from his people; for by sacrificing his children to Molek, he has defiled my sanctuary and profaned my holy name. 4 If the members of the community close their eyes when that man sacrifices one of his children to Molek and if they fail to put him to death, 5 I myself will set my face against him and his family and will cut them off from their people together with all who follow him in prostituting themselves to Molek.

6 “‘I will set my face against anyone who turns to mediums and spiritists to prostitute themselves by following them, and I will cut them off from their people.

7 “‘Consecrate yourselves and be holy, because I am the LORD your God. 8 Keep my

[a] 20 Or *be an inquiry* [b] 23 Hebrew *uncircumcised* [c] 36 An ephah was a dry measure having the capacity of about 3/5 of a bushel or about 22 liters. [d] 36 A hin was a liquid measure having the capacity of about 1 gallon or about 3.8 liters.

decrees and follow them. I am the LORD, who makes you holy.

9“ ‘Anyone who curses their father or mother is to be put to death. Because they have cursed their father or mother, their blood will be on their own head.

10“ ‘If a man commits adultery with another man’s wife—with the wife of his neighbor—both the adulterer and the adulteress are to be put to death.

11“ ‘If a man has sexual relations with his father’s wife, he has dishonored his father. Both the man and the woman are to be put to death; their blood will be on their own heads.

12“ ‘If a man has sexual relations with his daughter-in-law, both of them are to be put to death. What they have done is a perversion; their blood will be on their own heads.

13“ ‘If a man has sexual relations with a man as one does with a woman, both of them have done what is detestable. They are to be put to death; their blood will be on their own heads.

14“ ‘If a man marries both a woman and her mother, it is wicked. Both he and they must be burned in the fire, so that no wickedness will be among you.

15“ ‘If a man has sexual relations with an animal, he is to be put to death, and you must kill the animal.

16“ ‘If a woman approaches an animal to have sexual relations with it, kill both the woman and the animal. They are to be put to death; their blood will be on their own heads.

17“ ‘If a man marries his sister, the daughter of either his father or his mother, and they have sexual relations, it is a disgrace. They are to be publicly removed from their people. He has dishonored his sister and will be held responsible.

18“ ‘If a man has sexual relations with a woman during her monthly period, he has exposed the source of her flow, and she has also uncovered it. Both of them are to be cut off from their people.

19“ ‘Do not have sexual relations with the sister of either your mother or your father, for that would dishonor a close relative; both of you would be held responsible.

20“ ‘If a man has sexual relations with his aunt, he has dishonored his uncle. They will be held responsible; they will die childless.

21“ ‘If a man marries his brother’s wife, it is an act of impurity; he has dishonored his brother. They will be childless.

22“ ‘Keep all my decrees and laws and follow them, so that the land where I am bringing you to live may not vomit you out. 23You must not live according to the customs of the nations I am going to drive out before you. Because they did all these things, I abhorred them. 24But I said to you, “You will possess their land; I will give it to you as an inheritance, a land flowing with milk and honey.” I am the LORD your God, who has set you apart from the nations.

25“ ‘You must therefore make a distinction between clean and unclean animals and between unclean and clean birds. Do not defile yourselves by any animal or bird or anything that moves along the ground—those that I have set apart as unclean for you. 26You are to be holy to me because I, the LORD, am holy, and I have set you apart from the nations to be my own.

27“ ‘A man or woman who is a medium or spiritist among you must be put to death. You are to stone them; their blood will be on their own heads.’ ”

Rules for Priests

21 The LORD said to Moses, “Speak to the priests, the sons of Aaron, and say to them: ‘A priest must not make himself ceremonially unclean for any of his people who die, 2except for a close relative, such as his mother or father, his son or daughter, his brother, 3or an unmarried sister who is dependent on him since she has no husband—for her he may make himself unclean. 4He must not make himself unclean for people related to him by marriage,[a] and so defile himself.

5“ ‘Priests must not shave their heads or shave off the edges of their beards or cut their bodies. 6They must be holy to their God and must not profane the name of their God. Because they present the food offerings to the LORD, the food of their God, they are to be holy.

7“ ‘They must not marry women defiled by prostitution or divorced from their husbands, because priests are holy to their God. 8Regard them as holy, because they offer up the food of your God. Consider them holy,

[a] 4 Or *unclean as a leader among his people*

because I the LORD am holy—I who make
you holy.

9“ ‘If a priest’s daughter defiles herself by
becoming a prostitute, she disgraces her fa-
ther; she must be burned in the fire.

10“ ‘The high priest, the one among his
brothers who has had the anointing oil
poured on his head and who has been or-
dained to wear the priestly garments, must
not let his hair become unkempt[a] or tear his
clothes. 11He must not enter a place where
there is a dead body. He must not make him-
self unclean, even for his father or mother,
12nor leave the sanctuary of his God or des-
ecrate it, because he has been dedicated by
the anointing oil of his God. I am the LORD.

13“ ‘The woman he marries must be a vir-
gin. 14He must not marry a widow, a divorced
woman, or a woman defiled by prostitution,
but only a virgin from his own people, 15so
that he will not defile his offspring among
his people. I am the LORD, who makes him
holy.’ ”

16The LORD said to Moses, 17“Say to Aaron:
‘For the generations to come none of your de-
scendants who has a defect may come near
to offer the food of his God. 18No man who
has any defect may come near: no man who
is blind or lame, disfigured or deformed; 19no
man with a crippled foot or hand, 20or who
is a hunchback or a dwarf, or who has any
eye defect, or who has festering or running
sores or damaged testicles. 21No descendant
of Aaron the priest who has any defect is to
come near to present the food offerings to
the LORD. He has a defect; he must not come
near to offer the food of his God. 22He may
eat the most holy food of his God, as well as
the holy food; 23yet because of his defect, he
must not go near the curtain or approach the
altar, and so desecrate my sanctuary. I am
the LORD, who makes them holy.’ ”

24So Moses told this to Aaron and his sons
and to all the Israelites.

22 The LORD said to Moses, 2“Tell Aaron
and his sons to treat with respect the
sacred offerings the Israelites consecrate to
me, so they will not profane my holy name.
I am the LORD.

3“Say to them: ‘For the generations to
come, if any of your descendants is ceremo-
nially unclean and yet comes near the sa-
cred offerings that the Israelites consecrate
to the LORD, that person must be cut off from
my presence. I am the LORD.

4“ ‘If a descendant of Aaron has a defil-
ing skin disease[b] or a bodily discharge, he
may not eat the sacred offerings until he
is cleansed. He will also be unclean if he
touches something defiled by a corpse or by
anyone who has an emission of semen, 5or
if he touches any crawling thing that makes
him unclean, or any person who makes him
unclean, whatever the uncleanness may be.
6The one who touches any such thing will
be unclean till evening. He must not eat any
of the sacred offerings unless he has bathed
himself with water. 7When the sun goes
down, he will be clean, and after that he
may eat the sacred offerings, for they are his
food. 8He must not eat anything found dead
or torn by wild animals, and so become un-
clean through it. I am the LORD.

9“ ‘The priests are to perform my service
in such a way that they do not become guilty
and die for treating it with contempt. I am
the LORD, who makes them holy.

10“ ‘No one outside a priest’s family may
eat the sacred offering, nor may the guest of
a priest or his hired worker eat it. 11But if a
priest buys a slave with money, or if slaves
are born in his household, they may eat his
food. 12If a priest’s daughter marries anyone
other than a priest, she may not eat any of
the sacred contributions. 13But if a priest’s
daughter becomes a widow or is divorced,
yet has no children, and she returns to live
in her father’s household as in her youth, she
may eat her father’s food. No unauthorized
person, however, may eat it.

14“ ‘Anyone who eats a sacred offering by
mistake must make restitution to the priest
for the offering and add a fifth of the value
to it. 15The priests must not desecrate the
sacred offerings the Israelites present to the
LORD 16by allowing them to eat the sacred
offerings and so bring upon them guilt re-
quiring payment. I am the LORD, who makes
them holy.’ ”

Unacceptable Sacrifices

17The LORD said to Moses, 18“Speak to
Aaron and his sons and to all the Israelites
and say to them: ‘If any of you—whether an

[a] *10* Or *not uncover his head* [b] *4* The Hebrew word for *defiling skin disease,* traditionally translated “leprosy,” was used for various diseases affecting the skin.

Israelite or a foreigner residing in Israel—presents a gift for a burnt offering to the LORD, either to fulfill a vow or as a freewill offering, 19 you must present a male without defect from the cattle, sheep or goats in order that it may be accepted on your behalf. 20 Do not bring anything with a defect, because it will not be accepted on your behalf. 21 When anyone brings from the herd or flock a fellowship offering to the LORD to fulfill a special vow or as a freewill offering, it must be without defect or blemish to be acceptable. 22 Do not offer to the LORD the blind, the injured or the maimed, or anything with warts or festering or running sores. Do not place any of these on the altar as a food offering presented to the LORD. 23 You may, however, present as a freewill offering an ox[a] or a sheep that is deformed or stunted, but it will not be accepted in fulfillment of a vow. 24 You must not offer to the LORD an animal whose testicles are bruised, crushed, torn or cut. You must not do this in your own land, 25 and you must not accept such animals from the hand of a foreigner and offer them as the food of your God. They will not be accepted on your behalf, because they are deformed and have defects.'"

26 The LORD said to Moses, 27 "When a calf, a lamb or a goat is born, it is to remain with its mother for seven days. From the eighth day on, it will be acceptable as a food offering presented to the LORD. 28 Do not slaughter a cow or a sheep and its young on the same day.

29 "When you sacrifice a thank offering to the LORD, sacrifice it in such a way that it will be accepted on your behalf. 30 It must be eaten that same day; leave none of it till morning. I am the LORD.

31 "Keep my commands and follow them. I am the LORD. 32 Do not profane my holy name, for I must be acknowledged as holy by the Israelites. I am the LORD, who made you holy 33 and who brought you out of Egypt to be your God. I am the LORD."

The Appointed Festivals

23 The LORD said to Moses, 2 "Speak to the Israelites and say to them: 'These are my appointed festivals, the appointed festivals of the LORD, which you are to proclaim as sacred assemblies.

The Sabbath

3 " 'There are six days when you may work, but the seventh day is a day of sabbath rest, a day of sacred assembly. You are not to do any work; wherever you live, it is a sabbath to the LORD.

The Passover and the Festival of Unleavened Bread

4 " 'These are the LORD's appointed festivals, the sacred assemblies you are to proclaim at their appointed times: 5 The LORD's Passover begins at twilight on the fourteenth day of the first month. 6 On the fifteenth day of that month the LORD's Festival of Unleavened Bread begins; for seven days you must eat bread made without yeast. 7 On the first day hold a sacred assembly and do no regular work. 8 For seven days present a food offering to the LORD. And on the seventh day hold a sacred assembly and do no regular work.' "

Offering the Firstfruits

9 The LORD said to Moses, 10 "Speak to the Israelites and say to them: 'When you enter the land I am going to give you and you reap its harvest, bring to the priest a sheaf of the first grain you harvest. 11 He is to wave the sheaf before the LORD so it will be accepted on your behalf; the priest is to wave it on the day after the Sabbath. 12 On the day you wave the sheaf, you must sacrifice as a burnt offering to the LORD a lamb a year old without defect, 13 together with its grain offering of two-tenths of an ephah[b] of the finest flour mixed with olive oil—a food offering presented to the LORD, a pleasing aroma—and its drink offering of a quarter of a hin[c] of wine. 14 You must not eat any bread, or roasted or new grain, until the very day you bring this offering to your God. This is to be a lasting ordinance for the generations to come, wherever you live.

The Festival of Weeks

15 " 'From the day after the Sabbath, the day you brought the sheaf of the wave offering, count off seven full weeks. 16 Count off fifty days up to the day after the seventh Sabbath, and then present an offering of new grain to the LORD. 17 From wherever you

[a] *23* The Hebrew word can refer to either male or female. [b] *13* That is, probably about 7 pounds or about 3.2 kilograms; also in verse 17 [c] *13* That is, about 1 quart or about 1 liter

live, bring two loaves made of two-tenths of an ephah of the finest flour, baked with yeast, as a wave offering of firstfruits to the LORD. [18]Present with this bread seven male lambs, each a year old and without defect, one young bull and two rams. They will be a burnt offering to the LORD, together with their grain offerings and drink offerings — a food offering, an aroma pleasing to the LORD. [19]Then sacrifice one male goat for a sin offering[a] and two lambs, each a year old, for a fellowship offering. [20]The priest is to wave the two lambs before the LORD as a wave offering, together with the bread of the firstfruits. They are a sacred offering to the LORD for the priest. [21]On that same day you are to proclaim a sacred assembly and do no regular work. This is to be a lasting ordinance for the generations to come, wherever you live.

[22]" 'When you reap the harvest of your land, do not reap to the very edges of your field or gather the gleanings of your harvest. Leave them for the poor and for the foreigner residing among you. I am the LORD your God.' "

The Festival of Trumpets

[23]The LORD said to Moses, [24]"Say to the Israelites: 'On the first day of the seventh month you are to have a day of sabbath rest, a sacred assembly commemorated with trumpet blasts. [25]Do no regular work, but present a food offering to the LORD.' "

The Day of Atonement

[26]The LORD said to Moses, [27]"The tenth day of this seventh month is the Day of Atonement. Hold a sacred assembly and deny yourselves,[b] and present a food offering to the LORD. [28]Do not do any work on that day, because it is the Day of Atonement, when atonement is made for you before the LORD your God. [29]Those who do not deny themselves on that day must be cut off from their people. [30]I will destroy from among their people anyone who does any work on that day. [31]You shall do no work at all. This is to be a lasting ordinance for the generations to come, wherever you live. [32]It is a day of sabbath rest for you, and you must deny yourselves. From the evening of the ninth day of the month until the following evening you are to observe your sabbath."

The Festival of Tabernacles

[33]The LORD said to Moses, [34]"Say to the Israelites: 'On the fifteenth day of the seventh month the LORD's Festival of Tabernacles begins, and it lasts for seven days. [35]The first day is a sacred assembly; do no regular work. [36]For seven days present food offerings to the LORD, and on the eighth day hold a sacred assembly and present a food offering to the LORD. It is the closing special assembly; do no regular work.

[37](" 'These are the LORD's appointed festivals, which you are to proclaim as sacred assemblies for bringing food offerings to the LORD — the burnt offerings and grain offerings, sacrifices and drink offerings required for each day. [38]These offerings are in addition to those for the LORD's Sabbaths and[c] in addition to your gifts and whatever you have vowed and all the freewill offerings you give to the LORD.)

[39]" 'So beginning with the fifteenth day of the seventh month, after you have gathered the crops of the land, celebrate the festival to the LORD for seven days; the first day is a day of sabbath rest, and the eighth day also is a day of sabbath rest. [40]On the first day you are to take branches from luxuriant trees — from palms, willows and other leafy trees — and rejoice before the LORD your God for seven days. [41]Celebrate this as a festival to the LORD for seven days each year. This is to be a lasting ordinance for the generations to come; celebrate it in the seventh month. [42]Live in temporary shelters for seven days: All native-born Israelites are to live in such shelters [43]so your descendants will know that I had the Israelites live in temporary shelters when I brought them out of Egypt. I am the LORD your God.' "

[44]So Moses announced to the Israelites the appointed festivals of the LORD.

Olive Oil and Bread Set Before the LORD

24 The LORD said to Moses, [2]"Command the Israelites to bring you clear oil of pressed olives for the light so that the lamps may be kept burning continually. [3]Outside the curtain that shields the ark of

[a] 19 Or *purification offering* [b] 27 Or *and fast;* similarly in verses 29 and 32 [c] 38 Or *These festivals are in addition to the LORD's Sabbaths, and these offerings are*

the covenant law in the tent of meeting, Aaron is to tend the lamps before the LORD from evening till morning, continually. This is to be a lasting ordinance for the generations to come. [4]The lamps on the pure gold lampstand before the LORD must be tended continually.

[5]"Take the finest flour and bake twelve loaves of bread, using two-tenths of an ephah[a] for each loaf. [6]Arrange them in two stacks, six in each stack, on the table of pure gold before the LORD. [7]By each stack put some pure incense as a memorial[b] portion to represent the bread and to be a food offering presented to the LORD. [8]This bread is to be set out before the LORD regularly, Sabbath after Sabbath, on behalf of the Israelites, as a lasting covenant. [9]It belongs to Aaron and his sons, who are to eat it in the sanctuary area, because it is a most holy part of their perpetual share of the food offerings presented to the LORD."

A Blasphemer Put to Death

[10]Now the son of an Israelite mother and an Egyptian father went out among the Israelites, and a fight broke out in the camp between him and an Israelite. [11]The son of the Israelite woman blasphemed the Name with a curse; so they brought him to Moses. (His mother's name was Shelomith, the daughter of Dibri the Danite.) [12]They put him in custody until the will of the LORD should be made clear to them.

[13]Then the LORD said to Moses: [14]"Take the blasphemer outside the camp. All those who heard him are to lay their hands on his head, and the entire assembly is to stone him. [15]Say to the Israelites: 'Anyone who curses their God will be held responsible; [16]anyone who blasphemes the name of the LORD is to be put to death. The entire assembly must stone them. Whether foreigner or native-born, when they blaspheme the Name they are to be put to death.

[17]" 'Anyone who takes the life of a human being is to be put to death. [18]Anyone who takes the life of someone's animal must make restitution—life for life. [19]Anyone who injures their neighbor is to be injured in the same manner: [20]fracture for fracture, eye for eye, tooth for tooth. The one who has inflicted the injury must suffer the same injury. [21]Whoever kills an animal must make restitution, but whoever kills a human being is to be put to death. [22]You are to have the same law for the foreigner and the native-born. I am the LORD your God.' "

[23]Then Moses spoke to the Israelites, and they took the blasphemer outside the camp and stoned him. The Israelites did as the LORD commanded Moses.

The Sabbath Year

25 The LORD said to Moses at Mount Sinai, [2]"Speak to the Israelites and say to them: 'When you enter the land I am going to give you, the land itself must observe a sabbath to the LORD. [3]For six years sow your fields, and for six years prune your vineyards and gather their crops. [4]But in the seventh year the land is to have a year of sabbath rest, a sabbath to the LORD. Do not sow your fields or prune your vineyards. [5]Do not reap what grows of itself or harvest the grapes of your untended vines. The land is to have a year of rest. [6]Whatever the land yields during the sabbath year will be food for you—for yourself, your male and female servants, and the hired worker and temporary resident who live among you, [7]as well as for your livestock and the wild animals in your land. Whatever the land produces may be eaten.

The Year of Jubilee

[8]" 'Count off seven sabbath years—seven times seven years—so that the seven sabbath years amount to a period of forty-nine years. [9]Then have the trumpet sounded everywhere on the tenth day of the seventh month; on the Day of Atonement sound the trumpet throughout your land. [10]Consecrate the fiftieth year and proclaim liberty throughout the land to all its inhabitants. It shall be a jubilee for you; each of you is to return to your family property and to your own clan. [11]The fiftieth year shall be a jubilee for you; do not sow and do not reap what grows of itself or harvest the untended vines. [12]For it is a jubilee and is to be holy for you; eat only what is taken directly from the fields.

[13]" 'In this Year of Jubilee everyone is to return to their own property.

[14]" 'If you sell land to any of your own people or buy land from them, do not take advantage of each other. [15]You are to buy from

[a] 5 That is, probably about 7 pounds or about 3.2 kilograms [b] 7 Or *representative*

your own people on the basis of the number of years since the Jubilee. And they are to sell to you on the basis of the number of years left for harvesting crops. 16When the years are many, you are to increase the price, and when the years are few, you are to decrease the price, because what is really being sold to you is the number of crops. 17Do not take advantage of each other, but fear your God. I am the LORD your God.

18" 'Follow my decrees and be careful to obey my laws, and you will live safely in the land. 19Then the land will yield its fruit, and you will eat your fill and live there in safety. 20You may ask, "What will we eat in the seventh year if we do not plant or harvest our crops?" 21I will send you such a blessing in the sixth year that the land will yield enough for three years. 22While you plant during the eighth year, you will eat from the old crop and will continue to eat from it until the harvest of the ninth year comes in.

23" 'The land must not be sold permanently, because the land is mine and you reside in my land as foreigners and strangers. 24Throughout the land that you hold as a possession, you must provide for the redemption of the land.

25" 'If one of your fellow Israelites becomes poor and sells some of their property, their nearest relative is to come and redeem what they have sold. 26If, however, there is no one to redeem it for them but later on they prosper and acquire sufficient means to redeem it themselves, 27they are to determine the value for the years since they sold it and refund the balance to the one to whom they sold it; they can then go back to their own property. 28But if they do not acquire the means to repay, what was sold will remain in the possession of the buyer until the Year of Jubilee. It will be returned in the Jubilee, and they can then go back to their property.

29" 'Anyone who sells a house in a walled city retains the right of redemption a full year after its sale. During that time the seller may redeem it. 30If it is not redeemed before a full year has passed, the house in the walled city shall belong permanently to the buyer and the buyer's descendants. It is not to be returned in the Jubilee. 31But houses in villages without walls around them are to be considered as belonging to the open country. They can be redeemed, and they are to be returned in the Jubilee.

32" 'The Levites always have the right to redeem their houses in the Levitical towns, which they possess. 33So the property of the Levites is redeemable — that is, a house sold in any town they hold — and is to be returned in the Jubilee, because the houses in the towns of the Levites are their property among the Israelites. 34But the pastureland belonging to their towns must not be sold; it is their permanent possession.

35" 'If any of your fellow Israelites become poor and are unable to support themselves among you, help them as you would a foreigner and stranger, so they can continue to live among you. 36Do not take interest or any profit from them, but fear your God, so that they may continue to live among you. 37You must not lend them money at interest or sell them food at a profit. 38I am the LORD your God, who brought you out of Egypt to give you the land of Canaan and to be your God.

39" 'If any of your fellow Israelites become poor and sell themselves to you, do not make them work as slaves. 40They are to be treated as hired workers or temporary residents among you; they are to work for you until the Year of Jubilee. 41Then they and their children are to be released, and they will go back to their own clans and to the property of their ancestors. 42Because the Israelites are my servants, whom I brought out of Egypt, they must not be sold as slaves. 43Do not rule over them ruthlessly, but fear your God.

44" 'Your male and female slaves are to come from the nations around you; from them you may buy slaves. 45You may also buy some of the temporary residents living among you and members of their clans born in your country, and they will become your property. 46You can bequeath them to your children as inherited property and can make them slaves for life, but you must not rule over your fellow Israelites ruthlessly.

47" 'If a foreigner residing among you becomes rich and any of your fellow Israelites become poor and sell themselves to the foreigner or to a member of the foreigner's clan, 48they retain the right of redemption after they have sold themselves. One of their relatives may redeem them: 49An uncle or a cousin or any blood relative in their clan may redeem them. Or if they prosper, they may redeem themselves. 50They and their buyer are to count the time from the year they sold themselves up to the Year of Jubilee. The price for their release is to be based on the rate paid to a hired worker for that number of years. 51 If many years remain, they must pay for their redemption a larger share of the price paid for them. 52 If only a few years remain until the Year of Jubilee, they are to compute that and pay for their redemption accordingly. 53 They are to be treated as workers hired from year to year; you must see to it that those to whom they owe service do not rule over them ruthlessly.

54 “ ‘Even if someone is not redeemed in any of these ways, they and their children are to be released in the Year of Jubilee, 55 for the Israelites belong to me as servants. They are my servants, whom I brought out of Egypt. I am the LORD your God.

Reward for Obedience

26 “ ‘Do not make idols or set up an image or a sacred stone for yourselves, and do not place a carved stone in your land to bow down before it. I am the LORD your God.

2 “ ‘Observe my Sabbaths and have reverence for my sanctuary. I am the LORD.

3 “ ‘If you follow my decrees and are careful to obey my commands, 4 I will send you rain in its season, and the ground will yield its crops and the trees their fruit. 5 Your threshing will continue until grape harvest and the grape harvest will continue until planting, and you will eat all the food you want and live in safety in your land.

6 “ ‘I will grant peace in the land, and you will lie down and no one will make you afraid. I will remove wild beasts from the land, and the sword will not pass through your country. 7 You will pursue your enemies, and they will fall by the sword before you. 8 Five of you will chase a hundred, and a hundred of you will chase ten thousand, and your enemies will fall by the sword before you.

9 “ ‘I will look on you with favor and make you fruitful and increase your numbers, and I will keep my covenant with you. 10 You will still be eating last year’s harvest when you will have to move it out to make room for the new. 11 I will put my dwelling place[a] among you, and I will not abhor you. 12 I will walk among you and be your God, and you will be my people. 13 I am the LORD your God, who brought you out of Egypt so that you would no longer be slaves to the Egyptians; I broke the bars of your yoke and enabled you to walk with heads held high.

Punishment for Disobedience

14 “ ‘But if you will not listen to me and carry out all these commands, 15 and if you reject my decrees and abhor my laws and fail to carry out all my commands and so violate my covenant, 16 then I will do this to you: I will bring on you sudden terror, wasting diseases and fever that will destroy your sight and sap your strength. You will plant seed in vain, because your enemies will eat it. 17 I will set my face against you so that you will be defeated by your enemies; those who hate you will rule over you, and you will flee even when no one is pursuing you.

18 “ ‘If after all this you will not listen to me, I will punish you for your sins seven times over. 19 I will break down your stubborn pride and make the sky above you like iron and the ground beneath you like bronze. 20 Your strength will be spent in vain, because your soil will not yield its crops, nor will the trees of your land yield their fruit.

21 “ ‘If you remain hostile toward me and refuse to listen to me, I will multiply your afflictions seven times over, as your sins deserve. 22 I will send wild animals against you, and they will rob you of your children, destroy your cattle and make you so few in number that your roads will be deserted.

23 “ ‘If in spite of these things you do not accept my correction but continue to be hostile toward me, 24 I myself will be hostile toward you and will afflict you for your sins seven times over. 25 And I will bring the sword on you to avenge the breaking of the covenant. When you withdraw into your cities, I will send a plague among you, and you will be given into enemy hands. 26 When I cut off your supply of bread, ten women will be able to bake your bread in one oven, and they will dole out the bread by weight. You will eat, but you will not be satisfied.

27 “ ‘If in spite of this you still do not listen to me but continue to be hostile toward me, 28 then in my anger I will be hostile toward

[a] *11* Or *my tabernacle*

you, and I myself will punish you for your sins seven times over. 29 You will eat the flesh of your sons and the flesh of your daughters. 30 I will destroy your high places, cut down your incense altars and pile your dead bodies[a] on the lifeless forms of your idols, and I will abhor you. 31 I will turn your cities into ruins and lay waste your sanctuaries, and I will take no delight in the pleasing aroma of your offerings. 32 I myself will lay waste the land, so that your enemies who live there will be appalled. 33 I will scatter you among the nations and will draw out my sword and pursue you. Your land will be laid waste, and your cities will lie in ruins. 34 Then the land will enjoy its sabbath years all the time that it lies desolate and you are in the country of your enemies; then the land will rest and enjoy its sabbaths. 35 All the time that it lies desolate, the land will have the rest it did not have during the sabbaths you lived in it.

36 " 'As for those of you who are left, I will make their hearts so fearful in the lands of their enemies that the sound of a windblown leaf will put them to flight. They will run as though fleeing from the sword, and they will fall, even though no one is pursuing them. 37 They will stumble over one another as though fleeing from the sword, even though no one is pursuing them. So you will not be able to stand before your enemies. 38 You will perish among the nations; the land of your enemies will devour you. 39 Those of you who are left will waste away in the lands of their enemies because of their sins; also because of their ancestors' sins they will waste away.

40 " 'But if they will confess their sins and the sins of their ancestors — their unfaithfulness and their hostility toward me, 41 which made me hostile toward them so that I sent them into the land of their enemies — then when their uncircumcised hearts are humbled and they pay for their sin, 42 I will remember my covenant with Jacob and my covenant with Isaac and my covenant with Abraham, and I will remember the land. 43 For the land will be deserted by them and will enjoy its sabbaths while it lies desolate without them. They will pay for their sins because they rejected my laws and abhorred my decrees. 44 Yet in spite of this, when they are in the land of their enemies, I will not reject them or abhor them so as to destroy them completely, breaking my covenant with them. I am the LORD their God. 45 But for their sake I will remember the covenant with their ancestors whom I brought out of Egypt in the sight of the nations to be their God. I am the LORD.' "

46 These are the decrees, the laws and the regulations that the LORD established at Mount Sinai between himself and the Israelites through Moses.

Redeeming What Is the LORD's

27 The LORD said to Moses, 2 "Speak to the Israelites and say to them: 'If anyone makes a special vow to dedicate a person to the LORD by giving the equivalent value, 3 set the value of a male between the ages of twenty and sixty at fifty shekels[b] of silver, according to the sanctuary shekel[c]; 4 for a female, set her value at thirty shekels[d]; 5 for a person between the ages of five and twenty, set the value of a male at twenty shekels[e] and of a female at ten shekels[f]; 6 for a person between one month and five years, set the value of a male at five shekels[g] of silver and that of a female at three shekels[h] of silver; 7 for a person sixty years old or more, set the value of a male at fifteen shekels[i] and of a female at ten shekels. 8 If anyone making the vow is too poor to pay the specified amount, the person being dedicated is to be presented to the priest, who will set the value according to what the one making the vow can afford.

9 " 'If what they vowed is an animal that is acceptable as an offering to the LORD, such an animal given to the LORD becomes holy. 10 They must not exchange it or substitute a good one for a bad one, or a bad one for a good one; if they should substitute one animal for another, both it and the substitute become holy. 11 If what they vowed is a ceremonially unclean animal — one that is not acceptable as an offering to the LORD — the animal must be presented to the priest, 12 who will judge its quality as good or bad.

[a] *30* Or *your funeral offerings* [b] *3* That is, about 1 1/4 pounds or about 575 grams; also in verse 16 [c] *3* That is, about 2/5 ounce or about 12 grams; also in verse 25 [d] *4* That is, about 12 ounces or about 345 grams [e] *5* That is, about 8 ounces or about 230 grams [f] *5* That is, about 4 ounces or about 115 grams; also in verse 7 [g] *6* That is, about 2 ounces or about 58 grams [h] *6* That is, about 1 1/4 ounces or about 35 grams [i] *7* That is, about 6 ounces or about 175 grams

Whatever value the priest then sets, that is what it will be. 13If the owner wishes to redeem the animal, a fifth must be added to its value.

14" 'If anyone dedicates their house as something holy to the LORD, the priest will judge its quality as good or bad. Whatever value the priest then sets, so it will remain. 15If the one who dedicates their house wishes to redeem it, they must add a fifth to its value, and the house will again become theirs.

16" 'If anyone dedicates to the LORD part of their family land, its value is to be set according to the amount of seed required for it — fifty shekels of silver to a homer[a] of barley seed. 17If they dedicate a field during the Year of Jubilee, the value that has been set remains. 18But if they dedicate a field after the Jubilee, the priest will determine the value according to the number of years that remain until the next Year of Jubilee, and its set value will be reduced. 19If the one who dedicates the field wishes to redeem it, they must add a fifth to its value, and the field will again become theirs. 20If, however, they do not redeem the field, or if they have sold it to someone else, it can never be redeemed. 21When the field is released in the Jubilee, it will become holy, like a field devoted to the LORD; it will become priestly property.

22" 'If anyone dedicates to the LORD a field they have bought, which is not part of their family land, 23the priest will determine its value up to the Year of Jubilee, and the owner must pay its value on that day as something holy to the LORD. 24In the Year of Jubilee the field will revert to the person from whom it was bought, the one whose land it was. 25Every value is to be set according to the sanctuary shekel, twenty gerahs to the shekel.

26" 'No one, however, may dedicate the firstborn of an animal, since the firstborn already belongs to the LORD; whether an ox[b] or a sheep, it is the LORD's. 27If it is one of the unclean animals, it may be bought back at its set value, adding a fifth of the value to it. If it is not redeemed, it is to be sold at its set value.

28" 'But nothing that a person owns and devotes[c] to the LORD — whether a human being or an animal or family land — may be sold or redeemed; everything so devoted is most holy to the LORD.

29" 'No person devoted to destruction[d] may be ransomed; they are to be put to death.

30" 'A tithe of everything from the land, whether grain from the soil or fruit from the trees, belongs to the LORD; it is holy to the LORD. 31Whoever would redeem any of their tithe must add a fifth of the value to it. 32Every tithe of the herd and flock — every tenth animal that passes under the shepherd's rod — will be holy to the LORD. 33No one may pick out the good from the bad or make any substitution. If anyone does make a substitution, both the animal and its substitute become holy and cannot be redeemed.' "

34These are the commands the LORD gave Moses at Mount Sinai for the Israelites.

[a] *16* That is, probably about 300 pounds or about 135 kilograms [b] *26* The Hebrew word can refer to either male or female. [c] *28* The Hebrew term refers to the irrevocable giving over of things or persons to the LORD. [d] *29* The Hebrew term refers to the irrevocable giving over of things or persons to the LORD, often by totally destroying them.

NUMBERS

The Census

1 The LORD spoke to Moses in the tent of meeting in the Desert of Sinai on the first day of the second month of the second year after the Israelites came out of Egypt. He said:
2 "Take a census of the whole Israelite community by their clans and families, listing every man by name, one by one.
3 You and Aaron are to count according to their divisions all the men in Israel who are twenty years old or more and able to serve in the army.
4 One man from each tribe, each of them the head of his family, is to help you.
5 These are the names of the men who are to assist you:

from Reuben, Elizur son of Shedeur;
6 from Simeon, Shelumiel son of Zurishaddai;
7 from Judah, Nahshon son of Amminadab;
8 from Issachar, Nethanel son of Zuar;
9 from Zebulun, Eliab son of Helon;
10 from the sons of Joseph:
from Ephraim, Elishama son of Ammihud;
from Manasseh, Gamaliel son of Pedahzur;
11 from Benjamin, Abidan son of Gideoni;
12 from Dan, Ahiezer son of Ammishaddai;
13 from Asher, Pagiel son of Okran;
14 from Gad, Eliasaph son of Deuel;
15 from Naphtali, Ahira son of Enan."

16 These were the men appointed from the community, the leaders of their ancestral tribes. They were the heads of the clans of Israel.

17 Moses and Aaron took these men whose names had been specified,
18 and they called the whole community together on the first day of the second month. The people registered their ancestry by their clans and families, and the men twenty years old or more were listed by name, one by one,
19 as the LORD commanded Moses. And so he counted them in the Desert of Sinai:

20 From the descendants of Reuben the firstborn son of Israel:
All the men twenty years old or more who were able to serve in the army were listed by name, one by one, according to the records of their clans and families.
21 The number from the tribe of Reuben was 46,500.

22 From the descendants of Simeon:
All the men twenty years old or more who were able to serve in the army were counted and listed by name, one by one, according to the records of their clans and families.
23 The number from the tribe of Simeon was 59,300.

24 From the descendants of Gad:
All the men twenty years old or more who were able to serve in the army were listed by name, according to the records of their clans and families.
25 The number from the tribe of Gad was 45,650.

26 From the descendants of Judah:
All the men twenty years old or more who were able to serve in the army were listed by name, according to the records of their clans and families.
27 The number from the tribe of Judah was 74,600.

28 From the descendants of Issachar:
All the men twenty years old or more who were able to serve in the army were listed by name, according to the records of their clans and families.
29 The number from the tribe of Issachar was 54,400.

30 From the descendants of Zebulun:
All the men twenty years old or more who were able to serve in the army were listed by name, according to the records of their clans and families.
31 The number from the tribe of Zebulun was 57,400.

[32] From the sons of Joseph:
From the descendants of Ephraim:
All the men twenty years old or more who were able to serve in the army were listed by name, according to the records of their clans and families. [33] The number from the tribe of Ephraim was 40,500.

[34] From the descendants of Manasseh:
All the men twenty years old or more who were able to serve in the army were listed by name, according to the records of their clans and families. [35] The number from the tribe of Manasseh was 32,200.

[36] From the descendants of Benjamin:
All the men twenty years old or more who were able to serve in the army were listed by name, according to the records of their clans and families. [37] The number from the tribe of Benjamin was 35,400.

[38] From the descendants of Dan:
All the men twenty years old or more who were able to serve in the army were listed by name, according to the records of their clans and families. [39] The number from the tribe of Dan was 62,700.

[40] From the descendants of Asher:
All the men twenty years old or more who were able to serve in the army were listed by name, according to the records of their clans and families. [41] The number from the tribe of Asher was 41,500.

[42] From the descendants of Naphtali:
All the men twenty years old or more who were able to serve in the army were listed by name, according to the records of their clans and families. [43] The number from the tribe of Naphtali was 53,400.

[44] These were the men counted by Moses and Aaron and the twelve leaders of Israel, each one representing his family. [45] All the Israelites twenty years old or more who were able to serve in Israel's army were counted according to their families. [46] The total number was 603,550.

[47] The ancestral tribe of the Levites, however, was not counted along with the others. [48] The LORD had said to Moses: [49] "You must not count the tribe of Levi or include them in the census of the other Israelites. [50] Instead, appoint the Levites to be in charge of the tabernacle of the covenant law—over all its furnishings and everything belonging to it. They are to carry the tabernacle and all its furnishings; they are to take care of it and encamp around it. [51] Whenever the tabernacle is to move, the Levites are to take it down, and whenever the tabernacle is to be set up, the Levites shall do it. Anyone else who approaches it is to be put to death. [52] The Israelites are to set up their tents by divisions, each of them in their own camp under their standard. [53] The Levites, however, are to set up their tents around the tabernacle of the covenant law so that my wrath will not fall on the Israelite community. The Levites are to be responsible for the care of the tabernacle of the covenant law."

[54] The Israelites did all this just as the LORD commanded Moses.

The Arrangement of the Tribal Camps

2 The LORD said to Moses and Aaron: [2] "The Israelites are to camp around the tent of meeting some distance from it, each of them under their standard and holding the banners of their family."

[3] On the east, toward the sunrise, the divisions of the camp of Judah are to encamp under their standard. The leader of the people of Judah is Nahshon son of Amminadab. [4] His division numbers 74,600.

[5] The tribe of Issachar will camp next to them. The leader of the people of Issachar is Nethanel son of Zuar. [6] His division numbers 54,400.

[7] The tribe of Zebulun will be next. The leader of the people of Zebulun is Eliab son of Helon. [8] His division numbers 57,400.

[9] All the men assigned to the camp of Judah, according to their divisions, number 186,400. They will set out first.

[10] On the south will be the divisions of the camp of Reuben under their standard. The leader of the people of Reuben is Elizur son of Shedeur. [11] His division numbers 46,500.

[12] The tribe of Simeon will camp next

to them. The leader of the people of
Simeon is Shelumiel son of Zurishad-
dai. [13]His division numbers 59,300.
[14]The tribe of Gad will be next. The
leader of the people of Gad is Eliasaph
son of Deuel.[a] [15]His division numbers
45,650.
[16]All the men assigned to the camp
of Reuben, according to their divisions,
number 151,450. They will set out sec-
ond.

[17]Then the tent of meeting and the
camp of the Levites will set out in the
middle of the camps. They will set out
in the same order as they encamp, each
in their own place under their stan-
dard.

[18]On the west will be the divisions of
the camp of Ephraim under their stan-
dard. The leader of the people of Ephra-
im is Elishama son of Ammihud. [19]His
division numbers 40,500.
[20]The tribe of Manasseh will be next
to them. The leader of the people of
Manasseh is Gamaliel son of Pedahzur.
[21]His division numbers 32,200.
[22]The tribe of Benjamin will be next.
The leader of the people of Benjamin is
Abidan son of Gideoni. [23]His division
numbers 35,400.
[24]All the men assigned to the camp
of Ephraim, according to their divi-
sions, number 108,100. They will set
out third.

[25]On the north will be the divisions
of the camp of Dan under their stan-
dard. The leader of the people of Dan
is Ahiezer son of Ammishaddai. [26]His
division numbers 62,700.
[27]The tribe of Asher will camp next
to them. The leader of the people of
Asher is Pagiel son of Okran. [28]His di-
vision numbers 41,500.
[29]The tribe of Naphtali will be next.
The leader of the people of Naphtali is
Ahira son of Enan. [30]His division num-
bers 53,400.
[31]All the men assigned to the camp
of Dan number 157,600. They will set
out last, under their standards.

[32]These are the Israelites, counted
according to their families. All the men
in the camps, by their divisions, num-
ber 603,550. [33]The Levites, however,
were not counted along with the oth-
er Israelites, as the LORD commanded
Moses.

[34]So the Israelites did everything the
LORD commanded Moses; that is the way
they encamped under their standards, and
that is the way they set out, each of them
with their clan and family.

The Levites

3 This is the account of the family of
Aaron and Moses at the time the LORD
spoke to Moses at Mount Sinai.
[2]The names of the sons of Aaron were Na-
dab the firstborn and Abihu, Eleazar and Ith-
amar. [3]Those were the names of Aaron's sons,
the anointed priests, who were ordained to
serve as priests. [4]Nadab and Abihu, howev-
er, died before the LORD when they made an
offering with unauthorized fire before him
in the Desert of Sinai. They had no sons, so
Eleazar and Ithamar served as priests during
the lifetime of their father Aaron.
[5]The LORD said to Moses, [6]"Bring the
tribe of Levi and present them to Aaron the
priest to assist him. [7]They are to perform du-
ties for him and for the whole community at
the tent of meeting by doing the work of the
tabernacle. [8]They are to take care of all the
furnishings of the tent of meeting, fulfilling
the obligations of the Israelites by doing the
work of the tabernacle. [9]Give the Levites to
Aaron and his sons; they are the Israelites
who are to be given wholly to him.[b] [10]Ap-
point Aaron and his sons to serve as priests;
anyone else who approaches the sanctuary
is to be put to death."
[11]The LORD also said to Moses, [12]"I have
taken the Levites from among the Israelites
in place of the first male offspring of every
Israelite woman. The Levites are mine, [13]for
all the firstborn are mine. When I struck
down all the firstborn in Egypt, I set apart
for myself every firstborn in Israel, whether
human or animal. They are to be mine. I am
the LORD."

[a] *14* Many manuscripts of the Masoretic Text, Samaritan Pentateuch and Vulgate (see also 1:14); most manuscripts of the Masoretic Text *Reuel* [b] *9* Most manuscripts of the Masoretic Text; some manuscripts of the Masoretic Text, Samaritan Pentateuch and Septuagint (see also 8:16) *to me*

14 The LORD said to Moses in the Desert of
Sinai, 15 "Count the Levites by their families
and clans. Count every male a month old or
more." 16 So Moses counted them, as he was
commanded by the word of the LORD.

17 These were the names of the sons of
Levi:
Gershon, Kohath and Merari.
18 These were the names of the Gershon-
ite clans:
Libni and Shimei.
19 The Kohathite clans:
Amram, Izhar, Hebron and Uzziel.
20 The Merarite clans:
Mahli and Mushi.
These were the Levite clans, according to
their families.

21 To Gershon belonged the clans of the
Libnites and Shimeites; these were the Ger-
shonite clans. 22 The number of all the males
a month old or more who were counted
was 7,500. 23 The Gershonite clans were to
camp on the west, behind the tabernacle.
24 The leader of the families of the Gershon-
ites was Eliasaph son of Lael. 25 At the tent
of meeting the Gershonites were responsi-
ble for the care of the tabernacle and tent,
its coverings, the curtain at the entrance
to the tent of meeting, 26 the curtains of the
courtyard, the curtain at the entrance to the
courtyard surrounding the tabernacle and
altar, and the ropes — and everything relat-
ed to their use.

27 To Kohath belonged the clans of the
Amramites, Izharites, Hebronites and Uzzi-
elites; these were the Kohathite clans. 28 The
number of all the males a month old or more
was 8,600.[a] The Kohathites were responsible
for the care of the sanctuary. 29 The Kohath-
ite clans were to camp on the south side of
the tabernacle. 30 The leader of the families
of the Kohathite clans was Elizaphan son of
Uzziel. 31 They were responsible for the care
of the ark, the table, the lampstand, the al-
tars, the articles of the sanctuary used in
ministering, the curtain, and everything
related to their use. 32 The chief leader of the
Levites was Eleazar son of Aaron, the priest.
He was appointed over those who were re-
sponsible for the care of the sanctuary.

33 To Merari belonged the clans of the
Mahlites and the Mushites; these were the
Merarite clans. 34 The number of all the
males a month old or more who were count-
ed was 6,200. 35 The leader of the families of
the Merarite clans was Zuriel son of Abihail;
they were to camp on the north side of the
tabernacle. 36 The Merarites were appointed
to take care of the frames of the tabernacle,
its crossbars, posts, bases, all its equipment,
and everything related to their use, 37 as well
as the posts of the surrounding courtyard
with their bases, tent pegs and ropes.

38 Moses and Aaron and his sons were to
camp to the east of the tabernacle, toward
the sunrise, in front of the tent of meeting.
They were responsible for the care of the
sanctuary on behalf of the Israelites. Any-
one else who approached the sanctuary was
to be put to death.

39 The total number of Levites counted
at the LORD's command by Moses and Aar-
on according to their clans, including every
male a month old or more, was 22,000.

40 The LORD said to Moses, "Count all the
firstborn Israelite males who are a month
old or more and make a list of their names.
41 Take the Levites for me in place of all the
firstborn of the Israelites, and the livestock
of the Levites in place of all the firstborn of
the livestock of the Israelites. I am the LORD."

42 So Moses counted all the firstborn of
the Israelites, as the LORD commanded him.
43 The total number of firstborn males a month
old or more, listed by name, was 22,273.

44 The LORD also said to Moses, 45 "Take
the Levites in place of all the firstborn of Is-
rael, and the livestock of the Levites in place
of their livestock. The Levites are to be mine.
I am the LORD. 46 To redeem the 273 firstborn
Israelites who exceed the number of the Le-
vites, 47 collect five shekels[b] for each one,
according to the sanctuary shekel, which
weighs twenty gerahs. 48 Give the money for
the redemption of the additional Israelites to
Aaron and his sons."

49 So Moses collected the redemption
money from those who exceeded the num-
ber redeemed by the Levites. 50 From the

[a] *28* Hebrew; some Septuagint manuscripts *8,300*

[b] *47* That is, about 2 ounces or about 58 grams

firstborn of the Israelites he collected silver weighing 1,365 shekels,[a] according to the sanctuary shekel. 51 Moses gave the redemption money to Aaron and his sons, as he was commanded by the word of the LORD.

The Kohathites

4 The LORD said to Moses and Aaron: 2 "Take a census of the Kohathite branch of the Levites by their clans and families. 3 Count all the men from thirty to fifty years of age who come to serve in the work at the tent of meeting.

4 "This is the work of the Kohathites at the tent of meeting: the care of the most holy things. 5 When the camp is to move, Aaron and his sons are to go in and take down the shielding curtain and put it over the ark of the covenant law. 6 Then they are to cover the curtain with a durable leather,[b] spread a cloth of solid blue over that and put the poles in place.

7 "Over the table of the Presence they are to spread a blue cloth and put on it the plates, dishes and bowls, and the jars for drink offerings; the bread that is continually there is to remain on it. 8 They are to spread a scarlet cloth over them, cover that with the durable leather and put the poles in place.

9 "They are to take a blue cloth and cover the lampstand that is for light, together with its lamps, its wick trimmers and trays, and all its jars for the olive oil used to supply it. 10 Then they are to wrap it and all its accessories in a covering of the durable leather and put it on a carrying frame.

11 "Over the gold altar they are to spread a blue cloth and cover that with the durable leather and put the poles in place.

12 "They are to take all the articles used for ministering in the sanctuary, wrap them in a blue cloth, cover that with the durable leather and put them on a carrying frame.

13 "They are to remove the ashes from the bronze altar and spread a purple cloth over it. 14 Then they are to place on it all the utensils used for ministering at the altar, including the firepans, meat forks, shovels and sprinkling bowls. Over it they are to spread a covering of the durable leather and put the poles in place.

15 "After Aaron and his sons have finished covering the holy furnishings and all the holy articles, and when the camp is ready to move, only then are the Kohathites to come and do the carrying. But they must not touch the holy things or they will die. The Kohathites are to carry those things that are in the tent of meeting.

16 "Eleazar son of Aaron, the priest, is to have charge of the oil for the light, the fragrant incense, the regular grain offering and the anointing oil. He is to be in charge of the entire tabernacle and everything in it, including its holy furnishings and articles."

17 The LORD said to Moses and Aaron, 18 "See that the Kohathite tribal clans are not destroyed from among the Levites. 19 So that they may live and not die when they come near the most holy things, do this for them: Aaron and his sons are to go into the sanctuary and assign to each man his work and what he is to carry. 20 But the Kohathites must not go in to look at the holy things, even for a moment, or they will die."

The Gershonites

21 The LORD said to Moses, 22 "Take a census also of the Gershonites by their families and clans. 23 Count all the men from thirty to fifty years of age who come to serve in the work at the tent of meeting.

24 "This is the service of the Gershonite clans in their carrying and their other work: 25 They are to carry the curtains of the tabernacle, that is, the tent of meeting, its covering and its outer covering of durable leather, the curtains for the entrance to the tent of meeting, 26 the curtains of the courtyard surrounding the tabernacle and altar, the curtain for the entrance to the courtyard, the ropes and all the equipment used in the service of the tent. The Gershonites are to do all that needs to be done with these things. 27 All their service, whether carrying or doing other work, is to be done under the direction of Aaron and his sons. You shall assign to them as their responsibility all they are to carry. 28 This is the service of the Gershonite clans at the tent of meeting. Their duties are to be under the direction of Ithamar son of Aaron, the priest.

[a] *50* That is, about 35 pounds or about 16 kilograms also in verses 8, 10, 11, 12, 14 and 25

[b] *6* Possibly the hides of large aquatic mammals;

The Merarites

[29] "Count the Merarites by their clans and families. [30] Count all the men from thirty to fifty years of age who come to serve in the work at the tent of meeting. [31] As part of all their service at the tent, they are to carry the frames of the tabernacle, its crossbars, posts and bases, [32] as well as the posts of the surrounding courtyard with their bases, tent pegs, ropes, all their equipment and everything related to their use. Assign to each man the specific things he is to carry. [33] This is the service of the Merarite clans as they work at the tent of meeting under the direction of Ithamar son of Aaron, the priest."

The Numbering of the Levite Clans

[34] Moses, Aaron and the leaders of the community counted the Kohathites by their clans and families. [35] All the men from thirty to fifty years of age who came to serve in the work at the tent of meeting, [36] counted by clans, were 2,750. [37] This was the total of all those in the Kohathite clans who served at the tent of meeting. Moses and Aaron counted them according to the LORD's command through Moses.

[38] The Gershonites were counted by their clans and families. [39] All the men from thirty to fifty years of age who came to serve in the work at the tent of meeting, [40] counted by their clans and families, were 2,630. [41] This was the total of those in the Gershonite clans who served at the tent of meeting. Moses and Aaron counted them according to the LORD's command.

[42] The Merarites were counted by their clans and families. [43] All the men from thirty to fifty years of age who came to serve in the work at the tent of meeting, [44] counted by their clans, were 3,200. [45] This was the total of those in the Merarite clans. Moses and Aaron counted them according to the LORD's command through Moses.

[46] So Moses, Aaron and the leaders of Israel counted all the Levites by their clans and families. [47] All the men from thirty to fifty years of age who came to do the work of serving and carrying the tent of meeting [48] numbered 8,580. [49] At the LORD's command through Moses, each was assigned his work and told what to carry.

Thus they were counted, as the LORD commanded Moses.

The Purity of the Camp

5 The LORD said to Moses, [2] "Command the Israelites to send away from the camp anyone who has a defiling skin disease[a] or a discharge of any kind, or who is ceremonially unclean because of a dead body. [3] Send away male and female alike; send them outside the camp so they will not defile their camp, where I dwell among them." [4] The Israelites did so; they sent them outside the camp. They did just as the LORD had instructed Moses.

Restitution for Wrongs

[5] The LORD said to Moses, [6] "Say to the Israelites: 'Any man or woman who wrongs another in any way[b] and so is unfaithful to the LORD is guilty [7] and must confess the sin they have committed. They must make full restitution for the wrong they have done, add a fifth of the value to it and give it all to the person they have wronged. [8] But if that person has no close relative to whom restitution can be made for the wrong, the restitution belongs to the LORD and must be given to the priest, along with the ram with which atonement is made for the wrongdoer. [9] All the sacred contributions the Israelites bring to a priest will belong to him. [10] Sacred things belong to their owners, but what they give to the priest will belong to the priest.'"

The Test for an Unfaithful Wife

[11] Then the LORD said to Moses, [12] "Speak to the Israelites and say to them: 'If a man's wife goes astray and is unfaithful to him [13] so that another man has sexual relations with her, and this is hidden from her husband and her impurity is undetected (since there is no witness against her and she has not been caught in the act), [14] and if feelings of jealousy come over her husband and he suspects his wife and she is impure — or if he is jealous and suspects her even though she is not impure — [15] then he is to take his wife to the priest. He must also take an offering of a tenth of an ephah[c] of barley flour on

[a] *2* The Hebrew word for *defiling skin disease,* traditionally translated "leprosy," was used for various diseases affecting the skin. [b] *6* Or *woman who commits any wrong common to mankind* [c] *15* That is, probably about 3 1/2 pounds or about 1.6 kilograms

her behalf. He must not pour olive oil on it or
put incense on it, because it is a grain offer-
ing for jealousy, a reminder-offering to draw
attention to wrongdoing.
16 “ ‘The priest shall bring her and have her
stand before the LORD. 17 Then he shall take
some holy water in a clay jar and put some
dust from the tabernacle floor into the water.
18 After the priest has had the woman stand
before the LORD, he shall loosen her hair and
place in her hands the reminder-offering,
the grain offering for jealousy, while he him-
self holds the bitter water that brings a curse.
19 Then the priest shall put the woman under
oath and say to her, “If no other man has had
sexual relations with you and you have not
gone astray and become impure while mar-
ried to your husband, may this bitter water
that brings a curse not harm you. 20 But if you
have gone astray while married to your hus-
band and you have made yourself impure
by having sexual relations with a man other
than your husband” — 21 here the priest is to
put the woman under this curse — “may the
LORD cause you to become a curse[a] among
your people when he makes your womb mis-
carry and your abdomen swell. 22 May this
water that brings a curse enter your body
so that your abdomen swells or your womb
miscarries.”
“ ‘Then the woman is to say, “Amen. So
be it.”
23 “ ‘The priest is to write these curses on a
scroll and then wash them off into the bitter
water. 24 He shall make the woman drink the
bitter water that brings a curse, and this wa-
ter that brings a curse and causes bitter suf-
fering will enter her. 25 The priest is to take
from her hands the grain offering for jealou-
sy, wave it before the LORD and bring it to the
altar. 26 The priest is then to take a handful
of the grain offering as a memorial[b] offering
and burn it on the altar; after that, he is to
have the woman drink the water. 27 If she has
made herself impure and been unfaithful to
her husband, this will be the result: When
she is made to drink the water that brings
a curse and causes bitter suffering, it will
enter her, her abdomen will swell and her
womb will miscarry, and she will become
a curse. 28 If, however, the woman has not
made herself impure, but is clean, she will
be cleared of guilt and will be able to have
children.
29 “ ‘This, then, is the law of jealousy when
a woman goes astray and makes herself im-
pure while married to her husband, 30 or
when feelings of jealousy come over a man
because he suspects his wife. The priest is to
have her stand before the LORD and is to ap-
ply this entire law to her. 31 The husband will
be innocent of any wrongdoing, but the wom-
an will bear the consequences of her sin.’ ”

The Nazirite

6 The LORD said to Moses, 2 “Speak to the
Israelites and say to them: ‘If a man or
woman wants to make a special vow, a vow
of dedication to the LORD as a Nazirite, 3 they
must abstain from wine and other ferment-
ed drink and must not drink vinegar made
from wine or other fermented drink. They
must not drink grape juice or eat grapes or
raisins. 4 As long as they remain under their
Nazirite vow, they must not eat anything
that comes from the grapevine, not even the
seeds or skins.
5 “ ‘During the entire period of their Naz-
irite vow, no razor may be used on their
head. They must be holy until the period of
their dedication to the LORD is over; they
must let their hair grow long.
6 “ ‘Throughout the period of their dedi-
cation to the LORD, the Nazirite must not go
near a dead body. 7 Even if their own father
or mother or brother or sister dies, they must
not make themselves ceremonially unclean
on account of them, because the symbol
of their dedication to God is on their head.
8 Throughout the period of their dedication,
they are consecrated to the LORD.
9 “ ‘If someone dies suddenly in the Naz-
irite’s presence, thus defiling the hair that
symbolizes their dedication, they must
shave their head on the seventh day — the
day of their cleansing. 10 Then on the eighth
day they must bring two doves or two young
pigeons to the priest at the entrance to the
tent of meeting. 11 The priest is to offer one as
a sin offering[c] and the other as a burnt offer-
ing to make atonement for the Nazirite be-
cause they sinned by being in the presence
of the dead body. That same day they are to
consecrate their head again. 12 They must

[a] *21* That is, may he cause your name to be used in cursing (see Jer. 29:22); or, may others see that you are cursed; similarly in verse 27. [b] *26* Or *representative* [c] *11* Or *purification offering*; also in verses 14 and 16

rededicate themselves to the LORD for the same period of dedication and must bring a year-old male lamb as a guilt offering. The previous days do not count, because they became defiled during their period of dedication.

13“ ‘Now this is the law of the Nazirite when the period of their dedication is over. They are to be brought to the entrance to the tent of meeting. 14There they are to present their offerings to the LORD: a year-old male lamb without defect for a burnt offering, a year-old ewe lamb without defect for a sin offering, a ram without defect for a fellowship offering, 15together with their grain offerings and drink offerings, and a basket of bread made with the finest flour and without yeast—thick loaves with olive oil mixed in, and thin loaves brushed with olive oil.

16“ ‘The priest is to present all these before the LORD and make the sin offering and the burnt offering. 17He is to present the basket of unleavened bread and is to sacrifice the ram as a fellowship offering to the LORD, together with its grain offering and drink offering.

18“ ‘Then at the entrance to the tent of meeting, the Nazirite must shave off the hair that symbolizes their dedication. They are to take the hair and put it in the fire that is under the sacrifice of the fellowship offering.

19“ ‘After the Nazirite has shaved off the hair that symbolizes their dedication, the priest is to place in their hands a boiled shoulder of the ram, and one thick loaf and one thin loaf from the basket, both made without yeast. 20The priest shall then wave these before the LORD as a wave offering; they are holy and belong to the priest, together with the breast that was waved and the thigh that was presented. After that, the Nazirite may drink wine.

21“ ‘This is the law of the Nazirite who vows offerings to the LORD in accordance with their dedication, in addition to whatever else they can afford. They must fulfill the vows they have made, according to the law of the Nazirite.’ ”

The Priestly Blessing

22The LORD said to Moses, 23“Tell Aaron and his sons, ‘This is how you are to bless the Israelites. Say to them:

24“ ‘ “The LORD bless you
and keep you;
25the LORD make his face shine on you
and be gracious to you;
26the LORD turn his face toward you
and give you peace.” ’

27“So they will put my name on the Israelites, and I will bless them.”

Offerings at the Dedication of the Tabernacle

7 When Moses finished setting up the tabernacle, he anointed and consecrated it and all its furnishings. He also anointed and consecrated the altar and all its utensils. 2Then the leaders of Israel, the heads of families who were the tribal leaders in charge of those who were counted, made offerings. 3They brought as their gifts before the LORD six covered carts and twelve oxen—an ox from each leader and a cart from every two. These they presented before the tabernacle.

4The LORD said to Moses, 5“Accept these from them, that they may be used in the work at the tent of meeting. Give them to the Levites as each man's work requires.”

6So Moses took the carts and oxen and gave them to the Levites. 7He gave two carts and four oxen to the Gershonites, as their work required, 8and he gave four carts and eight oxen to the Merarites, as their work required. They were all under the direction of Ithamar son of Aaron, the priest. 9But Moses did not give any to the Kohathites, because they were to carry on their shoulders the holy things, for which they were responsible.

10When the altar was anointed, the leaders brought their offerings for its dedication and presented them before the altar. 11For the LORD had said to Moses, “Each day one leader is to bring his offering for the dedication of the altar.”

12The one who brought his offering on the first day was Nahshon son of Amminadab of the tribe of Judah.

13His offering was one silver plate weighing a hundred and thirty shekels[a] and one silver sprinkling bowl weighing seventy shekels,[b] both according to the sanctuary shekel, each filled with the finest flour mixed with olive oil as

[a] *13* That is, about 3 1/4 pounds or about 1.5 kilograms; also elsewhere in this chapter [b] *13* That is, about 1 3/4 pounds or about 800 grams; also elsewhere in this chapter

a grain offering; 14 one gold dish weigh-
ing ten shekels,[a] filled with incense;
15 one young bull, one ram and one
male lamb a year old for a burnt offer-
ing; 16 one male goat for a sin offering[b];
17 and two oxen, five rams, five male
goats and five male lambs a year old to
be sacrificed as a fellowship offering.
This was the offering of Nahshon son of
Amminadab.

18 On the second day Nethanel son of Zuar,
the leader of Issachar, brought his offering.
19 The offering he brought was one sil-
ver plate weighing a hundred and thir-
ty shekels and one silver sprinkling
bowl weighing seventy shekels, both
according to the sanctuary shekel, each
filled with the finest flour mixed with
olive oil as a grain offering; 20 one gold
dish weighing ten shekels, filled with
incense; 21 one young bull, one ram and
one male lamb a year old for a burnt
offering; 22 one male goat for a sin of-
fering; 23 and two oxen, five rams, five
male goats and five male lambs a year
old to be sacrificed as a fellowship of-
fering. This was the offering of Nethan-
el son of Zuar.

24 On the third day, Eliab son of Helon, the
leader of the people of Zebulun, brought his
offering.
25 His offering was one silver plate
weighing a hundred and thirty shekels
and one silver sprinkling bowl weigh-
ing seventy shekels, both according to
the sanctuary shekel, each filled with
the finest flour mixed with olive oil as
a grain offering; 26 one gold dish weigh-
ing ten shekels, filled with incense;
27 one young bull, one ram and one
male lamb a year old for a burnt offer-
ing; 28 one male goat for a sin offering;
29 and two oxen, five rams, five male
goats and five male lambs a year old
to be sacrificed as a fellowship offer-
ing. This was the offering of Eliab son
of Helon.

30 On the fourth day Elizur son of Shedeur,
the leader of the people of Reuben, brought
his offering.
31 His offering was one silver plate
weighing a hundred and thirty shekels
and one silver sprinkling bowl weigh-
ing seventy shekels, both according to
the sanctuary shekel, each filled with
the finest flour mixed with olive oil as
a grain offering; 32 one gold dish weigh-
ing ten shekels, filled with incense;
33 one young bull, one ram and one
male lamb a year old for a burnt offer-
ing; 34 one male goat for a sin offering;
35 and two oxen, five rams, five male
goats and five male lambs a year old to
be sacrificed as a fellowship offering.
This was the offering of Elizur son of
Shedeur.

36 On the fifth day Shelumiel son of Zuri-
shaddai, the leader of the people of Simeon,
brought his offering.
37 His offering was one silver plate
weighing a hundred and thirty shekels
and one silver sprinkling bowl weigh-
ing seventy shekels, both according to
the sanctuary shekel, each filled with
the finest flour mixed with olive oil as
a grain offering; 38 one gold dish weigh-
ing ten shekels, filled with incense;
39 one young bull, one ram and one
male lamb a year old for a burnt offer-
ing; 40 one male goat for a sin offering;
41 and two oxen, five rams, five male
goats and five male lambs a year old to
be sacrificed as a fellowship offering.
This was the offering of Shelumiel son
of Zurishaddai.

42 On the sixth day Eliasaph son of Deuel, the
leader of the people of Gad, brought his of-
fering.
43 His offering was one silver plate
weighing a hundred and thirty shekels
and one silver sprinkling bowl weigh-
ing seventy shekels, both according to
the sanctuary shekel, each filled with
the finest flour mixed with olive oil as
a grain offering; 44 one gold dish weigh-
ing ten shekels, filled with incense;
45 one young bull, one ram and one
male lamb a year old for a burnt offer-
ing; 46 one male goat for a sin offering;
47 and two oxen, five rams, five male
goats and five male lambs a year old to

[a] *14* That is, about 4 ounces or about 115 grams; also elsewhere in this chapter [b] *16* Or *purification offering*; also elsewhere in this chapter

be sacrificed as a fellowship offering.
This was the offering of Eliasaph son of
Deuel.

48 On the seventh day Elishama son of Am-
mihud, the leader of the people of Ephraim,
brought his offering.

49 His offering was one silver plate
weighing a hundred and thirty shekels
and one silver sprinkling bowl weigh-
ing seventy shekels, both according to
the sanctuary shekel, each filled with
the finest flour mixed with olive oil as
a grain offering; 50 one gold dish weigh-
ing ten shekels, filled with incense;
51 one young bull, one ram and one
male lamb a year old for a burnt offer-
ing; 52 one male goat for a sin offering;
53 and two oxen, five rams, five male
goats and five male lambs a year old to
be sacrificed as a fellowship offering.
This was the offering of Elishama son
of Ammihud.

54 On the eighth day Gamaliel son of Pedah-
zur, the leader of the people of Manasseh,
brought his offering.

55 His offering was one silver plate
weighing a hundred and thirty shekels
and one silver sprinkling bowl weigh-
ing seventy shekels, both according to
the sanctuary shekel, each filled with
the finest flour mixed with olive oil as
a grain offering; 56 one gold dish weigh-
ing ten shekels, filled with incense;
57 one young bull, one ram and one
male lamb a year old for a burnt offer-
ing; 58 one male goat for a sin offering;
59 and two oxen, five rams, five male
goats and five male lambs a year old to
be sacrificed as a fellowship offering.
This was the offering of Gamaliel son of
Pedahzur.

60 On the ninth day Abidan son of Gideo-
ni, the leader of the people of Benjamin,
brought his offering.

61 His offering was one silver plate
weighing a hundred and thirty shekels
and one silver sprinkling bowl weigh-
ing seventy shekels, both according to
the sanctuary shekel, each filled with
the finest flour mixed with olive oil as
a grain offering; 62 one gold dish weigh-
ing ten shekels, filled with incense;
63 one young bull, one ram and one
male lamb a year old for a burnt offer-
ing; 64 one male goat for a sin offering;
65 and two oxen, five rams, five male
goats and five male lambs a year old to
be sacrificed as a fellowship offering.
This was the offering of Abidan son of
Gideoni.

66 On the tenth day Ahiezer son of Ammi-
shaddai, the leader of the people of Dan,
brought his offering.

67 His offering was one silver plate
weighing a hundred and thirty shekels
and one silver sprinkling bowl weigh-
ing seventy shekels, both according to
the sanctuary shekel, each filled with
the finest flour mixed with olive oil as
a grain offering; 68 one gold dish weigh-
ing ten shekels, filled with incense;
69 one young bull, one ram and one
male lamb a year old for a burnt offer-
ing; 70 one male goat for a sin offering;
71 and two oxen, five rams, five male
goats and five male lambs a year old to
be sacrificed as a fellowship offering.
This was the offering of Ahiezer son of
Ammishaddai.

72 On the eleventh day Pagiel son of Okran,
the leader of the people of Asher, brought his
offering.

73 His offering was one silver plate
weighing a hundred and thirty shekels
and one silver sprinkling bowl weigh-
ing seventy shekels, both according to
the sanctuary shekel, each filled with
the finest flour mixed with olive oil as
a grain offering; 74 one gold dish weigh-
ing ten shekels, filled with incense;
75 one young bull, one ram and one
male lamb a year old for a burnt offer-
ing; 76 one male goat for a sin offering;
77 and two oxen, five rams, five male
goats and five male lambs a year old to
be sacrificed as a fellowship offering.
This was the offering of Pagiel son of
Okran.

78 On the twelfth day Ahira son of Enan, the
leader of the people of Naphtali, brought his
offering.

79 His offering was one silver plate
weighing a hundred and thirty shekels
and one silver sprinkling bowl weigh-
ing seventy shekels, both according to
the sanctuary shekel, each filled with

the finest flour mixed with olive oil as a grain offering; [80]one gold dish weighing ten shekels, filled with incense; [81]one young bull, one ram and one male lamb a year old for a burnt offering; [82]one male goat for a sin offering; [83]and two oxen, five rams, five male goats and five male lambs a year old to be sacrificed as a fellowship offering. This was the offering of Ahira son of Enan.

[84]These were the offerings of the Israelite leaders for the dedication of the altar when it was anointed: twelve silver plates, twelve silver sprinkling bowls and twelve gold dishes. [85]Each silver plate weighed a hundred and thirty shekels, and each sprinkling bowl seventy shekels. Altogether, the silver dishes weighed two thousand four hundred shekels,[a] according to the sanctuary shekel. [86]The twelve gold dishes filled with incense weighed ten shekels each, according to the sanctuary shekel. Altogether, the gold dishes weighed a hundred and twenty shekels.[b] [87]The total number of animals for the burnt offering came to twelve young bulls, twelve rams and twelve male lambs a year old, together with their grain offering. Twelve male goats were used for the sin offering. [88]The total number of animals for the sacrifice of the fellowship offering came to twenty-four oxen, sixty rams, sixty male goats and sixty male lambs a year old. These were the offerings for the dedication of the altar after it was anointed.

[89]When Moses entered the tent of meeting to speak with the LORD, he heard the voice speaking to him from between the two cherubim above the atonement cover on the ark of the covenant law. In this way the LORD spoke to him.

Setting Up the Lamps

8 The LORD said to Moses, [2]"Speak to Aaron and say to him, 'When you set up the lamps, see that all seven light up the area in front of the lampstand.' "

[3]Aaron did so; he set up the lamps so that they faced forward on the lampstand, just as the LORD commanded Moses. [4]This is how the lampstand was made: It was made of hammered gold—from its base to its blossoms. The lampstand was made exactly like the pattern the LORD had shown Moses.

The Setting Apart of the Levites

[5]The LORD said to Moses: [6]"Take the Levites from among all the Israelites and make them ceremonially clean. [7]To purify them, do this: Sprinkle the water of cleansing on them; then have them shave their whole bodies and wash their clothes. And so they will purify themselves. [8]Have them take a young bull with its grain offering of the finest flour mixed with olive oil; then you are to take a second young bull for a sin offering.[c] [9]Bring the Levites to the front of the tent of meeting and assemble the whole Israelite community. [10]You are to bring the Levites before the LORD, and the Israelites are to lay their hands on them. [11]Aaron is to present the Levites before the LORD as a wave offering from the Israelites, so that they may be ready to do the work of the LORD.

[12]"Then the Levites are to lay their hands on the heads of the bulls, using one for a sin offering to the LORD and the other for a burnt offering, to make atonement for the Levites. [13]Have the Levites stand in front of Aaron and his sons and then present them as a wave offering to the LORD. [14]In this way you are to set the Levites apart from the other Israelites, and the Levites will be mine.

[15]"After you have purified the Levites and presented them as a wave offering, they are to come to do their work at the tent of meeting. [16]They are the Israelites who are to be given wholly to me. I have taken them as my own in place of the firstborn, the first male offspring from every Israelite woman. [17]Every firstborn male in Israel, whether human or animal, is mine. When I struck down all the firstborn in Egypt, I set them apart for myself. [18]And I have taken the Levites in place of all the firstborn sons in Israel. [19]From among all the Israelites, I have given the Levites as gifts to Aaron and his sons to do the work at the tent of meeting on behalf of the Israelites and to make atonement for them so that no plague will strike the Israelites when they go near the sanctuary."

[20]Moses, Aaron and the whole Israelite community did with the Levites just as the

[a] *85* That is, about 60 pounds or about 28 kilograms [b] *86* That is, about 3 pounds or about 1.4 kilograms [c] *8* Or *purification offering;* also in verse 12

LORD commanded Moses. 21 The Levites pu-
rified themselves and washed their clothes.
Then Aaron presented them as a wave offer-
ing before the LORD and made atonement for
them to purify them. 22 After that, the Levites
came to do their work at the tent of meeting
under the supervision of Aaron and his sons.
They did with the Levites just as the LORD
commanded Moses.

23 The LORD said to Moses, 24 "This applies
to the Levites: Men twenty-five years old or
more shall come to take part in the work at
the tent of meeting, 25 but at the age of fifty,
they must retire from their regular service
and work no longer. 26 They may assist their
brothers in performing their duties at the
tent of meeting, but they themselves must
not do the work. This, then, is how you are
to assign the responsibilities of the Levites."

The Passover

9 The LORD spoke to Moses in the Desert
of Sinai in the first month of the second
year after they came out of Egypt. He said,
2 "Have the Israelites celebrate the Passover
at the appointed time. 3 Celebrate it at the ap-
pointed time, at twilight on the fourteenth
day of this month, in accordance with all its
rules and regulations."

4 So Moses told the Israelites to celebrate
the Passover, 5 and they did so in the Desert
of Sinai at twilight on the fourteenth day of
the first month. The Israelites did every-
thing just as the LORD commanded Moses.

6 But some of them could not celebrate
the Passover on that day because they were
ceremonially unclean on account of a dead
body. So they came to Moses and Aaron that
same day 7 and said to Moses, "We have be-
come unclean because of a dead body, but
why should we be kept from presenting the
LORD's offering with the other Israelites at
the appointed time?"

8 Moses answered them, "Wait until I find
out what the LORD commands concerning
you."

9 Then the LORD said to Moses, 10 "Tell
the Israelites: 'When any of you or your de-
scendants are unclean because of a dead
body or are away on a journey, they are still
to celebrate the LORD's Passover, 11 but they
are to do it on the fourteenth day of the sec-
ond month at twilight. They are to eat the
lamb, together with unleavened bread and
bitter herbs. 12 They must not leave any of it
till morning or break any of its bones. When
they celebrate the Passover, they must fol-
low all the regulations. 13 But if anyone who
is ceremonially clean and not on a journey
fails to celebrate the Passover, they must be
cut off from their people for not presenting
the LORD's offering at the appointed time.
They will bear the consequences of their sin.

14 " 'A foreigner residing among you is also
to celebrate the LORD's Passover in accor-
dance with its rules and regulations. You
must have the same regulations for both the
foreigner and the native-born.' "

The Cloud Above the Tabernacle

15 On the day the tabernacle, the tent of
the covenant law, was set up, the cloud cov-
ered it. From evening till morning the cloud
above the tabernacle looked like fire. 16 That
is how it continued to be; the cloud covered
it, and at night it looked like fire. 17 Whenever
the cloud lifted from above the tent, the Isra-
elites set out; wherever the cloud settled, the
Israelites encamped. 18 At the LORD's com-
mand the Israelites set out, and at his com-
mand they encamped. As long as the cloud
stayed over the tabernacle, they remained in
camp. 19 When the cloud remained over the
tabernacle a long time, the Israelites obeyed
the LORD's order and did not set out. 20 Some-
times the cloud was over the tabernacle
only a few days; at the LORD's command
they would encamp, and then at his com-
mand they would set out. 21 Sometimes the
cloud stayed only from evening till morn-
ing, and when it lifted in the morning, they
set out. Whether by day or by night, when-
ever the cloud lifted, they set out. 22 Wheth-
er the cloud stayed over the tabernacle for
two days or a month or a year, the Israelites
would remain in camp and not set out; but
when it lifted, they would set out. 23 At the
LORD's command they encamped, and at the
LORD's command they set out. They obeyed
the LORD's order, in accordance with his
command through Moses.

The Silver Trumpets

10 The LORD said to Moses: 2 "Make two
trumpets of hammered silver, and
use them for calling the community togeth-
er and for having the camps set out. 3 When
both are sounded, the whole community is

to assemble before you at the entrance to the tent of meeting. 4If only one is sounded, the leaders—the heads of the clans of Israel—are to assemble before you. 5When a trumpet blast is sounded, the tribes camping on the east are to set out. 6At the sounding of a second blast, the camps on the south are to set out. The blast will be the signal for setting out. 7To gather the assembly, blow the trumpets, but not with the signal for setting out.

8"The sons of Aaron, the priests, are to blow the trumpets. This is to be a lasting ordinance for you and the generations to come. 9When you go into battle in your own land against an enemy who is oppressing you, sound a blast on the trumpets. Then you will be remembered by the LORD your God and rescued from your enemies. 10Also at your times of rejoicing—your appointed festivals and New Moon feasts—you are to sound the trumpets over your burnt offerings and fellowship offerings, and they will be a memorial for you before your God. I am the LORD your God."

The Israelites Leave Sinai

11On the twentieth day of the second month of the second year, the cloud lifted from above the tabernacle of the covenant law. 12Then the Israelites set out from the Desert of Sinai and traveled from place to place until the cloud came to rest in the Desert of Paran. 13They set out, this first time, at the LORD's command through Moses.

14The divisions of the camp of Judah went first, under their standard. Nahshon son of Amminadab was in command. 15Nethanel son of Zuar was over the division of the tribe of Issachar, 16and Eliab son of Helon was over the division of the tribe of Zebulun. 17Then the tabernacle was taken down, and the Gershonites and Merarites, who carried it, set out.

18The divisions of the camp of Reuben went next, under their standard. Elizur son of Shedeur was in command. 19Shelumiel son of Zurishaddai was over the division of the tribe of Simeon, 20and Eliasaph son of Deuel was over the division of the tribe of Gad. 21Then the Kohathites set out, carrying the holy things. The tabernacle was to be set up before they arrived.

22The divisions of the camp of Ephraim went next, under their standard. Elishama son of Ammihud was in command. 23Gamaliel son of Pedahzur was over the division of the tribe of Manasseh, 24and Abidan son of Gideoni was over the division of the tribe of Benjamin.

25Finally, as the rear guard for all the units, the divisions of the camp of Dan set out under their standard. Ahiezer son of Ammishaddai was in command. 26Pagiel son of Okran was over the division of the tribe of Asher, 27and Ahira son of Enan was over the division of the tribe of Naphtali. 28This was the order of march for the Israelite divisions as they set out.

29Now Moses said to Hobab son of Reuel the Midianite, Moses' father-in-law, "We are setting out for the place about which the LORD said, 'I will give it to you.' Come with us and we will treat you well, for the LORD has promised good things to Israel."

30He answered, "No, I will not go; I am going back to my own land and my own people."

31But Moses said, "Please do not leave us. You know where we should camp in the wilderness, and you can be our eyes. 32If you come with us, we will share with you whatever good things the LORD gives us."

33So they set out from the mountain of the LORD and traveled for three days. The ark of the covenant of the LORD went before them during those three days to find them a place to rest. 34The cloud of the LORD was over them by day when they set out from the camp.

35Whenever the ark set out, Moses said,

"Rise up, LORD!
  May your enemies be scattered;
  may your foes flee before you."

36Whenever it came to rest, he said,

"Return, LORD,
  to the countless thousands of Israel."

Fire From the LORD

11 Now the people complained about their hardships in the hearing of the LORD, and when he heard them his anger was aroused. Then fire from the LORD burned among them and consumed some of the outskirts of the camp. 2When the people cried out to Moses, he prayed to the LORD and the fire died down. 3So that place was

called Taberah,[a] because fire from the LORD had burned among them.

Quail From the LORD

4The rabble with them began to crave other food, and again the Israelites started wailing and said, "If only we had meat to eat! 5We remember the fish we ate in Egypt at no cost—also the cucumbers, melons, leeks, onions and garlic. 6But now we have lost our appetite; we never see anything but this manna!"

7The manna was like coriander seed and looked like resin. 8The people went around gathering it, and then ground it in a hand mill or crushed it in a mortar. They cooked it in a pot or made it into loaves. And it tasted like something made with olive oil. 9When the dew settled on the camp at night, the manna also came down.

10Moses heard the people of every family wailing at the entrance to their tents. The LORD became exceedingly angry, and Moses was troubled. 11He asked the LORD, "Why have you brought this trouble on your servant? What have I done to displease you that you put the burden of all these people on me? 12Did I conceive all these people? Did I give them birth? Why do you tell me to carry them in my arms, as a nurse carries an infant, to the land you promised on oath to their ancestors? 13Where can I get meat for all these people? They keep wailing to me, 'Give us meat to eat!' 14I cannot carry all these people by myself; the burden is too heavy for me. 15If this is how you are going to treat me, please go ahead and kill me—if I have found favor in your eyes—and do not let me face my own ruin."

16The LORD said to Moses: "Bring me seventy of Israel's elders who are known to you as leaders and officials among the people. Have them come to the tent of meeting, that they may stand there with you. 17I will come down and speak with you there, and I will take some of the power of the Spirit that is on you and put it on them. They will share the burden of the people with you so that you will not have to carry it alone.

18"Tell the people: 'Consecrate yourselves in preparation for tomorrow, when you will eat meat. The LORD heard you when you wailed, "If only we had meat to eat! We were better off in Egypt!" Now the LORD will give you meat, and you will eat it. 19You will not eat it for just one day, or two days, or five, ten or twenty days, 20but for a whole month—until it comes out of your nostrils and you loathe it—because you have rejected the LORD, who is among you, and have wailed before him, saying, "Why did we ever leave Egypt?" ' "

21But Moses said, "Here I am among six hundred thousand men on foot, and you say, 'I will give them meat to eat for a whole month!' 22Would they have enough if flocks and herds were slaughtered for them? Would they have enough if all the fish in the sea were caught for them?"

23The LORD answered Moses, "Is the LORD's arm too short? Now you will see whether or not what I say will come true for you."

24So Moses went out and told the people what the LORD had said. He brought together seventy of their elders and had them stand around the tent. 25Then the LORD came down in the cloud and spoke with him, and he took some of the power of the Spirit that was on him and put it on the seventy elders. When the Spirit rested on them, they prophesied—but did not do so again.

26However, two men, whose names were Eldad and Medad, had remained in the camp. They were listed among the elders, but did not go out to the tent. Yet the Spirit also rested on them, and they prophesied in the camp. 27A young man ran and told Moses, "Eldad and Medad are prophesying in the camp."

28Joshua son of Nun, who had been Moses' aide since youth, spoke up and said, "Moses, my lord, stop them!"

29But Moses replied, "Are you jealous for my sake? I wish that all the LORD's people were prophets and that the LORD would put his Spirit on them!" 30Then Moses and the elders of Israel returned to the camp.

31Now a wind went out from the LORD and drove quail in from the sea. It scattered them up to two cubits[b] deep all around the camp, as far as a day's walk in any direction. 32All that day and night and all the next day the people went out and gathered quail. No

[a] 3 *Taberah* means *burning*. [b] 31 That is, about 3 feet or about 90 centimeters

one gathered less than ten homers.[a] Then
they spread them out all around the camp.
33 But while the meat was still between their
teeth and before it could be consumed, the
anger of the LORD burned against the peo-
ple, and he struck them with a severe plague.
34 Therefore the place was named Kibroth
Hattaavah,[b] because there they buried the
people who had craved other food.

35 From Kibroth Hattaavah the people
traveled to Hazeroth and stayed there.

Miriam and Aaron Oppose Moses

12 Miriam and Aaron began to talk
against Moses because of his Cush-
ite wife, for he had married a Cushite. 2 "Has
the LORD spoken only through Moses?" they
asked. "Hasn't he also spoken through us?"
And the LORD heard this.

3 (Now Moses was a very humble man,
more humble than anyone else on the face
of the earth.)

4 At once the LORD said to Moses, Aaron
and Miriam, "Come out to the tent of meet-
ing, all three of you." So the three of them
went out. 5 Then the LORD came down in a
pillar of cloud; he stood at the entrance to
the tent and summoned Aaron and Miriam.
When the two of them stepped forward, 6 he
said, "Listen to my words:

"When there is a prophet among you,
I, the LORD, reveal myself to them in visions,
I speak to them in dreams.
7 But this is not true of my servant Moses;
he is faithful in all my house.
8 With him I speak face to face,
clearly and not in riddles;
he sees the form of the LORD.
Why then were you not afraid
to speak against my servant Moses?"

9 The anger of the LORD burned against
them, and he left them.

10 When the cloud lifted from above the
tent, Miriam's skin was leprous[c]—it became
as white as snow. Aaron turned toward her
and saw that she had a defiling skin disease,
11 and he said to Moses, "Please, my lord, I
ask you not to hold against us the sin we have
so foolishly committed. 12 Do not let her be
like a stillborn infant coming from its moth-
er's womb with its flesh half eaten away."

13 So Moses cried out to the LORD, "Please,
God, heal her!"

14 The LORD replied to Moses, "If her fa-
ther had spit in her face, would she not have
been in disgrace for seven days? Confine her
outside the camp for seven days; after that
she can be brought back." 15 So Miriam was
confined outside the camp for seven days,
and the people did not move on till she was
brought back.

16 After that, the people left Hazeroth and
encamped in the Desert of Paran.

Exploring Canaan

13 The LORD said to Moses, 2 "Send some
men to explore the land of Canaan,
which I am giving to the Israelites. From
each ancestral tribe send one of its leaders."

3 So at the LORD's command Moses sent
them out from the Desert of Paran. All of
them were leaders of the Israelites. 4 These
are their names:

from the tribe of Reuben, Shammua son of Zakkur;
5 from the tribe of Simeon, Shaphat son of Hori;
6 from the tribe of Judah, Caleb son of Jephunneh;
7 from the tribe of Issachar, Igal son of Joseph;
8 from the tribe of Ephraim, Hoshea son of Nun;
9 from the tribe of Benjamin, Palti son of Raphu;
10 from the tribe of Zebulun, Gaddiel son of Sodi;
11 from the tribe of Manasseh (a tribe of Joseph), Gaddi son of Susi;
12 from the tribe of Dan, Ammiel son of Gemalli;
13 from the tribe of Asher, Sethur son of Michael;
14 from the tribe of Naphtali, Nahbi son of Vophsi;
15 from the tribe of Gad, Geuel son of Maki.

16 These are the names of the men Moses sent
to explore the land. (Moses gave Hoshea son
of Nun the name Joshua.)

17 When Moses sent them to explore Ca-
naan, he said, "Go up through the Negev and

[a] *32* That is, possibly about 1 3/4 tons or about 1.6 metric tons [b] *34* *Kibroth Hattaavah* means *graves of craving.* [c] *10* The Hebrew for *leprous* was used for various diseases affecting the skin.

on into the hill country. 18 See what the land
is like and whether the people who live there
are strong or weak, few or many. 19 What
kind of land do they live in? Is it good or bad?
What kind of towns do they live in? Are they
unwalled or fortified? 20 How is the soil? Is it
fertile or poor? Are there trees in it or not? Do
your best to bring back some of the fruit of
the land." (It was the season for the first ripe
grapes.)

21 So they went up and explored the land
from the Desert of Zin as far as Rehob, to-
ward Lebo Hamath. 22 They went up through
the Negev and came to Hebron, where Ahi-
man, Sheshai and Talmai, the descendants
of Anak, lived. (Hebron had been built sev-
en years before Zoan in Egypt.) 23 When they
reached the Valley of Eshkol,[a] they cut off
a branch bearing a single cluster of grapes.
Two of them carried it on a pole between
them, along with some pomegranates and
figs. 24 That place was called the Valley of
Eshkol because of the cluster of grapes the
Israelites cut off there. 25 At the end of forty
days they returned from exploring the land.

Report on the Exploration

26 They came back to Moses and Aaron and
the whole Israelite community at Kadesh in
the Desert of Paran. There they reported to
them and to the whole assembly and showed
them the fruit of the land. 27 They gave Mo-
ses this account: "We went into the land to
which you sent us, and it does flow with milk
and honey! Here is its fruit. 28 But the people
who live there are powerful, and the cities
are fortified and very large. We even saw de-
scendants of Anak there. 29 The Amalekites
live in the Negev; the Hittites, Jebusites and
Amorites live in the hill country; and the
Canaanites live near the sea and along the
Jordan."

30 Then Caleb silenced the people before
Moses and said, "We should go up and take
possession of the land, for we can certainly
do it."

31 But the men who had gone up with him
said, "We can't attack those people; they are
stronger than we are." 32 And they spread
among the Israelites a bad report about the
land they had explored. They said, "The land
we explored devours those living in it. All the
people we saw there are of great size. 33 We
saw the Nephilim there (the descendants of
Anak come from the Nephilim). We seemed
like grasshoppers in our own eyes, and we
looked the same to them."

The People Rebel

14 That night all the members of the
community raised their voices and
wept aloud. 2 All the Israelites grumbled
against Moses and Aaron, and the whole
assembly said to them, "If only we had died
in Egypt! Or in this wilderness! 3 Why is the
LORD bringing us to this land only to let us
fall by the sword? Our wives and children
will be taken as plunder. Wouldn't it be bet-
ter for us to go back to Egypt?" 4 And they
said to each other, "We should choose a lead-
er and go back to Egypt."

5 Then Moses and Aaron fell facedown in
front of the whole Israelite assembly gath-
ered there. 6 Joshua son of Nun and Caleb
son of Jephunneh, who were among those
who had explored the land, tore their clothes
7 and said to the entire Israelite assembly,
"The land we passed through and explored
is exceedingly good. 8 If the LORD is pleased
with us, he will lead us into that land, a land
flowing with milk and honey, and will give
it to us. 9 Only do not rebel against the LORD.
And do not be afraid of the people of the
land, because we will devour them. Their
protection is gone, but the LORD is with us.
Do not be afraid of them."

10 But the whole assembly talked about
stoning them. Then the glory of the LORD ap-
peared at the tent of meeting to all the Isra-
elites. 11 The LORD said to Moses, "How long
will these people treat me with contempt?
How long will they refuse to believe in me,
in spite of all the signs I have performed
among them? 12 I will strike them down with
a plague and destroy them, but I will make
you into a nation greater and stronger than
they."

13 Moses said to the LORD, "Then the
Egyptians will hear about it! By your power
you brought these people up from among
them. 14 And they will tell the inhabitants of
this land about it. They have already heard
that you, LORD, are with these people and
that you, LORD, have been seen face to face,
that your cloud stays over them, and that you
go before them in a pillar of cloud by day and

[a] 23 *Eshkol* means *cluster*; also in verse 24.

REVELATION SONG

Jennie Lee Riddle

Worthy is the Lamb who was slain
Holy, holy is he
Sing a new song to him who sits on
Heaven's Mercy Seat

Holy, Holy, Holy is the Lord, God Almighty
Who was and is and is to come
With all creation I sing
Praise to the King of Kings,
You are my everything. And I will adore you

Clothed in rainbows, of living color
Flashes of lightning, rolls of thunder
Blessing and honor, strength and glory and power be
To you, the only wise King

Filled with wonder, awestruck wonder
At the mention of your Name
Jesus, your Name is power, breath and living water
Such a marvelous mystery

THE INSPIRATION

The one who sat there had the appearance of jasper and ruby. A rainbow that shone like an emerald encircled the throne.

— Revelation 4:3

Read also: Ezekiel 1:26 – 28; Revelation 4:1 – 11

BEHIND THE SONG

The prophetic books of the Bible are an amazing source of worshipful texts. John, Ezekiel, Daniel and other prophets were given access to dreams and visions that most Christians never see. Their word pictures open our minds to the wonders of the supernatural and stir our hearts to join with the angels as they sing.

Jennie Lee Riddle is a wife, mother, teacher and worship leader. Although she had been privately writing songs for years, few people had heard them. One day, while caught up in the daily responsibilities of life (she says she had just changed her 20,446th diaper), she was moved to enter into worship at her home. Just before starting to make dinner for her family, she was inspired to sing a new song of worship.

"I put the baby down to play with his toys," she recalls, "picked up the guitar and began to play the four chords I had figured out how to play the day before. The Lord helped me paint what I was seeing through those passages — Revelation 4 and Ezekiel 1:26 – 28. 'Clothed in rainbows of living color, flashes of lightning, rolls of thunder ...' The melody stuck. It had the sound of heaven in it. The song wouldn't leave me, and I sang it for weeks."

Selah

The prophetic language of Revelation and Ezekiel can at times be difficult to understand. Though there are many schools of theological thought as to the symbolism and meaning of specific images, how do they make you feel? When you sing out in worship, do you ever imagine angels singing along? According to the Bible, someday that will happen.

A short time later, she introduced "Revelation Song" to her home church in Texas. The song took on a life of its own. It was recorded by new worship artist Kari Jobe and rocketed up the Christian radio charts as a hit for Phillips, Craig and Dean. This was the first song Riddle had composed, after learning only a handful of guitar chords, but it clearly struck a nerve within the church.

a pillar of fire by night. 15 If you put all these
people to death, leaving none alive, the na-
tions who have heard this report about you
will say, 16 'The LORD was not able to bring
these people into the land he promised them
on oath, so he slaughtered them in the wil-
derness.'

17 "Now may the Lord's strength be dis-
played, just as you have declared: 18 'The
LORD is slow to anger, abounding in love
and forgiving sin and rebellion. Yet he does
not leave the guilty unpunished; he punish-
es the children for the sin of the parents to
the third and fourth generation.' 19 In accor-
dance with your great love, forgive the sin
of these people, just as you have pardoned
them from the time they left Egypt until
now."

20 The LORD replied, "I have forgiven
them, as you asked. 21 Nevertheless, as sure-
ly as I live and as surely as the glory of the
LORD fills the whole earth, 22 not one of those
who saw my glory and the signs I performed
in Egypt and in the wilderness but who dis-
obeyed me and tested me ten times — 23 not
one of them will ever see the land I promised
on oath to their ancestors. No one who has
treated me with contempt will ever see it.
24 But because my servant Caleb has a differ-
ent spirit and follows me wholeheartedly, I
will bring him into the land he went to, and
his descendants will inherit it. 25 Since the
Amalekites and the Canaanites are living in
the valleys, turn back tomorrow and set out
toward the desert along the route to the Red
Sea.[a]"

26 The LORD said to Moses and Aaron:
27 "How long will this wicked community
grumble against me? I have heard the com-
plaints of these grumbling Israelites. 28 So
tell them, 'As surely as I live, declares the
LORD, I will do to you the very thing I heard
you say: 29 In this wilderness your bodies
will fall — every one of you twenty years old
or more who was counted in the census and
who has grumbled against me. 30 Not one of
you will enter the land I swore with uplift-
ed hand to make your home, except Caleb
son of Jephunneh and Joshua son of Nun.
31 As for your children that you said would
be taken as plunder, I will bring them in to
enjoy the land you have rejected. 32 But as
for you, your bodies will fall in this wilder-
ness. 33 Your children will be shepherds here
for forty years, suffering for your unfaith-
fulness, until the last of your bodies lies in
the wilderness. 34 For forty years — one year
for each of the forty days you explored the
land — you will suffer for your sins and know
what it is like to have me against you.' 35 I,
the LORD, have spoken, and I will surely do
these things to this whole wicked commu-
nity, which has banded together against me.
They will meet their end in this wilderness;
here they will die."

36 So the men Moses had sent to explore
the land, who returned and made the whole
community grumble against him by spread-
ing a bad report about it — 37 these men who
were responsible for spreading the bad re-
port about the land were struck down and
died of a plague before the LORD. 38 Of the
men who went to explore the land, only Josh-
ua son of Nun and Caleb son of Jephunneh
survived.

39 When Moses reported this to all the
Israelites, they mourned bitterly. 40 Early
the next morning they set out for the high-
est point in the hill country, saying, "Now
we are ready to go up to the land the LORD
promised. Surely we have sinned!"

41 But Moses said, "Why are you disobey-
ing the LORD's command? This will not suc-
ceed! 42 Do not go up, because the LORD is
not with you. You will be defeated by your
enemies, 43 for the Amalekites and the Ca-
naanites will face you there. Because you
have turned away from the LORD, he will not
be with you and you will fall by the sword."

44 Nevertheless, in their presumption they
went up toward the highest point in the hill
country, though neither Moses nor the ark of
the LORD's covenant moved from the camp.
45 Then the Amalekites and the Canaanites
who lived in that hill country came down
and attacked them and beat them down all
the way to Hormah.

Supplementary Offerings

15 The LORD said to Moses, 2 "Speak to
the Israelites and say to them: 'After
you enter the land I am giving you as a home
3 and you present to the LORD food offer-
ings from the herd or the flock, as an aroma

[a] 25 Or *the Sea of Reeds*

pleasing to the LORD—whether burnt offerings or sacrifices, for special vows or freewill offerings or festival offerings— 4then the person who brings an offering shall present to the LORD a grain offering of a tenth of an ephah[a] of the finest flour mixed with a quarter of a hin[b] of olive oil. 5With each lamb for the burnt offering or the sacrifice, prepare a quarter of a hin of wine as a drink offering.

6"'With a ram prepare a grain offering of two-tenths of an ephah[c] of the finest flour mixed with a third of a hin[d] of olive oil, 7and a third of a hin of wine as a drink offering. Offer it as an aroma pleasing to the LORD.

8"'When you prepare a young bull as a burnt offering or sacrifice, for a special vow or a fellowship offering to the LORD, 9bring with the bull a grain offering of three-tenths of an ephah[e] of the finest flour mixed with half a hin[f] of olive oil, 10and also bring half a hin of wine as a drink offering. This will be a food offering, an aroma pleasing to the LORD. 11Each bull or ram, each lamb or young goat, is to be prepared in this manner. 12Do this for each one, for as many as you prepare.

13"'Everyone who is native-born must do these things in this way when they present a food offering as an aroma pleasing to the LORD. 14For the generations to come, whenever a foreigner or anyone else living among you presents a food offering as an aroma pleasing to the LORD, they must do exactly as you do. 15The community is to have the same rules for you and for the foreigner residing among you; this is a lasting ordinance for the generations to come. You and the foreigner shall be the same before the LORD: 16The same laws and regulations will apply both to you and to the foreigner residing among you.'"

17The LORD said to Moses, 18"Speak to the Israelites and say to them: 'When you enter the land to which I am taking you 19and you eat the food of the land, present a portion as an offering to the LORD. 20Present a loaf from the first of your ground meal and present it as an offering from the threshing floor. 21Throughout the generations to come you are to give this offering to the LORD from the first of your ground meal.

Offerings for Unintentional Sins

22"'Now if you as a community unintentionally fail to keep any of these commands the LORD gave Moses— 23any of the LORD's commands to you through him, from the day the LORD gave them and continuing through the generations to come— 24and if this is done unintentionally without the community being aware of it, then the whole community is to offer a young bull for a burnt offering as an aroma pleasing to the LORD, along with its prescribed grain offering and drink offering, and a male goat for a sin offering.[g] 25The priest is to make atonement for the whole Israelite community, and they will be forgiven, for it was not intentional and they have presented to the LORD for their wrong a food offering and a sin offering. 26The whole Israelite community and the foreigners residing among them will be forgiven, because all the people were involved in the unintentional wrong.

27"'But if just one person sins unintentionally, that person must bring a year-old female goat for a sin offering. 28The priest is to make atonement before the LORD for the one who erred by sinning unintentionally, and when atonement has been made, that person will be forgiven. 29One and the same law applies to everyone who sins unintentionally, whether a native-born Israelite or a foreigner residing among you.

30"'But anyone who sins defiantly, whether native-born or foreigner, blasphemes the LORD and must be cut off from the people of Israel. 31Because they have despised the LORD's word and broken his commands, they must surely be cut off; their guilt remains on them.'"

The Sabbath-Breaker Put to Death

32While the Israelites were in the wilderness, a man was found gathering wood on the Sabbath day. 33Those who found him gathering wood brought him to Moses and Aaron and the whole assembly, 34and they kept him in custody, because it was not clear what should be done to him. 35Then the LORD said to Moses, "The man must die. The whole assembly must stone him outside the

[a] *4* That is, probably about 3 1/2 pounds or about 1.6 kilograms [b] *4* That is, about 1 quart or about 1 liter; also in verse 5 [c] *6* That is, probably about 7 pounds or about 3.2 kilograms [d] *6* That is, about 1 1/3 quarts or about 1.3 liters; also in verse 7 [e] *9* That is, probably about 11 pounds or about 5 kilograms [f] *9* That is, about 2 quarts or about 1.9 liters; also in verse 10 [g] *24* Or *purification offering*; also in verses 25 and 27

camp." 36So the assembly took him outside the camp and stoned him to death, as the LORD commanded Moses.

Tassels on Garments

37The LORD said to Moses, 38"Speak to the Israelites and say to them: 'Throughout the generations to come you are to make tassels on the corners of your garments, with a blue cord on each tassel. 39You will have these tassels to look at and so you will remember all the commands of the LORD, that you may obey them and not prostitute yourselves by chasing after the lusts of your own hearts and eyes. 40Then you will remember to obey all my commands and will be consecrated to your God. 41I am the LORD your God, who brought you out of Egypt to be your God. I am the LORD your God.' "

Korah, Dathan and Abiram

16 Korah son of Izhar, the son of Kohath, the son of Levi, and certain Reubenites—Dathan and Abiram, sons of Eliab, and On son of Peleth—became insolent[a] 2and rose up against Moses. With them were 250 Israelite men, well-known community leaders who had been appointed members of the council. 3They came as a group to oppose Moses and Aaron and said to them, "You have gone too far! The whole community is holy, every one of them, and the LORD is with them. Why then do you set yourselves above the LORD's assembly?"

4When Moses heard this, he fell facedown. 5Then he said to Korah and all his followers: "In the morning the LORD will show who belongs to him and who is holy, and he will have that person come near him. The man he chooses he will cause to come near him. 6You, Korah, and all your followers are to do this: Take censers 7and tomorrow put burning coals and incense in them before the LORD. The man the LORD chooses will be the one who is holy. You Levites have gone too far!"

8Moses also said to Korah, "Now listen, you Levites! 9Isn't it enough for you that the God of Israel has separated you from the rest of the Israelite community and brought you near himself to do the work at the LORD's tabernacle and to stand before the community and minister to them? 10He has brought you and all your fellow Levites near himself, but now you are trying to get the priesthood too. 11It is against the LORD that you and all your followers have banded together. Who is Aaron that you should grumble against him?"

12Then Moses summoned Dathan and Abiram, the sons of Eliab. But they said, "We will not come! 13Isn't it enough that you have brought us up out of a land flowing with milk and honey to kill us in the wilderness? And now you also want to lord it over us! 14Moreover, you haven't brought us into a land flowing with milk and honey or given us an inheritance of fields and vineyards. Do you want to treat these men like slaves[b]? No, we will not come!"

15Then Moses became very angry and said to the LORD, "Do not accept their offering. I have not taken so much as a donkey from them, nor have I wronged any of them."

16Moses said to Korah, "You and all your followers are to appear before the LORD tomorrow—you and they and Aaron. 17Each man is to take his censer and put incense in it—250 censers in all—and present it before the LORD. You and Aaron are to present your censers also." 18So each of them took his censer, put burning coals and incense in it, and stood with Moses and Aaron at the entrance to the tent of meeting. 19When Korah had gathered all his followers in opposition to them at the entrance to the tent of meeting, the glory of the LORD appeared to the entire assembly. 20The LORD said to Moses and Aaron, 21"Separate yourselves from this assembly so I can put an end to them at once."

22But Moses and Aaron fell facedown and cried out, "O God, the God who gives breath to all living things, will you be angry with the entire assembly when only one man sins?"

23Then the LORD said to Moses, 24"Say to the assembly, 'Move away from the tents of Korah, Dathan and Abiram.' "

25Moses got up and went to Dathan and Abiram, and the elders of Israel followed him. 26He warned the assembly, "Move back from the tents of these wicked men! Do not touch anything belonging to them, or you will be swept away because of all their sins."

[a] *1* Or *Peleth—took men* [b] *14* Or *to deceive these men*; Hebrew *Will you gouge out the eyes of these men*

[27]So they moved away from the tents of Korah, Dathan and Abiram. Dathan and Abiram had come out and were standing with their wives, children and little ones at the entrances to their tents.

[28]Then Moses said, "This is how you will know that the LORD has sent me to do all these things and that it was not my idea: [29]If these men die a natural death and suffer the fate of all mankind, then the LORD has not sent me. [30]But if the LORD brings about something totally new, and the earth opens its mouth and swallows them, with everything that belongs to them, and they go down alive into the realm of the dead, then you will know that these men have treated the LORD with contempt."

[31]As soon as he finished saying all this, the ground under them split apart [32]and the earth opened its mouth and swallowed them and their households, and all those associated with Korah, together with their possessions. [33]They went down alive into the realm of the dead, with everything they owned; the earth closed over them, and they perished and were gone from the community. [34]At their cries, all the Israelites around them fled, shouting, "The earth is going to swallow us too!"

[35]And fire came out from the LORD and consumed the 250 men who were offering the incense.

[36]The LORD said to Moses, [37]"Tell Eleazar son of Aaron, the priest, to remove the censers from the charred remains and scatter the coals some distance away, for the censers are holy— [38]the censers of the men who sinned at the cost of their lives. Hammer the censers into sheets to overlay the altar, for they were presented before the LORD and have become holy. Let them be a sign to the Israelites."

[39]So Eleazar the priest collected the bronze censers brought by those who had been burned to death, and he had them hammered out to overlay the altar, [40]as the LORD directed him through Moses. This was to remind the Israelites that no one except a descendant of Aaron should come to burn incense before the LORD, or he would become like Korah and his followers.

[41]The next day the whole Israelite community grumbled against Moses and Aaron. "You have killed the LORD's people," they said.

[42]But when the assembly gathered in opposition to Moses and Aaron and turned toward the tent of meeting, suddenly the cloud covered it and the glory of the LORD appeared. [43]Then Moses and Aaron went to the front of the tent of meeting, [44]and the LORD said to Moses, [45]"Get away from this assembly so I can put an end to them at once." And they fell facedown.

[46]Then Moses said to Aaron, "Take your censer and put incense in it, along with burning coals from the altar, and hurry to the assembly to make atonement for them. Wrath has come out from the LORD; the plague has started." [47]So Aaron did as Moses said, and ran into the midst of the assembly. The plague had already started among the people, but Aaron offered the incense and made atonement for them. [48]He stood between the living and the dead, and the plague stopped. [49]But 14,700 people died from the plague, in addition to those who had died because of Korah. [50]Then Aaron returned to Moses at the entrance to the tent of meeting, for the plague had stopped.[a]

The Budding of Aaron's Staff

17[b] The LORD said to Moses, [2]"Speak to the Israelites and get twelve staffs from them, one from the leader of each of their ancestral tribes. Write the name of each man on his staff. [3]On the staff of Levi write Aaron's name, for there must be one staff for the head of each ancestral tribe. [4]Place them in the tent of meeting in front of the ark of the covenant law, where I meet with you. [5]The staff belonging to the man I choose will sprout, and I will rid myself of this constant grumbling against you by the Israelites."

[6]So Moses spoke to the Israelites, and their leaders gave him twelve staffs, one for the leader of each of their ancestral tribes, and Aaron's staff was among them. [7]Moses placed the staffs before the LORD in the tent of the covenant law.

[8]The next day Moses entered the tent and saw that Aaron's staff, which represented the tribe of Levi, had not only sprouted but had budded, blossomed and produced almonds. [9]Then Moses brought out all the staffs from

[a] *50* In Hebrew texts 16:36-50 is numbered 17:1-15.

[b] In Hebrew texts 17:1-13 is numbered 17:16-28.

the LORD's presence to all the Israelites.
They looked at them, and each of the leaders
took his own staff.
10 The LORD said to Moses, "Put back Aar-
on's staff in front of the ark of the covenant
law, to be kept as a sign to the rebellious.
This will put an end to their grumbling
against me, so that they will not die." 11 Mo-
ses did just as the LORD commanded him.
12 The Israelites said to Moses, "We will
die! We are lost, we are all lost! 13 Anyone who
even comes near the tabernacle of the LORD
will die. Are we all going to die?"

Duties of Priests and Levites

18 The LORD said to Aaron, "You, your
sons and your family are to bear the
responsibility for offenses connected with
the sanctuary, and you and your sons alone
are to bear the responsibility for offenses
connected with the priesthood. 2 Bring your
fellow Levites from your ancestral tribe to
join you and assist you when you and your
sons minister before the tent of the covenant
law. 3 They are to be responsible to you and
are to perform all the duties of the tent, but
they must not go near the furnishings of the
sanctuary or the altar. Otherwise both they
and you will die. 4 They are to join you and be
responsible for the care of the tent of meet-
ing — all the work at the tent — and no one
else may come near where you are.
5 "You are to be responsible for the care
of the sanctuary and the altar, so that my
wrath will not fall on the Israelites again.
6 I myself have selected your fellow Levites
from among the Israelites as a gift to you,
dedicated to the LORD to do the work at the
tent of meeting. 7 But only you and your sons
may serve as priests in connection with ev-
erything at the altar and inside the curtain.
I am giving you the service of the priesthood
as a gift. Anyone else who comes near the
sanctuary is to be put to death."

Offerings for Priests and Levites

8 Then the LORD said to Aaron, "I myself
have put you in charge of the offerings pre-
sented to me; all the holy offerings the Is-
raelites give me I give to you and your sons
as your portion, your perpetual share. 9 You
are to have the part of the most holy offer-
ings that is kept from the fire. From all the
gifts they bring me as most holy offerings,
whether grain or sin[a] or guilt offerings, that
part belongs to you and your sons. 10 Eat it as
something most holy; every male shall eat it.
You must regard it as holy.
11 "This also is yours: whatever is set aside
from the gifts of all the wave offerings of the
Israelites. I give this to you and your sons
and daughters as your perpetual share. Ev-
eryone in your household who is ceremoni-
ally clean may eat it.
12 "I give you all the finest olive oil and all
the finest new wine and grain they give the
LORD as the firstfruits of their harvest. 13 All
the land's firstfruits that they bring to the
LORD will be yours. Everyone in your house-
hold who is ceremonially clean may eat it.
14 "Everything in Israel that is devoted[b] to
the LORD is yours. 15 The first offspring of ev-
ery womb, both human and animal, that is
offered to the LORD is yours. But you must re-
deem every firstborn son and every firstborn
male of unclean animals. 16 When they are a
month old, you must redeem them at the re-
demption price set at five shekels[c] of silver,
according to the sanctuary shekel, which
weighs twenty gerahs.
17 "But you must not redeem the firstborn
of a cow, a sheep or a goat; they are holy.
Splash their blood against the altar and burn
their fat as a food offering, an aroma pleas-
ing to the LORD. 18 Their meat is to be yours,
just as the breast of the wave offering and the
right thigh are yours. 19 Whatever is set aside
from the holy offerings the Israelites present
to the LORD I give to you and your sons and
daughters as your perpetual share. It is an
everlasting covenant of salt before the LORD
for both you and your offspring."
20 The LORD said to Aaron, "You will have
no inheritance in their land, nor will you
have any share among them; I am your share
and your inheritance among the Israelites.
21 "I give to the Levites all the tithes in Isra-
el as their inheritance in return for the work
they do while serving at the tent of meeting.
22 From now on the Israelites must not go
near the tent of meeting, or they will bear the
consequences of their sin and will die. 23 It
is the Levites who are to do the work at the
tent of meeting and bear the responsibility

[a] 9 Or *purification* [b] 14 The Hebrew term refers to the irrevocable giving over of things or persons to the LORD. [c] 16 That is, about 2 ounces or about 58 grams

for any offenses they commit against it. This is a lasting ordinance for the generations to come. They will receive no inheritance among the Israelites. [24]Instead, I give to the Levites as their inheritance the tithes that the Israelites present as an offering to the LORD. That is why I said concerning them: 'They will have no inheritance among the Israelites.' "

[25]The LORD said to Moses, [26]"Speak to the Levites and say to them: 'When you receive from the Israelites the tithe I give you as your inheritance, you must present a tenth of that tithe as the LORD's offering. [27]Your offering will be reckoned to you as grain from the threshing floor or juice from the winepress. [28]In this way you also will present an offering to the LORD from all the tithes you receive from the Israelites. From these tithes you must give the LORD's portion to Aaron the priest. [29]You must present as the LORD's portion the best and holiest part of everything given to you.'

[30]"Say to the Levites: 'When you present the best part, it will be reckoned to you as the product of the threshing floor or the winepress. [31]You and your households may eat the rest of it anywhere, for it is your wages for your work at the tent of meeting. [32]By presenting the best part of it you will not be guilty in this matter; then you will not defile the holy offerings of the Israelites, and you will not die.' "

The Water of Cleansing

19 The LORD said to Moses and Aaron: [2]"This is a requirement of the law that the LORD has commanded: Tell the Israelites to bring you a red heifer without defect or blemish and that has never been under a yoke. [3]Give it to Eleazar the priest; it is to be taken outside the camp and slaughtered in his presence. [4]Then Eleazar the priest is to take some of its blood on his finger and sprinkle it seven times toward the front of the tent of meeting. [5]While he watches, the heifer is to be burned — its hide, flesh, blood and intestines. [6]The priest is to take some cedar wood, hyssop and scarlet wool and throw them onto the burning heifer. [7]After that, the priest must wash his clothes and bathe himself with water. He may then come into the camp, but he will be ceremonially unclean till evening. [8]The man who burns it must also wash his clothes and bathe with water, and he too will be unclean till evening.

[9]"A man who is clean shall gather up the ashes of the heifer and put them in a ceremonially clean place outside the camp. They are to be kept by the Israelite community for use in the water of cleansing; it is for purification from sin. [10]The man who gathers up the ashes of the heifer must also wash his clothes, and he too will be unclean till evening. This will be a lasting ordinance both for the Israelites and for the foreigners residing among them.

[11]"Whoever touches a human corpse will be unclean for seven days. [12]They must purify themselves with the water on the third day and on the seventh day; then they will be clean. But if they do not purify themselves on the third and seventh days, they will not be clean. [13]If they fail to purify themselves after touching a human corpse, they defile the LORD's tabernacle. They must be cut off from Israel. Because the water of cleansing has not been sprinkled on them, they are unclean; their uncleanness remains on them.

[14]"This is the law that applies when a person dies in a tent: Anyone who enters the tent and anyone who is in it will be unclean for seven days, [15]and every open container without a lid fastened on it will be unclean.

[16]"Anyone out in the open who touches someone who has been killed with a sword or someone who has died a natural death, or anyone who touches a human bone or a grave, will be unclean for seven days.

[17]"For the unclean person, put some ashes from the burned purification offering into a jar and pour fresh water over them. [18]Then a man who is ceremonially clean is to take some hyssop, dip it in the water and sprinkle the tent and all the furnishings and the people who were there. He must also sprinkle anyone who has touched a human bone or a grave or anyone who has been killed or anyone who has died a natural death. [19]The man who is clean is to sprinkle those who are unclean on the third and seventh days, and on the seventh day he is to purify them. Those who are being cleansed must wash their clothes and bathe with water, and that evening they will be clean. [20]But if those who are unclean do not purify themselves, they must be cut off from the community,

because they have defiled the sanctuary of the LORD. The water of cleansing has not been sprinkled on them, and they are unclean. [21]This is a lasting ordinance for them.

"The man who sprinkles the water of cleansing must also wash his clothes, and anyone who touches the water of cleansing will be unclean till evening. [22]Anything that an unclean person touches becomes unclean, and anyone who touches it becomes unclean till evening."

Water From the Rock

20 In the first month the whole Israelite community arrived at the Desert of Zin, and they stayed at Kadesh. There Miriam died and was buried.

[2]Now there was no water for the community, and the people gathered in opposition to Moses and Aaron. [3]They quarreled with Moses and said, "If only we had died when our brothers fell dead before the LORD! [4]Why did you bring the LORD's community into this wilderness, that we and our livestock should die here? [5]Why did you bring us up out of Egypt to this terrible place? It has no grain or figs, grapevines or pomegranates. And there is no water to drink!"

[6]Moses and Aaron went from the assembly to the entrance to the tent of meeting and fell facedown, and the glory of the LORD appeared to them. [7]The LORD said to Moses, [8]"Take the staff, and you and your brother Aaron gather the assembly together. Speak to that rock before their eyes and it will pour out its water. You will bring water out of the rock for the community so they and their livestock can drink."

[9]So Moses took the staff from the LORD's presence, just as he commanded him. [10]He and Aaron gathered the assembly together in front of the rock and Moses said to them, "Listen, you rebels, must we bring you water out of this rock?" [11]Then Moses raised his arm and struck the rock twice with his staff. Water gushed out, and the community and their livestock drank.

[12]But the LORD said to Moses and Aaron, "Because you did not trust in me enough to honor me as holy in the sight of the Israelites, you will not bring this community into the land I give them."

[13]These were the waters of Meribah,[a] where the Israelites quarreled with the LORD and where he was proved holy among them.

Edom Denies Israel Passage

[14]Moses sent messengers from Kadesh to the king of Edom, saying:

> "This is what your brother Israel says: You know about all the hardships that have come on us. [15]Our ancestors went down into Egypt, and we lived there many years. The Egyptians mistreated us and our ancestors, [16]but when we cried out to the LORD, he heard our cry and sent an angel and brought us out of Egypt.
>
> "Now we are here at Kadesh, a town on the edge of your territory. [17]Please let us pass through your country. We will not go through any field or vineyard, or drink water from any well. We will travel along the King's Highway and not turn to the right or to the left until we have passed through your territory."

[18]But Edom answered:

> "You may not pass through here; if you try, we will march out and attack you with the sword."

[19]The Israelites replied:

> "We will go along the main road, and if we or our livestock drink any of your water, we will pay for it. We only want to pass through on foot—nothing else."

[20]Again they answered:

> "You may not pass through."

Then Edom came out against them with a large and powerful army. [21]Since Edom refused to let them go through their territory, Israel turned away from them.

The Death of Aaron

[22]The whole Israelite community set out from Kadesh and came to Mount Hor. [23]At Mount Hor, near the border of Edom, the LORD said to Moses and Aaron, [24]"Aaron will be gathered to his people. He will not enter the land I give the Israelites, because both

[a] 13 *Meribah* means *quarreling.*

of you rebelled against my command at the
waters of Meribah. 25 Get Aaron and his son
Eleazar and take them up Mount Hor. 26 Re-
move Aaron's garments and put them on his
son Eleazar, for Aaron will be gathered to his
people; he will die there."
27 Moses did as the LORD commanded:
They went up Mount Hor in the sight of the
whole community. 28 Moses removed Aaron's
garments and put them on his son Eleazar.
And Aaron died there on top of the moun-
tain. Then Moses and Eleazar came down
from the mountain, 29 and when the whole
community learned that Aaron had died, all
the Israelites mourned for him thirty days.

Arad Destroyed

21 When the Canaanite king of Arad,
who lived in the Negev, heard that Is-
rael was coming along the road to Atharim,
he attacked the Israelites and captured some
of them. 2 Then Israel made this vow to the
LORD: "If you will deliver these people into
our hands, we will totally destroy[a] their cit-
ies." 3 The LORD listened to Israel's plea and
gave the Canaanites over to them. They
completely destroyed them and their towns;
so the place was named Hormah.[b]

The Bronze Snake

4 They traveled from Mount Hor along the
route to the Red Sea,[c] to go around Edom.
But the people grew impatient on the way;
5 they spoke against God and against Moses,
and said, "Why have you brought us up out
of Egypt to die in the wilderness? There is no
bread! There is no water! And we detest this
miserable food!"
6 Then the LORD sent venomous snakes
among them; they bit the people and many
Israelites died. 7 The people came to Moses
and said, "We sinned when we spoke against
the LORD and against you. Pray that the
LORD will take the snakes away from us." So
Moses prayed for the people.
8 The LORD said to Moses, "Make a snake
and put it up on a pole; anyone who is bit-
ten can look at it and live." 9 So Moses made
a bronze snake and put it up on a pole. Then
when anyone was bitten by a snake and
looked at the bronze snake, they lived.

The Journey to Moab

10 The Israelites moved on and camped at
Oboth. 11 Then they set out from Oboth and
camped in Iye Abarim, in the wilderness
that faces Moab toward the sunrise. 12 From
there they moved on and camped in the Ze-
red Valley. 13 They set out from there and
camped alongside the Arnon, which is in the
wilderness extending into Amorite territory.
The Arnon is the border of Moab, between
Moab and the Amorites. 14 That is why the
Book of the Wars of the LORD says:

"... Zahab[d] in Suphah and the ravines,
the Arnon 15 and[e] the slopes of the
ravines
that lead to the settlement of Ar
and lie along the border of Moab."

16 From there they continued on to Beer, the
well where the LORD said to Moses, "Gath-
er the people together and I will give them
water."
17 Then Israel sang this song:

"Spring up, O well!
Sing about it,
18 about the well that the princes dug,
that the nobles of the people sank—
the nobles with scepters and staffs."

Then they went from the wilderness to Mat-
tanah, 19 from Mattanah to Nahaliel, from
Nahaliel to Bamoth, 20 and from Bamoth to
the valley in Moab where the top of Pisgah
overlooks the wasteland.

Defeat of Sihon and Og

21 Israel sent messengers to say to Sihon
king of the Amorites:

22 "Let us pass through your country.
We will not turn aside into any field or
vineyard, or drink water from any well.
We will travel along the King's Highway
until we have passed through your ter-
ritory."

23 But Sihon would not let Israel pass
through his territory. He mustered his en-
tire army and marched out into the wilder-
ness against Israel. When he reached Jahaz,
he fought with Israel. 24 Israel, however, put
him to the sword and took over his land from

[a] *2* The Hebrew term refers to the irrevocable giving over of things or persons to the LORD, often by totally destroying them; also in verse 3. [b] *3* *Hormah* means *destruction.* [c] *4* Or *the Sea of Reeds*
[d] *14* Septuagint; Hebrew *Waheb* [e] *14,15* Or *"I have been given from Suphah and the ravines / of the Arnon 15 to*

the Arnon to the Jabbok, but only as far as
the Ammonites, because their border was
fortified. 25Israel captured all the cities of
the Amorites and occupied them, includ-
ing Heshbon and all its surrounding settle-
ments. 26Heshbon was the city of Sihon king
of the Amorites, who had fought against the
former king of Moab and had taken from
him all his land as far as the Arnon.

27That is why the poets say:

"Come to Heshbon and let it be rebuilt;
 let Sihon's city be restored.

28"Fire went out from Heshbon,
 a blaze from the city of Sihon.
It consumed Ar of Moab,
 the citizens of Arnon's heights.
29Woe to you, Moab!
 You are destroyed, people of Chemosh!
He has given up his sons as fugitives
 and his daughters as captives
 to Sihon king of the Amorites.

30"But we have overthrown them;
 Heshbon's dominion has been
 destroyed all the way to Dibon.
We have demolished them as far as
 Nophah,
 which extends to Medeba."

31So Israel settled in the land of the Am-
orites.

32After Moses had sent spies to Jazer, the
Israelites captured its surrounding settle-
ments and drove out the Amorites who were
there. 33Then they turned and went up along
the road toward Bashan, and Og king of Ba-
shan and his whole army marched out to
meet them in battle at Edrei.

34The LORD said to Moses, "Do not be
afraid of him, for I have delivered him into
your hands, along with his whole army and
his land. Do to him what you did to Sihon king
of the Amorites, who reigned in Heshbon."

35So they struck him down, together with
his sons and his whole army, leaving them
no survivors. And they took possession of
his land.

Balak Summons Balaam

22 Then the Israelites traveled to the
plains of Moab and camped along
the Jordan across from Jericho.

2Now Balak son of Zippor saw all that Isra-
el had done to the Amorites, 3and Moab was
terrified because there were so many people.
Indeed, Moab was filled with dread because
of the Israelites.

4The Moabites said to the elders of Midi-
an, "This horde is going to lick up everything
around us, as an ox licks up the grass of the
field."

So Balak son of Zippor, who was king of
Moab at that time, 5sent messengers to sum-
mon Balaam son of Beor, who was at Pethor,
near the Euphrates River, in his native land.
Balak said:

"A people has come out of Egypt;
they cover the face of the land and have
settled next to me. 6Now come and put
a curse on these people, because they
are too powerful for me. Perhaps then
I will be able to defeat them and drive
them out of the land. For I know that
whoever you bless is blessed, and who-
ever you curse is cursed."

7The elders of Moab and Midian left, tak-
ing with them the fee for divination. When
they came to Balaam, they told him what Ba-
lak had said.

8"Spend the night here," Balaam said to
them, "and I will report back to you with the
answer the LORD gives me." So the Moabite
officials stayed with him.

9God came to Balaam and asked, "Who
are these men with you?"

10Balaam said to God, "Balak son of Zip-
por, king of Moab, sent me this message: 11'A
people that has come out of Egypt covers the
face of the land. Now come and put a curse
on them for me. Perhaps then I will be able to
fight them and drive them away.'"

12But God said to Balaam, "Do not go with
them. You must not put a curse on those peo-
ple, because they are blessed."

13The next morning Balaam got up and
said to Balak's officials, "Go back to your
own country, for the LORD has refused to let
me go with you."

14So the Moabite officials returned to
Balak and said, "Balaam refused to come
with us."

15Then Balak sent other officials, more
numerous and more distinguished than the
first. 16They came to Balaam and said:

"This is what Balak son of Zippor
says: Do not let anything keep you from
coming to me, 17because I will reward
you handsomely and do whatever you

say. Come and put a curse on these people for me."

18 But Balaam answered them, "Even if Balak gave me all the silver and gold in his palace, I could not do anything great or small to go beyond the command of the LORD my God. 19 Now spend the night here so that I can find out what else the LORD will tell me."

20 That night God came to Balaam and said, "Since these men have come to summon you, go with them, but do only what I tell you."

Balaam's Donkey

21 Balaam got up in the morning, saddled his donkey and went with the Moabite officials. 22 But God was very angry when he went, and the angel of the LORD stood in the road to oppose him. Balaam was riding on his donkey, and his two servants were with him. 23 When the donkey saw the angel of the LORD standing in the road with a drawn sword in his hand, it turned off the road into a field. Balaam beat it to get it back on the road.

24 Then the angel of the LORD stood in a narrow path through the vineyards, with walls on both sides. 25 When the donkey saw the angel of the LORD, it pressed close to the wall, crushing Balaam's foot against it. So he beat the donkey again.

26 Then the angel of the LORD moved on ahead and stood in a narrow place where there was no room to turn, either to the right or to the left. 27 When the donkey saw the angel of the LORD, it lay down under Balaam, and he was angry and beat it with his staff. 28 Then the LORD opened the donkey's mouth, and it said to Balaam, "What have I done to you to make you beat me these three times?"

29 Balaam answered the donkey, "You have made a fool of me! If only I had a sword in my hand, I would kill you right now."

30 The donkey said to Balaam, "Am I not your own donkey, which you have always ridden, to this day? Have I been in the habit of doing this to you?"

"No," he said.

31 Then the LORD opened Balaam's eyes, and he saw the angel of the LORD standing in the road with his sword drawn. So he bowed low and fell facedown.

32 The angel of the LORD asked him, "Why have you beaten your donkey these three times? I have come here to oppose you because your path is a reckless one before me.[a] 33 The donkey saw me and turned away from me these three times. If it had not turned away, I would certainly have killed you by now, but I would have spared it."

34 Balaam said to the angel of the LORD, "I have sinned. I did not realize you were standing in the road to oppose me. Now if you are displeased, I will go back."

35 The angel of the LORD said to Balaam, "Go with the men, but speak only what I tell you." So Balaam went with Balak's officials.

36 When Balak heard that Balaam was coming, he went out to meet him at the Moabite town on the Arnon border, at the edge of his territory. 37 Balak said to Balaam, "Did I not send you an urgent summons? Why didn't you come to me? Am I really not able to reward you?"

38 "Well, I have come to you now," Balaam replied. "But I can't say whatever I please. I must speak only what God puts in my mouth."

39 Then Balaam went with Balak to Kiriath Huzoth. 40 Balak sacrificed cattle and sheep, and gave some to Balaam and the officials who were with him. 41 The next morning Balak took Balaam up to Bamoth Baal, and from there he could see the outskirts of the Israelite camp.

Balaam's First Message

23 Balaam said, "Build me seven altars here, and prepare seven bulls and seven rams for me." 2 Balak did as Balaam said, and the two of them offered a bull and a ram on each altar.

3 Then Balaam said to Balak, "Stay here beside your offering while I go aside. Perhaps the LORD will come to meet with me. Whatever he reveals to me I will tell you." Then he went off to a barren height.

4 God met with him, and Balaam said, "I have prepared seven altars, and on each altar I have offered a bull and a ram."

5 The LORD put a word in Balaam's mouth and said, "Go back to Balak and give him this word."

[a] 32 The meaning of the Hebrew for this clause is uncertain.

[6]So he went back to him and found him
standing beside his offering, with all the
Moabite officials. [7]Then Balaam spoke his
message:

"Balak brought me from Aram,
the king of Moab from the eastern
mountains.
'Come,' he said, 'curse Jacob for me;
come, denounce Israel.'
[8]How can I curse
those whom God has not cursed?
How can I denounce
those whom the LORD has not
denounced?
[9]From the rocky peaks I see them,
from the heights I view them.
I see a people who live apart
and do not consider themselves one of
the nations.
[10]Who can count the dust of Jacob
or number even a fourth of Israel?
Let me die the death of the righteous,
and may my final end be like theirs!"

[11]Balak said to Balaam, "What have you
done to me? I brought you to curse my ene-
mies, but you have done nothing but bless
them!"
[12]He answered, "Must I not speak what
the LORD puts in my mouth?"

Balaam's Second Message

[13]Then Balak said to him, "Come with me
to another place where you can see them;
you will not see them all but only the out-
skirts of their camp. And from there, curse
them for me." [14]So he took him to the field
of Zophim on the top of Pisgah, and there
he built seven altars and offered a bull and a
ram on each altar.
[15]Balaam said to Balak, "Stay here beside
your offering while I meet with him over
there."
[16]The LORD met with Balaam and put a
word in his mouth and said, "Go back to Ba-
lak and give him this word."
[17]So he went to him and found him stand-
ing beside his offering, with the Moabite of-
ficials. Balak asked him, "What did the LORD
say?"
[18]Then he spoke his message:

"Arise, Balak, and listen;
hear me, son of Zippor.
[19]God is not human, that he should lie,
not a human being, that he should
change his mind.
Does he speak and then not act?
Does he promise and not fulfill?
[20]I have received a command to bless;
he has blessed, and I cannot
change it.
[21]"No misfortune is seen in Jacob,
no misery observed[a] in Israel.
The LORD their God is with them;
the shout of the King is among them.
[22]God brought them out of Egypt;
they have the strength of a wild ox.
[23]There is no divination against[b] Jacob,
no evil omens against[b] Israel.
It will now be said of Jacob
and of Israel, 'See what God has
done!'
[24]The people rise like a lioness;
they rouse themselves like a lion
that does not rest till it devours its prey
and drinks the blood of its victims."

[25]Then Balak said to Balaam, "Neither
curse them at all nor bless them at all!"
[26]Balaam answered, "Did I not tell you I
must do whatever the LORD says?"

Balaam's Third Message

[27]Then Balak said to Balaam, "Come, let
me take you to another place. Perhaps it will
please God to let you curse them for me from
there." [28]And Balak took Balaam to the top of
Peor, overlooking the wasteland.
[29]Balaam said, "Build me seven altars
here, and prepare seven bulls and seven
rams for me." [30]Balak did as Balaam had
said, and offered a bull and a ram on each
altar.

24 Now when Balaam saw that it
pleased the LORD to bless Israel, he
did not resort to divination as at other times,
but turned his face toward the wilderness.
[2]When Balaam looked out and saw Israel en-
camped tribe by tribe, the Spirit of God came
on him [3]and he spoke his message:

"The prophecy of Balaam son of Beor,
the prophecy of one whose eye sees
clearly,
[4]the prophecy of one who hears the words
of God,

[a] 21 Or *He has not looked on Jacob's offenses / or on the wrongs found* [b] 23 Or *in*

who sees a vision from the Almighty,[a]
who falls prostrate, and whose eyes are opened:

5 "How beautiful are your tents, Jacob,
your dwelling places, Israel!
6 "Like valleys they spread out,
like gardens beside a river,
like aloes planted by the LORD,
like cedars beside the waters.
7 Water will flow from their buckets;
their seed will have abundant water.

"Their king will be greater than Agag;
their kingdom will be exalted.
8 "God brought them out of Egypt;
they have the strength of a wild ox.
They devour hostile nations
and break their bones in pieces;
with their arrows they pierce them.
9 Like a lion they crouch and lie down,
like a lioness — who dares to rouse them?

"May those who bless you be blessed
and those who curse you be cursed!"

10 Then Balak's anger burned against Ba-
laam. He struck his hands together and said
to him, "I summoned you to curse my ene-
mies, but you have blessed them these three
times. 11 Now leave at once and go home! I
said I would reward you handsomely, but the
LORD has kept you from being rewarded."
12 Balaam answered Balak, "Did I not tell
the messengers you sent me, 13 'Even if Balak
gave me all the silver and gold in his palace,
I could not do anything of my own accord,
good or bad, to go beyond the command of
the LORD — and I must say only what the
LORD says'? 14 Now I am going back to my
people, but come, let me warn you of what
this people will do to your people in days to
come."

Balaam's Fourth Message

15 Then he spoke his message:

"The prophecy of Balaam son of Beor,
the prophecy of one whose eye sees clearly,
16 the prophecy of one who hears the words of God,
who has knowledge from the Most High,
who sees a vision from the Almighty,
who falls prostrate, and whose eyes are opened:

17 "I see him, but not now;
I behold him, but not near.
A star will come out of Jacob;
a scepter will rise out of Israel.
He will crush the foreheads of Moab,
the skulls[b] of[c] all the people of Sheth.[d]
18 Edom will be conquered;
Seir, his enemy, will be conquered,
but Israel will grow strong.
19 A ruler will come out of Jacob
and destroy the survivors of the city."

Balaam's Fifth Message

20 Then Balaam saw Amalek and spoke his
message:

"Amalek was first among the nations,
but their end will be utter destruction."

Balaam's Sixth Message

21 Then he saw the Kenites and spoke his
message:

"Your dwelling place is secure,
your nest is set in a rock;
22 yet you Kenites will be destroyed
when Ashur takes you captive."

Balaam's Seventh Message

23 Then he spoke his message:

"Alas! Who can live when God does this?[e]
24 Ships will come from the shores of Cyprus;
they will subdue Ashur and Eber,
but they too will come to ruin."

25 Then Balaam got up and returned
home, and Balak went his own way.

Moab Seduces Israel

25 While Israel was staying in Shittim,
the men began to indulge in sexual

[a] 4 Hebrew *Shaddai*; also in verse 16 [b] 17 Samaritan Pentateuch (see also Jer. 48:45); the meaning of the word in the Masoretic Text is uncertain. [c] 17 Or possibly *Moab, / batter* [d] 17 Or *all the noisy boasters* [e] 23 Masoretic Text; with a different word division of the Hebrew *The people from the islands will gather from the north.*

immorality with Moabite women, 2who in-
vited them to the sacrifices to their gods. The
people ate the sacrificial meal and bowed
down before these gods. 3So Israel yoked
themselves to the Baal of Peor. And the
LORD's anger burned against them.
4The LORD said to Moses, "Take all the
leaders of these people, kill them and expose
them in broad daylight before the LORD, so
that the LORD's fierce anger may turn away
from Israel."
5So Moses said to Israel's judges, "Each
of you must put to death those of your peo-
ple who have yoked themselves to the Baal
of Peor."
6Then an Israelite man brought into the
camp a Midianite woman right before the
eyes of Moses and the whole assembly of Is-
rael while they were weeping at the entrance
to the tent of meeting. 7When Phinehas son
of Eleazar, the son of Aaron, the priest, saw
this, he left the assembly, took a spear in his
hand 8and followed the Israelite into the
tent. He drove the spear into both of them,
right through the Israelite man and into the
woman's stomach. Then the plague against
the Israelites was stopped; 9but those who
died in the plague numbered 24,000.
10The LORD said to Moses, 11"Phinehas
son of Eleazar, the son of Aaron, the priest,
has turned my anger away from the Israel-
ites. Since he was as zealous for my honor
among them as I am, I did not put an end to
them in my zeal. 12Therefore tell him I am
making my covenant of peace with him.
13He and his descendants will have a cov-
enant of a lasting priesthood, because he
was zealous for the honor of his God and
made atonement for the Israelites."
14The name of the Israelite who was killed
with the Midianite woman was Zimri son of
Salu, the leader of a Simeonite family. 15And
the name of the Midianite woman who was
put to death was Kozbi daughter of Zur, a
tribal chief of a Midianite family.
16The LORD said to Moses, 17"Treat the
Midianites as enemies and kill them. 18They
treated you as enemies when they deceived
you in the Peor incident involving their sis-
ter Kozbi, the daughter of a Midianite leader,
the woman who was killed when the plague
came as a result of that incident."

The Second Census

26 After the plague the LORD said to
Moses and Eleazar son of Aaron, the
priest, 2"Take a census of the whole Israelite
community by families — all those twenty
years old or more who are able to serve in the
army of Israel." 3So on the plains of Moab by
the Jordan across from Jericho, Moses and
Eleazar the priest spoke with them and said,
4"Take a census of the men twenty years old
or more, as the LORD commanded Moses."

These were the Israelites who came out of
Egypt:

5The descendants of Reuben, the firstborn
son of Israel, were:

through Hanok, the Hanokite clan;
through Pallu, the Palluite clan;
6through Hezron, the Hezronite clan;
through Karmi, the Karmite clan.

7These were the clans of Reuben; those
numbered were 43,730.
8The son of Pallu was Eliab, 9and the sons
of Eliab were Nemuel, Dathan and Abiram.
The same Dathan and Abiram were the
community officials who rebelled against
Moses and Aaron and were among Korah's
followers when they rebelled against the
LORD. 10The earth opened its mouth and
swallowed them along with Korah, whose
followers died when the fire devoured the
250 men. And they served as a warning sign.
11The line of Korah, however, did not die out.
12The descendants of Simeon by their clans
were:

through Nemuel, the Nemuelite clan;
through Jamin, the Jaminite clan;
through Jakin, the Jakinite clan;
13through Zerah, the Zerahite clan;
through Shaul, the Shaulite clan.

14These were the clans of Simeon; those
numbered were 22,200.

15The descendants of Gad by their clans
were:

through Zephon, the Zephonite clan;
through Haggi, the Haggite clan;
through Shuni, the Shunite clan;
16through Ozni, the Oznite clan;
through Eri, the Erite clan;
17through Arodi,[a] the Arodite clan;
through Areli, the Arelite clan.

[a] 17 Samaritan Pentateuch and Syriac (see also Gen. 46:16); Masoretic Text *Arod*

[18]These were the clans of Gad; those numbered were 40,500.

[19]Er and Onan were sons of Judah, but they died in Canaan.
[20]The descendants of Judah by their clans were:
through Shelah, the Shelanite clan;
through Perez, the Perezite clan;
through Zerah, the Zerahite clan.
[21]The descendants of Perez were:
through Hezron, the Hezronite clan;
through Hamul, the Hamulite clan.
[22]These were the clans of Judah; those numbered were 76,500.

[23]The descendants of Issachar by their clans were:
through Tola, the Tolaite clan;
through Puah, the Puite[a] clan;
[24]through Jashub, the Jashubite clan;
through Shimron, the Shimronite clan.
[25]These were the clans of Issachar; those numbered were 64,300.

[26]The descendants of Zebulun by their clans were:
through Sered, the Seredite clan;
through Elon, the Elonite clan;
through Jahleel, the Jahleelite clan.
[27]These were the clans of Zebulun; those numbered were 60,500.

[28]The descendants of Joseph by their clans through Manasseh and Ephraim were:

[29]The descendants of Manasseh:
through Makir, the Makirite clan (Makir was the father of Gilead);
through Gilead, the Gileadite clan.
[30]These were the descendants of Gilead:
through Iezer, the Iezerite clan;
through Helek, the Helekite clan;
[31]through Asriel, the Asrielite clan;
through Shechem, the Shechemite clan;
[32]through Shemida, the Shemidaite clan;
through Hepher, the Hepherite clan.
[33](Zelophehad son of Hepher had no sons; he had only daughters, whose names were Mahlah, Noah, Hoglah, Milkah and Tirzah.)
[34]These were the clans of Manasseh; those numbered were 52,700.

[35]These were the descendants of Ephraim by their clans:
through Shuthelah, the Shuthelahite clan;
through Beker, the Bekerite clan;
through Tahan, the Tahanite clan.
[36]These were the descendants of Shuthelah:
through Eran, the Eranite clan.
[37]These were the clans of Ephraim; those numbered were 32,500.

These were the descendants of Joseph by their clans.

[38]The descendants of Benjamin by their clans were:
through Bela, the Belaite clan;
through Ashbel, the Ashbelite clan;
through Ahiram, the Ahiramite clan;
[39]through Shupham,[b] the Shuphamite clan;
through Hupham, the Huphamite clan.
[40]The descendants of Bela through Ard and Naaman were:
through Ard,[c] the Ardite clan;
through Naaman, the Naamite clan.
[41]These were the clans of Benjamin; those numbered were 45,600.

[42]These were the descendants of Dan by their clans:
through Shuham, the Shuhamite clan.
These were the clans of Dan: [43]All of them
were Shuhamite clans; and those numbered were 64,400.

[44]The descendants of Asher by their clans were:
through Imnah, the Imnite clan;
through Ishvi, the Ishvite clan;
through Beriah, the Beriite clan;
[45]and through the descendants of Beriah:
through Heber, the Heberite clan;
through Malkiel, the Malkielite clan.
[46](Asher had a daughter named Serah.)
[47]These were the clans of Asher; those numbered were 53,400.

[48]The descendants of Naphtali by their clans were:

[a] *23* Samaritan Pentateuch, Septuagint, Vulgate and Syriac (see also 1 Chron. 7:1); Masoretic Text *through Puvah, the Punite* [b] *39* A few manuscripts of the Masoretic Text, Samaritan Pentateuch, Vulgate and Syriac (see also Septuagint); most manuscripts of the Masoretic Text *Shephupham* [c] *40* Samaritan Pentateuch and Vulgate (see also Septuagint); Masoretic Text does not have *through Ard.*

through Jahzeel, the Jahzeelite clan;
through Guni, the Gunite clan;
49 through Jezer, the Jezerite clan;
through Shillem, the Shillemite clan.
50 These were the clans of Naphtali; those
numbered were 45,400.

51 The total number of the men of Israel was
601,730.

52 The LORD said to Moses, 53 "The land
is to be allotted to them as an inheritance
based on the number of names. 54 To a larg-
er group give a larger inheritance, and to a
smaller group a smaller one; each is to re-
ceive its inheritance according to the num-
ber of those listed. 55 Be sure that the land is
distributed by lot. What each group inherits
will be according to the names for its ances-
tral tribe. 56 Each inheritance is to be dis-
tributed by lot among the larger and smaller
groups."

57 These were the Levites who were counted
by their clans:
through Gershon, the Gershonite clan;
through Kohath, the Kohathite clan;
through Merari, the Merarite clan.
58 These also were Levite clans:
the Libnite clan,
the Hebronite clan,
the Mahlite clan,
the Mushite clan,
the Korahite clan.
(Kohath was the forefather of Amram;
59 the name of Amram's wife was Joch-
ebed, a descendant of Levi, who was
born to the Levites[a] in Egypt. To Am-
ram she bore Aaron, Moses and their
sister Miriam. 60 Aaron was the father
of Nadab and Abihu, Eleazar and Itha-
mar. 61 But Nadab and Abihu died when
they made an offering before the LORD
with unauthorized fire.)

62 All the male Levites a month old or more
numbered 23,000. They were not counted
along with the other Israelites because they
received no inheritance among them.

63 These are the ones counted by Moses
and Eleazar the priest when they count-
ed the Israelites on the plains of Moab by
the Jordan across from Jericho. 64 Not one
of them was among those counted by Mo-
ses and Aaron the priest when they counted
the Israelites in the Desert of Sinai. 65 For the
LORD had told those Israelites they would
surely die in the wilderness, and not one of
them was left except Caleb son of Jephunneh
and Joshua son of Nun.

Zelophehad's Daughters

27 The daughters of Zelophehad son of
Hepher, the son of Gilead, the son
of Makir, the son of Manasseh, belonged to
the clans of Manasseh son of Joseph. The
names of the daughters were Mahlah, Noah,
Hoglah, Milkah and Tirzah. They came for-
ward 2 and stood before Moses, Eleazar the
priest, the leaders and the whole assembly at
the entrance to the tent of meeting and said,
3 "Our father died in the wilderness. He was
not among Korah's followers, who banded
together against the LORD, but he died for
his own sin and left no sons. 4 Why should
our father's name disappear from his clan
because he had no son? Give us property
among our father's relatives."

5 So Moses brought their case before the
LORD, 6 and the LORD said to him, 7 "What
Zelophehad's daughters are saying is right.
You must certainly give them property as an
inheritance among their father's relatives
and give their father's inheritance to them.

8 "Say to the Israelites, 'If a man dies and
leaves no son, give his inheritance to his
daughter. 9 If he has no daughter, give his
inheritance to his brothers. 10 If he has no
brothers, give his inheritance to his father's
brothers. 11 If his father had no brothers, give
his inheritance to the nearest relative in his
clan, that he may possess it. This is to have
the force of law for the Israelites, as the LORD
commanded Moses.'"

Joshua to Succeed Moses

12 Then the LORD said to Moses, "Go up
this mountain in the Abarim Range and see
the land I have given the Israelites. 13 After
you have seen it, you too will be gathered to
your people, as your brother Aaron was, 14 for
when the community rebelled at the waters
in the Desert of Zin, both of you disobeyed
my command to honor me as holy before
their eyes." (These were the waters of Meri-
bah Kadesh, in the Desert of Zin.)

[a] 59 Or *Jochebed, a daughter of Levi, who was born to Levi*

15 Moses said to the LORD, 16 "May the
LORD, the God who gives breath to all living
things, appoint someone over this commu-
nity 17 to go out and come in before them, one
who will lead them out and bring them in,
so the LORD's people will not be like sheep
without a shepherd."

18 So the LORD said to Moses, "Take Josh-
ua son of Nun, a man in whom is the spirit
of leadership,[a] and lay your hand on him.
19 Have him stand before Eleazar the priest
and the entire assembly and commission
him in their presence. 20 Give him some of
your authority so the whole Israelite com-
munity will obey him. 21 He is to stand before
Eleazar the priest, who will obtain decisions
for him by inquiring of the Urim before the
LORD. At his command he and the entire
community of the Israelites will go out, and
at his command they will come in."

22 Moses did as the LORD commanded
him. He took Joshua and had him stand be-
fore Eleazar the priest and the whole assem-
bly. 23 Then he laid his hands on him and
commissioned him, as the LORD instructed
through Moses.

Daily Offerings

28 The LORD said to Moses, 2 "Give this
command to the Israelites and say to
them: 'Make sure that you present to me at
the appointed time my food offerings, as an
aroma pleasing to me.' 3 Say to them: 'This
is the food offering you are to present to the
LORD: two lambs a year old without defect,
as a regular burnt offering each day. 4 Offer
one lamb in the morning and the other at
twilight, 5 together with a grain offering of a
tenth of an ephah[b] of the finest flour mixed
with a quarter of a hin[c] of oil from pressed
olives. 6 This is the regular burnt offering
instituted at Mount Sinai as a pleasing aro-
ma, a food offering presented to the LORD.
7 The accompanying drink offering is to be
a quarter of a hin of fermented drink with
each lamb. Pour out the drink offering to
the LORD at the sanctuary. 8 Offer the second
lamb at twilight, along with the same kind
of grain offering and drink offering that you
offer in the morning. This is a food offering,
an aroma pleasing to the LORD.

Sabbath Offerings

9 " 'On the Sabbath day, make an offering
of two lambs a year old without defect, to-
gether with its drink offering and a grain of-
fering of two-tenths of an ephah[d] of the finest
flour mixed with olive oil. 10 This is the burnt
offering for every Sabbath, in addition to the
regular burnt offering and its drink offering.

Monthly Offerings

11 " 'On the first of every month, present to
the LORD a burnt offering of two young bulls,
one ram and seven male lambs a year old,
all without defect. 12 With each bull there is
to be a grain offering of three-tenths of an
ephah[e] of the finest flour mixed with oil;
with the ram, a grain offering of two-tenths
of an ephah of the finest flour mixed with oil;
13 and with each lamb, a grain offering of a
tenth of an ephah of the finest flour mixed
with oil. This is for a burnt offering, a pleas-
ing aroma, a food offering presented to the
LORD. 14 With each bull there is to be a drink
offering of half a hin[f] of wine; with the ram, a
third of a hin[g]; and with each lamb, a quarter
of a hin. This is the monthly burnt offering to
be made at each new moon during the year.
15 Besides the regular burnt offering with its
drink offering, one male goat is to be pre-
sented to the LORD as a sin offering.[h]

The Passover

16 " 'On the fourteenth day of the first
month the LORD's Passover is to be held.
17 On the fifteenth day of this month there
is to be a festival; for seven days eat bread
made without yeast. 18 On the first day hold
a sacred assembly and do no regular work.
19 Present to the LORD a food offering con-
sisting of a burnt offering of two young bulls,
one ram and seven male lambs a year old,
all without defect. 20 With each bull offer a
grain offering of three-tenths of an ephah
of the finest flour mixed with oil; with the
ram, two-tenths; 21 and with each of the sev-
en lambs, one-tenth. 22 Include one male

[a] *18* Or *the Spirit* [b] *5* That is, probably about 3 1/2 pounds or about 1.6 kilograms; also in verses 13, 21 and 29 [c] *5* That is, about 1 quart or about 1 liter; also in verses 7 and 14 [d] *9* That is, probably about 7 pounds or about 3.2 kilograms; also in verses 12, 20 and 28 [e] *12* That is, probably about 11 pounds or about 5 kilograms; also in verses 20 and 28 [f] *14* That is, about 2 quarts or about 1.9 liters [g] *14* That is, about 1 1/3 quarts or about 1.3 liters [h] *15* Or *purification offering*; also in verse 22

goat as a sin offering to make atonement for you. [23]Offer these in addition to the regular morning burnt offering. [24]In this way present the food offering every day for seven days as an aroma pleasing to the LORD; it is to be offered in addition to the regular burnt offering and its drink offering. [25]On the seventh day hold a sacred assembly and do no regular work.

The Festival of Weeks

[26]“ ‘On the day of firstfruits, when you present to the LORD an offering of new grain during the Festival of Weeks, hold a sacred assembly and do no regular work. [27]Present a burnt offering of two young bulls, one ram and seven male lambs a year old as an aroma pleasing to the LORD. [28]With each bull there is to be a grain offering of three-tenths of an ephah of the finest flour mixed with oil; with the ram, two-tenths; [29]and with each of the seven lambs, one-tenth. [30]Include one male goat to make atonement for you. [31]Offer these together with their drink offerings, in addition to the regular burnt offering and its grain offering. Be sure the animals are without defect.

The Festival of Trumpets

29 “ ‘On the first day of the seventh month hold a sacred assembly and do no regular work. It is a day for you to sound the trumpets. [2]As an aroma pleasing to the LORD, offer a burnt offering of one young bull, one ram and seven male lambs a year old, all without defect. [3]With the bull offer a grain offering of three-tenths of an ephah[a] of the finest flour mixed with olive oil; with the ram, two-tenths[b]; [4]and with each of the seven lambs, one-tenth.[c] [5]Include one male goat as a sin offering[d] to make atonement for you. [6]These are in addition to the monthly and daily burnt offerings with their grain offerings and drink offerings as specified. They are food offerings presented to the LORD, a pleasing aroma.

The Day of Atonement

[7]“ ‘On the tenth day of this seventh month hold a sacred assembly. You must deny yourselves[e] and do no work. [8]Present as an aroma pleasing to the LORD a burnt offering of one young bull, one ram and seven male lambs a year old, all without defect. [9]With the bull offer a grain offering of three-tenths of an ephah of the finest flour mixed with oil; with the ram, two-tenths; [10]and with each of the seven lambs, one-tenth. [11]Include one male goat as a sin offering, in addition to the sin offering for atonement and the regular burnt offering with its grain offering, and their drink offerings.

The Festival of Tabernacles

[12]“ ‘On the fifteenth day of the seventh month, hold a sacred assembly and do no regular work. Celebrate a festival to the LORD for seven days. [13]Present as an aroma pleasing to the LORD a food offering consisting of a burnt offering of thirteen young bulls, two rams and fourteen male lambs a year old, all without defect. [14]With each of the thirteen bulls offer a grain offering of three-tenths of an ephah of the finest flour mixed with oil; with each of the two rams, two-tenths; [15]and with each of the fourteen lambs, one-tenth. [16]Include one male goat as a sin offering, in addition to the regular burnt offering with its grain offering and drink offering.

[17]“ ‘On the second day offer twelve young bulls, two rams and fourteen male lambs a year old, all without defect. [18]With the bulls, rams and lambs, offer their grain offerings and drink offerings according to the number specified. [19]Include one male goat as a sin offering, in addition to the regular burnt offering with its grain offering, and their drink offerings.

[20]“ ‘On the third day offer eleven bulls, two rams and fourteen male lambs a year old, all without defect. [21]With the bulls, rams and lambs, offer their grain offerings and drink offerings according to the number specified. [22]Include one male goat as a sin offering, in addition to the regular burnt offering with its grain offering and drink offering.

[23]“ ‘On the fourth day offer ten bulls, two rams and fourteen male lambs a year old, all without defect. [24]With the bulls, rams and lambs, offer their grain offerings and drink

[a] 3 That is, probably about 11 pounds or about 5 kilograms; also in verses 9 and 14 [b] 3 That is, probably about 7 pounds or about 3.2 kilograms; also in verses 9 and 14 [c] 4 That is, probably about 3 1/2 pounds or about 1.6 kilograms; also in verses 10 and 15 [d] 5 Or *purification offering*; also elsewhere in this chapter [e] 7 Or *must fast*

offerings according to the number specified. [25]Include one male goat as a sin offering, in addition to the regular burnt offering with its grain offering and drink offering.

[26]" 'On the fifth day offer nine bulls, two rams and fourteen male lambs a year old, all without defect. [27]With the bulls, rams and lambs, offer their grain offerings and drink offerings according to the number specified. [28]Include one male goat as a sin offering, in addition to the regular burnt offering with its grain offering and drink offering.

[29]" 'On the sixth day offer eight bulls, two rams and fourteen male lambs a year old, all without defect. [30]With the bulls, rams and lambs, offer their grain offerings and drink offerings according to the number specified. [31]Include one male goat as a sin offering, in addition to the regular burnt offering with its grain offering and drink offering.

[32]" 'On the seventh day offer seven bulls, two rams and fourteen male lambs a year old, all without defect. [33]With the bulls, rams and lambs, offer their grain offerings and drink offerings according to the number specified. [34]Include one male goat as a sin offering, in addition to the regular burnt offering with its grain offering and drink offering.

[35]" 'On the eighth day hold a closing special assembly and do no regular work. [36]Present as an aroma pleasing to the LORD a food offering consisting of a burnt offering of one bull, one ram and seven male lambs a year old, all without defect. [37]With the bull, the ram and the lambs, offer their grain offerings and drink offerings according to the number specified. [38]Include one male goat as a sin offering, in addition to the regular burnt offering with its grain offering and drink offering.

[39]" 'In addition to what you vow and your freewill offerings, offer these to the LORD at your appointed festivals: your burnt offerings, grain offerings, drink offerings and fellowship offerings.' "

[40]Moses told the Israelites all that the LORD commanded him.[a]

Vows

30 [b] Moses said to the heads of the tribes of Israel: "This is what the LORD commands: [2]When a man makes a vow to the LORD or takes an oath to obligate himself by a pledge, he must not break his word but must do everything he said.

[3]"When a young woman still living in her father's household makes a vow to the LORD or obligates herself by a pledge [4]and her father hears about her vow or pledge but says nothing to her, then all her vows and every pledge by which she obligated herself will stand. [5]But if her father forbids her when he hears about it, none of her vows or the pledges by which she obligated herself will stand; the LORD will release her because her father has forbidden her.

[6]"If she marries after she makes a vow or after her lips utter a rash promise by which she obligates herself [7]and her husband hears about it but says nothing to her, then her vows or the pledges by which she obligated herself will stand. [8]But if her husband forbids her when he hears about it, he nullifies the vow that obligates her or the rash promise by which she obligates herself, and the LORD will release her.

[9]"Any vow or obligation taken by a widow or divorced woman will be binding on her.

[10]"If a woman living with her husband makes a vow or obligates herself by a pledge under oath [11]and her husband hears about it but says nothing to her and does not forbid her, then all her vows or the pledges by which she obligated herself will stand. [12]But if her husband nullifies them when he hears about them, then none of the vows or pledges that came from her lips will stand. Her husband has nullified them, and the LORD will release her. [13]Her husband may confirm or nullify any vow she makes or any sworn pledge to deny herself.[c] [14]But if her husband says nothing to her about it from day to day, then he confirms all her vows or the pledges binding on her. He confirms them by saying nothing to her when he hears about them. [15]If, however, he nullifies them some time after he hears about them, then he must bear the consequences of her wrongdoing."

[16]These are the regulations the LORD gave Moses concerning relationships between a man and his wife, and between a father and his young daughter still living at home.

[a] *40* In Hebrew texts this verse (29:40) is numbered 30:1. [b] In Hebrew texts 30:1-16 is numbered 30:2-17.
[c] *13* Or *to fast*

Vengeance on the Midianites

31 The LORD said to Moses, 2"Take vengeance on the Midianites for the Israelites. After that, you will be gathered to your people."

3So Moses said to the people, "Arm some of your men to go to war against the Midianites so that they may carry out the LORD's vengeance on them. 4Send into battle a thousand men from each of the tribes of Israel." 5So twelve thousand men armed for battle, a thousand from each tribe, were supplied from the clans of Israel. 6Moses sent them into battle, a thousand from each tribe, along with Phinehas son of Eleazar, the priest, who took with him articles from the sanctuary and the trumpets for signaling.

7They fought against Midian, as the LORD commanded Moses, and killed every man. 8Among their victims were Evi, Rekem, Zur, Hur and Reba — the five kings of Midian. They also killed Balaam son of Beor with the sword. 9The Israelites captured the Midianite women and children and took all the Midianite herds, flocks and goods as plunder. 10They burned all the towns where the Midianites had settled, as well as all their camps. 11They took all the plunder and spoils, including the people and animals, 12and brought the captives, spoils and plunder to Moses and Eleazar the priest and the Israelite assembly at their camp on the plains of Moab, by the Jordan across from Jericho.

13Moses, Eleazar the priest and all the leaders of the community went to meet them outside the camp. 14Moses was angry with the officers of the army — the commanders of thousands and commanders of hundreds — who returned from the battle.

15"Have you allowed all the women to live?" he asked them. 16"They were the ones who followed Balaam's advice and enticed the Israelites to be unfaithful to the LORD in the Peor incident, so that a plague struck the LORD's people. 17Now kill all the boys. And kill every woman who has slept with a man, 18but save for yourselves every girl who has never slept with a man.

19"Anyone who has killed someone or touched someone who was killed must stay outside the camp seven days. On the third and seventh days you must purify yourselves and your captives. 20Purify every garment as well as everything made of leather, goat hair or wood."

21Then Eleazar the priest said to the soldiers who had gone into battle, "This is what is required by the law that the LORD gave Moses: 22Gold, silver, bronze, iron, tin, lead 23and anything else that can withstand fire must be put through the fire, and then it will be clean. But it must also be purified with the water of cleansing. And whatever cannot withstand fire must be put through that water. 24On the seventh day wash your clothes and you will be clean. Then you may come into the camp."

Dividing the Spoils

25The LORD said to Moses, 26"You and Eleazar the priest and the family heads of the community are to count all the people and animals that were captured. 27Divide the spoils equally between the soldiers who took part in the battle and the rest of the community. 28From the soldiers who fought in the battle, set apart as tribute for the LORD one out of every five hundred, whether people, cattle, donkeys or sheep. 29Take this tribute from their half share and give it to Eleazar the priest as the LORD's part. 30From the Israelites' half, select one out of every fifty, whether people, cattle, donkeys, sheep or other animals. Give them to the Levites, who are responsible for the care of the LORD's tabernacle." 31So Moses and Eleazar the priest did as the LORD commanded Moses.

32The plunder remaining from the spoils that the soldiers took was 675,000 sheep, 3372,000 cattle, 3461,000 donkeys 35and 32,000 women who had never slept with a man.

36The half share of those who fought in the battle was:

337,500 sheep, 37of which the tribute for the LORD was 675;
3836,000 cattle, of which the tribute for the LORD was 72;
3930,500 donkeys, of which the tribute for the LORD was 61;
4016,000 people, of whom the tribute for the LORD was 32.

41Moses gave the tribute to Eleazar the priest as the LORD's part, as the LORD commanded Moses.

42The half belonging to the Israelites,

which Moses set apart from that of the fighting men — [43]the community's half — was 337,500 sheep, [44]36,000 cattle, [45]30,500 donkeys [46]and 16,000 people. [47]From the Israelites' half, Moses selected one out of every fifty people and animals, as the LORD commanded him, and gave them to the Levites, who were responsible for the care of the LORD's tabernacle.

[48]Then the officers who were over the units of the army — the commanders of thousands and commanders of hundreds — went to Moses [49]and said to him, "Your servants have counted the soldiers under our command, and not one is missing. [50]So we have brought as an offering to the LORD the gold articles each of us acquired — armlets, bracelets, signet rings, earrings and necklaces — to make atonement for ourselves before the LORD."

[51]Moses and Eleazar the priest accepted from them the gold — all the crafted articles. [52]All the gold from the commanders of thousands and commanders of hundreds that Moses and Eleazar presented as a gift to the LORD weighed 16,750 shekels.[a] [53]Each soldier had taken plunder for himself. [54]Moses and Eleazar the priest accepted the gold from the commanders of thousands and commanders of hundreds and brought it into the tent of meeting as a memorial for the Israelites before the LORD.

The Transjordan Tribes

32 The Reubenites and Gadites, who had very large herds and flocks, saw that the lands of Jazer and Gilead were suitable for livestock. [2]So they came to Moses and Eleazar the priest and to the leaders of the community, and said, [3]"Ataroth, Dibon, Jazer, Nimrah, Heshbon, Elealeh, Sebam, Nebo and Beon — [4]the land the LORD subdued before the people of Israel — are suitable for livestock, and your servants have livestock. [5]If we have found favor in your eyes," they said, "let this land be given to your servants as our possession. Do not make us cross the Jordan."

[6]Moses said to the Gadites and Reubenites, "Should your fellow Israelites go to war while you sit here? [7]Why do you discourage the Israelites from crossing over into the land the LORD has given them? [8]This is what your fathers did when I sent them from Kadesh Barnea to look over the land. [9]After they went up to the Valley of Eshkol and viewed the land, they discouraged the Israelites from entering the land the LORD had given them. [10]The LORD's anger was aroused that day and he swore this oath: [11]'Because they have not followed me wholeheartedly, not one of those who were twenty years old or more when they came up out of Egypt will see the land I promised on oath to Abraham, Isaac and Jacob — [12]not one except Caleb son of Jephunneh the Kenizzite and Joshua son of Nun, for they followed the LORD wholeheartedly.' [13]The LORD's anger burned against Israel and he made them wander in the wilderness forty years, until the whole generation of those who had done evil in his sight was gone.

[14]"And here you are, a brood of sinners, standing in the place of your fathers and making the LORD even more angry with Israel. [15]If you turn away from following him, he will again leave all this people in the wilderness, and you will be the cause of their destruction."

[16]Then they came up to him and said, "We would like to build pens here for our livestock and cities for our women and children. [17]But we will arm ourselves for battle[b] and go ahead of the Israelites until we have brought them to their place. Meanwhile our women and children will live in fortified cities, for protection from the inhabitants of the land. [18]We will not return to our homes until each of the Israelites has received their inheritance. [19]We will not receive any inheritance with them on the other side of the Jordan, because our inheritance has come to us on the east side of the Jordan."

[20]Then Moses said to them, "If you will do this — if you will arm yourselves before the LORD for battle [21]and if all of you who are armed cross over the Jordan before the LORD until he has driven his enemies out before him — [22]then when the land is subdued before the LORD, you may return and be free from your obligation to the LORD and to Israel. And this land will be your possession before the LORD.

[a] *52* That is, about 420 pounds or about 190 kilograms [b] *17* Septuagint; Hebrew *will be quick to arm ourselves*

23 "But if you fail to do this, you will be
sinning against the LORD; and you may be
sure that your sin will find you out. 24 Build
cities for your women and children, and
pens for your flocks, but do what you have
promised."

25 The Gadites and Reubenites said to Mo-
ses, "We your servants will do as our lord
commands. 26 Our children and wives, our
flocks and herds will remain here in the cit-
ies of Gilead. 27 But your servants, every man
who is armed for battle, will cross over to
fight before the LORD, just as our lord says."

28 Then Moses gave orders about them to
Eleazar the priest and Joshua son of Nun and
to the family heads of the Israelite tribes.
29 He said to them, "If the Gadites and Reu-
benites, every man armed for battle, cross
over the Jordan with you before the LORD,
then when the land is subdued before you,
you must give them the land of Gilead as
their possession. 30 But if they do not cross
over with you armed, they must accept their
possession with you in Canaan."

31 The Gadites and Reubenites answered,
"Your servants will do what the LORD has
said. 32 We will cross over before the LORD
into Canaan armed, but the property we in-
herit will be on this side of the Jordan."

33 Then Moses gave to the Gadites, the
Reubenites and the half-tribe of Manasseh
son of Joseph the kingdom of Sihon king of
the Amorites and the kingdom of Og king of
Bashan — the whole land with its cities and
the territory around them.

34 The Gadites built up Dibon, Ataroth,
Aroer, 35 Atroth Shophan, Jazer, Jogbehah,
36 Beth Nimrah and Beth Haran as fortified
cities, and built pens for their flocks. 37 And
the Reubenites rebuilt Heshbon, Elealeh
and Kiriathaim, 38 as well as Nebo and Baal
Meon (these names were changed) and Sib-
mah. They gave names to the cities they re-
built.

39 The descendants of Makir son of Ma-
nasseh went to Gilead, captured it and drove
out the Amorites who were there. 40 So Mo-
ses gave Gilead to the Makirites, the descen-
dants of Manasseh, and they settled there.
41 Jair, a descendant of Manasseh, captured
their settlements and called them Havvoth
Jair.[a] 42 And Nobah captured Kenath and its
surrounding settlements and called it No-
bah after himself.

Stages in Israel's Journey

33 Here are the stages in the journey
of the Israelites when they came out
of Egypt by divisions under the leadership of
Moses and Aaron. 2 At the LORD's command
Moses recorded the stages in their journey.
This is their journey by stages:

3 The Israelites set out from Ram-
eses on the fifteenth day of the first
month, the day after the Passover. They
marched out defiantly in full view of
all the Egyptians, 4 who were burying
all their firstborn, whom the LORD had
struck down among them; for the LORD
had brought judgment on their gods.

5 The Israelites left Rameses and
camped at Sukkoth.

6 They left Sukkoth and camped at
Etham, on the edge of the desert.

7 They left Etham, turned back to Pi
Hahiroth, to the east of Baal Zephon,
and camped near Migdol.

8 They left Pi Hahiroth[b] and passed
through the sea into the desert, and
when they had traveled for three days
in the Desert of Etham, they camped at
Marah.

9 They left Marah and went to Elim,
where there were twelve springs and
seventy palm trees, and they camped
there.

10 They left Elim and camped by the
Red Sea.[c]

11 They left the Red Sea and camped
in the Desert of Sin.

12 They left the Desert of Sin and
camped at Dophkah.

13 They left Dophkah and camped at
Alush.

14 They left Alush and camped at
Rephidim, where there was no water
for the people to drink.

15 They left Rephidim and camped in
the Desert of Sinai.

16 They left the Desert of Sinai and
camped at Kibroth Hattaavah.

[a] 41 Or *them the settlements of Jair* [b] 8 Many manuscripts of the Masoretic Text, Samaritan Pentateuch and Vulgate; most manuscripts of the Masoretic Text *left from before Hahiroth* [c] 10 Or *the Sea of Reeds*; also in verse 11

17 They left Kibroth Hattaavah and camped at Hazeroth.

18 They left Hazeroth and camped at Rithmah.

19 They left Rithmah and camped at Rimmon Perez.

20 They left Rimmon Perez and camped at Libnah.

21 They left Libnah and camped at Rissah.

22 They left Rissah and camped at Kehelathah.

23 They left Kehelathah and camped at Mount Shepher.

24 They left Mount Shepher and camped at Haradah.

25 They left Haradah and camped at Makheloth.

26 They left Makheloth and camped at Tahath.

27 They left Tahath and camped at Terah.

28 They left Terah and camped at Mithkah.

29 They left Mithkah and camped at Hashmonah.

30 They left Hashmonah and camped at Moseroth.

31 They left Moseroth and camped at Bene Jaakan.

32 They left Bene Jaakan and camped at Hor Haggidgad.

33 They left Hor Haggidgad and camped at Jotbathah.

34 They left Jotbathah and camped at Abronah.

35 They left Abronah and camped at Ezion Geber.

36 They left Ezion Geber and camped at Kadesh, in the Desert of Zin.

37 They left Kadesh and camped at
Mount Hor, on the border of Edom. 38 At
the LORD's command Aaron the priest
went up Mount Hor, where he died on
the first day of the fifth month of the
fortieth year after the Israelites came
out of Egypt. 39 Aaron was a hundred
and twenty-three years old when he
died on Mount Hor.

40 The Canaanite king of Arad, who lived in the Negev of Canaan, heard that the Israelites were coming.

41 They left Mount Hor and camped at Zalmonah.

42 They left Zalmonah and camped at Punon.

43 They left Punon and camped at Oboth.

44 They left Oboth and camped at Iye Abarim, on the border of Moab.

45 They left Iye Abarim and camped at Dibon Gad.

46 They left Dibon Gad and camped at Almon Diblathaim.

47 They left Almon Diblathaim and camped in the mountains of Abarim, near Nebo.

48 They left the mountains of Abarim
and camped on the plains of Moab by
the Jordan across from Jericho. 49 There
on the plains of Moab they camped
along the Jordan from Beth Jeshimoth
to Abel Shittim.

50 On the plains of Moab by the Jordan
across from Jericho the LORD said to Moses,
51 "Speak to the Israelites and say to them:
'When you cross the Jordan into Canaan,
52 drive out all the inhabitants of the land
before you. Destroy all their carved images
and their cast idols, and demolish all their
high places. 53 Take possession of the land
and settle in it, for I have given you the land
to possess. 54 Distribute the land by lot, ac-
cording to your clans. To a larger group give
a larger inheritance, and to a smaller group
a smaller one. Whatever falls to them by lot
will be theirs. Distribute it according to your
ancestral tribes.

55 " 'But if you do not drive out the inhabi-
tants of the land, those you allow to remain
will become barbs in your eyes and thorns in
your sides. They will give you trouble in the
land where you will live. 56 And then I will do
to you what I plan to do to them.' "

Boundaries of Canaan

34 The LORD said to Moses, 2 "Com-
mand the Israelites and say to them:
'When you enter Canaan, the land that will
be allotted to you as an inheritance is to have
these boundaries:

3 " 'Your southern side will include some of
the Desert of Zin along the border of Edom.
Your southern boundary will start in the
east from the southern end of the Dead Sea,
4 cross south of Scorpion Pass, continue on to
Zin and go south of Kadesh Barnea. Then it

will go to Hazar Addar and over to Azmon,
5 where it will turn, join the Wadi of Egypt
and end at the Mediterranean Sea.

6 "'Your western boundary will be the
coast of the Mediterranean Sea. This will be
your boundary on the west.

7 "'For your northern boundary, run a line
from the Mediterranean Sea to Mount Hor
8 and from Mount Hor to Lebo Hamath. Then
the boundary will go to Zedad, 9 continue to
Ziphron and end at Hazar Enan. This will be
your boundary on the north.

10 "'For your eastern boundary, run a line
from Hazar Enan to Shepham. 11 The bound-
ary will go down from Shepham to Riblah on
the east side of Ain and continue along the
slopes east of the Sea of Galilee.[a] 12 Then the
boundary will go down along the Jordan and
end at the Dead Sea.

"'This will be your land, with its bound-
aries on every side.'"

13 Moses commanded the Israelites: "As-
sign this land by lot as an inheritance. The
LORD has ordered that it be given to the nine
and a half tribes, 14 because the families of
the tribe of Reuben, the tribe of Gad and the
half-tribe of Manasseh have received their
inheritance. 15 These two and a half tribes
have received their inheritance east of the
Jordan across from Jericho, toward the sun-
rise."

16 The LORD said to Moses, 17 "These are
the names of the men who are to assign the
land for you as an inheritance: Eleazar the
priest and Joshua son of Nun. 18 And appoint
one leader from each tribe to help assign the
land. 19 These are their names:

Caleb son of Jephunneh,
from the tribe of Judah;
20 Shemuel son of Ammihud,
from the tribe of Simeon;
21 Elidad son of Kislon,
from the tribe of Benjamin;
22 Bukki son of Jogli,
the leader from the tribe of Dan;
23 Hanniel son of Ephod,
the leader from the tribe of Manas-
seh son of Joseph;
24 Kemuel son of Shiphtan,
the leader from the tribe of Ephraim
son of Joseph;
25 Elizaphan son of Parnak,
the leader from the tribe of Zebulun;
26 Paltiel son of Azzan,
the leader from the tribe of Issachar;
27 Ahihud son of Shelomi,
the leader from the tribe of Asher;
28 Pedahel son of Ammihud,
the leader from the tribe of Naphta-
li."

29 These are the men the LORD command-
ed to assign the inheritance to the Israelites
in the land of Canaan.

Towns for the Levites

35 On the plains of Moab by the Jordan
across from Jericho, the LORD said to
Moses, 2 "Command the Israelites to give the
Levites towns to live in from the inheritance
the Israelites will possess. And give them
pasturelands around the towns. 3 Then they
will have towns to live in and pasturelands
for the cattle they own and all their other
animals.

4 "The pasturelands around the towns
that you give the Levites will extend a thou-
sand cubits[b] from the town wall. 5 Outside
the town, measure two thousand cubits[c]
on the east side, two thousand on the south
side, two thousand on the west and two
thousand on the north, with the town in the
center. They will have this area as pasture-
land for the towns.

Cities of Refuge

6 "Six of the towns you give the Levites will
be cities of refuge, to which a person who has
killed someone may flee. In addition, give
them forty-two other towns. 7 In all you must
give the Levites forty-eight towns, togeth-
er with their pasturelands. 8 The towns you
give the Levites from the land the Israelites
possess are to be given in proportion to the
inheritance of each tribe: Take many towns
from a tribe that has many, but few from one
that has few."

9 Then the LORD said to Moses: 10 "Speak
to the Israelites and say to them: 'When you
cross the Jordan into Canaan, 11 select some
towns to be your cities of refuge, to which a
person who has killed someone accidental-
ly may flee. 12 They will be places of refuge

[a] *11* Hebrew *Kinnereth* [b] *4* That is, about 1,500 feet or about 450 meters [c] *5* That is, about 3,000 feet or about 900 meters

from the avenger, so that anyone accused of murder may not die before they stand trial before the assembly. [13]These six towns you give will be your cities of refuge. [14]Give three on this side of the Jordan and three in Canaan as cities of refuge. [15]These six towns will be a place of refuge for Israelites and for foreigners residing among them, so that anyone who has killed another accidentally can flee there.

[16]" 'If anyone strikes someone a fatal blow with an iron object, that person is a murderer; the murderer is to be put to death. [17]Or if anyone is holding a stone and strikes someone a fatal blow with it, that person is a murderer; the murderer is to be put to death. [18]Or if anyone is holding a wooden object and strikes someone a fatal blow with it, that person is a murderer; the murderer is to be put to death. [19]The avenger of blood shall put the murderer to death; when the avenger comes upon the murderer, the avenger shall put the murderer to death. [20]If anyone with malice aforethought shoves another or throws something at them intentionally so that they die [21]or if out of enmity one person hits another with their fist so that the other dies, that person is to be put to death; that person is a murderer. The avenger of blood shall put the murderer to death when they meet.

[22]" 'But if without enmity someone suddenly pushes another or throws something at them unintentionally [23]or, without seeing them, drops on them a stone heavy enough to kill them, and they die, then since that other person was not an enemy and no harm was intended, [24]the assembly must judge between the accused and the avenger of blood according to these regulations. [25]The assembly must protect the one accused of murder from the avenger of blood and send the accused back to the city of refuge to which they fled. The accused must stay there until the death of the high priest, who was anointed with the holy oil.

[26]" 'But if the accused ever goes outside the limits of the city of refuge to which they fled [27]and the avenger of blood finds them outside the city, the avenger of blood may kill the accused without being guilty of murder. [28]The accused must stay in the city of refuge until the death of the high priest; only after the death of the high priest may they return to their own property.

[29]" 'This is to have the force of law for you throughout the generations to come, wherever you live.

[30]" 'Anyone who kills a person is to be put to death as a murderer only on the testimony of witnesses. But no one is to be put to death on the testimony of only one witness.

[31]" 'Do not accept a ransom for the life of a murderer, who deserves to die. They are to be put to death.

[32]" 'Do not accept a ransom for anyone who has fled to a city of refuge and so allow them to go back and live on their own land before the death of the high priest.

[33]" 'Do not pollute the land where you are. Bloodshed pollutes the land, and atonement cannot be made for the land on which blood has been shed, except by the blood of the one who shed it. [34]Do not defile the land where you live and where I dwell, for I, the LORD, dwell among the Israelites.' "

Inheritance of Zelophehad's Daughters

36 The family heads of the clan of Gilead son of Makir, the son of Manasseh, who were from the clans of the descendants of Joseph, came and spoke before Moses and the leaders, the heads of the Israelite families. [2]They said, "When the LORD commanded my lord to give the land as an inheritance to the Israelites by lot, he ordered you to give the inheritance of our brother Zelophehad to his daughters. [3]Now suppose they marry men from other Israelite tribes; then their inheritance will be taken from our ancestral inheritance and added to that of the tribe they marry into. And so part of the inheritance allotted to us will be taken away. [4]When the Year of Jubilee for the Israelites comes, their inheritance will be added to that of the tribe into which they marry, and their property will be taken from the tribal inheritance of our ancestors."

[5]Then at the LORD's command Moses gave this order to the Israelites: "What the tribe of the descendants of Joseph is saying is right. [6]This is what the LORD commands for Zelophehad's daughters: They may marry anyone they please as long as they marry within their father's tribal clan. [7]No inheritance in Israel is to pass from one tribe to another, for every Israelite shall keep the tribal inheritance of their ancestors. [8]Every daughter who inherits land in any Israelite

tribe must marry someone in her father's
tribal clan, so that every Israelite will pos-
sess the inheritance of their ancestors. 9No
inheritance may pass from one tribe to an-
other, for each Israelite tribe is to keep the
land it inherits."

10So Zelophehad's daughters did as the
LORD commanded Moses. 11Zelophehad's
daughters — Mahlah, Tirzah, Hoglah, Mil-
kah and Noah — married their cousins on
their father's side. 12They married within the
clans of the descendants of Manasseh son of
Joseph, and their inheritance remained in
their father's tribe and clan.

13These are the commands and regula-
tions the LORD gave through Moses to the Is-
raelites on the plains of Moab by the Jordan
across from Jericho.

DEUTERONOMY

The Command to Leave Horeb

1 These are the words Moses spoke to all Israel in the wilderness east of the Jordan — that is, in the Arabah — opposite Suph, between Paran and Tophel, Laban, Hazeroth and Dizahab. 2(It takes eleven days to go from Horeb to Kadesh Barnea by the Mount Seir road.)

3In the fortieth year, on the first day of the eleventh month, Moses proclaimed to the Israelites all that the LORD had commanded him concerning them. 4This was after he had defeated Sihon king of the Amorites, who reigned in Heshbon, and at Edrei had defeated Og king of Bashan, who reigned in Ashtaroth.

5East of the Jordan in the territory of Moab, Moses began to expound this law, saying:

6The LORD our God said to us at Horeb, "You have stayed long enough at this mountain. 7Break camp and advance into the hill country of the Amorites; go to all the neighboring peoples in the Arabah, in the mountains, in the western foothills, in the Negev and along the coast, to the land of the Canaanites and to Lebanon, as far as the great river, the Euphrates. 8See, I have given you this land. Go in and take possession of the land the LORD swore he would give to your fathers — to Abraham, Isaac and Jacob — and to their descendants after them."

The Appointment of Leaders

9At that time I said to you, "You are too heavy a burden for me to carry alone. 10The LORD your God has increased your numbers so that today you are as numerous as the stars in the sky. 11May the LORD, the God of your ancestors, increase you a thousand times and bless you as he has promised! 12But how can I bear your problems and your burdens and your disputes all by myself? 13Choose some wise, understanding and respected men from each of your tribes, and I will set them over you."

14You answered me, "What you propose to do is good."

15So I took the leading men of your tribes, wise and respected men, and appointed them to have authority over you — as commanders of thousands, of hundreds, of fifties and of tens and as tribal officials. 16And I charged your judges at that time, "Hear the disputes between your people and judge fairly, whether the case is between two Israelites or between an Israelite and a foreigner residing among you. 17Do not show partiality in judging; hear both small and great alike. Do not be afraid of anyone, for judgment belongs to God. Bring me any case too hard for you, and I will hear it." 18And at that time I told you everything you were to do.

Spies Sent Out

19Then, as the LORD our God commanded us, we set out from Horeb and went toward the hill country of the Amorites through all that vast and dreadful wilderness that you have seen, and so we reached Kadesh Barnea. 20Then I said to you, "You have reached the hill country of the Amorites, which the LORD our God is giving us. 21See, the LORD your God has given you the land. Go up and take possession of it as the LORD, the God of your ancestors, told you. Do not be afraid; do not be discouraged."

22Then all of you came to me and said, "Let us send men ahead to spy out the land for us and bring back a report about the route we are to take and the towns we will come to."

23The idea seemed good to me; so I selected twelve of you, one man from each tribe. 24They left and went up into the hill country, and came to the Valley of Eshkol and explored it. 25Taking with them some of the fruit of the land, they brought it down to us and reported, "It is a good land that the LORD our God is giving us."

Rebellion Against the LORD

26 But you were unwilling to go up; you rebelled against the command of the LORD your God. 27 You grumbled in your tents and said, "The LORD hates us; so he brought us out of Egypt to deliver us into the hands of the Amorites to destroy us. 28 Where can we go? Our brothers have made our hearts melt in fear. They say, 'The people are stronger and taller than we are; the cities are large, with walls up to the sky. We even saw the Anakites there.' "

29 Then I said to you, "Do not be terrified; do not be afraid of them. 30 The LORD your God, who is going before you, will fight for you, as he did for you in Egypt, before your very eyes, 31 and in the wilderness. There you saw how the LORD your God carried you, as a father carries his son, all the way you went until you reached this place."

32 In spite of this, you did not trust in the LORD your God, 33 who went ahead of you on your journey, in fire by night and in a cloud by day, to search out places for you to camp and to show you the way you should go.

34 When the LORD heard what you said, he was angry and solemnly swore: 35 "No one from this evil generation shall see the good land I swore to give your ancestors, 36 except Caleb son of Jephunneh. He will see it, and I will give him and his descendants the land he set his feet on, because he followed the LORD wholeheartedly."

37 Because of you the LORD became angry with me also and said, "You shall not enter it, either. 38 But your assistant, Joshua son of Nun, will enter it. Encourage him, because he will lead Israel to inherit it. 39 And the little ones that you said would be taken captive, your children who do not yet know good from bad—they will enter the land. I will give it to them and they will take possession of it. 40 But as for you, turn around and set out toward the desert along the route to the Red Sea.[a]"

41 Then you replied, "We have sinned against the LORD. We will go up and fight, as the LORD our God commanded us." So every one of you put on his weapons, thinking it easy to go up into the hill country.

42 But the LORD said to me, "Tell them, 'Do not go up and fight, because I will not be with you. You will be defeated by your enemies.' "

43 So I told you, but you would not listen. You rebelled against the LORD's command and in your arrogance you marched up into the hill country. 44 The Amorites who lived in those hills came out against you; they chased you like a swarm of bees and beat you down from Seir all the way to Hormah. 45 You came back and wept before the LORD, but he paid no attention to your weeping and turned a deaf ear to you. 46 And so you stayed in Kadesh many days—all the time you spent there.

Wanderings in the Wilderness

2 Then we turned back and set out toward the wilderness along the route to the Red Sea,[a] as the LORD had directed me. For a long time we made our way around the hill country of Seir.

2 Then the LORD said to me, 3 "You have made your way around this hill country long enough; now turn north. 4 Give the people these orders: 'You are about to pass through the territory of your relatives the descendants of Esau, who live in Seir. They will be afraid of you, but be very careful. 5 Do not provoke them to war, for I will not give you any of their land, not even enough to put your foot on. I have given Esau the hill country of Seir as his own. 6 You are to pay them in silver for the food you eat and the water you drink.' "

7 The LORD your God has blessed you in all the work of your hands. He has watched over your journey through this vast wilderness. These forty years the LORD your God has been with you, and you have not lacked anything.

8 So we went on past our relatives the descendants of Esau, who live in Seir. We turned from the Arabah road, which comes up from Elath and Ezion Geber, and traveled along the desert road of Moab.

9 Then the LORD said to me, "Do not harass the Moabites or provoke them to war, for I will not give you any part of their land. I have given Ar to the descendants of Lot as a possession."

10 (The Emites used to live there—a people strong and numerous, and as tall as the Anakites. 11 Like the Anakites, they too were considered Rephaites, but the Moabites called them Emites. 12 Horites used to live in

[a] 40,1 Or *the Sea of Reeds*

Seir, but the descendants of Esau drove them out. They destroyed the Horites from before them and settled in their place, just as Israel did in the land the LORD gave them as their possession.)

13 And the LORD said, "Now get up and cross the Zered Valley." So we crossed the valley.

14 Thirty-eight years passed from the time we left Kadesh Barnea until we crossed the Zered Valley. By then, that entire generation of fighting men had perished from the camp, as the LORD had sworn to them. 15 The LORD's hand was against them until he had completely eliminated them from the camp.

16 Now when the last of these fighting men among the people had died, 17 the LORD said to me, 18 "Today you are to pass by the region of Moab at Ar. 19 When you come to the Ammonites, do not harass them or provoke them to war, for I will not give you possession of any land belonging to the Ammonites. I have given it as a possession to the descendants of Lot."

20 (That too was considered a land of the Rephaites, who used to live there; but the Ammonites called them Zamzummites. 21 They were a people strong and numerous, and as tall as the Anakites. The LORD destroyed them from before the Ammonites, who drove them out and settled in their place. 22 The LORD had done the same for the descendants of Esau, who lived in Seir, when he destroyed the Horites from before them. They drove them out and have lived in their place to this day. 23 And as for the Avvites who lived in villages as far as Gaza, the Caphtorites coming out from Caphtor[a] destroyed them and settled in their place.)

Defeat of Sihon King of Heshbon

24 "Set out now and cross the Arnon Gorge. See, I have given into your hand Sihon the Amorite, king of Heshbon, and his country. Begin to take possession of it and engage him in battle. 25 This very day I will begin to put the terror and fear of you on all the nations under heaven. They will hear reports of you and will tremble and be in anguish because of you."

26 From the Desert of Kedemoth I sent messengers to Sihon king of Heshbon offering peace and saying, 27 "Let us pass through your country. We will stay on the main road; we will not turn aside to the right or to the left. 28 Sell us food to eat and water to drink for their price in silver. Only let us pass through on foot— 29 as the descendants of Esau, who live in Seir, and the Moabites, who live in Ar, did for us—until we cross the Jordan into the land the LORD our God is giving us." 30 But Sihon king of Heshbon refused to let us pass through. For the LORD your God had made his spirit stubborn and his heart obstinate in order to give him into your hands, as he has now done.

31 The LORD said to me, "See, I have begun to deliver Sihon and his country over to you. Now begin to conquer and possess his land."

32 When Sihon and all his army came out to meet us in battle at Jahaz, 33 the LORD our God delivered him over to us and we struck him down, together with his sons and his whole army. 34 At that time we took all his towns and completely destroyed[b] them—men, women and children. We left no survivors. 35 But the livestock and the plunder from the towns we had captured we carried off for ourselves. 36 From Aroer on the rim of the Arnon Gorge, and from the town in the gorge, even as far as Gilead, not one town was too strong for us. The LORD our God gave us all of them. 37 But in accordance with the command of the LORD our God, you did not encroach on any of the land of the Ammonites, neither the land along the course of the Jabbok nor that around the towns in the hills.

Defeat of Og King of Bashan

3 Next we turned and went up along the road toward Bashan, and Og king of Bashan with his whole army marched out to meet us in battle at Edrei. 2 The LORD said to me, "Do not be afraid of him, for I have delivered him into your hands, along with his whole army and his land. Do to him what you did to Sihon king of the Amorites, who reigned in Heshbon."

3 So the LORD our God also gave into our hands Og king of Bashan and all his army. We struck them down, leaving no survivors. 4 At that time we took all his cities. There was not one of the sixty cities that we did not take

[a] 23 That is, Crete [b] 34 The Hebrew term refers to the irrevocable giving over of things or persons to the LORD, often by totally destroying them.

EVERLASTING GOD

Brenton Brown, Ken Riley

Strength will rise as we wait upon the Lord
We will wait upon the Lord, we will wait upon the Lord
Strength will rise as we wait upon the Lord
We will wait upon the Lord, we will wait upon the Lord

Our God, you reign forever
Our hope, our strong Deliverer

You are the everlasting God, the everlasting God
You do not faint, you won't grow weary
You're the defender of the weak, you comfort those in need
You lift us up on wings like eagles

THE INSPIRATION

Do you not know? Have you not heard? The LORD is the everlasting God, the Creator of the ends of the earth. He will not grow tired or weary, and his understanding no one can fathom. He gives strength to the weary and increases the power of the weak. Even youths grow tired and weary, and young men stumble and fall; but those who hope in the LORD will renew their strength. They will soar on wings like eagles; they will run and not grow weary, they will walk and not be faint. —Isaiah 40:28 – 31

BEHIND THE SONG

Worship leader Brenton Brown was at an artists' retreat, closing the day with some prayer and worship time, when the beginnings of "Everlasting God" were born. The powerful imagery of God, captured by the prophet Isaiah, came to mind as the lyrics flowed. Sometime later, Brown's friend Ken Riley played him a short bit of a song that he had been working on, which quickly became the pre-chorus for the song that would eventually be known as "Everlasting God."

Brown occasionally worked on the song but hadn't pulled it together yet when both he and his wife Jude were diagnosed with Chronic Fatigue Syndrome, a disease that challenged their ability to keep up their ministry work. Brown recommitted himself to finishing the song, as it perfectly articulated the weakness he was feeling.

"The chapter that it comes from, Isaiah 40, is an amazing chapter of promise and hope for those who wait on God," Brown explains. "Strength will rise. We will be lifted up and strengthened by him. It became a mission of mine to finish the song."

Brown did finish the song, with Riley's pre-chorus included, and right in the midst of his own personal weakness, God used this simple song to inspire millions of believers. It has been recorded by numerous artists, including a recording by worship leaders Chris Tomlin and Paul Baloche. For the Browns, however, it is still very personal and very powerful. "It's our theme song," he adds, "our anthem."

Selah

Is there anything in your life that is wearing you down? Are you relying on your own strength instead of the strength that comes from God?

Isaiah 40 has inspired worship in God's people for thousands of years. Whether read privately, spoken aloud or sung, these words inspire hope in the hopeless. Countless songs and hymns have been based on these verses and certainly more will be in the future.

Read Isaiah 40 and ask God to reveal any weaknesses in your faith. Write them down. Then commit yourself to letting him be your strength.

from them — the whole region of Argob, Og's kingdom in Bashan. 5All these cities were fortified with high walls and with gates and bars, and there were also a great many unwalled villages. 6We completely destroyed[a] them, as we had done with Sihon king of Heshbon, destroying[a] every city — men, women and children. 7But all the livestock and the plunder from their cities we carried off for ourselves.

8So at that time we took from these two kings of the Amorites the territory east of the Jordan, from the Arnon Gorge as far as Mount Hermon. 9(Hermon is called Sirion by the Sidonians; the Amorites call it Senir.) 10We took all the towns on the plateau, and all Gilead, and all Bashan as far as Salekah and Edrei, towns of Og's kingdom in Bashan. 11(Og king of Bashan was the last of the Rephaites. His bed was decorated with iron and was more than nine cubits long and four cubits wide.[b] It is still in Rabbah of the Ammonites.)

Division of the Land

12Of the land that we took over at that time, I gave the Reubenites and the Gadites the territory north of Aroer by the Arnon Gorge, including half the hill country of Gilead, together with its towns. 13The rest of Gilead and also all of Bashan, the kingdom of Og, I gave to the half-tribe of Manasseh. (The whole region of Argob in Bashan used to be known as a land of the Rephaites. 14Jair, a descendant of Manasseh, took the whole region of Argob as far as the border of the Geshurites and the Maakathites; it was named after him, so that to this day Bashan is called Havvoth Jair.[c]) 15And I gave Gilead to Makir. 16But to the Reubenites and the Gadites I gave the territory extending from Gilead down to the Arnon Gorge (the middle of the gorge being the border) and out to the Jabbok River, which is the border of the Ammonites. 17Its western border was the Jordan in the Arabah, from Kinnereth to the Sea of the Arabah (that is, the Dead Sea), below the slopes of Pisgah.

18I commanded you at that time: "The LORD your God has given you this land to take possession of it. But all your able-bodied men, armed for battle, must cross over ahead of the other Israelites. 19However, your wives, your children and your livestock (I know you have much livestock) may stay in the towns I have given you, 20until the LORD gives rest to your fellow Israelites as he has to you, and they too have taken over the land that the LORD your God is giving them across the Jordan. After that, each of you may go back to the possession I have given you."

Moses Forbidden to Cross the Jordan

21At that time I commanded Joshua: "You have seen with your own eyes all that the LORD your God has done to these two kings. The LORD will do the same to all the kingdoms over there where you are going. 22Do not be afraid of them; the LORD your God himself will fight for you."

23At that time I pleaded with the LORD: 24"Sovereign LORD, you have begun to show to your servant your greatness and your strong hand. For what god is there in heaven or on earth who can do the deeds and mighty works you do? 25Let me go over and see the good land beyond the Jordan — that fine hill country and Lebanon."

26But because of you the LORD was angry with me and would not listen to me. "That is enough," the LORD said. "Do not speak to me anymore about this matter. 27Go up to the top of Pisgah and look west and north and south and east. Look at the land with your own eyes, since you are not going to cross this Jordan. 28But commission Joshua, and encourage and strengthen him, for he will lead this people across and will cause them to inherit the land that you will see." 29So we stayed in the valley near Beth Peor.

Obedience Commanded

4 Now, Israel, hear the decrees and laws I am about to teach you. Follow them so that you may live and may go in and take possession of the land the LORD, the God of your ancestors, is giving you. 2Do not add to what I command you and do not subtract from it, but keep the commands of the LORD your God that I give you.

3You saw with your own eyes what the LORD did at Baal Peor. The LORD your God

[a] *6* The Hebrew term refers to the irrevocable giving over of things or persons to the LORD, often by totally destroying them. [b] *11* That is, about 14 feet long and 6 feet wide or about 4 meters long and 1.8 meters wide [c] *14* Or *called the settlements of Jair*

destroyed from among you everyone who followed the Baal of Peor, [4]but all of you who held fast to the LORD your God are still alive today.

[5]See, I have taught you decrees and laws as the LORD my God commanded me, so that you may follow them in the land you are entering to take possession of it. [6]Observe them carefully, for this will show your wisdom and understanding to the nations, who will hear about all these decrees and say, "Surely this great nation is a wise and understanding people." [7]What other nation is so great as to have their gods near them the way the LORD our God is near us whenever we pray to him? [8]And what other nation is so great as to have such righteous decrees and laws as this body of laws I am setting before you today?

[9]Only be careful, and watch yourselves closely so that you do not forget the things your eyes have seen or let them fade from your heart as long as you live. Teach them to your children and to their children after them. [10]Remember the day you stood before the LORD your God at Horeb, when he said to me, "Assemble the people before me to hear my words so that they may learn to revere me as long as they live in the land and may teach them to their children." [11]You came near and stood at the foot of the mountain while it blazed with fire to the very heavens, with black clouds and deep darkness. [12]Then the LORD spoke to you out of the fire. You heard the sound of words but saw no form; there was only a voice. [13]He declared to you his covenant, the Ten Commandments, which he commanded you to follow and then wrote them on two stone tablets. [14]And the LORD directed me at that time to teach you the decrees and laws you are to follow in the land that you are crossing the Jordan to possess.

Idolatry Forbidden

[15]You saw no form of any kind the day the LORD spoke to you at Horeb out of the fire. Therefore watch yourselves very carefully, [16]so that you do not become corrupt and make for yourselves an idol, an image of any shape, whether formed like a man or a woman, [17]or like any animal on earth or any bird that flies in the air, [18]or like any creature that moves along the ground or any fish in the waters below. [19]And when you look up to the sky and see the sun, the moon and the stars—all the heavenly array—do not be enticed into bowing down to them and worshiping things the LORD your God has apportioned to all the nations under heaven. [20]But as for you, the LORD took you and brought you out of the iron-smelting furnace, out of Egypt, to be the people of his inheritance, as you now are.

[21]The LORD was angry with me because of you, and he solemnly swore that I would not cross the Jordan and enter the good land the LORD your God is giving you as your inheritance. [22]I will die in this land; I will not cross the Jordan; but you are about to cross over and take possession of that good land. [23]Be careful not to forget the covenant of the LORD your God that he made with you; do not make for yourselves an idol in the form of anything the LORD your God has forbidden. [24]For the LORD your God is a consuming fire, a jealous God.

[25]After you have had children and grandchildren and have lived in the land a long time—if you then become corrupt and make any kind of idol, doing evil in the eyes of the LORD your God and arousing his anger, [26]I call the heavens and the earth as witnesses against you this day that you will quickly perish from the land that you are crossing the Jordan to possess. You will not live there long but will certainly be destroyed. [27]The LORD will scatter you among the peoples, and only a few of you will survive among the nations to which the LORD will drive you. [28]There you will worship man-made gods of wood and stone, which cannot see or hear or eat or smell. [29]But if from there you seek the LORD your God, you will find him if you seek him with all your heart and with all your soul. [30]When you are in distress and all these things have happened to you, then in later days you will return to the LORD your God and obey him. [31]For the LORD your God is a merciful God; he will not abandon or destroy you or forget the covenant with your ancestors, which he confirmed to them by oath.

The LORD Is God

[32]Ask now about the former days, long before your time, from the day God created human beings on the earth; ask from one end of the heavens to the other. Has anything so great as this ever happened, or has anything

like it ever been heard of? 33 Has any other people heard the voice of God[a] speaking out of fire, as you have, and lived? 34 Has any god ever tried to take for himself one nation out of another nation, by testings, by signs and wonders, by war, by a mighty hand and an outstretched arm, or by great and awesome deeds, like all the things the LORD your God did for you in Egypt before your very eyes?

35 You were shown these things so that you might know that the LORD is God; besides him there is no other. 36 From heaven he made you hear his voice to discipline you. On earth he showed you his great fire, and you heard his words from out of the fire. 37 Because he loved your ancestors and chose their descendants after them, he brought you out of Egypt by his Presence and his great strength, 38 to drive out before you nations greater and stronger than you and to bring you into their land to give it to you for your inheritance, as it is today.

39 Acknowledge and take to heart this day that the LORD is God in heaven above and on the earth below. There is no other. 40 Keep his decrees and commands, which I am giving you today, so that it may go well with you and your children after you and that you may live long in the land the LORD your God gives you for all time.

Cities of Refuge

41 Then Moses set aside three cities east of the Jordan, 42 to which anyone who had killed a person could flee if they had unintentionally killed a neighbor without malice aforethought. They could flee into one of these cities and save their life. 43 The cities were these: Bezer in the wilderness plateau, for the Reubenites; Ramoth in Gilead, for the Gadites; and Golan in Bashan, for the Manassites.

Introduction to the Law

44 This is the law Moses set before the Israelites. 45 These are the stipulations, decrees and laws Moses gave them when they came out of Egypt 46 and were in the valley near Beth Peor east of the Jordan, in the land of Sihon king of the Amorites, who reigned in Heshbon and was defeated by Moses and the Israelites as they came out of Egypt. 47 They took possession of his land and the land of Og king of Bashan, the two Amorite kings east of the Jordan. 48 This land extended from Aroer on the rim of the Arnon Gorge to Mount Sirion[b] (that is, Hermon), 49 and included all the Arabah east of the Jordan, as far as the Dead Sea,[c] below the slopes of Pisgah.

The Ten Commandments

5 Moses summoned all Israel and said:

Hear, Israel, the decrees and laws I declare in your hearing today. Learn them and be sure to follow them. 2 The LORD our God made a covenant with us at Horeb. 3 It was not with our ancestors[d] that the LORD made this covenant, but with us, with all of us who are alive here today. 4 The LORD spoke to you face to face out of the fire on the mountain. 5 (At that time I stood between the LORD and you to declare to you the word of the LORD, because you were afraid of the fire and did not go up the mountain.) And he said:

6 "I am the LORD your God, who brought you out of Egypt, out of the land of slavery.

7 "You shall have no other gods before[e] me.

8 "You shall not make for yourself an image in the form of anything in heaven above or on the earth beneath or in the waters below. 9 You shall not bow down to them or worship them; for I, the LORD your God, am a jealous God, punishing the children for the sin of the parents to the third and fourth generation of those who hate me, 10 but showing love to a thousand generations of those who love me and keep my commandments.

11 "You shall not misuse the name of the LORD your God, for the LORD will not hold anyone guiltless who misuses his name.

12 "Observe the Sabbath day by keeping it holy, as the LORD your God has commanded you. 13 Six days you shall labor and do all your work, 14 but the seventh day is a sabbath

[a] 33 Or *of a god* [b] 48 Syriac (see also 3:9); Hebrew *Siyon* [c] 49 Hebrew *the Sea of the Arabah*
[d] 3 Or *not only with our parents* [e] 7 Or *besides*

to the LORD your God. On it you
shall not do any work, neither you,
nor your son or daughter, nor your
male or female servant, nor your
ox, your donkey or any of your an-
imals, nor any foreigner residing
in your towns, so that your male
and female servants may rest,
as you do. 15 Remember that you
were slaves in Egypt and that the
LORD your God brought you out of
there with a mighty hand and an
outstretched arm. Therefore the
LORD your God has commanded
you to observe the Sabbath day.
16 "Honor your father and your mother,
as the LORD your God has com-
manded you, so that you may live
long and that it may go well with
you in the land the LORD your God
is giving you.
17 "You shall not murder.
18 "You shall not commit adultery.
19 "You shall not steal.
20 "You shall not give false testimony
against your neighbor.
21 "You shall not covet your neighbor's
wife. You shall not set your desire
on your neighbor's house or land,
his male or female servant, his ox
or donkey, or anything that be-
longs to your neighbor."

22 These are the commandments the LORD
proclaimed in a loud voice to your whole as-
sembly there on the mountain from out of
the fire, the cloud and the deep darkness;
and he added nothing more. Then he wrote
them on two stone tablets and gave them
to me.
23 When you heard the voice out of the
darkness, while the mountain was ablaze
with fire, all the leaders of your tribes and
your elders came to me. 24 And you said, "The
LORD our God has shown us his glory and his
majesty, and we have heard his voice from
the fire. Today we have seen that a person
can live even if God speaks with them. 25 But
now, why should we die? This great fire will
consume us, and we will die if we hear the
voice of the LORD our God any longer. 26 For
what mortal has ever heard the voice of the
living God speaking out of fire, as we have,
and survived? 27 Go near and listen to all that
the LORD our God says. Then tell us whatev-
er the LORD our God tells you. We will listen
and obey."
28 The LORD heard you when you spoke to
me, and the LORD said to me, "I have heard
what this people said to you. Everything
they said was good. 29 Oh, that their hearts
would be inclined to fear me and keep all my
commands always, so that it might go well
with them and their children forever!
30 "Go, tell them to return to their tents.
31 But you stay here with me so that I may
give you all the commands, decrees and
laws you are to teach them to follow in the
land I am giving them to possess."
32 So be careful to do what the LORD your
God has commanded you; do not turn aside
to the right or to the left. 33 Walk in obedience
to all that the LORD your God has command-
ed you, so that you may live and prosper and
prolong your days in the land that you will
possess.

Love the LORD Your God

6 These are the commands, decrees and
laws the LORD your God directed me
to teach you to observe in the land that you
are crossing the Jordan to possess, 2 so that
you, your children and their children after
them may fear the LORD your God as long as
you live by keeping all his decrees and com-
mands that I give you, and so that you may
enjoy long life. 3 Hear, Israel, and be careful
to obey so that it may go well with you and
that you may increase greatly in a land flow-
ing with milk and honey, just as the LORD,
the God of your ancestors, promised you.
4 Hear, O Israel: The LORD our God, the
LORD is one.[a] 5 Love the LORD your God with
all your heart and with all your soul and with
all your strength. 6 These commandments
that I give you today are to be on your hearts.
7 Impress them on your children. Talk about
them when you sit at home and when you
walk along the road, when you lie down
and when you get up. 8 Tie them as symbols
on your hands and bind them on your fore-
heads. 9 Write them on the doorframes of
your houses and on your gates.
10 When the LORD your God brings you

[a] 4 Or *The LORD our God is one LORD*; or *The LORD is our God, the LORD is one*; or *The LORD is our God, the LORD alone*

into the land he swore to your fathers, to Abraham, Isaac and Jacob, to give you—a land with large, flourishing cities you did not build, [11]houses filled with all kinds of good things you did not provide, wells you did not dig, and vineyards and olive groves you did not plant—then when you eat and are satisfied, [12]be careful that you do not forget the LORD, who brought you out of Egypt, out of the land of slavery.

[13]Fear the LORD your God, serve him only and take your oaths in his name. [14]Do not follow other gods, the gods of the peoples around you; [15]for the LORD your God, who is among you, is a jealous God and his anger will burn against you, and he will destroy you from the face of the land. [16]Do not put the LORD your God to the test as you did at Massah. [17]Be sure to keep the commands of the LORD your God and the stipulations and decrees he has given you. [18]Do what is right and good in the LORD's sight, so that it may go well with you and you may go in and take over the good land the LORD promised on oath to your ancestors, [19]thrusting out all your enemies before you, as the LORD said.

[20]In the future, when your son asks you, "What is the meaning of the stipulations, decrees and laws the LORD our God has commanded you?" [21]tell him: "We were slaves of Pharaoh in Egypt, but the LORD brought us out of Egypt with a mighty hand. [22]Before our eyes the LORD sent signs and wonders—great and terrible—on Egypt and Pharaoh and his whole household. [23]But he brought us out from there to bring us in and give us the land he promised on oath to our ancestors. [24]The LORD commanded us to obey all these decrees and to fear the LORD our God, so that we might always prosper and be kept alive, as is the case today. [25]And if we are careful to obey all this law before the LORD our God, as he has commanded us, that will be our righteousness."

Driving Out the Nations

7 When the LORD your God brings you into the land you are entering to possess and drives out before you many nations—the Hittites, Girgashites, Amorites, Canaanites, Perizzites, Hivites and Jebusites, seven nations larger and stronger than you—[2]and when the LORD your God has delivered them over to you and you have defeated them, then you must destroy them totally.[a] Make no treaty with them, and show them no mercy. [3]Do not intermarry with them. Do not give your daughters to their sons or take their daughters for your sons, [4]for they will turn your children away from following me to serve other gods, and the LORD's anger will burn against you and will quickly destroy you. [5]This is what you are to do to them: Break down their altars, smash their sacred stones, cut down their Asherah poles[b] and burn their idols in the fire. [6]For you are a people holy to the LORD your God. The LORD your God has chosen you out of all the peoples on the face of the earth to be his people, his treasured possession.

[7]The LORD did not set his affection on you and choose you because you were more numerous than other peoples, for you were the fewest of all peoples. [8]But it was because the LORD loved you and kept the oath he swore to your ancestors that he brought you out with a mighty hand and redeemed you from the land of slavery, from the power of Pharaoh king of Egypt. [9]Know therefore that the LORD your God is God; he is the faithful God, keeping his covenant of love to a thousand generations of those who love him and keep his commandments. [10]But

those who hate him he will repay to their
face by destruction;
he will not be slow to repay to their
face those who hate him.

[11]Therefore, take care to follow the commands, decrees and laws I give you today.

[12]If you pay attention to these laws and are careful to follow them, then the LORD your God will keep his covenant of love with you, as he swore to your ancestors. [13]He will love you and bless you and increase your numbers. He will bless the fruit of your womb, the crops of your land—your grain, new wine and olive oil—the calves of your herds and the lambs of your flocks in the land he swore to your ancestors to give you. [14]You will be blessed more than any other people; none of your men or women will

[a] 2 The Hebrew term refers to the irrevocable giving over of things or persons to the LORD, often by totally destroying them; also in verse 26. [b] 5 That is, wooden symbols of the goddess Asherah; here and elsewhere in Deuteronomy

be childless, nor will any of your livestock
be without young. 15The LORD will keep
you free from every disease. He will not in-
flict on you the horrible diseases you knew
in Egypt, but he will inflict them on all who
hate you. 16You must destroy all the peoples
the LORD your God gives over to you. Do not
look on them with pity and do not serve their
gods, for that will be a snare to you.

17You may say to yourselves, "These na-
tions are stronger than we are. How can we
drive them out?" 18But do not be afraid of
them; remember well what the LORD your
God did to Pharaoh and to all Egypt. 19You
saw with your own eyes the great trials, the
signs and wonders, the mighty hand and
outstretched arm, with which the LORD your
God brought you out. The LORD your God
will do the same to all the peoples you now
fear. 20Moreover, the LORD your God will
send the hornet among them until even the
survivors who hide from you have perished.
21Do not be terrified by them, for the LORD
your God, who is among you, is a great and
awesome God. 22The LORD your God will
drive out those nations before you, little by
little. You will not be allowed to eliminate
them all at once, or the wild animals will
multiply around you. 23But the LORD your
God will deliver them over to you, throwing
them into great confusion until they are de-
stroyed. 24He will give their kings into your
hand, and you will wipe out their names
from under heaven. No one will be able to
stand up against you; you will destroy them.
25The images of their gods you are to burn
in the fire. Do not covet the silver and gold
on them, and do not take it for yourselves, or
you will be ensnared by it, for it is detestable
to the LORD your God. 26Do not bring a de-
testable thing into your house or you, like it,
will be set apart for destruction. Regard it as
vile and utterly detest it, for it is set apart for
destruction.

Do Not Forget the LORD

8 Be careful to follow every command I
am giving you today, so that you may
live and increase and may enter and pos-
sess the land the LORD promised on oath to
your ancestors. 2Remember how the LORD
your God led you all the way in the wilder-
ness these forty years, to humble and test
you in order to know what was in your heart,
whether or not you would keep his com-
mands. 3He humbled you, causing you to
hunger and then feeding you with manna,
which neither you nor your ancestors had
known, to teach you that man does not live
on bread alone but on every word that comes
from the mouth of the LORD. 4Your clothes
did not wear out and your feet did not swell
during these forty years. 5Know then in your
heart that as a man disciplines his son, so
the LORD your God disciplines you.

6Observe the commands of the LORD your
God, walking in obedience to him and rever-
ing him. 7For the LORD your God is bringing
you into a good land — a land with brooks,
streams, and deep springs gushing out into
the valleys and hills; 8a land with wheat and
barley, vines and fig trees, pomegranates, ol-
ive oil and honey; 9a land where bread will
not be scarce and you will lack nothing; a
land where the rocks are iron and you can
dig copper out of the hills.

10When you have eaten and are satisfied,
praise the LORD your God for the good land
he has given you. 11Be careful that you do not
forget the LORD your God, failing to observe
his commands, his laws and his decrees that
I am giving you this day. 12Otherwise, when
you eat and are satisfied, when you build fine
houses and settle down, 13and when your
herds and flocks grow large and your silver
and gold increase and all you have is multi-
plied, 14then your heart will become proud
and you will forget the LORD your God, who
brought you out of Egypt, out of the land of
slavery. 15He led you through the vast and
dreadful wilderness, that thirsty and wa-
terless land, with its venomous snakes and
scorpions. He brought you water out of hard
rock. 16He gave you manna to eat in the wil-
derness, something your ancestors had nev-
er known, to humble and test you so that in
the end it might go well with you. 17You may
say to yourself, "My power and the strength
of my hands have produced this wealth for
me." 18But remember the LORD your God, for
it is he who gives you the ability to produce
wealth, and so confirms his covenant, which
he swore to your ancestors, as it is today.

19If you ever forget the LORD your God
and follow other gods and worship and
bow down to them, I testify against you to-
day that you will surely be destroyed. 20Like
the nations the LORD destroyed before you,

so you will be destroyed for not obeying the LORD your God.

Not Because of Israel's Righteousness

9 Hear, Israel: You are now about to cross the Jordan to go in and dispossess nations greater and stronger than you, with large cities that have walls up to the sky. 2The people are strong and tall—Anakites! You know about them and have heard it said: "Who can stand up against the Anakites?" 3But be assured today that the LORD your God is the one who goes across ahead of you like a devouring fire. He will destroy them; he will subdue them before you. And you will drive them out and annihilate them quickly, as the LORD has promised you.

4After the LORD your God has driven them out before you, do not say to yourself, "The LORD has brought me here to take possession of this land because of my righteousness." No, it is on account of the wickedness of these nations that the LORD is going to drive them out before you. 5It is not because of your righteousness or your integrity that you are going in to take possession of their land; but on account of the wickedness of these nations, the LORD your God will drive them out before you, to accomplish what he swore to your fathers, to Abraham, Isaac and Jacob. 6Understand, then, that it is not because of your righteousness that the LORD your God is giving you this good land to possess, for you are a stiff-necked people.

The Golden Calf

7Remember this and never forget how you aroused the anger of the LORD your God in the wilderness. From the day you left Egypt until you arrived here, you have been rebellious against the LORD. 8At Horeb you aroused the LORD's wrath so that he was angry enough to destroy you. 9When I went up on the mountain to receive the tablets of stone, the tablets of the covenant that the LORD had made with you, I stayed on the mountain forty days and forty nights; I ate no bread and drank no water. 10The LORD gave me two stone tablets inscribed by the finger of God. On them were all the commandments the LORD proclaimed to you on the mountain out of the fire, on the day of the assembly.

11At the end of the forty days and forty nights, the LORD gave me the two stone tablets, the tablets of the covenant. 12Then the LORD told me, "Go down from here at once, because your people whom you brought out of Egypt have become corrupt. They have turned away quickly from what I commanded them and have made an idol for themselves."

13And the LORD said to me, "I have seen this people, and they are a stiff-necked people indeed! 14Let me alone, so that I may destroy them and blot out their name from under heaven. And I will make you into a nation stronger and more numerous than they."

15So I turned and went down from the mountain while it was ablaze with fire. And the two tablets of the covenant were in my hands. 16When I looked, I saw that you had sinned against the LORD your God; you had made for yourselves an idol cast in the shape of a calf. You had turned aside quickly from the way that the LORD had commanded you. 17So I took the two tablets and threw them out of my hands, breaking them to pieces before your eyes.

18Then once again I fell prostrate before the LORD for forty days and forty nights; I ate no bread and drank no water, because of all the sin you had committed, doing what was evil in the LORD's sight and so arousing his anger. 19I feared the anger and wrath of the LORD, for he was angry enough with you to destroy you. But again the LORD listened to me. 20And the LORD was angry enough with Aaron to destroy him, but at that time I prayed for Aaron too. 21Also I took that sinful thing of yours, the calf you had made, and burned it in the fire. Then I crushed it and ground it to powder as fine as dust and threw the dust into a stream that flowed down the mountain.

22You also made the LORD angry at Taberah, at Massah and at Kibroth Hattaavah.

23And when the LORD sent you out from Kadesh Barnea, he said, "Go up and take possession of the land I have given you." But you rebelled against the command of the LORD your God. You did not trust him or obey him. 24You have been rebellious against the LORD ever since I have known you.

25I lay prostrate before the LORD those forty days and forty nights because the LORD had said he would destroy you. 26I prayed to

the LORD and said, "Sovereign LORD, do not
destroy your people, your own inheritance
that you redeemed by your great power and
brought out of Egypt with a mighty hand.
27Remember your servants Abraham, Isaac
and Jacob. Overlook the stubbornness of
this people, their wickedness and their sin.
28Otherwise, the country from which you
brought us will say, 'Because the LORD was
not able to take them into the land he had
promised them, and because he hated them,
he brought them out to put them to death in
the wilderness.' 29But they are your people,
your inheritance that you brought out by your
great power and your outstretched arm."

Tablets Like the First Ones

10 At that time the LORD said to me,
"Chisel out two stone tablets like the
first ones and come up to me on the moun-
tain. Also make a wooden ark.[a] 2I will write
on the tablets the words that were on the first
tablets, which you broke. Then you are to put
them in the ark."

3So I made the ark out of acacia wood and
chiseled out two stone tablets like the first
ones, and I went up on the mountain with
the two tablets in my hands. 4The LORD
wrote on these tablets what he had written
before, the Ten Commandments he had
proclaimed to you on the mountain, out of
the fire, on the day of the assembly. And the
LORD gave them to me. 5Then I came back
down the mountain and put the tablets in
the ark I had made, as the LORD command-
ed me, and they are there now.

6(The Israelites traveled from the wells
of Bene Jaakan to Moserah. There Aaron
died and was buried, and Eleazar his son
succeeded him as priest. 7From there they
traveled to Gudgodah and on to Jotbathah, a
land with streams of water. 8At that time the
LORD set apart the tribe of Levi to carry the
ark of the covenant of the LORD, to stand be-
fore the LORD to minister and to pronounce
blessings in his name, as they still do today.
9That is why the Levites have no share or in-
heritance among their fellow Israelites; the
LORD is their inheritance, as the LORD your
God told them.)

10Now I had stayed on the mountain forty
days and forty nights, as I did the first time,
and the LORD listened to me at this time also.
It was not his will to destroy you. 11"Go," the
LORD said to me, "and lead the people on
their way, so that they may enter and pos-
sess the land I swore to their ancestors to
give them."

Fear the LORD

12And now, Israel, what does the LORD
your God ask of you but to fear the LORD
your God, to walk in obedience to him, to
love him, to serve the LORD your God with
all your heart and with all your soul, 13and
to observe the LORD's commands and de-
crees that I am giving you today for your own
good?

14To the LORD your God belong the heav-
ens, even the highest heavens, the earth
and everything in it. 15Yet the LORD set his
affection on your ancestors and loved them,
and he chose you, their descendants, above
all the nations — as it is today. 16Circum-
cise your hearts, therefore, and do not be
stiff-necked any longer. 17For the LORD your
God is God of gods and Lord of lords, the
great God, mighty and awesome, who shows
no partiality and accepts no bribes. 18He de-
fends the cause of the fatherless and the wid-
ow, and loves the foreigner residing among
you, giving them food and clothing. 19And
you are to love those who are foreigners,
for you yourselves were foreigners in Egypt.
20Fear the LORD your God and serve him.
Hold fast to him and take your oaths in his
name. 21He is the one you praise; he is your
God, who performed for you those great and
awesome wonders you saw with your own
eyes. 22Your ancestors who went down into
Egypt were seventy in all, and now the LORD
your God has made you as numerous as the
stars in the sky.

Love and Obey the LORD

11 Love the LORD your God and keep his
requirements, his decrees, his laws
and his commands always. 2Remember to-
day that your children were not the ones
who saw and experienced the discipline of
the LORD your God: his majesty, his mighty
hand, his outstretched arm; 3the signs he
performed and the things he did in the heart
of Egypt, both to Pharaoh king of Egypt and

[a] *1* That is, a chest

to his whole country; [4]what he did to the Egyptian army, to its horses and chariots, how he overwhelmed them with the waters of the Red Sea[a] as they were pursuing you, and how the LORD brought lasting ruin on them. [5]It was not your children who saw what he did for you in the wilderness until you arrived at this place, [6]and what he did to Dathan and Abiram, sons of Eliab the Reubenite, when the earth opened its mouth right in the middle of all Israel and swallowed them up with their households, their tents and every living thing that belonged to them. [7]But it was your own eyes that saw all these great things the LORD has done.

[8]Observe therefore all the commands I am giving you today, so that you may have the strength to go in and take over the land that you are crossing the Jordan to possess, [9]and so that you may live long in the land the LORD swore to your ancestors to give to them and their descendants, a land flowing with milk and honey. [10]The land you are entering to take over is not like the land of Egypt, from which you have come, where you planted your seed and irrigated it by foot as in a vegetable garden. [11]But the land you are crossing the Jordan to take possession of is a land of mountains and valleys that drinks rain from heaven. [12]It is a land the LORD your God cares for; the eyes of the LORD your God are continually on it from the beginning of the year to its end.

[13]So if you faithfully obey the commands I am giving you today — to love the LORD your God and to serve him with all your heart and with all your soul — [14]then I will send rain on your land in its season, both autumn and spring rains, so that you may gather in your grain, new wine and olive oil. [15]I will provide grass in the fields for your cattle, and you will eat and be satisfied.

[16]Be careful, or you will be enticed to turn away and worship other gods and bow down to them. [17]Then the LORD's anger will burn against you, and he will shut up the heavens so that it will not rain and the ground will yield no produce, and you will soon perish from the good land the LORD is giving you. [18]Fix these words of mine in your hearts and minds; tie them as symbols on your hands and bind them on your foreheads. [19]Teach them to your children, talking about them when you sit at home and when you walk along the road, when you lie down and when you get up. [20]Write them on the doorframes of your houses and on your gates, [21]so that your days and the days of your children may be many in the land the LORD swore to give your ancestors, as many as the days that the heavens are above the earth.

[22]If you carefully observe all these commands I am giving you to follow — to love the LORD your God, to walk in obedience to him and to hold fast to him — [23]then the LORD will drive out all these nations before you, and you will dispossess nations larger and stronger than you. [24]Every place where you set your foot will be yours: Your territory will extend from the desert to Lebanon, and from the Euphrates River to the Mediterranean Sea. [25]No one will be able to stand against you. The LORD your God, as he promised you, will put the terror and fear of you on the whole land, wherever you go.

[26]See, I am setting before you today a blessing and a curse — [27]the blessing if you obey the commands of the LORD your God that I am giving you today; [28]the curse if you disobey the commands of the LORD your God and turn from the way that I command you today by following other gods, which you have not known. [29]When the LORD your God has brought you into the land you are entering to possess, you are to proclaim on Mount Gerizim the blessings, and on Mount Ebal the curses. [30]As you know, these mountains are across the Jordan, westward, toward the setting sun, near the great trees of Moreh, in the territory of those Canaanites living in the Arabah in the vicinity of Gilgal. [31]You are about to cross the Jordan to enter and take possession of the land the LORD your God is giving you. When you have taken it over and are living there, [32]be sure that you obey all the decrees and laws I am setting before you today.

The One Place of Worship

12 These are the decrees and laws you must be careful to follow in the land that the LORD, the God of your ancestors, has given you to possess — as long as you live in the land. [2]Destroy completely all the places on the high mountains, on the hills and under every spreading tree, where the nations

[a] 4 Or *the Sea of Reeds*

you are dispossessing worship their gods. [3]Break down their altars, smash their sacred stones and burn their Asherah poles in the fire; cut down the idols of their gods and wipe out their names from those places.

[4]You must not worship the LORD your God in their way. [5]But you are to seek the place the LORD your God will choose from among all your tribes to put his Name there for his dwelling. To that place you must go; [6]there bring your burnt offerings and sacrifices, your tithes and special gifts, what you have vowed to give and your freewill offerings, and the firstborn of your herds and flocks. [7]There, in the presence of the LORD your God, you and your families shall eat and shall rejoice in everything you have put your hand to, because the LORD your God has blessed you.

[8]You are not to do as we do here today, everyone doing as they see fit, [9]since you have not yet reached the resting place and the inheritance the LORD your God is giving you. [10]But you will cross the Jordan and settle in the land the LORD your God is giving you as an inheritance, and he will give you rest from all your enemies around you so that you will live in safety. [11]Then to the place the LORD your God will choose as a dwelling for his Name — there you are to bring everything I command you: your burnt offerings and sacrifices, your tithes and special gifts, and all the choice possessions you have vowed to the LORD. [12]And there rejoice before the LORD your God — you, your sons and daughters, your male and female servants, and the Levites from your towns who have no allotment or inheritance of their own. [13]Be careful not to sacrifice your burnt offerings anywhere you please. [14]Offer them only at the place the LORD will choose in one of your tribes, and there observe everything I command you.

[15]Nevertheless, you may slaughter your animals in any of your towns and eat as much of the meat as you want, as if it were gazelle or deer, according to the blessing the LORD your God gives you. Both the ceremonially unclean and the clean may eat it. [16]But you must not eat the blood; pour it out on the ground like water. [17]You must not eat in your own towns the tithe of your grain and new wine and olive oil, or the firstborn of your herds and flocks, or whatever you have vowed to give, or your freewill offerings or special gifts. [18]Instead, you are to eat them in the presence of the LORD your God at the place the LORD your God will choose — you, your sons and daughters, your male and female servants, and the Levites from your towns — and you are to rejoice before the LORD your God in everything you put your hand to. [19]Be careful not to neglect the Levites as long as you live in your land.

[20]When the LORD your God has enlarged your territory as he promised you, and you crave meat and say, "I would like some meat," then you may eat as much of it as you want. [21]If the place where the LORD your God chooses to put his Name is too far away from you, you may slaughter animals from the herds and flocks the LORD has given you, as I have commanded you, and in your own towns you may eat as much of them as you want. [22]Eat them as you would gazelle or deer. Both the ceremonially unclean and the clean may eat. [23]But be sure you do not eat the blood, because the blood is the life, and you must not eat the life with the meat. [24]You must not eat the blood; pour it out on the ground like water. [25]Do not eat it, so that it may go well with you and your children after you, because you will be doing what is right in the eyes of the LORD.

[26]But take your consecrated things and whatever you have vowed to give, and go to the place the LORD will choose. [27]Present your burnt offerings on the altar of the LORD your God, both the meat and the blood. The blood of your sacrifices must be poured beside the altar of the LORD your God, but you may eat the meat. [28]Be careful to obey all these regulations I am giving you, so that it may always go well with you and your children after you, because you will be doing what is good and right in the eyes of the LORD your God.

[29]The LORD your God will cut off before you the nations you are about to invade and dispossess. But when you have driven them out and settled in their land, [30]and after they have been destroyed before you, be careful not to be ensnared by inquiring about their gods, saying, "How do these nations serve their gods? We will do the same." [31]You must not worship the LORD your God in their way, because in worshiping their gods, they do all kinds of detestable things the LORD hates.

They even burn their sons and daughters in the fire as sacrifices to their gods.

32 See that you do all I command you; do not add to it or take away from it.[a]

Worshiping Other Gods

13 [b] If a prophet, or one who foretells by dreams, appears among you and announces to you a sign or wonder, 2 and if the sign or wonder spoken of takes place, and the prophet says, "Let us follow other gods" (gods you have not known) "and let us worship them," 3 you must not listen to the words of that prophet or dreamer. The LORD your God is testing you to find out whether you love him with all your heart and with all your soul. 4 It is the LORD your God you must follow, and him you must revere. Keep his commands and obey him; serve him and hold fast to him. 5 That prophet or dreamer must be put to death for inciting rebellion against the LORD your God, who brought you out of Egypt and redeemed you from the land of slavery. That prophet or dreamer tried to turn you from the way the LORD your God commanded you to follow. You must purge the evil from among you.

6 If your very own brother, or your son or daughter, or the wife you love, or your closest friend secretly entices you, saying, "Let us go and worship other gods" (gods that neither you nor your ancestors have known, 7 gods of the peoples around you, whether near or far, from one end of the land to the other), 8 do not yield to them or listen to them. Show them no pity. Do not spare them or shield them. 9 You must certainly put them to death. Your hand must be the first in putting them to death, and then the hands of all the people. 10 Stone them to death, because they tried to turn you away from the LORD your God, who brought you out of Egypt, out of the land of slavery. 11 Then all Israel will hear and be afraid, and no one among you will do such an evil thing again.

12 If you hear it said about one of the towns the LORD your God is giving you to live in 13 that troublemakers have arisen among you and have led the people of their town astray, saying, "Let us go and worship other gods" (gods you have not known), 14 then you must inquire, probe and investigate it thoroughly. And if it is true and it has been proved that this detestable thing has been done among you, 15 you must certainly put to the sword all who live in that town. You must destroy it completely,[c] both its people and its livestock. 16 You are to gather all the plunder of the town into the middle of the public square and completely burn the town and all its plunder as a whole burnt offering to the LORD your God. That town is to remain a ruin forever, never to be rebuilt, 17 and none of the condemned things[c] are to be found in your hands. Then the LORD will turn from his fierce anger, will show you mercy, and will have compassion on you. He will increase your numbers, as he promised on oath to your ancestors— 18 because you obey the LORD your God by keeping all his commands that I am giving you today and doing what is right in his eyes.

Clean and Unclean Food

14 You are the children of the LORD your God. Do not cut yourselves or shave the front of your heads for the dead, 2 for you are a people holy to the LORD your God. Out of all the peoples on the face of the earth, the LORD has chosen you to be his treasured possession.

3 Do not eat any detestable thing. 4 These are the animals you may eat: the ox, the sheep, the goat, 5 the deer, the gazelle, the roe deer, the wild goat, the ibex, the antelope and the mountain sheep.[d] 6 You may eat any animal that has a divided hoof and that chews the cud. 7 However, of those that chew the cud or that have a divided hoof you may not eat the camel, the rabbit or the hyrax. Although they chew the cud, they do not have a divided hoof; they are ceremonially unclean for you. 8 The pig is also unclean; although it has a divided hoof, it does not chew the cud. You are not to eat their meat or touch their carcasses.

9 Of all the creatures living in the water, you may eat any that has fins and scales. 10 But anything that does not have fins and scales you may not eat; for you it is unclean.

11 You may eat any clean bird. 12 But these

[a] *32* In Hebrew texts this verse (12:32) is numbered 13:1. [b] In Hebrew texts 13:1-18 is numbered 13:2-19.
[c] *15,17* The Hebrew term refers to the irrevocable giving over of things or persons to the LORD, often by totally destroying them. [d] *5* The precise identification of some of the birds and animals in this chapter is uncertain.

you may not eat: the eagle, the vulture, the black vulture, 13the red kite, the black kite, any kind of falcon, 14any kind of raven, 15the horned owl, the screech owl, the gull, any kind of hawk, 16the little owl, the great owl, the white owl, 17the desert owl, the osprey, the cormorant, 18the stork, any kind of heron, the hoopoe and the bat.

19All flying insects are unclean to you; do not eat them. 20But any winged creature that is clean you may eat.

21Do not eat anything you find already dead. You may give it to the foreigner residing in any of your towns, and they may eat it, or you may sell it to any other foreigner. But you are a people holy to the LORD your God.

Do not cook a young goat in its mother's milk.

Tithes

22Be sure to set aside a tenth of all that your fields produce each year. 23Eat the tithe of your grain, new wine and olive oil, and the firstborn of your herds and flocks in the presence of the LORD your God at the place he will choose as a dwelling for his Name, so that you may learn to revere the LORD your God always. 24But if that place is too distant and you have been blessed by the LORD your God and cannot carry your tithe (because the place where the LORD will choose to put his Name is so far away), 25then exchange your tithe for silver, and take the silver with you and go to the place the LORD your God will choose. 26Use the silver to buy whatever you like: cattle, sheep, wine or other fermented drink, or anything you wish. Then you and your household shall eat there in the presence of the LORD your God and rejoice. 27And do not neglect the Levites living in your towns, for they have no allotment or inheritance of their own.

28At the end of every three years, bring all the tithes of that year's produce and store it in your towns, 29so that the Levites (who have no allotment or inheritance of their own) and the foreigners, the fatherless and the widows who live in your towns may come and eat and be satisfied, and so that the LORD your God may bless you in all the work of your hands.

The Year for Canceling Debts

15 At the end of every seven years you must cancel debts. 2This is how it is to be done: Every creditor shall cancel any loan they have made to a fellow Israelite. They shall not require payment from anyone among their own people, because the LORD's time for canceling debts has been proclaimed. 3You may require payment from a foreigner, but you must cancel any debt your fellow Israelite owes you. 4However, there need be no poor people among you, for in the land the LORD your God is giving you to possess as your inheritance, he will richly bless you, 5if only you fully obey the LORD your God and are careful to follow all these commands I am giving you today. 6For the LORD your God will bless you as he has promised, and you will lend to many nations but will borrow from none. You will rule over many nations but none will rule over you.

7If anyone is poor among your fellow Israelites in any of the towns of the land the LORD your God is giving you, do not be hardhearted or tightfisted toward them. 8Rather, be openhanded and freely lend them whatever they need. 9Be careful not to harbor this wicked thought: "The seventh year, the year for canceling debts, is near," so that you do not show ill will toward the needy among your fellow Israelites and give them nothing. They may then appeal to the LORD against you, and you will be found guilty of sin. 10Give generously to them and do so without a grudging heart; then because of this the LORD your God will bless you in all your work and in everything you put your hand to. 11There will always be poor people in the land. Therefore I command you to be openhanded toward your fellow Israelites who are poor and needy in your land.

Freeing Servants

12If any of your people — Hebrew men or women — sell themselves to you and serve you six years, in the seventh year you must let them go free. 13And when you release them, do not send them away empty-handed. 14Supply them liberally from your flock, your threshing floor and your winepress. Give to them as the LORD your God has blessed you. 15Remember that you were slaves in Egypt and the LORD your God redeemed you. That is why I give you this command today.

16But if your servant says to you, "I do not want to leave you," because he loves you and your family and is well off with you, 17 then take an awl and push it through his earlobe into the door, and he will become your servant for life. Do the same for your female servant.

18 Do not consider it a hardship to set your servant free, because their service to you these six years has been worth twice as much as that of a hired hand. And the LORD your God will bless you in everything you do.

The Firstborn Animals

19 Set apart for the LORD your God every firstborn male of your herds and flocks. Do not put the firstborn of your cows to work, and do not shear the firstborn of your sheep. 20 Each year you and your family are to eat them in the presence of the LORD your God at the place he will choose. 21 If an animal has a defect, is lame or blind, or has any serious flaw, you must not sacrifice it to the LORD your God. 22 You are to eat it in your own towns. Both the ceremonially unclean and the clean may eat it, as if it were gazelle or deer. 23 But you must not eat the blood; pour it out on the ground like water.

The Passover

16 Observe the month of Aviv and celebrate the Passover of the LORD your God, because in the month of Aviv he brought you out of Egypt by night. 2 Sacrifice as the Passover to the LORD your God an animal from your flock or herd at the place the LORD will choose as a dwelling for his Name. 3 Do not eat it with bread made with yeast, but for seven days eat unleavened bread, the bread of affliction, because you left Egypt in haste—so that all the days of your life you may remember the time of your departure from Egypt. 4 Let no yeast be found in your possession in all your land for seven days. Do not let any of the meat you sacrifice on the evening of the first day remain until morning.

5 You must not sacrifice the Passover in any town the LORD your God gives you 6 except in the place he will choose as a dwelling for his Name. There you must sacrifice the Passover in the evening, when the sun goes down, on the anniversary[a] of your departure from Egypt. 7 Roast it and eat it at the place the LORD your God will choose. Then in the morning return to your tents. 8 For six days eat unleavened bread and on the seventh day hold an assembly to the LORD your God and do no work.

The Festival of Weeks

9 Count off seven weeks from the time you begin to put the sickle to the standing grain. 10 Then celebrate the Festival of Weeks to the LORD your God by giving a freewill offering in proportion to the blessings the LORD your God has given you. 11 And rejoice before the LORD your God at the place he will choose as a dwelling for his Name—you, your sons and daughters, your male and female servants, the Levites in your towns, and the foreigners, the fatherless and the widows living among you. 12 Remember that you were slaves in Egypt, and follow carefully these decrees.

The Festival of Tabernacles

13 Celebrate the Festival of Tabernacles for seven days after you have gathered the produce of your threshing floor and your winepress. 14 Be joyful at your festival—you, your sons and daughters, your male and female servants, and the Levites, the foreigners, the fatherless and the widows who live in your towns. 15 For seven days celebrate the festival to the LORD your God at the place the LORD will choose. For the LORD your God will bless you in all your harvest and in all the work of your hands, and your joy will be complete.

16 Three times a year all your men must appear before the LORD your God at the place he will choose: at the Festival of Unleavened Bread, the Festival of Weeks and the Festival of Tabernacles. No one should appear before the LORD empty-handed: 17 Each of you must bring a gift in proportion to the way the LORD your God has blessed you.

Judges

18 Appoint judges and officials for each of your tribes in every town the LORD your God is giving you, and they shall judge the people fairly. 19 Do not pervert justice or show partiality. Do not accept a bribe, for a bribe blinds the eyes of the wise and twists the words of the innocent. 20 Follow justice and justice alone, so that you may live and possess the land the LORD your God is giving you.

[a] 6 Or *down, at the time of day*

Worshiping Other Gods

21 Do not set up any wooden Asherah pole beside the altar you build to the LORD your God, 22 and do not erect a sacred stone, for these the LORD your God hates.

17 Do not sacrifice to the LORD your God an ox or a sheep that has any defect or flaw in it, for that would be detestable to him.

2 If a man or woman living among you in one of the towns the LORD gives you is found doing evil in the eyes of the LORD your God in violation of his covenant, 3 and contrary to my command has worshiped other gods, bowing down to them or to the sun or the moon or the stars in the sky, 4 and this has been brought to your attention, then you must investigate it thoroughly. If it is true and it has been proved that this detestable thing has been done in Israel, 5 take the man or woman who has done this evil deed to your city gate and stone that person to death. 6 On the testimony of two or three witnesses a person is to be put to death, but no one is to be put to death on the testimony of only one witness. 7 The hands of the witnesses must be the first in putting that person to death, and then the hands of all the people. You must purge the evil from among you.

Law Courts

8 If cases come before your courts that are too difficult for you to judge — whether bloodshed, lawsuits or assaults — take them to the place the LORD your God will choose. 9 Go to the Levitical priests and to the judge who is in office at that time. Inquire of them and they will give you the verdict. 10 You must act according to the decisions they give you at the place the LORD will choose. Be careful to do everything they instruct you to do. 11 Act according to whatever they teach you and the decisions they give you. Do not turn aside from what they tell you, to the right or to the left. 12 Anyone who shows contempt for the judge or for the priest who stands ministering there to the LORD your God is to be put to death. You must purge the evil from Israel. 13 All the people will hear and be afraid, and will not be contemptuous again.

The King

14 When you enter the land the LORD your God is giving you and have taken possession of it and settled in it, and you say, "Let us set a king over us like all the nations around us," 15 be sure to appoint over you a king the LORD your God chooses. He must be from among your fellow Israelites. Do not place a foreigner over you, one who is not an Israelite. 16 The king, moreover, must not acquire great numbers of horses for himself or make the people return to Egypt to get more of them, for the LORD has told you, "You are not to go back that way again." 17 He must not take many wives, or his heart will be led astray. He must not accumulate large amounts of silver and gold.

18 When he takes the throne of his kingdom, he is to write for himself on a scroll a copy of this law, taken from that of the Levitical priests. 19 It is to be with him, and he is to read it all the days of his life so that he may learn to revere the LORD his God and follow carefully all the words of this law and these decrees 20 and not consider himself better than his fellow Israelites and turn from the law to the right or to the left. Then he and his descendants will reign a long time over his kingdom in Israel.

Offerings for Priests and Levites

18 The Levitical priests — indeed, the whole tribe of Levi — are to have no allotment or inheritance with Israel. They shall live on the food offerings presented to the LORD, for that is their inheritance. 2 They shall have no inheritance among their fellow Israelites; the LORD is their inheritance, as he promised them.

3 This is the share due the priests from the people who sacrifice a bull or a sheep: the shoulder, the internal organs and the meat from the head. 4 You are to give them the firstfruits of your grain, new wine and olive oil, and the first wool from the shearing of your sheep, 5 for the LORD your God has chosen them and their descendants out of all your tribes to stand and minister in the LORD's name always.

6 If a Levite moves from one of your towns anywhere in Israel where he is living, and comes in all earnestness to the place the LORD will choose, 7 he may minister in the name of the LORD his God like all his fellow Levites who serve there in the presence of the LORD. 8 He is to share equally in their benefits, even though he has received money from the sale of family possessions.

Occult Practices

[9]When you enter the land the LORD your God is giving you, do not learn to imitate the detestable ways of the nations there. [10]Let no one be found among you who sacrifices their son or daughter in the fire, who practices divination or sorcery, interprets omens, engages in witchcraft, [11]or casts spells, or who is a medium or spiritist or who consults the dead. [12]Anyone who does these things is detestable to the LORD; because of these same detestable practices the LORD your God will drive out those nations before you. [13]You must be blameless before the LORD your God.

The Prophet

[14]The nations you will dispossess listen to those who practice sorcery or divination. But as for you, the LORD your God has not permitted you to do so. [15]The LORD your God will raise up for you a prophet like me from among you, from your fellow Israelites. You must listen to him. [16]For this is what you asked of the LORD your God at Horeb on the day of the assembly when you said, "Let us not hear the voice of the LORD our God nor see this great fire anymore, or we will die."

[17]The LORD said to me: "What they say is good. [18]I will raise up for them a prophet like you from among their fellow Israelites, and I will put my words in his mouth. He will tell them everything I command him. [19]I myself will call to account anyone who does not listen to my words that the prophet speaks in my name. [20]But a prophet who presumes to speak in my name anything I have not commanded, or a prophet who speaks in the name of other gods, is to be put to death."

[21]You may say to yourselves, "How can we know when a message has not been spoken by the LORD?" [22]If what a prophet proclaims in the name of the LORD does not take place or come true, that is a message the LORD has not spoken. That prophet has spoken presumptuously, so do not be alarmed.

Cities of Refuge

19 When the LORD your God has destroyed the nations whose land he is giving you, and when you have driven them out and settled in their towns and houses, [2]then set aside for yourselves three cities in the land the LORD your God is giving you to possess. [3]Determine the distances involved and divide into three parts the land the LORD your God is giving you as an inheritance, so that a person who kills someone may flee for refuge to one of these cities.

[4]This is the rule concerning anyone who kills a person and flees there for safety—anyone who kills a neighbor unintentionally, without malice aforethought. [5]For instance, a man may go into the forest with his neighbor to cut wood, and as he swings his ax to fell a tree, the head may fly off and hit his neighbor and kill him. That man may flee to one of these cities and save his life. [6]Otherwise, the avenger of blood might pursue him in a rage, overtake him if the distance is too great, and kill him even though he is not deserving of death, since he did it to his neighbor without malice aforethought. [7]This is why I command you to set aside for yourselves three cities.

[8]If the LORD your God enlarges your territory, as he promised on oath to your ancestors, and gives you the whole land he promised them, [9]because you carefully follow all these laws I command you today—to love the LORD your God and to walk always in obedience to him—then you are to set aside three more cities. [10]Do this so that innocent blood will not be shed in your land, which the LORD your God is giving you as your inheritance, and so that you will not be guilty of bloodshed.

[11]But if out of hate someone lies in wait, assaults and kills a neighbor, and then flees to one of these cities, [12]the killer shall be sent for by the town elders, be brought back from the city, and be handed over to the avenger of blood to die. [13]Show no pity. You must purge from Israel the guilt of shedding innocent blood, so that it may go well with you.

[14]Do not move your neighbor's boundary stone set up by your predecessors in the inheritance you receive in the land the LORD your God is giving you to possess.

Witnesses

[15]One witness is not enough to convict anyone accused of any crime or offense they may have committed. A matter must be established by the testimony of two or three witnesses.

[16]If a malicious witness takes the stand to accuse someone of a crime, [17]the two people involved in the dispute must stand in

the presence of the LORD before the priests and the judges who are in office at the time. 18 The judges must make a thorough investigation, and if the witness proves to be a liar, giving false testimony against a fellow Israelite, 19 then do to the false witness as that witness intended to do to the other party. You must purge the evil from among you. 20 The rest of the people will hear of this and be afraid, and never again will such an evil thing be done among you. 21 Show no pity: life for life, eye for eye, tooth for tooth, hand for hand, foot for foot.

Going to War

20 When you go to war against your enemies and see horses and chariots and an army greater than yours, do not be afraid of them, because the LORD your God, who brought you up out of Egypt, will be with you. 2 When you are about to go into battle, the priest shall come forward and address the army. 3 He shall say: "Hear, Israel: Today you are going into battle against your enemies. Do not be fainthearted or afraid; do not panic or be terrified by them. 4 For the LORD your God is the one who goes with you to fight for you against your enemies to give you victory."

5 The officers shall say to the army: "Has anyone built a new house and not yet begun to live in it? Let him go home, or he may die in battle and someone else may begin to live in it. 6 Has anyone planted a vineyard and not begun to enjoy it? Let him go home, or he may die in battle and someone else enjoy it. 7 Has anyone become pledged to a woman and not married her? Let him go home, or he may die in battle and someone else marry her." 8 Then the officers shall add, "Is anyone afraid or fainthearted? Let him go home so that his fellow soldiers will not become disheartened too." 9 When the officers have finished speaking to the army, they shall appoint commanders over it.

10 When you march up to attack a city, make its people an offer of peace. 11 If they accept and open their gates, all the people in it shall be subject to forced labor and shall work for you. 12 If they refuse to make peace and they engage you in battle, lay siege to that city. 13 When the LORD your God delivers it into your hand, put to the sword all the men in it. 14 As for the women, the children, the livestock and everything else in the city, you may take these as plunder for yourselves. And you may use the plunder the LORD your God gives you from your enemies. 15 This is how you are to treat all the cities that are at a distance from you and do not belong to the nations nearby.

16 However, in the cities of the nations the LORD your God is giving you as an inheritance, do not leave alive anything that breathes. 17 Completely destroy[a] them—the Hittites, Amorites, Canaanites, Perizzites, Hivites and Jebusites—as the LORD your God has commanded you. 18 Otherwise, they will teach you to follow all the detestable things they do in worshiping their gods, and you will sin against the LORD your God.

19 When you lay siege to a city for a long time, fighting against it to capture it, do not destroy its trees by putting an ax to them, because you can eat their fruit. Do not cut them down. Are the trees people, that you should besiege them?[b] 20 However, you may cut down trees that you know are not fruit trees and use them to build siege works until the city at war with you falls.

Atonement for an Unsolved Murder

21 If someone is found slain, lying in a field in the land the LORD your God is giving you to possess, and it is not known who the killer was, 2 your elders and judges shall go out and measure the distance from the body to the neighboring towns. 3 Then the elders of the town nearest the body shall take a heifer that has never been worked and has never worn a yoke 4 and lead it down to a valley that has not been plowed or planted and where there is a flowing stream. There in the valley they are to break the heifer's neck. 5 The Levitical priests shall step forward, for the LORD your God has chosen them to minister and to pronounce blessings in the name of the LORD and to decide all cases of dispute and assault. 6 Then all the elders of the town nearest the body shall wash their hands over the heifer whose neck was broken in the valley, 7 and they shall declare: "Our hands did not shed this blood, nor did our eyes see it done. 8 Accept this

[a] 17 The Hebrew term refers to the irrevocable giving over of things or persons to the LORD, often by totally destroying them. [b] 19 Or *down to use in the siege, for the fruit trees are for the benefit of people.*

atonement for your people Israel, whom you have redeemed, LORD, and do not hold your people guilty of the blood of an innocent person." Then the bloodshed will be atoned for, 9and you will have purged from yourselves the guilt of shedding innocent blood, since you have done what is right in the eyes of the LORD.

Marrying a Captive Woman

10When you go to war against your enemies and the LORD your God delivers them into your hands and you take captives, 11if you notice among the captives a beautiful woman and are attracted to her, you may take her as your wife. 12Bring her into your home and have her shave her head, trim her nails 13and put aside the clothes she was wearing when captured. After she has lived in your house and mourned her father and mother for a full month, then you may go to her and be her husband and she shall be your wife. 14If you are not pleased with her, let her go wherever she wishes. You must not sell her or treat her as a slave, since you have dishonored her.

The Right of the Firstborn

15If a man has two wives, and he loves one but not the other, and both bear him sons but the firstborn is the son of the wife he does not love, 16when he wills his property to his sons, he must not give the rights of the firstborn to the son of the wife he loves in preference to his actual firstborn, the son of the wife he does not love. 17He must acknowledge the son of his unloved wife as the firstborn by giving him a double share of all he has. That son is the first sign of his father's strength. The right of the firstborn belongs to him.

A Rebellious Son

18If someone has a stubborn and rebellious son who does not obey his father and mother and will not listen to them when they discipline him, 19his father and mother shall take hold of him and bring him to the elders at the gate of his town. 20They shall say to the elders, "This son of ours is stubborn and rebellious. He will not obey us. He is a glutton and a drunkard." 21Then all the men of his town are to stone him to death. You must purge the evil from among you. All Israel will hear of it and be afraid.

Various Laws

22If someone guilty of a capital offense is put to death and their body is exposed on a pole, 23you must not leave the body hanging on the pole overnight. Be sure to bury it that same day, because anyone who is hung on a pole is under God's curse. You must not desecrate the land the LORD your God is giving you as an inheritance.

22 If you see your fellow Israelite's ox or sheep straying, do not ignore it but be sure to take it back to its owner. 2If they do not live near you or if you do not know who owns it, take it home with you and keep it until they come looking for it. Then give it back. 3Do the same if you find their donkey or cloak or anything else they have lost. Do not ignore it.

4If you see your fellow Israelite's donkey or ox fallen on the road, do not ignore it. Help the owner get it to its feet.

5A woman must not wear men's clothing, nor a man wear women's clothing, for the LORD your God detests anyone who does this.

6If you come across a bird's nest beside the road, either in a tree or on the ground, and the mother is sitting on the young or on the eggs, do not take the mother with the young. 7You may take the young, but be sure to let the mother go, so that it may go well with you and you may have a long life.

8When you build a new house, make a parapet around your roof so that you may not bring the guilt of bloodshed on your house if someone falls from the roof.

9Do not plant two kinds of seed in your vineyard; if you do, not only the crops you plant but also the fruit of the vineyard will be defiled.[a]

10Do not plow with an ox and a donkey yoked together.

11Do not wear clothes of wool and linen woven together.

12Make tassels on the four corners of the cloak you wear.

Marriage Violations

13If a man takes a wife and, after sleeping with her, dislikes her 14and slanders her and gives her a bad name, saying, "I married

[a] 9 Or *be forfeited to the sanctuary*

this woman, but when I approached her, I did not find proof of her virginity," 15 then the young woman's father and mother shall bring to the town elders at the gate proof that she was a virgin. 16 Her father will say to the elders, "I gave my daughter in marriage to this man, but he dislikes her. 17 Now he has slandered her and said, 'I did not find your daughter to be a virgin.' But here is the proof of my daughter's virginity." Then her parents shall display the cloth before the elders of the town, 18 and the elders shall take the man and punish him. 19 They shall fine him a hundred shekels[a] of silver and give them to the young woman's father, because this man has given an Israelite virgin a bad name. She shall continue to be his wife; he must not divorce her as long as he lives.

20 If, however, the charge is true and no proof of the young woman's virginity can be found, 21 she shall be brought to the door of her father's house and there the men of her town shall stone her to death. She has done an outrageous thing in Israel by being promiscuous while still in her father's house. You must purge the evil from among you.

22 If a man is found sleeping with another man's wife, both the man who slept with her and the woman must die. You must purge the evil from Israel.

23 If a man happens to meet in a town a virgin pledged to be married and he sleeps with her, 24 you shall take both of them to the gate of that town and stone them to death — the young woman because she was in a town and did not scream for help, and the man because he violated another man's wife. You must purge the evil from among you.

25 But if out in the country a man happens to meet a young woman pledged to be married and rapes her, only the man who has done this shall die. 26 Do nothing to the woman; she has committed no sin deserving death. This case is like that of someone who attacks and murders a neighbor, 27 for the man found the young woman out in the country, and though the betrothed woman screamed, there was no one to rescue her.

28 If a man happens to meet a virgin who is not pledged to be married and rapes her and they are discovered, 29 he shall pay her father fifty shekels[b] of silver. He must marry the young woman, for he has violated her. He can never divorce her as long as he lives.

30 A man is not to marry his father's wife; he must not dishonor his father's bed.[c]

Exclusion From the Assembly

23 [d] No one who has been emasculated by crushing or cutting may enter the assembly of the LORD.

2 No one born of a forbidden marriage[e] nor any of their descendants may enter the assembly of the LORD, not even in the tenth generation.

3 No Ammonite or Moabite or any of their descendants may enter the assembly of the LORD, not even in the tenth generation. 4 For they did not come to meet you with bread and water on your way when you came out of Egypt, and they hired Balaam son of Beor from Pethor in Aram Naharaim[f] to pronounce a curse on you. 5 However, the LORD your God would not listen to Balaam but turned the curse into a blessing for you, because the LORD your God loves you. 6 Do not seek a treaty of friendship with them as long as you live.

7 Do not despise an Edomite, for the Edomites are related to you. Do not despise an Egyptian, because you resided as foreigners in their country. 8 The third generation of children born to them may enter the assembly of the LORD.

Uncleanness in the Camp

9 When you are encamped against your enemies, keep away from everything impure. 10 If one of your men is unclean because of a nocturnal emission, he is to go outside the camp and stay there. 11 But as evening approaches he is to wash himself, and at sunset he may return to the camp.

12 Designate a place outside the camp where you can go to relieve yourself. 13 As part of your equipment have something to dig with, and when you relieve yourself, dig a hole and cover up your excrement. 14 For the LORD your God moves about in your camp to protect you and to deliver your enemies to you. Your camp must be holy, so that he will not see among you anything indecent and turn away from you.

[a] *19* That is, about 2 1/2 pounds or about 1.2 kilograms [b] *29* That is, about 1 1/4 pounds or about 575 grams [c] *30* In Hebrew texts this verse (22:30) is numbered 23:1. [d] In Hebrew texts 23:1-25 is numbered 23:2-26. [e] *2* Or *one of illegitimate birth* [f] *4* That is, Northwest Mesopotamia

Miscellaneous Laws

15 If a slave has taken refuge with you, do not hand them over to their master. 16 Let them live among you wherever they like and in whatever town they choose. Do not oppress them.

17 No Israelite man or woman is to become a shrine prostitute. 18 You must not bring the earnings of a female prostitute or of a male prostitute[a] into the house of the LORD your God to pay any vow, because the LORD your God detests them both.

19 Do not charge a fellow Israelite interest, whether on money or food or anything else that may earn interest. 20 You may charge a foreigner interest, but not a fellow Israelite, so that the LORD your God may bless you in everything you put your hand to in the land you are entering to possess.

21 If you make a vow to the LORD your God, do not be slow to pay it, for the LORD your God will certainly demand it of you and you will be guilty of sin. 22 But if you refrain from making a vow, you will not be guilty. 23 Whatever your lips utter you must be sure to do, because you made your vow freely to the LORD your God with your own mouth.

24 If you enter your neighbor's vineyard, you may eat all the grapes you want, but do not put any in your basket. 25 If you enter your neighbor's grainfield, you may pick kernels with your hands, but you must not put a sickle to their standing grain.

24 If a man marries a woman who becomes displeasing to him because he finds something indecent about her, and he writes her a certificate of divorce, gives it to her and sends her from his house, 2 and if after she leaves his house she becomes the wife of another man, 3 and her second husband dislikes her and writes her a certificate of divorce, gives it to her and sends her from his house, or if he dies, 4 then her first husband, who divorced her, is not allowed to marry her again after she has been defiled. That would be detestable in the eyes of the LORD. Do not bring sin upon the land the LORD your God is giving you as an inheritance.

5 If a man has recently married, he must not be sent to war or have any other duty laid on him. For one year he is to be free to stay at home and bring happiness to the wife he has married.

6 Do not take a pair of millstones — not even the upper one — as security for a debt, because that would be taking a person's livelihood as security.

7 If someone is caught kidnapping a fellow Israelite and treating or selling them as a slave, the kidnapper must die. You must purge the evil from among you.

8 In cases of defiling skin diseases,[b] be very careful to do exactly as the Levitical priests instruct you. You must follow carefully what I have commanded them. 9 Remember what the LORD your God did to Miriam along the way after you came out of Egypt.

10 When you make a loan of any kind to your neighbor, do not go into their house to get what is offered to you as a pledge. 11 Stay outside and let the neighbor to whom you are making the loan bring the pledge out to you. 12 If the neighbor is poor, do not go to sleep with their pledge in your possession. 13 Return their cloak by sunset so that your neighbor may sleep in it. Then they will thank you, and it will be regarded as a righteous act in the sight of the LORD your God.

14 Do not take advantage of a hired worker who is poor and needy, whether that worker is a fellow Israelite or a foreigner residing in one of your towns. 15 Pay them their wages each day before sunset, because they are poor and are counting on it. Otherwise they may cry to the LORD against you, and you will be guilty of sin.

16 Parents are not to be put to death for their children, nor children put to death for their parents; each will die for their own sin.

17 Do not deprive the foreigner or the fatherless of justice, or take the cloak of the widow as a pledge. 18 Remember that you were slaves in Egypt and the LORD your God redeemed you from there. That is why I command you to do this.

19 When you are harvesting in your field and you overlook a sheaf, do not go back to get it. Leave it for the foreigner, the fatherless and the widow, so that the LORD your God may bless you in all the work of your hands. 20 When you beat the olives from your trees, do not go over the branches a second time.

[a] 18 Hebrew *of a dog* [b] 8 The Hebrew word for *defiling skin diseases*, traditionally translated "leprosy," was used for various diseases affecting the skin.

Leave what remains for the foreigner, the
fatherless and the widow. 21 When you har-
vest the grapes in your vineyard, do not go
over the vines again. Leave what remains for
the foreigner, the fatherless and the widow.
22 Remember that you were slaves in Egypt.
That is why I command you to do this.

25 When people have a dispute, they are
to take it to court and the judges will
decide the case, acquitting the innocent and
condemning the guilty. 2 If the guilty per-
son deserves to be beaten, the judge shall
make them lie down and have them flogged
in his presence with the number of lashes
the crime deserves, 3 but the judge must not
impose more than forty lashes. If the guilty
party is flogged more than that, your fellow
Israelite will be degraded in your eyes.

4 Do not muzzle an ox while it is treading
out the grain.

5 If brothers are living together and one
of them dies without a son, his widow must
not marry outside the family. Her husband's
brother shall take her and marry her and ful-
fill the duty of a brother-in-law to her. 6 The
first son she bears shall carry on the name of
the dead brother so that his name will not be
blotted out from Israel.

7 However, if a man does not want to mar-
ry his brother's wife, she shall go to the el-
ders at the town gate and say, "My husband's
brother refuses to carry on his brother's
name in Israel. He will not fulfill the duty
of a brother-in-law to me." 8 Then the elders
of his town shall summon him and talk to
him. If he persists in saying, "I do not want
to marry her," 9 his brother's widow shall go
up to him in the presence of the elders, take
off one of his sandals, spit in his face and say,
"This is what is done to the man who will not
build up his brother's family line." 10 That
man's line shall be known in Israel as The
Family of the Unsandaled.

11 If two men are fighting and the wife of
one of them comes to rescue her husband
from his assailant, and she reaches out and
seizes him by his private parts, 12 you shall
cut off her hand. Show her no pity.

13 Do not have two differing weights in
your bag—one heavy, one light. 14 Do not
have two differing measures in your house—
one large, one small. 15 You must have accu-
rate and honest weights and measures, so
that you may live long in the land the LORD
your God is giving you. 16 For the LORD your
God detests anyone who does these things,
anyone who deals dishonestly.

17 Remember what the Amalekites did
to you along the way when you came out of
Egypt. 18 When you were weary and worn
out, they met you on your journey and at-
tacked all who were lagging behind; they
had no fear of God. 19 When the LORD your
God gives you rest from all the enemies
around you in the land he is giving you to
possess as an inheritance, you shall blot out
the name of Amalek from under heaven. Do
not forget!

Firstfruits and Tithes

26 When you have entered the land the
LORD your God is giving you as an
inheritance and have taken possession of
it and settled in it, 2 take some of the first-
fruits of all that you produce from the soil
of the land the LORD your God is giving you
and put them in a basket. Then go to the
place the LORD your God will choose as a
dwelling for his Name 3 and say to the priest
in office at the time, "I declare today to the
LORD your God that I have come to the land
the LORD swore to our ancestors to give us."
4 The priest shall take the basket from your
hands and set it down in front of the altar of
the LORD your God. 5 Then you shall declare
before the LORD your God: "My father was a
wandering Aramean, and he went down into
Egypt with a few people and lived there and
became a great nation, powerful and numer-
ous. 6 But the Egyptians mistreated us and
made us suffer, subjecting us to harsh labor.
7 Then we cried out to the LORD, the God of
our ancestors, and the LORD heard our voice
and saw our misery, toil and oppression.
8 So the LORD brought us out of Egypt with a
mighty hand and an outstretched arm, with
great terror and with signs and wonders. 9 He
brought us to this place and gave us this land,
a land flowing with milk and honey; 10 and
now I bring the firstfruits of the soil that you,
LORD, have given me." Place the basket be-
fore the LORD your God and bow down be-
fore him. 11 Then you and the Levites and the
foreigners residing among you shall rejoice
in all the good things the LORD your God has
given to you and your household.

12 When you have finished setting aside a
tenth of all your produce in the third year, the

JESUS MESSIAH

Chris Tomlin, Daniel Carson, Jesse Reeves, Ed Cash

He became sin who knew no sin
That we might become his righteousness
He humbled himself and carried the cross
Love so amazing
Love so amazing

Jesus Messiah
Name above all names
Blessed Redeemer
Emmanuel
The rescue for sinners
The ransom from Heaven
Jesus Messiah
Lord of all

His body the bread, his blood the wine
Broken and poured out all for love
The whole earth trembled and the veil was torn
Love so amazing
Love so amazing

All our hope is in you
All our hope is in you
All the glory to you, God
The Light of the world

THE INSPIRATION

God made him who had no sin to be sin for us, so that in him we might become the righteousness of God. —2 Corinthians 5:21

BEHIND THE SONG

The Hebrew word *Messiah* evolved over centuries to mean "anointed one," "liberator" or "savior," but originally was not exclusively used to describe Jesus. The prophets Isaiah and Daniel, however, imbued this word with new and important meaning for God's people. There would be a redeemer, an anointed king who would deliver his people from their bondage once and for all.

Later, as the church expanded into Greek speaking cultures, the Hebrew word *Messiah* was translated as the Greek word *Christ*. The two mean the same thing. Jesus, the anointed Son of God, has the power to pay our ransom, to liberate us from our captivity to sin, and to deliver the church to God as an unblemished bride. It is not because of our goodness that he does this, but because of *his* goodness and *his* love. How we understand Jesus as Messiah has everything to do with how we understand our faith and our relationship with him.

Selah

How has Jesus been Messiah for you? From what has he saved you? Have you ever contemplated the unique aspects of Jesus that allow him to be Messiah? From a legal and spiritual perspective, recall some of the things that Jesus must be in order for him to have this saving power.

Daniel Carson, one of Chris Tomlin's band members, had the original idea for the chorus of this song. Tomlin heard it and the collaboration began. For Tomlin the song accomplished something he had been working on for years.

"For quite some time I wanted to write a song that included the word Messiah, Jesus as our Messiah," Tomlin explains. "I love that word, how beautiful that name sounds and what it means. Jesus is a great person, a great leader and a great man of faith, but when you say 'Messiah,' it really draws the line in the sand. It is a whole other level. You are saying he's the Anointed One. He's the chosen one, the very Son of God, and I wanted a song that really proclaimed that because that's who he is."

year of the tithe, you shall give it to the Levite,
the foreigner, the fatherless and the widow, so
that they may eat in your towns and be satis-
fied. 13Then say to the Lord your God: "I have
removed from my house the sacred portion
and have given it to the Levite, the foreigner,
the fatherless and the widow, according to
all you commanded. I have not turned aside
from your commands nor have I forgotten
any of them. 14I have not eaten any of the sa-
cred portion while I was in mourning, nor
have I removed any of it while I was unclean,
nor have I offered any of it to the dead. I have
obeyed the Lord my God; I have done ev-
erything you commanded me. 15Look down
from heaven, your holy dwelling place, and
bless your people Israel and the land you have
given us as you promised on oath to our an-
cestors, a land flowing with milk and honey."

Follow the Lord's Commands

16The Lord your God commands you this
day to follow these decrees and laws; careful-
ly observe them with all your heart and with
all your soul. 17You have declared this day
that the Lord is your God and that you will
walk in obedience to him, that you will keep
his decrees, commands and laws—that you
will listen to him. 18And the Lord has de-
clared this day that you are his people, his
treasured possession as he promised, and
that you are to keep all his commands. 19He
has declared that he will set you in praise,
fame and honor high above all the nations he
has made and that you will be a people holy
to the Lord your God, as he promised.

The Altar on Mount Ebal

27 Moses and the elders of Israel com-
manded the people: "Keep all these
commands that I give you today. 2When you
have crossed the Jordan into the land the
Lord your God is giving you, set up some
large stones and coat them with plaster.
3Write on them all the words of this law when
you have crossed over to enter the land the
Lord your God is giving you, a land flowing
with milk and honey, just as the Lord, the
God of your ancestors, promised you. 4And
when you have crossed the Jordan, set up
these stones on Mount Ebal, as I command
you today, and coat them with plaster. 5Build
there an altar to the Lord your God, an altar
of stones. Do not use any iron tool on them.
6Build the altar of the Lord your God with
fieldstones and offer burnt offerings on it to
the Lord your God. 7Sacrifice fellowship of-
ferings there, eating them and rejoicing in
the presence of the Lord your God. 8And
you shall write very clearly all the words of
this law on these stones you have set up."

Curses From Mount Ebal

9Then Moses and the Levitical priests
said to all Israel, "Be silent, Israel, and lis-
ten! You have now become the people of the
Lord your God. 10Obey the Lord your God
and follow his commands and decrees that
I give you today."

11On the same day Moses commanded
the people:

12When you have crossed the Jordan,
these tribes shall stand on Mount Gerizim
to bless the people: Simeon, Levi, Judah, Is-
sachar, Joseph and Benjamin. 13And these
tribes shall stand on Mount Ebal to pro-
nounce curses: Reuben, Gad, Asher, Zebu-
lun, Dan and Naphtali.

14The Levites shall recite to all the people
of Israel in a loud voice:

15"Cursed is anyone who makes an
idol—a thing detestable to the Lord,
the work of skilled hands—and sets it
up in secret."

Then all the people shall say,
"Amen!"

16"Cursed is anyone who dishonors
their father or mother."

Then all the people shall say,
"Amen!"

17"Cursed is anyone who moves their
neighbor's boundary stone."

Then all the people shall say,
"Amen!"

18"Cursed is anyone who leads the
blind astray on the road."

Then all the people shall say,
"Amen!"

19"Cursed is anyone who withholds
justice from the foreigner, the father-
less or the widow."

Then all the people shall say,
"Amen!"

20"Cursed is anyone who sleeps with
his father's wife, for he dishonors his fa-
ther's bed."

Then all the people shall say,
"Amen!"

21 “Cursed is anyone who has sexual relations with any animal.”

Then all the people shall say,
“Amen!”

22 “Cursed is anyone who sleeps with his sister, the daughter of his father or the daughter of his mother.”

Then all the people shall say,
“Amen!”

23 “Cursed is anyone who sleeps with his mother-in-law.”

Then all the people shall say,
“Amen!”

24 “Cursed is anyone who kills their neighbor secretly.”

Then all the people shall say,
“Amen!”

25 “Cursed is anyone who accepts a bribe to kill an innocent person.”

Then all the people shall say,
“Amen!”

26 “Cursed is anyone who does not uphold the words of this law by carrying them out.”

Then all the people shall say,
“Amen!”

Blessings for Obedience

28 If you fully obey the LORD your God and carefully follow all his commands I give you today, the LORD your God will set you high above all the nations on earth. 2 All these blessings will come on you and accompany you if you obey the LORD your God:

3 You will be blessed in the city and
blessed in the country.
4 The fruit of your womb will be
blessed, and the crops of your land
and the young of your livestock—the
calves of your herds and the lambs of
your flocks.
5 Your basket and your kneading
trough will be blessed.
6 You will be blessed when you come
in and blessed when you go out.

7 The LORD will grant that the enemies who rise up against you will be defeated before you. They will come at you from one direction but flee from you in seven.

8 The LORD will send a blessing on your barns and on everything you put your hand to. The LORD your God will bless you in the land he is giving you.

9 The LORD will establish you as his holy people, as he promised you on oath, if you keep the commands of the LORD your God and walk in obedience to him. 10 Then all the peoples on earth will see that you are called by the name of the LORD, and they will fear you. 11 The LORD will grant you abundant prosperity—in the fruit of your womb, the young of your livestock and the crops of your ground—in the land he swore to your ancestors to give you.

12 The LORD will open the heavens, the storehouse of his bounty, to send rain on your land in season and to bless all the work of your hands. You will lend to many nations but will borrow from none. 13 The LORD will make you the head, not the tail. If you pay attention to the commands of the LORD your God that I give you this day and carefully follow them, you will always be at the top, never at the bottom. 14 Do not turn aside from any of the commands I give you today, to the right or to the left, following other gods and serving them.

Curses for Disobedience

15 However, if you do not obey the LORD your God and do not carefully follow all his commands and decrees I am giving you today, all these curses will come on you and overtake you:

16 You will be cursed in the city and
cursed in the country.
17 Your basket and your kneading
trough will be cursed.
18 The fruit of your womb will be
cursed, and the crops of your land, and
the calves of your herds and the lambs
of your flocks.
19 You will be cursed when you come
in and cursed when you go out.

20 The LORD will send on you curses, confusion and rebuke in everything you put your hand to, until you are destroyed and come to sudden ruin because of the evil you have done in forsaking him.[a] 21 The LORD will plague you with diseases until he has destroyed you from the land you are entering

[a] *20* Hebrew *me*

to possess. 22The LORD will strike you with
wasting disease, with fever and inflamma-
tion, with scorching heat and drought, with
blight and mildew, which will plague you
until you perish. 23The sky over your head
will be bronze, the ground beneath you iron.
24The LORD will turn the rain of your coun-
try into dust and powder; it will come down
from the skies until you are destroyed.

25The LORD will cause you to be defeated
before your enemies. You will come at them
from one direction but flee from them in
seven, and you will become a thing of horror
to all the kingdoms on earth. 26Your carcass-
es will be food for all the birds and the wild
animals, and there will be no one to frighten
them away. 27The LORD will afflict you with
the boils of Egypt and with tumors, festering
sores and the itch, from which you cannot
be cured. 28The LORD will afflict you with
madness, blindness and confusion of mind.
29At midday you will grope about like a blind
person in the dark. You will be unsuccessful
in everything you do; day after day you will
be oppressed and robbed, with no one to res-
cue you.

30You will be pledged to be married to a
woman, but another will take her and rape
her. You will build a house, but you will not
live in it. You will plant a vineyard, but you
will not even begin to enjoy its fruit. 31Your
ox will be slaughtered before your eyes, but
you will eat none of it. Your donkey will be
forcibly taken from you and will not be re-
turned. Your sheep will be given to your
enemies, and no one will rescue them.
32Your sons and daughters will be given to
another nation, and you will wear out your
eyes watching for them day after day, pow-
erless to lift a hand. 33A people that you do
not know will eat what your land and labor
produce, and you will have nothing but cru-
el oppression all your days. 34The sights you
see will drive you mad. 35The LORD will af-
flict your knees and legs with painful boils
that cannot be cured, spreading from the
soles of your feet to the top of your head.

36The LORD will drive you and the king
you set over you to a nation unknown to you
or your ancestors. There you will worship
other gods, gods of wood and stone. 37You
will become a thing of horror, a byword and
an object of ridicule among all the peoples
where the LORD will drive you.

38You will sow much seed in the field but
you will harvest little, because locusts will
devour it. 39You will plant vineyards and cul-
tivate them but you will not drink the wine
or gather the grapes, because worms will eat
them. 40You will have olive trees throughout
your country but you will not use the oil, be-
cause the olives will drop off. 41You will have
sons and daughters but you will not keep
them, because they will go into captivity.
42Swarms of locusts will take over all your
trees and the crops of your land.

43The foreigners who reside among you
will rise above you higher and higher, but
you will sink lower and lower. 44They will
lend to you, but you will not lend to them.
They will be the head, but you will be the
tail.

45All these curses will come on you. They
will pursue you and overtake you until you
are destroyed, because you did not obey the
LORD your God and observe the commands
and decrees he gave you. 46They will be a
sign and a wonder to you and your descen-
dants forever. 47Because you did not serve
the LORD your God joyfully and gladly in
the time of prosperity, 48therefore in hunger
and thirst, in nakedness and dire poverty,
you will serve the enemies the LORD sends
against you. He will put an iron yoke on your
neck until he has destroyed you.

49The LORD will bring a nation against
you from far away, from the ends of the
earth, like an eagle swooping down, a nation
whose language you will not understand, 50a
fierce-looking nation without respect for the
old or pity for the young. 51They will devour
the young of your livestock and the crops of
your land until you are destroyed. They will
leave you no grain, new wine or olive oil, nor
any calves of your herds or lambs of your
flocks until you are ruined. 52They will lay
siege to all the cities throughout your land
until the high fortified walls in which you
trust fall down. They will besiege all the cit-
ies throughout the land the LORD your God
is giving you.

53Because of the suffering your enemy
will inflict on you during the siege, you will
eat the fruit of the womb, the flesh of the
sons and daughters the LORD your God has
given you. 54Even the most gentle and sen-
sitive man among you will have no compas-
sion on his own brother or the wife he loves

or his surviving children, [55]and he will not give to one of them any of the flesh of his children that he is eating. It will be all he has left because of the suffering your enemy will inflict on you during the siege of all your cities. [56]The most gentle and sensitive woman among you—so sensitive and gentle that she would not venture to touch the ground with the sole of her foot—will begrudge the husband she loves and her own son or daughter [57]the afterbirth from her womb and the children she bears. For in her dire need she intends to eat them secretly because of the suffering your enemy will inflict on you during the siege of your cities.

[58]If you do not carefully follow all the words of this law, which are written in this book, and do not revere this glorious and awesome name—the LORD your God—[59]the LORD will send fearful plagues on you and your descendants, harsh and prolonged disasters, and severe and lingering illnesses. [60]He will bring on you all the diseases of Egypt that you dreaded, and they will cling to you. [61]The LORD will also bring on you every kind of sickness and disaster not recorded in this Book of the Law, until you are destroyed. [62]You who were as numerous as the stars in the sky will be left but few in number, because you did not obey the LORD your God. [63]Just as it pleased the LORD to make you prosper and increase in number, so it will please him to ruin and destroy you. You will be uprooted from the land you are entering to possess.

[64]Then the LORD will scatter you among all nations, from one end of the earth to the other. There you will worship other gods—gods of wood and stone, which neither you nor your ancestors have known. [65]Among those nations you will find no repose, no resting place for the sole of your foot. There the LORD will give you an anxious mind, eyes weary with longing, and a despairing heart. [66]You will live in constant suspense, filled with dread both night and day, never sure of your life. [67]In the morning you will say, "If only it were evening!" and in the evening, "If only it were morning!"—because of the terror that will fill your hearts and the sights that your eyes will see. [68]The LORD will send you back in ships to Egypt on a journey I said you should never make again. There you will offer yourselves for sale to your enemies as male and female slaves, but no one will buy you.

Renewal of the Covenant

29[a] These are the terms of the covenant the LORD commanded Moses to make with the Israelites in Moab, in addition to the covenant he had made with them at Horeb.

[2]Moses summoned all the Israelites and said to them:

Your eyes have seen all that the LORD did in Egypt to Pharaoh, to all his officials and to all his land. [3]With your own eyes you saw those great trials, those signs and great wonders. [4]But to this day the LORD has not given you a mind that understands or eyes that see or ears that hear. [5]Yet the LORD says, "During the forty years that I led you through the wilderness, your clothes did not wear out, nor did the sandals on your feet. [6]You ate no bread and drank no wine or other fermented drink. I did this so that you might know that I am the LORD your God."

[7]When you reached this place, Sihon king of Heshbon and Og king of Bashan came out to fight against us, but we defeated them. [8]We took their land and gave it as an inheritance to the Reubenites, the Gadites and the half-tribe of Manasseh.

[9]Carefully follow the terms of this covenant, so that you may prosper in everything you do. [10]All of you are standing today in the presence of the LORD your God—your leaders and chief men, your elders and officials, and all the other men of Israel, [11]together with your children and your wives, and the foreigners living in your camps who chop your wood and carry your water. [12]You are standing here in order to enter into a covenant with the LORD your God, a covenant the LORD is making with you this day and sealing with an oath, [13]to confirm you this day as his people, that he may be your God as he promised you and as he swore to your fathers, Abraham, Isaac and Jacob. [14]I am making this covenant, with its oath, not only with you [15]who are standing here with us today in the presence of the LORD our God but also with those who are not here today.

[16]You yourselves know how we lived in

[a] In Hebrew texts 29:1 is numbered 28:69, and 29:2-29 is numbered 29:1-28.

Egypt and how we passed through the coun-
tries on the way here. 17You saw among them
their detestable images and idols of wood and
stone, of silver and gold. 18Make sure there is
no man or woman, clan or tribe among you
today whose heart turns away from the LORD
our God to go and worship the gods of those
nations; make sure there is no root among
you that produces such bitter poison.

19When such a person hears the words
of this oath and they invoke a blessing on
themselves, thinking, "I will be safe, even
though I persist in going my own way," they
will bring disaster on the watered land as
well as the dry. 20The LORD will never be
willing to forgive them; his wrath and zeal
will burn against them. All the curses writ-
ten in this book will fall on them, and the
LORD will blot out their names from under
heaven. 21The LORD will single them out
from all the tribes of Israel for disaster, ac-
cording to all the curses of the covenant
written in this Book of the Law.

22Your children who follow you in later
generations and foreigners who come from
distant lands will see the calamities that
have fallen on the land and the diseases with
which the LORD has afflicted it. 23The whole
land will be a burning waste of salt and sul-
fur — nothing planted, nothing sprouting,
no vegetation growing on it. It will be like
the destruction of Sodom and Gomorrah,
Admah and Zeboyim, which the LORD over-
threw in fierce anger. 24All the nations will
ask: "Why has the LORD done this to this
land? Why this fierce, burning anger?"

25And the answer will be: "It is because
this people abandoned the covenant of the
LORD, the God of their ancestors, the cov-
enant he made with them when he brought
them out of Egypt. 26They went off and wor-
shiped other gods and bowed down to them,
gods they did not know, gods he had not
given them. 27Therefore the LORD's anger
burned against this land, so that he brought
on it all the curses written in this book. 28In
furious anger and in great wrath the LORD
uprooted them from their land and thrust
them into another land, as it is now."

29The secret things belong to the LORD
our God, but the things revealed belong to
us and to our children forever, that we may
follow all the words of this law.

Prosperity After Turning to the LORD

30 When all these blessings and curs-
es I have set before you come on you
and you take them to heart wherever the
LORD your God disperses you among the
nations, 2and when you and your children
return to the LORD your God and obey him
with all your heart and with all your soul ac-
cording to everything I command you today,
3then the LORD your God will restore your
fortunes[a] and have compassion on you and
gather you again from all the nations where
he scattered you. 4Even if you have been
banished to the most distant land under
the heavens, from there the LORD your God
will gather you and bring you back. 5He will
bring you to the land that belonged to your
ancestors, and you will take possession of
it. He will make you more prosperous and
numerous than your ancestors. 6The LORD
your God will circumcise your hearts and
the hearts of your descendants, so that you
may love him with all your heart and with all
your soul, and live. 7The LORD your God will
put all these curses on your enemies who
hate and persecute you. 8You will again obey
the LORD and follow all his commands I am
giving you today. 9Then the LORD your God
will make you most prosperous in all the
work of your hands and in the fruit of your
womb, the young of your livestock and the
crops of your land. The LORD will again de-
light in you and make you prosperous, just as
he delighted in your ancestors, 10if you obey
the LORD your God and keep his commands
and decrees that are written in this Book of
the Law and turn to the LORD your God with
all your heart and with all your soul.

The Offer of Life or Death

11Now what I am commanding you today
is not too difficult for you or beyond your
reach. 12It is not up in heaven, so that you
have to ask, "Who will ascend into heaven to
get it and proclaim it to us so we may obey
it?" 13Nor is it beyond the sea, so that you
have to ask, "Who will cross the sea to get
it and proclaim it to us so we may obey it?"
14No, the word is very near you; it is in your
mouth and in your heart so you may obey it.

15See, I set before you today life and pros-
perity, death and destruction. 16For I com-
mand you today to love the LORD your God,

[a] 3 Or *will bring you back from captivity*

to walk in obedience to him, and to keep his commands, decrees and laws; then you will live and increase, and the LORD your God will bless you in the land you are entering to possess.

17But if your heart turns away and you are not obedient, and if you are drawn away to bow down to other gods and worship them, 18I declare to you this day that you will certainly be destroyed. You will not live long in the land you are crossing the Jordan to enter and possess.

19This day I call the heavens and the earth as witnesses against you that I have set before you life and death, blessings and curses. Now choose life, so that you and your children may live 20and that you may love the LORD your God, listen to his voice, and hold fast to him. For the LORD is your life, and he will give you many years in the land he swore to give to your fathers, Abraham, Isaac and Jacob.

Joshua to Succeed Moses

31 Then Moses went out and spoke these words to all Israel: 2"I am now a hundred and twenty years old and I am no longer able to lead you. The LORD has said to me, 'You shall not cross the Jordan.' 3The LORD your God himself will cross over ahead of you. He will destroy these nations before you, and you will take possession of their land. Joshua also will cross over ahead of you, as the LORD said. 4And the LORD will do to them what he did to Sihon and Og, the kings of the Amorites, whom he destroyed along with their land. 5The LORD will deliver them to you, and you must do to them all that I have commanded you. 6Be strong and courageous. Do not be afraid or terrified because of them, for the LORD your God goes with you; he will never leave you nor forsake you."

7Then Moses summoned Joshua and said to him in the presence of all Israel, "Be strong and courageous, for you must go with this people into the land that the LORD swore to their ancestors to give them, and you must divide it among them as their inheritance. 8The LORD himself goes before you and will be with you; he will never leave you nor forsake you. Do not be afraid; do not be discouraged."

Public Reading of the Law

9So Moses wrote down this law and gave it to the Levitical priests, who carried the ark of the covenant of the LORD, and to all the elders of Israel. 10Then Moses commanded them: "At the end of every seven years, in the year for canceling debts, during the Festival of Tabernacles, 11when all Israel comes to appear before the LORD your God at the place he will choose, you shall read this law before them in their hearing. 12Assemble the people — men, women and children, and the foreigners residing in your towns — so they can listen and learn to fear the LORD your God and follow carefully all the words of this law. 13Their children, who do not know this law, must hear it and learn to fear the LORD your God as long as you live in the land you are crossing the Jordan to possess."

Israel's Rebellion Predicted

14The LORD said to Moses, "Now the day of your death is near. Call Joshua and present yourselves at the tent of meeting, where I will commission him." So Moses and Joshua came and presented themselves at the tent of meeting.

15Then the LORD appeared at the tent in a pillar of cloud, and the cloud stood over the entrance to the tent. 16And the LORD said to Moses: "You are going to rest with your ancestors, and these people will soon prostitute themselves to the foreign gods of the land they are entering. They will forsake me and break the covenant I made with them. 17And in that day I will become angry with them and forsake them; I will hide my face from them, and they will be destroyed. Many disasters and calamities will come on them, and in that day they will ask, 'Have not these disasters come on us because our God is not with us?' 18And I will certainly hide my face in that day because of all their wickedness in turning to other gods.

19"Now write down this song and teach it to the Israelites and have them sing it, so that it may be a witness for me against them. 20When I have brought them into the land flowing with milk and honey, the land I promised on oath to their ancestors, and when they eat their fill and thrive, they will turn to other gods and worship them, rejecting me and breaking my covenant. 21And when many disasters and calamities come on them, this song will testify against them, because it will not be forgotten by their descendants. I know what they are disposed to

do, even before I bring them into the land I
promised them on oath." 22 So Moses wrote
down this song that day and taught it to the
Israelites.
23 The LORD gave this command to Josh-
ua son of Nun: "Be strong and courageous,
for you will bring the Israelites into the land
I promised them on oath, and I myself will
be with you."
24 After Moses finished writing in a book
the words of this law from beginning to end,
25 he gave this command to the Levites who
carried the ark of the covenant of the LORD:
26 "Take this Book of the Law and place it
beside the ark of the covenant of the LORD
your God. There it will remain as a witness
against you. 27 For I know how rebellious and
stiff-necked you are. If you have been rebel-
lious against the LORD while I am still alive
and with you, how much more will you rebel
after I die! 28 Assemble before me all the el-
ders of your tribes and all your officials, so
that I can speak these words in their hearing
and call the heavens and the earth to testi-
fy against them. 29 For I know that after my
death you are sure to become utterly corrupt
and to turn from the way I have command-
ed you. In days to come, disaster will fall on
you because you will do evil in the sight of
the LORD and arouse his anger by what your
hands have made."

The Song of Moses

30 And Moses recited the words of this
song from beginning to end in the hearing of
the whole assembly of Israel:

32 Listen, you heavens, and I will speak;
hear, you earth, the words of my mouth.
2 Let my teaching fall like rain
and my words descend like dew,
like showers on new grass,
like abundant rain on tender plants.

3 I will proclaim the name of the LORD.
Oh, praise the greatness of our God!
4 He is the Rock, his works are perfect,
and all his ways are just.
A faithful God who does no wrong,
upright and just is he.

5 They are corrupt and not his children;
to their shame they are a warped and crooked generation.
6 Is this the way you repay the LORD,
you foolish and unwise people?
Is he not your Father, your Creator,[a]
who made you and formed you?

7 Remember the days of old;
consider the generations long past.
Ask your father and he will tell you,
your elders, and they will explain to you.
8 When the Most High gave the nations their inheritance,
when he divided all mankind,
he set up boundaries for the peoples
according to the number of the sons of Israel.[b]
9 For the LORD's portion is his people,
Jacob his allotted inheritance.

10 In a desert land he found him,
in a barren and howling waste.
He shielded him and cared for him;
he guarded him as the apple of his eye,
11 like an eagle that stirs up its nest
and hovers over its young,
that spreads its wings to catch them
and carries them aloft.
12 The LORD alone led him;
no foreign god was with him.

13 He made him ride on the heights of the land
and fed him with the fruit of the fields.
He nourished him with honey from the rock,
and with oil from the flinty crag,
14 with curds and milk from herd and flock
and with fattened lambs and goats,
with choice rams of Bashan
and the finest kernels of wheat.
You drank the foaming blood of the grape.

15 Jeshurun[c] grew fat and kicked;
filled with food, they became heavy and sleek.
They abandoned the God who made them
and rejected the Rock their Savior.
16 They made him jealous with their foreign gods

[a] 6 Or *Father, who bought you* [b] 8 Masoretic Text; Dead Sea Scrolls (see also Septuagint) *sons of God*
[c] 15 *Jeshurun* means *the upright one,* that is, Israel.

and angered him with their detestable
idols.
17 They sacrificed to false gods, which are
not God —
gods they had not known,
gods that recently appeared,
gods your ancestors did not fear.
18 You deserted the Rock, who fathered you;
you forgot the God who gave you birth.

19 The LORD saw this and rejected them
because he was angered by his sons
and daughters.
20 "I will hide my face from them," he said,
"and see what their end will be;
for they are a perverse generation,
children who are unfaithful.
21 They made me jealous by what is no god
and angered me with their worthless
idols.
I will make them envious by those who
are not a people;
I will make them angry by a nation
that has no understanding.
22 For a fire will be kindled by my wrath,
one that burns down to the realm of
the dead below.
It will devour the earth and its harvests
and set afire the foundations of the
mountains.

23 "I will heap calamities on them
and spend my arrows against them.
24 I will send wasting famine against them,
consuming pestilence and deadly
plague;
I will send against them the fangs of wild
beasts,
the venom of vipers that glide in the
dust.
25 In the street the sword will make them
childless;
in their homes terror will reign.
The young men and young women will
perish,
the infants and those with gray hair.
26 I said I would scatter them
and erase their name from human
memory,
27 but I dreaded the taunt of the enemy,
lest the adversary misunderstand
and say, 'Our hand has triumphed;
the LORD has not done all this.' "
28 They are a nation without sense,
there is no discernment in them.
29 If only they were wise and would
understand this
and discern what their end will be!
30 How could one man chase a thousand,
or two put ten thousand to flight,
unless their Rock had sold them,
unless the LORD had given them up?
31 For their rock is not like our Rock,
as even our enemies concede.
32 Their vine comes from the vine of Sodom
and from the fields of Gomorrah.
Their grapes are filled with poison,
and their clusters with bitterness.
33 Their wine is the venom of serpents,
the deadly poison of cobras.

34 "Have I not kept this in reserve
and sealed it in my vaults?
35 It is mine to avenge; I will repay.
In due time their foot will slip;
their day of disaster is near
and their doom rushes upon them."

36 The LORD will vindicate his people
and relent concerning his servants
when he sees their strength is gone
and no one is left, slave or free.[a]
37 He will say: "Now where are their gods,
the rock they took refuge in,
38 the gods who ate the fat of their sacrifices
and drank the wine of their drink
offerings?
Let them rise up to help you!
Let them give you shelter!

39 "See now that I myself am he!
There is no god besides me.
I put to death and I bring to life,
I have wounded and I will heal,
and no one can deliver out of
my hand.
40 I lift my hand to heaven and solemnly
swear:
As surely as I live forever,
41 when I sharpen my flashing sword
and my hand grasps it in judgment,
I will take vengeance on my adversaries
and repay those who hate me.
42 I will make my arrows drunk with blood,
while my sword devours flesh:
the blood of the slain and the captives,
the heads of the enemy leaders."

[a] *36* Or *and they are without a ruler or leader*

43 Rejoice, you nations, with his people,[a,b]
for he will avenge the blood of his
servants;
he will take vengeance on his enemies
and make atonement for his land and
people.

44 Moses came with Joshua[c] son of Nun
and spoke all the words of this song in the
hearing of the people. 45 When Moses fin-
ished reciting all these words to all Isra-
el, 46 he said to them, "Take to heart all the
words I have solemnly declared to you this
day, so that you may command your chil-
dren to obey carefully all the words of this
law. 47 They are not just idle words for you—
they are your life. By them you will live long
in the land you are crossing the Jordan to
possess."

Moses to Die on Mount Nebo

48 On that same day the LORD told Moses,
49 "Go up into the Abarim Range to Mount
Nebo in Moab, across from Jericho, and view
Canaan, the land I am giving the Israelites
as their own possession. 50 There on the
mountain that you have climbed you will
die and be gathered to your people, just as
your brother Aaron died on Mount Hor and
was gathered to his people. 51 This is because
both of you broke faith with me in the pres-
ence of the Israelites at the waters of Meri-
bah Kadesh in the Desert of Zin and because
you did not uphold my holiness among the
Israelites. 52 Therefore, you will see the land
only from a distance; you will not enter the
land I am giving to the people of Israel."

Moses Blesses the Tribes

33 This is the blessing that Moses the
man of God pronounced on the Isra-
elites before his death. 2 He said:

"The LORD came from Sinai
and dawned over them from Seir;
he shone forth from Mount Paran.
He came with[d] myriads of holy ones
from the south, from his mountain
slopes.[e]
3 Surely it is you who love the people;
all the holy ones are in your hand.
At your feet they all bow down,
and from you receive instruction,
4 the law that Moses gave us,
the possession of the assembly of
Jacob.
5 He was king over Jeshurun[f]
when the leaders of the people
assembled,
along with the tribes of Israel.

6 "Let Reuben live and not die,
nor[g] his people be few."

7 And this he said about Judah:

"Hear, LORD, the cry of Judah;
bring him to his people.
With his own hands he defends his
cause.
Oh, be his help against his foes!"

8 About Levi he said:

"Your Thummim and Urim belong
to your faithful servant.
You tested him at Massah;
you contended with him at the waters
of Meribah.
9 He said of his father and mother,
'I have no regard for them.'
He did not recognize his brothers
or acknowledge his own children,
but he watched over your word
and guarded your covenant.
10 He teaches your precepts to Jacob
and your law to Israel.
He offers incense before you
and whole burnt offerings on your
altar.
11 Bless all his skills, LORD,
and be pleased with the work of his
hands.
Strike down those who rise against him,
his foes till they rise no more."

12 About Benjamin he said:

"Let the beloved of the LORD rest secure
in him,
for he shields him all day long,
and the one the LORD loves rests
between his shoulders."

13 About Joseph he said:

[a] 43 Or *Make his people rejoice, you nations* [b] 43 Masoretic Text; Dead Sea Scrolls (see also Septuagint) *people, / and let all the angels worship him, /* [c] 44 Hebrew *Hoshea,* a variant of *Joshua* [d] 2 Or *from* [e] 2 The meaning of the Hebrew for this phrase is uncertain. [f] 5 *Jeshurun* means *the upright one,* that is, Israel; also in verse 26. [g] 6 Or *but let*

"May the LORD bless his land
with the precious dew from heaven above
and with the deep waters that lie below;
14 with the best the sun brings forth
and the finest the moon can yield;
15 with the choicest gifts of the ancient mountains
and the fruitfulness of the everlasting hills;
16 with the best gifts of the earth and its fullness
and the favor of him who dwelt in the burning bush.
Let all these rest on the head of Joseph,
on the brow of the prince among[a] his brothers.
17 In majesty he is like a firstborn bull;
his horns are the horns of a wild ox.
With them he will gore the nations,
even those at the ends of the earth.
Such are the ten thousands of Ephraim;
such are the thousands of Manasseh."

18 About Zebulun he said:

"Rejoice, Zebulun, in your going out,
and you, Issachar, in your tents.
19 They will summon peoples to the mountain
and there offer the sacrifices of the righteous;
they will feast on the abundance of the seas,
on the treasures hidden in the sand."

20 About Gad he said:

"Blessed is he who enlarges Gad's domain!
Gad lives there like a lion,
tearing at arm or head.
21 He chose the best land for himself;
the leader's portion was kept for him.
When the heads of the people assembled,
he carried out the LORD's righteous will,
and his judgments concerning Israel."

22 About Dan he said:

"Dan is a lion's cub,
springing out of Bashan."

23 About Naphtali he said:

"Naphtali is abounding with the favor of the LORD
and is full of his blessing;
he will inherit southward to the lake."

24 About Asher he said:

"Most blessed of sons is Asher;
let him be favored by his brothers,
and let him bathe his feet in oil.
25 The bolts of your gates will be iron and bronze,
and your strength will equal your days.

26 "There is no one like the God of Jeshurun,
who rides across the heavens to help you
and on the clouds in his majesty.
27 The eternal God is your refuge,
and underneath are the everlasting arms.
He will drive out your enemies before you,
saying, 'Destroy them!'
28 So Israel will live in safety;
Jacob will dwell[b] secure
in a land of grain and new wine,
where the heavens drop dew.
29 Blessed are you, Israel!
Who is like you,
a people saved by the LORD?
He is your shield and helper
and your glorious sword.
Your enemies will cower before you,
and you will tread on their heights."

The Death of Moses

34 Then Moses climbed Mount Nebo
from the plains of Moab to the top of
Pisgah, across from Jericho. There the LORD
showed him the whole land — from Gilead to
Dan, 2 all of Naphtali, the territory of Ephra-
im and Manasseh, all the land of Judah as far
as the Mediterranean Sea, 3 the Negev and
the whole region from the Valley of Jericho,
the City of Palms, as far as Zoar. 4 Then the
LORD said to him, "This is the land I prom-
ised on oath to Abraham, Isaac and Jacob
when I said, 'I will give it to your descen-
dants.' I have let you see it with your eyes,
but you will not cross over into it."
5 And Moses the servant of the LORD died

[a] 16 Or *of the one separated from* [b] 28 Septuagint; Hebrew *Jacob's spring is*

there in Moab, as the LORD had said. 6He
buried him[a] in Moab, in the valley oppo-
site Beth Peor, but to this day no one knows
where his grave is. 7Moses was a hundred
and twenty years old when he died, yet his
eyes were not weak nor his strength gone.
8The Israelites grieved for Moses in the
plains of Moab thirty days, until the time of
weeping and mourning was over.

9Now Joshua son of Nun was filled with
the spirit[b] of wisdom because Moses had
laid his hands on him. So the Israelites lis-
tened to him and did what the LORD had
commanded Moses.

10Since then, no prophet has risen in Is-
rael like Moses, whom the LORD knew face
to face, 11who did all those signs and won-
ders the LORD sent him to do in Egypt — to
Pharaoh and to all his officials and to his
whole land. 12For no one has ever shown the
mighty power or performed the awesome
deeds that Moses did in the sight of all Israel.

[a] 6 Or *He was buried* [b] 9 Or *Spirit*

JOSHUA

Joshua Installed as Leader

1 After the death of Moses the servant of the LORD, the LORD said to Joshua son of Nun, Moses’ aide: 2“Moses my servant is dead. Now then, you and all these people, get ready to cross the Jordan River into the land I am about to give to them — to the Israelites. 3I will give you every place where you set your foot, as I promised Moses. 4Your territory will extend from the desert to Lebanon, and from the great river, the Euphrates — all the Hittite country — to the Mediterranean Sea in the west. 5No one will be able to stand against you all the days of your life. As I was with Moses, so I will be with you; I will never leave you nor forsake you. 6Be strong and courageous, because you will lead these people to inherit the land I swore to their ancestors to give them.

7“Be strong and very courageous. Be careful to obey all the law my servant Moses gave you; do not turn from it to the right or to the left, that you may be successful wherever you go. 8Keep this Book of the Law always on your lips; meditate on it day and night, so that you may be careful to do everything written in it. Then you will be prosperous and successful. 9Have I not commanded you? Be strong and courageous. Do not be afraid; do not be discouraged, for the LORD your God will be with you wherever you go.”

10So Joshua ordered the officers of the people: 11“Go through the camp and tell the people, ‘Get your provisions ready. Three days from now you will cross the Jordan here to go in and take possession of the land the LORD your God is giving you for your own.’ ”

12But to the Reubenites, the Gadites and the half-tribe of Manasseh, Joshua said, 13“Remember the command that Moses the servant of the LORD gave you after he said, ‘The LORD your God will give you rest by giving you this land.’ 14Your wives, your children and your livestock may stay in the land that Moses gave you east of the Jordan, but all your fighting men, ready for battle, must cross over ahead of your fellow Israelites. You are to help them 15until the LORD gives them rest, as he has done for you, and until they too have taken possession of the land the LORD your God is giving them. After that, you may go back and occupy your own land, which Moses the servant of the LORD gave you east of the Jordan toward the sunrise.”

16Then they answered Joshua, “Whatever you have commanded us we will do, and wherever you send us we will go. 17Just as we fully obeyed Moses, so we will obey you. Only may the LORD your God be with you as he was with Moses. 18Whoever rebels against your word and does not obey it, whatever you may command them, will be put to death. Only be strong and courageous!”

Rahab and the Spies

2 Then Joshua son of Nun secretly sent two spies from Shittim. “Go, look over the land,” he said, “especially Jericho.” So they went and entered the house of a prostitute named Rahab and stayed there.

2The king of Jericho was told, “Look, some of the Israelites have come here tonight to spy out the land.” 3So the king of Jericho sent this message to Rahab: “Bring out the men who came to you and entered your house, because they have come to spy out the whole land.”

4But the woman had taken the two men and hidden them. She said, “Yes, the men came to me, but I did not know where they had come from. 5At dusk, when it was time to close the city gate, they left. I don’t know which way they went. Go after them quickly. You may catch up with them.” 6(But she had taken them up to the roof and hidden them under the stalks of flax she had laid out on the roof.) 7So the men set out in pursuit of the spies on the road that leads to the fords of the Jordan, and as soon as the pursuers had gone out, the gate was shut.

8Before the spies lay down for the night,

she went up on the roof 9and said to them, "I know that the LORD has given you this land and that a great fear of you has fallen on us, so that all who live in this country are melting in fear because of you. 10We have heard how the LORD dried up the water of the Red Sea[a] for you when you came out of Egypt, and what you did to Sihon and Og, the two kings of the Amorites east of the Jordan, whom you completely destroyed.[b] 11When we heard of it, our hearts melted in fear and everyone's courage failed because of you, for the LORD your God is God in heaven above and on the earth below.

12"Now then, please swear to me by the LORD that you will show kindness to my family, because I have shown kindness to you. Give me a sure sign 13that you will spare the lives of my father and mother, my brothers and sisters, and all who belong to them — and that you will save us from death."

14"Our lives for your lives!" the men assured her. "If you don't tell what we are doing, we will treat you kindly and faithfully when the LORD gives us the land."

15So she let them down by a rope through the window, for the house she lived in was part of the city wall. 16She said to them, "Go to the hills so the pursuers will not find you. Hide yourselves there three days until they return, and then go on your way."

17Now the men had said to her, "This oath you made us swear will not be binding on us 18unless, when we enter the land, you have tied this scarlet cord in the window through which you let us down, and unless you have brought your father and mother, your brothers and all your family into your house. 19If any of them go outside your house into the street, their blood will be on their own heads; we will not be responsible. As for those who are in the house with you, their blood will be on our head if a hand is laid on them. 20But if you tell what we are doing, we will be released from the oath you made us swear."

21"Agreed," she replied. "Let it be as you say."

So she sent them away, and they departed. And she tied the scarlet cord in the window.

22When they left, they went into the hills and stayed there three days, until the pursuers had searched all along the road and returned without finding them. 23Then the two men started back. They went down out of the hills, forded the river and came to Joshua son of Nun and told him everything that had happened to them. 24They said to Joshua, "The LORD has surely given the whole land into our hands; all the people are melting in fear because of us."

Crossing the Jordan

3 Early in the morning Joshua and all the Israelites set out from Shittim and went to the Jordan, where they camped before crossing over. 2After three days the officers went throughout the camp, 3giving orders to the people: "When you see the ark of the covenant of the LORD your God, and the Levitical priests carrying it, you are to move out from your positions and follow it. 4Then you will know which way to go, since you have never been this way before. But keep a distance of about two thousand cubits[c] between you and the ark; do not go near it."

5Joshua told the people, "Consecrate yourselves, for tomorrow the LORD will do amazing things among you."

6Joshua said to the priests, "Take up the ark of the covenant and pass on ahead of the people." So they took it up and went ahead of them.

7And the LORD said to Joshua, "Today I will begin to exalt you in the eyes of all Israel, so they may know that I am with you as I was with Moses. 8Tell the priests who carry the ark of the covenant: 'When you reach the edge of the Jordan's waters, go and stand in the river.' "

9Joshua said to the Israelites, "Come here and listen to the words of the LORD your God. 10This is how you will know that the living God is among you and that he will certainly drive out before you the Canaanites, Hittites, Hivites, Perizzites, Girgashites, Amorites and Jebusites. 11See, the ark of the covenant of the Lord of all the earth will go into the Jordan ahead of you. 12Now then, choose twelve men from the tribes of Israel, one from each tribe. 13And as soon as the priests who carry the ark of the LORD — the Lord of all the earth — set foot in the Jordan, its waters flowing downstream will be cut off and stand up in a heap."

[a] 10 Or *the Sea of Reeds* [b] 10 The Hebrew term refers to the irrevocable giving over of things or persons to the LORD, often by totally destroying them. [c] 4 That is, about 3,000 feet or about 900 meters

14 So when the people broke camp to cross the Jordan, the priests carrying the ark of the covenant went ahead of them. 15 Now the Jordan is at flood stage all during harvest. Yet as soon as the priests who carried the ark reached the Jordan and their feet touched the water's edge, 16 the water from upstream stopped flowing. It piled up in a heap a great distance away, at a town called Adam in the vicinity of Zarethan, while the water flowing down to the Sea of the Arabah (that is, the Dead Sea) was completely cut off. So the people crossed over opposite Jericho. 17 The priests who carried the ark of the covenant of the LORD stopped in the middle of the Jordan and stood on dry ground, while all Israel passed by until the whole nation had completed the crossing on dry ground.

4 When the whole nation had finished crossing the Jordan, the LORD said to Joshua, 2 "Choose twelve men from among the people, one from each tribe, 3 and tell them to take up twelve stones from the middle of the Jordan, from right where the priests are standing, and carry them over with you and put them down at the place where you stay tonight."

4 So Joshua called together the twelve men he had appointed from the Israelites, one from each tribe, 5 and said to them, "Go over before the ark of the LORD your God into the middle of the Jordan. Each of you is to take up a stone on his shoulder, according to the number of the tribes of the Israelites, 6 to serve as a sign among you. In the future, when your children ask you, 'What do these stones mean?' 7 tell them that the flow of the Jordan was cut off before the ark of the covenant of the LORD. When it crossed the Jordan, the waters of the Jordan were cut off. These stones are to be a memorial to the people of Israel forever."

8 So the Israelites did as Joshua commanded them. They took twelve stones from the middle of the Jordan, according to the number of the tribes of the Israelites, as the LORD had told Joshua; and they carried them over with them to their camp, where they put them down. 9 Joshua set up the twelve stones that had been[a] in the middle of the Jordan at the spot where the priests who carried the ark of the covenant had stood. And they are there to this day.

10 Now the priests who carried the ark remained standing in the middle of the Jordan until everything the LORD had commanded Joshua was done by the people, just as Moses had directed Joshua. The people hurried over, 11 and as soon as all of them had crossed, the ark of the LORD and the priests came to the other side while the people watched. 12 The men of Reuben, Gad and the half-tribe of Manasseh crossed over, ready for battle, in front of the Israelites, as Moses had directed them. 13 About forty thousand armed for battle crossed over before the LORD to the plains of Jericho for war.

14 That day the LORD exalted Joshua in the sight of all Israel; and they stood in awe of him all the days of his life, just as they had stood in awe of Moses.

15 Then the LORD said to Joshua, 16 "Command the priests carrying the ark of the covenant law to come up out of the Jordan."

17 So Joshua commanded the priests, "Come up out of the Jordan."

18 And the priests came up out of the river carrying the ark of the covenant of the LORD. No sooner had they set their feet on the dry ground than the waters of the Jordan returned to their place and ran at flood stage as before.

19 On the tenth day of the first month the people went up from the Jordan and camped at Gilgal on the eastern border of Jericho. 20 And Joshua set up at Gilgal the twelve stones they had taken out of the Jordan. 21 He said to the Israelites, "In the future when your descendants ask their parents, 'What do these stones mean?' 22 tell them, 'Israel crossed the Jordan on dry ground.' 23 For the LORD your God dried up the Jordan before you until you had crossed over. The LORD your God did to the Jordan what he had done to the Red Sea[b] when he dried it up before us until we had crossed over. 24 He did this so that all the peoples of the earth might know that the hand of the LORD is powerful and so that you might always fear the LORD your God."

5 Now when all the Amorite kings west of the Jordan and all the Canaanite kings along the coast heard how the LORD had dried up the Jordan before the Israelites until they[c] had crossed over, their hearts melted

[a] 9 Or *Joshua also set up twelve stones* [b] 23 Or *the Sea of Reeds* [c] 1 Another textual tradition *we*

in fear and they no longer had the courage to
face the Israelites.

Circumcision and Passover at Gilgal

2At that time the LORD said to Joshua,
"Make flint knives and circumcise the Isra-
elites again." 3So Joshua made flint knives
and circumcised the Israelites at Gibeath
Haaraloth.[a]
4Now this is why he did so: All those who
came out of Egypt — all the men of military
age — died in the wilderness on the way af-
ter leaving Egypt. 5All the people that came
out had been circumcised, but all the peo-
ple born in the wilderness during the jour-
ney from Egypt had not. 6The Israelites had
moved about in the wilderness forty years
until all the men who were of military age
when they left Egypt had died, since they
had not obeyed the LORD. For the LORD had
sworn to them that they would not see the
land he had solemnly promised their an-
cestors to give us, a land flowing with milk
and honey. 7So he raised up their sons in
their place, and these were the ones Joshua
circumcised. They were still uncircumcised
because they had not been circumcised on
the way. 8And after the whole nation had
been circumcised, they remained where
they were in camp until they were healed.
9Then the LORD said to Joshua, "Today I
have rolled away the reproach of Egypt from
you." So the place has been called Gilgal[b] to
this day.
10On the evening of the fourteenth day of
the month, while camped at Gilgal on the
plains of Jericho, the Israelites celebrated
the Passover. 11The day after the Passover,
that very day, they ate some of the produce
of the land: unleavened bread and roasted
grain. 12The manna stopped the day after[c]
they ate this food from the land; there was no
longer any manna for the Israelites, but that
year they ate the produce of Canaan.

The Fall of Jericho

13Now when Joshua was near Jericho, he
looked up and saw a man standing in front of
him with a drawn sword in his hand. Joshua
went up to him and asked, "Are you for us or
for our enemies?"
14"Neither," he replied, "but as command-
er of the army of the LORD I have now come."
Then Joshua fell facedown to the ground in
reverence, and asked him, "What message
does my Lord[d] have for his servant?"
15The commander of the LORD's army re-
plied, "Take off your sandals, for the place
where you are standing is holy." And Joshua
did so.

6 Now the gates of Jericho were securely
barred because of the Israelites. No one
went out and no one came in.
2Then the LORD said to Joshua, "See, I
have delivered Jericho into your hands,
along with its king and its fighting men.
3March around the city once with all the
armed men. Do this for six days. 4Have sev-
en priests carry trumpets of rams' horns in
front of the ark. On the seventh day, march
around the city seven times, with the priests
blowing the trumpets. 5When you hear them
sound a long blast on the trumpets, have the
whole army give a loud shout; then the wall
of the city will collapse and the army will go
up, everyone straight in."
6So Joshua son of Nun called the priests
and said to them, "Take up the ark of the
covenant of the LORD and have seven priests
carry trumpets in front of it." 7And he or-
dered the army, "Advance! March around
the city, with an armed guard going ahead of
the ark of the LORD."
8When Joshua had spoken to the people,
the seven priests carrying the seven trum-
pets before the LORD went forward, blow-
ing their trumpets, and the ark of the LORD's
covenant followed them. 9The armed guard
marched ahead of the priests who blew the
trumpets, and the rear guard followed the
ark. All this time the trumpets were sound-
ing. 10But Joshua had commanded the army,
"Do not give a war cry, do not raise your voic-
es, do not say a word until the day I tell you
to shout. Then shout!" 11So he had the ark of
the LORD carried around the city, circling it
once. Then the army returned to camp and
spent the night there.
12Joshua got up early the next morning
and the priests took up the ark of the LORD.
13The seven priests carrying the seven trum-
pets went forward, marching before the ark
of the LORD and blowing the trumpets. The
armed men went ahead of them and the rear

[a] 3 *Gibeath Haaraloth* means *the hill of foreskins.* [b] 9 *Gilgal* sounds like the Hebrew for *roll.*
[c] 12 Or *the day* [d] 14 Or *lord*

guard followed the ark of the LORD, while the trumpets kept sounding. 14 So on the second day they marched around the city once and returned to the camp. They did this for six days.

15 On the seventh day, they got up at daybreak and marched around the city seven times in the same manner, except that on that day they circled the city seven times. 16 The seventh time around, when the priests sounded the trumpet blast, Joshua commanded the army, "Shout! For the LORD has given you the city! 17 The city and all that is in it are to be devoted[a] to the LORD. Only Rahab the prostitute and all who are with her in her house shall be spared, because she hid the spies we sent. 18 But keep away from the devoted things, so that you will not bring about your own destruction by taking any of them. Otherwise you will make the camp of Israel liable to destruction and bring trouble on it. 19 All the silver and gold and the articles of bronze and iron are sacred to the LORD and must go into his treasury."

20 When the trumpets sounded, the army shouted, and at the sound of the trumpet, when the men gave a loud shout, the wall collapsed; so everyone charged straight in, and they took the city. 21 They devoted the city to the LORD and destroyed with the sword every living thing in it — men and women, young and old, cattle, sheep and donkeys.

22 Joshua said to the two men who had spied out the land, "Go into the prostitute's house and bring her out and all who belong to her, in accordance with your oath to her." 23 So the young men who had done the spying went in and brought out Rahab, her father and mother, her brothers and sisters and all who belonged to her. They brought out her entire family and put them in a place outside the camp of Israel.

24 Then they burned the whole city and everything in it, but they put the silver and gold and the articles of bronze and iron into the treasury of the LORD's house. 25 But Joshua spared Rahab the prostitute, with her family and all who belonged to her, because she hid the men Joshua had sent as spies to Jericho — and she lives among the Israelites to this day.

26 At that time Joshua pronounced this solemn oath: "Cursed before the LORD is the one who undertakes to rebuild this city, Jericho:

"At the cost of his firstborn son
  he will lay its foundations;
at the cost of his youngest
  he will set up its gates."

27 So the LORD was with Joshua, and his fame spread throughout the land.

Achan's Sin

7 But the Israelites were unfaithful in regard to the devoted things[b]; Achan son of Karmi, the son of Zimri,[c] the son of Zerah, of the tribe of Judah, took some of them. So the LORD's anger burned against Israel.

2 Now Joshua sent men from Jericho to Ai, which is near Beth Aven to the east of Bethel, and told them, "Go up and spy out the region." So the men went up and spied out Ai.

3 When they returned to Joshua, they said, "Not all the army will have to go up against Ai. Send two or three thousand men to take it and do not weary the whole army, for only a few people live there." 4 So about three thousand went up; but they were routed by the men of Ai, 5 who killed about thirty-six of them. They chased the Israelites from the city gate as far as the stone quarries and struck them down on the slopes. At this the hearts of the people melted in fear and became like water.

6 Then Joshua tore his clothes and fell facedown to the ground before the ark of the LORD, remaining there till evening. The elders of Israel did the same, and sprinkled dust on their heads. 7 And Joshua said, "Alas, Sovereign LORD, why did you ever bring this people across the Jordan to deliver us into the hands of the Amorites to destroy us? If only we had been content to stay on the other side of the Jordan! 8 Pardon your servant, Lord. What can I say, now that Israel has been routed by its enemies? 9 The Canaanites and the other people of the country will hear about this and they will surround us

[a] *17* The Hebrew term refers to the irrevocable giving over of things or persons to the LORD, often by totally destroying them; also in verses 18 and 21. [b] *1* The Hebrew term refers to the irrevocable giving over of things or persons to the LORD, often by totally destroying them; also in verses 11, 12, 13 and 15. [c] *1* See Septuagint and 1 Chron. 2:6; Hebrew *Zabdi*; also in verses 17 and 18.

and wipe out our name from the earth. What
then will you do for your own great name?"

[10]The LORD said to Joshua, "Stand up!
What are you doing down on your face? [11]Is-
rael has sinned; they have violated my cov-
enant, which I commanded them to keep.
They have taken some of the devoted things;
they have stolen, they have lied, they have
put them with their own possessions. [12]That
is why the Israelites cannot stand against
their enemies; they turn their backs and
run because they have been made liable to
destruction. I will not be with you anymore
unless you destroy whatever among you is
devoted to destruction.

[13]"Go, consecrate the people. Tell them,
'Consecrate yourselves in preparation for to-
morrow; for this is what the LORD, the God of
Israel, says: There are devoted things among
you, Israel. You cannot stand against your
enemies until you remove them.

[14]" 'In the morning, present yourselves
tribe by tribe. The tribe the LORD chooses
shall come forward clan by clan; the clan
the LORD chooses shall come forward family
by family; and the family the LORD chooses
shall come forward man by man. [15]Whoev-
er is caught with the devoted things shall be
destroyed by fire, along with all that belongs
to him. He has violated the covenant of the
LORD and has done an outrageous thing in
Israel!' "

[16]Early the next morning Joshua had Is-
rael come forward by tribes, and Judah was
chosen. [17]The clans of Judah came forward,
and the Zerahites were chosen. He had the
clan of the Zerahites come forward by fam-
ilies, and Zimri was chosen. [18]Joshua had
his family come forward man by man, and
Achan son of Karmi, the son of Zimri, the
son of Zerah, of the tribe of Judah, was cho-
sen.

[19]Then Joshua said to Achan, "My son,
give glory to the LORD, the God of Israel, and
honor him. Tell me what you have done; do
not hide it from me."

[20]Achan replied, "It is true! I have sinned
against the LORD, the God of Israel. This is
what I have done: [21]When I saw in the plun-
der a beautiful robe from Babylonia,[a] two
hundred shekels[b] of silver and a bar of gold
weighing fifty shekels,[c] I coveted them and
took them. They are hidden in the ground
inside my tent, with the silver underneath."

[22]So Joshua sent messengers, and they
ran to the tent, and there it was, hidden in
his tent, with the silver underneath. [23]They
took the things from the tent, brought them
to Joshua and all the Israelites and spread
them out before the LORD.

[24]Then Joshua, together with all Israel,
took Achan son of Zerah, the silver, the robe,
the gold bar, his sons and daughters, his cat-
tle, donkeys and sheep, his tent and all that
he had, to the Valley of Achor. [25]Joshua said,
"Why have you brought this trouble on us?
The LORD will bring trouble on you today."

Then all Israel stoned him, and after
they had stoned the rest, they burned them.
[26]Over Achan they heaped up a large pile of
rocks, which remains to this day. Then the
LORD turned from his fierce anger. There-
fore that place has been called the Valley of
Achor[d] ever since.

Ai Destroyed

8 Then the LORD said to Joshua, "Do not
be afraid; do not be discouraged. Take
the whole army with you, and go up and at-
tack Ai. For I have delivered into your hands
the king of Ai, his people, his city and his
land. [2]You shall do to Ai and its king as you
did to Jericho and its king, except that you
may carry off their plunder and livestock for
yourselves. Set an ambush behind the city."

[3]So Joshua and the whole army moved
out to attack Ai. He chose thirty thousand
of his best fighting men and sent them out
at night [4]with these orders: "Listen care-
fully. You are to set an ambush behind the
city. Don't go very far from it. All of you be
on the alert. [5]I and all those with me will ad-
vance on the city, and when the men come
out against us, as they did before, we will flee
from them. [6]They will pursue us until we
have lured them away from the city, for they
will say, 'They are running away from us as
they did before.' So when we flee from them,
[7]you are to rise up from ambush and take the
city. The LORD your God will give it into your
hand. [8]When you have taken the city, set it
on fire. Do what the LORD has commanded.
See to it; you have my orders."

[a] 21 Hebrew *Shinar* [b] 21 That is, about 5 pounds or about 2.3 kilograms [c] 21 That is, about 1 1/4 pounds or about 575 grams [d] 26 *Achor* means *trouble.*

9 Then Joshua sent them off, and they went to the place of ambush and lay in wait between Bethel and Ai, to the west of Ai — but Joshua spent that night with the people.

10 Early the next morning Joshua mustered his army, and he and the leaders of Israel marched before them to Ai. 11 The entire force that was with him marched up and approached the city and arrived in front of it. They set up camp north of Ai, with the valley between them and the city. 12 Joshua had taken about five thousand men and set them in ambush between Bethel and Ai, to the west of the city. 13 So the soldiers took up their positions — with the main camp to the north of the city and the ambush to the west of it. That night Joshua went into the valley.

14 When the king of Ai saw this, he and all the men of the city hurried out early in the morning to meet Israel in battle at a certain place overlooking the Arabah. But he did not know that an ambush had been set against him behind the city. 15 Joshua and all Israel let themselves be driven back before them, and they fled toward the wilderness. 16 All the men of Ai were called to pursue them, and they pursued Joshua and were lured away from the city. 17 Not a man remained in Ai or Bethel who did not go after Israel. They left the city open and went in pursuit of Israel.

18 Then the LORD said to Joshua, "Hold out toward Ai the javelin that is in your hand, for into your hand I will deliver the city." So Joshua held out toward the city the javelin that was in his hand. 19 As soon as he did this, the men in the ambush rose quickly from their position and rushed forward. They entered the city and captured it and quickly set it on fire.

20 The men of Ai looked back and saw the smoke of the city rising up into the sky, but they had no chance to escape in any direction; the Israelites who had been fleeing toward the wilderness had turned back against their pursuers. 21 For when Joshua and all Israel saw that the ambush had taken the city and that smoke was going up from it, they turned around and attacked the men of Ai. 22 Those in the ambush also came out of the city against them, so that they were caught in the middle, with Israelites on both sides. Israel cut them down, leaving them neither survivors nor fugitives. 23 But they took the king of Ai alive and brought him to Joshua.

24 When Israel had finished killing all the men of Ai in the fields and in the wilderness where they had chased them, and when every one of them had been put to the sword, all the Israelites returned to Ai and killed those who were in it. 25 Twelve thousand men and women fell that day — all the people of Ai. 26 For Joshua did not draw back the hand that held out his javelin until he had destroyed[a] all who lived in Ai. 27 But Israel did carry off for themselves the livestock and plunder of this city, as the LORD had instructed Joshua.

28 So Joshua burned Ai[b] and made it a permanent heap of ruins, a desolate place to this day. 29 He impaled the body of the king of Ai on a pole and left it there until evening. At sunset, Joshua ordered them to take the body from the pole and throw it down at the entrance of the city gate. And they raised a large pile of rocks over it, which remains to this day.

The Covenant Renewed at Mount Ebal

30 Then Joshua built on Mount Ebal an altar to the LORD, the God of Israel, 31 as Moses the servant of the LORD had commanded the Israelites. He built it according to what is written in the Book of the Law of Moses — an altar of uncut stones, on which no iron tool had been used. On it they offered to the LORD burnt offerings and sacrificed fellowship offerings. 32 There, in the presence of the Israelites, Joshua wrote on stones a copy of the law of Moses. 33 All the Israelites, with their elders, officials and judges, were standing on both sides of the ark of the covenant of the LORD, facing the Levitical priests who carried it. Both the foreigners living among them and the native-born were there. Half of the people stood in front of Mount Gerizim and half of them in front of Mount Ebal, as Moses the servant of the LORD had formerly commanded when he gave instructions to bless the people of Israel.

34 Afterward, Joshua read all the words of the law — the blessings and the curses — just as it is written in the Book of the Law. 35 There was not a word of all that Moses had commanded that Joshua did not read

[a] *26* The Hebrew term refers to the irrevocable giving over of things or persons to the LORD, often by totally destroying them. [b] *28* *Ai* means *the ruin.*

to the whole assembly of Israel, including the women and children, and the foreigners who lived among them.

The Gibeonite Deception

9 Now when all the kings west of the Jordan heard about these things — the kings in the hill country, in the western foothills, and along the entire coast of the Mediterranean Sea as far as Lebanon (the kings of the Hittites, Amorites, Canaanites, Perizzites, Hivites and Jebusites) — [2]they came together to wage war against Joshua and Israel.

[3]However, when the people of Gibeon heard what Joshua had done to Jericho and Ai, [4]they resorted to a ruse: They went as a delegation whose donkeys were loaded[a] with worn-out sacks and old wineskins, cracked and mended. [5]They put worn and patched sandals on their feet and wore old clothes. All the bread of their food supply was dry and moldy. [6]Then they went to Joshua in the camp at Gilgal and said to him and the Israelites, "We have come from a distant country; make a treaty with us."

[7]The Israelites said to the Hivites, "But perhaps you live near us, so how can we make a treaty with you?"

[8]"We are your servants," they said to Joshua.

But Joshua asked, "Who are you and where do you come from?"

[9]They answered: "Your servants have come from a very distant country because of the fame of the LORD your God. For we have heard reports of him: all that he did in Egypt, [10]and all that he did to the two kings of the Amorites east of the Jordan — Sihon king of Heshbon, and Og king of Bashan, who reigned in Ashtaroth. [11]And our elders and all those living in our country said to us, 'Take provisions for your journey; go and meet them and say to them, "We are your servants; make a treaty with us."' [12]This bread of ours was warm when we packed it at home on the day we left to come to you. But now see how dry and moldy it is. [13]And these wineskins that we filled were new, but see how cracked they are. And our clothes and sandals are worn out by the very long journey."

[14]The Israelites sampled their provisions but did not inquire of the LORD. [15]Then Joshua made a treaty of peace with them to let them live, and the leaders of the assembly ratified it by oath.

[16]Three days after they made the treaty with the Gibeonites, the Israelites heard that they were neighbors, living near them. [17]So the Israelites set out and on the third day came to their cities: Gibeon, Kephirah, Beeroth and Kiriath Jearim. [18]But the Israelites did not attack them, because the leaders of the assembly had sworn an oath to them by the LORD, the God of Israel.

The whole assembly grumbled against the leaders, [19]but all the leaders answered, "We have given them our oath by the LORD, the God of Israel, and we cannot touch them now. [20]This is what we will do to them: We will let them live, so that God's wrath will not fall on us for breaking the oath we swore to them." [21]They continued, "Let them live, but let them be woodcutters and water carriers in the service of the whole assembly." So the leaders' promise to them was kept.

[22]Then Joshua summoned the Gibeonites and said, "Why did you deceive us by saying, 'We live a long way from you,' while actually you live near us? [23]You are now under a curse: You will never be released from service as woodcutters and water carriers for the house of my God."

[24]They answered Joshua, "Your servants were clearly told how the LORD your God had commanded his servant Moses to give you the whole land and to wipe out all its inhabitants from before you. So we feared for our lives because of you, and that is why we did this. [25]We are now in your hands. Do to us whatever seems good and right to you."

[26]So Joshua saved them from the Israelites, and they did not kill them. [27]That day he made the Gibeonites woodcutters and water carriers for the assembly, to provide for the needs of the altar of the LORD at the place the LORD would choose. And that is what they are to this day.

The Sun Stands Still

10 Now Adoni-Zedek king of Jerusalem heard that Joshua had taken Ai and

[a] 4 Most Hebrew manuscripts; some Hebrew manuscripts, Vulgate and Syriac (see also Septuagint) *They prepared provisions and loaded their donkeys*

totally destroyed[a] it, doing to Ai and its king
as he had done to Jericho and its king, and
that the people of Gibeon had made a trea-
ty of peace with Israel and had become their
allies. 2 He and his people were very much
alarmed at this, because Gibeon was an im-
portant city, like one of the royal cities; it was
larger than Ai, and all its men were good
fighters. 3 So Adoni-Zedek king of Jerusalem
appealed to Hoham king of Hebron, Piram
king of Jarmuth, Japhia king of Lachish and
Debir king of Eglon. 4 "Come up and help
me attack Gibeon," he said, "because it has
made peace with Joshua and the Israelites."

5 Then the five kings of the Amorites—
the kings of Jerusalem, Hebron, Jarmuth,
Lachish and Eglon—joined forces. They
moved up with all their troops and took up
positions against Gibeon and attacked it.

6 The Gibeonites then sent word to Josh-
ua in the camp at Gilgal: "Do not abandon
your servants. Come up to us quickly and
save us! Help us, because all the Amorite
kings from the hill country have joined forc-
es against us."

7 So Joshua marched up from Gilgal with
his entire army, including all the best fight-
ing men. 8 The LORD said to Joshua, "Do not
be afraid of them; I have given them into
your hand. Not one of them will be able to
withstand you."

9 After an all-night march from Gilgal,
Joshua took them by surprise. 10 The LORD
threw them into confusion before Israel,
so Joshua and the Israelites defeated them
completely at Gibeon. Israel pursued them
along the road going up to Beth Horon and
cut them down all the way to Azekah and
Makkedah. 11 As they fled before Israel on the
road down from Beth Horon to Azekah, the
LORD hurled large hailstones down on them,
and more of them died from the hail than
were killed by the swords of the Israelites.

12 On the day the LORD gave the Amorites
over to Israel, Joshua said to the LORD in the
presence of Israel:

"Sun, stand still over Gibeon,
  and you, moon, over the Valley of
    Aijalon."
13 So the sun stood still,
  and the moon stopped,
till the nation avenged itself on[b] its
    enemies,
as it is written in the Book of Jashar.

The sun stopped in the middle of the sky
and delayed going down about a full day.
14 There has never been a day like it before
or since, a day when the LORD listened to a
human being. Surely the LORD was fighting
for Israel!

15 Then Joshua returned with all Israel to
the camp at Gilgal.

Five Amorite Kings Killed

16 Now the five kings had fled and hidden
in the cave at Makkedah. 17 When Joshua was
told that the five kings had been found hid-
ing in the cave at Makkedah, 18 he said, "Roll
large rocks up to the mouth of the cave, and
post some men there to guard it. 19 But don't
stop; pursue your enemies! Attack them
from the rear and don't let them reach their
cities, for the LORD your God has given them
into your hand."

20 So Joshua and the Israelites defeated
them completely, but a few survivors man-
aged to reach their fortified cities. 21 The
whole army then returned safely to Joshua in
the camp at Makkedah, and no one uttered a
word against the Israelites.

22 Joshua said, "Open the mouth of the
cave and bring those five kings out to me."
23 So they brought the five kings out of the
cave—the kings of Jerusalem, Hebron, Jar-
muth, Lachish and Eglon. 24 When they
had brought these kings to Joshua, he sum-
moned all the men of Israel and said to the
army commanders who had come with him,
"Come here and put your feet on the necks
of these kings." So they came forward and
placed their feet on their necks.

25 Joshua said to them, "Do not be afraid;
do not be discouraged. Be strong and cou-
rageous. This is what the LORD will do to all
the enemies you are going to fight." 26 Then
Joshua put the kings to death and exposed
their bodies on five poles, and they were left
hanging on the poles until evening.

27 At sunset Joshua gave the order and they
took them down from the poles and threw
them into the cave where they had been hid-
ing. At the mouth of the cave they placed
large rocks, which are there to this day.

[a] *1* The Hebrew term refers to the irrevocable giving over of things or persons to the LORD, often by totally destroying them; also in verses 28, 35, 37, 39 and 40. [b] *13* Or *nation triumphed over*

Southern Cities Conquered

28 That day Joshua took Makkedah. He put the city and its king to the sword and totally destroyed everyone in it. He left no survivors. And he did to the king of Makkedah as he had done to the king of Jericho.

29 Then Joshua and all Israel with him moved on from Makkedah to Libnah and attacked it. 30 The LORD also gave that city and its king into Israel's hand. The city and everyone in it Joshua put to the sword. He left no survivors there. And he did to its king as he had done to the king of Jericho.

31 Then Joshua and all Israel with him moved on from Libnah to Lachish; he took up positions against it and attacked it. 32 The LORD gave Lachish into Israel's hands, and Joshua took it on the second day. The city and everyone in it he put to the sword, just as he had done to Libnah. 33 Meanwhile, Horam king of Gezer had come up to help Lachish, but Joshua defeated him and his army — until no survivors were left.

34 Then Joshua and all Israel with him moved on from Lachish to Eglon; they took up positions against it and attacked it. 35 They captured it that same day and put it to the sword and totally destroyed everyone in it, just as they had done to Lachish.

36 Then Joshua and all Israel with him went up from Eglon to Hebron and attacked it. 37 They took the city and put it to the sword, together with its king, its villages and everyone in it. They left no survivors. Just as at Eglon, they totally destroyed it and everyone in it.

38 Then Joshua and all Israel with him turned around and attacked Debir. 39 They took the city, its king and its villages, and put them to the sword. Everyone in it they totally destroyed. They left no survivors. They did to Debir and its king as they had done to Libnah and its king and to Hebron.

40 So Joshua subdued the whole region, including the hill country, the Negev, the western foothills and the mountain slopes, together with all their kings. He left no survivors. He totally destroyed all who breathed, just as the LORD, the God of Israel, had commanded. 41 Joshua subdued them from Kadesh Barnea to Gaza and from the whole region of Goshen to Gibeon. 42 All these kings and their lands Joshua conquered in one campaign, because the LORD, the God of Israel, fought for Israel.

43 Then Joshua returned with all Israel to the camp at Gilgal.

Northern Kings Defeated

11 When Jabin king of Hazor heard of this, he sent word to Jobab king of Madon, to the kings of Shimron and Akshaph, 2 and to the northern kings who were in the mountains, in the Arabah south of Kinnereth, in the western foothills and in Naphoth Dor on the west; 3 to the Canaanites in the east and west; to the Amorites, Hittites, Perizzites and Jebusites in the hill country; and to the Hivites below Hermon in the region of Mizpah. 4 They came out with all their troops and a large number of horses and chariots — a huge army, as numerous as the sand on the seashore. 5 All these kings joined forces and made camp together at the Waters of Merom to fight against Israel.

6 The LORD said to Joshua, "Do not be afraid of them, because by this time tomorrow I will hand all of them, slain, over to Israel. You are to hamstring their horses and burn their chariots."

7 So Joshua and his whole army came against them suddenly at the Waters of Merom and attacked them, 8 and the LORD gave them into the hand of Israel. They defeated them and pursued them all the way to Greater Sidon, to Misrephoth Maim, and to the Valley of Mizpah on the east, until no survivors were left. 9 Joshua did to them as the LORD had directed: He hamstrung their horses and burned their chariots.

10 At that time Joshua turned back and captured Hazor and put its king to the sword. (Hazor had been the head of all these kingdoms.) 11 Everyone in it they put to the sword. They totally destroyed[a] them, not sparing anyone that breathed, and he burned Hazor itself.

12 Joshua took all these royal cities and their kings and put them to the sword. He totally destroyed them, as Moses the servant of the LORD had commanded. 13 Yet Israel did not burn any of the cities built on their mounds — except Hazor, which Joshua burned. 14 The Israelites carried off for

[a] *11* The Hebrew term refers to the irrevocable giving over of things or persons to the LORD, often by totally destroying them; also in verses 12, 20 and 21.

themselves all the plunder and livestock of
these cities, but all the people they put to
the sword until they completely destroyed
them, not sparing anyone that breathed.
15 As the LORD commanded his servant Mo-
ses, so Moses commanded Joshua, and Josh-
ua did it; he left nothing undone of all that
the LORD commanded Moses.

16 So Joshua took this entire land: the hill
country, all the Negev, the whole region of
Goshen, the western foothills, the Arabah
and the mountains of Israel with their foot-
hills, 17 from Mount Halak, which rises to-
ward Seir, to Baal Gad in the Valley of Leb-
anon below Mount Hermon. He captured all
their kings and put them to death. 18 Joshua
waged war against all these kings for a long
time. 19 Except for the Hivites living in Gibe-
on, not one city made a treaty of peace with
the Israelites, who took them all in battle.
20 For it was the LORD himself who hardened
their hearts to wage war against Israel, so
that he might destroy them totally, extermi-
nating them without mercy, as the LORD had
commanded Moses.

21 At that time Joshua went and destroyed
the Anakites from the hill country: from He-
bron, Debir and Anab, from all the hill coun-
try of Judah, and from all the hill country of
Israel. Joshua totally destroyed them and
their towns. 22 No Anakites were left in Isra-
elite territory; only in Gaza, Gath and Ash-
dod did any survive.

23 So Joshua took the entire land, just as
the LORD had directed Moses, and he gave it
as an inheritance to Israel according to their
tribal divisions. Then the land had rest from
war.

List of Defeated Kings

12 These are the kings of the land whom
the Israelites had defeated and whose
territory they took over east of the Jordan,
from the Arnon Gorge to Mount Hermon,
including all the eastern side of the Arabah:

2 Sihon king of the Amorites, who
reigned in Heshbon.
He ruled from Aroer on the rim of
the Arnon Gorge — from the middle
of the gorge — to the Jabbok River,
which is the border of the Ammon-
ites. This included half of Gilead. 3 He
also ruled over the eastern Arabah
from the Sea of Galilee[a] to the Sea of
the Arabah (that is, the Dead Sea), to
Beth Jeshimoth, and then southward
below the slopes of Pisgah.

4 And the territory of Og king of Bashan,
one of the last of the Rephaites, who
reigned in Ashtaroth and Edrei.
5 He ruled over Mount Hermon, Sale-
kah, all of Bashan to the border of the
people of Geshur and Maakah, and
half of Gilead to the border of Sihon
king of Heshbon.

6 Moses, the servant of the LORD, and the
Israelites conquered them. And Moses the
servant of the LORD gave their land to the Reu-
benites, the Gadites and the half-tribe of Ma-
nasseh to be their possession.

7 Here is a list of the kings of the land that
Joshua and the Israelites conquered on the
west side of the Jordan, from Baal Gad in the
Valley of Lebanon to Mount Halak, which
rises toward Seir. Joshua gave their lands
as an inheritance to the tribes of Israel ac-
cording to their tribal divisions. 8 The lands
included the hill country, the western foot-
hills, the Arabah, the mountain slopes, the
wilderness and the Negev. These were the
lands of the Hittites, Amorites, Canaanites,
Perizzites, Hivites and Jebusites. These were
the kings:

9 the king of Jericho	one
the king of Ai (near Bethel)	one
10 the king of Jerusalem	one
the king of Hebron	one
11 the king of Jarmuth	one
the king of Lachish	one
12 the king of Eglon	one
the king of Gezer	one
13 the king of Debir	one
the king of Geder	one
14 the king of Hormah	one
the king of Arad	one
15 the king of Libnah	one
the king of Adullam	one
16 the king of Makkedah	one
the king of Bethel	one
17 the king of Tappuah	one
the king of Hepher	one
18 the king of Aphek	one
the king of Lasharon	one

[a] 3 Hebrew *Kinnereth*

19 the king of Madon one
the king of Hazor one
20 the king of Shimron Meron one
the king of Akshaph one
21 the king of Taanach one
the king of Megiddo one
22 the king of Kedesh one
the king of Jokneam in Carmel one
23 the king of Dor (in Naphoth Dor) one
the king of Goyim in Gilgal one
24 the king of Tirzah one
thirty-one kings in all.

Land Still to Be Taken

13 When Joshua had grown old, the
LORD said to him, "You are now very
old, and there are still very large areas of
land to be taken over.

2 "This is the land that remains: all the
regions of the Philistines and Geshu-
rites, 3 from the Shihor River on the east
of Egypt to the territory of Ekron on the
north, all of it counted as Canaanite
though held by the five Philistine rul-
ers in Gaza, Ashdod, Ashkelon, Gath
and Ekron; the territory of the Avvites
4 on the south; all the land of the Ca-
naanites, from Arah of the Sidonians as
far as Aphek and the border of the Am-
orites; 5 the area of Byblos; and all Leb-
anon to the east, from Baal Gad below
Mount Hermon to Lebo Hamath.

6 "As for all the inhabitants of the moun-
tain regions from Lebanon to Misrephoth
Maim, that is, all the Sidonians, I myself will
drive them out before the Israelites. Be sure
to allocate this land to Israel for an inheri-
tance, as I have instructed you, 7 and divide it
as an inheritance among the nine tribes and
half of the tribe of Manasseh."

Division of the Land East of the Jordan

8 The other half of Manasseh,[a] the Reuben-
ites and the Gadites had received the inher-
itance that Moses had given them east of the
Jordan, as he, the servant of the LORD, had
assigned it to them.

9 It extended from Aroer on the rim of
the Arnon Gorge, and from the town
in the middle of the gorge, and includ-
ed the whole plateau of Medeba as far
as Dibon, 10 and all the towns of Sihon
king of the Amorites, who ruled in
Heshbon, out to the border of the Am-
monites. 11 It also included Gilead, the
territory of the people of Geshur and
Maakah, all of Mount Hermon and all
Bashan as far as Salekah — 12 that is,
the whole kingdom of Og in Bashan,
who had reigned in Ashtaroth and Ed-
rei. (He was the last of the Rephaites.)
Moses had defeated them and tak-
en over their land. 13 But the Israelites
did not drive out the people of Geshur
and Maakah, so they continue to live
among the Israelites to this day.

14 But to the tribe of Levi he gave no inher-
itance, since the food offerings presented to
the LORD, the God of Israel, are their inheri-
tance, as he promised them.

15 This is what Moses had given to the tribe of
Reuben, according to its clans:

16 The territory from Aroer on the rim of
the Arnon Gorge, and from the town in
the middle of the gorge, and the whole
plateau past Medeba 17 to Heshbon and
all its towns on the plateau, including
Dibon, Bamoth Baal, Beth Baal Meon,
18 Jahaz, Kedemoth, Mephaath, 19 Kir-
iathaim, Sibmah, Zereth Shahar on the
hill in the valley, 20 Beth Peor, the slopes
of Pisgah, and Beth Jeshimoth — 21 all
the towns on the plateau and the entire
realm of Sihon king of the Amorites,
who ruled at Heshbon. Moses had de-
feated him and the Midianite chiefs,
Evi, Rekem, Zur, Hur and Reba — princ-
es allied with Sihon — who lived in that
country. 22 In addition to those slain
in battle, the Israelites had put to the
sword Balaam son of Beor, who prac-
ticed divination. 23 The boundary of the
Reubenites was the bank of the Jordan.
These towns and their villages were the
inheritance of the Reubenites, accord-
ing to their clans.

24 This is what Moses had given to the tribe of
Gad, according to its clans:

25 The territory of Jazer, all the towns of
Gilead and half the Ammonite coun-
try as far as Aroer, near Rabbah; 26 and

[a] 8 Hebrew *With it* (that is, with the other half of Manasseh)

48 In the hill country:
Shamir, Jattir, Sokoh, 49 Dannah, Kir-
iath Sannah (that is, Debir), 50 Anab,
Eshtemoh, Anim, 51 Goshen, Holon and
Giloh — eleven towns and their villages.
52 Arab, Dumah, Eshan, 53 Janim,
Beth Tappuah, Aphekah, 54 Humtah,
Kiriath Arba (that is, Hebron) and
Zior — nine towns and their villages.
55 Maon, Carmel, Ziph, Juttah, 56 Jez-
reel, Jokdeam, Zanoah, 57 Kain, Gibeah
and Timnah — ten towns and their vil-
lages.
58 Halhul, Beth Zur, Gedor, 59 Ma-
arath, Beth Anoth and Eltekon — six
towns and their villages.[a]
60 Kiriath Baal (that is, Kiriath Je-
arim) and Rabbah — two towns and
their villages.

61 In the wilderness:
Beth Arabah, Middin, Sekakah,
62 Nibshan, the City of Salt and En
Gedi — six towns and their villages.
63 Judah could not dislodge the Jebusites,
who were living in Jerusalem; to this day the
Jebusites live there with the people of Judah.

Allotment for Ephraim and Manasseh

16 The allotment for Joseph began
at the Jordan, east of the springs
of Jericho, and went up from there
through the desert into the hill country
of Bethel. 2 It went on from Bethel (that
is, Luz),[b] crossed over to the territory
of the Arkites in Ataroth, 3 descended
westward to the territory of the Japhle-
tites as far as the region of Lower Beth
Horon and on to Gezer, ending at the
Mediterranean Sea.
4 So Manasseh and Ephraim, the descen-
dants of Joseph, received their inheritance.

5 This was the territory of Ephraim, ac-
cording to its clans:

The boundary of their inheritance
went from Ataroth Addar in the east to
Upper Beth Horon 6 and continued to
the Mediterranean Sea. From Mikme-
thath on the north it curved eastward
to Taanath Shiloh, passing by it to Jano-
ah on the east. 7 Then it went down from
Janoah to Ataroth and Naarah, touched
Jericho and came out at the Jordan.
8 From Tappuah the border went west
to the Kanah Ravine and ended at the
Mediterranean Sea. This was the inher-
itance of the tribe of the Ephraimites,
according to its clans. 9 It also includ-
ed all the towns and their villages that
were set aside for the Ephraimites with-
in the inheritance of the Manassites.
10 They did not dislodge the Canaanites liv-
ing in Gezer; to this day the Canaanites live
among the people of Ephraim but are re-
quired to do forced labor.

17 This was the allotment for the tribe
of Manasseh as Joseph's firstborn,
that is, for Makir, Manasseh's firstborn. Ma-
kir was the ancestor of the Gileadites, who
had received Gilead and Bashan because
the Makirites were great soldiers. 2 So this
allotment was for the rest of the people of
Manasseh — the clans of Abiezer, Helek, As-
riel, Shechem, Hepher and Shemida. These
are the other male descendants of Manasseh
son of Joseph by their clans.
3 Now Zelophehad son of Hepher, the son
of Gilead, the son of Makir, the son of Manas-
seh, had no sons but only daughters, whose
names were Mahlah, Noah, Hoglah, Mil-
kah and Tirzah. 4 They went to Eleazar the
priest, Joshua son of Nun, and the leaders
and said, "The LORD commanded Moses to
give us an inheritance among our relatives."
So Joshua gave them an inheritance along
with the brothers of their father, according
to the LORD's command. 5 Manasseh's share
consisted of ten tracts of land besides Gilead
and Bashan east of the Jordan, 6 because the
daughters of the tribe of Manasseh received
an inheritance among the sons. The land of
Gilead belonged to the rest of the descen-
dants of Manasseh.

7 The territory of Manasseh extended
from Asher to Mikmethath east of She-
chem. The boundary ran southward
from there to include the people living
at En Tappuah. 8 (Manasseh had the
land of Tappuah, but Tappuah itself, on
the boundary of Manasseh, belonged
to the Ephraimites.) 9 Then the bound-
ary continued south to the Kanah Ra-
vine. There were towns belonging to

[a] 59 The Septuagint adds another district of eleven towns, including Tekoa and Ephrathah (Bethlehem).
[b] 2 Septuagint; Hebrew *Bethel to Luz*

YOUR GRACE IS ENOUGH

Matt Maher

Great is your faithfulness, oh God
You wrestle with the sinner's heart
You lead me by still waters into mercy
And nothing can keep us apart

So remember your people
Remember your children
Remember your promise, oh God

Your grace is enough
Your grace is enough
Your grace is enough for me

Great is your love and justice God
You use the weak to lead the strong
You lead us in the song of your salvation
And all your people sing along

THE INSPIRATION

[God] said to me, "My grace is sufficient for you, for my power is made perfect in weakness." Therefore I will boast all the more gladly about my weaknesses, so that Christ's power may rest on me.

—2 Corinthians 12:9

BEHIND THE SONG

There is a lot more to "Your Grace Is Enough" than a catchy chorus. In chapter 12 of Paul's second letter to the Corinthians, he explores the concept of personal weakness and the power of humility. He explains that to keep him humble, God allowed him to carry a "thorn in [his] flesh" (verse 7). No one knows exactly what this thorn was. Considering the context of the passages leading up to this verse, it is possible that Paul was referring to people who taught false doctrine and tempted the church to stray from the gospel. Whatever it was, the thorn was a constant reminder of Paul's weakness — "a messenger of Satan" (verse 7).

Paul also says that he asked God three times to remove the thorn, but God refused. Not only did God refuse, Paul says, God specifically told him that his grace would be sufficient for Paul's needs. Paul also adds this powerful promise to the end of the section: "For when I am weak, then I am strong" (verse 10). Here again, we encounter God's economy, one in which our own individual strength is shown to be nothing; it is only in the acceptance of our weakness that God can be strong in us.

Selah

Is there a "thorn in your flesh" that God has chosen not to remove? A difficult person, a source of persecution or another obstacle that makes you feel oppressed and weak? Spend some time thinking about the challenges to your faith, and then consider the ways God has allowed those "thorns" to keep you humble and usable for his purposes.

Worship leader Matt Maher was going through a challenging time when he spent some time reading through 2 Corinthians 12 and struggling with its meaning. "Paul talks about having a 'thorn in his flesh,'" Maher remembers, "and God's grace being sufficient in that. I thought, I'm not sure if I really believe that, but maybe if I write a song about it, and I sing it enough, it will sink in."

Maher did just that, penning "Your Grace Is Enough" and introducing it to churches and worship ministers around the world. Chris Tomlin first heard the song at a conference in Phoenix, Arizona.

"That chorus is massive," Tomlin observes. "You can see the people's hearts catch it and explode!"

The beauty of a song like this is that by singing it we remind ourselves that it's not about what we can do, but what Christ can do through us. "Like the criminal on the cross saying to Jesus, 'Remember me when you come into your kingdom,' I'm praying 'God, remember me. I'm nobody, but if you could remember who I am, maybe your grace would be sufficient in my life.' Of course God doesn't need to remember us," Maher adds. "[The song] is not really for him, it's for us!"

Ephraim lying among the towns of Ma-
nasseh, but the boundary of Manasseh
was the northern side of the ravine and
ended at the Mediterranean Sea. 10 On
the south the land belonged to Ephra-
im, on the north to Manasseh. The ter-
ritory of Manasseh reached the Medi-
terranean Sea and bordered Asher on
the north and Issachar on the east.

11 Within Issachar and Asher, Ma-
nasseh also had Beth Shan, Ibleam
and the people of Dor, Endor, Taanach
and Megiddo, together with their sur-
rounding settlements (the third in the
list is Naphoth[a]).

12 Yet the Manassites were not able to occu-
py these towns, for the Canaanites were de-
termined to live in that region. 13 However,
when the Israelites grew stronger, they sub-
jected the Canaanites to forced labor but did
not drive them out completely.

14 The people of Joseph said to Joshua,
"Why have you given us only one allotment
and one portion for an inheritance? We are a
numerous people, and the LORD has blessed
us abundantly."

15 "If you are so numerous," Joshua an-
swered, "and if the hill country of Ephraim
is too small for you, go up into the forest and
clear land for yourselves there in the land of
the Perizzites and Rephaites."

16 The people of Joseph replied, "The hill
country is not enough for us, and all the Ca-
naanites who live in the plain have chariots fit-
ted with iron, both those in Beth Shan and its
settlements and those in the Valley of Jezreel."

17 But Joshua said to the tribes of Joseph—
to Ephraim and Manasseh—"You are nu-
merous and very powerful. You will have
not only one allotment 18 but the forested hill
country as well. Clear it, and its farthest lim-
its will be yours; though the Canaanites have
chariots fitted with iron and though they are
strong, you can drive them out."

Division of the Rest of the Land

18 The whole assembly of the Israelites
gathered at Shiloh and set up the tent
of meeting there. The country was brought
under their control, 2 but there were still sev-
en Israelite tribes who had not yet received
their inheritance.

3 So Joshua said to the Israelites: "How
long will you wait before you begin to take
possession of the land that the LORD, the
God of your ancestors, has given you? 4 Ap-
point three men from each tribe. I will send
them out to make a survey of the land and
to write a description of it, according to the
inheritance of each. Then they will return
to me. 5 You are to divide the land into sev-
en parts. Judah is to remain in its territory
on the south and the tribes of Joseph in their
territory on the north. 6 After you have writ-
ten descriptions of the seven parts of the
land, bring them here to me and I will cast
lots for you in the presence of the LORD our
God. 7 The Levites, however, do not get a por-
tion among you, because the priestly service
of the LORD is their inheritance. And Gad,
Reuben and the half-tribe of Manasseh have
already received their inheritance on the
east side of the Jordan. Moses the servant of
the LORD gave it to them."

8 As the men started on their way to map
out the land, Joshua instructed them, "Go
and make a survey of the land and write a
description of it. Then return to me, and
I will cast lots for you here at Shiloh in the
presence of the LORD." 9 So the men left and
went through the land. They wrote its de-
scription on a scroll, town by town, in seven
parts, and returned to Joshua in the camp
at Shiloh. 10 Joshua then cast lots for them in
Shiloh in the presence of the LORD, and there
he distributed the land to the Israelites ac-
cording to their tribal divisions.

Allotment for Benjamin

11 The first lot came up for the tribe of Ben-
jamin according to its clans. Their allotted
territory lay between the tribes of Judah and
Joseph:

12 On the north side their boundary
began at the Jordan, passed the north-
ern slope of Jericho and headed west
into the hill country, coming out at the
wilderness of Beth Aven. 13 From there
it crossed to the south slope of Luz (that
is, Bethel) and went down to Ataroth
Addar on the hill south of Lower Beth
Horon.

14 From the hill facing Beth Horon on
the south the boundary turned south

[a] 11 That is, Naphoth Dor

along the western side and came out at
Kiriath Baal (that is, Kiriath Jearim), a
town of the people of Judah. This was
the western side.
[15]The southern side began at the
outskirts of Kiriath Jearim on the west,
and the boundary came out at the
spring of the waters of Nephtoah. [16]The
boundary went down to the foot of the
hill facing the Valley of Ben Hinnom,
north of the Valley of Rephaim. It con-
tinued down the Hinnom Valley along
the southern slope of the Jebusite city
and so to En Rogel. [17]It then curved
north, went to En Shemesh, contin-
ued to Geliloth, which faces the Pass of
Adummim, and ran down to the Stone
of Bohan son of Reuben. [18]It continued
to the northern slope of Beth Arabah[a]
and on down into the Arabah. [19]It then
went to the northern slope of Beth Hog-
lah and came out at the northern bay of
the Dead Sea, at the mouth of the Jor-
dan in the south. This was the southern
boundary.
[20]The Jordan formed the boundary
on the eastern side.
These were the boundaries that marked out
the inheritance of the clans of Benjamin on
all sides.

[21]The tribe of Benjamin, according to its
clans, had the following towns:
Jericho, Beth Hoglah, Emek Ke-
ziz, [22]Beth Arabah, Zemaraim, Beth-
el, [23]Avvim, Parah, Ophrah, [24]Kephar
Ammoni, Ophni and Geba — twelve
towns and their villages.
[25]Gibeon, Ramah, Beeroth, [26]Miz-
pah, Kephirah, Mozah, [27]Rekem, Irpe-
el, Taralah, [28]Zelah, Haeleph, the Jeb-
usite city (that is, Jerusalem), Gibeah
and Kiriath — fourteen towns and their
villages.
This was the inheritance of Benjamin for its
clans.

Allotment for Simeon

19 The second lot came out for the tribe
of Simeon according to its clans.
Their inheritance lay within the territory of
Judah. [2]It included:
Beersheba (or Sheba),[b] Moladah,
[3]Hazar Shual, Balah, Ezem, [4]Eltolad,
Bethul, Hormah, [5]Ziklag, Beth Marka-
both, Hazar Susah, [6]Beth Lebaoth and
Sharuhen — thirteen towns and their
villages;
[7]Ain, Rimmon, Ether and Ashan —
four towns and their villages — [8]and all
the villages around these towns as far
as Baalath Beer (Ramah in the Negev).
This was the inheritance of the tribe of the
Simeonites, according to its clans. [9]The in-
heritance of the Simeonites was taken from
the share of Judah, because Judah's portion
was more than they needed. So the Simeon-
ites received their inheritance within the
territory of Judah.

Allotment for Zebulun

[10]The third lot came up for Zebulun accord-
ing to its clans:
The boundary of their inheritance
went as far as Sarid. [11]Going west it ran
to Maralah, touched Dabbesheth, and
extended to the ravine near Jokneam.
[12]It turned east from Sarid toward the
sunrise to the territory of Kisloth Tabor
and went on to Daberath and up to Ja-
phia. [13]Then it continued eastward to
Gath Hepher and Eth Kazin; it came out
at Rimmon and turned toward Neah.
[14]There the boundary went around on
the north to Hannathon and ended at
the Valley of Iphtah El. [15]Included were
Kattath, Nahalal, Shimron, Idalah and
Bethlehem. There were twelve towns
and their villages.
[16]These towns and their villages were the in-
heritance of Zebulun, according to its clans.

Allotment for Issachar

[17]The fourth lot came out for Issachar accord-
ing to its clans. [18]Their territory included:
Jezreel, Kesulloth, Shunem, [19]Haph-
araim, Shion, Anaharath, [20]Rabbith,
Kishion, Ebez, [21]Remeth, En Gannim,
En Haddah and Beth Pazzez. [22]The
boundary touched Tabor, Shahazu-
mah and Beth Shemesh, and ended at
the Jordan. There were sixteen towns
and their villages.

[a] 18 Septuagint; Hebrew *slope facing the Arabah* [b] 2 Or *Beersheba, Sheba*; 1 Chron. 4:28 does not have *Sheba.*

23 These towns and their villages were the inheritance of the tribe of Issachar, according to its clans.

Allotment for Asher

24 The fifth lot came out for the tribe of Asher according to its clans. 25 Their territory included:

> Helkath, Hali, Beten, Akshaph, 26 Allammelek, Amad and Mishal. On the west the boundary touched Carmel and Shihor Libnath. 27 It then turned east toward Beth Dagon, touched Zebulun and the Valley of Iphtah El, and went north to Beth Emek and Neiel, passing Kabul on the left. 28 It went to Abdon,[a] Rehob, Hammon and Kanah, as far as Greater Sidon. 29 The boundary then turned back toward Ramah and went to the fortified city of Tyre, turned toward Hosah and came out at the Mediterranean Sea in the region of Akzib, 30 Ummah, Aphek and Rehob. There were twenty-two towns and their villages.

31 These towns and their villages were the inheritance of the tribe of Asher, according to its clans.

Allotment for Naphtali

32 The sixth lot came out for Naphtali according to its clans:

> 33 Their boundary went from Heleph and the large tree in Zaanannim, passing Adami Nekeb and Jabneel to Lakkum and ending at the Jordan. 34 The boundary ran west through Aznoth Tabor and came out at Hukkok. It touched Zebulun on the south, Asher on the west and the Jordan[b] on the east. 35 The fortified towns were Ziddim, Zer, Hammath, Rakkath, Kinnereth, 36 Adamah, Ramah, Hazor, 37 Kedesh, Edrei, En Hazor, 38 Iron, Migdal El, Horem, Beth Anath and Beth Shemesh. There were nineteen towns and their villages.

39 These towns and their villages were the inheritance of the tribe of Naphtali, according to its clans.

Allotment for Dan

40 The seventh lot came out for the tribe of Dan according to its clans. 41 The territory of their inheritance included:

> Zorah, Eshtaol, Ir Shemesh, 42 Shaalabbin, Aijalon, Ithlah, 43 Elon, Timnah, Ekron, 44 Eltekeh, Gibbethon, Baalath, 45 Jehud, Bene Berak, Gath Rimmon, 46 Me Jarkon and Rakkon, with the area facing Joppa.

47 (When the territory of the Danites was lost to them, they went up and attacked Leshem, took it, put it to the sword and occupied it. They settled in Leshem and named it Dan after their ancestor.) 48 These towns and their villages were the inheritance of the tribe of Dan, according to its clans.

Allotment for Joshua

49 When they had finished dividing the land into its allotted portions, the Israelites gave Joshua son of Nun an inheritance among them, 50 as the LORD had commanded. They gave him the town he asked for—Timnath Serah[c] in the hill country of Ephraim. And he built up the town and settled there.

51 These are the territories that Eleazar the priest, Joshua son of Nun and the heads of the tribal clans of Israel assigned by lot at Shiloh in the presence of the LORD at the entrance to the tent of meeting. And so they finished dividing the land.

Cities of Refuge

20 Then the LORD said to Joshua: 2 "Tell the Israelites to designate the cities of refuge, as I instructed you through Moses, 3 so that anyone who kills a person accidentally and unintentionally may flee there and find protection from the avenger of blood. 4 When they flee to one of these cities, they are to stand in the entrance of the city gate and state their case before the elders of that city. Then the elders are to admit the fugitive into their city and provide a place to live among them. 5 If the avenger of blood comes in pursuit, the elders must not surrender the fugitive, because the fugitive killed their neighbor unintentionally and without malice aforethought. 6 They are to stay in that city until they have stood trial before the assembly and until the death of the high priest who is serving at that time. Then they may

[a] *28* Some Hebrew manuscripts (see also 21:30); most Hebrew manuscripts *Ebron* [b] *34* Septuagint; Hebrew *west, and Judah, the Jordan,* [c] *50* Also known as *Timnath Heres* (see Judges 2:9)

go back to their own home in the town from
which they fled."
7So they set apart Kedesh in Galilee in the
hill country of Naphtali, Shechem in the hill
country of Ephraim, and Kiriath Arba (that
is, Hebron) in the hill country of Judah. 8East
of the Jordan (on the other side from Jericho)
they designated Bezer in the wilderness on
the plateau in the tribe of Reuben, Ramoth
in Gilead in the tribe of Gad, and Golan in
Bashan in the tribe of Manasseh. 9Any of the
Israelites or any foreigner residing among
them who killed someone accidentally
could flee to these designated cities and not
be killed by the avenger of blood prior to
standing trial before the assembly.

Towns for the Levites

21 Now the family heads of the Levites
approached Eleazar the priest, Josh-
ua son of Nun, and the heads of the other
tribal families of Israel 2at Shiloh in Canaan
and said to them, "The LORD commanded
through Moses that you give us towns to live
in, with pasturelands for our livestock." 3So,
as the LORD had commanded, the Israelites
gave the Levites the following towns and
pasturelands out of their own inheritance:
4The first lot came out for the Kohathites,
according to their clans. The Levites who
were descendants of Aaron the priest were
allotted thirteen towns from the tribes of Ju-
dah, Simeon and Benjamin. 5The rest of Ko-
hath's descendants were allotted ten towns
from the clans of the tribes of Ephraim, Dan
and half of Manasseh.
6The descendants of Gershon were al-
lotted thirteen towns from the clans of the
tribes of Issachar, Asher, Naphtali and the
half-tribe of Manasseh in Bashan.
7The descendants of Merari, according to
their clans, received twelve towns from the
tribes of Reuben, Gad and Zebulun.
8So the Israelites allotted to the Levites
these towns and their pasturelands, as the
LORD had commanded through Moses.
9From the tribes of Judah and Simeon
they allotted the following towns by name
10(these towns were assigned to the descen-
dants of Aaron who were from the Kohathite
clans of the Levites, because the first lot fell
to them):
11They gave them Kiriath Arba (that
is, Hebron), with its surrounding pas-
tureland, in the hill country of Judah.
(Arba was the forefather of Anak.) 12But
the fields and villages around the city
they had given to Caleb son of Jephun-
neh as his possession.
13So to the descendants of Aaron
the priest they gave Hebron (a city of
refuge for one accused of murder), Lib-
nah, 14Jattir, Eshtemoa, 15Holon, Debir,
16Ain, Juttah and Beth Shemesh, to-
gether with their pasturelands — nine
towns from these two tribes.
17And from the tribe of Benjamin
they gave them Gibeon, Geba, 18Ana-
thoth and Almon, together with their
pasturelands — four towns.
19The total number of towns for the priests,
the descendants of Aaron, came to thirteen,
together with their pasturelands.
20The rest of the Kohathite clans of the Le-
vites were allotted towns from the tribe of
Ephraim:
21In the hill country of Ephraim they
were given Shechem (a city of refuge
for one accused of murder) and Gezer,
22Kibzaim and Beth Horon, together
with their pasturelands — four towns.
23Also from the tribe of Dan they re-
ceived Eltekeh, Gibbethon, 24Aijalon
and Gath Rimmon, together with their
pasturelands — four towns.
25From half the tribe of Manas-
seh they received Taanach and Gath
Rimmon, together with their pasture-
lands — two towns.
26All these ten towns and their pasturelands
were given to the rest of the Kohathite clans.
27The Levite clans of the Gershonites were
given:
from the half-tribe of Manasseh,
Golan in Bashan (a city of refuge for one
accused of murder) and Be Eshterah,
together with their pasturelands — two
towns;
28from the tribe of Issachar,
Kishion, Daberath, 29Jarmuth and En
Gannim, together with their pasture-
lands — four towns;
30from the tribe of Asher,
Mishal, Abdon, 31Helkath and Rehob,
together with their pasturelands — four
towns;
32from the tribe of Naphtali,

Kedesh in Galilee (a city of refuge for
one accused of murder), Hammoth Dor
and Kartan, together with their pas-
turelands — three towns.
33 The total number of towns of the Gershon-
ite clans came to thirteen, together with
their pasturelands.

34 The Merarite clans (the rest of the Levites)
were given:
from the tribe of Zebulun,
Jokneam, Kartah, 35 Dimnah and Na-
halal, together with their pasture-
lands — four towns;
36 from the tribe of Reuben,
Bezer, Jahaz, 37 Kedemoth and Mepha-
ath, together with their pasturelands —
four towns;
38 from the tribe of Gad,
Ramoth in Gilead (a city of refuge for
one accused of murder), Mahanaim,
39 Heshbon and Jazer, together with
their pasturelands — four towns in all.
40 The total number of towns allotted to the
Merarite clans, who were the rest of the Le-
vites, came to twelve.

41 The towns of the Levites in the territory
held by the Israelites were forty-eight in all,
together with their pasturelands. 42 Each of
these towns had pasturelands surrounding
it; this was true for all these towns.

43 So the LORD gave Israel all the land he
had sworn to give their ancestors, and they
took possession of it and settled there. 44 The
LORD gave them rest on every side, just as he
had sworn to their ancestors. Not one of their
enemies withstood them; the LORD gave all
their enemies into their hands. 45 Not one of
all the LORD's good promises to Israel failed;
every one was fulfilled.

Eastern Tribes Return Home

22 Then Joshua summoned the Reu-
benites, the Gadites and the half-
tribe of Manasseh 2 and said to them, "You
have done all that Moses the servant of the
LORD commanded, and you have obeyed
me in everything I commanded. 3 For a long
time now — to this very day — you have not
deserted your fellow Israelites but have car-
ried out the mission the LORD your God gave
you. 4 Now that the LORD your God has giv-
en them rest as he promised, return to your
homes in the land that Moses the servant of
the LORD gave you on the other side of the
Jordan. 5 But be very careful to keep the com-
mandment and the law that Moses the ser-
vant of the LORD gave you: to love the LORD
your God, to walk in obedience to him, to
keep his commands, to hold fast to him and
to serve him with all your heart and with all
your soul."

6 Then Joshua blessed them and sent them
away, and they went to their homes. 7 (To the
half-tribe of Manasseh Moses had given
land in Bashan, and to the other half of the
tribe Joshua gave land on the west side of
the Jordan along with their fellow Israelites.)
When Joshua sent them home, he blessed
them, 8 saying, "Return to your homes with
your great wealth — with large herds of live-
stock, with silver, gold, bronze and iron, and
a great quantity of clothing — and divide the
plunder from your enemies with your fellow
Israelites."

9 So the Reubenites, the Gadites and the
half-tribe of Manasseh left the Israelites at
Shiloh in Canaan to return to Gilead, their
own land, which they had acquired in ac-
cordance with the command of the LORD
through Moses.

10 When they came to Geliloth near the
Jordan in the land of Canaan, the Reuben-
ites, the Gadites and the half-tribe of Ma-
nasseh built an imposing altar there by the
Jordan. 11 And when the Israelites heard that
they had built the altar on the border of Ca-
naan at Geliloth near the Jordan on the Is-
raelite side, 12 the whole assembly of Israel
gathered at Shiloh to go to war against them.

13 So the Israelites sent Phinehas son of El-
eazar, the priest, to the land of Gilead — to
Reuben, Gad and the half-tribe of Manas-
seh. 14 With him they sent ten of the chief
men, one from each of the tribes of Israel,
each the head of a family division among the
Israelite clans.

15 When they went to Gilead — to Reuben,
Gad and the half-tribe of Manasseh — they
said to them: 16 "The whole assembly of the
LORD says: 'How could you break faith with
the God of Israel like this? How could you
turn away from the LORD and build your-
selves an altar in rebellion against him now?
17 Was not the sin of Peor enough for us? Up to
this very day we have not cleansed ourselves
from that sin, even though a plague fell on
the community of the LORD! 18 And are you
now turning away from the LORD?

" 'If you rebel against the LORD today, tomorrow he will be angry with the whole community of Israel. 19 If the land you possess is defiled, come over to the LORD's land, where the LORD's tabernacle stands, and share the land with us. But do not rebel against the LORD or against us by building an altar for yourselves, other than the altar of the LORD our God. 20 When Achan son of Zerah was unfaithful in regard to the devoted things,[a] did not wrath come on the whole community of Israel? He was not the only one who died for his sin.' "

21 Then Reuben, Gad and the half-tribe of Manasseh replied to the heads of the clans of Israel: 22 "The Mighty One, God, the LORD! The Mighty One, God, the LORD! He knows! And let Israel know! If this has been in rebellion or disobedience to the LORD, do not spare us this day. 23 If we have built our own altar to turn away from the LORD and to offer burnt offerings and grain offerings, or to sacrifice fellowship offerings on it, may the LORD himself call us to account.

24 "No! We did it for fear that some day your descendants might say to ours, 'What do you have to do with the LORD, the God of Israel? 25 The LORD has made the Jordan a boundary between us and you — you Reubenites and Gadites! You have no share in the LORD.' So your descendants might cause ours to stop fearing the LORD.

26 "That is why we said, 'Let us get ready and build an altar — but not for burnt offerings or sacrifices.' 27 On the contrary, it is to be a witness between us and you and the generations that follow, that we will worship the LORD at his sanctuary with our burnt offerings, sacrifices and fellowship offerings. Then in the future your descendants will not be able to say to ours, 'You have no share in the LORD.'

28 "And we said, 'If they ever say this to us, or to our descendants, we will answer: Look at the replica of the LORD's altar, which our ancestors built, not for burnt offerings and sacrifices, but as a witness between us and you.'

29 "Far be it from us to rebel against the LORD and turn away from him today by building an altar for burnt offerings, grain offerings and sacrifices, other than the altar of the LORD our God that stands before his tabernacle."

30 When Phinehas the priest and the leaders of the community — the heads of the clans of the Israelites — heard what Reuben, Gad and Manasseh had to say, they were pleased. 31 And Phinehas son of Eleazar, the priest, said to Reuben, Gad and Manasseh, "Today we know that the LORD is with us, because you have not been unfaithful to the LORD in this matter. Now you have rescued the Israelites from the LORD's hand."

32 Then Phinehas son of Eleazar, the priest, and the leaders returned to Canaan from their meeting with the Reubenites and Gadites in Gilead and reported to the Israelites. 33 They were glad to hear the report and praised God. And they talked no more about going to war against them to devastate the country where the Reubenites and the Gadites lived.

34 And the Reubenites and the Gadites gave the altar this name: A Witness Between Us — that the LORD is God.

Joshua's Farewell to the Leaders

23 After a long time had passed and the LORD had given Israel rest from all their enemies around them, Joshua, by then a very old man, 2 summoned all Israel — their elders, leaders, judges and officials — and said to them: "I am very old. 3 You yourselves have seen everything the LORD your God has done to all these nations for your sake; it was the LORD your God who fought for you. 4 Remember how I have allotted as an inheritance for your tribes all the land of the nations that remain — the nations I conquered — between the Jordan and the Mediterranean Sea in the west. 5 The LORD your God himself will push them out for your sake. He will drive them out before you, and you will take possession of their land, as the LORD your God promised you.

6 "Be very strong; be careful to obey all that is written in the Book of the Law of Moses, without turning aside to the right or to the left. 7 Do not associate with these nations that remain among you; do not invoke the names of their gods or swear by them. You must not serve them or bow down to them. 8 But you are to hold fast to the LORD your God, as you have until now.

[a] 20 The Hebrew term refers to the irrevocable giving over of things or persons to the LORD, often by totally destroying them.

9"The LORD has driven out before you
great and powerful nations; to this day no
one has been able to withstand you. 10One of
you routs a thousand, because the LORD your
God fights for you, just as he promised. 11So
be very careful to love the LORD your God.

12"But if you turn away and ally yourselves
with the survivors of these nations that re-
main among you and if you intermarry with
them and associate with them, 13then you
may be sure that the LORD your God will no
longer drive out these nations before you. In-
stead, they will become snares and traps for
you, whips on your backs and thorns in your
eyes, until you perish from this good land,
which the LORD your God has given you.

14"Now I am about to go the way of all
the earth. You know with all your heart
and soul that not one of all the good prom-
ises the LORD your God gave you has failed.
Every promise has been fulfilled; not one
has failed. 15But just as all the good things
the LORD your God has promised you have
come to you, so he will bring on you all the
evil things he has threatened, until the
LORD your God has destroyed you from this
good land he has given you. 16If you violate
the covenant of the LORD your God, which
he commanded you, and go and serve oth-
er gods and bow down to them, the LORD's
anger will burn against you, and you will
quickly perish from the good land he has
given you."

The Covenant Renewed at Shechem

24 Then Joshua assembled all the tribes
of Israel at Shechem. He summoned
the elders, leaders, judges and officials of Is-
rael, and they presented themselves before
God.

2Joshua said to all the people, "This is
what the LORD, the God of Israel, says: 'Long
ago your ancestors, including Terah the fa-
ther of Abraham and Nahor, lived beyond
the Euphrates River and worshiped other
gods. 3But I took your father Abraham from
the land beyond the Euphrates and led him
throughout Canaan and gave him many de-
scendants. I gave him Isaac, 4and to Isaac
I gave Jacob and Esau. I assigned the hill
country of Seir to Esau, but Jacob and his
family went down to Egypt.

5" 'Then I sent Moses and Aaron, and I
afflicted the Egyptians by what I did there,
and I brought you out. 6When I brought your
people out of Egypt, you came to the sea, and
the Egyptians pursued them with chariots
and horsemen[a] as far as the Red Sea.[b] 7But
they cried to the LORD for help, and he put
darkness between you and the Egyptians;
he brought the sea over them and covered
them. You saw with your own eyes what I did
to the Egyptians. Then you lived in the wil-
derness for a long time.

8" 'I brought you to the land of the Am-
orites who lived east of the Jordan. They
fought against you, but I gave them into
your hands. I destroyed them from before
you, and you took possession of their land.
9When Balak son of Zippor, the king of
Moab, prepared to fight against Israel, he
sent for Balaam son of Beor to put a curse on
you. 10But I would not listen to Balaam, so he
blessed you again and again, and I delivered
you out of his hand.

11" 'Then you crossed the Jordan and came
to Jericho. The citizens of Jericho fought
against you, as did also the Amorites, Per-
izzites, Canaanites, Hittites, Girgashites,
Hivites and Jebusites, but I gave them into
your hands. 12I sent the hornet ahead of you,
which drove them out before you — also the
two Amorite kings. You did not do it with your
own sword and bow. 13So I gave you a land on
which you did not toil and cities you did not
build; and you live in them and eat from vine-
yards and olive groves that you did not plant.'

14"Now fear the LORD and serve him with
all faithfulness. Throw away the gods your
ancestors worshiped beyond the Euphra-
tes River and in Egypt, and serve the LORD.
15But if serving the LORD seems undesirable
to you, then choose for yourselves this day
whom you will serve, whether the gods your
ancestors served beyond the Euphrates, or
the gods of the Amorites, in whose land you
are living. But as for me and my household,
we will serve the LORD."

16Then the people answered, "Far be it
from us to forsake the LORD to serve other
gods! 17It was the LORD our God himself who
brought us and our parents up out of Egypt,
from that land of slavery, and performed
those great signs before our eyes. He pro-
tected us on our entire journey and among

[a] 6 Or *charioteers* [b] 6 Or *the Sea of Reeds*

all the nations through which we traveled.
[18]And the LORD drove out before us all the
nations, including the Amorites, who lived
in the land. We too will serve the LORD, be-
cause he is our God."

[19]Joshua said to the people, "You are not
able to serve the LORD. He is a holy God; he
is a jealous God. He will not forgive your re-
bellion and your sins. [20]If you forsake the
LORD and serve foreign gods, he will turn
and bring disaster on you and make an end
of you, after he has been good to you."

[21]But the people said to Joshua, "No! We
will serve the LORD."

[22]Then Joshua said, "You are witnesses
against yourselves that you have chosen to
serve the LORD."

"Yes, we are witnesses," they replied.

[23]"Now then," said Joshua, "throw away
the foreign gods that are among you and yield
your hearts to the LORD, the God of Israel."

[24]And the people said to Joshua, "We will
serve the LORD our God and obey him."

[25]On that day Joshua made a covenant
for the people, and there at Shechem he re-
affirmed for them decrees and laws. [26]And
Joshua recorded these things in the Book of
the Law of God. Then he took a large stone
and set it up there under the oak near the
holy place of the LORD.

[27]"See!" he said to all the people. "This
stone will be a witness against us. It has
heard all the words the LORD has said to us.
It will be a witness against you if you are un-
true to your God."

[28]Then Joshua dismissed the people, each
to their own inheritance.

Buried in the Promised Land

[29]After these things, Joshua son of Nun,
the servant of the LORD, died at the age of a
hundred and ten. [30]And they buried him in
the land of his inheritance, at Timnath Se-
rah[a] in the hill country of Ephraim, north of
Mount Gaash.

[31]Israel served the LORD throughout the
lifetime of Joshua and of the elders who out-
lived him and who had experienced every-
thing the LORD had done for Israel.

[32]And Joseph's bones, which the Israelites
had brought up from Egypt, were buried at
Shechem in the tract of land that Jacob bought
for a hundred pieces of silver[b] from the sons of
Hamor, the father of Shechem. This became
the inheritance of Joseph's descendants.

[33]And Eleazar son of Aaron died and was
buried at Gibeah, which had been allotted
to his son Phinehas in the hill country of
Ephraim.

[a] *30* Also known as *Timnath Heres* (see Judges 2:9) [b] *32* Hebrew *hundred kesitahs*; a kesitah was a unit of money of unknown weight and value.

JUDGES

Israel Fights the Remaining Canaanites

1 After the death of Joshua, the Israelites asked the LORD, "Who of us is to go up first to fight against the Canaanites?"

2 The LORD answered, "Judah shall go up; I have given the land into their hands."

3 The men of Judah then said to the Simeonites their fellow Israelites, "Come up with us into the territory allotted to us, to fight against the Canaanites. We in turn will go with you into yours." So the Simeonites went with them.

4 When Judah attacked, the LORD gave the Canaanites and Perizzites into their hands, and they struck down ten thousand men at Bezek. 5 It was there that they found Adoni-Bezek and fought against him, putting to rout the Canaanites and Perizzites. 6 Adoni-Bezek fled, but they chased him and caught him, and cut off his thumbs and big toes.

7 Then Adoni-Bezek said, "Seventy kings with their thumbs and big toes cut off have picked up scraps under my table. Now God has paid me back for what I did to them." They brought him to Jerusalem, and he died there.

8 The men of Judah attacked Jerusalem also and took it. They put the city to the sword and set it on fire.

9 After that, Judah went down to fight against the Canaanites living in the hill country, the Negev and the western foothills. 10 They advanced against the Canaanites living in Hebron (formerly called Kiriath Arba) and defeated Sheshai, Ahiman and Talmai. 11 From there they advanced against the people living in Debir (formerly called Kiriath Sepher).

12 And Caleb said, "I will give my daughter Aksah in marriage to the man who attacks and captures Kiriath Sepher." 13 Othniel son of Kenaz, Caleb's younger brother, took it; so Caleb gave his daughter Aksah to him in marriage.

14 One day when she came to Othniel, she urged him[a] to ask her father for a field. When she got off her donkey, Caleb asked her, "What can I do for you?"

15 She replied, "Do me a special favor. Since you have given me land in the Negev, give me also springs of water." So Caleb gave her the upper and lower springs.

16 The descendants of Moses' father-in-law, the Kenite, went up from the City of Palms[b] with the people of Judah to live among the inhabitants of the Desert of Judah in the Negev near Arad.

17 Then the men of Judah went with the Simeonites their fellow Israelites and attacked the Canaanites living in Zephath, and they totally destroyed[c] the city. Therefore it was called Hormah.[d] 18 Judah also took[e] Gaza, Ashkelon and Ekron—each city with its territory.

19 The LORD was with the men of Judah. They took possession of the hill country, but they were unable to drive the people from the plains, because they had chariots fitted with iron. 20 As Moses had promised, Hebron was given to Caleb, who drove from it the three sons of Anak. 21 The Benjamites, however, did not drive out the Jebusites, who were living in Jerusalem; to this day the Jebusites live there with the Benjamites.

22 Now the tribes of Joseph attacked Bethel, and the LORD was with them. 23 When they sent men to spy out Bethel (formerly called Luz), 24 the spies saw a man coming out of the city and they said to him, "Show us how to get into the city and we will see that you are treated well." 25 So he showed them, and they put the city to the sword but spared the man and his whole family. 26 He then went to the land of the Hittites, where he built a city and called it Luz, which is its name to this day.

27 But Manasseh did not drive out the

[a] *14* Hebrew; Septuagint and Vulgate *Othniel, he urged her* [b] *16* That is, Jericho [c] *17* The Hebrew term refers to the irrevocable giving over of things or persons to the LORD, often by totally destroying them. [d] *17* *Hormah* means *destruction.* [e] *18* Hebrew; Septuagint *Judah did not take*

people of Beth Shan or Taanach or Dor or Ibleam or Megiddo and their surrounding settlements, for the Canaanites were determined to live in that land. 28 When Israel became strong, they pressed the Canaanites into forced labor but never drove them out completely. 29 Nor did Ephraim drive out the Canaanites living in Gezer, but the Canaanites continued to live there among them. 30 Neither did Zebulun drive out the Canaanites living in Kitron or Nahalol, so these Canaanites lived among them, but Zebulun did subject them to forced labor. 31 Nor did Asher drive out those living in Akko or Sidon or Ahlab or Akzib or Helbah or Aphek or Rehob. 32 The Asherites lived among the Canaanite inhabitants of the land because they did not drive them out. 33 Neither did Naphtali drive out those living in Beth Shemesh or Beth Anath; but the Naphtalites too lived among the Canaanite inhabitants of the land, and those living in Beth Shemesh and Beth Anath became forced laborers for them. 34 The Amorites confined the Danites to the hill country, not allowing them to come down into the plain. 35 And the Amorites were determined also to hold out in Mount Heres, Aijalon and Shaalbim, but when the power of the tribes of Joseph increased, they too were pressed into forced labor. 36 The boundary of the Amorites was from Scorpion Pass to Sela and beyond

The Angel of the LORD at Bokim

2 The angel of the LORD went up from Gilgal to Bokim and said, "I brought you up out of Egypt and led you into the land I swore to give to your ancestors. I said, 'I will never break my covenant with you, 2 and you shall not make a covenant with the people of this land, but you shall break down their altars.' Yet you have disobeyed me. Why have you done this? 3 And I have also said, 'I will not drive them out before you; they will become traps for you, and their gods will become snares to you.' "

4 When the angel of the LORD had spoken these things to all the Israelites, the people wept aloud, 5 and they called that place Bokim.[a] There they offered sacrifices to the LORD.

Disobedience and Defeat

6 After Joshua had dismissed the Israelites, they went to take possession of the land, each to their own inheritance. 7 The people served the LORD throughout the lifetime of Joshua and of the elders who outlived him and who had seen all the great things the LORD had done for Israel.

8 Joshua son of Nun, the servant of the LORD, died at the age of a hundred and ten. 9 And they buried him in the land of his inheritance, at Timnath Heres[b] in the hill country of Ephraim, north of Mount Gaash.

10 After that whole generation had been gathered to their ancestors, another generation grew up who knew neither the LORD nor what he had done for Israel. 11 Then the Israelites did evil in the eyes of the LORD and served the Baals. 12 They forsook the LORD, the God of their ancestors, who had brought them out of Egypt. They followed and worshiped various gods of the peoples around them. They aroused the LORD's anger 13 because they forsook him and served Baal and the Ashtoreths. 14 In his anger against Israel the LORD gave them into the hands of raiders who plundered them. He sold them into the hands of their enemies all around, whom they were no longer able to resist. 15 Whenever Israel went out to fight, the hand of the LORD was against them to defeat them, just as he had sworn to them. They were in great distress.

16 Then the LORD raised up judges,[c] who saved them out of the hands of these raiders. 17 Yet they would not listen to their judges but prostituted themselves to other gods and worshiped them. They quickly turned from the ways of their ancestors, who had been obedient to the LORD's commands. 18 Whenever the LORD raised up a judge for them, he was with the judge and saved them out of the hands of their enemies as long as the judge lived; for the LORD relented because of their groaning under those who oppressed and afflicted them. 19 But when the judge died, the people returned to ways even more corrupt than those of their ancestors, following other gods and serving and worshiping them. They refused to give up their evil practices and stubborn ways.

[a] 5 *Bokim* means *weepers.* [b] 9 Also known as *Timnath Serah* (see Joshua 19:50 and 24:30)
[c] 16 Or *leaders;* similarly in verses 17-19

20 Therefore the LORD was very angry with Israel and said, "Because this nation has violated the covenant I ordained for their ancestors and has not listened to me, 21 I will no longer drive out before them any of the nations Joshua left when he died. 22 I will use them to test Israel and see whether they will keep the way of the LORD and walk in it as their ancestors did." 23 The LORD had allowed those nations to remain; he did not drive them out at once by giving them into the hands of Joshua.

3 These are the nations the LORD left to test all those Israelites who had not experienced any of the wars in Canaan 2 (he did this only to teach warfare to the descendants of the Israelites who had not had previous battle experience): 3 the five rulers of the Philistines, all the Canaanites, the Sidonians, and the Hivites living in the Lebanon mountains from Mount Baal Hermon to Lebo Hamath. 4 They were left to test the Israelites to see whether they would obey the LORD's commands, which he had given their ancestors through Moses.

5 The Israelites lived among the Canaanites, Hittites, Amorites, Perizzites, Hivites and Jebusites. 6 They took their daughters in marriage and gave their own daughters to their sons, and served their gods.

Othniel

7 The Israelites did evil in the eyes of the LORD; they forgot the LORD their God and served the Baals and the Asherahs. 8 The anger of the LORD burned against Israel so that he sold them into the hands of Cushan-Rishathaim king of Aram Naharaim,[a] to whom the Israelites were subject for eight years. 9 But when they cried out to the LORD, he raised up for them a deliverer, Othniel son of Kenaz, Caleb's younger brother, who saved them. 10 The Spirit of the LORD came on him, so that he became Israel's judge[b] and went to war. The LORD gave Cushan-Rishathaim king of Aram into the hands of Othniel, who overpowered him. 11 So the land had peace for forty years, until Othniel son of Kenaz died.

Ehud

12 Again the Israelites did evil in the eyes of the LORD, and because they did this evil the LORD gave Eglon king of Moab power over Israel. 13 Getting the Ammonites and Amalekites to join him, Eglon came and attacked Israel, and they took possession of the City of Palms.[c] 14 The Israelites were subject to Eglon king of Moab for eighteen years.

15 Again the Israelites cried out to the LORD, and he gave them a deliverer—Ehud, a left-handed man, the son of Gera the Benjamite. The Israelites sent him with tribute to Eglon king of Moab. 16 Now Ehud had made a double-edged sword about a cubit[d] long, which he strapped to his right thigh under his clothing. 17 He presented the tribute to Eglon king of Moab, who was a very fat man. 18 After Ehud had presented the tribute, he sent on their way those who had carried it. 19 But on reaching the stone images near Gilgal he himself went back to Eglon and said, "Your Majesty, I have a secret message for you."

The king said to his attendants, "Leave us!" And they all left.

20 Ehud then approached him while he was sitting alone in the upper room of his palace[e] and said, "I have a message from God for you." As the king rose from his seat, 21 Ehud reached with his left hand, drew the sword from his right thigh and plunged it into the king's belly. 22 Even the handle sank in after the blade, and his bowels discharged. Ehud did not pull the sword out, and the fat closed in over it. 23 Then Ehud went out to the porch[f]; he shut the doors of the upper room behind him and locked them.

24 After he had gone, the servants came and found the doors of the upper room locked. They said, "He must be relieving himself in the inner room of the palace." 25 They waited to the point of embarrassment, but when he did not open the doors of the room, they took a key and unlocked them. There they saw their lord fallen to the floor, dead.

26 While they waited, Ehud got away. He passed by the stone images and escaped to Seirah. 27 When he arrived there, he blew a trumpet in the hill country of Ephraim, and the Israelites went down with him from the hills, with him leading them.

[a] *8* That is, Northwest Mesopotamia [b] *10* Or *leader* [c] *13* That is, Jericho [d] *16* That is, about 18 inches or about 45 centimeters [e] *20* The meaning of the Hebrew for this word is uncertain; also in verse 24. [f] *23* The meaning of the Hebrew for this word is uncertain.

28 “Follow me,” he ordered, “for the LORD has given Moab, your enemy, into your hands.” So they followed him down and took possession of the fords of the Jordan that led to Moab; they allowed no one to cross over. 29 At that time they struck down about ten thousand Moabites, all vigorous and strong; not one escaped. 30 That day Moab was made subject to Israel, and the land had peace for eighty years.

Shamgar

31 After Ehud came Shamgar son of Anath, who struck down six hundred Philistines with an oxgoad. He too saved Israel.

Deborah

4 Again the Israelites did evil in the eyes of the LORD, now that Ehud was dead. 2 So the LORD sold them into the hands of Jabin king of Canaan, who reigned in Hazor. Sisera, the commander of his army, was based in Harosheth Haggoyim. 3 Because he had nine hundred chariots fitted with iron and had cruelly oppressed the Israelites for twenty years, they cried to the LORD for help.

4 Now Deborah, a prophet, the wife of Lappidoth, was leading[a] Israel at that time. 5 She held court under the Palm of Deborah between Ramah and Bethel in the hill country of Ephraim, and the Israelites went up to her to have their disputes decided. 6 She sent for Barak son of Abinoam from Kedesh in Naphtali and said to him, “The LORD, the God of Israel, commands you: ‘Go, take with you ten thousand men of Naphtali and Zebulun and lead them up to Mount Tabor. 7 I will lead Sisera, the commander of Jabin’s army, with his chariots and his troops to the Kishon River and give him into your hands.’ ”

8 Barak said to her, “If you go with me, I will go; but if you don’t go with me, I won’t go.”

9 “Certainly I will go with you,” said Deborah. “But because of the course you are taking, the honor will not be yours, for the LORD will deliver Sisera into the hands of a woman.” So Deborah went with Barak to Kedesh. 10 There Barak summoned Zebulun and Naphtali, and ten thousand men went up under his command. Deborah also went up with him.

11 Now Heber the Kenite had left the other Kenites, the descendants of Hobab, Moses’ brother-in-law,[b] and pitched his tent by the great tree in Zaanannim near Kedesh.

12 When they told Sisera that Barak son of Abinoam had gone up to Mount Tabor, 13 Sisera summoned from Harosheth Haggoyim to the Kishon River all his men and his nine hundred chariots fitted with iron.

14 Then Deborah said to Barak, “Go! This is the day the LORD has given Sisera into your hands. Has not the LORD gone ahead of you?” So Barak went down Mount Tabor, with ten thousand men following him. 15 At Barak’s advance, the LORD routed Sisera and all his chariots and army by the sword, and Sisera got down from his chariot and fled on foot.

16 Barak pursued the chariots and army as far as Harosheth Haggoyim, and all Sisera’s troops fell by the sword; not a man was left. 17 Sisera, meanwhile, fled on foot to the tent of Jael, the wife of Heber the Kenite, because there was an alliance between Jabin king of Hazor and the family of Heber the Kenite.

18 Jael went out to meet Sisera and said to him, “Come, my lord, come right in. Don’t be afraid.” So he entered her tent, and she covered him with a blanket.

19 “I’m thirsty,” he said. “Please give me some water.” She opened a skin of milk, gave him a drink, and covered him up.

20 “Stand in the doorway of the tent,” he told her. “If someone comes by and asks you, ‘Is anyone in there?’ say ‘No.’ ”

21 But Jael, Heber’s wife, picked up a tent peg and a hammer and went quietly to him while he lay fast asleep, exhausted. She drove the peg through his temple into the ground, and he died.

22 Just then Barak came by in pursuit of Sisera, and Jael went out to meet him. “Come,” she said, “I will show you the man you’re looking for.” So he went in with her, and there lay Sisera with the tent peg through his temple — dead.

23 On that day God subdued Jabin king of Canaan before the Israelites. 24 And the hand of the Israelites pressed harder and harder against Jabin king of Canaan until they destroyed him.

The Song of Deborah

5 On that day Deborah and Barak son of Abinoam sang this song:

[a] 4 Traditionally *judging* [b] 11 Or *father-in-law*

[2]"When the princes in Israel take the lead,
when the people willingly offer themselves —
praise the LORD!

[3]"Hear this, you kings! Listen, you rulers!
I, even I, will sing to[a] the LORD;
I will praise the LORD, the God of Israel, in song.

[4]"When you, LORD, went out from Seir,
when you marched from the land of Edom,
the earth shook, the heavens poured,
the clouds poured down water.
[5]The mountains quaked before the LORD,
the One of Sinai,
before the LORD, the God of Israel.

[6]"In the days of Shamgar son of Anath,
in the days of Jael, the highways were abandoned;
travelers took to winding paths.
[7]Villagers in Israel would not fight;
they held back until I, Deborah, arose,
until I arose, a mother in Israel.
[8]God chose new leaders
when war came to the city gates,
but not a shield or spear was seen
among forty thousand in Israel.
[9]My heart is with Israel's princes,
with the willing volunteers among the people.
Praise the LORD!

[10]"You who ride on white donkeys,
sitting on your saddle blankets,
and you who walk along the road,
consider [11]the voice of the singers[b] at the watering places.
They recite the victories of the LORD,
the victories of his villagers in Israel.

"Then the people of the LORD
went down to the city gates.
[12]'Wake up, wake up, Deborah!
Wake up, wake up, break out in song!
Arise, Barak!
Take captive your captives, son of Abinoam.'

[13]"The remnant of the nobles came down;
the people of the LORD came down to me against the mighty.
[14]Some came from Ephraim, whose roots were in Amalek;
Benjamin was with the people who followed you.
From Makir captains came down,
from Zebulun those who bear a commander's[b] staff.
[15]The princes of Issachar were with Deborah;
yes, Issachar was with Barak,
sent under his command into the valley.
In the districts of Reuben
there was much searching of heart.
[16]Why did you stay among the sheep pens[c]
to hear the whistling for the flocks?
In the districts of Reuben
there was much searching of heart.
[17]Gilead stayed beyond the Jordan.
And Dan, why did he linger by the ships?
Asher remained on the coast
and stayed in his coves.
[18]The people of Zebulun risked their very lives;
so did Naphtali on the terraced fields.

[19]"Kings came, they fought,
the kings of Canaan fought.
At Taanach, by the waters of Megiddo,
they took no plunder of silver.
[20]From the heavens the stars fought,
from their courses they fought against Sisera.
[21]The river Kishon swept them away,
the age-old river, the river Kishon.
March on, my soul; be strong!
[22]Then thundered the horses' hooves —
galloping, galloping go his mighty steeds.
[23]'Curse Meroz,' said the angel of the LORD.
'Curse its people bitterly,
because they did not come to help the LORD,
to help the LORD against the mighty.'

[24]"Most blessed of women be Jael,
the wife of Heber the Kenite,
most blessed of tent-dwelling women.
[25]He asked for water, and she gave him milk;

[a] 3 Or *of* [b] *11,14* The meaning of the Hebrew for this word is uncertain. [c] *16* Or *the campfires;* or *the saddlebags*

in a bowl fit for nobles she brought him
curdled milk.
26 Her hand reached for the tent peg,
her right hand for the workman's
hammer.
She struck Sisera, she crushed his head,
she shattered and pierced his temple.
27 At her feet he sank,
he fell; there he lay.
At her feet he sank, he fell;
where he sank, there he fell — dead.

28 "Through the window peered Sisera's
mother;
behind the lattice she cried out,
'Why is his chariot so long in coming?
Why is the clatter of his chariots
delayed?'
29 The wisest of her ladies answer her;
indeed, she keeps saying to herself,
30 'Are they not finding and dividing the
spoils:
a woman or two for each man,
colorful garments as plunder for Sisera,
colorful garments embroidered,
highly embroidered garments for my
neck —
all this as plunder?'

31 "So may all your enemies perish, LORD!
But may all who love you be like the
sun
when it rises in its strength."
Then the land had peace forty years.

Gideon

6 The Israelites did evil in the eyes of the
LORD, and for seven years he gave them
into the hands of the Midianites. 2 Because
the power of Midian was so oppressive, the
Israelites prepared shelters for themselves
in mountain clefts, caves and strongholds.
3 Whenever the Israelites planted their
crops, the Midianites, Amalekites and other
eastern peoples invaded the country. 4 They
camped on the land and ruined the crops all
the way to Gaza and did not spare a living
thing for Israel, neither sheep nor cattle nor
donkeys. 5 They came up with their livestock
and their tents like swarms of locusts. It was
impossible to count them or their camels;
they invaded the land to ravage it. 6 Midi-
an so impoverished the Israelites that they
cried out to the LORD for help.
7 When the Israelites cried out to the LORD
because of Midian, 8 he sent them a proph-
et, who said, "This is what the LORD, the
God of Israel, says: I brought you up out of
Egypt, out of the land of slavery. 9 I rescued
you from the hand of the Egyptians. And I
delivered you from the hand of all your op-
pressors; I drove them out before you and
gave you their land. 10 I said to you, 'I am the
LORD your God; do not worship the gods of
the Amorites, in whose land you live.' But
you have not listened to me."
11 The angel of the LORD came and sat
down under the oak in Ophrah that be-
longed to Joash the Abiezrite, where his son
Gideon was threshing wheat in a winepress
to keep it from the Midianites. 12 When the
angel of the LORD appeared to Gideon, he
said, "The LORD is with you, mighty warrior."
13 "Pardon me, my lord," Gideon replied,
"but if the LORD is with us, why has all this
happened to us? Where are all his wonders
that our ancestors told us about when they
said, 'Did not the LORD bring us up out of
Egypt?' But now the LORD has abandoned us
and given us into the hand of Midian."
14 The LORD turned to him and said, "Go in
the strength you have and save Israel out of
Midian's hand. Am I not sending you?"
15 "Pardon me, my lord," Gideon replied,
"but how can I save Israel? My clan is the
weakest in Manasseh, and I am the least in
my family."
16 The LORD answered, "I will be with you,
and you will strike down all the Midianites,
leaving none alive."
17 Gideon replied, "If now I have found fa-
vor in your eyes, give me a sign that it is real-
ly you talking to me. 18 Please do not go away
until I come back and bring my offering and
set it before you."
And the LORD said, "I will wait until you
return."
19 Gideon went inside, prepared a young
goat, and from an ephah[a] of flour he made
bread without yeast. Putting the meat in a
basket and its broth in a pot, he brought them
out and offered them to him under the oak.
20 The angel of God said to him, "Take
the meat and the unleavened bread, place

[a] *19* That is, probably about 36 pounds or about 16 kilograms

them on this rock, and pour out the broth."
And Gideon did so. 21 Then the angel of the
LORD touched the meat and the unleavened
bread with the tip of the staff that was in his
hand. Fire flared from the rock, consuming
the meat and the bread. And the angel of the
LORD disappeared. 22 When Gideon real-
ized that it was the angel of the LORD, he ex-
claimed, "Alas, Sovereign LORD! I have seen
the angel of the LORD face to face!"

23 But the LORD said to him, "Peace! Do not
be afraid. You are not going to die."

24 So Gideon built an altar to the LORD
there and called it The LORD Is Peace. To this
day it stands in Ophrah of the Abiezrites.

25 That same night the LORD said to him,
"Take the second bull from your father's
herd, the one seven years old.[a] Tear down
your father's altar to Baal and cut down
the Asherah pole[b] beside it. 26 Then build a
proper kind of[c] altar to the LORD your God
on the top of this height. Using the wood of
the Asherah pole that you cut down, offer the
second[d] bull as a burnt offering."

27 So Gideon took ten of his servants and
did as the LORD told him. But because he was
afraid of his family and the townspeople, he
did it at night rather than in the daytime.

28 In the morning when the people of the
town got up, there was Baal's altar, demol-
ished, with the Asherah pole beside it cut
down and the second bull sacrificed on the
newly built altar!

29 They asked each other, "Who did this?"

When they carefully investigated, they
were told, "Gideon son of Joash did it."

30 The people of the town demanded of
Joash, "Bring out your son. He must die, be-
cause he has broken down Baal's altar and
cut down the Asherah pole beside it."

31 But Joash replied to the hostile crowd
around him, "Are you going to plead Baal's
cause? Are you trying to save him? Who-
ever fights for him shall be put to death by
morning! If Baal really is a god, he can de-
fend himself when someone breaks down
his altar." 32 So because Gideon broke down
Baal's altar, they gave him the name Jerub-
Baal[e] that day, saying, "Let Baal contend
with him."

33 Now all the Midianites, Amalekites
and other eastern peoples joined forces and
crossed over the Jordan and camped in the
Valley of Jezreel. 34 Then the Spirit of the
LORD came on Gideon, and he blew a trum-
pet, summoning the Abiezrites to follow
him. 35 He sent messengers throughout Ma-
nasseh, calling them to arms, and also into
Asher, Zebulun and Naphtali, so that they
too went up to meet them.

36 Gideon said to God, "If you will save
Israel by my hand as you have promised—
37 look, I will place a wool fleece on the
threshing floor. If there is dew only on the
fleece and all the ground is dry, then I will
know that you will save Israel by my hand,
as you said." 38 And that is what happened.
Gideon rose early the next day; he squeezed
the fleece and wrung out the dew—a bowl-
ful of water.

39 Then Gideon said to God, "Do not be
angry with me. Let me make just one more
request. Allow me one more test with the
fleece, but this time make the fleece dry and
let the ground be covered with dew." 40 That
night God did so. Only the fleece was dry; all
the ground was covered with dew.

Gideon Defeats the Midianites

7 Early in the morning, Jerub-Baal (that
is, Gideon) and all his men camped at
the spring of Harod. The camp of Midian
was north of them in the valley near the hill
of Moreh. 2 The LORD said to Gideon, "You
have too many men. I cannot deliver Mid-
ian into their hands, or Israel would boast
against me, 'My own strength has saved me.'
3 Now announce to the army, 'Anyone who
trembles with fear may turn back and leave
Mount Gilead.'" So twenty-two thousand
men left, while ten thousand remained.

4 But the LORD said to Gideon, "There are
still too many men. Take them down to the
water, and I will thin them out for you there.
If I say, 'This one shall go with you,' he shall
go; but if I say, 'This one shall not go with
you,' he shall not go."

5 So Gideon took the men down to the
water. There the LORD told him, "Separate
those who lap the water with their tongues

[a] *25* Or *Take a full-grown, mature bull from your father's herd* [b] *25* That is, a wooden symbol of the goddess Asherah; also in verses 26, 28 and 30 [c] *26* Or *build with layers of stone an* [d] *26* Or *full-grown*; also in verse 28 [e] *32* *Jerub-Baal* probably means *let Baal contend.*

as a dog laps from those who kneel down to
drink." 6 Three hundred of them drank from
cupped hands, lapping like dogs. All the rest
got down on their knees to drink.

7 The LORD said to Gideon, "With the three
hundred men that lapped I will save you and
give the Midianites into your hands. Let all
the others go home." 8 So Gideon sent the
rest of the Israelites home but kept the three
hundred, who took over the provisions and
trumpets of the others.

Now the camp of Midian lay below him
in the valley. 9 During that night the LORD
said to Gideon, "Get up, go down against the
camp, because I am going to give it into your
hands. 10 If you are afraid to attack, go down
to the camp with your servant Purah 11 and
listen to what they are saying. Afterward,
you will be encouraged to attack the camp."
So he and Purah his servant went down to
the outposts of the camp. 12 The Midianites,
the Amalekites and all the other eastern
peoples had settled in the valley, thick as lo-
custs. Their camels could no more be count-
ed than the sand on the seashore.

13 Gideon arrived just as a man was telling
a friend his dream. "I had a dream," he was
saying. "A round loaf of barley bread came
tumbling into the Midianite camp. It struck
the tent with such force that the tent over-
turned and collapsed."

14 His friend responded, "This can be
nothing other than the sword of Gideon
son of Joash, the Israelite. God has given
the Midianites and the whole camp into his
hands."

15 When Gideon heard the dream and its
interpretation, he bowed down and wor-
shiped. He returned to the camp of Israel
and called out, "Get up! The LORD has given
the Midianite camp into your hands." 16 Di-
viding the three hundred men into three
companies, he placed trumpets and empty
jars in the hands of all of them, with torches
inside.

17 "Watch me," he told them. "Follow my
lead. When I get to the edge of the camp, do
exactly as I do. 18 When I and all who are with
me blow our trumpets, then from all around
the camp blow yours and shout, 'For the
LORD and for Gideon.'"

19 Gideon and the hundred men with him
reached the edge of the camp at the begin-
ning of the middle watch, just after they had
changed the guard. They blew their trum-
pets and broke the jars that were in their
hands. 20 The three companies blew the
trumpets and smashed the jars. Grasping
the torches in their left hands and holding
in their right hands the trumpets they were
to blow, they shouted, "A sword for the LORD
and for Gideon!" 21 While each man held his
position around the camp, all the Midianites
ran, crying out as they fled.

22 When the three hundred trumpets
sounded, the LORD caused the men through-
out the camp to turn on each other with their
swords. The army fled to Beth Shittah to-
ward Zererah as far as the border of Abel Me-
holah near Tabbath. 23 Israelites from Naph-
tali, Asher and all Manasseh were called out,
and they pursued the Midianites. 24 Gideon
sent messengers throughout the hill coun-
try of Ephraim, saying, "Come down against
the Midianites and seize the waters of the
Jordan ahead of them as far as Beth Barah."

So all the men of Ephraim were called out
and they seized the waters of the Jordan as
far as Beth Barah. 25 They also captured two
of the Midianite leaders, Oreb and Zeeb.
They killed Oreb at the rock of Oreb, and
Zeeb at the winepress of Zeeb. They pur-
sued the Midianites and brought the heads
of Oreb and Zeeb to Gideon, who was by the
Jordan.

Zebah and Zalmunna

8 Now the Ephraimites asked Gideon,
"Why have you treated us like this? Why
didn't you call us when you went to fight
Midian?" And they challenged him vigor-
ously.

2 But he answered them, "What have I ac-
complished compared to you? Aren't the
gleanings of Ephraim's grapes better than
the full grape harvest of Abiezer? 3 God gave
Oreb and Zeeb, the Midianite leaders, into
your hands. What was I able to do compared
to you?" At this, their resentment against
him subsided.

4 Gideon and his three hundred men, ex-
hausted yet keeping up the pursuit, came
to the Jordan and crossed it. 5 He said to
the men of Sukkoth, "Give my troops some
bread; they are worn out, and I am still pur-
suing Zebah and Zalmunna, the kings of
Midian."

6 But the officials of Sukkoth said, "Do you

already have the hands of Zebah and Zalmunna in your possession? Why should we give bread to your troops?"

[7]Then Gideon replied, "Just for that, when the LORD has given Zebah and Zalmunna into my hand, I will tear your flesh with desert thorns and briers."

[8]From there he went up to Peniel[a] and made the same request of them, but they answered as the men of Sukkoth had. [9]So he said to the men of Peniel, "When I return in triumph, I will tear down this tower."

[10]Now Zebah and Zalmunna were in Karkor with a force of about fifteen thousand men, all that were left of the armies of the eastern peoples; a hundred and twenty thousand swordsmen had fallen. [11]Gideon went up by the route of the nomads east of Nobah and Jogbehah and attacked the unsuspecting army. [12]Zebah and Zalmunna, the two kings of Midian, fled, but he pursued them and captured them, routing their entire army.

[13]Gideon son of Joash then returned from the battle by the Pass of Heres. [14]He caught a young man of Sukkoth and questioned him, and the young man wrote down for him the names of the seventy-seven officials of Sukkoth, the elders of the town. [15]Then Gideon came and said to the men of Sukkoth, "Here are Zebah and Zalmunna, about whom you taunted me by saying, 'Do you already have the hands of Zebah and Zalmunna in your possession? Why should we give bread to your exhausted men?' " [16]He took the elders of the town and taught the men of Sukkoth a lesson by punishing them with desert thorns and briers. [17]He also pulled down the tower of Peniel and killed the men of the town.

[18]Then he asked Zebah and Zalmunna, "What kind of men did you kill at Tabor?"

"Men like you," they answered, "each one with the bearing of a prince."

[19]Gideon replied, "Those were my brothers, the sons of my own mother. As surely as the LORD lives, if you had spared their lives, I would not kill you." [20]Turning to Jether, his oldest son, he said, "Kill them!" But Jether did not draw his sword, because he was only a boy and was afraid.

[21]Zebah and Zalmunna said, "Come, do it yourself. 'As is the man, so is his strength.' " So Gideon stepped forward and killed them, and took the ornaments off their camels' necks.

Gideon's Ephod

[22]The Israelites said to Gideon, "Rule over us — you, your son and your grandson — because you have saved us from the hand of Midian."

[23]But Gideon told them, "I will not rule over you, nor will my son rule over you. The LORD will rule over you." [24]And he said, "I do have one request, that each of you give me an earring from your share of the plunder." (It was the custom of the Ishmaelites to wear gold earrings.)

[25]They answered, "We'll be glad to give them." So they spread out a garment, and each of them threw a ring from his plunder onto it. [26]The weight of the gold rings he asked for came to seventeen hundred shekels,[b] not counting the ornaments, the pendants and the purple garments worn by the kings of Midian or the chains that were on their camels' necks. [27]Gideon made the gold into an ephod, which he placed in Ophrah, his town. All Israel prostituted themselves by worshiping it there, and it became a snare to Gideon and his family.

Gideon's Death

[28]Thus Midian was subdued before the Israelites and did not raise its head again. During Gideon's lifetime, the land had peace forty years.

[29]Jerub-Baal son of Joash went back home to live. [30]He had seventy sons of his own, for he had many wives. [31]His concubine, who lived in Shechem, also bore him a son, whom he named Abimelek. [32]Gideon son of Joash died at a good old age and was buried in the tomb of his father Joash in Ophrah of the Abiezrites.

[33]No sooner had Gideon died than the Israelites again prostituted themselves to the Baals. They set up Baal-Berith as their god [34]and did not remember the LORD their God, who had rescued them from the hands of all their enemies on every side. [35]They also failed to show any loyalty to the family of Jerub-Baal (that is, Gideon) in spite of all the good things he had done for them.

[a] *8* Hebrew *Penuel,* a variant of *Peniel;* also in verses 9 and 17 [b] *26* That is, about 43 pounds or about 20 kilograms

Abimelek

9 Abimelek son of Jerub-Baal went to his
mother's brothers in Shechem and said
to them and to all his mother's clan, 2"Ask all
the citizens of Shechem, 'Which is better for
you: to have all seventy of Jerub-Baal's sons
rule over you, or just one man?' Remember, I
am your flesh and blood."

3When the brothers repeated all this to
the citizens of Shechem, they were inclined
to follow Abimelek, for they said, "He is re-
lated to us." 4They gave him seventy shekels[a]
of silver from the temple of Baal-Berith, and
Abimelek used it to hire reckless scoundrels,
who became his followers. 5He went to his
father's home in Ophrah and on one stone
murdered his seventy brothers, the sons of
Jerub-Baal. But Jotham, the youngest son of
Jerub-Baal, escaped by hiding. 6Then all the
citizens of Shechem and Beth Millo gathered
beside the great tree at the pillar in Shechem
to crown Abimelek king.

7When Jotham was told about this, he
climbed up on the top of Mount Gerizim
and shouted to them, "Listen to me, citizens
of Shechem, so that God may listen to you.
8One day the trees went out to anoint a king
for themselves. They said to the olive tree,
'Be our king.'

9"But the olive tree answered, 'Should I
give up my oil, by which both gods and hu-
mans are honored, to hold sway over the
trees?'

10"Next, the trees said to the fig tree,
'Come and be our king.'

11"But the fig tree replied, 'Should I give
up my fruit, so good and sweet, to hold sway
over the trees?'

12"Then the trees said to the vine, 'Come
and be our king.'

13"But the vine answered, 'Should I give
up my wine, which cheers both gods and hu-
mans, to hold sway over the trees?'

14"Finally all the trees said to the thorn-
bush, 'Come and be our king.'

15"The thornbush said to the trees, 'If you
really want to anoint me king over you, come
and take refuge in my shade; but if not, then
let fire come out of the thornbush and con-
sume the cedars of Lebanon!'

16"Have you acted honorably and in good
faith by making Abimelek king? Have you
been fair to Jerub-Baal and his family? Have
you treated him as he deserves? 17Remem-
ber that my father fought for you and risked
his life to rescue you from the hand of Midi-
an. 18But today you have revolted against my
father's family. You have murdered his sev-
enty sons on a single stone and have made
Abimelek, the son of his female slave, king
over the citizens of Shechem because he is
related to you. 19So have you acted honor-
ably and in good faith toward Jerub-Baal and
his family today? If you have, may Abimelek
be your joy, and may you be his, too! 20But if
you have not, let fire come out from Abim-
elek and consume you, the citizens of She-
chem and Beth Millo, and let fire come out
from you, the citizens of Shechem and Beth
Millo, and consume Abimelek!"

21Then Jotham fled, escaping to Beer, and
he lived there because he was afraid of his
brother Abimelek.

22After Abimelek had governed Israel
three years, 23God stirred up animosity be-
tween Abimelek and the citizens of Shechem
so that they acted treacherously against
Abimelek. 24God did this in order that the
crime against Jerub-Baal's seventy sons, the
shedding of their blood, might be avenged
on their brother Abimelek and on the citi-
zens of Shechem, who had helped him mur-
der his brothers. 25In opposition to him these
citizens of Shechem set men on the hilltops
to ambush and rob everyone who passed by,
and this was reported to Abimelek.

26Now Gaal son of Ebed moved with his
clan into Shechem, and its citizens put their
confidence in him. 27After they had gone
out into the fields and gathered the grapes
and trodden them, they held a festival in the
temple of their god. While they were eating
and drinking, they cursed Abimelek. 28Then
Gaal son of Ebed said, "Who is Abimelek,
and why should we Shechemites be subject
to him? Isn't he Jerub-Baal's son, and isn't
Zebul his deputy? Serve the family of Ha-
mor, Shechem's father! Why should we serve
Abimelek? 29If only this people were under
my command! Then I would get rid of him. I
would say to Abimelek, 'Call out your whole
army!' "[b]

30When Zebul the governor of the city
heard what Gaal son of Ebed said, he was

[a] 4 That is, about 1 3/4 pounds or about 800 grams
[b] 29 Septuagint; Hebrew *him." Then he said to Abimelek, "Call out your whole army!"*

very angry. 31Under cover he sent messen-
gers to Abimelek, saying, “Gaal son of Ebed
and his clan have come to Shechem and are
stirring up the city against you. 32Now then,
during the night you and your men should
come and lie in wait in the fields. 33In the
morning at sunrise, advance against the city.
When Gaal and his men come out against
you, seize the opportunity to attack them.”

34So Abimelek and all his troops set out by
night and took up concealed positions near
Shechem in four companies. 35Now Gaal son
of Ebed had gone out and was standing at the
entrance of the city gate just as Abimelek and
his troops came out from their hiding place.

36When Gaal saw them, he said to Zebul,
“Look, people are coming down from the
tops of the mountains!”

Zebul replied, “You mistake the shadows
of the mountains for men.”

37But Gaal spoke up again: “Look, people
are coming down from the central hill,[a] and
a company is coming from the direction of
the diviners’ tree.”

38Then Zebul said to him, “Where is your
big talk now, you who said, ‘Who is Abime-
lek that we should be subject to him?’ Aren’t
these the men you ridiculed? Go out and
fight them!”

39So Gaal led out[b] the citizens of Shechem
and fought Abimelek. 40Abimelek chased
him all the way to the entrance of the gate,
and many were killed as they fled. 41Then
Abimelek stayed in Arumah, and Zebul
drove Gaal and his clan out of Shechem.

42The next day the people of Shechem
went out to the fields, and this was reported
to Abimelek. 43So he took his men, divided
them into three companies and set an am-
bush in the fields. When he saw the peo-
ple coming out of the city, he rose to attack
them. 44Abimelek and the companies with
him rushed forward to a position at the en-
trance of the city gate. Then two companies
attacked those in the fields and struck them
down. 45All that day Abimelek pressed his
attack against the city until he had captured
it and killed its people. Then he destroyed
the city and scattered salt over it.

46On hearing this, the citizens in the tow-
er of Shechem went into the stronghold of
the temple of El-Berith. 47When Abimelek
heard that they had assembled there, 48he
and all his men went up Mount Zalmon. He
took an ax and cut off some branches, which
he lifted to his shoulders. He ordered the
men with him, “Quick! Do what you have
seen me do!” 49So all the men cut branch-
es and followed Abimelek. They piled them
against the stronghold and set it on fire with
the people still inside. So all the people in
the tower of Shechem, about a thousand
men and women, also died.

50Next Abimelek went to Thebez and be-
sieged it and captured it. 51Inside the city,
however, was a strong tower, to which all
the men and women — all the people of the
city — had fled. They had locked themselves
in and climbed up on the tower roof. 52Abim-
elek went to the tower and attacked it. But as
he approached the entrance to the tower to
set it on fire, 53a woman dropped an upper
millstone on his head and cracked his skull.

54Hurriedly he called to his armor-bearer,
“Draw your sword and kill me, so that they
can’t say, ‘A woman killed him.’ ” So his ser-
vant ran him through, and he died. 55When
the Israelites saw that Abimelek was dead,
they went home.

56Thus God repaid the wickedness that
Abimelek had done to his father by murder-
ing his seventy brothers. 57God also made
the people of Shechem pay for all their wick-
edness. The curse of Jotham son of Jerub-
Baal came on them.

Tola

10 After the time of Abimelek, a man of
Issachar named Tola son of Puah, the
son of Dodo, rose to save Israel. He lived in
Shamir, in the hill country of Ephraim. 2He
led[c] Israel twenty-three years; then he died,
and was buried in Shamir.

Jair

3He was followed by Jair of Gilead, who
led Israel twenty-two years. 4He had thirty
sons, who rode thirty donkeys. They con-
trolled thirty towns in Gilead, which to this
day are called Havvoth Jair.[d] 5When Jair
died, he was buried in Kamon.

Jephthah

6Again the Israelites did evil in the eyes
of the LORD. They served the Baals and the

[a] 37 The Hebrew for this phrase means *the navel of the earth.* [b] 39 Or *Gaal went out in the sight of*
[c] 2 Traditionally *judged;* also in verse 3 [d] 4 Or *called the settlements of Jair*

Ashtoreths, and the gods of Aram, the gods of Sidon, the gods of Moab, the gods of the Ammonites and the gods of the Philistines. And because the Israelites forsook the LORD and no longer served him, 7he became angry with them. He sold them into the hands of the Philistines and the Ammonites, 8who that year shattered and crushed them. For eighteen years they oppressed all the Israelites on the east side of the Jordan in Gilead, the land of the Amorites. 9The Ammonites also crossed the Jordan to fight against Judah, Benjamin and Ephraim; Israel was in great distress. 10Then the Israelites cried out to the LORD, "We have sinned against you, forsaking our God and serving the Baals."

11The LORD replied, "When the Egyptians, the Amorites, the Ammonites, the Philistines, 12the Sidonians, the Amalekites and the Maonites[a] oppressed you and you cried to me for help, did I not save you from their hands? 13But you have forsaken me and served other gods, so I will no longer save you. 14Go and cry out to the gods you have chosen. Let them save you when you are in trouble!"

15But the Israelites said to the LORD, "We have sinned. Do with us whatever you think best, but please rescue us now." 16Then they got rid of the foreign gods among them and served the LORD. And he could bear Israel's misery no longer.

17When the Ammonites were called to arms and camped in Gilead, the Israelites assembled and camped at Mizpah. 18The leaders of the people of Gilead said to each other, "Whoever will take the lead in attacking the Ammonites will be head over all who live in Gilead."

11 Jephthah the Gileadite was a mighty warrior. His father was Gilead; his mother was a prostitute. 2Gilead's wife also bore him sons, and when they were grown up, they drove Jephthah away. "You are not going to get any inheritance in our family," they said, "because you are the son of another woman." 3So Jephthah fled from his brothers and settled in the land of Tob, where a gang of scoundrels gathered around him and followed him.

4Some time later, when the Ammonites were fighting against Israel, 5the elders of Gilead went to get Jephthah from the land of Tob. 6"Come," they said, "be our commander, so we can fight the Ammonites."

7Jephthah said to them, "Didn't you hate me and drive me from my father's house? Why do you come to me now, when you're in trouble?"

8The elders of Gilead said to him, "Nevertheless, we are turning to you now; come with us to fight the Ammonites, and you will be head over all of us who live in Gilead."

9Jephthah answered, "Suppose you take me back to fight the Ammonites and the LORD gives them to me — will I really be your head?"

10The elders of Gilead replied, "The LORD is our witness; we will certainly do as you say." 11So Jephthah went with the elders of Gilead, and the people made him head and commander over them. And he repeated all his words before the LORD in Mizpah.

12Then Jephthah sent messengers to the Ammonite king with the question: "What do you have against me that you have attacked my country?"

13The king of the Ammonites answered Jephthah's messengers, "When Israel came up out of Egypt, they took away my land from the Arnon to the Jabbok, all the way to the Jordan. Now give it back peaceably."

14Jephthah sent back messengers to the Ammonite king, 15saying:

"This is what Jephthah says: Israel did not take the land of Moab or the land of the Ammonites. 16But when they came up out of Egypt, Israel went through the wilderness to the Red Sea[b] and on to Kadesh. 17Then Israel sent messengers to the king of Edom, saying, 'Give us permission to go through your country,' but the king of Edom would not listen. They sent also to the king of Moab, and he refused. So Israel stayed at Kadesh.

18"Next they traveled through the wilderness, skirted the lands of Edom and Moab, passed along the eastern side of the country of Moab, and camped on the other side of the Arnon. They did not enter the territory of Moab, for the Arnon was its border.

19"Then Israel sent messengers to

[a] *12* Hebrew; some Septuagint manuscripts *Midianites* [b] *16* Or *the Sea of Reeds*

Sihon king of the Amorites, who ruled
in Heshbon, and said to him, 'Let us
pass through your country to our own
place.' 20 Sihon, however, did not trust
Israel[a] to pass through his territory. He
mustered all his troops and encamped
at Jahaz and fought with Israel.

21 "Then the LORD, the God of Israel,
gave Sihon and his whole army into Is-
rael's hands, and they defeated them.
Israel took over all the land of the Am-
orites who lived in that country, 22 cap-
turing all of it from the Arnon to the
Jabbok and from the desert to the Jor-
dan.

23 "Now since the LORD, the God of Is-
rael, has driven the Amorites out before
his people Israel, what right have you
to take it over? 24 Will you not take what
your god Chemosh gives you? Likewise,
whatever the LORD our God has given
us, we will possess. 25 Are you any better
than Balak son of Zippor, king of Moab?
Did he ever quarrel with Israel or fight
with them? 26 For three hundred years
Israel occupied Heshbon, Aroer, the
surrounding settlements and all the
towns along the Arnon. Why didn't you
retake them during that time? 27 I have
not wronged you, but you are doing me
wrong by waging war against me. Let
the LORD, the Judge, decide the dispute
this day between the Israelites and the
Ammonites."

28 The king of Ammon, however, paid no at-
tention to the message Jephthah sent him.

29 Then the Spirit of the LORD came on
Jephthah. He crossed Gilead and Manasseh,
passed through Mizpah of Gilead, and from
there he advanced against the Ammonites.
30 And Jephthah made a vow to the LORD:
"If you give the Ammonites into my hands,
31 whatever comes out of the door of my
house to meet me when I return in triumph
from the Ammonites will be the LORD's, and
I will sacrifice it as a burnt offering."

32 Then Jephthah went over to fight the
Ammonites, and the LORD gave them into
his hands. 33 He devastated twenty towns
from Aroer to the vicinity of Minnith, as far
as Abel Keramim. Thus Israel subdued Am-
mon.

34 When Jephthah returned to his home in
Mizpah, who should come out to meet him
but his daughter, dancing to the sound of
timbrels! She was an only child. Except for
her he had neither son nor daughter. 35 When
he saw her, he tore his clothes and cried, "Oh
no, my daughter! You have brought me down
and I am devastated. I have made a vow to
the LORD that I cannot break."

36 "My father," she replied, "you have giv-
en your word to the LORD. Do to me just
as you promised, now that the LORD has
avenged you of your enemies, the Ammon-
ites. 37 But grant me this one request," she
said. "Give me two months to roam the hills
and weep with my friends, because I will
never marry."

38 "You may go," he said. And he let her go
for two months. She and her friends went
into the hills and wept because she would
never marry. 39 After the two months, she re-
turned to her father, and he did to her as he
had vowed. And she was a virgin.

From this comes the Israelite tradition
40 that each year the young women of Isra-
el go out for four days to commemorate the
daughter of Jephthah the Gileadite.

Jephthah and Ephraim

12 The Ephraimite forces were called
out, and they crossed over to Zaphon.
They said to Jephthah, "Why did you go to
fight the Ammonites without calling us to
go with you? We're going to burn down your
house over your head."

2 Jephthah answered, "I and my peo-
ple were engaged in a great struggle with
the Ammonites, and although I called, you
didn't save me out of their hands. 3 When I
saw that you wouldn't help, I took my life in
my hands and crossed over to fight the Am-
monites, and the LORD gave me the victory
over them. Now why have you come up today
to fight me?"

4 Jephthah then called together the men
of Gilead and fought against Ephraim. The
Gileadites struck them down because the
Ephraimites had said, "You Gileadites are
renegades from Ephraim and Manasseh."
5 The Gileadites captured the fords of the Jor-
dan leading to Ephraim, and whenever a sur-
vivor of Ephraim said, "Let me cross over,"

[a] 20 Or *however, would not make an agreement for Israel*

the men of Gilead asked him, "Are you an Ephraimite?" If he replied, "No," [6]they said, "All right, say 'Shibboleth.'" If he said, "Sibboleth," because he could not pronounce the word correctly, they seized him and killed him at the fords of the Jordan. Forty-two thousand Ephraimites were killed at that time.

[7]Jephthah led[a] Israel six years. Then Jephthah the Gileadite died and was buried in a town in Gilead.

Ibzan, Elon and Abdon

[8]After him, Ibzan of Bethlehem led Israel. [9]He had thirty sons and thirty daughters. He gave his daughters away in marriage to those outside his clan, and for his sons he brought in thirty young women as wives from outside his clan. Ibzan led Israel seven years. [10]Then Ibzan died and was buried in Bethlehem.

[11]After him, Elon the Zebulunite led Israel ten years. [12]Then Elon died and was buried in Aijalon in the land of Zebulun.

[13]After him, Abdon son of Hillel, from Pirathon, led Israel. [14]He had forty sons and thirty grandsons, who rode on seventy donkeys. He led Israel eight years. [15]Then Abdon son of Hillel died and was buried at Pirathon in Ephraim, in the hill country of the Amalekites.

The Birth of Samson

13 Again the Israelites did evil in the eyes of the LORD, so the LORD delivered them into the hands of the Philistines for forty years.

[2]A certain man of Zorah, named Manoah, from the clan of the Danites, had a wife who was childless, unable to give birth. [3]The angel of the LORD appeared to her and said, "You are barren and childless, but you are going to become pregnant and give birth to a son. [4]Now see to it that you drink no wine or other fermented drink and that you do not eat anything unclean. [5]You will become pregnant and have a son whose head is never to be touched by a razor because the boy is to be a Nazirite, dedicated to God from the womb. He will take the lead in delivering Israel from the hands of the Philistines."

[6]Then the woman went to her husband and told him, "A man of God came to me. He looked like an angel of God, very awesome. I didn't ask him where he came from, and he didn't tell me his name. [7]But he said to me, 'You will become pregnant and have a son. Now then, drink no wine or other fermented drink and do not eat anything unclean, because the boy will be a Nazirite of God from the womb until the day of his death.'"

[8]Then Manoah prayed to the LORD: "Pardon your servant, Lord. I beg you to let the man of God you sent to us come again to teach us how to bring up the boy who is to be born."

[9]God heard Manoah, and the angel of God came again to the woman while she was out in the field; but her husband Manoah was not with her. [10]The woman hurried to tell her husband, "He's here! The man who appeared to me the other day!"

[11]Manoah got up and followed his wife. When he came to the man, he said, "Are you the man who talked to my wife?"

"I am," he said.

[12]So Manoah asked him, "When your words are fulfilled, what is to be the rule that governs the boy's life and work?"

[13]The angel of the LORD answered, "Your wife must do all that I have told her. [14]She must not eat anything that comes from the grapevine, nor drink any wine or other fermented drink nor eat anything unclean. She must do everything I have commanded her."

[15]Manoah said to the angel of the LORD, "We would like you to stay until we prepare a young goat for you."

[16]The angel of the LORD replied, "Even though you detain me, I will not eat any of your food. But if you prepare a burnt offering, offer it to the LORD." (Manoah did not realize that it was the angel of the LORD.)

[17]Then Manoah inquired of the angel of the LORD, "What is your name, so that we may honor you when your word comes true?"

[18]He replied, "Why do you ask my name? It is beyond understanding.[b]" [19]Then Manoah took a young goat, together with the grain offering, and sacrificed it on a rock to the LORD. And the LORD did an amazing thing while Manoah and his wife watched: [20]As

[a] 7 Traditionally *judged*; also in verses 8-14 [b] *18* Or *is wonderful*

the flame blazed up from the altar toward heaven, the angel of the LORD ascended in the flame. Seeing this, Manoah and his wife fell with their faces to the ground. 21When the angel of the LORD did not show himself again to Manoah and his wife, Manoah realized that it was the angel of the LORD.

22"We are doomed to die!" he said to his wife. "We have seen God!"

23But his wife answered, "If the LORD had meant to kill us, he would not have accepted a burnt offering and grain offering from our hands, nor shown us all these things or now told us this."

24The woman gave birth to a boy and named him Samson. He grew and the LORD blessed him, 25and the Spirit of the LORD began to stir him while he was in Mahaneh Dan, between Zorah and Eshtaol.

Samson's Marriage

14 Samson went down to Timnah and saw there a young Philistine woman. 2When he returned, he said to his father and mother, "I have seen a Philistine woman in Timnah; now get her for me as my wife."

3His father and mother replied, "Isn't there an acceptable woman among your relatives or among all our people? Must you go to the uncircumcised Philistines to get a wife?"

But Samson said to his father, "Get her for me. She's the right one for me." 4(His parents did not know that this was from the LORD, who was seeking an occasion to confront the Philistines; for at that time they were ruling over Israel.)

5Samson went down to Timnah together with his father and mother. As they approached the vineyards of Timnah, suddenly a young lion came roaring toward him. 6The Spirit of the LORD came powerfully upon him so that he tore the lion apart with his bare hands as he might have torn a young goat. But he told neither his father nor his mother what he had done. 7Then he went down and talked with the woman, and he liked her.

8Some time later, when he went back to marry her, he turned aside to look at the lion's carcass, and in it he saw a swarm of bees and some honey. 9He scooped out the honey with his hands and ate as he went along. When he rejoined his parents, he gave them some, and they too ate it. But he did not tell them that he had taken the honey from the lion's carcass.

10Now his father went down to see the woman. And there Samson held a feast, as was customary for young men. 11When the people saw him, they chose thirty men to be his companions.

12"Let me tell you a riddle," Samson said to them. "If you can give me the answer within the seven days of the feast, I will give you thirty linen garments and thirty sets of clothes. 13If you can't tell me the answer, you must give me thirty linen garments and thirty sets of clothes."

"Tell us your riddle," they said. "Let's hear it."

14He replied,

"Out of the eater, something to eat;
out of the strong, something sweet."

For three days they could not give the answer.

15On the fourth[a] day, they said to Samson's wife, "Coax your husband into explaining the riddle for us, or we will burn you and your father's household to death. Did you invite us here to steal our property?"

16Then Samson's wife threw herself on him, sobbing, "You hate me! You don't really love me. You've given my people a riddle, but you haven't told me the answer."

"I haven't even explained it to my father or mother," he replied, "so why should I explain it to you?" 17She cried the whole seven days of the feast. So on the seventh day he finally told her, because she continued to press him. She in turn explained the riddle to her people.

18Before sunset on the seventh day the men of the town said to him,

"What is sweeter than honey?
What is stronger than a lion?"

Samson said to them,

"If you had not plowed with my heifer,
you would not have solved my riddle."

19Then the Spirit of the LORD came powerfully upon him. He went down to Ashkelon,

[a] *15* Some Septuagint manuscripts and Syriac; Hebrew *seventh*

struck down thirty of their men, stripped
them of everything and gave their clothes to
those who had explained the riddle. Burning
with anger, he returned to his father's home.
20 And Samson's wife was given to one of his
companions who had attended him at the
feast.

Samson's Vengeance on the Philistines

15 Later on, at the time of wheat harvest, Samson took a young goat and
went to visit his wife. He said, "I'm going to
my wife's room." But her father would not let
him go in.
2 "I was so sure you hated her," he said,
"that I gave her to your companion. Isn't her
younger sister more attractive? Take her instead."
3 Samson said to them, "This time I have
a right to get even with the Philistines; I
will really harm them." 4 So he went out and
caught three hundred foxes and tied them
tail to tail in pairs. He then fastened a torch
to every pair of tails, 5 lit the torches and let
the foxes loose in the standing grain of the
Philistines. He burned up the shocks and
standing grain, together with the vineyards
and olive groves.
6 When the Philistines asked, "Who did
this?" they were told, "Samson, the Timnite's
son-in-law, because his wife was given to his
companion."
So the Philistines went up and burned
her and her father to death. 7 Samson said
to them, "Since you've acted like this, I
swear that I won't stop until I get my revenge on you." 8 He attacked them viciously and slaughtered many of them. Then he
went down and stayed in a cave in the rock
of Etam.
9 The Philistines went up and camped in
Judah, spreading out near Lehi. 10 The people of Judah asked, "Why have you come to
fight us?"
"We have come to take Samson prisoner,"
they answered, "to do to him as he did to us."
11 Then three thousand men from Judah
went down to the cave in the rock of Etam
and said to Samson, "Don't you realize that
the Philistines are rulers over us? What have
you done to us?"
He answered, "I merely did to them what
they did to me."
12 They said to him, "We've come to tie you
up and hand you over to the Philistines."
Samson said, "Swear to me that you won't
kill me yourselves."
13 "Agreed," they answered. "We will only
tie you up and hand you over to them. We
will not kill you." So they bound him with
two new ropes and led him up from the
rock. 14 As he approached Lehi, the Philistines came toward him shouting. The Spirit
of the LORD came powerfully upon him. The
ropes on his arms became like charred flax,
and the bindings dropped from his hands.
15 Finding a fresh jawbone of a donkey, he
grabbed it and struck down a thousand
men.
16 Then Samson said,

"With a donkey's jawbone
    I have made donkeys of them.[a]
With a donkey's jawbone
    I have killed a thousand men."

17 When he finished speaking, he threw away
the jawbone; and the place was called Ramath Lehi.[b]
18 Because he was very thirsty, he cried out
to the LORD, "You have given your servant
this great victory. Must I now die of thirst
and fall into the hands of the uncircumcised?" 19 Then God opened up the hollow
place in Lehi, and water came out of it. When
Samson drank, his strength returned and he
revived. So the spring was called En Hakkore,[c] and it is still there in Lehi.
20 Samson led[d] Israel for twenty years in
the days of the Philistines.

Samson and Delilah

16 One day Samson went to Gaza, where he saw a prostitute. He went in to
spend the night with her. 2 The people of Gaza
were told, "Samson is here!" So they surrounded the place and lay in wait for him all
night at the city gate. They made no move during the night, saying, "At dawn we'll kill him."
3 But Samson lay there only until the middle of the night. Then he got up and took
hold of the doors of the city gate, together
with the two posts, and tore them loose, bar

[a] 16 Or *made a heap or two*; the Hebrew for *donkey* sounds like the Hebrew for *heap*. [b] 17 *Ramath Lehi* means *jawbone hill*. [c] 19 *En Hakkore* means *caller's spring*. [d] 20 Traditionally *judged*

FOREVER

Chris Tomlin

Give thanks to the Lord our God and King
His love endures forever
For he is good, he is above all things
His love endures forever
Sing praise, sing praise

With a mighty hand and outstretched arm
His love endures forever
For the life that's been reborn
His love endures forever

Sing praise, sing praise
Sing praise, sing praise

Forever God is faithful
Forever God is strong
Forever God is with us
Forever

From the rising to the setting sun
His love endures forever
And by the grace of God we will carry on
His love endures forever

His love endures forever
His love endures forever
His love endures forever
Forever and ever

THE INSPIRATION

Give thanks to the Lord, *for he is good.* His love endures forever.

—Psalm 136:1

Read also: Psalm 89:1–2; 136:2–26

BEHIND THE SONG

Chris Tomlin was still in college at Texas A&M University when the idea for "Forever" first came to him.

"It started out of Psalm 136," he remembers. "I opened up the Scriptures and started reading, and it was written like no other psalm. After every line it would say 'His love endures forever.' I thought, There is a modern way of singing that.

While the verses came rather quickly, Tomlin knew the song wasn't complete. He kept trying to perfect the chorus but came up blank for a full four years.

"I was thinking, forever God is faithful, forever God is . . . and I just didn't have *that* word." Eventually Tomlin was working on the song at a youth camp when an unlikely contributor spoke up. "The whole week I was strumming this out and could not think of a word that would go there," he admits. "Jesse Reeves, my bass player, and his wife were in the other room all week and they kept hearing me playing this song over and over. Finally she opened the door and yelled, 'Chris, the word is *strong*' and closed the door. I just remember saying, 'That's it!' "

"Forever" has been sung millions of times since then. Around the world believers have confidently repeated that prayerful promise, "His love endures forever," just like the worshipers of old.

Selah

Consider the concept of "forever." It's impossible for a finite mind to fully contemplate the infinite, but take some time to think about it. What images come to mind? Now think about your current struggles. How do they look in light of the promise that God's love endures forever?

Your heart will always be distracted by immediate challenges, but if you periodically meditate on the vastness of God's goodness and love, you may start to see those challenges fade in comparison. Psalm 136 is a great passage to meditate on when you feel overwhelmed or scared.

and all. He lifted them to his shoulders and carried them to the top of the hill that faces Hebron.

4 Some time later, he fell in love with a woman in the Valley of Sorek whose name was Delilah. 5 The rulers of the Philistines went to her and said, "See if you can lure him into showing you the secret of his great strength and how we can overpower him so we may tie him up and subdue him. Each one of us will give you eleven hundred shekels[a] of silver."

6 So Delilah said to Samson, "Tell me the secret of your great strength and how you can be tied up and subdued."

7 Samson answered her, "If anyone ties me with seven fresh bowstrings that have not been dried, I'll become as weak as any other man."

8 Then the rulers of the Philistines brought her seven fresh bowstrings that had not been dried, and she tied him with them. 9 With men hidden in the room, she called to him, "Samson, the Philistines are upon you!" But he snapped the bowstrings as easily as a piece of string snaps when it comes close to a flame. So the secret of his strength was not discovered.

10 Then Delilah said to Samson, "You have made a fool of me; you lied to me. Come now, tell me how you can be tied."

11 He said, "If anyone ties me securely with new ropes that have never been used, I'll become as weak as any other man."

12 So Delilah took new ropes and tied him with them. Then, with men hidden in the room, she called to him, "Samson, the Philistines are upon you!" But he snapped the ropes off his arms as if they were threads.

13 Delilah then said to Samson, "All this time you have been making a fool of me and lying to me. Tell me how you can be tied."

He replied, "If you weave the seven braids of my head into the fabric on the loom and tighten it with the pin, I'll become as weak as any other man." So while he was sleeping, Delilah took the seven braids of his head, wove them into the fabric 14 and[b] tightened it with the pin.

Again she called to him, "Samson, the Philistines are upon you!" He awoke from his sleep and pulled up the pin and the loom, with the fabric.

15 Then she said to him, "How can you say, 'I love you,' when you won't confide in me? This is the third time you have made a fool of me and haven't told me the secret of your great strength." 16 With such nagging she prodded him day after day until he was sick to death of it.

17 So he told her everything. "No razor has ever been used on my head," he said, "because I have been a Nazirite dedicated to God from my mother's womb. If my head were shaved, my strength would leave me, and I would become as weak as any other man."

18 When Delilah saw that he had told her everything, she sent word to the rulers of the Philistines, "Come back once more; he has told me everything." So the rulers of the Philistines returned with the silver in their hands. 19 After putting him to sleep on her lap, she called for someone to shave off the seven braids of his hair, and so began to subdue him.[c] And his strength left him.

20 Then she called, "Samson, the Philistines are upon you!"

He awoke from his sleep and thought, "I'll go out as before and shake myself free." But he did not know that the LORD had left him.

21 Then the Philistines seized him, gouged out his eyes and took him down to Gaza. Binding him with bronze shackles, they set him to grinding grain in the prison. 22 But the hair on his head began to grow again after it had been shaved.

The Death of Samson

23 Now the rulers of the Philistines assembled to offer a great sacrifice to Dagon their god and to celebrate, saying, "Our god has delivered Samson, our enemy, into our hands."

24 When the people saw him, they praised their god, saying,

"Our god has delivered our enemy
  into our hands,
the one who laid waste our land
  and multiplied our slain."

25 While they were in high spirits, they shouted, "Bring out Samson to entertain us."

[a] 5 That is, about 28 pounds or about 13 kilograms [b] 13,14 Some Septuagint manuscripts; Hebrew *replied, "I can if you weave the seven braids of my head into the fabric on the loom." 14So she* [c] 19 Hebrew; some Septuagint manuscripts *and he began to weaken*

So they called Samson out of the prison, and he performed for them.

When they stood him among the pillars, 26 Samson said to the servant who held his hand, "Put me where I can feel the pillars that support the temple, so that I may lean against them." 27 Now the temple was crowded with men and women; all the rulers of the Philistines were there, and on the roof were about three thousand men and women watching Samson perform. 28 Then Samson prayed to the LORD, "Sovereign LORD, remember me. Please, God, strengthen me just once more, and let me with one blow get revenge on the Philistines for my two eyes." 29 Then Samson reached toward the two central pillars on which the temple stood. Bracing himself against them, his right hand on the one and his left hand on the other, 30 Samson said, "Let me die with the Philistines!" Then he pushed with all his might, and down came the temple on the rulers and all the people in it. Thus he killed many more when he died than while he lived.

31 Then his brothers and his father's whole family went down to get him. They brought him back and buried him between Zorah and Eshtaol in the tomb of Manoah his father. He had led[a] Israel twenty years.

Micah's Idols

17 Now a man named Micah from the hill country of Ephraim 2 said to his mother, "The eleven hundred shekels[b] of silver that were taken from you and about which I heard you utter a curse—I have that silver with me; I took it."

Then his mother said, "The LORD bless you, my son!"

3 When he returned the eleven hundred shekels of silver to his mother, she said, "I solemnly consecrate my silver to the LORD for my son to make an image overlaid with silver. I will give it back to you."

4 So after he returned the silver to his mother, she took two hundred shekels[c] of silver and gave them to a silversmith, who used them to make the idol. And it was put in Micah's house.

5 Now this man Micah had a shrine, and he made an ephod and some household gods and installed one of his sons as his priest. 6 In those days Israel had no king; everyone did as they saw fit.

7 A young Levite from Bethlehem in Judah, who had been living within the clan of Judah, 8 left that town in search of some other place to stay. On his way[d] he came to Micah's house in the hill country of Ephraim.

9 Micah asked him, "Where are you from?"

"I'm a Levite from Bethlehem in Judah," he said, "and I'm looking for a place to stay."

10 Then Micah said to him, "Live with me and be my father and priest, and I'll give you ten shekels[e] of silver a year, your clothes and your food." 11 So the Levite agreed to live with him, and the young man became like one of his sons to him. 12 Then Micah installed the Levite, and the young man became his priest and lived in his house. 13 And Micah said, "Now I know that the LORD will be good to me, since this Levite has become my priest."

The Danites Settle in Laish

18 In those days Israel had no king.

And in those days the tribe of the Danites was seeking a place of their own where they might settle, because they had not yet come into an inheritance among the tribes of Israel. 2 So the Danites sent five of their leading men from Zorah and Eshtaol to spy out the land and explore it. These men represented all the Danites. They told them, "Go, explore the land."

So they entered the hill country of Ephraim and came to the house of Micah, where they spent the night. 3 When they were near Micah's house, they recognized the voice of the young Levite; so they turned in there and asked him, "Who brought you here? What are you doing in this place? Why are you here?"

4 He told them what Micah had done for him, and said, "He has hired me and I am his priest."

5 Then they said to him, "Please inquire of God to learn whether our journey will be successful."

6 The priest answered them, "Go in peace. Your journey has the LORD's approval."

[a] *31* Traditionally *judged* [b] *2* That is, about 28 pounds or about 13 kilograms [c] *4* That is, about 5 pounds or about 2.3 kilograms [d] *8* Or *To carry on his profession* [e] *10* That is, about 4 ounces or about 115 grams

7So the five men left and came to Laish, where they saw that the people were living in safety, like the Sidonians, at peace and secure. And since their land lacked nothing, they were prosperous.[a] Also, they lived a long way from the Sidonians and had no relationship with anyone else.[b]

8When they returned to Zorah and Eshtaol, their fellow Danites asked them, "How did you find things?"

9They answered, "Come on, let's attack them! We have seen the land, and it is very good. Aren't you going to do something? Don't hesitate to go there and take it over. 10When you get there, you will find an unsuspecting people and a spacious land that God has put into your hands, a land that lacks nothing whatever."

11Then six hundred men of the Danites, armed for battle, set out from Zorah and Eshtaol. 12On their way they set up camp near Kiriath Jearim in Judah. This is why the place west of Kiriath Jearim is called Mahaneh Dan[c] to this day. 13From there they went on to the hill country of Ephraim and came to Micah's house.

14Then the five men who had spied out the land of Laish said to their fellow Danites, "Do you know that one of these houses has an ephod, some household gods and an image overlaid with silver? Now you know what to do." 15So they turned in there and went to the house of the young Levite at Micah's place and greeted him. 16The six hundred Danites, armed for battle, stood at the entrance of the gate. 17The five men who had spied out the land went inside and took the idol, the ephod and the household gods while the priest and the six hundred armed men stood at the entrance of the gate.

18When the five men went into Micah's house and took the idol, the ephod and the household gods, the priest said to them, "What are you doing?"

19They answered him, "Be quiet! Don't say a word. Come with us, and be our father and priest. Isn't it better that you serve a tribe and clan in Israel as priest rather than just one man's household?" 20The priest was very pleased. He took the ephod, the household gods and the idol and went along with the people. 21Putting their little children, their livestock and their possessions in front of them, they turned away and left.

22When they had gone some distance from Micah's house, the men who lived near Micah were called together and overtook the Danites. 23As they shouted after them, the Danites turned and said to Micah, "What's the matter with you that you called out your men to fight?"

24He replied, "You took the gods I made, and my priest, and went away. What else do I have? How can you ask, 'What's the matter with you?' "

25The Danites answered, "Don't argue with us, or some of the men may get angry and attack you, and you and your family will lose your lives." 26So the Danites went their way, and Micah, seeing that they were too strong for him, turned around and went back home.

27Then they took what Micah had made, and his priest, and went on to Laish, against a people at peace and secure. They attacked them with the sword and burned down their city. 28There was no one to rescue them because they lived a long way from Sidon and had no relationship with anyone else. The city was in a valley near Beth Rehob.

The Danites rebuilt the city and settled there. 29They named it Dan after their ancestor Dan, who was born to Israel — though the city used to be called Laish. 30There the Danites set up for themselves the idol, and Jonathan son of Gershom, the son of Moses,[d] and his sons were priests for the tribe of Dan until the time of the captivity of the land. 31They continued to use the idol Micah had made, all the time the house of God was in Shiloh.

A Levite and His Concubine

19 In those days Israel had no king.

Now a Levite who lived in a remote area in the hill country of Ephraim took a concubine from Bethlehem in Judah. 2But she was unfaithful to him. She left him and went back to her parents' home in Bethlehem, Judah. After she had been there four

[a] 7 The meaning of the Hebrew for this clause is uncertain. [b] 7 Hebrew; some Septuagint manuscripts *with the Arameans* [c] 12 *Mahaneh Dan* means *Dan's camp.* [d] 30 Many Hebrew manuscripts, some Septuagint manuscripts and Vulgate; many other Hebrew manuscripts and some other Septuagint manuscripts *Manasseh*

months, 3her husband went to her to per-
suade her to return. He had with him his
servant and two donkeys. She took him into
her parents' home, and when her father saw
him, he gladly welcomed him. 4His father-
in-law, the woman's father, prevailed on him
to stay; so he remained with him three days,
eating and drinking, and sleeping there.
5On the fourth day they got up early and
he prepared to leave, but the woman's father
said to his son-in-law, "Refresh yourself with
something to eat; then you can go." 6So the
two of them sat down to eat and drink to-
gether. Afterward the woman's father said,
"Please stay tonight and enjoy yourself."
7And when the man got up to go, his father-
in-law persuaded him, so he stayed there
that night. 8On the morning of the fifth day,
when he rose to go, the woman's father said,
"Refresh yourself. Wait till afternoon!" So
the two of them ate together.
9Then when the man, with his concubine
and his servant, got up to leave, his father-
in-law, the woman's father, said, "Now look,
it's almost evening. Spend the night here; the
day is nearly over. Stay and enjoy yourself.
Early tomorrow morning you can get up and
be on your way home." 10But, unwilling to
stay another night, the man left and went to-
ward Jebus (that is, Jerusalem), with his two
saddled donkeys and his concubine.
11When they were near Jebus and the day
was almost gone, the servant said to his mas-
ter, "Come, let's stop at this city of the Jebu-
sites and spend the night."
12His master replied, "No. We won't go
into any city whose people are not Israel-
ites. We will go on to Gibeah." 13He added,
"Come, let's try to reach Gibeah or Ramah
and spend the night in one of those places."
14So they went on, and the sun set as they
neared Gibeah in Benjamin. 15There they
stopped to spend the night. They went and
sat in the city square, but no one took them
in for the night.
16That evening an old man from the hill
country of Ephraim, who was living in Gib-
eah (the inhabitants of the place were Ben-
jamites), came in from his work in the fields.
17When he looked and saw the traveler in the
city square, the old man asked, "Where are
you going? Where did you come from?"
18He answered, "We are on our way from
Bethlehem in Judah to a remote area in the
hill country of Ephraim where I live. I have
been to Bethlehem in Judah and now I am
going to the house of the LORD.[a] No one has
taken me in for the night. 19We have both
straw and fodder for our donkeys and bread
and wine for ourselves your servants — me,
the woman and the young man with us. We
don't need anything."
20"You are welcome at my house," the
old man said. "Let me supply whatever you
need. Only don't spend the night in the
square." 21So he took him into his house and
fed his donkeys. After they had washed their
feet, they had something to eat and drink.
22While they were enjoying themselves,
some of the wicked men of the city sur-
rounded the house. Pounding on the door,
they shouted to the old man who owned the
house, "Bring out the man who came to your
house so we can have sex with him."
23The owner of the house went outside
and said to them, "No, my friends, don't be
so vile. Since this man is my guest, don't do
this outrageous thing. 24Look, here is my vir-
gin daughter, and his concubine. I will bring
them out to you now, and you can use them
and do to them whatever you wish. But as
for this man, don't do such an outrageous
thing."
25But the men would not listen to him.
So the man took his concubine and sent
her outside to them, and they raped her
and abused her throughout the night, and
at dawn they let her go. 26At daybreak the
woman went back to the house where her
master was staying, fell down at the door
and lay there until daylight.
27When her master got up in the morn-
ing and opened the door of the house and
stepped out to continue on his way, there
lay his concubine, fallen in the doorway of
the house, with her hands on the threshold.
28He said to her, "Get up; let's go." But there
was no answer. Then the man put her on his
donkey and set out for home.
29When he reached home, he took a knife
and cut up his concubine, limb by limb, into
twelve parts and sent them into all the areas
of Israel. 30Everyone who saw it was saying
to one another, "Such a thing has never been

[a] *18* Hebrew, Vulgate, Syriac and Targum; Septuagint *going home*

seen or done, not since the day the Israelites came up out of Egypt. Just imagine! We must do something! So speak up!"

The Israelites Punish the Benjamites

20 Then all Israel from Dan to Beersheba and from the land of Gilead came together as one and assembled before the LORD in Mizpah. 2 The leaders of all the people of the tribes of Israel took their places in the assembly of God's people, four hundred thousand men armed with swords. 3 (The Benjamites heard that the Israelites had gone up to Mizpah.) Then the Israelites said, "Tell us how this awful thing happened."

4 So the Levite, the husband of the murdered woman, said, "I and my concubine came to Gibeah in Benjamin to spend the night. 5 During the night the men of Gibeah came after me and surrounded the house, intending to kill me. They raped my concubine, and she died. 6 I took my concubine, cut her into pieces and sent one piece to each region of Israel's inheritance, because they committed this lewd and outrageous act in Israel. 7 Now, all you Israelites, speak up and tell me what you have decided to do."

8 All the men rose up together as one, saying, "None of us will go home. No, not one of us will return to his house. 9 But now this is what we'll do to Gibeah: We'll go up against it in the order decided by casting lots. 10 We'll take ten men out of every hundred from all the tribes of Israel, and a hundred from a thousand, and a thousand from ten thousand, to get provisions for the army. Then, when the army arrives at Gibeah[a] in Benjamin, it can give them what they deserve for this outrageous act done in Israel." 11 So all the Israelites got together and united as one against the city.

12 The tribes of Israel sent messengers throughout the tribe of Benjamin, saying, "What about this awful crime that was committed among you? 13 Now turn those wicked men of Gibeah over to us so that we may put them to death and purge the evil from Israel."

But the Benjamites would not listen to their fellow Israelites. 14 From their towns they came together at Gibeah to fight against the Israelites. 15 At once the Benjamites mobilized twenty-six thousand swordsmen from their towns, in addition to seven hundred able young men from those living in Gibeah. 16 Among all these soldiers there were seven hundred select troops who were left-handed, each of whom could sling a stone at a hair and not miss.

17 Israel, apart from Benjamin, mustered four hundred thousand swordsmen, all of them fit for battle.

18 The Israelites went up to Bethel[b] and inquired of God. They said, "Who of us is to go up first to fight against the Benjamites?"

The LORD replied, "Judah shall go first."

19 The next morning the Israelites got up and pitched camp near Gibeah. 20 The Israelites went out to fight the Benjamites and took up battle positions against them at Gibeah. 21 The Benjamites came out of Gibeah and cut down twenty-two thousand Israelites on the battlefield that day. 22 But the Israelites encouraged one another and again took up their positions where they had stationed themselves the first day. 23 The Israelites went up and wept before the LORD until evening, and they inquired of the LORD. They said, "Shall we go up again to fight against the Benjamites, our fellow Israelites?"

The LORD answered, "Go up against them."

24 Then the Israelites drew near to Benjamin the second day. 25 This time, when the Benjamites came out from Gibeah to oppose them, they cut down another eighteen thousand Israelites, all of them armed with swords.

26 Then all the Israelites, the whole army, went up to Bethel, and there they sat weeping before the LORD. They fasted that day until evening and presented burnt offerings and fellowship offerings to the LORD. 27 And the Israelites inquired of the LORD. (In those days the ark of the covenant of God was there, 28 with Phinehas son of Eleazar, the son of Aaron, ministering before it.) They asked, "Shall we go up again to fight against the Benjamites, our fellow Israelites, or not?"

The LORD responded, "Go, for tomorrow I will give them into your hands."

29 Then Israel set an ambush around

[a] *10* One Hebrew manuscript; most Hebrew manuscripts *Geba,* a variant of *Gibeah* [b] *18* Or *to the house of God*; also in verse 26

Gibeah. 30 They went up against the Benjamites on the third day and took up positions against Gibeah as they had done before. 31 The Benjamites came out to meet them and were drawn away from the city. They began to inflict casualties on the Israelites as before, so that about thirty men fell in the open field and on the roads — the one leading to Bethel and the other to Gibeah. 32 While the Benjamites were saying, "We are defeating them as before," the Israelites were saying, "Let's retreat and draw them away from the city to the roads."

33 All the men of Israel moved from their places and took up positions at Baal Tamar, and the Israelite ambush charged out of its place on the west[a] of Gibeah.[b] 34 Then ten thousand of Israel's able young men made a frontal attack on Gibeah. The fighting was so heavy that the Benjamites did not realize how near disaster was. 35 The LORD defeated Benjamin before Israel, and on that day the Israelites struck down 25,100 Benjamites, all armed with swords. 36 Then the Benjamites saw that they were beaten.

Now the men of Israel had given way before Benjamin, because they relied on the ambush they had set near Gibeah. 37 Those who had been in ambush made a sudden dash into Gibeah, spread out and put the whole city to the sword. 38 The Israelites had arranged with the ambush that they should send up a great cloud of smoke from the city, 39 and then the Israelites would counterattack.

The Benjamites had begun to inflict casualties on the Israelites (about thirty), and they said, "We are defeating them as in the first battle." 40 But when the column of smoke began to rise from the city, the Benjamites turned and saw the whole city going up in smoke. 41 Then the Israelites counterattacked, and the Benjamites were terrified, because they realized that disaster had come on them. 42 So they fled before the Israelites in the direction of the wilderness, but they could not escape the battle. And the Israelites who came out of the towns cut them down there. 43 They surrounded the Benjamites, chased them and easily[c] overran them in the vicinity of Gibeah on the east. 44 Eighteen thousand Benjamites fell, all of them valiant fighters. 45 As they turned and fled toward the wilderness to the rock of Rimmon, the Israelites cut down five thousand men along the roads. They kept pressing after the Benjamites as far as Gidom and struck down two thousand more.

46 On that day twenty-five thousand Benjamite swordsmen fell, all of them valiant fighters. 47 But six hundred of them turned and fled into the wilderness to the rock of Rimmon, where they stayed four months. 48 The men of Israel went back to Benjamin and put all the towns to the sword, including the animals and everything else they found. All the towns they came across they set on fire.

Wives for the Benjamites

21 The men of Israel had taken an oath at Mizpah: "Not one of us will give his daughter in marriage to a Benjamite."

2 The people went to Bethel,[d] where they sat before God until evening, raising their voices and weeping bitterly. 3 "LORD, God of Israel," they cried, "why has this happened to Israel? Why should one tribe be missing from Israel today?"

4 Early the next day the people built an altar and presented burnt offerings and fellowship offerings.

5 Then the Israelites asked, "Who from all the tribes of Israel has failed to assemble before the LORD?" For they had taken a solemn oath that anyone who failed to assemble before the LORD at Mizpah was to be put to death.

6 Now the Israelites grieved for the tribe of Benjamin, their fellow Israelites. "Today one tribe is cut off from Israel," they said. 7 "How can we provide wives for those who are left, since we have taken an oath by the LORD not to give them any of our daughters in marriage?" 8 Then they asked, "Which one of the tribes of Israel failed to assemble before the LORD at Mizpah?" They discovered that no one from Jabesh Gilead had come to the camp for the assembly. 9 For when they counted the people, they found that none of the people of Jabesh Gilead were there.

[a] *33* Some Septuagint manuscripts and Vulgate; the meaning of the Hebrew for this word is uncertain.
[b] *33* Hebrew *Geba,* a variant of *Gibeah*
[c] *45* The meaning of the Hebrew for this word is uncertain.
[d] *2* Or *to the house of God*

[10]So the assembly sent twelve thousand fighting men with instructions to go to Jabesh Gilead and put to the sword those living there, including the women and children. [11]"This is what you are to do," they said. "Kill every male and every woman who is not a virgin." [12]They found among the people living in Jabesh Gilead four hundred young women who had never slept with a man, and they took them to the camp at Shiloh in Canaan.

[13]Then the whole assembly sent an offer of peace to the Benjamites at the rock of Rimmon. [14]So the Benjamites returned at that time and were given the women of Jabesh Gilead who had been spared. But there were not enough for all of them.

[15]The people grieved for Benjamin, because the LORD had made a gap in the tribes of Israel. [16]And the elders of the assembly said, "With the women of Benjamin destroyed, how shall we provide wives for the men who are left? [17]The Benjamite survivors must have heirs," they said, "so that a tribe of Israel will not be wiped out. [18]We can't give them our daughters as wives, since we Israelites have taken this oath: 'Cursed be anyone who gives a wife to a Benjamite.' [19]But look, there is the annual festival of the LORD in Shiloh, which lies north of Bethel, east of the road that goes from Bethel to Shechem, and south of Lebonah."

[20]So they instructed the Benjamites, saying, "Go and hide in the vineyards [21]and watch. When the young women of Shiloh come out to join in the dancing, rush from the vineyards and each of you seize one of them to be your wife. Then return to the land of Benjamin. [22]When their fathers or brothers complain to us, we will say to them, 'Do us the favor of helping them, because we did not get wives for them during the war. You will not be guilty of breaking your oath because you did not give your daughters to them.'"

[23]So that is what the Benjamites did. While the young women were dancing, each man caught one and carried her off to be his wife. Then they returned to their inheritance and rebuilt the towns and settled in them.

[24]At that time the Israelites left that place and went home to their tribes and clans, each to his own inheritance.

[25]In those days Israel had no king; everyone did as they saw fit.

RUTH

Naomi Loses Her Husband and Sons

1 In the days when the judges ruled,[a] there was a famine in the land. So a man from Bethlehem in Judah, together with his wife and two sons, went to live for a while in the country of Moab. 2 The man's name was Elimelek, his wife's name was Naomi, and the names of his two sons were Mahlon and Kilion. They were Ephrathites from Bethlehem, Judah. And they went to Moab and lived there.

3 Now Elimelek, Naomi's husband, died, and she was left with her two sons. 4 They married Moabite women, one named Orpah and the other Ruth. After they had lived there about ten years, 5 both Mahlon and Kilion also died, and Naomi was left without her two sons and her husband.

Naomi and Ruth Return to Bethlehem

6 When Naomi heard in Moab that the LORD had come to the aid of his people by providing food for them, she and her daughters-in-law prepared to return home from there. 7 With her two daughters-in-law she left the place where she had been living and set out on the road that would take them back to the land of Judah.

8 Then Naomi said to her two daughters-in-law, "Go back, each of you, to your mother's home. May the LORD show you kindness, as you have shown kindness to your dead husbands and to me. 9 May the LORD grant that each of you will find rest in the home of another husband."

Then she kissed them goodbye and they wept aloud 10 and said to her, "We will go back with you to your people."

11 But Naomi said, "Return home, my daughters. Why would you come with me? Am I going to have any more sons, who could become your husbands? 12 Return home, my daughters; I am too old to have another husband. Even if I thought there was still hope for me — even if I had a husband tonight and then gave birth to sons — 13 would you wait until they grew up? Would you remain unmarried for them? No, my daughters. It is more bitter for me than for you, because the LORD's hand has turned against me!"

14 At this they wept aloud again. Then Orpah kissed her mother-in-law goodbye, but Ruth clung to her.

15 "Look," said Naomi, "your sister-in-law is going back to her people and her gods. Go back with her."

16 But Ruth replied, "Don't urge me to leave you or to turn back from you. Where you go I will go, and where you stay I will stay. Your people will be my people and your God my God. 17 Where you die I will die, and there I will be buried. May the LORD deal with me, be it ever so severely, if even death separates you and me." 18 When Naomi realized that Ruth was determined to go with her, she stopped urging her.

19 So the two women went on until they came to Bethlehem. When they arrived in Bethlehem, the whole town was stirred because of them, and the women exclaimed, "Can this be Naomi?"

20 "Don't call me Naomi,[b]" she told them. "Call me Mara,[c] because the Almighty[d] has made my life very bitter. 21 I went away full, but the LORD has brought me back empty. Why call me Naomi? The LORD has afflicted[e] me; the Almighty has brought misfortune upon me."

22 So Naomi returned from Moab accompanied by Ruth the Moabite, her daughter-in-law, arriving in Bethlehem as the barley harvest was beginning.

Ruth Meets Boaz in the Grain Field

2 Now Naomi had a relative on her husband's side, a man of standing from the clan of Elimelek, whose name was Boaz.

2 And Ruth the Moabite said to Naomi,

[a] 1 Traditionally *judged* [b] 20 *Naomi* means *pleasant.* [c] 20 *Mara* means *bitter.* [d] 20 Hebrew *Shaddai*; also in verse 21 [e] 21 Or *has testified against*

"Let me go to the fields and pick up the leftover grain behind anyone in whose eyes I find favor."

Naomi said to her, "Go ahead, my daughter." 3So she went out, entered a field and began to glean behind the harvesters. As it turned out, she was working in a field belonging to Boaz, who was from the clan of Elimelek.

4Just then Boaz arrived from Bethlehem and greeted the harvesters, "The LORD be with you!"

"The LORD bless you!" they answered.

5Boaz asked the overseer of his harvesters, "Who does that young woman belong to?"

6The overseer replied, "She is the Moabite who came back from Moab with Naomi. 7She said, 'Please let me glean and gather among the sheaves behind the harvesters.' She came into the field and has remained here from morning till now, except for a short rest in the shelter."

8So Boaz said to Ruth, "My daughter, listen to me. Don't go and glean in another field and don't go away from here. Stay here with the women who work for me. 9Watch the field where the men are harvesting, and follow along after the women. I have told the men not to lay a hand on you. And whenever you are thirsty, go and get a drink from the water jars the men have filled."

10At this, she bowed down with her face to the ground. She asked him, "Why have I found such favor in your eyes that you notice me—a foreigner?"

11Boaz replied, "I've been told all about what you have done for your mother-in-law since the death of your husband—how you left your father and mother and your homeland and came to live with a people you did not know before. 12May the LORD repay you for what you have done. May you be richly rewarded by the LORD, the God of Israel, under whose wings you have come to take refuge."

13"May I continue to find favor in your eyes, my lord," she said. "You have put me at ease by speaking kindly to your servant—though I do not have the standing of one of your servants."

14At mealtime Boaz said to her, "Come over here. Have some bread and dip it in the wine vinegar."

When she sat down with the harvesters, he offered her some roasted grain. She ate all she wanted and had some left over. 15As she got up to glean, Boaz gave orders to his men, "Let her gather among the sheaves and don't reprimand her. 16Even pull out some stalks for her from the bundles and leave them for her to pick up, and don't rebuke her."

17So Ruth gleaned in the field until evening. Then she threshed the barley she had gathered, and it amounted to about an ephah.[a] 18She carried it back to town, and her mother-in-law saw how much she had gathered. Ruth also brought out and gave her what she had left over after she had eaten enough.

19Her mother-in-law asked her, "Where did you glean today? Where did you work? Blessed be the man who took notice of you!"

Then Ruth told her mother-in-law about the one at whose place she had been working. "The name of the man I worked with today is Boaz," she said.

20"The LORD bless him!" Naomi said to her daughter-in-law. "He has not stopped showing his kindness to the living and the dead." She added, "That man is our close relative; he is one of our guardian-redeemers.[b]"

21Then Ruth the Moabite said, "He even said to me, 'Stay with my workers until they finish harvesting all my grain.'"

22Naomi said to Ruth her daughter-in-law, "It will be good for you, my daughter, to go with the women who work for him, because in someone else's field you might be harmed."

23So Ruth stayed close to the women of Boaz to glean until the barley and wheat harvests were finished. And she lived with her mother-in-law.

Ruth and Boaz at the Threshing Floor

3 One day Ruth's mother-in-law Naomi said to her, "My daughter, I must find a home[c] for you, where you will be well provided for. 2Now Boaz, with whose women you

[a] *17* That is, probably about 30 pounds or about 13 kilograms [b] *20* The Hebrew word for *guardian-redeemer* is a legal term for one who has the obligation to redeem a relative in serious difficulty (see Lev. 25:25-55). [c] *1* Hebrew *find rest* (see 1:9)

have worked, is a relative of ours. Tonight he will be winnowing barley on the threshing floor. 3 Wash, put on perfume, and get dressed in your best clothes. Then go down to the threshing floor, but don't let him know you are there until he has finished eating and drinking. 4 When he lies down, note the place where he is lying. Then go and uncover his feet and lie down. He will tell you what to do."

5 "I will do whatever you say," Ruth answered. 6 So she went down to the threshing floor and did everything her mother-in-law told her to do.

7 When Boaz had finished eating and drinking and was in good spirits, he went over to lie down at the far end of the grain pile. Ruth approached quietly, uncovered his feet and lay down. 8 In the middle of the night something startled the man; he turned—and there was a woman lying at his feet!

9 "Who are you?" he asked.

"I am your servant Ruth," she said. "Spread the corner of your garment over me, since you are a guardian-redeemer[a] of our family."

10 "The LORD bless you, my daughter," he replied. "This kindness is greater than that which you showed earlier: You have not run after the younger men, whether rich or poor. 11 And now, my daughter, don't be afraid. I will do for you all you ask. All the people of my town know that you are a woman of noble character. 12 Although it is true that I am a guardian-redeemer of our family, there is another who is more closely related than I. 13 Stay here for the night, and in the morning if he wants to do his duty as your guardian-redeemer, good; let him redeem you. But if he is not willing, as surely as the LORD lives I will do it. Lie here until morning."

14 So she lay at his feet until morning, but got up before anyone could be recognized; and he said, "No one must know that a woman came to the threshing floor."

15 He also said, "Bring me the shawl you are wearing and hold it out." When she did so, he poured into it six measures of barley and placed the bundle on her. Then he[b] went back to town.

16 When Ruth came to her mother-in-law, Naomi asked, "How did it go, my daughter?"

Then she told her everything Boaz had done for her 17 and added, "He gave me these six measures of barley, saying, 'Don't go back to your mother-in-law empty-handed.' "

18 Then Naomi said, "Wait, my daughter, until you find out what happens. For the man will not rest until the matter is settled today."

Boaz Marries Ruth

4 Meanwhile Boaz went up to the town gate and sat down there just as the guardian-redeemer[c] he had mentioned came along. Boaz said, "Come over here, my friend, and sit down." So he went over and sat down.

2 Boaz took ten of the elders of the town and said, "Sit here," and they did so. 3 Then he said to the guardian-redeemer, "Naomi, who has come back from Moab, is selling the piece of land that belonged to our relative Elimelek. 4 I thought I should bring the matter to your attention and suggest that you buy it in the presence of these seated here and in the presence of the elders of my people. If you will redeem it, do so. But if you[d] will not, tell me, so I will know. For no one has the right to do it except you, and I am next in line."

"I will redeem it," he said.

5 Then Boaz said, "On the day you buy the land from Naomi, you also acquire Ruth the Moabite, the[e] dead man's widow, in order to maintain the name of the dead with his property."

6 At this, the guardian-redeemer said, "Then I cannot redeem it because I might endanger my own estate. You redeem it yourself. I cannot do it."

7 (Now in earlier times in Israel, for the redemption and transfer of property to become final, one party took off his sandal and gave it

[a] 9 The Hebrew word for *guardian-redeemer* is a legal term for one who has the obligation to redeem a relative in serious difficulty (see Lev. 25:25-55); also in verses 12 and 13. [b] *15* Most Hebrew manuscripts; many Hebrew manuscripts, Vulgate and Syriac *she* [c] *1* The Hebrew word for *guardian-redeemer* is a legal term for one who has the obligation to redeem a relative in serious difficulty (see Lev. 25:25-55); also in verses 3, 6, 8 and 14. [d] *4* Many Hebrew manuscripts, Septuagint, Vulgate and Syriac; most Hebrew manuscripts *he* [e] *5* Vulgate and Syriac; Hebrew (see also Septuagint) *Naomi and from Ruth the Moabite, you acquire the*

to the other. This was the method of legaliz-
ing transactions in Israel.)
8 So the guardian-redeemer said to Boaz,
"Buy it yourself." And he removed his sandal.
9 Then Boaz announced to the elders and
all the people, "Today you are witnesses that
I have bought from Naomi all the property of
Elimelek, Kilion and Mahlon. 10 I have also ac-
quired Ruth the Moabite, Mahlon's widow, as
my wife, in order to maintain the name of the
dead with his property, so that his name will
not disappear from among his family or from
his hometown. Today you are witnesses!"
11 Then the elders and all the people at
the gate said, "We are witnesses. May the
LORD make the woman who is coming into
your home like Rachel and Leah, who to-
gether built up the family of Israel. May you
have standing in Ephrathah and be famous
in Bethlehem. 12 Through the offspring the
LORD gives you by this young woman, may
your family be like that of Perez, whom Ta-
mar bore to Judah."

Naomi Gains a Son

13 So Boaz took Ruth and she became his
wife. When he made love to her, the LORD
enabled her to conceive, and she gave birth
to a son. 14 The women said to Naomi: "Praise
be to the LORD, who this day has not left you
without a guardian-redeemer. May he be-
come famous throughout Israel! 15 He will
renew your life and sustain you in your old
age. For your daughter-in-law, who loves you
and who is better to you than seven sons, has
given him birth."
16 Then Naomi took the child in her arms
and cared for him. 17 The women living there
said, "Naomi has a son!" And they named
him Obed. He was the father of Jesse, the fa-
ther of David.

The Genealogy of David

18 This, then, is the family line of Perez:

Perez was the father of Hezron,
19 Hezron the father of Ram,
Ram the father of Amminadab,
20 Amminadab the father of Nahshon,
Nahshon the father of Salmon,[a]
21 Salmon the father of Boaz,
Boaz the father of Obed,
22 Obed the father of Jesse,
and Jesse the father of David.

[a] *20* A few Hebrew manuscripts, some Septuagint manuscripts and Vulgate (see also verse 21 and Septuagint of 1 Chron. 2:11); most Hebrew manuscripts *Salma*

1 SAMUEL

The Birth of Samuel

1 There was a certain man from Ramathaim, a Zuphite[a] from the hill country of Ephraim, whose name was Elkanah son of Jeroham, the son of Elihu, the son of Tohu, the son of Zuph, an Ephraimite. 2He had two wives; one was called Hannah and the other Peninnah. Peninnah had children, but Hannah had none.

3Year after year this man went up from his town to worship and sacrifice to the LORD Almighty at Shiloh, where Hophni and Phinehas, the two sons of Eli, were priests of the LORD. 4Whenever the day came for Elkanah to sacrifice, he would give portions of the meat to his wife Peninnah and to all her sons and daughters. 5But to Hannah he gave a double portion because he loved her, and the LORD had closed her womb. 6Because the LORD had closed Hannah's womb, her rival kept provoking her in order to irritate her. 7This went on year after year. Whenever Hannah went up to the house of the LORD, her rival provoked her till she wept and would not eat. 8Her husband Elkanah would say to her, "Hannah, why are you weeping? Why don't you eat? Why are you downhearted? Don't I mean more to you than ten sons?"

9Once when they had finished eating and drinking in Shiloh, Hannah stood up. Now Eli the priest was sitting on his chair by the doorpost of the LORD's house. 10In her deep anguish Hannah prayed to the LORD, weeping bitterly. 11And she made a vow, saying, "LORD Almighty, if you will only look on your servant's misery and remember me, and not forget your servant but give her a son, then I will give him to the LORD for all the days of his life, and no razor will ever be used on his head."

12As she kept on praying to the LORD, Eli observed her mouth. 13Hannah was praying in her heart, and her lips were moving but her voice was not heard. Eli thought she was drunk 14and said to her, "How long are you going to stay drunk? Put away your wine."

15"Not so, my lord," Hannah replied, "I am a woman who is deeply troubled. I have not been drinking wine or beer; I was pouring out my soul to the LORD. 16Do not take your servant for a wicked woman; I have been praying here out of my great anguish and grief."

17Eli answered, "Go in peace, and may the God of Israel grant you what you have asked of him."

18She said, "May your servant find favor in your eyes." Then she went her way and ate something, and her face was no longer downcast.

19Early the next morning they arose and worshiped before the LORD and then went back to their home at Ramah. Elkanah made love to his wife Hannah, and the LORD remembered her. 20So in the course of time Hannah became pregnant and gave birth to a son. She named him Samuel,[b] saying, "Because I asked the LORD for him."

Hannah Dedicates Samuel

21When her husband Elkanah went up with all his family to offer the annual sacrifice to the LORD and to fulfill his vow, 22Hannah did not go. She said to her husband, "After the boy is weaned, I will take him and present him before the LORD, and he will live there always."[c]

23"Do what seems best to you," her husband Elkanah told her. "Stay here until you have weaned him; only may the LORD make good his[d] word." So the woman stayed at home and nursed her son until she had weaned him.

24After he was weaned, she took the boy with her, young as he was, along with a

[a] *1* See Septuagint and 1 Chron. 6:26-27,33-35; or *from Ramathaim Zuphim.* [b] *20* *Samuel* sounds like the Hebrew for *heard by God.* [c] *22* Masoretic Text; Dead Sea Scrolls *always. I have dedicated him as a Nazirite—all the days of his life."* [d] *23* Masoretic Text; Dead Sea Scrolls, Septuagint and Syriac *your*

three-year-old bull,[a] an ephah[b] of flour and
a skin of wine, and brought him to the house
of the LORD at Shiloh. 25 When the bull had
been sacrificed, they brought the boy to Eli,
26 and she said to him, "Pardon me, my lord.
As surely as you live, I am the woman who
stood here beside you praying to the LORD.
27 I prayed for this child, and the LORD has
granted me what I asked of him. 28 So now
I give him to the LORD. For his whole life he
will be given over to the LORD." And he wor-
shiped the LORD there.

Hannah's Prayer

2 Then Hannah prayed and said:

"My heart rejoices in the LORD;
in the LORD my horn[c] is lifted high.
My mouth boasts over my enemies,
for I delight in your deliverance.

2 "There is no one holy like the LORD;
there is no one besides you;
there is no Rock like our God.

3 "Do not keep talking so proudly
or let your mouth speak such
arrogance,
for the LORD is a God who knows,
and by him deeds are weighed.

4 "The bows of the warriors are broken,
but those who stumbled are armed
with strength.
5 Those who were full hire themselves out
for food,
but those who were hungry are hungry
no more.
She who was barren has borne seven
children,
but she who has had many sons
pines away.

6 "The LORD brings death and makes alive;
he brings down to the grave and
raises up.
7 The LORD sends poverty and wealth;
he humbles and he exalts.
8 He raises the poor from the dust
and lifts the needy from the ash heap;
he seats them with princes
and has them inherit a throne of
honor.

"For the foundations of the earth are
the LORD's;
on them he has set the world.
9 He will guard the feet of his faithful
servants,
but the wicked will be silenced in the
place of darkness.

"It is not by strength that one prevails;
10 those who oppose the LORD will be
broken.
The Most High will thunder from heaven;
the LORD will judge the ends of the
earth.

"He will give strength to his king
and exalt the horn of his anointed."

11 Then Elkanah went home to Ramah, but
the boy ministered before the LORD under
Eli the priest.

Eli's Wicked Sons

12 Eli's sons were scoundrels; they had no
regard for the LORD. 13 Now it was the prac-
tice of the priests that, whenever any of the
people offered a sacrifice, the priest's ser-
vant would come with a three-pronged fork
in his hand while the meat was being boiled
14 and would plunge the fork into the pan or
kettle or caldron or pot. Whatever the fork
brought up the priest would take for him-
self. This is how they treated all the Israel-
ites who came to Shiloh. 15 But even before
the fat was burned, the priest's servant
would come and say to the person who was
sacrificing, "Give the priest some meat to
roast; he won't accept boiled meat from you,
but only raw."

16 If the person said to him, "Let the fat be
burned first, and then take whatever you
want," the servant would answer, "No, hand
it over now; if you don't, I'll take it by force."
17 This sin of the young men was very great
in the LORD's sight, for they[d] were treating
the LORD's offering with contempt.
18 But Samuel was ministering before
the LORD — a boy wearing a linen ephod.
19 Each year his mother made him a little
robe and took it to him when she went up
with her husband to offer the annual sac-
rifice. 20 Eli would bless Elkanah and his

[a] *24* Dead Sea Scrolls, Septuagint and Syriac; Masoretic Text *with three bulls* [b] *24* That is, probably about 36 pounds or about 16 kilograms [c] *1* *Horn* here symbolizes strength; also in verse 10. [d] *17* Dead Sea Scrolls and Septuagint; Masoretic Text *people*

wife, saying, "May the LORD give you children by this woman to take the place of the one she prayed for and gave to[a] the LORD." Then they would go home. 21 And the LORD was gracious to Hannah; she gave birth to three sons and two daughters. Meanwhile, the boy Samuel grew up in the presence of the LORD.

22 Now Eli, who was very old, heard about everything his sons were doing to all Israel and how they slept with the women who served at the entrance to the tent of meeting. 23 So he said to them, "Why do you do such things? I hear from all the people about these wicked deeds of yours. 24 No, my sons; the report I hear spreading among the LORD's people is not good. 25 If one person sins against another, God[b] may mediate for the offender; but if anyone sins against the LORD, who will intercede for them?" His sons, however, did not listen to their father's rebuke, for it was the LORD's will to put them to death.

26 And the boy Samuel continued to grow in stature and in favor with the LORD and with people.

Prophecy Against the House of Eli

27 Now a man of God came to Eli and said to him, "This is what the LORD says: 'Did I not clearly reveal myself to your ancestor's family when they were in Egypt under Pharaoh? 28 I chose your ancestor out of all the tribes of Israel to be my priest, to go up to my altar, to burn incense, and to wear an ephod in my presence. I also gave your ancestor's family all the food offerings presented by the Israelites. 29 Why do you[c] scorn my sacrifice and offering that I prescribed for my dwelling? Why do you honor your sons more than me by fattening yourselves on the choice parts of every offering made by my people Israel?'

30 "Therefore the LORD, the God of Israel, declares: 'I promised that members of your family would minister before me forever.' But now the LORD declares: 'Far be it from me! Those who honor me I will honor, but those who despise me will be disdained. 31 The time is coming when I will cut short your strength and the strength of your priestly house, so that no one in it will reach old age, 32 and you will see distress in my dwelling. Although good will be done to Israel, no one in your family line will ever reach old age. 33 Every one of you that I do not cut off from serving at my altar I will spare only to destroy your sight and sap your strength, and all your descendants will die in the prime of life.

34 "'And what happens to your two sons, Hophni and Phinehas, will be a sign to you—they will both die on the same day. 35 I will raise up for myself a faithful priest, who will do according to what is in my heart and mind. I will firmly establish his priestly house, and they will minister before my anointed one always. 36 Then everyone left in your family line will come and bow down before him for a piece of silver and a loaf of bread and plead, "Appoint me to some priestly office so I can have food to eat."'"

The LORD Calls Samuel

3 The boy Samuel ministered before the LORD under Eli. In those days the word of the LORD was rare; there were not many visions.

2 One night Eli, whose eyes were becoming so weak that he could barely see, was lying down in his usual place. 3 The lamp of God had not yet gone out, and Samuel was lying down in the house of the LORD, where the ark of God was. 4 Then the LORD called Samuel.

Samuel answered, "Here I am." 5 And he ran to Eli and said, "Here I am; you called me."

But Eli said, "I did not call; go back and lie down." So he went and lay down.

6 Again the LORD called, "Samuel!" And Samuel got up and went to Eli and said, "Here I am; you called me."

"My son," Eli said, "I did not call; go back and lie down."

7 Now Samuel did not yet know the LORD: The word of the LORD had not yet been revealed to him.

8 A third time the LORD called, "Samuel!" And Samuel got up and went to Eli and said, "Here I am; you called me."

Then Eli realized that the LORD was calling the boy. 9 So Eli told Samuel, "Go and lie down, and if he calls you, say, 'Speak, LORD,

[a] 20 Dead Sea Scrolls; Masoretic Text *and asked from* [b] 25 Or *the judges* [c] 29 The Hebrew is plural.

for your servant is listening.'" So Samuel went and lay down in his place.

10 The LORD came and stood there, calling as at the other times, "Samuel! Samuel!"

Then Samuel said, "Speak, for your servant is listening."

11 And the LORD said to Samuel: "See, I am about to do something in Israel that will make the ears of everyone who hears about it tingle. 12 At that time I will carry out against Eli everything I spoke against his family—from beginning to end. 13 For I told him that I would judge his family forever because of the sin he knew about; his sons blasphemed God,[a] and he failed to restrain them. 14 Therefore I swore to the house of Eli, 'The guilt of Eli's house will never be atoned for by sacrifice or offering.'"

15 Samuel lay down until morning and then opened the doors of the house of the LORD. He was afraid to tell Eli the vision, 16 but Eli called him and said, "Samuel, my son."

Samuel answered, "Here I am."

17 "What was it he said to you?" Eli asked. "Do not hide it from me. May God deal with you, be it ever so severely, if you hide from me anything he told you." 18 So Samuel told him everything, hiding nothing from him. Then Eli said, "He is the LORD; let him do what is good in his eyes."

19 The LORD was with Samuel as he grew up, and he let none of Samuel's words fall to the ground. 20 And all Israel from Dan to Beersheba recognized that Samuel was attested as a prophet of the LORD. 21 The LORD continued to appear at Shiloh, and there he revealed himself to Samuel through his word.

4 And Samuel's word came to all Israel.

The Philistines Capture the Ark

Now the Israelites went out to fight against the Philistines. The Israelites camped at Ebenezer, and the Philistines at Aphek. 2 The Philistines deployed their forces to meet Israel, and as the battle spread, Israel was defeated by the Philistines, who killed about four thousand of them on the battlefield. 3 When the soldiers returned to camp, the elders of Israel asked, "Why did the LORD bring defeat on us today before the Philistines? Let us bring the ark of the LORD's covenant from Shiloh, so that he may go with us and save us from the hand of our enemies."

4 So the people sent men to Shiloh, and they brought back the ark of the covenant of the LORD Almighty, who is enthroned between the cherubim. And Eli's two sons, Hophni and Phinehas, were there with the ark of the covenant of God.

5 When the ark of the LORD's covenant came into the camp, all Israel raised such a great shout that the ground shook. 6 Hearing the uproar, the Philistines asked, "What's all this shouting in the Hebrew camp?"

When they learned that the ark of the LORD had come into the camp, 7 the Philistines were afraid. "A god has[b] come into the camp," they said. "Oh no! Nothing like this has happened before. 8 We're doomed! Who will deliver us from the hand of these mighty gods? They are the gods who struck the Egyptians with all kinds of plagues in the wilderness. 9 Be strong, Philistines! Be men, or you will be subject to the Hebrews, as they have been to you. Be men, and fight!"

10 So the Philistines fought, and the Israelites were defeated and every man fled to his tent. The slaughter was very great; Israel lost thirty thousand foot soldiers. 11 The ark of God was captured, and Eli's two sons, Hophni and Phinehas, died.

Death of Eli

12 That same day a Benjamite ran from the battle line and went to Shiloh with his clothes torn and dust on his head. 13 When he arrived, there was Eli sitting on his chair by the side of the road, watching, because his heart feared for the ark of God. When the man entered the town and told what had happened, the whole town sent up a cry.

14 Eli heard the outcry and asked, "What is the meaning of this uproar?"

The man hurried over to Eli, 15 who was ninety-eight years old and whose eyes had failed so that he could not see. 16 He told Eli, "I have just come from the battle line; I fled from it this very day."

Eli asked, "What happened, my son?"

17 The man who brought the news replied,

[a] 13 An ancient Hebrew scribal tradition (see also Septuagint); Masoretic Text *sons made themselves contemptible* [b] 7 Or *"Gods have* (see Septuagint)

“Israel fled before the Philistines, and the
army has suffered heavy losses. Also your
two sons, Hophni and Phinehas, are dead,
and the ark of God has been captured.”
18When he mentioned the ark of God, Eli
fell backward off his chair by the side of the
gate. His neck was broken and he died, for he
was an old man, and he was heavy. He had
led[a] Israel forty years.
19His daughter-in-law, the wife of Phine-
has, was pregnant and near the time of deliv-
ery. When she heard the news that the ark of
God had been captured and that her father-
in-law and her husband were dead, she went
into labor and gave birth, but was overcome
by her labor pains. 20As she was dying, the
women attending her said, “Don’t despair;
you have given birth to a son.” But she did
not respond or pay any attention.
21She named the boy Ichabod,[b] saying,
“The Glory has departed from Israel” —be-
cause of the capture of the ark of God and the
deaths of her father-in-law and her husband.
22She said, “The Glory has departed from Is-
rael, for the ark of God has been captured.”

The Ark in Ashdod and Ekron

5 After the Philistines had captured the
ark of God, they took it from Ebene-
zer to Ashdod. 2Then they carried the ark
into Dagon’s temple and set it beside Da-
gon. 3When the people of Ashdod rose ear-
ly the next day, there was Dagon, fallen on
his face on the ground before the ark of the
LORD! They took Dagon and put him back
in his place. 4But the following morning
when they rose, there was Dagon, fallen on
his face on the ground before the ark of the
LORD! His head and hands had been broken
off and were lying on the threshold; only his
body remained. 5That is why to this day nei-
ther the priests of Dagon nor any others who
enter Dagon’s temple at Ashdod step on the
threshold.
6The LORD’s hand was heavy on the peo-
ple of Ashdod and its vicinity; he brought
devastation on them and afflicted them
with tumors.[c] 7When the people of Ashdod
saw what was happening, they said, “The ark
of the god of Israel must not stay here with
us, because his hand is heavy on us and on
Dagon our god.” 8So they called together all
the rulers of the Philistines and asked them,
“What shall we do with the ark of the god of
Israel?”
They answered, “Have the ark of the god
of Israel moved to Gath.” So they moved the
ark of the God of Israel.
9But after they had moved it, the LORD’s
hand was against that city, throwing it into
a great panic. He afflicted the people of the
city, both young and old, with an outbreak
of tumors.[d] 10So they sent the ark of God to
Ekron.
As the ark of God was entering Ekron,
the people of Ekron cried out, “They have
brought the ark of the god of Israel around to
us to kill us and our people.” 11So they called
together all the rulers of the Philistines and
said, “Send the ark of the god of Israel away;
let it go back to its own place, or it[e] will kill
us and our people.” For death had filled the
city with panic; God’s hand was very heavy
on it. 12Those who did not die were afflicted
with tumors, and the outcry of the city went
up to heaven.

The Ark Returned to Israel

6 When the ark of the LORD had been in
Philistine territory seven months, 2the
Philistines called for the priests and the di-
viners and said, “What shall we do with the
ark of the LORD? Tell us how we should send
it back to its place.”
3They answered, “If you return the ark of
the god of Israel, do not send it back to him
without a gift; by all means send a guilt offer-
ing to him. Then you will be healed, and you
will know why his hand has not been lifted
from you.”
4The Philistines asked, “What guilt offer-
ing should we send to him?”
They replied, “Five gold tumors and five
gold rats, according to the number of the
Philistine rulers, because the same plague
has struck both you and your rulers. 5Make
models of the tumors and of the rats that are
destroying the country, and give glory to Is-
rael’s god. Perhaps he will lift his hand from
you and your gods and your land. 6Why do

[a] *18* Traditionally *judged* [b] *21* *Ichabod* means *no glory.* [c] *6* Hebrew; Septuagint and Vulgate *tumors. And rats appeared in their land, and there was death and destruction throughout the city* [d] *9* Or *with tumors in the groin* (see Septuagint) [e] *11* Or *he*

you harden your hearts as the Egyptians and Pharaoh did? When Israel's god dealt harshly with them, did they not send the Israelites out so they could go on their way?

7 "Now then, get a new cart ready, with two cows that have calved and have never been yoked. Hitch the cows to the cart, but take their calves away and pen them up. 8 Take the ark of the LORD and put it on the cart, and in a chest beside it put the gold objects you are sending back to him as a guilt offering. Send it on its way, 9 but keep watching it. If it goes up to its own territory, toward Beth Shemesh, then the LORD has brought this great disaster on us. But if it does not, then we will know that it was not his hand that struck us but that it happened to us by chance."

10 So they did this. They took two such cows and hitched them to the cart and penned up their calves. 11 They placed the ark of the LORD on the cart and along with it the chest containing the gold rats and the models of the tumors. 12 Then the cows went straight up toward Beth Shemesh, keeping on the road and lowing all the way; they did not turn to the right or to the left. The rulers of the Philistines followed them as far as the border of Beth Shemesh.

13 Now the people of Beth Shemesh were harvesting their wheat in the valley, and when they looked up and saw the ark, they rejoiced at the sight. 14 The cart came to the field of Joshua of Beth Shemesh, and there it stopped beside a large rock. The people chopped up the wood of the cart and sacrificed the cows as a burnt offering to the LORD. 15 The Levites took down the ark of the LORD, together with the chest containing the gold objects, and placed them on the large rock. On that day the people of Beth Shemesh offered burnt offerings and made sacrifices to the LORD. 16 The five rulers of the Philistines saw all this and then returned that same day to Ekron.

17 These are the gold tumors the Philistines sent as a guilt offering to the LORD — one each for Ashdod, Gaza, Ashkelon, Gath and Ekron. 18 And the number of the gold rats was according to the number of Philistine towns belonging to the five rulers — the fortified towns with their country villages. The large rock on which the Levites set the ark of the LORD is a witness to this day in the field of Joshua of Beth Shemesh.

19 But God struck down some of the inhabitants of Beth Shemesh, putting seventy[a] of them to death because they looked into the ark of the LORD. The people mourned because of the heavy blow the LORD had dealt them. 20 And the people of Beth Shemesh asked, "Who can stand in the presence of the LORD, this holy God? To whom will the ark go up from here?"

21 Then they sent messengers to the people of Kiriath Jearim, saying, "The Philistines have returned the ark of the LORD. Come

7 down and take it up to your town." 1 So the men of Kiriath Jearim came and took up the ark of the LORD. They brought it to Abinadab's house on the hill and consecrated Eleazar his son to guard the ark of the LORD. 2 The ark remained at Kiriath Jearim a long time — twenty years in all.

Samuel Subdues the Philistines at Mizpah

Then all the people of Israel turned back to the LORD. 3 So Samuel said to all the Israelites, "If you are returning to the LORD with all your hearts, then rid yourselves of the foreign gods and the Ashtoreths and commit yourselves to the LORD and serve him only, and he will deliver you out of the hand of the Philistines." 4 So the Israelites put away their Baals and Ashtoreths, and served the LORD only.

5 Then Samuel said, "Assemble all Israel at Mizpah, and I will intercede with the LORD for you." 6 When they had assembled at Mizpah, they drew water and poured it out before the LORD. On that day they fasted and there they confessed, "We have sinned against the LORD." Now Samuel was serving as leader[b] of Israel at Mizpah.

7 When the Philistines heard that Israel had assembled at Mizpah, the rulers of the Philistines came up to attack them. When the Israelites heard of it, they were afraid because of the Philistines. 8 They said to Samuel, "Do not stop crying out to the LORD our God for us, that he may rescue us from the hand of the Philistines." 9 Then Samuel took a suckling lamb and sacrificed it as a whole burnt offering to the LORD. He cried out to

[a] *19* A few Hebrew manuscripts; most Hebrew manuscripts and Septuagint *50,070* [b] *6* Traditionally *judge;* also in verse 15

the LORD on Israel's behalf, and the LORD answered him.

10 While Samuel was sacrificing the burnt offering, the Philistines drew near to engage Israel in battle. But that day the LORD thundered with loud thunder against the Philistines and threw them into such a panic that they were routed before the Israelites. 11 The men of Israel rushed out of Mizpah and pursued the Philistines, slaughtering them along the way to a point below Beth Kar.

12 Then Samuel took a stone and set it up between Mizpah and Shen. He named it Ebenezer,[a] saying, "Thus far the LORD has helped us."

13 So the Philistines were subdued and they stopped invading Israel's territory. Throughout Samuel's lifetime, the hand of the LORD was against the Philistines. 14 The towns from Ekron to Gath that the Philistines had captured from Israel were restored to Israel, and Israel delivered the neighboring territory from the hands of the Philistines. And there was peace between Israel and the Amorites.

15 Samuel continued as Israel's leader all the days of his life. 16 From year to year he went on a circuit from Bethel to Gilgal to Mizpah, judging Israel in all those places. 17 But he always went back to Ramah, where his home was, and there he also held court for Israel. And he built an altar there to the LORD.

Israel Asks for a King

8 When Samuel grew old, he appointed his sons as Israel's leaders.[b] 2 The name of his firstborn was Joel and the name of his second was Abijah, and they served at Beersheba. 3 But his sons did not follow his ways. They turned aside after dishonest gain and accepted bribes and perverted justice.

4 So all the elders of Israel gathered together and came to Samuel at Ramah. 5 They said to him, "You are old, and your sons do not follow your ways; now appoint a king to lead[c] us, such as all the other nations have."

6 But when they said, "Give us a king to lead us," this displeased Samuel; so he prayed to the LORD. 7 And the LORD told him: "Listen to all that the people are saying to you; it is not you they have rejected, but they have rejected me as their king. 8 As they have done from the day I brought them up out of Egypt until this day, forsaking me and serving other gods, so they are doing to you. 9 Now listen to them; but warn them solemnly and let them know what the king who will reign over them will claim as his rights."

10 Samuel told all the words of the LORD to the people who were asking him for a king. 11 He said, "This is what the king who will reign over you will claim as his rights: He will take your sons and make them serve with his chariots and horses, and they will run in front of his chariots. 12 Some he will assign to be commanders of thousands and commanders of fifties, and others to plow his ground and reap his harvest, and still others to make weapons of war and equipment for his chariots. 13 He will take your daughters to be perfumers and cooks and bakers. 14 He will take the best of your fields and vineyards and olive groves and give them to his attendants. 15 He will take a tenth of your grain and of your vintage and give it to his officials and attendants. 16 Your male and female servants and the best of your cattle[d] and donkeys he will take for his own use. 17 He will take a tenth of your flocks, and you yourselves will become his slaves. 18 When that day comes, you will cry out for relief from the king you have chosen, but the LORD will not answer you in that day."

19 But the people refused to listen to Samuel. "No!" they said. "We want a king over us. 20 Then we will be like all the other nations, with a king to lead us and to go out before us and fight our battles."

21 When Samuel heard all that the people said, he repeated it before the LORD. 22 The LORD answered, "Listen to them and give them a king."

Then Samuel said to the Israelites, "Everyone go back to your own town."

Samuel Anoints Saul

9 There was a Benjamite, a man of standing, whose name was Kish son of Abiel, the son of Zeror, the son of Bekorath, the son of Aphiah of Benjamin. 2 Kish had a son named Saul, as handsome a young man as

[a] 12 *Ebenezer* means *stone of help.* [b] 1 Traditionally *judges* [c] 5 Traditionally *judge*; also in verses 6 and 20 [d] 16 Septuagint; Hebrew *young men*

could be found anywhere in Israel, and he
was a head taller than anyone else.
3 Now the donkeys belonging to Saul's fa-
ther Kish were lost, and Kish said to his son
Saul, "Take one of the servants with you and
go and look for the donkeys." 4 So he passed
through the hill country of Ephraim and
through the area around Shalisha, but they
did not find them. They went on into the dis-
trict of Shaalim, but the donkeys were not
there. Then he passed through the territory
of Benjamin, but they did not find them.
5 When they reached the district of Zuph,
Saul said to the servant who was with him,
"Come, let's go back, or my father will stop
thinking about the donkeys and start worry-
ing about us."
6 But the servant replied, "Look, in this
town there is a man of God; he is highly re-
spected, and everything he says comes true.
Let's go there now. Perhaps he will tell us
what way to take."
7 Saul said to his servant, "If we go, what
can we give the man? The food in our sacks
is gone. We have no gift to take to the man of
God. What do we have?"
8 The servant answered him again.
"Look," he said, "I have a quarter of a shekel[a]
of silver. I will give it to the man of God so
that he will tell us what way to take." 9 (For-
merly in Israel, if someone went to inquire of
God, they would say, "Come, let us go to the
seer," because the prophet of today used to
be called a seer.)
10 "Good," Saul said to his servant. "Come,
let's go." So they set out for the town where
the man of God was.
11 As they were going up the hill to the
town, they met some young women coming
out to draw water, and they asked them, "Is
the seer here?"
12 "He is," they answered. "He's ahead
of you. Hurry now; he has just come to our
town today, for the people have a sacrifice
at the high place. 13 As soon as you enter the
town, you will find him before he goes up to
the high place to eat. The people will not be-
gin eating until he comes, because he must
bless the sacrifice; afterward, those who are
invited will eat. Go up now; you should find
him about this time."
14 They went up to the town, and as they
were entering it, there was Samuel, coming
toward them on his way up to the high place.
15 Now the day before Saul came, the LORD
had revealed this to Samuel: 16 "About this
time tomorrow I will send you a man from
the land of Benjamin. Anoint him ruler over
my people Israel; he will deliver them from
the hand of the Philistines. I have looked on
my people, for their cry has reached me."
17 When Samuel caught sight of Saul, the
LORD said to him, "This is the man I spoke to
you about; he will govern my people."
18 Saul approached Samuel in the gateway
and asked, "Would you please tell me where
the seer's house is?"
19 "I am the seer," Samuel replied. "Go up
ahead of me to the high place, for today you
are to eat with me, and in the morning I will
send you on your way and will tell you all
that is in your heart. 20 As for the donkeys you
lost three days ago, do not worry about them;
they have been found. And to whom is all the
desire of Israel turned, if not to you and your
whole family line?"
21 Saul answered, "But am I not a Benja-
mite, from the smallest tribe of Israel, and is
not my clan the least of all the clans of the
tribe of Benjamin? Why do you say such a
thing to me?"
22 Then Samuel brought Saul and his ser-
vant into the hall and seated them at the
head of those who were invited — about
thirty in number. 23 Samuel said to the cook,
"Bring the piece of meat I gave you, the one I
told you to lay aside."
24 So the cook took up the thigh with what
was on it and set it in front of Saul. Samuel
said, "Here is what has been kept for you.
Eat, because it was set aside for you for this
occasion from the time I said, 'I have invited
guests.'" And Saul dined with Samuel that
day.
25 After they came down from the high
place to the town, Samuel talked with Saul
on the roof of his house. 26 They rose about
daybreak, and Samuel called to Saul on the
roof, "Get ready, and I will send you on your
way." When Saul got ready, he and Samuel
went outside together. 27 As they were going
down to the edge of the town, Samuel said
to Saul, "Tell the servant to go on ahead of
us" — and the servant did so — "but you stay

[a] *8* That is, about 1/10 ounce or about 3 grams

here for a while, so that I may give you a mes-
sage from God."

10 Then Samuel took a flask of ol-
ive oil and poured it on Saul's head
and kissed him, saying, "Has not the LORD
anointed you ruler over his inheritance?[a]
2When you leave me today, you will meet
two men near Rachel's tomb, at Zelzah on
the border of Benjamin. They will say to
you, 'The donkeys you set out to look for
have been found. And now your father has
stopped thinking about them and is wor-
ried about you. He is asking, "What shall I do
about my son?"'

3"Then you will go on from there until you
reach the great tree of Tabor. Three men go-
ing up to worship God at Bethel will meet
you there. One will be carrying three young
goats, another three loaves of bread, and an-
other a skin of wine. 4They will greet you and
offer you two loaves of bread, which you will
accept from them.

5"After that you will go to Gibeah of God,
where there is a Philistine outpost. As you
approach the town, you will meet a pro-
cession of prophets coming down from the
high place with lyres, timbrels, pipes and
harps being played before them, and they
will be prophesying. 6The Spirit of the LORD
will come powerfully upon you, and you
will prophesy with them; and you will be
changed into a different person. 7Once these
signs are fulfilled, do whatever your hand
finds to do, for God is with you.

8"Go down ahead of me to Gilgal. I will
surely come down to you to sacrifice burnt
offerings and fellowship offerings, but you
must wait seven days until I come to you and
tell you what you are to do."

Saul Made King

9As Saul turned to leave Samuel, God
changed Saul's heart, and all these signs
were fulfilled that day. 10When he and his
servant arrived at Gibeah, a procession of
prophets met him; the Spirit of God came
powerfully upon him, and he joined in their
prophesying. 11When all those who had for-
merly known him saw him prophesying with
the prophets, they asked each other, "What
is this that has happened to the son of Kish?
Is Saul also among the prophets?"

12A man who lived there answered, "And
who is their father?" So it became a saying:
"Is Saul also among the prophets?" 13After
Saul stopped prophesying, he went to the
high place.

14Now Saul's uncle asked him and his ser-
vant, "Where have you been?"

"Looking for the donkeys," he said. "But
when we saw they were not to be found, we
went to Samuel."

15Saul's uncle said, "Tell me what Samuel
said to you."

16Saul replied, "He assured us that the
donkeys had been found." But he did not tell
his uncle what Samuel had said about the
kingship.

17Samuel summoned the people of Israel
to the LORD at Mizpah 18and said to them,
"This is what the LORD, the God of Israel,
says: 'I brought Israel up out of Egypt, and I
delivered you from the power of Egypt and
all the kingdoms that oppressed you.' 19But
you have now rejected your God, who saves
you out of all your disasters and calamities.
And you have said, 'No, appoint a king over
us.' So now present yourselves before the
LORD by your tribes and clans."

20When Samuel had all Israel come for-
ward by tribes, the tribe of Benjamin was
taken by lot. 21Then he brought forward the
tribe of Benjamin, clan by clan, and Matri's
clan was taken. Finally Saul son of Kish was
taken. But when they looked for him, he was
not to be found. 22So they inquired further
of the LORD, "Has the man come here yet?"

And the LORD said, "Yes, he has hidden
himself among the supplies."

23They ran and brought him out, and as
he stood among the people he was a head
taller than any of the others. 24Samuel said
to all the people, "Do you see the man the
LORD has chosen? There is no one like him
among all the people."

Then the people shouted, "Long live the
king!"

25Samuel explained to the people the
rights and duties of kingship. He wrote them
down on a scroll and deposited it before the
LORD. Then Samuel dismissed the people to
go to their own homes.

26Saul also went to his home in Gibeah,

[a] *1* Hebrew; Septuagint and Vulgate *over his people Israel? You will reign over the LORD's people and save them from the power of their enemies round about. And this will be a sign to you that the LORD has anointed you ruler over his inheritance:*

accompanied by valiant men whose hearts God had touched. 27 But some scoundrels said, "How can this fellow save us?" They despised him and brought him no gifts. But Saul kept silent.

Saul Rescues the City of Jabesh

11 Nahash[a] the Ammonite went up and besieged Jabesh Gilead. And all the men of Jabesh said to him, "Make a treaty with us, and we will be subject to you."

2 But Nahash the Ammonite replied, "I will make a treaty with you only on the condition that I gouge out the right eye of every one of you and so bring disgrace on all Israel."

3 The elders of Jabesh said to him, "Give us seven days so we can send messengers throughout Israel; if no one comes to rescue us, we will surrender to you."

4 When the messengers came to Gibeah of Saul and reported these terms to the people, they all wept aloud. 5 Just then Saul was returning from the fields, behind his oxen, and he asked, "What is wrong with everyone? Why are they weeping?" Then they repeated to him what the men of Jabesh had said.

6 When Saul heard their words, the Spirit of God came powerfully upon him, and he burned with anger. 7 He took a pair of oxen, cut them into pieces, and sent the pieces by messengers throughout Israel, proclaiming, "This is what will be done to the oxen of anyone who does not follow Saul and Samuel." Then the terror of the LORD fell on the people, and they came out together as one. 8 When Saul mustered them at Bezek, the men of Israel numbered three hundred thousand and those of Judah thirty thousand.

9 They told the messengers who had come, "Say to the men of Jabesh Gilead, 'By the time the sun is hot tomorrow, you will be rescued.' " When the messengers went and reported this to the men of Jabesh, they were elated. 10 They said to the Ammonites, "Tomorrow we will surrender to you, and you can do to us whatever you like."

11 The next day Saul separated his men into three divisions; during the last watch of the night they broke into the camp of the Ammonites and slaughtered them until the heat of the day. Those who survived were scattered, so that no two of them were left together.

Saul Confirmed as King

12 The people then said to Samuel, "Who was it that asked, 'Shall Saul reign over us?' Turn these men over to us so that we may put them to death."

13 But Saul said, "No one will be put to death today, for this day the LORD has rescued Israel."

14 Then Samuel said to the people, "Come, let us go to Gilgal and there renew the kingship." 15 So all the people went to Gilgal and made Saul king in the presence of the LORD. There they sacrificed fellowship offerings before the LORD, and Saul and all the Israelites held a great celebration.

Samuel's Farewell Speech

12 Samuel said to all Israel, "I have listened to everything you said to me and have set a king over you. 2 Now you have a king as your leader. As for me, I am old and gray, and my sons are here with you. I have been your leader from my youth until this day. 3 Here I stand. Testify against me in the presence of the LORD and his anointed. Whose ox have I taken? Whose donkey have I taken? Whom have I cheated? Whom have I oppressed? From whose hand have I accepted a bribe to make me shut my eyes? If I have done any of these things, I will make it right."

4 "You have not cheated or oppressed us," they replied. "You have not taken anything from anyone's hand."

5 Samuel said to them, "The LORD is witness against you, and also his anointed is witness this day, that you have not found anything in my hand."

"He is witness," they said.

6 Then Samuel said to the people, "It is the LORD who appointed Moses and Aaron and brought your ancestors up out of Egypt. 7 Now then, stand here, because I am going

[a] *1* Masoretic Text; Dead Sea Scrolls *gifts. Now Nahash king of the Ammonites oppressed the Gadites and Reubenites severely. He gouged out all their right eyes and struck terror and dread in Israel. Not a man remained among the Israelites beyond the Jordan whose right eye was not gouged out by Nahash king of the Ammonites, except that seven thousand men fled from the Ammonites and entered Jabesh Gilead. About a month later,* [1]*Nahash*

to confront you with evidence before the LORD as to all the righteous acts performed by the LORD for you and your ancestors.

8 “After Jacob entered Egypt, they cried to the LORD for help, and the LORD sent Moses and Aaron, who brought your ancestors out of Egypt and settled them in this place.

9 “But they forgot the LORD their God; so he sold them into the hand of Sisera, the commander of the army of Hazor, and into the hands of the Philistines and the king of Moab, who fought against them. 10 They cried out to the LORD and said, ‘We have sinned; we have forsaken the LORD and served the Baals and the Ashtoreths. But now deliver us from the hands of our enemies, and we will serve you.’ 11 Then the LORD sent Jerub-Baal,[a] Barak,[b] Jephthah and Samuel,[c] and he delivered you from the hands of your enemies all around you, so that you lived in safety.

12 “But when you saw that Nahash king of the Ammonites was moving against you, you said to me, ‘No, we want a king to rule over us’—even though the LORD your God was your king. 13 Now here is the king you have chosen, the one you asked for; see, the LORD has set a king over you. 14 If you fear the LORD and serve and obey him and do not rebel against his commands, and if both you and the king who reigns over you follow the LORD your God—good! 15 But if you do not obey the LORD, and if you rebel against his commands, his hand will be against you, as it was against your ancestors.

16 “Now then, stand still and see this great thing the LORD is about to do before your eyes! 17 Is it not wheat harvest now? I will call on the LORD to send thunder and rain. And you will realize what an evil thing you did in the eyes of the LORD when you asked for a king.”

18 Then Samuel called on the LORD, and that same day the LORD sent thunder and rain. So all the people stood in awe of the LORD and of Samuel.

19 The people all said to Samuel, “Pray to the LORD your God for your servants so that we will not die, for we have added to all our other sins the evil of asking for a king.”

20 “Do not be afraid,” Samuel replied. “You have done all this evil; yet do not turn away from the LORD, but serve the LORD with all your heart. 21 Do not turn away after useless idols. They can do you no good, nor can they rescue you, because they are useless. 22 For the sake of his great name the LORD will not reject his people, because the LORD was pleased to make you his own. 23 As for me, far be it from me that I should sin against the LORD by failing to pray for you. And I will teach you the way that is good and right. 24 But be sure to fear the LORD and serve him faithfully with all your heart; consider what great things he has done for you. 25 Yet if you persist in doing evil, both you and your king will perish.”

Samuel Rebukes Saul

13 Saul was thirty[d] years old when he became king, and he reigned over Israel forty-[e] two years.

2 Saul chose three thousand men from Israel; two thousand were with him at Mikmash and in the hill country of Bethel, and a thousand were with Jonathan at Gibeah in Benjamin. The rest of the men he sent back to their homes.

3 Jonathan attacked the Philistine outpost at Geba, and the Philistines heard about it. Then Saul had the trumpet blown throughout the land and said, “Let the Hebrews hear!” 4 So all Israel heard the news: “Saul has attacked the Philistine outpost, and now Israel has become obnoxious to the Philistines.” And the people were summoned to join Saul at Gilgal.

5 The Philistines assembled to fight Israel, with three thousand[f] chariots, six thousand charioteers, and soldiers as numerous as the sand on the seashore. They went up and camped at Mikmash, east of Beth Aven. 6 When the Israelites saw that their situation was critical and that their army was hard pressed, they hid in caves and thickets, among the rocks, and in pits and cisterns. 7 Some Hebrews even crossed the Jordan to the land of Gad and Gilead.

Saul remained at Gilgal, and all the troops with him were quaking with fear. 8 He waited

[a] *11* Also called *Gideon* [b] *11* Some Septuagint manuscripts and Syriac; Hebrew *Bedan* [c] *11* Hebrew; some Septuagint manuscripts and Syriac *Samson* [d] *1* A few late manuscripts of the Septuagint; Hebrew does not have *thirty.* [e] *1* Probable reading of the original Hebrew text (see Acts 13:21); Masoretic Text does not have *forty-.* [f] *5* Some Septuagint manuscripts and Syriac; Hebrew *thirty thousand*

seven days, the time set by Samuel; but Sam-
uel did not come to Gilgal, and Saul's men
began to scatter. [9]So he said, "Bring me the
burnt offering and the fellowship offerings."
And Saul offered up the burnt offering. [10]Just
as he finished making the offering, Samuel
arrived, and Saul went out to greet him.

[11]"What have you done?" asked Samuel.

Saul replied, "When I saw that the men
were scattering, and that you did not come
at the set time, and that the Philistines were
assembling at Mikmash, [12]I thought, 'Now
the Philistines will come down against me
at Gilgal, and I have not sought the LORD's
favor.' So I felt compelled to offer the burnt
offering."

[13]"You have done a foolish thing," Sam-
uel said. "You have not kept the command
the LORD your God gave you; if you had, he
would have established your kingdom over
Israel for all time. [14]But now your kingdom
will not endure; the LORD has sought out a
man after his own heart and appointed him
ruler of his people, because you have not
kept the LORD's command."

[15]Then Samuel left Gilgal[a] and went up to
Gibeah in Benjamin, and Saul counted the
men who were with him. They numbered
about six hundred.

Israel Without Weapons

[16]Saul and his son Jonathan and the
men with them were staying in Gibeah[b] in
Benjamin, while the Philistines camped at
Mikmash. [17]Raiding parties went out from
the Philistine camp in three detachments.
One turned toward Ophrah in the vicinity
of Shual, [18]another toward Beth Horon, and
the third toward the borderland overlook-
ing the Valley of Zeboyim facing the wilder-
ness.

[19]Not a blacksmith could be found in the
whole land of Israel, because the Philistines
had said, "Otherwise the Hebrews will make
swords or spears!" [20]So all Israel went down
to the Philistines to have their plow points,
mattocks, axes and sickles[c] sharpened.
[21]The price was two-thirds of a shekel[d] for
sharpening plow points and mattocks, and
a third of a shekel[e] for sharpening forks and
axes and for repointing goads.

[22]So on the day of the battle not a soldier
with Saul and Jonathan had a sword or spear
in his hand; only Saul and his son Jonathan
had them.

Jonathan Attacks the Philistines

[23]Now a detachment of Philistines had
14 gone out to the pass at Mikmash. [1]One
day Jonathan son of Saul said to his
young armor-bearer, "Come, let's go over to
the Philistine outpost on the other side." But
he did not tell his father.

[2]Saul was staying on the outskirts of Gib-
eah under a pomegranate tree in Migron.
With him were about six hundred men,
[3]among whom was Ahijah, who was wearing
an ephod. He was a son of Ichabod's broth-
er Ahitub son of Phinehas, the son of Eli, the
LORD's priest in Shiloh. No one was aware
that Jonathan had left.

[4]On each side of the pass that Jonathan
intended to cross to reach the Philistine out-
post was a cliff; one was called Bozez and the
other Seneh. [5]One cliff stood to the north
toward Mikmash, the other to the south to-
ward Geba.

[6]Jonathan said to his young armor-bearer,
"Come, let's go over to the outpost of those
uncircumcised men. Perhaps the LORD will
act in our behalf. Nothing can hinder the
LORD from saving, whether by many or by
few."

[7]"Do all that you have in mind," his ar-
mor-bearer said. "Go ahead; I am with you
heart and soul."

[8]Jonathan said, "Come on, then; we will
cross over toward them and let them see us.
[9]If they say to us, 'Wait there until we come
to you,' we will stay where we are and not go
up to them. [10]But if they say, 'Come up to us,'
we will climb up, because that will be our
sign that the LORD has given them into our
hands."

[11]So both of them showed themselves to
the Philistine outpost. "Look!" said the Phi-
listines. "The Hebrews are crawling out of
the holes they were hiding in." [12]The men of

[a] *15* Hebrew; Septuagint *Gilgal and went his way; the rest of the people went after Saul to meet the army, and they went out of Gilgal* [b] *16* Two Hebrew manuscripts; most Hebrew manuscripts *Geba,* a variant of *Gibeah* [c] *20* Septuagint; Hebrew *plow points* [d] *21* That is, about 1/4 ounce or about 8 grams
[e] *21* That is, about 1/8 ounce or about 4 grams

the outpost shouted to Jonathan and his armor-bearer, "Come up to us and we'll teach you a lesson."

So Jonathan said to his armor-bearer, "Climb up after me; the LORD has given them into the hand of Israel."

13 Jonathan climbed up, using his hands and feet, with his armor-bearer right behind him. The Philistines fell before Jonathan, and his armor-bearer followed and killed behind him. 14 In that first attack Jonathan and his armor-bearer killed some twenty men in an area of about half an acre.

Israel Routs the Philistines

15 Then panic struck the whole army—those in the camp and field, and those in the outposts and raiding parties—and the ground shook. It was a panic sent by God.[a]

16 Saul's lookouts at Gibeah in Benjamin saw the army melting away in all directions. 17 Then Saul said to the men who were with him, "Muster the forces and see who has left us." When they did, it was Jonathan and his armor-bearer who were not there.

18 Saul said to Ahijah, "Bring the ark of God." (At that time it was with the Israelites.)[b] 19 While Saul was talking to the priest, the tumult in the Philistine camp increased more and more. So Saul said to the priest, "Withdraw your hand."

20 Then Saul and all his men assembled and went to the battle. They found the Philistines in total confusion, striking each other with their swords. 21 Those Hebrews who had previously been with the Philistines and had gone up with them to their camp went over to the Israelites who were with Saul and Jonathan. 22 When all the Israelites who had hidden in the hill country of Ephraim heard that the Philistines were on the run, they joined the battle in hot pursuit. 23 So on that day the LORD saved Israel, and the battle moved on beyond Beth Aven.

Jonathan Eats Honey

24 Now the Israelites were in distress that day, because Saul had bound the people under an oath, saying, "Cursed be anyone who eats food before evening comes, before I have avenged myself on my enemies!" So none of the troops tasted food.

25 The entire army entered the woods, and there was honey on the ground. 26 When they went into the woods, they saw the honey oozing out; yet no one put his hand to his mouth, because they feared the oath. 27 But Jonathan had not heard that his father had bound the people with the oath, so he reached out the end of the staff that was in his hand and dipped it into the honeycomb. He raised his hand to his mouth, and his eyes brightened.[c] 28 Then one of the soldiers told him, "Your father bound the army under a strict oath, saying, 'Cursed be anyone who eats food today!' That is why the men are faint."

29 Jonathan said, "My father has made trouble for the country. See how my eyes brightened when I tasted a little of this honey. 30 How much better it would have been if the men had eaten today some of the plunder they took from their enemies. Would not the slaughter of the Philistines have been even greater?"

31 That day, after the Israelites had struck down the Philistines from Mikmash to Aijalon, they were exhausted. 32 They pounced on the plunder and, taking sheep, cattle and calves, they butchered them on the ground and ate them, together with the blood. 33 Then someone said to Saul, "Look, the men are sinning against the LORD by eating meat that has blood in it."

"You have broken faith," he said. "Roll a large stone over here at once." 34 Then he said, "Go out among the men and tell them, 'Each of you bring me your cattle and sheep, and slaughter them here and eat them. Do not sin against the LORD by eating meat with blood still in it.' "

So everyone brought his ox that night and slaughtered it there. 35 Then Saul built an altar to the LORD; it was the first time he had done this.

36 Saul said, "Let us go down and pursue the Philistines by night and plunder them till dawn, and let us not leave one of them alive."

"Do whatever seems best to you," they replied.

But the priest said, "Let us inquire of God here."

37 So Saul asked God, "Shall I go down and

[a] 15 Or *a terrible panic* [b] 18 Hebrew; Septuagint *"Bring the ephod." (At that time he wore the ephod before the Israelites.)* [c] 27 Or *his strength was renewed*; similarly in verse 29

OPEN THE EYES OF MY HEART

Paul Baloche

Open the eyes of my heart, Lord
Open the eyes of my heart
I want to see you
I want to see you

Open the eyes of my heart, Lord
Open the eyes of my heart
I want to see you
I want to see you

To see you high and lifted up
Shining in the light of your glory
Pour out your power and love
As we sing holy, holy, holy

Holy, holy, holy
I want to see you

THE INSPIRATION

In the year that King Uzziah died, I saw the Lord, high and exalted, seated on a throne; and the train of his robe filled the temple.

—Isaiah 6:1

BEHIND THE SONG

Before and during times of worship, Paul Baloche often found himself repeating a certain prayer that he had heard one of his favorite Bible teachers, the late Dr. Bruce Morgan, start each of his services with. "Lord," Morgan would pray, "as we look into your Word tonight we ask that you open the eyes of our hearts and help us to comprehend and understand your mysteries. Amen." Baloche would sing the words to that prayer, extemporaneously modifying them to fit the cadence of a song.

After noticing how frequently that prayer showed up in his own worship times, Baloche was inspired to craft it into a song. During one of his personal quiet times he started to prayerfully consider who in the Bible had actually seen God. His mind was drawn to the prophet Isaiah, so he turned to Isaiah 6 and read about the glorious vision he had of seeing heaven.

"Isaiah saw the Lord," Baloche explains, "who was high and lifted up." The text is translated into English as "I saw the Lord, high and exalted, seated on a throne; and the train of his robe filled the temple." With what Baloche refers to as "the heart's imagination," he began to meditate on that line. Wondering about the experience Isaiah must have had, Baloche translated Isaiah 6:1 into a simple chorus that might serve as a prayer that God would help his people see with their hearts what they can't necessarily see with their eyes.

"I didn't sit down to write a song to sing," Baloche insists. "It was just something for our church to sing as we were crying out to God."

Selah

One of the powerful aspects of worship is the opportunity to recalibrate your heart to resonate with the heart of God. It is good to simply ask God to open the eyes of our hearts as we enter into his presence. When you approach God's Word, try to begin with a simple prayer that the Holy Spirit will open your eyes and your heart to the truth contained in God's Word.

pursue the Philistines? Will you give them into Israel's hand?" But God did not answer him that day.

38 Saul therefore said, "Come here, all you who are leaders of the army, and let us find out what sin has been committed today. 39 As surely as the LORD who rescues Israel lives, even if the guilt lies with my son Jonathan, he must die." But not one of them said a word.

40 Saul then said to all the Israelites, "You stand over there; I and Jonathan my son will stand over here."

"Do what seems best to you," they replied.

41 Then Saul prayed to the LORD, the God of Israel, "Why have you not answered your servant today? If the fault is in me or my son Jonathan, respond with Urim, but if the men of Israel are at fault,[a] respond with Thummim." Jonathan and Saul were taken by lot, and the men were cleared. 42 Saul said, "Cast the lot between me and Jonathan my son." And Jonathan was taken.

43 Then Saul said to Jonathan, "Tell me what you have done."

So Jonathan told him, "I tasted a little honey with the end of my staff. And now I must die!"

44 Saul said, "May God deal with me, be it ever so severely, if you do not die, Jonathan."

45 But the men said to Saul, "Should Jonathan die — he who has brought about this great deliverance in Israel? Never! As surely as the LORD lives, not a hair of his head will fall to the ground, for he did this today with God's help." So the men rescued Jonathan, and he was not put to death.

46 Then Saul stopped pursuing the Philistines, and they withdrew to their own land.

47 After Saul had assumed rule over Israel, he fought against their enemies on every side: Moab, the Ammonites, Edom, the kings[b] of Zobah, and the Philistines. Wherever he turned, he inflicted punishment on them.[c] 48 He fought valiantly and defeated the Amalekites, delivering Israel from the hands of those who had plundered them.

Saul's Family

49 Saul's sons were Jonathan, Ishvi and Malki-Shua. The name of his older daughter was Merab, and that of the younger was Michal. 50 His wife's name was Ahinoam daughter of Ahimaaz. The name of the commander of Saul's army was Abner son of Ner, and Ner was Saul's uncle. 51 Saul's father Kish and Abner's father Ner were sons of Abiel.

52 All the days of Saul there was bitter war with the Philistines, and whenever Saul saw a mighty or brave man, he took him into his service.

The LORD Rejects Saul as King

15 Samuel said to Saul, "I am the one the LORD sent to anoint you king over his people Israel; so listen now to the message from the LORD. 2 This is what the LORD Almighty says: 'I will punish the Amalekites for what they did to Israel when they waylaid them as they came up from Egypt. 3 Now go, attack the Amalekites and totally destroy[d] all that belongs to them. Do not spare them; put to death men and women, children and infants, cattle and sheep, camels and donkeys.'"

4 So Saul summoned the men and mustered them at Telaim — two hundred thousand foot soldiers and ten thousand from Judah. 5 Saul went to the city of Amalek and set an ambush in the ravine. 6 Then he said to the Kenites, "Go away, leave the Amalekites so that I do not destroy you along with them; for you showed kindness to all the Israelites when they came up out of Egypt." So the Kenites moved away from the Amalekites.

7 Then Saul attacked the Amalekites all the way from Havilah to Shur, near the eastern border of Egypt. 8 He took Agag king of the Amalekites alive, and all his people he totally destroyed with the sword. 9 But Saul and the army spared Agag and the best of the sheep and cattle, the fat calves[e] and lambs — everything that was good. These they were unwilling to destroy completely, but everything that was despised and weak they totally destroyed.

10 Then the word of the LORD came to Samuel: 11 "I regret that I have made Saul king, because he has turned away from me and has not carried out my instructions."

[a] 41 Septuagint; Hebrew does not have *"Why . . . at fault.* [b] 47 Masoretic Text; Dead Sea Scrolls and Septuagint *king* [c] 47 Hebrew; Septuagint *he was victorious* [d] 3 The Hebrew term refers to the irrevocable giving over of things or persons to the LORD, often by totally destroying them; also in verses 8, 9, 15, 18, 20 and 21. [e] 9 Or *the grown bulls*; the meaning of the Hebrew for this phrase is uncertain.

Samuel was angry, and he cried out to the LORD all that night.

12 Early in the morning Samuel got up and went to meet Saul, but he was told, "Saul has gone to Carmel. There he has set up a monument in his own honor and has turned and gone on down to Gilgal."

13 When Samuel reached him, Saul said, "The LORD bless you! I have carried out the LORD's instructions."

14 But Samuel said, "What then is this bleating of sheep in my ears? What is this lowing of cattle that I hear?"

15 Saul answered, "The soldiers brought them from the Amalekites; they spared the best of the sheep and cattle to sacrifice to the LORD your God, but we totally destroyed the rest."

16 "Enough!" Samuel said to Saul. "Let me tell you what the LORD said to me last night."

"Tell me," Saul replied.

17 Samuel said, "Although you were once small in your own eyes, did you not become the head of the tribes of Israel? The LORD anointed you king over Israel. 18 And he sent you on a mission, saying, 'Go and completely destroy those wicked people, the Amalekites; wage war against them until you have wiped them out.' 19 Why did you not obey the LORD? Why did you pounce on the plunder and do evil in the eyes of the LORD?"

20 "But I did obey the LORD," Saul said. "I went on the mission the LORD assigned me. I completely destroyed the Amalekites and brought back Agag their king. 21 The soldiers took sheep and cattle from the plunder, the best of what was devoted to God, in order to sacrifice them to the LORD your God at Gilgal."

22 But Samuel replied:

"Does the LORD delight in burnt offerings
and sacrifices
as much as in obeying the LORD?
To obey is better than sacrifice,
and to heed is better than the fat of
rams.
23 For rebellion is like the sin of
divination,
and arrogance like the evil of idolatry.
Because you have rejected the word of
the LORD,
he has rejected you as king."

24 Then Saul said to Samuel, "I have sinned. I violated the LORD's command and your instructions. I was afraid of the men and so I gave in to them. 25 Now I beg you, forgive my sin and come back with me, so that I may worship the LORD."

26 But Samuel said to him, "I will not go back with you. You have rejected the word of the LORD, and the LORD has rejected you as king over Israel!"

27 As Samuel turned to leave, Saul caught hold of the hem of his robe, and it tore. 28 Samuel said to him, "The LORD has torn the kingdom of Israel from you today and has given it to one of your neighbors—to one better than you. 29 He who is the Glory of Israel does not lie or change his mind; for he is not a human being, that he should change his mind."

30 Saul replied, "I have sinned. But please honor me before the elders of my people and before Israel; come back with me, so that I may worship the LORD your God." 31 So Samuel went back with Saul, and Saul worshiped the LORD.

32 Then Samuel said, "Bring me Agag king of the Amalekites."

Agag came to him in chains.[a] And he thought, "Surely the bitterness of death is past."

33 But Samuel said,

"As your sword has made women
childless,
so will your mother be childless
among women."

And Samuel put Agag to death before the LORD at Gilgal.

34 Then Samuel left for Ramah, but Saul went up to his home in Gibeah of Saul. 35 Until the day Samuel died, he did not go to see Saul again, though Samuel mourned for him. And the LORD regretted that he had made Saul king over Israel.

Samuel Anoints David

16 The LORD said to Samuel, "How long will you mourn for Saul, since I have rejected him as king over Israel? Fill your horn with oil and be on your way; I am sending you to Jesse of Bethlehem. I have chosen one of his sons to be king."

[a] *32* The meaning of the Hebrew for this phrase is uncertain.

2But Samuel said, "How can I go? If Saul hears about it, he will kill me."

The LORD said, "Take a heifer with you and say, 'I have come to sacrifice to the LORD.' 3Invite Jesse to the sacrifice, and I will show you what to do. You are to anoint for me the one I indicate."

4Samuel did what the LORD said. When he arrived at Bethlehem, the elders of the town trembled when they met him. They asked, "Do you come in peace?"

5Samuel replied, "Yes, in peace; I have come to sacrifice to the LORD. Consecrate yourselves and come to the sacrifice with me." Then he consecrated Jesse and his sons and invited them to the sacrifice.

6When they arrived, Samuel saw Eliab and thought, "Surely the LORD's anointed stands here before the LORD."

7But the LORD said to Samuel, "Do not consider his appearance or his height, for I have rejected him. The LORD does not look at the things people look at. People look at the outward appearance, but the LORD looks at the heart."

8Then Jesse called Abinadab and had him pass in front of Samuel. But Samuel said, "The LORD has not chosen this one either." 9Jesse then had Shammah pass by, but Samuel said, "Nor has the LORD chosen this one." 10Jesse had seven of his sons pass before Samuel, but Samuel said to him, "The LORD has not chosen these." 11So he asked Jesse, "Are these all the sons you have?"

"There is still the youngest," Jesse answered. "He is tending the sheep."

Samuel said, "Send for him; we will not sit down until he arrives."

12So he sent for him and had him brought in. He was glowing with health and had a fine appearance and handsome features.

Then the LORD said, "Rise and anoint him; this is the one."

13So Samuel took the horn of oil and anointed him in the presence of his brothers, and from that day on the Spirit of the LORD came powerfully upon David. Samuel then went to Ramah.

David in Saul's Service

14Now the Spirit of the LORD had departed from Saul, and an evil[a] spirit from the LORD tormented him.

15Saul's attendants said to him, "See, an evil spirit from God is tormenting you. 16Let our lord command his servants here to search for someone who can play the lyre. He will play when the evil spirit from God comes on you, and you will feel better."

17So Saul said to his attendants, "Find someone who plays well and bring him to me."

18One of the servants answered, "I have seen a son of Jesse of Bethlehem who knows how to play the lyre. He is a brave man and a warrior. He speaks well and is a fine-looking man. And the LORD is with him."

19Then Saul sent messengers to Jesse and said, "Send me your son David, who is with the sheep." 20So Jesse took a donkey loaded with bread, a skin of wine and a young goat and sent them with his son David to Saul.

21David came to Saul and entered his service. Saul liked him very much, and David became one of his armor-bearers. 22Then Saul sent word to Jesse, saying, "Allow David to remain in my service, for I am pleased with him."

23Whenever the spirit from God came on Saul, David would take up his lyre and play. Then relief would come to Saul; he would feel better, and the evil spirit would leave him.

David and Goliath

17 Now the Philistines gathered their forces for war and assembled at Sokoh in Judah. They pitched camp at Ephes Dammim, between Sokoh and Azekah. 2Saul and the Israelites assembled and camped in the Valley of Elah and drew up their battle line to meet the Philistines. 3The Philistines occupied one hill and the Israelites another, with the valley between them.

4A champion named Goliath, who was from Gath, came out of the Philistine camp. His height was six cubits and a span.[b] 5He had a bronze helmet on his head and wore a coat of scale armor of bronze weighing five thousand shekels[c]; 6on his legs he wore bronze greaves, and a bronze javelin was slung on his back. 7His spear shaft was like a weaver's rod, and its iron point weighed six hundred shekels.[d] His shield bearer went ahead of him.

[a] 14 Or *and a harmful*; similarly in verses 15, 16 and 23
[b] 4 That is, about 9 feet 9 inches or about 3 meters
[c] 5 That is, about 125 pounds or about 58 kilograms
[d] 7 That is, about 15 pounds or about 6.9 kilograms

8 Goliath stood and shouted to the ranks of Israel, "Why do you come out and line up for battle? Am I not a Philistine, and are you not the servants of Saul? Choose a man and have him come down to me. 9 If he is able to fight and kill me, we will become your subjects; but if I overcome him and kill him, you will become our subjects and serve us." 10 Then the Philistine said, "This day I defy the armies of Israel! Give me a man and let us fight each other." 11 On hearing the Philistine's words, Saul and all the Israelites were dismayed and terrified.

12 Now David was the son of an Ephrathite named Jesse, who was from Bethlehem in Judah. Jesse had eight sons, and in Saul's time he was very old. 13 Jesse's three oldest sons had followed Saul to the war: The firstborn was Eliab; the second, Abinadab; and the third, Shammah. 14 David was the youngest. The three oldest followed Saul, 15 but David went back and forth from Saul to tend his father's sheep at Bethlehem.

16 For forty days the Philistine came forward every morning and evening and took his stand.

17 Now Jesse said to his son David, "Take this ephah[a] of roasted grain and these ten loaves of bread for your brothers and hurry to their camp. 18 Take along these ten cheeses to the commander of their unit. See how your brothers are and bring back some assurance[b] from them. 19 They are with Saul and all the men of Israel in the Valley of Elah, fighting against the Philistines."

20 Early in the morning David left the flock in the care of a shepherd, loaded up and set out, as Jesse had directed. He reached the camp as the army was going out to its battle positions, shouting the war cry. 21 Israel and the Philistines were drawing up their lines facing each other. 22 David left his things with the keeper of supplies, ran to the battle lines and asked his brothers how they were. 23 As he was talking with them, Goliath, the Philistine champion from Gath, stepped out from his lines and shouted his usual defiance, and David heard it. 24 Whenever the Israelites saw the man, they all fled from him in great fear.

25 Now the Israelites had been saying, "Do you see how this man keeps coming out? He comes out to defy Israel. The king will give great wealth to the man who kills him. He will also give him his daughter in marriage and will exempt his family from taxes in Israel."

26 David asked the men standing near him, "What will be done for the man who kills this Philistine and removes this disgrace from Israel? Who is this uncircumcised Philistine that he should defy the armies of the living God?"

27 They repeated to him what they had been saying and told him, "This is what will be done for the man who kills him."

28 When Eliab, David's oldest brother, heard him speaking with the men, he burned with anger at him and asked, "Why have you come down here? And with whom did you leave those few sheep in the wilderness? I know how conceited you are and how wicked your heart is; you came down only to watch the battle."

29 "Now what have I done?" said David. "Can't I even speak?" 30 He then turned away to someone else and brought up the same matter, and the men answered him as before. 31 What David said was overheard and reported to Saul, and Saul sent for him.

32 David said to Saul, "Let no one lose heart on account of this Philistine; your servant will go and fight him."

33 Saul replied, "You are not able to go out against this Philistine and fight him; you are only a young man, and he has been a warrior from his youth."

34 But David said to Saul, "Your servant has been keeping his father's sheep. When a lion or a bear came and carried off a sheep from the flock, 35 I went after it, struck it and rescued the sheep from its mouth. When it turned on me, I seized it by its hair, struck it and killed it. 36 Your servant has killed both the lion and the bear; this uncircumcised Philistine will be like one of them, because he has defied the armies of the living God. 37 The LORD who rescued me from the paw of the lion and the paw of the bear will rescue me from the hand of this Philistine."

Saul said to David, "Go, and the LORD be with you."

38 Then Saul dressed David in his own tunic. He put a coat of armor on him and

[a] *17* That is, probably about 36 pounds or about 16 kilograms [b] *18* Or *some token*; or *some pledge of spoils*

a bronze helmet on his head. 39 David fas-
tened on his sword over the tunic and tried
walking around, because he was not used to
them.
“I cannot go in these,” he said to Saul,
“because I am not used to them.” So he took
them off. 40 Then he took his staff in his hand,
chose five smooth stones from the stream,
put them in the pouch of his shepherd’s bag
and, with his sling in his hand, approached
the Philistine.
41 Meanwhile, the Philistine, with his
shield bearer in front of him, kept com-
ing closer to David. 42 He looked David over
and saw that he was little more than a boy,
glowing with health and handsome, and he
despised him. 43 He said to David, “Am I a
dog, that you come at me with sticks?” And
the Philistine cursed David by his gods.
44 “Come here,” he said, “and I’ll give your
flesh to the birds and the wild animals!”
45 David said to the Philistine, “You come
against me with sword and spear and jav-
elin, but I come against you in the name of
the LORD Almighty, the God of the armies
of Israel, whom you have defied. 46 This day
the LORD will deliver you into my hands,
and I’ll strike you down and cut off your
head. This very day I will give the carcass-
es of the Philistine army to the birds and the
wild animals, and the whole world will know
that there is a God in Israel. 47 All those gath-
ered here will know that it is not by sword
or spear that the LORD saves; for the battle
is the LORD’s, and he will give all of you into
our hands.”
48 As the Philistine moved closer to attack
him, David ran quickly toward the battle
line to meet him. 49 Reaching into his bag
and taking out a stone, he slung it and struck
the Philistine on the forehead. The stone
sank into his forehead, and he fell facedown
on the ground.
50 So David triumphed over the Philistine
with a sling and a stone; without a sword in
his hand he struck down the Philistine and
killed him.
51 David ran and stood over him. He took
hold of the Philistine’s sword and drew it
from the sheath. After he killed him, he cut
off his head with the sword.
When the Philistines saw that their hero
was dead, they turned and ran. 52 Then the
men of Israel and Judah surged forward with
a shout and pursued the Philistines to the
entrance of Gath[a] and to the gates of Ekron.
Their dead were strewn along the Shaaraim
road to Gath and Ekron. 53 When the Israel-
ites returned from chasing the Philistines,
they plundered their camp.
54 David took the Philistine’s head and
brought it to Jerusalem; he put the Philis-
tine’s weapons in his own tent.
55 As Saul watched David going out to
meet the Philistine, he said to Abner, com-
mander of the army, “Abner, whose son is
that young man?”
Abner replied, “As surely as you live, Your
Majesty, I don’t know.”
56 The king said, “Find out whose son this
young man is.”
57 As soon as David returned from killing
the Philistine, Abner took him and brought
him before Saul, with David still holding the
Philistine’s head.
58 “Whose son are you, young man?” Saul
asked him.
David said, “I am the son of your servant
Jesse of Bethlehem.”

Saul’s Growing Fear of David

18 After David had finished talking
with Saul, Jonathan became one
in spirit with David, and he loved him as
himself. 2 From that day Saul kept David
with him and did not let him return home
to his family. 3 And Jonathan made a cov-
enant with David because he loved him as
himself. 4 Jonathan took off the robe he was
wearing and gave it to David, along with his
tunic, and even his sword, his bow and his
belt.
5 Whatever mission Saul sent him on, Da-
vid was so successful that Saul gave him a
high rank in the army. This pleased all the
troops, and Saul’s officers as well.
6 When the men were returning home af-
ter David had killed the Philistine, the wom-
en came out from all the towns of Israel to
meet King Saul with singing and dancing,
with joyful songs and with timbrels and
lyres. 7 As they danced, they sang:

“Saul has slain his thousands,
and David his tens of thousands.”

[a] 52 Some Septuagint manuscripts; Hebrew *of a valley*

8 Saul was very angry; this refrain displeased him greatly. "They have credited David with tens of thousands," he thought, "but me with only thousands. What more can he get but the kingdom?" 9 And from that time on Saul kept a close eye on David.

10 The next day an evil[a] spirit from God came forcefully on Saul. He was prophesying in his house, while David was playing the lyre, as he usually did. Saul had a spear in his hand 11 and he hurled it, saying to himself, "I'll pin David to the wall." But David eluded him twice.

12 Saul was afraid of David, because the LORD was with David but had departed from Saul. 13 So he sent David away from him and gave him command over a thousand men, and David led the troops in their campaigns. 14 In everything he did he had great success, because the LORD was with him. 15 When Saul saw how successful he was, he was afraid of him. 16 But all Israel and Judah loved David, because he led them in their campaigns.

17 Saul said to David, "Here is my older daughter Merab. I will give her to you in marriage; only serve me bravely and fight the battles of the LORD." For Saul said to himself, "I will not raise a hand against him. Let the Philistines do that!"

18 But David said to Saul, "Who am I, and what is my family or my clan in Israel, that I should become the king's son-in-law?" 19 So[b] when the time came for Merab, Saul's daughter, to be given to David, she was given in marriage to Adriel of Meholah.

20 Now Saul's daughter Michal was in love with David, and when they told Saul about it, he was pleased. 21 "I will give her to him," he thought, "so that she may be a snare to him and so that the hand of the Philistines may be against him." So Saul said to David, "Now you have a second opportunity to become my son-in-law."

22 Then Saul ordered his attendants: "Speak to David privately and say, 'Look, the king likes you, and his attendants all love you; now become his son-in-law.' "

23 They repeated these words to David. But David said, "Do you think it is a small matter to become the king's son-in-law? I'm only a poor man and little known."

24 When Saul's servants told him what David had said, 25 Saul replied, "Say to David, 'The king wants no other price for the bride than a hundred Philistine foreskins, to take revenge on his enemies.' " Saul's plan was to have David fall by the hands of the Philistines.

26 When the attendants told David these things, he was pleased to become the king's son-in-law. So before the allotted time elapsed, 27 David took his men with him and went out and killed two hundred Philistines and brought back their foreskins. They counted out the full number to the king so that David might become the king's son-in-law. Then Saul gave him his daughter Michal in marriage.

28 When Saul realized that the LORD was with David and that his daughter Michal loved David, 29 Saul became still more afraid of him, and he remained his enemy the rest of his days.

30 The Philistine commanders continued to go out to battle, and as often as they did, David met with more success than the rest of Saul's officers, and his name became well known.

Saul Tries to Kill David

19 Saul told his son Jonathan and all the attendants to kill David. But Jonathan had taken a great liking to David 2 and warned him, "My father Saul is looking for a chance to kill you. Be on your guard tomorrow morning; go into hiding and stay there. 3 I will go out and stand with my father in the field where you are. I'll speak to him about you and will tell you what I find out."

4 Jonathan spoke well of David to Saul his father and said to him, "Let not the king do wrong to his servant David; he has not wronged you, and what he has done has benefited you greatly. 5 He took his life in his hands when he killed the Philistine. The LORD won a great victory for all Israel, and you saw it and were glad. Why then would you do wrong to an innocent man like David by killing him for no reason?"

6 Saul listened to Jonathan and took this oath: "As surely as the LORD lives, David will not be put to death."

7 So Jonathan called David and told him

[a] 10 Or *a harmful* [b] 19 Or *However,*

the whole conversation. He brought him to Saul, and David was with Saul as before.

[8]Once more war broke out, and David went out and fought the Philistines. He struck them with such force that they fled before him.

[9]But an evil[a] spirit from the LORD came on Saul as he was sitting in his house with his spear in his hand. While David was playing the lyre, [10]Saul tried to pin him to the wall with his spear, but David eluded him as Saul drove the spear into the wall. That night David made good his escape.

[11]Saul sent men to David's house to watch it and to kill him in the morning. But Michal, David's wife, warned him, "If you don't run for your life tonight, tomorrow you'll be killed." [12]So Michal let David down through a window, and he fled and escaped. [13]Then Michal took an idol and laid it on the bed, covering it with a garment and putting some goats' hair at the head.

[14]When Saul sent the men to capture David, Michal said, "He is ill."

[15]Then Saul sent the men back to see David and told them, "Bring him up to me in his bed so that I may kill him." [16]But when the men entered, there was the idol in the bed, and at the head was some goats' hair.

[17]Saul said to Michal, "Why did you deceive me like this and send my enemy away so that he escaped?"

Michal told him, "He said to me, 'Let me get away. Why should I kill you?' "

[18]When David had fled and made his escape, he went to Samuel at Ramah and told him all that Saul had done to him. Then he and Samuel went to Naioth and stayed there. [19]Word came to Saul: "David is in Naioth at Ramah"; [20]so he sent men to capture him. But when they saw a group of prophets prophesying, with Samuel standing there as their leader, the Spirit of God came on Saul's men, and they also prophesied. [21]Saul was told about it, and he sent more men, and they prophesied too. Saul sent men a third time, and they also prophesied. [22]Finally, he himself left for Ramah and went to the great cistern at Seku. And he asked, "Where are Samuel and David?"

"Over in Naioth at Ramah," they said.

[23]So Saul went to Naioth at Ramah. But the Spirit of God came even on him, and he walked along prophesying until he came to Naioth. [24]He stripped off his garments, and he too prophesied in Samuel's presence. He lay naked all that day and all that night. This is why people say, "Is Saul also among the prophets?"

David and Jonathan

20 Then David fled from Naioth at Ramah and went to Jonathan and asked, "What have I done? What is my crime? How have I wronged your father, that he is trying to kill me?"

[2]"Never!" Jonathan replied. "You are not going to die! Look, my father doesn't do anything, great or small, without letting me know. Why would he hide this from me? It isn't so!"

[3]But David took an oath and said, "Your father knows very well that I have found favor in your eyes, and he has said to himself, 'Jonathan must not know this or he will be grieved.' Yet as surely as the LORD lives and as you live, there is only a step between me and death."

[4]Jonathan said to David, "Whatever you want me to do, I'll do for you."

[5]So David said, "Look, tomorrow is the New Moon feast, and I am supposed to dine with the king; but let me go and hide in the field until the evening of the day after tomorrow. [6]If your father misses me at all, tell him, 'David earnestly asked my permission to hurry to Bethlehem, his hometown, because an annual sacrifice is being made there for his whole clan.' [7]If he says, 'Very well,' then your servant is safe. But if he loses his temper, you can be sure that he is determined to harm me. [8]As for you, show kindness to your servant, for you have brought him into a covenant with you before the LORD. If I am guilty, then kill me yourself! Why hand me over to your father?"

[9]"Never!" Jonathan said. "If I had the least inkling that my father was determined to harm you, wouldn't I tell you?"

[10]David asked, "Who will tell me if your father answers you harshly?"

[11]"Come," Jonathan said, "let's go out into the field." So they went there together.

[12]Then Jonathan said to David, "I swear

[a] 9 Or *But a harmful*

by the LORD, the God of Israel, that I will
surely sound out my father by this time the
day after tomorrow! If he is favorably dis-
posed toward you, will I not send you word
and let you know? 13 But if my father intends
to harm you, may the LORD deal with Jona-
than, be it ever so severely, if I do not let you
know and send you away in peace. May the
LORD be with you as he has been with my fa-
ther. 14 But show me unfailing kindness like
the LORD's kindness as long as I live, so that
I may not be killed, 15 and do not ever cut off
your kindness from my family — not even
when the LORD has cut off every one of Da-
vid's enemies from the face of the earth."

16 So Jonathan made a covenant with the
house of David, saying, "May the LORD call
David's enemies to account." 17 And Jona-
than had David reaffirm his oath out of love
for him, because he loved him as he loved
himself.

18 Then Jonathan said to David, "To-
morrow is the New Moon feast. You will be
missed, because your seat will be empty.
19 The day after tomorrow, toward evening,
go to the place where you hid when this
trouble began, and wait by the stone Ezel.
20 I will shoot three arrows to the side of it, as
though I were shooting at a target. 21 Then I
will send a boy and say, 'Go, find the arrows.'
If I say to him, 'Look, the arrows are on this
side of you; bring them here,' then come, be-
cause, as surely as the LORD lives, you are
safe; there is no danger. 22 But if I say to the
boy, 'Look, the arrows are beyond you,' then
you must go, because the LORD has sent you
away. 23 And about the matter you and I dis-
cussed — remember, the LORD is witness be-
tween you and me forever."

24 So David hid in the field, and when the
New Moon feast came, the king sat down to
eat. 25 He sat in his customary place by the
wall, opposite Jonathan,[a] and Abner sat next
to Saul, but David's place was empty. 26 Saul
said nothing that day, for he thought, "Some-
thing must have happened to David to make
him ceremonially unclean — surely he is un-
clean." 27 But the next day, the second day of
the month, David's place was empty again.
Then Saul said to his son Jonathan, "Why
hasn't the son of Jesse come to the meal, ei-
ther yesterday or today?"

28 Jonathan answered, "David earnestly
asked me for permission to go to Bethlehem.
29 He said, 'Let me go, because our family
is observing a sacrifice in the town and my
brother has ordered me to be there. If I have
found favor in your eyes, let me get away
to see my brothers.' That is why he has not
come to the king's table."

30 Saul's anger flared up at Jonathan and
he said to him, "You son of a perverse and
rebellious woman! Don't I know that you
have sided with the son of Jesse to your own
shame and to the shame of the mother who
bore you? 31 As long as the son of Jesse lives
on this earth, neither you nor your kingdom
will be established. Now send someone to
bring him to me, for he must die!"

32 "Why should he be put to death? What
has he done?" Jonathan asked his father.
33 But Saul hurled his spear at him to kill
him. Then Jonathan knew that his father in-
tended to kill David.

34 Jonathan got up from the table in fierce
anger; on that second day of the feast he did
not eat, because he was grieved at his fa-
ther's shameful treatment of David.

35 In the morning Jonathan went out to
the field for his meeting with David. He had
a small boy with him, 36 and he said to the
boy, "Run and find the arrows I shoot." As
the boy ran, he shot an arrow beyond him.
37 When the boy came to the place where
Jonathan's arrow had fallen, Jonathan
called out after him, "Isn't the arrow beyond
you?" 38 Then he shouted, "Hurry! Go quick-
ly! Don't stop!" The boy picked up the ar-
row and returned to his master. 39 (The boy
knew nothing about all this; only Jonathan
and David knew.) 40 Then Jonathan gave
his weapons to the boy and said, "Go, carry
them back to town."

41 After the boy had gone, David got up
from the south side of the stone and bowed
down before Jonathan three times, with his
face to the ground. Then they kissed each
other and wept together — but David wept
the most.

42 Jonathan said to David, "Go in peace, for
we have sworn friendship with each other in
the name of the LORD, saying, 'The LORD is
witness between you and me, and between
your descendants and my descendants

[a] 25 Septuagint; Hebrew *wall. Jonathan arose*

forever.' " Then David left, and Jonathan went back to the town.[a]

David at Nob

21 [b] David went to Nob, to Ahimelek the priest. Ahimelek trembled when he met him, and asked, "Why are you alone? Why is no one with you?"

2 David answered Ahimelek the priest, "The king sent me on a mission and said to me, 'No one is to know anything about the mission I am sending you on.' As for my men, I have told them to meet me at a certain place. 3 Now then, what do you have on hand? Give me five loaves of bread, or whatever you can find."

4 But the priest answered David, "I don't have any ordinary bread on hand; however, there is some consecrated bread here — provided the men have kept themselves from women."

5 David replied, "Indeed women have been kept from us, as usual whenever[c] I set out. The men's bodies are holy even on missions that are not holy. How much more so today!" 6 So the priest gave him the consecrated bread, since there was no bread there except the bread of the Presence that had been removed from before the LORD and replaced by hot bread on the day it was taken away.

7 Now one of Saul's servants was there that day, detained before the LORD; he was Doeg the Edomite, Saul's chief shepherd.

8 David asked Ahimelek, "Don't you have a spear or a sword here? I haven't brought my sword or any other weapon, because the king's mission was urgent."

9 The priest replied, "The sword of Goliath the Philistine, whom you killed in the Valley of Elah, is here; it is wrapped in a cloth behind the ephod. If you want it, take it; there is no sword here but that one."

David said, "There is none like it; give it to me."

David at Gath

10 That day David fled from Saul and went to Achish king of Gath. 11 But the servants of Achish said to him, "Isn't this David, the king of the land? Isn't he the one they sing about in their dances:

" 'Saul has slain his thousands,
and David his tens of thousands'?"

12 David took these words to heart and was very much afraid of Achish king of Gath. 13 So he pretended to be insane in their presence; and while he was in their hands he acted like a madman, making marks on the doors of the gate and letting saliva run down his beard.

14 Achish said to his servants, "Look at the man! He is insane! Why bring him to me? 15 Am I so short of madmen that you have to bring this fellow here to carry on like this in front of me? Must this man come into my house?"

David at Adullam and Mizpah

22 David left Gath and escaped to the cave of Adullam. When his brothers and his father's household heard about it, they went down to him there. 2 All those who were in distress or in debt or discontented gathered around him, and he became their commander. About four hundred men were with him.

3 From there David went to Mizpah in Moab and said to the king of Moab, "Would you let my father and mother come and stay with you until I learn what God will do for me?" 4 So he left them with the king of Moab, and they stayed with him as long as David was in the stronghold.

5 But the prophet Gad said to David, "Do not stay in the stronghold. Go into the land of Judah." So David left and went to the forest of Hereth.

Saul Kills the Priests of Nob

6 Now Saul heard that David and his men had been discovered. And Saul was seated, spear in hand, under the tamarisk tree on the hill at Gibeah, with all his officials standing at his side. 7 He said to them, "Listen, men of Benjamin! Will the son of Jesse give all of you fields and vineyards? Will he make all of you commanders of thousands and commanders of hundreds? 8 Is that why you have all conspired against me? No one tells me when my son makes a covenant with the son of Jesse. None of you is concerned about me or tells me that my son has

[a] *42* In Hebrew texts this sentence (20:42b) is numbered 21:1. [b] In Hebrew texts 21:1-15 is numbered 21:2-16. [c] *5* Or *from us in the past few days since*

incited my servant to lie in wait for me, as he does today."

9 But Doeg the Edomite, who was standing with Saul's officials, said, "I saw the son of Jesse come to Ahimelek son of Ahitub at Nob. 10 Ahimelek inquired of the LORD for him; he also gave him provisions and the sword of Goliath the Philistine."

11 Then the king sent for the priest Ahimelek son of Ahitub and all the men of his family, who were the priests at Nob, and they all came to the king. 12 Saul said, "Listen now, son of Ahitub."

"Yes, my lord," he answered.

13 Saul said to him, "Why have you conspired against me, you and the son of Jesse, giving him bread and a sword and inquiring of God for him, so that he has rebelled against me and lies in wait for me, as he does today?"

14 Ahimelek answered the king, "Who of all your servants is as loyal as David the king's son-in-law, captain of your bodyguard and highly respected in your household? 15 Was that day the first time I inquired of God for him? Of course not! Let not the king accuse your servant or any of his father's family, for your servant knows nothing at all about this whole affair."

16 But the king said, "You will surely die, Ahimelek, you and your whole family."

17 Then the king ordered the guards at his side: "Turn and kill the priests of the LORD, because they too have sided with David. They knew he was fleeing, yet they did not tell me."

But the king's officials were unwilling to raise a hand to strike the priests of the LORD.

18 The king then ordered Doeg, "You turn and strike down the priests." So Doeg the Edomite turned and struck them down. That day he killed eighty-five men who wore the linen ephod. 19 He also put to the sword Nob, the town of the priests, with its men and women, its children and infants, and its cattle, donkeys and sheep.

20 But one son of Ahimelek son of Ahitub, named Abiathar, escaped and fled to join David. 21 He told David that Saul had killed the priests of the LORD. 22 Then David said to Abiathar, "That day, when Doeg the Edomite was there, I knew he would be sure to tell Saul. I am responsible for the death of your whole family. 23 Stay with me; don't be afraid. The man who wants to kill you is trying to kill me too. You will be safe with me."

David Saves Keilah

23 When David was told, "Look, the Philistines are fighting against Keilah and are looting the threshing floors," 2 he inquired of the LORD, saying, "Shall I go and attack these Philistines?"

The LORD answered him, "Go, attack the Philistines and save Keilah."

3 But David's men said to him, "Here in Judah we are afraid. How much more, then, if we go to Keilah against the Philistine forces!"

4 Once again David inquired of the LORD, and the LORD answered him, "Go down to Keilah, for I am going to give the Philistines into your hand." 5 So David and his men went to Keilah, fought the Philistines and carried off their livestock. He inflicted heavy losses on the Philistines and saved the people of Keilah. 6 (Now Abiathar son of Ahimelek had brought the ephod down with him when he fled to David at Keilah.)

Saul Pursues David

7 Saul was told that David had gone to Keilah, and he said, "God has delivered him into my hands, for David has imprisoned himself by entering a town with gates and bars." 8 And Saul called up all his forces for battle, to go down to Keilah to besiege David and his men.

9 When David learned that Saul was plotting against him, he said to Abiathar the priest, "Bring the ephod." 10 David said, "LORD, God of Israel, your servant has heard definitely that Saul plans to come to Keilah and destroy the town on account of me. 11 Will the citizens of Keilah surrender me to him? Will Saul come down, as your servant has heard? LORD, God of Israel, tell your servant."

And the LORD said, "He will."

12 Again David asked, "Will the citizens of Keilah surrender me and my men to Saul?"

And the LORD said, "They will."

13 So David and his men, about six hundred in number, left Keilah and kept moving from place to place. When Saul was told that David had escaped from Keilah, he did not go there.

14 David stayed in the wilderness strongholds and in the hills of the Desert of Ziph. Day after day Saul searched for him, but God did not give David into his hands.

[15]While David was at Horesh in the Desert of Ziph, he learned that[a] Saul had come out to take his life. [16]And Saul's son Jonathan went to David at Horesh and helped him find strength in God. [17]"Don't be afraid," he said. "My father Saul will not lay a hand on you. You will be king over Israel, and I will be second to you. Even my father Saul knows this." [18]The two of them made a covenant before the LORD. Then Jonathan went home, but David remained at Horesh.

[19]The Ziphites went up to Saul at Gibeah and said, "Is not David hiding among us in the strongholds at Horesh, on the hill of Hakilah, south of Jeshimon? [20]Now, Your Majesty, come down whenever it pleases you to do so, and we will be responsible for giving him into your hands."

[21]Saul replied, "The LORD bless you for your concern for me. [22]Go and get more information. Find out where David usually goes and who has seen him there. They tell me he is very crafty. [23]Find out about all the hiding places he uses and come back to me with definite information. Then I will go with you; if he is in the area, I will track him down among all the clans of Judah."

[24]So they set out and went to Ziph ahead of Saul. Now David and his men were in the Desert of Maon, in the Arabah south of Jeshimon. [25]Saul and his men began the search, and when David was told about it, he went down to the rock and stayed in the Desert of Maon. When Saul heard this, he went into the Desert of Maon in pursuit of David.

[26]Saul was going along one side of the mountain, and David and his men were on the other side, hurrying to get away from Saul. As Saul and his forces were closing in on David and his men to capture them, [27]a messenger came to Saul, saying, "Come quickly! The Philistines are raiding the land." [28]Then Saul broke off his pursuit of David and went to meet the Philistines. That is why they call this place Sela Hammahlekoth.[b] [29]And David went up from there and lived in the strongholds of En Gedi.[c]

David Spares Saul's Life

24[d] After Saul returned from pursuing the Philistines, he was told, "David is in the Desert of En Gedi." [2]So Saul took three thousand able young men from all Israel and set out to look for David and his men near the Crags of the Wild Goats.

[3]He came to the sheep pens along the way; a cave was there, and Saul went in to relieve himself. David and his men were far back in the cave. [4]The men said, "This is the day the LORD spoke of when he said[e] to you, 'I will give your enemy into your hands for you to deal with as you wish.' " Then David crept up unnoticed and cut off a corner of Saul's robe.

[5]Afterward, David was conscience-stricken for having cut off a corner of his robe. [6]He said to his men, "The LORD forbid that I should do such a thing to my master, the LORD's anointed, or lay my hand on him; for he is the anointed of the LORD." [7]With these words David sharply rebuked his men and did not allow them to attack Saul. And Saul left the cave and went his way.

[8]Then David went out of the cave and called out to Saul, "My lord the king!" When Saul looked behind him, David bowed down and prostrated himself with his face to the ground. [9]He said to Saul, "Why do you listen when men say, 'David is bent on harming you'? [10]This day you have seen with your own eyes how the LORD delivered you into my hands in the cave. Some urged me to kill you, but I spared you; I said, 'I will not lay my hand on my lord, because he is the LORD's anointed.' [11]See, my father, look at this piece of your robe in my hand! I cut off the corner of your robe but did not kill you. See that there is nothing in my hand to indicate that I am guilty of wrongdoing or rebellion. I have not wronged you, but you are hunting me down to take my life. [12]May the LORD judge between you and me. And may the LORD avenge the wrongs you have done to me, but my hand will not touch you. [13]As the old saying goes, 'From evildoers come evil deeds,' so my hand will not touch you.

[14]"Against whom has the king of Israel come out? Who are you pursuing? A dead dog? A flea? [15]May the LORD be our judge and decide between us. May he consider my cause and uphold it; may he vindicate me by delivering me from your hand."

[a] *15* Or *he was afraid because* [b] *28* *Sela Hammahlekoth* means *rock of parting.* [c] *29* In Hebrew texts this verse (23:29) is numbered 24:1. [d] In Hebrew texts 24:1-22 is numbered 24:2-23. [e] *4* Or *"Today the LORD is saying*

16When David finished saying this, Saul
asked, "Is that your voice, David my son?"
And he wept aloud. 17"You are more righ-
teous than I," he said. "You have treated me
well, but I have treated you badly. 18You have
just now told me about the good you did to
me; the LORD delivered me into your hands,
but you did not kill me. 19When a man finds
his enemy, does he let him get away un-
harmed? May the LORD reward you well for
the way you treated me today. 20I know that
you will surely be king and that the kingdom
of Israel will be established in your hands.
21Now swear to me by the LORD that you will
not kill off my descendants or wipe out my
name from my father's family."

22So David gave his oath to Saul. Then
Saul returned home, but David and his men
went up to the stronghold.

David, Nabal and Abigail

25 Now Samuel died, and all Israel as-
sembled and mourned for him, and
they buried him at his home in Ramah.
Then David moved down into the Desert of
Paran.[a]

2A certain man in Maon, who had proper-
ty there at Carmel, was very wealthy. He had
a thousand goats and three thousand sheep,
which he was shearing in Carmel. 3His name
was Nabal and his wife's name was Abigail.
She was an intelligent and beautiful woman,
but her husband was surly and mean in his
dealings — he was a Calebite.

4While David was in the wilderness, he
heard that Nabal was shearing sheep. 5So
he sent ten young men and said to them, "Go
up to Nabal at Carmel and greet him in my
name. 6Say to him: 'Long life to you! Good
health to you and your household! And good
health to all that is yours!

7" 'Now I hear that it is sheep-shearing
time. When your shepherds were with us, we
did not mistreat them, and the whole time
they were at Carmel nothing of theirs was
missing. 8Ask your own servants and they
will tell you. Therefore be favorable toward
my men, since we come at a festive time.
Please give your servants and your son Da-
vid whatever you can find for them.' "

9When David's men arrived, they gave
Nabal this message in David's name. Then
they waited.

10Nabal answered David's servants, "Who
is this David? Who is this son of Jesse? Many
servants are breaking away from their mas-
ters these days. 11Why should I take my
bread and water, and the meat I have slaugh-
tered for my shearers, and give it to men
coming from who knows where?"

12David's men turned around and went
back. When they arrived, they reported ev-
ery word. 13David said to his men, "Each of
you strap on your sword!" So they did, and
David strapped his on as well. About four
hundred men went up with David, while two
hundred stayed with the supplies.

14One of the servants told Abigail, Na-
bal's wife, "David sent messengers from the
wilderness to give our master his greetings,
but he hurled insults at them. 15Yet these
men were very good to us. They did not mis-
treat us, and the whole time we were out in
the fields near them nothing was missing.
16Night and day they were a wall around us
the whole time we were herding our sheep
near them. 17Now think it over and see what
you can do, because disaster is hanging over
our master and his whole household. He is
such a wicked man that no one can talk to
him."

18Abigail acted quickly. She took two hun-
dred loaves of bread, two skins of wine, five
dressed sheep, five seahs[b] of roasted grain,
a hundred cakes of raisins and two hundred
cakes of pressed figs, and loaded them on
donkeys. 19Then she told her servants, "Go
on ahead; I'll follow you." But she did not tell
her husband Nabal.

20As she came riding her donkey into a
mountain ravine, there were David and his
men descending toward her, and she met
them. 21David had just said, "It's been use-
less — all my watching over this fellow's
property in the wilderness so that nothing
of his was missing. He has paid me back evil
for good. 22May God deal with David,[c] be it
ever so severely, if by morning I leave alive
one male of all who belong to him!"

23When Abigail saw David, she quickly

[a] *1* Hebrew and some Septuagint manuscripts; other Septuagint manuscripts *Maon* [b] *18* That is, probably about 60 pounds or about 27 kilograms [c] *22* Some Septuagint manuscripts; Hebrew *with David's enemies*

got off her donkey and bowed down before
David with her face to the ground. 24She
fell at his feet and said: "Pardon your ser-
vant, my lord, and let me speak to you; hear
what your servant has to say. 25Please pay
no attention, my lord, to that wicked man
Nabal. He is just like his name—his name
means Fool, and folly goes with him. And as
for me, your servant, I did not see the men
my lord sent. 26And now, my lord, as surely
as the LORD your God lives and as you live,
since the LORD has kept you from blood-
shed and from avenging yourself with your
own hands, may your enemies and all who
are intent on harming my lord be like Nabal.
27And let this gift, which your servant has
brought to my lord, be given to the men who
follow you.

28"Please forgive your servant's presump-
tion. The LORD your God will certainly make
a lasting dynasty for my lord, because you
fight the LORD's battles, and no wrongdo-
ing will be found in you as long as you live.
29Even though someone is pursuing you
to take your life, the life of my lord will be
bound securely in the bundle of the living
by the LORD your God, but the lives of your
enemies he will hurl away as from the pock-
et of a sling. 30When the LORD has fulfilled
for my lord every good thing he promised
concerning him and has appointed him rul-
er over Israel, 31my lord will not have on his
conscience the staggering burden of need-
less bloodshed or of having avenged himself.
And when the LORD your God has brought
my lord success, remember your servant."

32David said to Abigail, "Praise be to the
LORD, the God of Israel, who has sent you
today to meet me. 33May you be blessed for
your good judgment and for keeping me
from bloodshed this day and from avenging
myself with my own hands. 34Otherwise, as
surely as the LORD, the God of Israel, lives,
who has kept me from harming you, if you
had not come quickly to meet me, not one
male belonging to Nabal would have been
left alive by daybreak."

35Then David accepted from her hand
what she had brought him and said, "Go
home in peace. I have heard your words and
granted your request."

36When Abigail went to Nabal, he was in
the house holding a banquet like that of a
king. He was in high spirits and very drunk.
So she told him nothing at all until day-
break. 37Then in the morning, when Nabal
was sober, his wife told him all these things,
and his heart failed him and he became like
a stone. 38About ten days later, the LORD
struck Nabal and he died.

39When David heard that Nabal was dead,
he said, "Praise be to the LORD, who has up-
held my cause against Nabal for treating
me with contempt. He has kept his servant
from doing wrong and has brought Nabal's
wrongdoing down on his own head."

Then David sent word to Abigail, ask-
ing her to become his wife. 40His servants
went to Carmel and said to Abigail, "David
has sent us to you to take you to become his
wife."

41She bowed down with her face to the
ground and said, "I am your servant and
am ready to serve you and wash the feet of
my lord's servants." 42Abigail quickly got on
a donkey and, attended by her five female
servants, went with David's messengers and
became his wife. 43David had also married
Ahinoam of Jezreel, and they both were his
wives. 44But Saul had given his daughter Mi-
chal, David's wife, to Paltiel[a] son of Laish,
who was from Gallim.

David Again Spares Saul's Life

26 The Ziphites went to Saul at Gibeah
and said, "Is not David hiding on the
hill of Hakilah, which faces Jeshimon?"

2So Saul went down to the Desert of Ziph,
with his three thousand select Israelite
troops, to search there for David. 3Saul made
his camp beside the road on the hill of Ha-
kilah facing Jeshimon, but David stayed in
the wilderness. When he saw that Saul had
followed him there, 4he sent out scouts and
learned that Saul had definitely arrived.

5Then David set out and went to the place
where Saul had camped. He saw where Saul
and Abner son of Ner, the commander of the
army, had lain down. Saul was lying inside
the camp, with the army encamped around
him.

6David then asked Ahimelek the Hittite
and Abishai son of Zeruiah, Joab's brother,
"Who will go down into the camp with me
to Saul?"

[a] *44* Hebrew *Palti,* a variant of *Paltiel*

"I'll go with you," said Abishai.

7So David and Abishai went to the army by night, and there was Saul, lying asleep inside the camp with his spear stuck in the ground near his head. Abner and the soldiers were lying around him.

8Abishai said to David, "Today God has delivered your enemy into your hands. Now let me pin him to the ground with one thrust of the spear; I won't strike him twice."

9But David said to Abishai, "Don't destroy him! Who can lay a hand on the LORD's anointed and be guiltless? 10As surely as the LORD lives," he said, "the LORD himself will strike him, or his time will come and he will die, or he will go into battle and perish. 11But the LORD forbid that I should lay a hand on the LORD's anointed. Now get the spear and water jug that are near his head, and let's go."

12So David took the spear and water jug near Saul's head, and they left. No one saw or knew about it, nor did anyone wake up. They were all sleeping, because the LORD had put them into a deep sleep.

13Then David crossed over to the other side and stood on top of the hill some distance away; there was a wide space between them. 14He called out to the army and to Abner son of Ner, "Aren't you going to answer me, Abner?"

Abner replied, "Who are you who calls to the king?"

15David said, "You're a man, aren't you? And who is like you in Israel? Why didn't you guard your lord the king? Someone came to destroy your lord the king. 16What you have done is not good. As surely as the LORD lives, you and your men must die, because you did not guard your master, the LORD's anointed. Look around you. Where are the king's spear and water jug that were near his head?"

17Saul recognized David's voice and said, "Is that your voice, David my son?"

David replied, "Yes it is, my lord the king." 18And he added, "Why is my lord pursuing his servant? What have I done, and what wrong am I guilty of? 19Now let my lord the king listen to his servant's words. If the LORD has incited you against me, then may he accept an offering. If, however, people have done it, may they be cursed before the LORD! They have driven me today from my share in the LORD's inheritance and have said, 'Go, serve other gods.' 20Now do not let my blood fall to the ground far from the presence of the LORD. The king of Israel has come out to look for a flea — as one hunts a partridge in the mountains."

21Then Saul said, "I have sinned. Come back, David my son. Because you considered my life precious today, I will not try to harm you again. Surely I have acted like a fool and have been terribly wrong."

22"Here is the king's spear," David answered. "Let one of your young men come over and get it. 23The LORD rewards everyone for their righteousness and faithfulness. The LORD delivered you into my hands today, but I would not lay a hand on the LORD's anointed. 24As surely as I valued your life today, so may the LORD value my life and deliver me from all trouble."

25Then Saul said to David, "May you be blessed, David my son; you will do great things and surely triumph."

So David went on his way, and Saul returned home.

David Among the Philistines

27 But David thought to himself, "One of these days I will be destroyed by the hand of Saul. The best thing I can do is to escape to the land of the Philistines. Then Saul will give up searching for me anywhere in Israel, and I will slip out of his hand."

2So David and the six hundred men with him left and went over to Achish son of Maok king of Gath. 3David and his men settled in Gath with Achish. Each man had his family with him, and David had his two wives: Ahinoam of Jezreel and Abigail of Carmel, the widow of Nabal. 4When Saul was told that David had fled to Gath, he no longer searched for him.

5Then David said to Achish, "If I have found favor in your eyes, let a place be assigned to me in one of the country towns, that I may live there. Why should your servant live in the royal city with you?"

6So on that day Achish gave him Ziklag, and it has belonged to the kings of Judah ever since. 7David lived in Philistine territory a year and four months.

8Now David and his men went up and raided the Geshurites, the Girzites and the Amalekites. (From ancient times these peoples had lived in the land extending to Shur and Egypt.) 9Whenever David attacked

an area, he did not leave a man or woman
alive, but took sheep and cattle, donkeys
and camels, and clothes. Then he returned
to Achish.
[10]When Achish asked, "Where did you go
raiding today?" David would say, "Against
the Negev of Judah" or "Against the Negev of
Jerahmeel" or "Against the Negev of the Ke-
nites." [11]He did not leave a man or woman
alive to be brought to Gath, for he thought,
"They might inform on us and say, 'This is
what David did.'" And such was his prac-
tice as long as he lived in Philistine territory.
[12]Achish trusted David and said to himself,
"He has become so obnoxious to his people,
the Israelites, that he will be my servant for
life."

28 In those days the Philistines gath-
ered their forces to fight against
Israel. Achish said to David, "You must un-
derstand that you and your men will accom-
pany me in the army."
[2]David said, "Then you will see for your-
self what your servant can do."
Achish replied, "Very well, I will make you
my bodyguard for life."

Saul and the Medium at Endor

[3]Now Samuel was dead, and all Israel had
mourned for him and buried him in his own
town of Ramah. Saul had expelled the medi-
ums and spiritists from the land.
[4]The Philistines assembled and came and
set up camp at Shunem, while Saul gathered
all Israel and set up camp at Gilboa. [5]When
Saul saw the Philistine army, he was afraid;
terror filled his heart. [6]He inquired of the
LORD, but the LORD did not answer him by
dreams or Urim or prophets. [7]Saul then said
to his attendants, "Find me a woman who is
a medium, so I may go and inquire of her."
"There is one in Endor," they said.
[8]So Saul disguised himself, putting on
other clothes, and at night he and two men
went to the woman. "Consult a spirit for
me," he said, "and bring up for me the one
I name."
[9]But the woman said to him, "Surely you
know what Saul has done. He has cut off the
mediums and spiritists from the land. Why
have you set a trap for my life to bring about
my death?"
[10]Saul swore to her by the LORD, "As surely
as the LORD lives, you will not be punished
for this."
[11]Then the woman asked, "Whom shall I
bring up for you?"
"Bring up Samuel," he said.
[12]When the woman saw Samuel, she cried
out at the top of her voice and said to Saul,
"Why have you deceived me? You are Saul!"
[13]The king said to her, "Don't be afraid.
What do you see?"
The woman said, "I see a ghostly figure[a]
coming up out of the earth."
[14]"What does he look like?" he asked.
"An old man wearing a robe is coming
up," she said.
Then Saul knew it was Samuel, and he
bowed down and prostrated himself with
his face to the ground.
[15]Samuel said to Saul, "Why have you dis-
turbed me by bringing me up?"
"I am in great distress," Saul said. "The
Philistines are fighting against me, and God
has departed from me. He no longer answers
me, either by prophets or by dreams. So I
have called on you to tell me what to do."
[16]Samuel said, "Why do you consult me,
now that the LORD has departed from you
and become your enemy? [17]The LORD has
done what he predicted through me. The
LORD has torn the kingdom out of your hands
and given it to one of your neighbors—to
David. [18]Because you did not obey the LORD
or carry out his fierce wrath against the Am-
alekites, the LORD has done this to you today.
[19]The LORD will deliver both Israel and you
into the hands of the Philistines, and tomor-
row you and your sons will be with me. The
LORD will also give the army of Israel into the
hands of the Philistines."
[20]Immediately Saul fell full length on the
ground, filled with fear because of Samuel's
words. His strength was gone, for he had eat-
en nothing all that day and all that night.
[21]When the woman came to Saul and saw
that he was greatly shaken, she said, "Look,
your servant has obeyed you. I took my life
in my hands and did what you told me to do.
[22]Now please listen to your servant and let
me give you some food so you may eat and
have the strength to go on your way."
[23]He refused and said, "I will not eat."

[a] *13* Or *see spirits*; or *see gods*

But his men joined the woman in urging him, and he listened to them. He got up from the ground and sat on the couch.

24 The woman had a fattened calf at the house, which she butchered at once. She took some flour, kneaded it and baked bread without yeast. 25 Then she set it before Saul and his men, and they ate. That same night they got up and left.

Achish Sends David Back to Ziklag

29 The Philistines gathered all their forces at Aphek, and Israel camped by the spring in Jezreel. 2 As the Philistine rulers marched with their units of hundreds and thousands, David and his men were marching at the rear with Achish. 3 The commanders of the Philistines asked, "What about these Hebrews?"

Achish replied, "Is this not David, who was an officer of Saul king of Israel? He has already been with me for over a year, and from the day he left Saul until now, I have found no fault in him."

4 But the Philistine commanders were angry with Achish and said, "Send the man back, that he may return to the place you assigned him. He must not go with us into battle, or he will turn against us during the fighting. How better could he regain his master's favor than by taking the heads of our own men? 5 Isn't this the David they sang about in their dances:

"'Saul has slain his thousands,
and David his tens of thousands'?"

6 So Achish called David and said to him, "As surely as the LORD lives, you have been reliable, and I would be pleased to have you serve with me in the army. From the day you came to me until today, I have found no fault in you, but the rulers don't approve of you. 7 Now turn back and go in peace; do nothing to displease the Philistine rulers."

8 "But what have I done?" asked David. "What have you found against your servant from the day I came to you until now? Why can't I go and fight against the enemies of my lord the king?"

9 Achish answered, "I know that you have been as pleasing in my eyes as an angel of God; nevertheless, the Philistine commanders have said, 'He must not go up with us into battle.' 10 Now get up early, along with your master's servants who have come with you, and leave in the morning as soon as it is light."

11 So David and his men got up early in the morning to go back to the land of the Philistines, and the Philistines went up to Jezreel.

David Destroys the Amalekites

30 David and his men reached Ziklag on the third day. Now the Amalekites had raided the Negev and Ziklag. They had attacked Ziklag and burned it, 2 and had taken captive the women and everyone else in it, both young and old. They killed none of them, but carried them off as they went on their way.

3 When David and his men reached Ziklag, they found it destroyed by fire and their wives and sons and daughters taken captive. 4 So David and his men wept aloud until they had no strength left to weep. 5 David's two wives had been captured — Ahinoam of Jezreel and Abigail, the widow of Nabal of Carmel. 6 David was greatly distressed because the men were talking of stoning him; each one was bitter in spirit because of his sons and daughters. But David found strength in the LORD his God.

7 Then David said to Abiathar the priest, the son of Ahimelek, "Bring me the ephod." Abiathar brought it to him, 8 and David inquired of the LORD, "Shall I pursue this raiding party? Will I overtake them?"

"Pursue them," he answered. "You will certainly overtake them and succeed in the rescue."

9 David and the six hundred men with him came to the Besor Valley, where some stayed behind. 10 Two hundred of them were too exhausted to cross the valley, but David and the other four hundred continued the pursuit.

11 They found an Egyptian in a field and brought him to David. They gave him water to drink and food to eat — 12 part of a cake of pressed figs and two cakes of raisins. He ate and was revived, for he had not eaten any food or drunk any water for three days and three nights.

13 David asked him, "Who do you belong to? Where do you come from?"

He said, "I am an Egyptian, the slave of an Amalekite. My master abandoned me when I became ill three days ago. 14 We raided the

Negev of the Kerethites, some territory belonging to Judah and the Negev of Caleb. And we burned Ziklag."

15 David asked him, "Can you lead me down to this raiding party?"

He answered, "Swear to me before God that you will not kill me or hand me over to my master, and I will take you down to them."

16 He led David down, and there they were, scattered over the countryside, eating, drinking and reveling because of the great amount of plunder they had taken from the land of the Philistines and from Judah. 17 David fought them from dusk until the evening of the next day, and none of them got away, except four hundred young men who rode off on camels and fled. 18 David recovered everything the Amalekites had taken, including his two wives. 19 Nothing was missing: young or old, boy or girl, plunder or anything else they had taken. David brought everything back. 20 He took all the flocks and herds, and his men drove them ahead of the other livestock, saying, "This is David's plunder."

21 Then David came to the two hundred men who had been too exhausted to follow him and who were left behind at the Besor Valley. They came out to meet David and the men with him. As David and his men approached, he asked them how they were. 22 But all the evil men and troublemakers among David's followers said, "Because they did not go out with us, we will not share with them the plunder we recovered. However, each man may take his wife and children and go."

23 David replied, "No, my brothers, you must not do that with what the LORD has given us. He has protected us and delivered into our hands the raiding party that came against us. 24 Who will listen to what you say? The share of the man who stayed with the supplies is to be the same as that of him who went down to the battle. All will share alike." 25 David made this a statute and ordinance for Israel from that day to this.

26 When David reached Ziklag, he sent some of the plunder to the elders of Judah, who were his friends, saying, "Here is a gift for you from the plunder of the LORD's enemies."

27 David sent it to those who were in Bethel, Ramoth Negev and Jattir; 28 to those in Aroer, Siphmoth, Eshtemoa 29 and Rakal; to those in the towns of the Jerahmeelites and the Kenites; 30 to those in Hormah, Bor Ashan, Athak 31 and Hebron; and to those in all the other places where he and his men had roamed.

Saul Takes His Life

31 Now the Philistines fought against Israel; the Israelites fled before them, and many fell dead on Mount Gilboa. 2 The Philistines were in hot pursuit of Saul and his sons, and they killed his sons Jonathan, Abinadab and Malki-Shua. 3 The fighting grew fierce around Saul, and when the archers overtook him, they wounded him critically.

4 Saul said to his armor-bearer, "Draw your sword and run me through, or these uncircumcised fellows will come and run me through and abuse me."

But his armor-bearer was terrified and would not do it; so Saul took his own sword and fell on it. 5 When the armor-bearer saw that Saul was dead, he too fell on his sword and died with him. 6 So Saul and his three sons and his armor-bearer and all his men died together that same day.

7 When the Israelites along the valley and those across the Jordan saw that the Israelite army had fled and that Saul and his sons had died, they abandoned their towns and fled. And the Philistines came and occupied them.

8 The next day, when the Philistines came to strip the dead, they found Saul and his three sons fallen on Mount Gilboa. 9 They cut off his head and stripped off his armor, and they sent messengers throughout the land of the Philistines to proclaim the news in the temple of their idols and among their people. 10 They put his armor in the temple of the Ashtoreths and fastened his body to the wall of Beth Shan.

11 When the people of Jabesh Gilead heard what the Philistines had done to Saul, 12 all their valiant men marched through the night to Beth Shan. They took down the bodies of Saul and his sons from the wall of Beth Shan and went to Jabesh, where they burned them. 13 Then they took their bones and buried them under a tamarisk tree at Jabesh, and they fasted seven days.

2 SAMUEL

David Hears of Saul's Death

1 After the death of Saul, David returned
from striking down the Amalekites and
stayed in Ziklag two days. 2 On the third day
a man arrived from Saul's camp with his
clothes torn and dust on his head. When he
came to David, he fell to the ground to pay
him honor.

3 "Where have you come from?" David
asked him.

He answered, "I have escaped from the Is-
raelite camp."

4 "What happened?" David asked.
"Tell me."

"The men fled from the battle," he replied.
"Many of them fell and died. And Saul and
his son Jonathan are dead."

5 Then David said to the young man who
brought him the report, "How do you know
that Saul and his son Jonathan are dead?"

6 "I happened to be on Mount Gilboa," the
young man said, "and there was Saul, lean-
ing on his spear, with the chariots and their
drivers in hot pursuit. 7 When he turned
around and saw me, he called out to me, and
I said, 'What can I do?'

8 "He asked me, 'Who are you?'

"'An Amalekite,' I answered.

9 "Then he said to me, 'Stand here by me
and kill me! I'm in the throes of death, but
I'm still alive.'

10 "So I stood beside him and killed him,
because I knew that after he had fallen he
could not survive. And I took the crown that
was on his head and the band on his arm and
have brought them here to my lord."

11 Then David and all the men with him
took hold of their clothes and tore them.
12 They mourned and wept and fasted till
evening for Saul and his son Jonathan, and
for the army of the LORD and for the nation of
Israel, because they had fallen by the sword.

13 David said to the young man who
brought him the report, "Where are you
from?"

"I am the son of a foreigner, an Amalek-
ite," he answered.

14 David asked him, "Why weren't you
afraid to lift your hand to destroy the LORD's
anointed?"

15 Then David called one of his men and
said, "Go, strike him down!" So he struck
him down, and he died. 16 For David had said
to him, "Your blood be on your own head.
Your own mouth testified against you when
you said, 'I killed the LORD's anointed.'"

David's Lament for Saul and Jonathan

17 David took up this lament concerning
Saul and his son Jonathan, 18 and he ordered
that the people of Judah be taught this la-
ment of the bow (it is written in the Book of
Jashar):

19 "A gazelle[a] lies slain on your heights,
Israel.
How the mighty have fallen!

20 "Tell it not in Gath,
proclaim it not in the streets of
Ashkelon,
lest the daughters of the Philistines be
glad,
lest the daughters of the
uncircumcised rejoice.

21 "Mountains of Gilboa,
may you have neither dew nor rain,
may no showers fall on your terraced
fields.[b]
For there the shield of the mighty was
despised,
the shield of Saul — no longer rubbed
with oil.

22 "From the blood of the slain,
from the flesh of the mighty,
the bow of Jonathan did not turn back,
the sword of Saul did not return
unsatisfied.
23 Saul and Jonathan —
in life they were loved and admired,

[a] *19 Gazelle* here symbolizes a human dignitary. [b] *21* Or / *nor fields that yield grain for offerings*

and in death they were not
parted.
They were swifter than eagles,
they were stronger than lions.

24 “Daughters of Israel,
weep for Saul,
who clothed you in scarlet and finery,
who adorned your garments with
ornaments of gold.

25 “How the mighty have fallen in battle!
Jonathan lies slain on your heights.
26 I grieve for you, Jonathan my brother;
you were very dear to me.
Your love for me was wonderful,
more wonderful than that of women.

27 “How the mighty have fallen!
The weapons of war have perished!”

David Anointed King Over Judah

2 In the course of time, David inquired
of the LORD. “Shall I go up to one of the
towns of Judah?” he asked.
The LORD said, “Go up.”
David asked, “Where shall I go?”
“To Hebron,” the LORD answered.
2 So David went up there with his two
wives, Ahinoam of Jezreel and Abigail, the
widow of Nabal of Carmel. 3 David also took
the men who were with him, each with his
family, and they settled in Hebron and its
towns. 4 Then the men of Judah came to He-
bron, and there they anointed David king
over the tribe of Judah.
When David was told that it was the men
from Jabesh Gilead who had buried Saul, 5 he
sent messengers to them to say to them, “The
LORD bless you for showing this kindness to
Saul your master by burying him. 6 May the
LORD now show you kindness and faithful-
ness, and I too will show you the same favor
because you have done this. 7 Now then, be
strong and brave, for Saul your master is
dead, and the people of Judah have anointed
me king over them.”

War Between the Houses of David and Saul

8 Meanwhile, Abner son of Ner, the com-
mander of Saul’s army, had taken Ish-Bo-
sheth son of Saul and brought him over to
Mahanaim. 9 He made him king over Gilead,
Ashuri and Jezreel, and also over Ephraim,
Benjamin and all Israel.
10 Ish-Bosheth son of Saul was forty years
old when he became king over Israel, and he
reigned two years. The tribe of Judah, how-
ever, remained loyal to David. 11 The length
of time David was king in Hebron over Judah
was seven years and six months.
12 Abner son of Ner, together with the men
of Ish-Bosheth son of Saul, left Mahanaim
and went to Gibeon. 13 Joab son of Zeruiah
and David’s men went out and met them at
the pool of Gibeon. One group sat down on
one side of the pool and one group on the
other side.
14 Then Abner said to Joab, “Let’s have
some of the young men get up and fight hand
to hand in front of us.”
“All right, let them do it,” Joab said.
15 So they stood up and were counted
off — twelve men for Benjamin and Ish-Bo-
sheth son of Saul, and twelve for David.
16 Then each man grabbed his opponent by
the head and thrust his dagger into his op-
ponent’s side, and they fell down together.
So that place in Gibeon was called Helkath
Hazzurim.[a]
17 The battle that day was very fierce, and
Abner and the Israelites were defeated by
David’s men.
18 The three sons of Zeruiah were there:
Joab, Abishai and Asahel. Now Asahel was
as fleet-footed as a wild gazelle. 19 He chased
Abner, turning neither to the right nor to the
left as he pursued him. 20 Abner looked be-
hind him and asked, “Is that you, Asahel?”
“It is,” he answered.
21 Then Abner said to him, “Turn aside
to the right or to the left; take on one of the
young men and strip him of his weapons.”
But Asahel would not stop chasing him.
22 Again Abner warned Asahel, “Stop
chasing me! Why should I strike you down?
How could I look your brother Joab in the
face?”
23 But Asahel refused to give up the pur-
suit; so Abner thrust the butt of his spear
into Asahel’s stomach, and the spear came
out through his back. He fell there and died
on the spot. And every man stopped when
he came to the place where Asahel had fallen
and died.

[a] 16 *Helkath Hazzurim* means *field of daggers* or *field of hostilities.*

24 But Joab and Abishai pursued Abner,
and as the sun was setting, they came to
the hill of Ammah, near Giah on the way to
the wasteland of Gibeon. 25 Then the men
of Benjamin rallied behind Abner. They
formed themselves into a group and took
their stand on top of a hill.

26 Abner called out to Joab, "Must the
sword devour forever? Don't you realize that
this will end in bitterness? How long before
you order your men to stop pursuing their
fellow Israelites?"

27 Joab answered, "As surely as God lives,
if you had not spoken, the men would have
continued pursuing them until morning."

28 So Joab blew the trumpet, and all the
troops came to a halt; they no longer pur-
sued Israel, nor did they fight anymore.

29 All that night Abner and his men
marched through the Arabah. They crossed
the Jordan, continued through the morning
hours[a] and came to Mahanaim.

30 Then Joab stopped pursuing Abner and
assembled the whole army. Besides Asahel,
nineteen of David's men were found miss-
ing. 31 But David's men had killed three hun-
dred and sixty Benjamites who were with
Abner. 32 They took Asahel and buried him
in his father's tomb at Bethlehem. Then Joab
and his men marched all night and arrived
at Hebron by daybreak.

3 The war between the house of Saul and
the house of David lasted a long time.
David grew stronger and stronger, while the
house of Saul grew weaker and weaker.

2 Sons were born to David in Hebron:

His firstborn was Amnon the son of
Ahinoam of Jezreel;
3 his second, Kileab the son of Abigail
the widow of Nabal of Carmel;
the third, Absalom the son of Maakah
daughter of Talmai king of Geshur;
4 the fourth, Adonijah the son of Hag-
gith;
the fifth, Shephatiah the son of Abital;
5 and the sixth, Ithream the son of Da-
vid's wife Eglah.
These were born to David in Hebron.

Abner Goes Over to David

6 During the war between the house of
Saul and the house of David, Abner had been
strengthening his own position in the house
of Saul. 7 Now Saul had had a concubine
named Rizpah daughter of Aiah. And Ish-
Bosheth said to Abner, "Why did you sleep
with my father's concubine?"

8 Abner was very angry because of what
Ish-Bosheth said. So he answered, "Am I a
dog's head—on Judah's side? This very day I
am loyal to the house of your father Saul and
to his family and friends. I haven't handed
you over to David. Yet now you accuse me
of an offense involving this woman! 9 May
God deal with Abner, be it ever so severely,
if I do not do for David what the LORD prom-
ised him on oath 10 and transfer the kingdom
from the house of Saul and establish David's
throne over Israel and Judah from Dan to
Beersheba." 11 Ish-Bosheth did not dare to
say another word to Abner, because he was
afraid of him.

12 Then Abner sent messengers on his be-
half to say to David, "Whose land is it? Make
an agreement with me, and I will help you
bring all Israel over to you."

13 "Good," said David. "I will make an
agreement with you. But I demand one thing
of you: Do not come into my presence unless
you bring Michal daughter of Saul when you
come to see me." 14 Then David sent messen-
gers to Ish-Bosheth son of Saul, demanding,
"Give me my wife Michal, whom I betrothed
to myself for the price of a hundred Philis-
tine foreskins."

15 So Ish-Bosheth gave orders and had her
taken away from her husband Paltiel son of
Laish. 16 Her husband, however, went with
her, weeping behind her all the way to Ba-
hurim. Then Abner said to him, "Go back
home!" So he went back.

17 Abner conferred with the elders of Israel
and said, "For some time you have wanted to
make David your king. 18 Now do it! For the
LORD promised David, 'By my servant David
I will rescue my people Israel from the hand
of the Philistines and from the hand of all
their enemies.'"

19 Abner also spoke to the Benjamites in
person. Then he went to Hebron to tell David
everything that Israel and the whole tribe of
Benjamin wanted to do. 20 When Abner, who
had twenty men with him, came to David at
Hebron, David prepared a feast for him and

[a] 29 See Septuagint; the meaning of the Hebrew for this phrase is uncertain.

his men. 21 Then Abner said to David, "Let me go at once and assemble all Israel for my lord the king, so that they may make a covenant with you, and that you may rule over all that your heart desires." So David sent Abner away, and he went in peace.

Joab Murders Abner

22 Just then David's men and Joab returned from a raid and brought with them a great deal of plunder. But Abner was no longer with David in Hebron, because David had sent him away, and he had gone in peace. 23 When Joab and all the soldiers with him arrived, he was told that Abner son of Ner had come to the king and that the king had sent him away and that he had gone in peace. 24 So Joab went to the king and said, "What have you done? Look, Abner came to you. Why did you let him go? Now he is gone! 25 You know Abner son of Ner; he came to deceive you and observe your movements and find out everything you are doing."

26 Joab then left David and sent messengers after Abner, and they brought him back from the cistern at Sirah. But David did not know it. 27 Now when Abner returned to Hebron, Joab took him aside into an inner chamber, as if to speak with him privately. And there, to avenge the blood of his brother Asahel, Joab stabbed him in the stomach, and he died.

28 Later, when David heard about this, he said, "I and my kingdom are forever innocent before the LORD concerning the blood of Abner son of Ner. 29 May his blood fall on the head of Joab and on his whole family! May Joab's family never be without someone who has a running sore or leprosy[a] or who leans on a crutch or who falls by the sword or who lacks food."

30 (Joab and his brother Abishai murdered Abner because he had killed their brother Asahel in the battle at Gibeon.)

31 Then David said to Joab and all the people with him, "Tear your clothes and put on sackcloth and walk in mourning in front of Abner." King David himself walked behind the bier. 32 They buried Abner in Hebron, and the king wept aloud at Abner's tomb. All the people wept also.

33 The king sang this lament for Abner:

"Should Abner have died as the lawless
die?
34 Your hands were not bound,
your feet were not fettered.
You fell as one falls before the wicked."

And all the people wept over him again.

35 Then they all came and urged David to eat something while it was still day; but David took an oath, saying, "May God deal with me, be it ever so severely, if I taste bread or anything else before the sun sets!"

36 All the people took note and were pleased; indeed, everything the king did pleased them. 37 So on that day all the people there and all Israel knew that the king had no part in the murder of Abner son of Ner.

38 Then the king said to his men, "Do you not realize that a commander and a great man has fallen in Israel this day? 39 And today, though I am the anointed king, I am weak, and these sons of Zeruiah are too strong for me. May the LORD repay the evildoer according to his evil deeds!"

Ish-Bosheth Murdered

4 When Ish-Bosheth son of Saul heard that Abner had died in Hebron, he lost courage, and all Israel became alarmed. 2 Now Saul's son had two men who were leaders of raiding bands. One was named Baanah and the other Rekab; they were sons of Rimmon the Beerothite from the tribe of Benjamin — Beeroth is considered part of Benjamin, 3 because the people of Beeroth fled to Gittaim and have resided there as foreigners to this day.

4 (Jonathan son of Saul had a son who was lame in both feet. He was five years old when the news about Saul and Jonathan came from Jezreel. His nurse picked him up and fled, but as she hurried to leave, he fell and became disabled. His name was Mephibosheth.)

5 Now Rekab and Baanah, the sons of Rimmon the Beerothite, set out for the house of Ish-Bosheth, and they arrived there in the heat of the day while he was taking his noonday rest. 6 They went into the inner part of the house as if to get some wheat, and they stabbed him in the stomach. Then Rekab and his brother Baanah slipped away.

7 They had gone into the house while he

[a] 29 The Hebrew for *leprosy* was used for various diseases affecting the skin.

was lying on the bed in his bedroom. After they stabbed and killed him, they cut off his head. Taking it with them, they traveled all night by way of the Arabah. [8]They brought the head of Ish-Bosheth to David at Hebron and said to the king, "Here is the head of Ish-Bosheth son of Saul, your enemy, who tried to kill you. This day the LORD has avenged my lord the king against Saul and his offspring."

[9]David answered Rekab and his brother Baanah, the sons of Rimmon the Beerothite, "As surely as the LORD lives, who has delivered me out of every trouble, [10]when someone told me, 'Saul is dead,' and thought he was bringing good news, I seized him and put him to death in Ziklag. That was the reward I gave him for his news! [11]How much more — when wicked men have killed an innocent man in his own house and on his own bed — should I not now demand his blood from your hand and rid the earth of you!"

[12]So David gave an order to his men, and they killed them. They cut off their hands and feet and hung the bodies by the pool in Hebron. But they took the head of Ish-Bosheth and buried it in Abner's tomb at Hebron.

David Becomes King Over Israel

5 All the tribes of Israel came to David at Hebron and said, "We are your own flesh and blood. [2]In the past, while Saul was king over us, you were the one who led Israel on their military campaigns. And the LORD said to you, 'You will shepherd my people Israel, and you will become their ruler.'"

[3]When all the elders of Israel had come to King David at Hebron, the king made a covenant with them at Hebron before the LORD, and they anointed David king over Israel.

[4]David was thirty years old when he became king, and he reigned forty years. [5]In Hebron he reigned over Judah seven years and six months, and in Jerusalem he reigned over all Israel and Judah thirty-three years.

David Conquers Jerusalem

[6]The king and his men marched to Jerusalem to attack the Jebusites, who lived there. The Jebusites said to David, "You will not get in here; even the blind and the lame can ward you off." They thought, "David cannot get in here." [7]Nevertheless, David captured the fortress of Zion — which is the City of David.

[8]On that day David had said, "Anyone who conquers the Jebusites will have to use the water shaft to reach those 'lame and blind' who are David's enemies.[a]" That is why they say, "The 'blind and lame' will not enter the palace."

[9]David then took up residence in the fortress and called it the City of David. He built up the area around it, from the terraces[b] inward. [10]And he became more and more powerful, because the LORD God Almighty was with him.

[11]Now Hiram king of Tyre sent envoys to David, along with cedar logs and carpenters and stonemasons, and they built a palace for David. [12]Then David knew that the LORD had established him as king over Israel and had exalted his kingdom for the sake of his people Israel.

[13]After he left Hebron, David took more concubines and wives in Jerusalem, and more sons and daughters were born to him. [14]These are the names of the children born to him there: Shammua, Shobab, Nathan, Solomon, [15]Ibhar, Elishua, Nepheg, Japhia, [16]Elishama, Eliada and Eliphelet.

David Defeats the Philistines

[17]When the Philistines heard that David had been anointed king over Israel, they went up in full force to search for him, but David heard about it and went down to the stronghold. [18]Now the Philistines had come and spread out in the Valley of Rephaim; [19]so David inquired of the LORD, "Shall I go and attack the Philistines? Will you deliver them into my hands?"

The LORD answered him, "Go, for I will surely deliver the Philistines into your hands."

[20]So David went to Baal Perazim, and there he defeated them. He said, "As waters break out, the LORD has broken out against my enemies before me." So that place was called Baal Perazim.[c] [21]The Philistines abandoned their idols there, and David and his men carried them off.

[22]Once more the Philistines came up and spread out in the Valley of Rephaim; [23]so

[a] 8 Or *are hated by David* [b] 9 Or *the Millo* [c] 20 *Baal Perazim* means *the lord who breaks out.*

David inquired of the LORD, and he answered, "Do not go straight up, but circle around behind them and attack them in front of the poplar trees. 24 As soon as you hear the sound of marching in the tops of the poplar trees, move quickly, because that will mean the LORD has gone out in front of you to strike the Philistine army." 25 So David did as the LORD commanded him, and he struck down the Philistines all the way from Gibeon[a] to Gezer.

The Ark Brought to Jerusalem

6 David again brought together all the able young men of Israel—thirty thousand. 2 He and all his men went to Baalah[b] in Judah to bring up from there the ark of God, which is called by the Name,[c] the name of the LORD Almighty, who is enthroned between the cherubim on the ark. 3 They set the ark of God on a new cart and brought it from the house of Abinadab, which was on the hill. Uzzah and Ahio, sons of Abinadab, were guiding the new cart 4 with the ark of God on it,[d] and Ahio was walking in front of it. 5 David and all Israel were celebrating with all their might before the LORD, with castanets,[e] harps, lyres, timbrels, sistrums and cymbals.

6 When they came to the threshing floor of Nakon, Uzzah reached out and took hold of the ark of God, because the oxen stumbled. 7 The LORD's anger burned against Uzzah because of his irreverent act; therefore God struck him down, and he died there beside the ark of God.

8 Then David was angry because the LORD's wrath had broken out against Uzzah, and to this day that place is called Perez Uzzah.[f]

9 David was afraid of the LORD that day and said, "How can the ark of the LORD ever come to me?" 10 He was not willing to take the ark of the LORD to be with him in the City of David. Instead, he took it to the house of Obed-Edom the Gittite. 11 The ark of the LORD remained in the house of Obed-Edom the Gittite for three months, and the LORD blessed him and his entire household.

12 Now King David was told, "The LORD has blessed the household of Obed-Edom and everything he has, because of the ark of God." So David went to bring up the ark of God from the house of Obed-Edom to the City of David with rejoicing. 13 When those who were carrying the ark of the LORD had taken six steps, he sacrificed a bull and a fattened calf. 14 Wearing a linen ephod, David was dancing before the LORD with all his might, 15 while he and all Israel were bringing up the ark of the LORD with shouts and the sound of trumpets.

16 As the ark of the LORD was entering the City of David, Michal daughter of Saul watched from a window. And when she saw King David leaping and dancing before the LORD, she despised him in her heart.

17 They brought the ark of the LORD and set it in its place inside the tent that David had pitched for it, and David sacrificed burnt offerings and fellowship offerings before the LORD. 18 After he had finished sacrificing the burnt offerings and fellowship offerings, he blessed the people in the name of the LORD Almighty. 19 Then he gave a loaf of bread, a cake of dates and a cake of raisins to each person in the whole crowd of Israelites, both men and women. And all the people went to their homes.

20 When David returned home to bless his household, Michal daughter of Saul came out to meet him and said, "How the king of Israel has distinguished himself today, going around half-naked in full view of the slave girls of his servants as any vulgar fellow would!"

21 David said to Michal, "It was before the LORD, who chose me rather than your father or anyone from his house when he appointed me ruler over the LORD's people Israel—I will celebrate before the LORD. 22 I will become even more undignified than this, and I will be humiliated in my own eyes. But by these slave girls you spoke of, I will be held in honor."

23 And Michal daughter of Saul had no children to the day of her death.

God's Promise to David

7 After the king was settled in his palace and the LORD had given him rest from

[a] *25* Septuagint (see also 1 Chron. 14:16); Hebrew *Geba* [b] *2* That is, Kiriath Jearim (see 1 Chron. 13:6) [c] *2* Hebrew; Septuagint and Vulgate do not have *the Name.* [d] *3,4* Dead Sea Scrolls and some Septuagint manuscripts; Masoretic Text *cart 4 and they brought it with the ark of God from the house of Abinadab, which was on the hill* [e] *5* Masoretic Text; Dead Sea Scrolls and Septuagint (see also 1 Chron. 13:8) *songs* [f] *8 Perez Uzzah* means *outbreak against Uzzah.*

all his enemies around him, [2]he said to Na-
than the prophet, "Here I am, living in a
house of cedar, while the ark of God remains
in a tent."
[3]Nathan replied to the king, "Whatever
you have in mind, go ahead and do it, for the
LORD is with you."
[4]But that night the word of the LORD came
to Nathan, saying:

[5]"Go and tell my servant David, 'This
is what the LORD says: Are you the one
to build me a house to dwell in? [6]I have
not dwelt in a house from the day I
brought the Israelites up out of Egypt to
this day. I have been moving from place
to place with a tent as my dwelling.
[7]Wherever I have moved with all the
Israelites, did I ever say to any of their
rulers whom I commanded to shep-
herd my people Israel, "Why have you
not built me a house of cedar?"'
[8]"Now then, tell my servant David,
'This is what the LORD Almighty says:
I took you from the pasture, from tend-
ing the flock, and appointed you rul-
er over my people Israel. [9]I have been
with you wherever you have gone, and
I have cut off all your enemies from be-
fore you. Now I will make your name
great, like the names of the greatest
men on earth. [10]And I will provide
a place for my people Israel and will
plant them so that they can have a
home of their own and no longer be
disturbed. Wicked people will not op-
press them anymore, as they did at the
beginning [11]and have done ever since
the time I appointed leaders[a] over my
people Israel. I will also give you rest
from all your enemies.
"'The LORD declares to you that the
LORD himself will establish a house for
you: [12]When your days are over and you
rest with your ancestors, I will raise up
your offspring to succeed you, your own
flesh and blood, and I will establish his
kingdom. [13]He is the one who will build
a house for my Name, and I will estab-
lish the throne of his kingdom forever.
[14]I will be his father, and he will be my
son. When he does wrong, I will punish
him with a rod wielded by men, with
floggings inflicted by human hands.
[15]But my love will never be taken away
from him, as I took it away from Saul,
whom I removed from before you.
[16]Your house and your kingdom will
endure forever before me[b]; your throne
will be established forever.'"

[17]Nathan reported to David all the words
of this entire revelation.

David's Prayer

[18]Then King David went in and sat before
the LORD, and he said:

"Who am I, Sovereign LORD, and
what is my family, that you have
brought me this far? [19]And as if this
were not enough in your sight, Sov-
ereign LORD, you have also spoken
about the future of the house of your
servant — and this decree, Sovereign
LORD, is for a mere human![c]
[20]"What more can David say to you?
For you know your servant, Sovereign
LORD. [21]For the sake of your word and
according to your will, you have done
this great thing and made it known to
your servant.
[22]"How great you are, Sovereign
LORD! There is no one like you, and
there is no God but you, as we have
heard with our own ears. [23]And who is
like your people Israel — the one nation
on earth that God went out to redeem
as a people for himself, and to make a
name for himself, and to perform great
and awesome wonders by driving out
nations and their gods from before
your people, whom you redeemed from
Egypt?[d] [24]You have established your
people Israel as your very own forever,
and you, LORD, have become their God.
[25]"And now, LORD God, keep forever
the promise you have made concerning
your servant and his house. Do as you
promised, [26]so that your name will be
great forever. Then people will say, 'The
LORD Almighty is God over Israel!' And

[a] *11* Traditionally *judges* [b] *16* Some Hebrew manuscripts and Septuagint; most Hebrew manuscripts *you* [c] *19* Or *for the human race* [d] *23* See Septuagint and 1 Chron. 17:21; Hebrew *wonders for your land and before your people, whom you redeemed from Egypt, from the nations and their gods.*

IN CHRIST ALONE

Stuart Townend, Keith Getty

In Christ alone my hope is found
He is my light, my strength, my song
This cornerstone, this solid ground
Firm through the fiercest drought and storm
What heights of love, what depths of peace
When fears are stilled, when strivings cease
My comforter, my all in all
Here in the love of Christ I stand

In Christ alone, who took on flesh
Fullness of God in helpless Babe
This gift of love and righteousness
Scorned by the ones he came to save
'Til on that cross as Jesus died
The wrath of God was satisfied
For every sin on him was laid
Here in the death of Christ I live

There in the ground his body lay
Light of the world by darkness slain
Then, bursting forth in glorious day
Up from the grave he rose again
And as he stands in victory
Sin's curse has lost its grip on me
For I am his and he is mine
Bought with the precious blood of Christ

No guilt in life, no fear in death
This is the power of Christ in me
From life's first cry to final breath
Jesus commands my destiny
No power of hell, no scheme of man
Can ever pluck me from his hand
'Til he returns or calls me home
Here in the power of Christ I'll stand

THE INSPIRATION

But whatever were gains to me I now consider loss for the sake of Christ. What is more, I consider everything a loss because of the surpassing worth of knowing Christ Jesus my Lord, for whose sake I have lost all things. I consider them garbage, that I may gain Christ and be found in him, not having a righteousness of my own that comes from the law, but that which is through faith in Christ — the righteousness that comes from God on the basis of faith. I want to know Christ — yes, to know the power of his resurrection and participation in his sufferings, becoming like him in his death, and so, somehow, attaining to the resurrection from the dead.

— Philippians 3:7 – 11

BEHIND THE SONG

English songwriter and worship leader Stuart Townend had never written songs with another person until his friend Keith Getty sent him a melody he had composed in the tradition of the great Irish hymns.

"It had a grandeur about it," Townend recalls. "I felt the lyrics should be a timeless theme commensurate with the melody." Townend began crafting lyrics that he felt were up to the emotional intensity of Getty's melody.

"As I wrote them," he explains, "the lyrics began to develop the whole theme of the life, death and resurrection of Christ." As he built the song verse by verse he felt himself getting more and more emotional about it. "I was contemplating the awesomeness of his sacrifice and what that means for us."

The crescendo of the song soars with the words "No guilt in life, no fear in death/This is the power of Christ in me!/From life's first cry to final breath/Jesus commands my destiny." Congregations around the world, in many different languages, experience a similar rush of emotion as they sing the words to this modern hymn.

"I think content is vitally important to our corporate worship," Townsend adds. "Sometimes great melodies are let down by indifferent or clichéd words. It's the writer's job to dig deep into the meaning of Scripture and express in poetic and memorable ways the truth he or she finds there. Songs remain in the mind in a way sermons do not, so songwriters have an important role and a huge responsibility."

Selah

The sacrifice of Christ is obviously at the heart of the Christian faith, but it can sometimes be overwhelming to contemplate. One of the great values of hymns and spiritual songs is that they help us comprehend vital truths in both rational and emotional ways.

Read through the lyrics of "In Christ Alone" and then read through Philippians 3:7–11. Consider how the apostle Paul grappled with the profound mystery of the cross. Invite the Holy Spirit to reveal to you any areas in your life that still need to be surrendered to God.

the house of your servant David will be established in your sight.

27 "LORD Almighty, God of Israel, you have revealed this to your servant, saying, 'I will build a house for you.' So your servant has found courage to pray this prayer to you. 28 Sovereign LORD, you are God! Your covenant is trustworthy, and you have promised these good things to your servant. 29 Now be pleased to bless the house of your servant, that it may continue forever in your sight; for you, Sovereign LORD, have spoken, and with your blessing the house of your servant will be blessed forever."

David's Victories

8 In the course of time, David defeated the Philistines and subdued them, and he took Metheg Ammah from the control of the Philistines.

2 David also defeated the Moabites. He made them lie down on the ground and measured them off with a length of cord. Every two lengths of them were put to death, and the third length was allowed to live. So the Moabites became subject to David and brought him tribute.

3 Moreover, David defeated Hadadezer son of Rehob, king of Zobah, when he went to restore his monument at[a] the Euphrates River. 4 David captured a thousand of his chariots, seven thousand charioteers[b] and twenty thousand foot soldiers. He hamstrung all but a hundred of the chariot horses.

5 When the Arameans of Damascus came to help Hadadezer king of Zobah, David struck down twenty-two thousand of them. 6 He put garrisons in the Aramean kingdom of Damascus, and the Arameans became subject to him and brought tribute. The LORD gave David victory wherever he went.

7 David took the gold shields that belonged to the officers of Hadadezer and brought them to Jerusalem. 8 From Tebah[c] and Berothai, towns that belonged to Hadadezer, King David took a great quantity of bronze.

9 When Tou[d] king of Hamath heard that David had defeated the entire army of Hadadezer, 10 he sent his son Joram[e] to King David to greet him and congratulate him on his victory in battle over Hadadezer, who had been at war with Tou. Joram brought with him articles of silver, of gold and of bronze.

11 King David dedicated these articles to the LORD, as he had done with the silver and gold from all the nations he had subdued: 12 Edom[f] and Moab, the Ammonites and the Philistines, and Amalek. He also dedicated the plunder taken from Hadadezer son of Rehob, king of Zobah.

13 And David became famous after he returned from striking down eighteen thousand Edomites[g] in the Valley of Salt.

14 He put garrisons throughout Edom, and all the Edomites became subject to David. The LORD gave David victory wherever he went.

David's Officials

15 David reigned over all Israel, doing what was just and right for all his people. 16 Joab son of Zeruiah was over the army; Jehoshaphat son of Ahilud was recorder; 17 Zadok son of Ahitub and Ahimelek son of Abiathar were priests; Seraiah was secretary; 18 Benaiah son of Jehoiada was over the Kerethites and Pelethites; and David's sons were priests.[h]

David and Mephibosheth

9 David asked, "Is there anyone still left of the house of Saul to whom I can show kindness for Jonathan's sake?"

2 Now there was a servant of Saul's household named Ziba. They summoned him to appear before David, and the king said to him, "Are you Ziba?"

"At your service," he replied.

3 The king asked, "Is there no one still alive from the house of Saul to whom I can show God's kindness?"

[a] *3* Or *his control along* [b] *4* Septuagint (see also Dead Sea Scrolls and 1 Chron. 18:4); Masoretic Text *captured seventeen hundred of his charioteers* [c] *8* See some Septuagint manuscripts (see also 1 Chron. 18:8); Hebrew *Betah.* [d] *9* Hebrew *Toi,* a variant of *Tou;* also in verse 10 [e] *10* A variant of *Hadoram* [f] *12* Some Hebrew manuscripts, Septuagint and Syriac (see also 1 Chron. 18:11); most Hebrew manuscripts *Aram* [g] *13* A few Hebrew manuscripts, Septuagint and Syriac (see also 1 Chron. 18:12); most Hebrew manuscripts *Aram* (that is, Arameans) [h] *18* Or *were chief officials* (see Septuagint and Targum; see also 1 Chron. 18:17)

Ziba answered the king, "There is still a
son of Jonathan; he is lame in both feet."
4 "Where is he?" the king asked.
Ziba answered, "He is at the house of Ma-
kir son of Ammiel in Lo Debar."
5 So King David had him brought from Lo
Debar, from the house of Makir son of Am-
miel.
6 When Mephibosheth son of Jonathan,
the son of Saul, came to David, he bowed
down to pay him honor.
David said, "Mephibosheth!"
"At your service," he replied.
7 "Don't be afraid," David said to him, "for
I will surely show you kindness for the sake
of your father Jonathan. I will restore to you
all the land that belonged to your grandfa-
ther Saul, and you will always eat at my ta-
ble."
8 Mephibosheth bowed down and said,
"What is your servant, that you should no-
tice a dead dog like me?"
9 Then the king summoned Ziba, Saul's
steward, and said to him, "I have given your
master's grandson everything that belonged
to Saul and his family. 10 You and your sons
and your servants are to farm the land for
him and bring in the crops, so that your
master's grandson may be provided for. And
Mephibosheth, grandson of your master,
will always eat at my table." (Now Ziba had
fifteen sons and twenty servants.)
11 Then Ziba said to the king, "Your ser-
vant will do whatever my lord the king com-
mands his servant to do." So Mephibosheth
ate at David's[a] table like one of the king's
sons.
12 Mephibosheth had a young son named
Mika, and all the members of Ziba's house-
hold were servants of Mephibosheth. 13 And
Mephibosheth lived in Jerusalem, because
he always ate at the king's table; he was lame
in both feet.

David Defeats the Ammonites

10 In the course of time, the king of the
Ammonites died, and his son Hanun
succeeded him as king. 2 David thought, "I
will show kindness to Hanun son of Nahash,
just as his father showed kindness to me." So
David sent a delegation to express his sym-
pathy to Hanun concerning his father.
When David's men came to the land of
the Ammonites, 3 the Ammonite command-
ers said to Hanun their lord, "Do you think
David is honoring your father by sending
envoys to you to express sympathy? Hasn't
David sent them to you only to explore the
city and spy it out and overthrow it?" 4 So Ha-
nun seized David's envoys, shaved off half of
each man's beard, cut off their garments at
the buttocks, and sent them away.
5 When David was told about this, he sent
messengers to meet the men, for they were
greatly humiliated. The king said, "Stay at
Jericho till your beards have grown, and
then come back."
6 When the Ammonites realized that they
had become obnoxious to David, they hired
twenty thousand Aramean foot soldiers
from Beth Rehob and Zobah, as well as the
king of Maakah with a thousand men, and
also twelve thousand men from Tob.
7 On hearing this, David sent Joab out
with the entire army of fighting men. 8 The
Ammonites came out and drew up in battle
formation at the entrance of their city gate,
while the Arameans of Zobah and Rehob
and the men of Tob and Maakah were by
themselves in the open country.
9 Joab saw that there were battle lines in
front of him and behind him; so he select-
ed some of the best troops in Israel and de-
ployed them against the Arameans. 10 He
put the rest of the men under the command
of Abishai his brother and deployed them
against the Ammonites. 11 Joab said, "If the
Arameans are too strong for me, then you are
to come to my rescue; but if the Ammonites
are too strong for you, then I will come to res-
cue you. 12 Be strong, and let us fight bravely
for our people and the cities of our God. The
LORD will do what is good in his sight."
13 Then Joab and the troops with him ad-
vanced to fight the Arameans, and they fled
before him. 14 When the Ammonites realized
that the Arameans were fleeing, they fled
before Abishai and went inside the city. So
Joab returned from fighting the Ammonites
and came to Jerusalem.
15 After the Arameans saw that they had
been routed by Israel, they regrouped.
16 Hadadezer had Arameans brought from
beyond the Euphrates River; they went to

[a] *11* Septuagint; Hebrew *my*

Helam, with Shobak the commander of Hadadezer's army leading them.

17 When David was told of this, he gathered all Israel, crossed the Jordan and went to Helam. The Arameans formed their battle lines to meet David and fought against him. 18 But they fled before Israel, and David killed seven hundred of their charioteers and forty thousand of their foot soldiers.[a] He also struck down Shobak the commander of their army, and he died there. 19 When all the kings who were vassals of Hadadezer saw that they had been routed by Israel, they made peace with the Israelites and became subject to them.

So the Arameans were afraid to help the Ammonites anymore.

David and Bathsheba

11 In the spring, at the time when kings go off to war, David sent Joab out with the king's men and the whole Israelite army. They destroyed the Ammonites and besieged Rabbah. But David remained in Jerusalem.

2 One evening David got up from his bed and walked around on the roof of the palace. From the roof he saw a woman bathing. The woman was very beautiful, 3 and David sent someone to find out about her. The man said, "She is Bathsheba, the daughter of Eliam and the wife of Uriah the Hittite." 4 Then David sent messengers to get her. She came to him, and he slept with her. (Now she was purifying herself from her monthly uncleanness.) Then she went back home. 5 The woman conceived and sent word to David, saying, "I am pregnant."

6 So David sent this word to Joab: "Send me Uriah the Hittite." And Joab sent him to David. 7 When Uriah came to him, David asked him how Joab was, how the soldiers were and how the war was going. 8 Then David said to Uriah, "Go down to your house and wash your feet." So Uriah left the palace, and a gift from the king was sent after him. 9 But Uriah slept at the entrance to the palace with all his master's servants and did not go down to his house.

10 David was told, "Uriah did not go home." So he asked Uriah, "Haven't you just come from a military campaign? Why didn't you go home?"

11 Uriah said to David, "The ark and Israel and Judah are staying in tents,[b] and my commander Joab and my lord's men are camped in the open country. How could I go to my house to eat and drink and make love to my wife? As surely as you live, I will not do such a thing!"

12 Then David said to him, "Stay here one more day, and tomorrow I will send you back." So Uriah remained in Jerusalem that day and the next. 13 At David's invitation, he ate and drank with him, and David made him drunk. But in the evening Uriah went out to sleep on his mat among his master's servants; he did not go home.

14 In the morning David wrote a letter to Joab and sent it with Uriah. 15 In it he wrote, "Put Uriah out in front where the fighting is fiercest. Then withdraw from him so he will be struck down and die."

16 So while Joab had the city under siege, he put Uriah at a place where he knew the strongest defenders were. 17 When the men of the city came out and fought against Joab, some of the men in David's army fell; moreover, Uriah the Hittite died.

18 Joab sent David a full account of the battle. 19 He instructed the messenger: "When you have finished giving the king this account of the battle, 20 the king's anger may flare up, and he may ask you, 'Why did you get so close to the city to fight? Didn't you know they would shoot arrows from the wall? 21 Who killed Abimelek son of Jerub-Besheth[c]? Didn't a woman drop an upper millstone on him from the wall, so that he died in Thebez? Why did you get so close to the wall?' If he asks you this, then say to him, 'Moreover, your servant Uriah the Hittite is dead.'"

22 The messenger set out, and when he arrived he told David everything Joab had sent him to say. 23 The messenger said to David, "The men overpowered us and came out against us in the open, but we drove them back to the entrance of the city gate. 24 Then the archers shot arrows at your servants from the wall, and some of the king's men died. Moreover, your servant Uriah the Hittite is dead."

[a] *18* Some Septuagint manuscripts (see also 1 Chron. 19:18); Hebrew *horsemen* [b] *11* Or *staying at Sukkoth* [c] *21* Also known as *Jerub-Baal* (that is, Gideon)

[25]David told the messenger, "Say this to Joab: 'Don't let this upset you; the sword devours one as well as another. Press the attack against the city and destroy it.' Say this to encourage Joab."

[26]When Uriah's wife heard that her husband was dead, she mourned for him. [27]After the time of mourning was over, David had her brought to his house, and she became his wife and bore him a son. But the thing David had done displeased the LORD.

Nathan Rebukes David

12 The LORD sent Nathan to David. When he came to him, he said, "There were two men in a certain town, one rich and the other poor. [2]The rich man had a very large number of sheep and cattle, [3]but the poor man had nothing except one little ewe lamb he had bought. He raised it, and it grew up with him and his children. It shared his food, drank from his cup and even slept in his arms. It was like a daughter to him.

[4]"Now a traveler came to the rich man, but the rich man refrained from taking one of his own sheep or cattle to prepare a meal for the traveler who had come to him. Instead, he took the ewe lamb that belonged to the poor man and prepared it for the one who had come to him."

[5]David burned with anger against the man and said to Nathan, "As surely as the LORD lives, the man who did this must die! [6]He must pay for that lamb four times over, because he did such a thing and had no pity."

[7]Then Nathan said to David, "You are the man! This is what the LORD, the God of Israel, says: 'I anointed you king over Israel, and I delivered you from the hand of Saul. [8]I gave your master's house to you, and your master's wives into your arms. I gave you all Israel and Judah. And if all this had been too little, I would have given you even more. [9]Why did you despise the word of the LORD by doing what is evil in his eyes? You struck down Uriah the Hittite with the sword and took his wife to be your own. You killed him with the sword of the Ammonites. [10]Now, therefore, the sword will never depart from your house, because you despised me and took the wife of Uriah the Hittite to be your own.'

[11]"This is what the LORD says: 'Out of your own household I am going to bring calamity on you. Before your very eyes I will take your wives and give them to one who is close to you, and he will sleep with your wives in broad daylight. [12]You did it in secret, but I will do this thing in broad daylight before all Israel.'"

[13]Then David said to Nathan, "I have sinned against the LORD."

Nathan replied, "The LORD has taken away your sin. You are not going to die. [14]But because by doing this you have shown utter contempt for[a] the LORD, the son born to you will die."

[15]After Nathan had gone home, the LORD struck the child that Uriah's wife had borne to David, and he became ill. [16]David pleaded with God for the child. He fasted and spent the nights lying in sackcloth[b] on the ground. [17]The elders of his household stood beside him to get him up from the ground, but he refused, and he would not eat any food with them.

[18]On the seventh day the child died. David's attendants were afraid to tell him that the child was dead, for they thought, "While the child was still living, he wouldn't listen to us when we spoke to him. How can we now tell him the child is dead? He may do something desperate."

[19]David noticed that his attendants were whispering among themselves, and he realized the child was dead. "Is the child dead?" he asked.

"Yes," they replied, "he is dead."

[20]Then David got up from the ground. After he had washed, put on lotions and changed his clothes, he went into the house of the LORD and worshiped. Then he went to his own house, and at his request they served him food, and he ate.

[21]His attendants asked him, "Why are you acting this way? While the child was alive, you fasted and wept, but now that the child is dead, you get up and eat!"

[22]He answered, "While the child was still alive, I fasted and wept. I thought, 'Who knows? The LORD may be gracious to me and let the child live.' [23]But now that he is dead, why should I go on fasting? Can I bring him back again? I will go to him, but he will not return to me."

[a] *14* An ancient Hebrew scribal tradition; Masoretic Text *for the enemies of* [b] *16* Dead Sea Scrolls and Septuagint; Masoretic Text does not have *in sackcloth*.

24 Then David comforted his wife Bathsheba, and he went to her and made love to her. She gave birth to a son, and they named him Solomon. The LORD loved him; 25 and because the LORD loved him, he sent word through Nathan the prophet to name him Jedidiah.[a]

26 Meanwhile Joab fought against Rabbah of the Ammonites and captured the royal citadel. 27 Joab then sent messengers to David, saying, "I have fought against Rabbah and taken its water supply. 28 Now muster the rest of the troops and besiege the city and capture it. Otherwise I will take the city, and it will be named after me."

29 So David mustered the entire army and went to Rabbah, and attacked and captured it. 30 David took the crown from their king's[b] head, and it was placed on his own head. It weighed a talent[c] of gold, and it was set with precious stones. David took a great quantity of plunder from the city 31 and brought out the people who were there, consigning them to labor with saws and with iron picks and axes, and he made them work at brickmaking.[d] David did this to all the Ammonite towns. Then he and his entire army returned to Jerusalem.

Amnon and Tamar

13 In the course of time, Amnon son of David fell in love with Tamar, the beautiful sister of Absalom son of David.

2 Amnon became so obsessed with his sister Tamar that he made himself ill. She was a virgin, and it seemed impossible for him to do anything to her.

3 Now Amnon had an adviser named Jonadab son of Shimeah, David's brother. Jonadab was a very shrewd man. 4 He asked Amnon, "Why do you, the king's son, look so haggard morning after morning? Won't you tell me?"

Amnon said to him, "I'm in love with Tamar, my brother Absalom's sister."

5 "Go to bed and pretend to be ill," Jonadab said. "When your father comes to see you, say to him, 'I would like my sister Tamar to come and give me something to eat. Let her prepare the food in my sight so I may watch her and then eat it from her hand.'"

6 So Amnon lay down and pretended to be ill. When the king came to see him, Amnon said to him, "I would like my sister Tamar to come and make some special bread in my sight, so I may eat from her hand."

7 David sent word to Tamar at the palace: "Go to the house of your brother Amnon and prepare some food for him." 8 So Tamar went to the house of her brother Amnon, who was lying down. She took some dough, kneaded it, made the bread in his sight and baked it. 9 Then she took the pan and served him the bread, but he refused to eat.

"Send everyone out of here," Amnon said. So everyone left him. 10 Then Amnon said to Tamar, "Bring the food here into my bedroom so I may eat from your hand." And Tamar took the bread she had prepared and brought it to her brother Amnon in his bedroom. 11 But when she took it to him to eat, he grabbed her and said, "Come to bed with me, my sister."

12 "No, my brother!" she said to him. "Don't force me! Such a thing should not be done in Israel! Don't do this wicked thing. 13 What about me? Where could I get rid of my disgrace? And what about you? You would be like one of the wicked fools in Israel. Please speak to the king; he will not keep me from being married to you." 14 But he refused to listen to her, and since he was stronger than she, he raped her.

15 Then Amnon hated her with intense hatred. In fact, he hated her more than he had loved her. Amnon said to her, "Get up and get out!"

16 "No!" she said to him. "Sending me away would be a greater wrong than what you have already done to me."

But he refused to listen to her. 17 He called his personal servant and said, "Get this woman out of my sight and bolt the door after her." 18 So his servant put her out and bolted the door after her. She was wearing an ornate[e] robe, for this was the kind of garment the virgin daughters of the king wore. 19 Tamar put ashes on her head and tore the ornate robe she was wearing. She put her hands on her head and went away, weeping aloud as she went.

20 Her brother Absalom said to her, "Has

[a] *25 Jedidiah* means *loved by the LORD.* [b] *30* Or *from Milkom's* (that is, Molek's) [c] *30* That is, about 75 pounds or about 34 kilograms [d] *31* The meaning of the Hebrew for this clause is uncertain.
[e] *18* The meaning of the Hebrew for this word is uncertain; also in verse 19.

that Amnon, your brother, been with you? Be quiet for now, my sister; he is your brother. Don't take this thing to heart." And Tamar lived in her brother Absalom's house, a desolate woman.
[21]When King David heard all this, he was furious. [22]And Absalom never said a word to Amnon, either good or bad; he hated Amnon because he had disgraced his sister Tamar.

Absalom Kills Amnon

[23]Two years later, when Absalom's sheepshearers were at Baal Hazor near the border of Ephraim, he invited all the king's sons to come there. [24]Absalom went to the king and
said, "Your servant has had shearers come. Will the king and his attendants please join me?"
[25]"No, my son," the king replied. "All of us should not go; we would only be a burden to you." Although Absalom urged him, he still refused to go but gave him his blessing.
[26]Then Absalom said, "If not, please let my brother Amnon come with us."

The king asked him, "Why should he go with you?" [27]But Absalom urged him, so he sent with him Amnon and the rest of the king's sons.
[28]Absalom ordered his men, "Listen! When Amnon is in high spirits from drinking wine and I say to you, 'Strike Amnon down,' then kill him. Don't be afraid. Haven't I given you this order? Be strong and brave."
[29]So Absalom's men did to Amnon what Absalom had ordered. Then all the king's sons got up, mounted their mules and fled.
[30]While they were on their way, the report came to David: "Absalom has struck down all the king's sons; not one of them is left."
[31]The king stood up, tore his clothes and lay down on the ground; and all his attendants stood by with their clothes torn.
[32]But Jonadab son of Shimeah, David's brother, said, "My lord should not think that they killed all the princes; only Amnon is dead. This has been Absalom's express intention ever since the day Amnon raped his sister Tamar. [33]My lord the king should not be concerned about the report that all the king's sons are dead. Only Amnon is dead."
[34]Meanwhile, Absalom had fled.

Now the man standing watch looked up and saw many people on the road west of him, coming down the side of the hill. The watchman went and told the king, "I see men in the direction of Horonaim, on the side of the hill."[a]
[35]Jonadab said to the king, "See, the king's sons have come; it has happened just as your servant said."
[36]As he finished speaking, the king's sons came in, wailing loudly. The king, too, and all his attendants wept very bitterly.
[37]Absalom fled and went to Talmai son of Ammihud, the king of Geshur. But King David mourned many days for his son.
[38]After Absalom fled and went to Geshur, he stayed there three years. [39]And King David longed to go to Absalom, for he was consoled concerning Amnon's death.

Absalom Returns to Jerusalem

14 Joab son of Zeruiah knew that the king's heart longed for Absalom.
[2]So Joab sent someone to Tekoa and had a wise woman brought from there. He said to her, "Pretend you are in mourning. Dress in mourning clothes, and don't use any cosmetic lotions. Act like a woman who has spent many days grieving for the dead. [3]Then go to the king and speak these words to him." And Joab put the words in her mouth.
[4]When the woman from Tekoa went[b] to the king, she fell with her face to the ground to pay him honor, and she said, "Help me, Your Majesty!"
[5]The king asked her, "What is troubling you?"

She said, "I am a widow; my husband is dead. [6]I your servant had two sons. They got into a fight with each other in the field, and no one was there to separate them. One struck the other and killed him. [7]Now the whole clan has risen up against your servant; they say, 'Hand over the one who struck his brother down, so that we may put him to death for the life of his brother whom he killed; then we will get rid of the heir as well.' They would put out the only burning coal I have left, leaving my husband neither name nor descendant on the face of the earth."
[8]The king said to the woman, "Go home, and I will issue an order in your behalf."

[a] *34* Septuagint; Hebrew does not have this sentence.
[b] *4* Many Hebrew manuscripts, Septuagint, Vulgate and Syriac; most Hebrew manuscripts *spoke*

9 But the woman from Tekoa said to him, "Let my lord the king pardon me and my family, and let the king and his throne be without guilt."

10 The king replied, "If anyone says anything to you, bring them to me, and they will not bother you again."

11 She said, "Then let the king invoke the LORD his God to prevent the avenger of blood from adding to the destruction, so that my son will not be destroyed."

"As surely as the LORD lives," he said, "not one hair of your son's head will fall to the ground."

12 Then the woman said, "Let your servant speak a word to my lord the king."

"Speak," he replied.

13 The woman said, "Why then have you devised a thing like this against the people of God? When the king says this, does he not convict himself, for the king has not brought back his banished son? 14 Like water spilled on the ground, which cannot be recovered, so we must die. But that is not what God desires; rather, he devises ways so that a banished person does not remain banished from him.

15 "And now I have come to say this to my lord the king because the people have made me afraid. Your servant thought, 'I will speak to the king; perhaps he will grant his servant's request. 16 Perhaps the king will agree to deliver his servant from the hand of the man who is trying to cut off both me and my son from God's inheritance.'

17 "And now your servant says, 'May the word of my lord the king secure my inheritance, for my lord the king is like an angel of God in discerning good and evil. May the LORD your God be with you.' "

18 Then the king said to the woman, "Don't keep from me the answer to what I am going to ask you."

"Let my lord the king speak," the woman said.

19 The king asked, "Isn't the hand of Joab with you in all this?"

The woman answered, "As surely as you live, my lord the king, no one can turn to the right or to the left from anything my lord the king says. Yes, it was your servant Joab who instructed me to do this and who put all these words into the mouth of your servant. 20 Your servant Joab did this to change the present situation. My lord has wisdom like that of an angel of God—he knows everything that happens in the land."

21 The king said to Joab, "Very well, I will do it. Go, bring back the young man Absalom."

22 Joab fell with his face to the ground to pay him honor, and he blessed the king. Joab said, "Today your servant knows that he has found favor in your eyes, my lord the king, because the king has granted his servant's request."

23 Then Joab went to Geshur and brought Absalom back to Jerusalem. 24 But the king said, "He must go to his own house; he must not see my face." So Absalom went to his own house and did not see the face of the king.

25 In all Israel there was not a man so highly praised for his handsome appearance as Absalom. From the top of his head to the sole of his foot there was no blemish in him. 26 Whenever he cut the hair of his head—he used to cut his hair once a year because it became too heavy for him—he would weigh it, and its weight was two hundred shekels[a] by the royal standard.

27 Three sons and a daughter were born to Absalom. His daughter's name was Tamar, and she became a beautiful woman.

28 Absalom lived two years in Jerusalem without seeing the king's face. 29 Then Absalom sent for Joab in order to send him to the king, but Joab refused to come to him. So he sent a second time, but he refused to come. 30 Then he said to his servants, "Look, Joab's field is next to mine, and he has barley there. Go and set it on fire." So Absalom's servants set the field on fire.

31 Then Joab did go to Absalom's house, and he said to him, "Why have your servants set my field on fire?"

32 Absalom said to Joab, "Look, I sent word to you and said, 'Come here so I can send you to the king to ask, "Why have I come from Geshur? It would be better for me if I were still there!"' Now then, I want to see the king's face, and if I am guilty of anything, let him put me to death."

33 So Joab went to the king and told him this. Then the king summoned Absalom, and he came in and bowed down with his face to the ground before the king. And the king kissed Absalom.

[a] *26* That is, about 5 pounds or about 2.3 kilograms

Absalom's Conspiracy

15 In the course of time, Absalom provided himself with a chariot and horses and with fifty men to run ahead of him. 2 He would get up early and stand by the side of the road leading to the city gate. Whenever anyone came with a complaint to be placed before the king for a decision, Absalom would call out to him, "What town are you from?" He would answer, "Your servant is from one of the tribes of Israel." 3 Then Absalom would say to him, "Look, your claims are valid and proper, but there is no representative of the king to hear you." 4 And Absalom would add, "If only I were appointed judge in the land! Then everyone who has a complaint or case could come to me and I would see that they receive justice."

5 Also, whenever anyone approached him to bow down before him, Absalom would reach out his hand, take hold of him and kiss him. 6 Absalom behaved in this way toward all the Israelites who came to the king asking for justice, and so he stole the hearts of the people of Israel.

7 At the end of four[a] years, Absalom said to the king, "Let me go to Hebron and fulfill a vow I made to the LORD. 8 While your servant was living at Geshur in Aram, I made this vow: 'If the LORD takes me back to Jerusalem, I will worship the LORD in Hebron.[b]' "

9 The king said to him, "Go in peace." So he went to Hebron.

10 Then Absalom sent secret messengers throughout the tribes of Israel to say, "As soon as you hear the sound of the trumpets, then say, 'Absalom is king in Hebron.' " 11 Two hundred men from Jerusalem had accompanied Absalom. They had been invited as guests and went quite innocently, knowing nothing about the matter. 12 While Absalom was offering sacrifices, he also sent for Ahithophel the Gilonite, David's counselor, to come from Giloh, his hometown. And so the conspiracy gained strength, and Absalom's following kept on increasing.

David Flees

13 A messenger came and told David, "The hearts of the people of Israel are with Absalom."

14 Then David said to all his officials who were with him in Jerusalem, "Come! We must flee, or none of us will escape from Absalom. We must leave immediately, or he will move quickly to overtake us and bring ruin on us and put the city to the sword."

15 The king's officials answered him, "Your servants are ready to do whatever our lord the king chooses."

16 The king set out, with his entire household following him; but he left ten concubines to take care of the palace. 17 So the king set out, with all the people following him, and they halted at the edge of the city. 18 All his men marched past him, along with all the Kerethites and Pelethites; and all the six hundred Gittites who had accompanied him from Gath marched before the king.

19 The king said to Ittai the Gittite, "Why should you come along with us? Go back and stay with King Absalom. You are a foreigner, an exile from your homeland. 20 You came only yesterday. And today shall I make you wander about with us, when I do not know where I am going? Go back, and take your people with you. May the LORD show you kindness and faithfulness."[c]

21 But Ittai replied to the king, "As surely as the LORD lives, and as my lord the king lives, wherever my lord the king may be, whether it means life or death, there will your servant be."

22 David said to Ittai, "Go ahead, march on." So Ittai the Gittite marched on with all his men and the families that were with him.

23 The whole countryside wept aloud as all the people passed by. The king also crossed the Kidron Valley, and all the people moved on toward the wilderness.

24 Zadok was there, too, and all the Levites who were with him were carrying the ark of the covenant of God. They set down the ark of God, and Abiathar offered sacrifices until all the people had finished leaving the city.

25 Then the king said to Zadok, "Take the ark of God back into the city. If I find favor in the LORD's eyes, he will bring me back and let me see it and his dwelling place again. 26 But if he says, 'I am not pleased with you,' then I am ready; let him do to me whatever seems good to him."

[a] *7* Some Septuagint manuscripts, Syriac and Josephus; Hebrew *forty* [b] *8* Some Septuagint manuscripts; Hebrew does not have *in Hebron.* [c] *20* Septuagint; Hebrew *May kindness and faithfulness be with you*

27 The king also said to Zadok the priest, "Do you understand? Go back to the city with my blessing. Take your son Ahimaaz with you, and also Abiathar's son Jonathan. You and Abiathar return with your two sons. 28 I will wait at the fords in the wilderness until word comes from you to inform me." 29 So Zadok and Abiathar took the ark of God back to Jerusalem and stayed there.

30 But David continued up the Mount of Olives, weeping as he went; his head was covered and he was barefoot. All the people with him covered their heads too and were weeping as they went up. 31 Now David had been told, "Ahithophel is among the conspirators with Absalom." So David prayed, "LORD, turn Ahithophel's counsel into foolishness."

32 When David arrived at the summit, where people used to worship God, Hushai the Arkite was there to meet him, his robe torn and dust on his head. 33 David said to him, "If you go with me, you will be a burden to me. 34 But if you return to the city and say to Absalom, 'Your Majesty, I will be your servant; I was your father's servant in the past, but now I will be your servant,' then you can help me by frustrating Ahithophel's advice. 35 Won't the priests Zadok and Abiathar be there with you? Tell them anything you hear in the king's palace. 36 Their two sons, Ahimaaz son of Zadok and Jonathan son of Abiathar, are there with them. Send them to me with anything you hear."

37 So Hushai, David's confidant, arrived at Jerusalem as Absalom was entering the city.

David and Ziba

16 When David had gone a short distance beyond the summit, there was Ziba, the steward of Mephibosheth, waiting to meet him. He had a string of donkeys saddled and loaded with two hundred loaves of bread, a hundred cakes of raisins, a hundred cakes of figs and a skin of wine.

2 The king asked Ziba, "Why have you brought these?"

Ziba answered, "The donkeys are for the king's household to ride on, the bread and fruit are for the men to eat, and the wine is to refresh those who become exhausted in the wilderness."

3 The king then asked, "Where is your master's grandson?"

Ziba said to him, "He is staying in Jerusalem, because he thinks, 'Today the Israelites will restore to me my grandfather's kingdom.' "

4 Then the king said to Ziba, "All that belonged to Mephibosheth is now yours."

"I humbly bow," Ziba said. "May I find favor in your eyes, my lord the king."

Shimei Curses David

5 As King David approached Bahurim, a man from the same clan as Saul's family came out from there. His name was Shimei son of Gera, and he cursed as he came out. 6 He pelted David and all the king's officials with stones, though all the troops and the special guard were on David's right and left. 7 As he cursed, Shimei said, "Get out, get out, you murderer, you scoundrel! 8 The LORD has repaid you for all the blood you shed in the household of Saul, in whose place you have reigned. The LORD has given the kingdom into the hands of your son Absalom. You have come to ruin because you are a murderer!"

9 Then Abishai son of Zeruiah said to the king, "Why should this dead dog curse my lord the king? Let me go over and cut off his head."

10 But the king said, "What does this have to do with you, you sons of Zeruiah? If he is cursing because the LORD said to him, 'Curse David,' who can ask, 'Why do you do this?' "

11 David then said to Abishai and all his officials, "My son, my own flesh and blood, is trying to kill me. How much more, then, this Benjamite! Leave him alone; let him curse, for the LORD has told him to. 12 It may be that the LORD will look upon my misery and restore to me his covenant blessing instead of his curse today."

13 So David and his men continued along the road while Shimei was going along the hillside opposite him, cursing as he went and throwing stones at him and showering him with dirt. 14 The king and all the people with him arrived at their destination exhausted. And there he refreshed himself.

The Advice of Ahithophel and Hushai

15 Meanwhile, Absalom and all the men of Israel came to Jerusalem, and Ahithophel was with him. 16 Then Hushai the Arkite, David's

confidant, went to Absalom and said to him,
"Long live the king! Long live the king!"
17 Absalom said to Hushai, "So this is
the love you show your friend? If he's your
friend, why didn't you go with him?"
18 Hushai said to Absalom, "No, the one
chosen by the LORD, by these people, and
by all the men of Israel—his I will be, and I
will remain with him. 19 Furthermore, whom
should I serve? Should I not serve the son? Just
as I served your father, so I will serve you."
20 Absalom said to Ahithophel, "Give us
your advice. What should we do?"
21 Ahithophel answered, "Sleep with your
father's concubines whom he left to take
care of the palace. Then all Israel will hear
that you have made yourself obnoxious to
your father, and the hands of everyone with
you will be more resolute." 22 So they pitched
a tent for Absalom on the roof, and he slept
with his father's concubines in the sight of
all Israel.
23 Now in those days the advice Ahitho-
phel gave was like that of one who inquires of
God. That was how both David and Absalom
regarded all of Ahithophel's advice.

17 Ahithophel said to Absalom, "I would[a]
choose twelve thousand men and set
out tonight in pursuit of David. 2 I would at-
tack him while he is weary and weak. I would
strike him with terror, and then all the peo-
ple with him will flee. I would strike down
only the king 3 and bring all the people back
to you. The death of the man you seek will
mean the return of all; all the people will be
unharmed." 4 This plan seemed good to Ab-
salom and to all the elders of Israel.
5 But Absalom said, "Summon also Hushai
the Arkite, so we can hear what he has to say
as well." 6 When Hushai came to him, Absa-
lom said, "Ahithophel has given this advice.
Should we do what he says? If not, give us
your opinion."
7 Hushai replied to Absalom, "The advice
Ahithophel has given is not good this time.
8 You know your father and his men; they are
fighters, and as fierce as a wild bear robbed
of her cubs. Besides, your father is an expe-
rienced fighter; he will not spend the night
with the troops. 9 Even now, he is hidden in a
cave or some other place. If he should attack
your troops first,[b] whoever hears about it
will say, 'There has been a slaughter among
the troops who follow Absalom.' 10 Then
even the bravest soldier, whose heart is like
the heart of a lion, will melt with fear, for all
Israel knows that your father is a fighter and
that those with him are brave.
11 "So I advise you: Let all Israel, from Dan
to Beersheba—as numerous as the sand on
the seashore—be gathered to you, with you
yourself leading them into battle. 12 Then we
will attack him wherever he may be found,
and we will fall on him as dew settles on the
ground. Neither he nor any of his men will be
left alive. 13 If he withdraws into a city, then
all Israel will bring ropes to that city, and we
will drag it down to the valley until not so
much as a pebble is left."
14 Absalom and all the men of Israel said,
"The advice of Hushai the Arkite is better than
that of Ahithophel." For the LORD had deter-
mined to frustrate the good advice of Ahith-
ophel in order to bring disaster on Absalom.
15 Hushai told Zadok and Abiathar, the
priests, "Ahithophel has advised Absalom
and the elders of Israel to do such and such,
but I have advised them to do so and so.
16 Now send a message at once and tell Da-
vid, 'Do not spend the night at the fords in
the wilderness; cross over without fail, or
the king and all the people with him will be
swallowed up.'"
17 Jonathan and Ahimaaz were staying at
En Rogel. A female servant was to go and in-
form them, and they were to go and tell King
David, for they could not risk being seen en-
tering the city. 18 But a young man saw them
and told Absalom. So the two of them left at
once and went to the house of a man in Ba-
hurim. He had a well in his courtyard, and
they climbed down into it. 19 His wife took a
covering and spread it out over the opening
of the well and scattered grain over it. No one
knew anything about it.
20 When Absalom's men came to the wom-
an at the house, they asked, "Where are
Ahimaaz and Jonathan?"
The woman answered them, "They crossed
over the brook."[c] The men searched but found
no one, so they returned to Jerusalem.
21 After they had gone, the two climbed
out of the well and went to inform King Da-
vid. They said to him, "Set out and cross the

[a] *1* Or *Let me* [b] *9* Or *When some of the men fall at the first attack* [c] *20* Or *"They passed by the sheep pen toward the water."*

river at once; Ahithophel has advised such
and such against you." 22So David and all the
people with him set out and crossed the Jor-
dan. By daybreak, no one was left who had
not crossed the Jordan.

23When Ahithophel saw that his advice
had not been followed, he saddled his don-
key and set out for his house in his home-
town. He put his house in order and then
hanged himself. So he died and was buried
in his father's tomb.

Absalom's Death

24David went to Mahanaim, and Absalom
crossed the Jordan with all the men of Isra-
el. 25Absalom had appointed Amasa over the
army in place of Joab. Amasa was the son of
Jether,[a] an Ishmaelite[b] who had married Ab-
igail,[c] the daughter of Nahash and sister of
Zeruiah the mother of Joab. 26The Israelites
and Absalom camped in the land of Gilead.

27When David came to Mahanaim, Shobi
son of Nahash from Rabbah of the Ammon-
ites, and Makir son of Ammiel from Lo De-
bar, and Barzillai the Gileadite from Rogelim
28brought bedding and bowls and articles of
pottery. They also brought wheat and barley,
flour and roasted grain, beans and lentils,[d]
29honey and curds, sheep, and cheese from
cows' milk for David and his people to eat. For
they said, "The people have become exhaust-
ed and hungry and thirsty in the wilderness."

18 David mustered the men who were
with him and appointed over them
commanders of thousands and command-
ers of hundreds. 2David sent out his troops,
a third under the command of Joab, a third
under Joab's brother Abishai son of Zeruiah,
and a third under Ittai the Gittite. The king
told the troops, "I myself will surely march
out with you."

3But the men said, "You must not go out;
if we are forced to flee, they won't care about
us. Even if half of us die, they won't care; but
you are worth ten thousand of us.[e] It would
be better now for you to give us support from
the city."

4The king answered, "I will do whatever
seems best to you."

So the king stood beside the gate while all
his men marched out in units of hundreds
and of thousands. 5The king commanded
Joab, Abishai and Ittai, "Be gentle with the
young man Absalom for my sake." And all
the troops heard the king giving orders con-
cerning Absalom to each of the command-
ers.

6David's army marched out of the city to
fight Israel, and the battle took place in the
forest of Ephraim. 7There Israel's troops
were routed by David's men, and the casual-
ties that day were great—twenty thousand
men. 8The battle spread out over the whole
countryside, and the forest swallowed up
more men that day than the sword.

9Now Absalom happened to meet Da-
vid's men. He was riding his mule, and as
the mule went under the thick branches of
a large oak, Absalom's hair got caught in the
tree. He was left hanging in midair, while the
mule he was riding kept on going.

10When one of the men saw what had
happened, he told Joab, "I just saw Absalom
hanging in an oak tree."

11Joab said to the man who had told him
this, "What! You saw him? Why didn't you
strike him to the ground right there? Then
I would have had to give you ten shekels[f] of
silver and a warrior's belt."

12But the man replied, "Even if a thousand
shekels[g] were weighed out into my hands, I
would not lay a hand on the king's son. In
our hearing the king commanded you and
Abishai and Ittai, 'Protect the young man
Absalom for my sake.[h]' 13And if I had put
my life in jeopardy[i]—and nothing is hidden
from the king—you would have kept your
distance from me."

14Joab said, "I'm not going to wait like this
for you." So he took three javelins in his hand
and plunged them into Absalom's heart
while Absalom was still alive in the oak tree.
15And ten of Joab's armor-bearers surround-
ed Absalom, struck him and killed him.

[a] 25 Hebrew *Ithra*, a variant of *Jether* [b] 25 Some Septuagint manuscripts (see also 1 Chron. 2:17); Hebrew and other Septuagint manuscripts *Israelite* [c] 25 Hebrew *Abigal*, a variant of *Abigail* [d] 28 Most Septuagint manuscripts and Syriac; Hebrew *lentils, and roasted grain* [e] 3 Two Hebrew manuscripts, some Septuagint manuscripts and Vulgate; most Hebrew manuscripts *care; for now there are ten thousand like us* [f] 11 That is, about 4 ounces or about 115 grams [g] 12 That is, about 25 pounds or about 12 kilograms [h] 12 A few Hebrew manuscripts, Septuagint, Vulgate and Syriac; most Hebrew manuscripts may be translated *Absalom, whoever you may be.* [i] 13 Or *Otherwise, if I had acted treacherously toward him*

16 Then Joab sounded the trumpet, and
the troops stopped pursuing Israel, for Joab
halted them. 17 They took Absalom, threw
him into a big pit in the forest and piled up a
large heap of rocks over him. Meanwhile, all
the Israelites fled to their homes.

18 During his lifetime Absalom had taken a
pillar and erected it in the King's Valley as a
monument to himself, for he thought, "I have
no son to carry on the memory of my name."
He named the pillar after himself, and it is
called Absalom's Monument to this day.

David Mourns

19 Now Ahimaaz son of Zadok said, "Let
me run and take the news to the king that the
LORD has vindicated him by delivering him
from the hand of his enemies."

20 "You are not the one to take the news to-
day," Joab told him. "You may take the news
another time, but you must not do so today,
because the king's son is dead."

21 Then Joab said to a Cushite, "Go, tell
the king what you have seen." The Cushite
bowed down before Joab and ran off.

22 Ahimaaz son of Zadok again said to
Joab, "Come what may, please let me run be-
hind the Cushite."

But Joab replied, "My son, why do you
want to go? You don't have any news that will
bring you a reward."

23 He said, "Come what may, I want to
run."

So Joab said, "Run!" Then Ahimaaz ran by
way of the plain[a] and outran the Cushite.

24 While David was sitting between the
inner and outer gates, the watchman went
up to the roof of the gateway by the wall. As
he looked out, he saw a man running alone.
25 The watchman called out to the king and
reported it.

The king said, "If he is alone, he must have
good news." And the runner came closer and
closer.

26 Then the watchman saw another run-
ner, and he called down to the gatekeeper,
"Look, another man running alone!"

The king said, "He must be bringing good
news, too."

27 The watchman said, "It seems to me
that the first one runs like Ahimaaz son of
Zadok."

"He's a good man," the king said. "He
comes with good news."

28 Then Ahimaaz called out to the king,
"All is well!" He bowed down before the king
with his face to the ground and said, "Praise
be to the LORD your God! He has delivered
up those who lifted their hands against my
lord the king."

29 The king asked, "Is the young man Ab-
salom safe?"

Ahimaaz answered, "I saw great confu-
sion just as Joab was about to send the king's
servant and me, your servant, but I don't
know what it was."

30 The king said, "Stand aside and wait
here." So he stepped aside and stood there.

31 Then the Cushite arrived and said, "My
lord the king, hear the good news! The LORD
has vindicated you today by delivering you
from the hand of all who rose up against you."

32 The king asked the Cushite, "Is the
young man Absalom safe?"

The Cushite replied, "May the enemies of
my lord the king and all who rise up to harm
you be like that young man."

33 The king was shaken. He went up to the
room over the gateway and wept. As he went,
he said: "O my son Absalom! My son, my son
Absalom! If only I had died instead of you—
O Absalom, my son, my son!"[b]

19[c] Joab was told, "The king is weeping
and mourning for Absalom." 2 And
for the whole army the victory that day was
turned into mourning, because on that day
the troops heard it said, "The king is grieving
for his son." 3 The men stole into the city that
day as men steal in who are ashamed when
they flee from battle. 4 The king covered his
face and cried aloud, "O my son Absalom!
O Absalom, my son, my son!"

5 Then Joab went into the house to the
king and said, "Today you have humiliated
all your men, who have just saved your life
and the lives of your sons and daughters and
the lives of your wives and concubines. 6 You
love those who hate you and hate those who
love you. You have made it clear today that
the commanders and their men mean noth-
ing to you. I see that you would be pleased if
Absalom were alive today and all of us were
dead. 7 Now go out and encourage your men.
I swear by the LORD that if you don't go out,

[a] *23* That is, the plain of the Jordan [b] *33* In Hebrew texts this verse (18:33) is numbered 19:1.
[c] In Hebrew texts 19:1-43 is numbered 19:2-44

not a man will be left with you by nightfall. This will be worse for you than all the calamities that have come on you from your youth till now."

8 So the king got up and took his seat in the gateway. When the men were told, "The king is sitting in the gateway," they all came before him.

Meanwhile, the Israelites had fled to their homes.

David Returns to Jerusalem

9 Throughout the tribes of Israel, all the people were arguing among themselves, saying, "The king delivered us from the hand of our enemies; he is the one who rescued us from the hand of the Philistines. But now he has fled the country to escape from Absalom; 10 and Absalom, whom we anointed to rule over us, has died in battle. So why do you say nothing about bringing the king back?"

11 King David sent this message to Zadok and Abiathar, the priests: "Ask the elders of Judah, 'Why should you be the last to bring the king back to his palace, since what is being said throughout Israel has reached the king at his quarters? 12 You are my relatives, my own flesh and blood. So why should you be the last to bring back the king?' 13 And say to Amasa, 'Are you not my own flesh and blood? May God deal with me, be it ever so severely, if you are not the commander of my army for life in place of Joab.'"

14 He won over the hearts of the men of Judah so that they were all of one mind. They sent word to the king, "Return, you and all your men." 15 Then the king returned and went as far as the Jordan.

Now the men of Judah had come to Gilgal to go out and meet the king and bring him across the Jordan. 16 Shimei son of Gera, the Benjamite from Bahurim, hurried down with the men of Judah to meet King David. 17 With him were a thousand Benjamites, along with Ziba, the steward of Saul's household, and his fifteen sons and twenty servants. They rushed to the Jordan, where the king was. 18 They crossed at the ford to take the king's household over and to do whatever he wished.

When Shimei son of Gera crossed the Jordan, he fell prostrate before the king 19 and said to him, "May my lord not hold me guilty. Do not remember how your servant did wrong on the day my lord the king left Jerusalem. May the king put it out of his mind. 20 For I your servant know that I have sinned, but today I have come here as the first from the tribes of Joseph to come down and meet my lord the king."

21 Then Abishai son of Zeruiah said, "Shouldn't Shimei be put to death for this? He cursed the LORD's anointed."

22 David replied, "What does this have to do with you, you sons of Zeruiah? What right do you have to interfere? Should anyone be put to death in Israel today? Don't I know that today I am king over Israel?" 23 So the king said to Shimei, "You shall not die." And the king promised him on oath.

24 Mephibosheth, Saul's grandson, also went down to meet the king. He had not taken care of his feet or trimmed his mustache or washed his clothes from the day the king left until the day he returned safely. 25 When he came from Jerusalem to meet the king, the king asked him, "Why didn't you go with me, Mephibosheth?"

26 He said, "My lord the king, since I your servant am lame, I said, 'I will have my donkey saddled and will ride on it, so I can go with the king.' But Ziba my servant betrayed me. 27 And he has slandered your servant to my lord the king. My lord the king is like an angel of God; so do whatever you wish. 28 All my grandfather's descendants deserved nothing but death from my lord the king, but you gave your servant a place among those who eat at your table. So what right do I have to make any more appeals to the king?"

29 The king said to him, "Why say more? I order you and Ziba to divide the land."

30 Mephibosheth said to the king, "Let him take everything, now that my lord the king has returned home safely."

31 Barzillai the Gileadite also came down from Rogelim to cross the Jordan with the king and to send him on his way from there. 32 Now Barzillai was very old, eighty years of age. He had provided for the king during his stay in Mahanaim, for he was a very wealthy man. 33 The king said to Barzillai, "Cross over with me and stay with me in Jerusalem, and I will provide for you."

34 But Barzillai answered the king, "How many more years will I live, that I should go up to Jerusalem with the king? 35 I am now

eighty years old. Can I tell the difference between what is enjoyable and what is not? Can your servant taste what he eats and drinks? Can I still hear the voices of male and female singers? Why should your servant be an added burden to my lord the king?
[36]Your servant will cross over the Jordan with the king for a short distance, but why should the king reward me in this way?
[37]Let your servant return, that I may die in my own town near the tomb of my father and mother. But here is your servant Kimham. Let him cross over with my lord the king. Do for him whatever you wish."

[38]The king said, "Kimham shall cross over with me, and I will do for him whatever you wish. And anything you desire from me I will do for you."

[39]So all the people crossed the Jordan, and then the king crossed over. The king kissed Barzillai and bid him farewell, and Barzillai returned to his home.

[40]When the king crossed over to Gilgal, Kimham crossed with him. All the troops of Judah and half the troops of Israel had taken the king over.

[41]Soon all the men of Israel were coming to the king and saying to him, "Why did our brothers, the men of Judah, steal the king away and bring him and his household across the Jordan, together with all his men?"

[42]All the men of Judah answered the men of Israel, "We did this because the king is closely related to us. Why are you angry about it? Have we eaten any of the king's provisions? Have we taken anything for ourselves?"

[43]Then the men of Israel answered the men of Judah, "We have ten shares in the king; so we have a greater claim on David than you have. Why then do you treat us with contempt? Weren't we the first to speak of bringing back our king?"

But the men of Judah pressed their claims even more forcefully than the men of Israel.

Sheba Rebels Against David

20 Now a troublemaker named Sheba son of Bikri, a Benjamite, happened to be there. He sounded the trumpet and shouted,

"We have no share in David,
no part in Jesse's son!
Every man to his tent, Israel!"

[2]So all the men of Israel deserted David to follow Sheba son of Bikri. But the men of Judah stayed by their king all the way from the Jordan to Jerusalem.

[3]When David returned to his palace in Jerusalem, he took the ten concubines he had left to take care of the palace and put them in a house under guard. He provided for them but had no sexual relations with them. They were kept in confinement till the day of their death, living as widows.

[4]Then the king said to Amasa, "Summon the men of Judah to come to me within three days, and be here yourself."
[5]But when Amasa went to summon Judah, he took longer than the time the king had set for him.

[6]David said to Abishai, "Now Sheba son of Bikri will do us more harm than Absalom did. Take your master's men and pursue him, or he will find fortified cities and escape from us."[a]
[7]So Joab's men and the Kerethites and Pelethites and all the mighty warriors went out under the command of Abishai. They marched out from Jerusalem to pursue Sheba son of Bikri.

[8]While they were at the great rock in Gibeon, Amasa came to meet them. Joab was wearing his military tunic, and strapped over it at his waist was a belt with a dagger in its sheath. As he stepped forward, it dropped out of its sheath.

[9]Joab said to Amasa, "How are you, my brother?" Then Joab took Amasa by the beard with his right hand to kiss him.
[10]Amasa was not on his guard against the dagger in Joab's hand, and Joab plunged it into his belly, and his intestines spilled out on the ground. Without being stabbed again, Amasa died. Then Joab and his brother Abishai pursued Sheba son of Bikri.

[11]One of Joab's men stood beside Amasa and said, "Whoever favors Joab, and whoever is for David, let him follow Joab!"
[12]Amasa lay wallowing in his blood in the middle of the road, and the man saw that all the troops came to a halt there. When he realized that everyone who came up to Amasa stopped, he dragged him from the road into a field and threw a garment over him.
[13]After Amasa

[a] 6 Or *and do us serious injury*

had been removed from the road, everyone
went on with Joab to pursue Sheba son of
Bikri.
14 Sheba passed through all the tribes of
Israel to Abel Beth Maakah and through the
entire region of the Bikrites,[a] who gathered
together and followed him. 15 All the troops
with Joab came and besieged Sheba in Abel
Beth Maakah. They built a siege ramp up to
the city, and it stood against the outer forti-
fications. While they were battering the wall
to bring it down, 16 a wise woman called from
the city, "Listen! Listen! Tell Joab to come
here so I can speak to him." 17 He went to-
ward her, and she asked, "Are you Joab?"
"I am," he answered.
She said, "Listen to what your servant has
to say."
"I'm listening," he said.
18 She continued, "Long ago they used to
say, 'Get your answer at Abel,' and that set-
tled it. 19 We are the peaceful and faithful in
Israel. You are trying to destroy a city that is
a mother in Israel. Why do you want to swal-
low up the LORD's inheritance?"
20 "Far be it from me!" Joab replied, "Far be
it from me to swallow up or destroy! 21 That
is not the case. A man named Sheba son of
Bikri, from the hill country of Ephraim, has
lifted up his hand against the king, against
David. Hand over this one man, and I'll
withdraw from the city."
The woman said to Joab, "His head will be
thrown to you from the wall."
22 Then the woman went to all the peo-
ple with her wise advice, and they cut off
the head of Sheba son of Bikri and threw it
to Joab. So he sounded the trumpet, and his
men dispersed from the city, each returning
to his home. And Joab went back to the king
in Jerusalem.

David's Officials

23 Joab was over Israel's entire army; Be-
naiah son of Jehoiada was over the Kereth-
ites and Pelethites; 24 Adoniram[b] was in
charge of forced labor; Jehoshaphat son of
Ahilud was recorder; 25 Sheva was secretary;
Zadok and Abiathar were priests; 26 and Ira
the Jairite[c] was David's priest.

The Gibeonites Avenged

21 During the reign of David, there was
a famine for three successive years;
so David sought the face of the LORD. The
LORD said, "It is on account of Saul and his
blood-stained house; it is because he put the
Gibeonites to death."
2 The king summoned the Gibeonites and
spoke to them. (Now the Gibeonites were
not a part of Israel but were survivors of the
Amorites; the Israelites had sworn to spare
them, but Saul in his zeal for Israel and Ju-
dah had tried to annihilate them.) 3 David
asked the Gibeonites, "What shall I do for
you? How shall I make atonement so that you
will bless the LORD's inheritance?"
4 The Gibeonites answered him, "We have
no right to demand silver or gold from Saul
or his family, nor do we have the right to put
anyone in Israel to death."
"What do you want me to do for you?" Da-
vid asked.
5 They answered the king, "As for the man
who destroyed us and plotted against us so
that we have been decimated and have no
place anywhere in Israel, 6 let seven of his
male descendants be given to us to be killed
and their bodies exposed before the LORD at
Gibeah of Saul — the LORD's chosen one."
So the king said, "I will give them to you."
7 The king spared Mephibosheth son of
Jonathan, the son of Saul, because of the
oath before the LORD between David and
Jonathan son of Saul. 8 But the king took
Armoni and Mephibosheth, the two sons
of Aiah's daughter Rizpah, whom she had
borne to Saul, together with the five sons
of Saul's daughter Merab,[d] whom she had
borne to Adriel son of Barzillai the Meho-
lathite. 9 He handed them over to the Gibe-
onites, who killed them and exposed their
bodies on a hill before the LORD. All seven
of them fell together; they were put to death
during the first days of the harvest, just as
the barley harvest was beginning.
10 Rizpah daughter of Aiah took sackcloth
and spread it out for herself on a rock. From
the beginning of the harvest till the rain
poured down from the heavens on the bod-
ies, she did not let the birds touch them by

[a] *14* See Septuagint and Vulgate; Hebrew *Berites.* [b] *24* Some Septuagint manuscripts (see also 1 Kings 4:6 and 5:14); Hebrew *Adoram* [c] *26* Hebrew; some Septuagint manuscripts and Syriac (see also 23:38) *Ithrite* [d] *8* Two Hebrew manuscripts, some Septuagint manuscripts and Syriac (see also 1 Samuel 18:19); most Hebrew and Septuagint manuscripts *Michal*

day or the wild animals by night. 11 When
David was told what Aiah's daughter Rizpah,
Saul's concubine, had done, 12 he went and
took the bones of Saul and his son Jonathan
from the citizens of Jabesh Gilead. (They had
stolen their bodies from the public square at
Beth Shan, where the Philistines had hung
them after they struck Saul down on Gil-
boa.) 13 David brought the bones of Saul and
his son Jonathan from there, and the bones
of those who had been killed and exposed
were gathered up.
14 They buried the bones of Saul and his
son Jonathan in the tomb of Saul's father
Kish, at Zela in Benjamin, and did every-
thing the king commanded. After that, God
answered prayer in behalf of the land.

Wars Against the Philistines

15 Once again there was a battle between
the Philistines and Israel. David went down
with his men to fight against the Philis-
tines, and he became exhausted. 16 And Ish-
bi-Benob, one of the descendants of Rapha,
whose bronze spearhead weighed three
hundred shekels[a] and who was armed with
a new sword, said he would kill David. 17 But
Abishai son of Zeruiah came to David's res-
cue; he struck the Philistine down and killed
him. Then David's men swore to him, say-
ing, "Never again will you go out with us to
battle, so that the lamp of Israel will not be
extinguished."
18 In the course of time, there was anoth-
er battle with the Philistines, at Gob. At that
time Sibbekai the Hushathite killed Saph,
one of the descendants of Rapha.
19 In another battle with the Philistines at
Gob, Elhanan son of Jair[b] the Bethlehemite
killed the brother of[c] Goliath the Gittite, who
had a spear with a shaft like a weaver's rod.
20 In still another battle, which took place
at Gath, there was a huge man with six fin-
gers on each hand and six toes on each
foot — twenty-four in all. He also was de-
scended from Rapha. 21 When he taunted
Israel, Jonathan son of Shimeah, David's
brother, killed him.
22 These four were descendants of Rapha
in Gath, and they fell at the hands of David
and his men.

David's Song of Praise

22 David sang to the LORD the words of
this song when the LORD delivered
him from the hand of all his enemies and
from the hand of Saul. 2 He said:

"The LORD is my rock, my fortress and my
deliverer;
3 my God is my rock, in whom I take
refuge,
my shield[d] and the horn[e] of my
salvation.
He is my stronghold, my refuge and my
savior —
from violent people you save me.

4 "I called to the LORD, who is worthy of
praise,
and have been saved from my
enemies.
5 The waves of death swirled about me;
the torrents of destruction
overwhelmed me.
6 The cords of the grave coiled around me;
the snares of death confronted me.

7 "In my distress I called to the LORD;
I called out to my God.
From his temple he heard my voice;
my cry came to his ears.
8 The earth trembled and quaked,
the foundations of the heavens[f]
shook;
they trembled because he was angry.
9 Smoke rose from his nostrils;
consuming fire came from his mouth,
burning coals blazed out of it.
10 He parted the heavens and came down;
dark clouds were under his feet.
11 He mounted the cherubim and flew;
he soared[g] on the wings of the wind.
12 He made darkness his canopy around
him —
the dark[h] rain clouds of the sky.
13 Out of the brightness of his presence
bolts of lightning blazed forth.
14 The LORD thundered from heaven;
the voice of the Most High resounded.

[a] *16* That is, about 7 1/2 pounds or about 3.5 kilograms [b] *19* See 1 Chron. 20:5; Hebrew *Jaare-Oregim.* [c] *19* See 1 Chron. 20:5; Hebrew does not have *the brother of.* [d] *3* Or *sovereign* [e] *3* *Horn* here symbolizes strength. [f] *8* Hebrew; Vulgate and Syriac (see also Psalm 18:7) *mountains* [g] *11* Many Hebrew manuscripts (see also Psalm 18:10); most Hebrew manuscripts *appeared* [h] *12* Septuagint (see also Psalm 18:11); Hebrew *massed*

15 He shot his arrows and scattered the enemy,
with great bolts of lightning he routed them.
16 The valleys of the sea were exposed
and the foundations of the earth laid bare
at the rebuke of the LORD,
at the blast of breath from his nostrils.

17 "He reached down from on high and took hold of me;
he drew me out of deep waters.
18 He rescued me from my powerful enemy,
from my foes, who were too strong for me.
19 They confronted me in the day of my disaster,
but the LORD was my support.
20 He brought me out into a spacious place;
he rescued me because he delighted in me.

21 "The LORD has dealt with me according to my righteousness;
according to the cleanness of my hands he has rewarded me.
22 For I have kept the ways of the LORD;
I am not guilty of turning from my God.
23 All his laws are before me;
I have not turned away from his decrees.
24 I have been blameless before him
and have kept myself from sin.
25 The LORD has rewarded me according to my righteousness,
according to my cleanness[a] in his sight.

26 "To the faithful you show yourself faithful,
to the blameless you show yourself blameless,
27 to the pure you show yourself pure,
but to the devious you show yourself shrewd.
28 You save the humble,
but your eyes are on the haughty to bring them low.
29 You, LORD, are my lamp;
the LORD turns my darkness into light.
30 With your help I can advance against a troop[b];
with my God I can scale a wall.

31 "As for God, his way is perfect:
The LORD's word is flawless;
he shields all who take refuge in him.
32 For who is God besides the LORD?
And who is the Rock except our God?
33 It is God who arms me with strength[c]
and keeps my way secure.
34 He makes my feet like the feet of a deer;
he causes me to stand on the heights.
35 He trains my hands for battle;
my arms can bend a bow of bronze.
36 You make your saving help my shield;
your help has made[d] me great.
37 You provide a broad path for my feet,
so that my ankles do not give way.

38 "I pursued my enemies and crushed them;
I did not turn back till they were destroyed.
39 I crushed them completely, and they could not rise;
they fell beneath my feet.
40 You armed me with strength for battle;
you humbled my adversaries before me.
41 You made my enemies turn their backs in flight,
and I destroyed my foes.
42 They cried for help, but there was no one to save them —
to the LORD, but he did not answer.
43 I beat them as fine as the dust of the earth;
I pounded and trampled them like mud in the streets.

44 "You have delivered me from the attacks of the peoples;
you have preserved me as the head of nations.
People I did not know now serve me,
45 foreigners cower before me;
as soon as they hear of me, they obey me.
46 They all lose heart;
they come trembling[e] from their strongholds.

[a] 25 Hebrew; Septuagint and Vulgate (see also Psalm 18:24) *to the cleanness of my hands* [b] 30 Or *can run through a barricade* [c] 33 Dead Sea Scrolls, some Septuagint manuscripts, Vulgate and Syriac (see also Psalm 18:32); Masoretic Text *who is my strong refuge* [d] 36 Dead Sea Scrolls; Masoretic Text *shield; / you stoop down to make* [e] 46 Some Septuagint manuscripts and Vulgate (see also Psalm 18:45); Masoretic Text *they arm themselves*

[47]"The LORD lives! Praise be to my Rock!
Exalted be my God, the Rock, my
Savior!
[48]He is the God who avenges me,
who puts the nations under me,
[49]who sets me free from my enemies.
You exalted me above my foes;
from a violent man you rescued me.
[50]Therefore I will praise you, LORD, among
the nations;
I will sing the praises of your name.

[51]"He gives his king great victories;
he shows unfailing kindness to his
anointed,
to David and his descendants
forever."

David's Last Words

23 These are the last words of David:

"The inspired utterance of David son
of Jesse,
the utterance of the man exalted by the
Most High,
the man anointed by the God of Jacob,
the hero of Israel's songs:

[2]"The Spirit of the LORD spoke through me;
his word was on my tongue.
[3]The God of Israel spoke,
the Rock of Israel said to me:
'When one rules over people in
righteousness,
when he rules in the fear of God,
[4]he is like the light of morning at sunrise
on a cloudless morning,
like the brightness after rain
that brings grass from the earth.'

[5]"If my house were not right with God,
surely he would not have made with
me an everlasting covenant,
arranged and secured in every part;
surely he would not bring to fruition my
salvation
and grant me my every desire.
[6]But evil men are all to be cast aside like
thorns,
which are not gathered with the hand.
[7]Whoever touches thorns
uses a tool of iron or the shaft of
a spear;
they are burned up where they lie."

David's Mighty Warriors

[8]These are the names of David's mighty
warriors:
Josheb-Basshebeth,[a] a Tahkemonite,[b] was
chief of the Three; he raised his spear against
eight hundred men, whom he killed[c] in one
encounter.
[9]Next to him was Eleazar son of Dodai
the Ahohite. As one of the three mighty war-
riors, he was with David when they taunted
the Philistines gathered at Pas Dammim[d] for
battle. Then the Israelites retreated, [10]but
Eleazar stood his ground and struck down
the Philistines till his hand grew tired and
froze to the sword. The LORD brought about
a great victory that day. The troops returned
to Eleazar, but only to strip the dead.
[11]Next to him was Shammah son of Agee
the Hararite. When the Philistines banded
together at a place where there was a field
full of lentils, Israel's troops fled from them.
[12]But Shammah took his stand in the mid-
dle of the field. He defended it and struck
the Philistines down, and the LORD brought
about a great victory.
[13]During harvest time, three of the thir-
ty chief warriors came down to David at the
cave of Adullam, while a band of Philistines
was encamped in the Valley of Rephaim.
[14]At that time David was in the stronghold,
and the Philistine garrison was at Beth-
lehem. [15]David longed for water and said,
"Oh, that someone would get me a drink of
water from the well near the gate of Bethle-
hem!" [16]So the three mighty warriors broke
through the Philistine lines, drew water
from the well near the gate of Bethlehem
and carried it back to David. But he refused
to drink it; instead, he poured it out before
the LORD. [17]"Far be it from me, LORD, to do
this!" he said. "Is it not the blood of men who
went at the risk of their lives?" And David
would not drink it.
Such were the exploits of the three mighty
warriors.

[a] 8 Hebrew; some Septuagint manuscripts suggest *Ish-Bosheth,* that is, *Esh-Baal* (see also 1 Chron. 11:11 *Jashobeam*). [b] 8 Probably a variant of *Hakmonite* (see 1 Chron. 11:11) [c] 8 Some Septuagint manuscripts (see also 1 Chron. 11:11); Hebrew and other Septuagint manuscripts *Three; it was Adino the Eznite who killed eight hundred men* [d] 9 See 1 Chron. 11:13; Hebrew *gathered there.*

18 Abishai the brother of Joab son of Zer-
uiah was chief of the Three.[a] He raised his
spear against three hundred men, whom he
killed, and so he became as famous as the
Three. 19 Was he not held in greater honor
than the Three? He became their command-
er, even though he was not included among
them.

20 Benaiah son of Jehoiada, a valiant fight-
er from Kabzeel, performed great exploits.
He struck down Moab's two mightiest war-
riors. He also went down into a pit on a
snowy day and killed a lion. 21 And he struck
down a huge Egyptian. Although the Egyp-
tian had a spear in his hand, Benaiah went
against him with a club. He snatched the
spear from the Egyptian's hand and killed
him with his own spear. 22 Such were the
exploits of Benaiah son of Jehoiada; he too
was as famous as the three mighty warriors.
23 He was held in greater honor than any of
the Thirty, but he was not included among
the Three. And David put him in charge of
his bodyguard.

24 Among the Thirty were:
Asahel the brother of Joab,
Elhanan son of Dodo from Bethlehem,
25 Shammah the Harodite,
Elika the Harodite,
26 Helez the Paltite,
Ira son of Ikkesh from Tekoa,
27 Abiezer from Anathoth,
Sibbekai[b] the Hushathite,
28 Zalmon the Ahohite,
Maharai the Netophathite,
29 Heled[c] son of Baanah the Netophathite,
Ithai son of Ribai from Gibeah in Benjamin,
30 Benaiah the Pirathonite,
Hiddai[d] from the ravines of Gaash,
31 Abi-Albon the Arbathite,
Azmaveth the Barhumite,
32 Eliahba the Shaalbonite,
the sons of Jashen,
Jonathan 33 son of[e] Shammah the Hararite,
Ahiam son of Sharar[f] the Hararite,
34 Eliphelet son of Ahasbai the Maakathite,
Eliam son of Ahithophel the Gilonite,
35 Hezro the Carmelite,
Paarai the Arbite,
36 Igal son of Nathan from Zobah,
the son of Hagri,[g]
37 Zelek the Ammonite,
Naharai the Beerothite, the armor-bearer of Joab son of Zeruiah,
38 Ira the Ithrite,
Gareb the Ithrite
39 and Uriah the Hittite.
There were thirty-seven in all.

David Enrolls the Fighting Men

24 Again the anger of the LORD burned
against Israel, and he incited David
against them, saying, "Go and take a census
of Israel and Judah."

2 So the king said to Joab and the army
commanders[h] with him, "Go throughout the
tribes of Israel from Dan to Beersheba and
enroll the fighting men, so that I may know
how many there are."

3 But Joab replied to the king, "May the
LORD your God multiply the troops a hun-
dred times over, and may the eyes of my lord
the king see it. But why does my lord the king
want to do such a thing?"

4 The king's word, however, overruled
Joab and the army commanders; so they left
the presence of the king to enroll the fighting
men of Israel.

5 After crossing the Jordan, they camped
near Aroer, south of the town in the gorge,
and then went through Gad and on to Jazer.
6 They went to Gilead and the region of Tah-
tim Hodshi, and on to Dan Jaan and around
toward Sidon. 7 Then they went toward the
fortress of Tyre and all the towns of the Hi-
vites and Canaanites. Finally, they went on
to Beersheba in the Negev of Judah.

[a] *18* Most Hebrew manuscripts (see also 1 Chron. 11:20); two Hebrew manuscripts and Syriac *Thirty*
[b] *27* Some Septuagint manuscripts (see also 21:18; 1 Chron. 11:29); Hebrew *Mebunnai*
[c] *29* Some Hebrew manuscripts and Vulgate (see also 1 Chron. 11:30); most Hebrew manuscripts *Heleb*
[d] *30* Hebrew; some Septuagint manuscripts (see also 1 Chron. 11:32) *Hurai*
[e] *33* Some Septuagint manuscripts (see also 1 Chron. 11:34); Hebrew does not have *son of.*
[f] *33* Hebrew; some Septuagint manuscripts (see also 1 Chron. 11:35) *Sakar*
[g] *36* Some Septuagint manuscripts (see also 1 Chron. 11:38); Hebrew *Haggadi*
[h] *2* Septuagint (see also verse 4 and 1 Chron. 21:2); Hebrew *Joab the army commander*

8 After they had gone through the entire land, they came back to Jerusalem at the end of nine months and twenty days.

9 Joab reported the number of the fighting men to the king: In Israel there were eight hundred thousand able-bodied men who could handle a sword, and in Judah five hundred thousand.

10 David was conscience-stricken after he had counted the fighting men, and he said to the LORD, "I have sinned greatly in what I have done. Now, LORD, I beg you, take away the guilt of your servant. I have done a very foolish thing."

11 Before David got up the next morning, the word of the LORD had come to Gad the prophet, David's seer: 12 "Go and tell David, 'This is what the LORD says: I am giving you three options. Choose one of them for me to carry out against you.' "

13 So Gad went to David and said to him, "Shall there come on you three[a] years of famine in your land? Or three months of fleeing from your enemies while they pursue you? Or three days of plague in your land? Now then, think it over and decide how I should answer the one who sent me."

14 David said to Gad, "I am in deep distress. Let us fall into the hands of the LORD, for his mercy is great; but do not let me fall into human hands."

15 So the LORD sent a plague on Israel from that morning until the end of the time designated, and seventy thousand of the people from Dan to Beersheba died. 16 When the angel stretched out his hand to destroy Jerusalem, the LORD relented concerning the disaster and said to the angel who was afflicting the people, "Enough! Withdraw your hand." The angel of the LORD was then at the threshing floor of Araunah the Jebusite.

17 When David saw the angel who was striking down the people, he said to the LORD, "I have sinned; I, the shepherd,[b] have done wrong. These are but sheep. What have they done? Let your hand fall on me and my family."

David Builds an Altar

18 On that day Gad went to David and said to him, "Go up and build an altar to the LORD on the threshing floor of Araunah the Jebusite." 19 So David went up, as the LORD had commanded through Gad. 20 When Araunah looked and saw the king and his officials coming toward him, he went out and bowed down before the king with his face to the ground.

21 Araunah said, "Why has my lord the king come to his servant?"

"To buy your threshing floor," David answered, "so I can build an altar to the LORD, that the plague on the people may be stopped."

22 Araunah said to David, "Let my lord the king take whatever he wishes and offer it up. Here are oxen for the burnt offering, and here are threshing sledges and ox yokes for the wood. 23 Your Majesty, Araunah[c] gives all this to the king." Araunah also said to him, "May the LORD your God accept you."

24 But the king replied to Araunah, "No, I insist on paying you for it. I will not sacrifice to the LORD my God burnt offerings that cost me nothing."

So David bought the threshing floor and the oxen and paid fifty shekels[d] of silver for them. 25 David built an altar to the LORD there and sacrificed burnt offerings and fellowship offerings. Then the LORD answered his prayer in behalf of the land, and the plague on Israel was stopped.

[a] *13* Septuagint (see also 1 Chron. 21:12); Hebrew *seven* [b] *17* Dead Sea Scrolls and Septuagint; Masoretic Text does not have *the shepherd.* [c] *23* Some Hebrew manuscripts and Septuagint; most Hebrew manuscripts *King Araunah* [d] *24* That is, about 1 1/4 pounds or about 575 grams

1 KINGS

Adonijah Sets Himself Up as King

1 When King David was very old, he could
not keep warm even when they put cov-
ers over him. [2]So his attendants said to him,
"Let us look for a young virgin to serve the
king and take care of him. She can lie be-
side him so that our lord the king may keep
warm."
[3]Then they searched throughout Israel
for a beautiful young woman and found Abi-
shag, a Shunammite, and brought her to the
king. [4]The woman was very beautiful; she
took care of the king and waited on him, but
the king had no sexual relations with her.
[5]Now Adonijah, whose mother was Hag-
gith, put himself forward and said, "I will be
king." So he got chariots and horses[a] ready,
with fifty men to run ahead of him. [6](His fa-
ther had never rebuked him by asking, "Why
do you behave as you do?" He was also very
handsome and was born next after Absalom.)
[7]Adonijah conferred with Joab son of
Zeruiah and with Abiathar the priest, and
they gave him their support. [8]But Zadok the
priest, Benaiah son of Jehoiada, Nathan the
prophet, Shimei and Rei and David's special
guard did not join Adonijah.
[9]Adonijah then sacrificed sheep, cattle
and fattened calves at the Stone of Zoheleth
near En Rogel. He invited all his brothers,
the king's sons, and all the royal officials of
Judah, [10]but he did not invite Nathan the
prophet or Benaiah or the special guard or
his brother Solomon.
[11]Then Nathan asked Bathsheba, Solo-
mon's mother, "Have you not heard that Ad-
onijah, the son of Haggith, has become king,
and our lord David knows nothing about it?
[12]Now then, let me advise you how you can
save your own life and the life of your son
Solomon. [13]Go in to King David and say to
him, 'My lord the king, did you not swear to
me your servant: "Surely Solomon your son
shall be king after me, and he will sit on my
throne"? Why then has Adonijah become
king?' [14]While you are still there talking to
the king, I will come in and add my word to
what you have said."
[15]So Bathsheba went to see the aged king
in his room, where Abishag the Shunam-
mite was attending him. [16]Bathsheba bowed
down, prostrating herself before the king.
"What is it you want?" the king asked.
[17]She said to him, "My lord, you yourself
swore to me your servant by the LORD your
God: 'Solomon your son shall be king af-
ter me, and he will sit on my throne.' [18]But
now Adonijah has become king, and you,
my lord the king, do not know about it. [19]He
has sacrificed great numbers of cattle, fat-
tened calves, and sheep, and has invited all
the king's sons, Abiathar the priest and Joab
the commander of the army, but he has not
invited Solomon your servant. [20]My lord
the king, the eyes of all Israel are on you, to
learn from you who will sit on the throne of
my lord the king after him. [21]Otherwise, as
soon as my lord the king is laid to rest with
his ancestors, I and my son Solomon will be
treated as criminals."
[22]While she was still speaking with the
king, Nathan the prophet arrived. [23]And the
king was told, "Nathan the prophet is here."
So he went before the king and bowed with
his face to the ground.
[24]Nathan said, "Have you, my lord the
king, declared that Adonijah shall be king
after you, and that he will sit on your throne?
[25]Today he has gone down and sacrificed
great numbers of cattle, fattened calves, and
sheep. He has invited all the king's sons, the
commanders of the army and Abiathar the
priest. Right now they are eating and drink-
ing with him and saying, 'Long live King Ado-
nijah!' [26]But me your servant, and Zadok the
priest, and Benaiah son of Jehoiada, and your
servant Solomon he did not invite. [27]Is this
something my lord the king has done with-
out letting his servants know who should sit
on the throne of my lord the king after him?"

[a] 5 Or *charioteers*

David Makes Solomon King

28 Then King David said, "Call in Bathshe-
ba." So she came into the king's presence
and stood before him.
29 The king then took an oath: "As surely
as the LORD lives, who has delivered me out
of every trouble, 30 I will surely carry out this
very day what I swore to you by the LORD,
the God of Israel: Solomon your son shall be
king after me, and he will sit on my throne
in my place."
31 Then Bathsheba bowed down with her
face to the ground, prostrating herself before
the king, and said, "May my lord King David
live forever!"
32 King David said, "Call in Zadok the
priest, Nathan the prophet and Benaiah son
of Jehoiada." When they came before the
king, 33 he said to them: "Take your lord's
servants with you and have Solomon my son
mount my own mule and take him down to
Gihon. 34 There have Zadok the priest and
Nathan the prophet anoint him king over Is-
rael. Blow the trumpet and shout, 'Long live
King Solomon!' 35 Then you are to go up with
him, and he is to come and sit on my throne
and reign in my place. I have appointed him
ruler over Israel and Judah."
36 Benaiah son of Jehoiada answered the
king, "Amen! May the LORD, the God of my
lord the king, so declare it. 37 As the LORD
was with my lord the king, so may he be with
Solomon to make his throne even greater
than the throne of my lord King David!"
38 So Zadok the priest, Nathan the prophet,
Benaiah son of Jehoiada, the Kerethites and
the Pelethites went down and had Solomon
mount King David's mule, and they escort-
ed him to Gihon. 39 Zadok the priest took the
horn of oil from the sacred tent and anointed
Solomon. Then they sounded the trumpet
and all the people shouted, "Long live King
Solomon!" 40 And all the people went up after
him, playing pipes and rejoicing greatly, so
that the ground shook with the sound.
41 Adonijah and all the guests who were
with him heard it as they were finishing their
feast. On hearing the sound of the trumpet,
Joab asked, "What's the meaning of all the
noise in the city?"
42 Even as he was speaking, Jonathan son
of Abiathar the priest arrived. Adonijah said,
"Come in. A worthy man like you must be
bringing good news."
43 "Not at all!" Jonathan answered. "Our
lord King David has made Solomon king.
44 The king has sent with him Zadok the
priest, Nathan the prophet, Benaiah son
of Jehoiada, the Kerethites and the Pele-
thites, and they have put him on the king's
mule, 45 and Zadok the priest and Nathan
the prophet have anointed him king at Gi-
hon. From there they have gone up cheer-
ing, and the city resounds with it. That's the
noise you hear. 46 Moreover, Solomon has
taken his seat on the royal throne. 47 Also,
the royal officials have come to congratulate
our lord King David, saying, 'May your God
make Solomon's name more famous than
yours and his throne greater than yours!'
And the king bowed in worship on his bed
48 and said, 'Praise be to the LORD, the God
of Israel, who has allowed my eyes to see a
successor on my throne today.'"
49 At this, all Adonijah's guests rose in
alarm and dispersed. 50 But Adonijah, in fear
of Solomon, went and took hold of the horns
of the altar. 51 Then Solomon was told, "Ado-
nijah is afraid of King Solomon and is cling-
ing to the horns of the altar. He says, 'Let
King Solomon swear to me today that he will
not put his servant to death with the sword.'"
52 Solomon replied, "If he shows himself
to be worthy, not a hair of his head will fall
to the ground; but if evil is found in him, he
will die." 53 Then King Solomon sent men,
and they brought him down from the al-
tar. And Adonijah came and bowed down
to King Solomon, and Solomon said, "Go to
your home."

David's Charge to Solomon

2 When the time drew near for David to
die, he gave a charge to Solomon his son.
2 "I am about to go the way of all the
earth," he said. "So be strong, act like a man,
3 and observe what the LORD your God re-
quires: Walk in obedience to him, and keep
his decrees and commands, his laws and
regulations, as written in the Law of Moses.
Do this so that you may prosper in all you do
and wherever you go 4 and that the LORD may
keep his promise to me: 'If your descendants
watch how they live, and if they walk faith-
fully before me with all their heart and soul,
you will never fail to have a successor on the
throne of Israel.'
5 "Now you yourself know what Joab son of

Zeruiah did to me—what he did to the two
commanders of Israel's armies, Abner son of
Ner and Amasa son of Jether. He killed them,
shedding their blood in peacetime as if in
battle, and with that blood he stained the
belt around his waist and the sandals on his
feet. 6Deal with him according to your wis-
dom, but do not let his gray head go down to
the grave in peace.

7"But show kindness to the sons of Bar-
zillai of Gilead and let them be among those
who eat at your table. They stood by me
when I fled from your brother Absalom.

8"And remember, you have with you
Shimei son of Gera, the Benjamite from Ba-
hurim, who called down bitter curses on me
the day I went to Mahanaim. When he came
down to meet me at the Jordan, I swore to
him by the LORD: 'I will not put you to death
by the sword.' 9But now, do not consider him
innocent. You are a man of wisdom; you will
know what to do to him. Bring his gray head
down to the grave in blood."

10Then David rested with his ancestors
and was buried in the City of David. 11He
had reigned forty years over Israel—seven
years in Hebron and thirty-three in Jerusa-
lem. 12So Solomon sat on the throne of his
father David, and his rule was firmly estab-
lished.

Solomon's Throne Established

13Now Adonijah, the son of Haggith, went
to Bathsheba, Solomon's mother. Bathsheba
asked him, "Do you come peacefully?"

He answered, "Yes, peacefully." 14Then he
added, "I have something to say to you."

"You may say it," she replied.

15"As you know," he said, "the kingdom
was mine. All Israel looked to me as their
king. But things changed, and the kingdom
has gone to my brother; for it has come to
him from the LORD. 16Now I have one re-
quest to make of you. Do not refuse me."

"You may make it," she said.

17So he continued, "Please ask King Sol-
omon—he will not refuse you—to give me
Abishag the Shunammite as my wife."

18"Very well," Bathsheba replied, "I will
speak to the king for you."

19When Bathsheba went to King Solo-
mon to speak to him for Adonijah, the king
stood up to meet her, bowed down to her
and sat down on his throne. He had a throne
brought for the king's mother, and she sat
down at his right hand.

20"I have one small request to make of
you," she said. "Do not refuse me."

The king replied, "Make it, my mother; I
will not refuse you."

21So she said, "Let Abishag the Shunam-
mite be given in marriage to your brother
Adonijah."

22King Solomon answered his mother,
"Why do you request Abishag the Shunam-
mite for Adonijah? You might as well request
the kingdom for him—after all, he is my old-
er brother—yes, for him and for Abiathar
the priest and Joab son of Zeruiah!"

23Then King Solomon swore by the LORD:
"May God deal with me, be it ever so severe-
ly, if Adonijah does not pay with his life for
this request! 24And now, as surely as the
LORD lives—he who has established me se-
curely on the throne of my father David and
has founded a dynasty for me as he prom-
ised—Adonijah shall be put to death today!"
25So King Solomon gave orders to Benaiah
son of Jehoiada, and he struck down Adoni-
jah and he died.

26To Abiathar the priest the king said, "Go
back to your fields in Anathoth. You deserve
to die, but I will not put you to death now, be-
cause you carried the ark of the Sovereign
LORD before my father David and shared
all my father's hardships." 27So Solomon re-
moved Abiathar from the priesthood of the
LORD, fulfilling the word the LORD had spo-
ken at Shiloh about the house of Eli.

28When the news reached Joab, who had
conspired with Adonijah though not with
Absalom, he fled to the tent of the LORD and
took hold of the horns of the altar. 29King
Solomon was told that Joab had fled to the
tent of the LORD and was beside the altar.
Then Solomon ordered Benaiah son of Jehoi-
ada, "Go, strike him down!"

30So Benaiah entered the tent of the LORD
and said to Joab, "The king says, 'Come out!'"

But he answered, "No, I will die here."

Benaiah reported to the king, "This is how
Joab answered me."

31Then the king commanded Benaiah,
"Do as he says. Strike him down and bury
him, and so clear me and my whole family
of the guilt of the innocent blood that Joab
shed. 32The LORD will repay him for the blood
he shed, because without my father David

knowing it he attacked two men and killed them with the sword. Both of them — Abner son of Ner, commander of Israel's army, and Amasa son of Jether, commander of Judah's army — were better men and more upright than he. 33 May the guilt of their blood rest on the head of Joab and his descendants forever. But on David and his descendants, his house and his throne, may there be the LORD's peace forever."

34 So Benaiah son of Jehoiada went up and struck down Joab and killed him, and he was buried at his home out in the country. 35 The king put Benaiah son of Jehoiada over the army in Joab's position and replaced Abiathar with Zadok the priest.

36 Then the king sent for Shimei and said to him, "Build yourself a house in Jerusalem and live there, but do not go anywhere else. 37 The day you leave and cross the Kidron Valley, you can be sure you will die; your blood will be on your own head."

38 Shimei answered the king, "What you say is good. Your servant will do as my lord the king has said." And Shimei stayed in Jerusalem for a long time.

39 But three years later, two of Shimei's slaves ran off to Achish son of Maakah, king of Gath, and Shimei was told, "Your slaves are in Gath." 40 At this, he saddled his donkey and went to Achish at Gath in search of his slaves. So Shimei went away and brought the slaves back from Gath.

41 When Solomon was told that Shimei had gone from Jerusalem to Gath and had returned, 42 the king summoned Shimei and said to him, "Did I not make you swear by the LORD and warn you, 'On the day you leave to go anywhere else, you can be sure you will die'? At that time you said to me, 'What you say is good. I will obey.' 43 Why then did you not keep your oath to the LORD and obey the command I gave you?"

44 The king also said to Shimei, "You know in your heart all the wrong you did to my father David. Now the LORD will repay you for your wrongdoing. 45 But King Solomon will be blessed, and David's throne will remain secure before the LORD forever."

46 Then the king gave the order to Benaiah son of Jehoiada, and he went out and struck Shimei down and he died.

The kingdom was now established in Solomon's hands.

Solomon Asks for Wisdom

3 Solomon made an alliance with Pharaoh king of Egypt and married his daughter. He brought her to the City of David until he finished building his palace and the temple of the LORD, and the wall around Jerusalem. 2 The people, however, were still sacrificing at the high places, because a temple had not yet been built for the Name of the LORD. 3 Solomon showed his love for the LORD by walking according to the instructions given him by his father David, except that he offered sacrifices and burned incense on the high places.

4 The king went to Gibeon to offer sacrifices, for that was the most important high place, and Solomon offered a thousand burnt offerings on that altar. 5 At Gibeon the LORD appeared to Solomon during the night in a dream, and God said, "Ask for whatever you want me to give you."

6 Solomon answered, "You have shown great kindness to your servant, my father David, because he was faithful to you and righteous and upright in heart. You have continued this great kindness to him and have given him a son to sit on his throne this very day.

7 "Now, LORD my God, you have made your servant king in place of my father David. But I am only a little child and do not know how to carry out my duties. 8 Your servant is here among the people you have chosen, a great people, too numerous to count or number. 9 So give your servant a discerning heart to govern your people and to distinguish between right and wrong. For who is able to govern this great people of yours?"

10 The Lord was pleased that Solomon had asked for this. 11 So God said to him, "Since you have asked for this and not for long life or wealth for yourself, nor have asked for the death of your enemies but for discernment in administering justice, 12 I will do what you have asked. I will give you a wise and discerning heart, so that there will never have been anyone like you, nor will there ever be. 13 Moreover, I will give you what you have not asked for — both wealth and honor — so that in your lifetime you will have no equal among kings. 14 And if you walk in obedience to me and keep my decrees and commands as David your father did, I will give you a long life." 15 Then Solomon awoke — and he realized it had been a dream.

He returned to Jerusalem, stood before the ark of the Lord's covenant and sacrificed burnt offerings and fellowship offerings. Then he gave a feast for all his court.

A Wise Ruling

16Now two prostitutes came to the king
and stood before him. 17One of them said,
"Pardon me, my lord. This woman and I live in the same house, and I had a baby while
she was there with me. 18The third day after
my child was born, this woman also had a baby. We were alone; there was no one in the house but the two of us.

19"During the night this woman's son
died because she lay on him. 20So she got
up in the middle of the night and took my son from my side while I your servant was asleep. She put him by her breast and put
her dead son by my breast. 21The next morn-
ing, I got up to nurse my son — and he was dead! But when I looked at him closely in the morning light, I saw that it wasn't the son I had borne."

22The other woman said, "No! The living one is my son; the dead one is yours."

But the first one insisted, "No! The dead one is yours; the living one is mine." And so they argued before the king.

23The king said, "This one says, 'My son is alive and your son is dead,' while that one says, 'No! Your son is dead and mine is alive.'"

24Then the king said, "Bring me a sword."
So they brought a sword for the king. 25He
then gave an order: "Cut the living child in two and give half to one and half to the other."

26The woman whose son was alive was deeply moved out of love for her son and said to the king, "Please, my lord, give her the living baby! Don't kill him!"

But the other said, "Neither I nor you shall have him. Cut him in two!"

27Then the king gave his ruling: "Give the living baby to the first woman. Do not kill him; she is his mother."

28When all Israel heard the verdict the king had given, they held the king in awe, because they saw that he had wisdom from God to administer justice.

Solomon's Officials and Governors

4 So King Solomon ruled over all Israel.
2And these were his chief officials:

Azariah son of Zadok — the priest;
3Elihoreph and Ahijah, sons of Shisha — secretaries;
Jehoshaphat son of Ahilud — recorder;
4Benaiah son of Jehoiada — commander in chief;
Zadok and Abiathar — priests;
5Azariah son of Nathan — in charge of the district governors;
Zabud son of Nathan — a priest and adviser to the king;
6Ahishar — palace administrator;
Adoniram son of Abda — in charge of forced labor.

7Solomon had twelve district governors
over all Israel, who supplied provisions for the king and the royal household. Each one had to provide supplies for one month in the
year. 8These are their names:

Ben-Hur — in the hill country of Ephraim;
9Ben-Deker — in Makaz, Shaalbim, Beth Shemesh and Elon Bethhanan;
10Ben-Hesed — in Arubboth (Sokoh and all the land of Hepher were his);
11Ben-Abinadab — in Naphoth Dor (he was married to Taphath daughter of Solomon);
12Baana son of Ahilud — in Taanach and Megiddo, and in all of Beth Shan next to Zarethan below Jezreel, from Beth Shan to Abel Meholah across to Jokmeam;
13Ben-Geber — in Ramoth Gilead (the settlements of Jair son of Manasseh in Gilead were his, as well as the region of Argob in Bashan and its sixty large walled cities with bronze gate bars);
14Ahinadab son of Iddo — in Mahanaim;
15Ahimaaz — in Naphtali (he had married Basemath daughter of Solomon);
16Baana son of Hushai — in Asher and in Aloth;
17Jehoshaphat son of Paruah — in Issachar;
18Shimei son of Ela — in Benjamin;
19Geber son of Uri — in Gilead (the country of Sihon king of the Amorites and the country of Og king of Bashan). He was the only governor over the district.

Solomon's Daily Provisions

20 The people of Judah and Israel were as numerous as the sand on the seashore; they ate, they drank and they were happy. 21 And Solomon ruled over all the kingdoms from the Euphrates River to the land of the Philistines, as far as the border of Egypt. These countries brought tribute and were Solomon's subjects all his life.

22 Solomon's daily provisions were thirty cors[a] of the finest flour and sixty cors[b] of meal, 23 ten head of stall-fed cattle, twenty of pasture-fed cattle and a hundred sheep and goats, as well as deer, gazelles, roebucks and choice fowl. 24 For he ruled over all the kingdoms west of the Euphrates River, from Tiphsah to Gaza, and had peace on all sides. 25 During Solomon's lifetime Judah and Israel, from Dan to Beersheba, lived in safety, everyone under their own vine and under their own fig tree.

26 Solomon had four[c] thousand stalls for chariot horses, and twelve thousand horses.[d]

27 The district governors, each in his month, supplied provisions for King Solomon and all who came to the king's table. They saw to it that nothing was lacking. 28 They also brought to the proper place their quotas of barley and straw for the chariot horses and the other horses.

Solomon's Wisdom

29 God gave Solomon wisdom and very great insight, and a breadth of understanding as measureless as the sand on the seashore. 30 Solomon's wisdom was greater than the wisdom of all the people of the East, and greater than all the wisdom of Egypt. 31 He was wiser than anyone else, including Ethan the Ezrahite—wiser than Heman, Kalkol and Darda, the sons of Mahol. And his fame spread to all the surrounding nations. 32 He spoke three thousand proverbs and his songs numbered a thousand and five. 33 He spoke about plant life, from the cedar of Lebanon to the hyssop that grows out of walls. He also spoke about animals and birds, reptiles and fish. 34 From all nations people came to listen to Solomon's wisdom, sent by all the kings of the world, who had heard of his wisdom.[e]

Preparations for Building the Temple

5 [f] When Hiram king of Tyre heard that Solomon had been anointed king to succeed his father David, he sent his envoys to Solomon, because he had always been on friendly terms with David. 2 Solomon sent back this message to Hiram:

3 "You know that because of the wars waged against my father David from all sides, he could not build a temple for the Name of the LORD his God until the LORD put his enemies under his feet. 4 But now the LORD my God has given me rest on every side, and there is no adversary or disaster. 5 I intend, therefore, to build a temple for the Name of the LORD my God, as the LORD told my father David, when he said, 'Your son whom I will put on the throne in your place will build the temple for my Name.'

6 "So give orders that cedars of Lebanon be cut for me. My men will work with yours, and I will pay you for your men whatever wages you set. You know that we have no one so skilled in felling timber as the Sidonians."

7 When Hiram heard Solomon's message, he was greatly pleased and said, "Praise be to the LORD today, for he has given David a wise son to rule over this great nation."

8 So Hiram sent word to Solomon:

"I have received the message you sent me and will do all you want in providing the cedar and juniper logs. 9 My men will haul them down from Lebanon to the Mediterranean Sea, and I will float them as rafts by sea to the place you specify. There I will separate them and you can take them away. And you are to grant my wish by providing food for my royal household."

10 In this way Hiram kept Solomon supplied with all the cedar and juniper logs he wanted, 11 and Solomon gave Hiram twenty

[a] *22* That is, probably about 5 1/2 tons or about 5 metric tons [b] *22* That is, probably about 11 tons or about 10 metric tons [c] *26* Some Septuagint manuscripts (see also 2 Chron. 9:25); Hebrew *forty* [d] *26* Or *charioteers* [e] *34* In Hebrew texts 4:21-34 is numbered 5:1-14. [f] In Hebrew texts 5:1-18 is numbered 5:15-32.

thousand cors[a] of wheat as food for his household, in addition to twenty thousand baths[b,c] of pressed olive oil. Solomon continued to do this for Hiram year after year. 12 The LORD gave Solomon wisdom, just as he had promised him. There were peaceful relations between Hiram and Solomon, and the two of them made a treaty.

13 King Solomon conscripted laborers from all Israel — thirty thousand men. 14 He sent them off to Lebanon in shifts of ten thousand a month, so that they spent one month in Lebanon and two months at home. Adoniram was in charge of the forced labor. 15 Solomon had seventy thousand carriers and eighty thousand stonecutters in the hills, 16 as well as thirty-three hundred[d] foremen who supervised the project and directed the workers. 17 At the king's command they removed from the quarry large blocks of high-grade stone to provide a foundation of dressed stone for the temple. 18 The craftsmen of Solomon and Hiram and workers from Byblos cut and prepared the timber and stone for the building of the temple.

Solomon Builds the Temple

6 In the four hundred and eightieth[e] year after the Israelites came out of Egypt, in the fourth year of Solomon's reign over Israel, in the month of Ziv, the second month, he began to build the temple of the LORD.

2 The temple that King Solomon built for the LORD was sixty cubits long, twenty wide and thirty high.[f] 3 The portico at the front of the main hall of the temple extended the width of the temple, that is twenty cubits,[g] and projected ten cubits[h] from the front of the temple. 4 He made narrow windows high up in the temple walls. 5 Against the walls of the main hall and inner sanctuary he built a structure around the building, in which there were side rooms. 6 The lowest floor was five cubits[i] wide, the middle floor six cubits[j] and the third floor seven.[k] He made offset ledges around the outside of the temple so that nothing would be inserted into the temple walls.

7 In building the temple, only blocks dressed at the quarry were used, and no hammer, chisel or any other iron tool was heard at the temple site while it was being built.

8 The entrance to the lowest[l] floor was on the south side of the temple; a stairway led up to the middle level and from there to the third. 9 So he built the temple and completed it, roofing it with beams and cedar planks. 10 And he built the side rooms all along the temple. The height of each was five cubits, and they were attached to the temple by beams of cedar.

11 The word of the LORD came to Solomon: 12 "As for this temple you are building, if you follow my decrees, observe my laws and keep all my commands and obey them, I will fulfill through you the promise I gave to David your father. 13 And I will live among the Israelites and will not abandon my people Israel."

14 So Solomon built the temple and completed it. 15 He lined its interior walls with cedar boards, paneling them from the floor of the temple to the ceiling, and covered the floor of the temple with planks of juniper. 16 He partitioned off twenty cubits at the rear of the temple with cedar boards from floor to ceiling to form within the temple an inner sanctuary, the Most Holy Place. 17 The main hall in front of this room was forty cubits[m] long. 18 The inside of the temple was cedar, carved with gourds and open flowers. Everything was cedar; no stone was to be seen.

19 He prepared the inner sanctuary within the temple to set the ark of the covenant of the LORD there. 20 The inner sanctuary was twenty cubits long, twenty wide and twenty high. He overlaid the inside with pure gold, and he also overlaid the altar of cedar. 21 Solomon covered the inside of the temple with pure gold, and he extended gold chains across the front of the inner sanctuary, which

[a] *11* That is, probably about 3,600 tons or about 3,250 metric tons [b] *11* Septuagint (see also 2 Chron. 2:10); Hebrew *twenty cors* [c] *11* That is, about 120,000 gallons or about 440,000 liters [d] *16* Hebrew; some Septuagint manuscripts (see also 2 Chron. 2:2,18) *thirty-six hundred* [e] *1* Hebrew; Septuagint *four hundred and fortieth* [f] *2* That is, about 90 feet long, 30 feet wide and 45 feet high or about 27 meters long, 9 meters wide and 14 meters high [g] *3* That is, about 30 feet or about 9 meters; also in verses 16 and 20 [h] *3* That is, about 15 feet or about 4.5 meters; also in verses 23-26 [i] *6* That is, about 7 1/2 feet or about 2.3 meters; also in verses 10 and 24 [j] *6* That is, about 9 feet or about 2.7 meters [k] *6* That is, about 11 feet or about 3.2 meters [l] *8* Septuagint; Hebrew *middle* [m] *17* That is, about 60 feet or about 18 meters

was overlaid with gold. 22So he overlaid the whole interior with gold. He also overlaid with gold the altar that belonged to the inner sanctuary.

23For the inner sanctuary he made a pair of cherubim out of olive wood, each ten cubits high. 24One wing of the first cherub was five cubits long, and the other wing five cubits — ten cubits from wing tip to wing tip. 25The second cherub also measured ten cubits, for the two cherubim were identical in size and shape. 26The height of each cherub was ten cubits. 27He placed the cherubim inside the innermost room of the temple, with their wings spread out. The wing of one cherub touched one wall, while the wing of the other touched the other wall, and their wings touched each other in the middle of the room. 28He overlaid the cherubim with gold.

29On the walls all around the temple, in both the inner and outer rooms, he carved cherubim, palm trees and open flowers. 30He also covered the floors of both the inner and outer rooms of the temple with gold.

31For the entrance to the inner sanctuary he made doors out of olive wood that were one fifth of the width of the sanctuary. 32And on the two olive-wood doors he carved cherubim, palm trees and open flowers, and overlaid the cherubim and palm trees with hammered gold. 33In the same way, for the entrance to the main hall he made doorframes out of olive wood that were one fourth of the width of the hall. 34He also made two doors out of juniper wood, each having two leaves that turned in sockets. 35He carved cherubim, palm trees and open flowers on them and overlaid them with gold hammered evenly over the carvings.

36And he built the inner courtyard of three courses of dressed stone and one course of trimmed cedar beams.

37The foundation of the temple of the LORD was laid in the fourth year, in the month of Ziv. 38In the eleventh year in the month of Bul, the eighth month, the temple was finished in all its details according to its specifications. He had spent seven years building it.

Solomon Builds His Palace

7 It took Solomon thirteen years, however, to complete the construction of his palace. 2He built the Palace of the Forest of Lebanon a hundred cubits long, fifty wide and thirty high,[a] with four rows of cedar columns supporting trimmed cedar beams. 3It was roofed with cedar above the beams that rested on the columns — forty-five beams, fifteen to a row. 4Its windows were placed high in sets of three, facing each other. 5All the doorways had rectangular frames; they were in the front part in sets of three, facing each other.[b]

6He made a colonnade fifty cubits long and thirty wide.[c] In front of it was a portico, and in front of that were pillars and an overhanging roof.

7He built the throne hall, the Hall of Justice, where he was to judge, and he covered it with cedar from floor to ceiling.[d] 8And the palace in which he was to live, set farther back, was similar in design. Solomon also made a palace like this hall for Pharaoh's daughter, whom he had married.

9All these structures, from the outside to the great courtyard and from foundation to eaves, were made of blocks of high-grade stone cut to size and smoothed on their inner and outer faces. 10The foundations were laid with large stones of good quality, some measuring ten cubits[e] and some eight.[f] 11Above were high-grade stones, cut to size, and cedar beams. 12The great courtyard was surrounded by a wall of three courses of dressed stone and one course of trimmed cedar beams, as was the inner courtyard of the temple of the LORD with its portico.

The Temple's Furnishings

13King Solomon sent to Tyre and brought Huram,[g] 14whose mother was a widow from the tribe of Naphtali and whose father was from Tyre and a skilled craftsman in bronze. Huram was filled with wisdom, with understanding and with knowledge to do all kinds of bronze work. He came to King Solomon and did all the work assigned to him.

[a] *2* That is, about 150 feet long, 75 feet wide and 45 feet high or about 45 meters long, 23 meters wide and 14 meters high [b] *5* The meaning of the Hebrew for this verse is uncertain. [c] *6* That is, about 75 feet long and 45 feet wide or about 23 meters long and 14 meters wide [d] *7* Vulgate and Syriac; Hebrew *floor* [e] *10* That is, about 15 feet or about 4.5 meters; also in verse 23 [f] *10* That is, about 12 feet or about 3.6 meters [g] *13* Hebrew *Hiram,* a variant of *Huram*; also in verses 40 and 45

HOLY IS THE LORD

Chris Tomlin, Louie Giglio

We stand and lift up our hands
For the joy of the Lord is our strength
We bow down and worship him now
How great, how awesome is he

And together we sing
Everyone sing

Holy is the Lord God Almighty
The earth is filled with his glory
Holy is the Lord God Almighty
The earth is filled with his glory
The earth is filled with his glory

It is rising up all around
It's the anthem of the Lord's renown

THE INSPIRATION

And they were calling to one another: "Holy, holy, holy is the L*ORD Almighty; the whole earth is full of his glory."*

—Isaiah 6:3

Read also: Nehemiah 8; Revelation 5:13

BEHIND THE SONG

The song, "Holy Is the Lord" was inspired by a passage in Isaiah and by a story found in the book of Nehemiah. Chris Tomlin had been reading Isaiah 6 and was struck by the angels' worship of God.

"I've always been intrigued by the passage," he recalls, "that says the angels call back to one another, seraphim and cherubim, and they say, 'Holy, holy, holy is the Lord God Almighty. The whole earth is filled with his glory.' So I just started singing that back and forth, just that simple chorus."

A couple of days later Tomlin was with Louie Giglio, the founder and leader of the Passion movement as they prepared for a Passion event. Giglio, an avid Bible reader, student and teacher, frequently contributes lyrical ideas for Tomlin's songs. The two have collaborated on numerous compositions over the years. When Tomlin shared the chorus for "Holy Is the Lord," Giglio was immediately inspired.

Giglio had been reading Nehemiah 8 and saw some excellent parallels between that account and the worship that the Passion team desired to bring to college students. Both Giglio and Tomlin were fascinated by the descriptions of the Israelites lifting their hands in praise and then bowing down with their faces to the ground. "It's interesting how those two postures of worship came rushing together," Giglio says. Then a certain phrase started resonating in his heart. "It's rising up, all around. It's the anthem of the Lord's renown." The idea of making Jesus famous in the world was at the heart of Passion's ministry to college students.

Selah

The angels covered their faces and their feet as they sang to God. Why do you suppose they did this? Think about your own worship for a minute. Is it primarily a mental exercise or something more? What does your posture reflect about your beliefs and feelings about God?

15 He cast two bronze pillars, each eighteen cubits high and twelve cubits in circumference.[a] 16 He also made two capitals of cast bronze to set on the tops of the pillars; each capital was five cubits[b] high. 17 A network of interwoven chains adorned the capitals on top of the pillars, seven for each capital. 18 He made pomegranates in two rows[c] encircling each network to decorate the capitals on top of the pillars.[d] He did the same for each capital. 19 The capitals on top of the pillars in the portico were in the shape of lilies, four cubits[e] high. 20 On the capitals of both pillars, above the bowl-shaped part next to the network, were the two hundred pomegranates in rows all around. 21 He erected the pillars at the portico of the temple. The pillar to the south he named Jakin[f] and the one to the north Boaz.[g] 22 The capitals on top were in the shape of lilies. And so the work on the pillars was completed.

23 He made the Sea of cast metal, circular in shape, measuring ten cubits from rim to rim and five cubits high. It took a line of thirty cubits[h] to measure around it. 24 Below the rim, gourds encircled it—ten to a cubit. The gourds were cast in two rows in one piece with the Sea.

25 The Sea stood on twelve bulls, three facing north, three facing west, three facing south and three facing east. The Sea rested on top of them, and their hindquarters were toward the center. 26 It was a handbreadth[i] in thickness, and its rim was like the rim of a cup, like a lily blossom. It held two thousand baths.[j]

27 He also made ten movable stands of bronze; each was four cubits long, four wide and three high.[k] 28 This is how the stands were made: They had side panels attached to uprights. 29 On the panels between the uprights were lions, bulls and cherubim—and on the uprights as well. Above and below the lions and bulls were wreaths of hammered work. 30 Each stand had four bronze wheels with bronze axles, and each had a basin resting on four supports, cast with wreaths on each side. 31 On the inside of the stand there was an opening that had a circular frame one cubit[l] deep. This opening was round, and with its basework it measured a cubit and a half.[m] Around its opening there was engraving. The panels of the stands were square, not round. 32 The four wheels were under the panels, and the axles of the wheels were attached to the stand. The diameter of each wheel was a cubit and a half. 33 The wheels were made like chariot wheels; the axles, rims, spokes and hubs were all of cast metal.

34 Each stand had four handles, one on each corner, projecting from the stand. 35 At the top of the stand there was a circular band half a cubit[n] deep. The supports and panels were attached to the top of the stand. 36 He engraved cherubim, lions and palm trees on the surfaces of the supports and on the panels, in every available space, with wreaths all around. 37 This is the way he made the ten stands. They were all cast in the same molds and were identical in size and shape.

38 He then made ten bronze basins, each holding forty baths[o] and measuring four cubits across, one basin to go on each of the ten stands. 39 He placed five of the stands on the south side of the temple and five on the north. He placed the Sea on the south side, at the southeast corner of the temple. 40 He also made the pots[p] and shovels and sprinkling bowls.

So Huram finished all the work he had undertaken for King Solomon in the temple of the LORD:

[a] *15* That is, about 27 feet high and 18 feet in circumference or about 8.1 meters high and 5.4 meters in circumference [b] *16* That is, about 7 1/2 feet or about 2.3 meters; also in verse 23 [c] *18* Two Hebrew manuscripts and Septuagint; most Hebrew manuscripts *made the pillars, and there were two rows* [d] *18* Many Hebrew manuscripts and Syriac; most Hebrew manuscripts *pomegranates* [e] *19* That is, about 6 feet or about 1.8 meters; also in verse 38 [f] *21* *Jakin* probably means *he establishes.* [g] *21* *Boaz* probably means *in him is strength.* [h] *23* That is, about 45 feet or about 14 meters [i] *26* That is, about 3 inches or about 7.5 centimeters [j] *26* That is, about 12,000 gallons or about 44,000 liters; the Septuagint does not have this sentence. [k] *27* That is, about 6 feet long and wide and about 4 1/2 feet high or about 1.8 meters long and wide and 1.4 meters high [l] *31* That is, about 18 inches or about 45 centimeters [m] *31* That is, about 2 1/4 feet or about 68 centimeters; also in verse 32 [n] *35* That is, about 9 inches or about 23 centimeters [o] *38* That is, about 240 gallons or about 880 liters [p] *40* Many Hebrew manuscripts, Septuagint, Syriac and Vulgate (see also verse 45 and 2 Chron. 4:11); many other Hebrew manuscripts *basins*

41 the two pillars;
the two bowl-shaped capitals on top of
the pillars;
the two sets of network decorating the
two bowl-shaped capitals on top of
the pillars;
42 the four hundred pomegranates for
the two sets of network (two rows of
pomegranates for each network dec-
orating the bowl-shaped capitals on
top of the pillars);
43 the ten stands with their ten basins;
44 the Sea and the twelve bulls under it;
45 the pots, shovels and sprinkling bowls.

All these objects that Huram made for
King Solomon for the temple of the LORD
were of burnished bronze. 46 The king had
them cast in clay molds in the plain of the
Jordan between Sukkoth and Zarethan.
47 Solomon left all these things unweighed,
because there were so many; the weight of
the bronze was not determined.
48 Solomon also made all the furnishings
that were in the LORD's temple:

the golden altar;
the golden table on which was the
bread of the Presence;
49 the lampstands of pure gold (five on the
right and five on the left, in front of
the inner sanctuary);
the gold floral work and lamps and
tongs;
50 the pure gold basins, wick trimmers,
sprinkling bowls, dishes and cen-
sers;
and the gold sockets for the doors of
the innermost room, the Most Holy
Place, and also for the doors of the
main hall of the temple.

51 When all the work King Solomon had
done for the temple of the LORD was fin-
ished, he brought in the things his father Da-
vid had dedicated — the silver and gold and
the furnishings — and he placed them in the
treasuries of the LORD's temple.

The Ark Brought to the Temple

8 Then King Solomon summoned into his
presence at Jerusalem the elders of Isra-
el, all the heads of the tribes and the chiefs
of the Israelite families, to bring up the ark
of the LORD's covenant from Zion, the City
of David. 2 All the Israelites came together
to King Solomon at the time of the festival in
the month of Ethanim, the seventh month.
3 When all the elders of Israel had ar-
rived, the priests took up the ark, 4 and they
brought up the ark of the LORD and the tent
of meeting and all the sacred furnishings in
it. The priests and Levites carried them up,
5 and King Solomon and the entire assembly
of Israel that had gathered about him were
before the ark, sacrificing so many sheep
and cattle that they could not be recorded or
counted.
6 The priests then brought the ark of the
LORD's covenant to its place in the inner
sanctuary of the temple, the Most Holy Place,
and put it beneath the wings of the cheru-
bim. 7 The cherubim spread their wings over
the place of the ark and overshadowed the
ark and its carrying poles. 8 These poles were
so long that their ends could be seen from
the Holy Place in front of the inner sanctu-
ary, but not from outside the Holy Place; and
they are still there today. 9 There was nothing
in the ark except the two stone tablets that
Moses had placed in it at Horeb, where the
LORD made a covenant with the Israelites af-
ter they came out of Egypt.
10 When the priests withdrew from the
Holy Place, the cloud filled the temple of the
LORD. 11 And the priests could not perform
their service because of the cloud, for the
glory of the LORD filled his temple.
12 Then Solomon said, "The LORD has said
that he would dwell in a dark cloud; 13 I have
indeed built a magnificent temple for you, a
place for you to dwell forever."
14 While the whole assembly of Israel was
standing there, the king turned around and
blessed them. 15 Then he said:

"Praise be to the LORD, the God of
Israel, who with his own hand has ful-
filled what he promised with his own
mouth to my father David. For he said,
16 'Since the day I brought my people
Israel out of Egypt, I have not chosen a
city in any tribe of Israel to have a tem-
ple built so that my Name might be
there, but I have chosen David to rule
my people Israel.'
17 "My father David had it in his heart
to build a temple for the Name of the
LORD, the God of Israel. 18 But the LORD

said to my father David, 'You did well
to have it in your heart to build a tem-
ple for my Name. 19 Nevertheless, you
are not the one to build the temple, but
your son, your own flesh and blood—
he is the one who will build the temple
for my Name.'

20 "The LORD has kept the promise
he made: I have succeeded David my
father and now I sit on the throne of
Israel, just as the LORD promised, and
I have built the temple for the Name
of the LORD, the God of Israel. 21 I have
provided a place there for the ark, in
which is the covenant of the LORD that
he made with our ancestors when he
brought them out of Egypt."

Solomon's Prayer of Dedication

22 Then Solomon stood before the altar of
the LORD in front of the whole assembly of
Israel, spread out his hands toward heaven
23 and said:

"LORD, the God of Israel, there is no
God like you in heaven above or on
earth below—you who keep your cov-
enant of love with your servants who
continue wholeheartedly in your way.
24 You have kept your promise to your
servant David my father; with your
mouth you have promised and with
your hand you have fulfilled it—as it
is today.

25 "Now LORD, the God of Israel, keep
for your servant David my father the
promises you made to him when you
said, 'You shall never fail to have a suc-
cessor to sit before me on the throne
of Israel, if only your descendants are
careful in all they do to walk before
me faithfully as you have done.' 26 And
now, God of Israel, let your word that
you promised your servant David my
father come true.

27 "But will God really dwell on
earth? The heavens, even the high-
est heaven, cannot contain you. How
much less this temple I have built! 28 Yet
give attention to your servant's prayer
and his plea for mercy, LORD my God.
Hear the cry and the prayer that your
servant is praying in your presence this
day. 29 May your eyes be open toward
this temple night and day, this place
of which you said, 'My Name shall be
there,' so that you will hear the prayer
your servant prays toward this place.
30 Hear the supplication of your servant
and of your people Israel when they
pray toward this place. Hear from heav-
en, your dwelling place, and when you
hear, forgive.

31 "When anyone wrongs their neigh-
bor and is required to take an oath and
they come and swear the oath before
your altar in this temple, 32 then hear
from heaven and act. Judge between
your servants, condemning the guilty
by bringing down on their heads what
they have done, and vindicating the in-
nocent by treating them in accordance
with their innocence.

33 "When your people Israel have
been defeated by an enemy because
they have sinned against you, and
when they turn back to you and give
praise to your name, praying and mak-
ing supplication to you in this temple,
34 then hear from heaven and forgive
the sin of your people Israel and bring
them back to the land you gave to their
ancestors.

35 "When the heavens are shut up
and there is no rain because your peo-
ple have sinned against you, and when
they pray toward this place and give
praise to your name and turn from
their sin because you have afflicted
them, 36 then hear from heaven and for-
give the sin of your servants, your peo-
ple Israel. Teach them the right way to
live, and send rain on the land you gave
your people for an inheritance.

37 "When famine or plague comes to
the land, or blight or mildew, locusts
or grasshoppers, or when an enemy
besieges them in any of their cities,
whatever disaster or disease may come,
38 and when a prayer or plea is made by
anyone among your people Israel—be-
ing aware of the afflictions of their own
hearts, and spreading out their hands
toward this temple— 39 then hear from
heaven, your dwelling place. Forgive
and act; deal with everyone accord-
ing to all they do, since you know their
hearts (for you alone know every human

heart), 40 so that they will fear you all the time they live in the land you gave our ancestors.

41 "As for the foreigner who does not belong to your people Israel but has come from a distant land because of your name— 42 for they will hear of your great name and your mighty hand and your outstretched arm—when they come and pray toward this temple, 43 then hear from heaven, your dwelling place. Do whatever the foreigner asks of you, so that all the peoples of the earth may know your name and fear you, as do your own people Israel, and may know that this house I have built bears your Name.

44 "When your people go to war against their enemies, wherever you send them, and when they pray to the LORD toward the city you have chosen and the temple I have built for your Name, 45 then hear from heaven their prayer and their plea, and uphold their cause.

46 "When they sin against you—for there is no one who does not sin—and you become angry with them and give them over to their enemies, who take them captive to their own lands, far away or near; 47 and if they have a change of heart in the land where they are held captive, and repent and plead with you in the land of their captors and say, 'We have sinned, we have done wrong, we have acted wickedly'; 48 and if they turn back to you with all their heart and soul in the land of their enemies who took them captive, and pray to you toward the land you gave their ancestors, toward the city you have chosen and the temple I have built for your Name; 49 then from heaven, your dwelling place, hear their prayer and their plea, and uphold their cause. 50 And forgive your people, who have sinned against you; forgive all the offenses they have committed against you, and cause their captors to show them mercy; 51 for they are your people and your inheritance, whom you brought out of Egypt, out of that iron-smelting furnace.

52 "May your eyes be open to your servant's plea and to the plea of your people Israel, and may you listen to them whenever they cry out to you. 53 For you singled them out from all the nations of the world to be your own inheritance, just as you declared through your servant Moses when you, Sovereign LORD, brought our ancestors out of Egypt."

54 When Solomon had finished all these prayers and supplications to the LORD, he rose from before the altar of the LORD, where he had been kneeling with his hands spread out toward heaven. 55 He stood and blessed the whole assembly of Israel in a loud voice, saying:

56 "Praise be to the LORD, who has given rest to his people Israel just as he promised. Not one word has failed of all the good promises he gave through his servant Moses. 57 May the LORD our God be with us as he was with our ancestors; may he never leave us nor forsake us. 58 May he turn our hearts to him, to walk in obedience to him and keep the commands, decrees and laws he gave our ancestors. 59 And may these words of mine, which I have prayed before the LORD, be near to the LORD our God day and night, that he may uphold the cause of his servant and the cause of his people Israel according to each day's need, 60 so that all the peoples of the earth may know that the LORD is God and that there is no other. 61 And may your hearts be fully committed to the LORD our God, to live by his decrees and obey his commands, as at this time."

The Dedication of the Temple

62 Then the king and all Israel with him offered sacrifices before the LORD. 63 Solomon offered a sacrifice of fellowship offerings to the LORD: twenty-two thousand cattle and a hundred and twenty thousand sheep and goats. So the king and all the Israelites dedicated the temple of the LORD.

64 On that same day the king consecrated the middle part of the courtyard in front of the temple of the LORD, and there he offered burnt offerings, grain offerings and the fat of the fellowship offerings, because the bronze altar that stood before the LORD was too

small to hold the burnt offerings, the grain offerings and the fat of the fellowship offerings.

[65]So Solomon observed the festival at that time, and all Israel with him — a vast assembly, people from Lebo Hamath to the Wadi of Egypt. They celebrated it before the LORD our God for seven days and seven days more, fourteen days in all. [66]On the following day he sent the people away. They blessed the king and then went home, joyful and glad in heart for all the good things the LORD had done for his servant David and his people Israel.

The LORD Appears to Solomon

9 When Solomon had finished building the temple of the LORD and the royal palace, and had achieved all he had desired to do, [2]the LORD appeared to him a second time, as he had appeared to him at Gibeon. [3]The LORD said to him:

"I have heard the prayer and plea you have made before me; I have consecrated this temple, which you have built, by putting my Name there forever. My eyes and my heart will always be there.

[4]"As for you, if you walk before me faithfully with integrity of heart and uprightness, as David your father did, and do all I command and observe my decrees and laws, [5]I will establish your royal throne over Israel forever, as I promised David your father when I said, 'You shall never fail to have a successor on the throne of Israel.'

[6]"But if you[a] or your descendants turn away from me and do not observe the commands and decrees I have given you[a] and go off to serve other gods and worship them, [7]then I will cut off Israel from the land I have given them and will reject this temple I have consecrated for my Name. Israel will then become a byword and an object of ridicule among all peoples. [8]This temple will become a heap of rubble. All[b] who pass by will be appalled and will scoff and say, 'Why has the LORD done such a thing to this land and to this temple?' [9]People will answer, 'Because they have forsaken the LORD their God, who brought their ancestors out of Egypt, and have embraced other gods, worshiping and serving them — that is why the LORD brought all this disaster on them.' "

Solomon's Other Activities

[10]At the end of twenty years, during which Solomon built these two buildings — the temple of the LORD and the royal palace — [11]King Solomon gave twenty towns in Galilee to Hiram king of Tyre, because Hiram had supplied him with all the cedar and juniper and gold he wanted. [12]But when Hiram went from Tyre to see the towns that Solomon had given him, he was not pleased with them. [13]"What kind of towns are these you have given me, my brother?" he asked. And he called them the Land of Kabul,[c] a name they have to this day. [14]Now Hiram had sent to the king 120 talents[d] of gold.

[15]Here is the account of the forced labor King Solomon conscripted to build the LORD's temple, his own palace, the terraces,[e] the wall of Jerusalem, and Hazor, Megiddo and Gezer. [16](Pharaoh king of Egypt had attacked and captured Gezer. He had set it on fire. He killed its Canaanite inhabitants and then gave it as a wedding gift to his daughter, Solomon's wife. [17]And Solomon rebuilt Gezer.) He built up Lower Beth Horon, [18]Baalath, and Tadmor[f] in the desert, within his land, [19]as well as all his store cities and the towns for his chariots and for his horses[g] — whatever he desired to build in Jerusalem, in Lebanon and throughout all the territory he ruled.

[20]There were still people left from the Amorites, Hittites, Perizzites, Hivites and Jebusites (these peoples were not Israelites). [21]Solomon conscripted the descendants of all these peoples remaining in the land — whom the Israelites could not exterminate[h] — to serve as slave labor, as it is to this day. [22]But Solomon did not make slaves of any of the Israelites; they were his fighting

[a] 6 The Hebrew is plural. [b] 8 See some Septuagint manuscripts, Old Latin, Syriac, Arabic and Targum; Hebrew *And though this temple is now imposing, all* [c] 13 *Kabul* sounds like the Hebrew for *good-for-nothing.* [d] 14 That is, about 4 1/2 tons or about 4 metric tons [e] 15 Or *the Millo;* also in verse 24 [f] 18 The Hebrew may also be read *Tamar.* [g] 19 Or *charioteers* [h] 21 The Hebrew term refers to the irrevocable giving over of things or persons to the LORD, often by totally destroying them.

men, his government officials, his officers,
his captains, and the commanders of his
chariots and charioteers. 23They were also
the chief officials in charge of Solomon's
projects — 550 officials supervising those
who did the work.
24After Pharaoh's daughter had come up
from the City of David to the palace Solo-
mon had built for her, he constructed the
terraces.
25Three times a year Solomon sacrificed
burnt offerings and fellowship offerings on
the altar he had built for the LORD, burning
incense before the LORD along with them,
and so fulfilled the temple obligations.
26King Solomon also built ships at Ezion
Geber, which is near Elath in Edom, on the
shore of the Red Sea.[a] 27And Hiram sent his
men — sailors who knew the sea — to serve
in the fleet with Solomon's men. 28They
sailed to Ophir and brought back 420 tal-
ents[b] of gold, which they delivered to King
Solomon.

The Queen of Sheba Visits Solomon

10 When the queen of Sheba heard
about the fame of Solomon and his
relationship to the LORD, she came to test
Solomon with hard questions. 2Arriving at
Jerusalem with a very great caravan — with
camels carrying spices, large quantities of
gold, and precious stones — she came to Sol-
omon and talked with him about all that she
had on her mind. 3Solomon answered all her
questions; nothing was too hard for the king
to explain to her. 4When the queen of She-
ba saw all the wisdom of Solomon and the
palace he had built, 5the food on his table,
the seating of his officials, the attending ser-
vants in their robes, his cupbearers, and the
burnt offerings he made at[c] the temple of the
LORD, she was overwhelmed.
6She said to the king, "The report I heard
in my own country about your achieve-
ments and your wisdom is true. 7But I did
not believe these things until I came and
saw with my own eyes. Indeed, not even half
was told me; in wisdom and wealth you have
far exceeded the report I heard. 8How happy
your people must be! How happy your offi-
cials, who continually stand before you and
hear your wisdom! 9Praise be to the LORD
your God, who has delighted in you and
placed you on the throne of Israel. Because
of the LORD's eternal love for Israel, he has
made you king to maintain justice and righ-
teousness."
10And she gave the king 120 talents[d] of
gold, large quantities of spices, and precious
stones. Never again were so many spices
brought in as those the queen of Sheba gave
to King Solomon.
11(Hiram's ships brought gold from Ophir;
and from there they brought great cargoes
of almugwood[e] and precious stones. 12The
king used the almugwood to make supports[f]
for the temple of the LORD and for the royal
palace, and to make harps and lyres for the
musicians. So much almugwood has never
been imported or seen since that day.)
13King Solomon gave the queen of Sheba
all she desired and asked for, besides what
he had given her out of his royal bounty.
Then she left and returned with her retinue
to her own country.

Solomon's Splendor

14The weight of the gold that Solomon re-
ceived yearly was 666 talents,[g] 15not includ-
ing the revenues from merchants and trad-
ers and from all the Arabian kings and the
governors of the territories.
16King Solomon made two hundred large
shields of hammered gold; six hundred
shekels[h] of gold went into each shield. 17He
also made three hundred small shields of
hammered gold, with three minas[i] of gold in
each shield. The king put them in the Palace
of the Forest of Lebanon.
18Then the king made a great throne cov-
ered with ivory and overlaid with fine gold.
19The throne had six steps, and its back had
a rounded top. On both sides of the seat were
armrests, with a lion standing beside each of
them. 20Twelve lions stood on the six steps,
one at either end of each step. Nothing like it

[a] 26 Or *the Sea of Reeds* [b] 28 That is, about 16 tons or about 14 metric tons [c] 5 Or *the ascent by which he went up to* [d] 10 That is, about 4 1/2 tons or about 4 metric tons [e] 11 Probably a variant of *algumwood;* also in verse 12 [f] 12 The meaning of the Hebrew for this word is uncertain. [g] 14 That is, about 25 tons or about 23 metric tons [h] 16 That is, about 15 pounds or about 6.9 kilograms; also in verse 29 [i] 17 That is, about 3 3/4 pounds or about 1.7 kilograms; or perhaps reference is to double minas, that is, about 7 1/2 pounds or about 3.5 kilograms.

had ever been made for any other kingdom.
21 All King Solomon's goblets were gold, and
all the household articles in the Palace of the
Forest of Lebanon were pure gold. Nothing
was made of silver, because silver was con-
sidered of little value in Solomon's days.
22 The king had a fleet of trading ships[a] at sea
along with the ships of Hiram. Once every
three years it returned, carrying gold, silver
and ivory, and apes and baboons.

23 King Solomon was greater in riches and
wisdom than all the other kings of the earth.
24 The whole world sought audience with
Solomon to hear the wisdom God had put
in his heart. 25 Year after year, everyone who
came brought a gift — articles of silver and
gold, robes, weapons and spices, and horses
and mules.

26 Solomon accumulated chariots and
horses; he had fourteen hundred chariots
and twelve thousand horses,[b] which he kept
in the chariot cities and also with him in Je-
rusalem. 27 The king made silver as common
in Jerusalem as stones, and cedar as plen-
tiful as sycamore-fig trees in the foothills.
28 Solomon's horses were imported from
Egypt and from Kue[c] — the royal merchants
purchased them from Kue at the current
price. 29 They imported a chariot from Egypt
for six hundred shekels of silver, and a horse
for a hundred and fifty.[d] They also exported
them to all the kings of the Hittites and of the
Arameans.

Solomon's Wives

11 King Solomon, however, loved many
foreign women besides Pharaoh's
daughter — Moabites, Ammonites, Edom-
ites, Sidonians and Hittites. 2 They were from
nations about which the LORD had told the Is-
raelites, "You must not intermarry with them,
because they will surely turn your hearts af-
ter their gods." Nevertheless, Solomon held
fast to them in love. 3 He had seven hundred
wives of royal birth and three hundred con-
cubines, and his wives led him astray. 4 As
Solomon grew old, his wives turned his heart
after other gods, and his heart was not fully
devoted to the LORD his God, as the heart of
David his father had been. 5 He followed Ash-
toreth the goddess of the Sidonians, and Mo-
lek the detestable god of the Ammonites. 6 So
Solomon did evil in the eyes of the LORD; he
did not follow the LORD completely, as David
his father had done.

7 On a hill east of Jerusalem, Solomon built
a high place for Chemosh the detestable god
of Moab, and for Molek the detestable god of
the Ammonites. 8 He did the same for all his
foreign wives, who burned incense and of-
fered sacrifices to their gods.

9 The LORD became angry with Solomon
because his heart had turned away from the
LORD, the God of Israel, who had appeared to
him twice. 10 Although he had forbidden Sol-
omon to follow other gods, Solomon did not
keep the LORD's command. 11 So the LORD
said to Solomon, "Since this is your attitude
and you have not kept my covenant and my
decrees, which I commanded you, I will
most certainly tear the kingdom away from
you and give it to one of your subordinates.
12 Nevertheless, for the sake of David your
father, I will not do it during your lifetime. I
will tear it out of the hand of your son. 13 Yet
I will not tear the whole kingdom from him,
but will give him one tribe for the sake of Da-
vid my servant and for the sake of Jerusalem,
which I have chosen."

Solomon's Adversaries

14 Then the LORD raised up against Solo-
mon an adversary, Hadad the Edomite, from
the royal line of Edom. 15 Earlier when David
was fighting with Edom, Joab the command-
er of the army, who had gone up to bury the
dead, had struck down all the men in Edom.
16 Joab and all the Israelites stayed there for
six months, until they had destroyed all the
men in Edom. 17 But Hadad, still only a boy,
fled to Egypt with some Edomite officials
who had served his father. 18 They set out
from Midian and went to Paran. Then tak-
ing people from Paran with them, they went
to Egypt, to Pharaoh king of Egypt, who gave
Hadad a house and land and provided him
with food.

19 Pharaoh was so pleased with Hadad
that he gave him a sister of his own wife,
Queen Tahpenes, in marriage. 20 The sister of
Tahpenes bore him a son named Genubath,
whom Tahpenes brought up in the royal pal-
ace. There Genubath lived with Pharaoh's
own children.

[a] 22 Hebrew *of ships of Tarshish* [b] 26 Or *charioteers* [c] 28 Probably *Cilicia* [d] 29 That is, about 3 3/4 pounds or about 1.7 kilograms

21 While he was in Egypt, Hadad heard that David rested with his ancestors and that Joab the commander of the army was also dead. Then Hadad said to Pharaoh, "Let me go, that I may return to my own country."

22 "What have you lacked here that you want to go back to your own country?" Pharaoh asked.

"Nothing," Hadad replied, "but do let me go!"

23 And God raised up against Solomon another adversary, Rezon son of Eliada, who had fled from his master, Hadadezer king of Zobah. 24 When David destroyed Zobah's army, Rezon gathered a band of men around him and became their leader; they went to Damascus, where they settled and took control. 25 Rezon was Israel's adversary as long as Solomon lived, adding to the trouble caused by Hadad. So Rezon ruled in Aram and was hostile toward Israel.

Jeroboam Rebels Against Solomon

26 Also, Jeroboam son of Nebat rebelled against the king. He was one of Solomon's officials, an Ephraimite from Zeredah, and his mother was a widow named Zeruah.

27 Here is the account of how he rebelled against the king: Solomon had built the terraces[a] and had filled in the gap in the wall of the city of David his father. 28 Now Jeroboam was a man of standing, and when Solomon saw how well the young man did his work he put him in charge of the whole labor force of the tribes of Joseph.

29 About that time Jeroboam was going out of Jerusalem, and Ahijah the prophet of Shiloh met him on the way, wearing a new cloak. The two of them were alone out in the country, 30 and Ahijah took hold of the new cloak he was wearing and tore it into twelve pieces. 31 Then he said to Jeroboam, "Take ten pieces for yourself, for this is what the Lord, the God of Israel, says: 'See, I am going to tear the kingdom out of Solomon's hand and give you ten tribes. 32 But for the sake of my servant David and the city of Jerusalem, which I have chosen out of all the tribes of Israel, he will have one tribe. 33 I will do this because they have[b] forsaken me and worshiped Ashtoreth the goddess of the Sidonians, Chemosh the god of the Moabites, and Molek the god of the Ammonites, and have not walked in obedience to me, nor done what is right in my eyes, nor kept my decrees and laws as David, Solomon's father, did.

34 " 'But I will not take the whole kingdom out of Solomon's hand; I have made him ruler all the days of his life for the sake of David my servant, whom I chose and who obeyed my commands and decrees. 35 I will take the kingdom from his son's hands and give you ten tribes. 36 I will give one tribe to his son so that David my servant may always have a lamp before me in Jerusalem, the city where I chose to put my Name. 37 However, as for you, I will take you, and you will rule over all that your heart desires; you will be king over Israel. 38 If you do whatever I command you and walk in obedience to me and do what is right in my eyes by obeying my decrees and commands, as David my servant did, I will be with you. I will build you a dynasty as enduring as the one I built for David and will give Israel to you. 39 I will humble David's descendants because of this, but not forever.' "

40 Solomon tried to kill Jeroboam, but Jeroboam fled to Egypt, to Shishak the king, and stayed there until Solomon's death.

Solomon's Death

41 As for the other events of Solomon's reign—all he did and the wisdom he displayed—are they not written in the book of the annals of Solomon? 42 Solomon reigned in Jerusalem over all Israel forty years. 43 Then he rested with his ancestors and was buried in the city of David his father. And Rehoboam his son succeeded him as king.

Israel Rebels Against Rehoboam

12 Rehoboam went to Shechem, for all Israel had gone there to make him king. 2 When Jeroboam son of Nebat heard this (he was still in Egypt, where he had fled from King Solomon), he returned from[c] Egypt. 3 So they sent for Jeroboam, and he and the whole assembly of Israel went to Rehoboam and said to him: 4 "Your father put a heavy yoke on us, but now lighten the harsh labor and the heavy yoke he put on us, and we will serve you."

5 Rehoboam answered, "Go away for three

[a] 27 Or *the Millo* [b] 33 Hebrew; Septuagint, Vulgate and Syriac *because he has* [c] 2 Or *he remained in*

days and then come back to me." So the peo-
ple went away.
[6]Then King Rehoboam consulted the el-
ders who had served his father Solomon dur-
ing his lifetime. "How would you advise me
to answer these people?" he asked.
[7]They replied, "If today you will be a ser-
vant to these people and serve them and give
them a favorable answer, they will always be
your servants."
[8]But Rehoboam rejected the advice the
elders gave him and consulted the young
men who had grown up with him and were
serving him. [9]He asked them, "What is your
advice? How should we answer these people
who say to me, 'Lighten the yoke your father
put on us'?"
[10]The young men who had grown up with
him replied, "These people have said to you,
'Your father put a heavy yoke on us, but make
our yoke lighter.' Now tell them, 'My little
finger is thicker than my father's waist. [11]My
father laid on you a heavy yoke; I will make
it even heavier. My father scourged you with
whips; I will scourge you with scorpions.'"
[12]Three days later Jeroboam and all the
people returned to Rehoboam, as the king
had said, "Come back to me in three days."
[13]The king answered the people harshly.
Rejecting the advice given him by the el-
ders, [14]he followed the advice of the young
men and said, "My father made your yoke
heavy; I will make it even heavier. My father
scourged you with whips; I will scourge you
with scorpions." [15]So the king did not listen
to the people, for this turn of events was from
the LORD, to fulfill the word the LORD had
spoken to Jeroboam son of Nebat through
Ahijah the Shilonite.
[16]When all Israel saw that the king refused
to listen to them, they answered the king:

"What share do we have in David,
what part in Jesse's son?
To your tents, Israel!
Look after your own house, David!"

So the Israelites went home. [17]But as for the
Israelites who were living in the towns of Ju-
dah, Rehoboam still ruled over them.
[18]King Rehoboam sent out Adoniram,[a]
who was in charge of forced labor, but all
Israel stoned him to death. King Rehobo-
am, however, managed to get into his char-
iot and escape to Jerusalem. [19]So Israel has
been in rebellion against the house of David
to this day.
[20]When all the Israelites heard that Jer-
oboam had returned, they sent and called
him to the assembly and made him king over
all Israel. Only the tribe of Judah remained
loyal to the house of David.
[21]When Rehoboam arrived in Jerusalem,
he mustered all Judah and the tribe of Benja-
min — a hundred and eighty thousand able
young men — to go to war against Israel and
to regain the kingdom for Rehoboam son of
Solomon.
[22]But this word of God came to Shema-
iah the man of God: [23]"Say to Rehoboam
son of Solomon king of Judah, to all Judah
and Benjamin, and to the rest of the people,
[24]'This is what the LORD says: Do not go up
to fight against your brothers, the Israelites.
Go home, every one of you, for this is my do-
ing.'" So they obeyed the word of the LORD
and went home again, as the LORD had or-
dered.

Golden Calves at Bethel and Dan

[25]Then Jeroboam fortified Shechem in
the hill country of Ephraim and lived there.
From there he went out and built up Peniel.[b]
[26]Jeroboam thought to himself, "The
kingdom will now likely revert to the house
of David. [27]If these people go up to offer sac-
rifices at the temple of the LORD in Jerusa-
lem, they will again give their allegiance to
their lord, Rehoboam king of Judah. They
will kill me and return to King Rehoboam."
[28]After seeking advice, the king made two
golden calves. He said to the people, "It is too
much for you to go up to Jerusalem. Here are
your gods, Israel, who brought you up out of
Egypt." [29]One he set up in Bethel, and the
other in Dan. [30]And this thing became a sin;
the people came to worship the one at Bethel
and went as far as Dan to worship the other.[c]
[31]Jeroboam built shrines on high places
and appointed priests from all sorts of peo-
ple, even though they were not Levites. [32]He
instituted a festival on the fifteenth day of the
eighth month, like the festival held in Judah,

[a] *18* Some Septuagint manuscripts and Syriac (see also 4:6 and 5:14); Hebrew *Adoram* [b] *25* Hebrew *Penuel,* a variant of *Peniel* [c] *30* Probable reading of the original Hebrew text; Masoretic Text *people went to the one as far as Dan*

and offered sacrifices on the altar. This he did in Bethel, sacrificing to the calves he had made. And at Bethel he also installed priests at the high places he had made. [33]On the fifteenth day of the eighth month, a month of his own choosing, he offered sacrifices on the altar he had built at Bethel. So he instituted the festival for the Israelites and went up to the altar to make offerings.

The Man of God From Judah

13 By the word of the LORD a man of God came from Judah to Bethel, as Jeroboam was standing by the altar to make an offering. [2]By the word of the LORD he cried out against the altar: "Altar, altar! This is what the LORD says: 'A son named Josiah will be born to the house of David. On you he will sacrifice the priests of the high places who make offerings here, and human bones will be burned on you.' " [3]That same day the man of God gave a sign: "This is the sign the LORD has declared: The altar will be split apart and the ashes on it will be poured out."

[4]When King Jeroboam heard what the man of God cried out against the altar at Bethel, he stretched out his hand from the altar and said, "Seize him!" But the hand he stretched out toward the man shriveled up, so that he could not pull it back. [5]Also, the altar was split apart and its ashes poured out according to the sign given by the man of God by the word of the LORD.

[6]Then the king said to the man of God, "Intercede with the LORD your God and pray for me that my hand may be restored." So the man of God interceded with the LORD, and the king's hand was restored and became as it was before.

[7]The king said to the man of God, "Come home with me for a meal, and I will give you a gift."

[8]But the man of God answered the king, "Even if you were to give me half your possessions, I would not go with you, nor would I eat bread or drink water here. [9]For I was commanded by the word of the LORD: 'You must not eat bread or drink water or return by the way you came.' " [10]So he took another road and did not return by the way he had come to Bethel.

[11]Now there was a certain old prophet living in Bethel, whose sons came and told him all that the man of God had done there that day. They also told their father what he had said to the king. [12]Their father asked them, "Which way did he go?" And his sons showed him which road the man of God from Judah had taken. [13]So he said to his sons, "Saddle the donkey for me." And when they had saddled the donkey for him, he mounted it [14]and rode after the man of God. He found him sitting under an oak tree and asked, "Are you the man of God who came from Judah?"

"I am," he replied.

[15]So the prophet said to him, "Come home with me and eat."

[16]The man of God said, "I cannot turn back and go with you, nor can I eat bread or drink water with you in this place. [17]I have been told by the word of the LORD: 'You must not eat bread or drink water there or return by the way you came.' "

[18]The old prophet answered, "I too am a prophet, as you are. And an angel said to me by the word of the LORD: 'Bring him back with you to your house so that he may eat bread and drink water.' " (But he was lying to him.) [19]So the man of God returned with him and ate and drank in his house.

[20]While they were sitting at the table, the word of the LORD came to the old prophet who had brought him back. [21]He cried out to the man of God who had come from Judah, "This is what the LORD says: 'You have defied the word of the LORD and have not kept the command the LORD your God gave you. [22]You came back and ate bread and drank water in the place where he told you not to eat or drink. Therefore your body will not be buried in the tomb of your ancestors.' "

[23]When the man of God had finished eating and drinking, the prophet who had brought him back saddled his donkey for him. [24]As he went on his way, a lion met him on the road and killed him, and his body was left lying on the road, with both the donkey and the lion standing beside it. [25]Some people who passed by saw the body lying there, with the lion standing beside the body, and they went and reported it in the city where the old prophet lived.

[26]When the prophet who had brought him back from his journey heard of it, he said, "It is the man of God who defied the word of the LORD. The LORD has given him over to the lion, which has mauled him and killed him, as the word of the LORD had warned him."

27 The prophet said to his sons, "Saddle
the donkey for me," and they did so. 28 Then
he went out and found the body lying on the
road, with the donkey and the lion standing
beside it. The lion had neither eaten the body
nor mauled the donkey. 29 So the prophet
picked up the body of the man of God, laid
it on the donkey, and brought it back to his
own city to mourn for him and bury him.
30 Then he laid the body in his own tomb,
and they mourned over him and said, "Alas,
my brother!"

31 After burying him, he said to his sons,
"When I die, bury me in the grave where the
man of God is buried; lay my bones beside
his bones. 32 For the message he declared
by the word of the LORD against the altar
in Bethel and against all the shrines on the
high places in the towns of Samaria will cer-
tainly come true."

33 Even after this, Jeroboam did not
change his evil ways, but once more ap-
pointed priests for the high places from all
sorts of people. Anyone who wanted to be-
come a priest he consecrated for the high
places. 34 This was the sin of the house of Jer-
oboam that led to its downfall and to its de-
struction from the face of the earth.

Ahijah's Prophecy Against Jeroboam

14 At that time Abijah son of Jeroboam
became ill, 2 and Jeroboam said to his
wife, "Go, disguise yourself, so you won't be
recognized as the wife of Jeroboam. Then go
to Shiloh. Ahijah the prophet is there — the
one who told me I would be king over this
people. 3 Take ten loaves of bread with you,
some cakes and a jar of honey, and go to him.
He will tell you what will happen to the boy."
4 So Jeroboam's wife did what he said and
went to Ahijah's house in Shiloh.

Now Ahijah could not see; his sight was
gone because of his age. 5 But the LORD had
told Ahijah, "Jeroboam's wife is coming to
ask you about her son, for he is ill, and you
are to give her such and such an answer.
When she arrives, she will pretend to be
someone else."

6 So when Ahijah heard the sound of her
footsteps at the door, he said, "Come in, wife
of Jeroboam. Why this pretense? I have been
sent to you with bad news. 7 Go, tell Jeroboam
that this is what the LORD, the God of Israel,
says: 'I raised you up from among the people
and appointed you ruler over my people Isra-
el. 8 I tore the kingdom away from the house
of David and gave it to you, but you have not
been like my servant David, who kept my
commands and followed me with all his
heart, doing only what was right in my eyes.
9 You have done more evil than all who lived
before you. You have made for yourself other
gods, idols made of metal; you have aroused
my anger and turned your back on me.

10 " 'Because of this, I am going to bring
disaster on the house of Jeroboam. I will cut
off from Jeroboam every last male in Israel —
slave or free.[a] I will burn up the house of Jer-
oboam as one burns dung, until it is all gone.
11 Dogs will eat those belonging to Jeroboam
who die in the city, and the birds will feed on
those who die in the country. The LORD has
spoken!'

12 "As for you, go back home. When you set
foot in your city, the boy will die. 13 All Israel
will mourn for him and bury him. He is the
only one belonging to Jeroboam who will
be buried, because he is the only one in the
house of Jeroboam in whom the LORD, the
God of Israel, has found anything good.

14 "The LORD will raise up for himself a
king over Israel who will cut off the family
of Jeroboam. Even now this is beginning to
happen.[b] 15 And the LORD will strike Israel, so
that it will be like a reed swaying in the wa-
ter. He will uproot Israel from this good land
that he gave to their ancestors and scatter
them beyond the Euphrates River, because
they aroused the LORD's anger by making
Asherah poles.[c] 16 And he will give Israel up
because of the sins Jeroboam has committed
and has caused Israel to commit."

17 Then Jeroboam's wife got up and left
and went to Tirzah. As soon as she stepped
over the threshold of the house, the boy died.
18 They buried him, and all Israel mourned
for him, as the LORD had said through his
servant the prophet Ahijah.

19 The other events of Jeroboam's reign,
his wars and how he ruled, are written in
the book of the annals of the kings of Israel.
20 He reigned for twenty-two years and then
rested with his ancestors. And Nadab his son
succeeded him as king.

[a] *10* Or *Israel — every ruler or leader* [b] *14* The meaning of the Hebrew for this sentence is uncertain.
[c] *15* That is, wooden symbols of the goddess Asherah; here and elsewhere in 1 Kings

Rehoboam King of Judah

21 Rehoboam son of Solomon was king in Judah. He was forty-one years old when he became king, and he reigned seventeen years in Jerusalem, the city the LORD had chosen out of all the tribes of Israel in which to put his Name. His mother's name was Naamah; she was an Ammonite.

22 Judah did evil in the eyes of the LORD. By the sins they committed they stirred up his jealous anger more than those who were before them had done. 23 They also set up for themselves high places, sacred stones and Asherah poles on every high hill and under every spreading tree. 24 There were even male shrine prostitutes in the land; the people engaged in all the detestable practices of the nations the LORD had driven out before the Israelites.

25 In the fifth year of King Rehoboam, Shishak king of Egypt attacked Jerusalem. 26 He carried off the treasures of the temple of the LORD and the treasures of the royal palace. He took everything, including all the gold shields Solomon had made. 27 So King Rehoboam made bronze shields to replace them and assigned these to the commanders of the guard on duty at the entrance to the royal palace. 28 Whenever the king went to the LORD's temple, the guards bore the shields, and afterward they returned them to the guardroom.

29 As for the other events of Rehoboam's reign, and all he did, are they not written in the book of the annals of the kings of Judah? 30 There was continual warfare between Rehoboam and Jeroboam. 31 And Rehoboam rested with his ancestors and was buried with them in the City of David. His mother's name was Naamah; she was an Ammonite. And Abijah[a] his son succeeded him as king.

Abijah King of Judah

15 In the eighteenth year of the reign of Jeroboam son of Nebat, Abijah[b] became king of Judah, 2 and he reigned in Jerusalem three years. His mother's name was Maakah daughter of Abishalom.[c]

3 He committed all the sins his father had done before him; his heart was not fully devoted to the LORD his God, as the heart of David his forefather had been. 4 Nevertheless, for David's sake the LORD his God gave him a lamp in Jerusalem by raising up a son to succeed him and by making Jerusalem strong. 5 For David had done what was right in the eyes of the LORD and had not failed to keep any of the LORD's commands all the days of his life — except in the case of Uriah the Hittite.

6 There was war between Abijah[d] and Jeroboam throughout Abijah's lifetime. 7 As for the other events of Abijah's reign, and all he did, are they not written in the book of the annals of the kings of Judah? There was war between Abijah and Jeroboam. 8 And Abijah rested with his ancestors and was buried in the City of David. And Asa his son succeeded him as king.

Asa King of Judah

9 In the twentieth year of Jeroboam king of Israel, Asa became king of Judah, 10 and he reigned in Jerusalem forty-one years. His grandmother's name was Maakah daughter of Abishalom.

11 Asa did what was right in the eyes of the LORD, as his father David had done. 12 He expelled the male shrine prostitutes from the land and got rid of all the idols his ancestors had made. 13 He even deposed his grandmother Maakah from her position as queen mother, because she had made a repulsive image for the worship of Asherah. Asa cut it down and burned it in the Kidron Valley. 14 Although he did not remove the high places, Asa's heart was fully committed to the LORD all his life. 15 He brought into the temple of the LORD the silver and gold and the articles that he and his father had dedicated.

16 There was war between Asa and Baasha king of Israel throughout their reigns. 17 Baasha king of Israel went up against Judah and fortified Ramah to prevent anyone from leaving or entering the territory of Asa king of Judah.

18 Asa then took all the silver and gold that was left in the treasuries of the LORD's temple and of his own palace. He entrusted it to his officials and sent them to Ben-Hadad son

[a] *31* Some Hebrew manuscripts and Septuagint (see also 2 Chron. 12:16); most Hebrew manuscripts *Abijam* [b] *1* Some Hebrew manuscripts and Septuagint (see also 2 Chron. 12:16); most Hebrew manuscripts *Abijam*; also in verses 7 and 8 [c] *2* A variant of *Absalom*; also in verse 10 [d] *6* Some Hebrew manuscripts and Syriac *Abijam* (that is Abijah); most Hebrew manuscripts *Rehoboam*

of Tabrimmon, the son of Hezion, the king of
Aram, who was ruling in Damascus. 19“Let
there be a treaty between me and you,” he
said, “as there was between my father and
your father. See, I am sending you a gift of
silver and gold. Now break your treaty with
Baasha king of Israel so he will withdraw
from me.”

20Ben-Hadad agreed with King Asa and
sent the commanders of his forces against
the towns of Israel. He conquered Ijon, Dan,
Abel Beth Maakah and all Kinnereth in addi-
tion to Naphtali. 21When Baasha heard this,
he stopped building Ramah and withdrew to
Tirzah. 22Then King Asa issued an order to
all Judah — no one was exempt — and they
carried away from Ramah the stones and
timber Baasha had been using there. With
them King Asa built up Geba in Benjamin,
and also Mizpah.

23As for all the other events of Asa’s reign,
all his achievements, all he did and the cit-
ies he built, are they not written in the book
of the annals of the kings of Judah? In his
old age, however, his feet became diseased.
24Then Asa rested with his ancestors and
was buried with them in the city of his father
David. And Jehoshaphat his son succeeded
him as king.

Nadab King of Israel

25Nadab son of Jeroboam became king of
Israel in the second year of Asa king of Ju-
dah, and he reigned over Israel two years.
26He did evil in the eyes of the LORD, follow-
ing the ways of his father and committing
the same sin his father had caused Israel to
commit.

27Baasha son of Ahijah from the tribe of
Issachar plotted against him, and he struck
him down at Gibbethon, a Philistine town,
while Nadab and all Israel were besieging it.
28Baasha killed Nadab in the third year of Asa
king of Judah and succeeded him as king.

29As soon as he began to reign, he killed
Jeroboam’s whole family. He did not leave
Jeroboam anyone that breathed, but de-
stroyed them all, according to the word of
the LORD given through his servant Ahijah
the Shilonite. 30This happened because of
the sins Jeroboam had committed and had
caused Israel to commit, and because he
aroused the anger of the LORD, the God of
Israel.

31As for the other events of Nadab’s reign,
and all he did, are they not written in the
book of the annals of the kings of Israel?
32There was war between Asa and Baasha
king of Israel throughout their reigns.

Baasha King of Israel

33In the third year of Asa king of Judah,
Baasha son of Ahijah became king of all Is-
rael in Tirzah, and he reigned twenty-four
years. 34He did evil in the eyes of the LORD,
following the ways of Jeroboam and com-
mitting the same sin Jeroboam had caused
Israel to commit.

16 Then the word of the LORD came to
Jehu son of Hanani concerning Ba-
asha: 2“I lifted you up from the dust and
appointed you ruler over my people Israel,
but you followed the ways of Jeroboam and
caused my people Israel to sin and to arouse
my anger by their sins. 3So I am about to
wipe out Baasha and his house, and I will
make your house like that of Jeroboam son of
Nebat. 4Dogs will eat those belonging to Ba-
asha who die in the city, and birds will feed
on those who die in the country.”

5As for the other events of Baasha’s reign,
what he did and his achievements, are they
not written in the book of the annals of the
kings of Israel? 6Baasha rested with his an-
cestors and was buried in Tirzah. And Elah
his son succeeded him as king.

7Moreover, the word of the LORD came
through the prophet Jehu son of Hanani to
Baasha and his house, because of all the evil
he had done in the eyes of the LORD, arous-
ing his anger by the things he did, becoming
like the house of Jeroboam — and also be-
cause he destroyed it.

Elah King of Israel

8In the twenty-sixth year of Asa king of Ju-
dah, Elah son of Baasha became king of Isra-
el, and he reigned in Tirzah two years.

9Zimri, one of his officials, who had com-
mand of half his chariots, plotted against
him. Elah was in Tirzah at the time, get-
ting drunk in the home of Arza, the palace
administrator at Tirzah. 10Zimri came in,
struck him down and killed him in the twen-
ty-seventh year of Asa king of Judah. Then he
succeeded him as king.

11As soon as he began to reign and was
seated on the throne, he killed off Baasha’s

whole family. He did not spare a single male, whether relative or friend. 12 So Zimri destroyed the whole family of Baasha, in accordance with the word of the LORD spoken against Baasha through the prophet Jehu— 13 because of all the sins Baasha and his son Elah had committed and had caused Israel to commit, so that they aroused the anger of the LORD, the God of Israel, by their worthless idols.

14 As for the other events of Elah's reign, and all he did, are they not written in the book of the annals of the kings of Israel?

Zimri King of Israel

15 In the twenty-seventh year of Asa king of Judah, Zimri reigned in Tirzah seven days. The army was encamped near Gibbethon, a Philistine town. 16 When the Israelites in the camp heard that Zimri had plotted against the king and murdered him, they proclaimed Omri, the commander of the army, king over Israel that very day there in the camp. 17 Then Omri and all the Israelites with him withdrew from Gibbethon and laid siege to Tirzah. 18 When Zimri saw that the city was taken, he went into the citadel of the royal palace and set the palace on fire around him. So he died, 19 because of the sins he had committed, doing evil in the eyes of the LORD and following the ways of Jeroboam and committing the same sin Jeroboam had caused Israel to commit.

20 As for the other events of Zimri's reign, and the rebellion he carried out, are they not written in the book of the annals of the kings of Israel?

Omri King of Israel

21 Then the people of Israel were split into two factions; half supported Tibni son of Ginath for king, and the other half supported Omri. 22 But Omri's followers proved stronger than those of Tibni son of Ginath. So Tibni died and Omri became king.

23 In the thirty-first year of Asa king of Judah, Omri became king of Israel, and he reigned twelve years, six of them in Tirzah. 24 He bought the hill of Samaria from Shemer for two talents[a] of silver and built a city on the hill, calling it Samaria, after Shemer, the name of the former owner of the hill.

25 But Omri did evil in the eyes of the LORD and sinned more than all those before him. 26 He followed completely the ways of Jeroboam son of Nebat, committing the same sin Jeroboam had caused Israel to commit, so that they aroused the anger of the LORD, the God of Israel, by their worthless idols.

27 As for the other events of Omri's reign, what he did and the things he achieved, are they not written in the book of the annals of the kings of Israel? 28 Omri rested with his ancestors and was buried in Samaria. And Ahab his son succeeded him as king.

Ahab Becomes King of Israel

29 In the thirty-eighth year of Asa king of Judah, Ahab son of Omri became king of Israel, and he reigned in Samaria over Israel twenty-two years. 30 Ahab son of Omri did more evil in the eyes of the LORD than any of those before him. 31 He not only considered it trivial to commit the sins of Jeroboam son of Nebat, but he also married Jezebel daughter of Ethbaal king of the Sidonians, and began to serve Baal and worship him. 32 He set up an altar for Baal in the temple of Baal that he built in Samaria. 33 Ahab also made an Asherah pole and did more to arouse the anger of the LORD, the God of Israel, than did all the kings of Israel before him.

34 In Ahab's time, Hiel of Bethel rebuilt Jericho. He laid its foundations at the cost of his firstborn son Abiram, and he set up its gates at the cost of his youngest son Segub, in accordance with the word of the LORD spoken by Joshua son of Nun.

Elijah Announces a Great Drought

17 Now Elijah the Tishbite, from Tishbe[b] in Gilead, said to Ahab, "As the LORD, the God of Israel, lives, whom I serve, there will be neither dew nor rain in the next few years except at my word."

Elijah Fed by Ravens

2 Then the word of the LORD came to Elijah: 3 "Leave here, turn eastward and hide in the Kerith Ravine, east of the Jordan. 4 You will drink from the brook, and I have directed the ravens to supply you with food there."

5 So he did what the LORD had told him. He went to the Kerith Ravine, east of the Jordan,

[a] *24* That is, about 150 pounds or about 68 kilograms

[b] *1* Or *Tishbite, of the settlers*

and stayed there. 6 The ravens brought him
bread and meat in the morning and bread
and meat in the evening, and he drank from
the brook.

Elijah and the Widow at Zarephath

7 Some time later the brook dried up be-
cause there had been no rain in the land.
8 Then the word of the LORD came to him:
9 "Go at once to Zarephath in the region of
Sidon and stay there. I have directed a wid-
ow there to supply you with food." 10 So he
went to Zarephath. When he came to the
town gate, a widow was there gathering
sticks. He called to her and asked, "Would
you bring me a little water in a jar so I may
have a drink?" 11 As she was going to get it,
he called, "And bring me, please, a piece of
bread."

12 "As surely as the LORD your God lives,"
she replied, "I don't have any bread — only a
handful of flour in a jar and a little olive oil
in a jug. I am gathering a few sticks to take
home and make a meal for myself and my
son, that we may eat it — and die."

13 Elijah said to her, "Don't be afraid.
Go home and do as you have said. But first
make a small loaf of bread for me from what
you have and bring it to me, and then make
something for yourself and your son. 14 For
this is what the LORD, the God of Israel, says:
'The jar of flour will not be used up and the
jug of oil will not run dry until the day the
LORD sends rain on the land.' "

15 She went away and did as Elijah had told
her. So there was food every day for Elijah
and for the woman and her family. 16 For the
jar of flour was not used up and the jug of oil
did not run dry, in keeping with the word of
the LORD spoken by Elijah.

17 Some time later the son of the wom-
an who owned the house became ill. He
grew worse and worse, and finally stopped
breathing. 18 She said to Elijah, "What do you
have against me, man of God? Did you come
to remind me of my sin and kill my son?"

19 "Give me your son," Elijah replied. He
took him from her arms, carried him to the
upper room where he was staying, and laid
him on his bed. 20 Then he cried out to the
LORD, "LORD my God, have you brought
tragedy even on this widow I am staying
with, by causing her son to die?" 21 Then he
stretched himself out on the boy three times
and cried out to the LORD, "LORD my God, let
this boy's life return to him!"

22 The LORD heard Elijah's cry, and the
boy's life returned to him, and he lived.
23 Elijah picked up the child and carried him
down from the room into the house. He gave
him to his mother and said, "Look, your son
is alive!"

24 Then the woman said to Elijah, "Now
I know that you are a man of God and that
the word of the LORD from your mouth is the
truth."

Elijah and Obadiah

18 After a long time, in the third year,
the word of the LORD came to Elijah:
"Go and present yourself to Ahab, and I will
send rain on the land." 2 So Elijah went to
present himself to Ahab.

Now the famine was severe in Samaria,
3 and Ahab had summoned Obadiah, his
palace administrator. (Obadiah was a de-
vout believer in the LORD. 4 While Jezebel
was killing off the LORD's prophets, Obadi-
ah had taken a hundred prophets and hid-
den them in two caves, fifty in each, and had
supplied them with food and water.) 5 Ahab
had said to Obadiah, "Go through the land
to all the springs and valleys. Maybe we
can find some grass to keep the horses and
mules alive so we will not have to kill any of
our animals." 6 So they divided the land they
were to cover, Ahab going in one direction
and Obadiah in another.

7 As Obadiah was walking along, Elijah
met him. Obadiah recognized him, bowed
down to the ground, and said, "Is it really
you, my lord Elijah?"

8 "Yes," he replied. "Go tell your master,
'Elijah is here.' "

9 "What have I done wrong," asked Obadi-
ah, "that you are handing your servant over
to Ahab to be put to death? 10 As surely as the
LORD your God lives, there is not a nation
or kingdom where my master has not sent
someone to look for you. And whenever a na-
tion or kingdom claimed you were not there,
he made them swear they could not find
you. 11 But now you tell me to go to my mas-
ter and say, 'Elijah is here.' 12 I don't know
where the Spirit of the LORD may carry you
when I leave you. If I go and tell Ahab and
he doesn't find you, he will kill me. Yet I your
servant have worshiped the LORD since my

youth. [13]Haven't you heard, my lord, what I did while Jezebel was killing the prophets of the LORD? I hid a hundred of the LORD's prophets in two caves, fifty in each, and supplied them with food and water. [14]And now you tell me to go to my master and say, 'Elijah is here.' He will kill me!"

[15]Elijah said, "As the LORD Almighty lives, whom I serve, I will surely present myself to Ahab today."

Elijah on Mount Carmel

[16]So Obadiah went to meet Ahab and told him, and Ahab went to meet Elijah. [17]When he saw Elijah, he said to him, "Is that you, you troubler of Israel?"

[18]"I have not made trouble for Israel," Elijah replied. "But you and your father's family have. You have abandoned the LORD's commands and have followed the Baals. [19]Now summon the people from all over Israel to meet me on Mount Carmel. And bring the four hundred and fifty prophets of Baal and the four hundred prophets of Asherah, who eat at Jezebel's table."

[20]So Ahab sent word throughout all Israel and assembled the prophets on Mount Carmel. [21]Elijah went before the people and said, "How long will you waver between two opinions? If the LORD is God, follow him; but if Baal is God, follow him."

But the people said nothing.

[22]Then Elijah said to them, "I am the only one of the LORD's prophets left, but Baal has four hundred and fifty prophets. [23]Get two bulls for us. Let Baal's prophets choose one for themselves, and let them cut it into pieces and put it on the wood but not set fire to it. I will prepare the other bull and put it on the wood but not set fire to it. [24]Then you call on the name of your god, and I will call on the name of the LORD. The god who answers by fire—he is God."

Then all the people said, "What you say is good."

[25]Elijah said to the prophets of Baal, "Choose one of the bulls and prepare it first, since there are so many of you. Call on the name of your god, but do not light the fire." [26]So they took the bull given them and prepared it.

Then they called on the name of Baal from morning till noon. "Baal, answer us!" they shouted. But there was no response; no one answered. And they danced around the altar they had made.

[27]At noon Elijah began to taunt them. "Shout louder!" he said. "Surely he is a god! Perhaps he is deep in thought, or busy, or traveling. Maybe he is sleeping and must be awakened." [28]So they shouted louder and slashed themselves with swords and spears, as was their custom, until their blood flowed. [29]Midday passed, and they continued their frantic prophesying until the time for the evening sacrifice. But there was no response, no one answered, no one paid attention.

[30]Then Elijah said to all the people, "Come here to me." They came to him, and he repaired the altar of the LORD, which had been torn down. [31]Elijah took twelve stones, one for each of the tribes descended from Jacob, to whom the word of the LORD had come, saying, "Your name shall be Israel." [32]With the stones he built an altar in the name of the LORD, and he dug a trench around it large enough to hold two seahs[a] of seed. [33]He arranged the wood, cut the bull into pieces and laid it on the wood. Then he said to them, "Fill four large jars with water and pour it on the offering and on the wood."

[34]"Do it again," he said, and they did it again.

"Do it a third time," he ordered, and they did it the third time. [35]The water ran down around the altar and even filled the trench.

[36]At the time of sacrifice, the prophet Elijah stepped forward and prayed: "LORD, the God of Abraham, Isaac and Israel, let it be known today that you are God in Israel and that I am your servant and have done all these things at your command. [37]Answer me, LORD, answer me, so these people will know that you, LORD, are God, and that you are turning their hearts back again."

[38]Then the fire of the LORD fell and burned up the sacrifice, the wood, the stones and the soil, and also licked up the water in the trench.

[39]When all the people saw this, they fell prostrate and cried, "The LORD—he is God! The LORD—he is God!"

[40]Then Elijah commanded them, "Seize the prophets of Baal. Don't let anyone get

[a] 32 That is, probably about 24 pounds or about 11 kilograms

away!" They seized them, and Elijah had them brought down to the Kishon Valley and slaughtered there.

[41]And Elijah said to Ahab, "Go, eat and drink, for there is the sound of a heavy rain." [42]So Ahab went off to eat and drink, but Elijah climbed to the top of Carmel, bent down to the ground and put his face between his knees.

[43]"Go and look toward the sea," he told his servant. And he went up and looked.

"There is nothing there," he said.

Seven times Elijah said, "Go back."

[44]The seventh time the servant reported, "A cloud as small as a man's hand is rising from the sea."

So Elijah said, "Go and tell Ahab, 'Hitch up your chariot and go down before the rain stops you.'"

[45]Meanwhile, the sky grew black with clouds, the wind rose, a heavy rain started falling and Ahab rode off to Jezreel. [46]The power of the LORD came on Elijah and, tucking his cloak into his belt, he ran ahead of Ahab all the way to Jezreel.

Elijah Flees to Horeb

19 Now Ahab told Jezebel everything Elijah had done and how he had killed all the prophets with the sword. [2]So Jezebel sent a messenger to Elijah to say, "May the gods deal with me, be it ever so severely, if by this time tomorrow I do not make your life like that of one of them."

[3]Elijah was afraid[a] and ran for his life. When he came to Beersheba in Judah, he left his servant there, [4]while he himself went a day's journey into the wilderness. He came to a broom bush, sat down under it and prayed that he might die. "I have had enough, LORD," he said. "Take my life; I am no better than my ancestors." [5]Then he lay down under the bush and fell asleep.

All at once an angel touched him and said, "Get up and eat." [6]He looked around, and there by his head was some bread baked over hot coals, and a jar of water. He ate and drank and then lay down again.

[7]The angel of the LORD came back a second time and touched him and said, "Get up and eat, for the journey is too much for you." [8]So he got up and ate and drank. Strengthened by that food, he traveled forty days and forty nights until he reached Horeb, the mountain of God. [9]There he went into a cave and spent the night.

The LORD Appears to Elijah

And the word of the LORD came to him: "What are you doing here, Elijah?"

[10]He replied, "I have been very zealous for the LORD God Almighty. The Israelites have rejected your covenant, torn down your altars, and put your prophets to death with the sword. I am the only one left, and now they are trying to kill me too."

[11]The LORD said, "Go out and stand on the mountain in the presence of the LORD, for the LORD is about to pass by."

Then a great and powerful wind tore the mountains apart and shattered the rocks before the LORD, but the LORD was not in the wind. After the wind there was an earthquake, but the LORD was not in the earthquake. [12]After the earthquake came a fire, but the LORD was not in the fire. And after the fire came a gentle whisper. [13]When Elijah heard it, he pulled his cloak over his face and went out and stood at the mouth of the cave.

Then a voice said to him, "What are you doing here, Elijah?"

[14]He replied, "I have been very zealous for the LORD God Almighty. The Israelites have rejected your covenant, torn down your altars, and put your prophets to death with the sword. I am the only one left, and now they are trying to kill me too."

[15]The LORD said to him, "Go back the way you came, and go to the Desert of Damascus. When you get there, anoint Hazael king over Aram. [16]Also, anoint Jehu son of Nimshi king over Israel, and anoint Elisha son of Shaphat from Abel Meholah to succeed you as prophet. [17]Jehu will put to death any who escape the sword of Hazael, and Elisha will put to death any who escape the sword of Jehu. [18]Yet I reserve seven thousand in Israel—all whose knees have not bowed down to Baal and whose mouths have not kissed him."

The Call of Elisha

[19]So Elijah went from there and found Elisha son of Shaphat. He was plowing with

[a] 3 Or *Elijah saw*

twelve yoke of oxen, and he himself was driving the twelfth pair. Elijah went up to him and threw his cloak around him. 20Elisha then left his oxen and ran after Elijah. "Let me kiss my father and mother goodbye," he said, "and then I will come with you."

"Go back," Elijah replied. "What have I done to you?"

21So Elisha left him and went back. He took his yoke of oxen and slaughtered them. He burned the plowing equipment to cook the meat and gave it to the people, and they ate. Then he set out to follow Elijah and became his servant.

Ben-Hadad Attacks Samaria

20 Now Ben-Hadad king of Aram mustered his entire army. Accompanied by thirty-two kings with their horses and chariots, he went up and besieged Samaria and attacked it. 2He sent messengers into the city to Ahab king of Israel, saying, "This is what Ben-Hadad says: 3'Your silver and gold are mine, and the best of your wives and children are mine.'"

4The king of Israel answered, "Just as you say, my lord the king. I and all I have are yours."

5The messengers came again and said, "This is what Ben-Hadad says: 'I sent to demand your silver and gold, your wives and your children. 6But about this time tomorrow I am going to send my officials to search your palace and the houses of your officials. They will seize everything you value and carry it away.'"

7The king of Israel summoned all the elders of the land and said to them, "See how this man is looking for trouble! When he sent for my wives and my children, my silver and my gold, I did not refuse him."

8The elders and the people all answered, "Don't listen to him or agree to his demands."

9So he replied to Ben-Hadad's messengers, "Tell my lord the king, 'Your servant will do all you demanded the first time, but this demand I cannot meet.'" They left and took the answer back to Ben-Hadad.

10Then Ben-Hadad sent another message to Ahab: "May the gods deal with me, be it ever so severely, if enough dust remains in Samaria to give each of my men a handful."

11The king of Israel answered, "Tell him: 'One who puts on his armor should not boast like one who takes it off.'"

12Ben-Hadad heard this message while he and the kings were drinking in their tents,[a] and he ordered his men: "Prepare to attack." So they prepared to attack the city.

Ahab Defeats Ben-Hadad

13Meanwhile a prophet came to Ahab king of Israel and announced, "This is what the LORD says: 'Do you see this vast army? I will give it into your hand today, and then you will know that I am the LORD.'"

14"But who will do this?" asked Ahab.

The prophet replied, "This is what the LORD says: 'The junior officers under the provincial commanders will do it.'"

"And who will start the battle?" he asked.

The prophet answered, "You will."

15So Ahab summoned the 232 junior officers under the provincial commanders. Then he assembled the rest of the Israelites, 7,000 in all. 16They set out at noon while Ben-Hadad and the 32 kings allied with him were in their tents getting drunk. 17The junior officers under the provincial commanders went out first.

Now Ben-Hadad had dispatched scouts, who reported, "Men are advancing from Samaria."

18He said, "If they have come out for peace, take them alive; if they have come out for war, take them alive."

19The junior officers under the provincial commanders marched out of the city with the army behind them 20and each one struck down his opponent. At that, the Arameans fled, with the Israelites in pursuit. But Ben-Hadad king of Aram escaped on horseback with some of his horsemen. 21The king of Israel advanced and overpowered the horses and chariots and inflicted heavy losses on the Arameans.

22Afterward, the prophet came to the king of Israel and said, "Strengthen your position and see what must be done, because next spring the king of Aram will attack you again."

23Meanwhile, the officials of the king of Aram advised him, "Their gods are gods of the hills. That is why they were too strong for

a 12 Or *in Sukkoth*; also in verse 16

us. But if we fight them on the plains, surely we will be stronger than they. 24 Do this: Remove all the kings from their commands and replace them with other officers. 25 You must also raise an army like the one you lost—horse for horse and chariot for chariot—so we can fight Israel on the plains. Then surely we will be stronger than they." He agreed with them and acted accordingly.

26 The next spring Ben-Hadad mustered the Arameans and went up to Aphek to fight against Israel. 27 When the Israelites were also mustered and given provisions, they marched out to meet them. The Israelites camped opposite them like two small flocks of goats, while the Arameans covered the countryside.

28 The man of God came up and told the king of Israel, "This is what the LORD says: 'Because the Arameans think the LORD is a god of the hills and not a god of the valleys, I will deliver this vast army into your hands, and you will know that I am the LORD.' "

29 For seven days they camped opposite each other, and on the seventh day the battle was joined. The Israelites inflicted a hundred thousand casualties on the Aramean foot soldiers in one day. 30 The rest of them escaped to the city of Aphek, where the wall collapsed on twenty-seven thousand of them. And Ben-Hadad fled to the city and hid in an inner room.

31 His officials said to him, "Look, we have heard that the kings of Israel are merciful. Let us go to the king of Israel with sackcloth around our waists and ropes around our heads. Perhaps he will spare your life."

32 Wearing sackcloth around their waists and ropes around their heads, they went to the king of Israel and said, "Your servant Ben-Hadad says: 'Please let me live.' "

The king answered, "Is he still alive? He is my brother."

33 The men took this as a good sign and were quick to pick up his word. "Yes, your brother Ben-Hadad!" they said.

"Go and get him," the king said. When Ben-Hadad came out, Ahab had him come up into his chariot.

34 "I will return the cities my father took from your father," Ben-Hadad offered. "You may set up your own market areas in Damascus, as my father did in Samaria."

Ahab said, "On the basis of a treaty I will set you free." So he made a treaty with him, and let him go.

A Prophet Condemns Ahab

35 By the word of the LORD one of the company of the prophets said to his companion, "Strike me with your weapon," but he refused.

36 So the prophet said, "Because you have not obeyed the LORD, as soon as you leave me a lion will kill you." And after the man went away, a lion found him and killed him.

37 The prophet found another man and said, "Strike me, please." So the man struck him and wounded him. 38 Then the prophet went and stood by the road waiting for the king. He disguised himself with his headband down over his eyes. 39 As the king passed by, the prophet called out to him, "Your servant went into the thick of the battle, and someone came to me with a captive and said, 'Guard this man. If he is missing, it will be your life for his life, or you must pay a talent[a] of silver.' 40 While your servant was busy here and there, the man disappeared."

"That is your sentence," the king of Israel said. "You have pronounced it yourself."

41 Then the prophet quickly removed the headband from his eyes, and the king of Israel recognized him as one of the prophets. 42 He said to the king, "This is what the LORD says: 'You have set free a man I had determined should die.[b] Therefore it is your life for his life, your people for his people.' " 43 Sullen and angry, the king of Israel went to his palace in Samaria.

Naboth's Vineyard

21 Some time later there was an incident involving a vineyard belonging to Naboth the Jezreelite. The vineyard was in Jezreel, close to the palace of Ahab king of Samaria. 2 Ahab said to Naboth, "Let me have your vineyard to use for a vegetable garden, since it is close to my palace. In exchange I will give you a better vineyard or, if you prefer, I will pay you whatever it is worth."

3 But Naboth replied, "The LORD forbid that I should give you the inheritance of my ancestors."

[a] *39* That is, about 75 pounds or about 34 kilograms

[b] *42* The Hebrew term refers to the irrevocable giving over of things or persons to the LORD, often by totally destroying them.

4So Ahab went home, sullen and angry because Naboth the Jezreelite had said, "I will not give you the inheritance of my ancestors." He lay on his bed sulking and refused to eat.

5His wife Jezebel came in and asked him, "Why are you so sullen? Why won't you eat?"

6He answered her, "Because I said to Naboth the Jezreelite, 'Sell me your vineyard; or if you prefer, I will give you another vineyard in its place.' But he said, 'I will not give you my vineyard.'"

7Jezebel his wife said, "Is this how you act as king over Israel? Get up and eat! Cheer up. I'll get you the vineyard of Naboth the Jezreelite."

8So she wrote letters in Ahab's name, placed his seal on them, and sent them to the elders and nobles who lived in Naboth's city with him. 9In those letters she wrote:

> "Proclaim a day of fasting and seat Naboth in a prominent place among the people. 10But seat two scoundrels opposite him and have them bring charges that he has cursed both God and the king. Then take him out and stone him to death."

11So the elders and nobles who lived in Naboth's city did as Jezebel directed in the letters she had written to them. 12They proclaimed a fast and seated Naboth in a prominent place among the people. 13Then two scoundrels came and sat opposite him and brought charges against Naboth before the people, saying, "Naboth has cursed both God and the king." So they took him outside the city and stoned him to death. 14Then they sent word to Jezebel: "Naboth has been stoned to death."

15As soon as Jezebel heard that Naboth had been stoned to death, she said to Ahab, "Get up and take possession of the vineyard of Naboth the Jezreelite that he refused to sell you. He is no longer alive, but dead." 16When Ahab heard that Naboth was dead, he got up and went down to take possession of Naboth's vineyard.

17Then the word of the LORD came to Elijah the Tishbite: 18"Go down to meet Ahab king of Israel, who rules in Samaria. He is now in Naboth's vineyard, where he has gone to take possession of it. 19Say to him, 'This is what the LORD says: Have you not murdered a man and seized his property?' Then say to him, 'This is what the LORD says: In the place where dogs licked up Naboth's blood, dogs will lick up your blood—yes, yours!'"

20Ahab said to Elijah, "So you have found me, my enemy!"

"I have found you," he answered, "because you have sold yourself to do evil in the eyes of the LORD. 21He says, 'I am going to bring disaster on you. I will wipe out your descendants and cut off from Ahab every last male in Israel—slave or free.[a] 22I will make your house like that of Jeroboam son of Nebat and that of Baasha son of Ahijah, because you have aroused my anger and have caused Israel to sin.'

23"And also concerning Jezebel the LORD says: 'Dogs will devour Jezebel by the wall of[b] Jezreel.'

24"Dogs will eat those belonging to Ahab who die in the city, and the birds will feed on those who die in the country."

25(There was never anyone like Ahab, who sold himself to do evil in the eyes of the LORD, urged on by Jezebel his wife. 26He behaved in the vilest manner by going after idols, like the Amorites the LORD drove out before Israel.)

27When Ahab heard these words, he tore his clothes, put on sackcloth and fasted. He lay in sackcloth and went around meekly.

28Then the word of the LORD came to Elijah the Tishbite: 29"Have you noticed how Ahab has humbled himself before me? Because he has humbled himself, I will not bring this disaster in his day, but I will bring it on his house in the days of his son."

Micaiah Prophesies Against Ahab

22 For three years there was no war between Aram and Israel. 2But in the third year Jehoshaphat king of Judah went down to see the king of Israel. 3The king of Israel had said to his officials, "Don't you know that Ramoth Gilead belongs to us and yet we are doing nothing to retake it from the king of Aram?"

4So he asked Jehoshaphat, "Will you go with me to fight against Ramoth Gilead?"

[a] 21 Or *Israel—every ruler or leader* [b] 23 Most Hebrew manuscripts; a few Hebrew manuscripts, Vulgate and Syriac (see also 2 Kings 9:26) *the plot of ground at*

Jehoshaphat replied to the king of Israel, "I am as you are, my people as your people, my horses as your horses." 5 But Jehoshaphat also said to the king of Israel, "First seek the counsel of the LORD."

6 So the king of Israel brought together the prophets — about four hundred men — and asked them, "Shall I go to war against Ramoth Gilead, or shall I refrain?"

"Go," they answered, "for the Lord will give it into the king's hand."

7 But Jehoshaphat asked, "Is there no longer a prophet of the LORD here whom we can inquire of?"

8 The king of Israel answered Jehoshaphat, "There is still one prophet through whom we can inquire of the LORD, but I hate him because he never prophesies anything good about me, but always bad. He is Micaiah son of Imlah."

"The king should not say such a thing," Jehoshaphat replied.

9 So the king of Israel called one of his officials and said, "Bring Micaiah son of Imlah at once."

10 Dressed in their royal robes, the king of Israel and Jehoshaphat king of Judah were sitting on their thrones at the threshing floor by the entrance of the gate of Samaria, with all the prophets prophesying before them. 11 Now Zedekiah son of Kenaanah had made iron horns and he declared, "This is what the LORD says: 'With these you will gore the Arameans until they are destroyed.'"

12 All the other prophets were prophesying the same thing. "Attack Ramoth Gilead and be victorious," they said, "for the LORD will give it into the king's hand."

13 The messenger who had gone to summon Micaiah said to him, "Look, the other prophets without exception are predicting success for the king. Let your word agree with theirs, and speak favorably."

14 But Micaiah said, "As surely as the LORD lives, I can tell him only what the LORD tells me."

15 When he arrived, the king asked him, "Micaiah, shall we go to war against Ramoth Gilead, or not?"

"Attack and be victorious," he answered, "for the LORD will give it into the king's hand."

16 The king said to him, "How many times must I make you swear to tell me nothing but the truth in the name of the LORD?"

17 Then Micaiah answered, "I saw all Israel scattered on the hills like sheep without a shepherd, and the LORD said, 'These people have no master. Let each one go home in peace.'"

18 The king of Israel said to Jehoshaphat, "Didn't I tell you that he never prophesies anything good about me, but only bad?"

19 Micaiah continued, "Therefore hear the word of the LORD: I saw the LORD sitting on his throne with all the multitudes of heaven standing around him on his right and on his left. 20 And the LORD said, 'Who will entice Ahab into attacking Ramoth Gilead and going to his death there?'

"One suggested this, and another that. 21 Finally, a spirit came forward, stood before the LORD and said, 'I will entice him.'

22 "'By what means?' the LORD asked.

"'I will go out and be a deceiving spirit in the mouths of all his prophets,' he said.

"'You will succeed in enticing him,' said the LORD. 'Go and do it.'

23 "So now the LORD has put a deceiving spirit in the mouths of all these prophets of yours. The LORD has decreed disaster for you."

24 Then Zedekiah son of Kenaanah went up and slapped Micaiah in the face. "Which way did the spirit from[a] the LORD go when he went from me to speak to you?" he asked.

25 Micaiah replied, "You will find out on the day you go to hide in an inner room."

26 The king of Israel then ordered, "Take Micaiah and send him back to Amon the ruler of the city and to Joash the king's son 27 and say, 'This is what the king says: Put this fellow in prison and give him nothing but bread and water until I return safely.'"

28 Micaiah declared, "If you ever return safely, the LORD has not spoken through me." Then he added, "Mark my words, all you people!"

Ahab Killed at Ramoth Gilead

29 So the king of Israel and Jehoshaphat king of Judah went up to Ramoth Gilead. 30 The king of Israel said to Jehoshaphat, "I will enter the battle in disguise, but you wear

a 24 Or *Spirit of*

your royal robes." So the king of Israel disguised himself and went into battle.

31 Now the king of Aram had ordered his thirty-two chariot commanders, "Do not fight with anyone, small or great, except the king of Israel." 32 When the chariot commanders saw Jehoshaphat, they thought, "Surely this is the king of Israel." So they turned to attack him, but when Jehoshaphat cried out, 33 the chariot commanders saw that he was not the king of Israel and stopped pursuing him.

34 But someone drew his bow at random and hit the king of Israel between the sections of his armor. The king told his chariot driver, "Wheel around and get me out of the fighting. I've been wounded." 35 All day long the battle raged, and the king was propped up in his chariot facing the Arameans. The blood from his wound ran onto the floor of the chariot, and that evening he died. 36 As the sun was setting, a cry spread through the army: "Every man to his town. Every man to his land!"

37 So the king died and was brought to Samaria, and they buried him there. 38 They washed the chariot at a pool in Samaria (where the prostitutes bathed),[a] and the dogs licked up his blood, as the word of the LORD had declared.

39 As for the other events of Ahab's reign, including all he did, the palace he built and adorned with ivory, and the cities he fortified, are they not written in the book of the annals of the kings of Israel? 40 Ahab rested with his ancestors. And Ahaziah his son succeeded him as king.

Jehoshaphat King of Judah

41 Jehoshaphat son of Asa became king of Judah in the fourth year of Ahab king of Israel. 42 Jehoshaphat was thirty-five years old when he became king, and he reigned in Jerusalem twenty-five years. His mother's name was Azubah daughter of Shilhi. 43 In everything he followed the ways of his father Asa and did not stray from them; he did what was right in the eyes of the LORD. The high places, however, were not removed, and the people continued to offer sacrifices and burn incense there.[b] 44 Jehoshaphat was also at peace with the king of Israel.

45 As for the other events of Jehoshaphat's reign, the things he achieved and his military exploits, are they not written in the book of the annals of the kings of Judah? 46 He rid the land of the rest of the male shrine prostitutes who remained there even after the reign of his father Asa. 47 There was then no king in Edom; a provincial governor ruled.

48 Now Jehoshaphat built a fleet of trading ships[c] to go to Ophir for gold, but they never set sail — they were wrecked at Ezion Geber. 49 At that time Ahaziah son of Ahab said to Jehoshaphat, "Let my men sail with yours," but Jehoshaphat refused.

50 Then Jehoshaphat rested with his ancestors and was buried with them in the city of David his father. And Jehoram his son succeeded him as king.

Ahaziah King of Israel

51 Ahaziah son of Ahab became king of Israel in Samaria in the seventeenth year of Jehoshaphat king of Judah, and he reigned over Israel two years. 52 He did evil in the eyes of the LORD, because he followed the ways of his father and mother and of Jeroboam son of Nebat, who caused Israel to sin. 53 He served and worshiped Baal and aroused the anger of the LORD, the God of Israel, just as his father had done.

[a] 38 Or *Samaria and cleaned the weapons* [b] 43 In Hebrew texts this sentence (22:43b) is numbered 22:44, and 22:44-53 is numbered 22:45-54. [c] 48 Hebrew *of ships of Tarshish*

2 KINGS

The LORD's Judgment on Ahaziah

1 After Ahab's death, Moab rebelled against Israel. 2 Now Ahaziah had fallen through the lattice of his upper room in Samaria and injured himself. So he sent messengers, saying to them, "Go and consult Baal-Zebub, the god of Ekron, to see if I will recover from this injury."

3 But the angel of the LORD said to Elijah the Tishbite, "Go up and meet the messengers of the king of Samaria and ask them, 'Is it because there is no God in Israel that you are going off to consult Baal-Zebub, the god of Ekron?' 4 Therefore this is what the LORD says: 'You will not leave the bed you are lying on. You will certainly die!' " So Elijah went.

5 When the messengers returned to the king, he asked them, "Why have you come back?"

6 "A man came to meet us," they replied. "And he said to us, 'Go back to the king who sent you and tell him, "This is what the LORD says: Is it because there is no God in Israel that you are sending messengers to consult Baal-Zebub, the god of Ekron? Therefore you will not leave the bed you are lying on. You will certainly die!" ' "

7 The king asked them, "What kind of man was it who came to meet you and told you this?"

8 They replied, "He had a garment of hair[a] and had a leather belt around his waist."

The king said, "That was Elijah the Tishbite."

9 Then he sent to Elijah a captain with his company of fifty men. The captain went up to Elijah, who was sitting on the top of a hill, and said to him, "Man of God, the king says, 'Come down!' "

10 Elijah answered the captain, "If I am a man of God, may fire come down from heaven and consume you and your fifty men!" Then fire fell from heaven and consumed the captain and his men.

11 At this the king sent to Elijah another captain with his fifty men. The captain said to him, "Man of God, this is what the king says, 'Come down at once!' "

12 "If I am a man of God," Elijah replied, "may fire come down from heaven and consume you and your fifty men!" Then the fire of God fell from heaven and consumed him and his fifty men.

13 So the king sent a third captain with his fifty men. This third captain went up and fell on his knees before Elijah. "Man of God," he begged, "please have respect for my life and the lives of these fifty men, your servants! 14 See, fire has fallen from heaven and consumed the first two captains and all their men. But now have respect for my life!"

15 The angel of the LORD said to Elijah, "Go down with him; do not be afraid of him." So Elijah got up and went down with him to the king.

16 He told the king, "This is what the LORD says: Is it because there is no God in Israel for you to consult that you have sent messengers to consult Baal-Zebub, the god of Ekron? Because you have done this, you will never leave the bed you are lying on. You will certainly die!" 17 So he died, according to the word of the LORD that Elijah had spoken.

Because Ahaziah had no son, Joram[b] succeeded him as king in the second year of Jehoram son of Jehoshaphat king of Judah. 18 As for all the other events of Ahaziah's reign, and what he did, are they not written in the book of the annals of the kings of Israel?

Elijah Taken Up to Heaven

2 When the LORD was about to take Elijah up to heaven in a whirlwind, Elijah and Elisha were on their way from Gilgal. 2 Elijah said to Elisha, "Stay here; the LORD has sent me to Bethel."

But Elisha said, "As surely as the LORD lives and as you live, I will not leave you." So they went down to Bethel.

[a] 8 Or *He was a hairy man* [b] 17 Hebrew *Jehoram*, a variant of *Joram*

3The company of the prophets at Bethel
came out to Elisha and asked, "Do you know
that the LORD is going to take your master
from you today?"
"Yes, I know," Elisha replied, "so be quiet."
4Then Elijah said to him, "Stay here, Eli-
sha; the LORD has sent me to Jericho."
And he replied, "As surely as the LORD
lives and as you live, I will not leave you." So
they went to Jericho.
5The company of the prophets at Jericho
went up to Elisha and asked him, "Do you
know that the LORD is going to take your
master from you today?"
"Yes, I know," he replied, "so be quiet."
6Then Elijah said to him, "Stay here; the
LORD has sent me to the Jordan."
And he replied, "As surely as the LORD
lives and as you live, I will not leave you." So
the two of them walked on.
7Fifty men from the company of the
prophets went and stood at a distance, fac-
ing the place where Elijah and Elisha had
stopped at the Jordan. 8Elijah took his cloak,
rolled it up and struck the water with it. The
water divided to the right and to the left, and
the two of them crossed over on dry ground.
9When they had crossed, Elijah said to
Elisha, "Tell me, what can I do for you before
I am taken from you?"
"Let me inherit a double portion of your
spirit," Elisha replied.
10"You have asked a difficult thing," Elijah
said, "yet if you see me when I am taken from
you, it will be yours—otherwise, it will not."
11As they were walking along and talk-
ing together, suddenly a chariot of fire and
horses of fire appeared and separated the
two of them, and Elijah went up to heaven
in a whirlwind. 12Elisha saw this and cried
out, "My father! My father! The chariots and
horsemen of Israel!" And Elisha saw him no
more. Then he took hold of his garment and
tore it in two.
13Elisha then picked up Elijah's cloak
that had fallen from him and went back and
stood on the bank of the Jordan. 14He took
the cloak that had fallen from Elijah and
struck the water with it. "Where now is the
LORD, the God of Elijah?" he asked. When he
struck the water, it divided to the right and to
the left, and he crossed over.
15The company of the prophets from Jeri-
cho, who were watching, said, "The spirit of
Elijah is resting on Elisha." And they went to
meet him and bowed to the ground before
him. 16"Look," they said, "we your servants
have fifty able men. Let them go and look for
your master. Perhaps the Spirit of the LORD
has picked him up and set him down on
some mountain or in some valley."
"No," Elisha replied, "do not send them."
17But they persisted until he was too em-
barrassed to refuse. So he said, "Send them."
And they sent fifty men, who searched for
three days but did not find him. 18When they
returned to Elisha, who was staying in Jer-
icho, he said to them, "Didn't I tell you not
to go?"

Healing of the Water

19The people of the city said to Elisha,
"Look, our lord, this town is well situated, as
you can see, but the water is bad and the land
is unproductive."
20"Bring me a new bowl," he said, "and put
salt in it." So they brought it to him.
21Then he went out to the spring and
threw the salt into it, saying, "This is what
the LORD says: 'I have healed this water.
Never again will it cause death or make the
land unproductive.'" 22And the water has
remained pure to this day, according to the
word Elisha had spoken.

Elisha Is Jeered

23From there Elisha went up to Bethel. As
he was walking along the road, some boys
came out of the town and jeered at him.
"Get out of here, baldy!" they said. "Get out
of here, baldy!" 24He turned around, looked
at them and called down a curse on them in
the name of the LORD. Then two bears came
out of the woods and mauled forty-two of
the boys. 25And he went on to Mount Carmel
and from there returned to Samaria.

Moab Revolts

3 Joram[a] son of Ahab became king of Is-
rael in Samaria in the eighteenth year of
Jehoshaphat king of Judah, and he reigned
twelve years. 2He did evil in the eyes of the
LORD, but not as his father and mother had
done. He got rid of the sacred stone of Baal

[a] *1* Hebrew *Jehoram,* a variant of *Joram;* also in verse 6

that his father had made. 3Nevertheless he clung to the sins of Jeroboam son of Nebat, which he had caused Israel to commit; he did not turn away from them.

4Now Mesha king of Moab raised sheep, and he had to pay the king of Israel a tribute of a hundred thousand lambs and the wool of a hundred thousand rams. 5But after Ahab died, the king of Moab rebelled against the king of Israel. 6So at that time King Joram set out from Samaria and mobilized all Israel. 7He also sent this message to Jehoshaphat king of Judah: "The king of Moab has rebelled against me. Will you go with me to fight against Moab?"

"I will go with you," he replied. "I am as you are, my people as your people, my horses as your horses."

8"By what route shall we attack?" he asked.

"Through the Desert of Edom," he answered.

9So the king of Israel set out with the king of Judah and the king of Edom. After a roundabout march of seven days, the army had no more water for themselves or for the animals with them.

10"What!" exclaimed the king of Israel. "Has the LORD called us three kings together only to deliver us into the hands of Moab?"

11But Jehoshaphat asked, "Is there no prophet of the LORD here, through whom we may inquire of the LORD?"

An officer of the king of Israel answered, "Elisha son of Shaphat is here. He used to pour water on the hands of Elijah.[a]"

12Jehoshaphat said, "The word of the LORD is with him." So the king of Israel and Jehoshaphat and the king of Edom went down to him.

13Elisha said to the king of Israel, "Why do you want to involve me? Go to the prophets of your father and the prophets of your mother."

"No," the king of Israel answered, "because it was the LORD who called us three kings together to deliver us into the hands of Moab."

14Elisha said, "As surely as the LORD Almighty lives, whom I serve, if I did not have respect for the presence of Jehoshaphat king of Judah, I would not pay any attention to you. 15But now bring me a harpist."

While the harpist was playing, the hand of the LORD came on Elisha 16and he said, "This is what the LORD says: I will fill this valley with pools of water. 17For this is what the LORD says: You will see neither wind nor rain, yet this valley will be filled with water, and you, your cattle and your other animals will drink. 18This is an easy thing in the eyes of the LORD; he will also deliver Moab into your hands. 19You will overthrow every fortified city and every major town. You will cut down every good tree, stop up all the springs, and ruin every good field with stones."

20The next morning, about the time for offering the sacrifice, there it was—water flowing from the direction of Edom! And the land was filled with water.

21Now all the Moabites had heard that the kings had come to fight against them; so every man, young and old, who could bear arms was called up and stationed on the border. 22When they got up early in the morning, the sun was shining on the water. To the Moabites across the way, the water looked red—like blood. 23"That's blood!" they said. "Those kings must have fought and slaughtered each other. Now to the plunder, Moab!"

24But when the Moabites came to the camp of Israel, the Israelites rose up and fought them until they fled. And the Israelites invaded the land and slaughtered the Moabites. 25They destroyed the towns, and each man threw a stone on every good field until it was covered. They stopped up all the springs and cut down every good tree. Only Kir Hareseth was left with its stones in place, but men armed with slings surrounded it and attacked it.

26When the king of Moab saw that the battle had gone against him, he took with him seven hundred swordsmen to break through to the king of Edom, but they failed. 27Then he took his firstborn son, who was to succeed him as king, and offered him as a sacrifice on the city wall. The fury against Israel was great; they withdrew and returned to their own land.

The Widow's Olive Oil

4 The wife of a man from the company of the prophets cried out to Elisha, "Your servant my husband is dead, and you know

[a] *11* That is, he was Elijah's personal servant.

that he revered the LORD. But now his creditor
is coming to take my two boys as his slaves."
2Elisha replied to her, "How can I help you?
Tell me, what do you have in your house?"
"Your servant has nothing there at all,"
she said, "except a small jar of olive oil."
3Elisha said, "Go around and ask all your
neighbors for empty jars. Don't ask for just a
few. 4Then go inside and shut the door be-
hind you and your sons. Pour oil into all the
jars, and as each is filled, put it to one side."
5She left him and shut the door behind
her and her sons. They brought the jars to
her and she kept pouring. 6When all the jars
were full, she said to her son, "Bring me an-
other one."
But he replied, "There is not a jar left."
Then the oil stopped flowing.
7She went and told the man of God, and he
said, "Go, sell the oil and pay your debts. You
and your sons can live on what is left."

The Shunammite's Son Restored to Life

8One day Elisha went to Shunem. And
a well-to-do woman was there, who urged
him to stay for a meal. So whenever he came
by, he stopped there to eat. 9She said to her
husband, "I know that this man who often
comes our way is a holy man of God. 10Let's
make a small room on the roof and put in it a
bed and a table, a chair and a lamp for him.
Then he can stay there whenever he comes
to us."
11One day when Elisha came, he went up
to his room and lay down there. 12He said to
his servant Gehazi, "Call the Shunammite."
So he called her, and she stood before him.
13Elisha said to him, "Tell her, 'You have
gone to all this trouble for us. Now what can
be done for you? Can we speak on your be-
half to the king or the commander of the
army?'"
She replied, "I have a home among my
own people."
14"What can be done for her?" Elisha
asked.
Gehazi said, "She has no son, and her hus-
band is old."
15Then Elisha said, "Call her." So he called
her, and she stood in the doorway. 16"About
this time next year," Elisha said, "you will
hold a son in your arms."
"No, my lord!" she objected. "Please, man
of God, don't mislead your servant!"

17But the woman became pregnant, and
the next year about that same time she gave
birth to a son, just as Elisha had told her.
18The child grew, and one day he went out
to his father, who was with the reapers. 19He
said to his father, "My head! My head!"
His father told a servant, "Carry him to his
mother." 20After the servant had lifted him
up and carried him to his mother, the boy
sat on her lap until noon, and then he died.
21She went up and laid him on the bed of the
man of God, then shut the door and went out.
22She called her husband and said,
"Please send me one of the servants and a
donkey so I can go to the man of God quickly
and return."
23"Why go to him today?" he asked. "It's
not the New Moon or the Sabbath."
"That's all right," she said.
24She saddled the donkey and said to her
servant, "Lead on; don't slow down for me
unless I tell you." 25So she set out and came
to the man of God at Mount Carmel.
When he saw her in the distance, the man
of God said to his servant Gehazi, "Look!
There's the Shunammite! 26Run to meet her
and ask her, 'Are you all right? Is your hus-
band all right? Is your child all right?'"
"Everything is all right," she said.
27When she reached the man of God at the
mountain, she took hold of his feet. Gehazi
came over to push her away, but the man of
God said, "Leave her alone! She is in bitter
distress, but the LORD has hidden it from me
and has not told me why."
28"Did I ask you for a son, my lord?"
she said. "Didn't I tell you, 'Don't raise my
hopes'?"
29Elisha said to Gehazi, "Tuck your cloak
into your belt, take my staff in your hand
and run. Don't greet anyone you meet, and
if anyone greets you, do not answer. Lay my
staff on the boy's face."
30But the child's mother said, "As surely as
the LORD lives and as you live, I will not leave
you." So he got up and followed her.
31Gehazi went on ahead and laid the staff
on the boy's face, but there was no sound or
response. So Gehazi went back to meet Elisha
and told him, "The boy has not awakened."
32When Elisha reached the house, there
was the boy lying dead on his couch. 33He
went in, shut the door on the two of them
and prayed to the LORD. 34Then he got on

the bed and lay on the boy, mouth to mouth,
eyes to eyes, hands to hands. As he stretched
himself out on him, the boy's body grew
warm. 35 Elisha turned away and walked
back and forth in the room and then got on
the bed and stretched out on him once more.
The boy sneezed seven times and opened his
eyes.

36 Elisha summoned Gehazi and said,
"Call the Shunammite." And he did. When
she came, he said, "Take your son." 37 She
came in, fell at his feet and bowed to the
ground. Then she took her son and went out.

Death in the Pot

38 Elisha returned to Gilgal and there was
a famine in that region. While the company
of the prophets was meeting with him, he
said to his servant, "Put on the large pot and
cook some stew for these prophets."

39 One of them went out into the fields
to gather herbs and found a wild vine and
picked as many of its gourds as his garment
could hold. When he returned, he cut them
up into the pot of stew, though no one knew
what they were. 40 The stew was poured out
for the men, but as they began to eat it, they
cried out, "Man of God, there is death in the
pot!" And they could not eat it.

41 Elisha said, "Get some flour." He put it
into the pot and said, "Serve it to the people
to eat." And there was nothing harmful in
the pot.

Feeding of a Hundred

42 A man came from Baal Shalishah,
bringing the man of God twenty loaves of
barley bread baked from the first ripe grain,
along with some heads of new grain. "Give it
to the people to eat," Elisha said.

43 "How can I set this before a hundred
men?" his servant asked.

But Elisha answered, "Give it to the people
to eat. For this is what the LORD says: 'They
will eat and have some left over.'" 44 Then
he set it before them, and they ate and had
some left over, according to the word of the
LORD.

Naaman Healed of Leprosy

5 Now Naaman was commander of the
army of the king of Aram. He was a great
man in the sight of his master and highly re-
garded, because through him the LORD had
given victory to Aram. He was a valiant sol-
dier, but he had leprosy.[a]

2 Now bands of raiders from Aram had
gone out and had taken captive a young girl
from Israel, and she served Naaman's wife.
3 She said to her mistress, "If only my master
would see the prophet who is in Samaria! He
would cure him of his leprosy."

4 Naaman went to his master and told him
what the girl from Israel had said. 5 "By all
means, go," the king of Aram replied. "I will
send a letter to the king of Israel." So Naaman
left, taking with him ten talents[b] of silver,
six thousand shekels[c] of gold and ten sets of
clothing. 6 The letter that he took to the king
of Israel read: "With this letter I am sending
my servant Naaman to you so that you may
cure him of his leprosy."

7 As soon as the king of Israel read the let-
ter, he tore his robes and said, "Am I God?
Can I kill and bring back to life? Why does
this fellow send someone to me to be cured
of his leprosy? See how he is trying to pick a
quarrel with me!"

8 When Elisha the man of God heard that
the king of Israel had torn his robes, he sent
him this message: "Why have you torn your
robes? Have the man come to me and he will
know that there is a prophet in Israel." 9 So
Naaman went with his horses and chariots
and stopped at the door of Elisha's house.
10 Elisha sent a messenger to say to him, "Go,
wash yourself seven times in the Jordan, and
your flesh will be restored and you will be
cleansed."

11 But Naaman went away angry and said,
"I thought that he would surely come out to
me and stand and call on the name of the
LORD his God, wave his hand over the spot
and cure me of my leprosy. 12 Are not Abana
and Pharpar, the rivers of Damascus, better
than all the waters of Israel? Couldn't I wash
in them and be cleansed?" So he turned and
went off in a rage.

13 Naaman's servants went to him and
said, "My father, if the prophet had told you
to do some great thing, would you not have
done it? How much more, then, when he tells
you, 'Wash and be cleansed'!" 14 So he went
down and dipped himself in the Jordan sev-

[a] *1* The Hebrew for *leprosy* was used for various diseases affecting the skin; also in verses 3, 6, 7, 11 and 27.
[b] *5* That is, about 750 pounds or about 340 kilograms
[c] *5* That is, about 150 pounds or about 69 kilograms

en times, as the man of God had told him,
and his flesh was restored and became clean
like that of a young boy.
[15]Then Naaman and all his attendants
went back to the man of God. He stood be-
fore him and said, "Now I know that there is
no God in all the world except in Israel. So
please accept a gift from your servant."
[16]The prophet answered, "As surely as the
LORD lives, whom I serve, I will not accept
a thing." And even though Naaman urged
him, he refused.
[17]"If you will not," said Naaman, "please
let me, your servant, be given as much earth
as a pair of mules can carry, for your ser-
vant will never again make burnt offerings
and sacrifices to any other god but the LORD.
[18]But may the LORD forgive your servant for
this one thing: When my master enters the
temple of Rimmon to bow down and he is
leaning on my arm and I have to bow there
also—when I bow down in the temple of
Rimmon, may the LORD forgive your servant
for this."
[19]"Go in peace," Elisha said.
After Naaman had traveled some dis-
tance, [20]Gehazi, the servant of Elisha the
man of God, said to himself, "My master
was too easy on Naaman, this Aramean, by
not accepting from him what he brought. As
surely as the LORD lives, I will run after him
and get something from him."
[21]So Gehazi hurried after Naaman. When
Naaman saw him running toward him, he
got down from the chariot to meet him. "Is
everything all right?" he asked.
[22]"Everything is all right," Gehazi an-
swered. "My master sent me to say, 'Two
young men from the company of the proph-
ets have just come to me from the hill coun-
try of Ephraim. Please give them a talent[a] of
silver and two sets of clothing.'"
[23]"By all means, take two talents," said
Naaman. He urged Gehazi to accept them,
and then tied up the two talents of silver in
two bags, with two sets of clothing. He gave
them to two of his servants, and they carried
them ahead of Gehazi. [24]When Gehazi came
to the hill, he took the things from the ser-
vants and put them away in the house. He
sent the men away and they left.
[25]When he went in and stood before his
master, Elisha asked him, "Where have you
been, Gehazi?"
"Your servant didn't go anywhere," Geha-
zi answered.
[26]But Elisha said to him, "Was not my
spirit with you when the man got down from
his chariot to meet you? Is this the time to
take money or to accept clothes—or olive
groves and vineyards, or flocks and herds, or
male and female slaves? [27]Naaman's lepro-
sy will cling to you and to your descendants
forever." Then Gehazi went from Elisha's
presence and his skin was leprous—it had
become as white as snow.

An Axhead Floats

6 The company of the prophets said to
Elisha, "Look, the place where we meet
with you is too small for us. [2]Let us go to the
Jordan, where each of us can get a pole; and
let us build a place there for us to meet."
And he said, "Go."
[3]Then one of them said, "Won't you please
come with your servants?"
"I will," Elisha replied. [4]And he went with
them.
They went to the Jordan and began to cut
down trees. [5]As one of them was cutting
down a tree, the iron axhead fell into the wa-
ter. "Oh no, my lord!" he cried out. "It was bor-
rowed!"
[6]The man of God asked, "Where did it
fall?" When he showed him the place, Eli-
sha cut a stick and threw it there, and made
the iron float. [7]"Lift it out," he said. Then the
man reached out his hand and took it.

Elisha Traps Blinded Arameans

[8]Now the king of Aram was at war with
Israel. After conferring with his officers, he
said, "I will set up my camp in such and such
a place."
[9]The man of God sent word to the king
of Israel: "Beware of passing that place, be-
cause the Arameans are going down there."
[10]So the king of Israel checked on the place
indicated by the man of God. Time and
again Elisha warned the king, so that he was
on his guard in such places.
[11]This enraged the king of Aram. He sum-
moned his officers and demanded of them,
"Tell me! Which of us is on the side of the
king of Israel?"

[a] 22 That is, about 75 pounds or about 34 kilograms

12 "None of us, my lord the king," said one
of his officers, "but Elisha, the prophet who
is in Israel, tells the king of Israel the very
words you speak in your bedroom."

13 "Go, find out where he is," the king or-
dered, "so I can send men and capture him."
The report came back: "He is in Dothan."
14 Then he sent horses and chariots and a
strong force there. They went by night and
surrounded the city.

15 When the servant of the man of God
got up and went out early the next morning,
an army with horses and chariots had sur-
rounded the city. "Oh no, my lord! What shall
we do?" the servant asked.

16 "Don't be afraid," the prophet answered.
"Those who are with us are more than those
who are with them."

17 And Elisha prayed, "Open his eyes,
LORD, so that he may see." Then the LORD
opened the servant's eyes, and he looked
and saw the hills full of horses and chariots
of fire all around Elisha.

18 As the enemy came down toward him,
Elisha prayed to the LORD, "Strike this army
with blindness." So he struck them with
blindness, as Elisha had asked.

19 Elisha told them, "This is not the road
and this is not the city. Follow me, and I will
lead you to the man you are looking for." And
he led them to Samaria.

20 After they entered the city, Elisha said,
"LORD, open the eyes of these men so they
can see." Then the LORD opened their eyes
and they looked, and there they were, inside
Samaria.

21 When the king of Israel saw them, he
asked Elisha, "Shall I kill them, my father?
Shall I kill them?"

22 "Do not kill them," he answered.
"Would you kill those you have captured
with your own sword or bow? Set food and
water before them so that they may eat and
drink and then go back to their master." 23 So
he prepared a great feast for them, and after
they had finished eating and drinking, he
sent them away, and they returned to their
master. So the bands from Aram stopped
raiding Israel's territory.

Famine in Besieged Samaria

24 Some time later, Ben-Hadad king of Aram
mobilized his entire army and marched up
and laid siege to Samaria. 25 There was a great
famine in the city; the siege lasted so long that
a donkey's head sold for eighty shekels[a] of sil-
ver, and a quarter of a cab[b] of seed pods[c] for
five shekels.[d]

26 As the king of Israel was passing by on
the wall, a woman cried to him, "Help me,
my lord the king!"

27 The king replied, "If the LORD does not
help you, where can I get help for you? From
the threshing floor? From the winepress?"
28 Then he asked her, "What's the matter?"

She answered, "This woman said to me,
'Give up your son so we may eat him today,
and tomorrow we'll eat my son.' 29 So we
cooked my son and ate him. The next day I
said to her, 'Give up your son so we may eat
him,' but she had hidden him."

30 When the king heard the woman's
words, he tore his robes. As he went along
the wall, the people looked, and they saw
that, under his robes, he had sackcloth on
his body. 31 He said, "May God deal with me,
be it ever so severely, if the head of Elisha son
of Shaphat remains on his shoulders today!"

32 Now Elisha was sitting in his house, and
the elders were sitting with him. The king
sent a messenger ahead, but before he ar-
rived, Elisha said to the elders, "Don't you
see how this murderer is sending someone
to cut off my head? Look, when the messen-
ger comes, shut the door and hold it shut
against him. Is not the sound of his master's
footsteps behind him?" 33 While he was still
talking to them, the messenger came down
to him.

The king said, "This disaster is from the
LORD. Why should I wait for the LORD any
longer?"

7 Elisha replied, "Hear the word of the
LORD. This is what the LORD says: About
this time tomorrow, a seah[e] of the finest
flour will sell for a shekel[f] and two seahs[g] of
barley for a shekel at the gate of Samaria."

2 The officer on whose arm the king was
leaning said to the man of God, "Look, even

[a] *25* That is, about 2 pounds or about 920 grams [b] *25* That is, probably about 1/4 pound or about 100 grams [c] *25* Or *of doves' dung* [d] *25* That is, about 2 ounces or about 58 grams [e] *1* That is, probably about 12 pounds or about 5.5 kilograms of flour; also in verses 16 and 18 [f] *1* That is, about 2/5 ounce or about 12 grams; also in verses 16 and 18 [g] *1* That is, probably about 20 pounds or about 9 kilograms of barley; also in verses 16 and 18

if the LORD should open the floodgates of the heavens, could this happen?"

"You will see it with your own eyes," answered Elisha, "but you will not eat any of it!"

The Siege Lifted

[3]Now there were four men with leprosy[a] at the entrance of the city gate. They said to each other, "Why stay here until we die? [4]If we say, 'We'll go into the city'—the famine is there, and we will die. And if we stay here, we will die. So let's go over to the camp of the Arameans and surrender. If they spare us, we live; if they kill us, then we die."

[5]At dusk they got up and went to the camp of the Arameans. When they reached the edge of the camp, no one was there, [6]for the Lord had caused the Arameans to hear the sound of chariots and horses and a great army, so that they said to one another, "Look, the king of Israel has hired the Hittite and Egyptian kings to attack us!" [7]So they got up and fled in the dusk and abandoned their tents and their horses and donkeys. They left the camp as it was and ran for their lives.

[8]The men who had leprosy reached the edge of the camp, entered one of the tents and ate and drank. Then they took silver, gold and clothes, and went off and hid them. They returned and entered another tent and took some things from it and hid them also.

[9]Then they said to each other, "What we're doing is not right. This is a day of good news and we are keeping it to ourselves. If we wait until daylight, punishment will overtake us. Let's go at once and report this to the royal palace."

[10]So they went and called out to the city gatekeepers and told them, "We went into the Aramean camp and no one was there—not a sound of anyone—only tethered horses and donkeys, and the tents left just as they were." [11]The gatekeepers shouted the news, and it was reported within the palace.

[12]The king got up in the night and said to his officers, "I will tell you what the Arameans have done to us. They know we are starving; so they have left the camp to hide in the countryside, thinking, 'They will surely come out, and then we will take them alive and get into the city.'"

[13]One of his officers answered, "Have some men take five of the horses that are left in the city. Their plight will be like that of all the Israelites left here—yes, they will only be like all these Israelites who are doomed. So let us send them to find out what happened."

[14]So they selected two chariots with their horses, and the king sent them after the Aramean army. He commanded the drivers, "Go and find out what has happened." [15]They followed them as far as the Jordan, and they found the whole road strewn with the clothing and equipment the Arameans had thrown away in their headlong flight. So the messengers returned and reported to the king. [16]Then the people went out and plundered the camp of the Arameans. So a seah of the finest flour sold for a shekel, and two seahs of barley sold for a shekel, as the LORD had said.

[17]Now the king had put the officer on whose arm he leaned in charge of the gate, and the people trampled him in the gateway, and he died, just as the man of God had foretold when the king came down to his house. [18]It happened as the man of God had said to the king: "About this time tomorrow, a seah of the finest flour will sell for a shekel and two seahs of barley for a shekel at the gate of Samaria."

[19]The officer had said to the man of God, "Look, even if the LORD should open the floodgates of the heavens, could this happen?" The man of God had replied, "You will see it with your own eyes, but you will not eat any of it!" [20]And that is exactly what happened to him, for the people trampled him in the gateway, and he died.

The Shunammite's Land Restored

8 Now Elisha had said to the woman whose son he had restored to life, "Go away with your family and stay for a while wherever you can, because the LORD has decreed a famine in the land that will last seven years." [2]The woman proceeded to do as the man of God said. She and her family went away and stayed in the land of the Philistines seven years.

[3]At the end of the seven years she came back from the land of the Philistines and

[a] 3 The Hebrew for *leprosy* was used for various diseases affecting the skin; also in verse 8.

went to appeal to the king for her house and land. 4The king was talking to Gehazi, the servant of the man of God, and had said, "Tell me about all the great things Elisha has done." 5Just as Gehazi was telling the king how Elisha had restored the dead to life, the woman whose son Elisha had brought back to life came to appeal to the king for her house and land.

Gehazi said, "This is the woman, my lord the king, and this is her son whom Elisha restored to life." 6The king asked the woman about it, and she told him.

Then he assigned an official to her case and said to him, "Give back everything that belonged to her, including all the income from her land from the day she left the country until now."

Hazael Murders Ben-Hadad

7Elisha went to Damascus, and Ben-Hadad king of Aram was ill. When the king was told, "The man of God has come all the way up here," 8he said to Hazael, "Take a gift with you and go to meet the man of God. Consult the LORD through him; ask him, 'Will I recover from this illness?' "

9Hazael went to meet Elisha, taking with him as a gift forty camel-loads of all the finest wares of Damascus. He went in and stood before him, and said, "Your son Ben-Hadad king of Aram has sent me to ask, 'Will I recover from this illness?' "

10Elisha answered, "Go and say to him, 'You will certainly recover.' Nevertheless,[a] the LORD has revealed to me that he will in fact die." 11He stared at him with a fixed gaze until Hazael was embarrassed. Then the man of God began to weep.

12"Why is my lord weeping?" asked Hazael.

"Because I know the harm you will do to the Israelites," he answered. "You will set fire to their fortified places, kill their young men with the sword, dash their little children to the ground, and rip open their pregnant women."

13Hazael said, "How could your servant, a mere dog, accomplish such a feat?"

"The LORD has shown me that you will become king of Aram," answered Elisha.

14Then Hazael left Elisha and returned to his master. When Ben-Hadad asked, "What did Elisha say to you?" Hazael replied, "He told me that you would certainly recover." 15But the next day he took a thick cloth, soaked it in water and spread it over the king's face, so that he died. Then Hazael succeeded him as king.

Jehoram King of Judah

16In the fifth year of Joram son of Ahab king of Israel, when Jehoshaphat was king of Judah, Jehoram son of Jehoshaphat began his reign as king of Judah. 17He was thirty-two years old when he became king, and he reigned in Jerusalem eight years. 18He followed the ways of the kings of Israel, as the house of Ahab had done, for he married a daughter of Ahab. He did evil in the eyes of the LORD. 19Nevertheless, for the sake of his servant David, the LORD was not willing to destroy Judah. He had promised to maintain a lamp for David and his descendants forever.

20In the time of Jehoram, Edom rebelled against Judah and set up its own king. 21So Jehoram[b] went to Zair with all his chariots. The Edomites surrounded him and his chariot commanders, but he rose up and broke through by night; his army, however, fled back home. 22To this day Edom has been in rebellion against Judah. Libnah revolted at the same time.

23As for the other events of Jehoram's reign, and all he did, are they not written in the book of the annals of the kings of Judah? 24Jehoram rested with his ancestors and was buried with them in the City of David. And Ahaziah his son succeeded him as king.

Ahaziah King of Judah

25In the twelfth year of Joram son of Ahab king of Israel, Ahaziah son of Jehoram king of Judah began to reign. 26Ahaziah was twenty-two years old when he became king, and he reigned in Jerusalem one year. His mother's name was Athaliah, a granddaughter of Omri king of Israel. 27He followed the ways of the house of Ahab and did evil in the eyes of the LORD, as the house of Ahab had done, for he was related by marriage to Ahab's family.

28Ahaziah went with Joram son of Ahab to war against Hazael king of Aram at Ramoth

[a] *10* The Hebrew may also be read *Go and say, 'You will certainly not recover,' for.* [b] *21* Hebrew *Joram,* a variant of *Jehoram;* also in verses 23 and 24

Gilead. The Arameans wounded Joram; 29so
King Joram returned to Jezreel to recover
from the wounds the Arameans had inflict-
ed on him at Ramoth[a] in his battle with Haz-
ael king of Aram.
Then Ahaziah son of Jehoram king of Ju-
dah went down to Jezreel to see Joram son of
Ahab, because he had been wounded.

Jehu Anointed King of Israel

9 The prophet Elisha summoned a man
from the company of the prophets and
said to him, "Tuck your cloak into your belt,
take this flask of olive oil with you and go to
Ramoth Gilead. 2When you get there, look
for Jehu son of Jehoshaphat, the son of Nim-
shi. Go to him, get him away from his com-
panions and take him into an inner room.
3Then take the flask and pour the oil on his
head and declare, 'This is what the LORD
says: I anoint you king over Israel.' Then
open the door and run; don't delay!"
4So the young prophet went to Ramoth
Gilead. 5When he arrived, he found the army
officers sitting together. "I have a message
for you, commander," he said.
"For which of us?" asked Jehu.
"For you, commander," he replied.
6Jehu got up and went into the house.
Then the prophet poured the oil on Jehu's
head and declared, "This is what the LORD,
the God of Israel, says: 'I anoint you king over
the LORD's people Israel. 7You are to destroy
the house of Ahab your master, and I will
avenge the blood of my servants the proph-
ets and the blood of all the LORD's servants
shed by Jezebel. 8The whole house of Ahab
will perish. I will cut off from Ahab every last
male in Israel — slave or free.[b] 9I will make
the house of Ahab like the house of Jerobo-
am son of Nebat and like the house of Baasha
son of Ahijah. 10As for Jezebel, dogs will de-
vour her on the plot of ground at Jezreel, and
no one will bury her.' " Then he opened the
door and ran.
11When Jehu went out to his fellow offi-
cers, one of them asked him, "Is everything
all right? Why did this maniac come to you?"
"You know the man and the sort of things
he says," Jehu replied.
12"That's not true!" they said. "Tell us."
Jehu said, "Here is what he told me: 'This
is what the LORD says: I anoint you king over
Israel.' "
13They quickly took their cloaks and
spread them under him on the bare steps.
Then they blew the trumpet and shouted,
"Jehu is king!"

Jehu Kills Joram and Ahaziah

14So Jehu son of Jehoshaphat, the son of
Nimshi, conspired against Joram. (Now Jo-
ram and all Israel had been defending Ra-
moth Gilead against Hazael king of Aram,
15but King Joram[c] had returned to Jezreel
to recover from the wounds the Arameans
had inflicted on him in the battle with Haz-
ael king of Aram.) Jehu said, "If you desire
to make me king, don't let anyone slip out
of the city to go and tell the news in Jezre-
el." 16Then he got into his chariot and rode
to Jezreel, because Joram was resting there
and Ahaziah king of Judah had gone down
to see him.
17When the lookout standing on the tower
in Jezreel saw Jehu's troops approaching, he
called out, "I see some troops coming."
"Get a horseman," Joram ordered. "Send
him to meet them and ask, 'Do you come in
peace?' "
18The horseman rode off to meet Jehu and
said, "This is what the king says: 'Do you
come in peace?' "
"What do you have to do with peace?"
Jehu replied. "Fall in behind me."
The lookout reported, "The messenger
has reached them, but he isn't coming back."
19So the king sent out a second horseman.
When he came to them he said, "This is what
the king says: 'Do you come in peace?' "
Jehu replied, "What do you have to do
with peace? Fall in behind me."
20The lookout reported, "He has reached
them, but he isn't coming back either. The
driving is like that of Jehu son of Nimshi —
he drives like a maniac."
21"Hitch up my chariot," Joram ordered.
And when it was hitched up, Joram king of
Israel and Ahaziah king of Judah rode out,
each in his own chariot, to meet Jehu. They
met him at the plot of ground that had be-
longed to Naboth the Jezreelite. 22When Jo-
ram saw Jehu he asked, "Have you come in
peace, Jehu?"

[a] 29 Hebrew *Ramah,* a variant of *Ramoth* [b] 8 Or *Israel — every ruler or leader* [c] 15 Hebrew *Jehoram,* a variant of *Joram;* also in verses 17 and 21-24

HOW HE LOVES

John Mark McMillan

He is jealous for me
Loves like a hurricane, I am a tree
Bending beneath the weight of his wind and mercy
When all of a sudden
I am unaware of these afflictions eclipsed by glory
And I realize just how beautiful you are
And how great your affections are for me

And oh, how he loves us, oh
Oh, how he loves us
How he loves us all

He loves us
Oh, how he loves us
Oh, how he loves us
Oh, how he loves

We are his portion and he is our prize
Drawn to redemption by the grace in his eyes
If grace is an ocean, we're all sinking
So Heaven meets earth like a sloppy wet kiss (alt. unforeseen kiss)
And my heart turns violently inside of my chest
I don't have time to maintain these regrets
When I think about the way

THE INSPIRATION

God is love. — 1 John 4:8

Read also: 1 Corinthians 13; 1 John 4:7–21

BEHIND THE SONG

"Love can be such a non-word sometimes," says John Mark McMillan, a worship leader and songwriter who has reached a large segment of the church with his evocative, emotional and intense style of worship music. His song "How He Loves" may seem simple on the surface, but a look inside the heart of the song reveals tension, confusion, pain and loss.

After suddenly losing a close friend in a car accident, mourning and pain led McMillan to attempt something he thought might not be possible: writing a song about God's love.

"It's difficult to use the word 'love' in a song, because what does it really mean?" McMillan asks. So he did the only thing he knew how to do — he processed the concept poetically. With Scriptures such as 1 John 4 and 1 Corinthians 13 guiding him, he proceeded to paint word pictures about the overwhelming, powerful, unconditional love God lavishes on his children.

"The love I'm singing about is not a pretty, clean, Hollywood love," he adds. "It's a love that is willing to love things that are messy." Like the psalmists of old, McMillan laid his heart bare and found that God could take it. "He could love me through that," he realized. "He wasn't offended because I was angry."

McMillan continues, "This song isn't a celebration of weakness and anger, it's a celebration of a God who wants to be a part of our lives through those things. Despite who we are he wants to be a part of us; to be a part of our family and our community. That's the kind of love I'm talking about."

Selah

Reread 1 Corinthians 13 and 1 John 4:7 – 21, and compare the love of God to the love of the world. Can you think of better words to describe these "loves"?

The Bible says God is love, the author of love, and we cannot love without him. As challenging as this concept may be, it is one of the most important aspects of being a member of the family of God.

"How can there be peace," Jehu replied,
"as long as all the idolatry and witchcraft of
your mother Jezebel abound?"
23 Joram turned about and fled, calling out
to Ahaziah, "Treachery, Ahaziah!"
24 Then Jehu drew his bow and shot Joram
between the shoulders. The arrow pierced
his heart and he slumped down in his char-
iot. 25 Jehu said to Bidkar, his chariot officer,
"Pick him up and throw him on the field
that belonged to Naboth the Jezreelite. Re-
member how you and I were riding togeth-
er in chariots behind Ahab his father when
the LORD spoke this prophecy against him:
26 'Yesterday I saw the blood of Naboth and
the blood of his sons, declares the LORD, and
I will surely make you pay for it on this plot of
ground, declares the LORD.'[a] Now then, pick
him up and throw him on that plot, in accor-
dance with the word of the LORD."
27 When Ahaziah king of Judah saw what
had happened, he fled up the road to Beth
Haggan.[b] Jehu chased him, shouting, "Kill
him too!" They wounded him in his chariot
on the way up to Gur near Ibleam, but he es-
caped to Megiddo and died there. 28 His ser-
vants took him by chariot to Jerusalem and
buried him with his ancestors in his tomb
in the City of David. 29 (In the eleventh year
of Joram son of Ahab, Ahaziah had become
king of Judah.)

Jezebel Killed

30 Then Jehu went to Jezreel. When Jezebel
heard about it, she put on eye makeup, ar-
ranged her hair and looked out of a window.
31 As Jehu entered the gate, she asked, "Have
you come in peace, you Zimri, you murderer
of your master?"[c]
32 He looked up at the window and called
out, "Who is on my side? Who?" Two or three
eunuchs looked down at him. 33 "Throw her
down!" Jehu said. So they threw her down,
and some of her blood spattered the wall and
the horses as they trampled her underfoot.
34 Jehu went in and ate and drank. "Take
care of that cursed woman," he said, "and
bury her, for she was a king's daughter."
35 But when they went out to bury her, they
found nothing except her skull, her feet and
her hands. 36 They went back and told Jehu,
who said, "This is the word of the LORD that
he spoke through his servant Elijah the Tish-
bite: On the plot of ground at Jezreel dogs
will devour Jezebel's flesh.[d] 37 Jezebel's body
will be like dung on the ground in the plot
at Jezreel, so that no one will be able to say,
'This is Jezebel.'"

Ahab's Family Killed

10 Now there were in Samaria seventy
sons of the house of Ahab. So Jehu
wrote letters and sent them to Samaria: to
the officials of Jezreel,[e] to the elders and to
the guardians of Ahab's children. He said,
2 "You have your master's sons with you and
you have chariots and horses, a fortified
city and weapons. Now as soon as this letter
reaches you, 3 choose the best and most wor-
thy of your master's sons and set him on his
father's throne. Then fight for your master's
house."
4 But they were terrified and said, "If two
kings could not resist him, how can we?"
5 So the palace administrator, the city gov-
ernor, the elders and the guardians sent this
message to Jehu: "We are your servants and
we will do anything you say. We will not ap-
point anyone as king; you do whatever you
think best."
6 Then Jehu wrote them a second letter,
saying, "If you are on my side and will obey
me, take the heads of your master's sons and
come to me in Jezreel by this time tomorrow."
Now the royal princes, seventy of them,
were with the leading men of the city, who
were rearing them. 7 When the letter ar-
rived, these men took the princes and
slaughtered all seventy of them. They put
their heads in baskets and sent them to Jehu
in Jezreel. 8 When the messenger arrived, he
told Jehu, "They have brought the heads of
the princes."
Then Jehu ordered, "Put them in two piles
at the entrance of the city gate until morning."
9 The next morning Jehu went out. He
stood before all the people and said, "You
are innocent. It was I who conspired against
my master and killed him, but who killed
all these? 10 Know, then, that not a word
the LORD has spoken against the house of
Ahab will fail. The LORD has done what he

[a] *26* See 1 Kings 21:19. [b] *27* Or *fled by way of the garden house* [c] *31* Or *"Was there peace for Zimri, who murdered his master?"* [d] *36* See 1 Kings 21:23. [e] *1* Hebrew; some Septuagint manuscripts and Vulgate *of the city*

announced through his servant Elijah." 11 So Jehu killed everyone in Jezreel who remained of the house of Ahab, as well as all his chief men, his close friends and his priests, leaving him no survivor.

12 Jehu then set out and went toward Samaria. At Beth Eked of the Shepherds, 13 he met some relatives of Ahaziah king of Judah and asked, "Who are you?"

They said, "We are relatives of Ahaziah, and we have come down to greet the families of the king and of the queen mother."

14 "Take them alive!" he ordered. So they took them alive and slaughtered them by the well of Beth Eked—forty-two of them. He left no survivor.

15 After he left there, he came upon Jehonadab son of Rekab, who was on his way to meet him. Jehu greeted him and said, "Are you in accord with me, as I am with you?"

"I am," Jehonadab answered.

"If so," said Jehu, "give me your hand." So he did, and Jehu helped him up into the chariot. 16 Jehu said, "Come with me and see my zeal for the LORD." Then he had him ride along in his chariot.

17 When Jehu came to Samaria, he killed all who were left there of Ahab's family; he destroyed them, according to the word of the LORD spoken to Elijah.

Servants of Baal Killed

18 Then Jehu brought all the people together and said to them, "Ahab served Baal a little; Jehu will serve him much. 19 Now summon all the prophets of Baal, all his servants and all his priests. See that no one is missing, because I am going to hold a great sacrifice for Baal. Anyone who fails to come will no longer live." But Jehu was acting deceptively in order to destroy the servants of Baal.

20 Jehu said, "Call an assembly in honor of Baal." So they proclaimed it. 21 Then he sent word throughout Israel, and all the servants of Baal came; not one stayed away. They crowded into the temple of Baal until it was full from one end to the other. 22 And Jehu said to the keeper of the wardrobe, "Bring robes for all the servants of Baal." So he brought out robes for them.

23 Then Jehu and Jehonadab son of Rekab went into the temple of Baal. Jehu said to the servants of Baal, "Look around and see that no one who serves the LORD is here with you—only servants of Baal." 24 So they went in to make sacrifices and burnt offerings. Now Jehu had posted eighty men outside with this warning: "If one of you lets any of the men I am placing in your hands escape, it will be your life for his life."

25 As soon as Jehu had finished making the burnt offering, he ordered the guards and officers: "Go in and kill them; let no one escape." So they cut them down with the sword. The guards and officers threw the bodies out and then entered the inner shrine of the temple of Baal. 26 They brought the sacred stone out of the temple of Baal and burned it. 27 They demolished the sacred stone of Baal and tore down the temple of Baal, and people have used it for a latrine to this day.

28 So Jehu destroyed Baal worship in Israel. 29 However, he did not turn away from the sins of Jeroboam son of Nebat, which he had caused Israel to commit—the worship of the golden calves at Bethel and Dan.

30 The LORD said to Jehu, "Because you have done well in accomplishing what is right in my eyes and have done to the house of Ahab all I had in mind to do, your descendants will sit on the throne of Israel to the fourth generation." 31 Yet Jehu was not careful to keep the law of the LORD, the God of Israel, with all his heart. He did not turn away from the sins of Jeroboam, which he had caused Israel to commit.

32 In those days the LORD began to reduce the size of Israel. Hazael overpowered the Israelites throughout their territory 33 east of the Jordan in all the land of Gilead (the region of Gad, Reuben and Manasseh), from Aroer by the Arnon Gorge through Gilead to Bashan.

34 As for the other events of Jehu's reign, all he did, and all his achievements, are they not written in the book of the annals of the kings of Israel?

35 Jehu rested with his ancestors and was buried in Samaria. And Jehoahaz his son succeeded him as king. 36 The time that Jehu reigned over Israel in Samaria was twenty-eight years.

Athaliah and Joash

11 When Athaliah the mother of Ahaziah saw that her son was dead, she proceeded to destroy the whole royal family.

2But Jehosheba, the daughter of King Jehoram[a] and sister of Ahaziah, took Joash son of Ahaziah and stole him away from among the royal princes, who were about to be murdered. She put him and his nurse in a bedroom to hide him from Athaliah; so he was not killed. 3He remained hidden with his nurse at the temple of the LORD for six years while Athaliah ruled the land.

4In the seventh year Jehoiada sent for the commanders of units of a hundred, the Carites and the guards and had them brought to him at the temple of the LORD. He made a covenant with them and put them under oath at the temple of the LORD. Then he showed them the king's son. 5He commanded them, saying, "This is what you are to do: You who are in the three companies that are going on duty on the Sabbath — a third of you guarding the royal palace, 6a third at the Sur Gate, and a third at the gate behind the guard, who take turns guarding the temple — 7and you who are in the other two companies that normally go off Sabbath duty are all to guard the temple for the king. 8Station yourselves around the king, each of you with weapon in hand. Anyone who approaches your ranks[b] is to be put to death. Stay close to the king wherever he goes."

9The commanders of units of a hundred did just as Jehoiada the priest ordered. Each one took his men — those who were going on duty on the Sabbath and those who were going off duty — and came to Jehoiada the priest. 10Then he gave the commanders the spears and shields that had belonged to King David and that were in the temple of the LORD. 11The guards, each with weapon in hand, stationed themselves around the king — near the altar and the temple, from the south side to the north side of the temple.

12Jehoiada brought out the king's son and put the crown on him; he presented him with a copy of the covenant and proclaimed him king. They anointed him, and the people clapped their hands and shouted, "Long live the king!"

13When Athaliah heard the noise made by the guards and the people, she went to the people at the temple of the LORD. 14She looked and there was the king, standing by the pillar, as the custom was. The officers and the trumpeters were beside the king, and all the people of the land were rejoicing and blowing trumpets. Then Athaliah tore her robes and called out, "Treason! Treason!"

15Jehoiada the priest ordered the commanders of units of a hundred, who were in charge of the troops: "Bring her out between the ranks[c] and put to the sword anyone who follows her." For the priest had said, "She must not be put to death in the temple of the LORD." 16So they seized her as she reached the place where the horses enter the palace grounds, and there she was put to death.

17Jehoiada then made a covenant between the LORD and the king and people that they would be the LORD's people. He also made a covenant between the king and the people. 18All the people of the land went to the temple of Baal and tore it down. They smashed the altars and idols to pieces and killed Mattan the priest of Baal in front of the altars.

Then Jehoiada the priest posted guards at the temple of the LORD. 19He took with him the commanders of hundreds, the Carites, the guards and all the people of the land, and together they brought the king down from the temple of the LORD and went into the palace, entering by way of the gate of the guards. The king then took his place on the royal throne. 20All the people of the land rejoiced, and the city was calm, because Athaliah had been slain with the sword at the palace.

21Joash[d] was seven years old when he began to reign.[e]

Joash Repairs the Temple

12[f] In the seventh year of Jehu, Joash[g] became king, and he reigned in Jerusalem forty years. His mother's name was Zibiah; she was from Beersheba. 2Joash did what was right in the eyes of the LORD all the years Jehoiada the priest instructed him. 3The high places, however, were not removed; the people continued to offer sacrifices and burn incense there.

4Joash said to the priests, "Collect all the

[a] *2* Hebrew *Joram,* a variant of *Jehoram* [b] *8* Or *approaches the precincts* [c] *15* Or *out from the precincts* [d] *21* Hebrew *Jehoash,* a variant of *Joash* [e] *21* In Hebrew texts this verse (11:21) is numbered 12:1. [f] In Hebrew texts 12:1-21 is numbered 12:2-22. [g] *1* Hebrew *Jehoash,* a variant of *Joash*; also in verses 2, 4, 6, 7 and 18

money that is brought as sacred offerings
to the temple of the LORD — the money col-
lected in the census, the money received
from personal vows and the money brought
voluntarily to the temple. 5 Let every priest
receive the money from one of the treasur-
ers, then use it to repair whatever damage is
found in the temple."

6 But by the twenty-third year of King Jo-
ash the priests still had not repaired the
temple. 7 Therefore King Joash summoned
Jehoiada the priest and the other priests and
asked them, "Why aren't you repairing the
damage done to the temple? Take no more
money from your treasurers, but hand it
over for repairing the temple." 8 The priests
agreed that they would not collect any more
money from the people and that they would
not repair the temple themselves.

9 Jehoiada the priest took a chest and
bored a hole in its lid. He placed it beside
the altar, on the right side as one enters the
temple of the LORD. The priests who guarded
the entrance put into the chest all the money
that was brought to the temple of the LORD.
10 Whenever they saw that there was a large
amount of money in the chest, the royal sec-
retary and the high priest came, counted the
money that had been brought into the tem-
ple of the LORD and put it into bags. 11 When
the amount had been determined, they gave
the money to the men appointed to super-
vise the work on the temple. With it they
paid those who worked on the temple of the
LORD — the carpenters and builders, 12 the
masons and stonecutters. They purchased
timber and blocks of dressed stone for the
repair of the temple of the LORD, and met all
the other expenses of restoring the temple.

13 The money brought into the temple
was not spent for making silver basins, wick
trimmers, sprinkling bowls, trumpets or any
other articles of gold or silver for the temple
of the LORD; 14 it was paid to the workers, who
used it to repair the temple. 15 They did not
require an accounting from those to whom
they gave the money to pay the workers, be-
cause they acted with complete honesty.
16 The money from the guilt offerings and sin
offerings[a] was not brought into the temple of
the LORD; it belonged to the priests.

17 About this time Hazael king of Aram
went up and attacked Gath and captured it.
Then he turned to attack Jerusalem. 18 But
Joash king of Judah took all the sacred ob-
jects dedicated by his predecessors — Je-
hoshaphat, Jehoram and Ahaziah, the kings
of Judah — and the gifts he himself had ded-
icated and all the gold found in the treasur-
ies of the temple of the LORD and of the royal
palace, and he sent them to Hazael king of
Aram, who then withdrew from Jerusalem.

19 As for the other events of the reign of
Joash, and all he did, are they not written
in the book of the annals of the kings of Ju-
dah? 20 His officials conspired against him
and assassinated him at Beth Millo, on the
road down to Silla. 21 The officials who mur-
dered him were Jozabad son of Shimeath
and Jehozabad son of Shomer. He died and
was buried with his ancestors in the City of
David. And Amaziah his son succeeded him
as king.

Jehoahaz King of Israel

13 In the twenty-third year of Joash son
of Ahaziah king of Judah, Jehoahaz
son of Jehu became king of Israel in Samar-
ia, and he reigned seventeen years. 2 He did
evil in the eyes of the LORD by following the
sins of Jeroboam son of Nebat, which he
had caused Israel to commit, and he did not
turn away from them. 3 So the LORD's anger
burned against Israel, and for a long time he
kept them under the power of Hazael king of
Aram and Ben-Hadad his son.

4 Then Jehoahaz sought the LORD's favor,
and the LORD listened to him, for he saw
how severely the king of Aram was oppress-
ing Israel. 5 The LORD provided a deliverer
for Israel, and they escaped from the power
of Aram. So the Israelites lived in their own
homes as they had before. 6 But they did not
turn away from the sins of the house of Jer-
oboam, which he had caused Israel to com-
mit; they continued in them. Also, the Ashe-
rah pole[b] remained standing in Samaria.

7 Nothing had been left of the army of Je-
hoahaz except fifty horsemen, ten chariots
and ten thousand foot soldiers, for the king
of Aram had destroyed the rest and made
them like the dust at threshing time.

8 As for the other events of the reign of Je-
hoahaz, all he did and his achievements, are

[a] 16 Or *purification offerings* [b] 6 That is, a wooden symbol of the goddess Asherah; here and elsewhere in 2 Kings

they not written in the book of the annals of the kings of Israel? 9 Jehoahaz rested with his ancestors and was buried in Samaria. And Jehoash[a] his son succeeded him as king.

Jehoash King of Israel

10 In the thirty-seventh year of Joash king of Judah, Jehoash son of Jehoahaz became king of Israel in Samaria, and he reigned sixteen years. 11 He did evil in the eyes of the LORD and did not turn away from any of the sins of Jeroboam son of Nebat, which he had caused Israel to commit; he continued in them.

12 As for the other events of the reign of Jehoash, all he did and his achievements, including his war against Amaziah king of Judah, are they not written in the book of the annals of the kings of Israel? 13 Jehoash rested with his ancestors, and Jeroboam succeeded him on the throne. Jehoash was buried in Samaria with the kings of Israel.

14 Now Elisha had been suffering from the illness from which he died. Jehoash king of Israel went down to see him and wept over him. "My father! My father!" he cried. "The chariots and horsemen of Israel!"

15 Elisha said, "Get a bow and some arrows," and he did so. 16 "Take the bow in your hands," he said to the king of Israel. When he had taken it, Elisha put his hands on the king's hands.

17 "Open the east window," he said, and he opened it. "Shoot!" Elisha said, and he shot. "The LORD's arrow of victory, the arrow of victory over Aram!" Elisha declared. "You will completely destroy the Arameans at Aphek."

18 Then he said, "Take the arrows," and the king took them. Elisha told him, "Strike the ground." He struck it three times and stopped. 19 The man of God was angry with him and said, "You should have struck the ground five or six times; then you would have defeated Aram and completely destroyed it. But now you will defeat it only three times."

20 Elisha died and was buried.

Now Moabite raiders used to enter the country every spring. 21 Once while some Israelites were burying a man, suddenly they saw a band of raiders; so they threw the man's body into Elisha's tomb. When the body touched Elisha's bones, the man came to life and stood up on his feet.

22 Hazael king of Aram oppressed Israel throughout the reign of Jehoahaz. 23 But the LORD was gracious to them and had compassion and showed concern for them because of his covenant with Abraham, Isaac and Jacob. To this day he has been unwilling to destroy them or banish them from his presence.

24 Hazael king of Aram died, and Ben-Hadad his son succeeded him as king. 25 Then Jehoash son of Jehoahaz recaptured from Ben-Hadad son of Hazael the towns he had taken in battle from his father Jehoahaz. Three times Jehoash defeated him, and so he recovered the Israelite towns.

Amaziah King of Judah

14 In the second year of Jehoash[b] son of Jehoahaz king of Israel, Amaziah son of Joash king of Judah began to reign. 2 He was twenty-five years old when he became king, and he reigned in Jerusalem twenty-nine years. His mother's name was Jehoaddan; she was from Jerusalem. 3 He did what was right in the eyes of the LORD, but not as his father David had done. In everything he followed the example of his father Joash. 4 The high places, however, were not removed; the people continued to offer sacrifices and burn incense there.

5 After the kingdom was firmly in his grasp, he executed the officials who had murdered his father the king. 6 Yet he did not put the children of the assassins to death, in accordance with what is written in the Book of the Law of Moses where the LORD commanded: "Parents are not to be put to death for their children, nor children put to death for their parents; each will die for their own sin."[c]

7 He was the one who defeated ten thousand Edomites in the Valley of Salt and captured Sela in battle, calling it Joktheel, the name it has to this day.

8 Then Amaziah sent messengers to Jehoash son of Jehoahaz, the son of Jehu, king of Israel, with the challenge: "Come, let us face each other in battle."

9 But Jehoash king of Israel replied to Amaziah king of Judah: "A thistle in Lebanon sent

[a] 9 Hebrew *Joash,* a variant of *Jehoash*; also in verses 12-14 and 25 [b] 1 Hebrew *Joash,* a variant of *Jehoash*; also in verses 13, 23 and 27 [c] 6 Deut. 24:16

a message to a cedar in Lebanon, 'Give your
daughter to my son in marriage.' Then a wild
beast in Lebanon came along and trampled
the thistle underfoot. 10You have indeed de-
feated Edom and now you are arrogant. Glo-
ry in your victory, but stay at home! Why ask
for trouble and cause your own downfall and
that of Judah also?"

11Amaziah, however, would not listen, so
Jehoash king of Israel attacked. He and Am-
aziah king of Judah faced each other at Beth
Shemesh in Judah. 12Judah was routed by
Israel, and every man fled to his home. 13Je-
hoash king of Israel captured Amaziah king
of Judah, the son of Joash, the son of Ahazi-
ah, at Beth Shemesh. Then Jehoash went to
Jerusalem and broke down the wall of Jeru-
salem from the Ephraim Gate to the Corner
Gate — a section about four hundred cubits
long.[a] 14He took all the gold and silver and
all the articles found in the temple of the
LORD and in the treasuries of the royal pal-
ace. He also took hostages and returned to
Samaria.

15As for the other events of the reign of Je-
hoash, what he did and his achievements,
including his war against Amaziah king of
Judah, are they not written in the book of the
annals of the kings of Israel? 16Jehoash rest-
ed with his ancestors and was buried in Sa-
maria with the kings of Israel. And Jeroboam
his son succeeded him as king.

17Amaziah son of Joash king of Judah
lived for fifteen years after the death of Je-
hoash son of Jehoahaz king of Israel. 18As for
the other events of Amaziah's reign, are they
not written in the book of the annals of the
kings of Judah?

19They conspired against him in Jerusa-
lem, and he fled to Lachish, but they sent
men after him to Lachish and killed him
there. 20He was brought back by horse and
was buried in Jerusalem with his ancestors,
in the City of David.

21Then all the people of Judah took Aza-
riah,[b] who was sixteen years old, and made
him king in place of his father Amaziah.
22He was the one who rebuilt Elath and re-
stored it to Judah after Amaziah rested with
his ancestors.

Jeroboam II King of Israel

23In the fifteenth year of Amaziah son of
Joash king of Judah, Jeroboam son of Jeho-
ash king of Israel became king in Samaria,
and he reigned forty-one years. 24He did evil
in the eyes of the LORD and did not turn away
from any of the sins of Jeroboam son of Ne-
bat, which he had caused Israel to commit.
25He was the one who restored the bound-
aries of Israel from Lebo Hamath to the
Dead Sea,[c] in accordance with the word of
the LORD, the God of Israel, spoken through
his servant Jonah son of Amittai, the prophet
from Gath Hepher.

26The LORD had seen how bitterly ev-
eryone in Israel, whether slave or free, was
suffering;[d] there was no one to help them.
27And since the LORD had not said he would
blot out the name of Israel from under heav-
en, he saved them by the hand of Jeroboam
son of Jehoash.

28As for the other events of Jeroboam's
reign, all he did, and his military achieve-
ments, including how he recovered for Isra-
el both Damascus and Hamath, which had
belonged to Judah, are they not written in
the book of the annals of the kings of Isra-
el? 29Jeroboam rested with his ancestors, the
kings of Israel. And Zechariah his son suc-
ceeded him as king.

Azariah King of Judah

15 In the twenty-seventh year of Jero-
boam king of Israel, Azariah[e] son of
Amaziah king of Judah began to reign. 2He
was sixteen years old when he became king,
and he reigned in Jerusalem fifty-two years.
His mother's name was Jekoliah; she was
from Jerusalem. 3He did what was right in
the eyes of the LORD, just as his father Am-
aziah had done. 4The high places, however,
were not removed; the people continued to
offer sacrifices and burn incense there.

5The LORD afflicted the king with lepro-
sy[f] until the day he died, and he lived in a
separate house.[g] Jotham the king's son had
charge of the palace and governed the peo-
ple of the land.

6As for the other events of Azariah's reign,
and all he did, are they not written in the

[a] *13* That is, about 600 feet or about 180 meters [b] *21* Also called *Uzziah* [c] *25* Hebrew *the Sea of the Arabah* [d] *26* Or *Israel was suffering. They were without a ruler or leader, and* [e] *1* Also called *Uzziah*; also in verses 6, 7, 8, 17, 23 and 27 [f] *5* The Hebrew for *leprosy* was used for various diseases affecting the skin. [g] *5* Or *in a house where he was relieved of responsibilities*

book of the annals of the kings of Judah?
7 Azariah rested with his ancestors and was
buried near them in the City of David. And
Jotham his son succeeded him as king.

Zechariah King of Israel

8 In the thirty-eighth year of Azariah
king of Judah, Zechariah son of Jeroboam
became king of Israel in Samaria, and he
reigned six months. 9 He did evil in the eyes
of the LORD, as his predecessors had done.
He did not turn away from the sins of Jerobo-
am son of Nebat, which he had caused Israel
to commit.

10 Shallum son of Jabesh conspired against
Zechariah. He attacked him in front of the
people,[a] assassinated him and succeeded
him as king. 11 The other events of Zechari-
ah's reign are written in the book of the an-
nals of the kings of Israel. 12 So the word of
the LORD spoken to Jehu was fulfilled: "Your
descendants will sit on the throne of Israel to
the fourth generation."[b]

Shallum King of Israel

13 Shallum son of Jabesh became king in
the thirty-ninth year of Uzziah king of Ju-
dah, and he reigned in Samaria one month.
14 Then Menahem son of Gadi went from Tir-
zah up to Samaria. He attacked Shallum son
of Jabesh in Samaria, assassinated him and
succeeded him as king.

15 The other events of Shallum's reign,
and the conspiracy he led, are written in the
book of the annals of the kings of Israel.

16 At that time Menahem, starting out
from Tirzah, attacked Tiphsah and everyone
in the city and its vicinity, because they re-
fused to open their gates. He sacked Tiphsah
and ripped open all the pregnant women.

Menahem King of Israel

17 In the thirty-ninth year of Azariah king
of Judah, Menahem son of Gadi became
king of Israel, and he reigned in Samaria ten
years. 18 He did evil in the eyes of the LORD.
During his entire reign he did not turn away
from the sins of Jeroboam son of Nebat,
which he had caused Israel to commit.

19 Then Pul[c] king of Assyria invaded the
land, and Menahem gave him a thousand
talents[d] of silver to gain his support and
strengthen his own hold on the kingdom.
20 Menahem exacted this money from Israel.
Every wealthy person had to contribute fif-
ty shekels[e] of silver to be given to the king of
Assyria. So the king of Assyria withdrew and
stayed in the land no longer.

21 As for the other events of Menahem's
reign, and all he did, are they not written in
the book of the annals of the kings of Israel?
22 Menahem rested with his ancestors. And
Pekahiah his son succeeded him as king.

Pekahiah King of Israel

23 In the fiftieth year of Azariah king of
Judah, Pekahiah son of Menahem became
king of Israel in Samaria, and he reigned two
years. 24 Pekahiah did evil in the eyes of the
LORD. He did not turn away from the sins of
Jeroboam son of Nebat, which he had caused
Israel to commit. 25 One of his chief officers,
Pekah son of Remaliah, conspired against
him. Taking fifty men of Gilead with him,
he assassinated Pekahiah, along with Argob
and Arieh, in the citadel of the royal palace
at Samaria. So Pekah killed Pekahiah and
succeeded him as king.

26 The other events of Pekahiah's reign,
and all he did, are written in the book of the
annals of the kings of Israel.

Pekah King of Israel

27 In the fifty-second year of Azariah king
of Judah, Pekah son of Remaliah became
king of Israel in Samaria, and he reigned
twenty years. 28 He did evil in the eyes of the
LORD. He did not turn away from the sins of
Jeroboam son of Nebat, which he had caused
Israel to commit.

29 In the time of Pekah king of Israel, Tig-
lath-Pileser king of Assyria came and took
Ijon, Abel Beth Maakah, Janoah, Kedesh and
Hazor. He took Gilead and Galilee, includ-
ing all the land of Naphtali, and deported
the people to Assyria. 30 Then Hoshea son of
Elah conspired against Pekah son of Rema-
liah. He attacked and assassinated him, and
then succeeded him as king in the twentieth
year of Jotham son of Uzziah.

31 As for the other events of Pekah's reign,

[a] *10* Hebrew; some Septuagint manuscripts *in Ibleam* [b] *12* 2 Kings 10:30 [c] *19* Also called *Tiglath-Pileser* [d] *19* That is, about 38 tons or about 34 metric tons [e] *20* That is, about 1 1/4 pounds or about 575 grams

and all he did, are they not written in the book of the annals of the kings of Israel?

Jotham King of Judah

[32]In the second year of Pekah son of Remaliah king of Israel, Jotham son of Uzziah king of Judah began to reign. [33]He was twenty-five years old when he became king, and he reigned in Jerusalem sixteen years. His mother's name was Jerusha daughter of Zadok. [34]He did what was right in the eyes of the LORD, just as his father Uzziah had done. [35]The high places, however, were not removed; the people continued to offer sacrifices and burn incense there. Jotham rebuilt the Upper Gate of the temple of the LORD.

[36]As for the other events of Jotham's reign, and what he did, are they not written in the book of the annals of the kings of Judah? [37](In those days the LORD began to send Rezin king of Aram and Pekah son of Remaliah against Judah.) [38]Jotham rested with his ancestors and was buried with them in the City of David, the city of his father. And Ahaz his son succeeded him as king.

Ahaz King of Judah

16 In the seventeenth year of Pekah son of Remaliah, Ahaz son of Jotham king of Judah began to reign. [2]Ahaz was twenty years old when he became king, and he reigned in Jerusalem sixteen years. Unlike David his father, he did not do what was right in the eyes of the LORD his God. [3]He followed the ways of the kings of Israel and even sacrificed his son in the fire, engaging in the detestable practices of the nations the LORD had driven out before the Israelites. [4]He offered sacrifices and burned incense at the high places, on the hilltops and under every spreading tree.

[5]Then Rezin king of Aram and Pekah son of Remaliah king of Israel marched up to fight against Jerusalem and besieged Ahaz, but they could not overpower him. [6]At that time, Rezin king of Aram recovered Elath for Aram by driving out the people of Judah. Edomites then moved into Elath and have lived there to this day.

[7]Ahaz sent messengers to say to Tiglath-Pileser king of Assyria, "I am your servant and vassal. Come up and save me out of the hand of the king of Aram and of the king of Israel, who are attacking me." [8]And Ahaz took the silver and gold found in the temple of the LORD and in the treasuries of the royal palace and sent it as a gift to the king of Assyria. [9]The king of Assyria complied by attacking Damascus and capturing it. He deported its inhabitants to Kir and put Rezin to death.

[10]Then King Ahaz went to Damascus to meet Tiglath-Pileser king of Assyria. He saw an altar in Damascus and sent to Uriah the priest a sketch of the altar, with detailed plans for its construction. [11]So Uriah the priest built an altar in accordance with all the plans that King Ahaz had sent from Damascus and finished it before King Ahaz returned. [12]When the king came back from Damascus and saw the altar, he approached it and presented offerings[a] on it. [13]He offered up his burnt offering and grain offering, poured out his drink offering, and splashed the blood of his fellowship offerings against the altar. [14]As for the bronze altar that stood before the LORD, he brought it from the front of the temple — from between the new altar and the temple of the LORD — and put it on the north side of the new altar.

[15]King Ahaz then gave these orders to Uriah the priest: "On the large new altar, offer the morning burnt offering and the evening grain offering, the king's burnt offering and his grain offering, and the burnt offering of all the people of the land, and their grain offering and their drink offering. Splash against this altar the blood of all the burnt offerings and sacrifices. But I will use the bronze altar for seeking guidance." [16]And Uriah the priest did just as King Ahaz had ordered.

[17]King Ahaz cut off the side panels and removed the basins from the movable stands. He removed the Sea from the bronze bulls that supported it and set it on a stone base. [18]He took away the Sabbath canopy[b] that had been built at the temple and removed the royal entryway outside the temple of the LORD, in deference to the king of Assyria.

[19]As for the other events of the reign of Ahaz, and what he did, are they not written in the book of the annals of the kings of Judah? [20]Ahaz rested with his ancestors and was buried with them in the City of David.

[a] 12 Or *and went up* [b] 18 Or *the dais of his throne* (see Septuagint)

And Hezekiah his son succeeded him as king.

Hoshea Last King of Israel

17 In the twelfth year of Ahaz king of Judah, Hoshea son of Elah became king of Israel in Samaria, and he reigned nine years. 2He did evil in the eyes of the LORD, but not like the kings of Israel who preceded him.

3Shalmaneser king of Assyria came up to attack Hoshea, who had been Shalmaneser's vassal and had paid him tribute. 4But the king of Assyria discovered that Hoshea was a traitor, for he had sent envoys to So[a] king of Egypt, and he no longer paid tribute to the king of Assyria, as he had done year by year. Therefore Shalmaneser seized him and put him in prison. 5The king of Assyria invaded the entire land, marched against Samaria and laid siege to it for three years. 6In the ninth year of Hoshea, the king of Assyria captured Samaria and deported the Israelites to Assyria. He settled them in Halah, in Gozan on the Habor River and in the towns of the Medes.

Israel Exiled Because of Sin

7All this took place because the Israelites had sinned against the LORD their God, who had brought them up out of Egypt from under the power of Pharaoh king of Egypt. They worshiped other gods 8and followed the practices of the nations the LORD had driven out before them, as well as the practices that the kings of Israel had introduced. 9The Israelites secretly did things against the LORD their God that were not right. From watchtower to fortified city they built themselves high places in all their towns. 10They set up sacred stones and Asherah poles on every high hill and under every spreading tree. 11At every high place they burned incense, as the nations whom the LORD had driven out before them had done. They did wicked things that aroused the LORD's anger. 12They worshiped idols, though the LORD had said, "You shall not do this."[b] 13The LORD warned Israel and Judah through all his prophets and seers: "Turn from your evil ways. Observe my commands and decrees, in accordance with the entire Law that I commanded your ancestors to obey and that I delivered to you through my servants the prophets."

14But they would not listen and were as stiff-necked as their ancestors, who did not trust in the LORD their God. 15They rejected his decrees and the covenant he had made with their ancestors and the statutes he had warned them to keep. They followed worthless idols and themselves became worthless. They imitated the nations around them although the LORD had ordered them, "Do not do as they do."

16They forsook all the commands of the LORD their God and made for themselves two idols cast in the shape of calves, and an Asherah pole. They bowed down to all the starry hosts, and they worshiped Baal. 17They sacrificed their sons and daughters in the fire. They practiced divination and sought omens and sold themselves to do evil in the eyes of the LORD, arousing his anger.

18So the LORD was very angry with Israel and removed them from his presence. Only the tribe of Judah was left, 19and even Judah did not keep the commands of the LORD their God. They followed the practices Israel had introduced. 20Therefore the LORD rejected all the people of Israel; he afflicted them and gave them into the hands of plunderers, until he thrust them from his presence.

21When he tore Israel away from the house of David, they made Jeroboam son of Nebat their king. Jeroboam enticed Israel away from following the LORD and caused them to commit a great sin. 22The Israelites persisted in all the sins of Jeroboam and did not turn away from them 23until the LORD removed them from his presence, as he had warned through all his servants the prophets. So the people of Israel were taken from their homeland into exile in Assyria, and they are still there.

Samaria Resettled

24The king of Assyria brought people from Babylon, Kuthah, Avva, Hamath and Sepharvaim and settled them in the towns of Samaria to replace the Israelites. They took over Samaria and lived in its towns. 25When they first lived there, they did not worship the LORD; so he sent lions among them and they killed some of the people. 26It was reported

[a] 4 *So* is probably an abbreviation for *Osorkon*. [b] 12 Exodus 20:4,5

to the king of Assyria: "The people you de-
ported and resettled in the towns of Samaria
do not know what the god of that country re-
quires. He has sent lions among them, which
are killing them off, because the people do
not know what he requires."

[27]Then the king of Assyria gave this or-
der: "Have one of the priests you took cap-
tive from Samaria go back to live there and
teach the people what the god of the land re-
quires." [28]So one of the priests who had been
exiled from Samaria came to live in Bethel
and taught them how to worship the LORD.

[29]Nevertheless, each national group
made its own gods in the several towns
where they settled, and set them up in the
shrines the people of Samaria had made at
the high places. [30]The people from Babylon
made Sukkoth Benoth, those from Kuthah
made Nergal, and those from Hamath made
Ashima; [31]the Avvites made Nibhaz and Tar-
tak, and the Sepharvites burned their chil-
dren in the fire as sacrifices to Adrammelek
and Anammelek, the gods of Sepharvaim.
[32]They worshiped the LORD, but they also
appointed all sorts of their own people to
officiate for them as priests in the shrines at
the high places. [33]They worshiped the LORD,
but they also served their own gods in accor-
dance with the customs of the nations from
which they had been brought.

[34]To this day they persist in their former
practices. They neither worship the LORD
nor adhere to the decrees and regulations,
the laws and commands that the LORD gave
the descendants of Jacob, whom he named
Israel. [35]When the LORD made a covenant
with the Israelites, he commanded them:
"Do not worship any other gods or bow down
to them, serve them or sacrifice to them.
[36]But the LORD, who brought you up out of
Egypt with mighty power and outstretched
arm, is the one you must worship. To him
you shall bow down and to him offer sacri-
fices. [37]You must always be careful to keep
the decrees and regulations, the laws and
commands he wrote for you. Do not worship
other gods. [38]Do not forget the covenant I
have made with you, and do not worship
other gods. [39]Rather, worship the LORD your
God; it is he who will deliver you from the
hand of all your enemies."

[40]They would not listen, however, but per-
sisted in their former practices. [41]Even while
these people were worshiping the LORD,
they were serving their idols. To this day
their children and grandchildren continue
to do as their ancestors did.

Hezekiah King of Judah

18 In the third year of Hoshea son of
Elah king of Israel, Hezekiah son
of Ahaz king of Judah began to reign. [2]He
was twenty-five years old when he became
king, and he reigned in Jerusalem twenty-
nine years. His mother's name was Abijah[a]
daughter of Zechariah. [3]He did what was
right in the eyes of the LORD, just as his fa-
ther David had done. [4]He removed the high
places, smashed the sacred stones and cut
down the Asherah poles. He broke into piec-
es the bronze snake Moses had made, for up
to that time the Israelites had been burning
incense to it. (It was called Nehushtan.[b])

[5]Hezekiah trusted in the LORD, the God of
Israel. There was no one like him among all
the kings of Judah, either before him or after
him. [6]He held fast to the LORD and did not
stop following him; he kept the commands
the LORD had given Moses. [7]And the LORD
was with him; he was successful in what-
ever he undertook. He rebelled against the
king of Assyria and did not serve him. [8]From
watchtower to fortified city, he defeated the
Philistines, as far as Gaza and its territory.

[9]In King Hezekiah's fourth year, which
was the seventh year of Hoshea son of Elah
king of Israel, Shalmaneser king of Assyria
marched against Samaria and laid siege to
it. [10]At the end of three years the Assyrians
took it. So Samaria was captured in Hezeki-
ah's sixth year, which was the ninth year of
Hoshea king of Israel. [11]The king of Assyria
deported Israel to Assyria and settled them
in Halah, in Gozan on the Habor River and
in towns of the Medes. [12]This happened be-
cause they had not obeyed the LORD their
God, but had violated his covenant — all that
Moses the servant of the LORD commanded.
They neither listened to the commands nor
carried them out.

[13]In the fourteenth year of King Hezeki-
ah's reign, Sennacherib king of Assyria at-
tacked all the fortified cities of Judah and

[a] 2 Hebrew *Abi,* a variant of *Abijah* [b] 4 *Nehushtan* sounds like the Hebrew for both *bronze* and *snake.*

captured them. 14So Hezekiah king of Judah
sent this message to the king of Assyria at La-
chish: "I have done wrong. Withdraw from
me, and I will pay whatever you demand of
me." The king of Assyria exacted from Heze-
kiah king of Judah three hundred talents[a] of
silver and thirty talents[b] of gold. 15So Heze-
kiah gave him all the silver that was found in
the temple of the LORD and in the treasuries
of the royal palace.
16At this time Hezekiah king of Judah
stripped off the gold with which he had cov-
ered the doors and doorposts of the temple of
the LORD, and gave it to the king of Assyria.

Sennacherib Threatens Jerusalem

17The king of Assyria sent his supreme
commander, his chief officer and his field
commander with a large army, from Lachish
to King Hezekiah at Jerusalem. They came
up to Jerusalem and stopped at the aqueduct
of the Upper Pool, on the road to the Washer-
man's Field. 18They called for the king; and
Eliakim son of Hilkiah the palace adminis-
trator, Shebna the secretary, and Joah son of
Asaph the recorder went out to them.
19The field commander said to them, "Tell
Hezekiah:

> "'This is what the great king, the
> king of Assyria, says: On what are you
> basing this confidence of yours? 20You
> say you have the counsel and the might
> for war—but you speak only empty
> words. On whom are you depending,
> that you rebel against me? 21Look, I
> know you are depending on Egypt, that
> splintered reed of a staff, which pierc-
> es the hand of anyone who leans on
> it! Such is Pharaoh king of Egypt to all
> who depend on him. 22But if you say to
> me, "We are depending on the LORD
> our God"—isn't he the one whose high
> places and altars Hezekiah removed,
> saying to Judah and Jerusalem, "You
> must worship before this altar in Jeru-
> salem"?
>
> 23"'Come now, make a bargain with
> my master, the king of Assyria: I will
> give you two thousand horses—if you
> can put riders on them! 24How can
> you repulse one officer of the least of
> my master's officials, even though you
> are depending on Egypt for chariots
> and horsemen[c]? 25Furthermore, have
> I come to attack and destroy this place
> without word from the LORD? The LORD
> himself told me to march against this
> country and destroy it.'"

26Then Eliakim son of Hilkiah, and Sheb-
na and Joah said to the field commander,
"Please speak to your servants in Aramaic,
since we understand it. Don't speak to us in
Hebrew in the hearing of the people on the
wall."
27But the commander replied, "Was it
only to your master and you that my master
sent me to say these things, and not to the
people sitting on the wall—who, like you,
will have to eat their own excrement and
drink their own urine?"
28Then the commander stood and called
out in Hebrew, "Hear the word of the great
king, the king of Assyria! 29This is what the
king says: Do not let Hezekiah deceive you.
He cannot deliver you from my hand. 30Do
not let Hezekiah persuade you to trust in the
LORD when he says, 'The LORD will surely
deliver us; this city will not be given into the
hand of the king of Assyria.'
31"Do not listen to Hezekiah. This is what
the king of Assyria says: Make peace with me
and come out to me. Then each of you will
eat fruit from your own vine and fig tree and
drink water from your own cistern, 32until I
come and take you to a land like your own—
a land of grain and new wine, a land of bread
and vineyards, a land of olive trees and hon-
ey. Choose life and not death!
"Do not listen to Hezekiah, for he is mis-
leading you when he says, 'The LORD will
deliver us.' 33Has the god of any nation ever
delivered his land from the hand of the king
of Assyria? 34Where are the gods of Hamath
and Arpad? Where are the gods of Sepharva-
im, Hena and Ivvah? Have they rescued Sa-
maria from my hand? 35Who of all the gods
of these countries has been able to save his
land from me? How then can the LORD deliv-
er Jerusalem from my hand?"
36But the people remained silent and said
nothing in reply, because the king had com-
manded, "Do not answer him."

[a] *14* That is, about 11 tons or about 10 metric tons [b] *14* That is, about 1 ton or about 1 metric ton
[c] *24* Or *charioteers*

37 Then Eliakim son of Hilkiah the palace administrator, Shebna the secretary, and Joah son of Asaph the recorder went to Hezekiah, with their clothes torn, and told him what the field commander had said.

Jerusalem's Deliverance Foretold

19 When King Hezekiah heard this, he tore his clothes and put on sackcloth and went into the temple of the LORD. 2 He sent Eliakim the palace administrator, Shebna the secretary and the leading priests, all wearing sackcloth, to the prophet Isaiah son of Amoz. 3 They told him, "This is what Hezekiah says: This day is a day of distress and rebuke and disgrace, as when children come to the moment of birth and there is no strength to deliver them. 4 It may be that the LORD your God will hear all the words of the field commander, whom his master, the king of Assyria, has sent to ridicule the living God, and that he will rebuke him for the words the LORD your God has heard. Therefore pray for the remnant that still survives."

5 When King Hezekiah's officials came to Isaiah, 6 Isaiah said to them, "Tell your master, 'This is what the LORD says: Do not be afraid of what you have heard — those words with which the underlings of the king of Assyria have blasphemed me. 7 Listen! When he hears a certain report, I will make him want to return to his own country, and there I will have him cut down with the sword.'"

8 When the field commander heard that the king of Assyria had left Lachish, he withdrew and found the king fighting against Libnah.

9 Now Sennacherib received a report that Tirhakah, the king of Cush,[a] was marching out to fight against him. So he again sent messengers to Hezekiah with this word: 10 "Say to Hezekiah king of Judah: Do not let the god you depend on deceive you when he says, 'Jerusalem will not be given into the hands of the king of Assyria.' 11 Surely you have heard what the kings of Assyria have done to all the countries, destroying them completely. And will you be delivered? 12 Did the gods of the nations that were destroyed by my predecessors deliver them — the gods of Gozan, Harran, Rezeph and the people of Eden who were in Tel Assar? 13 Where is the king of Hamath or the king of Arpad? Where are the kings of Lair, Sepharvaim, Hena and Ivvah?"

Hezekiah's Prayer

14 Hezekiah received the letter from the messengers and read it. Then he went up to the temple of the LORD and spread it out before the LORD. 15 And Hezekiah prayed to the LORD: "LORD, the God of Israel, enthroned between the cherubim, you alone are God over all the kingdoms of the earth. You have made heaven and earth. 16 Give ear, LORD, and hear; open your eyes, LORD, and see; listen to the words Sennacherib has sent to ridicule the living God.

17 "It is true, LORD, that the Assyrian kings have laid waste these nations and their lands. 18 They have thrown their gods into the fire and destroyed them, for they were not gods but only wood and stone, fashioned by human hands. 19 Now, LORD our God, deliver us from his hand, so that all the kingdoms of the earth may know that you alone, LORD, are God."

Isaiah Prophesies Sennacherib's Fall

20 Then Isaiah son of Amoz sent a message to Hezekiah: "This is what the LORD, the God of Israel, says: I have heard your prayer concerning Sennacherib king of Assyria. 21 This is the word that the LORD has spoken against him:

"'Virgin Daughter Zion
despises you and mocks you.
Daughter Jerusalem
tosses her head as you flee.
22 Who is it you have ridiculed and blasphemed?
Against whom have you raised your voice
and lifted your eyes in pride?
Against the Holy One of Israel!
23 By your messengers
you have ridiculed the Lord.
And you have said,
"With my many chariots
I have ascended the heights of the mountains,
the utmost heights of Lebanon.
I have cut down its tallest cedars,
the choicest of its junipers.

[a] 9 That is, the upper Nile region

I have reached its remotest parts,
the finest of its forests.
24 I have dug wells in foreign lands
and drunk the water there.
With the soles of my feet
I have dried up all the streams of
Egypt."

25 " 'Have you not heard?
Long ago I ordained it.
In days of old I planned it;
now I have brought it to pass,
that you have turned fortified cities
into piles of stone.
26 Their people, drained of power,
are dismayed and put to shame.
They are like plants in the field,
like tender green shoots,
like grass sprouting on the roof,
scorched before it grows up.

27 " 'But I know where you are
and when you come and go
and how you rage against me.
28 Because you rage against me
and because your insolence has
reached my ears,
I will put my hook in your nose
and my bit in your mouth,
and I will make you return
by the way you came.'

29 "This will be the sign for you, Hezekiah:

"This year you will eat what grows by
itself,
and the second year what springs from
that.
But in the third year sow and reap,
plant vineyards and eat their fruit.
30 Once more a remnant of the kingdom of
Judah
will take root below and bear fruit
above.
31 For out of Jerusalem will come a
remnant,
and out of Mount Zion a band of
survivors.

"The zeal of the LORD Almighty will accomplish this.

32 "Therefore this is what the LORD says concerning the king of Assyria:

" 'He will not enter this city
or shoot an arrow here.
He will not come before it with shield
or build a siege ramp against it.
33 By the way that he came he will return;
he will not enter this city,
declares the LORD.
34 I will defend this city and save it,
for my sake and for the sake of David
my servant.' "

35 That night the angel of the LORD went out
and put to death a hundred and eighty-five
thousand in the Assyrian camp. When the
people got up the next morning—there were
all the dead bodies! 36 So Sennacherib king
of Assyria broke camp and withdrew. He re-
turned to Nineveh and stayed there.
37 One day, while he was worshiping in the
temple of his god Nisrok, his sons Adramme-
lek and Sharezer killed him with the sword,
and they escaped to the land of Ararat. And
Esarhaddon his son succeeded him as king.

Hezekiah's Illness

20 In those days Hezekiah became ill
and was at the point of death. The
prophet Isaiah son of Amoz went to him and
said, "This is what the LORD says: Put your
house in order, because you are going to die;
you will not recover."
2 Hezekiah turned his face to the wall and
prayed to the LORD, 3 "Remember, LORD,
how I have walked before you faithfully and
with wholehearted devotion and have done
what is good in your eyes." And Hezekiah
wept bitterly.
4 Before Isaiah had left the middle court,
the word of the LORD came to him: 5 "Go
back and tell Hezekiah, the ruler of my peo-
ple, 'This is what the LORD, the God of your
father David, says: I have heard your prayer
and seen your tears; I will heal you. On the
third day from now you will go up to the tem-
ple of the LORD. 6 I will add fifteen years to
your life. And I will deliver you and this city
from the hand of the king of Assyria. I will
defend this city for my sake and for the sake
of my servant David.' "
7 Then Isaiah said, "Prepare a poultice of
figs." They did so and applied it to the boil,
and he recovered.
8 Hezekiah had asked Isaiah, "What will
be the sign that the LORD will heal me and
that I will go up to the temple of the LORD on
the third day from now?"

[9]Isaiah answered, "This is the LORD's sign to you that the LORD will do what he has promised: Shall the shadow go forward ten steps, or shall it go back ten steps?"

[10]"It is a simple matter for the shadow to go forward ten steps," said Hezekiah. "Rather, have it go back ten steps."

[11]Then the prophet Isaiah called on the LORD, and the LORD made the shadow go back the ten steps it had gone down on the stairway of Ahaz.

Envoys From Babylon

[12]At that time Marduk-Baladan son of Baladan king of Babylon sent Hezekiah letters and a gift, because he had heard of Hezekiah's illness. [13]Hezekiah received the envoys and showed them all that was in his storehouses — the silver, the gold, the spices and the fine olive oil — his armory and everything found among his treasures. There was nothing in his palace or in all his kingdom that Hezekiah did not show them.

[14]Then Isaiah the prophet went to King Hezekiah and asked, "What did those men say, and where did they come from?"

"From a distant land," Hezekiah replied. "They came from Babylon."

[15]The prophet asked, "What did they see in your palace?"

"They saw everything in my palace," Hezekiah said. "There is nothing among my treasures that I did not show them."

[16]Then Isaiah said to Hezekiah, "Hear the word of the LORD: [17]The time will surely come when everything in your palace, and all that your predecessors have stored up until this day, will be carried off to Babylon. Nothing will be left, says the LORD. [18]And some of your descendants, your own flesh and blood who will be born to you, will be taken away, and they will become eunuchs in the palace of the king of Babylon."

[19]"The word of the LORD you have spoken is good," Hezekiah replied. For he thought, "Will there not be peace and security in my lifetime?"

[20]As for the other events of Hezekiah's reign, all his achievements and how he made the pool and the tunnel by which he brought water into the city, are they not written in the book of the annals of the kings of Judah? [21]Hezekiah rested with his ancestors. And Manasseh his son succeeded him as king.

Manasseh King of Judah

21 Manasseh was twelve years old when he became king, and he reigned in Jerusalem fifty-five years. His mother's name was Hephzibah. [2]He did evil in the eyes of the LORD, following the detestable practices of the nations the LORD had driven out before the Israelites. [3]He rebuilt the high places his father Hezekiah had destroyed; he also erected altars to Baal and made an Asherah pole, as Ahab king of Israel had done. He bowed down to all the starry hosts and worshiped them. [4]He built altars in the temple of the LORD, of which the LORD had said, "In Jerusalem I will put my Name." [5]In the two courts of the temple of the LORD, he built altars to all the starry hosts. [6]He sacrificed his own son in the fire, practiced divination, sought omens, and consulted mediums and spiritists. He did much evil in the eyes of the LORD, arousing his anger.

[7]He took the carved Asherah pole he had made and put it in the temple, of which the LORD had said to David and to his son Solomon, "In this temple and in Jerusalem, which I have chosen out of all the tribes of Israel, I will put my Name forever. [8]I will not again make the feet of the Israelites wander from the land I gave their ancestors, if only they will be careful to do everything I commanded them and will keep the whole Law that my servant Moses gave them." [9]But the people did not listen. Manasseh led them astray, so that they did more evil than the nations the LORD had destroyed before the Israelites.

[10]The LORD said through his servants the prophets: [11]"Manasseh king of Judah has committed these detestable sins. He has done more evil than the Amorites who preceded him and has led Judah into sin with his idols. [12]Therefore this is what the LORD, the God of Israel, says: I am going to bring such disaster on Jerusalem and Judah that the ears of everyone who hears of it will tingle. [13]I will stretch out over Jerusalem the measuring line used against Samaria and the plumb line used against the house of Ahab. I will wipe out Jerusalem as one wipes a dish, wiping it and turning it upside down. [14]I will forsake the remnant of my inheritance and give them into the hands of enemies. They will be looted and plundered by all their enemies; [15]they have done evil in

my eyes and have aroused my anger from the day their ancestors came out of Egypt until this day."

16 Moreover, Manasseh also shed so much innocent blood that he filled Jerusalem from end to end—besides the sin that he had caused Judah to commit, so that they did evil in the eyes of the LORD.

17 As for the other events of Manasseh's reign, and all he did, including the sin he committed, are they not written in the book of the annals of the kings of Judah? 18 Manasseh rested with his ancestors and was buried in his palace garden, the garden of Uzza. And Amon his son succeeded him as king.

Amon King of Judah

19 Amon was twenty-two years old when he became king, and he reigned in Jerusalem two years. His mother's name was Meshullemeth daughter of Haruz; she was from Jotbah. 20 He did evil in the eyes of the LORD, as his father Manasseh had done. 21 He followed completely the ways of his father, worshiping the idols his father had worshiped, and bowing down to them. 22 He forsook the LORD, the God of his ancestors, and did not walk in obedience to him.

23 Amon's officials conspired against him and assassinated the king in his palace. 24 Then the people of the land killed all who had plotted against King Amon, and they made Josiah his son king in his place.

25 As for the other events of Amon's reign, and what he did, are they not written in the book of the annals of the kings of Judah? 26 He was buried in his tomb in the garden of Uzza. And Josiah his son succeeded him as king.

The Book of the Law Found

22 Josiah was eight years old when he became king, and he reigned in Jerusalem thirty-one years. His mother's name was Jedidah daughter of Adaiah; she was from Bozkath. 2 He did what was right in the eyes of the LORD and followed completely the ways of his father David, not turning aside to the right or to the left.

3 In the eighteenth year of his reign, King Josiah sent the secretary, Shaphan son of Azaliah, the son of Meshullam, to the temple of the LORD. He said: 4 "Go up to Hilkiah the high priest and have him get ready the money that has been brought into the temple of the LORD, which the doorkeepers have collected from the people. 5 Have them entrust it to the men appointed to supervise the work on the temple. And have these men pay the workers who repair the temple of the LORD— 6 the carpenters, the builders and the masons. Also have them purchase timber and dressed stone to repair the temple. 7 But they need not account for the money entrusted to them, because they are honest in their dealings."

8 Hilkiah the high priest said to Shaphan the secretary, "I have found the Book of the Law in the temple of the LORD." He gave it to Shaphan, who read it. 9 Then Shaphan the secretary went to the king and reported to him: "Your officials have paid out the money that was in the temple of the LORD and have entrusted it to the workers and supervisors at the temple." 10 Then Shaphan the secretary informed the king, "Hilkiah the priest has given me a book." And Shaphan read from it in the presence of the king.

11 When the king heard the words of the Book of the Law, he tore his robes. 12 He gave these orders to Hilkiah the priest, Ahikam son of Shaphan, Akbor son of Micaiah, Shaphan the secretary and Asaiah the king's attendant: 13 "Go and inquire of the LORD for me and for the people and for all Judah about what is written in this book that has been found. Great is the LORD's anger that burns against us because those who have gone before us have not obeyed the words of this book; they have not acted in accordance with all that is written there concerning us."

14 Hilkiah the priest, Ahikam, Akbor, Shaphan and Asaiah went to speak to the prophet Huldah, who was the wife of Shallum son of Tikvah, the son of Harhas, keeper of the wardrobe. She lived in Jerusalem, in the New Quarter.

15 She said to them, "This is what the LORD, the God of Israel, says: Tell the man who sent you to me, 16 'This is what the LORD says: I am going to bring disaster on this place and its people, according to everything written in the book the king of Judah has read. 17 Because they have forsaken me and burned incense to other gods and aroused my anger by all the idols their hands have made,[a] my anger will burn against this place and will not

[a] 17 Or *by everything they have done*

be quenched.' [18]Tell the king of Judah, who sent you to inquire of the LORD, 'This is what the LORD, the God of Israel, says concerning the words you heard: [19]Because your heart was responsive and you humbled yourself before the LORD when you heard what I have spoken against this place and its people — that they would become a curse[a] and be laid waste — and because you tore your robes and wept in my presence, I also have heard you, declares the LORD. [20]Therefore I will gather you to your ancestors, and you will be buried in peace. Your eyes will not see all the disaster I am going to bring on this place.' "

So they took her answer back to the king.

Josiah Renews the Covenant

23 Then the king called together all the elders of Judah and Jerusalem. [2]He went up to the temple of the LORD with the people of Judah, the inhabitants of Jerusalem, the priests and the prophets — all the people from the least to the greatest. He read in their hearing all the words of the Book of the Covenant, which had been found in the temple of the LORD. [3]The king stood by the pillar and renewed the covenant in the presence of the LORD — to follow the LORD and keep his commands, statutes and decrees with all his heart and all his soul, thus confirming the words of the covenant written in this book. Then all the people pledged themselves to the covenant.

[4]The king ordered Hilkiah the high priest, the priests next in rank and the doorkeepers to remove from the temple of the LORD all the articles made for Baal and Asherah and all the starry hosts. He burned them outside Jerusalem in the fields of the Kidron Valley and took the ashes to Bethel. [5]He did away with the idolatrous priests appointed by the kings of Judah to burn incense on the high places of the towns of Judah and on those around Jerusalem — those who burned incense to Baal, to the sun and moon, to the constellations and to all the starry hosts. [6]He took the Asherah pole from the temple of the LORD to the Kidron Valley outside Jerusalem and burned it there. He ground it to powder and scattered the dust over the graves of the common people. [7]He also tore down the quarters of the male shrine prostitutes that were in the temple of the LORD, the quarters where women did weaving for Asherah.

[8]Josiah brought all the priests from the towns of Judah and desecrated the high places, from Geba to Beersheba, where the priests had burned incense. He broke down the gateway at the entrance of the Gate of Joshua, the city governor, which was on the left of the city gate. [9]Although the priests of the high places did not serve at the altar of the LORD in Jerusalem, they ate unleavened bread with their fellow priests.

[10]He desecrated Topheth, which was in the Valley of Ben Hinnom, so no one could use it to sacrifice their son or daughter in the fire to Molek. [11]He removed from the entrance to the temple of the LORD the horses that the kings of Judah had dedicated to the sun. They were in the court[b] near the room of an official named Nathan-Melek. Josiah then burned the chariots dedicated to the sun.

[12]He pulled down the altars the kings of Judah had erected on the roof near the upper room of Ahaz, and the altars Manasseh had built in the two courts of the temple of the LORD. He removed them from there, smashed them to pieces and threw the rubble into the Kidron Valley. [13]The king also desecrated the high places that were east of Jerusalem on the south of the Hill of Corruption — the ones Solomon king of Israel had built for Ashtoreth the vile goddess of the Sidonians, for Chemosh the vile god of Moab, and for Molek the detestable god of the people of Ammon. [14]Josiah smashed the sacred stones and cut down the Asherah poles and covered the sites with human bones.

[15]Even the altar at Bethel, the high place made by Jeroboam son of Nebat, who had caused Israel to sin — even that altar and high place he demolished. He burned the high place and ground it to powder, and burned the Asherah pole also. [16]Then Josiah looked around, and when he saw the tombs that were there on the hillside, he had the bones removed from them and burned on the altar to defile it, in accordance with the word of the LORD proclaimed by the man of God who foretold these things.

[17]The king asked, "What is that tombstone I see?"

[a] *19* That is, their names would be used in cursing (see Jer. 29:22); or, others would see that they are cursed. [b] *11* The meaning of the Hebrew for this word is uncertain.

The people of the city said, “It marks the tomb of the man of God who came from Judah and pronounced against the altar of Bethel the very things you have done to it.”

18 “Leave it alone,” he said. “Don’t let anyone disturb his bones.” So they spared his bones and those of the prophet who had come from Samaria.

19 Just as he had done at Bethel, Josiah removed all the shrines at the high places that the kings of Israel had built in the towns of Samaria and that had aroused the LORD’s anger. 20 Josiah slaughtered all the priests of those high places on the altars and burned human bones on them. Then he went back to Jerusalem.

21 The king gave this order to all the people: “Celebrate the Passover to the LORD your God, as it is written in this Book of the Covenant.” 22 Neither in the days of the judges who led Israel nor in the days of the kings of Israel and the kings of Judah had any such Passover been observed. 23 But in the eighteenth year of King Josiah, this Passover was celebrated to the LORD in Jerusalem.

24 Furthermore, Josiah got rid of the mediums and spiritists, the household gods, the idols and all the other detestable things seen in Judah and Jerusalem. This he did to fulfill the requirements of the law written in the book that Hilkiah the priest had discovered in the temple of the LORD. 25 Neither before nor after Josiah was there a king like him who turned to the LORD as he did—with all his heart and with all his soul and with all his strength, in accordance with all the Law of Moses.

26 Nevertheless, the LORD did not turn away from the heat of his fierce anger, which burned against Judah because of all that Manasseh had done to arouse his anger. 27 So the LORD said, “I will remove Judah also from my presence as I removed Israel, and I will reject Jerusalem, the city I chose, and this temple, about which I said, ‘My Name shall be there.’[a]”

28 As for the other events of Josiah’s reign, and all he did, are they not written in the book of the annals of the kings of Judah?

29 While Josiah was king, Pharaoh Necho king of Egypt went up to the Euphrates River to help the king of Assyria. King Josiah marched out to meet him in battle, but Necho faced him and killed him at Megiddo. 30 Josiah’s servants brought his body in a chariot from Megiddo to Jerusalem and buried him in his own tomb. And the people of the land took Jehoahaz son of Josiah and anointed him and made him king in place of his father.

Jehoahaz King of Judah

31 Jehoahaz was twenty-three years old when he became king, and he reigned in Jerusalem three months. His mother’s name was Hamutal daughter of Jeremiah; she was from Libnah. 32 He did evil in the eyes of the LORD, just as his predecessors had done. 33 Pharaoh Necho put him in chains at Riblah in the land of Hamath so that he might not reign in Jerusalem, and he imposed on Judah a levy of a hundred talents[b] of silver and a talent[c] of gold. 34 Pharaoh Necho made Eliakim son of Josiah king in place of his father Josiah and changed Eliakim’s name to Jehoiakim. But he took Jehoahaz and carried him off to Egypt, and there he died. 35 Jehoiakim paid Pharaoh Necho the silver and gold he demanded. In order to do so, he taxed the land and exacted the silver and gold from the people of the land according to their assessments.

Jehoiakim King of Judah

36 Jehoiakim was twenty-five years old when he became king, and he reigned in Jerusalem eleven years. His mother’s name was Zebidah daughter of Pedaiah; she was from Rumah. 37 And he did evil in the eyes of the LORD, just as his predecessors had done.

24 During Jehoiakim’s reign, Nebuchadnezzar king of Babylon invaded the land, and Jehoiakim became his vassal for three years. But then he turned against Nebuchadnezzar and rebelled. 2 The LORD sent Babylonian,[d] Aramean, Moabite and Ammonite raiders against him to destroy Judah, in accordance with the word of the LORD proclaimed by his servants the prophets. 3 Surely these things happened to Judah according to the LORD’s command, in order to remove them from his presence because of the sins of Manasseh and all he had done, 4 including the shedding of innocent blood. For he had

[a] *27* 1 Kings 8:29 [b] *33* That is, about 3 3/4 tons or about 3.4 metric tons [c] *33* That is, about 75 pounds or about 34 kilograms [d] *2* Or *Chaldean*

filled Jerusalem with innocent blood, and
the LORD was not willing to forgive.
5As for the other events of Jehoiakim's
reign, and all he did, are they not written in
the book of the annals of the kings of Judah?
6Jehoiakim rested with his ancestors. And
Jehoiachin his son succeeded him as king.
7The king of Egypt did not march out from
his own country again, because the king of
Babylon had taken all his territory, from the
Wadi of Egypt to the Euphrates River.

Jehoiachin King of Judah

8Jehoiachin was eighteen years old when
he became king, and he reigned in Jerusalem three months. His mother's name was
Nehushta daughter of Elnathan; she was
from Jerusalem. 9He did evil in the eyes of
the LORD, just as his father had done.
10At that time the officers of Nebuchadnezzar king of Babylon advanced on Jerusalem and laid siege to it, 11and Nebuchadnezzar himself came up to the city while his
officers were besieging it. 12Jehoiachin king
of Judah, his mother, his attendants, his nobles and his officials all surrendered to him.

In the eighth year of the reign of the king
of Babylon, he took Jehoiachin prisoner. 13As
the LORD had declared, Nebuchadnezzar removed the treasures from the temple of the
LORD and from the royal palace, and cut up
the gold articles that Solomon king of Israel
had made for the temple of the LORD. 14He
carried all Jerusalem into exile: all the officers
and fighting men, and all the skilled workers
and artisans—a total of ten thousand. Only
the poorest people of the land were left.
15Nebuchadnezzar took Jehoiachin captive to Babylon. He also took from Jerusalem
to Babylon the king's mother, his wives, his
officials and the prominent people of the
land. 16The king of Babylon also deported to
Babylon the entire force of seven thousand
fighting men, strong and fit for war, and a
thousand skilled workers and artisans. 17He
made Mattaniah, Jehoiachin's uncle, king in
his place and changed his name to Zedekiah.

Zedekiah King of Judah

18Zedekiah was twenty-one years old
when he became king, and he reigned in
Jerusalem eleven years. His mother's name
was Hamutal daughter of Jeremiah; she was
from Libnah. 19He did evil in the eyes of the
LORD, just as Jehoiakim had done. 20It was
because of the LORD's anger that all this happened to Jerusalem and Judah, and in the
end he thrust them from his presence.

The Fall of Jerusalem

Now Zedekiah rebelled against the king
of Babylon.

25 So in the ninth year of Zedekiah's
reign, on the tenth day of the tenth
month, Nebuchadnezzar king of Babylon
marched against Jerusalem with his whole
army. He encamped outside the city and
built siege works all around it. 2The city was
kept under siege until the eleventh year of
King Zedekiah.
3By the ninth day of the fourth[a] month
the famine in the city had become so severe
that there was no food for the people to eat.
4Then the city wall was broken through, and
the whole army fled at night through the
gate between the two walls near the king's
garden, though the Babylonians[b] were surrounding the city. They fled toward the Arabah,[c] 5but the Babylonian[d] army pursued
the king and overtook him in the plains of
Jericho. All his soldiers were separated from
him and scattered, 6and he was captured.

He was taken to the king of Babylon at
Riblah, where sentence was pronounced
on him. 7They killed the sons of Zedekiah
before his eyes. Then they put out his eyes,
bound him with bronze shackles and took
him to Babylon.
8On the seventh day of the fifth month,
in the nineteenth year of Nebuchadnezzar
king of Babylon, Nebuzaradan commander
of the imperial guard, an official of the king
of Babylon, came to Jerusalem. 9He set fire to
the temple of the LORD, the royal palace and
all the houses of Jerusalem. Every important
building he burned down. 10The whole Babylonian army under the commander of the
imperial guard broke down the walls around
Jerusalem. 11Nebuzaradan the commander
of the guard carried into exile the people
who remained in the city, along with the rest
of the populace and those who had deserted

[a] 3 Probable reading of the original Hebrew text (see Jer. 52:6); Masoretic Text does not have *fourth*.
[b] 4 Or *Chaldeans*; also in verses 13, 25 and 26 [c] 4 Or *the Jordan Valley* [d] 5 Or *Chaldean*; also in verses 10 and 24

to the king of Babylon. [12]But the commander left behind some of the poorest people of the land to work the vineyards and fields.

[13]The Babylonians broke up the bronze pillars, the movable stands and the bronze Sea that were at the temple of the LORD and they carried the bronze to Babylon. [14]They also took away the pots, shovels, wick trimmers, dishes and all the bronze articles used in the temple service. [15]The commander of the imperial guard took away the censers and sprinkling bowls — all that were made of pure gold or silver.

[16]The bronze from the two pillars, the Sea and the movable stands, which Solomon had made for the temple of the LORD, was more than could be weighed. [17]Each pillar was eighteen cubits[a] high. The bronze capital on top of one pillar was three cubits[b] high and was decorated with a network and pomegranates of bronze all around. The other pillar, with its network, was similar.

[18]The commander of the guard took as prisoners Seraiah the chief priest, Zephaniah the priest next in rank and the three doorkeepers. [19]Of those still in the city, he took the officer in charge of the fighting men, and five royal advisers. He also took the secretary who was chief officer in charge of conscripting the people of the land and sixty of the conscripts who were found in the city. [20]Nebuzaradan the commander took them all and brought them to the king of Babylon at Riblah. [21]There at Riblah, in the land of Hamath, the king had them executed.

So Judah went into captivity, away from her land.

[22]Nebuchadnezzar king of Babylon appointed Gedaliah son of Ahikam, the son of Shaphan, to be over the people he had left behind in Judah. [23]When all the army officers and their men heard that the king of Babylon had appointed Gedaliah as governor, they came to Gedaliah at Mizpah — Ishmael son of Nethaniah, Johanan son of Kareah, Seraiah son of Tanhumeth the Netophathite, Jaazaniah the son of the Maakathite, and their men. [24]Gedaliah took an oath to reassure them and their men. "Do not be afraid of the Babylonian officials," he said. "Settle down in the land and serve the king of Babylon, and it will go well with you."

[25]In the seventh month, however, Ishmael son of Nethaniah, the son of Elishama, who was of royal blood, came with ten men and assassinated Gedaliah and also the men of Judah and the Babylonians who were with him at Mizpah. [26]At this, all the people from the least to the greatest, together with the army officers, fled to Egypt for fear of the Babylonians.

Jehoiachin Released

[27]In the thirty-seventh year of the exile of Jehoiachin king of Judah, in the year Awel-Marduk became king of Babylon, he released Jehoiachin king of Judah from prison. He did this on the twenty-seventh day of the twelfth month. [28]He spoke kindly to him and gave him a seat of honor higher than those of the other kings who were with him in Babylon. [29]So Jehoiachin put aside his prison clothes and for the rest of his life ate regularly at the king's table. [30]Day by day the king gave Jehoiachin a regular allowance as long as he lived.

[a] *17* That is, about 27 feet or about 8.1 meters [b] *17* That is, about 4 1/2 feet or about 1.4 meters

1 CHRONICLES

Historical Records From Adam to Abraham

To Noah's Sons

1 Adam, Seth, Enosh, 2 Kenan, Mahalalel, Jared, 3 Enoch, Methuselah, Lamech, Noah.

4 The sons of Noah:[a]
Shem, Ham and Japheth.

The Japhethites

5 The sons[b] of Japheth:
Gomer, Magog, Madai, Javan, Tubal, Meshek and Tiras.
6 The sons of Gomer:
Ashkenaz, Riphath[c] and Togarmah.
7 The sons of Javan:
Elishah, Tarshish, the Kittites and the Rodanites.

The Hamites

8 The sons of Ham:
Cush, Egypt, Put and Canaan.
9 The sons of Cush:
Seba, Havilah, Sabta, Raamah and Sabteka.
The sons of Raamah:
Sheba and Dedan.
10 Cush was the father[d] of
Nimrod, who became a mighty warrior on earth.
11 Egypt was the father of
the Ludites, Anamites, Lehabites, Naphtuhites, 12 Pathrusites, Kasluhites (from whom the Philistines came) and Caphtorites.
13 Canaan was the father of
Sidon his firstborn,[e] and of the Hittites, 14 Jebusites, Amorites, Girgashites, 15 Hivites, Arkites, Sinites, 16 Arvadites, Zemarites and Hamathites.

The Semites

17 The sons of Shem:
Elam, Ashur, Arphaxad, Lud and Aram.
The sons of Aram:[f]
Uz, Hul, Gether and Meshek.
18 Arphaxad was the father of Shelah,
and Shelah the father of Eber.
19 Two sons were born to Eber:
One was named Peleg,[g] because in his time the earth was divided; his brother was named Joktan.
20 Joktan was the father of
Almodad, Sheleph, Hazarmaveth, Jerah, 21 Hadoram, Uzal, Diklah, 22 Obal,[h] Abimael, Sheba, 23 Ophir, Havilah and Jobab. All these were sons of Joktan.

24 Shem, Arphaxad,[i] Shelah,
25 Eber, Peleg, Reu,
26 Serug, Nahor, Terah
27 and Abram (that is, Abraham).

The Family of Abraham

28 The sons of Abraham:
Isaac and Ishmael.

Descendants of Hagar

29 These were their descendants:
Nebaioth the firstborn of Ishmael, Kedar, Adbeel, Mibsam, 30 Mishma, Dumah, Massa, Hadad, Tema, 31 Jetur, Naphish and Kedemah. These were the sons of Ishmael.

[a] 4 Septuagint; Hebrew does not have this line. [b] 5 *Sons* may mean *descendants* or *successors* or *nations*; also in verses 6-9, 17 and 23. [c] 6 Many Hebrew manuscripts and Vulgate (see also Septuagint and Gen. 10:3); most Hebrew manuscripts *Diphath* [d] 10 *Father* may mean *ancestor* or *predecessor* or *founder*; also in verses 11, 13, 18 and 20. [e] 13 Or *of the Sidonians, the foremost* [f] 17 One Hebrew manuscript and some Septuagint manuscripts (see also Gen. 10:23); most Hebrew manuscripts do not have this line. [g] 19 *Peleg* means *division.* [h] 22 Some Hebrew manuscripts and Syriac (see also Gen. 10:28); most Hebrew manuscripts *Ebal* [i] 24 Hebrew; some Septuagint manuscripts *Arphaxad, Cainan* (see also note at Gen. 11:10)

Descendants of Keturah

[32]The sons born to Keturah, Abraham's concubine:
Zimran, Jokshan, Medan, Midian, Ishbak and Shuah.
The sons of Jokshan:
Sheba and Dedan.
[33]The sons of Midian:
Ephah, Epher, Hanok, Abida and Eldaah.
All these were descendants of Keturah.

Descendants of Sarah

[34]Abraham was the father of Isaac.
The sons of Isaac:
Esau and Israel.

Esau's Sons

[35]The sons of Esau:
Eliphaz, Reuel, Jeush, Jalam and Korah.
[36]The sons of Eliphaz:
Teman, Omar, Zepho,[a] Gatam and Kenaz;
by Timna: Amalek.[b]
[37]The sons of Reuel:
Nahath, Zerah, Shammah and Mizzah.

The People of Seir in Edom

[38]The sons of Seir:
Lotan, Shobal, Zibeon, Anah, Dishon, Ezer and Dishan.
[39]The sons of Lotan:
Hori and Homam. Timna was Lotan's sister.
[40]The sons of Shobal:
Alvan,[c] Manahath, Ebal, Shepho and Onam.
The sons of Zibeon:
Aiah and Anah.
[41]The son of Anah:
Dishon.
The sons of Dishon:
Hemdan,[d] Eshban, Ithran and Keran.
[42]The sons of Ezer:
Bilhan, Zaavan and Akan.[e]
The sons of Dishan[f]:
Uz and Aran.

The Rulers of Edom

[43]These were the kings who reigned in Edom before any Israelite king reigned:
Bela son of Beor, whose city was named Dinhabah.
[44]When Bela died, Jobab son of Zerah from Bozrah succeeded him as king.
[45]When Jobab died, Husham from the land of the Temanites succeeded him as king.
[46]When Husham died, Hadad son of Bedad, who defeated Midian in the country of Moab, succeeded him as king. His city was named Avith.
[47]When Hadad died, Samlah from Masrekah succeeded him as king.
[48]When Samlah died, Shaul from Rehoboth on the river[g] succeeded him as king.
[49]When Shaul died, Baal-Hanan son of Akbor succeeded him as king.
[50]When Baal-Hanan died, Hadad succeeded him as king. His city was named Pau,[h] and his wife's name was Mehetabel daughter of Matred, the daughter of Me-Zahab. [51]Hadad also died.

The chiefs of Edom were:
Timna, Alvah, Jetheth, [52]Oholibamah, Elah, Pinon, [53]Kenaz, Teman, Mibzar, [54]Magdiel and Iram. These were the chiefs of Edom.

Israel's Sons

2 These were the sons of Israel:
Reuben, Simeon, Levi, Judah, Issachar, Zebulun, [2]Dan, Joseph, Benjamin, Naphtali, Gad and Asher.

Judah

To Hezron's Sons

[3]The sons of Judah:
Er, Onan and Shelah. These three

[a] *36* Many Hebrew manuscripts, some Septuagint manuscripts and Syriac (see also Gen. 36:11); most Hebrew manuscripts *Zephi* [b] *36* Some Septuagint manuscripts (see also Gen. 36:12); Hebrew *Gatam, Kenaz, Timna and Amalek* [c] *40* Many Hebrew manuscripts and some Septuagint manuscripts (see also Gen. 36:23); most Hebrew manuscripts *Alian* [d] *41* Many Hebrew manuscripts and some Septuagint manuscripts (see also Gen. 36:26); most Hebrew manuscripts *Hamran* [e] *42* Many Hebrew and Septuagint manuscripts (see also Gen. 36:27); most Hebrew manuscripts *Zaavan, Jaakan* [f] *42* See Gen. 36:28; Hebrew *Dishon,* a variant of *Dishan* [g] *48* Possibly the Euphrates [h] *50* Many Hebrew manuscripts, some Septuagint manuscripts, Vulgate and Syriac (see also Gen. 36:39); most Hebrew manuscripts *Pai*

were born to him by a Canaanite
woman, the daughter of Shua. Er,
Judah's firstborn, was wicked in the
LORD's sight; so the LORD put him to
death. [4]Judah's daughter-in-law Ta-
mar bore Perez and Zerah to Judah.
He had five sons in all.

[5]The sons of Perez:
Hezron and Hamul.
[6]The sons of Zerah:
Zimri, Ethan, Heman, Kalkol and
Darda[a]—five in all.
[7]The son of Karmi:
Achar,[b] who brought trouble on Isra-
el by violating the ban on taking de-
voted things.[c]
[8]The son of Ethan:
Azariah.
[9]The sons born to Hezron were:
Jerahmeel, Ram and Caleb.[d]

From Ram Son of Hezron

[10]Ram was the father of
Amminadab, and Amminadab the
father of Nahshon, the leader of the
people of Judah. [11]Nahshon was
the father of Salmon,[e] Salmon the
father of Boaz, [12]Boaz the father of
Obed and Obed the father of Jesse.
[13]Jesse was the father of
Eliab his firstborn; the second son
was Abinadab, the third Shim-
ea, [14]the fourth Nethanel, the fifth
Raddai, [15]the sixth Ozem and the
seventh David. [16]Their sisters were
Zeruiah and Abigail. Zeruiah's three
sons were Abishai, Joab and Asahel.
[17]Abigail was the mother of Amasa,
whose father was Jether the Ishma-
elite.

Caleb Son of Hezron

[18]Caleb son of Hezron had children by
his wife Azubah (and by Jerioth).
These were her sons: Jesher, Shobab
and Ardon. [19]When Azubah died,
Caleb married Ephrath, who bore
him Hur. [20]Hur was the father of Uri,
and Uri the father of Bezalel.
[21]Later, Hezron, when he was sixty years
old, married the daughter of Ma-
kir the father of Gilead. He made
love to her, and she bore him Se-
gub. [22]Segub was the father of Jair,
who controlled twenty-three towns
in Gilead. [23](But Geshur and Aram
captured Havvoth Jair,[f] as well as
Kenath with its surrounding settle-
ments—sixty towns.) All these were
descendants of Makir the father of
Gilead.

[24]After Hezron died in Caleb Ephrathah,
Abijah the wife of Hezron bore him
Ashhur the father[g] of Tekoa.

Jerahmeel Son of Hezron

[25]The sons of Jerahmeel the firstborn of
Hezron:
Ram his firstborn, Bunah, Oren,
Ozem and[h] Ahijah. [26]Jerahmeel had
another wife, whose name was Ata-
rah; she was the mother of Onam.
[27]The sons of Ram the firstborn of Jerah-
meel:
Maaz, Jamin and Eker.
[28]The sons of Onam:
Shammai and Jada.
The sons of Shammai:
Nadab and Abishur.
[29]Abishur's wife was named Abihail, who
bore him Ahban and Molid.
[30]The sons of Nadab:
Seled and Appaim. Seled died with-
out children.
[31]The son of Appaim:
Ishi, who was the father of Sheshan.
Sheshan was the father of Ahlai.
[32]The sons of Jada, Shammai's brother:
Jether and Jonathan. Jether died
without children.
[33]The sons of Jonathan:
Peleth and Zaza.
These were the descendants of Jerah-
meel.

[a] *6* Many Hebrew manuscripts, some Septuagint manuscripts and Syriac (see also 1 Kings 4:31); most Hebrew manuscripts *Dara* [b] *7* *Achar* means *trouble*; *Achar* is called *Achan* in Joshua.
[c] *7* The Hebrew term refers to the irrevocable giving over of things or persons to the LORD, often by totally destroying them. [d] *9* Hebrew *Kelubai*, a variant of *Caleb* [e] *11* Septuagint (see also Ruth 4:21); Hebrew *Salma* [f] *23* Or *captured the settlements of Jair* [g] *24* *Father* may mean *civic leader* or *military leader*; also in verses 42, 45, 49-52 and possibly elsewhere. [h] *25* Or *Oren and Ozem, by*

34 Sheshan had no sons — only daughters.
He had an Egyptian servant named
Jarha. 35 Sheshan gave his daughter
in marriage to his servant Jarha, and
she bore him Attai.
36 Attai was the father of Nathan,
Nathan the father of Zabad,
37 Zabad the father of Ephlal,
Ephlal the father of Obed,
38 Obed the father of Jehu,
Jehu the father of Azariah,
39 Azariah the father of Helez,
Helez the father of Eleasah,
40 Eleasah the father of Sismai,
Sismai the father of Shallum,
41 Shallum the father of Jekamiah,
and Jekamiah the father of Elishama.

The Clans of Caleb

42 The sons of Caleb the brother of Jerahmeel:
Mesha his firstborn, who was the father of Ziph, and his son Mareshah,[a]
who was the father of Hebron.
43 The sons of Hebron:
Korah, Tappuah, Rekem and Shema.
44 Shema was the father of Raham,
and Raham the father of Jorkeam.
Rekem was the father of Shammai.
45 The son of Shammai was Maon,
and Maon was the father of Beth Zur.
46 Caleb's concubine Ephah was the
mother of Haran, Moza and Gazez.
Haran was the father of Gazez.
47 The sons of Jahdai:
Regem, Jotham, Geshan, Pelet,
Ephah and Shaaph.
48 Caleb's concubine Maakah was the
mother of Sheber and Tirhanah.
49 She also gave birth to Shaaph the
father of Madmannah and to Sheva
the father of Makbenah and Gibea.
Caleb's daughter was Aksah. 50 These
were the descendants of Caleb.

The sons of Hur the firstborn of Ephrathah:
Shobal the father of Kiriath Jearim,
51 Salma the father of Bethlehem,
and Hareph the father of Beth Gader.
52 The descendants of Shobal the father of
Kiriath Jearim were:
Haroeh, half the Manahathites,
53 and the clans of Kiriath Jearim: the
Ithrites, Puthites, Shumathites and
Mishraites. From these descended
the Zorathites and Eshtaolites.
54 The descendants of Salma:
Bethlehem, the Netophathites, Atroth Beth Joab, half the Manahathites, the Zorites, 55 and the clans of
scribes[b] who lived at Jabez: the Tirathites, Shimeathites and Sucathites. These are the Kenites who came from Hammath, the father of the Rekabites.[c]

The Sons of David

3 These were the sons of David born to him in Hebron:
The firstborn was Amnon the son of Ahinoam of Jezreel;
the second, Daniel the son of Abigail of Carmel;
2 the third, Absalom the son of Maakah daughter of Talmai king of Geshur;
the fourth, Adonijah the son of Haggith;
3 the fifth, Shephatiah the son of Abital;
and the sixth, Ithream, by his wife Eglah.
4 These six were born to David in Hebron, where he reigned seven years and six months.
David reigned in Jerusalem thirty-three
years, 5 and these were the children born to
him there:
Shammua,[d] Shobab, Nathan and
Solomon. These four were by Bathsheba[e] daughter of Ammiel. 6 There
were also Ibhar, Elishua,[f] Eliphelet,
7 Nogah, Nepheg, Japhia, 8 Elishama, Eliada and Eliphelet — nine in
all. 9 All these were the sons of David,
besides his sons by his concubines.
And Tamar was their sister.

The Kings of Judah

10 Solomon's son was Rehoboam,
Abijah his son,

[a] *42* The meaning of the Hebrew for this phrase is uncertain. [b] *55* Or *of the Sopherites* [c] *55* Or *father of Beth Rekab* [d] *5* Hebrew *Shimea*, a variant of *Shammua* [e] *5* One Hebrew manuscript and Vulgate (see also Septuagint and 2 Samuel 11:3); most Hebrew manuscripts *Bathshua* [f] *6* Two Hebrew manuscripts (see also 2 Samuel 5:15 and 1 Chron. 14:5); most Hebrew manuscripts *Elishama*

Asa his son,
Jehoshaphat his son,
[11] Jehoram[a] his son,
Ahaziah his son,
Joash his son,
[12] Amaziah his son,
Azariah his son,
Jotham his son,
[13] Ahaz his son,
Hezekiah his son,
Manasseh his son,
[14] Amon his son,
Josiah his son.

[15] The sons of Josiah:
Johanan the firstborn,
Jehoiakim the second son,
Zedekiah the third,
Shallum the fourth.

[16] The successors of Jehoiakim:
Jehoiachin[b] his son,
and Zedekiah.

The Royal Line After the Exile

[17] The descendants of Jehoiachin the captive:
Shealtiel his son, [18] Malkiram, Pedaiah, Shenazzar, Jekamiah, Hoshama and Nedabiah.

[19] The sons of Pedaiah:
Zerubbabel and Shimei.
The sons of Zerubbabel:
Meshullam and Hananiah.
Shelomith was their sister.
[20] There were also five others:
Hashubah, Ohel, Berekiah, Hasadiah and Jushab-Hesed.

[21] The descendants of Hananiah:
Pelatiah and Jeshaiah, and the sons of Rephaiah, of Arnan, of Obadiah and of Shekaniah.

[22] The descendants of Shekaniah:
Shemaiah and his sons:
Hattush, Igal, Bariah, Neariah and Shaphat — six in all.

[23] The sons of Neariah:
Elioenai, Hizkiah and Azrikam — three in all.

[24] The sons of Elioenai:
Hodaviah, Eliashib, Pelaiah, Akkub, Johanan, Delaiah and Anani — seven in all.

Other Clans of Judah

4 The descendants of Judah:
Perez, Hezron, Karmi, Hur and Shobal.

[2] Reaiah son of Shobal was the father of Jahath, and Jahath the father of Ahumai and Lahad. These were the clans of the Zorathites.

[3] These were the sons[c] of Etam:
Jezreel, Ishma and Idbash. Their sister was named Hazzelelponi. [4] Penuel was the father of Gedor, and Ezer the father of Hushah.
These were the descendants of Hur, the firstborn of Ephrathah and father[d] of Bethlehem.

[5] Ashhur the father of Tekoa had two wives, Helah and Naarah.

[6] Naarah bore him Ahuzzam, Hepher, Temeni and Haahashtari. These were the descendants of Naarah.

[7] The sons of Helah:
Zereth, Zohar, Ethnan, [8] and Koz, who was the father of Anub and Hazzobebah and of the clans of Aharhel son of Harum.

[9] Jabez was more honorable than his
brothers. His mother had named him Jabez,[e]
saying, "I gave birth to him in pain." [10] Jabez
cried out to the God of Israel, "Oh, that you
would bless me and enlarge my territory! Let
your hand be with me, and keep me from
harm so that I will be free from pain." And
God granted his request.

[11] Kelub, Shuhah's brother, was the father of Mehir, who was the father of Eshton. [12] Eshton was the father of Beth Rapha, Paseah and Tehinnah the father of Ir Nahash.[f] These were the men of Rekah.

[13] The sons of Kenaz:
Othniel and Seraiah.
The sons of Othniel:
Hathath and Meonothai.[g] [14] Meonothai was the father of Ophrah.

[a] *11* Hebrew *Joram,* a variant of *Jehoram* [b] *16* Hebrew *Jeconiah,* a variant of *Jehoiachin;* also in verse 17 [c] *3* Some Septuagint manuscripts (see also Vulgate); Hebrew *father* [d] *4* *Father* may mean *civic leader* or *military leader;* also in verses 12, 14, 17, 18 and possibly elsewhere. [e] *9* *Jabez* sounds like the Hebrew for *pain.* [f] *12* Or *of the city of Nahash* [g] *13* Some Septuagint manuscripts and Vulgate; Hebrew does not have *and Meonothai.*

Seraiah was the father of Joab,
the father of Ge Harashim.[a] It was
called this because its people were
skilled workers.

15 The sons of Caleb son of Jephunneh:
Iru, Elah and Naam.
The son of Elah:
Kenaz.

16 The sons of Jehallelel:
Ziph, Ziphah, Tiria and Asarel.

17 The sons of Ezrah:
Jether, Mered, Epher and Jalon. One
of Mered's wives gave birth to Miri-
am, Shammai and Ishbah the father
of Eshtemoa. 18 (His wife from the
tribe of Judah gave birth to Jered the
father of Gedor, Heber the father of
Soko, and Jekuthiel the father of Za-
noah.) These were the children of
Pharaoh's daughter Bithiah, whom
Mered had married.

19 The sons of Hodiah's wife, the sister of
Naham:
the father of Keilah the Garmite, and
Eshtemoa the Maakathite.

20 The sons of Shimon:
Amnon, Rinnah, Ben-Hanan and Ti-
lon.
The descendants of Ishi:
Zoheth and Ben-Zoheth.

21 The sons of Shelah son of Judah:
Er the father of Lekah, Laadah the fa-
ther of Mareshah and the clans of the
linen workers at Beth Ashbea, 22 Jo-
kim, the men of Kozeba, and Joash
and Saraph, who ruled in Moab and
Jashubi Lehem. (These records are
from ancient times.) 23 They were the
potters who lived at Netaim and Ge-
derah; they stayed there and worked
for the king.

Simeon

24 The descendants of Simeon:
Nemuel, Jamin, Jarib, Zerah and
Shaul;
25 Shallum was Shaul's son, Mibsam
his son and Mishma his son.

26 The descendants of Mishma:
Hammuel his son, Zakkur his son
and Shimei his son.

27 Shimei had sixteen sons and six daugh-
ters, but his brothers did not have many chil-
dren; so their entire clan did not become as
numerous as the people of Judah. 28 They
lived in Beersheba, Moladah, Hazar Shual,
29 Bilhah, Ezem, Tolad, 30 Bethuel, Hormah,
Ziklag, 31 Beth Markaboth, Hazar Susim,
Beth Biri and Shaaraim. These were their
towns until the reign of David. 32 Their sur-
rounding villages were Etam, Ain, Rimmon,
Token and Ashan — five towns — 33 and all
the villages around these towns as far as Ba-
alath.[b] These were their settlements. And
they kept a genealogical record.

34 Meshobab, Jamlech, Joshah son of
Amaziah, 35 Joel, Jehu son of Joshibi-
ah, the son of Seraiah, the son of Asiel,
36 also Elioenai, Jaakobah, Jeshohaiah,
Asaiah, Adiel, Jesimiel, Benaiah, 37 and
Ziza son of Shiphi, the son of Allon, the
son of Jedaiah, the son of Shimri, the
son of Shemaiah.

38 The men listed above by name were
leaders of their clans. Their families in-
creased greatly, 39 and they went to the out-
skirts of Gedor to the east of the valley in
search of pasture for their flocks. 40 They
found rich, good pasture, and the land was
spacious, peaceful and quiet. Some Hamites
had lived there formerly.

41 The men whose names were listed came
in the days of Hezekiah king of Judah. They
attacked the Hamites in their dwellings
and also the Meunites who were there and
completely destroyed[c] them, as is evident
to this day. Then they settled in their place,
because there was pasture for their flocks.
42 And five hundred of these Simeonites, led
by Pelatiah, Neariah, Rephaiah and Uzziel,
the sons of Ishi, invaded the hill country of
Seir. 43 They killed the remaining Amalekites
who had escaped, and they have lived there
to this day.

Reuben

5 The sons of Reuben the firstborn of Is-
rael (he was the firstborn, but when he
defiled his father's marriage bed, his rights
as firstborn were given to the sons of Joseph

[a] *14* *Ge Harashim* means *valley of skilled workers.* [b] *33* Some Septuagint manuscripts (see also Joshua 19:8); Hebrew *Baal* [c] *41* The Hebrew term refers to the irrevocable giving over of things or persons to the LORD, often by totally destroying them.

son of Israel; so he could not be listed in the genealogical record in accordance with his birthright, 2 and though Judah was the strongest of his brothers and a ruler came from him, the rights of the firstborn belonged to Joseph) — 3 the sons of Reuben the firstborn of Israel:

Hanok, Pallu, Hezron and Karmi.

4 The descendants of Joel:

Shemaiah his son, Gog his son,
Shimei his son, 5 Micah his son,
Reaiah his son, Baal his son,
6 and Beerah his son, whom Tiglath-Pileser[a] king of Assyria took into exile. Beerah was a leader of the Reubenites.

7 Their relatives by clans, listed according to their genealogical records:

Jeiel the chief, Zechariah, 8 and Bela son of Azaz, the son of Shema, the son of Joel. They settled in the area from Aroer to Nebo and Baal Meon. 9 To the east they occupied the land up to the edge of the desert that extends to the Euphrates River, because their livestock had increased in Gilead.

10 During Saul's reign they waged war against the Hagrites, who were defeated at their hands; they occupied the dwellings of the Hagrites throughout the entire region east of Gilead.

Gad

11 The Gadites lived next to them in Bashan, as far as Salekah:

12 Joel was the chief, Shapham the second, then Janai and Shaphat, in Bashan.

13 Their relatives, by families, were:

Michael, Meshullam, Sheba, Jorai, Jakan, Zia and Eber — seven in all.

14 These were the sons of Abihail son of Huri, the son of Jaroah, the son of Gilead, the son of Michael, the son of Jeshishai, the son of Jahdo, the son of Buz.

15 Ahi son of Abdiel, the son of Guni, was head of their family.

16 The Gadites lived in Gilead, in Bashan and its outlying villages, and on all the pasturelands of Sharon as far as they extended.

17 All these were entered in the genealogical records during the reigns of Jotham king of Judah and Jeroboam king of Israel.

18 The Reubenites, the Gadites and the half-tribe of Manasseh had 44,760 men ready for military service — able-bodied men who could handle shield and sword, who could use a bow, and who were trained for battle. 19 They waged war against the Hagrites, Jetur, Naphish and Nodab. 20 They were helped in fighting them, and God delivered the Hagrites and all their allies into their hands, because they cried out to him during the battle. He answered their prayers, because they trusted in him. 21 They seized the livestock of the Hagrites — fifty thousand camels, two hundred fifty thousand sheep and two thousand donkeys. They also took one hundred thousand people captive, 22 and many others fell slain, because the battle was God's. And they occupied the land until the exile.

The Half-Tribe of Manasseh

23 The people of the half-tribe of Manasseh were numerous; they settled in the land from Bashan to Baal Hermon, that is, to Senir (Mount Hermon).

24 These were the heads of their families: Epher, Ishi, Eliel, Azriel, Jeremiah, Hodaviah and Jahdiel. They were brave warriors, famous men, and heads of their families. 25 But they were unfaithful to the God of their ancestors and prostituted themselves to the gods of the peoples of the land, whom God had destroyed before them. 26 So the God of Israel stirred up the spirit of Pul king of Assyria (that is, Tiglath-Pileser king of Assyria), who took the Reubenites, the Gadites and the half-tribe of Manasseh into exile. He took them to Halah, Habor, Hara and the river of Gozan, where they are to this day.

Levi

6 [b] The sons of Levi:

Gershon, Kohath and Merari.

2 The sons of Kohath:

Amram, Izhar, Hebron and Uzziel.

3 The children of Amram:

Aaron, Moses and Miriam.

[a] 6 Hebrew *Tilgath-Pilneser,* a variant of *Tiglath-Pileser*; also in verse 26 [b] In Hebrew texts 6:1-15 is numbered 5:27-41, and 6:16-81 is numbered 6:1-66.

The sons of Aaron:
Nadab, Abihu, Eleazar and Ithamar.
4 Eleazar was the father of Phinehas,
Phinehas the father of Abishua,
5 Abishua the father of Bukki,
Bukki the father of Uzzi,
6 Uzzi the father of Zerahiah,
Zerahiah the father of Meraioth,
7 Meraioth the father of Amariah,
Amariah the father of Ahitub,
8 Ahitub the father of Zadok,
Zadok the father of Ahimaaz,
9 Ahimaaz the father of Azariah,
Azariah the father of Johanan,
10 Johanan the father of Azariah (it was he who served as priest in the temple Solomon built in Jerusalem),
11 Azariah the father of Amariah,
Amariah the father of Ahitub,
12 Ahitub the father of Zadok,
Zadok the father of Shallum,
13 Shallum the father of Hilkiah,
Hilkiah the father of Azariah,
14 Azariah the father of Seraiah,
and Seraiah the father of Jozadak.[a]
15 Jozadak was deported when the LORD sent Judah and Jerusalem into exile by the hand of Nebuchadnezzar.

16 The sons of Levi:
Gershon,[b] Kohath and Merari.
17 These are the names of the sons of Gershon:
Libni and Shimei.
18 The sons of Kohath:
Amram, Izhar, Hebron and Uzziel.
19 The sons of Merari:
Mahli and Mushi.
These are the clans of the Levites listed according to their fathers:
20 Of Gershon:
Libni his son, Jahath his son,
Zimmah his son, 21 Joah his son,
Iddo his son, Zerah his son
and Jeatherai his son.
22 The descendants of Kohath:
Amminadab his son, Korah his son,
Assir his son, 23 Elkanah his son,
Ebiasaph his son, Assir his son,
24 Tahath his son, Uriel his son,
Uzziah his son and Shaul his son.
25 The descendants of Elkanah:
Amasai, Ahimoth,
26 Elkanah his son,[c] Zophai his son,
Nahath his son, 27 Eliab his son,
Jeroham his son, Elkanah his son
and Samuel his son.[d]
28 The sons of Samuel:
Joel[e] the firstborn
and Abijah the second son.
29 The descendants of Merari:
Mahli, Libni his son,
Shimei his son, Uzzah his son,
30 Shimea his son, Haggiah his son
and Asaiah his son.

The Temple Musicians

31 These are the men David put in charge of the music in the house of the LORD after the ark came to rest there. 32 They ministered with music before the tabernacle, the tent of meeting, until Solomon built the temple of the LORD in Jerusalem. They performed their duties according to the regulations laid down for them.

33 Here are the men who served, together with their sons:
From the Kohathites:
Heman, the musician,
the son of Joel, the son of Samuel,
34 the son of Elkanah, the son of Jeroham,
the son of Eliel, the son of Toah,
35 the son of Zuph, the son of Elkanah,
the son of Mahath, the son of Amasai,
36 the son of Elkanah, the son of Joel,
the son of Azariah, the son of Zephaniah,
37 the son of Tahath, the son of Assir,
the son of Ebiasaph, the son of Korah,
38 the son of Izhar, the son of Kohath,
the son of Levi, the son of Israel;
39 and Heman's associate Asaph, who served at his right hand:
Asaph son of Berekiah, the son of Shimea,
40 the son of Michael, the son of Baaseiah,[f]

[a] *14* Hebrew *Jehozadak*, a variant of *Jozadak*; also in verse 15 [b] *16* Hebrew *Gershom*, a variant of *Gershon*; also in verses 17, 20, 43, 62 and 71 [c] *26* Some Hebrew manuscripts, Septuagint and Syriac; most Hebrew manuscripts *Ahimoth* [26] *and Elkanah. The sons of Elkanah:* [d] *27* Some Septuagint manuscripts (see also 1 Samuel 1:19,20 and 1 Chron. 6:33,34); Hebrew does not have *and Samuel his son.* [e] *28* Some Septuagint manuscripts and Syriac (see also 1 Samuel 8:2 and 1 Chron. 6:33); Hebrew does not have *Joel.* [f] *40* Most Hebrew manuscripts; some Hebrew manuscripts, one Septuagint manuscript and Syriac *Maaseiah*

the son of Malkijah, [41]the son of Ethni,
the son of Zerah, the son of Adaiah,
[42]the son of Ethan, the son of Zimmah,
the son of Shimei, [43]the son of Jahath,
the son of Gershon, the son of Levi;
[44]and from their associates, the Merarites, at his left hand:
Ethan son of Kishi, the son of Abdi,
the son of Malluk, [45]the son of Hashabiah,
the son of Amaziah, the son of Hilkiah,
[46]the son of Amzi, the son of Bani,
the son of Shemer, [47]the son of Mahli,
the son of Mushi, the son of Merari,
the son of Levi.

[48]Their fellow Levites were assigned to all
the other duties of the tabernacle, the house
of God. [49]But Aaron and his descendants
were the ones who presented offerings on
the altar of burnt offering and on the altar of
incense in connection with all that was done
in the Most Holy Place, making atonement
for Israel, in accordance with all that Moses
the servant of God had commanded.

[50]These were the descendants of Aaron:
Eleazar his son, Phinehas his son,
Abishua his son, [51]Bukki his son,
Uzzi his son, Zerahiah his son,
[52]Meraioth his son, Amariah his son,
Ahitub his son, [53]Zadok his son
and Ahimaaz his son.

[54]These were the locations of their settlements allotted as their territory (they were assigned to the descendants of Aaron who were from the Kohathite clan, because the first lot was for them):

[55]They were given Hebron in Judah
with its surrounding pasturelands.
[56]But the fields and villages around the
city were given to Caleb son of Jephunneh.
[57]So the descendants of Aaron were
given Hebron (a city of refuge), and Libnah,[a] Jattir, Eshtemoa, [58]Hilen, Debir,
[59]Ashan, Juttah[b] and Beth Shemesh,
together with their pasturelands.
[60]And from the tribe of Benjamin they
were given Gibeon,[c] Geba, Alemeth
and Anathoth, together with their pasturelands.

The total number of towns distributed among the Kohathite clans came to thirteen.

[61]The rest of Kohath's descendants were
allotted ten towns from the clans of half the
tribe of Manasseh.

[62]The descendants of Gershon, clan by
clan, were allotted thirteen towns from the
tribes of Issachar, Asher and Naphtali, and
from the part of the tribe of Manasseh that
is in Bashan.

[63]The descendants of Merari, clan by
clan, were allotted twelve towns from the
tribes of Reuben, Gad and Zebulun.

[64]So the Israelites gave the Levites these
towns and their pasturelands. [65]From the
tribes of Judah, Simeon and Benjamin they
allotted the previously named towns.

[66]Some of the Kohathite clans were given as their territory towns from the tribe of
Ephraim.

[67]In the hill country of Ephraim they
were given Shechem (a city of refuge),
and Gezer,[d] [68]Jokmeam, Beth Horon,
[69]Aijalon and Gath Rimmon, together
with their pasturelands.

[70]And from half the tribe of Manasseh the Israelites gave Aner and Bileam, together with their pasturelands,
to the rest of the Kohathite clans.

[71]The Gershonites received the following:
From the clan of the half-tribe of Manasseh
they received Golan in Bashan and
also Ashtaroth, together with their
pasturelands;
[72]from the tribe of Issachar
they received Kedesh, Daberath,
[73]Ramoth and Anem, together with
their pasturelands;
[74]from the tribe of Asher
they received Mashal, Abdon, [75]Hukok and Rehob, together with their
pasturelands;
[76]and from the tribe of Naphtali
they received Kedesh in Galilee,
Hammon and Kiriathaim, together
with their pasturelands.

[a] 57 See Joshua 21:13; Hebrew *given the cities of refuge: Hebron, Libnah.* [b] 59 Syriac (see also Septuagint and Joshua 21:16); Hebrew does not have *Juttah.* [c] 60 See Joshua 21:17; Hebrew does not have *Gibeon.* [d] 67 See Joshua 21:21; Hebrew *given the cities of refuge: Shechem, Gezer.*

77 The Merarites (the rest of the Levites) received the following:
From the tribe of Zebulun
they received Jokneam, Kartah,[a] Rimmono and Tabor, together with their pasturelands;
78 from the tribe of Reuben across the Jordan east of Jericho
they received Bezer in the wilderness, Jahzah,
79 Kedemoth and Mephaath, together with their pasturelands;
80 and from the tribe of Gad
they received Ramoth in Gilead, Mahanaim,
81 Heshbon and Jazer, together with their pasturelands.

Issachar

7 The sons of Issachar:
Tola, Puah, Jashub and Shimron — four in all.
2 The sons of Tola:
Uzzi, Rephaiah, Jeriel, Jahmai, Ibsam and Samuel — heads of their families. During the reign of David, the descendants of Tola listed as fighting men in their genealogy numbered 22,600.
3 The son of Uzzi:
Izrahiah.
The sons of Izrahiah:
Michael, Obadiah, Joel and Ishiah. All five of them were chiefs.
4 According to their family genealogy, they had 36,000 men ready for battle, for they had many wives and children.
5 The relatives who were fighting men belonging to all the clans of Issachar, as listed in their genealogy, were 87,000 in all.

Benjamin

6 Three sons of Benjamin:
Bela, Beker and Jediael.
7 The sons of Bela:
Ezbon, Uzzi, Uzziel, Jerimoth and Iri, heads of families — five in all. Their genealogical record listed 22,034 fighting men.
8 The sons of Beker:
Zemirah, Joash, Eliezer, Elioenai, Omri, Jeremoth, Abijah, Anathoth and Alemeth. All these were the sons of Beker.
9 Their genealogical record listed the heads of families and 20,200 fighting men.
10 The son of Jediael:
Bilhan.
The sons of Bilhan:
Jeush, Benjamin, Ehud, Kenaanah, Zethan, Tarshish and Ahishahar.
11 All these sons of Jediael were heads of families. There were 17,200 fighting men ready to go out to war.
12 The Shuppites and Huppites were the descendants of Ir, and the Hushites[b] the descendants of Aher.

Naphtali

13 The sons of Naphtali:
Jahziel, Guni, Jezer and Shillem[c] — the descendants of Bilhah.

Manasseh

14 The descendants of Manasseh:
Asriel was his descendant through his Aramean concubine. She gave birth to Makir the father of Gilead.
15 Makir took a wife from among the Huppites and Shuppites. His sister's name was Maakah.
Another descendant was named Zelophehad, who had only daughters.
16 Makir's wife Maakah gave birth to a son and named him Peresh. His brother was named Sheresh, and his sons were Ulam and Rakem.
17 The son of Ulam:
Bedan.
These were the sons of Gilead son of Makir, the son of Manasseh.
18 His sister Hammoleketh gave birth to Ishhod, Abiezer and Mahlah.
19 The sons of Shemida were:
Ahian, Shechem, Likhi and Aniam.

Ephraim

20 The descendants of Ephraim:
Shuthelah, Bered his son,
Tahath his son, Eleadah his son,

[a] 77 See Septuagint and Joshua 21:34; Hebrew does not have *Jokneam, Kartah.* [b] 12 Or *Ir. The sons of Dan: Hushim,* (see Gen. 46:23); Hebrew does not have *The sons of Dan.* [c] 13 Some Hebrew and Septuagint manuscripts (see also Gen. 46:24 and Num. 26:49); most Hebrew manuscripts *Shallum*

Tahath his son, [21]Zabad his son
and Shuthelah his son.

Ezer and Elead were killed by the na-
tive-born men of Gath, when they went
down to seize their livestock. [22]Their fa-
ther Ephraim mourned for them many
days, and his relatives came to comfort
him. [23]Then he made love to his wife
again, and she became pregnant and
gave birth to a son. He named him Beri-
ah,[a] because there had been misfortune
in his family. [24]His daughter was Shee-
rah, who built Lower and Upper Beth
Horon as well as Uzzen Sheerah.

[25]Rephah was his son, Resheph his son,[b]
Telah his son, Tahan his son,
[26]Ladan his son, Ammihud his son,
Elishama his son, [27]Nun his son
and Joshua his son.

[28]Their lands and settlements included
Bethel and its surrounding villages, Naaran
to the east, Gezer and its villages to the west,
and Shechem and its villages all the way to
Ayyah and its villages. [29]Along the borders
of Manasseh were Beth Shan, Taanach, Me-
giddo and Dor, together with their villages.
The descendants of Joseph son of Israel lived
in these towns.

Asher

[30]The sons of Asher:
Imnah, Ishvah, Ishvi and Beriah.
Their sister was Serah.
[31]The sons of Beriah:
Heber and Malkiel, who was the fa-
ther of Birzaith.
[32]Heber was the father of Japhlet, Shomer
and Hotham and of their sister Shua.
[33]The sons of Japhlet:
Pasak, Bimhal and Ashvath.
These were Japhlet's sons.
[34]The sons of Shomer:
Ahi, Rohgah,[c] Hubbah and Aram.
[35]The sons of his brother Helem:
Zophah, Imna, Shelesh and Amal.
[36]The sons of Zophah:
Suah, Harnepher, Shual, Beri, Im-
rah, [37]Bezer, Hod, Shamma, Shil-
shah, Ithran[d] and Beera.
[38]The sons of Jether:
Jephunneh, Pispah and Ara.
[39]The sons of Ulla:
Arah, Hanniel and Rizia.

[40]All these were descendants of Asher —
heads of families, choice men, brave war-
riors and outstanding leaders. The number
of men ready for battle, as listed in their ge-
nealogy, was 26,000.

The Genealogy of Saul the Benjamite

8 Benjamin was the father of Bela his first-
born,
Ashbel the second son, Aharah the
third,
[2]Nohah the fourth and Rapha the fifth.
[3]The sons of Bela were:
Addar, Gera, Abihud,[e] [4]Abishua, Na-
aman, Ahoah, [5]Gera, Shephuphan
and Huram.
[6]These were the descendants of Ehud,
who were heads of families of those
living in Geba and were deported to
Manahath:
[7]Naaman, Ahijah, and Gera, who de-
ported them and who was the father
of Uzza and Ahihud.
[8]Sons were born to Shaharaim in Moab
after he had divorced his wives Hu-
shim and Baara. [9]By his wife Ho-
desh he had Jobab, Zibia, Mesha,
Malkam, [10]Jeuz, Sakia and Mirmah.
These were his sons, heads of fami-
lies. [11]By Hushim he had Abitub and
Elpaal.
[12]The sons of Elpaal:
Eber, Misham, Shemed (who built
Ono and Lod with its surrounding
villages), [13]and Beriah and Shema,
who were heads of families of those
living in Aijalon and who drove out
the inhabitants of Gath.
[14]Ahio, Shashak, Jeremoth, [15]Zebadiah,
Arad, Eder, [16]Michael, Ishpah and
Joha were the sons of Beriah.
[17]Zebadiah, Meshullam, Hizki, Heber,
[18]Ishmerai, Izliah and Jobab were
the sons of Elpaal.
[19]Jakim, Zikri, Zabdi, [20]Elienai, Zillethai,
Eliel, [21]Adaiah, Beraiah and Shim-
rath were the sons of Shimei.
[22]Ishpan, Eber, Eliel, [23]Abdon, Zikri, Ha-
nan, [24]Hananiah, Elam, Anthothijah,

[a] *23* *Beriah* sounds like the Hebrew for *misfortune.* [b] *25* Some Septuagint manuscripts; Hebrew does not have *his son.* [c] *34* Or *of his brother Shomer: Rohgah* [d] *37* Possibly a variant of *Jether*
[e] *3* Or *Gera the father of Ehud*

YOU ARE MY KING (AMAZING LOVE)

Billy Foote

I'm forgiven because you were forsaken
I'm accepted; you were condemned
I'm alive and well, your Spirit is within me
Because you died and rose again

Amazing love, how can it be
That you, my King, should die for me
Amazing love, I know it's true
It's my joy to honor you
In all I do, I honor you
You are my King, you are my King
Jesus, you are my King, you are my King

THE INSPIRATION

Jesus said, "Father, forgive them, for they do not know what they are doing." And they divided up his clothes by casting lots.

—Luke 23:34

Read also: 1 John 3:1

BEHIND THE SONG

Billy James Foote is an iterant teacher and worship leader from Texas who has been serving churches and camps since the mid-1990s. "You Are My King (Amazing Love)" was one of the first songs Foote composed. While many of the songs from the early days of the modern worship era focused on describing God in familiar, accessible terms, Foote's simple song carefully ties Jesus' atoning sacrifice for our sin to his role as the King of kings.

"I remember sitting at a night of worship," Foote says, "and the Holy Spirit was reminding me that I was forgiven and accepted. Christ was forsaken and condemned so that I might have life. The first half of the verse just came to me as I sat there." Foote finished the song a few days later and brought it to a group he was serving. "The first time that I led worship with the song was very moving. It was a joy to see people connect with it and be able to bless the Lord as Savior and King."

The verses lay out the propositional and positional truth that Jesus took on the weight of our sin, and the chorus offers the heartfelt response to that realization; "You are my king!"

Selah

Wonder is a critical part of worship. We cheapen words like "amazing" by throwing them around easily, but when you think about it, the idea that Jesus, the King of kings, would take on our sin, be forsaken by the Father and die a brutal death in our place is nothing short of amazing!

Have you recognized Jesus as your king recently? It may seem rhetorical, and God certainly takes on many roles (father, friend, healer, shepherd, just to name a few), but don't forget about his kingship. Can you think of any ways you could more fully worship Jesus as your king?

[25]Iphdeiah and Penuel were the sons of Shashak.
[26]Shamsherai, Shehariah, Athaliah, [27]Jaareshiah, Elijah and Zikri were the sons of Jeroham.

[28]All these were heads of families, chiefs as listed in their genealogy, and they lived in Jerusalem.

[29]Jeiel[a] the father[b] of Gibeon lived in Gibeon.
His wife's name was Maakah, [30]and his firstborn son was Abdon, followed by Zur, Kish, Baal, Ner,[c] Nadab, [31]Gedor, Ahio, Zeker [32]and Mikloth, who was the father of Shimeah.
They too lived near their relatives in Jerusalem.
[33]Ner was the father of Kish, Kish the father of Saul, and Saul the father of Jonathan, Malki-Shua, Abinadab and Esh-Baal.[d]
[34]The son of Jonathan:
Merib-Baal,[e] who was the father of Micah.
[35]The sons of Micah:
Pithon, Melek, Tarea and Ahaz.
[36]Ahaz was the father of Jehoaddah, Jehoaddah was the father of Alemeth, Azmaveth and Zimri, and Zimri was
the father of Moza. [37]Moza was the father of Binea; Raphah was his son, Eleasah his son and Azel his son.
[38]Azel had six sons, and these were their names:
Azrikam, Bokeru, Ishmael, Sheariah, Obadiah and Hanan. All these were the sons of Azel.
[39]The sons of his brother Eshek:
Ulam his firstborn, Jeush the second
son and Eliphelet the third. [40]The
sons of Ulam were brave warriors who could handle the bow. They had many sons and grandsons — 150 in all.

All these were the descendants of Benjamin.

9 All Israel was listed in the genealogies recorded in the book of the kings of Israel and Judah. They were taken captive to Babylon because of their unfaithfulness.

The People in Jerusalem

[2]Now the first to resettle on their own property in their own towns were some Israelites, priests, Levites and temple servants.

[3]Those from Judah, from Benjamin, and from Ephraim and Manasseh who lived in Jerusalem were:

[4]Uthai son of Ammihud, the son of Omri, the son of Imri, the son of Bani, a descendant of Perez son of Judah.
[5]Of the Shelanites[f]:
Asaiah the firstborn and his sons.
[6]Of the Zerahites:
Jeuel.
The people from Judah numbered 690.
[7]Of the Benjamites:
Sallu son of Meshullam, the son of Hodaviah, the son of Hassenuah;
[8]Ibneiah son of Jeroham; Elah son of Uzzi, the son of Mikri; and Meshullam son of Shephatiah, the son of Reuel, the son of Ibnijah.
[9]The people from Benjamin, as listed in their genealogy, numbered 956. All these men were heads of their families.
[10]Of the priests:
Jedaiah; Jehoiarib; Jakin;
[11]Azariah son of Hilkiah, the son of Meshullam, the son of Zadok, the son of Meraioth, the son of Ahitub, the official in charge of the house of God;
[12]Adaiah son of Jeroham, the son of Pashhur, the son of Malkijah; and Maasai son of Adiel, the son of Jahzerah, the son of Meshullam, the son of Meshillemith, the son of Immer.
[13]The priests, who were heads of families, numbered 1,760. They were able men, responsible for ministering in the house of God.
[14]Of the Levites:
Shemaiah son of Hasshub, the son of Azrikam, the son of Hashabiah,
a Merarite; [15]Bakbakkar, Heresh,
Galal and Mattaniah son of Mika, the son of Zikri, the son of Asaph;
[16]Obadiah son of Shemaiah, the son

[a] *29* Some Septuagint manuscripts (see also 9:35); Hebrew does not have *Jeiel.* [b] *29* *Father* may mean *civic leader* or *military leader.* [c] *30* Some Septuagint manuscripts (see also 9:36); Hebrew does not have *Ner.* [d] *33* Also known as *Ish-Bosheth* [e] *34* Also known as *Mephibosheth* [f] *5* See Num. 26:20; Hebrew *Shilonites.*

of Galal, the son of Jeduthun; and Berekiah son of Asa, the son of Elkanah, who lived in the villages of the Netophathites.

17 The gatekeepers:

Shallum, Akkub, Talmon, Ahiman and their fellow Levites, Shallum their chief 18 being stationed at the King's Gate on the east, up to the present time. These were the gatekeepers belonging to the camp of the Levites. 19 Shallum son of Kore, the son of Ebiasaph, the son of Korah, and his fellow gatekeepers from his family (the Korahites) were responsible for guarding the thresholds of the tent just as their ancestors had been responsible for guarding the entrance to the dwelling of the LORD. 20 In earlier times Phinehas son of Eleazar was the official in charge of the gatekeepers, and the LORD was with him. 21 Zechariah son of Meshelemiah was the gatekeeper at the entrance to the tent of meeting.

22 Altogether, those chosen to be gatekeepers at the thresholds numbered 212 They were registered by genealogy in their villages. The gatekeepers had been assigned to their positions of trust by David and Samuel the seer. 23 They and their descendants were in charge of guarding the gates of the house of the LORD — the house called the tent of meeting. 24 The gatekeepers were on the four sides: east, west, north and south. 25 Their fellow Levites in their villages had to come from time to time and share their duties for seven-day periods. 26 But the four principal gatekeepers, who were Levites, were entrusted with the responsibility for the rooms and treasuries in the house of God. 27 They would spend the night stationed around the house of God, because they had to guard it; and they had charge of the key for opening it each morning.

28 Some of them were in charge of the articles used in the temple service; they counted them when they were brought in and when they were taken out. 29 Others were assigned to take care of the furnishings and all the other articles of the sanctuary, as well as the special flour and wine, and the olive oil, incense and spices. 30 But some of the priests took care of mixing the spices. 31 A Levite named Mattithiah, the firstborn son of Shallum the Korahite, was entrusted with the responsibility for baking the offering bread. 32 Some of the Kohathites, their fellow Levites, were in charge of preparing for every Sabbath the bread set out on the table.

33 Those who were musicians, heads of Levite families, stayed in the rooms of the temple and were exempt from other duties because they were responsible for the work day and night.

34 All these were heads of Levite families, chiefs as listed in their genealogy, and they lived in Jerusalem.

The Genealogy of Saul

35 Jeiel the father[a] of Gibeon lived in Gibeon.

His wife's name was Maakah, 36 and his firstborn son was Abdon, followed by Zur, Kish, Baal, Ner, Nadab, 37 Gedor, Ahio, Zechariah and Mikloth. 38 Mikloth was the father of Shimeam. They too lived near their relatives in Jerusalem.

39 Ner was the father of Kish, Kish the father of Saul, and Saul the father of Jonathan, Malki-Shua, Abinadab and Esh-Baal.[b]

40 The son of Jonathan:

Merib-Baal,[c] who was the father of Micah.

41 The sons of Micah:

Pithon, Melek, Tahrea and Ahaz.[d]

42 Ahaz was the father of Jadah, Jadah[e] was the father of Alemeth, Azmaveth and Zimri, and Zimri was the father of Moza. 43 Moza was the father of Binea; Rephaiah was his son, Eleasah his son and Azel his son.

44 Azel had six sons, and these were their names:

Azrikam, Bokeru, Ishmael, Sheariah, Obadiah and Hanan. These were the sons of Azel.

[a] *35 Father* may mean *civic leader* or *military leader.* [b] *39* Also known as *Ish-Bosheth* [c] *40* Also known as *Mephibosheth* [d] *41* Vulgate and Syriac (see also Septuagint and 8:35); Hebrew does not have *and Ahaz.* [e] *42* Some Hebrew manuscripts and Septuagint (see also 8:36); most Hebrew manuscripts *Jarah, Jarah*

Saul Takes His Life

10 Now the Philistines fought against
Israel; the Israelites fled before them,
and many fell dead on Mount Gilboa. 2The
Philistines were in hot pursuit of Saul and
his sons, and they killed his sons Jonathan,
Abinadab and Malki-Shua. 3The fighting
grew fierce around Saul, and when the ar-
chers overtook him, they wounded him.
4Saul said to his armor-bearer, "Draw your
sword and run me through, or these uncir-
cumcised fellows will come and abuse me."
But his armor-bearer was terrified and
would not do it; so Saul took his own sword
and fell on it. 5When the armor-bearer saw
that Saul was dead, he too fell on his sword
and died. 6So Saul and his three sons died,
and all his house died together.
7When all the Israelites in the valley saw
that the army had fled and that Saul and his
sons had died, they abandoned their towns
and fled. And the Philistines came and oc-
cupied them.
8The next day, when the Philistines came
to strip the dead, they found Saul and his
sons fallen on Mount Gilboa. 9They stripped
him and took his head and his armor, and
sent messengers throughout the land of the
Philistines to proclaim the news among
their idols and their people. 10They put his
armor in the temple of their gods and hung
up his head in the temple of Dagon.
11When all the inhabitants of Jabesh Gil-
ead heard what the Philistines had done to
Saul, 12all their valiant men went and took
the bodies of Saul and his sons and brought
them to Jabesh. Then they buried their
bones under the great tree in Jabesh, and
they fasted seven days.
13Saul died because he was unfaithful to
the LORD; he did not keep the word of the
LORD and even consulted a medium for
guidance, 14and did not inquire of the LORD.
So the LORD put him to death and turned the
kingdom over to David son of Jesse.

David Becomes King Over Israel

11 All Israel came together to David at
Hebron and said, "We are your own
flesh and blood. 2In the past, even while
Saul was king, you were the one who led Is-
rael on their military campaigns. And the
LORD your God said to you, 'You will shep-
herd my people Israel, and you will become
their ruler.' "
3When all the elders of Israel had come to
King David at Hebron, he made a covenant
with them at Hebron before the LORD, and
they anointed David king over Israel, as the
LORD had promised through Samuel.

David Conquers Jerusalem

4David and all the Israelites marched to
Jerusalem (that is, Jebus). The Jebusites who
lived there 5said to David, "You will not get
in here." Nevertheless, David captured the
fortress of Zion — which is the City of David.
6David had said, "Whoever leads the
attack on the Jebusites will become com-
mander-in-chief." Joab son of Zeruiah went
up first, and so he received the command.
7David then took up residence in the for-
tress, and so it was called the City of David.
8He built up the city around it, from the ter-
races[a] to the surrounding wall, while Joab
restored the rest of the city. 9And David be-
came more and more powerful, because the
LORD Almighty was with him.

David's Mighty Warriors

10These were the chiefs of David's mighty
warriors — they, together with all Israel, gave
his kingship strong support to extend it over
the whole land, as the LORD had promised —
11this is the list of David's mighty warriors:
Jashobeam,[b] a Hakmonite, was chief of
the officers[c]; he raised his spear against
three hundred men, whom he killed in one
encounter.
12Next to him was Eleazar son of Dodai
the Ahohite, one of the three mighty war-
riors. 13He was with David at Pas Dammim
when the Philistines gathered there for bat-
tle. At a place where there was a field full of
barley, the troops fled from the Philistines.
14But they took their stand in the middle of
the field. They defended it and struck the
Philistines down, and the LORD brought
about a great victory.
15Three of the thirty chiefs came down
to David to the rock at the cave of Adullam,
while a band of Philistines was encamped

[a] 8 Or *the Millo* [b] 11 Possibly a variant of *Jashob-Baal* [c] 11 Or *Thirty*; some Septuagint manuscripts *Three* (see also 2 Samuel 23:8)

in the Valley of Rephaim. [16]At that time Da-
vid was in the stronghold, and the Philistine
garrison was at Bethlehem. [17]David longed
for water and said, "Oh, that someone would
get me a drink of water from the well near
the gate of Bethlehem!" [18]So the Three broke
through the Philistine lines, drew water
from the well near the gate of Bethlehem
and carried it back to David. But he refused
to drink it; instead, he poured it out to the
LORD. [19]"God forbid that I should do this!" he
said. "Should I drink the blood of these men
who went at the risk of their lives?" Because
they risked their lives to bring it back, David
would not drink it.

Such were the exploits of the three mighty warriors.

[20]Abishai the brother of Joab was chief of
the Three. He raised his spear against three
hundred men, whom he killed, and so he be-
came as famous as the Three. [21]He was dou-
bly honored above the Three and became
their commander, even though he was not
included among them.

[22]Benaiah son of Jehoiada, a valiant
fighter from Kabzeel, performed great ex-
ploits. He struck down Moab's two might-
iest warriors. He also went down into a pit
on a snowy day and killed a lion. [23]And he
struck down an Egyptian who was five cu-
bits[a] tall. Although the Egyptian had a spear
like a weaver's rod in his hand, Benaiah went
against him with a club. He snatched the
spear from the Egyptian's hand and killed
him with his own spear. [24]Such were the
exploits of Benaiah son of Jehoiada; he too
was as famous as the three mighty warriors.
[25]He was held in greater honor than any of
the Thirty, but he was not included among
the Three. And David put him in charge of
his bodyguard.

[26]The mighty warriors were:
Asahel the brother of Joab,
Elhanan son of Dodo from Bethlehem,
[27]Shammoth the Harorite,
Helez the Pelonite,
[28]Ira son of Ikkesh from Tekoa,
Abiezer from Anathoth,
[29]Sibbekai the Hushathite,
Ilai the Ahohite,
[30]Maharai the Netophathite,
Heled son of Baanah the Netophathite,
[31]Ithai son of Ribai from Gibeah in Benjamin,
Benaiah the Pirathonite,
[32]Hurai from the ravines of Gaash,
Abiel the Arbathite,
[33]Azmaveth the Baharumite,
Eliahba the Shaalbonite,
[34]the sons of Hashem the Gizonite,
Jonathan son of Shagee the Hararite,
[35]Ahiam son of Sakar the Hararite,
Eliphal son of Ur,
[36]Hepher the Mekerathite,
Ahijah the Pelonite,
[37]Hezro the Carmelite,
Naarai son of Ezbai,
[38]Joel the brother of Nathan,
Mibhar son of Hagri,
[39]Zelek the Ammonite,
Naharai the Berothite, the armor-bearer of Joab son of Zeruiah,
[40]Ira the Ithrite,
Gareb the Ithrite,
[41]Uriah the Hittite,
Zabad son of Ahlai,
[42]Adina son of Shiza the Reubenite, who was chief of the Reubenites, and the thirty with him,
[43]Hanan son of Maakah,
Joshaphat the Mithnite,
[44]Uzzia the Ashterathite,
Shama and Jeiel the sons of Hotham the Aroerite,
[45]Jediael son of Shimri,
his brother Joha the Tizite,
[46]Eliel the Mahavite,
Jeribai and Joshaviah the sons of Elnaam,
Ithmah the Moabite,
[47]Eliel, Obed and Jaasiel the Mezobaite.

Warriors Join David

12 These were the men who came to Da-
vid at Ziklag, while he was banished
from the presence of Saul son of Kish (they
were among the warriors who helped him
in battle; [2]they were armed with bows and
were able to shoot arrows or to sling stones
right-handed or left-handed; they were rela-
tives of Saul from the tribe of Benjamin):

[3]Ahiezer their chief and Joash the sons
of Shemaah the Gibeathite; Jeziel and

[a] *23* That is, about 7 feet 6 inches or about 2.3 meters

Pelet the sons of Azmaveth; Berakah,
Jehu the Anathothite, 4 and Ishmaiah
the Gibeonite, a mighty warrior among
the Thirty, who was a leader of the
Thirty; Jeremiah, Jahaziel, Johanan,
Jozabad the Gederathite,[a] 5 Eluzai, Jer-
imoth, Bealiah, Shemariah and Sheph-
atiah the Haruphite; 6 Elkanah, Ishiah,
Azarel, Joezer and Jashobeam the Ko-
rahites; 7 and Joelah and Zebadiah the
sons of Jeroham from Gedor.

8 Some Gadites defected to David at his
stronghold in the wilderness. They were
brave warriors, ready for battle and able
to handle the shield and spear. Their faces
were the faces of lions, and they were as swift
as gazelles in the mountains.

9 Ezer was the chief,
Obadiah the second in command, Eliab the third,
10 Mishmannah the fourth, Jeremiah the fifth,
11 Attai the sixth, Eliel the seventh,
12 Johanan the eighth, Elzabad the ninth,
13 Jeremiah the tenth and Makbannai the eleventh.

14 These Gadites were army commanders;
the least was a match for a hundred, and the
greatest for a thousand. 15 It was they who
crossed the Jordan in the first month when
it was overflowing all its banks, and they put
to flight everyone living in the valleys, to the
east and to the west.

16 Other Benjamites and some men from
Judah also came to David in his stronghold.
17 David went out to meet them and said to
them, "If you have come to me in peace to
help me, I am ready for you to join me. But if
you have come to betray me to my enemies
when my hands are free from violence, may
the God of our ancestors see it and judge you."

18 Then the Spirit came on Amasai, chief of
the Thirty, and he said:

"We are yours, David!
We are with you, son of Jesse!
Success, success to you,
and success to those who help you,
for your God will help you."

So David received them and made them
leaders of his raiding bands.

19 Some of the tribe of Manasseh defected
to David when he went with the Philistines
to fight against Saul. (He and his men did not
help the Philistines because, after consulta-
tion, their rulers sent him away. They said,
"It will cost us our heads if he deserts to his
master Saul.") 20 When David went to Ziklag,
these were the men of Manasseh who de-
fected to him: Adnah, Jozabad, Jediael, Mi-
chael, Jozabad, Elihu and Zillethai, leaders
of units of a thousand in Manasseh. 21 They
helped David against raiding bands, for all
of them were brave warriors, and they were
commanders in his army. 22 Day after day
men came to help David, until he had a great
army, like the army of God.[b]

Others Join David at Hebron

23 These are the numbers of the men
armed for battle who came to David at He-
bron to turn Saul's kingdom over to him, as
the LORD had said:

24 from Judah, carrying shield and spear—6,800 armed for battle;
25 from Simeon, warriors ready for battle—7,100;
26 from Levi—4,600, 27 including Jehoi-
ada, leader of the family of Aaron,
with 3,700 men, 28 and Zadok, a brave
young warrior, with 22 officers from his family;
29 from Benjamin, Saul's tribe—3,000, most of whom had remained loyal to Saul's house until then;
30 from Ephraim, brave warriors, famous in their own clans—20,800;
31 from half the tribe of Manasseh, designated by name to come and make David king—18,000;
32 from Issachar, men who understood the times and knew what Israel should do—200 chiefs, with all their relatives under their command;
33 from Zebulun, experienced soldiers prepared for battle with every type of weapon, to help David with undivided loyalty—50,000;
34 from Naphtali—1,000 officers, together with 37,000 men carrying shields and spears;
35 from Dan, ready for battle—28,600;

[a] 4 In Hebrew texts the second half of this verse (*Jeremiah . . . Gederathite*) is numbered 12:5, and 12:5-40 is numbered 12:6-41. [b] 22 Or *a great and mighty army*

36 from Asher, experienced soldiers pre-
pared for battle—40,000;
37 and from east of the Jordan, from Reu-
ben, Gad and the half-tribe of Ma-
nasseh, armed with every type of
weapon—120,000.
38 All these were fighting men who vol-
unteered to serve in the ranks. They came
to Hebron fully determined to make David
king over all Israel. All the rest of the Isra-
elites were also of one mind to make Da-
vid king. 39 The men spent three days there
with David, eating and drinking, for their
families had supplied provisions for them.
40 Also, their neighbors from as far away as
Issachar, Zebulun and Naphtali came bring-
ing food on donkeys, camels, mules and
oxen. There were plentiful supplies of flour,
fig cakes, raisin cakes, wine, olive oil, cattle
and sheep, for there was joy in Israel.

Bringing Back the Ark

13 David conferred with each of his of-
ficers, the commanders of thousands
and commanders of hundreds. 2 He then said
to the whole assembly of Israel, "If it seems
good to you and if it is the will of the LORD
our God, let us send word far and wide to the
rest of our people throughout the territories
of Israel, and also to the priests and Levites
who are with them in their towns and pas-
turelands, to come and join us. 3 Let us bring
the ark of our God back to us, for we did not
inquire of[a] it[b] during the reign of Saul." 4 The
whole assembly agreed to do this, because it
seemed right to all the people.
5 So David assembled all Israel, from the
Shihor River in Egypt to Lebo Hamath, to
bring the ark of God from Kiriath Jearim.
6 David and all Israel went to Baalah of Judah
(Kiriath Jearim) to bring up from there the
ark of God the LORD, who is enthroned be-
tween the cherubim—the ark that is called
by the Name.
7 They moved the ark of God from Abina-
dab's house on a new cart, with Uzzah and
Ahio guiding it. 8 David and all the Israelites
were celebrating with all their might before
God, with songs and with harps, lyres, tim-
brels, cymbals and trumpets.
9 When they came to the threshing floor
of Kidon, Uzzah reached out his hand to
steady the ark, because the oxen stumbled.
10 The LORD's anger burned against Uzzah,
and he struck him down because he had put
his hand on the ark. So he died there before
God.
11 Then David was angry because the
LORD's wrath had broken out against Uzzah,
and to this day that place is called Perez Uz-
zah.[c]
12 David was afraid of God that day and
asked, "How can I ever bring the ark of God
to me?" 13 He did not take the ark to be with
him in the City of David. Instead, he took it
to the house of Obed-Edom the Gittite. 14 The
ark of God remained with the family of
Obed-Edom in his house for three months,
and the LORD blessed his household and ev-
erything he had.

David's House and Family

14 Now Hiram king of Tyre sent messen-
gers to David, along with cedar logs,
stonemasons and carpenters to build a pal-
ace for him. 2 And David knew that the LORD
had established him as king over Israel and
that his kingdom had been highly exalted for
the sake of his people Israel.
3 In Jerusalem David took more wives and
became the father of more sons and daugh-
ters. 4 These are the names of the children
born to him there: Shammua, Shobab, Na-
than, Solomon, 5 Ibhar, Elishua, Elpelet,
6 Nogah, Nepheg, Japhia, 7 Elishama, Beelia-
da[d] and Eliphelet.

David Defeats the Philistines

8 When the Philistines heard that David
had been anointed king over all Israel, they
went up in full force to search for him, but
David heard about it and went out to meet
them. 9 Now the Philistines had come and
raided the Valley of Rephaim; 10 so David
inquired of God: "Shall I go and attack the
Philistines? Will you deliver them into my
hands?"
The LORD answered him, "Go, I will deliv-
er them into your hands."
11 So David and his men went up to Baal
Perazim, and there he defeated them. He
said, "As waters break out, God has broken
out against my enemies by my hand." So
that place was called Baal Perazim.[e] 12 The

[a] 3 Or *we neglected* [b] 3 Or *him* [c] 11 *Perez Uzzah* means *outbreak against Uzzah.* [d] 7 A variant of *Eliada* [e] 11 *Baal Perazim* means *the lord who breaks out.*

Philistines had abandoned their gods there,
and David gave orders to burn them in the
fire.
13 Once more the Philistines raided the
valley; 14 so David inquired of God again,
and God answered him, "Do not go directly
after them, but circle around them and at-
tack them in front of the poplar trees. 15 As
soon as you hear the sound of marching in
the tops of the poplar trees, move out to bat-
tle, because that will mean God has gone out
in front of you to strike the Philistine army."
16 So David did as God commanded him, and
they struck down the Philistine army, all the
way from Gibeon to Gezer.
17 So David's fame spread throughout ev-
ery land, and the LORD made all the nations
fear him.

The Ark Brought to Jerusalem

15 After David had constructed build-
ings for himself in the City of David,
he prepared a place for the ark of God and
pitched a tent for it. 2 Then David said, "No
one but the Levites may carry the ark of God,
because the LORD chose them to carry the
ark of the LORD and to minister before him
forever."
3 David assembled all Israel in Jerusalem
to bring up the ark of the LORD to the place
he had prepared for it. 4 He called together
the descendants of Aaron and the Levites:
5 From the descendants of Kohath,
Uriel the leader and 120 relatives;
6 from the descendants of Merari,
Asaiah the leader and 220 relatives;
7 from the descendants of Gershon,[a]
Joel the leader and 130 relatives;
8 from the descendants of Elizaphan,
Shemaiah the leader and 200 rela-
tives;
9 from the descendants of Hebron,
Eliel the leader and 80 relatives;
10 from the descendants of Uzziel,
Amminadab the leader and 112 rela-
tives.
11 Then David summoned Zadok and Abi-
athar the priests, and Uriel, Asaiah, Joel,
Shemaiah, Eliel and Amminadab the Le-
vites. 12 He said to them, "You are the heads
of the Levitical families; you and your fellow
Levites are to consecrate yourselves and
bring up the ark of the LORD, the God of Isra-
el, to the place I have prepared for it. 13 It was
because you, the Levites, did not bring it up
the first time that the LORD our God broke
out in anger against us. We did not inquire
of him about how to do it in the prescribed
way." 14 So the priests and Levites consecrat-
ed themselves in order to bring up the ark of
the LORD, the God of Israel. 15 And the Le-
vites carried the ark of God with the poles on
their shoulders, as Moses had commanded
in accordance with the word of the LORD.
16 David told the leaders of the Levites to
appoint their fellow Levites as musicians to
make a joyful sound with musical instru-
ments: lyres, harps and cymbals.
17 So the Levites appointed Heman son of
Joel; from his relatives, Asaph son of Bereki-
ah; and from their relatives the Merarites,
Ethan son of Kushaiah; 18 and with them
their relatives next in rank: Zechariah,[b] Ja-
aziel, Shemiramoth, Jehiel, Unni, Eliab, Be-
naiah, Maaseiah, Mattithiah, Eliphelehu,
Mikneiah, Obed-Edom and Jeiel,[c] the gate-
keepers.
19 The musicians Heman, Asaph and
Ethan were to sound the bronze cymbals;
20 Zechariah, Jaaziel,[d] Shemiramoth, Jehiel,
Unni, Eliab, Maaseiah and Benaiah were to
play the lyres according to *alamoth*,[e] 21 and
Mattithiah, Eliphelehu, Mikneiah, Obed-
Edom, Jeiel and Azaziah were to play the
harps, directing according to *sheminith*.[e]
22 Kenaniah the head Levite was in charge of
the singing; that was his responsibility be-
cause he was skillful at it.
23 Berekiah and Elkanah were to be door-
keepers for the ark. 24 Shebaniah, Joshaphat,
Nethanel, Amasai, Zechariah, Benaiah and
Eliezer the priests were to blow trumpets be-
fore the ark of God. Obed-Edom and Jehiah
were also to be doorkeepers for the ark.
25 So David and the elders of Israel and the
commanders of units of a thousand went to
bring up the ark of the covenant of the LORD
from the house of Obed-Edom, with rejoic-
ing. 26 Because God had helped the Levites
who were carrying the ark of the covenant of

[a] *7* Hebrew *Gershom*, a variant of *Gershon* [b] *18* Three Hebrew manuscripts and most Septuagint manuscripts (see also verse 20 and 16:5); most Hebrew manuscripts *Zechariah son and* or *Zechariah, Ben and* [c] *18* Hebrew; Septuagint (see also verse 21) *Jeiel and Azaziah* [d] *20* See verse 18; Hebrew *Aziel*, a variant of *Jaaziel*. [e] *20,21* Probably a musical term

the LORD, seven bulls and seven rams were
sacrificed. 27 Now David was clothed in a
robe of fine linen, as were all the Levites who
were carrying the ark, and as were the musi-
cians, and Kenaniah, who was in charge of
the singing of the choirs. David also wore a
linen ephod. 28 So all Israel brought up the
ark of the covenant of the LORD with shouts,
with the sounding of rams' horns and trum-
pets, and of cymbals, and the playing of lyres
and harps.

29 As the ark of the covenant of the LORD
was entering the City of David, Michal
daughter of Saul watched from a window.
And when she saw King David dancing and
celebrating, she despised him in her heart.

Ministering Before the Ark

16 They brought the ark of God and
set it inside the tent that David had
pitched for it, and they presented burnt of-
ferings and fellowship offerings before God.
2 After David had finished sacrificing the
burnt offerings and fellowship offerings, he
blessed the people in the name of the LORD.
3 Then he gave a loaf of bread, a cake of dates
and a cake of raisins to each Israelite man
and woman.

4 He appointed some of the Levites to
minister before the ark of the LORD, to ex-
tol,[a] thank, and praise the LORD, the God
of Israel: 5 Asaph was the chief, and next to
him in rank were Zechariah, then Jaaziel,[b]
Shemiramoth, Jehiel, Mattithiah, Eliab, Be-
naiah, Obed-Edom and Jeiel. They were to
play the lyres and harps, Asaph was to sound
the cymbals, 6 and Benaiah and Jahaziel the
priests were to blow the trumpets regularly
before the ark of the covenant of God.

7 That day David first appointed Asaph
and his associates to give praise to the LORD
in this manner:

8 Give praise to the LORD, proclaim his
name;
make known among the nations what
he has done.
9 Sing to him, sing praise to him;
tell of all his wonderful acts.
10 Glory in his holy name;
let the hearts of those who seek the
LORD rejoice.
11 Look to the LORD and his strength;
seek his face always.

12 Remember the wonders he has done,
his miracles, and the judgments he
pronounced,
13 you his servants, the descendants of
Israel,
his chosen ones, the children of Jacob.
14 He is the LORD our God;
his judgments are in all the earth.

15 He remembers[c] his covenant forever,
the promise he made, for a thousand
generations,
16 the covenant he made with Abraham,
the oath he swore to Isaac.
17 He confirmed it to Jacob as a decree,
to Israel as an everlasting covenant:
18 "To you I will give the land of Canaan
as the portion you will inherit."

19 When they were but few in number,
few indeed, and strangers in it,
20 they[d] wandered from nation to nation,
from one kingdom to another.
21 He allowed no one to oppress them;
for their sake he rebuked kings:
22 "Do not touch my anointed ones;
do my prophets no harm."

23 Sing to the LORD, all the earth;
proclaim his salvation day after day.
24 Declare his glory among the nations,
his marvelous deeds among all
peoples.

25 For great is the LORD and most worthy of
praise;
he is to be feared above all gods.
26 For all the gods of the nations are idols,
but the LORD made the heavens.
27 Splendor and majesty are before him;
strength and joy are in his dwelling
place.

28 Ascribe to the LORD, all you families of
nations,
ascribe to the LORD glory and strength.
29 Ascribe to the LORD the glory due his
name;

[a] *4* Or *petition*; or *invoke* [b] *5* See 15:18,20 Hebrew *Jeiel*, possibly another name for *Jaaziel*.
[c] *15* Some Septuagint manuscripts (see also Psalm 105:8); Hebrew *Remember* [d] *18-20* One Hebrew manuscript, Septuagint and Vulgate (see also Psalm 105:12); most Hebrew manuscripts *inherit, / 19 though you are but few in number, / few indeed, and strangers in it." / 20 They*

bring an offering and come before
him.
Worship the LORD in the splendor of his[a]
holiness.
30 Tremble before him, all the earth!
The world is firmly established; it
cannot be moved.

31 Let the heavens rejoice, let the earth be
glad;
let them say among the nations, "The
LORD reigns!"
32 Let the sea resound, and all that is in it;
let the fields be jubilant, and
everything in them!
33 Let the trees of the forest sing,
let them sing for joy before the LORD,
for he comes to judge the earth.

34 Give thanks to the LORD, for he is good;
his love endures forever.
35 Cry out, "Save us, God our Savior;
gather us and deliver us from the
nations,
that we may give thanks to your holy
name,
and glory in your praise."
36 Praise be to the LORD, the God of Israel,
from everlasting to everlasting.

Then all the people said "Amen" and "Praise
the LORD."

37 David left Asaph and his associates be-
fore the ark of the covenant of the LORD to
minister there regularly, according to each
day's requirements. 38 He also left Obed-
Edom and his sixty-eight associates to min-
ister with them. Obed-Edom son of Jedu-
thun, and also Hosah, were gatekeepers.
39 David left Zadok the priest and his fel-
low priests before the tabernacle of the LORD
at the high place in Gibeon 40 to present
burnt offerings to the LORD on the altar of
burnt offering regularly, morning and eve-
ning, in accordance with everything written
in the Law of the LORD, which he had given
Israel. 41 With them were Heman and Jedu-
thun and the rest of those chosen and des-
ignated by name to give thanks to the LORD,
"for his love endures forever." 42 Heman and
Jeduthun were responsible for the sound-
ing of the trumpets and cymbals and for the
playing of the other instruments for sacred
song. The sons of Jeduthun were stationed at
the gate.
43 Then all the people left, each for their
own home, and David returned home to
bless his family.

God's Promise to David

17 After David was settled in his palace,
he said to Nathan the prophet, "Here
I am, living in a house of cedar, while the ark
of the covenant of the LORD is under a tent."
2 Nathan replied to David, "Whatever you
have in mind, do it, for God is with you."
3 But that night the word of God came to
Nathan, saying:

4 "Go and tell my servant David, 'This
is what the LORD says: You are not the
one to build me a house to dwell in. 5 I
have not dwelt in a house from the day
I brought Israel up out of Egypt to this
day. I have moved from one tent site
to another, from one dwelling place to
another. 6 Wherever I have moved with
all the Israelites, did I ever say to any of
their leaders[b] whom I commanded to
shepherd my people, "Why have you
not built me a house of cedar?" '
7 "Now then, tell my servant David,
'This is what the LORD Almighty says:
I took you from the pasture, from tend-
ing the flock, and appointed you rul-
er over my people Israel. 8 I have been
with you wherever you have gone, and
I have cut off all your enemies from be-
fore you. Now I will make your name
like the names of the greatest men on
earth. 9 And I will provide a place for
my people Israel and will plant them so
that they can have a home of their own
and no longer be disturbed. Wicked
people will not oppress them anymore,
as they did at the beginning 10 and have
done ever since the time I appointed
leaders over my people Israel. I will also
subdue all your enemies.

" 'I declare to you that the LORD will
build a house for you: 11 When your days
are over and you go to be with your an-
cestors, I will raise up your offspring to
succeed you, one of your own sons, and
I will establish his kingdom. 12 He is the
one who will build a house for me, and I

[a] 29 Or *LORD with the splendor of*
[b] 6 Traditionally *judges*; also in verse 10

will establish his throne forever. [13]I will be his father, and he will be my son. I will never take my love away from him, as I took it away from your predecessor. [14]I will set him over my house and my kingdom forever; his throne will be established forever.'"

[15]Nathan reported to David all the words of this entire revelation.

David's Prayer

[16]Then King David went in and sat before the LORD, and he said:

"Who am I, LORD God, and what is my family, that you have brought me this far? [17]And as if this were not enough in your sight, my God, you have spoken about the future of the house of your servant. You, LORD God, have looked on me as though I were the most exalted of men.

[18]"What more can David say to you for honoring your servant? For you know your servant, [19]LORD. For the sake of your servant and according to your will, you have done this great thing and made known all these great promises.

[20]"There is no one like you, LORD, and there is no God but you, as we have heard with our own ears. [21]And who is like your people Israel — the one nation on earth whose God went out to redeem a people for himself, and to make a name for yourself, and to perform great and awesome wonders by driving out nations from before your people, whom you redeemed from Egypt? [22]You made your people Israel your very own forever, and you, LORD, have become their God.

[23]"And now, LORD, let the promise you have made concerning your servant and his house be established forever. Do as you promised, [24]so that it will be established and that your name will be great forever. Then people will say, 'The LORD Almighty, the God over Israel, is Israel's God!' And the house of your servant David will be established before you.

[25]"You, my God, have revealed to your servant that you will build a house for him. So your servant has found courage to pray to you. [26]You, LORD, are God! You have promised these good things to your servant. [27]Now you have been pleased to bless the house of your servant, that it may continue forever in your sight; for you, LORD, have blessed it, and it will be blessed forever."

David's Victories

18 In the course of time, David defeated the Philistines and subdued them, and he took Gath and its surrounding villages from the control of the Philistines.

[2]David also defeated the Moabites, and they became subject to him and brought him tribute.

[3]Moreover, David defeated Hadadezer king of Zobah, in the vicinity of Hamath, when he went to set up his monument at[a] the Euphrates River. [4]David captured a thousand of his chariots, seven thousand charioteers and twenty thousand foot soldiers. He hamstrung all but a hundred of the chariot horses.

[5]When the Arameans of Damascus came to help Hadadezer king of Zobah, David struck down twenty-two thousand of them. [6]He put garrisons in the Aramean kingdom of Damascus, and the Arameans became subject to him and brought him tribute. The LORD gave David victory wherever he went.

[7]David took the gold shields carried by the officers of Hadadezer and brought them to Jerusalem. [8]From Tebah[b] and Kun, towns that belonged to Hadadezer, David took a great quantity of bronze, which Solomon used to make the bronze Sea, the pillars and various bronze articles.

[9]When Tou king of Hamath heard that David had defeated the entire army of Hadadezer king of Zobah, [10]he sent his son Hadoram to King David to greet him and congratulate him on his victory in battle over Hadadezer, who had been at war with Tou. Hadoram brought all kinds of articles of gold, of silver and of bronze.

[11]King David dedicated these articles to the LORD, as he had done with the silver and gold he had taken from all these nations:

[a] 3 Or *to restore his control over* [b] 8 Hebrew *Tibhath,* a variant of *Tebah*

Edom and Moab, the Ammonites and the Philistines, and Amalek.

[12]Abishai son of Zeruiah struck down eighteen thousand Edomites in the Valley of Salt. [13]He put garrisons in Edom, and all the Edomites became subject to David. The LORD gave David victory wherever he went.

David's Officials

[14]David reigned over all Israel, doing what was just and right for all his people. [15]Joab son of Zeruiah was over the army; Jehoshaphat son of Ahilud was recorder; [16]Zadok son of Ahitub and Ahimelek[a] son of Abiathar were priests; Shavsha was secretary; [17]Benaiah son of Jehoiada was over the Kerethites and Pelethites; and David's sons were chief officials at the king's side.

David Defeats the Ammonites

19 In the course of time, Nahash king of the Ammonites died, and his son succeeded him as king. [2]David thought, "I will show kindness to Hanun son of Nahash, because his father showed kindness to me." So David sent a delegation to express his sympathy to Hanun concerning his father.

When David's envoys came to Hanun in the land of the Ammonites to express sympathy to him, [3]the Ammonite commanders said to Hanun, "Do you think David is honoring your father by sending envoys to you to express sympathy? Haven't his envoys come to you only to explore and spy out the country and overthrow it?" [4]So Hanun seized David's envoys, shaved them, cut off their garments at the buttocks, and sent them away.

[5]When someone came and told David about the men, he sent messengers to meet them, for they were greatly humiliated. The king said, "Stay at Jericho till your beards have grown, and then come back."

[6]When the Ammonites realized that they had become obnoxious to David, Hanun and the Ammonites sent a thousand talents[b] of silver to hire chariots and charioteers from Aram Naharaim,[c] Aram Maakah and Zobah. [7]They hired thirty-two thousand chariots and charioteers, as well as the king of Maakah with his troops, who came and camped near Medeba, while the Ammonites were mustered from their towns and moved out for battle.

[8]On hearing this, David sent Joab out with the entire army of fighting men. [9]The Ammonites came out and drew up in battle formation at the entrance to their city, while the kings who had come were by themselves in the open country.

[10]Joab saw that there were battle lines in front of him and behind him; so he selected some of the best troops in Israel and deployed them against the Arameans. [11]He put the rest of the men under the command of Abishai his brother, and they were deployed against the Ammonites. [12]Joab said, "If the Arameans are too strong for me, then you are to rescue me; but if the Ammonites are too strong for you, then I will rescue you. [13]Be strong, and let us fight bravely for our people and the cities of our God. The LORD will do what is good in his sight."

[14]Then Joab and the troops with him advanced to fight the Arameans, and they fled before him. [15]When the Ammonites realized that the Arameans were fleeing, they too fled before his brother Abishai and went inside the city. So Joab went back to Jerusalem.

[16]After the Arameans saw that they had been routed by Israel, they sent messengers and had Arameans brought from beyond the Euphrates River, with Shophak the commander of Hadadezer's army leading them.

[17]When David was told of this, he gathered all Israel and crossed the Jordan; he advanced against them and formed his battle lines opposite them. David formed his lines to meet the Arameans in battle, and they fought against him. [18]But they fled before Israel, and David killed seven thousand of their charioteers and forty thousand of their foot soldiers. He also killed Shophak the commander of their army.

[19]When the vassals of Hadadezer saw that they had been routed by Israel, they made peace with David and became subject to him.

So the Arameans were not willing to help the Ammonites anymore.

The Capture of Rabbah

20 In the spring, at the time when kings go off to war, Joab led out the armed forces. He laid waste the land of the Ammonites and went to Rabbah and besieged

[a] *16* Some Hebrew manuscripts, Vulgate and Syriac (see also 2 Samuel 8:17); most Hebrew manuscripts *Abimelek* [b] *6* That is, about 38 tons or about 34 metric tons [c] *6* That is, Northwest Mesopotamia

it, but David remained in Jerusalem. Joab attacked Rabbah and left it in ruins. 2David took the crown from the head of their king[a]—its weight was found to be a talent[b] of gold, and it was set with precious stones—and it was placed on David's head. He took a great quantity of plunder from the city 3and brought out the people who were there, consigning them to labor with saws and with iron picks and axes. David did this to all the Ammonite towns. Then David and his entire army returned to Jerusalem.

War With the Philistines

4In the course of time, war broke out with the Philistines, at Gezer. At that time Sibbekai the Hushathite killed Sippai, one of the descendants of the Rephaites, and the Philistines were subjugated.

5In another battle with the Philistines, Elhanan son of Jair killed Lahmi the brother of Goliath the Gittite, who had a spear with a shaft like a weaver's rod.

6In still another battle, which took place at Gath, there was a huge man with six fingers on each hand and six toes on each foot—twenty-four in all. He also was descended from Rapha. 7When he taunted Israel, Jonathan son of Shimea, David's brother, killed him.

8These were descendants of Rapha in Gath, and they fell at the hands of David and his men.

David Counts the Fighting Men

21 Satan rose up against Israel and incited David to take a census of Israel. 2So David said to Joab and the commanders of the troops, "Go and count the Israelites from Beersheba to Dan. Then report back to me so that I may know how many there are."

3But Joab replied, "May the LORD multiply his troops a hundred times over. My lord the king, are they not all my lord's subjects? Why does my lord want to do this? Why should he bring guilt on Israel?"

4The king's word, however, overruled Joab; so Joab left and went throughout Israel and then came back to Jerusalem. 5Joab reported the number of the fighting men to David: In all Israel there were one million one hundred thousand men who could handle a sword, including four hundred and seventy thousand in Judah.

6But Joab did not include Levi and Benjamin in the numbering, because the king's command was repulsive to him. 7This command was also evil in the sight of God; so he punished Israel.

8Then David said to God, "I have sinned greatly by doing this. Now, I beg you, take away the guilt of your servant. I have done a very foolish thing."

9The LORD said to Gad, David's seer, 10"Go and tell David, 'This is what the LORD says: I am giving you three options. Choose one of them for me to carry out against you.'"

11So Gad went to David and said to him, "This is what the LORD says: 'Take your choice: 12three years of famine, three months of being swept away[c] before your enemies, with their swords overtaking you, or three days of the sword of the LORD—days of plague in the land, with the angel of the LORD ravaging every part of Israel.' Now then, decide how I should answer the one who sent me."

13David said to Gad, "I am in deep distress. Let me fall into the hands of the LORD, for his mercy is very great; but do not let me fall into human hands."

14So the LORD sent a plague on Israel, and seventy thousand men of Israel fell dead. 15And God sent an angel to destroy Jerusalem. But as the angel was doing so, the LORD saw it and relented concerning the disaster and said to the angel who was destroying the people, "Enough! Withdraw your hand." The angel of the LORD was then standing at the threshing floor of Araunah[d] the Jebusite.

16David looked up and saw the angel of the LORD standing between heaven and earth, with a drawn sword in his hand extended over Jerusalem. Then David and the elders, clothed in sackcloth, fell facedown.

17David said to God, "Was it not I who ordered the fighting men to be counted? I, the shepherd,[e] have sinned and done wrong. These are but sheep. What have they done? LORD my God, let your hand fall on me and

[a] 2 Or *of Milkom,* that is, Molek [b] 2 That is, about 75 pounds or about 34 kilograms [c] 12 Hebrew; Septuagint and Vulgate (see also 2 Samuel 24:13) *of fleeing* [d] 15 Hebrew *Ornan,* a variant of *Araunah;* also in verses 18-28 [e] 17 Probable reading of the original Hebrew text (see 2 Samuel 24:17 and note); Masoretic Text does not have *the shepherd.*

my family, but do not let this plague remain on your people."

David Builds an Altar

18 Then the angel of the LORD ordered Gad to tell David to go up and build an altar to the LORD on the threshing floor of Araunah the Jebusite. 19 So David went up in obedience to the word that Gad had spoken in the name of the LORD.

20 While Araunah was threshing wheat, he turned and saw the angel; his four sons who were with him hid themselves. 21 Then David approached, and when Araunah looked and saw him, he left the threshing floor and bowed down before David with his face to the ground.

22 David said to him, "Let me have the site of your threshing floor so I can build an altar to the LORD, that the plague on the people may be stopped. Sell it to me at the full price."

23 Araunah said to David, "Take it! Let my lord the king do whatever pleases him. Look, I will give the oxen for the burnt offerings, the threshing sledges for the wood, and the wheat for the grain offering. I will give all this."

24 But King David replied to Araunah, "No, I insist on paying the full price. I will not take for the LORD what is yours, or sacrifice a burnt offering that costs me nothing."

25 So David paid Araunah six hundred shekels[a] of gold for the site. 26 David built an altar to the LORD there and sacrificed burnt offerings and fellowship offerings. He called on the LORD, and the LORD answered him with fire from heaven on the altar of burnt offering.

27 Then the LORD spoke to the angel, and he put his sword back into its sheath. 28 At that time, when David saw that the LORD had answered him on the threshing floor of Araunah the Jebusite, he offered sacrifices there. 29 The tabernacle of the LORD, which Moses had made in the wilderness, and the altar of burnt offering were at that time on the high place at Gibeon. 30 But David could not go before it to inquire of God, because he was afraid of the sword of the angel of the LORD.

22

Then David said, "The house of the LORD God is to be here, and also the altar of burnt offering for Israel."

Preparations for the Temple

2 So David gave orders to assemble the foreigners residing in Israel, and from among them he appointed stonecutters to prepare dressed stone for building the house of God. 3 He provided a large amount of iron to make nails for the doors of the gateways and for the fittings, and more bronze than could be weighed. 4 He also provided more cedar logs than could be counted, for the Sidonians and Tyrians had brought large numbers of them to David.

5 David said, "My son Solomon is young and inexperienced, and the house to be built for the LORD should be of great magnificence and fame and splendor in the sight of all the nations. Therefore I will make preparations for it." So David made extensive preparations before his death.

6 Then he called for his son Solomon and charged him to build a house for the LORD, the God of Israel. 7 David said to Solomon: "My son, I had it in my heart to build a house for the Name of the LORD my God. 8 But this word of the LORD came to me: 'You have shed much blood and have fought many wars. You are not to build a house for my Name, because you have shed much blood on the earth in my sight. 9 But you will have a son who will be a man of peace and rest, and I will give him rest from all his enemies on every side. His name will be Solomon,[b] and I will grant Israel peace and quiet during his reign. 10 He is the one who will build a house for my Name. He will be my son, and I will be his father. And I will establish the throne of his kingdom over Israel forever.'

11 "Now, my son, the LORD be with you, and may you have success and build the house of the LORD your God, as he said you would. 12 May the LORD give you discretion and understanding when he puts you in command over Israel, so that you may keep the law of the LORD your God. 13 Then you will have success if you are careful to observe the decrees and laws that the LORD gave Moses for

[a] *25* That is, about 15 pounds or about 6.9 kilograms

[b] *9* *Solomon* sounds like and may be derived from the Hebrew for *peace*.

Israel. Be strong and courageous. Do not be afraid or discouraged.

14 “I have taken great pains to provide for the temple of the LORD a hundred thousand talents[a] of gold, a million talents[b] of silver, quantities of bronze and iron too great to be weighed, and wood and stone. And you may add to them. 15 You have many workers: stonecutters, masons and carpenters, as well as those skilled in every kind of work 16 in gold and silver, bronze and iron—craftsmen beyond number. Now begin the work, and the LORD be with you.”

17 Then David ordered all the leaders of Israel to help his son Solomon. 18 He said to them, “Is not the LORD your God with you? And has he not granted you rest on every side? For he has given the inhabitants of the land into my hands, and the land is subject to the LORD and to his people. 19 Now devote your heart and soul to seeking the LORD your God. Begin to build the sanctuary of the LORD God, so that you may bring the ark of the covenant of the LORD and the sacred articles belonging to God into the temple that will be built for the Name of the LORD.”

The Levites

23 When David was old and full of years, he made his son Solomon king over Israel.

2 He also gathered together all the leaders of Israel, as well as the priests and Levites. 3 The Levites thirty years old or more were counted, and the total number of men was thirty-eight thousand. 4 David said, “Of these, twenty-four thousand are to be in charge of the work of the temple of the LORD and six thousand are to be officials and judges. 5 Four thousand are to be gatekeepers and four thousand are to praise the LORD with the musical instruments I have provided for that purpose.”

6 David separated the Levites into divisions corresponding to the sons of Levi: Gershon, Kohath and Merari.

Gershonites

7 Belonging to the Gershonites:
Ladan and Shimei.
8 The sons of Ladan:
Jehiel the first, Zetham and Joel—three in all.
9 The sons of Shimei:
Shelomoth, Haziel and Haran—three in all.
These were the heads of the families of Ladan.
10 And the sons of Shimei:
Jahath, Ziza,[c] Jeush and Beriah.
These were the sons of Shimei—four in all.
11 Jahath was the first and Ziza the second, but Jeush and Beriah did not have many sons; so they were counted as one family with one assignment.

Kohathites

12 The sons of Kohath:
Amram, Izhar, Hebron and Uzziel—four in all.
13 The sons of Amram:
Aaron and Moses.
Aaron was set apart, he and his descendants forever, to consecrate the most holy things, to offer sacrifices before the LORD, to minister before him and to pronounce blessings in his name forever. 14 The sons of Moses the man of God were counted as part of the tribe of Levi.
15 The sons of Moses:
Gershom and Eliezer.
16 The descendants of Gershom:
Shubael was the first.
17 The descendants of Eliezer:
Rehabiah was the first.
Eliezer had no other sons, but the sons of Rehabiah were very numerous.
18 The sons of Izhar:
Shelomith was the first.
19 The sons of Hebron:
Jeriah the first, Amariah the second, Jahaziel the third and Jekameam the fourth.
20 The sons of Uzziel:
Micah the first and Ishiah the second.

Merarites

21 The sons of Merari:
Mahli and Mushi.

[a] *14* That is, about 3,750 tons or about 3,400 metric tons [b] *14* That is, about 37,500 tons or about 34,000 metric tons [c] *10* One Hebrew manuscript, Septuagint and Vulgate (see also verse 11); most Hebrew manuscripts *Zina*

The sons of Mahli:
Eleazar and Kish.
22 Eleazar died without having sons: he
had only daughters. Their cousins,
the sons of Kish, married them.
23 The sons of Mushi:
Mahli, Eder and Jerimoth — three in
all.

24 These were the descendants of Levi
by their families — the heads of families as
they were registered under their names and
counted individually, that is, the workers
twenty years old or more who served in the
temple of the LORD. 25 For David had said,
"Since the LORD, the God of Israel, has grant-
ed rest to his people and has come to dwell
in Jerusalem forever, 26 the Levites no longer
need to carry the tabernacle or any of the ar-
ticles used in its service." 27 According to the
last instructions of David, the Levites were
counted from those twenty years old or more.
28 The duty of the Levites was to help Aar-
on's descendants in the service of the tem-
ple of the LORD: to be in charge of the court-
yards, the side rooms, the purification of all
sacred things and the performance of other
duties at the house of God. 29 They were in
charge of the bread set out on the table, the
special flour for the grain offerings, the thin
loaves made without yeast, the baking and
the mixing, and all measurements of quan-
tity and size. 30 They were also to stand every
morning to thank and praise the LORD. They
were to do the same in the evening 31 and
whenever burnt offerings were present-
ed to the LORD on the Sabbaths, at the New
Moon feasts and at the appointed festivals.
They were to serve before the LORD regular-
ly in the proper number and in the way pre-
scribed for them.
32 And so the Levites carried out their re-
sponsibilities for the tent of meeting, for the
Holy Place and, under their relatives the de-
scendants of Aaron, for the service of the
temple of the LORD.

The Divisions of Priests

24 These were the divisions of the de-
scendants of Aaron:
The sons of Aaron were Nadab, Abihu, El-
eazar and Ithamar. 2 But Nadab and Abihu
died before their father did, and they had no
sons; so Eleazar and Ithamar served as the
priests. 3 With the help of Zadok a descendant
of Eleazar and Ahimelek a descendant of Ith-
amar, David separated them into divisions for
their appointed order of ministering. 4 A larg-
er number of leaders were found among Elea-
zar's descendants than among Ithamar's, and
they were divided accordingly: sixteen heads
of families from Eleazar's descendants and
eight heads of families from Ithamar's de-
scendants. 5 They divided them impartially
by casting lots, for there were officials of the
sanctuary and officials of God among the de-
scendants of both Eleazar and Ithamar.
6 The scribe Shemaiah son of Nethanel,
a Levite, recorded their names in the pres-
ence of the king and of the officials: Zadok
the priest, Ahimelek son of Abiathar and the
heads of families of the priests and of the Le-
vites — one family being taken from Eleazar
and then one from Ithamar.

7 The first lot fell to Jehoiarib,
the second to Jedaiah,
8 the third to Harim,
the fourth to Seorim,
9 the fifth to Malkijah,
the sixth to Mijamin,
10 the seventh to Hakkoz,
the eighth to Abijah,
11 the ninth to Jeshua,
the tenth to Shekaniah,
12 the eleventh to Eliashib,
the twelfth to Jakim,
13 the thirteenth to Huppah,
the fourteenth to Jeshebeab,
14 the fifteenth to Bilgah,
the sixteenth to Immer,
15 the seventeenth to Hezir,
the eighteenth to Happizzez,
16 the nineteenth to Pethahiah,
the twentieth to Jehezkel,
17 the twenty-first to Jakin,
the twenty-second to Gamul,
18 the twenty-third to Delaiah
and the twenty-fourth to Maaziah.

19 This was their appointed order of min-
istering when they entered the temple of the
LORD, according to the regulations prescribed
for them by their ancestor Aaron, as the LORD,
the God of Israel, had commanded him.

The Rest of the Levites

20 As for the rest of the descendants of Levi:
from the sons of Amram: Shubael;
from the sons of Shubael: Jehdeiah.

21 As for Rehabiah, from his sons:
Ishiah was the first.
22 From the Izharites: Shelomoth;
from the sons of Shelomoth: Jahath.
23 The sons of Hebron: Jeriah the first,[a]
Amariah the second, Jahaziel the
third and Jekameam the fourth.
24 The son of Uzziel: Micah;
from the sons of Micah: Shamir.
25 The brother of Micah: Ishiah;
from the sons of Ishiah: Zechariah.
26 The sons of Merari: Mahli and Mushi.
The son of Jaaziah: Beno.
27 The sons of Merari:
from Jaaziah: Beno, Shoham, Zakkur
and Ibri.
28 From Mahli: Eleazar, who had no sons.
29 From Kish: the son of Kish:
Jerahmeel.
30 And the sons of Mushi: Mahli, Eder and
Jerimoth.

These were the Levites, according to their
families. 31 They also cast lots, just as their
relatives the descendants of Aaron did, in
the presence of King David and of Zadok,
Ahimelek, and the heads of families of the
priests and of the Levites. The families of
the oldest brother were treated the same as
those of the youngest.

The Musicians

25 David, together with the command-
ers of the army, set apart some of the
sons of Asaph, Heman and Jeduthun for the
ministry of prophesying, accompanied by
harps, lyres and cymbals. Here is the list of
the men who performed this service:

2 From the sons of Asaph:
Zakkur, Joseph, Nethaniah and Asare-
lah. The sons of Asaph were under the
supervision of Asaph, who prophesied
under the king's supervision.
3 As for Jeduthun, from his sons:
Gedaliah, Zeri, Jeshaiah, Shimei,[b]
Hashabiah and Mattithiah, six in all,
under the supervision of their father Je-
duthun, who prophesied, using the harp
in thanking and praising the LORD.
4 As for Heman, from his sons:
Bukkiah, Mattaniah, Uzziel, Shuba-
el and Jerimoth; Hananiah, Hanani,
Eliathah, Giddalti and Romamti-Ezer;
Joshbekashah, Mallothi, Hothir and
Mahazioth. 5 (All these were sons of
Heman the king's seer. They were giv-
en him through the promises of God to
exalt him. God gave Heman fourteen
sons and three daughters.)

6 All these men were under the supervi-
sion of their father for the music of the tem-
ple of the LORD, with cymbals, lyres and
harps, for the ministry at the house of God.
Asaph, Jeduthun and Heman were under
the supervision of the king. 7 Along with their
relatives—all of them trained and skilled in
music for the LORD—they numbered 288.
8 Young and old alike, teacher as well as stu-
dent, cast lots for their duties.

9 The first lot, which was for Asaph,
fell to Joseph,
his sons and relatives[c] 12[d]
the second to Gedaliah,
him and his relatives and sons 12
10 the third to Zakkur,
his sons and relatives 12
11 the fourth to Izri,[e]
his sons and relatives 12
12 the fifth to Nethaniah,
his sons and relatives 12
13 the sixth to Bukkiah,
his sons and relatives 12
14 the seventh to Jesarelah,[f]
his sons and relatives 12
15 the eighth to Jeshaiah,
his sons and relatives 12
16 the ninth to Mattaniah,
his sons and relatives 12
17 the tenth to Shimei,
his sons and relatives 12
18 the eleventh to Azarel,[g]
his sons and relatives 12
19 the twelfth to Hashabiah,
his sons and relatives 12
20 the thirteenth to Shubael,
his sons and relatives 12
21 the fourteenth to Mattithiah,
his sons and relatives 12

[a] *23* Two Hebrew manuscripts and some Septuagint manuscripts (see also 23:19); most Hebrew manuscripts *The sons of Jeriah:* [b] *3* One Hebrew manuscript and some Septuagint manuscripts (see also verse 17); most Hebrew manuscripts do not have *Shimei.* [c] *9* See Septuagint; Hebrew does not have *his sons and relatives.* [d] *9* See the total in verse 7; Hebrew does not have *twelve.* [e] *11* A variant of *Zeri* [f] *14* A variant of *Asarelah* [g] *18* A variant of *Uzziel*

[22] the fifteenth to Jerimoth,
his sons and relatives 12
[23] the sixteenth to Hananiah,
his sons and relatives 12
[24] the seventeenth to Joshbekashah,
his sons and relatives 12
[25] the eighteenth to Hanani,
his sons and relatives 12
[26] the nineteenth to Mallothi,
his sons and relatives 12
[27] the twentieth to Eliathah,
his sons and relatives 12
[28] the twenty-first to Hothir,
his sons and relatives 12
[29] the twenty-second to Giddalti,
his sons and relatives 12
[30] the twenty-third to Mahazioth,
his sons and relatives 12
[31] the twenty-fourth to Romamti-Ezer,
his sons and relatives 12.

The Gatekeepers

26 The divisions of the gatekeepers:

From the Korahites: Meshelemiah son of Kore, one of the sons of Asaph.
[2] Meshelemiah had sons:
Zechariah the firstborn,
Jediael the second,
Zebadiah the third,
Jathniel the fourth,
[3] Elam the fifth,
Jehohanan the sixth
and Eliehoenai the seventh.
[4] Obed-Edom also had sons:
Shemaiah the firstborn,
Jehozabad the second,
Joah the third,
Sakar the fourth,
Nethanel the fifth,
[5] Ammiel the sixth,
Issachar the seventh
and Peullethai the eighth.
(For God had blessed Obed-Edom.)

[6] Obed-Edom's son Shemaiah also had
sons, who were leaders in their father's family because they were very
capable men. [7] The sons of Shemaiah: Othni, Rephael, Obed and Elzabad; his relatives Elihu and Semakiah were also able men. [8] All these
were descendants of Obed-Edom; they and their sons and their relatives were capable men with the strength to do the work — descendants of Obed-Edom, 62 in all.
[9] Meshelemiah had sons and relatives,
who were able men — 18 in all.

[10] Hosah the Merarite had sons: Shimri the first (although he was not the firstborn, his father had appointed
him the first), [11] Hilkiah the second,
Tabaliah the third and Zechariah the fourth. The sons and relatives of Hosah were 13 in all.
[12] These divisions of the gatekeepers, through their leaders, had duties for ministering in the temple of the LORD, just as their
relatives had. [13] Lots were cast for each gate,
according to their families, young and old alike.
[14] The lot for the East Gate fell to Shelemiah.[a] Then lots were cast for his son Zechariah, a wise counselor, and the lot for the
North Gate fell to him. [15] The lot for the South
Gate fell to Obed-Edom, and the lot for the storehouse fell to his sons. [16] The lots for the
West Gate and the Shalleketh Gate on the upper road fell to Shuppim and Hosah.

Guard was alongside of guard: [17] There
were six Levites a day on the east, four a day on the north, four a day on the south and two at a time at the storehouse. [18] As for the
court[b] to the west, there were four at the road and two at the court[b] itself.
[19] These were the divisions of the gatekeepers who were descendants of Korah and Merari.

The Treasurers and Other Officials

[20] Their fellow Levites were[c] in charge of
the treasuries of the house of God and the treasuries for the dedicated things.
[21] The descendants of Ladan, who were Gershonites through Ladan and who were heads of families belonging to Ladan the Gershonite, were Jehieli, [22] the sons of Jehieli, Zetham
and his brother Joel. They were in charge of the treasuries of the temple of the LORD.
[23] From the Amramites, the Izharites, the
Hebronites and the Uzzielites:

[a] 14 A variant of *Meshelemiah* [b] 18 The meaning of the Hebrew for this word is uncertain.
[c] 20 Septuagint; Hebrew *As for the Levites, Ahijah was*

that you may possess this good land and
pass it on as an inheritance to your descen-
dants forever.

9 “And you, my son Solomon, acknowledge
the God of your father, and serve him with
wholehearted devotion and with a willing
mind, for the LORD searches every heart and
understands every desire and every thought.
If you seek him, he will be found by you; but
if you forsake him, he will reject you forever.
10 Consider now, for the LORD has chosen you
to build a house as the sanctuary. Be strong
and do the work.”

11 Then David gave his son Solomon the
plans for the portico of the temple, its build-
ings, its storerooms, its upper parts, its in-
ner rooms and the place of atonement. 12 He
gave him the plans of all that the Spirit had
put in his mind for the courts of the temple
of the LORD and all the surrounding rooms,
for the treasuries of the temple of God and
for the treasuries for the dedicated things.
13 He gave him instructions for the divisions
of the priests and Levites, and for all the
work of serving in the temple of the LORD,
as well as for all the articles to be used in its
service. 14 He designated the weight of gold
for all the gold articles to be used in various
kinds of service, and the weight of silver for
all the silver articles to be used in various
kinds of service: 15 the weight of gold for the
gold lampstands and their lamps, with the
weight for each lampstand and its lamps;
and the weight of silver for each silver lamp-
stand and its lamps, according to the use
of each lampstand; 16 the weight of gold for
each table for consecrated bread; the weight
of silver for the silver tables; 17 the weight
of pure gold for the forks, sprinkling bowls
and pitchers; the weight of gold for each gold
dish; the weight of silver for each silver dish;
18 and the weight of the refined gold for the
altar of incense. He also gave him the plan
for the chariot, that is, the cherubim of gold
that spread their wings and overshadow the
ark of the covenant of the LORD.

19 “All this,” David said, “I have in writing
as a result of the LORD’s hand on me, and he
enabled me to understand all the details of
the plan.”

20 David also said to Solomon his son, “Be
strong and courageous, and do the work. Do
not be afraid or discouraged, for the LORD
God, my God, is with you. He will not fail
you or forsake you until all the work for the
service of the temple of the LORD is finished.
21 The divisions of the priests and Levites are
ready for all the work on the temple of God,
and every willing person skilled in any craft
will help you in all the work. The officials
and all the people will obey your every com-
mand.”

Gifts for Building the Temple

29 Then King David said to the whole
assembly: “My son Solomon, the one
whom God has chosen, is young and inex-
perienced. The task is great, because this
palatial structure is not for man but for the
LORD God. 2 With all my resources I have
provided for the temple of my God — gold
for the gold work, silver for the silver, bronze
for the bronze, iron for the iron and wood for
the wood, as well as onyx for the settings,
turquoise,[a] stones of various colors, and all
kinds of fine stone and marble — all of these
in large quantities. 3 Besides, in my devotion
to the temple of my God I now give my per-
sonal treasures of gold and silver for the tem-
ple of my God, over and above everything I
have provided for this holy temple: 4 three
thousand talents[b] of gold (gold of Ophir) and
seven thousand talents[c] of refined silver, for
the overlaying of the walls of the buildings,
5 for the gold work and the silver work, and
for all the work to be done by the craftsmen.
Now, who is willing to consecrate them-
selves to the LORD today?”

6 Then the leaders of families, the officers
of the tribes of Israel, the commanders of
thousands and commanders of hundreds,
and the officials in charge of the king’s work
gave willingly. 7 They gave toward the work on
the temple of God five thousand talents[d] and
ten thousand darics[e] of gold, ten thousand
talents[f] of silver, eighteen thousand talents[g]
of bronze and a hundred thousand talents[h]
of iron. 8 Anyone who had precious stones
gave them to the treasury of the temple of the

[a] *2* The meaning of the Hebrew for this word is uncertain. [b] *4* That is, about 110 tons or about 100 metric tons [c] *4* That is, about 260 tons or about 235 metric tons [d] *7* That is, about 190 tons or about 170 metric tons [e] *7* That is, about 185 pounds or about 84 kilograms [f] *7* That is, about 380 tons or about 340 metric tons [g] *7* That is, about 675 tons or about 610 metric tons [h] *7* That is, about 3,800 tons or about 3,400 metric tons

LORD in the custody of Jehiel the Gershonite.
9The people rejoiced at the willing response
of their leaders, for they had given freely and
wholeheartedly to the LORD. David the king
also rejoiced greatly.

David's Prayer

10David praised the LORD in the presence
of the whole assembly, saying,

"Praise be to you, LORD,
the God of our father Israel,
from everlasting to everlasting.
11Yours, LORD, is the greatness and the
power
and the glory and the majesty and the
splendor,
for everything in heaven and earth is
yours.
Yours, LORD, is the kingdom;
you are exalted as head over all.
12Wealth and honor come from you;
you are the ruler of all things.
In your hands are strength and power
to exalt and give strength to all.
13Now, our God, we give you thanks,
and praise your glorious name.

14"But who am I, and who are my people,
that we should be able to give as generous-
ly as this? Everything comes from you, and
we have given you only what comes from
your hand. 15We are foreigners and strang-
ers in your sight, as were all our ancestors.
Our days on earth are like a shadow, with-
out hope. 16LORD our God, all this abun-
dance that we have provided for building
you a temple for your Holy Name comes
from your hand, and all of it belongs to you.
17I know, my God, that you test the heart and
are pleased with integrity. All these things I
have given willingly and with honest intent.
And now I have seen with joy how willing-
ly your people who are here have given to
you. 18LORD, the God of our fathers Abra-
ham, Isaac and Israel, keep these desires
and thoughts in the hearts of your people
forever, and keep their hearts loyal to you.
19And give my son Solomon the wholeheart-
ed devotion to keep your commands, stat-
utes and decrees and to do everything to
build the palatial structure for which I have
provided."

20Then David said to the whole assem-
bly, "Praise the LORD your God." So they all
praised the LORD, the God of their fathers;
they bowed down, prostrating themselves
before the LORD and the king.

Solomon Acknowledged as King

21The next day they made sacrifices to
the LORD and presented burnt offerings
to him: a thousand bulls, a thousand rams
and a thousand male lambs, together with
their drink offerings, and other sacrifices
in abundance for all Israel. 22They ate and
drank with great joy in the presence of the
LORD that day.

Then they acknowledged Solomon son of
David as king a second time, anointing him
before the LORD to be ruler and Zadok to be
priest. 23So Solomon sat on the throne of the
LORD as king in place of his father David. He
prospered and all Israel obeyed him. 24All
the officers and warriors, as well as all of
King David's sons, pledged their submission
to King Solomon.

25The LORD highly exalted Solomon in the
sight of all Israel and bestowed on him roy-
al splendor such as no king over Israel ever
had before.

The Death of David

26David son of Jesse was king over all Is-
rael. 27He ruled over Israel forty years — sev-
en in Hebron and thirty-three in Jerusalem.
28He died at a good old age, having enjoyed
long life, wealth and honor. His son Solomon
succeeded him as king.

29As for the events of King David's reign,
from beginning to end, they are written in
the records of Samuel the seer, the records
of Nathan the prophet and the records of
Gad the seer, 30together with the details of
his reign and power, and the circumstanc-
es that surrounded him and Israel and the
kingdoms of all the other lands.

2 CHRONICLES

Solomon Asks for Wisdom

1 Solomon son of David established himself firmly over his kingdom, for the LORD his God was with him and made him exceedingly great.

[2]Then Solomon spoke to all Israel — to the commanders of thousands and commanders of hundreds, to the judges and to all the leaders in Israel, the heads of families — [3]and Solomon and the whole assembly went to the high place at Gibeon, for God's tent of meeting was there, which Moses the LORD's servant had made in the wilderness. [4]Now David had brought up the ark of God from Kiriath Jearim to the place he had prepared for it, because he had pitched a tent for it in Jerusalem. [5]But the bronze altar that Bezalel son of Uri, the son of Hur, had made was in Gibeon in front of the tabernacle of the LORD; so Solomon and the assembly inquired of him there. [6]Solomon went up to the bronze altar before the LORD in the tent of meeting and offered a thousand burnt offerings on it.

[7]That night God appeared to Solomon and said to him, "Ask for whatever you want me to give you."

[8]Solomon answered God, "You have shown great kindness to David my father and have made me king in his place. [9]Now, LORD God, let your promise to my father David be confirmed, for you have made me king over a people who are as numerous as the dust of the earth. [10]Give me wisdom and knowledge, that I may lead this people, for who is able to govern this great people of yours?"

[11]God said to Solomon, "Since this is your heart's desire and you have not asked for wealth, possessions or honor, nor for the death of your enemies, and since you have not asked for a long life but for wisdom and knowledge to govern my people over whom I have made you king, [12]therefore wisdom and knowledge will be given you. And I will also give you wealth, possessions and honor, such as no king who was before you ever had and none after you will have."

[13]Then Solomon went to Jerusalem from the high place at Gibeon, from before the tent of meeting. And he reigned over Israel.

[14]Solomon accumulated chariots and horses; he had fourteen hundred chariots and twelve thousand horses,[a] which he kept in the chariot cities and also with him in Jerusalem. [15]The king made silver and gold as common in Jerusalem as stones, and cedar as plentiful as sycamore-fig trees in the foothills. [16]Solomon's horses were imported from Egypt and from Kue[b] — the royal merchants purchased them from Kue at the current price. [17]They imported a chariot from Egypt for six hundred shekels[c] of silver, and a horse for a hundred and fifty.[d] They also exported them to all the kings of the Hittites and of the Arameans.

Preparations for Building the Temple

2[e] Solomon gave orders to build a temple for the Name of the LORD and a royal palace for himself. [2]He conscripted 70,000 men as carriers and 80,000 as stonecutters in the hills and 3,600 as foremen over them.

[3]Solomon sent this message to Hiram[f] king of Tyre:

"Send me cedar logs as you did for my father David when you sent him cedar to build a palace to live in. [4]Now I am about to build a temple for the Name of the LORD my God and to dedicate it to him for burning fragrant incense before him, for setting out the consecrated bread regularly, and for making burnt offerings every morning and evening and on the Sabbaths, at the New Moons and at the appointed

[a] *14* Or *charioteers* [b] *16* Probably Cilicia [c] *17* That is, about 15 pounds or about 6.9 kilograms [d] *17* That is, about 3 3/4 pounds or about 1.7 kilograms [e] In Hebrew texts 2:1 is numbered 1:18, and 2:2-18 is numbered 2:1-17. [f] *3* Hebrew *Huram,* a variant of *Hiram*; also in verses 11 and 12

festivals of the LORD our God. This is a lasting ordinance for Israel.

5 "The temple I am going to build will be great, because our God is greater than all other gods. 6 But who is able to build a temple for him, since the heavens, even the highest heavens, cannot contain him? Who then am I to build a temple for him, except as a place to burn sacrifices before him?

7 "Send me, therefore, a man skilled to work in gold and silver, bronze and iron, and in purple, crimson and blue yarn, and experienced in the art of engraving, to work in Judah and Jerusalem with my skilled workers, whom my father David provided.

8 "Send me also cedar, juniper and algum[a] logs from Lebanon, for I know that your servants are skilled in cutting timber there. My servants will work with yours 9 to provide me with plenty of lumber, because the temple I build must be large and magnificent. 10 I will give your servants, the woodsmen who cut the timber, twenty thousand cors[b] of ground wheat, twenty thousand cors[c] of barley, twenty thousand baths[d] of wine and twenty thousand baths of olive oil."

11 Hiram king of Tyre replied by letter to Solomon:

"Because the LORD loves his people, he has made you their king."

12 And Hiram added:

"Praise be to the LORD, the God of Israel, who made heaven and earth! He has given King David a wise son, endowed with intelligence and discernment, who will build a temple for the LORD and a palace for himself.

13 "I am sending you Huram-Abi, a man of great skill, 14 whose mother was from Dan and whose father was from Tyre. He is trained to work in gold and silver, bronze and iron, stone and wood, and with purple and blue and crimson yarn and fine linen. He is experienced in all kinds of engraving and can execute any design given to him. He will work with your skilled workers and with those of my lord, David your father.

15 "Now let my lord send his servants the wheat and barley and the olive oil and wine he promised, 16 and we will cut all the logs from Lebanon that you need and will float them as rafts by sea down to Joppa. You can then take them up to Jerusalem."

17 Solomon took a census of all the foreigners residing in Israel, after the census his father David had taken; and they were found to be 153,600. 18 He assigned 70,000 of them to be carriers and 80,000 to be stonecutters in the hills, with 3,600 foremen over them to keep the people working.

Solomon Builds the Temple

3 Then Solomon began to build the temple of the LORD in Jerusalem on Mount Moriah, where the LORD had appeared to his father David. It was on the threshing floor of Araunah[e] the Jebusite, the place provided by David. 2 He began building on the second day of the second month in the fourth year of his reign.

3 The foundation Solomon laid for building the temple of God was sixty cubits long and twenty cubits wide[f] (using the cubit of the old standard). 4 The portico at the front of the temple was twenty cubits[g] long across the width of the building and twenty[h] cubits high.

He overlaid the inside with pure gold. 5 He paneled the main hall with juniper and covered it with fine gold and decorated it with palm tree and chain designs. 6 He adorned the temple with precious stones. And the gold he used was gold of Parvaim. 7 He overlaid the ceiling beams, doorframes, walls and doors of the temple with gold, and he carved cherubim on the walls.

[a] *8* Probably a variant of *almug* [b] *10* That is, probably about 3,600 tons or about 3,200 metric tons of wheat [c] *10* That is, probably about 3,000 tons or about 2,700 metric tons of barley [d] *10* That is, about 120,000 gallons or about 440,000 liters [e] *1* Hebrew *Ornan,* a variant of *Araunah* [f] *3* That is, about 90 feet long and 30 feet wide or about 27 meters long and 9 meters wide [g] *4* That is, about 30 feet or about 9 meters; also in verses 8, 11 and 13 [h] *4* Some Septuagint and Syriac manuscripts; Hebrew *and a hundred and twenty*

8 He built the Most Holy Place, its length
corresponding to the width of the temple—
twenty cubits long and twenty cubits wide.
He overlaid the inside with six hundred tal-
ents[a] of fine gold. 9 The gold nails weighed
fifty shekels.[b] He also overlaid the upper
parts with gold.

10 For the Most Holy Place he made a pair
of sculptured cherubim and overlaid them
with gold. 11 The total wingspan of the cher-
ubim was twenty cubits. One wing of the first
cherub was five cubits[c] long and touched the
temple wall, while its other wing, also five
cubits long, touched the wing of the other
cherub. 12 Similarly one wing of the second
cherub was five cubits long and touched the
other temple wall, and its other wing, also
five cubits long, touched the wing of the first
cherub. 13 The wings of these cherubim ex-
tended twenty cubits. They stood on their
feet, facing the main hall.[d]

14 He made the curtain of blue, purple and
crimson yarn and fine linen, with cherubim
worked into it.

15 For the front of the temple he made
two pillars, which together were thirty-five
cubits[e] long, each with a capital five cubits
high. 16 He made interwoven chains[f] and put
them on top of the pillars. He also made a
hundred pomegranates and attached them
to the chains. 17 He erected the pillars in the
front of the temple, one to the south and one
to the north. The one to the south he named
Jakin[g] and the one to the north Boaz.[h]

The Temple's Furnishings

4 He made a bronze altar twenty cubits
long, twenty cubits wide and ten cubits
high.[i] 2 He made the Sea of cast metal, circu-
lar in shape, measuring ten cubits from rim
to rim and five cubits[j] high. It took a line of
thirty cubits[k] to measure around it. 3 Below
the rim, figures of bulls encircled it—ten to
a cubit.[l] The bulls were cast in two rows in
one piece with the Sea.

4 The Sea stood on twelve bulls, three fac-
ing north, three facing west, three facing
south and three facing east. The Sea rested
on top of them, and their hindquarters were
toward the center. 5 It was a handbreadth[m] in
thickness, and its rim was like the rim of a
cup, like a lily blossom. It held three thou-
sand baths.[n]

6 He then made ten basins for washing and
placed five on the south side and five on the
north. In them the things to be used for the
burnt offerings were rinsed, but the Sea was
to be used by the priests for washing.

7 He made ten gold lampstands accord-
ing to the specifications for them and placed
them in the temple, five on the south side
and five on the north.

8 He made ten tables and placed them in
the temple, five on the south side and five
on the north. He also made a hundred gold
sprinkling bowls.

9 He made the courtyard of the priests,
and the large court and the doors for the
court, and overlaid the doors with bronze.
10 He placed the Sea on the south side, at the
southeast corner.

11 And Huram also made the pots and
shovels and sprinkling bowls.

So Huram finished the work he had un-
dertaken for King Solomon in the temple of
God:

12 the two pillars;
the two bowl-shaped capitals on top of
the pillars;
the two sets of network decorating the
two bowl-shaped capitals on top of
the pillars;
13 the four hundred pomegranates for
the two sets of network (two rows
of pomegranates for each network,
decorating the bowl-shaped capitals
on top of the pillars);
14 the stands with their basins;
15 the Sea and the twelve bulls under it;
16 the pots, shovels, meat forks and all re-
lated articles.

[a] *8* That is, about 23 tons or about 21 metric tons [b] *9* That is, about 1 1/4 pounds or about 575 grams [c] *11* That is, about 7 1/2 feet or about 2.3 meters; also in verse 15 [d] *13* Or *facing inward* [e] *15* That is, about 53 feet or about 16 meters [f] *16* Or possibly *made chains in the inner sanctuary*; the meaning of the Hebrew for this phrase is uncertain. [g] *17* *Jakin* probably means *he establishes.* [h] *17* *Boaz* probably means *in him is strength.* [i] *1* That is, about 30 feet long and wide and 15 feet high or about 9 meters long and wide and 4.5 meters high [j] *2* That is, about 7 1/2 feet or about 2.3 meters [k] *2* That is, about 45 feet or about 14 meters [l] *3* That is, about 18 inches or about 45 centimeters [m] *5* That is, about 3 inches or about 7.5 centimeters [n] *5* That is, about 18,000 gallons or about 66,000 liters

FROM THE INSIDE OUT

Joel Houston

A thousand times I've failed
Still your mercy remains
And should I stumble again
Still I'm caught in your grace
Everlasting
Your light will shine when all else fades
Never-ending
Your glory goes beyond all fame

Your will above all else
My purpose remains
The art of losing myself
In bringing you praise
Everlasting
Your light will shine when all else fades
Never-ending
Your glory goes beyond all fame

In my heart in my soul
I give you control
Consume me from the inside out Lord
Let justice and praise
Become my embrace
To love you from the inside out

Everlasting
Your light will shine when all else fades
Never-ending
Your glory goes beyond all fame
And the cry of my heart
Is to bring you praise
From the inside out
Lord my soul cries out

THE INSPIRATION

The sun will no more be your light by day, nor will the brightness of the moon shine on you, for the LORD will be your everlasting light, and your God will be your glory. —Isaiah 60:19

BEHIND THE SONG

For Joel Houston, a worship leader and songwriter at Hillsong Church in Australia, "From the Inside Out" was one of the most difficult songs he had ever written. While he captured the melody and accompaniment quickly, the lyrics were more elusive.

"I could close my eyes, and I could hear people singing it," Houston recounts. "I just wasn't entirely sure what they were signing."

While on tour with Hillsong United, Houston practiced the song with the band but still felt unsettled as to its final lyrics. Finally, with about 30 minutes left until it was time to record the song, Houston excused himself to go to a quiet place and desperately sought the Lord's guidance. Then, in a matter of minutes, every word fell into place.

"Sometimes I feel like God holds things back to the point where you trust him to come through," Houston says.

Interestingly enough, the lyrics paint a powerful picture of the tension between what is and what is yet to come. Much like Isaiah 60, the words of "From the Inside Out" describe the preeminent light of God that is in no way compromised by the shadows of this world. Houston himself longs to be transformed internally so that his worship will be pleasing to God. It's about imagining the kingdom of Heaven coming to earth and setting everything right and then committing to allowing the personal transformation necessary to be an agent of that change in the world.

Selah

It's one thing to sing worship songs; it's another to pour them out of a worshipful heart. If your worship feels dry and forced, try addressing the condition of your heart by inviting the Holy Spirit to shine a light into any darkened corners where selfishness, fear or sin may be hiding.

When your heart becomes aligned with the heart of God in worship, you will invariably find more than just songs pouring out of your life. What kinds of character traits do you notice in others and how do their actions suggest to you that they are being transformed from within?

All the objects that Huram-Abi made for
King Solomon for the temple of the LORD
were of polished bronze. 17 The king had
them cast in clay molds in the plain of the
Jordan between Sukkoth and Zarethan.[a]
18 All these things that Solomon made
amounted to so much that the weight of the
bronze could not be calculated.

19 Solomon also made all the furnishings
that were in God's temple:

the golden altar;
the tables on which was the bread of the
Presence;
20 the lampstands of pure gold with their
lamps, to burn in front of the inner
sanctuary as prescribed;
21 the gold floral work and lamps and
tongs (they were solid gold);
22 the pure gold wick trimmers, sprin-
kling bowls, dishes and censers; and
the gold doors of the temple: the in-
ner doors to the Most Holy Place and
the doors of the main hall.

5 When all the work Solomon had done
for the temple of the LORD was finished,
he brought in the things his father David
had dedicated — the silver and gold and all
the furnishings — and he placed them in the
treasuries of God's temple.

The Ark Brought to the Temple

2 Then Solomon summoned to Jerusalem
the elders of Israel, all the heads of the tribes
and the chiefs of the Israelite families, to
bring up the ark of the LORD's covenant from
Zion, the City of David. 3 And all the Israel-
ites came together to the king at the time of
the festival in the seventh month.

4 When all the elders of Israel had ar-
rived, the Levites took up the ark, 5 and they
brought up the ark and the tent of meeting
and all the sacred furnishings in it. The Le-
vitical priests carried them up; 6 and King
Solomon and the entire assembly of Israel
that had gathered about him were before
the ark, sacrificing so many sheep and cattle
that they could not be recorded or counted.

7 The priests then brought the ark of
the LORD's covenant to its place in the in-
ner sanctuary of the temple, the Most Holy
Place, and put it beneath the wings of the
cherubim. 8 The cherubim spread their
wings over the place of the ark and covered
the ark and its carrying poles. 9 These poles
were so long that their ends, extending from
the ark, could be seen from in front of the in-
ner sanctuary, but not from outside the Holy
Place; and they are still there today. 10 There
was nothing in the ark except the two tablets
that Moses had placed in it at Horeb, where
the LORD made a covenant with the Israel-
ites after they came out of Egypt.

11 The priests then withdrew from the Holy
Place. All the priests who were there had
consecrated themselves, regardless of their
divisions. 12 All the Levites who were musi-
cians — Asaph, Heman, Jeduthun and their
sons and relatives — stood on the east side
of the altar, dressed in fine linen and playing
cymbals, harps and lyres. They were accom-
panied by 120 priests sounding trumpets.
13 The trumpeters and musicians joined in
unison to give praise and thanks to the LORD.
Accompanied by trumpets, cymbals and
other instruments, the singers raised their
voices in praise to the LORD and sang:

"He is good;
his love endures forever."

Then the temple of the LORD was filled
with the cloud, 14 and the priests could not
perform their service because of the cloud,
for the glory of the LORD filled the temple of
God.

6 Then Solomon said, "The LORD has said
that he would dwell in a dark cloud; 2 I
have built a magnificent temple for you, a
place for you to dwell forever."

3 While the whole assembly of Israel was
standing there, the king turned around and
blessed them. 4 Then he said:

"Praise be to the LORD, the God of
Israel, who with his hands has fulfilled
what he promised with his mouth to my
father David. For he said, 5 'Since the
day I brought my people out of Egypt,
I have not chosen a city in any tribe of
Israel to have a temple built so that my
Name might be there, nor have I cho-
sen anyone to be ruler over my people
Israel. 6 But now I have chosen Jerusa-
lem for my Name to be there, and I have
chosen David to rule my people Israel.'

[a] 17 Hebrew *Zeredatha,* a variant of *Zarethan*

7 "My father David had it in his heart to build a temple for the Name of the LORD, the God of Israel. 8 But the LORD said to my father David, 'You did well to have it in your heart to build a temple for my Name. 9 Nevertheless, you are not the one to build the temple, but your son, your own flesh and blood—he is the one who will build the temple for my Name.'

10 "The LORD has kept the promise he made. I have succeeded David my father and now I sit on the throne of Israel, just as the LORD promised, and I have built the temple for the Name of the LORD, the God of Israel. 11 There I have placed the ark, in which is the covenant of the LORD that he made with the people of Israel."

Solomon's Prayer of Dedication

12 Then Solomon stood before the altar of the LORD in front of the whole assembly of Israel and spread out his hands. 13 Now he had made a bronze platform, five cubits long, five cubits wide and three cubits high,[a] and had placed it in the center of the outer court. He stood on the platform and then knelt down before the whole assembly of Israel and spread out his hands toward heaven. 14 He said:

"LORD, the God of Israel, there is no God like you in heaven or on earth—you who keep your covenant of love with your servants who continue wholeheartedly in your way. 15 You have kept your promise to your servant David my father; with your mouth you have promised and with your hand you have fulfilled it—as it is today.

16 "Now, LORD, the God of Israel, keep for your servant David my father the promises you made to him when you said, 'You shall never fail to have a successor to sit before me on the throne of Israel, if only your descendants are careful in all they do to walk before me according to my law, as you have done.' 17 And now, LORD, the God of Israel, let your word that you promised your servant David come true.

18 "But will God really dwell on earth with humans? The heavens, even the highest heavens, cannot contain you. How much less this temple I have built! 19 Yet, LORD my God, give attention to your servant's prayer and his plea for mercy. Hear the cry and the prayer that your servant is praying in your presence. 20 May your eyes be open toward this temple day and night, this place of which you said you would put your Name there. May you hear the prayer your servant prays toward this place. 21 Hear the supplications of your servant and of your people Israel when they pray toward this place. Hear from heaven, your dwelling place; and when you hear, forgive.

22 "When anyone wrongs their neighbor and is required to take an oath and they come and swear the oath before your altar in this temple, 23 then hear from heaven and act. Judge between your servants, condemning the guilty and bringing down on their heads what they have done, and vindicating the innocent by treating them in accordance with their innocence.

24 "When your people Israel have been defeated by an enemy because they have sinned against you and when they turn back and give praise to your name, praying and making supplication before you in this temple, 25 then hear from heaven and forgive the sin of your people Israel and bring them back to the land you gave to them and their ancestors.

26 "When the heavens are shut up and there is no rain because your people have sinned against you, and when they pray toward this place and give praise to your name and turn from their sin because you have afflicted them, 27 then hear from heaven and forgive the sin of your servants, your people Israel. Teach them the right way to live, and send rain on the land you gave your people for an inheritance.

28 "When famine or plague comes to the land, or blight or mildew, locusts or grasshoppers, or when enemies besiege

[a] 13 That is, about 7 1/2 feet long and wide and 4 1/2 feet high or about 2.3 meters long and wide and 1.4 meters high

them in any of their cities, whatever disaster or disease may come, 29 and when a prayer or plea is made by anyone among your people Israel — being aware of their afflictions and pains, and spreading out their hands toward this temple — 30 then hear from heaven, your dwelling place. Forgive, and deal with everyone according to all they do, since you know their hearts (for you alone know the human heart), 31 so that they will fear you and walk in obedience to you all the time they live in the land you gave our ancestors.

32 "As for the foreigner who does not belong to your people Israel but has come from a distant land because of your great name and your mighty hand and your outstretched arm — when they come and pray toward this temple, 33 then hear from heaven, your dwelling place. Do whatever the foreigner asks of you, so that all the peoples of the earth may know your name and fear you, as do your own people Israel, and may know that this house I have built bears your Name.

34 "When your people go to war against their enemies, wherever you send them, and when they pray to you toward this city you have chosen and the temple I have built for your Name, 35 then hear from heaven their prayer and their plea, and uphold their cause.

36 "When they sin against you — for there is no one who does not sin — and you become angry with them and give them over to the enemy, who takes them captive to a land far away or near; 37 and if they have a change of heart in the land where they are held captive, and repent and plead with you in the land of their captivity and say, 'We have sinned, we have done wrong and acted wickedly'; 38 and if they turn back to you with all their heart and soul in the land of their captivity where they were taken, and pray toward the land you gave their ancestors, toward the city you have chosen and toward the temple I have built for your Name; 39 then from heaven, your dwelling place, hear their prayer and their pleas, and uphold their cause. And forgive your people, who have sinned against you.

40 "Now, my God, may your eyes be open and your ears attentive to the prayers offered in this place.

41 "Now arise, LORD God, and come
to your resting place,
you and the ark of your might.
May your priests, LORD God, be
clothed with salvation,
may your faithful people
rejoice in your goodness.
42 LORD God, do not reject your
anointed one.
Remember the great love
promised to David your
servant."

The Dedication of the Temple

7 When Solomon finished praying, fire came down from heaven and consumed the burnt offering and the sacrifices, and the glory of the LORD filled the temple. 2 The priests could not enter the temple of the LORD because the glory of the LORD filled it. 3 When all the Israelites saw the fire coming down and the glory of the LORD above the temple, they knelt on the pavement with their faces to the ground, and they worshiped and gave thanks to the LORD, saying,

"He is good;
his love endures forever."

4 Then the king and all the people offered sacrifices before the LORD. 5 And King Solomon offered a sacrifice of twenty-two thousand head of cattle and a hundred and twenty thousand sheep and goats. So the king and all the people dedicated the temple of God. 6 The priests took their positions, as did the Levites with the LORD's musical instruments, which King David had made for praising the LORD and which were used when he gave thanks, saying, "His love endures forever." Opposite the Levites, the priests blew their trumpets, and all the Israelites were standing.

7 Solomon consecrated the middle part of the courtyard in front of the temple of the LORD, and there he offered burnt offerings and the fat of the fellowship offerings, because the bronze altar he had made could not hold the burnt offerings, the grain offerings and the fat portions.

8 So Solomon observed the festival at that time for seven days, and all Israel with

him—a vast assembly, people from Lebo
Hamath to the Wadi of Egypt. 9On the eighth
day they held an assembly, for they had cel-
ebrated the dedication of the altar for seven
days and the festival for seven days more.
10On the twenty-third day of the seventh
month he sent the people to their homes,
joyful and glad in heart for the good things
the LORD had done for David and Solomon
and for his people Israel.

The LORD Appears to Solomon

11When Solomon had finished the tem-
ple of the LORD and the royal palace, and
had succeeded in carrying out all he had in
mind to do in the temple of the LORD and in
his own palace, 12the LORD appeared to him
at night and said:

> "I have heard your prayer and have
> chosen this place for myself as a temple
> for sacrifices.
> 13"When I shut up the heavens so
> that there is no rain, or command lo-
> custs to devour the land or send a
> plague among my people, 14if my peo-
> ple, who are called by my name, will
> humble themselves and pray and seek
> my face and turn from their wicked
> ways, then I will hear from heaven,
> and I will forgive their sin and will heal
> their land. 15Now my eyes will be open
> and my ears attentive to the prayers
> offered in this place. 16I have chosen
> and consecrated this temple so that my
> Name may be there forever. My eyes
> and my heart will always be there.
> 17"As for you, if you walk before me
> faithfully as David your father did, and
> do all I command, and observe my de-
> crees and laws, 18I will establish your
> royal throne, as I covenanted with Da-
> vid your father when I said, 'You shall
> never fail to have a successor to rule
> over Israel.'
> 19"But if you[a] turn away and forsake
> the decrees and commands I have giv-
> en you[a] and go off to serve other gods
> and worship them, 20then I will uproot
> Israel from my land, which I have given
> them, and will reject this temple I have
> consecrated for my Name. I will make
> it a byword and an object of ridicule
> among all peoples. 21This temple will
> become a heap of rubble. All[b] who pass
> by will be appalled and say, 'Why has
> the LORD done such a thing to this land
> and to this temple?' 22People will an-
> swer, 'Because they have forsaken the
> LORD, the God of their ancestors, who
> brought them out of Egypt, and have
> embraced other gods, worshiping and
> serving them—that is why he brought
> all this disaster on them.'"

Solomon's Other Activities

8 At the end of twenty years, during which
Solomon built the temple of the LORD
and his own palace, 2Solomon rebuilt the
villages that Hiram[c] had given him, and set-
tled Israelites in them. 3Solomon then went
to Hamath Zobah and captured it. 4He also
built up Tadmor in the desert and all the
store cities he had built in Hamath. 5He re-
built Upper Beth Horon and Lower Beth Ho-
ron as fortified cities, with walls and with
gates and bars, 6as well as Baalath and all
his store cities, and all the cities for his char-
iots and for his horses[d]—whatever he de-
sired to build in Jerusalem, in Lebanon and
throughout all the territory he ruled.

7There were still people left from the
Hittites, Amorites, Perizzites, Hivites and
Jebusites (these people were not Israelites).
8Solomon conscripted the descendants of all
these people remaining in the land—whom
the Israelites had not destroyed—to serve
as slave labor, as it is to this day. 9But Solo-
mon did not make slaves of the Israelites for
his work; they were his fighting men, com-
manders of his captains, and commanders
of his chariots and charioteers. 10They were
also King Solomon's chief officials—two
hundred and fifty officials supervising the
men.

11Solomon brought Pharaoh's daughter
up from the City of David to the palace he
had built for her, for he said, "My wife must
not live in the palace of David king of Israel,
because the places the ark of the LORD has
entered are holy."

12On the altar of the LORD that he had built

[a] *19* The Hebrew is plural. [b] *21* See some Septuagint manuscripts, Old Latin, Syriac, Arabic and Targum; Hebrew *And though this temple is now so imposing, all* [c] *2* Hebrew *Huram,* a variant of *Hiram;* also in verse 18 [d] *6* Or *charioteers*

in front of the portico, Solomon sacrificed burnt offerings to the LORD, [13]according to the daily requirement for offerings commanded by Moses for the Sabbaths, the New Moons and the three annual festivals—the Festival of Unleavened Bread, the Festival of Weeks and the Festival of Tabernacles. [14]In keeping with the ordinance of his father David, he appointed the divisions of the priests for their duties, and the Levites to lead the praise and to assist the priests according to each day's requirement. He also appointed the gatekeepers by divisions for the various gates, because this was what David the man of God had ordered. [15]They did not deviate from the king's commands to the priests or to the Levites in any matter, including that of the treasuries.

[16]All Solomon's work was carried out, from the day the foundation of the temple of the LORD was laid until its completion. So the temple of the LORD was finished.

[17]Then Solomon went to Ezion Geber and Elath on the coast of Edom. [18]And Hiram sent him ships commanded by his own men, sailors who knew the sea. These, with Solomon's men, sailed to Ophir and brought back four hundred and fifty talents[a] of gold, which they delivered to King Solomon.

The Queen of Sheba Visits Solomon

9 When the queen of Sheba heard of Solomon's fame, she came to Jerusalem to test him with hard questions. Arriving with a very great caravan—with camels carrying spices, large quantities of gold, and precious stones—she came to Solomon and talked with him about all she had on her mind. [2]Solomon answered all her questions; nothing was too hard for him to explain to her. [3]When the queen of Sheba saw the wisdom of Solomon, as well as the palace he had built, [4]the food on his table, the seating of his officials, the attending servants in their robes, the cupbearers in their robes and the burnt offerings he made at[b] the temple of the LORD, she was overwhelmed.

[5]She said to the king, "The report I heard in my own country about your achievements and your wisdom is true. [6]But I did not believe what they said until I came and saw with my own eyes. Indeed, not even half the greatness of your wisdom was told me; you have far exceeded the report I heard. [7]How happy your people must be! How happy your officials, who continually stand before you and hear your wisdom! [8]Praise be to the LORD your God, who has delighted in you and placed you on his throne as king to rule for the LORD your God. Because of the love of your God for Israel and his desire to uphold them forever, he has made you king over them, to maintain justice and righteousness."

[9]Then she gave the king 120 talents[c] of gold, large quantities of spices, and precious stones. There had never been such spices as those the queen of Sheba gave to King Solomon.

[10](The servants of Hiram and the servants of Solomon brought gold from Ophir; they also brought algumwood[d] and precious stones. [11]The king used the algumwood to make steps for the temple of the LORD and for the royal palace, and to make harps and lyres for the musicians. Nothing like them had ever been seen in Judah.)

[12]King Solomon gave the queen of Sheba all she desired and asked for; he gave her more than she had brought to him. Then she left and returned with her retinue to her own country.

Solomon's Splendor

[13]The weight of the gold that Solomon received yearly was 666 talents,[e] [14]not including the revenues brought in by merchants and traders. Also all the kings of Arabia and the governors of the territories brought gold and silver to Solomon.

[15]King Solomon made two hundred large shields of hammered gold; six hundred shekels[f] of hammered gold went into each shield. [16]He also made three hundred small shields of hammered gold, with three hundred shekels[g] of gold in each shield. The king put them in the Palace of the Forest of Lebanon.

[17]Then the king made a great throne covered with ivory and overlaid with pure

[a] *18* That is, about 17 tons or about 15 metric tons [b] *4* Or *and the ascent by which he went up to* [c] *9* That is, about 4 1/2 tons or about 4 metric tons [d] *10* Probably a variant of *almugwood* [e] *13* That is, about 25 tons or about 23 metric tons [f] *15* That is, about 15 pounds or about 6.9 kilograms [g] *16* That is, about 7 1/2 pounds or about 3.5 kilograms

gold. 18 The throne had six steps, and a footstool of gold was attached to it. On both sides of the seat were armrests, with a lion standing beside each of them. 19 Twelve lions stood on the six steps, one at either end of each step. Nothing like it had ever been made for any other kingdom. 20 All King Solomon's goblets were gold, and all the household articles in the Palace of the Forest of Lebanon were pure gold. Nothing was made of silver, because silver was considered of little value in Solomon's day. 21 The king had a fleet of trading ships[a] manned by Hiram's[b] servants. Once every three years it returned, carrying gold, silver and ivory, and apes and baboons.

22 King Solomon was greater in riches and wisdom than all the other kings of the earth. 23 All the kings of the earth sought audience with Solomon to hear the wisdom God had put in his heart. 24 Year after year, everyone who came brought a gift—articles of silver and gold, and robes, weapons and spices, and horses and mules.

25 Solomon had four thousand stalls for horses and chariots, and twelve thousand horses,[c] which he kept in the chariot cities and also with him in Jerusalem. 26 He ruled over all the kings from the Euphrates River to the land of the Philistines, as far as the border of Egypt. 27 The king made silver as common in Jerusalem as stones, and cedar as plentiful as sycamore-fig trees in the foothills. 28 Solomon's horses were imported from Egypt and from all other countries.

Solomon's Death

29 As for the other events of Solomon's reign, from beginning to end, are they not written in the records of Nathan the prophet, in the prophecy of Ahijah the Shilonite and in the visions of Iddo the seer concerning Jeroboam son of Nebat? 30 Solomon reigned in Jerusalem over all Israel forty years. 31 Then he rested with his ancestors and was buried in the city of David his father. And Rehoboam his son succeeded him as king.

Israel Rebels Against Rehoboam

10 Rehoboam went to Shechem, for all Israel had gone there to make him king. 2 When Jeroboam son of Nebat heard this (he was in Egypt, where he had fled from King Solomon), he returned from Egypt. 3 So they sent for Jeroboam, and he and all Israel went to Rehoboam and said to him: 4 "Your father put a heavy yoke on us, but now lighten the harsh labor and the heavy yoke he put on us, and we will serve you."

5 Rehoboam answered, "Come back to me in three days." So the people went away.

6 Then King Rehoboam consulted the elders who had served his father Solomon during his lifetime. "How would you advise me to answer these people?" he asked.

7 They replied, "If you will be kind to these people and please them and give them a favorable answer, they will always be your servants."

8 But Rehoboam rejected the advice the elders gave him and consulted the young men who had grown up with him and were serving him. 9 He asked them, "What is your advice? How should we answer these people who say to me, 'Lighten the yoke your father put on us'?"

10 The young men who had grown up with him replied, "The people have said to you, 'Your father put a heavy yoke on us, but make our yoke lighter.' Now tell them, 'My little finger is thicker than my father's waist. 11 My father laid on you a heavy yoke; I will make it even heavier. My father scourged you with whips; I will scourge you with scorpions.' "

12 Three days later Jeroboam and all the people returned to Rehoboam, as the king had said, "Come back to me in three days." 13 The king answered them harshly. Rejecting the advice of the elders, 14 he followed the advice of the young men and said, "My father made your yoke heavy; I will make it even heavier. My father scourged you with whips; I will scourge you with scorpions." 15 So the king did not listen to the people, for this turn of events was from God, to fulfill the word the LORD had spoken to Jeroboam son of Nebat through Ahijah the Shilonite.

16 When all Israel saw that the king refused to listen to them, they answered the king:

"What share do we have in David,
  what part in Jesse's son?
To your tents, Israel!
  Look after your own house, David!"

[a] 21 Hebrew *of ships that could go to Tarshish* [b] 21 Hebrew *Huram,* a variant of *Hiram*
[c] 25 Or *charioteers*

So all the Israelites went home. [17]But as for the Israelites who were living in the towns of Judah, Rehoboam still ruled over them.

[18]King Rehoboam sent out Adoniram,[a] who was in charge of forced labor, but the Israelites stoned him to death. King Rehoboam, however, managed to get into his chariot and escape to Jerusalem. [19]So Israel has been in rebellion against the house of David to this day.

11 When Rehoboam arrived in Jerusalem, he mustered Judah and Benjamin — a hundred and eighty thousand able young men — to go to war against Israel and to regain the kingdom for Rehoboam.

[2]But this word of the LORD came to Shemaiah the man of God: [3]"Say to Rehoboam son of Solomon king of Judah and to all Israel in Judah and Benjamin, [4]'This is what the LORD says: Do not go up to fight against your fellow Israelites. Go home, every one of you, for this is my doing.' " So they obeyed the words of the LORD and turned back from marching against Jeroboam.

Rehoboam Fortifies Judah

[5]Rehoboam lived in Jerusalem and built up towns for defense in Judah: [6]Bethlehem, Etam, Tekoa, [7]Beth Zur, Soko, Adullam, [8]Gath, Mareshah, Ziph, [9]Adoraim, Lachish, Azekah, [10]Zorah, Aijalon and Hebron. These were fortified cities in Judah and Benjamin. [11]He strengthened their defenses and put commanders in them, with supplies of food, olive oil and wine. [12]He put shields and spears in all the cities, and made them very strong. So Judah and Benjamin were his.

[13]The priests and Levites from all their districts throughout Israel sided with him. [14]The Levites even abandoned their pasturelands and property and came to Judah and Jerusalem, because Jeroboam and his sons had rejected them as priests of the LORD [15]when he appointed his own priests for the high places and for the goat and calf idols he had made. [16]Those from every tribe of Israel who set their hearts on seeking the LORD, the God of Israel, followed the Levites to Jerusalem to offer sacrifices to the LORD, the God of their ancestors. [17]They strengthened the kingdom of Judah and supported Rehoboam son of Solomon three years, following the ways of David and Solomon during this time.

Rehoboam's Family

[18]Rehoboam married Mahalath, who was the daughter of David's son Jerimoth and of Abihail, the daughter of Jesse's son Eliab. [19]She bore him sons: Jeush, Shemariah and Zaham. [20]Then he married Maakah daughter of Absalom, who bore him Abijah, Attai, Ziza and Shelomith. [21]Rehoboam loved Maakah daughter of Absalom more than any of his other wives and concubines. In all, he had eighteen wives and sixty concubines, twenty-eight sons and sixty daughters.

[22]Rehoboam appointed Abijah son of Maakah as crown prince among his brothers, in order to make him king. [23]He acted wisely, dispersing some of his sons throughout the districts of Judah and Benjamin, and to all the fortified cities. He gave them abundant provisions and took many wives for them.

Shishak Attacks Jerusalem

12 After Rehoboam's position as king was established and he had become strong, he and all Israel[b] with him abandoned the law of the LORD. [2]Because they had been unfaithful to the LORD, Shishak king of Egypt attacked Jerusalem in the fifth year of King Rehoboam. [3]With twelve hundred chariots and sixty thousand horsemen and the innumerable troops of Libyans, Sukkites and Cushites[c] that came with him from Egypt, [4]he captured the fortified cities of Judah and came as far as Jerusalem.

[5]Then the prophet Shemaiah came to Rehoboam and to the leaders of Judah who had assembled in Jerusalem for fear of Shishak, and he said to them, "This is what the LORD says, 'You have abandoned me; therefore, I now abandon you to Shishak.' "

[6]The leaders of Israel and the king humbled themselves and said, "The LORD is just."

[7]When the LORD saw that they humbled themselves, this word of the LORD came to Shemaiah: "Since they have humbled themselves, I will not destroy them but will soon give them deliverance. My wrath will not be poured out on Jerusalem through Shishak.

[a] *18* Hebrew *Hadoram,* a variant of *Adoniram* [b] *1* That is, Judah, as frequently in 2 Chronicles
[c] *3* That is, people from the upper Nile region

[8]They will, however, become subject to him, so that they may learn the difference between serving me and serving the kings of other lands."

[9]When Shishak king of Egypt attacked Jerusalem, he carried off the treasures of the temple of the LORD and the treasures of the royal palace. He took everything, including the gold shields Solomon had made. [10]So King Rehoboam made bronze shields to replace them and assigned these to the commanders of the guard on duty at the entrance to the royal palace. [11]Whenever the king went to the LORD's temple, the guards went with him, bearing the shields, and afterward they returned them to the guardroom.

[12]Because Rehoboam humbled himself, the LORD's anger turned from him, and he was not totally destroyed. Indeed, there was some good in Judah.

[13]King Rehoboam established himself firmly in Jerusalem and continued as king. He was forty-one years old when he became king, and he reigned seventeen years in Jerusalem, the city the LORD had chosen out of all the tribes of Israel in which to put his Name. His mother's name was Naamah; she was an Ammonite. [14]He did evil because he had not set his heart on seeking the LORD.

[15]As for the events of Rehoboam's reign, from beginning to end, are they not written in the records of Shemaiah the prophet and of Iddo the seer that deal with genealogies? There was continual warfare between Rehoboam and Jeroboam. [16]Rehoboam rested with his ancestors and was buried in the City of David. And Abijah his son succeeded him as king.

Abijah King of Judah

13 In the eighteenth year of the reign of Jeroboam, Abijah became king of Judah, [2]and he reigned in Jerusalem three years. His mother's name was Maakah,[a] a daughter[b] of Uriel of Gibeah.

There was war between Abijah and Jeroboam. [3]Abijah went into battle with an army of four hundred thousand able fighting men, and Jeroboam drew up a battle line against him with eight hundred thousand able troops.

[4]Abijah stood on Mount Zemaraim, in the hill country of Ephraim, and said, "Jeroboam and all Israel, listen to me! [5]Don't you know that the LORD, the God of Israel, has given the kingship of Israel to David and his descendants forever by a covenant of salt? [6]Yet Jeroboam son of Nebat, an official of Solomon son of David, rebelled against his master. [7]Some worthless scoundrels gathered around him and opposed Rehoboam son of Solomon when he was young and indecisive and not strong enough to resist them.

[8]"And now you plan to resist the kingdom of the LORD, which is in the hands of David's descendants. You are indeed a vast army and have with you the golden calves that Jeroboam made to be your gods. [9]But didn't you drive out the priests of the LORD, the sons of Aaron, and the Levites, and make priests of your own as the peoples of other lands do? Whoever comes to consecrate himself with a young bull and seven rams may become a priest of what are not gods.

[10]"As for us, the LORD is our God, and we have not forsaken him. The priests who serve the LORD are sons of Aaron, and the Levites assist them. [11]Every morning and evening they present burnt offerings and fragrant incense to the LORD. They set out the bread on the ceremonially clean table and light the lamps on the gold lampstand every evening. We are observing the requirements of the LORD our God. But you have forsaken him. [12]God is with us; he is our leader. His priests with their trumpets will sound the battle cry against you. People of Israel, do not fight against the LORD, the God of your ancestors, for you will not succeed."

[13]Now Jeroboam had sent troops around to the rear, so that while he was in front of Judah the ambush was behind them. [14]Judah turned and saw that they were being attacked at both front and rear. Then they cried out to the LORD. The priests blew their trumpets [15]and the men of Judah raised the battle cry. At the sound of their battle cry, God routed Jeroboam and all Israel before Abijah and Judah. [16]The Israelites fled before Judah, and God delivered them into their hands. [17]Abijah and his troops inflicted heavy losses on them, so that there were five

[a] 2 Most Septuagint manuscripts and Syriac (see also 11:20 and 1 Kings 15:2); Hebrew *Micaiah*
[b] 2 Or *granddaughter*

hundred thousand casualties among Israel's
able men. 18 The Israelites were subdued on
that occasion, and the people of Judah were
victorious because they relied on the LORD,
the God of their ancestors.
19 Abijah pursued Jeroboam and took
from him the towns of Bethel, Jeshanah
and Ephron, with their surrounding villag-
es. 20 Jeroboam did not regain power during
the time of Abijah. And the LORD struck him
down and he died.
21 But Abijah grew in strength. He married
fourteen wives and had twenty-two sons and
sixteen daughters.
22 The other events of Abijah's reign, what
he did and what he said, are written in the
annotations of the prophet Iddo.

14 [a] And Abijah rested with his ancestors
and was buried in the City of David.
Asa his son succeeded him as king, and in
his days the country was at peace for ten
years.

Asa King of Judah

2 Asa did what was good and right in the
eyes of the LORD his God. 3 He removed the
foreign altars and the high places, smashed
the sacred stones and cut down the Asherah
poles.[b] 4 He commanded Judah to seek the
LORD, the God of their ancestors, and to obey
his laws and commands. 5 He removed the
high places and incense altars in every town
in Judah, and the kingdom was at peace un-
der him. 6 He built up the fortified cities of
Judah, since the land was at peace. No one
was at war with him during those years, for
the LORD gave him rest.
7 "Let us build up these towns," he said
to Judah, "and put walls around them, with
towers, gates and bars. The land is still ours,
because we have sought the LORD our God;
we sought him and he has given us rest on
every side." So they built and prospered.
8 Asa had an army of three hundred thou-
sand men from Judah, equipped with large
shields and with spears, and two hundred
and eighty thousand from Benjamin, armed
with small shields and with bows. All these
were brave fighting men.
9 Zerah the Cushite marched out against
them with an army of thousands upon thou-
sands and three hundred chariots, and
came as far as Mareshah. 10 Asa went out to
meet him, and they took up battle positions
in the Valley of Zephathah near Mareshah.
11 Then Asa called to the LORD his God
and said, "LORD, there is no one like you to
help the powerless against the mighty. Help
us, LORD our God, for we rely on you, and in
your name we have come against this vast
army. LORD, you are our God; do not let mere
mortals prevail against you."
12 The LORD struck down the Cushites be-
fore Asa and Judah. The Cushites fled, 13 and
Asa and his army pursued them as far as Ge-
rar. Such a great number of Cushites fell that
they could not recover; they were crushed
before the LORD and his forces. The men of
Judah carried off a large amount of plunder.
14 They destroyed all the villages around Ge-
rar, for the terror of the LORD had fallen on
them. They looted all these villages, since
there was much plunder there. 15 They also
attacked the camps of the herders and car-
ried off droves of sheep and goats and cam-
els. Then they returned to Jerusalem.

Asa's Reform

15 The Spirit of God came on Azariah
son of Oded. 2 He went out to meet
Asa and said to him, "Listen to me, Asa and
all Judah and Benjamin. The LORD is with
you when you are with him. If you seek him,
he will be found by you, but if you forsake
him, he will forsake you. 3 For a long time
Israel was without the true God, without a
priest to teach and without the law. 4 But in
their distress they turned to the LORD, the
God of Israel, and sought him, and he was
found by them. 5 In those days it was not safe
to travel about, for all the inhabitants of the
lands were in great turmoil. 6 One nation
was being crushed by another and one city
by another, because God was troubling them
with every kind of distress. 7 But as for you,
be strong and do not give up, for your work
will be rewarded."
8 When Asa heard these words and the
prophecy of Azariah son of[c] Oded the prophet,
he took courage. He removed the detestable
idols from the whole land of Judah and Ben-
jamin and from the towns he had captured

[a] In Hebrew texts 14:1 is numbered 13:23, and 14:2-15 is numbered 14:1-14. [b] 3 That is, wooden symbols of the goddess Asherah; here and elsewhere in 2 Chronicles [c] 8 Vulgate and Syriac (see also Septuagint and verse 1); Hebrew does not have *Azariah son of*.

in the hills of Ephraim. He repaired the altar
of the LORD that was in front of the portico of
the LORD's temple.

9 Then he assembled all Judah and Ben-
jamin and the people from Ephraim, Ma-
nasseh and Simeon who had settled among
them, for large numbers had come over to
him from Israel when they saw that the LORD
his God was with him.

10 They assembled at Jerusalem in the
third month of the fifteenth year of Asa's
reign. 11 At that time they sacrificed to the
LORD seven hundred head of cattle and sev-
en thousand sheep and goats from the plun-
der they had brought back. 12 They entered
into a covenant to seek the LORD, the God of
their ancestors, with all their heart and soul.
13 All who would not seek the LORD, the God
of Israel, were to be put to death, whether
small or great, man or woman. 14 They took
an oath to the LORD with loud acclama-
tion, with shouting and with trumpets and
horns. 15 All Judah rejoiced about the oath
because they had sworn it wholeheartedly.
They sought God eagerly, and he was found
by them. So the LORD gave them rest on ev-
ery side.

16 King Asa also deposed his grandmother
Maakah from her position as queen moth-
er, because she had made a repulsive image
for the worship of Asherah. Asa cut it down,
broke it up and burned it in the Kidron Val-
ley. 17 Although he did not remove the high
places from Israel, Asa's heart was fully com-
mitted to the LORD all his life. 18 He brought
into the temple of God the silver and gold
and the articles that he and his father had
dedicated.

19 There was no more war until the thirty-
fifth year of Asa's reign.

Asa's Last Years

16 In the thirty-sixth year of Asa's reign
Baasha king of Israel went up against
Judah and fortified Ramah to prevent any-
one from leaving or entering the territory of
Asa king of Judah.

2 Asa then took the silver and gold out of
the treasuries of the LORD's temple and of his
own palace and sent it to Ben-Hadad king of
Aram, who was ruling in Damascus. 3 "Let
there be a treaty between me and you," he
said, "as there was between my father and
your father. See, I am sending you silver and
gold. Now break your treaty with Baasha
king of Israel so he will withdraw from me."

4 Ben-Hadad agreed with King Asa and
sent the commanders of his forces against
the towns of Israel. They conquered Ijon,
Dan, Abel Maim[a] and all the store cities
of Naphtali. 5 When Baasha heard this, he
stopped building Ramah and abandoned
his work. 6 Then King Asa brought all the
men of Judah, and they carried away from
Ramah the stones and timber Baasha had
been using. With them he built up Geba and
Mizpah.

7 At that time Hanani the seer came to Asa
king of Judah and said to him: "Because you
relied on the king of Aram and not on the
LORD your God, the army of the king of Aram
has escaped from your hand. 8 Were not the
Cushites[b] and Libyans a mighty army with
great numbers of chariots and horsemen[c]?
Yet when you relied on the LORD, he deliv-
ered them into your hand. 9 For the eyes
of the LORD range throughout the earth to
strengthen those whose hearts are fully
committed to him. You have done a foolish
thing, and from now on you will be at war."

10 Asa was angry with the seer because of
this; he was so enraged that he put him in
prison. At the same time Asa brutally op-
pressed some of the people.

11 The events of Asa's reign, from begin-
ning to end, are written in the book of the
kings of Judah and Israel. 12 In the thirty-
ninth year of his reign Asa was afflicted with
a disease in his feet. Though his disease was
severe, even in his illness he did not seek
help from the LORD, but only from the phy-
sicians. 13 Then in the forty-first year of his
reign Asa died and rested with his ancestors.
14 They buried him in the tomb that he had
cut out for himself in the City of David. They
laid him on a bier covered with spices and
various blended perfumes, and they made a
huge fire in his honor.

Jehoshaphat King of Judah

17 Jehoshaphat his son succeeded him
as king and strengthened himself
against Israel. 2 He stationed troops in all the
fortified cities of Judah and put garrisons in

[a] 4 Also known as *Abel Beth Maakah* [b] 8 That is, people from the upper Nile region
[c] 8 Or *charioteers*

Judah and in the towns of Ephraim that his father Asa had captured.

3The LORD was with Jehoshaphat because he followed the ways of his father David before him. He did not consult the Baals 4but sought the God of his father and followed his commands rather than the practices of Israel. 5The LORD established the kingdom under his control; and all Judah brought gifts to Jehoshaphat, so that he had great wealth and honor. 6His heart was devoted to the ways of the LORD; furthermore, he removed the high places and the Asherah poles from Judah.

7In the third year of his reign he sent his officials Ben-Hail, Obadiah, Zechariah, Nethanel and Micaiah to teach in the towns of Judah. 8With them were certain Levites — Shemaiah, Nethaniah, Zebadiah, Asahel, Shemiramoth, Jehonathan, Adonijah, Tobijah and Tob-Adonijah — and the priests Elishama and Jehoram. 9They taught throughout Judah, taking with them the Book of the Law of the LORD; they went around to all the towns of Judah and taught the people.

10The fear of the LORD fell on all the kingdoms of the lands surrounding Judah, so that they did not go to war against Jehoshaphat. 11Some Philistines brought Jehoshaphat gifts and silver as tribute, and the Arabs brought him flocks: seven thousand seven hundred rams and seven thousand seven hundred goats.

12Jehoshaphat became more and more powerful; he built forts and store cities in Judah 13and had large supplies in the towns of Judah. He also kept experienced fighting men in Jerusalem. 14Their enrollment by families was as follows:

From Judah, commanders of units of 1,000:
Adnah the commander, with 300,000 fighting men;
15next, Jehohanan the commander, with 280,000;
16next, Amasiah son of Zikri, who volunteered himself for the service of the LORD, with 200,000.

17From Benjamin:
Eliada, a valiant soldier, with 200,000 men armed with bows and shields;
18next, Jehozabad, with 180,000 men armed for battle.

19These were the men who served the king, besides those he stationed in the fortified cities throughout Judah.

Micaiah Prophesies Against Ahab

18 Now Jehoshaphat had great wealth and honor, and he allied himself with Ahab by marriage. 2Some years later he went down to see Ahab in Samaria. Ahab slaughtered many sheep and cattle for him and the people with him and urged him to attack Ramoth Gilead. 3Ahab king of Israel asked Jehoshaphat king of Judah, "Will you go with me against Ramoth Gilead?"

Jehoshaphat replied, "I am as you are, and my people as your people; we will join you in the war." 4But Jehoshaphat also said to the king of Israel, "First seek the counsel of the LORD."

5So the king of Israel brought together the prophets — four hundred men — and asked them, "Shall we go to war against Ramoth Gilead, or shall I not?"

"Go," they answered, "for God will give it into the king's hand."

6But Jehoshaphat asked, "Is there no longer a prophet of the LORD here whom we can inquire of?"

7The king of Israel answered Jehoshaphat, "There is still one prophet through whom we can inquire of the LORD, but I hate him because he never prophesies anything good about me, but always bad. He is Micaiah son of Imlah."

"The king should not say such a thing," Jehoshaphat replied.

8So the king of Israel called one of his officials and said, "Bring Micaiah son of Imlah at once."

9Dressed in their royal robes, the king of Israel and Jehoshaphat king of Judah were sitting on their thrones at the threshing floor by the entrance of the gate of Samaria, with all the prophets prophesying before them. 10Now Zedekiah son of Kenaanah had made iron horns, and he declared, "This is what the LORD says: 'With these you will gore the Arameans until they are destroyed.' "

11All the other prophets were prophesying the same thing. "Attack Ramoth Gilead and be victorious," they said, "for the LORD will give it into the king's hand."

12The messenger who had gone to summon Micaiah said to him, "Look, the other

prophets without exception are predicting
success for the king. Let your word agree
with theirs, and speak favorably."

13 But Micaiah said, "As surely as the LORD
lives, I can tell him only what my God says."

14 When he arrived, the king asked him,
"Micaiah, shall we go to war against Ramoth
Gilead, or shall I not?"

"Attack and be victorious," he answered,
"for they will be given into your hand."

15 The king said to him, "How many times
must I make you swear to tell me nothing but
the truth in the name of the LORD?"

16 Then Micaiah answered, "I saw all Isra-
el scattered on the hills like sheep without
a shepherd, and the LORD said, 'These peo-
ple have no master. Let each one go home in
peace.'"

17 The king of Israel said to Jehoshaphat,
"Didn't I tell you that he never prophesies
anything good about me, but only bad?"

18 Micaiah continued, "Therefore hear the
word of the LORD: I saw the LORD sitting on
his throne with all the multitudes of heaven
standing on his right and on his left. 19 And
the LORD said, 'Who will entice Ahab king of
Israel into attacking Ramoth Gilead and go-
ing to his death there?'

"One suggested this, and another that.
20 Finally, a spirit came forward, stood before
the LORD and said, 'I will entice him.'

"'By what means?' the LORD asked.

21 "'I will go and be a deceiving spirit in
the mouths of all his prophets,' he said.

"'You will succeed in enticing him,' said
the LORD. 'Go and do it.'

22 "So now the LORD has put a deceiv-
ing spirit in the mouths of these prophets
of yours. The LORD has decreed disaster for
you."

23 Then Zedekiah son of Kenaanah went
up and slapped Micaiah in the face. "Which
way did the spirit from[a] the LORD go when
he went from me to speak to you?" he asked.

24 Micaiah replied, "You will find out on
the day you go to hide in an inner room."

25 The king of Israel then ordered, "Take
Micaiah and send him back to Amon the
ruler of the city and to Joash the king's son,
26 and say, 'This is what the king says: Put
this fellow in prison and give him nothing
but bread and water until I return safely.'"

27 Micaiah declared, "If you ever return
safely, the LORD has not spoken through
me." Then he added, "Mark my words, all
you people!"

Ahab Killed at Ramoth Gilead

28 So the king of Israel and Jehoshaphat
king of Judah went up to Ramoth Gilead.
29 The king of Israel said to Jehoshaphat, "I
will enter the battle in disguise, but you wear
your royal robes." So the king of Israel dis-
guised himself and went into battle.

30 Now the king of Aram had ordered his
chariot commanders, "Do not fight with
anyone, small or great, except the king of Is-
rael." 31 When the chariot commanders saw
Jehoshaphat, they thought, "This is the king
of Israel." So they turned to attack him, but
Jehoshaphat cried out, and the LORD helped
him. God drew them away from him, 32 for
when the chariot commanders saw that he
was not the king of Israel, they stopped pur-
suing him.

33 But someone drew his bow at random
and hit the king of Israel between the breast-
plate and the scale armor. The king told the
chariot driver, "Wheel around and get me
out of the fighting. I've been wounded." 34 All
day long the battle raged, and the king of Is-
rael propped himself up in his chariot facing
the Arameans until evening. Then at sunset
he died.

19 When Jehoshaphat king of Judah re-
turned safely to his palace in Jerusa-
lem, 2 Jehu the seer, the son of Hanani, went
out to meet him and said to the king, "Should
you help the wicked and love[b] those who
hate the LORD? Because of this, the wrath of
the LORD is on you. 3 There is, however, some
good in you, for you have rid the land of the
Asherah poles and have set your heart on
seeking God."

Jehoshaphat Appoints Judges

4 Jehoshaphat lived in Jerusalem, and he
went out again among the people from Be-
ersheba to the hill country of Ephraim and
turned them back to the LORD, the God of
their ancestors. 5 He appointed judges in the
land, in each of the fortified cities of Judah.
6 He told them, "Consider carefully what you
do, because you are not judging for mere

[a] 23 Or *Spirit of* [b] 2 Or *and make alliances with*

mortals but for the LORD, who is with you whenever you give a verdict. 7Now let the fear of the LORD be on you. Judge carefully, for with the LORD our God there is no injustice or partiality or bribery."

8In Jerusalem also, Jehoshaphat appointed some of the Levites, priests and heads of Israelite families to administer the law of the LORD and to settle disputes. And they lived in Jerusalem. 9He gave them these orders: "You must serve faithfully and wholeheartedly in the fear of the LORD. 10In every case that comes before you from your people who live in the cities — whether bloodshed or other concerns of the law, commands, decrees or regulations — you are to warn them not to sin against the LORD; otherwise his wrath will come on you and your people. Do this, and you will not sin.

11"Amariah the chief priest will be over you in any matter concerning the LORD, and Zebadiah son of Ishmael, the leader of the tribe of Judah, will be over you in any matter concerning the king, and the Levites will serve as officials before you. Act with courage, and may the LORD be with those who do well."

Jehoshaphat Defeats Moab and Ammon

20 After this, the Moabites and Ammonites with some of the Meunites[a] came to wage war against Jehoshaphat.

2Some people came and told Jehoshaphat, "A vast army is coming against you from Edom,[b] from the other side of the Dead Sea. It is already in Hazezon Tamar" (that is, En Gedi). 3Alarmed, Jehoshaphat resolved to inquire of the LORD, and he proclaimed a fast for all Judah. 4The people of Judah came together to seek help from the LORD; indeed, they came from every town in Judah to seek him.

5Then Jehoshaphat stood up in the assembly of Judah and Jerusalem at the temple of the LORD in the front of the new courtyard 6and said:

"LORD, the God of our ancestors,
are you not the God who is in heaven?
You rule over all the kingdoms of the
nations. Power and might are in your
hand, and no one can withstand you.
7Our God, did you not drive out the
inhabitants of this land before your
people Israel and give it forever to the
descendants of Abraham your friend?
8They have lived in it and have built in
it a sanctuary for your Name, saying,
9'If calamity comes upon us, whether the sword of judgment, or plague
or famine, we will stand in your presence before this temple that bears your
Name and will cry out to you in our distress, and you will hear us and save us.'

10"But now here are men from Ammon, Moab and Mount Seir, whose territory you would not allow Israel to invade when they came from Egypt; so they turned away from them and did not destroy them. 11See how they are repaying us by coming to drive us out of the possession you gave us as an inheritance. 12Our God, will you not judge them? For we have no power to face this vast army that is attacking us. We do not know what to do, but our eyes are on you."

13All the men of Judah, with their wives and children and little ones, stood there before the LORD.

14Then the Spirit of the LORD came on Jahaziel son of Zechariah, the son of Benaiah, the son of Jeiel, the son of Mattaniah, a Levite and descendant of Asaph, as he stood in the assembly.

15He said: "Listen, King Jehoshaphat and all who live in Judah and Jerusalem! This is what the LORD says to you: 'Do not be afraid or discouraged because of this vast army. For the battle is not yours, but God's. 16Tomorrow march down against them. They will be climbing up by the Pass of Ziz, and you will find them at the end of the gorge in the Desert of Jeruel. 17You will not have to fight this battle. Take up your positions; stand firm and see the deliverance the LORD will give you, Judah and Jerusalem. Do not be afraid; do not be discouraged. Go out to face them tomorrow, and the LORD will be with you.' "

18Jehoshaphat bowed down with his face to the ground, and all the people of Judah and Jerusalem fell down in worship before the LORD. 19Then some Levites from the

[a] *1* Some Septuagint manuscripts; Hebrew *Ammonites*
[b] *2* One Hebrew manuscript; most Hebrew manuscripts, Septuagint and Vulgate *Aram*

Kohathites and Korahites stood up and praised the LORD, the God of Israel, with a very loud voice.

[20]Early in the morning they left for the Desert of Tekoa. As they set out, Jehoshaphat stood and said, "Listen to me, Judah and people of Jerusalem! Have faith in the LORD your God and you will be upheld; have faith in his prophets and you will be successful." [21]After consulting the people, Jehoshaphat appointed men to sing to the LORD and to praise him for the splendor of his[a] holiness as they went out at the head of the army, saying:

"Give thanks to the LORD,
for his love endures forever."

[22]As they began to sing and praise, the LORD set ambushes against the men of Ammon and Moab and Mount Seir who were invading Judah, and they were defeated. [23]The Ammonites and Moabites rose up against the men from Mount Seir to destroy and annihilate them. After they finished slaughtering the men from Seir, they helped to destroy one another.

[24]When the men of Judah came to the place that overlooks the desert and looked toward the vast army, they saw only dead bodies lying on the ground; no one had escaped. [25]So Jehoshaphat and his men went to carry off their plunder, and they found among them a great amount of equipment and clothing[b] and also articles of value—more than they could take away. There was so much plunder that it took three days to collect it. [26]On the fourth day they assembled in the Valley of Berakah, where they praised the LORD. This is why it is called the Valley of Berakah[c] to this day.

[27]Then, led by Jehoshaphat, all the men of Judah and Jerusalem returned joyfully to Jerusalem, for the LORD had given them cause to rejoice over their enemies. [28]They entered Jerusalem and went to the temple of the LORD with harps and lyres and trumpets.

[29]The fear of God came on all the surrounding kingdoms when they heard how the LORD had fought against the enemies of Israel. [30]And the kingdom of Jehoshaphat was at peace, for his God had given him rest on every side.

The End of Jehoshaphat's Reign

[31]So Jehoshaphat reigned over Judah. He was thirty-five years old when he became king of Judah, and he reigned in Jerusalem twenty-five years. His mother's name was Azubah daughter of Shilhi. [32]He followed the ways of his father Asa and did not stray from them; he did what was right in the eyes of the LORD. [33]The high places, however, were not removed, and the people still had not set their hearts on the God of their ancestors.

[34]The other events of Jehoshaphat's reign, from beginning to end, are written in the annals of Jehu son of Hanani, which are recorded in the book of the kings of Israel.

[35]Later, Jehoshaphat king of Judah made an alliance with Ahaziah king of Israel, whose ways were wicked. [36]He agreed with him to construct a fleet of trading ships.[d] After these were built at Ezion Geber, [37]Eliezer son of Dodavahu of Mareshah prophesied against Jehoshaphat, saying, "Because you have made an alliance with Ahaziah, the LORD will destroy what you have made." The ships were wrecked and were not able to set sail to trade.[e]

21 Then Jehoshaphat rested with his ancestors and was buried with them in the City of David. And Jehoram his son succeeded him as king. [2]Jehoram's brothers, the sons of Jehoshaphat, were Azariah, Jehiel, Zechariah, Azariahu, Michael and Shephatiah. All these were sons of Jehoshaphat king of Israel.[f] [3]Their father had given them many gifts of silver and gold and articles of value, as well as fortified cities in Judah, but he had given the kingdom to Jehoram because he was his firstborn son.

Jehoram King of Judah

[4]When Jehoram established himself firmly over his father's kingdom, he put all his brothers to the sword along with some of the officials of Israel. [5]Jehoram was thirty-two years old when he became king, and he reigned in Jerusalem eight years. [6]He followed the ways of the kings of Israel, as the house of Ahab had done, for he married a daughter of Ahab. He did evil in the eyes of

[a] 21 Or *him with the splendor of* [b] 25 Some Hebrew manuscripts and Vulgate; most Hebrew manuscripts *corpses* [c] 26 *Berakah* means *praise.* [d] 36 Hebrew *of ships that could go to Tarshish* [e] 37 Hebrew *sail for Tarshish* [f] 2 That is, Judah, as frequently in 2 Chronicles

the LORD. 7Nevertheless, because of the covenant the LORD had made with David, the LORD was not willing to destroy the house of David. He had promised to maintain a lamp for him and his descendants forever.

8In the time of Jehoram, Edom rebelled against Judah and set up its own king. 9So Jehoram went there with his officers and all his chariots. The Edomites surrounded him and his chariot commanders, but he rose up and broke through by night. 10To this day Edom has been in rebellion against Judah.

Libnah revolted at the same time, because Jehoram had forsaken the LORD, the God of his ancestors. 11He had also built high places on the hills of Judah and had caused the people of Jerusalem to prostitute themselves and had led Judah astray.

12Jehoram received a letter from Elijah the prophet, which said:

> "This is what the LORD, the God of your father David, says: 'You have not followed the ways of your father Jehoshaphat or of Asa king of Judah. 13But you have followed the ways of the kings of Israel, and you have led Judah and the people of Jerusalem to prostitute themselves, just as the house of Ahab did. You have also murdered your own brothers, members of your own family, men who were better than you. 14So now the LORD is about to strike your people, your sons, your wives and everything that is yours, with a heavy blow. 15You yourself will be very ill with a lingering disease of the bowels, until the disease causes your bowels to come out.' "

16The LORD aroused against Jehoram the hostility of the Philistines and of the Arabs who lived near the Cushites. 17They attacked Judah, invaded it and carried off all the goods found in the king's palace, together with his sons and wives. Not a son was left to him except Ahaziah,[a] the youngest.

18After all this, the LORD afflicted Jehoram with an incurable disease of the bowels. 19In the course of time, at the end of the second year, his bowels came out because of the disease, and he died in great pain. His people made no funeral fire in his honor, as they had for his predecessors.

20Jehoram was thirty-two years old when he became king, and he reigned in Jerusalem eight years. He passed away, to no one's regret, and was buried in the City of David, but not in the tombs of the kings.

Ahaziah King of Judah

22 The people of Jerusalem made Ahaziah, Jehoram's youngest son, king in his place, since the raiders, who came with the Arabs into the camp, had killed all the older sons. So Ahaziah son of Jehoram king of Judah began to reign.

2Ahaziah was twenty-two[b] years old when he became king, and he reigned in Jerusalem one year. His mother's name was Athaliah, a granddaughter of Omri.

3He too followed the ways of the house of Ahab, for his mother encouraged him to act wickedly. 4He did evil in the eyes of the LORD, as the house of Ahab had done, for after his father's death they became his advisers, to his undoing. 5He also followed their counsel when he went with Joram[c] son of Ahab king of Israel to wage war against Hazael king of Aram at Ramoth Gilead. The Arameans wounded Joram; 6so he returned to Jezreel to recover from the wounds they had inflicted on him at Ramoth[d] in his battle with Hazael king of Aram.

Then Ahaziah[e] son of Jehoram king of Judah went down to Jezreel to see Joram son of Ahab because he had been wounded.

7Through Ahaziah's visit to Joram, God brought about Ahaziah's downfall. When Ahaziah arrived, he went out with Joram to meet Jehu son of Nimshi, whom the LORD had anointed to destroy the house of Ahab. 8While Jehu was executing judgment on the house of Ahab, he found the officials of Judah and the sons of Ahaziah's relatives, who had been attending Ahaziah, and he killed them. 9He then went in search of Ahaziah, and his men captured him while he was hiding in Samaria. He was brought to Jehu and put to death. They buried him, for they said, "He was a son of Jehoshaphat, who sought

[a] *17* Hebrew *Jehoahaz,* a variant of *Ahaziah* [b] *2* Some Septuagint manuscripts and Syriac (see also 2 Kings 8:26); Hebrew *forty-two* [c] *5* Hebrew *Jehoram,* a variant of *Joram*; also in verses 6 and 7 [d] *6* Hebrew *Ramah,* a variant of *Ramoth* [e] *6* Some Hebrew manuscripts, Septuagint, Vulgate and Syriac (see also 2 Kings 8:29); most Hebrew manuscripts *Azariah*

the LORD with all his heart." So there was
no one in the house of Ahaziah powerful
enough to retain the kingdom.

Athaliah and Joash

[10]When Athaliah the mother of Ahaziah
saw that her son was dead, she proceeded to
destroy the whole royal family of the house
of Judah. [11]But Jehosheba,[a] the daughter of
King Jehoram, took Joash son of Ahaziah
and stole him away from among the roy-
al princes who were about to be murdered
and put him and his nurse in a bedroom.
Because Jehosheba,[a] the daughter of King
Jehoram and wife of the priest Jehoiada, was
Ahaziah's sister, she hid the child from Atha-
liah so she could not kill him. [12]He remained
hidden with them at the temple of God for six
years while Athaliah ruled the land.

23 In the seventh year Jehoiada showed
his strength. He made a covenant
with the commanders of units of a hundred:
Azariah son of Jeroham, Ishmael son of Je-
hohanan, Azariah son of Obed, Maaseiah
son of Adaiah, and Elishaphat son of Zikri.
[2]They went throughout Judah and gathered
the Levites and the heads of Israelite fami-
lies from all the towns. When they came to
Jerusalem, [3]the whole assembly made a cov-
enant with the king at the temple of God.

Jehoiada said to them, "The king's son
shall reign, as the LORD promised concern-
ing the descendants of David. [4]Now this is
what you are to do: A third of you priests and
Levites who are going on duty on the Sab-
bath are to keep watch at the doors, [5]a third
of you at the royal palace and a third at the
Foundation Gate, and all the others are to be
in the courtyards of the temple of the LORD.
[6]No one is to enter the temple of the LORD
except the priests and Levites on duty; they
may enter because they are consecrated, but
all the others are to observe the LORD's com-
mand not to enter.[b] [7]The Levites are to sta-
tion themselves around the king, each with
weapon in hand. Anyone who enters the
temple is to be put to death. Stay close to the
king wherever he goes."

[8]The Levites and all the men of Judah did
just as Jehoiada the priest ordered. Each one
took his men — those who were going on
duty on the Sabbath and those who were
going off duty — for Jehoiada the priest had
not released any of the divisions. [9]Then he
gave the commanders of units of a hundred
the spears and the large and small shields
that had belonged to King David and that
were in the temple of God. [10]He stationed all
the men, each with his weapon in his hand,
around the king — near the altar and the
temple, from the south side to the north side
of the temple.

[11]Jehoiada and his sons brought out the
king's son and put the crown on him; they
presented him with a copy of the covenant
and proclaimed him king. They anointed
him and shouted, "Long live the king!"

[12]When Athaliah heard the noise of the
people running and cheering the king, she
went to them at the temple of the LORD. [13]She
looked, and there was the king, standing by
his pillar at the entrance. The officers and
the trumpeters were beside the king, and
all the people of the land were rejoicing and
blowing trumpets, and musicians with their
instruments were leading the praises. Then
Athaliah tore her robes and shouted, "Trea-
son! Treason!"

[14]Jehoiada the priest sent out the com-
manders of units of a hundred, who were
in charge of the troops, and said to them:
"Bring her out between the ranks[c] and put
to the sword anyone who follows her." For
the priest had said, "Do not put her to death
at the temple of the LORD." [15]So they seized
her as she reached the entrance of the Horse
Gate on the palace grounds, and there they
put her to death.

[16]Jehoiada then made a covenant that he,
the people and the king[d] would be the LORD's
people. [17]All the people went to the temple of
Baal and tore it down. They smashed the al-
tars and idols and killed Mattan the priest of
Baal in front of the altars.

[18]Then Jehoiada placed the oversight of
the temple of the LORD in the hands of the
Levitical priests, to whom David had made
assignments in the temple, to present the
burnt offerings of the LORD as written in the
Law of Moses, with rejoicing and singing,
as David had ordered. [19]He also stationed
gatekeepers at the gates of the LORD's temple

[a] *11* Hebrew *Jehoshabeath,* a variant of *Jehosheba* [b] *6* Or *are to stand guard where the LORD has assigned them* [c] *14* Or *out from the precincts* [d] *16* Or *covenant between the LORD and the people and the king that they* (see 2 Kings 11:17)

so that no one who was in any way unclean
might enter.
20 He took with him the commanders of
hundreds, the nobles, the rulers of the peo-
ple and all the people of the land and brought
the king down from the temple of the LORD.
They went into the palace through the Upper
Gate and seated the king on the royal throne.
21 All the people of the land rejoiced, and the
city was calm, because Athaliah had been
slain with the sword.

Joash Repairs the Temple

24 Joash was seven years old when he
became king, and he reigned in Je-
rusalem forty years. His mother's name was
Zibiah; she was from Beersheba. 2 Joash did
what was right in the eyes of the LORD all
the years of Jehoiada the priest. 3 Jehoiada
chose two wives for him, and he had sons
and daughters.
4 Some time later Joash decided to restore
the temple of the LORD. 5 He called together
the priests and Levites and said to them, "Go
to the towns of Judah and collect the mon-
ey due annually from all Israel, to repair the
temple of your God. Do it now." But the Le-
vites did not act at once.
6 Therefore the king summoned Jehoi-
ada the chief priest and said to him, "Why
haven't you required the Levites to bring in
from Judah and Jerusalem the tax imposed
by Moses the servant of the LORD and by
the assembly of Israel for the tent of the cov-
enant law?"
7 Now the sons of that wicked woman
Athaliah had broken into the temple of God
and had used even its sacred objects for the
Baals.
8 At the king's command, a chest was
made and placed outside, at the gate of the
temple of the LORD. 9 A proclamation was
then issued in Judah and Jerusalem that
they should bring to the LORD the tax that
Moses the servant of God had required of Is-
rael in the wilderness. 10 All the officials and
all the people brought their contributions
gladly, dropping them into the chest until it
was full. 11 Whenever the chest was brought
in by the Levites to the king's officials and
they saw that there was a large amount of
money, the royal secretary and the officer of
the chief priest would come and empty the
chest and carry it back to its place. They did
this regularly and collected a great amount
of money. 12 The king and Jehoiada gave it to
those who carried out the work required for
the temple of the LORD. They hired masons
and carpenters to restore the LORD's temple,
and also workers in iron and bronze to repair
the temple.
13 The men in charge of the work were
diligent, and the repairs progressed under
them. They rebuilt the temple of God ac-
cording to its original design and reinforced
it. 14 When they had finished, they brought
the rest of the money to the king and Jehoi-
ada, and with it were made articles for the
LORD's temple: articles for the service and
for the burnt offerings, and also dishes and
other objects of gold and silver. As long as Je-
hoiada lived, burnt offerings were presented
continually in the temple of the LORD.
15 Now Jehoiada was old and full of years,
and he died at the age of a hundred and thir-
ty. 16 He was buried with the kings in the City
of David, because of the good he had done in
Israel for God and his temple.

The Wickedness of Joash

17 After the death of Jehoiada, the officials
of Judah came and paid homage to the king,
and he listened to them. 18 They abandoned
the temple of the LORD, the God of their an-
cestors, and worshiped Asherah poles and
idols. Because of their guilt, God's anger
came on Judah and Jerusalem. 19 Although
the LORD sent prophets to the people to
bring them back to him, and though they
testified against them, they would not listen.
20 Then the Spirit of God came on Zechari-
ah son of Jehoiada the priest. He stood before
the people and said, "This is what God says:
'Why do you disobey the LORD's commands?
You will not prosper. Because you have for-
saken the LORD, he has forsaken you.' "
21 But they plotted against him, and by or-
der of the king they stoned him to death in
the courtyard of the LORD's temple. 22 King
Joash did not remember the kindness Zech-
ariah's father Jehoiada had shown him but
killed his son, who said as he lay dying, "May
the LORD see this and call you to account."
23 At the turn of the year,[a] the army of

[a] *23* Probably in the spring

Aram marched against Joash; it invaded Judah and Jerusalem and killed all the leaders of the people. They sent all the plunder to their king in Damascus. 24 Although the Aramean army had come with only a few men, the LORD delivered into their hands a much larger army. Because Judah had forsaken the LORD, the God of their ancestors, judgment was executed on Joash. 25 When the Arameans withdrew, they left Joash severely wounded. His officials conspired against him for murdering the son of Jehoiada the priest, and they killed him in his bed. So he died and was buried in the City of David, but not in the tombs of the kings.

26 Those who conspired against him were Zabad,[a] son of Shimeath an Ammonite woman, and Jehozabad, son of Shimrith[b] a Moabite woman. 27 The account of his sons, the many prophecies about him, and the record of the restoration of the temple of God are written in the annotations on the book of the kings. And Amaziah his son succeeded him as king.

Amaziah King of Judah

25 Amaziah was twenty-five years old when he became king, and he reigned in Jerusalem twenty-nine years. His mother's name was Jehoaddan; she was from Jerusalem. 2 He did what was right in the eyes of the LORD, but not wholeheartedly. 3 After the kingdom was firmly in his control, he executed the officials who had murdered his father the king. 4 Yet he did not put their children to death, but acted in accordance with what is written in the Law, in the Book of Moses, where the LORD commanded: "Parents shall not be put to death for their children, nor children be put to death for their parents; each will die for their own sin."[c]

5 Amaziah called the people of Judah together and assigned them according to their families to commanders of thousands and commanders of hundreds for all Judah and Benjamin. He then mustered those twenty years old or more and found that there were three hundred thousand men fit for military service, able to handle the spear and shield. 6 He also hired a hundred thousand fighting men from Israel for a hundred talents[d] of silver.

7 But a man of God came to him and said, "Your Majesty, these troops from Israel must not march with you, for the LORD is not with Israel — not with any of the people of Ephraim. 8 Even if you go and fight courageously in battle, God will overthrow you before the enemy, for God has the power to help or to overthrow."

9 Amaziah asked the man of God, "But what about the hundred talents I paid for these Israelite troops?"

The man of God replied, "The LORD can give you much more than that."

10 So Amaziah dismissed the troops who had come to him from Ephraim and sent them home. They were furious with Judah and left for home in a great rage.

11 Amaziah then marshaled his strength and led his army to the Valley of Salt, where he killed ten thousand men of Seir. 12 The army of Judah also captured ten thousand men alive, took them to the top of a cliff and threw them down so that all were dashed to pieces.

13 Meanwhile the troops that Amaziah had sent back and had not allowed to take part in the war raided towns belonging to Judah from Samaria to Beth Horon. They killed three thousand people and carried off great quantities of plunder.

14 When Amaziah returned from slaughtering the Edomites, he brought back the gods of the people of Seir. He set them up as his own gods, bowed down to them and burned sacrifices to them. 15 The anger of the LORD burned against Amaziah, and he sent a prophet to him, who said, "Why do you consult this people's gods, which could not save their own people from your hand?"

16 While he was still speaking, the king said to him, "Have we appointed you an adviser to the king? Stop! Why be struck down?"

So the prophet stopped but said, "I know that God has determined to destroy you, because you have done this and have not listened to my counsel."

17 After Amaziah king of Judah consulted his advisers, he sent this challenge to Jehoash[e] son of Jehoahaz, the son of Jehu, king of Israel: "Come, let us face each other in battle."

[a] *26* A variant of *Jozabad* [b] *26* A variant of *Shomer* [c] *4* Deut. 24:16 [d] *6* That is, about 3 3/4 tons or about 3.4 metric tons; also in verse 9 [e] *17* Hebrew *Joash,* a variant of *Jehoash;* also in verses 18, 21, 23 and 25

18 But Jehoash king of Israel replied to Amaziah king of Judah: "A thistle in Lebanon sent a message to a cedar in Lebanon, 'Give your daughter to my son in marriage.' Then a wild beast in Lebanon came along and trampled the thistle underfoot. 19 You say to yourself that you have defeated Edom, and now you are arrogant and proud. But stay at home! Why ask for trouble and cause your own downfall and that of Judah also?"

20 Amaziah, however, would not listen, for God so worked that he might deliver them into the hands of Jehoash, because they sought the gods of Edom. 21 So Jehoash king of Israel attacked. He and Amaziah king of Judah faced each other at Beth Shemesh in Judah. 22 Judah was routed by Israel, and every man fled to his home. 23 Jehoash king of Israel captured Amaziah king of Judah, the son of Joash, the son of Ahaziah,[a] at Beth Shemesh. Then Jehoash brought him to Jerusalem and broke down the wall of Jerusalem from the Ephraim Gate to the Corner Gate — a section about four hundred cubits[b] long. 24 He took all the gold and silver and all the articles found in the temple of God that had been in the care of Obed-Edom, together with the palace treasures and the hostages, and returned to Samaria.

25 Amaziah son of Joash king of Judah lived for fifteen years after the death of Jehoash son of Jehoahaz king of Israel. 26 As for the other events of Amaziah's reign, from beginning to end, are they not written in the book of the kings of Judah and Israel? 27 From the time that Amaziah turned away from following the LORD, they conspired against him in Jerusalem and he fled to Lachish, but they sent men after him to Lachish and killed him there. 28 He was brought back by horse and was buried with his ancestors in the City of Judah.[c]

Uzziah King of Judah

26 Then all the people of Judah took Uzziah,[d] who was sixteen years old, and made him king in place of his father Amaziah. 2 He was the one who rebuilt Elath and restored it to Judah after Amaziah rested with his ancestors.

3 Uzziah was sixteen years old when he became king, and he reigned in Jerusalem fifty-two years. His mother's name was Jekoliah; she was from Jerusalem. 4 He did what was right in the eyes of the LORD, just as his father Amaziah had done. 5 He sought God during the days of Zechariah, who instructed him in the fear[e] of God. As long as he sought the LORD, God gave him success.

6 He went to war against the Philistines and broke down the walls of Gath, Jabneh and Ashdod. He then rebuilt towns near Ashdod and elsewhere among the Philistines. 7 God helped him against the Philistines and against the Arabs who lived in Gur Baal and against the Meunites. 8 The Ammonites brought tribute to Uzziah, and his fame spread as far as the border of Egypt, because he had become very powerful.

9 Uzziah built towers in Jerusalem at the Corner Gate, at the Valley Gate and at the angle of the wall, and he fortified them. 10 He also built towers in the wilderness and dug many cisterns, because he had much livestock in the foothills and in the plain. He had people working his fields and vineyards in the hills and in the fertile lands, for he loved the soil.

11 Uzziah had a well-trained army, ready to go out by divisions according to their numbers as mustered by Jeiel the secretary and Maaseiah the officer under the direction of Hananiah, one of the royal officials. 12 The total number of family leaders over the fighting men was 2,600. 13 Under their command was an army of 307,500 men trained for war, a powerful force to support the king against his enemies. 14 Uzziah provided shields, spears, helmets, coats of armor, bows and slingstones for the entire army. 15 In Jerusalem he made devices invented for use on the towers and on the corner defenses so that soldiers could shoot arrows and hurl large stones from the walls. His fame spread far and wide, for he was greatly helped until he became powerful.

16 But after Uzziah became powerful, his pride led to his downfall. He was unfaithful to the LORD his God, and entered the temple of the LORD to burn incense on the altar

[a] *23* Hebrew *Jehoahaz,* a variant of *Ahaziah* [b] *23* That is, about 600 feet or about 180 meters
[c] *28* Most Hebrew manuscripts; some Hebrew manuscripts, Septuagint, Vulgate and Syriac (see also 2 Kings 14:20) *David* [d] *1* Also called *Azariah* [e] *5* Many Hebrew manuscripts, Septuagint and Syriac; other Hebrew manuscripts *vision*

of incense. 17 Azariah the priest with eighty other courageous priests of the LORD followed him in. 18 They confronted King Uzziah and said, "It is not right for you, Uzziah, to burn incense to the LORD. That is for the priests, the descendants of Aaron, who have been consecrated to burn incense. Leave the sanctuary, for you have been unfaithful; and you will not be honored by the LORD God."

19 Uzziah, who had a censer in his hand ready to burn incense, became angry. While he was raging at the priests in their presence before the incense altar in the LORD's temple, leprosy[a] broke out on his forehead. 20 When Azariah the chief priest and all the other priests looked at him, they saw that he had leprosy on his forehead, so they hurried him out. Indeed, he himself was eager to leave, because the LORD had afflicted him.

21 King Uzziah had leprosy until the day he died. He lived in a separate house[b]—leprous, and banned from the temple of the LORD. Jotham his son had charge of the palace and governed the people of the land.

22 The other events of Uzziah's reign, from beginning to end, are recorded by the prophet Isaiah son of Amoz. 23 Uzziah rested with his ancestors and was buried near them in a cemetery that belonged to the kings, for people said, "He had leprosy." And Jotham his son succeeded him as king.

Jotham King of Judah

27 Jotham was twenty-five years old when he became king, and he reigned in Jerusalem sixteen years. His mother's name was Jerusha daughter of Zadok. 2 He did what was right in the eyes of the LORD, just as his father Uzziah had done, but unlike him he did not enter the temple of the LORD. The people, however, continued their corrupt practices. 3 Jotham rebuilt the Upper Gate of the temple of the LORD and did extensive work on the wall at the hill of Ophel. 4 He built towns in the hill country of Judah and forts and towers in the wooded areas.

5 Jotham waged war against the king of the Ammonites and conquered them. That year the Ammonites paid him a hundred talents[c] of silver, ten thousand cors[d] of wheat and ten thousand cors[e] of barley. The Ammonites brought him the same amount also in the second and third years.

6 Jotham grew powerful because he walked steadfastly before the LORD his God.

7 The other events in Jotham's reign, including all his wars and the other things he did, are written in the book of the kings of Israel and Judah. 8 He was twenty-five years old when he became king, and he reigned in Jerusalem sixteen years. 9 Jotham rested with his ancestors and was buried in the City of David. And Ahaz his son succeeded him as king.

Ahaz King of Judah

28 Ahaz was twenty years old when he became king, and he reigned in Jerusalem sixteen years. Unlike David his father, he did not do what was right in the eyes of the LORD. 2 He followed the ways of the kings of Israel and also made idols for worshiping the Baals. 3 He burned sacrifices in the Valley of Ben Hinnom and sacrificed his children in the fire, engaging in the detestable practices of the nations the LORD had driven out before the Israelites. 4 He offered sacrifices and burned incense at the high places, on the hilltops and under every spreading tree.

5 Therefore the LORD his God delivered him into the hands of the king of Aram. The Arameans defeated him and took many of his people as prisoners and brought them to Damascus.

He was also given into the hands of the king of Israel, who inflicted heavy casualties on him. 6 In one day Pekah son of Remaliah killed a hundred and twenty thousand soldiers in Judah—because Judah had forsaken the LORD, the God of their ancestors. 7 Zikri, an Ephraimite warrior, killed Maaseiah the king's son, Azrikam the officer in charge of the palace, and Elkanah, second to the king. 8 The men of Israel took captive from their fellow Israelites who were from Judah two hundred thousand wives, sons and daughters. They also took a great deal of plunder, which they carried back to Samaria.

9 But a prophet of the LORD named Oded was there, and he went out to meet the army

[a] *19* The Hebrew for *leprosy* was used for various diseases affecting the skin; also in verses 20, 21 and 23.
[b] *21* Or *in a house where he was relieved of responsibilities*
[c] *5* That is, about 3 3/4 tons or about 3.4 metric tons
[d] *5* That is, probably about 1,800 tons or about 1,600 metric tons of wheat
[e] *5* That is, probably about 1,500 tons or about 1,350 metric tons of barley

HOSANNA

Brooke Ligerwood

I see the King of glory
Coming on the clouds with fire
The whole earth shakes
The whole earth shakes yeah
I see his love and mercy
Washing over all our sin
The people sing
The people sing

Hosanna, hosanna
Hosanna in the highest
Hosanna, hosanna
Hosanna in the highest

I see a generation
Rising up to take their place
With selfless faith
With selfless faith
I see a near revival
Stirring as we pray and seek
We're on our knees
We're on our knees

Heal my heart and make it clean
Open up my eyes to the things unseen
Show me how to love like you have loved me
Break my heart for what breaks yours
Everything I am for your Kingdom's cause
As I walk from earth into eternity

THE INSPIRATION

The crowds that went ahead of [Jesus] and those that followed shouted, "Hosanna to the Son of David!" "Blessed is he who comes in the name of the Lord!" "Hosanna in the highest heaven!"

—Matthew 21:9

Read also: Mark 11:9–10; John 12:13

BEHIND THE SONG

Brooke Ligerwood has been a frequent worship leader and songwriter at Hillsong Church in Australia for many years, but composing "Hosanna" was a unique experience for her.

"I wrote the verses and the bridge very easily in my bedroom at home," she says, "but the chorus was still missing. There was this big gap after the lyric says 'the people sing, the people sing.' I asked, 'What do the people sing, Lord?'"

Ligerwood found a quiet room with a piano and began playing the parts she had completed and waited for the chorus to arrive. Finally, it did. She started singing the word *Hosanna*, borrowed from the crowds as they waved their palm branches and sang praise to Jesus at his Triumphal Entry into Jerusalem.

"Jesus had resolutely set out for Jerusalem where he was about to die on the cross for our sin," Ligerwood explains. "In verse 9 it says that those who went before and those who followed after all cried, 'Hosanna.' *Hosanna* is an ancient Hebrew word that literally means 'praise, save us!'"

Ligerwood found a unique perspective on a few words, seeing herself and her generation as "ones who came after."

"'Hosanna' has been sung for thousands of years," she adds, "for generations that have gone before us. And it will also be sung by generations yet to come. It's an eternal cry of praise."

Selah

The song "Hosanna" starts with a vision of the return of Christ and then explores the idea of a coming revival. The song joins generations of believers who have cried out "save us!" Have there been times in your life when your worship consisted primarily as a plea for help from God?

We know that many of the same crowd members who chanted "Hosanna" as Jesus entered Jerusalem chanted "Crucify him!" just a week later. Oh, how fickle the human heart can be when our expectations are not met! Can you think of times in your life when Jesus has not seemed to do what you expected of him? How did you respond?

when it returned to Samaria. He said to them, "Because the LORD, the God of your ancestors, was angry with Judah, he gave them into your hand. But you have slaughtered them in a rage that reaches to heaven. 10 And now you intend to make the men and women of Judah and Jerusalem your slaves. But aren't you also guilty of sins against the LORD your God? 11 Now listen to me! Send back your fellow Israelites you have taken as prisoners, for the LORD's fierce anger rests on you."

12 Then some of the leaders in Ephraim—Azariah son of Jehohanan, Berekiah son of Meshillemoth, Jehizkiah son of Shallum, and Amasa son of Hadlai—confronted those who were arriving from the war. 13 "You must not bring those prisoners here," they said, "or we will be guilty before the LORD. Do you intend to add to our sin and guilt? For our guilt is already great, and his fierce anger rests on Israel."

14 So the soldiers gave up the prisoners and plunder in the presence of the officials and all the assembly. 15 The men designated by name took the prisoners, and from the plunder they clothed all who were naked. They provided them with clothes and sandals, food and drink, and healing balm. All those who were weak they put on donkeys. So they took them back to their fellow Israelites at Jericho, the City of Palms, and returned to Samaria.

16 At that time King Ahaz sent to the kings[a] of Assyria for help. 17 The Edomites had again come and attacked Judah and carried away prisoners, 18 while the Philistines had raided towns in the foothills and in the Negev of Judah. They captured and occupied Beth Shemesh, Aijalon and Gederoth, as well as Soko, Timnah and Gimzo, with their surrounding villages. 19 The LORD had humbled Judah because of Ahaz king of Israel,[b] for he had promoted wickedness in Judah and had been most unfaithful to the LORD. 20 Tiglath-Pileser[c] king of Assyria came to him, but he gave him trouble instead of help. 21 Ahaz took some of the things from the temple of the LORD and from the royal palace and from the officials and presented them to the king of Assyria, but that did not help him.

22 In his time of trouble King Ahaz became even more unfaithful to the LORD. 23 He offered sacrifices to the gods of Damascus, who had defeated him; for he thought, "Since the gods of the kings of Aram have helped them, I will sacrifice to them so they will help me." But they were his downfall and the downfall of all Israel.

24 Ahaz gathered together the furnishings from the temple of God and cut them in pieces. He shut the doors of the LORD's temple and set up altars at every street corner in Jerusalem. 25 In every town in Judah he built high places to burn sacrifices to other gods and aroused the anger of the LORD, the God of his ancestors.

26 The other events of his reign and all his ways, from beginning to end, are written in the book of the kings of Judah and Israel. 27 Ahaz rested with his ancestors and was buried in the city of Jerusalem, but he was not placed in the tombs of the kings of Israel. And Hezekiah his son succeeded him as king.

Hezekiah Purifies the Temple

29 Hezekiah was twenty-five years old when he became king, and he reigned in Jerusalem twenty-nine years. His mother's name was Abijah daughter of Zechariah. 2 He did what was right in the eyes of the LORD, just as his father David had done.

3 In the first month of the first year of his reign, he opened the doors of the temple of the LORD and repaired them. 4 He brought in the priests and the Levites, assembled them in the square on the east side 5 and said: "Listen to me, Levites! Consecrate yourselves now and consecrate the temple of the LORD, the God of your ancestors. Remove all defilement from the sanctuary. 6 Our parents were unfaithful; they did evil in the eyes of the LORD our God and forsook him. They turned their faces away from the LORD's dwelling place and turned their backs on him. 7 They also shut the doors of the portico and put out the lamps. They did not burn incense or present any burnt offerings at the sanctuary to the God of Israel. 8 Therefore, the anger of the LORD has fallen on Judah and Jerusalem; he has made them an object of dread and

[a] *16* Most Hebrew manuscripts; one Hebrew manuscript, Septuagint and Vulgate (see also 2 Kings 16:7) *king* [b] *19* That is, Judah, as frequently in 2 Chronicles [c] *20* Hebrew *Tilgath-Pilneser,* a variant of *Tiglath-Pileser*

horror and scorn, as you can see with your own eyes. 9This is why our fathers have fallen by the sword and why our sons and daughters and our wives are in captivity. 10Now I intend to make a covenant with the LORD, the God of Israel, so that his fierce anger will turn away from us. 11My sons, do not be negligent now, for the LORD has chosen you to stand before him and serve him, to minister before him and to burn incense."

12Then these Levites set to work:

from the Kohathites,
  Mahath son of Amasai and Joel son of Azariah;
from the Merarites,
  Kish son of Abdi and Azariah son of Jehallelel;
from the Gershonites,
  Joah son of Zimmah and Eden son of Joah;
13from the descendants of Elizaphan,
  Shimri and Jeiel;
from the descendants of Asaph,
  Zechariah and Mattaniah;
14from the descendants of Heman,
  Jehiel and Shimei;
from the descendants of Jeduthun,
  Shemaiah and Uzziel.

15When they had assembled their fellow Levites and consecrated themselves, they went in to purify the temple of the LORD, as the king had ordered, following the word of the LORD. 16The priests went into the sanctuary of the LORD to purify it. They brought out to the courtyard of the LORD's temple everything unclean that they found in the temple of the LORD. The Levites took it and carried it out to the Kidron Valley. 17They began the consecration on the first day of the first month, and by the eighth day of the month they reached the portico of the LORD. For eight more days they consecrated the temple of the LORD itself, finishing on the sixteenth day of the first month.

18Then they went in to King Hezekiah and reported: "We have purified the entire temple of the LORD, the altar of burnt offering with all its utensils, and the table for setting out the consecrated bread, with all its articles. 19We have prepared and consecrated all the articles that King Ahaz removed in his unfaithfulness while he was king. They are now in front of the LORD's altar."

20Early the next morning King Hezekiah gathered the city officials together and went up to the temple of the LORD. 21They brought seven bulls, seven rams, seven male lambs and seven male goats as a sin offering[a] for the kingdom, for the sanctuary and for Judah. The king commanded the priests, the descendants of Aaron, to offer these on the altar of the LORD. 22So they slaughtered the bulls, and the priests took the blood and splashed it against the altar; next they slaughtered the rams and splashed their blood against the altar; then they slaughtered the lambs and splashed their blood against the altar. 23The goats for the sin offering were brought before the king and the assembly, and they laid their hands on them. 24The priests then slaughtered the goats and presented their blood on the altar for a sin offering to atone for all Israel, because the king had ordered the burnt offering and the sin offering for all Israel.

25He stationed the Levites in the temple of the LORD with cymbals, harps and lyres in the way prescribed by David and Gad the king's seer and Nathan the prophet; this was commanded by the LORD through his prophets. 26So the Levites stood ready with David's instruments, and the priests with their trumpets.

27Hezekiah gave the order to sacrifice the burnt offering on the altar. As the offering began, singing to the LORD began also, accompanied by trumpets and the instruments of David king of Israel. 28The whole assembly bowed in worship, while the musicians played and the trumpets sounded. All this continued until the sacrifice of the burnt offering was completed.

29When the offerings were finished, the king and everyone present with him knelt down and worshiped. 30King Hezekiah and his officials ordered the Levites to praise the LORD with the words of David and of Asaph the seer. So they sang praises with gladness and bowed down and worshiped.

31Then Hezekiah said, "You have now dedicated yourselves to the LORD. Come and bring sacrifices and thank offerings to the temple of the LORD." So the assembly brought sacrifices and thank offerings, and all whose hearts were willing brought burnt offerings.

[a] 21 Or *purification offering*; also in verses 23 and 24

[32]The number of burnt offerings the assembly brought was seventy bulls, a hundred rams and two hundred male lambs — all of them for burnt offerings to the LORD. [33]The animals consecrated as sacrifices amounted to six hundred bulls and three thousand sheep and goats. [34]The priests, however, were too few to skin all the burnt offerings; so their relatives the Levites helped them until the task was finished and until other priests had been consecrated, for the Levites had been more conscientious in consecrating themselves than the priests had been. [35]There were burnt offerings in abundance, together with the fat of the fellowship offerings and the drink offerings that accompanied the burnt offerings.

So the service of the temple of the LORD was reestablished. [36]Hezekiah and all the people rejoiced at what God had brought about for his people, because it was done so quickly.

Hezekiah Celebrates the Passover

30 Hezekiah sent word to all Israel and Judah and also wrote letters to Ephraim and Manasseh, inviting them to come to the temple of the LORD in Jerusalem and celebrate the Passover to the LORD, the God of Israel. [2]The king and his officials and the whole assembly in Jerusalem decided to celebrate the Passover in the second month. [3]They had not been able to celebrate it at the regular time because not enough priests had consecrated themselves and the people had not assembled in Jerusalem. [4]The plan seemed right both to the king and to the whole assembly. [5]They decided to send a proclamation throughout Israel, from Beersheba to Dan, calling the people to come to Jerusalem and celebrate the Passover to the LORD, the God of Israel. It had not been celebrated in large numbers according to what was written.

[6]At the king's command, couriers went throughout Israel and Judah with letters from the king and from his officials, which read:

"People of Israel, return to the LORD,
the God of Abraham, Isaac and Israel,
that he may return to you who are left,
who have escaped from the hand of the
kings of Assyria. [7]Do not be like your
parents and your fellow Israelites, who
were unfaithful to the LORD, the God of
their ancestors, so that he made them
an object of horror, as you see. [8]Do not
be stiff-necked, as your ancestors were;
submit to the LORD. Come to his sanctuary, which he has consecrated forever. Serve the LORD your God, so that his
fierce anger will turn away from you.
[9]If you return to the LORD, then your
fellow Israelites and your children will
be shown compassion by their captors and will return to this land, for the
LORD your God is gracious and compassionate. He will not turn his face
from you if you return to him."

[10]The couriers went from town to town in Ephraim and Manasseh, as far as Zebulun, but people scorned and ridiculed them. [11]Nevertheless, some from Asher, Manasseh and Zebulun humbled themselves and went to Jerusalem. [12]Also in Judah the hand of God was on the people to give them unity of mind to carry out what the king and his officials had ordered, following the word of the LORD.

[13]A very large crowd of people assembled in Jerusalem to celebrate the Festival of Unleavened Bread in the second month. [14]They removed the altars in Jerusalem and cleared away the incense altars and threw them into the Kidron Valley.

[15]They slaughtered the Passover lamb on the fourteenth day of the second month. The priests and the Levites were ashamed and consecrated themselves and brought burnt offerings to the temple of the LORD. [16]Then they took up their regular positions as prescribed in the Law of Moses the man of God. The priests splashed against the altar the blood handed to them by the Levites. [17]Since many in the crowd had not consecrated themselves, the Levites had to kill the Passover lambs for all those who were not ceremonially clean and could not consecrate their lambs[a] to the LORD. [18]Although most of the many people who came from Ephraim, Manasseh, Issachar and Zebulun had not purified themselves, yet they ate the Passover, contrary to what was written. But Hezekiah prayed for them, saying, "May the

[a] 17 Or *consecrate themselves*

LORD, who is good, pardon everyone [19]who sets their heart on seeking God—the LORD, the God of their ancestors—even if they are not clean according to the rules of the sanctuary." [20]And the LORD heard Hezekiah and healed the people.

[21]The Israelites who were present in Jerusalem celebrated the Festival of Unleavened Bread for seven days with great rejoicing, while the Levites and priests praised the LORD every day with resounding instruments dedicated to the LORD.[a]

[22]Hezekiah spoke encouragingly to all the Levites, who showed good understanding of the service of the LORD. For the seven days they ate their assigned portion and offered fellowship offerings and praised[b] the LORD, the God of their ancestors.

[23]The whole assembly then agreed to celebrate the festival seven more days; so for another seven days they celebrated joyfully. [24]Hezekiah king of Judah provided a thousand bulls and seven thousand sheep and goats for the assembly, and the officials provided them with a thousand bulls and ten thousand sheep and goats. A great number of priests consecrated themselves. [25]The entire assembly of Judah rejoiced, along with the priests and Levites and all who had assembled from Israel, including the foreigners who had come from Israel and also those who resided in Judah. [26]There was great joy in Jerusalem, for since the days of Solomon son of David king of Israel there had been nothing like this in Jerusalem. [27]The priests and the Levites stood to bless the people, and God heard them, for their prayer reached heaven, his holy dwelling place.

31 When all this had ended, the Israelites who were there went out to the towns of Judah, smashed the sacred stones and cut down the Asherah poles. They destroyed the high places and the altars throughout Judah and Benjamin and in Ephraim and Manasseh. After they had destroyed all of them, the Israelites returned to their own towns and to their own property.

Contributions for Worship

[2]Hezekiah assigned the priests and Levites to divisions—each of them according to their duties as priests or Levites—to offer burnt offerings and fellowship offerings, to minister, to give thanks and to sing praises at the gates of the LORD's dwelling. [3]The king contributed from his own possessions for the morning and evening burnt offerings and for the burnt offerings on the Sabbaths, at the New Moons and at the appointed festivals as written in the Law of the LORD. [4]He ordered the people living in Jerusalem to give the portion due the priests and Levites so they could devote themselves to the Law of the LORD. [5]As soon as the order went out, the Israelites generously gave the firstfruits of their grain, new wine, olive oil and honey and all that the fields produced. They brought a great amount, a tithe of everything. [6]The people of Israel and Judah who lived in the towns of Judah also brought a tithe of their herds and flocks and a tithe of the holy things dedicated to the LORD their God, and they piled them in heaps. [7]They began doing this in the third month and finished in the seventh month. [8]When Hezekiah and his officials came and saw the heaps, they praised the LORD and blessed his people Israel.

[9]Hezekiah asked the priests and Levites about the heaps; [10]and Azariah the chief priest, from the family of Zadok, answered, "Since the people began to bring their contributions to the temple of the LORD, we have had enough to eat and plenty to spare, because the LORD has blessed his people, and this great amount is left over."

[11]Hezekiah gave orders to prepare storerooms in the temple of the LORD, and this was done. [12]Then they faithfully brought in the contributions, tithes and dedicated gifts. Konaniah, a Levite, was the overseer in charge of these things, and his brother Shimei was next in rank. [13]Jehiel, Azaziah, Nahath, Asahel, Jerimoth, Jozabad, Eliel, Ismakiah, Mahath and Benaiah were assistants of Konaniah and Shimei his brother. All these served by appointment of King Hezekiah and Azariah the official in charge of the temple of God.

[14]Kore son of Imnah the Levite, keeper of the East Gate, was in charge of the freewill offerings given to God, distributing the contributions made to the LORD and also the consecrated gifts. [15]Eden, Miniamin,

[a] 21 Or *priests sang to the LORD every day, accompanied by the LORD's instruments of praise* [b] 22 Or *and confessed their sins to*

Jeshua, Shemaiah, Amariah and Shekaniah assisted him faithfully in the towns of the priests, distributing to their fellow priests according to their divisions, old and young alike.

[16]In addition, they distributed to the males three years old or more whose names were in the genealogical records — all who would enter the temple of the LORD to perform the daily duties of their various tasks, according to their responsibilities and their
divisions. [17]And they distributed to the priests enrolled by their families in the genealogical records and likewise to the Levites twenty years old or more, according to their
responsibilities and their divisions. [18]They included all the little ones, the wives, and the sons and daughters of the whole community listed in these genealogical records. For they were faithful in consecrating themselves.

[19]As for the priests, the descendants of Aaron, who lived on the farmlands around their towns or in any other towns, men were designated by name to distribute portions to every male among them and to all who were recorded in the genealogies of the Levites.

[20]This is what Hezekiah did throughout Judah, doing what was good and right and
faithful before the LORD his God. [21]In everything that he undertook in the service of God's temple and in obedience to the law and the commands, he sought his God and worked wholeheartedly. And so he prospered.

Sennacherib Threatens Jerusalem

32 After all that Hezekiah had so faithfully done, Sennacherib king of Assyria came and invaded Judah. He laid siege to the fortified cities, thinking to con-
quer them for himself. [2]When Hezekiah saw that Sennacherib had come and that he in-
tended to wage war against Jerusalem, [3]he consulted with his officials and military staff about blocking off the water from the springs outside the city, and they helped
him. [4]They gathered a large group of people who blocked all the springs and the stream that flowed through the land. "Why should the kings[a] of Assyria come and find plenty
of water?" they said. [5]Then he worked hard repairing all the broken sections of the wall and building towers on it. He built another wall outside that one and reinforced the terraces[b] of the City of David. He also made large numbers of weapons and shields.

[6]He appointed military officers over the people and assembled them before him in the square at the city gate and encouraged
them with these words: [7]"Be strong and courageous. Do not be afraid or discouraged because of the king of Assyria and the vast army with him, for there is a greater power
with us than with him. [8]With him is only the arm of flesh, but with us is the LORD our God to help us and to fight our battles." And the people gained confidence from what Hezekiah the king of Judah said.

[9]Later, when Sennacherib king of Assyria and all his forces were laying siege to Lachish, he sent his officers to Jerusalem with this message for Hezekiah king of Judah and for all the people of Judah who were there:

> [10]"This is what Sennacherib king of Assyria says: On what are you basing your confidence, that you remain in Je-
> rusalem under siege? [11]When Hezekiah says, 'The LORD our God will save us from the hand of the king of Assyria,' he is misleading you, to let you die of hun-
> ger and thirst. [12]Did not Hezekiah himself remove this god's high places and altars, saying to Judah and Jerusalem, 'You must worship before one altar and burn sacrifices on it'?
>
> [13]"Do you not know what I and my predecessors have done to all the peoples of the other lands? Were the gods of those nations ever able to deliver their
> land from my hand? [14]Who of all the gods of these nations that my predecessors destroyed has been able to save his people from me? How then can your
> god deliver you from my hand? [15]Now do not let Hezekiah deceive you and mislead you like this. Do not believe him, for no god of any nation or kingdom has been able to deliver his people from my hand or the hand of my predecessors. How much less will your god deliver you from my hand!"

[16]Sennacherib's officers spoke further against the LORD God and against his servant

[a] 4 Hebrew; Septuagint and Syriac *king* [b] 5 Or *the Millo*

Hezekiah. 17 The king also wrote letters ridiculing the LORD, the God of Israel, and saying this against him: "Just as the gods of the peoples of the other lands did not rescue their people from my hand, so the god of Hezekiah will not rescue his people from my hand." 18 Then they called out in Hebrew to the people of Jerusalem who were on the wall, to terrify them and make them afraid in order to capture the city. 19 They spoke about the God of Jerusalem as they did about the gods of the other peoples of the world — the work of human hands.

20 King Hezekiah and the prophet Isaiah son of Amoz cried out in prayer to heaven about this. 21 And the LORD sent an angel, who annihilated all the fighting men and the commanders and officers in the camp of the Assyrian king. So he withdrew to his own land in disgrace. And when he went into the temple of his god, some of his sons, his own flesh and blood, cut him down with the sword.

22 So the LORD saved Hezekiah and the people of Jerusalem from the hand of Sennacherib king of Assyria and from the hand of all others. He took care of them[a] on every side. 23 Many brought offerings to Jerusalem for the LORD and valuable gifts for Hezekiah king of Judah. From then on he was highly regarded by all the nations.

Hezekiah's Pride, Success and Death

24 In those days Hezekiah became ill and was at the point of death. He prayed to the LORD, who answered him and gave him a miraculous sign. 25 But Hezekiah's heart was proud and he did not respond to the kindness shown him; therefore the LORD's wrath was on him and on Judah and Jerusalem. 26 Then Hezekiah repented of the pride of his heart, as did the people of Jerusalem; therefore the LORD's wrath did not come on them during the days of Hezekiah.

27 Hezekiah had very great wealth and honor, and he made treasuries for his silver and gold and for his precious stones, spices, shields and all kinds of valuables. 28 He also made buildings to store the harvest of grain, new wine and olive oil; and he made stalls for various kinds of cattle, and pens for the flocks. 29 He built villages and acquired great numbers of flocks and herds, for God had given him very great riches.

30 It was Hezekiah who blocked the upper outlet of the Gihon spring and channeled the water down to the west side of the City of David. He succeeded in everything he undertook. 31 But when envoys were sent by the rulers of Babylon to ask him about the miraculous sign that had occurred in the land, God left him to test him and to know everything that was in his heart.

32 The other events of Hezekiah's reign and his acts of devotion are written in the vision of the prophet Isaiah son of Amoz in the book of the kings of Judah and Israel. 33 Hezekiah rested with his ancestors and was buried on the hill where the tombs of David's descendants are. All Judah and the people of Jerusalem honored him when he died. And Manasseh his son succeeded him as king.

Manasseh King of Judah

33 Manasseh was twelve years old when he became king, and he reigned in Jerusalem fifty-five years. 2 He did evil in the eyes of the LORD, following the detestable practices of the nations the LORD had driven out before the Israelites. 3 He rebuilt the high places his father Hezekiah had demolished; he also erected altars to the Baals and made Asherah poles. He bowed down to all the starry hosts and worshiped them. 4 He built altars in the temple of the LORD, of which the LORD had said, "My Name will remain in Jerusalem forever." 5 In both courts of the temple of the LORD, he built altars to all the starry hosts. 6 He sacrificed his children in the fire in the Valley of Ben Hinnom, practiced divination and witchcraft, sought omens, and consulted mediums and spiritists. He did much evil in the eyes of the LORD, arousing his anger.

7 He took the image he had made and put it in God's temple, of which God had said to David and to his son Solomon, "In this temple and in Jerusalem, which I have chosen out of all the tribes of Israel, I will put my Name forever. 8 I will not again make the feet of the Israelites leave the land I assigned to your ancestors, if only they will be careful to do everything I commanded them concerning all the laws, decrees and regulations

[a] 22 Hebrew; Septuagint and Vulgate *He gave them rest*

given through Moses." [9]But Manasseh led Judah and the people of Jerusalem astray, so that they did more evil than the nations the LORD had destroyed before the Israelites.

[10]The LORD spoke to Manasseh and his people, but they paid no attention. [11]So the LORD brought against them the army commanders of the king of Assyria, who took Manasseh prisoner, put a hook in his nose, bound him with bronze shackles and took him to Babylon. [12]In his distress he sought the favor of the LORD his God and humbled himself greatly before the God of his ancestors. [13]And when he prayed to him, the LORD was moved by his entreaty and listened to his plea; so he brought him back to Jerusalem and to his kingdom. Then Manasseh knew that the LORD is God.

[14]Afterward he rebuilt the outer wall of the City of David, west of the Gihon spring in the valley, as far as the entrance of the Fish Gate and encircling the hill of Ophel; he also made it much higher. He stationed military commanders in all the fortified cities in Judah.

[15]He got rid of the foreign gods and removed the image from the temple of the LORD, as well as all the altars he had built on the temple hill and in Jerusalem; and he threw them out of the city. [16]Then he restored the altar of the LORD and sacrificed fellowship offerings and thank offerings on it, and told Judah to serve the LORD, the God of Israel. [17]The people, however, continued to sacrifice at the high places, but only to the LORD their God.

[18]The other events of Manasseh's reign, including his prayer to his God and the words the seers spoke to him in the name of the LORD, the God of Israel, are written in the annals of the kings of Israel.[a] [19]His prayer and how God was moved by his entreaty, as well as all his sins and unfaithfulness, and the sites where he built high places and set up Asherah poles and idols before he humbled himself — all these are written in the records of the seers.[b] [20]Manasseh rested with his ancestors and was buried in his palace. And Amon his son succeeded him as king.

Amon King of Judah

[21]Amon was twenty-two years old when he became king, and he reigned in Jerusalem two years. [22]He did evil in the eyes of the LORD, as his father Manasseh had done. Amon worshiped and offered sacrifices to all the idols Manasseh had made. [23]But unlike his father Manasseh, he did not humble himself before the LORD; Amon increased his guilt.

[24]Amon's officials conspired against him and assassinated him in his palace. [25]Then the people of the land killed all who had plotted against King Amon, and they made Josiah his son king in his place.

Josiah's Reforms

34 Josiah was eight years old when he became king, and he reigned in Jerusalem thirty-one years. [2]He did what was right in the eyes of the LORD and followed the ways of his father David, not turning aside to the right or to the left.

[3]In the eighth year of his reign, while he was still young, he began to seek the God of his father David. In his twelfth year he began to purge Judah and Jerusalem of high places, Asherah poles and idols. [4]Under his direction the altars of the Baals were torn down; he cut to pieces the incense altars that were above them, and smashed the Asherah poles and the idols. These he broke to pieces and scattered over the graves of those who had sacrificed to them. [5]He burned the bones of the priests on their altars, and so he purged Judah and Jerusalem. [6]In the towns of Manasseh, Ephraim and Simeon, as far as Naphtali, and in the ruins around them, [7]he tore down the altars and the Asherah poles and crushed the idols to powder and cut to pieces all the incense altars throughout Israel. Then he went back to Jerusalem.

[8]In the eighteenth year of Josiah's reign, to purify the land and the temple, he sent Shaphan son of Azaliah and Maaseiah the ruler of the city, with Joah son of Joahaz, the recorder, to repair the temple of the LORD his God.

[9]They went to Hilkiah the high priest and gave him the money that had been brought into the temple of God, which the Levites who were the gatekeepers had collected from the people of Manasseh, Ephraim and the entire remnant of Israel and from all the people of Judah and Benjamin and the

[a] *18* That is, Judah, as frequently in 2 Chronicles [b] *19* One Hebrew manuscript and Septuagint; most Hebrew manuscripts *of Hozai*

inhabitants of Jerusalem. 10Then they entrusted it to the men appointed to supervise the work on the LORD's temple. These men paid the workers who repaired and restored the temple. 11They also gave money to the carpenters and builders to purchase dressed stone, and timber for joists and beams for the buildings that the kings of Judah had allowed to fall into ruin.

12The workers labored faithfully. Over them to direct them were Jahath and Obadiah, Levites descended from Merari, and Zechariah and Meshullam, descended from Kohath. The Levites — all who were skilled in playing musical instruments — 13had charge of the laborers and supervised all the workers from job to job. Some of the Levites were secretaries, scribes and gatekeepers.

The Book of the Law Found

14While they were bringing out the money that had been taken into the temple of the LORD, Hilkiah the priest found the Book of the Law of the LORD that had been given through Moses. 15Hilkiah said to Shaphan the secretary, "I have found the Book of the Law in the temple of the LORD." He gave it to Shaphan.

16Then Shaphan took the book to the king and reported to him: "Your officials are doing everything that has been committed to them. 17They have paid out the money that was in the temple of the LORD and have entrusted it to the supervisors and workers." 18Then Shaphan the secretary informed the king, "Hilkiah the priest has given me a book." And Shaphan read from it in the presence of the king.

19When the king heard the words of the Law, he tore his robes. 20He gave these orders to Hilkiah, Ahikam son of Shaphan, Abdon son of Micah,[a] Shaphan the secretary and Asaiah the king's attendant: 21"Go and inquire of the LORD for me and for the remnant in Israel and Judah about what is written in this book that has been found. Great is the LORD's anger that is poured out on us because those who have gone before us have not kept the word of the LORD; they have not acted in accordance with all that is written in this book."

22Hilkiah and those the king had sent with him[b] went to speak to the prophet Huldah, who was the wife of Shallum son of Tokhath,[c] the son of Hasrah,[d] keeper of the wardrobe. She lived in Jerusalem, in the New Quarter.

23She said to them, "This is what the LORD, the God of Israel, says: Tell the man who sent you to me, 24'This is what the LORD says: I am going to bring disaster on this place and its people — all the curses written in the book that has been read in the presence of the king of Judah. 25Because they have forsaken me and burned incense to other gods and aroused my anger by all that their hands have made,[e] my anger will be poured out on this place and will not be quenched.' 26Tell the king of Judah, who sent you to inquire of the LORD, 'This is what the LORD, the God of Israel, says concerning the words you heard: 27Because your heart was responsive and you humbled yourself before God when you heard what he spoke against this place and its people, and because you humbled yourself before me and tore your robes and wept in my presence, I have heard you, declares the LORD. 28Now I will gather you to your ancestors, and you will be buried in peace. Your eyes will not see all the disaster I am going to bring on this place and on those who live here.' "

So they took her answer back to the king.

29Then the king called together all the elders of Judah and Jerusalem. 30He went up to the temple of the LORD with the people of Judah, the inhabitants of Jerusalem, the priests and the Levites — all the people from the least to the greatest. He read in their hearing all the words of the Book of the Covenant, which had been found in the temple of the LORD. 31The king stood by his pillar and renewed the covenant in the presence of the LORD — to follow the LORD and keep his commands, statutes and decrees with all his heart and all his soul, and to obey the words of the covenant written in this book.

32Then he had everyone in Jerusalem and Benjamin pledge themselves to it; the people of Jerusalem did this in accordance with the covenant of God, the God of their ancestors.

33Josiah removed all the detestable idols

[a] 20 Also called *Akbor son of Micaiah* [b] 22 One Hebrew manuscript, Vulgate and Syriac; most Hebrew manuscripts do not have *had sent with him.* [c] 22 Also called *Tikvah* [d] 22 Also called *Harhas*
[e] 25 Or *by everything they have done*

from all the territory belonging to the Israelites, and he had all who were present in Israel serve the LORD their God. As long as he lived, they did not fail to follow the LORD, the God of their ancestors.

Josiah Celebrates the Passover

35 Josiah celebrated the Passover to the LORD in Jerusalem, and the Passover lamb was slaughtered on the fourteenth day of the first month. [2]He appointed the priests to their duties and encouraged them in the service of the LORD's temple. [3]He said to the Levites, who instructed all Israel and who had been consecrated to the LORD: "Put the sacred ark in the temple that Solomon son of David king of Israel built. It is not to be carried about on your shoulders. Now serve the LORD your God and his people Israel. [4]Prepare yourselves by families in your divisions, according to the instructions written by David king of Israel and by his son Solomon.

[5]"Stand in the holy place with a group of Levites for each subdivision of the families of your fellow Israelites, the lay people. [6]Slaughter the Passover lambs, consecrate yourselves and prepare the lambs for your fellow Israelites, doing what the LORD commanded through Moses."

[7]Josiah provided for all the lay people who were there a total of thirty thousand lambs and goats for the Passover offerings, and also three thousand cattle — all from the king's own possessions.

[8]His officials also contributed voluntarily to the people and the priests and Levites. Hilkiah, Zechariah and Jehiel, the officials in charge of God's temple, gave the priests twenty-six hundred Passover offerings and three hundred cattle. [9]Also Konaniah along with Shemaiah and Nethanel, his brothers, and Hashabiah, Jeiel and Jozabad, the leaders of the Levites, provided five thousand Passover offerings and five hundred head of cattle for the Levites.

[10]The service was arranged and the priests stood in their places with the Levites in their divisions as the king had ordered. [11]The Passover lambs were slaughtered, and the priests splashed against the altar the blood handed to them, while the Levites skinned the animals. [12]They set aside the burnt offerings to give them to the subdivisions of the families of the people to offer to the LORD, as it is written in the Book of Moses. They did the same with the cattle. [13]They roasted the Passover animals over the fire as prescribed, and boiled the holy offerings in pots, caldrons and pans and served them quickly to all the people. [14]After this, they made preparations for themselves and for the priests, because the priests, the descendants of Aaron, were sacrificing the burnt offerings and the fat portions until nightfall. So the Levites made preparations for themselves and for the Aaronic priests.

[15]The musicians, the descendants of Asaph, were in the places prescribed by David, Asaph, Heman and Jeduthun the king's seer. The gatekeepers at each gate did not need to leave their posts, because their fellow Levites made the preparations for them.

[16]So at that time the entire service of the LORD was carried out for the celebration of the Passover and the offering of burnt offerings on the altar of the LORD, as King Josiah had ordered. [17]The Israelites who were present celebrated the Passover at that time and observed the Festival of Unleavened Bread for seven days. [18]The Passover had not been observed like this in Israel since the days of the prophet Samuel; and none of the kings of Israel had ever celebrated such a Passover as did Josiah, with the priests, the Levites and all Judah and Israel who were there with the people of Jerusalem. [19]This Passover was celebrated in the eighteenth year of Josiah's reign.

The Death of Josiah

[20]After all this, when Josiah had set the temple in order, Necho king of Egypt went up to fight at Carchemish on the Euphrates, and Josiah marched out to meet him in battle. [21]But Necho sent messengers to him, saying, "What quarrel is there, king of Judah, between you and me? It is not you I am attacking at this time, but the house with which I am at war. God has told me to hurry; so stop opposing God, who is with me, or he will destroy you."

[22]Josiah, however, would not turn away from him, but disguised himself to engage him in battle. He would not listen to what Necho had said at God's command but went to fight him on the plain of Megiddo.

[23]Archers shot King Josiah, and he told his

officers, "Take me away; I am badly wounded." [24]So they took him out of his chariot, put him in his other chariot and brought him to Jerusalem, where he died. He was buried in the tombs of his ancestors, and all Judah and Jerusalem mourned for him.

[25]Jeremiah composed laments for Josiah, and to this day all the male and female singers commemorate Josiah in the laments. These became a tradition in Israel and are written in the Laments.

[26]The other events of Josiah's reign and his acts of devotion in accordance with what is written in the Law of the LORD— [27]all the events, from beginning to end, are written in
36 the book of the kings of Israel and Judah. [1]And the people of the land took Jehoahaz son of Josiah and made him king in Jerusalem in place of his father.

Jehoahaz King of Judah

[2]Jehoahaz[a] was twenty-three years old when he became king, and he reigned in Jerusalem three months. [3]The king of Egypt dethroned him in Jerusalem and imposed on Judah a levy of a hundred talents[b] of silver and a talent[c] of gold. [4]The king of Egypt made Eliakim, a brother of Jehoahaz, king over Judah and Jerusalem and changed Eliakim's name to Jehoiakim. But Necho took Eliakim's brother Jehoahaz and carried him off to Egypt.

Jehoiakim King of Judah

[5]Jehoiakim was twenty-five years old when he became king, and he reigned in Jerusalem eleven years. He did evil in the eyes of the LORD his God. [6]Nebuchadnezzar king of Babylon attacked him and bound him with bronze shackles to take him to Babylon. [7]Nebuchadnezzar also took to Babylon articles from the temple of the LORD and put them in his temple[d] there.

[8]The other events of Jehoiakim's reign, the detestable things he did and all that was found against him, are written in the book of the kings of Israel and Judah. And Jehoiachin his son succeeded him as king.

Jehoiachin King of Judah

[9]Jehoiachin was eighteen[e] years old when he became king, and he reigned in Jerusalem three months and ten days. He did evil in the eyes of the LORD. [10]In the spring, King Nebuchadnezzar sent for him and brought him to Babylon, together with articles of value from the temple of the LORD, and he made Jehoiachin's uncle,[f] Zedekiah, king over Judah and Jerusalem.

Zedekiah King of Judah

[11]Zedekiah was twenty-one years old when he became king, and he reigned in Jerusalem eleven years. [12]He did evil in the eyes of the LORD his God and did not humble himself before Jeremiah the prophet, who spoke the word of the LORD. [13]He also rebelled against King Nebuchadnezzar, who had made him take an oath in God's name. He became stiff-necked and hardened his heart and would not turn to the LORD, the God of Israel. [14]Furthermore, all the leaders of the priests and the people became more and more unfaithful, following all the detestable practices of the nations and defiling the temple of the LORD, which he had consecrated in Jerusalem.

The Fall of Jerusalem

[15]The LORD, the God of their ancestors, sent word to them through his messengers again and again, because he had pity on his people and on his dwelling place. [16]But they mocked God's messengers, despised his words and scoffed at his prophets until the wrath of the LORD was aroused against his people and there was no remedy. [17]He brought up against them the king of the Babylonians,[g] who killed their young men with the sword in the sanctuary, and did not spare young men or young women, the elderly or the infirm. God gave them all into the hands of Nebuchadnezzar. [18]He carried to Babylon all the articles from the temple of God, both large and small, and the treasures of the LORD's temple and the treasures of the king and his officials. [19]They set fire to God's temple and broke down the wall of Jerusalem; they burned all the palaces and destroyed everything of value there.

[20]He carried into exile to Babylon the remnant, who escaped from the sword, and

[a] *2* Hebrew *Joahaz,* a variant of *Jehoahaz;* also in verse 4 [b] *3* That is, about 3 3/4 tons or about 3.4 metric tons [c] *3* That is, about 75 pounds or about 34 kilograms [d] *7* Or *palace* [e] *9* One Hebrew manuscript, some Septuagint manuscripts and Syriac (see also 2 Kings 24:8); most Hebrew manuscripts *eight* [f] *10* Hebrew *brother,* that is, relative (see 2 Kings 24:17) [g] *17* Or *Chaldeans*

they became servants to him and his successors until the kingdom of Persia came to power. [21]The land enjoyed its sabbath rests; all the time of its desolation it rested, until the seventy years were completed in fulfillment of the word of the LORD spoken by Jeremiah.

[22]In the first year of Cyrus king of Persia, in order to fulfill the word of the LORD spoken by Jeremiah, the LORD moved the heart of Cyrus king of Persia to make a proclamation throughout his realm and also to put it in writing:

[23]"This is what Cyrus king of Persia says:

"'The LORD, the God of heaven, has given me all the kingdoms of the earth and he has appointed me to build a temple for him at Jerusalem in Judah. Any of his people among you may go up, and may the LORD their God be with them.'"

EZRA

Cyrus Helps the Exiles to Return

1 In the first year of Cyrus king of Persia,
in order to fulfill the word of the LORD
spoken by Jeremiah, the LORD moved the
heart of Cyrus king of Persia to make a proc-
lamation throughout his realm and also to
put it in writing:

2 “This is what Cyrus king of Persia says:
“ ‘The LORD, the God of heaven, has
given me all the kingdoms of the earth
and he has appointed me to build a
temple for him at Jerusalem in Judah.
3 Any of his people among you may go
up to Jerusalem in Judah and build the
temple of the LORD, the God of Israel,
the God who is in Jerusalem, and may
their God be with them. 4 And in any
locality where survivors may now be
living, the people are to provide them
with silver and gold, with goods and
livestock, and with freewill offerings
for the temple of God in Jerusalem.’ ”

5 Then the family heads of Judah and
Benjamin, and the priests and Levites — ev-
eryone whose heart God had moved — pre-
pared to go up and build the house of the
LORD in Jerusalem. 6 All their neighbors as-
sisted them with articles of silver and gold,
with goods and livestock, and with valuable
gifts, in addition to all the freewill offerings.
7 Moreover, King Cyrus brought out the
articles belonging to the temple of the LORD,
which Nebuchadnezzar had carried away
from Jerusalem and had placed in the tem-
ple of his god.[a] 8 Cyrus king of Persia had
them brought by Mithredath the treasurer,
who counted them out to Sheshbazzar the
prince of Judah.
9 This was the inventory:

gold dishes	30
silver dishes	1,000
silver pans[b]	29
10 gold bowls	30
matching silver bowls	410
other articles	1,000

11 In all, there were 5,400 articles of gold
and of silver. Sheshbazzar brought all these
along with the exiles when they came up
from Babylon to Jerusalem.

The List of the Exiles Who Returned

2 Now these are the people of the prov-
ince who came up from the captivity of
the exiles, whom Nebuchadnezzar king of
Babylon had taken captive to Babylon (they
returned to Jerusalem and Judah, each to
their own town, 2 in company with Zerubba-
bel, Joshua, Nehemiah, Seraiah, Reelaiah,
Mordecai, Bilshan, Mispar, Bigvai, Rehum
and Baanah):

The list of the men of the people of Is-
rael:

3 the descendants of Parosh	2,172
4 of Shephatiah	372
5 of Arah	775
6 of Pahath-Moab (through the line of Jeshua and Joab)	2,812
7 of Elam	1,254
8 of Zattu	945
9 of Zakkai	760
10 of Bani	642
11 of Bebai	623
12 of Azgad	1,222
13 of Adonikam	666
14 of Bigvai	2,056
15 of Adin	454
16 of Ater (through Hezekiah)	98
17 of Bezai	323
18 of Jorah	112
19 of Hashum	223
20 of Gibbar	95
21 the men of Bethlehem	123
22 of Netophah	56
23 of Anathoth	128
24 of Azmaveth	42

[a] 7 Or *gods* [b] 9 The meaning of the Hebrew for this word is uncertain.

[25] of Kiriath Jearim,[a] Kephirah and Beeroth 743
[26] of Ramah and Geba 621
[27] of Mikmash 122
[28] of Bethel and Ai 223
[29] of Nebo 52
[30] of Magbish 156
[31] of the other Elam 1,254
[32] of Harim 320
[33] of Lod, Hadid and Ono 725
[34] of Jericho 345
[35] of Senaah 3,630

[36] The priests:

the descendants of Jedaiah (through the family of Jeshua) 973
[37] of Immer 1,052
[38] of Pashhur 1,247
[39] of Harim 1,017

[40] The Levites:

the descendants of Jeshua and Kadmiel (of the line of Hodaviah) 74

[41] The musicians:

the descendants of Asaph 128

[42] The gatekeepers of the temple:

the descendants of
Shallum, Ater, Talmon,
Akkub, Hatita and Shobai 139

[43] The temple servants:

the descendants of
Ziha, Hasupha, Tabbaoth,
[44] Keros, Siaha, Padon,
[45] Lebanah, Hagabah, Akkub,
[46] Hagab, Shalmai, Hanan,
[47] Giddel, Gahar, Reaiah,
[48] Rezin, Nekoda, Gazzam,
[49] Uzza, Paseah, Besai,
[50] Asnah, Meunim, Nephusim,
[51] Bakbuk, Hakupha, Harhur,
[52] Bazluth, Mehida, Harsha,
[53] Barkos, Sisera, Temah,
[54] Neziah and Hatipha

[55] The descendants of the servants of Solomon:

the descendants of
Sotai, Hassophereth, Peruda,
[56] Jaala, Darkon, Giddel,
[57] Shephatiah, Hattil,
Pokereth-Hazzebaim and Ami

[58] The temple servants and the descendants of the servants of Solomon 392

[59] The following came up from the
towns of Tel Melah, Tel Harsha, Kerub,
Addon and Immer, but they could not
show that their families were descend-
ed from Israel:

[60] The descendants of
Delaiah, Tobiah and Nekoda 652

[61] And from among the priests:

The descendants of
Hobaiah, Hakkoz and Barzillai (a man who had married a daughter of Barzillai the Gileadite and was called by that name).

[62] These searched for their family rec-
ords, but they could not find them and
so were excluded from the priesthood
as unclean. [63] The governor ordered
them not to eat any of the most sacred
food until there was a priest minister-
ing with the Urim and Thummim.

[64] The whole company numbered
42,360, [65] besides their 7,337 male and
female slaves; and they also had 200
male and female singers. [66] They had
736 horses, 245 mules, [67] 435 camels
and 6,720 donkeys.

[68] When they arrived at the house of the
LORD in Jerusalem, some of the heads of the
families gave freewill offerings toward the re-
building of the house of God on its site. [69] Ac-
cording to their ability they gave to the trea-
sury for this work 61,000 darics[b] of gold, 5,000
minas[c] of silver and 100 priestly garments.

[70] The priests, the Levites, the musicians,
the gatekeepers and the temple servants set-
tled in their own towns, along with some of
the other people, and the rest of the Israelites
settled in their towns.

Rebuilding the Altar

3 When the seventh month came and the
Israelites had settled in their towns, the

[a] *25* See Septuagint (see also Neh. 7:29); Hebrew *Kiriath Arim.* [b] *69* That is, about 1,100 pounds or about 500 kilograms [c] *69* That is, about 3 tons or about 2.8 metric tons

people assembled together as one in Jerusa-
lem. [2]Then Joshua son of Jozadak and his fel-
low priests and Zerubbabel son of Shealtiel
and his associates began to build the altar of
the God of Israel to sacrifice burnt offerings
on it, in accordance with what is written in
the Law of Moses the man of God. [3]Despite
their fear of the peoples around them, they
built the altar on its foundation and sacri-
ficed burnt offerings on it to the LORD, both
the morning and evening sacrifices. [4]Then
in accordance with what is written, they
celebrated the Festival of Tabernacles with
the required number of burnt offerings pre-
scribed for each day. [5]After that, they pre-
sented the regular burnt offerings, the New
Moon sacrifices and the sacrifices for all the
appointed sacred festivals of the LORD, as
well as those brought as freewill offerings
to the LORD. [6]On the first day of the seventh
month they began to offer burnt offerings
to the LORD, though the foundation of the
LORD's temple had not yet been laid.

Rebuilding the Temple

[7]Then they gave money to the masons and
carpenters, and gave food and drink and ol-
ive oil to the people of Sidon and Tyre, so that
they would bring cedar logs by sea from Leb-
anon to Joppa, as authorized by Cyrus king
of Persia.

[8]In the second month of the second year
after their arrival at the house of God in Je-
rusalem, Zerubbabel son of Shealtiel, Josh-
ua son of Jozadak and the rest of the people
(the priests and the Levites and all who had
returned from the captivity to Jerusalem)
began the work. They appointed Levites
twenty years old and older to supervise the
building of the house of the LORD. [9]Joshua
and his sons and brothers and Kadmiel and
his sons (descendants of Hodaviah[a]) and the
sons of Henadad and their sons and broth-
ers — all Levites — joined together in super-
vising those working on the house of God.

[10]When the builders laid the foundation
of the temple of the LORD, the priests in their
vestments and with trumpets, and the Le-
vites (the sons of Asaph) with cymbals, took
their places to praise the LORD, as prescribed
by David king of Israel. [11]With praise and
thanksgiving they sang to the LORD:

"He is good;
his love toward Israel endures forever."

And all the people gave a great shout of
praise to the LORD, because the foundation
of the house of the LORD was laid. [12]But many
of the older priests and Levites and family
heads, who had seen the former temple, wept
aloud when they saw the foundation of this
temple being laid, while many others shout-
ed for joy. [13]No one could distinguish the
sound of the shouts of joy from the sound of
weeping, because the people made so much
noise. And the sound was heard far away.

Opposition to the Rebuilding

4 When the enemies of Judah and Ben-
jamin heard that the exiles were build-
ing a temple for the LORD, the God of Israel,
[2]they came to Zerubbabel and to the heads
of the families and said, "Let us help you
build because, like you, we seek your God
and have been sacrificing to him since the
time of Esarhaddon king of Assyria, who
brought us here."

[3]But Zerubbabel, Joshua and the rest of
the heads of the families of Israel answered,
"You have no part with us in building a tem-
ple to our God. We alone will build it for the
LORD, the God of Israel, as King Cyrus, the
king of Persia, commanded us."

[4]Then the peoples around them set out
to discourage the people of Judah and make
them afraid to go on building.[b] [5]They bribed
officials to work against them and frustrate
their plans during the entire reign of Cyrus
king of Persia and down to the reign of Dari-
us king of Persia.

Later Opposition Under Xerxes and Artaxerxes

[6]At the beginning of the reign of Xerxes,[c]
they lodged an accusation against the peo-
ple of Judah and Jerusalem.

[7]And in the days of Artaxerxes king of
Persia, Bishlam, Mithredath, Tabeel and the
rest of his associates wrote a letter to Arta-
xerxes. The letter was written in Aramaic
script and in the Aramaic language.[d,e]

[8]Rehum the commanding officer and
Shimshai the secretary wrote a letter against
Jerusalem to Artaxerxes the king as follows:

[a] 9 Hebrew *Yehudah,* a variant of *Hodaviah* [b] 4 Or *and troubled them as they built* [c] 6 Hebrew *Ahasuerus* [d] 7 Or *written in Aramaic and translated* [e] 7 The text of 4:8 - 6:18 is in Aramaic.

[9]Rehum the commanding officer and Shimshai the secretary, together with the rest of their associates—the judges, officials and administrators over the people from Persia, Uruk and Babylon, the Elamites of Susa, [10]and the other people whom the great and honorable Ashurbanipal deported and settled in the city of Samaria and elsewhere in Trans-Euphrates.

[11](This is a copy of the letter they sent him.)

To King Artaxerxes,

From your servants in Trans-Euphrates:

[12]The king should know that the people who came up to us from you have gone to Jerusalem and are rebuilding that rebellious and wicked city. They are restoring the walls and repairing the foundations.

[13]Furthermore, the king should know that if this city is built and its walls are restored, no more taxes, tribute or duty will be paid, and eventually the royal revenues will suffer.[a] [14]Now since we are under obligation to the palace and it is not proper for us to see the king dishonored, we are sending this message to inform the king, [15]so that a search may be made in the archives of your predecessors. In these records you will find that this city is a rebellious city, troublesome to kings and provinces, a place with a long history of sedition. That is why this city was destroyed. [16]We inform the king that if this city is built and its walls are restored, you will be left with nothing in Trans-Euphrates.

[17]The king sent this reply:

To Rehum the commanding officer, Shimshai the secretary and the rest of their associates living in Samaria and elsewhere in Trans-Euphrates:

Greetings.

[18]The letter you sent us has been read and translated in my presence. [19]I issued an order and a search was made, and it was found that this city has a long history of revolt against kings and has been a place of rebellion and sedition. [20]Jerusalem has had powerful kings ruling over the whole of Trans-Euphrates, and taxes, tribute and duty were paid to them. [21]Now issue an order to these men to stop work, so that this city will not be rebuilt until I so order. [22]Be careful not to neglect this matter. Why let this threat grow, to the detriment of the royal interests?

[23]As soon as the copy of the letter of King Artaxerxes was read to Rehum and Shimshai the secretary and their associates, they went immediately to the Jews in Jerusalem and compelled them by force to stop.

[24]Thus the work on the house of God in Jerusalem came to a standstill until the second year of the reign of Darius king of Persia.

Tattenai's Letter to Darius

5 Now Haggai the prophet and Zechariah the prophet, a descendant of Iddo, prophesied to the Jews in Judah and Jerusalem in the name of the God of Israel, who was over them. [2]Then Zerubbabel son of Shealtiel and Joshua son of Jozadak set to work to rebuild the house of God in Jerusalem. And the prophets of God were with them, supporting them.

[3]At that time Tattenai, governor of Trans-Euphrates, and Shethar-Bozenai and their associates went to them and asked, "Who authorized you to rebuild this temple and to finish it?" [4]They[b] also asked, "What are the names of those who are constructing this building?" [5]But the eye of their God was watching over the elders of the Jews, and they were not stopped until a report could go to Darius and his written reply be received.

[6]This is a copy of the letter that Tattenai, governor of Trans-Euphrates, and Shethar-Bozenai and their associates, the officials of Trans-Euphrates, sent to King Darius. [7]The report they sent him read as follows:

To King Darius:

Cordial greetings.

[8]The king should know that we went to the district of Judah, to the temple of

[a] *13* The meaning of the Aramaic for this clause is uncertain. [b] *4* See Septuagint; Aramaic *We.*

the great God. The people are building it with large stones and placing the timbers in the walls. The work is being carried on with diligence and is making rapid progress under their direction.

[9]We questioned the elders and asked them, "Who authorized you to rebuild this temple and to finish it?" [10]We also asked them their names, so that we could write down the names of their leaders for your information.

[11]This is the answer they gave us:

"We are the servants of the God of heaven and earth, and we are rebuilding the temple that was built many years ago, one that a great king of Israel built and finished. [12]But because our ancestors angered the God of heaven, he gave them into the hands of Nebuchadnezzar the Chaldean, king of Babylon, who destroyed this temple and deported the people to Babylon.

[13]"However, in the first year of Cyrus king of Babylon, King Cyrus issued a decree to rebuild this house of God. [14]He even removed from the temple[a] of Babylon the gold and silver articles of the house of God, which Nebuchadnezzar had taken from the temple in Jerusalem and brought to the temple[a] in Babylon. Then King Cyrus gave them to a man named Sheshbazzar, whom he had appointed governor, [15]and he told him, 'Take these articles and go and deposit them in the temple in Jerusalem. And rebuild the house of God on its site.'

[16]"So this Sheshbazzar came and laid the foundations of the house of God in Jerusalem. From that day to the present it has been under construction but is not yet finished."

[17]Now if it pleases the king, let a search be made in the royal archives of Babylon to see if King Cyrus did in fact issue a decree to rebuild this house of God in Jerusalem. Then let the king send us his decision in this matter.

The Decree of Darius

6 King Darius then issued an order, and they searched in the archives stored in the treasury at Babylon. [2]A scroll was found in the citadel of Ecbatana in the province of Media, and this was written on it:

Memorandum:

[3]In the first year of King Cyrus, the king issued a decree concerning the temple of God in Jerusalem:

Let the temple be rebuilt as a place to present sacrifices, and let its foundations be laid. It is to be sixty cubits[b] high and sixty cubits wide, [4]with three courses of large stones and one of timbers. The costs are to be paid by the royal treasury. [5]Also, the gold and silver articles of the house of God, which Nebuchadnezzar took from the temple in Jerusalem and brought to Babylon, are to be returned to their places in the temple in Jerusalem; they are to be deposited in the house of God.

[6]Now then, Tattenai, governor of Trans-Euphrates, and Shethar-Bozenai and you other officials of that province, stay away from there. [7]Do not interfere with the work on this temple of God. Let the governor of the Jews and the Jewish elders rebuild this house of God on its site.

[8]Moreover, I hereby decree what you are to do for these elders of the Jews in the construction of this house of God:

Their expenses are to be fully paid out of the royal treasury, from the revenues of Trans-Euphrates, so that the work will not stop. [9]Whatever is needed—young bulls, rams, male lambs for burnt offerings to the God of heaven, and wheat, salt, wine and olive oil, as requested by the priests in Jerusalem—must be given them daily without fail, [10]so that they may offer sacrifices pleasing to the God of heaven and pray for the well-being of the king and his sons.

[11]Furthermore, I decree that if anyone defies this edict, a beam is to be pulled from their house and they are to be impaled on it. And for this crime their house is to be made a pile of rubble. [12]May God, who has caused his Name to dwell there, overthrow any

[a] *14* Or *palace* [b] *3* That is, about 90 feet or about 27 meters

king or people who lifts a hand to
change this decree or to destroy this
temple in Jerusalem.

I Darius have decreed it. Let it be car-
ried out with diligence.

Completion and Dedication of the Temple

13Then, because of the decree King Da-
rius had sent, Tattenai, governor of Trans-
Euphrates, and Shethar-Bozenai and their
associates carried it out with diligence. 14So
the elders of the Jews continued to build and
prosper under the preaching of Haggai the
prophet and Zechariah, a descendant of Iddo.
They finished building the temple according
to the command of the God of Israel and the
decrees of Cyrus, Darius and Artaxerxes,
kings of Persia. 15The temple was complet-
ed on the third day of the month Adar, in the
sixth year of the reign of King Darius.

16Then the people of Israel — the priests,
the Levites and the rest of the exiles — cel-
ebrated the dedication of the house of God
with joy. 17For the dedication of this house
of God they offered a hundred bulls, two
hundred rams, four hundred male lambs
and, as a sin offering[a] for all Israel, twelve
male goats, one for each of the tribes of Is-
rael. 18And they installed the priests in their
divisions and the Levites in their groups for
the service of God at Jerusalem, according to
what is written in the Book of Moses.

The Passover

19On the fourteenth day of the first month,
the exiles celebrated the Passover. 20The
priests and Levites had purified themselves
and were all ceremonially clean. The Le-
vites slaughtered the Passover lamb for all
the exiles, for their relatives the priests and
for themselves. 21So the Israelites who had
returned from the exile ate it, together with
all who had separated themselves from the
unclean practices of their Gentile neighbors
in order to seek the LORD, the God of Israel.
22For seven days they celebrated with joy the
Festival of Unleavened Bread, because the
LORD had filled them with joy by changing
the attitude of the king of Assyria so that he
assisted them in the work on the house of
God, the God of Israel.

Ezra Comes to Jerusalem

7 After these things, during the reign of
Artaxerxes king of Persia, Ezra son of
Seraiah, the son of Azariah, the son of Hil-
kiah, 2the son of Shallum, the son of Zadok,
the son of Ahitub, 3the son of Amariah, the
son of Azariah, the son of Meraioth, 4the son
of Zerahiah, the son of Uzzi, the son of Buk-
ki, 5the son of Abishua, the son of Phinehas,
the son of Eleazar, the son of Aaron the chief
priest — 6this Ezra came up from Babylon.
He was a teacher well versed in the Law of
Moses, which the LORD, the God of Israel,
had given. The king had granted him ev-
erything he asked, for the hand of the LORD
his God was on him. 7Some of the Israelites,
including priests, Levites, musicians, gate-
keepers and temple servants, also came up
to Jerusalem in the seventh year of King Ar-
taxerxes.

8Ezra arrived in Jerusalem in the fifth
month of the seventh year of the king. 9He
had begun his journey from Babylon on the
first day of the first month, and he arrived in
Jerusalem on the first day of the fifth month,
for the gracious hand of his God was on him.
10For Ezra had devoted himself to the study
and observance of the Law of the LORD, and
to teaching its decrees and laws in Israel.

King Artaxerxes' Letter to Ezra

11This is a copy of the letter King Artaxer-
xes had given to Ezra the priest, a teacher of
the Law, a man learned in matters concern-
ing the commands and decrees of the LORD
for Israel:

12Artaxerxes, king of kings,

To Ezra the priest, teacher of the Law of
the God of heaven:

Greetings.

13Now I decree that any of the Isra-
elites in my kingdom, including priests
and Levites, who volunteer to go to Je-
rusalem with you, may go. 14You are
sent by the king and his seven advisers
to inquire about Judah and Jerusalem
with regard to the Law of your God,
which is in your hand. 15Moreover,
you are to take with you the silver and
gold that the king and his advisers have

[a] *17* Or *purification offering*

freely given to the God of Israel, whose
dwelling is in Jerusalem, 16together
with all the silver and gold you may ob-
tain from the province of Babylon, as
well as the freewill offerings of the peo-
ple and priests for the temple of their
God in Jerusalem. 17With this money
be sure to buy bulls, rams and male
lambs, together with their grain offer-
ings and drink offerings, and sacrifice
them on the altar of the temple of your
God in Jerusalem.
18You and your fellow Israelites may
then do whatever seems best with the
rest of the silver and gold, in accor-
dance with the will of your God. 19De-
liver to the God of Jerusalem all the
articles entrusted to you for worship in
the temple of your God. 20And anything
else needed for the temple of your God
that you are responsible to supply, you
may provide from the royal treasury.
21Now I, King Artaxerxes, decree
that all the treasurers of Trans-Eu-
phrates are to provide with diligence
whatever Ezra the priest, the teacher of
the Law of the God of heaven, may ask
of you — 22up to a hundred talents[a] of
silver, a hundred cors[b] of wheat, a hun-
dred baths[c] of wine, a hundred baths[c]
of olive oil, and salt without limit.
23Whatever the God of heaven has pre-
scribed, let it be done with diligence for
the temple of the God of heaven. Why
should his wrath fall on the realm of the
king and of his sons? 24You are also to
know that you have no authority to im-
pose taxes, tribute or duty on any of the
priests, Levites, musicians, gatekeep-
ers, temple servants or other workers at
this house of God.
25And you, Ezra, in accordance with
the wisdom of your God, which you
possess, appoint magistrates and judg-
es to administer justice to all the peo-
ple of Trans-Euphrates — all who know
the laws of your God. And you are to
teach any who do not know them.
26Whoever does not obey the law of
your God and the law of the king must
surely be punished by death, banish-
ment, confiscation of property, or im-
prisonment.[d]
27Praise be to the LORD, the God of our an-
cestors, who has put it into the king's heart to
bring honor to the house of the LORD in Je-
rusalem in this way 28and who has extended
his good favor to me before the king and his
advisers and all the king's powerful officials.
Because the hand of the LORD my God was
on me, I took courage and gathered leaders
from Israel to go up with me.

List of the Family Heads Returning With Ezra

8 These are the family heads and those
registered with them who came up with
me from Babylon during the reign of King
Artaxerxes:

2of the descendants of Phinehas, Ger-
shom;
of the descendants of Ithamar, Daniel;
of the descendants of David, Hattush
3of the descendants of Shekaniah;

of the descendants of Parosh, Zechari-
ah, and with him were registered 150
men;
4of the descendants of Pahath-Moab,
Eliehoenai son of Zerahiah, and with
him 200 men;
5of the descendants of Zattu,[e] Shekani-
ah son of Jahaziel, and with him 300
men;
6of the descendants of Adin, Ebed son of
Jonathan, and with him 50 men;
7of the descendants of Elam, Jeshaiah
son of Athaliah, and with him 70
men;
8of the descendants of Shephatiah, Zeb-
adiah son of Michael, and with him
80 men;
9of the descendants of Joab, Obadiah
son of Jehiel, and with him 218 men;
10of the descendants of Bani,[f] Shelomith
son of Josiphiah, and with him 160
men;
11of the descendants of Bebai, Zechariah
son of Bebai, and with him 28 men;

[a] *22* That is, about 3 3/4 tons or about 3.4 metric tons [b] *22* That is, probably about 18 tons or about 16 metric tons [c] *22* That is, about 600 gallons or about 2,200 liters [d] *26* The text of 7:12-26 is in Aramaic. [e] *5* Some Septuagint manuscripts (also 1 Esdras 8:32); Hebrew does not have *Zattu.* [f] *10* Some Septuagint manuscripts (also 1 Esdras 8:36); Hebrew does not have *Bani.*

12 of the descendants of Azgad, Johanan
son of Hakkatan, and with him 110
men;
13 of the descendants of Adonikam, the
last ones, whose names were Eliph-
elet, Jeuel and Shemaiah, and with
them 60 men;
14 of the descendants of Bigvai, Uthai and
Zakkur, and with them 70 men.

The Return to Jerusalem

15 I assembled them at the canal that flows
toward Ahava, and we camped there three
days. When I checked among the people and
the priests, I found no Levites there. 16 So I
summoned Eliezer, Ariel, Shemaiah, Elna-
than, Jarib, Elnathan, Nathan, Zechariah
and Meshullam, who were leaders, and Joi-
arib and Elnathan, who were men of learn-
ing, 17 and I ordered them to go to Iddo, the
leader in Kasiphia. I told them what to say to
Iddo and his fellow Levites, the temple ser-
vants in Kasiphia, so that they might bring
attendants to us for the house of our God.
18 Because the gracious hand of our God was
on us, they brought us Sherebiah, a capable
man, from the descendants of Mahli son of
Levi, the son of Israel, and Sherebiah's sons
and brothers, 18 in all; 19 and Hashabiah, to-
gether with Jeshaiah from the descendants
of Merari, and his brothers and nephews, 20
in all. 20 They also brought 220 of the temple
servants — a body that David and the offi-
cials had established to assist the Levites.
All were registered by name.

21 There, by the Ahava Canal, I proclaimed
a fast, so that we might humble ourselves be-
fore our God and ask him for a safe journey
for us and our children, with all our posses-
sions. 22 I was ashamed to ask the king for
soldiers and horsemen to protect us from
enemies on the road, because we had told
the king, "The gracious hand of our God is
on everyone who looks to him, but his great
anger is against all who forsake him." 23 So
we fasted and petitioned our God about this,
and he answered our prayer.

24 Then I set apart twelve of the leading
priests, namely, Sherebiah, Hashabiah and
ten of their brothers, 25 and I weighed out to
them the offering of silver and gold and the
articles that the king, his advisers, his offi-
cials and all Israel present there had donat-
ed for the house of our God. 26 I weighed out
to them 650 talents[a] of silver, silver articles
weighing 100 talents,[b] 100 talents[b] of gold,
27 20 bowls of gold valued at 1,000 darics,[c]
and two fine articles of polished bronze, as
precious as gold.

28 I said to them, "You as well as these arti-
cles are consecrated to the LORD. The silver
and gold are a freewill offering to the LORD,
the God of your ancestors. 29 Guard them
carefully until you weigh them out in the
chambers of the house of the LORD in Jeru-
salem before the leading priests and the Le-
vites and the family heads of Israel." 30 Then
the priests and Levites received the silver
and gold and sacred articles that had been
weighed out to be taken to the house of our
God in Jerusalem.

31 On the twelfth day of the first month we
set out from the Ahava Canal to go to Jeru-
salem. The hand of our God was on us, and
he protected us from enemies and bandits
along the way. 32 So we arrived in Jerusalem,
where we rested three days.

33 On the fourth day, in the house of our
God, we weighed out the silver and gold and
the sacred articles into the hands of Mere-
moth son of Uriah, the priest. Eleazar son of
Phinehas was with him, and so were the Le-
vites Jozabad son of Jeshua and Noadiah son
of Binnui. 34 Everything was accounted for
by number and weight, and the entire weight
was recorded at that time.

35 Then the exiles who had returned from
captivity sacrificed burnt offerings to the
God of Israel: twelve bulls for all Israel, nine-
ty-six rams, seventy-seven male lambs and,
as a sin offering,[d] twelve male goats. All this
was a burnt offering to the LORD. 36 They also
delivered the king's orders to the royal sa-
traps and to the governors of Trans-Euphra-
tes, who then gave assistance to the people
and to the house of God.

Ezra's Prayer About Intermarriage

9 After these things had been done, the
leaders came to me and said, "The peo-
ple of Israel, including the priests and the Le-
vites, have not kept themselves separate from
the neighboring peoples with their detest-
able practices, like those of the Canaanites,

[a] 26 That is, about 24 tons or about 22 metric tons [b] 26 That is, about 3 3/4 tons or about 3.4 metric tons
[c] 27 That is, about 19 pounds or about 8.4 kilograms [d] 35 Or *purification offering*

Hittites, Perizzites, Jebusites, Ammonites, Moabites, Egyptians and Amorites. [2]They have taken some of their daughters as wives for themselves and their sons, and have mingled the holy race with the peoples around them. And the leaders and officials have led the way in this unfaithfulness."

[3]When I heard this, I tore my tunic and cloak, pulled hair from my head and beard and sat down appalled. [4]Then everyone who trembled at the words of the God of Israel gathered around me because of this unfaithfulness of the exiles. And I sat there appalled until the evening sacrifice.

[5]Then, at the evening sacrifice, I rose from my self-abasement, with my tunic and cloak torn, and fell on my knees with my hands spread out to the LORD my God [6]and prayed:

"I am too ashamed and disgraced my God, to lift up my face to you, because our sins are higher than our heads and our guilt has reached to the heavens. [7]From the days of our ancestors until now, our guilt has been great. Because of our sins, we and our kings and our priests have been subjected to the sword and captivity, to pillage and humiliation at the hand of foreign kings, as it is today.

[8]"But now, for a brief moment, the LORD our God has been gracious in leaving us a remnant and giving us a firm place[a] in his sanctuary, and so our God gives light to our eyes and a little relief in our bondage. [9]Though we are slaves, our God has not forsaken us in our bondage. He has shown us kindness in the sight of the kings of Persia: He has granted us new life to rebuild the house of our God and repair its ruins, and he has given us a wall of protection in Judah and Jerusalem.

[10]"But now, our God, what can we say after this? For we have forsaken the commands [11]you gave through your servants the prophets when you said: 'The land you are entering to possess is a land polluted by the corruption of its peoples. By their detestable practices they have filled it with their impurity from one end to the other. [12]Therefore, do not give your daughters in marriage to their sons or take their daughters for your sons. Do not seek a treaty of friendship with them at any time, that you may be strong and eat the good things of the land and leave it to your children as an everlasting inheritance.'

[13]"What has happened to us is a result of our evil deeds and our great guilt, and yet, our God, you have punished us less than our sins deserved and have given us a remnant like this. [14]Shall we then break your commands again and intermarry with the peoples who commit such detestable practices? Would you not be angry enough with us to destroy us, leaving us no remnant or survivor? [15]LORD, the God of Israel, you are righteous! We are left this day as a remnant. Here we are before you in our guilt, though because of it not one of us can stand in your presence."

The People's Confession of Sin

10 While Ezra was praying and confessing, weeping and throwing himself down before the house of God, a large crowd of Israelites—men, women and children—gathered around him. They too wept bitterly. [2]Then Shekaniah son of Jehiel, one of the descendants of Elam, said to Ezra, "We have been unfaithful to our God by marrying foreign women from the peoples around us. But in spite of this, there is still hope for Israel. [3]Now let us make a covenant before our God to send away all these women and their children, in accordance with the counsel of my lord and of those who fear the commands of our God. Let it be done according to the Law. [4]Rise up; this matter is in your hands. We will support you, so take courage and do it."

[5]So Ezra rose up and put the leading priests and Levites and all Israel under oath to do what had been suggested. And they took the oath. [6]Then Ezra withdrew from before the house of God and went to the room of Jehohanan son of Eliashib. While he was there, he ate no food and drank no water, because he continued to mourn over the unfaithfulness of the exiles.

[7]A proclamation was then issued throughout Judah and Jerusalem for all the exiles to assemble in Jerusalem. [8]Anyone who failed

[a] 8 Or *a foothold*

to appear within three days would forfeit all his property, in accordance with the decision of the officials and elders, and would himself be expelled from the assembly of the exiles.

9Within the three days, all the men of Ju-
dah and Benjamin had gathered in Jerusalem. And on the twentieth day of the ninth month, all the people were sitting in the square before the house of God, greatly distressed by the occasion and because of the
rain. 10Then Ezra the priest stood up and said to them, "You have been unfaithful; you have married foreign women, adding to Is-
rael's guilt. 11Now honor[a] the LORD, the God of your ancestors, and do his will. Separate yourselves from the peoples around you and from your foreign wives."

12The whole assembly responded with a loud voice: "You are right! We must do as
you say. 13But there are many people here and it is the rainy season; so we cannot stand outside. Besides, this matter cannot be taken care of in a day or two, because we have
sinned greatly in this thing. 14Let our officials act for the whole assembly. Then let everyone in our towns who has married a foreign woman come at a set time, along with the elders and judges of each town, until the fierce anger of our God in this matter is
turned away from us." 15Only Jonathan son of Asahel and Jahzeiah son of Tikvah, supported by Meshullam and Shabbethai the Levite, opposed this.

16So the exiles did as was proposed. Ezra the priest selected men who were family heads, one from each family division, and all of them designated by name. On the first day of the tenth month they sat down to in-
vestigate the cases, 17and by the first day of the first month they finished dealing with all the men who had married foreign women.

Those Guilty of Intermarriage

18Among the descendants of the priests, the following had married foreign women:

From the descendants of Joshua son of Jozadak, and his brothers: Maaseiah, Eliezer, Jarib and Gedaliah.
19(They all gave their hands in pledge to put away their wives, and for their guilt they each presented a ram from the flock as a guilt offering.)

20From the descendants of Immer:
Hanani and Zebadiah.

21From the descendants of Harim:
Maaseiah, Elijah, Shemaiah, Jehiel and Uzziah.

22From the descendants of Pashhur:
Elioenai, Maaseiah, Ishmael, Nethanel, Jozabad and Elasah.

23Among the Levites:

Jozabad, Shimei, Kelaiah (that is, Kelita), Pethahiah, Judah and Eliezer.

24From the musicians:
Eliashib.

From the gatekeepers:
Shallum, Telem and Uri.

25And among the other Israelites:

From the descendants of Parosh:
Ramiah, Izziah, Malkijah, Mijamin, Eleazar, Malkijah and Benaiah.

26From the descendants of Elam:
Mattaniah, Zechariah, Jehiel, Abdi, Jeremoth and Elijah.

27From the descendants of Zattu:
Elioenai, Eliashib, Mattaniah, Jeremoth, Zabad and Aziza.

28From the descendants of Bebai:
Jehohanan, Hananiah, Zabbai and Athlai.

29From the descendants of Bani:
Meshullam, Malluk, Adaiah, Jashub, Sheal and Jeremoth.

30From the descendants of Pahath-Moab:
Adna, Kelal, Benaiah, Maaseiah, Mattaniah, Bezalel, Binnui and Manasseh.

31From the descendants of Harim:
Eliezer, Ishijah, Malkijah, Shemaiah, Shimeon,
32Benjamin, Malluk and Shemariah.

33From the descendants of Hashum:
Mattenai, Mattattah, Zabad, Eliphelet, Jeremai, Manasseh and Shimei.

34From the descendants of Bani:
Maadai, Amram, Uel,
35Benaiah, Bedeiah, Keluhi,
36Vaniah, Meremoth, Eliashib,
37Mattaniah, Mattenai and Jaasu.

[a] *11* Or *Now make confession to*

38 From the descendants of Binnui:[a]
Shimei, 39 Shelemiah, Nathan, Ada-
iah, 40 Maknadebai, Shashai, Sharai,
41 Azarel, Shelemiah, Shemariah,
42 Shallum, Amariah and Joseph.
43 From the descendants of Nebo:
Jeiel, Mattithiah, Zabad, Zebina, Jad-
dai, Joel and Benaiah.

44 All these had married foreign women,
and some of them had children by these
wives.[b]

[a] 37,38 See Septuagint (also 1 Esdras 9:34); Hebrew *Jaasu* [38] *and Bani and Binnui,* [b] 44 Or *and they sent them away with their children*

NEHEMIAH

Nehemiah's Prayer

1 The words of Nehemiah son of Hakaliah:

In the month of Kislev in the twentieth
year, while I was in the citadel of Susa, 2 Ha-
nani, one of my brothers, came from Judah
with some other men, and I questioned them
about the Jewish remnant that had survived
the exile, and also about Jerusalem.
3 They said to me, "Those who survived
the exile and are back in the province are in
great trouble and disgrace. The wall of Je-
rusalem is broken down, and its gates have
been burned with fire."
4 When I heard these things, I sat down
and wept. For some days I mourned and
fasted and prayed before the God of heaven.
5 Then I said:

"LORD, the God of heaven, the great
and awesome God, who keeps his cov-
enant of love with those who love him
and keep his commandments, 6 let your
ear be attentive and your eyes open to
hear the prayer your servant is praying
before you day and night for your ser-
vants, the people of Israel. I confess the
sins we Israelites, including myself and
my father's family, have committed
against you. 7 We have acted very wick-
edly toward you. We have not obeyed
the commands, decrees and laws you
gave your servant Moses.
8 "Remember the instruction you
gave your servant Moses, saying, 'If you
are unfaithful, I will scatter you among
the nations, 9 but if you return to me
and obey my commands, then even if
your exiled people are at the farthest
horizon, I will gather them from there
and bring them to the place I have cho-
sen as a dwelling for my Name.'
10 "They are your servants and your
people, whom you redeemed by your
great strength and your mighty hand.
11 Lord, let your ear be attentive to the
prayer of this your servant and to the
prayer of your servants who delight in
revering your name. Give your servant
success today by granting him favor in
the presence of this man."

I was cupbearer to the king.

Artaxerxes Sends Nehemiah to Jerusalem

2 In the month of Nisan in the twentieth
year of King Artaxerxes, when wine was
brought for him, I took the wine and gave it
to the king. I had not been sad in his pres-
ence before, 2 so the king asked me, "Why
does your face look so sad when you are
not ill? This can be nothing but sadness of
heart."
I was very much afraid, 3 but I said to the
king, "May the king live forever! Why should
my face not look sad when the city where my
ancestors are buried lies in ruins, and its
gates have been destroyed by fire?"
4 The king said to me, "What is it you want?"
Then I prayed to the God of heaven, 5 and I
answered the king, "If it pleases the king and
if your servant has found favor in his sight,
let him send me to the city in Judah where
my ancestors are buried so that I can re-
build it."
6 Then the king, with the queen sitting
beside him, asked me, "How long will your
journey take, and when will you get back?"
It pleased the king to send me; so I set a time.
7 I also said to him, "If it pleases the king,
may I have letters to the governors of Trans-
Euphrates, so that they will provide me safe-
conduct until I arrive in Judah? 8 And may
I have a letter to Asaph, keeper of the roy-
al park, so he will give me timber to make
beams for the gates of the citadel by the tem-
ple and for the city wall and for the residence
I will occupy?" And because the gracious
hand of my God was on me, the king granted
my requests. 9 So I went to the governors of
Trans-Euphrates and gave them the king's
letters. The king had also sent army officers
and cavalry with me.

[10]When Sanballat the Horonite and Tobiah the Ammonite official heard about this, they were very much disturbed that someone had come to promote the welfare of the Israelites.

Nehemiah Inspects Jerusalem's Walls

[11]I went to Jerusalem, and after staying there three days [12]I set out during the night with a few others. I had not told anyone what my God had put in my heart to do for Jerusalem. There were no mounts with me except the one I was riding on.

[13]By night I went out through the Valley Gate toward the Jackal[a] Well and the Dung Gate, examining the walls of Jerusalem, which had been broken down, and its gates, which had been destroyed by fire. [14]Then I moved on toward the Fountain Gate and the King's Pool, but there was not enough room for my mount to get through; [15]so I went up the valley by night, examining the wall. Finally, I turned back and reentered through the Valley Gate. [16]The officials did not know where I had gone or what I was doing, because as yet I had said nothing to the Jews or the priests or nobles or officials or any others who would be doing the work.

[17]Then I said to them, "You see the trouble we are in: Jerusalem lies in ruins, and its gates have been burned with fire. Come, let us rebuild the wall of Jerusalem, and we will no longer be in disgrace." [18]I also told them about the gracious hand of my God on me and what the king had said to me.

They replied, "Let us start rebuilding." So they began this good work.

[19]But when Sanballat the Horonite, Tobiah the Ammonite official and Geshem the Arab heard about it, they mocked and ridiculed us. "What is this you are doing?" they asked. "Are you rebelling against the king?"

[20]I answered them by saying, "The God of heaven will give us success. We his servants will start rebuilding, but as for you, you have no share in Jerusalem or any claim or historic right to it."

Builders of the Wall

3 Eliashib the high priest and his fellow priests went to work and rebuilt the Sheep Gate. They dedicated it and set its doors in place, building as far as the Tower of the Hundred, which they dedicated, and as far as the Tower of Hananel. [2]The men of Jericho built the adjoining section, and Zakkur son of Imri built next to them.

[3]The Fish Gate was rebuilt by the sons of Hassenaah. They laid its beams and put its doors and bolts and bars in place. [4]Meremoth son of Uriah, the son of Hakkoz, repaired the next section. Next to him Meshullam son of Berekiah, the son of Meshezabel, made repairs, and next to him Zadok son of Baana also made repairs. [5]The next section was repaired by the men of Tekoa, but their nobles would not put their shoulders to the work under their supervisors.[b]

[6]The Jeshanah[c] Gate was repaired by Joiada son of Paseah and Meshullam son of Besodeiah. They laid its beams and put its doors with their bolts and bars in place. [7]Next to them, repairs were made by men from Gibeon and Mizpah — Melatiah of Gibeon and Jadon of Meronoth — places under the authority of the governor of Trans-Euphrates. [8]Uzziel son of Harhaiah, one of the goldsmiths, repaired the next section; and Hananiah, one of the perfume-makers, made repairs next to that. They restored Jerusalem as far as the Broad Wall. [9]Rephaiah son of Hur, ruler of a half-district of Jerusalem, repaired the next section. [10]Adjoining this, Jedaiah son of Harumaph made repairs opposite his house, and Hattush son of Hashabneiah made repairs next to him. [11]Malkijah son of Harim and Hasshub son of Pahath-Moab repaired another section and the Tower of the Ovens. [12]Shallum son of Hallohesh, ruler of a half-district of Jerusalem, repaired the next section with the help of his daughters.

[13]The Valley Gate was repaired by Hanun and the residents of Zanoah. They rebuilt it and put its doors with their bolts and bars in place. They also repaired a thousand cubits[d] of the wall as far as the Dung Gate.

[14]The Dung Gate was repaired by Malkijah son of Rekab, ruler of the district of Beth Hakkerem. He rebuilt it and put its doors with their bolts and bars in place.

[15]The Fountain Gate was repaired by Shallun son of Kol-Hozeh, ruler of the district of

[a] *13* Or *Serpent* or *Fig* [b] *5* Or *their Lord* or *the governor* [c] *6* Or *Old* [d] *13* That is, about 1,500 feet or about 450 meters

Mizpah. He rebuilt it, roofing it over and put-
ting its doors and bolts and bars in place. He
also repaired the wall of the Pool of Siloam,[a]
by the King's Garden, as far as the steps going
down from the City of David. 16Beyond him,
Nehemiah son of Azbuk, ruler of a half-dis-
trict of Beth Zur, made repairs up to a point
opposite the tombs[b] of David, as far as the
artificial pool and the House of the Heroes.

17Next to him, the repairs were made by
the Levites under Rehum son of Bani. Beside
him, Hashabiah, ruler of half the district of
Keilah, carried out repairs for his district.
18Next to him, the repairs were made by their
fellow Levites under Binnui[c] son of Hena-
dad, ruler of the other half-district of Kei-
lah. 19Next to him, Ezer son of Jeshua, ruler
of Mizpah, repaired another section, from a
point facing the ascent to the armory as far
as the angle of the wall. 20Next to him, Bar-
uch son of Zabbai zealously repaired anoth-
er section, from the angle to the entrance of
the house of Eliashib the high priest. 21Next
to him, Meremoth son of Uriah, the son of
Hakkoz, repaired another section, from the
entrance of Eliashib's house to the end of it.

22The repairs next to him were made by
the priests from the surrounding region.
23Beyond them, Benjamin and Hasshub
made repairs in front of their house; and
next to them, Azariah son of Maaseiah, the
son of Ananiah, made repairs beside his
house. 24Next to him, Binnui son of Hena-
dad repaired another section, from Azari-
ah's house to the angle and the corner, 25and
Palal son of Uzai worked opposite the angle
and the tower projecting from the upper
palace near the court of the guard. Next to
him, Pedaiah son of Parosh 26and the tem-
ple servants living on the hill of Ophel made
repairs up to a point opposite the Water Gate
toward the east and the projecting tower.
27Next to them, the men of Tekoa repaired
another section, from the great projecting
tower to the wall of Ophel.

28Above the Horse Gate, the priests made
repairs, each in front of his own house.
29Next to them, Zadok son of Immer made
repairs opposite his house. Next to him,
Shemaiah son of Shekaniah, the guard at
the East Gate, made repairs. 30Next to him,
Hananiah son of Shelemiah, and Hanun, the
sixth son of Zalaph, repaired another sec-
tion. Next to them, Meshullam son of Bereki-
ah made repairs opposite his living quarters.
31Next to him, Malkijah, one of the gold-
smiths, made repairs as far as the house of
the temple servants and the merchants, op-
posite the Inspection Gate, and as far as the
room above the corner; 32and between the
room above the corner and the Sheep Gate
the goldsmiths and merchants made repairs.

Opposition to the Rebuilding

4[d] When Sanballat heard that we were
rebuilding the wall, he became angry
and was greatly incensed. He ridiculed the
Jews, 2and in the presence of his associates
and the army of Samaria, he said, "What
are those feeble Jews doing? Will they re-
store their wall? Will they offer sacrifices?
Will they finish in a day? Can they bring the
stones back to life from those heaps of rub-
ble — burned as they are?"

3Tobiah the Ammonite, who was at his
side, said, "What they are building — even a
fox climbing up on it would break down their
wall of stones!"

4Hear us, our God, for we are despised.
Turn their insults back on their own heads.
Give them over as plunder in a land of cap-
tivity. 5Do not cover up their guilt or blot
out their sins from your sight, for they have
thrown insults in the face of[e] the builders.

6So we rebuilt the wall till all of it reached
half its height, for the people worked with all
their heart.

7But when Sanballat, Tobiah, the Arabs,
the Ammonites and the people of Ashdod
heard that the repairs to Jerusalem's walls
had gone ahead and that the gaps were being
closed, they were very angry. 8They all plot-
ted together to come and fight against Jeru-
salem and stir up trouble against it. 9But we
prayed to our God and posted a guard day
and night to meet this threat.

10Meanwhile, the people in Judah said,
"The strength of the laborers is giving out,

[a] *15* Hebrew *Shelah,* a variant of *Shiloah,* that is, Siloam [b] *16* Hebrew; Septuagint, some Vulgate manuscripts and Syriac *tomb* [c] *18* Two Hebrew manuscripts and Syriac (see also Septuagint and verse 24); most Hebrew manuscripts *Bavvai* [d] In Hebrew texts 4:1-6 is numbered 3:33-38, and 4:7-23 is numbered 4:1-17. [e] *5* Or *have aroused your anger before*

and there is so much rubble that we cannot rebuild the wall."

11 Also our enemies said, "Before they know it or see us, we will be right there among them and will kill them and put an end to the work."

12 Then the Jews who lived near them came and told us ten times over, "Wherever you turn, they will attack us."

13 Therefore I stationed some of the people behind the lowest points of the wall at the exposed places, posting them by families, with their swords, spears and bows. 14 After I looked things over, I stood up and said to the nobles, the officials and the rest of the people, "Don't be afraid of them. Remember the Lord, who is great and awesome, and fight for your families, your sons and your daughters, your wives and your homes."

15 When our enemies heard that we were aware of their plot and that God had frustrated it, we all returned to the wall, each to our own work.

16 From that day on, half of my men did the work, while the other half were equipped with spears, shields, bows and armor. The officers posted themselves behind all the people of Judah 17 who were building the wall. Those who carried materials did their work with one hand and held a weapon in the other, 18 and each of the builders wore his sword at his side as he worked. But the man who sounded the trumpet stayed with me.

19 Then I said to the nobles, the officials and the rest of the people, "The work is extensive and spread out, and we are widely separated from each other along the wall. 20 Wherever you hear the sound of the trumpet, join us there. Our God will fight for us!"

21 So we continued the work with half the men holding spears, from the first light of dawn till the stars came out. 22 At that time I also said to the people, "Have every man and his helper stay inside Jerusalem at night, so they can serve us as guards by night and as workers by day." 23 Neither I nor my brothers nor my men nor the guards with me took off our clothes; each had his weapon, even when he went for water.[a]

Nehemiah Helps the Poor

5 Now the men and their wives raised a great outcry against their fellow Jews. 2 Some were saying, "We and our sons and daughters are numerous; in order for us to eat and stay alive, we must get grain."

3 Others were saying, "We are mortgaging our fields, our vineyards and our homes to get grain during the famine."

4 Still others were saying, "We have had to borrow money to pay the king's tax on our fields and vineyards. 5 Although we are of the same flesh and blood as our fellow Jews and though our children are as good as theirs, yet we have to subject our sons and daughters to slavery. Some of our daughters have already been enslaved, but we are powerless, because our fields and our vineyards belong to others."

6 When I heard their outcry and these charges, I was very angry. 7 I pondered them in my mind and then accused the nobles and officials. I told them, "You are charging your own people interest!" So I called together a large meeting to deal with them 8 and said: "As far as possible, we have bought back our fellow Jews who were sold to the Gentiles. Now you are selling your own people, only for them to be sold back to us!" They kept quiet, because they could find nothing to say.

9 So I continued, "What you are doing is not right. Shouldn't you walk in the fear of our God to avoid the reproach of our Gentile enemies? 10 I and my brothers and my men are also lending the people money and grain. But let us stop charging interest! 11 Give back to them immediately their fields, vineyards, olive groves and houses, and also the interest you are charging them — one percent of the money, grain, new wine and olive oil."

12 "We will give it back," they said. "And we will not demand anything more from them. We will do as you say."

Then I summoned the priests and made the nobles and officials take an oath to do what they had promised. 13 I also shook out the folds of my robe and said, "In this way may God shake out of their house and possessions anyone who does not keep this promise. So may such a person be shaken out and emptied!"

At this the whole assembly said, "Amen," and praised the LORD. And the people did as they had promised.

14 Moreover, from the twentieth year of

[a] 23 The meaning of the Hebrew for this clause is uncertain.

GLORY TO GOD FOREVER

Steve Fee, Vicki Beeching

Before the world was made
Before you spoke it to be
You were the King of kings
Yeah you were, yeah you were
And now you're reigning still
Enthroned above all things
Angels and saints cry out
We join them as we sing

Glory to God
Glory to God
Glory to God forever

Creator God you gave
Me breath so I could praise
Your great and matchless name
All my days, all my days
So let my whole life be
A blazing offering
A life that shouts and sings
The greatness of the King

Take my life and let it be
All for you and for your glory
Take my life and let it be yours

THE INSPIRATION

"He must become greater; I must become less." —John 3:30

BEHIND THE STORY

The sentiment behind the triumphant song, "Glory to God Forever," may seem simple at first, but at the heart of this crowd-pleaser is the absolute essence of the Christian life.

"It's a simple song with a massive thought," says Steve Fee, who wrote the song with worship leader and artist Vicky Beeching. "Embedded in the song is this prayer. It says 'take my life and let it be all for you and for your glory.' It's a huge prayer!"

For Fee it's a prayer that is especially powerful in our culture right now. "God, save me from letting my life be about myself," Fee adds. "That's the 'gospel' of our culture: take your life, make it as big as possible and get everything you can for yourself — that's not what I want my life to be about. I want my life to be about God's glory, God's grandness and my purpose in the story of God."

Selah

Think about the Christian influencers in your life, the people who have really shown you what it means to love God. Write down the characteristics of people who bring glory to God in visible and tangible ways.

King Artaxerxes, when I was appointed to be their governor in the land of Judah, until his thirty-second year — twelve years — neither I nor my brothers ate the food allotted to the governor. 15 But the earlier governors — those preceding me — placed a heavy burden on the people and took forty shekels[a] of silver from them in addition to food and wine. Their assistants also lorded it over the people. But out of reverence for God I did not act like that. 16 Instead, I devoted myself to the work on this wall. All my men were assembled there for the work; we[b] did not acquire any land.

17 Furthermore, a hundred and fifty Jews and officials ate at my table, as well as those who came to us from the surrounding nations. 18 Each day one ox, six choice sheep and some poultry were prepared for me, and every ten days an abundant supply of wine of all kinds. In spite of all this, I never demanded the food allotted to the governor, because the demands were heavy on these people.

19 Remember me with favor, my God, for all I have done for these people.

Further Opposition to the Rebuilding

6 When word came to Sanballat, Tobiah, Geshem the Arab and the rest of our enemies that I had rebuilt the wall and not a gap was left in it — though up to that time I had not set the doors in the gates — 2 Sanballat and Geshem sent me this message: "Come, let us meet together in one of the villages[c] on the plain of Ono."

But they were scheming to harm me; 3 so I sent messengers to them with this reply: "I am carrying on a great project and cannot go down. Why should the work stop while I leave it and go down to you?" 4 Four times they sent me the same message, and each time I gave them the same answer.

5 Then, the fifth time, Sanballat sent his aide to me with the same message, and in his hand was an unsealed letter 6 in which was written:

> "It is reported among the nations — and Geshem[d] says it is true — that you and the Jews are plotting to revolt, and therefore you are building the wall. Moreover, according to these reports you are about to become their king 7 and have even appointed prophets to make this proclamation about you in Jerusalem: 'There is a king in Judah!' Now this report will get back to the king; so come, let us meet together."

8 I sent him this reply: "Nothing like what you are saying is happening; you are just making it up out of your head."

9 They were all trying to frighten us, thinking, "Their hands will get too weak for the work, and it will not be completed."

But I prayed, "Now strengthen my hands."

10 One day I went to the house of Shemaiah son of Delaiah, the son of Mehetabel, who was shut in at his home. He said, "Let us meet in the house of God, inside the temple, and let us close the temple doors, because men are coming to kill you — by night they are coming to kill you."

11 But I said, "Should a man like me run away? Or should someone like me go into the temple to save his life? I will not go!" 12 I realized that God had not sent him, but that he had prophesied against me because Tobiah and Sanballat had hired him. 13 He had been hired to intimidate me so that I would commit a sin by doing this, and then they would give me a bad name to discredit me.

14 Remember Tobiah and Sanballat, my God, because of what they have done; remember also the prophet Noadiah and how she and the rest of the prophets have been trying to intimidate me. 15 So the wall was completed on the twenty-fifth of Elul, in fifty-two days.

Opposition to the Completed Wall

16 When all our enemies heard about this, all the surrounding nations were afraid and lost their self-confidence, because they realized that this work had been done with the help of our God.

17 Also, in those days the nobles of Judah were sending many letters to Tobiah, and replies from Tobiah kept coming to them. 18 For many in Judah were under oath to him, since he was son-in-law to Shekaniah son of Arah, and his son Jehohanan had married the daughter of Meshullam son of Berekiah. 19 Moreover, they kept reporting to me his

[a] *15* That is, about 1 pound or about 460 grams [b] *16* Most Hebrew manuscripts; some Hebrew manuscripts, Septuagint, Vulgate and Syriac *I* [c] *2* Or *in Kephirim* [d] *6* Hebrew *Gashmu,* a variant of *Geshem*

good deeds and then telling him what I said.
And Tobiah sent letters to intimidate me.

7 After the wall had been rebuilt and I had
set the doors in place, the gatekeepers,
the musicians and the Levites were appoint-
ed. [2]I put in charge of Jerusalem my broth-
er Hanani, along with Hananiah the com-
mander of the citadel, because he was a man
of integrity and feared God more than most
people do. [3]I said to them, "The gates of Je-
rusalem are not to be opened until the sun is
hot. While the gatekeepers are still on duty,
have them shut the doors and bar them. Also
appoint residents of Jerusalem as guards,
some at their posts and some near their own
houses."

The List of the Exiles Who Returned

[4]Now the city was large and spacious, but
there were few people in it, and the houses
had not yet been rebuilt. [5]So my God put it
into my heart to assemble the nobles, the
officials and the common people for regis-
tration by families. I found the genealogical
record of those who had been the first to re-
turn. This is what I found written there:

[6]These are the people of the prov-
ince who came up from the captivity of
the exiles whom Nebuchadnezzar king
of Babylon had taken captive (they re-
turned to Jerusalem and Judah, each
to his own town, [7]in company with Ze-
rubbabel, Joshua, Nehemiah, Azariah,
Raamiah, Nahamani, Mordecai, Bil-
shan, Mispereth, Bigvai, Nehum and
Baanah):

The list of the men of Israel:

[8]the descendants of Parosh 2,172
[9]of Shephatiah 372
[10]of Arah 652
[11]of Pahath-Moab (through
the line of Jeshua and Joab) 2 818
[12]of Elam 1 254
[13]of Zattu 845
[14]of Zakkai 760
[15]of Binnui 648
[16]of Bebai 628
[17]of Azgad 2,322
[18]of Adonikam 667
[19]of Bigvai 2,067
[20]of Adin 655
[21]of Ater (through Hezekiah) 98
[22]of Hashum 328
[23]of Bezai 324
[24]of Hariph 112
[25]of Gibeon 95

[26]the men of Bethlehem and
Netophah 188
[27]of Anathoth 128
[28]of Beth Azmaveth 42
[29]of Kiriath Jearim, Kephirah
and Beeroth 743
[30]of Ramah and Geba 621
[31]of Mikmash 122
[32]of Bethel and Ai 123
[33]of the other Nebo 52
[34]of the other Elam 1,254
[35]of Harim 320
[36]of Jericho 345
[37]of Lod, Hadid and Ono 721
[38]of Senaah 3,930

[39]The priests:

the descendants of Jedaiah
(through the family of Jeshua) 973
[40]of Immer 1,052
[41]of Pashhur 1,247
[42]of Harim 1,017

[43]The Levites:

the descendants of Jeshua
(through Kadmiel through
the line of Hodaviah) 74

[44]The musicians:

the descendants of Asaph 148

[45]The gatekeepers:

the descendants of
Shallum, Ater, Talmon,
Akkub, Hatita and Shobai 138

[46]The temple servants:

the descendants of
Ziha, Hasupha, Tabbaoth,
[47]Keros, Sia, Padon,
[48]Lebana, Hagaba, Shalmai,
[49]Hanan, Giddel, Gahar,
[50]Reaiah, Rezin, Nekoda,
[51]Gazzam, Uzza, Paseah,
[52]Besai, Meunim, Nephusim,
[53]Bakbuk, Hakupha, Harhur,
[54]Bazluth, Mehida, Harsha,
[55]Barkos, Sisera, Temah,
[56]Neziah and Hatipha

[57]The descendants of the servants of
Solomon:

the descendants of
Sotai, Sophereth, Perida,
58 Jaala, Darkon, Giddel,
59 Shephatiah, Hattil,
Pokereth-Hazzebaim and Amon

60 The temple servants and the descendants of the servants of Solomon 392

61 The following came up from the towns of Tel Melah, Tel Harsha, Kerub, Addon and Immer, but they could not show that their families were descended from Israel:

62 the descendants of
Delaiah, Tobiah and Nekoda 642

63 And from among the priests:

the descendants of
Hobaiah, Hakkoz and Barzillai (a man who had married a daughter of Barzillai the Gileadite and was called by that name).

64 These searched for their family records, but they could not find them and so were excluded from the priesthood as unclean. 65 The governor, therefore, ordered them not to eat any of the most sacred food until there should be a priest ministering with the Urim and Thummim.

66 The whole company numbered 42,360, 67 besides their 7,337 male and female slaves; and they also had 245 male and female singers. 68 There were 736 horses, 245 mules,[a] 69 435 camels and 6,720 donkeys.

70 Some of the heads of the families contributed to the work. The governor gave to the treasury 1,000 darics[b] of gold, 50 bowls and 530 garments for priests. 71 Some of the heads of the families gave to the treasury for the work 20,000 darics[c] of gold and 2,200 minas[d] of silver. 72 The total given by the rest of the people was 20,000 darics of gold, 2,000 minas[e] of silver and 67 garments for priests.

73 The priests, the Levites, the gatekeepers, the musicians and the temple servants, along with certain of the people and the rest of the Israelites, settled in their own towns.

Ezra Reads the Law

8 When the seventh month came and the Israelites had settled in their towns, 1 all the people came together as one in the square before the Water Gate. They told Ezra the teacher of the Law to bring out the Book of the Law of Moses, which the LORD had commanded for Israel.

2 So on the first day of the seventh month Ezra the priest brought the Law before the assembly, which was made up of men and women and all who were able to understand. 3 He read it aloud from daybreak till noon as he faced the square before the Water Gate in the presence of the men, women and others who could understand. And all the people listened attentively to the Book of the Law.

4 Ezra the teacher of the Law stood on a high wooden platform built for the occasion. Beside him on his right stood Mattithiah, Shema, Anaiah, Uriah, Hilkiah and Maaseiah; and on his left were Pedaiah, Mishael, Malkijah, Hashum, Hashbaddanah, Zechariah and Meshullam.

5 Ezra opened the book. All the people could see him because he was standing above them; and as he opened it, the people all stood up. 6 Ezra praised the LORD, the great God; and all the people lifted their hands and responded, "Amen! Amen!" Then they bowed down and worshiped the LORD with their faces to the ground.

7 The Levites — Jeshua, Bani, Sherebiah, Jamin, Akkub, Shabbethai, Hodiah, Maaseiah, Kelita, Azariah, Jozabad, Hanan and Pelaiah — instructed the people in the Law while the people were standing there. 8 They read from the Book of the Law of God, making it clear[f] and giving the meaning so that the people understood what was being read.

9 Then Nehemiah the governor, Ezra the priest and teacher of the Law, and the Levites who were instructing the people said to them all, "This day is holy to the LORD your

[a] *68* Some Hebrew manuscripts (see also Ezra 2:66); most Hebrew manuscripts do not have this verse.
[b] *70* That is, about 19 pounds or about 8.4 kilograms
[c] *71* That is, about 375 pounds or about 170 kilograms; also in verse 72
[d] *71* That is, about 1 1/3 tons or about 1.2 metric tons
[e] *72* That is, about 1 1/4 tons or about 1.1 metric tons
[f] *8* Or *God, translating it*

God. Do not mourn or weep." For all the people had been weeping as they listened to the words of the Law.

10 Nehemiah said, "Go and enjoy choice food and sweet drinks, and send some to those who have nothing prepared. This day is holy to our Lord. Do not grieve, for the joy of the LORD is your strength."

11 The Levites calmed all the people, saying, "Be still, for this is a holy day. Do not grieve."

12 Then all the people went away to eat and drink, to send portions of food and to celebrate with great joy, because they now understood the words that had been made known to them.

13 On the second day of the month, the heads of all the families, along with the priests and the Levites, gathered around Ezra the teacher to give attention to the words of the Law. 14 They found written in the Law, which the LORD had commanded through Moses, that the Israelites were to live in temporary shelters during the festival of the seventh month 15 and that they should proclaim this word and spread it throughout their towns and in Jerusalem: "Go out into the hill country and bring back branches from olive and wild olive trees, and from myrtles, palms and shade trees, to make temporary shelters"—as it is written.[a]

16 So the people went out and brought back branches and built themselves temporary shelters on their own roofs, in their courtyards, in the courts of the house of God and in the square by the Water Gate and the one by the Gate of Ephraim. 17 The whole company that had returned from exile built temporary shelters and lived in them. From the days of Joshua son of Nun until that day, the Israelites had not celebrated it like this. And their joy was very great.

18 Day after day, from the first day to the last, Ezra read from the Book of the Law of God. They celebrated the festival for seven days, and on the eighth day, in accordance with the regulation, there was an assembly.

The Israelites Confess Their Sins

9 On the twenty-fourth day of the same month, the Israelites gathered together, fasting and wearing sackcloth and putting dust on their heads. 2 Those of Israelite descent had separated themselves from all foreigners. They stood in their places and confessed their sins and the sins of their ancestors. 3 They stood where they were and read from the Book of the Law of the LORD their God for a quarter of the day, and spent another quarter in confession and in worshiping the LORD their God. 4 Standing on the stairs of the Levites were Jeshua, Bani, Kadmiel, Shebaniah, Bunni, Sherebiah, Bani and Kenani. They cried out with loud voices to the LORD their God. 5 And the Levites—Jeshua, Kadmiel, Bani, Hashabneiah, Sherebiah, Hodiah, Shebaniah and Pethahiah—said: "Stand up and praise the LORD your God, who is from everlasting to everlasting.[b]"

"Blessed be your glorious name, and may it be exalted above all blessing and praise. 6 You alone are the LORD. You made the heavens, even the highest heavens, and all their starry host, the earth and all that is on it, the seas and all that is in them. You give life to everything, and the multitudes of heaven worship you.

7 "You are the LORD God, who chose Abram and brought him out of Ur of the Chaldeans and named him Abraham. 8 You found his heart faithful to you, and you made a covenant with him to give to his descendants the land of the Canaanites, Hittites, Amorites, Perizzites, Jebusites and Girgashites. You have kept your promise because you are righteous.

9 "You saw the suffering of our ancestors in Egypt; you heard their cry at the Red Sea.[c] 10 You sent signs and wonders against Pharaoh, against all his officials and all the people of his land, for you knew how arrogantly the Egyptians treated them. You made a name for yourself, which remains to this day. 11 You divided the sea before them, so that they passed through it on dry ground, but you hurled their pursuers into the depths, like a stone into mighty waters. 12 By day you led them with a pillar of cloud, and by night with a pillar of fire to give them light on the way they were to take.

[a] 15 See Lev. 23:37-40. [b] 5 Or *God for ever and ever* [c] 9 Or *the Sea of Reeds*

13 "You came down on Mount Sinai; you spoke to them from heaven. You gave them regulations and laws that are just and right, and decrees and commands that are good. 14 You made known to them your holy Sabbath and gave them commands, decrees and laws through your servant Moses. 15 In their hunger you gave them bread from heaven and in their thirst you brought them water from the rock; you told them to go in and take possession of the land you had sworn with uplifted hand to give them.

16 "But they, our ancestors, became arrogant and stiff-necked, and they did not obey your commands. 17 They refused to listen and failed to remember the miracles you performed among them. They became stiff-necked and in their rebellion appointed a leader in order to return to their slavery. But you are a forgiving God, gracious and compassionate, slow to anger and abounding in love. Therefore you did not desert them, 18 even when they cast for themselves an image of a calf and said, 'This is your god, who brought you up out of Egypt,' or when they committed awful blasphemies.

19 "Because of your great compassion you did not abandon them in the wilderness. By day the pillar of cloud did not fail to guide them on their path, nor the pillar of fire by night to shine on the way they were to take. 20 You gave your good Spirit to instruct them. You did not withhold your manna from their mouths, and you gave them water for their thirst. 21 For forty years you sustained them in the wilderness; they lacked nothing, their clothes did not wear out nor did their feet become swollen.

22 "You gave them kingdoms and nations, allotting to them even the remotest frontiers. They took over the country of Sihon[a] king of Heshbon and the country of Og king of Bashan. 23 You made their children as numerous as the stars in the sky, and you brought them into the land that you told their parents to enter and possess. 24 Their children went in and took possession of the land. You subdued before them the Canaanites, who lived in the land; you gave the Canaanites into their hands, along with their kings and the peoples of the land, to deal with them as they pleased. 25 They captured fortified cities and fertile land; they took possession of houses filled with all kinds of good things, wells already dug, vineyards, olive groves and fruit trees in abundance. They ate to the full and were well-nourished; they reveled in your great goodness.

26 "But they were disobedient and rebelled against you; they turned their backs on your law. They killed your prophets, who had warned them in order to turn them back to you; they committed awful blasphemies. 27 So you delivered them into the hands of their enemies, who oppressed them. But when they were oppressed they cried out to you. From heaven you heard them, and in your great compassion you gave them deliverers, who rescued them from the hand of their enemies.

28 "But as soon as they were at rest, they again did what was evil in your sight. Then you abandoned them to the hand of their enemies so that they ruled over them. And when they cried out to you again, you heard from heaven, and in your compassion you delivered them time after time.

29 "You warned them in order to turn them back to your law, but they became arrogant and disobeyed your commands. They sinned against your ordinances, of which you said, 'The person who obeys them will live by them.' Stubbornly they turned their backs on you, became stiff-necked and refused to listen. 30 For many years you were patient with them. By your Spirit you warned them through your prophets. Yet they paid no attention, so you gave them into the hands of the neighboring peoples. 31 But in your great mercy you did not put an end to them or abandon them, for you are a gracious and merciful God.

32 "Now therefore, our God, the great

[a] *22* One Hebrew manuscript and Septuagint; most Hebrew manuscripts *Sihon, that is, the country of the*

God, mighty and awesome, who keeps
his covenant of love, do not let all this
hardship seem trifling in your eyes —
the hardship that has come on us, on
our kings and leaders, on our priests
and prophets, on our ancestors and all
your people, from the days of the kings
of Assyria until today. 33 In all that has
happened to us, you have remained
righteous; you have acted faithfully,
while we acted wickedly. 34 Our kings,
our leaders, our priests and our ances-
tors did not follow your law; they did
not pay attention to your commands or
the statutes you warned them to keep.
35 Even while they were in their king-
dom, enjoying your great goodness to
them in the spacious and fertile land
you gave them, they did not serve you
or turn from their evil ways.

36 "But see, we are slaves today, slaves
in the land you gave our ancestors so
they could eat its fruit and the other
good things it produces. 37 Because of
our sins, its abundant harvest goes to
the kings you have placed over us. They
rule over our bodies and our cattle as
they please. We are in great distress.

The Agreement of the People

38 "In view of all this, we are making a
binding agreement, putting it in writing,
and our leaders, our Levites and our priests
are affixing their seals to it."[a]

10

[b] Those who sealed it were:

Nehemiah the governor, the son of Hakaliah.

Zedekiah, 2 Seraiah, Azariah, Jeremiah,
3 Pashhur, Amariah, Malkijah,
4 Hattush, Shebaniah, Malluk,
5 Harim, Meremoth, Obadiah,
6 Daniel, Ginnethon, Baruch,
7 Meshullam, Abijah, Mijamin,
8 Maaziah, Bilgai and Shemaiah.
These were the priests.

9 The Levites:

Jeshua son of Azaniah, Binnui of the sons of Henadad, Kadmiel,
10 and their associates: Shebaniah,
Hodiah, Kelita, Pelaiah, Hanan,
11 Mika, Rehob, Hashabiah,
12 Zakkur, Sherebiah, Shebaniah,
13 Hodiah, Bani and Beninu.

14 The leaders of the people:

Parosh, Pahath-Moab, Elam, Zattu, Bani,
15 Bunni, Azgad, Bebai,
16 Adonijah, Bigvai, Adin,
17 Ater, Hezekiah, Azzur,
18 Hodiah, Hashum, Bezai,
19 Hariph, Anathoth, Nebai,
20 Magpiash, Meshullam, Hezir,
21 Meshezabel, Zadok, Jaddua,
22 Pelatiah, Hanan, Anaiah,
23 Hoshea, Hananiah, Hasshub,
24 Hallohesh, Pilha, Shobek,
25 Rehum, Hashabnah, Maaseiah,
26 Ahiah, Hanan, Anan,
27 Malluk, Harim and Baanah.

28 "The rest of the people — priests,
Levites, gatekeepers, musicians, tem-
ple servants and all who separated
themselves from the neighboring peo-
ples for the sake of the Law of God, to-
gether with their wives and all their
sons and daughters who are able to un-
derstand — 29 all these now join their
fellow Israelites the nobles, and bind
themselves with a curse and an oath
to follow the Law of God given through
Moses the servant of God and to obey
carefully all the commands, regula-
tions and decrees of the LORD our Lord.

30 "We promise not to give our daugh-
ters in marriage to the peoples around
us or take their daughters for our sons.

31 "When the neighboring peoples
bring merchandise or grain to sell on
the Sabbath, we will not buy from them
on the Sabbath or on any holy day. Ev-
ery seventh year we will forgo working
the land and will cancel all debts.

32 "We assume the responsibility for
carrying out the commands to give a
third of a shekel[c] each year for the ser-
vice of the house of our God: 33 for the
bread set out on the table; for the regular

[a] 38 In Hebrew texts this verse (9:38) is numbered 10:1.
[b] In Hebrew texts 10:1-39 is numbered 10:2-40.
[c] 32 That is, about 1/8 ounce or about 4 grams

grain offerings and burnt offerings; for
the offerings on the Sabbaths, at the New
Moon feasts and at the appointed festi-
vals; for the holy offerings; for sin offer-
ings[a] to make atonement for Israel; and
for all the duties of the house of our God.
34 “We — the priests, the Levites
and the people — have cast lots to de-
termine when each of our families is
to bring to the house of our God at set
times each year a contribution of wood
to burn on the altar of the LORD our
God, as it is written in the Law.
35 “We also assume responsibility for
bringing to the house of the LORD each
year the firstfruits of our crops and of
every fruit tree.
36 “As it is also written in the Law, we
will bring the firstborn of our sons and
of our cattle, of our herds and of our
flocks to the house of our God, to the
priests ministering there.
37 “Moreover, we will bring to the
storerooms of the house of our God, to
the priests, the first of our ground meal,
of our grain offerings, of the fruit of all
our trees and of our new wine and ol-
ive oil. And we will bring a tithe of our
crops to the Levites, for it is the Levites
who collect the tithes in all the towns
where we work. 38 A priest descended
from Aaron is to accompany the Le-
vites when they receive the tithes, and
the Levites are to bring a tenth of the
tithes up to the house of our God, to the
storerooms of the treasury. 39 The peo-
ple of Israel, including the Levites, are
to bring their contributions of grain,
new wine and olive oil to the store-
rooms, where the articles for the sanc-
tuary and for the ministering priests,
the gatekeepers and the musicians are
also kept.

“We will not neglect the house of our
God.”

The New Residents of Jerusalem

11 Now the leaders of the people settled
in Jerusalem. The rest of the people
cast lots to bring one out of every ten of them
to live in Jerusalem, the holy city, while the
remaining nine were to stay in their own
towns. 2 The people commended all who vol-
unteered to live in Jerusalem.

3 These are the provincial leaders who
settled in Jerusalem (now some Israelites,
priests, Levites, temple servants and de-
scendants of Solomon’s servants lived in the
towns of Judah, each on their own property in
the various towns, 4 while other people from
both Judah and Benjamin lived in Jerusalem):

From the descendants of Judah:

Athaiah son of Uzziah, the son of Zech-
ariah, the son of Amariah, the son of
Shephatiah, the son of Mahalalel, a de-
scendant of Perez; 5 and Maaseiah son
of Baruch, the son of Kol-Hozeh, the
son of Hazaiah, the son of Adaiah, the
son of Joiarib, the son of Zechariah, a
descendant of Shelah. 6 The descen-
dants of Perez who lived in Jerusalem
totaled 468 men of standing.

7 From the descendants of Benjamin:

Sallu son of Meshullam, the son of Joed,
the son of Pedaiah, the son of Kolaiah,
the son of Maaseiah, the son of Ithiel,
the son of Jeshaiah, 8 and his follow-
ers, Gabbai and Sallai — 928 men. 9 Joel
son of Zikri was their chief officer, and
Judah son of Hassenuah was over the
New Quarter of the city.

10 From the priests:

Jedaiah; the son of Joiarib; Jakin; 11 Se-
raiah son of Hilkiah, the son of Me-
shullam, the son of Zadok, the son of
Meraioth, the son of Ahitub, the official
in charge of the house of God, 12 and
their associates, who carried on work
for the temple — 822 men; Adaiah son
of Jeroham, the son of Pelaliah, the
son of Amzi, the son of Zechariah, the
son of Pashhur, the son of Malkijah,
13 and his associates, who were heads
of families — 242 men; Amashsai son
of Azarel, the son of Ahzai, the son of
Meshillemoth, the son of Immer, 14 and
his[b] associates, who were men of stand-
ing — 128. Their chief officer was Zab-
diel son of Haggedolim.

15 From the Levites:

Shemaiah son of Hasshub, the son of
Azrikam, the son of Hashabiah, the son

[a] 33 Or *purification offerings* [b] 14 Most Septuagint manuscripts; Hebrew *their*

of Bunni; [16]Shabbethai and Jozabad,
two of the heads of the Levites, who had
charge of the outside work of the house
of God; [17]Mattaniah son of Mika, the son
of Zabdi, the son of Asaph, the director
who led in thanksgiving and prayer;
Bakbukiah, second among his asso-
ciates; and Abda son of Shammua, the
son of Galal, the son of Jeduthun. [18]The
Levites in the holy city totaled 284.

[19]The gatekeepers:

Akkub, Talmon and their associates,
who kept watch at the gates — 172 men.

[20]The rest of the Israelites, with the priests
and Levites, were in all the towns of Judah,
each on their ancestral property.
[21]The temple servants lived on the hill of
Ophel, and Ziha and Gishpa were in charge
of them.
[22]The chief officer of the Levites in Jerusa-
lem was Uzzi son of Bani, the son of Hasha-
biah, the son of Mattaniah, the son of Mika.
Uzzi was one of Asaph's descendants, who
were the musicians responsible for the ser-
vice of the house of God. [23]The musicians
were under the king's orders, which regulat-
ed their daily activity.
[24]Pethahiah son of Meshezabel, one of
the descendants of Zerah son of Judah, was
the king's agent in all affairs relating to the
people.
[25]As for the villages with their fields, some
of the people of Judah lived in Kiriath Arba
and its surrounding settlements, in Dibon
and its settlements, in Jekabzeel and its vil-
lages, [26]in Jeshua, in Moladah, in Beth Pelet,
[27]in Hazar Shual, in Beersheba and its set-
tlements, [28]in Ziklag, in Mekonah and its
settlements, [29]in En Rimmon, in Zorah, in
Jarmuth, [30]Zanoah, Adullam and their vil-
lages, in Lachish and its fields, and in Aze-
kah and its settlements. So they were living
all the way from Beersheba to the Valley of
Hinnom.
[31]The descendants of the Benjamites from
Geba lived in Mikmash, Aija, Bethel and its
settlements, [32]in Anathoth, Nob and Anani-
ah, [33]in Hazor, Ramah and Gittaim, [34]in Ha-
did, Zeboim and Neballat, [35]in Lod and Ono,
and in Ge Harashim.
[36]Some of the divisions of the Levites of
Judah settled in Benjamin.

Priests and Levites

12 These were the priests and Levites
who returned with Zerubbabel son
of Shealtiel and with Joshua:

Seraiah, Jeremiah, Ezra,
[2]Amariah, Malluk, Hattush,
[3]Shekaniah, Rehum, Meremoth,
[4]Iddo, Ginnethon,[a] Abijah,
[5]Mijamin,[b] Moadiah, Bilgah,
[6]Shemaiah, Joiarib, Jedaiah,
[7]Sallu, Amok, Hilkiah and Jedaiah.

These were the leaders of the priests and
their associates in the days of Joshua.
[8]The Levites were Jeshua, Binnui, Kad-
miel, Sherebiah, Judah, and also Mattani-
ah, who, together with his associates, was in
charge of the songs of thanksgiving. [9]Bakbu-
kiah and Unni, their associates, stood oppo-
site them in the services.
[10]Joshua was the father of Joiakim, Joia-
kim the father of Eliashib, Eliashib the father
of Joiada, [11]Joiada the father of Jonathan,
and Jonathan the father of Jaddua.
[12]In the days of Joiakim, these were the
heads of the priestly families:

of Seraiah's family, Meraiah;
of Jeremiah's, Hananiah;
[13]of Ezra's, Meshullam;
of Amariah's, Jehohanan;
[14]of Malluk's, Jonathan;
of Shekaniah's,[c] Joseph;
[15]of Harim's, Adna;
of Meremoth's,[d] Helkai;
[16]of Iddo's, Zechariah;
of Ginnethon's, Meshullam;
[17]of Abijah's, Zikri;
of Miniamin's and of Moadiah's, Piltai;
[18]of Bilgah's, Shammua;
of Shemaiah's, Jehonathan;
[19]of Joiarib's, Mattenai;
of Jedaiah's, Uzzi;
[20]of Sallu's, Kallai;
of Amok's, Eber;
[21]of Hilkiah's, Hashabiah;
of Jedaiah's, Nethanel.

[a] *4* Many Hebrew manuscripts and Vulgate (see also verse 16); most Hebrew manuscripts *Ginnethoi*
[b] *5* A variant of *Miniamin* [c] *14* Very many Hebrew manuscripts, some Septuagint manuscripts and Syriac (see also verse 3); most Hebrew manuscripts *Shebaniah's* [d] *15* Some Septuagint manuscripts (see also verse 3); Hebrew *Meraioth's*

22 The family heads of the Levites in the
days of Eliashib, Joiada, Johanan and Jad-
dua, as well as those of the priests, were re-
corded in the reign of Darius the Persian.
23 The family heads among the descendants
of Levi up to the time of Johanan son of Elia-
shib were recorded in the book of the annals.
24 And the leaders of the Levites were Hasha-
biah, Sherebiah, Jeshua son of Kadmiel, and
their associates, who stood opposite them to
give praise and thanksgiving, one section
responding to the other, as prescribed by
David the man of God.

25 Mattaniah, Bakbukiah, Obadiah, Me-
shullam, Talmon and Akkub were gatekeep-
ers who guarded the storerooms at the gates.
26 They served in the days of Joiakim son of
Joshua, the son of Jozadak, and in the days
of Nehemiah the governor and of Ezra the
priest, the teacher of the Law.

Dedication of the Wall of Jerusalem

27 At the dedication of the wall of Jerusalem,
the Levites were sought out from where they
lived and were brought to Jerusalem to cel-
ebrate joyfully the dedication with songs of
thanksgiving and with the music of cymbals,
harps and lyres. 28 The musicians also were
brought together from the region around Je-
rusalem—from the villages of the Netopha-
thites, 29 from Beth Gilgal, and from the area
of Geba and Azmaveth, for the musicians had
built villages for themselves around Jerusa-
lem. 30 When the priests and Levites had pu-
rified themselves ceremonially, they purified
the people, the gates and the wall.

31 I had the leaders of Judah go up on top
of[a] the wall. I also assigned two large choirs
to give thanks. One was to proceed on top
of[b] the wall to the right, toward the Dung
Gate. 32 Hoshaiah and half the leaders of Ju-
dah followed them, 33 along with Azariah,
Ezra, Meshullam, 34 Judah, Benjamin, She-
maiah, Jeremiah, 35 as well as some priests
with trumpets, and also Zechariah son of
Jonathan, the son of Shemaiah, the son of
Mattaniah, the son of Micaiah, the son of
Zakkur, the son of Asaph, 36 and his associ-
ates—Shemaiah, Azarel, Milalai, Gilalai,
Maai, Nethanel, Judah and Hanani—with
musical instruments prescribed by David
the man of God. Ezra the teacher of the Law
led the procession. 37 At the Fountain Gate
they continued directly up the steps of the
City of David on the ascent to the wall and
passed above the site of David's palace to the
Water Gate on the east.

38 The second choir proceeded in the oppo-
site direction. I followed them on top of[c] the
wall, together with half the people—past the
Tower of the Ovens to the Broad Wall, 39 over
the Gate of Ephraim, the Jeshanah[d] Gate, the
Fish Gate, the Tower of Hananel and the Tow-
er of the Hundred, as far as the Sheep Gate. At
the Gate of the Guard they stopped.

40 The two choirs that gave thanks then
took their places in the house of God; so did
I, together with half the officials, 41 as well as
the priests—Eliakim, Maaseiah, Miniamin,
Micaiah, Elioenai, Zechariah and Hanani-
ah with their trumpets— 42 and also Maa-
seiah, Shemaiah, Eleazar, Uzzi, Jehohanan,
Malkijah, Elam and Ezer. The choirs sang
under the direction of Jezrahiah. 43 And on
that day they offered great sacrifices, re-
joicing because God had given them great
joy. The women and children also rejoiced.
The sound of rejoicing in Jerusalem could be
heard far away.

44 At that time men were appointed to be
in charge of the storerooms for the contribu-
tions, firstfruits and tithes. From the fields
around the towns they were to bring into the
storerooms the portions required by the Law
for the priests and the Levites, for Judah was
pleased with the ministering priests and Le-
vites. 45 They performed the service of their
God and the service of purification, as did
also the musicians and gatekeepers, accord-
ing to the commands of David and his son Sol-
omon. 46 For long ago, in the days of David and
Asaph, there had been directors for the musi-
cians and for the songs of praise and thanks-
giving to God. 47 So in the days of Zerubbabel
and of Nehemiah, all Israel contributed the
daily portions for the musicians and the gate-
keepers. They also set aside the portion for
the other Levites, and the Levites set aside the
portion for the descendants of Aaron.

Nehemiah's Final Reforms

13 On that day the Book of Moses was
read aloud in the hearing of the peo-
ple and there it was found written that no
Ammonite or Moabite should ever be ad-
mitted into the assembly of God, 2 because

[a] *31* Or *go alongside* [b] *31* Or *proceed alongside* [c] *38* Or *them alongside* [d] *39* Or *Old*

they had not met the Israelites with food and water but had hired Balaam to call a curse down on them. (Our God, however, turned the curse into a blessing.) 3When the people heard this law, they excluded from Israel all who were of foreign descent.

4Before this, Eliashib the priest had been put in charge of the storerooms of the house of our God. He was closely associated with Tobiah, 5and he had provided him with a large room formerly used to store the grain offerings and incense and temple articles, and also the tithes of grain, new wine and olive oil prescribed for the Levites, musicians and gatekeepers, as well as the contributions for the priests.

6But while all this was going on, I was not in Jerusalem, for in the thirty-second year of Artaxerxes king of Babylon I had returned to the king. Some time later I asked his permission 7and came back to Jerusalem. Here I learned about the evil thing Eliashib had done in providing Tobiah a room in the courts of the house of God. 8I was greatly displeased and threw all Tobiah's household goods out of the room. 9I gave orders to purify the rooms, and then I put back into them the equipment of the house of God, with the grain offerings and the incense.

10I also learned that the portions assigned to the Levites had not been given to them, and that all the Levites and musicians responsible for the service had gone back to their own fields. 11So I rebuked the officials and asked them, "Why is the house of God neglected?" Then I called them together and stationed them at their posts.

12All Judah brought the tithes of grain, new wine and olive oil into the storerooms. 13I put Shelemiah the priest, Zadok the scribe, and a Levite named Pedaiah in charge of the storerooms and made Hanan son of Zakkur, the son of Mattaniah, their assistant, because they were considered trustworthy. They were made responsible for distributing the supplies to their fellow Levites.

14Remember me for this, my God, and do not blot out what I have so faithfully done for the house of my God and its services.

15In those days I saw people in Judah treading winepresses on the Sabbath and bringing in grain and loading it on donkeys, together with wine, grapes, figs and all other kinds of loads. And they were bringing all this into Jerusalem on the Sabbath. Therefore I warned them against selling food on that day. 16People from Tyre who lived in Jerusalem were bringing in fish and all kinds of merchandise and selling them in Jerusalem on the Sabbath to the people of Judah. 17I rebuked the nobles of Judah and said to them, "What is this wicked thing you are doing—desecrating the Sabbath day? 18Didn't your ancestors do the same things, so that our God brought all this calamity on us and on this city? Now you are stirring up more wrath against Israel by desecrating the Sabbath."

19When evening shadows fell on the gates of Jerusalem before the Sabbath, I ordered the doors to be shut and not opened until the Sabbath was over. I stationed some of my own men at the gates so that no load could be brought in on the Sabbath day. 20Once or twice the merchants and sellers of all kinds of goods spent the night outside Jerusalem. 21But I warned them and said, "Why do you spend the night by the wall? If you do this again, I will arrest you." From that time on they no longer came on the Sabbath. 22Then I commanded the Levites to purify themselves and go and guard the gates in order to keep the Sabbath day holy.

Remember me for this also, my God, and show mercy to me according to your great love.

23Moreover, in those days I saw men of Judah who had married women from Ashdod, Ammon and Moab. 24Half of their children spoke the language of Ashdod or the language of one of the other peoples, and did not know how to speak the language of Judah. 25I rebuked them and called curses down on them. I beat some of the men and pulled out their hair. I made them take an oath in God's name and said: "You are not to give your daughters in marriage to their sons, nor are you to take their daughters in marriage for your sons or for yourselves. 26Was it not because of marriages like these that Solomon king of Israel sinned? Among the many nations there was no king like him. He was loved by his God, and God made him king over all Israel, but even he was led into sin by foreign women. 27Must we hear now that you too are doing all this terrible wickedness and are being unfaithful to our God by marrying foreign women?"

[28]One of the sons of Joiada son of Eliashib
the high priest was son-in-law to Sanballat
the Horonite. And I drove him away from me.

[29]Remember them, my God, because they
defiled the priestly office and the covenant
of the priesthood and of the Levites.

[30]So I purified the priests and the Levites
of everything foreign, and assigned them
duties, each to his own task. [31]I also made
provision for contributions of wood at desig-
nated times, and for the firstfruits.

Remember me with favor, my God.

ESTHER

Queen Vashti Deposed

1 This is what happened during the time of Xerxes,[a] the Xerxes who ruled over 127 provinces stretching from India to Cush[b]: [2]At that time King Xerxes reigned from his royal throne in the citadel of Susa, [3]and in the third year of his reign he gave a banquet for all his nobles and officials. The military leaders of Persia and Media, the princes, and the nobles of the provinces were present.

[4]For a full 180 days he displayed the vast wealth of his kingdom and the splendor and glory of his majesty. [5]When these days were over, the king gave a banquet, lasting seven days, in the enclosed garden of the king's palace, for all the people from the least to the greatest who were in the citadel of Susa. [6]The garden had hangings of white and blue linen, fastened with cords of white linen and purple material to silver rings on marble pillars. There were couches of gold and silver on a mosaic pavement of porphyry, marble, mother-of-pearl and other costly stones. [7]Wine was served in goblets of gold, each one different from the other, and the royal wine was abundant, in keeping with the king's liberality. [8]By the king's command each guest was allowed to drink with no restrictions, for the king instructed all the wine stewards to serve each man what he wished.

[9]Queen Vashti also gave a banquet for the women in the royal palace of King Xerxes.

[10]On the seventh day, when King Xerxes was in high spirits from wine, he commanded the seven eunuchs who served him — Mehuman, Biztha, Harbona, Bigtha, Abagtha, Zethar and Karkas — [11]to bring before him Queen Vashti, wearing her royal crown, in order to display her beauty to the people and nobles, for she was lovely to look at. [12]But when the attendants delivered the king's command, Queen Vashti refused to come. Then the king became furious and burned with anger.

[13]Since it was customary for the king to consult experts in matters of law and justice, he spoke with the wise men who understood the times [14]and were closest to the king — Karshena, Shethar, Admatha, Tarshish, Meres, Marsena and Memukan, the seven nobles of Persia and Media who had special access to the king and were highest in the kingdom.

[15]"According to law, what must be done to Queen Vashti?" he asked. "She has not obeyed the command of King Xerxes that the eunuchs have taken to her."

[16]Then Memukan replied in the presence of the king and the nobles, "Queen Vashti has done wrong, not only against the king but also against all the nobles and the peoples of all the provinces of King Xerxes. [17]For the queen's conduct will become known to all the women, and so they will despise their husbands and say, 'King Xerxes commanded Queen Vashti to be brought before him, but she would not come.' [18]This very day the Persian and Median women of the nobility who have heard about the queen's conduct will respond to all the king's nobles in the same way. There will be no end of disrespect and discord.

[19]"Therefore, if it pleases the king, let him issue a royal decree and let it be written in the laws of Persia and Media, which cannot be repealed, that Vashti is never again to enter the presence of King Xerxes. Also let the king give her royal position to someone else who is better than she. [20]Then when the king's edict is proclaimed throughout all his vast realm, all the women will respect their husbands, from the least to the greatest."

[21]The king and his nobles were pleased with this advice, so the king did as Memukan proposed. [22]He sent dispatches to all parts of the kingdom, to each province in its own script and to each people in their own language, proclaiming that every man should be ruler over his own household, using his native tongue.

[a] *1* Hebrew *Ahasuerus*; here and throughout Esther

[b] *1* That is, the upper Nile region

Esther Made Queen

2 Later when King Xerxes' fury had subsided, he remembered Vashti and what she had done and what he had decreed about her. 2 Then the king's personal attendants proposed, "Let a search be made for beautiful young virgins for the king. 3 Let the king appoint commissioners in every province of his realm to bring all these beautiful young women into the harem at the citadel of Susa. Let them be placed under the care of Hegai, the king's eunuch, who is in charge of the women; and let beauty treatments be given to them. 4 Then let the young woman who pleases the king be queen instead of Vashti." This advice appealed to the king, and he followed it.

5 Now there was in the citadel of Susa a Jew of the tribe of Benjamin, named Mordecai son of Jair, the son of Shimei, the son of Kish, 6 who had been carried into exile from Jerusalem by Nebuchadnezzar king of Babylon, among those taken captive with Jehoiachin[a] king of Judah. 7 Mordecai had a cousin named Hadassah, whom he had brought up because she had neither father nor mother. This young woman, who was also known as Esther, had a lovely figure and was beautiful. Mordecai had taken her as his own daughter when her father and mother died.

8 When the king's order and edict had been proclaimed, many young women were brought to the citadel of Susa and put under the care of Hegai. Esther also was taken to the king's palace and entrusted to Hegai, who had charge of the harem. 9 She pleased him and won his favor. Immediately he provided her with her beauty treatments and special food. He assigned to her seven female attendants selected from the king's palace and moved her and her attendants into the best place in the harem.

10 Esther had not revealed her nationality and family background, because Mordecai had forbidden her to do so. 11 Every day he walked back and forth near the courtyard of the harem to find out how Esther was and what was happening to her.

12 Before a young woman's turn came to go in to King Xerxes, she had to complete twelve months of beauty treatments prescribed for the women, six months with oil of myrrh and six with perfumes and cosmetics. 13 And this is how she would go to the king: Anything she wanted was given her to take with her from the harem to the king's palace. 14 In the evening she would go there and in the morning return to another part of the harem to the care of Shaashgaz, the king's eunuch who was in charge of the concubines. She would not return to the king unless he was pleased with her and summoned her by name.

15 When the turn came for Esther (the young woman Mordecai had adopted, the daughter of his uncle Abihail) to go to the king, she asked for nothing other than what Hegai, the king's eunuch who was in charge of the harem, suggested. And Esther won the favor of everyone who saw her. 16 She was taken to King Xerxes in the royal residence in the tenth month, the month of Tebeth, in the seventh year of his reign.

17 Now the king was attracted to Esther more than to any of the other women, and she won his favor and approval more than any of the other virgins. So he set a royal crown on her head and made her queen instead of Vashti. 18 And the king gave a great banquet, Esther's banquet, for all his nobles and officials. He proclaimed a holiday throughout the provinces and distributed gifts with royal liberality.

Mordecai Uncovers a Conspiracy

19 When the virgins were assembled a second time, Mordecai was sitting at the king's gate. 20 But Esther had kept secret her family background and nationality just as Mordecai had told her to do, for she continued to follow Mordecai's instructions as she had done when he was bringing her up.

21 During the time Mordecai was sitting at the king's gate, Bigthana[b] and Teresh, two of the king's officers who guarded the doorway, became angry and conspired to assassinate King Xerxes. 22 But Mordecai found out about the plot and told Queen Esther, who in turn reported it to the king, giving credit to Mordecai. 23 And when the report was investigated and found to be true, the two officials were impaled on poles. All this was recorded in the book of the annals in the presence of the king.

[a] 6 Hebrew *Jeconiah,* a variant of *Jehoiachin* [b] 21 Hebrew *Bigthan,* a variant of *Bigthana*

Haman's Plot to Destroy the Jews

3 After these events, King Xerxes honored Haman son of Hammedatha, the Agagite, elevating him and giving him a seat of honor higher than that of all the other nobles. [2]All the royal officials at the king's gate knelt down and paid honor to Haman, for the king had commanded this concerning him. But Mordecai would not kneel down or pay him honor.

[3]Then the royal officials at the king's gate asked Mordecai, "Why do you disobey the king's command?" [4]Day after day they spoke to him but he refused to comply. Therefore they told Haman about it to see whether Mordecai's behavior would be tolerated, for he had told them he was a Jew.

[5]When Haman saw that Mordecai would not kneel down or pay him honor, he was enraged. [6]Yet having learned who Mordecai's people were, he scorned the idea of killing only Mordecai. Instead Haman looked for a way to destroy all Mordecai's people, the Jews, throughout the whole kingdom of Xerxes.

[7]In the twelfth year of King Xerxes, in the first month, the month of Nisan, the *pur* (that is, the lot) was cast in the presence of Haman to select a day and month. And the lot fell on[a] the twelfth month, the month of Adar.

[8]Then Haman said to King Xerxes, "There is a certain people dispersed among the peoples in all the provinces of your kingdom who keep themselves separate. Their customs are different from those of all other people, and they do not obey the king's laws; it is not in the king's best interest to tolerate them. [9]If it pleases the king, let a decree be issued to destroy them, and I will give ten thousand talents[b] of silver to the king's administrators for the royal treasury."

[10]So the king took his signet ring from his finger and gave it to Haman son of Hammedatha, the Agagite, the enemy of the Jews. [11]"Keep the money," the king said to Haman, "and do with the people as you please."

[12]Then on the thirteenth day of the first month the royal secretaries were summoned. They wrote out in the script of each province and in the language of each people all Haman's orders to the king's satraps, the governors of the various provinces and the nobles of the various peoples. These were written in the name of King Xerxes himself and sealed with his own ring. [13]Dispatches were sent by couriers to all the king's provinces with the order to destroy, kill and annihilate all the Jews—young and old, women and children—on a single day, the thirteenth day of the twelfth month, the month of Adar, and to plunder their goods. [14]A copy of the text of the edict was to be issued as law in every province and made known to the people of every nationality so they would be ready for that day.

[15]The couriers went out, spurred on by the king's command, and the edict was issued in the citadel of Susa. The king and Haman sat down to drink, but the city of Susa was bewildered.

Mordecai Persuades Esther to Help

4 When Mordecai learned of all that had been done, he tore his clothes, put on sackcloth and ashes, and went out into the city, wailing loudly and bitterly. [2]But he went only as far as the king's gate, because no one clothed in sackcloth was allowed to enter it. [3]In every province to which the edict and order of the king came, there was great mourning among the Jews, with fasting, weeping and wailing. Many lay in sackcloth and ashes.

[4]When Esther's eunuchs and female attendants came and told her about Mordecai, she was in great distress. She sent clothes for him to put on instead of his sackcloth, but he would not accept them. [5]Then Esther summoned Hathak, one of the king's eunuchs assigned to attend her, and ordered him to find out what was troubling Mordecai and why.

[6]So Hathak went out to Mordecai in the open square of the city in front of the king's gate. [7]Mordecai told him everything that had happened to him, including the exact amount of money Haman had promised to pay into the royal treasury for the destruction of the Jews. [8]He also gave him a copy of the text of the edict for their annihilation, which had been published in Susa, to show to Esther and explain it to her, and he told him to instruct her to go into the king's

[a] 7 Septuagint; Hebrew does not have *And the lot fell on.* [b] 9 That is, about 375 tons or about 340 metric tons

presence to beg for mercy and plead with
him for her people.
9 Hathak went back and reported to Es-
ther what Mordecai had said. 10 Then she
instructed him to say to Mordecai, 11 "All the
king's officials and the people of the royal
provinces know that for any man or woman
who approaches the king in the inner court
without being summoned the king has but
one law: that they be put to death unless
the king extends the gold scepter to them
and spares their lives. But thirty days have
passed since I was called to go to the king."
12 When Esther's words were reported to
Mordecai, 13 he sent back this answer: "Do
not think that because you are in the king's
house you alone of all the Jews will escape.
14 For if you remain silent at this time, relief
and deliverance for the Jews will arise from
another place, but you and your father's fam-
ily will perish. And who knows but that you
have come to your royal position for such a
time as this?"
15 Then Esther sent this reply to Mordecai:
16 "Go, gather together all the Jews who are in
Susa, and fast for me. Do not eat or drink for
three days, night or day. I and my attendants
will fast as you do. When this is done, I will
go to the king, even though it is against the
law. And if I perish, I perish."
17 So Mordecai went away and carried out
all of Esther's instructions.

Esther's Request to the King

5 On the third day Esther put on her royal
robes and stood in the inner court of the
palace, in front of the king's hall. The king
was sitting on his royal throne in the hall,
facing the entrance. 2 When he saw Queen
Esther standing in the court, he was pleased
with her and held out to her the gold scepter
that was in his hand. So Esther approached
and touched the tip of the scepter.
3 Then the king asked, "What is it, Queen
Esther? What is your request? Even up to half
the kingdom, it will be given you."
4 "If it pleases the king," replied Esther, "let
the king, together with Haman, come today
to a banquet I have prepared for him."
5 "Bring Haman at once," the king said, "so
that we may do what Esther asks."
So the king and Haman went to the ban-
quet Esther had prepared. 6 As they were
drinking wine, the king again asked Esther,
"Now what is your petition? It will be given
you. And what is your request? Even up to
half the kingdom, it will be granted."
7 Esther replied, "My petition and my re-
quest is this: 8 If the king regards me with
favor and if it pleases the king to grant my
petition and fulfill my request, let the king
and Haman come tomorrow to the banquet I
will prepare for them. Then I will answer the
king's question."

Haman's Rage Against Mordecai

9 Haman went out that day happy and in
high spirits. But when he saw Mordecai at
the king's gate and observed that he neither
rose nor showed fear in his presence, he was
filled with rage against Mordecai. 10 Never-
theless, Haman restrained himself and went
home.
Calling together his friends and Zeresh,
his wife, 11 Haman boasted to them about his
vast wealth, his many sons, and all the ways
the king had honored him and how he had
elevated him above the other nobles and of-
ficials. 12 "And that's not all," Haman added.
"I'm the only person Queen Esther invited to
accompany the king to the banquet she gave.
And she has invited me along with the king
tomorrow. 13 But all this gives me no satisfac-
tion as long as I see that Jew Mordecai sitting
at the king's gate."
14 His wife Zeresh and all his friends said
to him, "Have a pole set up, reaching to a
height of fifty cubits,[a] and ask the king in
the morning to have Mordecai impaled on
it. Then go with the king to the banquet and
enjoy yourself." This suggestion delighted
Haman, and he had the pole set up.

Mordecai Honored

6 That night the king could not sleep; so
he ordered the book of the chronicles,
the record of his reign, to be brought in and
read to him. 2 It was found recorded there
that Mordecai had exposed Bigthana and
Teresh, two of the king's officers who guard-
ed the doorway, who had conspired to assas-
sinate King Xerxes.
3 "What honor and recognition has Mor-
decai received for this?" the king asked.
"Nothing has been done for him," his at-
tendants answered.

[a] *14* That is, about 75 feet or about 23 meters

[4]The king said, "Who is in the court?" Now Haman had just entered the outer court of the palace to speak to the king about impaling Mordecai on the pole he had set up for him.

[5]His attendants answered, "Haman is standing in the court."

"Bring him in," the king ordered.

[6]When Haman entered, the king asked him, "What should be done for the man the king delights to honor?"

Now Haman thought to himself, "Who is there that the king would rather honor than me?" [7]So he answered the king, "For the man the king delights to honor, [8]have them bring a royal robe the king has worn and a horse the king has ridden, one with a royal crest placed on its head. [9]Then let the robe and horse be entrusted to one of the king's most noble princes. Let them robe the man the king delights to honor, and lead him on the horse through the city streets, proclaiming before him, 'This is what is done for the man the king delights to honor!' "

[10]"Go at once," the king commanded Haman. "Get the robe and the horse and do just as you have suggested for Mordecai the Jew, who sits at the king's gate. Do not neglect anything you have recommended."

[11]So Haman got the robe and the horse. He robed Mordecai, and led him on horseback through the city streets, proclaiming before him, "This is what is done for the man the king delights to honor!"

[12]Afterward Mordecai returned to the king's gate. But Haman rushed home, with his head covered in grief, [13]and told Zeresh his wife and all his friends everything that had happened to him.

His advisers and his wife Zeresh said to him, "Since Mordecai, before whom your downfall has started, is of Jewish origin, you cannot stand against him — you will surely come to ruin!" [14]While they were still talking with him, the king's eunuchs arrived and hurried Haman away to the banquet Esther had prepared.

Haman Impaled

7 So the king and Haman went to Queen Esther's banquet, [2]and as they were drinking wine on the second day, the king again asked, "Queen Esther, what is your petition? It will be given you. What is your request? Even up to half the kingdom, it will be granted."

[3]Then Queen Esther answered, "If I have found favor with you, Your Majesty, and if it pleases you, grant me my life — this is my petition. And spare my people — this is my request. [4]For I and my people have been sold to be destroyed, killed and annihilated. If we had merely been sold as male and female slaves, I would have kept quiet, because no such distress would justify disturbing the king.[a]"

[5]King Xerxes asked Queen Esther, "Who is he? Where is he — the man who has dared to do such a thing?"

[6]Esther said, "An adversary and enemy! This vile Haman!"

Then Haman was terrified before the king and queen. [7]The king got up in a rage, left his wine and went out into the palace garden. But Haman, realizing that the king had already decided his fate, stayed behind to beg Queen Esther for his life.

[8]Just as the king returned from the palace garden to the banquet hall, Haman was falling on the couch where Esther was reclining.

The king exclaimed, "Will he even molest the queen while she is with me in the house?"

As soon as the word left the king's mouth, they covered Haman's face. [9]Then Harbona, one of the eunuchs attending the king, said, "A pole reaching to a height of fifty cubits[b] stands by Haman's house. He had it set up for Mordecai, who spoke up to help the king."

The king said, "Impale him on it!" [10]So they impaled Haman on the pole he had set up for Mordecai. Then the king's fury subsided.

The King's Edict in Behalf of the Jews

8 That same day King Xerxes gave Queen Esther the estate of Haman, the enemy of the Jews. And Mordecai came into the presence of the king, for Esther had told how he was related to her. [2]The king took off his signet ring, which he had reclaimed from Haman, and presented it to Mordecai. And Esther appointed him over Haman's estate.

[3]Esther again pleaded with the king, falling at his feet and weeping. She begged him to

[a] 4 Or *quiet, but the compensation our adversary offers cannot be compared with the loss the king would suffer* [b] 9 That is, about 75 feet or about 23 meters

put an end to the evil plan of Haman the Agagite, which he had devised against the Jews. 4 Then the king extended the gold scepter to Esther and she arose and stood before him.

5 "If it pleases the king," she said, "and if he regards me with favor and thinks it the right thing to do, and if he is pleased with me, let an order be written overruling the dispatches that Haman son of Hammedatha, the Agagite, devised and wrote to destroy the Jews in all the king's provinces. 6 For how can I bear to see disaster fall on my people? How can I bear to see the destruction of my family?"

7 King Xerxes replied to Queen Esther and to Mordecai the Jew, "Because Haman attacked the Jews, I have given his estate to Esther, and they have impaled him on the pole he set up. 8 Now write another decree in the king's name in behalf of the Jews as seems best to you, and seal it with the king's signet ring—for no document written in the king's name and sealed with his ring can be revoked."

9 At once the royal secretaries were summoned—on the twenty-third day of the third month, the month of Sivan. They wrote out all Mordecai's orders to the Jews, and to the satraps, governors and nobles of the 127 provinces stretching from India to Cush.[a] These orders were written in the script of each province and the language of each people and also to the Jews in their own script and language. 10 Mordecai wrote in the name of King Xerxes, sealed the dispatches with the king's signet ring, and sent them by mounted couriers, who rode fast horses especially bred for the king.

11 The king's edict granted the Jews in every city the right to assemble and protect themselves; to destroy, kill and annihilate the armed men of any nationality or province who might attack them and their women and children,[b] and to plunder the property of their enemies. 12 The day appointed for the Jews to do this in all the provinces of King Xerxes was the thirteenth day of the twelfth month, the month of Adar. 13 A copy of the text of the edict was to be issued as law in every province and made known to the people of every nationality so that the Jews would be ready on that day to avenge themselves on their enemies.

14 The couriers, riding the royal horses, went out, spurred on by the king's command, and the edict was issued in the citadel of Susa.

The Triumph of the Jews

15 When Mordecai left the king's presence, he was wearing royal garments of blue and white, a large crown of gold and a purple robe of fine linen. And the city of Susa held a joyous celebration. 16 For the Jews it was a time of happiness and joy, gladness and honor. 17 In every province and in every city to which the edict of the king came, there was joy and gladness among the Jews, with feasting and celebrating. And many people of other nationalities became Jews because fear of the Jews had seized them.

9 On the thirteenth day of the twelfth month, the month of Adar, the edict commanded by the king was to be carried out. On this day the enemies of the Jews had hoped to overpower them, but now the tables were turned and the Jews got the upper hand over those who hated them. 2 The Jews assembled in their cities in all the provinces of King Xerxes to attack those determined to destroy them. No one could stand against them, because the people of all the other nationalities were afraid of them. 3 And all the nobles of the provinces, the satraps, the governors and the king's administrators helped the Jews, because fear of Mordecai had seized them. 4 Mordecai was prominent in the palace; his reputation spread throughout the provinces, and he became more and more powerful.

5 The Jews struck down all their enemies with the sword, killing and destroying them, and they did what they pleased to those who hated them. 6 In the citadel of Susa, the Jews killed and destroyed five hundred men. 7 They also killed Parshandatha, Dalphon, Aspatha, 8 Poratha, Adalia, Aridatha, 9 Parmashta, Arisai, Aridai and Vaizatha, 10 the ten sons of Haman son of Hammedatha, the enemy of the Jews. But they did not lay their hands on the plunder.

11 The number of those killed in the citadel of Susa was reported to the king that same day. 12 The king said to Queen Esther, "The Jews have killed and destroyed five hundred men and the ten sons of Haman in

[a] 9 That is, the upper Nile region [b] 11 Or *province, together with their women and children, who might attack them;*

the citadel of Susa. What have they done in the rest of the king's provinces? Now what is your petition? It will be given you. What is your request? It will also be granted."

[13]"If it pleases the king," Esther answered, "give the Jews in Susa permission to carry out this day's edict tomorrow also, and let Haman's ten sons be impaled on poles."

[14]So the king commanded that this be done. An edict was issued in Susa, and they impaled the ten sons of Haman. [15]The Jews in Susa came together on the fourteenth day of the month of Adar, and they put to death in Susa three hundred men, but they did not lay their hands on the plunder.

[16]Meanwhile, the remainder of the Jews who were in the king's provinces also assembled to protect themselves and get relief from their enemies. They killed seventy-five thousand of them but did not lay their hands on the plunder. [17]This happened on the thirteenth day of the month of Adar, and on the fourteenth they rested and made it a day of feasting and joy.

[18]The Jews in Susa, however, had assembled on the thirteenth and fourteenth, and then on the fifteenth they rested and made it a day of feasting and joy.

[19]That is why rural Jews — those living in villages — observe the fourteenth of the month of Adar as a day of joy and feasting, a day for giving presents to each other.

Purim Established

[20]Mordecai recorded these events, and he sent letters to all the Jews throughout the provinces of King Xerxes, near and far, [21]to have them celebrate annually the fourteenth and fifteenth days of the month of Adar [22]as the time when the Jews got relief from their enemies, and as the month when their sorrow was turned into joy and their mourning into a day of celebration. He wrote them to observe the days as days of feasting and joy and giving presents of food to one another and gifts to the poor.

[23]So the Jews agreed to continue the celebration they had begun, doing what Mordecai had written to them. [24]For Haman son of Hammedatha, the Agagite, the enemy of all the Jews, had plotted against the Jews to destroy them and had cast the *pur* (that is, the lot) for their ruin and destruction. [25]But when the plot came to the king's attention,[a] he issued written orders that the evil scheme Haman had devised against the Jews should come back onto his own head, and that he and his sons should be impaled on poles. [26](Therefore these days were called Purim, from the word *pur*.) Because of everything written in this letter and because of what they had seen and what had happened to them, [27]the Jews took it on themselves to establish the custom that they and their descendants and all who join them should without fail observe these two days every year, in the way prescribed and at the time appointed. [28]These days should be remembered and observed in every generation by every family, and in every province and in every city. And these days of Purim should never fail to be celebrated by the Jews — nor should the memory of these days die out among their descendants.

[29]So Queen Esther, daughter of Abihail, along with Mordecai the Jew, wrote with full authority to confirm this second letter concerning Purim. [30]And Mordecai sent letters to all the Jews in the 127 provinces of Xerxes' kingdom — words of goodwill and assurance — [31]to establish these days of Purim at their designated times, as Mordecai the Jew and Queen Esther had decreed for them, and as they had established for themselves and their descendants in regard to their times of fasting and lamentation. [32]Esther's decree confirmed these regulations about Purim, and it was written down in the records.

The Greatness of Mordecai

10 King Xerxes imposed tribute throughout the empire, to its distant shores. [2]And all his acts of power and might, together with a full account of the greatness of Mordecai, whom the king had promoted, are they not written in the book of the annals of the kings of Media and Persia? [3]Mordecai the Jew was second in rank to King Xerxes, preeminent among the Jews, and held in high esteem by his many fellow Jews, because he worked for the good of his people and spoke up for the welfare of all the Jews.

[a] 25 Or *when Esther came before the king*

JOB

Prologue

1 In the land of Uz there lived a man whose
name was Job. This man was blameless
and upright; he feared God and shunned
evil. 2He had seven sons and three daugh-
ters, 3and he owned seven thousand sheep,
three thousand camels, five hundred yoke
of oxen and five hundred donkeys, and had
a large number of servants. He was the great-
est man among all the people of the East.

4His sons used to hold feasts in their
homes on their birthdays, and they would
invite their three sisters to eat and drink with
them. 5When a period of feasting had run its
course, Job would make arrangements for
them to be purified. Early in the morning he
would sacrifice a burnt offering for each of
them, thinking, "Perhaps my children have
sinned and cursed God in their hearts." This
was Job's regular custom.

6One day the angels[a] came to present
themselves before the LORD, and Satan[b] also
came with them. 7The LORD said to Satan,
"Where have you come from?"

Satan answered the LORD, "From roaming
throughout the earth, going back and forth
on it."

8Then the LORD said to Satan, "Have you
considered my servant Job? There is no one
on earth like him; he is blameless and up-
right, a man who fears God and shuns evil."

9"Does Job fear God for nothing?" Satan
replied. 10"Have you not put a hedge around
him and his household and everything he
has? You have blessed the work of his hands,
so that his flocks and herds are spread
throughout the land. 11But now stretch out
your hand and strike everything he has, and
he will surely curse you to your face."

12The LORD said to Satan, "Very well,
then, everything he has is in your power, but
on the man himself do not lay a finger."

Then Satan went out from the presence of
the LORD.

13One day when Job's sons and daughters
were feasting and drinking wine at the old-
est brother's house, 14a messenger came to
Job and said, "The oxen were plowing and
the donkeys were grazing nearby, 15and the
Sabeans attacked and made off with them.
They put the servants to the sword, and I am
the only one who has escaped to tell you!"

16While he was still speaking, another
messenger came and said, "The fire of God
fell from the heavens and burned up the
sheep and the servants, and I am the only
one who has escaped to tell you!"

17While he was still speaking, another
messenger came and said, "The Chalde-
ans formed three raiding parties and swept
down on your camels and made off with
them. They put the servants to the sword,
and I am the only one who has escaped to
tell you!"

18While he was still speaking, yet anoth-
er messenger came and said, "Your sons and
daughters were feasting and drinking wine
at the oldest brother's house, 19when sud-
denly a mighty wind swept in from the des-
ert and struck the four corners of the house.
It collapsed on them and they are dead, and I
am the only one who has escaped to tell you!"

20At this, Job got up and tore his robe and
shaved his head. Then he fell to the ground
in worship 21and said:

"Naked I came from my mother's womb,
  and naked I will depart.[c]
The LORD gave and the LORD has taken
  away;
  may the name of the LORD be praised."

22In all this, Job did not sin by charging
God with wrongdoing.

2 On another day the angels[a] came to pre-
sent themselves before the LORD, and
Satan also came with them to present him-
self before him. 2And the LORD said to Satan,
"Where have you come from?"

Satan answered the LORD, "From roaming

[a] 6,1 Hebrew *the sons of God* [b] 6 Hebrew *satan* means *adversary.* [c] 21 Or *will return there*

throughout the earth, going back and forth
on it."
3 Then the LORD said to Satan, "Have you
considered my servant Job? There is no one
on earth like him; he is blameless and up-
right, a man who fears God and shuns evil.
And he still maintains his integrity, though
you incited me against him to ruin him with-
out any reason."
4 "Skin for skin!" Satan replied. "A man
will give all he has for his own life. 5 But now
stretch out your hand and strike his flesh
and bones, and he will surely curse you to
your face."
6 The LORD said to Satan, "Very well, then,
he is in your hands; but you must spare his
life."
7 So Satan went out from the presence of
the LORD and afflicted Job with painful sores
from the soles of his feet to the crown of his
head. 8 Then Job took a piece of broken pot-
tery and scraped himself with it as he sat
among the ashes.
9 His wife said to him, "Are you still main-
taining your integrity? Curse God and die!"
10 He replied, "You are talking like a fool-
ish[a] woman. Shall we accept good from God,
and not trouble?"
In all this, Job did not sin in what he said.

11 When Job's three friends, Eliphaz the
Temanite, Bildad the Shuhite and Zophar
the Naamathite, heard about all the troubles
that had come upon him, they set out from
their homes and met together by agreement
to go and sympathize with him and comfort
him. 12 When they saw him from a distance,
they could hardly recognize him; they be-
gan to weep aloud, and they tore their robes
and sprinkled dust on their heads. 13 Then
they sat on the ground with him for seven
days and seven nights. No one said a word
to him, because they saw how great his suf-
fering was.

Job Speaks

3 After this, Job opened his mouth and
cursed the day of his birth. 2 He said:

3 "May the day of my birth perish,
and the night that said, 'A boy is conceived!'
4 That day—may it turn to darkness;
may God above not care about it;
may no light shine on it.
5 May gloom and utter darkness claim it once more;
may a cloud settle over it;
may blackness overwhelm it.
6 That night—may thick darkness seize it;
may it not be included among the days of the year
nor be entered in any of the months.
7 May that night be barren;
may no shout of joy be heard in it.
8 May those who curse days[b] curse that day,
those who are ready to rouse Leviathan.
9 May its morning stars become dark;
may it wait for daylight in vain
and not see the first rays of dawn,
10 for it did not shut the doors of the womb on me
to hide trouble from my eyes.

11 "Why did I not perish at birth,
and die as I came from the womb?
12 Why were there knees to receive me
and breasts that I might be nursed?
13 For now I would be lying down in peace;
I would be asleep and at rest
14 with kings and rulers of the earth,
who built for themselves places now lying in ruins,
15 with princes who had gold,
who filled their houses with silver.
16 Or why was I not hidden away in the ground like a stillborn child,
like an infant who never saw the light of day?
17 There the wicked cease from turmoil,
and there the weary are at rest.
18 Captives also enjoy their ease;
they no longer hear the slave driver's shout.
19 The small and the great are there,
and the slaves are freed from their owners.

20 "Why is light given to those in misery,
and life to the bitter of soul,
21 to those who long for death that does not come,
who search for it more than for hidden treasure,

[a] 10 The Hebrew word rendered *foolish* denotes moral deficiency. [b] 8 Or *curse the sea*

[22] who are filled with gladness
and rejoice when they reach the grave?
[23] Why is life given to a man
whose way is hidden,
whom God has hedged in?
[24] For sighing has become my daily food;
my groans pour out like water.
[25] What I feared has come upon me;
what I dreaded has happened to me.
[26] I have no peace, no quietness;
I have no rest, but only turmoil."

Eliphaz

4 Then Eliphaz the Temanite replied:

[2] "If someone ventures a word with you,
will you be impatient?
But who can keep from speaking?
[3] Think how you have instructed many,
how you have strengthened feeble
hands.
[4] Your words have supported those who
stumbled;
you have strengthened faltering knees.
[5] But now trouble comes to you, and you
are discouraged;
it strikes you, and you are dismayed.
[6] Should not your piety be your confidence
and your blameless ways your hope?

[7] "Consider now: Who, being innocent, has
ever perished?
Where were the upright ever
destroyed?
[8] As I have observed, those who plow evil
and those who sow trouble reap it.
[9] At the breath of God they perish;
at the blast of his anger they are no
more.
[10] The lions may roar and growl,
yet the teeth of the great lions are
broken.
[11] The lion perishes for lack of prey,
and the cubs of the lioness are
scattered.

[12] "A word was secretly brought to me,
my ears caught a whisper of it.
[13] Amid disquieting dreams in the night,
when deep sleep falls on people,
[14] fear and trembling seized me
and made all my bones shake.
[15] A spirit glided past my face,
and the hair on my body stood on end.
[16] It stopped,
but I could not tell what it was.
A form stood before my eyes,
and I heard a hushed voice:
[17] 'Can a mortal be more righteous than
God?
Can even a strong man be more pure
than his Maker?
[18] If God places no trust in his servants,
if he charges his angels with error,
[19] how much more those who live in houses
of clay,
whose foundations are in the dust,
who are crushed more readily than a
moth!
[20] Between dawn and dusk they are broken
to pieces;
unnoticed, they perish forever.
[21] Are not the cords of their tent pulled up,
so that they die without wisdom?'

5 "Call if you will, but who will answer
you?
To which of the holy ones will you
turn?
[2] Resentment kills a fool,
and envy slays the simple.
[3] I myself have seen a fool taking root,
but suddenly his house was cursed.
[4] His children are far from safety,
crushed in court without a defender.
[5] The hungry consume his harvest,
taking it even from among thorns,
and the thirsty pant after his wealth.
[6] For hardship does not spring from the
soil,
nor does trouble sprout from the
ground.
[7] Yet man is born to trouble
as surely as sparks fly upward.

[8] "But if I were you, I would appeal to God;
I would lay my cause before him.
[9] He performs wonders that cannot be
fathomed,
miracles that cannot be counted.
[10] He provides rain for the earth;
he sends water on the countryside.
[11] The lowly he sets on high,
and those who mourn are lifted to
safety.
[12] He thwarts the plans of the crafty,
so that their hands achieve no success.
[13] He catches the wise in their craftiness,
and the schemes of the wily are swept
away.

[14] Darkness comes upon them in the daytime;
at noon they grope as in the night.
[15] He saves the needy from the sword in their mouth;
he saves them from the clutches of the powerful.
[16] So the poor have hope,
and injustice shuts its mouth.

[17] "Blessed is the one whom God corrects;
so do not despise the discipline of the Almighty.[a]
[18] For he wounds, but he also binds up;
he injures, but his hands also heal.
[19] From six calamities he will rescue you;
in seven no harm will touch you.
[20] In famine he will deliver you from death,
and in battle from the stroke of the sword.
[21] You will be protected from the lash of the tongue,
and need not fear when destruction comes.
[22] You will laugh at destruction and famine,
and need not fear the wild animals.
[23] For you will have a covenant with the stones of the field,
and the wild animals will be at peace with you.
[24] You will know that your tent is secure;
you will take stock of your property and find nothing missing.
[25] You will know that your children will be many,
and your descendants like the grass of the earth.
[26] You will come to the grave in full vigor,
like sheaves gathered in season.

[27] "We have examined this, and it is true.
So hear it and apply it to yourself."

Job

6 Then Job replied:

[2] "If only my anguish could be weighed
and all my misery be placed on the scales!
[3] It would surely outweigh the sand of the seas —
no wonder my words have been impetuous.
[4] The arrows of the Almighty are in me,
my spirit drinks in their poison;
God's terrors are marshaled against me.
[5] Does a wild donkey bray when it has grass,
or an ox bellow when it has fodder?
[6] Is tasteless food eaten without salt,
or is there flavor in the sap of the mallow[b]?
[7] I refuse to touch it;
such food makes me ill.

[8] "Oh, that I might have my request,
that God would grant what I hope for,
[9] that God would be willing to crush me,
to let loose his hand and cut off my life!
[10] Then I would still have this consolation —
my joy in unrelenting pain —
that I had not denied the words of the Holy One.

[11] "What strength do I have, that I should still hope?
What prospects, that I should be patient?
[12] Do I have the strength of stone?
Is my flesh bronze?
[13] Do I have any power to help myself,
now that success has been driven from me?

[14] "Anyone who withholds kindness from a friend
forsakes the fear of the Almighty.
[15] But my brothers are as undependable as intermittent streams,
as the streams that overflow
[16] when darkened by thawing ice
and swollen with melting snow,
[17] but that stop flowing in the dry season,
and in the heat vanish from their channels.
[18] Caravans turn aside from their routes;
they go off into the wasteland and perish.
[19] The caravans of Tema look for water,
the traveling merchants of Sheba look in hope.
[20] They are distressed, because they had been confident;
they arrive there, only to be disappointed.

[a] *17* Hebrew *Shaddai*; here and throughout Job

[b] *6* The meaning of the Hebrew for this phrase is uncertain.

HOSANNA (PRAISE IS RISING)

Brenton Brown, Paul Baloche

Praise is rising, eyes are turning to you
We turn to you
Hope is stirring, hearts are yearning for you
We long for you

'Cause when we see you we find strength
To face the day
And in your presence all our fears are
Washed away, washed away

Hosanna, hosanna
You are the God who saves us
Worthy of all our praises

Hear the sound of hearts returning to you
We turn to you
In your kingdom broken lives are made new
You make all things new

Hosanna, hosanna
You are the God who saves us
Worthy of all our praises
Hosanna, hosanna
Come have your way among us
We welcome you here Lord Jesus

THE INSPIRATION

The crowds that went ahead of him and those that followed shouted, "Hosanna to the Son of David!" "Blessed is he who comes in the name of the Lord!" "Hosanna in the highest heaven!"

—Matthew 21:9

Read also: Psalm 146:7–10

BEHIND THE SONG

Paul Baloche and Brenton Brown are both worship leaders and songwriters, and they are also close friends. Several years ago they took their families on vacation and spent a week together. But even when the goal is rest and relaxation, worshipers tend to worship.

"We were sitting around after dinner," Brown remembers, "passing the guitar person to person and there was a groove that [Paul] came up with that we really liked. The lyrics just came out 'praise is rising as we're turning to you' and the picture was of worship, of what's happening during worship."

The two remembered one of the only scenes of worship described in the New Testament that is not in the book of Revelation. It was the moment of Jesus' Triumphal Entry into Jerusalem on Palm Sunday when the great crowds of people sang, "Hosanna in the highest!"

"*Hosanna* is a great word because it used to mean 'save us,' but now it also means 'we praise you.' So it's got this dual meaning of 'help us God' and 'thank you God,' or 'we praise you God,' which I think are the two sort of basic prayers of worship."

Selah

Brenton Brown identifies the two main prayers of worship as "praise you God" and "help us God." Does that ring true in your worship? Think about the goals you have for worship. Can you list them? One of the last lines of the song says, "Come have your way among us." If Jesus was to fully have his way with you and your faith community, would anything change?

21 Now you too have proved to be of no help;
you see something dreadful and are afraid.
22 Have I ever said, 'Give something on my behalf,
pay a ransom for me from your wealth,
23 deliver me from the hand of the enemy,
rescue me from the clutches of the ruthless'?

24 "Teach me, and I will be quiet;
show me where I have been wrong.
25 How painful are honest words!
But what do your arguments prove?
26 Do you mean to correct what I say,
and treat my desperate words as wind?
27 You would even cast lots for the fatherless
and barter away your friend.

28 "But now be so kind as to look at me.
Would I lie to your face?
29 Relent, do not be unjust;
reconsider, for my integrity is at stake.[a]
30 Is there any wickedness on my lips?
Can my mouth not discern malice?

7 "Do not mortals have hard service on earth?
Are not their days like those of hired laborers?
2 Like a slave longing for the evening shadows,
or a hired laborer waiting to be paid,
3 so I have been allotted months of futility,
and nights of misery have been assigned to me.
4 When I lie down I think, 'How long before I get up?'
The night drags on, and I toss and turn until dawn.
5 My body is clothed with worms and scabs,
my skin is broken and festering.

6 "My days are swifter than a weaver's shuttle,
and they come to an end without hope.
7 Remember, O God, that my life is but a breath;
my eyes will never see happiness again.
8 The eye that now sees me will see me no longer;
you will look for me, but I will be no more.
9 As a cloud vanishes and is gone,
so one who goes down to the grave does not return.
10 He will never come to his house again;
his place will know him no more.

11 "Therefore I will not keep silent;
I will speak out in the anguish of my spirit,
I will complain in the bitterness of my soul.
12 Am I the sea, or the monster of the deep,
that you put me under guard?
13 When I think my bed will comfort me
and my couch will ease my complaint,
14 even then you frighten me with dreams
and terrify me with visions,
15 so that I prefer strangling and death,
rather than this body of mine.
16 I despise my life; I would not live forever.
Let me alone; my days have no meaning.

17 "What is mankind that you make so much of them,
that you give them so much attention,
18 that you examine them every morning
and test them every moment?
19 Will you never look away from me,
or let me alone even for an instant?
20 If I have sinned, what have I done to you,
you who see everything we do?
Why have you made me your target?
Have I become a burden to you?[b]
21 Why do you not pardon my offenses
and forgive my sins?
For I will soon lie down in the dust;
you will search for me, but I will be no more."

Bildad

8 Then Bildad the Shuhite replied:

2 "How long will you say such things?
Your words are a blustering wind.
3 Does God pervert justice?
Does the Almighty pervert what is right?
4 When your children sinned against him,
he gave them over to the penalty of their sin.
5 But if you will seek God earnestly
and plead with the Almighty,

[a] 29 Or *my righteousness still stands* [b] 20 A few manuscripts of the Masoretic Text, an ancient Hebrew scribal tradition and Septuagint; most manuscripts of the Masoretic Text *I have become a burden to myself.*

[6]if you are pure and upright,
even now he will rouse himself on your behalf
and restore you to your prosperous state.
[7]Your beginnings will seem humble,
so prosperous will your future be.

[8]"Ask the former generation
and find out what their ancestors learned,
[9]for we were born only yesterday and know nothing,
and our days on earth are but a shadow.
[10]Will they not instruct you and tell you?
Will they not bring forth words from their understanding?
[11]Can papyrus grow tall where there is no marsh?
Can reeds thrive without water?
[12]While still growing and uncut,
they wither more quickly than grass.
[13]Such is the destiny of all who forget God;
so perishes the hope of the godless.
[14]What they trust in is fragile[a];
what they rely on is a spider's web.
[15]They lean on the web, but it gives way;
they cling to it, but it does not hold.
[16]They are like a well-watered plant in the sunshine,
spreading its shoots over the garden;
[17]it entwines its roots around a pile of rocks
and looks for a place among the stones.
[18]But when it is torn from its spot,
that place disowns it and says, 'I never saw you.'
[19]Surely its life withers away,
and[b] from the soil other plants grow.

[20]"Surely God does not reject one who is blameless
or strengthen the hands of evildoers.
[21]He will yet fill your mouth with laughter
and your lips with shouts of joy.
[22]Your enemies will be clothed in shame,
and the tents of the wicked will be no more."

Job

9 Then Job replied:

[2]"Indeed, I know that this is true.
But how can mere mortals prove their innocence before God?
[3]Though they wished to dispute with him,
they could not answer him one time out of a thousand.
[4]His wisdom is profound, his power is vast.
Who has resisted him and come out unscathed?
[5]He moves mountains without their knowing it
and overturns them in his anger.
[6]He shakes the earth from its place
and makes its pillars tremble.
[7]He speaks to the sun and it does not shine;
he seals off the light of the stars.
[8]He alone stretches out the heavens
and treads on the waves of the sea.
[9]He is the Maker of the Bear[c] and Orion,
the Pleiades and the constellations of the south.
[10]He performs wonders that cannot be fathomed,
miracles that cannot be counted.
[11]When he passes me, I cannot see him;
when he goes by, I cannot perceive him.
[12]If he snatches away, who can stop him?
Who can say to him, 'What are you doing?'
[13]God does not restrain his anger;
even the cohorts of Rahab cowered at his feet.

[14]"How then can I dispute with him?
How can I find words to argue with him?
[15]Though I were innocent, I could not answer him;
I could only plead with my Judge for mercy.
[16]Even if I summoned him and he responded,
I do not believe he would give me a hearing.
[17]He would crush me with a storm
and multiply my wounds for no reason.

[a] 14 The meaning of the Hebrew for this word is uncertain. [b] 19 Or *Surely all the joy it has / is that*
[c] 9 Or *of Leo*

18 He would not let me catch my breath
but would overwhelm me with misery.
19 If it is a matter of strength, he is mighty!
And if it is a matter of justice, who can
challenge him[a]?
20 Even if I were innocent, my mouth would
condemn me;
if I were blameless, it would pronounce
me guilty.

21 "Although I am blameless,
I have no concern for myself;
I despise my own life.
22 It is all the same; that is why I say,
'He destroys both the blameless and
the wicked.'
23 When a scourge brings sudden death,
he mocks the despair of the innocent.
24 When a land falls into the hands of the
wicked,
he blindfolds its judges.
If it is not he, then who is it?

25 "My days are swifter than a runner;
they fly away without a glimpse of joy.
26 They skim past like boats of papyrus,
like eagles swooping down on their
prey.
27 If I say, 'I will forget my complaint,
I will change my expression, and
smile,'
28 I still dread all my sufferings,
for I know you will not hold me
innocent.
29 Since I am already found guilty,
why should I struggle in vain?
30 Even if I washed myself with soap
and my hands with cleansing powder,
31 you would plunge me into a slime pit
so that even my clothes would detest
me.

32 "He is not a mere mortal like me that I
might answer him,
that we might confront each other in
court.
33 If only there were someone to mediate
between us,
someone to bring us together,
34 someone to remove God's rod from me,
so that his terror would frighten me no
more.
35 Then I would speak up without fear of
him,
but as it now stands with me,
I cannot.

10 "I loathe my very life;
therefore I will give free rein to my
complaint
and speak out in the bitterness of
my soul.
2 I say to God: Do not declare me guilty,
but tell me what charges you have
against me.
3 Does it please you to oppress me,
to spurn the work of your hands,
while you smile on the plans of the
wicked?
4 Do you have eyes of flesh?
Do you see as a mortal sees?
5 Are your days like those of a mortal
or your years like those of a strong
man,
6 that you must search out my faults
and probe after my sin —
7 though you know that I am not guilty
and that no one can rescue me from
your hand?

8 "Your hands shaped me and made me.
Will you now turn and destroy me?
9 Remember that you molded me like clay.
Will you now turn me to dust again?
10 Did you not pour me out like milk
and curdle me like cheese,
11 clothe me with skin and flesh
and knit me together with bones and
sinews?
12 You gave me life and showed me
kindness,
and in your providence watched over
my spirit.

13 "But this is what you concealed in your
heart,
and I know that this was in your
mind:
14 If I sinned, you would be watching me
and would not let my offense go
unpunished.
15 If I am guilty — woe to me!
Even if I am innocent, I cannot lift my
head,
for I am full of shame
and drowned in[b] my affliction.
16 If I hold my head high, you stalk me like
a lion

[a] 19 See Septuagint; Hebrew *me.* [b] 15 Or *and aware of*

and again display your awesome
power against me.
[17]You bring new witnesses against me
and increase your anger toward me;
your forces come against me wave
upon wave.

[18]"Why then did you bring me out of the
womb?
I wish I had died before any eye saw me.
[19]If only I had never come into being,
or had been carried straight from the
womb to the grave!
[20]Are not my few days almost over?
Turn away from me so I can have a
moment's joy
[21]before I go to the place of no return,
to the land of gloom and utter
darkness,
[22]to the land of deepest night,
of utter darkness and disorder,
where even the light is like darkness."

Zophar

11 Then Zophar the Naamathite replied:

[2]"Are all these words to go unanswered?
Is this talker to be vindicated?
[3]Will your idle talk reduce others to
silence?
Will no one rebuke you when you
mock?
[4]You say to God, 'My beliefs are flawless
and I am pure in your sight.'
[5]Oh, how I wish that God would speak,
that he would open his lips against you
[6]and disclose to you the secrets of
wisdom,
for true wisdom has two sides.
Know this: God has even forgotten
some of your sin.

[7]"Can you fathom the mysteries of God?
Can you probe the limits of the
Almighty?
[8]They are higher than the heavens
above—what can you do?
They are deeper than the depths
below—what can you know?
[9]Their measure is longer than the earth
and wider than the sea.

[10]"If he comes along and confines you in
prison
and convenes a court, who can oppose
him?
[11]Surely he recognizes deceivers;
and when he sees evil, does he not take
note?
[12]But the witless can no more become wise
than a wild donkey's colt can be born
human.[a]

[13]"Yet if you devote your heart to him
and stretch out your hands to him,
[14]if you put away the sin that is in your
hand
and allow no evil to dwell in your tent,
[15]then, free of fault, you will lift up your
face;
you will stand firm and without fear.
[16]You will surely forget your trouble,
recalling it only as waters gone by.
[17]Life will be brighter than noonday,
and darkness will become like
morning.
[18]You will be secure, because there
is hope;
you will look about you and take your
rest in safety.
[19]You will lie down, with no one to make
you afraid,
and many will court your favor.
[20]But the eyes of the wicked will fail,
and escape will elude them;
their hope will become a dying gasp."

Job

12 Then Job replied:

[2]"Doubtless you are the only people who
matter,
and wisdom will die with you!
[3]But I have a mind as well as you;
I am not inferior to you.
Who does not know all these things?

[4]"I have become a laughingstock to my
friends,
though I called on God and he
answered—
a mere laughingstock, though
righteous and blameless!
[5]Those who are at ease have contempt for
misfortune
as the fate of those whose feet are
slipping.

[a] 12 Or *wild donkey can be born tame*

[6]The tents of marauders are undisturbed,
and those who provoke God are secure —
those God has in his hand.[a]

[7]"But ask the animals, and they will teach you,
or the birds in the sky, and they will tell you;
[8]or speak to the earth, and it will teach you,
or let the fish in the sea inform you.
[9]Which of all these does not know
that the hand of the LORD has done this?
[10]In his hand is the life of every creature
and the breath of all mankind.
[11]Does not the ear test words
as the tongue tastes food?
[12]Is not wisdom found among the aged?
Does not long life bring understanding?

[13]"To God belong wisdom and power;
counsel and understanding are his.
[14]What he tears down cannot be rebuilt;
those he imprisons cannot be released.
[15]If he holds back the waters, there is drought;
if he lets them loose, they devastate the land.
[16]To him belong strength and insight;
both deceived and deceiver are his.
[17]He leads rulers away stripped
and makes fools of judges.
[18]He takes off the shackles put on by kings
and ties a loincloth[b] around their waist.
[19]He leads priests away stripped
and overthrows officials long established.
[20]He silences the lips of trusted advisers
and takes away the discernment of elders.
[21]He pours contempt on nobles
and disarms the mighty.
[22]He reveals the deep things of darkness
and brings utter darkness into the light.
[23]He makes nations great, and destroys them;
he enlarges nations, and disperses them.
[24]He deprives the leaders of the earth of their reason;
he makes them wander in a trackless waste.
[25]They grope in darkness with no light;
he makes them stagger like drunkards.

13 "My eyes have seen all this,
my ears have heard and understood it.
[2]What you know, I also know;
I am not inferior to you.
[3]But I desire to speak to the Almighty
and to argue my case with God.
[4]You, however, smear me with lies;
you are worthless physicians, all of you!
[5]If only you would be altogether silent!
For you, that would be wisdom.
[6]Hear now my argument;
listen to the pleas of my lips.
[7]Will you speak wickedly on God's behalf?
Will you speak deceitfully for him?
[8]Will you show him partiality?
Will you argue the case for God?
[9]Would it turn out well if he examined you?
Could you deceive him as you might deceive a mortal?
[10]He would surely call you to account
if you secretly showed partiality.
[11]Would not his splendor terrify you?
Would not the dread of him fall on you?
[12]Your maxims are proverbs of ashes;
your defenses are defenses of clay.

[13]"Keep silent and let me speak;
then let come to me what may.
[14]Why do I put myself in jeopardy
and take my life in my hands?
[15]Though he slay me, yet will I hope in him;
I will surely[c] defend my ways to his face.
[16]Indeed, this will turn out for my deliverance,
for no godless person would dare come before him!
[17]Listen carefully to what I say;
let my words ring in your ears.
[18]Now that I have prepared my case,
I know I will be vindicated.

[a] 6 Or *those whose god is in their own hand* [b] 18 Or *shackles of kings / and ties a belt* [c] 15 Or *He will surely slay me; I have no hope — / yet I will*

19 Can anyone bring charges against me?
If so, I will be silent and die.

20 "Only grant me these two things, God,
and then I will not hide from you:
21 Withdraw your hand far from me,
and stop frightening me with your terrors.
22 Then summon me and I will answer,
or let me speak, and you reply to me.
23 How many wrongs and sins have I committed?
Show me my offense and my sin.
24 Why do you hide your face
and consider me your enemy?
25 Will you torment a windblown leaf?
Will you chase after dry chaff?
26 For you write down bitter things against me
and make me reap the sins of my youth.
27 You fasten my feet in shackles;
you keep close watch on all my paths
by putting marks on the soles of my feet.

28 "So man wastes away like something rotten,
like a garment eaten by moths.

14 "Mortals, born of woman,
are of few days and full of trouble.
2 They spring up like flowers and wither away;
like fleeting shadows, they do not endure.
3 Do you fix your eye on them?
Will you bring them[a] before you for judgment?
4 Who can bring what is pure from the impure?
No one!
5 A person's days are determined;
you have decreed the number of his months
and have set limits he cannot exceed.
6 So look away from him and let him alone,
till he has put in his time like a hired laborer.

7 "At least there is hope for a tree:
If it is cut down, it will sprout again,
and its new shoots will not fail.
8 Its roots may grow old in the ground
and its stump die in the soil,
9 yet at the scent of water it will bud
and put forth shoots like a plant.
10 But a man dies and is laid low;
he breathes his last and is no more.
11 As the water of a lake dries up
or a riverbed becomes parched and dry,
12 so he lies down and does not rise;
till the heavens are no more, people will not awake
or be roused from their sleep.

13 "If only you would hide me in the grave
and conceal me till your anger has passed!
If only you would set me a time
and then remember me!
14 If someone dies, will they live again?
All the days of my hard service
I will wait for my renewal[b] to come.
15 You will call and I will answer you;
you will long for the creature your hands have made.
16 Surely then you will count my steps
but not keep track of my sin.
17 My offenses will be sealed up in a bag;
you will cover over my sin.

18 "But as a mountain erodes and crumbles
and as a rock is moved from its place,
19 as water wears away stones
and torrents wash away the soil,
so you destroy a person's hope.
20 You overpower them once for all, and they are gone;
you change their countenance and send them away.
21 If their children are honored, they do not know it;
if their offspring are brought low, they do not see it.
22 They feel but the pain of their own bodies
and mourn only for themselves."

Eliphaz

15 Then Eliphaz the Temanite replied:

2 "Would a wise person answer with empty notions
or fill their belly with the hot east wind?
3 Would they argue with useless words,
with speeches that have no value?

[a] 3 Septuagint, Vulgate and Syriac; Hebrew *me*
[b] 14 Or *release*

[4] But you even undermine piety
and hinder devotion to God.
[5] Your sin prompts your mouth;
you adopt the tongue of the crafty.
[6] Your own mouth condemns you, not mine;
your own lips testify against you.

[7] "Are you the first man ever born?
Were you brought forth before the hills?
[8] Do you listen in on God's council?
Do you have a monopoly on wisdom?
[9] What do you know that we do not know?
What insights do you have that we do not have?
[10] The gray-haired and the aged are on our side,
men even older than your father.
[11] Are God's consolations not enough for you,
words spoken gently to you?
[12] Why has your heart carried you away,
and why do your eyes flash,
[13] so that you vent your rage against God
and pour out such words from your mouth?

[14] "What are mortals, that they could be pure,
or those born of woman, that they could be righteous?
[15] If God places no trust in his holy ones,
if even the heavens are not pure in his eyes,
[16] how much less mortals, who are vile and corrupt,
who drink up evil like water!

[17] "Listen to me and I will explain to you;
let me tell you what I have seen,
[18] what the wise have declared,
hiding nothing received from their ancestors
[19] (to whom alone the land was given
when no foreigners moved among them):
[20] All his days the wicked man suffers torment,
the ruthless man through all the years stored up for him.
[21] Terrifying sounds fill his ears;
when all seems well, marauders attack him.
[22] He despairs of escaping the realm of darkness;
he is marked for the sword.
[23] He wanders about for food like a vulture;
he knows the day of darkness is at hand.
[24] Distress and anguish fill him with terror;
troubles overwhelm him, like a king poised to attack,
[25] because he shakes his fist at God
and vaunts himself against the Almighty,
[26] defiantly charging against him
with a thick, strong shield.

[27] "Though his face is covered with fat
and his waist bulges with flesh,
[28] he will inhabit ruined towns
and houses where no one lives,
houses crumbling to rubble.
[29] He will no longer be rich and his wealth will not endure,
nor will his possessions spread over the land.
[30] He will not escape the darkness;
a flame will wither his shoots,
and the breath of God's mouth will carry him away.
[31] Let him not deceive himself by trusting what is worthless,
for he will get nothing in return.
[32] Before his time he will wither,
and his branches will not flourish.
[33] He will be like a vine stripped of its unripe grapes,
like an olive tree shedding its blossoms.
[34] For the company of the godless will be barren,
and fire will consume the tents of those who love bribes.
[35] They conceive trouble and give birth to evil;
their womb fashions deceit."

Job

16 Then Job replied:

[2] "I have heard many things like these;
you are miserable comforters, all of you!
[3] Will your long-winded speeches never end?
What ails you that you keep on arguing?
[4] I also could speak like you,
if you were in my place;

I could make fine speeches against you
and shake my head at you.
5 But my mouth would encourage you;
comfort from my lips would bring you relief.

6 "Yet if I speak, my pain is not relieved;
and if I refrain, it does not go away.
7 Surely, God, you have worn me out;
you have devastated my entire household.
8 You have shriveled me up — and it has become a witness;
my gauntness rises up and testifies against me.
9 God assails me and tears me in his anger
and gnashes his teeth at me;
my opponent fastens on me his piercing eyes.
10 People open their mouths to jeer at me;
they strike my cheek in scorn
and unite together against me.
11 God has turned me over to the ungodly
and thrown me into the clutches of the wicked.
12 All was well with me, but he shattered me;
he seized me by the neck and crushed me.
He has made me his target;
13 his archers surround me.
Without pity, he pierces my kidneys
and spills my gall on the ground.
14 Again and again he bursts upon me;
he rushes at me like a warrior.

15 "I have sewed sackcloth over my skin
and buried my brow in the dust.
16 My face is red with weeping,
dark shadows ring my eyes;
17 yet my hands have been free of violence
and my prayer is pure.

18 "Earth, do not cover my blood;
may my cry never be laid to rest!
19 Even now my witness is in heaven;
my advocate is on high.
20 My intercessor is my friend[a]
as my eyes pour out tears to God;
21 on behalf of a man he pleads with God
as one pleads for a friend.

22 "Only a few years will pass
before I take the path of no return.

17 1 My spirit is broken,
my days are cut short,
the grave awaits me.
2 Surely mockers surround me;
my eyes must dwell on their hostility.

3 "Give me, O God, the pledge you demand.
Who else will put up security for me?
4 You have closed their minds to understanding;
therefore you will not let them triumph.
5 If anyone denounces their friends for reward,
the eyes of their children will fail.

6 "God has made me a byword to everyone,
a man in whose face people spit.
7 My eyes have grown dim with grief;
my whole frame is but a shadow.
8 The upright are appalled at this;
the innocent are aroused against the ungodly.
9 Nevertheless, the righteous will hold to their ways,
and those with clean hands will grow stronger.

10 "But come on, all of you, try again!
I will not find a wise man among you.
11 My days have passed, my plans are shattered.
Yet the desires of my heart
12 turn night into day;
in the face of the darkness light is near.
13 If the only home I hope for is the grave,
if I spread out my bed in the realm of darkness,
14 if I say to corruption, 'You are my father,'
and to the worm, 'My mother' or 'My sister,'
15 where then is my hope —
who can see any hope for me?
16 Will it go down to the gates of death?
Will we descend together into the dust?"

Bildad

18 Then Bildad the Shuhite replied:

2 "When will you end these speeches?
Be sensible, and then we can talk.
3 Why are we regarded as cattle
and considered stupid in your sight?

[a] 20 Or *My friends treat me with scorn*

[4]You who tear yourself to pieces in your anger,
is the earth to be abandoned for your sake?
Or must the rocks be moved from their place?
[5]"The lamp of a wicked man is snuffed out;
the flame of his fire stops burning.
[6]The light in his tent becomes dark;
the lamp beside him goes out.
[7]The vigor of his step is weakened;
his own schemes throw him down.
[8]His feet thrust him into a net;
he wanders into its mesh.
[9]A trap seizes him by the heel;
a snare holds him fast.
[10]A noose is hidden for him on the ground;
a trap lies in his path.
[11]Terrors startle him on every side
and dog his every step.
[12]Calamity is hungry for him;
disaster is ready for him when he falls.
[13]It eats away parts of his skin;
death's firstborn devours his limbs.
[14]He is torn from the security of his tent
and marched off to the king of terrors.
[15]Fire resides[a] in his tent;
burning sulfur is scattered over his dwelling.
[16]His roots dry up below
and his branches wither above.
[17]The memory of him perishes from the earth;
he has no name in the land.
[18]He is driven from light into the realm of darkness
and is banished from the world.
[19]He has no offspring or descendants among his people,
no survivor where once he lived.
[20]People of the west are appalled at his fate;
those of the east are seized with horror.
[21]Surely such is the dwelling of an evil man;
such is the place of one who does not know God."

Job

19

Then Job replied:

[2]"How long will you torment me
and crush me with words?
[3]Ten times now you have reproached me;
shamelessly you attack me.
[4]If it is true that I have gone astray,
my error remains my concern alone.
[5]If indeed you would exalt yourselves above me
and use my humiliation against me,
[6]then know that God has wronged me
and drawn his net around me.

[7]"Though I cry, 'Violence!' I get no response;
though I call for help, there is no justice.
[8]He has blocked my way so I cannot pass;
he has shrouded my paths in darkness.
[9]He has stripped me of my honor
and removed the crown from my head.
[10]He tears me down on every side till I am gone;
he uproots my hope like a tree.
[11]His anger burns against me;
he counts me among his enemies.
[12]His troops advance in force;
they build a siege ramp against me
and encamp around my tent.

[13]"He has alienated my family from me;
my acquaintances are completely estranged from me.
[14]My relatives have gone away;
my closest friends have forgotten me.
[15]My guests and my female servants count me a foreigner;
they look on me as on a stranger.
[16]I summon my servant, but he does not answer,
though I beg him with my own mouth.
[17]My breath is offensive to my wife;
I am loathsome to my own family.
[18]Even the little boys scorn me;
when I appear, they ridicule me.
[19]All my intimate friends detest me;
those I love have turned against me.
[20]I am nothing but skin and bones;
I have escaped only by the skin of my teeth.[b]

[21]"Have pity on me, my friends, have pity,
for the hand of God has struck me.
[22]Why do you pursue me as God does?
Will you never get enough of my flesh?

[23]"Oh, that my words were recorded,
that they were written on a scroll,

[a] 15 Or *Nothing he had remains* [b] 20 Or *only by my gums*

[24] that they were inscribed with an iron tool
on[a] lead,
or engraved in rock forever!
[25] I know that my redeemer[b] lives,
and that in the end he will stand on the
earth.[c]
[26] And after my skin has been destroyed,
yet[d] in[e] my flesh I will see God;
[27] I myself will see him
with my own eyes — I, and not another.
How my heart yearns within me!
[28] "If you say, 'How we will hound him,
since the root of the trouble lies in
him,[f]'
[29] you should fear the sword yourselves;
for wrath will bring punishment by the
sword,
and then you will know that there is
judgment.[g]"

Zophar

20 Then Zophar the Naamathite replied:

[2] "My troubled thoughts prompt me to
answer
because I am greatly disturbed.
[3] I hear a rebuke that dishonors me,
and my understanding inspires me
to reply.

[4] "Surely you know how it has been from
of old,
ever since mankind[h] was placed on
the earth,
[5] that the mirth of the wicked is brief,
the joy of the godless lasts but a
moment.
[6] Though the pride of the godless person
reaches to the heavens
and his head touches the clouds,
[7] he will perish forever, like his own
dung;
those who have seen him will say,
'Where is he?'
[8] Like a dream he flies away, no more to
be found,
banished like a vision of the night.
[9] The eye that saw him will not see him
again;
his place will look on him no more.
[10] His children must make amends to the
poor;
his own hands must give back his
wealth.
[11] The youthful vigor that fills his bones
will lie with him in the dust.

[12] "Though evil is sweet in his mouth
and he hides it under his tongue,
[13] though he cannot bear to let it go
and lets it linger in his mouth,
[14] yet his food will turn sour in his
stomach;
it will become the venom of serpents
within him.
[15] He will spit out the riches he swallowed;
God will make his stomach vomit
them up.
[16] He will suck the poison of serpents;
the fangs of an adder will kill him.
[17] He will not enjoy the streams,
the rivers flowing with honey and
cream.
[18] What he toiled for he must give back
uneaten;
he will not enjoy the profit from his
trading.
[19] For he has oppressed the poor and left
them destitute;
he has seized houses he did not build.

[20] "Surely he will have no respite from his
craving;
he cannot save himself by his treasure.
[21] Nothing is left for him to devour;
his prosperity will not endure.
[22] In the midst of his plenty, distress will
overtake him;
the full force of misery will come upon
him.
[23] When he has filled his belly,
God will vent his burning anger
against him
and rain down his blows on him.
[24] Though he flees from an iron weapon,
a bronze-tipped arrow pierces him.
[25] He pulls it out of his back,
the gleaming point out of his liver.
Terrors will come over him;
[26] total darkness lies in wait for his
treasures.

[a] 24 Or *and* [b] 25 Or *vindicator* [c] 25 Or *on my grave* [d] 26 Or *And after I awake, / though this body has been destroyed, / then* [e] 26 Or *destroyed, / apart from* [f] 28 Many Hebrew manuscripts, Septuagint and Vulgate; most Hebrew manuscripts *me* [g] 29 Or *sword, / that you may come to know the Almighty* [h] 4 Or *Adam*

A fire unfanned will consume him
and devour what is left in his tent.
27 The heavens will expose his guilt;
the earth will rise up against him.
28 A flood will carry off his house,
rushing waters[a] on the day of God's
wrath.
29 Such is the fate God allots the wicked,
the heritage appointed for them
by God."

Job

21 Then Job replied:

2 "Listen carefully to my words;
let this be the consolation you give me.
3 Bear with me while I speak,
and after I have spoken, mock on.

4 "Is my complaint directed to a human
being?
Why should I not be impatient?
5 Look at me and be appalled;
clap your hand over your mouth.
6 When I think about this, I am terrified;
trembling seizes my body.
7 Why do the wicked live on,
growing old and increasing in power?
8 They see their children established
around them,
their offspring before their eyes.
9 Their homes are safe and free from fear;
the rod of God is not on them.
10 Their bulls never fail to breed;
their cows calve and do not miscarry.
11 They send forth their children as a flock;
their little ones dance about.
12 They sing to the music of timbrel and
lyre;
they make merry to the sound of the
pipe.
13 They spend their years in prosperity
and go down to the grave in peace.[b]
14 Yet they say to God, 'Leave us alone!
We have no desire to know your ways.
15 Who is the Almighty, that we should
serve him?
What would we gain by praying to
him?'
16 But their prosperity is not in their own
hands,
so I stand aloof from the plans of the
wicked.

17 "Yet how often is the lamp of the wicked
snuffed out?
How often does calamity come upon
them,
the fate God allots in his anger?
18 How often are they like straw before the
wind,
like chaff swept away by a gale?
19 It is said, 'God stores up the punishment
of the wicked for their children.'
Let him repay the wicked, so that they
themselves will experience it!
20 Let their own eyes see their destruction;
let them drink the cup of the wrath of
the Almighty.
21 For what do they care about the families
they leave behind
when their allotted months come to an
end?

22 "Can anyone teach knowledge to God,
since he judges even the highest?
23 One person dies in full vigor,
completely secure and at ease,
24 well nourished in body,[c]
bones rich with marrow.
25 Another dies in bitterness of soul,
never having enjoyed anything good.
26 Side by side they lie in the dust,
and worms cover them both.

27 "I know full well what you are thinking,
the schemes by which you would
wrong me.
28 You say, 'Where now is the house of the
great,
the tents where the wicked lived?'
29 Have you never questioned those who
travel?
Have you paid no regard to their
accounts—
30 that the wicked are spared from the day
of calamity,
that they are delivered from[d] the day
of wrath?
31 Who denounces their conduct to their
face?
Who repays them for what they have
done?

[a] 28 Or *The possessions in his house will be carried off, / washed away* [b] 13 Or *in an instant*
[c] 24 The meaning of the Hebrew for this word is uncertain. [d] 30 Or *wicked are reserved for the day of calamity, / that they are brought forth to*

[32]They are carried to the grave,
and watch is kept over their tombs.
[33]The soil in the valley is sweet to them;
everyone follows after them,
and a countless throng goes[a] before
them.
[34]"So how can you console me with your
nonsense?
Nothing is left of your answers but
falsehood!"

Eliphaz

22 Then Eliphaz the Temanite replied:

[2]"Can a man be of benefit to God?
Can even a wise person benefit him?
[3]What pleasure would it give the Almighty
if you were righteous?
What would he gain if your ways were
blameless?

[4]"Is it for your piety that he rebukes you
and brings charges against you?
[5]Is not your wickedness great?
Are not your sins endless?
[6]You demanded security from your
relatives for no reason;
you stripped people of their clothing,
leaving them naked.
[7]You gave no water to the weary
and you withheld food from the
hungry,
[8]though you were a powerful man,
owning land —
an honored man, living on it.
[9]And you sent widows away empty-
handed
and broke the strength of the
fatherless.
[10]That is why snares are all around you,
why sudden peril terrifies you,
[11]why it is so dark you cannot see,
and why a flood of water covers you.

[12]"Is not God in the heights of heaven?
And see how lofty are the highest stars!
[13]Yet you say, 'What does God know?
Does he judge through such darkness?
[14]Thick clouds veil him, so he does not
see us
as he goes about in the vaulted
heavens.'
[15]Will you keep to the old path
that the wicked have trod?
[16]They were carried off before their time,
their foundations washed away by a
flood.
[17]They said to God, 'Leave us alone!
What can the Almighty do to us?'
[18]Yet it was he who filled their houses with
good things,
so I stand aloof from the plans of the
wicked.
[19]The righteous see their ruin and rejoice;
the innocent mock them, saying,
[20]'Surely our foes are destroyed,
and fire devours their wealth.'

[21]"Submit to God and be at peace with him;
in this way prosperity will come
to you.
[22]Accept instruction from his mouth
and lay up his words in your heart.
[23]If you return to the Almighty, you will
be restored:
If you remove wickedness far from
your tent
[24]and assign your nuggets to the dust,
your gold of Ophir to the rocks in the
ravines,
[25]then the Almighty will be your gold,
the choicest silver for you.
[26]Surely then you will find delight in the
Almighty
and will lift up your face to God.
[27]You will pray to him, and he will hear
you,
and you will fulfill your vows.
[28]What you decide on will be done,
and light will shine on your ways.
[29]When people are brought low and you
say, 'Lift them up!'
then he will save the downcast.
[30]He will deliver even one who is not
innocent,
who will be delivered through the
cleanness of your hands."

Job

23 Then Job replied:

[2]"Even today my complaint is bitter;
his hand[b] is heavy in spite of[c] my
groaning.

[a] 33 Or *them, / as a countless throng went* [b] 2 Septuagint and Syriac; Hebrew / *the hand on me*
[c] 2 Or *heavy on me in*

[3] If only I knew where to find him;
if only I could go to his dwelling!
[4] I would state my case before him
and fill my mouth with arguments.
[5] I would find out what he would answer me,
and consider what he would say to me.
[6] Would he vigorously oppose me?
No, he would not press charges
against me.
[7] There the upright can establish their
innocence before him,
and there I would be delivered forever
from my judge.

[8] "But if I go to the east, he is not there;
if I go to the west, I do not find him.
[9] When he is at work in the north, I do not
see him;
when he turns to the south, I catch no
glimpse of him.
[10] But he knows the way that I take;
when he has tested me, I will come
forth as gold.
[11] My feet have closely followed his steps;
I have kept to his way without turning
aside.
[12] I have not departed from the commands
of his lips;
I have treasured the words of his
mouth more than my daily bread.

[13] "But he stands alone, and who can
oppose him?
He does whatever he pleases.
[14] He carries out his decree against me,
and many such plans he still has in
store.
[15] That is why I am terrified before him;
when I think of all this, I fear him.
[16] God has made my heart faint;
the Almighty has terrified me.
[17] Yet I am not silenced by the darkness,
by the thick darkness that covers
my face.

24 "Why does the Almighty not set
times for judgment?
Why must those who know him look in
vain for such days?
[2] There are those who move boundary
stones;
they pasture flocks they have stolen.
[3] They drive away the orphan's donkey
and take the widow's ox in pledge.
[4] They thrust the needy from the path
and force all the poor of the land into
hiding.
[5] Like wild donkeys in the desert,
the poor go about their labor of
foraging food;
the wasteland provides food for their
children.
[6] They gather fodder in the fields
and glean in the vineyards of the
wicked.
[7] Lacking clothes, they spend the night
naked;
they have nothing to cover themselves
in the cold.
[8] They are drenched by mountain rains
and hug the rocks for lack of shelter.
[9] The fatherless child is snatched from the
breast;
the infant of the poor is seized for a
debt.
[10] Lacking clothes, they go about naked;
they carry the sheaves, but still go
hungry.
[11] They crush olives among the terraces[a];
they tread the winepresses, yet suffer
thirst.
[12] The groans of the dying rise from the city,
and the souls of the wounded cry out
for help.
But God charges no one with
wrongdoing.

[13] "There are those who rebel against
the light,
who do not know its ways
or stay in its paths.
[14] When daylight is gone, the murderer
rises up,
kills the poor and needy,
and in the night steals forth like a thief.
[15] The eye of the adulterer watches for dusk;
he thinks, 'No eye will see me,'
and he keeps his face concealed.
[16] In the dark, thieves break into houses,
but by day they shut themselves in;
they want nothing to do with the light.
[17] For all of them, midnight is their
morning;
they make friends with the terrors
of darkness.

[18] "Yet they are foam on the surface of
the water;

[a] *11* The meaning of the Hebrew for this word is uncertain.

their portion of the land is cursed,
so that no one goes to the vineyards.
19 As heat and drought snatch away the melted snow,
so the grave snatches away those who have sinned.
20 The womb forgets them,
the worm feasts on them;
the wicked are no longer remembered
but are broken like a tree.
21 They prey on the barren and childless woman,
and to the widow they show no kindness.
22 But God drags away the mighty by his power;
though they become established, they have no assurance of life.
23 He may let them rest in a feeling of security,
but his eyes are on their ways.
24 For a little while they are exalted, and then they are gone;
they are brought low and gathered up like all others;
they are cut off like heads of grain.

25 "If this is not so, who can prove me false
and reduce my words to nothing?"

Bildad

25 Then Bildad the Shuhite replied:

2 "Dominion and awe belong to God;
he establishes order in the heights of heaven.
3 Can his forces be numbered?
On whom does his light not rise?
4 How then can a mortal be righteous before God?
How can one born of woman be pure?
5 If even the moon is not bright
and the stars are not pure in his eyes,
6 how much less a mortal, who is but a maggot —
a human being, who is only a worm!"

Job

26 Then Job replied:

2 "How you have helped the powerless!
How you have saved the arm that is feeble!
3 What advice you have offered to one without wisdom!
And what great insight you have displayed!
4 Who has helped you utter these words?
And whose spirit spoke from your mouth?

5 "The dead are in deep anguish,
those beneath the waters and all that live in them.
6 The realm of the dead is naked before God;
Destruction[a] lies uncovered.
7 He spreads out the northern skies over empty space;
he suspends the earth over nothing.
8 He wraps up the waters in his clouds,
yet the clouds do not burst under their weight.
9 He covers the face of the full moon,
spreading his clouds over it.
10 He marks out the horizon on the face of the waters
for a boundary between light and darkness.
11 The pillars of the heavens quake,
aghast at his rebuke.
12 By his power he churned up the sea;
by his wisdom he cut Rahab to pieces.
13 By his breath the skies became fair;
his hand pierced the gliding serpent.
14 And these are but the outer fringe of his works;
how faint the whisper we hear of him!
Who then can understand the thunder of his power?"

Job's Final Word to His Friends

27 And Job continued his discourse:

2 "As surely as God lives, who has denied me justice,
the Almighty, who has made my life bitter,
3 as long as I have life within me,
the breath of God in my nostrils,
4 my lips will not say anything wicked,
and my tongue will not utter lies.
5 I will never admit you are in the right;
till I die, I will not deny my integrity.
6 I will maintain my innocence and never let go of it;

[a] 6 Hebrew *Abaddon*

my conscience will not reproach me as long as I live.

7 "May my enemy be like the wicked,
my adversary like the unjust!
8 For what hope have the godless when they are cut off,
when God takes away their life?
9 Does God listen to their cry
when distress comes upon them?
10 Will they find delight in the Almighty?
Will they call on God at all times?

11 "I will teach you about the power of God;
the ways of the Almighty I will not conceal.
12 You have all seen this yourselves.
Why then this meaningless talk?

13 "Here is the fate God allots to the wicked,
the heritage a ruthless man receives from the Almighty:
14 However many his children, their fate is the sword;
his offspring will never have enough to eat.
15 The plague will bury those who survive him,
and their widows will not weep for them.
16 Though he heaps up silver like dust
and clothes like piles of clay,
17 what he lays up the righteous will wear,
and the innocent will divide his silver.
18 The house he builds is like a moth's cocoon,
like a hut made by a watchman.
19 He lies down wealthy, but will do so no more;
when he opens his eyes, all is gone.
20 Terrors overtake him like a flood;
a tempest snatches him away in the night.
21 The east wind carries him off, and he is gone;
it sweeps him out of his place.
22 It hurls itself against him without mercy
as he flees headlong from its power.
23 It claps its hands in derision
and hisses him out of his place."

Interlude: Where Wisdom Is Found

28 There is a mine for silver
and a place where gold is refined.
2 Iron is taken from the earth,
and copper is smelted from ore.
3 Mortals put an end to the darkness;
they search out the farthest recesses
for ore in the blackest darkness.
4 Far from human dwellings they cut a shaft,
in places untouched by human feet;
far from other people they dangle and sway.
5 The earth, from which food comes,
is transformed below as by fire;
6 lapis lazuli comes from its rocks,
and its dust contains nuggets of gold.
7 No bird of prey knows that hidden path,
no falcon's eye has seen it.
8 Proud beasts do not set foot on it,
and no lion prowls there.
9 People assault the flinty rock with their hands
and lay bare the roots of the mountains.
10 They tunnel through the rock;
their eyes see all its treasures.
11 They search[a] the sources of the rivers
and bring hidden things to light.

12 But where can wisdom be found?
Where does understanding dwell?
13 No mortal comprehends its worth;
it cannot be found in the land of the living.
14 The deep says, "It is not in me";
the sea says, "It is not with me."
15 It cannot be bought with the finest gold,
nor can its price be weighed out in silver.
16 It cannot be bought with the gold of Ophir,
with precious onyx or lapis lazuli.
17 Neither gold nor crystal can compare with it,
nor can it be had for jewels of gold.
18 Coral and jasper are not worthy of mention;
the price of wisdom is beyond rubies.
19 The topaz of Cush cannot compare with it;
it cannot be bought with pure gold.

20 Where then does wisdom come from?
Where does understanding dwell?
21 It is hidden from the eyes of every living thing,

[a] *11* Septuagint, Aquila and Vulgate; Hebrew *They dam up*

concealed even from the birds in
the sky.
22 Destruction[a] and Death say,
"Only a rumor of it has reached our
ears."
23 God understands the way to it
and he alone knows where it dwells,
24 for he views the ends of the earth
and sees everything under the
heavens.
25 When he established the force of
the wind
and measured out the waters,
26 when he made a decree for the rain
and a path for the thunderstorm,
27 then he looked at wisdom and
appraised it;
he confirmed it and tested it.
28 And he said to the human race,
"The fear of the Lord—that is wisdom,
and to shun evil is understanding."

Job's Final Defense

29 Job continued his discourse:

2 "How I long for the months gone by,
for the days when God watched
over me,
3 when his lamp shone on my head
and by his light I walked through
darkness!
4 Oh, for the days when I was in my prime,
when God's intimate friendship
blessed my house,
5 when the Almighty was still with me
and my children were around me,
6 when my path was drenched with cream
and the rock poured out for me
streams of olive oil.

7 "When I went to the gate of the city
and took my seat in the public square,
8 the young men saw me and stepped
aside
and the old men rose to their feet;
9 the chief men refrained from speaking
and covered their mouths with their
hands;
10 the voices of the nobles were hushed,
and their tongues stuck to the roof of
their mouths.
11 Whoever heard me spoke well of me,
and those who saw me commended me,
12 because I rescued the poor who cried
for help,
and the fatherless who had none to
assist them.
13 The one who was dying blessed me;
I made the widow's heart sing.
14 I put on righteousness as my clothing;
justice was my robe and my turban.
15 I was eyes to the blind
and feet to the lame.
16 I was a father to the needy;
I took up the case of the stranger.
17 I broke the fangs of the wicked
and snatched the victims from their
teeth.

18 "I thought, 'I will die in my own house,
my days as numerous as the grains
of sand.
19 My roots will reach to the water,
and the dew will lie all night on my
branches.
20 My glory will not fade;
the bow will be ever new in my hand.'

21 "People listened to me expectantly,
waiting in silence for my counsel.
22 After I had spoken, they spoke no more;
my words fell gently on their ears.
23 They waited for me as for showers
and drank in my words as the spring
rain.
24 When I smiled at them, they scarcely
believed it;
the light of my face was precious
to them.[b]
25 I chose the way for them and sat as their
chief;
I dwelt as a king among his troops;
I was like one who comforts
mourners.

30 "But now they mock me,
men younger than I,
whose fathers I would have disdained
to put with my sheep dogs.
2 Of what use was the strength of their
hands to me,
since their vigor had gone from
them?
3 Haggard from want and hunger,
they roamed[c] the parched land
in desolate wastelands at night.
4 In the brush they gathered salt herbs,

[a] 22 Hebrew *Abaddon* [b] 24 The meaning of the Hebrew for this clause is uncertain. [c] 3 Or *gnawed*

and their food[a] was the root of the
broom bush.
5 They were banished from human society,
shouted at as if they were thieves.
6 They were forced to live in the dry stream
beds,
among the rocks and in holes in the
ground.
7 They brayed among the bushes
and huddled in the undergrowth.
8 A base and nameless brood,
they were driven out of the land.

9 "And now those young men mock me
in song;
I have become a byword among them.
10 They detest me and keep their distance;
they do not hesitate to spit in my face.
11 Now that God has unstrung my bow and
afflicted me,
they throw off restraint in my
presence.
12 On my right the tribe[b] attacks;
they lay snares for my feet,
they build their siege ramps
against me.
13 They break up my road;
they succeed in destroying me.
'No one can help him,' they say.
14 They advance as through a gaping
breach;
amid the ruins they come rolling in.
15 Terrors overwhelm me;
my dignity is driven away as by the
wind,
my safety vanishes like a cloud.

16 "And now my life ebbs away;
days of suffering grip me.
17 Night pierces my bones;
my gnawing pains never rest.
18 In his great power God becomes like
clothing to me[c];
he binds me like the neck of my
garment.
19 He throws me into the mud,
and I am reduced to dust and ashes.

20 "I cry out to you, God, but you do not
answer;
I stand up, but you merely look at me.
21 You turn on me ruthlessly;
with the might of your hand you
attack me.
22 You snatch me up and drive me before
the wind;
you toss me about in the storm.
23 I know you will bring me down to death,
to the place appointed for all the
living.

24 "Surely no one lays a hand on a broken
man
when he cries for help in his distress.
25 Have I not wept for those in trouble?
Has not my soul grieved for the poor?
26 Yet when I hoped for good, evil came;
when I looked for light, then came
darkness.
27 The churning inside me never stops;
days of suffering confront me.
28 I go about blackened, but not by the sun;
I stand up in the assembly and cry
for help.
29 I have become a brother of jackals,
a companion of owls.
30 My skin grows black and peels;
my body burns with fever.
31 My lyre is tuned to mourning,
and my pipe to the sound of wailing.

31 "I made a covenant with my eyes
not to look lustfully at a young
woman.
2 For what is our lot from God above,
our heritage from the Almighty on
high?
3 Is it not ruin for the wicked,
disaster for those who do wrong?
4 Does he not see my ways
and count my every step?

5 "If I have walked with falsehood
or my foot has hurried after deceit—
6 let God weigh me in honest scales
and he will know that I am
blameless—
7 if my steps have turned from the path,
if my heart has been led by my eyes,
or if my hands have been defiled,
8 then may others eat what I have sown,
and may my crops be uprooted.

9 "If my heart has been enticed by a
woman,
or if I have lurked at my neighbor's
door,

[a] 4 Or *fuel* [b] 12 The meaning of the Hebrew for this word is uncertain. [c] 18 Hebrew; Septuagint *power he grasps my clothing*

[10] then may my wife grind another man's
grain,
and may other men sleep with her.
[11] For that would have been wicked,
a sin to be judged.
[12] It is a fire that burns to Destruction[a];
it would have uprooted my harvest.

[13] "If I have denied justice to any of my
servants,
whether male or female,
when they had a grievance against me,
[14] what will I do when God confronts me?
What will I answer when called to
account?
[15] Did not he who made me in the womb
make them?
Did not the same one form us both
within our mothers?

[16] "If I have denied the desires of the poor
or let the eyes of the widow grow
weary,
[17] if I have kept my bread to myself,
not sharing it with the fatherless—
[18] but from my youth I reared them as a
father would,
and from my birth I guided the
widow—
[19] if I have seen anyone perishing for lack of
clothing,
or the needy without garments,
[20] and their hearts did not bless me
for warming them with the fleece from
my sheep,
[21] if I have raised my hand against the
fatherless,
knowing that I had influence in court,
[22] then let my arm fall from the shoulder,
let it be broken off at the joint.
[23] For I dreaded destruction from God,
and for fear of his splendor I could not
do such things.

[24] "If I have put my trust in gold
or said to pure gold, 'You are my
security,'
[25] if I have rejoiced over my great wealth,
the fortune my hands had gained,
[26] if I have regarded the sun in its radiance
or the moon moving in splendor,
[27] so that my heart was secretly enticed
and my hand offered them a kiss of
homage,
[28] then these also would be sins to be
judged,
for I would have been unfaithful to
God on high.

[29] "If I have rejoiced at my enemy's
misfortune
or gloated over the trouble that came
to him—
[30] I have not allowed my mouth to sin
by invoking a curse against their life—
[31] if those of my household have never said,
'Who has not been filled with Job's
meat?'—
[32] but no stranger had to spend the night in
the street,
for my door was always open to the
traveler—
[33] if I have concealed my sin as people do,[b]
by hiding my guilt in my heart
[34] because I so feared the crowd
and so dreaded the contempt of the
clans
that I kept silent and would not go
outside—

[35] ("Oh, that I had someone to hear me!
I sign now my defense—let the
Almighty answer me;
let my accuser put his indictment in
writing.
[36] Surely I would wear it on my shoulder,
I would put it on like a crown.
[37] I would give him an account of my every
step;
I would present it to him as to a
ruler.)—

[38] "if my land cries out against me
and all its furrows are wet with tears,
[39] if I have devoured its yield without
payment
or broken the spirit of its tenants,
[40] then let briers come up instead of wheat
and stinkweed instead of barley."

The words of Job are ended.

Elihu

32 So these three men stopped answer-
ing Job, because he was righteous in
his own eyes. [2] But Elihu son of Barakel the
Buzite, of the family of Ram, became very
angry with Job for justifying himself rather

[a] 12 Hebrew *Abaddon* [b] 33 Or *as Adam did*

THE STAND

Joel Houston

You stood before creation
Eternity in your hand
You spoke the earth into motion
My soul now to stand

You stood before my failure
And carried the cross for my shame
My sin weighed upon your shoulders
My soul now to stand

So what can I say
And what can I do
But offer this heart O God
Completely to you

So I'll walk upon salvation
Your Spirit alive in me
My life to declare your promise
My soul now to stand

So I'll stand
With arms high and heart abandoned
In awe of the One who gave it all
I'll stand
My soul Lord to you surrendered
All I am is yours

THE INSPIRATION

LORD, I have heard of your fame; I stand in awe of your deeds, LORD. Repeat them in our day, in our time make them known; in wrath remember mercy. —Habakkuk 3:2

BEHIND THE SONG

Joel Houston was leading worship at a special prayer gathering for the young people of Hillsong Church in Australia when a time of musical worship spontaneously broke out. The people sang this anthem at the top of their lungs: "I'll stand, with arms high and heart abandoned, in awe of the One who gave it all." Houston rushed to record the song somewhere, afraid he'd forget it. He ended up recording it on his phone, which he then lost.

Eight months later a similar spontaneous worship time happened and this same song — which Houston had long forgotten all about — was sung again.

"It's a song of response to God in worship about who he is and what he's done," Houston explains. "It's actually a metaphor for our hearts. It's a song of surrender, and I kind of like that — that paradox of God. It really is a posture of saying, 'I'm going to stand. I'm going to surrender to you God; all that I am because you stood for me. You created it all. You stood for me on the cross. What can I say? What can I do? I'm just going to stand for who you are. I'm going to stand up and be counted when it comes to living my life for you.'"

Selah

Sometimes worship requires us to take a stand. Maybe it's about living out our faith in the workplace or at school. Maybe it causes us to say "no" to poverty, injustice or complacency in Jesus' name.

The prophet Habakkuk said to the Lord, "I have heard of your fame; I stand in awe of your deeds." Would Habakkuk have heard of the Lord's deeds if he had encountered you? Is there an area of your life or an issue in your community on which God has been calling you to take a stand?

than God. [3] He was also angry with the three
friends, because they had found no way to
refute Job, and yet had condemned him.[a]
[4] Now Elihu had waited before speaking to
Job because they were older than he. [5] But
when he saw that the three men had nothing
more to say, his anger was aroused.

[6] So Elihu son of Barakel the Buzite said:

"I am young in years,
and you are old;
that is why I was fearful,
not daring to tell you what I know.
[7] I thought, 'Age should speak;
advanced years should teach wisdom.'
[8] But it is the spirit[b] in a person,
the breath of the Almighty, that gives
them understanding.
[9] It is not only the old[c] who are wise,
not only the aged who understand
what is right.

[10] "Therefore I say: Listen to me;
I too will tell you what I know.
[11] I waited while you spoke,
I listened to your reasoning;
while you were searching for words,
[12] I gave you my full attention.
But not one of you has proved Job wrong;
none of you has answered his
arguments.
[13] Do not say, 'We have found wisdom;
let God, not a man, refute him.'
[14] But Job has not marshaled his words
against me,
and I will not answer him with your
arguments.

[15] "They are dismayed and have no more
to say;
words have failed them.
[16] Must I wait, now that they are silent,
now that they stand there with no
reply?
[17] I too will have my say;
I too will tell what I know.
[18] For I am full of words,
and the spirit within me compels me;
[19] inside I am like bottled-up wine,
like new wineskins ready to burst.
[20] I must speak and find relief;
I must open my lips and reply.
[21] I will show no partiality,
nor will I flatter anyone;
[22] for if I were skilled in flattery,
my Maker would soon take me away.

33 "But now, Job, listen to my words;
pay attention to everything I say.
[2] I am about to open my mouth;
my words are on the tip of my tongue.
[3] My words come from an upright heart;
my lips sincerely speak what I know.
[4] The Spirit of God has made me;
the breath of the Almighty gives
me life.
[5] Answer me then, if you can;
stand up and argue your case
before me.
[6] I am the same as you in God's sight;
I too am a piece of clay.
[7] No fear of me should alarm you,
nor should my hand be heavy on you.

[8] "But you have said in my hearing—
I heard the very words—
[9] 'I am pure, I have done no wrong;
I am clean and free from sin.
[10] Yet God has found fault with me;
he considers me his enemy.
[11] He fastens my feet in shackles;
he keeps close watch on all my paths.'

[12] "But I tell you, in this you are not right,
for God is greater than any mortal.
[13] Why do you complain to him
that he responds to no one's words[d]?
[14] For God does speak—now one way, now
another—
though no one perceives it.
[15] In a dream, in a vision of the night,
when deep sleep falls on people
as they slumber in their beds,
[16] he may speak in their ears
and terrify them with warnings,
[17] to turn them from wrongdoing
and keep them from pride,
[18] to preserve them from the pit,
their lives from perishing by the
sword.[e]

[19] "Or someone may be chastened on a bed
of pain
with constant distress in their bones,

[a] 3 Masoretic Text; an ancient Hebrew scribal tradition *Job, and so had condemned God* [b] 8 Or *Spirit*; also in verse 18 [c] 9 Or *many*; or *great* [d] 13 Or *that he does not answer for any of his actions*
[e] 18 Or *from crossing the river*

[20] so that their body finds food repulsive
and their soul loathes the choicest meal.
[21] Their flesh wastes away to nothing,
and their bones, once hidden, now stick out.
[22] They draw near to the pit,
and their life to the messengers of death.[a]
[23] Yet if there is an angel at their side,
a messenger, one out of a thousand,
sent to tell them how to be upright,
[24] and he is gracious to that person and says to God,
'Spare them from going down to the pit;
I have found a ransom for them —
[25] let their flesh be renewed like a child's;
let them be restored as in the days of their youth' —
[26] then that person can pray to God and find favor with him,
they will see God's face and shout for joy;
he will restore them to full well-being.
[27] And they will go to others and say,
'I have sinned, I have perverted what is right,
but I did not get what I deserved.
[28] God has delivered me from going down to the pit,
and I shall live to enjoy the light of life.'

[29] "God does all these things to a person —
twice, even three times —
[30] to turn them back from the pit,
that the light of life may shine on them.

[31] "Pay attention, Job, and listen to me;
be silent, and I will speak.
[32] If you have anything to say, answer me;
speak up, for I want to vindicate you.
[33] But if not, then listen to me;
be silent, and I will teach you wisdom."

34

Then Elihu said:

[2] "Hear my words, you wise men;
listen to me, you men of learning.
[3] For the ear tests words
as the tongue tastes food.
[4] Let us discern for ourselves what is right;
let us learn together what is good.

[5] "Job says, 'I am innocent,
but God denies me justice.
[6] Although I am right,
I am considered a liar;
although I am guiltless,
his arrow inflicts an incurable wound.'
[7] Is there anyone like Job,
who drinks scorn like water?
[8] He keeps company with evildoers;
he associates with the wicked.
[9] For he says, 'There is no profit
in trying to please God.'

[10] "So listen to me, you men of understanding.
Far be it from God to do evil,
from the Almighty to do wrong.
[11] He repays everyone for what they have done;
he brings on them what their conduct deserves.
[12] It is unthinkable that God would do wrong,
that the Almighty would pervert justice.
[13] Who appointed him over the earth?
Who put him in charge of the whole world?
[14] If it were his intention
and he withdrew his spirit[b] and breath,
[15] all humanity would perish together
and mankind would return to the dust.

[16] "If you have understanding, hear this;
listen to what I say.
[17] Can someone who hates justice govern?
Will you condemn the just and mighty One?
[18] Is he not the One who says to kings, 'You are worthless,'
and to nobles, 'You are wicked,'
[19] who shows no partiality to princes
and does not favor the rich over the poor,
for they are all the work of his hands?
[20] They die in an instant, in the middle of the night;
the people are shaken and they pass away;
the mighty are removed without human hand.

[21] "His eyes are on the ways of mortals;
he sees their every step.

[a] 22 Or *to the place of the dead* [b] 14 Or *Spirit*

22 There is no deep shadow, no utter
darkness,
where evildoers can hide.
23 God has no need to examine people
further,
that they should come before him for
judgment.
24 Without inquiry he shatters the mighty
and sets up others in their place.
25 Because he takes note of their deeds,
he overthrows them in the night and
they are crushed.
26 He punishes them for their wickedness
where everyone can see them,
27 because they turned from following him
and had no regard for any of his ways.
28 They caused the cry of the poor to come
before him,
so that he heard the cry of the needy.
29 But if he remains silent, who can
condemn him?
If he hides his face, who can see him?
Yet he is over individual and nation alike,
30 to keep the godless from ruling,
from laying snares for the people.

31 "Suppose someone says to God,
'I am guilty but will offend no more.
32 Teach me what I cannot see;
if I have done wrong, I will not do so
again.'
33 Should God then reward you on your
terms,
when you refuse to repent?
You must decide, not I;
so tell me what you know.

34 "Men of understanding declare,
wise men who hear me say to me,
35 'Job speaks without knowledge;
his words lack insight.'
36 Oh, that Job might be tested to the
utmost
for answering like a wicked man!
37 To his sin he adds rebellion;
scornfully he claps his hands
among us
and multiplies his words against God."

35

Then Elihu said:

2 "Do you think this is just?
You say, 'I am in the right, not God.'
3 Yet you ask him, 'What profit is it to me,[a]
and what do I gain by not sinning?'

4 "I would like to reply to you
and to your friends with you.
5 Look up at the heavens and see;
gaze at the clouds so high above you.
6 If you sin, how does that affect him?
If your sins are many, what does that
do to him?
7 If you are righteous, what do you give
to him,
or what does he receive from your
hand?
8 Your wickedness only affects humans
like yourself,
and your righteousness only other
people.

9 "People cry out under a load of
oppression;
they plead for relief from the arm of the
powerful.
10 But no one says, 'Where is God my Maker,
who gives songs in the night,
11 who teaches us more than he teaches[b]
the beasts of the earth
and makes us wiser than[c] the birds in
the sky?'
12 He does not answer when people cry out
because of the arrogance of the
wicked.
13 Indeed, God does not listen to their
empty plea;
the Almighty pays no attention to it.
14 How much less, then, will he listen
when you say that you do not see him,
that your case is before him
and you must wait for him,
15 and further, that his anger never
punishes
and he does not take the least notice of
wickedness.[d]
16 So Job opens his mouth with empty talk;
without knowledge he multiplies
words."

36

Elihu continued:

2 "Bear with me a little longer and I will
show you
that there is more to be said in God's
behalf.

[a] 3 Or *you* [b] 10,11 Or *night,* / [11]*who teaches us by* [c] 11 Or *us wise by* [d] 15 Symmachus, Theodotion and Vulgate; the meaning of the Hebrew for this word is uncertain.

³I get my knowledge from afar;
I will ascribe justice to my Maker.
⁴Be assured that my words are not false;
one who has perfect knowledge is with you.

⁵"God is mighty, but despises no one;
he is mighty, and firm in his purpose.
⁶He does not keep the wicked alive
but gives the afflicted their rights.
⁷He does not take his eyes off the righteous;
he enthrones them with kings
and exalts them forever.
⁸But if people are bound in chains,
held fast by cords of affliction,
⁹he tells them what they have done —
that they have sinned arrogantly.
¹⁰He makes them listen to correction
and commands them to repent of their evil.
¹¹If they obey and serve him,
they will spend the rest of their days in prosperity
and their years in contentment.
¹²But if they do not listen,
they will perish by the sword[a]
and die without knowledge.

¹³"The godless in heart harbor resentment;
even when he fetters them, they do not cry for help.
¹⁴They die in their youth,
among male prostitutes of the shrines.
¹⁵But those who suffer he delivers in their suffering;
he speaks to them in their affliction.

¹⁶"He is wooing you from the jaws of distress
to a spacious place free from restriction,
to the comfort of your table laden with choice food.
¹⁷But now you are laden with the judgment due the wicked;
judgment and justice have taken hold of you.
¹⁸Be careful that no one entices you by riches;
do not let a large bribe turn you aside.
¹⁹Would your wealth or even all your mighty efforts
sustain you so you would not be in distress?
²⁰Do not long for the night,
to drag people away from their homes.[b]
²¹Beware of turning to evil,
which you seem to prefer to affliction.

²²"God is exalted in his power.
Who is a teacher like him?
²³Who has prescribed his ways for him,
or said to him, 'You have done wrong'?
²⁴Remember to extol his work,
which people have praised in song.
²⁵All humanity has seen it;
mortals gaze on it from afar.
²⁶How great is God — beyond our understanding!
The number of his years is past finding out.

²⁷"He draws up the drops of water,
which distill as rain to the streams[c];
²⁸the clouds pour down their moisture
and abundant showers fall on mankind.
²⁹Who can understand how he spreads out the clouds,
how he thunders from his pavilion?
³⁰See how he scatters his lightning about him,
bathing the depths of the sea.
³¹This is the way he governs[d] the nations
and provides food in abundance.
³²He fills his hands with lightning
and commands it to strike its mark.
³³His thunder announces the coming storm;
even the cattle make known its approach.[e]

37 "At this my heart pounds
and leaps from its place.
²Listen! Listen to the roar of his voice,
to the rumbling that comes from his mouth.
³He unleashes his lightning beneath the whole heaven
and sends it to the ends of the earth.
⁴After that comes the sound of his roar;

[a] 12 Or *will cross the river* [b] 20 The meaning of the Hebrew for verses 18-20 is uncertain.
[c] 27 Or *distill from the mist as rain* [d] 31 Or *nourishes* [e] 33 Or *announces his coming — / the One zealous against evil*

he thunders with his majestic
voice.
When his voice resounds,
he holds nothing back.
5 God's voice thunders in marvelous ways;
he does great things beyond our
understanding.
6 He says to the snow, 'Fall on the earth,'
and to the rain shower, 'Be a mighty
downpour.'
7 So that everyone he has made may know
his work,
he stops all people from their labor.[a]
8 The animals take cover;
they remain in their dens.
9 The tempest comes out from its chamber,
the cold from the driving winds.
10 The breath of God produces ice,
and the broad waters become frozen.
11 He loads the clouds with moisture;
he scatters his lightning through them.
12 At his direction they swirl around
over the face of the whole earth
to do whatever he commands them.
13 He brings the clouds to punish people,
or to water his earth and show his love.

14 "Listen to this, Job;
stop and consider God's wonders.
15 Do you know how God controls the
clouds
and makes his lightning flash?
16 Do you know how the clouds hang
poised,
those wonders of him who has perfect
knowledge?
17 You who swelter in your clothes
when the land lies hushed under the
south wind,
18 can you join him in spreading out the
skies,
hard as a mirror of cast bronze?

19 "Tell us what we should say to him;
we cannot draw up our case because of
our darkness.
20 Should he be told that I want to speak?
Would anyone ask to be swallowed up?
21 Now no one can look at the sun,
bright as it is in the skies
after the wind has swept them clean.
22 Out of the north he comes in golden
splendor;
God comes in awesome majesty.
23 The Almighty is beyond our reach and
exalted in power;
in his justice and great righteousness,
he does not oppress.
24 Therefore, people revere him,
for does he not have regard for all the
wise in heart?[b]"

The LORD Speaks

38 Then the LORD spoke to Job out of the
storm. He said:

2 "Who is this that obscures my plans
with words without knowledge?
3 Brace yourself like a man;
I will question you,
and you shall answer me.

4 "Where were you when I laid the earth's
foundation?
Tell me, if you understand.
5 Who marked off its dimensions? Surely
you know!
Who stretched a measuring line
across it?
6 On what were its footings set,
or who laid its cornerstone —
7 while the morning stars sang together
and all the angels[c] shouted for joy?

8 "Who shut up the sea behind doors
when it burst forth from the womb,
9 when I made the clouds its garment
and wrapped it in thick darkness,
10 when I fixed limits for it
and set its doors and bars in place,
11 when I said, 'This far you may come and
no farther;
here is where your proud waves halt'?

12 "Have you ever given orders to the
morning,
or shown the dawn its place,
13 that it might take the earth by the edges
and shake the wicked out of it?
14 The earth takes shape like clay under
a seal;
its features stand out like those of a
garment.
15 The wicked are denied their light,
and their upraised arm is broken.

16 "Have you journeyed to the springs of
the sea

[a] 7 Or *work, / he fills all people with fear by his power* [b] 24 Or *for he does not have regard for any who think they are wise.* [c] 7 Hebrew *the sons of God*

or walked in the recesses of the
deep?
17 Have the gates of death been shown
to you?
Have you seen the gates of the deepest
darkness?
18 Have you comprehended the vast
expanses of the earth?
Tell me, if you know all this.

19 "What is the way to the abode of light?
And where does darkness reside?
20 Can you take them to their places?
Do you know the paths to their
dwellings?
21 Surely you know, for you were already
born!
You have lived so many years!

22 "Have you entered the storehouses of
the snow
or seen the storehouses of the hail,
23 which I reserve for times of trouble,
for days of war and battle?
24 What is the way to the place where the
lightning is dispersed,
or the place where the east winds are
scattered over the earth?
25 Who cuts a channel for the torrents
of rain,
and a path for the thunderstorm,
26 to water a land where no one lives,
an uninhabited desert,
27 to satisfy a desolate wasteland
and make it sprout with grass?
28 Does the rain have a father?
Who fathers the drops of dew?
29 From whose womb comes the ice?
Who gives birth to the frost from the
heavens
30 when the waters become hard as stone,
when the surface of the deep is frozen?

31 "Can you bind the chains[a] of the
Pleiades?
Can you loosen Orion's belt?
32 Can you bring forth the constellations in
their seasons[b]
or lead out the Bear[c] with its cubs?
33 Do you know the laws of the heavens?
Can you set up God's[d] dominion over
the earth?

34 "Can you raise your voice to the clouds
and cover yourself with a flood of
water?
35 Do you send the lightning bolts on
their way?
Do they report to you, 'Here we are'?
36 Who gives the ibis wisdom[e]
or gives the rooster understanding?[f]
37 Who has the wisdom to count the clouds?
Who can tip over the water jars of the
heavens
38 when the dust becomes hard
and the clods of earth stick together?

39 "Do you hunt the prey for the lioness
and satisfy the hunger of the lions
40 when they crouch in their dens
or lie in wait in a thicket?
41 Who provides food for the raven
when its young cry out to God
and wander about for lack of food?

39

"Do you know when the mountain
goats give birth?
Do you watch when the doe bears her
fawn?
2 Do you count the months till they bear?
Do you know the time they give birth?
3 They crouch down and bring forth their
young;
their labor pains are ended.
4 Their young thrive and grow strong in
the wilds;
they leave and do not return.

5 "Who let the wild donkey go free?
Who untied its ropes?
6 I gave it the wasteland as its home,
the salt flats as its habitat.
7 It laughs at the commotion in the town;
it does not hear a driver's shout.
8 It ranges the hills for its pasture
and searches for any green thing.

9 "Will the wild ox consent to serve you?
Will it stay by your manger at night?
10 Can you hold it to the furrow with a
harness?
Will it till the valleys behind you?
11 Will you rely on it for its great strength?
Will you leave your heavy work to it?
12 Can you trust it to haul in your grain
and bring it to your threshing floor?

[a] 31 Septuagint; Hebrew *beauty* [b] 32 Or *the morning star in its season* [c] 32 Or *out Leo*
[d] 33 Or *their* [e] 36 That is, wisdom about the flooding of the Nile [f] 36 That is, understanding of when to crow; the meaning of the Hebrew for this verse is uncertain.

13 "The wings of the ostrich flap joyfully,
though they cannot compare
with the wings and feathers of the
stork.
14 She lays her eggs on the ground
and lets them warm in the sand,
15 unmindful that a foot may crush them,
that some wild animal may trample
them.
16 She treats her young harshly, as if they
were not hers;
she cares not that her labor was in
vain,
17 for God did not endow her with wisdom
or give her a share of good sense.
18 Yet when she spreads her feathers to run,
she laughs at horse and rider.

19 "Do you give the horse its strength
or clothe its neck with a flowing mane?
20 Do you make it leap like a locust,
striking terror with its proud snorting?
21 It paws fiercely, rejoicing in its strength,
and charges into the fray.
22 It laughs at fear, afraid of nothing;
it does not shy away from the sword.
23 The quiver rattles against its side,
along with the flashing spear and
lance.
24 In frenzied excitement it eats up the
ground;
it cannot stand still when the trumpet
sounds.
25 At the blast of the trumpet it snorts, 'Aha!'
It catches the scent of battle from afar,
the shout of commanders and the
battle cry.

26 "Does the hawk take flight by your
wisdom
and spread its wings toward the south?
27 Does the eagle soar at your command
and build its nest on high?
28 It dwells on a cliff and stays there at
night;
a rocky crag is its stronghold.
29 From there it looks for food;
its eyes detect it from afar.
30 Its young ones feast on blood,
and where the slain are, there it is."

40 The LORD said to Job:

2 "Will the one who contends with the
Almighty correct him?
Let him who accuses God answer him!"

3 Then Job answered the LORD:

4 "I am unworthy — how can I reply to you?
I put my hand over my mouth.
5 I spoke once, but I have no answer —
twice, but I will say no more."

6 Then the LORD spoke to Job out of the
storm:

7 "Brace yourself like a man;
I will question you,
and you shall answer me.

8 "Would you discredit my justice?
Would you condemn me to justify
yourself?
9 Do you have an arm like God's,
and can your voice thunder like his?
10 Then adorn yourself with glory and
splendor,
and clothe yourself in honor and
majesty.
11 Unleash the fury of your wrath,
look at all who are proud and bring
them low,
12 look at all who are proud and humble
them,
crush the wicked where they stand.
13 Bury them all in the dust together;
shroud their faces in the grave.
14 Then I myself will admit to you
that your own right hand can save you.

15 "Look at Behemoth,
which I made along with you
and which feeds on grass like an ox.
16 What strength it has in its loins,
what power in the muscles of its belly!
17 Its tail sways like a cedar;
the sinews of its thighs are close-knit.
18 Its bones are tubes of bronze,
its limbs like rods of iron.
19 It ranks first among the works of God,
yet its Maker can approach it with his
sword.
20 The hills bring it their produce,
and all the wild animals play nearby.
21 Under the lotus plants it lies,
hidden among the reeds in the marsh.
22 The lotuses conceal it in their shadow;
the poplars by the stream surround it.
23 A raging river does not alarm it;
it is secure, though the Jordan should
surge against its mouth.

[24] Can anyone capture it by the eyes,
or trap it and pierce its nose?

41 [a] "Can you pull in Leviathan with a fishhook
or tie down its tongue with a rope?
[2] Can you put a cord through its nose
or pierce its jaw with a hook?
[3] Will it keep begging you for mercy?
Will it speak to you with gentle words?
[4] Will it make an agreement with you
for you to take it as your slave for life?
[5] Can you make a pet of it like a bird
or put it on a leash for the young women in your house?
[6] Will traders barter for it?
Will they divide it up among the merchants?
[7] Can you fill its hide with harpoons
or its head with fishing spears?
[8] If you lay a hand on it,
you will remember the struggle and never do it again!
[9] Any hope of subduing it is false;
the mere sight of it is overpowering.
[10] No one is fierce enough to rouse it.
Who then is able to stand against me?
[11] Who has a claim against me that I must pay?
Everything under heaven belongs to me.

[12] "I will not fail to speak of Leviathan's limbs,
its strength and its graceful form.
[13] Who can strip off its outer coat?
Who can penetrate its double coat of armor[b]?
[14] Who dares open the doors of its mouth,
ringed about with fearsome teeth?
[15] Its back has[c] rows of shields
tightly sealed together;
[16] each is so close to the next
that no air can pass between.
[17] They are joined fast to one another;
they cling together and cannot be parted.
[18] Its snorting throws out flashes of light;
its eyes are like the rays of dawn.
[19] Flames stream from its mouth;
sparks of fire shoot out.
[20] Smoke pours from its nostrils
as from a boiling pot over burning reeds.
[21] Its breath sets coals ablaze,
and flames dart from its mouth.
[22] Strength resides in its neck;
dismay goes before it.
[23] The folds of its flesh are tightly joined;
they are firm and immovable.
[24] Its chest is hard as rock,
hard as a lower millstone.
[25] When it rises up, the mighty are terrified;
they retreat before its thrashing.
[26] The sword that reaches it has no effect,
nor does the spear or the dart or the javelin.
[27] Iron it treats like straw
and bronze like rotten wood.
[28] Arrows do not make it flee;
slingstones are like chaff to it.
[29] A club seems to it but a piece of straw;
it laughs at the rattling of the lance.
[30] Its undersides are jagged potsherds,
leaving a trail in the mud like a threshing sledge.
[31] It makes the depths churn like a boiling caldron
and stirs up the sea like a pot of ointment.
[32] It leaves a glistening wake behind it;
one would think the deep had white hair.
[33] Nothing on earth is its equal —
a creature without fear.
[34] It looks down on all that are haughty;
it is king over all that are proud."

Job

42 Then Job replied to the LORD:

[2] "I know that you can do all things;
no purpose of yours can be thwarted.
[3] You asked, 'Who is this that obscures my plans without knowledge?'
Surely I spoke of things I did not understand,
things too wonderful for me to know.

[4] "You said, 'Listen now, and I will speak;
I will question you,
and you shall answer me.'

[a] In Hebrew texts 41:1-8 is numbered 40:25-32, and 41:9-34 is numbered 41:1-26. [b] *13* Septuagint; Hebrew *double bridle* [c] *15* Or *Its pride is its*

5 My ears had heard of you
but now my eyes have seen you.
6 Therefore I despise myself
and repent in dust and ashes."

Epilogue

7 After the LORD had said these things to
Job, he said to Eliphaz the Temanite, "I am
angry with you and your two friends, be-
cause you have not spoken the truth about
me, as my servant Job has. 8 So now take sev-
en bulls and seven rams and go to my ser-
vant Job and sacrifice a burnt offering for
yourselves. My servant Job will pray for you,
and I will accept his prayer and not deal with
you according to your folly. You have not
spoken the truth about me, as my servant
Job has." 9 So Eliphaz the Temanite, Bildad
the Shuhite and Zophar the Naamathite did
what the LORD told them; and the LORD ac-
cepted Job's prayer.

10 After Job had prayed for his friends,
the LORD restored his fortunes and gave
him twice as much as he had before. 11 All
his brothers and sisters and everyone who
had known him before came and ate with
him in his house. They comforted and con-
soled him over all the trouble the LORD had
brought on him, and each one gave him a
piece of silver[a] and a gold ring.

12 The LORD blessed the latter part of Job's
life more than the former part. He had four-
teen thousand sheep, six thousand camels,
a thousand yoke of oxen and a thousand
donkeys. 13 And he also had seven sons and
three daughters. 14 The first daughter he
named Jemimah, the second Keziah and
the third Keren-Happuch. 15 Nowhere in all
the land were there found women as beau-
tiful as Job's daughters, and their father
granted them an inheritance along with
their brothers.

16 After this, Job lived a hundred and forty
years; he saw his children and their children
to the fourth generation. 17 And so Job died,
an old man and full of years.

[a] 11 Hebrew *him a kesitah;* a kesitah was a unit of money of unknown weight and value.

PSALMS

BOOK I

Psalms 1–41

Psalm 1

[1] Blessed is the one
who does not walk in step with the wicked
or stand in the way that sinners take
or sit in the company of mockers,
[2] but whose delight is in the law of the LORD,
and who meditates on his law day and night.
[3] That person is like a tree planted by streams of water,
which yields its fruit in season
and whose leaf does not wither—
whatever they do prospers.

[4] Not so the wicked!
They are like chaff
that the wind blows away.
[5] Therefore the wicked will not stand in the judgment,
nor sinners in the assembly of the righteous.

[6] For the LORD watches over the way of the righteous,
but the way of the wicked leads to destruction.

Psalm 2

[1] Why do the nations conspire[a]
and the peoples plot in vain?
[2] The kings of the earth rise up
and the rulers band together
against the LORD and against his anointed, saying,
[3] "Let us break their chains
and throw off their shackles."

[4] The One enthroned in heaven laughs;
the Lord scoffs at them.
[5] He rebukes them in his anger
and terrifies them in his wrath, saying,
[6] "I have installed my king
on Zion, my holy mountain."

[7] I will proclaim the LORD's decree:

He said to me, "You are my son;
today I have become your father.
[8] Ask me,
and I will make the nations your inheritance,
the ends of the earth your possession.
[9] You will break them with a rod of iron[b];
you will dash them to pieces like pottery."

[10] Therefore, you kings, be wise;
be warned, you rulers of the earth.
[11] Serve the LORD with fear
and celebrate his rule with trembling.
[12] Kiss his son, or he will be angry
and your way will lead to your destruction,
for his wrath can flare up in a moment.
Blessed are all who take refuge in him.

Psalm 3[c]

A psalm of David. When he fled from his son Absalom.

[1] LORD, how many are my foes!
How many rise up against me!
[2] Many are saying of me,
"God will not deliver him."[d]

[3] But you, LORD, are a shield around me,
my glory, the One who lifts my head high.
[4] I call out to the LORD,
and he answers me from his holy mountain.

[5] I lie down and sleep;
I wake again, because the LORD sustains me.

[a] *1* Hebrew; Septuagint *rage* [b] 9 Or *will rule them with an iron scepter* (see Septuagint and Syriac) [c] In Hebrew texts 3:1-8 is numbered 3:2-9. [d] *2* The Hebrew has *Selah* (a word of uncertain meaning) here and at the end of verses 4 and 8.

6 I will not fear though tens of thousands
assail me on every side.

7 Arise, LORD!
Deliver me, my God!
Strike all my enemies on the jaw;
break the teeth of the wicked.

8 From the LORD comes deliverance.
May your blessing be on your people.

Psalm 4[a]

For the director of music.
With stringed instruments. A psalm of David.

1 Answer me when I call to you,
my righteous God.
Give me relief from my distress;
have mercy on me and hear my prayer.

2 How long will you people turn my glory
into shame?
How long will you love delusions and
seek false gods[b]?[c]
3 Know that the LORD has set apart his
faithful servant for himself;
the LORD hears when I call to him.

4 Tremble and[d] do not sin;
when you are on your beds,
search your hearts and be silent.
5 Offer the sacrifices of the righteous
and trust in the LORD.

6 Many, LORD, are asking, "Who will bring
us prosperity?"
Let the light of your face shine on us.
7 Fill my heart with joy
when their grain and new wine abound.

8 In peace I will lie down and sleep,
for you alone, LORD,
make me dwell in safety.

Psalm 5[e]

For the director of music. For pipes.
A psalm of David.

1 Listen to my words, LORD,
consider my lament.
2 Hear my cry for help,
my King and my God,
for to you I pray.

3 In the morning, LORD, you hear my
voice;
in the morning I lay my requests
before you
and wait expectantly.
4 For you are not a God who is pleased with
wickedness;
with you, evil people are not welcome.
5 The arrogant cannot stand
in your presence.
You hate all who do wrong;
6 you destroy those who tell lies.
The bloodthirsty and deceitful
you, LORD, detest.
7 But I, by your great love,
can come into your house;
in reverence I bow down
toward your holy temple.

8 Lead me, LORD, in your righteousness
because of my enemies —
make your way straight before me.
9 Not a word from their mouth can be
trusted;
their heart is filled with malice.
Their throat is an open grave;
with their tongues they tell lies.
10 Declare them guilty, O God!
Let their intrigues be their downfall.
Banish them for their many sins,
for they have rebelled against you.
11 But let all who take refuge in you be glad;
let them ever sing for joy.
Spread your protection over them,
that those who love your name may
rejoice in you.

12 Surely, LORD, you bless the righteous;
you surround them with your favor as
with a shield.

Psalm 6[f]

For the director of music. With stringed instruments. According to sheminith.[g]
A psalm of David.

1 LORD, do not rebuke me in your anger
or discipline me in your wrath.
2 Have mercy on me, LORD, for I am faint;
heal me, LORD, for my bones are in
agony.
3 My soul is in deep anguish.
How long, LORD, how long?

[a] In Hebrew texts 4:1-8 is numbered 4:2-9. [b] 2 Or *seek lies* [c] 2 The Hebrew has *Selah* (a word of uncertain meaning) here and at the end of verse 4. [d] 4 Or *In your anger* (see Septuagint) [e] In Hebrew texts 5:1-12 is numbered 5:2-13. [f] In Hebrew texts 6:1-10 is numbered 6:2-11. [g] Title: Probably a musical term

[4] Turn, LORD, and deliver me;
save me because of your unfailing love.
[5] Among the dead no one proclaims
your name.
Who praises you from the grave?

[6] I am worn out from my groaning.

All night long I flood my bed with weeping
and drench my couch with tears.
[7] My eyes grow weak with sorrow;
they fail because of all my foes.

[8] Away from me, all you who do evil,
for the LORD has heard my weeping.
[9] The LORD has heard my cry for mercy;
the LORD accepts my prayer.
[10] All my enemies will be overwhelmed
with shame and anguish;
they will turn back and suddenly be
put to shame.

Psalm 7[a]

A shiggaion[b] *of David,*
which he sang to the LORD concerning
Cush, a Benjamite.

[1] LORD my God, I take refuge in you;
save and deliver me from all who
pursue me,
[2] or they will tear me apart like a lion
and rip me to pieces with no one to
rescue me.

[3] LORD my God, if I have done this
and there is guilt on my hands—
[4] if I have repaid my ally with evil
or without cause have robbed my foe—
[5] then let my enemy pursue and
overtake me;
let him trample my life to the ground
and make me sleep in the dust.[c]

[6] Arise, LORD, in your anger;
rise up against the rage of my enemies.
Awake, my God; decree justice.
[7] Let the assembled peoples gather
around you,
while you sit enthroned over them
on high.
[8] Let the LORD judge the peoples.
Vindicate me, LORD, according to my
righteousness,
according to my integrity, O Most High.
[9] Bring to an end the violence of the wicked
and make the righteous secure—
you, the righteous God
who probes minds and hearts.

[10] My shield[d] is God Most High,
who saves the upright in heart.
[11] God is a righteous judge,
a God who displays his wrath every day.
[12] If he does not relent,
he[e] will sharpen his sword;
he will bend and string his bow.
[13] He has prepared his deadly weapons;
he makes ready his flaming arrows.

[14] Whoever is pregnant with evil
conceives trouble and gives birth to
disillusionment.
[15] Whoever digs a hole and scoops it out
falls into the pit they have made.
[16] The trouble they cause recoils on them;
their violence comes down on their
own heads.

[17] I will give thanks to the LORD because of
his righteousness;
I will sing the praises of the name of
the LORD Most High.

Psalm 8[f]

For the director of music. According to gittith.[g]
A psalm of David.

[1] LORD, our Lord,
how majestic is your name in all the
earth!

You have set your glory
in the heavens.
[2] Through the praise of children and
infants
you have established a stronghold
against your enemies,
to silence the foe and the avenger.
[3] When I consider your heavens,
the work of your fingers,
the moon and the stars,
which you have set in place,
[4] what is mankind that you are mindful of
them,
human beings that you care for them?[h]

[a] In Hebrew texts 7:1-17 is numbered 7:2-18. [b] Title: Probably a literary or musical term [c] 5 The Hebrew has *Selah* (a word of uncertain meaning) here. [d] 10 Or *sovereign* [e] 12 Or *If anyone does not repent, / God* [f] In Hebrew texts 8:1-9 is numbered 8:2-10. [g] Title: Probably a musical term
[h] 4 Or *what is a human being that you are mindful of him, / a son of man that you care for him?*

[5]You have made them[a] a little lower than
the angels[b]
and crowned them[a] with glory and
honor.
[6]You made them rulers over the works of
your hands;
you put everything under their[c] feet:
[7]all flocks and herds,
and the animals of the wild,
[8]the birds in the sky,
and the fish in the sea,
all that swim the paths of the seas.

[9]LORD, our Lord,
how majestic is your name in all
the earth!

Psalm 9[d,e]

For the director of music.
To the tune of "The Death of the Son."
A psalm of David.

[1]I will give thanks to you, LORD, with all
my heart;
I will tell of all your wonderful deeds.
[2]I will be glad and rejoice in you;
I will sing the praises of your name,
O Most High.

[3]My enemies turn back;
they stumble and perish before you.
[4]For you have upheld my right and my
cause,
sitting enthroned as the righteous
judge.
[5]You have rebuked the nations and
destroyed the wicked;
you have blotted out their name for
ever and ever.
[6]Endless ruin has overtaken my enemies,
you have uprooted their cities;
even the memory of them has
perished.

[7]The LORD reigns forever;
he has established his throne for
judgment.
[8]He rules the world in righteousness
and judges the peoples with equity.
[9]The LORD is a refuge for the oppressed,
a stronghold in times of trouble.
[10]Those who know your name trust in you,
for you, LORD, have never forsaken
those who seek you.

[11]Sing the praises of the LORD, enthroned
in Zion;
proclaim among the nations what he
has done.
[12]For he who avenges blood remembers;
he does not ignore the cries of the
afflicted.

[13]LORD, see how my enemies persecute me!
Have mercy and lift me up from the
gates of death,
[14]that I may declare your praises
in the gates of Daughter Zion,
and there rejoice in your salvation.

[15]The nations have fallen into the pit they
have dug;
their feet are caught in the net they
have hidden.
[16]The LORD is known by his acts of justice;
the wicked are ensnared by the work of
their hands.[f]
[17]The wicked go down to the realm of
the dead,
all the nations that forget God.
[18]But God will never forget the needy;
the hope of the afflicted will never
perish.

[19]Arise, LORD, do not let mortals triumph;
let the nations be judged in your
presence.
[20]Strike them with terror, LORD;
let the nations know they are only
mortal.

Psalm 10[d]

[1]Why, LORD, do you stand far off?
Why do you hide yourself in times of
trouble?

[2]In his arrogance the wicked man hunts
down the weak,
who are caught in the schemes he
devises.
[3]He boasts about the cravings of his
heart;

[a] 5 Or *him* [b] 5 Or *than God* [c] 6 Or *made him ruler . . . ; / . . . his* [d] Psalms 9 and 10 may originally have been a single acrostic poem in which alternating lines began with the successive letters of the Hebrew alphabet. In the Septuagint they constitute one psalm. [e] In Hebrew texts 9:1-20 is numbered 9:2-21. [f] 16 The Hebrew has *Higgaion* and *Selah* (words of uncertain meaning) here; *Selah* occurs also at the end of verse 20.

he blesses the greedy and reviles the
LORD.
4 In his pride the wicked man does not
seek him;
in all his thoughts there is no room
for God.
5 His ways are always prosperous;
your laws are rejected by[a] him;
he sneers at all his enemies.
6 He says to himself, "Nothing will ever
shake me."
He swears, "No one will ever do me
harm."

7 His mouth is full of lies and threats;
trouble and evil are under his tongue.
8 He lies in wait near the villages;
from ambush he murders the
innocent.
His eyes watch in secret for his victims;
9 like a lion in cover he lies in wait.
He lies in wait to catch the helpless;
he catches the helpless and drags them
off in his net.
10 His victims are crushed, they collapse;
they fall under his strength.
11 He says to himself, "God will never notice;
he covers his face and never sees."

12 Arise, LORD! Lift up your hand, O God.
Do not forget the helpless.
13 Why does the wicked man revile God?
Why does he say to himself,
"He won't call me to account"?
14 But you, God, see the trouble of the
afflicted;
you consider their grief and take it
in hand.
The victims commit themselves to you;
you are the helper of the fatherless.
15 Break the arm of the wicked man;
call the evildoer to account for his
wickedness
that would not otherwise be found out.

16 The LORD is King for ever and ever;
the nations will perish from his land.
17 You, LORD, hear the desire of the
afflicted;
you encourage them, and you listen to
their cry,
18 defending the fatherless and the
oppressed,
so that mere earthly mortals
will never again strike terror.

Psalm 11

For the director of music. Of David.

1 In the LORD I take refuge.
How then can you say to me:
"Flee like a bird to your mountain.
2 For look, the wicked bend their bows;
they set their arrows against the
strings
to shoot from the shadows
at the upright in heart.
3 When the foundations are being
destroyed,
what can the righteous do?"

4 The LORD is in his holy temple;
the LORD is on his heavenly throne.
He observes everyone on earth;
his eyes examine them.
5 The LORD examines the righteous,
but the wicked, those who love
violence,
he hates with a passion.
6 On the wicked he will rain
fiery coals and burning sulfur;
a scorching wind will be their lot.

7 For the LORD is righteous,
he loves justice;
the upright will see his face.

Psalm 12[b]

For the director of music.
According to sheminith.[c] *A psalm of David.*

1 Help, LORD, for no one is faithful anymore;
those who are loyal have vanished
from the human race.
2 Everyone lies to their neighbor;
they flatter with their lips
but harbor deception in their hearts.

3 May the LORD silence all flattering lips
and every boastful tongue —
4 those who say,
"By our tongues we will prevail;
our own lips will defend us — who is
lord over us?"

5 "Because the poor are plundered and the
needy groan,

[a] 5 See Septuagint; Hebrew / *they are haughty, and your laws are far from* [b] In Hebrew texts 12:1-8 is numbered 12:2-9. [c] Title: Probably a musical term

WE FALL DOWN

Chris Tomlin

We fall down, we lay our crowns
At the feet of Jesus
The greatness of mercy and love
At the feet of Jesus

And we cry holy, holy, holy
And we cry holy, holy, holy
And we cry holy, holy, holy is the Lamb

THE INSPIRATION

"'Holy, holy, holy is the Lord God Almighty,' who was, and is, and is to come."
— Revelation 4:8

Read also: Isaiah 6:3; Psalm 51:1; Revelation 4:1 – 11

BEHIND THE SONG

In 1998, Chris Tomlin was an independent musician who traveled around Texas leading worship at various camps. One week he found himself at a camp where Louie Giglio was teaching a lesson based on Revelation 4, in which the apostle John shares a vision of worship happening around the throne of God. Tomlin was deeply moved.

"This is reality," he says. "It's not what will be, way off in the future, or what was. This is what's happening right now."

When the evening was over Tomlin went to his room, opened his Bible and began singing right from the text. At about 3:00 a.m. he decided he needed to play the song immediately for Giglio, whom he had just met and who happened to be staying in the room next door. Fortunately Giglio, though surprised to be awakened by the camp singer, allowed him to sing the song. When Tomlin finished, Giglio stared at him, eventually saying something that caught the young artist completely off guard. "Chris," he said, "I think the whole world is going to sing that song."

"I was just hoping we could sing it tomorrow at camp." Tomlin laughed. "I don't know anything about the whole world!"

The song did go on to become one of the most widely sung worship songs in the history of the church. The song also marked the beginning of a working relationship between Tomlin and Giglio that continues to this day.

Tomlin fully recognizes that the Lord arranged the meeting between him and Giglio at the camp and delivered that song. "God will put you where he wants to," he confesses. "He'll move mountains to put you where he wants you."

Selah

At the heart of the fantastic images in Revelation 4 is the act of worship. We know from the text that the incredible, supernatural creatures that surround the throne of God sing this same, simple chorus: "Holy, holy, holy." If you feel that you have no words to express your worship, try speaking or singing the text of Revelation 4 and know that you are truly singing with the angels.

I will now arise," says the LORD.
"I will protect them from those who malign them."
[6] And the words of the LORD are flawless,
like silver purified in a crucible,
like gold[a] refined seven times.

[7] You, LORD, will keep the needy safe
and will protect us forever from the wicked,
[8] who freely strut about
when what is vile is honored by the human race.

Psalm 13[b]

For the director of music. A psalm of David.

[1] How long, LORD? Will you forget me forever?
How long will you hide your face from me?
[2] How long must I wrestle with my thoughts
and day after day have sorrow in my heart?
How long will my enemy triumph over me?

[3] Look on me and answer, LORD my God.
Give light to my eyes, or I will sleep in death,
[4] and my enemy will say, "I have overcome him,"
and my foes will rejoice when I fall.

[5] But I trust in your unfailing love;
my heart rejoices in your salvation.
[6] I will sing the LORD's praise,
for he has been good to me.

Psalm 14

For the director of music. Of David.

[1] The fool[c] says in his heart,
"There is no God."
They are corrupt, their deeds are vile;
there is no one who does good.

[2] The LORD looks down from heaven on all mankind
to see if there are any who understand,
any who seek God.
[3] All have turned away, all have become corrupt;
there is no one who does good,
not even one.

[4] Do all these evildoers know nothing?

They devour my people as though eating bread;
they never call on the LORD.
[5] But there they are, overwhelmed with dread,
for God is present in the company of the righteous.
[6] You evildoers frustrate the plans of the poor,
but the LORD is their refuge.

[7] Oh, that salvation for Israel would come out of Zion!
When the LORD restores his people,
let Jacob rejoice and Israel be glad!

Psalm 15

A psalm of David.

[1] LORD, who may dwell in your sacred tent?
Who may live on your holy mountain?

[2] The one whose walk is blameless,
who does what is righteous,
who speaks the truth from their heart;
[3] whose tongue utters no slander,
who does no wrong to a neighbor,
and casts no slur on others;
[4] who despises a vile person
but honors those who fear the LORD;
who keeps an oath even when it hurts,
and does not change their mind;
[5] who lends money to the poor without interest;
who does not accept a bribe against the innocent.

Whoever does these things
will never be shaken.

Psalm 16

A miktam[d] of David.

[1] Keep me safe, my God,
for in you I take refuge.

[2] I say to the LORD, "You are my Lord;
apart from you I have no good thing."

[a] *6* Probable reading of the original Hebrew text; Masoretic Text *earth* [b] In Hebrew texts 13:1-6 is numbered 13:2-6. [c] *1* The Hebrew words rendered *fool* in Psalms denote one who is morally deficient. [d] Title: Probably a literary or musical term

[3] I say of the holy people who are in the land,
"They are the noble ones in whom is all my delight."
[4] Those who run after other gods will suffer more and more.
I will not pour out libations of blood to such gods
or take up their names on my lips.

[5] LORD, you alone are my portion and my cup;
you make my lot secure.
[6] The boundary lines have fallen for me in pleasant places;
surely I have a delightful inheritance.
[7] I will praise the LORD, who counsels me;
even at night my heart instructs me.
[8] I keep my eyes always on the LORD.
With him at my right hand, I will not be shaken.

[9] Therefore my heart is glad and my tongue rejoices;
my body also will rest secure,
[10] because you will not abandon me to the realm of the dead,
nor will you let your faithful[a] one see decay.
[11] You make known to me the path of life
you will fill me with joy in your presence,
with eternal pleasures at your right hand.

Psalm 17

A prayer of David.

[1] Hear me, LORD, my plea is just;
listen to my cry.
Hear my prayer—
it does not rise from deceitful lips.
[2] Let my vindication come from you;
may your eyes see what is right.

[3] Though you probe my heart,
though you examine me at night and test me,
you will find that I have planned no evil;
my mouth has not transgressed.
[4] Though people tried to bribe me,
I have kept myself from the ways of the violent
through what your lips have commanded.

[5] My steps have held to your paths;
my feet have not stumbled.

[6] I call on you, my God, for you will answer me;
turn your ear to me and hear my prayer.
[7] Show me the wonders of your great love,
you who save by your right hand
those who take refuge in you from their foes.
[8] Keep me as the apple of your eye;
hide me in the shadow of your wings
[9] from the wicked who are out to destroy me,
from my mortal enemies who surround me.

[10] They close up their callous hearts,
and their mouths speak with arrogance.
[11] They have tracked me down, they now surround me,
with eyes alert, to throw me to the ground.
[12] They are like a lion hungry for prey,
like a fierce lion crouching in cover.

[13] Rise up, LORD, confront them, bring them down;
with your sword rescue me from the wicked.
[14] By your hand save me from such people, LORD,
from those of this world whose reward is in this life.
May what you have stored up for the wicked fill their bellies;
may their children gorge themselves on it,
and may there be leftovers for their little ones.

[15] As for me, I will be vindicated and will see your face;
when I awake, I will be satisfied with seeing your likeness.

Psalm 18[b]

For the director of music. Of David the servant of the LORD. He sang to the LORD the words of this song when the LORD delivered him from the hand of all his enemies and from the hand of Saul. He said:

[1] I love you, LORD, my strength.

[2] The LORD is my rock, my fortress and my deliverer;

[a] *10* Or *holy* [b] In Hebrew texts 18:1-50 is numbered 18:2-51.

my God is my rock, in whom I take
refuge,
my shield[a] and the horn[b] of my
salvation, my stronghold.

[3] I called to the LORD, who is worthy of
praise,
and I have been saved from my
enemies.
[4] The cords of death entangled me;
the torrents of destruction
overwhelmed me.
[5] The cords of the grave coiled around me;
the snares of death confronted me.

[6] In my distress I called to the LORD;
I cried to my God for help.
From his temple he heard my voice;
my cry came before him, into his ears.
[7] The earth trembled and quaked,
and the foundations of the mountains
shook;
they trembled because he was angry.
[8] Smoke rose from his nostrils;
consuming fire came from his mouth,
burning coals blazed out of it.
[9] He parted the heavens and came down;
dark clouds were under his feet.
[10] He mounted the cherubim and flew;
he soared on the wings of the wind.
[11] He made darkness his covering, his
canopy around him—
the dark rain clouds of the sky.
[12] Out of the brightness of his presence
clouds advanced,
with hailstones and bolts of lightning.
[13] The LORD thundered from heaven;
the voice of the Most High resounded.[c]
[14] He shot his arrows and scattered the
enemy,
with great bolts of lightning he routed
them.
[15] The valleys of the sea were exposed
and the foundations of the earth laid
bare
at your rebuke, LORD,
at the blast of breath from your
nostrils.

[16] He reached down from on high and took
hold of me;
he drew me out of deep waters.
[17] He rescued me from my powerful enemy,
from my foes, who were too strong
for me.
[18] They confronted me in the day of my
disaster,
but the LORD was my support.
[19] He brought me out into a spacious place;
he rescued me because he delighted
in me.

[20] The LORD has dealt with me according to
my righteousness;
according to the cleanness of my
hands he has rewarded me.
[21] For I have kept the ways of the LORD;
I am not guilty of turning from my God.
[22] All his laws are before me;
I have not turned away from his
decrees.
[23] I have been blameless before him
and have kept myself from sin.
[24] The LORD has rewarded me according to
my righteousness,
according to the cleanness of my
hands in his sight.

[25] To the faithful you show yourself faithful,
to the blameless you show yourself
blameless,
[26] to the pure you show yourself pure,
but to the devious you show yourself
shrewd.
[27] You save the humble
but bring low those whose eyes are
haughty.
[28] You, LORD, keep my lamp burning;
my God turns my darkness into light.
[29] With your help I can advance against
a troop[d];
with my God I can scale a wall.

[30] As for God, his way is perfect:
The LORD's word is flawless;
he shields all who take refuge in him.
[31] For who is God besides the LORD?
And who is the Rock except our God?
[32] It is God who arms me with strength
and keeps my way secure.
[33] He makes my feet like the feet of a deer;
he causes me to stand on the heights.
[34] He trains my hands for battle;
my arms can bend a bow of bronze.

[a] 2 Or *sovereign* [b] 2 *Horn* here symbolizes strength. [c] 13 Some Hebrew manuscripts and Septuagint (see also 2 Samuel 22:14); most Hebrew manuscripts *resounded, / amid hailstones and bolts of lightning* [d] 29 Or *can run through a barricade*

[35]You make your saving help my shield,
and your right hand sustains me;
your help has made me great.
[36]You provide a broad path for my feet,
so that my ankles do not give way.

[37]I pursued my enemies and overtook them;
I did not turn back till they were destroyed.
[38]I crushed them so that they could not rise;
they fell beneath my feet.
[39]You armed me with strength for battle;
you humbled my adversaries before me.
[40]You made my enemies turn their backs in flight,
and I destroyed my foes.
[41]They cried for help, but there was no one to save them—
to the LORD, but he did not answer.
[42]I beat them as fine as windblown dust;
I trampled them[a] like mud in the streets.
[43]You have delivered me from the attacks of the people;
you have made me the head of nations.
People I did not know now serve me,
44 foreigners cower before me;
as soon as they hear of me, they obey me.
[45]They all lose heart;
they come trembling from their strongholds.

[46]The LORD lives! Praise be to my Rock!
Exalted be God my Savior!
[47]He is the God who avenges me,
who subdues nations under me,
48 who saves me from my enemies.
You exalted me above my foes;
from a violent man you rescued me.
[49]Therefore I will praise you, LORD, among the nations;
I will sing the praises of your name.

[50]He gives his king great victories;
he shows unfailing love to his anointed,
to David and to his descendants forever.

Psalm 19[b]

For the director of music. A psalm of David.

[1]The heavens declare the glory of God;
the skies proclaim the work of his hands.
[2]Day after day they pour forth speech;
night after night they reveal knowledge.
[3]They have no speech, they use no words;
no sound is heard from them.
[4]Yet their voice[c] goes out into all the earth,
their words to the ends of the world.
In the heavens God has pitched a tent for the sun.
5 It is like a bridegroom coming out of his chamber,
like a champion rejoicing to run his course.
[6]It rises at one end of the heavens
and makes its circuit to the other;
nothing is deprived of its warmth.

[7]The law of the LORD is perfect,
refreshing the soul.
The statutes of the LORD are trustworthy,
making wise the simple.
[8]The precepts of the LORD are right,
giving joy to the heart.
The commands of the LORD are radiant,
giving light to the eyes.
[9]The fear of the LORD is pure,
enduring forever.
The decrees of the LORD are firm,
and all of them are righteous.

[10]They are more precious than gold,
than much pure gold;
they are sweeter than honey,
than honey from the honeycomb.
[11]By them your servant is warned;
in keeping them there is great reward.
[12]But who can discern their own errors?
Forgive my hidden faults.
[13]Keep your servant also from willful sins;
may they not rule over me.
Then I will be blameless,
innocent of great transgression.

[14]May these words of my mouth and this meditation of my heart
be pleasing in your sight,
LORD, my Rock and my Redeemer.

[a] *42* Many Hebrew manuscripts, Septuagint, Syriac and Targum (see also 2 Samuel 22:43); Masoretic Text *I poured them out* [b] In Hebrew texts 19:1-14 is numbered 19:2-15. [c] *4* Septuagint, Jerome and Syriac; Hebrew *measuring line*

Psalm 20[a]

For the director of music. A psalm of David.

1 May the LORD answer you when you are
in distress;
may the name of the God of Jacob
protect you.
2 May he send you help from the sanctuary
and grant you support from Zion.
3 May he remember all your sacrifices
and accept your burnt offerings.[b]
4 May he give you the desire of your heart
and make all your plans succeed.
5 May we shout for joy over your victory
and lift up our banners in the name of
our God.

May the LORD grant all your requests.

6 Now this I know:
The LORD gives victory to his anointed.
He answers him from his heavenly
sanctuary
with the victorious power of his right
hand.
7 Some trust in chariots and some in
horses,
but we trust in the name of the LORD
our God.
8 They are brought to their knees and fall,
but we rise up and stand firm.
9 LORD, give victory to the king!
Answer us when we call!

Psalm 21[c]

For the director of music. A psalm of David.

1 The king rejoices in your strength, LORD.
How great is his joy in the victories
you give!
2 You have granted him his heart's desire
and have not withheld the request of
his lips.[b]
3 You came to greet him with rich blessings
and placed a crown of pure gold on his
head.
4 He asked you for life, and you gave it
to him—
length of days, for ever and ever.
5 Through the victories you gave, his glory
is great;
you have bestowed on him splendor
and majesty.
6 Surely you have granted him unending
blessings
and made him glad with the joy of your
presence.
7 For the king trusts in the LORD;
through the unfailing love of the Most
High
he will not be shaken.

8 Your hand will lay hold on all your
enemies;
your right hand will seize your foes.
9 When you appear for battle,
you will burn them up as in a blazing
furnace.
The LORD will swallow them up in his
wrath,
and his fire will consume them.
10 You will destroy their descendants from
the earth,
their posterity from mankind.
11 Though they plot evil against you
and devise wicked schemes, they
cannot succeed.
12 You will make them turn their backs
when you aim at them with drawn
bow.

13 Be exalted in your strength, LORD;
we will sing and praise your might.

Psalm 22[d]

For the director of music. To the tune of "The Doe of the Morning." A psalm of David.

1 My God, my God, why have you
forsaken me?
Why are you so far from saving me,
so far from my cries of anguish?
2 My God, I cry out by day, but you do not
answer,
by night, but I find no rest.[e]

3 Yet you are enthroned as the Holy One;
you are the one Israel praises.[f]
4 In you our ancestors put their trust;
they trusted and you delivered them.
5 To you they cried out and were saved;
in you they trusted and were not put
to shame.

[a] In Hebrew texts 20:1-9 is numbered 20:2-10. [b] *3,2* The Hebrew has *Selah* (a word of uncertain meaning) here. [c] In Hebrew texts 21:1-13 is numbered 21:2-14. [d] In Hebrew texts 22:1-31 is numbered 22:2-32. [e] *2* Or *night, and am not silent* [f] *3* Or *Yet you are holy, / enthroned on the praises of Israel*

6 But I am a worm and not a man,
scorned by everyone, despised by the people.
7 All who see me mock me;
they hurl insults, shaking their heads.
8 "He trusts in the LORD," they say,
"let the LORD rescue him.
Let him deliver him,
since he delights in him."

9 Yet you brought me out of the womb;
you made me trust in you, even at my mother's breast.
10 From birth I was cast on you;
from my mother's womb you have been my God.

11 Do not be far from me,
for trouble is near
and there is no one to help.

12 Many bulls surround me;
strong bulls of Bashan encircle me.
13 Roaring lions that tear their prey
open their mouths wide against me.
14 I am poured out like water,
and all my bones are out of joint.
My heart has turned to wax;
it has melted within me.
15 My mouth[a] is dried up like a potsherd,
and my tongue sticks to the roof of my mouth;
you lay me in the dust of death.

16 Dogs surround me,
a pack of villains encircles me;
they pierce[b] my hands and my feet.
17 All my bones are on display;
people stare and gloat over me.
18 They divide my clothes among them
and cast lots for my garment.

19 But you, LORD, do not be far from me.
You are my strength; come quickly to help me.
20 Deliver me from the sword,
my precious life from the power of the dogs.
21 Rescue me from the mouth of the lions;
save me from the horns of the wild oxen.

22 I will declare your name to my people;
in the assembly I will praise you.
23 You who fear the LORD, praise him!
All you descendants of Jacob, honor him!
Revere him, all you descendants of Israel!
24 For he has not despised or scorned
the suffering of the afflicted one;
he has not hidden his face from him
but has listened to his cry for help.

25 From you comes the theme of my praise
in the great assembly;
before those who fear you[c] I will fulfill my vows.
26 The poor will eat and be satisfied;
those who seek the LORD will praise him—
may your hearts live forever!
27 All the ends of the earth
will remember and turn to the LORD,
and all the families of the nations
will bow down before him,
28 for dominion belongs to the LORD
and he rules over the nations.

29 All the rich of the earth will feast and worship;
all who go down to the dust will kneel before him—
those who cannot keep themselves alive.
30 Posterity will serve him;
future generations will be told about the Lord.
31 They will proclaim his righteousness,
declaring to a people yet unborn:
He has done it!

Psalm 23

A psalm of David.

1 The LORD is my shepherd, I lack nothing.
2 He makes me lie down in green pastures,
he leads me beside quiet waters,
3 he refreshes my soul.
He guides me along the right paths
for his name's sake.

[a] *15* Probable reading of the original Hebrew text; Masoretic Text *strength* [b] *16* Dead Sea Scrolls and some manuscripts of the Masoretic Text, Septuagint and Syriac; most manuscripts of the Masoretic Text *me, / like a lion* [c] *25* Hebrew *him*

[4]Even though I walk
through the darkest valley,[a]
I will fear no evil,
for you are with me;
your rod and your staff,
they comfort me.

[5]You prepare a table before me
in the presence of my enemies.
You anoint my head with oil;
my cup overflows.
[6]Surely your goodness and love will
follow me
all the days of my life,
and I will dwell in the house of the LORD
forever.

Psalm 24

Of David. A psalm.

[1]The earth is the LORD's, and everything
in it,
the world, and all who live in it;
[2]for he founded it on the seas
and established it on the waters.

[3]Who may ascend the mountain of the
LORD?
Who may stand in his holy place?
[4]The one who has clean hands and a
pure heart,
who does not trust in an idol
or swear by a false god.[b]

[5]They will receive blessing from the LORD
and vindication from God their Savior.
[6]Such is the generation of those who
seek him,
who seek your face, God of Jacob.[c,d]

[7]Lift up your heads, you gates;
be lifted up, you ancient doors,
that the King of glory may come in.
[8]Who is this King of glory?
The LORD strong and mighty,
the LORD mighty in battle.
[9]Lift up your heads, you gates;
lift them up, you ancient doors,
that the King of glory may come in.
[10]Who is he, this King of glory?
The LORD Almighty—
he is the King of glory.

Psalm 25[e]

Of David.

[1]In you, LORD my God,
I put my trust.

[2]I trust in you;
do not let me be put to shame,
nor let my enemies triumph over me.
[3]No one who hopes in you
will ever be put to shame,
but shame will come on those
who are treacherous without cause.

[4]Show me your ways, LORD,
teach me your paths.
[5]Guide me in your truth and teach me,
for you are God my Savior,
and my hope is in you all day long.
[6]Remember, LORD, your great mercy
and love,
for they are from of old.
[7]Do not remember the sins of my youth
and my rebellious ways;
according to your love remember me,
for you, LORD, are good.

[8]Good and upright is the LORD;
therefore he instructs sinners in
his ways.
[9]He guides the humble in what is right
and teaches them his way.
[10]All the ways of the LORD are loving and
faithful
toward those who keep the demands of
his covenant.
[11]For the sake of your name, LORD,
forgive my iniquity, though it is great.

[12]Who, then, are those who fear the LORD?
He will instruct them in the ways they
should choose.[f]
[13]They will spend their days in prosperity,
and their descendants will inherit
the land.
[14]The LORD confides in those who fear him;
he makes his covenant known
to them.
[15]My eyes are ever on the LORD,
for only he will release my feet from
the snare.

[a] 4 Or *the valley of the shadow of death* [b] 4 Or *swear falsely* [c] 6 Two Hebrew manuscripts and Syriac (see also Septuagint); most Hebrew manuscripts *face, Jacob* [d] 6 The Hebrew has *Selah* (a word of uncertain meaning) here and at the end of verse 10. [e] This psalm is an acrostic poem, the verses of which begin with the successive letters of the Hebrew alphabet. [f] 12 Or *ways he chooses*

[16]Turn to me and be gracious to me,
for I am lonely and afflicted.
[17]Relieve the troubles of my heart
and free me from my anguish.
[18]Look on my affliction and my distress
and take away all my sins.
[19]See how numerous are my enemies
and how fiercely they hate me!

[20]Guard my life and rescue me;
do not let me be put to shame,
for I take refuge in you.
[21]May integrity and uprightness
protect me,
because my hope, LORD,[a] is in you.

[22]Deliver Israel, O God,
from all their troubles!

Psalm 26

Of David.

[1]Vindicate me, LORD,
for I have led a blameless life;
I have trusted in the LORD
and have not faltered.
[2]Test me, LORD, and try me,
examine my heart and my mind;
[3]for I have always been mindful of your
unfailing love
and have lived in reliance on your
faithfulness.

[4]I do not sit with the deceitful,
nor do I associate with hypocrites.
[5]I abhor the assembly of evildoers
and refuse to sit with the wicked.
[6]I wash my hands in innocence,
and go about your altar, LORD,
[7]proclaiming aloud your praise
and telling of all your wonderful deeds.

[8]LORD, I love the house where you live,
the place where your glory dwells.
[9]Do not take away my soul along with
sinners,
my life with those who are
bloodthirsty,
[10]in whose hands are wicked schemes,
whose right hands are full of bribes.
[11]I lead a blameless life;
deliver me and be merciful to me.

[12]My feet stand on level ground;
in the great congregation I will praise
the LORD.

Psalm 27

Of David.

[1]The LORD is my light and my salvation —
whom shall I fear?
The LORD is the stronghold of my life —
of whom shall I be afraid?

[2]When the wicked advance against me
to devour[b] me,
it is my enemies and my foes
who will stumble and fall.
[3]Though an army besiege me,
my heart will not fear;
though war break out against me,
even then I will be confident.

[4]One thing I ask from the LORD,
this only do I seek:
that I may dwell in the house of the LORD
all the days of my life,
to gaze on the beauty of the LORD
and to seek him in his temple.
[5]For in the day of trouble
he will keep me safe in his dwelling;
he will hide me in the shelter of his
sacred tent
and set me high upon a rock.

[6]Then my head will be exalted
above the enemies who surround me;
at his sacred tent I will sacrifice with
shouts of joy;
I will sing and make music to the
LORD.

[7]Hear my voice when I call, LORD;
be merciful to me and answer me.
[8]My heart says of you, "Seek his face!"
Your face, LORD, I will seek.
[9]Do not hide your face from me,
do not turn your servant away in anger;
you have been my helper.
Do not reject me or forsake me,
God my Savior.
[10]Though my father and mother
forsake me,
the LORD will receive me.
[11]Teach me your way, LORD;
lead me in a straight path
because of my oppressors.

[a] *21* Septuagint; Hebrew does not have *LORD.* [b] *2* Or *slander*

[12] Do not turn me over to the desire of
my foes,
for false witnesses rise up against me,
spouting malicious accusations.

[13] I remain confident of this:
I will see the goodness of the LORD
in the land of the living.
[14] Wait for the LORD;
be strong and take heart
and wait for the LORD.

Psalm 28

Of David.

[1] To you, LORD, I call;
you are my Rock,
do not turn a deaf ear to me.
For if you remain silent,
I will be like those who go down to
the pit.
[2] Hear my cry for mercy
as I call to you for help,
as I lift up my hands
toward your Most Holy Place.
[3] Do not drag me away with the wicked,
with those who do evil,
who speak cordially with their neighbors
but harbor malice in their hearts.
[4] Repay them for their deeds
and for their evil work;
repay them for what their hands have
done
and bring back on them what they
deserve.

[5] Because they have no regard for the
deeds of the LORD
and what his hands have done,
he will tear them down
and never build them up again.

[6] Praise be to the LORD,
for he has heard my cry for mercy.
[7] The LORD is my strength and my shield;
my heart trusts in him, and he
helps me.
My heart leaps for joy,
and with my song I praise him.

[8] The LORD is the strength of his people,
a fortress of salvation for his anointed
one.
[9] Save your people and bless your
inheritance;
be their shepherd and carry them
forever.

Psalm 29

A psalm of David.

[1] Ascribe to the LORD, you heavenly
beings,
ascribe to the LORD glory and strength.
[2] Ascribe to the LORD the glory due his
name;
worship the LORD in the splendor of
his[a] holiness.

[3] The voice of the LORD is over the waters;
the God of glory thunders,
the LORD thunders over the mighty
waters.
[4] The voice of the LORD is powerful;
the voice of the LORD is majestic.
[5] The voice of the LORD breaks the cedars;
the LORD breaks in pieces the cedars
of Lebanon.
[6] He makes Lebanon leap like a calf,
Sirion[b] like a young wild ox.
[7] The voice of the LORD strikes
with flashes of lightning.
[8] The voice of the LORD shakes the desert;
the LORD shakes the Desert of Kadesh.
[9] The voice of the LORD twists the oaks[c]
and strips the forests bare.
And in his temple all cry, "Glory!"
[10] The LORD sits enthroned over the flood;
the LORD is enthroned as King forever.
[11] The LORD gives strength to his people;
the LORD blesses his people with
peace.

Psalm 30[d]

A psalm. A song.
For the dedication of the temple.[e] Of David.

[1] I will exalt you, LORD,
for you lifted me out of the depths
and did not let my enemies gloat
over me.
[2] LORD my God, I called to you for help,
and you healed me.
[3] You, LORD, brought me up from the realm
of the dead;

[a] 2 Or *LORD with the splendor of* [b] 6 That is, Mount Hermon [c] 9 Or *LORD makes the deer give birth*
[d] In Hebrew texts 30:1-12 is numbered 30:2-13. [e] Title: Or *palace*

you spared me from going down to
the pit.

[4] Sing the praises of the LORD, you his
faithful people;
praise his holy name.
[5] For his anger lasts only a moment,
but his favor lasts a lifetime;
weeping may stay for the night,
but rejoicing comes in the morning.

[6] When I felt secure, I said,
"I will never be shaken."
[7] LORD, when you favored me,
you made my royal mountain[a] stand
firm;
but when you hid your face,
I was dismayed.

[8] To you, LORD, I called;
to the Lord I cried for mercy:
[9] "What is gained if I am silenced,
if I go down to the pit?
Will the dust praise you?
Will it proclaim your faithfulness?
[10] Hear, LORD, and be merciful to me;
LORD, be my help."

[11] You turned my wailing into dancing;
you removed my sackcloth and clothed
me with joy,
[12] that my heart may sing your praises and
not be silent.
LORD my God, I will praise you forever.

Psalm 31[b]

For the director of music.
A psalm of David.

[1] In you, LORD, I have taken refuge;
let me never be put to shame;
deliver me in your righteousness.
[2] Turn your ear to me,
come quickly to my rescue;
be my rock of refuge,
a strong fortress to save me.
[3] Since you are my rock and my fortress,
for the sake of your name lead and
guide me.
[4] Keep me free from the trap that is set
for me,
for you are my refuge.
[5] Into your hands I commit my spirit;
deliver me, LORD, my faithful God.

[6] I hate those who cling to worthless idols;
as for me, I trust in the LORD.
[7] I will be glad and rejoice in your love,
for you saw my affliction
and knew the anguish of my soul.
[8] You have not given me into the hands of
the enemy
but have set my feet in a spacious
place.

[9] Be merciful to me, LORD, for I am in
distress;
my eyes grow weak with sorrow,
my soul and body with grief.
[10] My life is consumed by anguish
and my years by groaning;
my strength fails because of my
affliction,[c]
and my bones grow weak.
[11] Because of all my enemies,
I am the utter contempt of my
neighbors
and an object of dread to my closest
friends—
those who see me on the street flee
from me.
[12] I am forgotten as though I were dead;
I have become like broken pottery.
[13] For I hear many whispering,
"Terror on every side!"
They conspire against me
and plot to take my life.

[14] But I trust in you, LORD;
I say, "You are my God."
[15] My times are in your hands;
deliver me from the hands of my
enemies,
from those who pursue me.
[16] Let your face shine on your servant;
save me in your unfailing love.
[17] Let me not be put to shame, LORD,
for I have cried out to you;
but let the wicked be put to shame
and be silent in the realm of the dead.
[18] Let their lying lips be silenced,
for with pride and contempt
they speak arrogantly against the
righteous.

[19] How abundant are the good things
that you have stored up for those who
fear you,
that you bestow in the sight of all,
on those who take refuge in you.

[a] 7 That is, Mount Zion [b] In Hebrew texts 31:1-24 is numbered 31:2-25. [c] 10 Or *guilt*

[20]In the shelter of your presence you
hide them
from all human intrigues;
you keep them safe in your dwelling
from accusing tongues.

[21]Praise be to the LORD,
for he showed me the wonders of
his love
when I was in a city under siege.
[22]In my alarm I said,
"I am cut off from your sight!"
Yet you heard my cry for mercy
when I called to you for help.

[23]Love the LORD, all his faithful people!
The LORD preserves those who are true
to him,
but the proud he pays back in full.
[24]Be strong and take heart,
all you who hope in the LORD.

Psalm 32

Of David. A maskil.[a]

[1]Blessed is the one
whose transgressions are forgiven,
whose sins are covered.
[2]Blessed is the one
whose sin the LORD does not count
against them
and in whose spirit is no deceit.

[3]When I kept silent,
my bones wasted away
through my groaning all day long.
[4]For day and night
your hand was heavy on me;
my strength was sapped
as in the heat of summer.[b]

[5]Then I acknowledged my sin to you
and did not cover up my iniquity.
I said, "I will confess
my transgressions to the LORD."
And you forgave
the guilt of my sin.

[6]Therefore let all the faithful pray to you
while you may be found;
surely the rising of the mighty waters
will not reach them.
[7]You are my hiding place;
you will protect me from trouble
and surround me with songs of
deliverance.

[8]I will instruct you and teach you in the
way you should go;
I will counsel you with my loving eye
on you.
[9]Do not be like the horse or the mule,
which have no understanding
but must be controlled by bit and bridle
or they will not come to you.
[10]Many are the woes of the wicked,
but the LORD's unfailing love
surrounds the one who trusts in him.

[11]Rejoice in the LORD and be glad, you
righteous;
sing, all you who are upright in heart!

Psalm 33

[1]Sing joyfully to the LORD, you righteous;
it is fitting for the upright to praise
him.
[2]Praise the LORD with the harp;
make music to him on the ten-stringed
lyre.
[3]Sing to him a new song;
play skillfully, and shout for joy.
[4]For the word of the LORD is right and true;
he is faithful in all he does.
[5]The LORD loves righteousness and
justice;
the earth is full of his unfailing love.

[6]By the word of the LORD the heavens were
made,
their starry host by the breath of his
mouth.
[7]He gathers the waters of the sea into jars[c];
he puts the deep into storehouses.
[8]Let all the earth fear the LORD;
let all the people of the world revere
him.
[9]For he spoke, and it came to be;
he commanded, and it stood firm.

[10]The LORD foils the plans of the nations;
he thwarts the purposes of the
peoples.
[11]But the plans of the LORD stand firm
forever,
the purposes of his heart through all
generations.

[a] Title: Probably a literary or musical term [b] *4* The Hebrew has *Selah* (a word of uncertain meaning) here and at the end of verses 5 and 7. [c] *7* Or *sea as into a heap*

[12] Blessed is the nation whose God is the
LORD,
the people he chose for his
inheritance.
[13] From heaven the LORD looks down
and sees all mankind;
[14] from his dwelling place he watches
all who live on earth—
[15] he who forms the hearts of all,
who considers everything they do.

[16] No king is saved by the size of his army;
no warrior escapes by his great
strength.
[17] A horse is a vain hope for deliverance;
despite all its great strength it cannot
save.
[18] But the eyes of the LORD are on those who
fear him,
on those whose hope is in his unfailing
love,
[19] to deliver them from death
and keep them alive in famine.

[20] We wait in hope for the LORD;
he is our help and our shield.
[21] In him our hearts rejoice,
for we trust in his holy name.
[22] May your unfailing love be with us, LORD,
even as we put our hope in you.

Psalm 34[a,b]

Of David. When he pretended to be insane before Abimelek, who drove him away, and he left.

[1] I will extol the LORD at all times;
his praise will always be on my lips.
[2] I will glory in the LORD;
let the afflicted hear and rejoice.
[3] Glorify the LORD with me;
let us exalt his name together.

[4] I sought the LORD, and he answered me;
he delivered me from all my fears.
[5] Those who look to him are radiant;
their faces are never covered with
shame.
[6] This poor man called, and the LORD
heard him;
he saved him out of all his troubles.
[7] The angel of the LORD encamps around
those who fear him,
and he delivers them.

[8] Taste and see that the LORD is good;
blessed is the one who takes refuge
in him.
[9] Fear the LORD, you his holy people,
for those who fear him lack nothing.
[10] The lions may grow weak and hungry,
but those who seek the LORD lack no
good thing.
[11] Come, my children, listen to me;
I will teach you the fear of the LORD.
[12] Whoever of you loves life
and desires to see many good days,
[13] keep your tongue from evil
and your lips from telling lies.
[14] Turn from evil and do good;
seek peace and pursue it.

[15] The eyes of the LORD are on the
righteous,
and his ears are attentive to their cry;
[16] but the face of the LORD is against those
who do evil,
to blot out their name from the earth.

[17] The righteous cry out, and the LORD
hears them;
he delivers them from all their
troubles.
[18] The LORD is close to the brokenhearted
and saves those who are crushed in
spirit.

[19] The righteous person may have many
troubles,
but the LORD delivers him from
them all;
[20] he protects all his bones,
not one of them will be broken.

[21] Evil will slay the wicked;
the foes of the righteous will be
condemned.
[22] The LORD will rescue his servants;
no one who takes refuge in him will be
condemned.

Psalm 35

Of David.

[1] Contend, LORD, with those who contend
with me;
fight against those who fight against me.
[2] Take up shield and armor;
arise and come to my aid.

[a] This psalm is an acrostic poem, the verses of which begin with the successive letters of the Hebrew alphabet. [b] In Hebrew texts 34:1-22 is numbered 34:2-23.

[3]Brandish spear and javelin[a]
against those who pursue me.
Say to me,
"I am your salvation."

[4]May those who seek my life
be disgraced and put to shame;
may those who plot my ruin
be turned back in dismay.
[5]May they be like chaff before the wind,
with the angel of the LORD driving
them away;
[6]may their path be dark and slippery,
with the angel of the LORD pursuing
them.

[7]Since they hid their net for me without
cause
and without cause dug a pit for me,
[8]may ruin overtake them by surprise —
may the net they hid entangle them,
may they fall into the pit, to their ruin.
[9]Then my soul will rejoice in the LORD
and delight in his salvation.
[10]My whole being will exclaim,
"Who is like you, LORD?
You rescue the poor from those too
strong for them,
the poor and needy from those who
rob them."

[11]Ruthless witnesses come forward;
they question me on things I know
nothing about.
[12]They repay me evil for good
and leave me like one bereaved.
[13]Yet when they were ill, I put on sackcloth
and humbled myself with fasting.
When my prayers returned to me
unanswered,
[14] I went about mourning
as though for my friend or brother.
I bowed my head in grief
as though weeping for my mother.
[15]But when I stumbled, they gathered
in glee;
assailants gathered against me
without my knowledge.
They slandered me without ceasing.
[16]Like the ungodly they maliciously
mocked;[b]
they gnashed their teeth at me.

[17]How long, Lord, will you look on?
Rescue me from their ravages,
my precious life from these lions.
[18]I will give you thanks in the great
assembly;
among the throngs I will praise you.
[19]Do not let those gloat over me
who are my enemies without cause;
do not let those who hate me without
reason
maliciously wink the eye.
[20]They do not speak peaceably,
but devise false accusations
against those who live quietly in
the land.
[21]They sneer at me and say, "Aha! Aha!
With our own eyes we have seen it."
[22]LORD, you have seen this; do not be silent.
Do not be far from me, Lord.
[23]Awake, and rise to my defense!
Contend for me, my God and Lord.
[24]Vindicate me in your righteousness,
LORD my God;
do not let them gloat over me.
[25]Do not let them think, "Aha, just what
we wanted!"
or say, "We have swallowed him up."

[26]May all who gloat over my distress
be put to shame and confusion;
may all who exalt themselves over me
be clothed with shame and disgrace.
[27]May those who delight in my vindication
shout for joy and gladness;
may they always say, "The LORD be
exalted,
who delights in the well-being of his
servant."
[28]My tongue will proclaim your
righteousness,
your praises all day long.

Psalm 36[c]

For the director of music.
Of David the servant of the LORD.

[1]I have a message from God in my heart
concerning the sinfulness of the
wicked:[d]
There is no fear of God
before their eyes.

[a] 3 Or *and block the way* [b] 16 Septuagint; Hebrew may mean *Like an ungodly circle of mockers,* [c] In Hebrew texts 36:1-12 is numbered 36:2-13. [d] 1 Or *A message from God: The transgression of the wicked / resides in their hearts.*

[2] In their own eyes they flatter themselves
too much to detect or hate their sin.
[3] The words of their mouths are wicked
and deceitful;
they fail to act wisely or do good.
[4] Even on their beds they plot evil;
they commit themselves to a sinful
course
and do not reject what is wrong.

[5] Your love, LORD, reaches to the heavens,
your faithfulness to the skies.
[6] Your righteousness is like the highest
mountains,
your justice like the great deep.
You, LORD, preserve both people and
animals.
[7] How priceless is your unfailing love,
O God!
People take refuge in the shadow of
your wings.
[8] They feast on the abundance of your
house;
you give them drink from your river
of delights.
[9] For with you is the fountain of life;
in your light we see light.

[10] Continue your love to those who
know you,
your righteousness to the upright in
heart.
[11] May the foot of the proud not come
against me,
nor the hand of the wicked drive
me away.
[12] See how the evildoers lie fallen—
thrown down, not able to rise!

Psalm 37[a]

Of David.

[1] Do not fret because of those who are evil
or be envious of those who do wrong;
[2] for like the grass they will soon wither,
like green plants they will soon die
away.

[3] Trust in the LORD and do good;
dwell in the land and enjoy safe
pasture.
[4] Take delight in the LORD,
and he will give you the desires of your
heart.

[5] Commit your way to the LORD;
trust in him and he will do this:
[6] He will make your righteous reward
shine like the dawn,
your vindication like the noonday sun.

[7] Be still before the LORD
and wait patiently for him;
do not fret when people succeed in
their ways,
when they carry out their wicked
schemes.

[8] Refrain from anger and turn from wrath;
do not fret—it leads only to evil.
[9] For those who are evil will be destroyed,
but those who hope in the LORD will
inherit the land.

[10] A little while, and the wicked will be no
more;
though you look for them, they will not
be found.
[11] But the meek will inherit the land
and enjoy peace and prosperity.

[12] The wicked plot against the righteous
and gnash their teeth at them;
[13] but the Lord laughs at the wicked,
for he knows their day is coming.

[14] The wicked draw the sword
and bend the bow
to bring down the poor and needy,
to slay those whose ways are upright.
[15] But their swords will pierce their own
hearts,
and their bows will be broken.

[16] Better the little that the righteous have
than the wealth of many wicked;
[17] for the power of the wicked will be
broken,
but the LORD upholds the righteous.

[18] The blameless spend their days under the
LORD's care,
and their inheritance will endure
forever.
[19] In times of disaster they will not wither;
in days of famine they will enjoy
plenty.

[20] But the wicked will perish:
Though the LORD's enemies are like
the flowers of the field,

[a] This psalm is an acrostic poem, the stanzas of which begin with the successive letters of the Hebrew alphabet.

GOD OF WONDERS

Marc Byrd, Steve Hindalong

Lord of all creation
Of water, earth and sky
The heavens are your tabernacle
Glory to the Lord on high

God of wonders beyond our galaxy
You are holy, holy
The universe declares your majesty
You are holy, holy

Lord of heaven and earth
Lord of heaven and earth

Early in the morning
I will celebrate the light
And as I stumble in the darkness
I will call your name by night

Hallelujah! To the Lord of heaven and earth

THE INSPIRATION

Many, Lord my God, are the wonders you have done, the things you planned for us. None can compare with you; were I to speak and tell of your deeds, they would be too many to declare.

—Psalm 40:5

Read also: Exodus 15:11

BEHIND THE SONG

For the attentive believer, cues to worship are everywhere. Marc Byrd had been the front man of a successful rock band (Common Children) and was experiencing some confusing times when he found the inspiration for "God of Wonders."

"I took my car and drove out to a lake in Hot Springs National Park one night," he remembers. "I was upset about some things and was definitely not in the mood to worship, but when I looked up into the night sky I was overwhelmed by the vastness of God's creation. Suddenly my problems and doubts seemed incredibly small."

Byrd was moved to write a song very different from his usual style. He came up with the beginnings of "God of Wonders" and then connected with his friend Steve Hindalong, a songwriter, producer and member of the alternative Christian band The Choir. Hindalong was working on an album that would pull together a disparate group of Christian artists to worship and celebrate community in a fresh new way. He helped Byrd finish the song and then included it on the first *City on a Hill* album. The recording featured Mac Powell of Third Day, Leigh Nash of Sixpence None the Richer, and Cliff and Danielle Young of Caedmon's Call. With its evocative verses and sweeping melody, "God of Wonders" quickly became a favorite on Christian radio and in churches around the world.

Selah

With so many distractions in our lives, it is frightfully easy to become oblivious to the wonder that surrounds us. The truth is that if we learn to open our eyes again we will be overwhelmed with evidence of God's goodness, creativity and majesty.

What are some of the most amazing things you have ever seen? Make a list of the things that have inspired awe and wonder in you. If you begin to feel dry or uninspired, or if you find it hard to engage in worship, revisit the wonders of your past or discover some new ones.

they will be consumed, they will go up
in smoke.

21 The wicked borrow and do not repay,
but the righteous give generously;
22 those the LORD blesses will inherit the
land,
but those he curses will be destroyed.

23 The LORD makes firm the steps
of the one who delights in him;
24 though he may stumble, he will not fall,
for the LORD upholds him with his
hand.

25 I was young and now I am old,
yet I have never seen the righteous
forsaken
or their children begging bread.
26 They are always generous and lend
freely;
their children will be a blessing.[a]

27 Turn from evil and do good;
then you will dwell in the land forever.
28 For the LORD loves the just
and will not forsake his faithful ones.

Wrongdoers will be completely
destroyed[b];
the offspring of the wicked will perish.
29 The righteous will inherit the land
and dwell in it forever.

30 The mouths of the righteous utter
wisdom,
and their tongues speak what is just.
31 The law of their God is in their hearts;
their feet do not slip.

32 The wicked lie in wait for the righteous,
intent on putting them to death;
33 but the LORD will not leave them in the
power of the wicked
or let them be condemned when
brought to trial.

34 Hope in the LORD
and keep his way.
He will exalt you to inherit the land;
when the wicked are destroyed, you
will see it.

35 I have seen a wicked and ruthless man
flourishing like a luxuriant native tree,
36 but he soon passed away and was no more;
though I looked for him, he could not
be found.

37 Consider the blameless, observe the
upright;
a future awaits those who seek peace.[c]
38 But all sinners will be destroyed;
there will be no future[d] for the wicked.

39 The salvation of the righteous comes
from the LORD;
he is their stronghold in time of
trouble.
40 The LORD helps them and delivers them;
he delivers them from the wicked and
saves them,
because they take refuge in him.

Psalm 38[e]

A psalm of David. A petition.

1 LORD, do not rebuke me in your anger
or discipline me in your wrath.
2 Your arrows have pierced me,
and your hand has come down on me.
3 Because of your wrath there is no health
in my body;
there is no soundness in my bones
because of my sin.
4 My guilt has overwhelmed me
like a burden too heavy to bear.

5 My wounds fester and are loathsome
because of my sinful folly.
6 I am bowed down and brought very low;
all day long I go about mourning.
7 My back is filled with searing pain;
there is no health in my body.
8 I am feeble and utterly crushed;
I groan in anguish of heart.

9 All my longings lie open before you,
Lord;
my sighing is not hidden from you.
10 My heart pounds, my strength fails me;
even the light has gone from my eyes.
11 My friends and companions avoid me
because of my wounds;
my neighbors stay far away.
12 Those who want to kill me set their
traps,

[a] 26 Or *freely; / the names of their children will be used in blessings* (see Gen. 48:20); or *freely; / others will see that their children are blessed* [b] 28 See Septuagint; Hebrew *They will be protected forever*
[c] 37 Or *upright; / those who seek peace will have posterity* [d] 38 Or *posterity* [e] In Hebrew texts 38:1-22 is numbered 38:2-23.

those who would harm me talk of
my ruin;
all day long they scheme and lie.
13 I am like the deaf, who cannot hear,
like the mute, who cannot speak;
14 I have become like one who does
not hear,
whose mouth can offer no reply.
15 LORD, I wait for you;
you will answer, Lord my God.
16 For I said, "Do not let them gloat
or exalt themselves over me when my
feet slip."
17 For I am about to fall,
and my pain is ever with me.
18 I confess my iniquity;
I am troubled by my sin.
19 Many have become my enemies without
cause[a];
those who hate me without reason are
numerous.
20 Those who repay my good with evil
lodge accusations against me,
though I seek only to do what is good.

21 LORD, do not forsake me;
do not be far from me, my God.
22 Come quickly to help me,
my Lord and my Savior.

Psalm 39[b]

For the director of music.
For Jeduthun. A psalm of David.

1 I said, "I will watch my ways
and keep my tongue from sin;
I will put a muzzle on my mouth
while in the presence of the wicked."
2 So I remained utterly silent,
not even saying anything good.
But my anguish increased;
3 my heart grew hot within me.
While I meditated, the fire burned;
then I spoke with my tongue:

4 "Show me, LORD, my life's end
and the number of my days;
let me know how fleeting my life is.
5 You have made my days a mere
handbreadth;
the span of my years is as nothing
before you.
Everyone is but a breath,
even those who seem secure.[c]
6 "Surely everyone goes around like a mere
phantom;
in vain they rush about, heaping up
wealth
without knowing whose it will
finally be.

7 "But now, Lord, what do I look for?
My hope is in you.
8 Save me from all my transgressions;
do not make me the scorn of fools.
9 I was silent; I would not open my mouth,
for you are the one who has done this.
10 Remove your scourge from me;
I am overcome by the blow of your
hand.
11 When you rebuke and discipline anyone
for their sin,
you consume their wealth like a
moth—
surely everyone is but a breath.

12 "Hear my prayer, LORD,
listen to my cry for help;
do not be deaf to my weeping.
I dwell with you as a foreigner,
a stranger, as all my ancestors were.
13 Look away from me, that I may enjoy life
again
before I depart and am no more."

Psalm 40[d]

For the director of music.
Of David. A psalm.

1 I waited patiently for the LORD;
he turned to me and heard my cry.
2 He lifted me out of the slimy pit,
out of the mud and mire;
he set my feet on a rock
and gave me a firm place to stand.
3 He put a new song in my mouth,
a hymn of praise to our God.
Many will see and fear the LORD
and put their trust in him.

4 Blessed is the one
who trusts in the LORD,
who does not look to the proud,
to those who turn aside to false gods.[e]

[a] 19 One Dead Sea Scrolls manuscript; Masoretic Text *my vigorous enemies* [b] In Hebrew texts 39:1-13 is numbered 39:2-14. [c] 5 The Hebrew has *Selah* (a word of uncertain meaning) here and at the end of verse 11. [d] In Hebrew texts 40:1-17 is numbered 40:2-18. [e] 4 Or *to lies*

[5]Many, LORD my God,
are the wonders you have done,
the things you planned for us.
None can compare with you;
were I to speak and tell of your deeds,
they would be too many to declare.

[6]Sacrifice and offering you did not desire —
but my ears you have opened[a] —
burnt offerings and sin offerings[b] you did not require.
[7]Then I said, "Here I am, I have come —
it is written about me in the scroll.[c]
[8]I desire to do your will, my God;
your law is within my heart."

[9]I proclaim your saving acts in the great assembly;
I do not seal my lips, LORD,
as you know.
[10]I do not hide your righteousness in my heart;
I speak of your faithfulness and your saving help.
I do not conceal your love and your faithfulness
from the great assembly.

[11]Do not withhold your mercy from me, LORD;
may your love and faithfulness always protect me.
[12]For troubles without number surround me;
my sins have overtaken me, and I cannot see.
They are more than the hairs of my head,
and my heart fails within me.
[13]Be pleased to save me, LORD;
come quickly, LORD, to help me.

[14]May all who want to take my life
be put to shame and confusion;
may all who desire my ruin
be turned back in disgrace.
[15]May those who say to me, "Aha! Aha!"
be appalled at their own shame.
[16]But may all who seek you
rejoice and be glad in you;
may those who long for your saving help always say,
"The LORD is great!"

[17]But as for me, I am poor and needy;
may the Lord think of me.
You are my help and my deliverer;
you are my God, do not delay.

Psalm 41[d]

For the director of music. A psalm of David.

[1]Blessed are those who have regard for the weak;
the LORD delivers them in times of trouble.
[2]The LORD protects and preserves them —
they are counted among the blessed in the land —
he does not give them over to the desire of their foes.
[3]The LORD sustains them on their sickbed
and restores them from their bed of illness.

[4]I said, "Have mercy on me, LORD;
heal me, for I have sinned against you."
[5]My enemies say of me in malice,
"When will he die and his name perish?"
[6]When one of them comes to see me,
he speaks falsely, while his heart gathers slander;
then he goes out and spreads it around.

[7]All my enemies whisper together against me;
they imagine the worst for me, saying,
[8]"A vile disease has afflicted him;
he will never get up from the place where he lies."
[9]Even my close friend,
someone I trusted,
one who shared my bread,
has turned[e] against me.

[10]But may you have mercy on me, LORD;
raise me up, that I may repay them.
[11]I know that you are pleased with me,
for my enemy does not triumph over me.
[12]Because of my integrity you uphold me
and set me in your presence forever.

[13]Praise be to the LORD, the God of Israel,
from everlasting to everlasting.
Amen and Amen.

[a] 6 Hebrew; some Septuagint manuscripts *but a body you have prepared for me* [b] 6 Or *purification offerings* [c] 7 Or *come / with the scroll written for me* [d] In Hebrew texts 41:1-13 is numbered 41:2-14.
[e] 9 Hebrew *has lifted up his heel*

BOOK II

Psalms 42–72

Psalm 42[a,b]

For the director of music.
A maskil[c] *of the Sons of Korah.*

1 As the deer pants for streams of water,
so my soul pants for you, my God.
2 My soul thirsts for God, for the living God.
When can I go and meet with God?
3 My tears have been my food
day and night,
while people say to me all day long,
"Where is your God?"
4 These things I remember
as I pour out my soul:
how I used to go to the house of God
under the protection of the
Mighty One[d]
with shouts of joy and praise
among the festive throng.

5 Why, my soul, are you downcast?
Why so disturbed within me?
Put your hope in God,
for I will yet praise him,
my Savior and my God.

6 My soul is downcast within me;
therefore I will remember you
from the land of the Jordan,
the heights of Hermon — from Mount
Mizar.
7 Deep calls to deep
in the roar of your waterfalls;
all your waves and breakers
have swept over me.

8 By day the LORD directs his love,
at night his song is with me —
a prayer to the God of my life.

9 I say to God my Rock,
"Why have you forgotten me?
Why must I go about mourning,
oppressed by the enemy?"
10 My bones suffer mortal agony
as my foes taunt me,
saying to me all day long,
"Where is your God?"

11 Why, my soul, are you downcast?
Why so disturbed within me?
Put your hope in God,
for I will yet praise him,
my Savior and my God.

Psalm 43[a]

1 Vindicate me, my God,
and plead my cause
against an unfaithful nation.
Rescue me from those who are
deceitful and wicked.
2 You are God my stronghold.
Why have you rejected me?
Why must I go about mourning,
oppressed by the enemy?
3 Send me your light and your faithful care,
let them lead me;
let them bring me to your holy
mountain,
to the place where you dwell.
4 Then I will go to the altar of God,
to God, my joy and my delight.
I will praise you with the lyre,
O God, my God.

5 Why, my soul, are you downcast?
Why so disturbed within me?
Put your hope in God,
for I will yet praise him,
my Savior and my God.

Psalm 44[e]

For the director of music.
Of the Sons of Korah. A maskil.[c]

1 We have heard it with our ears, O God;
our ancestors have told us
what you did in their days,
in days long ago.
2 With your hand you drove out the nations
and planted our ancestors;
you crushed the peoples
and made our ancestors flourish.
3 It was not by their sword that they won
the land,
nor did their arm bring them victory;
it was your right hand, your arm,
and the light of your face, for you
loved them.

[a] In many Hebrew manuscripts Psalms 42 and 43 constitute one psalm. [b] In Hebrew texts 42:1-11 is numbered 42:2-12. [c] Title: Probably a literary or musical term [d] 4 See Septuagint and Syriac; the meaning of the Hebrew for this line is uncertain. [e] In Hebrew texts 44:1-26 is numbered 44:2-27.

[4] You are my King and my God,
who decrees[a] victories for Jacob.
[5] Through you we push back our enemies;
through your name we trample
our foes.
[6] I put no trust in my bow,
my sword does not bring me victory;
[7] but you give us victory over our enemies,
you put our adversaries to shame.
[8] In God we make our boast all day long,
and we will praise your name forever.[b]

[9] But now you have rejected and
humbled us;
you no longer go out with our armies.
[10] You made us retreat before the enemy,
and our adversaries have plundered us.
[11] You gave us up to be devoured like sheep
and have scattered us among the
nations.
[12] You sold your people for a pittance,
gaining nothing from their sale.

[13] You have made us a reproach to our
neighbors,
the scorn and derision of those
around us.
[14] You have made us a byword among the
nations;
the peoples shake their heads at us.
[15] I live in disgrace all day long,
and my face is covered with shame
[16] at the taunts of those who reproach and
revile me,
because of the enemy, who is bent on
revenge.

[17] All this came upon us,
though we had not forgotten you;
we had not been false to your
covenant.
[18] Our hearts had not turned back;
our feet had not strayed from your
path.
[19] But you crushed us and made us a haunt
for jackals;
you covered us over with deep
darkness.

[20] If we had forgotten the name of our God
or spread out our hands to a foreign
god,
[21] would not God have discovered it,
since he knows the secrets of the
heart?
[22] Yet for your sake we face death all day long;
we are considered as sheep to be
slaughtered.

[23] Awake, Lord! Why do you sleep?
Rouse yourself! Do not reject us forever.
[24] Why do you hide your face
and forget our misery and oppression?
[25] We are brought down to the dust;
our bodies cling to the ground.
[26] Rise up and help us;
rescue us because of your unfailing
love.

Psalm 45[c]

For the director of music. To the tune of "Lilies." Of the Sons of Korah. A maskil.[d] *A wedding song.*

[1] My heart is stirred by a noble theme
as I recite my verses for the king;
my tongue is the pen of a skillful writer.

[2] You are the most excellent of men
and your lips have been anointed with
grace,
since God has blessed you forever.

[3] Gird your sword on your side, you
mighty one;
clothe yourself with splendor and
majesty.
[4] In your majesty ride forth victoriously
in the cause of truth, humility and
justice;
let your right hand achieve awesome
deeds.
[5] Let your sharp arrows pierce the hearts of
the king's enemies;
let the nations fall beneath your feet.
[6] Your throne, O God,[e] will last for ever
and ever;
a scepter of justice will be the scepter
of your kingdom.
[7] You love righteousness and hate
wickedness;
therefore God, your God, has set you
above your companions
by anointing you with the oil of joy.

[a] *4* Septuagint, Aquila and Syriac; Hebrew *King, O God; / command* [b] *8* The Hebrew has *Selah* (a word of uncertain meaning) here. [c] In Hebrew texts 45:1-17 is numbered 45:2-18. [d] Title: Probably a literary or musical term [e] *6* Here the king is addressed as God's representative.

[8]All your robes are fragrant with myrrh
and aloes and cassia;
from palaces adorned with ivory
the music of the strings makes you
glad.
[9]Daughters of kings are among your
honored women;
at your right hand is the royal bride in
gold of Ophir.

[10]Listen, daughter, and pay careful
attention:
Forget your people and your father's
house.
[11]Let the king be enthralled by your
beauty;
honor him, for he is your lord.
[12]The city of Tyre will come with a gift,[a]
people of wealth will seek your favor.
[13]All glorious is the princess within her
chamber;
her gown is interwoven with gold.
[14]In embroidered garments she is led to
the king;
her virgin companions follow her—
those brought to be with her.
[15]Led in with joy and gladness,
they enter the palace of the king.

[16]Your sons will take the place of your
fathers;
you will make them princes
throughout the land.

[17]I will perpetuate your memory through
all generations;
therefore the nations will praise you
for ever and ever.

Psalm 46[b]

For the director of music. Of the Sons of Korah.
According to alamoth.[c] *A song.*

[1]God is our refuge and strength,
an ever-present help in trouble.
[2]Therefore we will not fear, though the
earth give way
and the mountains fall into the heart
of the sea,
[3]though its waters roar and foam
and the mountains quake with their
surging.[d]

[4]There is a river whose streams make glad
the city of God,
the holy place where the Most High
dwells.
[5]God is within her, she will not fall;
God will help her at break of day.
[6]Nations are in uproar, kingdoms fall;
he lifts his voice, the earth melts.

[7]The LORD Almighty is with us;
the God of Jacob is our fortress.

[8]Come and see what the LORD has done,
the desolations he has brought on
the earth.
[9]He makes wars cease
to the ends of the earth.
He breaks the bow and shatters the
spear;
he burns the shields[e] with fire.
[10]He says, "Be still, and know that I
am God;
I will be exalted among the nations,
I will be exalted in the earth."

[11]The LORD Almighty is with us;
the God of Jacob is our fortress.

Psalm 47[f]

For the director of music.
Of the Sons of Korah. A psalm.

[1]Clap your hands, all you nations;
shout to God with cries of joy.

[2]For the LORD Most High is awesome,
the great King over all the earth.
[3]He subdued nations under us,
peoples under our feet.
[4]He chose our inheritance for us,
the pride of Jacob, whom he loved.[g]

[5]God has ascended amid shouts of joy,
the LORD amid the sounding of
trumpets.
[6]Sing praises to God, sing praises;
sing praises to our King, sing praises.
[7]For God is the King of all the earth;
sing to him a psalm of praise.

[8]God reigns over the nations;
God is seated on his holy throne.
[9]The nobles of the nations assemble
as the people of the God of Abraham,

[a] *12* Or *A Tyrian robe is among the gifts* [b] In Hebrew texts 46:1-11 is numbered 46:2-12. [c] Title: Probably a musical term [d] *3* The Hebrew has *Selah* (a word of uncertain meaning) here and at the end of verses 7 and 11. [e] *9* Or *chariots* [f] In Hebrew texts 47:1-9 is numbered 47:2-10. [g] *4* The Hebrew has *Selah* (a word of uncertain meaning) here.

for the kings[a] of the earth belong to God;
he is greatly exalted.

Psalm 48[b]

A song. A psalm of the Sons of Korah.

1 Great is the LORD, and most worthy of praise,
in the city of our God, his holy mountain.

2 Beautiful in its loftiness,
the joy of the whole earth,
like the heights of Zaphon[c] is Mount Zion,
the city of the Great King.
3 God is in her citadels;
he has shown himself to be her fortress.

4 When the kings joined forces,
when they advanced together,
5 they saw her and were astounded;
they fled in terror.
6 Trembling seized them there,
pain like that of a woman in labor.
7 You destroyed them like ships of Tarshish
shattered by an east wind.

8 As we have heard,
so we have seen
in the city of the LORD Almighty,
in the city of our God:
God makes her secure
forever.[d]

9 Within your temple, O God,
we meditate on your unfailing love.
10 Like your name, O God,
your praise reaches to the ends of the earth;
your right hand is filled with righteousness.
11 Mount Zion rejoices,
the villages of Judah are glad
because of your judgments.

12 Walk about Zion, go around her,
count her towers,
13 consider well her ramparts,
view her citadels,
that you may tell of them
to the next generation.

14 For this God is our God for ever and ever;
he will be our guide even to the end.

Psalm 49[e]

For the director of music.
Of the Sons of Korah. A psalm.

1 Hear this, all you peoples;
listen, all who live in this world,
2 both low and high,
rich and poor alike:
3 My mouth will speak words of wisdom;
the meditation of my heart will give you understanding.
4 I will turn my ear to a proverb;
with the harp I will expound my riddle:

5 Why should I fear when evil days come,
when wicked deceivers surround me—
6 those who trust in their wealth
and boast of their great riches?
7 No one can redeem the life of another
or give to God a ransom for them—
8 the ransom for a life is costly,
no payment is ever enough—
9 so that they should live on forever
and not see decay.
10 For all can see that the wise die,
that the foolish and the senseless also perish,
leaving their wealth to others.
11 Their tombs will remain their houses[f] forever,
their dwellings for endless generations,
though they had[g] named lands after themselves.

12 People, despite their wealth, do not endure;
they are like the beasts that perish.

13 This is the fate of those who trust in themselves,
and of their followers, who approve their sayings.[h]
14 They are like sheep and are destined to die;
death will be their shepherd

[a] 9 Or *shields* [b] In Hebrew texts 48:1-14 is numbered 48:2-15. [c] 2 *Zaphon* was the most sacred mountain of the Canaanites. [d] 8 The Hebrew has *Selah* (a word of uncertain meaning) here. [e] In Hebrew texts 49:1-20 is numbered 49:2-21. [f] 11 Septuagint and Syriac; Hebrew *In their thoughts their houses will remain* [g] 11 Or *generations, / for they have* [h] 13 The Hebrew has *Selah* (a word of uncertain meaning) here and at the end of verse 15.

(but the upright will prevail over them
in the morning).
Their forms will decay in the grave,
far from their princely mansions.
15 But God will redeem me from the realm
of the dead;
he will surely take me to himself.
16 Do not be overawed when others grow
rich,
when the splendor of their houses
increases;
17 for they will take nothing with them
when they die,
their splendor will not descend
with them.
18 Though while they live they count
themselves blessed —
and people praise you when you
prosper —
19 they will join those who have gone
before them,
who will never again see the light
of life.

20 People who have wealth but lack
understanding
are like the beasts that perish.

Psalm 50

A psalm of Asaph.

1 The Mighty One, God, the LORD,
speaks and summons the earth
from the rising of the sun to where
it sets.
2 From Zion, perfect in beauty,
God shines forth.
3 Our God comes
and will not be silent;
a fire devours before him,
and around him a tempest rages.
4 He summons the heavens above,
and the earth, that he may judge
his people:
5 "Gather to me this consecrated
people,
who made a covenant with me by
sacrifice."
6 And the heavens proclaim his
righteousness,
for he is a God of justice.[a,b]

7 "Listen, my people, and I will speak;
I will testify against you, Israel:
I am God, your God.
8 I bring no charges against you
concerning your sacrifices
or concerning your burnt offerings,
which are ever before me.
9 I have no need of a bull from your stall
or of goats from your pens,
10 for every animal of the forest is mine,
and the cattle on a thousand hills.
11 I know every bird in the mountains,
and the insects in the fields are
mine.
12 If I were hungry I would not tell you,
for the world is mine, and all that is
in it.
13 Do I eat the flesh of bulls
or drink the blood of goats?

14 "Sacrifice thank offerings to God,
fulfill your vows to the Most High,
15 and call on me in the day of trouble;
I will deliver you, and you will
honor me."

16 But to the wicked person, God says:

"What right have you to recite my laws
or take my covenant on your lips?
17 You hate my instruction
and cast my words behind you.
18 When you see a thief, you join
with him;
you throw in your lot with
adulterers.
19 You use your mouth for evil
and harness your tongue to deceit.
20 You sit and testify against your brother
and slander your own mother's son.
21 When you did these things and I kept
silent,
you thought I was exactly[c] like you.
But I now arraign you
and set my accusations before you.

22 "Consider this, you who forget God,
or I will tear you to pieces, with no one
to rescue you:
23 Those who sacrifice thank offerings
honor me,
and to the blameless[d] I will show my
salvation."

[a] 6 With a different word division of the Hebrew; Masoretic Text *for God himself is judge* [b] 6 The Hebrew has *Selah* (a word of uncertain meaning) here. [c] 21 Or *thought the 'I AM' was* [d] 23 Probable reading of the original Hebrew text; the meaning of the Masoretic Text for this phrase is uncertain.

Psalm 51[a]

For the director of music. A psalm of David. When the prophet Nathan came to him after David had committed adultery with Bathsheba.

1 Have mercy on me, O God,
according to your unfailing love;
according to your great compassion
blot out my transgressions.
2 Wash away all my iniquity
and cleanse me from my sin.

3 For I know my transgressions,
and my sin is always before me.
4 Against you, you only, have I sinned
and done what is evil in your sight;
so you are right in your verdict
and justified when you judge.
5 Surely I was sinful at birth,
sinful from the time my mother
conceived me.
6 Yet you desired faithfulness even in
the womb;
you taught me wisdom in that secret
place.

7 Cleanse me with hyssop, and I will be
clean;
wash me, and I will be whiter than
snow.
8 Let me hear joy and gladness;
let the bones you have crushed rejoice.
9 Hide your face from my sins
and blot out all my iniquity.

10 Create in me a pure heart, O God,
and renew a steadfast spirit within me.
11 Do not cast me from your presence
or take your Holy Spirit from me.
12 Restore to me the joy of your salvation
and grant me a willing spirit, to
sustain me.

13 Then I will teach transgressors your ways,
so that sinners will turn back to you.
14 Deliver me from the guilt of bloodshed,
O God,
you who are God my Savior,
and my tongue will sing of your
righteousness.
15 Open my lips, Lord,
and my mouth will declare your
praise.
16 You do not delight in sacrifice, or I would
bring it;
you do not take pleasure in burnt
offerings.
17 My sacrifice, O God, is[b] a broken spirit;
a broken and contrite heart
you, God, will not despise.

18 May it please you to prosper Zion,
to build up the walls of Jerusalem.
19 Then you will delight in the sacrifices of
the righteous,
in burnt offerings offered whole;
then bulls will be offered on your altar.

Psalm 52[c]

For the director of music. A maskil[d] *of David. When Doeg the Edomite had gone to Saul and told him: "David has gone to the house of Ahimelek."*

1 Why do you boast of evil, you mighty
hero?
Why do you boast all day long,
you who are a disgrace in the eyes
of God?
2 You who practice deceit,
your tongue plots destruction;
it is like a sharpened razor.
3 You love evil rather than good,
falsehood rather than speaking the
truth.[e]
4 You love every harmful word,
you deceitful tongue!

5 Surely God will bring you down to
everlasting ruin:
He will snatch you up and pluck you
from your tent;
he will uproot you from the land of
the living.
6 The righteous will see and fear;
they will laugh at you, saying,
7 "Here now is the man
who did not make God his stronghold
but trusted in his great wealth
and grew strong by destroying others!"

8 But I am like an olive tree
flourishing in the house of God;
I trust in God's unfailing love
for ever and ever.
9 For what you have done I will always
praise you

[a] In Hebrew texts 51:1-19 is numbered 51:3-21. [b] 17 Or *The sacrifices of God are* [c] In Hebrew texts 52:1-9 is numbered 52:3-11. [d] Title: Probably a literary or musical term [e] 3 The Hebrew has *Selah* (a word of uncertain meaning) here and at the end of verse 5.

in the presence of your faithful
people.
And I will hope in your name,
for your name is good.

Psalm 53[a]

For the director of music.
According to mahalath.[b] *A* maskil[c] *of David.*

1 The fool says in his heart,
"There is no God."
They are corrupt, and their ways are vile;
there is no one who does good.

2 God looks down from heaven
on all mankind
to see if there are any who understand,
any who seek God.
3 Everyone has turned away, all have
become corrupt;
there is no one who does good,
not even one.

4 Do all these evildoers know nothing?

They devour my people as though eating
bread;
they never call on God.
5 But there they are, overwhelmed with
dread,
where there was nothing to dread.
God scattered the bones of those who
attacked you;
you put them to shame, for God
despised them.

6 Oh, that salvation for Israel would come
out of Zion!
When God restores his people,
let Jacob rejoice and Israel be glad!

Psalm 54[d]

For the director of music.
With stringed instruments. A maskil[c] *of David.*
When the Ziphites had gone to Saul and said,
"Is not David hiding among us?"

1 Save me, O God, by your name;
vindicate me by your might.
2 Hear my prayer, O God;
listen to the words of my mouth.

3 Arrogant foes are attacking me;
ruthless people are trying to kill me—
people without regard for God.[e]

4 Surely God is my help;
the Lord is the one who sustains me.

5 Let evil recoil on those who slander me;
in your faithfulness destroy them.

6 I will sacrifice a freewill offering to you;
I will praise your name, LORD, for it
is good.
7 You have delivered me from all my
troubles,
and my eyes have looked in triumph
on my foes.

Psalm 55[f]

For the director of music. With stringed
instruments. A maskil[c] *of David.*

1 Listen to my prayer, O God,
do not ignore my plea;
2 hear me and answer me.
My thoughts trouble me and I am
distraught
3 because of what my enemy is saying,
because of the threats of the wicked;
for they bring down suffering on me
and assail me in their anger.

4 My heart is in anguish within me;
the terrors of death have fallen on me.
5 Fear and trembling have beset me;
horror has overwhelmed me.
6 I said, "Oh, that I had the wings of
a dove!
I would fly away and be at rest.
7 I would flee far away
and stay in the desert;[g]
8 I would hurry to my place of shelter,
far from the tempest and storm."

9 Lord, confuse the wicked, confound
their words,
for I see violence and strife in the city.
10 Day and night they prowl about on its
walls;
malice and abuse are within it.
11 Destructive forces are at work in the city;
threats and lies never leave its streets.

[a] In Hebrew texts 53:1-6 is numbered 53:2-7. [b] Title: Probably a musical term [c] Title: Probably a literary or musical term [d] In Hebrew texts 54:1-7 is numbered 54:3-9. [e] *3* The Hebrew has *Selah* (a word of uncertain meaning) here. [f] In Hebrew texts 55:1-23 is numbered 55:2-24. [g] 7 The Hebrew has *Selah* (a word of uncertain meaning) here and in the middle of verse 19.

[12] If an enemy were insulting me,
I could endure it;
if a foe were rising against me,
I could hide.
[13] But it is you, a man like myself,
my companion, my close friend,
[14] with whom I once enjoyed sweet
fellowship
at the house of God,
as we walked about
among the worshipers.

[15] Let death take my enemies by surprise;
let them go down alive to the realm of
the dead,
for evil finds lodging among them.

[16] As for me, I call to God,
and the LORD saves me.
[17] Evening, morning and noon
I cry out in distress,
and he hears my voice.
[18] He rescues me unharmed
from the battle waged against me,
even though many oppose me.
[19] God, who is enthroned from of old,
who does not change —
he will hear them and humble them,
because they have no fear of God.

[20] My companion attacks his friends;
he violates his covenant.
[21] His talk is smooth as butter,
yet war is in his heart;
his words are more soothing than oil,
yet they are drawn swords.

[22] Cast your cares on the LORD
and he will sustain you;
he will never let
the righteous be shaken.
[23] But you, God, will bring down the wicked
into the pit of decay;
the bloodthirsty and deceitful
will not live out half their days.

But as for me, I trust in you.

Psalm 56[a]

For the director of music. To the tune of "A Dove on Distant Oaks." Of David. A miktam.[b] *When the Philistines had seized him in Gath.*

[1] Be merciful to me, my God,
for my enemies are in hot pursuit;
all day long they press their
attack.
[2] My adversaries pursue me all day long;
in their pride many are attacking me.

[3] When I am afraid, I put my trust in you.
[4] In God, whose word I praise —
in God I trust and am not afraid.
What can mere mortals do to me?

[5] All day long they twist my words;
all their schemes are for my ruin.
[6] They conspire, they lurk,
they watch my steps,
hoping to take my life.
[7] Because of their wickedness do not[c] let
them escape;
in your anger, God, bring the nations
down.

[8] Record my misery;
list my tears on your scroll[d] —
are they not in your record?
[9] Then my enemies will turn back
when I call for help.
By this I will know that God is for me.

[10] In God, whose word I praise,
in the LORD, whose word I praise —
[11] in God I trust and am not afraid.
What can man do to me?

[12] I am under vows to you, my God;
I will present my thank offerings
to you.
[13] For you have delivered me from death
and my feet from stumbling,
that I may walk before God
in the light of life.

Psalm 57[e]

For the director of music. To the tune of "Do Not Destroy." Of David. A miktam.[b] *When he had fled from Saul into the cave.*

[1] Have mercy on me, my God, have mercy
on me,
for in you I take refuge.
I will take refuge in the shadow of your
wings
until the disaster has passed.

[2] I cry out to God Most High,
to God, who vindicates me.

[a] In Hebrew texts 56:1-13 is numbered 56:2-14. [b] Title: Probably a literary or musical term
[c] 7 Probable reading of the original Hebrew text; Masoretic Text does not have *do not.* [d] 8 Or *misery; / put my tears in your wineskin* [e] In Hebrew texts 57:1-11 is numbered 57:2-12.

[3]He sends from heaven and saves me,
rebuking those who hotly pursue
me —[a]
God sends forth his love and his
faithfulness.

[4]I am in the midst of lions;
I am forced to dwell among ravenous
beasts —
men whose teeth are spears and arrows,
whose tongues are sharp swords.

[5]Be exalted, O God, above the heavens;
let your glory be over all the earth.

[6]They spread a net for my feet —
I was bowed down in distress.
They dug a pit in my path —
but they have fallen into it themselves.

[7]My heart, O God, is steadfast,
my heart is steadfast;
I will sing and make music.
[8]Awake, my soul!
Awake, harp and lyre!
I will awaken the dawn.

[9]I will praise you, Lord, among the
nations;
I will sing of you among the peoples.
[10]For great is your love, reaching to the
heavens;
your faithfulness reaches to the skies.

[11]Be exalted, O God, above the heavens;
let your glory be over all the earth.

Psalm 58[b]

For the director of music. To the tune of "Do Not Destroy." Of David. A miktam.[c]

[1]Do you rulers indeed speak justly?
Do you judge people with equity?
[2]No, in your heart you devise injustice,
and your hands mete out violence on
the earth.

[3]Even from birth the wicked go astray;
from the womb they are wayward,
spreading lies.
[4]Their venom is like the venom of a snake,
like that of a cobra that has stopped
its ears,
[5]that will not heed the tune of the
charmer,
however skillful the enchanter
may be.

[6]Break the teeth in their mouths, O God;
LORD, tear out the fangs of those
lions!
[7]Let them vanish like water that flows
away;
when they draw the bow, let their
arrows fall short.
[8]May they be like a slug that melts away as
it moves along,
like a stillborn child that never sees
the sun.

[9]Before your pots can feel the heat of the
thorns —
whether they be green or dry — the
wicked will be swept away.[d]
[10]The righteous will be glad when they are
avenged,
when they dip their feet in the blood of
the wicked.
[11]Then people will say,
"Surely the righteous still are
rewarded;
surely there is a God who judges the
earth."

Psalm 59[e]

For the director of music. To the tune of "Do Not Destroy." Of David. A miktam.[c] *When Saul had sent men to watch David's house in order to kill him.*

[1]Deliver me from my enemies, O God;
be my fortress against those who are
attacking me.
[2]Deliver me from evildoers
and save me from those who are after
my blood.

[3]See how they lie in wait for me!
Fierce men conspire against me
for no offense or sin of mine, LORD.
[4]I have done no wrong, yet they are ready
to attack me.
Arise to help me; look on my plight!
[5]You, LORD God Almighty,
you who are the God of Israel,

[a] 3 The Hebrew has *Selah* (a word of uncertain meaning) here and at the end of verse 6. [b] In Hebrew texts 58:1-11 is numbered 58:2-12. [c] Title: Probably a literary or musical term [d] 9 The meaning of the Hebrew for this verse is uncertain. [e] In Hebrew texts 59:1-17 is numbered 59:2-18.

rouse yourself to punish all the
nations;
show no mercy to wicked traitors.[a]

6 They return at evening,
snarling like dogs,
and prowl about the city.
7 See what they spew from their
mouths —
the words from their lips are sharp
as swords,
and they think, "Who can hear us?"
8 But you laugh at them, LORD;
you scoff at all those nations.

9 You are my strength, I watch for you;
you, God, are my fortress,
10 my God on whom I can rely.

God will go before me
and will let me gloat over those who
slander me.
11 But do not kill them, Lord our shield,[b]
or my people will forget.
In your might uproot them
and bring them down.
12 For the sins of their mouths,
for the words of their lips,
let them be caught in their pride.
For the curses and lies they utter,
13 consume them in your wrath,
consume them till they are no
more.
Then it will be known to the ends of
the earth
that God rules over Jacob.

14 They return at evening,
snarling like dogs,
and prowl about the city.
15 They wander about for food
and howl if not satisfied.
16 But I will sing of your strength,
in the morning I will sing of your
love;
for you are my fortress,
my refuge in times of trouble.

17 You are my strength, I sing praise
to you;
you, God, are my fortress,
my God on whom I can rely.

Psalm 60[c]

For the director of music. To the tune of "The Lily of the Covenant." A miktam[d] *of David. For teaching. When he fought Aram Naharaim[e] and Aram Zobah,[f] and when Joab returned and struck down twelve thousand Edomites in the Valley of Salt.*

1 You have rejected us, God, and burst
upon us;
you have been angry — now restore us!
2 You have shaken the land and torn it
open;
mend its fractures, for it is quaking.
3 You have shown your people desperate
times;
you have given us wine that makes us
stagger.
4 But for those who fear you, you have
raised a banner
to be unfurled against the bow.[g]

5 Save us and help us with your right hand,
that those you love may be delivered.
6 God has spoken from his sanctuary:
"In triumph I will parcel out Shechem
and measure off the Valley of Sukkoth.
7 Gilead is mine, and Manasseh is mine;
Ephraim is my helmet,
Judah is my scepter.
8 Moab is my washbasin,
on Edom I toss my sandal;
over Philistia I shout in triumph."
9 Who will bring me to the fortified city?
Who will lead me to Edom?
10 Is it not you, God, you who have now
rejected us
and no longer go out with our armies?
11 Give us aid against the enemy,
for human help is worthless.
12 With God we will gain the victory,
and he will trample down our enemies.

Psalm 61[h]

For the director of music. With stringed instruments. Of David.

1 Hear my cry, O God;
listen to my prayer.

2 From the ends of the earth I call to you,
I call as my heart grows faint;

[a] 5 The Hebrew has *Selah* (a word of uncertain meaning) here and at the end of verse 13. [b] 11 Or *sovereign*
[c] In Hebrew texts 60:1-12 is numbered 60:3-14. [d] Title: Probably a literary or musical term [e] Title: That is, Arameans of Northwest Mesopotamia [f] Title: That is, Arameans of central Syria [g] 4 The Hebrew has *Selah* (a word of uncertain meaning) here. [h] In Hebrew texts 61:1-8 is numbered 61:2-9.

lead me to the rock that is higher
than I.
3 For you have been my refuge,
a strong tower against the foe.

4 I long to dwell in your tent forever
and take refuge in the shelter of your
wings.[a]
5 For you, God, have heard my vows;
you have given me the heritage of
those who fear your name.

6 Increase the days of the king's life,
his years for many generations.
7 May he be enthroned in God's presence
forever;
appoint your love and faithfulness to
protect him.

8 Then I will ever sing in praise of your
name
and fulfill my vows day after day.

Psalm 62[b]

For the director of music.
For Jeduthun. A psalm of David.

1 Truly my soul finds rest in God;
my salvation comes from him.
2 Truly he is my rock and my salvation;
he is my fortress, I will never be
shaken.

3 How long will you assault me?
Would all of you throw me down —
this leaning wall, this tottering fence?
4 Surely they intend to topple me
from my lofty place;
they take delight in lies.
With their mouths they bless,
but in their hearts they curse.[c]

5 Yes, my soul, find rest in God;
my hope comes from him.
6 Truly he is my rock and my salvation;
he is my fortress, I will not be shaken.
7 My salvation and my honor depend
on God[d];
he is my mighty rock, my refuge.
8 Trust in him at all times, you people;
pour out your hearts to him,
for God is our refuge.

9 Surely the lowborn are but a breath,
the highborn are but a lie.
If weighed on a balance, they are
nothing;
together they are only a breath.
10 Do not trust in extortion
or put vain hope in stolen goods;
though your riches increase,
do not set your heart on them.

11 One thing God has spoken,
two things I have heard:
"Power belongs to you, God,
12 and with you, Lord, is unfailing love";
and, "You reward everyone
according to what they have done."

Psalm 63[e]

A psalm of David.
When he was in the Desert of Judah.

1 You, God, are my God,
earnestly I seek you;
I thirst for you,
my whole being longs for you,
in a dry and parched land
where there is no water.

2 I have seen you in the sanctuary
and beheld your power and your
glory.
3 Because your love is better than life,
my lips will glorify you.
4 I will praise you as long as I live,
and in your name I will lift up my
hands.
5 I will be fully satisfied as with the richest
of foods;
with singing lips my mouth will
praise you.

6 On my bed I remember you;
I think of you through the watches of
the night.
7 Because you are my help,
I sing in the shadow of your wings.
8 I cling to you;
your right hand upholds me.

9 Those who want to kill me will be
destroyed;
they will go down to the depths of
the earth.
10 They will be given over to the sword
and become food for jackals.

[a] 4 The Hebrew has *Selah* (a word of uncertain meaning) here. [b] In Hebrew texts 62:1-12 is numbered 62:2-13. [c] 4 The Hebrew has *Selah* (a word of uncertain meaning) here and at the end of verse 8. [d] 7 Or / *God Most High is my salvation and my honor* [e] In Hebrew texts 63:1-11 is numbered 63:2-12.

THE HEART OF WORSHIP

Matt Redman

When the music fades, all is stripped away
And I simply come
Longing just to bring something that's of worth
That will bless your heart

I'll bring you more than a song
For a song in itself is not what you have required
You search much deeper within
Through the way things appear
You're looking into my heart

I'm coming back to the heart of worship
And it's all about you, it's all about you Jesus
I'm sorry, Lord, for the thing I've made it
When it's all about you, it's all about you Jesus

King of endless worth no one could express
How much you deserve
Though I'm weak and poor all I have is yours
Every single breath

THE INSPIRATION

Ascribe to the LORD the glory due his name; worship the LORD in the splendor of his holiness.

—Psalm 29:2

Read also: Philippians 3:8

BEHIND THE SONG

One Sunday in the late 1990s, Mike Pilavachi, the pastor of Soul Survivor Watford church in England, did something radical. This young, vibrant church had been built on worship and, in many ways, was thriving.

"We spent a lot of time in our meetings approaching God with music," Soul Survivor worship leader Matt Redman recounts. "And yet something seemed to be missing — there was a dynamic that used to be there but wasn't anymore."

Pilavachi shocked the congregation when he decided to pull the plug, literally, on the worship music.

"He decided to get rid of the sound system and band for a season," Redman adds. "We gathered together with just our voices. His point was that we'd lost our way in worship, and that the way to get back to the heart would be to strip everything away."

The experience inspired Redman to craft a worship song that would remind his fellow church members, and himself, about the importance of not letting the trappings of worship get in the way of worship. The result was a quiet, simple song called "The Heart of Worship," which became the title track of Redman's first album of worship music.

While Christians around the world certainly had no idea what had led to the crafting of "The Heart of Worship," they certainly embraced it. In many ways the song became a touchstone for the growing "modern worship" movement. Now, well over a decade since its debut, this powerful song still rings like a bell.

Selah

Mike Pilavachi removed the musical accompaniment for his church's worship music in an effort to help his congregation focus on what matters most in worship. It's a good habit to periodically take inventory of your Christian life to make sure you haven't picked up any unnecessary baggage that might keep you from best accomplishing your calling. Are there any things in your life that you need to evaluate or "pull the plug" on? What steps are you going to take?

[11] But the king will rejoice in God;
all who swear by God will glory in him,
while the mouths of liars will be silenced.

Psalm 64[a]

For the director of music.
A psalm of David.

[1] Hear me, my God, as I voice my complaint;
protect my life from the threat of the enemy.

[2] Hide me from the conspiracy of the wicked,
from the plots of evildoers.
[3] They sharpen their tongues like swords
and aim cruel words like deadly arrows.
[4] They shoot from ambush at the innocent;
they shoot suddenly, without fear.

[5] They encourage each other in evil plans,
they talk about hiding their snares;
they say, "Who will see it[b]?"
[6] They plot injustice and say,
"We have devised a perfect plan!"
Surely the human mind and heart are cunning.

[7] But God will shoot them with his arrows;
they will suddenly be struck down.
[8] He will turn their own tongues against them
and bring them to ruin;
all who see them will shake their heads in scorn.
[9] All people will fear;
they will proclaim the works of God
and ponder what he has done.

[10] The righteous will rejoice in the LORD
and take refuge in him;
all the upright in heart will glory in him!

Psalm 65[c]

For the director of music.
A psalm of David. A song.

[1] Praise awaits[d] you, our God, in Zion;
to you our vows will be fulfilled.
[2] You who answer prayer,
to you all people will come.
[3] When we were overwhelmed by sins,
you forgave[e] our transgressions.
[4] Blessed are those you choose
and bring near to live in your courts!
We are filled with the good things of your house,
of your holy temple.

[5] You answer us with awesome and righteous deeds,
God our Savior,
the hope of all the ends of the earth
and of the farthest seas,
[6] who formed the mountains by your power,
having armed yourself with strength,
[7] who stilled the roaring of the seas,
the roaring of their waves,
and the turmoil of the nations.
[8] The whole earth is filled with awe at your wonders;
where morning dawns, where evening fades,
you call forth songs of joy.

[9] You care for the land and water it;
you enrich it abundantly.
The streams of God are filled with water
to provide the people with grain,
for so you have ordained it.[f]
[10] You drench its furrows and level its ridges;
you soften it with showers and bless its crops.
[11] You crown the year with your bounty,
and your carts overflow with abundance.
[12] The grasslands of the wilderness overflow;
the hills are clothed with gladness.
[13] The meadows are covered with flocks
and the valleys are mantled with grain;
they shout for joy and sing.

Psalm 66

For the director of music. A song. A psalm.

[1] Shout for joy to God, all the earth!
[2] Sing the glory of his name;
make his praise glorious.

[a] In Hebrew texts 64:1-10 is numbered 64:2-11. [b] 5 Or *us* [c] In Hebrew texts 65:1-13 is numbered 65:2-14. [d] *1* Or *befits*; the meaning of the Hebrew for this word is uncertain. [e] *3* Or *made atonement for* [f] *9* Or *for that is how you prepare the land*

[3] Say to God, "How awesome are your
deeds!
So great is your power
that your enemies cringe before you.
[4] All the earth bows down to you;
they sing praise to you,
they sing the praises of your name."[a]

[5] Come and see what God has done,
his awesome deeds for mankind!
[6] He turned the sea into dry land,
they passed through the waters on
foot—
come, let us rejoice in him.
[7] He rules forever by his power,
his eyes watch the nations—
let not the rebellious rise up
against him.
[8] Praise our God, all peoples,
let the sound of his praise be heard;
[9] he has preserved our lives
and kept our feet from slipping.
[10] For you, God, tested us;
you refined us like silver.
[11] You brought us into prison
and laid burdens on our backs.
[12] You let people ride over our heads;
we went through fire and water,
but you brought us to a place of
abundance.

[13] I will come to your temple with burnt
offerings
and fulfill my vows to you—
[14] vows my lips promised and my mouth
spoke
when I was in trouble.
[15] I will sacrifice fat animals to you
and an offering of rams;
I will offer bulls and goats.
[16] Come and hear, all you who fear God;
let me tell you what he has done for me.
[17] I cried out to him with my mouth;
his praise was on my tongue.
[18] If I had cherished sin in my heart,
the Lord would not have listened;
[19] but God has surely listened
and has heard my prayer.
[20] Praise be to God,
who has not rejected my prayer
or withheld his love from me!

Psalm 67[b]

For the director of music. With stringed instruments. A psalm. A song.

[1] May God be gracious to us and bless us
and make his face shine on us—[c]
[2] so that your ways may be known on
earth,
your salvation among all nations.

[3] May the peoples praise you, God;
may all the peoples praise you.
[4] May the nations be glad and sing for joy,
for you rule the peoples with equity
and guide the nations of the earth.
[5] May the peoples praise you, God;
may all the peoples praise you.

[6] The land yields its harvest;
God, our God, blesses us.
[7] May God bless us still,
so that all the ends of the earth will
fear him.

Psalm 68[d]

For the director of music. Of David. A psalm. A song.

[1] May God arise, may his enemies be
scattered;
may his foes flee before him.
[2] May you blow them away like smoke—
as wax melts before the fire,
may the wicked perish before God.
[3] But may the righteous be glad
and rejoice before God;
may they be happy and joyful.

[4] Sing to God, sing in praise of his name,
extol him who rides on the clouds[e];
rejoice before him—his name is
the LORD.
[5] A father to the fatherless, a defender of
widows,
is God in his holy dwelling.
[6] God sets the lonely in families,[f]
he leads out the prisoners with
singing;
but the rebellious live in a sun-
scorched land.

[7] When you, God, went out before your
people,

[a] 4 The Hebrew has *Selah* (a word of uncertain meaning) here and at the end of verses 7 and 15. [b] In Hebrew texts 67:1-7 is numbered 67:2-8. [c] 1 The Hebrew has *Selah* (a word of uncertain meaning) here and at the end of verse 4. [d] In Hebrew texts 68:1-35 is numbered 68:2-36. [e] 4 Or *name, / prepare the way for him who rides through the deserts* [f] 6 Or *the desolate in a homeland*

when you marched through the wilderness,[a]
8 the earth shook, the heavens poured down rain,
before God, the One of Sinai,
before God, the God of Israel.
9 You gave abundant showers, O God;
you refreshed your weary inheritance.
10 Your people settled in it,
and from your bounty, God, you provided for the poor.

11 The Lord announces the word,
and the women who proclaim it are a mighty throng:
12 "Kings and armies flee in haste;
the women at home divide the plunder.
13 Even while you sleep among the sheep pens,[b]
the wings of my dove are sheathed with silver,
its feathers with shining gold."
14 When the Almighty[c] scattered the kings in the land,
it was like snow fallen on Mount Zalmon.

15 Mount Bashan, majestic mountain,
Mount Bashan, rugged mountain,
16 why gaze in envy, you rugged mountain,
at the mountain where God chooses to reign,
where the LORD himself will dwell forever?
17 The chariots of God are tens of thousands
and thousands of thousands;
the Lord has come from Sinai into his sanctuary.[d]
18 When you ascended on high,
you took many captives;
you received gifts from people,
even from[e] the rebellious—
that you,[f] LORD God, might dwell there.

19 Praise be to the Lord, to God our Savior,
who daily bears our burdens.
20 Our God is a God who saves;
from the Sovereign LORD comes escape from death.

21 Surely God will crush the heads of his enemies,
the hairy crowns of those who go on in their sins.
22 The Lord says, "I will bring them from Bashan;
I will bring them from the depths of the sea,
23 that your feet may wade in the blood of your foes,
while the tongues of your dogs have their share."

24 Your procession, God, has come into view,
the procession of my God and King into the sanctuary.
25 In front are the singers, after them the musicians;
with them are the young women playing the timbrels.
26 Praise God in the great congregation;
praise the LORD in the assembly of Israel.
27 There is the little tribe of Benjamin, leading them,
there the great throng of Judah's princes,
and there the princes of Zebulun and of Naphtali.

28 Summon your power, God[g];
show us your strength, our God, as you have done before.
29 Because of your temple at Jerusalem
kings will bring you gifts.
30 Rebuke the beast among the reeds,
the herd of bulls among the calves of the nations.
Humbled, may the beast bring bars of silver.
Scatter the nations who delight in war.
31 Envoys will come from Egypt;
Cush[h] will submit herself to God.

32 Sing to God, you kingdoms of the earth,
sing praise to the Lord,
33 to him who rides across the highest heavens, the ancient heavens,
who thunders with mighty voice.

[a] *7* The Hebrew has *Selah* (a word of uncertain meaning) here and at the end of verses 19 and 32.
[b] *13* Or *the campfires;* or *the saddlebags* [c] *14* Hebrew *Shaddai* [d] *17* Probable reading of the original Hebrew text; Masoretic Text *Lord is among them at Sinai in holiness* [e] *18* Or *gifts for people, / even* [f] *18* Or *they* [g] *28* Many Hebrew manuscripts, Septuagint and Syriac; most Hebrew manuscripts *Your God has summoned power for you* [h] *31* That is, the upper Nile region

[34] Proclaim the power of God,
whose majesty is over Israel,
whose power is in the heavens.
[35] You, God, are awesome in your sanctuary;
the God of Israel gives power and strength to his people.

Praise be to God!

Psalm 69[a]

For the director of music.
To the tune of "Lilies." Of David.

[1] Save me, O God,
for the waters have come up to my neck.
[2] I sink in the miry depths,
where there is no foothold.
I have come into the deep waters;
the floods engulf me.
[3] I am worn out calling for help;
my throat is parched.
My eyes fail,
looking for my God.
[4] Those who hate me without reason
outnumber the hairs of my head;
many are my enemies without cause,
those who seek to destroy me.
I am forced to restore
what I did not steal.

[5] You, God, know my folly;
my guilt is not hidden from you.

[6] Lord, the LORD Almighty,
may those who hope in you
not be disgraced because of me;
God of Israel,
may those who seek you
not be put to shame because of me.
[7] For I endure scorn for your sake,
and shame covers my face.
[8] I am a foreigner to my own family,
a stranger to my own mother's children;
[9] for zeal for your house consumes me,
and the insults of those who insult you fall on me.
[10] When I weep and fast,
I must endure scorn;
[11] when I put on sackcloth,
people make sport of me.
[12] Those who sit at the gate mock me,
and I am the song of the drunkards.
[13] But I pray to you, LORD,
in the time of your favor;
in your great love, O God,
answer me with your sure salvation.
[14] Rescue me from the mire,
do not let me sink;
deliver me from those who hate me,
from the deep waters.
[15] Do not let the floodwaters engulf me
or the depths swallow me up
or the pit close its mouth over me.

[16] Answer me, LORD, out of the goodness of your love;
in your great mercy turn to me.
[17] Do not hide your face from your servant;
answer me quickly, for I am in trouble.
[18] Come near and rescue me;
deliver me because of my foes.

[19] You know how I am scorned, disgraced and shamed;
all my enemies are before you.
[20] Scorn has broken my heart
and has left me helpless;
I looked for sympathy, but there was none,
for comforters, but I found none.
[21] They put gall in my food
and gave me vinegar for my thirst.

[22] May the table set before them become a snare;
may it become retribution and[b] a trap.
[23] May their eyes be darkened so they cannot see,
and their backs be bent forever.
[24] Pour out your wrath on them;
let your fierce anger overtake them.
[25] May their place be deserted;
let there be no one to dwell in their tents.
[26] For they persecute those you wound
and talk about the pain of those you hurt.
[27] Charge them with crime upon crime;
do not let them share in your salvation.
[28] May they be blotted out of the book of life
and not be listed with the righteous.

[29] But as for me, afflicted and in pain —
may your salvation, God, protect me.

[a] In Hebrew texts 69:1-36 is numbered 69:2-37.
[b] 22 Or *snare / and their fellowship become*

[30] I will praise God's name in song
and glorify him with thanksgiving.
[31] This will please the LORD more than an ox,
more than a bull with its horns and hooves.
[32] The poor will see and be glad —
you who seek God, may your hearts live!
[33] The LORD hears the needy
and does not despise his captive people.

[34] Let heaven and earth praise him,
the seas and all that move in them,
[35] for God will save Zion
and rebuild the cities of Judah.
Then people will settle there and possess it;
[36] the children of his servants will inherit it,
and those who love his name will dwell there.

Psalm 70[a]

For the director of music. Of David. A petition.

[1] Hasten, O God, to save me;
come quickly, LORD, to help me.
[2] May those who want to take my life
be put to shame and confusion;
may all who desire my ruin
be turned back in disgrace.
[3] May those who say to me, "Aha! Aha!"
turn back because of their shame.
[4] But may all who seek you
rejoice and be glad in you;
may those who long for your saving help
always say,
"The LORD is great!"

[5] But as for me, I am poor and needy;
come quickly to me, O God.
You are my help and my deliverer;
LORD, do not delay.

Psalm 71

[1] In you, LORD, I have taken refuge;
let me never be put to shame.
[2] In your righteousness, rescue me and deliver me;
turn your ear to me and save me.
[3] Be my rock of refuge,
to which I can always go;
give the command to save me,
for you are my rock and my fortress.
[4] Deliver me, my God, from the hand of the wicked,
from the grasp of those who are evil and cruel.

[5] For you have been my hope, Sovereign LORD,
my confidence since my youth.
[6] From birth I have relied on you;
you brought me forth from my mother's womb.
I will ever praise you.
[7] I have become a sign to many;
you are my strong refuge.
[8] My mouth is filled with your praise,
declaring your splendor all day long.
[9] Do not cast me away when I am old;
do not forsake me when my strength is gone.
[10] For my enemies speak against me;
those who wait to kill me conspire together.
[11] They say, "God has forsaken him;
pursue him and seize him,
for no one will rescue him."
[12] Do not be far from me, my God;
come quickly, God, to help me.
[13] May my accusers perish in shame;
may those who want to harm me
be covered with scorn and disgrace.

[14] As for me, I will always have hope;
I will praise you more and more.

[15] My mouth will tell of your righteous deeds,
of your saving acts all day long —
though I know not how to relate them all.
[16] I will come and proclaim your mighty acts, Sovereign LORD;
I will proclaim your righteous deeds, yours alone.
[17] Since my youth, God, you have taught me,
and to this day I declare your marvelous deeds.
[18] Even when I am old and gray,
do not forsake me, my God,
till I declare your power to the next generation,

[a] In Hebrew texts 70:1-5 is numbered 70:2-6.

your mighty acts to all who are to come.

19 Your righteousness, God, reaches to the heavens,
you who have done great things.
Who is like you, God?
20 Though you have made me see troubles,
many and bitter,
you will restore my life again;
from the depths of the earth
you will again bring me up.
21 You will increase my honor
and comfort me once more.

22 I will praise you with the harp
for your faithfulness, my God;
I will sing praise to you with the lyre,
Holy One of Israel.
23 My lips will shout for joy
when I sing praise to you—
I whom you have delivered.
24 My tongue will tell of your righteous acts
all day long,
for those who wanted to harm me
have been put to shame and confusion.

Psalm 72

Of Solomon.

1 Endow the king with your justice, O God,
the royal son with your righteousness.
2 May he judge your people in righteousness,
your afflicted ones with justice.

3 May the mountains bring prosperity to the people,
the hills the fruit of righteousness.
4 May he defend the afflicted among the people
and save the children of the needy;
may he crush the oppressor.
5 May he endure[a] as long as the sun,
as long as the moon, through all generations.
6 May he be like rain falling on a mown field,
like showers watering the earth.
7 In his days may the righteous flourish
and prosperity abound till the moon is no more.

8 May he rule from sea to sea
and from the River[b] to the ends of the earth.
9 May the desert tribes bow before him
and his enemies lick the dust.
10 May the kings of Tarshish and of distant shores
bring tribute to him.
May the kings of Sheba and Seba
present him gifts.
11 May all kings bow down to him
and all nations serve him.
12 For he will deliver the needy who cry out,
the afflicted who have no one to help.
13 He will take pity on the weak and the needy
and save the needy from death.
14 He will rescue them from oppression and violence,
for precious is their blood in his sight.

15 Long may he live!
May gold from Sheba be given him.
May people ever pray for him
and bless him all day long.
16 May grain abound throughout the land;
on the tops of the hills may it sway.
May the crops flourish like Lebanon
and thrive[c] like the grass of the field.
17 May his name endure forever;
may it continue as long as the sun.

Then all nations will be blessed through him,[d]
and they will call him blessed.

18 Praise be to the LORD God, the God of Israel,
who alone does marvelous deeds.
19 Praise be to his glorious name forever;
may the whole earth be filled with his glory.
Amen and Amen.

20 This concludes the prayers of David son of Jesse.

[a] 5 Septuagint; Hebrew *You will be feared* [b] 8 That is, the Euphrates [c] *16* Probable reading of the original Hebrew text; Masoretic Text *Lebanon, / from the city* [d] *17* Or *will use his name in blessings* (see Gen. 48:20)

BOOK III

Psalms 73–89

Psalm 73

A psalm of Asaph.

[1] Surely God is good to Israel,
to those who are pure in heart.

[2] But as for me, my feet had almost slipped;
I had nearly lost my foothold.
[3] For I envied the arrogant
when I saw the prosperity of the wicked.

[4] They have no struggles;
their bodies are healthy and strong.[a]
[5] They are free from common human burdens;
they are not plagued by human ills.
[6] Therefore pride is their necklace;
they clothe themselves with violence.
[7] From their callous hearts comes iniquity[b];
their evil imaginations have no limits.
[8] They scoff, and speak with malice;
with arrogance they threaten oppression.
[9] Their mouths lay claim to heaven,
and their tongues take possession of the earth.
[10] Therefore their people turn to them
and drink up waters in abundance.[c]
[11] They say, "How would God know?
Does the Most High know anything?"

[12] This is what the wicked are like—
always free of care, they go on amassing wealth.

[13] Surely in vain I have kept my heart pure
and have washed my hands in innocence.
[14] All day long I have been afflicted,
and every morning brings new punishments.

[15] If I had spoken out like that,
I would have betrayed your children.
[16] When I tried to understand all this,
it troubled me deeply
[17] till I entered the sanctuary of God;
then I understood their final destiny.

[18] Surely you place them on slippery ground;
you cast them down to ruin.
[19] How suddenly are they destroyed,
completely swept away by terrors!
[20] They are like a dream when one awakes;
when you arise, Lord,
you will despise them as fantasies.

[21] When my heart was grieved
and my spirit embittered,
[22] I was senseless and ignorant;
I was a brute beast before you.

[23] Yet I am always with you;
you hold me by my right hand.
[24] You guide me with your counsel,
and afterward you will take me into glory.
[25] Whom have I in heaven but you?
And earth has nothing I desire besides you.
[26] My flesh and my heart may fail,
but God is the strength of my heart
and my portion forever.

[27] Those who are far from you will perish;
you destroy all who are unfaithful to you.
[28] But as for me, it is good to be near God.
I have made the Sovereign LORD my refuge;
I will tell of all your deeds.

Psalm 74

A maskil[d] of Asaph.

[1] O God, why have you rejected us forever?
Why does your anger smolder against the sheep of your pasture?
[2] Remember the nation you purchased long ago,
the people of your inheritance, whom you redeemed—
Mount Zion, where you dwelt.
[3] Turn your steps toward these everlasting ruins,
all this destruction the enemy has brought on the sanctuary.

[4] Your foes roared in the place where you met with us;
they set up their standards as signs.

[a] 4 With a different word division of the Hebrew; Masoretic Text *struggles at their death; / their bodies are healthy* [b] 7 Syriac (see also Septuagint); Hebrew *Their eyes bulge with fat* [c] 10 The meaning of the Hebrew for this verse is uncertain. [d] Title: Probably a literary or musical term

5 They behaved like men wielding axes
to cut through a thicket of trees.
6 They smashed all the carved paneling
with their axes and hatchets.
7 They burned your sanctuary to the ground;
they defiled the dwelling place of your Name.
8 They said in their hearts, "We will crush them completely!"
They burned every place where God was worshiped in the land.
9 We are given no signs from God;
no prophets are left,
and none of us knows how long this will be.
10 How long will the enemy mock you, God?
Will the foe revile your name forever?
11 Why do you hold back your hand, your right hand?
Take it from the folds of your garment and destroy them!

12 But God is my King from long ago;
he brings salvation on the earth.

13 It was you who split open the sea by your power;
you broke the heads of the monster in the waters.
14 It was you who crushed the heads of Leviathan
and gave it as food to the creatures of the desert.
15 It was you who opened up springs and streams;
you dried up the ever-flowing rivers.
16 The day is yours, and yours also the night;
you established the sun and moon.
17 It was you who set all the boundaries of the earth;
you made both summer and winter.

18 Remember how the enemy has mocked you, LORD,
how foolish people have reviled your name.
19 Do not hand over the life of your dove to wild beasts;
do not forget the lives of your afflicted people forever.
20 Have regard for your covenant,
because haunts of violence fill the dark places of the land.
21 Do not let the oppressed retreat in disgrace;
may the poor and needy praise your name.
22 Rise up, O God, and defend your cause;
remember how fools mock you all day long.
23 Do not ignore the clamor of your adversaries,
the uproar of your enemies, which rises continually.

Psalm 75[a]

For the director of music.
To the tune of "Do Not Destroy."
A psalm of Asaph. A song.

1 We praise you, God,
we praise you, for your Name is near;
people tell of your wonderful deeds.

2 You say, "I choose the appointed time;
it is I who judge with equity.
3 When the earth and all its people quake,
it is I who hold its pillars firm.[b]
4 To the arrogant I say, 'Boast no more,'
and to the wicked, 'Do not lift up your horns.[c]
5 Do not lift your horns against heaven;
do not speak so defiantly.' "
6 No one from the east or the west
or from the desert can exalt themselves.
7 It is God who judges:
He brings one down, he exalts another.
8 In the hand of the LORD is a cup
full of foaming wine mixed with spices;
he pours it out, and all the wicked of the earth
drink it down to its very dregs.

9 As for me, I will declare this forever;
I will sing praise to the God of Jacob,
10 who says, "I will cut off the horns of all the wicked,
but the horns of the righteous will be lifted up."

[a] In Hebrew texts 75:1-10 is numbered 75:2-11. [b] 3 The Hebrew has *Selah* (a word of uncertain meaning) here. [c] 4 *Horns* here symbolize strength; also in verses 5 and 10.

Psalm 76[a]

For the director of music. With stringed instruments. A psalm of Asaph. A song.

1 God is renowned in Judah;
in Israel his name is great.
2 His tent is in Salem,
his dwelling place in Zion.
3 There he broke the flashing arrows,
the shields and the swords, the weapons of war.[b]

4 You are radiant with light,
more majestic than mountains rich with game.
5 The valiant lie plundered,
they sleep their last sleep;
not one of the warriors
can lift his hands.
6 At your rebuke, God of Jacob,
both horse and chariot lie still.

7 It is you alone who are to be feared.
Who can stand before you when you are angry?
8 From heaven you pronounced judgment,
and the land feared and was quiet—
9 when you, God, rose up to judge,
to save all the afflicted of the land.
10 Surely your wrath against mankind brings you praise,
and the survivors of your wrath are restrained.[c]

11 Make vows to the LORD your God and fulfill them;
let all the neighboring lands
bring gifts to the One to be feared.
12 He breaks the spirit of rulers;
he is feared by the kings of the earth.

Psalm 77[d]

For the director of music. For Jeduthun. Of Asaph. A psalm.

1 I cried out to God for help;
I cried out to God to hear me.
2 When I was in distress, I sought the Lord;
at night I stretched out untiring hands,
and I would not be comforted.

3 I remembered you, God, and I groaned;
I meditated, and my spirit grew faint.[e]
4 You kept my eyes from closing;
I was too troubled to speak.
5 I thought about the former days,
the years of long ago;
6 I remembered my songs in the night.
My heart meditated and my spirit asked:

7 "Will the Lord reject forever?
Will he never show his favor again?
8 Has his unfailing love vanished forever?
Has his promise failed for all time?
9 Has God forgotten to be merciful?
Has he in anger withheld his compassion?"

10 Then I thought, "To this I will appeal:
the years when the Most High stretched out his right hand.
11 I will remember the deeds of the LORD;
yes, I will remember your miracles of long ago.
12 I will consider all your works
and meditate on all your mighty deeds."

13 Your ways, God, are holy.
What god is as great as our God?
14 You are the God who performs miracles;
you display your power among the peoples.
15 With your mighty arm you redeemed your people,
the descendants of Jacob and Joseph.

16 The waters saw you, God,
the waters saw you and writhed;
the very depths were convulsed.
17 The clouds poured down water,
the heavens resounded with thunder;
your arrows flashed back and forth.
18 Your thunder was heard in the whirlwind,
your lightning lit up the world;
the earth trembled and quaked.
19 Your path led through the sea,
your way through the mighty waters,
though your footprints were not seen.

20 You led your people like a flock
by the hand of Moses and Aaron.

[a] In Hebrew texts 76:1-12 is numbered 76:2-13. [b] *3* The Hebrew has *Selah* (a word of uncertain meaning) here and at the end of verse 9. [c] *10* Or *Surely the wrath of mankind brings you praise, / and with the remainder of wrath you arm yourself* [d] In Hebrew texts 77:1-20 is numbered 77:2-21. [e] *3* The Hebrew has *Selah* (a word of uncertain meaning) here and at the end of verses 9 and 15.

Psalm 78

A maskil[a] of Asaph.

[1] My people, hear my teaching;
listen to the words of my mouth.
[2] I will open my mouth with a parable;
I will utter hidden things, things from of old—
[3] things we have heard and known,
things our ancestors have told us.
[4] We will not hide them from their descendants;
we will tell the next generation
the praiseworthy deeds of the LORD,
his power, and the wonders he has done.
[5] He decreed statutes for Jacob
and established the law in Israel,
which he commanded our ancestors
to teach their children,
[6] so the next generation would know them,
even the children yet to be born,
and they in turn would tell their children.
[7] Then they would put their trust in God
and would not forget his deeds
but would keep his commands.
[8] They would not be like their ancestors—
a stubborn and rebellious generation,
whose hearts were not loyal to God,
whose spirits were not faithful to him.

[9] The men of Ephraim, though armed with bows,
turned back on the day of battle;
[10] they did not keep God's covenant
and refused to live by his law.
[11] They forgot what he had done,
the wonders he had shown them.
[12] He did miracles in the sight of their ancestors
in the land of Egypt, in the region of Zoan.
[13] He divided the sea and led them through;
he made the water stand up like a wall.
[14] He guided them with the cloud by day
and with light from the fire all night.
[15] He split the rocks in the wilderness
and gave them water as abundant as the seas;
[16] he brought streams out of a rocky crag
and made water flow down like rivers.

[17] But they continued to sin against him,
rebelling in the wilderness against the Most High.
[18] They willfully put God to the test
by demanding the food they craved.
[19] They spoke against God;
they said, "Can God really
spread a table in the wilderness?
[20] True, he struck the rock,
and water gushed out,
streams flowed abundantly,
but can he also give us bread?
Can he supply meat for his people?"
[21] When the LORD heard them, he was furious;
his fire broke out against Jacob,
and his wrath rose against Israel,
[22] for they did not believe in God
or trust in his deliverance.
[23] Yet he gave a command to the skies above
and opened the doors of the heavens;
[24] he rained down manna for the people to eat,
he gave them the grain of heaven.
[25] Human beings ate the bread of angels;
he sent them all the food they could eat.
[26] He let loose the east wind from the heavens
and by his power made the south wind blow.
[27] He rained meat down on them like dust,
birds like sand on the seashore.
[28] He made them come down inside their camp,
all around their tents.
[29] They ate till they were gorged—
he had given them what they craved.
[30] But before they turned from what they craved,
even while the food was still in their mouths,
[31] God's anger rose against them;
he put to death the sturdiest among them,
cutting down the young men of Israel.
[32] In spite of all this, they kept on sinning;
in spite of his wonders, they did not believe.
[33] So he ended their days in futility
and their years in terror.
[34] Whenever God slew them, they would seek him;
they eagerly turned to him again.

[a] Title: Probably a literary or musical term

35 They remembered that God was their Rock,
that God Most High was their Redeemer.
36 But then they would flatter him with their mouths,
lying to him with their tongues;
37 their hearts were not loyal to him,
they were not faithful to his covenant.
38 Yet he was merciful;
he forgave their iniquities
and did not destroy them.
Time after time he restrained his anger
and did not stir up his full wrath.
39 He remembered that they were but flesh,
a passing breeze that does not return.

40 How often they rebelled against him in the wilderness
and grieved him in the wasteland!
41 Again and again they put God to the test;
they vexed the Holy One of Israel.
42 They did not remember his power —
the day he redeemed them from the oppressor,
43 the day he displayed his signs in Egypt,
his wonders in the region of Zoan.
44 He turned their river into blood;
they could not drink from their streams.
45 He sent swarms of flies that devoured them,
and frogs that devastated them.
46 He gave their crops to the grasshopper,
their produce to the locust.
47 He destroyed their vines with hail
and their sycamore-figs with sleet.
48 He gave over their cattle to the hail,
their livestock to bolts of lightning.
49 He unleashed against them his hot anger,
his wrath, indignation and hostility —
a band of destroying angels.
50 He prepared a path for his anger;
he did not spare them from death
but gave them over to the plague.
51 He struck down all the firstborn of Egypt,
the firstfruits of manhood in the tents of Ham.
52 But he brought his people out like a flock;
he led them like sheep through the wilderness.
53 He guided them safely, so they were unafraid;
but the sea engulfed their enemies.
54 And so he brought them to the border of his holy land,
to the hill country his right hand had taken.
55 He drove out nations before them
and allotted their lands to them as an inheritance;
he settled the tribes of Israel in their homes.

56 But they put God to the test
and rebelled against the Most High;
they did not keep his statutes.
57 Like their ancestors they were disloyal and faithless,
as unreliable as a faulty bow.
58 They angered him with their high places;
they aroused his jealousy with their idols.
59 When God heard them, he was furious;
he rejected Israel completely.
60 He abandoned the tabernacle of Shiloh,
the tent he had set up among humans.
61 He sent the ark of his might into captivity,
his splendor into the hands of the enemy.
62 He gave his people over to the sword;
he was furious with his inheritance.
63 Fire consumed their young men,
and their young women had no wedding songs;
64 their priests were put to the sword,
and their widows could not weep.

65 Then the Lord awoke as from sleep,
as a warrior wakes from the stupor of wine.
66 He beat back his enemies;
he put them to everlasting shame.
67 Then he rejected the tents of Joseph,
he did not choose the tribe of Ephraim;
68 but he chose the tribe of Judah,
Mount Zion, which he loved.
69 He built his sanctuary like the heights,
like the earth that he established forever.
70 He chose David his servant
and took him from the sheep pens;
71 from tending the sheep he brought him
to be the shepherd of his people Jacob,
of Israel his inheritance.
72 And David shepherded them with integrity of heart;
with skillful hands he led them.

Psalm 79

A psalm of Asaph.

1 O God, the nations have invaded your
inheritance;
they have defiled your holy temple,
they have reduced Jerusalem to
rubble.
2 They have left the dead bodies of your
servants
as food for the birds of the sky,
the flesh of your own people for the
animals of the wild.
3 They have poured out blood like water
all around Jerusalem,
and there is no one to bury the dead.
4 We are objects of contempt to our
neighbors,
of scorn and derision to those
around us.

5 How long, LORD? Will you be angry
forever?
How long will your jealousy burn
like fire?
6 Pour out your wrath on the nations
that do not acknowledge you,
on the kingdoms
that do not call on your name;
7 for they have devoured Jacob
and devastated his homeland.

8 Do not hold against us the sins of past
generations;
may your mercy come quickly to
meet us,
for we are in desperate need.
9 Help us, God our Savior,
for the glory of your name;
deliver us and forgive our sins
for your name's sake.
10 Why should the nations say,
"Where is their God?"

Before our eyes, make known among the
nations
that you avenge the outpoured blood
of your servants.
11 May the groans of the prisoners come
before you;
with your strong arm preserve those
condemned to die.
12 Pay back into the laps of our neighbors
seven times
the contempt they have hurled at
you, Lord.
13 Then we your people, the sheep of your
pasture,
will praise you forever;
from generation to generation
we will proclaim your praise.

Psalm 80[a]

For the director of music. To the tune of "The Lilies of the Covenant." Of Asaph. A psalm.

1 Hear us, Shepherd of Israel,
you who lead Joseph like a flock.
You who sit enthroned between the
cherubim,
shine forth 2 before Ephraim,
Benjamin and Manasseh.
Awaken your might;
come and save us.

3 Restore us, O God;
make your face shine on us,
that we may be saved.

4 How long, LORD God Almighty,
will your anger smolder
against the prayers of your people?
5 You have fed them with the bread of
tears;
you have made them drink tears by
the bowlful.
6 You have made us an object of derision[b]
to our neighbors,
and our enemies mock us.

7 Restore us, God Almighty;
make your face shine on us,
that we may be saved.

8 You transplanted a vine from Egypt;
you drove out the nations and
planted it.
9 You cleared the ground for it,
and it took root and filled the land.
10 The mountains were covered with its
shade,
the mighty cedars with its branches.
11 Its branches reached as far as the Sea,[c]
its shoots as far as the River.[d]

12 Why have you broken down its walls
so that all who pass by pick its grapes?
13 Boars from the forest ravage it,
and insects from the fields feed on it.

[a] In Hebrew texts 80:1-19 is numbered 80:2-20. [b] *6* Probable reading of the original Hebrew text; Masoretic Text *contention* [c] *11* Probably the Mediterranean [d] *11* That is, the Euphrates

[14] Return to us, God Almighty!
Look down from heaven and see!
Watch over this vine,
[15] the root your right hand has planted,
the son[a] you have raised up for yourself.

[16] Your vine is cut down, it is burned with fire;
at your rebuke your people perish.
[17] Let your hand rest on the man at your right hand,
the son of man you have raised up for yourself.
[18] Then we will not turn away from you;
revive us, and we will call on your name.

[19] Restore us, LORD God Almighty;
make your face shine on us,
that we may be saved.

Psalm 81[b]

For the director of music. According to gittith.[c] *Of Asaph.*

[1] Sing for joy to God our strength;
shout aloud to the God of Jacob!
[2] Begin the music, strike the timbrel,
play the melodious harp and lyre.
[3] Sound the ram's horn at the New Moon,
and when the moon is full, on the day of our festival;
[4] this is a decree for Israel,
an ordinance of the God of Jacob.
[5] When God went out against Egypt,
he established it as a statute for Joseph.

I heard an unknown voice say:

[6] "I removed the burden from their shoulders;
their hands were set free from the basket.
[7] In your distress you called and I rescued you,
I answered you out of a thundercloud;
I tested you at the waters of Meribah.[d]
[8] Hear me, my people, and I will warn you—
if you would only listen to me, Israel!
[9] You shall have no foreign god among you;
you shall not worship any god other than me.
[10] I am the LORD your God,
who brought you up out of Egypt.
Open wide your mouth and I will fill it.

[11] "But my people would not listen to me;
Israel would not submit to me.
[12] So I gave them over to their stubborn hearts
to follow their own devices.

[13] "If my people would only listen to me,
if Israel would only follow my ways,
[14] how quickly I would subdue their enemies
and turn my hand against their foes!
[15] Those who hate the LORD would cringe before him,
and their punishment would last forever.
[16] But you would be fed with the finest of wheat;
with honey from the rock I would satisfy you."

Psalm 82

A psalm of Asaph.

[1] God presides in the great assembly;
he renders judgment among the "gods":

[2] "How long will you[e] defend the unjust
and show partiality to the wicked?[d]
[3] Defend the weak and the fatherless;
uphold the cause of the poor and the oppressed.
[4] Rescue the weak and the needy;
deliver them from the hand of the wicked.

[5] "The 'gods' know nothing, they understand nothing.
They walk about in darkness;
all the foundations of the earth are shaken.

[6] "I said, 'You are "gods";
you are all sons of the Most High.'
[7] But you will die like mere mortals;
you will fall like every other ruler."
[8] Rise up, O God, judge the earth,
for all the nations are your inheritance.

[a] *15* Or *branch* [b] In Hebrew texts 81:1-16 is numbered 81:2-17. [c] Title: Probably a musical term
[d] *7,2* The Hebrew has *Selah* (a word of uncertain meaning) here. [e] *2* The Hebrew is plural.

Psalm 83[a]

A song. A psalm of Asaph.

1 O God, do not remain silent;
do not turn a deaf ear,
do not stand aloof, O God.
2 See how your enemies growl,
how your foes rear their heads.
3 With cunning they conspire against your people;
they plot against those you cherish.
4 "Come," they say, "let us destroy them as a nation,
so that Israel's name is remembered no more."

5 With one mind they plot together;
they form an alliance against you—
6 the tents of Edom and the Ishmaelites,
of Moab and the Hagrites,
7 Byblos, Ammon and Amalek,
Philistia, with the people of Tyre.
8 Even Assyria has joined them
to reinforce Lot's descendants.[b]

9 Do to them as you did to Midian,
as you did to Sisera and Jabin at the river Kishon,
10 who perished at Endor
and became like dung on the ground
11 Make their nobles like Oreb and Zeeb,
all their princes like Zebah and Zalmunna,
12 who said, "Let us take possession
of the pasturelands of God."

13 Make them like tumbleweed, my God,
like chaff before the wind.
14 As fire consumes the forest
or a flame sets the mountains ablaze,
15 so pursue them with your tempest
and terrify them with your storm.
16 Cover their faces with shame, LORD,
so that they will seek your name.

17 May they ever be ashamed and dismayed;
may they perish in disgrace.
18 Let them know that you, whose name is the LORD—
that you alone are the Most High over all the earth.

Psalm 84[c]

For the director of music. According to gittith.[d] *Of the Sons of Korah. A psalm.*

1 How lovely is your dwelling place,
LORD Almighty!
2 My soul yearns, even faints,
for the courts of the LORD;
my heart and my flesh cry out
for the living God.
3 Even the sparrow has found a home,
and the swallow a nest for herself,
where she may have her young—
a place near your altar,
LORD Almighty, my King and my God.
4 Blessed are those who dwell in your house;
they are ever praising you.[e]

5 Blessed are those whose strength is in you,
whose hearts are set on pilgrimage.
6 As they pass through the Valley of Baka,
they make it a place of springs;
the autumn rains also cover it with pools.[f]
7 They go from strength to strength,
till each appears before God in Zion.

8 Hear my prayer, LORD God Almighty;
listen to me, God of Jacob.
9 Look on our shield,[g] O God;
look with favor on your anointed one.

10 Better is one day in your courts
than a thousand elsewhere;
I would rather be a doorkeeper in the house of my God
than dwell in the tents of the wicked.
11 For the LORD God is a sun and shield;
the LORD bestows favor and honor;
no good thing does he withhold
from those whose walk is blameless.

12 LORD Almighty,
blessed is the one who trusts in you.

[a] In Hebrew texts 83:1-18 is numbered 83:2-19. [b] 8 The Hebrew has *Selah* (a word of uncertain meaning) here. [c] In Hebrew texts 84:1-12 is numbered 84:2-13. [d] Title: Probably a musical term [e] 4 The Hebrew has *Selah* (a word of uncertain meaning) here and at the end of verse 8. [f] 6 Or *blessings* [g] 9 Or *sovereign*

YOU NEVER LET GO

Matt Redman, Beth Redman

Even though I walk through the valley of the shadow of death
Your perfect love is casting out fear
And even when I'm caught in the middle of the storms of this life
I won't turn back
I know you are near

And I will fear no evil
For my God is with me
And if my God is with me
Whom then shall I fear
Whom then shall I fear

Oh no, you never let go
Through the calm and through the storm
Oh no, you never let go
In ev'ry high and ev'ry low
Oh no, you never let go
Lord, you never let go of me

And I can see a light that is coming for the heart that holds on
A glorious light beyond all compare
And there will be an end to these troubles
But until that day comes
We'll live to know you here on the earth

Yes, I can see a light that is coming
For the heart that holds on
And there will be an end to these troubles
But until that day comes
Still I will praise you
Still I will praise you

THE INSPIRATION

Even though I walk through the darkest valley, I will fear no evil, for you are with me; your rod and your staff, they comfort me.

—Psalm 23:4

Read also: Deuteronomy 31:6

BEHIND THE SONG

When Matt and Beth Redman crafted the worship anthem "You Never Let Go," it came from painful personal tragedy — the miscarriage of a baby. And the Redman's emotions and faith were rocked not only by personal tragedy but also by terrorist attacks in their hometown of London. The couple dove into Psalm 23 for comfort and guidance. There they found the words of King David, a man who was no stranger to heartache and who turned to God for solace. This desperate faith pulses through every stanza of this powerful song.

"It was a depressing and dark time," Matt Redman admits. But the beautiful truth of God's love, protection and guidance had never been more vivid. Redman entitled the album on which "You Never Let Go" appeared *Beautiful News* because, "It truly is beautiful news."

As with other Redman compositions, "You Never Let Go" fills an important need in the modern worship songbook. Instead of ignoring the hard times in life or dismissing them with platitudes, "You Never Let Go" follows right in David's footsteps, acknowledging these dark times and insistently pointing through the clouds to the light on the other side.

Selah

Psalm 23 is undoubtedly one of the most quoted passages in the Bible. As you read through these verses, are there any phrases, words or stanzas that jump out at you — perhaps for the first time?

Read again the lyrics of "You Never Let Go" and sing along, thinking about the elements of your own "valley of death" and ask God to give you a glimpse of his glory behind your clouds.

Psalm 85[a]

For the director of music.
Of the Sons of Korah. A psalm.

1 You, LORD, showed favor to your land;
you restored the fortunes of Jacob.
2 You forgave the iniquity of your people
and covered all their sins.[b]
3 You set aside all your wrath
and turned from your fierce anger.

4 Restore us again, God our Savior,
and put away your displeasure toward us.
5 Will you be angry with us forever?
Will you prolong your anger through all generations?
6 Will you not revive us again,
that your people may rejoice in you?
7 Show us your unfailing love, LORD,
and grant us your salvation.

8 I will listen to what God the LORD says;
he promises peace to his people, his faithful servants —
but let them not turn to folly.
9 Surely his salvation is near those who fear him,
that his glory may dwell in our land.

10 Love and faithfulness meet together;
righteousness and peace kiss each other.
11 Faithfulness springs forth from the earth,
and righteousness looks down from heaven.
12 The LORD will indeed give what is good,
and our land will yield its harvest.
13 Righteousness goes before him
and prepares the way for his steps.

Psalm 86

A prayer of David.

1 Hear me, LORD, and answer me,
for I am poor and needy.
2 Guard my life, for I am faithful to you;
save your servant who trusts in you.
You are my God; 3 have mercy on me, Lord,
for I call to you all day long.
4 Bring joy to your servant, Lord,
for I put my trust in you.

5 You, Lord, are forgiving and good,
abounding in love to all who call to you.
6 Hear my prayer, LORD;
listen to my cry for mercy.
7 When I am in distress, I call to you,
because you answer me.

8 Among the gods there is none like you, Lord;
no deeds can compare with yours.
9 All the nations you have made
will come and worship before you, Lord;
they will bring glory to your name.
10 For you are great and do marvelous deeds;
you alone are God.

11 Teach me your way, LORD,
that I may rely on your faithfulness;
give me an undivided heart,
that I may fear your name.
12 I will praise you, Lord my God, with all my heart;
I will glorify your name forever.
13 For great is your love toward me;
you have delivered me from the depths,
from the realm of the dead.

14 Arrogant foes are attacking me, O God;
ruthless people are trying to kill me —
they have no regard for you.
15 But you, Lord, are a compassionate and gracious God,
slow to anger, abounding in love and faithfulness.
16 Turn to me and have mercy on me;
show your strength in behalf of your servant;
save me, because I serve you
just as my mother did.
17 Give me a sign of your goodness,
that my enemies may see it and be put to shame,
for you, LORD, have helped me and comforted me.

Psalm 87

Of the Sons of Korah. A psalm. A song.

1 He has founded his city on the holy mountain.

[a] In Hebrew texts 85:1-13 is numbered 85:2-14. [b] 2 The Hebrew has *Selah* (a word of uncertain meaning) here.

[2] The LORD loves the gates of Zion
more than all the other dwellings of Jacob.
[3] Glorious things are said of you,
city of God:[a]
[4] "I will record Rahab[b] and Babylon
among those who acknowledge me—
Philistia too, and Tyre, along with Cush[c]—
and will say, 'This one was born in Zion.'"[d]
[5] Indeed, of Zion it will be said,
"This one and that one were born in her,
and the Most High himself will establish her."
[6] The LORD will write in the register of the peoples:
"This one was born in Zion."
[7] As they make music they will sing,
"All my fountains are in you."

Psalm 88[e]

A song. A psalm of the Sons of Korah. For the director of music. According to mahalath leannoth.[f] *A* maskil[g] *of Heman the Ezrahite.*

[1] LORD, you are the God who saves me;
day and night I cry out to you.
[2] May my prayer come before you;
turn your ear to my cry.

[3] I am overwhelmed with troubles
and my life draws near to death.
[4] I am counted among those who go down to the pit;
I am like one without strength.
[5] I am set apart with the dead,
like the slain who lie in the grave,
whom you remember no more,
who are cut off from your care.

[6] You have put me in the lowest pit,
in the darkest depths.
[7] Your wrath lies heavily on me;
you have overwhelmed me with all your waves.[h]
[8] You have taken from me my closest friends
and have made me repulsive to them.
I am confined and cannot escape;
[9] my eyes are dim with grief.

I call to you, LORD, every day;
I spread out my hands to you.
[10] Do you show your wonders to the dead?
Do their spirits rise up and praise you?
[11] Is your love declared in the grave,
your faithfulness in Destruction[i]?
[12] Are your wonders known in the place of darkness,
or your righteous deeds in the land of oblivion?

[13] But I cry to you for help, LORD;
in the morning my prayer comes before you.
[14] Why, LORD, do you reject me
and hide your face from me?

[15] From my youth I have suffered and been close to death;
I have borne your terrors and am in despair.
[16] Your wrath has swept over me;
your terrors have destroyed me.
[17] All day long they surround me like a flood;
they have completely engulfed me.
[18] You have taken from me friend and neighbor—
darkness is my closest friend.

Psalm 89[j]

A maskil[g] *of Ethan the Ezrahite.*

[1] I will sing of the LORD's great love forever;
with my mouth I will make your faithfulness known
through all generations.
[2] I will declare that your love stands firm forever,
that you have established your faithfulness in heaven itself.
[3] You said, "I have made a covenant with my chosen one,

[a] *3* The Hebrew has *Selah* (a word of uncertain meaning) here and at the end of verse 6. [b] *4* A poetic name for Egypt [c] *4* That is, the upper Nile region [d] *4* Or *"I will record concerning those who acknowledge me: / 'This one was born in Zion.' / Hear this, Rahab and Babylon, / and you too, Philistia, Tyre and Cush."* [e] In Hebrew texts 88:1-18 is numbered 88:2-19. [f] Title: Possibly a tune, "The Suffering of Affliction" [g] Title: Probably a literary or musical term [h] *7* The Hebrew has *Selah* (a word of uncertain meaning) here and at the end of verse 10. [i] *11* Hebrew *Abaddon* [j] In Hebrew texts 89:1-52 is numbered 89:2-53.

I have sworn to David my servant,
4 'I will establish your line forever
and make your throne firm through all generations.' "[a]

5 The heavens praise your wonders, LORD,
your faithfulness too, in the assembly of the holy ones.
6 For who in the skies above can compare with the LORD?
Who is like the LORD among the heavenly beings?
7 In the council of the holy ones God is greatly feared;
he is more awesome than all who surround him.
8 Who is like you, LORD God Almighty?
You, LORD, are mighty, and your faithfulness surrounds you.

9 You rule over the surging sea;
when its waves mount up, you still them.
10 You crushed Rahab like one of the slain;
with your strong arm you scattered your enemies.
11 The heavens are yours, and yours also the earth;
you founded the world and all that is in it.
12 You created the north and the south;
Tabor and Hermon sing for joy at your name.
13 Your arm is endowed with power;
your hand is strong, your right hand exalted.

14 Righteousness and justice are the foundation of your throne;
love and faithfulness go before you.
15 Blessed are those who have learned to acclaim you,
who walk in the light of your presence, LORD.
16 They rejoice in your name all day long;
they celebrate your righteousness.
17 For you are their glory and strength,
and by your favor you exalt our horn.[b]
18 Indeed, our shield[c] belongs to the LORD,
our king to the Holy One of Israel.

19 Once you spoke in a vision,
to your faithful people you said:
"I have bestowed strength on a warrior;
I have raised up a young man from among the people.
20 I have found David my servant;
with my sacred oil I have anointed him.
21 My hand will sustain him;
surely my arm will strengthen him.
22 The enemy will not get the better of him;
the wicked will not oppress him.
23 I will crush his foes before him
and strike down his adversaries.
24 My faithful love will be with him,
and through my name his horn[d] will be exalted.
25 I will set his hand over the sea,
his right hand over the rivers.
26 He will call out to me, 'You are my Father,
my God, the Rock my Savior.'
27 And I will appoint him to be my firstborn,
the most exalted of the kings of the earth.
28 I will maintain my love to him forever,
and my covenant with him will never fail.
29 I will establish his line forever,
his throne as long as the heavens endure.

30 "If his sons forsake my law
and do not follow my statutes,
31 if they violate my decrees
and fail to keep my commands,
32 I will punish their sin with the rod,
their iniquity with flogging;
33 but I will not take my love from him,
nor will I ever betray my faithfulness.
34 I will not violate my covenant
or alter what my lips have uttered.
35 Once for all, I have sworn by my holiness—
and I will not lie to David—
36 that his line will continue forever
and his throne endure before me like the sun;
37 it will be established forever like the moon,
the faithful witness in the sky."

38 But you have rejected, you have spurned,
you have been very angry with your anointed one.

[a] *4* The Hebrew has *Selah* (a word of uncertain meaning) here and at the end of verses 37, 45 and 48.
[b] *17 Horn* here symbolizes strong one. [c] *18* Or *sovereign* [d] *24 Horn* here symbolizes strength.

[39] You have renounced the covenant with
your servant
and have defiled his crown in the
dust.
[40] You have broken through all his walls
and reduced his strongholds to ruins.
[41] All who pass by have plundered him;
he has become the scorn of his
neighbors.
[42] You have exalted the right hand of his foes;
you have made all his enemies rejoice.
[43] Indeed, you have turned back the edge of
his sword
and have not supported him in battle.
[44] You have put an end to his splendor
and cast his throne to the ground.
[45] You have cut short the days of his youth;
you have covered him with a mantle
of shame.
[46] How long, LORD? Will you hide yourself
forever?
How long will your wrath burn like fire?
[47] Remember how fleeting is my life.
For what futility you have created all
humanity!
[48] Who can live and not see death,
or who can escape the power of the
grave?
[49] Lord, where is your former great love,
which in your faithfulness you swore
to David?
[50] Remember, Lord, how your servant has[a]
been mocked,
how I bear in my heart the taunts of all
the nations,
[51] the taunts with which your enemies,
LORD, have mocked,
with which they have mocked every
step of your anointed one.

[52] Praise be to the LORD forever!
Amen and Amen.

BOOK IV

Psalms 90–106

Psalm 90

A prayer of Moses the man of God.

[1] Lord, you have been our dwelling place
throughout all generations.
[2] Before the mountains were born
or you brought forth the whole world,
from everlasting to everlasting you
are God.

[3] You turn people back to dust,
saying, "Return to dust, you mortals."
[4] A thousand years in your sight
are like a day that has just gone by,
or like a watch in the night.
[5] Yet you sweep people away in the sleep of
death —
they are like the new grass of the
morning:
[6] In the morning it springs up new,
but by evening it is dry and withered.

[7] We are consumed by your anger
and terrified by your indignation.
[8] You have set our iniquities before you,
our secret sins in the light of your
presence.
[9] All our days pass away under your wrath;
we finish our years with a moan.
[10] Our days may come to seventy years,
or eighty, if our strength endures;
yet the best of them are but trouble and
sorrow,
for they quickly pass, and we fly away.
[11] If only we knew the power of your anger!
Your wrath is as great as the fear that is
your due.
[12] Teach us to number our days,
that we may gain a heart of wisdom.

[13] Relent, LORD! How long will it be?
Have compassion on your servants.
[14] Satisfy us in the morning with your
unfailing love,
that we may sing for joy and be glad all
our days.
[15] Make us glad for as many days as you
have afflicted us,
for as many years as we have seen
trouble.
[16] May your deeds be shown to your
servants,
your splendor to their children.

[17] May the favor[b] of the Lord our God rest
on us;
establish the work of our hands
for us —
yes, establish the work of our hands.

[a] 50 Or *your servants have* [b] 17 Or *beauty*

Psalm 91

[1] Whoever dwells in the shelter of the Most High
will rest in the shadow of the Almighty.[a]
[2] I will say of the LORD, "He is my refuge and my fortress,
my God, in whom I trust."

[3] Surely he will save you
from the fowler's snare
and from the deadly pestilence.
[4] He will cover you with his feathers,
and under his wings you will find refuge;
his faithfulness will be your shield and rampart.
[5] You will not fear the terror of night,
nor the arrow that flies by day,
[6] nor the pestilence that stalks in the darkness,
nor the plague that destroys at midday.
[7] A thousand may fall at your side,
ten thousand at your right hand,
but it will not come near you.
[8] You will only observe with your eyes
and see the punishment of the wicked.

[9] If you say, "The LORD is my refuge,"
and you make the Most High your dwelling,
[10] no harm will overtake you,
no disaster will come near your tent.
[11] For he will command his angels concerning you
to guard you in all your ways;
[12] they will lift you up in their hands,
so that you will not strike your foot against a stone.
[13] You will tread on the lion and the cobra;
you will trample the great lion and the serpent.

[14] "Because he[b] loves me," says the LORD, "I will rescue him;
I will protect him, for he acknowledges my name.
[15] He will call on me, and I will answer him;
I will be with him in trouble,
I will deliver him and honor him.
[16] With long life I will satisfy him
and show him my salvation."

Psalm 92[c]

A psalm. A song. For the Sabbath day.

[1] It is good to praise the LORD
and make music to your name, O Most High,
[2] proclaiming your love in the morning
and your faithfulness at night,
[3] to the music of the ten-stringed lyre
and the melody of the harp.

[4] For you make me glad by your deeds, LORD;
I sing for joy at what your hands have done.
[5] How great are your works, LORD,
how profound your thoughts!
[6] Senseless people do not know,
fools do not understand,
[7] that though the wicked spring up like grass
and all evildoers flourish,
they will be destroyed forever.

[8] But you, LORD, are forever exalted.

[9] For surely your enemies, LORD,
surely your enemies will perish;
all evildoers will be scattered.
[10] You have exalted my horn[d] like that of a wild ox;
fine oils have been poured on me.
[11] My eyes have seen the defeat of my adversaries;
my ears have heard the rout of my wicked foes.

[12] The righteous will flourish like a palm tree,
they will grow like a cedar of Lebanon;
[13] planted in the house of the LORD,
they will flourish in the courts of our God.
[14] They will still bear fruit in old age,
they will stay fresh and green,
[15] proclaiming, "The LORD is upright;
he is my Rock, and there is no wickedness in him."

Psalm 93

[1] The LORD reigns, he is robed in majesty;
the LORD is robed in majesty and armed with strength;

[a] *1* Hebrew *Shaddai* [b] *14* That is, probably the king [c] In Hebrew texts 92:1-15 is numbered 92:2-16.
[d] *10* *Horn* here symbolizes strength.

indeed, the world is established, firm
and secure.
[2] Your throne was established long ago;
you are from all eternity.

[3] The seas have lifted up, LORD,
the seas have lifted up their voice;
the seas have lifted up their pounding
waves.
[4] Mightier than the thunder of the great
waters,
mightier than the breakers of the
sea—
the LORD on high is mighty.

[5] Your statutes, LORD, stand firm;
holiness adorns your house
for endless days.

Psalm 94

[1] The LORD is a God who avenges.
O God who avenges, shine forth.
[2] Rise up, Judge of the earth;
pay back to the proud what they
deserve.
[3] How long, LORD, will the wicked,
how long will the wicked be jubilant?

[4] They pour out arrogant words;
all the evildoers are full of boasting.
[5] They crush your people, LORD;
they oppress your inheritance.
[6] They slay the widow and the foreigner;
they murder the fatherless.
[7] They say, "The LORD does not see;
the God of Jacob takes no notice."

[8] Take notice, you senseless ones among
the people;
you fools, when will you become wise?
[9] Does he who fashioned the ear not hear?
Does he who formed the eye not see?
[10] Does he who disciplines nations not
punish?
Does he who teaches mankind lack
knowledge?
[11] The LORD knows all human plans;
he knows that they are futile.

[12] Blessed is the one you discipline, LORD,
the one you teach from your law;
[13] you grant them relief from days of
trouble,
till a pit is dug for the wicked.
[14] For the LORD will not reject his people;
he will never forsake his inheritance.
[15] Judgment will again be founded on
righteousness,
and all the upright in heart will
follow it.

[16] Who will rise up for me against the
wicked?
Who will take a stand for me against
evildoers?
[17] Unless the LORD had given me help,
I would soon have dwelt in the silence
of death.
[18] When I said, "My foot is slipping,"
your unfailing love, LORD,
supported me.
[19] When anxiety was great within me,
your consolation brought me joy.

[20] Can a corrupt throne be allied with
you—
a throne that brings on misery by its
decrees?
[21] The wicked band together against the
righteous
and condemn the innocent to death.
[22] But the LORD has become my fortress,
and my God the rock in whom I take
refuge.
[23] He will repay them for their sins
and destroy them for their
wickedness;
the LORD our God will destroy them.

Psalm 95

[1] Come, let us sing for joy to the LORD;
let us shout aloud to the Rock of our
salvation.
[2] Let us come before him with
thanksgiving
and extol him with music and song.

[3] For the LORD is the great God,
the great King above all gods.
[4] In his hand are the depths of the earth,
and the mountain peaks belong to
him.
[5] The sea is his, for he made it,
and his hands formed the dry land.

[6] Come, let us bow down in worship,
let us kneel before the LORD our
Maker;
[7] for he is our God
and we are the people of his pasture,
the flock under his care.

Today, if only you would hear his voice,
[8] "Do not harden your hearts as you did at Meribah,[a]
as you did that day at Massah[b] in the wilderness,
[9] where your ancestors tested me;
they tried me, though they had seen what I did.
[10] For forty years I was angry with that generation;
I said, 'They are a people whose hearts go astray,
and they have not known my ways.'
[11] So I declared on oath in my anger,
'They shall never enter my rest.' "

Psalm 96

[1] Sing to the LORD a new song;
sing to the LORD, all the earth.
[2] Sing to the LORD, praise his name;
proclaim his salvation day after day.
[3] Declare his glory among the nations,
his marvelous deeds among all peoples.

[4] For great is the LORD and most worthy of praise;
he is to be feared above all gods.
[5] For all the gods of the nations are idols,
but the LORD made the heavens.
[6] Splendor and majesty are before him;
strength and glory are in his sanctuary.

[7] Ascribe to the LORD, all you families of nations,
ascribe to the LORD glory and strength.
[8] Ascribe to the LORD the glory due his name;
bring an offering and come into his courts.
[9] Worship the LORD in the splendor of his[c] holiness;
tremble before him, all the earth.
[10] Say among the nations, "The LORD reigns."
The world is firmly established, it cannot be moved;
he will judge the peoples with equity.

[11] Let the heavens rejoice, let the earth be glad;
let the sea resound, and all that is in it.
[12] Let the fields be jubilant, and everything in them;
let all the trees of the forest sing for joy.
[13] Let all creation rejoice before the LORD,
for he comes,
he comes to judge the earth.
He will judge the world in righteousness
and the peoples in his faithfulness.

Psalm 97

[1] The LORD reigns, let the earth be glad;
let the distant shores rejoice.
[2] Clouds and thick darkness surround him;
righteousness and justice are the foundation of his throne.
[3] Fire goes before him
and consumes his foes on every side.
[4] His lightning lights up the world;
the earth sees and trembles.
[5] The mountains melt like wax before the LORD,
before the Lord of all the earth.
[6] The heavens proclaim his righteousness,
and all peoples see his glory.

[7] All who worship images are put to shame,
those who boast in idols—
worship him, all you gods!

[8] Zion hears and rejoices
and the villages of Judah are glad
because of your judgments, LORD.
[9] For you, LORD, are the Most High over all the earth;
you are exalted far above all gods.
[10] Let those who love the LORD hate evil,
for he guards the lives of his faithful ones
and delivers them from the hand of the wicked.
[11] Light shines[d] on the righteous
and joy on the upright in heart.
[12] Rejoice in the LORD, you who are righteous,
and praise his holy name.

Psalm 98

A psalm.

[1] Sing to the LORD a new song,
for he has done marvelous things;

[a] 8 *Meribah* means *quarreling.* [b] 8 *Massah* means *testing.* [c] 9 Or *LORD with the splendor of* [d] 11 One Hebrew manuscript and ancient versions (see also 112:4); most Hebrew manuscripts *Light is sown*

his right hand and his holy arm
have worked salvation for him.
[2]The LORD has made his salvation known
and revealed his righteousness to the nations.
[3]He has remembered his love
and his faithfulness to Israel;
all the ends of the earth have seen
the salvation of our God.

[4]Shout for joy to the LORD, all the earth,
burst into jubilant song with music;
[5]make music to the LORD with the harp,
with the harp and the sound of singing,
[6]with trumpets and the blast of the ram's horn—
shout for joy before the LORD, the King.

[7]Let the sea resound, and everything in it,
the world, and all who live in it.
[8]Let the rivers clap their hands,
let the mountains sing together for joy;
[9]let them sing before the LORD,
for he comes to judge the earth.
He will judge the world in righteousness
and the peoples with equity.

Psalm 99

[1]The LORD reigns,
let the nations tremble;
he sits enthroned between the cherubim,
let the earth shake.
[2]Great is the LORD in Zion;
he is exalted over all the nations.
[3]Let them praise your great and awesome name—
he is holy.

[4]The King is mighty, he loves justice—
you have established equity;
in Jacob you have done
what is just and right.
[5]Exalt the LORD our God
and worship at his footstool;
he is holy.

[6]Moses and Aaron were among his priests,
Samuel was among those who called on his name;
they called on the LORD
and he answered them.
[7]He spoke to them from the pillar of cloud;
they kept his statutes and the decrees
he gave them.

[8]LORD our God,
you answered them;
you were to Israel a forgiving God,
though you punished their misdeeds.[a]
[9]Exalt the LORD our God
and worship at his holy mountain,
for the LORD our God is holy.

Psalm 100

A psalm. For giving grateful praise.

[1]Shout for joy to the LORD, all the earth.
[2]Worship the LORD with gladness;
come before him with joyful songs.
[3]Know that the LORD is God.
It is he who made us, and we are his[b];
we are his people, the sheep of his pasture.

[4]Enter his gates with thanksgiving
and his courts with praise;
give thanks to him and praise his name.
[5]For the LORD is good and his love endures forever;
his faithfulness continues through all generations.

Psalm 101

Of David. A psalm.

[1]I will sing of your love and justice;
to you, LORD, I will sing praise.
[2]I will be careful to lead a blameless life—
when will you come to me?

I will conduct the affairs of my house
with a blameless heart.
[3]I will not look with approval
on anything that is vile.

I hate what faithless people do;
I will have no part in it.
[4]The perverse of heart shall be far from me;
I will have nothing to do with what is evil.

[5]Whoever slanders their neighbor in secret,
I will put to silence;
whoever has haughty eyes and a proud heart,
I will not tolerate.

[a] 8 Or *God, / an avenger of the wrongs done to them*
[b] 3 Or *and not we ourselves*

[6] My eyes will be on the faithful in the land,
that they may dwell with me;
the one whose walk is blameless
will minister to me.

[7] No one who practices deceit
will dwell in my house;
no one who speaks falsely
will stand in my presence.

[8] Every morning I will put to silence
all the wicked in the land;
I will cut off every evildoer
from the city of the LORD.

Psalm 102[a]

A prayer of an afflicted person who has grown weak and pours out a lament before the LORD.

[1] Hear my prayer, LORD;
let my cry for help come to you.
[2] Do not hide your face from me
when I am in distress.
Turn your ear to me;
when I call, answer me quickly.
[3] For my days vanish like smoke;
my bones burn like glowing embers.
[4] My heart is blighted and withered like grass;
I forget to eat my food.
[5] In my distress I groan aloud
and am reduced to skin and bones.
[6] I am like a desert owl,
like an owl among the ruins.
[7] I lie awake; I have become
like a bird alone on a roof.
[8] All day long my enemies taunt me;
those who rail against me use my name as a curse.
[9] For I eat ashes as my food
and mingle my drink with tears
[10] because of your great wrath,
for you have taken me up and thrown me aside.
[11] My days are like the evening shadow;
I wither away like grass.

[12] But you, LORD, sit enthroned forever;
your renown endures through all generations.
[13] You will arise and have compassion on Zion,
for it is time to show favor to her;
the appointed time has come.
[14] For her stones are dear to your servants;
her very dust moves them to pity.
[15] The nations will fear the name of the LORD,
all the kings of the earth will revere your glory.
[16] For the LORD will rebuild Zion
and appear in his glory.
[17] He will respond to the prayer of the destitute;
he will not despise their plea.

[18] Let this be written for a future generation,
that a people not yet created may praise the LORD:
[19] "The LORD looked down from his sanctuary on high,
from heaven he viewed the earth,
[20] to hear the groans of the prisoners
and release those condemned to death."
[21] So the name of the LORD will be declared in Zion
and his praise in Jerusalem
[22] when the peoples and the kingdoms
assemble to worship the LORD.

[23] In the course of my life[b] he broke my strength;
he cut short my days.
[24] So I said:
"Do not take me away, my God, in the midst of my days;
your years go on through all generations.
[25] In the beginning you laid the foundations of the earth,
and the heavens are the work of your hands.
[26] They will perish, but you remain;
they will all wear out like a garment.
Like clothing you will change them
and they will be discarded.
[27] But you remain the same,
and your years will never end.
[28] The children of your servants will live in your presence;
their descendants will be established before you."

[a] In Hebrew texts 102:1-28 is numbered 102:2-29. [b] 23 Or *By his power*

Psalm 103

Of David.

[1] Praise the LORD, my soul;
all my inmost being, praise his holy name.
[2] Praise the LORD, my soul,
and forget not all his benefits—
[3] who forgives all your sins
and heals all your diseases,
[4] who redeems your life from the pit
and crowns you with love and compassion,
[5] who satisfies your desires with good things
so that your youth is renewed like the eagle's.

[6] The LORD works righteousness
and justice for all the oppressed.

[7] He made known his ways to Moses,
his deeds to the people of Israel:
[8] The LORD is compassionate and gracious,
slow to anger, abounding in love.
[9] He will not always accuse,
nor will he harbor his anger forever;
[10] he does not treat us as our sins deserve
or repay us according to our iniquities.
[11] For as high as the heavens are above the earth,
so great is his love for those who fear him;
[12] as far as the east is from the west,
so far has he removed our transgressions from us.

[13] As a father has compassion on his children,
so the LORD has compassion on those who fear him;
[14] for he knows how we are formed,
he remembers that we are dust.
[15] The life of mortals is like grass,
they flourish like a flower of the field;
[16] the wind blows over it and it is gone,
and its place remembers it no more.
[17] But from everlasting to everlasting
the LORD's love is with those who fear him,
and his righteousness with their children's children—
[18] with those who keep his covenant
and remember to obey his precepts.
[19] The LORD has established his throne in heaven,
and his kingdom rules over all.

[20] Praise the LORD, you his angels,
you mighty ones who do his bidding,
who obey his word.
[21] Praise the LORD, all his heavenly hosts,
you his servants who do his will.
[22] Praise the LORD, all his works
everywhere in his dominion.

Praise the LORD, my soul.

Psalm 104

[1] Praise the LORD, my soul.

LORD my God, you are very great;
you are clothed with splendor and majesty.

[2] The LORD wraps himself in light as with a garment;
he stretches out the heavens like a tent
[3] and lays the beams of his upper chambers on their waters.
He makes the clouds his chariot
and rides on the wings of the wind.
[4] He makes winds his messengers,[a]
flames of fire his servants.

[5] He set the earth on its foundations;
it can never be moved.
[6] You covered it with the watery depths as with a garment;
the waters stood above the mountains.
[7] But at your rebuke the waters fled,
at the sound of your thunder they took to flight;
[8] they flowed over the mountains,
they went down into the valleys,
to the place you assigned for them.
[9] You set a boundary they cannot cross;
never again will they cover the earth.

[10] He makes springs pour water into the ravines;
it flows between the mountains.
[11] They give water to all the beasts of the field;
the wild donkeys quench their thirst.
[12] The birds of the sky nest by the waters;
they sing among the branches.
[13] He waters the mountains from his upper chambers;

[a] 4 Or *angels*

the land is satisfied by the fruit of
his work.
[14] He makes grass grow for the cattle,
and plants for people to cultivate —
bringing forth food from the earth:
[15] wine that gladdens human hearts,
oil to make their faces shine,
and bread that sustains their hearts.
[16] The trees of the LORD are well watered,
the cedars of Lebanon that he planted.
[17] There the birds make their nests;
the stork has its home in the junipers.
[18] The high mountains belong to the wild
goats;
the crags are a refuge for the hyrax.

[19] He made the moon to mark the seasons,
and the sun knows when to go down.
[20] You bring darkness, it becomes night,
and all the beasts of the forest prowl.
[21] The lions roar for their prey
and seek their food from God.
[22] The sun rises, and they steal away;
they return and lie down in their dens.
[23] Then people go out to their work,
to their labor until evening.

[24] How many are your works, LORD!
In wisdom you made them all;
the earth is full of your creatures.
[25] There is the sea, vast and spacious,
teeming with creatures beyond
number —
living things both large and small.
[26] There the ships go to and fro,
and Leviathan, which you formed to
frolic there.

[27] All creatures look to you
to give them their food at the proper
time.
[28] When you give it to them,
they gather it up;
when you open your hand,
they are satisfied with good things.
[29] When you hide your face,
they are terrified;
when you take away their breath,
they die and return to the dust.
[30] When you send your Spirit,
they are created,
and you renew the face of the ground.

[31] May the glory of the LORD endure forever;
may the LORD rejoice in his works —
[32] he who looks at the earth, and it trembles,
who touches the mountains, and they
smoke.

[33] I will sing to the LORD all my life;
I will sing praise to my God as long as
I live.
[34] May my meditation be pleasing to him,
as I rejoice in the LORD.
[35] But may sinners vanish from the earth
and the wicked be no more.

Praise the LORD, my soul.

Praise the LORD.[a]

Psalm 105

[1] Give praise to the LORD, proclaim his
name;
make known among the nations what
he has done.
[2] Sing to him, sing praise to him;
tell of all his wonderful acts.
[3] Glory in his holy name;
let the hearts of those who seek the
LORD rejoice.
[4] Look to the LORD and his strength;
seek his face always.

[5] Remember the wonders he has done,
his miracles, and the judgments he
pronounced,
[6] you his servants, the descendants of
Abraham,
his chosen ones, the children of Jacob.
[7] He is the LORD our God;
his judgments are in all the earth.

[8] He remembers his covenant forever,
the promise he made, for a thousand
generations,
[9] the covenant he made with Abraham,
the oath he swore to Isaac.
[10] He confirmed it to Jacob as a decree,
to Israel as an everlasting covenant:
[11] "To you I will give the land of Canaan
as the portion you will inherit."

[12] When they were but few in number,
few indeed, and strangers in it,
[13] they wandered from nation to nation,
from one kingdom to another.
[14] He allowed no one to oppress them;
for their sake he rebuked kings:
[15] "Do not touch my anointed ones;
do my prophets no harm."

[a] 35 Hebrew *Hallelu Yah*; in the Septuagint this line stands at the beginning of Psalm 105.

[16]He called down famine on the land
and destroyed all their supplies
of food;
[17]and he sent a man before them—
Joseph, sold as a slave.
[18]They bruised his feet with shackles,
his neck was put in irons,
[19]till what he foretold came to pass,
till the word of the LORD proved
him true.
[20]The king sent and released him,
the ruler of peoples set him free.
[21]He made him master of his household,
ruler over all he possessed,
[22]to instruct his princes as he pleased
and teach his elders wisdom.

[23]Then Israel entered Egypt;
Jacob resided as a foreigner in the land
of Ham.
[24]The LORD made his people very fruitful;
he made them too numerous for their
foes,
[25]whose hearts he turned to hate his
people,
to conspire against his servants.
[26]He sent Moses his servant,
and Aaron, whom he had chosen.
[27]They performed his signs among them,
his wonders in the land of Ham.
[28]He sent darkness and made the land
dark—
for had they not rebelled against his
words?
[29]He turned their waters into blood,
causing their fish to die.
[30]Their land teemed with frogs,
which went up into the bedrooms of
their rulers.
[31]He spoke, and there came swarms of flies,
and gnats throughout their country.
[32]He turned their rain into hail,
with lightning throughout their land;
[33]he struck down their vines and fig trees
and shattered the trees of their
country.
[34]He spoke, and the locusts came,
grasshoppers without number;
[35]they ate up every green thing in their land,
ate up the produce of their soil.
[36]Then he struck down all the firstborn in
their land,
the firstfruits of all their manhood.
[37]He brought out Israel, laden with silver
and gold,
and from among their tribes no one
faltered.
[38]Egypt was glad when they left,
because dread of Israel had fallen
on them.

[39]He spread out a cloud as a covering,
and a fire to give light at night.
[40]They asked, and he brought them quail;
he fed them well with the bread of
heaven.
[41]He opened the rock, and water gushed
out;
it flowed like a river in the desert.

[42]For he remembered his holy promise
given to his servant Abraham.
[43]He brought out his people with rejoicing,
his chosen ones with shouts of joy;
[44]he gave them the lands of the nations,
and they fell heir to what others had
toiled for—
[45]that they might keep his precepts
and observe his laws.

Praise the LORD.[a]

Psalm 106

[1]Praise the LORD.[b]

Give thanks to the LORD, for he is good;
his love endures forever.

[2]Who can proclaim the mighty acts of
the LORD
or fully declare his praise?
[3]Blessed are those who act justly,
who always do what is right.

[4]Remember me, LORD, when you show
favor to your people,
come to my aid when you save them,
[5]that I may enjoy the prosperity of your
chosen ones,
that I may share in the joy of your
nation
and join your inheritance in giving
praise.

[6]We have sinned, even as our ancestors
did;
we have done wrong and acted
wickedly.
[7]When our ancestors were in Egypt,

[a] 45 Hebrew *Hallelu Yah* [b] 1 Hebrew *Hallelu Yah*; also in verse 48

they gave no thought to your miracles;
they did not remember your many kindnesses,
and they rebelled by the sea, the Red Sea.[a]
8 Yet he saved them for his name's sake,
to make his mighty power known.
9 He rebuked the Red Sea, and it dried up;
he led them through the depths as through a desert.
10 He saved them from the hand of the foe;
from the hand of the enemy he redeemed them.
11 The waters covered their adversaries;
not one of them survived.
12 Then they believed his promises
and sang his praise.

13 But they soon forgot what he had done
and did not wait for his plan to unfold.
14 In the desert they gave in to their craving;
in the wilderness they put God to the test.
15 So he gave them what they asked for,
but sent a wasting disease among them.

16 In the camp they grew envious of Moses
and of Aaron, who was consecrated to the LORD.
17 The earth opened up and swallowed Dathan;
it buried the company of Abiram.
18 Fire blazed among their followers;
a flame consumed the wicked.
19 At Horeb they made a calf
and worshiped an idol cast from metal.
20 They exchanged their glorious God
for an image of a bull, which eats grass.
21 They forgot the God who saved them,
who had done great things in Egypt,
22 miracles in the land of Ham
and awesome deeds by the Red Sea.
23 So he said he would destroy them—
had not Moses, his chosen one,
stood in the breach before him
to keep his wrath from destroying them.

24 Then they despised the pleasant land;
they did not believe his promise.
25 They grumbled in their tents
and did not obey the LORD.
26 So he swore to them with uplifted hand
that he would make them fall in the wilderness,
27 make their descendants fall among the nations
and scatter them throughout the lands.
28 They yoked themselves to the Baal of Peor
and ate sacrifices offered to lifeless gods;
29 they aroused the LORD's anger by their wicked deeds,
and a plague broke out among them.
30 But Phinehas stood up and intervened,
and the plague was checked.
31 This was credited to him as righteousness
for endless generations to come.
32 By the waters of Meribah they angered the LORD,
and trouble came to Moses because of them;
33 for they rebelled against the Spirit of God,
and rash words came from Moses' lips.[b]

34 They did not destroy the peoples
as the LORD had commanded them,
35 but they mingled with the nations
and adopted their customs.
36 They worshiped their idols,
which became a snare to them.
37 They sacrificed their sons
and their daughters to false gods.
38 They shed innocent blood,
the blood of their sons and daughters,
whom they sacrificed to the idols of Canaan,
and the land was desecrated by their blood.
39 They defiled themselves by what they did;
by their deeds they prostituted themselves.

40 Therefore the LORD was angry with his people
and abhorred his inheritance.
41 He gave them into the hands of the nations,
and their foes ruled over them.
42 Their enemies oppressed them
and subjected them to their power.
43 Many times he delivered them,
but they were bent on rebellion
and they wasted away in their sin.

[a] 7 Or *the Sea of Reeds*; also in verses 9 and 22 [b] 33 Or *against his spirit, / and rash words came from his lips*

[44] Yet he took note of their distress
when he heard their cry;
[45] for their sake he remembered his covenant
and out of his great love he relented.
[46] He caused all who held them captive
to show them mercy.

[47] Save us, LORD our God,
and gather us from the nations,
that we may give thanks to your holy name
and glory in your praise.

[48] Praise be to the LORD, the God of Israel,
from everlasting to everlasting.

Let all the people say, "Amen!"

Praise the LORD.

BOOK V

Psalms 107–150

Psalm 107

[1] Give thanks to the LORD, for he is good;
his love endures forever.

[2] Let the redeemed of the LORD tell their story—
those he redeemed from the hand of the foe,
[3] those he gathered from the lands,
from east and west, from north and south.[a]

[4] Some wandered in desert wastelands,
finding no way to a city where they could settle.
[5] They were hungry and thirsty,
and their lives ebbed away.
[6] Then they cried out to the LORD in their trouble,
and he delivered them from their distress.
[7] He led them by a straight way
to a city where they could settle.
[8] Let them give thanks to the LORD for his unfailing love
and his wonderful deeds for mankind,
[9] for he satisfies the thirsty
and fills the hungry with good things.

[10] Some sat in darkness, in utter darkness,
prisoners suffering in iron chains,
[11] because they rebelled against God's commands
and despised the plans of the Most High.
[12] So he subjected them to bitter labor;
they stumbled, and there was no one to help.
[13] Then they cried to the LORD in their trouble,
and he saved them from their distress.
[14] He brought them out of darkness, the utter darkness,
and broke away their chains.
[15] Let them give thanks to the LORD for his unfailing love
and his wonderful deeds for mankind,
[16] for he breaks down gates of bronze
and cuts through bars of iron.

[17] Some became fools through their rebellious ways
and suffered affliction because of their iniquities.
[18] They loathed all food
and drew near the gates of death.
[19] Then they cried to the LORD in their trouble,
and he saved them from their distress.
[20] He sent out his word and healed them;
he rescued them from the grave.
[21] Let them give thanks to the LORD for his unfailing love
and his wonderful deeds for mankind.
[22] Let them sacrifice thank offerings
and tell of his works with songs of joy.

[23] Some went out on the sea in ships;
they were merchants on the mighty waters.
[24] They saw the works of the LORD,
his wonderful deeds in the deep.
[25] For he spoke and stirred up a tempest
that lifted high the waves.
[26] They mounted up to the heavens and went down to the depths;
in their peril their courage melted away.
[27] They reeled and staggered like drunkards;
they were at their wits' end.
[28] Then they cried out to the LORD in their trouble,
and he brought them out of their distress.

[a] 3 Hebrew *north and the sea*

[29] He stilled the storm to a whisper;
the waves of the sea[a] were hushed.
[30] They were glad when it grew calm,
and he guided them to their desired haven.
[31] Let them give thanks to the LORD for his unfailing love
and his wonderful deeds for mankind.
[32] Let them exalt him in the assembly of the people
and praise him in the council of the elders.

[33] He turned rivers into a desert,
flowing springs into thirsty ground,
[34] and fruitful land into a salt waste,
because of the wickedness of those who lived there.
[35] He turned the desert into pools of water
and the parched ground into flowing springs;
[36] there he brought the hungry to live,
and they founded a city where they could settle.
[37] They sowed fields and planted vineyards
that yielded a fruitful harvest;
[38] he blessed them, and their numbers greatly increased,
and he did not let their herds diminish.

[39] Then their numbers decreased, and they were humbled
by oppression, calamity and sorrow;
[40] he who pours contempt on nobles
made them wander in a trackless waste.
[41] But he lifted the needy out of their affliction
and increased their families like flocks.
[42] The upright see and rejoice,
but all the wicked shut their mouths.

[43] Let the one who is wise heed these things
and ponder the loving deeds of the LORD.

Psalm 108[b]

A song. A psalm of David.

[1] My heart, O God, is steadfast;
I will sing and make music with all my soul.
[2] Awake, harp and lyre!
I will awaken the dawn.
[3] I will praise you, LORD, among the nations;
I will sing of you among the peoples.
[4] For great is your love, higher than the heavens;
your faithfulness reaches to the skies.
[5] Be exalted, O God, above the heavens;
let your glory be over all the earth.

[6] Save us and help us with your right hand,
that those you love may be delivered.
[7] God has spoken from his sanctuary:
"In triumph I will parcel out Shechem
and measure off the Valley of Sukkoth.
[8] Gilead is mine, Manasseh is mine;
Ephraim is my helmet,
Judah is my scepter.
[9] Moab is my washbasin,
on Edom I toss my sandal;
over Philistia I shout in triumph."

[10] Who will bring me to the fortified city?
Who will lead me to Edom?
[11] Is it not you, God, you who have rejected us
and no longer go out with our armies?
[12] Give us aid against the enemy,
for human help is worthless.
[13] With God we will gain the victory,
and he will trample down our enemies.

Psalm 109

For the director of music. Of David. A psalm.

[1] My God, whom I praise,
do not remain silent,
[2] for people who are wicked and deceitful
have opened their mouths against me;
they have spoken against me with lying tongues.
[3] With words of hatred they surround me;
they attack me without cause.
[4] In return for my friendship they accuse me,
but I am a man of prayer.
[5] They repay me evil for good,
and hatred for my friendship.

[6] Appoint someone evil to oppose my enemy;
let an accuser stand at his right hand.

[a] 29 Dead Sea Scrolls; Masoretic Text / *their waves*
[b] In Hebrew texts 108:1-13 is numbered 108:2-14.

[7] When he is tried, let him be found guilty,
and may his prayers condemn him.
[8] May his days be few;
may another take his place of leadership.
[9] May his children be fatherless
and his wife a widow.
[10] May his children be wandering beggars;
may they be driven[a] from their ruined homes.
[11] May a creditor seize all he has;
may strangers plunder the fruits of his labor.
[12] May no one extend kindness to him
or take pity on his fatherless children.
[13] May his descendants be cut off,
their names blotted out from the next generation.
[14] May the iniquity of his fathers be remembered before the LORD;
may the sin of his mother never be blotted out.
[15] May their sins always remain before the LORD,
that he may blot out their name from the earth.

[16] For he never thought of doing a kindness,
but hounded to death the poor
and the needy and the brokenhearted.
[17] He loved to pronounce a curse—
may it come back on him.
He found no pleasure in blessing—
may it be far from him.
[18] He wore cursing as his garment;
it entered into his body like water,
into his bones like oil.
[19] May it be like a cloak wrapped about him,
like a belt tied forever around him.
[20] May this be the LORD's payment to my accusers,
to those who speak evil of me.

[21] But you, Sovereign LORD,
help me for your name's sake;
out of the goodness of your love,
deliver me.
[22] For I am poor and needy,
and my heart is wounded within me.
[23] I fade away like an evening shadow;
I am shaken off like a locust.
[24] My knees give way from fasting;
my body is thin and gaunt.
[25] I am an object of scorn to my accusers;
when they see me, they shake their heads.

[26] Help me, LORD my God;
save me according to your unfailing love.
[27] Let them know that it is your hand,
that you, LORD, have done it.
[28] While they curse, may you bless;
may those who attack me be put to shame,
but may your servant rejoice.
[29] May my accusers be clothed with disgrace
and wrapped in shame as in a cloak.

[30] With my mouth I will greatly extol the LORD;
in the great throng of worshipers I will praise him.
[31] For he stands at the right hand of the needy,
to save their lives from those who would condemn them.

Psalm 110

Of David. A psalm.

[1] The LORD says to my lord:[b]

"Sit at my right hand
until I make your enemies
a footstool for your feet."

[2] The LORD will extend your mighty scepter from Zion, saying,
"Rule in the midst of your enemies!"
[3] Your troops will be willing
on your day of battle.
Arrayed in holy splendor,
your young men will come to you
like dew from the morning's womb.[c]

[4] The LORD has sworn
and will not change his mind:
"You are a priest forever,
in the order of Melchizedek."

[5] The Lord is at your right hand[d];
he will crush kings on the day of his wrath.
[6] He will judge the nations, heaping up the dead
and crushing the rulers of the whole earth.

[a] 10 Septuagint; Hebrew *sought* [b] 1 Or *Lord* [c] 3 The meaning of the Hebrew for this sentence is uncertain. [d] 5 Or *My lord is at your right hand, LORD*

BEAUTIFUL ONE

Tim Hughes

Wonderful, so wonderful is your unfailing love
Your cross has spoken mercy over me
No eye has seen, no ear has heard
No heart could fully know
How glorious, how beautiful you are

Beautiful One I love, beautiful One I adore
Beautiful One my soul must sing

Powerful, so powerful, your glory fills the skies
Your mighty works displayed for all to see
The beauty of your majesty
Awakes my heart to sing
How marvelous, how wonderful you are

You opened my eyes to your wonders anew
You captured my heart with this love
'Cause nothing on earth is as beautiful as you

My soul, my soul must sing
My soul, my soul must sing
My soul, my soul must sing
Beautiful One

THE INSPIRATION

He grew up before him like a tender shoot, and like a root out of dry ground. He had no beauty or majesty to attract us to him, nothing in his appearance that we should desire him. —Isaiah 53:2

Read also: 1 Corinthians 2:9

BEHIND THE SONG

When Tim Hughes set out to write a song about the beauty of Jesus, he expected it to be a slow, intimate song. But by the time he had finished, "Beautiful One" had become an upbeat anthem. With its driving beat and epic melody, it has become a favorite of young people and college students around the world.

Lyrically, Hughes' heart went to Isaiah 53, a fascinating and important bit of Messianic prophecy. In describing the coming Messiah or "Savior," Isaiah poetically foretells that the great rescuer will not look physically attractive: "He had no beauty or majesty to attract us to him, nothing in his appearance that we should desire him." Hughes was struck by the significance of this verse. "It kind of just shocked me."

Isaiah goes on to warn Israel that her deliverer will be scorned, abused and even killed as a sacrifice for his people. No, his beauty would not be externally visible; it must be seen by faith. Of course Jesus fulfilled every letter of this prophecy.

Selah

When Jesus came to earth, most people did not recognize him as the Messiah. Despite Isaiah's clear prophecy, God's chosen people were looking for someone famous, politically powerful and attractive in other ways. Jesus was right in front of them, and they missed him completely. Many Christians still have mistaken ideas of who Jesus is or what he looks like. What are some common misunderstandings about Jesus' identity and mission? Can you identify any such errors in your own heart and mind?

[7] He will drink from a brook along the way,[a]
and so he will lift his head high.

Psalm 111[b]

[1] Praise the LORD.[c]

I will extol the LORD with all my heart
in the council of the upright and in the assembly.

[2] Great are the works of the LORD;
they are pondered by all who delight in them.
[3] Glorious and majestic are his deeds,
and his righteousness endures forever.
[4] He has caused his wonders to be remembered;
the LORD is gracious and compassionate.
[5] He provides food for those who fear him;
he remembers his covenant forever.

[6] He has shown his people the power of his works,
giving them the lands of other nations.
[7] The works of his hands are faithful and just;
all his precepts are trustworthy.
[8] They are established for ever and ever,
enacted in faithfulness and uprightness.
[9] He provided redemption for his people;
he ordained his covenant forever —
holy and awesome is his name.

[10] The fear of the LORD is the beginning of wisdom;
all who follow his precepts have good understanding.
To him belongs eternal praise.

Psalm 112[b]

[1] Praise the LORD.[c]

Blessed are those who fear the LORD,
who find great delight in his commands.

[2] Their children will be mighty in the land;
the generation of the upright will be blessed.
[3] Wealth and riches are in their houses,
and their righteousness endures forever.
[4] Even in darkness light dawns for the upright,
for those who are gracious and compassionate and righteous.
[5] Good will come to those who are generous and lend freely,
who conduct their affairs with justice.

[6] Surely the righteous will never be shaken;
they will be remembered forever.
[7] They will have no fear of bad news;
their hearts are steadfast, trusting in the LORD.
[8] Their hearts are secure, they will have no fear;
in the end they will look in triumph on their foes.
[9] They have freely scattered their gifts to the poor,
their righteousness endures forever;
their horn[d] will be lifted high in honor.

[10] The wicked will see and be vexed,
they will gnash their teeth and waste away;
the longings of the wicked will come to nothing.

Psalm 113

[1] Praise the LORD.[e]

Praise the LORD, you his servants;
praise the name of the LORD.
[2] Let the name of the LORD be praised,
both now and forevermore.
[3] From the rising of the sun to the place where it sets,
the name of the LORD is to be praised.

[4] The LORD is exalted over all the nations,
his glory above the heavens.
[5] Who is like the LORD our God,
the One who sits enthroned on high,
[6] who stoops down to look
on the heavens and the earth?

[7] He raises the poor from the dust
and lifts the needy from the ash heap;
[8] he seats them with princes,
with the princes of his people.

[a] *7* The meaning of the Hebrew for this clause is uncertain. [b] This psalm is an acrostic poem, the lines of which begin with the successive letters of the Hebrew alphabet. [c] *1* Hebrew *Hallelu Yah* [d] *9* *Horn* here symbolizes dignity. [e] *1* Hebrew *Hallelu Yah*; also in verse 9

9 He settles the childless woman in her
home
as a happy mother of children.

Praise the LORD.

Psalm 114

1 When Israel came out of Egypt,
Jacob from a people of foreign tongue,
2 Judah became God's sanctuary,
Israel his dominion.

3 The sea looked and fled,
the Jordan turned back;
4 the mountains leaped like rams,
the hills like lambs.

5 Why was it, sea, that you fled?
Why, Jordan, did you turn back?
6 Why, mountains, did you leap like rams,
you hills, like lambs?

7 Tremble, earth, at the presence of the
Lord,
at the presence of the God of Jacob,
8 who turned the rock into a pool,
the hard rock into springs of water.

Psalm 115

1 Not to us, LORD, not to us
but to your name be the glory,
because of your love and faithfulness.

2 Why do the nations say,
"Where is their God?"
3 Our God is in heaven;
he does whatever pleases him.
4 But their idols are silver and gold,
made by human hands.
5 They have mouths, but cannot speak,
eyes, but cannot see.
6 They have ears, but cannot hear,
noses, but cannot smell.
7 They have hands, but cannot feel,
feet, but cannot walk,
nor can they utter a sound with their
throats.
8 Those who make them will be like them,
and so will all who trust in them.

9 All you Israelites, trust in the LORD—
he is their help and shield.
10 House of Aaron, trust in the LORD—
he is their help and shield.
11 You who fear him, trust in the LORD—
he is their help and shield.

12 The LORD remembers us and will
bless us:
He will bless his people Israel,
he will bless the house of Aaron,
13 he will bless those who fear the LORD—
small and great alike.

14 May the LORD cause you to flourish,
both you and your children.
15 May you be blessed by the LORD,
the Maker of heaven and earth.

16 The highest heavens belong to the LORD,
but the earth he has given to mankind.
17 It is not the dead who praise the LORD,
those who go down to the place of
silence;
18 it is we who extol the LORD,
both now and forevermore.

Praise the LORD.[a]

Psalm 116

1 I love the LORD, for he heard my voice;
he heard my cry for mercy.
2 Because he turned his ear to me,
I will call on him as long as I live.

3 The cords of death entangled me,
the anguish of the grave came over me;
I was overcome by distress and sorrow.
4 Then I called on the name of the LORD:
"LORD, save me!"

5 The LORD is gracious and righteous;
our God is full of compassion.
6 The LORD protects the unwary;
when I was brought low, he saved me.

7 Return to your rest, my soul,
for the LORD has been good to you.

8 For you, LORD, have delivered me from
death,
my eyes from tears,
my feet from stumbling,
9 that I may walk before the LORD
in the land of the living.

10 I trusted in the LORD when I said,
"I am greatly afflicted";
11 in my alarm I said,
"Everyone is a liar."

[a] *18* Hebrew *Hallelu Yah*

[12] What shall I return to the LORD
for all his goodness to me?

[13] I will lift up the cup of salvation
and call on the name of the LORD.
[14] I will fulfill my vows to the LORD
in the presence of all his people.

[15] Precious in the sight of the LORD
is the death of his faithful servants.
[16] Truly I am your servant, LORD;
I serve you just as my mother did;
you have freed me from my chains.

[17] I will sacrifice a thank offering to you
and call on the name of the LORD.
[18] I will fulfill my vows to the LORD
in the presence of all his people,
[19] in the courts of the house of the LORD—
in your midst, Jerusalem.

Praise the LORD.[a]

Psalm 117

[1] Praise the LORD, all you nations;
extol him, all you peoples.
[2] For great is his love toward us,
and the faithfulness of the LORD
endures forever.

Praise the LORD.[a]

Psalm 118

[1] Give thanks to the LORD, for he is good;
his love endures forever.

[2] Let Israel say:
"His love endures forever."
[3] Let the house of Aaron say:
"His love endures forever."
[4] Let those who fear the LORD say:
"His love endures forever."

[5] When hard pressed, I cried to the LORD;
he brought me into a spacious place.
[6] The LORD is with me; I will not be afraid.
What can mere mortals do to me?
[7] The LORD is with me; he is my helper.
I look in triumph on my enemies.

[8] It is better to take refuge in the LORD
than to trust in humans.
[9] It is better to take refuge in the LORD
than to trust in princes.
[10] All the nations surrounded me,
but in the name of the LORD I cut
them down.
[11] They surrounded me on every side,
but in the name of the LORD I cut them
down.
[12] They swarmed around me like bees,
but they were consumed as quickly as
burning thorns;
in the name of the LORD I cut them
down.
[13] I was pushed back and about to fall,
but the LORD helped me.
[14] The LORD is my strength and my
defense[b];
he has become my salvation.

[15] Shouts of joy and victory
resound in the tents of the righteous:
"The LORD's right hand has done mighty
things!
[16] The LORD's right hand is lifted high;
the LORD's right hand has done mighty
things!"
[17] I will not die but live,
and will proclaim what the LORD has
done.
[18] The LORD has chastened me severely,
but he has not given me over to death.
[19] Open for me the gates of the righteous;
I will enter and give thanks to the
LORD.
[20] This is the gate of the LORD
through which the righteous may
enter.
[21] I will give you thanks, for you answered
me;
you have become my salvation.

[22] The stone the builders rejected
has become the cornerstone;
[23] the LORD has done this,
and it is marvelous in our eyes.
[24] The LORD has done it this very day;
let us rejoice today and be glad.

[25] LORD, save us!
LORD, grant us success!

[26] Blessed is he who comes in the name of
the LORD.
From the house of the LORD we bless
you.[c]
[27] The LORD is God,
and he has made his light shine on us.

[a] *19,2* Hebrew *Hallelu Yah* [b] *14* Or *song* [c] *26* The Hebrew is plural.

With boughs in hand, join in the festal procession
up[a] to the horns of the altar.

28 You are my God, and I will praise you;
you are my God, and I will exalt you.

29 Give thanks to the LORD, for he is good;
his love endures forever.

Psalm 119[b]

א Aleph

1 Blessed are those whose ways are blameless,
who walk according to the law of the LORD.
2 Blessed are those who keep his statutes
and seek him with all their heart—
3 they do no wrong
but follow his ways.
4 You have laid down precepts
that are to be fully obeyed.
5 Oh, that my ways were steadfast
in obeying your decrees!
6 Then I would not be put to shame
when I consider all your commands.
7 I will praise you with an upright heart
as I learn your righteous laws.
8 I will obey your decrees;
do not utterly forsake me.

ב Beth

9 How can a young person stay on the path of purity?
By living according to your word.
10 I seek you with all my heart;
do not let me stray from your commands.
11 I have hidden your word in my heart
that I might not sin against you.
12 Praise be to you, LORD;
teach me your decrees.
13 With my lips I recount
all the laws that come from your mouth.
14 I rejoice in following your statutes
as one rejoices in great riches.
15 I meditate on your precepts
and consider your ways.
16 I delight in your decrees;
I will not neglect your word.

ג Gimel

17 Be good to your servant while I live,
that I may obey your word.
18 Open my eyes that I may see
wonderful things in your law.
19 I am a stranger on earth;
do not hide your commands from me.
20 My soul is consumed with longing
for your laws at all times.
21 You rebuke the arrogant, who are accursed,
those who stray from your commands.
22 Remove from me their scorn and contempt,
for I keep your statutes.
23 Though rulers sit together and slander me,
your servant will meditate on your decrees.
24 Your statutes are my delight;
they are my counselors.

ד Daleth

25 I am laid low in the dust;
preserve my life according to your word.
26 I gave an account of my ways and you answered me;
teach me your decrees.
27 Cause me to understand the way of your precepts,
that I may meditate on your wonderful deeds.
28 My soul is weary with sorrow;
strengthen me according to your word.
29 Keep me from deceitful ways;
be gracious to me and teach me your law.
30 I have chosen the way of faithfulness;
I have set my heart on your laws.
31 I hold fast to your statutes, LORD;
do not let me be put to shame.
32 I run in the path of your commands,
for you have broadened my understanding.

ה He

33 Teach me, LORD, the way of your decrees,
that I may follow it to the end.[c]
34 Give me understanding, so that I may keep your law
and obey it with all my heart.

[a] 27 Or *Bind the festal sacrifice with ropes / and take it* [b] This psalm is an acrostic poem, the stanzas of which begin with successive letters of the Hebrew alphabet; moreover, the verses of each stanza begin with the same letter of the Hebrew alphabet. [c] 33 Or *follow it for its reward*

[35] Direct me in the path of your commands,
for there I find delight.
[36] Turn my heart toward your statutes
and not toward selfish gain.
[37] Turn my eyes away from worthless
things;
preserve my life according to your
word.[a]
[38] Fulfill your promise to your servant,
so that you may be feared.
[39] Take away the disgrace I dread,
for your laws are good.
[40] How I long for your precepts!
In your righteousness preserve my life.

ו Waw

[41] May your unfailing love come to me,
LORD,
your salvation, according to your
promise;
[42] then I can answer anyone who taunts me,
for I trust in your word.
[43] Never take your word of truth from my
mouth,
for I have put my hope in your laws.
[44] I will always obey your law,
for ever and ever.
[45] I will walk about in freedom,
for I have sought out your precepts.
[46] I will speak of your statutes before kings
and will not be put to shame,
[47] for I delight in your commands
because I love them.
[48] I reach out for your commands, which I
love,
that I may meditate on your decrees.

ז Zayin

[49] Remember your word to your servant,
for you have given me hope.
[50] My comfort in my suffering is this:
Your promise preserves my life.
[51] The arrogant mock me unmercifully,
but I do not turn from your law.
[52] I remember, LORD, your ancient laws,
and I find comfort in them.
[53] Indignation grips me because of the
wicked,
who have forsaken your law.
[54] Your decrees are the theme of my song
wherever I lodge.
[55] In the night, LORD, I remember your
name,
that I may keep your law.
[56] This has been my practice:
I obey your precepts.

ח Heth

[57] You are my portion, LORD;
I have promised to obey your words.
[58] I have sought your face with all my heart;
be gracious to me according to your
promise.
[59] I have considered my ways
and have turned my steps to your
statutes.
[60] I will hasten and not delay
to obey your commands.
[61] Though the wicked bind me with ropes,
I will not forget your law.
[62] At midnight I rise to give you thanks
for your righteous laws.
[63] I am a friend to all who fear you,
to all who follow your precepts.
[64] The earth is filled with your love, LORD;
teach me your decrees.

ט Teth

[65] Do good to your servant
according to your word, LORD.
[66] Teach me knowledge and good judgment,
for I trust your commands.
[67] Before I was afflicted I went astray,
but now I obey your word.
[68] You are good, and what you do is good;
teach me your decrees.
[69] Though the arrogant have smeared me
with lies,
I keep your precepts with all my heart.
[70] Their hearts are callous and unfeeling,
but I delight in your law.
[71] It was good for me to be afflicted
so that I might learn your decrees.
[72] The law from your mouth is more
precious to me
than thousands of pieces of silver and
gold.

י Yodh

[73] Your hands made me and formed me;
give me understanding to learn your
commands.

[a] 37 Two manuscripts of the Masoretic Text and Dead Sea Scrolls; most manuscripts of the Masoretic Text *life in your way*

[74] May those who fear you rejoice when
they see me,
for I have put my hope in your word.
[75] I know, LORD, that your laws are
righteous,
and that in faithfulness you have
afflicted me.
[76] May your unfailing love be my comfort,
according to your promise to your
servant.
[77] Let your compassion come to me that I
may live,
for your law is my delight.
[78] May the arrogant be put to shame for
wronging me without cause;
but I will meditate on your precepts.
[79] May those who fear you turn to me,
those who understand your statutes.
[80] May I wholeheartedly follow your decrees,
that I may not be put to shame.

כ Kaph

[81] My soul faints with longing for your
salvation,
but I have put my hope in your word.
[82] My eyes fail, looking for your promise;
I say, "When will you comfort me?"
[83] Though I am like a wineskin in the smoke,
I do not forget your decrees.
[84] How long must your servant wait?
When will you punish my persecutors?
[85] The arrogant dig pits to trap me,
contrary to your law.
[86] All your commands are trustworthy;
help me, for I am being persecuted
without cause.
[87] They almost wiped me from the earth,
but I have not forsaken your precepts.
[88] In your unfailing love preserve my life,
that I may obey the statutes of your
mouth.

ל Lamedh

[89] Your word, LORD, is eternal;
it stands firm in the heavens.
[90] Your faithfulness continues through all
generations;
you established the earth, and it
endures.
[91] Your laws endure to this day,
for all things serve you.
[92] If your law had not been my delight,
I would have perished in my
affliction.
[93] I will never forget your precepts,
for by them you have preserved my life.
[94] Save me, for I am yours;
I have sought out your precepts.
[95] The wicked are waiting to destroy me,
but I will ponder your statutes.
[96] To all perfection I see a limit,
but your commands are boundless.

מ Mem

[97] Oh, how I love your law!
I meditate on it all day long.
[98] Your commands are always with me
and make me wiser than my enemies.
[99] I have more insight than all my teachers,
for I meditate on your statutes.
[100] I have more understanding than the
elders,
for I obey your precepts.
[101] I have kept my feet from every evil path
so that I might obey your word.
[102] I have not departed from your laws,
for you yourself have taught me.
[103] How sweet are your words to my taste,
sweeter than honey to my mouth!
[104] I gain understanding from your
precepts;
therefore I hate every wrong path.

נ Nun

[105] Your word is a lamp for my feet,
a light on my path.
[106] I have taken an oath and confirmed it,
that I will follow your righteous laws.
[107] I have suffered much;
preserve my life, LORD, according to
your word.
[108] Accept, LORD, the willing praise of my
mouth,
and teach me your laws.
[109] Though I constantly take my life in my
hands,
I will not forget your law.
[110] The wicked have set a snare for me,
but I have not strayed from your
precepts.
[111] Your statutes are my heritage forever;
they are the joy of my heart.
[112] My heart is set on keeping your decrees
to the very end.[a]

[a] *112* Or *decrees / for their enduring reward*

ס Samekh

113 I hate double-minded people,
but I love your law.
114 You are my refuge and my shield;
I have put my hope in your word.
115 Away from me, you evildoers,
that I may keep the commands of
my God!
116 Sustain me, my God, according to your
promise, and I will live;
do not let my hopes be dashed.
117 Uphold me, and I will be delivered;
I will always have regard for your
decrees.
118 You reject all who stray from your
decrees,
for their delusions come to nothing.
119 All the wicked of the earth you discard
like dross;
therefore I love your statutes.
120 My flesh trembles in fear of you;
I stand in awe of your laws.

ע Ayin

121 I have done what is righteous and just;
do not leave me to my oppressors.
122 Ensure your servant's well-being;
do not let the arrogant oppress me.
123 My eyes fail, looking for your salvation,
looking for your righteous promise.
124 Deal with your servant according to
your love
and teach me your decrees.
125 I am your servant; give me discernment
that I may understand your statutes.
126 It is time for you to act, LORD;
your law is being broken.
127 Because I love your commands
more than gold, more than pure gold,
128 and because I consider all your precepts
right,
I hate every wrong path.

פ Pe

129 Your statutes are wonderful;
therefore I obey them.
130 The unfolding of your words gives light;
it gives understanding to the simple.
131 I open my mouth and pant,
longing for your commands.
132 Turn to me and have mercy on me,
as you always do to those who love
your name.
133 Direct my footsteps according to your
word;
let no sin rule over me.
134 Redeem me from human oppression,
that I may obey your precepts.
135 Make your face shine on your servant
and teach me your decrees.
136 Streams of tears flow from my eyes,
for your law is not obeyed.

צ Tsadhe

137 You are righteous, LORD,
and your laws are right.
138 The statutes you have laid down are
righteous;
they are fully trustworthy.
139 My zeal wears me out,
for my enemies ignore your words.
140 Your promises have been thoroughly
tested,
and your servant loves them.
141 Though I am lowly and despised,
I do not forget your precepts.
142 Your righteousness is everlasting
and your law is true.
143 Trouble and distress have come
upon me,
but your commands give me delight.
144 Your statutes are always righteous;
give me understanding that I may live.

ק Qoph

145 I call with all my heart; answer me,
LORD,
and I will obey your decrees.
146 I call out to you; save me
and I will keep your statutes.
147 I rise before dawn and cry for help;
I have put my hope in your word.
148 My eyes stay open through the watches
of the night,
that I may meditate on your promises.
149 Hear my voice in accordance with your
love;
preserve my life, LORD, according to
your laws.
150 Those who devise wicked schemes are
near,
but they are far from your law.
151 Yet you are near, LORD,
and all your commands are true.
152 Long ago I learned from your statutes
that you established them to last
forever.

ר Resh

153 Look on my suffering and deliver me,
for I have not forgotten your law.
154 Defend my cause and redeem me;
preserve my life according to your promise.
155 Salvation is far from the wicked,
for they do not seek out your decrees
156 Your compassion, LORD, is great;
preserve my life according to your laws.
157 Many are the foes who persecute me,
but I have not turned from your statutes.
158 I look on the faithless with loathing,
for they do not obey your word.
159 See how I love your precepts;
preserve my life, LORD, in accordance with your love.
160 All your words are true;
all your righteous laws are eternal.

ש Sin and Shin

161 Rulers persecute me without cause,
but my heart trembles at your word.
162 I rejoice in your promise
like one who finds great spoil.
163 I hate and detest falsehood
but I love your law.
164 Seven times a day I praise you
for your righteous laws.
165 Great peace have those who love your law,
and nothing can make them stumble.
166 I wait for your salvation, LORD,
and I follow your commands.
167 I obey your statutes,
for I love them greatly.
168 I obey your precepts and your statutes,
for all my ways are known to you.

ת Taw

169 May my cry come before you, LORD;
give me understanding according to your word.
170 May my supplication come before you;
deliver me according to your promise.
171 May my lips overflow with praise,
for you teach me your decrees.
172 May my tongue sing of your word,
for all your commands are righteous.
173 May your hand be ready to help me,
for I have chosen your precepts.
174 I long for your salvation, LORD,
and your law gives me delight.
175 Let me live that I may praise you,
and may your laws sustain me.
176 I have strayed like a lost sheep.
Seek your servant,
for I have not forgotten your commands.

Psalm 120

A song of ascents.

1 I call on the LORD in my distress,
and he answers me.
2 Save me, LORD,
from lying lips
and from deceitful tongues.

3 What will he do to you,
and what more besides,
you deceitful tongue?
4 He will punish you with a warrior's sharp arrows,
with burning coals of the broom bush.

5 Woe to me that I dwell in Meshek,
that I live among the tents of Kedar!
6 Too long have I lived
among those who hate peace.
7 I am for peace;
but when I speak, they are for war.

Psalm 121

A song of ascents.

1 I lift up my eyes to the mountains—
where does my help come from?
2 My help comes from the LORD,
the Maker of heaven and earth.

3 He will not let your foot slip—
he who watches over you will not slumber;
4 indeed, he who watches over Israel
will neither slumber nor sleep.

5 The LORD watches over you—
the LORD is your shade at your right hand;
6 the sun will not harm you by day,
nor the moon by night.

7 The LORD will keep you from all harm—
he will watch over your life;
8 the LORD will watch over your coming and going
both now and forevermore.

Psalm 122

A song of ascents. Of David.

[1] I rejoiced with those who said to me,
"Let us go to the house of the LORD."
[2] Our feet are standing
in your gates, Jerusalem.

[3] Jerusalem is built like a city
that is closely compacted together.
[4] That is where the tribes go up —
the tribes of the LORD —
to praise the name of the LORD
according to the statute given to Israel.
[5] There stand the thrones for judgment,
the thrones of the house of David.

[6] Pray for the peace of Jerusalem:
"May those who love you be secure.
[7] May there be peace within your walls
and security within your citadels."
[8] For the sake of my family and friends,
I will say, "Peace be within you."
[9] For the sake of the house of the LORD
our God,
I will seek your prosperity.

Psalm 123

A song of ascents.

[1] I lift up my eyes to you,
to you who sit enthroned in heaven.
[2] As the eyes of slaves look to the hand of
their master,
as the eyes of a female slave look to the
hand of her mistress,
so our eyes look to the LORD our God,
till he shows us his mercy.

[3] Have mercy on us, LORD, have mercy
on us,
for we have endured no end of
contempt.
[4] We have endured no end
of ridicule from the arrogant,
of contempt from the proud.

Psalm 124

A song of ascents. Of David.

[1] If the LORD had not been on our side —
let Israel say —
[2] if the LORD had not been on our side
when people attacked us,
[3] they would have swallowed us alive
when their anger flared against us;
[4] the flood would have engulfed us,
the torrent would have swept over us,
[5] the raging waters
would have swept us away.

[6] Praise be to the LORD,
who has not let us be torn by their teeth.
[7] We have escaped like a bird
from the fowler's snare;
the snare has been broken,
and we have escaped.
[8] Our help is in the name of the LORD,
the Maker of heaven and earth.

Psalm 125

A song of ascents.

[1] Those who trust in the LORD are like
Mount Zion,
which cannot be shaken but endures
forever.
[2] As the mountains surround Jerusalem,
so the LORD surrounds his people
both now and forevermore.

[3] The scepter of the wicked will not remain
over the land allotted to the righteous,
for then the righteous might use
their hands to do evil.

[4] LORD, do good to those who are good,
to those who are upright in heart.
[5] But those who turn to crooked ways
the LORD will banish with the evildoers.

Peace be on Israel.

Psalm 126

A song of ascents.

[1] When the LORD restored the fortunes
of[a] Zion,
we were like those who dreamed.[b]
[2] Our mouths were filled with laughter,
our tongues with songs of joy.
Then it was said among the nations,
"The LORD has done great things for
them."
[3] The LORD has done great things for us,
and we are filled with joy.

[4] Restore our fortunes,[c] LORD,
like streams in the Negev.

[a] 1 Or *LORD brought back the captives to* [b] 1 Or *those restored to health* [c] 4 Or *Bring back our captives*

5 Those who sow with tears
will reap with songs of joy.
6 Those who go out weeping,
carrying seed to sow,
will return with songs of joy,
carrying sheaves with them.

Psalm 127

A song of ascents. Of Solomon.

1 Unless the LORD builds the house,
the builders labor in vain.
Unless the LORD watches over the city,
the guards stand watch in vain.
2 In vain you rise early
and stay up late,
toiling for food to eat —
for he grants sleep to[a] those he loves.
3 Children are a heritage from the LORD,
offspring a reward from him.
4 Like arrows in the hands of a warrior
are children born in one's youth.
5 Blessed is the man
whose quiver is full of them.
They will not be put to shame
when they contend with their opponents in court.

Psalm 128

A song of ascents.

1 Blessed are all who fear the LORD,
who walk in obedience to him.
2 You will eat the fruit of your labor;
blessings and prosperity will be yours.
3 Your wife will be like a fruitful vine
within your house;
your children will be like olive shoots
around your table.
4 Yes, this will be the blessing
for the man who fears the LORD.

5 May the LORD bless you from Zion;
may you see the prosperity of Jerusalem
all the days of your life.
6 May you live to see your children's children —
peace be on Israel.

[a] 2 Or *eat — / for while they sleep he provides for*

Psalm 129

A song of ascents.

1 "They have greatly oppressed me from my youth,"
let Israel say;
2 "they have greatly oppressed me from my youth,
but they have not gained the victory over me.
3 Plowmen have plowed my back
and made their furrows long.
4 But the LORD is righteous;
he has cut me free from the cords of the wicked."

5 May all who hate Zion
be turned back in shame.
6 May they be like grass on the roof,
which withers before it can grow;
7 a reaper cannot fill his hands with it,
nor one who gathers fill his arms.
8 May those who pass by not say to them,
"The blessing of the LORD be on you;
we bless you in the name of the LORD."

Psalm 130

A song of ascents.

1 Out of the depths I cry to you, LORD;
2 Lord, hear my voice.
Let your ears be attentive
to my cry for mercy.
3 If you, LORD, kept a record of sins,
Lord, who could stand?
4 But with you there is forgiveness,
so that we can, with reverence, serve you.

5 I wait for the LORD, my whole being waits,
and in his word I put my hope.
6 I wait for the Lord
more than watchmen wait for the morning,
more than watchmen wait for the morning.

7 Israel, put your hope in the LORD,
for with the LORD is unfailing love
and with him is full redemption.
8 He himself will redeem Israel
from all their sins.

Psalm 131

A song of ascents. Of David.

[1] My heart is not proud, LORD,
my eyes are not haughty;
I do not concern myself with great matters
or things too wonderful for me.
[2] But I have calmed and quieted myself,
I am like a weaned child with its mother;
like a weaned child I am content.

[3] Israel, put your hope in the LORD
both now and forevermore.

Psalm 132

A song of ascents.

[1] LORD, remember David
and all his self-denial.

[2] He swore an oath to the LORD,
he made a vow to the Mighty One of Jacob:
[3] "I will not enter my house
or go to my bed,
[4] I will allow no sleep to my eyes
or slumber to my eyelids,
[5] till I find a place for the LORD,
a dwelling for the Mighty One of Jacob."

[6] We heard it in Ephrathah,
we came upon it in the fields of Jaar:[a]
[7] "Let us go to his dwelling place,
let us worship at his footstool, saying,
[8] 'Arise, LORD, and come to your resting place,
you and the ark of your might.
[9] May your priests be clothed with your righteousness;
may your faithful people sing for joy.' "

[10] For the sake of your servant David,
do not reject your anointed one.

[11] The LORD swore an oath to David,
a sure oath he will not revoke:
"One of your own descendants
I will place on your throne.
[12] If your sons keep my covenant
and the statutes I teach them,
then their sons will sit
on your throne for ever and ever."

[13] For the LORD has chosen Zion,
he has desired it for his dwelling, saying,
[14] "This is my resting place for ever and ever;
here I will sit enthroned, for I have desired it.
[15] I will bless her with abundant provisions;
her poor I will satisfy with food.
[16] I will clothe her priests with salvation,
and her faithful people will ever sing for joy.

[17] "Here I will make a horn[b] grow for David
and set up a lamp for my anointed one.
[18] I will clothe his enemies with shame,
but his head will be adorned with a radiant crown."

Psalm 133

A song of ascents. Of David.

[1] How good and pleasant it is
when God's people live together in unity!
[2] It is like precious oil poured on the head,
running down on the beard,
running down on Aaron's beard,
down on the collar of his robe.
[3] It is as if the dew of Hermon
were falling on Mount Zion.
For there the LORD bestows his blessing,
even life forevermore.

Psalm 134

A song of ascents.

[1] Praise the LORD, all you servants of the LORD
who minister by night in the house of the LORD.
[2] Lift up your hands in the sanctuary
and praise the LORD.
[3] May the LORD bless you from Zion,
he who is the Maker of heaven and earth.

Psalm 135

[1] Praise the LORD.[c]

Praise the name of the LORD;
praise him, you servants of the LORD,

[a] 6 Or *heard of it in Ephrathah, / we found it in the fields of Jearim.* (See 1 Chron. 13:5,6) (And no quotation marks around verses 7-9) [b] 17 *Horn* here symbolizes strong one, that is, king. [c] 1 Hebrew *Hallelu Yah;* also in verses 3 and 21

[2]you who minister in the house of the
LORD,
in the courts of the house of our God.

[3]Praise the LORD, for the LORD is good;
sing praise to his name, for that is
pleasant.
[4]For the LORD has chosen Jacob to be
his own,
Israel to be his treasured possession.

[5]I know that the LORD is great,
that our Lord is greater than all gods.
[6]The LORD does whatever pleases him,
in the heavens and on the earth,
in the seas and all their depths.
[7]He makes clouds rise from the ends of
the earth;
he sends lightning with the rain
and brings out the wind from his
storehouses.

[8]He struck down the firstborn of Egypt,
the firstborn of people and animals.
[9]He sent his signs and wonders into your
midst, Egypt,
against Pharaoh and all his servants.
[10]He struck down many nations
and killed mighty kings —
[11]Sihon king of the Amorites,
Og king of Bashan,
and all the kings of Canaan —
[12]and he gave their land as an inheritance,
an inheritance to his people Israel.

[13]Your name, LORD, endures forever,
your renown, LORD, through all
generations.
[14]For the LORD will vindicate his people
and have compassion on his servants.

[15]The idols of the nations are silver and gold,
made by human hands.
[16]They have mouths, but cannot speak,
eyes, but cannot see.
[17]They have ears, but cannot hear,
nor is there breath in their mouths.
[18]Those who make them will be like them,
and so will all who trust in them.

[19]All you Israelites, praise the LORD;
house of Aaron, praise the LORD;
[20]house of Levi, praise the LORD;
you who fear him, praise the LORD.
[21]Praise be to the LORD from Zion,
to him who dwells in Jerusalem.

Praise the LORD.

Psalm 136

[1]Give thanks to the LORD, for he is good.
His love endures forever.
[2]Give thanks to the God of gods.
His love endures forever.
[3]Give thanks to the Lord of lords:
His love endures forever.

[4]to him who alone does great wonders,
His love endures forever.
[5]who by his understanding made the
heavens,
His love endures forever.
[6]who spread out the earth upon the waters,
His love endures forever.
[7]who made the great lights —
His love endures forever.
[8]the sun to govern the day,
His love endures forever.
[9]the moon and stars to govern the night;
His love endures forever.

[10]to him who struck down the firstborn
of Egypt
His love endures forever.
[11]and brought Israel out from among them
His love endures forever.
[12]with a mighty hand and outstretched
arm;
His love endures forever.

[13]to him who divided the Red Sea[a] asunder
His love endures forever.
[14]and brought Israel through the midst of it,
His love endures forever.
[15]but swept Pharaoh and his army into the
Red Sea;
His love endures forever.

[16]to him who led his people through the
wilderness;
His love endures forever.

[17]to him who struck down great kings,
His love endures forever.
[18]and killed mighty kings —
His love endures forever.
[19]Sihon king of the Amorites
His love endures forever.
[20]and Og king of Bashan —
His love endures forever.
[21]and gave their land as an inheritance,
His love endures forever.
[22]an inheritance to his servant Israel.
His love endures forever.

[a] *13* Or *the Sea of Reeds*; also in verse 15

YOUR NAME

Paul Baloche, Glenn Packiam

As morning dawns and evening fades
You inspire songs of praise
That rise from earth to touch your heart and glorify your Name

Your Name is a strong and mighty tower
Your Name is a shelter like no other
Your Name, let the nations sing it louder
'Cause nothing has the power to save
But your Name

Jesus, in your Name we pray
Come and fill our hearts today
Lord, give us strength to live for you and glorify your Name

THE INSPIRATION

The name of the LORD is a fortified tower; the righteous run to it and are safe. —Proverbs 18:10

Read also: Psalm 7:17; Psalm 18:49; Psalm 65:8

BEHIND THE SONG

Paul Baloche was visiting with his friend and fellow worship leader Glenn Packiam in Colorado when the song "Your Name" came to them. While many songwriters meet for co-writing sessions that can run for three or four hours, Baloche has always preferred a more organic approach.

"I feel that it's better to go in and sing some familiar worship songs, read Scripture and pray together," Baloche explains, "and then to see if anything rises up."

On that particular day Baloche was improvising on the piano while Packiam read aloud from the Bible. When he read Psalm 65:8, Baloche latched onto an idea. "It says 'where morning dawns, where evening fades, you call forth songs of joy.' I said, 'That sounds like the beginning of a song, doesn't it?' "

As the two began to pray through the book of Psalms, other Scripture passages came to mind. The idea of focusing on the "name of the Lord" quickly became their guiding theme. Baloche then remembered Proverbs 18:10, which describes God as a "fortified tower." Soon this simple, but powerful song was well on its way to completion.

"This is why it's important to hide the Word of God in your heart," Baloche adds. "In Colossians [3:16] … it says [essentially] to let the Word of God dwell in you richly and out of that will come psalms, hymns and spiritual songs."

For Baloche and many other worship songwriters it is this kind of organic expression rooted in authentic worship experiences that are the most exciting part of the work they do.

Selah

Throughout the Bible, the names of people represent their character. "Lord" is described as the "name above all names" (see Philippians 2:9). It represents all that the Lord is and does. When the psalmist says that the "name of the Lord is a fortified tower," it means that the Lord is a mighty protector who cannot be reached or brought down. God becomes personal to us through his name. How is God like a fortified tower in your life? How does God protect you? What does it mean to "call on the name of the Lord"? What does it mean to do something "in the name of the Lord"?

[23] He remembered us in our low estate
His love endures forever.
[24] and freed us from our enemies.
His love endures forever.
[25] He gives food to every creature.
His love endures forever.
[26] Give thanks to the God of heaven.
His love endures forever.

Psalm 137

[1] By the rivers of Babylon we sat and wept
when we remembered Zion.
[2] There on the poplars
we hung our harps,
[3] for there our captors asked us for songs,
our tormentors demanded songs
of joy;
they said, "Sing us one of the songs
of Zion!"
[4] How can we sing the songs of the LORD
while in a foreign land?
[5] If I forget you, Jerusalem,
may my right hand forget its skill.
[6] May my tongue cling to the roof of my
mouth
if I do not remember you,
if I do not consider Jerusalem
my highest joy.
[7] Remember, LORD, what the Edomites did
on the day Jerusalem fell.
"Tear it down," they cried,
"tear it down to its foundations!"
[8] Daughter Babylon, doomed to
destruction,
happy is the one who repays you
according to what you have done to us.
[9] Happy is the one who seizes your infants
and dashes them against the rocks.

Psalm 138

Of David.

[1] I will praise you, LORD, with all my heart;
before the "gods" I will sing your
praise.
[2] I will bow down toward your holy temple
and will praise your name
for your unfailing love and your
faithfulness,
for you have so exalted your solemn
decree
that it surpasses your fame.
[3] When I called, you answered me;
you greatly emboldened me.
[4] May all the kings of the earth praise you,
LORD,
when they hear what you have
decreed.
[5] May they sing of the ways of the LORD,
for the glory of the LORD is great.
[6] Though the LORD is exalted, he looks
kindly on the lowly;
though lofty, he sees them from afar.
[7] Though I walk in the midst of trouble,
you preserve my life.
You stretch out your hand against the
anger of my foes;
with your right hand you save me.
[8] The LORD will vindicate me;
your love, LORD, endures forever—
do not abandon the works of your
hands.

Psalm 139

For the director of music.
Of David. A psalm.

[1] You have searched me, LORD,
and you know me.
[2] You know when I sit and when I rise;
you perceive my thoughts from afar.
[3] You discern my going out and my lying
down;
you are familiar with all my ways.
[4] Before a word is on my tongue
you, LORD, know it completely.
[5] You hem me in behind and before,
and you lay your hand upon me.
[6] Such knowledge is too wonderful for me,
too lofty for me to attain.

[7] Where can I go from your Spirit?
Where can I flee from your presence?
[8] If I go up to the heavens, you are there;
if I make my bed in the depths, you are
there.
[9] If I rise on the wings of the dawn,
if I settle on the far side of the sea,
[10] even there your hand will guide me,
your right hand will hold me fast.
[11] If I say, "Surely the darkness will hide me
and the light become night around me,"
[12] even the darkness will not be dark to you;
the night will shine like the day,
for darkness is as light to you.

[13]For you created my inmost being;
you knit me together in my mother's womb.
[14]I praise you because I am fearfully and wonderfully made;
your works are wonderful,
I know that full well.
[15]My frame was not hidden from you
when I was made in the secret place,
when I was woven together in the depths of the earth.
[16]Your eyes saw my unformed body;
all the days ordained for me were written in your book
before one of them came to be.
[17]How precious to me are your thoughts,[a] God!
How vast is the sum of them!
[18]Were I to count them,
they would outnumber the grains of sand—
when I awake, I am still with you.

[19]If only you, God, would slay the wicked!
Away from me, you who are bloodthirsty!
[20]They speak of you with evil intent;
your adversaries misuse your name.
[21]Do I not hate those who hate you, LORD,
and abhor those who are in rebellion against you?
[22]I have nothing but hatred for them;
I count them my enemies.
[23]Search me, God, and know my heart;
test me and know my anxious thoughts.
[24]See if there is any offensive way in me,
and lead me in the way everlasting.

Psalm 140[b]

For the director of music.
A psalm of David.

[1]Rescue me, LORD, from evildoers;
protect me from the violent,
[2]who devise evil plans in their hearts
and stir up war every day.
[3]They make their tongues as sharp as a serpent's;
the poison of vipers is on their lips.[c]

[4]Keep me safe, LORD, from the hands of the wicked;
protect me from the violent,
who devise ways to trip my feet.
[5]The arrogant have hidden a snare for me;
they have spread out the cords of their net
and have set traps for me along my path.

[6]I say to the LORD, "You are my God."
Hear, LORD, my cry for mercy.
[7]Sovereign LORD, my strong deliverer,
you shield my head in the day of battle.
[8]Do not grant the wicked their desires, LORD;
do not let their plans succeed.

[9]Those who surround me proudly rear their heads;
may the mischief of their lips engulf them.
[10]May burning coals fall on them;
may they be thrown into the fire,
into miry pits, never to rise.
[11]May slanderers not be established in the land;
may disaster hunt down the violent.

[12]I know that the LORD secures justice for the poor
and upholds the cause of the needy.
[13]Surely the righteous will praise your name,
and the upright will live in your presence.

Psalm 141

A psalm of David.

[1]I call to you, LORD, come quickly to me;
hear me when I call to you.
[2]May my prayer be set before you like incense;
may the lifting up of my hands be like the evening sacrifice.

[3]Set a guard over my mouth, LORD;
keep watch over the door of my lips.
[4]Do not let my heart be drawn to what is evil
so that I take part in wicked deeds
along with those who are evildoers;
do not let me eat their delicacies.

[5]Let a righteous man strike me—that is a kindness;

[a] 17 Or *How amazing are your thoughts concerning me* [b] In Hebrew texts 140:1-13 is numbered 140:2-14.
[c] 3 The Hebrew has *Selah* (a word of uncertain meaning) here and at the end of verses 5 and 8.

let him rebuke me—that is oil on
my head.
My head will not refuse it,
for my prayer will still be against the
deeds of evildoers.

6 Their rulers will be thrown down from
the cliffs,
and the wicked will learn that my
words were well spoken.
7 They will say, "As one plows and breaks
up the earth,
so our bones have been scattered at
the mouth of the grave."
8 But my eyes are fixed on you, Sovereign
LORD;
in you I take refuge—do not give me
over to death.
9 Keep me safe from the traps set by
evildoers,
from the snares they have laid for me.
10 Let the wicked fall into their own nets,
while I pass by in safety.

Psalm 142[a]

A maskil[b] *of David. When he was in the cave. A prayer.*

1 I cry aloud to the LORD;
I lift up my voice to the LORD for mercy.
2 I pour out before him my complaint;
before him I tell my trouble.

3 When my spirit grows faint within me,
it is you who watch over my way.
In the path where I walk
people have hidden a snare for me.
4 Look and see, there is no one at my right
hand;
no one is concerned for me.
I have no refuge;
no one cares for my life.

5 I cry to you, LORD;
I say, "You are my refuge,
my portion in the land of the living."

6 Listen to my cry,
for I am in desperate need;
rescue me from those who pursue me,
for they are too strong for me.
7 Set me free from my prison,
that I may praise your name.

Then the righteous will gather about me
because of your goodness to me.

Psalm 143

A psalm of David.

1 LORD, hear my prayer,
listen to my cry for mercy;
in your faithfulness and righteousness
come to my relief.
2 Do not bring your servant into
judgment,
for no one living is righteous before
you.
3 The enemy pursues me,
he crushes me to the ground;
he makes me dwell in the darkness
like those long dead.
4 So my spirit grows faint within me;
my heart within me is dismayed.
5 I remember the days of long ago;
I meditate on all your works
and consider what your hands have
done.
6 I spread out my hands to you;
I thirst for you like a parched land.[c]
7 Answer me quickly, LORD;
my spirit fails.
Do not hide your face from me
or I will be like those who go down to
the pit.
8 Let the morning bring me word of your
unfailing love,
for I have put my trust in you.
Show me the way I should go,
for to you I entrust my life.
9 Rescue me from my enemies, LORD,
for I hide myself in you.
10 Teach me to do your will,
for you are my God;
may your good Spirit
lead me on level ground.

11 For your name's sake, LORD, preserve
my life;
in your righteousness, bring me out
of trouble.
12 In your unfailing love, silence my
enemies;
destroy all my foes,
for I am your servant.

[a] In Hebrew texts 142:1-7 is numbered 142:2-8. [b] Title: Probably a literary or musical term [c] 6 The Hebrew has *Selah* (a word of uncertain meaning) here.

Psalm 144

Of David.

[1] Praise be to the LORD my Rock,
who trains my hands for war,
my fingers for battle.
[2] He is my loving God and my fortress,
my stronghold and my deliverer,
my shield, in whom I take refuge,
who subdues peoples[a] under me.

[3] LORD, what are human beings that you
care for them,
mere mortals that you think of them?
[4] They are like a breath;
their days are like a fleeting shadow.

[5] Part your heavens, LORD, and come
down;
touch the mountains, so that they
smoke.
[6] Send forth lightning and scatter the
enemy;
shoot your arrows and rout them.
[7] Reach down your hand from on high;
deliver me and rescue me
from the mighty waters,
from the hands of foreigners
[8] whose mouths are full of lies,
whose right hands are deceitful.

[9] I will sing a new song to you, my God;
on the ten-stringed lyre I will make
music to you,
[10] to the One who gives victory to kings,
who delivers his servant David.

From the deadly sword [11] deliver me;
rescue me from the hands of foreigners
whose mouths are full of lies,
whose right hands are deceitful.

[12] Then our sons in their youth
will be like well-nurtured plants,
and our daughters will be like pillars
carved to adorn a palace.
[13] Our barns will be filled
with every kind of provision.
Our sheep will increase by thousands,
by tens of thousands in our fields;
[14] our oxen will draw heavy loads.[b]
There will be no breaching of walls,
no going into captivity,
no cry of distress in our streets.
[15] Blessed is the people of whom this is true;
blessed is the people whose God is the
LORD.

Psalm 145[c]

A psalm of praise. Of David.

[1] I will exalt you, my God the King;
I will praise your name for ever and
ever.
[2] Every day I will praise you
and extol your name for ever and ever.

[3] Great is the LORD and most worthy of
praise;
his greatness no one can fathom.
[4] One generation commends your works to
another;
they tell of your mighty acts.
[5] They speak of the glorious splendor of
your majesty—
and I will meditate on your wonderful
works.[d]
[6] They tell of the power of your awesome
works—
and I will proclaim your great deeds.
[7] They celebrate your abundant goodness
and joyfully sing of your
righteousness.

[8] The LORD is gracious and compassionate,
slow to anger and rich in love.
[9] The LORD is good to all;
he has compassion on all he has
made.
[10] All your works praise you, LORD;
your faithful people extol you.
[11] They tell of the glory of your kingdom
and speak of your might,
[12] so that all people may know of your
mighty acts
and the glorious splendor of your
kingdom.
[13] Your kingdom is an everlasting kingdom,
and your dominion endures through
all generations.

[a] *2* Many manuscripts of the Masoretic Text, Dead Sea Scrolls, Aquila, Jerome and Syriac; most manuscripts of the Masoretic Text *subdues my people* [b] *14* Or *our chieftains will be firmly established* [c] This psalm is an acrostic poem, the verses of which (including verse 13b) begin with the successive letters of the Hebrew alphabet. [d] *5* Dead Sea Scrolls and Syriac (see also Septuagint); Masoretic Text *On the glorious splendor of your majesty / and on your wonderful works I will meditate*

The LORD is trustworthy in all he
promises
and faithful in all he does.[a]
14 The LORD upholds all who fall
and lifts up all who are bowed down.
15 The eyes of all look to you,
and you give them their food at the
proper time.
16 You open your hand
and satisfy the desires of every living
thing.

17 The LORD is righteous in all his ways
and faithful in all he does.
18 The LORD is near to all who call on him,
to all who call on him in truth.
19 He fulfills the desires of those who fear
him;
he hears their cry and saves them.
20 The LORD watches over all who love him,
but all the wicked he will destroy.

21 My mouth will speak in praise of the LORD.
Let every creature praise his holy name
for ever and ever.

Psalm 146

1 Praise the LORD.[b]

Praise the LORD, my soul.

2 I will praise the LORD all my life;
I will sing praise to my God as long as
I live.
3 Do not put your trust in princes,
in human beings, who cannot save.
4 When their spirit departs, they return to
the ground;
on that very day their plans come to
nothing.
5 Blessed are those whose help is the God
of Jacob,
whose hope is in the LORD their God.

6 He is the Maker of heaven and earth,
the sea, and everything in them—
he remains faithful forever.
7 He upholds the cause of the oppressed
and gives food to the hungry.
The LORD sets prisoners free,
8 the LORD gives sight to the blind,
the LORD lifts up those who are bowed
down,
the LORD loves the righteous.
9 The LORD watches over the foreigner
and sustains the fatherless and the
widow,
but he frustrates the ways of the
wicked.

10 The LORD reigns forever,
your God, O Zion, for all generations.

Praise the LORD.

Psalm 147

1 Praise the LORD.[c]

How good it is to sing praises to our God,
how pleasant and fitting to praise him!

2 The LORD builds up Jerusalem;
he gathers the exiles of Israel.
3 He heals the brokenhearted
and binds up their wounds.
4 He determines the number of the stars
and calls them each by name.
5 Great is our Lord and mighty in power;
his understanding has no limit.
6 The LORD sustains the humble
but casts the wicked to the ground.

7 Sing to the LORD with grateful praise;
make music to our God on the harp.

8 He covers the sky with clouds;
he supplies the earth with rain
and makes grass grow on the hills.
9 He provides food for the cattle
and for the young ravens when they
call.

10 His pleasure is not in the strength of the
horse,
nor his delight in the legs of the
warrior;
11 the LORD delights in those who fear him,
who put their hope in his unfailing
love.

12 Extol the LORD, Jerusalem;
praise your God, Zion.

13 He strengthens the bars of your gates
and blesses your people within you.
14 He grants peace to your borders
and satisfies you with the finest of
wheat.

[a] *13* One manuscript of the Masoretic Text, Dead Sea Scrolls and Syriac (see also Septuagint); most manuscripts of the Masoretic Text do not have the last two lines of verse 13. [b] *1* Hebrew *Hallelu Yah*; also in verse 10 [c] *1* Hebrew *Hallelu Yah*; also in verse 20

15 He sends his command to the earth;
his word runs swiftly.
16 He spreads the snow like wool
and scatters the frost like ashes.
17 He hurls down his hail like pebbles.
Who can withstand his icy blast?
18 He sends his word and melts them;
he stirs up his breezes, and the
waters flow.

19 He has revealed his word to Jacob,
his laws and decrees to Israel.
20 He has done this for no other nation;
they do not know his laws.[a]

Praise the LORD.

Psalm 148

1 Praise the LORD.[b]

Praise the LORD from the heavens;
praise him in the heights above.
2 Praise him, all his angels;
praise him, all his heavenly hosts.
3 Praise him, sun and moon;
praise him, all you shining stars.
4 Praise him, you highest heavens
and you waters above the skies.

5 Let them praise the name of the LORD,
for at his command they were
created,
6 and he established them for ever and
ever—
he issued a decree that will never pass
away.

7 Praise the LORD from the earth,
you great sea creatures and all ocean
depths,
8 lightning and hail, snow and clouds,
stormy winds that do his bidding,
9 you mountains and all hills,
fruit trees and all cedars,
10 wild animals and all cattle,
small creatures and flying birds,
11 kings of the earth and all nations,
you princes and all rulers on earth,
12 young men and women,
old men and children.

13 Let them praise the name of the LORD,
for his name alone is exalted;
his splendor is above the earth and the
heavens.
14 And he has raised up for his people a
horn,[c]
the praise of all his faithful servants,
of Israel, the people close to his heart.

Praise the LORD.

Psalm 149

1 Praise the LORD.[d]

Sing to the LORD a new song,
his praise in the assembly of his
faithful people.

2 Let Israel rejoice in their Maker;
let the people of Zion be glad in their
King.
3 Let them praise his name with dancing
and make music to him with timbrel
and harp.
4 For the LORD takes delight in his
people;
he crowns the humble with victory.
5 Let his faithful people rejoice in this
honor
and sing for joy on their beds.

6 May the praise of God be in their
mouths
and a double-edged sword in their
hands,
7 to inflict vengeance on the nations
and punishment on the peoples,
8 to bind their kings with fetters,
their nobles with shackles of iron,
9 to carry out the sentence written against
them—
this is the glory of all his faithful
people.

Praise the LORD.

Psalm 150

1 Praise the LORD.[e]

Praise God in his sanctuary;
praise him in his mighty heavens.
2 Praise him for his acts of power;
praise him for his surpassing
greatness.

[a] *20* Masoretic Text; Dead Sea Scrolls and Septuagint *nation; / he has not made his laws known to them*
[b] *1* Hebrew *Hallelu Yah*; also in verse 14 [c] *14* *Horn* here symbolizes strength. [d] *1* Hebrew *Hallelu Yah*; also in verse 9 [e] *1* Hebrew *Hallelu Yah*; also in verse 6

3 Praise him with the sounding of the trumpet,
praise him with the harp and lyre,
4 praise him with timbrel and dancing,
praise him with the strings and pipe,
5 praise him with the clash of cymbals,
praise him with resounding cymbals.

6 Let everything that has breath praise the LORD.

Praise the LORD.

PROVERBS

Purpose and Theme

1 The proverbs of Solomon son of David, king of Israel:

[2] for gaining wisdom and instruction;
for understanding words of insight;
[3] for receiving instruction in prudent behavior,
doing what is right and just and fair;
[4] for giving prudence to those who are simple,[a]
knowledge and discretion to the young—
[5] let the wise listen and add to their learning,
and let the discerning get guidance—
[6] for understanding proverbs and parables,
the sayings and riddles of the wise.[b]

[7] The fear of the LORD is the beginning of knowledge,
but fools[c] despise wisdom and instruction.

Prologue: Exhortations to Embrace Wisdom

Warning Against the Invitation of Sinful Men

[8] Listen, my son, to your father's instruction
and do not forsake your mother's teaching.
[9] They are a garland to grace your head
and a chain to adorn your neck.

[10] My son, if sinful men entice you,
do not give in to them.
[11] If they say, "Come along with us;
let's lie in wait for innocent blood,
let's ambush some harmless soul;
[12] let's swallow them alive, like the grave,
and whole, like those who go down to the pit;
[13] we will get all sorts of valuable things
and fill our houses with plunder;
[14] cast lots with us;
we will all share the loot"—
[15] my son, do not go along with them,
do not set foot on their paths;
[16] for their feet rush into evil,
they are swift to shed blood.
[17] How useless to spread a net
where every bird can see it!
[18] These men lie in wait for their own blood;
they ambush only themselves!
[19] Such are the paths of all who go after ill-gotten gain;
it takes away the life of those who get it.

Wisdom's Rebuke

[20] Out in the open wisdom calls aloud,
she raises her voice in the public square;
[21] on top of the wall[d] she cries out,
at the city gate she makes her speech:

[22] "How long will you who are simple love your simple ways?
How long will mockers delight in mockery
and fools hate knowledge?
[23] Repent at my rebuke!
Then I will pour out my thoughts to you,
I will make known to you my teachings.
[24] But since you refuse to listen when I call
and no one pays attention when I stretch out my hand,
[25] since you disregard all my advice
and do not accept my rebuke,
[26] I in turn will laugh when disaster strikes you;
I will mock when calamity overtakes you—
[27] when calamity overtakes you like a storm,

[a] *4* The Hebrew word rendered *simple* in Proverbs denotes a person who is gullible, without moral direction and inclined to evil. [b] *6* Or *understanding a proverb, namely, a parable, / and the sayings of the wise, their riddles* [c] *7* The Hebrew words rendered *fool* in Proverbs, and often elsewhere in the Old Testament, denote a person who is morally deficient. [d] *21* Septuagint; Hebrew */ at noisy street corners*

when disaster sweeps over you like a whirlwind,
when distress and trouble overwhelm you.

28 "Then they will call to me but I will not answer;
they will look for me but will not find me,
29 since they hated knowledge
and did not choose to fear the LORD.
30 Since they would not accept my advice
and spurned my rebuke,
31 they will eat the fruit of their ways
and be filled with the fruit of their schemes.
32 For the waywardness of the simple will kill them,
and the complacency of fools will destroy them;
33 but whoever listens to me will live in safety
and be at ease, without fear of harm."

Moral Benefits of Wisdom

2 My son, if you accept my words
and store up my commands within you,
2 turning your ear to wisdom
and applying your heart to understanding—
3 indeed, if you call out for insight
and cry aloud for understanding,
4 and if you look for it as for silver
and search for it as for hidden treasure,
5 then you will understand the fear of the LORD
and find the knowledge of God.
6 For the LORD gives wisdom;
from his mouth come knowledge and understanding.
7 He holds success in store for the upright,
he is a shield to those whose walk is blameless,
8 for he guards the course of the just
and protects the way of his faithful ones.
9 Then you will understand what is right and just
and fair—every good path.
10 For wisdom will enter your heart,
and knowledge will be pleasant to your soul.
11 Discretion will protect you,
and understanding will guard you.
12 Wisdom will save you from the ways of wicked men,
from men whose words are perverse,
13 who have left the straight paths
to walk in dark ways,
14 who delight in doing wrong
and rejoice in the perverseness of evil,
15 whose paths are crooked
and who are devious in their ways.
16 Wisdom will save you also from the adulterous woman,
from the wayward woman with her seductive words,
17 who has left the partner of her youth
and ignored the covenant she made before God.[a]
18 Surely her house leads down to death
and her paths to the spirits of the dead.
19 None who go to her return
or attain the paths of life.
20 Thus you will walk in the ways of the good
and keep to the paths of the righteous.
21 For the upright will live in the land,
and the blameless will remain in it;
22 but the wicked will be cut off from the land,
and the unfaithful will be torn from it.

Wisdom Bestows Well-Being

3 My son, do not forget my teaching,
but keep my commands in your heart,
2 for they will prolong your life many years
and bring you peace and prosperity.
3 Let love and faithfulness never leave you;
bind them around your neck,
write them on the tablet of your heart.
4 Then you will win favor and a good name
in the sight of God and man.
5 Trust in the LORD with all your heart
and lean not on your own understanding;
6 in all your ways submit to him,
and he will make your paths straight.[b]
7 Do not be wise in your own eyes;
fear the LORD and shun evil.
8 This will bring health to your body
and nourishment to your bones.
9 Honor the LORD with your wealth,
with the firstfruits of all your crops;

[a] 17 Or *covenant of her God* [b] 6 Or *will direct your paths*

10 then your barns will be filled to
overflowing,
and your vats will brim over with
new wine.

11 My son, do not despise the LORD's
discipline,
and do not resent his rebuke,
12 because the LORD disciplines those
he loves,
as a father the son he delights in.[a]

13 Blessed are those who find wisdom,
those who gain understanding,
14 for she is more profitable than silver
and yields better returns than gold.
15 She is more precious than rubies;
nothing you desire can compare
with her.
16 Long life is in her right hand;
in her left hand are riches and honor.
17 Her ways are pleasant ways,
and all her paths are peace.
18 She is a tree of life to those who take hold
of her;
those who hold her fast will be
blessed.

19 By wisdom the LORD laid the earth's
foundations,
by understanding he set the heavens
in place;
20 by his knowledge the watery depths were
divided,
and the clouds let drop the dew.

21 My son, do not let wisdom and
understanding out of your sight
preserve sound judgment and
discretion;
22 they will be life for you,
an ornament to grace your neck.
23 Then you will go on your way in safety,
and your foot will not stumble.
24 When you lie down, you will not be
afraid;
when you lie down, your sleep will be
sweet.
25 Have no fear of sudden disaster
or of the ruin that overtakes the
wicked,
26 for the LORD will be at your side
and will keep your foot from being
snared.

27 Do not withhold good from those to
whom it is due,
when it is in your power to act.
28 Do not say to your neighbor,
"Come back tomorrow and I'll give it
to you" —
when you already have it with you.
29 Do not plot harm against your neighbor,
who lives trustfully near you.
30 Do not accuse anyone for no reason —
when they have done you no harm.

31 Do not envy the violent
or choose any of their ways.

32 For the LORD detests the perverse
but takes the upright into his
confidence.
33 The LORD's curse is on the house of the
wicked,
but he blesses the home of the
righteous.
34 He mocks proud mockers
but shows favor to the humble and
oppressed.
35 The wise inherit honor,
but fools get only shame.

Get Wisdom at Any Cost

4 Listen, my sons, to a father's
instruction;
pay attention and gain understanding.
2 I give you sound learning,
so do not forsake my teaching.
3 For I too was a son to my father,
still tender, and cherished by my
mother.
4 Then he taught me, and he said to me,
"Take hold of my words with all your
heart;
keep my commands, and you will live.
5 Get wisdom, get understanding;
do not forget my words or turn away
from them.
6 Do not forsake wisdom, and she will
protect you;
love her, and she will watch over you.
7 The beginning of wisdom is this: Get[b]
wisdom.
Though it cost all you have,[c] get
understanding.
8 Cherish her, and she will exalt you;
embrace her, and she will honor you.

[a] *12* Hebrew; Septuagint *loves, / and he chastens everyone he accepts as his child* [b] *7* Or *Wisdom is supreme; therefore get* [c] *7* Or *wisdom. / Whatever else you get*

[9]She will give you a garland to grace
your head
and present you with a glorious crown."

[10]Listen, my son, accept what I say,
and the years of your life will be many.
[11]I instruct you in the way of wisdom
and lead you along straight paths.
[12]When you walk, your steps will not be
hampered;
when you run, you will not stumble.
[13]Hold on to instruction, do not let it go;
guard it well, for it is your life.
[14]Do not set foot on the path of the wicked
or walk in the way of evildoers.
[15]Avoid it, do not travel on it;
turn from it and go on your way.
[16]For they cannot rest until they do evil;
they are robbed of sleep till they make
someone stumble.
[17]They eat the bread of wickedness
and drink the wine of violence.

[18]The path of the righteous is like the
morning sun,
shining ever brighter till the full light
of day.
[19]But the way of the wicked is like deep
darkness;
they do not know what makes them
stumble.

[20]My son, pay attention to what I say;
turn your ear to my words.
[21]Do not let them out of your sight,
keep them within your heart;
[22]for they are life to those who find them
and health to one's whole body.
[23]Above all else, guard your heart,
for everything you do flows from it.
[24]Keep your mouth free of perversity;
keep corrupt talk far from your lips.
[25]Let your eyes look straight ahead;
fix your gaze directly before you.
[26]Give careful thought to the[a] paths for
your feet
and be steadfast in all your ways.
[27]Do not turn to the right or the left;
keep your foot from evil.

Warning Against Adultery

5 My son, pay attention to my wisdom,
turn your ear to my words of insight,
[2]that you may maintain discretion
and your lips may preserve knowledge.
[3]For the lips of the adulterous woman drip
honey,
and her speech is smoother than oil;
[4]but in the end she is bitter as gall,
sharp as a double-edged sword.
[5]Her feet go down to death;
her steps lead straight to the grave.
[6]She gives no thought to the way of life;
her paths wander aimlessly, but she
does not know it.

[7]Now then, my sons, listen to me;
do not turn aside from what I say.
[8]Keep to a path far from her,
do not go near the door of her house,
[9]lest you lose your honor to others
and your dignity[b] to one who is cruel,
[10]lest strangers feast on your wealth
and your toil enrich the house of
another.
[11]At the end of your life you will groan,
when your flesh and body are spent.
[12]You will say, "How I hated discipline!
How my heart spurned correction!
[13]I would not obey my teachers
or turn my ear to my instructors.
[14]And I was soon in serious trouble
in the assembly of God's people."

[15]Drink water from your own cistern,
running water from your own well.
[16]Should your springs overflow in the
streets,
your streams of water in the public
squares?
[17]Let them be yours alone,
never to be shared with strangers.
[18]May your fountain be blessed,
and may you rejoice in the wife of your
youth.
[19]A loving doe, a graceful deer—
may her breasts satisfy you always,
may you ever be intoxicated with
her love.
[20]Why, my son, be intoxicated with another
man's wife?
Why embrace the bosom of a wayward
woman?

[21]For your ways are in full view of the LORD,
and he examines all your paths.
[22]The evil deeds of the wicked ensnare
them;
the cords of their sins hold them fast.

[a] 26 Or *Make level* [b] 9 Or *years*

[23] For lack of discipline they will die,
led astray by their own great folly.

Warnings Against Folly

6 My son, if you have put up security for
your neighbor,
if you have shaken hands in pledge for
a stranger,
[2] you have been trapped by what you said,
ensnared by the words of your mouth.
[3] So do this, my son, to free yourself,
since you have fallen into your
neighbor's hands:
Go — to the point of exhaustion — [a]
and give your neighbor no rest!
[4] Allow no sleep to your eyes,
no slumber to your eyelids.
[5] Free yourself, like a gazelle from the
hand of the hunter,
like a bird from the snare of the fowler.

[6] Go to the ant, you sluggard;
consider its ways and be wise!
[7] It has no commander,
no overseer or ruler,
[8] yet it stores its provisions in summer
and gathers its food at harvest.

[9] How long will you lie there, you sluggard?
When will you get up from your sleep?
[10] A little sleep, a little slumber,
a little folding of the hands to rest —
[11] and poverty will come on you like a thief
and scarcity like an armed man.

[12] A troublemaker and a villain,
who goes about with a corrupt mouth,
[13] who winks maliciously with his eye,
signals with his feet
and motions with his fingers,
[14] who plots evil with deceit in his
heart —
he always stirs up conflict.
[15] Therefore disaster will overtake him in
an instant;
he will suddenly be destroyed —
without remedy.

[16] There are six things the LORD hates,
seven that are detestable to him:
[17] haughty eyes,
a lying tongue,
hands that shed innocent blood,
[18] a heart that devises wicked schemes,
feet that are quick to rush into evil,
[19] a false witness who pours out lies
and a person who stirs up conflict in
the community.

Warning Against Adultery

[20] My son, keep your father's command
and do not forsake your mother's
teaching.
[21] Bind them always on your heart;
fasten them around your neck.
[22] When you walk, they will guide you;
when you sleep, they will watch over
you;
when you awake, they will speak to you.
[23] For this command is a lamp,
this teaching is a light,
and correction and instruction
are the way to life,
[24] keeping you from your neighbor's wife,
from the smooth talk of a wayward
woman.

[25] Do not lust in your heart after her beauty
or let her captivate you with her eyes.
[26] For a prostitute can be had for a loaf of
bread,
but another man's wife preys on your
very life.
[27] Can a man scoop fire into his lap
without his clothes being burned?
[28] Can a man walk on hot coals
without his feet being scorched?
[29] So is he who sleeps with another man's
wife;
no one who touches her will go
unpunished.

[30] People do not despise a thief if he steals
to satisfy his hunger when he is
starving.
[31] Yet if he is caught, he must pay sevenfold,
though it costs him all the wealth of
his house.
[32] But a man who commits adultery has
no sense;
whoever does so destroys himself.
[33] Blows and disgrace are his lot,
and his shame will never be wiped
away.

[34] For jealousy arouses a husband's fury,
and he will show no mercy when he
takes revenge.

[a] 3 Or *Go and humble yourself,*

SING TO THE KING

Billy Foote, Charles Silvester Horne

Sing to the King who is coming to reign
Glory to Jesus, the Lamb that was slain
Life and salvation his empire shall bring
And joy to the nations, when Jesus is King

Come, let us sing a song
A song declaring that we belong to Jesus
He is all we need
Lift up a heart of praise
Sing now with voices raised to Jesus
Sing to the King

For his returning we watch and we pray
We will be ready the dawn of that day
We'll join in singing with all the redeemed
'Cause Satan is vanquished and Jesus is King

THE INSPIRATION

I charge you to keep this command without spot or blame until the appearing of our Lord Jesus Christ, which God will bring about in his own time — God, the blessed and only Ruler, the King of kings and Lord of lords, who alone is immortal and who lives in unapproachable light, whom no one has seen or can see. To him be honor and might forever. Amen. — 1 Timothy 6:13 – 16

Read also: Psalm 45:6 – 7

BEHIND THE SONG

Many of the most popular modern worship songs are updates of older hymns. Changes in language usage, melodic sensibilities and even instrumentation have led to the evolution of hymns and spiritual songs for thousands of years; that tradition is alive and well in the contemporary worship community.

Worship leader Billy Foote was looking through an old Baptist hymnal one day when he came across "Sing We the King," a hymn that immediately grabbed his attention. "I thought the lyrics of the first verse were amazing," he recalls. "I took a melody that I had previously written and it fit the verse perfectly." Foote wrote an original chorus and combined other pieces of the hymn's original verses into a second verse. He changed the title to "Sing to the King" because the original title just felt awkward. "Please don't hate me," he laughs, "but 'Sing *We* the King' just sounds strange."

The result is a triumphant, regal song with lyrics that are theologically rich as well as melodic, and a rhythmic structure that is memorable and accessible. "What excites me most about this song is that Charles Silvester Horne's inspired lyrics are not forgotten," Foote adds. "His words remind us that one day every knee will bow and every tongue will confess that Jesus alone is King!"

Selah

Considering how fallible most human kings have been, it can be difficult to imagine singing to a king by choice. But the truth is that the human heart deeply longs to be led, inspired and protected by a perfect leader. The royal language used throughout the Old Testament and even by Paul in his letter to Timothy, points to God Almighty as the one true King we all long to serve.

And how does this King of kings treat us? With nothing less than perfect love, unending faithfulness, lavish grace and life-saving sacrifice. No human king could be better than that.

[35] He will not accept any compensation;
he will refuse a bribe, however great
it is.

Warning Against the Adulterous Woman

7 My son, keep my words
and store up my commands within you.
[2] Keep my commands and you will live;
guard my teachings as the apple of
your eye.
[3] Bind them on your fingers;
write them on the tablet of your heart.
[4] Say to wisdom, "You are my sister,"
and to insight, "You are my relative."
[5] They will keep you from the adulterous
woman,
from the wayward woman with her
seductive words.

[6] At the window of my house
I looked down through the lattice.
[7] I saw among the simple,
I noticed among the young men,
a youth who had no sense.
[8] He was going down the street near her
corner,
walking along in the direction of her
house
[9] at twilight, as the day was fading,
as the dark of night set in.

[10] Then out came a woman to meet him,
dressed like a prostitute and with
crafty intent.
[11] (She is unruly and defiant,
her feet never stay at home;
[12] now in the street, now in the squares,
at every corner she lurks.)
[13] She took hold of him and kissed him
and with a brazen face she said:

[14] "Today I fulfilled my vows,
and I have food from my fellowship
offering at home.
[15] So I came out to meet you;
I looked for you and have found you!
[16] I have covered my bed
with colored linens from Egypt.
[17] I have perfumed my bed
with myrrh, aloes and cinnamon.
[18] Come, let's drink deeply of love till
morning;
let's enjoy ourselves with love!
[19] My husband is not at home;
he has gone on a long journey.
[20] He took his purse filled with money
and will not be home till full moon."

[21] With persuasive words she led him
astray;
she seduced him with her smooth talk.
[22] All at once he followed her
like an ox going to the slaughter,
like a deer[a] stepping into a noose[b]
[23] till an arrow pierces his liver,
like a bird darting into a snare,
little knowing it will cost him his life.

[24] Now then, my sons, listen to me;
pay attention to what I say.
[25] Do not let your heart turn to her ways
or stray into her paths.
[26] Many are the victims she has brought
down;
her slain are a mighty throng.
[27] Her house is a highway to the grave,
leading down to the chambers of
death.

Wisdom's Call

8 Does not wisdom call out?
Does not understanding raise her
voice?
[2] At the highest point along the way,
where the paths meet, she takes her
stand;
[3] beside the gate leading into the city,
at the entrance, she cries aloud:
[4] "To you, O people, I call out;
I raise my voice to all mankind.
[5] You who are simple, gain prudence;
you who are foolish, set your hearts
on it.[c]
[6] Listen, for I have trustworthy things
to say;
I open my lips to speak what is right.
[7] My mouth speaks what is true,
for my lips detest wickedness.
[8] All the words of my mouth are just;
none of them is crooked or perverse.
[9] To the discerning all of them are right;
they are upright to those who have
found knowledge.
[10] Choose my instruction instead of silver,
knowledge rather than choice gold,

[a] 22 Syriac (see also Septuagint); Hebrew *fool* [b] 22 The meaning of the Hebrew for this line is uncertain. [c] 5 Septuagint; Hebrew *foolish, instruct your minds*

11 for wisdom is more precious than rubies,
and nothing you desire can compare with her.

12 "I, wisdom, dwell together with prudence;
I possess knowledge and discretion.
13 To fear the LORD is to hate evil;
I hate pride and arrogance,
evil behavior and perverse speech.
14 Counsel and sound judgment are mine;
I have insight, I have power.
15 By me kings reign
and rulers issue decrees that are just;
16 by me princes govern,
and nobles — all who rule on earth.[a]
17 I love those who love me,
and those who seek me find me.
18 With me are riches and honor,
enduring wealth and prosperity.
19 My fruit is better than fine gold;
what I yield surpasses choice silver.
20 I walk in the way of righteousness,
along the paths of justice,
21 bestowing a rich inheritance on those who love me
and making their treasuries full.

22 "The LORD brought me forth as the first of his works,[b,c]
before his deeds of old;
23 I was formed long ages ago,
at the very beginning, when the world came to be.
24 When there were no watery depths, I was given birth,
when there were no springs overflowing with water;
25 before the mountains were settled in place,
before the hills, I was given birth,
26 before he made the world or its fields
or any of the dust of the earth.
27 I was there when he set the heavens in place,
when he marked out the horizon on the face of the deep,
28 when he established the clouds above
and fixed securely the fountains of the deep,
29 when he gave the sea its boundary
so the waters would not overstep his command,
and when he marked out the foundations of the earth.
30 Then I was constantly[d] at his side.
I was filled with delight day after day,
rejoicing always in his presence,
31 rejoicing in his whole world
and delighting in mankind.

32 "Now then, my children, listen to me;
blessed are those who keep my ways.
33 Listen to my instruction and be wise;
do not disregard it.
34 Blessed are those who listen to me,
watching daily at my doors,
waiting at my doorway.
35 For those who find me find life
and receive favor from the LORD.
36 But those who fail to find me harm themselves;
all who hate me love death."

Invitations of Wisdom and Folly

9 Wisdom has built her house;
she has set up[e] its seven pillars.
2 She has prepared her meat and mixed her wine;
she has also set her table.
3 She has sent out her servants, and she calls
from the highest point of the city,
4 "Let all who are simple come to my house!"
To those who have no sense she says,
5 "Come, eat my food
and drink the wine I have mixed.
6 Leave your simple ways and you will live;
walk in the way of insight."

7 Whoever corrects a mocker invites insults;
whoever rebukes the wicked incurs abuse.
8 Do not rebuke mockers or they will hate you;
rebuke the wise and they will love you.
9 Instruct the wise and they will be wiser still;

[a] 16 Some Hebrew manuscripts and Septuagint; other Hebrew manuscripts *all righteous rulers*
[b] 22 Or *way*; or *dominion* [c] 22 Or *The LORD possessed me at the beginning of his work*; or *The LORD brought me forth at the beginning of his work* [d] 30 Or *was the artisan*; or *was a little child*
[e] 1 Septuagint, Syriac and Targum; Hebrew *has hewn out*

teach the righteous and they will add
to their learning.

[10]The fear of the LORD is the beginning of
wisdom,
and knowledge of the Holy One is
understanding.
[11]For through wisdom[a] your days will
be many,
and years will be added to your life.
[12]If you are wise, your wisdom will reward
you;
if you are a mocker, you alone will
suffer.

[13]Folly is an unruly woman;
she is simple and knows nothing.
[14]She sits at the door of her house,
on a seat at the highest point of the
city,
[15]calling out to those who pass by,
who go straight on their way,
[16]"Let all who are simple come to my
house!"
To those who have no sense she says,
[17]"Stolen water is sweet;
food eaten in secret is delicious!"
[18]But little do they know that the dead are
there,
that her guests are deep in the realm of
the dead.

Proverbs of Solomon

10 The proverbs of Solomon:

A wise son brings joy to his father,
but a foolish son brings grief to his
mother.
[2]Ill-gotten treasures have no lasting value,
but righteousness delivers from death.

[3]The LORD does not let the righteous go
hungry,
but he thwarts the craving of the
wicked.

[4]Lazy hands make for poverty,
but diligent hands bring wealth.

[5]He who gathers crops in summer is a
prudent son,
but he who sleeps during harvest is a
disgraceful son.

[6]Blessings crown the head of the
righteous,
but violence overwhelms the mouth of
the wicked.[b]

[7]The name of the righteous is used in
blessings,[c]
but the name of the wicked will rot.

[8]The wise in heart accept commands,
but a chattering fool comes to ruin.
[9]Whoever walks in integrity walks
securely,
but whoever takes crooked paths will
be found out.

[10]Whoever winks maliciously causes grief,
and a chattering fool comes to ruin.

[11]The mouth of the righteous is a fountain
of life,
but the mouth of the wicked conceals
violence.

[12]Hatred stirs up conflict,
but love covers over all wrongs.

[13]Wisdom is found on the lips of the
discerning,
but a rod is for the back of one who has
no sense.

[14]The wise store up knowledge,
but the mouth of a fool invites ruin.

[15]The wealth of the rich is their fortified
city,
but poverty is the ruin of the poor.

[16]The wages of the righteous is life,
but the earnings of the wicked are sin
and death.

[17]Whoever heeds discipline shows the way
to life,
but whoever ignores correction leads
others astray.

[18]Whoever conceals hatred with lying lips
and spreads slander is a fool.

[19]Sin is not ended by multiplying words,
but the prudent hold their tongues.

[20]The tongue of the righteous is choice
silver,
but the heart of the wicked is of little
value.

[a] *11* Septuagint, Syriac and Targum; Hebrew *me* [b] *6* Or *righteous, / but the mouth of the wicked conceals violence* [c] *7* See Gen. 48:20.

21 The lips of the righteous nourish many,
but fools die for lack of sense.

22 The blessing of the LORD brings wealth,
without painful toil for it.

23 A fool finds pleasure in wicked schemes,
but a person of understanding delights
in wisdom.

24 What the wicked dread will overtake
them;
what the righteous desire will be
granted.

25 When the storm has swept by, the wicked
are gone,
but the righteous stand firm forever.

26 As vinegar to the teeth and smoke to the
eyes,
so are sluggards to those who send
them.

27 The fear of the LORD adds length to life,
but the years of the wicked are cut
short.

28 The prospect of the righteous is joy,
but the hopes of the wicked come to
nothing.

29 The way of the LORD is a refuge for the
blameless,
but it is the ruin of those who do evil.

30 The righteous will never be uprooted
but the wicked will not remain in
the land.

31 From the mouth of the righteous comes
the fruit of wisdom,
but a perverse tongue will be silenced.

32 The lips of the righteous know what finds
favor,
but the mouth of the wicked only what
is perverse.

11 The LORD detests dishonest scales,
but accurate weights find favor with
him.

2 When pride comes, then comes disgrace,
but with humility comes wisdom.

3 The integrity of the upright guides them,
but the unfaithful are destroyed by
their duplicity.

4 Wealth is worthless in the day of wrath,
but righteousness delivers from death.

5 The righteousness of the blameless
makes their paths straight,
but the wicked are brought down by
their own wickedness.

6 The righteousness of the upright delivers
them,
but the unfaithful are trapped by evil
desires.

7 Hopes placed in mortals die with them;
all the promise of[a] their power comes
to nothing.

8 The righteous person is rescued from
trouble,
and it falls on the wicked instead.

9 With their mouths the godless destroy
their neighbors,
but through knowledge the righteous
escape.

10 When the righteous prosper, the city
rejoices;
when the wicked perish, there are
shouts of joy.

11 Through the blessing of the upright a city
is exalted,
but by the mouth of the wicked it is
destroyed.

12 Whoever derides their neighbor has no
sense,
but the one who has understanding
holds their tongue.

13 A gossip betrays a confidence,
but a trustworthy person keeps a
secret.

14 For lack of guidance a nation falls,
but victory is won through many
advisers.

15 Whoever puts up security for a stranger
will surely suffer,
but whoever refuses to shake hands in
pledge is safe.

16 A kindhearted woman gains honor,
but ruthless men gain only wealth.

17 Those who are kind benefit themselves,
but the cruel bring ruin on themselves.

[a] 7 Two Hebrew manuscripts; most Hebrew manuscripts, Vulgate, Syriac and Targum *When the wicked die, their hope perishes; / all they expected from*

[18] A wicked person earns deceptive wages,
but the one who sows righteousness
reaps a sure reward.

[19] Truly the righteous attain life,
but whoever pursues evil finds death.

[20] The LORD detests those whose hearts are
perverse,
but he delights in those whose ways
are blameless.

[21] Be sure of this: The wicked will not go
unpunished,
but those who are righteous will go free.

[22] Like a gold ring in a pig's snout
is a beautiful woman who shows no
discretion.

[23] The desire of the righteous ends only in
good,
but the hope of the wicked only in
wrath.

[24] One person gives freely, yet gains even
more;
another withholds unduly, but comes
to poverty.

[25] A generous person will prosper;
whoever refreshes others will be
refreshed.

[26] People curse the one who hoards grain,
but they pray God's blessing on the one
who is willing to sell.

[27] Whoever seeks good finds favor,
but evil comes to one who searches
for it.

[28] Those who trust in their riches will fall,
but the righteous will thrive like a
green leaf.

[29] Whoever brings ruin on their family will
inherit only wind,
and the fool will be servant to the wise.

[30] The fruit of the righteous is a tree of life,
and the one who is wise saves lives.

[31] If the righteous receive their due on
earth,
how much more the ungodly and the
sinner!

12 Whoever loves discipline loves
knowledge,
but whoever hates correction is stupid.

[2] Good people obtain favor from the LORD,
but he condemns those who devise
wicked schemes.

[3] No one can be established through
wickedness,
but the righteous cannot be uprooted.

[4] A wife of noble character is her husband's
crown,
but a disgraceful wife is like decay in
his bones.

[5] The plans of the righteous are just,
but the advice of the wicked is
deceitful.

[6] The words of the wicked lie in wait for
blood,
but the speech of the upright rescues
them.

[7] The wicked are overthrown and are no
more,
but the house of the righteous stands
firm.

[8] A person is praised according to their
prudence,
and one with a warped mind is
despised.

[9] Better to be a nobody and yet have a
servant
than pretend to be somebody and have
no food.

[10] The righteous care for the needs of their
animals,
but the kindest acts of the wicked are
cruel.

[11] Those who work their land will have
abundant food,
but those who chase fantasies have no
sense.

[12] The wicked desire the stronghold of
evildoers,
but the root of the righteous endures.

[13] Evildoers are trapped by their sinful talk,
and so the innocent escape trouble.

[14] From the fruit of their lips people are
filled with good things,
and the work of their hands brings
them reward.

[15] The way of fools seems right to them,
but the wise listen to advice.

16 Fools show their annoyance at once,
but the prudent overlook an insult.

17 An honest witness tells the truth,
but a false witness tells lies.

18 The words of the reckless pierce like swords,
but the tongue of the wise brings healing.

19 Truthful lips endure forever,
but a lying tongue lasts only a moment.

20 Deceit is in the hearts of those who plot evil,
but those who promote peace have joy.

21 No harm overtakes the righteous,
but the wicked have their fill of trouble.

22 The LORD detests lying lips,
but he delights in people who are trustworthy.

23 The prudent keep their knowledge to themselves,
but a fool's heart blurts out folly.

24 Diligent hands will rule,
but laziness ends in forced labor.

25 Anxiety weighs down the heart,
but a kind word cheers it up.

26 The righteous choose their friends carefully,
but the way of the wicked leads them astray.

27 The lazy do not roast[a] any game,
but the diligent feed on the riches of the hunt.

28 In the way of righteousness there is life;
along that path is immortality.

13 A wise son heeds his father's instruction,
but a mocker does not respond to rebukes.

2 From the fruit of their lips people enjoy good things,
but the unfaithful have an appetite for violence.

3 Those who guard their lips preserve their lives,
but those who speak rashly will come to ruin.

4 A sluggard's appetite is never filled,
but the desires of the diligent are fully satisfied.

5 The righteous hate what is false,
but the wicked make themselves a stench
and bring shame on themselves.

6 Righteousness guards the person of integrity,
but wickedness overthrows the sinner.

7 One person pretends to be rich, yet has nothing;
another pretends to be poor, yet has great wealth.

8 A person's riches may ransom their life,
but the poor cannot respond to threatening rebukes.

9 The light of the righteous shines brightly,
but the lamp of the wicked is snuffed out.

10 Where there is strife, there is pride,
but wisdom is found in those who take advice.

11 Dishonest money dwindles away,
but whoever gathers money little by little makes it grow.

12 Hope deferred makes the heart sick,
but a longing fulfilled is a tree of life.

13 Whoever scorns instruction will pay for it,
but whoever respects a command is rewarded.

14 The teaching of the wise is a fountain of life,
turning a person from the snares of death.

15 Good judgment wins favor,
but the way of the unfaithful leads to their destruction.[b]

16 All who are prudent act with[c] knowledge,
but fools expose their folly.

[a] *27* The meaning of the Hebrew for this word is uncertain. [b] *15* Septuagint and Syriac; the meaning of the Hebrew for this phrase is uncertain. [c] *16* Or *prudent protect themselves through*

[17]A wicked messenger falls into trouble,
but a trustworthy envoy brings healing.

[18]Whoever disregards discipline comes to poverty and shame,
but whoever heeds correction is honored.

[19]A longing fulfilled is sweet to the soul,
but fools detest turning from evil.

[20]Walk with the wise and become wise,
for a companion of fools suffers harm.

[21]Trouble pursues the sinner,
but the righteous are rewarded with good things.

[22]A good person leaves an inheritance for their children's children,
but a sinner's wealth is stored up for the righteous.

[23]An unplowed field produces food for the poor,
but injustice sweeps it away.

[24]Whoever spares the rod hates their children,
but the one who loves their children is careful to discipline them.

[25]The righteous eat to their hearts' content,
but the stomach of the wicked goes hungry.

14 The wise woman builds her house,
but with her own hands the foolish one tears hers down.

[2]Whoever fears the LORD walks uprightly,
but those who despise him are devious in their ways.

[3]A fool's mouth lashes out with pride,
but the lips of the wise protect them.

[4]Where there are no oxen, the manger is empty,
but from the strength of an ox come abundant harvests.

[5]An honest witness does not deceive,
but a false witness pours out lies.

[6]The mocker seeks wisdom and finds none,
but knowledge comes easily to the discerning.

[7]Stay away from a fool,
for you will not find knowledge on their lips.

[8]The wisdom of the prudent is to give thought to their ways,
but the folly of fools is deception.

[9]Fools mock at making amends for sin,
but goodwill is found among the upright.

[10]Each heart knows its own bitterness,
and no one else can share its joy.

[11]The house of the wicked will be destroyed,
but the tent of the upright will flourish.

[12]There is a way that appears to be right,
but in the end it leads to death.

[13]Even in laughter the heart may ache,
and rejoicing may end in grief.

[14]The faithless will be fully repaid for their ways,
and the good rewarded for theirs.

[15]The simple believe anything,
but the prudent give thought to their steps.

[16]The wise fear the LORD and shun evil,
but a fool is hotheaded and yet feels secure.

[17]A quick-tempered person does foolish things,
and the one who devises evil schemes is hated.

[18]The simple inherit folly,
but the prudent are crowned with knowledge.

[19]Evildoers will bow down in the presence of the good,
and the wicked at the gates of the righteous.

[20]The poor are shunned even by their neighbors,
but the rich have many friends.

[21]It is a sin to despise one's neighbor,
but blessed is the one who is kind to the needy.

[22]Do not those who plot evil go astray?

But those who plan what is good find[a]
love and faithfulness.

23 All hard work brings a profit,
but mere talk leads only to poverty.

24 The wealth of the wise is their crown,
but the folly of fools yields folly.

25 A truthful witness saves lives,
but a false witness is deceitful.

26 Whoever fears the LORD has a secure
fortress,
and for their children it will be a refuge.

27 The fear of the LORD is a fountain of life,
turning a person from the snares of
death.

28 A large population is a king's glory,
but without subjects a prince is ruined.

29 Whoever is patient has great
understanding,
but one who is quick-tempered
displays folly.

30 A heart at peace gives life to the body,
but envy rots the bones.

31 Whoever oppresses the poor shows
contempt for their Maker,
but whoever is kind to the needy
honors God.

32 When calamity comes, the wicked are
brought down,
but even in death the righteous seek
refuge in God.

33 Wisdom reposes in the heart of the
discerning
and even among fools she lets herself
be known.[b]

34 Righteousness exalts a nation,
but sin condemns any people.

35 A king delights in a wise servant,
but a shameful servant arouses
his fury.

15 A gentle answer turns away wrath,
but a harsh word stirs up anger.

2 The tongue of the wise adorns
knowledge,
but the mouth of the fool gushes folly.

3 The eyes of the LORD are everywhere,
keeping watch on the wicked and the
good.

4 The soothing tongue is a tree of life,
but a perverse tongue crushes the spirit.

5 A fool spurns a parent's discipline,
but whoever heeds correction shows
prudence.

6 The house of the righteous contains great
treasure,
but the income of the wicked brings
ruin.

7 The lips of the wise spread knowledge,
but the hearts of fools are not upright.

8 The LORD detests the sacrifice of the
wicked,
but the prayer of the upright pleases
him.

9 The LORD detests the way of the wicked,
but he loves those who pursue
righteousness.

10 Stern discipline awaits anyone who
leaves the path;
the one who hates correction will die.

11 Death and Destruction[c] lie open before
the LORD —
how much more do human hearts!

12 Mockers resent correction,
so they avoid the wise.

13 A happy heart makes the face cheerful,
but heartache crushes the spirit.

14 The discerning heart seeks knowledge,
but the mouth of a fool feeds on folly.

15 All the days of the oppressed are
wretched,
but the cheerful heart has a continual
feast.

16 Better a little with the fear of the LORD
than great wealth with turmoil.

17 Better a small serving of vegetables with
love
than a fattened calf with hatred.

18 A hot-tempered person stirs up conflict,
but the one who is patient calms a
quarrel.

[a] 22 Or *show* [b] 33 Hebrew; Septuagint and Syriac *discerning / but in the heart of fools she is not known*
[c] 11 Hebrew *Abaddon*

[19] The way of the sluggard is blocked with thorns,
but the path of the upright is a highway.

[20] A wise son brings joy to his father,
but a foolish man despises his mother.

[21] Folly brings joy to one who has no sense,
but whoever has understanding keeps a straight course.

[22] Plans fail for lack of counsel,
but with many advisers they succeed.

[23] A person finds joy in giving an apt reply —
and how good is a timely word!

[24] The path of life leads upward for the prudent
to keep them from going down to the realm of the dead.

[25] The LORD tears down the house of the proud,
but he sets the widow's boundary stones in place.

[26] The LORD detests the thoughts of the wicked,
but gracious words are pure in his sight.

[27] The greedy bring ruin to their households,
but the one who hates bribes will live.

[28] The heart of the righteous weighs its answers,
but the mouth of the wicked gushes evil.

[29] The LORD is far from the wicked,
but he hears the prayer of the righteous.

[30] Light in a messenger's eyes brings joy to the heart,
and good news gives health to the bones.

[31] Whoever heeds life-giving correction
will be at home among the wise.

[32] Those who disregard discipline despise themselves,
but the one who heeds correction gains understanding.

[33] Wisdom's instruction is to fear the LORD,
and humility comes before honor.

16

To humans belong the plans of the heart,
but from the LORD comes the proper answer of the tongue.

[2] All a person's ways seem pure to them,
but motives are weighed by the LORD.

[3] Commit to the LORD whatever you do,
and he will establish your plans.

[4] The LORD works out everything to its proper end —
even the wicked for a day of disaster.

[5] The LORD detests all the proud of heart.
Be sure of this: They will not go unpunished.

[6] Through love and faithfulness sin is atoned for;
through the fear of the LORD evil is avoided.

[7] When the LORD takes pleasure in anyone's way,
he causes their enemies to make peace with them.

[8] Better a little with righteousness
than much gain with injustice.

[9] In their hearts humans plan their course,
but the LORD establishes their steps.

[10] The lips of a king speak as an oracle,
and his mouth does not betray justice.

[11] Honest scales and balances belong to the LORD;
all the weights in the bag are of his making.

[12] Kings detest wrongdoing,
for a throne is established through righteousness.

[13] Kings take pleasure in honest lips;
they value the one who speaks what is right.

[14] A king's wrath is a messenger of death,
but the wise will appease it.

[15] When a king's face brightens, it means life;
his favor is like a rain cloud in spring.

[16] How much better to get wisdom than gold,
to get insight rather than silver!

[17] The highway of the upright avoids evil;
those who guard their ways preserve their lives.

[18] Pride goes before destruction,
a haughty spirit before a fall.

[19] Better to be lowly in spirit along with the oppressed
than to share plunder with the proud.

[20] Whoever gives heed to instruction prospers,[a]
and blessed is the one who trusts in the LORD.

[21] The wise in heart are called discerning,
and gracious words promote instruction.[b]

[22] Prudence is a fountain of life to the prudent,
but folly brings punishment to fools.

[23] The hearts of the wise make their mouths prudent,
and their lips promote instruction.[c]

[24] Gracious words are a honeycomb,
sweet to the soul and healing to the bones.

[25] There is a way that appears to be right,
but in the end it leads to death.

[26] The appetite of laborers works for them;
their hunger drives them on.

[27] A scoundrel plots evil,
and on their lips it is like a scorching fire.

[28] A perverse person stirs up conflict,
and a gossip separates close friends.

[29] A violent person entices their neighbor
and leads them down a path that is not good.

[30] Whoever winks with their eye is plotting perversity;
whoever purses their lips is bent on evil.

[31] Gray hair is a crown of splendor;
it is attained in the way of righteousness.

[32] Better a patient person than a warrior,
one with self-control than one who takes a city.

[33] The lot is cast into the lap,
but its every decision is from the LORD.

17

Better a dry crust with peace and quiet
than a house full of feasting, with strife.

[2] A prudent servant will rule over a disgraceful son
and will share the inheritance as one of the family.

[3] The crucible for silver and the furnace for gold,
but the LORD tests the heart.

[4] A wicked person listens to deceitful lips;
a liar pays attention to a destructive tongue.

[5] Whoever mocks the poor shows contempt for their Maker;
whoever gloats over disaster will not go unpunished.

[6] Children's children are a crown to the aged,
and parents are the pride of their children.

[7] Eloquent lips are unsuited to a godless fool—
how much worse lying lips to a ruler!

[8] A bribe is seen as a charm by the one who gives it;
they think success will come at every turn.

[9] Whoever would foster love covers over an offense,
but whoever repeats the matter separates close friends.

[10] A rebuke impresses a discerning person
more than a hundred lashes a fool.

[11] Evildoers foster rebellion against God;
the messenger of death will be sent against them.

[12] Better to meet a bear robbed of her cubs
than a fool bent on folly.

[13] Evil will never leave the house
of one who pays back evil for good.

[a] 20 Or *whoever speaks prudently finds what is good*
[c] 23 Or *prudent / and make their lips persuasive*
[b] 21 Or *words make a person persuasive*

[14] Starting a quarrel is like breaching a dam;
so drop the matter before a dispute breaks out.

[15] Acquitting the guilty and condemning the innocent —
the LORD detests them both.

[16] Why should fools have money in hand to buy wisdom,
when they are not able to understand it?

[17] A friend loves at all times,
and a brother is born for a time of adversity.

[18] One who has no sense shakes hands in pledge
and puts up security for a neighbor.

[19] Whoever loves a quarrel loves sin;
whoever builds a high gate invites destruction.

[20] One whose heart is corrupt does not prosper;
one whose tongue is perverse falls into trouble.

[21] To have a fool for a child brings grief;
there is no joy for the parent of a godless fool.

[22] A cheerful heart is good medicine,
but a crushed spirit dries up the bones.

[23] The wicked accept bribes in secret
to pervert the course of justice.

[24] A discerning person keeps wisdom in view,
but a fool's eyes wander to the ends of the earth.

[25] A foolish son brings grief to his father
and bitterness to the mother who bore him.

[26] If imposing a fine on the innocent is not good,
surely to flog honest officials is not right.

[27] The one who has knowledge uses words with restraint,
and whoever has understanding is even-tempered.

[28] Even fools are thought wise if they keep silent,
and discerning if they hold their tongues.

18

An unfriendly person pursues selfish ends
and against all sound judgment starts quarrels.

[2] Fools find no pleasure in understanding
but delight in airing their own opinions.

[3] When wickedness comes, so does contempt,
and with shame comes reproach.

[4] The words of the mouth are deep waters,
but the fountain of wisdom is a rushing stream.

[5] It is not good to be partial to the wicked
and so deprive the innocent of justice.

[6] The lips of fools bring them strife,
and their mouths invite a beating.

[7] The mouths of fools are their undoing,
and their lips are a snare to their very lives.

[8] The words of a gossip are like choice morsels;
they go down to the inmost parts.

[9] One who is slack in his work
is brother to one who destroys.

[10] The name of the LORD is a fortified tower;
the righteous run to it and are safe.

[11] The wealth of the rich is their fortified city;
they imagine it a wall too high to scale.

[12] Before a downfall the heart is haughty,
but humility comes before honor.

[13] To answer before listening —
that is folly and shame.

[14] The human spirit can endure in sickness,
but a crushed spirit who can bear?

[15] The heart of the discerning acquires knowledge,
for the ears of the wise seek it out.

[16] A gift opens the way
and ushers the giver into the presence of the great.

[17] In a lawsuit the first to speak seems right,
until someone comes forward and cross-examines.

[18] Casting the lot settles disputes
and keeps strong opponents apart.

[19] A brother wronged is more unyielding
than a fortified city;
disputes are like the barred gates of
a citadel.

[20] From the fruit of their mouth a person's
stomach is filled;
with the harvest of their lips they are
satisfied.

[21] The tongue has the power of life and
death,
and those who love it will eat
its fruit.

[22] He who finds a wife finds what is good
and receives favor from the LORD.

[23] The poor plead for mercy,
but the rich answer harshly.

[24] One who has unreliable friends soon
comes to ruin,
but there is a friend who sticks closer
than a brother.

19 Better the poor whose walk is
blameless
than a fool whose lips are perverse.

[2] Desire without knowledge is not good—
how much more will hasty feet miss
the way!

[3] A person's own folly leads to their ruin,
yet their heart rages against the LORD.

[4] Wealth attracts many friends,
but even the closest friend of the poor
person deserts them.

[5] A false witness will not go unpunished,
and whoever pours out lies will not
go free.

[6] Many curry favor with a ruler,
and everyone is the friend of one who
gives gifts.

[7] The poor are shunned by all their
relatives—
how much more do their friends avoid
them!
Though the poor pursue them with
pleading,
they are nowhere to be found.[a]

[8] The one who gets wisdom loves life;
the one who cherishes understanding
will soon prosper.

[9] A false witness will not go unpunished,
and whoever pours out lies will perish.

[10] It is not fitting for a fool to live in luxury—
how much worse for a slave to rule over
princes!

[11] A person's wisdom yields patience;
it is to one's glory to overlook an offense.

[12] A king's rage is like the roar of a lion,
but his favor is like dew on the grass.

[13] A foolish child is a father's ruin,
and a quarrelsome wife is like
the constant dripping of a leaky roof.

[14] Houses and wealth are inherited from
parents,
but a prudent wife is from the LORD.

[15] Laziness brings on deep sleep,
and the shiftless go hungry.

[16] Whoever keeps commandments keeps
their life,
but whoever shows contempt for their
ways will die.

[17] Whoever is kind to the poor lends to the
LORD,
and he will reward them for what they
have done.

[18] Discipline your children, for in that there
is hope;
do not be a willing party to their death.

[19] A hot-tempered person must pay the
penalty;
rescue them, and you will have to do
it again.

[20] Listen to advice and accept discipline,
and at the end you will be counted
among the wise.

[21] Many are the plans in a person's heart,
but it is the LORD's purpose that
prevails.

[22] What a person desires is unfailing love[b];
better to be poor than a liar.

[23] The fear of the LORD leads to life;
then one rests content, untouched by
trouble.

[a] 7 The meaning of the Hebrew for this sentence is uncertain. [b] 22 Or *Greed is a person's shame*

[24] A sluggard buries his hand in the dish;
he will not even bring it back to his mouth!

[25] Flog a mocker, and the simple will learn prudence;
rebuke the discerning, and they will gain knowledge.

[26] Whoever robs their father and drives out their mother
is a child who brings shame and disgrace.

[27] Stop listening to instruction, my son,
and you will stray from the words of knowledge.

[28] A corrupt witness mocks at justice,
and the mouth of the wicked gulps down evil.

[29] Penalties are prepared for mockers,
and beatings for the backs of fools.

20 Wine is a mocker and beer a brawler;
whoever is led astray by them is not wise.

[2] A king's wrath strikes terror like the roar of a lion;
those who anger him forfeit their lives.

[3] It is to one's honor to avoid strife,
but every fool is quick to quarrel.

[4] Sluggards do not plow in season;
so at harvest time they look but find nothing.

[5] The purposes of a person's heart are deep waters,
but one who has insight draws them out.

[6] Many claim to have unfailing love,
but a faithful person who can find?

[7] The righteous lead blameless lives;
blessed are their children after them.

[8] When a king sits on his throne to judge,
he winnows out all evil with his eyes.

[9] Who can say, "I have kept my heart pure;
I am clean and without sin"?

[10] Differing weights and differing measures—
the LORD detests them both.

[11] Even small children are known by their actions,
so is their conduct really pure and upright?

[12] Ears that hear and eyes that see—
the LORD has made them both.

[13] Do not love sleep or you will grow poor;
stay awake and you will have food to spare.

[14] "It's no good, it's no good!" says the buyer—
then goes off and boasts about the purchase.

[15] Gold there is, and rubies in abundance,
but lips that speak knowledge are a rare jewel.

[16] Take the garment of one who puts up security for a stranger;
hold it in pledge if it is done for an outsider.

[17] Food gained by fraud tastes sweet,
but one ends up with a mouth full of gravel.

[18] Plans are established by seeking advice;
so if you wage war, obtain guidance.

[19] A gossip betrays a confidence;
so avoid anyone who talks too much.

[20] If someone curses their father or mother,
their lamp will be snuffed out in pitch darkness.

[21] An inheritance claimed too soon
will not be blessed at the end.

[22] Do not say, "I'll pay you back for this wrong!"
Wait for the LORD, and he will avenge you.

[23] The LORD detests differing weights,
and dishonest scales do not please him.

[24] A person's steps are directed by the LORD.
How then can anyone understand their own way?

[25] It is a trap to dedicate something rashly
and only later to consider one's vows.

[26] A wise king winnows out the wicked;
he drives the threshing wheel over them.

27 The human spirit is[a] the lamp of the LORD
that sheds light on one's inmost being.

28 Love and faithfulness keep a king safe;
through love his throne is made secure.

29 The glory of young men is their strength,
gray hair the splendor of the old.

30 Blows and wounds scrub away evil,
and beatings purge the inmost being.

21 In the LORD's hand the king's heart is a stream of water
that he channels toward all who please him.

2 A person may think their own ways are right,
but the LORD weighs the heart.

3 To do what is right and just
is more acceptable to the LORD than sacrifice.

4 Haughty eyes and a proud heart—
the unplowed field of the wicked—
produce sin.

5 The plans of the diligent lead to profit
as surely as haste leads to poverty.

6 A fortune made by a lying tongue
is a fleeting vapor and a deadly snare.[b]

7 The violence of the wicked will drag them away,
for they refuse to do what is right.

8 The way of the guilty is devious,
but the conduct of the innocent is upright.

9 Better to live on a corner of the roof
than share a house with a quarrelsome wife.

10 The wicked crave evil;
their neighbors get no mercy from them.

11 When a mocker is punished, the simple gain wisdom;
by paying attention to the wise they get knowledge.

12 The Righteous One[c] takes note of the house of the wicked
and brings the wicked to ruin.

13 Whoever shuts their ears to the cry of the poor
will also cry out and not be answered.

14 A gift given in secret soothes anger,
and a bribe concealed in the cloak pacifies great wrath.

15 When justice is done, it brings joy to the righteous
but terror to evildoers.

16 Whoever strays from the path of prudence
comes to rest in the company of the dead.

17 Whoever loves pleasure will become poor;
whoever loves wine and olive oil will never be rich.

18 The wicked become a ransom for the righteous,
and the unfaithful for the upright.

19 Better to live in a desert
than with a quarrelsome and nagging wife.

20 The wise store up choice food and olive oil,
but fools gulp theirs down.

21 Whoever pursues righteousness and love
finds life, prosperity[d] and honor.

22 One who is wise can go up against the city of the mighty
and pull down the stronghold in which they trust.

23 Those who guard their mouths and their tongues
keep themselves from calamity.

24 The proud and arrogant person—"Mocker" is his name—
behaves with insolent fury.

25 The craving of a sluggard will be the death of him,
because his hands refuse to work.

26 All day long he craves for more,
but the righteous give without sparing.

27 The sacrifice of the wicked is detestable—

[a] 27 Or *A person's words are* [b] 6 Some Hebrew manuscripts, Septuagint and Vulgate; most Hebrew manuscripts *vapor for those who seek death* [c] 12 Or *The righteous person* [d] 21 Or *righteousness*

how much more so when brought with
evil intent!

28 A false witness will perish,
but a careful listener will testify
successfully.

29 The wicked put up a bold front,
but the upright give thought to their
ways.

30 There is no wisdom, no insight, no plan
that can succeed against the LORD.

31 The horse is made ready for the day of
battle,
but victory rests with the LORD.

22 A good name is more desirable than
great riches;
to be esteemed is better than silver
or gold.

2 Rich and poor have this in common:
The LORD is the Maker of them all.

3 The prudent see danger and take refuge,
but the simple keep going and pay the
penalty.

4 Humility is the fear of the LORD;
its wages are riches and honor and life.

5 In the paths of the wicked are snares and
pitfalls,
but those who would preserve their life
stay far from them.

6 Start children off on the way they
should go,
and even when they are old they will
not turn from it.

7 The rich rule over the poor,
and the borrower is slave to the lender.

8 Whoever sows injustice reaps calamity,
and the rod they wield in fury will be
broken.

9 The generous will themselves be blessed,
for they share their food with the poor.

10 Drive out the mocker, and out goes strife;
quarrels and insults are ended.

11 One who loves a pure heart and who
speaks with grace
will have the king for a friend.

12 The eyes of the LORD keep watch over
knowledge,
but he frustrates the words of the
unfaithful.

13 The sluggard says, "There's a lion outside!
I'll be killed in the public square!"

14 The mouth of an adulterous woman is a
deep pit;
a man who is under the LORD's wrath
falls into it.

15 Folly is bound up in the heart of a child,
but the rod of discipline will drive it
far away.

16 One who oppresses the poor to increase
his wealth
and one who gives gifts to the rich—
both come to poverty.

Thirty Sayings of the Wise

Saying 1

17 Pay attention and turn your ear to the
sayings of the wise;
apply your heart to what I teach,
18 for it is pleasing when you keep them in
your heart
and have all of them ready on your
lips.
19 So that your trust may be in the LORD,
I teach you today, even you.
20 Have I not written thirty sayings for you,
sayings of counsel and knowledge,
21 teaching you to be honest and to speak
the truth,
so that you bring back truthful reports
to those you serve?

Saying 2

22 Do not exploit the poor because they
are poor
and do not crush the needy in court,
23 for the LORD will take up their case
and will exact life for life.

Saying 3

24 Do not make friends with a hot-tempered
person,
do not associate with one easily
angered,
25 or you may learn their ways
and get yourself ensnared.

Saying 4

26 Do not be one who shakes hands in
pledge
or puts up security for debts;

[27] if you lack the means to pay,
your very bed will be snatched from under you.

Saying 5

[28] Do not move an ancient boundary stone
set up by your ancestors.

Saying 6

[29] Do you see someone skilled in their work?
They will serve before kings;
they will not serve before officials of low rank.

Saying 7

23 When you sit to dine with a ruler,
note well what[a] is before you,
[2] and put a knife to your throat
if you are given to gluttony.
[3] Do not crave his delicacies,
for that food is deceptive.

Saying 8

[4] Do not wear yourself out to get rich;
do not trust your own cleverness.
[5] Cast but a glance at riches, and they are gone,
for they will surely sprout wings
and fly off to the sky like an eagle.

Saying 9

[6] Do not eat the food of a begrudging host,
do not crave his delicacies;
[7] for he is the kind of person
who is always thinking about the cost.[b]
"Eat and drink," he says to you,
but his heart is not with you.
[8] You will vomit up the little you have eaten
and will have wasted your compliments.

Saying 10

[9] Do not speak to fools,
for they will scorn your prudent words.

Saying 11

[10] Do not move an ancient boundary stone
or encroach on the fields of the fatherless,
[11] for their Defender is strong;
he will take up their case against you.

Saying 12

[12] Apply your heart to instruction
and your ears to words of knowledge.

Saying 13

[13] Do not withhold discipline from a child;
if you punish them with the rod, they will not die.
[14] Punish them with the rod
and save them from death.

Saying 14

[15] My son, if your heart is wise,
then my heart will be glad indeed;
[16] my inmost being will rejoice
when your lips speak what is right.

Saying 15

[17] Do not let your heart envy sinners,
but always be zealous for the fear of the LORD.
[18] There is surely a future hope for you,
and your hope will not be cut off.

Saying 16

[19] Listen, my son, and be wise,
and set your heart on the right path:
[20] Do not join those who drink too much wine
or gorge themselves on meat,
[21] for drunkards and gluttons become poor,
and drowsiness clothes them in rags.

Saying 17

[22] Listen to your father, who gave you life,
and do not despise your mother when she is old.
[23] Buy the truth and do not sell it—
wisdom, instruction and insight as well.
[24] The father of a righteous child has great joy;
a man who fathers a wise son rejoices in him.
[25] May your father and mother rejoice;
may she who gave you birth be joyful!

Saying 18

[26] My son, give me your heart
and let your eyes delight in my ways,
[27] for an adulterous woman is a deep pit,
and a wayward wife is a narrow well.

[a] 1 Or *who* [b] 7 Or *for as he thinks within himself, / so he is*; or *for as he puts on a feast, / so he is*

[28] Like a bandit she lies in wait
and multiplies the unfaithful
among men.

Saying 19

[29] Who has woe? Who has sorrow?
Who has strife? Who has complaints?
Who has needless bruises? Who has
bloodshot eyes?
[30] Those who linger over wine,
who go to sample bowls of mixed wine.
[31] Do not gaze at wine when it is red,
when it sparkles in the cup,
when it goes down smoothly!
[32] In the end it bites like a snake
and poisons like a viper.
[33] Your eyes will see strange sights,
and your mind will imagine confusing
things.
[34] You will be like one sleeping on the high
seas,
lying on top of the rigging.
[35] "They hit me," you will say, "but I'm not
hurt!
They beat me, but I don't feel it!
When will I wake up
so I can find another drink?"

Saying 20

24 Do not envy the wicked,
do not desire their company;
[2] for their hearts plot violence,
and their lips talk about making
trouble.

Saying 21

[3] By wisdom a house is built,
and through understanding it is
established;
[4] through knowledge its rooms are filled
with rare and beautiful treasures.

Saying 22

[5] The wise prevail through great power,
and those who have knowledge muster
their strength.
[6] Surely you need guidance to wage war,
and victory is won through many
advisers.

Saying 23

[7] Wisdom is too high for fools;
in the assembly at the gate they must
not open their mouths.

Saying 24

[8] Whoever plots evil
will be known as a schemer.
[9] The schemes of folly are sin,
and people detest a mocker.

Saying 25

[10] If you falter in a time of trouble,
how small is your strength!
[11] Rescue those being led away to death;
hold back those staggering toward
slaughter.
[12] If you say, "But we knew nothing about
this,"
does not he who weighs the heart
perceive it?
Does not he who guards your life
know it?
Will he not repay everyone according
to what they have done?

Saying 26

[13] Eat honey, my son, for it is good;
honey from the comb is sweet to your
taste.
[14] Know also that wisdom is like honey for
you:
If you find it, there is a future hope
for you,
and your hope will not be cut off.

Saying 27

[15] Do not lurk like a thief near the house of
the righteous,
do not plunder their dwelling place;
[16] for though the righteous fall seven times,
they rise again,
but the wicked stumble when calamity
strikes.

Saying 28

[17] Do not gloat when your enemy falls;
when they stumble, do not let your
heart rejoice,
[18] or the LORD will see and disapprove
and turn his wrath away from
them.

Saying 29

[19] Do not fret because of evildoers
or be envious of the wicked,
[20] for the evildoer has no future hope,
and the lamp of the wicked will be
snuffed out.

Saying 30

21 Fear the LORD and the king, my son,
and do not join with rebellious officials,
22 for those two will send sudden destruction on them,
and who knows what calamities they can bring?

Further Sayings of the Wise

23 These also are sayings of the wise:

To show partiality in judging is not good:
24 Whoever says to the guilty, "You are innocent,"
will be cursed by peoples and denounced by nations.
25 But it will go well with those who convict the guilty,
and rich blessing will come on them.

26 An honest answer
is like a kiss on the lips.

27 Put your outdoor work in order
and get your fields ready;
after that, build your house.

28 Do not testify against your neighbor without cause—
would you use your lips to mislead?
29 Do not say, "I'll do to them as they have done to me;
I'll pay them back for what they did."

30 I went past the field of a sluggard,
past the vineyard of someone who has no sense;
31 thorns had come up everywhere,
the ground was covered with weeds,
and the stone wall was in ruins.
32 I applied my heart to what I observed
and learned a lesson from what I saw:
33 A little sleep, a little slumber,
a little folding of the hands to rest—
34 and poverty will come on you like a thief
and scarcity like an armed man.

More Proverbs of Solomon

25 These are more proverbs of Solomon, compiled by the men of Hezekiah king of Judah:

2 It is the glory of God to conceal a matter;
to search out a matter is the glory of kings.
3 As the heavens are high and the earth is deep,
so the hearts of kings are unsearchable.

4 Remove the dross from the silver,
and a silversmith can produce a vessel;
5 remove wicked officials from the king's presence,
and his throne will be established through righteousness.

6 Do not exalt yourself in the king's presence,
and do not claim a place among his great men;
7 it is better for him to say to you, "Come up here,"
than for him to humiliate you before his nobles.

What you have seen with your eyes
8 do not bring[a] hastily to court,
for what will you do in the end
if your neighbor puts you to shame?

9 If you take your neighbor to court,
do not betray another's confidence,
10 or the one who hears it may shame you
and the charge against you will stand.

11 Like apples[b] of gold in settings of silver
is a ruling rightly given.
12 Like an earring of gold or an ornament of fine gold
is the rebuke of a wise judge to a listening ear.

13 Like a snow-cooled drink at harvest time
is a trustworthy messenger to the one who sends him;
he refreshes the spirit of his master.
14 Like clouds and wind without rain
is one who boasts of gifts never given.

15 Through patience a ruler can be persuaded,
and a gentle tongue can break a bone.

16 If you find honey, eat just enough—
too much of it, and you will vomit.
17 Seldom set foot in your neighbor's house—
too much of you, and they will hate you.

[a] 7,8 Or *nobles / on whom you had set your eyes. / [8]Do not go* [b] 11 Or possibly *apricots*

[18]Like a club or a sword or a sharp arrow
is one who gives false testimony
against a neighbor.
[19]Like a broken tooth or a lame foot
is reliance on the unfaithful in a time
of trouble.
[20]Like one who takes away a garment on a
cold day,
or like vinegar poured on a wound,
is one who sings songs to a heavy
heart.

[21]If your enemy is hungry, give him food
to eat;
if he is thirsty, give him water to drink.
[22]In doing this, you will heap burning coals
on his head,
and the LORD will reward you.

[23]Like a north wind that brings unexpected
rain
is a sly tongue — which provokes a
horrified look.

[24]Better to live on a corner of the roof
than share a house with a quarrelsome
wife.

[25]Like cold water to a weary soul
is good news from a distant land.
[26]Like a muddied spring or a polluted well
are the righteous who give way to the
wicked.

[27]It is not good to eat too much honey,
nor is it honorable to search out
matters that are too deep.

[28]Like a city whose walls are broken
through
is a person who lacks self-control.

26 Like snow in summer or rain in
harvest,
honor is not fitting for a fool.
[2]Like a fluttering sparrow or a darting
swallow,
an undeserved curse does not come
to rest.
[3]A whip for the horse, a bridle for the
donkey,
and a rod for the backs of fools!
[4]Do not answer a fool according to his folly,
or you yourself will be just like him.
[5]Answer a fool according to his folly,
or he will be wise in his own eyes.
[6]Sending a message by the hands of a fool
is like cutting off one's feet or drinking
poison.
[7]Like the useless legs of one who is lame
is a proverb in the mouth of a fool.
[8]Like tying a stone in a sling
is the giving of honor to a fool.
[9]Like a thornbush in a drunkard's hand
is a proverb in the mouth of a fool.
[10]Like an archer who wounds at random
is one who hires a fool or any passer-by.
[11]As a dog returns to its vomit,
so fools repeat their folly.
[12]Do you see a person wise in their own
eyes?
There is more hope for a fool than
for them.

[13]A sluggard says, "There's a lion in the
road,
a fierce lion roaming the streets!"
[14]As a door turns on its hinges,
so a sluggard turns on his bed.
[15]A sluggard buries his hand in the dish;
he is too lazy to bring it back to his
mouth.
[16]A sluggard is wiser in his own eyes
than seven people who answer
discreetly.

[17]Like one who grabs a stray dog by
the ears
is someone who rushes into a quarrel
not their own.

[18]Like a maniac shooting
flaming arrows of death
[19]is one who deceives their neighbor
and says, "I was only joking!"

[20]Without wood a fire goes out;
without a gossip a quarrel dies down.
[21]As charcoal to embers and as wood
to fire,
so is a quarrelsome person for kindling
strife.
[22]The words of a gossip are like choice
morsels;
they go down to the inmost parts.

[23]Like a coating of silver dross on
earthenware
are fervent[a] lips with an evil heart.
[24]Enemies disguise themselves with their
lips,
but in their hearts they harbor deceit.

[a] 23 Hebrew; Septuagint *smooth*

[25] Though their speech is charming, do not
believe them,
for seven abominations fill their hearts.
[26] Their malice may be concealed by
deception,
but their wickedness will be exposed
in the assembly.
[27] Whoever digs a pit will fall into it;
if someone rolls a stone, it will roll back
on them.
[28] A lying tongue hates those it hurts,
and a flattering mouth works ruin.

27 Do not boast about tomorrow,
for you do not know what a day may
bring.

[2] Let someone else praise you, and not
your own mouth;
an outsider, and not your own lips.

[3] Stone is heavy and sand a burden,
but a fool's provocation is heavier
than both.

[4] Anger is cruel and fury overwhelming,
but who can stand before jealousy?

[5] Better is open rebuke
than hidden love.

[6] Wounds from a friend can be trusted,
but an enemy multiplies kisses.

[7] One who is full loathes honey from the
comb,
but to the hungry even what is bitter
tastes sweet.

[8] Like a bird that flees its nest
is anyone who flees from home.

[9] Perfume and incense bring joy to the
heart,
and the pleasantness of a friend
springs from their heartfelt advice.

[10] Do not forsake your friend or a friend of
your family,
and do not go to your relative's house
when disaster strikes you—
better a neighbor nearby than a
relative far away.

[11] Be wise, my son, and bring joy to my
heart;
then I can answer anyone who treats
me with contempt.

[12] The prudent see danger and take refuge,
but the simple keep going and pay
the penalty.

[13] Take the garment of one who puts up
security for a stranger;
hold it in pledge if it is done for an
outsider.

[14] If anyone loudly blesses their neighbor
early in the morning,
it will be taken as a curse.

[15] A quarrelsome wife is like the dripping
of a leaky roof in a rainstorm;
[16] restraining her is like restraining
the wind
or grasping oil with the hand.

[17] As iron sharpens iron,
so one person sharpens another.

[18] The one who guards a fig tree will eat
its fruit,
and whoever protects their master will
be honored.

[19] As water reflects the face,
so one's life reflects the heart.[a]

[20] Death and Destruction[b] are never
satisfied,
and neither are human eyes.

[21] The crucible for silver and the furnace
for gold,
but people are tested by their praise.

[22] Though you grind a fool in a mortar,
grinding them like grain with a pestle,
you will not remove their folly
from them.

[23] Be sure you know the condition of your
flocks,
give careful attention to your herds;
[24] for riches do not endure forever,
and a crown is not secure for all
generations.
[25] When the hay is removed and new
growth appears
and the grass from the hills is
gathered in,
[26] the lambs will provide you with clothing,
and the goats with the price of a field.
[27] You will have plenty of goats' milk to feed
your family
and to nourish your female servants.

[a] 19 Or *so others reflect your heart back to you* [b] 20 Hebrew *Abaddon*

28 The wicked flee though no one pursues,
but the righteous are as bold as a lion.

2 When a country is rebellious, it has many rulers,
but a ruler with discernment and knowledge maintains order.

3 A ruler[a] who oppresses the poor
is like a driving rain that leaves no crops.

4 Those who forsake instruction praise the wicked,
but those who heed it resist them.

5 Evildoers do not understand what is right,
but those who seek the LORD understand it fully.

6 Better the poor whose walk is blameless
than the rich whose ways are perverse.

7 A discerning son heeds instruction,
but a companion of gluttons disgraces his father.

8 Whoever increases wealth by taking interest or profit from the poor
amasses it for another, who will be kind to the poor.

9 If anyone turns a deaf ear to my instruction,
even their prayers are detestable.

10 Whoever leads the upright along an evil path
will fall into their own trap,
but the blameless will receive a good inheritance.

11 The rich are wise in their own eyes;
one who is poor and discerning sees how deluded they are.

12 When the righteous triumph, there is great elation;
but when the wicked rise to power, people go into hiding.

13 Whoever conceals their sins does not prosper,
but the one who confesses and renounces them finds mercy.

14 Blessed is the one who always trembles before God,
but whoever hardens their heart falls into trouble.

15 Like a roaring lion or a charging bear
is a wicked ruler over a helpless people.

16 A tyrannical ruler practices extortion,
but one who hates ill-gotten gain will enjoy a long reign.

17 Anyone tormented by the guilt of murder
will seek refuge in the grave;
let no one hold them back.

18 The one whose walk is blameless is kept safe,
but the one whose ways are perverse will fall into the pit.[b]

19 Those who work their land will have abundant food,
but those who chase fantasies will have their fill of poverty.

20 A faithful person will be richly blessed,
but one eager to get rich will not go unpunished.

21 To show partiality is not good —
yet a person will do wrong for a piece of bread.

22 The stingy are eager to get rich
and are unaware that poverty awaits them.

23 Whoever rebukes a person will in the end gain favor
rather than one who has a flattering tongue.

24 Whoever robs their father or mother
and says, "It's not wrong,"
is partner to one who destroys.

25 The greedy stir up conflict,
but those who trust in the LORD will prosper.

26 Those who trust in themselves are fools,
but those who walk in wisdom are kept safe.

27 Those who give to the poor will lack nothing,
but those who close their eyes to them receive many curses.

[a] 3 Or *A poor person* [b] 18 Syriac (see Septuagint); Hebrew *into one*

28 When the wicked rise to power, people go
into hiding;
but when the wicked perish, the
righteous thrive.

29 Whoever remains stiff-necked after
many rebukes
will suddenly be destroyed—without
remedy.

2 When the righteous thrive, the people
rejoice;
when the wicked rule, the people groan.

3 A man who loves wisdom brings joy to
his father,
but a companion of prostitutes
squanders his wealth.

4 By justice a king gives a country stability,
but those who are greedy for[a] bribes
tear it down.

5 Those who flatter their neighbors
are spreading nets for their feet.

6 Evildoers are snared by their own sin,
but the righteous shout for joy and
are glad.

7 The righteous care about justice for the
poor,
but the wicked have no such concern.

8 Mockers stir up a city,
but the wise turn away anger.

9 If a wise person goes to court with a fool,
the fool rages and scoffs, and there is
no peace.

10 The bloodthirsty hate a person of
integrity
and seek to kill the upright.

11 Fools give full vent to their rage,
but the wise bring calm in the end.

12 If a ruler listens to lies,
all his officials become wicked.

13 The poor and the oppressor have this in
common:
The LORD gives sight to the eyes of both.

14 If a king judges the poor with fairness,
his throne will be established forever.

15 A rod and a reprimand impart wisdom,
but a child left undisciplined disgraces
its mother.

16 When the wicked thrive, so does sin,
but the righteous will see their
downfall.

17 Discipline your children, and they will
give you peace;
they will bring you the delights you
desire.

18 Where there is no revelation, people cast
off restraint;
but blessed is the one who heeds
wisdom's instruction.

19 Servants cannot be corrected by mere
words;
though they understand, they will not
respond.

20 Do you see someone who speaks in haste?
There is more hope for a fool than for
them.

21 A servant pampered from youth
will turn out to be insolent.

22 An angry person stirs up conflict,
and a hot-tempered person commits
many sins.

23 Pride brings a person low,
but the lowly in spirit gain honor.

24 The accomplices of thieves are their own
enemies;
they are put under oath and dare not
testify.

25 Fear of man will prove to be a snare,
but whoever trusts in the LORD is
kept safe.

26 Many seek an audience with a ruler,
but it is from the LORD that one gets
justice.

27 The righteous detest the dishonest;
the wicked detest the upright.

Sayings of Agur

30 The sayings of Agur son of Jakeh—
an inspired utterance.

This man's utterance to Ithiel:

"I am weary, God,
but I can prevail.[b]
2 Surely I am only a brute, not a man;
I do not have human understanding.

[a] 4 Or *who give* [b] 1 With a different word division of the Hebrew; Masoretic Text *utterance to Ithiel, / to Ithiel and Ukal:*

HOW DEEP THE FATHER'S LOVE FOR US

Stuart Townend

How deep the Father's love
for us
How vast beyond all measure
That he should give his only Son
To make a wretch his treasure
How great the pain of
searing loss
The Father turns his face away
As wounds which mar the
Chosen One
Bring many sons to glory

Behold the Man upon the cross
My sin upon his shoulders
Ashamed, I hear my
mocking voice
Call out among the scoffers

It was my sin that held him there
Until it was accomplished
His dying breath has brought
me life
I know that it is finished

I will not boast in anything
No gifts, no power, no wisdom
But I will boast in Jesus Christ
His death and resurrection
Why should I gain from
his reward?
I cannot give an answer
But this I know with all my heart
His wounds have paid
my ransom

THE INSPIRATION

Because of his great love for us, God, who is rich in mercy, made us alive with Christ even when we were dead in transgressions — it is by grace you have been saved. And God raised us up with Christ and seated us with him in the heavenly realms in Christ Jesus, in order that in the coming ages he might show the incomparable riches of his grace, expressed in his kindness to us in Christ Jesus. For it is by grace you have been saved, through faith — and this is not from yourselves, it is the gift of God — not by works, so that no one can boast.

— Ephesians 2:4 - 9

Read also: Isaiah 53:12

BEHIND THE SONG

While the modern music vernacular lends itself well to memorability and accessibility, it often does so by simplifying the lyrics — reducing the number of words in a song and repeating how often they are used. This format is very useful in many ways, but it does have its limitations. Several contemporary worship writers have been stretching the boundaries of the genre, crafting songs with expansive lyrics and deeper theology.

As a songwriter and worship leader, Stuart Townend longed for richer content in his worship times, and he often turned to ancient hymns. He eventually decided that one need not sacrifice the richness of the hymn in order to create accessible, contemporary songs. One of his first compositions was "How Deep the Father's Love for Us," a song that helped to usher in the "modern hymn" era. "I really wanted to write something that was more hymn-like," Townend explains. "I wondered why we didn't have songs full of poetic, powerful language these days. So I set out to write them."

"The melody came very quickly," Townend continues. "I actually feared that because it came so easily, I must have borrowed it from somewhere. Then, as I was contemplating the power of the cross, the lyrics just began to spill out."

Selah

The lyrics of "How Deep the Father's Love for Us" read like poetry, even without musical accompaniment. Read through Ephesians 2:4–9 and then read and recite the lyrics to this song, or sing along to a recording. Allow your imagination and your heart to meditate on the wonder of God the Father's complete love for us, his children. How does reflection on the glory of Christ's sacrifice deepen your understanding of God's love?

[3] I have not learned wisdom,
nor have I attained to the knowledge of the Holy One.
[4] Who has gone up to heaven and come down?
Whose hands have gathered up the wind?
Who has wrapped up the waters in a cloak?
Who has established all the ends of the earth?
What is his name, and what is the name of his son?
Surely you know!

[5] "Every word of God is flawless;
he is a shield to those who take refuge in him.
[6] Do not add to his words,
or he will rebuke you and prove you a liar.

[7] "Two things I ask of you, LORD;
do not refuse me before I die:
[8] Keep falsehood and lies far from me;
give me neither poverty nor riches,
but give me only my daily bread.
[9] Otherwise, I may have too much and disown you
and say, 'Who is the LORD?'
Or I may become poor and steal,
and so dishonor the name of my God.

[10] "Do not slander a servant to their master,
or they will curse you, and you will pay for it.

[11] "There are those who curse their fathers
and do not bless their mothers;
[12] those who are pure in their own eyes
and yet are not cleansed of their filth;
[13] those whose eyes are ever so haughty,
whose glances are so disdainful;
[14] those whose teeth are swords
and whose jaws are set with knives
to devour the poor from the earth
and the needy from among mankind.

[15] "The leech has two daughters.
'Give! Give!' they cry.

"There are three things that are never satisfied,
four that never say, 'Enough!':
[16] the grave, the barren womb,
land, which is never satisfied with water,
and fire, which never says, 'Enough!'

[17] "The eye that mocks a father,
that scorns an aged mother,
will be pecked out by the ravens of the valley,
will be eaten by the vultures.

[18] "There are three things that are too amazing for me,
four that I do not understand:
[19] the way of an eagle in the sky,
the way of a snake on a rock,
the way of a ship on the high seas,
and the way of a man with a young woman.

[20] "This is the way of an adulterous woman:
She eats and wipes her mouth
and says, 'I've done nothing wrong.'

[21] "Under three things the earth trembles,
under four it cannot bear up:
[22] a servant who becomes king,
a godless fool who gets plenty to eat,
[23] a contemptible woman who gets married,
and a servant who displaces her mistress.

[24] "Four things on earth are small,
yet they are extremely wise:
[25] Ants are creatures of little strength,
yet they store up their food in the summer;
[26] hyraxes are creatures of little power,
yet they make their home in the crags;
[27] locusts have no king,
yet they advance together in ranks;
[28] a lizard can be caught with the hand,
yet it is found in kings' palaces.

[29] "There are three things that are stately in their stride,
four that move with stately bearing:
[30] a lion, mighty among beasts,
who retreats before nothing;
[31] a strutting rooster, a he-goat,
and a king secure against revolt.[a]

[32] "If you play the fool and exalt yourself,
or if you plan evil,
clap your hand over your mouth!

[a] *31* The meaning of the Hebrew for this phrase is uncertain.

[33] For as churning cream produces butter,
and as twisting the nose produces blood,
so stirring up anger produces strife."

Sayings of King Lemuel

31 The sayings of King Lemuel — an inspired utterance his mother taught him.

[2] Listen, my son! Listen, son of my womb!
Listen, my son, the answer to my prayers!
[3] Do not spend your strength[a] on women,
your vigor on those who ruin kings.
[4] It is not for kings, Lemuel —
it is not for kings to drink wine,
not for rulers to crave beer,
[5] lest they drink and forget what has been decreed,
and deprive all the oppressed of their rights.
[6] Let beer be for those who are perishing,
wine for those who are in anguish!
[7] Let them drink and forget their poverty
and remember their misery no more.

[8] Speak up for those who cannot speak for themselves,
for the rights of all who are destitute.
[9] Speak up and judge fairly;
defend the rights of the poor and needy.

Epilogue: The Wife of Noble Character

[10] [b]A wife of noble character who can find?
She is worth far more than rubies.
[11] Her husband has full confidence in her
and lacks nothing of value.
[12] She brings him good, not harm,
all the days of her life.
[13] She selects wool and flax
and works with eager hands.
[14] She is like the merchant ships,
bringing her food from afar.
[15] She gets up while it is still night;
she provides food for her family
and portions for her female servants.
[16] She considers a field and buys it;
out of her earnings she plants a vineyard.
[17] She sets about her work vigorously;
her arms are strong for her tasks.
[18] She sees that her trading is profitable,
and her lamp does not go out at night.
[19] In her hand she holds the distaff
and grasps the spindle with her fingers.
[20] She opens her arms to the poor
and extends her hands to the needy.
[21] When it snows, she has no fear for her household;
for all of them are clothed in scarlet.
[22] She makes coverings for her bed;
she is clothed in fine linen and purple.
[23] Her husband is respected at the city gate,
where he takes his seat among the elders of the land.
[24] She makes linen garments and sells them,
and supplies the merchants with sashes.
[25] She is clothed with strength and dignity;
she can laugh at the days to come.
[26] She speaks with wisdom,
and faithful instruction is on her tongue.
[27] She watches over the affairs of her household
and does not eat the bread of idleness.
[28] Her children arise and call her blessed;
her husband also, and he praises her:
[29] "Many women do noble things,
but you surpass them all."
[30] Charm is deceptive, and beauty is fleeting;
but a woman who fears the LORD is to be praised.
[31] Honor her for all that her hands have done,
and let her works bring her praise at the city gate.

[a] 3 Or *wealth* [b] 10 Verses 10-31 are an acrostic poem, the verses of which begin with the successive letters of the Hebrew alphabet.

ECCLESIASTES

Everything Is Meaningless

1 The words of the Teacher,[a] son of David, king in Jerusalem:

[2] "Meaningless! Meaningless!"
says the Teacher.
"Utterly meaningless!
Everything is meaningless."
[3] What do people gain from all their labors
at which they toil under the sun?
[4] Generations come and generations go,
but the earth remains forever.
[5] The sun rises and the sun sets,
and hurries back to where it rises.
[6] The wind blows to the south
and turns to the north;
round and round it goes,
ever returning on its course.
[7] All streams flow into the sea,
yet the sea is never full.
To the place the streams come from,
there they return again.
[8] All things are wearisome,
more than one can say.
The eye never has enough of seeing,
nor the ear its fill of hearing.
[9] What has been will be again,
what has been done will be done again;
there is nothing new under the sun.
[10] Is there anything of which one can say,
"Look! This is something new"?
It was here already, long ago;
it was here before our time.
[11] No one remembers the former
generations,
and even those yet to come
will not be remembered
by those who follow them.

Wisdom Is Meaningless

[12] I, the Teacher, was king over Israel in Jerusalem. [13] I applied my mind to study and to explore by wisdom all that is done under the heavens. What a heavy burden God has laid on mankind! [14] I have seen all the things that are done under the sun; all of them are meaningless, a chasing after the wind.

[15] What is crooked cannot be straightened;
what is lacking cannot be counted.

[16] I said to myself, "Look, I have increased in wisdom more than anyone who has ruled over Jerusalem before me; I have experienced much of wisdom and knowledge." [17] Then I applied myself to the understanding of wisdom, and also of madness and folly, but I learned that this, too, is a chasing after the wind.

[18] For with much wisdom comes much
sorrow;
the more knowledge, the more grief.

Pleasures Are Meaningless

2 I said to myself, "Come now, I will test you with pleasure to find out what is good." But that also proved to be meaningless. [2] "Laughter," I said, "is madness. And what does pleasure accomplish?" [3] I tried cheering myself with wine, and embracing folly—my mind still guiding me with wisdom. I wanted to see what was good for people to do under the heavens during the few days of their lives.

[4] I undertook great projects: I built houses for myself and planted vineyards. [5] I made gardens and parks and planted all kinds of fruit trees in them. [6] I made reservoirs to water groves of flourishing trees. [7] I bought male and female slaves and had other slaves who were born in my house. I also owned more herds and flocks than anyone in Jerusalem before me. [8] I amassed silver and gold for myself, and the treasure of kings and provinces. I acquired male and female singers, and a harem[b] as well—the delights of a man's heart. [9] I became greater by far than anyone in Jerusalem before me. In all this my wisdom stayed with me.

[a] *1* Or *the leader of the assembly*; also in verses 2 and 12 [b] *8* The meaning of the Hebrew for this phrase is uncertain.

10 I denied myself nothing my eyes desired;
I refused my heart no pleasure.
My heart took delight in all my labor,
and this was the reward for all my toil.
11 Yet when I surveyed all that my hands
had done
and what I had toiled to achieve,
everything was meaningless, a chasing
after the wind;
nothing was gained under the sun.

Wisdom and Folly Are Meaningless

12 Then I turned my thoughts to consider
wisdom,
and also madness and folly.
What more can the king's successor do
than what has already been done?
13 I saw that wisdom is better than folly,
just as light is better than darkness.
14 The wise have eyes in their heads,
while the fool walks in the darkness;
but I came to realize
that the same fate overtakes them
both.

15 Then I said to myself,

"The fate of the fool will overtake me
also.
What then do I gain by being wise?"
I said to myself,
"This too is meaningless."
16 For the wise, like the fool, will not be long
remembered;
the days have already come when both
have been forgotten.
Like the fool, the wise too must die!

Toil Is Meaningless

17 So I hated life, because the work that is
done under the sun was grievous to me. All
of it is meaningless, a chasing after the wind.
18 I hated all the things I had toiled for under
the sun, because I must leave them to the
one who comes after me. 19 And who knows
whether that person will be wise or foolish?
Yet they will have control over all the fruit of
my toil into which I have poured my effort
and skill under the sun. This too is mean-
ingless. 20 So my heart began to despair over
all my toilsome labor under the sun. 21 For a
person may labor with wisdom, knowledge
and skill, and then they must leave all they
own to another who has not toiled for it. This
too is meaningless and a great misfortune.
22 What do people get for all the toil and anx-
ious striving with which they labor under
the sun? 23 All their days their work is grief
and pain; even at night their minds do not
rest. This too is meaningless.

24 A person can do nothing better than to
eat and drink and find satisfaction in their
own toil. This too, I see, is from the hand
of God, 25 for without him, who can eat or
find enjoyment? 26 To the person who pleas-
es him, God gives wisdom, knowledge and
happiness, but to the sinner he gives the task
of gathering and storing up wealth to hand it
over to the one who pleases God. This too is
meaningless, a chasing after the wind.

A Time for Everything

3 There is a time for everything,
and a season for every activity under
the heavens:

2 a time to be born and a time to die,
a time to plant and a time to uproot,
3 a time to kill and a time to heal,
a time to tear down and a time to
build,
4 a time to weep and a time to laugh,
a time to mourn and a time to dance,
5 a time to scatter stones and a time to
gather them,
a time to embrace and a time to refrain
from embracing,
6 a time to search and a time to give up,
a time to keep and a time to throw
away,
7 a time to tear and a time to mend,
a time to be silent and a time to speak,
8 a time to love and a time to hate,
a time for war and a time for peace.

9 What do workers gain from their toil?
10 I have seen the burden God has laid on
the human race. 11 He has made everything
beautiful in its time. He has also set eternity
in the human heart; yet[a] no one can fathom
what God has done from beginning to end.
12 I know that there is nothing better for peo-
ple than to be happy and to do good while
they live. 13 That each of them may eat and
drink, and find satisfaction in all their toil —
this is the gift of God. 14 I know that every-
thing God does will endure forever; nothing

[a] 11 Or *also placed ignorance in the human heart, so that*

can be added to it and nothing taken from it. God does it so that people will fear him.

15 Whatever is has already been,
and what will be has been before;
and God will call the past to account.[a]

16 And I saw something else under the sun:

In the place of judgment—wickedness
was there,
in the place of justice—wickedness
was there.

17 I said to myself,

"God will bring into judgment
both the righteous and the wicked,
for there will be a time for every activity,
a time to judge every deed."

18 I also said to myself, "As for humans,
God tests them so that they may see that
they are like the animals. 19 Surely the fate
of human beings is like that of the animals;
the same fate awaits them both: As one dies,
so dies the other. All have the same breath[b];
humans have no advantage over animals.
Everything is meaningless. 20 All go to the
same place; all come from dust, and to dust
all return. 21 Who knows if the human spirit
rises upward and if the spirit of the animal
goes down into the earth?"

22 So I saw that there is nothing better for
a person than to enjoy their work, because
that is their lot. For who can bring them to
see what will happen after them?

Oppression, Toil, Friendlessness

4 Again I looked and saw all the oppression that was taking place under the sun:

I saw the tears of the oppressed—
and they have no comforter;
power was on the side of their
oppressors—
and they have no comforter.
2 And I declared that the dead,
who had already died,
are happier than the living,
who are still alive.
3 But better than both
is the one who has never been born,
who has not seen the evil
that is done under the sun.

4 And I saw that all toil and all achieve-
ment spring from one person's envy of an-
other. This too is meaningless, a chasing
after the wind.

5 Fools fold their hands
and ruin themselves.
6 Better one handful with tranquillity
than two handfuls with toil
and chasing after the wind.

7 Again I saw something meaningless un-
der the sun:

8 There was a man all alone;
he had neither son nor brother.
There was no end to his toil,
yet his eyes were not content with
his wealth.
"For whom am I toiling," he asked,
"and why am I depriving myself of
enjoyment?"
This too is meaningless—
a miserable business!

9 Two are better than one,
because they have a good return for
their labor:
10 If either of them falls down,
one can help the other up.
But pity anyone who falls
and has no one to help them up.
11 Also, if two lie down together, they will
keep warm.
But how can one keep warm
alone?
12 Though one may be overpowered,
two can defend themselves.
A cord of three strands is not quickly
broken.

Advancement Is Meaningless

13 Better a poor but wise youth than an old
but foolish king who no longer knows how to
heed a warning. 14 The youth may have come
from prison to the kingship, or he may have
been born in poverty within his kingdom.
15 I saw that all who lived and walked under
the sun followed the youth, the king's suc-
cessor. 16 There was no end to all the people
who were before them. But those who came
later were not pleased with the successor.
This too is meaningless, a chasing after the
wind.

[a] 15 Or *God calls back the past* [b] 19 Or *spirit*

Fulfill Your Vow to God

5[a] Guard your steps when you go to the house of God. Go near to listen rather than to offer the sacrifice of fools, who do not know that they do wrong.

2 Do not be quick with your mouth,
do not be hasty in your heart
to utter anything before God.
God is in heaven
and you are on earth,
so let your words be few.
3 A dream comes when there are many cares,
and many words mark the speech of a fool.

4 When you make a vow to God, do not delay to fulfill it. He has no pleasure in fools;
fulfill your vow. 5 It is better not to make a
vow than to make one and not fulfill it. 6 Do
not let your mouth lead you into sin. And do not protest to the temple messenger, "My vow was a mistake." Why should God be angry at what you say and destroy the work
of your hands? 7 Much dreaming and many words are meaningless. Therefore fear God.

Riches Are Meaningless

8 If you see the poor oppressed in a district, and justice and rights denied, do not be surprised at such things; for one official is eyed by a higher one, and over them both are
others higher still. 9 The increase from the
land is taken by all; the king himself profits from the fields.

10 Whoever loves money never has enough;
whoever loves wealth is never satisfied with their income.
This too is meaningless.

11 As goods increase,
so do those who consume them.
And what benefit are they to the owners
except to feast their eyes on them?

12 The sleep of a laborer is sweet,
whether they eat little or much,
but as for the rich, their abundance
permits them no sleep.

13 I have seen a grievous evil under the sun:

wealth hoarded to the harm of its owners,
14 or wealth lost through some misfortune,
so that when they have children
there is nothing left for them to inherit.
15 Everyone comes naked from their mother's womb,
and as everyone comes, so they depart.
They take nothing from their toil
that they can carry in their hands.

16 This too is a grievous evil:

As everyone comes, so they depart,
and what do they gain,
since they toil for the wind?
17 All their days they eat in darkness,
with great frustration, affliction and anger.

18 This is what I have observed to be good:
that it is appropriate for a person to eat, to drink and to find satisfaction in their toilsome labor under the sun during the few days of life God has given them—for this is
their lot. 19 Moreover, when God gives someone wealth and possessions, and the ability to enjoy them, to accept their lot and be happy in their toil—this is a gift of God. 20 They
seldom reflect on the days of their life, because God keeps them occupied with gladness of heart.

6 I have seen another evil under the sun, and it weighs heavily on mankind:
2 God gives some people wealth, possessions and honor, so that they lack nothing their hearts desire, but God does not grant them the ability to enjoy them, and strangers enjoy them instead. This is meaningless, a grievous evil.

3 A man may have a hundred children and live many years; yet no matter how long he lives, if he cannot enjoy his prosperity and does not receive proper burial, I say
that a stillborn child is better off than he. 4 It
comes without meaning, it departs in darkness, and in darkness its name is shrouded.
5 Though it never saw the sun or knew anything, it has more rest than does that man—
6 even if he lives a thousand years twice over but fails to enjoy his prosperity. Do not all go to the same place?

7 Everyone's toil is for their mouth,
yet their appetite is never satisfied.

[a] In Hebrew texts 5:1 is numbered 4:17, and 5:2-20 is numbered 5:1-19.

[8]What advantage have the wise over fools?
What do the poor gain
by knowing how to conduct themselves before others?
[9]Better what the eye sees
than the roving of the appetite.
This too is meaningless,
a chasing after the wind.

[10]Whatever exists has already been named,
and what humanity is has been known;
no one can contend
with someone who is stronger.
[11]The more the words,
the less the meaning,
and how does that profit anyone?

[12]For who knows what is good for a person
in life, during the few and meaningless days
they pass through like a shadow? Who can
tell them what will happen under the sun af-
ter they are gone?

Wisdom

7 A good name is better than fine perfume,
and the day of death better than the day of birth.
[2]It is better to go to a house of mourning
than to go to a house of feasting,
for death is the destiny of everyone;
the living should take this to heart.
[3]Frustration is better than laughter,
because a sad face is good for the heart.
[4]The heart of the wise is in the house of mourning,
but the heart of fools is in the house of pleasure.
[5]It is better to heed the rebuke of a wise person
than to listen to the song of fools.
[6]Like the crackling of thorns under the pot,
so is the laughter of fools.
This too is meaningless.

[7]Extortion turns a wise person into a fool,
and a bribe corrupts the heart.

[8]The end of a matter is better than its beginning,
and patience is better than pride.
[9]Do not be quickly provoked in your spirit,
for anger resides in the lap of fools.

[10]Do not say, "Why were the old days better than these?"
For it is not wise to ask such questions.

[11]Wisdom, like an inheritance, is a good thing
and benefits those who see the sun.
[12]Wisdom is a shelter
as money is a shelter,
but the advantage of knowledge is this:
Wisdom preserves those who have it.

[13]Consider what God has done:

Who can straighten
what he has made crooked?
[14]When times are good, be happy;
but when times are bad, consider this:
God has made the one
as well as the other.
Therefore, no one can discover
anything about their future.

[15]In this meaningless life of mine I have
seen both of these:

the righteous perishing in their righteousness,
and the wicked living long in their wickedness.
[16]Do not be overrighteous,
neither be overwise —
why destroy yourself?
[17]Do not be overwicked,
and do not be a fool —
why die before your time?
[18]It is good to grasp the one
and not let go of the other.
Whoever fears God will avoid all extremes.[a]

[19]Wisdom makes one wise person more powerful
than ten rulers in a city.

[20]Indeed, there is no one on earth who is righteous,
no one who does what is right and never sins.

[21]Do not pay attention to every word people say,
or you may hear your servant cursing you —

[a] 18 Or *will follow them both*

22 for you know in your heart
that many times you yourself have
cursed others.

23 All this I tested by wisdom and I said,

"I am determined to be wise" —
but this was beyond me.
24 Whatever exists is far off and most
profound —
who can discover it?
25 So I turned my mind to understand,
to investigate and to search out
wisdom and the scheme of things
and to understand the stupidity of
wickedness
and the madness of folly.

26 I find more bitter than death
the woman who is a snare,
whose heart is a trap
and whose hands are chains.
The man who pleases God will escape
her,
but the sinner she will ensnare.

27 "Look," says the Teacher,[a] "this is what I have discovered:

"Adding one thing to another to discover
the scheme of things —
28 while I was still searching
but not finding —
I found one upright man among a
thousand,
but not one upright woman among
them all.
29 This only have I found:
God created mankind upright,
but they have gone in search of many
schemes."

8 Who is like the wise?
Who knows the explanation of things?
A person's wisdom brightens their face
and changes its hard appearance.

Obey the King

2 Obey the king's command, I say, because
you took an oath before God. 3 Do not be in
a hurry to leave the king's presence. Do not
stand up for a bad cause, for he will do whatev-
er he pleases. 4 Since a king's word is supreme,
who can say to him, "What are you doing?"

5 Whoever obeys his command will come
to no harm,
and the wise heart will know the
proper time and procedure.
6 For there is a proper time and procedure
for every matter,
though a person may be weighed down
by misery.

7 Since no one knows the future,
who can tell someone else what is to
come?
8 As no one has power over the wind to
contain it,
so[b] no one has power over the time of
their death.
As no one is discharged in time of war,
so wickedness will not release those
who practice it.

9 All this I saw, as I applied my mind to
everything done under the sun. There is a
time when a man lords it over others to his
own[c] hurt. 10 Then too, I saw the wicked bur-
ied — those who used to come and go from
the holy place and receive praise[d] in the city
where they did this. This too is meaningless.
11 When the sentence for a crime is not
quickly carried out, people's hearts are
filled with schemes to do wrong. 12 Although
a wicked person who commits a hundred
crimes may live a long time, I know that it
will go better with those who fear God, who
are reverent before him. 13 Yet because the
wicked do not fear God, it will not go well
with them, and their days will not lengthen
like a shadow.
14 There is something else meaningless
that occurs on earth: the righteous who get
what the wicked deserve, and the wicked
who get what the righteous deserve. This
too, I say, is meaningless. 15 So I commend
the enjoyment of life, because there is noth-
ing better for a person under the sun than to
eat and drink and be glad. Then joy will ac-
company them in their toil all the days of the
life God has given them under the sun.
16 When I applied my mind to know wis-
dom and to observe the labor that is done
on earth — people getting no sleep day or
night — 17 then I saw all that God has done.
No one can comprehend what goes on under

[a] 27 Or *the leader of the assembly* [b] 8 Or *over the human spirit to retain it, / and so* [c] 9 Or *to their*
[d] 10 Some Hebrew manuscripts and Septuagint (Aquila); most Hebrew manuscripts *and are forgotten*

the sun. Despite all their efforts to search it out, no one can discover its meaning. Even if the wise claim they know, they cannot really comprehend it.

A Common Destiny for All

9 So I reflected on all this and concluded that the righteous and the wise and what they do are in God's hands, but no one knows whether love or hate awaits them.
2 All share a common destiny — the righteous and the wicked, the good and the bad,[a] the clean and the unclean, those who offer sacrifices and those who do not.

As it is with the good,
so with the sinful;
as it is with those who take oaths,
so with those who are afraid to take them.

3 This is the evil in everything that happens under the sun: The same destiny overtakes all. The hearts of people, moreover, are full of evil and there is madness in their hearts while they live, and afterward they join the dead.
4 Anyone who is among the living has hope[b] — even a live dog is better off than a dead lion!

5 For the living know that they will die,
but the dead know nothing;
they have no further reward,
and even their name is forgotten.
6 Their love, their hate
and their jealousy have long since vanished;
never again will they have a part
in anything that happens under the sun.

7 Go, eat your food with gladness, and drink your wine with a joyful heart, for God has already approved what you do.
8 Always be clothed in white, and always anoint your head with oil.
9 Enjoy life with your wife, whom you love, all the days of this meaningless life that God has given you under the sun — all your meaningless days. For this is your lot in life and in your toilsome labor under the sun.
10 Whatever your hand finds to do, do it with all your might, for in the realm of the dead, where you are going, there is neither working nor planning nor knowledge nor wisdom.

11 I have seen something else under the sun:

The race is not to the swift
or the battle to the strong,
nor does food come to the wise
or wealth to the brilliant
or favor to the learned;
but time and chance happen to them all.

12 Moreover, no one knows when their hour will come:

As fish are caught in a cruel net,
or birds are taken in a snare,
so people are trapped by evil times
that fall unexpectedly upon them.

Wisdom Better Than Folly

13 I also saw under the sun this example of wisdom that greatly impressed me:
14 There was once a small city with only a few people in it. And a powerful king came against it, surrounded it and built huge siege works against it.
15 Now there lived in that city a man poor but wise, and he saved the city by his wisdom. But nobody remembered that poor man.
16 So I said, "Wisdom is better than strength." But the poor man's wisdom is despised, and his words are no longer heeded.

17 The quiet words of the wise are more to be heeded
than the shouts of a ruler of fools.
18 Wisdom is better than weapons of war,
but one sinner destroys much good.

10 As dead flies give perfume a bad smell,
so a little folly outweighs wisdom and honor.
2 The heart of the wise inclines to the right,
but the heart of the fool to the left.
3 Even as fools walk along the road,
they lack sense
and show everyone how stupid they are.
4 If a ruler's anger rises against you,
do not leave your post;
calmness can lay great offenses to rest.

5 There is an evil I have seen under the sun,
the sort of error that arises from a ruler:

[a] 2 Septuagint (Aquila), Vulgate and Syriac; Hebrew does not have *and the bad.* [b] 4 Or *What then is to be chosen? With all who live, there is hope*

[6] Fools are put in many high positions
while the rich occupy the low ones.
[7] I have seen slaves on horseback,
while princes go on foot like slaves.

[8] Whoever digs a pit may fall into it;
whoever breaks through a wall may be bitten by a snake.
[9] Whoever quarries stones may be injured by them;
whoever splits logs may be endangered by them.

[10] If the ax is dull
and its edge unsharpened,
more strength is needed,
but skill will bring success.

[11] If a snake bites before it is charmed,
the charmer receives no fee.

[12] Words from the mouth of the wise are gracious,
but fools are consumed by their own lips.
[13] At the beginning their words are folly;
at the end they are wicked madness —
[14] and fools multiply words.

No one knows what is coming —
who can tell someone else what will happen after them?

[15] The toil of fools wearies them;
they do not know the way to town.

[16] Woe to the land whose king was a servant[a]
and whose princes feast in the morning.
[17] Blessed is the land whose king is of noble birth
and whose princes eat at a proper time —
for strength and not for drunkenness.

[18] Through laziness, the rafters sag;
because of idle hands, the house leaks.

[19] A feast is made for laughter,
wine makes life merry,
and money is the answer for everything.

[20] Do not revile the king even in your thoughts,
or curse the rich in your bedroom,
because a bird in the sky may carry your words,
and a bird on the wing may report what you say.

Invest in Many Ventures

11 Ship your grain across the sea;
after many days you may receive a return.
[2] Invest in seven ventures, yes, in eight;
you do not know what disaster may come upon the land.

[3] If clouds are full of water,
they pour rain on the earth.
Whether a tree falls to the south or to the north,
in the place where it falls, there it will lie.
[4] Whoever watches the wind will not plant;
whoever looks at the clouds will not reap.
[5] As you do not know the path of the wind,
or how the body is formed[b] in a mother's womb,
so you cannot understand the work of God,
the Maker of all things.
[6] Sow your seed in the morning,
and at evening let your hands not be idle,
for you do not know which will succeed,
whether this or that,
or whether both will do equally well.

Remember Your Creator While Young

[7] Light is sweet,
and it pleases the eyes to see the sun.
[8] However many years anyone may live,
let them enjoy them all.
But let them remember the days of darkness,
for there will be many.
Everything to come is meaningless.

[9] You who are young, be happy while you are young,
and let your heart give you joy in the days of your youth.
Follow the ways of your heart
and whatever your eyes see,
but know that for all these things
God will bring you into judgment.

[a] 16 Or *king is a child* [b] 5 Or *know how life* (or *the spirit*) */ enters the body being formed*

[10] So then, banish anxiety from your heart
and cast off the troubles of your body,
for youth and vigor are meaningless.

12 Remember your Creator
in the days of your youth,
before the days of trouble come
and the years approach when you
will say,
"I find no pleasure in them" —
[2] before the sun and the light
and the moon and the stars grow dark,
and the clouds return after the rain;
[3] when the keepers of the house tremble,
and the strong men stoop,
when the grinders cease because they
are few,
and those looking through the
windows grow dim;
[4] when the doors to the street are closed
and the sound of grinding fades;
when people rise up at the sound of birds,
but all their songs grow faint;
[5] when people are afraid of heights
and of dangers in the streets;
when the almond tree blossoms
and the grasshopper drags itself along
and desire no longer is stirred.
Then people go to their eternal home
and mourners go about the streets.
[6] Remember him — before the silver cord is
severed,
and the golden bowl is broken;
before the pitcher is shattered at the
spring,
and the wheel broken at the well,
[7] and the dust returns to the ground it
came from,
and the spirit returns to God who
gave it.

[8] "Meaningless! Meaningless!" says the
Teacher.[a]
"Everything is meaningless!"

The Conclusion of the Matter

[9] Not only was the Teacher wise, but he
also imparted knowledge to the people. He
pondered and searched out and set in order
many proverbs. [10] The Teacher searched to
find just the right words, and what he wrote
was upright and true.

[11] The words of the wise are like goads,
their collected sayings like firmly embedded
nails — given by one shepherd.[b] [12] Be warned,
my son, of anything in addition to them.

Of making many books there is no end,
and much study wearies the body.

[13] Now all has been heard;
here is the conclusion of the matter:
Fear God and keep his commandments,
for this is the duty of all mankind.
[14] For God will bring every deed into
judgment,
including every hidden thing,
whether it is good or evil.

[a] 8 Or *the leader of the assembly*; also in verses 9 and 10 [b] 11 Or *Shepherd*

SONG OF SONGS

1 Solomon's Song of Songs.

She[a]

[2] Let him kiss me with the kisses of his
mouth —
for your love is more delightful than
wine.
[3] Pleasing is the fragrance of your
perfumes;
your name is like perfume poured out.
No wonder the young women love you!
[4] Take me away with you — let us hurry!
Let the king bring me into his
chambers.

Friends

We rejoice and delight in you[b];
we will praise your love more than
wine.

She

How right they are to adore you!

[5] Dark am I, yet lovely,
daughters of Jerusalem,
dark like the tents of Kedar,
like the tent curtains of Solomon.[c]
[6] Do not stare at me because I am dark,
because I am darkened by the sun.
My mother's sons were angry with me
and made me take care of the
vineyards;
my own vineyard I had to neglect.
[7] Tell me, you whom I love,
where you graze your flock
and where you rest your sheep at
midday.
Why should I be like a veiled woman
beside the flocks of your friends?

Friends

[8] If you do not know, most beautiful of
women,
follow the tracks of the sheep
and graze your young goats
by the tents of the shepherds.

He

[9] I liken you, my darling, to a mare
among Pharaoh's chariot horses.
[10] Your cheeks are beautiful with
earrings,
your neck with strings of jewels.
[11] We will make you earrings of gold,
studded with silver.

She

[12] While the king was at his table,
my perfume spread its fragrance.
[13] My beloved is to me a sachet of myrrh
resting between my breasts.
[14] My beloved is to me a cluster of henna
blossoms
from the vineyards of En Gedi.

He

[15] How beautiful you are, my darling!
Oh, how beautiful!
Your eyes are doves.

She

[16] How handsome you are, my beloved!
Oh, how charming!
And our bed is verdant.

He

[17] The beams of our house are cedars;
our rafters are firs.

She[d]

2 I am a rose[e] of Sharon,
a lily of the valleys.

He

[2] Like a lily among thorns
is my darling among the young
women.

[a] The main male and female speakers (identified primarily on the basis of the gender of the relevant Hebrew forms) are indicated by the captions *He* and *She* respectively. The words of others are marked *Friends*. In some instances the divisions and their captions are debatable. [b] 4 The Hebrew is masculine singular. [c] 5 Or *Salma* [d] Or *He* [e] 1 Probably a member of the crocus family

She

3 Like an apple[a] tree among the trees of
the forest
is my beloved among the young men.
I delight to sit in his shade,
and his fruit is sweet to my taste.
4 Let him lead me to the banquet hall,
and let his banner over me be love.
5 Strengthen me with raisins,
refresh me with apples,
for I am faint with love.
6 His left arm is under my head,
and his right arm embraces me.
7 Daughters of Jerusalem, I charge you
by the gazelles and by the does of
the field:
Do not arouse or awaken love
until it so desires.

8 Listen! My beloved!
Look! Here he comes,
leaping across the mountains,
bounding over the hills.
9 My beloved is like a gazelle or a young
stag.
Look! There he stands behind our wall,
gazing through the windows,
peering through the lattice.
10 My beloved spoke and said to me,
"Arise, my darling,
my beautiful one, come with me.
11 See! The winter is past;
the rains are over and gone.
12 Flowers appear on the earth;
the season of singing has come,
the cooing of doves
is heard in our land.
13 The fig tree forms its early fruit;
the blossoming vines spread their
fragrance.
Arise, come, my darling;
my beautiful one, come with me."

He

14 My dove in the clefts of the rock,
in the hiding places on the
mountainside,
show me your face,
let me hear your voice;
for your voice is sweet,
and your face is lovely.
15 Catch for us the foxes,
the little foxes
that ruin the vineyards,
our vineyards that are in bloom.

She

16 My beloved is mine and I am his;
he browses among the lilies.
17 Until the day breaks
and the shadows flee,
turn, my beloved,
and be like a gazelle
or like a young stag
on the rugged hills.[b]

3 All night long on my bed
I looked for the one my heart loves;
I looked for him but did not find him.
2 I will get up now and go about the city,
through its streets and squares;
I will search for the one my heart loves.
So I looked for him but did not find him.
3 The watchmen found me
as they made their rounds in the city.
"Have you seen the one my heart
loves?"
4 Scarcely had I passed them
when I found the one my heart loves.
I held him and would not let him go
till I had brought him to my mother's
house,
to the room of the one who
conceived me.
5 Daughters of Jerusalem, I charge you
by the gazelles and by the does of
the field:
Do not arouse or awaken love
until it so desires.

6 Who is this coming up from the
wilderness
like a column of smoke,
perfumed with myrrh and incense
made from all the spices of the
merchant?
7 Look! It is Solomon's carriage,
escorted by sixty warriors,
the noblest of Israel,
8 all of them wearing the sword,
all experienced in battle,
each with his sword at his side,
prepared for the terrors of the night.
9 King Solomon made for himself the
carriage;
he made it of wood from Lebanon.

[a] 3 Or possibly *apricot*; here and elsewhere in Song of Songs [b] 17 Or *the hills of Bether*

10 Its posts he made of silver,
its base of gold.
Its seat was upholstered with purple,
its interior inlaid with love.
Daughters of Jerusalem, 11 come out,
and look, you daughters of Zion.
Look[a] on King Solomon wearing a crown,
the crown with which his mother
crowned him
on the day of his wedding,
the day his heart rejoiced.

He

4 How beautiful you are, my darling!
Oh, how beautiful!
Your eyes behind your veil are doves.
Your hair is like a flock of goats
descending from the hills of Gilead.
2 Your teeth are like a flock of sheep just
shorn,
coming up from the washing.
Each has its twin;
not one of them is alone.
3 Your lips are like a scarlet ribbon;
your mouth is lovely.
Your temples behind your veil
are like the halves of a pomegranate.
4 Your neck is like the tower of David,
built with courses of stone[b];
on it hang a thousand shields,
all of them shields of warriors.
5 Your breasts are like two fawns,
like twin fawns of a gazelle
that browse among the lilies.
6 Until the day breaks
and the shadows flee,
I will go to the mountain of myrrh
and to the hill of incense.
7 You are altogether beautiful, my darling;
there is no flaw in you.

8 Come with me from Lebanon, my bride,
come with me from Lebanon.
Descend from the crest of Amana,
from the top of Senir, the summit of
Hermon,
from the lions' dens
and the mountain haunts of leopards.
9 You have stolen my heart, my sister, my
bride;
you have stolen my heart
with one glance of your eyes,
with one jewel of your necklace.
10 How delightful is your love, my sister, my
bride!
How much more pleasing is your love
than wine,
and the fragrance of your perfume
more than any spice!
11 Your lips drop sweetness as the
honeycomb, my bride;
milk and honey are under your tongue.
The fragrance of your garments
is like the fragrance of Lebanon.
12 You are a garden locked up, my sister,
my bride;
you are a spring enclosed, a sealed
fountain.
13 Your plants are an orchard of
pomegranates
with choice fruits,
with henna and nard,
14 nard and saffron,
calamus and cinnamon,
with every kind of incense tree,
with myrrh and aloes
and all the finest spices.
15 You are[c] a garden fountain,
a well of flowing water
streaming down from Lebanon.

She

16 Awake, north wind,
and come, south wind!
Blow on my garden,
that its fragrance may spread
everywhere.
Let my beloved come into his garden
and taste its choice fruits.

He

5 I have come into my garden, my sister,
my bride;
I have gathered my myrrh with my
spice.
I have eaten my honeycomb and my
honey;
I have drunk my wine and my milk.

Friends

Eat, friends, and drink;
drink your fill of love.

She

2 I slept but my heart was awake.
Listen! My beloved is knocking:

[a] 10,11 Or *interior lovingly inlaid / by the daughters of Jerusalem. / [11]Come out, you daughters of Zion, / and look* [b] 4 The meaning of the Hebrew for this phrase is uncertain. [c] 15 Or *I am* (spoken by *She*)

"Open to me, my sister, my darling,
my dove, my flawless one.
My head is drenched with dew,
my hair with the dampness of the night."
3 I have taken off my robe —
must I put it on again?
I have washed my feet —
must I soil them again?
4 My beloved thrust his hand through the latch-opening;
my heart began to pound for him.
5 I arose to open for my beloved,
and my hands dripped with myrrh,
my fingers with flowing myrrh,
on the handles of the bolt.
6 I opened for my beloved,
but my beloved had left; he was gone.
My heart sank at his departure.[a]
I looked for him but did not find him.
I called him but he did not answer.
7 The watchmen found me
as they made their rounds in the city.
They beat me, they bruised me;
they took away my cloak,
those watchmen of the walls!
8 Daughters of Jerusalem, I charge you —
if you find my beloved,
what will you tell him?
Tell him I am faint with love.

Friends

9 How is your beloved better than others,
most beautiful of women?
How is your beloved better than others,
that you so charge us?

She

10 My beloved is radiant and ruddy,
outstanding among ten thousand.
11 His head is purest gold;
his hair is wavy
and black as a raven.
12 His eyes are like doves
by the water streams,
washed in milk,
mounted like jewels.
13 His cheeks are like beds of spice
yielding perfume.
His lips are like lilies
dripping with myrrh.
14 His arms are rods of gold
set with topaz.
His body is like polished ivory
decorated with lapis lazuli.
15 His legs are pillars of marble
set on bases of pure gold.
His appearance is like Lebanon,
choice as its cedars.
16 His mouth is sweetness itself;
he is altogether lovely.
This is my beloved, this is my friend,
daughters of Jerusalem.

Friends

6 Where has your beloved gone,
most beautiful of women?
Which way did your beloved turn,
that we may look for him with you?

She

2 My beloved has gone down to his garden,
to the beds of spices,
to browse in the gardens
and to gather lilies.
3 I am my beloved's and my beloved is mine;
he browses among the lilies.

He

4 You are as beautiful as Tirzah, my darling,
as lovely as Jerusalem,
as majestic as troops with banners.
5 Turn your eyes from me;
they overwhelm me.
Your hair is like a flock of goats
descending from Gilead.
6 Your teeth are like a flock of sheep
coming up from the washing.
Each has its twin,
not one of them is missing.
7 Your temples behind your veil
are like the halves of a pomegranate.
8 Sixty queens there may be,
and eighty concubines,
and virgins beyond number;
9 but my dove, my perfect one, is unique,
the only daughter of her mother,
the favorite of the one who bore her.
The young women saw her and called her blessed;
the queens and concubines praised her.

Friends

10 Who is this that appears like the dawn,
fair as the moon, bright as the sun,
majestic as the stars in procession?

[a] 6 Or *heart had gone out to him when he spoke*

He

11 I went down to the grove of nut trees
to look at the new growth in the valley,
to see if the vines had budded
or the pomegranates were in bloom.
12 Before I realized it,
my desire set me among the royal
chariots of my people.[a]

Friends

13 Come back, come back, O Shulammite;
come back, come back, that we may
gaze on you!

He

Why would you gaze on the Shulammite
as on the dance of Mahanaim?[b]

7 [c] How beautiful your sandaled feet,
O prince's daughter!
Your graceful legs are like jewels,
the work of an artist's hands.
2 Your navel is a rounded goblet
that never lacks blended wine.
Your waist is a mound of wheat
encircled by lilies.
3 Your breasts are like two fawns,
like twin fawns of a gazelle.
4 Your neck is like an ivory tower.
Your eyes are the pools of Heshbon
by the gate of Bath Rabbim.
Your nose is like the tower of Lebanon
looking toward Damascus.
5 Your head crowns you like Mount Carmel.
Your hair is like royal tapestry;
the king is held captive by its tresses.
6 How beautiful you are and how pleasing,
my love, with your delights!
7 Your stature is like that of the palm,
and your breasts like clusters of fruit.
8 I said, "I will climb the palm tree;
I will take hold of its fruit."
May your breasts be like clusters of
grapes on the vine,
the fragrance of your breath like apples,
9 and your mouth like the best wine.

She

May the wine go straight to my beloved,
flowing gently over lips and teeth.[d]
10 I belong to my beloved,
and his desire is for me.
11 Come, my beloved, let us go to the
countryside,
let us spend the night in the villages.[e]
12 Let us go early to the vineyards
to see if the vines have budded,
if their blossoms have opened,
and if the pomegranates are in
bloom—
there I will give you my love.
13 The mandrakes send out their fragrance,
and at our door is every delicacy,
both new and old,
that I have stored up for you, my
beloved.

8 If only you were to me like a brother,
who was nursed at my mother's
breasts!
Then, if I found you outside,
I would kiss you,
and no one would despise me.
2 I would lead you
and bring you to my mother's house—
she who has taught me.
I would give you spiced wine to drink,
the nectar of my pomegranates.
3 His left arm is under my head
and his right arm embraces me.
4 Daughters of Jerusalem, I charge you:
Do not arouse or awaken love
until it so desires.

Friends

5 Who is this coming up from the
wilderness
leaning on her beloved?

She

Under the apple tree I roused you;
there your mother conceived you,
there she who was in labor gave you
birth.
6 Place me like a seal over your heart,
like a seal on your arm;
for love is as strong as death,
its jealousy[f] unyielding as the grave.
It burns like blazing fire,
like a mighty flame.[g]

[a] 12 Or *among the chariots of Amminadab*; or *among the chariots of the people of the prince* [b] 13 In Hebrew texts this verse (6:13) is numbered 7:1. [c] In Hebrew texts 7:1-13 is numbered 7:2-14. [d] 9 Septuagint, Aquila, Vulgate and Syriac; Hebrew *lips of sleepers* [e] 11 Or *the henna bushes* [f] 6 Or *ardor* [g] 6 Or *fire, / like the very flame of the* LORD

7 Many waters cannot quench love;
rivers cannot sweep it away.
If one were to give
all the wealth of one's house for love,
it[a] would be utterly scorned.

Friends

8 We have a little sister,
and her breasts are not yet grown.
What shall we do for our sister
on the day she is spoken for?
9 If she is a wall,
we will build towers of silver on her.
If she is a door,
we will enclose her with panels of cedar.

She

10 I am a wall,
and my breasts are like towers.
Thus I have become in his eyes
like one bringing contentment.
11 Solomon had a vineyard in Baal
Hamon;
he let out his vineyard to tenants.
Each was to bring for its fruit
a thousand shekels[b] of silver.
12 But my own vineyard is mine to give;
the thousand shekels are for you,
Solomon,
and two hundred[c] are for those who
tend its fruit.

He

13 You who dwell in the gardens
with friends in attendance,
let me hear your voice!

She

14 Come away, my beloved,
and be like a gazelle
or like a young stag
on the spice-laden mountains.

[a] *7* Or *he* [b] *11* That is, about 25 pounds or about 12 kilograms; also in verse 12 [c] *12* That is, about 5 pounds or about 2.3 kilograms

ISAIAH

1 The vision concerning Judah and Jerusalem that Isaiah son of Amoz saw during the reigns of Uzziah, Jotham, Ahaz and Hezekiah, kings of Judah.

A Rebellious Nation

2 Hear me, you heavens! Listen, earth!
For the LORD has spoken:
"I reared children and brought them up,
but they have rebelled against me.
3 The ox knows its master,
the donkey its owner's manger,
but Israel does not know,
my people do not understand."

4 Woe to the sinful nation,
a people whose guilt is great,
a brood of evildoers,
children given to corruption!
They have forsaken the LORD;
they have spurned the Holy One of Israel
and turned their backs on him.

5 Why should you be beaten anymore?
Why do you persist in rebellion?
Your whole head is injured,
your whole heart afflicted.
6 From the sole of your foot to the top of your head
there is no soundness —
only wounds and welts
and open sores,
not cleansed or bandaged
or soothed with olive oil.

7 Your country is desolate,
your cities burned with fire;
your fields are being stripped by foreigners
right before you,
laid waste as when overthrown by strangers.
8 Daughter Zion is left
like a shelter in a vineyard,
like a hut in a cucumber field,
like a city under siege.
9 Unless the LORD Almighty
had left us some survivors,
we would have become like Sodom,
we would have been like Gomorrah.

10 Hear the word of the LORD,
you rulers of Sodom;
listen to the instruction of our God,
you people of Gomorrah!
11 "The multitude of your sacrifices —
what are they to me?" says the LORD.
"I have more than enough of burnt offerings,
of rams and the fat of fattened animals;
I have no pleasure
in the blood of bulls and lambs and goats.
12 When you come to appear before me,
who has asked this of you,
this trampling of my courts?
13 Stop bringing meaningless offerings!
Your incense is detestable to me.
New Moons, Sabbaths and convocations —
I cannot bear your worthless assemblies.
14 Your New Moon feasts and your appointed festivals
I hate with all my being.
They have become a burden to me;
I am weary of bearing them.
15 When you spread out your hands in prayer,
I hide my eyes from you;
even when you offer many prayers,
I am not listening.

Your hands are full of blood!

16 Wash and make yourselves clean.
Take your evil deeds out of my sight;
stop doing wrong.
17 Learn to do right; seek justice.
Defend the oppressed.[a]
Take up the cause of the fatherless;
plead the case of the widow.

[a] 17 Or *justice. / Correct the oppressor*

18 "Come now, let us settle the matter,"
says the LORD.
"Though your sins are like scarlet,
they shall be as white as snow;
though they are red as crimson,
they shall be like wool.
19 If you are willing and obedient,
you will eat the good things of the land;
20 but if you resist and rebel,
you will be devoured by the sword."
For the mouth of the LORD has spoken.

21 See how the faithful city
has become a prostitute!
She once was full of justice;
righteousness used to dwell in her—
but now murderers!
22 Your silver has become dross,
your choice wine is diluted with water.
23 Your rulers are rebels,
partners with thieves;
they all love bribes
and chase after gifts.
They do not defend the cause of the fatherless;
the widow's case does not come before them.
24 Therefore the Lord, the LORD Almighty,
the Mighty One of Israel, declares:
"Ah! I will vent my wrath on my foes
and avenge myself on my enemies.
25 I will turn my hand against you;[a]
I will thoroughly purge away your dross
and remove all your impurities.
26 I will restore your leaders as in days of old,
your rulers as at the beginning.
Afterward you will be called
the City of Righteousness,
the Faithful City."

27 Zion will be delivered with justice,
her penitent ones with righteousness.
28 But rebels and sinners will both be broken,
and those who forsake the LORD will perish.

29 "You will be ashamed because of the sacred oaks
in which you have delighted;
you will be disgraced because of the gardens
that you have chosen.
30 You will be like an oak with fading leaves,
like a garden without water.
31 The mighty man will become tinder
and his work a spark;
both will burn together,
with no one to quench the fire."

The Mountain of the LORD

2 This is what Isaiah son of Amoz saw concerning Judah and Jerusalem:

2 In the last days

the mountain of the LORD's temple will be established
as the highest of the mountains;
it will be exalted above the hills,
and all nations will stream to it.

3 Many peoples will come and say,

"Come, let us go up to the mountain of the LORD,
to the temple of the God of Jacob.
He will teach us his ways,
so that we may walk in his paths."
The law will go out from Zion,
the word of the LORD from Jerusalem.
4 He will judge between the nations
and will settle disputes for many peoples.
They will beat their swords into plowshares
and their spears into pruning hooks.
Nation will not take up sword against nation,
nor will they train for war anymore.

5 Come, descendants of Jacob,
let us walk in the light of the LORD.

The Day of the LORD

6 You, LORD, have abandoned your people,
the descendants of Jacob.
They are full of superstitions from the East;
they practice divination like the Philistines
and embrace pagan customs.
7 Their land is full of silver and gold;
there is no end to their treasures.
Their land is full of horses;
there is no end to their chariots.

[a] 25 That is, against Jerusalem

[8] Their land is full of idols;
they bow down to the work of their hands,
to what their fingers have made.
[9] So people will be brought low
and everyone humbled —
do not forgive them.[a]

[10] Go into the rocks, hide in the ground
from the fearful presence of the LORD
and the splendor of his majesty!
[11] The eyes of the arrogant will be humbled
and human pride brought low;
the LORD alone will be exalted in that day.

[12] The LORD Almighty has a day in store
for all the proud and lofty,
for all that is exalted
(and they will be humbled),
[13] for all the cedars of Lebanon, tall and lofty,
and all the oaks of Bashan,
[14] for all the towering mountains
and all the high hills,
[15] for every lofty tower
and every fortified wall,
[16] for every trading ship[b]
and every stately vessel.
[17] The arrogance of man will be brought low
and human pride humbled;
the LORD alone will be exalted in that day,
[18] and the idols will totally disappear.

[19] People will flee to caves in the rocks
and to holes in the ground
from the fearful presence of the LORD
and the splendor of his majesty,
when he rises to shake the earth.
[20] In that day people will throw away
to the moles and bats
their idols of silver and idols of gold,
which they made to worship.
[21] They will flee to caverns in the rocks
and to the overhanging crags
from the fearful presence of the LORD
and the splendor of his majesty,
when he rises to shake the earth.

[22] Stop trusting in mere humans,
who have but a breath in their nostrils.
Why hold them in esteem?

Judgment on Jerusalem and Judah

3 See now, the Lord,
the LORD Almighty,
is about to take from Jerusalem and Judah
both supply and support:
all supplies of food and all supplies of water,
[2] the hero and the warrior,
the judge and the prophet,
the diviner and the elder,
[3] the captain of fifty and the man of rank,
the counselor, skilled craftsman and clever enchanter.

[4] "I will make mere youths their officials;
children will rule over them."

[5] People will oppress each other —
man against man, neighbor against neighbor.
The young will rise up against the old,
the nobody against the honored.
[6] A man will seize one of his brothers
in his father's house, and say,
"You have a cloak, you be our leader;
take charge of this heap of ruins!"
[7] But in that day he will cry out,
"I have no remedy.
I have no food or clothing in my house;
do not make me the leader of the people."

[8] Jerusalem staggers,
Judah is falling;
their words and deeds are against the LORD,
defying his glorious presence.
[9] The look on their faces testifies against them;
they parade their sin like Sodom;
they do not hide it.
Woe to them!
They have brought disaster upon themselves.

[10] Tell the righteous it will be well with them,
for they will enjoy the fruit of their deeds.
[11] Woe to the wicked!
Disaster is upon them!
They will be paid back
for what their hands have done.

[a] 9 Or *not raise them up* [b] 16 Hebrew *every ship of Tarshish*

INDESCRIBABLE

Laura Story, Jesse Reeves

From the highest of heights to the depths of the sea
Creation's revealing your majesty
From the colors of fall to the fragrance of spring
Every creature unique in the song that it sings
All exclaiming

Indescribable, uncontainable
You placed the stars in the sky and you know them by name
You are amazing, God
And all powerful, untamable
Awestruck we fall to our knees as we humbly proclaim
You are amazing, God

Who has told every lightning bolt where it should go
Or seen heavenly store houses laden with snow?
Who imagined the sun and gives source to its light
Yet conceals it to bring us the coolness of night?
None can fathom

Indescribable, uncontainable
You placed the stars in the sky and you know them by name
You are amazing, God
And all powerful, untamable
Awestruck we fall to our knees as we humbly proclaim
You are amazing, God
You are amazing, God

THE INSPIRATION

He determines the number of the stars and calls them each by name. Great is our Lord and mighty in power; his understanding has no limit. —Psalm 147:4–5

Read also: Psalm 95:4–5

BEHIND THE SONG

It is impossible for the finite mind to comprehend the infinite, so it is not surprising that we struggle to describe the God who created and sustains us. Worship, however, invites us to try. It's not hard to imagine God gazing in parental joy as he hears his children attempting to describe his greatness. While our understanding of the magnitude of God is limited this side of eternity, he does provide us with ways in which to know and glorify him.

Laura Story had been writing songs for years when she came up with the inspiration for "Indescribable." "I was driving in my car through the Smoky Mountains in North Carolina," Story recalls, "and it was one of those days when the leaves were changing and the sun was setting. I wanted to worship. I wanted to sing. But at first, no words came out. That's when I started thinking about this idea of God being indescribable — that our words are just so feeble in describing him."

Selah

Both Psalm 95 and 147 contain vivid word pictures that stretch the imagination, allowing us room to conceive of the vast goodness of God. Spend some time thinking and reflecting on the aspects of God's nature, character or behavior that prompt you to worship him. How long does it take to get to the end of your ability to describe him?

Worship leaders and song writers are given the task of helping people to articulate the worship that is in their hearts, even when that sentiment is that no words will ever quite describe just how awesome God is.

[12]Youths oppress my people,
women rule over them.
My people, your guides lead you astray;
they turn you from the path.

[13]The LORD takes his place in court;
he rises to judge the people.
[14]The LORD enters into judgment
against the elders and leaders of his
people:
"It is you who have ruined my vineyard;
the plunder from the poor is in your
houses.
[15]What do you mean by crushing my
people
and grinding the faces of the poor?"
declares the Lord,
the LORD Almighty.

[16]The LORD says,
"The women of Zion are haughty,
walking along with outstretched necks,
flirting with their eyes,
strutting along with swaying hips,
with ornaments jingling on their
ankles.
[17]Therefore the Lord will bring sores on the
heads of the women of Zion;
the LORD will make their scalps bald."

[18]In that day the Lord will snatch away
their finery: the bangles and headbands
and crescent necklaces, [19]the earrings and
bracelets and veils, [20]the headdresses and
anklets and sashes, the perfume bottles and
charms, [21]the signet rings and nose rings,
[22]the fine robes and the capes and cloaks,
the purses [23]and mirrors, and the linen gar-
ments and tiaras and shawls.

[24]Instead of fragrance there will be a stench;
instead of a sash, a rope;
instead of well-dressed hair, baldness;
instead of fine clothing, sackcloth;
instead of beauty, branding.
[25]Your men will fall by the sword,
your warriors in battle.
[26]The gates of Zion will lament and mourn;
destitute, she will sit on the ground.

4 [1]In that day seven women
will take hold of one man
and say, "We will eat our own food
and provide our own clothes;
only let us be called by your name.
Take away our disgrace!"

The Branch of the LORD

[2]In that day the Branch of the LORD will
be beautiful and glorious, and the fruit of the
land will be the pride and glory of the sur-
vivors in Israel. [3]Those who are left in Zion,
who remain in Jerusalem, will be called
holy, all who are recorded among the living
in Jerusalem. [4]The Lord will wash away the
filth of the women of Zion; he will cleanse
the bloodstains from Jerusalem by a spir-
it[a] of judgment and a spirit[a] of fire. [5]Then
the LORD will create over all of Mount Zion
and over those who assemble there a cloud
of smoke by day and a glow of flaming fire
by night; over everything the glory[b] will be a
canopy. [6]It will be a shelter and shade from
the heat of the day, and a refuge and hiding
place from the storm and rain.

The Song of the Vineyard

5 I will sing for the one I love
a song about his vineyard:
My loved one had a vineyard
on a fertile hillside.
[2]He dug it up and cleared it of stones
and planted it with the choicest vines.
He built a watchtower in it
and cut out a winepress as well.
Then he looked for a crop of good grapes,
but it yielded only bad fruit.

[3]"Now you dwellers in Jerusalem and
people of Judah,
judge between me and my vineyard.
[4]What more could have been done for my
vineyard
than I have done for it?
When I looked for good grapes,
why did it yield only bad?
[5]Now I will tell you
what I am going to do to my vineyard:
I will take away its hedge,
and it will be destroyed;
I will break down its wall,
and it will be trampled.
[6]I will make it a wasteland,
neither pruned nor cultivated,
and briers and thorns will grow there.
I will command the clouds
not to rain on it."

[7]The vineyard of the LORD Almighty
is the nation of Israel,

[a] 4 Or *the Spirit* [b] 5 Or *over all the glory there*

and the people of Judah
are the vines he delighted in.
And he looked for justice, but saw
bloodshed;
for righteousness, but heard cries of
distress.

Woes and Judgments

8 Woe to you who add house to house
and join field to field
till no space is left
and you live alone in the land.

9 The LORD Almighty has declared in my
hearing:

"Surely the great houses will become
desolate,
the fine mansions left without
occupants.
10 A ten-acre vineyard will produce only a
bath[a] of wine;
a homer[b] of seed will yield only an
ephah[c] of grain."
11 Woe to those who rise early in the
morning
to run after their drinks,
who stay up late at night
till they are inflamed with wine.
12 They have harps and lyres at their
banquets,
pipes and timbrels and wine,
but they have no regard for the deeds of
the LORD,
no respect for the work of his hands.
13 Therefore my people will go into exile
for lack of understanding;
those of high rank will die of hunger
and the common people will be
parched with thirst.
14 Therefore Death expands its jaws,
opening wide its mouth;
into it will descend their nobles and
masses
with all their brawlers and revelers.
15 So people will be brought low
and everyone humbled,
the eyes of the arrogant humbled.
16 But the LORD Almighty will be exalted by
his justice,
and the holy God will be proved holy
by his righteous acts.
17 Then sheep will graze as in their own
pasture;
lambs will feed[d] among the ruins of
the rich.
18 Woe to those who draw sin along with
cords of deceit,
and wickedness as with cart ropes,
19 to those who say, "Let God hurry;
let him hasten his work
so we may see it.
The plan of the Holy One of Israel—
let it approach, let it come into view,
so we may know it."
20 Woe to those who call evil good
and good evil,
who put darkness for light
and light for darkness,
who put bitter for sweet
and sweet for bitter.
21 Woe to those who are wise in their
own eyes
and clever in their own sight.
22 Woe to those who are heroes at drinking
wine
and champions at mixing drinks,
23 who acquit the guilty for a bribe,
but deny justice to the innocent.
24 Therefore, as tongues of fire lick up straw
and as dry grass sinks down in the
flames,
so their roots will decay
and their flowers blow away like dust;
for they have rejected the law of the LORD
Almighty
and spurned the word of the Holy One
of Israel.
25 Therefore the LORD's anger burns against
his people;
his hand is raised and he strikes them
down.
The mountains shake,
and the dead bodies are like refuse in
the streets.

Yet for all this, his anger is not turned
away,
his hand is still upraised.
26 He lifts up a banner for the distant
nations,

[a] *10* That is, about 6 gallons or about 22 liters [b] *10* That is, probably about 360 pounds or about 160 kilograms [c] *10* That is, probably about 36 pounds or about 16 kilograms [d] *17* Septuagint; Hebrew */ strangers will eat*

he whistles for those at the ends of the
earth.
Here they come,
swiftly and speedily!
27 Not one of them grows tired or stumbles,
not one slumbers or sleeps;
not a belt is loosened at the waist,
not a sandal strap is broken.
28 Their arrows are sharp,
all their bows are strung;
their horses' hooves seem like flint,
their chariot wheels like a whirlwind.
29 Their roar is like that of the lion,
they roar like young lions;
they growl as they seize their prey
and carry it off with no one to rescue.
30 In that day they will roar over it
like the roaring of the sea.
And if one looks at the land,
there is only darkness and distress;
even the sun will be darkened by
clouds.

Isaiah's Commission

6 In the year that King Uzziah died, I saw
the Lord, high and exalted, seated on a
throne; and the train of his robe filled the
temple. 2 Above him were seraphim, each
with six wings: With two wings they covered
their faces, with two they covered their feet,
and with two they were flying. 3 And they
were calling to one another:

"Holy, holy, holy is the LORD Almighty;
the whole earth is full of his glory."

4 At the sound of their voices the doorposts
and thresholds shook and the temple was
filled with smoke.

5 "Woe to me!" I cried. "I am ruined! For I
am a man of unclean lips, and I live among
a people of unclean lips, and my eyes have
seen the King, the LORD Almighty."

6 Then one of the seraphim flew to me
with a live coal in his hand, which he had
taken with tongs from the altar. 7 With it he
touched my mouth and said, "See, this has
touched your lips; your guilt is taken away
and your sin atoned for."

8 Then I heard the voice of the Lord say-
ing, "Whom shall I send? And who will go
for us?"

And I said, "Here am I. Send me!"
9 He said, "Go and tell this people:
" 'Be ever hearing, but never
understanding;
be ever seeing, but never perceiving.'
10 Make the heart of this people calloused;
make their ears dull
and close their eyes.[a]
Otherwise they might see with their eyes,
hear with their ears,
understand with their hearts,
and turn and be healed."

11 Then I said, "For how long, Lord?"
And he answered:

"Until the cities lie ruined
and without inhabitant,
until the houses are left deserted
and the fields ruined and ravaged,
12 until the LORD has sent everyone far
away
and the land is utterly forsaken.
13 And though a tenth remains in the land,
it will again be laid waste.
But as the terebinth and oak
leave stumps when they are cut down,
so the holy seed will be the stump in
the land."

The Sign of Immanuel

7 When Ahaz son of Jotham, the son of
Uzziah, was king of Judah, King Rezin of
Aram and Pekah son of Remaliah king of Is-
rael marched up to fight against Jerusalem,
but they could not overpower it.

2 Now the house of David was told, "Aram
has allied itself with[b] Ephraim"; so the hearts
of Ahaz and his people were shaken, as the
trees of the forest are shaken by the wind.

3 Then the LORD said to Isaiah, "Go out,
you and your son Shear-Jashub,[c] to meet
Ahaz at the end of the aqueduct of the Upper
Pool, on the road to the Launderer's Field.
4 Say to him, 'Be careful, keep calm and don't
be afraid. Do not lose heart because of these
two smoldering stubs of firewood — because
of the fierce anger of Rezin and Aram and of
the son of Remaliah. 5 Aram, Ephraim and
Remaliah's son have plotted your ruin, say-
ing, 6 "Let us invade Judah; let us tear it apart
and divide it among ourselves, and make the

[a] 9,10 Hebrew; Septuagint *'You will be ever hearing, but never understanding; / you will be ever seeing, but never perceiving.' / [10]This people's heart has become calloused; / they hardly hear with their ears, / and they have closed their eyes* [b] 2 Or *has set up camp in* [c] 3 *Shear-Jashub* means *a remnant will return.*

son of Tabeel king over it." 7 Yet this is what
the Sovereign LORD says:

"'It will not take place,
it will not happen,
8 for the head of Aram is Damascus,
and the head of Damascus is only
Rezin.
Within sixty-five years
Ephraim will be too shattered to be a
people.
9 The head of Ephraim is Samaria,
and the head of Samaria is only
Remaliah's son.
If you do not stand firm in your faith,
you will not stand at all.'"

10 Again the LORD spoke to Ahaz, 11 "Ask
the LORD your God for a sign, whether in the
deepest depths or in the highest heights."
12 But Ahaz said, "I will not ask; I will not
put the LORD to the test."
13 Then Isaiah said, "Hear now, you house
of David! Is it not enough to try the patience
of humans? Will you try the patience of my
God also? 14 Therefore the Lord himself will
give you[a] a sign: The virgin[b] will conceive
and give birth to a son, and[c] will call him
Immanuel.[d] 15 He will be eating curds and
honey when he knows enough to reject the
wrong and choose the right, 16 for before the
boy knows enough to reject the wrong and
choose the right, the land of the two kings
you dread will be laid waste. 17 The LORD will
bring on you and on your people and on the
house of your father a time unlike any since
Ephraim broke away from Judah — he will
bring the king of Assyria."

Assyria, the LORD's Instrument

18 In that day the LORD will whistle for
flies from the Nile delta in Egypt and for
bees from the land of Assyria. 19 They will all
come and settle in the steep ravines and in
the crevices in the rocks, on all the thorn-
bushes and at all the water holes. 20 In that
day the Lord will use a razor hired from be-
yond the Euphrates River — the king of As-
syria — to shave your head and private parts,
and to cut off your beard also. 21 In that day, a
person will keep alive a young cow and two
goats. 22 And because of the abundance of
the milk they give, there will be curds to eat.
All who remain in the land will eat curds and
honey. 23 In that day, in every place where
there were a thousand vines worth a thou-
sand silver shekels,[e] there will be only briers
and thorns. 24 Hunters will go there with bow
and arrow, for the land will be covered with
briers and thorns. 25 As for all the hills once
cultivated by the hoe, you will no longer go
there for fear of the briers and thorns; they
will become places where cattle are turned
loose and where sheep run.

Isaiah and His Children as Signs

8 The LORD said to me, "Take a large
scroll and write on it with an ordinary
pen: Maher-Shalal-Hash-Baz."[f] 2 So I called
in Uriah the priest and Zechariah son of Je-
berekiah as reliable witnesses for me. 3 Then
I made love to the prophetess, and she con-
ceived and gave birth to a son. And the LORD
said to me, "Name him Maher-Shalal-Hash-
Baz. 4 For before the boy knows how to say
'My father' or 'My mother,' the wealth of Da-
mascus and the plunder of Samaria will be
carried off by the king of Assyria."
5 The LORD spoke to me again:

6 "Because this people has rejected
the gently flowing waters of Shiloah
and rejoices over Rezin
and the son of Remaliah,
7 therefore the Lord is about to bring
against them
the mighty floodwaters of the
Euphrates —
the king of Assyria with all his pomp.
It will overflow all its channels,
run over all its banks
8 and sweep on into Judah, swirling over it,
passing through it and reaching up to
the neck.
Its outspread wings will cover the
breadth of your land,
Immanuel[d]!"

9 Raise the war cry,[g] you nations, and be
shattered!
Listen, all you distant lands.

[a] 14 The Hebrew is plural. [b] 14 Or *young woman* [c] 14 Masoretic Text; Dead Sea Scrolls *son, and he* or *son, and they* [d] 14,8 *Immanuel* means *God with us.* [e] 23 That is, about 25 pounds or about 12 kilograms [f] 1 *Maher-Shalal-Hash-Baz* means *quick to the plunder, swift to the spoil;* also in verse 3.
[g] 9 Or *Do your worst*

Prepare for battle, and be shattered!
Prepare for battle, and be shattered!
10 Devise your strategy, but it will be thwarted;
propose your plan, but it will not stand,
for God is with us.[a]

11 This is what the LORD says to me with his strong hand upon me, warning me not to follow the way of this people:

12 "Do not call conspiracy
everything this people calls a conspiracy;
do not fear what they fear,
and do not dread it.
13 The LORD Almighty is the one you are to regard as holy,
he is the one you are to fear,
he is the one you are to dread.
14 He will be a holy place;
for both Israel and Judah he will be
a stone that causes people to stumble
and a rock that makes them fall.
And for the people of Jerusalem he will be
a trap and a snare.
15 Many of them will stumble;
they will fall and be broken,
they will be snared and captured."

16 Bind up this testimony of warning
and seal up God's instruction among my disciples.
17 I will wait for the LORD,
who is hiding his face from the descendants of Jacob.
I will put my trust in him.

18 Here am I, and the children the LORD has given me. We are signs and symbols in Israel from the LORD Almighty, who dwells on Mount Zion.

The Darkness Turns to Light

19 When someone tells you to consult mediums and spiritists, who whisper and mutter, should not a people inquire of their God? Why consult the dead on behalf of the living?
20 Consult God's instruction and the testimony of warning. If anyone does not speak according to this word, they have no light of dawn. 21 Distressed and hungry, they will roam through the land; when they are famished, they will become enraged and, looking upward, will curse their king and their God. 22 Then they will look toward the earth and see only distress and darkness and fearful gloom, and they will be thrust into utter darkness.

9 [b] Nevertheless, there will be no more gloom for those who were in distress. In the past he humbled the land of Zebulun and the land of Naphtali, but in the future he will honor Galilee of the nations, by the Way of the Sea, beyond the Jordan —

2 The people walking in darkness
have seen a great light;
on those living in the land of deep darkness
a light has dawned.
3 You have enlarged the nation
and increased their joy;
they rejoice before you
as people rejoice at the harvest,
as warriors rejoice
when dividing the plunder.
4 For as in the day of Midian's defeat,
you have shattered
the yoke that burdens them,
the bar across their shoulders,
the rod of their oppressor.
5 Every warrior's boot used in battle
and every garment rolled in blood
will be destined for burning,
will be fuel for the fire.
6 For to us a child is born,
to us a son is given,
and the government will be on his shoulders.
And he will be called
Wonderful Counselor, Mighty God,
Everlasting Father, Prince of Peace.
7 Of the greatness of his government and peace
there will be no end.
He will reign on David's throne
and over his kingdom,
establishing and upholding it
with justice and righteousness
from that time on and forever.
The zeal of the LORD Almighty
will accomplish this.

The LORD's Anger Against Israel

8 The Lord has sent a message against Jacob;
it will fall on Israel.

[a] 10 Hebrew *Immanuel* [b] In Hebrew texts 9:1 is numbered 8:23, and 9:2-21 is numbered 9:1-20.

9 All the people will know it—
Ephraim and the inhabitants of Samaria—
who say with pride
and arrogance of heart,
10 "The bricks have fallen down,
but we will rebuild with dressed stone;
the fig trees have been felled,
but we will replace them with cedars."
11 But the LORD has strengthened Rezin's foes against them
and has spurred their enemies on.
12 Arameans from the east and Philistines from the west
have devoured Israel with open mouth.

Yet for all this, his anger is not turned away,
his hand is still upraised.

13 But the people have not returned to him who struck them,
nor have they sought the LORD Almighty.
14 So the LORD will cut off from Israel both head and tail,
both palm branch and reed in a single day;
15 the elders and dignitaries are the head,
the prophets who teach lies are the tail.
16 Those who guide this people mislead them,
and those who are guided are led astray.
17 Therefore the Lord will take no pleasure in the young men,
nor will he pity the fatherless and widows,
for everyone is ungodly and wicked,
every mouth speaks folly.

Yet for all this, his anger is not turned away,
his hand is still upraised.

18 Surely wickedness burns like a fire;
it consumes briers and thorns,
it sets the forest thickets ablaze,
so that it rolls upward in a column of smoke.
19 By the wrath of the LORD Almighty
the land will be scorched
and the people will be fuel for the fire;
they will not spare one another.
20 On the right they will devour,
but still be hungry;
on the left they will eat,
but not be satisfied.
Each will feed on the flesh of their own offspring[a]:
21 Manasseh will feed on Ephraim, and Ephraim on Manasseh;
together they will turn against Judah.

Yet for all this, his anger is not turned away,
his hand is still upraised.

10 Woe to those who make unjust laws,
to those who issue oppressive decrees,
2 to deprive the poor of their rights
and withhold justice from the oppressed of my people,
making widows their prey
and robbing the fatherless.
3 What will you do on the day of reckoning,
when disaster comes from afar?
To whom will you run for help?
Where will you leave your riches?
4 Nothing will remain but to cringe among the captives
or fall among the slain.

Yet for all this, his anger is not turned away,
his hand is still upraised.

God's Judgment on Assyria

5 "Woe to the Assyrian, the rod of my anger,
in whose hand is the club of my wrath!
6 I send him against a godless nation,
I dispatch him against a people who anger me,
to seize loot and snatch plunder,
and to trample them down like mud in the streets.
7 But this is not what he intends,
this is not what he has in mind;
his purpose is to destroy,
to put an end to many nations.
8 'Are not my commanders all kings?' he says.
9 'Has not Kalno fared like Carchemish?

[a] 20 Or *arm*

Is not Hamath like Arpad,
and Samaria like Damascus?
10 As my hand seized the kingdoms of the idols,
kingdoms whose images excelled those of Jerusalem and Samaria—
11 shall I not deal with Jerusalem and her images
as I dealt with Samaria and her idols?' "

12 When the Lord has finished all his work
against Mount Zion and Jerusalem, he will
say, "I will punish the king of Assyria for the
willful pride of his heart and the haughty
look in his eyes. 13 For he says:

" 'By the strength of my hand I have done this,
and by my wisdom, because I have understanding.
I removed the boundaries of nations,
I plundered their treasures;
like a mighty one I subdued[a] their kings.
14 As one reaches into a nest,
so my hand reached for the wealth of the nations;
as people gather abandoned eggs,
so I gathered all the countries;
not one flapped a wing,
or opened its mouth to chirp.' "
15 Does the ax raise itself above the person who swings it,
or the saw boast against the one who uses it?
As if a rod were to wield the person who lifts it up,
or a club brandish the one who is not wood!
16 Therefore, the Lord, the LORD Almighty,
will send a wasting disease upon his sturdy warriors;
under his pomp a fire will be kindled
like a blazing flame.
17 The Light of Israel will become a fire,
their Holy One a flame;
in a single day it will burn and consume
his thorns and his briers.
18 The splendor of his forests and fertile fields
it will completely destroy,
as when a sick person wastes away.
19 And the remaining trees of his forests will be so few
that a child could write them down.

The Remnant of Israel

20 In that day the remnant of Israel,
the survivors of Jacob,
will no longer rely on him
who struck them down
but will truly rely on the LORD,
the Holy One of Israel.
21 A remnant will return,[b] a remnant of Jacob
will return to the Mighty God.
22 Though your people be like the sand by the sea, Israel,
only a remnant will return.
Destruction has been decreed,
overwhelming and righteous.
23 The Lord, the LORD Almighty, will carry out
the destruction decreed upon the whole land.

24 Therefore this is what the Lord, the
LORD Almighty, says:

"My people who live in Zion,
do not be afraid of the Assyrians,
who beat you with a rod
and lift up a club against you, as Egypt did.
25 Very soon my anger against you will end
and my wrath will be directed to their destruction."

26 The LORD Almighty will lash them with a whip,
as when he struck down Midian at the rock of Oreb;
and he will raise his staff over the waters,
as he did in Egypt.
27 In that day their burden will be lifted from your shoulders,
their yoke from your neck;
the yoke will be broken
because you have grown so fat.[c]

28 They enter Aiath;
they pass through Migron;
they store supplies at Mikmash.
29 They go over the pass, and say,
"We will camp overnight at Geba."

[a] *13* Or *treasures; / I subdued the mighty,* [b] *21* Hebrew *shear-jashub* (see 7:3 and note); also in verse 22
[c] *27* Hebrew; Septuagint *broken / from your shoulders*

Ramah trembles;
Gibeah of Saul flees.
30 Cry out, Daughter Gallim!
Listen, Laishah!
Poor Anathoth!
31 Madmenah is in flight;
the people of Gebim take cover.
32 This day they will halt at Nob;
they will shake their fist
at the mount of Daughter Zion,
at the hill of Jerusalem.

33 See, the Lord, the LORD Almighty,
will lop off the boughs with great
power.
The lofty trees will be felled,
the tall ones will be brought low.
34 He will cut down the forest thickets with
an ax;
Lebanon will fall before the Mighty
One.

The Branch From Jesse

11 A shoot will come up from the stump
of Jesse;
from his roots a Branch will bear fruit.
2 The Spirit of the LORD will rest on him—
the Spirit of wisdom and of
understanding,
the Spirit of counsel and of might,
the Spirit of the knowledge and fear of
the LORD—
3 and he will delight in the fear of the
LORD.

He will not judge by what he sees with
his eyes,
or decide by what he hears with his
ears;
4 but with righteousness he will judge the
needy,
with justice he will give decisions for
the poor of the earth.
He will strike the earth with the rod of his
mouth;
with the breath of his lips he will slay
the wicked.
5 Righteousness will be his belt
and faithfulness the sash around his
waist.

6 The wolf will live with the lamb,
the leopard will lie down with the goat,
the calf and the lion and the yearling[a]
together;
and a little child will lead them.
7 The cow will feed with the bear,
their young will lie down together,
and the lion will eat straw like the ox.
8 The infant will play near the cobra's den,
and the young child will put its hand
into the viper's nest.
9 They will neither harm nor destroy
on all my holy mountain,
for the earth will be filled with the
knowledge of the LORD
as the waters cover the sea.

10 In that day the Root of Jesse will stand as
a banner for the peoples; the nations will ral-
ly to him, and his resting place will be glori-
ous. 11 In that day the Lord will reach out his
hand a second time to reclaim the surviving
remnant of his people from Assyria, from
Lower Egypt, from Upper Egypt, from Cush,[b]
from Elam, from Babylonia,[c] from Hamath
and from the islands of the Mediterranean.

12 He will raise a banner for the nations
and gather the exiles of Israel;
he will assemble the scattered people of
Judah
from the four quarters of the earth.
13 Ephraim's jealousy will vanish,
and Judah's enemies[d] will be
destroyed;
Ephraim will not be jealous of Judah,
nor Judah hostile toward Ephraim.
14 They will swoop down on the slopes of
Philistia to the west;
together they will plunder the people
to the east.
They will subdue Edom and Moab,
and the Ammonites will be subject to
them.
15 The LORD will dry up
the gulf of the Egyptian sea;
with a scorching wind he will sweep his
hand
over the Euphrates River.
He will break it up into seven streams
so that anyone can cross over in
sandals.
16 There will be a highway for the remnant
of his people
that is left from Assyria,

[a] 6 Hebrew; Septuagint *lion will feed* [b] 11 That is, the upper Nile region [c] 11 Hebrew *Shinar*
[d] 13 Or *hostility*

as there was for Israel
when they came up from Egypt.

Songs of Praise

12 In that day you will say:

"I will praise you, LORD.
Although you were angry with me,
your anger has turned away
and you have comforted me.
2 Surely God is my salvation;
I will trust and not be afraid.
The LORD, the LORD himself, is my
strength and my defense[a];
he has become my salvation."
3 With joy you will draw water
from the wells of salvation.

4 In that day you will say:

"Give praise to the LORD, proclaim his
name;
make known among the nations what
he has done,
and proclaim that his name is exalted.
5 Sing to the LORD, for he has done glorious
things;
let this be known to all the world.
6 Shout aloud and sing for joy, people of
Zion,
for great is the Holy One of Israel
among you."

A Prophecy Against Babylon

13 A prophecy against Babylon that Isa-
iah son of Amoz saw:

2 Raise a banner on a bare hilltop,
shout to them;
beckon to them
to enter the gates of the nobles.
3 I have commanded those I prepared for
battle;
I have summoned my warriors to carry
out my wrath—
those who rejoice in my triumph.
4 Listen, a noise on the mountains,
like that of a great multitude!
Listen, an uproar among the kingdoms,
like nations massing together!
The LORD Almighty is mustering
an army for war.
5 They come from faraway lands,
from the ends of the heavens—
the LORD and the weapons of his wrath—
to destroy the whole country.
6 Wail, for the day of the LORD is near;
it will come like destruction from the
Almighty.[b]
7 Because of this, all hands will go limp,
every heart will melt with fear.
8 Terror will seize them,
pain and anguish will grip them;
they will writhe like a woman in labor.
They will look aghast at each other,
their faces aflame.
9 See, the day of the LORD is coming
—a cruel day, with wrath and fierce
anger—
to make the land desolate
and destroy the sinners within it.
10 The stars of heaven and their
constellations
will not show their light.
The rising sun will be darkened
and the moon will not give its light.
11 I will punish the world for its evil,
the wicked for their sins.
I will put an end to the arrogance of the
haughty
and will humble the pride of the
ruthless.
12 I will make people scarcer than pure
gold,
more rare than the gold of Ophir.
13 Therefore I will make the heavens
tremble;
and the earth will shake from its place
at the wrath of the LORD Almighty,
in the day of his burning anger.
14 Like a hunted gazelle,
like sheep without a shepherd,
they will all return to their own people,
they will flee to their native land.
15 Whoever is captured will be thrust
through;
all who are caught will fall by the
sword.
16 Their infants will be dashed to pieces
before their eyes;
their houses will be looted and their
wives violated.
17 See, I will stir up against them the Medes,
who do not care for silver
and have no delight in gold.

[a] 2 Or *song* [b] 6 Hebrew *Shaddai*

[18] Their bows will strike down the young
men;
they will have no mercy on infants
nor will they look with compassion on
children.
[19] Babylon, the jewel of kingdoms,
the pride and glory of the
Babylonians,[a]
will be overthrown by God
like Sodom and Gomorrah.
[20] She will never be inhabited
or lived in through all generations;
there no nomads will pitch their tents
there no shepherds will rest their
flocks.
[21] But desert creatures will lie there,
jackals will fill her houses;
there the owls will dwell,
and there the wild goats will leap
about.
[22] Hyenas will inhabit her strongholds,
jackals her luxurious palaces.
Her time is at hand,
and her days will not be prolonged.

14 The LORD will have compassion on
Jacob;
once again he will choose Israel
and will settle them in their own land.
Foreigners will join them
and unite with the descendants of
Jacob.
[2] Nations will take them
and bring them to their own place.
And Israel will take possession of the
nations
and make them male and female
servants in the LORD's land.
They will make captives of their captors
and rule over their oppressors.

[3] On the day the LORD gives you relief from
your suffering and turmoil and from the
harsh labor forced on you, [4] you will take up
this taunt against the king of Babylon:

How the oppressor has come to an end!
How his fury[b] has ended!
[5] The LORD has broken the rod of the
wicked,
the scepter of the rulers,
[6] which in anger struck down peoples
with unceasing blows,
and in fury subdued nations
with relentless aggression.
[7] All the lands are at rest and at peace;
they break into singing.
[8] Even the junipers and the cedars of
Lebanon
gloat over you and say,
"Now that you have been laid low,
no one comes to cut us down."

[9] The realm of the dead below is all astir
to meet you at your coming;
it rouses the spirits of the departed to
greet you—
all those who were leaders in the world;
it makes them rise from their thrones—
all those who were kings over the
nations.
[10] They will all respond,
they will say to you,
"You also have become weak, as we are;
you have become like us."
[11] All your pomp has been brought down to
the grave,
along with the noise of your harps;
maggots are spread out beneath you
and worms cover you.

[12] How you have fallen from heaven,
morning star, son of the dawn!
You have been cast down to the earth,
you who once laid low the nations!
[13] You said in your heart,
"I will ascend to the heavens;
I will raise my throne
above the stars of God;
I will sit enthroned on the mount of
assembly,
on the utmost heights of Mount
Zaphon.[c]
[14] I will ascend above the tops of the clouds;
I will make myself like the Most High."
[15] But you are brought down to the realm of
the dead,
to the depths of the pit.
[16] Those who see you stare at you,
they ponder your fate:
"Is this the man who shook the earth
and made kingdoms tremble,

[a] *19* Or *Chaldeans* [b] *4* Dead Sea Scrolls, Septuagint and Syriac; the meaning of the word in the Masoretic Text is uncertain. [c] *13* Or *of the north*; Zaphon was the most sacred mountain of the Canaanites.

17 the man who made the world a
wilderness,
who overthrew its cities
and would not let his captives go
home?"

18 All the kings of the nations lie in state,
each in his own tomb.
19 But you are cast out of your tomb
like a rejected branch;
you are covered with the slain,
with those pierced by the sword,
those who descend to the stones of
the pit.
Like a corpse trampled underfoot,
20 you will not join them in burial,
for you have destroyed your land
and killed your people.

Let the offspring of the wicked
never be mentioned again.
21 Prepare a place to slaughter his children
for the sins of their ancestors;
they are not to rise to inherit the land
and cover the earth with their cities.

22 "I will rise up against them,"
declares the LORD Almighty.
"I will wipe out Babylon's name and
survivors,
her offspring and descendants,"
declares the LORD.
23 "I will turn her into a place for owls
and into swampland;
I will sweep her with the broom of
destruction,"
declares the LORD Almighty.

24 The LORD Almighty has sworn,

"Surely, as I have planned, so it will be,
and as I have purposed, so it will
happen.
25 I will crush the Assyrian in my land;
on my mountains I will trample him
down.
His yoke will be taken from my people,
and his burden removed from their
shoulders."

26 This is the plan determined for the whole
world;
this is the hand stretched out over all
nations.
27 For the LORD Almighty has purposed,
and who can thwart him?
His hand is stretched out, and who can
turn it back?

A Prophecy Against the Philistines

28 This prophecy came in the year King
Ahaz died:

29 Do not rejoice, all you Philistines,
that the rod that struck you is broken;
from the root of that snake will spring up
a viper,
its fruit will be a darting, venomous
serpent.
30 The poorest of the poor will find pasture,
and the needy will lie down in safety.
But your root I will destroy by famine;
it will slay your survivors.

31 Wail, you gate! Howl, you city!
Melt away, all you Philistines!
A cloud of smoke comes from the north,
and there is not a straggler in its ranks.
32 What answer shall be given
to the envoys of that nation?
"The LORD has established Zion,
and in her his afflicted people will find
refuge."

A Prophecy Against Moab

15 A prophecy against Moab:

Ar in Moab is ruined,
destroyed in a night!
Kir in Moab is ruined,
destroyed in a night!
2 Dibon goes up to its temple,
to its high places to weep;
Moab wails over Nebo and Medeba.
Every head is shaved
and every beard cut off.
3 In the streets they wear sackcloth;
on the roofs and in the public squares
they all wail,
prostrate with weeping.
4 Heshbon and Elealeh cry out,
their voices are heard all the way to
Jahaz.
Therefore the armed men of Moab
cry out,
and their hearts are faint.

5 My heart cries out over Moab;
her fugitives flee as far as Zoar,
as far as Eglath Shelishiyah.
They go up the hill to Luhith,
weeping as they go;

on the road to Horonaim
they lament their destruction.
[6]The waters of Nimrim are dried up
and the grass is withered;
the vegetation is gone
and nothing green is left.
[7]So the wealth they have acquired and
stored up
they carry away over the Ravine of the
Poplars.
[8]Their outcry echoes along the border
of Moab;
their wailing reaches as far as Eglaim,
their lamentation as far as Beer Elim.
[9]The waters of Dimon[a] are full of blood,
but I will bring still more upon
Dimon[a]—
a lion upon the fugitives of Moab
and upon those who remain in the
land.

16 Send lambs as tribute
to the ruler of the land,
from Sela, across the desert,
to the mount of Daughter Zion.
[2]Like fluttering birds
pushed from the nest,
so are the women of Moab
at the fords of the Arnon.

[3]"Make up your mind," Moab says.
"Render a decision.
Make your shadow like night—
at high noon.
Hide the fugitives,
do not betray the refugees.
[4]Let the Moabite fugitives stay with you;
be their shelter from the destroyer."

The oppressor will come to an end,
and destruction will cease;
the aggressor will vanish from the land.
[5]In love a throne will be established;
in faithfulness a man will sit on it—
one from the house[b] of David—
one who in judging seeks justice
and speeds the cause of righteousness.

[6]We have heard of Moab's pride—
how great is her arrogance!—
of her conceit, her pride and her
insolence;
but her boasts are empty.
[7]Therefore the Moabites wail,
they wail together for Moab.
Lament and grieve
for the raisin cakes of Kir Hareseth.
[8]The fields of Heshbon wither,
the vines of Sibmah also.
The rulers of the nations
have trampled down the choicest
vines,
which once reached Jazer
and spread toward the desert.
Their shoots spread out
and went as far as the sea.[c]
[9]So I weep, as Jazer weeps,
for the vines of Sibmah.
Heshbon and Elealeh,
I drench you with tears!
The shouts of joy over your ripened fruit
and over your harvests have been
stilled.
[10]Joy and gladness are taken away from the
orchards;
no one sings or shouts in the
vineyards;
no one treads out wine at the presses,
for I have put an end to the shouting.
[11]My heart laments for Moab like a harp,
my inmost being for Kir Hareseth.
[12]When Moab appears at her high place,
she only wears herself out;
when she goes to her shrine to pray,
it is to no avail.

[13]This is the word the LORD has already
spoken concerning Moab. [14]But now the
LORD says: "Within three years, as a servant
bound by contract would count them, Mo-
ab's splendor and all her many people will
be despised, and her survivors will be very
few and feeble."

A Prophecy Against Damascus

17 A prophecy against Damascus:

"See, Damascus will no longer be a city
but will become a heap of ruins.
[2]The cities of Aroer will be deserted
and left to flocks, which will lie down,
with no one to make them afraid.
[3]The fortified city will disappear from
Ephraim,
and royal power from Damascus;

[a] 9 *Dimon,* a wordplay on *Dibon* (see verse 2), sounds like the Hebrew for *blood.* [b] 5 Hebrew *tent*
[c] 8 Probably the Dead Sea

the remnant of Aram will be
like the glory of the Israelites,"
declares the LORD Almighty.

4 "In that day the glory of Jacob will fade;
the fat of his body will waste away.
5 It will be as when reapers harvest the standing grain,
gathering the grain in their arms —
as when someone gleans heads of grain
in the Valley of Rephaim.
6 Yet some gleanings will remain,
as when an olive tree is beaten,
leaving two or three olives on the topmost branches,
four or five on the fruitful boughs,"
declares the LORD, the God of Israel.

7 In that day people will look to their Maker
and turn their eyes to the Holy One of Israel.
8 They will not look to the altars,
the work of their hands,
and they will have no regard for the Asherah poles[a]
and the incense altars their fingers have made.

9 In that day their strong cities, which they
left because of the Israelites, will be like
places abandoned to thickets and under-
growth. And all will be desolation.

10 You have forgotten God your Savior;
you have not remembered the Rock,
your fortress.
Therefore, though you set out the finest plants
and plant imported vines,
11 though on the day you set them out, you make them grow,
and on the morning when you plant them, you bring them to bud,
yet the harvest will be as nothing
in the day of disease and incurable pain.

12 Woe to the many nations that rage —
they rage like the raging sea!
Woe to the peoples who roar —
they roar like the roaring of great waters!
13 Although the peoples roar like the roar of surging waters,
when he rebukes them they flee far away,
driven before the wind like chaff on the hills,
like tumbleweed before a gale.
14 In the evening, sudden terror!
Before the morning, they are gone!
This is the portion of those who loot us,
the lot of those who plunder us.

A Prophecy Against Cush

18 Woe to the land of whirring wings[b]
along the rivers of Cush,[c]
2 which sends envoys by sea
in papyrus boats over the water.

Go, swift messengers,
to a people tall and smooth-skinned,
to a people feared far and wide,
an aggressive nation of strange speech,
whose land is divided by rivers.

3 All you people of the world,
you who live on the earth,
when a banner is raised on the mountains,
you will see it,
and when a trumpet sounds,
you will hear it.
4 This is what the LORD says to me:
"I will remain quiet and will look on
from my dwelling place,
like shimmering heat in the sunshine,
like a cloud of dew in the heat of harvest."
5 For, before the harvest, when the blossom is gone
and the flower becomes a ripening grape,
he will cut off the shoots with pruning knives,
and cut down and take away the spreading branches.
6 They will all be left to the mountain birds of prey
and to the wild animals;
the birds will feed on them all summer,
the wild animals all winter.

7 At that time gifts will be brought to the
LORD Almighty

[a] *8* That is, wooden symbols of the goddess Asherah [b] *1* Or *of locusts* [c] *1* That is, the upper Nile region

from a people tall and smooth-skinned,
from a people feared far and wide,
an aggressive nation of strange speech,
whose land is divided by rivers —
the gifts will be brought to Mount Zion, the place of the Name of the LORD Almighty.

A Prophecy Against Egypt

19 A prophecy against Egypt:

See, the LORD rides on a swift cloud
and is coming to Egypt.
The idols of Egypt tremble before him,
and the hearts of the Egyptians melt
with fear.

2 "I will stir up Egyptian against
Egyptian —
brother will fight against brother,
neighbor against neighbor,
city against city,
kingdom against kingdom.
3 The Egyptians will lose heart,
and I will bring their plans to nothing;
they will consult the idols and the spirits
of the dead,
the mediums and the spiritists.
4 I will hand the Egyptians over
to the power of a cruel master,
and a fierce king will rule over them,"
declares the Lord, the LORD Almighty.

5 The waters of the river will dry up,
and the riverbed will be parched
and dry.
6 The canals will stink;
the streams of Egypt will dwindle and
dry up.
The reeds and rushes will wither,
7 also the plants along the Nile,
at the mouth of the river.
Every sown field along the Nile
will become parched, will blow away
and be no more.
8 The fishermen will groan and lament,
all who cast hooks into the Nile;
those who throw nets on the water
will pine away.
9 Those who work with combed flax will
despair,
the weavers of fine linen will lose
hope.
10 The workers in cloth will be dejected,
and all the wage earners will be sick
at heart.

11 The officials of Zoan are nothing but
fools;
the wise counselors of Pharaoh give
senseless advice.
How can you say to Pharaoh,
"I am one of the wise men,
a disciple of the ancient kings"?
12 Where are your wise men now?
Let them show you and make known
what the LORD Almighty
has planned against Egypt.
13 The officials of Zoan have become fools,
the leaders of Memphis are deceived;
the cornerstones of her peoples
have led Egypt astray.
14 The LORD has poured into them
a spirit of dizziness;
they make Egypt stagger in all that she
does,
as a drunkard staggers around in his
vomit.
15 There is nothing Egypt can do —
head or tail, palm branch or reed.

16 In that day the Egyptians will become
weaklings. They will shudder with fear at the
uplifted hand that the LORD Almighty rais-
es against them. 17 And the land of Judah will
bring terror to the Egyptians; everyone to
whom Judah is mentioned will be terrified,
because of what the LORD Almighty is plan-
ning against them.
18 In that day five cities in Egypt will speak
the language of Canaan and swear alle-
giance to the LORD Almighty. One of them
will be called the City of the Sun.[a]
19 In that day there will be an altar to the
LORD in the heart of Egypt, and a monument
to the LORD at its border. 20 It will be a sign
and witness to the LORD Almighty in the
land of Egypt. When they cry out to the LORD
because of their oppressors, he will send
them a savior and defender, and he will res-
cue them. 21 So the LORD will make himself
known to the Egyptians, and in that day they
will acknowledge the LORD. They will wor-
ship with sacrifices and grain offerings; they
will make vows to the LORD and keep them.

[a] 18 Some manuscripts of the Masoretic Text, Dead Sea Scrolls, Symmachus and Vulgate; most manuscripts of the Masoretic Text *City of Destruction*

22 The LORD will strike Egypt with a plague;
he will strike them and heal them. They will
turn to the LORD, and he will respond to
their pleas and heal them.
23 In that day there will be a highway from
Egypt to Assyria. The Assyrians will go to
Egypt and the Egyptians to Assyria. The
Egyptians and Assyrians will worship to-
gether.
24 In that day Israel will be the third,
along with Egypt and Assyria, a blessing[a] on
the earth.
25 The LORD Almighty will bless
them, saying, "Blessed be Egypt my people,
Assyria my handiwork, and Israel my inher-
itance."

A Prophecy Against Egypt and Cush

20 In the year that the supreme com-
mander, sent by Sargon king of As-
syria, came to Ashdod and attacked and
captured it —
2 at that time the LORD spoke
through Isaiah son of Amoz. He said to him,
"Take off the sackcloth from your body and
the sandals from your feet." And he did so,
going around stripped and barefoot.
3 Then the LORD said, "Just as my servant
Isaiah has gone stripped and barefoot for
three years, as a sign and portent against
Egypt and Cush,[b]
4 so the king of Assyria will
lead away stripped and barefoot the Egyp-
tian captives and Cushite exiles, young and
old, with buttocks bared — to Egypt's shame.
5 Those who trusted in Cush and boasted in
Egypt will be dismayed and put to shame.
6 In that day the people who live on this coast
will say, 'See what has happened to those we
relied on, those we fled to for help and de-
liverance from the king of Assyria! How then
can we escape?' "

A Prophecy Against Babylon

21 A prophecy against the Desert by the
Sea:

Like whirlwinds sweeping through the
southland,
an invader comes from the desert,
from a land of terror.

2 A dire vision has been shown to me:
The traitor betrays, the looter takes
loot.
Elam, attack! Media, lay siege!
I will bring to an end all the groaning
she caused.

3 At this my body is racked with pain,
pangs seize me, like those of a woman
in labor;
I am staggered by what I hear,
I am bewildered by what I see.
4 My heart falters,
fear makes me tremble;
the twilight I longed for
has become a horror to me.

5 They set the tables,
they spread the rugs,
they eat, they drink!
Get up, you officers,
oil the shields!

6 This is what the Lord says to me:

"Go, post a lookout
and have him report what he sees.
7 When he sees chariots
with teams of horses,
riders on donkeys
or riders on camels,
let him be alert,
fully alert."

8 And the lookout[c] shouted,

"Day after day, my lord, I stand on the
watchtower;
every night I stay at my post.
9 Look, here comes a man in a chariot
with a team of horses.
And he gives back the answer:
'Babylon has fallen, has fallen!
All the images of its gods
lie shattered on the ground!' "

10 My people who are crushed on the
threshing floor,
I tell you what I have heard
from the LORD Almighty,
from the God of Israel.

A Prophecy Against Edom

11 A prophecy against Dumah[d]:

Someone calls to me from Seir,
"Watchman, what is left of the night?
Watchman, what is left of the night?"

[a] *24* Or *Assyria, whose names will be used in blessings* (see Gen. 48:20); or *Assyria, who will be seen by others as blessed* [b] *3* That is, the upper Nile region; also in verse 5 [c] *8* Dead Sea Scrolls and Syriac; Masoretic Text *A lion* [d] *11* *Dumah*, a wordplay on *Edom*, means *silence* or *stillness*.

[12]The watchman replies,
"Morning is coming, but also the night.
If you would ask, then ask;
and come back yet again."

A Prophecy Against Arabia

[13]A prophecy against Arabia:

You caravans of Dedanites,
who camp in the thickets of Arabia,
14 bring water for the thirsty;
you who live in Tema,
bring food for the fugitives.
[15]They flee from the sword,
from the drawn sword,
from the bent bow
and from the heat of battle.

[16]This is what the Lord says to me: "Within one year, as a servant bound by contract
would count it, all the splendor of Kedar
will come to an end. [17]The survivors of the
archers, the warriors of Kedar, will be few."
The LORD, the God of Israel, has spoken.

A Prophecy About Jerusalem

22 A prophecy against the Valley of Vision:

What troubles you now,
that you have all gone up on the roofs,
[2]you town so full of commotion,
you city of tumult and revelry?
Your slain were not killed by the sword,
nor did they die in battle.
[3]All your leaders have fled together;
they have been captured without using the bow.
All you who were caught were taken prisoner together,
having fled while the enemy was still far away.
[4]Therefore I said, "Turn away from me;
let me weep bitterly.
Do not try to console me
over the destruction of my people."

[5]The Lord, the LORD Almighty, has a day
of tumult and trampling and terror
in the Valley of Vision,
a day of battering down walls
and of crying out to the mountains.
[6]Elam takes up the quiver,
with her charioteers and horses;
Kir uncovers the shield.
[7]Your choicest valleys are full of chariots,
and horsemen are posted at the city gates.
[8]The Lord stripped away the defenses of Judah,
and you looked in that day
to the weapons in the Palace of the Forest.
[9]You saw that the walls of the City of David
were broken through in many places;
you stored up water
in the Lower Pool.
[10]You counted the buildings in Jerusalem
and tore down houses to strengthen the wall.
[11]You built a reservoir between the two walls
for the water of the Old Pool,
but you did not look to the One who made it,
or have regard for the One who planned it long ago.

[12]The Lord, the LORD Almighty,
called you on that day
to weep and to wail,
to tear out your hair and put on sackcloth.
[13]But see, there is joy and revelry,
slaughtering of cattle and killing of sheep,
eating of meat and drinking of wine!
"Let us eat and drink," you say,
"for tomorrow we die!"

[14]The LORD Almighty has revealed this in my hearing: "Till your dying day this sin will not be atoned for," says the Lord, the LORD Almighty.

[15]This is what the Lord, the LORD Almighty, says:

"Go, say to this steward,
to Shebna the palace administrator:
[16]What are you doing here and who gave you permission
to cut out a grave for yourself here,
hewing your grave on the height
and chiseling your resting place in the rock?

[17]"Beware, the LORD is about to take firm hold of you
and hurl you away, you mighty man.

[18] He will roll you up tightly like a ball
and throw you into a large country.
There you will die
and there the chariots you were so proud of
will become a disgrace to your master's house.
[19] I will depose you from your office,
and you will be ousted from your position.

[20] "In that day I will summon my servant,
Eliakim son of Hilkiah. [21] I will clothe him
with your robe and fasten your sash around
him and hand your authority over to him.
He will be a father to those who live in Je-
rusalem and to the people of Judah. [22] I will
place on his shoulder the key to the house of
David; what he opens no one can shut, and
what he shuts no one can open. [23] I will drive
him like a peg into a firm place; he will be-
come a seat[a] of honor for the house of his
father. [24] All the glory of his family will hang
on him: its offspring and offshoots—all its
lesser vessels, from the bowls to all the jars.

[25] "In that day," declares the LORD Al-
mighty, "the peg driven into the firm place
will give way; it will be sheared off and will
fall, and the load hanging on it will be cut
down." The LORD has spoken.

A Prophecy Against Tyre

23 A prophecy against Tyre:

Wail, you ships of Tarshish!
For Tyre is destroyed
and left without house or harbor.
From the land of Cyprus
word has come to them.

[2] Be silent, you people of the island
and you merchants of Sidon,
whom the seafarers have enriched.
[3] On the great waters
came the grain of the Shihor;
the harvest of the Nile[b] was the revenue of Tyre,
and she became the marketplace of the nations.

[4] Be ashamed, Sidon, and you fortress of the sea,
for the sea has spoken:
"I have neither been in labor nor given birth;
I have neither reared sons nor brought up daughters."
[5] When word comes to Egypt,
they will be in anguish at the report from Tyre.

[6] Cross over to Tarshish;
wail, you people of the island.
[7] Is this your city of revelry,
the old, old city,
whose feet have taken her
to settle in far-off lands?
[8] Who planned this against Tyre,
the bestower of crowns,
whose merchants are princes,
whose traders are renowned in the earth?
[9] The LORD Almighty planned it,
to bring down her pride in all her splendor
and to humble all who are renowned on the earth.

[10] Till[c] your land as they do along the Nile,
Daughter Tarshish,
for you no longer have a harbor.
[11] The LORD has stretched out his hand over the sea
and made its kingdoms tremble.
He has given an order concerning Phoenicia
that her fortresses be destroyed.
[12] He said, "No more of your reveling,
Virgin Daughter Sidon, now crushed!

"Up, cross over to Cyprus;
even there you will find no rest."
[13] Look at the land of the Babylonians,[d]
this people that is now of no account!
The Assyrians have made it
a place for desert creatures;
they raised up their siege towers,
they stripped its fortresses bare
and turned it into a ruin.

[14] Wail, you ships of Tarshish;
your fortress is destroyed!

[15] At that time Tyre will be forgotten for
seventy years, the span of a king's life. But at

[a] 23 Or *throne* [b] 2,3 Masoretic Text; Dead Sea Scrolls *Sidon, / who cross over the sea; / your envoys* [3] *are on the great waters. / The grain of the Shihor, / the harvest of the Nile,* [c] 10 Dead Sea Scrolls and some Septuagint manuscripts; Masoretic Text *Go through* [d] 13 Or *Chaldeans*

the end of these seventy years, it will happen
to Tyre as in the song of the prostitute:

16 "Take up a harp, walk through the city,
you forgotten prostitute;
play the harp well, sing many a song,
so that you will be remembered."

17 At the end of seventy years, the LORD
will deal with Tyre. She will return to her
lucrative prostitution and will ply her trade
with all the kingdoms on the face of the
earth. 18 Yet her profit and her earnings will
be set apart for the LORD; they will not be
stored up or hoarded. Her profits will go to
those who live before the LORD, for abundant food and fine clothes.

The LORD's Devastation of the Earth

24 See, the LORD is going to lay waste the earth
and devastate it;
he will ruin its face
and scatter its inhabitants—
2 it will be the same
for priest as for people,
for the master as for his servant,
for the mistress as for her servant,
for seller as for buyer,
for borrower as for lender,
for debtor as for creditor.
3 The earth will be completely laid waste
and totally plundered.
The LORD has spoken this word.

4 The earth dries up and withers,
the world languishes and withers,
the heavens languish with the earth.
5 The earth is defiled by its people;
they have disobeyed the laws,
violated the statutes
and broken the everlasting covenant.
6 Therefore a curse consumes the earth;
its people must bear their guilt.
Therefore earth's inhabitants are burned up,
and very few are left.
7 The new wine dries up and the vine withers;
all the merrymakers groan.
8 The joyful timbrels are stilled,
the noise of the revelers has stopped,
the joyful harp is silent.
9 No longer do they drink wine with a song;
the beer is bitter to its drinkers.
10 The ruined city lies desolate;
the entrance to every house is barred.
11 In the streets they cry out for wine;
all joy turns to gloom,
all joyful sounds are banished from the earth.
12 The city is left in ruins,
its gate is battered to pieces.
13 So will it be on the earth
and among the nations,
as when an olive tree is beaten,
or as when gleanings are left after the grape harvest.

14 They raise their voices, they shout for joy;
from the west they acclaim the LORD's majesty.
15 Therefore in the east give glory to the LORD;
exalt the name of the LORD, the God of Israel,
in the islands of the sea.
16 From the ends of the earth we hear singing:
"Glory to the Righteous One."

But I said, "I waste away, I waste away!
Woe to me!
The treacherous betray!
With treachery the treacherous betray!"
17 Terror and pit and snare await you,
people of the earth.
18 Whoever flees at the sound of terror
will fall into a pit;
whoever climbs out of the pit
will be caught in a snare.

The floodgates of the heavens are opened,
the foundations of the earth shake.
19 The earth is broken up,
the earth is split asunder,
the earth is violently shaken.
20 The earth reels like a drunkard,
it sways like a hut in the wind;
so heavy upon it is the guilt of its rebellion
that it falls—never to rise again.

21 In that day the LORD will punish
the powers in the heavens above
and the kings on the earth below.
22 They will be herded together
like prisoners bound in a dungeon;

they will be shut up in prison
and be punished[a] after many days.
23 The moon will be dismayed,
the sun ashamed;
for the LORD Almighty will reign
on Mount Zion and in Jerusalem,
and before its elders — with great glory.

Praise to the LORD

25 LORD, you are my God;
I will exalt you and praise your name,
for in perfect faithfulness
you have done wonderful things,
things planned long ago.
2 You have made the city a heap of rubble,
the fortified town a ruin,
the foreigners' stronghold a city no more;
it will never be rebuilt.
3 Therefore strong peoples will honor you;
cities of ruthless nations will revere you.
4 You have been a refuge for the poor,
a refuge for the needy in their distress,
a shelter from the storm
and a shade from the heat.
For the breath of the ruthless
is like a storm driving against a wall
5 and like the heat of the desert.
You silence the uproar of foreigners;
as heat is reduced by the shadow of a cloud,
so the song of the ruthless is stilled.

6 On this mountain the LORD Almighty will prepare
a feast of rich food for all peoples,
a banquet of aged wine —
the best of meats and the finest of wines.
7 On this mountain he will destroy
the shroud that enfolds all peoples,
the sheet that covers all nations;
8 he will swallow up death forever.
The Sovereign LORD will wipe away the tears
from all faces;
he will remove his people's disgrace
from all the earth.
The LORD has spoken.
9 In that day they will say,

"Surely this is our God;
we trusted in him, and he saved us.
This is the LORD, we trusted in him;
let us rejoice and be glad in his salvation."
10 The hand of the LORD will rest on this mountain;
but Moab will be trampled in their land
as straw is trampled down in the manure.
11 They will stretch out their hands in it,
as swimmers stretch out their hands to swim.
God will bring down their pride
despite the cleverness[b] of their hands.
12 He will bring down your high fortified walls
and lay them low;
he will bring them down to the ground,
to the very dust.

A Song of Praise

26 In that day this song will be sung in the land of Judah:

We have a strong city;
God makes salvation
its walls and ramparts.
2 Open the gates
that the righteous nation may enter,
the nation that keeps faith.
3 You will keep in perfect peace
those whose minds are steadfast,
because they trust in you.
4 Trust in the LORD forever,
for the LORD, the LORD himself, is the Rock eternal.
5 He humbles those who dwell on high,
he lays the lofty city low;
he levels it to the ground
and casts it down to the dust.
6 Feet trample it down —
the feet of the oppressed,
the footsteps of the poor.

7 The path of the righteous is level;
you, the Upright One, make the way of the righteous smooth.
8 Yes, LORD, walking in the way of your laws,[c]
we wait for you;
your name and renown
are the desire of our hearts.

[a] 22 Or *released* [b] 11 The meaning of the Hebrew for this word is uncertain. [c] 8 Or *judgments*

[9]My soul yearns for you in the night;
in the morning my spirit longs for you.
When your judgments come upon the earth,
the people of the world learn righteousness.
[10]But when grace is shown to the wicked,
they do not learn righteousness;
even in a land of uprightness they go on doing evil
and do not regard the majesty of the LORD.
[11]LORD, your hand is lifted high,
but they do not see it.
Let them see your zeal for your people and be put to shame;
let the fire reserved for your enemies consume them.

[12]LORD, you establish peace for us;
all that we have accomplished you have done for us.
[13]LORD our God, other lords besides you have ruled over us,
but your name alone do we honor.
[14]They are now dead, they live no more;
their spirits do not rise.
You punished them and brought them to ruin;
you wiped out all memory of them.
[15]You have enlarged the nation, LORD;
you have enlarged the nation.
You have gained glory for yourself;
you have extended all the borders of the land.

[16]LORD, they came to you in their distress;
when you disciplined them,
they could barely whisper a prayer.[a]
[17]As a pregnant woman about to give birth
writhes and cries out in her pain,
so were we in your presence, LORD.
[18]We were with child, we writhed in labor,
but we gave birth to wind.
We have not brought salvation to the earth,
and the people of the world have not come to life.

[19]But your dead will live, LORD;
their bodies will rise —
let those who dwell in the dust
wake up and shout for joy —
your dew is like the dew of the morning;
the earth will give birth to her dead.

[20]Go, my people, enter your rooms
and shut the doors behind you;
hide yourselves for a little while
until his wrath has passed by.
[21]See, the LORD is coming out of his dwelling
to punish the people of the earth for their sins.
The earth will disclose the blood shed on it;
the earth will conceal its slain no longer.

Deliverance of Israel

27 In that day,

the LORD will punish with his sword —
his fierce, great and powerful sword —
Leviathan the gliding serpent,
Leviathan the coiling serpent;
he will slay the monster of the sea.

[2]In that day —
"Sing about a fruitful vineyard:
[3]I, the LORD, watch over it;
I water it continually.
I guard it day and night
so that no one may harm it.
[4]I am not angry.
If only there were briers and thorns confronting me!
I would march against them in battle;
I would set them all on fire.
[5]Or else let them come to me for refuge;
let them make peace with me,
yes, let them make peace with me."

[6]In days to come Jacob will take root,
Israel will bud and blossom
and fill all the world with fruit.

[7]Has the LORD struck her
as he struck down those who struck her?
Has she been killed
as those were killed who killed her?
[8]By warfare[b] and exile you contend with her —
with his fierce blast he drives her out,
as on a day the east wind blows.

[a] *16* The meaning of the Hebrew for this clause is uncertain. [b] *8* See Septuagint; the meaning of the Hebrew for this word is uncertain.

BEAUTIFUL THINGS

Michael Gungor, Lisa Gungor

All this pain
I wonder if I'll ever find my way
I wonder if my life
Could really
Change at all

All this earth
Could all that is lost
Ever be found
Could a garden come up from this
Ground at all

You make beautiful things
You make beautiful things
Out of the dust
You make beautiful things
You make beautiful things out of us

All around
Hope is springing up
From this old ground
Out of chaos life is being
Found in you

You make me new
You are making me new

THE INSPIRATION

"See, I will create new heavens and a new earth. The former things will not be remembered, nor will they come to mind."

—Isaiah 65:17

BEHIND THE SONG

Pain is rarely the subject of contemporary worship songs, but "Beautiful Things" by Michael and Lisa Gungor is no ordinary worship song. Through their band, Gungor, Michael and Lisa stretch musical and thematic boundaries with each new record and every live appearance. Every Gungor song is worshipful in its own way, but "Beautiful Things," a plaintive observation of God's ability to bring order to chaos and healing to wounds, is exceptional.

"We had been seeing a lot of pain in the world and had been experiencing a lot of it in ourselves and in our community," Michael explains. "This is a song that acknowledges the pain. But there is also a ray of hope within that pain — that God is not distanced from it but is very present with us. He is able to take the dust and breathe life into pain and suffering and make something beautiful — even out of the things that look the most chaotic and ugly."

The prophet Isaiah spoke for God when God promised that, in time, he would make all things new. Isaiah spoke of a time when people would not even remember the pain of this world. There would be no tears. Everything broken about this world would be healed; everything dead would be resurrected.

Some Christians struggle with articulating their pain and brokenness. They may feel that expressing those emotions betrays a lack of faith on their part. Are there wounds in your past that prevent you from fully entering into worship? Sing or speak the lyrics to "Beautiful Things," and read the passage from Isaiah. Then ask God to help you express your woundedness and receive his healing and comfort.

[9]By this, then, will Jacob's guilt be
atoned for,
and this will be the full fruit of the
removal of his sin:
When he makes all the altar stones
to be like limestone crushed to pieces,
no Asherah poles[a] or incense altars
will be left standing.
[10]The fortified city stands desolate,
an abandoned settlement, forsaken
like the wilderness;
there the calves graze,
there they lie down;
they strip its branches bare.
[11]When its twigs are dry, they are
broken off
and women come and make fires with
them.
For this is a people without
understanding;
so their Maker has no compassion on
them,
and their Creator shows them no favor.

[12]In that day the LORD will thresh from
the flowing Euphrates to the Wadi of Egypt,
and you, Israel, will be gathered up one by
one. [13]And in that day a great trumpet will
sound. Those who were perishing in Assyr-
ia and those who were exiled in Egypt will
come and worship the LORD on the holy
mountain in Jerusalem.

Woe to the Leaders of Ephraim and Judah

28 Woe to that wreath, the pride of
Ephraim's drunkards,
to the fading flower, his glorious
beauty,
set on the head of a fertile valley —
to that city, the pride of those laid low
by wine!
[2]See, the Lord has one who is powerful
and strong.
Like a hailstorm and a destructive
wind,
like a driving rain and a flooding
downpour,
he will throw it forcefully to the
ground.
[3]That wreath, the pride of Ephraim's
drunkards,
will be trampled underfoot.
[4]That fading flower, his glorious beauty,
set on the head of a fertile valley,
will be like figs ripe before harvest —
as soon as people see them and take
them in hand,
they swallow them.

[5]In that day the LORD Almighty
will be a glorious crown,
a beautiful wreath
for the remnant of his people.
[6]He will be a spirit of justice
to the one who sits in judgment,
a source of strength
to those who turn back the battle at
the gate.

[7]And these also stagger from wine
and reel from beer:
Priests and prophets stagger from beer
and are befuddled with wine;
they reel from beer,
they stagger when seeing visions,
they stumble when rendering
decisions.
[8]All the tables are covered with vomit
and there is not a spot without filth.

[9]"Who is it he is trying to teach?
To whom is he explaining his message?
To children weaned from their milk,
to those just taken from the breast?
[10]For it is:
Do this, do that,
a rule for this, a rule for that[b];
a little here, a little there."

[11]Very well then, with foreign lips and
strange tongues
God will speak to this people,
[12]to whom he said,
"This is the resting place, let the
weary rest";
and, "This is the place of repose" —
but they would not listen.
[13]So then, the word of the LORD to them
will become:
Do this, do that,
a rule for this, a rule for that;
a little here, a little there —
so that as they go they will fall
backward;

[a] 9 That is, wooden symbols of the goddess Asherah
[b] *10* Hebrew / *sav lasav sav lasav / kav lakav kav lakav* (probably meaningless sounds mimicking the prophet's words); also in verse 13

they will be injured and snared and
captured.
[14]Therefore hear the word of the LORD, you
scoffers
who rule this people in Jerusalem.
[15]You boast, "We have entered into a
covenant with death,
with the realm of the dead we have
made an agreement.
When an overwhelming scourge
sweeps by,
it cannot touch us,
for we have made a lie our refuge
and falsehood[a] our hiding place."

[16]So this is what the Sovereign LORD says:

"See, I lay a stone in Zion, a tested stone,
a precious cornerstone for a sure
foundation;
the one who relies on it
will never be stricken with panic.
[17]I will make justice the measuring line
and righteousness the plumb line;
hail will sweep away your refuge, the lie,
and water will overflow your hiding
place.
[18]Your covenant with death will be
annulled;
your agreement with the realm of the
dead will not stand.
When the overwhelming scourge
sweeps by,
you will be beaten down by it.
[19]As often as it comes it will carry you away;
morning after morning, by day and
by night,
it will sweep through."

The understanding of this message
will bring sheer terror.
[20]The bed is too short to stretch out on,
the blanket too narrow to wrap
around you.
[21]The LORD will rise up as he did at Mount
Perazim,
he will rouse himself as in the Valley of
Gibeon —
to do his work, his strange work,
and perform his task, his alien task.
[22]Now stop your mocking,
or your chains will become heavier;
the Lord, the LORD Almighty, has told me
of the destruction decreed against the
whole land.

[23]Listen and hear my voice;
pay attention and hear what I say.
[24]When a farmer plows for planting, does
he plow continually?
Does he keep on breaking up and
working the soil?
[25]When he has leveled the surface,
does he not sow caraway and scatter
cumin?
Does he not plant wheat in its place,[b]
barley in its plot,[b]
and spelt in its field?
[26]His God instructs him
and teaches him the right way.

[27]Caraway is not threshed with a sledge,
nor is the wheel of a cart rolled over
cumin;
caraway is beaten out with a rod,
and cumin with a stick.
[28]Grain must be ground to make bread;
so one does not go on threshing it
forever.
The wheels of a threshing cart may be
rolled over it,
but one does not use horses to grind
grain.
[29]All this also comes from the LORD
Almighty,
whose plan is wonderful,
whose wisdom is magnificent.

Woe to David's City

29 Woe to you, Ariel, Ariel,
the city where David settled!
Add year to year
and let your cycle of festivals go on.
[2]Yet I will besiege Ariel;
she will mourn and lament,
she will be to me like an altar hearth.[c]
[3]I will encamp against you on all sides;
I will encircle you with towers
and set up my siege works against you.
[4]Brought low, you will speak from the
ground;
your speech will mumble out of the
dust.
Your voice will come ghostlike from the
earth;

[a] 15 Or *false gods* [b] 25 The meaning of the Hebrew for this word is uncertain. [c] 2 The Hebrew for *altar hearth* sounds like the Hebrew for *Ariel.*

out of the dust your speech will
whisper.

[5] But your many enemies will become like
fine dust,
the ruthless hordes like blown chaff.
Suddenly, in an instant,
[6] the LORD Almighty will come
with thunder and earthquake and great
noise,
with windstorm and tempest and
flames of a devouring fire.
[7] Then the hordes of all the nations that
fight against Ariel,
that attack her and her fortress and
besiege her,
will be as it is with a dream,
with a vision in the night—
[8] as when a hungry person dreams of
eating,
but awakens hungry still;
as when a thirsty person dreams of
drinking,
but awakens faint and thirsty still.
So will it be with the hordes of all the
nations
that fight against Mount Zion.

[9] Be stunned and amazed,
blind yourselves and be sightless;
be drunk, but not from wine,
stagger, but not from beer.
[10] The LORD has brought over you a deep
sleep:
He has sealed your eyes (the prophets);
he has covered your heads (the seers).

[11] For you this whole vision is nothing
but words sealed in a scroll. And if you give
the scroll to someone who can read, and
say, "Read this, please," they will answer, "I
can't; it is sealed." [12] Or if you give the scroll
to someone who cannot read, and say, "Read
this, please," they will answer, "I don't know
how to read."

[13] The Lord says:

"These people come near to me with
their mouth
and honor me with their lips,
but their hearts are far from me.
Their worship of me
is based on merely human rules they
have been taught.[a]
[14] Therefore once more I will astound these
people
with wonder upon wonder;
the wisdom of the wise will perish,
the intelligence of the intelligent will
vanish."
[15] Woe to those who go to great depths
to hide their plans from the LORD,
who do their work in darkness and think,
"Who sees us? Who will know?"
[16] You turn things upside down,
as if the potter were thought to be like
the clay!
Shall what is formed say to the one who
formed it,
"You did not make me"?
Can the pot say to the potter,
"You know nothing"?

[17] In a very short time, will not Lebanon be
turned into a fertile field
and the fertile field seem like a forest?
[18] In that day the deaf will hear the words of
the scroll,
and out of gloom and darkness
the eyes of the blind will see.
[19] Once more the humble will rejoice in the
LORD;
the needy will rejoice in the Holy One
of Israel.
[20] The ruthless will vanish,
the mockers will disappear,
and all who have an eye for evil will be
cut down—
[21] those who with a word make someone
out to be guilty,
who ensnare the defender in court
and with false testimony deprive the
innocent of justice.

[22] Therefore this is what the LORD, who re-
deemed Abraham, says to the descendants
of Jacob:

"No longer will Jacob be ashamed;
no longer will their faces grow pale.
[23] When they see among them their
children,
the work of my hands,
they will keep my name holy;
they will acknowledge the holiness of
the Holy One of Jacob,
and will stand in awe of the God of
Israel.

[a] *13* Hebrew; Septuagint *They worship me in vain; / their teachings are merely human rules*

[24]Those who are wayward in spirit will
gain understanding;
those who complain will accept
instruction."

Woe to the Obstinate Nation

30 "Woe to the obstinate children,"
declares the LORD,
"to those who carry out plans that are not
mine,
forming an alliance, but not by my
Spirit,
heaping sin upon sin;
[2]who go down to Egypt
without consulting me;
who look for help to Pharaoh's protection,
to Egypt's shade for refuge.
[3]But Pharaoh's protection will be to your
shame,
Egypt's shade will bring you disgrace.
[4]Though they have officials in Zoan
and their envoys have arrived in
Hanes,
[5]everyone will be put to shame
because of a people useless to them,
who bring neither help nor advantage,
but only shame and disgrace."

[6]A prophecy concerning the animals of
the Negev:

Through a land of hardship and distress,
of lions and lionesses,
of adders and darting snakes,
the envoys carry their riches on donkeys'
backs,
their treasures on the humps of
camels,
to that unprofitable nation,
[7] to Egypt, whose help is utterly useless.
Therefore I call her
Rahab the Do-Nothing.
[8]Go now, write it on a tablet for them,
inscribe it on a scroll,
that for the days to come
it may be an everlasting witness.
[9]For these are rebellious people, deceitful
children,
children unwilling to listen to the
LORD's instruction.
[10]They say to the seers,
"See no more visions!"
and to the prophets,
"Give us no more visions of what
is right!
Tell us pleasant things,
prophesy illusions.
[11]Leave this way,
get off this path,
and stop confronting us
with the Holy One of Israel!"

[12]Therefore this is what the Holy One of
Israel says:

"Because you have rejected this message,
relied on oppression
and depended on deceit,
[13]this sin will become for you
like a high wall, cracked and bulging,
that collapses suddenly, in an instant.
[14]It will break in pieces like pottery,
shattered so mercilessly
that among its pieces not a fragment will
be found
for taking coals from a hearth
or scooping water out of a cistern."

[15]This is what the Sovereign LORD, the
Holy One of Israel, says:

"In repentance and rest is your salvation,
in quietness and trust is your strength,
but you would have none of it.
[16]You said, 'No, we will flee on horses.'
Therefore you will flee!
You said, 'We will ride off on swift
horses.'
Therefore your pursuers will be swift!
[17]A thousand will flee
at the threat of one;
at the threat of five
you will all flee away,
till you are left
like a flagstaff on a mountaintop,
like a banner on a hill."

[18]Yet the LORD longs to be gracious to you;
therefore he will rise up to show you
compassion.
For the LORD is a God of justice.
Blessed are all who wait for him!

[19]People of Zion, who live in Jerusalem,
you will weep no more. How gracious he
will be when you cry for help! As soon as he
hears, he will answer you. [20]Although the
Lord gives you the bread of adversity and
the water of affliction, your teachers will be
hidden no more; with your own eyes you will
see them. [21]Whether you turn to the right or
to the left, your ears will hear a voice behind

you, saying, "This is the way; walk in it."
22Then you will desecrate your idols overlaid with silver and your images covered with gold; you will throw them away like a menstrual cloth and say to them, "Away with you!"

23He will also send you rain for the seed you sow in the ground, and the food that comes from the land will be rich and plentiful. In that day your cattle will graze in broad
meadows. 24The oxen and donkeys that work the soil will eat fodder and mash, spread out
with fork and shovel. 25In the day of great slaughter, when the towers fall, streams of water will flow on every high mountain and
every lofty hill. 26The moon will shine like the sun, and the sunlight will be seven times brighter, like the light of seven full days, when the LORD binds up the bruises of his people and heals the wounds he inflicted.

27See, the Name of the LORD comes from afar,
with burning anger and dense clouds of smoke;
his lips are full of wrath,
and his tongue is a consuming fire.
28His breath is like a rushing torrent,
rising up to the neck.
He shakes the nations in the sieve of destruction;
he places in the jaws of the peoples
a bit that leads them astray.
29And you will sing
as on the night you celebrate a holy festival;
your hearts will rejoice
as when people playing pipes go up
to the mountain of the LORD,
to the Rock of Israel.
30The LORD will cause people to hear his majestic voice
and will make them see his arm coming down
with raging anger and consuming fire,
with cloudburst, thunderstorm and hail.
31The voice of the LORD will shatter Assyria;
with his rod he will strike them down.
32Every stroke the LORD lays on them
with his punishing club
will be to the music of timbrels and harps,
as he fights them in battle with the blows of his arm.
33Topheth has long been prepared;
it has been made ready for the king.
Its fire pit has been made deep and wide,
with an abundance of fire and wood;
the breath of the LORD,
like a stream of burning sulfur,
sets it ablaze.

Woe to Those Who Rely on Egypt

31 Woe to those who go down to Egypt for help,
who rely on horses,
who trust in the multitude of their chariots
and in the great strength of their horsemen,
but do not look to the Holy One of Israel,
or seek help from the LORD.
2Yet he too is wise and can bring disaster;
he does not take back his words.
He will rise up against that wicked nation,
against those who help evildoers.
3But the Egyptians are mere mortals and not God;
their horses are flesh and not spirit.
When the LORD stretches out his hand,
those who help will stumble,
those who are helped will fall;
all will perish together.

4This is what the LORD says to me:

"As a lion growls,
a great lion over its prey—
and though a whole band of shepherds
is called together against it,
it is not frightened by their shouts
or disturbed by their clamor—
so the LORD Almighty will come down
to do battle on Mount Zion and on its heights.
5Like birds hovering overhead,
the LORD Almighty will shield Jerusalem;
he will shield it and deliver it,
he will 'pass over' it and will rescue it."

6Return, you Israelites, to the One you
have so greatly revolted against. 7For in that
day every one of you will reject the idols of silver and gold your sinful hands have made.

8 "Assyria will fall by no human sword;
a sword, not of mortals, will devour them.
They will flee before the sword
and their young men will be put to forced labor.
9 Their stronghold will fall because of terror;
at the sight of the battle standard their commanders will panic,"
declares the LORD,
whose fire is in Zion,
whose furnace is in Jerusalem.

The Kingdom of Righteousness

32 See, a king will reign in righteousness
and rulers will rule with justice.
2 Each one will be like a shelter from the wind
and a refuge from the storm,
like streams of water in the desert
and the shadow of a great rock in a thirsty land.
3 Then the eyes of those who see will no longer be closed,
and the ears of those who hear will listen.
4 The fearful heart will know and understand,
and the stammering tongue will be fluent and clear.
5 No longer will the fool be called noble
nor the scoundrel be highly respected.
6 For fools speak folly,
their hearts are bent on evil:
They practice ungodliness
and spread error concerning the LORD;
the hungry they leave empty
and from the thirsty they withhold water.
7 Scoundrels use wicked methods,
they make up evil schemes
to destroy the poor with lies,
even when the plea of the needy is just.
8 But the noble make noble plans,
and by noble deeds they stand.

The Women of Jerusalem

9 You women who are so complacent,
rise up and listen to me;
you daughters who feel secure,
hear what I have to say!
10 In little more than a year
you who feel secure will tremble;
the grape harvest will fail,
and the harvest of fruit will not come.
11 Tremble, you complacent women;
shudder, you daughters who feel secure!
Strip off your fine clothes
and wrap yourselves in rags.
12 Beat your breasts for the pleasant fields,
for the fruitful vines
13 and for the land of my people,
a land overgrown with thorns and briers —
yes, mourn for all houses of merriment
and for this city of revelry.
14 The fortress will be abandoned,
the noisy city deserted;
citadel and watchtower will become a wasteland forever,
the delight of donkeys, a pasture for flocks,
15 till the Spirit is poured on us from on high,
and the desert becomes a fertile field,
and the fertile field seems like a forest.
16 The LORD's justice will dwell in the desert,
his righteousness live in the fertile field.
17 The fruit of that righteousness will be peace;
its effect will be quietness and confidence forever.
18 My people will live in peaceful dwelling places,
in secure homes,
in undisturbed places of rest.
19 Though hail flattens the forest
and the city is leveled completely,
20 how blessed you will be,
sowing your seed by every stream,
and letting your cattle and donkeys range free.

Distress and Help

33 Woe to you, destroyer,
you who have not been destroyed!
Woe to you, betrayer,
you who have not been betrayed!
When you stop destroying,
you will be destroyed;
when you stop betraying,
you will be betrayed.

2 LORD, be gracious to us;
we long for you.

Be our strength every morning,
our salvation in time of distress.
3 At the uproar of your army, the peoples flee;
when you rise up, the nations scatter.
4 Your plunder, O nations, is harvested as by young locusts;
like a swarm of locusts people pounce on it.

5 The LORD is exalted, for he dwells on high;
he will fill Zion with his justice and righteousness.
6 He will be the sure foundation for your times,
a rich store of salvation and wisdom and knowledge;
the fear of the LORD is the key to this treasure.[a]

7 Look, their brave men cry aloud in the streets;
the envoys of peace weep bitterly.
8 The highways are deserted,
no travelers are on the roads.
The treaty is broken,
its witnesses[b] are despised,
no one is respected.
9 The land dries up and wastes away,
Lebanon is ashamed and withers;
Sharon is like the Arabah,
and Bashan and Carmel drop their leaves.

10 "Now will I arise," says the LORD.
"Now will I be exalted;
now will I be lifted up.
11 You conceive chaff,
you give birth to straw;
your breath is a fire that consumes you.
12 The peoples will be burned to ashes;
like cut thornbushes they will be set ablaze."

13 You who are far away, hear what I have done;
you who are near, acknowledge my power!
14 The sinners in Zion are terrified;
trembling grips the godless:
"Who of us can dwell with the consuming fire?
Who of us can dwell with everlasting burning?"
15 Those who walk righteously
and speak what is right,
who reject gain from extortion
and keep their hands from accepting bribes,
who stop their ears against plots of murder
and shut their eyes against contemplating evil—
16 they are the ones who will dwell on the heights,
whose refuge will be the mountain fortress.
Their bread will be supplied,
and water will not fail them.
17 Your eyes will see the king in his beauty
and view a land that stretches afar.
18 In your thoughts you will ponder the former terror:
"Where is that chief officer?
Where is the one who took the revenue?
Where is the officer in charge of the towers?"
19 You will see those arrogant people no more,
people whose speech is obscure,
whose language is strange and incomprehensible.

20 Look on Zion, the city of our festivals;
your eyes will see Jerusalem,
a peaceful abode, a tent that will not be moved;
its stakes will never be pulled up,
nor any of its ropes broken.
21 There the LORD will be our Mighty One.
It will be like a place of broad rivers and streams.
No galley with oars will ride them,
no mighty ship will sail them.
22 For the LORD is our judge,
the LORD is our lawgiver,
the LORD is our king;
it is he who will save us.

23 Your rigging hangs loose:
The mast is not held secure,
the sail is not spread.
Then an abundance of spoils will be divided
and even the lame will carry off plunder.

[a] 6 Or *is a treasure from him* [b] 8 Dead Sea Scrolls; Masoretic Text / *the cities*

[24]No one living in Zion will say, "I am ill";
and the sins of those who dwell there
will be forgiven.

Judgment Against the Nations

34 Come near, you nations, and listen;
pay attention, you peoples!
Let the earth hear, and all that is in it,
the world, and all that comes out of it!
[2]The LORD is angry with all nations;
his wrath is on all their armies.
He will totally destroy[a] them,
he will give them over to slaughter.
[3]Their slain will be thrown out,
their dead bodies will stink;
the mountains will be soaked with
their blood.
[4]All the stars in the sky will be dissolved
and the heavens rolled up like a scroll;
all the starry host will fall
like withered leaves from the vine,
like shriveled figs from the fig tree.

[5]My sword has drunk its fill in the
heavens;
see, it descends in judgment on Edom,
the people I have totally destroyed.
[6]The sword of the LORD is bathed in blood,
it is covered with fat—
the blood of lambs and goats,
fat from the kidneys of rams.
For the LORD has a sacrifice in Bozrah
and a great slaughter in the land of
Edom.
[7]And the wild oxen will fall with them,
the bull calves and the great bulls.
Their land will be drenched with blood,
and the dust will be soaked with fat.

[8]For the LORD has a day of vengeance,
a year of retribution, to uphold Zion's
cause.
[9]Edom's streams will be turned into pitch,
her dust into burning sulfur;
her land will become blazing pitch!
[10]It will not be quenched night or day;
its smoke will rise forever.
From generation to generation it will lie
desolate;
no one will ever pass through it again.
[11]The desert owl[b] and screech owl[b] will
possess it;
the great owl[b] and the raven will nest
there.
God will stretch out over Edom
the measuring line of chaos
and the plumb line of desolation.
[12]Her nobles will have nothing there to be
called a kingdom,
all her princes will vanish away.
[13]Thorns will overrun her citadels,
nettles and brambles her strongholds.
She will become a haunt for jackals,
a home for owls.
[14]Desert creatures will meet with hyenas,
and wild goats will bleat to each other;
there the night creatures will also lie
down
and find for themselves places of rest.
[15]The owl will nest there and lay eggs,
she will hatch them, and care for her
young
under the shadow of her wings;
there also the falcons will gather,
each with its mate.

[16]Look in the scroll of the LORD and read:

None of these will be missing,
not one will lack her mate.
For it is his mouth that has given the
order,
and his Spirit will gather them
together.
[17]He allots their portions;
his hand distributes them by measure.
They will possess it forever
and dwell there from generation to
generation.

Joy of the Redeemed

35 The desert and the parched land
will be glad;
the wilderness will rejoice and
blossom.
Like the crocus, [2]it will burst into bloom;
it will rejoice greatly and shout for joy.
The glory of Lebanon will be given to it,
the splendor of Carmel and Sharon;
they will see the glory of the LORD,
the splendor of our God.

[3]Strengthen the feeble hands,
steady the knees that give way;
[4]say to those with fearful hearts,

[a] *2* The Hebrew term refers to the irrevocable giving over of things or persons to the LORD, often by totally destroying them; also in verse 5. [b] *11* The precise identification of these birds is uncertain.

"Be strong, do not fear;
your God will come,
he will come with vengeance;
with divine retribution
he will come to save you."

5 Then will the eyes of the blind be opened
and the ears of the deaf unstopped.
6 Then will the lame leap like a deer,
and the mute tongue shout for joy.
Water will gush forth in the wilderness
and streams in the desert.
7 The burning sand will become a pool,
the thirsty ground bubbling springs.
In the haunts where jackals once lay,
grass and reeds and papyrus will grow.

8 And a highway will be there;
it will be called the Way of Holiness;
it will be for those who walk on
that Way.
The unclean will not journey on it;
wicked fools will not go about on it.
9 No lion will be there,
nor any ravenous beast;
they will not be found there.
But only the redeemed will walk there,
10 and those the LORD has rescued will
return.
They will enter Zion with singing;
everlasting joy will crown their heads.
Gladness and joy will overtake them,
and sorrow and sighing will flee away.

Sennacherib Threatens Jerusalem

36 In the fourteenth year of King Hez-
ekiah's reign, Sennacherib king of
Assyria attacked all the fortified cities of
Judah and captured them. 2 Then the king
of Assyria sent his field commander with a
large army from Lachish to King Hezekiah at
Jerusalem. When the commander stopped at
the aqueduct of the Upper Pool, on the road
to the Launderer's Field, 3 Eliakim son of Hil-
kiah the palace administrator, Shebna the
secretary, and Joah son of Asaph the record-
er went out to him.

4 The field commander said to them, "Tell
Hezekiah:

"'This is what the great king, the
king of Assyria, says: On what are you
basing this confidence of yours? 5 You
say you have counsel and might for
war—but you speak only empty words.
On whom are you depending, that you
rebel against me? 6 Look, I know you
are depending on Egypt, that splint-
ered reed of a staff, which pierces the
hand of anyone who leans on it! Such
is Pharaoh king of Egypt to all who de-
pend on him. 7 But if you say to me, "We
are depending on the LORD our God"—
isn't he the one whose high places and
altars Hezekiah removed, saying to Ju-
dah and Jerusalem, "You must worship
before this altar"?

8 "'Come now, make a bargain with
my master, the king of Assyria: I will
give you two thousand horses—if you
can put riders on them! 9 How then can
you repulse one officer of the least of
my master's officials, even though you
are depending on Egypt for chariots
and horsemen[a]? 10 Furthermore, have
I come to attack and destroy this land
without the LORD? The LORD himself
told me to march against this country
and destroy it.'"

11 Then Eliakim, Shebna and Joah said to
the field commander, "Please speak to your
servants in Aramaic, since we understand it.
Don't speak to us in Hebrew in the hearing of
the people on the wall."

12 But the commander replied, "Was it
only to your master and you that my master
sent me to say these things, and not to the
people sitting on the wall—who, like you,
will have to eat their own excrement and
drink their own urine?"

13 Then the commander stood and called
out in Hebrew, "Hear the words of the great
king, the king of Assyria! 14 This is what the
king says: Do not let Hezekiah deceive you.
He cannot deliver you! 15 Do not let Hezeki-
ah persuade you to trust in the LORD when
he says, 'The LORD will surely deliver us; this
city will not be given into the hand of the
king of Assyria.'

16 "Do not listen to Hezekiah. This is what
the king of Assyria says: Make peace with me
and come out to me. Then each of you will
eat fruit from your own vine and fig tree and
drink water from your own cistern, 17 until I
come and take you to a land like your own—
a land of grain and new wine, a land of bread
and vineyards.

[a] 9 Or *charioteers*

18 "Do not let Hezekiah mislead you when
he says, 'The LORD will deliver us.' Have
the gods of any nations ever delivered their
lands from the hand of the king of Assyria?
19 Where are the gods of Hamath and Arpad?
Where are the gods of Sepharvaim? Have
they rescued Samaria from my hand? 20 Who
of all the gods of these countries have been
able to save their lands from me? How then
can the LORD deliver Jerusalem from my
hand?"

21 But the people remained silent and said
nothing in reply, because the king had com-
manded, "Do not answer him."

22 Then Eliakim son of Hilkiah the palace
administrator, Shebna the secretary and
Joah son of Asaph the recorder went to Hez-
ekiah, with their clothes torn, and told him
what the field commander had said.

Jerusalem's Deliverance Foretold

37 When King Hezekiah heard this,
he tore his clothes and put on sack-
cloth and went into the temple of the LORD.
2 He sent Eliakim the palace administra-
tor, Shebna the secretary, and the leading
priests, all wearing sackcloth, to the prophet
Isaiah son of Amoz. 3 They told him, "This is
what Hezekiah says: This day is a day of dis-
tress and rebuke and disgrace, as when chil-
dren come to the moment of birth and there
is no strength to deliver them. 4 It may be that
the LORD your God will hear the words of
the field commander, whom his master, the
king of Assyria, has sent to ridicule the liv-
ing God, and that he will rebuke him for the
words the LORD your God has heard. There-
fore pray for the remnant that still survives."

5 When King Hezekiah's officials came to
Isaiah, 6 Isaiah said to them, "Tell your mas-
ter, 'This is what the LORD says: Do not be
afraid of what you have heard — those words
with which the underlings of the king of As-
syria have blasphemed me. 7 Listen! When
he hears a certain report, I will make him
want to return to his own country, and there
I will have him cut down with the sword.'"

8 When the field commander heard that
the king of Assyria had left Lachish, he with-
drew and found the king fighting against
Libnah.

9 Now Sennacherib received a report that
Tirhakah, the king of Cush,[a] was marching
out to fight against him. When he heard it, he
sent messengers to Hezekiah with this word:
10 "Say to Hezekiah king of Judah: Do not let
the god you depend on deceive you when he
says, 'Jerusalem will not be given into the
hands of the king of Assyria.' 11 Surely you
have heard what the kings of Assyria have
done to all the countries, destroying them
completely. And will you be delivered? 12 Did
the gods of the nations that were destroyed
by my predecessors deliver them — the gods
of Gozan, Harran, Rezeph and the people of
Eden who were in Tel Assar? 13 Where is the
king of Hamath or the king of Arpad? Where
are the kings of Lair, Sepharvaim, Hena and
Ivvah?"

Hezekiah's Prayer

14 Hezekiah received the letter from the
messengers and read it. Then he went up to
the temple of the LORD and spread it out be-
fore the LORD. 15 And Hezekiah prayed to the
LORD: 16 "LORD Almighty, the God of Israel,
enthroned between the cherubim, you alone
are God over all the kingdoms of the earth.
You have made heaven and earth. 17 Give ear,
LORD, and hear; open your eyes, LORD, and
see; listen to all the words Sennacherib has
sent to ridicule the living God.

18 "It is true, LORD, that the Assyrian kings
have laid waste all these peoples and their
lands. 19 They have thrown their gods into
the fire and destroyed them, for they were
not gods but only wood and stone, fashioned
by human hands. 20 Now, LORD our God, de-
liver us from his hand, so that all the king-
doms of the earth may know that you, LORD,
are the only God.[b]"

Sennacherib's Fall

21 Then Isaiah son of Amoz sent a message
to Hezekiah: "This is what the LORD, the God
of Israel, says: Because you have prayed to
me concerning Sennacherib king of Assyr-
ia, 22 this is the word the LORD has spoken
against him:

"Virgin Daughter Zion
    despises and mocks you.
Daughter Jerusalem
    tosses her head as you flee.

[a] 9 That is, the upper Nile region [b] 20 Dead Sea Scrolls (see also 2 Kings 19:19); Masoretic Text *you alone are the LORD*

23 Who is it you have ridiculed and
blasphemed?
Against whom have you raised your
voice
and lifted your eyes in pride?
Against the Holy One of Israel!
24 By your messengers
you have ridiculed the Lord.
And you have said,
'With my many chariots
I have ascended the heights of the
mountains,
the utmost heights of Lebanon.
I have cut down its tallest cedars,
the choicest of its junipers.
I have reached its remotest heights,
the finest of its forests.
25 I have dug wells in foreign lands[a]
and drunk the water there.
With the soles of my feet
I have dried up all the streams of
Egypt.'
26 "Have you not heard?
Long ago I ordained it.
In days of old I planned it;
now I have brought it to pass,
that you have turned fortified cities
into piles of stone.
27 Their people, drained of power,
are dismayed and put to shame.
They are like plants in the field,
like tender green shoots,
like grass sprouting on the roof,
scorched[b] before it grows up.

28 "But I know where you are
and when you come and go
and how you rage against me.
29 Because you rage against me
and because your insolence has
reached my ears,
I will put my hook in your nose
and my bit in your mouth,
and I will make you return
by the way you came.

30 "This will be the sign for you, Hezekiah:

"This year you will eat what grows by
itself,
and the second year what springs
from that.
But in the third year sow and reap,
plant vineyards and eat their fruit.
31 Once more a remnant of the kingdom of
Judah
will take root below and bear fruit
above.
32 For out of Jerusalem will come a
remnant,
and out of Mount Zion a band of
survivors.
The zeal of the LORD Almighty
will accomplish this.

33 "Therefore this is what the LORD says
concerning the king of Assyria:

"He will not enter this city
or shoot an arrow here.
He will not come before it with shield
or build a siege ramp against it.
34 By the way that he came he will return;
he will not enter this city,"
declares the LORD.
35 "I will defend this city and save it,
for my sake and for the sake of David
my servant!"

36 Then the angel of the LORD went out and
put to death a hundred and eighty-five thou-
sand in the Assyrian camp. When the peo-
ple got up the next morning—there were all
the dead bodies! 37 So Sennacherib king of
Assyria broke camp and withdrew. He re-
turned to Nineveh and stayed there.
38 One day, while he was worshiping in the
temple of his god Nisrok, his sons Adramme-
lek and Sharezer killed him with the sword,
and they escaped to the land of Ararat. And
Esarhaddon his son succeeded him as king.

Hezekiah's Illness

38 In those days Hezekiah became ill
and was at the point of death. The
prophet Isaiah son of Amoz went to him and
said, "This is what the LORD says: Put your
house in order, because you are going to die;
you will not recover."
2 Hezekiah turned his face to the wall and
prayed to the LORD, 3 "Remember, LORD,
how I have walked before you faithfully and
with wholehearted devotion and have done
what is good in your eyes." And Hezekiah
wept bitterly.

[a] 25 Dead Sea Scrolls (see also 2 Kings 19:24); Masoretic Text does not have *in foreign lands.* [b] 27 Some manuscripts of the Masoretic Text, Dead Sea Scrolls and some Septuagint manuscripts (see also 2 Kings 19:26); most manuscripts of the Masoretic Text *roof / and terraced fields*

[4]Then the word of the LORD came to Isa-
iah: [5]"Go and tell Hezekiah, 'This is what the
LORD, the God of your father David, says: I
have heard your prayer and seen your tears;
I will add fifteen years to your life. [6]And I will
deliver you and this city from the hand of the
king of Assyria. I will defend this city.
[7]" 'This is the LORD's sign to you that the
LORD will do what he has promised: [8]I will
make the shadow cast by the sun go back the
ten steps it has gone down on the stairway
of Ahaz.' " So the sunlight went back the ten
steps it had gone down.

[9]A writing of Hezekiah king of Judah after
his illness and recovery:

[10]I said, "In the prime of my life
must I go through the gates of death
and be robbed of the rest of my years?"
[11]I said, "I will not again see the LORD
himself
in the land of the living;
no longer will I look on my fellow man,
or be with those who now dwell in this
world.
[12]Like a shepherd's tent my house
has been pulled down and taken
from me.
Like a weaver I have rolled up my life,
and he has cut me off from the loom;
day and night you made an end of me.
[13]I waited patiently till dawn,
but like a lion he broke all my bones;
day and night you made an end of me.
[14]I cried like a swift or thrush,
I moaned like a mourning dove.
My eyes grew weak as I looked to the
heavens.
I am being threatened; Lord, come to
my aid!"

[15]But what can I say?
He has spoken to me, and he himself
has done this.
I will walk humbly all my years
because of this anguish of my soul.
[16]Lord, by such things people live;
and my spirit finds life in them too.
You restored me to health
and let me live.
[17]Surely it was for my benefit
that I suffered such anguish.
In your love you kept me
from the pit of destruction;
you have put all my sins
behind your back.
[18]For the grave cannot praise you,
death cannot sing your praise;
those who go down to the pit
cannot hope for your faithfulness.
[19]The living, the living—they praise you,
as I am doing today;
parents tell their children
about your faithfulness.

[20]The LORD will save me,
and we will sing with stringed
instruments
all the days of our lives
in the temple of the LORD.

[21]Isaiah had said, "Prepare a poultice of
figs and apply it to the boil, and he will re-
cover."
[22]Hezekiah had asked, "What will be the
sign that I will go up to the temple of the
LORD?"

Envoys From Babylon

39 At that time Marduk-Baladan son of
Baladan king of Babylon sent Heze-
kiah letters and a gift, because he had heard
of his illness and recovery. [2]Hezekiah re-
ceived the envoys gladly and showed them
what was in his storehouses—the silver, the
gold, the spices, the fine olive oil—his entire
armory and everything found among his
treasures. There was nothing in his palace
or in all his kingdom that Hezekiah did not
show them.
[3]Then Isaiah the prophet went to King
Hezekiah and asked, "What did those men
say, and where did they come from?"
"From a distant land," Hezekiah replied.
"They came to me from Babylon."
[4]The prophet asked, "What did they see in
your palace?"
"They saw everything in my palace," Hez-
ekiah said. "There is nothing among my
treasures that I did not show them."
[5]Then Isaiah said to Hezekiah, "Hear the
word of the LORD Almighty: [6]The time will
surely come when everything in your pal-
ace and all that your predecessors have
stored up until this day, will be carried off to
Babylon. Nothing will be left, says the LORD.
[7]And some of your descendants, your own
flesh and blood who will be born to you, will

be taken away, and they will become eunuchs in the palace of the king of Babylon."
8 "The word of the LORD you have spoken is good," Hezekiah replied. For he thought, "There will be peace and security in my lifetime."

Comfort for God's People

40 Comfort, comfort my people,
says your God.
2 Speak tenderly to Jerusalem,
and proclaim to her
that her hard service has been completed,
that her sin has been paid for,
that she has received from the LORD's hand
double for all her sins.

3 A voice of one calling:
"In the wilderness prepare
the way for the LORD[a];
make straight in the desert
a highway for our God.[b]
4 Every valley shall be raised up,
every mountain and hill made low;
the rough ground shall become level,
the rugged places a plain.
5 And the glory of the LORD will be revealed,
and all people will see it together.
For the mouth of the LORD has spoken."

6 A voice says, "Cry out."
And I said, "What shall I cry?"

"All people are like grass,
and all their faithfulness is like the flowers of the field.
7 The grass withers and the flowers fall,
because the breath of the LORD blows on them.
Surely the people are grass.
8 The grass withers and the flowers fall,
but the word of our God endures forever."

9 You who bring good news to Zion,
go up on a high mountain.
You who bring good news to Jerusalem,[c]
lift up your voice with a shout,
lift it up, do not be afraid;
say to the towns of Judah,
"Here is your God!"
10 See, the Sovereign LORD comes with power,
and he rules with a mighty arm.
See, his reward is with him,
and his recompense accompanies him.
11 He tends his flock like a shepherd:
He gathers the lambs in his arms
and carries them close to his heart;
he gently leads those that have young.

12 Who has measured the waters in the hollow of his hand,
or with the breadth of his hand marked off the heavens?
Who has held the dust of the earth in a basket,
or weighed the mountains on the scales
and the hills in a balance?
13 Who can fathom the Spirit[d] of the LORD,
or instruct the LORD as his counselor?
14 Whom did the LORD consult to enlighten him,
and who taught him the right way?
Who was it that taught him knowledge,
or showed him the path of understanding?

15 Surely the nations are like a drop in a bucket;
they are regarded as dust on the scales;
he weighs the islands as though they were fine dust.
16 Lebanon is not sufficient for altar fires,
nor its animals enough for burnt offerings.
17 Before him all the nations are as nothing;
they are regarded by him as worthless
and less than nothing.

18 With whom, then, will you compare God?
To what image will you liken him?
19 As for an idol, a metalworker casts it,
and a goldsmith overlays it with gold
and fashions silver chains for it.
20 A person too poor to present such an offering
selects wood that will not rot;
they look for a skilled worker
to set up an idol that will not topple.

[a] 3 Or *A voice of one calling in the wilderness: / "Prepare the way for the LORD* [b] 3 Hebrew; Septuagint *make straight the paths of our God* [c] 9 Or *Zion, bringer of good news, / go up on a high mountain. / Jerusalem, bringer of good news* [d] 13 Or *mind*

21 Do you not know?
Have you not heard?
Has it not been told you from the beginning?
Have you not understood since the earth was founded?
22 He sits enthroned above the circle of the earth,
and its people are like grasshoppers.
He stretches out the heavens like a canopy,
and spreads them out like a tent to live in.
23 He brings princes to naught
and reduces the rulers of this world to nothing.
24 No sooner are they planted,
no sooner are they sown,
no sooner do they take root in the ground,
than he blows on them and they wither,
and a whirlwind sweeps them away like chaff.

25 "To whom will you compare me?
Or who is my equal?" says the Holy One.
26 Lift up your eyes and look to the heavens:
Who created all these?
He who brings out the starry host one by one
and calls forth each of them by name.
Because of his great power and mighty strength,
not one of them is missing.

27 Why do you complain, Jacob?
Why do you say, Israel,
"My way is hidden from the LORD;
my cause is disregarded by my God"?
28 Do you not know?
Have you not heard?
The LORD is the everlasting God,
the Creator of the ends of the earth.
He will not grow tired or weary,
and his understanding no one can fathom.
29 He gives strength to the weary
and increases the power of the weak.
30 Even youths grow tired and weary,
and young men stumble and fall;
31 but those who hope in the LORD
will renew their strength.
They will soar on wings like eagles;
they will run and not grow weary,
they will walk and not be faint.

The Helper of Israel

41 "Be silent before me, you islands!
Let the nations renew their strength!
Let them come forward and speak;
let us meet together at the place of judgment.

2 "Who has stirred up one from the east,
calling him in righteousness to his service[a]?
He hands nations over to him
and subdues kings before him.
He turns them to dust with his sword,
to windblown chaff with his bow.
3 He pursues them and moves on unscathed,
by a path his feet have not traveled before.
4 Who has done this and carried it through,
calling forth the generations from the beginning?
I, the LORD—with the first of them
and with the last—I am he."

5 The islands have seen it and fear;
the ends of the earth tremble.
They approach and come forward;
6 they help each other
and say to their companions, "Be strong!"
7 The metalworker encourages the goldsmith,
and the one who smooths with the hammer
spurs on the one who strikes the anvil.
One says of the welding, "It is good."
The other nails down the idol so it will not topple.

8 "But you, Israel, my servant,
Jacob, whom I have chosen,
you descendants of Abraham my friend,
9 I took you from the ends of the earth,
from its farthest corners I called you.
I said, 'You are my servant';
I have chosen you and have not rejected you.

[a] 2 Or *east, / whom victory meets at every step*

[10] So do not fear, for I am with you;
do not be dismayed, for I am your God.
I will strengthen you and help you;
I will uphold you with my righteous right hand.

[11] "All who rage against you
will surely be ashamed and disgraced;
those who oppose you
will be as nothing and perish.
[12] Though you search for your enemies,
you will not find them.
Those who wage war against you
will be as nothing at all.
[13] For I am the LORD your God
who takes hold of your right hand
and says to you, Do not fear;
I will help you.
[14] Do not be afraid, you worm Jacob,
little Israel, do not fear,
for I myself will help you," declares the LORD,
your Redeemer, the Holy One of Israel.
[15] "See, I will make you into a threshing sledge,
new and sharp, with many teeth.
You will thresh the mountains and crush them,
and reduce the hills to chaff.
[16] You will winnow them, the wind will pick them up,
and a gale will blow them away.
But you will rejoice in the LORD
and glory in the Holy One of Israel.

[17] "The poor and needy search for water,
but there is none;
their tongues are parched with thirst.
But I the LORD will answer them;
I, the God of Israel, will not forsake them.
[18] I will make rivers flow on barren heights,
and springs within the valleys.
I will turn the desert into pools of water,
and the parched ground into springs.
[19] I will put in the desert
the cedar and the acacia, the myrtle and the olive.
I will set junipers in the wasteland,
the fir and the cypress together,
[20] so that people may see and know,
may consider and understand,
that the hand of the LORD has done this,
that the Holy One of Israel has created it.

[21] "Present your case," says the LORD.
"Set forth your arguments," says Jacob's King.
[22] "Tell us, you idols,
what is going to happen.
Tell us what the former things were,
so that we may consider them
and know their final outcome.
Or declare to us the things to come,
[23] tell us what the future holds,
so we may know that you are gods.
Do something, whether good or bad,
so that we will be dismayed and filled with fear.
[24] But you are less than nothing
and your works are utterly worthless;
whoever chooses you is detestable.

[25] "I have stirred up one from the north, and he comes —
one from the rising sun who calls on my name.
He treads on rulers as if they were mortar,
as if he were a potter treading the clay.
[26] Who told of this from the beginning, so we could know,
or beforehand, so we could say, 'He was right'?
No one told of this,
no one foretold it,
no one heard any words from you.
[27] I was the first to tell Zion, 'Look, here they are!'
I gave to Jerusalem a messenger of good news.
[28] I look but there is no one —
no one among the gods to give counsel,
no one to give answer when I ask them.
[29] See, they are all false!
Their deeds amount to nothing;
their images are but wind and confusion.

The Servant of the LORD

42 "Here is my servant, whom I uphold,
my chosen one in whom I delight;
I will put my Spirit on him,
and he will bring justice to the nations.
[2] He will not shout or cry out,
or raise his voice in the streets.
[3] A bruised reed he will not break,
and a smoldering wick he will not snuff out.

In faithfulness he will bring forth justice;
4 he will not falter or be discouraged
till he establishes justice on earth.
In his teaching the islands will put
their hope."

5 This is what God the LORD says—
the Creator of the heavens, who stretches
them out,
who spreads out the earth with all that
springs from it,
who gives breath to its people,
and life to those who walk on it:
6 "I, the LORD, have called you in
righteousness;
I will take hold of your hand.
I will keep you and will make you
to be a covenant for the people
and a light for the Gentiles,
7 to open eyes that are blind,
to free captives from prison
and to release from the dungeon those
who sit in darkness.

8 "I am the LORD; that is my name!
I will not yield my glory to another
or my praise to idols.
9 See, the former things have taken place,
and new things I declare;
before they spring into being
I announce them to you."

Song of Praise to the LORD

10 Sing to the LORD a new song,
his praise from the ends of the earth,
you who go down to the sea, and all that
is in it,
you islands, and all who live in them.
11 Let the wilderness and its towns raise
their voices;
let the settlements where Kedar lives
rejoice.
Let the people of Sela sing for joy;
let them shout from the mountaintops.
12 Let them give glory to the LORD
and proclaim his praise in the islands.
13 The LORD will march out like a
champion,
like a warrior he will stir up his zeal;
with a shout he will raise the battle cry
and will triumph over his enemies.

14 "For a long time I have kept silent,
I have been quiet and held myself back.
But now, like a woman in childbirth,
I cry out, I gasp and pant.
15 I will lay waste the mountains and hills
and dry up all their vegetation;
I will turn rivers into islands
and dry up the pools.
16 I will lead the blind by ways they have not
known,
along unfamiliar paths I will guide
them;
I will turn the darkness into light before
them
and make the rough places smooth.
These are the things I will do;
I will not forsake them.
17 But those who trust in idols,
who say to images, 'You are our gods,'
will be turned back in utter shame.

Israel Blind and Deaf

18 "Hear, you deaf;
look, you blind, and see!
19 Who is blind but my servant,
and deaf like the messenger I send?
Who is blind like the one in covenant
with me,
blind like the servant of the LORD?
20 You have seen many things, but you pay
no attention;
your ears are open, but you do not
listen."
21 It pleased the LORD
for the sake of his righteousness
to make his law great and glorious.
22 But this is a people plundered and looted,
all of them trapped in pits
or hidden away in prisons.
They have become plunder,
with no one to rescue them;
they have been made loot,
with no one to say, "Send them back."

23 Which of you will listen to this
or pay close attention in time to come?
24 Who handed Jacob over to become loot,
and Israel to the plunderers?
Was it not the LORD,
against whom we have sinned?
For they would not follow his ways;
they did not obey his law.
25 So he poured out on them his burning
anger,
the violence of war.
It enveloped them in flames, yet they did
not understand;
it consumed them, but they did not
take it to heart.

Israel's Only Savior

43 But now, this is what the LORD says—
he who created you, Jacob,
he who formed you, Israel:
"Do not fear, for I have redeemed you;
I have summoned you by name; you are mine.
2 When you pass through the waters,
I will be with you;
and when you pass through the rivers,
they will not sweep over you.
When you walk through the fire,
you will not be burned;
the flames will not set you ablaze.
3 For I am the LORD your God,
the Holy One of Israel, your Savior;
I give Egypt for your ransom,
Cush[a] and Seba in your stead.
4 Since you are precious and honored in my sight,
and because I love you,
I will give people in exchange for you,
nations in exchange for your life.
5 Do not be afraid, for I am with you;
I will bring your children from the east
and gather you from the west.
6 I will say to the north, 'Give them up!'
and to the south, 'Do not hold them back.'
Bring my sons from afar
and my daughters from the ends of the earth—
7 everyone who is called by my name,
whom I created for my glory,
whom I formed and made."

8 Lead out those who have eyes but are blind,
who have ears but are deaf.
9 All the nations gather together
and the peoples assemble.
Which of their gods foretold this
and proclaimed to us the former things?
Let them bring in their witnesses to prove they were right,
so that others may hear and say, "It is true."
10 "You are my witnesses," declares the LORD,
"and my servant whom I have chosen,
so that you may know and believe me
and understand that I am he.
Before me no god was formed,
nor will there be one after me.
11 I, even I, am the LORD,
and apart from me there is no savior.
12 I have revealed and saved and proclaimed—
I, and not some foreign god among you.
You are my witnesses," declares the LORD, "that I am God.
13 Yes, and from ancient days I am he.
No one can deliver out of my hand.
When I act, who can reverse it?"

God's Mercy and Israel's Unfaithfulness

14 This is what the LORD says—
your Redeemer, the Holy One of Israel:
"For your sake I will send to Babylon
and bring down as fugitives all the Babylonians,[b]
in the ships in which they took pride.
15 I am the LORD, your Holy One,
Israel's Creator, your King."

16 This is what the LORD says—
he who made a way through the sea,
a path through the mighty waters,
17 who drew out the chariots and horses,
the army and reinforcements together,
and they lay there, never to rise again,
extinguished, snuffed out like a wick:
18 "Forget the former things;
do not dwell on the past.
19 See, I am doing a new thing!
Now it springs up; do you not perceive it?
I am making a way in the wilderness
and streams in the wasteland.
20 The wild animals honor me,
the jackals and the owls,
because I provide water in the wilderness
and streams in the wasteland,
to give drink to my people, my chosen,
21 the people I formed for myself
that they may proclaim my praise.

22 "Yet you have not called on me, Jacob,
you have not wearied yourselves for[c] me, Israel.
23 You have not brought me sheep for burnt offerings,
nor honored me with your sacrifices.
I have not burdened you with grain offerings

[a] 3 That is, the upper Nile region [b] 14 Or *Chaldeans* [c] 22 Or *Jacob; / surely you have grown weary of*

nor wearied you with demands for
incense.
24 You have not bought any fragrant
calamus for me,
or lavished on me the fat of your
sacrifices.
But you have burdened me with your sins
and wearied me with your offenses.
25 "I, even I, am he who blots out
your transgressions, for my own
sake,
and remembers your sins no more.
26 Review the past for me,
let us argue the matter together;
state the case for your innocence.
27 Your first father sinned;
those I sent to teach you rebelled
against me.
28 So I disgraced the dignitaries of your
temple;
I consigned Jacob to destruction[a]
and Israel to scorn.

Israel the Chosen

44 "But now listen, Jacob, my servant,
Israel, whom I have chosen.
2 This is what the LORD says —
he who made you, who formed you in
the womb,
and who will help you:
Do not be afraid, Jacob, my servant,
Jeshurun,[b] whom I have chosen.
3 For I will pour water on the thirsty land,
and streams on the dry ground;
I will pour out my Spirit on your
offspring,
and my blessing on your descendants.
4 They will spring up like grass in a
meadow,
like poplar trees by flowing streams.
5 Some will say, 'I belong to the LORD';
others will call themselves by the
name of Jacob;
still others will write on their hand, 'The
LORD's,'
and will take the name Israel.

The LORD, Not Idols

6 "This is what the LORD says —
Israel's King and Redeemer, the LORD
Almighty:
I am the first and I am the last;
apart from me there is no God.
7 Who then is like me? Let him proclaim it.
Let him declare and lay out before me
what has happened since I established
my ancient people,
and what is yet to come —
yes, let them foretell what will come.
8 Do not tremble, do not be afraid.
Did I not proclaim this and foretell it
long ago?
You are my witnesses. Is there any God
besides me?
No, there is no other Rock; I know
not one."

9 All who make idols are nothing,
and the things they treasure are
worthless.
Those who would speak up for them are
blind;
they are ignorant, to their own shame.
10 Who shapes a god and casts an idol,
which can profit nothing?
11 People who do that will be put to shame;
such craftsmen are only human
beings.
Let them all come together and take their
stand;
they will be brought down to terror
and shame.

12 The blacksmith takes a tool
and works with it in the coals;
he shapes an idol with hammers,
he forges it with the might of his arm.
He gets hungry and loses his strength;
he drinks no water and grows faint.
13 The carpenter measures with a line
and makes an outline with a
marker;
he roughs it out with chisels
and marks it with compasses.
He shapes it in human form,
human form in all its glory,
that it may dwell in a shrine.
14 He cut down cedars,
or perhaps took a cypress or oak.
He let it grow among the trees of the
forest,
or planted a pine, and the rain made
it grow.

[a] *28* The Hebrew term refers to the irrevocable giving over of things or persons to the LORD, often by totally destroying them. [b] *2* *Jeshurun* means *the upright one*, that is, Israel.

[15] It is used as fuel for burning;
some of it he takes and warms himself,
he kindles a fire and bakes bread.
But he also fashions a god and worships it;
he makes an idol and bows down to it.
[16] Half of the wood he burns in the fire;
over it he prepares his meal,
he roasts his meat and eats his fill.
He also warms himself and says,
"Ah! I am warm; I see the fire."
[17] From the rest he makes a god, his idol;
he bows down to it and worships.
He prays to it and says,
"Save me! You are my god!"
[18] They know nothing, they understand nothing;
their eyes are plastered over so they cannot see,
and their minds closed so they cannot understand.
[19] No one stops to think,
no one has the knowledge or understanding to say,
"Half of it I used for fuel;
I even baked bread over its coals,
I roasted meat and I ate.
Shall I make a detestable thing from what is left?
Shall I bow down to a block of wood?"
[20] Such a person feeds on ashes; a deluded heart misleads him;
he cannot save himself, or say,
"Is not this thing in my right hand a lie?"

[21] "Remember these things, Jacob,
for you, Israel, are my servant.
I have made you, you are my servant;
Israel, I will not forget you.
[22] I have swept away your offenses like a cloud,
your sins like the morning mist.
Return to me,
for I have redeemed you."

[23] Sing for joy, you heavens, for the LORD has done this;
shout aloud, you earth beneath.
Burst into song, you mountains,
you forests and all your trees,
for the LORD has redeemed Jacob,
he displays his glory in Israel.

Jerusalem to Be Inhabited

[24] "This is what the LORD says—
your Redeemer, who formed you in the womb:

I am the LORD,
the Maker of all things,
who stretches out the heavens,
who spreads out the earth by myself,
[25] who foils the signs of false prophets
and makes fools of diviners,
who overthrows the learning of the wise
and turns it into nonsense,
[26] who carries out the words of his servants
and fulfills the predictions of his messengers,

who says of Jerusalem, 'It shall be inhabited,'
of the towns of Judah, 'They shall be rebuilt,'
and of their ruins, 'I will restore them,'
[27] who says to the watery deep, 'Be dry,
and I will dry up your streams,'
[28] who says of Cyrus, 'He is my shepherd
and will accomplish all that I please;
he will say of Jerusalem, "Let it be rebuilt,"
and of the temple, "Let its foundations be laid." '

45 "This is what the LORD says to his anointed,
to Cyrus, whose right hand I take hold of
to subdue nations before him
and to strip kings of their armor,
to open doors before him
so that gates will not be shut:
[2] I will go before you
and will level the mountains[a];
I will break down gates of bronze
and cut through bars of iron.
[3] I will give you hidden treasures,
riches stored in secret places,
so that you may know that I am the LORD,
the God of Israel, who summons you by name.
[4] For the sake of Jacob my servant,
of Israel my chosen,
I summon you by name
and bestow on you a title of honor,
though you do not acknowledge me.

[a] 2 Dead Sea Scrolls and Septuagint; the meaning of the word in the Masoretic Text is uncertain.

5 I am the LORD, and there is no other;
apart from me there is no God.
I will strengthen you,
though you have not acknowledged me,
6 so that from the rising of the sun
to the place of its setting
people may know there is none
besides me.
I am the LORD, and there is no other.
7 I form the light and create darkness,
I bring prosperity and create disaster;
I, the LORD, do all these things.

8 "You heavens above, rain down my
righteousness;
let the clouds shower it down.
Let the earth open wide,
let salvation spring up,
let righteousness flourish with it;
I, the LORD, have created it.

9 "Woe to those who quarrel with their
Maker,
those who are nothing but potsherds
among the potsherds on the ground.
Does the clay say to the potter,
'What are you making?'
Does your work say,
'The potter has no hands'?
10 Woe to the one who says to a father,
'What have you begotten?'
or to a mother,
'What have you brought to birth?'

11 "This is what the LORD says—
the Holy One of Israel, and its Maker:
Concerning things to come,
do you question me about my children,
or give me orders about the work of
my hands?
12 It is I who made the earth
and created mankind on it.
My own hands stretched out the heavens;
I marshaled their starry hosts.
13 I will raise up Cyrus[a] in my
righteousness:
I will make all his ways straight.
He will rebuild my city
and set my exiles free,
but not for a price or reward,
says the LORD Almighty."

14 This is what the LORD says:

"The products of Egypt and the
merchandise of Cush,[b]
and those tall Sabeans—
they will come over to you
and will be yours;
they will trudge behind you,
coming over to you in chains.
They will bow down before you
and plead with you, saying,
'Surely God is with you, and there is no
other;
there is no other god.' "

15 Truly you are a God who has been hiding
himself,
the God and Savior of Israel.
16 All the makers of idols will be put to
shame and disgraced;
they will go off into disgrace together.
17 But Israel will be saved by the LORD
with an everlasting salvation;
you will never be put to shame or
disgraced,
to ages everlasting.

18 For this is what the LORD says—
he who created the heavens,
he is God;
he who fashioned and made the earth,
he founded it;
he did not create it to be empty,
but formed it to be inhabited—
he says:
"I am the LORD,
and there is no other.
19 I have not spoken in secret,
from somewhere in a land of darkness;
I have not said to Jacob's descendants,
'Seek me in vain.'
I, the LORD, speak the truth;
I declare what is right.

20 "Gather together and come;
assemble, you fugitives from the
nations.
Ignorant are those who carry about idols
of wood,
who pray to gods that cannot save.
21 Declare what is to be, present it—
let them take counsel together.
Who foretold this long ago,
who declared it from the distant past?
Was it not I, the LORD?
And there is no God apart from me,
a righteous God and a Savior;
there is none but me.

[a] 13 Hebrew *him* [b] 14 That is, the upper Nile region

[22] "Turn to me and be saved,
all you ends of the earth;
for I am God, and there is no other.
[23] By myself I have sworn,
my mouth has uttered in all integrity
a word that will not be revoked:
Before me every knee will bow;
by me every tongue will swear.
[24] They will say of me, 'In the LORD alone
are deliverance and strength.'"
All who have raged against him
will come to him and be put to shame.
[25] But all the descendants of Israel
will find deliverance in the LORD
and will make their boast in him.

Gods of Babylon

46 Bel bows down, Nebo stoops low;
their idols are borne by beasts of burden.[a]
The images that are carried about are burdensome,
a burden for the weary.
[2] They stoop and bow down together;
unable to rescue the burden,
they themselves go off into captivity.

[3] "Listen to me, you descendants of Jacob,
all the remnant of the people of Israel,
you whom I have upheld since your birth,
and have carried since you were born.
[4] Even to your old age and gray hairs
I am he, I am he who will sustain you.
I have made you and I will carry you;
I will sustain you and I will rescue you.

[5] "With whom will you compare me or count me equal?
To whom will you liken me that we may be compared?
[6] Some pour out gold from their bags
and weigh out silver on the scales;
they hire a goldsmith to make it into a god,
and they bow down and worship it.
[7] They lift it to their shoulders and carry it;
they set it up in its place, and there it stands.
From that spot it cannot move.
Even though someone cries out to it, it cannot answer;
it cannot save them from their troubles.

[8] "Remember this, keep it in mind,
take it to heart, you rebels.
[9] Remember the former things, those of long ago;
I am God, and there is no other;
I am God, and there is none like me.
[10] I make known the end from the beginning,
from ancient times, what is still to come.
I say, 'My purpose will stand,
and I will do all that I please.'
[11] From the east I summon a bird of prey;
from a far-off land, a man to fulfill my purpose.
What I have said, that I will bring about;
what I have planned, that I will do.
[12] Listen to me, you stubborn-hearted,
you who are now far from my righteousness.
[13] I am bringing my righteousness near,
it is not far away;
and my salvation will not be delayed.
I will grant salvation to Zion,
my splendor to Israel.

The Fall of Babylon

47 "Go down, sit in the dust,
Virgin Daughter Babylon;
sit on the ground without a throne,
queen city of the Babylonians.[b]
No more will you be called
tender or delicate.
[2] Take millstones and grind flour;
take off your veil.
Lift up your skirts, bare your legs,
and wade through the streams.
[3] Your nakedness will be exposed
and your shame uncovered.
I will take vengeance;
I will spare no one."
[4] Our Redeemer — the LORD Almighty is his name —
is the Holy One of Israel.

[5] "Sit in silence, go into darkness,
queen city of the Babylonians;
no more will you be called
queen of kingdoms.
[6] I was angry with my people
and desecrated my inheritance;
I gave them into your hand,
and you showed them no mercy.

[a] *1* Or *are but beasts and cattle* [b] *1* Or *Chaldeans;* also in verse 5

Even on the aged
you laid a very heavy yoke.
7 You said, 'I am forever —
the eternal queen!'
But you did not consider these things
or reflect on what might happen.

8 "Now then, listen, you lover of pleasure,
lounging in your security
and saying to yourself,
'I am, and there is none besides me.
I will never be a widow
or suffer the loss of children.'
9 Both of these will overtake you
in a moment, on a single day:
loss of children and widowhood.
They will come upon you in full measure,
in spite of your many sorceries
and all your potent spells.
10 You have trusted in your wickedness
and have said, 'No one sees me.'
Your wisdom and knowledge mislead you
when you say to yourself,
'I am, and there is none besides me.'
11 Disaster will come upon you,
and you will not know how to conjure
it away.
A calamity will fall upon you
that you cannot ward off with a
ransom;
a catastrophe you cannot foresee
will suddenly come upon you.

12 "Keep on, then, with your magic spells
and with your many sorceries,
which you have labored at since
childhood.
Perhaps you will succeed,
perhaps you will cause terror.
13 All the counsel you have received has
only worn you out!
Let your astrologers come forward,
those stargazers who make predictions
month by month,
let them save you from what is coming
upon you.
14 Surely they are like stubble;
the fire will burn them up.
They cannot even save themselves
from the power of the flame.
These are not coals for warmth;
this is not a fire to sit by.
15 That is all they are to you —
these you have dealt with
and labored with since childhood.
All of them go on in their error;
there is not one that can save you.

Stubborn Israel

48 "Listen to this, you descendants
of Jacob,
you who are called by the name of
Israel
and come from the line of Judah,
you who take oaths in the name of the
LORD
and invoke the God of Israel —
but not in truth or righteousness —
2 you who call yourselves citizens of the
holy city
and claim to rely on the God of Israel —
the LORD Almighty is his name:
3 I foretold the former things long ago,
my mouth announced them and I
made them known;
then suddenly I acted, and they came
to pass.
4 For I knew how stubborn you were;
your neck muscles were iron,
your forehead was bronze.
5 Therefore I told you these things long ago;
before they happened I announced
them to you
so that you could not say,
'My images brought them about;
my wooden image and metal god
ordained them.'
6 You have heard these things; look at
them all.
Will you not admit them?

"From now on I will tell you of new
things,
of hidden things unknown to you.
7 They are created now, and not long ago;
you have not heard of them before
today.
So you cannot say,
'Yes, I knew of them.'
8 You have neither heard nor understood;
from of old your ears have not been
open.
Well do I know how treacherous you are;
you were called a rebel from birth.
9 For my own name's sake I delay my
wrath;
for the sake of my praise I hold it back
from you,
so as not to destroy you completely.

[10] See, I have refined you, though not as silver;
I have tested you in the furnace of affliction.
[11] For my own sake, for my own sake, I do this.
How can I let myself be defamed?
I will not yield my glory to another.

Israel Freed

[12] "Listen to me, Jacob,
Israel, whom I have called:
I am he;
I am the first and I am the last.
[13] My own hand laid the foundations of the earth,
and my right hand spread out the heavens;
when I summon them,
they all stand up together.

[14] "Come together, all of you, and listen:
Which of the idols has foretold these things?
The LORD's chosen ally
will carry out his purpose against Babylon;
his arm will be against the Babylonians.[a]
[15] I, even I, have spoken;
yes, I have called him.
I will bring him,
and he will succeed in his mission.

[16] "Come near me and listen to this:

"From the first announcement I have not spoken in secret;
at the time it happens, I am there."

And now the Sovereign LORD has sent me,
endowed with his Spirit.

[17] This is what the LORD says —
your Redeemer, the Holy One of Israel:
"I am the LORD your God,
who teaches you what is best for you,
who directs you in the way you should go.
[18] If only you had paid attention to my commands,
your peace would have been like a river,
your well-being like the waves of the sea.
[19] Your descendants would have been like the sand,
your children like its numberless grains;
their name would never be blotted out
nor destroyed from before me."

[20] Leave Babylon,
flee from the Babylonians!
Announce this with shouts of joy
and proclaim it.
Send it out to the ends of the earth;
say, "The LORD has redeemed his servant Jacob."
[21] They did not thirst when he led them through the deserts;
he made water flow for them from the rock;
he split the rock
and water gushed out.

[22] "There is no peace," says the LORD, "for the wicked."

The Servant of the LORD

49 Listen to me, you islands;
hear this, you distant nations:
Before I was born the LORD called me;
from my mother's womb he has spoken my name.
[2] He made my mouth like a sharpened sword,
in the shadow of his hand he hid me;
he made me into a polished arrow
and concealed me in his quiver.
[3] He said to me, "You are my servant,
Israel, in whom I will display my splendor."
[4] But I said, "I have labored in vain;
I have spent my strength for nothing at all.
Yet what is due me is in the LORD's hand,
and my reward is with my God."

[5] And now the LORD says —
he who formed me in the womb to be his servant
to bring Jacob back to him
and gather Israel to himself,
for I am[b] honored in the eyes of the LORD
and my God has been my strength —
[6] he says:
"It is too small a thing for you to be my servant

[a] 14 Or *Chaldeans*; also in verse 20 [b] 5 Or *him, / but Israel would not be gathered; / yet I will be*

to restore the tribes of Jacob
and bring back those of Israel I have kept.
I will also make you a light for the Gentiles,
that my salvation may reach to the ends of the earth."

[7] This is what the LORD says—
the Redeemer and Holy One of Israel—
to him who was despised and abhorred by the nation,
to the servant of rulers:
"Kings will see you and stand up,
princes will see and bow down,
because of the LORD, who is faithful,
the Holy One of Israel, who has chosen you."

Restoration of Israel

[8] This is what the LORD says:

"In the time of my favor I will answer you,
and in the day of salvation I will help you;
I will keep you and will make you
to be a covenant for the people,
to restore the land
and to reassign its desolate inheritances,
[9] to say to the captives, 'Come out,'
and to those in darkness, 'Be free!'

"They will feed beside the roads
and find pasture on every barren hill.
[10] They will neither hunger nor thirst,
nor will the desert heat or the sun beat down on them.
He who has compassion on them will guide them
and lead them beside springs of water.
[11] I will turn all my mountains into roads,
and my highways will be raised up.
[12] See, they will come from afar—
some from the north, some from the west,
some from the region of Aswan.[a]"

[13] Shout for joy, you heavens;
rejoice, you earth;
burst into song, you mountains!
For the LORD comforts his people
and will have compassion on his afflicted ones.

[14] But Zion said, "The LORD has forsaken me,
the Lord has forgotten me."

[15] "Can a mother forget the baby at her breast
and have no compassion on the child she has borne?
Though she may forget,
I will not forget you!
[16] See, I have engraved you on the palms of my hands;
your walls are ever before me.
[17] Your children hasten back,
and those who laid you waste depart from you.
[18] Lift up your eyes and look around;
all your children gather and come to you.
As surely as I live," declares the LORD,
"you will wear them all as ornaments;
you will put them on, like a bride.

[19] "Though you were ruined and made desolate
and your land laid waste,
now you will be too small for your people,
and those who devoured you will be far away.
[20] The children born during your bereavement
will yet say in your hearing,
'This place is too small for us;
give us more space to live in.'
[21] Then you will say in your heart,
'Who bore me these?
I was bereaved and barren;
I was exiled and rejected.
Who brought these up?
I was left all alone,
but these—where have they come from?'"

[22] This is what the Sovereign LORD says:

"See, I will beckon to the nations,
I will lift up my banner to the peoples;
they will bring your sons in their arms
and carry your daughters on their hips.
[23] Kings will be your foster fathers,
and their queens your nursing mothers.
They will bow down before you with their faces to the ground;
they will lick the dust at your feet.

[a] *12* Dead Sea Scrolls; Masoretic Text *Sinim*

Then you will know that I am the LORD;
those who hope in me will not be disappointed."

24 Can plunder be taken from warriors,
or captives be rescued from the fierce[a]?

25 But this is what the LORD says:

"Yes, captives will be taken from warriors,
and plunder retrieved from the fierce;
I will contend with those who contend with you,
and your children I will save.
26 I will make your oppressors eat their own flesh;
they will be drunk on their own blood, as with wine.
Then all mankind will know
that I, the LORD, am your Savior,
your Redeemer, the Mighty One of Jacob."

Israel's Sin and the Servant's Obedience

50 This is what the LORD says:

"Where is your mother's certificate of divorce
with which I sent her away?
Or to which of my creditors
did I sell you?
Because of your sins you were sold;
because of your transgressions your mother was sent away.
2 When I came, why was there no one?
When I called, why was there no one to answer?
Was my arm too short to deliver you?
Do I lack the strength to rescue you?
By a mere rebuke I dry up the sea,
I turn rivers into a desert;
their fish rot for lack of water
and die of thirst.
3 I clothe the heavens with darkness
and make sackcloth its covering."

4 The Sovereign LORD has given me a well-instructed tongue,
to know the word that sustains the weary.
He wakens me morning by morning,
wakens my ear to listen like one being instructed.
5 The Sovereign LORD has opened my ears;
I have not been rebellious,
I have not turned away.
6 I offered my back to those who beat me,
my cheeks to those who pulled out my beard;
I did not hide my face
from mocking and spitting.
7 Because the Sovereign LORD helps me,
I will not be disgraced.
Therefore have I set my face like flint,
and I know I will not be put to shame.
8 He who vindicates me is near.
Who then will bring charges against me?
Let us face each other!
Who is my accuser?
Let him confront me!
9 It is the Sovereign LORD who helps me.
Who will condemn me?
They will all wear out like a garment;
the moths will eat them up.

10 Who among you fears the LORD
and obeys the word of his servant?
Let the one who walks in the dark,
who has no light,
trust in the name of the LORD
and rely on their God.
11 But now, all you who light fires
and provide yourselves with flaming torches,
go, walk in the light of your fires
and of the torches you have set ablaze.
This is what you shall receive from my hand:
You will lie down in torment.

Everlasting Salvation for Zion

51 "Listen to me, you who pursue righteousness
and who seek the LORD:
Look to the rock from which you were cut
and to the quarry from which you were hewn;
2 look to Abraham, your father,
and to Sarah, who gave you birth.
When I called him he was only one man,
and I blessed him and made him many.
3 The LORD will surely comfort Zion

[a] 24 Dead Sea Scrolls, Vulgate and Syriac (see also Septuagint and verse 25); Masoretic Text *righteous*

and will look with compassion on all
her ruins;
he will make her deserts like Eden,
her wastelands like the garden of the
LORD.
Joy and gladness will be found in her,
thanksgiving and the sound of singing.

4 "Listen to me, my people;
hear me, my nation:
Instruction will go out from me;
my justice will become a light to
the nations.
5 My righteousness draws near speedily,
my salvation is on the way,
and my arm will bring justice to the
nations.
The islands will look to me
and wait in hope for my arm.
6 Lift up your eyes to the heavens,
look at the earth beneath;
the heavens will vanish like smoke,
the earth will wear out like a garment
and its inhabitants die like flies.
But my salvation will last forever,
my righteousness will never fail.

7 "Hear me, you who know what is right,
you people who have taken my
instruction to heart:
Do not fear the reproach of mere mortals
or be terrified by their insults.
8 For the moth will eat them up like a
garment;
the worm will devour them like wool.
But my righteousness will last forever,
my salvation through all generations."

9 Awake, awake, arm of the LORD,
clothe yourself with strength!
Awake, as in days gone by,
as in generations of old.
Was it not you who cut Rahab to pieces,
who pierced that monster through?
10 Was it not you who dried up the sea,
the waters of the great deep,
who made a road in the depths of the sea
so that the redeemed might cross
over?
11 Those the LORD has rescued will return.
They will enter Zion with singing;
everlasting joy will crown their heads.
Gladness and joy will overtake them,
and sorrow and sighing will flee away.

12 "I, even I, am he who comforts you.
Who are you that you fear mere
mortals,
human beings who are but grass,
13 that you forget the LORD your Maker,
who stretches out the heavens
and who lays the foundations of the
earth,
that you live in constant terror every day
because of the wrath of the oppressor,
who is bent on destruction?
For where is the wrath of the oppressor?
14 The cowering prisoners will soon be
set free;
they will not die in their dungeon,
nor will they lack bread.
15 For I am the LORD your God,
who stirs up the sea so that its waves
roar —
the LORD Almighty is his name.
16 I have put my words in your mouth
and covered you with the shadow of
my hand —
I who set the heavens in place,
who laid the foundations of the earth,
and who say to Zion, 'You are my
people.' "

The Cup of the LORD's Wrath

17 Awake, awake!
Rise up, Jerusalem,
you who have drunk from the hand of the
LORD
the cup of his wrath,
you who have drained to its dregs
the goblet that makes people stagger.
18 Among all the children she bore
there was none to guide her;
among all the children she reared
there was none to take her by the hand.
19 These double calamities have come
upon you —
who can comfort you? —
ruin and destruction, famine and
sword —
who can[a] console you?
20 Your children have fainted;
they lie at every street corner,
like antelope caught in a net.
They are filled with the wrath of the
LORD,
with the rebuke of your God.

[a] *19* Dead Sea Scrolls, Septuagint, Vulgate and Syriac; Masoretic Text / *how can I*

HAPPY DAY

Tim Hughes, Ben Cantelon

The greatest day in history
Death is beaten, you have rescued me
Sing it out, Jesus is alive
The empty cross, the empty grave
Life eternal, you have won the day
Shout it out, Jesus is alive, he's alive

And oh, happy day, happy day
You washed my sin away
Oh, happy day, happy day
I'll never be the same
Forever I am changed

When I stand in that place
Free at last, meeting face to face
I am yours, Jesus, you are mine
Endless joy, perfect peace
Earthly pain finally will cease
Celebrate, Jesus is alive, he's alive

Oh, what a glorious day
What a glorious way
That you have saved me
And oh, what a glorious day
What a glorious name
Yeah

THE INSPIRATION

The angel said to the women, "Do not be afraid, for I know that you are looking for Jesus, who was crucified. He is not here; he has risen, just as he said. Come and see the place where he lay."

— Matthew 28:5 – 6

BEHIND THE SONG

Due to its peppy feel and straightforward, upbeat lyric, it may be easy to think of "Happy Day" by Tim Hughes as a lightweight worship song. But the truth is that this infectious tune is the result of an intentional effort by Hughes to fill a gap he noticed in the modern worship songbook.

"A while ago I was having a conversation with a theologian friend of mine," Hughes explains. "He was challenging me with the assertion that there was a lack of new songs that spoke of the resurrection of Christ. That got me thinking. At the time I was reading *The Empty Cross of Jesus* by Michael Green. I stumbled across a challenge that Michelangelo once posed to fellow artists who were forever depicting Christ's death on the cross, 'Paint him instead the Lord of life.' With all these thoughts buzzing in my head, I picked up my guitar and began to worship. As I fumbled around with some chords and melodies, a verse was forming. I then sang out the chorus, 'Oh happy day, happy day, you washed my sin away. Oh happy day, happy day, I'll never be the same.' "

The song was completed when Hughes brought it to a band rehearsal and his keyboardist, Ben Cantalon, (also a strong worship writer) composed the bridge. The song is increasingly known and loved by Christians around the world; it is a favorite at Easter and throughout the year.

"The verses aim to fill our lips with the truth and joy of all that Christ has done for us," Hughes adds. "My desire, by the time the chorus is reached, is that hearts explode with praise."

Selah

Put yourself in the shoes of the disciples, or Mary and Martha, on that first Easter morning. All your hopes and dreams seem to have died, and then suddenly, are alive again! What thoughts and emotions does contemplating the resurrection evoke for you? What do those thoughts and emotions lead you to do? How does the resurrection shape your life?

[21] Therefore hear this, you afflicted one,
made drunk, but not with wine.
[22] This is what your Sovereign LORD says,
your God, who defends his people:
"See, I have taken out of your hand
the cup that made you stagger;
from that cup, the goblet of my wrath,
you will never drink again.
[23] I will put it into the hands of your
tormentors,
who said to you,
'Fall prostrate that we may walk on you.'
And you made your back like the ground,
like a street to be walked on."

52 Awake, awake, Zion,
clothe yourself with strength!
Put on your garments of splendor,
Jerusalem, the holy city.
The uncircumcised and defiled
will not enter you again.
[2] Shake off your dust;
rise up, sit enthroned, Jerusalem.
Free yourself from the chains on your
neck,
Daughter Zion, now a captive.

[3] For this is what the LORD says:

"You were sold for nothing,
and without money you will be
redeemed."

[4] For this is what the Sovereign LORD says:

"At first my people went down to Egypt
to live;
lately, Assyria has oppressed them.

[5] "And now what do I have here?" declares
the LORD.

"For my people have been taken away for
nothing,
and those who rule them mock,[a]"
declares the LORD.

"And all day long
my name is constantly blasphemed.
[6] Therefore my people will know my name;
therefore in that day they will know
that it is I who foretold it.
Yes, it is I."

[7] How beautiful on the mountains
are the feet of those who bring good
news,
who proclaim peace,
who bring good tidings,
who proclaim salvation,
who say to Zion,
"Your God reigns!"
[8] Listen! Your watchmen lift up their voices;
together they shout for joy.
When the LORD returns to Zion,
they will see it with their own eyes.
[9] Burst into songs of joy together,
you ruins of Jerusalem,
for the LORD has comforted his people,
he has redeemed Jerusalem.
[10] The LORD will lay bare his holy arm
in the sight of all the nations,
and all the ends of the earth will see
the salvation of our God.

[11] Depart, depart, go out from there!
Touch no unclean thing!
Come out from it and be pure,
you who carry the articles of the
LORD's house.
[12] But you will not leave in haste
or go in flight;
for the LORD will go before you,
the God of Israel will be your rear
guard.

The Suffering and Glory of the Servant

[13] See, my servant will act wisely[b];
he will be raised and lifted up and
highly exalted.
[14] Just as there were many who were
appalled at him[c]—
his appearance was so disfigured
beyond that of any human being
and his form marred beyond human
likeness—
[15] so he will sprinkle many nations,[d]
and kings will shut their mouths
because of him.
For what they were not told, they will see,
and what they have not heard, they
will understand.

53 Who has believed our message
and to whom has the arm of the
LORD been revealed?
[2] He grew up before him like a tender
shoot,
and like a root out of dry ground.

[a] 5 Dead Sea Scrolls and Vulgate; Masoretic Text *wail* [b] 13 Or *will prosper* [c] 14 Hebrew *you*
[d] 15 Or *so will many nations be amazed at him* (see also Septuagint)

He had no beauty or majesty to attract us
to him,
nothing in his appearance that we
should desire him.
3 He was despised and rejected by
mankind,
a man of suffering, and familiar with
pain.
Like one from whom people hide their
faces
he was despised, and we held him in
low esteem.

4 Surely he took up our pain
and bore our suffering,
yet we considered him punished by God,
stricken by him, and afflicted.
5 But he was pierced for our transgressions,
he was crushed for our iniquities;
the punishment that brought us peace
was on him,
and by his wounds we are healed.
6 We all, like sheep, have gone astray,
each of us has turned to our own way;
and the LORD has laid on him
the iniquity of us all.
7 He was oppressed and afflicted,
yet he did not open his mouth;
he was led like a lamb to the slaughter,
and as a sheep before its shearers is
silent,
so he did not open his mouth.
8 By oppression[a] and judgment he was
taken away.
Yet who of his generation protested?
For he was cut off from the land of the
living;
for the transgression of my people he
was punished.[b]
9 He was assigned a grave with the wicked,
and with the rich in his death,
though he had done no violence,
nor was any deceit in his mouth.

10 Yet it was the LORD's will to crush him
and cause him to suffer,
and though the LORD makes[c] his life
an offering for sin,
he will see his offspring and prolong his
days,
and the will of the LORD will prosper in
his hand.
11 After he has suffered,
he will see the light of life[d] and be
satisfied[e];
by his knowledge[f] my righteous servant
will justify many,
and he will bear their iniquities.
12 Therefore I will give him a portion among
the great,[g]
and he will divide the spoils with the
strong,[h]
because he poured out his life unto
death,
and was numbered with the
transgressors.
For he bore the sin of many,
and made intercession for the
transgressors.

The Future Glory of Zion

54 "Sing, barren woman,
you who never bore a child;
burst into song, shout for joy,
you who were never in labor;
because more are the children of the
desolate woman
than of her who has a husband,"
says the LORD.

2 "Enlarge the place of your tent,
stretch your tent curtains wide,
do not hold back;
lengthen your cords,
strengthen your stakes.
3 For you will spread out to the right and to
the left;
your descendants will dispossess
nations
and settle in their desolate cities.
4 "Do not be afraid; you will not be put to
shame.
Do not fear disgrace; you will not be
humiliated.
You will forget the shame of your youth
and remember no more the reproach
of your widowhood.
5 For your Maker is your husband—
the LORD Almighty is his name—

[a] 8 Or *From arrest* [b] 8 Or *generation considered / that he was cut off from the land of the living, / that he was punished for the transgression of my people?* [c] 10 Hebrew *though you make* [d] 11 Dead Sea Scrolls (see also Septuagint); Masoretic Text does not have *the light of life.* [e] 11 Or (with Masoretic Text) *11 He will see the fruit of his suffering / and will be satisfied* [f] 11 Or *by knowledge of him* [g] 12 Or *many* [h] 12 Or *numerous*

the Holy One of Israel is your Redeemer;
he is called the God of all the
earth.
6 The LORD will call you back
as if you were a wife deserted and
distressed in spirit—
a wife who married young,
only to be rejected," says your God.
7 "For a brief moment I abandoned you,
but with deep compassion I will bring
you back.
8 In a surge of anger
I hid my face from you for a moment,
but with everlasting kindness
I will have compassion on you,"
says the LORD your Redeemer.

9 "To me this is like the days of Noah,
when I swore that the waters of Noah
would never again cover the
earth.
So now I have sworn not to be angry
with you,
never to rebuke you again.
10 Though the mountains be shaken
and the hills be removed,
yet my unfailing love for you will not be
shaken
nor my covenant of peace be
removed,"
says the LORD, who has compassion
on you.

11 "Afflicted city, lashed by storms and not
comforted,
I will rebuild you with stones of
turquoise,[a]
your foundations with lapis lazuli.
12 I will make your battlements of rubies,
your gates of sparkling jewels,
and all your walls of precious stones.
13 All your children will be taught by the
LORD,
and great will be their peace.
14 In righteousness you will be established:
Tyranny will be far from you;
you will have nothing to fear.
Terror will be far removed;
it will not come near you.
15 If anyone does attack you, it will not be
my doing;
whoever attacks you will surrender
to you.

16 "See, it is I who created the blacksmith
who fans the coals into flame
and forges a weapon fit for its work.
And it is I who have created the destroyer
to wreak havoc;
17 no weapon forged against you will
prevail,
and you will refute every tongue that
accuses you.
This is the heritage of the servants of the
LORD,
and this is their vindication from me,"
declares the LORD.

Invitation to the Thirsty

55 "Come, all you who are thirsty,
come to the waters;
and you who have no money,
come, buy and eat!
Come, buy wine and milk
without money and without cost.
2 Why spend money on what is not bread,
and your labor on what does not
satisfy?
Listen, listen to me, and eat what is good,
and you will delight in the richest
of fare.
3 Give ear and come to me;
listen, that you may live.
I will make an everlasting covenant
with you,
my faithful love promised to David.
4 See, I have made him a witness to the
peoples,
a ruler and commander of the peoples.
5 Surely you will summon nations you
know not,
and nations you do not know will come
running to you,
because of the LORD your God,
the Holy One of Israel,
for he has endowed you with
splendor."

6 Seek the LORD while he may be found;
call on him while he is near.
7 Let the wicked forsake their ways
and the unrighteous their thoughts.
Let them turn to the LORD, and he will
have mercy on them,
and to our God, for he will freely
pardon.

[a] 11 The meaning of the Hebrew for this word is uncertain.

[8] "For my thoughts are not your thoughts,
neither are your ways my ways,"
declares the LORD.
[9] "As the heavens are higher than the earth,
so are my ways higher than your ways
and my thoughts than your thoughts.
[10] As the rain and the snow
come down from heaven,
and do not return to it
without watering the earth
and making it bud and flourish,
so that it yields seed for the sower and bread for the eater,
[11] so is my word that goes out from my mouth:
It will not return to me empty,
but will accomplish what I desire
and achieve the purpose for which I sent it.
[12] You will go out in joy
and be led forth in peace;
the mountains and hills
will burst into song before you,
and all the trees of the field
will clap their hands.
[13] Instead of the thornbush will grow the juniper,
and instead of briers the myrtle will grow.
This will be for the LORD's renown,
for an everlasting sign,
that will endure forever."

Salvation for Others

56 This is what the LORD says:

"Maintain justice
and do what is right,
for my salvation is close at hand
and my righteousness will soon be revealed.
[2] Blessed is the one who does this—
the person who holds it fast,
who keeps the Sabbath without desecrating it,
and keeps their hands from doing any evil."
[3] Let no foreigner who is bound to the LORD say,
"The LORD will surely exclude me from his people."
And let no eunuch complain,
"I am only a dry tree."

[4] For this is what the LORD says:

"To the eunuchs who keep my Sabbaths,
who choose what pleases me
and hold fast to my covenant—
[5] to them I will give within my temple and its walls
a memorial and a name
better than sons and daughters;
I will give them an everlasting name
that will endure forever.
[6] And foreigners who bind themselves to the LORD
to minister to him,
to love the name of the LORD,
and to be his servants,
all who keep the Sabbath without desecrating it
and who hold fast to my covenant—
[7] these I will bring to my holy mountain
and give them joy in my house of prayer.
Their burnt offerings and sacrifices
will be accepted on my altar;
for my house will be called
a house of prayer for all nations."
[8] The Sovereign LORD declares—
he who gathers the exiles of Israel:
"I will gather still others to them
besides those already gathered."

God's Accusation Against the Wicked

[9] Come, all you beasts of the field,
come and devour, all you beasts of the forest!
[10] Israel's watchmen are blind,
they all lack knowledge;
they are all mute dogs,
they cannot bark;
they lie around and dream,
they love to sleep.
[11] They are dogs with mighty appetites;
they never have enough.
They are shepherds who lack understanding;
they all turn to their own way,
they seek their own gain.
[12] "Come," each one cries, "let me get wine!
Let us drink our fill of beer!
And tomorrow will be like today,
or even far better."

57 The righteous perish,
and no one takes it to heart;
the devout are taken away,
and no one understands
that the righteous are taken away
to be spared from evil.
2 Those who walk uprightly
enter into peace;
they find rest as they lie in death.

3 "But you—come here, you children of a sorceress,
you offspring of adulterers and prostitutes!
4 Who are you mocking?
At whom do you sneer
and stick out your tongue?
Are you not a brood of rebels,
the offspring of liars?
5 You burn with lust among the oaks
and under every spreading tree;
you sacrifice your children in the ravines
and under the overhanging crags.
6 The idols among the smooth stones of the ravines are your portion;
indeed, they are your lot.
Yes, to them you have poured out drink offerings
and offered grain offerings.
In view of all this, should I relent?
7 You have made your bed on a high and lofty hill;
there you went up to offer your sacrifices.
8 Behind your doors and your doorposts
you have put your pagan symbols.
Forsaking me, you uncovered your bed,
you climbed into it and opened it wide;
you made a pact with those whose beds you love,
and you looked with lust on their naked bodies.
9 You went to Molek[a] with olive oil
and increased your perfumes.
You sent your ambassadors[b] far away;
you descended to the very realm of the dead!
10 You wearied yourself by such going about,
but you would not say, 'It is hopeless.'
You found renewal of your strength,
and so you did not faint.

11 "Whom have you so dreaded and feared
that you have not been true to me,
and have neither remembered me
nor taken this to heart?
Is it not because I have long been silent
that you do not fear me?
12 I will expose your righteousness and your works,
and they will not benefit you.
13 When you cry out for help,
let your collection of idols save you!
The wind will carry all of them off,
a mere breath will blow them away.
But whoever takes refuge in me
will inherit the land
and possess my holy mountain."

Comfort for the Contrite

14 And it will be said:

"Build up, build up, prepare the road!
Remove the obstacles out of the way of my people."
15 For this is what the high and exalted One says—
he who lives forever, whose name is holy:
"I live in a high and holy place,
but also with the one who is contrite and lowly in spirit,
to revive the spirit of the lowly
and to revive the heart of the contrite.
16 I will not accuse them forever,
nor will I always be angry,
for then they would faint away because of me—
the very people I have created.
17 I was enraged by their sinful greed;
I punished them, and hid my face in anger,
yet they kept on in their willful ways.
18 I have seen their ways, but I will heal them;
I will guide them and restore comfort to Israel's mourners,
19 creating praise on their lips.
Peace, peace, to those far and near,"
says the LORD. "And I will heal them."
20 But the wicked are like the tossing sea,
which cannot rest,
whose waves cast up mire and mud.
21 "There is no peace," says my God, "for the wicked."

[a] 9 Or *to the king* [b] 9 Or *idols*

True Fasting

58 "Shout it aloud, do not hold back.
Raise your voice like a trumpet.
Declare to my people their rebellion
and to the descendants of Jacob their sins.
2 For day after day they seek me out;
they seem eager to know my ways,
as if they were a nation that does what is right
and has not forsaken the commands of its God.
They ask me for just decisions
and seem eager for God to come near them.
3 'Why have we fasted,' they say,
'and you have not seen it?
Why have we humbled ourselves,
and you have not noticed?'

"Yet on the day of your fasting, you do as you please
and exploit all your workers.
4 Your fasting ends in quarreling and strife,
and in striking each other with wicked fists.
You cannot fast as you do today
and expect your voice to be heard on high.
5 Is this the kind of fast I have chosen,
only a day for people to humble themselves?
Is it only for bowing one's head like a reed
and for lying in sackcloth and ashes?
Is that what you call a fast,
a day acceptable to the LORD?
6 "Is not this the kind of fasting I have chosen:
to loose the chains of injustice
and untie the cords of the yoke,
to set the oppressed free
and break every yoke?
7 Is it not to share your food with the hungry
and to provide the poor wanderer with shelter—
when you see the naked, to clothe them,
and not to turn away from your own flesh and blood?
8 Then your light will break forth like the dawn,
and your healing will quickly appear;
then your righteousness[a] will go before you,
and the glory of the LORD will be your rear guard.
9 Then you will call, and the LORD will answer;
you will cry for help, and he will say: Here am I.

"If you do away with the yoke of oppression,
with the pointing finger and malicious talk,
10 and if you spend yourselves in behalf of the hungry
and satisfy the needs of the oppressed,
then your light will rise in the darkness,
and your night will become like the noonday.
11 The LORD will guide you always;
he will satisfy your needs in a sun-scorched land
and will strengthen your frame.
You will be like a well-watered garden,
like a spring whose waters never fail.
12 Your people will rebuild the ancient ruins
and will raise up the age-old foundations;
you will be called Repairer of Broken Walls,
Restorer of Streets with Dwellings.
13 "If you keep your feet from breaking the Sabbath
and from doing as you please on my holy day,
if you call the Sabbath a delight
and the LORD's holy day honorable,
and if you honor it by not going your own way
and not doing as you please or speaking idle words,
14 then you will find your joy in the LORD,
and I will cause you to ride in triumph on the heights of the land
and to feast on the inheritance of your father Jacob."
For the mouth of the LORD has spoken.

Sin, Confession and Redemption

59 Surely the arm of the LORD is not too short to save,
nor his ear too dull to hear.

[a] 8 Or *your righteous One*

[2]But your iniquities have separated
you from your God;
your sins have hidden his face from you,
so that he will not hear.
[3]For your hands are stained with blood,
your fingers with guilt.
Your lips have spoken falsely,
and your tongue mutters wicked things.
[4]No one calls for justice;
no one pleads a case with integrity.
They rely on empty arguments, they
utter lies;
they conceive trouble and give birth
to evil.
[5]They hatch the eggs of vipers
and spin a spider's web.
Whoever eats their eggs will die,
and when one is broken, an adder is
hatched.
[6]Their cobwebs are useless for clothing;
they cannot cover themselves with
what they make.
Their deeds are evil deeds,
and acts of violence are in their hands.
[7]Their feet rush into sin;
they are swift to shed innocent blood.
They pursue evil schemes;
acts of violence mark their ways.
[8]The way of peace they do not know;
there is no justice in their paths.
They have turned them into crooked
roads;
no one who walks along them will
know peace.

[9]So justice is far from us,
and righteousness does not reach us.
We look for light, but all is darkness;
for brightness, but we walk in deep
shadows.
[10]Like the blind we grope along the wall,
feeling our way like people without
eyes.
At midday we stumble as if it were
twilight;
among the strong, we are like the dead.
[11]We all growl like bears;
we moan mournfully like doves.
We look for justice, but find none;
for deliverance, but it is far away.
[12]For our offenses are many in your sight,
and our sins testify against us.
Our offenses are ever with us,
and we acknowledge our iniquities:
[13]rebellion and treachery against the LORD,
turning our backs on our God,
inciting revolt and oppression,
uttering lies our hearts have
conceived.
[14]So justice is driven back,
and righteousness stands at a distance;
truth has stumbled in the streets,
honesty cannot enter.
[15]Truth is nowhere to be found,
and whoever shuns evil becomes
a prey.

The LORD looked and was displeased
that there was no justice.
[16]He saw that there was no one,
he was appalled that there was no one
to intervene;
so his own arm achieved salvation
for him,
and his own righteousness sustained
him.
[17]He put on righteousness as his
breastplate,
and the helmet of salvation on his
head;
he put on the garments of vengeance
and wrapped himself in zeal as in
a cloak.
[18]According to what they have done,
so will he repay
wrath to his enemies
and retribution to his foes;
he will repay the islands their due.
[19]From the west, people will fear the name
of the LORD,
and from the rising of the sun, they
will revere his glory.
For he will come like a pent-up flood
that the breath of the LORD drives
along.[a]

[20]"The Redeemer will come to Zion,
to those in Jacob who repent of
their sins,"
declares the LORD.

[21]"As for me, this is my covenant with
them," says the LORD. "My Spirit, who is on
you, will not depart from you, and my words
that I have put in your mouth will always be
on your lips, on the lips of your children and

[a] 19 Or *When enemies come in like a flood, / the Spirit of the LORD will put them to flight*

on the lips of their descendants — from this time on and forever," says the LORD.

The Glory of Zion

60 "Arise, shine, for your light has come,
and the glory of the LORD rises upon you.
2 See, darkness covers the earth
and thick darkness is over the peoples,
but the LORD rises upon you
and his glory appears over you.
3 Nations will come to your light,
and kings to the brightness of your dawn.

4 "Lift up your eyes and look about you:
All assemble and come to you;
your sons come from afar,
and your daughters are carried on the hip.
5 Then you will look and be radiant,
your heart will throb and swell with joy;
the wealth on the seas will be brought to you,
to you the riches of the nations will come.
6 Herds of camels will cover your land,
young camels of Midian and Ephah.
And all from Sheba will come,
bearing gold and incense
and proclaiming the praise of the LORD.
7 All Kedar's flocks will be gathered to you,
the rams of Nebaioth will serve you;
they will be accepted as offerings on my altar,
and I will adorn my glorious temple.

8 "Who are these that fly along like clouds,
like doves to their nests?
9 Surely the islands look to me;
in the lead are the ships of Tarshish,[a]
bringing your children from afar,
with their silver and gold,
to the honor of the LORD your God,
the Holy One of Israel,
for he has endowed you with splendor.

10 "Foreigners will rebuild your walls,
and their kings will serve you.
Though in anger I struck you,
in favor I will show you compassion.
11 Your gates will always stand open,
they will never be shut, day or night,
so that people may bring you the wealth of the nations —
their kings led in triumphal procession.
12 For the nation or kingdom that will not serve you will perish;
it will be utterly ruined.

13 "The glory of Lebanon will come to you,
the juniper, the fir and the cypress together,
to adorn my sanctuary;
and I will glorify the place for my feet.
14 The children of your oppressors will come bowing before you;
all who despise you will bow down at your feet
and will call you the City of the LORD,
Zion of the Holy One of Israel.

15 "Although you have been forsaken and hated,
with no one traveling through,
I will make you the everlasting pride
and the joy of all generations.
16 You will drink the milk of nations
and be nursed at royal breasts.
Then you will know that I, the LORD, am your Savior,
your Redeemer, the Mighty One of Jacob.
17 Instead of bronze I will bring you gold,
and silver in place of iron.
Instead of wood I will bring you bronze,
and iron in place of stones.
I will make peace your governor
and well-being your ruler.
18 No longer will violence be heard in your land,
nor ruin or destruction within your borders,
but you will call your walls Salvation
and your gates Praise.
19 The sun will no more be your light by day,
nor will the brightness of the moon shine on you,
for the LORD will be your everlasting light,
and your God will be your glory.
20 Your sun will never set again,
and your moon will wane no more;

[a] 9 Or *the trading ships*

the LORD will be your everlasting light,
and your days of sorrow will end.
21 Then all your people will be righteous
and they will possess the land forever.
They are the shoot I have planted,
the work of my hands,
for the display of my splendor.
22 The least of you will become a thousand,
the smallest a mighty nation.
I am the LORD;
in its time I will do this swiftly."

The Year of the LORD's Favor

61 The Spirit of the Sovereign LORD is on me,
because the LORD has anointed me
to proclaim good news to the poor.
He has sent me to bind up the brokenhearted,
to proclaim freedom for the captives
and release from darkness for the prisoners,[a]
2 to proclaim the year of the LORD's favor
and the day of vengeance of our God,
to comfort all who mourn,
3 and provide for those who grieve in Zion—
to bestow on them a crown of beauty
instead of ashes,
the oil of joy
instead of mourning,
and a garment of praise
instead of a spirit of despair.
They will be called oaks of righteousness,
a planting of the LORD
for the display of his splendor.

4 They will rebuild the ancient ruins
and restore the places long devastated;
they will renew the ruined cities
that have been devastated for generations.
5 Strangers will shepherd your flocks;
foreigners will work your fields and vineyards.
6 And you will be called priests of the LORD,
you will be named ministers of our God.
You will feed on the wealth of nations,
and in their riches you will boast.

7 Instead of your shame
you will receive a double portion,
and instead of disgrace
you will rejoice in your inheritance.
And so you will inherit a double portion in your land,
and everlasting joy will be yours.

8 "For I, the LORD, love justice;
I hate robbery and wrongdoing.
In my faithfulness I will reward my people
and make an everlasting covenant with them.
9 Their descendants will be known among the nations
and their offspring among the peoples.
All who see them will acknowledge
that they are a people the LORD has blessed."

10 I delight greatly in the LORD;
my soul rejoices in my God.
For he has clothed me with garments of salvation
and arrayed me in a robe of his righteousness,
as a bridegroom adorns his head like a priest,
and as a bride adorns herself with her jewels.
11 For as the soil makes the sprout come up
and a garden causes seeds to grow,
so the Sovereign LORD will make righteousness
and praise spring up before all nations.

Zion's New Name

62 For Zion's sake I will not keep silent,
for Jerusalem's sake I will not remain quiet,
till her vindication shines out like the dawn,
her salvation like a blazing torch.
2 The nations will see your vindication,
and all kings your glory;
you will be called by a new name
that the mouth of the LORD will bestow.
3 You will be a crown of splendor in the LORD's hand,
a royal diadem in the hand of your God.
4 No longer will they call you Deserted,
or name your land Desolate.

[a] 1 Hebrew; Septuagint *the blind*

But you will be called Hephzibah,[a]
and your land Beulah[b];
for the LORD will take delight in you,
and your land will be married.
5 As a young man marries a young woman,
so will your Builder marry you;
as a bridegroom rejoices over his bride,
so will your God rejoice over you.

6 I have posted watchmen on your walls,
Jerusalem;
they will never be silent day or night.
You who call on the LORD,
give yourselves no rest,
7 and give him no rest till he establishes
Jerusalem
and makes her the praise of the earth.

8 The LORD has sworn by his right hand
and by his mighty arm:
"Never again will I give your grain
as food for your enemies,
and never again will foreigners drink the
new wine
for which you have toiled;
9 but those who harvest it will eat it
and praise the LORD,
and those who gather the grapes will
drink it
in the courts of my sanctuary."

10 Pass through, pass through the gates!
Prepare the way for the people.
Build up, build up the highway!
Remove the stones.
Raise a banner for the nations.

11 The LORD has made proclamation
to the ends of the earth:
"Say to Daughter Zion,
'See, your Savior comes!
See, his reward is with him,
and his recompense accompanies
him.' "
12 They will be called the Holy People,
the Redeemed of the LORD;
and you will be called Sought After,
the City No Longer Deserted.

God's Day of Vengeance and Redemption

63 Who is this coming from Edom,
from Bozrah, with his garments
stained crimson?
Who is this, robed in splendor,
striding forward in the greatness of his
strength?

"It is I, proclaiming victory,
mighty to save."

2 Why are your garments red,
like those of one treading the
winepress?

3 "I have trodden the winepress alone;
from the nations no one was with me.
I trampled them in my anger
and trod them down in my wrath;
their blood spattered my garments,
and I stained all my clothing.
4 It was for me the day of vengeance;
the year for me to redeem had come.
5 I looked, but there was no one to help,
I was appalled that no one gave
support;
so my own arm achieved salvation
for me,
and my own wrath sustained me.
6 I trampled the nations in my anger;
in my wrath I made them drunk
and poured their blood on the
ground."

Praise and Prayer

7 I will tell of the kindnesses of the LORD,
the deeds for which he is to be praised,
according to all the LORD has done
for us—
yes, the many good things
he has done for Israel,
according to his compassion and
many kindnesses.
8 He said, "Surely they are my people,
children who will be true to me";
and so he became their Savior.
9 In all their distress he too was distressed,
and the angel of his presence saved
them.[c]
In his love and mercy he redeemed
them;
he lifted them up and carried them
all the days of old.
10 Yet they rebelled
and grieved his Holy Spirit.
So he turned and became their enemy
and he himself fought against them.

[a] 4 *Hephzibah* means *my delight is in her.* [b] 4 *Beulah* means *married.* [c] 9 Or *Savior* [9]*in their distress. / It was no envoy or angel / but his own presence that saved them*

11 Then his people recalled[a] the days of old,
the days of Moses and his people —
where is he who brought them through the sea,
with the shepherd of his flock?
Where is he who set
his Holy Spirit among them,
12 who sent his glorious arm of power
to be at Moses' right hand,
who divided the waters before them,
to gain for himself everlasting renown,
13 who led them through the depths?
Like a horse in open country,
they did not stumble;
14 like cattle that go down to the plain,
they were given rest by the Spirit of the LORD.
This is how you guided your people
to make for yourself a glorious name.

15 Look down from heaven and see,
from your lofty throne, holy and glorious.
Where are your zeal and your might?
Your tenderness and compassion are withheld from us.
16 But you are our Father,
though Abraham does not know us
or Israel acknowledge us;
you, LORD, are our Father,
our Redeemer from of old is your name.
17 Why, LORD, do you make us wander from your ways
and harden our hearts so we do not revere you?
Return for the sake of your servants,
the tribes that are your inheritance.
18 For a little while your people possessed your holy place,
but now our enemies have trampled down your sanctuary.
19 We are yours from of old;
but you have not ruled over them,
they have not been called[b] by your name.

64 [c] Oh, that you would rend the heavens and come down,
that the mountains would tremble before you!
2 As when fire sets twigs ablaze
and causes water to boil,
come down to make your name known to your enemies
and cause the nations to quake before you!
3 For when you did awesome things that we did not expect,
you came down, and the mountains trembled before you.
4 Since ancient times no one has heard,
no ear has perceived,
no eye has seen any God besides you,
who acts on behalf of those who wait for him.
5 You come to the help of those who gladly do right,
who remember your ways.
But when we continued to sin against them,
you were angry.
How then can we be saved?
6 All of us have become like one who is unclean,
and all our righteous acts are like filthy rags;
we all shrivel up like a leaf,
and like the wind our sins sweep us away.
7 No one calls on your name
or strives to lay hold of you;
for you have hidden your face from us
and have given us over to[d] our sins.

8 Yet you, LORD, are our Father.
We are the clay, you are the potter;
we are all the work of your hand.
9 Do not be angry beyond measure, LORD;
do not remember our sins forever.
Oh, look on us, we pray,
for we are all your people.
10 Your sacred cities have become a wasteland;
even Zion is a wasteland, Jerusalem a desolation.
11 Our holy and glorious temple, where our ancestors praised you,
has been burned with fire,
and all that we treasured lies in ruins.
12 After all this, LORD, will you hold yourself back?

[a] 11 Or *But may he recall* [b] 19 Or *We are like those you have never ruled, / like those never called* [c] In Hebrew texts 64:1 is numbered 63:19b, and 64:2-12 is numbered 64:1-11. [d] 7 Septuagint, Syriac and Targum; Hebrew *have made us melt because of*

Will you keep silent and punish us
beyond measure?

Judgment and Salvation

65 "I revealed myself to those who did
not ask for me;
I was found by those who did not
seek me.
To a nation that did not call on my name,
I said, 'Here am I, here am I.'
2 All day long I have held out my hands
to an obstinate people,
who walk in ways not good,
pursuing their own imaginations —
3 a people who continually provoke me
to my very face,
offering sacrifices in gardens
and burning incense on altars of brick;
4 who sit among the graves
and spend their nights keeping secret
vigil;
who eat the flesh of pigs,
and whose pots hold broth of impure
meat;
5 who say, 'Keep away; don't come near me,
for I am too sacred for you!'
Such people are smoke in my nostrils,
a fire that keeps burning all day.

6 "See, it stands written before me:
I will not keep silent but will pay back
in full;
I will pay it back into their laps —
7 both your sins and the sins of your
ancestors,"
says the LORD.
"Because they burned sacrifices on the
mountains
and defied me on the hills,
I will measure into their laps
the full payment for their former
deeds."

8 This is what the LORD says:

"As when juice is still found in a cluster
of grapes
and people say, 'Don't destroy it,
there is still a blessing in it,'
so will I do in behalf of my servants;
I will not destroy them all.
9 I will bring forth descendants from
Jacob,
and from Judah those who will possess
my mountains;
my chosen people will inherit them,
and there will my servants live.
10 Sharon will become a pasture for flocks,
and the Valley of Achor a resting place
for herds,
for my people who seek me.
11 "But as for you who forsake the LORD
and forget my holy mountain,
who spread a table for Fortune
and fill bowls of mixed wine for
Destiny,
12 I will destine you for the sword,
and all of you will fall in the slaughter;
for I called but you did not answer,
I spoke but you did not listen.
You did evil in my sight
and chose what displeases me."

13 Therefore this is what the Sovereign
LORD says:

"My servants will eat,
but you will go hungry;
my servants will drink,
but you will go thirsty;
my servants will rejoice,
but you will be put to shame.
14 My servants will sing
out of the joy of their hearts,
but you will cry out
from anguish of heart
and wail in brokenness of spirit.
15 You will leave your name
for my chosen ones to use in their
curses;
the Sovereign LORD will put you to death,
but to his servants he will give another
name.
16 Whoever invokes a blessing in the land
will do so by the one true God;
whoever takes an oath in the land
will swear by the one true God.
For the past troubles will be forgotten
and hidden from my eyes.

New Heavens and a New Earth

17 "See, I will create
new heavens and a new earth.
The former things will not be
remembered,
nor will they come to mind.
18 But be glad and rejoice forever
in what I will create,
for I will create Jerusalem to be a delight
and its people a joy.

[19] I will rejoice over Jerusalem
and take delight in my people;
the sound of weeping and of crying
will be heard in it no more.

[20] "Never again will there be in it
an infant who lives but a few days,
or an old man who does not live out
his years;
the one who dies at a hundred
will be thought a mere child;
the one who fails to reach[a] a hundred
will be considered accursed.
[21] They will build houses and dwell in
them;
they will plant vineyards and eat
their fruit.
[22] No longer will they build houses and
others live in them,
or plant and others eat.
For as the days of a tree,
so will be the days of my people;
my chosen ones will long enjoy
the work of their hands.
[23] They will not labor in vain,
nor will they bear children doomed to
misfortune;
for they will be a people blessed by
the LORD,
they and their descendants with them.
[24] Before they call I will answer;
while they are still speaking I will hear.
[25] The wolf and the lamb will feed together,
and the lion will eat straw like the ox,
and dust will be the serpent's food.
They will neither harm nor destroy
on all my holy mountain,"
says the LORD.

Judgment and Hope

66 This is what the LORD says:

"Heaven is my throne,
and the earth is my footstool.
Where is the house you will build for me?
Where will my resting place be?
[2] Has not my hand made all these things,
and so they came into being?"
declares the LORD.

"These are the ones I look on with favor:
those who are humble and contrite in
spirit,
and who tremble at my word.
[3] But whoever sacrifices a bull
is like one who kills a person,
and whoever offers a lamb
is like one who breaks a dog's neck;
whoever makes a grain offering
is like one who presents pig's blood,
and whoever burns memorial incense
is like one who worships an idol.
They have chosen their own ways,
and they delight in their
abominations;
[4] so I also will choose harsh treatment
for them
and will bring on them what they
dread.
For when I called, no one answered,
when I spoke, no one listened.
They did evil in my sight
and chose what displeases me."

[5] Hear the word of the LORD,
you who tremble at his word:
"Your own people who hate you,
and exclude you because of my name,
have said,
'Let the LORD be glorified,
that we may see your joy!'
Yet they will be put to shame.
[6] Hear that uproar from the city,
hear that noise from the temple!
It is the sound of the LORD
repaying his enemies all they deserve.

[7] "Before she goes into labor,
she gives birth;
before the pains come upon her,
she delivers a son.
[8] Who has ever heard of such things?
Who has ever seen things like this?
Can a country be born in a day
or a nation be brought forth in a
moment?
Yet no sooner is Zion in labor
than she gives birth to her children.
[9] Do I bring to the moment of birth
and not give delivery?" says the LORD.
"Do I close up the womb
when I bring to delivery?" says
your God.
[10] "Rejoice with Jerusalem and be glad
for her,
all you who love her;

[a] 20 Or *the sinner who reaches*

rejoice greatly with her,
all you who mourn over her.
11 For you will nurse and be satisfied
at her comforting breasts;
you will drink deeply
and delight in her overflowing
abundance."

12 For this is what the LORD says:

"I will extend peace to her like a river,
and the wealth of nations like a
flooding stream;
you will nurse and be carried on her arm
and dandled on her knees.
13 As a mother comforts her child,
so will I comfort you;
and you will be comforted over
Jerusalem."

14 When you see this, your heart will rejoice
and you will flourish like grass;
the hand of the LORD will be made
known to his servants,
but his fury will be shown to his foes.
15 See, the LORD is coming with fire,
and his chariots are like a whirlwind;
he will bring down his anger with fury,
and his rebuke with flames of fire.
16 For with fire and with his sword
the LORD will execute judgment on all
people,
and many will be those slain by the
LORD.

17 "Those who consecrate and purify
themselves to go into the gardens, following
one who is among those who eat the flesh of
pigs, rats and other unclean things—they
will meet their end together with the one
they follow," declares the LORD.
18 "And I, because of what they have
planned and done, am about to come[a] and
gather the people of all nations and languag-
es, and they will come and see my glory.
19 "I will set a sign among them, and I
will send some of those who survive to the
nations—to Tarshish, to the Libyans[b] and
Lydians (famous as archers), to Tubal and
Greece, and to the distant islands that have
not heard of my fame or seen my glory. They
will proclaim my glory among the nations.
20 And they will bring all your people, from
all the nations, to my holy mountain in Jeru-
salem as an offering to the LORD—on hors-
es, in chariots and wagons, and on mules
and camels," says the LORD. "They will bring
them, as the Israelites bring their grain of-
ferings, to the temple of the LORD in ceremo-
nially clean vessels. 21 And I will select some
of them also to be priests and Levites," says
the LORD.

22 "As the new heavens and the new earth
that I make will endure before me," declares
the LORD, "so will your name and descen-
dants endure. 23 From one New Moon to an-
other and from one Sabbath to another, all
mankind will come and bow down before
me," says the LORD. 24 "And they will go out
and look on the dead bodies of those who re-
belled against me; the worms that eat them
will not die, the fire that burns them will not
be quenched, and they will be loathsome to
all mankind."

[a] *18* The meaning of the Hebrew for this clause is uncertain [b] *19* Some Septuagint manuscripts *Put* (Libyans); Hebrew *Pul*

JEREMIAH

1 The words of Jeremiah son of Hilkiah,
one of the priests at Anathoth in the ter-
ritory of Benjamin. 2 The word of the LORD
came to him in the thirteenth year of the
reign of Josiah son of Amon king of Judah,
3 and through the reign of Jehoiakim son of
Josiah king of Judah, down to the fifth month
of the eleventh year of Zedekiah son of Josi-
ah king of Judah, when the people of Jerusa-
lem went into exile.

The Call of Jeremiah

4 The word of the LORD came to me, saying,

5 "Before I formed you in the womb
I knew[a] you,
before you were born I set you apart;
I appointed you as a prophet to the
nations."

6 "Alas, Sovereign LORD," I said, "I do not
know how to speak; I am too young."
7 But the LORD said to me, "Do not say, 'I
am too young.' You must go to everyone I
send you to and say whatever I command
you. 8 Do not be afraid of them, for I am with
you and will rescue you," declares the LORD.
9 Then the LORD reached out his hand and
touched my mouth and said to me, "I have
put my words in your mouth. 10 See, today I
appoint you over nations and kingdoms to
uproot and tear down, to destroy and over-
throw, to build and to plant."
11 The word of the LORD came to me:
"What do you see, Jeremiah?"
"I see the branch of an almond tree," I re-
plied.
12 The LORD said to me, "You have seen
correctly, for I am watching[b] to see that my
word is fulfilled."
13 The word of the LORD came to me again:
"What do you see?"
"I see a pot that is boiling," I answered. "It
is tilting toward us from the north."
14 The LORD said to me, "From the north di-
saster will be poured out on all who live in the
land. 15 I am about to summon all the peoples
of the northern kingdoms," declares the LORD.

"Their kings will come and set up their
thrones
in the entrance of the gates of
Jerusalem;
they will come against all her
surrounding walls
and against all the towns of Judah.
16 I will pronounce my judgments on my
people
because of their wickedness in
forsaking me,
in burning incense to other gods
and in worshiping what their hands
have made.

17 "Get yourself ready! Stand up and say to
them whatever I command you. Do not be
terrified by them, or I will terrify you before
them. 18 Today I have made you a fortified
city, an iron pillar and a bronze wall to stand
against the whole land — against the kings of
Judah, its officials, its priests and the people
of the land. 19 They will fight against you but
will not overcome you, for I am with you and
will rescue you," declares the LORD.

Israel Forsakes God

2 The word of the LORD came to me: 2 "Go
and proclaim in the hearing of Jerusalem:

"This is what the LORD says:

" 'I remember the devotion of your youth,
how as a bride you loved me
and followed me through the wilderness,
through a land not sown.
3 Israel was holy to the LORD,
the firstfruits of his harvest;
all who devoured her were held guilty,
and disaster overtook them,' "
declares the LORD.

4 Hear the word of the LORD, you
descendants of Jacob,
all you clans of Israel.

[a] 5 Or *chose* [b] 12 The Hebrew for *watching* sounds like the Hebrew for *almond tree.*

[5]This is what the LORD says:

"What fault did your ancestors find
in me,
that they strayed so far from me?
They followed worthless idols
and became worthless themselves.
[6]They did not ask, 'Where is the LORD,
who brought us up out of Egypt
and led us through the barren
wilderness,
through a land of deserts and
ravines,
a land of drought and utter darkness,
a land where no one travels and no
one lives?'
[7]I brought you into a fertile land
to eat its fruit and rich produce.
But you came and defiled my land
and made my inheritance detestable.
[8]The priests did not ask,
'Where is the LORD?'
Those who deal with the law did not
know me;
the leaders rebelled against me.
The prophets prophesied by Baal,
following worthless idols.

[9]"Therefore I bring charges against you
again,"
declares the LORD.
"And I will bring charges against your
children's children.
[10]Cross over to the coasts of Cyprus and
look,
send to Kedar[a] and observe closely;
see if there has ever been anything
like this:
[11]Has a nation ever changed its gods?
(Yet they are not gods at all.)
But my people have exchanged their
glorious God
for worthless idols.
[12]Be appalled at this, you heavens,
and shudder with great horror,"
declares the LORD.
[13]"My people have committed two sins:
They have forsaken me,
the spring of living water,
and have dug their own cisterns,
broken cisterns that cannot hold water.
[14]Is Israel a servant, a slave by birth?
Why then has he become plunder?
[15]Lions have roared;
they have growled at him.
They have laid waste his land;
his towns are burned and deserted.
[16]Also, the men of Memphis and
Tahpanhes
have cracked your skull.
[17]Have you not brought this on yourselves
by forsaking the LORD your God
when he led you in the way?
[18]Now why go to Egypt
to drink water from the Nile[b]?
And why go to Assyria
to drink water from the Euphrates?
[19]Your wickedness will punish you;
your backsliding will rebuke you.
Consider then and realize
how evil and bitter it is for you
when you forsake the LORD your God
and have no awe of me,"
declares the Lord,
the LORD Almighty.

[20]"Long ago you broke off your yoke
and tore off your bonds;
you said, 'I will not serve you!'
Indeed, on every high hill
and under every spreading tree
you lay down as a prostitute.
[21]I had planted you like a choice vine
of sound and reliable stock.
How then did you turn against me
into a corrupt, wild vine?
[22]Although you wash yourself with soap
and use an abundance of cleansing
powder,
the stain of your guilt is still before
me,"
declares the Sovereign LORD.
[23]"How can you say, 'I am not defiled;
I have not run after the Baals'?
See how you behaved in the valley;
consider what you have done.
You are a swift she-camel
running here and there,
[24]a wild donkey accustomed to the desert,
sniffing the wind in her craving—
in her heat who can restrain her?
Any males that pursue her need not tire
themselves;
at mating time they will find her.
[25]Do not run until your feet are bare
and your throat is dry.

[a] *10* In the Syro-Arabian desert [b] *18* Hebrew *Shihor;* that is, a branch of the Nile

But you said, 'It's no use!
I love foreign gods,
and I must go after them.'

26 "As a thief is disgraced when he is caught,
so the people of Israel are disgraced—
they, their kings and their officials,
their priests and their prophets.
27 They say to wood, 'You are my father,'
and to stone, 'You gave me birth.'
They have turned their backs to me
and not their faces;
yet when they are in trouble, they say,
'Come and save us!'
28 Where then are the gods you made for yourselves?
Let them come if they can save you
when you are in trouble!
For you, Judah, have as many gods
as you have towns.

29 "Why do you bring charges against me?
You have all rebelled against me,"
declares the LORD.
30 "In vain I punished your people;
they did not respond to correction.
Your sword has devoured your prophets
like a ravenous lion.

31 "You of this generation, consider the word of the LORD:

"Have I been a desert to Israel
or a land of great darkness?
Why do my people say, 'We are free to roam;
we will come to you no more'?
32 Does a young woman forget her jewelry,
a bride her wedding ornaments?
Yet my people have forgotten me,
days without number.
33 How skilled you are at pursuing love!
Even the worst of women can learn
from your ways.
34 On your clothes is found
the lifeblood of the innocent poor,
though you did not catch them
breaking in.
Yet in spite of all this
35 you say, 'I am innocent;
he is not angry with me.'
But I will pass judgment on you
because you say, 'I have not sinned.'
36 Why do you go about so much,
changing your ways?
You will be disappointed by Egypt
as you were by Assyria.
37 You will also leave that place
with your hands on your head,
for the LORD has rejected those you trust;
you will not be helped by them.

3 "If a man divorces his wife
and she leaves him and marries
another man,
should he return to her again?
Would not the land be completely
defiled?
But you have lived as a prostitute with
many lovers—
would you now return to me?"
declares the LORD.
2 "Look up to the barren heights and see.
Is there any place where you have not
been ravished?
By the roadside you sat waiting for lovers,
sat like a nomad in the desert.
You have defiled the land
with your prostitution and
wickedness.
3 Therefore the showers have been
withheld,
and no spring rains have fallen.
Yet you have the brazen look of a
prostitute;
you refuse to blush with shame.
4 Have you not just called to me:
'My Father, my friend from my youth,
5 will you always be angry?
Will your wrath continue forever?'
This is how you talk,
but you do all the evil you can."

Unfaithful Israel

6 During the reign of King Josiah, the LORD
said to me, "Have you seen what faithless Is-
rael has done? She has gone up on every high
hill and under every spreading tree and has
committed adultery there. 7 I thought that
after she had done all this she would return
to me but she did not, and her unfaithful sis-
ter Judah saw it. 8 I gave faithless Israel her
certificate of divorce and sent her away be-
cause of all her adulteries. Yet I saw that her
unfaithful sister Judah had no fear; she also
went out and committed adultery. 9 Because
Israel's immorality mattered so little to her,
she defiled the land and committed adultery
with stone and wood. 10 In spite of all this,

her unfaithful sister Judah did not return to
me with all her heart, but only in pretense,"
declares the LORD.

[11] The LORD said to me, "Faithless Israel is
more righteous than unfaithful Judah. [12] Go,
proclaim this message toward the north:

"'Return, faithless Israel,' declares
the LORD,
'I will frown on you no longer,
for I am faithful,' declares the LORD,
'I will not be angry forever.
[13] Only acknowledge your guilt—
you have rebelled against the LORD
your God,
you have scattered your favors to foreign
gods
under every spreading tree,
and have not obeyed me,'"
declares the LORD.

[14] "Return, faithless people," declares the
LORD, "for I am your husband. I will choose
you—one from a town and two from a
clan—and bring you to Zion. [15] Then I will
give you shepherds after my own heart, who
will lead you with knowledge and under-
standing. [16] In those days, when your num-
bers have increased greatly in the land," de-
clares the LORD, "people will no longer say,
'The ark of the covenant of the LORD.' It will
never enter their minds or be remembered;
it will not be missed, nor will another one
be made. [17] At that time they will call Jerusa-
lem The Throne of the LORD, and all nations
will gather in Jerusalem to honor the name
of the LORD. No longer will they follow the
stubbornness of their evil hearts. [18] In those
days the people of Judah will join the people
of Israel, and together they will come from a
northern land to the land I gave your ances-
tors as an inheritance.

[19] "I myself said,

"'How gladly would I treat you like my
children
and give you a pleasant land,
the most beautiful inheritance of any
nation.'
I thought you would call me 'Father'
and not turn away from following me.
[20] But like a woman unfaithful to her
husband,
so you, Israel, have been unfaithful
to me,"
declares the LORD.

[21] A cry is heard on the barren heights,
the weeping and pleading of the
people of Israel,
because they have perverted their ways
and have forgotten the LORD
their God.

[22] "Return, faithless people;
I will cure you of backsliding."

"Yes, we will come to you,
for you are the LORD our God.
[23] Surely the idolatrous commotion on
the hills
and mountains is a deception;
surely in the LORD our God
is the salvation of Israel.
[24] From our youth shameful gods have
consumed
the fruits of our ancestors' labor—
their flocks and herds,
their sons and daughters.
[25] Let us lie down in our shame,
and let our disgrace cover us.
We have sinned against the LORD
our God,
both we and our ancestors;
from our youth till this day
we have not obeyed the LORD
our God."

4 "If you, Israel, will return,
then return to me,"
declares the LORD.
"If you put your detestable idols out of
my sight
and no longer go astray,
[2] and if in a truthful, just and righteous
way
you swear, 'As surely as the LORD lives,'
then the nations will invoke blessings
by him
and in him they will boast."

[3] This is what the LORD says to the people
of Judah and to Jerusalem:

"Break up your unplowed ground
and do not sow among thorns.
[4] Circumcise yourselves to the LORD,
circumcise your hearts,
you people of Judah and inhabitants of
Jerusalem,
or my wrath will flare up and burn like
fire
because of the evil you have done—
burn with no one to quench it.

Disaster From the North

5 "Announce in Judah and proclaim in
Jerusalem and say:
'Sound the trumpet throughout the
land!'
Cry aloud and say:
'Gather together!
Let us flee to the fortified cities!'
6 Raise the signal to go to Zion!
Flee for safety without delay!
For I am bringing disaster from the north,
even terrible destruction."

7 A lion has come out of his lair;
a destroyer of nations has set out.
He has left his place
to lay waste your land.
Your towns will lie in ruins
without inhabitant.
8 So put on sackcloth,
lament and wail,
for the fierce anger of the LORD
has not turned away from us.

9 "In that day," declares the LORD,
"the king and the officials will lose
heart,
the priests will be horrified,
and the prophets will be appalled."

10 Then I said, "Alas, Sovereign LORD! How
completely you have deceived this peo-
ple and Jerusalem by saying, 'You will have
peace,' when the sword is at our throats!"
11 At that time this people and Jerusalem
will be told, "A scorching wind from the bar-
ren heights in the desert blows toward my
people, but not to winnow or cleanse; 12 a
wind too strong for that comes from me. Now
I pronounce my judgments against them."

13 Look! He advances like the clouds,
his chariots come like a whirlwind,
his horses are swifter than eagles.
Woe to us! We are ruined!
14 Jerusalem, wash the evil from your heart
and be saved.
How long will you harbor wicked
thoughts?
15 A voice is announcing from Dan,
proclaiming disaster from the hills of
Ephraim.
16 "Tell this to the nations,
proclaim concerning Jerusalem:
'A besieging army is coming from a
distant land,
raising a war cry against the cities of
Judah.
17 They surround her like men guarding
a field,
because she has rebelled against me,'"
declares the LORD.
18 "Your own conduct and actions
have brought this on you.
This is your punishment.
How bitter it is!
How it pierces to the heart!"

19 Oh, my anguish, my anguish!
I writhe in pain.
Oh, the agony of my heart!
My heart pounds within me,
I cannot keep silent.
For I have heard the sound of the
trumpet;
I have heard the battle cry.
20 Disaster follows disaster;
the whole land lies in ruins.
In an instant my tents are destroyed,
my shelter in a moment.
21 How long must I see the battle standard
and hear the sound of the trumpet?

22 "My people are fools;
they do not know me.
They are senseless children;
they have no understanding.
They are skilled in doing evil;
they know not how to do good."

23 I looked at the earth,
and it was formless and empty;
and at the heavens,
and their light was gone.
24 I looked at the mountains,
and they were quaking;
all the hills were swaying.
25 I looked, and there were no people;
every bird in the sky had flown away.
26 I looked, and the fruitful land was a
desert;
all its towns lay in ruins
before the LORD, before his fierce anger.

27 This is what the LORD says:

"The whole land will be ruined,
though I will not destroy it completely.
28 Therefore the earth will mourn
and the heavens above grow dark,
because I have spoken and will not
relent,
I have decided and will not turn back."

[29] At the sound of horsemen and archers
every town takes to flight.
Some go into the thickets;
some climb up among the rocks.
All the towns are deserted;
no one lives in them.

[30] What are you doing, you devastated one?
Why dress yourself in scarlet
and put on jewels of gold?
Why highlight your eyes with makeup?
You adorn yourself in vain.
Your lovers despise you;
they want to kill you.

[31] I hear a cry as of a woman in labor,
a groan as of one bearing her first child —
the cry of Daughter Zion gasping for breath,
stretching out her hands and saying,
"Alas! I am fainting;
my life is given over to murderers."

Not One Is Upright

5 "Go up and down the streets of Jerusalem,
look around and consider,
search through her squares.
If you can find but one person
who deals honestly and seeks the truth,
I will forgive this city.
[2] Although they say, 'As surely as the LORD lives,'
still they are swearing falsely."
[3] LORD, do not your eyes look for truth?
You struck them, but they felt no pain;
you crushed them, but they refused correction.
They made their faces harder than stone
and refused to repent.
[4] I thought, "These are only the poor;
they are foolish,
for they do not know the way of the LORD,
the requirements of their God.
[5] So I will go to the leaders
and speak to them;
surely they know the way of the LORD,
the requirements of their God."
But with one accord they too had broken off the yoke
and torn off the bonds.
[6] Therefore a lion from the forest will attack them,
a wolf from the desert will ravage them,
a leopard will lie in wait near their towns
to tear to pieces any who venture out,
for their rebellion is great
and their backslidings many.

[7] "Why should I forgive you?
Your children have forsaken me
and sworn by gods that are not gods.
I supplied all their needs,
yet they committed adultery
and thronged to the houses of prostitutes.
[8] They are well-fed, lusty stallions,
each neighing for another man's wife.
[9] Should I not punish them for this?"
declares the LORD.
"Should I not avenge myself
on such a nation as this?

[10] "Go through her vineyards and ravage them,
but do not destroy them completely.
Strip off her branches,
for these people do not belong to the LORD.
[11] The people of Israel and the people of Judah
have been utterly unfaithful to me,"
declares the LORD.

[12] They have lied about the LORD;
they said, "He will do nothing!
No harm will come to us;
we will never see sword or famine.
[13] The prophets are but wind
and the word is not in them;
so let what they say be done to them."

[14] Therefore this is what the LORD God Almighty says:

"Because the people have spoken these words,
I will make my words in your mouth a fire
and these people the wood it consumes.
[15] People of Israel," declares the LORD,
"I am bringing a distant nation against you —
an ancient and enduring nation,
a people whose language you do not know,
whose speech you do not understand.

[16]Their quivers are like an open grave;
all of them are mighty warriors.
[17]They will devour your harvests and food,
devour your sons and daughters;
they will devour your flocks and herds,
devour your vines and fig trees.
With the sword they will destroy
the fortified cities in which you trust.

[18]"Yet even in those days," declares the
LORD, "I will not destroy you completely.
[19]And when the people ask, 'Why has the
LORD our God done all this to us?' you will
tell them, 'As you have forsaken me and
served foreign gods in your own land, so
now you will serve foreigners in a land not
your own.'

[20]"Announce this to the descendants
of Jacob
and proclaim it in Judah:
[21]Hear this, you foolish and senseless
people,
who have eyes but do not see,
who have ears but do not hear:
[22]Should you not fear me?" declares
the LORD.
"Should you not tremble in my
presence?
I made the sand a boundary for the sea,
an everlasting barrier it cannot cross.
The waves may roll, but they cannot
prevail;
they may roar, but they cannot cross it.
[23]But these people have stubborn and
rebellious hearts;
they have turned aside and gone away.
[24]They do not say to themselves,
'Let us fear the LORD our God,
who gives autumn and spring rains in
season,
who assures us of the regular weeks
of harvest.'
[25]Your wrongdoings have kept these away;
your sins have deprived you of good.

[26]"Among my people are the wicked
who lie in wait like men who snare
birds
and like those who set traps to catch
people.
[27]Like cages full of birds,
their houses are full of deceit;
they have become rich and powerful
[28] and have grown fat and sleek.
Their evil deeds have no limit;
they do not seek justice.
They do not promote the case of the
fatherless;
they do not defend the just cause of
the poor.
[29]Should I not punish them for this?"
declares the LORD.
"Should I not avenge myself
on such a nation as this?
[30]"A horrible and shocking thing
has happened in the land:
[31]The prophets prophesy lies,
the priests rule by their own authority,
and my people love it this way.
But what will you do in the end?

Jerusalem Under Siege

6 "Flee for safety, people of Benjamin!
Flee from Jerusalem!
Sound the trumpet in Tekoa!
Raise the signal over Beth Hakkerem!
For disaster looms out of the north,
even terrible destruction.
[2]I will destroy Daughter Zion,
so beautiful and delicate.
[3]Shepherds with their flocks will come
against her;
they will pitch their tents around her,
each tending his own portion."

[4]"Prepare for battle against her!
Arise, let us attack at noon!
But, alas, the daylight is fading,
and the shadows of evening grow long.
[5]So arise, let us attack at night
and destroy her fortresses!"

[6]This is what the LORD Almighty says:

"Cut down the trees
and build siege ramps against
Jerusalem.
This city must be punished;
it is filled with oppression.
[7]As a well pours out its water,
so she pours out her wickedness.
Violence and destruction resound
in her;
her sickness and wounds are ever
before me.
[8]Take warning, Jerusalem,
or I will turn away from you
and make your land desolate
so no one can live in it."

[9]This is what the LORD Almighty says:

"Let them glean the remnant of Israel
as thoroughly as a vine;
pass your hand over the branches again,
like one gathering grapes."
[10]To whom can I speak and give warning?
Who will listen to me?
Their ears are closed[a]
so they cannot hear.
The word of the LORD is offensive
to them;
they find no pleasure in it.
[11]But I am full of the wrath of the LORD,
and I cannot hold it in.

"Pour it out on the children in the street
and on the young men gathered
together;
both husband and wife will be caught
in it,
and the old, those weighed down with
years.
[12]Their houses will be turned over to
others,
together with their fields and their
wives,
when I stretch out my hand
against those who live in the land,"
declares the LORD.
[13]"From the least to the greatest,
all are greedy for gain;
prophets and priests alike,
all practice deceit.
[14]They dress the wound of my people
as though it were not serious.
'Peace, peace,' they say,
when there is no peace.
[15]Are they ashamed of their detestable
conduct?
No, they have no shame at all;
they do not even know how to blush.
So they will fall among the fallen;
they will be brought down when I
punish them,"
says the LORD.
[16]This is what the LORD says:

"Stand at the crossroads and look;
ask for the ancient paths,
ask where the good way is, and walk in it,
and you will find rest for your souls.
But you said, 'We will not walk in it.'
[17]I appointed watchmen over you and said,
'Listen to the sound of the trumpet!'
But you said, 'We will not listen.'
[18]Therefore hear, you nations;
you who are witnesses,
observe what will happen to them.
[19]Hear, you earth:
I am bringing disaster on this people,
the fruit of their schemes,
because they have not listened to my
words
and have rejected my law.
[20]What do I care about incense from Sheba
or sweet calamus from a distant land?
Your burnt offerings are not acceptable;
your sacrifices do not please me."
[21]Therefore this is what the LORD says:
"I will put obstacles before this people.
Parents and children alike will
stumble over them;
neighbors and friends will perish."
[22]This is what the LORD says:

"Look, an army is coming
from the land of the north;
a great nation is being stirred up
from the ends of the earth.
[23]They are armed with bow and spear;
they are cruel and show no mercy.
They sound like the roaring sea
as they ride on their horses;
they come like men in battle formation
to attack you, Daughter Zion."
[24]We have heard reports about them,
and our hands hang limp.
Anguish has gripped us,
pain like that of a woman in labor.
[25]Do not go out to the fields
or walk on the roads,
for the enemy has a sword,
and there is terror on every side.
[26]Put on sackcloth, my people,
and roll in ashes;
mourn with bitter wailing
as for an only son,
for suddenly the destroyer
will come upon us.

[27]"I have made you a tester of metals
and my people the ore,
that you may observe
and test their ways.

[a] *10* Hebrew *uncircumcised*

28 They are all hardened rebels,
going about to slander.
They are bronze and iron;
they all act corruptly.
29 The bellows blow fiercely
to burn away the lead with fire,
but the refining goes on in vain;
the wicked are not purged out.
30 They are called rejected silver,
because the LORD has rejected them."

False Religion Worthless

7 This is the word that came to Jeremiah
from the LORD: 2 "Stand at the gate of the
LORD's house and there proclaim this mes-
sage:

" 'Hear the word of the LORD, all you peo-
ple of Judah who come through these gates
to worship the LORD. 3 This is what the LORD
Almighty, the God of Israel, says: Reform
your ways and your actions, and I will let
you live in this place. 4 Do not trust in de-
ceptive words and say, "This is the temple of
the LORD, the temple of the LORD, the tem-
ple of the LORD!" 5 If you really change your
ways and your actions and deal with each
other justly, 6 if you do not oppress the for-
eigner, the fatherless or the widow and do
not shed innocent blood in this place, and
if you do not follow other gods to your own
harm, 7 then I will let you live in this place,
in the land I gave your ancestors for ever and
ever. 8 But look, you are trusting in deceptive
words that are worthless.

9 " 'Will you steal and murder, commit
adultery and perjury,[a] burn incense to Baal
and follow other gods you have not known,
10 and then come and stand before me in this
house, which bears my Name, and say, "We
are safe" — safe to do all these detestable
things? 11 Has this house, which bears my
Name, become a den of robbers to you? But I
have been watching! declares the LORD.

12 " 'Go now to the place in Shiloh where I
first made a dwelling for my Name, and see
what I did to it because of the wickedness of
my people Israel. 13 While you were doing all
these things, declares the LORD, I spoke to
you again and again, but you did not listen; I
called you, but you did not answer. 14 There-
fore, what I did to Shiloh I will now do to the
house that bears my Name, the temple you
trust in, the place I gave to you and your an-
cestors. 15 I will thrust you from my presence,
just as I did all your fellow Israelites, the peo-
ple of Ephraim.'

16 "So do not pray for this people nor offer
any plea or petition for them; do not plead
with me, for I will not listen to you. 17 Do you
not see what they are doing in the towns of
Judah and in the streets of Jerusalem? 18 The
children gather wood, the fathers light the
fire, and the women knead the dough and
make cakes to offer to the Queen of Heaven.
They pour out drink offerings to other gods
to arouse my anger. 19 But am I the one they
are provoking? declares the LORD. Are they
not rather harming themselves, to their own
shame?

20 " 'Therefore this is what the Sovereign
LORD says: My anger and my wrath will be
poured out on this place — on man and
beast, on the trees of the field and on the
crops of your land — and it will burn and not
be quenched.

21 " 'This is what the LORD Almighty, the
God of Israel, says: Go ahead, add your burnt
offerings to your other sacrifices and eat
the meat yourselves! 22 For when I brought
your ancestors out of Egypt and spoke to
them, I did not just give them commands
about burnt offerings and sacrifices, 23 but
I gave them this command: Obey me, and I
will be your God and you will be my people.
Walk in obedience to all I command you,
that it may go well with you. 24 But they did
not listen or pay attention; instead, they fol-
lowed the stubborn inclinations of their evil
hearts. They went backward and not for-
ward. 25 From the time your ancestors left
Egypt until now, day after day, again and
again I sent you my servants the prophets.
26 But they did not listen to me or pay atten-
tion. They were stiff-necked and did more
evil than their ancestors.'

27 "When you tell them all this, they will
not listen to you; when you call to them, they
will not answer. 28 Therefore say to them,
'This is the nation that has not obeyed the
LORD its God or responded to correction.
Truth has perished; it has vanished from
their lips.

29 " 'Cut off your hair and throw it away;
take up a lament on the barren heights, for

[a] 9 Or *and swear by false gods*

the LORD has rejected and abandoned this
generation that is under his wrath.

The Valley of Slaughter

[30] "'The people of Judah have done evil in
my eyes, declares the LORD. They have set
up their detestable idols in the house that
bears my Name and have defiled it. [31] They
have built the high places of Topheth in the
Valley of Ben Hinnom to burn their sons
and daughters in the fire—something I did
not command, nor did it enter my mind.
[32] So beware, the days are coming, declares
the LORD, when people will no longer call it
Topheth or the Valley of Ben Hinnom, but
the Valley of Slaughter, for they will bury
the dead in Topheth until there is no more
room. [33] Then the carcasses of this people
will become food for the birds and the wild
animals, and there will be no one to fright-
en them away. [34] I will bring an end to the
sounds of joy and gladness and to the voices
of bride and bridegroom in the towns of Ju-
dah and the streets of Jerusalem, for the land
will become desolate.

8 "'At that time, declares the LORD, the
bones of the kings and officials of Judah,
the bones of the priests and prophets, and
the bones of the people of Jerusalem will be
removed from their graves. [2] They will be ex-
posed to the sun and the moon and all the
stars of the heavens, which they have loved
and served and which they have followed
and consulted and worshiped. They will not
be gathered up or buried, but will be like
dung lying on the ground. [3] Wherever I ban-
ish them, all the survivors of this evil nation
will prefer death to life, declares the LORD
Almighty.'

Sin and Punishment

[4] "Say to them, 'This is what the LORD says:

"'When people fall down, do they not
get up?
When someone turns away, do they
not return?
[5] Why then have these people turned
away?
Why does Jerusalem always turn away?
They cling to deceit;
they refuse to return.
[6] I have listened attentively,
but they do not say what is right.
None of them repent of their wickedness,
saying, "What have I done?"
Each pursues their own course
like a horse charging into battle.
[7] Even the stork in the sky
knows her appointed seasons,
and the dove, the swift and the thrush
observe the time of their migration.
But my people do not know
the requirements of the LORD.

[8] "'How can you say, "We are wise,
for we have the law of the LORD,"
when actually the lying pen of the
scribes
has handled it falsely?
[9] The wise will be put to shame;
they will be dismayed and trapped.
Since they have rejected the word of
the LORD,
what kind of wisdom do they have?
[10] Therefore I will give their wives to
other men
and their fields to new owners.
From the least to the greatest,
all are greedy for gain;
prophets and priests alike,
all practice deceit.
[11] They dress the wound of my people
as though it were not serious.
"Peace, peace," they say,
when there is no peace.
[12] Are they ashamed of their detestable
conduct?
No, they have no shame at all;
they do not even know how to blush.
So they will fall among the fallen;
they will be brought down when they
are punished,
says the LORD.

[13] "'I will take away their harvest,
declares the LORD.
There will be no grapes on the vine.
There will be no figs on the tree,
and their leaves will wither.
What I have given them
will be taken from them.[a]'"
[14] Why are we sitting here?
Gather together!
Let us flee to the fortified cities
and perish there!

[a] 13 The meaning of the Hebrew for this sentence is uncertain.

For the LORD our God has doomed us
to perish
and given us poisoned water to drink,
because we have sinned against him.
15 We hoped for peace
but no good has come,
for a time of healing
but there is only terror.
16 The snorting of the enemy's horses
is heard from Dan;
at the neighing of their stallions
the whole land trembles.
They have come to devour
the land and everything in it,
the city and all who live there.

17 "See, I will send venomous snakes
among you,
vipers that cannot be charmed,
and they will bite you,"
declares the LORD.

18 You who are my Comforter[a] in sorrow,
my heart is faint within me.
19 Listen to the cry of my people
from a land far away:
"Is the LORD not in Zion?
Is her King no longer there?"

"Why have they aroused my anger with
their images,
with their worthless foreign idols?"

20 "The harvest is past,
the summer has ended,
and we are not saved."

21 Since my people are crushed, I am
crushed;
I mourn, and horror grips me.
22 Is there no balm in Gilead?
Is there no physician there?
Why then is there no healing
for the wound of my people?

9[b] 1 Oh, that my head were a spring of
water
and my eyes a fountain of tears!
I would weep day and night
for the slain of my people.
2 Oh, that I had in the desert
a lodging place for travelers,
so that I might leave my people
and go away from them;
for they are all adulterers,
a crowd of unfaithful people.

3 "They make ready their tongue
like a bow, to shoot lies;
it is not by truth
that they triumph[c] in the land.
They go from one sin to another;
they do not acknowledge me,"
declares the LORD.
4 "Beware of your friends;
do not trust anyone in your clan.
For every one of them is a deceiver,[d]
and every friend a slanderer.
5 Friend deceives friend,
and no one speaks the truth.
They have taught their tongues to lie;
they weary themselves with sinning.
6 You[e] live in the midst of deception;
in their deceit they refuse to
acknowledge me,"
declares the LORD.

7 Therefore this is what the LORD Almighty
says:

"See, I will refine and test them,
for what else can I do
because of the sin of my people?
8 Their tongue is a deadly arrow;
it speaks deceitfully.
With their mouths they all speak
cordially to their neighbors,
but in their hearts they set traps for
them.
9 Should I not punish them for this?"
declares the LORD.
"Should I not avenge myself
on such a nation as this?"

10 I will weep and wail for the mountains
and take up a lament concerning the
wilderness grasslands.
They are desolate and untraveled,
and the lowing of cattle is not
heard.
The birds have all fled
and the animals are gone.

11 "I will make Jerusalem a heap of ruins,
a haunt of jackals;
and I will lay waste the towns of Judah
so no one can live there."

[a] *18* The meaning of the Hebrew for this word is uncertain. [b] In Hebrew texts 9:1 is numbered 8:23, and 9:2-26 is numbered 9:1-25. [c] *3* Or *lies; / they are not valiant for truth* [d] *4* Or *a deceiving Jacob* [e] *6* That is, Jeremiah (the Hebrew is singular)

12 Who is wise enough to understand this?
Who has been instructed by the LORD and
can explain it? Why has the land been ru-
ined and laid waste like a desert that no one
can cross?
13 The LORD said, "It is because they have
forsaken my law, which I set before them;
they have not obeyed me or followed my
law. 14 Instead, they have followed the stub-
bornness of their hearts; they have followed
the Baals, as their ancestors taught them."
15 Therefore this is what the LORD Almighty,
the God of Israel, says: "See, I will make this
people eat bitter food and drink poisoned
water. 16 I will scatter them among nations
that neither they nor their ancestors have
known, and I will pursue them with the
sword until I have made an end of them."

17 This is what the LORD Almighty says:

"Consider now! Call for the wailing
women to come;
send for the most skillful of them.
18 Let them come quickly
and wail over us
till our eyes overflow with tears
and water streams from our eyelids.
19 The sound of wailing is heard from
Zion:
'How ruined we are!
How great is our shame!
We must leave our land
because our houses are in ruins.' "

20 Now, you women, hear the word of
the LORD;
open your ears to the words of his
mouth.
Teach your daughters how to wail;
teach one another a lament.
21 Death has climbed in through our
windows
and has entered our fortresses;
it has removed the children from the
streets
and the young men from the public
squares.

22 Say, "This is what the LORD declares:

" 'Dead bodies will lie
like dung on the open field,
like cut grain behind the reaper,
with no one to gather them.' "

23 This is what the LORD says:

"Let not the wise boast of their wisdom
or the strong boast of their strength
or the rich boast of their riches,
24 but let the one who boasts boast about
this:
that they have the understanding to
know me,
that I am the LORD, who exercises
kindness,
justice and righteousness on earth,
for in these I delight,"
declares the LORD.

25 "The days are coming," declares the
LORD, "when I will punish all who are cir-
cumcised only in the flesh— 26 Egypt, Ju-
dah, Edom, Ammon, Moab and all who live
in the wilderness in distant places.[a] For all
these nations are really uncircumcised, and
even the whole house of Israel is uncircum-
cised in heart."

God and Idols

10 Hear what the LORD says to you, peo-
ple of Israel. 2 This is what the LORD
says:

"Do not learn the ways of the nations
or be terrified by signs in the heavens,
though the nations are terrified by
them.
3 For the practices of the peoples are
worthless;
they cut a tree out of the forest,
and a craftsman shapes it with his
chisel.
4 They adorn it with silver and gold;
they fasten it with hammer and nails
so it will not totter.
5 Like a scarecrow in a cucumber field,
their idols cannot speak;
they must be carried
because they cannot walk.
Do not fear them;
they can do no harm
nor can they do any good."

6 No one is like you, LORD;
you are great,
and your name is mighty in power.
7 Who should not fear you,
King of the nations?
This is your due.

[a] 26 Or *wilderness and who clip the hair by their foreheads*

BETTER IS ONE DAY

Matt Redman

How lovely is your dwelling place
O Lord Almighty
For my soul longs and even faints for you
For here my heart is satisfied
Within your presence
I sing beneath the shadow of your wings

Better is one day in your courts
Better is one day in your house
Better is one day in your courts
Than thousands elsewhere

One thing I ask and I would seek
To see your beauty
To find you in the place your glory dwells

My heart and flesh cry out
For you, the living God
Your Spirit's water to my soul
I've tasted and I've seen
Come once again to me
I will draw near to you
I will draw near to you

THE INSPIRATION

Better is one day in your courts than a thousand elsewhere; I would rather be a doorkeeper in the house of my God than dwell in the tents of the wicked. For the LORD God is a sun and shield; the LORD bestows favor and honor; no good thing does he withhold from those whose walk is blameless. — Psalm 84:10 – 11

Read also: Psalm 42; Psalm 94

BEHIND THE SONG

Self-preservation and the pursuit of comfort are certainly two of the most powerful instincts in the human experience. Most of us know that they are empty goals if accomplished outside the perfect will and wisdom of God, but many of us still struggle for those things. There is no such thing, however, as safety or provision outside of his care, and within his care, there is no risk of harm or need.

Matt Redman had some ideas he wanted to deliver in song but no song he knew contained them. "It was the end of the service, and I was meeting quite powerfully with God," he recalls. "I opened my Bible to Psalm 94, 'How lovely is your dwelling place,' and just started singing it out. Then I got to this little refrain: 'Better is one day in your courts/Better is one day in your house/Better is one day in your courts than thousands elsewhere.' Then I went home and built the song around that."

Selah

In the line, "To find you in the place your glory dwells," Redman is referring to the *shekina* glory of God, the presence that filled the Most Holy Place in the tabernacle. Since sin cannot exist in God's presence, most of the Israelites were not allowed into this powerful place (see 1 Chronicles 6:9). Only the high priest could enter, and only once per year when he would make an atoning sacrifice for the sins of the people, an obvious look forward to the work that Jesus would do on the cross. Jesus' sacrifice made it possible for us to meet God on any day and at any time. Have you experienced times when you desperately wanted to sense God's presence? What practices do you engage in daily so that you can meet with Jesus?

Among all the wise leaders of the nations
and in all their kingdoms,
there is no one like you.

8 They are all senseless and foolish;
they are taught by worthless wooden idols.
9 Hammered silver is brought from Tarshish
and gold from Uphaz.
What the craftsman and goldsmith have made
is then dressed in blue and purple—
all made by skilled workers.
10 But the LORD is the true God;
he is the living God, the eternal King.
When he is angry, the earth trembles;
the nations cannot endure his wrath.

11 "Tell them this: 'These gods, who did not make the heavens and the earth, will perish from the earth and from under the heavens.' "[a]

12 But God made the earth by his power;
he founded the world by his wisdom
and stretched out the heavens by his understanding.
13 When he thunders, the waters in the heavens roar;
he makes clouds rise from the ends of the earth.
He sends lightning with the rain
and brings out the wind from his storehouses.

14 Everyone is senseless and without knowledge;
every goldsmith is shamed by his idols.
The images he makes are a fraud;
they have no breath in them.
15 They are worthless, the objects of mockery;
when their judgment comes, they will perish.
16 He who is the Portion of Jacob is not like these,
for he is the Maker of all things,
including Israel, the people of his inheritance—
the LORD Almighty is his name.

Coming Destruction

17 Gather up your belongings to leave the land,
you who live under siege.
18 For this is what the LORD says:
"At this time I will hurl out
those who live in this land;
I will bring distress on them
so that they may be captured."

19 Woe to me because of my injury!
My wound is incurable!
Yet I said to myself,
"This is my sickness, and I must endure it."
20 My tent is destroyed;
all its ropes are snapped.
My children are gone from me and are no more;
no one is left now to pitch my tent
or to set up my shelter.
21 The shepherds are senseless
and do not inquire of the LORD;
so they do not prosper
and all their flock is scattered.
22 Listen! The report is coming—
a great commotion from the land of the north!
It will make the towns of Judah desolate,
a haunt of jackals.

Jeremiah's Prayer

23 LORD, I know that people's lives are not their own;
it is not for them to direct their steps.
24 Discipline me, LORD, but only in due measure—
not in your anger,
or you will reduce me to nothing.
25 Pour out your wrath on the nations
that do not acknowledge you,
on the peoples who do not call on your name.
For they have devoured Jacob;
they have devoured him completely
and destroyed his homeland.

The Covenant Is Broken

11 This is the word that came to Jere-
miah from the LORD: 2 "Listen to the
terms of this covenant and tell them to the
people of Judah and to those who live in Je-
rusalem. 3 Tell them that this is what the
LORD, the God of Israel, says: 'Cursed is the
one who does not obey the terms of this cov-
enant— 4 the terms I commanded your an-
cestors when I brought them out of Egypt,

[a] 11 The text of this verse is in Aramaic.

out of the iron-smelting furnace.' I said,
'Obey me and do everything I command
you, and you will be my people, and I will
be your God. 5 Then I will fulfill the oath I
swore to your ancestors, to give them a land
flowing with milk and honey'—the land you
possess today."

I answered, "Amen, LORD."

6 The LORD said to me, "Proclaim all
these words in the towns of Judah and in the
streets of Jerusalem: 'Listen to the terms of
this covenant and follow them. 7 From the
time I brought your ancestors up from Egypt
until today, I warned them again and again,
saying, "Obey me." 8 But they did not lis-
ten or pay attention; instead, they followed
the stubbornness of their evil hearts. So I
brought on them all the curses of the cov-
enant I had commanded them to follow but
that they did not keep.'"

9 Then the LORD said to me, "There is a
conspiracy among the people of Judah and
those who live in Jerusalem. 10 They have
returned to the sins of their ancestors, who
refused to listen to my words. They have
followed other gods to serve them. Both Is-
rael and Judah have broken the covenant I
made with their ancestors. 11 Therefore this
is what the LORD says: 'I will bring on them a
disaster they cannot escape. Although they
cry out to me, I will not listen to them. 12 The
towns of Judah and the people of Jerusalem
will go and cry out to the gods to whom they
burn incense, but they will not help them at
all when disaster strikes. 13 You, Judah, have
as many gods as you have towns; and the al-
tars you have set up to burn incense to that
shameful god Baal are as many as the streets
of Jerusalem.'

14 "Do not pray for this people or offer any
plea or petition for them, because I will not
listen when they call to me in the time of
their distress.

15 "What is my beloved doing in my temple
as she, with many others, works out
her evil schemes?
Can consecrated meat avert your
punishment?
When you engage in your wickedness,
then you rejoice.[a]"

16 The LORD called you a thriving olive tree
with fruit beautiful in form.
But with the roar of a mighty storm
he will set it on fire,
and its branches will be broken.

17 The LORD Almighty, who planted you, has
decreed disaster for you, because the peo-
ple of both Israel and Judah have done evil
and aroused my anger by burning incense
to Baal.

Plot Against Jeremiah

18 Because the LORD revealed their plot
to me, I knew it, for at that time he showed
me what they were doing. 19 I had been like
a gentle lamb led to the slaughter; I did not
realize that they had plotted against me,
saying,

"Let us destroy the tree and its fruit;
let us cut him off from the land of the
living,
that his name be remembered no
more."

20 But you, LORD Almighty, who judge
righteously
and test the heart and mind,
let me see your vengeance on them,
for to you I have committed my cause.

21 Therefore this is what the LORD says
about the people of Anathoth who are
threatening to kill you, saying, "Do not
prophesy in the name of the LORD or you will
die by our hands"— 22 therefore this is what
the LORD Almighty says: "I will punish them.
Their young men will die by the sword, their
sons and daughters by famine. 23 Not even a
remnant will be left to them, because I will
bring disaster on the people of Anathoth in
the year of their punishment."

Jeremiah's Complaint

12 You are always righteous, LORD,
when I bring a case before you.
Yet I would speak with you about your
justice:
Why does the way of the wicked
prosper?
Why do all the faithless live at ease?
2 You have planted them, and they have
taken root;
they grow and bear fruit.
You are always on their lips
but far from their hearts.

[a] 15 Or *Could consecrated meat avert your punishment? / Then you would rejoice*

3 Yet you know me, LORD;
you see me and test my thoughts
about you.
Drag them off like sheep to be butchered!
Set them apart for the day of slaughter!
4 How long will the land lie parched
and the grass in every field be
withered?
Because those who live in it are wicked,
the animals and birds have perished.
Moreover, the people are saying,
"He will not see what happens to us."

God's Answer

5 "If you have raced with men on foot
and they have worn you out,
how can you compete with horses?
If you stumble[a] in safe country,
how will you manage in the thickets
by[b] the Jordan?
6 Your relatives, members of your own
family—
even they have betrayed you;
they have raised a loud cry against
you.
Do not trust them,
though they speak well of you.

7 "I will forsake my house,
abandon my inheritance;
I will give the one I love
into the hands of her enemies.
8 My inheritance has become to me
like a lion in the forest.
She roars at me;
therefore I hate her.
9 Has not my inheritance become to me
like a speckled bird of prey
that other birds of prey surround and
attack?
Go and gather all the wild beasts;
bring them to devour.
10 Many shepherds will ruin my vineyard
and trample down my field;
they will turn my pleasant field
into a desolate wasteland.
11 It will be made a wasteland,
parched and desolate before me;
the whole land will be laid waste
because there is no one who cares.
12 Over all the barren heights in the desert
destroyers will swarm,
for the sword of the LORD will devour
from one end of the land to the other;
no one will be safe.
13 They will sow wheat but reap thorns;
they will wear themselves out but gain
nothing.
They will bear the shame of their harvest
because of the LORD's fierce anger."

14 This is what the LORD says: "As for all my
wicked neighbors who seize the inheritance
I gave my people Israel, I will uproot them
from their lands and I will uproot the people
of Judah from among them. 15 But after I up-
root them, I will again have compassion and
will bring each of them back to their own
inheritance and their own country. 16 And
if they learn well the ways of my people and
swear by my name, saying, 'As surely as the
LORD lives'—even as they once taught my
people to swear by Baal—then they will be
established among my people. 17 But if any
nation does not listen, I will completely up-
root and destroy it," declares the LORD.

A Linen Belt

13 This is what the LORD said to me: "Go
and buy a linen belt and put it around
your waist, but do not let it touch water." 2 So
I bought a belt, as the LORD directed, and put
it around my waist.
3 Then the word of the LORD came to me a
second time: 4 "Take the belt you bought and
are wearing around your waist, and go now
to Perath[c] and hide it there in a crevice in the
rocks." 5 So I went and hid it at Perath, as the
LORD told me.
6 Many days later the LORD said to me,
"Go now to Perath and get the belt I told you
to hide there." 7 So I went to Perath and dug
up the belt and took it from the place where
I had hidden it, but now it was ruined and
completely useless.
8 Then the word of the LORD came to me:
9 "This is what the LORD says: 'In the same
way I will ruin the pride of Judah and the
great pride of Jerusalem. 10 These wicked
people, who refuse to listen to my words,
who follow the stubbornness of their hearts
and go after other gods to serve and wor-
ship them, will be like this belt—completely
useless! 11 For as a belt is bound around the
waist, so I bound all the people of Israel and
all the people of Judah to me,' declares the

[a] 5 Or *you feel secure only* [b] 5 Or *the flooding of* [c] 4 Or possibly *to the Euphrates*; similarly in verses 5-7

LORD, 'to be my people for my renown and
praise and honor. But they have not listened.'

Wineskins

12 "Say to them: 'This is what the LORD, the
God of Israel, says: Every wineskin should
be filled with wine.' And if they say to you,
'Don't we know that every wineskin should
be filled with wine?' 13 then tell them, 'This
is what the LORD says: I am going to fill with
drunkenness all who live in this land, in-
cluding the kings who sit on David's throne,
the priests, the prophets and all those liv-
ing in Jerusalem. 14 I will smash them one
against the other, parents and children
alike, declares the LORD. I will allow no pity
or mercy or compassion to keep me from de-
stroying them.' "

Threat of Captivity

15 Hear and pay attention,
do not be arrogant,
for the LORD has spoken.
16 Give glory to the LORD your God
before he brings the darkness,
before your feet stumble
on the darkening hills.
You hope for light,
but he will turn it to utter darkness
and change it to deep gloom.
17 If you do not listen,
I will weep in secret
because of your pride;
my eyes will weep bitterly,
overflowing with tears,
because the LORD's flock will be taken
captive.

18 Say to the king and to the queen mother,
"Come down from your thrones,
for your glorious crowns
will fall from your heads."
19 The cities in the Negev will be shut up,
and there will be no one to open them.
All Judah will be carried into exile,
carried completely away.

20 Look up and see
those who are coming from the north.
Where is the flock that was entrusted
to you,
the sheep of which you boasted?
21 What will you say when the LORD sets
over you
those you cultivated as your special
allies?
Will not pain grip you
like that of a woman in labor?
22 And if you ask yourself,
"Why has this happened to me?" —
it is because of your many sins
that your skirts have been torn off
and your body mistreated.
23 Can an Ethiopian[a] change his skin
or a leopard its spots?
Neither can you do good
who are accustomed to doing evil.

24 "I will scatter you like chaff
driven by the desert wind.
25 This is your lot,
the portion I have decreed for you,"
declares the LORD,
"because you have forgotten me
and trusted in false gods.
26 I will pull up your skirts over your face
that your shame may be seen —
27 your adulteries and lustful neighings,
your shameless prostitution!
I have seen your detestable acts
on the hills and in the fields.
Woe to you, Jerusalem!
How long will you be unclean?"

Drought, Famine, Sword

14 This is the word of the LORD that
came to Jeremiah concerning the
drought:

2 "Judah mourns,
her cities languish;
they wail for the land,
and a cry goes up from Jerusalem.
3 The nobles send their servants for water;
they go to the cisterns
but find no water.
They return with their jars unfilled;
dismayed and despairing,
they cover their heads.
4 The ground is cracked
because there is no rain in the land;
the farmers are dismayed
and cover their heads.
5 Even the doe in the field
deserts her newborn fawn
because there is no grass.
6 Wild donkeys stand on the barren
heights

[a] 23 Hebrew *Cushite* (probably a person from the upper Nile region)

and pant like jackals;
their eyes fail
for lack of food."

7 Although our sins testify against us,
do something, LORD, for the sake of your name.
For we have often rebelled;
we have sinned against you.
8 You who are the hope of Israel,
its Savior in times of distress,
why are you like a stranger in the land,
like a traveler who stays only a night?
9 Why are you like a man taken by surprise,
like a warrior powerless to save?
You are among us, LORD,
and we bear your name;
do not forsake us!

10 This is what the LORD says about this
people:

"They greatly love to wander;
they do not restrain their feet.
So the LORD does not accept them;
he will now remember their wickedness
and punish them for their sins."

11 Then the LORD said to me, "Do not pray
for the well-being of this people. 12 Although
they fast, I will not listen to their cry; though
they offer burnt offerings and grain offer-
ings, I will not accept them. Instead, I will
destroy them with the sword, famine and
plague."
13 But I said, "Alas, Sovereign LORD! The
prophets keep telling them, 'You will not
see the sword or suffer famine. Indeed, I will
give you lasting peace in this place.' "
14 Then the LORD said to me, "The proph-
ets are prophesying lies in my name. I have
not sent them or appointed them or spoken
to them. They are prophesying to you false
visions, divinations, idolatries[a] and the de-
lusions of their own minds. 15 Therefore this
is what the LORD says about the prophets
who are prophesying in my name: I did not
send them, yet they are saying, 'No sword
or famine will touch this land.' Those same
prophets will perish by sword and famine.
16 And the people they are prophesying to
will be thrown out into the streets of Jerusa-
lem because of the famine and sword. There
will be no one to bury them, their wives,
their sons and their daughters. I will pour
out on them the calamity they deserve.

17 "Speak this word to them:

" 'Let my eyes overflow with tears
night and day without ceasing;
for the Virgin Daughter, my people,
has suffered a grievous wound,
a crushing blow.
18 If I go into the country,
I see those slain by the sword;
if I go into the city,
I see the ravages of famine.
Both prophet and priest
have gone to a land they know not.' "

19 Have you rejected Judah completely?
Do you despise Zion?
Why have you afflicted us
so that we cannot be healed?
We hoped for peace
but no good has come,
for a time of healing
but there is only terror.
20 We acknowledge our wickedness, LORD,
and the guilt of our ancestors;
we have indeed sinned against you.
21 For the sake of your name do not despise us;
do not dishonor your glorious throne.
Remember your covenant with us
and do not break it.
22 Do any of the worthless idols of the nations bring rain?
Do the skies themselves send down showers?
No, it is you, LORD our God.
Therefore our hope is in you,
for you are the one who does all this.

15 Then the LORD said to me: "Even if
Moses and Samuel were to stand be-
fore me, my heart would not go out to this
people. Send them away from my presence!
Let them go! 2 And if they ask you, 'Where
shall we go?' tell them, 'This is what the
LORD says:

" 'Those destined for death, to death;
those for the sword, to the sword;
those for starvation, to starvation;
those for captivity, to captivity.'

[a] 14 Or *visions, worthless divinations*

[3]"I will send four kinds of destroyers
against them," declares the LORD, "the
sword to kill and the dogs to drag away and
the birds and the wild animals to devour and
destroy. [4]I will make them abhorrent to all
the kingdoms of the earth because of what
Manasseh son of Hezekiah king of Judah did
in Jerusalem.

[5]"Who will have pity on you, Jerusalem?
Who will mourn for you?
Who will stop to ask how you are?
[6]You have rejected me," declares the LORD.
"You keep on backsliding.
So I will reach out and destroy you;
I am tired of holding back.
[7]I will winnow them with a winnowing
fork
at the city gates of the land.
I will bring bereavement and destruction
on my people,
for they have not changed their ways.
[8]I will make their widows more numerous
than the sand of the sea.
At midday I will bring a destroyer
against the mothers of their young men;
suddenly I will bring down on them
anguish and terror.
[9]The mother of seven will grow faint
and breathe her last.
Her sun will set while it is still day;
she will be disgraced and humiliated.
I will put the survivors to the sword
before their enemies,"
declares the LORD.

[10]Alas, my mother, that you gave me
birth,
a man with whom the whole land
strives and contends!
I have neither lent nor borrowed,
yet everyone curses me.

[11]The LORD said,

"Surely I will deliver you for a good
purpose;
surely I will make your enemies plead
with you
in times of disaster and times of
distress.

[12]"Can a man break iron —
iron from the north — or bronze?
[13]"Your wealth and your treasures
I will give as plunder, without charge,
because of all your sins
throughout your country.
[14]I will enslave you to your enemies
in[a] a land you do not know,
for my anger will kindle a fire
that will burn against you."

[15]LORD, you understand;
remember me and care for me.
Avenge me on my persecutors.
You are long-suffering — do not take me
away;
think of how I suffer reproach for
your sake.
[16]When your words came, I ate them;
they were my joy and my heart's
delight,
for I bear your name,
LORD God Almighty.
[17]I never sat in the company of revelers,
never made merry with them;
I sat alone because your hand was
on me
and you had filled me with
indignation.
[18]Why is my pain unending
and my wound grievous and
incurable?
You are to me like a deceptive brook,
like a spring that fails.

[19]Therefore this is what the LORD says:

"If you repent, I will restore you
that you may serve me;
if you utter worthy, not worthless,
words,
you will be my spokesman.
Let this people turn to you,
but you must not turn to them.
[20]I will make you a wall to this people,
a fortified wall of bronze;
they will fight against you
but will not overcome you,
for I am with you
to rescue and save you,"
declares the LORD.
[21]"I will save you from the hands of the
wicked
and deliver you from the grasp of
the cruel."

[a] *14* Some Hebrew manuscripts, Septuagint and Syriac (see also 17:4); most Hebrew manuscripts *I will cause your enemies to bring you / into*

Day of Disaster

16 Then the word of the LORD came to
me: 2 “You must not marry and have
sons or daughters in this place.” 3 For this
is what the LORD says about the sons and
daughters born in this land and about the
women who are their mothers and the men
who are their fathers: 4 “They will die of
deadly diseases. They will not be mourned
or buried but will be like dung lying on the
ground. They will perish by sword and fam-
ine, and their dead bodies will become food
for the birds and the wild animals.”

5 For this is what the LORD says: “Do not
enter a house where there is a funeral meal;
do not go to mourn or show sympathy, be-
cause I have withdrawn my blessing, my love
and my pity from this people,” declares the
LORD. 6 “Both high and low will die in this
land. They will not be buried or mourned,
and no one will cut themselves or shave their
head for the dead. 7 No one will offer food to
comfort those who mourn for the dead — not
even for a father or a mother — nor will any-
one give them a drink to console them.

8 “And do not enter a house where there is
feasting and sit down to eat and drink. 9 For
this is what the LORD Almighty, the God of
Israel, says: Before your eyes and in your
days I will bring an end to the sounds of joy
and gladness and to the voices of bride and
bridegroom in this place.

10 “When you tell these people all this and
they ask you, ‘Why has the LORD decreed
such a great disaster against us? What wrong
have we done? What sin have we commit-
ted against the LORD our God?’ 11 then say to
them, ‘It is because your ancestors forsook
me,’ declares the LORD, ‘and followed other
gods and served and worshiped them. They
forsook me and did not keep my law. 12 But
you have behaved more wickedly than your
ancestors. See how all of you are following
the stubbornness of your evil hearts instead
of obeying me. 13 So I will throw you out of
this land into a land neither you nor your an-
cestors have known, and there you will serve
other gods day and night, for I will show you
no favor.’

14 “However, the days are coming,” de-
clares the LORD, “when it will no longer
be said, ‘As surely as the LORD lives, who
brought the Israelites up out of Egypt,’ 15 but
it will be said, ‘As surely as the LORD lives,
who brought the Israelites up out of the
land of the north and out of all the countries
where he had banished them.’ For I will re-
store them to the land I gave their ancestors.

16 “But now I will send for many fisher-
men,” declares the LORD, “and they will
catch them. After that I will send for many
hunters, and they will hunt them down on
every mountain and hill and from the crev-
ices of the rocks. 17 My eyes are on all their
ways; they are not hidden from me, nor is
their sin concealed from my eyes. 18 I will re-
pay them double for their wickedness and
their sin, because they have defiled my land
with the lifeless forms of their vile images
and have filled my inheritance with their
detestable idols.”

19 LORD, my strength and my fortress,
my refuge in time of distress,
to you the nations will come
from the ends of the earth and say,
“Our ancestors possessed nothing but
false gods,
worthless idols that did them no good.
20 Do people make their own gods?
Yes, but they are not gods!”

21 “Therefore I will teach them —
this time I will teach them
my power and might.
Then they will know
that my name is the LORD.

17 “Judah’s sin is engraved with an iron
tool,
inscribed with a flint point,
on the tablets of their hearts
and on the horns of their altars.
2 Even their children remember
their altars and Asherah poles[a]
beside the spreading trees
and on the high hills.
3 My mountain in the land
and your[b] wealth and all your
treasures
I will give away as plunder,
together with your high places,
because of sin throughout your
country.
4 Through your own fault you will lose
the inheritance I gave you.

[a] 2 That is, wooden symbols of the goddess Asherah

[b] 2,3 Or *hills* / [3] *and the mountains of the land.* / *Your*

I will enslave you to your enemies
in a land you do not know,
for you have kindled my anger,
and it will burn forever."

5 This is what the LORD says:

"Cursed is the one who trusts in man,
who draws strength from mere flesh
and whose heart turns away from the LORD.
6 That person will be like a bush in the wastelands;
they will not see prosperity when it comes.
They will dwell in the parched places of the desert,
in a salt land where no one lives.

7 "But blessed is the one who trusts in the LORD,
whose confidence is in him.
8 They will be like a tree planted by the water
that sends out its roots by the stream.
It does not fear when heat comes;
its leaves are always green.
It has no worries in a year of drought
and never fails to bear fruit."

9 The heart is deceitful above all things
and beyond cure.
Who can understand it?
10 "I the LORD search the heart
and examine the mind,
to reward each person according to their conduct,
according to what their deeds deserve."

11 Like a partridge that hatches eggs it did not lay
are those who gain riches by unjust means.
When their lives are half gone, their riches will desert them,
and in the end they will prove to be fools.

12 A glorious throne, exalted from the beginning,
is the place of our sanctuary.
13 LORD, you are the hope of Israel;
all who forsake you will be put to shame.
Those who turn away from you will be written in the dust
because they have forsaken the LORD,
the spring of living water.

14 Heal me, LORD, and I will be healed;
save me and I will be saved,
for you are the one I praise.
15 They keep saying to me,
"Where is the word of the LORD?
Let it now be fulfilled!"
16 I have not run away from being your shepherd;
you know I have not desired the day of despair.
What passes my lips is open before you.
17 Do not be a terror to me;
you are my refuge in the day of disaster.
18 Let my persecutors be put to shame,
but keep me from shame;
let them be terrified,
but keep me from terror.
Bring on them the day of disaster;
destroy them with double destruction.

Keeping the Sabbath Day Holy

19 This is what the LORD said to me: "Go
and stand at the Gate of the People,[a] through
which the kings of Judah go in and out; stand
also at all the other gates of Jerusalem. 20 Say
to them, 'Hear the word of the LORD, you
kings of Judah and all people of Judah and
everyone living in Jerusalem who come
through these gates. 21 This is what the LORD
says: Be careful not to carry a load on the
Sabbath day or bring it through the gates of
Jerusalem. 22 Do not bring a load out of your
houses or do any work on the Sabbath, but
keep the Sabbath day holy, as I commanded your ancestors. 23 Yet they did not listen
or pay attention; they were stiff-necked and
would not listen or respond to discipline.
24 But if you are careful to obey me, declares
the LORD, and bring no load through the
gates of this city on the Sabbath, but keep
the Sabbath day holy by not doing any work
on it, 25 then kings who sit on David's throne
will come through the gates of this city with
their officials. They and their officials will
come riding in chariots and on horses, accompanied by the men of Judah and those

[a] *19* Or *Army*

living in Jerusalem, and this city will be in-
habited forever. 26 People will come from the
towns of Judah and the villages around Je-
rusalem, from the territory of Benjamin and
the western foothills, from the hill country
and the Negev, bringing burnt offerings and
sacrifices, grain offerings and incense, and
bringing thank offerings to the house of the
LORD. 27 But if you do not obey me to keep the
Sabbath day holy by not carrying any load
as you come through the gates of Jerusalem
on the Sabbath day, then I will kindle an un-
quenchable fire in the gates of Jerusalem
that will consume her fortresses.' "

At the Potter's House

18 This is the word that came to Jere-
miah from the LORD: 2 "Go down to
the potter's house, and there I will give you
my message." 3 So I went down to the pot-
ter's house, and I saw him working at the
wheel. 4 But the pot he was shaping from the
clay was marred in his hands; so the pot-
ter formed it into another pot, shaping it as
seemed best to him.

5 Then the word of the LORD came to me.
6 He said, "Can I not do with you, Israel, as
this potter does?" declares the LORD. "Like
clay in the hand of the potter, so are you in
my hand, Israel. 7 If at any time I announce
that a nation or kingdom is to be uprooted,
torn down and destroyed, 8 and if that na-
tion I warned repents of its evil, then I will
relent and not inflict on it the disaster I had
planned. 9 And if at another time I announce
that a nation or kingdom is to be built up and
planted, 10 and if it does evil in my sight and
does not obey me, then I will reconsider the
good I had intended to do for it.

11 "Now therefore say to the people of Ju-
dah and those living in Jerusalem, 'This is
what the LORD says: Look! I am preparing a
disaster for you and devising a plan against
you. So turn from your evil ways, each one of
you, and reform your ways and your actions.'
12 But they will reply, 'It's no use. We will con-
tinue with our own plans; we will all follow
the stubbornness of our evil hearts.' "

13 Therefore this is what the LORD says:

"Inquire among the nations:
 Who has ever heard anything like this?
A most horrible thing has been done
 by Virgin Israel.
14 Does the snow of Lebanon
 ever vanish from its rocky slopes?
Do its cool waters from distant sources
 ever stop flowing?[a]
15 Yet my people have forgotten me;
 they burn incense to worthless idols,
which made them stumble in their ways,
 in the ancient paths.
They made them walk in byways,
 on roads not built up.
16 Their land will be an object of horror
 and of lasting scorn;
all who pass by will be appalled
 and will shake their heads.
17 Like a wind from the east,
 I will scatter them before their
 enemies;
I will show them my back and not my face
 in the day of their disaster."

18 They said, "Come, let's make plans
against Jeremiah; for the teaching of the law
by the priest will not cease, nor will coun-
sel from the wise, nor the word from the
prophets. So come, let's attack him with our
tongues and pay no attention to anything he
says."

19 Listen to me, LORD;
 hear what my accusers are saying!
20 Should good be repaid with evil?
 Yet they have dug a pit for me.
Remember that I stood before you
 and spoke in their behalf
 to turn your wrath away from them.
21 So give their children over to famine;
 hand them over to the power of the
 sword.
Let their wives be made childless and
 widows;
 let their men be put to death,
 their young men slain by the sword in
 battle.
22 Let a cry be heard from their houses
 when you suddenly bring invaders
 against them,
for they have dug a pit to capture me
 and have hidden snares for my feet.
23 But you, LORD, know
 all their plots to kill me.
Do not forgive their crimes
 or blot out their sins from your sight.

[a] *14* The meaning of the Hebrew for this sentence is uncertain.

Let them be overthrown before you;
deal with them in the time of your
anger.

19 This is what the LORD says: "Go and
buy a clay jar from a potter. Take
along some of the elders of the people and
of the priests 2and go out to the Valley of
Ben Hinnom, near the entrance of the Pot-
sherd Gate. There proclaim the words I tell
you, 3and say, 'Hear the word of the LORD,
you kings of Judah and people of Jerusalem.
This is what the LORD Almighty, the God of
Israel, says: Listen! I am going to bring a di-
saster on this place that will make the ears
of everyone who hears of it tingle. 4For they
have forsaken me and made this a place of
foreign gods; they have burned incense in it
to gods that neither they nor their ancestors
nor the kings of Judah ever knew, and they
have filled this place with the blood of the
innocent. 5They have built the high places
of Baal to burn their children in the fire as
offerings to Baal — something I did not com-
mand or mention, nor did it enter my mind.
6So beware, the days are coming, declares
the LORD, when people will no longer call
this place Topheth or the Valley of Ben Hin-
nom, but the Valley of Slaughter.

7" 'In this place I will ruin[a] the plans of Ju-
dah and Jerusalem. I will make them fall by
the sword before their enemies, at the hands
of those who want to kill them, and I will
give their carcasses as food to the birds and
the wild animals. 8I will devastate this city
and make it an object of horror and scorn; all
who pass by will be appalled and will scoff
because of all its wounds. 9I will make them
eat the flesh of their sons and daughters, and
they will eat one another's flesh because
their enemies will press the siege so hard
against them to destroy them.'

10"Then break the jar while those who go
with you are watching, 11and say to them,
'This is what the LORD Almighty says: I will
smash this nation and this city just as this
potter's jar is smashed and cannot be re-
paired. They will bury the dead in Topheth
until there is no more room. 12This is what
I will do to this place and to those who live
here, declares the LORD. I will make this city
like Topheth. 13The houses in Jerusalem
and those of the kings of Judah will be de-
filed like this place, Topheth — all the hous-
es where they burned incense on the roofs
to all the starry hosts and poured out drink
offerings to other gods.' "

14Jeremiah then returned from Topheth,
where the LORD had sent him to prophesy,
and stood in the court of the LORD's temple
and said to all the people, 15"This is what
the LORD Almighty, the God of Israel, says:
'Listen! I am going to bring on this city and
all the villages around it every disaster I
pronounced against them, because they
were stiff-necked and would not listen to my
words.' "

Jeremiah and Pashhur

20 When the priest Pashhur son of Im-
mer, the official in charge of the tem-
ple of the LORD, heard Jeremiah prophesying
these things, 2he had Jeremiah the prophet
beaten and put in the stocks at the Up-
per Gate of Benjamin at the LORD's temple.
3The next day, when Pashhur released him
from the stocks, Jeremiah said to him, "The
LORD's name for you is not Pashhur, but Ter-
ror on Every Side. 4For this is what the LORD
says: 'I will make you a terror to yourself and
to all your friends; with your own eyes you
will see them fall by the sword of their en-
emies. I will give all Judah into the hands
of the king of Babylon, who will carry them
away to Babylon or put them to the sword.
5I will deliver all the wealth of this city into
the hands of their enemies — all its prod-
ucts, all its valuables and all the treasures
of the kings of Judah. They will take it away
as plunder and carry it off to Babylon. 6And
you, Pashhur, and all who live in your house
will go into exile to Babylon. There you will
die and be buried, you and all your friends to
whom you have prophesied lies.' "

Jeremiah's Complaint

7You deceived[b] me, LORD, and I was
deceived[b];
you overpowered me and prevailed.
I am ridiculed all day long;
everyone mocks me.
8Whenever I speak, I cry out
proclaiming violence and
destruction.

[a] 7 The Hebrew for *ruin* sounds like the Hebrew for *jar* (see verses 1 and 10). [b] 7 Or *persuaded*

So the word of the LORD has brought me
insult and reproach all day long.
9 But if I say, "I will not mention his word
or speak anymore in his name,"
his word is in my heart like a fire,
a fire shut up in my bones.
I am weary of holding it in;
indeed, I cannot.
10 I hear many whispering,
"Terror on every side!
Denounce him! Let's denounce
him!"
All my friends
are waiting for me to slip, saying,
"Perhaps he will be deceived;
then we will prevail over him
and take our revenge on him."

11 But the LORD is with me like a mighty
warrior;
so my persecutors will stumble and
not prevail.
They will fail and be thoroughly
disgraced;
their dishonor will never be forgotten.
12 LORD Almighty, you who examine the
righteous
and probe the heart and mind,
let me see your vengeance on them,
for to you I have committed my cause.

13 Sing to the LORD!
Give praise to the LORD!
He rescues the life of the needy
from the hands of the wicked.

14 Cursed be the day I was born!
May the day my mother bore me not be
blessed!
15 Cursed be the man who brought my
father the news,
who made him very glad, saying,
"A child is born to you — a son!"
16 May that man be like the towns
the LORD overthrew without pity.
May he hear wailing in the morning,
a battle cry at noon.
17 For he did not kill me in the womb,
with my mother as my grave,
her womb enlarged forever.
18 Why did I ever come out of the womb
to see trouble and sorrow
and to end my days in shame?

God Rejects Zedekiah's Request

21 The word came to Jeremiah from the
LORD when King Zedekiah sent to
him Pashhur son of Malkijah and the priest
Zephaniah son of Maaseiah. They said: 2 "In-
quire now of the LORD for us because Nebu-
chadnezzar[a] king of Babylon is attacking us.
Perhaps the LORD will perform wonders for
us as in times past so that he will withdraw
from us."
3 But Jeremiah answered them, "Tell Zed-
ekiah, 4 'This is what the LORD, the God of
Israel, says: I am about to turn against you
the weapons of war that are in your hands,
which you are using to fight the king of Bab-
ylon and the Babylonians[b] who are outside
the wall besieging you. And I will gather
them inside this city. 5 I myself will fight
against you with an outstretched hand and
a mighty arm in furious anger and in great
wrath. 6 I will strike down those who live in
this city — both man and beast — and they
will die of a terrible plague. 7 After that, de-
clares the LORD, I will give Zedekiah king
of Judah, his officials and the people in this
city who survive the plague, sword and fam-
ine, into the hands of Nebuchadnezzar king
of Babylon and to their enemies who want
to kill them. He will put them to the sword;
he will show them no mercy or pity or com-
passion.'
8 "Furthermore, tell the people, 'This is
what the LORD says: See, I am setting be-
fore you the way of life and the way of death.
9 Whoever stays in this city will die by the
sword, famine or plague. But whoever goes
out and surrenders to the Babylonians who
are besieging you will live; they will escape
with their lives. 10 I have determined to do
this city harm and not good, declares the
LORD. It will be given into the hands of the
king of Babylon, and he will destroy it with
fire.'
11 "Moreover, say to the royal house of Ju-
dah, 'Hear the word of the LORD. 12 This is
what the LORD says to you, house of David:

"'Administer justice every morning;
rescue from the hand of the oppressor
the one who has been robbed,
or my wrath will break out and burn
like fire

[a] 2 Hebrew *Nebuchadrezzar,* of which *Nebuchadnezzar* is a variant; here and often in Jeremiah and Ezekiel [b] 4 Or *Chaldeans;* also in verse 9

because of the evil you have done —
burn with no one to quench it.
[13] I am against you, Jerusalem,
you who live above this valley
on the rocky plateau, declares the
LORD —
you who say, "Who can come against us?
Who can enter our refuge?"
[14] I will punish you as your deeds deserve,
declares the LORD.
I will kindle a fire in your forests
that will consume everything
around you.'"

Judgment Against Wicked Kings

22 This is what the LORD says: "Go
down to the palace of the king of Ju-
dah and proclaim this message there: [2] 'Hear
the word of the LORD to you, king of Judah,
you who sit on David's throne — you, your
officials and your people who come through
these gates. [3] This is what the LORD says:
Do what is just and right. Rescue from the
hand of the oppressor the one who has been
robbed. Do no wrong or violence to the for-
eigner, the fatherless or the widow, and do
not shed innocent blood in this place. [4] For
if you are careful to carry out these com-
mands, then kings who sit on David's throne
will come through the gates of this palace,
riding in chariots and on horses, accompa-
nied by their officials and their people. [5] But
if you do not obey these commands, declares
the LORD, I swear by myself that this palace
will become a ruin.'"

[6] For this is what the LORD says about the
palace of the king of Judah:

"Though you are like Gilead to me,
like the summit of Lebanon,
I will surely make you like a wasteland,
like towns not inhabited.
[7] I will send destroyers against you,
each man with his weapons,
and they will cut up your fine cedar
beams
and throw them into the fire.

[8] "People from many nations will pass
by this city and will ask one another, 'Why
has the LORD done such a thing to this great
city?' [9] And the answer will be: 'Because
they have forsaken the covenant of the LORD
their God and have worshiped and served
other gods.'"

[10] Do not weep for the dead king or mourn
his loss;
rather, weep bitterly for him who is
exiled,
because he will never return
nor see his native land again.

[11] For this is what the LORD says about Shal-
lum[a] son of Josiah, who succeeded his fa-
ther as king of Judah but has gone from this
place: "He will never return. [12] He will die in
the place where they have led him captive;
he will not see this land again."

[13] "Woe to him who builds his palace by
unrighteousness,
his upper rooms by injustice,
making his own people work for nothing,
not paying them for their labor.
[14] He says, 'I will build myself a great palace
with spacious upper rooms.'
So he makes large windows in it,
panels it with cedar
and decorates it in red.

[15] "Does it make you a king
to have more and more cedar?
Did not your father have food and drink?
He did what was right and just,
so all went well with him.
[16] He defended the cause of the poor
and needy,
and so all went well.
Is that not what it means to know me?"
declares the LORD.
[17] "But your eyes and your heart
are set only on dishonest gain,
on shedding innocent blood
and on oppression and extortion."

[18] Therefore this is what the LORD says about
Jehoiakim son of Josiah king of Judah:

"They will not mourn for him:
'Alas, my brother! Alas, my sister!'
They will not mourn for him:
'Alas, my master! Alas, his splendor!'
[19] He will have the burial of a donkey —
dragged away and thrown
outside the gates of Jerusalem."

[20] "Go up to Lebanon and cry out,
let your voice be heard in Bashan,

[a] 11 Also called *Jehoahaz*

cry out from Abarim,
for all your allies are crushed.
21 I warned you when you felt secure,
but you said, 'I will not listen!'
This has been your way from your youth;
you have not obeyed me.
22 The wind will drive all your shepherds
away,
and your allies will go into exile.
Then you will be ashamed and disgraced
because of all your wickedness.
23 You who live in 'Lebanon,[a]'
who are nestled in cedar buildings,
how you will groan when pangs come
upon you,
pain like that of a woman in labor!

24 "As surely as I live," declares the LORD,
"even if you, Jehoiachin[b] son of Jehoiakim
king of Judah, were a signet ring on my right
hand, I would still pull you off. 25 I will deliv-
er you into the hands of those who want to
kill you, those you fear — Nebuchadnezzar
king of Babylon and the Babylonians.[c] 26 I
will hurl you and the mother who gave you
birth into another country, where neither of
you was born, and there you both will die.
27 You will never come back to the land you
long to return to."

28 Is this man Jehoiachin a despised,
broken pot,
an object no one wants?
Why will he and his children be
hurled out,
cast into a land they do not know?
29 O land, land, land,
hear the word of the LORD!
30 This is what the LORD says:
"Record this man as if childless,
a man who will not prosper in his
lifetime,
for none of his offspring will prosper,
none will sit on the throne of David
or rule anymore in Judah."

The Righteous Branch

23 "Woe to the shepherds who are de-
stroying and scattering the sheep
of my pasture!" declares the LORD. 2 There-
fore this is what the LORD, the God of Israel,
says to the shepherds who tend my people:
"Because you have scattered my flock and
driven them away and have not bestowed
care on them, I will bestow punishment on
you for the evil you have done," declares the
LORD. 3 "I myself will gather the remnant of
my flock out of all the countries where I have
driven them and will bring them back to
their pasture, where they will be fruitful and
increase in number. 4 I will place shepherds
over them who will tend them, and they will
no longer be afraid or terrified, nor will any
be missing," declares the LORD.

5 "The days are coming," declares the
LORD,
"when I will raise up for David[d] a
righteous Branch,
a King who will reign wisely
and do what is just and right in
the land.
6 In his days Judah will be saved
and Israel will live in safety.
This is the name by which he will
be called:
The LORD Our Righteous Savior.

7 "So then, the days are coming," declares
the LORD, "when people will no longer say,
'As surely as the LORD lives, who brought the
Israelites up out of Egypt,' 8 but they will say,
'As surely as the LORD lives, who brought the
descendants of Israel up out of the land of
the north and out of all the countries where
he had banished them.' Then they will live in
their own land."

Lying Prophets

9 Concerning the prophets:

My heart is broken within me;
all my bones tremble.
I am like a drunken man,
like a strong man overcome by wine,
because of the LORD
and his holy words.
10 The land is full of adulterers;
because of the curse[e] the land lies
parched
and the pastures in the wilderness are
withered.
The prophets follow an evil course
and use their power unjustly.

[a] *23* That is, the palace in Jerusalem (see 1 Kings 7:2) [b] *24* Hebrew *Koniah,* a variant of *Jehoiachin*; also in verse 28 [c] *25* Or *Chaldeans* [d] *5* Or *up from David's line* [e] *10* Or *because of these things*

11 "Both prophet and priest are godless;
even in my temple I find their
wickedness,"
declares the LORD.
12 "Therefore their path will become
slippery;
they will be banished to darkness
and there they will fall.
I will bring disaster on them
in the year they are punished,"
declares the LORD.

13 "Among the prophets of Samaria
I saw this repulsive thing:
They prophesied by Baal
and led my people Israel astray.
14 And among the prophets of Jerusalem
I have seen something horrible:
They commit adultery and live a lie.
They strengthen the hands of evildoers,
so that not one of them turns from
their wickedness.
They are all like Sodom to me;
the people of Jerusalem are like
Gomorrah."

15 Therefore this is what the LORD Al-
mighty says concerning the prophets:

"I will make them eat bitter food
and drink poisoned water,
because from the prophets of Jerusalem
ungodliness has spread throughout
the land."

16 This is what the LORD Almighty says:
"Do not listen to what the prophets are
prophesying to you;
they fill you with false hopes.
They speak visions from their own
minds,
not from the mouth of the LORD.
17 They keep saying to those who
despise me,
'The LORD says: You will have peace.'
And to all who follow the stubbornness of
their hearts
they say, 'No harm will come to you.'
18 But which of them has stood in the
council of the LORD
to see or to hear his word?
Who has listened and heard his word?
19 See, the storm of the LORD
will burst out in wrath,
a whirlwind swirling down
on the heads of the wicked.
20 The anger of the LORD will not turn back
until he fully accomplishes
the purposes of his heart.
In days to come
you will understand it clearly.
21 I did not send these prophets,
yet they have run with their message;
I did not speak to them,
yet they have prophesied.
22 But if they had stood in my council,
they would have proclaimed my words
to my people
and would have turned them from their
evil ways
and from their evil deeds.

23 "Am I only a God nearby,"
declares the LORD,
"and not a God far away?
24 Who can hide in secret places
so that I cannot see them?"
declares the LORD.
"Do not I fill heaven and earth?"
declares the LORD.

25 "I have heard what the prophets say who
prophesy lies in my name. They say, 'I had a
dream! I had a dream!'
26 How long will this
continue in the hearts of these lying proph-
ets, who prophesy the delusions of their own
minds?
27 They think the dreams they tell
one another will make my people forget my
name, just as their ancestors forgot my name
through Baal worship.
28 Let the prophet who
has a dream recount the dream, but let the
one who has my word speak it faithfully. For
what has straw to do with grain?" declares
the LORD.
29 "Is not my word like fire," de-
clares the LORD, "and like a hammer that
breaks a rock in pieces?

30 "Therefore," declares the LORD, "I am
against the prophets who steal from one an-
other words supposedly from me.
31 Yes," de-
clares the LORD, "I am against the prophets
who wag their own tongues and yet declare,
'The LORD declares.'
32 Indeed, I am against
those who prophesy false dreams," declares
the LORD. "They tell them and lead my peo-
ple astray with their reckless lies, yet I did not
send or appoint them. They do not benefit
these people in the least," declares the LORD.

False Prophecy

33 "When these people, or a prophet or a
priest, ask you, 'What is the message from

the LORD?' say to them, 'What message? I will forsake you, declares the LORD.' 34 If a prophet or a priest or anyone else claims, 'This is a message from the LORD,' I will punish them and their household. 35 This is what each of you keeps saying to your friends and other Israelites: 'What is the LORD's answer?' or 'What has the LORD spoken?' 36 But you must not mention 'a message from the LORD' again, because each one's word becomes their own message. So you distort the words of the living God, the LORD Almighty, our God. 37 This is what you keep saying to a prophet: 'What is the LORD's answer to you?' or 'What has the LORD spoken?' 38 Although you claim, 'This is a message from the LORD,' this is what the LORD says: You used the words, 'This is a message from the LORD,' even though I told you that you must not claim, 'This is a message from the LORD.' 39 Therefore, I will surely forget you and cast you out of my presence along with the city I gave to you and your ancestors. 40 I will bring on you everlasting disgrace — everlasting shame that will not be forgotten."

Two Baskets of Figs

24 After Jehoiachin[a] son of Jehoiakim king of Judah and the officials, the skilled workers and the artisans of Judah were carried into exile from Jerusalem to Babylon by Nebuchadnezzar king of Babylon, the LORD showed me two baskets of figs placed in front of the temple of the LORD. 2 One basket had very good figs, like those that ripen early; the other basket had very bad figs, so bad they could not be eaten.

3 Then the LORD asked me, "What do you see, Jeremiah?"

"Figs," I answered. "The good ones are very good, but the bad ones are so bad they cannot be eaten."

4 Then the word of the LORD came to me: 5 "This is what the LORD, the God of Israel, says: 'Like these good figs, I regard as good the exiles from Judah, whom I sent away from this place to the land of the Babylonians.[b] 6 My eyes will watch over them for their good, and I will bring them back to this land. I will build them up and not tear them down; I will plant them and not uproot them. 7 I will give them a heart to know me, that I am the LORD. They will be my people, and I will be their God, for they will return to me with all their heart.

8 " 'But like the bad figs, which are so bad they cannot be eaten,' says the LORD, 'so will I deal with Zedekiah king of Judah, his officials and the survivors from Jerusalem, whether they remain in this land or live in Egypt. 9 I will make them abhorrent and an offense to all the kingdoms of the earth, a reproach and a byword, a curse[c] and an object of ridicule, wherever I banish them. 10 I will send the sword, famine and plague against them until they are destroyed from the land I gave to them and their ancestors.' "

Seventy Years of Captivity

25 The word came to Jeremiah concerning all the people of Judah in the fourth year of Jehoiakim son of Josiah king of Judah, which was the first year of Nebuchadnezzar king of Babylon. 2 So Jeremiah the prophet said to all the people of Judah and to all those living in Jerusalem: 3 For twenty-three years — from the thirteenth year of Josiah son of Amon king of Judah until this very day — the word of the LORD has come to me and I have spoken to you again and again, but you have not listened.

4 And though the LORD has sent all his servants the prophets to you again and again, you have not listened or paid any attention. 5 They said, "Turn now, each of you, from your evil ways and your evil practices, and you can stay in the land the LORD gave to you and your ancestors for ever and ever. 6 Do not follow other gods to serve and worship them; do not arouse my anger with what your hands have made. Then I will not harm you."

7 "But you did not listen to me," declares the LORD, "and you have aroused my anger with what your hands have made, and you have brought harm to yourselves."

8 Therefore the LORD Almighty says this: "Because you have not listened to my words, 9 I will summon all the peoples of the north and my servant Nebuchadnezzar king of Babylon," declares the LORD, "and I will bring them against this land and its inhabitants and against all the surrounding nations.

[a] *1* Hebrew *Jeconiah,* a variant of *Jehoiachin* [b] *5* Or *Chaldeans* [c] *9* That is, their names will be used in cursing (see 29:22); or, others will see that they are cursed.

I will completely destroy[a] them and make
them an object of horror and scorn, and an
everlasting ruin. 10 I will banish from them
the sounds of joy and gladness, the voices
of bride and bridegroom, the sound of mill-
stones and the light of the lamp. 11 This whole
country will become a desolate wasteland,
and these nations will serve the king of Bab-
ylon seventy years.

12 "But when the seventy years are ful-
filled, I will punish the king of Babylon and
his nation, the land of the Babylonians,[b] for
their guilt," declares the LORD, "and will
make it desolate forever. 13 I will bring on
that land all the things I have spoken against
it, all that are written in this book and proph-
esied by Jeremiah against all the nations.
14 They themselves will be enslaved by many
nations and great kings; I will repay them ac-
cording to their deeds and the work of their
hands."

The Cup of God's Wrath

15 This is what the LORD, the God of Isra-
el, said to me: "Take from my hand this cup
filled with the wine of my wrath and make
all the nations to whom I send you drink it.
16 When they drink it, they will stagger and
go mad because of the sword I will send
among them."

17 So I took the cup from the LORD's hand
and made all the nations to whom he sent
me drink it: 18 Jerusalem and the towns of
Judah, its kings and officials, to make them
a ruin and an object of horror and scorn, a
curse[c] — as they are today; 19 Pharaoh king of
Egypt, his attendants, his officials and all his
people, 20 and all the foreign people there; all
the kings of Uz; all the kings of the Philis-
tines (those of Ashkelon, Gaza, Ekron, and
the people left at Ashdod); 21 Edom, Moab
and Ammon; 22 all the kings of Tyre and Si-
don; the kings of the coastlands across the
sea; 23 Dedan, Tema, Buz and all who are in
distant places[d]; 24 all the kings of Arabia and
all the kings of the foreign people who live
in the wilderness; 25 all the kings of Zimri,
Elam and Media; 26 and all the kings of the
north, near and far, one after the other — all
the kingdoms on the face of the earth. And
after all of them, the king of Sheshak[e] will
drink it too.

27 "Then tell them, 'This is what the LORD
Almighty, the God of Israel, says: Drink, get
drunk and vomit, and fall to rise no more be-
cause of the sword I will send among you.'
28 But if they refuse to take the cup from
your hand and drink, tell them, 'This is what
the LORD Almighty says: You must drink it!
29 See, I am beginning to bring disaster on
the city that bears my Name, and will you
indeed go unpunished? You will not go un-
punished, for I am calling down a sword on
all who live on the earth, declares the LORD
Almighty.'

30 "Now prophesy all these words against
them and say to them:

" 'The LORD will roar from on high;
he will thunder from his holy dwelling
and roar mightily against his land.
He will shout like those who tread the
grapes,
shout against all who live on the earth.
31 The tumult will resound to the ends of
the earth,
for the LORD will bring charges against
the nations;
he will bring judgment on all mankind
and put the wicked to the sword,' "
declares the LORD.

32 This is what the LORD Almighty says:

"Look! Disaster is spreading
from nation to nation;
a mighty storm is rising
from the ends of the earth."

33 At that time those slain by the LORD will be
everywhere — from one end of the earth to
the other. They will not be mourned or gath-
ered up or buried, but will be like dung lying
on the ground.

34 Weep and wail, you shepherds;
roll in the dust, you leaders of the flock.
For your time to be slaughtered has come;
you will fall like the best of the rams.[f]
35 The shepherds will have nowhere to flee,
the leaders of the flock no place to
escape.

[a] 9 The Hebrew term refers to the irrevocable giving over of things or persons to the LORD, often by totally destroying them. [b] 12 Or *Chaldeans* [c] 18 That is, their names to be used in cursing (see 29:22); or, to be seen by others as cursed [d] 23 Or *who clip the hair by their foreheads* [e] 26 *Sheshak* is a cryptogram for Babylon. [f] 34 Septuagint; Hebrew *fall and be shattered like fine pottery*

36 Hear the cry of the shepherds,
the wailing of the leaders of the flock,
for the LORD is destroying their
pasture.
37 The peaceful meadows will be laid waste
because of the fierce anger of the
LORD.
38 Like a lion he will leave his lair,
and their land will become desolate
because of the sword[a] of the oppressor
and because of the LORD's fierce anger.

Jeremiah Threatened With Death

26 Early in the reign of Jehoiakim son of
Josiah king of Judah, this word came
from the LORD: 2 "This is what the LORD says:
Stand in the courtyard of the LORD's house
and speak to all the people of the towns of Ju-
dah who come to worship in the house of the
LORD. Tell them everything I command you;
do not omit a word. 3 Perhaps they will lis-
ten and each will turn from their evil ways.
Then I will relent and not inflict on them the
disaster I was planning because of the evil
they have done. 4 Say to them, 'This is what
the LORD says: If you do not listen to me and
follow my law, which I have set before you,
5 and if you do not listen to the words of my
servants the prophets, whom I have sent to
you again and again (though you have not
listened), 6 then I will make this house like
Shiloh and this city a curse[b] among all the
nations of the earth.'"

7 The priests, the prophets and all the peo-
ple heard Jeremiah speak these words in
the house of the LORD. 8 But as soon as Jer-
emiah finished telling all the people every-
thing the LORD had commanded him to say,
the priests, the prophets and all the people
seized him and said, "You must die! 9 Why do
you prophesy in the LORD's name that this
house will be like Shiloh and this city will be
desolate and deserted?" And all the people
crowded around Jeremiah in the house of
the LORD.

10 When the officials of Judah heard about
these things, they went up from the royal
palace to the house of the LORD and took
their places at the entrance of the New Gate
of the LORD's house. 11 Then the priests and
the prophets said to the officials and all the
people, "This man should be sentenced to
death because he has prophesied against
this city. You have heard it with your own
ears!"

12 Then Jeremiah said to all the officials
and all the people: "The LORD sent me to
prophesy against this house and this city
all the things you have heard. 13 Now re-
form your ways and your actions and obey
the LORD your God. Then the LORD will re-
lent and not bring the disaster he has pro-
nounced against you. 14 As for me, I am in
your hands; do with me whatever you think
is good and right. 15 Be assured, however,
that if you put me to death, you will bring the
guilt of innocent blood on yourselves and
on this city and on those who live in it, for in
truth the LORD has sent me to you to speak
all these words in your hearing."

16 Then the officials and all the people
said to the priests and the prophets, "This
man should not be sentenced to death! He
has spoken to us in the name of the LORD our
God."

17 Some of the elders of the land stepped
forward and said to the entire assembly of
people, 18 "Micah of Moresheth prophesied
in the days of Hezekiah king of Judah. He
told all the people of Judah, 'This is what the
LORD Almighty says:

"'Zion will be plowed like a field,
Jerusalem will become a heap of
rubble,
the temple hill a mound overgrown
with thickets.'[c]

19 "Did Hezekiah king of Judah or anyone
else in Judah put him to death? Did not Hez-
ekiah fear the LORD and seek his favor? And
did not the LORD relent, so that he did not
bring the disaster he pronounced against
them? We are about to bring a terrible disas-
ter on ourselves!"

20 (Now Uriah son of Shemaiah from Kir-
iath Jearim was another man who prophe-
sied in the name of the LORD; he prophesied
the same things against this city and this
land as Jeremiah did. 21 When King Jehoia-
kim and all his officers and officials heard
his words, the king was determined to put
him to death. But Uriah heard of it and fled

[a] *38* Some Hebrew manuscripts and Septuagint (see also 46:16 and 50:16); most Hebrew manuscripts *anger* [b] *6* That is, its name will be used in cursing (see 29:22); or, others will see that it is cursed.
[c] *18* Micah 3:12

in fear to Egypt. [22]King Jehoiakim, however, sent Elnathan son of Akbor to Egypt, along with some other men. [23]They brought Uriah out of Egypt and took him to King Jehoiakim, who had him struck down with a sword and his body thrown into the burial place of the common people.)

[24]Furthermore, Ahikam son of Shaphan supported Jeremiah, and so he was not handed over to the people to be put to death.

Judah to Serve Nebuchadnezzar

27 Early in the reign of Zedekiah[a] son of Josiah king of Judah, this word came to Jeremiah from the LORD: [2]This is what the LORD said to me: "Make a yoke out of straps and crossbars and put it on your neck. [3]Then send word to the kings of Edom, Moab, Ammon, Tyre and Sidon through the envoys who have come to Jerusalem to Zedekiah king of Judah. [4]Give them a message for their masters and say, 'This is what the LORD Almighty, the God of Israel, says: "Tell this to your masters: [5]With my great power and outstretched arm I made the earth and its people and the animals that are on it, and I give it to anyone I please. [6]Now I will give all your countries into the hands of my servant Nebuchadnezzar king of Babylon; I will make even the wild animals subject to him. [7]All nations will serve him and his son and his grandson until the time for his land comes; then many nations and great kings will subjugate him.

[8]"'"If, however, any nation or kingdom will not serve Nebuchadnezzar king of Babylon or bow its neck under his yoke, I will punish that nation with the sword, famine and plague, declares the LORD, until I destroy it by his hand. [9]So do not listen to your prophets, your diviners, your interpreters of dreams, your mediums or your sorcerers who tell you, 'You will not serve the king of Babylon.' [10]They prophesy lies to you that will only serve to remove you far from your lands; I will banish you and you will perish. [11]But if any nation will bow its neck under the yoke of the king of Babylon and serve him, I will let that nation remain in its own land to till it and to live there, declares the LORD."'"

[12]I gave the same message to Zedekiah king of Judah. I said, "Bow your neck under the yoke of the king of Babylon; serve him and his people, and you will live. [13]Why will you and your people die by the sword, famine and plague with which the LORD has threatened any nation that will not serve the king of Babylon? [14]Do not listen to the words of the prophets who say to you, 'You will not serve the king of Babylon,' for they are prophesying lies to you. [15]'I have not sent them,' declares the LORD. 'They are prophesying lies in my name. Therefore, I will banish you and you will perish, both you and the prophets who prophesy to you.'"

[16]Then I said to the priests and all these people, "This is what the LORD says: Do not listen to the prophets who say, 'Very soon now the articles from the LORD's house will be brought back from Babylon.' They are prophesying lies to you. [17]Do not listen to them. Serve the king of Babylon, and you will live. Why should this city become a ruin? [18]If they are prophets and have the word of the LORD, let them plead with the LORD Almighty that the articles remaining in the house of the LORD and in the palace of the king of Judah and in Jerusalem not be taken to Babylon. [19]For this is what the LORD Almighty says about the pillars, the bronze Sea, the movable stands and the other articles that are left in this city, [20]which Nebuchadnezzar king of Babylon did not take away when he carried Jehoiachin[b] son of Jehoiakim king of Judah into exile from Jerusalem to Babylon, along with all the nobles of Judah and Jerusalem — [21]yes, this is what the LORD Almighty, the God of Israel, says about the things that are left in the house of the LORD and in the palace of the king of Judah and in Jerusalem: [22]'They will be taken to Babylon and there they will remain until the day I come for them,' declares the LORD. 'Then I will bring them back and restore them to this place.'"

The False Prophet Hananiah

28 In the fifth month of that same year, the fourth year, early in the reign of Zedekiah king of Judah, the prophet Hananiah son of Azzur, who was from Gibeon, said

[a] *1* A few Hebrew manuscripts and Syriac (see also 27:3,12 and 28:1); most Hebrew manuscripts *Jehoiakim* (Most Septuagint manuscripts do not have this verse.) [b] *20* Hebrew *Jeconiah,* a variant of *Jehoiachin*

to me in the house of the LORD in the presence of the priests and all the people: [2]"This is what the LORD Almighty, the God of Israel, says: 'I will break the yoke of the king of Babylon. [3]Within two years I will bring back to this place all the articles of the LORD's house that Nebuchadnezzar king of Babylon removed from here and took to Babylon. [4]I will also bring back to this place Jehoiachin[a] son of Jehoiakim king of Judah and all the other exiles from Judah who went to Babylon,' declares the LORD, 'for I will break the yoke of the king of Babylon.' "

[5]Then the prophet Jeremiah replied to the prophet Hananiah before the priests and all the people who were standing in the house of the LORD. [6]He said, "Amen! May the LORD do so! May the LORD fulfill the words you have prophesied by bringing the articles of the LORD's house and all the exiles back to this place from Babylon. [7]Nevertheless, listen to what I have to say in your hearing and in the hearing of all the people: [8]From early times the prophets who preceded you and me have prophesied war, disaster and plague against many countries and great kingdoms. [9]But the prophet who prophesies peace will be recognized as one truly sent by the LORD only if his prediction comes true."

[10]Then the prophet Hananiah took the yoke off the neck of the prophet Jeremiah and broke it, [11]and he said before all the people, "This is what the LORD says: 'In the same way I will break the yoke of Nebuchadnezzar king of Babylon off the neck of all the nations within two years.' " At this, the prophet Jeremiah went on his way.

[12]After the prophet Hananiah had broken the yoke off the neck of the prophet Jeremiah, the word of the LORD came to Jeremiah: [13]"Go and tell Hananiah, 'This is what the LORD says: You have broken a wooden yoke, but in its place you will get a yoke of iron. [14]This is what the LORD Almighty, the God of Israel, says: I will put an iron yoke on the necks of all these nations to make them serve Nebuchadnezzar king of Babylon, and they will serve him. I will even give him control over the wild animals.' "

[15]Then the prophet Jeremiah said to Hananiah the prophet, "Listen, Hananiah! The LORD has not sent you, yet you have persuaded this nation to trust in lies. [16]Therefore this is what the LORD says: 'I am about to remove you from the face of the earth. This very year you are going to die, because you have preached rebellion against the LORD.' "

[17]In the seventh month of that same year, Hananiah the prophet died.

A Letter to the Exiles

29 This is the text of the letter that the prophet Jeremiah sent from Jerusalem to the surviving elders among the exiles and to the priests, the prophets and all the other people Nebuchadnezzar had carried into exile from Jerusalem to Babylon. [2](This was after King Jehoiachin[a] and the queen mother, the court officials and the leaders of Judah and Jerusalem, the skilled workers and the artisans had gone into exile from Jerusalem.) [3]He entrusted the letter to Elasah son of Shaphan and to Gemariah son of Hilkiah, whom Zedekiah king of Judah sent to King Nebuchadnezzar in Babylon. It said:

> [4]This is what the LORD Almighty, the God of Israel, says to all those I carried into exile from Jerusalem to Babylon: [5]"Build houses and settle down; plant gardens and eat what they produce. [6]Marry and have sons and daughters; find wives for your sons and give your daughters in marriage, so that they too may have sons and daughters. Increase in number there; do not decrease. [7]Also, seek the peace and prosperity of the city to which I have carried you into exile. Pray to the LORD for it, because if it prospers, you too will prosper." [8]Yes, this is what the LORD Almighty, the God of Israel, says: "Do not let the prophets and diviners among you deceive you. Do not listen to the dreams you encourage them to have. [9]They are prophesying lies to you in my name. I have not sent them," declares the LORD.
>
> [10]This is what the LORD says: "When seventy years are completed for Babylon, I will come to you and fulfill my good promise to bring you back to this place. [11]For I know the plans I have for you," declares the LORD, "plans to prosper you and not to harm you, plans to give you hope and a future. [12]Then you

[a] 4,2 Hebrew *Jeconiah,* a variant of *Jehoiachin*

will call on me and come and pray to me, and I will listen to you. [13]You will seek me and find me when you seek me with all your heart. [14]I will be found by you," declares the LORD, "and will bring you back from captivity.[a] I will gather you from all the nations and places where I have banished you," declares the LORD, "and will bring you back to the place from which I carried you into exile."

[15]You may say, "The LORD has raised up prophets for us in Babylon," [16]but this is what the LORD says about the king who sits on David's throne and all the people who remain in this city, your fellow citizens who did not go with you into exile — [17]yes, this is what the LORD Almighty says: "I will send the sword, famine and plague against them and I will make them like figs that are so bad they cannot be eaten. [18]I will pursue them with the sword, famine and plague and will make them abhorrent to all the kingdoms of the earth, a curse[b] and an object of horror, of scorn and reproach, among all the nations where I drive them. [19]For they have not listened to my words," declares the LORD, "words that I sent to them again and again by my servants the prophets. And you exiles have not listened either," declares the LORD.

[20]Therefore, hear the word of the LORD, all you exiles whom I have sent away from Jerusalem to Babylon. [21]This is what the LORD Almighty, the God of Israel, says about Ahab son of Kolaiah and Zedekiah son of Maaseiah, who are prophesying lies to you in my name: "I will deliver them into the hands of Nebuchadnezzar king of Babylon, and he will put them to death before your very eyes. [22]Because of them, all the exiles from Judah who are in Babylon will use this curse: 'May the LORD treat you like Zedekiah and Ahab, whom the king of Babylon burned in the fire.' [23]For they have done outrageous things in Israel; they have committed adultery with their neighbors' wives, and in my name they have uttered lies — which I did not authorize. I knew it and am a witness to it," declares the LORD.

Message to Shemaiah

[24]Tell Shemaiah the Nehelamite, [25]"This is what the LORD Almighty, the God of Israel, says: You sent letters in your own name to all the people in Jerusalem, to the priest Zephaniah son of Maaseiah, and to all the other priests. You said to Zephaniah, [26]'The LORD has appointed you priest in place of Jehoiada to be in charge of the house of the LORD; you should put any maniac who acts like a prophet into the stocks and neck-irons. [27]So why have you not reprimanded Jeremiah from Anathoth, who poses as a prophet among you? [28]He has sent this message to us in Babylon: It will be a long time. Therefore build houses and settle down; plant gardens and eat what they produce.' "

[29]Zephaniah the priest, however, read the letter to Jeremiah the prophet. [30]Then the word of the LORD came to Jeremiah: [31]"Send this message to all the exiles: 'This is what the LORD says about Shemaiah the Nehelamite: Because Shemaiah has prophesied to you, even though I did not send him, and has persuaded you to trust in lies, [32]this is what the LORD says: I will surely punish Shemaiah the Nehelamite and his descendants. He will have no one left among this people, nor will he see the good things I will do for my people, declares the LORD, because he has preached rebellion against me.' "

Restoration of Israel

30 This is the word that came to Jeremiah from the LORD: [2]"This is what the LORD, the God of Israel, says: 'Write in a book all the words I have spoken to you. [3]The days are coming,' declares the LORD, 'when I will bring my people Israel and Judah back from captivity[c] and restore them to the land I gave their ancestors to possess,' says the LORD."

[4]These are the words the LORD spoke concerning Israel and Judah: [5]"This is what the LORD says:

" 'Cries of fear are heard —
terror, not peace.
[6]Ask and see:
Can a man bear children?

[a] 14 Or *will restore your fortunes* [b] 18 That is, their names will be used in cursing (see verse 22); or, others will see that they are cursed. [c] 3 Or *will restore the fortunes of my people Israel and Judah*

Then why do I see every strong man
with his hands on his stomach like a woman in labor,
every face turned deathly pale?
7 How awful that day will be!
No other will be like it.
It will be a time of trouble for Jacob,
but he will be saved out of it.

8 " 'In that day,' declares the LORD Almighty,
'I will break the yoke off their necks
and will tear off their bonds;
no longer will foreigners enslave them.
9 Instead, they will serve the LORD their God
and David their king,
whom I will raise up for them.

10 " 'So do not be afraid, Jacob my servant;
do not be dismayed, Israel,'
declares the LORD.
'I will surely save you out of a distant place,
your descendants from the land of their exile.
Jacob will again have peace and security,
and no one will make him afraid.
11 I am with you and will save you,'
declares the LORD.
'Though I completely destroy all the nations
among which I scatter you,
I will not completely destroy you.
I will discipline you but only in due measure;
I will not let you go entirely unpunished.'

12 "This is what the LORD says:

" 'Your wound is incurable,
your injury beyond healing.
13 There is no one to plead your cause,
no remedy for your sore,
no healing for you.
14 All your allies have forgotten you;
they care nothing for you.
I have struck you as an enemy would
and punished you as would the cruel,
because your guilt is so great
and your sins so many.
15 Why do you cry out over your wound,
your pain that has no cure?
Because of your great guilt and many sins
I have done these things to you.

16 " 'But all who devour you will be devoured;
all your enemies will go into exile.
Those who plunder you will be plundered;
all who make spoil of you I will despoil.
17 But I will restore you to health
and heal your wounds,'
declares the LORD,
'because you are called an outcast,
Zion for whom no one cares.'

18 "This is what the LORD says:

" 'I will restore the fortunes of Jacob's tents
and have compassion on his dwellings;
the city will be rebuilt on her ruins,
and the palace will stand in its proper place.
19 From them will come songs of thanksgiving
and the sound of rejoicing.
I will add to their numbers,
and they will not be decreased;
I will bring them honor,
and they will not be disdained.
20 Their children will be as in days of old,
and their community will be established before me;
I will punish all who oppress them.
21 Their leader will be one of their own;
their ruler will arise from among them.
I will bring him near and he will come close to me —
for who is he who will devote himself
to be close to me?'
declares the LORD.
22 " 'So you will be my people,
and I will be your God.' "

23 See, the storm of the LORD
will burst out in wrath,
a driving wind swirling down
on the heads of the wicked.
24 The fierce anger of the LORD will not turn back
until he fully accomplishes
the purposes of his heart.
In days to come
you will understand this.

31 "At that time," declares the LORD, "I will be the God of all the families of Israel, and they will be my people."

[2]This is what the LORD says:

"The people who survive the sword
will find favor in the wilderness;
I will come to give rest to Israel."

[3]The LORD appeared to us in the past,[a]
saying:

"I have loved you with an everlasting
love;
I have drawn you with unfailing
kindness.
[4]I will build you up again,
and you, Virgin Israel, will be rebuilt.
Again you will take up your timbrels
and go out to dance with the joyful.
[5]Again you will plant vineyards
on the hills of Samaria;
the farmers will plant them
and enjoy their fruit.
[6]There will be a day when watchmen
cry out
on the hills of Ephraim,
'Come, let us go up to Zion,
to the LORD our God.'"

[7]This is what the LORD says:

"Sing with joy for Jacob;
shout for the foremost of the nations.
Make your praises heard, and say,
'LORD, save your people,
the remnant of Israel.'
[8]See, I will bring them from the land of
the north
and gather them from the ends of the
earth.
Among them will be the blind and the
lame,
expectant mothers and women in
labor;
a great throng will return.
[9]They will come with weeping;
they will pray as I bring them back.
I will lead them beside streams of water
on a level path where they will not
stumble,
because I am Israel's father,
and Ephraim is my firstborn son.
[10]"Hear the word of the LORD, you
nations;
proclaim it in distant coastlands:
'He who scattered Israel will gather them
and will watch over his flock like a
shepherd.'
[11]For the LORD will deliver Jacob
and redeem them from the hand of
those stronger than they.
[12]They will come and shout for joy on the
heights of Zion;
they will rejoice in the bounty of the
LORD—
the grain, the new wine and the olive oil,
the young of the flocks and herds.
They will be like a well-watered garden,
and they will sorrow no more.
[13]Then young women will dance and
be glad,
young men and old as well.
I will turn their mourning into gladness;
I will give them comfort and joy
instead of sorrow.
[14]I will satisfy the priests with abundance,
and my people will be filled with my
bounty,"
declares the LORD.

[15]This is what the LORD says:

"A voice is heard in Ramah,
mourning and great weeping,
Rachel weeping for her children
and refusing to be comforted,
because they are no more."
[16]This is what the LORD says:

"Restrain your voice from weeping
and your eyes from tears,
for your work will be rewarded,"
declares the LORD.
"They will return from the land of the
enemy.
[17]So there is hope for your descendants,"
declares the LORD.
"Your children will return to their own
land.

[18]"I have surely heard Ephraim's moaning:
'You disciplined me like an unruly
calf,
and I have been disciplined.
Restore me, and I will return,
because you are the LORD my God.
[19]After I strayed,
I repented;
after I came to understand,
I beat my breast.

[a] 3 Or *LORD has appeared to us from afar*

I was ashamed and humiliated
because I bore the disgrace of my youth.'
20 Is not Ephraim my dear son,
the child in whom I delight?
Though I often speak against him,
I still remember him.
Therefore my heart yearns for him;
I have great compassion for him,"
declares the LORD.

21 "Set up road signs;
put up guideposts.
Take note of the highway,
the road that you take.
Return, Virgin Israel,
return to your towns.
22 How long will you wander,
unfaithful Daughter Israel?
The LORD will create a new thing on earth—
the woman will return to[a] the man."

23 This is what the LORD Almighty, the God
of Israel, says: "When I bring them back from
captivity,[b] the people in the land of Judah
and in its towns will once again use these
words: 'The LORD bless you, you prosperous
city, you sacred mountain.' 24 People will live
together in Judah and all its towns—farm-
ers and those who move about with their
flocks. 25 I will refresh the weary and satisfy
the faint."

26 At this I awoke and looked around. My
sleep had been pleasant to me.

27 "The days are coming," declares the
LORD, "when I will plant the kingdoms of
Israel and Judah with the offspring of peo-
ple and of animals. 28 Just as I watched over
them to uproot and tear down, and to over-
throw, destroy and bring disaster, so I will
watch over them to build and to plant," de-
clares the LORD. 29 "In those days people will
no longer say,

'The parents have eaten sour grapes,
and the children's teeth are set on edge.'

30 Instead, everyone will die for their own
sin; whoever eats sour grapes—their own
teeth will be set on edge.

31 "The days are coming," declares the LORD,
"when I will make a new covenant
with the people of Israel
and with the people of Judah.
32 It will not be like the covenant
I made with their ancestors
when I took them by the hand
to lead them out of Egypt,
because they broke my covenant,
though I was a husband to[c] them,[d]"
declares the LORD.
33 "This is the covenant I will make with the people of Israel
after that time," declares the LORD.
"I will put my law in their minds
and write it on their hearts.
I will be their God,
and they will be my people.
34 No longer will they teach their neighbor,
or say to one another, 'Know the LORD,'
because they will all know me,
from the least of them to the greatest,"
declares the LORD.
"For I will forgive their wickedness
and will remember their sins no more."

35 This is what the LORD says,

he who appoints the sun
to shine by day,
who decrees the moon and stars
to shine by night,
who stirs up the sea
so that its waves roar—
the LORD Almighty is his name:
36 "Only if these decrees vanish from my sight,"
declares the LORD,
"will Israel ever cease
being a nation before me."

37 This is what the LORD says:

"Only if the heavens above can be measured
and the foundations of the earth below be searched out
will I reject all the descendants of Israel
because of all they have done,"
declares the LORD.

38 "The days are coming," declares the
LORD, "when this city will be rebuilt for me
from the Tower of Hananel to the Corner
Gate. 39 The measuring line will stretch from

[a] 22 Or *will protect* [b] 23 Or *I restore their fortunes away from* [d] 32 Or *was their master* [c] 32 Hebrew; Septuagint and Syriac / *and I turned*

there straight to the hill of Gareb and then turn to Goah. [40]The whole valley where dead bodies and ashes are thrown, and all the terraces out to the Kidron Valley on the east as far as the corner of the Horse Gate, will be holy to the LORD. The city will never again be uprooted or demolished."

Jeremiah Buys a Field

32 This is the word that came to Jeremiah from the LORD in the tenth year of Zedekiah king of Judah, which was the eighteenth year of Nebuchadnezzar. [2]The army of the king of Babylon was then besieging Jerusalem, and Jeremiah the prophet was confined in the courtyard of the guard in the royal palace of Judah.

[3]Now Zedekiah king of Judah had imprisoned him there, saying, "Why do you prophesy as you do? You say, 'This is what the LORD says: I am about to give this city into the hands of the king of Babylon, and he will capture it. [4]Zedekiah king of Judah will not escape the Babylonians[a] but will certainly be given into the hands of the king of Babylon, and will speak with him face to face and see him with his own eyes. [5]He will take Zedekiah to Babylon, where he will remain until I deal with him, declares the LORD. If you fight against the Babylonians, you will not succeed.'"

[6]Jeremiah said, "The word of the LORD came to me: [7]Hanamel son of Shallum your uncle is going to come to you and say, 'Buy my field at Anathoth, because as nearest relative it is your right and duty to buy it.'

[8]"Then, just as the LORD had said, my cousin Hanamel came to me in the courtyard of the guard and said, 'Buy my field at Anathoth in the territory of Benjamin. Since it is your right to redeem it and possess it, buy it for yourself.'

"I knew that this was the word of the LORD; [9]so I bought the field at Anathoth from my cousin Hanamel and weighed out for him seventeen shekels[b] of silver. [10]I signed and sealed the deed, had it witnessed, and weighed out the silver on the scales. [11]I took the deed of purchase — the sealed copy containing the terms and conditions, as well as the unsealed copy — [12]and I gave this deed to Baruch son of Neriah, the son of Mahseiah, in the presence of my cousin Hanamel and of the witnesses who had signed the deed and of all the Jews sitting in the courtyard of the guard.

[13]"In their presence I gave Baruch these instructions: [14]'This is what the LORD Almighty, the God of Israel, says: Take these documents, both the sealed and unsealed copies of the deed of purchase, and put them in a clay jar so they will last a long time. [15]For this is what the LORD Almighty, the God of Israel, says: Houses, fields and vineyards will again be bought in this land.'

[16]"After I had given the deed of purchase to Baruch son of Neriah, I prayed to the LORD:

> [17]"Ah, Sovereign LORD, you have made the heavens and the earth by your great power and outstretched arm. Nothing is too hard for you. [18]You show love to thousands but bring the punishment for the parents' sins into the laps of their children after them. Great and mighty God, whose name is the LORD Almighty, [19]great are your purposes and mighty are your deeds. Your eyes are open to the ways of all mankind; you reward each person according to their conduct and as their deeds deserve. [20]You performed signs and wonders in Egypt and have continued them to this day, in Israel and among all mankind, and have gained the renown that is still yours. [21]You brought your people Israel out of Egypt with signs and wonders, by a mighty hand and an outstretched arm and with great terror. [22]You gave them this land you had sworn to give their ancestors, a land flowing with milk and honey. [23]They came in and took possession of it, but they did not obey you or follow your law; they did not do what you commanded them to do. So you brought all this disaster on them.
>
> [24]"See how the siege ramps are built up to take the city. Because of the sword, famine and plague, the city will be given into the hands of the Babylonians who are attacking it. What you said has happened, as you now see. [25]And though the city will be given into the

[a] *4* Or *Chaldeans*; also in verses 5, 24, 25, 28, 29 and 43 [b] *9* That is, about 7 ounces or about 200 grams

hands of the Babylonians, you, Sov-
ereign LORD, say to me, 'Buy the field
with silver and have the transaction
witnessed.'"

26 Then the word of the LORD came to Jere-
miah: 27 "I am the LORD, the God of all man-
kind. Is anything too hard for me? 28 There-
fore this is what the LORD says: I am about to
give this city into the hands of the Babyloni-
ans and to Nebuchadnezzar king of Babylon,
who will capture it. 29 The Babylonians who
are attacking this city will come in and set it
on fire; they will burn it down, along with the
houses where the people aroused my anger
by burning incense on the roofs to Baal and
by pouring out drink offerings to other gods.
30 "The people of Israel and Judah have
done nothing but evil in my sight from their
youth; indeed, the people of Israel have done
nothing but arouse my anger with what
their hands have made, declares the LORD.
31 From the day it was built until now, this
city has so aroused my anger and wrath that
I must remove it from my sight. 32 The people
of Israel and Judah have provoked me by all
the evil they have done — they, their kings
and officials, their priests and prophets, the
people of Judah and those living in Jerusa-
lem. 33 They turned their backs to me and
not their faces; though I taught them again
and again, they would not listen or respond
to discipline. 34 They set up their vile imag-
es in the house that bears my Name and de-
filed it. 35 They built high places for Baal in
the Valley of Ben Hinnom to sacrifice their
sons and daughters to Molek, though I never
commanded — nor did it enter my mind —
that they should do such a detestable thing
and so make Judah sin.
36 "You are saying about this city, 'By the
sword, famine and plague it will be given
into the hands of the king of Babylon'; but
this is what the LORD, the God of Israel, says:
37 I will surely gather them from all the lands
where I banish them in my furious anger and
great wrath; I will bring them back to this
place and let them live in safety. 38 They will
be my people, and I will be their God. 39 I will
give them singleness of heart and action,
so that they will always fear me and that all
will then go well for them and for their chil-
dren after them. 40 I will make an everlasting
covenant with them: I will never stop doing
good to them, and I will inspire them to fear
me, so that they will never turn away from
me. 41 I will rejoice in doing them good and
will assuredly plant them in this land with
all my heart and soul.
42 "This is what the LORD says: As I have
brought all this great calamity on this peo-
ple, so I will give them all the prosperity I
have promised them. 43 Once more fields
will be bought in this land of which you say,
'It is a desolate waste, without people or an-
imals, for it has been given into the hands of
the Babylonians.' 44 Fields will be bought for
silver, and deeds will be signed, sealed and
witnessed in the territory of Benjamin, in
the villages around Jerusalem, in the towns
of Judah and in the towns of the hill country,
of the western foothills and of the Negev, be-
cause I will restore their fortunes,[a] declares
the LORD."

Promise of Restoration

33 While Jeremiah was still confined in
the courtyard of the guard, the word
of the LORD came to him a second time:
2 "This is what the LORD says, he who made
the earth, the LORD who formed it and estab-
lished it — the LORD is his name: 3 'Call to me
and I will answer you and tell you great and
unsearchable things you do not know.' 4 For
this is what the LORD, the God of Israel, says
about the houses in this city and the royal
palaces of Judah that have been torn down
to be used against the siege ramps and the
sword 5 in the fight with the Babylonians[b]:
'They will be filled with the dead bodies of
the people I will slay in my anger and wrath.
I will hide my face from this city because of
all its wickedness.
6 " 'Nevertheless, I will bring health and
healing to it; I will heal my people and will
let them enjoy abundant peace and securi-
ty. 7 I will bring Judah and Israel back from
captivity[c] and will rebuild them as they were
before. 8 I will cleanse them from all the sin
they have committed against me and will
forgive all their sins of rebellion against me.
9 Then this city will bring me renown, joy,
praise and honor before all nations on earth

[a] 44 Or *will bring them back from captivity and Israel*
[b] 5 Or *Chaldeans*
[c] 7 Or *will restore the fortunes of Judah*

that hear of all the good things I do for it; and they will be in awe and will tremble at the abundant prosperity and peace I provide for it.'

10 "This is what the LORD says: 'You say about this place, "It is a desolate waste, without people or animals." Yet in the towns of Judah and the streets of Jerusalem that are deserted, inhabited by neither people nor animals, there will be heard once more 11 the sounds of joy and gladness, the voices of bride and bridegroom, and the voices of those who bring thank offerings to the house of the LORD, saying,

"Give thanks to the LORD Almighty,
for the LORD is good;
his love endures forever."

For I will restore the fortunes of the land as they were before,' says the LORD.

12 "This is what the LORD Almighty says: 'In this place, desolate and without people or animals—in all its towns there will again be pastures for shepherds to rest their flocks. 13 In the towns of the hill country, of the western foothills and of the Negev, in the territory of Benjamin, in the villages around Jerusalem and in the towns of Judah, flocks will again pass under the hand of the one who counts them,' says the LORD.

14 " 'The days are coming,' declares the LORD, 'when I will fulfill the good promise I made to the people of Israel and Judah.

15 " 'In those days and at that time
I will make a righteous Branch sprout
from David's line;
he will do what is just and right in the
land.
16 In those days Judah will be saved
and Jerusalem will live in safety.
This is the name by which it[a] will be
called:
The LORD Our Righteous Savior.'

17 For this is what the LORD says: 'David will never fail to have a man to sit on the throne of Israel, 18 nor will the Levitical priests ever fail to have a man to stand before me continually to offer burnt offerings, to burn grain offerings and to present sacrifices.' "

19 The word of the LORD came to Jeremiah: 20 "This is what the LORD says: 'If you can break my covenant with the day and my covenant with the night, so that day and night no longer come at their appointed time, 21 then my covenant with David my servant—and my covenant with the Levites who are priests ministering before me—can be broken and David will no longer have a descendant to reign on his throne. 22 I will make the descendants of David my servant and the Levites who minister before me as countless as the stars in the sky and as measureless as the sand on the seashore.' "

23 The word of the LORD came to Jeremiah: 24 "Have you not noticed that these people are saying, 'The LORD has rejected the two kingdoms[b] he chose'? So they despise my people and no longer regard them as a nation. 25 This is what the LORD says: 'If I have not made my covenant with day and night and established the laws of heaven and earth, 26 then I will reject the descendants of Jacob and David my servant and will not choose one of his sons to rule over the descendants of Abraham, Isaac and Jacob. For I will restore their fortunes[c] and have compassion on them.' "

Warning to Zedekiah

34 While Nebuchadnezzar king of Babylon and all his army and all the kingdoms and peoples in the empire he ruled were fighting against Jerusalem and all its surrounding towns, this word came to Jeremiah from the LORD: 2 "This is what the LORD, the God of Israel, says: Go to Zedekiah king of Judah and tell him, 'This is what the LORD says: I am about to give this city into the hands of the king of Babylon, and he will burn it down. 3 You will not escape from his grasp but will surely be captured and given into his hands. You will see the king of Babylon with your own eyes, and he will speak with you face to face. And you will go to Babylon.

4 " 'Yet hear the LORD's promise to you, Zedekiah king of Judah. This is what the LORD says concerning you: You will not die by the sword; 5 you will die peacefully. As people made a funeral fire in honor of your predecessors, the kings who ruled before you, so they will make a fire in your honor and lament, "Alas, master!" I myself make this promise, declares the LORD.' "

[a] *16* Or *he* [b] *24* Or *families* [c] *26* Or *will bring them back from captivity*

FOREVER REIGN

Reuben Morgan, Jason Ingram

You are good you are good
When there's nothing good in me
You are love you are love
On display for all to see
You are light you are light
When the darkness closes in
You are hope you are hope
You have covered all my sin

You are peace you are peace
When my fear is crippling
You are true you are true
Even in my wandering
You are joy you are joy
You're the reason that I sing
You are life you are life
In you death has lost its sting

Oh I'm running to your arms
I'm running to your arms
The riches of your love
Will always be enough
Nothing compares to
your embrace
Light of the world forever reign

You are more you are more
Than my words will ever say
You are Lord you are Lord
All creation will proclaim
You are here you are here
In your presence I'm made whole
You are God you are God
Of all else I'm letting go

My heart will sing
No other Name
Jesus
Jesus

THE INSPIRATION

The people walking in darkness have seen a great light; on those living in the land of deep darkness a light has dawned [. . .] For to us a child is born, to us a son is given, and the government will be on his shoulders. And he will be called Wonderful Counselor, Mighty God, Everlasting Father, Prince of Peace. Of the greatness of his government and peace there will be no end. He will reign on David's throne and over his kingdom, establishing and upholding it with justice and righteousness from that time on and forever. The zeal of the LORD Almighty will accomplish this. —Isaiah 9:2, 6–7

Read also: Lamentations 5:19

BEHIND THE SONG

Juxtaposition is an important literary tool in Scripture and often helps to create powerful moments of personal worship. Many examples of worship in the Bible include statements of confession, lament or even protest, all while acknowledging the goodness of God. Christians are caught, as many writers have noted, between the "now" and the "not yet."

Hillsong's Reuben Morgan and Jason Ingram explored these ideas when they wrote this song. Morgan explains, "Jason and I have become really good friends and we were just hanging out and writing a bit and he had this idea: 'You are good, you are good when there's nothing good in me.' I liked the feel of it." The result is a uniquely personal worship song that works in group settings as well. Morgan immediately clicked with the idea and dove right in, taking the confessional tone even further.

Confession is a critical and often neglected aspect of personal worship. We cannot approach God's throne of grace if we are not honest and repentant about our sin. In the ancient book of Isaiah, the prophet details the faithlessness of God's people and the judgment and suffering that would result because they had wandered far from God. And Isaiah sees all too well his own sinfulness in the light of the holiness of God: "'Woe to me!' I cried. 'I am ruined! For I am a man of unclean lips, and I live among a people of unclean lips, and my eyes have seen the King, the LORD Almighty'" (Isaiah 6:5).

In your prayer time, do you speak of your struggles to God? It can be especially powerful to confess your own failures and sin when detailing your trials.

Reread the entire chapter of Isaiah 9, a section of prophecy that directly references the coming of Christ. Consider the darkness of the world the prophet Isaiah called home, as well as the darkness of the culture in which we live. In what ways do you long to recognize God's presence and work in your world?

[6]Then Jeremiah the prophet told all this to
Zedekiah king of Judah, in Jerusalem, [7]while
the army of the king of Babylon was fighting
against Jerusalem and the other cities of Ju-
dah that were still holding out — Lachish
and Azekah. These were the only fortified
cities left in Judah.

Freedom for Slaves

[8]The word came to Jeremiah from the
LORD after King Zedekiah had made a cov-
enant with all the people in Jerusalem to
proclaim freedom for the slaves. [9]Every-
one was to free their Hebrew slaves, both
male and female; no one was to hold a fel-
low Hebrew in bondage. [10]So all the officials
and people who entered into this covenant
agreed that they would free their male and
female slaves and no longer hold them in
bondage. They agreed, and set them free.
[11]But afterward they changed their minds
and took back the slaves they had freed and
enslaved them again.

[12]Then the word of the LORD came to Jer-
emiah: [13]"This is what the LORD, the God
of Israel, says: I made a covenant with your
ancestors when I brought them out of Egypt,
out of the land of slavery. I said, [14]'Every sev-
enth year each of you must free any fellow
Hebrews who have sold themselves to you.
After they have served you six years, you
must let them go free.'[a] Your ancestors, how-
ever, did not listen to me or pay attention to
me. [15]Recently you repented and did what
is right in my sight: Each of you proclaimed
freedom to your own people. You even made
a covenant before me in the house that
bears my Name. [16]But now you have turned
around and profaned my name; each of you
has taken back the male and female slaves
you had set free to go where they wished.
You have forced them to become your slaves
again.

[17]"Therefore this is what the LORD says:
You have not obeyed me; you have not pro-
claimed freedom to your own people. So I
now proclaim 'freedom' for you, declares
the LORD — 'freedom' to fall by the sword,
plague and famine. I will make you abhor-
rent to all the kingdoms of the earth. [18]Those
who have violated my covenant and have
not fulfilled the terms of the covenant they
made before me, I will treat like the calf they
cut in two and then walked between its piec-
es. [19]The leaders of Judah and Jerusalem, the
court officials, the priests and all the people
of the land who walked between the pieces
of the calf, [20]I will deliver into the hands of
their enemies who want to kill them. Their
dead bodies will become food for the birds
and the wild animals.

[21]"I will deliver Zedekiah king of Judah
and his officials into the hands of their en-
emies who want to kill them, to the army of
the king of Babylon, which has withdrawn
from you. [22]I am going to give the order, de-
clares the LORD, and I will bring them back
to this city. They will fight against it, take it
and burn it down. And I will lay waste the
towns of Judah so no one can live there."

The Rekabites

35 This is the word that came to Jeremi-
ah from the LORD during the reign of
Jehoiakim son of Josiah king of Judah: [2]"Go
to the Rekabite family and invite them to
come to one of the side rooms of the house of
the LORD and give them wine to drink."

[3]So I went to get Jaazaniah son of Jeremi-
ah, the son of Habazziniah, and his brothers
and all his sons — the whole family of the
Rekabites. [4]I brought them into the house of
the LORD, into the room of the sons of Hanan
son of Igdaliah the man of God. It was next to
the room of the officials, which was over that
of Maaseiah son of Shallum the doorkeep-
er. [5]Then I set bowls full of wine and some
cups before the Rekabites and said to them,
"Drink some wine."

[6]But they replied, "We do not drink wine,
because our forefather Jehonadab[b] son of
Rekab gave us this command: 'Neither you
nor your descendants must ever drink wine.
[7]Also you must never build houses, sow seed
or plant vineyards; you must never have any
of these things, but must always live in tents.
Then you will live a long time in the land
where you are nomads.' [8]We have obeyed
everything our forefather Jehonadab son of
Rekab commanded us. Neither we nor our
wives nor our sons and daughters have ever
drunk wine [9]or built houses to live in or had
vineyards, fields or crops. [10]We have lived in
tents and have fully obeyed everything our

[a] *14* Deut. 15:12 [b] *6* Hebrew *Jonadab*, a variant of *Jehonadab*; here and often in this chapter

forefather Jehonadab commanded us. 11But
when Nebuchadnezzar king of Babylon in-
vaded this land, we said, 'Come, we must go
to Jerusalem to escape the Babylonian[a] and
Aramean armies.' So we have remained in
Jerusalem."

12Then the word of the LORD came to Jer-
emiah, saying: 13"This is what the LORD Al-
mighty, the God of Israel, says: Go and tell
the people of Judah and those living in Jeru-
salem, 'Will you not learn a lesson and obey
my words?' declares the LORD. 14'Jehonadab
son of Rekab ordered his descendants not
to drink wine and this command has been
kept. To this day they do not drink wine, be-
cause they obey their forefather's command.
But I have spoken to you again and again, yet
you have not obeyed me. 15Again and again
I sent all my servants the prophets to you.
They said, "Each of you must turn from your
wicked ways and reform your actions; do not
follow other gods to serve them. Then you
will live in the land I have given to you and
your ancestors." But you have not paid atten-
tion or listened to me. 16The descendants of
Jehonadab son of Rekab have carried out the
command their forefather gave them, but
these people have not obeyed me.'

17"Therefore this is what the LORD God
Almighty, the God of Israel, says: 'Listen! I
am going to bring on Judah and on every-
one living in Jerusalem every disaster I pro-
nounced against them. I spoke to them, but
they did not listen; I called to them, but they
did not answer.' "

18Then Jeremiah said to the family of the
Rekabites, "This is what the LORD Almighty,
the God of Israel, says: 'You have obeyed the
command of your forefather Jehonadab and
have followed all his instructions and have
done everything he ordered.' 19Therefore
this is what the LORD Almighty, the God of
Israel, says: 'Jehonadab son of Rekab will
never fail to have a descendant to serve me.' "

Jehoiakim Burns Jeremiah's Scroll

36 In the fourth year of Jehoiakim son of
Josiah king of Judah, this word came
to Jeremiah from the LORD: 2"Take a scroll
and write on it all the words I have spoken to
you concerning Israel, Judah and all the oth-
er nations from the time I began speaking to
you in the reign of Josiah till now. 3Perhaps
when the people of Judah hear about every
disaster I plan to inflict on them, they will
each turn from their wicked ways; then I will
forgive their wickedness and their sin."

4So Jeremiah called Baruch son of Neriah,
and while Jeremiah dictated all the words
the LORD had spoken to him, Baruch wrote
them on the scroll. 5Then Jeremiah told Bar-
uch, "I am restricted; I am not allowed to go
to the LORD's temple. 6So you go to the house
of the LORD on a day of fasting and read to
the people from the scroll the words of the
LORD that you wrote as I dictated. Read them
to all the people of Judah who come in from
their towns. 7Perhaps they will bring their
petition before the LORD and will each turn
from their wicked ways, for the anger and
wrath pronounced against this people by the
LORD are great."

8Baruch son of Neriah did everything
Jeremiah the prophet told him to do; at the
LORD's temple he read the words of the LORD
from the scroll. 9In the ninth month of the
fifth year of Jehoiakim son of Josiah king of
Judah, a time of fasting before the LORD was
proclaimed for all the people in Jerusalem
and those who had come from the towns of
Judah. 10From the room of Gemariah son
of Shaphan the secretary, which was in the
upper courtyard at the entrance of the New
Gate of the temple, Baruch read to all the
people at the LORD's temple the words of Jer-
emiah from the scroll.

11When Micaiah son of Gemariah, the son
of Shaphan, heard all the words of the LORD
from the scroll, 12he went down to the secre-
tary's room in the royal palace, where all the
officials were sitting: Elishama the secre-
tary, Delaiah son of Shemaiah, Elnathan son
of Akbor, Gemariah son of Shaphan, Zede-
kiah son of Hananiah, and all the other offi-
cials. 13After Micaiah told them everything
he had heard Baruch read to the people from
the scroll, 14all the officials sent Jehudi son
of Nethaniah, the son of Shelemiah, the son
of Cushi, to say to Baruch, "Bring the scroll
from which you have read to the people and
come." So Baruch son of Neriah went to
them with the scroll in his hand. 15They said
to him, "Sit down, please, and read it to us."

So Baruch read it to them. 16When they

[a] 11 Or *Chaldean*

heard all these words, they looked at each
other in fear and said to Baruch, "We must re-
port all these words to the king." 17 Then they
asked Baruch, "Tell us, how did you come to
write all this? Did Jeremiah dictate it?"
18 "Yes," Baruch replied, "he dictated all
these words to me, and I wrote them in ink
on the scroll."
19 Then the officials said to Baruch, "You
and Jeremiah, go and hide. Don't let anyone
know where you are."
20 After they put the scroll in the room of
Elishama the secretary, they went to the king
in the courtyard and reported everything to
him. 21 The king sent Jehudi to get the scroll,
and Jehudi brought it from the room of Elish-
ama the secretary and read it to the king and
all the officials standing beside him. 22 It was
the ninth month and the king was sitting in
the winter apartment, with a fire burning in
the firepot in front of him. 23 Whenever Je-
hudi had read three or four columns of the
scroll, the king cut them off with a scribe's
knife and threw them into the firepot, un-
til the entire scroll was burned in the fire.
24 The king and all his attendants who heard
all these words showed no fear, nor did they
tear their clothes. 25 Even though Elnathan,
Delaiah and Gemariah urged the king not to
burn the scroll, he would not listen to them.
26 Instead, the king commanded Jerahmeel,
a son of the king, Seraiah son of Azriel and
Shelemiah son of Abdeel to arrest Baruch
the scribe and Jeremiah the prophet. But the
LORD had hidden them.
27 After the king burned the scroll con-
taining the words that Baruch had written
at Jeremiah's dictation, the word of the LORD
came to Jeremiah: 28 "Take another scroll
and write on it all the words that were on the
first scroll, which Jehoiakim king of Judah
burned up. 29 Also tell Jehoiakim king of Ju-
dah, 'This is what the LORD says: You burned
that scroll and said, "Why did you write on
it that the king of Babylon would certainly
come and destroy this land and wipe from
it both man and beast?" 30 Therefore this is
what the LORD says about Jehoiakim king
of Judah: He will have no one to sit on the
throne of David; his body will be thrown out
and exposed to the heat by day and the frost
by night. 31 I will punish him and his chil-
dren and his attendants for their wicked-
ness; I will bring on them and those living in
Jerusalem and the people of Judah every di-
saster I pronounced against them, because
they have not listened.' "
32 So Jeremiah took another scroll and
gave it to the scribe Baruch son of Neriah,
and as Jeremiah dictated, Baruch wrote on
it all the words of the scroll that Jehoiakim
king of Judah had burned in the fire. And
many similar words were added to them.

Jeremiah in Prison

37 Zedekiah son of Josiah was made
king of Judah by Nebuchadnezzar
king of Babylon; he reigned in place of Jehoi-
achin[a] son of Jehoiakim. 2 Neither he nor his
attendants nor the people of the land paid
any attention to the words the LORD had spo-
ken through Jeremiah the prophet.
3 King Zedekiah, however, sent Jehukal
son of Shelemiah with the priest Zephani-
ah son of Maaseiah to Jeremiah the prophet
with this message: "Please pray to the LORD
our God for us."
4 Now Jeremiah was free to come and go
among the people, for he had not yet been
put in prison. 5 Pharaoh's army had marched
out of Egypt, and when the Babylonians[b]
who were besieging Jerusalem heard the re-
port about them, they withdrew from Jeru-
salem.
6 Then the word of the LORD came to Jere-
miah the prophet: 7 "This is what the LORD,
the God of Israel, says: Tell the king of Judah,
who sent you to inquire of me, 'Pharaoh's
army, which has marched out to support
you, will go back to its own land, to Egypt.
8 Then the Babylonians will return and at-
tack this city; they will capture it and burn
it down.'
9 "This is what the LORD says: Do not de-
ceive yourselves, thinking, 'The Babylo-
nians will surely leave us.' They will not!
10 Even if you were to defeat the entire Bab-
ylonian[c] army that is attacking you and only
wounded men were left in their tents, they
would come out and burn this city down."
11 After the Babylonian army had with-
drawn from Jerusalem because of Pharaoh's

[a] *1* Hebrew *Koniah,* a variant of *Jehoiachin* [b] *5* Or *Chaldeans;* also in verses 8, 9, 13 and 14
[c] *10* Or *Chaldean;* also in verse 11

army, 12 Jeremiah started to leave the city to go to the territory of Benjamin to get his share of the property among the people there. 13 But when he reached the Benjamin Gate, the captain of the guard, whose name was Irijah son of Shelemiah, the son of Hananiah, arrested him and said, "You are deserting to the Babylonians!"

14 "That's not true!" Jeremiah said. "I am not deserting to the Babylonians." But Irijah would not listen to him; instead, he arrested Jeremiah and brought him to the officials. 15 They were angry with Jeremiah and had him beaten and imprisoned in the house of Jonathan the secretary, which they had made into a prison.

16 Jeremiah was put into a vaulted cell in a dungeon, where he remained a long time. 17 Then King Zedekiah sent for him and had him brought to the palace, where he asked him privately, "Is there any word from the LORD?"

"Yes," Jeremiah replied, "you will be delivered into the hands of the king of Babylon."

18 Then Jeremiah said to King Zedekiah, "What crime have I committed against you or your attendants or this people, that you have put me in prison? 19 Where are your prophets who prophesied to you, 'The king of Babylon will not attack you or this land'? 20 But now, my lord the king, please listen. Let me bring my petition before you: Do not send me back to the house of Jonathan the secretary, or I will die there."

21 King Zedekiah then gave orders for Jeremiah to be placed in the courtyard of the guard and given a loaf of bread from the street of the bakers each day until all the bread in the city was gone. So Jeremiah remained in the courtyard of the guard.

Jeremiah Thrown Into a Cistern

38 Shephatiah son of Mattan, Gedaliah son of Pashhur, Jehukal[a] son of Shelemiah, and Pashhur son of Malkijah heard what Jeremiah was telling all the people when he said, 2 "This is what the LORD says: 'Whoever stays in this city will die by the sword, famine or plague, but whoever goes over to the Babylonians[b] will live. They will escape with their lives; they will live.' 3 And this is what the LORD says: 'This city will certainly be given into the hands of the army of the king of Babylon, who will capture it.' "

4 Then the officials said to the king, "This man should be put to death. He is discouraging the soldiers who are left in this city, as well as all the people, by the things he is saying to them. This man is not seeking the good of these people but their ruin."

5 "He is in your hands," King Zedekiah answered. "The king can do nothing to oppose you."

6 So they took Jeremiah and put him into the cistern of Malkijah, the king's son, which was in the courtyard of the guard. They lowered Jeremiah by ropes into the cistern; it had no water in it, only mud, and Jeremiah sank down into the mud.

7 But Ebed-Melek, a Cushite,[c] an official[d] in the royal palace, heard that they had put Jeremiah into the cistern. While the king was sitting in the Benjamin Gate, 8 Ebed-Melek went out of the palace and said to him, 9 "My lord the king, these men have acted wickedly in all they have done to Jeremiah the prophet. They have thrown him into a cistern, where he will starve to death when there is no longer any bread in the city."

10 Then the king commanded Ebed-Melek the Cushite, "Take thirty men from here with you and lift Jeremiah the prophet out of the cistern before he dies."

11 So Ebed-Melek took the men with him and went to a room under the treasury in the palace. He took some old rags and worn-out clothes from there and let them down with ropes to Jeremiah in the cistern. 12 Ebed-Melek the Cushite said to Jeremiah, "Put these old rags and worn-out clothes under your arms to pad the ropes." Jeremiah did so, 13 and they pulled him up with the ropes and lifted him out of the cistern. And Jeremiah remained in the courtyard of the guard.

Zedekiah Questions Jeremiah Again

14 Then King Zedekiah sent for Jeremiah the prophet and had him brought to the third entrance to the temple of the LORD. "I am going to ask you something," the king said to Jeremiah. "Do not hide anything from me."

[a] *1* Hebrew *Jukal,* a variant of *Jehukal* [b] *2* Or *Chaldeans;* also in verses 18, 19 and 23 [c] *7* Probably from the upper Nile region [d] *7* Or *a eunuch*

15 Jeremiah said to Zedekiah, "If I give you an answer, will you not kill me? Even if I did give you counsel, you would not listen to me."

16 But King Zedekiah swore this oath secretly to Jeremiah: "As surely as the LORD lives, who has given us breath, I will neither kill you nor hand you over to those who want to kill you."

17 Then Jeremiah said to Zedekiah, "This is what the LORD God Almighty, the God of Israel, says: 'If you surrender to the officers of the king of Babylon, your life will be spared and this city will not be burned down; you and your family will live. 18 But if you will not surrender to the officers of the king of Babylon, this city will be given into the hands of the Babylonians and they will burn it down; you yourself will not escape from them.'"

19 King Zedekiah said to Jeremiah, "I am afraid of the Jews who have gone over to the Babylonians, for the Babylonians may hand me over to them and they will mistreat me."

20 "They will not hand you over," Jeremiah replied. "Obey the LORD by doing what I tell you. Then it will go well with you, and your life will be spared. 21 But if you refuse to surrender, this is what the LORD has revealed to me: 22 All the women left in the palace of the king of Judah will be brought out to the officials of the king of Babylon. Those women will say to you:

"'They misled you and overcame you—
  those trusted friends of yours.
Your feet are sunk in the mud;
  your friends have deserted you.'

23 "All your wives and children will be brought out to the Babylonians. You yourself will not escape from their hands but will be captured by the king of Babylon; and this city will[a] be burned down."

24 Then Zedekiah said to Jeremiah, "Do not let anyone know about this conversation, or you may die. 25 If the officials hear that I talked with you, and they come to you and say, 'Tell us what you said to the king and what the king said to you; do not hide it from us or we will kill you,' 26 then tell them, 'I was pleading with the king not to send me back to Jonathan's house to die there.'"

27 All the officials did come to Jeremiah and question him, and he told them everything the king had ordered him to say. So they said no more to him, for no one had heard his conversation with the king.

28 And Jeremiah remained in the courtyard of the guard until the day Jerusalem was captured.

The Fall of Jerusalem

39 This is how Jerusalem was taken: 1 In the ninth year of Zedekiah king of Judah, in the tenth month, Nebuchadnezzar king of Babylon marched against Jerusalem with his whole army and laid siege to it. 2 And on the ninth day of the fourth month of Zedekiah's eleventh year, the city wall was broken through. 3 Then all the officials of the king of Babylon came and took seats in the Middle Gate: Nergal-Sharezer of Samgar, Nebo-Sarsekim a chief officer, Nergal-Sharezer a high official and all the other officials of the king of Babylon. 4 When Zedekiah king of Judah and all the soldiers saw them, they fled; they left the city at night by way of the king's garden, through the gate between the two walls, and headed toward the Arabah.[b]

5 But the Babylonian[c] army pursued them and overtook Zedekiah in the plains of Jericho. They captured him and took him to Nebuchadnezzar king of Babylon at Riblah in the land of Hamath, where he pronounced sentence on him. 6 There at Riblah the king of Babylon slaughtered the sons of Zedekiah before his eyes and also killed all the nobles of Judah. 7 Then he put out Zedekiah's eyes and bound him with bronze shackles to take him to Babylon.

8 The Babylonians[d] set fire to the royal palace and the houses of the people and broke down the walls of Jerusalem. 9 Nebuzaradan commander of the imperial guard carried into exile to Babylon the people who remained in the city, along with those who had gone over to him, and the rest of the people. 10 But Nebuzaradan the commander of the guard left behind in the land of Judah some of the poor people, who owned nothing; and at that time he gave them vineyards and fields.

11 Now Nebuchadnezzar king of Babylon had given these orders about Jeremiah through Nebuzaradan commander of the

[a] 23 Or *and you will cause this city to* [b] 4 Or *the Jordan Valley* [c] 5 Or *Chaldean* [d] 8 Or *Chaldeans*

imperial guard: [12]“Take him and look after
him; don’t harm him but do for him what-
ever he asks.” [13]So Nebuzaradan the com-
mander of the guard, Nebushazban a chief
officer, Nergal-Sharezer a high official and
all the other officers of the king of Babylon
[14]sent and had Jeremiah taken out of the
courtyard of the guard. They turned him
over to Gedaliah son of Ahikam, the son of
Shaphan, to take him back to his home. So he
remained among his own people.

[15]While Jeremiah had been confined in
the courtyard of the guard, the word of the
LORD came to him: [16]“Go and tell Ebed-Me-
lek the Cushite, ‘This is what the LORD Al-
mighty, the God of Israel, says: I am about
to fulfill my words against this city—words
concerning disaster, not prosperity. At that
time they will be fulfilled before your eyes.
[17]But I will rescue you on that day, declares
the LORD; you will not be given into the
hands of those you fear. [18]I will save you; you
will not fall by the sword but will escape with
your life, because you trust in me, declares
the LORD.’ ”

Jeremiah Freed

40 The word came to Jeremiah from the
LORD after Nebuzaradan command-
er of the imperial guard had released him at
Ramah. He had found Jeremiah bound in
chains among all the captives from Jerusa-
lem and Judah who were being carried into
exile to Babylon. [2]When the commander of
the guard found Jeremiah, he said to him,
“The LORD your God decreed this disas-
ter for this place. [3]And now the LORD has
brought it about; he has done just as he said
he would. All this happened because you
people sinned against the LORD and did not
obey him. [4]But today I am freeing you from
the chains on your wrists. Come with me to
Babylon, if you like, and I will look after you;
but if you do not want to, then don’t come.
Look, the whole country lies before you; go
wherever you please.” [5]However, before Jer-
emiah turned to go,[a] Nebuzaradan added,
“Go back to Gedaliah son of Ahikam, the son
of Shaphan, whom the king of Babylon has
appointed over the towns of Judah, and live
with him among the people, or go anywhere
else you please.”

Then the commander gave him provi-
sions and a present and let him go. [6]So Jer-
emiah went to Gedaliah son of Ahikam at
Mizpah and stayed with him among the
people who were left behind in the land.

Gedaliah Assassinated

[7]When all the army officers and their men
who were still in the open country heard that
the king of Babylon had appointed Gedali-
ah son of Ahikam as governor over the land
and had put him in charge of the men, wom-
en and children who were the poorest in
the land and who had not been carried into
exile to Babylon, [8]they came to Gedaliah at
Mizpah—Ishmael son of Nethaniah, Joha-
nan and Jonathan the sons of Kareah, Sera-
iah son of Tanhumeth, the sons of Ephai the
Netophathite, and Jaazaniah[b] the son of the
Maakathite, and their men. [9]Gedaliah son
of Ahikam, the son of Shaphan, took an oath
to reassure them and their men. “Do not be
afraid to serve the Babylonians,[c]” he said.
“Settle down in the land and serve the king
of Babylon, and it will go well with you. [10]I
myself will stay at Mizpah to represent you
before the Babylonians who come to us, but
you are to harvest the wine, summer fruit
and olive oil, and put them in your storage
jars, and live in the towns you have taken
over.”

[11]When all the Jews in Moab, Ammon,
Edom and all the other countries heard that
the king of Babylon had left a remnant in
Judah and had appointed Gedaliah son of
Ahikam, the son of Shaphan, as governor
over them, [12]they all came back to the land
of Judah, to Gedaliah at Mizpah, from all the
countries where they had been scattered.
And they harvested an abundance of wine
and summer fruit.

[13]Johanan son of Kareah and all the army
officers still in the open country came to
Gedaliah at Mizpah [14]and said to him,
“Don’t you know that Baalis king of the Am-
monites has sent Ishmael son of Nethaniah
to take your life?” But Gedaliah son of Ahi-
kam did not believe them.

[15]Then Johanan son of Kareah said pri-
vately to Gedaliah in Mizpah, “Let me go
and kill Ishmael son of Nethaniah, and no

[a] 5 Or *Jeremiah answered* [b] 8 Hebrew *Jezaniah,* a variant of *Jaazaniah* [c] 9 Or *Chaldeans*; also in verse 10

one will know it. Why should he take your life and cause all the Jews who are gathered around you to be scattered and the remnant of Judah to perish?"

16 But Gedaliah son of Ahikam said to Johanan son of Kareah, "Don't do such a thing! What you are saying about Ishmael is not true."

41 In the seventh month Ishmael son of Nethaniah, the son of Elishama, who was of royal blood and had been one of the king's officers, came with ten men to Gedaliah son of Ahikam at Mizpah. While they were eating together there, 2 Ishmael son of Nethaniah and the ten men who were with him got up and struck down Gedaliah son of Ahikam, the son of Shaphan, with the sword, killing the one whom the king of Babylon had appointed as governor over the land. 3 Ishmael also killed all the men of Judah who were with Gedaliah at Mizpah, as well as the Babylonian[a] soldiers who were there.

4 The day after Gedaliah's assassination, before anyone knew about it, 5 eighty men who had shaved off their beards, torn their clothes and cut themselves came from Shechem, Shiloh and Samaria, bringing grain offerings and incense with them to the house of the LORD. 6 Ishmael son of Nethaniah went out from Mizpah to meet them, weeping as he went. When he met them, he said, "Come to Gedaliah son of Ahikam." 7 When they went into the city, Ishmael son of Nethaniah and the men who were with him slaughtered them and threw them into a cistern. 8 But ten of them said to Ishmael, "Don't kill us! We have wheat and barley, olive oil and honey, hidden in a field." So he let them alone and did not kill them with the others. 9 Now the cistern where he threw all the bodies of the men he had killed along with Gedaliah was the one King Asa had made as part of his defense against Baasha king of Israel. Ishmael son of Nethaniah filled it with the dead.

10 Ishmael made captives of all the rest of the people who were in Mizpah — the king's daughters along with all the others who were left there, over whom Nebuzaradan commander of the imperial guard had appointed Gedaliah son of Ahikam. Ishmael son of Nethaniah took them captive and set out to cross over to the Ammonites.

11 When Johanan son of Kareah and all the army officers who were with him heard about all the crimes Ishmael son of Nethaniah had committed, 12 they took all their men and went to fight Ishmael son of Nethaniah. They caught up with him near the great pool in Gibeon. 13 When all the people Ishmael had with him saw Johanan son of Kareah and the army officers who were with him, they were glad. 14 All the people Ishmael had taken captive at Mizpah turned and went over to Johanan son of Kareah. 15 But Ishmael son of Nethaniah and eight of his men escaped from Johanan and fled to the Ammonites.

Flight to Egypt

16 Then Johanan son of Kareah and all the army officers who were with him led away all the people of Mizpah who had survived, whom Johanan had recovered from Ishmael son of Nethaniah after Ishmael had assassinated Gedaliah son of Ahikam — the soldiers, women, children and court officials he had recovered from Gibeon. 17 And they went on, stopping at Geruth Kimham near Bethlehem on their way to Egypt 18 to escape the Babylonians.[b] They were afraid of them because Ishmael son of Nethaniah had killed Gedaliah son of Ahikam, whom the king of Babylon had appointed as governor over the land.

42 Then all the army officers, including Johanan son of Kareah and Jezaniah[c] son of Hoshaiah, and all the people from the least to the greatest approached 2 Jeremiah the prophet and said to him, "Please hear our petition and pray to the LORD your God for this entire remnant. For as you now see, though we were once many, now only a few are left. 3 Pray that the LORD your God will tell us where we should go and what we should do."

4 "I have heard you," replied Jeremiah the prophet. "I will certainly pray to the LORD your God as you have requested; I will tell you everything the LORD says and will keep nothing back from you."

5 Then they said to Jeremiah, "May the LORD be a true and faithful witness against us if we do not act in accordance with everything the LORD your God sends you to tell us.

[a] *3* Or *Chaldean* [b] *18* Or *Chaldeans* [c] *1* Hebrew; Septuagint (see also 43:2) *Azariah*

6Whether it is favorable or unfavorable, we will obey the LORD our God, to whom we are sending you, so that it will go well with us, for we will obey the LORD our God."

7Ten days later the word of the LORD came to Jeremiah. 8So he called together Johanan son of Kareah and all the army officers who were with him and all the people from the least to the greatest. 9He said to them, "This is what the LORD, the God of Israel, to whom you sent me to present your petition, says: 10'If you stay in this land, I will build you up and not tear you down; I will plant you and not uproot you, for I have relented concerning the disaster I have inflicted on you. 11Do not be afraid of the king of Babylon, whom you now fear. Do not be afraid of him, declares the LORD, for I am with you and will save you and deliver you from his hands. 12I will show you compassion so that he will have compassion on you and restore you to your land.'

13"However, if you say, 'We will not stay in this land,' and so disobey the LORD your God, 14and if you say, 'No, we will go and live in Egypt, where we will not see war or hear the trumpet or be hungry for bread,' 15then hear the word of the LORD, you remnant of Judah. This is what the LORD Almighty, the God of Israel, says: 'If you are determined to go to Egypt and you do go to settle there, 16then the sword you fear will overtake you there, and the famine you dread will follow you into Egypt, and there you will die. 17Indeed, all who are determined to go to Egypt to settle there will die by the sword, famine and plague; not one of them will survive or escape the disaster I will bring on them.' 18This is what the LORD Almighty, the God of Israel, says: 'As my anger and wrath have been poured out on those who lived in Jerusalem, so will my wrath be poured out on you when you go to Egypt. You will be a curse[a] and an object of horror, a curse[a] and an object of reproach; you will never see this place again.'

19"Remnant of Judah, the LORD has told you, 'Do not go to Egypt.' Be sure of this: I warn you today 20that you made a fatal mistake when you sent me to the LORD your God and said, 'Pray to the LORD our God for us; tell us everything he says and we will do it.' 21I have told you today, but you still have not obeyed the LORD your God in all he sent me to tell you. 22So now, be sure of this: You will die by the sword, famine and plague in the place where you want to go to settle."

43 When Jeremiah had finished telling the people all the words of the LORD their God—everything the LORD had sent him to tell them— 2Azariah son of Hoshaiah and Johanan son of Kareah and all the arrogant men said to Jeremiah, "You are lying! The LORD our God has not sent you to say, 'You must not go to Egypt to settle there.' 3But Baruch son of Neriah is inciting you against us to hand us over to the Babylonians,[b] so they may kill us or carry us into exile to Babylon."

4So Johanan son of Kareah and all the army officers and all the people disobeyed the LORD's command to stay in the land of Judah. 5Instead, Johanan son of Kareah and all the army officers led away all the remnant of Judah who had come back to live in the land of Judah from all the nations where they had been scattered. 6They also led away all those whom Nebuzaradan commander of the imperial guard had left with Gedaliah son of Ahikam, the son of Shaphan—the men, the women, the children and the king's daughters. And they took Jeremiah the prophet and Baruch son of Neriah along with them. 7So they entered Egypt in disobedience to the LORD and went as far as Tahpanhes.

8In Tahpanhes the word of the LORD came to Jeremiah: 9"While the Jews are watching, take some large stones with you and bury them in clay in the brick pavement at the entrance to Pharaoh's palace in Tahpanhes. 10Then say to them, 'This is what the LORD Almighty, the God of Israel, says: I will send for my servant Nebuchadnezzar king of Babylon, and I will set his throne over these stones I have buried here; he will spread his royal canopy above them. 11He will come and attack Egypt, bringing death to those destined for death, captivity to those destined for captivity, and the sword to those destined for the sword. 12He will set fire to the temples of the gods of Egypt; he will burn their temples and take their gods captive. As a shepherd picks his garment clean of lice, so he will pick Egypt clean and depart. 13There in the temple of the sun[c] in Egypt he will

[a] *18* That is, your name will be used in cursing (see 29:22); or, others will see that you are cursed.
[b] *3* Or *Chaldeans* [c] *13* Or *in Heliopolis*

demolish the sacred pillars and will burn down the temples of the gods of Egypt.' "

Disaster Because of Idolatry

44 This word came to Jeremiah concerning all the Jews living in Lower Egypt — in Migdol, Tahpanhes and Memphis — and in Upper Egypt: 2 "This is what the LORD Almighty, the God of Israel, says: You saw the great disaster I brought on Jerusalem and on all the towns of Judah. Today they lie deserted and in ruins 3 because of the evil they have done. They aroused my anger by burning incense to and worshiping other gods that neither they nor you nor your ancestors ever knew. 4 Again and again I sent my servants the prophets, who said, 'Do not do this detestable thing that I hate!' 5 But they did not listen or pay attention; they did not turn from their wickedness or stop burning incense to other gods. 6 Therefore, my fierce anger was poured out; it raged against the towns of Judah and the streets of Jerusalem and made them the desolate ruins they are today.

7 "Now this is what the LORD God Almighty, the God of Israel, says: Why bring such great disaster on yourselves by cutting off from Judah the men and women, the children and infants, and so leave yourselves without a remnant? 8 Why arouse my anger with what your hands have made, burning incense to other gods in Egypt, where you have come to live? You will destroy yourselves and make yourselves a curse[a] and an object of reproach among all the nations on earth. 9 Have you forgotten the wickedness committed by your ancestors and by the kings and queens of Judah and the wickedness committed by you and your wives in the land of Judah and the streets of Jerusalem? 10 To this day they have not humbled themselves or shown reverence, nor have they followed my law and the decrees I set before you and your ancestors.

11 "Therefore this is what the LORD Almighty, the God of Israel, says: I am determined to bring disaster on you and to destroy all Judah. 12 I will take away the remnant of Judah who were determined to go to Egypt to settle there. They will all perish in Egypt; they will fall by the sword or die from famine. From the least to the greatest, they will die by sword or famine. They will become a curse and an object of horror, a curse and an object of reproach. 13 I will punish those who live in Egypt with the sword, famine and plague, as I punished Jerusalem. 14 None of the remnant of Judah who have gone to live in Egypt will escape or survive to return to the land of Judah, to which they long to return and live; none will return except a few fugitives."

15 Then all the men who knew that their wives were burning incense to other gods, along with all the women who were present — a large assembly — and all the people living in Lower and Upper Egypt, said to Jeremiah, 16 "We will not listen to the message you have spoken to us in the name of the LORD! 17 We will certainly do everything we said we would: We will burn incense to the Queen of Heaven and will pour out drink offerings to her just as we and our ancestors, our kings and our officials did in the towns of Judah and in the streets of Jerusalem. At that time we had plenty of food and were well off and suffered no harm. 18 But ever since we stopped burning incense to the Queen of Heaven and pouring out drink offerings to her, we have had nothing and have been perishing by sword and famine."

19 The women added, "When we burned incense to the Queen of Heaven and poured out drink offerings to her, did not our husbands know that we were making cakes impressed with her image and pouring out drink offerings to her?"

20 Then Jeremiah said to all the people, both men and women, who were answering him, 21 "Did not the LORD remember and call to mind the incense burned in the towns of Judah and the streets of Jerusalem by you and your ancestors, your kings and your officials and the people of the land? 22 When the LORD could no longer endure your wicked actions and the detestable things you did, your land became a curse and a desolate waste without inhabitants, as it is today. 23 Because you have burned incense and have sinned against the LORD and have not obeyed him or followed his law or his decrees or his stipulations, this disaster has come upon you, as you now see."

[a] 8 That is, your name will be used in cursing (see 29:22); or, others will see that you are cursed; also in verse 12; similarly in verse 22.

[24]Then Jeremiah said to all the people,
including the women, "Hear the word of
the LORD, all you people of Judah in Egypt.
[25]This is what the LORD Almighty, the God
of Israel, says: You and your wives have done
what you said you would do when you prom-
ised, 'We will certainly carry out the vows we
made to burn incense and pour out drink of-
ferings to the Queen of Heaven.'

"Go ahead then, do what you promised!
Keep your vows! [26]But hear the word of the
LORD, all you Jews living in Egypt: 'I swear
by my great name,' says the LORD, 'that no
one from Judah living anywhere in Egypt
will ever again invoke my name or swear, "As
surely as the Sovereign LORD lives." [27]For I
am watching over them for harm, not for
good; the Jews in Egypt will perish by sword
and famine until they are all destroyed.
[28]Those who escape the sword and return
to the land of Judah from Egypt will be very
few. Then the whole remnant of Judah who
came to live in Egypt will know whose word
will stand — mine or theirs.

[29]" 'This will be the sign to you that I will
punish you in this place,' declares the LORD,
'so that you will know that my threats of
harm against you will surely stand.' [30]This
is what the LORD says: 'I am going to deliv-
er Pharaoh Hophra king of Egypt into the
hands of his enemies who want to kill him,
just as I gave Zedekiah king of Judah into the
hands of Nebuchadnezzar king of Babylon,
the enemy who wanted to kill him.' "

A Message to Baruch

45 When Baruch son of Neriah wrote
on a scroll the words Jeremiah the
prophet dictated in the fourth year of Jehoi-
akim son of Josiah king of Judah, Jeremiah
said this to Baruch: [2]"This is what the LORD,
the God of Israel, says to you, Baruch: [3]You
said, 'Woe to me! The LORD has added sor-
row to my pain; I am worn out with groaning
and find no rest.' [4]But the LORD has told me
to say to you, 'This is what the LORD says: I
will overthrow what I have built and uproot
what I have planted, throughout the earth.
[5]Should you then seek great things for your-
self? Do not seek them. For I will bring di-
saster on all people, declares the LORD, but
wherever you go I will let you escape with
your life.' "

A Message About Egypt

46 This is the word of the LORD that
came to Jeremiah the prophet con-
cerning the nations:

[2]Concerning Egypt:

This is the message against the army of
Pharaoh Necho king of Egypt, which was de-
feated at Carchemish on the Euphrates Riv-
er by Nebuchadnezzar king of Babylon in the
fourth year of Jehoiakim son of Josiah king
of Judah:

[3]"Prepare your shields, both large and
small,
and march out for battle!
[4]Harness the horses,
mount the steeds!
Take your positions
with helmets on!
Polish your spears,
put on your armor!
[5]What do I see?
They are terrified,
they are retreating,
their warriors are defeated.
They flee in haste
without looking back,
and there is terror on every side,"
declares the LORD.
[6]"The swift cannot flee
nor the strong escape.
In the north by the River Euphrates
they stumble and fall.

[7]"Who is this that rises like the Nile,
like rivers of surging waters?
[8]Egypt rises like the Nile,
like rivers of surging waters.
She says, 'I will rise and cover the earth;
I will destroy cities and their people.'
[9]Charge, you horses!
Drive furiously, you charioteers!
March on, you warriors — men of Cush[a]
and Put who carry shields,
men of Lydia who draw the bow.
[10]But that day belongs to the Lord, the
LORD Almighty —
a day of vengeance, for vengeance on
his foes.
The sword will devour till it is satisfied,
till it has quenched its thirst with
blood.

[a] 9 That is, the upper Nile region

For the Lord, the LORD Almighty, will
offer sacrifice
in the land of the north by the River
Euphrates.

11 "Go up to Gilead and get balm,
Virgin Daughter Egypt.
But you try many medicines in vain;
there is no healing for you.
12 The nations will hear of your shame;
your cries will fill the earth.
One warrior will stumble over another;
both will fall down together."

13 This is the message the LORD spoke to
Jeremiah the prophet about the coming of
Nebuchadnezzar king of Babylon to attack
Egypt:

14 "Announce this in Egypt, and proclaim it
in Migdol;
proclaim it also in Memphis and
Tahpanhes:
'Take your positions and get ready,
for the sword devours those around
you.'
15 Why will your warriors be laid low?
They cannot stand, for the LORD
will push them down.
16 They will stumble repeatedly;
they will fall over each other.
They will say, 'Get up, let us go back
to our own people and our native
lands,
away from the sword of the oppressor.'
17 There they will exclaim,
'Pharaoh king of Egypt is only a loud
noise;
he has missed his opportunity.'

18 "As surely as I live," declares the King,
whose name is the LORD Almighty,
"one will come who is like Tabor among
the mountains,
like Carmel by the sea.
19 Pack your belongings for exile,
you who live in Egypt,
for Memphis will be laid waste
and lie in ruins without inhabitant.

20 "Egypt is a beautiful heifer,
but a gadfly is coming
against her from the north.
21 The mercenaries in her ranks
are like fattened calves.
They too will turn and flee together,
they will not stand their ground,
for the day of disaster is coming upon
them,
the time for them to be punished.
22 Egypt will hiss like a fleeing serpent
as the enemy advances in force;
they will come against her with axes,
like men who cut down trees.
23 They will chop down her forest,"
declares the LORD,
"dense though it be.
They are more numerous than locusts,
they cannot be counted.
24 Daughter Egypt will be put to shame,
given into the hands of the people of
the north."

25 The LORD Almighty, the God of Israel,
says: "I am about to bring punishment on
Amon god of Thebes, on Pharaoh, on Egypt
and her gods and her kings, and on those
who rely on Pharaoh. 26 I will give them into
the hands of those who want to kill them—
Nebuchadnezzar king of Babylon and his of-
ficers. Later, however, Egypt will be inhabit-
ed as in times past," declares the LORD.

27 "Do not be afraid, Jacob my servant;
do not be dismayed, Israel.
I will surely save you out of a distant
place,
your descendants from the land of
their exile.
Jacob will again have peace and security,
and no one will make him afraid.
28 Do not be afraid, Jacob my servant,
for I am with you," declares the LORD.
"Though I completely destroy all the
nations
among which I scatter you,
I will not completely destroy you.
I will discipline you but only in due
measure;
I will not let you go entirely
unpunished."

A Message About the Philistines

47 This is the word of the LORD that
came to Jeremiah the prophet con-
cerning the Philistines before Pharaoh at-
tacked Gaza:

2 This is what the LORD says:

"See how the waters are rising in the
north;

they will become an overflowing
torrent.
They will overflow the land and
everything in it,
the towns and those who live in them.
The people will cry out;
all who dwell in the land will wail
3 at the sound of the hooves of galloping
steeds,
at the noise of enemy chariots
and the rumble of their wheels.
Parents will not turn to help their
children;
their hands will hang limp.
4 For the day has come
to destroy all the Philistines
and to remove all survivors
who could help Tyre and Sidon.
The LORD is about to destroy the
Philistines,
the remnant from the coasts of
Caphtor.[a]
5 Gaza will shave her head in mourning;
Ashkelon will be silenced.
You remnant on the plain,
how long will you cut yourselves?

6 " 'Alas, sword of the LORD,
how long till you rest?
Return to your sheath;
cease and be still.'
7 But how can it rest
when the LORD has commanded it,
when he has ordered it
to attack Ashkelon and the coast?"

A Message About Moab

48 Concerning Moab:

This is what the LORD Almighty, the God of Israel, says:

"Woe to Nebo, for it will be ruined.
Kiriathaim will be disgraced and
captured;
the stronghold[b] will be disgraced and
shattered.
2 Moab will be praised no more;
in Heshbon[c] people will plot her
downfall:
'Come, let us put an end to that nation.'
You, the people of Madmen,[d] will also be
silenced;
the sword will pursue you.
3 Cries of anguish arise from Horonaim,
cries of great havoc and destruction.
4 Moab will be broken;
her little ones will cry out.[e]
5 They go up the hill to Luhith,
weeping bitterly as they go;
on the road down to Horonaim
anguished cries over the destruction
are heard.
6 Flee! Run for your lives;
become like a bush[f] in the desert.
7 Since you trust in your deeds and riches,
you too will be taken captive,
and Chemosh will go into exile,
together with his priests and officials.
8 The destroyer will come against every
town,
and not a town will escape.
The valley will be ruined
and the plateau destroyed,
because the LORD has spoken.
9 Put salt on Moab,
for she will be laid waste[g];
her towns will become desolate,
with no one to live in them.

10 "A curse on anyone who is lax in doing
the LORD's work!
A curse on anyone who keeps their
sword from bloodshed!

11 "Moab has been at rest from youth,
like wine left on its dregs,
not poured from one jar to another—
she has not gone into exile.
So she tastes as she did,
and her aroma is unchanged.
12 But days are coming,"
declares the LORD,
"when I will send men who pour from
pitchers,
and they will pour her out;
they will empty her pitchers
and smash her jars.
13 Then Moab will be ashamed of
Chemosh,
as Israel was ashamed
when they trusted in Bethel.

14 "How can you say, 'We are warriors,
men valiant in battle'?

[a] 4 That is, Crete [b] 1 Or *captured; / Misgab* [c] 2 The Hebrew for *Heshbon* sounds like the Hebrew for *plot.* [d] 2 The name of the Moabite town Madmen sounds like the Hebrew for *be silenced.* [e] 4 Hebrew; Septuagint / *proclaim it to Zoar* [f] 6 Or *like Aroer* [g] 9 Or *Give wings to Moab, / for she will fly away*

[15] Moab will be destroyed and her towns
invaded;
her finest young men will go down in
the slaughter,"
declares the King, whose name is the
LORD Almighty.
[16] "The fall of Moab is at hand;
her calamity will come quickly.
[17] Mourn for her, all who live around her,
all who know her fame;
say, 'How broken is the mighty scepter,
how broken the glorious staff!'

[18] "Come down from your glory
and sit on the parched ground,
you inhabitants of Daughter Dibon,
for the one who destroys Moab
will come up against you
and ruin your fortified cities.
[19] Stand by the road and watch,
you who live in Aroer.
Ask the man fleeing and the woman
escaping,
ask them, 'What has happened?'
[20] Moab is disgraced, for she is shattered.
Wail and cry out!
Announce by the Arnon
that Moab is destroyed.
[21] Judgment has come to the plateau —
to Holon, Jahzah and Mephaath,
22 to Dibon, Nebo and Beth Diblathaim,
23 to Kiriathaim, Beth Gamul and Beth
Meon,
24 to Kerioth and Bozrah —
to all the towns of Moab, far and near.
[25] Moab's horn[a] is cut off;
her arm is broken,"
declares the LORD.

[26] "Make her drunk,
for she has defied the LORD.
Let Moab wallow in her vomit;
let her be an object of ridicule.
[27] Was not Israel the object of your
ridicule?
Was she caught among thieves,
that you shake your head in scorn
whenever you speak of her?
[28] Abandon your towns and dwell among
the rocks,
you who live in Moab.
Be like a dove that makes its nest
at the mouth of a cave.

[29] "We have heard of Moab's pride —
how great is her arrogance! —
of her insolence, her pride, her conceit
and the haughtiness of her heart.
[30] I know her insolence but it is futile,"
declares the LORD,
"and her boasts accomplish nothing.
[31] Therefore I wail over Moab,
for all Moab I cry out,
I moan for the people of Kir Hareseth.
[32] I weep for you, as Jazer weeps,
you vines of Sibmah.
Your branches spread as far as the sea[b];
they reached as far as[c] Jazer.
The destroyer has fallen
on your ripened fruit and grapes.
[33] Joy and gladness are gone
from the orchards and fields of
Moab.
I have stopped the flow of wine from the
presses;
no one treads them with shouts of joy.
Although there are shouts,
they are not shouts of joy.

[34] "The sound of their cry rises
from Heshbon to Elealeh and Jahaz,
from Zoar as far as Horonaim and Eglath
Shelishiyah,
for even the waters of Nimrim are
dried up.
[35] In Moab I will put an end
to those who make offerings on the
high places
and burn incense to their gods,"
declares the LORD.

[36] "So my heart laments for Moab like the
music of a pipe;
it laments like a pipe for the people of
Kir Hareseth.
The wealth they acquired is gone.
[37] Every head is shaved
and every beard cut off;
every hand is slashed
and every waist is covered with
sackcloth.
[38] On all the roofs in Moab
and in the public squares
there is nothing but mourning,
for I have broken Moab
like a jar that no one wants,"
declares the LORD.

[a] 25 *Horn* here symbolizes strength. [b] 32 Probably the Dead Sea [c] 32 Two Hebrew manuscripts and Septuagint; most Hebrew manuscripts *as far as the Sea of*

[39] "How shattered she is! How they wail!
How Moab turns her back in shame!
Moab has become an object of ridicule,
an object of horror to all those
around her."

[40] This is what the LORD says:

"Look! An eagle is swooping down,
spreading its wings over Moab.
[41] Kerioth[a] will be captured
and the strongholds taken.
In that day the hearts of Moab's warriors
will be like the heart of a woman in
labor.
[42] Moab will be destroyed as a nation
because she defied the LORD.
[43] Terror and pit and snare await you,
you people of Moab,"
declares the LORD.
[44] "Whoever flees from the terror
will fall into a pit,
whoever climbs out of the pit
will be caught in a snare;
for I will bring on Moab
the year of her punishment,"
declares the LORD.

[45] "In the shadow of Heshbon
the fugitives stand helpless,
for a fire has gone out from Heshbon,
a blaze from the midst of Sihon;
it burns the foreheads of Moab,
the skulls of the noisy boasters.
[46] Woe to you, Moab!
The people of Chemosh are destroyed;
your sons are taken into exile
and your daughters into captivity.
[47] "Yet I will restore the fortunes of Moab
in days to come,"
declares the LORD.

Here ends the judgment on Moab.

A Message About Ammon

49 Concerning the Ammonites:

This is what the LORD says:

"Has Israel no sons?
Has Israel no heir?
Why then has Molek[b] taken possession
of Gad?
Why do his people live in its towns?
[2] But the days are coming,"
declares the LORD,
"when I will sound the battle cry
against Rabbah of the Ammonites;
it will become a mound of ruins,
and its surrounding villages will be set
on fire.
Then Israel will drive out
those who drove her out,"
says the LORD.
[3] "Wail, Heshbon, for Ai is destroyed!
Cry out, you inhabitants of Rabbah!
Put on sackcloth and mourn;
rush here and there inside the walls,
for Molek will go into exile,
together with his priests and officials.
[4] Why do you boast of your valleys,
boast of your valleys so fruitful?
Unfaithful Daughter Ammon,
you trust in your riches and say,
'Who will attack me?'
[5] I will bring terror on you
from all those around you,"
declares the Lord,
the LORD Almighty.
"Every one of you will be driven away,
and no one will gather the fugitives.
[6] "Yet afterward, I will restore the fortunes
of the Ammonites,"
declares the LORD.

A Message About Edom

[7] Concerning Edom:

This is what the LORD Almighty says:

"Is there no longer wisdom in Teman?
Has counsel perished from the
prudent?
Has their wisdom decayed?
[8] Turn and flee, hide in deep caves,
you who live in Dedan,
for I will bring disaster on Esau
at the time when I punish him.
[9] If grape pickers came to you,
would they not leave a few grapes?
If thieves came during the night,
would they not steal only as much as
they wanted?
[10] But I will strip Esau bare;
I will uncover his hiding places,
so that he cannot conceal himself.
His armed men are destroyed,

[a] 41 Or *The cities* [b] 1 Or *their king*; also in verse 3

also his allies and neighbors,
so there is no one to say,
11 'Leave your fatherless children; I will keep them alive.
Your widows too can depend on me.' "

12 This is what the LORD says: "If those who
do not deserve to drink the cup must drink it,
why should you go unpunished? You will not
go unpunished, but must drink it. 13 I swear
by myself," declares the LORD, "that Bozrah
will become a ruin and a curse,[a] an object of
horror and reproach; and all its towns will be
in ruins forever."

14 I have heard a message from the LORD;
an envoy was sent to the nations to say,
"Assemble yourselves to attack it!
Rise up for battle!"

15 "Now I will make you small among the nations,
despised by mankind.
16 The terror you inspire
and the pride of your heart have deceived you,
you who live in the clefts of the rocks,
who occupy the heights of the hill.
Though you build your nest as high as the eagle's,
from there I will bring you down,"
declares the LORD.
17 "Edom will become an object of horror;
all who pass by will be appalled and will scoff
because of all its wounds.
18 As Sodom and Gomorrah were overthrown,
along with their neighboring towns,"
says the LORD,
"so no one will live there;
no people will dwell in it.

19 "Like a lion coming up from Jordan's thickets
to a rich pastureland,
I will chase Edom from its land in an instant.
Who is the chosen one I will appoint for this?
Who is like me and who can challenge me?
And what shepherd can stand against me?"
20 Therefore, hear what the LORD has planned against Edom,
what he has purposed against those who live in Teman:
The young of the flock will be dragged away;
their pasture will be appalled at their fate.
21 At the sound of their fall the earth will tremble;
their cry will resound to the Red Sea.[b]
22 Look! An eagle will soar and swoop down,
spreading its wings over Bozrah.
In that day the hearts of Edom's warriors
will be like the heart of a woman in labor.

A Message About Damascus

23 Concerning Damascus:

"Hamath and Arpad are dismayed,
for they have heard bad news.
They are disheartened,
troubled like[c] the restless sea.
24 Damascus has become feeble,
she has turned to flee
and panic has gripped her;
anguish and pain have seized her,
pain like that of a woman in labor.
25 Why has the city of renown not been abandoned,
the town in which I delight?
26 Surely, her young men will fall in the streets;
all her soldiers will be silenced in that day,"
declares the LORD Almighty.
27 "I will set fire to the walls of Damascus;
it will consume the fortresses of Ben-Hadad."

A Message About Kedar and Hazor

28 Concerning Kedar and the kingdoms of
Hazor, which Nebuchadnezzar king of Bab-
ylon attacked:

This is what the LORD says:

"Arise, and attack Kedar
and destroy the people of the East.
29 Their tents and their flocks will be taken;
their shelters will be carried off
with all their goods and camels.

[a] *13* That is, its name will be used in cursing (see 29:22); or, others will see that it is cursed. [b] *21* Or *the Sea of Reeds* [c] *23* Hebrew *on* or *by*

People will shout to them,
'Terror on every side!'

30 "Flee quickly away!
Stay in deep caves, you who live in Hazor,"
declares the LORD.
"Nebuchadnezzar king of Babylon has plotted against you;
he has devised a plan against you.

31 "Arise and attack a nation at ease,
which lives in confidence,"
declares the LORD,
"a nation that has neither gates nor bars;
its people live far from danger.
32 Their camels will become plunder,
and their large herds will be spoils of war.
I will scatter to the winds those who are in distant places[a]
and will bring disaster on them from every side,"
declares the LORD.
33 "Hazor will become a haunt of jackals,
a desolate place forever.
No one will live there;
no people will dwell in it."

A Message About Elam

34 This is the word of the LORD that came
to Jeremiah the prophet concerning Elam,
early in the reign of Zedekiah king of Judah:

35 This is what the LORD Almighty says:

"See, I will break the bow of Elam,
the mainstay of their might.
36 I will bring against Elam the four winds
from the four quarters of heaven;
I will scatter them to the four winds,
and there will not be a nation
where Elam's exiles do not go.
37 I will shatter Elam before their foes,
before those who want to kill them;
I will bring disaster on them,
even my fierce anger,"
declares the LORD.
"I will pursue them with the sword
until I have made an end of them.
38 I will set my throne in Elam
and destroy her king and officials,"
declares the LORD.

39 "Yet I will restore the fortunes of Elam
in days to come,"
declares the LORD.

A Message About Babylon

50 This is the word the LORD spoke
through Jeremiah the prophet con-
cerning Babylon and the land of the Babylo-
nians[b]:

2 "Announce and proclaim among the nations,
lift up a banner and proclaim it;
keep nothing back, but say,
'Babylon will be captured;
Bel will be put to shame,
Marduk filled with terror.
Her images will be put to shame
and her idols filled with terror.'
3 A nation from the north will attack her
and lay waste her land.
No one will live in it;
both people and animals will flee away.

4 "In those days, at that time,"
declares the LORD,
"the people of Israel and the people of Judah together
will go in tears to seek the LORD their God.
5 They will ask the way to Zion
and turn their faces toward it.
They will come and bind themselves to the LORD
in an everlasting covenant
that will not be forgotten.

6 "My people have been lost sheep;
their shepherds have led them astray
and caused them to roam on the mountains.
They wandered over mountain and hill
and forgot their own resting place.
7 Whoever found them devoured them;
their enemies said, 'We are not guilty,
for they sinned against the LORD, their verdant pasture,
the LORD, the hope of their ancestors.'

8 "Flee out of Babylon;
leave the land of the Babylonians,
and be like the goats that lead the flock.

[a] 32 Or *who clip the hair by their foreheads* [b] 1 Or *Chaldeans*; also in verses 8, 25, 35 and 45

9 For I will stir up and bring against
Babylon
an alliance of great nations from the
land of the north.
They will take up their positions
against her,
and from the north she will be
captured.
Their arrows will be like skilled warriors
who do not return empty-handed.
10 So Babylonia[a] will be plundered;
all who plunder her will have their fill,"
declares the LORD.

11 "Because you rejoice and are glad,
you who pillage my inheritance,
because you frolic like a heifer threshing
grain
and neigh like stallions,
12 your mother will be greatly ashamed;
she who gave you birth will be
disgraced.
She will be the least of the nations —
a wilderness, a dry land, a desert.
13 Because of the LORD's anger she will not
be inhabited
but will be completely desolate.
All who pass Babylon will be appalled;
they will scoff because of all her
wounds.

14 "Take up your positions around Babylon,
all you who draw the bow.
Shoot at her! Spare no arrows,
for she has sinned against the LORD.
15 Shout against her on every side!
She surrenders, her towers fall,
her walls are torn down.
Since this is the vengeance of the LORD,
take vengeance on her;
do to her as she has done to others.
16 Cut off from Babylon the sower,
and the reaper with his sickle at
harvest.
Because of the sword of the oppressor
let everyone return to their own
people,
let everyone flee to their own land.

17 "Israel is a scattered flock
that lions have chased away.
The first to devour them
was the king of Assyria;
the last to crush their bones
was Nebuchadnezzar king of
Babylon."

18 Therefore this is what the LORD Al-
mighty, the God of Israel, says:

"I will punish the king of Babylon and
his land
as I punished the king of Assyria.
19 But I will bring Israel back to their own
pasture,
and they will graze on Carmel and
Bashan;
their appetite will be satisfied
on the hills of Ephraim and Gilead.
20 In those days, at that time,"
declares the LORD,
"search will be made for Israel's guilt,
but there will be none,
and for the sins of Judah,
but none will be found,
for I will forgive the remnant I spare.

21 "Attack the land of Merathaim
and those who live in Pekod.
Pursue, kill and completely destroy[b]
them,"
declares the LORD.
"Do everything I have commanded
you.
22 The noise of battle is in the land,
the noise of great destruction!
23 How broken and shattered
is the hammer of the whole earth!
How desolate is Babylon
among the nations!
24 I set a trap for you, Babylon,
and you were caught before you
knew it;
you were found and captured
because you opposed the LORD.
25 The LORD has opened his arsenal
and brought out the weapons of his
wrath,
for the Sovereign LORD Almighty has
work to do
in the land of the Babylonians.
26 Come against her from afar.
Break open her granaries;
pile her up like heaps of grain.
Completely destroy her
and leave her no remnant.

[a] *10* Or *Chaldea* [b] *21* The Hebrew term refers to the irrevocable giving over of things or persons to the LORD, often by totally destroying them; also in verse 26.

[27] Kill all her young bulls;
let them go down to the slaughter!
Woe to them! For their day has come,
the time for them to be punished.
[28] Listen to the fugitives and refugees from Babylon
declaring in Zion
how the LORD our God has taken vengeance,
vengeance for his temple.

[29] "Summon archers against Babylon,
all those who draw the bow.
Encamp all around her;
let no one escape.
Repay her for her deeds;
do to her as she has done.
For she has defied the LORD,
the Holy One of Israel.
[30] Therefore, her young men will fall in the streets;
all her soldiers will be silenced in that day,"
declares the LORD.
[31] "See, I am against you, you arrogant one,"
declares the Lord, the LORD Almighty,
"for your day has come,
the time for you to be punished.
[32] The arrogant one will stumble and fall
and no one will help her up;
I will kindle a fire in her towns
that will consume all who are around her."

[33] This is what the LORD Almighty says:
"The people of Israel are oppressed,
and the people of Judah as well.
All their captors hold them fast,
refusing to let them go.
[34] Yet their Redeemer is strong;
the LORD Almighty is his name.
He will vigorously defend their cause
so that he may bring rest to their land,
but unrest to those who live in Babylon.

[35] "A sword against the Babylonians!"
declares the LORD—
"against those who live in Babylon
and against her officials and wise men!
[36] A sword against her false prophets!
They will become fools.
A sword against her warriors!
They will be filled with terror.
[37] A sword against her horses and chariots
and all the foreigners in her ranks!
They will become weaklings.
A sword against her treasures!
They will be plundered.
[38] A drought on[a] her waters!
They will dry up.
For it is a land of idols,
idols that will go mad with terror.

[39] "So desert creatures and hyenas will live there,
and there the owl will dwell.
It will never again be inhabited
or lived in from generation to generation.
[40] As I overthrew Sodom and Gomorrah
along with their neighboring towns,"
declares the LORD,
"so no one will live there;
no people will dwell in it.

[41] "Look! An army is coming from the north;
a great nation and many kings
are being stirred up from the ends of the earth.
[42] They are armed with bows and spears;
they are cruel and without mercy.
They sound like the roaring sea
as they ride on their horses;
they come like men in battle formation
to attack you, Daughter Babylon.
[43] The king of Babylon has heard reports about them,
and his hands hang limp.
Anguish has gripped him,
pain like that of a woman in labor.
[44] Like a lion coming up from Jordan's thickets
to a rich pastureland,
I will chase Babylon from its land in an instant.
Who is the chosen one I will appoint for this?
Who is like me and who can challenge me?
And what shepherd can stand against me?"

[45] Therefore, hear what the LORD has planned against Babylon,
what he has purposed against the land of the Babylonians:

[a] 38 Or *A sword against*

The young of the flock will be dragged
away;
their pasture will be appalled at
their fate.
46 At the sound of Babylon's capture the
earth will tremble;
its cry will resound among the nations.

51 This is what the LORD says:

"See, I will stir up the spirit of a destroyer
against Babylon and the people of Leb
Kamai.[a]
2 I will send foreigners to Babylon
to winnow her and to devastate
her land;
they will oppose her on every side
in the day of her disaster.
3 Let not the archer string his bow,
nor let him put on his armor.
Do not spare her young men;
completely destroy[b] her army.
4 They will fall down slain in Babylon,[c]
fatally wounded in her streets.
5 For Israel and Judah have not been
forsaken
by their God, the LORD Almighty,
though their land[d] is full of guilt
before the Holy One of Israel.

6 "Flee from Babylon!
Run for your lives!
Do not be destroyed because of
her sins.
It is time for the LORD's vengeance;
he will repay her what she deserves.
7 Babylon was a gold cup in the LORD's
hand;
she made the whole earth drunk.
The nations drank her wine;
therefore they have now gone mad.
8 Babylon will suddenly fall and be broken.
Wail over her!
Get balm for her pain;
perhaps she can be healed.

9 " 'We would have healed Babylon,
but she cannot be healed;
let us leave her and each go to our own
land,
for her judgment reaches to the skies,
it rises as high as the heavens.'
10 " 'The LORD has vindicated us;
come, let us tell in Zion
what the LORD our God has done.'

11 "Sharpen the arrows,
take up the shields!
The LORD has stirred up the kings of
the Medes,
because his purpose is to destroy
Babylon.
The LORD will take vengeance,
vengeance for his temple.
12 Lift up a banner against the walls of
Babylon!
Reinforce the guard,
station the watchmen,
prepare an ambush!
The LORD will carry out his purpose,
his decree against the people of
Babylon.
13 You who live by many waters
and are rich in treasures,
your end has come,
the time for you to be destroyed.
14 The LORD Almighty has sworn by
himself:
I will surely fill you with troops, as
with a swarm of locusts,
and they will shout in triumph
over you.

15 "He made the earth by his power;
he founded the world by his wisdom
and stretched out the heavens by his
understanding.
16 When he thunders, the waters in the
heavens roar;
he makes clouds rise from the ends of
the earth.
He sends lightning with the rain
and brings out the wind from his
storehouses.

17 "Everyone is senseless and without
knowledge;
every goldsmith is shamed by his idols.
The images he makes are a fraud;
they have no breath in them.
18 They are worthless, the objects of
mockery;
when their judgment comes, they will
perish.

[a] *1 Leb Kamai* is a cryptogram for Chaldea, that is, Babylonia. [b] *3* The Hebrew term refers to the irrevocable giving over of things or persons to the LORD, often by totally destroying them.
[c] *4* Or *Chaldea* [d] *5* Or *Almighty, / and the land of the Babylonians*

[19] He who is the Portion of Jacob is not like these,
for he is the Maker of all things,
including the people of his inheritance—
the LORD Almighty is his name.

[20] "You are my war club,
my weapon for battle—
with you I shatter nations,
with you I destroy kingdoms,
[21] with you I shatter horse and rider,
with you I shatter chariot and driver,
[22] with you I shatter man and woman,
with you I shatter old man and youth,
with you I shatter young man and young woman,
[23] with you I shatter shepherd and flock,
with you I shatter farmer and oxen,
with you I shatter governors and officials.

[24] "Before your eyes I will repay Babylon
and all who live in Babylonia[a] for all the
wrong they have done in Zion," declares the
LORD.

[25] "I am against you, you destroying mountain,
you who destroy the whole earth,"
declares the LORD.
"I will stretch out my hand against you,
roll you off the cliffs,
and make you a burned-out mountain.
[26] No rock will be taken from you for a cornerstone,
nor any stone for a foundation,
for you will be desolate forever,"
declares the LORD.
[27] "Lift up a banner in the land!
Blow the trumpet among the nations!
Prepare the nations for battle against her;
summon against her these kingdoms:
Ararat, Minni and Ashkenaz.
Appoint a commander against her;
send up horses like a swarm of locusts.
[28] Prepare the nations for battle against her—
the kings of the Medes,
their governors and all their officials,
and all the countries they rule.
[29] The land trembles and writhes,
for the LORD's purposes against Babylon stand—
to lay waste the land of Babylon
so that no one will live there.
[30] Babylon's warriors have stopped fighting;
they remain in their strongholds.
Their strength is exhausted;
they have become weaklings.
Her dwellings are set on fire;
the bars of her gates are broken.
[31] One courier follows another
and messenger follows messenger
to announce to the king of Babylon
that his entire city is captured,
[32] the river crossings seized,
the marshes set on fire,
and the soldiers terrified."

[33] This is what the LORD Almighty, the
God of Israel, says:

"Daughter Babylon is like a threshing floor
at the time it is trampled;
the time to harvest her will soon come."

[34] "Nebuchadnezzar king of Babylon has devoured us,
he has thrown us into confusion,
he has made us an empty jar.
Like a serpent he has swallowed us
and filled his stomach with our delicacies,
and then has spewed us out.
[35] May the violence done to our flesh[b] be on Babylon,"
say the inhabitants of Zion.
"May our blood be on those who live in Babylonia,"
says Jerusalem.

[36] Therefore this is what the LORD says:

"See, I will defend your cause
and avenge you;
I will dry up her sea
and make her springs dry.
[37] Babylon will be a heap of ruins,
a haunt of jackals,
an object of horror and scorn,
a place where no one lives.
[38] Her people all roar like young lions,
they growl like lion cubs.
[39] But while they are aroused,
I will set out a feast for them
and make them drunk,

[a] *24* Or *Chaldea*; also in verse 35 [b] *35* Or *done to us and to our children*

so that they shout with laughter —
then sleep forever and not awake,"
declares the LORD.
40 "I will bring them down
like lambs to the slaughter,
like rams and goats.

41 "How Sheshak[a] will be captured,
the boast of the whole earth seized!
How desolate Babylon will be
among the nations!
42 The sea will rise over Babylon;
its roaring waves will cover her.
43 Her towns will be desolate,
a dry and desert land,
a land where no one lives,
through which no one travels.
44 I will punish Bel in Babylon
and make him spew out what he has
swallowed.
The nations will no longer stream
to him.
And the wall of Babylon will fall.

45 "Come out of her, my people!
Run for your lives!
Run from the fierce anger of the LORD.
46 Do not lose heart or be afraid
when rumors are heard in the land;
one rumor comes this year, another
the next,
rumors of violence in the land
and of ruler against ruler.
47 For the time will surely come
when I will punish the idols of
Babylon;
her whole land will be disgraced
and her slain will all lie fallen
within her.
48 Then heaven and earth and all that is in
them
will shout for joy over Babylon,
for out of the north
destroyers will attack her,"
declares the LORD.

49 "Babylon must fall because of Israel's
slain,
just as the slain in all the earth
have fallen because of Babylon.
50 You who have escaped the sword,
leave and do not linger!
Remember the LORD in a distant land,
and call to mind Jerusalem."

51 "We are disgraced,
for we have been insulted
and shame covers our faces,
because foreigners have entered
the holy places of the LORD's house."

52 "But days are coming," declares the LORD,
"when I will punish her idols,
and throughout her land
the wounded will groan.
53 Even if Babylon ascends to the heavens
and fortifies her lofty stronghold,
I will send destroyers against her,"
declares the LORD.

54 "The sound of a cry comes from Babylon,
the sound of great destruction
from the land of the Babylonians.[b]
55 The LORD will destroy Babylon;
he will silence her noisy din.
Waves of enemies will rage like great
waters;
the roar of their voices will resound.
56 A destroyer will come against Babylon;
her warriors will be captured,
and their bows will be broken.
For the LORD is a God of retribution;
he will repay in full.
57 I will make her officials and wise men
drunk,
her governors, officers and warriors
as well;
they will sleep forever and not awake,"
declares the King, whose name is the
LORD Almighty.

58 This is what the LORD Almighty says:

"Babylon's thick wall will be leveled
and her high gates set on fire;
the peoples exhaust themselves for
nothing,
the nations' labor is only fuel for the
flames."

59 This is the message Jeremiah the proph-
et gave to the staff officer Seraiah son of Ne-
riah, the son of Mahseiah, when he went
to Babylon with Zedekiah king of Judah in
the fourth year of his reign. 60 Jeremiah had
written on a scroll about all the disasters
that would come upon Babylon — all that
had been recorded concerning Babylon.
61 He said to Seraiah, "When you get to Bab-
ylon, see that you read all these words aloud.

[a] 41 *Sheshak* is a cryptogram for Babylon. [b] 54 Or *Chaldeans*

[62]Then say, 'LORD, you have said you will destroy this place, so that neither people nor animals will live in it; it will be desolate forever.' [63]When you finish reading this scroll, tie a stone to it and throw it into the Euphrates. [64]Then say, 'So will Babylon sink to rise no more because of the disaster I will bring on her. And her people will fall.' "

The words of Jeremiah end here.

The Fall of Jerusalem

52 Zedekiah was twenty-one years old when he became king, and he reigned in Jerusalem eleven years. His mother's name was Hamutal daughter of Jeremiah; she was from Libnah. [2]He did evil in the eyes of the LORD, just as Jehoiakim had done. [3]It was because of the LORD's anger that all this happened to Jerusalem and Judah, and in the end he thrust them from his presence.

Now Zedekiah rebelled against the king of Babylon.

[4]So in the ninth year of Zedekiah's reign, on the tenth day of the tenth month, Nebuchadnezzar king of Babylon marched against Jerusalem with his whole army. They encamped outside the city and built siege works all around it. [5]The city was kept under siege until the eleventh year of King Zedekiah.

[6]By the ninth day of the fourth month the famine in the city had become so severe that there was no food for the people to eat. [7]Then the city wall was broken through, and the whole army fled. They left the city at night through the gate between the two walls near the king's garden, though the Babylonians[a] were surrounding the city. They fled toward the Arabah,[b] [8]but the Babylonian[c] army pursued King Zedekiah and overtook him in the plains of Jericho. All his soldiers were separated from him and scattered, [9]and he was captured.

He was taken to the king of Babylon at Riblah in the land of Hamath, where he pronounced sentence on him. [10]There at Riblah the king of Babylon killed the sons of Zedekiah before his eyes; he also killed all the officials of Judah. [11]Then he put out Zedekiah's eyes, bound him with bronze shackles and took him to Babylon, where he put him in prison till the day of his death.

[12]On the tenth day of the fifth month, in the nineteenth year of Nebuchadnezzar king of Babylon, Nebuzaradan commander of the imperial guard, who served the king of Babylon, came to Jerusalem. [13]He set fire to the temple of the LORD, the royal palace and all the houses of Jerusalem. Every important building he burned down. [14]The whole Babylonian army, under the commander of the imperial guard, broke down all the walls around Jerusalem. [15]Nebuzaradan the commander of the guard carried into exile some of the poorest people and those who remained in the city, along with the rest of the craftsmen[d] and those who had deserted to the king of Babylon. [16]But Nebuzaradan left behind the rest of the poorest people of the land to work the vineyards and fields.

[17]The Babylonians broke up the bronze pillars, the movable stands and the bronze Sea that were at the temple of the LORD and they carried all the bronze to Babylon. [18]They also took away the pots, shovels, wick trimmers, sprinkling bowls, dishes and all the bronze articles used in the temple service. [19]The commander of the imperial guard took away the basins, censers, sprinkling bowls, pots, lampstands, dishes and bowls used for drink offerings—all that were made of pure gold or silver.

[20]The bronze from the two pillars, the Sea and the twelve bronze bulls under it, and the movable stands, which King Solomon had made for the temple of the LORD, was more than could be weighed. [21]Each pillar was eighteen cubits high and twelve cubits in circumference[e]; each was four fingers thick, and hollow. [22]The bronze capital on top of one pillar was five cubits[f] high and was decorated with a network and pomegranates of bronze all around. The other pillar, with its pomegranates, was similar. [23]There were ninety-six pomegranates on the sides; the total number of pomegranates above the surrounding network was a hundred.

[24]The commander of the guard took as

[a] 7 Or *Chaldeans*; also in verse 17 [b] 7 Or *the Jordan Valley* [c] 8 Or *Chaldean*; also in verse 14
[d] 15 Or *the populace* [e] 21 That is, about 27 feet high and 18 feet in circumference or about 8.1 meters high and 5.4 meters in circumference [f] 22 That is, about 7 1/2 feet or about 2.3 meters

prisoners Seraiah the chief priest, Zepha-
niah the priest next in rank and the three
doorkeepers. [25]Of those still in the city, he
took the officer in charge of the fighting
men, and seven royal advisers. He also took
the secretary who was chief officer in charge
of conscripting the people of the land, six-
ty of whom were found in the city. [26]Neb-
uzaradan the commander took them all
and brought them to the king of Babylon at
Riblah. [27]There at Riblah, in the land of Ha-
math, the king had them executed.

So Judah went into captivity, away from
her land. [28]This is the number of the people
Nebuchadnezzar carried into exile:

in the seventh year, 3,023 Jews;
[29]in Nebuchadnezzar's eighteenth year,
832 people from Jerusalem;
[30]in his twenty-third year,
745 Jews taken into exile by Nebuzaradan the commander of the imperial guard.

There were 4,600 people in all.

Jehoiachin Released

[31]In the thirty-seventh year of the ex-
ile of Jehoiachin king of Judah, in the year
Awel-Marduk became king of Babylon, on
the twenty-fifth day of the twelfth month, he
released Jehoiachin king of Judah and freed
him from prison. [32]He spoke kindly to him
and gave him a seat of honor higher than
those of the other kings who were with him in
Babylon. [33]So Jehoiachin put aside his prison
clothes and for the rest of his life ate regular-
ly at the king's table. [34]Day by day the king of
Babylon gave Jehoiachin a regular allowance
as long as he lived, till the day of his death.

LAMENTATIONS

1[a] How deserted lies the city,
once so full of people!
How like a widow is she,
who once was great among the nations!
She who was queen among the provinces
has now become a slave.

[2] Bitterly she weeps at night,
tears are on her cheeks.
Among all her lovers
there is no one to comfort her.
All her friends have betrayed her;
they have become her enemies.

[3] After affliction and harsh labor,
Judah has gone into exile.
She dwells among the nations;
she finds no resting place.
All who pursue her have overtaken her
in the midst of her distress.

[4] The roads to Zion mourn,
for no one comes to her appointed festivals.
All her gateways are desolate,
her priests groan,
her young women grieve,
and she is in bitter anguish.

[5] Her foes have become her masters;
her enemies are at ease.
The LORD has brought her grief
because of her many sins.
Her children have gone into exile,
captive before the foe.

[6] All the splendor has departed
from Daughter Zion.
Her princes are like deer
that find no pasture;
in weakness they have fled
before the pursuer.

[7] In the days of her affliction and wandering
Jerusalem remembers all the treasures
that were hers in days of old.
When her people fell into enemy hands,
there was no one to help her.
Her enemies looked at her
and laughed at her destruction.

[8] Jerusalem has sinned greatly
and so has become unclean.
All who honored her despise her,
for they have all seen her naked;
she herself groans
and turns away.

[9] Her filthiness clung to her skirts;
she did not consider her future.
Her fall was astounding;
there was none to comfort her.
"Look, LORD, on my affliction,
for the enemy has triumphed."

[10] The enemy laid hands
on all her treasures;
she saw pagan nations
enter her sanctuary—
those you had forbidden
to enter your assembly.

[11] All her people groan
as they search for bread;
they barter their treasures for food
to keep themselves alive.
"Look, LORD, and consider,
for I am despised."

[12] "Is it nothing to you, all you who pass by?
Look around and see.
Is any suffering like my suffering
that was inflicted on me,
that the LORD brought on me
in the day of his fierce anger?

[13] "From on high he sent fire,
sent it down into my bones.
He spread a net for my feet
and turned me back.
He made me desolate,
faint all the day long.

[a] This chapter is an acrostic poem, the verses of which begin with the successive letters of the Hebrew alphabet.

14 "My sins have been bound into a yoke[a];
by his hands they were woven
together.
They have been hung on my neck,
and the Lord has sapped my strength.
He has given me into the hands
of those I cannot withstand.

15 "The Lord has rejected
all the warriors in my midst;
he has summoned an army against me
to[b] crush my young men.
In his winepress the Lord has trampled
Virgin Daughter Judah.

16 "This is why I weep
and my eyes overflow with tears.
No one is near to comfort me,
no one to restore my spirit.
My children are destitute
because the enemy has prevailed."

17 Zion stretches out her hands,
but there is no one to comfort her.
The LORD has decreed for Jacob
that his neighbors become his foes;
Jerusalem has become
an unclean thing among them.

18 "The LORD is righteous,
yet I rebelled against his command.
Listen, all you peoples;
look on my suffering.
My young men and young women
have gone into exile.

19 "I called to my allies
but they betrayed me.
My priests and my elders
perished in the city
while they searched for food
to keep themselves alive.

20 "See, LORD, how distressed I am!
I am in torment within,
and in my heart I am disturbed,
for I have been most rebellious.
Outside, the sword bereaves;
inside, there is only death.

21 "People have heard my groaning,
but there is no one to comfort me.
All my enemies have heard of my
distress;
they rejoice at what you have
done.
May you bring the day you have
announced
so they may become like me.

22 "Let all their wickedness come
before you;
deal with them
as you have dealt with me
because of all my sins.
My groans are many
and my heart is faint."

2[c] How the Lord has covered Daughter
Zion
with the cloud of his anger[d]!
He has hurled down the splendor of
Israel
from heaven to earth;
he has not remembered his footstool
in the day of his anger.

2 Without pity the Lord has swallowed up
all the dwellings of Jacob;
in his wrath he has torn down
the strongholds of Daughter Judah.
He has brought her kingdom and its
princes
down to the ground in dishonor.

3 In fierce anger he has cut off
every horn[e,f] of Israel.
He has withdrawn his right hand
at the approach of the enemy.
He has burned in Jacob like a flaming fire
that consumes everything around it.

4 Like an enemy he has strung his bow;
his right hand is ready.
Like a foe he has slain
all who were pleasing to the eye;
he has poured out his wrath like fire
on the tent of Daughter Zion.

5 The Lord is like an enemy;
he has swallowed up Israel.
He has swallowed up all her palaces
and destroyed her strongholds.
He has multiplied mourning and
lamentation
for Daughter Judah.

[a] *14* Most Hebrew manuscripts; many Hebrew manuscripts and Septuagint *He kept watch over my sins*
[b] *15* Or *has set a time for me / when he will*
[c] This chapter is an acrostic poem, the verses of which begin with the successive letters of the Hebrew alphabet.
[d] *1* Or *How the Lord in his anger / has treated Daughter Zion with contempt*
[e] *3* Or *off / all the strength*; or *every king*
[f] *3* *Horn* here symbolizes strength.

[6] He has laid waste his dwelling like a garden;
he has destroyed his place of meeting.
The LORD has made Zion forget
her appointed festivals and her Sabbaths;
in his fierce anger he has spurned
both king and priest.

[7] The Lord has rejected his altar
and abandoned his sanctuary.
He has given the walls of her palaces
into the hands of the enemy;
they have raised a shout in the house of the LORD
as on the day of an appointed festival.

[8] The LORD determined to tear down
the wall around Daughter Zion.
He stretched out a measuring line
and did not withhold his hand from destroying.
He made ramparts and walls lament;
together they wasted away.

[9] Her gates have sunk into the ground;
their bars he has broken and destroyed.
Her king and her princes are exiled
among the nations,
the law is no more,
and her prophets no longer find
visions from the LORD.

[10] The elders of Daughter Zion
sit on the ground in silence;
they have sprinkled dust on their heads
and put on sackcloth.
The young women of Jerusalem
have bowed their heads to the ground.

[11] My eyes fail from weeping,
I am in torment within;
my heart is poured out on the ground
because my people are destroyed,
because children and infants faint
in the streets of the city.

[12] They say to their mothers,
"Where is bread and wine?"
as they faint like the wounded
in the streets of the city,
as their lives ebb away
in their mothers' arms.

[13] What can I say for you?
With what can I compare you,
Daughter Jerusalem?
To what can I liken you,
that I may comfort you,
Virgin Daughter Zion?
Your wound is as deep as the sea.
Who can heal you?

[14] The visions of your prophets
were false and worthless;
they did not expose your sin
to ward off your captivity.
The prophecies they gave you
were false and misleading.

[15] All who pass your way
clap their hands at you;
they scoff and shake their heads
at Daughter Jerusalem:
"Is this the city that was called
the perfection of beauty,
the joy of the whole earth?"

[16] All your enemies open their mouths
wide against you;
they scoff and gnash their teeth
and say, "We have swallowed her up.
This is the day we have waited for;
we have lived to see it."

[17] The LORD has done what he planned;
he has fulfilled his word,
which he decreed long ago.
He has overthrown you without pity,
he has let the enemy gloat over you,
he has exalted the horn[a] of your foes.

[18] The hearts of the people
cry out to the Lord.
You walls of Daughter Zion,
let your tears flow like a river
day and night;
give yourself no relief,
your eyes no rest.

[19] Arise, cry out in the night,
as the watches of the night begin;
pour out your heart like water
in the presence of the Lord.
Lift up your hands to him
for the lives of your children,
who faint from hunger
at every street corner.

[20] "Look, LORD, and consider:

[a] *17 Horn* here symbolizes strength.

Whom have you ever treated like this?
Should women eat their offspring,
the children they have cared for?
Should priest and prophet be killed
in the sanctuary of the Lord?

21 "Young and old lie together
in the dust of the streets;
my young men and young women
have fallen by the sword.
You have slain them in the day of your
anger;
you have slaughtered them
without pity.

22 "As you summon to a feast day,
so you summoned against me terrors
on every side.
In the day of the LORD's anger
no one escaped or survived;
those I cared for and reared
my enemy has destroyed."

3 [a] I am the man who has seen affliction
by the rod of the LORD's wrath.
2 He has driven me away and made me walk
in darkness rather than light;
3 indeed, he has turned his hand
against me
again and again, all day long.

4 He has made my skin and my flesh
grow old
and has broken my bones.
5 He has besieged me and surrounded me
with bitterness and hardship.
6 He has made me dwell in darkness
like those long dead.

7 He has walled me in so I cannot escape;
he has weighed me down with chains.
8 Even when I call out or cry for help,
he shuts out my prayer.
9 He has barred my way with blocks
of stone;
he has made my paths crooked.

10 Like a bear lying in wait,
like a lion in hiding,
11 he dragged me from the path and
mangled me
and left me without help.
12 He drew his bow
and made me the target for his arrows.
13 He pierced my heart
with arrows from his quiver.
14 I became the laughingstock of all my
people;
they mock me in song all day long.
15 He has filled me with bitter herbs
and given me gall to drink.

16 He has broken my teeth with gravel;
he has trampled me in the dust.
17 I have been deprived of peace;
I have forgotten what prosperity is.
18 So I say, "My splendor is gone
and all that I had hoped from the LORD."

19 I remember my affliction and my
wandering,
the bitterness and the gall.
20 I well remember them,
and my soul is downcast within me.
21 Yet this I call to mind
and therefore I have hope:

22 Because of the LORD's great love we are
not consumed,
for his compassions never fail.
23 They are new every morning;
great is your faithfulness.
24 I say to myself, "The LORD is my portion;
therefore I will wait for him."

25 The LORD is good to those whose hope is
in him,
to the one who seeks him;
26 it is good to wait quietly
for the salvation of the LORD.
27 It is good for a man to bear the yoke
while he is young.

28 Let him sit alone in silence,
for the LORD has laid it on him.
29 Let him bury his face in the dust—
there may yet be hope.
30 Let him offer his cheek to one who would
strike him,
and let him be filled with disgrace.

31 For no one is cast off
by the Lord forever.
32 Though he brings grief, he will show
compassion,
so great is his unfailing love.
33 For he does not willingly bring affliction
or grief to anyone.

[a] This chapter is an acrostic poem; the verses of each stanza begin with the successive letters of the Hebrew alphabet, and the verses within each stanza begin with the same letter.

[34]To crush underfoot
all prisoners in the land,
[35]to deny people their rights
before the Most High,
[36]to deprive them of justice —
would not the Lord see such things?

[37]Who can speak and have it happen
if the Lord has not decreed it?
[38]Is it not from the mouth of the Most High
that both calamities and good things
come?
[39]Why should the living complain
when punished for their sins?

[40]Let us examine our ways and test them,
and let us return to the LORD.
[41]Let us lift up our hearts and our hands
to God in heaven, and say:
[42]"We have sinned and rebelled
and you have not forgiven.

[43]"You have covered yourself with anger
and pursued us;
you have slain without pity.
[44]You have covered yourself with a cloud
so that no prayer can get through.
[45]You have made us scum and refuse
among the nations.

[46]"All our enemies have opened their
mouths
wide against us.
[47]We have suffered terror and pitfalls,
ruin and destruction."
[48]Streams of tears flow from my eyes
because my people are destroyed.

[49]My eyes will flow unceasingly,
without relief,
[50]until the LORD looks down
from heaven and sees.
[51]What I see brings grief to my soul
because of all the women of my city.

[52]Those who were my enemies without
cause
hunted me like a bird.
[53]They tried to end my life in a pit
and threw stones at me;
[54]the waters closed over my head,
and I thought I was about to perish.

[55]I called on your name, LORD,
from the depths of the pit.
[56]You heard my plea: "Do not close
your ears
to my cry for relief."
[57]You came near when I called you,
and you said, "Do not fear."

[58]You, Lord, took up my case;
you redeemed my life.
[59]LORD, you have seen the wrong done
to me.
Uphold my cause!
[60]You have seen the depth of their
vengeance,
all their plots against me.

[61]LORD, you have heard their insults,
all their plots against me —
[62]what my enemies whisper and mutter
against me all day long.
[63]Look at them! Sitting or standing,
they mock me in their songs.

[64]Pay them back what they deserve,
LORD,
for what their hands have done.
[65]Put a veil over their hearts,
and may your curse be on them!
[66]Pursue them in anger and destroy them
from under the heavens of the LORD.

4 [a]How the gold has lost its luster,
the fine gold become dull!
The sacred gems are scattered
at every street corner.

[2]How the precious children of Zion,
once worth their weight in gold,
are now considered as pots of clay,
the work of a potter's hands!

[3]Even jackals offer their breasts
to nurse their young,
but my people have become
heartless
like ostriches in the desert.

[4]Because of thirst the infant's tongue
sticks to the roof of its mouth;
the children beg for bread,
but no one gives it to them.

[5]Those who once ate delicacies
are destitute in the streets.
Those brought up in royal purple
now lie on ash heaps.

[a] This chapter is an acrostic poem, the verses of which begin with the successive letters of the Hebrew alphabet.

[6] The punishment of my people
is greater than that of Sodom,
which was overthrown in a moment
without a hand turned to help her.

[7] Their princes were brighter than snow
and whiter than milk,
their bodies more ruddy than rubies,
their appearance like lapis lazuli.

[8] But now they are blacker than soot;
they are not recognized in the streets.
Their skin has shriveled on their bones;
it has become as dry as a stick.

[9] Those killed by the sword are better off
than those who die of famine;
racked with hunger, they waste away
for lack of food from the field.

[10] With their own hands compassionate
women
have cooked their own children,
who became their food
when my people were destroyed.

[11] The LORD has given full vent to his wrath;
he has poured out his fierce anger.
He kindled a fire in Zion
that consumed her foundations.

[12] The kings of the earth did not believe,
nor did any of the peoples of the world,
that enemies and foes could enter
the gates of Jerusalem.

[13] But it happened because of the sins of her
prophets
and the iniquities of her priests,
who shed within her
the blood of the righteous.

[14] Now they grope through the streets
as if they were blind.
They are so defiled with blood
that no one dares to touch their
garments.

[15] "Go away! You are unclean!" people cry
to them.
"Away! Away! Don't touch us!"
When they flee and wander about,
people among the nations say,
"They can stay here no longer."

[16] The LORD himself has scattered them;
he no longer watches over them.
The priests are shown no honor,
the elders no favor.

[17] Moreover, our eyes failed,
looking in vain for help;
from our towers we watched
for a nation that could not save us.

[18] People stalked us at every step,
so we could not walk in our streets.
Our end was near, our days were
numbered,
for our end had come.

[19] Our pursuers were swifter
than eagles in the sky;
they chased us over the mountains
and lay in wait for us in the desert.

[20] The LORD's anointed, our very life breath,
was caught in their traps.
We thought that under his shadow
we would live among the nations.

[21] Rejoice and be glad, Daughter Edom,
you who live in the land of Uz.
But to you also the cup will be passed;
you will be drunk and stripped naked.

[22] Your punishment will end, Daughter
Zion;
he will not prolong your exile.
But he will punish your sin, Daughter
Edom,
and expose your wickedness.

5 Remember, LORD, what has happened
to us;
look, and see our disgrace.
[2] Our inheritance has been turned over to
strangers,
our homes to foreigners.
[3] We have become fatherless,
our mothers are widows.
[4] We must buy the water we drink;
our wood can be had only at a price.
[5] Those who pursue us are at our heels;
we are weary and find no rest.
[6] We submitted to Egypt and Assyria
to get enough bread.
[7] Our ancestors sinned and are no more,
and we bear their punishment.
[8] Slaves rule over us,
and there is no one to free us from
their hands.
[9] We get our bread at the risk of our lives
because of the sword in the desert.
[10] Our skin is hot as an oven,
feverish from hunger.

11 Women have been violated in Zion,
and virgins in the towns of Judah.
12 Princes have been hung up by their
hands;
elders are shown no respect.
13 Young men toil at the millstones;
boys stagger under loads of wood.
14 The elders are gone from the city gate;
the young men have stopped their
music.
15 Joy is gone from our hearts;
our dancing has turned to mourning.
16 The crown has fallen from our head.
Woe to us, for we have sinned!
17 Because of this our hearts are faint,
because of these things our eyes
grow dim
18 for Mount Zion, which lies desolate,
with jackals prowling over it.

19 You, LORD, reign forever;
your throne endures from generation
to generation.
20 Why do you always forget us?
Why do you forsake us so long?
21 Restore us to yourself, LORD, that we may
return;
renew our days as of old
22 unless you have utterly rejected us
and are angry with us beyond
measure.

SING SING SING

Chris Tomlin, Jesse Reeves, Matt Gilder, Daniel Carson, Travis Nunn

Sing, sing, sing
And make music with the heavens
We will sing, sing, sing
Grateful that you hear us
When we shout your praise
Lift high the name of Jesus

What's not to love about you?
Heaven and earth adore you
Kings and kingdoms bow down
Son of God, you are the One
You are the One we're living for

You are the love that frees us
You are the light that leads us
Like a fire burning
Son of God, you are the One
You are the One we're living for

THE INSPIRATION

Sing praises to God, sing praises; sing praises to our King, sing praises. — Psalm 47:6

BEHIND THE SONG

Of all the songs Chris Tomlin has written, "Sing, Sing, Sing" is the only one to which his whole band has contributed. Tomlin has used it to open many of his worship concerts over the last several years. "It's a pretty simple song," Tomlin admits, "but it's really energetic. It's one of those really great songs to open up a night with." As a result, this rousing song really gets crowds going.

As with several of his songs, "Sing, Sing, Sing" includes intrinsic instructions within the lyrics. It's an effective tool for leading worship that goes all the way back to Old Testament times. The book of Psalms is full of instructive worship songs — from suggested instruments to suggested postures (raising hands, falling prostrate, etc.). It can be very helpful to actually encourage the congregation or the individual to do something with their body that reflects the praise coming from their heart.

Selah

How do you approach worship when you really don't feel like worshiping? Don't feel alone! Every believer has found themselves in a congregation, mouthing the words, but unable to really enter in.

At times like these, a song like "Sing, Sing, Sing" is great for helping us to overcome our negative emotions and distractions. As simple as the lyric is, it's convincing that Jesus is absolutely worth singing about, and often our emotions catch up with the truth as we sing.

EZEKIEL

Ezekiel's Inaugural Vision

1 In my thirtieth year, in the fourth month
on the fifth day, while I was among the
exiles by the Kebar River, the heavens were
opened and I saw visions of God.
2 On the fifth of the month — it was the
fifth year of the exile of King Jehoiachin —
3 the word of the LORD came to Ezekiel the
priest, the son of Buzi, by the Kebar River in
the land of the Babylonians.[a] There the hand
of the LORD was on him.
4 I looked, and I saw a windstorm com-
ing out of the north — an immense cloud
with flashing lightning and surrounded by
brilliant light. The center of the fire looked
like glowing metal, 5 and in the fire was what
looked like four living creatures. In appear-
ance their form was human, 6 but each of
them had four faces and four wings. 7 Their
legs were straight; their feet were like those
of a calf and gleamed like burnished bronze.
8 Under their wings on their four sides they
had human hands. All four of them had fac-
es and wings, 9 and the wings of one touched
the wings of another. Each one went straight
ahead; they did not turn as they moved.
10 Their faces looked like this: Each of the
four had the face of a human being, and on
the right side each had the face of a lion, and
on the left the face of an ox; each also had
the face of an eagle. 11 Such were their faces.
They each had two wings spreading out up-
ward, each wing touching that of the crea-
ture on either side; and each had two other
wings covering its body. 12 Each one went
straight ahead. Wherever the spirit would
go, they would go, without turning as they
went. 13 The appearance of the living crea-
tures was like burning coals of fire or like
torches. Fire moved back and forth among
the creatures; it was bright, and lightning
flashed out of it. 14 The creatures sped back
and forth like flashes of lightning.
15 As I looked at the living creatures, I saw
a wheel on the ground beside each creature
with its four faces. 16 This was the appear-
ance and structure of the wheels: They spar-
kled like topaz, and all four looked alike.
Each appeared to be made like a wheel in-
tersecting a wheel. 17 As they moved, they
would go in any one of the four directions the
creatures faced; the wheels did not change
direction as the creatures went. 18 Their rims
were high and awesome, and all four rims
were full of eyes all around.
19 When the living creatures moved,
the wheels beside them moved; and when
the living creatures rose from the ground,
the wheels also rose. 20 Wherever the spir-
it would go, they would go, and the wheels
would rise along with them, because the
spirit of the living creatures was in the
wheels. 21 When the creatures moved, they
also moved; when the creatures stood still,
they also stood still; and when the creatures
rose from the ground, the wheels rose along
with them, because the spirit of the living
creatures was in the wheels.
22 Spread out above the heads of the liv-
ing creatures was what looked something
like a vault, sparkling like crystal, and awe-
some. 23 Under the vault their wings were
stretched out one toward the other, and each
had two wings covering its body. 24 When the
creatures moved, I heard the sound of their
wings, like the roar of rushing waters, like
the voice of the Almighty,[b] like the tumult of
an army. When they stood still, they lowered
their wings.
25 Then there came a voice from above
the vault over their heads as they stood with
lowered wings. 26 Above the vault over their
heads was what looked like a throne of lapis
lazuli, and high above on the throne was a
figure like that of a man. 27 I saw that from
what appeared to be his waist up he looked
like glowing metal, as if full of fire, and that
from there down he looked like fire; and
brilliant light surrounded him. 28 Like the

[a] 3 Or *Chaldeans* [b] 24 Hebrew *Shaddai*

appearance of a rainbow in the clouds on a rainy day, so was the radiance around him.

This was the appearance of the likeness of the glory of the LORD. When I saw it, I fell facedown, and I heard the voice of one speaking.

Ezekiel's Call to Be a Prophet

2 He said to me, "Son of man,[a] stand up on your feet and I will speak to you." [2]As he spoke, the Spirit came into me and raised me to my feet, and I heard him speaking to me.

[3]He said: "Son of man, I am sending you to the Israelites, to a rebellious nation that has rebelled against me; they and their ancestors have been in revolt against me to this very day. [4]The people to whom I am sending you are obstinate and stubborn. Say to them, 'This is what the Sovereign LORD says.' [5]And whether they listen or fail to listen—for they are a rebellious people—they will know that a prophet has been among them. [6]And you, son of man, do not be afraid of them or their words. Do not be afraid, though briers and thorns are all around you and you live among scorpions. Do not be afraid of what they say or be terrified by them, though they are a rebellious people. [7]You must speak my words to them, whether they listen or fail to listen, for they are rebellious. [8]But you, son of man, listen to what I say to you. Do not rebel like that rebellious people; open your mouth and eat what I give you."

[9]Then I looked, and I saw a hand stretched out to me. In it was a scroll, [10]which he unrolled before me. On both sides of it were written words of lament and mourning and woe.

3 And he said to me, "Son of man, eat what is before you, eat this scroll; then go and speak to the people of Israel." [2]So I opened my mouth, and he gave me the scroll to eat.

[3]Then he said to me, "Son of man, eat this scroll I am giving you and fill your stomach with it." So I ate it, and it tasted as sweet as honey in my mouth.

[4]He then said to me: "Son of man, go now to the people of Israel and speak my words to them. [5]You are not being sent to a people of obscure speech and strange language, but to the people of Israel—[6]not to many peoples of obscure speech and strange language, whose words you cannot understand. Surely if I had sent you to them, they would have listened to you. [7]But the people of Israel are not willing to listen to you because they are not willing to listen to me, for all the Israelites are hardened and obstinate. [8]But I will make you as unyielding and hardened as they are. [9]I will make your forehead like the hardest stone, harder than flint. Do not be afraid of them or terrified by them, though they are a rebellious people."

[10]And he said to me, "Son of man, listen carefully and take to heart all the words I speak to you. [11]Go now to your people in exile and speak to them. Say to them, 'This is what the Sovereign LORD says,' whether they listen or fail to listen."

[12]Then the Spirit lifted me up, and I heard behind me a loud rumbling sound as the glory of the LORD rose from the place where it was standing.[b] [13]It was the sound of the wings of the living creatures brushing against each other and the sound of the wheels beside them, a loud rumbling sound. [14]The Spirit then lifted me up and took me away, and I went in bitterness and in the anger of my spirit, with the strong hand of the LORD on me. [15]I came to the exiles who lived at Tel Aviv near the Kebar River. And there, where they were living, I sat among them for seven days—deeply distressed.

Ezekiel's Task as Watchman

[16]At the end of seven days the word of the LORD came to me: [17]"Son of man, I have made you a watchman for the people of Israel; so hear the word I speak and give them warning from me. [18]When I say to a wicked person, 'You will surely die,' and you do not warn them or speak out to dissuade them from their evil ways in order to save their life, that wicked person will die for[c] their sin, and I will hold you accountable for their blood. [19]But if you do warn the wicked person and they do not turn from their wickedness or from their evil ways, they will die for their sin; but you will have saved yourself.

[20]"Again, when a righteous person turns

[a] *1* The Hebrew phrase *ben adam* means *human being.* The phrase *son of man* is retained as a form of address here and throughout Ezekiel because of its possible association with "Son of Man" in the New Testament. [b] *12* Probable reading of the original Hebrew text; Masoretic Text *sound—may the glory of the LORD be praised from his place* [c] *18* Or *in*; also in verses 19 and 20

from their righteousness and does evil, and I put a stumbling block before them, they will die. Since you did not warn them, they will die for their sin. The righteous things that person did will not be remembered, and I will hold you accountable for their blood.
[21]But if you do warn the righteous person not to sin and they do not sin, they will surely live because they took warning, and you will have saved yourself."

[22]The hand of the LORD was on me there, and he said to me, "Get up and go out to the plain, and there I will speak to you."
[23]So I got up and went out to the plain. And the glory of the LORD was standing there, like the glory I had seen by the Kebar River, and I fell facedown.

[24]Then the Spirit came into me and raised me to my feet. He spoke to me and said: "Go, shut yourself inside your house.
[25]And you, son of man, they will tie with ropes; you will be bound so that you cannot go out among the people.
[26]I will make your tongue stick to the roof of your mouth so that you will be silent and unable to rebuke them, for they are a rebellious people.
[27]But when I speak to you, I will open your mouth and you shall say to them, 'This is what the Sovereign LORD says.' Whoever will listen let them listen, and whoever will refuse let them refuse; for they are a rebellious people.

Siege of Jerusalem Symbolized

4 "Now, son of man, take a block of clay, put it in front of you and draw the city of Jerusalem on it.
[2]Then lay siege to it: Erect siege works against it, build a ramp up to it, set up camps against it and put battering rams around it.
[3]Then take an iron pan, place it as an iron wall between you and the city and turn your face toward it. It will be under siege, and you shall besiege it. This will be a sign to the people of Israel.

[4]"Then lie on your left side and put the sin of the people of Israel upon yourself.[a] You are to bear their sin for the number of days you lie on your side.
[5]I have assigned you the same number of days as the years of their sin. So for 390 days you will bear the sin of the people of Israel.

[6]"After you have finished this, lie down again, this time on your right side, and bear the sin of the people of Judah. I have assigned you 40 days, a day for each year.
[7]Turn your face toward the siege of Jerusalem and with bared arm prophesy against her.
[8]I will tie you up with ropes so that you cannot turn from one side to the other until you have finished the days of your siege.

[9]"Take wheat and barley, beans and lentils, millet and spelt; put them in a storage jar and use them to make bread for yourself. You are to eat it during the 390 days you lie on your side.
[10]Weigh out twenty shekels[b] of food to eat each day and eat it at set times.
[11]Also measure out a sixth of a hin[c] of water and drink it at set times.
[12]Eat the food as you would a loaf of barley bread; bake it in the sight of the people, using human excrement for fuel."
[13]The LORD said, "In this way the people of Israel will eat defiled food among the nations where I will drive them."

[14]Then I said, "Not so, Sovereign LORD! I have never defiled myself. From my youth until now I have never eaten anything found dead or torn by wild animals. No impure meat has ever entered my mouth."

[15]"Very well," he said, "I will let you bake your bread over cow dung instead of human excrement."

[16]He then said to me: "Son of man, I am about to cut off the food supply in Jerusalem. The people will eat rationed food in anxiety and drink rationed water in despair,
[17]for food and water will be scarce. They will be appalled at the sight of each other and will waste away because of[d] their sin.

God's Razor of Judgment

5 "Now, son of man, take a sharp sword and use it as a barber's razor to shave your head and your beard. Then take a set of scales and divide up the hair.
[2]When the days of your siege come to an end, burn a third of the hair inside the city. Take a third and strike it with the sword all around the city. And scatter a third to the wind. For I will pursue them with drawn sword.
[3]But take a few hairs and tuck them away in the folds of your garment.
[4]Again, take a few of these and throw them into the fire and burn them up. A fire will spread from there to all Israel.

[a] *4* Or *upon your side* [b] *10* That is, about 8 ounces or about 230 grams [c] *11* That is, about 2/3 quart or about 0.6 liter [d] *17* Or *away in*

5 “This is what the Sovereign LORD says: This is Jerusalem, which I have set in the center of the nations, with countries all around her. 6 Yet in her wickedness she has rebelled against my laws and decrees more than the nations and countries around her. She has rejected my laws and has not followed my decrees.

7 “Therefore this is what the Sovereign LORD says: You have been more unruly than the nations around you and have not followed my decrees or kept my laws. You have not even[a] conformed to the standards of the nations around you.

8 “Therefore this is what the Sovereign LORD says: I myself am against you, Jerusalem, and I will inflict punishment on you in the sight of the nations. 9 Because of all your detestable idols, I will do to you what I have never done before and will never do again. 10 Therefore in your midst parents will eat their children, and children will eat their parents. I will inflict punishment on you and will scatter all your survivors to the winds. 11 Therefore as surely as I live, declares the Sovereign LORD, because you have defiled my sanctuary with all your vile images and detestable practices, I myself will shave you; I will not look on you with pity or spare you. 12 A third of your people will die of the plague or perish by famine inside you; a third will fall by the sword outside your walls; and a third I will scatter to the winds and pursue with drawn sword.

13 “Then my anger will cease and my wrath against them will subside, and I will be avenged. And when I have spent my wrath on them, they will know that I the LORD have spoken in my zeal.

14 “I will make you a ruin and a reproach among the nations around you, in the sight of all who pass by. 15 You will be a reproach and a taunt, a warning and an object of horror to the nations around you when I inflict punishment on you in anger and in wrath and with stinging rebuke. I the LORD have spoken. 16 When I shoot at you with my deadly and destructive arrows of famine, I will shoot to destroy you. I will bring more and more famine upon you and cut off your supply of food. 17 I will send famine and wild beasts against you, and they will leave you childless. Plague and bloodshed will sweep through you, and I will bring the sword against you. I the LORD have spoken.”

Doom for the Mountains of Israel

6 The word of the LORD came to me: 2 “Son of man, set your face against the mountains of Israel; prophesy against them 3 and say: ‘You mountains of Israel, hear the word of the Sovereign LORD. This is what the Sovereign LORD says to the mountains and hills, to the ravines and valleys: I am about to bring a sword against you, and I will destroy your high places. 4 Your altars will be demolished and your incense altars will be smashed; and I will slay your people in front of your idols. 5 I will lay the dead bodies of the Israelites in front of their idols, and I will scatter your bones around your altars. 6 Wherever you live, the towns will be laid waste and the high places demolished, so that your altars will be laid waste and devastated, your idols smashed and ruined, your incense altars broken down, and what you have made wiped out. 7 Your people will fall slain among you, and you will know that I am the LORD.

8 “ ‘But I will spare some, for some of you will escape the sword when you are scattered among the lands and nations. 9 Then in the nations where they have been carried captive, those who escape will remember me — how I have been grieved by their adulterous hearts, which have turned away from me, and by their eyes, which have lusted after their idols. They will loathe themselves for the evil they have done and for all their detestable practices. 10 And they will know that I am the LORD; I did not threaten in vain to bring this calamity on them.

11 “ ‘This is what the Sovereign LORD says: Strike your hands together and stamp your feet and cry out “Alas!” because of all the wicked and detestable practices of the people of Israel, for they will fall by the sword, famine and plague. 12 One who is far away will die of the plague, and one who is near will fall by the sword, and anyone who survives and is spared will die of famine. So will I pour out my wrath on them. 13 And they will know that I am the LORD, when their people lie slain among their idols around their altars, on

[a] 7 Most Hebrew manuscripts; some Hebrew manuscripts and Syriac *You have*

every high hill and on all the mountaintops,
under every spreading tree and every leafy
oak—places where they offered fragrant in-
cense to all their idols. 14 And I will stretch out
my hand against them and make the land a
desolate waste from the desert to Diblah[a]—
wherever they live. Then they will know that
I am the LORD.'"

The End Has Come

7 The word of the LORD came to me: 2 "Son
of man, this is what the Sovereign LORD
says to the land of Israel:

"'The end! The end has come
upon the four corners of the land!
3 The end is now upon you,
and I will unleash my anger against
you.
I will judge you according to your
conduct
and repay you for all your detestable
practices.
4 I will not look on you with pity;
I will not spare you.
I will surely repay you for your conduct
and for the detestable practices
among you.

"'Then you will know that I am the LORD.'

5 "This is what the Sovereign LORD says:

"'Disaster! Unheard-of[b] disaster!
See, it comes!
6 The end has come!
The end has come!
It has roused itself against you.
See, it comes!
7 Doom has come upon you,
upon you who dwell in the land.
The time has come! The day is near!
There is panic, not joy, on the
mountains.
8 I am about to pour out my wrath on you
and spend my anger against you.
I will judge you according to your
conduct
and repay you for all your detestable
practices.
9 I will not look on you with pity;
I will not spare you.
I will repay you for your conduct
and for the detestable practices
among you.

"'Then you will know that it is I the LORD
who strikes you.

10 "'See, the day!
See, it comes!
Doom has burst forth,
the rod has budded,
arrogance has blossomed!
11 Violence has arisen,[c]
a rod to punish the wicked.
None of the people will be left,
none of that crowd—
none of their wealth,
nothing of value.
12 The time has come!
The day has arrived!
Let not the buyer rejoice
nor the seller grieve,
for my wrath is on the whole crowd.
13 The seller will not recover
the property that was sold—
as long as both buyer and seller live.
For the vision concerning the whole
crowd
will not be reversed.
Because of their sins, not one of them
will preserve their life.

14 "'They have blown the trumpet,
they have made all things ready,
but no one will go into battle,
for my wrath is on the whole crowd.
15 Outside is the sword;
inside are plague and famine.
Those in the country
will die by the sword;
those in the city
will be devoured by famine and
plague.
16 The fugitives who escape
will flee to the mountains.
Like doves of the valleys,
they will all moan,
each for their own sins.
17 Every hand will go limp;
every leg will be wet with urine.
18 They will put on sackcloth
and be clothed with terror.
Every face will be covered with shame,
and every head will be shaved.

[a] 14 Most Hebrew manuscripts; a few Hebrew manuscripts *Riblah* [b] 5 Most Hebrew manuscripts; some Hebrew manuscripts and Syriac *Disaster after* [c] 11 Or *The violent one has become*

[19] "'They will throw their silver into the
streets,
and their gold will be treated as a thing
unclean.
Their silver and gold
will not be able to deliver them
in the day of the LORD's wrath.
It will not satisfy their hunger
or fill their stomachs,
for it has caused them to stumble
into sin.
[20] They took pride in their beautiful jewelry
and used it to make their detestable
idols.
They made it into vile images;
therefore I will make it a thing unclean
for them.
[21] I will give their wealth as plunder to
foreigners
and as loot to the wicked of the earth,
who will defile it.
[22] I will turn my face away from the people,
and robbers will desecrate the place
I treasure.
They will enter it
and will defile it.

[23] "'Prepare chains!
For the land is full of bloodshed,
and the city is full of violence.
[24] I will bring the most wicked of nations
to take possession of their houses.
I will put an end to the pride of the
mighty,
and their sanctuaries will be
desecrated.
[25] When terror comes,
they will seek peace in vain.
[26] Calamity upon calamity will come,
and rumor upon rumor.
They will go searching for a vision from
the prophet,
priestly instruction in the law will
cease,
the counsel of the elders will come to
an end.
[27] The king will mourn,
the prince will be clothed with
despair,
and the hands of the people of the land
will tremble.
I will deal with them according to their
conduct,
and by their own standards I will
judge them.

"'Then they will know that I am the LORD.'"

Idolatry in the Temple

8 In the sixth year, in the sixth month on
the fifth day, while I was sitting in my
house and the elders of Judah were sitting
before me, the hand of the Sovereign LORD
came on me there. [2] I looked, and I saw a fig-
ure like that of a man.[a] From what appeared
to be his waist down he was like fire, and
from there up his appearance was as bright
as glowing metal. [3] He stretched out what
looked like a hand and took me by the hair
of my head. The Spirit lifted me up between
earth and heaven and in visions of God he
took me to Jerusalem, to the entrance of the
north gate of the inner court, where the idol
that provokes to jealousy stood. [4] And there
before me was the glory of the God of Israel,
as in the vision I had seen in the plain.

[5] Then he said to me, "Son of man, look to-
ward the north." So I looked, and in the en-
trance north of the gate of the altar I saw this
idol of jealousy.

[6] And he said to me, "Son of man, do you
see what they are doing—the utterly de-
testable things the Israelites are doing here,
things that will drive me far from my sanc-
tuary? But you will see things that are even
more detestable."

[7] Then he brought me to the entrance to
the court. I looked, and I saw a hole in the
wall. [8] He said to me, "Son of man, now dig
into the wall." So I dug into the wall and saw
a doorway there.

[9] And he said to me, "Go in and see the
wicked and detestable things they are do-
ing here." [10] So I went in and looked, and I
saw portrayed all over the walls all kinds
of crawling things and unclean animals
and all the idols of Israel. [11] In front of them
stood seventy elders of Israel, and Jaazaniah
son of Shaphan was standing among them.
Each had a censer in his hand, and a fragrant
cloud of incense was rising.

[12] He said to me, "Son of man, have you
seen what the elders of Israel are doing in
the darkness, each at the shrine of his own
idol? They say, 'The LORD does not see us;
the LORD has forsaken the land.'" [13] Again,

[a] 2 Or *saw a fiery figure*

he said, "You will see them doing things that are even more detestable."

[14]Then he brought me to the entrance of the north gate of the house of the LORD, and I saw women sitting there, mourning the god Tammuz. [15]He said to me, "Do you see this, son of man? You will see things that are even more detestable than this."

[16]He then brought me into the inner court of the house of the LORD, and there at the entrance to the temple, between the portico and the altar, were about twenty-five men. With their backs toward the temple of the LORD and their faces toward the east, they were bowing down to the sun in the east.

[17]He said to me, "Have you seen this, son of man? Is it a trivial matter for the people of Judah to do the detestable things they are doing here? Must they also fill the land with violence and continually arouse my anger? Look at them putting the branch to their nose! [18]Therefore I will deal with them in anger; I will not look on them with pity or spare them. Although they shout in my ears, I will not listen to them."

Judgment on the Idolaters

9 Then I heard him call out in a loud voice, "Bring near those who are appointed to execute judgment on the city, each with a weapon in his hand." [2]And I saw six men coming from the direction of the upper gate, which faces north, each with a deadly weapon in his hand. With them was a man clothed in linen who had a writing kit at his side. They came in and stood beside the bronze altar.

[3]Now the glory of the God of Israel went up from above the cherubim, where it had been, and moved to the threshold of the temple. Then the LORD called to the man clothed in linen who had the writing kit at his side [4]and said to him, "Go throughout the city of Jerusalem and put a mark on the foreheads of those who grieve and lament over all the detestable things that are done in it."

[5]As I listened, he said to the others, "Follow him through the city and kill, without showing pity or compassion. [6]Slaughter the old men, the young men and women, the mothers and children, but do not touch anyone who has the mark. Begin at my sanctuary." So they began with the old men who were in front of the temple.

[7]Then he said to them, "Defile the temple and fill the courts with the slain. Go!" So they went out and began killing throughout the city. [8]While they were killing and I was left alone, I fell facedown, crying out, "Alas, Sovereign LORD! Are you going to destroy the entire remnant of Israel in this outpouring of your wrath on Jerusalem?"

[9]He answered me, "The sin of the people of Israel and Judah is exceedingly great; the land is full of bloodshed and the city is full of injustice. They say, 'The LORD has forsaken the land; the LORD does not see.' [10]So I will not look on them with pity or spare them, but I will bring down on their own heads what they have done."

[11]Then the man in linen with the writing kit at his side brought back word, saying, "I have done as you commanded."

God's Glory Departs From the Temple

10 I looked, and I saw the likeness of a throne of lapis lazuli above the vault that was over the heads of the cherubim. [2]The LORD said to the man clothed in linen, "Go in among the wheels beneath the cherubim. Fill your hands with burning coals from among the cherubim and scatter them over the city." And as I watched, he went in.

[3]Now the cherubim were standing on the south side of the temple when the man went in, and a cloud filled the inner court. [4]Then the glory of the LORD rose from above the cherubim and moved to the threshold of the temple. The cloud filled the temple, and the court was full of the radiance of the glory of the LORD. [5]The sound of the wings of the cherubim could be heard as far away as the outer court, like the voice of God Almighty[a] when he speaks.

[6]When the LORD commanded the man in linen, "Take fire from among the wheels, from among the cherubim," the man went in and stood beside a wheel. [7]Then one of the cherubim reached out his hand to the fire that was among them. He took up some of it and put it into the hands of the man in linen, who took it and went out. [8](Under the wings of the cherubim could be seen what looked like human hands.)

[a] 5 Hebrew *El-Shaddai*

[9]I looked, and I saw beside the cherubim four wheels, one beside each of the cherubim; the wheels sparkled like topaz. [10]As for their appearance, the four of them looked alike; each was like a wheel intersecting a wheel. [11]As they moved, they would go in any one of the four directions the cherubim faced; the wheels did not turn about[a] as the cherubim went. The cherubim went in whatever direction the head faced, without turning as they went. [12]Their entire bodies, including their backs, their hands and their wings, were completely full of eyes, as were their four wheels. [13]I heard the wheels being called "the whirling wheels." [14]Each of the cherubim had four faces: One face was that of a cherub, the second the face of a human being, the third the face of a lion, and the fourth the face of an eagle.

[15]Then the cherubim rose upward. These were the living creatures I had seen by the Kebar River. [16]When the cherubim moved, the wheels beside them moved; and when the cherubim spread their wings to rise from the ground, the wheels did not leave their side. [17]When the cherubim stood still, they also stood still; and when the cherubim rose, they rose with them, because the spirit of the living creatures was in them.

[18]Then the glory of the LORD departed from over the threshold of the temple and stopped above the cherubim. [19]While I watched, the cherubim spread their wings and rose from the ground, and as they went, the wheels went with them. They stopped at the entrance of the east gate of the LORD's house, and the glory of the God of Israel was above them.

[20]These were the living creatures I had seen beneath the God of Israel by the Kebar River, and I realized that they were cherubim. [21]Each had four faces and four wings, and under their wings was what looked like human hands. [22]Their faces had the same appearance as those I had seen by the Kebar River. Each one went straight ahead.

God's Sure Judgment on Jerusalem

11 Then the Spirit lifted me up and brought me to the gate of the house of the LORD that faces east. There at the entrance of the gate were twenty-five men, and I saw among them Jaazaniah son of Azzur and Pelatiah son of Benaiah, leaders of the people. [2]The LORD said to me, "Son of man, these are the men who are plotting evil and giving wicked advice in this city. [3]They say, 'Haven't our houses been recently rebuilt? This city is a pot, and we are the meat in it.' [4]Therefore prophesy against them; prophesy, son of man."

[5]Then the Spirit of the LORD came on me, and he told me to say: "This is what the LORD says: That is what you are saying, you leaders in Israel, but I know what is going through your mind. [6]You have killed many people in this city and filled its streets with the dead.

[7]"Therefore this is what the Sovereign LORD says: The bodies you have thrown there are the meat and this city is the pot, but I will drive you out of it. [8]You fear the sword, and the sword is what I will bring against you, declares the Sovereign LORD. [9]I will drive you out of the city and deliver you into the hands of foreigners and inflict punishment on you. [10]You will fall by the sword, and I will execute judgment on you at the borders of Israel. Then you will know that I am the LORD. [11]This city will not be a pot for you, nor will you be the meat in it; I will execute judgment on you at the borders of Israel. [12]And you will know that I am the LORD, for you have not followed my decrees or kept my laws but have conformed to the standards of the nations around you."

[13]Now as I was prophesying, Pelatiah son of Benaiah died. Then I fell facedown and cried out in a loud voice, "Alas, Sovereign LORD! Will you completely destroy the remnant of Israel?"

The Promise of Israel's Return

[14]The word of the LORD came to me: [15]"Son of man, the people of Jerusalem have said of your fellow exiles and all the other Israelites, 'They are far away from the LORD; this land was given to us as our possession.'

[16]"Therefore say: 'This is what the Sovereign LORD says: Although I sent them far away among the nations and scattered them among the countries, yet for a little while I have been a sanctuary for them in the countries where they have gone.'

[a] *11* Or *aside*

[17]"Therefore say: 'This is what the Sovereign LORD says: I will gather you from the nations and bring you back from the countries where you have been scattered, and I will give you back the land of Israel again.'

[18]"They will return to it and remove all its vile images and detestable idols. [19]I will give them an undivided heart and put a new spirit in them; I will remove from them their heart of stone and give them a heart of flesh. [20]Then they will follow my decrees and be careful to keep my laws. They will be my people, and I will be their God. [21]But as for those whose hearts are devoted to their vile images and detestable idols, I will bring down on their own heads what they have done, declares the Sovereign LORD."

[22]Then the cherubim, with the wheels beside them, spread their wings, and the glory of the God of Israel was above them. [23]The glory of the LORD went up from within the city and stopped above the mountain east of it. [24]The Spirit lifted me up and brought me to the exiles in Babylonia[a] in the vision given by the Spirit of God.

Then the vision I had seen went up from me, [25]and I told the exiles everything the LORD had shown me.

The Exile Symbolized

12 The word of the LORD came to me: [2]"Son of man, you are living among a rebellious people. They have eyes to see but do not see and ears to hear but do not hear, for they are a rebellious people.

[3]"Therefore, son of man, pack your belongings for exile and in the daytime, as they watch, set out and go from where you are to another place. Perhaps they will understand, though they are a rebellious people. [4]During the daytime, while they watch, bring out your belongings packed for exile. Then in the evening, while they are watching, go out like those who go into exile. [5]While they watch, dig through the wall and take your belongings out through it. [6]Put them on your shoulder as they are watching and carry them out at dusk. Cover your face so that you cannot see the land, for I have made you a sign to the Israelites."

[7]So I did as I was commanded. During the day I brought out my things packed for exile. Then in the evening I dug through the wall with my hands. I took my belongings out at dusk, carrying them on my shoulders while they watched.

[8]In the morning the word of the LORD came to me: [9]"Son of man, did not the Israelites, that rebellious people, ask you, 'What are you doing?'

[10]"Say to them, 'This is what the Sovereign LORD says: This prophecy concerns the prince in Jerusalem and all the Israelites who are there.' [11]Say to them, 'I am a sign to you.'

"As I have done, so it will be done to them. They will go into exile as captives.

[12]"The prince among them will put his things on his shoulder at dusk and leave, and a hole will be dug in the wall for him to go through. He will cover his face so that he cannot see the land. [13]I will spread my net for him, and he will be caught in my snare; I will bring him to Babylonia, the land of the Chaldeans, but he will not see it, and there he will die. [14]I will scatter to the winds all those around him—his staff and all his troops—and I will pursue them with drawn sword.

[15]"They will know that I am the LORD, when I disperse them among the nations and scatter them through the countries. [16]But I will spare a few of them from the sword, famine and plague, so that in the nations where they go they may acknowledge all their detestable practices. Then they will know that I am the LORD."

[17]The word of the LORD came to me: [18]"Son of man, tremble as you eat your food, and shudder in fear as you drink your water. [19]Say to the people of the land: 'This is what the Sovereign LORD says about those living in Jerusalem and in the land of Israel: They will eat their food in anxiety and drink their water in despair, for their land will be stripped of everything in it because of the violence of all who live there. [20]The inhabited towns will be laid waste and the land will be desolate. Then you will know that I am the LORD.'"

There Will Be No Delay

[21]The word of the LORD came to me: [22]"Son of man, what is this proverb you have in the land of Israel: 'The days go by and every

[a] 24 Or *Chaldea*

vision comes to nothing'? 23 Say to them, 'This is what the Sovereign LORD says: I am going to put an end to this proverb, and they will no longer quote it in Israel.' Say to them, 'The days are near when every vision will be fulfilled. 24 For there will be no more false visions or flattering divinations among the people of Israel. 25 But I the LORD will speak what I will, and it shall be fulfilled without delay. For in your days, you rebellious people, I will fulfill whatever I say, declares the Sovereign LORD.' "

26 The word of the LORD came to me: 27 "Son of man, the Israelites are saying, 'The vision he sees is for many years from now, and he prophesies about the distant future.'

28 "Therefore say to them, 'This is what the Sovereign LORD says: None of my words will be delayed any longer; whatever I say will be fulfilled, declares the Sovereign LORD.' "

False Prophets Condemned

13 The word of the LORD came to me: 2 "Son of man, prophesy against the prophets of Israel who are now prophesying. Say to those who prophesy out of their own imagination: 'Hear the word of the LORD! 3 This is what the Sovereign LORD says: Woe to the foolish[a] prophets who follow their own spirit and have seen nothing! 4 Your prophets, Israel, are like jackals among ruins. 5 You have not gone up to the breaches in the wall to repair it for the people of Israel so that it will stand firm in the battle on the day of the LORD. 6 Their visions are false and their divinations a lie. Even though the LORD has not sent them, they say, "The LORD declares," and expect him to fulfill their words. 7 Have you not seen false visions and uttered lying divinations when you say, "The LORD declares," though I have not spoken?

8 " 'Therefore this is what the Sovereign LORD says: Because of your false words and lying visions, I am against you, declares the Sovereign LORD. 9 My hand will be against the prophets who see false visions and utter lying divinations. They will not belong to the council of my people or be listed in the records of Israel, nor will they enter the land of Israel. Then you will know that I am the Sovereign LORD.

10 " 'Because they lead my people astray, saying, "Peace," when there is no peace, and because, when a flimsy wall is built, they cover it with whitewash, 11 therefore tell those who cover it with whitewash that it is going to fall. Rain will come in torrents, and I will send hailstones hurtling down, and violent winds will burst forth. 12 When the wall collapses, will people not ask you, "Where is the whitewash you covered it with?"

13 " 'Therefore this is what the Sovereign LORD says: In my wrath I will unleash a violent wind, and in my anger hailstones and torrents of rain will fall with destructive fury. 14 I will tear down the wall you have covered with whitewash and will level it to the ground so that its foundation will be laid bare. When it[b] falls, you will be destroyed in it; and you will know that I am the LORD. 15 So I will pour out my wrath against the wall and against those who covered it with whitewash. I will say to you, "The wall is gone and so are those who whitewashed it, 16 those prophets of Israel who prophesied to Jerusalem and saw visions of peace for her when there was no peace, declares the Sovereign LORD." '

17 "Now, son of man, set your face against the daughters of your people who prophesy out of their own imagination. Prophesy against them 18 and say, 'This is what the Sovereign LORD says: Woe to the women who sew magic charms on all their wrists and make veils of various lengths for their heads in order to ensnare people. Will you ensnare the lives of my people but preserve your own? 19 You have profaned me among my people for a few handfuls of barley and scraps of bread. By lying to my people, who listen to lies, you have killed those who should not have died and have spared those who should not live.

20 " 'Therefore this is what the Sovereign LORD says: I am against your magic charms with which you ensnare people like birds and I will tear them from your arms; I will set free the people that you ensnare like birds. 21 I will tear off your veils and save my people from your hands, and they will no longer fall prey to your power. Then you will know that I am the LORD. 22 Because you disheartened the righteous with your lies, when I had brought them no grief, and

[a] 3 Or *wicked* [b] 14 Or *the city*

because you encouraged the wicked not to turn from their evil ways and so save their lives, [23]therefore you will no longer see false visions or practice divination. I will save my people from your hands. And then you will know that I am the LORD.' "

Idolaters Condemned

14 Some of the elders of Israel came to me and sat down in front of me. [2]Then the word of the LORD came to me: [3]"Son of man, these men have set up idols in their hearts and put wicked stumbling blocks before their faces. Should I let them inquire of me at all? [4]Therefore speak to them and tell them, 'This is what the Sovereign LORD says: When any of the Israelites set up idols in their hearts and put a wicked stumbling block before their faces and then go to a prophet, I the LORD will answer them myself in keeping with their great idolatry. [5]I will do this to recapture the hearts of the people of Israel, who have all deserted me for their idols.'

[6]"Therefore say to the people of Israel, 'This is what the Sovereign LORD says: Repent! Turn from your idols and renounce all your detestable practices!

[7]" 'When any of the Israelites or any foreigner residing in Israel separate themselves from me and set up idols in their hearts and put a wicked stumbling block before their faces and then go to a prophet to inquire of me, I the LORD will answer them myself. [8]I will set my face against them and make them an example and a byword. I will remove them from my people. Then you will know that I am the LORD.

[9]" 'And if the prophet is enticed to utter a prophecy, I the LORD have enticed that prophet, and I will stretch out my hand against him and destroy him from among my people Israel. [10]They will bear their guilt—the prophet will be as guilty as the one who consults him. [11]Then the people of Israel will no longer stray from me, nor will they defile themselves anymore with all their sins. They will be my people, and I will be their God, declares the Sovereign LORD.' "

Jerusalem's Judgment Inescapable

[12]The word of the LORD came to me: [13]"Son of man, if a country sins against me by being unfaithful and I stretch out my hand against it to cut off its food supply and send famine upon it and kill its people and their animals, [14]even if these three men—Noah, Daniel[a] and Job—were in it, they could save only themselves by their righteousness, declares the Sovereign LORD.

[15]"Or if I send wild beasts through that country and they leave it childless and it becomes desolate so that no one can pass through it because of the beasts, [16]as surely as I live, declares the Sovereign LORD, even if these three men were in it, they could not save their own sons or daughters. They alone would be saved, but the land would be desolate.

[17]"Or if I bring a sword against that country and say, 'Let the sword pass throughout the land,' and I kill its people and their animals, [18]as surely as I live, declares the Sovereign LORD, even if these three men were in it, they could not save their own sons or daughters. They alone would be saved.

[19]"Or if I send a plague into that land and pour out my wrath on it through bloodshed, killing its people and their animals, [20]as surely as I live, declares the Sovereign LORD, even if Noah, Daniel and Job were in it, they could save neither son nor daughter. They would save only themselves by their righteousness.

[21]"For this is what the Sovereign LORD says: How much worse will it be when I send against Jerusalem my four dreadful judgments—sword and famine and wild beasts and plague—to kill its men and their animals! [22]Yet there will be some survivors—sons and daughters who will be brought out of it. They will come to you, and when you see their conduct and their actions, you will be consoled regarding the disaster I have brought on Jerusalem—every disaster I have brought on it. [23]You will be consoled when you see their conduct and their actions, for you will know that I have done nothing in it without cause, declares the Sovereign LORD."

Jerusalem as a Useless Vine

15 The word of the LORD came to me: [2]"Son of man, how is the wood of a vine different from that of a branch from any

[a] *14* Or *Danel,* a man of renown in ancient literature; also in verse 20

of the trees in the forest? 3Is wood ever tak-
en from it to make anything useful? Do they
make pegs from it to hang things on? 4And af-
ter it is thrown on the fire as fuel and the fire
burns both ends and chars the middle, is it
then useful for anything? 5If it was not useful
for anything when it was whole, how much
less can it be made into something useful
when the fire has burned it and it is charred?
6"Therefore this is what the Sovereign
LORD says: As I have given the wood of the
vine among the trees of the forest as fuel for
the fire, so will I treat the people living in
Jerusalem. 7I will set my face against them.
Although they have come out of the fire, the
fire will yet consume them. And when I set
my face against them, you will know that I
am the LORD. 8I will make the land desolate
because they have been unfaithful, declares
the Sovereign LORD."

Jerusalem as an Adulterous Wife

16 The word of the LORD came to me:
2"Son of man, confront Jerusalem
with her detestable practices 3and say, 'This
is what the Sovereign LORD says to Jerusa-
lem: Your ancestry and birth were in the
land of the Canaanites; your father was an
Amorite and your mother a Hittite. 4On the
day you were born your cord was not cut,
nor were you washed with water to make
you clean, nor were you rubbed with salt or
wrapped in cloths. 5No one looked on you
with pity or had compassion enough to do
any of these things for you. Rather, you were
thrown out into the open field, for on the day
you were born you were despised.
6" 'Then I passed by and saw you kicking
about in your blood, and as you lay there in
your blood I said to you, "Live!"[a] 7I made you
grow like a plant of the field. You grew and
developed and entered puberty. Your breasts
had formed and your hair had grown, yet
you were stark naked.
8" 'Later I passed by, and when I looked
at you and saw that you were old enough for
love, I spread the corner of my garment over
you and covered your naked body. I gave you
my solemn oath and entered into a covenant
with you, declares the Sovereign LORD, and
you became mine.
9" 'I bathed you with water and washed
the blood from you and put ointments on
you. 10I clothed you with an embroidered
dress and put sandals of fine leather on you.
I dressed you in fine linen and covered you
with costly garments. 11I adorned you with
jewelry: I put bracelets on your arms and
a necklace around your neck, 12and I put
a ring on your nose, earrings on your ears
and a beautiful crown on your head. 13So
you were adorned with gold and silver; your
clothes were of fine linen and costly fabric
and embroidered cloth. Your food was hon-
ey, olive oil and the finest flour. You became
very beautiful and rose to be a queen. 14And
your fame spread among the nations on ac-
count of your beauty, because the splendor I
had given you made your beauty perfect, de-
clares the Sovereign LORD.
15" 'But you trusted in your beauty and
used your fame to become a prostitute. You
lavished your favors on anyone who passed
by and your beauty became his. 16You took
some of your garments to make gaudy high
places, where you carried on your prosti-
tution. You went to him, and he possessed
your beauty.[b] 17You also took the fine jew-
elry I gave you, the jewelry made of my gold
and silver, and you made for yourself male
idols and engaged in prostitution with them.
18And you took your embroidered clothes
to put on them, and you offered my oil and
incense before them. 19Also the food I pro-
vided for you — the flour, olive oil and honey
I gave you to eat — you offered as fragrant in-
cense before them. That is what happened,
declares the Sovereign LORD.
20" 'And you took your sons and daughters
whom you bore to me and sacrificed them as
food to the idols. Was your prostitution not
enough? 21You slaughtered my children and
sacrificed them to the idols. 22In all your de-
testable practices and your prostitution you
did not remember the days of your youth,
when you were naked and bare, kicking
about in your blood.
23" 'Woe! Woe to you, declares the Sover-
eign LORD. In addition to all your other wick-
edness, 24you built a mound for yourself and
made a lofty shrine in every public square.
25At every street corner you built your lofty

[a] 6 A few Hebrew manuscripts, Septuagint and Syriac; most Hebrew manuscripts repeat *and as you lay there in your blood I said to you, "Live!"* [b] 16 The meaning of the Hebrew for this sentence is uncertain.

shrines and degraded your beauty, spread-
ing your legs with increasing promiscuity
to anyone who passed by. 26You engaged in
prostitution with the Egyptians, your neigh-
bors with large genitals, and aroused my an-
ger with your increasing promiscuity. 27So I
stretched out my hand against you and re-
duced your territory; I gave you over to the
greed of your enemies, the daughters of the
Philistines, who were shocked by your lewd
conduct. 28You engaged in prostitution with
the Assyrians too, because you were insa-
tiable; and even after that, you still were not
satisfied. 29Then you increased your pro-
miscuity to include Babylonia,[a] a land of
merchants, but even with this you were not
satisfied.

30" 'I am filled with fury against you,[b] de-
clares the Sovereign LORD, when you do all
these things, acting like a brazen prosti-
tute! 31When you built your mounds at every
street corner and made your lofty shrines in
every public square, you were unlike a pros-
titute, because you scorned payment.

32" 'You adulterous wife! You prefer
strangers to your own husband! 33All pros-
titutes receive gifts, but you give gifts to all
your lovers, bribing them to come to you
from everywhere for your illicit favors. 34So
in your prostitution you are the opposite of
others; no one runs after you for your favors.
You are the very opposite, for you give pay-
ment and none is given to you.

35" 'Therefore, you prostitute, hear the
word of the LORD! 36This is what the Sov-
ereign LORD says: Because you poured out
your lust and exposed your naked body in
your promiscuity with your lovers, and be-
cause of all your detestable idols, and be-
cause you gave them your children's blood,
37therefore I am going to gather all your lov-
ers, with whom you found pleasure, those
you loved as well as those you hated. I will
gather them against you from all around and
will strip you in front of them, and they will
see you stark naked. 38I will sentence you
to the punishment of women who commit
adultery and who shed blood; I will bring on
you the blood vengeance of my wrath and
jealous anger. 39Then I will deliver you into
the hands of your lovers, and they will tear
down your mounds and destroy your lofty
shrines. They will strip you of your clothes
and take your fine jewelry and leave you
stark naked. 40They will bring a mob against
you, who will stone you and hack you to piec-
es with their swords. 41They will burn down
your houses and inflict punishment on you
in the sight of many women. I will put a stop
to your prostitution, and you will no longer
pay your lovers. 42Then my wrath against
you will subside and my jealous anger will
turn away from you; I will be calm and no
longer angry.

43" 'Because you did not remember the
days of your youth but enraged me with all
these things, I will surely bring down on
your head what you have done, declares the
Sovereign LORD. Did you not add lewdness
to all your other detestable practices?

44" 'Everyone who quotes proverbs will
quote this proverb about you: "Like moth-
er, like daughter." 45You are a true daughter
of your mother, who despised her husband
and her children; and you are a true sister of
your sisters, who despised their husbands
and their children. Your mother was a Hit-
tite and your father an Amorite. 46Your older
sister was Samaria, who lived to the north of
you with her daughters; and your younger
sister, who lived to the south of you with her
daughters, was Sodom. 47You not only fol-
lowed their ways and copied their detestable
practices, but in all your ways you soon be-
came more depraved than they. 48As surely
as I live, declares the Sovereign LORD, your
sister Sodom and her daughters never did
what you and your daughters have done.

49" 'Now this was the sin of your sister Sod-
om: She and her daughters were arrogant,
overfed and unconcerned; they did not help
the poor and needy. 50They were haughty
and did detestable things before me. There-
fore I did away with them as you have seen.
51Samaria did not commit half the sins you
did. You have done more detestable things
than they, and have made your sisters seem
righteous by all these things you have done.
52Bear your disgrace, for you have furnished
some justification for your sisters. Because
your sins were more vile than theirs, they
appear more righteous than you. So then,
be ashamed and bear your disgrace, for you
have made your sisters appear righteous.

53" 'However, I will restore the fortunes
of Sodom and her daughters and of Samaria

[a] 29 Or *Chaldea* [b] 30 Or *How feverish is your heart,*

and her daughters, and your fortunes along with them, [54]so that you may bear your disgrace and be ashamed of all you have done in giving them comfort. [55]And your sisters, Sodom with her daughters and Samaria with her daughters, will return to what they were before; and you and your daughters will return to what you were before. [56]You would not even mention your sister Sodom in the day of your pride, [57]before your wickedness was uncovered. Even so, you are now scorned by the daughters of Edom[a] and all her neighbors and the daughters of the Philistines—all those around you who despise you. [58]You will bear the consequences of your lewdness and your detestable practices, declares the LORD.

[59]" 'This is what the Sovereign LORD says: I will deal with you as you deserve, because you have despised my oath by breaking the covenant. [60]Yet I will remember the covenant I made with you in the days of your youth, and I will establish an everlasting covenant with you. [61]Then you will remember your ways and be ashamed when you receive your sisters, both those who are older than you and those who are younger. I will give them to you as daughters, but not on the basis of my covenant with you. [62]So I will establish my covenant with you, and you will know that I am the LORD. [63]Then, when I make atonement for you for all you have done, you will remember and be ashamed and never again open your mouth because of your humiliation, declares the Sovereign LORD.' "

Two Eagles and a Vine

17 The word of the LORD came to me: [2]"Son of man, set forth an allegory and tell it to the Israelites as a parable. [3]Say to them, 'This is what the Sovereign LORD says: A great eagle with powerful wings, long feathers and full plumage of varied colors came to Lebanon. Taking hold of the top of a cedar, [4]he broke off its topmost shoot and carried it away to a land of merchants, where he planted it in a city of traders.

[5]" 'He took one of the seedlings of the land and put it in fertile soil. He planted it like a willow by abundant water, [6]and it sprouted and became a low, spreading vine. Its branches turned toward him, but its roots remained under it. So it became a vine and produced branches and put out leafy boughs.

[7]" 'But there was another great eagle with powerful wings and full plumage. The vine now sent out its roots toward him from the plot where it was planted and stretched out its branches to him for water. [8]It had been planted in good soil by abundant water so that it would produce branches, bear fruit and become a splendid vine.'

[9]"Say to them, 'This is what the Sovereign LORD says: Will it thrive? Will it not be uprooted and stripped of its fruit so that it withers? All its new growth will wither. It will not take a strong arm or many people to pull it up by the roots. [10]It has been planted, but will it thrive? Will it not wither completely when the east wind strikes it—wither away in the plot where it grew?' "

[11]Then the word of the LORD came to me: [12]"Say to this rebellious people, 'Do you not know what these things mean?' Say to them: 'The king of Babylon went to Jerusalem and carried off her king and her nobles, bringing them back with him to Babylon. [13]Then he took a member of the royal family and made a treaty with him, putting him under oath. He also carried away the leading men of the land, [14]so that the kingdom would be brought low, unable to rise again, surviving only by keeping his treaty. [15]But the king rebelled against him by sending his envoys to Egypt to get horses and a large army. Will he succeed? Will he who does such things escape? Will he break the treaty and yet escape?

[16]" 'As surely as I live, declares the Sovereign LORD, he shall die in Babylon, in the land of the king who put him on the throne, whose oath he despised and whose treaty he broke. [17]Pharaoh with his mighty army and great horde will be of no help to him in war, when ramps are built and siege works erected to destroy many lives. [18]He despised the oath by breaking the covenant. Because he had given his hand in pledge and yet did all these things, he shall not escape.

[19]" 'Therefore this is what the Sovereign LORD says: As surely as I live, I will repay him for despising my oath and breaking my covenant. [20]I will spread my net for him, and

[a] 57 Many Hebrew manuscripts and Syriac; most Hebrew manuscripts, Septuagint and Vulgate *Aram*

he will be caught in my snare. I will bring
him to Babylon and execute judgment on
him there because he was unfaithful to me.
21 All his choice troops will fall by the sword,
and the survivors will be scattered to the
winds. Then you will know that I the LORD
have spoken.

22 "'This is what the Sovereign LORD says:
I myself will take a shoot from the very top of
a cedar and plant it; I will break off a tender
sprig from its topmost shoots and plant it on
a high and lofty mountain. 23 On the moun-
tain heights of Israel I will plant it; it will pro-
duce branches and bear fruit and become a
splendid cedar. Birds of every kind will nest
in it; they will find shelter in the shade of its
branches. 24 All the trees of the forest will
know that I the LORD bring down the tall tree
and make the low tree grow tall. I dry up the
green tree and make the dry tree flourish.

"'I the LORD have spoken, and I will
do it.'"

The One Who Sins Will Die

18 The word of the LORD came to me:
2 "What do you people mean by quot-
ing this proverb about the land of Israel:

> "'The parents eat sour grapes,
> and the children's teeth are set on
> edge'?

3 "As surely as I live, declares the Sover-
eign LORD, you will no longer quote this
proverb in Israel. 4 For everyone belongs to
me, the parent as well as the child—both
alike belong to me. The one who sins is the
one who will die.

> 5 "Suppose there is a righteous man
> who does what is just and right.
> 6 He does not eat at the mountain shrines
> or look to the idols of Israel.
> He does not defile his neighbor's wife
> or have sexual relations with a woman
> during her period.
> 7 He does not oppress anyone,
> but returns what he took in pledge
> for a loan.
> He does not commit robbery
> but gives his food to the hungry
> and provides clothing for the naked.
> 8 He does not lend to them at interest
> or take a profit from them.
> He withholds his hand from doing wrong
> and judges fairly between two parties.
> 9 He follows my decrees
> and faithfully keeps my laws.
> That man is righteous;
> he will surely live,
> declares the Sovereign LORD.

10 "Suppose he has a violent son, who
sheds blood or does any of these other
things[a] 11 (though the father has done none
of them):

> "He eats at the mountain shrines.
> He defiles his neighbor's wife.
> 12 He oppresses the poor and needy.
> He commits robbery.
> He does not return what he took in
> pledge.
> He looks to the idols.
> He does detestable things.
> 13 He lends at interest and takes a profit.

Will such a man live? He will not! Because he
has done all these detestable things, he is to
be put to death; his blood will be on his own
head.

14 "But suppose this son has a son who sees
all the sins his father commits, and though
he sees them, he does not do such things:

> 15 "He does not eat at the mountain shrines
> or look to the idols of Israel.
> He does not defile his neighbor's wife.
> 16 He does not oppress anyone
> or require a pledge for a loan.
> He does not commit robbery
> but gives his food to the hungry
> and provides clothing for the naked.
> 17 He withholds his hand from mistreating
> the poor
> and takes no interest or profit
> from them.
> He keeps my laws and follows my
> decrees.

He will not die for his father's sin; he will
surely live. 18 But his father will die for his
own sin, because he practiced extortion,
robbed his brother and did what was wrong
among his people.

19 "Yet you ask, 'Why does the son not
share the guilt of his father?' Since the son
has done what is just and right and has been
careful to keep all my decrees, he will surely

[a] 10 Or *things to a brother*

live. [20]The one who sins is the one who will
die. The child will not share the guilt of the
parent, nor will the parent share the guilt of
the child. The righteousness of the righteous
will be credited to them, and the wickedness
of the wicked will be charged against them.
[21]"But if a wicked person turns away
from all the sins they have committed and
keeps all my decrees and does what is just
and right, that person will surely live; they
will not die. [22]None of the offenses they have
committed will be remembered against
them. Because of the righteous things they
have done, they will live. [23]Do I take any
pleasure in the death of the wicked? declares the Sovereign LORD. Rather, am I not
pleased when they turn from their ways and
live?
[24]"But if a righteous person turns from
their righteousness and commits sin and
does the same detestable things the wicked
person does, will they live? None of the righteous things that person has done will be
remembered. Because of the unfaithfulness
they are guilty of and because of the sins
they have committed, they will die.
[25]"Yet you say, 'The way of the Lord is
not just.' Hear, you Israelites: Is my way unjust? Is it not your ways that are unjust? [26]If
a righteous person turns from their righteousness and commits sin, they will die for
it; because of the sin they have committed
they will die. [27]But if a wicked person turns
away from the wickedness they have committed and does what is just and right, they
will save their life. [28]Because they consider
all the offenses they have committed and
turn away from them, that person will surely live; they will not die. [29]Yet the Israelites
say, 'The way of the Lord is not just.' Are my
ways unjust, people of Israel? Is it not your
ways that are unjust?
[30]"Therefore, you Israelites, I will judge
each of you according to your own ways,
declares the Sovereign LORD. Repent! Turn
away from all your offenses; then sin will
not be your downfall. [31]Rid yourselves of all
the offenses you have committed, and get a
new heart and a new spirit. Why will you die,
people of Israel? [32]For I take no pleasure in
the death of anyone, declares the Sovereign
LORD. Repent and live!

A Lament Over Israel's Princes

19 "Take up a lament concerning the princes of Israel [2]and say:

"'What a lioness was your mother
among the lions!
She lay down among them
and reared her cubs.
[3]She brought up one of her cubs,
and he became a strong lion.
He learned to tear the prey
and he became a man-eater.
[4]The nations heard about him,
and he was trapped in their pit.
They led him with hooks
to the land of Egypt.

[5]"'When she saw her hope unfulfilled,
her expectation gone,
she took another of her cubs
and made him a strong lion.
[6]He prowled among the lions,
for he was now a strong lion.
He learned to tear the prey
and he became a man-eater.
[7]He broke down[a] their strongholds
and devastated their towns.
The land and all who were in it
were terrified by his roaring.
[8]Then the nations came against him,
those from regions round about.
They spread their net for him,
and he was trapped in their pit.
[9]With hooks they pulled him into a cage
and brought him to the king of Babylon.
They put him in prison,
so his roar was heard no longer
on the mountains of Israel.

[10]"'Your mother was like a vine in your vineyard[b]
planted by the water;
it was fruitful and full of branches
because of abundant water.
[11]Its branches were strong,
fit for a ruler's scepter.
It towered high
above the thick foliage,
conspicuous for its height
and for its many branches.
[12]But it was uprooted in fury
and thrown to the ground.

[a] 7 Targum (see Septuagint); Hebrew *He knew* manuscripts *your blood*

[b] 10 Two Hebrew manuscripts; most Hebrew

The east wind made it shrivel,
  it was stripped of its fruit;
its strong branches withered
  and fire consumed them.
13 Now it is planted in the desert,
  in a dry and thirsty land.
14 Fire spread from one of its main[a]
    branches
  and consumed its fruit.
No strong branch is left on it
  fit for a ruler's scepter.'

"This is a lament and is to be used as a la-
ment."

Rebellious Israel Purged

20 In the seventh year, in the fifth
month on the tenth day, some of the
elders of Israel came to inquire of the LORD,
and they sat down in front of me.
2 Then the word of the LORD came to me:
3 "Son of man, speak to the elders of Israel
and say to them, 'This is what the Sovereign
LORD says: Have you come to inquire of me?
As surely as I live, I will not let you inquire of
me, declares the Sovereign LORD.'
4 "Will you judge them? Will you judge
them, son of man? Then confront them with
the detestable practices of their ancestors
5 and say to them: 'This is what the Sover-
eign LORD says: On the day I chose Israel,
I swore with uplifted hand to the descen-
dants of Jacob and revealed myself to them
in Egypt. With uplifted hand I said to them,
"I am the LORD your God." 6 On that day I
swore to them that I would bring them out
of Egypt into a land I had searched out for
them, a land flowing with milk and honey,
the most beautiful of all lands. 7 And I said to
them, "Each of you, get rid of the vile images
you have set your eyes on, and do not defile
yourselves with the idols of Egypt. I am the
LORD your God."
8 " 'But they rebelled against me and
would not listen to me; they did not get rid
of the vile images they had set their eyes on,
nor did they forsake the idols of Egypt. So I
said I would pour out my wrath on them and
spend my anger against them in Egypt. 9 But
for the sake of my name, I brought them out
of Egypt. I did it to keep my name from being
profaned in the eyes of the nations among
whom they lived and in whose sight I had re-
vealed myself to the Israelites. 10 Therefore I
led them out of Egypt and brought them into
the wilderness. 11 I gave them my decrees
and made known to them my laws, by which
the person who obeys them will live. 12 Also
I gave them my Sabbaths as a sign between
us, so they would know that I the LORD made
them holy.
13 " 'Yet the people of Israel rebelled
against me in the wilderness. They did not
follow my decrees but rejected my laws — by
which the person who obeys them will live —
and they utterly desecrated my Sabbaths. So
I said I would pour out my wrath on them
and destroy them in the wilderness. 14 But for
the sake of my name I did what would keep
it from being profaned in the eyes of the na-
tions in whose sight I had brought them out.
15 Also with uplifted hand I swore to them in
the wilderness that I would not bring them
into the land I had given them — a land flow-
ing with milk and honey, the most beautiful
of all lands — 16 because they rejected my
laws and did not follow my decrees and des-
ecrated my Sabbaths. For their hearts were
devoted to their idols. 17 Yet I looked on them
with pity and did not destroy them or put
an end to them in the wilderness. 18 I said to
their children in the wilderness, "Do not fol-
low the statutes of your parents or keep their
laws or defile yourselves with their idols. 19 I
am the LORD your God; follow my decrees
and be careful to keep my laws. 20 Keep my
Sabbaths holy, that they may be a sign be-
tween us. Then you will know that I am the
LORD your God."
21 " 'But the children rebelled against me:
They did not follow my decrees, they were
not careful to keep my laws, of which I said,
"The person who obeys them will live by
them," and they desecrated my Sabbaths.
So I said I would pour out my wrath on them
and spend my anger against them in the wil-
derness. 22 But I withheld my hand, and for
the sake of my name I did what would keep
it from being profaned in the eyes of the na-
tions in whose sight I had brought them out.
23 Also with uplifted hand I swore to them
in the wilderness that I would disperse
them among the nations and scatter them
through the countries, 24 because they had
not obeyed my laws but had rejected my de-
crees and desecrated my Sabbaths, and their

[a] 14 Or *from under its*

eyes lusted after their parents' idols. 25 So I
gave them other statutes that were not good
and laws through which they could not live;
26 I defiled them through their gifts — the
sacrifice of every firstborn — that I might fill
them with horror so they would know that I
am the LORD.'
27 "Therefore, son of man, speak to the
people of Israel and say to them, 'This is
what the Sovereign LORD says: In this also
your ancestors blasphemed me by being un-
faithful to me: 28 When I brought them into
the land I had sworn to give them and they
saw any high hill or any leafy tree, there they
offered their sacrifices, made offerings that
aroused my anger, presented their fragrant
incense and poured out their drink offerings.
29 Then I said to them: What is this high place
you go to?' " (It is called Bamah[a] to this day.)

Rebellious Israel Renewed

30 "Therefore say to the Israelites: 'This is
what the Sovereign LORD says: Will you de-
file yourselves the way your ancestors did
and lust after their vile images? 31 When
you offer your gifts — the sacrifice of your
children in the fire — you continue to de-
file yourselves with all your idols to this day.
Am I to let you inquire of me, you Israelites?
As surely as I live, declares the Sovereign
LORD, I will not let you inquire of me.
32 " 'You say, "We want to be like the na-
tions, like the peoples of the world, who
serve wood and stone." But what you have in
mind will never happen. 33 As surely as I live,
declares the Sovereign LORD, I will reign
over you with a mighty hand and an out-
stretched arm and with outpoured wrath.
34 I will bring you from the nations and gath-
er you from the countries where you have
been scattered — with a mighty hand and
an outstretched arm and with outpoured
wrath. 35 I will bring you into the wilderness
of the nations and there, face to face, I will
execute judgment upon you. 36 As I judged
your ancestors in the wilderness of the land
of Egypt, so I will judge you, declares the
Sovereign LORD. 37 I will take note of you as
you pass under my rod, and I will bring you
into the bond of the covenant. 38 I will purge
you of those who revolt and rebel against me.
Although I will bring them out of the land
where they are living, yet they will not enter
the land of Israel. Then you will know that I
am the LORD.
39 " 'As for you, people of Israel, this is what
the Sovereign LORD says: Go and serve your
idols, every one of you! But afterward you
will surely listen to me and no longer pro-
fane my holy name with your gifts and idols.
40 For on my holy mountain, the high moun-
tain of Israel, declares the Sovereign LORD,
there in the land all the people of Israel will
serve me, and there I will accept them. There
I will require your offerings and your choice
gifts,[b] along with all your holy sacrifices. 41 I
will accept you as fragrant incense when I
bring you out from the nations and gather
you from the countries where you have been
scattered, and I will be proved holy through
you in the sight of the nations. 42 Then you
will know that I am the LORD, when I bring
you into the land of Israel, the land I had
sworn with uplifted hand to give to your
ancestors. 43 There you will remember your
conduct and all the actions by which you
have defiled yourselves, and you will loathe
yourselves for all the evil you have done.
44 You will know that I am the LORD, when I
deal with you for my name's sake and not ac-
cording to your evil ways and your corrupt
practices, you people of Israel, declares the
Sovereign LORD.' "

Prophecy Against the South

45 The word of the LORD came to me:
46 "Son of man, set your face toward the
south; preach against the south and proph-
esy against the forest of the southland. 47 Say
to the southern forest: 'Hear the word of the
LORD. This is what the Sovereign LORD says:
I am about to set fire to you, and it will con-
sume all your trees, both green and dry. The
blazing flame will not be quenched, and ev-
ery face from south to north will be scorched
by it. 48 Everyone will see that I the LORD
have kindled it; it will not be quenched.' "
49 Then I said, "Sovereign LORD, they are
saying of me, 'Isn't he just telling parables?' "[c]

Babylon as God's Sword of Judgment

21 [d] The word of the LORD came to me:
2 "Son of man, set your face against
Jerusalem and preach against the sanctuary.

[a] 29 *Bamah* means *high place.* [b] 40 Or *and the gifts of your firstfruits* [c] 49 In Hebrew texts 20:45-49 is numbered 21:1-5. [d] In Hebrew texts 21:1-32 is numbered 21:6-37.

Prophesy against the land of Israel 3and say to
her: 'This is what the LORD says: I am against
you. I will draw my sword from its sheath and
cut off from you both the righteous and the
wicked. 4Because I am going to cut off the
righteous and the wicked, my sword will be
unsheathed against everyone from south to
north. 5Then all people will know that I the
LORD have drawn my sword from its sheath; it
will not return again.'

6"Therefore groan, son of man! Groan
before them with broken heart and bitter
grief. 7And when they ask you, 'Why are you
groaning?' you shall say, 'Because of the
news that is coming. Every heart will melt
with fear and every hand go limp; every spir-
it will become faint and every leg will be wet
with urine.' It is coming! It will surely take
place, declares the Sovereign LORD."

8The word of the LORD came to me: 9"Son
of man, prophesy and say, 'This is what the
Lord says:

"'A sword, a sword,
  sharpened and polished—
10sharpened for the slaughter,
  polished to flash like lightning!

"'Shall we rejoice in the scepter of my roy-
al son? The sword despises every such stick.

11"'The sword is appointed to be polished,
  to be grasped with the hand;
it is sharpened and polished,
  made ready for the hand of the slayer.
12Cry out and wail, son of man,
  for it is against my people;
  it is against all the princes of Israel.
They are thrown to the sword
  along with my people.
Therefore beat your breast.

13"'Testing will surely come. And what if
even the scepter, which the sword despises,
does not continue? declares the Sovereign
LORD.'

14"So then, son of man, prophesy
  and strike your hands together.
Let the sword strike twice,
  even three times.
It is a sword for slaughter—
  a sword for great slaughter,
  closing in on them from every side.
15So that hearts may melt with fear
  and the fallen be many,
I have stationed the sword for slaughter[a]
  at all their gates.
Look! It is forged to strike like lightning,
  it is grasped for slaughter.
16Slash to the right, you sword,
  then to the left,
  wherever your blade is turned.
17I too will strike my hands together,
  and my wrath will subside.
I the LORD have spoken."

18The word of the LORD came to me:
19"Son of man, mark out two roads for the
sword of the king of Babylon to take, both
starting from the same country. Make a
signpost where the road branches off to
the city. 20Mark out one road for the sword
to come against Rabbah of the Ammonites
and another against Judah and fortified Je-
rusalem. 21For the king of Babylon will stop
at the fork in the road, at the junction of the
two roads, to seek an omen: He will cast lots
with arrows, he will consult his idols, he will
examine the liver. 22Into his right hand will
come the lot for Jerusalem, where he is to
set up battering rams, to give the command
to slaughter, to sound the battle cry, to set
battering rams against the gates, to build a
ramp and to erect siege works. 23It will seem
like a false omen to those who have sworn al-
legiance to him, but he will remind them of
their guilt and take them captive.

24"Therefore this is what the Sover-
eign LORD says: 'Because you people have
brought to mind your guilt by your open re-
bellion, revealing your sins in all that you
do—because you have done this, you will be
taken captive.

25"'You profane and wicked prince of Is-
rael, whose day has come, whose time of
punishment has reached its climax, 26this is
what the Sovereign LORD says: Take off the
turban, remove the crown. It will not be as
it was: The lowly will be exalted and the ex-
alted will be brought low. 27A ruin! A ruin! I
will make it a ruin! The crown will not be re-
stored until he to whom it rightfully belongs
shall come; to him I will give it.'

28"And you, son of man, prophesy and say,
'This is what the Sovereign LORD says about
the Ammonites and their insults:

[a] *15* Septuagint; the meaning of the Hebrew for this word is uncertain.

" 'A sword, a sword,
drawn for the slaughter,
polished to consume
and to flash like lightning!
29 Despite false visions concerning you
and lying divinations about you,
it will be laid on the necks
of the wicked who are to be slain,
whose day has come,
whose time of punishment has
reached its climax.

30 " 'Let the sword return to its sheath.
In the place where you were created,
in the land of your ancestry,
I will judge you.
31 I will pour out my wrath on you
and breathe out my fiery anger
against you;
I will deliver you into the hands of
brutal men,
men skilled in destruction.
32 You will be fuel for the fire,
your blood will be shed in your land,
you will be remembered no more;
for I the LORD have spoken.' "

Judgment on Jerusalem's Sins

22 The word of the LORD came to me:
2 "Son of man, will you judge her? Will you
judge this city of bloodshed? Then confront
her with all her detestable practices 3 and
say: 'This is what the Sovereign LORD says:
You city that brings on herself doom by shed-
ding blood in her midst and defiles herself
by making idols, 4 you have become guilty
because of the blood you have shed and have
become defiled by the idols you have made.
You have brought your days to a close, and
the end of your years has come. Therefore I
will make you an object of scorn to the na-
tions and a laughingstock to all the coun-
tries. 5 Those who are near and those who are
far away will mock you, you infamous city,
full of turmoil.
6 " 'See how each of the princes of Israel
who are in you uses his power to shed blood.
7 In you they have treated father and mother
with contempt; in you they have oppressed
the foreigner and mistreated the fatherless
and the widow. 8 You have despised my holy
things and desecrated my Sabbaths. 9 In you
are slanderers who are bent on shedding
blood; in you are those who eat at the moun-
tain shrines and commit lewd acts. 10 In you
are those who dishonor their father's bed;
in you are those who violate women dur-
ing their period, when they are ceremoni-
ally unclean. 11 In you one man commits a
detestable offense with his neighbor's wife,
another shamefully defiles his daughter-in-
law, and another violates his sister, his own
father's daughter. 12 In you are people who
accept bribes to shed blood; you take inter-
est and make a profit from the poor. You ex-
tort unjust gain from your neighbors. And
you have forgotten me, declares the Sover-
eign LORD.
13 " 'I will surely strike my hands togeth-
er at the unjust gain you have made and
at the blood you have shed in your midst.
14 Will your courage endure or your hands be
strong in the day I deal with you? I the LORD
have spoken, and I will do it. 15 I will dis-
perse you among the nations and scatter you
through the countries; and I will put an end
to your uncleanness. 16 When you have been
defiled[a] in the eyes of the nations, you will
know that I am the LORD.' "
17 Then the word of the LORD came to me:
18 "Son of man, the people of Israel have be-
come dross to me; all of them are the copper,
tin, iron and lead left inside a furnace. They
are but the dross of silver. 19 Therefore this is
what the Sovereign LORD says: 'Because you
have all become dross, I will gather you into
Jerusalem. 20 As silver, copper, iron, lead and
tin are gathered into a furnace to be melted
with a fiery blast, so will I gather you in my
anger and my wrath and put you inside the
city and melt you. 21 I will gather you and I
will blow on you with my fiery wrath, and
you will be melted inside her. 22 As silver is
melted in a furnace, so you will be melted in-
side her, and you will know that I the LORD
have poured out my wrath on you.' "
23 Again the word of the LORD came to
me: 24 "Son of man, say to the land, 'You
are a land that has not been cleansed or
rained on in the day of wrath.' 25 There is a
conspiracy of her princes[b] within her like
a roaring lion tearing its prey; they devour
people, take treasures and precious things
and make many widows within her. 26 Her

[a] 16 Or *When I have allotted you your inheritance* [b] 25 Septuagint; Hebrew *prophets*

priests do violence to my law and profane my holy things; they do not distinguish between the holy and the common; they teach that there is no difference between the unclean and the clean; and they shut their eyes to the keeping of my Sabbaths, so that I am profaned among them. 27 Her officials within her are like wolves tearing their prey; they shed blood and kill people to make unjust gain. 28 Her prophets whitewash these deeds for them by false visions and lying divinations. They say, 'This is what the Sovereign LORD says' — when the LORD has not spoken. 29 The people of the land practice extortion and commit robbery; they oppress the poor and needy and mistreat the foreigner, denying them justice.

30 "I looked for someone among them who would build up the wall and stand before me in the gap on behalf of the land so I would not have to destroy it, but I found no one. 31 So I will pour out my wrath on them and consume them with my fiery anger, bringing down on their own heads all they have done, declares the Sovereign LORD."

Two Adulterous Sisters

23 The word of the LORD came to me: 2 "Son of man, there were two women, daughters of the same mother. 3 They became prostitutes in Egypt, engaging in prostitution from their youth. In that land their breasts were fondled and their virgin bosoms caressed. 4 The older was named Oholah, and her sister was Oholibah. They were mine and gave birth to sons and daughters. Oholah is Samaria, and Oholibah is Jerusalem.

5 "Oholah engaged in prostitution while she was still mine; and she lusted after her lovers, the Assyrians — warriors 6 clothed in blue, governors and commanders, all of them handsome young men, and mounted horsemen. 7 She gave herself as a prostitute to all the elite of the Assyrians and defiled herself with all the idols of everyone she lusted after. 8 She did not give up the prostitution she began in Egypt, when during her youth men slept with her, caressed her virgin bosom and poured out their lust on her.

9 "Therefore I delivered her into the hands of her lovers, the Assyrians, for whom she lusted. 10 They stripped her naked, took away her sons and daughters and killed her with the sword. She became a byword among women, and punishment was inflicted on her.

11 "Her sister Oholibah saw this, yet in her lust and prostitution she was more depraved than her sister. 12 She too lusted after the Assyrians — governors and commanders, warriors in full dress, mounted horsemen, all handsome young men. 13 I saw that she too defiled herself; both of them went the same way.

14 "But she carried her prostitution still further. She saw men portrayed on a wall, figures of Chaldeans[a] portrayed in red, 15 with belts around their waists and flowing turbans on their heads; all of them looked like Babylonian chariot officers, natives of Chaldea.[b] 16 As soon as she saw them, she lusted after them and sent messengers to them in Chaldea. 17 Then the Babylonians came to her, to the bed of love, and in their lust they defiled her. After she had been defiled by them, she turned away from them in disgust. 18 When she carried on her prostitution openly and exposed her naked body, I turned away from her in disgust, just as I had turned away from her sister. 19 Yet she became more and more promiscuous as she recalled the days of her youth, when she was a prostitute in Egypt. 20 There she lusted after her lovers, whose genitals were like those of donkeys and whose emission was like that of horses. 21 So you longed for the lewdness of your youth, when in Egypt your bosom was caressed and your young breasts fondled.[c]

22 "Therefore, Oholibah, this is what the Sovereign LORD says: I will stir up your lovers against you, those you turned away from in disgust, and I will bring them against you from every side — 23 the Babylonians and all the Chaldeans, the men of Pekod and Shoa and Koa, and all the Assyrians with them, handsome young men, all of them governors and commanders, chariot officers and men of high rank, all mounted on horses. 24 They will come against you with weapons,[d] chariots and wagons and with a throng of people; they will take up positions against you on every side with large and small shields and

[a] *14* Or *Babylonians* [b] *15* Or *Babylonia*; also in verse 16 [c] *21* Syriac (see also verse 3); Hebrew *caressed because of your young breasts* [d] *24* The meaning of the Hebrew for this word is uncertain.

with helmets. I will turn you over to them for punishment, and they will punish you according to their standards. 25 I will direct my jealous anger against you, and they will deal with you in fury. They will cut off your noses and your ears, and those of you who are left will fall by the sword. They will take away your sons and daughters, and those of you who are left will be consumed by fire. 26 They will also strip you of your clothes and take your fine jewelry. 27 So I will put a stop to the lewdness and prostitution you began in Egypt. You will not look on these things with longing or remember Egypt anymore.

28 "For this is what the Sovereign LORD says: I am about to deliver you into the hands of those you hate, to those you turned away from in disgust. 29 They will deal with you in hatred and take away everything you have worked for. They will leave you stark naked, and the shame of your prostitution will be exposed. Your lewdness and promiscuity 30 have brought this on you, because you lusted after the nations and defiled yourself with their idols. 31 You have gone the way of your sister; so I will put her cup into your hand.

32 "This is what the Sovereign LORD says:

"You will drink your sister's cup,
a cup large and deep;
it will bring scorn and derision,
for it holds so much.
33 You will be filled with drunkenness and sorrow,
the cup of ruin and desolation,
the cup of your sister Samaria.
34 You will drink it and drain it dry
and chew on its pieces —
and you will tear your breasts.

I have spoken, declares the Sovereign LORD.

35 "Therefore this is what the Sovereign LORD says: Since you have forgotten me and turned your back on me, you must bear the consequences of your lewdness and prostitution."

36 The LORD said to me: "Son of man, will you judge Oholah and Oholibah? Then confront them with their detestable practices, 37 for they have committed adultery and blood is on their hands. They committed adultery with their idols; they even sacrificed their children, whom they bore to me, as food for them. 38 They have also done this to me: At that same time they defiled my sanctuary and desecrated my Sabbaths. 39 On the very day they sacrificed their children to their idols, they entered my sanctuary and desecrated it. That is what they did in my house.

40 "They even sent messengers for men who came from far away, and when they arrived you bathed yourself for them, applied eye makeup and put on your jewelry. 41 You sat on an elegant couch, with a table spread before it on which you had placed the incense and olive oil that belonged to me.

42 "The noise of a carefree crowd was around her; drunkards were brought from the desert along with men from the rabble, and they put bracelets on the wrists of the woman and her sister and beautiful crowns on their heads. 43 Then I said about the one worn out by adultery, 'Now let them use her as a prostitute, for that is all she is.' 44 And they slept with her. As men sleep with a prostitute, so they slept with those lewd women, Oholah and Oholibah. 45 But righteous judges will sentence them to the punishment of women who commit adultery and shed blood, because they are adulterous and blood is on their hands.

46 "This is what the Sovereign LORD says: Bring a mob against them and give them over to terror and plunder. 47 The mob will stone them and cut them down with their swords; they will kill their sons and daughters and burn down their houses.

48 "So I will put an end to lewdness in the land, that all women may take warning and not imitate you. 49 You will suffer the penalty for your lewdness and bear the consequences of your sins of idolatry. Then you will know that I am the Sovereign LORD."

Jerusalem as a Cooking Pot

24 In the ninth year, in the tenth month on the tenth day, the word of the LORD came to me: 2 "Son of man, record this date, this very date, because the king of Babylon has laid siege to Jerusalem this very day. 3 Tell this rebellious people a parable and say to them: 'This is what the Sovereign LORD says:

" 'Put on the cooking pot; put it on
and pour water into it.

[4]Put into it the pieces of meat,
all the choice pieces — the leg and the
shoulder.
Fill it with the best of these bones;
[5] take the pick of the flock.
Pile wood beneath it for the bones;
bring it to a boil
and cook the bones in it.

[6]" 'For this is what the Sovereign LORD says:

" 'Woe to the city of bloodshed,
to the pot now encrusted,
whose deposit will not go away!
Take the meat out piece by piece
in whatever order it comes.

[7]" 'For the blood she shed is in her midst:
She poured it on the bare rock;
she did not pour it on the ground,
where the dust would cover it.
[8]To stir up wrath and take revenge
I put her blood on the bare rock,
so that it would not be covered.

[9]" 'Therefore this is what the Sovereign LORD
says:

" 'Woe to the city of bloodshed!
I, too, will pile the wood high.
[10]So heap on the wood
and kindle the fire.
Cook the meat well,
mixing in the spices;
and let the bones be charred.
[11]Then set the empty pot on the coals
till it becomes hot and its copper
glows,
so that its impurities may be melted
and its deposit burned away.
[12]It has frustrated all efforts;
its heavy deposit has not been
removed,
not even by fire.

[13]" 'Now your impurity is lewdness. Be-
cause I tried to cleanse you but you would
not be cleansed from your impurity, you will
not be clean again until my wrath against
you has subsided.

[14]" 'I the LORD have spoken. The time has
come for me to act. I will not hold back; I will
not have pity, nor will I relent. You will be
judged according to your conduct and your
actions, declares the Sovereign LORD.' "

[a] 23 Or *away in*

Ezekiel's Wife Dies

[15]The word of the LORD came to me:
[16]"Son of man, with one blow I am about to
take away from you the delight of your eyes.
Yet do not lament or weep or shed any tears.
[17]Groan quietly; do not mourn for the dead.
Keep your turban fastened and your san-
dals on your feet; do not cover your mus-
tache and beard or eat the customary food
of mourners."

[18]So I spoke to the people in the morning,
and in the evening my wife died. The next
morning I did as I had been commanded.

[19]Then the people asked me, "Won't you
tell us what these things have to do with us?
Why are you acting like this?"

[20]So I said to them, "The word of the
LORD came to me: [21]Say to the people of Is-
rael, 'This is what the Sovereign LORD says:
I am about to desecrate my sanctuary — the
stronghold in which you take pride, the de-
light of your eyes, the object of your affec-
tion. The sons and daughters you left behind
will fall by the sword. [22]And you will do as
I have done. You will not cover your mus-
tache and beard or eat the customary food
of mourners. [23]You will keep your turbans
on your heads and your sandals on your
feet. You will not mourn or weep but will
waste away because of[a] your sins and groan
among yourselves. [24]Ezekiel will be a sign to
you; you will do just as he has done. When
this happens, you will know that I am the
Sovereign LORD.'

[25]"And you, son of man, on the day I take
away their stronghold, their joy and glory,
the delight of their eyes, their heart's desire,
and their sons and daughters as well — [26]on
that day a fugitive will come to tell you the
news. [27]At that time your mouth will be
opened; you will speak with him and will no
longer be silent. So you will be a sign to them,
and they will know that I am the LORD."

A Prophecy Against Ammon

25 The word of the LORD came to me:
[2]"Son of man, set your face against
the Ammonites and prophesy against them.
[3]Say to them, 'Hear the word of the Sover-
eign LORD. This is what the Sovereign LORD
says: Because you said "Aha!" over my sanc-
tuary when it was desecrated and over the

land of Israel when it was laid waste and over the people of Judah when they went into exile, [4]therefore I am going to give you to the people of the East as a possession. They will set up their camps and pitch their tents among you; they will eat your fruit and drink your milk. [5]I will turn Rabbah into a pasture for camels and Ammon into a resting place for sheep. Then you will know that I am the LORD. [6]For this is what the Sovereign LORD says: Because you have clapped your hands and stamped your feet, rejoicing with all the malice of your heart against the land of Israel, [7]therefore I will stretch out my hand against you and give you as plunder to the nations. I will wipe you out from among the nations and exterminate you from the countries. I will destroy you, and you will know that I am the LORD.' "

A Prophecy Against Moab

[8]"This is what the Sovereign LORD says: 'Because Moab and Seir said, "Look, Judah has become like all the other nations," [9]therefore I will expose the flank of Moab, beginning at its frontier towns—Beth Jeshimoth, Baal Meon and Kiriathaim—the glory of that land. [10]I will give Moab along with the Ammonites to the people of the East as a possession, so that the Ammonites will not be remembered among the nations; [11]and I will inflict punishment on Moab. Then they will know that I am the LORD.' "

A Prophecy Against Edom

[12]"This is what the Sovereign LORD says: 'Because Edom took revenge on Judah and became very guilty by doing so, [13]therefore this is what the Sovereign LORD says: I will stretch out my hand against Edom and kill both man and beast. I will lay it waste, and from Teman to Dedan they will fall by the sword. [14]I will take vengeance on Edom by the hand of my people Israel, and they will deal with Edom in accordance with my anger and my wrath; they will know my vengeance, declares the Sovereign LORD.' "

A Prophecy Against Philistia

[15]"This is what the Sovereign LORD says: 'Because the Philistines acted in vengeance and took revenge with malice in their hearts, and with ancient hostility sought to destroy Judah, [16]therefore this is what the Sovereign LORD says: I am about to stretch out my hand against the Philistines, and I will wipe out the Kerethites and destroy those remaining along the coast. [17]I will carry out great vengeance on them and punish them in my wrath. Then they will know that I am the LORD, when I take vengeance on them.' "

A Prophecy Against Tyre

26 In the eleventh month of the twelfth[a] year, on the first day of the month, the word of the LORD came to me: [2]"Son of man, because Tyre has said of Jerusalem, 'Aha! The gate to the nations is broken, and its doors have swung open to me; now that she lies in ruins I will prosper,' [3]therefore this is what the Sovereign LORD says: I am against you, Tyre, and I will bring many nations against you, like the sea casting up its waves. [4]They will destroy the walls of Tyre and pull down her towers; I will scrape away her rubble and make her a bare rock. [5]Out in the sea she will become a place to spread fishnets, for I have spoken, declares the Sovereign LORD. She will become plunder for the nations, [6]and her settlements on the mainland will be ravaged by the sword. Then they will know that I am the LORD.

[7]"For this is what the Sovereign LORD says: From the north I am going to bring against Tyre Nebuchadnezzar[b] king of Babylon, king of kings, with horses and chariots, with horsemen and a great army. [8]He will ravage your settlements on the mainland with the sword; he will set up siege works against you, build a ramp up to your walls and raise his shields against you. [9]He will direct the blows of his battering rams against your walls and demolish your towers with his weapons. [10]His horses will be so many that they will cover you with dust. Your walls will tremble at the noise of the warhorses, wagons and chariots when he enters your gates as men enter a city whose walls have been broken through. [11]The hooves of his horses will trample all your streets; he will kill your people with the sword, and your strong pillars will fall to the ground. [12]They will plunder your wealth and loot your merchandise;

[a] *1* Probable reading of the original Hebrew text; Masoretic Text does not have *month of the twelfth.*
[b] *7* Hebrew *Nebuchadrezzar,* of which *Nebuchadnezzar* is a variant; here and often in Ezekiel and Jeremiah

ENOUGH

Chris Tomlin, Louie Giglio

All of you is more than enough for all of me
For ev'ry thirst and ev'ry need
You satisfy me with your love
And all I have in you is more than enough

You're my supply, my breath of life
Still more awesome than I know
You're my reward, worth living for
Still more awesome than I know

You're my sacrifice of greatest price
Still more awesome than I know
You're my coming King, you are ev'rything
Still more awesome than I know

More than all I want, more than all I need
You are more than enough for me
More than all I know, more than all I can
You are more than enough

THE INSPIRATION

[God] said to me, "My grace is sufficient for you, for my power is made perfect in weakness." Therefore I will boast all the more gladly about my weaknesses, so that Christ's power may rest on me.

— 2 Corinthians 12:9

BEHIND THE SONG

"Enough" started out as a scrap of paper Louie Giglio tore out of his journal and handed to Chris Tomlin. Giglio had been thinking about Christ's sufficiency, and a few lines came to him. "Whatever it is that we're up against," Giglio thought, "whatever it is that's going on in our lives [. . .] not only is Christ enough for us, but he's really more than enough."

Tomlin took those first few lines and fleshed them out into a full song. He immediately resonated with the thoughts and feelings Giglio was leaning into. "In our feeble attempt to say 'God, you're enough for me. You're more than enough for me'—even *that* is an understatement. God is still more awesome than I can ever know and could ever imagine, and that's just so cool. God is everything to us and still he's more than that."

A few days later, the two men were together in Giglio's kitchen and Tomlin sang the song for him. "The song came from Louie," Tomlin adds. "It's a page of his journal put to music in a good way." For his part, Giglio quickly deflects the credit. "There's a little kernel in there of where I started," he recognizes, "and pretty much everything else in there is where Chris and the Lord ended up with it."

Selah

In 2 Corinthians 12, Paul advises the church on how to deal with trials, difficulties and challenges. The crux of the whole chapter is that it turns our natural human notions of self-sufficiency upside-down. The Lord tells Paul, "My grace is sufficient for you, for my power is made perfect in weakness."

It is comforting to know that in God's economy, our weakness allows his strength to support us. Have you been struggling with your weaknesses? Consider the lyrics of "Enough," line by line, and contemplate the completeness of God. Rest in that knowledge, and if you don't "feel" it yet, try singing it a few times. List some of the ways God has given you strength and see how your perspective changes.

they will break down your walls and demolish your fine houses and throw your stones, timber and rubble into the sea.
[13]I will put an end to your noisy songs, and the music of your harps will be heard no more.
[14]I will make you a bare rock, and you will become a place to spread fishnets. You will never be rebuilt, for I the LORD have spoken, declares the Sovereign LORD.

[15]"This is what the Sovereign LORD says to Tyre: Will not the coastlands tremble at the sound of your fall, when the wounded groan and the slaughter takes place in you?
[16]Then all the princes of the coast will step down from their thrones and lay aside their robes and take off their embroidered garments. Clothed with terror, they will sit on the ground, trembling every moment, appalled at you.
[17]Then they will take up a lament concerning you and say to you:

"'How you are destroyed, city of renown,
peopled by men of the sea!
You were a power on the seas,
you and your citizens;
you put your terror
on all who lived there.
[18]Now the coastlands tremble
on the day of your fall;
the islands in the sea
are terrified at your collapse.'

[19]"This is what the Sovereign LORD says: When I make you a desolate city, like cities no longer inhabited, and when I bring the ocean depths over you and its vast waters cover you,
[20]then I will bring you down with those who go down to the pit, to the people of long ago. I will make you dwell in the earth below, as in ancient ruins, with those who go down to the pit, and you will not return or take your place[a] in the land of the living.
[21]I will bring you to a horrible end and you will be no more. You will be sought, but you will never again be found, declares the Sovereign LORD."

A Lament Over Tyre

27 The word of the LORD came to me:
[2]"Son of man, take up a lament concerning Tyre.
[3]Say to Tyre, situated at the gateway to the sea, merchant of peoples on many coasts, 'This is what the Sovereign LORD says:

"'You say, Tyre,
"I am perfect in beauty."
[4]Your domain was on the high seas;
your builders brought your beauty to perfection.
[5]They made all your timbers
of juniper from Senir[b];
they took a cedar from Lebanon
to make a mast for you.
[6]Of oaks from Bashan
they made your oars;
of cypress wood[c] from the coasts of Cyprus
they made your deck, adorned with ivory.
[7]Fine embroidered linen from Egypt was your sail
and served as your banner;
your awnings were of blue and purple
from the coasts of Elishah.
[8]Men of Sidon and Arvad were your oarsmen;
your skilled men, Tyre, were aboard as your sailors.
[9]Veteran craftsmen of Byblos were on board
as shipwrights to caulk your seams.
All the ships of the sea and their sailors
came alongside to trade for your wares.
[10]"'Men of Persia, Lydia and Put
served as soldiers in your army.
They hung their shields and helmets on your walls,
bringing you splendor.
[11]Men of Arvad and Helek
guarded your walls on every side;
men of Gammad
were in your towers.
They hung their shields around your walls;
they brought your beauty to perfection.

[12]"'Tarshish did business with you because of your great wealth of goods; they exchanged silver, iron, tin and lead for your merchandise.
[13]"'Greece, Tubal and Meshek did business

[a] *20* Septuagint; Hebrew *return, and I will give glory*
[b] *5* That is, Mount Hermon
[c] *6* Targum; the Masoretic Text has a different division of the consonants.

with you; they traded human beings and articles of bronze for your wares.
[14]"'Men of Beth Togarmah exchanged chariot horses, cavalry horses and mules for your merchandise.
[15]"'The men of Rhodes[a] traded with you, and many coastlands were your customers; they paid you with ivory tusks and ebony.
[16]"'Aram[b] did business with you because of your many products; they exchanged turquoise, purple fabric, embroidered work, fine linen, coral and rubies for your merchandise.
[17]"'Judah and Israel traded with you; they exchanged wheat from Minnith and confections,[c] honey, olive oil and balm for your wares.
[18]"'Damascus did business with you because of your many products and great wealth of goods. They offered wine from Helbon, wool from Zahar [19]and casks of wine from Izal in exchange for your wares: wrought iron, cassia and calamus.
[20]"'Dedan traded in saddle blankets with you.
[21]"'Arabia and all the princes of Kedar were your customers; they did business with you in lambs, rams and goats.
[22]"'The merchants of Sheba and Raamah traded with you; for your merchandise they exchanged the finest of all kinds of spices and precious stones, and gold.
[23]"'Harran, Kanneh and Eden and merchants of Sheba, Ashur and Kilmad traded with you. [24]In your marketplace they traded with you beautiful garments, blue fabric, embroidered work and multicolored rugs with cords twisted and tightly knotted.

[25]"'The ships of Tarshish serve
as carriers for your wares.
You are filled with heavy cargo
as you sail the sea.
[26]Your oarsmen take you
out to the high seas.
But the east wind will break you to pieces
far out at sea.
[27]Your wealth, merchandise and wares,
your mariners, sailors and
shipwrights,
your merchants and all your soldiers,
and everyone else on board
will sink into the heart of the sea
on the day of your shipwreck.
[28]The shorelands will quake
when your sailors cry out.
[29]All who handle the oars
will abandon their ships;
the mariners and all the sailors
will stand on the shore.
[30]They will raise their voice
and cry bitterly over you;
they will sprinkle dust on their heads
and roll in ashes.
[31]They will shave their heads because
of you
and will put on sackcloth.
They will weep over you with anguish
of soul
and with bitter mourning.
[32]As they wail and mourn over you,
they will take up a lament concerning
you:
"Who was ever silenced like Tyre,
surrounded by the sea?"
[33]When your merchandise went out on the
seas,
you satisfied many nations;
with your great wealth and your wares
you enriched the kings of the earth.
[34]Now you are shattered by the sea
in the depths of the waters;
your wares and all your company
have gone down with you.
[35]All who live in the coastlands
are appalled at you;
their kings shudder with horror
and their faces are distorted with fear.
[36]The merchants among the nations scoff
at you;
you have come to a horrible end
and will be no more.'"

A Prophecy Against the King of Tyre

28 The word of the LORD came to me: [2]"Son of man, say to the ruler of Tyre, 'This is what the Sovereign LORD says:

"'In the pride of your heart
you say, "I am a god;
I sit on the throne of a god
in the heart of the seas."
But you are a mere mortal and
not a god,

[a] *15* Septuagint; Hebrew *Dedan* [b] *16* Most Hebrew manuscripts; some Hebrew manuscripts and Syriac *Edom* [c] *17* The meaning of the Hebrew for this word is uncertain.

though you think you are as wise as
a god.
3 Are you wiser than Daniel[a]?
Is no secret hidden from you?
4 By your wisdom and understanding
you have gained wealth for yourself
and amassed gold and silver
in your treasuries.
5 By your great skill in trading
you have increased your wealth,
and because of your wealth
your heart has grown proud.

6 " 'Therefore this is what the Sovereign
LORD says:

" 'Because you think you are wise,
as wise as a god,
7 I am going to bring foreigners against
you,
the most ruthless of nations;
they will draw their swords against your
beauty and wisdom
and pierce your shining splendor.
8 They will bring you down to the pit,
and you will die a violent death
in the heart of the seas.
9 Will you then say, "I am a god,"
in the presence of those who kill you?
You will be but a mortal, not a god,
in the hands of those who slay you.
10 You will die the death of the
uncircumcised
at the hands of foreigners.

I have spoken, declares the Sovereign
LORD.' "

11 The word of the LORD came to me:
12 "Son of man, take up a lament concerning
the king of Tyre and say to him: 'This is what
the Sovereign LORD says:

" 'You were the seal of perfection,
full of wisdom and perfect in beauty.
13 You were in Eden,
the garden of God;
every precious stone adorned you:
carnelian, chrysolite and emerald,
topaz, onyx and jasper,
lapis lazuli, turquoise and beryl.[b]
Your settings and mountings[c] were made
of gold;
on the day you were created they were
prepared.
14 You were anointed as a guardian cherub,
for so I ordained you.
You were on the holy mount of God;
you walked among the fiery stones.
15 You were blameless in your ways
from the day you were created
till wickedness was found in you.
16 Through your widespread trade
you were filled with violence,
and you sinned.
So I drove you in disgrace from the
mount of God,
and I expelled you, guardian cherub,
from among the fiery stones.
17 Your heart became proud
on account of your beauty,
and you corrupted your wisdom
because of your splendor.
So I threw you to the earth;
I made a spectacle of you before
kings.
18 By your many sins and dishonest trade
you have desecrated your sanctuaries.
So I made a fire come out from you,
and it consumed you,
and I reduced you to ashes on the ground
in the sight of all who were watching.
19 All the nations who knew you
are appalled at you;
you have come to a horrible end
and will be no more.' "

A Prophecy Against Sidon

20 The word of the LORD came to me:
21 "Son of man, set your face against Sidon;
prophesy against her 22 and say: 'This is what
the Sovereign LORD says:

" 'I am against you, Sidon,
and among you I will display my glory.
You will know that I am the LORD,
when I inflict punishment on you
and within you am proved to be holy.
23 I will send a plague upon you
and make blood flow in your streets.
The slain will fall within you,
with the sword against you on
every side.
Then you will know that I am the LORD.

[a] 3 Or *Danel*, a man of renown in ancient literature [b] 13 The precise identification of some of these precious stones is uncertain. [c] 13 The meaning of the Hebrew for this phrase is uncertain.

[24]“ ‘No longer will the people of Israel have malicious neighbors who are painful briers and sharp thorns. Then they will know that I am the Sovereign LORD.

[25]“ ‘This is what the Sovereign LORD says: When I gather the people of Israel from the nations where they have been scattered, I will be proved holy through them in the sight of the nations. Then they will live in their own land, which I gave to my servant Jacob. [26]They will live there in safety and will build houses and plant vineyards; they will live in safety when I inflict punishment on all their neighbors who maligned them. Then they will know that I am the LORD their God.’ ”

A Prophecy Against Egypt

Judgment on Pharaoh

29 In the tenth year, in the tenth month on the twelfth day, the word of the LORD came to me: [2]“Son of man, set your face against Pharaoh king of Egypt and prophesy against him and against all Egypt. [3]Speak to him and say: ‘This is what the Sovereign LORD says:

“ ‘I am against you, Pharaoh king of Egypt,
you great monster lying among your streams.
You say, “The Nile belongs to me;
I made it for myself.”
[4]But I will put hooks in your jaws
and make the fish of your streams stick to your scales.
I will pull you out from among your streams,
with all the fish sticking to your scales.
[5]I will leave you in the desert,
you and all the fish of your streams.
You will fall on the open field
and not be gathered or picked up.
I will give you as food
to the beasts of the earth and the birds of the sky.

[6]Then all who live in Egypt will know that I am the LORD.

“ ‘You have been a staff of reed for the people of Israel. [7]When they grasped you with their hands, you splintered and you tore open their shoulders; when they leaned on you, you broke and their backs were wrenched.[a]

[8]“ ‘Therefore this is what the Sovereign LORD says: I will bring a sword against you and kill both man and beast. [9]Egypt will become a desolate wasteland. Then they will know that I am the LORD.

“ ‘Because you said, “The Nile is mine; I made it,” [10]therefore I am against you and against your streams, and I will make the land of Egypt a ruin and a desolate waste from Migdol to Aswan, as far as the border of Cush.[b] [11]The foot of neither man nor beast will pass through it; no one will live there for forty years. [12]I will make the land of Egypt desolate among devastated lands, and her cities will lie desolate forty years among ruined cities. And I will disperse the Egyptians among the nations and scatter them through the countries.

[13]“ ‘Yet this is what the Sovereign LORD says: At the end of forty years I will gather the Egyptians from the nations where they were scattered. [14]I will bring them back from captivity and return them to Upper Egypt, the land of their ancestry. There they will be a lowly kingdom. [15]It will be the lowliest of kingdoms and will never again exalt itself above the other nations. I will make it so weak that it will never again rule over the nations. [16]Egypt will no longer be a source of confidence for the people of Israel but will be a reminder of their sin in turning to her for help. Then they will know that I am the Sovereign LORD.’ ”

Nebuchadnezzar’s Reward

[17]In the twenty-seventh year, in the first month on the first day, the word of the LORD came to me: [18]“Son of man, Nebuchadnezzar king of Babylon drove his army in a hard campaign against Tyre; every head was rubbed bare and every shoulder made raw. Yet he and his army got no reward from the campaign he led against Tyre. [19]Therefore this is what the Sovereign LORD says: I am going to give Egypt to Nebuchadnezzar king of Babylon, and he will carry off its wealth. He will loot and plunder the land as pay for his army. [20]I have given him Egypt as a reward for his efforts because he and his army did it for me, declares the Sovereign LORD.

[21]“On that day I will make a horn[c] grow for the Israelites, and I will open your mouth

[a] 7 Syriac (see also Septuagint and Vulgate); Hebrew *and you caused their backs to stand* [b] 10 That is, the upper Nile region [c] 21 *Horn* here symbolizes strength.

among them. Then they will know that I am the LORD."

A Lament Over Egypt

30 The word of the LORD came to me: 2"Son of man, prophesy and say: 'This is what the Sovereign LORD says:

"'Wail and say,
"Alas for that day!"
3 For the day is near,
the day of the LORD is near—
a day of clouds,
a time of doom for the nations.
4 A sword will come against Egypt,
and anguish will come upon Cush.[a]
When the slain fall in Egypt,
her wealth will be carried away
and her foundations torn down.

5 Cush and Libya, Lydia and all Arabia, Kub and the people of the covenant land will fall by the sword along with Egypt.

6"'This is what the LORD says:

"'The allies of Egypt will fall
and her proud strength will fail.
From Migdol to Aswan
they will fall by the sword within her,
declares the Sovereign LORD.
7"'They will be desolate
among desolate lands,
and their cities will lie
among ruined cities.
8 Then they will know that I am the LORD,
when I set fire to Egypt
and all her helpers are crushed.

9"'On that day messengers will go out from me in ships to frighten Cush out of her complacency. Anguish will take hold of them on the day of Egypt's doom, for it is sure to come.

10"'This is what the Sovereign LORD says:

"'I will put an end to the hordes of Egypt
by the hand of Nebuchadnezzar king
of Babylon.
11 He and his army—the most ruthless of
nations—
will be brought in to destroy the land.
They will draw their swords against
Egypt
and fill the land with the slain.
12 I will dry up the waters of the Nile
and sell the land to an evil nation;
by the hand of foreigners
I will lay waste the land and
everything in it.

I the LORD have spoken.

13"'This is what the Sovereign LORD says:

"'I will destroy the idols
and put an end to the images in
Memphis.
No longer will there be a prince in Egypt,
and I will spread fear throughout
the land.
14 I will lay waste Upper Egypt,
set fire to Zoan
and inflict punishment on Thebes.
15 I will pour out my wrath on Pelusium,
the stronghold of Egypt,
and wipe out the hordes of Thebes.
16 I will set fire to Egypt;
Pelusium will writhe in agony.
Thebes will be taken by storm;
Memphis will be in constant distress.
17 The young men of Heliopolis and
Bubastis
will fall by the sword,
and the cities themselves will go into
captivity.
18 Dark will be the day at Tahpanhes
when I break the yoke of Egypt;
there her proud strength will come to
an end.
She will be covered with clouds,
and her villages will go into captivity.
19 So I will inflict punishment on Egypt,
and they will know that I am the
LORD.'"

Pharaoh's Arms Are Broken

20 In the eleventh year, in the first month
on the seventh day, the word of the LORD
came to me: 21"Son of man, I have broken
the arm of Pharaoh king of Egypt. It has
not been bound up to be healed or put in a
splint so that it may become strong enough
to hold a sword. 22 Therefore this is what the
Sovereign LORD says: I am against Pharaoh
king of Egypt. I will break both his arms,
the good arm as well as the broken one, and
make the sword fall from his hand. 23 I will
disperse the Egyptians among the nations

[a] 4 That is, the upper Nile region; also in verses 5 and 9

and scatter them through the countries. [24]I will strengthen the arms of the king of Babylon and put my sword in his hand, but I will break the arms of Pharaoh, and he will groan before him like a mortally wounded man. [25]I will strengthen the arms of the king of Babylon, but the arms of Pharaoh will fall limp. Then they will know that I am the LORD, when I put my sword into the hand of the king of Babylon and he brandishes it against Egypt. [26]I will disperse the Egyptians among the nations and scatter them through the countries. Then they will know that I am the LORD."

Pharaoh as a Felled Cedar of Lebanon

31 In the eleventh year, in the third month on the first day, the word of the LORD came to me: [2]"Son of man, say to Pharaoh king of Egypt and to his hordes:

" 'Who can be compared with you in
majesty?
[3]Consider Assyria, once a cedar in
Lebanon,
with beautiful branches
overshadowing the forest;
it towered on high,
its top above the thick foliage.
[4]The waters nourished it,
deep springs made it grow tall;
their streams flowed
all around its base
and sent their channels
to all the trees of the field.
[5]So it towered higher
than all the trees of the field;
its boughs increased
and its branches grew long,
spreading because of abundant
waters.
[6]All the birds of the sky
nested in its boughs,
all the animals of the wild
gave birth under its branches;
all the great nations
lived in its shade.
[7]It was majestic in beauty,
with its spreading boughs,
for its roots went down
to abundant waters.
[8]The cedars in the garden of God
could not rival it,
nor could the junipers
equal its boughs,
nor could the plane trees
compare with its branches —
no tree in the garden of God
could match its beauty.
[9]I made it beautiful
with abundant branches,
the envy of all the trees of Eden
in the garden of God.

[10]" 'Therefore this is what the Sovereign LORD says: Because the great cedar towered over the thick foliage, and because it was proud of its height, [11]I gave it into the hands of the ruler of the nations, for him to deal with according to its wickedness. I cast it aside, [12]and the most ruthless of foreign nations cut it down and left it. Its boughs fell on the mountains and in all the valleys; its branches lay broken in all the ravines of the land. All the nations of the earth came out from under its shade and left it. [13]All the birds settled on the fallen tree, and all the wild animals lived among its branches. [14]Therefore no other trees by the waters are ever to tower proudly on high, lifting their tops above the thick foliage. No other trees so well-watered are ever to reach such a height; they are all destined for death, for the earth below, among mortals who go down to the realm of the dead.

[15]" 'This is what the Sovereign LORD says: On the day it was brought down to the realm of the dead I covered the deep springs with mourning for it; I held back its streams, and its abundant waters were restrained. Because of it I clothed Lebanon with gloom, and all the trees of the field withered away. [16]I made the nations tremble at the sound of its fall when I brought it down to the realm of the dead to be with those who go down to the pit. Then all the trees of Eden, the choicest and best of Lebanon, the well-watered trees, were consoled in the earth below. [17]They too, like the great cedar, had gone down to the realm of the dead, to those killed by the sword, along with the armed men who lived in its shade among the nations.

[18]" 'Which of the trees of Eden can be compared with you in splendor and majesty? Yet you, too, will be brought down with the trees of Eden to the earth below; you will lie among the uncircumcised, with those killed by the sword.

" This is Pharaoh and all his hordes, declares the Sovereign LORD.' "

A Lament Over Pharaoh

32 In the twelfth year, in the twelfth month on the first day, the word of the LORD came to me: [2] "Son of man, take up a lament concerning Pharaoh king of Egypt and say to him:

" 'You are like a lion among the nations;
you are like a monster in the seas
thrashing about in your streams,
churning the water with your feet
and muddying the streams.

[3] " 'This is what the Sovereign LORD says:

" 'With a great throng of people
I will cast my net over you,
and they will haul you up in my net.
[4] I will throw you on the land
and hurl you on the open field.
I will let all the birds of the sky settle
on you
and all the animals of the wild gorge
themselves on you.
[5] I will spread your flesh on the mountains
and fill the valleys with your remains.
[6] I will drench the land with your flowing
blood
all the way to the mountains,
and the ravines will be filled with your
flesh.
[7] When I snuff you out, I will cover the
heavens
and darken their stars;
I will cover the sun with a cloud,
and the moon will not give its light.
[8] All the shining lights in the heavens
I will darken over you;
I will bring darkness over your land,
declares the Sovereign LORD.
[9] I will trouble the hearts of many peoples
when I bring about your destruction
among the nations,
among[a] lands you have not known.
[10] I will cause many peoples to be appalled
at you,
and their kings will shudder with
horror because of you
when I brandish my sword before them.
On the day of your downfall
each of them will tremble
every moment for his life.

[11] " 'For this is what the Sovereign LORD says:

" 'The sword of the king of Babylon
will come against you.
[12] I will cause your hordes to fall
by the swords of mighty men —
the most ruthless of all nations.
They will shatter the pride of Egypt,
and all her hordes will be overthrown.
[13] I will destroy all her cattle
from beside abundant waters
no longer to be stirred by the foot of man
or muddied by the hooves of cattle.
[14] Then I will let her waters settle
and make her streams flow like oil,
declares the Sovereign LORD.
[15] When I make Egypt desolate
and strip the land of everything in it,
when I strike down all who live there,
then they will know that I am the LORD.'

[16] "This is the lament they will chant for her. The daughters of the nations will chant it; for Egypt and all her hordes they will chant it, declares the Sovereign LORD."

Egypt's Descent Into the Realm of the Dead

[17] In the twelfth year, on the fifteenth day
of the month, the word of the LORD came
to me: [18] "Son of man, wail for the hordes of
Egypt and consign to the earth below both
her and the daughters of mighty nations,
along with those who go down to the pit.
[19] Say to them, 'Are you more favored than
others? Go down and be laid among the un-
circumcised.' [20] They will fall among those
killed by the sword. The sword is drawn;
let her be dragged off with all her hordes.
[21] From within the realm of the dead the
mighty leaders will say of Egypt and her al-
lies, 'They have come down and they lie with
the uncircumcised, with those killed by the
sword.'

[22] "Assyria is there with her whole army;
she is surrounded by the graves of all her
slain, all who have fallen by the sword.
[23] Their graves are in the depths of the pit
and her army lies around her grave. All who
had spread terror in the land of the living are
slain, fallen by the sword.

[24] "Elam is there, with all her hordes
around her grave. All of them are slain, fall-
en by the sword. All who had spread terror in
the land of the living went down uncircum-
cised to the earth below. They bear their

[a] 9 Hebrew; Septuagint *bring you into captivity among the nations, / to*

shame with those who go down to the pit. 25 A bed is made for her among the slain, with all her hordes around her grave. All of them are uncircumcised, killed by the sword. Because their terror had spread in the land of the living, they bear their shame with those who go down to the pit; they are laid among the slain.

26 "Meshek and Tubal are there, with all their hordes around their graves. All of them are uncircumcised, killed by the sword because they spread their terror in the land of the living. 27 But they do not lie with the fallen warriors of old,[a] who went down to the realm of the dead with their weapons of war—their swords placed under their heads and their shields[b] resting on their bones—though these warriors also had terrorized the land of the living.

28 "You too, Pharaoh, will be broken and will lie among the uncircumcised, with those killed by the sword.

29 "Edom is there, her kings and all her princes; despite their power, they are laid with those killed by the sword. They lie with the uncircumcised, with those who go down to the pit.

30 "All the princes of the north and all the Sidonians are there; they went down with the slain in disgrace despite the terror caused by their power. They lie uncircumcised with those killed by the sword and bear their shame with those who go down to the pit.

31 "Pharaoh—he and all his army—will see them and he will be consoled for all his hordes that were killed by the sword, declares the Sovereign LORD. 32 Although I had him spread terror in the land of the living, Pharaoh and all his hordes will be laid among the uncircumcised, with those killed by the sword, declares the Sovereign LORD."

Renewal of Ezekiel's Call as Watchman

33 The word of the LORD came to me: 2 "Son of man, speak to your people and say to them: 'When I bring the sword against a land, and the people of the land choose one of their men and make him their watchman, 3 and he sees the sword coming against the land and blows the trumpet to warn the people, 4 then if anyone hears the trumpet but does not heed the warning and the sword comes and takes their life, their blood will be on their own head. 5 Since they heard the sound of the trumpet but did not heed the warning, their blood will be on their own head. If they had heeded the warning, they would have saved themselves. 6 But if the watchman sees the sword coming and does not blow the trumpet to warn the people and the sword comes and takes someone's life, that person's life will be taken because of their sin, but I will hold the watchman accountable for their blood.'

7 "Son of man, I have made you a watchman for the people of Israel; so hear the word I speak and give them warning from me. 8 When I say to the wicked, 'You wicked person, you will surely die,' and you do not speak out to dissuade them from their ways, that wicked person will die for[c] their sin, and I will hold you accountable for their blood. 9 But if you do warn the wicked person to turn from their ways and they do not do so, they will die for their sin, though you yourself will be saved.

10 "Son of man, say to the Israelites, 'This is what you are saying: "Our offenses and sins weigh us down, and we are wasting away because of[d] them. How then can we live?"' 11 Say to them, 'As surely as I live, declares the Sovereign LORD, I take no pleasure in the death of the wicked, but rather that they turn from their ways and live. Turn! Turn from your evil ways! Why will you die, people of Israel?'

12 "Therefore, son of man, say to your people, 'If someone who is righteous disobeys, that person's former righteousness will count for nothing. And if someone who is wicked repents, that person's former wickedness will not bring condemnation. The righteous person who sins will not be allowed to live even though they were formerly righteous.' 13 If I tell a righteous person that they will surely live, but then they trust in their righteousness and do evil, none of the righteous things that person has done will be remembered; they will die for the evil they have done. 14 And if I say to a wicked person, 'You will surely die,' but they then turn away from their sin and do what is just and right— 15 if they give back what

[a] 27 Septuagint; Hebrew *warriors who were uncircumcised* [b] 27 Probable reading of the original Hebrew text; Masoretic Text *punishment* [c] 8 Or *in*; also in verse 9 [d] 10 Or *away in*

they took in pledge for a loan, return what they have stolen, follow the decrees that give life, and do no evil — that person will surely live; they will not die. 16None of the sins that person has committed will be remembered against them. They have done what is just and right; they will surely live.

17"Yet your people say, 'The way of the Lord is not just.' But it is their way that is not just. 18If a righteous person turns from their righteousness and does evil, they will die for it. 19And if a wicked person turns away from their wickedness and does what is just and right, they will live by doing so. 20Yet you Israelites say, 'The way of the Lord is not just.' But I will judge each of you according to your own ways."

Jerusalem's Fall Explained

21In the twelfth year of our exile, in the tenth month on the fifth day, a man who had escaped from Jerusalem came to me and said, "The city has fallen!" 22Now the evening before the man arrived, the hand of the LORD was on me, and he opened my mouth before the man came to me in the morning. So my mouth was opened and I was no longer silent.

23Then the word of the LORD came to me: 24"Son of man, the people living in those ruins in the land of Israel are saying, 'Abraham was only one man, yet he possessed the land. But we are many; surely the land has been given to us as our possession.' 25Therefore say to them, 'This is what the Sovereign LORD says: Since you eat meat with the blood still in it and look to your idols and shed blood, should you then possess the land? 26You rely on your sword, you do detestable things, and each of you defiles his neighbor's wife. Should you then possess the land?'

27"Say this to them: 'This is what the Sovereign LORD says: As surely as I live, those who are left in the ruins will fall by the sword, those out in the country I will give to the wild animals to be devoured, and those in strongholds and caves will die of a plague. 28I will make the land a desolate waste, and her proud strength will come to an end, and the mountains of Israel will become desolate so that no one will cross them. 29Then they will know that I am the LORD, when I have made the land a desolate waste because of all the detestable things they have done.'

30"As for you, son of man, your people are talking together about you by the walls and at the doors of the houses, saying to each other, 'Come and hear the message that has come from the LORD.' 31My people come to you, as they usually do, and sit before you to hear your words, but they do not put them into practice. Their mouths speak of love, but their hearts are greedy for unjust gain. 32Indeed, to them you are nothing more than one who sings love songs with a beautiful voice and plays an instrument well, for they hear your words but do not put them into practice.

33"When all this comes true — and it surely will — then they will know that a prophet has been among them."

The LORD Will Be Israel's Shepherd

34 The word of the LORD came to me: 2"Son of man, prophesy against the shepherds of Israel; prophesy and say to them: 'This is what the Sovereign LORD says: Woe to you shepherds of Israel who only take care of yourselves! Should not shepherds take care of the flock? 3You eat the curds, clothe yourselves with the wool and slaughter the choice animals, but you do not take care of the flock. 4You have not strengthened the weak or healed the sick or bound up the injured. You have not brought back the strays or searched for the lost. You have ruled them harshly and brutally. 5So they were scattered because there was no shepherd, and when they were scattered they became food for all the wild animals. 6My sheep wandered over all the mountains and on every high hill. They were scattered over the whole earth, and no one searched or looked for them.

7" 'Therefore, you shepherds, hear the word of the LORD: 8As surely as I live, declares the Sovereign LORD, because my flock lacks a shepherd and so has been plundered and has become food for all the wild animals, and because my shepherds did not search for my flock but cared for themselves rather than for my flock, 9therefore, you shepherds, hear the word of the LORD: 10This is what the Sovereign LORD says: I am against the shepherds and will hold them accountable for my flock. I will remove them from tending the flock so that the shepherds can no longer feed themselves. I will rescue

my flock from their mouths, and it will no
longer be food for them.
11 " 'For this is what the Sovereign LORD
says: I myself will search for my sheep and
look after them. 12 As a shepherd looks after
his scattered flock when he is with them, so
will I look after my sheep. I will rescue them
from all the places where they were scat-
tered on a day of clouds and darkness. 13 I
will bring them out from the nations and
gather them from the countries, and I will
bring them into their own land. I will pas-
ture them on the mountains of Israel, in the
ravines and in all the settlements in the land.
14 I will tend them in a good pasture, and the
mountain heights of Israel will be their graz-
ing land. There they will lie down in good
grazing land, and there they will feed in a
rich pasture on the mountains of Israel. 15 I
myself will tend my sheep and have them lie
down, declares the Sovereign LORD. 16 I will
search for the lost and bring back the strays.
I will bind up the injured and strengthen the
weak, but the sleek and the strong I will de-
stroy. I will shepherd the flock with justice.
17 " 'As for you, my flock, this is what the
Sovereign LORD says: I will judge between
one sheep and another, and between rams
and goats. 18 Is it not enough for you to feed
on the good pasture? Must you also tram-
ple the rest of your pasture with your feet?
Is it not enough for you to drink clear water?
Must you also muddy the rest with your feet?
19 Must my flock feed on what you have tram-
pled and drink what you have muddied with
your feet?
20 " 'Therefore this is what the Sovereign
LORD says to them: See, I myself will judge
between the fat sheep and the lean sheep.
21 Because you shove with flank and shoul-
der, butting all the weak sheep with your
horns until you have driven them away,
22 I will save my flock, and they will no lon-
ger be plundered. I will judge between one
sheep and another. 23 I will place over them
one shepherd, my servant David, and he will
tend them; he will tend them and be their
shepherd. 24 I the LORD will be their God,
and my servant David will be prince among
them. I the LORD have spoken.
25 " 'I will make a covenant of peace with
them and rid the land of savage beasts so
that they may live in the wilderness and
sleep in the forests in safety. 26 I will make
them and the places surrounding my hill a
blessing.[a] I will send down showers in sea-
son; there will be showers of blessing. 27 The
trees will yield their fruit and the ground
will yield its crops; the people will be secure
in their land. They will know that I am the
LORD, when I break the bars of their yoke
and rescue them from the hands of those
who enslaved them. 28 They will no longer be
plundered by the nations, nor will wild an-
imals devour them. They will live in safety,
and no one will make them afraid. 29 I will
provide for them a land renowned for its
crops, and they will no longer be victims of
famine in the land or bear the scorn of the
nations. 30 Then they will know that I, the
LORD their God, am with them and that
they, the Israelites, are my people, declares
the Sovereign LORD. 31 You are my sheep, the
sheep of my pasture, and I am your God, de-
clares the Sovereign LORD.' "

A Prophecy Against Edom

35 The word of the LORD came to me:
2 "Son of man, set your face against
Mount Seir; prophesy against it 3 and say:
'This is what the Sovereign LORD says: I am
against you, Mount Seir, and I will stretch
out my hand against you and make you a
desolate waste. 4 I will turn your towns into
ruins and you will be desolate. Then you will
know that I am the LORD.
5 " 'Because you harbored an ancient hos-
tility and delivered the Israelites over to the
sword at the time of their calamity, the time
their punishment reached its climax, 6 there-
fore as surely as I live, declares the Sovereign
LORD, I will give you over to bloodshed and
it will pursue you. Since you did not hate
bloodshed, bloodshed will pursue you. 7 I
will make Mount Seir a desolate waste and
cut off from it all who come and go. 8 I will fill
your mountains with the slain; those killed
by the sword will fall on your hills and in
your valleys and in all your ravines. 9 I will
make you desolate forever; your towns will
not be inhabited. Then you will know that I
am the LORD.
10 " 'Because you have said, "These two
nations and countries will be ours and we

[a] 26 Or *I will cause them and the places surrounding my hill to be named in blessings* (see Gen. 48:20); or *I will cause them and the places surrounding my hill to be seen as blessed*

will take possession of them," even though I the LORD was there, [11]therefore as surely as I live, declares the Sovereign LORD, I will treat you in accordance with the anger and jealousy you showed in your hatred of them and I will make myself known among them when I judge you. [12]Then you will know that I the LORD have heard all the contemptible things you have said against the mountains of Israel. You said, "They have been laid waste and have been given over to us to devour." [13]You boasted against me and spoke against me without restraint, and I heard it. [14]This is what the Sovereign LORD says: While the whole earth rejoices, I will make you desolate. [15]Because you rejoiced when the inheritance of Israel became desolate, that is how I will treat you. You will be desolate, Mount Seir, you and all of Edom. Then they will know that I am the LORD.' "

Hope for the Mountains of Israel

36 "Son of man, prophesy to the mountains of Israel and say, 'Mountains of Israel, hear the word of the LORD. [2]This is what the Sovereign LORD says: The enemy said of you, "Aha! The ancient heights have become our possession." ' [3]Therefore prophesy and say, 'This is what the Sovereign LORD says: Because they ravaged and crushed you from every side so that you became the possession of the rest of the nations and the object of people's malicious talk and slander, [4]therefore, mountains of Israel, hear the word of the Sovereign LORD: This is what the Sovereign LORD says to the mountains and hills, to the ravines and valleys, to the desolate ruins and the deserted towns that have been plundered and ridiculed by the rest of the nations around you— [5]this is what the Sovereign LORD says: In my burning zeal I have spoken against the rest of the nations, and against all Edom, for with glee and with malice in their hearts they made my land their own possession so that they might plunder its pastureland.' [6]Therefore prophesy concerning the land of Israel and say to the mountains and hills, to the ravines and valleys: 'This is what the Sovereign LORD says: I speak in my jealous wrath because you have suffered the scorn of the nations. [7]Therefore this is what the Sovereign LORD says: I swear with uplifted hand that the nations around you will also suffer scorn.

[8]" 'But you, mountains of Israel, will produce branches and fruit for my people Israel, for they will soon come home. [9]I am concerned for you and will look on you with favor; you will be plowed and sown, [10]and I will cause many people to live on you—yes, all of Israel. The towns will be inhabited and the ruins rebuilt. [11]I will increase the number of people and animals living on you, and they will be fruitful and become numerous. I will settle people on you as in the past and will make you prosper more than before. Then you will know that I am the LORD. [12]I will cause people, my people Israel, to live on you. They will possess you, and you will be their inheritance; you will never again deprive them of their children.

[13]" 'This is what the Sovereign LORD says: Because some say to you, "You devour people and deprive your nation of its children," [14]therefore you will no longer devour people or make your nation childless, declares the Sovereign LORD. [15]No longer will I make you hear the taunts of the nations, and no longer will you suffer the scorn of the peoples or cause your nation to fall, declares the Sovereign LORD.' "

Israel's Restoration Assured

[16]Again the word of the LORD came to me: [17]"Son of man, when the people of Israel were living in their own land, they defiled it by their conduct and their actions. Their conduct was like a woman's monthly uncleanness in my sight. [18]So I poured out my wrath on them because they had shed blood in the land and because they had defiled it with their idols. [19]I dispersed them among the nations, and they were scattered through the countries; I judged them according to their conduct and their actions. [20]And wherever they went among the nations they profaned my holy name, for it was said of them, 'These are the LORD's people, and yet they had to leave his land.' [21]I had concern for my holy name, which the people of Israel profaned among the nations where they had gone.

[22]"Therefore say to the Israelites, 'This is what the Sovereign LORD says: It is not for your sake, people of Israel, that I am going to do these things, but for the sake of my holy name, which you have profaned among the nations where you have gone. [23]I will

show the holiness of my great name, which
has been profaned among the nations, the
name you have profaned among them. Then
the nations will know that I am the LORD,
declares the Sovereign LORD, when I am
proved holy through you before their eyes.
24 "'For I will take you out of the nations;
I will gather you from all the countries and
bring you back into your own land. 25 I will
sprinkle clean water on you, and you will be
clean; I will cleanse you from all your im-
purities and from all your idols. 26 I will give
you a new heart and put a new spirit in you; I
will remove from you your heart of stone and
give you a heart of flesh. 27 And I will put my
Spirit in you and move you to follow my de-
crees and be careful to keep my laws. 28 Then
you will live in the land I gave your ances-
tors; you will be my people, and I will be
your God. 29 I will save you from all your un-
cleanness. I will call for the grain and make
it plentiful and will not bring famine upon
you. 30 I will increase the fruit of the trees
and the crops of the field, so that you will no
longer suffer disgrace among the nations be-
cause of famine. 31 Then you will remember
your evil ways and wicked deeds, and you
will loathe yourselves for your sins and de-
testable practices. 32 I want you to know that I
am not doing this for your sake, declares the
Sovereign LORD. Be ashamed and disgraced
for your conduct, people of Israel!
33 "'This is what the Sovereign LORD says:
On the day I cleanse you from all your sins,
I will resettle your towns, and the ruins will
be rebuilt. 34 The desolate land will be culti-
vated instead of lying desolate in the sight
of all who pass through it. 35 They will say,
"This land that was laid waste has become
like the garden of Eden; the cities that were
lying in ruins, desolate and destroyed, are
now fortified and inhabited." 36 Then the na-
tions around you that remain will know that
I the LORD have rebuilt what was destroyed
and have replanted what was desolate. I the
LORD have spoken, and I will do it.'
37 "This is what the Sovereign LORD says:
Once again I will yield to Israel's plea and
do this for them: I will make their people as
numerous as sheep, 38 as numerous as the
flocks for offerings at Jerusalem during her
appointed festivals. So will the ruined cities
be filled with flocks of people. Then they will
know that I am the LORD."

The Valley of Dry Bones

37 The hand of the LORD was on me, and
he brought me out by the Spirit of the
LORD and set me in the middle of a valley; it
was full of bones. 2 He led me back and forth
among them, and I saw a great many bones
on the floor of the valley, bones that were
very dry. 3 He asked me, "Son of man, can
these bones live?"
I said, "Sovereign LORD, you alone know."
4 Then he said to me, "Prophesy to these
bones and say to them, 'Dry bones, hear the
word of the LORD! 5 This is what the Sover-
eign LORD says to these bones: I will make
breath[a] enter you, and you will come to life.
6 I will attach tendons to you and make flesh
come upon you and cover you with skin;
I will put breath in you, and you will come
to life. Then you will know that I am the
LORD.'"
7 So I prophesied as I was commanded.
And as I was prophesying, there was a noise,
a rattling sound, and the bones came togeth-
er, bone to bone. 8 I looked, and tendons and
flesh appeared on them and skin covered
them, but there was no breath in them.
9 Then he said to me, "Prophesy to the
breath; prophesy, son of man, and say to
it, 'This is what the Sovereign LORD says:
Come, breath, from the four winds and
breathe into these slain, that they may live.'"
10 So I prophesied as he commanded me, and
breath entered them; they came to life and
stood up on their feet—a vast army.
11 Then he said to me: "Son of man, these
bones are the people of Israel. They say, 'Our
bones are dried up and our hope is gone; we
are cut off.' 12 Therefore prophesy and say to
them: 'This is what the Sovereign LORD says:
My people, I am going to open your graves
and bring you up from them; I will bring you
back to the land of Israel. 13 Then you, my
people, will know that I am the LORD, when
I open your graves and bring you up from
them. 14 I will put my Spirit in you and you
will live, and I will settle you in your own
land. Then you will know that I the LORD
have spoken, and I have done it, declares the
LORD.'"

[a] 5 The Hebrew for this word can also mean *wind* or *spirit* (see verses 6-14).

One Nation Under One King

15 The word of the LORD came to me: 16 "Son of man, take a stick of wood and write on it, 'Belonging to Judah and the Israelites associated with him.' Then take another stick of wood, and write on it, 'Belonging to Joseph (that is, to Ephraim) and all the Israelites associated with him.' 17 Join them together into one stick so that they will become one in your hand.

18 "When your people ask you, 'Won't you tell us what you mean by this?' 19 say to them, 'This is what the Sovereign LORD says: I am going to take the stick of Joseph—which is in Ephraim's hand—and of the Israelite tribes associated with him, and join it to Judah's stick. I will make them into a single stick of wood, and they will become one in my hand.' 20 Hold before their eyes the sticks you have written on 21 and say to them, 'This is what the Sovereign LORD says: I will take the Israelites out of the nations where they have gone. I will gather them from all around and bring them back into their own land. 22 I will make them one nation in the land, on the mountains of Israel. There will be one king over all of them and they will never again be two nations or be divided into two kingdoms. 23 They will no longer defile themselves with their idols and vile images or with any of their offenses, for I will save them from all their sinful backsliding,[a] and I will cleanse them. They will be my people, and I will be their God.

24 " 'My servant David will be king over them, and they will all have one shepherd. They will follow my laws and be careful to keep my decrees. 25 They will live in the land I gave to my servant Jacob, the land where your ancestors lived. They and their children and their children's children will live there forever, and David my servant will be their prince forever. 26 I will make a covenant of peace with them; it will be an everlasting covenant. I will establish them and increase their numbers, and I will put my sanctuary among them forever. 27 My dwelling place will be with them; I will be their God, and they will be my people. 28 Then the nations will know that I the LORD make Israel holy, when my sanctuary is among them forever.' "

The LORD's Great Victory Over the Nations

38 The word of the LORD came to me: 2 "Son of man, set your face against Gog, of the land of Magog, the chief prince of[b] Meshek and Tubal; prophesy against him 3 and say: 'This is what the Sovereign LORD says: I am against you, Gog, chief prince of[c] Meshek and Tubal. 4 I will turn you around, put hooks in your jaws and bring you out with your whole army—your horses, your horsemen fully armed, and a great horde with large and small shields, all of them brandishing their swords. 5 Persia, Cush[d] and Put will be with them, all with shields and helmets, 6 also Gomer with all its troops, and Beth Togarmah from the far north with all its troops—the many nations with you.

7 " 'Get ready; be prepared, you and all the hordes gathered about you, and take command of them. 8 After many days you will be called to arms. In future years you will invade a land that has recovered from war, whose people were gathered from many nations to the mountains of Israel, which had long been desolate. They had been brought out from the nations, and now all of them live in safety. 9 You and all your troops and the many nations with you will go up, advancing like a storm; you will be like a cloud covering the land.

10 " 'This is what the Sovereign LORD says: On that day thoughts will come into your mind and you will devise an evil scheme. 11 You will say, "I will invade a land of unwalled villages; I will attack a peaceful and unsuspecting people—all of them living without walls and without gates and bars. 12 I will plunder and loot and turn my hand against the resettled ruins and the people gathered from the nations, rich in livestock and goods, living at the center of the land.[e]" 13 Sheba and Dedan and the merchants of Tarshish and all her villages[f] will say to you, "Have you come to plunder? Have you gathered your hordes to loot, to carry off silver and gold, to take away livestock and goods and to seize much plunder?" '

14 "Therefore, son of man, prophesy and say to Gog: 'This is what the Sovereign LORD

[a] *23* Many Hebrew manuscripts (see also Septuagint); most Hebrew manuscripts *all their dwelling places where they sinned* [b] *2* Or *the prince of Rosh,* [c] *3* Or *Gog, prince of Rosh,* [d] *5* That is, the upper Nile region [e] *12* The Hebrew for this phrase means *the navel of the earth.* [f] *13* Or *her strong lions*

says: In that day, when my people Israel are living in safety, will you not take notice of it? 15 You will come from your place in the far north, you and many nations with you, all of them riding on horses, a great horde, a mighty army. 16 You will advance against my people Israel like a cloud that covers the land. In days to come, Gog, I will bring you against my land, so that the nations may know me when I am proved holy through you before their eyes.

17 “ ‘This is what the Sovereign LORD says: You are the one I spoke of in former days by my servants the prophets of Israel. At that time they prophesied for years that I would bring you against them. 18 This is what will happen in that day: When Gog attacks the land of Israel, my hot anger will be aroused, declares the Sovereign LORD. 19 In my zeal and fiery wrath I declare that at that time there shall be a great earthquake in the land of Israel. 20 The fish in the sea, the birds in the sky, the beasts of the field, every creature that moves along the ground, and all the people on the face of the earth will tremble at my presence. The mountains will be overturned, the cliffs will crumble and every wall will fall to the ground. 21 I will summon a sword against Gog on all my mountains, declares the Sovereign LORD. Every man’s sword will be against his brother. 22 I will execute judgment on him with plague and bloodshed; I will pour down torrents of rain, hailstones and burning sulfur on him and on his troops and on the many nations with him. 23 And so I will show my greatness and my holiness, and I will make myself known in the sight of many nations. Then they will know that I am the LORD.’

39 “Son of man, prophesy against Gog and say: ‘This is what the Sovereign LORD says: I am against you, Gog, chief prince of[a] Meshek and Tubal. 2 I will turn you around and drag you along. I will bring you from the far north and send you against the mountains of Israel. 3 Then I will strike your bow from your left hand and make your arrows drop from your right hand. 4 On the mountains of Israel you will fall, you and all your troops and the nations with you. I will give you as food to all kinds of carrion birds and to the wild animals. 5 You will fall in the open field, for I have spoken, declares the Sovereign LORD. 6 I will send fire on Magog and on those who live in safety in the coastlands, and they will know that I am the LORD.

7 “ ‘I will make known my holy name among my people Israel. I will no longer let my holy name be profaned, and the nations will know that I the LORD am the Holy One in Israel. 8 It is coming! It will surely take place, declares the Sovereign LORD. This is the day I have spoken of.

9 “ ‘Then those who live in the towns of Israel will go out and use the weapons for fuel and burn them up — the small and large shields, the bows and arrows, the war clubs and spears. For seven years they will use them for fuel. 10 They will not need to gather wood from the fields or cut it from the forests, because they will use the weapons for fuel. And they will plunder those who plundered them and loot those who looted them, declares the Sovereign LORD.

11 “ ‘On that day I will give Gog a burial place in Israel, in the valley of those who travel east of the Sea. It will block the way of travelers, because Gog and all his hordes will be buried there. So it will be called the Valley of Hamon Gog.[b]

12 “ ‘For seven months the Israelites will be burying them in order to cleanse the land. 13 All the people of the land will bury them, and the day I display my glory will be a memorable day for them, declares the Sovereign LORD. 14 People will be continually employed in cleansing the land. They will spread out across the land and, along with others, they will bury any bodies that are lying on the ground.

“ ‘After the seven months they will carry out a more detailed search. 15 As they go through the land, anyone who sees a human bone will leave a marker beside it until the gravediggers bury it in the Valley of Hamon Gog, 16 near a town called Hamonah.[c] And so they will cleanse the land.’

17 “Son of man, this is what the Sovereign LORD says: Call out to every kind of bird and all the wild animals: ‘Assemble and come together from all around to the sacrifice I am preparing for you, the great sacrifice on the mountains of Israel. There you will eat flesh

[a] *1* Or *Gog, prince of Rosh,* [b] *11* *Hamon Gog* means *hordes of Gog.* [c] *16* *Hamonah* means *horde.*

and drink blood. 18You will eat the flesh of mighty men and drink the blood of the princes of the earth as if they were rams and lambs, goats and bulls—all of them fattened animals from Bashan. 19At the sacrifice I am preparing for you, you will eat fat till you are glutted and drink blood till you are drunk. 20At my table you will eat your fill of horses and riders, mighty men and soldiers of every kind,' declares the Sovereign LORD.

21"I will display my glory among the nations, and all the nations will see the punishment I inflict and the hand I lay on them. 22From that day forward the people of Israel will know that I am the LORD their God. 23And the nations will know that the people of Israel went into exile for their sin, because they were unfaithful to me. So I hid my face from them and handed them over to their enemies, and they all fell by the sword. 24I dealt with them according to their uncleanness and their offenses, and I hid my face from them.

25"Therefore this is what the Sovereign LORD says: I will now restore the fortunes of Jacob[a] and will have compassion on all the people of Israel, and I will be zealous for my holy name. 26They will forget their shame and all the unfaithfulness they showed toward me when they lived in safety in their land with no one to make them afraid. 27When I have brought them back from the nations and have gathered them from the countries of their enemies, I will be proved holy through them in the sight of many nations. 28Then they will know that I am the LORD their God, for though I sent them into exile among the nations, I will gather them to their own land, not leaving any behind. 29I will no longer hide my face from them, for I will pour out my Spirit on the people of Israel, declares the Sovereign LORD."

The Temple Area Restored

40 In the twenty-fifth year of our exile, at the beginning of the year, on the tenth of the month, in the fourteenth year after the fall of the city—on that very day the hand of the LORD was on me and he took me there. 2In visions of God he took me to the land of Israel and set me on a very high mountain, on whose south side were some buildings that looked like a city. 3He took me there, and I saw a man whose appearance was like bronze; he was standing in the gateway with a linen cord and a measuring rod in his hand. 4The man said to me, "Son of man, look carefully and listen closely and pay attention to everything I am going to show you, for that is why you have been brought here. Tell the people of Israel everything you see."

The East Gate to the Outer Court

5I saw a wall completely surrounding the temple area. The length of the measuring rod in the man's hand was six long cubits,[b] each of which was a cubit and a handbreadth. He measured the wall; it was one measuring rod thick and one rod high.

6Then he went to the east gate. He climbed its steps and measured the threshold of the gate; it was one rod deep. 7The alcoves for the guards were one rod long and one rod wide, and the projecting walls between the alcoves were five cubits[c] thick. And the threshold of the gate next to the portico facing the temple was one rod deep.

8Then he measured the portico of the gateway; 9it[d] was eight cubits[e] deep and its jambs were two cubits[f] thick. The portico of the gateway faced the temple.

10Inside the east gate were three alcoves on each side; the three had the same measurements, and the faces of the projecting walls on each side had the same measurements. 11Then he measured the width of the entrance of the gateway; it was ten cubits and its length was thirteen cubits.[g] 12In front of each alcove was a wall one cubit high, and the alcoves were six cubits square. 13Then he measured the gateway from the top of the rear wall of one alcove to the top of the opposite one; the distance was twenty-five

[a] 25 Or *now bring Jacob back from captivity* [b] 5 That is, about 11 feet or about 3.2 meters; also in verse 12. The long cubit of about 21 inches or about 53 centimeters is the basic unit of measurement of length throughout chapters 40–48. [c] 7 That is, about 8 3/4 feet or about 2.7 meters; also in verse 48 [d] 8,9 Many Hebrew manuscripts, Septuagint, Vulgate and Syriac; most Hebrew manuscripts *gateway facing the temple; it was one rod deep. 9Then he measured the portico of the gateway; it* [e] 9 That is, about 14 feet or about 4.2 meters [f] 9 That is, about 3 1/2 feet or about 1 meter [g] 11 That is, about 18 feet wide and 23 feet long or about 5.3 meters wide and 6.9 meters long

cubits[a] from one parapet opening to the opposite one. 14 He measured along the faces of the projecting walls all around the inside of the gateway — sixty cubits.[b] The measurement was up to the portico[c] facing the courtyard.[d] 15 The distance from the entrance of the gateway to the far end of its portico was fifty cubits.[e] 16 The alcoves and the projecting walls inside the gateway were surmounted by narrow parapet openings all around, as was the portico; the openings all around faced inward. The faces of the projecting walls were decorated with palm trees.

The Outer Court

17 Then he brought me into the outer court. There I saw some rooms and a pavement that had been constructed all around the court; there were thirty rooms along the pavement. 18 It abutted the sides of the gateways and was as wide as they were long; this was the lower pavement. 19 Then he measured the distance from the inside of the lower gateway to the outside of the inner court; it was a hundred cubits[f] on the east side as well as on the north.

The North Gate

20 Then he measured the length and width of the north gate, leading into the outer court. 21 Its alcoves — three on each side — its projecting walls and its portico had the same measurements as those of the first gateway. It was fifty cubits long and twenty-five cubits wide. 22 Its openings, its portico and its palm tree decorations had the same measurements as those of the gate facing east. Seven steps led up to it, with its portico opposite them. 23 There was a gate to the inner court facing the north gate, just as there was on the east. He measured from one gate to the opposite one; it was a hundred cubits.

The South Gate

24 Then he led me to the south side and I saw the south gate. He measured its jambs and its portico, and they had the same measurements as the others. 25 The gateway and its portico had narrow openings all around, like the openings of the others. It was fifty cubits long and twenty-five cubits wide. 26 Seven steps led up to it, with its portico opposite them; it had palm tree decorations on the faces of the projecting walls on each side. 27 The inner court also had a gate facing south, and he measured from this gate to the outer gate on the south side; it was a hundred cubits.

The Gates to the Inner Court

28 Then he brought me into the inner court through the south gate, and he measured the south gate; it had the same measurements as the others. 29 Its alcoves, its projecting walls and its portico had the same measurements as the others. The gateway and its portico had openings all around. It was fifty cubits long and twenty-five cubits wide. 30 (The porticoes of the gateways around the inner court were twenty-five cubits wide and five cubits deep.) 31 Its portico faced the outer court; palm trees decorated its jambs, and eight steps led up to it.

32 Then he brought me to the inner court on the east side, and he measured the gateway; it had the same measurements as the others. 33 Its alcoves, its projecting walls and its portico had the same measurements as the others. The gateway and its portico had openings all around. It was fifty cubits long and twenty-five cubits wide. 34 Its portico faced the outer court; palm trees decorated the jambs on either side, and eight steps led up to it.

35 Then he brought me to the north gate and measured it. It had the same measurements as the others, 36 as did its alcoves, its projecting walls and its portico, and it had openings all around. It was fifty cubits long and twenty-five cubits wide. 37 Its portico[g] faced the outer court; palm trees decorated the jambs on either side, and eight steps led up to it.

The Rooms for Preparing Sacrifices

38 A room with a doorway was by the portico in each of the inner gateways, where the burnt offerings were washed. 39 In the

[a] *13* That is, about 44 feet or about 13 meters; also in verses 21, 25, 29, 30, 33 and 36 [b] *14* That is, about 105 feet or about 32 meters [c] *14* Septuagint; Hebrew *projecting wall* [d] *14* The meaning of the Hebrew for this verse is uncertain. [e] *15* That is, about 88 feet or about 27 meters; also in verses 21, 25, 29, 33 and 36 [f] *19* That is, about 175 feet or about 53 meters; also in verses 23, 27 and 47 [g] *37* Septuagint (see also verses 31 and 34); Hebrew *jambs*

portico of the gateway were two tables on each side, on which the burnt offerings, sin offerings[a] and guilt offerings were slaughtered. 40By the outside wall of the portico of the gateway, near the steps at the entrance of the north gateway were two tables, and on the other side of the steps were two tables. 41So there were four tables on one side of the gateway and four on the other — eight tables in all — on which the sacrifices were slaughtered. 42There were also four tables of dressed stone for the burnt offerings, each a cubit and a half long, a cubit and a half wide and a cubit high.[b] On them were placed the utensils for slaughtering the burnt offerings and the other sacrifices. 43And double-pronged hooks, each a handbreadth[c] long, were attached to the wall all around. The tables were for the flesh of the offerings.

The Rooms for the Priests

44Outside the inner gate, within the inner court, were two rooms, one[d] at the side of the north gate and facing south, and another at the side of the south[e] gate and facing north. 45He said to me, "The room facing south is for the priests who guard the temple, 46and the room facing north is for the priests who guard the altar. These are the sons of Zadok, who are the only Levites who may draw near to the LORD to minister before him."

47Then he measured the court: It was square — a hundred cubits long and a hundred cubits wide. And the altar was in front of the temple.

The New Temple

48He brought me to the portico of the temple and measured the jambs of the portico; they were five cubits wide on either side. The width of the entrance was fourteen cubits[f] and its projecting walls were[g] three cubits[h] wide on either side. 49The portico was twenty cubits[i] wide, and twelve[j] cubits[k] from front to back. It was reached by a flight of stairs,[l] and there were pillars on each side of the jambs.

41 Then the man brought me to the main hall and measured the jambs; the width of the jambs was six cubits[m] on each side.[n] 2The entrance was ten cubits[o] wide, and the projecting walls on each side of it were five cubits[p] wide. He also measured the main hall; it was forty cubits long and twenty cubits wide.[q]

3Then he went into the inner sanctuary and measured the jambs of the entrance; each was two cubits[r] wide. The entrance was six cubits wide, and the projecting walls on each side of it were seven cubits[s] wide. 4And he measured the length of the inner sanctuary; it was twenty cubits, and its width was twenty cubits across the end of the main hall. He said to me, "This is the Most Holy Place."

5Then he measured the wall of the temple; it was six cubits thick, and each side room around the temple was four cubits[t] wide. 6The side rooms were on three levels, one above another, thirty on each level. There were ledges all around the wall of the temple to serve as supports for the side rooms, so that the supports were not inserted into the wall of the temple. 7The side rooms all around the temple were wider at each successive level. The structure surrounding the temple was built in ascending stages, so that the rooms widened as one went upward. A stairway went up from the lowest floor to the top floor through the middle floor.

8I saw that the temple had a raised base all around it, forming the foundation of the side rooms. It was the length of the rod, six long cubits. 9The outer wall of the side rooms was five cubits thick. The open area between the side rooms of the temple 10and

[a] 39 Or *purification offerings* [b] 42 That is, about 2 2/3 feet long and wide and 21 inches high or about 80 centimeters long and wide and 53 centimeters high [c] 43 That is, about 3 1/2 inches or about 9 centimeters [d] 44 Septuagint; Hebrew *were rooms for singers, which were* [e] 44 Septuagint; Hebrew *east* [f] 48 That is, about 25 feet or about 7.4 meters [g] 48 Septuagint; Hebrew *entrance was* [h] 48 That is, about 5 1/4 feet or about 1.6 meters [i] 49 That is, about 35 feet or about 11 meters [j] 49 Septuagint; Hebrew *eleven* [k] 49 That is, about 21 feet or about 6.4 meters [l] 49 Hebrew; Septuagint *Ten steps led up to it* [m] 1 That is, about 11 feet or about 3.2 meters; also in verses 3, 5 and 8 [n] 1 One Hebrew manuscript and Septuagint; most Hebrew manuscripts *side, the width of the tent* [o] 2 That is, about 18 feet or about 5.3 meters [p] 2 That is, about 8 3/4 feet or about 2.7 meters; also in verses 9, 11 and 12 [q] 2 That is, about 70 feet long and 35 feet wide or about 21 meters long and 11 meters wide [r] 3 That is, about 3 1/2 feet or about 1.1 meters; also in verse 22 [s] 3 That is, about 12 feet or about 3.7 meters [t] 5 That is, about 7 feet or about 2.1 meters

the priests' rooms was twenty cubits wide all around the temple. [11]There were entrances to the side rooms from the open area, one on the north and another on the south; and the base adjoining the open area was five cubits wide all around.

[12]The building facing the temple courtyard on the west side was seventy cubits[a] wide. The wall of the building was five cubits thick all around, and its length was ninety cubits.[b]

[13]Then he measured the temple; it was a hundred cubits[c] long, and the temple courtyard and the building with its walls were also a hundred cubits long. [14]The width of the temple courtyard on the east, including the front of the temple, was a hundred cubits.

[15]Then he measured the length of the building facing the courtyard at the rear of the temple, including its galleries on each side; it was a hundred cubits.

The main hall, the inner sanctuary and the portico facing the court, [16]as well as the thresholds and the narrow windows and galleries around the three of them—everything beyond and including the threshold was covered with wood. The floor, the wall up to the windows, and the windows were covered. [17]In the space above the outside of the entrance to the inner sanctuary and on the walls at regular intervals all around the inner and outer sanctuary [18]were carved cherubim and palm trees. Palm trees alternated with cherubim. Each cherub had two faces: [19]the face of a human being toward the palm tree on one side and the face of a lion toward the palm tree on the other. They were carved all around the whole temple. [20]From the floor to the area above the entrance, cherubim and palm trees were carved on the wall of the main hall.

[21]The main hall had a rectangular doorframe, and the one at the front of the Most Holy Place was similar. [22]There was a wooden altar three cubits[d] high and two cubits square[e]; its corners, its base[f] and its sides were of wood. The man said to me, "This is the table that is before the LORD." [23]Both the main hall and the Most Holy Place had double doors. [24]Each door had two leaves—two hinged leaves for each door. [25]And on the doors of the main hall were carved cherubim and palm trees like those carved on the walls, and there was a wooden overhang on the front of the portico. [26]On the sidewalls of the portico were narrow windows with palm trees carved on each side. The side rooms of the temple also had overhangs.

The Rooms for the Priests

42 Then the man led me northward into the outer court and brought me to the rooms opposite the temple courtyard and opposite the outer wall on the north side. [2]The building whose door faced north was a hundred cubits long and fifty cubits wide.[g] [3]Both in the section twenty cubits[h] from the inner court and in the section opposite the pavement of the outer court, gallery faced gallery at the three levels. [4]In front of the rooms was an inner passageway ten cubits wide and a hundred cubits[i] long.[j] Their doors were on the north. [5]Now the upper rooms were narrower, for the galleries took more space from them than from the rooms on the lower and middle floors of the building. [6]The rooms on the top floor had no pillars, as the courts had; so they were smaller in floor space than those on the lower and middle floors. [7]There was an outer wall parallel to the rooms and the outer court; it extended in front of the rooms for fifty cubits. [8]While the row of rooms on the side next to the outer court was fifty cubits long, the row on the side nearest the sanctuary was a hundred cubits long. [9]The lower rooms had an entrance on the east side as one enters them from the outer court.

[10]On the south side[k] along the length of the wall of the outer court, adjoining the temple courtyard and opposite the outer wall, were rooms [11]with a passageway in front of them. These were like the rooms on the north; they had the same length and width, with similar exits and dimensions.

[a] *12* That is, about 123 feet or about 37 meters [b] *12* That is, about 158 feet or about 48 meters [c] *13* That is, about 175 feet or about 53 meters; also in verses 14 and 15 [d] *22* That is, about 5 1/4 feet or about 1.5 meters [e] *22* Septuagint; Hebrew *long* [f] *22* Septuagint; Hebrew *length* [g] *2* That is, about 175 feet long and 88 feet wide or about 53 meters long and 27 meters wide [h] *3* That is, about 35 feet or about 11 meters [i] *4* Septuagint and Syriac; Hebrew *and one cubit* [j] *4* That is, about 18 feet wide and 175 feet long or about 5.3 meters wide and 53 meters long [k] *10* Septuagint; Hebrew *Eastward*

Similar to the doorways on the north 12were the doorways of the rooms on the south. There was a doorway at the beginning of the passageway that was parallel to the corresponding wall extending eastward, by which one enters the rooms.

13Then he said to me, "The north and south rooms facing the temple courtyard are the priests' rooms, where the priests who approach the LORD will eat the most holy offerings. There they will put the most holy offerings — the grain offerings, the sin offerings[a] and the guilt offerings — for the place is holy. 14Once the priests enter the holy precincts, they are not to go into the outer court until they leave behind the garments in which they minister, for these are holy. They are to put on other clothes before they go near the places that are for the people."

15When he had finished measuring what was inside the temple area, he led me out by the east gate and measured the area all around: 16He measured the east side with the measuring rod; it was five hundred cubits.[b,c] 17He measured the north side; it was five hundred cubits[d] by the measuring rod. 18He measured the south side; it was five hundred cubits by the measuring rod. 19Then he turned to the west side and measured; it was five hundred cubits by the measuring rod. 20So he measured the area on all four sides. It had a wall around it, five hundred cubits long and five hundred cubits wide, to separate the holy from the common.

God's Glory Returns to the Temple

43 Then the man brought me to the gate facing east, 2and I saw the glory of the God of Israel coming from the east. His voice was like the roar of rushing waters, and the land was radiant with his glory. 3The vision I saw was like the vision I had seen when he[e] came to destroy the city and like the visions I had seen by the Kebar River, and I fell facedown. 4The glory of the LORD entered the temple through the gate facing east. 5Then the Spirit lifted me up and brought me into the inner court, and the glory of the LORD filled the temple.

6While the man was standing beside me, I heard someone speaking to me from inside the temple. 7He said: "Son of man, this is the place of my throne and the place for the soles of my feet. This is where I will live among the Israelites forever. The people of Israel will never again defile my holy name — neither they nor their kings — by their prostitution and the funeral offerings[f] for their kings at their death.[g] 8When they placed their threshold next to my threshold and their doorposts beside my doorposts, with only a wall between me and them, they defiled my holy name by their detestable practices. So I destroyed them in my anger. 9Now let them put away from me their prostitution and the funeral offerings for their kings, and I will live among them forever.

10"Son of man, describe the temple to the people of Israel, that they may be ashamed of their sins. Let them consider its perfection, 11and if they are ashamed of all they have done, make known to them the design of the temple — its arrangement, its exits and entrances — its whole design and all its regulations[h] and laws. Write these down before them so that they may be faithful to its design and follow all its regulations.

12"This is the law of the temple: All the surrounding area on top of the mountain will be most holy. Such is the law of the temple.

The Great Altar Restored

13"These are the measurements of the altar in long cubits,[i] that cubit being a cubit and a handbreadth: Its gutter is a cubit deep and a cubit wide, with a rim of one span[j] around the edge. And this is the height of the altar: 14From the gutter on the ground up to the lower ledge that goes around the altar it is two cubits high, and the ledge is a cubit wide.[k] From this lower ledge to the upper ledge that goes around the altar it is four

[a] *13* Or *purification offerings* [b] *16* See Septuagint of verse 17; Hebrew *rods*; also in verses 18 and 19.
[c] *16* Five hundred cubits equal about 875 feet or about 265 meters; also in verses 17, 18 and 19.
[d] *17* Septuagint; Hebrew *rods* [e] *3* Some Hebrew manuscripts and Vulgate; most Hebrew manuscripts *I*
[f] *7* Or *the memorial monuments*; also in verse 9 [g] *7* Or *their high places* [h] *11* Some Hebrew manuscripts and Septuagint; most Hebrew manuscripts *regulations and its whole design* [i] *13* That is, about 21 inches or about 53 centimeters; also in verses 14 and 17. The long cubit is the basic unit for linear measurement throughout Ezekiel 40 – 48. [j] *13* That is, about 11 inches or about 27 centimeters
[k] *14* That is, about 3 1/2 feet high and 1 3/4 feet wide or about 105 centimeters high and 53 centimeters wide

cubits high, and that ledge is also a cubit wide.[a] [15]Above that, the altar hearth is four cubits high, and four horns project upward from the hearth. [16]The altar hearth is square, twelve cubits[b] long and twelve cubits wide. [17]The upper ledge also is square, fourteen cubits[c] long and fourteen cubits wide. All around the altar is a gutter of one cubit with a rim of half a cubit.[d] The steps of the altar face east."

[18]Then he said to me, "Son of man, this is what the Sovereign LORD says: These will be the regulations for sacrificing burnt offerings and splashing blood against the altar when it is built: [19]You are to give a young bull as a sin offering[e] to the Levitical priests of the family of Zadok, who come near to minister before me, declares the Sovereign LORD. [20]You are to take some of its blood and put it on the four horns of the altar and on the four corners of the upper ledge and all around the rim, and so purify the altar and make atonement for it. [21]You are to take the bull for the sin offering and burn it in the designated part of the temple area outside the sanctuary.

[22]"On the second day you are to offer a male goat without defect for a sin offering, and the altar is to be purified as it was purified with the bull. [23]When you have finished purifying it, you are to offer a young bull and a ram from the flock, both without defect. [24]You are to offer them before the LORD, and the priests are to sprinkle salt on them and sacrifice them as a burnt offering to the LORD.

[25]"For seven days you are to provide a male goat daily for a sin offering; you are also to provide a young bull and a ram from the flock, both without defect. [26]For seven days they are to make atonement for the altar and cleanse it; thus they will dedicate it. [27]At the end of these days, from the eighth day on, the priests are to present your burnt offerings and fellowship offerings on the altar. Then I will accept you, declares the Sovereign LORD."

The Priesthood Restored

44 Then the man brought me back to the outer gate of the sanctuary, the one facing east, and it was shut. [2]The LORD said to me, "This gate is to remain shut. It must not be opened; no one may enter through it. It is to remain shut because the LORD, the God of Israel, has entered through it. [3]The prince himself is the only one who may sit inside the gateway to eat in the presence of the LORD. He is to enter by way of the portico of the gateway and go out the same way."

[4]Then the man brought me by way of the north gate to the front of the temple. I looked and saw the glory of the LORD filling the temple of the LORD, and I fell facedown.

[5]The LORD said to me, "Son of man, look carefully, listen closely and give attention to everything I tell you concerning all the regulations and instructions regarding the temple of the LORD. Give attention to the entrance to the temple and all the exits of the sanctuary. [6]Say to rebellious Israel, 'This is what the Sovereign LORD says: Enough of your detestable practices, people of Israel! [7]In addition to all your other detestable practices, you brought foreigners uncircumcised in heart and flesh into my sanctuary, desecrating my temple while you offered me food, fat and blood, and you broke my covenant. [8]Instead of carrying out your duty in regard to my holy things, you put others in charge of my sanctuary. [9]This is what the Sovereign LORD says: No foreigner uncircumcised in heart and flesh is to enter my sanctuary, not even the foreigners who live among the Israelites.

[10]" 'The Levites who went far from me when Israel went astray and who wandered from me after their idols must bear the consequences of their sin. [11]They may serve in my sanctuary, having charge of the gates of the temple and serving in it; they may slaughter the burnt offerings and sacrifices for the people and stand before the people and serve them. [12]But because they served them in the presence of their idols and made the people of Israel fall into sin, therefore I have sworn with uplifted hand that they must bear the consequences of their sin, declares the Sovereign LORD. [13]They are not to come near to serve me as priests or come near any of my holy things or my most holy offerings; they must bear the shame of their

[a] *14* That is, about 7 feet high and 1 3/4 feet wide or about 2.1 meters high and 53 centimeters wide
[b] *16* That is, about 21 feet or about 6.4 meters [c] *17* That is, about 25 feet or about 7.4 meters [d] *17* That is, about 11 inches or about 27 centimeters [e] *19* Or *purification offering*; also in verses 21, 22 and 25

detestable practices. 14And I will appoint
them to guard the temple for all the work
that is to be done in it.

15" 'But the Levitical priests, who are de-
scendants of Zadok and who guarded my
sanctuary when the Israelites went astray
from me, are to come near to minister be-
fore me; they are to stand before me to of-
fer sacrifices of fat and blood, declares the
Sovereign LORD. 16They alone are to enter
my sanctuary; they alone are to come near
my table to minister before me and serve me
as guards.

17" 'When they enter the gates of the inner
court, they are to wear linen clothes; they
must not wear any woolen garment while
ministering at the gates of the inner court or
inside the temple. 18They are to wear linen
turbans on their heads and linen undergar-
ments around their waists. They must not
wear anything that makes them perspire.
19When they go out into the outer court
where the people are, they are to take off the
clothes they have been ministering in and
are to leave them in the sacred rooms, and
put on other clothes, so that the people are
not consecrated through contact with their
garments.

20" 'They must not shave their heads or let
their hair grow long, but they are to keep the
hair of their heads trimmed. 21No priest is to
drink wine when he enters the inner court.
22They must not marry widows or divorced
women; they may marry only virgins of Isra-
elite descent or widows of priests. 23They are
to teach my people the difference between
the holy and the common and show them
how to distinguish between the unclean and
the clean.

24" 'In any dispute, the priests are to serve
as judges and decide it according to my or-
dinances. They are to keep my laws and my
decrees for all my appointed festivals, and
they are to keep my Sabbaths holy.

25" 'A priest must not defile himself by
going near a dead person; however, if the
dead person was his father or mother, son or
daughter, brother or unmarried sister, then
he may defile himself. 26After he is cleansed,
he must wait seven days. 27On the day he
goes into the inner court of the sanctuary to
minister in the sanctuary, he is to offer a sin
offering[a] for himself, declares the Sovereign
LORD.

28" 'I am to be the only inheritance the
priests have. You are to give them no pos-
session in Israel; I will be their possession.
29They will eat the grain offerings, the sin
offerings and the guilt offerings; and every-
thing in Israel devoted[b] to the LORD will be-
long to them. 30The best of all the firstfruits
and of all your special gifts will belong to the
priests. You are to give them the first portion
of your ground meal so that a blessing may
rest on your household. 31The priests must
not eat anything, whether bird or animal,
found dead or torn by wild animals.

Israel Fully Restored

45 " 'When you allot the land as an in-
heritance, you are to present to the
LORD a portion of the land as a sacred dis-
trict, 25,000 cubits[c] long and 20,000[d] cubits[e]
wide; the entire area will be holy. 2Of this,
a section 500 cubits[f] square is to be for the
sanctuary, with 50 cubits[g] around it for open
land. 3In the sacred district, measure off a
section 25,000 cubits long and 10,000 cubits[h]
wide. In it will be the sanctuary, the Most
Holy Place. 4It will be the sacred portion of
the land for the priests, who minister in the
sanctuary and who draw near to minister
before the LORD. It will be a place for their
houses as well as a holy place for the sanctu-
ary. 5An area 25,000 cubits long and 10,000
cubits wide will belong to the Levites, who
serve in the temple, as their possession for
towns to live in.[i]

6" 'You are to give the city as its property
an area 5,000 cubits[j] wide and 25,000 cubits
long, adjoining the sacred portion; it will be-
long to all Israel.

7" 'The prince will have the land border-
ing each side of the area formed by the sa-
cred district and the property of the city. It
will extend westward from the west side and

[a] *27* Or *purification offering*; also in verse 29 [b] *29* The Hebrew term refers to the irrevocable giving over of things or persons to the LORD. [c] *1* That is, about 8 miles or about 13 kilometers; also in verses 3, 5 and 6 [d] *1* Septuagint (see also verses 3 and 5 and 48:9); Hebrew *10,000* [e] *1* That is, about 6 1/2 miles or about 11 kilometers [f] *2* That is, about 875 feet or about 265 meters [g] *2* That is, about 88 feet or about 27 meters [h] *3* That is, about 3 1/3 miles or about 5.3 kilometers; also in verse 5 [i] *5* Septuagint; Hebrew *temple; they will have as their possession 20 rooms* [j] *6* That is, about 1 2/3 miles or about 2.7 kilometers

eastward from the east side, running length-
wise from the western to the eastern border
parallel to one of the tribal portions. [8]This
land will be his possession in Israel. And my
princes will no longer oppress my people but
will allow the people of Israel to possess the
land according to their tribes.
[9]" 'This is what the Sovereign LORD says:
You have gone far enough, princes of Israel!
Give up your violence and oppression and
do what is just and right. Stop dispossess-
ing my people, declares the Sovereign LORD.
[10]You are to use accurate scales, an accurate
ephah[a] and an accurate bath.[b] [11]The ephah
and the bath are to be the same size, the bath
containing a tenth of a homer and the ephah
a tenth of a homer; the homer is to be the
standard measure for both. [12]The shekel[c] is
to consist of twenty gerahs. Twenty shekels
plus twenty-five shekels plus fifteen shekels
equal one mina.[d]
[13]" 'This is the special gift you are to of-
fer: a sixth of an ephah[e] from each homer
of wheat and a sixth of an ephah[f] from each
homer of barley. [14]The prescribed portion of
olive oil, measured by the bath, is a tenth of
a bath[g] from each cor (which consists of ten
baths or one homer, for ten baths are equiv-
alent to a homer). [15]Also one sheep is to be
taken from every flock of two hundred from
the well-watered pastures of Israel. These
will be used for the grain offerings, burnt
offerings and fellowship offerings to make
atonement for the people, declares the Sov-
ereign LORD. [16]All the people of the land will
be required to give this special offering to
the prince in Israel. [17]It will be the duty of
the prince to provide the burnt offerings,
grain offerings and drink offerings at the fes-
tivals, the New Moons and the Sabbaths — at
all the appointed festivals of Israel. He will
provide the sin offerings,[h] grain offerings,
burnt offerings and fellowship offerings to
make atonement for the Israelites.
[18]" 'This is what the Sovereign LORD says:
In the first month on the first day you are to
take a young bull without defect and purify
the sanctuary. [19]The priest is to take some
of the blood of the sin offering and put it on
the doorposts of the temple, on the four cor-
ners of the upper ledge of the altar and on the
gateposts of the inner court. [20]You are to do
the same on the seventh day of the month for
anyone who sins unintentionally or through
ignorance; so you are to make atonement for
the temple.
[21]" 'In the first month on the fourteenth
day you are to observe the Passover, a fes-
tival lasting seven days, during which you
shall eat bread made without yeast. [22]On
that day the prince is to provide a bull as a
sin offering for himself and for all the peo-
ple of the land. [23]Every day during the sev-
en days of the festival he is to provide sev-
en bulls and seven rams without defect as
a burnt offering to the LORD, and a male
goat for a sin offering. [24]He is to provide as a
grain offering an ephah for each bull and an
ephah for each ram, along with a hin[i] of olive
oil for each ephah.
[25]" 'During the seven days of the festival,
which begins in the seventh month on the
fifteenth day, he is to make the same provi-
sion for sin offerings, burnt offerings, grain
offerings and oil.

46 " 'This is what the Sovereign LORD
says: The gate of the inner court fac-
ing east is to be shut on the six working days,
but on the Sabbath day and on the day of the
New Moon it is to be opened. [2]The prince is
to enter from the outside through the por-
tico of the gateway and stand by the gate-
post. The priests are to sacrifice his burnt
offering and his fellowship offerings. He
is to bow down in worship at the thresh-
old of the gateway and then go out, but the
gate will not be shut until evening. [3]On the
Sabbaths and New Moons the people of
the land are to worship in the presence of
the LORD at the entrance of that gateway.
[4]The burnt offering the prince brings to the
LORD on the Sabbath day is to be six male
lambs and a ram, all without defect. [5]The
grain offering given with the ram is to be an

[a] *10* An ephah was a dry measure having the capacity of about 3/5 bushel or about 22 liters. [b] *10* A bath was a liquid measure equaling about 6 gallons or about 22 liters. [c] *12* A shekel weighed about 2/5 ounce or about 12 grams. [d] *12* That is, 60 shekels; the common mina was 50 shekels. Sixty shekels were about 1 1/2 pounds or about 690 grams. [e] *13* That is, probably about 6 pounds or about 2.7 kilograms [f] *13* That is, probably about 5 pounds or about 2.3 kilograms [g] *14* That is, about 2 1/2 quarts or about 2.2 liters [h] *17* Or *purification offerings;* also in verses 19, 22, 23 and 25 [i] *24* That is, about 1 gallon or about 3.8 liters

ephah,[a] and the grain offering with the lambs is to be as much as he pleases, along with a hin[b] of olive oil for each ephah. 6 On the day of the New Moon he is to offer a young bull, six lambs and a ram, all without defect. 7 He is to provide as a grain offering one ephah with the bull, one ephah with the ram, and with the lambs as much as he wants to give, along with a hin of oil for each ephah. 8 When the prince enters, he is to go in through the portico of the gateway, and he is to come out the same way.

9 " 'When the people of the land come before the LORD at the appointed festivals, whoever enters by the north gate to worship is to go out the south gate; and whoever enters by the south gate is to go out the north gate. No one is to return through the gate by which they entered, but each is to go out the opposite gate. 10 The prince is to be among them, going in when they go in and going out when they go out. 11 At the feasts and the appointed festivals, the grain offering is to be an ephah with a bull, an ephah with a ram, and with the lambs as much as he pleases, along with a hin of oil for each ephah.

12 " 'When the prince provides a freewill offering to the LORD—whether a burnt offering or fellowship offerings—the gate facing east is to be opened for him. He shall offer his burnt offering or his fellowship offerings as he does on the Sabbath day. Then he shall go out, and after he has gone out, the gate will be shut.

13 " 'Every day you are to provide a year-old lamb without defect for a burnt offering to the LORD; morning by morning you shall provide it. 14 You are also to provide with it morning by morning a grain offering, consisting of a sixth of an ephah[c] with a third of a hin[d] of oil to moisten the flour. The presenting of this grain offering to the LORD is a lasting ordinance. 15 So the lamb and the grain offering and the oil shall be provided morning by morning for a regular burnt offering.

16 " 'This is what the Sovereign LORD says: If the prince makes a gift from his inheritance to one of his sons, it will also belong to his descendants; it is to be their property by inheritance. 17 If, however, he makes a gift from his inheritance to one of his servants, the servant may keep it until the year of freedom; then it will revert to the prince. His inheritance belongs to his sons only; it is theirs. 18 The prince must not take any of the inheritance of the people, driving them off their property. He is to give his sons their inheritance out of his own property, so that not one of my people will be separated from their property.' "

19 Then the man brought me through the entrance at the side of the gate to the sacred rooms facing north, which belonged to the priests, and showed me a place at the western end. 20 He said to me, "This is the place where the priests are to cook the guilt offering and the sin offering[e] and bake the grain offering, to avoid bringing them into the outer court and consecrating the people."

21 He then brought me to the outer court and led me around to its four corners, and I saw in each corner another court. 22 In the four corners of the outer court were enclosed[f] courts, forty cubits long and thirty cubits wide;[g] each of the courts in the four corners was the same size. 23 Around the inside of each of the four courts was a ledge of stone, with places for fire built all around under the ledge. 24 He said to me, "These are the kitchens where those who minister at the temple are to cook the sacrifices of the people."

The River From the Temple

47 The man brought me back to the entrance to the temple, and I saw water coming out from under the threshold of the temple toward the east (for the temple faced east). The water was coming down from under the south side of the temple, south of the altar. 2 He then brought me out through the north gate and led me around the outside to the outer gate facing east, and the water was trickling from the south side.

3 As the man went eastward with a measuring line in his hand, he measured off a

[a] *5* That is, probably about 35 pounds or about 16 kilograms; also in verses 7 and 11 [b] *5* That is, about 1 gallon or about 3.8 liters; also in verses 7 and 11 [c] *14* That is, probably about 6 pounds or about 2.7 kilograms [d] *14* That is, about 1 1/2 quarts or about 1.3 liters [e] *20* Or *purification offering* [f] *22* The meaning of the Hebrew for this word is uncertain. [g] *22* That is, about 70 feet long and 53 feet wide or about 21 meters long and 16 meters wide

thousand cubits[a] and then led me through
water that was ankle-deep. 4He measured
off another thousand cubits and led me
through water that was knee-deep. He mea-
sured off another thousand and led me
through water that was up to the waist. 5He
measured off another thousand, but now it
was a river that I could not cross, because
the water had risen and was deep enough
to swim in — a river that no one could cross.
6He asked me, "Son of man, do you see this?"

Then he led me back to the bank of the
river. 7When I arrived there, I saw a great
number of trees on each side of the river.
8He said to me, "This water flows toward the
eastern region and goes down into the Ar-
abah,[b] where it enters the Dead Sea. When
it empties into the sea, the salty water there
becomes fresh. 9Swarms of living creatures
will live wherever the river flows. There
will be large numbers of fish, because this
water flows there and makes the salt water
fresh; so where the river flows everything
will live. 10Fishermen will stand along the
shore; from En Gedi to En Eglaim there will
be places for spreading nets. The fish will be
of many kinds — like the fish of the Mediter-
ranean Sea. 11But the swamps and marshes
will not become fresh; they will be left for
salt. 12Fruit trees of all kinds will grow on
both banks of the river. Their leaves will not
wither, nor will their fruit fail. Every month
they will bear fruit, because the water from
the sanctuary flows to them. Their fruit will
serve for food and their leaves for healing."

The Boundaries of the Land

13This is what the Sovereign LORD says:
"These are the boundaries of the land that
you will divide among the twelve tribes of Is-
rael as their inheritance, with two portions
for Joseph. 14You are to divide it equally
among them. Because I swore with uplifted
hand to give it to your ancestors, this land
will become your inheritance.

15"This is to be the boundary of the land:

"On the north side it will run from the Med-
iterranean Sea by the Hethlon road past
Lebo Hamath to Zedad, 16Berothah[c]
and Sibraim (which lies on the border
between Damascus and Hamath), as far
as Hazer Hattikon, which is on the bor-
der of Hauran. 17The boundary will ex-
tend from the sea to Hazar Enan,[d] along
the northern border of Damascus, with
the border of Hamath to the north. This
will be the northern boundary.

18"On the east side the boundary will run
between Hauran and Damascus, along
the Jordan between Gilead and the
land of Israel, to the Dead Sea and as
far as Tamar.[e] This will be the eastern
boundary.

19"On the south side it will run from Tamar
as far as the waters of Meribah Kadesh,
then along the Wadi of Egypt to the
Mediterranean Sea. This will be the
southern boundary.

20"On the west side, the Mediterranean Sea
will be the boundary to a point oppo-
site Lebo Hamath. This will be the
western boundary.

21"You are to distribute this land among
yourselves according to the tribes of Isra-
el. 22You are to allot it as an inheritance for
yourselves and for the foreigners residing
among you and who have children. You are
to consider them as native-born Israelites;
along with you they are to be allotted an
inheritance among the tribes of Israel. 23In
whatever tribe a foreigner resides, there you
are to give them their inheritance," declares
the Sovereign LORD.

The Division of the Land

48 "These are the tribes, listed by name:
At the northern frontier, Dan will
have one portion; it will follow the Hethlon
road to Lebo Hamath; Hazar Enan and the
northern border of Damascus next to Ha-
math will be part of its border from the east
side to the west side.

2"Asher will have one portion; it will bor-
der the territory of Dan from east to west.

3"Naphtali will have one portion; it will
border the territory of Asher from east to west.

4"Manasseh will have one portion; it will
border the territory of Naphtali from east to
west.

[a] *3* That is, about 1,700 feet or about 530 meters [b] *8* Or *the Jordan Valley* [c] *15,16* See Septuagint and 48:1; Hebrew *road to go into Zedad, 16Hamath, Berothah.* [d] *17* Hebrew *Enon,* a variant of *Enan*
[e] *18* See Syriac; Hebrew *Israel. You will measure to the Dead Sea.*

GIVE US CLEAN HANDS

Charlie Hall

We bow our hearts, we bend our knees
Oh Spirit come and make us humble
We turn our eyes from evil things
Oh Lord we cast down our idols

Give us clean hands
Give us pure hearts
Let us not lift our souls to another

And O God, let us be
A generation that seeks
That seeks your face
O God of Jacob

THE INSPIRATION

Who may ascend the mountain of the LORD? Who may stand in his holy place? The one who has clean hands and a pure heart, who does not trust in an idol or swear by a false god. —Psalm 24:3–4

BEHIND THE SONG

Charlie Hall occasionally sits down, opens his Bible and asks God to "push something out" that would change his heart. One day while doing this, he came across Psalm 24 and gravitated toward its language and meaning. "I came across the part," Hall recalls, "where it says 'Who may ascend to the hill of the Lord,' and 'Who may stand in his holy place? The one who has clean hands and a pure heart,' who doesn't love anyone else more than God. Man, that was for me!"

A couple of verses later the chapter describes a generation that would seek after God. "The generation that seeks after him are those who don't speak out of falsehood and who love him with their hearts, minds, souls, strength," Hall adds. Hall's heart resonated with this challenge, and the song that grew from Psalm 24 has become a rallying cry for worshipers around the world.

For Hall this habit of essentially setting Scripture to music is very important to his own spiritual journey. "A Scripture will hit me," he says, "and I just try to sing it—not even really to write a song, but to just sing what he's written to me back to him. I'm saying 'hey, Lord, I'm agreeing with this and I want to sing it to you.'"

Selah

Although the melodies are lost to history, many Bible historians believe that a good number of the psalms were originally set to music. In this way Hall and many other contemporary worship writers follow in ancient footsteps.

Because of the way music functions in the brain (and many believe, the spirit) it reinforces phrases and ideas in our memory. Singing Scripture to music is one of the best ways to commit it to memory. What are some of the Scriptures you've learned by singing them? How different was that experience from memorizing Scripture without music?

5 “Ephraim will have one portion; it will
border the territory of Manasseh from east
to west.

6 “Reuben will have one portion; it will
border the territory of Ephraim from east to
west.

7 “Judah will have one portion; it will bor-
der the territory of Reuben from east to west.

8 “Bordering the territory of Judah from
east to west will be the portion you are to
present as a special gift. It will be 25,000 cu-
bits[a] wide, and its length from east to west
will equal one of the tribal portions; the
sanctuary will be in the center of it.

9 “The special portion you are to offer
to the LORD will be 25,000 cubits long and
10,000 cubits[b] wide. 10 This will be the sacred
portion for the priests. It will be 25,000 cubits
long on the north side, 10,000 cubits wide on
the west side, 10,000 cubits wide on the east
side and 25,000 cubits long on the south side.
In the center of it will be the sanctuary of
the LORD. 11 This will be for the consecrated
priests, the Zadokites, who were faithful in
serving me and did not go astray as the Le-
vites did when the Israelites went astray. 12 It
will be a special gift to them from the sacred
portion of the land, a most holy portion, bor-
dering the territory of the Levites.

13 “Alongside the territory of the priests,
the Levites will have an allotment 25,000
cubits long and 10,000 cubits wide. Its total
length will be 25,000 cubits and its width
10,000 cubits. 14 They must not sell or ex-
change any of it. This is the best of the land
and must not pass into other hands, because
it is holy to the LORD.

15 “The remaining area, 5,000 cubits[c] wide
and 25,000 cubits long, will be for the com-
mon use of the city, for houses and for pas-
tureland. The city will be in the center of it
16 and will have these measurements: the
north side 4,500 cubits,[d] the south side 4,500
cubits, the east side 4,500 cubits, and the
west side 4,500 cubits. 17 The pastureland for
the city will be 250 cubits[e] on the north, 250
cubits on the south, 250 cubits on the east,
and 250 cubits on the west. 18 What remains
of the area, bordering on the sacred portion
and running the length of it, will be 10,000
cubits on the east side and 10,000 cubits on
the west side. Its produce will supply food for
the workers of the city. 19 The workers from
the city who farm it will come from all the
tribes of Israel. 20 The entire portion will be a
square, 25,000 cubits on each side. As a spe-
cial gift you will set aside the sacred portion,
along with the property of the city.

21 “What remains on both sides of the area
formed by the sacred portion and the prop-
erty of the city will belong to the prince. It
will extend eastward from the 25,000 cubits
of the sacred portion to the eastern border,
and westward from the 25,000 cubits to the
western border. Both these areas running
the length of the tribal portions will belong
to the prince, and the sacred portion with
the temple sanctuary will be in the center
of them. 22 So the property of the Levites and
the property of the city will lie in the center of
the area that belongs to the prince. The area
belonging to the prince will lie between the
border of Judah and the border of Benjamin.

23 “As for the rest of the tribes: Benjamin
will have one portion; it will extend from the
east side to the west side.

24 “Simeon will have one portion; it will
border the territory of Benjamin from east
to west.

25 “Issachar will have one portion; it will
border the territory of Simeon from east to
west.

26 “Zebulun will have one portion; it will
border the territory of Issachar from east to
west.

27 “Gad will have one portion; it will border
the territory of Zebulun from east to west.

28 “The southern boundary of Gad will run
south from Tamar to the waters of Meribah
Kadesh, then along the Wadi of Egypt to the
Mediterranean Sea.

29 “This is the land you are to allot as an
inheritance to the tribes of Israel, and these
will be their portions,” declares the Sover-
eign LORD.

The Gates of the New City

30 “These will be the exits of the city: Be-
ginning on the north side, which is 4,500 cu-
bits long, 31 the gates of the city will be named

[a] *8* That is, about 8 miles or about 13 kilometers; also in verses 9, 10, 13, 15, 20 and 21 [b] *9* That is, about 3 1/3 miles or about 5.3 kilometers; also in verses 10, 13 and 18 [c] *15* That is, about 1 2/3 miles or about 2.7 kilometers [d] *16* That is, about 1 1/2 miles or about 2.4 kilometers; also in verses 30, 32, 33 and 34 [e] *17* That is, about 440 feet or about 135 meters

after the tribes of Israel. The three gates on the north side will be the gate of Reuben, the gate of Judah and the gate of Levi.

[32] "On the east side, which is 4,500 cubits long, will be three gates: the gate of Joseph, the gate of Benjamin and the gate of Dan.

[33] "On the south side, which measures 4,500 cubits, will be three gates: the gate of Simeon, the gate of Issachar and the gate of Zebulun.

[34] "On the west side, which is 4,500 cubits long, will be three gates: the gate of Gad, the gate of Asher and the gate of Naphtali.

[35] "The distance all around will be 18,000 cubits.[a]

"And the name of the city from that time on will be:

THE LORD IS THERE."

[a] *35* That is, about 6 miles or about 9.5 kilometers

DANIEL

Daniel's Training in Babylon

1 In the third year of the reign of Jehoiakim king of Judah, Nebuchadnezzar king of Babylon came to Jerusalem and besieged it. [2]And the Lord delivered Jehoiakim king of Judah into his hand, along with some of the articles from the temple of God. These he carried off to the temple of his god in Babylonia[a] and put in the treasure house of his god.

[3]Then the king ordered Ashpenaz, chief of his court officials, to bring into the king's service some of the Israelites from the royal family and the nobility— [4]young men without any physical defect, handsome, showing aptitude for every kind of learning, well informed, quick to understand, and qualified to serve in the king's palace. He was to teach them the language and literature of the Babylonians.[b] [5]The king assigned them a daily amount of food and wine from the king's table. They were to be trained for three years, and after that they were to enter the king's service.

[6]Among those who were chosen were some from Judah: Daniel, Hananiah, Mishael and Azariah. [7]The chief official gave them new names: to Daniel, the name Belteshazzar; to Hananiah, Shadrach; to Mishael, Meshach; and to Azariah, Abednego.

[8]But Daniel resolved not to defile himself with the royal food and wine, and he asked the chief official for permission not to defile himself this way. [9]Now God had caused the official to show favor and compassion to Daniel, [10]but the official told Daniel, "I am afraid of my lord the king, who has assigned your[c] food and drink. Why should he see you looking worse than the other young men your age? The king would then have my head because of you."

[11]Daniel then said to the guard whom the chief official had appointed over Daniel, Hananiah, Mishael and Azariah, [12]"Please test your servants for ten days: Give us nothing but vegetables to eat and water to drink. [13]Then compare our appearance with that of the young men who eat the royal food, and treat your servants in accordance with what you see." [14]So he agreed to this and tested them for ten days.

[15]At the end of the ten days they looked healthier and better nourished than any of the young men who ate the royal food. [16]So the guard took away their choice food and the wine they were to drink and gave them vegetables instead.

[17]To these four young men God gave knowledge and understanding of all kinds of literature and learning. And Daniel could understand visions and dreams of all kinds.

[18]At the end of the time set by the king to bring them into his service, the chief official presented them to Nebuchadnezzar. [19]The king talked with them, and he found none equal to Daniel, Hananiah, Mishael and Azariah; so they entered the king's service. [20]In every matter of wisdom and understanding about which the king questioned them, he found them ten times better than all the magicians and enchanters in his whole kingdom.

[21]And Daniel remained there until the first year of King Cyrus.

Nebuchadnezzar's Dream

2 In the second year of his reign, Nebuchadnezzar had dreams; his mind was troubled and he could not sleep. [2]So the king summoned the magicians, enchanters, sorcerers and astrologers[d] to tell him what he had dreamed. When they came in and stood before the king, [3]he said to them, "I have had a dream that troubles me and I want to know what it means.[e]"

[4]Then the astrologers answered the king,[f]

[a] 2 Hebrew *Shinar* [b] 4 Or *Chaldeans* [c] 10 The Hebrew for *your* and *you* in this verse is plural.
[d] 2 Or *Chaldeans*; also in verses 4, 5 and 10 [e] 3 Or *was* [f] 4 At this point the Hebrew text has *in Aramaic*, indicating that the text from here through the end of chapter 7 is in Aramaic.

"May the king live forever! Tell your servants
the dream, and we will interpret it."
[5]The king replied to the astrologers, "This
is what I have firmly decided: If you do not
tell me what my dream was and interpret it, I
will have you cut into pieces and your hous-
es turned into piles of rubble. [6]But if you tell
me the dream and explain it, you will receive
from me gifts and rewards and great honor.
So tell me the dream and interpret it for me."
[7]Once more they replied, "Let the king
tell his servants the dream, and we will in-
terpret it."
[8]Then the king answered, "I am certain
that you are trying to gain time, because you
realize that this is what I have firmly decid-
ed: [9]If you do not tell me the dream, there is
only one penalty for you. You have conspired
to tell me misleading and wicked things,
hoping the situation will change. So then,
tell me the dream, and I will know that you
can interpret it for me."
[10]The astrologers answered the king,
"There is no one on earth who can do what
the king asks! No king, however great and
mighty, has ever asked such a thing of any
magician or enchanter or astrologer. [11]What
the king asks is too difficult. No one can re-
veal it to the king except the gods, and they
do not live among humans."
[12]This made the king so angry and furious
that he ordered the execution of all the wise
men of Babylon. [13]So the decree was issued
to put the wise men to death, and men were
sent to look for Daniel and his friends to put
them to death.
[14]When Arioch, the commander of the
king's guard, had gone out to put to death
the wise men of Babylon, Daniel spoke to
him with wisdom and tact. [15]He asked the
king's officer, "Why did the king issue such
a harsh decree?" Arioch then explained the
matter to Daniel. [16]At this, Daniel went in to
the king and asked for time, so that he might
interpret the dream for him.
[17]Then Daniel returned to his house and
explained the matter to his friends Hanani-
ah, Mishael and Azariah. [18]He urged them
to plead for mercy from the God of heaven
concerning this mystery, so that he and his
friends might not be executed with the rest
of the wise men of Babylon. [19]During the
night the mystery was revealed to Daniel
in a vision. Then Daniel praised the God of
heaven [20]and said:

"Praise be to the name of God for ever
and ever;
wisdom and power are his.
[21]He changes times and seasons;
he deposes kings and raises up others.
He gives wisdom to the wise
and knowledge to the discerning.
[22]He reveals deep and hidden things;
he knows what lies in darkness,
and light dwells with him.
[23]I thank and praise you, God of my
ancestors:
You have given me wisdom and power,
you have made known to me what we
asked of you,
you have made known to us the dream
of the king."

Daniel Interprets the Dream

[24]Then Daniel went to Arioch, whom the
king had appointed to execute the wise men
of Babylon, and said to him, "Do not execute
the wise men of Babylon. Take me to the
king, and I will interpret his dream for him."
[25]Arioch took Daniel to the king at once
and said, "I have found a man among the ex-
iles from Judah who can tell the king what
his dream means."
[26]The king asked Daniel (also called Bel-
teshazzar), "Are you able to tell me what I
saw in my dream and interpret it?"
[27]Daniel replied, "No wise man, enchant-
er, magician or diviner can explain to the
king the mystery he has asked about, [28]but
there is a God in heaven who reveals mys-
teries. He has shown King Nebuchadnez-
zar what will happen in days to come. Your
dream and the visions that passed through
your mind as you were lying in bed are these:
[29]"As Your Majesty was lying there, your
mind turned to things to come, and the re-
vealer of mysteries showed you what is go-
ing to happen. [30]As for me, this mystery has
been revealed to me, not because I have
greater wisdom than anyone else alive, but
so that Your Majesty may know the interpre-
tation and that you may understand what
went through your mind.
[31]"Your Majesty looked, and there before
you stood a large statue — an enormous, daz-
zling statue, awesome in appearance. [32]The
head of the statue was made of pure gold, its
chest and arms of silver, its belly and thighs
of bronze, [33]its legs of iron, its feet partly of

iron and partly of baked clay. [34]While you were watching, a rock was cut out, but not by human hands. It struck the statue on its feet of iron and clay and smashed them. [35]Then the iron, the clay, the bronze, the silver and the gold were all broken to pieces and became like chaff on a threshing floor in the summer. The wind swept them away without leaving a trace. But the rock that struck the statue became a huge mountain and filled the whole earth.

[36]"This was the dream, and now we will interpret it to the king. [37]Your Majesty, you are the king of kings. The God of heaven has given you dominion and power and might and glory; [38]in your hands he has placed all mankind and the beasts of the field and the birds in the sky. Wherever they live, he has made you ruler over them all. You are that head of gold.

[39]"After you, another kingdom will arise, inferior to yours. Next, a third kingdom, one of bronze, will rule over the whole earth. [40]Finally, there will be a fourth kingdom, strong as iron—for iron breaks and smashes everything—and as iron breaks things to pieces, so it will crush and break all the others. [41]Just as you saw that the feet and toes were partly of baked clay and partly of iron, so this will be a divided kingdom; yet it will have some of the strength of iron in it, even as you saw iron mixed with clay. [42]As the toes were partly iron and partly clay, so this kingdom will be partly strong and partly brittle. [43]And just as you saw the iron mixed with baked clay, so the people will be a mixture and will not remain united, any more than iron mixes with clay.

[44]"In the time of those kings, the God of heaven will set up a kingdom that will never be destroyed, nor will it be left to another people. It will crush all those kingdoms and bring them to an end, but it will itself endure forever. [45]This is the meaning of the vision of the rock cut out of a mountain, but not by human hands—a rock that broke the iron, the bronze, the clay, the silver and the gold to pieces.

"The great God has shown the king what will take place in the future. The dream is true and its interpretation is trustworthy."

[46]Then King Nebuchadnezzar fell prostrate before Daniel and paid him honor and ordered that an offering and incense be presented to him. [47]The king said to Daniel, "Surely your God is the God of gods and the Lord of kings and a revealer of mysteries, for you were able to reveal this mystery."

[48]Then the king placed Daniel in a high position and lavished many gifts on him. He made him ruler over the entire province of Babylon and placed him in charge of all its wise men. [49]Moreover, at Daniel's request the king appointed Shadrach, Meshach and Abednego administrators over the province of Babylon, while Daniel himself remained at the royal court.

The Image of Gold and the Blazing Furnace

3 King Nebuchadnezzar made an image of gold, sixty cubits high and six cubits wide,[a] and set it up on the plain of Dura in the province of Babylon. [2]He then summoned the satraps, prefects, governors, advisers, treasurers, judges, magistrates and all the other provincial officials to come to the dedication of the image he had set up. [3]So the satraps, prefects, governors, advisers, treasurers, judges, magistrates and all the other provincial officials assembled for the dedication of the image that King Nebuchadnezzar had set up, and they stood before it.

[4]Then the herald loudly proclaimed, "Nations and peoples of every language, this is what you are commanded to do: [5]As soon as you hear the sound of the horn, flute, zither, lyre, harp, pipe and all kinds of music, you must fall down and worship the image of gold that King Nebuchadnezzar has set up. [6]Whoever does not fall down and worship will immediately be thrown into a blazing furnace."

[7]Therefore, as soon as they heard the sound of the horn, flute, zither, lyre, harp and all kinds of music, all the nations and peoples of every language fell down and worshiped the image of gold that King Nebuchadnezzar had set up.

[8]At this time some astrologers[b] came forward and denounced the Jews. [9]They said to

[a] *1* That is, about 90 feet high and 9 feet wide or about 27 meters high and 2.7 meters wide
[b] *8* Or *Chaldeans*

King Nebuchadnezzar, "May the king live
forever! 10Your Majesty has issued a decree
that everyone who hears the sound of the
horn, flute, zither, lyre, harp, pipe and all
kinds of music must fall down and worship
the image of gold, 11and that whoever does
not fall down and worship will be thrown
into a blazing furnace. 12But there are some
Jews whom you have set over the affairs of
the province of Babylon — Shadrach, Meshach and Abednego — who pay no attention to you, Your Majesty. They neither serve
your gods nor worship the image of gold you
have set up."

13Furious with rage, Nebuchadnezzar
summoned Shadrach, Meshach and Abednego. So these men were brought before the
king, 14and Nebuchadnezzar said to them,
"Is it true, Shadrach, Meshach and Abednego, that you do not serve my gods or worship
the image of gold I have set up? 15Now when
you hear the sound of the horn, flute, zither, lyre, harp, pipe and all kinds of music, if
you are ready to fall down and worship the
image I made, very good. But if you do not
worship it, you will be thrown immediately
into a blazing furnace. Then what god will
be able to rescue you from my hand?"

16Shadrach, Meshach and Abednego replied to him, "King Nebuchadnezzar, we do
not need to defend ourselves before you in
this matter. 17If we are thrown into the blazing furnace, the God we serve is able to deliver us from it, and he will deliver us[a] from
Your Majesty's hand. 18But even if he does
not, we want you to know, Your Majesty, that
we will not serve your gods or worship the
image of gold you have set up."

19Then Nebuchadnezzar was furious with
Shadrach, Meshach and Abednego, and his
attitude toward them changed. He ordered
the furnace heated seven times hotter than
usual 20and commanded some of the strongest soldiers in his army to tie up Shadrach,
Meshach and Abednego and throw them
into the blazing furnace. 21So these men,
wearing their robes, trousers, turbans and
other clothes, were bound and thrown into
the blazing furnace. 22The king's command
was so urgent and the furnace so hot that
the flames of the fire killed the soldiers who
took up Shadrach, Meshach and Abednego,
23and these three men, firmly tied, fell into
the blazing furnace.

24Then King Nebuchadnezzar leaped to
his feet in amazement and asked his advisers, "Weren't there three men that we tied up
and threw into the fire?"

They replied, "Certainly, Your Majesty."

25He said, "Look! I see four men walking
around in the fire, unbound and unharmed,
and the fourth looks like a son of the gods."

26Nebuchadnezzar then approached the
opening of the blazing furnace and shouted, "Shadrach, Meshach and Abednego, servants of the Most High God, come out! Come
here!"

So Shadrach, Meshach and Abednego
came out of the fire, 27and the satraps, prefects, governors and royal advisers crowded
around them. They saw that the fire had not
harmed their bodies, nor was a hair of their
heads singed; their robes were not scorched,
and there was no smell of fire on them.

28Then Nebuchadnezzar said, "Praise be
to the God of Shadrach, Meshach and Abednego, who has sent his angel and rescued his
servants! They trusted in him and defied the
king's command and were willing to give
up their lives rather than serve or worship
any god except their own God. 29Therefore
I decree that the people of any nation or language who say anything against the God of
Shadrach, Meshach and Abednego be cut
into pieces and their houses be turned into
piles of rubble, for no other god can save in
this way."

30Then the king promoted Shadrach, Meshach and Abednego in the province of Babylon.

Nebuchadnezzar's Dream of a Tree

4 [b] King Nebuchadnezzar,

To the nations and peoples of every
language, who live in all the earth:

May you prosper greatly!

2It is my pleasure to tell you about
the miraculous signs and wonders
that the Most High God has performed
for me.

3How great are his signs,
how mighty his wonders!

[a] 17 Or *If the God we serve is able to deliver us, then he will deliver us from the blazing furnace and*
[b] In Aramaic texts 4:1-3 is numbered 3:31-33, and 4:4-37 is numbered 4:1-34.

His kingdom is an eternal
kingdom;
his dominion endures from
generation to generation.

4 I, Nebuchadnezzar, was at home in
my palace, contented and prosperous.
5 I had a dream that made me afraid.
As I was lying in bed, the images and
visions that passed through my mind
terrified me. 6 So I commanded that
all the wise men of Babylon be brought
before me to interpret the dream for
me. 7 When the magicians, enchant-
ers, astrologers[a] and diviners came,
I told them the dream, but they could
not interpret it for me. 8 Finally, Daniel
came into my presence and I told him
the dream. (He is called Belteshazzar,
after the name of my god, and the spirit
of the holy gods is in him.)

9 I said, "Belteshazzar, chief of the
magicians, I know that the spirit of the
holy gods is in you, and no mystery is
too difficult for you. Here is my dream;
interpret it for me. 10 These are the vi-
sions I saw while lying in bed: I looked,
and there before me stood a tree in the
middle of the land. Its height was enor-
mous. 11 The tree grew large and strong
and its top touched the sky; it was visi-
ble to the ends of the earth. 12 Its leaves
were beautiful, its fruit abundant, and
on it was food for all. Under it the wild
animals found shelter, and the birds
lived in its branches; from it every crea-
ture was fed.

13 "In the visions I saw while lying in
bed, I looked, and there before me was
a holy one, a messenger,[b] coming down
from heaven. 14 He called in a loud
voice: 'Cut down the tree and trim off its
branches; strip off its leaves and scatter
its fruit. Let the animals flee from un-
der it and the birds from its branches.
15 But let the stump and its roots, bound
with iron and bronze, remain in the
ground, in the grass of the field.

" 'Let him be drenched with the dew
of heaven, and let him live with the an-
imals among the plants of the earth.
16 Let his mind be changed from that of
a man and let him be given the mind
of an animal, till seven times[c] pass by
for him.

17 " 'The decision is announced by
messengers, the holy ones declare the
verdict, so that the living may know
that the Most High is sovereign over all
kingdoms on earth and gives them to
anyone he wishes and sets over them
the lowliest of people.'

18 "This is the dream that I, King Neb-
uchadnezzar, had. Now, Belteshazzar,
tell me what it means, for none of the
wise men in my kingdom can interpret
it for me. But you can, because the spirit
of the holy gods is in you."

Daniel Interprets the Dream

19 Then Daniel (also called Belte-
shazzar) was greatly perplexed for a
time, and his thoughts terrified him. So
the king said, "Belteshazzar, do not let
the dream or its meaning alarm you."

Belteshazzar answered, "My lord, if
only the dream applied to your enemies
and its meaning to your adversaries!
20 The tree you saw, which grew large
and strong, with its top touching the
sky, visible to the whole earth, 21 with
beautiful leaves and abundant fruit,
providing food for all, giving shelter to
the wild animals, and having nesting
places in its branches for the birds —
22 Your Majesty, you are that tree! You
have become great and strong; your
greatness has grown until it reaches
the sky, and your dominion extends to
distant parts of the earth.

23 "Your Majesty saw a holy one, a
messenger, coming down from heav-
en and saying, 'Cut down the tree and
destroy it, but leave the stump, bound
with iron and bronze, in the grass of
the field, while its roots remain in the
ground. Let him be drenched with the
dew of heaven; let him live with the
wild animals, until seven times pass by
for him.'

24 "This is the interpretation, Your
Majesty, and this is the decree the
Most High has issued against my lord
the king: 25 You will be driven away
from people and will live with the wild

[a] 7 Or *Chaldeans* [b] 13 Or *watchman*; also in verses 17 and 23 [c] 16 Or *years*; also in verses 23, 25 and 32

animals; you will eat grass like the ox
and be drenched with the dew of heav-
en. Seven times will pass by for you un-
til you acknowledge that the Most High
is sovereign over all kingdoms on earth
and gives them to anyone he wishes.
26 The command to leave the stump of
the tree with its roots means that your
kingdom will be restored to you when
you acknowledge that Heaven rules.
27 Therefore, Your Majesty, be pleased
to accept my advice: Renounce your
sins by doing what is right, and your
wickedness by being kind to the op-
pressed. It may be that then your pros-
perity will continue."

The Dream Is Fulfilled

28 All this happened to King Nebu-
chadnezzar. 29 Twelve months later, as
the king was walking on the roof of the
royal palace of Babylon, 30 he said, "Is
not this the great Babylon I have built
as the royal residence, by my mighty
power and for the glory of my majesty?"
31 Even as the words were on his lips,
a voice came from heaven, "This is what
is decreed for you, King Nebuchadnez-
zar: Your royal authority has been tak-
en from you. 32 You will be driven away
from people and will live with the wild
animals; you will eat grass like the ox.
Seven times will pass by for you until
you acknowledge that the Most High is
sovereign over all kingdoms on earth
and gives them to anyone he wishes."
33 Immediately what had been said
about Nebuchadnezzar was fulfilled.
He was driven away from people and
ate grass like the ox. His body was
drenched with the dew of heaven until
his hair grew like the feathers of an ea-
gle and his nails like the claws of a bird.

34 At the end of that time, I, Nebu-
chadnezzar, raised my eyes toward
heaven, and my sanity was restored.
Then I praised the Most High; I honored
and glorified him who lives forever.

His dominion is an eternal dominion;
his kingdom endures from generation
to generation.
35 All the peoples of the earth
are regarded as nothing.
He does as he pleases
with the powers of heaven
and the peoples of the earth.
No one can hold back his hand
or say to him: "What have you done?"

36 At the same time that my sanity
was restored, my honor and splendor
were returned to me for the glory of
my kingdom. My advisers and nobles
sought me out, and I was restored to
my throne and became even greater
than before. 37 Now I, Nebuchadnez-
zar, praise and exalt and glorify the
King of heaven, because everything he
does is right and all his ways are just.
And those who walk in pride he is able
to humble.

The Writing on the Wall

5 King Belshazzar gave a great banquet
for a thousand of his nobles and drank
wine with them. 2 While Belshazzar was
drinking his wine, he gave orders to bring in
the gold and silver goblets that Nebuchad-
nezzar his father[a] had taken from the temple
in Jerusalem, so that the king and his nobles,
his wives and his concubines might drink
from them. 3 So they brought in the gold gob-
lets that had been taken from the temple of
God in Jerusalem, and the king and his no-
bles, his wives and his concubines drank
from them. 4 As they drank the wine, they
praised the gods of gold and silver, of bronze,
iron, wood and stone.
5 Suddenly the fingers of a human hand
appeared and wrote on the plaster of the
wall, near the lampstand in the royal palace.
The king watched the hand as it wrote. 6 His
face turned pale and he was so frightened
that his legs became weak and his knees
were knocking.
7 The king summoned the enchanters,
astrologers[b] and diviners. Then he said to
these wise men of Babylon, "Whoever reads
this writing and tells me what it means will
be clothed in purple and have a gold chain
placed around his neck, and he will be made
the third highest ruler in the kingdom."
8 Then all the king's wise men came in,
but they could not read the writing or tell the

[a] 2 Or *ancestor*; or *predecessor*; also in verses 11, 13 and 18 [b] 7 Or *Chaldeans*; also in verse 11

king what it meant. 9 So King Belshazzar became even more terrified and his face grew more pale. His nobles were baffled.

10 The queen,[a] hearing the voices of the king and his nobles, came into the banquet hall. "May the king live forever!" she said. "Don't be alarmed! Don't look so pale! 11 There is a man in your kingdom who has the spirit of the holy gods in him. In the time of your father he was found to have insight and intelligence and wisdom like that of the gods. Your father, King Nebuchadnezzar, appointed him chief of the magicians, enchanters, astrologers and diviners. 12 He did this because Daniel, whom the king called Belteshazzar, was found to have a keen mind and knowledge and understanding, and also the ability to interpret dreams, explain riddles and solve difficult problems. Call for Daniel, and he will tell you what the writing means."

13 So Daniel was brought before the king, and the king said to him, "Are you Daniel, one of the exiles my father the king brought from Judah? 14 I have heard that the spirit of the gods is in you and that you have insight, intelligence and outstanding wisdom. 15 The wise men and enchanters were brought before me to read this writing and tell me what it means, but they could not explain it. 16 Now I have heard that you are able to give interpretations and to solve difficult problems. If you can read this writing and tell me what it means, you will be clothed in purple and have a gold chain placed around your neck, and you will be made the third highest ruler in the kingdom."

17 Then Daniel answered the king, "You may keep your gifts for yourself and give your rewards to someone else. Nevertheless, I will read the writing for the king and tell him what it means.

18 "Your Majesty, the Most High God gave your father Nebuchadnezzar sovereignty and greatness and glory and splendor. 19 Because of the high position he gave him, all the nations and peoples of every language dreaded and feared him. Those the king wanted to put to death, he put to death; those he wanted to spare, he spared; those he wanted to promote, he promoted; and those he wanted to humble, he humbled. 20 But when his heart became arrogant and hardened with pride, he was deposed from his royal throne and stripped of his glory. 21 He was driven away from people and given the mind of an animal; he lived with the wild donkeys and ate grass like the ox; and his body was drenched with the dew of heaven, until he acknowledged that the Most High God is sovereign over all kingdoms on earth and sets over them anyone he wishes.

22 "But you, Belshazzar, his son,[b] have not humbled yourself, though you knew all this. 23 Instead, you have set yourself up against the Lord of heaven. You had the goblets from his temple brought to you, and you and your nobles, your wives and your concubines drank wine from them. You praised the gods of silver and gold, of bronze, iron, wood and stone, which cannot see or hear or understand. But you did not honor the God who holds in his hand your life and all your ways. 24 Therefore he sent the hand that wrote the inscription.

25 "This is the inscription that was written:

MENE, MENE, TEKEL, PARSIN

26 "Here is what these words mean:

Mene[c]: God has numbered the days of your reign and brought it to an end.

27 *Tekel*[d]: You have been weighed on the scales and found wanting.

28 *Peres*[e]: Your kingdom is divided and given to the Medes and Persians."

29 Then at Belshazzar's command, Daniel was clothed in purple, a gold chain was placed around his neck, and he was proclaimed the third highest ruler in the kingdom.

30 That very night Belshazzar, king of the Babylonians,[f] was slain, 31 and Darius the Mede took over the kingdom, at the age of sixty-two.[g]

[a] *10* Or *queen mother* [b] *22* Or *descendant;* or *successor* [c] *26* *Mene* can mean *numbered* or *mina* (a unit of money). [d] *27* *Tekel* can mean *weighed* or *shekel.* [e] *28* *Peres* (the singular of *Parsin*) can mean *divided* or *Persia* or *a half mina* or *a half shekel.* [f] *30* Or *Chaldeans* [g] *31* In Aramaic texts this verse (5:31) is numbered 6:1.

Daniel in the Den of Lions

6 [a] It pleased Darius to appoint 120 satraps to rule throughout the kingdom, [2]with three administrators over them, one of whom was Daniel. The satraps were made accountable to them so that the king might not suffer loss. [3]Now Daniel so distinguished himself among the administrators and the satraps by his exceptional qualities that the king planned to set him over the whole kingdom. [4]At this, the administrators and the satraps tried to find grounds for charges against Daniel in his conduct of government affairs, but they were unable to do so. They could find no corruption in him, because he was trustworthy and neither corrupt nor negligent. [5]Finally these men said, "We will never find any basis for charges against this man Daniel unless it has something to do with the law of his God."

[6]So these administrators and satraps went as a group to the king and said: "May King Darius live forever! [7]The royal administrators, prefects, satraps, advisers and governors have all agreed that the king should issue an edict and enforce the decree that anyone who prays to any god or human being during the next thirty days, except to you, Your Majesty, shall be thrown into the lions' den. [8]Now, Your Majesty, issue the decree and put it in writing so that it cannot be altered — in accordance with the law of the Medes and Persians, which cannot be repealed." [9]So King Darius put the decree in writing.

[10]Now when Daniel learned that the decree had been published, he went home to his upstairs room where the windows opened toward Jerusalem. Three times a day he got down on his knees and prayed, giving thanks to his God, just as he had done before. [11]Then these men went as a group and found Daniel praying and asking God for help. [12]So they went to the king and spoke to him about his royal decree: "Did you not publish a decree that during the next thirty days anyone who prays to any god or human being except to you, Your Majesty, would be thrown into the lions' den?"

The king answered, "The decree stands — in accordance with the law of the Medes and Persians, which cannot be repealed."

[13]Then they said to the king, "Daniel, who is one of the exiles from Judah, pays no attention to you, Your Majesty, or to the decree you put in writing. He still prays three times a day." [14]When the king heard this, he was greatly distressed; he was determined to rescue Daniel and made every effort until sundown to save him.

[15]Then the men went as a group to King Darius and said to him, "Remember, Your Majesty, that according to the law of the Medes and Persians no decree or edict that the king issues can be changed."

[16]So the king gave the order, and they brought Daniel and threw him into the lions' den. The king said to Daniel, "May your God, whom you serve continually, rescue you!"

[17]A stone was brought and placed over the mouth of the den, and the king sealed it with his own signet ring and with the rings of his nobles, so that Daniel's situation might not be changed. [18]Then the king returned to his palace and spent the night without eating and without any entertainment being brought to him. And he could not sleep.

[19]At the first light of dawn, the king got up and hurried to the lions' den. [20]When he came near the den, he called to Daniel in an anguished voice, "Daniel, servant of the living God, has your God, whom you serve continually, been able to rescue you from the lions?"

[21]Daniel answered, "May the king live forever! [22]My God sent his angel, and he shut the mouths of the lions. They have not hurt me, because I was found innocent in his sight. Nor have I ever done any wrong before you, Your Majesty."

[23]The king was overjoyed and gave orders to lift Daniel out of the den. And when Daniel was lifted from the den, no wound was found on him, because he had trusted in his God.

[24]At the king's command, the men who had falsely accused Daniel were brought in and thrown into the lions' den, along with their wives and children. And before they reached the floor of the den, the lions overpowered them and crushed all their bones.

[25]Then King Darius wrote to all the nations and peoples of every language in all the earth:

[a] In Aramaic texts 6:1-28 is numbered 6:2-29.

“May you prosper greatly!

26 “I issue a decree that in every part
of my kingdom people must fear and
reverence the God of Daniel.

“For he is the living God
and he endures forever;
his kingdom will not be destroyed,
his dominion will never end.
27 He rescues and he saves;
he performs signs and wonders
in the heavens and on the earth.
He has rescued Daniel
from the power of the lions.”

28 So Daniel prospered during the reign of
Darius and the reign of Cyrus[a] the Persian.

Daniel’s Dream of Four Beasts

7 In the first year of Belshazzar king of
Babylon, Daniel had a dream, and vi-
sions passed through his mind as he was ly-
ing in bed. He wrote down the substance of
his dream.

2 Daniel said: “In my vision at night I
looked, and there before me were the four
winds of heaven churning up the great sea.
3 Four great beasts, each different from the
others, came up out of the sea.

4 “The first was like a lion, and it had the
wings of an eagle. I watched until its wings
were torn off and it was lifted from the
ground so that it stood on two feet like a hu-
man being, and the mind of a human was
given to it.

5 “And there before me was a second beast,
which looked like a bear. It was raised up on
one of its sides, and it had three ribs in its
mouth between its teeth. It was told, ‘Get up
and eat your fill of flesh!’

6 “After that, I looked, and there before
me was another beast, one that looked like
a leopard. And on its back it had four wings
like those of a bird. This beast had four
heads, and it was given authority to rule.

7 “After that, in my vision at night I looked,
and there before me was a fourth beast—
terrifying and frightening and very power-
ful. It had large iron teeth; it crushed and de-
voured its victims and trampled underfoot
whatever was left. It was different from all
the former beasts, and it had ten horns.

8 “While I was thinking about the horns,
there before me was another horn, a little
one, which came up among them; and three
of the first horns were uprooted before it.
This horn had eyes like the eyes of a human
being and a mouth that spoke boastfully.

9 “As I looked,

“thrones were set in place,
and the Ancient of Days took his seat.
His clothing was as white as snow;
the hair of his head was white like
wool.
His throne was flaming with fire,
and its wheels were all ablaze.
10 A river of fire was flowing,
coming out from before him.
Thousands upon thousands attended
him;
ten thousand times ten thousand
stood before him.
The court was seated,
and the books were opened.

11 “Then I continued to watch because of
the boastful words the horn was speaking. I
kept looking until the beast was slain and its
body destroyed and thrown into the blazing
fire. 12 (The other beasts had been stripped of
their authority, but were allowed to live for a
period of time.)

13 “In my vision at night I looked, and
there before me was one like a son of man,[b]
coming with the clouds of heaven. He ap-
proached the Ancient of Days and was led
into his presence. 14 He was given authority,
glory and sovereign power; all nations and
peoples of every language worshiped him.
His dominion is an everlasting dominion
that will not pass away, and his kingdom is
one that will never be destroyed.

The Interpretation of the Dream

15 “I, Daniel, was troubled in spirit, and
the visions that passed through my mind
disturbed me. 16 I approached one of those
standing there and asked him the meaning
of all this.

“So he told me and gave me the inter-
pretation of these things: 17 ‘The four great
beasts are four kings that will rise from the
earth. 18 But the holy people of the Most High

[a] 28 Or *Darius, that is, the reign of Cyrus* [b] 13 The Aramaic phrase *bar enash* means *human being.* The phrase *son of man* is retained here because of its use in the New Testament as a title of Jesus, probably based largely on this verse.

will receive the kingdom and will possess it
forever — yes, for ever and ever.'
19 "Then I wanted to know the meaning of
the fourth beast, which was different from
all the others and most terrifying, with its
iron teeth and bronze claws — the beast that
crushed and devoured its victims and tram-
pled underfoot whatever was left. 20 I also
wanted to know about the ten horns on its
head and about the other horn that came up,
before which three of them fell — the horn
that looked more imposing than the others
and that had eyes and a mouth that spoke
boastfully. 21 As I watched, this horn was wag-
ing war against the holy people and defeating
them, 22 until the Ancient of Days came and
pronounced judgment in favor of the holy
people of the Most High, and the time came
when they possessed the kingdom.
23 "He gave me this explanation: 'The
fourth beast is a fourth kingdom that will
appear on earth. It will be different from
all the other kingdoms and will devour the
whole earth, trampling it down and crush-
ing it. 24 The ten horns are ten kings who will
come from this kingdom. After them anoth-
er king will arise, different from the earlier
ones; he will subdue three kings. 25 He will
speak against the Most High and oppress his
holy people and try to change the set times
and the laws. The holy people will be deliv-
ered into his hands for a time, times and half
a time.[a]
26 " 'But the court will sit, and his power
will be taken away and completely destroyed
forever. 27 Then the sovereignty, power and
greatness of all the kingdoms under heaven
will be handed over to the holy people of the
Most High. His kingdom will be an everlast-
ing kingdom, and all rulers will worship and
obey him.'
28 "This is the end of the matter. I, Daniel,
was deeply troubled by my thoughts, and
my face turned pale, but I kept the matter to
myself."

Daniel's Vision of a Ram and a Goat

8 In the third year of King Belshazzar's
reign, I, Daniel, had a vision, after the
one that had already appeared to me. 2 In
my vision I saw myself in the citadel of Susa
in the province of Elam; in the vision I was
beside the Ulai Canal. 3 I looked up, and
there before me was a ram with two horns,
standing beside the canal, and the horns
were long. One of the horns was longer than
the other but grew up later. 4 I watched the
ram as it charged toward the west and the
north and the south. No animal could stand
against it, and none could rescue from its
power. It did as it pleased and became great.
5 As I was thinking about this, sudden-
ly a goat with a prominent horn between
its eyes came from the west, crossing the
whole earth without touching the ground.
6 It came toward the two-horned ram I had
seen standing beside the canal and charged
at it in great rage. 7 I saw it attack the ram fu-
riously, striking the ram and shattering its
two horns. The ram was powerless to stand
against it; the goat knocked it to the ground
and trampled on it, and none could rescue
the ram from its power. 8 The goat became
very great, but at the height of its power the
large horn was broken off, and in its place
four prominent horns grew up toward the
four winds of heaven.
9 Out of one of them came another horn,
which started small but grew in power to the
south and to the east and toward the Beau-
tiful Land. 10 It grew until it reached the host
of the heavens, and it threw some of the star-
ry host down to the earth and trampled on
them. 11 It set itself up to be as great as the
commander of the army of the LORD; it took
away the daily sacrifice from the LORD, and
his sanctuary was thrown down. 12 Because
of rebellion, the LORD's people[b] and the dai-
ly sacrifice were given over to it. It prospered
in everything it did, and truth was thrown to
the ground.
13 Then I heard a holy one speaking, and
another holy one said to him, "How long will
it take for the vision to be fulfilled — the vi-
sion concerning the daily sacrifice, the re-
bellion that causes desolation, the surrender
of the sanctuary and the trampling under-
foot of the LORD's people?"
14 He said to me, "It will take 2,300 eve-
nings and mornings; then the sanctuary will
be reconsecrated."

The Interpretation of the Vision

15 While I, Daniel, was watching the vision
and trying to understand it, there before me

[a] 25 Or *for a year, two years and half a year* [b] 12 Or *rebellion, the armies*

stood one who looked like a man. 16And I
heard a man's voice from the Ulai calling,
"Gabriel, tell this man the meaning of the
vision."

17As he came near the place where I was
standing, I was terrified and fell prostrate.
"Son of man,"[a] he said to me, "understand
that the vision concerns the time of the end."

18While he was speaking to me, I was in a
deep sleep, with my face to the ground. Then
he touched me and raised me to my feet.

19He said: "I am going to tell you what will
happen later in the time of wrath, because
the vision concerns the appointed time of
the end.[b] 20The two-horned ram that you
saw represents the kings of Media and Per-
sia. 21The shaggy goat is the king of Greece,
and the large horn between its eyes is the
first king. 22The four horns that replaced the
one that was broken off represent four king-
doms that will emerge from his nation but
will not have the same power.

23"In the latter part of their reign, when
rebels have become completely wicked, a
fierce-looking king, a master of intrigue, will
arise. 24He will become very strong, but not
by his own power. He will cause astounding
devastation and will succeed in whatever he
does. He will destroy those who are mighty,
the holy people. 25He will cause deceit to
prosper, and he will consider himself super-
ior. When they feel secure, he will destroy
many and take his stand against the Prince
of princes. Yet he will be destroyed, but not
by human power.

26"The vision of the evenings and morn-
ings that has been given you is true, but seal
up the vision, for it concerns the distant fu-
ture."

27I, Daniel, was worn out. I lay exhaust-
ed for several days. Then I got up and went
about the king's business. I was appalled by
the vision; it was beyond understanding.

Daniel's Prayer

9 In the first year of Darius son of Xerxes[c]
(a Mede by descent), who was made rul-
er over the Babylonian[d] kingdom — 2in the
first year of his reign, I, Daniel, understood
from the Scriptures, according to the word of
the LORD given to Jeremiah the prophet, that
the desolation of Jerusalem would last sev-
enty years. 3So I turned to the Lord God and
pleaded with him in prayer and petition, in
fasting, and in sackcloth and ashes.

4I prayed to the LORD my God and con-
fessed:

"Lord, the great and awesome God,
who keeps his covenant of love with
those who love him and keep his com-
mandments, 5we have sinned and done
wrong. We have been wicked and have
rebelled; we have turned away from
your commands and laws. 6We have
not listened to your servants the proph-
ets, who spoke in your name to our
kings, our princes and our ancestors,
and to all the people of the land.

7"Lord, you are righteous, but this
day we are covered with shame — the
people of Judah and the inhabitants of
Jerusalem and all Israel, both near and
far, in all the countries where you have
scattered us because of our unfaith-
fulness to you. 8We and our kings, our
princes and our ancestors are covered
with shame, LORD, because we have
sinned against you. 9The Lord our God
is merciful and forgiving, even though
we have rebelled against him; 10we
have not obeyed the LORD our God
or kept the laws he gave us through
his servants the prophets. 11All Israel
has transgressed your law and turned
away, refusing to obey you.

"Therefore the curses and sworn
judgments written in the Law of Moses,
the servant of God, have been poured
out on us, because we have sinned
against you. 12You have fulfilled the
words spoken against us and against
our rulers by bringing on us great di-
saster. Under the whole heaven noth-
ing has ever been done like what has
been done to Jerusalem. 13Just as it is
written in the Law of Moses, all this di-
saster has come on us, yet we have not
sought the favor of the LORD our God by
turning from our sins and giving atten-
tion to your truth. 14The LORD did not

[a] *17* The Hebrew phrase *ben adam* means *human being*. The phrase *son of man* is retained as a form of address here because of its possible association with "Son of Man" in the New Testament.
[b] *19* Or *because the end will be at the appointed time* [c] *1* Hebrew *Ahasuerus* [d] *1* Or *Chaldean*

hesitate to bring the disaster on us, for the LORD our God is righteous in everything he does; yet we have not obeyed him.

15 "Now, Lord our God, who brought your people out of Egypt with a mighty hand and who made for yourself a name that endures to this day, we have sinned, we have done wrong. 16 Lord, in keeping with all your righteous acts, turn away your anger and your wrath from Jerusalem, your city, your holy hill. Our sins and the iniquities of our ancestors have made Jerusalem and your people an object of scorn to all those around us.

17 "Now, our God, hear the prayers and petitions of your servant. For your sake, Lord, look with favor on your desolate sanctuary. 18 Give ear, our God, and hear; open your eyes and see the desolation of the city that bears your Name. We do not make requests of you because we are righteous, but because of your great mercy. 19 Lord, listen! Lord, forgive! Lord, hear and act! For your sake, my God, do not delay, because your city and your people bear your Name."

The Seventy "Sevens"

20 While I was speaking and praying, confessing my sin and the sin of my people Israel and making my request to the LORD my God for his holy hill— 21 while I was still in prayer, Gabriel, the man I had seen in the earlier vision, came to me in swift flight about the time of the evening sacrifice. 22 He instructed me and said to me, "Daniel, I have now come to give you insight and understanding. 23 As soon as you began to pray, a word went out, which I have come to tell you, for you are highly esteemed. Therefore, consider the word and understand the vision:

24 "Seventy 'sevens'[a] are decreed for your people and your holy city to finish[b] transgression, to put an end to sin, to atone for wickedness, to bring in everlasting righteousness, to seal up vision and prophecy and to anoint the Most Holy Place.[c]

25 "Know and understand this: From the time the word goes out to restore and rebuild Jerusalem until the Anointed One,[d] the ruler, comes, there will be seven 'sevens,' and sixty-two 'sevens.' It will be rebuilt with streets and a trench, but in times of trouble. 26 After the sixty-two 'sevens,' the Anointed One will be put to death and will have nothing.[e] The people of the ruler who will come will destroy the city and the sanctuary. The end will come like a flood: War will continue until the end, and desolations have been decreed. 27 He will confirm a covenant with many for one 'seven.'[f] In the middle of the 'seven'[f] he will put an end to sacrifice and offering. And at the temple[g] he will set up an abomination that causes desolation, until the end that is decreed is poured out on him."[h][i]

Daniel's Vision of a Man

10 In the third year of Cyrus king of Persia, a revelation was given to Daniel (who was called Belteshazzar). Its message was true and it concerned a great war.[j] The understanding of the message came to him in a vision.

2 At that time I, Daniel, mourned for three weeks. 3 I ate no choice food; no meat or wine touched my lips; and I used no lotions at all until the three weeks were over.

4 On the twenty-fourth day of the first month, as I was standing on the bank of the great river, the Tigris, 5 I looked up and there before me was a man dressed in linen, with a belt of fine gold from Uphaz around his waist. 6 His body was like topaz, his face like lightning, his eyes like flaming torches, his arms and legs like the gleam of burnished bronze, and his voice like the sound of a multitude.

7 I, Daniel, was the only one who saw the vision; those who were with me did not see it, but such terror overwhelmed them that they fled and hid themselves. 8 So I was left alone, gazing at this great vision; I had no strength left, my face turned deathly pale and I was helpless. 9 Then I heard him speaking, and as I listened to him, I fell into a deep sleep, my face to the ground.

[a] 24 Or *'weeks'*; also in verses 25 and 26 [b] 24 Or *restrain* [c] 24 Or *the most holy One* [d] 25 Or *an anointed one*; also in verse 26 [e] 26 Or *death and will have no one*; or *death, but not for himself* [f] 27 Or *'week'* [g] 27 Septuagint and Theodotion; Hebrew *wing* [h] 27 Or *it* [i] 27 Or *And one who causes desolation will come upon the wing of the abominable temple, until the end that is decreed is poured out on the desolated city* [j] 1 Or *true and burdensome*

10 A hand touched me and set me trembling on my hands and knees. 11 He said, "Daniel, you who are highly esteemed, consider carefully the words I am about to speak to you, and stand up, for I have now been sent to you." And when he said this to me, I stood up trembling.

12 Then he continued, "Do not be afraid, Daniel. Since the first day that you set your mind to gain understanding and to humble yourself before your God, your words were heard, and I have come in response to them. 13 But the prince of the Persian kingdom resisted me twenty-one days. Then Michael, one of the chief princes, came to help me, because I was detained there with the king of Persia. 14 Now I have come to explain to you what will happen to your people in the future, for the vision concerns a time yet to come."

15 While he was saying this to me, I bowed with my face toward the ground and was speechless. 16 Then one who looked like a man[a] touched my lips, and I opened my mouth and began to speak. I said to the one standing before me, "I am overcome with anguish because of the vision, my lord, and I feel very weak. 17 How can I, your servant, talk with you, my lord? My strength is gone and I can hardly breathe."

18 Again the one who looked like a man touched me and gave me strength. 19 "Do not be afraid, you who are highly esteemed," he said. "Peace! Be strong now; be strong."

When he spoke to me, I was strengthened and said, "Speak, my lord, since you have given me strength."

20 So he said, "Do you know why I have come to you? Soon I will return to fight against the prince of Persia, and when I go, the prince of Greece will come; 21 but first I will tell you what is written in the Book of Truth. (No one supports me against them except Michael, your prince.

11 1 And in the first year of Darius the Mede, I took my stand to support and protect him.)

The Kings of the South and the North

2 "Now then, I tell you the truth: Three more kings will arise in Persia, and then a fourth, who will be far richer than all the others. When he has gained power by his wealth, he will stir up everyone against the kingdom of Greece. 3 Then a mighty king will arise, who will rule with great power and do as he pleases. 4 After he has arisen, his empire will be broken up and parceled out toward the four winds of heaven. It will not go to his descendants, nor will it have the power he exercised, because his empire will be uprooted and given to others.

5 "The king of the South will become strong, but one of his commanders will become even stronger than he and will rule his own kingdom with great power. 6 After some years, they will become allies. The daughter of the king of the South will go to the king of the North to make an alliance, but she will not retain her power, and he and his power[b] will not last. In those days she will be betrayed, together with her royal escort and her father[c] and the one who supported her.

7 "One from her family line will arise to take her place. He will attack the forces of the king of the North and enter his fortress; he will fight against them and be victorious. 8 He will also seize their gods, their metal images and their valuable articles of silver and gold and carry them off to Egypt. For some years he will leave the king of the North alone. 9 Then the king of the North will invade the realm of the king of the South but will retreat to his own country. 10 His sons will prepare for war and assemble a great army, which will sweep on like an irresistible flood and carry the battle as far as his fortress.

11 "Then the king of the South will march out in a rage and fight against the king of the North, who will raise a large army, but it will be defeated. 12 When the army is carried off, the king of the South will be filled with pride and will slaughter many thousands, yet he will not remain triumphant. 13 For the king of the North will muster another army, larger than the first; and after several years, he will advance with a huge army fully equipped.

14 "In those times many will rise against the king of the South. Those who are violent among your own people will rebel in fulfillment of the vision, but without success.

[a] *16* Most manuscripts of the Masoretic Text; one manuscript of the Masoretic Text, Dead Sea Scrolls and Septuagint *Then something that looked like a human hand* [b] *6* Or *offspring* [c] *6* Or *child* (see Vulgate and Syriac)

15 Then the king of the North will come and
build up siege ramps and will capture a forti-
fied city. The forces of the South will be pow-
erless to resist; even their best troops will not
have the strength to stand. 16 The invader
will do as he pleases; no one will be able to
stand against him. He will establish himself
in the Beautiful Land and will have the pow-
er to destroy it. 17 He will determine to come
with the might of his entire kingdom and will
make an alliance with the king of the South.
And he will give him a daughter in marriage
in order to overthrow the kingdom, but his
plans[a] will not succeed or help him. 18 Then
he will turn his attention to the coastlands
and will take many of them, but a command-
er will put an end to his insolence and will
turn his insolence back on him. 19 After this,
he will turn back toward the fortresses of his
own country but will stumble and fall, to be
seen no more.

20 "His successor will send out a tax collec-
tor to maintain the royal splendor. In a few
years, however, he will be destroyed, yet not
in anger or in battle.

21 "He will be succeeded by a contempt-
ible person who has not been given the hon-
or of royalty. He will invade the kingdom
when its people feel secure, and he will seize
it through intrigue. 22 Then an overwhelm-
ing army will be swept away before him;
both it and a prince of the covenant will
be destroyed. 23 After coming to an agree-
ment with him, he will act deceitfully, and
with only a few people he will rise to pow-
er. 24 When the richest provinces feel secure,
he will invade them and will achieve what
neither his fathers nor his forefathers did.
He will distribute plunder, loot and wealth
among his followers. He will plot the over-
throw of fortresses — but only for a time.

25 "With a large army he will stir up his
strength and courage against the king of the
South. The king of the South will wage war
with a large and very powerful army, but he
will not be able to stand because of the plots
devised against him. 26 Those who eat from
the king's provisions will try to destroy him;
his army will be swept away, and many will
fall in battle. 27 The two kings, with their
hearts bent on evil, will sit at the same table
and lie to each other, but to no avail, because
an end will still come at the appointed time.
28 The king of the North will return to his
own country with great wealth, but his heart
will be set against the holy covenant. He will
take action against it and then return to his
own country.

29 "At the appointed time he will invade
the South again, but this time the outcome
will be different from what it was before.
30 Ships of the western coastlands will op-
pose him, and he will lose heart. Then he
will turn back and vent his fury against the
holy covenant. He will return and show favor
to those who forsake the holy covenant.

31 "His armed forces will rise up to dese-
crate the temple fortress and will abolish
the daily sacrifice. Then they will set up the
abomination that causes desolation. 32 With
flattery he will corrupt those who have vio-
lated the covenant, but the people who know
their God will firmly resist him.

33 "Those who are wise will instruct many,
though for a time they will fall by the sword
or be burned or captured or plundered.
34 When they fall, they will receive a little
help, and many who are not sincere will join
them. 35 Some of the wise will stumble, so
that they may be refined, purified and made
spotless until the time of the end, for it will
still come at the appointed time.

The King Who Exalts Himself

36 "The king will do as he pleases. He will
exalt and magnify himself above every god
and will say unheard-of things against the
God of gods. He will be successful until the
time of wrath is completed, for what has
been determined must take place. 37 He will
show no regard for the gods of his ancestors
or for the one desired by women, nor will he
regard any god, but will exalt himself above
them all. 38 Instead of them, he will honor a
god of fortresses; a god unknown to his an-
cestors he will honor with gold and silver,
with precious stones and costly gifts. 39 He
will attack the mightiest fortresses with the
help of a foreign god and will greatly honor
those who acknowledge him. He will make
them rulers over many people and will dis-
tribute the land at a price.[b]

40 "At the time of the end the king of the
South will engage him in battle, and the

[a] 17 Or *but she* [b] 39 Or *land for a reward*

king of the North will storm out against him
with chariots and cavalry and a great fleet
of ships. He will invade many countries
and sweep through them like a flood. 41 He
will also invade the Beautiful Land. Many
countries will fall, but Edom, Moab and the
leaders of Ammon will be delivered from his
hand. 42 He will extend his power over many
countries; Egypt will not escape. 43 He will
gain control of the treasures of gold and sil-
ver and all the riches of Egypt, with the Lib-
yans and Cushites[a] in submission. 44 But re-
ports from the east and the north will alarm
him, and he will set out in a great rage to de-
stroy and annihilate many. 45 He will pitch
his royal tents between the seas at[b] the beau-
tiful holy mountain. Yet he will come to his
end, and no one will help him.

The End Times

12 "At that time Michael, the great
prince who protects your people,
will arise. There will be a time of distress
such as has not happened from the begin-
ning of nations until then. But at that time
your people — everyone whose name is
found written in the book — will be deliv-
ered. 2 Multitudes who sleep in the dust of
the earth will awake: some to everlasting
life, others to shame and everlasting con-
tempt. 3 Those who are wise[c] will shine like
the brightness of the heavens, and those
who lead many to righteousness, like the
stars for ever and ever. 4 But you, Daniel, roll
up and seal the words of the scroll until the
time of the end. Many will go here and there
to increase knowledge."

5 Then I, Daniel, looked, and there before
me stood two others, one on this bank of the
river and one on the opposite bank. 6 One of
them said to the man clothed in linen, who
was above the waters of the river, "How long
will it be before these astonishing things are
fulfilled?"

7 The man clothed in linen, who was
above the waters of the river, lifted his right
hand and his left hand toward heaven, and
I heard him swear by him who lives forever,
saying, "It will be for a time, times and half
a time.[d] When the power of the holy people
has been finally broken, all these things will
be completed."

8 I heard, but I did not understand. So I
asked, "My lord, what will the outcome of all
this be?"

9 He replied, "Go your way, Daniel, be-
cause the words are rolled up and sealed
until the time of the end. 10 Many will be pu-
rified, made spotless and refined, but the
wicked will continue to be wicked. None of
the wicked will understand, but those who
are wise will understand.

11 "From the time that the daily sacrifice is
abolished and the abomination that causes
desolation is set up, there will be 1,290 days.
12 Blessed is the one who waits for and reach-
es the end of the 1,335 days.

13 "As for you, go your way till the end. You
will rest, and then at the end of the days you
will rise to receive your allotted inheritance."

[a] *43* That is, people from the upper Nile region [b] *45* Or *the sea and* [c] *3* Or *who impart wisdom*
[d] *7* Or *a year, two years and half a year*

HOSEA

1 The word of the LORD that came to Hosea son of Beeri during the reigns of Uzziah, Jotham, Ahaz and Hezekiah, kings of Judah, and during the reign of Jeroboam son of Jehoash[a] king of Israel:

Hosea's Wife and Children

2 When the LORD began to speak through Hosea, the LORD said to him, "Go, marry a promiscuous woman and have children with her, for like an adulterous wife this land is guilty of unfaithfulness to the LORD." 3 So he married Gomer daughter of Diblaim, and she conceived and bore him a son.

4 Then the LORD said to Hosea, "Call him Jezreel, because I will soon punish the house of Jehu for the massacre at Jezreel, and I will put an end to the kingdom of Israel. 5 In that day I will break Israel's bow in the Valley of Jezreel."

6 Gomer conceived again and gave birth to a daughter. Then the LORD said to Hosea, "Call her Lo-Ruhamah (which means "not loved"), for I will no longer show love to Israel, that I should at all forgive them. 7 Yet I will show love to Judah; and I will save them—not by bow, sword or battle, or by horses and horsemen, but I, the LORD their God, will save them."

8 After she had weaned Lo-Ruhamah, Gomer had another son. 9 Then the LORD said, "Call him Lo-Ammi (which means "not my people"), for you are not my people, and I am not your God.[b]

10 "Yet the Israelites will be like the sand on the seashore, which cannot be measured or counted. In the place where it was said to them, 'You are not my people,' they will be called 'children of the living God.' 11 The people of Judah and the people of Israel will come together; they will appoint one leader and will come up out of the land, for great will be the day of Jezreel.[c]

2[d] "Say of your brothers, 'My people,' and of your sisters, 'My loved one.'

Israel Punished and Restored

2 "Rebuke your mother, rebuke her,
for she is not my wife,
and I am not her husband.
Let her remove the adulterous look from her face
and the unfaithfulness from between her breasts.
3 Otherwise I will strip her naked
and make her as bare as on the day she was born;
I will make her like a desert,
turn her into a parched land,
and slay her with thirst.
4 I will not show my love to her children,
because they are the children of adultery.
5 Their mother has been unfaithful
and has conceived them in disgrace.
She said, 'I will go after my lovers,
who give me my food and my water,
my wool and my linen, my olive oil and my drink.'
6 Therefore I will block her path with thornbushes;
I will wall her in so that she cannot find her way.
7 She will chase after her lovers but not catch them;
she will look for them but not find them.
Then she will say,
'I will go back to my husband as at first,
for then I was better off than now.'
8 She has not acknowledged that I was the one
who gave her the grain, the new wine and oil,
who lavished on her the silver and gold—
which they used for Baal.

9 "Therefore I will take away my grain when it ripens,
and my new wine when it is ready.

[a] *1* Hebrew *Joash,* a variant of *Jehoash* [b] *9* Or *your I AM* [c] *11* In Hebrew texts 1:10,11 is numbered 2:1,2. [d] In Hebrew texts 2:1-23 is numbered 2:3-25.

I will take back my wool and my linen,
intended to cover her naked body.
10 So now I will expose her lewdness
before the eyes of her lovers;
no one will take her out of my hands.
11 I will stop all her celebrations:
her yearly festivals, her New Moons,
her Sabbath days — all her appointed
festivals.
12 I will ruin her vines and her fig trees,
which she said were her pay from her
lovers;
I will make them a thicket,
and wild animals will devour them.
13 I will punish her for the days
she burned incense to the Baals;
she decked herself with rings and
jewelry,
and went after her lovers,
but me she forgot,"
declares the LORD.

14 "Therefore I am now going to allure her;
I will lead her into the wilderness
and speak tenderly to her.
15 There I will give her back her vineyards,
and will make the Valley of Achor[a] a
door of hope.
There she will respond[b] as in the days of
her youth,
as in the day she came up out of Egypt.

16 "In that day," declares the LORD,
"you will call me 'my husband';
you will no longer call me 'my master.[c]'
17 I will remove the names of the Baals from
her lips;
no longer will their names be invoked.
18 In that day I will make a covenant for
them
with the beasts of the field, the birds in
the sky
and the creatures that move along the
ground.
Bow and sword and battle
I will abolish from the land,
so that all may lie down in safety.
19 I will betroth you to me forever;
I will betroth you in[d] righteousness
and justice,
in[d] love and compassion.
20 I will betroth you in[d] faithfulness,
and you will acknowledge the LORD.

21 "In that day I will respond,"
declares the LORD —
"I will respond to the skies,
and they will respond to the earth;
22 and the earth will respond to the grain,
the new wine and the olive oil,
and they will respond to Jezreel.[e]
23 I will plant her for myself in the land;
I will show my love to the one I called
'Not my loved one.[f]'
I will say to those called 'Not my people,[g]'
'You are my people';
and they will say, 'You are my God.' "

Hosea's Reconciliation With His Wife

3 The LORD said to me, "Go, show your
love to your wife again, though she is
loved by another man and is an adulteress.
Love her as the LORD loves the Israelites,
though they turn to other gods and love the
sacred raisin cakes."
2 So I bought her for fifteen shekels[h] of sil-
ver and about a homer and a lethek[i] of bar-
ley. 3 Then I told her, "You are to live with me
many days; you must not be a prostitute or
be intimate with any man, and I will behave
the same way toward you."
4 For the Israelites will live many days
without king or prince, without sacrifice or
sacred stones, without ephod or household
gods. 5 Afterward the Israelites will return
and seek the LORD their God and David their
king. They will come trembling to the LORD
and to his blessings in the last days.

The Charge Against Israel

4 Hear the word of the LORD, you
Israelites,
because the LORD has a charge
to bring
against you who live in the land:
"There is no faithfulness, no love,
no acknowledgment of God in
the land.
2 There is only cursing,[j] lying and murder,
stealing and adultery;

[a] 15 *Achor* means *trouble.* [b] 15 Or *sing* [c] 16 Hebrew *baal* [d] 19,20 Or *with* [e] 22 *Jezreel* means *God plants.* [f] 23 Hebrew *Lo-Ruhamah* (see 1:6) [g] 23 Hebrew *Lo-Ammi* (see 1:9) [h] 2 That is, about 6 ounces or about 170 grams [i] 2 A homer and a lethek possibly weighed about 430 pounds or about 195 kilograms. [j] 2 That is, to pronounce a curse on

they break all bounds,
and bloodshed follows bloodshed.
[3] Because of this the land dries up,
and all who live in it waste away;
the beasts of the field, the birds in the sky
and the fish in the sea are swept away.

[4] "But let no one bring a charge,
let no one accuse another,
for your people are like those
who bring charges against a priest.
[5] You stumble day and night,
and the prophets stumble with you.
So I will destroy your mother —
[6] my people are destroyed from lack of knowledge.

"Because you have rejected knowledge,
I also reject you as my priests;
because you have ignored the law of your God,
I also will ignore your children.
[7] The more priests there were,
the more they sinned against me;
they exchanged their glorious God[a] for something disgraceful.
[8] They feed on the sins of my people
and relish their wickedness.
[9] And it will be: Like people, like priests.
I will punish both of them for their ways
and repay them for their deeds.

[10] "They will eat but not have enough;
they will engage in prostitution but not flourish,
because they have deserted the LORD
to give themselves [11] to prostitution;
old wine and new wine
take away their understanding.
[12] My people consult a wooden idol,
and a diviner's rod speaks to them.
A spirit of prostitution leads them astray;
they are unfaithful to their God.
[13] They sacrifice on the mountaintops
and burn offerings on the hills,
under oak, poplar and terebinth,
where the shade is pleasant.
Therefore your daughters turn to prostitution
and your daughters-in-law to adultery.

[14] "I will not punish your daughters
when they turn to prostitution,
nor your daughters-in-law
when they commit adultery,
because the men themselves consort with harlots
and sacrifice with shrine prostitutes —
a people without understanding will come to ruin!

[15] "Though you, Israel, commit adultery,
do not let Judah become guilty.

"Do not go to Gilgal;
do not go up to Beth Aven.[b]
And do not swear, 'As surely as the LORD lives!'
[16] The Israelites are stubborn,
like a stubborn heifer.
How then can the LORD pasture them
like lambs in a meadow?
[17] Ephraim is joined to idols;
leave him alone!
[18] Even when their drinks are gone,
they continue their prostitution;
their rulers dearly love shameful ways.
[19] A whirlwind will sweep them away,
and their sacrifices will bring them shame.

Judgment Against Israel

5 "Hear this, you priests!
Pay attention, you Israelites!
Listen, royal house!
This judgment is against you:
You have been a snare at Mizpah,
a net spread out on Tabor.
[2] The rebels are knee-deep in slaughter.
I will discipline all of them.
[3] I know all about Ephraim;
Israel is not hidden from me.
Ephraim, you have now turned to prostitution;
Israel is corrupt.

[4] "Their deeds do not permit them
to return to their God.
A spirit of prostitution is in their heart;
they do not acknowledge the LORD.
[5] Israel's arrogance testifies against them;
the Israelites, even Ephraim, stumble in their sin;
Judah also stumbles with them.

[a] 7 Syriac (see also an ancient Hebrew scribal tradition); Masoretic Text *me; / I will exchange their glory*
[b] 15 *Beth Aven* means *house of wickedness* (a derogatory name for Bethel, which means *house of God*).

[6]When they go with their flocks and herds
to seek the LORD,
they will not find him;
he has withdrawn himself from them.
[7]They are unfaithful to the LORD;
they give birth to illegitimate children.
When they celebrate their New Moon
feasts,
he will devour[a] their fields.

[8]"Sound the trumpet in Gibeah,
the horn in Ramah.
Raise the battle cry in Beth Aven[b];
lead on, Benjamin.
[9]Ephraim will be laid waste
on the day of reckoning.
Among the tribes of Israel
I proclaim what is certain.
[10]Judah's leaders are like those
who move boundary stones.
I will pour out my wrath on them
like a flood of water.
[11]Ephraim is oppressed,
trampled in judgment,
intent on pursuing idols.[c]
[12]I am like a moth to Ephraim,
like rot to the people of Judah.

[13]"When Ephraim saw his sickness,
and Judah his sores,
then Ephraim turned to Assyria,
and sent to the great king for help.
But he is not able to cure you,
not able to heal your sores.
[14]For I will be like a lion to Ephraim,
like a great lion to Judah.
I will tear them to pieces and go away;
I will carry them off, with no one to
rescue them.
[15]Then I will return to my lair
until they have borne their guilt
and seek my face—
in their misery
they will earnestly seek me."

Israel Unrepentant

6 "Come, let us return to the LORD.
He has torn us to pieces
but he will heal us;
he has injured us
but he will bind up our wounds.
[2]After two days he will revive us;
on the third day he will restore us,
that we may live in his presence.
[3]Let us acknowledge the LORD;
let us press on to acknowledge him.
As surely as the sun rises,
he will appear;
he will come to us like the winter rains,
like the spring rains that water the
earth."

[4]"What can I do with you, Ephraim?
What can I do with you, Judah?
Your love is like the morning mist,
like the early dew that disappears.
[5]Therefore I cut you in pieces with my
prophets,
I killed you with the words of my
mouth—
then my judgments go forth like
the sun.[d]
[6]For I desire mercy, not sacrifice,
and acknowledgment of God rather
than burnt offerings.
[7]As at Adam,[e] they have broken the
covenant;
they were unfaithful to me there.
[8]Gilead is a city of evildoers,
stained with footprints of blood.
[9]As marauders lie in ambush for a victim,
so do bands of priests;
they murder on the road to Shechem,
carrying out their wicked schemes.
[10]I have seen a horrible thing in Israel:
There Ephraim is given to prostitution,
Israel is defiled.

[11]"Also for you, Judah,
a harvest is appointed.

"Whenever I would restore the fortunes
of my people,
7 [1]whenever I would heal Israel,
the sins of Ephraim are exposed
and the crimes of Samaria revealed.
They practice deceit,
thieves break into houses,
bandits rob in the streets;
[2]but they do not realize
that I remember all their evil deeds.
Their sins engulf them;
they are always before me.

[a] 7 Or *Now their New Moon feasts / will devour them and* [b] 8 *Beth Aven* means *house of wickedness* (a derogatory name for Bethel, which means *house of God*). [c] 11 The meaning of the Hebrew for this word is uncertain. [d] 5 The meaning of the Hebrew for this line is uncertain. [e] 7 Or *Like Adam*; or *Like human beings*

3 "They delight the king with their
wickedness,
the princes with their lies.
4 They are all adulterers,
burning like an oven
whose fire the baker need not stir
from the kneading of the dough till
it rises.
5 On the day of the festival of our king
the princes become inflamed with
wine,
and he joins hands with the mockers.
6 Their hearts are like an oven;
they approach him with intrigue.
Their passion smolders all night;
in the morning it blazes like a
flaming fire.
7 All of them are hot as an oven;
they devour their rulers.
All their kings fall,
and none of them calls on me.

8 "Ephraim mixes with the nations;
Ephraim is a flat loaf not turned over.
9 Foreigners sap his strength,
but he does not realize it.
His hair is sprinkled with gray,
but he does not notice.
10 Israel's arrogance testifies against him,
but despite all this
he does not return to the LORD his God
or search for him.
11 "Ephraim is like a dove,
easily deceived and senseless —
now calling to Egypt,
now turning to Assyria.
12 When they go, I will throw my net over
them;
I will pull them down like the birds in
the sky.
When I hear them flocking together,
I will catch them.
13 Woe to them,
because they have strayed from me!
Destruction to them,
because they have rebelled
against me!
I long to redeem them
but they speak about me falsely.
14 They do not cry out to me from their
hearts
but wail on their beds.
They slash themselves,[a] appealing to
their gods
for grain and new wine,
but they turn away from me.
15 I trained them and strengthened
their arms,
but they plot evil against me.
16 They do not turn to the Most High;
they are like a faulty bow.
Their leaders will fall by the sword
because of their insolent words.
For this they will be ridiculed
in the land of Egypt.

Israel to Reap the Whirlwind

8 "Put the trumpet to your lips!
An eagle is over the house of the LORD
because the people have broken my
covenant
and rebelled against my law.
2 Israel cries out to me,
'Our God, we acknowledge you!'
3 But Israel has rejected what is good;
an enemy will pursue him.
4 They set up kings without my consent;
they choose princes without my
approval.
With their silver and gold
they make idols for themselves
to their own destruction.
5 Samaria, throw out your calf-idol!
My anger burns against them.
How long will they be incapable of
purity?
6 They are from Israel!
This calf — a metalworker has made it;
it is not God.
It will be broken in pieces,
that calf of Samaria.

7 "They sow the wind
and reap the whirlwind.
The stalk has no head;
it will produce no flour.
Were it to yield grain,
foreigners would swallow it up.
8 Israel is swallowed up;
now she is among the nations
like something no one wants.
9 For they have gone up to Assyria
like a wild donkey wandering alone.
Ephraim has sold herself to lovers.

[a] 14 Some Hebrew manuscripts and Septuagint; most Hebrew manuscripts *They gather together*

10 Although they have sold themselves
among the nations,
I will now gather them together.
They will begin to waste away
under the oppression of the mighty
king.

11 "Though Ephraim built many altars for
sin offerings,
these have become altars for sinning.
12 I wrote for them the many things of
my law,
but they regarded them as something
foreign.
13 Though they offer sacrifices as gifts
to me,
and though they eat the meat,
the LORD is not pleased with them.
Now he will remember their wickedness
and punish their sins:
They will return to Egypt.
14 Israel has forgotten their Maker
and built palaces;
Judah has fortified many towns.
But I will send fire on their cities
that will consume their fortresses."

Punishment for Israel

9 Do not rejoice, Israel;
do not be jubilant like the other
nations.
For you have been unfaithful to your God;
you love the wages of a prostitute
at every threshing floor.
2 Threshing floors and winepresses will
not feed the people;
the new wine will fail them.
3 They will not remain in the LORD's land;
Ephraim will return to Egypt
and eat unclean food in Assyria.
4 They will not pour out wine offerings to
the LORD,
nor will their sacrifices please him.
Such sacrifices will be to them like the
bread of mourners;
all who eat them will be unclean.
This food will be for themselves;
it will not come into the temple of
the LORD.

5 What will you do on the day of your
appointed festivals,
on the feast days of the LORD?
6 Even if they escape from destruction,
Egypt will gather them,
and Memphis will bury them.
Their treasures of silver will be taken
over by briers,
and thorns will overrun their tents.
7 The days of punishment are coming,
the days of reckoning are at hand.
Let Israel know this.
Because your sins are so many
and your hostility so great,
the prophet is considered a fool,
the inspired person a maniac.
8 The prophet, along with my God,
is the watchman over Ephraim,[a]
yet snares await him on all his paths,
and hostility in the house of his God.
9 They have sunk deep into corruption,
as in the days of Gibeah.
God will remember their wickedness
and punish them for their sins.

10 "When I found Israel,
it was like finding grapes in the desert;
when I saw your ancestors,
it was like seeing the early fruit on the
fig tree.
But when they came to Baal Peor,
they consecrated themselves to that
shameful idol
and became as vile as the thing they
loved.
11 Ephraim's glory will fly away like a bird —
no birth, no pregnancy, no conception.
12 Even if they rear children,
I will bereave them of every one.
Woe to them
when I turn away from them!
13 I have seen Ephraim, like Tyre,
planted in a pleasant place.
But Ephraim will bring out
their children to the slayer."

14 Give them, LORD —
what will you give them?
Give them wombs that miscarry
and breasts that are dry.

15 "Because of all their wickedness in Gilgal,
I hated them there.
Because of their sinful deeds,
I will drive them out of my house.
I will no longer love them;
all their leaders are rebellious.

[a] 8 Or *The prophet is the watchman over Ephraim, / the people of my God*

16 Ephraim is blighted,
their root is withered,
they yield no fruit.
Even if they bear children,
I will slay their cherished offspring."
17 My God will reject them
because they have not obeyed him;
they will be wanderers among the
nations.

10 Israel was a spreading vine;
he brought forth fruit for himself.
As his fruit increased,
he built more altars;
as his land prospered,
he adorned his sacred stones.
2 Their heart is deceitful,
and now they must bear their guilt.
The LORD will demolish their altars
and destroy their sacred stones.
3 Then they will say, "We have no king
because we did not revere the LORD.
But even if we had a king,
what could he do for us?"
4 They make many promises,
take false oaths
and make agreements;
therefore lawsuits spring up
like poisonous weeds in a plowed field.
5 The people who live in Samaria fear
for the calf-idol of Beth Aven.[a]
Its people will mourn over it,
and so will its idolatrous priests,
those who had rejoiced over its
splendor,
because it is taken from them into
exile.
6 It will be carried to Assyria
as tribute for the great king.
Ephraim will be disgraced;
Israel will be ashamed of its foreign
alliances.
7 Samaria's king will be destroyed,
swept away like a twig on the surface
of the waters.
8 The high places of wickedness[b] will be
destroyed —
it is the sin of Israel.
Thorns and thistles will grow up
and cover their altars.
Then they will say to the mountains,
"Cover us!"
and to the hills, "Fall on us!"
9 "Since the days of Gibeah, you have
sinned, Israel,
and there you have remained.[c]
Will not war again overtake
the evildoers in Gibeah?
10 When I please, I will punish them;
nations will be gathered against them
to put them in bonds for their
double sin.
11 Ephraim is a trained heifer
that loves to thresh;
so I will put a yoke
on her fair neck.
I will drive Ephraim,
Judah must plow,
and Jacob must break up the ground.
12 Sow righteousness for yourselves,
reap the fruit of unfailing love,
and break up your unplowed ground;
for it is time to seek the LORD,
until he comes
and showers his righteousness on you.
13 But you have planted wickedness,
you have reaped evil,
you have eaten the fruit of deception.
Because you have depended on your own
strength
and on your many warriors,
14 the roar of battle will rise against your
people,
so that all your fortresses will be
devastated —
as Shalman devastated Beth Arbel on the
day of battle,
when mothers were dashed to the
ground with their children.
15 So will it happen to you, Bethel,
because your wickedness is great.
When that day dawns,
the king of Israel will be completely
destroyed.

God's Love for Israel

11 "When Israel was a child, I loved
him,
and out of Egypt I called my son.
2 But the more they were called,

[a] 5 *Beth Aven* means *house of wickedness* (a derogatory name for Bethel, which means *house of God*).
[b] 8 Hebrew *aven,* a reference to Beth Aven (a derogatory name for Bethel); see verse 5. [c] 9 Or *there a stand was taken*

the more they went away
from me.[a]
They sacrificed to the Baals
and they burned incense to images.
[3] It was I who taught Ephraim to walk,
taking them by the arms;
but they did not realize
it was I who healed them.
[4] I led them with cords of human kindness,
with ties of love.
To them I was like one who lifts
a little child to the cheek,
and I bent down to feed them.

[5] "Will they not return to Egypt
and will not Assyria rule over them
because they refuse to repent?
[6] A sword will flash in their cities;
it will devour their false prophets
and put an end to their plans.
[7] My people are determined to turn
from me.
Even though they call me God Most
High,
I will by no means exalt them.

[8] "How can I give you up, Ephraim?
How can I hand you over, Israel?
How can I treat you like Admah?
How can I make you like Zeboyim?
My heart is changed within me;
all my compassion is aroused.
[9] I will not carry out my fierce anger,
nor will I devastate Ephraim again.
For I am God, and not a man —
the Holy One among you.
I will not come against their cities.
[10] They will follow the LORD;
he will roar like a lion.
When he roars,
his children will come trembling from
the west.
[11] They will come from Egypt,
trembling like sparrows,
from Assyria, fluttering like doves.
I will settle them in their homes,"
declares the LORD.

Israel's Sin

[12] Ephraim has surrounded me with lies,
Israel with deceit.
And Judah is unruly against God,
even against the faithful
Holy One.[b]

12[c] [1] Ephraim feeds on the wind;
he pursues the east wind all day
and multiplies lies and violence.
He makes a treaty with Assyria
and sends olive oil to Egypt.
[2] The LORD has a charge to bring against
Judah;
he will punish Jacob[d] according to
his ways
and repay him according to his deeds.
[3] In the womb he grasped his brother's
heel;
as a man he struggled with God.
[4] He struggled with the angel and
overcame him;
he wept and begged for his favor.
He found him at Bethel
and talked with him there —
[5] the LORD God Almighty,
the LORD is his name!
[6] But you must return to your God;
maintain love and justice,
and wait for your God always.

[7] The merchant uses dishonest scales
and loves to defraud.
[8] Ephraim boasts,
"I am very rich; I have become wealthy.
With all my wealth they will not find
in me
any iniquity or sin."

[9] "I have been the LORD your God
ever since you came out of Egypt;
I will make you live in tents again,
as in the days of your appointed
festivals.
[10] I spoke to the prophets,
gave them many visions
and told parables through them."

[11] Is Gilead wicked?
Its people are worthless!
Do they sacrifice bulls in Gilgal?
Their altars will be like piles of
stones
on a plowed field.
[12] Jacob fled to the country of Aram[e];
Israel served to get a wife,
and to pay for her he tended sheep.

[a] *2* Septuagint; Hebrew *them* [b] *12* In Hebrew texts this verse (11:12) is numbered 12:1. [c] In Hebrew texts 12:1-14 is numbered 12:2-15. [d] *2* *Jacob* means *he grasps the heel*, a Hebrew idiom for *he takes advantage of* or *he deceives.* [e] *12* That is, Northwest Mesopotamia

[13]The LORD used a prophet to bring Israel
up from Egypt,
by a prophet he cared for him.
[14]But Ephraim has aroused his bitter
anger;
his Lord will leave on him the guilt of
his bloodshed
and will repay him for his contempt.

The LORD's Anger Against Israel

13 When Ephraim spoke, people
trembled;
he was exalted in Israel.
But he became guilty of Baal worship
and died.
[2]Now they sin more and more;
they make idols for themselves from
their silver,
cleverly fashioned images,
all of them the work of craftsmen.
It is said of these people,
"They offer human sacrifices!
They kiss[a] calf-idols!"
[3]Therefore they will be like the morning
mist,
like the early dew that disappears,
like chaff swirling from a threshing
floor,
like smoke escaping through a
window.

[4]"But I have been the LORD your God
ever since you came out of Egypt.
You shall acknowledge no God but me,
no Savior except me.
[5]I cared for you in the wilderness,
in the land of burning heat.
[6]When I fed them, they were satisfied;
when they were satisfied, they became
proud;
then they forgot me.
[7]So I will be like a lion to them,
like a leopard I will lurk by the path.
[8]Like a bear robbed of her cubs,
I will attack them and rip them open;
like a lion I will devour them —
a wild animal will tear them apart.

[9]"You are destroyed, Israel,
because you are against me, against
your helper.
[10]Where is your king, that he may save you?
Where are your rulers in all your
towns,
of whom you said,
'Give me a king and princes'?
[11]So in my anger I gave you a king,
and in my wrath I took him away.
[12]The guilt of Ephraim is stored up,
his sins are kept on record.
[13]Pains as of a woman in childbirth come
to him,
but he is a child without wisdom;
when the time arrives,
he doesn't have the sense to come out
of the womb.

[14]"I will deliver this people from the power
of the grave;
I will redeem them from death.
Where, O death, are your plagues?
Where, O grave, is your destruction?

"I will have no compassion,
15 even though he thrives among his
brothers.
An east wind from the LORD will come,
blowing in from the desert;
his spring will fail
and his well dry up.
His storehouse will be plundered
of all its treasures.
[16]The people of Samaria must bear their
guilt,
because they have rebelled against
their God.
They will fall by the sword;
their little ones will be dashed to the
ground,
their pregnant women ripped open."[b]

Repentance to Bring Blessing

14[c] Return, Israel, to the LORD your
God.
Your sins have been your downfall!
[2]Take words with you
and return to the LORD.
Say to him:
"Forgive all our sins
and receive us graciously,
that we may offer the fruit of our lips.[d]
[3]Assyria cannot save us;
we will not mount warhorses.
We will never again say 'Our gods'

[a] 2 Or *"Men who sacrifice / kiss* [b] 16 In Hebrew texts this verse (13:16) is numbered 14:1. [c] In Hebrew texts 14:1-9 is numbered 14:2-10. [d] 2 Or *offer our lips as sacrifices of bulls*

CHRIST IS RISEN

Matt Maher, Mia Fields

Let no one caught in sin remain
Inside the lie of inward shame
But fix our eyes upon the cross
And run to him
Who showed great love
And bled for us
Freely you've bled for us

Christ is risen from the dead
Trampling over death by death
Come awake, come awake
Come and rise up from the grave

Christ is risen from the dead
We are one with him again
Come awake, come awake
Come and rise up from the grave

Beneath the weight of all our sin
You bowed to none but
heaven's will

No scheme of hell
No scoffer's crown
No burden great
Can hold you down

In strength you reign
Forever let your church proclaim

O death, where is your sting?
O hell, where is your victory?
O church, come stand in the light
The glory of God has defeated
the night
O death, where is your sting?
O hell, where is your victory?
O church, come stand in the light
Our God is not dead
He's alive! He's alive!

THE INSPIRATION

"Where, O death, is your victory? Where, O death, is your sting?"

— 1 Corinthians 15:55

BEHIND THE SONG

Matt Maher finds inspiration for songs in unusual places. One of his friends, a Ukrainian priest, told him about an amazing sermon from the fourth century, and Maher immediately resonated with its message.

"There was a priest named John Chrysostom," Maher explains. "His nickname was 'The Golden Tongue' because he was such a great preacher. One year on Easter, he preached a homily with the message; 'Christ is risen from the dead, trampling over death by death and redeeming us from the grave.' " Maher was so moved by both the original Chrysostom message and the passion of his Ukrainian friend as he told him about it, that he began to explore the concept within the context of a worship song for Easter.

"The whole song is about the cross — the death and the resurrection of Christ," Maher adds. "Hell thought it had swallowed another victim; just another human being, but it swallowed God Incarnate. So God literally used death to destroy death and that's something only God can do!"

The song ends by triumphantly proclaiming "He's alive! He's alive!" "It's a refutation of modernism in a way," Maher admits. "There's this whole notion in these times that religion is obsolete or God is dead. He is not dead. He's alive!"

Selah

The center of the gospel is the death and resurrection of Jesus, but it is all too easy for us — and our worship — to focus on other things. History is riddled with examples of people adding to, or taking away from, the simplicity of the gospel. Some even wonder if it matters whether or not Jesus rose from the dead. First Corinthians 15 is an incredible study on the centrality of the resurrection.

Read and pray through this chapter. Note the confidence Paul has in his message. Follow the logical path of his reasoning and notice how worshipful his words become as he practically shouts from the page regarding the glory of the resurrection! Consider the impact of Jesus' resurrection and celebrate. Every day is Easter for the believing Christian.

to what our own hands have made,
for in you the fatherless find
compassion."

4 "I will heal their waywardness
and love them freely,
for my anger has turned away
from them.
5 I will be like the dew to Israel;
he will blossom like a lily.
Like a cedar of Lebanon
he will send down his roots;
6 his young shoots will grow.
His splendor will be like an olive tree,
his fragrance like a cedar of Lebanon.
7 People will dwell again in his shade;
they will flourish like the grain,
they will blossom like the vine —
Israel's fame will be like the wine
of Lebanon.
8 Ephraim, what more have I[a] to do
with idols?
I will answer him and care
for him.
I am like a flourishing juniper;
your fruitfulness comes from me."

9 Who is wise? Let them realize these
things.
Who is discerning? Let them
understand.
The ways of the LORD are right;
the righteous walk in them,
but the rebellious stumble in them.

[a] 8 Or Hebrew; Septuagint *What more has Ephraim*

JOEL

1 The word of the LORD that came to Joel son of Pethuel.

An Invasion of Locusts

2 Hear this, you elders;
listen, all who live in the land.
Has anything like this ever happened in your days
or in the days of your ancestors?
3 Tell it to your children,
and let your children tell it to their children,
and their children to the next generation.
4 What the locust swarm has left
the great locusts have eaten;
what the great locusts have left
the young locusts have eaten;
what the young locusts have left
other locusts[a] have eaten.

5 Wake up, you drunkards, and weep!
Wail, all you drinkers of wine;
wail because of the new wine,
for it has been snatched from your lips.
6 A nation has invaded my land,
a mighty army without number;
it has the teeth of a lion,
the fangs of a lioness.
7 It has laid waste my vines
and ruined my fig trees.
It has stripped off their bark
and thrown it away,
leaving their branches white.

8 Mourn like a virgin in sackcloth
grieving for the betrothed of her youth.
9 Grain offerings and drink offerings
are cut off from the house of the LORD.
The priests are in mourning,
those who minister before the LORD.
10 The fields are ruined,
the ground is dried up;
the grain is destroyed,
the new wine is dried up,
the olive oil fails.

11 Despair, you farmers,
wail, you vine growers;
grieve for the wheat and the barley,
because the harvest of the field is destroyed.
12 The vine is dried up
and the fig tree is withered;
the pomegranate, the palm and the apple[b] tree —
all the trees of the field — are dried up.
Surely the people's joy
is withered away.

A Call to Lamentation

13 Put on sackcloth, you priests, and mourn;
wail, you who minister before the altar.
Come, spend the night in sackcloth,
you who minister before my God;
for the grain offerings and drink offerings
are withheld from the house of your God.
14 Declare a holy fast;
call a sacred assembly.
Summon the elders
and all who live in the land
to the house of the LORD your God,
and cry out to the LORD.

15 Alas for that day!
For the day of the LORD is near;
it will come like destruction from the Almighty.[c]

16 Has not the food been cut off
before our very eyes —
joy and gladness
from the house of our God?
17 The seeds are shriveled
beneath the clods.[d]
The storehouses are in ruins,
the granaries have been broken down,
for the grain has dried up.
18 How the cattle moan!
The herds mill about

[a] *4* The precise meaning of the four Hebrew words used here for locusts is uncertain. [b] *12* Or possibly *apricot* [c] *15* Hebrew *Shaddai* [d] *17* The meaning of the Hebrew for this word is uncertain.

because they have no pasture;
even the flocks of sheep are suffering.

19 To you, LORD, I call,
for fire has devoured the pastures in the wilderness
and flames have burned up all the trees of the field.
20 Even the wild animals pant for you;
the streams of water have dried up
and fire has devoured the pastures in the wilderness.

An Army of Locusts

2 Blow the trumpet in Zion;
sound the alarm on my holy hill.

Let all who live in the land tremble,
for the day of the LORD is coming.
It is close at hand—
2 a day of darkness and gloom,
a day of clouds and blackness.
Like dawn spreading across the mountains
a large and mighty army comes,
such as never was in ancient times
nor ever will be in ages to come.

3 Before them fire devours,
behind them a flame blazes.
Before them the land is like the garden of Eden,
behind them, a desert waste—
nothing escapes them.
4 They have the appearance of horses;
they gallop along like cavalry.
5 With a noise like that of chariots
they leap over the mountaintops,
like a crackling fire consuming stubble,
like a mighty army drawn up for battle.

6 At the sight of them, nations are in anguish;
every face turns pale.
7 They charge like warriors;
they scale walls like soldiers.
They all march in line,
not swerving from their course.
8 They do not jostle each other;
each marches straight ahead.
They plunge through defenses
without breaking ranks.
9 They rush upon the city;
they run along the wall.
They climb into the houses;
like thieves they enter through the windows.

10 Before them the earth shakes,
the heavens tremble,
the sun and moon are darkened,
and the stars no longer shine.
11 The LORD thunders
at the head of his army;
his forces are beyond number,
and mighty is the army that obeys his command.
The day of the LORD is great;
it is dreadful.
Who can endure it?

Rend Your Heart

12 "Even now," declares the LORD,
"return to me with all your heart,
with fasting and weeping and mourning."

13 Rend your heart
and not your garments.
Return to the LORD your God,
for he is gracious and compassionate,
slow to anger and abounding in love,
and he relents from sending calamity.
14 Who knows? He may turn and relent
and leave behind a blessing—
grain offerings and drink offerings
for the LORD your God.

15 Blow the trumpet in Zion,
declare a holy fast,
call a sacred assembly.
16 Gather the people,
consecrate the assembly;
bring together the elders,
gather the children,
those nursing at the breast.
Let the bridegroom leave his room
and the bride her chamber.
17 Let the priests, who minister before the LORD,
weep between the portico and the altar.
Let them say, "Spare your people, LORD.
Do not make your inheritance an object of scorn,
a byword among the nations.
Why should they say among the peoples,
'Where is their God?'"

The LORD's Answer

18 Then the LORD was jealous for his land
and took pity on his people.

19 The LORD replied[a] to them:

"I am sending you grain, new wine and
olive oil,
enough to satisfy you fully;
never again will I make you
an object of scorn to the nations.

20 "I will drive the northern horde far
from you,
pushing it into a parched and barren
land;
its eastern ranks will drown in the
Dead Sea
and its western ranks in the
Mediterranean Sea.
And its stench will go up;
its smell will rise."

Surely he has done great things!
21 Do not be afraid, land of Judah;
be glad and rejoice.
Surely the LORD has done great things!
22 Do not be afraid, you wild animals,
for the pastures in the wilderness are
becoming green.
The trees are bearing their fruit;
the fig tree and the vine yield their
riches.
23 Be glad, people of Zion,
rejoice in the LORD your God,
for he has given you the autumn rains
because he is faithful.
He sends you abundant showers,
both autumn and spring rains, as
before.
24 The threshing floors will be filled with
grain;
the vats will overflow with new wine
and oil.

25 "I will repay you for the years the locusts
have eaten —
the great locust and the young
locust,
the other locusts and the locust
swarm[b] —
my great army that I sent among you.
26 You will have plenty to eat, until you
are full,
and you will praise the name of the
LORD your God,
who has worked wonders for you;
never again will my people be shamed.
27 Then you will know that I am in Israel,
that I am the LORD your God,
and that there is no other;
never again will my people be shamed.

The Day of the LORD

28 "And afterward,
I will pour out my Spirit on all people.
Your sons and daughters will prophesy,
your old men will dream dreams,
your young men will see visions.
29 Even on my servants, both men and
women,
I will pour out my Spirit in those days.
30 I will show wonders in the heavens
and on the earth,
blood and fire and billows of smoke.
31 The sun will be turned to darkness
and the moon to blood
before the coming of the great and
dreadful day of the LORD.
32 And everyone who calls
on the name of the LORD will be
saved;
for on Mount Zion and in Jerusalem
there will be deliverance,
as the LORD has said,
even among the survivors
whom the LORD calls.[c]

The Nations Judged

3 [d] "In those days and at that time,
when I restore the fortunes of Judah
and Jerusalem,
2 I will gather all nations
and bring them down to the Valley of
Jehoshaphat.[e]
There I will put them on trial
for what they did to my inheritance,
my people Israel,
because they scattered my people among
the nations
and divided up my land.

[a] *18,19* Or *LORD will be jealous . . . / and take pity . . . / [19]The LORD will reply* [b] *25* The precise meaning of the four Hebrew words used here for locusts is uncertain. [c] *32* In Hebrew texts 2:28-32 is numbered 3:1-5. [d] In Hebrew texts 3:1-21 is numbered 4:1-21. [e] *2* *Jehoshaphat* means *the LORD judges*; also in verse 12.

[3] They cast lots for my people
and traded boys for prostitutes;
they sold girls for wine to drink.

[4] "Now what have you against me, Tyre
and Sidon and all you regions of Philistia?
Are you repaying me for something I have
done? If you are paying me back, I will swift-
ly and speedily return on your own heads
what you have done. [5] For you took my silver
and my gold and carried off my finest trea-
sures to your temples.[a] [6] You sold the people
of Judah and Jerusalem to the Greeks, that
you might send them far from their home-
land.

[7] "See, I am going to rouse them out of the
places to which you sold them, and I will re-
turn on your own heads what you have done.
[8] I will sell your sons and daughters to the
people of Judah, and they will sell them to
the Sabeans, a nation far away." The LORD
has spoken.

[9] Proclaim this among the nations:
Prepare for war!
Rouse the warriors!
Let all the fighting men draw near and attack.
[10] Beat your plowshares into swords
and your pruning hooks into spears.
Let the weakling say,
"I am strong!"
[11] Come quickly, all you nations from every side,
and assemble there.

Bring down your warriors, LORD!

[12] "Let the nations be roused;
let them advance into the Valley of Jehoshaphat,
for there I will sit
to judge all the nations on every side.
[13] Swing the sickle,
for the harvest is ripe.
Come, trample the grapes,
for the winepress is full
and the vats overflow—
so great is their wickedness!"

[14] Multitudes, multitudes
in the valley of decision!
For the day of the LORD is near
in the valley of decision.
[15] The sun and moon will be darkened,
and the stars no longer shine.
[16] The LORD will roar from Zion
and thunder from Jerusalem;
the earth and the heavens will tremble.
But the LORD will be a refuge for his people,
a stronghold for the people of Israel.

Blessings for God's People

[17] "Then you will know that I, the LORD your God,
dwell in Zion, my holy hill.
Jerusalem will be holy;
never again will foreigners invade her.

[18] "In that day the mountains will drip new wine,
and the hills will flow with milk;
all the ravines of Judah will run with water.
A fountain will flow out of the LORD's house
and will water the valley of acacias.[b]
[19] But Egypt will be desolate,
Edom a desert waste,
because of violence done to the people of Judah,
in whose land they shed innocent blood.
[20] Judah will be inhabited forever
and Jerusalem through all generations.
[21] Shall I leave their innocent blood unavenged?
No, I will not."

The LORD dwells in Zion!

[a] 5 Or *palaces* [b] 18 Or *Valley of Shittim*

AMOS

1 The words of Amos, one of the shepherds of Tekoa — the vision he saw concerning Israel two years before the earthquake, when Uzziah was king of Judah and Jeroboam son of Jehoash[a] was king of Israel.
2 He said:

"The LORD roars from Zion
and thunders from Jerusalem;
the pastures of the shepherds dry up,
and the top of Carmel withers."

Judgment on Israel's Neighbors

3 This is what the LORD says:

"For three sins of Damascus,
even for four, I will not relent.
Because she threshed Gilead
with sledges having iron teeth,
4 I will send fire on the house of Hazael
that will consume the fortresses of Ben-Hadad.
5 I will break down the gate of Damascus;
I will destroy the king who is in[b] the Valley of Aven[c]
and the one who holds the scepter in Beth Eden.
The people of Aram will go into exile to Kir,"
says the LORD.

6 This is what the LORD says:

"For three sins of Gaza,
even for four, I will not relent.
Because she took captive whole communities
and sold them to Edom,
7 I will send fire on the walls of Gaza
that will consume her fortresses.
8 I will destroy the king[d] of Ashdod
and the one who holds the scepter in Ashkelon.
I will turn my hand against Ekron,
till the last of the Philistines are dead,"
says the Sovereign LORD.

9 This is what the LORD says:

"For three sins of Tyre,
even for four, I will not relent.
Because she sold whole communities of captives to Edom,
disregarding a treaty of brotherhood,
10 I will send fire on the walls of Tyre
that will consume her fortresses."

11 This is what the LORD says:

"For three sins of Edom,
even for four, I will not relent.
Because he pursued his brother with a sword
and slaughtered the women of the land,
because his anger raged continually
and his fury flamed unchecked,
12 I will send fire on Teman
that will consume the fortresses of Bozrah."

13 This is what the LORD says:

"For three sins of Ammon,
even for four, I will not relent.
Because he ripped open the pregnant women of Gilead
in order to extend his borders,
14 I will set fire to the walls of Rabbah
that will consume her fortresses
amid war cries on the day of battle,
amid violent winds on a stormy day.
15 Her king[e] will go into exile,
he and his officials together,"
says the LORD.

2 This is what the LORD says:

"For three sins of Moab,
even for four, I will not relent.
Because he burned to ashes
the bones of Edom's king,
2 I will send fire on Moab

[a] *1* Hebrew *Joash,* a variant of *Jehoash* [b] *5* Or *the inhabitants of* [c] *5* *Aven* means *wickedness.*
[d] *8* Or *inhabitants* [e] *15* Or / *Molek*

that will consume the fortresses of
Kerioth.[a]
Moab will go down in great tumult
amid war cries and the blast of the
trumpet.
3 I will destroy her ruler
and kill all her officials with him,"
says the LORD.

4 This is what the LORD says:

"For three sins of Judah,
even for four, I will not relent.
Because they have rejected the law of
the LORD
and have not kept his decrees,
because they have been led astray by
false gods,[b]
the gods[c] their ancestors followed,
5 I will send fire on Judah
that will consume the fortresses of
Jerusalem."

Judgment on Israel

6 This is what the LORD says:

"For three sins of Israel,
even for four, I will not relent.
They sell the innocent for silver,
and the needy for a pair of sandals.
7 They trample on the heads of the poor
as on the dust of the ground
and deny justice to the oppressed.
Father and son use the same girl
and so profane my holy name.
8 They lie down beside every altar
on garments taken in pledge.
In the house of their god
they drink wine taken as fines.

9 "Yet I destroyed the Amorites before
them,
though they were tall as the cedars
and strong as the oaks.
I destroyed their fruit above
and their roots below.
10 I brought you up out of Egypt
and led you forty years in the
wilderness
to give you the land of the Amorites.

11 "I also raised up prophets from among
your children
and Nazirites from among your
youths.
Is this not true, people of Israel?"
declares the LORD.
12 "But you made the Nazirites drink wine
and commanded the prophets not
to prophesy.

13 "Now then, I will crush you
as a cart crushes when loaded with
grain.
14 The swift will not escape,
the strong will not muster their
strength,
and the warrior will not save his life.
15 The archer will not stand his ground,
the fleet-footed soldier will not get
away,
and the horseman will not save his
life.
16 Even the bravest warriors
will flee naked on that day,"
declares the LORD.

Witnesses Summoned Against Israel

3 Hear this word, people of Israel, the
word the LORD has spoken against
you — against the whole family I brought up
out of Egypt:

2 "You only have I chosen
of all the families of the earth;
therefore I will punish you
for all your sins."

3 Do two walk together
unless they have agreed to do so?
4 Does a lion roar in the thicket
when it has no prey?
Does it growl in its den
when it has caught nothing?
5 Does a bird swoop down to a trap on
the ground
when no bait is there?
Does a trap spring up from the ground
if it has not caught anything?
6 When a trumpet sounds in a city,
do not the people tremble?
When disaster comes to a city,
has not the LORD caused it?

7 Surely the Sovereign LORD does nothing
without revealing his plan
to his servants the prophets.

8 The lion has roared —
who will not fear?

[a] 2 Or *of her cities* [b] 4 Or *by lies* [c] 4 Or *lies*

The Sovereign LORD has spoken —
who can but prophesy?

[9] Proclaim to the fortresses of Ashdod
and to the fortresses of Egypt:
"Assemble yourselves on the mountains
of Samaria;
see the great unrest within her
and the oppression among her people."
[10] "They do not know how to do right,"
declares the LORD,
"who store up in their fortresses
what they have plundered and looted."

[11] Therefore this is what the Sovereign
LORD says:

"An enemy will overrun your land,
pull down your strongholds
and plunder your fortresses."

[12] This is what the LORD says:

"As a shepherd rescues from the lion's
mouth
only two leg bones or a piece of an ear,
so will the Israelites living in Samaria be
rescued,
with only the head of a bed
and a piece of fabric[a] from a couch.[b]"

[13] "Hear this and testify against the de-
scendants of Jacob," declares the Lord, the
LORD God Almighty.

[14] "On the day I punish Israel for her sins,
I will destroy the altars of Bethel;
the horns of the altar will be cut off
and fall to the ground.
[15] I will tear down the winter house
along with the summer house;
the houses adorned with ivory will be
destroyed
and the mansions will be demolished,"
declares the LORD.

Israel Has Not Returned to God

4 Hear this word, you cows of Bashan on
Mount Samaria,
you women who oppress the poor and
crush the needy
and say to your husbands, "Bring us
some drinks!"
[2] The Sovereign LORD has sworn by his
holiness:
"The time will surely come
when you will be taken away with hooks,
the last of you with fishhooks.[c]
[3] You will each go straight out
through breaches in the wall,
and you will be cast out toward
Harmon,[d]"
declares the LORD.

[4] "Go to Bethel and sin;
go to Gilgal and sin yet more.
Bring your sacrifices every morning,
your tithes every three years.[e]
[5] Burn leavened bread as a thank offering
and brag about your freewill
offerings —
boast about them, you Israelites,
for this is what you love to do,"
declares the Sovereign LORD.

[6] "I gave you empty stomachs in every city
and lack of bread in every town,
yet you have not returned to me,"
declares the LORD.

[7] "I also withheld rain from you
when the harvest was still three
months away.
I sent rain on one town,
but withheld it from another.
One field had rain;
another had none and dried up.
[8] People staggered from town to town for
water
but did not get enough to drink,
yet you have not returned to me,"
declares the LORD.

[9] "Many times I struck your gardens and
vineyards,
destroying them with blight and
mildew.
Locusts devoured your fig and olive
trees,
yet you have not returned to me,"
declares the LORD.

[10] "I sent plagues among you
as I did to Egypt.
I killed your young men with the sword,
along with your captured horses.

[a] *12* The meaning of the Hebrew for this phrase is uncertain. [b] *12* Or *Israelites be rescued, / those who sit in Samaria / on the edge of their beds / and in Damascus on their couches.* [c] *2* Or *away in baskets, / the last of you in fish baskets* [d] *3* Masoretic Text; with a different word division of the Hebrew (see Septuagint) *out, you mountain of oppression* [e] *4* Or *days*

I filled your nostrils with the stench of
your camps,
yet you have not returned to me,"
declares the LORD.

[11] "I overthrew some of you
as I overthrew Sodom and
Gomorrah.
You were like a burning stick snatched
from the fire,
yet you have not returned to me,"
declares the LORD.

[12] "Therefore this is what I will do to you,
Israel,
and because I will do this to you,
Israel,
prepare to meet your God."

[13] He who forms the mountains,
who creates the wind,
and who reveals his thoughts to
mankind,
who turns dawn to darkness,
and treads on the heights of the
earth —
the LORD God Almighty is his name.

A Lament and Call to Repentance

5 Hear this word, Israel, this lament I take
up concerning you:

[2] "Fallen is Virgin Israel,
never to rise again,
deserted in her own land,
with no one to lift her up."

[3] This is what the Sovereign LORD says to
Israel:

"Your city that marches out a thousand
strong
will have only a hundred left;
your town that marches out a hundred
strong
will have only ten left."

[4] This is what the LORD says to Israel:

"Seek me and live;
[5] do not seek Bethel,
do not go to Gilgal,
do not journey to Beersheba.
For Gilgal will surely go into exile,
and Bethel will be reduced to
nothing.[a]"

[6] Seek the LORD and live,
or he will sweep through the tribes of
Joseph like a fire;
it will devour them,
and Bethel will have no one to
quench it.

[7] There are those who turn justice into
bitterness
and cast righteousness to the ground.

[8] He who made the Pleiades and Orion,
who turns midnight into dawn
and darkens day into night,
who calls for the waters of the sea
and pours them out over the face of
the land —
the LORD is his name.
[9] With a blinding flash he destroys the
stronghold
and brings the fortified city to ruin.

[10] There are those who hate the one who
upholds justice in court
and detest the one who tells the truth.

[11] You levy a straw tax on the poor
and impose a tax on their grain.
Therefore, though you have built stone
mansions,
you will not live in them;
though you have planted lush vineyards,
you will not drink their wine.
[12] For I know how many are your offenses
and how great your sins.
There are those who oppress the
innocent and take bribes
and deprive the poor of justice in the
courts.
[13] Therefore the prudent keep quiet in
such times,
for the times are evil.

[14] Seek good, not evil,
that you may live.
Then the LORD God Almighty will be
with you,
just as you say he is.
[15] Hate evil, love good;
maintain justice in the courts.
Perhaps the LORD God Almighty will
have mercy
on the remnant of Joseph.

[16] Therefore this is what the Lord, the LORD
God Almighty, says:

[a] 5 Hebrew *aven,* a reference to Beth Aven (a derogatory name for Bethel); see Hosea 4:15.

"There will be wailing in all the streets
and cries of anguish in every public square.
The farmers will be summoned to weep
and the mourners to wail.
17 There will be wailing in all the vineyards,
for I will pass through your midst,"
says the LORD.

The Day of the LORD

18 Woe to you who long
for the day of the LORD!
Why do you long for the day of the LORD?
That day will be darkness, not light.
19 It will be as though a man fled from a lion
only to meet a bear,
as though he entered his house
and rested his hand on the wall
only to have a snake bite him.
20 Will not the day of the LORD be darkness, not light—
pitch-dark, without a ray of brightness?

21 "I hate, I despise your religious festivals;
your assemblies are a stench to me.
22 Even though you bring me burnt offerings and grain offerings,
I will not accept them.
Though you bring choice fellowship offerings,
I will have no regard for them.
23 Away with the noise of your songs!
I will not listen to the music of your harps.
24 But let justice roll on like a river,
righteousness like a never-failing stream!

25 "Did you bring me sacrifices and offerings
forty years in the wilderness, people of Israel?
26 You have lifted up the shrine of your king,
the pedestal of your idols,
the star of your god[a]—
which you made for yourselves.
27 Therefore I will send you into exile beyond Damascus,"
says the LORD, whose name is God Almighty.

Woe to the Complacent

6 Woe to you who are complacent in Zion,
and to you who feel secure on Mount Samaria,
you notable men of the foremost nation,
to whom the people of Israel come!
2 Go to Kalneh and look at it;
go from there to great Hamath,
and then go down to Gath in Philistia.
Are they better off than your two kingdoms?
Is their land larger than yours?
3 You put off the day of disaster
and bring near a reign of terror.
4 You lie on beds adorned with ivory
and lounge on your couches.
You dine on choice lambs
and fattened calves.
5 You strum away on your harps like David
and improvise on musical instruments.
6 You drink wine by the bowlful
and use the finest lotions,
but you do not grieve over the ruin of Joseph.
7 Therefore you will be among the first to go into exile;
your feasting and lounging will end.

The LORD Abhors the Pride of Israel

8 The Sovereign LORD has sworn by him-
self—the LORD God Almighty declares:

"I abhor the pride of Jacob
and detest his fortresses;
I will deliver up the city
and everything in it."

9 If ten people are left in one house, they
too will die. 10 And if the relative who comes
to carry the bodies out of the house to burn
them[b] asks anyone who might be hiding
there, "Is anyone else with you?" and he
says, "No," then he will go on to say, "Hush!
We must not mention the name of the LORD."

11 For the LORD has given the command,
and he will smash the great house into pieces
and the small house into bits.

[a] 26 Or *lifted up Sakkuth your king / and Kaiwan your idols, / your star-gods*; Septuagint *lifted up the shrine of Molek / and the star of your god Rephan, / their idols* [b] 10 Or *to make a funeral fire in honor of the dead*

[12]Do horses run on the rocky crags?
Does one plow the sea[a] with oxen?
But you have turned justice into poison
and the fruit of righteousness into bitterness—
[13]you who rejoice in the conquest of Lo Debar[b]
and say, "Did we not take Karnaim[c]
by our own strength?"

[14]For the LORD God Almighty declares,
"I will stir up a nation against you, Israel,
that will oppress you all the way
from Lebo Hamath to the valley of the Arabah."

Locusts, Fire and a Plumb Line

7 This is what the Sovereign LORD showed
me: He was preparing swarms of locusts
after the king's share had been harvested
and just as the late crops were coming up.
[2]When they had stripped the land clean, I
cried out, "Sovereign LORD, forgive! How can
Jacob survive? He is so small!"
[3]So the LORD relented.
"This will not happen," the LORD said.
[4]This is what the Sovereign LORD showed
me: The Sovereign LORD was calling for
judgment by fire; it dried up the great deep
and devoured the land. [5]Then I cried out,
"Sovereign LORD, I beg you, stop! How can
Jacob survive? He is so small!"
[6]So the LORD relented.
"This will not happen either," the Sovereign LORD said.

[7]This is what he showed me: The Lord was
standing by a wall that had been built true
to plumb,[d] with a plumb line[e] in his hand.
[8]And the LORD asked me, "What do you see,
Amos?"
"A plumb line," I replied.
Then the Lord said, "Look, I am setting a
plumb line among my people Israel; I will
spare them no longer.

[9]"The high places of Isaac will be destroyed
and the sanctuaries of Israel will be ruined;
with my sword I will rise against the house of Jeroboam."

Amos and Amaziah

[10]Then Amaziah the priest of Bethel sent a
message to Jeroboam king of Israel: "Amos is
raising a conspiracy against you in the very
heart of Israel. The land cannot bear all his
words. [11]For this is what Amos is saying:

" 'Jeroboam will die by the sword,
and Israel will surely go into exile,
away from their native land.' "

[12]Then Amaziah said to Amos, "Get out,
you seer! Go back to the land of Judah. Earn
your bread there and do your prophesying
there. [13]Don't prophesy anymore at Bethel,
because this is the king's sanctuary and the
temple of the kingdom."
[14]Amos answered Amaziah, "I was neither a prophet nor the son of a prophet, but I
was a shepherd, and I also took care of sycamore-fig trees. [15]But the LORD took me from
tending the flock and said to me, 'Go, prophesy to my people Israel.' [16]Now then, hear
the word of the LORD. You say,

" 'Do not prophesy against Israel,
and stop preaching against the descendants of Isaac.'

[17]"Therefore this is what the LORD says:

" 'Your wife will become a prostitute in the city,
and your sons and daughters will fall by the sword.
Your land will be measured and divided up,
and you yourself will die in a pagan[f] country.
And Israel will surely go into exile,
away from their native land.' "

A Basket of Ripe Fruit

8 This is what the Sovereign LORD showed
me: a basket of ripe fruit. [2]"What do you
see, Amos?" he asked.
"A basket of ripe fruit," I answered.
Then the LORD said to me, "The time is
ripe for my people Israel; I will spare them
no longer.

[a] 12 With a different word division of the Hebrew; Masoretic Text *plow there* [b] 13 *Lo Debar* means *nothing.* [c] 13 *Karnaim* means *horns; horn* here symbolizes strength. [d] 7 The meaning of the Hebrew for this phrase is uncertain. [e] 7 The meaning of the Hebrew for this phrase is uncertain; also in verse 8. [f] 17 Hebrew *an unclean*

[3]"In that day," declares the Sovereign
LORD, "the songs in the temple will turn to
wailing.[a] Many, many bodies — flung every-
where! Silence!"

[4]Hear this, you who trample the needy
and do away with the poor of the land,

[5]saying,

"When will the New Moon be over
that we may sell grain,
and the Sabbath be ended
that we may market wheat?" —
skimping on the measure,
boosting the price
and cheating with dishonest scales,
[6]buying the poor with silver
and the needy for a pair of sandals,
selling even the sweepings with the
wheat.

[7]The LORD has sworn by himself, the
Pride of Jacob: "I will never forget anything
they have done.

[8]"Will not the land tremble for this,
and all who live in it mourn?
The whole land will rise like the Nile;
it will be stirred up and then sink
like the river of Egypt.

[9]"In that day," declares the Sovereign
LORD,

"I will make the sun go down at noon
and darken the earth in broad
daylight.
[10]I will turn your religious festivals into
mourning
and all your singing into weeping.
I will make all of you wear sackcloth
and shave your heads.
I will make that time like mourning for
an only son
and the end of it like a bitter day.

[11]"The days are coming," declares the
Sovereign LORD,
"when I will send a famine through the
land —
not a famine of food or a thirst for water,
but a famine of hearing the words of
the LORD.
[12]People will stagger from sea to sea
and wander from north to east,
searching for the word of the LORD,
but they will not find it.

[13]"In that day

"the lovely young women and strong
young men
will faint because of thirst.
[14]Those who swear by the sin of Samaria —
who say, 'As surely as your god lives,
Dan,'
or, 'As surely as the god[b] of Beersheba
lives' —
they will fall, never to rise again."

Israel to Be Destroyed

9 I saw the Lord standing by the altar, and
he said:

"Strike the tops of the pillars
so that the thresholds shake.
Bring them down on the heads of all the
people;
those who are left I will kill with the
sword.
Not one will get away,
none will escape.
[2]Though they dig down to the depths
below,
from there my hand will take them.
Though they climb up to the heavens
above,
from there I will bring them down.
[3]Though they hide themselves on the top
of Carmel,
there I will hunt them down and seize
them.
Though they hide from my eyes at the
bottom of the sea,
there I will command the serpent to
bite them.
[4]Though they are driven into exile by their
enemies,
there I will command the sword to
slay them.

"I will keep my eye on them
for harm and not for good."

[5]The Lord, the LORD Almighty —
he touches the earth and it melts,
and all who live in it mourn;
the whole land rises like the Nile,
then sinks like the river of Egypt;

[a] 3 Or *"the temple singers will wail* [b] 14 Hebrew *the way*

[6]he builds his lofty palace[a] in the heavens
and sets its foundation[b] on the earth;
he calls for the waters of the sea
and pours them out over the face of the land—
the LORD is his name.

[7]"Are not you Israelites
the same to me as the Cushites[c]?"
declares the LORD.
"Did I not bring Israel up from Egypt,
the Philistines from Caphtor[d]
and the Arameans from Kir?

[8]"Surely the eyes of the Sovereign LORD
are on the sinful kingdom.
I will destroy it
from the face of the earth.
Yet I will not totally destroy
the descendants of Jacob,"
declares the LORD.
[9]"For I will give the command,
and I will shake the people of Israel
among all the nations
as grain is shaken in a sieve,
and not a pebble will reach the ground.
[10]All the sinners among my people
will die by the sword,
all those who say,
'Disaster will not overtake or meet us.'

Israel's Restoration

[11]"In that day
"I will restore David's fallen shelter—
I will repair its broken walls
and restore its ruins—
and will rebuild it as it used to be,
[12]so that they may possess the remnant of Edom
and all the nations that bear my name,[e]"
declares the LORD, who will do these things.

[13]"The days are coming," declares the
LORD,

"when the reaper will be overtaken by the plowman
and the planter by the one treading grapes.
New wine will drip from the mountains
and flow from all the hills,
14 and I will bring my people Israel back from exile.[f]

"They will rebuild the ruined cities and live in them.
They will plant vineyards and drink their wine;
they will make gardens and eat their fruit.
[15]I will plant Israel in their own land,
never again to be uprooted
from the land I have given them,"
says the LORD your God.

[a] 6 The meaning of the Hebrew for this phrase is uncertain. [b] 6 The meaning of the Hebrew for this word is uncertain. [c] 7 That is, people from the upper Nile region [d] 7 That is, Crete [e] 12 Hebrew; Septuagint *so that the remnant of people / and all the nations that bear my name may seek me*
[f] 14 Or *will restore the fortunes of my people Israel*

OBADIAH

Obadiah's Vision

1 The vision of Obadiah.

This is what the Sovereign LORD says about Edom—

We have heard a message from the LORD:
An envoy was sent to the nations to say,
"Rise, let us go against her for battle"—

2 "See, I will make you small among the nations;
you will be utterly despised.
3 The pride of your heart has deceived you,
you who live in the clefts of the rocks[a]
and make your home on the heights,
you who say to yourself,
'Who can bring me down to the ground?'
4 Though you soar like the eagle
and make your nest among the stars,
from there I will bring you down,"
declares the LORD.
5 "If thieves came to you,
if robbers in the night—
oh, what a disaster awaits you!—
would they not steal only as much as they wanted?
If grape pickers came to you,
would they not leave a few grapes?
6 But how Esau will be ransacked,
his hidden treasures pillaged!
7 All your allies will force you to the border;
your friends will deceive and overpower you;
those who eat your bread will set a trap for you,[b]
but you will not detect it.

8 "In that day," declares the LORD,
"will I not destroy the wise men of Edom,
those of understanding in the mountains of Esau?
9 Your warriors, Teman, will be terrified,
and everyone in Esau's mountains
will be cut down in the slaughter.
10 Because of the violence against your brother Jacob,
you will be covered with shame;
you will be destroyed forever.
11 On the day you stood aloof
while strangers carried off his wealth
and foreigners entered his gates
and cast lots for Jerusalem,
you were like one of them.
12 You should not gloat over your brother
in the day of his misfortune,
nor rejoice over the people of Judah
in the day of their destruction,
nor boast so much
in the day of their trouble.
13 You should not march through the gates of my people
in the day of their disaster,
nor gloat over them in their calamity
in the day of their disaster,
nor seize their wealth
in the day of their disaster.
14 You should not wait at the crossroads
to cut down their fugitives,
nor hand over their survivors
in the day of their trouble.

15 "The day of the LORD is near
for all nations.
As you have done, it will be done to you;
your deeds will return upon your own head.
16 Just as you drank on my holy hill,
so all the nations will drink continually;
they will drink and drink
and be as if they had never been.
17 But on Mount Zion will be deliverance;
it will be holy,
and Jacob will possess his inheritance.
18 Jacob will be a fire
and Joseph a flame;

[a] 3 Or *of Sela* [b] 7 The meaning of the Hebrew for this clause is uncertain.

Esau will be stubble,
and they will set him on fire and destroy him.
There will be no survivors
from Esau."
The LORD has spoken.

19 People from the Negev will occupy
the mountains of Esau,
and people from the foothills will possess
the land of the Philistines.
They will occupy the fields of Ephraim
and Samaria,
and Benjamin will possess
Gilead.
20 This company of Israelite exiles who
are in Canaan
will possess the land as far as
Zarephath;
the exiles from Jerusalem who are in
Sepharad
will possess the towns of the Negev.
21 Deliverers will go up on[a] Mount Zion
to govern the mountains of Esau.
And the kingdom will be the LORD's.

[a] 21 Or *from*

JONAH

Jonah Flees From the LORD

1 The word of the LORD came to Jonah son of Amittai: 2 "Go to the great city of Nineveh and preach against it, because its wickedness has come up before me."

3 But Jonah ran away from the LORD and headed for Tarshish. He went down to Joppa, where he found a ship bound for that port. After paying the fare, he went aboard and sailed for Tarshish to flee from the LORD.

4 Then the LORD sent a great wind on the sea, and such a violent storm arose that the ship threatened to break up. 5 All the sailors were afraid and each cried out to his own god. And they threw the cargo into the sea to lighten the ship.

But Jonah had gone below deck, where he lay down and fell into a deep sleep. 6 The captain went to him and said, "How can you sleep? Get up and call on your god! Maybe he will take notice of us so that we will not perish."

7 Then the sailors said to each other, "Come, let us cast lots to find out who is responsible for this calamity." They cast lots and the lot fell on Jonah. 8 So they asked him, "Tell us, who is responsible for making all this trouble for us? What kind of work do you do? Where do you come from? What is your country? From what people are you?"

9 He answered, "I am a Hebrew and I worship the LORD, the God of heaven, who made the sea and the dry land."

10 This terrified them and they asked, "What have you done?" (They knew he was running away from the LORD, because he had already told them so.)

11 The sea was getting rougher and rougher. So they asked him, "What should we do to you to make the sea calm down for us?"

12 "Pick me up and throw me into the sea," he replied, "and it will become calm. I know that it is my fault that this great storm has come upon you."

13 Instead, the men did their best to row back to land. But they could not, for the sea grew even wilder than before. 14 Then they cried out to the LORD, "Please, LORD, do not let us die for taking this man's life. Do not hold us accountable for killing an innocent man, for you, LORD, have done as you pleased." 15 Then they took Jonah and threw him overboard, and the raging sea grew calm. 16 At this the men greatly feared the LORD, and they offered a sacrifice to the LORD and made vows to him.

Jonah's Prayer

17 Now the LORD provided a huge fish to swallow Jonah, and Jonah was in the belly of
2[a] the fish three days and three nights.
1 From inside the fish Jonah prayed to the LORD his God. 2 He said:

"In my distress I called to the LORD,
 and he answered me.
From deep in the realm of the dead I
 called for help,
 and you listened to my cry.
3 You hurled me into the depths,
 into the very heart of the seas,
 and the currents swirled about me;
all your waves and breakers
 swept over me.
4 I said, 'I have been banished
 from your sight;
yet I will look again
 toward your holy temple.'
5 The engulfing waters threatened me,[b]
 the deep surrounded me;
 seaweed was wrapped around
 my head.
6 To the roots of the mountains I sank
 down;
 the earth beneath barred me in
 forever.
But you, LORD my God,
 brought my life up from the pit.

7 "When my life was ebbing away,
 I remembered you, LORD,

[a] In Hebrew texts 2:1 is numbered 1:17, and 2:1-10 is numbered 2:2-11. [b] 5 Or *waters were at my throat*

and my prayer rose to you,
to your holy temple.

8 “Those who cling to worthless idols
turn away from God’s love for them.
9 But I, with shouts of grateful praise,
will sacrifice to you.
What I have vowed I will make good.
I will say, ‘Salvation comes from
the LORD.’ ”

10 And the LORD commanded the fish, and
it vomited Jonah onto dry land.

Jonah Goes to Nineveh

3 Then the word of the LORD came to Jo-
nah a second time: 2 “Go to the great city
of Nineveh and proclaim to it the message I
give you.”

3 Jonah obeyed the word of the LORD and
went to Nineveh. Now Nineveh was a very
large city; it took three days to go through it.
4 Jonah began by going a day’s journey into
the city, proclaiming, “Forty more days and
Nineveh will be overthrown.” 5 The Nine-
vites believed God. A fast was proclaimed,
and all of them, from the greatest to the least,
put on sackcloth.

6 When Jonah’s warning reached the king
of Nineveh, he rose from his throne, took off
his royal robes, covered himself with sack-
cloth and sat down in the dust. 7 This is the
proclamation he issued in Nineveh:

“By the decree of the king and his nobles:

Do not let people or animals, herds
or flocks, taste anything; do not let
them eat or drink. 8 But let people and
animals be covered with sackcloth.
Let everyone call urgently on God. Let
them give up their evil ways and their
violence. 9 Who knows? God may yet re-
lent and with compassion turn from his
fierce anger so that we will not perish.”

10 When God saw what they did and how
they turned from their evil ways, he relented
and did not bring on them the destruction he
had threatened.

Jonah’s Anger at the LORD’s Compassion

4 But to Jonah this seemed very wrong,
and he became angry. 2 He prayed to the
LORD, “Isn’t this what I said, LORD, when I
was still at home? That is what I tried to fore-
stall by fleeing to Tarshish. I knew that you
are a gracious and compassionate God, slow
to anger and abounding in love, a God who
relents from sending calamity. 3 Now, LORD,
take away my life, for it is better for me to die
than to live.”

4 But the LORD replied, “Is it right for you
to be angry?”

5 Jonah had gone out and sat down at a
place east of the city. There he made himself
a shelter, sat in its shade and waited to see
what would happen to the city. 6 Then the
LORD God provided a leafy plant[a] and made
it grow up over Jonah to give shade for his
head to ease his discomfort, and Jonah was
very happy about the plant. 7 But at dawn
the next day God provided a worm, which
chewed the plant so that it withered. 8 When
the sun rose, God provided a scorching east
wind, and the sun blazed on Jonah’s head
so that he grew faint. He wanted to die, and
said, “It would be better for me to die than
to live.”

9 But God said to Jonah, “Is it right for you
to be angry about the plant?”

“It is,” he said. “And I’m so angry I wish I
were dead.”

10 But the LORD said, “You have been con-
cerned about this plant, though you did not
tend it or make it grow. It sprang up over-
night and died overnight. 11 And should I
not have concern for the great city of Nine-
veh, in which there are more than a hundred
and twenty thousand people who cannot tell
their right hand from their left—and also
many animals?”

[a] 6 The precise identification of this plant is uncertain; also in verses 7, 9 and 10.

MICAH

1 The word of the LORD that came to Micah of Moresheth during the reigns of Jotham, Ahaz and Hezekiah, kings of Judah — the vision he saw concerning Samaria and Jerusalem.

[2] Hear, you peoples, all of you,
listen, earth and all who live in it,
that the Sovereign LORD may bear witness against you,
the Lord from his holy temple.

Judgment Against Samaria and Jerusalem

[3] Look! The LORD is coming from his dwelling place;
he comes down and treads on the heights of the earth.
[4] The mountains melt beneath him
and the valleys split apart,
like wax before the fire,
like water rushing down a slope.
[5] All this is because of Jacob's transgression,
because of the sins of the people of Israel.
What is Jacob's transgression?
Is it not Samaria?
What is Judah's high place?
Is it not Jerusalem?

[6] "Therefore I will make Samaria a heap of rubble,
a place for planting vineyards.
I will pour her stones into the valley
and lay bare her foundations.
[7] All her idols will be broken to pieces;
all her temple gifts will be burned with fire;
I will destroy all her images.
Since she gathered her gifts from the wages of prostitutes,
as the wages of prostitutes they will again be used."

Weeping and Mourning

[8] Because of this I will weep and wail;
I will go about barefoot and naked.
I will howl like a jackal
and moan like an owl.
[9] For Samaria's plague is incurable;
it has spread to Judah.
It has reached the very gate of my people,
even to Jerusalem itself.
[10] Tell it not in Gath[a];
weep not at all.
In Beth Ophrah[b]
roll in the dust.
[11] Pass by naked and in shame,
you who live in Shaphir.[c]
Those who live in Zaanan[d]
will not come out.
Beth Ezel is in mourning;
it no longer protects you.
[12] Those who live in Maroth[e] writhe in pain,
waiting for relief,
because disaster has come from the LORD,
even to the gate of Jerusalem.
[13] You who live in Lachish,
harness fast horses to the chariot.
You are where the sin of Daughter Zion began,
for the transgressions of Israel were found in you.
[14] Therefore you will give parting gifts
to Moresheth Gath.
The town of Akzib[f] will prove deceptive
to the kings of Israel.
[15] I will bring a conqueror against you
who live in Mareshah.[g]
The nobles of Israel
will flee to Adullam.
[16] Shave your head in mourning
for the children in whom you delight;
make yourself as bald as the vulture,
for they will go from you into exile.

[a] 10 *Gath* sounds like the Hebrew for *tell.* [b] 10 *Beth Ophrah* means *house of dust.* [c] 11 *Shaphir* means *pleasant.* [d] 11 *Zaanan* sounds like the Hebrew for *come out.* [e] 12 *Maroth* sounds like the Hebrew for *bitter.* [f] 14 *Akzib* means *deception.* [g] 15 *Mareshah* sounds like the Hebrew for *conqueror.*

Human Plans and God's Plans

2 Woe to those who plan iniquity,
to those who plot evil on their beds!
At morning's light they carry it out
because it is in their power to do it.
[2] They covet fields and seize them,
and houses, and take them.
They defraud people of their homes,
they rob them of their inheritance.

[3] Therefore, the LORD says:

"I am planning disaster against this people,
from which you cannot save yourselves.
You will no longer walk proudly,
for it will be a time of calamity.
[4] In that day people will ridicule you;
they will taunt you with this mournful song:
'We are utterly ruined;
my people's possession is divided up.
He takes it from me!
He assigns our fields to traitors.' "

[5] Therefore you will have no one in the assembly of the LORD
to divide the land by lot.

False Prophets

[6] "Do not prophesy," their prophets say.
"Do not prophesy about these things;
disgrace will not overtake us."
[7] You descendants of Jacob, should it be said,
"Does the LORD become[a] impatient?
Does he do such things?"

"Do not my words do good
to the one whose ways are upright?
[8] Lately my people have risen up
like an enemy.
You strip off the rich robe
from those who pass by without a care,
like men returning from battle.
[9] You drive the women of my people
from their pleasant homes.
You take away my blessing
from their children forever.
[10] Get up, go away!
For this is not your resting place,
because it is defiled,
it is ruined, beyond all remedy.
[11] If a liar and deceiver comes and says,
'I will prophesy for you plenty of wine and beer,'
that would be just the prophet for this people!

Deliverance Promised

[12] "I will surely gather all of you, Jacob;
I will surely bring together the remnant of Israel.
I will bring them together like sheep in a pen,
like a flock in its pasture;
the place will throng with people.
[13] The One who breaks open the way will go up before them;
they will break through the gate and go out.
Their King will pass through before them,
the LORD at their head."

Leaders and Prophets Rebuked

3 Then I said,

"Listen, you leaders of Jacob,
you rulers of Israel.
Should you not embrace justice,
[2] you who hate good and love evil;
who tear the skin from my people
and the flesh from their bones;
[3] who eat my people's flesh,
strip off their skin
and break their bones in pieces;
who chop them up like meat for the pan,
like flesh for the pot?"

[4] Then they will cry out to the LORD,
but he will not answer them.
At that time he will hide his face from them
because of the evil they have done.

[5] This is what the LORD says:

"As for the prophets
who lead my people astray,
they proclaim 'peace'
if they have something to eat,
but prepare to wage war against anyone
who refuses to feed them.
[6] Therefore night will come over you,
without visions,
and darkness, without divination.

[a] 7 Or *Is the Spirit of the LORD*

The sun will set for the prophets,
and the day will go dark for them.
7 The seers will be ashamed
and the diviners disgraced.
They will all cover their faces
because there is no answer
from God."
8 But as for me, I am filled with power,
with the Spirit of the LORD,
and with justice and might,
to declare to Jacob his transgression,
to Israel his sin.

9 Hear this, you leaders of Jacob,
you rulers of Israel,
who despise justice
and distort all that is right;
10 who build Zion with bloodshed,
and Jerusalem with wickedness.
11 Her leaders judge for a bribe,
her priests teach for a price,
and her prophets tell fortunes for
money.
Yet they look for the LORD's support
and say,
"Is not the LORD among us?
No disaster will come upon us."
12 Therefore because of you,
Zion will be plowed like a field,
Jerusalem will become a heap of rubble,
the temple hill a mound overgrown
with thickets.

The Mountain of the LORD

4 In the last days

the mountain of the LORD's temple will
be established
as the highest of the mountains;
it will be exalted above the hills,
and peoples will stream to it.

2 Many nations will come and say,

"Come, let us go up to the mountain of
the LORD,
to the temple of the God of Jacob.
He will teach us his ways,
so that we may walk in his paths."
The law will go out from Zion,
the word of the LORD from Jerusalem.
3 He will judge between many peoples
and will settle disputes for strong
nations far and wide.
They will beat their swords into
plowshares
and their spears into pruning hooks.
Nation will not take up sword against
nation,
nor will they train for war anymore.
4 Everyone will sit under their own vine
and under their own fig tree,
and no one will make them afraid,
for the LORD Almighty has spoken.
5 All the nations may walk
in the name of their gods,
but we will walk in the name of the LORD
our God for ever and ever.

The LORD's Plan

6 "In that day," declares the LORD,

"I will gather the lame;
I will assemble the exiles
and those I have brought to grief.
7 I will make the lame my remnant,
those driven away a strong nation.
The LORD will rule over them in Mount
Zion
from that day and forever.
8 As for you, watchtower of the flock,
stronghold[a] of Daughter Zion,
the former dominion will be restored to
you;
kingship will come to Daughter
Jerusalem."

9 Why do you now cry aloud—
have you no king[b]?
Has your ruler[c] perished,
that pain seizes you like that of a
woman in labor?
10 Writhe in agony, Daughter Zion,
like a woman in labor,
for now you must leave the city
to camp in the open field.
You will go to Babylon;
there you will be rescued.
There the LORD will redeem you
out of the hand of your enemies.

11 But now many nations
are gathered against you.
They say, "Let her be defiled,
let our eyes gloat over Zion!"
12 But they do not know
the thoughts of the LORD;
they do not understand his plan,

[a] 8 Or *hill* [b] 9 Or *King* [c] 9 Or *Ruler*

that he has gathered them like sheaves
to the threshing floor.
13 "Rise and thresh, Daughter Zion,
for I will give you horns of iron;
I will give you hooves of bronze,
and you will break to pieces many
nations."
You will devote their ill-gotten gains to
the LORD,
their wealth to the Lord of all the earth.

A Promised Ruler From Bethlehem

5[a] Marshal your troops now, city of
troops,
for a siege is laid against us.
They will strike Israel's ruler
on the cheek with a rod.

2 "But you, Bethlehem Ephrathah,
though you are small among the clans[b]
of Judah,
out of you will come for me
one who will be ruler over Israel,
whose origins are from of old,
from ancient times."

3 Therefore Israel will be abandoned
until the time when she who is in labor
bears a son,
and the rest of his brothers return
to join the Israelites.

4 He will stand and shepherd his flock
in the strength of the LORD,
in the majesty of the name of the LORD
his God.
And they will live securely, for then his
greatness
will reach to the ends of the earth.

5 And he will be our peace
when the Assyrians invade our land
and march through our fortresses.
We will raise against them seven
shepherds,
even eight commanders,
6 who will rule[c] the land of Assyria with
the sword,
the land of Nimrod with drawn
sword.[d]
He will deliver us from the Assyrians
when they invade our land
and march across our borders.

7 The remnant of Jacob will be
in the midst of many peoples
like dew from the LORD,
like showers on the grass,
which do not wait for anyone
or depend on man.
8 The remnant of Jacob will be among
the nations,
in the midst of many peoples,
like a lion among the beasts of the forest,
like a young lion among flocks of
sheep,
which mauls and mangles as it goes,
and no one can rescue.
9 Your hand will be lifted up in triumph
over your enemies,
and all your foes will be destroyed.

10 "In that day," declares the LORD,

"I will destroy your horses from
among you
and demolish your chariots.
11 I will destroy the cities of your land
and tear down all your strongholds.
12 I will destroy your witchcraft
and you will no longer cast spells.
13 I will destroy your idols
and your sacred stones from
among you;
you will no longer bow down
to the work of your hands.
14 I will uproot from among you your
Asherah poles[e]
when I demolish your cities.
15 I will take vengeance in anger and wrath
on the nations that have not
obeyed me."

The LORD's Case Against Israel

6 Listen to what the LORD says:

"Stand up, plead my case before the
mountains;
let the hills hear what you have to say.

2 "Hear, you mountains, the LORD's
accusation;
listen, you everlasting foundations of
the earth.
For the LORD has a case against his
people;
he is lodging a charge against Israel.

[a] In Hebrew texts 5:1 is numbered 4:14, and 5:2-15 is numbered 5:1-14. [b] 2 Or *rulers* [c] 6 Or *crush* [d] 6 Or *Nimrod in its gates* [e] 14 That is, wooden symbols of the goddess Asherah

[3] "My people, what have I done to you?
How have I burdened you? Answer me.
[4] I brought you up out of Egypt
and redeemed you from the land of slavery.
I sent Moses to lead you,
also Aaron and Miriam.
[5] My people, remember
what Balak king of Moab plotted
and what Balaam son of Beor answered.
Remember your journey from Shittim to Gilgal,
that you may know the righteous acts of the LORD."

[6] With what shall I come before the LORD
and bow down before the exalted God?
Shall I come before him with burnt offerings,
with calves a year old?
[7] Will the LORD be pleased with thousands of rams,
with ten thousand rivers of olive oil?
Shall I offer my firstborn for my transgression,
the fruit of my body for the sin of my soul?
[8] He has shown you, O mortal, what is good.
And what does the LORD require of you?
To act justly and to love mercy
and to walk humbly[a] with your God.

Israel's Guilt and Punishment

[9] Listen! The LORD is calling to the city —
and to fear your name is wisdom —
"Heed the rod and the One who appointed it.[b]
[10] Am I still to forget your ill-gotten treasures, you wicked house,
and the short ephah,[c] which is accursed?
[11] Shall I acquit someone with dishonest scales,
with a bag of false weights?
[12] Your rich people are violent;
your inhabitants are liars
and their tongues speak deceitfully.
[13] Therefore, I have begun to destroy you,
to ruin[d] you because of your sins.
[14] You will eat but not be satisfied;
your stomach will still be empty.[e]
You will store up but save nothing,
because what you save[f] I will give to the sword.
[15] You will plant but not harvest;
you will press olives but not use the oil,
you will crush grapes but not drink the wine.
[16] You have observed the statutes of Omri
and all the practices of Ahab's house;
you have followed their traditions.
Therefore I will give you over to ruin
and your people to derision;
you will bear the scorn of the nations.[g]"

Israel's Misery

7 What misery is mine!
I am like one who gathers summer fruit
at the gleaning of the vineyard;
there is no cluster of grapes to eat,
none of the early figs that I crave.
[2] The faithful have been swept from the land;
not one upright person remains.
Everyone lies in wait to shed blood;
they hunt each other with nets.
[3] Both hands are skilled in doing evil;
the ruler demands gifts,
the judge accepts bribes,
the powerful dictate what they desire —
they all conspire together.
[4] The best of them is like a brier,
the most upright worse than a thorn hedge.
The day God visits you has come,
the day your watchmen sound the alarm.
Now is the time of your confusion.
[5] Do not trust a neighbor;
put no confidence in a friend.
Even with the woman who lies in your embrace
guard the words of your lips.
[6] For a son dishonors his father,
a daughter rises up against her mother,

[a] *8* Or *prudently* [b] *9* The meaning of the Hebrew for this line is uncertain. [c] *10* An ephah was a dry measure. [d] *13* Or *Therefore, I will make you ill and destroy you; / I will ruin* [e] *14* The meaning of the Hebrew for this word is uncertain. [f] *14* Or *You will press toward birth but not give birth, / and what you bring to birth* [g] *16* Septuagint; Hebrew *scorn due my people*

GIVE THANKS

Henry Smith

Give thanks with a grateful heart
Give thanks to the Holy One
Give thanks because he's given Jesus Christ, his Son
Give thanks with a grateful heart
Give thanks to the Holy One
Give thanks because he's given Jesus Christ, his Son

And now, let the weak say, "I am strong"
Let the poor say, "I am rich"
Because of what the Lord has done for us
Give thanks

THE INSPIRATION

Be filled with the Spirit, speaking to one another with psalms, hymns, and songs from the Spirit. Sing and make music from your heart to the Lord, always giving thanks to God the Father for everything, in the name of our Lord Jesus Christ. — Ephesians 5:18 – 20

Read also: Joel 3:10; 2 Corinthians 9:15; 1 Thessalonians 5:18

BEHIND THE SONG

Henry Smith has written over 300 songs during his lifetime, but only one of them has ever been published. But that song, "Give Thanks," has been one of the most popular and beloved worship songs of the last 30 years!

Smith had been writing hymns and spiritual songs for many years when he penned "Give Thanks" in 1978. His pastor in Williamsburg, Virginia, taught a sermon one Sunday that highlighted how Jesus made himself poor so that we could gain untold riches in him. Smith thought that sounded like a good idea for a song and proceeded to craft this powerful but simple chorus. He and his soon-to-be wife Cindy sang the song a number of times over the coming weeks. A young military couple heard it, learned it and took it with them when they returned to Germany. "As far as I know that is how my song got to Europe," Smith explains. "It did a lot of traveling before Integrity Music published it."

Eight years later, "Give Thanks" was recorded by Integrity's Hosanna! Music. The song was listed as "author unknown," but a friend of Smith's recognized it and brought the error to his attention. Integrity gratefully signed a publishing agreement with Smith, and the song quickly became known around the world. At one point, it was one of the three most frequently sung songs in American churches!

Selah

Gratitude is a critical aspect of the spiritual life of any growing believer. Giving thanks causes us to constantly be aware of all that God blesses us with: Good health, friends, children, a home and even just a simple meal can illicit sincere thanksgiving. But time spent contemplating the ultimate goodness of God—his forgiveness, grace and mercy—takes us beyond thanksgiving to worship and adoration.

Keep a running list of blessings for which you can give thanks. Consider how writing down your blessings helps you express gratitude to God and leads you into worship.

a daughter-in-law against her mother-in-law—
a man's enemies are the members of his own household.

[7] But as for me, I watch in hope for the LORD,
I wait for God my Savior;
my God will hear me.

Israel Will Rise

[8] Do not gloat over me, my enemy!
Though I have fallen, I will rise.
Though I sit in darkness,
the LORD will be my light.
[9] Because I have sinned against him,
I will bear the LORD's wrath,
until he pleads my case
and upholds my cause.
He will bring me out into the light;
I will see his righteousness.
[10] Then my enemy will see it
and will be covered with shame,
she who said to me,
"Where is the LORD your God?"
My eyes will see her downfall;
even now she will be trampled underfoot
like mire in the streets.

[11] The day for building your walls will come,
the day for extending your boundaries.
[12] In that day people will come to you
from Assyria and the cities of Egypt,
even from Egypt to the Euphrates
and from sea to sea
and from mountain to mountain.
[13] The earth will become desolate because of its inhabitants,
as the result of their deeds.

Prayer and Praise

[14] Shepherd your people with your staff,
the flock of your inheritance,
which lives by itself in a forest,
in fertile pasturelands.[a]
Let them feed in Bashan and Gilead
as in days long ago.

[15] "As in the days when you came out of Egypt,
I will show them my wonders."
[16] Nations will see and be ashamed,
deprived of all their power.
They will put their hands over their mouths
and their ears will become deaf.
[17] They will lick dust like a snake,
like creatures that crawl on the ground.
They will come trembling out of their dens;
they will turn in fear to the LORD our God
and will be afraid of you.
[18] Who is a God like you,
who pardons sin and forgives the transgression
of the remnant of his inheritance?
You do not stay angry forever
but delight to show mercy.
[19] You will again have compassion on us;
you will tread our sins underfoot
and hurl all our iniquities into the depths of the sea.
[20] You will be faithful to Jacob,
and show love to Abraham,
as you pledged on oath to our ancestors
in days long ago.

[a] 14 Or *in the middle of Carmel*

NAHUM

1 A prophecy concerning Nineveh. The book of the vision of Nahum the Elkoshite.

The LORD's Anger Against Nineveh

[2]The LORD is a jealous and avenging God;
the LORD takes vengeance and is filled with wrath.
The LORD takes vengeance on his foes
and vents his wrath against his enemies.
[3]The LORD is slow to anger but great in power;
the LORD will not leave the guilty unpunished.
His way is in the whirlwind and the storm,
and clouds are the dust of his feet.
[4]He rebukes the sea and dries it up;
he makes all the rivers run dry.
Bashan and Carmel wither
and the blossoms of Lebanon fade.
[5]The mountains quake before him
and the hills melt away.
The earth trembles at his presence,
the world and all who live in it.
[6]Who can withstand his indignation?
Who can endure his fierce anger?
His wrath is poured out like fire;
the rocks are shattered before him.

[7]The LORD is good,
a refuge in times of trouble.
He cares for those who trust in him,
[8] but with an overwhelming flood
he will make an end of Nineveh;
he will pursue his foes into the realm of darkness.

[9]Whatever they plot against the LORD
he will bring[a] to an end;
trouble will not come a second time.
[10]They will be entangled among thorns
and drunk from their wine;
they will be consumed like dry stubble.[b]
[11]From you, Nineveh, has one come forth
who plots evil against the LORD
and devises wicked plans.

[12]This is what the LORD says:

"Although they have allies and are numerous,
they will be destroyed and pass away.
Although I have afflicted you, Judah,
I will afflict you no more.
[13]Now I will break their yoke from your neck
and tear your shackles away."

[14]The LORD has given a command concerning you, Nineveh:
"You will have no descendants to bear your name.
I will destroy the images and idols
that are in the temple of your gods.
I will prepare your grave,
for you are vile."

[15]Look, there on the mountains,
the feet of one who brings good news,
who proclaims peace!
Celebrate your festivals, Judah,
and fulfill your vows.
No more will the wicked invade you;
they will be completely destroyed.[c]

Nineveh to Fall

2 [d]An attacker advances against you, Nineveh.
Guard the fortress,
watch the road,
brace yourselves,
marshal all your strength!

[2]The LORD will restore the splendor of Jacob
like the splendor of Israel,

[a] 9 Or *What do you foes plot against the LORD? / He will bring it* [b] 10 The meaning of the Hebrew for this verse is uncertain. [c] *15* In Hebrew texts this verse (1:15) is numbered 2:1. [d] In Hebrew texts 2:1-13 is numbered 2:2-14.

though destroyers have laid them waste
and have ruined their vines.

3 The shields of the soldiers are red;
the warriors are clad in scarlet.
The metal on the chariots flashes
on the day they are made ready;
the spears of juniper are brandished.[a]
4 The chariots storm through the streets,
rushing back and forth through the squares.
They look like flaming torches;
they dart about like lightning.

5 Nineveh summons her picked troops,
yet they stumble on their way.
They dash to the city wall;
the protective shield is put in place.
6 The river gates are thrown open
and the palace collapses.
7 It is decreed[b] that Nineveh
be exiled and carried away.
Her female slaves moan like doves
and beat on their breasts.
8 Nineveh is like a pool
whose water is draining away.
"Stop! Stop!" they cry,
but no one turns back.
9 Plunder the silver!
Plunder the gold!
The supply is endless,
the wealth from all its treasures!
10 She is pillaged, plundered, stripped!
Hearts melt, knees give way,
bodies tremble, every face grows pale.

11 Where now is the lions' den,
the place where they fed their young,
where the lion and lioness went,
and the cubs, with nothing to fear?
12 The lion killed enough for his cubs
and strangled the prey for his mate,
filling his lairs with the kill
and his dens with the prey.

13 "I am against you,"
declares the LORD Almighty.
"I will burn up your chariots in smoke,
and the sword will devour your young lions.
I will leave you no prey on the earth.
The voices of your messengers
will no longer be heard."

Woe to Nineveh

3 Woe to the city of blood,
full of lies,
full of plunder,
never without victims!
2 The crack of whips,
the clatter of wheels,
galloping horses
and jolting chariots!
3 Charging cavalry,
flashing swords
and glittering spears!
Many casualties,
piles of dead,
bodies without number,
people stumbling over the corpses—
4 all because of the wanton lust of a prostitute,
alluring, the mistress of sorceries,
who enslaved nations by her prostitution
and peoples by her witchcraft.

5 "I am against you," declares the LORD Almighty.
"I will lift your skirts over your face.
I will show the nations your nakedness
and the kingdoms your shame.
6 I will pelt you with filth,
I will treat you with contempt
and make you a spectacle.
7 All who see you will flee from you and say,
'Nineveh is in ruins—who will mourn for her?'
Where can I find anyone to comfort you?"

8 Are you better than Thebes,
situated on the Nile,
with water around her?
The river was her defense,
the waters her wall.
9 Cush[c] and Egypt were her boundless strength;
Put and Libya were among her allies.
10 Yet she was taken captive
and went into exile.
Her infants were dashed to pieces
at every street corner.
Lots were cast for her nobles,
and all her great men were put in chains.

[a] 3 Hebrew; Septuagint and Syriac *ready; / the horsemen rush to and fro.* [b] 7 The meaning of the Hebrew for this word is uncertain. [c] 9 That is, the upper Nile region

[11] You too will become drunk;
you will go into hiding
and seek refuge from the enemy.

[12] All your fortresses are like fig trees
with their first ripe fruit;
when they are shaken,
the figs fall into the mouth of the
eater.

[13] Look at your troops—
they are all weaklings.
The gates of your land
are wide open to your enemies;
fire has consumed the bars of
your gates.

[14] Draw water for the siege,
strengthen your defenses!
Work the clay,
tread the mortar,
repair the brickwork!

[15] There the fire will consume you;
the sword will cut you down—
they will devour you like a swarm
of locusts.
Multiply like grasshoppers,
multiply like locusts!

[16] You have increased the number of your
merchants
till they are more numerous than the
stars in the sky,
but like locusts they strip the land
and then fly away.

[17] Your guards are like locusts,
your officials like swarms of locusts
that settle in the walls on a cold day—
but when the sun appears they fly away,
and no one knows where.

[18] King of Assyria, your shepherds[a] slumber;
your nobles lie down to rest.
Your people are scattered on the
mountains
with no one to gather them.

[19] Nothing can heal you;
your wound is fatal.
All who hear the news about you
clap their hands at your fall,
for who has not felt
your endless cruelty?

[a] *18* That is, rulers

HABAKKUK

1 The prophecy that Habakkuk the prophet received.

Habakkuk's Complaint

[2] How long, LORD, must I call for help,
but you do not listen?
Or cry out to you, "Violence!"
but you do not save?
[3] Why do you make me look at injustice?
Why do you tolerate wrongdoing?
Destruction and violence are before me;
there is strife, and conflict abounds.
[4] Therefore the law is paralyzed,
and justice never prevails.
The wicked hem in the righteous,
so that justice is perverted.

The LORD's Answer

[5] "Look at the nations and watch —
and be utterly amazed.
For I am going to do something in
your days
that you would not believe,
even if you were told.
[6] I am raising up the Babylonians,[a]
that ruthless and impetuous people,
who sweep across the whole earth
to seize dwellings not their own.
[7] They are a feared and dreaded people;
they are a law to themselves
and promote their own honor.
[8] Their horses are swifter than leopards,
fiercer than wolves at dusk.
Their cavalry gallops headlong;
their horsemen come from afar.
They fly like an eagle swooping to
devour;
[9] they all come intent on violence.
Their hordes[b] advance like a desert
wind
and gather prisoners like sand.
[10] They mock kings
and scoff at rulers.
They laugh at all fortified cities;
by building earthen ramps they
capture them.
[11] Then they sweep past like the wind and
go on —
guilty people, whose own strength is
their god."

Habakkuk's Second Complaint

[12] LORD, are you not from everlasting?
My God, my Holy One, you[c] will
never die.
You, LORD, have appointed them to
execute judgment;
you, my Rock, have ordained them to
punish.
[13] Your eyes are too pure to look on evil;
you cannot tolerate wrongdoing.
Why then do you tolerate the
treacherous?
Why are you silent while the wicked
swallow up those more righteous than
themselves?
[14] You have made people like the fish in
the sea,
like the sea creatures that have no
ruler.
[15] The wicked foe pulls all of them up
with hooks,
he catches them in his net,
he gathers them up in his dragnet;
and so he rejoices and is glad.
[16] Therefore he sacrifices to his net
and burns incense to his dragnet,
for by his net he lives in luxury
and enjoys the choicest food.
[17] Is he to keep on emptying his net,
destroying nations without
mercy?

2 I will stand at my watch
and station myself on the ramparts;
I will look to see what he will say to me,
and what answer I am to give to this
complaint.[d]

[a] 6 Or *Chaldeans* [b] 9 The meaning of the Hebrew for this word is uncertain. [c] 12 An ancient Hebrew scribal tradition; Masoretic Text *we* [d] 1 Or *and what to answer when I am rebuked*

The LORD's Answer

[2]Then the LORD replied:

"Write down the revelation
and make it plain on tablets
so that a herald[a] may run with it.
[3]For the revelation awaits an appointed time;
it speaks of the end
and will not prove false.
Though it linger, wait for it;
it[b] will certainly come
and will not delay.

[4]"See, the enemy is puffed up;
his desires are not upright —
but the righteous person will live by his faithfulness[c] —
[5]indeed, wine betrays him;
he is arrogant and never at rest.
Because he is as greedy as the grave
and like death is never satisfied,
he gathers to himself all the nations
and takes captive all the peoples.

[6]"Will not all of them taunt him with ridicule and scorn, saying,

"'Woe to him who piles up stolen goods
and makes himself wealthy by extortion!
How long must this go on?'
[7]Will not your creditors suddenly arise?
Will they not wake up and make you tremble?
Then you will become their prey.
[8]Because you have plundered many nations,
the peoples who are left will plunder you.
For you have shed human blood;
you have destroyed lands and cities
and everyone in them.

[9]"Woe to him who builds his house by unjust gain,
setting his nest on high
to escape the clutches of ruin!
[10]You have plotted the ruin of many peoples,
shaming your own house and forfeiting your life.
[11]The stones of the wall will cry out,
and the beams of the woodwork will echo it.

[12]"Woe to him who builds a city with bloodshed
and establishes a town by injustice!
[13]Has not the LORD Almighty determined
that the people's labor is only fuel for the fire,
that the nations exhaust themselves for nothing?
[14]For the earth will be filled with the knowledge of the glory of the LORD
as the waters cover the sea.

[15]"Woe to him who gives drink to his neighbors,
pouring it from the wineskin till they are drunk,
so that he can gaze on their naked bodies!
[16]You will be filled with shame instead of glory.
Now it is your turn! Drink and let your nakedness be exposed[d]!
The cup from the LORD's right hand is coming around to you,
and disgrace will cover your glory.
[17]The violence you have done to Lebanon will overwhelm you,
and your destruction of animals will terrify you.
For you have shed human blood;
you have destroyed lands and cities
and everyone in them.

[18]"Of what value is an idol carved by a craftsman?
Or an image that teaches lies?
For the one who makes it trusts in his own creation;
he makes idols that cannot speak.
[19]Woe to him who says to wood, 'Come to life!'
Or to lifeless stone, 'Wake up!'
Can it give guidance?
It is covered with gold and silver;
there is no breath in it."

[20]The LORD is in his holy temple;
let all the earth be silent before him.

[a] 2 Or *so that whoever reads it* [b] 3 Or *Though he linger, wait for him; / he* [c] 4 Or *faith*
[d] 16 Masoretic Text; Dead Sea Scrolls, Aquila, Vulgate and Syriac (see also Septuagint) *and stagger*

Habakkuk's Prayer

3 A prayer of Habakkuk the prophet. On *shigionoth.*[a]

[2] LORD, I have heard of your fame;
I stand in awe of your deeds, LORD.
Repeat them in our day,
in our time make them known;
in wrath remember mercy.

[3] God came from Teman,
the Holy One from Mount Paran.[b]
His glory covered the heavens
and his praise filled the earth.
[4] His splendor was like the sunrise;
rays flashed from his hand,
where his power was hidden.
[5] Plague went before him;
pestilence followed his steps.
[6] He stood, and shook the earth;
he looked, and made the nations
tremble.
The ancient mountains crumbled
and the age-old hills collapsed —
but he marches on forever.
[7] I saw the tents of Cushan in distress,
the dwellings of Midian in anguish.

[8] Were you angry with the rivers, LORD?
Was your wrath against the streams?
Did you rage against the sea
when you rode your horses
and your chariots to victory?
[9] You uncovered your bow,
you called for many arrows.
You split the earth with rivers;
[10] the mountains saw you and writhed.
Torrents of water swept by;
the deep roared
and lifted its waves on high.
[11] Sun and moon stood still in the heavens
at the glint of your flying arrows,
at the lightning of your flashing spear.
[12] In wrath you strode through the earth
and in anger you threshed the nations.
[13] You came out to deliver your people,
to save your anointed one.
You crushed the leader of the land of
wickedness,
you stripped him from head to foot.
[14] With his own spear you pierced his head
when his warriors stormed out to
scatter us,
gloating as though about to devour
the wretched who were in hiding.
[15] You trampled the sea with your horses,
churning the great waters.

[16] I heard and my heart pounded,
my lips quivered at the sound;
decay crept into my bones,
and my legs trembled.
Yet I will wait patiently for the day of
calamity
to come on the nation invading us.
[17] Though the fig tree does not bud
and there are no grapes on the vines,
though the olive crop fails
and the fields produce no food,
though there are no sheep in the pen
and no cattle in the stalls,
[18] yet I will rejoice in the LORD,
I will be joyful in God my Savior.

[19] The Sovereign LORD is my strength;
he makes my feet like the feet of a deer,
he enables me to tread on the heights.

For the director of music. On my stringed
instruments.

[a] *1* Probably a literary or musical term [b] *3* The Hebrew has *Selah* (a word of uncertain meaning) here and at the middle of verse 9 and at the end of verse 13.

ZEPHANIAH

1 The word of the LORD that came to
Zephaniah son of Cushi, the son of Gedaliah, the son of Amariah, the son of Hezekiah, during the reign of Josiah son of Amon king of Judah:

Judgment on the Whole Earth in the Day of the LORD

2 "I will sweep away everything
from the face of the earth,"
declares the LORD.
3 "I will sweep away both man and beast;
I will sweep away the birds in the sky
and the fish in the sea —
and the idols that cause the wicked to stumble."[a]

"When I destroy all mankind
on the face of the earth,"
declares the LORD,
4 "I will stretch out my hand against Judah
and against all who live in Jerusalem.
I will destroy every remnant of Baal worship in this place,
the very names of the idolatrous priests —
5 those who bow down on the roofs
to worship the starry host,
those who bow down and swear by the LORD
and who also swear by Molek,[b]
6 those who turn back from following the LORD
and neither seek the LORD nor inquire of him."

7 Be silent before the Sovereign LORD,
for the day of the LORD is near.
The LORD has prepared a sacrifice;
he has consecrated those he has invited.
8 "On the day of the LORD's sacrifice
I will punish the officials
and the king's sons
and all those clad
in foreign clothes.
9 On that day I will punish
all who avoid stepping on the threshold,[c]
who fill the temple of their gods
with violence and deceit.

10 "On that day,"
declares the LORD,
"a cry will go up from the Fish Gate,
wailing from the New Quarter,
and a loud crash from the hills.
11 Wail, you who live in the market district[d];
all your merchants will be wiped out,
all who trade with[e] silver will be destroyed.
12 At that time I will search Jerusalem with lamps
and punish those who are complacent,
who are like wine left on its dregs,
who think, 'The LORD will do nothing,
either good or bad.'
13 Their wealth will be plundered,
their houses demolished.
Though they build houses,
they will not live in them;
though they plant vineyards,
they will not drink the wine."

14 The great day of the LORD is near —
near and coming quickly.
The cry on the day of the LORD is bitter;
the Mighty Warrior shouts his battle cry.
15 That day will be a day of wrath —
a day of distress and anguish,
a day of trouble and ruin,
a day of darkness and gloom,
a day of clouds and blackness —
16 a day of trumpet and battle cry
against the fortified cities
and against the corner towers.

[a] 3 The meaning of the Hebrew for this line is uncertain. [b] 5 Hebrew *Malkam* [c] 9 See 1 Samuel 5:5.
[d] 11 Or *the Mortar* [e] 11 Or *in*

17 "I will bring such distress on all people
that they will grope about like those
who are blind,
because they have sinned against
the LORD.
Their blood will be poured out like dust
and their entrails like dung.
18 Neither their silver nor their gold
will be able to save them
on the day of the LORD's wrath."

In the fire of his jealousy
the whole earth will be consumed,
for he will make a sudden end
of all who live on the earth.

Judah and Jerusalem Judged Along With the Nations

Judah Summoned to Repent

2 Gather together, gather yourselves
together,
you shameful nation,
2 before the decree takes effect
and that day passes like windblown
chaff,
before the LORD's fierce anger
comes upon you,
before the day of the LORD's wrath
comes upon you.
3 Seek the LORD, all you humble of
the land,
you who do what he commands.
Seek righteousness, seek humility;
perhaps you will be sheltered
on the day of the LORD's anger.

Philistia

4 Gaza will be abandoned
and Ashkelon left in ruins.
At midday Ashdod will be emptied
and Ekron uprooted.
5 Woe to you who live by the sea,
you Kerethite people;
the word of the LORD is against you,
Canaan, land of the Philistines.
He says, "I will destroy you,
and none will be left."
6 The land by the sea will become pastures
having wells for shepherds
and pens for flocks.
7 That land will belong
to the remnant of the people of Judah;
there they will find pasture.
In the evening they will lie down
in the houses of Ashkelon.
The LORD their God will care for them;
he will restore their fortunes.[a]

Moab and Ammon

8 "I have heard the insults of Moab
and the taunts of the Ammonites,
who insulted my people
and made threats against their land.
9 Therefore, as surely as I live,"
declares the LORD Almighty,
the God of Israel,
"surely Moab will become like Sodom,
the Ammonites like Gomorrah—
a place of weeds and salt pits,
a wasteland forever.
The remnant of my people will plunder
them;
the survivors of my nation will inherit
their land."

10 This is what they will get in return for
their pride,
for insulting and mocking
the people of the LORD Almighty.
11 The LORD will be awesome to them
when he destroys all the gods of the
earth.
Distant nations will bow down to him,
all of them in their own lands.

Cush

12 "You Cushites,[b] too,
will be slain by my sword."

Assyria

13 He will stretch out his hand against
the north
and destroy Assyria,
leaving Nineveh utterly desolate
and dry as the desert.
14 Flocks and herds will lie down there,
creatures of every kind.
The desert owl and the screech owl
will roost on her columns.
Their hooting will echo through the
windows,
rubble will fill the doorways,
the beams of cedar will be
exposed.
15 This is the city of revelry
that lived in safety.

[a] 7 Or *will bring back their captives* [b] 12 That is, people from the upper Nile region

She said to herself,
"I am the one! And there is none besides me."
What a ruin she has become,
a lair for wild beasts!
All who pass by her scoff
and shake their fists.

Jerusalem

3 Woe to the city of oppressors,
rebellious and defiled!
2 She obeys no one,
she accepts no correction.
She does not trust in the LORD,
she does not draw near to her God.
3 Her officials within her
are roaring lions;
her rulers are evening wolves,
who leave nothing for the morning.
4 Her prophets are unprincipled;
they are treacherous people.
Her priests profane the sanctuary
and do violence to the law.
5 The LORD within her is righteous;
he does no wrong.
Morning by morning he dispenses his justice,
and every new day he does not fail,
yet the unrighteous know no shame.

Jerusalem Remains Unrepentant

6 "I have destroyed nations;
their strongholds are demolished.
I have left their streets deserted,
with no one passing through.
Their cities are laid waste;
they are deserted and empty.
7 Of Jerusalem I thought,
'Surely you will fear me
and accept correction!'
Then her place of refuge[a] would not be destroyed,
nor all my punishments come upon[b] her.
But they were still eager
to act corruptly in all they did.
8 Therefore wait for me,"
declares the LORD,
"for the day I will stand up to testify.[c]
I have decided to assemble the nations,
to gather the kingdoms
and to pour out my wrath on them—
all my fierce anger.
The whole world will be consumed
by the fire of my jealous anger.

Restoration of Israel's Remnant

9 "Then I will purify the lips of the peoples,
that all of them may call on the name of the LORD
and serve him shoulder to shoulder.
10 From beyond the rivers of Cush[d]
my worshipers, my scattered people,
will bring me offerings.
11 On that day you, Jerusalem, will not be put to shame
for all the wrongs you have done to me,
because I will remove from you
your arrogant boasters.
Never again will you be haughty
on my holy hill.
12 But I will leave within you
the meek and humble.
The remnant of Israel
will trust in the name of the LORD.
13 They will do no wrong;
they will tell no lies.
A deceitful tongue
will not be found in their mouths.
They will eat and lie down
and no one will make them afraid."

14 Sing, Daughter Zion;
shout aloud, Israel!
Be glad and rejoice with all your heart,
Daughter Jerusalem!
15 The LORD has taken away your punishment,
he has turned back your enemy.
The LORD, the King of Israel, is with you;
never again will you fear any harm.
16 On that day
they will say to Jerusalem,
"Do not fear, Zion;
do not let your hands hang limp.
17 The LORD your God is with you,
the Mighty Warrior who saves.
He will take great delight in you;
in his love he will no longer rebuke you,
but will rejoice over you with singing."

18 "I will remove from you

[a] 7 Or *her sanctuary* [b] 7 Or *all those I appointed over to plunder* [c] 8 Septuagint and Syriac; Hebrew *will rise up* [d] 10 That is, the upper Nile region

all who mourn over the loss of your
appointed festivals,
which is a burden and reproach
for you.
19 At that time I will deal
with all who oppressed you.
I will rescue the lame;
I will gather the exiles.
I will give them praise and honor
in every land where they have suffered
shame.
20 At that time I will gather you;
at that time I will bring you home.
I will give you honor and praise
among all the peoples of the earth
when I restore your fortunes[a]
before your very eyes,"
says the LORD.

[a] 20 Or *I bring back your captives*

HAGGAI

A Call to Build the House of the LORD

1 In the second year of King Darius, on the
first day of the sixth month, the word of
the LORD came through the prophet Hag-
gai to Zerubbabel son of Shealtiel, governor
of Judah, and to Joshua son of Jozadak, the
high priest:
2 This is what the LORD Almighty says:
"These people say, 'The time has not yet
come to rebuild the LORD's house.' "
3 Then the word of the LORD came through
the prophet Haggai: 4 "Is it a time for you
yourselves to be living in your paneled hous-
es, while this house remains a ruin?"
5 Now this is what the LORD Almighty says:
"Give careful thought to your ways. 6 You
have planted much, but harvested little. You
eat, but never have enough. You drink, but
never have your fill. You put on clothes, but
are not warm. You earn wages, only to put
them in a purse with holes in it."
7 This is what the LORD Almighty says:
"Give careful thought to your ways. 8 Go up
into the mountains and bring down timber
and build my house, so that I may take plea-
sure in it and be honored," says the LORD.
9 "You expected much, but see, it turned out
to be little. What you brought home, I blew
away. Why?" declares the LORD Almighty.
"Because of my house, which remains a
ruin, while each of you is busy with your own
house. 10 Therefore, because of you the heav-
ens have withheld their dew and the earth
its crops. 11 I called for a drought on the fields
and the mountains, on the grain, the new
wine, the olive oil and everything else the
ground produces, on people and livestock,
and on all the labor of your hands."

12 Then Zerubbabel son of Shealtiel, Josh-
ua son of Jozadak, the high priest, and the
whole remnant of the people obeyed the
voice of the LORD their God and the message
of the prophet Haggai, because the LORD
their God had sent him. And the people
feared the LORD.
13 Then Haggai, the LORD's messenger,
gave this message of the LORD to the people:
"I am with you," declares the LORD. 14 So the
LORD stirred up the spirit of Zerubbabel son
of Shealtiel, governor of Judah, and the spirit
of Joshua son of Jozadak, the high priest, and
the spirit of the whole remnant of the people.
They came and began to work on the house
of the LORD Almighty, their God, 15 on the
twenty-fourth day of the sixth month.

The Promised Glory of the New House

2 In the second year of King Darius, 1 on
the twenty-first day of the seventh
month, the word of the LORD came through
the prophet Haggai: 2 "Speak to Zerubbabel
son of Shealtiel, governor of Judah, to Joshua
son of Jozadak,[a] the high priest, and to the
remnant of the people. Ask them, 3 'Who of
you is left who saw this house in its former
glory? How does it look to you now? Does
it not seem to you like nothing? 4 But now
be strong, Zerubbabel,' declares the LORD.
'Be strong, Joshua son of Jozadak, the high
priest. Be strong, all you people of the land,'
declares the LORD, 'and work. For I am with
you,' declares the LORD Almighty. 5 'This is
what I covenanted with you when you came
out of Egypt. And my Spirit remains among
you. Do not fear.'
6 "This is what the LORD Almighty says: 'In
a little while I will once more shake the heav-
ens and the earth, the sea and the dry land.
7 I will shake all nations, and what is desired
by all nations will come, and I will fill this
house with glory,' says the LORD Almighty.
8 'The silver is mine and the gold is mine,'
declares the LORD Almighty. 9 'The glory of
this present house will be greater than the
glory of the former house,' says the LORD Al-
mighty. 'And in this place I will grant peace,'
declares the LORD Almighty."

[a] 2 Hebrew *Jehozadak*, a variant of *Jozadak*; also in verse 4

Blessings for a Defiled People

10On the twenty-fourth day of the ninth
month, in the second year of Darius, the
word of the LORD came to the prophet Hag-
gai: 11"This is what the LORD Almighty says:
'Ask the priests what the law says: 12If some-
one carries consecrated meat in the fold of
their garment, and that fold touches some
bread or stew, some wine, olive oil or other
food, does it become consecrated?'"

The priests answered, "No."

13Then Haggai said, "If a person defiled
by contact with a dead body touches one of
these things, does it become defiled?"

"Yes," the priests replied, "it becomes de-
filed."

14Then Haggai said, "'So it is with this
people and this nation in my sight,' declares
the LORD. 'Whatever they do and whatever
they offer there is defiled.

15"'Now give careful thought to this from
this day on[a]—consider how things were
before one stone was laid on another in the
LORD's temple. 16When anyone came to a
heap of twenty measures, there were only
ten. When anyone went to a wine vat to draw
fifty measures, there were only twenty. 17I
struck all the work of your hands with blight,
mildew and hail, yet you did not return to
me,' declares the LORD. 18'From this day
on, from this twenty-fourth day of the ninth
month, give careful thought to the day when
the foundation of the LORD's temple was
laid. Give careful thought: 19Is there yet any
seed left in the barn? Until now, the vine and
the fig tree, the pomegranate and the olive
tree have not borne fruit.

"'From this day on I will bless you.'"

Zerubbabel the LORD's Signet Ring

20The word of the LORD came to Haggai a
second time on the twenty-fourth day of the
month: 21"Tell Zerubbabel governor of Ju-
dah that I am going to shake the heavens and
the earth. 22I will overturn royal thrones and
shatter the power of the foreign kingdoms. I
will overthrow chariots and their drivers;
horses and their riders will fall, each by the
sword of his brother.

23"'On that day,' declares the LORD Al-
mighty, 'I will take you, my servant Zerubba-
bel son of Shealtiel,' declares the LORD, 'and
I will make you like my signet ring, for I have
chosen you,' declares the LORD Almighty."

[a] 15 Or *to the days past*

ZECHARIAH

A Call to Return to the LORD

1 In the eighth month of the second year
of Darius, the word of the LORD came to
the prophet Zechariah son of Berekiah, the
son of Iddo:
2“The LORD was very angry with your
ancestors. 3Therefore tell the people: This
is what the LORD Almighty says: ‘Return to
me,’ declares the LORD Almighty, ‘and I will
return to you,’ says the LORD Almighty. 4Do
not be like your ancestors, to whom the ear-
lier prophets proclaimed: This is what the
LORD Almighty says: ‘Turn from your evil
ways and your evil practices.’ But they would
not listen or pay attention to me, declares the
LORD. 5Where are your ancestors now? And
the prophets, do they live forever? 6But did
not my words and my decrees, which I com-
manded my servants the prophets, overtake
your ancestors?
“Then they repented and said, ‘The LORD
Almighty has done to us what our ways and
practices deserve, just as he determined
to do.’ ”

The Man Among the Myrtle Trees

7On the twenty-fourth day of the eleventh
month, the month of Shebat, in the second
year of Darius, the word of the LORD came to
the prophet Zechariah son of Berekiah, the
son of Iddo.
8During the night I had a vision, and
there before me was a man mounted on a
red horse. He was standing among the myr-
tle trees in a ravine. Behind him were red,
brown and white horses.
9I asked, “What are these, my lord?”
The angel who was talking with me an-
swered, “I will show you what they are.”
10Then the man standing among the myr-
tle trees explained, “They are the ones the
LORD has sent to go throughout the earth.”
11And they reported to the angel of the
LORD who was standing among the myrtle
trees, “We have gone throughout the earth
and found the whole world at rest and in
peace.”
12Then the angel of the LORD said, “LORD
Almighty, how long will you withhold mer-
cy from Jerusalem and from the towns of
Judah, which you have been angry with
these seventy years?” 13So the LORD spoke
kind and comforting words to the angel who
talked with me.
14Then the angel who was speaking to me
said, “Proclaim this word: This is what the
LORD Almighty says: ‘I am very jealous for
Jerusalem and Zion, 15and I am very angry
with the nations that feel secure. I was only
a little angry, but they went too far with the
punishment.’
16“Therefore this is what the LORD says:
‘I will return to Jerusalem with mercy, and
there my house will be rebuilt. And the mea-
suring line will be stretched out over Jerusa-
lem,’ declares the LORD Almighty.
17“Proclaim further: This is what the
LORD Almighty says: ‘My towns will again
overflow with prosperity, and the LORD will
again comfort Zion and choose Jerusalem.’ ”

Four Horns and Four Craftsmen

18Then I looked up, and there before me
were four horns. 19I asked the angel who was
speaking to me, “What are these?”
He answered me, “These are the horns
that scattered Judah, Israel and Jerusalem.”
20Then the LORD showed me four crafts-
men. 21I asked, “What are these coming
to do?”
He answered, “These are the horns that
scattered Judah so that no one could raise
their head, but the craftsmen have come to
terrify them and throw down these horns of
the nations who lifted up their horns against
the land of Judah to scatter its people.”[a]

A Man With a Measuring Line

2 [b] Then I looked up, and there before me
was a man with a measuring line in his
hand. 2I asked, “Where are you going?”

[a] *21* In Hebrew texts 1:18-21 is numbered 2:1-4. [b] In Hebrew texts 2:1-13 is numbered 2:5-17.

He answered me, "To measure Jerusalem, to find out how wide and how long it is."

3 While the angel who was speaking to me was leaving, another angel came to meet him 4 and said to him: "Run, tell that young man, 'Jerusalem will be a city without walls because of the great number of people and animals in it. 5 And I myself will be a wall of fire around it,' declares the LORD, 'and I will be its glory within.'

6 "Come! Come! Flee from the land of the north," declares the LORD, "for I have scattered you to the four winds of heaven," declares the LORD.

7 "Come, Zion! Escape, you who live in Daughter Babylon!" 8 For this is what the LORD Almighty says: "After the Glorious One has sent me against the nations that have plundered you — for whoever touches you touches the apple of his eye — 9 I will surely raise my hand against them so that their slaves will plunder them.[a] Then you will know that the LORD Almighty has sent me.

10 "Shout and be glad, Daughter Zion. For I am coming, and I will live among you," declares the LORD. 11 "Many nations will be joined with the LORD in that day and will become my people. I will live among you and you will know that the LORD Almighty has sent me to you. 12 The LORD will inherit Judah as his portion in the holy land and will again choose Jerusalem. 13 Be still before the LORD, all mankind, because he has roused himself from his holy dwelling."

Clean Garments for the High Priest

3 Then he showed me Joshua the high priest standing before the angel of the LORD, and Satan[b] standing at his right side to accuse him. 2 The LORD said to Satan, "The LORD rebuke you, Satan! The LORD, who has chosen Jerusalem, rebuke you! Is not this man a burning stick snatched from the fire?"

3 Now Joshua was dressed in filthy clothes as he stood before the angel. 4 The angel said to those who were standing before him, "Take off his filthy clothes."

Then he said to Joshua, "See, I have taken away your sin, and I will put fine garments on you."

5 Then I said, "Put a clean turban on his head." So they put a clean turban on his head and clothed him, while the angel of the LORD stood by.

6 The angel of the LORD gave this charge to Joshua: 7 "This is what the LORD Almighty says: 'If you will walk in obedience to me and keep my requirements, then you will govern my house and have charge of my courts, and I will give you a place among these standing here.

8 "'Listen, High Priest Joshua, you and your associates seated before you, who are men symbolic of things to come: I am going to bring my servant, the Branch. 9 See, the stone I have set in front of Joshua! There are seven eyes[c] on that one stone, and I will engrave an inscription on it,' says the LORD Almighty, 'and I will remove the sin of this land in a single day.

10 "'In that day each of you will invite your neighbor to sit under your vine and fig tree,' declares the LORD Almighty."

The Gold Lampstand and the Two Olive Trees

4 Then the angel who talked with me returned and woke me up, like someone awakened from sleep. 2 He asked me, "What do you see?"

I answered, "I see a solid gold lampstand with a bowl at the top and seven lamps on it, with seven channels to the lamps. 3 Also there are two olive trees by it, one on the right of the bowl and the other on its left."

4 I asked the angel who talked with me, "What are these, my lord?"

5 He answered, "Do you not know what these are?"

"No, my lord," I replied.

6 So he said to me, "This is the word of the LORD to Zerubbabel: 'Not by might nor by power, but by my Spirit,' says the LORD Almighty.

7 "What are you, mighty mountain? Before Zerubbabel you will become level ground. Then he will bring out the capstone to shouts of 'God bless it! God bless it!'"

8 Then the word of the LORD came to me: 9 "The hands of Zerubbabel have laid the foundation of this temple; his hands will also complete it. Then you will know that the LORD Almighty has sent me to you.

[a] 8,9 Or *says after . . . eye:* 9"*I . . . plunder them."* [b] *1* Hebrew *satan* means *adversary.* [c] 9 Or *facets*

10 “Who dares despise the day of small things, since the seven eyes of the LORD that range throughout the earth will rejoice when they see the chosen capstone[a] in the hand of Zerubbabel?”

11 Then I asked the angel, “What are these two olive trees on the right and the left of the lampstand?”

12 Again I asked him, “What are these two olive branches beside the two gold pipes that pour out golden oil?”

13 He replied, “Do you not know what these are?”

“No, my lord,” I said.

14 So he said, “These are the two who are anointed to[b] serve the Lord of all the earth.”

The Flying Scroll

5 I looked again, and there before me was a flying scroll.

2 He asked me, “What do you see?”

I answered, “I see a flying scroll, twenty cubits long and ten cubits wide.[c]”

3 And he said to me, “This is the curse that is going out over the whole land; for according to what it says on one side, every thief will be banished, and according to what it says on the other, everyone who swears falsely will be banished. 4 The LORD Almighty declares, ‘I will send it out, and it will enter the house of the thief and the house of anyone who swears falsely by my name. It will remain in that house and destroy it completely, both its timbers and its stones.’ ”

The Woman in a Basket

5 Then the angel who was speaking to me came forward and said to me, “Look up and see what is appearing.”

6 I asked, “What is it?”

He replied, “It is a basket.” And he added, “This is the iniquity[d] of the people throughout the land.”

7 Then the cover of lead was raised, and there in the basket sat a woman! 8 He said, “This is wickedness,” and he pushed her back into the basket and pushed its lead cover down on it.

9 Then I looked up — and there before me were two women, with the wind in their wings! They had wings like those of a stork, and they lifted up the basket between heaven and earth.

10 “Where are they taking the basket?” I asked the angel who was speaking to me.

11 He replied, “To the country of Babylonia[e] to build a house for it. When the house is ready, the basket will be set there in its place.”

Four Chariots

6 I looked up again, and there before me were four chariots coming out from between two mountains — mountains of bronze. 2 The first chariot had red horses, the second black, 3 the third white, and the fourth dappled — all of them powerful. 4 I asked the angel who was speaking to me, “What are these, my lord?”

5 The angel answered me, “These are the four spirits[f] of heaven, going out from standing in the presence of the Lord of the whole world. 6 The one with the black horses is going toward the north country, the one with the white horses toward the west,[g] and the one with the dappled horses toward the south.”

7 When the powerful horses went out, they were straining to go throughout the earth. And he said, “Go throughout the earth!” So they went throughout the earth.

8 Then he called to me, “Look, those going toward the north country have given my Spirit[h] rest in the land of the north.”

A Crown for Joshua

9 The word of the LORD came to me: 10 “Take silver and gold from the exiles Heldai, Tobijah and Jedaiah, who have arrived from Babylon. Go the same day to the house of Josiah son of Zephaniah. 11 Take the silver and gold and make a crown, and set it on the head of the high priest, Joshua son of Jozadak.[i] 12 Tell him this is what the LORD Almighty says: ‘Here is the man whose name is the Branch, and he will branch out from his place and build the temple of the LORD. 13 It is he who will build the temple of the LORD, and he will be clothed with majesty and will sit and rule on his throne. And he[j] will be a priest on his throne. And there will be harmony between the two.’

[a] 10 Or *the plumb line* [b] 14 Or *two who bring oil and* [c] 2 That is, about 30 feet long and 15 feet wide or about 9 meters long and 4.5 meters wide [d] 6 Or *appearance* [e] 11 Hebrew *Shinar* [f] 5 Or *winds* [g] 6 Or *horses after them* [h] 8 Or *spirit* [i] 11 Hebrew *Jehozadak*, a variant of *Jozadak* [j] 13 Or *there*

14The crown will be given to Heldai,[a] Tobijah, Jedaiah and Hen[b] son of Zephaniah as a memorial in the temple of the LORD. 15Those who are far away will come and help to build the temple of the LORD, and you will know that the LORD Almighty has sent me to you. This will happen if you diligently obey the LORD your God."

Justice and Mercy, Not Fasting

7 In the fourth year of King Darius, the word of the LORD came to Zechariah on the fourth day of the ninth month, the month of Kislev. 2The people of Bethel had sent Sharezer and Regem-Melek, together with their men, to entreat the LORD 3by asking the priests of the house of the LORD Almighty and the prophets, "Should I mourn and fast in the fifth month, as I have done for so many years?"

4Then the word of the LORD Almighty came to me: 5"Ask all the people of the land and the priests, 'When you fasted and mourned in the fifth and seventh months for the past seventy years, was it really for me that you fasted? 6And when you were eating and drinking, were you not just feasting for yourselves? 7Are these not the words the LORD proclaimed through the earlier prophets when Jerusalem and its surrounding towns were at rest and prosperous, and the Negev and the western foothills were settled?' "

8And the word of the LORD came again to Zechariah: 9"This is what the LORD Almighty said: 'Administer true justice; show mercy and compassion to one another. 10Do not oppress the widow or the fatherless, the foreigner or the poor. Do not plot evil against each other.'

11"But they refused to pay attention; stubbornly they turned their backs and covered their ears. 12They made their hearts as hard as flint and would not listen to the law or to the words that the LORD Almighty had sent by his Spirit through the earlier prophets. So the LORD Almighty was very angry.

13" 'When I called, they did not listen; so when they called, I would not listen,' says the LORD Almighty. 14'I scattered them with a whirlwind among all the nations, where they were strangers. The land they left behind them was so desolate that no one traveled through it. This is how they made the pleasant land desolate.' "

The LORD Promises to Bless Jerusalem

8 The word of the LORD Almighty came to me.

2This is what the LORD Almighty says: "I am very jealous for Zion; I am burning with jealousy for her."

3This is what the LORD says: "I will return to Zion and dwell in Jerusalem. Then Jerusalem will be called the Faithful City, and the mountain of the LORD Almighty will be called the Holy Mountain."

4This is what the LORD Almighty says: "Once again men and women of ripe old age will sit in the streets of Jerusalem, each of them with cane in hand because of their age. 5The city streets will be filled with boys and girls playing there."

6This is what the LORD Almighty says: "It may seem marvelous to the remnant of this people at that time, but will it seem marvelous to me?" declares the LORD Almighty.

7This is what the LORD Almighty says: "I will save my people from the countries of the east and the west. 8I will bring them back to live in Jerusalem; they will be my people, and I will be faithful and righteous to them as their God."

9This is what the LORD Almighty says: "Now hear these words, 'Let your hands be strong so that the temple may be built.' This is also what the prophets said who were present when the foundation was laid for the house of the LORD Almighty. 10Before that time there were no wages for people or hire for animals. No one could go about their business safely because of their enemies, since I had turned everyone against their neighbor. 11But now I will not deal with the remnant of this people as I did in the past," declares the LORD Almighty.

12"The seed will grow well, the vine will yield its fruit, the ground will produce its crops, and the heavens will drop their dew. I will give all these things as an inheritance to the remnant of this people. 13Just as you, Judah and Israel, have been a curse[c] among

[a] *14* Syriac; Hebrew *Helem* [b] *14* Or *and the gracious one, the* [c] *13* That is, your name has been used in cursing (see Jer. 29:22); or, you have been regarded as under a curse.

the nations, so I will save you, and you will
be a blessing.[a] Do not be afraid, but let your
hands be strong."
14 This is what the LORD Almighty says:
"Just as I had determined to bring disas-
ter on you and showed no pity when your
ancestors angered me," says the LORD Al-
mighty, 15 "so now I have determined to do
good again to Jerusalem and Judah. Do not
be afraid. 16 These are the things you are to
do: Speak the truth to each other, and ren-
der true and sound judgment in your courts;
17 do not plot evil against each other, and do
not love to swear falsely. I hate all this," de-
clares the LORD.
18 The word of the LORD Almighty came
to me.
19 This is what the LORD Almighty says:
"The fasts of the fourth, fifth, seventh and
tenth months will become joyful and glad
occasions and happy festivals for Judah.
Therefore love truth and peace."
20 This is what the LORD Almighty says:
"Many peoples and the inhabitants of many
cities will yet come, 21 and the inhabitants
of one city will go to another and say, 'Let
us go at once to entreat the LORD and seek
the LORD Almighty. I myself am going.'
22 And many peoples and powerful nations
will come to Jerusalem to seek the LORD Al-
mighty and to entreat him."
23 This is what the LORD Almighty says:
"In those days ten people from all languages
and nations will take firm hold of one Jew by
the hem of his robe and say, 'Let us go with
you, because we have heard that God is with
you.'"

Judgment on Israel's Enemies

9 A prophecy:

The word of the LORD is against the land
of Hadrak
and will come to rest on Damascus —
for the eyes of all people and all the tribes
of Israel
are on the LORD — [b]
2 and on Hamath too, which borders on it,
and on Tyre and Sidon, though they
are very skillful.
3 Tyre has built herself a stronghold;
she has heaped up silver like dust,
and gold like the dirt of the streets.
4 But the Lord will take away her
possessions
and destroy her power on the sea,
and she will be consumed by fire.
5 Ashkelon will see it and fear;
Gaza will writhe in agony,
and Ekron too, for her hope will wither.
Gaza will lose her king
and Ashkelon will be deserted.
6 A mongrel people will occupy Ashdod,
and I will put an end to the pride of the
Philistines.
7 I will take the blood from their mouths,
the forbidden food from between their
teeth.
Those who are left will belong to our God
and become a clan in Judah,
and Ekron will be like the Jebusites.
8 But I will encamp at my temple
to guard it against marauding forces.
Never again will an oppressor overrun
my people,
for now I am keeping watch.

The Coming of Zion's King

9 Rejoice greatly, Daughter Zion!
Shout, Daughter Jerusalem!
See, your king comes to you,
righteous and victorious,
lowly and riding on a donkey,
on a colt, the foal of a donkey.
10 I will take away the chariots from
Ephraim
and the warhorses from Jerusalem,
and the battle bow will be broken.
He will proclaim peace to the nations.
His rule will extend from sea to sea
and from the River[c] to the ends of
the earth.
11 As for you, because of the blood of my
covenant with you,
I will free your prisoners from the
waterless pit.
12 Return to your fortress, you prisoners
of hope;
even now I announce that I will restore
twice as much to you.
13 I will bend Judah as I bend my bow
and fill it with Ephraim.

[a] 13 Or *and your name will be used in blessings* (see Gen. 48:20); or *and you will be seen as blessed*
[b] 1 Or *Damascus. / For the eye of the LORD is on all people, / as well as on the tribes of Israel,*
[c] 10 That is, the Euphrates

I will rouse your sons, Zion,
against your sons, Greece,
and make you like a warrior's sword.

The LORD Will Appear

14 Then the LORD will appear over them;
his arrow will flash like lightning.
The Sovereign LORD will sound the trumpet;
he will march in the storms of the south,
15 and the LORD Almighty will shield them.
They will destroy
and overcome with slingstones.
They will drink and roar as with wine;
they will be full like a bowl
used for sprinkling[a] the corners of the altar.
16 The LORD their God will save his people on that day
as a shepherd saves his flock.
They will sparkle in his land
like jewels in a crown.
17 How attractive and beautiful they will be!
Grain will make the young men thrive,
and new wine the young women.

The LORD Will Care for Judah

10 Ask the LORD for rain in the springtime;
it is the LORD who sends the thunderstorms.
He gives showers of rain to all people,
and plants of the field to everyone.
2 The idols speak deceitfully,
diviners see visions that lie;
they tell dreams that are false,
they give comfort in vain.
Therefore the people wander like sheep
oppressed for lack of a shepherd.

3 "My anger burns against the shepherds,
and I will punish the leaders;
for the LORD Almighty will care
for his flock, the people of Judah,
and make them like a proud horse in battle.
4 From Judah will come the cornerstone,
from him the tent peg,
from him the battle bow,
from him every ruler.
5 Together they[b] will be like warriors in battle
trampling their enemy into the mud of the streets.
They will fight because the LORD is with them,
and they will put the enemy horsemen to shame.

6 "I will strengthen Judah
and save the tribes of Joseph.
I will restore them
because I have compassion on them.
They will be as though
I had not rejected them,
for I am the LORD their God
and I will answer them.
7 The Ephraimites will become like warriors,
and their hearts will be glad as with wine.
Their children will see it and be joyful;
their hearts will rejoice in the LORD.
8 I will signal for them
and gather them in.
Surely I will redeem them;
they will be as numerous as before.
9 Though I scatter them among the peoples,
yet in distant lands they will remember me.
They and their children will survive,
and they will return.
10 I will bring them back from Egypt
and gather them from Assyria.
I will bring them to Gilead and Lebanon,
and there will not be room enough for them.
11 They will pass through the sea of trouble;
the surging sea will be subdued
and all the depths of the Nile will dry up.
Assyria's pride will be brought down
and Egypt's scepter will pass away.
12 I will strengthen them in the LORD
and in his name they will live securely,"
declares the LORD.

11 Open your doors, Lebanon,
so that fire may devour your cedars!
2 Wail, you juniper, for the cedar has fallen;
the stately trees are ruined!

[a] 15 Or *bowl, / like* [b] 4,5 Or *ruler, all of them together. / [5]They*

Wail, oaks of Bashan;
  the dense forest has been cut down!
3 Listen to the wail of the shepherds;
  their rich pastures are destroyed!
Listen to the roar of the lions;
  the lush thicket of the Jordan is ruined!

Two Shepherds

4 This is what the LORD my God says:
"Shepherd the flock marked for slaughter.
5 Their buyers slaughter them and go un-
punished. Those who sell them say, 'Praise
the LORD, I am rich!' Their own shepherds
do not spare them. 6 For I will no longer have
pity on the people of the land," declares the
LORD. "I will give everyone into the hands
of their neighbors and their king. They will
devastate the land, and I will not rescue any-
one from their hands."

7 So I shepherded the flock marked for
slaughter, particularly the oppressed of the
flock. Then I took two staffs and called one
Favor and the other Union, and I shepherded
the flock. 8 In one month I got rid of the three
shepherds.

The flock detested me, and I grew weary
of them 9 and said, "I will not be your shep-
herd. Let the dying die, and the perishing
perish. Let those who are left eat one anoth-
er's flesh."

10 Then I took my staff called Favor and
broke it, revoking the covenant I had made
with all the nations. 11 It was revoked on that
day, and so the oppressed of the flock who
were watching me knew it was the word of
the LORD.

12 I told them, "If you think it best, give me
my pay; but if not, keep it." So they paid me
thirty pieces of silver.

13 And the LORD said to me, "Throw it to
the potter" — the handsome price at which
they valued me! So I took the thirty pieces
of silver and threw them to the potter at the
house of the LORD.

14 Then I broke my second staff called
Union, breaking the family bond between
Judah and Israel.

15 Then the LORD said to me, "Take again
the equipment of a foolish shepherd. 16 For
I am going to raise up a shepherd over the
land who will not care for the lost, or seek
the young, or heal the injured, or feed the
healthy, but will eat the meat of the choice
sheep, tearing off their hooves.

17 "Woe to the worthless shepherd,
  who deserts the flock!
May the sword strike his arm and his
    right eye!
  May his arm be completely withered,
  his right eye totally blinded!"

Jerusalem's Enemies to Be Destroyed

12 A prophecy: The word of the LORD
concerning Israel.

The LORD, who stretches out the heavens,
who lays the foundation of the earth, and
who forms the human spirit within a person,
declares: 2 "I am going to make Jerusalem a
cup that sends all the surrounding peoples
reeling. Judah will be besieged as well as Je-
rusalem. 3 On that day, when all the nations
of the earth are gathered against her, I will
make Jerusalem an immovable rock for all
the nations. All who try to move it will in-
jure themselves. 4 On that day I will strike
every horse with panic and its rider with
madness," declares the LORD. "I will keep a
watchful eye over Judah, but I will blind all
the horses of the nations. 5 Then the clans of
Judah will say in their hearts, 'The people of
Jerusalem are strong, because the LORD Al-
mighty is their God.'

6 "On that day I will make the clans of Ju-
dah like a firepot in a woodpile, like a flam-
ing torch among sheaves. They will consume
all the surrounding peoples right and left,
but Jerusalem will remain intact in her place.

7 "The LORD will save the dwellings of Ju-
dah first, so that the honor of the house of
David and of Jerusalem's inhabitants may
not be greater than that of Judah. 8 On that
day the LORD will shield those who live in
Jerusalem, so that the feeblest among them
will be like David, and the house of David
will be like God, like the angel of the LORD
going before them. 9 On that day I will set
out to destroy all the nations that attack Je-
rusalem.

Mourning for the One They Pierced

10 "And I will pour out on the house of Da-
vid and the inhabitants of Jerusalem a spir-
it[a] of grace and supplication. They will look
on[b] me, the one they have pierced, and they

[a] 10 Or *the Spirit* [b] 10 Or *to*

HE IS EXALTED

Twila Paris

He is exalted, the King is exalted on high
And I will praise him
He is exalted, forever exalted and
I will praise his Name

For he is the Lord
Forever his truth shall reign
Heaven and earth rejoice in his holy Name
He is exalted, the King is exalted on high

THE INSPIRATION

I will praise you, LORD, with all my heart; before the "gods" I will sing your praise. I will bow down toward your holy temple and will praise your name for your unfailing love and your faithfulness.

— Psalm 138:1 – 2

Read also: Psalm 95:3; Psalm 105:3; Psalm 145

BEHIND THE SONG

Twila Paris has been a successful Christian songwriter since the early 1980s, but for her, the ultimate purpose of her work is much higher than radio singles, album sales or concert tours.

"I have always felt," Paris shares, "that not only the ability to write songs, but the songs themselves, are gifts from God. So I also feel that when one of those songs is returned to God in worship by any one of his children it is the highest and most appropriate purpose that song can find."

Several of Paris's songs have done just that. Many worship leaders and students of contemporary worship recognize the simple chorus, "He Is Exalted," as an important moment in the evolution of modern worship. But for Paris, all of the accolades pale in comparison to seeing the song move people to lift the name of Jesus.

Paris recalls one of the first times she realized that the songs she was giving back to the Lord were catching on around the world. "A missionary friend of mine came home from Brazil and told me that 'He is Exalted' was being sung by the churches there. He also told me that many of the worship bands included talented jazz musicians. Once they got started, they would sing the song over and over in a joyful celebration. I can still vividly see him dancing around my kitchen as he sang 'Ele E Exaltado' in Portuguese in an effort to show me the exuberance with which the brothers and sisters in Brazil offered the song back to the Lord in worship."

Selah

The word "exalt" means to lift up, to intensify, to draw attention to or to celebrate. Think about the things that are exalted in our culture. People love to lift up the name and symbols of everything from sports teams to national flags. In worship, believers are called to lift the name of Jesus above all other banners.

What are some things that you exalt on a daily or weekly basis? Can those around you tell what you love by the things you exalt? Can they tell that your first love is the Lord?

will mourn for him as one mourns for an only child, and grieve bitterly for him as one grieves for a firstborn son. 11 On that day the weeping in Jerusalem will be as great as the weeping of Hadad Rimmon in the plain of Megiddo. 12 The land will mourn, each clan by itself, with their wives by themselves: the clan of the house of David and their wives, the clan of the house of Nathan and their wives, 13 the clan of the house of Levi and their wives, the clan of Shimei and their wives, 14 and all the rest of the clans and their wives.

Cleansing From Sin

13 "On that day a fountain will be opened to the house of David and the inhabitants of Jerusalem, to cleanse them from sin and impurity.

2 "On that day, I will banish the names of the idols from the land, and they will be remembered no more," declares the LORD Almighty. "I will remove both the prophets and the spirit of impurity from the land. 3 And if anyone still prophesies, their father and mother, to whom they were born, will say to them, 'You must die, because you have told lies in the LORD's name.' Then their own parents will stab the one who prophesies.

4 "On that day every prophet will be ashamed of their prophetic vision. They will not put on a prophet's garment of hair in order to deceive. 5 Each will say, 'I am not a prophet. I am a farmer; the land has been my livelihood since my youth.[a]' 6 If someone asks, 'What are these wounds on your body[b]?' they will answer, 'The wounds I was given at the house of my friends.'

The Shepherd Struck, the Sheep Scattered

7 "Awake, sword, against my shepherd,
  against the man who is close to me!"
  declares the LORD Almighty.
"Strike the shepherd,
  and the sheep will be scattered,
  and I will turn my hand against the
    little ones.
8 In the whole land," declares the LORD,
  "two-thirds will be struck down and
    perish;
  yet one-third will be left in it.
9 This third I will put into the fire;
  I will refine them like silver
  and test them like gold.
They will call on my name
  and I will answer them;
I will say, 'They are my people,'
  and they will say, 'The LORD is
    our God.'"

The LORD Comes and Reigns

14 A day of the LORD is coming, Jerusalem, when your possessions will be plundered and divided up within your very walls.

2 I will gather all the nations to Jerusalem to fight against it; the city will be captured, the houses ransacked, and the women raped. Half of the city will go into exile, but the rest of the people will not be taken from the city. 3 Then the LORD will go out and fight against those nations, as he fights on a day of battle. 4 On that day his feet will stand on the Mount of Olives, east of Jerusalem, and the Mount of Olives will be split in two from east to west, forming a great valley, with half of the mountain moving north and half moving south. 5 You will flee by my mountain valley, for it will extend to Azel. You will flee as you fled from the earthquake[c] in the days of Uzziah king of Judah. Then the LORD my God will come, and all the holy ones with him.

6 On that day there will be neither sunlight nor cold, frosty darkness. 7 It will be a unique day—a day known only to the LORD—with no distinction between day and night. When evening comes, there will be light.

8 On that day living water will flow out from Jerusalem, half of it east to the Dead Sea and half of it west to the Mediterranean Sea, in summer and in winter.

9 The LORD will be king over the whole earth. On that day there will be one LORD, and his name the only name.

10 The whole land, from Geba to Rimmon, south of Jerusalem, will become like the Arabah. But Jerusalem will be raised up high from the Benjamin Gate to the site of the First Gate, to the Corner Gate, and from the Tower of Hananel to the royal winepresses, and will remain in its place. 11 It will be inhabited;

[a] 5 Or *farmer; a man sold me in my youth* [b] 6 Or *wounds between your hands* [c] 5 Or *5 My mountain valley will be blocked and will extend to Azel. It will be blocked as it was blocked because of the earthquake*

never again will it be destroyed. Jerusalem
will be secure.
[12]This is the plague with which the LORD
will strike all the nations that fought against
Jerusalem: Their flesh will rot while they are
still standing on their feet, their eyes will rot
in their sockets, and their tongues will rot in
their mouths. [13]On that day people will be
stricken by the LORD with great panic. They
will seize each other by the hand and attack
one another. [14]Judah too will fight at Jeru-
salem. The wealth of all the surrounding
nations will be collected — great quantities
of gold and silver and clothing. [15]A similar
plague will strike the horses and mules, the
camels and donkeys, and all the animals in
those camps.
[16]Then the survivors from all the nations
that have attacked Jerusalem will go up year
after year to worship the King, the LORD Al-
mighty, and to celebrate the Festival of Tab-
ernacles. [17]If any of the peoples of the earth
do not go up to Jerusalem to worship the
King, the LORD Almighty, they will have no
rain. [18]If the Egyptian people do not go up
and take part, they will have no rain. The
LORD[a] will bring on them the plague he in-
flicts on the nations that do not go up to cele-
brate the Festival of Tabernacles. [19]This will
be the punishment of Egypt and the punish-
ment of all the nations that do not go up to
celebrate the Festival of Tabernacles.
[20]On that day HOLY TO THE LORD will be
inscribed on the bells of the horses, and the
cooking pots in the LORD's house will be like
the sacred bowls in front of the altar. [21]Ev-
ery pot in Jerusalem and Judah will be holy
to the LORD Almighty, and all who come to
sacrifice will take some of the pots and cook
in them. And on that day there will no lon-
ger be a Canaanite[b] in the house of the LORD
Almighty.

[a] 18 Or *part, then the LORD* [b] 21 Or *merchant*

MALACHI

1 A prophecy: The word of the LORD to Israel through Malachi.[a]

Israel Doubts God's Love

2 "I have loved you," says the LORD.

"But you ask, 'How have you loved us?'

"Was not Esau Jacob's brother?" declares the LORD. "Yet I have loved Jacob, 3 but Esau I have hated, and I have turned his hill country into a wasteland and left his inheritance to the desert jackals."

4 Edom may say, "Though we have been crushed, we will rebuild the ruins."

But this is what the LORD Almighty says: "They may build, but I will demolish. They will be called the Wicked Land, a people always under the wrath of the LORD. 5 You will see it with your own eyes and say, 'Great is the LORD—even beyond the borders of Israel!'

Breaking Covenant Through Blemished Sacrifices

6 "A son honors his father, and a slave his master. If I am a father, where is the honor due me? If I am a master, where is the respect due me?" says the LORD Almighty.

"It is you priests who show contempt for my name.

"But you ask, 'How have we shown contempt for your name?'

7 "By offering defiled food on my altar.

"But you ask, 'How have we defiled you?'

"By saying that the LORD's table is contemptible. 8 When you offer blind animals for sacrifice, is that not wrong? When you sacrifice lame or diseased animals, is that not wrong? Try offering them to your governor! Would he be pleased with you? Would he accept you?" says the LORD Almighty.

9 "Now plead with God to be gracious to us. With such offerings from your hands, will he accept you?"—says the LORD Almighty.

10 "Oh, that one of you would shut the temple doors, so that you would not light useless fires on my altar! I am not pleased with you," says the LORD Almighty, "and I will accept no offering from your hands. 11 My name will be great among the nations, from where the sun rises to where it sets. In every place incense and pure offerings will be brought to me, because my name will be great among the nations," says the LORD Almighty.

12 "But you profane it by saying, 'The Lord's table is defiled,' and, 'Its food is contemptible.' 13 And you say, 'What a burden!' and you sniff at it contemptuously," says the LORD Almighty.

"When you bring injured, lame or diseased animals and offer them as sacrifices, should I accept them from your hands?" says the LORD. 14 "Cursed is the cheat who has an acceptable male in his flock and vows to give it, but then sacrifices a blemished animal to the Lord. For I am a great king," says the LORD Almighty, "and my name is to be feared among the nations.

Additional Warning to the Priests

2 "And now, you priests, this warning is for you. 2 If you do not listen, and if you do not resolve to honor my name," says the LORD Almighty, "I will send a curse on you, and I will curse your blessings. Yes, I have already cursed them, because you have not resolved to honor me.

3 "Because of you I will rebuke your descendants[b]; I will smear on your faces the dung from your festival sacrifices, and you will be carried off with it. 4 And you will know that I have sent you this warning so that my covenant with Levi may continue," says the LORD Almighty. 5 "My covenant was with him, a covenant of life and peace, and I gave them to him; this called for reverence and he revered me and stood in awe of my name. 6 True instruction was in his mouth and nothing false was found on his lips. He walked with me in peace and uprightness, and turned many from sin.

[a] 1 *Malachi* means *my messenger.* [b] 3 Or *will blight your grain*

7 "For the lips of a priest ought to preserve knowledge, because he is the messenger of the LORD Almighty and people seek instruction from his mouth. 8 But you have turned from the way and by your teaching have caused many to stumble; you have violated the covenant with Levi," says the LORD Almighty. 9 "So I have caused you to be despised and humiliated before all the people, because you have not followed my ways but have shown partiality in matters of the law."

Breaking Covenant Through Divorce

10 Do we not all have one Father[a]? Did not one God create us? Why do we profane the covenant of our ancestors by being unfaithful to one another?

11 Judah has been unfaithful. A detestable thing has been committed in Israel and in Jerusalem: Judah has desecrated the sanctuary the LORD loves by marrying women who worship a foreign god. 12 As for the man who does this, whoever he may be, may the LORD remove him from the tents of Jacob[b]—even though he brings an offering to the LORD Almighty.

13 Another thing you do: You flood the LORD's altar with tears. You weep and wail because he no longer looks with favor on your offerings or accepts them with pleasure from your hands. 14 You ask, "Why?" It is because the LORD is the witness between you and the wife of your youth. You have been unfaithful to her, though she is your partner, the wife of your marriage covenant.

15 Has not the one God made you? You belong to him in body and spirit. And what does the one God seek? Godly offspring.[c] So be on your guard, and do not be unfaithful to the wife of your youth.

16 "The man who hates and divorces his wife," says the LORD, the God of Israel, "does violence to the one he should protect,"[d] says the LORD Almighty.

So be on your guard, and do not be unfaithful.

Breaking Covenant Through Injustice

17 You have wearied the LORD with your words.

"How have we wearied him?" you ask.

By saying, "All who do evil are good in the eyes of the LORD, and he is pleased with them" or "Where is the God of justice?"

3 "I will send my messenger, who will prepare the way before me. Then suddenly the Lord you are seeking will come to his temple; the messenger of the covenant, whom you desire, will come," says the LORD Almighty.

2 But who can endure the day of his coming? Who can stand when he appears? For he will be like a refiner's fire or a launderer's soap. 3 He will sit as a refiner and purifier of silver; he will purify the Levites and refine them like gold and silver. Then the LORD will have men who will bring offerings in righteousness, 4 and the offerings of Judah and Jerusalem will be acceptable to the LORD, as in days gone by, as in former years.

5 "So I will come to put you on trial. I will be quick to testify against sorcerers, adulterers and perjurers, against those who defraud laborers of their wages, who oppress the widows and the fatherless, and deprive the foreigners among you of justice, but do not fear me," says the LORD Almighty.

Breaking Covenant by Withholding Tithes

6 "I the LORD do not change. So you, the descendants of Jacob, are not destroyed. 7 Ever since the time of your ancestors you have turned away from my decrees and have not kept them. Return to me, and I will return to you," says the LORD Almighty.

"But you ask, 'How are we to return?'

8 "Will a mere mortal rob God? Yet you rob me.

"But you ask, 'How are we robbing you?'

"In tithes and offerings. 9 You are under a curse—your whole nation—because you are robbing me. 10 Bring the whole tithe into the storehouse, that there may be food in my house. Test me in this," says the LORD Almighty, "and see if I will not throw open the floodgates of heaven and pour out so much blessing that there will not be room enough to store it. 11 I will prevent pests from devouring your crops, and the vines in your fields

[a] 10 Or *father* [b] 12 Or *12 May the LORD remove from the tents of Jacob anyone who gives testimony in behalf of the man who does this* [c] 15 The meaning of the Hebrew for the first part of this verse is uncertain. [d] 16 Or *"I hate divorce," says the LORD, the God of Israel, "because the man who divorces his wife covers his garment with violence,"*

will not drop their fruit before it is ripe," says
the Lord Almighty. 12 "Then all the nations
will call you blessed, for yours will be a de-
lightful land," says the Lord Almighty.

Israel Speaks Arrogantly Against God

13 "You have spoken arrogantly against
me," says the Lord.

"Yet you ask, 'What have we said against
you?'

14 "You have said, 'It is futile to serve God.
What do we gain by carrying out his require-
ments and going about like mourners before
the Lord Almighty? 15 But now we call the
arrogant blessed. Certainly evildoers pros-
per, and even when they put God to the test,
they get away with it.' "

The Faithful Remnant

16 Then those who feared the Lord talked
with each other, and the Lord listened and
heard. A scroll of remembrance was written
in his presence concerning those who feared
the Lord and honored his name.

17 "On the day when I act," says the Lord Al-
mighty, "they will be my treasured possession.
I will spare them, just as a father has compas-
sion and spares his son who serves him. 18 And
you will again see the distinction between the
righteous and the wicked, between those who
serve God and those who do not.

Judgment and Covenant Renewal

4 [a] "Surely the day is coming; it will burn
like a furnace. All the arrogant and
every evildoer will be stubble, and the day
that is coming will set them on fire," says
the Lord Almighty. "Not a root or a branch
will be left to them. 2 But for you who revere
my name, the sun of righteousness will rise
with healing in its rays. And you will go out
and frolic like well-fed calves. 3 Then you will
trample on the wicked; they will be ashes
under the soles of your feet on the day when
I act," says the Lord Almighty.

4 "Remember the law of my servant Moses,
the decrees and laws I gave him at Horeb for
all Israel.

5 "See, I will send the prophet Elijah to you
before that great and dreadful day of the Lord
comes. 6 He will turn the hearts of the parents
to their children, and the hearts of the chil-
dren to their parents; or else I will come and
strike the land with total destruction."

[a] In Hebrew texts 4:1-6 is numbered 3:19-24.

THE NEW TESTAMENT

MATTHEW

The Genealogy of Jesus the Messiah

1 This is the genealogy[a] of Jesus the Messiah[b] the son of David, the son of Abraham:

2 Abraham was the father of Isaac,
Isaac the father of Jacob,
Jacob the father of Judah and his brothers,
3 Judah the father of Perez and Zerah, whose mother was Tamar,
Perez the father of Hezron,
Hezron the father of Ram,
4 Ram the father of Amminadab,
Amminadab the father of Nahshon,
Nahshon the father of Salmon,
5 Salmon the father of Boaz, whose mother was Rahab,
Boaz the father of Obed, whose mother was Ruth,
Obed the father of Jesse,
6 and Jesse the father of King David.

David was the father of Solomon, whose mother had been Uriah's wife,
7 Solomon the father of Rehoboam,
Rehoboam the father of Abijah,
Abijah the father of Asa,
8 Asa the father of Jehoshaphat,
Jehoshaphat the father of Jehoram,
Jehoram the father of Uzziah,
9 Uzziah the father of Jotham,
Jotham the father of Ahaz,
Ahaz the father of Hezekiah,
10 Hezekiah the father of Manasseh,
Manasseh the father of Amon,
Amon the father of Josiah,
11 and Josiah the father of Jeconiah[c] and his brothers at the time of the exile to Babylon.

12 After the exile to Babylon:
Jeconiah was the father of Shealtiel,
Shealtiel the father of Zerubbabel,
13 Zerubbabel the father of Abihud,
Abihud the father of Eliakim,
Eliakim the father of Azor,
14 Azor the father of Zadok,
Zadok the father of Akim,
Akim the father of Elihud,
15 Elihud the father of Eleazar,
Eleazar the father of Matthan,
Matthan the father of Jacob,
16 and Jacob the father of Joseph, the husband of Mary, and Mary was the mother of Jesus who is called the Messiah.

17 Thus there were fourteen generations
in all from Abraham to David, fourteen from
David to the exile to Babylon, and fourteen
from the exile to the Messiah.

Joseph Accepts Jesus as His Son

18 This is how the birth of Jesus the Messiah
came about[d]: His mother Mary was pledged
to be married to Joseph, but before they
came together, she was found to be pregnant
through the Holy Spirit. 19 Because Joseph
her husband was faithful to the law, and yet[e]
did not want to expose her to public disgrace,
he had in mind to divorce her quietly.
20 But after he had considered this, an an-
gel of the Lord appeared to him in a dream
and said, "Joseph son of David, do not be
afraid to take Mary home as your wife, be-
cause what is conceived in her is from the
Holy Spirit. 21 She will give birth to a son, and
you are to give him the name Jesus,[f] because
he will save his people from their sins."
22 All this took place to fulfill what the
Lord had said through the prophet: 23 "The
virgin will conceive and give birth to a son,
and they will call him Immanuel"[g] (which
means "God with us").
24 When Joseph woke up, he did what the

[a] *1* Or *is an account of the origin* [b] *1* Or *Jesus Christ. Messiah* (Hebrew) and *Christ* (Greek) both mean *Anointed One*; also in verse 18. [c] *11* That is, Jehoiachin; also in verse 12 [d] *18* Or *The origin of Jesus the Messiah was like this* [e] *19* Or *was a righteous man and* [f] *21* *Jesus* is the Greek form of *Joshua*, which means *the LORD saves.* [g] *23* Isaiah 7:14

angel of the Lord had commanded him and took Mary home as his wife. 25 But he did not consummate their marriage until she gave birth to a son. And he gave him the name Jesus.

The Magi Visit the Messiah

2 After Jesus was born in Bethlehem in Judea, during the time of King Herod, Magi[a] from the east came to Jerusalem 2 and asked, "Where is the one who has been born king of the Jews? We saw his star when it rose and have come to worship him."

3 When King Herod heard this he was disturbed, and all Jerusalem with him. 4 When he had called together all the people's chief priests and teachers of the law, he asked them where the Messiah was to be born. 5 "In Bethlehem in Judea," they replied, "for this is what the prophet has written:

6 " 'But you, Bethlehem, in the land of Judah,
are by no means least among the rulers of Judah;
for out of you will come a ruler
who will shepherd my people Israel.'[b]"

7 Then Herod called the Magi secretly and found out from them the exact time the star had appeared. 8 He sent them to Bethlehem and said, "Go and search carefully for the child. As soon as you find him, report to me, so that I too may go and worship him."

9 After they had heard the king, they went on their way, and the star they had seen when it rose went ahead of them until it stopped over the place where the child was. 10 When they saw the star, they were overjoyed. 11 On coming to the house, they saw the child with his mother Mary, and they bowed down and worshiped him. Then they opened their treasures and presented him with gifts of gold, frankincense and myrrh. 12 And having been warned in a dream not to go back to Herod, they returned to their country by another route.

The Escape to Egypt

13 When they had gone, an angel of the Lord appeared to Joseph in a dream. "Get up," he said, "take the child and his mother and escape to Egypt. Stay there until I tell you, for Herod is going to search for the child to kill him."

14 So he got up, took the child and his mother during the night and left for Egypt, 15 where he stayed until the death of Herod. And so was fulfilled what the Lord had said through the prophet: "Out of Egypt I called my son."[c]

16 When Herod realized that he had been outwitted by the Magi, he was furious, and he gave orders to kill all the boys in Bethlehem and its vicinity who were two years old and under, in accordance with the time he had learned from the Magi. 17 Then what was said through the prophet Jeremiah was fulfilled:

18 "A voice is heard in Ramah,
weeping and great mourning,
Rachel weeping for her children
and refusing to be comforted,
because they are no more."[d]

The Return to Nazareth

19 After Herod died, an angel of the Lord appeared in a dream to Joseph in Egypt 20 and said, "Get up, take the child and his mother and go to the land of Israel, for those who were trying to take the child's life are dead."

21 So he got up, took the child and his mother and went to the land of Israel. 22 But when he heard that Archelaus was reigning in Judea in place of his father Herod, he was afraid to go there. Having been warned in a dream, he withdrew to the district of Galilee, 23 and he went and lived in a town called Nazareth. So was fulfilled what was said through the prophets, that he would be called a Nazarene.

John the Baptist Prepares the Way

3 In those days John the Baptist came, preaching in the wilderness of Judea 2 and saying, "Repent, for the kingdom of heaven has come near." 3 This is he who was spoken of through the prophet Isaiah:

"A voice of one calling in the wilderness,
'Prepare the way for the Lord,
make straight paths for him.' "[e]

4 John's clothes were made of camel's hair, and he had a leather belt around his waist.

[a] *1* Traditionally *wise men* [b] *6* Micah 5:2,4 [c] *15* Hosea 11:1 [d] *18* Jer. 31:15 [e] *3* Isaiah 40:3

His food was locusts and wild honey. 5Peo-
ple went out to him from Jerusalem and all
Judea and the whole region of the Jordan.
6Confessing their sins, they were baptized
by him in the Jordan River.
7But when he saw many of the Pharisees
and Sadducees coming to where he was bap-
tizing, he said to them: "You brood of vipers!
Who warned you to flee from the coming
wrath? 8Produce fruit in keeping with re-
pentance. 9And do not think you can say
to yourselves, 'We have Abraham as our fa-
ther.' I tell you that out of these stones God
can raise up children for Abraham. 10The ax
is already at the root of the trees, and every
tree that does not produce good fruit will be
cut down and thrown into the fire.
11"I baptize you with[a] water for repen-
tance. But after me comes one who is more
powerful than I, whose sandals I am not
worthy to carry. He will baptize you with[a]
the Holy Spirit and fire. 12His winnow-
ing fork is in his hand, and he will clear his
threshing floor, gathering his wheat into
the barn and burning up the chaff with un-
quenchable fire."

The Baptism of Jesus

13Then Jesus came from Galilee to the Jor-
dan to be baptized by John. 14But John tried
to deter him, saying, "I need to be baptized
by you, and do you come to me?"
15Jesus replied, "Let it be so now; it is
proper for us to do this to fulfill all righ-
teousness." Then John consented.
16As soon as Jesus was baptized, he went
up out of the water. At that moment heaven
was opened, and he saw the Spirit of God
descending like a dove and alighting on
him. 17And a voice from heaven said, "This
is my Son, whom I love; with him I am well
pleased."

Jesus Is Tested in the Wilderness

4 Then Jesus was led by the Spirit into the
wilderness to be tempted[b] by the devil.
2After fasting forty days and forty nights, he
was hungry. 3The tempter came to him and
said, "If you are the Son of God, tell these
stones to become bread."
4Jesus answered, "It is written: 'Man shall
not live on bread alone, but on every word
that comes from the mouth of God.'[c]"
5Then the devil took him to the holy city
and had him stand on the highest point of
the temple. 6"If you are the Son of God," he
said, "throw yourself down. For it is written:

"'He will command his angels
concerning you,
and they will lift you up in their hands,
so that you will not strike your foot
against a stone.'[d]"

7Jesus answered him, "It is also written:
'Do not put the Lord your God to the test.'[e]"
8Again, the devil took him to a very high
mountain and showed him all the kingdoms
of the world and their splendor. 9"All this I
will give you," he said, "if you will bow down
and worship me."
10Jesus said to him, "Away from me, Satan!
For it is written: 'Worship the Lord your God,
and serve him only.'[f]"
11Then the devil left him, and angels
came and attended him.

Jesus Begins to Preach

12When Jesus heard that John had been
put in prison, he withdrew to Galilee.
13Leaving Nazareth, he went and lived in Ca-
pernaum, which was by the lake in the area
of Zebulun and Naphtali— 14to fulfill what
was said through the prophet Isaiah:

15"Land of Zebulun and land of Naphtali,
the Way of the Sea, beyond the Jordan,
Galilee of the Gentiles—
16the people living in darkness
have seen a great light;
on those living in the land of the shadow
of death
a light has dawned."[g]

17From that time on Jesus began to
preach, "Repent, for the kingdom of heaven
has come near."

Jesus Calls His First Disciples

18As Jesus was walking beside the Sea of
Galilee, he saw two brothers, Simon called
Peter and his brother Andrew. They were
casting a net into the lake, for they were fish-
ermen. 19"Come, follow me," Jesus said, "and

[a] *11* Or *in* [b] *1* The Greek for *tempted* can also mean *tested.* [c] *4* Deut. 8:3 [d] *6* Psalm 91:11,12
[e] *7* Deut. 6:16 [f] *10* Deut. 6:13 [g] *16* Isaiah 9:1,2

I will send you out to fish for people." 20 At once they left their nets and followed him.

21 Going on from there, he saw two other brothers, James son of Zebedee and his brother John. They were in a boat with their father Zebedee, preparing their nets. Jesus called them, 22 and immediately they left the boat and their father and followed him.

Jesus Heals the Sick

23 Jesus went throughout Galilee, teaching in their synagogues, proclaiming the good news of the kingdom, and healing every disease and sickness among the people. 24 News about him spread all over Syria, and people brought to him all who were ill with various diseases, those suffering severe pain, the demon-possessed, those having seizures, and the paralyzed; and he healed them. 25 Large crowds from Galilee, the Decapolis,[a] Jerusalem, Judea and the region across the Jordan followed him.

Introduction to the Sermon on the Mount

5 Now when Jesus saw the crowds, he went up on a mountainside and sat down. His disciples came to him, 2 and he began to teach them.

The Beatitudes

He said:

3 "Blessed are the poor in spirit,
for theirs is the kingdom of heaven.
4 Blessed are those who mourn,
for they will be comforted.
5 Blessed are the meek,
for they will inherit the earth.
6 Blessed are those who hunger and thirst
for righteousness,
for they will be filled.
7 Blessed are the merciful,
for they will be shown mercy.
8 Blessed are the pure in heart,
for they will see God.
9 Blessed are the peacemakers,
for they will be called children of God.
10 Blessed are those who are persecuted
because of righteousness,
for theirs is the kingdom of heaven.

11 "Blessed are you when people insult you, persecute you and falsely say all kinds of evil against you because of me. 12 Rejoice and be glad, because great is your reward in heaven, for in the same way they persecuted the prophets who were before you.

Salt and Light

13 "You are the salt of the earth. But if the salt loses its saltiness, how can it be made salty again? It is no longer good for anything, except to be thrown out and trampled underfoot.

14 "You are the light of the world. A town built on a hill cannot be hidden. 15 Neither do people light a lamp and put it under a bowl. Instead they put it on its stand, and it gives light to everyone in the house. 16 In the same way, let your light shine before others, that they may see your good deeds and glorify your Father in heaven.

The Fulfillment of the Law

17 "Do not think that I have come to abolish the Law or the Prophets; I have not come to abolish them but to fulfill them. 18 For truly I tell you, until heaven and earth disappear, not the smallest letter, not the least stroke of a pen, will by any means disappear from the Law until everything is accomplished. 19 Therefore anyone who sets aside one of the least of these commands and teaches others accordingly will be called least in the kingdom of heaven, but whoever practices and teaches these commands will be called great in the kingdom of heaven. 20 For I tell you that unless your righteousness surpasses that of the Pharisees and the teachers of the law, you will certainly not enter the kingdom of heaven.

Murder

21 "You have heard that it was said to the people long ago, 'You shall not murder,[b] and anyone who murders will be subject to judgment.' 22 But I tell you that anyone who is angry with a brother or sister[c,d] will be subject to judgment. Again, anyone who says to a brother or sister, 'Raca,'[e] is answerable to the court. And anyone who says, 'You fool!' will be in danger of the fire of hell.

[a] 25 That is, the Ten Cities [b] 21 Exodus 20:13 [c] 22 The Greek word for *brother or sister* (*adelphos*) refers here to a fellow disciple, whether man or woman; also in verse 23. [d] 22 Some manuscripts *brother or sister without cause* [e] 22 An Aramaic term of contempt

23 “Therefore, if you are offering your gift
at the altar and there remember that your
brother or sister has something against you,
24 leave your gift there in front of the altar.
First go and be reconciled to them; then
come and offer your gift.
25 “Settle matters quickly with your adver-
sary who is taking you to court. Do it while
you are still together on the way, or your ad-
versary may hand you over to the judge, and
the judge may hand you over to the officer,
and you may be thrown into prison. 26 Truly
I tell you, you will not get out until you have
paid the last penny.

Adultery

27 “You have heard that it was said, ‘You
shall not commit adultery.’[a] 28 But I tell you
that anyone who looks at a woman lustful-
ly has already committed adultery with her
in his heart. 29 If your right eye causes you to
stumble, gouge it out and throw it away. It is
better for you to lose one part of your body
than for your whole body to be thrown into
hell. 30 And if your right hand causes you to
stumble, cut it off and throw it away. It is bet-
ter for you to lose one part of your body than
for your whole body to go into hell.

Divorce

31 “It has been said, ‘Anyone who divorc-
es his wife must give her a certificate of di-
vorce.’[b] 32 But I tell you that anyone who
divorces his wife, except for sexual immo-
rality, makes her the victim of adultery, and
anyone who marries a divorced woman
commits adultery.

Oaths

33 “Again, you have heard that it was said
to the people long ago, ‘Do not break your
oath, but fulfill to the Lord the vows you have
made.’ 34 But I tell you, do not swear an oath
at all: either by heaven, for it is God’s throne;
35 or by the earth, for it is his footstool; or by
Jerusalem, for it is the city of the Great King.
36 And do not swear by your head, for you
cannot make even one hair white or black.
37 All you need to say is simply ‘Yes’ or ‘No’;
anything beyond this comes from the evil
one.[c]

Eye for Eye

38 “You have heard that it was said, ‘Eye for
eye, and tooth for tooth.’[d] 39 But I tell you, do
not resist an evil person. If anyone slaps you
on the right cheek, turn to them the other
cheek also. 40 And if anyone wants to sue you
and take your shirt, hand over your coat as
well. 41 If anyone forces you to go one mile, go
with them two miles. 42 Give to the one who
asks you, and do not turn away from the one
who wants to borrow from you.

Love for Enemies

43 “You have heard that it was said, ‘Love
your neighbor[e] and hate your enemy.’ 44 But
I tell you, love your enemies and pray for
those who persecute you, 45 that you may be
children of your Father in heaven. He causes
his sun to rise on the evil and the good, and
sends rain on the righteous and the unrigh-
teous. 46 If you love those who love you, what
reward will you get? Are not even the tax col-
lectors doing that? 47 And if you greet only
your own people, what are you doing more
than others? Do not even pagans do that?
48 Be perfect, therefore, as your heavenly Fa-
ther is perfect.

Giving to the Needy

6 “Be careful not to practice your righ-
teousness in front of others to be seen
by them. If you do, you will have no reward
from your Father in heaven.
2 “So when you give to the needy, do not
announce it with trumpets, as the hyp-
ocrites do in the synagogues and on the
streets, to be honored by others. Truly I tell
you, they have received their reward in full.
3 But when you give to the needy, do not let
your left hand know what your right hand is
doing, 4 so that your giving may be in secret.
Then your Father, who sees what is done in
secret, will reward you.

Prayer

5 “And when you pray, do not be like the
hypocrites, for they love to pray standing in
the synagogues and on the street corners to
be seen by others. Truly I tell you, they have
received their reward in full. 6 But when you
pray, go into your room, close the door and

[a] *27* Exodus 20:14 [b] *31* Deut. 24:1 [c] *37* Or *from evil* [d] *38* Exodus 21:24; Lev. 24:20; Deut. 19:21
[e] *43* Lev. 19:18

pray to your Father, who is unseen. Then
your Father, who sees what is done in secret,
will reward you. 7 And when you pray, do not
keep on babbling like pagans, for they think
they will be heard because of their many
words. 8 Do not be like them, for your Father
knows what you need before you ask him.

9 "This, then, is how you should pray:

"'Our Father in heaven,
hallowed be your name,
10 your kingdom come,
your will be done,
on earth as it is in heaven.
11 Give us today our daily bread.
12 And forgive us our debts,
as we also have forgiven our debtors.
13 And lead us not into temptation,[a]
but deliver us from the evil one.[b]'

14 For if you forgive other people when they
sin against you, your heavenly Father will
also forgive you. 15 But if you do not forgive
others their sins, your Father will not forgive
your sins.

Fasting

16 "When you fast, do not look somber as
the hypocrites do, for they disfigure their
faces to show others they are fasting. Truly
I tell you, they have received their reward
in full. 17 But when you fast, put oil on your
head and wash your face, 18 so that it will not
be obvious to others that you are fasting, but
only to your Father, who is unseen; and your
Father, who sees what is done in secret, will
reward you.

Treasures in Heaven

19 "Do not store up for yourselves treasures
on earth, where moths and vermin destroy,
and where thieves break in and steal. 20 But
store up for yourselves treasures in heaven,
where moths and vermin do not destroy,
and where thieves do not break in and steal.
21 For where your treasure is, there your
heart will be also.

22 "The eye is the lamp of the body. If your
eyes are healthy,[c] your whole body will be
full of light. 23 But if your eyes are unhealthy,[d]
your whole body will be full of darkness. If
then the light within you is darkness, how
great is that darkness!

24 "No one can serve two masters. Either
you will hate the one and love the other, or
you will be devoted to the one and despise
the other. You cannot serve both God and
money.

Do Not Worry

25 "Therefore I tell you, do not worry about
your life, what you will eat or drink; or about
your body, what you will wear. Is not life
more than food, and the body more than
clothes? 26 Look at the birds of the air; they
do not sow or reap or store away in barns,
and yet your heavenly Father feeds them.
Are you not much more valuable than they?
27 Can any one of you by worrying add a sin-
gle hour to your life[e]?

28 "And why do you worry about clothes?
See how the flowers of the field grow. They
do not labor or spin. 29 Yet I tell you that
not even Solomon in all his splendor was
dressed like one of these. 30 If that is how God
clothes the grass of the field, which is here
today and tomorrow is thrown into the fire,
will he not much more clothe you—you of
little faith? 31 So do not worry, saying, 'What
shall we eat?' or 'What shall we drink?' or
'What shall we wear?' 32 For the pagans run
after all these things, and your heavenly Fa-
ther knows that you need them. 33 But seek
first his kingdom and his righteousness, and
all these things will be given to you as well.
34 Therefore do not worry about tomorrow,
for tomorrow will worry about itself. Each
day has enough trouble of its own.

Judging Others

7 "Do not judge, or you too will be judged.
2 For in the same way you judge others,
you will be judged, and with the measure
you use, it will be measured to you.

3 "Why do you look at the speck of sawdust
in your brother's eye and pay no attention
to the plank in your own eye? 4 How can you
say to your brother, 'Let me take the speck
out of your eye,' when all the time there is a
plank in your own eye? 5 You hypocrite, first
take the plank out of your own eye, and then

[a] *13* The Greek for *temptation* can also mean *testing.* [b] *13* Or *from evil*; some late manuscripts *one, / for yours is the kingdom and the power and the glory forever. Amen.* [c] *22* The Greek for *healthy* here implies *generous.* [d] *23* The Greek for *unhealthy* here implies *stingy.* [e] *27* Or *single cubit to your height*

you will see clearly to remove the speck from
your brother's eye.
6 "Do not give dogs what is sacred; do not
throw your pearls to pigs. If you do, they may
trample them under their feet, and turn and
tear you to pieces.

Ask, Seek, Knock

7 "Ask and it will be given to you; seek and
you will find; knock and the door will be
opened to you. 8 For everyone who asks re-
ceives; the one who seeks finds; and to the
one who knocks, the door will be opened.
9 "Which of you, if your son asks for bread,
will give him a stone? 10 Or if he asks for a
fish, will give him a snake? 11 If you, then,
though you are evil, know how to give good
gifts to your children, how much more will
your Father in heaven give good gifts to
those who ask him! 12 So in everything, do to
others what you would have them do to you,
for this sums up the Law and the Prophets.

The Narrow and Wide Gates

13 "Enter through the narrow gate. For
wide is the gate and broad is the road
that leads to destruction, and many enter
through it. 14 But small is the gate and nar-
row the road that leads to life, and only a few
find it.

True and False Prophets

15 "Watch out for false prophets. They
come to you in sheep's clothing, but inward-
ly they are ferocious wolves. 16 By their fruit
you will recognize them. Do people pick
grapes from thornbushes, or figs from this-
tles? 17 Likewise, every good tree bears good
fruit, but a bad tree bears bad fruit. 18 A good
tree cannot bear bad fruit, and a bad tree
cannot bear good fruit. 19 Every tree that
does not bear good fruit is cut down and
thrown into the fire. 20 Thus, by their fruit
you will recognize them.

True and False Disciples

21 "Not everyone who says to me, 'Lord,
Lord,' will enter the kingdom of heaven, but
only the one who does the will of my Father
who is in heaven. 22 Many will say to me on
that day, 'Lord, Lord, did we not prophesy in
your name and in your name drive out de-
mons and in your name perform many mira-
cles?' 23 Then I will tell them plainly, 'I never
knew you. Away from me, you evildoers!'

The Wise and Foolish Builders

24 "Therefore everyone who hears these
words of mine and puts them into practice
is like a wise man who built his house on the
rock. 25 The rain came down, the streams
rose, and the winds blew and beat against
that house; yet it did not fall, because it had
its foundation on the rock. 26 But everyone
who hears these words of mine and does
not put them into practice is like a foolish
man who built his house on sand. 27 The rain
came down, the streams rose, and the winds
blew and beat against that house, and it fell
with a great crash."

28 When Jesus had finished saying these
things, the crowds were amazed at his teach-
ing, 29 because he taught as one who had au-
thority, and not as their teachers of the law.

Jesus Heals a Man With Leprosy

8 When Jesus came down from the moun-
tainside, large crowds followed him. 2 A
man with leprosy[a] came and knelt before
him and said, "Lord, if you are willing, you
can make me clean."
3 Jesus reached out his hand and touched
the man. "I am willing," he said. "Be clean!"
Immediately he was cleansed of his leprosy.
4 Then Jesus said to him, "See that you don't
tell anyone. But go, show yourself to the
priest and offer the gift Moses commanded,
as a testimony to them."

The Faith of the Centurion

5 When Jesus had entered Capernaum,
a centurion came to him, asking for help.
6 "Lord," he said, "my servant lies at home
paralyzed, suffering terribly."
7 Jesus said to him, "Shall I come and heal
him?"
8 The centurion replied, "Lord, I do not de-
serve to have you come under my roof. But
just say the word, and my servant will be
healed. 9 For I myself am a man under au-
thority, with soldiers under me. I tell this
one, 'Go,' and he goes; and that one, 'Come,'
and he comes. I say to my servant, 'Do this,'
and he does it."

[a] 2 The Greek word traditionally translated *leprosy* was used for various diseases affecting the skin.

10 When Jesus heard this, he was amazed
and said to those following him, "Truly I
tell you, I have not found anyone in Isra-
el with such great faith. 11 I say to you that
many will come from the east and the west,
and will take their places at the feast with
Abraham, Isaac and Jacob in the kingdom
of heaven. 12 But the subjects of the kingdom
will be thrown outside, into the darkness,
where there will be weeping and gnashing
of teeth."

13 Then Jesus said to the centurion, "Go!
Let it be done just as you believed it would."
And his servant was healed at that moment.

Jesus Heals Many

14 When Jesus came into Peter's house, he
saw Peter's mother-in-law lying in bed with
a fever. 15 He touched her hand and the fever
left her, and she got up and began to wait on
him.

16 When evening came, many who were
demon-possessed were brought to him,
and he drove out the spirits with a word and
healed all the sick. 17 This was to fulfill what
was spoken through the prophet Isaiah:

> "He took up our infirmities
> and bore our diseases."[a]

The Cost of Following Jesus

18 When Jesus saw the crowd around him,
he gave orders to cross to the other side of the
lake. 19 Then a teacher of the law came to him
and said, "Teacher, I will follow you wherev-
er you go."

20 Jesus replied, "Foxes have dens and
birds have nests, but the Son of Man has no
place to lay his head."

21 Another disciple said to him, "Lord, first
let me go and bury my father."

22 But Jesus told him, "Follow me, and let
the dead bury their own dead."

Jesus Calms the Storm

23 Then he got into the boat and his dis-
ciples followed him. 24 Suddenly a furious
storm came up on the lake, so that the waves
swept over the boat. But Jesus was sleeping.
25 The disciples went and woke him, saying,
"Lord, save us! We're going to drown!"

26 He replied, "You of little faith, why are
you so afraid?" Then he got up and rebuked
the winds and the waves, and it was com-
pletely calm.

27 The men were amazed and asked,
"What kind of man is this? Even the winds
and the waves obey him!"

Jesus Restores Two Demon-Possessed Men

28 When he arrived at the other side in the
region of the Gadarenes,[b] two demon-pos-
sessed men coming from the tombs met him.
They were so violent that no one could pass
that way. 29 "What do you want with us, Son
of God?" they shouted. "Have you come here
to torture us before the appointed time?"

30 Some distance from them a large herd
of pigs was feeding. 31 The demons begged
Jesus, "If you drive us out, send us into the
herd of pigs."

32 He said to them, "Go!" So they came out
and went into the pigs, and the whole herd
rushed down the steep bank into the lake
and died in the water. 33 Those tending the
pigs ran off, went into the town and reported
all this, including what had happened to the
demon-possessed men. 34 Then the whole
town went out to meet Jesus. And when they
saw him, they pleaded with him to leave
their region.

Jesus Forgives and Heals a Paralyzed Man

9 Jesus stepped into a boat, crossed over
and came to his own town. 2 Some men
brought to him a paralyzed man, lying on a
mat. When Jesus saw their faith, he said to
the man, "Take heart, son; your sins are for-
given."

3 At this, some of the teachers of the law
said to themselves, "This fellow is blas-
pheming!"

4 Knowing their thoughts, Jesus said,
"Why do you entertain evil thoughts in your
hearts? 5 Which is easier: to say, 'Your sins
are forgiven,' or to say, 'Get up and walk'?
6 But I want you to know that the Son of Man
has authority on earth to forgive sins." So he
said to the paralyzed man, "Get up, take your
mat and go home." 7 Then the man got up
and went home. 8 When the crowd saw this,
they were filled with awe; and they praised
God, who had given such authority to man.

[a] *17* Isaiah 53:4 (see Septuagint) [b] *28* Some manuscripts *Gergesenes;* other manuscripts *Gerasenes*

The Calling of Matthew

9 As Jesus went on from there, he saw a
man named Matthew sitting at the tax col-
lector's booth. "Follow me," he told him, and
Matthew got up and followed him.
10 While Jesus was having dinner at Mat-
thew's house, many tax collectors and sin-
ners came and ate with him and his disci-
ples. 11 When the Pharisees saw this, they
asked his disciples, "Why does your teacher
eat with tax collectors and sinners?"
12 On hearing this, Jesus said, "It is not
the healthy who need a doctor, but the sick.
13 But go and learn what this means: 'I desire
mercy, not sacrifice.'[a] For I have not come to
call the righteous, but sinners."

Jesus Questioned About Fasting

14 Then John's disciples came and asked
him, "How is it that we and the Pharisees fast
often, but your disciples do not fast?"
15 Jesus answered, "How can the guests
of the bridegroom mourn while he is with
them? The time will come when the bride-
groom will be taken from them; then they
will fast.
16 "No one sews a patch of unshrunk cloth
on an old garment, for the patch will pull
away from the garment, making the tear
worse. 17 Neither do people pour new wine
into old wineskins. If they do, the skins will
burst; the wine will run out and the wine-
skins will be ruined. No, they pour new
wine into new wineskins, and both are pre-
served."

Jesus Raises a Dead Girl and Heals a Sick Woman

18 While he was saying this, a synagogue
leader came and knelt before him and said,
"My daughter has just died. But come and
put your hand on her, and she will live."
19 Jesus got up and went with him, and so did
his disciples.
20 Just then a woman who had been sub-
ject to bleeding for twelve years came up be-
hind him and touched the edge of his cloak.
21 She said to herself, "If I only touch his
cloak, I will be healed."
22 Jesus turned and saw her. "Take heart,
daughter," he said, "your faith has healed
you." And the woman was healed at that mo-
ment.
23 When Jesus entered the synagogue
leader's house and saw the noisy crowd and
people playing pipes, 24 he said, "Go away.
The girl is not dead but asleep." But they
laughed at him. 25 After the crowd had been
put outside, he went in and took the girl by
the hand, and she got up. 26 News of this
spread through all that region.

Jesus Heals the Blind and the Mute

27 As Jesus went on from there, two blind
men followed him, calling out, "Have mercy
on us, Son of David!"
28 When he had gone indoors, the blind
men came to him, and he asked them, "Do
you believe that I am able to do this?"
"Yes, Lord," they replied.
29 Then he touched their eyes and said,
"According to your faith let it be done to you";
30 and their sight was restored. Jesus warned
them sternly, "See that no one knows about
this." 31 But they went out and spread the
news about him all over that region.
32 While they were going out, a man who
was demon-possessed and could not talk
was brought to Jesus. 33 And when the de-
mon was driven out, the man who had been
mute spoke. The crowd was amazed and
said, "Nothing like this has ever been seen
in Israel."
34 But the Pharisees said, "It is by the
prince of demons that he drives out demons."

The Workers Are Few

35 Jesus went through all the towns and
villages, teaching in their synagogues, pro-
claiming the good news of the kingdom and
healing every disease and sickness. 36 When
he saw the crowds, he had compassion on
them, because they were harassed and help-
less, like sheep without a shepherd. 37 Then
he said to his disciples, "The harvest is plen-
tiful but the workers are few. 38 Ask the Lord
of the harvest, therefore, to send out workers
into his harvest field."

Jesus Sends Out the Twelve

10 Jesus called his twelve disciples to
him and gave them authority to drive
out impure spirits and to heal every disease
and sickness.
2 These are the names of the twelve apos-
tles: first, Simon (who is called Peter) and

[a] 13 Hosea 6:6

his brother Andrew; James son of Zebedee,
and his brother John; 3 Philip and Bartholo-
mew; Thomas and Matthew the tax collec-
tor; James son of Alphaeus, and Thaddaeus;
4 Simon the Zealot and Judas Iscariot, who
betrayed him.

5 These twelve Jesus sent out with the fol-
lowing instructions: "Do not go among the
Gentiles or enter any town of the Samar-
itans. 6 Go rather to the lost sheep of Isra-
el. 7 As you go, proclaim this message: 'The
kingdom of heaven has come near.' 8 Heal
the sick, raise the dead, cleanse those who
have leprosy,[a] drive out demons. Freely you
have received; freely give.

9 "Do not get any gold or silver or copper to
take with you in your belts — 10 no bag for the
journey or extra shirt or sandals or a staff,
for the worker is worth his keep. 11 Whatev-
er town or village you enter, search there for
some worthy person and stay at their house
until you leave. 12 As you enter the home, give
it your greeting. 13 If the home is deserving,
let your peace rest on it; if it is not, let your
peace return to you. 14 If anyone will not wel-
come you or listen to your words, leave that
home or town and shake the dust off your
feet. 15 Truly I tell you, it will be more bear-
able for Sodom and Gomorrah on the day of
judgment than for that town.

16 "I am sending you out like sheep among
wolves. Therefore be as shrewd as snakes
and as innocent as doves. 17 Be on your
guard; you will be handed over to the local
councils and be flogged in the synagogues.
18 On my account you will be brought before
governors and kings as witnesses to them
and to the Gentiles. 19 But when they arrest
you, do not worry about what to say or how to
say it. At that time you will be given what to
say, 20 for it will not be you speaking, but the
Spirit of your Father speaking through you.

21 "Brother will betray brother to death,
and a father his child; children will rebel
against their parents and have them put to
death. 22 You will be hated by everyone be-
cause of me, but the one who stands firm to
the end will be saved. 23 When you are per-
secuted in one place, flee to another. Truly I
tell you, you will not finish going through the
towns of Israel before the Son of Man comes.

24 "The student is not above the teacher,
nor a servant above his master. 25 It is enough
for students to be like their teachers, and ser-
vants like their masters. If the head of the
house has been called Beelzebul, how much
more the members of his household!

26 "So do not be afraid of them, for there
is nothing concealed that will not be dis-
closed, or hidden that will not be made
known. 27 What I tell you in the dark, speak
in the daylight; what is whispered in your
ear, proclaim from the roofs. 28 Do not be
afraid of those who kill the body but can-
not kill the soul. Rather, be afraid of the One
who can destroy both soul and body in hell.
29 Are not two sparrows sold for a penny? Yet
not one of them will fall to the ground out-
side your Father's care.[b] 30 And even the very
hairs of your head are all numbered. 31 So
don't be afraid; you are worth more than
many sparrows.

32 "Whoever acknowledges me before oth-
ers, I will also acknowledge before my Fa-
ther in heaven. 33 But whoever disowns me
before others, I will disown before my Father
in heaven.

34 "Do not suppose that I have come to
bring peace to the earth. I did not come to
bring peace, but a sword. 35 For I have come
to turn

"'a man against his father,
a daughter against her mother,
a daughter-in-law against her mother-
in-law —
36 a man's enemies will be the members
of his own household.'[c]

37 "Anyone who loves their father or moth-
er more than me is not worthy of me; anyone
who loves their son or daughter more than
me is not worthy of me. 38 Whoever does not
take up their cross and follow me is not wor-
thy of me. 39 Whoever finds their life will lose
it, and whoever loses their life for my sake
will find it.

40 "Anyone who welcomes you welcomes
me, and anyone who welcomes me wel-
comes the one who sent me. 41 Whoever wel-
comes a prophet as a prophet will receive a
prophet's reward, and whoever welcomes a
righteous person as a righteous person will
receive a righteous person's reward. 42 And if

[a] *8* The Greek word traditionally translated *leprosy* was used for various diseases affecting the skin.
[b] *29* Or *will*; or *knowledge* [c] *36* Micah 7:6

anyone gives even a cup of cold water to one of these little ones who is my disciple, truly I tell you, that person will certainly not lose their reward."

Jesus and John the Baptist

11 After Jesus had finished instructing his twelve disciples, he went on from there to teach and preach in the towns of Galilee.[a]

2 When John, who was in prison, heard about the deeds of the Messiah, he sent his disciples 3 to ask him, "Are you the one who is to come, or should we expect someone else?"

4 Jesus replied, "Go back and report to John what you hear and see: 5 The blind receive sight, the lame walk, those who have leprosy[b] are cleansed, the deaf hear, the dead are raised, and the good news is proclaimed to the poor. 6 Blessed is anyone who does not stumble on account of me."

7 As John's disciples were leaving, Jesus began to speak to the crowd about John: "What did you go out into the wilderness to see? A reed swayed by the wind? 8 If not, what did you go out to see? A man dressed in fine clothes? No, those who wear fine clothes are in kings' palaces. 9 Then what did you go out to see? A prophet? Yes, I tell you, and more than a prophet. 10 This is the one about whom it is written:

"'I will send my messenger ahead
of you,
who will prepare your way
before you.'[c]

11 Truly I tell you, among those born of women there has not risen anyone greater than John the Baptist; yet whoever is least in the kingdom of heaven is greater than he. 12 From the days of John the Baptist until now, the kingdom of heaven has been subjected to violence,[d] and violent people have been raiding it. 13 For all the Prophets and the Law prophesied until John. 14 And if you are willing to accept it, he is the Elijah who was to come. 15 Whoever has ears, let them hear.

16 "To what can I compare this generation? They are like children sitting in the marketplaces and calling out to others:

17 "'We played the pipe for you,
and you did not dance;
we sang a dirge,
and you did not mourn.'

18 For John came neither eating nor drinking, and they say, 'He has a demon.' 19 The Son of Man came eating and drinking, and they say, 'Here is a glutton and a drunkard, a friend of tax collectors and sinners.' But wisdom is proved right by her deeds."

Woe on Unrepentant Towns

20 Then Jesus began to denounce the towns in which most of his miracles had been performed, because they did not repent. 21 "Woe to you, Chorazin! Woe to you, Bethsaida! For if the miracles that were performed in you had been performed in Tyre and Sidon, they would have repented long ago in sackcloth and ashes. 22 But I tell you, it will be more bearable for Tyre and Sidon on the day of judgment than for you. 23 And you, Capernaum, will you be lifted to the heavens? No, you will go down to Hades.[e] For if the miracles that were performed in you had been performed in Sodom, it would have remained to this day. 24 But I tell you that it will be more bearable for Sodom on the day of judgment than for you."

The Father Revealed in the Son

25 At that time Jesus said, "I praise you, Father, Lord of heaven and earth, because you have hidden these things from the wise and learned, and revealed them to little children. 26 Yes, Father, for this is what you were pleased to do.

27 "All things have been committed to me by my Father. No one knows the Son except the Father, and no one knows the Father except the Son and those to whom the Son chooses to reveal him.

28 "Come to me, all you who are weary and burdened, and I will give you rest. 29 Take my yoke upon you and learn from me, for I am gentle and humble in heart, and you will find rest for your souls. 30 For my yoke is easy and my burden is light."

Jesus Is Lord of the Sabbath

12 At that time Jesus went through the grainfields on the Sabbath. His disciples were hungry and began to pick some heads of grain and eat them. 2 When the

[a] *1* Greek *in their towns* [b] *5* The Greek word traditionally translated *leprosy* was used for various diseases affecting the skin. [c] *10* Mal. 3:1 [d] *12* Or *been forcefully advancing* [e] *23* That is, the realm of the dead

Pharisees saw this, they said to him, "Look!
Your disciples are doing what is unlawful on
the Sabbath."
3He answered, "Haven't you read what
David did when he and his companions were
hungry? 4He entered the house of God, and
he and his companions ate the consecrated
bread — which was not lawful for them to do,
but only for the priests. 5Or haven't you read
in the Law that the priests on Sabbath duty in
the temple desecrate the Sabbath and yet are
innocent? 6I tell you that something greater
than the temple is here. 7If you had known
what these words mean, 'I desire mercy, not
sacrifice,'[a] you would not have condemned
the innocent. 8For the Son of Man is Lord of
the Sabbath."
9Going on from that place, he went into
their synagogue, 10and a man with a shriv-
eled hand was there. Looking for a reason to
bring charges against Jesus, they asked him,
"Is it lawful to heal on the Sabbath?"
11He said to them, "If any of you has a
sheep and it falls into a pit on the Sabbath,
will you not take hold of it and lift it out?
12How much more valuable is a person than
a sheep! Therefore it is lawful to do good on
the Sabbath."
13Then he said to the man, "Stretch out
your hand." So he stretched it out and it was
completely restored, just as sound as the
other. 14But the Pharisees went out and plot-
ted how they might kill Jesus.

God's Chosen Servant

15Aware of this, Jesus withdrew from that
place. A large crowd followed him, and he
healed all who were ill. 16He warned them
not to tell others about him. 17This was to
fulfill what was spoken through the proph-
et Isaiah:

18 "Here is my servant whom I have chosen,
the one I love, in whom I delight;
I will put my Spirit on him,
and he will proclaim justice to the
nations.
19 He will not quarrel or cry out;
no one will hear his voice in the
streets.
20 A bruised reed he will not break,
and a smoldering wick he will not
snuff out,
till he has brought justice through to
victory.
21 In his name the nations will put
their hope."[b]

Jesus and Beelzebul

22Then they brought him a demon-pos-
sessed man who was blind and mute, and
Jesus healed him, so that he could both talk
and see. 23All the people were astonished
and said, "Could this be the Son of David?"
24But when the Pharisees heard this, they
said, "It is only by Beelzebul, the prince of
demons, that this fellow drives out demons."
25Jesus knew their thoughts and said to
them, "Every kingdom divided against itself
will be ruined, and every city or household
divided against itself will not stand. 26If Sa-
tan drives out Satan, he is divided against
himself. How then can his kingdom stand?
27And if I drive out demons by Beelzebul,
by whom do your people drive them out?
So then, they will be your judges. 28But if
it is by the Spirit of God that I drive out de-
mons, then the kingdom of God has come
upon you.
29"Or again, how can anyone enter a
strong man's house and carry off his posses-
sions unless he first ties up the strong man?
Then he can plunder his house.
30"Whoever is not with me is against me,
and whoever does not gather with me scat-
ters. 31And so I tell you, every kind of sin
and slander can be forgiven, but blasphe-
my against the Spirit will not be forgiven.
32Anyone who speaks a word against the
Son of Man will be forgiven, but anyone
who speaks against the Holy Spirit will not
be forgiven, either in this age or in the age
to come.
33"Make a tree good and its fruit will be
good, or make a tree bad and its fruit will be
bad, for a tree is recognized by its fruit. 34You
brood of vipers, how can you who are evil
say anything good? For the mouth speaks
what the heart is full of. 35A good man brings
good things out of the good stored up in him,
and an evil man brings evil things out of the
evil stored up in him. 36But I tell you that
everyone will have to give account on the
day of judgment for every empty word they
have spoken. 37For by your words you will

[a] *7* Hosea 6:6 [b] *21* Isaiah 42:1-4

be acquitted, and by your words you will be
condemned."

The Sign of Jonah

38 Then some of the Pharisees and teach-
ers of the law said to him, "Teacher, we want
to see a sign from you."

39 He answered, "A wicked and adulter-
ous generation asks for a sign! But none will
be given it except the sign of the prophet Jo-
nah. 40 For as Jonah was three days and three
nights in the belly of a huge fish, so the Son
of Man will be three days and three nights in
the heart of the earth. 41 The men of Nineveh
will stand up at the judgment with this gen-
eration and condemn it; for they repented at
the preaching of Jonah, and now something
greater than Jonah is here. 42 The Queen of
the South will rise at the judgment with this
generation and condemn it; for she came
from the ends of the earth to listen to Solo-
mon's wisdom, and now something greater
than Solomon is here.

43 "When an impure spirit comes out of a
person, it goes through arid places seeking
rest and does not find it. 44 Then it says, 'I will
return to the house I left.' When it arrives,
it finds the house unoccupied, swept clean
and put in order. 45 Then it goes and takes
with it seven other spirits more wicked than
itself, and they go in and live there. And the
final condition of that person is worse than
the first. That is how it will be with this wick-
ed generation."

Jesus' Mother and Brothers

46 While Jesus was still talking to the
crowd, his mother and brothers stood out-
side, wanting to speak to him. 47 Someone
told him, "Your mother and brothers are
standing outside, wanting to speak to you."

48 He replied to him, "Who is my mother,
and who are my brothers?" 49 Pointing to his
disciples, he said, "Here are my mother and
my brothers. 50 For whoever does the will of
my Father in heaven is my brother and sister
and mother."

The Parable of the Sower

13 That same day Jesus went out of the
house and sat by the lake. 2 Such
large crowds gathered around him that he
got into a boat and sat in it, while all the peo-
ple stood on the shore. 3 Then he told them
many things in parables, saying: "A farmer
went out to sow his seed. 4 As he was scatter-
ing the seed, some fell along the path, and
the birds came and ate it up. 5 Some fell on
rocky places, where it did not have much
soil. It sprang up quickly, because the soil
was shallow. 6 But when the sun came up,
the plants were scorched, and they withered
because they had no root. 7 Other seed fell
among thorns, which grew up and choked
the plants. 8 Still other seed fell on good soil,
where it produced a crop — a hundred, six-
ty or thirty times what was sown. 9 Whoever
has ears, let them hear."

10 The disciples came to him and asked,
"Why do you speak to the people in para-
bles?"

11 He replied, "Because the knowledge of
the secrets of the kingdom of heaven has
been given to you, but not to them. 12 Who-
ever has will be given more, and they will
have an abundance. Whoever does not have,
even what they have will be taken from
them. 13 This is why I speak to them in par-
ables:

"Though seeing, they do not see;
though hearing, they do not hear or
understand.

14 In them is fulfilled the prophecy of Isaiah:

" 'You will be ever hearing but never
understanding;
you will be ever seeing but never
perceiving.
15 For this people's heart has become
calloused;
they hardly hear with their ears,
and they have closed their eyes.
Otherwise they might see with their eyes,
hear with their ears,
understand with their hearts
and turn, and I would heal them.'[a]

16 But blessed are your eyes because they see,
and your ears because they hear. 17 For truly
I tell you, many prophets and righteous peo-
ple longed to see what you see but did not
see it, and to hear what you hear but did not
hear it.

[a] *15* Isaiah 6:9,10 (see Septuagint)

18 “Listen then to what the parable of
the sower means: 19 When anyone hears
the message about the kingdom and does
not understand it, the evil one comes and
snatches away what was sown in their heart.
This is the seed sown along the path. 20 The
seed falling on rocky ground refers to some-
one who hears the word and at once receives
it with joy. 21 But since they have no root, they
last only a short time. When trouble or per-
secution comes because of the word, they
quickly fall away. 22 The seed falling among
the thorns refers to someone who hears the
word, but the worries of this life and the de-
ceitfulness of wealth choke the word, mak-
ing it unfruitful. 23 But the seed falling on
good soil refers to someone who hears the
word and understands it. This is the one who
produces a crop, yielding a hundred, sixty or
thirty times what was sown.”

The Parable of the Weeds

24 Jesus told them another parable: “The
kingdom of heaven is like a man who sowed
good seed in his field. 25 But while everyone
was sleeping, his enemy came and sowed
weeds among the wheat, and went away.
26 When the wheat sprouted and formed
heads, then the weeds also appeared.

27 “The owner’s servants came to him and
said, ‘Sir, didn’t you sow good seed in your
field? Where then did the weeds come from?’

28 “ ‘An enemy did this,’ he replied.

“The servants asked him, ‘Do you want us
to go and pull them up?’

29 “ ‘No,’ he answered, ‘because while you
are pulling the weeds, you may uproot the
wheat with them. 30 Let both grow together
until the harvest. At that time I will tell the
harvesters: First collect the weeds and tie
them in bundles to be burned; then gather
the wheat and bring it into my barn.’ ”

The Parables of the Mustard Seed and the Yeast

31 He told them another parable: “The
kingdom of heaven is like a mustard seed,
which a man took and planted in his field.
32 Though it is the smallest of all seeds, yet
when it grows, it is the largest of garden
plants and becomes a tree, so that the birds
come and perch in its branches.”

33 He told them still another parable: “The
kingdom of heaven is like yeast that a woman
took and mixed into about sixty pounds[a] of
flour until it worked all through the dough.”

34 Jesus spoke all these things to the crowd
in parables; he did not say anything to them
without using a parable. 35 So was fulfilled
what was spoken through the prophet:

“I will open my mouth in parables,
I will utter things hidden since the
creation of the world.”[b]

The Parable of the Weeds Explained

36 Then he left the crowd and went into the
house. His disciples came to him and said,
“Explain to us the parable of the weeds in the
field.”

37 He answered, “The one who sowed the
good seed is the Son of Man. 38 The field is
the world, and the good seed stands for the
people of the kingdom. The weeds are the
people of the evil one, 39 and the enemy who
sows them is the devil. The harvest is the end
of the age, and the harvesters are angels.

40 “As the weeds are pulled up and burned
in the fire, so it will be at the end of the age.
41 The Son of Man will send out his angels,
and they will weed out of his kingdom ev-
erything that causes sin and all who do evil.
42 They will throw them into the blazing
furnace, where there will be weeping and
gnashing of teeth. 43 Then the righteous will
shine like the sun in the kingdom of their Fa-
ther. Whoever has ears, let them hear.

The Parables of the Hidden Treasure and the Pearl

44 “The kingdom of heaven is like treasure
hidden in a field. When a man found it, he
hid it again, and then in his joy went and sold
all he had and bought that field.

45 “Again, the kingdom of heaven is like a
merchant looking for fine pearls. 46 When he
found one of great value, he went away and
sold everything he had and bought it.

The Parable of the Net

47 “Once again, the kingdom of heaven
is like a net that was let down into the lake
and caught all kinds of fish. 48 When it was
full, the fishermen pulled it up on the shore.
Then they sat down and collected the good

[a] *33* Or about 27 kilograms [b] *35* Psalm 78:2

fish in baskets, but threw the bad away.
[49]This is how it will be at the end of the age.
The angels will come and separate the wick-
ed from the righteous [50]and throw them
into the blazing furnace, where there will be
weeping and gnashing of teeth.

[51]"Have you understood all these things?"
Jesus asked.

"Yes," they replied.

[52]He said to them, "Therefore every teach-
er of the law who has become a disciple in
the kingdom of heaven is like the owner of a
house who brings out of his storeroom new
treasures as well as old."

A Prophet Without Honor

[53]When Jesus had finished these para-
bles, he moved on from there. [54]Coming to
his hometown, he began teaching the people
in their synagogue, and they were amazed.
"Where did this man get this wisdom and
these miraculous powers?" they asked.
[55]"Isn't this the carpenter's son? Isn't his
mother's name Mary, and aren't his brothers
James, Joseph, Simon and Judas? [56]Aren't all
his sisters with us? Where then did this man
get all these things?" [57]And they took offense
at him.

But Jesus said to them, "A prophet is not without honor except in his own town and in his own home."

[58]And he did not do many miracles there because of their lack of faith.

John the Baptist Beheaded

14 At that time Herod the tetrarch heard
the reports about Jesus, [2]and he said
to his attendants, "This is John the Baptist;
he has risen from the dead! That is why miraculous powers are at work in him."

[3]Now Herod had arrested John and bound
him and put him in prison because of Hero-
dias, his brother Philip's wife, [4]for John had
been saying to him: "It is not lawful for you to
have her." [5]Herod wanted to kill John, but he
was afraid of the people, because they considered John a prophet.

[6]On Herod's birthday the daughter of He-
rodias danced for the guests and pleased
Herod so much [7]that he promised with
an oath to give her whatever she asked.
[8]Prompted by her mother, she said, "Give me
here on a platter the head of John the Bap-
tist." [9]The king was distressed, but because
of his oaths and his dinner guests, he or-
dered that her request be granted [10]and had
John beheaded in the prison. [11]His head was
brought in on a platter and given to the girl,
who carried it to her mother. [12]John's disci-
ples came and took his body and buried it.
Then they went and told Jesus.

Jesus Feeds the Five Thousand

[13]When Jesus heard what had happened,
he withdrew by boat privately to a solitary
place. Hearing of this, the crowds followed
him on foot from the towns. [14]When Jesus
landed and saw a large crowd, he had compassion on them and healed their sick.

[15]As evening approached, the disciples
came to him and said, "This is a remote
place, and it's already getting late. Send the
crowds away, so they can go to the villages
and buy themselves some food."

[16]Jesus replied, "They do not need to go
away. You give them something to eat."

[17]"We have here only five loaves of bread
and two fish," they answered.

[18]"Bring them here to me," he said. [19]And
he directed the people to sit down on the
grass. Taking the five loaves and the two fish
and looking up to heaven, he gave thanks
and broke the loaves. Then he gave them to
the disciples, and the disciples gave them
to the people. [20]They all ate and were satis-
fied, and the disciples picked up twelve bas-
ketfuls of broken pieces that were left over.
[21]The number of those who ate was about
five thousand men, besides women and children.

Jesus Walks on the Water

[22]Immediately Jesus made the disciples
get into the boat and go on ahead of him
to the other side, while he dismissed the
crowd. [23]After he had dismissed them, he
went up on a mountainside by himself to
pray. Later that night, he was there alone,
[24]and the boat was already a considerable
distance from land, buffeted by the waves
because the wind was against it.

[25]Shortly before dawn Jesus went out to
them, walking on the lake. [26]When the disci-
ples saw him walking on the lake, they were
terrified. "It's a ghost," they said, and cried
out in fear.

[27]But Jesus immediately said to them:
"Take courage! It is I. Don't be afraid."

28 “Lord, if it’s you,” Peter replied, “tell me
to come to you on the water.”
29 “Come,” he said.
Then Peter got down out of the boat,
walked on the water and came toward Jesus.
30 But when he saw the wind, he was afraid
and, beginning to sink, cried out, “Lord,
save me!”
31 Immediately Jesus reached out his hand
and caught him. “You of little faith,” he said,
“why did you doubt?”
32 And when they climbed into the boat,
the wind died down. 33 Then those who were
in the boat worshiped him, saying, “Truly
you are the Son of God.”
34 When they had crossed over, they land-
ed at Gennesaret. 35 And when the men of
that place recognized Jesus, they sent word
to all the surrounding country. People
brought all their sick to him 36 and begged
him to let the sick just touch the edge of his
cloak, and all who touched it were healed.

That Which Defiles

15 Then some Pharisees and teachers of
the law came to Jesus from Jerusalem
and asked, 2 “Why do your disciples break
the tradition of the elders? They don’t wash
their hands before they eat!”
3 Jesus replied, “And why do you break the
command of God for the sake of your tradi-
tion? 4 For God said, ‘Honor your father and
mother’[a] and ‘Anyone who curses their fa-
ther or mother is to be put to death.’[b] 5 But
you say that if anyone declares that what
might have been used to help their father or
mother is ‘devoted to God,’ 6 they are not to
‘honor their father or mother’ with it. Thus
you nullify the word of God for the sake of
your tradition. 7 You hypocrites! Isaiah was
right when he prophesied about you:

8 “ ‘These people honor me with their
lips,
but their hearts are far from me.
9 They worship me in vain;
their teachings are merely human
rules.’[c]”

10 Jesus called the crowd to him and said,
“Listen and understand. 11 What goes into
someone’s mouth does not defile them, but
what comes out of their mouth, that is what
defiles them.”
12 Then the disciples came to him and
asked, “Do you know that the Pharisees were
offended when they heard this?”
13 He replied, “Every plant that my heav-
enly Father has not planted will be pulled
up by the roots. 14 Leave them; they are blind
guides.[d] If the blind lead the blind, both will
fall into a pit.”
15 Peter said, “Explain the parable to us.”
16 “Are you still so dull?” Jesus asked them.
17 “Don’t you see that whatever enters the
mouth goes into the stomach and then out
of the body? 18 But the things that come out
of a person’s mouth come from the heart,
and these defile them. 19 For out of the heart
come evil thoughts — murder, adultery, sex-
ual immorality, theft, false testimony, slan-
der. 20 These are what defile a person; but
eating with unwashed hands does not defile
them.”

The Faith of a Canaanite Woman

21 Leaving that place, Jesus withdrew to
the region of Tyre and Sidon. 22 A Canaanite
woman from that vicinity came to him, cry-
ing out, “Lord, Son of David, have mercy on
me! My daughter is demon-possessed and
suffering terribly.”
23 Jesus did not answer a word. So his dis-
ciples came to him and urged him, “Send her
away, for she keeps crying out after us.”
24 He answered, “I was sent only to the lost
sheep of Israel.”
25 The woman came and knelt before him.
“Lord, help me!” she said.
26 He replied, “It is not right to take the
children’s bread and toss it to the dogs.”
27 “Yes it is, Lord,” she said. “Even the dogs
eat the crumbs that fall from their master’s
table.”
28 Then Jesus said to her, “Woman, you
have great faith! Your request is granted.”
And her daughter was healed at that mo-
ment.

Jesus Feeds the Four Thousand

29 Jesus left there and went along the Sea
of Galilee. Then he went up on a mountain-
side and sat down. 30 Great crowds came to

[a] *4* Exodus 20:12; Deut. 5:16 [b] *4* Exodus 21:17; Lev. 20:9 [c] *9* Isaiah 29:13 [d] *14* Some manuscripts *blind guides of the blind*

him, bringing the lame, the blind, the crip-
pled, the mute and many others, and laid
them at his feet; and he healed them. 31 The
people were amazed when they saw the
mute speaking, the crippled made well, the
lame walking and the blind seeing. And they
praised the God of Israel.
32 Jesus called his disciples to him and
said, "I have compassion for these people;
they have already been with me three days
and have nothing to eat. I do not want to
send them away hungry, or they may col-
lapse on the way."
33 His disciples answered, "Where could
we get enough bread in this remote place to
feed such a crowd?"
34 "How many loaves do you have?" Jesus
asked.
"Seven," they replied, "and a few small
fish."
35 He told the crowd to sit down on the
ground. 36 Then he took the seven loaves and
the fish, and when he had given thanks, he
broke them and gave them to the disciples,
and they in turn to the people. 37 They all
ate and were satisfied. Afterward the disci-
ples picked up seven basketfuls of broken
pieces that were left over. 38 The number of
those who ate was four thousand men, be-
sides women and children. 39 After Jesus had
sent the crowd away, he got into the boat and
went to the vicinity of Magadan.

The Demand for a Sign

16 The Pharisees and Sadducees came
to Jesus and tested him by asking
him to show them a sign from heaven.
2 He replied, "When evening comes, you
say, 'It will be fair weather, for the sky is
red,' 3 and in the morning, 'Today it will be
stormy, for the sky is red and overcast.' You
know how to interpret the appearance of the
sky, but you cannot interpret the signs of the
times.[a] 4 A wicked and adulterous generation
looks for a sign, but none will be given it ex-
cept the sign of Jonah." Jesus then left them
and went away.

The Yeast of the Pharisees and Sadducees

5 When they went across the lake, the dis-
ciples forgot to take bread. 6 "Be careful,"
Jesus said to them. "Be on your guard against
the yeast of the Pharisees and Sadducees."
7 They discussed this among themselves
and said, "It is because we didn't bring any
bread."
8 Aware of their discussion, Jesus asked,
"You of little faith, why are you talking
among yourselves about having no bread?
9 Do you still not understand? Don't you re-
member the five loaves for the five thousand,
and how many basketfuls you gathered? 10 Or
the seven loaves for the four thousand, and
how many basketfuls you gathered? 11 How
is it you don't understand that I was not talk-
ing to you about bread? But be on your guard
against the yeast of the Pharisees and Sad-
ducees." 12 Then they understood that he was
not telling them to guard against the yeast
used in bread, but against the teaching of the
Pharisees and Sadducees.

Peter Declares That Jesus Is the Messiah

13 When Jesus came to the region of Caesa-
rea Philippi, he asked his disciples, "Who do
people say the Son of Man is?"
14 They replied, "Some say John the Bap-
tist; others say Elijah; and still others, Jere-
miah or one of the prophets."
15 "But what about you?" he asked. "Who
do you say I am?"
16 Simon Peter answered, "You are the
Messiah, the Son of the living God."
17 Jesus replied, "Blessed are you, Simon
son of Jonah, for this was not revealed to you
by flesh and blood, but by my Father in heav-
en. 18 And I tell you that you are Peter,[b] and
on this rock I will build my church, and the
gates of Hades[c] will not overcome it. 19 I will
give you the keys of the kingdom of heaven;
whatever you bind on earth will be[d] bound
in heaven, and whatever you loose on earth
will be[d] loosed in heaven." 20 Then he or-
dered his disciples not to tell anyone that he
was the Messiah.

Jesus Predicts His Death

21 From that time on Jesus began to ex-
plain to his disciples that he must go to Jeru-
salem and suffer many things at the hands of
the elders, the chief priests and the teachers

[a] 2,3 Some early manuscripts do not have *When evening comes . . . of the times.* [b] 18 The Greek word for *Peter* means *rock.* [c] 18 That is, the realm of the dead [d] 19 Or *will have been*

of the law, and that he must be killed and on the third day be raised to life.

22 Peter took him aside and began to rebuke him. "Never, Lord!" he said. "This shall never happen to you!"

23 Jesus turned and said to Peter, "Get behind me, Satan! You are a stumbling block to me; you do not have in mind the concerns of God, but merely human concerns."

24 Then Jesus said to his disciples, "Whoever wants to be my disciple must deny themselves and take up their cross and follow me. 25 For whoever wants to save their life[a] will lose it, but whoever loses their life for me will find it. 26 What good will it be for someone to gain the whole world, yet forfeit their soul? Or what can anyone give in exchange for their soul? 27 For the Son of Man is going to come in his Father's glory with his angels, and then he will reward each person according to what they have done.

28 "Truly I tell you, some who are standing here will not taste death before they see the Son of Man coming in his kingdom."

The Transfiguration

17 After six days Jesus took with him Peter, James and John the brother of James, and led them up a high mountain by themselves. 2 There he was transfigured before them. His face shone like the sun, and his clothes became as white as the light. 3 Just then there appeared before them Moses and Elijah, talking with Jesus.

4 Peter said to Jesus, "Lord, it is good for us to be here. If you wish, I will put up three shelters — one for you, one for Moses and one for Elijah."

5 While he was still speaking, a bright cloud covered them, and a voice from the cloud said, "This is my Son, whom I love; with him I am well pleased. Listen to him!"

6 When the disciples heard this, they fell facedown to the ground, terrified. 7 But Jesus came and touched them. "Get up," he said. "Don't be afraid." 8 When they looked up, they saw no one except Jesus.

9 As they were coming down the mountain, Jesus instructed them, "Don't tell anyone what you have seen, until the Son of Man has been raised from the dead."

10 The disciples asked him, "Why then do the teachers of the law say that Elijah must come first?"

11 Jesus replied, "To be sure, Elijah comes and will restore all things. 12 But I tell you, Elijah has already come, and they did not recognize him, but have done to him everything they wished. In the same way the Son of Man is going to suffer at their hands." 13 Then the disciples understood that he was talking to them about John the Baptist.

Jesus Heals a Demon-Possessed Boy

14 When they came to the crowd, a man approached Jesus and knelt before him. 15 "Lord, have mercy on my son," he said. "He has seizures and is suffering greatly. He often falls into the fire or into the water. 16 I brought him to your disciples, but they could not heal him."

17 "You unbelieving and perverse generation," Jesus replied, "how long shall I stay with you? How long shall I put up with you? Bring the boy here to me." 18 Jesus rebuked the demon, and it came out of the boy, and he was healed at that moment.

19 Then the disciples came to Jesus in private and asked, "Why couldn't we drive it out?"

20 He replied, "Because you have so little faith. Truly I tell you, if you have faith as small as a mustard seed, you can say to this mountain, 'Move from here to there,' and it will move. Nothing will be impossible for you." [21][b]

Jesus Predicts His Death a Second Time

22 When they came together in Galilee, he said to them, "The Son of Man is going to be delivered into the hands of men. 23 They will kill him, and on the third day he will be raised to life." And the disciples were filled with grief.

The Temple Tax

24 After Jesus and his disciples arrived in Capernaum, the collectors of the two-drachma temple tax came to Peter and asked, "Doesn't your teacher pay the temple tax?"

25 "Yes, he does," he replied.

[a] *25* The Greek word means either *life* or *soul*; also in verse 26. [b] *21* Some manuscripts include here words similar to Mark 9:29.

When Peter came into the house, Jesus
was the first to speak. “What do you think,
Simon?” he asked. “From whom do the kings
of the earth collect duty and taxes — from
their own children or from others?”
26 “From others,” Peter answered.
“Then the children are exempt,” Jesus said
to him. 27 “But so that we may not cause of-
fense, go to the lake and throw out your line.
Take the first fish you catch; open its mouth
and you will find a four-drachma coin. Take
it and give it to them for my tax and yours.”

The Greatest in the Kingdom of Heaven

18 At that time the disciples came to
Jesus and asked, “Who, then, is the
greatest in the kingdom of heaven?”
2 He called a little child to him, and placed
the child among them. 3 And he said: “Truly I
tell you, unless you change and become like
little children, you will never enter the king-
dom of heaven. 4 Therefore, whoever takes
the lowly position of this child is the great-
est in the kingdom of heaven. 5 And whoever
welcomes one such child in my name wel-
comes me.

Causing to Stumble

6 “If anyone causes one of these little
ones — those who believe in me — to stum-
ble, it would be better for them to have a
large millstone hung around their neck and
to be drowned in the depths of the sea. 7 Woe
to the world because of the things that cause
people to stumble! Such things must come,
but woe to the person through whom they
come! 8 If your hand or your foot causes you
to stumble, cut it off and throw it away. It is
better for you to enter life maimed or crip-
pled than to have two hands or two feet and
be thrown into eternal fire. 9 And if your
eye causes you to stumble, gouge it out and
throw it away. It is better for you to enter life
with one eye than to have two eyes and be
thrown into the fire of hell.

The Parable of the Wandering Sheep

10 “See that you do not despise one of these
little ones. For I tell you that their angels in
heaven always see the face of my Father in
heaven. [11][a]
12 “What do you think? If a man owns a
hundred sheep, and one of them wanders
away, will he not leave the ninety-nine on
the hills and go to look for the one that wan-
dered off? 13 And if he finds it, truly I tell you,
he is happier about that one sheep than
about the ninety-nine that did not wander
off. 14 In the same way your Father in heav-
en is not willing that any of these little ones
should perish.

Dealing With Sin in the Church

15 “If your brother or sister[b] sins,[c] go and
point out their fault, just between the two of
you. If they listen to you, you have won them
over. 16 But if they will not listen, take one or
two others along, so that ‘every matter may
be established by the testimony of two or
three witnesses.’[d] 17 If they still refuse to lis-
ten, tell it to the church; and if they refuse to
listen even to the church, treat them as you
would a pagan or a tax collector.
18 “Truly I tell you, whatever you bind on
earth will be[e] bound in heaven, and what-
ever you loose on earth will be[e] loosed in
heaven.
19 “Again, truly I tell you that if two of you
on earth agree about anything they ask for, it
will be done for them by my Father in heav-
en. 20 For where two or three gather in my
name, there am I with them.”

The Parable of the Unmerciful Servant

21 Then Peter came to Jesus and asked,
“Lord, how many times shall I forgive my
brother or sister who sins against me? Up to
seven times?”
22 Jesus answered, “I tell you, not seven
times, but seventy-seven times.[f]
23 “Therefore, the kingdom of heaven is
like a king who wanted to settle accounts
with his servants. 24 As he began the settle-
ment, a man who owed him ten thousand
bags of gold[g] was brought to him. 25 Since he
was not able to pay, the master ordered that
he and his wife and his children and all that
he had be sold to repay the debt.

[a] *11* Some manuscripts include here the words of Luke 19:10. [b] *15* The Greek word for *brother or sister* (*adelphos*) refers here to a fellow disciple, whether man or woman; also in verses 21 and 35. [c] *15* Some manuscripts *sins against you* [d] *16* Deut. 19:15 [e] *18* Or *will have been* [f] *22* Or *seventy times seven* [g] *24* Greek *ten thousand talents*; a talent was worth about 20 years of a day laborer's wages.

THY WORD

Amy Grant, Michael W. Smith

Thy Word is a lamp unto my feet
And a light unto my path
Thy Word is a lamp unto my feet
And a light unto my path

When I feel afraid
And I think I've lost my way
Still you're there right beside me
Nothing will I fear
As long as you are near
Please be near me to the end

I will not forget
Your love for me and yet
My heart forever is wandering
Jesus be my guide
And hold me to your side
I will love you to the end

THE INSPIRATION

Your word is a lamp for my feet, a light on my path.

— Psalm 119:105

BEHIND THE SONG

Amy Grant came to contemporary Christian music in the early 1980s with a fresh, youthful sound that became a favorite on Christian radio and even in many churches. Her 1984 album, *Straight Ahead*, featured a simple but lasting arrangement of Psalm 119:115 that both cemented the text of that passage into millions of people's memories and contextualized it with personal reflection. Its accessible melody and memorable phrasing made it a favorite chorus with many youth groups, college ministries and Sunday services. Even now, some 30 years later, it remains an incredibly popular song with an ever important message.

Grant's good friend and co-writer Michael W. Smith recalls the night the song was written while the two were working on her album. "One night Amy left the studio to go back to her cabin and got totally lost — and you don't want to get lost up there; there are bears and mountain lions around. So finally, she saw a lantern in a window and just kept stumbling towards the light until she walked right up to it and saw that it was her cabin." The experience inspired her to pen the entire song that night, artfully connecting the feeling of being lost in the woods with every Christian's need for the written Word of God as a light for their darkened path through life.

Selah

The secret to using the Bible effectively is really no secret at all. Psalm 119:11 tells us that the psalmist "[hid] God's word in his heart," and in Paul's second letter to Timothy, he instructs the young pastor to "correctly handle[s] the word of truth" (2 Timothy 2:15). The Scriptures, like any tool, must be worked with, put into practice and applied frequently if real skill in living them out is to be developed. We should not wait until we are in the dark to take advantage of this amazing light.

When life gets confusing, do you turn to the Word of God for guidance? Have you found the Bible to be a guiding light during a dark or confusing time in your life? Recall some of those times. How did knowing Scripture help you during those times?

26“At this the servant fell on his knees be-
fore him. ‘Be patient with me,’ he begged,
‘and I will pay back everything.’ 27The ser-
vant’s master took pity on him, canceled the
debt and let him go.

28“But when that servant went out, he
found one of his fellow servants who owed
him a hundred silver coins.[a] He grabbed
him and began to choke him. ‘Pay back what
you owe me!’ he demanded.

29“His fellow servant fell to his knees and
begged him, ‘Be patient with me, and I will
pay it back.’

30“But he refused. Instead, he went off
and had the man thrown into prison un-
til he could pay the debt. 31When the other
servants saw what had happened, they were
outraged and went and told their master ev-
erything that had happened.

32“Then the master called the servant in.
‘You wicked servant,’ he said, ‘I canceled all
that debt of yours because you begged me to.
33Shouldn’t you have had mercy on your fel-
low servant just as I had on you?’ 34In anger
his master handed him over to the jailers to
be tortured, until he should pay back all he
owed.

35“This is how my heavenly Father will
treat each of you unless you forgive your
brother or sister from your heart.”

Divorce

19 When Jesus had finished saying
these things, he left Galilee and went
into the region of Judea to the other side of
the Jordan. 2Large crowds followed him, and
he healed them there.

3Some Pharisees came to him to test him.
They asked, “Is it lawful for a man to divorce
his wife for any and every reason?”

4“Haven’t you read,” he replied, “that at
the beginning the Creator ‘made them male
and female,’[b] 5and said, ‘For this reason a
man will leave his father and mother and be
united to his wife, and the two will become
one flesh’[c]? 6So they are no longer two, but
one flesh. Therefore what God has joined to-
gether, let no one separate.”

7“Why then,” they asked, “did Moses com-
mand that a man give his wife a certificate of
divorce and send her away?”

8Jesus replied, “Moses permitted you to
divorce your wives because your hearts were
hard. But it was not this way from the begin-
ning. 9I tell you that anyone who divorces his
wife, except for sexual immorality, and mar-
ries another woman commits adultery.”

10The disciples said to him, “If this is the
situation between a husband and wife, it is
better not to marry.”

11Jesus replied, “Not everyone can accept
this word, but only those to whom it has been
given. 12For there are eunuchs who were
born that way, and there are eunuchs who
have been made eunuchs by others — and
there are those who choose to live like eu-
nuchs for the sake of the kingdom of heav-
en. The one who can accept this should ac-
cept it.”

The Little Children and Jesus

13Then people brought little children to
Jesus for him to place his hands on them
and pray for them. But the disciples rebuked
them.

14Jesus said, “Let the little children come
to me, and do not hinder them, for the king-
dom of heaven belongs to such as these.”
15When he had placed his hands on them, he
went on from there.

The Rich and the Kingdom of God

16Just then a man came up to Jesus and
asked, “Teacher, what good thing must I do
to get eternal life?”

17“Why do you ask me about what is
good?” Jesus replied. “There is only One who
is good. If you want to enter life, keep the
commandments.”

18“Which ones?” he inquired.

Jesus replied, “ ‘You shall not murder,
you shall not commit adultery, you shall
not steal, you shall not give false testimony,
19honor your father and mother,’[d] and ‘love
your neighbor as yourself.’[e]”

20“All these I have kept,” the young man
said. “What do I still lack?”

21Jesus answered, “If you want to be per-
fect, go, sell your possessions and give to the
poor, and you will have treasure in heaven.
Then come, follow me.”

22When the young man heard this, he
went away sad, because he had great wealth.

[a] *28* Greek *a hundred denarii*; a denarius was the usual daily wage of a day laborer (see 20:2).
[b] *4* Gen. 1:27 [c] *5* Gen. 2:24 [d] *19* Exodus 20:12-16; Deut. 5:16-20 [e] *19* Lev. 19:18

23Then Jesus said to his disciples, "Truly I
tell you, it is hard for someone who is rich to
enter the kingdom of heaven. 24Again I tell
you, it is easier for a camel to go through the
eye of a needle than for someone who is rich
to enter the kingdom of God."
25When the disciples heard this, they
were greatly astonished and asked, "Who
then can be saved?"
26Jesus looked at them and said, "With
man this is impossible, but with God all
things are possible."
27Peter answered him, "We have left ev-
erything to follow you! What then will there
be for us?"
28Jesus said to them, "Truly I tell you, at the
renewal of all things, when the Son of Man
sits on his glorious throne, you who have
followed me will also sit on twelve thrones,
judging the twelve tribes of Israel. 29And ev-
eryone who has left houses or brothers or sis-
ters or father or mother or wife[a] or children
or fields for my sake will receive a hundred
times as much and will inherit eternal life.
30But many who are first will be last, and
many who are last will be first.

The Parable of the Workers in the Vineyard

20 "For the kingdom of heaven is like a
landowner who went out early in the
morning to hire workers for his vineyard.
2He agreed to pay them a denarius[b] for the
day and sent them into his vineyard.
3"About nine in the morning he went out
and saw others standing in the marketplace
doing nothing. 4He told them, 'You also go
and work in my vineyard, and I will pay you
whatever is right.' 5So they went.
"He went out again about noon and about
three in the afternoon and did the same
thing. 6About five in the afternoon he went
out and found still others standing around.
He asked them, 'Why have you been stand-
ing here all day long doing nothing?'
7"'Because no one has hired us,' they an-
swered.
"He said to them, 'You also go and work in
my vineyard.'
8"When evening came, the owner of the
vineyard said to his foreman, 'Call the work-
ers and pay them their wages, beginning
with the last ones hired and going on to the
first.'
9"The workers who were hired about five
in the afternoon came and each received a
denarius. 10So when those came who were
hired first, they expected to receive more.
But each one of them also received a denar-
ius. 11When they received it, they began to
grumble against the landowner. 12'These
who were hired last worked only one hour,'
they said, 'and you have made them equal
to us who have borne the burden of the work
and the heat of the day.'
13"But he answered one of them, 'I am not
being unfair to you, friend. Didn't you agree
to work for a denarius? 14Take your pay and
go. I want to give the one who was hired last
the same as I gave you. 15Don't I have the
right to do what I want with my own money?
Or are you envious because I am generous?'
16"So the last will be first, and the first will
be last."

Jesus Predicts His Death a Third Time

17Now Jesus was going up to Jerusalem.
On the way, he took the Twelve aside and
said to them, 18"We are going up to Jerusa-
lem, and the Son of Man will be delivered
over to the chief priests and the teachers of
the law. They will condemn him to death
19and will hand him over to the Gentiles to
be mocked and flogged and crucified. On
the third day he will be raised to life!"

A Mother's Request

20Then the mother of Zebedee's sons
came to Jesus with her sons and, kneeling
down, asked a favor of him.
21"What is it you want?" he asked.
She said, "Grant that one of these two sons
of mine may sit at your right and the other at
your left in your kingdom."
22"You don't know what you are asking,"
Jesus said to them. "Can you drink the cup I
am going to drink?"
"We can," they answered.
23Jesus said to them, "You will indeed
drink from my cup, but to sit at my right or
left is not for me to grant. These places be-
long to those for whom they have been pre-
pared by my Father."

[a] 29 Some manuscripts do not have *or wife*. [b] 2 A denarius was the usual daily wage of a day laborer.

24 When the ten heard about this, they
were indignant with the two brothers.
25 Jesus called them together and said, "You
know that the rulers of the Gentiles lord
it over them, and their high officials exer-
cise authority over them. 26 Not so with you.
Instead, whoever wants to become great
among you must be your servant, 27 and who-
ever wants to be first must be your slave—
28 just as the Son of Man did not come to be
served, but to serve, and to give his life as a
ransom for many."

Two Blind Men Receive Sight

29 As Jesus and his disciples were leaving
Jericho, a large crowd followed him. 30 Two
blind men were sitting by the roadside, and
when they heard that Jesus was going by,
they shouted, "Lord, Son of David, have mer-
cy on us!"
31 The crowd rebuked them and told them
to be quiet, but they shouted all the louder,
"Lord, Son of David, have mercy on us!"
32 Jesus stopped and called them. "What
do you want me to do for you?" he asked.
33 "Lord," they answered, "we want our
sight."
34 Jesus had compassion on them and
touched their eyes. Immediately they re-
ceived their sight and followed him.

Jesus Comes to Jerusalem as King

21 As they approached Jerusalem and
came to Bethphage on the Mount of
Olives, Jesus sent two disciples, 2 saying to
them, "Go to the village ahead of you, and at
once you will find a donkey tied there, with
her colt by her. Untie them and bring them to
me. 3 If anyone says anything to you, say that
the Lord needs them, and he will send them
right away."
4 This took place to fulfill what was spoken
through the prophet:

5 "Say to Daughter Zion,
'See, your king comes to you,
gentle and riding on a donkey,
and on a colt, the foal of
a donkey.'"[a]

6 The disciples went and did as Jesus had
instructed them. 7 They brought the don-
key and the colt and placed their cloaks on
them for Jesus to sit on. 8 A very large crowd
spread their cloaks on the road, while others
cut branches from the trees and spread them
on the road. 9 The crowds that went ahead of
him and those that followed shouted,

"Hosanna[b] to the Son of David!"
"Blessed is he who comes in the name of
the Lord!"[c]
"Hosanna[b] in the highest heaven!"

10 When Jesus entered Jerusalem, the
whole city was stirred and asked, "Who is
this?"
11 The crowds answered, "This is Jesus,
the prophet from Nazareth in Galilee."

Jesus at the Temple

12 Jesus entered the temple courts and
drove out all who were buying and selling
there. He overturned the tables of the mon-
ey changers and the benches of those selling
doves. 13 "It is written," he said to them, "'My
house will be called a house of prayer,'[d] but
you are making it 'a den of robbers.'"[e]
14 The blind and the lame came to him at
the temple, and he healed them. 15 But when
the chief priests and the teachers of the law
saw the wonderful things he did and the
children shouting in the temple courts, "Ho-
sanna to the Son of David," they were indig-
nant.
16 "Do you hear what these children are
saying?" they asked him.
"Yes," replied Jesus, "have you never read,

"'From the lips of children and infants
you, Lord, have called forth your
praise'[f]?"

17 And he left them and went out of the city
to Bethany, where he spent the night.

Jesus Curses a Fig Tree

18 Early in the morning, as Jesus was on his
way back to the city, he was hungry. 19 See-
ing a fig tree by the road, he went up to it but
found nothing on it except leaves. Then he
said to it, "May you never bear fruit again!"
Immediately the tree withered.
20 When the disciples saw this, they were
amazed. "How did the fig tree wither so
quickly?" they asked.

[a] 5 Zech. 9:9 [b] 9 A Hebrew expression meaning "Save!" which became an exclamation of praise; also in verse 15 [c] 9 Psalm 118:25,26 [d] 13 Isaiah 56:7 [e] 13 Jer. 7:11 [f] 16 Psalm 8:2 (see Septuagint)

21 Jesus replied, "Truly I tell you, if you
have faith and do not doubt, not only can you
do what was done to the fig tree, but also you
can say to this mountain, 'Go, throw yourself
into the sea,' and it will be done. 22 If you be-
lieve, you will receive whatever you ask for
in prayer."

The Authority of Jesus Questioned

23 Jesus entered the temple courts, and,
while he was teaching, the chief priests and
the elders of the people came to him. "By what
authority are you doing these things?" they
asked. "And who gave you this authority?"
24 Jesus replied, "I will also ask you one
question. If you answer me, I will tell you
by what authority I am doing these things.
25 John's baptism — where did it come from?
Was it from heaven, or of human origin?"
They discussed it among themselves and
said, "If we say, 'From heaven,' he will ask,
'Then why didn't you believe him?' 26 But if
we say, 'Of human origin' — we are afraid of
the people, for they all hold that John was a
prophet."
27 So they answered Jesus, "We don't know."
Then he said, "Neither will I tell you by
what authority I am doing these things.

The Parable of the Two Sons

28 "What do you think? There was a man
who had two sons. He went to the first and
said, 'Son, go and work today in the vineyard.'
29 " 'I will not,' he answered, but later he
changed his mind and went.
30 "Then the father went to the other son
and said the same thing. He answered, 'I
will, sir,' but he did not go.
31 "Which of the two did what his father
wanted?"
"The first," they answered.
Jesus said to them, "Truly I tell you, the
tax collectors and the prostitutes are enter-
ing the kingdom of God ahead of you. 32 For
John came to you to show you the way of
righteousness, and you did not believe him,
but the tax collectors and the prostitutes did.
And even after you saw this, you did not re-
pent and believe him.

The Parable of the Tenants

33 "Listen to another parable: There was a
landowner who planted a vineyard. He put
a wall around it, dug a winepress in it and
built a watchtower. Then he rented the vine-
yard to some farmers and moved to another
place. 34 When the harvest time approached,
he sent his servants to the tenants to collect
his fruit.
35 "The tenants seized his servants; they
beat one, killed another, and stoned a third.
36 Then he sent other servants to them, more
than the first time, and the tenants treated
them the same way. 37 Last of all, he sent his
son to them. 'They will respect my son,' he
said.
38 "But when the tenants saw the son, they
said to each other, 'This is the heir. Come,
let's kill him and take his inheritance.' 39 So
they took him and threw him out of the vine-
yard and killed him.
40 "Therefore, when the owner of the vine-
yard comes, what will he do to those tenants?"
41 "He will bring those wretches to a
wretched end," they replied, "and he will
rent the vineyard to other tenants, who will
give him his share of the crop at harvest
time."
42 Jesus said to them, "Have you never read
in the Scriptures:

" 'The stone the builders rejected
has become the cornerstone;
the Lord has done this,
and it is marvelous in our eyes'[a]?

43 "Therefore I tell you that the kingdom of
God will be taken away from you and given
to a people who will produce its fruit. 44 Any-
one who falls on this stone will be broken
to pieces; anyone on whom it falls will be
crushed."[b]
45 When the chief priests and the Phar-
isees heard Jesus' parables, they knew he
was talking about them. 46 They looked for a
way to arrest him, but they were afraid of the
crowd because the people held that he was
a prophet.

The Parable of the Wedding Banquet

22 Jesus spoke to them again in para-
bles, saying: 2 "The kingdom of heav-
en is like a king who prepared a wedding
banquet for his son. 3 He sent his servants to
those who had been invited to the banquet to
tell them to come, but they refused to come.

[a] 42 Psalm 118:22,23 [b] 44 Some manuscripts do not have verse 44.

4"Then he sent some more servants and
said, 'Tell those who have been invited that
I have prepared my dinner: My oxen and
fattened cattle have been butchered, and
everything is ready. Come to the wedding
banquet.'
5"But they paid no attention and went
off — one to his field, another to his busi-
ness. 6The rest seized his servants, mistreat-
ed them and killed them. 7The king was en-
raged. He sent his army and destroyed those
murderers and burned their city.
8"Then he said to his servants, 'The wed-
ding banquet is ready, but those I invited
did not deserve to come. 9So go to the street
corners and invite to the banquet anyone
you find.' 10So the servants went out into
the streets and gathered all the people they
could find, the bad as well as the good, and
the wedding hall was filled with guests.
11"But when the king came in to see the
guests, he noticed a man there who was not
wearing wedding clothes. 12He asked, 'How
did you get in here without wedding clothes,
friend?' The man was speechless.
13"Then the king told the attendants, 'Tie
him hand and foot, and throw him outside,
into the darkness, where there will be weep-
ing and gnashing of teeth.'
14"For many are invited, but few are cho-
sen."

Paying the Imperial Tax to Caesar

15Then the Pharisees went out and laid
plans to trap him in his words. 16They sent
their disciples to him along with the Hero-
dians. "Teacher," they said, "we know that
you are a man of integrity and that you teach
the way of God in accordance with the truth.
You aren't swayed by others, because you
pay no attention to who they are. 17Tell us
then, what is your opinion? Is it right to pay
the imperial tax[a] to Caesar or not?"
18But Jesus, knowing their evil intent,
said, "You hypocrites, why are you trying to
trap me? 19Show me the coin used for pay-
ing the tax." They brought him a denarius,
20and he asked them, "Whose image is this?
And whose inscription?"
21"Caesar's," they replied.
Then he said to them, "So give back to Cae-
sar what is Caesar's, and to God what is God's."
22When they heard this, they were amazed.
So they left him and went away.

Marriage at the Resurrection

23That same day the Sadducees, who say
there is no resurrection, came to him with
a question. 24"Teacher," they said, "Moses
told us that if a man dies without having
children, his brother must marry the widow
and raise up offspring for him. 25Now there
were seven brothers among us. The first one
married and died, and since he had no chil-
dren, he left his wife to his brother. 26The
same thing happened to the second and
third brother, right on down to the seventh.
27Finally, the woman died. 28Now then, at
the resurrection, whose wife will she be of
the seven, since all of them were married to
her?"
29Jesus replied, "You are in error because
you do not know the Scriptures or the pow-
er of God. 30At the resurrection people will
neither marry nor be given in marriage; they
will be like the angels in heaven. 31But about
the resurrection of the dead — have you not
read what God said to you, 32'I am the God
of Abraham, the God of Isaac, and the God
of Jacob'[b]? He is not the God of the dead but
of the living."
33When the crowds heard this, they were
astonished at his teaching.

The Greatest Commandment

34Hearing that Jesus had silenced the Sad-
ducees, the Pharisees got together. 35One of
them, an expert in the law, tested him with
this question: 36"Teacher, which is the great-
est commandment in the Law?"
37Jesus replied: " 'Love the Lord your God
with all your heart and with all your soul
and with all your mind.'[c] 38This is the first
and greatest commandment. 39And the sec-
ond is like it: 'Love your neighbor as your-
self.'[d] 40All the Law and the Prophets hang
on these two commandments."

Whose Son Is the Messiah?

41While the Pharisees were gathered to-
gether, Jesus asked them, 42"What do you
think about the Messiah? Whose son is he?"
"The son of David," they replied.
43He said to them, "How is it then that

[a] *17* A special tax levied on subject peoples, not on Roman citizens [b] *32* Exodus 3:6 [c] *37* Deut. 6:5
[d] *39* Lev. 19:18

David, speaking by the Spirit, calls him
'Lord'? For he says,

44 " 'The Lord said to my Lord:
"Sit at my right hand
until I put your enemies
under your feet." '[a]

45 If then David calls him 'Lord,' how can he
be his son?" 46 No one could say a word in re-
ply, and from that day on no one dared to ask
him any more questions.

A Warning Against Hypocrisy

23 Then Jesus said to the crowds and to
his disciples: 2 "The teachers of the
law and the Pharisees sit in Moses' seat. 3 So
you must be careful to do everything they
tell you. But do not do what they do, for they
do not practice what they preach. 4 They tie
up heavy, cumbersome loads and put them
on other people's shoulders, but they them-
selves are not willing to lift a finger to move
them.

5 "Everything they do is done for people to
see: They make their phylacteries[b] wide and
the tassels on their garments long; 6 they
love the place of honor at banquets and the
most important seats in the synagogues;
7 they love to be greeted with respect in the
marketplaces and to be called 'Rabbi' by
others.

8 "But you are not to be called 'Rabbi,' for
you have one Teacher, and you are all broth-
ers. 9 And do not call anyone on earth 'fa-
ther,' for you have one Father, and he is in
heaven. 10 Nor are you to be called instruc-
tors, for you have one Instructor, the Mes-
siah. 11 The greatest among you will be your
servant. 12 For those who exalt themselves
will be humbled, and those who humble
themselves will be exalted.

Seven Woes on the Teachers of the Law and the Pharisees

13 "Woe to you, teachers of the law and
Pharisees, you hypocrites! You shut the door
of the kingdom of heaven in people's faces.
You yourselves do not enter, nor will you let
those enter who are trying to. [14][c]

15 "Woe to you, teachers of the law and
Pharisees, you hypocrites! You travel over
land and sea to win a single convert, and
when you have succeeded, you make them
twice as much a child of hell as you are.

16 "Woe to you, blind guides! You say, 'If
anyone swears by the temple, it means noth-
ing; but anyone who swears by the gold of
the temple is bound by that oath.' 17 You
blind fools! Which is greater: the gold, or the
temple that makes the gold sacred? 18 You
also say, 'If anyone swears by the altar, it
means nothing; but anyone who swears by
the gift on the altar is bound by that oath.'
19 You blind men! Which is greater: the gift,
or the altar that makes the gift sacred?
20 Therefore, anyone who swears by the altar
swears by it and by everything on it. 21 And
anyone who swears by the temple swears by
it and by the one who dwells in it. 22 And any-
one who swears by heaven swears by God's
throne and by the one who sits on it.

23 "Woe to you, teachers of the law and
Pharisees, you hypocrites! You give a tenth
of your spices—mint, dill and cumin. But
you have neglected the more important mat-
ters of the law—justice, mercy and faithful-
ness. You should have practiced the latter,
without neglecting the former. 24 You blind
guides! You strain out a gnat but swallow a
camel.

25 "Woe to you, teachers of the law and
Pharisees, you hypocrites! You clean the
outside of the cup and dish, but inside they
are full of greed and self-indulgence. 26 Blind
Pharisee! First clean the inside of the cup
and dish, and then the outside also will be
clean.

27 "Woe to you, teachers of the law and
Pharisees, you hypocrites! You are like
whitewashed tombs, which look beautiful
on the outside but on the inside are full of the
bones of the dead and everything unclean.
28 In the same way, on the outside you appear
to people as righteous but on the inside you
are full of hypocrisy and wickedness.

29 "Woe to you, teachers of the law and
Pharisees, you hypocrites! You build tombs
for the prophets and decorate the graves
of the righteous. 30 And you say, 'If we had
lived in the days of our ancestors, we would
not have taken part with them in shedding
the blood of the prophets.' 31 So you testify

[a] *44* Psalm 110:1 [b] *5* That is, boxes containing Scripture verses, worn on forehead and arm
[c] *14* Some manuscripts include here words similar to Mark 12:40 and Luke 20:47.

against yourselves that you are the descendants of those who murdered the prophets. [32]Go ahead, then, and complete what your ancestors started!

[33]"You snakes! You brood of vipers! How will you escape being condemned to hell? [34]Therefore I am sending you prophets and sages and teachers. Some of them you will kill and crucify; others you will flog in your synagogues and pursue from town to town. [35]And so upon you will come all the righteous blood that has been shed on earth, from the blood of righteous Abel to the blood of Zechariah son of Berekiah, whom you murdered between the temple and the altar. [36]Truly I tell you, all this will come on this generation.

[37]"Jerusalem, Jerusalem, you who kill the prophets and stone those sent to you, how often I have longed to gather your children together, as a hen gathers her chicks under her wings, and you were not willing. [38]Look, your house is left to you desolate. [39]For I tell you, you will not see me again until you say, 'Blessed is he who comes in the name of the Lord.'[a]"

The Destruction of the Temple and Signs of the End Times

24 Jesus left the temple and was walking away when his disciples came up to him to call his attention to its buildings. [2]"Do you see all these things?" he asked. "Truly I tell you, not one stone here will be left on another; every one will be thrown down."

[3]As Jesus was sitting on the Mount of Olives, the disciples came to him privately. "Tell us," they said, "when will this happen, and what will be the sign of your coming and of the end of the age?"

[4]Jesus answered: "Watch out that no one deceives you. [5]For many will come in my name, claiming, 'I am the Messiah,' and will deceive many. [6]You will hear of wars and rumors of wars, but see to it that you are not alarmed. Such things must happen, but the end is still to come. [7]Nation will rise against nation, and kingdom against kingdom. There will be famines and earthquakes in various places. [8]All these are the beginning of birth pains.

[9]"Then you will be handed over to be persecuted and put to death, and you will be hated by all nations because of me. [10]At that time many will turn away from the faith and will betray and hate each other, [11]and many false prophets will appear and deceive many people. [12]Because of the increase of wickedness, the love of most will grow cold, [13]but the one who stands firm to the end will be saved. [14]And this gospel of the kingdom will be preached in the whole world as a testimony to all nations, and then the end will come.

[15]"So when you see standing in the holy place 'the abomination that causes desolation,'[b] spoken of through the prophet Daniel—let the reader understand— [16]then let those who are in Judea flee to the mountains. [17]Let no one on the housetop go down to take anything out of the house. [18]Let no one in the field go back to get their cloak. [19]How dreadful it will be in those days for pregnant women and nursing mothers! [20]Pray that your flight will not take place in winter or on the Sabbath. [21]For then there will be great distress, unequaled from the beginning of the world until now—and never to be equaled again.

[22]"If those days had not been cut short, no one would survive, but for the sake of the elect those days will be shortened. [23]At that time if anyone says to you, 'Look, here is the Messiah!' or, 'There he is!' do not believe it. [24]For false messiahs and false prophets will appear and perform great signs and wonders to deceive, if possible, even the elect. [25]See, I have told you ahead of time.

[26]"So if anyone tells you, 'There he is, out in the wilderness,' do not go out; or, 'Here he is, in the inner rooms,' do not believe it. [27]For as lightning that comes from the east is visible even in the west, so will be the coming of the Son of Man. [28]Wherever there is a carcass, there the vultures will gather.

[29]"Immediately after the distress of those days

"'the sun will be darkened,
  and the moon will not give
    its light;
the stars will fall from the sky,
  and the heavenly bodies will be
    shaken.'[c]

[a] *39* Psalm 118:26 [b] *15* Daniel 9:27; 11:31; 12:11 [c] *29* Isaiah 13:10; 34:4

30 "Then will appear the sign of the Son of Man in heaven. And then all the peoples of the earth[a] will mourn when they see the Son of Man coming on the clouds of heaven, with power and great glory.[b] 31 And he will send his angels with a loud trumpet call, and they will gather his elect from the four winds, from one end of the heavens to the other.

32 "Now learn this lesson from the fig tree: As soon as its twigs get tender and its leaves come out, you know that summer is near. 33 Even so, when you see all these things, you know that it[c] is near, right at the door. 34 Truly I tell you, this generation will certainly not pass away until all these things have happened. 35 Heaven and earth will pass away, but my words will never pass away.

The Day and Hour Unknown

36 "But about that day or hour no one knows, not even the angels in heaven, nor the Son,[d] but only the Father. 37 As it was in the days of Noah, so it will be at the coming of the Son of Man. 38 For in the days before the flood, people were eating and drinking, marrying and giving in marriage, up to the day Noah entered the ark; 39 and they knew nothing about what would happen until the flood came and took them all away. That is how it will be at the coming of the Son of Man. 40 Two men will be in the field; one will be taken and the other left. 41 Two women will be grinding with a hand mill; one will be taken and the other left.

42 "Therefore keep watch, because you do not know on what day your Lord will come. 43 But understand this: If the owner of the house had known at what time of night the thief was coming, he would have kept watch and would not have let his house be broken into. 44 So you also must be ready, because the Son of Man will come at an hour when you do not expect him.

45 "Who then is the faithful and wise servant, whom the master has put in charge of the servants in his household to give them their food at the proper time? 46 It will be good for that servant whose master finds him doing so when he returns. 47 Truly I tell you, he will put him in charge of all his possessions. 48 But suppose that servant is wicked and says to himself, 'My master is staying away a long time,' 49 and he then begins to beat his fellow servants and to eat and drink with drunkards. 50 The master of that servant will come on a day when he does not expect him and at an hour he is not aware of. 51 He will cut him to pieces and assign him a place with the hypocrites, where there will be weeping and gnashing of teeth.

The Parable of the Ten Virgins

25 "At that time the kingdom of heaven will be like ten virgins who took their lamps and went out to meet the bridegroom. 2 Five of them were foolish and five were wise. 3 The foolish ones took their lamps but did not take any oil with them. 4 The wise ones, however, took oil in jars along with their lamps. 5 The bridegroom was a long time in coming, and they all became drowsy and fell asleep.

6 "At midnight the cry rang out: 'Here's the bridegroom! Come out to meet him!'

7 "Then all the virgins woke up and trimmed their lamps. 8 The foolish ones said to the wise, 'Give us some of your oil; our lamps are going out.'

9 "'No,' they replied, 'there may not be enough for both us and you. Instead, go to those who sell oil and buy some for yourselves.'

10 "But while they were on their way to buy the oil, the bridegroom arrived. The virgins who were ready went in with him to the wedding banquet. And the door was shut.

11 "Later the others also came. 'Lord, Lord,' they said, 'open the door for us!'

12 "But he replied, 'Truly I tell you, I don't know you.'

13 "Therefore keep watch, because you do not know the day or the hour.

The Parable of the Bags of Gold

14 "Again, it will be like a man going on a journey, who called his servants and entrusted his wealth to them. 15 To one he gave five bags of gold, to another two bags, and to another one bag,[e] each according to his ability. Then he went on his journey. 16 The man who had received five bags of gold went at once and put his money to work and gained five

[a] 30 Or *the tribes of the land* [b] 30 See Daniel 7:13-14. [c] 33 Or *he* [d] 36 Some manuscripts do not have *nor the Son.* [e] 15 Greek *five talents . . . two talents . . . one talent*; also throughout this parable; a talent was worth about 20 years of a day laborer's wage.

bags more. 17 So also, the one with two bags
of gold gained two more. 18 But the man who
had received one bag went off, dug a hole in
the ground and hid his master's money.
19 "After a long time the master of those
servants returned and settled accounts with
them. 20 The man who had received five bags
of gold brought the other five. 'Master,' he
said, 'you entrusted me with five bags of
gold. See, I have gained five more.'
21 "His master replied, 'Well done, good
and faithful servant! You have been faithful
with a few things; I will put you in charge of
many things. Come and share your master's
happiness!'
22 "The man with two bags of gold also
came. 'Master,' he said, 'you entrusted me
with two bags of gold; see, I have gained two
more.'
23 "His master replied, 'Well done, good
and faithful servant! You have been faithful
with a few things; I will put you in charge of
many things. Come and share your master's
happiness!'
24 "Then the man who had received one
bag of gold came. 'Master,' he said, 'I knew
that you are a hard man, harvesting where
you have not sown and gathering where
you have not scattered seed. 25 So I was
afraid and went out and hid your gold in the
ground. See, here is what belongs to you.'
26 "His master replied, 'You wicked, lazy
servant! So you knew that I harvest where I
have not sown and gather where I have not
scattered seed? 27 Well then, you should have
put my money on deposit with the bankers,
so that when I returned I would have re-
ceived it back with interest.
28 " 'So take the bag of gold from him and
give it to the one who has ten bags. 29 For
whoever has will be given more, and they
will have an abundance. Whoever does not
have, even what they have will be taken from
them. 30 And throw that worthless servant
outside, into the darkness, where there will
be weeping and gnashing of teeth.'

The Sheep and the Goats

31 "When the Son of Man comes in his glo-
ry, and all the angels with him, he will sit on
his glorious throne. 32 All the nations will be
gathered before him, and he will separate
the people one from another as a shepherd
separates the sheep from the goats. 33 He will
put the sheep on his right and the goats on
his left.
34 "Then the King will say to those on his
right, 'Come, you who are blessed by my Fa-
ther; take your inheritance, the kingdom
prepared for you since the creation of the
world. 35 For I was hungry and you gave me
something to eat, I was thirsty and you gave
me something to drink, I was a stranger and
you invited me in, 36 I needed clothes and
you clothed me, I was sick and you looked
after me, I was in prison and you came to
visit me.'
37 "Then the righteous will answer him,
'Lord, when did we see you hungry and feed
you, or thirsty and give you something to
drink? 38 When did we see you a stranger and
invite you in, or needing clothes and clothe
you? 39 When did we see you sick or in prison
and go to visit you?'
40 "The King will reply, 'Truly I tell you,
whatever you did for one of the least of these
brothers and sisters of mine, you did for me.'
41 "Then he will say to those on his left,
'Depart from me, you who are cursed, into
the eternal fire prepared for the devil and his
angels. 42 For I was hungry and you gave me
nothing to eat, I was thirsty and you gave me
nothing to drink, 43 I was a stranger and you
did not invite me in, I needed clothes and
you did not clothe me, I was sick and in pris-
on and you did not look after me.'
44 "They also will answer, 'Lord, when did
we see you hungry or thirsty or a stranger or
needing clothes or sick or in prison, and did
not help you?'
45 "He will reply, 'Truly I tell you, whatever
you did not do for one of the least of these,
you did not do for me.'
46 "Then they will go away to eternal pun-
ishment, but the righteous to eternal life."

The Plot Against Jesus

26 When Jesus had finished saying all
these things, he said to his disci-
ples, 2 "As you know, the Passover is two days
away—and the Son of Man will be handed
over to be crucified."
3 Then the chief priests and the elders of
the people assembled in the palace of the
high priest, whose name was Caiaphas, 4 and
they schemed to arrest Jesus secretly and kill
him. 5 "But not during the festival," they said,
"or there may be a riot among the people."

Jesus Anointed at Bethany

6 While Jesus was in Bethany in the home
of Simon the Leper, 7 a woman came to him
with an alabaster jar of very expensive per-
fume, which she poured on his head as he
was reclining at the table.
8 When the disciples saw this, they were
indignant. "Why this waste?" they asked.
9 "This perfume could have been sold at a
high price and the money given to the poor."
10 Aware of this, Jesus said to them, "Why
are you bothering this woman? She has done
a beautiful thing to me. 11 The poor you will
always have with you,[a] but you will not al-
ways have me. 12 When she poured this per-
fume on my body, she did it to prepare me
for burial. 13 Truly I tell you, wherever this
gospel is preached throughout the world,
what she has done will also be told, in mem-
ory of her."

Judas Agrees to Betray Jesus

14 Then one of the Twelve — the one called
Judas Iscariot — went to the chief priests
15 and asked, "What are you willing to give
me if I deliver him over to you?" So they
counted out for him thirty pieces of silver.
16 From then on Judas watched for an oppor-
tunity to hand him over.

The Last Supper

17 On the first day of the Festival of Unleav-
ened Bread, the disciples came to Jesus and
asked, "Where do you want us to make prep-
arations for you to eat the Passover?"
18 He replied, "Go into the city to a cer-
tain man and tell him, 'The Teacher says: My
appointed time is near. I am going to cele-
brate the Passover with my disciples at your
house.' " 19 So the disciples did as Jesus had
directed them and prepared the Passover.
20 When evening came, Jesus was reclin-
ing at the table with the Twelve. 21 And while
they were eating, he said, "Truly I tell you,
one of you will betray me."
22 They were very sad and began to say to
him one after the other, "Surely you don't
mean me, Lord?"
23 Jesus replied, "The one who has dipped
his hand into the bowl with me will betray
me. 24 The Son of Man will go just as it is writ-
ten about him. But woe to that man who be-
trays the Son of Man! It would be better for
him if he had not been born."
25 Then Judas, the one who would betray
him, said, "Surely you don't mean me, Rab-
bi?"
Jesus answered, "You have said so."
26 While they were eating, Jesus took
bread, and when he had given thanks, he
broke it and gave it to his disciples, saying,
"Take and eat; this is my body."
27 Then he took a cup, and when he had
given thanks, he gave it to them, saying,
"Drink from it, all of you. 28 This is my blood
of the[b] covenant, which is poured out for
many for the forgiveness of sins. 29 I tell you, I
will not drink from this fruit of the vine from
now on until that day when I drink it new
with you in my Father's kingdom."
30 When they had sung a hymn, they went
out to the Mount of Olives.

Jesus Predicts Peter's Denial

31 Then Jesus told them, "This very night
you will all fall away on account of me, for
it is written:

" 'I will strike the shepherd,
and the sheep of the flock will be
scattered.'[c]

32 But after I have risen, I will go ahead of you
into Galilee."
33 Peter replied, "Even if all fall away on
account of you, I never will."
34 "Truly I tell you," Jesus answered, "this
very night, before the rooster crows, you will
disown me three times."
35 But Peter declared, "Even if I have to die
with you, I will never disown you." And all
the other disciples said the same.

Gethsemane

36 Then Jesus went with his disciples to
a place called Gethsemane, and he said to
them, "Sit here while I go over there and
pray." 37 He took Peter and the two sons of
Zebedee along with him, and he began to
be sorrowful and troubled. 38 Then he said
to them, "My soul is overwhelmed with sor-
row to the point of death. Stay here and keep
watch with me."
39 Going a little farther, he fell with his face
to the ground and prayed, "My Father, if it is

[a] *11* See Deut. 15:11. [b] *28* Some manuscripts *the new* [c] *31* Zech. 13:7

possible, may this cup be taken from me. Yet not as I will, but as you will."

[40]Then he returned to his disciples and found them sleeping. "Couldn't you men keep watch with me for one hour?" he asked Peter. [41]"Watch and pray so that you will not fall into temptation. The spirit is willing, but the flesh is weak."

[42]He went away a second time and prayed, "My Father, if it is not possible for this cup to be taken away unless I drink it, may your will be done."

[43]When he came back, he again found them sleeping, because their eyes were heavy. [44]So he left them and went away once more and prayed the third time, saying the same thing.

[45]Then he returned to the disciples and said to them, "Are you still sleeping and resting? Look, the hour has come, and the Son of Man is delivered into the hands of sinners. [46]Rise! Let us go! Here comes my betrayer!"

Jesus Arrested

[47]While he was still speaking, Judas, one of the Twelve, arrived. With him was a large crowd armed with swords and clubs, sent from the chief priests and the elders of the people. [48]Now the betrayer had arranged a signal with them: "The one I kiss is the man; arrest him." [49]Going at once to Jesus, Judas said, "Greetings, Rabbi!" and kissed him.

[50]Jesus replied, "Do what you came for, friend."[a]

Then the men stepped forward, seized Jesus and arrested him. [51]With that, one of Jesus' companions reached for his sword, drew it out and struck the servant of the high priest, cutting off his ear.

[52]"Put your sword back in its place," Jesus said to him, "for all who draw the sword will die by the sword. [53]Do you think I cannot call on my Father, and he will at once put at my disposal more than twelve legions of angels? [54]But how then would the Scriptures be fulfilled that say it must happen in this way?"

[55]In that hour Jesus said to the crowd, "Am I leading a rebellion, that you have come out with swords and clubs to capture me? Every day I sat in the temple courts teaching, and you did not arrest me. [56]But this has all taken place that the writings of the prophets might be fulfilled." Then all the disciples deserted him and fled.

Jesus Before the Sanhedrin

[57]Those who had arrested Jesus took him to Caiaphas the high priest, where the teachers of the law and the elders had assembled. [58]But Peter followed him at a distance, right up to the courtyard of the high priest. He entered and sat down with the guards to see the outcome.

[59]The chief priests and the whole Sanhedrin were looking for false evidence against Jesus so that they could put him to death. [60]But they did not find any, though many false witnesses came forward.

Finally two came forward [61]and declared, "This fellow said, 'I am able to destroy the temple of God and rebuild it in three days.' "

[62]Then the high priest stood up and said to Jesus, "Are you not going to answer? What is this testimony that these men are bringing against you?" [63]But Jesus remained silent.

The high priest said to him, "I charge you under oath by the living God: Tell us if you are the Messiah, the Son of God."

[64]"You have said so," Jesus replied. "But I say to all of you: From now on you will see the Son of Man sitting at the right hand of the Mighty One and coming on the clouds of heaven."[b]

[65]Then the high priest tore his clothes and said, "He has spoken blasphemy! Why do we need any more witnesses? Look, now you have heard the blasphemy. [66]What do you think?"

"He is worthy of death," they answered.

[67]Then they spit in his face and struck him with their fists. Others slapped him [68]and said, "Prophesy to us, Messiah. Who hit you?"

Peter Disowns Jesus

[69]Now Peter was sitting out in the courtyard, and a servant girl came to him. "You also were with Jesus of Galilee," she said.

[70]But he denied it before them all. "I don't know what you're talking about," he said.

[71]Then he went out to the gateway, where another servant girl saw him and said to the people there, "This fellow was with Jesus of Nazareth."

[a] 50 Or *"Why have you come, friend?"* [b] 64 See Psalm 110:1; Daniel 7:13.

72 He denied it again, with an oath: "I don't know the man!"

73 After a little while, those standing there went up to Peter and said, "Surely you are one of them; your accent gives you away."

74 Then he began to call down curses, and he swore to them, "I don't know the man!"

Immediately a rooster crowed. 75 Then Peter remembered the word Jesus had spoken: "Before the rooster crows, you will disown me three times." And he went outside and wept bitterly.

Judas Hangs Himself

27 Early in the morning, all the chief priests and the elders of the people made their plans how to have Jesus executed. 2 So they bound him, led him away and handed him over to Pilate the governor.

3 When Judas, who had betrayed him, saw that Jesus was condemned, he was seized with remorse and returned the thirty pieces of silver to the chief priests and the elders. 4 "I have sinned," he said, "for I have betrayed innocent blood."

"What is that to us?" they replied. "That's your responsibility."

5 So Judas threw the money into the temple and left. Then he went away and hanged himself.

6 The chief priests picked up the coins and said, "It is against the law to put this into the treasury, since it is blood money." 7 So they decided to use the money to buy the potter's field as a burial place for foreigners. 8 That is why it has been called the Field of Blood to this day. 9 Then what was spoken by Jeremiah the prophet was fulfilled: "They took the thirty pieces of silver, the price set on him by the people of Israel, 10 and they used them to buy the potter's field, as the Lord commanded me."[a]

Jesus Before Pilate

11 Meanwhile Jesus stood before the governor, and the governor asked him, "Are you the king of the Jews?"

"You have said so," Jesus replied.

12 When he was accused by the chief priests and the elders, he gave no answer. 13 Then Pilate asked him, "Don't you hear the testimony they are bringing against you?" 14 But Jesus made no reply, not even to a single charge—to the great amazement of the governor.

15 Now it was the governor's custom at the festival to release a prisoner chosen by the crowd. 16 At that time they had a well-known prisoner whose name was Jesus[b] Barabbas. 17 So when the crowd had gathered, Pilate asked them, "Which one do you want me to release to you: Jesus Barabbas, or Jesus who is called the Messiah?" 18 For he knew it was out of self-interest that they had handed Jesus over to him.

19 While Pilate was sitting on the judge's seat, his wife sent him this message: "Don't have anything to do with that innocent man, for I have suffered a great deal today in a dream because of him."

20 But the chief priests and the elders persuaded the crowd to ask for Barabbas and to have Jesus executed.

21 "Which of the two do you want me to release to you?" asked the governor.

"Barabbas," they answered.

22 "What shall I do, then, with Jesus who is called the Messiah?" Pilate asked.

They all answered, "Crucify him!"

23 "Why? What crime has he committed?" asked Pilate.

But they shouted all the louder, "Crucify him!"

24 When Pilate saw that he was getting nowhere, but that instead an uproar was starting, he took water and washed his hands in front of the crowd. "I am innocent of this man's blood," he said. "It is your responsibility!"

25 All the people answered, "His blood is on us and on our children!"

26 Then he released Barabbas to them. But he had Jesus flogged, and handed him over to be crucified.

The Soldiers Mock Jesus

27 Then the governor's soldiers took Jesus into the Praetorium and gathered the whole company of soldiers around him. 28 They stripped him and put a scarlet robe on him, 29 and then twisted together a crown of thorns and set it on his head. They put a staff in his right hand. Then they knelt in front of him and mocked him. "Hail, king of the Jews!" they said. 30 They spit on him, and

[a] *10* See Zech. 11:12,13; Jer. 19:1-13; 32:6-9. [b] *16* Many manuscripts do not have *Jesus*; also in verse 17.

took the staff and struck him on the head
again and again. 31 After they had mocked
him, they took off the robe and put his own
clothes on him. Then they led him away to
crucify him.

The Crucifixion of Jesus

32 As they were going out, they met a
man from Cyrene, named Simon, and they
forced him to carry the cross. 33 They came
to a place called Golgotha (which means
"the place of the skull"). 34 There they of-
fered Jesus wine to drink, mixed with gall;
but after tasting it, he refused to drink it.
35 When they had crucified him, they divid-
ed up his clothes by casting lots. 36 And sit-
ting down, they kept watch over him there.
37 Above his head they placed the written
charge against him: THIS IS JESUS, THE KING
OF THE JEWS.

38 Two rebels were crucified with him,
one on his right and one on his left. 39 Those
who passed by hurled insults at him, shak-
ing their heads 40 and saying, "You who are
going to destroy the temple and build it in
three days, save yourself! Come down from
the cross, if you are the Son of God!" 41 In
the same way the chief priests, the teach-
ers of the law and the elders mocked him.
42 "He saved others," they said, "but he can't
save himself! He's the king of Israel! Let him
come down now from the cross, and we will
believe in him. 43 He trusts in God. Let God
rescue him now if he wants him, for he said,
'I am the Son of God.'" 44 In the same way
the rebels who were crucified with him also
heaped insults on him.

The Death of Jesus

45 From noon until three in the afternoon
darkness came over all the land. 46 About
three in the afternoon Jesus cried out in a
loud voice, *"Eli, Eli,*[a] *lema sabachthani?"*
(which means "My God, my God, why have
you forsaken me?").[b]

47 When some of those standing there
heard this, they said, "He's calling Elijah."

48 Immediately one of them ran and got a
sponge. He filled it with wine vinegar, put
it on a staff, and offered it to Jesus to drink.
49 The rest said, "Now leave him alone. Let's
see if Elijah comes to save him."

50 And when Jesus had cried out again in a
loud voice, he gave up his spirit.

51 At that moment the curtain of the tem-
ple was torn in two from top to bottom. The
earth shook, the rocks split 52 and the tombs
broke open. The bodies of many holy peo-
ple who had died were raised to life. 53 They
came out of the tombs after Jesus' resur-
rection and[c] went into the holy city and ap-
peared to many people.

54 When the centurion and those with
him who were guarding Jesus saw the earth-
quake and all that had happened, they were
terrified, and exclaimed, "Surely he was the
Son of God!"

55 Many women were there, watching from
a distance. They had followed Jesus from
Galilee to care for his needs. 56 Among them
were Mary Magdalene, Mary the mother of
James and Joseph,[d] and the mother of Zeb-
edee's sons.

The Burial of Jesus

57 As evening approached, there came
a rich man from Arimathea, named Jo-
seph, who had himself become a disciple of
Jesus. 58 Going to Pilate, he asked for Jesus'
body, and Pilate ordered that it be given to
him. 59 Joseph took the body, wrapped it in a
clean linen cloth, 60 and placed it in his own
new tomb that he had cut out of the rock. He
rolled a big stone in front of the entrance to
the tomb and went away. 61 Mary Magdalene
and the other Mary were sitting there oppo-
site the tomb.

The Guard at the Tomb

62 The next day, the one after Preparation
Day, the chief priests and the Pharisees went
to Pilate. 63 "Sir," they said, "we remember
that while he was still alive that deceiver
said, 'After three days I will rise again.' 64 So
give the order for the tomb to be made se-
cure until the third day. Otherwise, his dis-
ciples may come and steal the body and tell
the people that he has been raised from the
dead. This last deception will be worse than
the first."

65 "Take a guard," Pilate answered. "Go,
make the tomb as secure as you know how."
66 So they went and made the tomb secure by

[a] 46 Some manuscripts *Eloi, Eloi* [b] 46 Psalm 22:1 [c] 53 Or *tombs, and after Jesus' resurrection they*
[d] 56 Greek *Joses*, a variant of *Joseph*

putting a seal on the stone and posting the
guard.

Jesus Has Risen

28 After the Sabbath, at dawn on the first
day of the week, Mary Magdalene
and the other Mary went to look at the tomb.
[2]There was a violent earthquake, for an
angel of the Lord came down from heaven
and, going to the tomb, rolled back the stone
and sat on it. [3]His appearance was like light-
ning, and his clothes were white as snow.
[4]The guards were so afraid of him that they
shook and became like dead men.
[5]The angel said to the women, "Do not
be afraid, for I know that you are looking for
Jesus, who was crucified. [6]He is not here; he
has risen, just as he said. Come and see the
place where he lay. [7]Then go quickly and tell
his disciples: 'He has risen from the dead
and is going ahead of you into Galilee. There
you will see him.' Now I have told you."
[8]So the women hurried away from the
tomb, afraid yet filled with joy, and ran to
tell his disciples. [9]Suddenly Jesus met them.
"Greetings," he said. They came to him,
clasped his feet and worshiped him. [10]Then
Jesus said to them, "Do not be afraid. Go and
tell my brothers to go to Galilee; there they
will see me."

The Guards' Report

[11]While the women were on their way,
some of the guards went into the city and
reported to the chief priests everything that
had happened. [12]When the chief priests
had met with the elders and devised a plan,
they gave the soldiers a large sum of money,
[13]telling them, "You are to say, 'His disciples
came during the night and stole him away
while we were asleep.' [14]If this report gets to
the governor, we will satisfy him and keep
you out of trouble." [15]So the soldiers took the
money and did as they were instructed. And
this story has been widely circulated among
the Jews to this very day.

The Great Commission

[16]Then the eleven disciples went to Gal-
ilee, to the mountain where Jesus had told
them to go. [17]When they saw him, they
worshiped him; but some doubted. [18]Then
Jesus came to them and said, "All authori-
ty in heaven and on earth has been given to
me. [19]Therefore go and make disciples of all
nations, baptizing them in the name of the
Father and of the Son and of the Holy Spir-
it, [20]and teaching them to obey everything I
have commanded you. And surely I am with
you always, to the very end of the age."

MARK

John the Baptist Prepares the Way

1 The beginning of the good news about Jesus the Messiah,[a] the Son of God,[b] 2 as it is written in Isaiah the prophet:

> "I will send my messenger ahead of you,
> who will prepare your way"[c] —
> 3 "a voice of one calling in the wilderness,
> 'Prepare the way for the Lord,
> make straight paths for him.'"[d]

4 And so John the Baptist appeared in the wilderness, preaching a baptism of repentance for the forgiveness of sins. 5 The whole Judean countryside and all the people of Jerusalem went out to him. Confessing their sins, they were baptized by him in the Jordan River. 6 John wore clothing made of camel's hair, with a leather belt around his waist, and he ate locusts and wild honey. 7 And this was his message: "After me comes the one more powerful than I, the straps of whose sandals I am not worthy to stoop down and untie. 8 I baptize you with[e] water, but he will baptize you with[e] the Holy Spirit."

The Baptism and Testing of Jesus

9 At that time Jesus came from Nazareth in Galilee and was baptized by John in the Jordan. 10 Just as Jesus was coming up out of the water, he saw heaven being torn open and the Spirit descending on him like a dove. 11 And a voice came from heaven: "You are my Son, whom I love; with you I am well pleased."

12 At once the Spirit sent him out into the wilderness, 13 and he was in the wilderness forty days, being tempted[f] by Satan. He was with the wild animals, and angels attended him.

Jesus Announces the Good News

14 After John was put in prison, Jesus went into Galilee, proclaiming the good news of God. 15 "The time has come," he said. "The kingdom of God has come near. Repent and believe the good news!"

Jesus Calls His First Disciples

16 As Jesus walked beside the Sea of Galilee, he saw Simon and his brother Andrew casting a net into the lake, for they were fishermen. 17 "Come, follow me," Jesus said, "and I will send you out to fish for people." 18 At once they left their nets and followed him.

19 When he had gone a little farther, he saw James son of Zebedee and his brother John in a boat, preparing their nets. 20 Without delay he called them, and they left their father Zebedee in the boat with the hired men and followed him.

Jesus Drives Out an Impure Spirit

21 They went to Capernaum, and when the Sabbath came, Jesus went into the synagogue and began to teach. 22 The people were amazed at his teaching, because he taught them as one who had authority, not as the teachers of the law. 23 Just then a man in their synagogue who was possessed by an impure spirit cried out, 24 "What do you want with us, Jesus of Nazareth? Have you come to destroy us? I know who you are — the Holy One of God!"

25 "Be quiet!" said Jesus sternly. "Come out of him!" 26 The impure spirit shook the man violently and came out of him with a shriek.

27 The people were all so amazed that they asked each other, "What is this? A new teaching — and with authority! He even gives orders to impure spirits and they obey him." 28 News about him spread quickly over the whole region of Galilee.

Jesus Heals Many

29 As soon as they left the synagogue, they went with James and John to the home of

[a] *1* Or *Jesus Christ. Messiah* (Hebrew) and *Christ* (Greek) both mean *Anointed One.* [b] *1* Some manuscripts do not have *the Son of God.* [c] *2* Mal. 3:1 [d] *3* Isaiah 40:3 [e] *8* Or *in* [f] *13* The Greek for *tempted* can also mean *tested.*

Simon and Andrew. [30]Simon's mother-in-
law was in bed with a fever, and they imme-
diately told Jesus about her. [31]So he went to
her, took her hand and helped her up. The
fever left her and she began to wait on them.
[32]That evening after sunset the people
brought to Jesus all the sick and demon-
possessed. [33]The whole town gathered at
the door, [34]and Jesus healed many who had
various diseases. He also drove out many de-
mons, but he would not let the demons speak
because they knew who he was.

Jesus Prays in a Solitary Place

[35]Very early in the morning, while it was
still dark, Jesus got up, left the house and
went off to a solitary place, where he prayed.
[36]Simon and his companions went to look
for him, [37]and when they found him, they
exclaimed: "Everyone is looking for you!"
[38]Jesus replied, "Let us go somewhere
else — to the nearby villages — so I can preach
there also. That is why I have come." [39]So he
traveled throughout Galilee, preaching in
their synagogues and driving out demons.

Jesus Heals a Man With Leprosy

[40]A man with leprosy[a] came to him and
begged him on his knees, "If you are willing,
you can make me clean."
[41]Jesus was indignant.[b] He reached out
his hand and touched the man. "I am will-
ing," he said. "Be clean!" [42]Immediately the
leprosy left him and he was cleansed.
[43]Jesus sent him away at once with a
strong warning: [44]"See that you don't tell
this to anyone. But go, show yourself to the
priest and offer the sacrifices that Moses
commanded for your cleansing, as a testi-
mony to them." [45]Instead he went out and
began to talk freely, spreading the news. As
a result, Jesus could no longer enter a town
openly but stayed outside in lonely places.
Yet the people still came to him from every-
where.

Jesus Forgives and Heals a Paralyzed Man

2 A few days later, when Jesus again en-
tered Capernaum, the people heard that
he had come home. [2]They gathered in such
large numbers that there was no room left,
not even outside the door, and he preached
the word to them. [3]Some men came, bring-
ing to him a paralyzed man, carried by four
of them. [4]Since they could not get him to
Jesus because of the crowd, they made an
opening in the roof above Jesus by digging
through it and then lowered the mat the man
was lying on. [5]When Jesus saw their faith, he
said to the paralyzed man, "Son, your sins
are forgiven."
[6]Now some teachers of the law were sit-
ting there, thinking to themselves, [7]"Why
does this fellow talk like that? He's blas-
pheming! Who can forgive sins but God
alone?"
[8]Immediately Jesus knew in his spir-
it that this was what they were thinking in
their hearts, and he said to them, "Why are
you thinking these things? [9]Which is easi-
er: to say to this paralyzed man, 'Your sins
are forgiven,' or to say, 'Get up, take your mat
and walk'? [10]But I want you to know that the
Son of Man has authority on earth to forgive
sins." So he said to the man, [11]"I tell you, get
up, take your mat and go home." [12]He got up,
took his mat and walked out in full view of
them all. This amazed everyone and they
praised God, saying, "We have never seen
anything like this!"

Jesus Calls Levi and Eats With Sinners

[13]Once again Jesus went out beside the
lake. A large crowd came to him, and he be-
gan to teach them. [14]As he walked along, he
saw Levi son of Alphaeus sitting at the tax
collector's booth. "Follow me," Jesus told
him, and Levi got up and followed him.
[15]While Jesus was having dinner at Levi's
house, many tax collectors and sinners were
eating with him and his disciples, for there
were many who followed him. [16]When the
teachers of the law who were Pharisees saw
him eating with the sinners and tax collec-
tors, they asked his disciples: "Why does he
eat with tax collectors and sinners?"
[17]On hearing this, Jesus said to them, "It
is not the healthy who need a doctor, but the
sick. I have not come to call the righteous,
but sinners."

[a] 40 The Greek word traditionally translated *leprosy* was used for various diseases affecting the skin.
[b] 41 Many manuscripts *Jesus was filled with compassion*

Jesus Questioned About Fasting

[18]Now John's disciples and the Pharisees were fasting. Some people came and asked Jesus, "How is it that John's disciples and the disciples of the Pharisees are fasting, but yours are not?"

[19]Jesus answered, "How can the guests of the bridegroom fast while he is with them? They cannot, so long as they have him with them. [20]But the time will come when the bridegroom will be taken from them, and on that day they will fast.

[21]"No one sews a patch of unshrunk cloth on an old garment. Otherwise, the new piece will pull away from the old, making the tear worse. [22]And no one pours new wine into old wineskins. Otherwise, the wine will burst the skins, and both the wine and the wineskins will be ruined. No, they pour new wine into new wineskins."

Jesus Is Lord of the Sabbath

[23]One Sabbath Jesus was going through the grainfields, and as his disciples walked along, they began to pick some heads of grain. [24]The Pharisees said to him, "Look, why are they doing what is unlawful on the Sabbath?"

[25]He answered, "Have you never read what David did when he and his companions were hungry and in need? [26]In the days of Abiathar the high priest, he entered the house of God and ate the consecrated bread, which is lawful only for priests to eat. And he also gave some to his companions."

[27]Then he said to them, "The Sabbath was made for man, not man for the Sabbath. [28]So the Son of Man is Lord even of the Sabbath."

Jesus Heals on the Sabbath

3 Another time Jesus went into the synagogue, and a man with a shriveled hand was there. [2]Some of them were looking for a reason to accuse Jesus, so they watched him closely to see if he would heal him on the Sabbath. [3]Jesus said to the man with the shriveled hand, "Stand up in front of everyone."

[4]Then Jesus asked them, "Which is lawful on the Sabbath: to do good or to do evil, to save life or to kill?" But they remained silent.

[5]He looked around at them in anger and, deeply distressed at their stubborn hearts, said to the man, "Stretch out your hand." He stretched it out, and his hand was completely restored. [6]Then the Pharisees went out and began to plot with the Herodians how they might kill Jesus.

Crowds Follow Jesus

[7]Jesus withdrew with his disciples to the lake, and a large crowd from Galilee followed. [8]When they heard about all he was doing, many people came to him from Judea, Jerusalem, Idumea, and the regions across the Jordan and around Tyre and Sidon. [9]Because of the crowd he told his disciples to have a small boat ready for him, to keep the people from crowding him. [10]For he had healed many, so that those with diseases were pushing forward to touch him. [11]Whenever the impure spirits saw him, they fell down before him and cried out, "You are the Son of God." [12]But he gave them strict orders not to tell others about him.

Jesus Appoints the Twelve

[13]Jesus went up on a mountainside and called to him those he wanted, and they came to him. [14]He appointed twelve[a] that they might be with him and that he might send them out to preach [15]and to have authority to drive out demons. [16]These are the twelve he appointed: Simon (to whom he gave the name Peter), [17]James son of Zebedee and his brother John (to them he gave the name Boanerges, which means "sons of thunder"), [18]Andrew, Philip, Bartholomew, Matthew, Thomas, James son of Alphaeus, Thaddaeus, Simon the Zealot [19]and Judas Iscariot, who betrayed him.

Jesus Accused by His Family and by Teachers of the Law

[20]Then Jesus entered a house, and again a crowd gathered, so that he and his disciples were not even able to eat. [21]When his family[b] heard about this, they went to take charge of him, for they said, "He is out of his mind."

[22]And the teachers of the law who came down from Jerusalem said, "He is possessed by Beelzebul! By the prince of demons he is driving out demons."

[23]So Jesus called them over to him and

[a] 14 Some manuscripts *twelve — designating them apostles —* [b] 21 Or *his associates*

began to speak to them in parables: "How can Satan drive out Satan? 24If a kingdom is divided against itself, that kingdom cannot stand. 25If a house is divided against itself, that house cannot stand. 26And if Satan opposes himself and is divided, he cannot stand; his end has come. 27In fact, no one can enter a strong man's house without first tying him up. Then he can plunder the strong man's house. 28Truly I tell you, people can be forgiven all their sins and every slander they utter, 29but whoever blasphemes against the Holy Spirit will never be forgiven; they are guilty of an eternal sin."

30He said this because they were saying, "He has an impure spirit."

31Then Jesus' mother and brothers arrived. Standing outside, they sent someone in to call him. 32A crowd was sitting around him, and they told him, "Your mother and brothers are outside looking for you."

33"Who are my mother and my brothers?" he asked.

34Then he looked at those seated in a circle around him and said, "Here are my mother and my brothers! 35Whoever does God's will is my brother and sister and mother."

The Parable of the Sower

4 Again Jesus began to teach by the lake. The crowd that gathered around him was so large that he got into a boat and sat in it out on the lake, while all the people were along the shore at the water's edge. 2He taught them many things by parables, and in his teaching said: 3"Listen! A farmer went out to sow his seed. 4As he was scattering the seed, some fell along the path, and the birds came and ate it up. 5Some fell on rocky places, where it did not have much soil. It sprang up quickly, because the soil was shallow. 6But when the sun came up, the plants were scorched, and they withered because they had no root. 7Other seed fell among thorns, which grew up and choked the plants, so that they did not bear grain. 8Still other seed fell on good soil. It came up, grew and produced a crop, some multiplying thirty, some sixty, some a hundred times."

9Then Jesus said, "Whoever has ears to hear, let them hear."

10When he was alone, the Twelve and the others around him asked him about the parables. 11He told them, "The secret of the kingdom of God has been given to you. But to those on the outside everything is said in parables 12so that,

"'they may be ever seeing but never
perceiving,
and ever hearing but never
understanding;
otherwise they might turn and be
forgiven!'[a]"

13Then Jesus said to them, "Don't you understand this parable? How then will you understand any parable? 14The farmer sows the word. 15Some people are like seed along the path, where the word is sown. As soon as they hear it, Satan comes and takes away the word that was sown in them. 16Others, like seed sown on rocky places, hear the word and at once receive it with joy. 17But since they have no root, they last only a short time. When trouble or persecution comes because of the word, they quickly fall away. 18Still others, like seed sown among thorns, hear the word; 19but the worries of this life, the deceitfulness of wealth and the desires for other things come in and choke the word, making it unfruitful. 20Others, like seed sown on good soil, hear the word, accept it, and produce a crop—some thirty, some sixty, some a hundred times what was sown."

A Lamp on a Stand

21He said to them, "Do you bring in a lamp to put it under a bowl or a bed? Instead, don't you put it on its stand? 22For whatever is hidden is meant to be disclosed, and whatever is concealed is meant to be brought out into the open. 23If anyone has ears to hear, let them hear."

24"Consider carefully what you hear," he continued. "With the measure you use, it will be measured to you—and even more. 25Whoever has will be given more; whoever does not have, even what they have will be taken from them."

The Parable of the Growing Seed

26He also said, "This is what the kingdom of God is like. A man scatters seed on the ground 27Night and day, whether he sleeps

[a] 12 Isaiah 6:9,10

or gets up, the seed sprouts and grows, though he does not know how. [28]All by itself the soil produces grain — first the stalk, then the head, then the full kernel in the head. [29]As soon as the grain is ripe, he puts the sickle to it, because the harvest has come."

The Parable of the Mustard Seed

[30]Again he said, "What shall we say the kingdom of God is like, or what parable shall we use to describe it? [31]It is like a mustard seed, which is the smallest of all seeds on earth. [32]Yet when planted, it grows and becomes the largest of all garden plants, with such big branches that the birds can perch in its shade."

[33]With many similar parables Jesus spoke the word to them, as much as they could understand. [34]He did not say anything to them without using a parable. But when he was alone with his own disciples, he explained everything.

Jesus Calms the Storm

[35]That day when evening came, he said to his disciples, "Let us go over to the other side." [36]Leaving the crowd behind, they took him along, just as he was, in the boat. There were also other boats with him. [37]A furious squall came up, and the waves broke over the boat, so that it was nearly swamped. [38]Jesus was in the stern, sleeping on a cushion. The disciples woke him and said to him, "Teacher, don't you care if we drown?"

[39]He got up, rebuked the wind and said to the waves, "Quiet! Be still!" Then the wind died down and it was completely calm.

[40]He said to his disciples, "Why are you so afraid? Do you still have no faith?"

[41]They were terrified and asked each other, "Who is this? Even the wind and the waves obey him!"

Jesus Restores a Demon-Possessed Man

5 They went across the lake to the region of the Gerasenes.[a] [2]When Jesus got out of the boat, a man with an impure spirit came from the tombs to meet him. [3]This man lived in the tombs, and no one could bind him anymore, not even with a chain. [4]For he had often been chained hand and foot, but he tore the chains apart and broke the irons on his feet. No one was strong enough to subdue him. [5]Night and day among the tombs and in the hills he would cry out and cut himself with stones.

[6]When he saw Jesus from a distance, he ran and fell on his knees in front of him. [7]He shouted at the top of his voice, "What do you want with me, Jesus, Son of the Most High God? In God's name don't torture me!" [8]For Jesus had said to him, "Come out of this man, you impure spirit!"

[9]Then Jesus asked him, "What is your name?"

"My name is Legion," he replied, "for we are many." [10]And he begged Jesus again and again not to send them out of the area.

[11]A large herd of pigs was feeding on the nearby hillside. [12]The demons begged Jesus, "Send us among the pigs; allow us to go into them." [13]He gave them permission, and the impure spirits came out and went into the pigs. The herd, about two thousand in number, rushed down the steep bank into the lake and were drowned.

[14]Those tending the pigs ran off and reported this in the town and countryside, and the people went out to see what had happened. [15]When they came to Jesus, they saw the man who had been possessed by the legion of demons, sitting there, dressed and in his right mind; and they were afraid. [16]Those who had seen it told the people what had happened to the demon-possessed man — and told about the pigs as well. [17]Then the people began to plead with Jesus to leave their region.

[18]As Jesus was getting into the boat, the man who had been demon-possessed begged to go with him. [19]Jesus did not let him, but said, "Go home to your own people and tell them how much the Lord has done for you, and how he has had mercy on you." [20]So the man went away and began to tell in the Decapolis[b] how much Jesus had done for him. And all the people were amazed.

Jesus Raises a Dead Girl and Heals a Sick Woman

[21]When Jesus had again crossed over by boat to the other side of the lake, a large crowd gathered around him while he was by

[a] *1* Some manuscripts *Gadarenes;* other manuscripts *Gergesenes*
[b] *20* That is, the Ten Cities

the lake. [22]Then one of the synagogue leaders, named Jairus, came, and when he saw Jesus, he fell at his feet. [23]He pleaded earnestly with him, "My little daughter is dying. Please come and put your hands on her so that she will be healed and live." [24]So Jesus went with him.

A large crowd followed and pressed around him. [25]And a woman was there who had been subject to bleeding for twelve years. [26]She had suffered a great deal under the care of many doctors and had spent all she had, yet instead of getting better she grew worse. [27]When she heard about Jesus, she came up behind him in the crowd and touched his cloak, [28]because she thought, "If I just touch his clothes, I will be healed." [29]Immediately her bleeding stopped and she felt in her body that she was freed from her suffering.

[30]At once Jesus realized that power had gone out from him. He turned around in the crowd and asked, "Who touched my clothes?"

[31]"You see the people crowding against you," his disciples answered, "and yet you can ask, 'Who touched me?' "

[32]But Jesus kept looking around to see who had done it. [33]Then the woman, knowing what had happened to her, came and fell at his feet and, trembling with fear, told him the whole truth. [34]He said to her, "Daughter, your faith has healed you. Go in peace and be freed from your suffering."

[35]While Jesus was still speaking, some people came from the house of Jairus, the synagogue leader. "Your daughter is dead," they said. "Why bother the teacher anymore?"

[36]Overhearing[a] what they said, Jesus told him, "Don't be afraid; just believe."

[37]He did not let anyone follow him except Peter, James and John the brother of James. [38]When they came to the home of the synagogue leader, Jesus saw a commotion, with people crying and wailing loudly. [39]He went in and said to them, "Why all this commotion and wailing? The child is not dead but asleep." [40]But they laughed at him.

After he put them all out, he took the child's father and mother and the disciples who were with him, and went in where the child was. [41]He took her by the hand and said to her, *"Talitha koum!"* (which means "Little girl, I say to you, get up!"). [42]Immediately the girl stood up and began to walk around (she was twelve years old). At this they were completely astonished. [43]He gave strict orders not to let anyone know about this, and told them to give her something to eat.

A Prophet Without Honor

6 Jesus left there and went to his hometown, accompanied by his disciples. [2]When the Sabbath came, he began to teach in the synagogue, and many who heard him were amazed.

"Where did this man get these things?" they asked. "What's this wisdom that has been given him? What are these remarkable miracles he is performing? [3]Isn't this the carpenter? Isn't this Mary's son and the brother of James, Joseph,[b] Judas and Simon? Aren't his sisters here with us?" And they took offense at him.

[4]Jesus said to them, "A prophet is not without honor except in his own town, among his relatives and in his own home." [5]He could not do any miracles there, except lay his hands on a few sick people and heal them. [6]He was amazed at their lack of faith.

Jesus Sends Out the Twelve

Then Jesus went around teaching from village to village. [7]Calling the Twelve to him, he began to send them out two by two and gave them authority over impure spirits.

[8]These were his instructions: "Take nothing for the journey except a staff—no bread, no bag, no money in your belts. [9]Wear sandals but not an extra shirt. [10]Whenever you enter a house, stay there until you leave that town. [11]And if any place will not welcome you or listen to you, leave that place and shake the dust off your feet as a testimony against them."

[12]They went out and preached that people should repent. [13]They drove out many demons and anointed many sick people with oil and healed them.

John the Baptist Beheaded

[14]King Herod heard about this, for Jesus' name had become well known. Some were saying,[c] "John the Baptist has been raised

[a] 36 Or *Ignoring* [b] 3 Greek *Joses*, a variant of *Joseph* [c] 14 Some early manuscripts *He was saying*

from the dead, and that is why miraculous powers are at work in him."

15 Others said, "He is Elijah."

And still others claimed, "He is a prophet, like one of the prophets of long ago."

16 But when Herod heard this, he said, "John, whom I beheaded, has been raised from the dead!"

17 For Herod himself had given orders to have John arrested, and he had him bound and put in prison. He did this because of Herodias, his brother Philip's wife, whom he had married. 18 For John had been saying to Herod, "It is not lawful for you to have your brother's wife." 19 So Herodias nursed a grudge against John and wanted to kill him. But she was not able to, 20 because Herod feared John and protected him, knowing him to be a righteous and holy man. When Herod heard John, he was greatly puzzled[a]; yet he liked to listen to him.

21 Finally the opportune time came. On his birthday Herod gave a banquet for his high officials and military commanders and the leading men of Galilee. 22 When the daughter of[b] Herodias came in and danced, she pleased Herod and his dinner guests.

The king said to the girl, "Ask me for anything you want, and I'll give it to you." 23 And he promised her with an oath, "Whatever you ask I will give you, up to half my kingdom."

24 She went out and said to her mother, "What shall I ask for?"

"The head of John the Baptist," she answered.

25 At once the girl hurried in to the king with the request: "I want you to give me right now the head of John the Baptist on a platter."

26 The king was greatly distressed, but because of his oaths and his dinner guests, he did not want to refuse her. 27 So he immediately sent an executioner with orders to bring John's head. The man went, beheaded John in the prison, 28 and brought back his head on a platter. He presented it to the girl, and she gave it to her mother. 29 On hearing of this, John's disciples came and took his body and laid it in a tomb.

Jesus Feeds the Five Thousand

30 The apostles gathered around Jesus and reported to him all they had done and taught. 31 Then, because so many people were coming and going that they did not even have a chance to eat, he said to them, "Come with me by yourselves to a quiet place and get some rest."

32 So they went away by themselves in a boat to a solitary place. 33 But many who saw them leaving recognized them and ran on foot from all the towns and got there ahead of them. 34 When Jesus landed and saw a large crowd, he had compassion on them, because they were like sheep without a shepherd. So he began teaching them many things.

35 By this time it was late in the day, so his disciples came to him. "This is a remote place," they said, "and it's already very late. 36 Send the people away so that they can go to the surrounding countryside and villages and buy themselves something to eat."

37 But he answered, "You give them something to eat."

They said to him, "That would take more than half a year's wages[c]! Are we to go and spend that much on bread and give it to them to eat?"

38 "How many loaves do you have?" he asked. "Go and see."

When they found out, they said, "Five—and two fish."

39 Then Jesus directed them to have all the people sit down in groups on the green grass. 40 So they sat down in groups of hundreds and fifties. 41 Taking the five loaves and the two fish and looking up to heaven, he gave thanks and broke the loaves. Then he gave them to his disciples to distribute to the people. He also divided the two fish among them all. 42 They all ate and were satisfied, 43 and the disciples picked up twelve basketfuls of broken pieces of bread and fish. 44 The number of the men who had eaten was five thousand.

Jesus Walks on the Water

45 Immediately Jesus made his disciples get into the boat and go on ahead of him to Bethsaida, while he dismissed the crowd. 46 After leaving them, he went up on a mountainside to pray.

47 Later that night, the boat was in the middle of the lake, and he was alone on land. 48 He saw the disciples straining at the oars,

[a] 20 Some early manuscripts *he did many things*
[b] 22 Some early manuscripts *When his daughter*
[c] 37 Greek *take two hundred denarii*

because the wind was against them. Shortly before dawn he went out to them, walking on the lake. He was about to pass by them, [49]but when they saw him walking on the lake, they thought he was a ghost. They cried out, [50]because they all saw him and were terrified.

Immediately he spoke to them and said, "Take courage! It is I. Don't be afraid." [51]Then he climbed into the boat with them, and the wind died down. They were completely amazed, [52]for they had not understood about the loaves; their hearts were hardened.

[53]When they had crossed over, they landed at Gennesaret and anchored there. [54]As soon as they got out of the boat, people recognized Jesus. [55]They ran throughout that whole region and carried the sick on mats to wherever they heard he was. [56]And wherever he went—into villages, towns or countryside—they placed the sick in the marketplaces. They begged him to let them touch even the edge of his cloak, and all who touched it were healed.

That Which Defiles

7 The Pharisees and some of the teachers of the law who had come from Jerusalem gathered around Jesus [2]and saw some of his disciples eating food with hands that were defiled, that is, unwashed. [3](The Pharisees and all the Jews do not eat unless they give their hands a ceremonial washing, holding to the tradition of the elders. [4]When they come from the marketplace they do not eat unless they wash. And they observe many other traditions, such as the washing of cups, pitchers and kettles.[a])

[5]So the Pharisees and teachers of the law asked Jesus, "Why don't your disciples live according to the tradition of the elders instead of eating their food with defiled hands?"

[6]He replied, "Isaiah was right when he prophesied about you hypocrites; as it is written:

"'These people honor me with their lips,
but their hearts are far from me.
[7]They worship me in vain;
their teachings are merely human
rules.'[b]

[8]You have let go of the commands of God and are holding on to human traditions."

[9]And he continued, "You have a fine way of setting aside the commands of God in order to observe[c] your own traditions! [10]For Moses said, 'Honor your father and mother,'[d] and, 'Anyone who curses their father or mother is to be put to death.'[e] [11]But you say that if anyone declares that what might have been used to help their father or mother is Corban (that is, devoted to God)— [12]then you no longer let them do anything for their father or mother. [13]Thus you nullify the word of God by your tradition that you have handed down. And you do many things like that."

[14]Again Jesus called the crowd to him and said, "Listen to me, everyone, and understand this. [15]Nothing outside a person can defile them by going into them. Rather, it is what comes out of a person that defiles them." [16][f]

[17]After he had left the crowd and entered the house, his disciples asked him about this parable. [18]"Are you so dull?" he asked. "Don't you see that nothing that enters a person from the outside can defile them? [19]For it doesn't go into their heart but into their stomach, and then out of the body." (In saying this, Jesus declared all foods clean.)

[20]He went on: "What comes out of a person is what defiles them. [21]For it is from within, out of a person's heart, that evil thoughts come—sexual immorality, theft, murder, [22]adultery, greed, malice, deceit, lewdness, envy, slander, arrogance and folly. [23]All these evils come from inside and defile a person."

Jesus Honors a Syrophoenician Woman's Faith

[24]Jesus left that place and went to the vicinity of Tyre.[g] He entered a house and did not want anyone to know it; yet he could not keep his presence secret. [25]In fact, as soon as she heard about him, a woman whose little daughter was possessed by an impure spirit came and fell at his feet. [26]The woman was a Greek, born in Syrian Phoenicia. She begged Jesus to drive the demon out of her daughter.

[27]"First let the children eat all they want,"

[a] *4* Some early manuscripts *pitchers, kettles and dining couches* [b] *6,7* Isaiah 29:13 [c] *9* Some manuscripts *set up* [d] *10* Exodus 20:12; Deut. 5:16 [e] *10* Exodus 21:17; Lev. 20:9 [f] *16* Some manuscripts include here the words of 4:23. [g] *24* Many early manuscripts *Tyre and Sidon*

he told her, "for it is not right to take the chil-
dren's bread and toss it to the dogs."
28 "Lord," she replied, "even the dogs un-
der the table eat the children's crumbs."
29 Then he told her, "For such a reply, you
may go; the demon has left your daughter."
30 She went home and found her child ly-
ing on the bed, and the demon gone.

Jesus Heals a Deaf and Mute Man

31 Then Jesus left the vicinity of Tyre and
went through Sidon, down to the Sea of Gal-
ilee and into the region of the Decapolis.[a]
32 There some people brought to him a man
who was deaf and could hardly talk, and
they begged Jesus to place his hand on him.
33 After he took him aside, away from the
crowd, Jesus put his fingers into the man's
ears. Then he spit and touched the man's
tongue. 34 He looked up to heaven and with a
deep sigh said to him, *"Ephphatha!"* (which
means "Be opened!"). 35 At this, the man's
ears were opened, his tongue was loosened
and he began to speak plainly.
36 Jesus commanded them not to tell any-
one. But the more he did so, the more they
kept talking about it. 37 People were over-
whelmed with amazement. "He has done
everything well," they said. "He even makes
the deaf hear and the mute speak."

Jesus Feeds the Four Thousand

8 During those days another large crowd
gathered. Since they had nothing to eat,
Jesus called his disciples to him and said, 2 "I
have compassion for these people; they have
already been with me three days and have
nothing to eat. 3 If I send them home hungry,
they will collapse on the way, because some
of them have come a long distance."
4 His disciples answered, "But where in
this remote place can anyone get enough
bread to feed them?"
5 "How many loaves do you have?" Jesus
asked.
"Seven," they replied.
6 He told the crowd to sit down on the
ground. When he had taken the seven loaves
and given thanks, he broke them and gave
them to his disciples to distribute to the peo-
ple, and they did so. 7 They had a few small
fish as well; he gave thanks for them also and
told the disciples to distribute them. 8 The
people ate and were satisfied. Afterward the
disciples picked up seven basketfuls of bro-
ken pieces that were left over. 9 About four
thousand were present. After he had sent
them away, 10 he got into the boat with his
disciples and went to the region of Dalma-
nutha.
11 The Pharisees came and began to ques-
tion Jesus. To test him, they asked him for a
sign from heaven. 12 He sighed deeply and
said, "Why does this generation ask for a
sign? Truly I tell you, no sign will be given
to it." 13 Then he left them, got back into the
boat and crossed to the other side.

The Yeast of the Pharisees and Herod

14 The disciples had forgotten to bring
bread, except for one loaf they had with them
in the boat. 15 "Be careful," Jesus warned
them. "Watch out for the yeast of the Phar-
isees and that of Herod."
16 They discussed this with one another
and said, "It is because we have no bread."
17 Aware of their discussion, Jesus asked
them: "Why are you talking about having no
bread? Do you still not see or understand?
Are your hearts hardened? 18 Do you have
eyes but fail to see, and ears but fail to hear?
And don't you remember? 19 When I broke
the five loaves for the five thousand, how
many basketfuls of pieces did you pick up?"
"Twelve," they replied.
20 "And when I broke the seven loaves for
the four thousand, how many basketfuls of
pieces did you pick up?"
They answered, "Seven."
21 He said to them, "Do you still not under-
stand?"

Jesus Heals a Blind Man at Bethsaida

22 They came to Bethsaida, and some peo-
ple brought a blind man and begged Jesus to
touch him. 23 He took the blind man by the
hand and led him outside the village. When
he had spit on the man's eyes and put his
hands on him, Jesus asked, "Do you see any-
thing?"
24 He looked up and said, "I see people;
they look like trees walking around."
25 Once more Jesus put his hands on the
man's eyes. Then his eyes were opened, his

[a] *31* That is, the Ten Cities

sight was restored, and he saw everything
clearly. 26Jesus sent him home, saying,
"Don't even go into[a] the village."

Peter Declares That Jesus Is the Messiah

27Jesus and his disciples went on to the
villages around Caesarea Philippi. On the
way he asked them, "Who do people say
I am?"
28They replied, "Some say John the Bap-
tist; others say Elijah; and still others, one of
the prophets."
29"But what about you?" he asked. "Who
do you say I am?"
Peter answered, "You are the Messiah."
30Jesus warned them not to tell anyone
about him.

Jesus Predicts His Death

31He then began to teach them that the
Son of Man must suffer many things and be
rejected by the elders, the chief priests and
the teachers of the law, and that he must be
killed and after three days rise again. 32He
spoke plainly about this, and Peter took him
aside and began to rebuke him.
33But when Jesus turned and looked at his
disciples, he rebuked Peter. "Get behind me,
Satan!" he said. "You do not have in mind
the concerns of God, but merely human con-
cerns."

The Way of the Cross

34Then he called the crowd to him along
with his disciples and said: "Whoever wants
to be my disciple must deny themselves and
take up their cross and follow me. 35For who-
ever wants to save their life[b] will lose it, but
whoever loses their life for me and for the
gospel will save it. 36What good is it for some-
one to gain the whole world, yet forfeit their
soul? 37Or what can anyone give in exchange
for their soul? 38If anyone is ashamed of me
and my words in this adulterous and sinful
generation, the Son of Man will be ashamed
of them when he comes in his Father's glory
with the holy angels."
9 And he said to them, "Truly I tell you,
some who are standing here will not
taste death before they see that the kingdom
of God has come with power."

The Transfiguration

2After six days Jesus took Peter, James and
John with him and led them up a high moun-
tain, where they were all alone. There he was
transfigured before them. 3His clothes be-
came dazzling white, whiter than anyone in
the world could bleach them. 4And there ap-
peared before them Elijah and Moses, who
were talking with Jesus.
5Peter said to Jesus, "Rabbi, it is good for
us to be here. Let us put up three shelters—
one for you, one for Moses and one for Eli-
jah." 6(He did not know what to say, they
were so frightened.)
7Then a cloud appeared and covered
them, and a voice came from the cloud:
"This is my Son, whom I love. Listen to him!"
8Suddenly, when they looked around,
they no longer saw anyone with them except
Jesus.
9As they were coming down the moun-
tain, Jesus gave them orders not to tell any-
one what they had seen until the Son of Man
had risen from the dead. 10They kept the
matter to themselves, discussing what "ris-
ing from the dead" meant.
11And they asked him, "Why do the teach-
ers of the law say that Elijah must come
first?"
12Jesus replied, "To be sure, Elijah does
come first, and restores all things. Why then
is it written that the Son of Man must suffer
much and be rejected? 13But I tell you, Elijah
has come, and they have done to him every-
thing they wished, just as it is written about
him."

Jesus Heals a Boy Possessed by an Impure Spirit

14When they came to the other disciples,
they saw a large crowd around them and the
teachers of the law arguing with them. 15As
soon as all the people saw Jesus, they were
overwhelmed with wonder and ran to greet
him.
16"What are you arguing with them
about?" he asked.
17A man in the crowd answered, "Teacher,
I brought you my son, who is possessed by a
spirit that has robbed him of speech. 18When-
ever it seizes him, it throws him to the ground.

[a] 26 Some manuscripts *go and tell anyone in* the village
[b] 35 The Greek word means either *life* or *soul*; also in verses 36 and 37.

He foams at the mouth, gnashes his teeth and
becomes rigid. I asked your disciples to drive
out the spirit, but they could not.”
19“You unbelieving generation,” Jesus re-
plied, “how long shall I stay with you? How
long shall I put up with you? Bring the boy
to me.”
20So they brought him. When the spir-
it saw Jesus, it immediately threw the boy
into a convulsion. He fell to the ground and
rolled around, foaming at the mouth.
21Jesus asked the boy’s father, “How long
has he been like this?”
“From childhood,” he answered. 22“It has
often thrown him into fire or water to kill
him. But if you can do anything, take pity on
us and help us.”
23“ ‘If you can’?” said Jesus. “Everything is
possible for one who believes.”
24Immediately the boy’s father exclaimed,
“I do believe; help me overcome my unbelief!”
25When Jesus saw that a crowd was run-
ning to the scene, he rebuked the impure
spirit. “You deaf and mute spirit,” he said, “I
command you, come out of him and never
enter him again.”
26The spirit shrieked, convulsed him vi-
olently and came out. The boy looked so
much like a corpse that many said, “He’s
dead.” 27But Jesus took him by the hand and
lifted him to his feet, and he stood up.
28After Jesus had gone indoors, his disci-
ples asked him privately, “Why couldn’t we
drive it out?”
29He replied, “This kind can come out
only by prayer.[a]”

Jesus Predicts His Death a Second Time

30They left that place and passed through
Galilee. Jesus did not want anyone to know
where they were, 31because he was teaching
his disciples. He said to them, “The Son of
Man is going to be delivered into the hands
of men. They will kill him, and after three
days he will rise.” 32But they did not under-
stand what he meant and were afraid to ask
him about it.
33They came to Capernaum. When he was
in the house, he asked them, “What were you
arguing about on the road?” 34But they kept
quiet because on the way they had argued
about who was the greatest.
35Sitting down, Jesus called the Twelve
and said, “Anyone who wants to be first must
be the very last, and the servant of all.”
36He took a little child whom he placed
among them. Taking the child in his arms,
he said to them, 37“Whoever welcomes one
of these little children in my name welcomes
me; and whoever welcomes me does not wel-
come me but the one who sent me.”

Whoever Is Not Against Us Is for Us

38“Teacher,” said John, “we saw someone
driving out demons in your name and we told
him to stop, because he was not one of us.”
39“Do not stop him,” Jesus said. “For no
one who does a miracle in my name can in
the next moment say anything bad about
me, 40for whoever is not against us is for
us. 41Truly I tell you, anyone who gives you
a cup of water in my name because you be-
long to the Messiah will certainly not lose
their reward.

Causing to Stumble

42“If anyone causes one of these little
ones — those who believe in me — to stum-
ble, it would be better for them if a large
millstone were hung around their neck and
they were thrown into the sea. 43If your hand
causes you to stumble, cut it off. It is better
for you to enter life maimed than with two
hands to go into hell, where the fire never
goes out. [44][b] 45And if your foot causes you
to stumble, cut it off. It is better for you to
enter life crippled than to have two feet and
be thrown into hell. [46][b] 47And if your eye
causes you to stumble, pluck it out. It is bet-
ter for you to enter the kingdom of God with
one eye than to have two eyes and be thrown
into hell, 48where

> “ ‘the worms that eat them do not die,
> and the fire is not quenched.’[c]

49Everyone will be salted with fire.
50“Salt is good, but if it loses its saltiness,
how can you make it salty again? Have salt
among yourselves, and be at peace with each
other.”

Divorce

10 Jesus then left that place and went
into the region of Judea and across

[a] 29 Some manuscripts *prayer and fasting* [b] 44,46 Some manuscripts include here the words of verse 48. [c] 48 Isaiah 66:24

the Jordan. Again crowds of people came to
him, and as was his custom, he taught them.
2 Some Pharisees came and tested him by
asking, "Is it lawful for a man to divorce his
wife?"
3 "What did Moses command you?" he re-
plied.
4 They said, "Moses permitted a man to
write a certificate of divorce and send her
away."
5 "It was because your hearts were hard
that Moses wrote you this law," Jesus re-
plied. 6 "But at the beginning of creation
God 'made them male and female.'[a] 7 'For
this reason a man will leave his father and
mother and be united to his wife,[b] 8 and the
two will become one flesh.'[c] So they are no
longer two, but one flesh. 9 Therefore what
God has joined together, let no one sepa-
rate."
10 When they were in the house again, the
disciples asked Jesus about this. 11 He an-
swered, "Anyone who divorces his wife and
marries another woman commits adultery
against her. 12 And if she divorces her hus-
band and marries another man, she com-
mits adultery."

The Little Children and Jesus

13 People were bringing little children to
Jesus for him to place his hands on them, but
the disciples rebuked them. 14 When Jesus
saw this, he was indignant. He said to them,
"Let the little children come to me, and do
not hinder them, for the kingdom of God be-
longs to such as these. 15 Truly I tell you, any-
one who will not receive the kingdom of God
like a little child will never enter it." 16 And
he took the children in his arms, placed his
hands on them and blessed them.

The Rich and the Kingdom of God

17 As Jesus started on his way, a man ran
up to him and fell on his knees before him.
"Good teacher," he asked, "what must I do to
inherit eternal life?"
18 "Why do you call me good?" Jesus an-
swered. "No one is good — except God alone.
19 You know the commandments: 'You shall
not murder, you shall not commit adultery,
you shall not steal, you shall not give false
testimony, you shall not defraud, honor your
father and mother.'[d]"
20 "Teacher," he declared, "all these I have
kept since I was a boy."
21 Jesus looked at him and loved him. "One
thing you lack," he said. "Go, sell everything
you have and give to the poor, and you will
have treasure in heaven. Then come, fol-
low me."
22 At this the man's face fell. He went away
sad, because he had great wealth.
23 Jesus looked around and said to his dis-
ciples, "How hard it is for the rich to enter the
kingdom of God!"
24 The disciples were amazed at his words.
But Jesus said again, "Children, how hard it
is[e] to enter the kingdom of God! 25 It is easier
for a camel to go through the eye of a nee-
dle than for someone who is rich to enter the
kingdom of God."
26 The disciples were even more amazed,
and said to each other, "Who then can be
saved?"
27 Jesus looked at them and said, "With
man this is impossible, but not with God; all
things are possible with God."
28 Then Peter spoke up, "We have left ev-
erything to follow you!"
29 "Truly I tell you," Jesus replied, "no
one who has left home or brothers or sis-
ters or mother or father or children or fields
for me and the gospel 30 will fail to receive a
hundred times as much in this present age:
homes, brothers, sisters, mothers, children
and fields — along with persecutions — and
in the age to come eternal life. 31 But many
who are first will be last, and the last first."

Jesus Predicts His Death a Third Time

32 They were on their way up to Jerusalem,
with Jesus leading the way, and the disciples
were astonished, while those who followed
were afraid. Again he took the Twelve aside
and told them what was going to happen to
him. 33 "We are going up to Jerusalem," he
said, "and the Son of Man will be delivered
over to the chief priests and the teachers of
the law. They will condemn him to death and
will hand him over to the Gentiles, 34 who
will mock him and spit on him, flog him and
kill him. Three days later he will rise."

[a] *6* Gen. 1:27 [b] *7* Some early manuscripts do not have *and be united to his wife.* [c] *8* Gen. 2:24
[d] *19* Exodus 20:12-16; Deut. 5:16-20 [e] *24* Some manuscripts *is for those who trust in riches*

The Request of James and John

35 Then James and John, the sons of Zebedee, came to him. "Teacher," they said, "we want you to do for us whatever we ask."

36 "What do you want me to do for you?" he asked.

37 They replied, "Let one of us sit at your right and the other at your left in your glory."

38 "You don't know what you are asking," Jesus said. "Can you drink the cup I drink or be baptized with the baptism I am baptized with?"

39 "We can," they answered.

Jesus said to them, "You will drink the cup I drink and be baptized with the baptism I am baptized with, 40 but to sit at my right or left is not for me to grant. These places belong to those for whom they have been prepared."

41 When the ten heard about this, they became indignant with James and John. 42 Jesus called them together and said, "You know that those who are regarded as rulers of the Gentiles lord it over them, and their high officials exercise authority over them. 43 Not so with you. Instead, whoever wants to become great among you must be your servant, 44 and whoever wants to be first must be slave of all. 45 For even the Son of Man did not come to be served, but to serve, and to give his life as a ransom for many."

Blind Bartimaeus Receives His Sight

46 Then they came to Jericho. As Jesus and his disciples, together with a large crowd, were leaving the city, a blind man, Bartimaeus (which means "son of Timaeus"), was sitting by the roadside begging. 47 When he heard that it was Jesus of Nazareth, he began to shout, "Jesus, Son of David, have mercy on me!"

48 Many rebuked him and told him to be quiet, but he shouted all the more, "Son of David, have mercy on me!"

49 Jesus stopped and said, "Call him."

So they called to the blind man, "Cheer up! On your feet! He's calling you." 50 Throwing his cloak aside, he jumped to his feet and came to Jesus.

51 "What do you want me to do for you?" Jesus asked him.

The blind man said, "Rabbi, I want to see."

52 "Go," said Jesus, "your faith has healed you." Immediately he received his sight and followed Jesus along the road.

Jesus Comes to Jerusalem as King

11 As they approached Jerusalem and came to Bethphage and Bethany at the Mount of Olives, Jesus sent two of his disciples, 2 saying to them, "Go to the village ahead of you, and just as you enter it, you will find a colt tied there, which no one has ever ridden. Untie it and bring it here. 3 If anyone asks you, 'Why are you doing this?' say, 'The Lord needs it and will send it back here shortly.'"

4 They went and found a colt outside in the street, tied at a doorway. As they untied it, 5 some people standing there asked, "What are you doing, untying that colt?" 6 They answered as Jesus had told them to, and the people let them go. 7 When they brought the colt to Jesus and threw their cloaks over it, he sat on it. 8 Many people spread their cloaks on the road, while others spread branches they had cut in the fields. 9 Those who went ahead and those who followed shouted,

"Hosanna![a]"

"Blessed is he who comes in the name of
the Lord!"[b]

10 "Blessed is the coming kingdom of our
father David!"

"Hosanna in the highest heaven!"

11 Jesus entered Jerusalem and went into the temple courts. He looked around at everything, but since it was already late, he went out to Bethany with the Twelve.

Jesus Curses a Fig Tree and Clears the Temple Courts

12 The next day as they were leaving Bethany, Jesus was hungry. 13 Seeing in the distance a fig tree in leaf, he went to find out if it had any fruit. When he reached it, he found nothing but leaves, because it was not the season for figs. 14 Then he said to the tree, "May no one ever eat fruit from you again." And his disciples heard him say it.

15 On reaching Jerusalem, Jesus entered the temple courts and began driving out

[a] 9 A Hebrew expression meaning "Save!" which became an exclamation of praise; also in verse 10
[b] 9 Psalm 118:25,26

those who were buying and selling there. He
overturned the tables of the money chang-
ers and the benches of those selling doves,
16and would not allow anyone to carry mer-
chandise through the temple courts. 17And
as he taught them, he said, "Is it not written:
'My house will be called a house of prayer for
all nations'[a]? But you have made it 'a den of
robbers.'[b]"

18The chief priests and the teachers of the
law heard this and began looking for a way
to kill him, for they feared him, because the
whole crowd was amazed at his teaching.

19When evening came, Jesus and his dis-
ciples[c] went out of the city.

20In the morning, as they went along, they
saw the fig tree withered from the roots. 21Pe-
ter remembered and said to Jesus, "Rabbi,
look! The fig tree you cursed has withered!"

22"Have faith in God," Jesus answered.
23"Truly[d] I tell you, if anyone says to this
mountain, 'Go, throw yourself into the
sea,' and does not doubt in their heart but
believes that what they say will happen, it
will be done for them. 24Therefore I tell you,
whatever you ask for in prayer, believe that
you have received it, and it will be yours.
25And when you stand praying, if you hold
anything against anyone, forgive them, so
that your Father in heaven may forgive you
your sins." [26][e]

The Authority of Jesus Questioned

27They arrived again in Jerusalem, and
while Jesus was walking in the temple courts,
the chief priests, the teachers of the law and
the elders came to him. 28"By what author-
ity are you doing these things?" they asked.
"And who gave you authority to do this?"

29Jesus replied, "I will ask you one ques-
tion. Answer me, and I will tell you by what
authority I am doing these things. 30John's
baptism — was it from heaven, or of human
origin? Tell me!"

31They discussed it among themselves
and said, "If we say, 'From heaven,' he will
ask, 'Then why didn't you believe him?'
32But if we say, 'Of human origin' . . ." (They
feared the people, for everyone held that
John really was a prophet.)

33So they answered Jesus, "We don't know."
Jesus said, "Neither will I tell you by what
authority I am doing these things."

The Parable of the Tenants

12 Jesus then began to speak to them
in parables: "A man planted a vine-
yard. He put a wall around it, dug a pit for
the winepress and built a watchtower. Then
he rented the vineyard to some farmers and
moved to another place. 2At harvest time he
sent a servant to the tenants to collect from
them some of the fruit of the vineyard. 3But
they seized him, beat him and sent him
away empty-handed. 4Then he sent another
servant to them; they struck this man on the
head and treated him shamefully. 5He sent
still another, and that one they killed. He
sent many others; some of them they beat,
others they killed.

6"He had one left to send, a son, whom he
loved. He sent him last of all, saying, 'They
will respect my son.'

7"But the tenants said to one another,
'This is the heir. Come, let's kill him, and
the inheritance will be ours.' 8So they took
him and killed him, and threw him out of the
vineyard.

9"What then will the owner of the vine-
yard do? He will come and kill those tenants
and give the vineyard to others. 10Haven't
you read this passage of Scripture:

"'The stone the builders rejected
has become the cornerstone;
11the Lord has done this,
and it is marvelous in our eyes'[f]?"

12Then the chief priests, the teachers of
the law and the elders looked for a way to
arrest him because they knew he had spo-
ken the parable against them. But they were
afraid of the crowd; so they left him and went
away.

Paying the Imperial Tax to Caesar

13Later they sent some of the Pharisees
and Herodians to Jesus to catch him in his
words. 14They came to him and said, "Teach-
er, we know that you are a man of integrity.
You aren't swayed by others, because you pay

[a] *17* Isaiah 56:7 [b] *17* Jer. 7:11 [c] *19* Some early manuscripts *came, Jesus* [d] *22,23* Some early manuscripts *"If you have faith in God," Jesus answered, 23"truly* [e] *26* Some manuscripts include here words similar to Matt. 6:15. [f] *11* Psalm 118:22,23

no attention to who they are; but you teach the way of God in accordance with the truth. Is it right to pay the imperial tax[a] to Caesar or not? 15 Should we pay or shouldn't we?"

But Jesus knew their hypocrisy. "Why are you trying to trap me?" he asked. "Bring me a denarius and let me look at it." 16 They brought the coin, and he asked them, "Whose image is this? And whose inscription?"

"Caesar's," they replied.

17 Then Jesus said to them, "Give back to Caesar what is Caesar's and to God what is God's."

And they were amazed at him.

Marriage at the Resurrection

18 Then the Sadducees, who say there is no resurrection, came to him with a question. 19 "Teacher," they said, "Moses wrote for us that if a man's brother dies and leaves a wife but no children, the man must marry the widow and raise up offspring for his brother. 20 Now there were seven brothers. The first one married and died without leaving any children. 21 The second one married the widow, but he also died, leaving no child. It was the same with the third. 22 In fact, none of the seven left any children. Last of all, the woman died too. 23 At the resurrection[b] whose wife will she be, since the seven were married to her?"

24 Jesus replied, "Are you not in error because you do not know the Scriptures or the power of God? 25 When the dead rise, they will neither marry nor be given in marriage; they will be like the angels in heaven. 26 Now about the dead rising—have you not read in the Book of Moses, in the account of the burning bush, how God said to him, 'I am the God of Abraham, the God of Isaac, and the God of Jacob'[c]? 27 He is not the God of the dead, but of the living. You are badly mistaken!"

The Greatest Commandment

28 One of the teachers of the law came and heard them debating. Noticing that Jesus had given them a good answer, he asked him, "Of all the commandments, which is the most important?"

29 "The most important one," answered Jesus, "is this: 'Hear, O Israel: The Lord our God, the Lord is one.[d] 30 Love the Lord your God with all your heart and with all your soul and with all your mind and with all your strength.'[e] 31 The second is this: 'Love your neighbor as yourself.'[f] There is no commandment greater than these."

32 "Well said, teacher," the man replied. "You are right in saying that God is one and there is no other but him. 33 To love him with all your heart, with all your understanding and with all your strength, and to love your neighbor as yourself is more important than all burnt offerings and sacrifices."

34 When Jesus saw that he had answered wisely, he said to him, "You are not far from the kingdom of God." And from then on no one dared ask him any more questions.

Whose Son Is the Messiah?

35 While Jesus was teaching in the temple courts, he asked, "Why do the teachers of the law say that the Messiah is the son of David? 36 David himself, speaking by the Holy Spirit, declared:

"'The Lord said to my Lord:
"Sit at my right hand
until I put your enemies
under your feet."'[g]

37 David himself calls him 'Lord.' How then can he be his son?"

The large crowd listened to him with delight.

Warning Against the Teachers of the Law

38 As he taught, Jesus said, "Watch out for the teachers of the law. They like to walk around in flowing robes and be greeted with respect in the marketplaces, 39 and have the most important seats in the synagogues and the places of honor at banquets. 40 They devour widows' houses and for a show make lengthy prayers. These men will be punished most severely."

The Widow's Offering

41 Jesus sat down opposite the place where the offerings were put and watched the crowd putting their money into the temple treasury. Many rich people threw in large

[a] *14* A special tax levied on subject peoples, not on Roman citizens [b] *23* Some manuscripts *resurrection, when people rise from the dead,* [c] *26* Exodus 3:6 [d] *29* Or *The Lord our God is one Lord* [e] *30* Deut. 6:4,5 [f] *31* Lev. 19:18 [g] *36* Psalm 110:1

amounts. 42 But a poor widow came and put in two very small copper coins, worth only a few cents.

43 Calling his disciples to him, Jesus said, "Truly I tell you, this poor widow has put more into the treasury than all the others. 44 They all gave out of their wealth; but she, out of her poverty, put in everything — all she had to live on."

The Destruction of the Temple and Signs of the End Times

13 As Jesus was leaving the temple, one of his disciples said to him, "Look, Teacher! What massive stones! What magnificent buildings!"

2 "Do you see all these great buildings?" replied Jesus. "Not one stone here will be left on another; every one will be thrown down."

3 As Jesus was sitting on the Mount of Olives opposite the temple, Peter, James, John and Andrew asked him privately, 4 "Tell us, when will these things happen? And what will be the sign that they are all about to be fulfilled?"

5 Jesus said to them: "Watch out that no one deceives you. 6 Many will come in my name, claiming, 'I am he,' and will deceive many. 7 When you hear of wars and rumors of wars, do not be alarmed. Such things must happen, but the end is still to come. 8 Nation will rise against nation, and kingdom against kingdom. There will be earthquakes in various places, and famines. These are the beginning of birth pains.

9 "You must be on your guard. You will be handed over to the local councils and flogged in the synagogues. On account of me you will stand before governors and kings as witnesses to them. 10 And the gospel must first be preached to all nations. 11 Whenever you are arrested and brought to trial, do not worry beforehand about what to say. Just say whatever is given you at the time, for it is not you speaking, but the Holy Spirit.

12 "Brother will betray brother to death, and a father his child. Children will rebel against their parents and have them put to death. 13 Everyone will hate you because of me, but the one who stands firm to the end will be saved.

14 "When you see 'the abomination that causes desolation'[a] standing where it[b] does not belong — let the reader understand — then let those who are in Judea flee to the mountains. 15 Let no one on the housetop go down or enter the house to take anything out. 16 Let no one in the field go back to get their cloak. 17 How dreadful it will be in those days for pregnant women and nursing mothers! 18 Pray that this will not take place in winter, 19 because those will be days of distress unequaled from the beginning, when God created the world, until now — and never to be equaled again.

20 "If the Lord had not cut short those days, no one would survive. But for the sake of the elect, whom he has chosen, he has shortened them. 21 At that time if anyone says to you, 'Look, here is the Messiah!' or, 'Look, there he is!' do not believe it. 22 For false messiahs and false prophets will appear and perform signs and wonders to deceive, if possible, even the elect. 23 So be on your guard; I have told you everything ahead of time.

24 "But in those days, following that distress,

" 'the sun will be darkened,
  and the moon will not give its light;
25 the stars will fall from the sky,
  and the heavenly bodies will be
    shaken.'[c]

26 "At that time people will see the Son of Man coming in clouds with great power and glory. 27 And he will send his angels and gather his elect from the four winds, from the ends of the earth to the ends of the heavens.

28 "Now learn this lesson from the fig tree: As soon as its twigs get tender and its leaves come out, you know that summer is near. 29 Even so, when you see these things happening, you know that it[b] is near, right at the door. 30 Truly I tell you, this generation will certainly not pass away until all these things have happened. 31 Heaven and earth will pass away, but my words will never pass away.

The Day and Hour Unknown

32 "But about that day or hour no one knows, not even the angels in heaven, nor the Son, but only the Father. 33 Be on guard!

[a] *14* Daniel 9:27; 11:31; 12:11 [b] *14,29* Or *he* [c] *25* Isaiah 13:10; 34:4

SOON AND VERY SOON

Andraé Crouch

Soon and very soon
We are going to see the King
Soon and very soon
We are going to see the King
Soon and very soon
We are going to see the King
Hallelujah, hallelujah
We are going to see the King

No more crying there
We are going to see the King
Hallelujah, hallelujah
We are going to see the King
No more dying there
We are going to see the King
No more dying there
Hallelujah, hallelujah
We are going to see the King
Hallelujah, hallelujah

Should there be any rivers we must cross
Should there be any mountains we must climb
God will supply all the strength that we need
Give us grace 'til we reach the other side
We have come from every nation
God knows each of us by name
Jesus took his blood and he washed our sins
And he washed them all away
Yes, there are some of us
Who have laid down our lives
But we all shall live again
On the other side
Hallelujah.
Ooh, ooh, ooh, ooh, ooh, ah

THE INSPIRATION

He who testifies to these things says, "Yes, I am coming soon." Amen. Come, Lord Jesus. The grace of the Lord Jesus be with God's people. Amen.

—Revelation 22:20–21

BEHIND THE SONG

Andraé Crouch is a pastor, songwriter, producer and artist who has had an immense impact on the Christian music world over the last 50 years. His unique style of songwriting and performing brought African-American and white audiences together like no artist before or since. "Soon and Very Soon" — one of his most popular congregational songs — has been beloved for so long that many people believe it is an old hymn. The song was actually written in 1976, however, and has been recorded many times since then.

"Soon and Very Soon" employs the simple style of traditional spiritual, from its easy-to-learn lyrics and rhythmic patterns to its hopeful message. Spirituals often used music to deliver and to reinforce hopeful messages of future relief from the temporal suffering and bondage experienced by slaves and other oppressed people. "Soon and Very Soon" is certainly no exception. The lyric features resolute optimism about a coming deliverance from this world of tears, death and oppression.

Selah

When you feel oppressed, challenged or even hopeless, try singing this wonderfully simple and yet profound song. The struggles of this life are temporary, and soon all believers will be in the presence of the King of kings. He will redeem creation and set all wrongs right. While the Bible tells us relatively little about the exact details of heaven, it is clear that it is a place where there is no sorrow, no mourning, no loss and no pain. But in the meantime, God supplies us with strength and grace to live for him "'til we reach the other side"

If there are things in your life that you are eager to leave behind before you leave the earth, try placing them before the King Jesus and inviting him to help you in those areas. You can even add your own verses to this song, detailing the things you look forward to leaving behind when you enter glory.

Be alert[a]! You do not know when that time
will come. 34 It's like a man going away: He
leaves his house and puts his servants in
charge, each with their assigned task, and
tells the one at the door to keep watch.
35 "Therefore keep watch because you do
not know when the owner of the house will
come back—whether in the evening, or at
midnight, or when the rooster crows, or at
dawn. 36 If he comes suddenly, do not let him
find you sleeping. 37 What I say to you, I say to
everyone: 'Watch!'"

Jesus Anointed at Bethany

14 Now the Passover and the Festival of
Unleavened Bread were only two days
away, and the chief priests and the teachers
of the law were scheming to arrest Jesus se-
cretly and kill him. 2 "But not during the festi-
val," they said, "or the people may riot."
3 While he was in Bethany, reclining at
the table in the home of Simon the Leper, a
woman came with an alabaster jar of very
expensive perfume, made of pure nard. She
broke the jar and poured the perfume on his
head.
4 Some of those present were saying in-
dignantly to one another, "Why this waste of
perfume? 5 It could have been sold for more
than a year's wages[b] and the money given to
the poor." And they rebuked her harshly.
6 "Leave her alone," said Jesus. "Why are
you bothering her? She has done a beautiful
thing to me. 7 The poor you will always have
with you,[c] and you can help them any time
you want. But you will not always have me.
8 She did what she could. She poured per-
fume on my body beforehand to prepare
for my burial. 9 Truly I tell you, wherever the
gospel is preached throughout the world,
what she has done will also be told, in mem-
ory of her."
10 Then Judas Iscariot, one of the Twelve,
went to the chief priests to betray Jesus to
them. 11 They were delighted to hear this and
promised to give him money. So he watched
for an opportunity to hand him over.

The Last Supper

12 On the first day of the Festival of Un-
leavened Bread, when it was customary to
sacrifice the Passover lamb, Jesus' disciples
asked him, "Where do you want us to go and
make preparations for you to eat the Pass-
over?"
13 So he sent two of his disciples, telling
them, "Go into the city, and a man carry-
ing a jar of water will meet you. Follow him.
14 Say to the owner of the house he enters,
'The Teacher asks: Where is my guest room,
where I may eat the Passover with my disci-
ples?' 15 He will show you a large room up-
stairs, furnished and ready. Make prepara-
tions for us there."
16 The disciples left, went into the city and
found things just as Jesus had told them. So
they prepared the Passover.
17 When evening came, Jesus arrived with
the Twelve. 18 While they were reclining at
the table eating, he said, "Truly I tell you,
one of you will betray me—one who is eat-
ing with me."
19 They were saddened, and one by one
they said to him, "Surely you don't mean me?"
20 "It is one of the Twelve," he replied, "one
who dips bread into the bowl with me. 21 The
Son of Man will go just as it is written about
him. But woe to that man who betrays the
Son of Man! It would be better for him if he
had not been born."
22 While they were eating, Jesus took
bread, and when he had given thanks, he
broke it and gave it to his disciples, saying,
"Take it; this is my body."
23 Then he took a cup, and when he had
given thanks, he gave it to them, and they all
drank from it.
24 "This is my blood of the[d] covenant,
which is poured out for many," he said to
them. 25 "Truly I tell you, I will not drink
again from the fruit of the vine until that day
when I drink it new in the kingdom of God."
26 When they had sung a hymn, they went
out to the Mount of Olives.

Jesus Predicts Peter's Denial

27 "You will all fall away," Jesus told them,
"for it is written:

"'I will strike the shepherd,
and the sheep will be scattered.'[e]

28 But after I have risen, I will go ahead of you
into Galilee."

[a] *33* Some manuscripts *alert and pray* [b] *5* Greek *than three hundred denarii* [c] *7* See Deut. 15:11.
[d] *24* Some manuscripts *the new* [e] *27* Zech. 13:7

29 Peter declared, "Even if all fall away, I
will not."
30 "Truly I tell you," Jesus answered, "to-
day—yes, tonight—before the rooster
crows twice[a] you yourself will disown me
three times."
31 But Peter insisted emphatically, "Even
if I have to die with you, I will never disown
you." And all the others said the same.

Gethsemane

32 They went to a place called Gethsema-
ne, and Jesus said to his disciples, "Sit here
while I pray." 33 He took Peter, James and
John along with him, and he began to be
deeply distressed and troubled. 34 "My soul
is overwhelmed with sorrow to the point of
death," he said to them. "Stay here and keep
watch."
35 Going a little farther, he fell to the
ground and prayed that if possible the hour
might pass from him. 36 "*Abba*,[b] Father," he
said, "everything is possible for you. Take
this cup from me. Yet not what I will, but
what you will."
37 Then he returned to his disciples and
found them sleeping. "Simon," he said to Pe-
ter, "are you asleep? Couldn't you keep watch
for one hour? 38 Watch and pray so that you
will not fall into temptation. The spirit is
willing, but the flesh is weak."
39 Once more he went away and prayed the
same thing. 40 When he came back, he again
found them sleeping, because their eyes
were heavy. They did not know what to say
to him.
41 Returning the third time, he said to
them, "Are you still sleeping and resting?
Enough! The hour has come. Look, the Son
of Man is delivered into the hands of sinners.
42 Rise! Let us go! Here comes my betrayer!"

Jesus Arrested

43 Just as he was speaking, Judas, one of
the Twelve, appeared. With him was a crowd
armed with swords and clubs, sent from the
chief priests, the teachers of the law, and the
elders.
44 Now the betrayer had arranged a signal
with them: "The one I kiss is the man; arrest
him and lead him away under guard." 45 Go-
ing at once to Jesus, Judas said, "Rabbi!" and
kissed him. 46 The men seized Jesus and ar-
rested him. 47 Then one of those standing
near drew his sword and struck the servant
of the high priest, cutting off his ear.
48 "Am I leading a rebellion," said Jesus,
"that you have come out with swords and
clubs to capture me? 49 Every day I was with
you, teaching in the temple courts, and you
did not arrest me. But the Scriptures must
be fulfilled." 50 Then everyone deserted him
and fled.
51 A young man, wearing nothing but a lin-
en garment, was following Jesus. When they
seized him, 52 he fled naked, leaving his gar-
ment behind.

Jesus Before the Sanhedrin

53 They took Jesus to the high priest, and
all the chief priests, the elders and the teach-
ers of the law came together. 54 Peter fol-
lowed him at a distance, right into the court-
yard of the high priest. There he sat with the
guards and warmed himself at the fire.
55 The chief priests and the whole Sanhe-
drin were looking for evidence against Jesus
so that they could put him to death, but they
did not find any. 56 Many testified falsely
against him, but their statements did not
agree.
57 Then some stood up and gave this false
testimony against him: 58 "We heard him say,
'I will destroy this temple made with human
hands and in three days will build another,
not made with hands.'" 59 Yet even then their
testimony did not agree.
60 Then the high priest stood up before
them and asked Jesus, "Are you not going to
answer? What is this testimony that these
men are bringing against you?" 61 But Jesus
remained silent and gave no answer.
Again the high priest asked him, "Are you
the Messiah, the Son of the Blessed One?"
62 "I am," said Jesus. "And you will see the
Son of Man sitting at the right hand of the
Mighty One and coming on the clouds of
heaven."
63 The high priest tore his clothes. "Why
do we need any more witnesses?" he asked.
64 "You have heard the blasphemy. What do
you think?"
They all condemned him as worthy of
death. 65 Then some began to spit at him;

[a] *30* Some early manuscripts do not have *twice*. [b] *36* Aramaic for *father*

they blindfolded him, struck him with their
fists, and said, "Prophesy!" And the guards
took him and beat him.

Peter Disowns Jesus

66 While Peter was below in the courtyard,
one of the servant girls of the high priest
came by. 67 When she saw Peter warming
himself, she looked closely at him.
"You also were with that Nazarene, Jesus,"
she said.
68 But he denied it. "I don't know or under-
stand what you're talking about," he said,
and went out into the entryway.[a]
69 When the servant girl saw him there,
she said again to those standing around,
"This fellow is one of them." 70 Again he de-
nied it.
After a little while, those standing near
said to Peter, "Surely you are one of them, for
you are a Galilean."
71 He began to call down curses, and he
swore to them, "I don't know this man you're
talking about."
72 Immediately the rooster crowed the
second time.[b] Then Peter remembered the
word Jesus had spoken to him: "Before the
rooster crows twice[c] you will disown me
three times." And he broke down and wept.

Jesus Before Pilate

15 Very early in the morning, the chief
priests, with the elders, the teachers
of the law and the whole Sanhedrin, made
their plans. So they bound Jesus, led him
away and handed him over to Pilate.
2 "Are you the king of the Jews?" asked Pi-
late.
"You have said so," Jesus replied.
3 The chief priests accused him of many
things. 4 So again Pilate asked him, "Aren't
you going to answer? See how many things
they are accusing you of."
5 But Jesus still made no reply, and Pilate
was amazed.
6 Now it was the custom at the festival to
release a prisoner whom the people request-
ed. 7 A man called Barabbas was in prison
with the insurrectionists who had com-
mitted murder in the uprising. 8 The crowd
came up and asked Pilate to do for them
what he usually did.
9 "Do you want me to release to you the
king of the Jews?" asked Pilate, 10 knowing it
was out of self-interest that the chief priests
had handed Jesus over to him. 11 But the
chief priests stirred up the crowd to have Pi-
late release Barabbas instead.
12 "What shall I do, then, with the one you
call the king of the Jews?" Pilate asked them.
13 "Crucify him!" they shouted.
14 "Why? What crime has he committed?"
asked Pilate.
But they shouted all the louder, "Crucify
him!"
15 Wanting to satisfy the crowd, Pilate
released Barabbas to them. He had Jesus
flogged, and handed him over to be crucified.

The Soldiers Mock Jesus

16 The soldiers led Jesus away into the
palace (that is, the Praetorium) and called
together the whole company of soldiers.
17 They put a purple robe on him, then twist-
ed together a crown of thorns and set it on
him. 18 And they began to call out to him,
"Hail, king of the Jews!" 19 Again and again
they struck him on the head with a staff and
spit on him. Falling on their knees, they
paid homage to him. 20 And when they had
mocked him, they took off the purple robe
and put his own clothes on him. Then they
led him out to crucify him.

The Crucifixion of Jesus

21 A certain man from Cyrene, Simon, the
father of Alexander and Rufus, was pass-
ing by on his way in from the country, and
they forced him to carry the cross. 22 They
brought Jesus to the place called Golgo-
tha (which means "the place of the skull").
23 Then they offered him wine mixed with
myrrh, but he did not take it. 24 And they cru-
cified him. Dividing up his clothes, they cast
lots to see what each would get.
25 It was nine in the morning when they
crucified him. 26 The written notice of the
charge against him read: THE KING OF THE
JEWS.
27 They crucified two rebels with him, one
on his right and one on his left. [28][d] 29 Those
who passed by hurled insults at him, shaking

[a] 68 Some early manuscripts *entryway and the rooster crowed* [b] 72 Some early manuscripts do not have *the second time.* [c] 72 Some early manuscripts do not have *twice.* [d] 28 Some manuscripts include here words similar to Luke 22:37.

their heads and saying, "So! You who are go-
ing to destroy the temple and build it in three
days, [30]come down from the cross and save
yourself!" [31]In the same way the chief priests
and the teachers of the law mocked him
among themselves. "He saved others," they
said, "but he can't save himself! [32]Let this
Messiah, this king of Israel, come down now
from the cross, that we may see and believe."
Those crucified with him also heaped insults
on him.

The Death of Jesus

[33]At noon, darkness came over the whole
land until three in the afternoon. [34]And at
three in the afternoon Jesus cried out in a
loud voice, *"Eloi, Eloi, lema sabachthani?"*
(which means "My God, my God, why have
you forsaken me?").[a]

[35]When some of those standing near
heard this, they said, "Listen, he's calling
Elijah."

[36]Someone ran, filled a sponge with wine
vinegar, put it on a staff, and offered it to
Jesus to drink. "Now leave him alone. Let's
see if Elijah comes to take him down," he
said.

[37]With a loud cry, Jesus breathed his last.

[38]The curtain of the temple was torn in
two from top to bottom. [39]And when the cen-
turion, who stood there in front of Jesus, saw
how he died,[b] he said, "Surely this man was
the Son of God!"

[40]Some women were watching from a dis-
tance. Among them were Mary Magdalene,
Mary the mother of James the younger and
of Joseph,[c] and Salome. [41]In Galilee these
women had followed him and cared for his
needs. Many other women who had come up
with him to Jerusalem were also there.

The Burial of Jesus

[42]It was Preparation Day (that is, the
day before the Sabbath). So as evening ap-
proached, [43]Joseph of Arimathea, a promi-
nent member of the Council, who was him-
self waiting for the kingdom of God, went
boldly to Pilate and asked for Jesus' body.
[44]Pilate was surprised to hear that he was
already dead. Summoning the centuri-
on, he asked him if Jesus had already died.
[45]When he learned from the centurion that
it was so, he gave the body to Joseph. [46]So
Joseph bought some linen cloth, took down
the body, wrapped it in the linen, and placed
it in a tomb cut out of rock. Then he rolled
a stone against the entrance of the tomb.
[47]Mary Magdalene and Mary the mother of
Joseph saw where he was laid.

Jesus Has Risen

16 When the Sabbath was over, Mary
Magdalene, Mary the mother of
James, and Salome bought spices so that they
might go to anoint Jesus' body. [2]Very early on
the first day of the week, just after sunrise,
they were on their way to the tomb [3]and they
asked each other, "Who will roll the stone
away from the entrance of the tomb?"

[4]But when they looked up, they saw that
the stone, which was very large, had been
rolled away. [5]As they entered the tomb,
they saw a young man dressed in a white
robe sitting on the right side, and they were
alarmed.

[6]"Don't be alarmed," he said. "You are
looking for Jesus the Nazarene, who was
crucified. He has risen! He is not here. See
the place where they laid him. [7]But go, tell
his disciples and Peter, 'He is going ahead of
you into Galilee. There you will see him, just
as he told you.' "

[8]Trembling and bewildered, the wom-
en went out and fled from the tomb. They
said nothing to anyone, because they were
afraid.[d]

[The earliest manuscripts and some other
ancient witnesses do not have verses 9–20.]

*[9]When Jesus rose early on the first day of the
week, he appeared first to Mary Magdalene, out of
whom he had driven seven demons. [10]She went and
told those who had been with him and who were
mourning and weeping. [11]When they heard that
Jesus was alive and that she had seen him, they did
not believe it.*

[a] *34* Psalm 22:1 [b] *39* Some manuscripts *saw that he died with such a cry* [c] *40* Greek *Joses,* a variant of *Joseph*; also in verse 47 [d] *8* Some manuscripts have the following ending between verses 8 and 9, and one manuscript has it after verse 8 (omitting verses 9-20): *Then they quickly reported all these instructions to those around Peter. After this, Jesus himself also sent out through them from east to west the sacred and imperishable proclamation of eternal salvation. Amen.*

*[12] Afterward Jesus appeared in a different form to
two of them while they were walking in the country.
[13] These returned and reported it to the rest; but they
did not believe them either.*

*[14] Later Jesus appeared to the Eleven as they were
eating; he rebuked them for their lack of faith and
their stubborn refusal to believe those who had seen
him after he had risen.*

*[15] He said to them, "Go into all the world and
preach the gospel to all creation. [16] Whoever be-
lieves and is baptized will be saved, but whoever
does not believe will be condemned. [17] And these
signs will accompany those who believe: In my
name they will drive out demons; they will speak in
new tongues; [18] they will pick up snakes with their
hands; and when they drink deadly poison, it will
not hurt them at all; they will place their hands on
sick people, and they will get well."*

*[19] After the Lord Jesus had spoken to them, he
was taken up into heaven and he sat at the right
hand of God. [20] Then the disciples went out and
preached everywhere, and the Lord worked with
them and confirmed his word by the signs that ac-
companied it.*

LUKE

Introduction

1 Many have undertaken to draw up an
account of the things that have been
fulfilled[a] among us, 2just as they were hand-
ed down to us by those who from the first
were eyewitnesses and servants of the word.
3With this in mind, since I myself have care-
fully investigated everything from the be-
ginning, I too decided to write an orderly
account for you, most excellent Theophilus,
4so that you may know the certainty of the
things you have been taught.

The Birth of John the Baptist Foretold

5In the time of Herod king of Judea there
was a priest named Zechariah, who be-
longed to the priestly division of Abijah; his
wife Elizabeth was also a descendant of Aar-
on. 6Both of them were righteous in the sight
of God, observing all the Lord's commands
and decrees blamelessly. 7But they were
childless because Elizabeth was not able to
conceive, and they were both very old.

8Once when Zechariah's division was
on duty and he was serving as priest before
God, 9he was chosen by lot, according to
the custom of the priesthood, to go into the
temple of the Lord and burn incense. 10And
when the time for the burning of incense
came, all the assembled worshipers were
praying outside.

11Then an angel of the Lord appeared to
him, standing at the right side of the altar of
incense. 12When Zechariah saw him, he was
startled and was gripped with fear. 13But the
angel said to him: "Do not be afraid, Zecha-
riah; your prayer has been heard. Your wife
Elizabeth will bear you a son, and you are to
call him John. 14He will be a joy and delight
to you, and many will rejoice because of his
birth, 15for he will be great in the sight of the
Lord. He is never to take wine or other fer-
mented drink, and he will be filled with the
Holy Spirit even before he is born. 16He will
bring back many of the people of Israel to the
Lord their God. 17And he will go on before
the Lord, in the spirit and power of Elijah, to
turn the hearts of the parents to their chil-
dren and the disobedient to the wisdom of
the righteous — to make ready a people pre-
pared for the Lord."

18Zechariah asked the angel, "How can I
be sure of this? I am an old man and my wife
is well along in years."

19The angel said to him, "I am Gabriel.
I stand in the presence of God, and I have
been sent to speak to you and to tell you this
good news. 20And now you will be silent and
not able to speak until the day this happens,
because you did not believe my words, which
will come true at their appointed time."

21Meanwhile, the people were waiting for
Zechariah and wondering why he stayed so
long in the temple. 22When he came out, he
could not speak to them. They realized he
had seen a vision in the temple, for he kept
making signs to them but remained unable
to speak.

23When his time of service was complet-
ed, he returned home. 24After this his wife
Elizabeth became pregnant and for five
months remained in seclusion. 25"The Lord
has done this for me," she said. "In these
days he has shown his favor and taken away
my disgrace among the people."

The Birth of Jesus Foretold

26In the sixth month of Elizabeth's preg-
nancy, God sent the angel Gabriel to Naza-
reth, a town in Galilee, 27to a virgin pledged
to be married to a man named Joseph, a de-
scendant of David. The virgin's name was
Mary. 28The angel went to her and said,
"Greetings, you who are highly favored! The
Lord is with you."

29Mary was greatly troubled at his words
and wondered what kind of greeting this
might be. 30But the angel said to her, "Do
not be afraid, Mary; you have found favor
with God. 31You will conceive and give birth

[a] *1* Or *been surely believed*

to a son, and you are to call him Jesus. 32 He
will be great and will be called the Son of
the Most High. The Lord God will give him
the throne of his father David, 33 and he will
reign over Jacob's descendants forever; his
kingdom will never end."

34 "How will this be," Mary asked the an-
gel, "since I am a virgin?"

35 The angel answered, "The Holy Spirit
will come on you, and the power of the Most
High will overshadow you. So the holy one to
be born will be called[a] the Son of God. 36 Even
Elizabeth your relative is going to have a
child in her old age, and she who was said to
be unable to conceive is in her sixth month.
37 For no word from God will ever fail."

38 "I am the Lord's servant," Mary an-
swered. "May your word to me be fulfilled."
Then the angel left her.

Mary Visits Elizabeth

39 At that time Mary got ready and hur-
ried to a town in the hill country of Judea,
40 where she entered Zechariah's home and
greeted Elizabeth. 41 When Elizabeth heard
Mary's greeting, the baby leaped in her
womb, and Elizabeth was filled with the
Holy Spirit. 42 In a loud voice she exclaimed:
"Blessed are you among women, and blessed
is the child you will bear! 43 But why am I so
favored, that the mother of my Lord should
come to me? 44 As soon as the sound of your
greeting reached my ears, the baby in my
womb leaped for joy. 45 Blessed is she who
has believed that the Lord would fulfill his
promises to her!"

Mary's Song

46 And Mary said:

"My soul glorifies the Lord
47 and my spirit rejoices in God my
Savior,
48 for he has been mindful
of the humble state of his servant.
From now on all generations will call
me blessed,
49 for the Mighty One has done great
things for me—
holy is his name.
50 His mercy extends to those who
fear him,
from generation to generation.
51 He has performed mighty deeds with
his arm;
he has scattered those who are proud
in their inmost thoughts.
52 He has brought down rulers from their
thrones
but has lifted up the humble.
53 He has filled the hungry with good things
but has sent the rich away empty.
54 He has helped his servant Israel,
remembering to be merciful
55 to Abraham and his descendants forever,
just as he promised our ancestors."

56 Mary stayed with Elizabeth for about
three months and then returned home.

The Birth of John the Baptist

57 When it was time for Elizabeth to have
her baby, she gave birth to a son. 58 Her
neighbors and relatives heard that the Lord
had shown her great mercy, and they shared
her joy.

59 On the eighth day they came to circum-
cise the child, and they were going to name
him after his father Zechariah, 60 but his
mother spoke up and said, "No! He is to be
called John."

61 They said to her, "There is no one among
your relatives who has that name."

62 Then they made signs to his father,
to find out what he would like to name the
child. 63 He asked for a writing tablet, and
to everyone's astonishment he wrote, "His
name is John." 64 Immediately his mouth was
opened and his tongue set free, and he be-
gan to speak, praising God. 65 All the neigh-
bors were filled with awe, and throughout
the hill country of Judea people were talk-
ing about all these things. 66 Everyone who
heard this wondered about it, asking, "What
then is this child going to be?" For the Lord's
hand was with him.

Zechariah's Song

67 His father Zechariah was filled with the
Holy Spirit and prophesied:

68 "Praise be to the Lord, the God of Israel,
because he has come to his people and
redeemed them.
69 He has raised up a horn[b] of salvation
for us
in the house of his servant David

[a] 35 Or *So the child to be born will be called holy,* [b] 69 *Horn* here symbolizes a strong king.

[70] (as he said through his holy prophets
of long ago),
[71] salvation from our enemies
and from the hand of all who
hate us—
[72] to show mercy to our ancestors
and to remember his holy covenant,
[73] the oath he swore to our father
Abraham:
[74] to rescue us from the hand of our
enemies,
and to enable us to serve him without
fear
[75] in holiness and righteousness before
him all our days.

[76] And you, my child, will be called a
prophet of the Most High;
for you will go on before the Lord to
prepare the way for him,
[77] to give his people the knowledge of
salvation
through the forgiveness of their sins,
[78] because of the tender mercy of our God,
by which the rising sun will come to
us from heaven
[79] to shine on those living in darkness
and in the shadow of death,
to guide our feet into the path
of peace."

[80] And the child grew and became strong
in spirit[a]; and he lived in the wilderness un-
til he appeared publicly to Israel.

The Birth of Jesus

2 In those days Caesar Augustus issued a
decree that a census should be taken of
the entire Roman world. [2] (This was the first
census that took place while[b] Quirinius was
governor of Syria.) [3] And everyone went to
their own town to register.

[4] So Joseph also went up from the town of
Nazareth in Galilee to Judea, to Bethlehem
the town of David, because he belonged to
the house and line of David. [5] He went there
to register with Mary, who was pledged to be
married to him and was expecting a child.
[6] While they were there, the time came for
the baby to be born, [7] and she gave birth to
her firstborn, a son. She wrapped him in
cloths and placed him in a manger, because
there was no guest room available for them.

[8] And there were shepherds living out in
the fields nearby, keeping watch over their
flocks at night. [9] An angel of the Lord ap-
peared to them, and the glory of the Lord
shone around them, and they were terri-
fied. [10] But the angel said to them, "Do not be
afraid. I bring you good news that will cause
great joy for all the people. [11] Today in the
town of David a Savior has been born to you;
he is the Messiah, the Lord. [12] This will be a
sign to you: You will find a baby wrapped in
cloths and lying in a manger."

[13] Suddenly a great company of the heav-
enly host appeared with the angel, praising
God and saying,

[14] "Glory to God in the highest heaven,
and on earth peace to those on whom
his favor rests."

[15] When the angels had left them and gone
into heaven, the shepherds said to one an-
other, "Let's go to Bethlehem and see this
thing that has happened, which the Lord has
told us about."

[16] So they hurried off and found Mary
and Joseph, and the baby, who was lying
in the manger. [17] When they had seen him,
they spread the word concerning what had
been told them about this child, [18] and all
who heard it were amazed at what the shep-
herds said to them. [19] But Mary treasured up
all these things and pondered them in her
heart. [20] The shepherds returned, glorifying
and praising God for all the things they had
heard and seen, which were just as they had
been told.

[21] On the eighth day, when it was time to
circumcise the child, he was named Jesus,
the name the angel had given him before he
was conceived.

Jesus Presented in the Temple

[22] When the time came for the purifica-
tion rites required by the Law of Moses, Jo-
seph and Mary took him to Jerusalem to pre-
sent him to the Lord [23] (as it is written in the
Law of the Lord, "Every firstborn male is to
be consecrated to the Lord"[c]), [24] and to of-
fer a sacrifice in keeping with what is said in
the Law of the Lord: "a pair of doves or two
young pigeons."[d]

[25] Now there was a man in Jerusalem called

[a] *80* Or *in the Spirit* [b] *2* Or *This census took place before* [c] *23* Exodus 13:2,12 [d] *24* Lev. 12:8

Simeon, who was righteous and devout. He was waiting for the consolation of Israel, and the Holy Spirit was on him. [26]It had been revealed to him by the Holy Spirit that he would not die before he had seen the Lord's Messiah. [27]Moved by the Spirit, he went into the temple courts. When the parents brought in the child Jesus to do for him what the custom of the Law required, [28]Simeon took him in his arms and praised God, saying:

29 "Sovereign Lord, as you have promised,
you may now dismiss[a] your servant
in peace.
30 For my eyes have seen your salvation,
31 which you have prepared in the
sight of all nations:
32 a light for revelation to the Gentiles,
and the glory of your people
Israel."

[33]The child's father and mother marveled at what was said about him. [34]Then Simeon blessed them and said to Mary, his mother: "This child is destined to cause the falling and rising of many in Israel, and to be a sign that will be spoken against, [35]so that the thoughts of many hearts will be revealed. And a sword will pierce your own soul too."

[36]There was also a prophet, Anna, the daughter of Penuel, of the tribe of Asher. She was very old; she had lived with her husband seven years after her marriage, [37]and then was a widow until she was eighty-four.[b] She never left the temple but worshiped night and day, fasting and praying. [38]Coming up to them at that very moment, she gave thanks to God and spoke about the child to all who were looking forward to the redemption of Jerusalem.

[39]When Joseph and Mary had done everything required by the Law of the Lord, they returned to Galilee to their own town of Nazareth. [40]And the child grew and became strong; he was filled with wisdom, and the grace of God was on him.

The Boy Jesus at the Temple

[41]Every year Jesus' parents went to Jerusalem for the Festival of the Passover. [42]When he was twelve years old, they went up to the festival, according to the custom. [43]After the festival was over, while his parents were returning home, the boy Jesus stayed behind in Jerusalem, but they were unaware of it. [44]Thinking he was in their company, they traveled on for a day. Then they began looking for him among their relatives and friends. [45]When they did not find him, they went back to Jerusalem to look for him. [46]After three days they found him in the temple courts, sitting among the teachers, listening to them and asking them questions. [47]Everyone who heard him was amazed at his understanding and his answers. [48]When his parents saw him, they were astonished. His mother said to him, "Son, why have you treated us like this? Your father and I have been anxiously searching for you."

[49]"Why were you searching for me?" he asked. "Didn't you know I had to be in my Father's house?"[c] [50]But they did not understand what he was saying to them.

[51]Then he went down to Nazareth with them and was obedient to them. But his mother treasured all these things in her heart. [52]And Jesus grew in wisdom and stature, and in favor with God and man.

John the Baptist Prepares the Way

3 In the fifteenth year of the reign of Tiberius Caesar—when Pontius Pilate was governor of Judea, Herod tetrarch of Galilee, his brother Philip tetrarch of Iturea and Traconitis, and Lysanias tetrarch of Abilene— [2]during the high-priesthood of Annas and Caiaphas, the word of God came to John son of Zechariah in the wilderness. [3]He went into all the country around the Jordan, preaching a baptism of repentance for the forgiveness of sins. [4]As it is written in the book of the words of Isaiah the prophet:

"A voice of one calling in the
wilderness,
'Prepare the way for the Lord,
make straight paths for him.
5 Every valley shall be filled in,
every mountain and hill made low.
The crooked roads shall become
straight,
the rough ways smooth.
6 And all people will see God's
salvation.'"[d]

[a] 29 Or *promised, / now dismiss* [b] 37 Or *then had been a widow for eighty-four years.* [c] 49 Or *be about my Father's business* [d] 6 Isaiah 40:3-5

7 John said to the crowds coming out to be
baptized by him, "You brood of vipers! Who
warned you to flee from the coming wrath?
8 Produce fruit in keeping with repentance.
And do not begin to say to yourselves, 'We
have Abraham as our father.' For I tell you
that out of these stones God can raise up
children for Abraham. 9 The ax is already at
the root of the trees, and every tree that does
not produce good fruit will be cut down and
thrown into the fire."

10 "What should we do then?" the crowd
asked.

11 John answered, "Anyone who has two
shirts should share with the one who has
none, and anyone who has food should do
the same."

12 Even tax collectors came to be baptized.
"Teacher," they asked, "what should we do?"

13 "Don't collect any more than you are re-
quired to," he told them.

14 Then some soldiers asked him, "And
what should we do?"

He replied, "Don't extort money and don't
accuse people falsely — be content with your
pay."

15 The people were waiting expectant-
ly and were all wondering in their hearts if
John might possibly be the Messiah. 16 John
answered them all, "I baptize you with[a] wa-
ter. But one who is more powerful than I will
come, the straps of whose sandals I am not
worthy to untie. He will baptize you with[a]
the Holy Spirit and fire. 17 His winnowing
fork is in his hand to clear his threshing floor
and to gather the wheat into his barn, but he
will burn up the chaff with unquenchable
fire." 18 And with many other words John ex-
horted the people and proclaimed the good
news to them.

19 But when John rebuked Herod the te-
trarch because of his marriage to Herodi-
as, his brother's wife, and all the other evil
things he had done, 20 Herod added this to
them all: He locked John up in prison.

The Baptism and Genealogy of Jesus

21 When all the people were being bap-
tized, Jesus was baptized too. And as he was
praying, heaven was opened 22 and the Holy
Spirit descended on him in bodily form like
a dove. And a voice came from heaven: "You
are my Son, whom I love; with you I am well
pleased."

23 Now Jesus himself was about thirty
years old when he began his ministry. He
was the son, so it was thought, of Joseph,

the son of Heli, 24 the son of Matthat,
the son of Levi, the son of Melki,
the son of Jannai, the son of Joseph,
25 the son of Mattathias, the son of Amos,
the son of Nahum, the son of Esli,
the son of Naggai, 26 the son of Maath,
the son of Mattathias, the son of Semein,
the son of Josek, the son of Joda,
27 the son of Joanan, the son of Rhesa,
the son of Zerubbabel, the son of Sheal-
tiel,
the son of Neri, 28 the son of Melki,
the son of Addi, the son of Cosam,
the son of Elmadam, the son of Er,
29 the son of Joshua, the son of Eliezer,
the son of Jorim, the son of Matthat,
the son of Levi, 30 the son of Simeon,
the son of Judah, the son of Joseph,
the son of Jonam, the son of Eliakim,
31 the son of Melea, the son of Menna,
the son of Mattatha, the son of Nathan,
the son of David, 32 the son of Jesse,
the son of Obed, the son of Boaz,
the son of Salmon,[b] the son of Nahshon,
33 the son of Amminadab, the son of Ram,[c]
the son of Hezron, the son of Perez,
the son of Judah, 34 the son of Jacob,
the son of Isaac, the son of Abraham,
the son of Terah, the son of Nahor,
35 the son of Serug, the son of Reu,
the son of Peleg, the son of Eber,
the son of Shelah, 36 the son of Cainan,
the son of Arphaxad, the son of Shem,
the son of Noah, the son of Lamech,
37 the son of Methuselah, the son of Enoch,
the son of Jared, the son of Mahalalel,
the son of Kenan, 38 the son of Enosh,
the son of Seth, the son of Adam,
the son of God.

Jesus Is Tested in the Wilderness

4 Jesus, full of the Holy Spirit, left the Jor-
dan and was led by the Spirit into the
wilderness, 2 where for forty days he was
tempted[d] by the devil. He ate nothing during

[a] *16* Or *in* [b] *32* Some early manuscripts *Sala the son of Arni*; other manuscripts vary widely. [c] *33* Some manuscripts *Amminadab, the son of Admin,* [d] *2* The Greek for *tempted* can also mean *tested.*

those days, and at the end of them he was
hungry.
3 The devil said to him, "If you are the Son
of God, tell this stone to become bread."
4 Jesus answered, "It is written: 'Man shall
not live on bread alone.'[a]"
5 The devil led him up to a high place and
showed him in an instant all the kingdoms
of the world. 6 And he said to him, "I will give
you all their authority and splendor; it has
been given to me, and I can give it to any-
one I want to. 7 If you worship me, it will all
be yours."
8 Jesus answered, "It is written: 'Worship
the Lord your God and serve him only.'[b]"
9 The devil led him to Jerusalem and had
him stand on the highest point of the tem-
ple. "If you are the Son of God," he said,
"throw yourself down from here. 10 For it is
written:

"'He will command his angels
concerning you
to guard you carefully;
11 they will lift you up in their hands,
so that you will not strike your foot
against a stone.'[c]"

12 Jesus answered, "It is said: 'Do not put
the Lord your God to the test.'[d]"
13 When the devil had finished all this
tempting, he left him until an opportune
time.

Jesus Rejected at Nazareth

14 Jesus returned to Galilee in the pow-
er of the Spirit, and news about him spread
through the whole countryside. 15 He was
teaching in their synagogues, and everyone
praised him.
16 He went to Nazareth, where he had
been brought up, and on the Sabbath day he
went into the synagogue, as was his custom.
He stood up to read, 17 and the scroll of the
prophet Isaiah was handed to him. Unroll-
ing it, he found the place where it is written:

18 "The Spirit of the Lord is on me,
because he has anointed me
to proclaim good news to the poor.
He has sent me to proclaim freedom for
the prisoners
and recovery of sight for the blind,
to set the oppressed free,
19 to proclaim the year of the Lord's
favor."[e]

20 Then he rolled up the scroll, gave it back
to the attendant and sat down. The eyes of
everyone in the synagogue were fastened on
him. 21 He began by saying to them, "Today
this scripture is fulfilled in your hearing."
22 All spoke well of him and were amazed
at the gracious words that came from his
lips. "Isn't this Joseph's son?" they asked.
23 Jesus said to them, "Surely you will
quote this proverb to me: 'Physician, heal
yourself!' And you will tell me, 'Do here in
your hometown what we have heard that you
did in Capernaum.'"
24 "Truly I tell you," he continued, "no
prophet is accepted in his hometown. 25 I
assure you that there were many widows
in Israel in Elijah's time, when the sky was
shut for three and a half years and there was
a severe famine throughout the land. 26 Yet
Elijah was not sent to any of them, but to a
widow in Zarephath in the region of Sidon.
27 And there were many in Israel with lepro-
sy[f] in the time of Elisha the prophet, yet not
one of them was cleansed — only Naaman
the Syrian."
28 All the people in the synagogue were
furious when they heard this. 29 They got up,
drove him out of the town, and took him to
the brow of the hill on which the town was
built, in order to throw him off the cliff. 30 But
he walked right through the crowd and went
on his way.

Jesus Drives Out an Impure Spirit

31 Then he went down to Capernaum,
a town in Galilee, and on the Sabbath he
taught the people. 32 They were amazed at
his teaching, because his words had au-
thority.
33 In the synagogue there was a man pos-
sessed by a demon, an impure spirit. He
cried out at the top of his voice, 34 "Go away!
What do you want with us, Jesus of Naza-
reth? Have you come to destroy us? I know
who you are — the Holy One of God!"
35 "Be quiet!" Jesus said sternly. "Come

[a] *4* Deut. 8:3 [b] *8* Deut. 6:13 [c] *11* Psalm 91:11,12 [d] *12* Deut. 6:16 [e] *19* Isaiah 61:1,2 (see Septuagint); Isaiah 58:6 [f] *27* The Greek word traditionally translated *leprosy* was used for various diseases affecting the skin.

out of him!" Then the demon threw the man
down before them all and came out without
injuring him.
[36]All the people were amazed and said to
each other, "What words these are! With au-
thority and power he gives orders to impure
spirits and they come out!" [37]And the news
about him spread throughout the surround-
ing area.

Jesus Heals Many

[38]Jesus left the synagogue and went to the
home of Simon. Now Simon's mother-in-law
was suffering from a high fever, and they
asked Jesus to help her. [39]So he bent over her
and rebuked the fever, and it left her. She got
up at once and began to wait on them.
[40]At sunset, the people brought to Jesus
all who had various kinds of sickness, and
laying his hands on each one, he healed
them. [41]Moreover, demons came out of
many people, shouting, "You are the Son of
God!" But he rebuked them and would not
allow them to speak, because they knew he
was the Messiah.
[42]At daybreak, Jesus went out to a solitary
place. The people were looking for him and
when they came to where he was, they tried
to keep him from leaving them. [43]But he
said, "I must proclaim the good news of the
kingdom of God to the other towns also, be-
cause that is why I was sent." [44]And he kept
on preaching in the synagogues of Judea.

Jesus Calls His First Disciples

5 One day as Jesus was standing by the
Lake of Gennesaret,[a] the people were
crowding around him and listening to the
word of God. [2]He saw at the water's edge two
boats, left there by the fishermen, who were
washing their nets. [3]He got into one of the
boats, the one belonging to Simon, and asked
him to put out a little from shore. Then he sat
down and taught the people from the boat.
[4]When he had finished speaking, he said
to Simon, "Put out into deep water, and let
down the nets for a catch."
[5]Simon answered, "Master, we've worked
hard all night and haven't caught anything.
But because you say so, I will let down the
nets."
[6]When they had done so, they caught such
a large number of fish that their nets began
to break. [7]So they signaled their partners in
the other boat to come and help them, and
they came and filled both boats so full that
they began to sink.
[8]When Simon Peter saw this, he fell at
Jesus' knees and said, "Go away from me,
Lord; I am a sinful man!" [9]For he and all his
companions were astonished at the catch of
fish they had taken, [10]and so were James and
John, the sons of Zebedee, Simon's partners.
Then Jesus said to Simon, "Don't be
afraid; from now on you will fish for people."
[11]So they pulled their boats up on shore, left
everything and followed him.

Jesus Heals a Man With Leprosy

[12]While Jesus was in one of the towns, a
man came along who was covered with lep-
rosy.[b] When he saw Jesus, he fell with his
face to the ground and begged him, "Lord,
if you are willing, you can make me clean."
[13]Jesus reached out his hand and touched
the man. "I am willing," he said. "Be clean!"
And immediately the leprosy left him.
[14]Then Jesus ordered him, "Don't tell any-
one, but go, show yourself to the priest and
offer the sacrifices that Moses commanded
for your cleansing, as a testimony to them."
[15]Yet the news about him spread all the
more, so that crowds of people came to hear
him and to be healed of their sicknesses.
[16]But Jesus often withdrew to lonely places
and prayed.

Jesus Forgives and Heals a Paralyzed Man

[17]One day Jesus was teaching, and Phar-
isees and teachers of the law were sitting
there. They had come from every village
of Galilee and from Judea and Jerusalem.
And the power of the Lord was with Jesus
to heal the sick. [18]Some men came carrying
a paralyzed man on a mat and tried to take
him into the house to lay him before Jesus.
[19]When they could not find a way to do this
because of the crowd, they went up on the
roof and lowered him on his mat through
the tiles into the middle of the crowd, right
in front of Jesus.

[a] *1* That is, the Sea of Galilee [b] *12* The Greek word traditionally translated *leprosy* was used for various diseases affecting the skin.

[20]When Jesus saw their faith, he said,
"Friend, your sins are forgiven."
[21]The Pharisees and the teachers of the
law began thinking to themselves, "Who is
this fellow who speaks blasphemy? Who can
forgive sins but God alone?"
[22]Jesus knew what they were thinking
and asked, "Why are you thinking these
things in your hearts? [23]Which is easier: to
say, 'Your sins are forgiven,' or to say, 'Get up
and walk'? [24]But I want you to know that the
Son of Man has authority on earth to forgive
sins." So he said to the paralyzed man, "I tell
you, get up, take your mat and go home."
[25]Immediately he stood up in front of them,
took what he had been lying on and went
home praising God. [26]Everyone was amazed
and gave praise to God. They were filled with
awe and said, "We have seen remarkable
things today."

Jesus Calls Levi and Eats With Sinners

[27]After this, Jesus went out and saw a tax
collector by the name of Levi sitting at his
tax booth. "Follow me," Jesus said to him,
[28]and Levi got up, left everything and fol-
lowed him.
[29]Then Levi held a great banquet for Jesus
at his house, and a large crowd of tax col-
lectors and others were eating with them.
[30]But the Pharisees and the teachers of the
law who belonged to their sect complained
to his disciples, "Why do you eat and drink
with tax collectors and sinners?"
[31]Jesus answered them, "It is not the
healthy who need a doctor, but the sick. [32]I
have not come to call the righteous, but sin-
ners to repentance."

Jesus Questioned About Fasting

[33]They said to him, "John's disciples often
fast and pray, and so do the disciples of the
Pharisees, but yours go on eating and drink-
ing."
[34]Jesus answered, "Can you make the
friends of the bridegroom fast while he is
with them? [35]But the time will come when
the bridegroom will be taken from them; in
those days they will fast."
[36]He told them this parable: "No one tears
a piece out of a new garment to patch an old
one. Otherwise, they will have torn the new
garment, and the patch from the new will not
match the old. [37]And no one pours new wine
into old wineskins. Otherwise, the new wine
will burst the skins; the wine will run out
and the wineskins will be ruined. [38]No, new
wine must be poured into new wineskins.
[39]And no one after drinking old wine wants
the new, for they say, 'The old is better.'"

Jesus Is Lord of the Sabbath

6 One Sabbath Jesus was going through
the grainfields, and his disciples be-
gan to pick some heads of grain, rub them in
their hands and eat the kernels. [2]Some of the
Pharisees asked, "Why are you doing what is
unlawful on the Sabbath?"
[3]Jesus answered them, "Have you nev-
er read what David did when he and his
companions were hungry? [4]He entered the
house of God, and taking the consecrated
bread, he ate what is lawful only for priests
to eat. And he also gave some to his compan-
ions." [5]Then Jesus said to them, "The Son of
Man is Lord of the Sabbath."
[6]On another Sabbath he went into the
synagogue and was teaching, and a man was
there whose right hand was shriveled. [7]The
Pharisees and the teachers of the law were
looking for a reason to accuse Jesus, so they
watched him closely to see if he would heal
on the Sabbath. [8]But Jesus knew what they
were thinking and said to the man with the
shriveled hand, "Get up and stand in front of
everyone." So he got up and stood there.
[9]Then Jesus said to them, "I ask you,
which is lawful on the Sabbath: to do good or
to do evil, to save life or to destroy it?"
[10]He looked around at them all, and then
said to the man, "Stretch out your hand."
He did so, and his hand was completely re-
stored. [11]But the Pharisees and the teachers
of the law were furious and began to dis-
cuss with one another what they might do
to Jesus.

The Twelve Apostles

[12]One of those days Jesus went out to a
mountainside to pray, and spent the night
praying to God. [13]When morning came, he
called his disciples to him and chose twelve
of them, whom he also designated apostles:
[14]Simon (whom he named Peter), his brother
Andrew, James, John, Philip, Bartholomew,
[15]Matthew, Thomas, James son of Alphae-
us, Simon who was called the Zealot, [16]Judas

son of James, and Judas Iscariot, who became a traitor.

Blessings and Woes

17 He went down with them and stood on a level place. A large crowd of his disciples was there and a great number of people from all over Judea, from Jerusalem, and from the coastal region around Tyre and Sidon, 18 who had come to hear him and to be healed of their diseases. Those troubled by impure spirits were cured, 19 and the people all tried to touch him, because power was coming from him and healing them all.

20 Looking at his disciples, he said:

"Blessed are you who are poor,
for yours is the kingdom of God.
21 Blessed are you who hunger now,
for you will be satisfied.
Blessed are you who weep now,
for you will laugh.
22 Blessed are you when people hate you,
when they exclude you and insult you
and reject your name as evil,
because of the Son of Man.

23 "Rejoice in that day and leap for joy, because great is your reward in heaven. For that is how their ancestors treated the prophets.

24 "But woe to you who are rich,
for you have already received your
comfort.
25 Woe to you who are well fed now,
for you will go hungry.
Woe to you who laugh now,
for you will mourn and weep.
26 Woe to you when everyone speaks well
of you,
for that is how their ancestors treated
the false prophets.

Love for Enemies

27 "But to you who are listening I say: Love your enemies, do good to those who hate you, 28 bless those who curse you, pray for those who mistreat you. 29 If someone slaps you on one cheek, turn to them the other also. If someone takes your coat, do not withhold your shirt from them. 30 Give to everyone who asks you, and if anyone takes what belongs to you, do not demand it back. 31 Do to others as you would have them do to you.

32 "If you love those who love you, what credit is that to you? Even sinners love those who love them. 33 And if you do good to those who are good to you, what credit is that to you? Even sinners do that. 34 And if you lend to those from whom you expect repayment, what credit is that to you? Even sinners lend to sinners, expecting to be repaid in full. 35 But love your enemies, do good to them, and lend to them without expecting to get anything back. Then your reward will be great, and you will be children of the Most High, because he is kind to the ungrateful and wicked. 36 Be merciful, just as your Father is merciful.

Judging Others

37 "Do not judge, and you will not be judged. Do not condemn, and you will not be condemned. Forgive, and you will be forgiven. 38 Give, and it will be given to you. A good measure, pressed down, shaken together and running over, will be poured into your lap. For with the measure you use, it will be measured to you."

39 He also told them this parable: "Can the blind lead the blind? Will they not both fall into a pit? 40 The student is not above the teacher, but everyone who is fully trained will be like their teacher.

41 "Why do you look at the speck of sawdust in your brother's eye and pay no attention to the plank in your own eye? 42 How can you say to your brother, 'Brother, let me take the speck out of your eye,' when you yourself fail to see the plank in your own eye? You hypocrite, first take the plank out of your eye, and then you will see clearly to remove the speck from your brother's eye.

A Tree and Its Fruit

43 "No good tree bears bad fruit, nor does a bad tree bear good fruit. 44 Each tree is recognized by its own fruit. People do not pick figs from thornbushes, or grapes from briers. 45 A good man brings good things out of the good stored up in his heart, and an evil man brings evil things out of the evil stored up in his heart. For the mouth speaks what the heart is full of.

The Wise and Foolish Builders

46 "Why do you call me, 'Lord, Lord,' and do not do what I say? 47 As for everyone who

comes to me and hears my words and puts them into practice, I will show you what they are like. 48They are like a man building a house, who dug down deep and laid the foundation on rock. When a flood came, the torrent struck that house but could not shake it, because it was well built. 49But the one who hears my words and does not put them into practice is like a man who built a house on the ground without a foundation. The moment the torrent struck that house, it collapsed and its destruction was complete."

The Faith of the Centurion

7 When Jesus had finished saying all this to the people who were listening, he entered Capernaum. 2There a centurion's servant, whom his master valued highly, was sick and about to die. 3The centurion heard of Jesus and sent some elders of the Jews to him, asking him to come and heal his servant. 4When they came to Jesus, they pleaded earnestly with him, "This man deserves to have you do this, 5because he loves our nation and has built our synagogue." 6So Jesus went with them.

He was not far from the house when the centurion sent friends to say to him: "Lord, don't trouble yourself, for I do not deserve to have you come under my roof. 7That is why I did not even consider myself worthy to come to you. But say the word, and my servant will be healed. 8For I myself am a man under authority, with soldiers under me. I tell this one, 'Go,' and he goes; and that one, 'Come,' and he comes. I say to my servant, 'Do this,' and he does it."

9When Jesus heard this, he was amazed at him, and turning to the crowd following him, he said, "I tell you, I have not found such great faith even in Israel." 10Then the men who had been sent returned to the house and found the servant well.

Jesus Raises a Widow's Son

11Soon afterward, Jesus went to a town called Nain, and his disciples and a large crowd went along with him. 12As he approached the town gate, a dead person was being carried out — the only son of his mother, and she was a widow. And a large crowd from the town was with her. 13When the Lord saw her, his heart went out to her and he said, "Don't cry."

14Then he went up and touched the bier they were carrying him on, and the bearers stood still. He said, "Young man, I say to you, get up!" 15The dead man sat up and began to talk, and Jesus gave him back to his mother.

16They were all filled with awe and praised God. "A great prophet has appeared among us," they said. "God has come to help his people." 17This news about Jesus spread throughout Judea and the surrounding country.

Jesus and John the Baptist

18John's disciples told him about all these things. Calling two of them, 19he sent them to the Lord to ask, "Are you the one who is to come, or should we expect someone else?"

20When the men came to Jesus, they said, "John the Baptist sent us to you to ask, 'Are you the one who is to come, or should we expect someone else?' "

21At that very time Jesus cured many who had diseases, sicknesses and evil spirits, and gave sight to many who were blind. 22So he replied to the messengers, "Go back and report to John what you have seen and heard: The blind receive sight, the lame walk, those who have leprosy[a] are cleansed, the deaf hear, the dead are raised, and the good news is proclaimed to the poor. 23Blessed is anyone who does not stumble on account of me."

24After John's messengers left, Jesus began to speak to the crowd about John: "What did you go out into the wilderness to see? A reed swayed by the wind? 25If not, what did you go out to see? A man dressed in fine clothes? No, those who wear expensive clothes and indulge in luxury are in palaces. 26But what did you go out to see? A prophet? Yes, I tell you, and more than a prophet. 27This is the one about whom it is written:

" 'I will send my messenger ahead of you,
who will prepare your way before you.'[b]

28I tell you, among those born of women there is no one greater than John; yet the one who is least in the kingdom of God is greater than he."

[a] 22 The Greek word traditionally translated *leprosy* was used for various diseases affecting the skin.
[b] 27 Mal. 3:1

29 (All the people, even the tax collectors, when they heard Jesus' words, acknowledged that God's way was right, because they had been baptized by John. 30 But the Pharisees and the experts in the law rejected God's purpose for themselves, because they had not been baptized by John.)

31 Jesus went on to say, "To what, then, can I compare the people of this generation? What are they like? 32 They are like children sitting in the marketplace and calling out to each other:

"'We played the pipe for you,
  and you did not dance;
we sang a dirge,
  and you did not cry.'

33 For John the Baptist came neither eating bread nor drinking wine, and you say, 'He has a demon.' 34 The Son of Man came eating and drinking, and you say, 'Here is a glutton and a drunkard, a friend of tax collectors and sinners.' 35 But wisdom is proved right by all her children."

Jesus Anointed by a Sinful Woman

36 When one of the Pharisees invited Jesus to have dinner with him, he went to the Pharisee's house and reclined at the table. 37 A woman in that town who lived a sinful life learned that Jesus was eating at the Pharisee's house, so she came there with an alabaster jar of perfume. 38 As she stood behind him at his feet weeping, she began to wet his feet with her tears. Then she wiped them with her hair, kissed them and poured perfume on them.

39 When the Pharisee who had invited him saw this, he said to himself, "If this man were a prophet, he would know who is touching him and what kind of woman she is — that she is a sinner."

40 Jesus answered him, "Simon, I have something to tell you."

"Tell me, teacher," he said.

41 "Two people owed money to a certain moneylender. One owed him five hundred denarii,[a] and the other fifty. 42 Neither of them had the money to pay him back, so he forgave the debts of both. Now which of them will love him more?"

43 Simon replied, "I suppose the one who had the bigger debt forgiven."

"You have judged correctly," Jesus said.

44 Then he turned toward the woman and said to Simon, "Do you see this woman? I came into your house. You did not give me any water for my feet, but she wet my feet with her tears and wiped them with her hair. 45 You did not give me a kiss, but this woman, from the time I entered, has not stopped kissing my feet. 46 You did not put oil on my head, but she has poured perfume on my feet. 47 Therefore, I tell you, her many sins have been forgiven — as her great love has shown. But whoever has been forgiven little loves little."

48 Then Jesus said to her, "Your sins are forgiven."

49 The other guests began to say among themselves, "Who is this who even forgives sins?"

50 Jesus said to the woman, "Your faith has saved you; go in peace."

The Parable of the Sower

8 After this, Jesus traveled about from one town and village to another, proclaiming the good news of the kingdom of God. The Twelve were with him, 2 and also some women who had been cured of evil spirits and diseases: Mary (called Magdalene) from whom seven demons had come out; 3 Joanna the wife of Chuza, the manager of Herod's household; Susanna; and many others. These women were helping to support them out of their own means.

4 While a large crowd was gathering and people were coming to Jesus from town after town, he told this parable: 5 "A farmer went out to sow his seed. As he was scattering the seed, some fell along the path; it was trampled on, and the birds ate it up. 6 Some fell on rocky ground, and when it came up, the plants withered because they had no moisture. 7 Other seed fell among thorns, which grew up with it and choked the plants. 8 Still other seed fell on good soil. It came up and yielded a crop, a hundred times more than was sown."

When he said this, he called out, "Whoever has ears to hear, let them hear."

9 His disciples asked him what this parable meant. 10 He said, "The knowledge of the secrets of the kingdom of God has been given

[a] *41* A denarius was the usual daily wage of a day laborer (see Matt. 20:2).

to you, but to others I speak in parables, so that,

> “ ‘though seeing, they may not see;
> though hearing, they may not
> understand.’[a]

11 “This is the meaning of the parable: The seed is the word of God. 12 Those along the path are the ones who hear, and then the devil comes and takes away the word from their hearts, so that they may not believe and be saved. 13 Those on the rocky ground are the ones who receive the word with joy when they hear it, but they have no root. They believe for a while, but in the time of testing they fall away. 14 The seed that fell among thorns stands for those who hear, but as they go on their way they are choked by life’s worries, riches and pleasures, and they do not mature. 15 But the seed on good soil stands for those with a noble and good heart, who hear the word, retain it, and by persevering produce a crop.

A Lamp on a Stand

16 “No one lights a lamp and hides it in a clay jar or puts it under a bed. Instead, they put it on a stand, so that those who come in can see the light. 17 For there is nothing hidden that will not be disclosed, and nothing concealed that will not be known or brought out into the open. 18 Therefore consider carefully how you listen. Whoever has will be given more; whoever does not have, even what they think they have will be taken from them.”

Jesus’ Mother and Brothers

19 Now Jesus’ mother and brothers came to see him, but they were not able to get near him because of the crowd. 20 Someone told him, “Your mother and brothers are standing outside, wanting to see you.”

21 He replied, “My mother and brothers are those who hear God’s word and put it into practice.”

Jesus Calms the Storm

22 One day Jesus said to his disciples, “Let us go over to the other side of the lake.” So they got into a boat and set out. 23 As they sailed, he fell asleep. A squall came down on the lake, so that the boat was being swamped, and they were in great danger.

24 The disciples went and woke him, saying, “Master, Master, we’re going to drown!”

He got up and rebuked the wind and the raging waters; the storm subsided, and all was calm. 25 “Where is your faith?” he asked his disciples.

In fear and amazement they asked one another, “Who is this? He commands even the winds and the water, and they obey him.”

Jesus Restores a Demon-Possessed Man

26 They sailed to the region of the Gerasenes,[b] which is across the lake from Galilee. 27 When Jesus stepped ashore, he was met by a demon-possessed man from the town. For a long time this man had not worn clothes or lived in a house, but had lived in the tombs. 28 When he saw Jesus, he cried out and fell at his feet, shouting at the top of his voice, “What do you want with me, Jesus, Son of the Most High God? I beg you, don’t torture me!” 29 For Jesus had commanded the impure spirit to come out of the man. Many times it had seized him, and though he was chained hand and foot and kept under guard, he had broken his chains and had been driven by the demon into solitary places.

30 Jesus asked him, “What is your name?”

“Legion,” he replied, because many demons had gone into him. 31 And they begged Jesus repeatedly not to order them to go into the Abyss.

32 A large herd of pigs was feeding there on the hillside. The demons begged Jesus to let them go into the pigs, and he gave them permission. 33 When the demons came out of the man, they went into the pigs, and the herd rushed down the steep bank into the lake and was drowned.

34 When those tending the pigs saw what had happened, they ran off and reported this in the town and countryside, 35 and the people went out to see what had happened. When they came to Jesus, they found the man from whom the demons had gone out, sitting at Jesus’ feet, dressed and in his right mind; and they were afraid. 36 Those who had seen it told the people how the demon-possessed

[a] *10* Isaiah 6:9 [b] *26* Some manuscripts *Gadarenes*; other manuscripts *Gergesenes*; also in verse 37

man had been cured. [37]Then all the people
of the region of the Gerasenes asked Jesus
to leave them, because they were overcome
with fear. So he got into the boat and left.
[38]The man from whom the demons had
gone out begged to go with him, but Jesus
sent him away, saying, [39]"Return home and
tell how much God has done for you." So the
man went away and told all over town how
much Jesus had done for him.

Jesus Raises a Dead Girl and Heals a Sick Woman

[40]Now when Jesus returned, a crowd wel-
comed him, for they were all expecting him.
[41]Then a man named Jairus, a synagogue
leader, came and fell at Jesus' feet, pleading
with him to come to his house [42]because his
only daughter, a girl of about twelve, was
dying.

As Jesus was on his way, the crowds al-
most crushed him. [43]And a woman was
there who had been subject to bleeding for
twelve years,[a] but no one could heal her.
[44]She came up behind him and touched
the edge of his cloak, and immediately her
bleeding stopped.

[45]"Who touched me?" Jesus asked.

When they all denied it, Peter said, "Mas-
ter, the people are crowding and pressing
against you."

[46]But Jesus said, "Someone touched me; I
know that power has gone out from me."

[47]Then the woman, seeing that she could
not go unnoticed, came trembling and fell at
his feet. In the presence of all the people, she
told why she had touched him and how she
had been instantly healed. [48]Then he said to
her, "Daughter, your faith has healed you. Go
in peace."

[49]While Jesus was still speaking, some-
one came from the house of Jairus, the syn-
agogue leader. "Your daughter is dead," he
said. "Don't bother the teacher anymore."

[50]Hearing this, Jesus said to Jairus, "Don't
be afraid; just believe, and she will be
healed."

[51]When he arrived at the house of Jairus,
he did not let anyone go in with him except
Peter, John and James, and the child's father
and mother. [52]Meanwhile, all the people
were wailing and mourning for her. "Stop
wailing," Jesus said. "She is not dead but
asleep."

[53]They laughed at him, knowing that she
was dead. [54]But he took her by the hand
and said, "My child, get up!" [55]Her spirit re-
turned, and at once she stood up. Then Jesus
told them to give her something to eat. [56]Her
parents were astonished, but he ordered
them not to tell anyone what had happened.

Jesus Sends Out the Twelve

9 When Jesus had called the Twelve to-
gether, he gave them power and au-
thority to drive out all demons and to cure
diseases, [2]and he sent them out to proclaim
the kingdom of God and to heal the sick. [3]He
told them: "Take nothing for the journey—
no staff, no bag, no bread, no money, no ex-
tra shirt. [4]Whatever house you enter, stay
there until you leave that town. [5]If people do
not welcome you, leave their town and shake
the dust off your feet as a testimony against
them." [6]So they set out and went from village
to village, proclaiming the good news and
healing people everywhere.

[7]Now Herod the tetrarch heard about all
that was going on. And he was perplexed be-
cause some were saying that John had been
raised from the dead, [8]others that Elijah had
appeared, and still others that one of the
prophets of long ago had come back to life.
[9]But Herod said, "I beheaded John. Who,
then, is this I hear such things about?" And
he tried to see him.

Jesus Feeds the Five Thousand

[10]When the apostles returned, they re-
ported to Jesus what they had done. Then he
took them with him and they withdrew by
themselves to a town called Bethsaida, [11]but
the crowds learned about it and followed
him. He welcomed them and spoke to them
about the kingdom of God, and healed those
who needed healing.

[12]Late in the afternoon the Twelve came
to him and said, "Send the crowd away so
they can go to the surrounding villages and
countryside and find food and lodging, be-
cause we are in a remote place here."

[13]He replied, "You give them something
to eat."

They answered, "We have only five loaves

[a] *43* Many manuscripts *years, and she had spent all she had on doctors*

of bread and two fish — unless we go and buy food for all this crowd." 14(About five thousand men were there.)

But he said to his disciples, "Have them sit down in groups of about fifty each." 15The disciples did so, and everyone sat down. 16Taking the five loaves and the two fish and looking up to heaven, he gave thanks and broke them. Then he gave them to the disciples to distribute to the people. 17They all ate and were satisfied, and the disciples picked up twelve basketfuls of broken pieces that were left over.

Peter Declares That Jesus Is the Messiah

18Once when Jesus was praying in private and his disciples were with him, he asked them, "Who do the crowds say I am?"

19They replied, "Some say John the Baptist; others say Elijah; and still others, that one of the prophets of long ago has come back to life."

20"But what about you?" he asked. "Who do you say I am?"

Peter answered, "God's Messiah."

Jesus Predicts His Death

21Jesus strictly warned them not to tell this to anyone. 22And he said, "The Son of Man must suffer many things and be rejected by the elders, the chief priests and the teachers of the law, and he must be killed and on the third day be raised to life."

23Then he said to them all: "Whoever wants to be my disciple must deny themselves and take up their cross daily and follow me. 24For whoever wants to save their life will lose it, but whoever loses their life for me will save it. 25What good is it for someone to gain the whole world, and yet lose or forfeit their very self? 26Whoever is ashamed of me and my words, the Son of Man will be ashamed of them when he comes in his glory and in the glory of the Father and of the holy angels.

27"Truly I tell you, some who are standing here will not taste death before they see the kingdom of God."

The Transfiguration

28About eight days after Jesus said this, he took Peter, John and James with him and went up onto a mountain to pray. 29As he was praying, the appearance of his face changed, and his clothes became as bright as a flash of lightning. 30Two men, Moses and Elijah, appeared in glorious splendor, talking with Jesus. 31They spoke about his departure,[a] which he was about to bring to fulfillment at Jerusalem. 32Peter and his companions were very sleepy, but when they became fully awake, they saw his glory and the two men standing with him. 33As the men were leaving Jesus, Peter said to him, "Master, it is good for us to be here. Let us put up three shelters — one for you, one for Moses and one for Elijah." (He did not know what he was saying.)

34While he was speaking, a cloud appeared and covered them, and they were afraid as they entered the cloud. 35A voice came from the cloud, saying, "This is my Son, whom I have chosen; listen to him." 36When the voice had spoken, they found that Jesus was alone. The disciples kept this to themselves and did not tell anyone at that time what they had seen.

Jesus Heals a Demon-Possessed Boy

37The next day, when they came down from the mountain, a large crowd met him. 38A man in the crowd called out, "Teacher, I beg you to look at my son, for he is my only child. 39A spirit seizes him and he suddenly screams; it throws him into convulsions so that he foams at the mouth. It scarcely ever leaves him and is destroying him. 40I begged your disciples to drive it out, but they could not."

41"You unbelieving and perverse generation," Jesus replied, "how long shall I stay with you and put up with you? Bring your son here."

42Even while the boy was coming, the demon threw him to the ground in a convulsion. But Jesus rebuked the impure spirit, healed the boy and gave him back to his father. 43And they were all amazed at the greatness of God.

Jesus Predicts His Death a Second Time

While everyone was marveling at all that Jesus did, he said to his disciples, 44"Listen carefully to what I am about to tell you: The Son of Man is going to be delivered into the

[a] *31* Greek *exodos*

hands of men." 45 But they did not understand what this meant. It was hidden from them, so that they did not grasp it, and they were afraid to ask him about it.

46 An argument started among the disciples as to which of them would be the greatest. 47 Jesus, knowing their thoughts, took a little child and had him stand beside him. 48 Then he said to them, "Whoever welcomes this little child in my name welcomes me; and whoever welcomes me welcomes the one who sent me. For it is the one who is least among you all who is the greatest."

49 "Master," said John, "we saw someone driving out demons in your name and we tried to stop him, because he is not one of us."

50 "Do not stop him," Jesus said, "for whoever is not against you is for you."

Samaritan Opposition

51 As the time approached for him to be taken up to heaven, Jesus resolutely set out for Jerusalem. 52 And he sent messengers on ahead, who went into a Samaritan village to get things ready for him; 53 but the people there did not welcome him, because he was heading for Jerusalem. 54 When the disciples James and John saw this, they asked, "Lord, do you want us to call fire down from heaven to destroy them[a]?" 55 But Jesus turned and rebuked them. 56 Then he and his disciples went to another village.

The Cost of Following Jesus

57 As they were walking along the road, a man said to him, "I will follow you wherever you go."

58 Jesus replied, "Foxes have dens and birds have nests, but the Son of Man has no place to lay his head."

59 He said to another man, "Follow me."

But he replied, "Lord, first let me go and bury my father."

60 Jesus said to him, "Let the dead bury their own dead, but you go and proclaim the kingdom of God."

61 Still another said, "I will follow you, Lord; but first let me go back and say goodbye to my family."

62 Jesus replied, "No one who puts a hand to the plow and looks back is fit for service in the kingdom of God."

Jesus Sends Out the Seventy-Two

10 After this the Lord appointed seventy-two[b] others and sent them two by two ahead of him to every town and place where he was about to go. 2 He told them, "The harvest is plentiful, but the workers are few. Ask the Lord of the harvest, therefore, to send out workers into his harvest field. 3 Go! I am sending you out like lambs among wolves. 4 Do not take a purse or bag or sandals; and do not greet anyone on the road.

5 "When you enter a house, first say, 'Peace to this house.' 6 If someone who promotes peace is there, your peace will rest on them; if not, it will return to you. 7 Stay there, eating and drinking whatever they give you, for the worker deserves his wages. Do not move around from house to house.

8 "When you enter a town and are welcomed, eat what is offered to you. 9 Heal the sick who are there and tell them, 'The kingdom of God has come near to you.' 10 But when you enter a town and are not welcomed, go into its streets and say, 11 'Even the dust of your town we wipe from our feet as a warning to you. Yet be sure of this: The kingdom of God has come near.' 12 I tell you, it will be more bearable on that day for Sodom than for that town.

13 "Woe to you, Chorazin! Woe to you, Bethsaida! For if the miracles that were performed in you had been performed in Tyre and Sidon, they would have repented long ago, sitting in sackcloth and ashes. 14 But it will be more bearable for Tyre and Sidon at the judgment than for you. 15 And you, Capernaum, will you be lifted to the heavens? No, you will go down to Hades.[c]

16 "Whoever listens to you listens to me; whoever rejects you rejects me; but whoever rejects me rejects him who sent me."

17 The seventy-two returned with joy and said, "Lord, even the demons submit to us in your name."

18 He replied, "I saw Satan fall like lightning from heaven. 19 I have given you authority to trample on snakes and scorpions and to overcome all the power of the enemy; nothing will harm you. 20 However, do not

[a] 54 Some manuscripts *them, just as Elijah did*
[b] 1 Some manuscripts *seventy*; also in verse 17
[c] 15 That is, the realm of the dead

rejoice that the spirits submit to you, but re-
joice that your names are written in heaven."
21 At that time Jesus, full of joy through the
Holy Spirit, said, "I praise you, Father, Lord
of heaven and earth, because you have hid-
den these things from the wise and learned,
and revealed them to little children. Yes, Fa-
ther, for this is what you were pleased to do.
22 "All things have been committed to me
by my Father. No one knows who the Son is
except the Father, and no one knows who the
Father is except the Son and those to whom
the Son chooses to reveal him."
23 Then he turned to his disciples and said
privately, "Blessed are the eyes that see what
you see. 24 For I tell you that many prophets
and kings wanted to see what you see but did
not see it, and to hear what you hear but did
not hear it."

The Parable of the Good Samaritan

25 On one occasion an expert in the law
stood up to test Jesus. "Teacher," he asked,
"what must I do to inherit eternal life?"
26 "What is written in the Law?" he replied.
"How do you read it?"
27 He answered, " 'Love the Lord your God
with all your heart and with all your soul
and with all your strength and with all your
mind'[a]; and, 'Love your neighbor as your-
self.'[b]"
28 "You have answered correctly," Jesus re-
plied. "Do this and you will live."
29 But he wanted to justify himself, so he
asked Jesus, "And who is my neighbor?"
30 In reply Jesus said: "A man was going
down from Jerusalem to Jericho, when he
was attacked by robbers. They stripped him
of his clothes, beat him and went away, leav-
ing him half dead. 31 A priest happened to be
going down the same road, and when he saw
the man, he passed by on the other side. 32 So
too, a Levite, when he came to the place and
saw him, passed by on the other side. 33 But
a Samaritan, as he traveled, came where the
man was; and when he saw him, he took pity
on him. 34 He went to him and bandaged his
wounds, pouring on oil and wine. Then he
put the man on his own donkey, brought him
to an inn and took care of him. 35 The next
day he took out two denarii[c] and gave them
to the innkeeper. 'Look after him,' he said,
'and when I return, I will reimburse you for
any extra expense you may have.'
36 "Which of these three do you think
was a neighbor to the man who fell into the
hands of robbers?"
37 The expert in the law replied, "The one
who had mercy on him."
Jesus told him, "Go and do likewise."

At the Home of Martha and Mary

38 As Jesus and his disciples were on their
way, he came to a village where a woman
named Martha opened her home to him.
39 She had a sister called Mary, who sat at the
Lord's feet listening to what he said. 40 But
Martha was distracted by all the prepara-
tions that had to be made. She came to him
and asked, "Lord, don't you care that my sis-
ter has left me to do the work by myself? Tell
her to help me!"
41 "Martha, Martha," the Lord answered,
"you are worried and upset about many
things, 42 but few things are needed — or
indeed only one.[d] Mary has chosen what is
better, and it will not be taken away from
her."

Jesus' Teaching on Prayer

11 One day Jesus was praying in a cer-
tain place. When he finished, one of
his disciples said to him, "Lord, teach us to
pray, just as John taught his disciples."
2 He said to them, "When you pray, say:

" 'Father,[e]
hallowed be your name,
your kingdom come.[f]
3 Give us each day our daily bread.
4 Forgive us our sins,
for we also forgive everyone who sins
against us.[g]
And lead us not into temptation.[h]' "

5 Then Jesus said to them, "Suppose you
have a friend, and you go to him at mid-
night and say, 'Friend, lend me three loaves
of bread; 6 a friend of mine on a journey has
come to me, and I have no food to offer him.'

[a] *27* Deut. 6:5 [b] *27* Lev. 19:18 [c] *35* A denarius was the usual daily wage of a day laborer (see Matt. 20:2). [d] *42* Some manuscripts *but only one thing is needed* [e] *2* Some manuscripts *Our Father in heaven* [f] *2* Some manuscripts *come. May your will be done on earth as it is in heaven.* [g] *4* Greek *everyone who is indebted to us* [h] *4* Some manuscripts *temptation, but deliver us from the evil one*

7And suppose the one inside answers, 'Don't bother me. The door is already locked, and my children and I are in bed. I can't get up and give you anything.' 8I tell you, even though he will not get up and give you the bread because of friendship, yet because of your shameless audacity[a] he will surely get up and give you as much as you need.

9"So I say to you: Ask and it will be given to you; seek and you will find; knock and the door will be opened to you. 10For everyone who asks receives; the one who seeks finds; and to the one who knocks, the door will be opened.

11"Which of you fathers, if your son asks for[b] a fish, will give him a snake instead? 12Or if he asks for an egg, will give him a scorpion? 13If you then, though you are evil, know how to give good gifts to your children, how much more will your Father in heaven give the Holy Spirit to those who ask him!"

Jesus and Beelzebul

14Jesus was driving out a demon that was mute. When the demon left, the man who had been mute spoke, and the crowd was amazed. 15But some of them said, "By Beelzebul, the prince of demons, he is driving out demons." 16Others tested him by asking for a sign from heaven.

17Jesus knew their thoughts and said to them: "Any kingdom divided against itself will be ruined, and a house divided against itself will fall. 18If Satan is divided against himself, how can his kingdom stand? I say this because you claim that I drive out demons by Beelzebul. 19Now if I drive out demons by Beelzebul, by whom do your followers drive them out? So then, they will be your judges. 20But if I drive out demons by the finger of God, then the kingdom of God has come upon you.

21"When a strong man, fully armed, guards his own house, his possessions are safe. 22But when someone stronger attacks and overpowers him, he takes away the armor in which the man trusted and divides up his plunder.

23"Whoever is not with me is against me, and whoever does not gather with me scatters.

24"When an impure spirit comes out of a person, it goes through arid places seeking rest and does not find it. Then it says, 'I will return to the house I left.' 25When it arrives, it finds the house swept clean and put in order. 26Then it goes and takes seven other spirits more wicked than itself, and they go in and live there. And the final condition of that person is worse than the first."

27As Jesus was saying these things, a woman in the crowd called out, "Blessed is the mother who gave you birth and nursed you."

28He replied, "Blessed rather are those who hear the word of God and obey it."

The Sign of Jonah

29As the crowds increased, Jesus said, "This is a wicked generation. It asks for a sign, but none will be given it except the sign of Jonah. 30For as Jonah was a sign to the Ninevites, so also will the Son of Man be to this generation. 31The Queen of the South will rise at the judgment with the people of this generation and condemn them, for she came from the ends of the earth to listen to Solomon's wisdom; and now something greater than Solomon is here. 32The men of Nineveh will stand up at the judgment with this generation and condemn it, for they repented at the preaching of Jonah; and now something greater than Jonah is here.

The Lamp of the Body

33"No one lights a lamp and puts it in a place where it will be hidden, or under a bowl. Instead they put it on its stand, so that those who come in may see the light. 34Your eye is the lamp of your body. When your eyes are healthy,[c] your whole body also is full of light. But when they are unhealthy,[d] your body also is full of darkness. 35See to it, then, that the light within you is not darkness. 36Therefore, if your whole body is full of light, and no part of it dark, it will be just as full of light as when a lamp shines its light on you."

Woes on the Pharisees and the Experts in the Law

37When Jesus had finished speaking, a Pharisee invited him to eat with him; so he went in and reclined at the table. 38But the Pharisee was surprised when he noticed that Jesus did not first wash before the meal.

[a] *8* Or *yet to preserve his good name* [b] *11* Some manuscripts *for bread, will give him a stone? Or if he asks for* [c] *34* The Greek for *healthy* here implies *generous.* [d] *34* The Greek for *unhealthy* here implies *stingy.*

39 Then the Lord said to him, "Now then, you Pharisees clean the outside of the cup and dish, but inside you are full of greed and wickedness. 40 You foolish people! Did not the one who made the outside make the inside also? 41 But now as for what is inside you — be generous to the poor, and everything will be clean for you.

42 "Woe to you Pharisees, because you give God a tenth of your mint, rue and all other kinds of garden herbs, but you neglect justice and the love of God. You should have practiced the latter without leaving the former undone.

43 "Woe to you Pharisees, because you love the most important seats in the synagogues and respectful greetings in the marketplaces.

44 "Woe to you, because you are like unmarked graves, which people walk over without knowing it."

45 One of the experts in the law answered him, "Teacher, when you say these things, you insult us also."

46 Jesus replied, "And you experts in the law, woe to you, because you load people down with burdens they can hardly carry, and you yourselves will not lift one finger to help them.

47 "Woe to you, because you build tombs for the prophets, and it was your ancestors who killed them. 48 So you testify that you approve of what your ancestors did; they killed the prophets, and you build their tombs. 49 Because of this, God in his wisdom said, 'I will send them prophets and apostles, some of whom they will kill and others they will persecute.' 50 Therefore this generation will be held responsible for the blood of all the prophets that has been shed since the beginning of the world, 51 from the blood of Abel to the blood of Zechariah, who was killed between the altar and the sanctuary. Yes, I tell you, this generation will be held responsible for it all.

52 "Woe to you experts in the law, because you have taken away the key to knowledge. You yourselves have not entered, and you have hindered those who were entering."

53 When Jesus went outside, the Pharisees and the teachers of the law began to oppose him fiercely and to besiege him with questions, 54 waiting to catch him in something he might say.

Warnings and Encouragements

12 Meanwhile, when a crowd of many thousands had gathered, so that they were trampling on one another, Jesus began to speak first to his disciples, saying: "Be[a] on your guard against the yeast of the Pharisees, which is hypocrisy. 2 There is nothing concealed that will not be disclosed, or hidden that will not be made known. 3 What you have said in the dark will be heard in the daylight, and what you have whispered in the ear in the inner rooms will be proclaimed from the roofs.

4 "I tell you, my friends, do not be afraid of those who kill the body and after that can do no more. 5 But I will show you whom you should fear: Fear him who, after your body has been killed, has authority to throw you into hell. Yes, I tell you, fear him. 6 Are not five sparrows sold for two pennies? Yet not one of them is forgotten by God. 7 Indeed, the very hairs of your head are all numbered. Don't be afraid; you are worth more than many sparrows.

8 "I tell you, whoever publicly acknowledges me before others, the Son of Man will also acknowledge before the angels of God. 9 But whoever disowns me before others will be disowned before the angels of God. 10 And everyone who speaks a word against the Son of Man will be forgiven, but anyone who blasphemes against the Holy Spirit will not be forgiven.

11 "When you are brought before synagogues, rulers and authorities, do not worry about how you will defend yourselves or what you will say, 12 for the Holy Spirit will teach you at that time what you should say."

The Parable of the Rich Fool

13 Someone in the crowd said to him, "Teacher, tell my brother to divide the inheritance with me."

14 Jesus replied, "Man, who appointed me a judge or an arbiter between you?" 15 Then he said to them, "Watch out! Be on your guard against all kinds of greed; life does not consist in an abundance of possessions."

16 And he told them this parable: "The ground of a certain rich man yielded an abundant harvest. 17 He thought to himself, 'What shall I do? I have no place to store my crops.'

[a] 1 Or *speak to his disciples, saying: "First of all, be*

18 “Then he said, ‘This is what I’ll do. I will tear down my barns and build bigger ones, and there I will store my surplus grain. 19 And I’ll say to myself, “You have plenty of grain laid up for many years. Take life easy; eat, drink and be merry.” ’

20 “But God said to him, ‘You fool! This very night your life will be demanded from you. Then who will get what you have prepared for yourself?’

21 “This is how it will be with whoever stores up things for themselves but is not rich toward God.”

Do Not Worry

22 Then Jesus said to his disciples: “Therefore I tell you, do not worry about your life, what you will eat; or about your body, what you will wear. 23 For life is more than food, and the body more than clothes. 24 Consider the ravens: They do not sow or reap, they have no storeroom or barn; yet God feeds them. And how much more valuable you are than birds! 25 Who of you by worrying can add a single hour to your life[a]? 26 Since you cannot do this very little thing, why do you worry about the rest?

27 “Consider how the wild flowers grow. They do not labor or spin. Yet I tell you, not even Solomon in all his splendor was dressed like one of these. 28 If that is how God clothes the grass of the field, which is here today, and tomorrow is thrown into the fire, how much more will he clothe you — you of little faith! 29 And do not set your heart on what you will eat or drink; do not worry about it. 30 For the pagan world runs after all such things, and your Father knows that you need them. 31 But seek his kingdom, and these things will be given to you as well.

32 “Do not be afraid, little flock, for your Father has been pleased to give you the kingdom. 33 Sell your possessions and give to the poor. Provide purses for yourselves that will not wear out, a treasure in heaven that will never fail, where no thief comes near and no moth destroys. 34 For where your treasure is, there your heart will be also.

Watchfulness

35 “Be dressed ready for service and keep your lamps burning, 36 like servants waiting for their master to return from a wedding banquet, so that when he comes and knocks they can immediately open the door for him. 37 It will be good for those servants whose master finds them watching when he comes. Truly I tell you, he will dress himself to serve, will have them recline at the table and will come and wait on them. 38 It will be good for those servants whose master finds them ready, even if he comes in the middle of the night or toward daybreak. 39 But understand this: If the owner of the house had known at what hour the thief was coming, he would not have let his house be broken into. 40 You also must be ready, because the Son of Man will come at an hour when you do not expect him.”

41 Peter asked, “Lord, are you telling this parable to us, or to everyone?”

42 The Lord answered, “Who then is the faithful and wise manager, whom the master puts in charge of his servants to give them their food allowance at the proper time? 43 It will be good for that servant whom the master finds doing so when he returns. 44 Truly I tell you, he will put him in charge of all his possessions. 45 But suppose the servant says to himself, ‘My master is taking a long time in coming,’ and he then begins to beat the other servants, both men and women, and to eat and drink and get drunk. 46 The master of that servant will come on a day when he does not expect him and at an hour he is not aware of. He will cut him to pieces and assign him a place with the unbelievers.

47 “The servant who knows the master’s will and does not get ready or does not do what the master wants will be beaten with many blows. 48 But the one who does not know and does things deserving punishment will be beaten with few blows. From everyone who has been given much, much will be demanded; and from the one who has been entrusted with much, much more will be asked.

Not Peace but Division

49 “I have come to bring fire on the earth, and how I wish it were already kindled! 50 But I have a baptism to undergo, and what constraint I am under until it is completed! 51 Do you think I came to bring peace on

[a] 25 Or *single cubit to your height*

earth? No, I tell you, but division. [52]From now on there will be five in one family divided against each other, three against two and two against three. [53]They will be divided, father against son and son against father, mother against daughter and daughter against mother, mother-in-law against daughter-in-law and daughter-in-law against mother-in-law."

Interpreting the Times

[54]He said to the crowd: "When you see a cloud rising in the west, immediately you say, 'It's going to rain,' and it does. [55]And when the south wind blows, you say, 'It's going to be hot,' and it is. [56]Hypocrites! You know how to interpret the appearance of the earth and the sky. How is it that you don't know how to interpret this present time?

[57]"Why don't you judge for yourselves what is right? [58]As you are going with your adversary to the magistrate, try hard to be reconciled on the way, or your adversary may drag you off to the judge, and the judge turn you over to the officer, and the officer throw you into prison. [59]I tell you, you will not get out until you have paid the last penny."

Repent or Perish

13 Now there were some present at that time who told Jesus about the Galileans whose blood Pilate had mixed with their sacrifices. [2]Jesus answered, "Do you think that these Galileans were worse sinners than all the other Galileans because they suffered this way? [3]I tell you, no! But unless you repent, you too will all perish. [4]Or those eighteen who died when the tower in Siloam fell on them—do you think they were more guilty than all the others living in Jerusalem? [5]I tell you, no! But unless you repent, you too will all perish."

[6]Then he told this parable: "A man had a fig tree growing in his vineyard, and he went to look for fruit on it but did not find any. [7]So he said to the man who took care of the vineyard, 'For three years now I've been coming to look for fruit on this fig tree and haven't found any. Cut it down! Why should it use up the soil?'

[8]"'Sir,' the man replied, 'leave it alone for one more year, and I'll dig around it and fertilize it. [9]If it bears fruit next year, fine! If not, then cut it down.'"

Jesus Heals a Crippled Woman on the Sabbath

[10]On a Sabbath Jesus was teaching in one of the synagogues, [11]and a woman was there who had been crippled by a spirit for eighteen years. She was bent over and could not straighten up at all. [12]When Jesus saw her, he called her forward and said to her, "Woman, you are set free from your infirmity." [13]Then he put his hands on her, and immediately she straightened up and praised God.

[14]Indignant because Jesus had healed on the Sabbath, the synagogue leader said to the people, "There are six days for work. So come and be healed on those days, not on the Sabbath."

[15]The Lord answered him, "You hypocrites! Doesn't each of you on the Sabbath untie your ox or donkey from the stall and lead it out to give it water? [16]Then should not this woman, a daughter of Abraham, whom Satan has kept bound for eighteen long years, be set free on the Sabbath day from what bound her?"

[17]When he said this, all his opponents were humiliated, but the people were delighted with all the wonderful things he was doing.

The Parables of the Mustard Seed and the Yeast

[18]Then Jesus asked, "What is the kingdom of God like? What shall I compare it to? [19]It is like a mustard seed, which a man took and planted in his garden. It grew and became a tree, and the birds perched in its branches."

[20]Again he asked, "What shall I compare the kingdom of God to? [21]It is like yeast that a woman took and mixed into about sixty pounds[a] of flour until it worked all through the dough."

The Narrow Door

[22]Then Jesus went through the towns and villages, teaching as he made his way to Jerusalem. [23]Someone asked him, "Lord, are only a few people going to be saved?"

He said to them, [24]"Make every effort to enter through the narrow door, because

[a] *21* Or about 27 kilograms

many, I tell you, will try to enter and will not be able to. 25Once the owner of the house gets up and closes the door, you will stand outside knocking and pleading, 'Sir, open the door for us.'

"But he will answer, 'I don't know you or where you come from.'

26"Then you will say, 'We ate and drank with you, and you taught in our streets.'

27"But he will reply, 'I don't know you or where you come from. Away from me, all you evildoers!'

28"There will be weeping there, and gnashing of teeth, when you see Abraham, Isaac and Jacob and all the prophets in the kingdom of God, but you yourselves thrown out. 29People will come from east and west and north and south, and will take their places at the feast in the kingdom of God. 30Indeed there are those who are last who will be first, and first who will be last."

Jesus' Sorrow for Jerusalem

31At that time some Pharisees came to Jesus and said to him, "Leave this place and go somewhere else. Herod wants to kill you."

32He replied, "Go tell that fox, 'I will keep on driving out demons and healing people today and tomorrow, and on the third day I will reach my goal.' 33In any case, I must press on today and tomorrow and the next day—for surely no prophet can die outside Jerusalem!

34"Jerusalem, Jerusalem, you who kill the prophets and stone those sent to you, how often I have longed to gather your children together, as a hen gathers her chicks under her wings, and you were not willing. 35Look, your house is left to you desolate. I tell you, you will not see me again until you say, 'Blessed is he who comes in the name of the Lord.'[a]"

Jesus at a Pharisee's House

14 One Sabbath, when Jesus went to eat in the house of a prominent Pharisee, he was being carefully watched. 2There in front of him was a man suffering from abnormal swelling of his body. 3Jesus asked the Pharisees and experts in the law, "Is it lawful to heal on the Sabbath or not?" 4But they remained silent. So taking hold of the man, he healed him and sent him on his way.

5Then he asked them, "If one of you has a child[b] or an ox that falls into a well on the Sabbath day, will you not immediately pull it out?" 6And they had nothing to say.

7When he noticed how the guests picked the places of honor at the table, he told them this parable: 8"When someone invites you to a wedding feast, do not take the place of honor, for a person more distinguished than you may have been invited. 9If so, the host who invited both of you will come and say to you, 'Give this person your seat.' Then, humiliated, you will have to take the least important place. 10But when you are invited, take the lowest place, so that when your host comes, he will say to you, 'Friend, move up to a better place.' Then you will be honored in the presence of all the other guests. 11For all those who exalt themselves will be humbled, and those who humble themselves will be exalted."

12Then Jesus said to his host, "When you give a luncheon or dinner, do not invite your friends, your brothers or sisters, your relatives, or your rich neighbors; if you do, they may invite you back and so you will be repaid. 13But when you give a banquet, invite the poor, the crippled, the lame, the blind, 14and you will be blessed. Although they cannot repay you, you will be repaid at the resurrection of the righteous."

The Parable of the Great Banquet

15When one of those at the table with him heard this, he said to Jesus, "Blessed is the one who will eat at the feast in the kingdom of God."

16Jesus replied: "A certain man was preparing a great banquet and invited many guests. 17At the time of the banquet he sent his servant to tell those who had been invited, 'Come, for everything is now ready.'

18"But they all alike began to make excuses. The first said, 'I have just bought a field, and I must go and see it. Please excuse me.'

19"Another said, 'I have just bought five yoke of oxen, and I'm on my way to try them out. Please excuse me.'

20"Still another said, 'I just got married, so I can't come.'

21"The servant came back and reported this to his master. Then the owner of the

[a] 35 Psalm 118:26 [b] 5 Some manuscripts *donkey*

house became angry and ordered his servant, 'Go out quickly into the streets and alleys of the town and bring in the poor, the crippled, the blind and the lame.'

22 " 'Sir,' the servant said, 'what you ordered has been done, but there is still room.'

23 "Then the master told his servant, 'Go out to the roads and country lanes and compel them to come in, so that my house will be full. 24 I tell you, not one of those who were invited will get a taste of my banquet.' "

The Cost of Being a Disciple

25 Large crowds were traveling with Jesus, and turning to them he said: 26 "If anyone comes to me and does not hate father and mother, wife and children, brothers and sisters — yes, even their own life — such a person cannot be my disciple. 27 And whoever does not carry their cross and follow me cannot be my disciple.

28 "Suppose one of you wants to build a tower. Won't you first sit down and estimate the cost to see if you have enough money to complete it? 29 For if you lay the foundation and are not able to finish it, everyone who sees it will ridicule you, 30 saying, 'This person began to build and wasn't able to finish.'

31 "Or suppose a king is about to go to war against another king. Won't he first sit down and consider whether he is able with ten thousand men to oppose the one coming against him with twenty thousand? 32 If he is not able, he will send a delegation while the other is still a long way off and will ask for terms of peace. 33 In the same way, those of you who do not give up everything you have cannot be my disciples.

34 "Salt is good, but if it loses its saltiness, how can it be made salty again? 35 It is fit neither for the soil nor for the manure pile; it is thrown out.

"Whoever has ears to hear, let them hear."

The Parable of the Lost Sheep

15 Now the tax collectors and sinners were all gathering around to hear Jesus. 2 But the Pharisees and the teachers of the law muttered, "This man welcomes sinners and eats with them."

3 Then Jesus told them this parable: 4 "Suppose one of you has a hundred sheep and loses one of them. Doesn't he leave the ninety-nine in the open country and go after the lost sheep until he finds it? 5 And when he finds it, he joyfully puts it on his shoulders 6 and goes home. Then he calls his friends and neighbors together and says, 'Rejoice with me; I have found my lost sheep.' 7 I tell you that in the same way there will be more rejoicing in heaven over one sinner who repents than over ninety-nine righteous persons who do not need to repent.

The Parable of the Lost Coin

8 "Or suppose a woman has ten silver coins[a] and loses one. Doesn't she light a lamp, sweep the house and search carefully until she finds it? 9 And when she finds it, she calls her friends and neighbors together and says, 'Rejoice with me; I have found my lost coin.' 10 In the same way, I tell you, there is rejoicing in the presence of the angels of God over one sinner who repents."

The Parable of the Lost Son

11 Jesus continued: "There was a man who had two sons. 12 The younger one said to his father, 'Father, give me my share of the estate.' So he divided his property between them.

13 "Not long after that, the younger son got together all he had, set off for a distant country and there squandered his wealth in wild living. 14 After he had spent everything, there was a severe famine in that whole country, and he began to be in need. 15 So he went and hired himself out to a citizen of that country, who sent him to his fields to feed pigs. 16 He longed to fill his stomach with the pods that the pigs were eating, but no one gave him anything.

17 "When he came to his senses, he said, 'How many of my father's hired servants have food to spare, and here I am starving to death! 18 I will set out and go back to my father and say to him: Father, I have sinned against heaven and against you. 19 I am no longer worthy to be called your son; make me like one of your hired servants.' 20 So he got up and went to his father.

"But while he was still a long way off, his father saw him and was filled with compassion for him; he ran to his son, threw his arms around him and kissed him.

[a] 8 Greek *ten drachmas,* each worth about a day's wages

[21]"The son said to him, 'Father, I have sinned against heaven and against you. I am no longer worthy to be called your son.'

[22]"But the father said to his servants, 'Quick! Bring the best robe and put it on him. Put a ring on his finger and sandals on his feet. [23]Bring the fattened calf and kill it. Let's have a feast and celebrate. [24]For this son of mine was dead and is alive again; he was lost and is found.' So they began to celebrate.

[25]"Meanwhile, the older son was in the field. When he came near the house, he heard music and dancing. [26]So he called one of the servants and asked him what was going on. [27]'Your brother has come,' he replied, 'and your father has killed the fattened calf because he has him back safe and sound.'

[28]"The older brother became angry and refused to go in. So his father went out and pleaded with him. [29]But he answered his father, 'Look! All these years I've been slaving for you and never disobeyed your orders. Yet you never gave me even a young goat so I could celebrate with my friends. [30]But when this son of yours who has squandered your property with prostitutes comes home, you kill the fattened calf for him!'

[31]"'My son,' the father said, 'you are always with me, and everything I have is yours. [32]But we had to celebrate and be glad, because this brother of yours was dead and is alive again; he was lost and is found.'"

The Parable of the Shrewd Manager

16 Jesus told his disciples: "There was a rich man whose manager was accused of wasting his possessions. [2]So he called him in and asked him, 'What is this I hear about you? Give an account of your management, because you cannot be manager any longer.'

[3]"The manager said to himself, 'What shall I do now? My master is taking away my job. I'm not strong enough to dig, and I'm ashamed to beg— [4]I know what I'll do so that, when I lose my job here, people will welcome me into their houses.'

[5]"So he called in each one of his master's debtors. He asked the first, 'How much do you owe my master?'

[6]"'Nine hundred gallons[a] of olive oil,' he replied.

"The manager told him, 'Take your bill, sit down quickly, and make it four hundred and fifty.'

[7]"Then he asked the second, 'And how much do you owe?'

"'A thousand bushels[b] of wheat,' he replied.

"He told him, 'Take your bill and make it eight hundred.'

[8]"The master commended the dishonest manager because he had acted shrewdly. For the people of this world are more shrewd in dealing with their own kind than are the people of the light. [9]I tell you, use worldly wealth to gain friends for yourselves, so that when it is gone, you will be welcomed into eternal dwellings.

[10]"Whoever can be trusted with very little can also be trusted with much, and whoever is dishonest with very little will also be dishonest with much. [11]So if you have not been trustworthy in handling worldly wealth, who will trust you with true riches? [12]And if you have not been trustworthy with someone else's property, who will give you property of your own?

[13]"No one can serve two masters. Either you will hate the one and love the other, or you will be devoted to the one and despise the other. You cannot serve both God and money."

[14]The Pharisees, who loved money, heard all this and were sneering at Jesus. [15]He said to them, "You are the ones who justify yourselves in the eyes of others, but God knows your hearts. What people value highly is detestable in God's sight.

Additional Teachings

[16]"The Law and the Prophets were proclaimed until John. Since that time, the good news of the kingdom of God is being preached, and everyone is forcing their way into it. [17]It is easier for heaven and earth to disappear than for the least stroke of a pen to drop out of the Law.

[18]"Anyone who divorces his wife and marries another woman commits adultery, and the man who marries a divorced woman commits adultery.

The Rich Man and Lazarus

[19]"There was a rich man who was dressed in purple and fine linen and lived in luxury

[a] 6 Or about 3,000 liters [b] 7 Or about 30 tons

every day. 20At his gate was laid a beggar named Lazarus, covered with sores 21and longing to eat what fell from the rich man's table. Even the dogs came and licked his sores.

22"The time came when the beggar died and the angels carried him to Abraham's side. The rich man also died and was buried. 23In Hades, where he was in torment, he looked up and saw Abraham far away, with Lazarus by his side. 24So he called to him, 'Father Abraham, have pity on me and send Lazarus to dip the tip of his finger in water and cool my tongue, because I am in agony in this fire.'

25"But Abraham replied, 'Son, remember that in your lifetime you received your good things, while Lazarus received bad things, but now he is comforted here and you are in agony. 26And besides all this, between us and you a great chasm has been set in place, so that those who want to go from here to you cannot, nor can anyone cross over from there to us.'

27"He answered, 'Then I beg you, father, send Lazarus to my family, 28for I have five brothers. Let him warn them, so that they will not also come to this place of torment.'

29"Abraham replied, 'They have Moses and the Prophets; let them listen to them.'

30" 'No, father Abraham,' he said, 'but if someone from the dead goes to them, they will repent.'

31"He said to him, 'If they do not listen to Moses and the Prophets, they will not be convinced even if someone rises from the dead.' "

Sin, Faith, Duty

17 Jesus said to his disciples: "Things that cause people to stumble are bound to come, but woe to anyone through whom they come. 2It would be better for them to be thrown into the sea with a millstone tied around their neck than to cause one of these little ones to stumble. 3So watch yourselves.

"If your brother or sister[a] sins against you, rebuke them; and if they repent, forgive them. 4Even if they sin against you seven times in a day and seven times come back to you saying 'I repent,' you must forgive them."

5The apostles said to the Lord, "Increase our faith!"

6He replied, "If you have faith as small as a mustard seed, you can say to this mulberry tree, 'Be uprooted and planted in the sea,' and it will obey you.

7"Suppose one of you has a servant plowing or looking after the sheep. Will he say to the servant when he comes in from the field, 'Come along now and sit down to eat'? 8Won't he rather say, 'Prepare my supper, get yourself ready and wait on me while I eat and drink; after that you may eat and drink'? 9Will he thank the servant because he did what he was told to do? 10So you also, when you have done everything you were told to do, should say, 'We are unworthy servants; we have only done our duty.' "

Jesus Heals Ten Men With Leprosy

11Now on his way to Jerusalem, Jesus traveled along the border between Samaria and Galilee. 12As he was going into a village, ten men who had leprosy[b] met him. They stood at a distance 13and called out in a loud voice, "Jesus, Master, have pity on us!"

14When he saw them, he said, "Go, show yourselves to the priests." And as they went, they were cleansed.

15One of them, when he saw he was healed, came back, praising God in a loud voice. 16He threw himself at Jesus' feet and thanked him — and he was a Samaritan.

17Jesus asked, "Were not all ten cleansed? Where are the other nine? 18Has no one returned to give praise to God except this foreigner?" 19Then he said to him, "Rise and go; your faith has made you well."

The Coming of the Kingdom of God

20Once, on being asked by the Pharisees when the kingdom of God would come, Jesus replied, "The coming of the kingdom of God is not something that can be observed, 21nor will people say, 'Here it is,' or 'There it is,' because the kingdom of God is in your midst."[c]

22Then he said to his disciples, "The time is coming when you will long to see one of the days of the Son of Man, but you will not see it. 23People will tell you, 'There he is!'

[a] 3 The Greek word for *brother or sister* (*adelphos*) refers here to a fellow disciple, whether man or woman.
[b] 12 The Greek word traditionally translated *leprosy* was used for various diseases affecting the skin.
[c] 21 Or *is within you*

or 'Here he is!' Do not go running off after them. [24]For the Son of Man in his day[a] will be like the lightning, which flashes and lights up the sky from one end to the other. [25]But first he must suffer many things and be rejected by this generation.

[26]"Just as it was in the days of Noah, so also will it be in the days of the Son of Man. [27]People were eating, drinking, marrying and being given in marriage up to the day Noah entered the ark. Then the flood came and destroyed them all.

[28]"It was the same in the days of Lot. People were eating and drinking, buying and selling, planting and building. [29]But the day Lot left Sodom, fire and sulfur rained down from heaven and destroyed them all.

[30]"It will be just like this on the day the Son of Man is revealed. [31]On that day no one who is on the housetop, with possessions inside, should go down to get them. Likewise, no one in the field should go back for anything. [32]Remember Lot's wife! [33]Whoever tries to keep their life will lose it, and whoever loses their life will preserve it. [34]I tell you, on that night two people will be in one bed; one will be taken and the other left. [35]Two women will be grinding grain together; one will be taken and the other left." [36][b]

[37]"Where, Lord?" they asked.

He replied, "Where there is a dead body, there the vultures will gather."

The Parable of the Persistent Widow

18 Then Jesus told his disciples a parable to show them that they should always pray and not give up. [2]He said: "In a certain town there was a judge who neither feared God nor cared what people thought. [3]And there was a widow in that town who kept coming to him with the plea, 'Grant me justice against my adversary.'

[4]"For some time he refused. But finally he said to himself, 'Even though I don't fear God or care what people think, [5]yet because this widow keeps bothering me, I will see that she gets justice, so that she won't eventually come and attack me!'"

[6]And the Lord said, "Listen to what the unjust judge says. [7]And will not God bring about justice for his chosen ones, who cry out to him day and night? Will he keep putting them off? [8]I tell you, he will see that they get justice, and quickly. However, when the Son of Man comes, will he find faith on the earth?"

The Parable of the Pharisee and the Tax Collector

[9]To some who were confident of their own righteousness and looked down on everyone else, Jesus told this parable: [10]"Two men went up to the temple to pray, one a Pharisee and the other a tax collector. [11]The Pharisee stood by himself and prayed: 'God, I thank you that I am not like other people — robbers, evildoers, adulterers — or even like this tax collector. [12]I fast twice a week and give a tenth of all I get.'

[13]"But the tax collector stood at a distance. He would not even look up to heaven, but beat his breast and said, 'God, have mercy on me, a sinner.'

[14]"I tell you that this man, rather than the other, went home justified before God. For all those who exalt themselves will be humbled, and those who humble themselves will be exalted."

The Little Children and Jesus

[15]People were also bringing babies to Jesus for him to place his hands on them. When the disciples saw this, they rebuked them. [16]But Jesus called the children to him and said, "Let the little children come to me, and do not hinder them, for the kingdom of God belongs to such as these. [17]Truly I tell you, anyone who will not receive the kingdom of God like a little child will never enter it."

The Rich and the Kingdom of God

[18]A certain ruler asked him, "Good teacher, what must I do to inherit eternal life?"

[19]"Why do you call me good?" Jesus answered. "No one is good — except God alone. [20]You know the commandments: 'You shall not commit adultery, you shall not murder, you shall not steal, you shall not give false testimony, honor your father and mother.'[c]"

[21]"All these I have kept since I was a boy," he said.

[a] *24* Some manuscripts do not have *in his day.* [b] *36* Some manuscripts include here words similar to Matt. 24:40. [c] *20* Exodus 20:12-16; Deut. 5:16-20

22 When Jesus heard this, he said to him, "You still lack one thing. Sell everything you have and give to the poor, and you will have treasure in heaven. Then come, follow me."

23 When he heard this, he became very sad, because he was very wealthy. 24 Jesus looked at him and said, "How hard it is for the rich to enter the kingdom of God! 25 Indeed, it is easier for a camel to go through the eye of a needle than for someone who is rich to enter the kingdom of God."

26 Those who heard this asked, "Who then can be saved?"

27 Jesus replied, "What is impossible with man is possible with God."

28 Peter said to him, "We have left all we had to follow you!"

29 "Truly I tell you," Jesus said to them, "no one who has left home or wife or brothers or sisters or parents or children for the sake of the kingdom of God 30 will fail to receive many times as much in this age, and in the age to come eternal life."

Jesus Predicts His Death a Third Time

31 Jesus took the Twelve aside and told them, "We are going up to Jerusalem, and everything that is written by the prophets about the Son of Man will be fulfilled. 32 He will be delivered over to the Gentiles. They will mock him, insult him and spit on him; 33 they will flog him and kill him. On the third day he will rise again."

34 The disciples did not understand any of this. Its meaning was hidden from them, and they did not know what he was talking about.

A Blind Beggar Receives His Sight

35 As Jesus approached Jericho, a blind man was sitting by the roadside begging. 36 When he heard the crowd going by, he asked what was happening. 37 They told him, "Jesus of Nazareth is passing by."

38 He called out, "Jesus, Son of David, have mercy on me!"

39 Those who led the way rebuked him and told him to be quiet, but he shouted all the more, "Son of David, have mercy on me!"

40 Jesus stopped and ordered the man to be brought to him. When he came near, Jesus asked him, 41 "What do you want me to do for you?"

"Lord, I want to see," he replied.

42 Jesus said to him, "Receive your sight; your faith has healed you." 43 Immediately he received his sight and followed Jesus, praising God. When all the people saw it, they also praised God.

Zacchaeus the Tax Collector

19 Jesus entered Jericho and was passing through. 2 A man was there by the name of Zacchaeus; he was a chief tax collector and was wealthy. 3 He wanted to see who Jesus was, but because he was short he could not see over the crowd. 4 So he ran ahead and climbed a sycamore-fig tree to see him, since Jesus was coming that way.

5 When Jesus reached the spot, he looked up and said to him, "Zacchaeus, come down immediately. I must stay at your house today." 6 So he came down at once and welcomed him gladly.

7 All the people saw this and began to mutter, "He has gone to be the guest of a sinner."

8 But Zacchaeus stood up and said to the Lord, "Look, Lord! Here and now I give half of my possessions to the poor, and if I have cheated anybody out of anything, I will pay back four times the amount."

9 Jesus said to him, "Today salvation has come to this house, because this man, too, is a son of Abraham. 10 For the Son of Man came to seek and to save the lost."

The Parable of the Ten Minas

11 While they were listening to this, he went on to tell them a parable, because he was near Jerusalem and the people thought that the kingdom of God was going to appear at once. 12 He said: "A man of noble birth went to a distant country to have himself appointed king and then to return. 13 So he called ten of his servants and gave them ten minas.[a] 'Put this money to work,' he said, 'until I come back.'

14 "But his subjects hated him and sent a delegation after him to say, 'We don't want this man to be our king.'

15 "He was made king, however, and returned home. Then he sent for the servants to whom he had given the money, in order to find out what they had gained with it.

16 "The first one came and said, 'Sir, your mina has earned ten more.'

[a] *13* A mina was about three months' wages.

17 " 'Well done, my good servant!' his mas-
ter replied. 'Because you have been trust-
worthy in a very small matter, take charge of
ten cities.'
18 "The second came and said, 'Sir, your
mina has earned five more.'
19 "His master answered, 'You take charge
of five cities.'
20 "Then another servant came and said,
'Sir, here is your mina; I have kept it laid
away in a piece of cloth. 21 I was afraid of you,
because you are a hard man. You take out
what you did not put in and reap what you
did not sow.'
22 "His master replied, 'I will judge you by
your own words, you wicked servant! You
knew, did you, that I am a hard man, taking
out what I did not put in, and reaping what I
did not sow? 23 Why then didn't you put my
money on deposit, so that when I came back,
I could have collected it with interest?'
24 "Then he said to those standing by,
'Take his mina away from him and give it to
the one who has ten minas.'
25 " 'Sir,' they said, 'he already has ten!'
26 "He replied, 'I tell you that to everyone
who has, more will be given, but as for the
one who has nothing, even what they have
will be taken away. 27 But those enemies of
mine who did not want me to be king over
them — bring them here and kill them in
front of me.' "

Jesus Comes to Jerusalem as King

28 After Jesus had said this, he went on
ahead, going up to Jerusalem. 29 As he ap-
proached Bethphage and Bethany at the hill
called the Mount of Olives, he sent two of his
disciples, saying to them, 30 "Go to the village
ahead of you, and as you enter it, you will
find a colt tied there, which no one has ever
ridden. Untie it and bring it here. 31 If anyone
asks you, 'Why are you untying it?' say, 'The
Lord needs it.' "
32 Those who were sent ahead went and
found it just as he had told them. 33 As they
were untying the colt, its owners asked
them, "Why are you untying the colt?"
34 They replied, "The Lord needs it."
35 They brought it to Jesus, threw their
cloaks on the colt and put Jesus on it. 36 As
he went along, people spread their cloaks on
the road.

37 When he came near the place where
the road goes down the Mount of Olives, the
whole crowd of disciples began joyfully to
praise God in loud voices for all the miracles
they had seen:

38 "Blessed is the king who comes in the
name of the Lord!"[a]

"Peace in heaven and glory in the highest!"

39 Some of the Pharisees in the crowd said
to Jesus, "Teacher, rebuke your disciples!"
40 "I tell you," he replied, "if they keep qui-
et, the stones will cry out."
41 As he approached Jerusalem and saw
the city, he wept over it 42 and said, "If you,
even you, had only known on this day what
would bring you peace — but now it is hid-
den from your eyes. 43 The days will come
upon you when your enemies will build an
embankment against you and encircle you
and hem you in on every side. 44 They will
dash you to the ground, you and the chil-
dren within your walls. They will not leave
one stone on another, because you did not
recognize the time of God's coming to you."

Jesus at the Temple

45 When Jesus entered the temple courts,
he began to drive out those who were selling.
46 "It is written," he said to them, " 'My house
will be a house of prayer'[b]; but you have
made it 'a den of robbers.'[c]"
47 Every day he was teaching at the temple.
But the chief priests, the teachers of the law
and the leaders among the people were try-
ing to kill him. 48 Yet they could not find any
way to do it, because all the people hung on
his words.

The Authority of Jesus Questioned

20 One day as Jesus was teaching the
people in the temple courts and pro-
claiming the good news, the chief priests
and the teachers of the law, together with
the elders, came up to him. 2 "Tell us by what
authority you are doing these things," they
said. "Who gave you this authority?"
3 He replied, "I will also ask you a ques-
tion. Tell me: 4 John's baptism — was it from
heaven, or of human origin?"
5 They discussed it among themselves and
said, "If we say, 'From heaven,' he will ask,

[a] 38 Psalm 118:26 [b] 46 Isaiah 56:7 [c] 46 Jer. 7:11

'Why didn't you believe him?' 6But if we say, 'Of human origin,' all the people will stone us, because they are persuaded that John was a prophet."

7So they answered, "We don't know where it was from."

8Jesus said, "Neither will I tell you by what authority I am doing these things."

The Parable of the Tenants

9He went on to tell the people this parable: "A man planted a vineyard, rented it to some farmers and went away for a long time. 10At harvest time he sent a servant to the tenants so they would give him some of the fruit of the vineyard. But the tenants beat him and sent him away empty-handed. 11He sent another servant, but that one also they beat and treated shamefully and sent away empty-handed. 12He sent still a third, and they wounded him and threw him out.

13"Then the owner of the vineyard said, 'What shall I do? I will send my son, whom I love; perhaps they will respect him.'

14"But when the tenants saw him, they talked the matter over. 'This is the heir,' they said. 'Let's kill him, and the inheritance will be ours.' 15So they threw him out of the vineyard and killed him.

"What then will the owner of the vineyard do to them? 16He will come and kill those tenants and give the vineyard to others."

When the people heard this, they said, "God forbid!"

17Jesus looked directly at them and asked, "Then what is the meaning of that which is written:

> " 'The stone the builders rejected
> has become the cornerstone'[a]?

18Everyone who falls on that stone will be broken to pieces; anyone on whom it falls will be crushed."

19The teachers of the law and the chief priests looked for a way to arrest him immediately, because they knew he had spoken this parable against them. But they were afraid of the people.

Paying Taxes to Caesar

20Keeping a close watch on him, they sent spies, who pretended to be sincere. They hoped to catch Jesus in something he said, so that they might hand him over to the power and authority of the governor. 21So the spies questioned him: "Teacher, we know that you speak and teach what is right, and that you do not show partiality but teach the way of God in accordance with the truth. 22Is it right for us to pay taxes to Caesar or not?"

23He saw through their duplicity and said to them, 24"Show me a denarius. Whose image and inscription are on it?"

"Caesar's," they replied.

25He said to them, "Then give back to Caesar what is Caesar's, and to God what is God's."

26They were unable to trap him in what he had said there in public. And astonished by his answer, they became silent.

The Resurrection and Marriage

27Some of the Sadducees, who say there is no resurrection, came to Jesus with a question. 28"Teacher," they said, "Moses wrote for us that if a man's brother dies and leaves a wife but no children, the man must marry the widow and raise up offspring for his brother. 29Now there were seven brothers. The first one married a woman and died childless. 30The second 31and then the third married her, and in the same way the seven died, leaving no children. 32Finally, the woman died too. 33Now then, at the resurrection whose wife will she be, since the seven were married to her?"

34Jesus replied, "The people of this age marry and are given in marriage. 35But those who are considered worthy of taking part in the age to come and in the resurrection from the dead will neither marry nor be given in marriage, 36and they can no longer die; for they are like the angels. They are God's children, since they are children of the resurrection. 37But in the account of the burning bush, even Moses showed that the dead rise, for he calls the Lord 'the God of Abraham, and the God of Isaac, and the God of Jacob.'[b] 38He is not the God of the dead, but of the living, for to him all are alive."

39Some of the teachers of the law responded, "Well said, teacher!" 40And no one dared to ask him any more questions.

[a] *17* Psalm 118:22 [b] *37* Exodus 3:6

Whose Son Is the Messiah?

[41]Then Jesus said to them, "Why is it said that the Messiah is the son of David? [42]David himself declares in the Book of Psalms:

"'The Lord said to my Lord:
"Sit at my right hand
[43]until I make your enemies
a footstool for your feet."'[a]

[44]David calls him 'Lord.' How then can he be his son?"

Warning Against the Teachers of the Law

[45]While all the people were listening, Jesus said to his disciples, [46]"Beware of the teachers of the law. They like to walk around in flowing robes and love to be greeted with respect in the marketplaces and have the most important seats in the synagogues and the places of honor at banquets. [47]They devour widows' houses and for a show make lengthy prayers. These men will be punished most severely."

The Widow's Offering

21 As Jesus looked up, he saw the rich putting their gifts into the temple treasury. [2]He also saw a poor widow put in two very small copper coins. [3]"Truly I tell you," he said, "this poor widow has put in more than all the others. [4]All these people gave their gifts out of their wealth; but she out of her poverty put in all she had to live on."

The Destruction of the Temple and Signs of the End Times

[5]Some of his disciples were remarking about how the temple was adorned with beautiful stones and with gifts dedicated to God. But Jesus said, [6]"As for what you see here, the time will come when not one stone will be left on another; every one of them will be thrown down."

[7]"Teacher," they asked, "when will these things happen? And what will be the sign that they are about to take place?"

[8]He replied: "Watch out that you are not deceived. For many will come in my name, claiming, 'I am he,' and, 'The time is near.' Do not follow them. [9]When you hear of wars and uprisings, do not be frightened. These things must happen first, but the end will not come right away."

[10]Then he said to them: "Nation will rise against nation, and kingdom against kingdom. [11]There will be great earthquakes, famines and pestilences in various places, and fearful events and great signs from heaven.

[12]"But before all this, they will seize you and persecute you. They will hand you over to synagogues and put you in prison, and you will be brought before kings and governors, and all on account of my name. [13]And so you will bear testimony to me. [14]But make up your mind not to worry beforehand how you will defend yourselves. [15]For I will give you words and wisdom that none of your adversaries will be able to resist or contradict. [16]You will be betrayed even by parents, brothers and sisters, relatives and friends, and they will put some of you to death. [17]Everyone will hate you because of me. [18]But not a hair of your head will perish. [19]Stand firm, and you will win life.

[20]"When you see Jerusalem being surrounded by armies, you will know that its desolation is near. [21]Then let those who are in Judea flee to the mountains, let those in the city get out, and let those in the country not enter the city. [22]For this is the time of punishment in fulfillment of all that has been written. [23]How dreadful it will be in those days for pregnant women and nursing mothers! There will be great distress in the land and wrath against this people. [24]They will fall by the sword and will be taken as prisoners to all the nations. Jerusalem will be trampled on by the Gentiles until the times of the Gentiles are fulfilled.

[25]"There will be signs in the sun, moon and stars. On the earth, nations will be in anguish and perplexity at the roaring and tossing of the sea. [26]People will faint from terror, apprehensive of what is coming on the world, for the heavenly bodies will be shaken. [27]At that time they will see the Son of Man coming in a cloud with power and great glory. [28]When these things begin to take place, stand up and lift up your heads, because your redemption is drawing near."

[a] *43* Psalm 110:1

O LORD, YOU'RE BEAUTIFUL

Keith Green

Oh, Lord, you're beautiful
Your face is all I seek
For when your eyes are on this child
Your grace abounds to me

I wanna take your word
And shine it all around
But first help me just to live it, Lord
And when I'm doing well
Help me to never seek the crown
For my reward is giving glory to you

Oh, Lord, please light the fire
That once burned bright and clear
Replace the lamp of my first love
That burns with holy fear

THE INSPIRATION

My heart says of you, "Seek his face!" Your face, LORD, I will seek.

— Psalm 27:8

Read also: Isaiah 52:7; 1 Chronicles 16:11

BEHIND THE SONG

Keith and Melody Green came to faith in Christ during a time of revival known as the Jesus Movement of the late 1960s and early 1970s. Keith had aspired to be a pop singer in the style of Elton John before accepting Christ, who transformed Green into a powerful teacher and musical evangelist. Green eventually became a composer, singer and innovator of music that would later become known as Contemporary Christian Music. His concerts were more about teaching and worshiping than entertaining. He passionately devoted himself to his ministry until he lost his life in a small plane crash in 1982.

Melody remembers the morning Keith wrote "O Lord, You're Beautiful." "We had squeezed his old upright piano into our bedroom," she recalls. "We had no room for it anywhere else because our small house was packed with a dozen people we'd taken in off the streets. Very early one morning, I heard Keith playing softly, trying not to wake me. I pretended to still be asleep, not wanting to interrupt the precious moment. I kept my eyes closed and listened. It was one of the most beautiful songs I'd ever heard! Keith was singing it directly to the Lord from his heart, with a tender brokenness in his voice. I believe Keith was seeing God's beauty as he sought his face."

Keith Green's legacy of music and ministry continue to this day with new generations discovering his heartfelt, Biblically passionate songs and listening to recordings of his Bible studies. "Above all, Keith was a true worshiper," Melody adds. "This song touched him so much that he even wept while recording it in the studio."

Selah

The words of "O Lord, You're Beautiful" echo prayers found throughout the Bible. Most spiritual giants of the faith, at one time or another, have needed God's help to seek his face. If you find that your spiritual hunger wanes from time to time, you are in good company.

If you feel that the fire of your faith that once burned bright and clear has become dull, reach out to God and ask him to help you want him more. God loves to answer that prayer!

29 He told them this parable: "Look at the fig tree and all the trees. 30 When they sprout leaves, you can see for yourselves and know that summer is near. 31 Even so, when you see these things happening, you know that the kingdom of God is near.

32 "Truly I tell you, this generation will certainly not pass away until all these things have happened. 33 Heaven and earth will pass away, but my words will never pass away.

34 "Be careful, or your hearts will be weighed down with carousing, drunkenness and the anxieties of life, and that day will close on you suddenly like a trap. 35 For it will come on all those who live on the face of the whole earth. 36 Be always on the watch, and pray that you may be able to escape all that is about to happen, and that you may be able to stand before the Son of Man."

37 Each day Jesus was teaching at the temple, and each evening he went out to spend the night on the hill called the Mount of Olives, 38 and all the people came early in the morning to hear him at the temple.

Judas Agrees to Betray Jesus

22 Now the Festival of Unleavened Bread, called the Passover, was approaching, 2 and the chief priests and the teachers of the law were looking for some way to get rid of Jesus, for they were afraid of the people. 3 Then Satan entered Judas, called Iscariot, one of the Twelve. 4 And Judas went to the chief priests and the officers of the temple guard and discussed with them how he might betray Jesus. 5 They were delighted and agreed to give him money. 6 He consented, and watched for an opportunity to hand Jesus over to them when no crowd was present.

The Last Supper

7 Then came the day of Unleavened Bread on which the Passover lamb had to be sacrificed. 8 Jesus sent Peter and John, saying, "Go and make preparations for us to eat the Passover."

9 "Where do you want us to prepare for it?" they asked.

10 He replied, "As you enter the city, a man carrying a jar of water will meet you. Follow him to the house that he enters, 11 and say to the owner of the house, 'The Teacher asks: Where is the guest room, where I may eat the Passover with my disciples?' 12 He will show you a large room upstairs, all furnished. Make preparations there."

13 They left and found things just as Jesus had told them. So they prepared the Passover.

14 When the hour came, Jesus and his apostles reclined at the table. 15 And he said to them, "I have eagerly desired to eat this Passover with you before I suffer. 16 For I tell you, I will not eat it again until it finds fulfillment in the kingdom of God."

17 After taking the cup, he gave thanks and said, "Take this and divide it among you. 18 For I tell you I will not drink again from the fruit of the vine until the kingdom of God comes."

19 And he took bread, gave thanks and broke it, and gave it to them, saying, "This is my body given for you; do this in remembrance of me."

20 In the same way, after the supper he took the cup, saying, "This cup is the new covenant in my blood, which is poured out for you.[a] 21 But the hand of him who is going to betray me is with mine on the table. 22 The Son of Man will go as it has been decreed. But woe to that man who betrays him!" 23 They began to question among themselves which of them it might be who would do this.

24 A dispute also arose among them as to which of them was considered to be greatest. 25 Jesus said to them, "The kings of the Gentiles lord it over them; and those who exercise authority over them call themselves Benefactors. 26 But you are not to be like that. Instead, the greatest among you should be like the youngest, and the one who rules like the one who serves. 27 For who is greater, the one who is at the table or the one who serves? Is it not the one who is at the table? But I am among you as one who serves. 28 You are those who have stood by me in my trials. 29 And I confer on you a kingdom, just as my Father conferred one on me, 30 so that you may eat and drink at my table in my kingdom and sit on thrones, judging the twelve tribes of Israel.

[a] *19,20* Some manuscripts do not have *given for you . . . poured out for you.*

31 "Simon, Simon, Satan has asked to sift all of you as wheat. 32 But I have prayed for you, Simon, that your faith may not fail. And when you have turned back, strengthen your brothers."

33 But he replied, "Lord, I am ready to go with you to prison and to death."

34 Jesus answered, "I tell you, Peter, before the rooster crows today, you will deny three times that you know me."

35 Then Jesus asked them, "When I sent you without purse, bag or sandals, did you lack anything?"

"Nothing," they answered.

36 He said to them, "But now if you have a purse, take it, and also a bag; and if you don't have a sword, sell your cloak and buy one. 37 It is written: 'And he was numbered with the transgressors'[a]; and I tell you that this must be fulfilled in me. Yes, what is written about me is reaching its fulfillment."

38 The disciples said, "See, Lord, here are two swords."

"That's enough!" he replied.

Jesus Prays on the Mount of Olives

39 Jesus went out as usual to the Mount of Olives, and his disciples followed him. 40 On reaching the place, he said to them, "Pray that you will not fall into temptation." 41 He withdrew about a stone's throw beyond them, knelt down and prayed, 42 "Father, if you are willing, take this cup from me; yet not my will, but yours be done." 43 An angel from heaven appeared to him and strengthened him. 44 And being in anguish, he prayed more earnestly, and his sweat was like drops of blood falling to the ground.[b]

45 When he rose from prayer and went back to the disciples, he found them asleep, exhausted from sorrow. 46 "Why are you sleeping?" he asked them. "Get up and pray so that you will not fall into temptation."

Jesus Arrested

47 While he was still speaking a crowd came up, and the man who was called Judas, one of the Twelve, was leading them. He approached Jesus to kiss him, 48 but Jesus asked him, "Judas, are you betraying the Son of Man with a kiss?"

49 When Jesus' followers saw what was going to happen, they said, "Lord, should we strike with our swords?" 50 And one of them struck the servant of the high priest, cutting off his right ear.

51 But Jesus answered, "No more of this!" And he touched the man's ear and healed him.

52 Then Jesus said to the chief priests, the officers of the temple guard, and the elders, who had come for him, "Am I leading a rebellion, that you have come with swords and clubs? 53 Every day I was with you in the temple courts, and you did not lay a hand on me. But this is your hour—when darkness reigns."

Peter Disowns Jesus

54 Then seizing him, they led him away and took him into the house of the high priest. Peter followed at a distance. 55 And when some there had kindled a fire in the middle of the courtyard and had sat down together, Peter sat down with them. 56 A servant girl saw him seated there in the firelight. She looked closely at him and said, "This man was with him."

57 But he denied it. "Woman, I don't know him," he said.

58 A little later someone else saw him and said, "You also are one of them."

"Man, I am not!" Peter replied.

59 About an hour later another asserted, "Certainly this fellow was with him, for he is a Galilean."

60 Peter replied, "Man, I don't know what you're talking about!" Just as he was speaking, the rooster crowed. 61 The Lord turned and looked straight at Peter. Then Peter remembered the word the Lord had spoken to him: "Before the rooster crows today, you will disown me three times." 62 And he went outside and wept bitterly.

The Guards Mock Jesus

63 The men who were guarding Jesus began mocking and beating him. 64 They blindfolded him and demanded, "Prophesy! Who hit you?" 65 And they said many other insulting things to him.

Jesus Before Pilate and Herod

66 At daybreak the council of the elders of the people, both the chief priests and the

[a] *37* Isaiah 53:12 [b] *43,44* Many early manuscripts do not have verses 43 and 44.

teachers of the law, met together, and Jesus was led before them. [67]“If you are the Messiah,” they said, “tell us.”

Jesus answered, “If I tell you, you will not believe me, [68]and if I asked you, you would not answer. [69]But from now on, the Son of Man will be seated at the right hand of the mighty God.”

[70]They all asked, “Are you then the Son of God?”

He replied, “You say that I am.”

[71]Then they said, “Why do we need any more testimony? We have heard it from his own lips.”

23 Then the whole assembly rose and led him off to Pilate. [2]And they began to accuse him, saying, “We have found this man subverting our nation. He opposes payment of taxes to Caesar and claims to be Messiah, a king.”

[3]So Pilate asked Jesus, “Are you the king of the Jews?”

“You have said so,” Jesus replied.

[4]Then Pilate announced to the chief priests and the crowd, “I find no basis for a charge against this man.”

[5]But they insisted, “He stirs up the people all over Judea by his teaching. He started in Galilee and has come all the way here.”

[6]On hearing this, Pilate asked if the man was a Galilean. [7]When he learned that Jesus was under Herod’s jurisdiction, he sent him to Herod, who was also in Jerusalem at that time.

[8]When Herod saw Jesus, he was greatly pleased, because for a long time he had been wanting to see him. From what he had heard about him, he hoped to see him perform a sign of some sort. [9]He plied him with many questions, but Jesus gave him no answer. [10]The chief priests and the teachers of the law were standing there, vehemently accusing him. [11]Then Herod and his soldiers ridiculed and mocked him. Dressing him in an elegant robe, they sent him back to Pilate. [12]That day Herod and Pilate became friends — before this they had been enemies.

[13]Pilate called together the chief priests, the rulers and the people, [14]and said to them, “You brought me this man as one who was inciting the people to rebellion. I have examined him in your presence and have found no basis for your charges against him. [15]Neither has Herod, for he sent him back to us; as you can see, he has done nothing to deserve death. [16]Therefore, I will punish him and then release him.” [17][a]

[18]But the whole crowd shouted, “Away with this man! Release Barabbas to us!” [19](Barabbas had been thrown into prison for an insurrection in the city, and for murder.)

[20]Wanting to release Jesus, Pilate appealed to them again. [21]But they kept shouting, “Crucify him! Crucify him!”

[22]For the third time he spoke to them: “Why? What crime has this man committed? I have found in him no grounds for the death penalty. Therefore I will have him punished and then release him.”

[23]But with loud shouts they insistently demanded that he be crucified, and their shouts prevailed. [24]So Pilate decided to grant their demand. [25]He released the man who had been thrown into prison for insurrection and murder, the one they asked for, and surrendered Jesus to their will.

The Crucifixion of Jesus

[26]As the soldiers led him away, they seized Simon from Cyrene, who was on his way in from the country, and put the cross on him and made him carry it behind Jesus. [27]A large number of people followed him, including women who mourned and wailed for him. [28]Jesus turned and said to them, “Daughters of Jerusalem, do not weep for me; weep for yourselves and for your children. [29]For the time will come when you will say, ‘Blessed are the childless women, the wombs that never bore and the breasts that never nursed!’ [30]Then

“ ‘they will say to the mountains, “Fall on us!”
and to the hills, “Cover us!” ’[b]

[31]For if people do these things when the tree is green, what will happen when it is dry?”

[32]Two other men, both criminals, were also led out with him to be executed. [33]When they came to the place called the Skull, they crucified him there, along with the criminals — one on his right, the other on his left. [34]Jesus said, “Father, forgive

[a] *17* Some manuscripts include here words similar to Matt. 27:15 and Mark 15:6. [b] *30* Hosea 10:8

them, for they do not know what they are
doing."[a] And they divided up his clothes by
casting lots.
35 The people stood watching, and the
rulers even sneered at him. They said, "He
saved others; let him save himself if he is
God's Messiah, the Chosen One."
36 The soldiers also came up and mocked
him. They offered him wine vinegar 37 and
said, "If you are the king of the Jews, save
yourself."
38 There was a written notice above him,
which read: THIS IS THE KING OF THE JEWS.
39 One of the criminals who hung there
hurled insults at him: "Aren't you the Messi-
ah? Save yourself and us!"
40 But the other criminal rebuked him.
"Don't you fear God," he said, "since you are
under the same sentence? 41 We are pun-
ished justly, for we are getting what our
deeds deserve. But this man has done noth-
ing wrong."
42 Then he said, "Jesus, remember me
when you come into your kingdom.[b]"
43 Jesus answered him, "Truly I tell you, to-
day you will be with me in paradise."

The Death of Jesus

44 It was now about noon, and darkness
came over the whole land until three in
the afternoon, 45 for the sun stopped shin-
ing. And the curtain of the temple was torn
in two. 46 Jesus called out with a loud voice,
"Father, into your hands I commit my spir-
it."[c] When he had said this, he breathed his
last.
47 The centurion, seeing what had hap-
pened, praised God and said, "Surely this
was a righteous man." 48 When all the people
who had gathered to witness this sight saw
what took place, they beat their breasts and
went away. 49 But all those who knew him,
including the women who had followed him
from Galilee, stood at a distance, watching
these things.

The Burial of Jesus

50 Now there was a man named Joseph, a
member of the Council, a good and upright
man, 51 who had not consented to their de-
cision and action. He came from the Jude-
an town of Arimathea, and he himself was
waiting for the kingdom of God. 52 Going
to Pilate, he asked for Jesus' body. 53 Then
he took it down, wrapped it in linen cloth
and placed it in a tomb cut in the rock, one
in which no one had yet been laid. 54 It was
Preparation Day, and the Sabbath was about
to begin.
55 The women who had come with Jesus
from Galilee followed Joseph and saw the
tomb and how his body was laid in it. 56 Then
they went home and prepared spices and
perfumes. But they rested on the Sabbath in
obedience to the commandment.

Jesus Has Risen

24 On the first day of the week, very
early in the morning, the women
took the spices they had prepared and went
to the tomb. 2 They found the stone rolled
away from the tomb, 3 but when they en-
tered, they did not find the body of the Lord
Jesus. 4 While they were wondering about
this, suddenly two men in clothes that
gleamed like lightning stood beside them.
5 In their fright the women bowed down
with their faces to the ground, but the men
said to them, "Why do you look for the liv-
ing among the dead? 6 He is not here; he has
risen! Remember how he told you, while he
was still with you in Galilee: 7 'The Son of
Man must be delivered over to the hands of
sinners, be crucified and on the third day be
raised again.' " 8 Then they remembered his
words.
9 When they came back from the tomb,
they told all these things to the Eleven and
to all the others. 10 It was Mary Magdalene,
Joanna, Mary the mother of James, and the
others with them who told this to the apos-
tles. 11 But they did not believe the women,
because their words seemed to them like
nonsense. 12 Peter, however, got up and ran to
the tomb. Bending over, he saw the strips of
linen lying by themselves, and he went away,
wondering to himself what had happened.

On the Road to Emmaus

13 Now that same day two of them were go-
ing to a village called Emmaus, about seven
miles[d] from Jerusalem. 14 They were talking

[a] *34* Some early manuscripts do not have this sentence. [b] *42* Some manuscripts *come with your kingly power* [c] *46* Psalm 31:5 [d] *13* Or about 11 kilometers

with each other about everything that had happened. [15]As they talked and discussed these things with each other, Jesus himself came up and walked along with them; [16]but they were kept from recognizing him.

[17]He asked them, "What are you discussing together as you walk along?"

They stood still, their faces downcast. [18]One of them, named Cleopas, asked him, "Are you the only one visiting Jerusalem who does not know the things that have happened there in these days?"

[19]"What things?" he asked.

"About Jesus of Nazareth," they replied. "He was a prophet, powerful in word and deed before God and all the people. [20]The chief priests and our rulers handed him over to be sentenced to death, and they crucified him; [21]but we had hoped that he was the one who was going to redeem Israel. And what is more, it is the third day since all this took place. [22]In addition, some of our women amazed us. They went to the tomb early this morning [23]but didn't find his body. They came and told us that they had seen a vision of angels, who said he was alive. [24]Then some of our companions went to the tomb and found it just as the women had said, but they did not see Jesus."

[25]He said to them, "How foolish you are, and how slow to believe all that the prophets have spoken! [26]Did not the Messiah have to suffer these things and then enter his glory?" [27]And beginning with Moses and all the Prophets, he explained to them what was said in all the Scriptures concerning himself.

[28]As they approached the village to which they were going, Jesus continued on as if he were going farther. [29]But they urged him strongly, "Stay with us, for it is nearly evening; the day is almost over." So he went in to stay with them.

[30]When he was at the table with them, he took bread, gave thanks, broke it and began to give it to them. [31]Then their eyes were opened and they recognized him, and he disappeared from their sight. [32]They asked each other, "Were not our hearts burning within us while he talked with us on the road and opened the Scriptures to us?"

[33]They got up and returned at once to Jerusalem. There they found the Eleven and those with them, assembled together [34]and saying, "It is true! The Lord has risen and has appeared to Simon." [35]Then the two told what had happened on the way, and how Jesus was recognized by them when he broke the bread.

Jesus Appears to the Disciples

[36]While they were still talking about this, Jesus himself stood among them and said to them, "Peace be with you."

[37]They were startled and frightened, thinking they saw a ghost. [38]He said to them, "Why are you troubled, and why do doubts rise in your minds? [39]Look at my hands and my feet. It is I myself! Touch me and see; a ghost does not have flesh and bones, as you see I have."

[40]When he had said this, he showed them his hands and feet. [41]And while they still did not believe it because of joy and amazement, he asked them, "Do you have anything here to eat?" [42]They gave him a piece of broiled fish, [43]and he took it and ate it in their presence.

[44]He said to them, "This is what I told you while I was still with you: Everything must be fulfilled that is written about me in the Law of Moses, the Prophets and the Psalms."

[45]Then he opened their minds so they could understand the Scriptures. [46]He told them, "This is what is written: The Messiah will suffer and rise from the dead on the third day, [47]and repentance for the forgiveness of sins will be preached in his name to all nations, beginning at Jerusalem. [48]You are witnesses of these things. [49]I am going to send you what my Father has promised; but stay in the city until you have been clothed with power from on high."

The Ascension of Jesus

[50]When he had led them out to the vicinity of Bethany, he lifted up his hands and blessed them. [51]While he was blessing them, he left them and was taken up into heaven. [52]Then they worshiped him and returned to Jerusalem with great joy. [53]And they stayed continually at the temple, praising God.

JOHN

The Word Became Flesh

1 In the beginning was the Word, and the Word was with God, and the Word was God. 2He was with God in the beginning. 3Through him all things were made; without him nothing was made that has been made. 4In him was life, and that life was the light of all mankind. 5The light shines in the darkness, and the darkness has not overcome[a] it.

6There was a man sent from God whose name was John. 7He came as a witness to testify concerning that light, so that through him all might believe. 8He himself was not the light; he came only as a witness to the light.

9The true light that gives light to everyone was coming into the world. 10He was in the world, and though the world was made through him, the world did not recognize him. 11He came to that which was his own, but his own did not receive him. 12Yet to all who did receive him, to those who believed in his name, he gave the right to become children of God— 13children born not of natural descent, nor of human decision or a husband's will, but born of God.

14The Word became flesh and made his dwelling among us. We have seen his glory, the glory of the one and only Son, who came from the Father, full of grace and truth.

15(John testified concerning him. He cried out, saying, "This is the one I spoke about when I said, 'He who comes after me has surpassed me because he was before me.' ") 16Out of his fullness we have all received grace in place of grace already given. 17For the law was given through Moses; grace and truth came through Jesus Christ. 18No one has ever seen God, but the one and only Son, who is himself God and[b] is in closest relationship with the Father, has made him known.

John the Baptist Denies Being the Messiah

19Now this was John's testimony when the Jewish leaders[c] in Jerusalem sent priests and Levites to ask him who he was. 20He did not fail to confess, but confessed freely, "I am not the Messiah."

21They asked him, "Then who are you? Are you Elijah?"

He said, "I am not."

"Are you the Prophet?"

He answered, "No."

22Finally they said, "Who are you? Give us an answer to take back to those who sent us. What do you say about yourself?"

23John replied in the words of Isaiah the prophet, "I am the voice of one calling in the wilderness, 'Make straight the way for the Lord.' "[d]

24Now the Pharisees who had been sent 25questioned him, "Why then do you baptize if you are not the Messiah, nor Elijah, nor the Prophet?"

26"I baptize with[e] water," John replied, "but among you stands one you do not know. 27He is the one who comes after me, the straps of whose sandals I am not worthy to untie."

28This all happened at Bethany on the other side of the Jordan, where John was baptizing.

John Testifies About Jesus

29The next day John saw Jesus coming toward him and said, "Look, the Lamb of God, who takes away the sin of the world! 30This is the one I meant when I said, 'A man who comes after me has surpassed me because he was before me.' 31I myself did not know him, but the reason I came baptizing with water was that he might be revealed to Israel."

32Then John gave this testimony: "I saw

[a] 5 Or *understood* [b] 18 Some manuscripts *but the only Son, who* [c] 19 The Greek term traditionally translated *the Jews* (*hoi Ioudaioi*) refers here and elsewhere in John's Gospel to those Jewish leaders who opposed Jesus; also in 5:10, 15, 16; 7:1, 11, 13; 9:22; 18:14, 28, 36; 19:7, 12, 31, 38; 20:19. [d] 23 Isaiah 40:3 [e] 26 Or *in*; also in verses 31 and 33 (twice)

the Spirit come down from heaven as a dove
and remain on him. 33 And I myself did not
know him, but the one who sent me to bap-
tize with water told me, 'The man on whom
you see the Spirit come down and remain
is the one who will baptize with the Holy
Spirit.' 34 I have seen and I testify that this is
God's Chosen One."[a]

John's Disciples Follow Jesus

35 The next day John was there again with
two of his disciples. 36 When he saw Jesus
passing by, he said, "Look, the Lamb of God!"
37 When the two disciples heard him say
this, they followed Jesus. 38 Turning around,
Jesus saw them following and asked, "What
do you want?"

They said, "Rabbi" (which means "Teach-
er"), "where are you staying?"

39 "Come," he replied, "and you will see."

So they went and saw where he was stay-
ing, and they spent that day with him. It was
about four in the afternoon.

40 Andrew, Simon Peter's brother, was one
of the two who heard what John had said and
who had followed Jesus. 41 The first thing
Andrew did was to find his brother Simon
and tell him, "We have found the Messiah"
(that is, the Christ). 42 And he brought him to
Jesus.

Jesus looked at him and said, "You are Si-
mon son of John. You will be called Cephas"
(which, when translated, is Peter[b]).

Jesus Calls Philip and Nathanael

43 The next day Jesus decided to leave for
Galilee. Finding Philip, he said to him, "Fol-
low me."

44 Philip, like Andrew and Peter, was
from the town of Bethsaida. 45 Philip found
Nathanael and told him, "We have found
the one Moses wrote about in the Law, and
about whom the prophets also wrote — Jesus
of Nazareth, the son of Joseph."

46 "Nazareth! Can anything good come
from there?" Nathanael asked.

"Come and see," said Philip.

47 When Jesus saw Nathanael approach-
ing, he said of him, "Here truly is an Israelite
in whom there is no deceit."

48 "How do you know me?" Nathanael
asked.

Jesus answered, "I saw you while you were
still under the fig tree before Philip called
you."

49 Then Nathanael declared, "Rabbi, you
are the Son of God; you are the king of Isra-
el."

50 Jesus said, "You believe[c] because I told
you I saw you under the fig tree. You will see
greater things than that." 51 He then added,
"Very truly I tell you,[d] you[d] will see 'heaven
open, and the angels of God ascending and
descending on'[e] the Son of Man."

Jesus Changes Water Into Wine

2 On the third day a wedding took place
at Cana in Galilee. Jesus' mother was
there, 2 and Jesus and his disciples had also
been invited to the wedding. 3 When the
wine was gone, Jesus' mother said to him,
"They have no more wine."

4 "Woman,[f] why do you involve me?" Jesus
replied. "My hour has not yet come."

5 His mother said to the servants, "Do
whatever he tells you."

6 Nearby stood six stone water jars, the kind
used by the Jews for ceremonial washing,
each holding from twenty to thirty gallons.[g]

7 Jesus said to the servants, "Fill the jars
with water"; so they filled them to the brim.

8 Then he told them, "Now draw some out
and take it to the master of the banquet."

They did so, 9 and the master of the ban-
quet tasted the water that had been turned
into wine. He did not realize where it had
come from, though the servants who had
drawn the water knew. Then he called the
bridegroom aside 10 and said, "Everyone
brings out the choice wine first and then the
cheaper wine after the guests have had too
much to drink; but you have saved the best
till now."

11 What Jesus did here in Cana of Galilee
was the first of the signs through which he
revealed his glory; and his disciples believed
in him.

12 After this he went down to Capernaum
with his mother and brothers and his disci-
ples. There they stayed for a few days.

[a] *34* See Isaiah 42:1; many manuscripts *is the Son of God.* [b] *42* *Cephas* (Aramaic) and *Peter* (Greek) both mean *rock.* [c] *50* Or *Do you believe . . . ?* [d] *51* The Greek is plural. [e] *51* Gen. 28:12 [f] *4* The Greek for *Woman* does not denote any disrespect. [g] *6* Or from about 75 to about 115 liters

Jesus Clears the Temple Courts

13 When it was almost time for the Jewish Passover, Jesus went up to Jerusalem. 14 In the temple courts he found people selling cattle, sheep and doves, and others sitting at tables exchanging money. 15 So he made a whip out of cords, and drove all from the temple courts, both sheep and cattle; he scattered the coins of the money changers and overturned their tables. 16 To those who sold doves he said, "Get these out of here! Stop turning my Father's house into a market!" 17 His disciples remembered that it is written: "Zeal for your house will consume me."[a]

18 The Jews then responded to him, "What sign can you show us to prove your authority to do all this?"

19 Jesus answered them, "Destroy this temple, and I will raise it again in three days."

20 They replied, "It has taken forty-six years to build this temple, and you are going to raise it in three days?" 21 But the temple he had spoken of was his body. 22 After he was raised from the dead, his disciples recalled what he had said. Then they believed the scripture and the words that Jesus had spoken.

23 Now while he was in Jerusalem at the Passover Festival, many people saw the signs he was performing and believed in his name.[b] 24 But Jesus would not entrust himself to them, for he knew all people. 25 He did not need any testimony about mankind, for he knew what was in each person.

Jesus Teaches Nicodemus

3 Now there was a Pharisee, a man named Nicodemus who was a member of the Jewish ruling council. 2 He came to Jesus at night and said, "Rabbi, we know that you are a teacher who has come from God. For no one could perform the signs you are doing if God were not with him."

3 Jesus replied, "Very truly I tell you, no one can see the kingdom of God unless they are born again.[c]"

4 "How can someone be born when they are old?" Nicodemus asked. "Surely they cannot enter a second time into their mother's womb to be born!"

5 Jesus answered, "Very truly I tell you, no one can enter the kingdom of God unless they are born of water and the Spirit. 6 Flesh gives birth to flesh, but the Spirit[d] gives birth to spirit. 7 You should not be surprised at my saying, 'You[e] must be born again.' 8 The wind blows wherever it pleases. You hear its sound, but you cannot tell where it comes from or where it is going. So it is with everyone born of the Spirit."[f]

9 "How can this be?" Nicodemus asked.

10 "You are Israel's teacher," said Jesus, "and do you not understand these things? 11 Very truly I tell you, we speak of what we know, and we testify to what we have seen, but still you people do not accept our testimony. 12 I have spoken to you of earthly things and you do not believe; how then will you believe if I speak of heavenly things? 13 No one has ever gone into heaven except the one who came from heaven — the Son of Man.[g] 14 Just as Moses lifted up the snake in the wilderness, so the Son of Man must be lifted up,[h] 15 that everyone who believes may have eternal life in him."[i]

16 For God so loved the world that he gave his one and only Son, that whoever believes in him shall not perish but have eternal life. 17 For God did not send his Son into the world to condemn the world, but to save the world through him. 18 Whoever believes in him is not condemned, but whoever does not believe stands condemned already because they have not believed in the name of God's one and only Son. 19 This is the verdict: Light has come into the world, but people loved darkness instead of light because their deeds were evil. 20 Everyone who does evil hates the light, and will not come into the light for fear that their deeds will be exposed. 21 But whoever lives by the truth comes into the light, so that it may be seen plainly that what they have done has been done in the sight of God.

John Testifies Again About Jesus

22 After this, Jesus and his disciples went out into the Judean countryside, where he

[a] *17* Psalm 69:9 [b] *23* Or *in him* [c] *3* The Greek for *again* also means *from above*; also in verse 7.
[d] *6* Or *but spirit* [e] *7* The Greek is plural. [f] *8* The Greek for *Spirit* is the same as that for *wind*.
[g] *13* Some manuscripts *Man, who is in heaven* [h] *14* The Greek for *lifted up* also means *exalted*.
[i] *15* Some interpreters end the quotation with verse 21.

spent some time with them, and baptized. [23]Now John also was baptizing at Aenon near Salim, because there was plenty of water, and people were coming and being baptized. [24](This was before John was put in prison.) [25]An argument developed between some of John's disciples and a certain Jew over the matter of ceremonial washing. [26]They came to John and said to him, "Rabbi, that man who was with you on the other side of the Jordan — the one you testified about — look, he is baptizing, and everyone is going to him."

[27]To this John replied, "A person can receive only what is given them from heaven. [28]You yourselves can testify that I said, 'I am not the Messiah but am sent ahead of him.' [29]The bride belongs to the bridegroom. The friend who attends the bridegroom waits and listens for him, and is full of joy when he hears the bridegroom's voice. That joy is mine, and it is now complete. [30]He must become greater; I must become less."[a]

[31]The one who comes from above is above all; the one who is from the earth belongs to the earth, and speaks as one from the earth. The one who comes from heaven is above all. [32]He testifies to what he has seen and heard, but no one accepts his testimony. [33]Whoever has accepted it has certified that God is truthful. [34]For the one whom God has sent speaks the words of God, for God[b] gives the Spirit without limit. [35]The Father loves the Son and has placed everything in his hands. [36]Whoever believes in the Son has eternal life, but whoever rejects the Son will not see life, for God's wrath remains on them.

Jesus Talks With a Samaritan Woman

4 Now Jesus learned that the Pharisees had heard that he was gaining and baptizing more disciples than John — [2]although in fact it was not Jesus who baptized, but his disciples. [3]So he left Judea and went back once more to Galilee.

[4]Now he had to go through Samaria. [5]So he came to a town in Samaria called Sychar, near the plot of ground Jacob had given to his son Joseph. [6]Jacob's well was there, and Jesus, tired as he was from the journey, sat down by the well. It was about noon.

[7]When a Samaritan woman came to draw water, Jesus said to her, "Will you give me a drink?" [8](His disciples had gone into the town to buy food.)

[9]The Samaritan woman said to him, "You are a Jew and I am a Samaritan woman. How can you ask me for a drink?" (For Jews do not associate with Samaritans.[c])

[10]Jesus answered her, "If you knew the gift of God and who it is that asks you for a drink, you would have asked him and he would have given you living water."

[11]"Sir," the woman said, "you have nothing to draw with and the well is deep. Where can you get this living water? [12]Are you greater than our father Jacob, who gave us the well and drank from it himself, as did also his sons and his livestock?"

[13]Jesus answered, "Everyone who drinks this water will be thirsty again, [14]but whoever drinks the water I give them will never thirst. Indeed, the water I give them will become in them a spring of water welling up to eternal life."

[15]The woman said to him, "Sir, give me this water so that I won't get thirsty and have to keep coming here to draw water."

[16]He told her, "Go, call your husband and come back."

[17]"I have no husband," she replied.

Jesus said to her, "You are right when you say you have no husband. [18]The fact is, you have had five husbands, and the man you now have is not your husband. What you have just said is quite true."

[19]"Sir," the woman said, "I can see that you are a prophet. [20]Our ancestors worshiped on this mountain, but you Jews claim that the place where we must worship is in Jerusalem."

[21]"Woman," Jesus replied, "believe me, a time is coming when you will worship the Father neither on this mountain nor in Jerusalem. [22]You Samaritans worship what you do not know; we worship what we do know, for salvation is from the Jews. [23]Yet a time is coming and has now come when the true worshipers will worship the Father in the Spirit and in truth, for they are the kind of worshipers the Father seeks. [24]God is spirit, and his worshipers must worship in the Spirit and in truth."

[a] *30* Some interpreters end the quotation with verse 36. [b] *34* Greek *he* [c] *9* Or *do not use dishes Samaritans have used*

25 The woman said, "I know that Messiah"
(called Christ) "is coming. When he comes,
he will explain everything to us."
26 Then Jesus declared, "I, the one speak-
ing to you — I am he."

The Disciples Rejoin Jesus

27 Just then his disciples returned and
were surprised to find him talking with a
woman. But no one asked, "What do you
want?" or "Why are you talking with her?"
28 Then, leaving her water jar, the woman
went back to the town and said to the peo-
ple, 29 "Come, see a man who told me every-
thing I ever did. Could this be the Messiah?"
30 They came out of the town and made their
way toward him.
31 Meanwhile his disciples urged him,
"Rabbi, eat something."
32 But he said to them, "I have food to eat
that you know nothing about."
33 Then his disciples said to each other,
"Could someone have brought him food?"
34 "My food," said Jesus, "is to do the will
of him who sent me and to finish his work.
35 Don't you have a saying, 'It's still four
months until harvest'? I tell you, open your
eyes and look at the fields! They are ripe
for harvest. 36 Even now the one who reaps
draws a wage and harvests a crop for eter-
nal life, so that the sower and the reaper may
be glad together. 37 Thus the saying 'One
sows and another reaps' is true. 38 I sent you
to reap what you have not worked for. Oth-
ers have done the hard work, and you have
reaped the benefits of their labor."

Many Samaritans Believe

39 Many of the Samaritans from that town
believed in him because of the woman's tes-
timony, "He told me everything I ever did."
40 So when the Samaritans came to him, they
urged him to stay with them, and he stayed
two days. 41 And because of his words many
more became believers.
42 They said to the woman, "We no lon-
ger believe just because of what you said;
now we have heard for ourselves, and we
know that this man really is the Savior of the
world."

Jesus Heals an Official's Son

43 After the two days he left for Galilee.
44 (Now Jesus himself had pointed out that
a prophet has no honor in his own country.)
45 When he arrived in Galilee, the Galileans
welcomed him. They had seen all that he
had done in Jerusalem at the Passover Festi-
val, for they also had been there.
46 Once more he visited Cana in Galilee,
where he had turned the water into wine.
And there was a certain royal official whose
son lay sick at Capernaum. 47 When this
man heard that Jesus had arrived in Galilee
from Judea, he went to him and begged him
to come and heal his son, who was close to
death.
48 "Unless you people see signs and won-
ders," Jesus told him, "you will never be-
lieve."
49 The royal official said, "Sir, come down
before my child dies."
50 "Go," Jesus replied, "your son will live."
The man took Jesus at his word and de-
parted. 51 While he was still on the way, his
servants met him with the news that his boy
was living. 52 When he inquired as to the
time when his son got better, they said to
him, "Yesterday, at one in the afternoon, the
fever left him."
53 Then the father realized that this was
the exact time at which Jesus had said to
him, "Your son will live." So he and his whole
household believed.
54 This was the second sign Jesus per-
formed after coming from Judea to Galilee.

The Healing at the Pool

5 Some time later, Jesus went up to Jerusa-
lem for one of the Jewish festivals. 2 Now
there is in Jerusalem near the Sheep Gate a
pool, which in Aramaic is called Bethesda[a]
and which is surrounded by five covered col-
onnades. 3 Here a great number of disabled
people used to lie — the blind, the lame, the
paralyzed. [4][b] 5 One who was there had been
an invalid for thirty-eight years. 6 When
Jesus saw him lying there and learned that
he had been in this condition for a long time,
he asked him, "Do you want to get well?"

[a] 2 Some manuscripts *Bethzatha;* other manuscripts *Bethsaida* [b] 3,4 Some manuscripts include here, wholly or in part, *paralyzed — and they waited for the moving of the waters. [4]From time to time an angel of the Lord would come down and stir up the waters. The first one into the pool after each such disturbance would be cured of whatever disease they had.*

7 “Sir,” the invalid replied, “I have no one
to help me into the pool when the water is
stirred. While I am trying to get in, someone
else goes down ahead of me.”
8 Then Jesus said to him, “Get up! Pick up
your mat and walk.” 9 At once the man was
cured; he picked up his mat and walked.

The day on which this took place was a
Sabbath, 10 and so the Jewish leaders said to
the man who had been healed, “It is the Sab-
bath; the law forbids you to carry your mat.”
11 But he replied, “The man who made
me well said to me, ‘Pick up your mat and
walk.’ ”
12 So they asked him, “Who is this fellow
who told you to pick it up and walk?”
13 The man who was healed had no idea
who it was, for Jesus had slipped away into
the crowd that was there.
14 Later Jesus found him at the temple and
said to him, “See, you are well again. Stop
sinning or something worse may happen to
you.” 15 The man went away and told the Jew-
ish leaders that it was Jesus who had made
him well.

The Authority of the Son

16 So, because Jesus was doing these things
on the Sabbath, the Jewish leaders began to
persecute him. 17 In his defense Jesus said to
them, “My Father is always at his work to this
very day, and I too am working.” 18 For this
reason they tried all the more to kill him; not
only was he breaking the Sabbath, but he
was even calling God his own Father, mak-
ing himself equal with God.
19 Jesus gave them this answer: “Very truly
I tell you, the Son can do nothing by himself;
he can do only what he sees his Father do-
ing, because whatever the Father does the
Son also does. 20 For the Father loves the Son
and shows him all he does. Yes, and he will
show him even greater works than these, so
that you will be amazed. 21 For just as the Fa-
ther raises the dead and gives them life, even
so the Son gives life to whom he is pleased
to give it. 22 Moreover, the Father judges no
one, but has entrusted all judgment to the
Son, 23 that all may honor the Son just as they
honor the Father. Whoever does not honor
the Son does not honor the Father, who sent
him.
24 “Very truly I tell you, whoever hears
my word and believes him who sent me has
eternal life and will not be judged but has
crossed over from death to life. 25 Very truly I
tell you, a time is coming and has now come
when the dead will hear the voice of the Son
of God and those who hear will live. 26 For
as the Father has life in himself, so he has
granted the Son also to have life in himself.
27 And he has given him authority to judge
because he is the Son of Man.
28 “Do not be amazed at this, for a time is
coming when all who are in their graves will
hear his voice 29 and come out — those who
have done what is good will rise to live, and
those who have done what is evil will rise to
be condemned. 30 By myself I can do noth-
ing; I judge only as I hear, and my judgment
is just, for I seek not to please myself but him
who sent me.

Testimonies About Jesus

31 “If I testify about myself, my testimony
is not true. 32 There is another who testifies
in my favor, and I know that his testimony
about me is true.
33 “You have sent to John and he has testi-
fied to the truth. 34 Not that I accept human
testimony; but I mention it that you may be
saved. 35 John was a lamp that burned and
gave light, and you chose for a time to enjoy
his light.
36 “I have testimony weightier than that of
John. For the works that the Father has giv-
en me to finish — the very works that I am
doing — testify that the Father has sent me.
37 And the Father who sent me has himself
testified concerning me. You have never
heard his voice nor seen his form, 38 nor does
his word dwell in you, for you do not believe
the one he sent. 39 You study[a] the Scriptures
diligently because you think that in them
you have eternal life. These are the very
Scriptures that testify about me, 40 yet you
refuse to come to me to have life.
41 “I do not accept glory from human be-
ings, 42 but I know you. I know that you do not
have the love of God in your hearts. 43 I have
come in my Father’s name, and you do not
accept me; but if someone else comes in his
own name, you will accept him. 44 How can
you believe since you accept glory from one

[a] 39 Or 39 *Study*

another but do not seek the glory that comes
from the only God[a]?
45“But do not think I will accuse you be-
fore the Father. Your accuser is Moses, on
whom your hopes are set. 46If you believed
Moses, you would believe me, for he wrote
about me. 47But since you do not believe
what he wrote, how are you going to believe
what I say?”

Jesus Feeds the Five Thousand

6 Some time after this, Jesus crossed to
the far shore of the Sea of Galilee (that
is, the Sea of Tiberias), 2and a great crowd
of people followed him because they saw
the signs he had performed by healing the
sick. 3Then Jesus went up on a mountainside
and sat down with his disciples. 4The Jewish
Passover Festival was near.
5When Jesus looked up and saw a great
crowd coming toward him, he said to Philip,
“Where shall we buy bread for these people
to eat?” 6He asked this only to test him, for he
already had in mind what he was going to do.
7Philip answered him, “It would take
more than half a year’s wages[b] to buy enough
bread for each one to have a bite!”
8Another of his disciples, Andrew, Si-
mon Peter’s brother, spoke up, 9“Here is a
boy with five small barley loaves and two
small fish, but how far will they go among so
many?”
10Jesus said, “Have the people sit down.”
There was plenty of grass in that place, and
they sat down (about five thousand men
were there). 11Jesus then took the loaves,
gave thanks, and distributed to those who
were seated as much as they wanted. He did
the same with the fish.
12When they had all had enough to eat, he
said to his disciples, “Gather the pieces that
are left over. Let nothing be wasted.” 13So
they gathered them and filled twelve baskets
with the pieces of the five barley loaves left
over by those who had eaten.
14After the people saw the sign Jesus per-
formed, they began to say, “Surely this is
the Prophet who is to come into the world.”
15Jesus, knowing that they intended to come
and make him king by force, withdrew again
to a mountain by himself.

Jesus Walks on the Water

16When evening came, his disciples went
down to the lake, 17where they got into a boat
and set off across the lake for Capernaum. By
now it was dark, and Jesus had not yet joined
them. 18A strong wind was blowing and the
waters grew rough. 19When they had rowed
about three or four miles,[c] they saw Jesus
approaching the boat, walking on the wa-
ter; and they were frightened. 20But he said
to them, “It is I; don’t be afraid.” 21Then they
were willing to take him into the boat, and
immediately the boat reached the shore
where they were heading.
22The next day the crowd that had stayed
on the opposite shore of the lake realized
that only one boat had been there, and that
Jesus had not entered it with his disciples,
but that they had gone away alone. 23Then
some boats from Tiberias landed near the
place where the people had eaten the bread
after the Lord had given thanks. 24Once the
crowd realized that neither Jesus nor his dis-
ciples were there, they got into the boats and
went to Capernaum in search of Jesus.

Jesus the Bread of Life

25When they found him on the other side
of the lake, they asked him, “Rabbi, when did
you get here?”
26Jesus answered, “Very truly I tell you,
you are looking for me, not because you saw
the signs I performed but because you ate
the loaves and had your fill. 27Do not work
for food that spoils, but for food that endures
to eternal life, which the Son of Man will give
you. For on him God the Father has placed
his seal of approval.”
28Then they asked him, “What must we do
to do the works God requires?”
29Jesus answered, “The work of God is
this: to believe in the one he has sent.”
30So they asked him, “What sign then will
you give that we may see it and believe you?
What will you do? 31Our ancestors ate the
manna in the wilderness; as it is written: ‘He
gave them bread from heaven to eat.’[d]”
32Jesus said to them, “Very truly I tell you,
it is not Moses who has given you the bread
from heaven, but it is my Father who gives
you the true bread from heaven. 33For the

[a] *44* Some early manuscripts *the Only One* [b] *7* Greek *take two hundred denarii* [c] *19* Or about 5 or 6 kilometers [d] *31* Exodus 16:4; Neh. 9:15; Psalm 78:24,25

bread of God is the bread that comes down from heaven and gives life to the world."

34 "Sir," they said, "always give us this bread."

35 Then Jesus declared, "I am the bread of life. Whoever comes to me will never go hungry, and whoever believes in me will never be thirsty. 36 But as I told you, you have seen me and still you do not believe. 37 All those the Father gives me will come to me, and whoever comes to me I will never drive away. 38 For I have come down from heaven not to do my will but to do the will of him who sent me. 39 And this is the will of him who sent me, that I shall lose none of all those he has given me, but raise them up at the last day. 40 For my Father's will is that everyone who looks to the Son and believes in him shall have eternal life, and I will raise them up at the last day."

41 At this the Jews there began to grumble about him because he said, "I am the bread that came down from heaven." 42 They said, "Is this not Jesus, the son of Joseph, whose father and mother we know? How can he now say, 'I came down from heaven'?"

43 "Stop grumbling among yourselves," Jesus answered. 44 "No one can come to me unless the Father who sent me draws them, and I will raise them up at the last day. 45 It is written in the Prophets: 'They will all be taught by God.'[a] Everyone who has heard the Father and learned from him comes to me. 46 No one has seen the Father except the one who is from God; only he has seen the Father. 47 Very truly I tell you, the one who believes has eternal life. 48 I am the bread of life. 49 Your ancestors ate the manna in the wilderness, yet they died. 50 But here is the bread that comes down from heaven, which anyone may eat and not die. 51 I am the living bread that came down from heaven. Whoever eats this bread will live forever. This bread is my flesh, which I will give for the life of the world."

52 Then the Jews began to argue sharply among themselves, "How can this man give us his flesh to eat?"

53 Jesus said to them, "Very truly I tell you, unless you eat the flesh of the Son of Man and drink his blood, you have no life in you. 54 Whoever eats my flesh and drinks my blood has eternal life, and I will raise them up at the last day. 55 For my flesh is real food and my blood is real drink. 56 Whoever eats my flesh and drinks my blood remains in me, and I in them. 57 Just as the living Father sent me and I live because of the Father, so the one who feeds on me will live because of me. 58 This is the bread that came down from heaven. Your ancestors ate manna and died, but whoever feeds on this bread will live forever." 59 He said this while teaching in the synagogue in Capernaum.

Many Disciples Desert Jesus

60 On hearing it, many of his disciples said, "This is a hard teaching. Who can accept it?"

61 Aware that his disciples were grumbling about this, Jesus said to them, "Does this offend you? 62 Then what if you see the Son of Man ascend to where he was before! 63 The Spirit gives life; the flesh counts for nothing. The words I have spoken to you — they are full of the Spirit[b] and life. 64 Yet there are some of you who do not believe." For Jesus had known from the beginning which of them did not believe and who would betray him. 65 He went on to say, "This is why I told you that no one can come to me unless the Father has enabled them."

66 From this time many of his disciples turned back and no longer followed him.

67 "You do not want to leave too, do you?" Jesus asked the Twelve.

68 Simon Peter answered him, "Lord, to whom shall we go? You have the words of eternal life. 69 We have come to believe and to know that you are the Holy One of God."

70 Then Jesus replied, "Have I not chosen you, the Twelve? Yet one of you is a devil!" 71 (He meant Judas, the son of Simon Iscariot, who, though one of the Twelve, was later to betray him.)

Jesus Goes to the Festival of Tabernacles

7 After this, Jesus went around in Galilee. He did not want[c] to go about in Judea because the Jewish leaders there were looking for a way to kill him. 2 But when the Jewish Festival of Tabernacles was near, 3 Jesus' brothers said to him, "Leave Galilee and go to Judea, so that your disciples there may see

[a] *45* Isaiah 54:13 [b] *63* Or *are Spirit*; or *are spirit* [c] *1* Some manuscripts *not have authority*

the works you do. 4 No one who wants to be-
come a public figure acts in secret. Since you
are doing these things, show yourself to the
world." 5 For even his own brothers did not
believe in him.

6 Therefore Jesus told them, "My time is
not yet here; for you any time will do. 7 The
world cannot hate you, but it hates me be-
cause I testify that its works are evil. 8 You
go to the festival. I am not[a] going up to this
festival, because my time has not yet fully
come." 9 After he had said this, he stayed in
Galilee.

10 However, after his brothers had left for
the festival, he went also, not publicly, but
in secret. 11 Now at the festival the Jewish
leaders were watching for Jesus and asking,
"Where is he?"

12 Among the crowds there was wide-
spread whispering about him. Some said,
"He is a good man."

Others replied, "No, he deceives the peo-
ple." 13 But no one would say anything pub-
licly about him for fear of the leaders.

Jesus Teaches at the Festival

14 Not until halfway through the festival
did Jesus go up to the temple courts and be-
gin to teach. 15 The Jews there were amazed
and asked, "How did this man get such
learning without having been taught?"

16 Jesus answered, "My teaching is not
my own. It comes from the one who sent
me. 17 Anyone who chooses to do the will
of God will find out whether my teaching
comes from God or whether I speak on my
own. 18 Whoever speaks on their own does
so to gain personal glory, but he who seeks
the glory of the one who sent him is a man
of truth; there is nothing false about him.
19 Has not Moses given you the law? Yet not
one of you keeps the law. Why are you trying
to kill me?"

20 "You are demon-possessed," the crowd
answered. "Who is trying to kill you?"

21 Jesus said to them, "I did one miracle,
and you are all amazed. 22 Yet, because Mo-
ses gave you circumcision (though actually
it did not come from Moses, but from the pa-
triarchs), you circumcise a boy on the Sab-
bath. 23 Now if a boy can be circumcised on
the Sabbath so that the law of Moses may not
be broken, why are you angry with me for
healing a man's whole body on the Sabbath?
24 Stop judging by mere appearances, but in-
stead judge correctly."

Division Over Who Jesus Is

25 At that point some of the people of Jeru-
salem began to ask, "Isn't this the man they
are trying to kill? 26 Here he is, speaking pub-
licly, and they are not saying a word to him.
Have the authorities really concluded that
he is the Messiah? 27 But we know where this
man is from; when the Messiah comes, no
one will know where he is from."

28 Then Jesus, still teaching in the temple
courts, cried out, "Yes, you know me, and
you know where I am from. I am not here
on my own authority, but he who sent me is
true. You do not know him, 29 but I know him
because I am from him and he sent me."

30 At this they tried to seize him, but no
one laid a hand on him, because his hour
had not yet come. 31 Still, many in the crowd
believed in him. They said, "When the Mes-
siah comes, will he perform more signs than
this man?"

32 The Pharisees heard the crowd whis-
pering such things about him. Then the
chief priests and the Pharisees sent temple
guards to arrest him.

33 Jesus said, "I am with you for only a
short time, and then I am going to the one
who sent me. 34 You will look for me, but you
will not find me; and where I am, you cannot
come."

35 The Jews said to one another, "Where
does this man intend to go that we cannot
find him? Will he go where our people live
scattered among the Greeks, and teach the
Greeks? 36 What did he mean when he said,
'You will look for me, but you will not find
me,' and 'Where I am, you cannot come'?"

37 On the last and greatest day of the festi-
val, Jesus stood and said in a loud voice, "Let
anyone who is thirsty come to me and drink.
38 Whoever believes in me, as Scripture has
said, rivers of living water will flow from
within them."[b] 39 By this he meant the Spirit,
whom those who believed in him were lat-
er to receive. Up to that time the Spirit had

[a] 8 Some manuscripts *not yet* [b] 37,38 Or *me. And let anyone drink* 38 *who believes in me." As Scripture has said, "Out of him* (or *them*) *will flow rivers of living water."*

not been given, since Jesus had not yet been
glorified.
40 On hearing his words, some of the peo-
ple said, "Surely this man is the Prophet."
41 Others said, "He is the Messiah."
Still others asked, "How can the Messi-
ah come from Galilee? 42 Does not Scripture
say that the Messiah will come from David's
descendants and from Bethlehem, the town
where David lived?" 43 Thus the people were
divided because of Jesus. 44 Some wanted to
seize him, but no one laid a hand on him.

Unbelief of the Jewish Leaders

45 Finally the temple guards went back
to the chief priests and the Pharisees, who
asked them, "Why didn't you bring him in?"
46 "No one ever spoke the way this man
does," the guards replied.
47 "You mean he has deceived you also?"
the Pharisees retorted. 48 "Have any of the
rulers or of the Pharisees believed in him?
49 No! But this mob that knows nothing of the
law — there is a curse on them."
50 Nicodemus, who had gone to Jesus ear-
lier and who was one of their own number,
asked, 51 "Does our law condemn a man
without first hearing him to find out what he
has been doing?"
52 They replied, "Are you from Galilee, too?
Look into it, and you will find that a prophet
does not come out of Galilee."

[The earliest manuscripts and many other ancient witnesses do not have John 7:53 — 8:11. A few manuscripts include these verses, wholly or in part, after John 7:36, John 21:25, Luke 21:38 or Luke 24:53.]

8 *53 Then they all went home, 1 but Jesus went to*
the Mount of Olives.
2 At dawn he appeared again in the temple
courts, where all the people gathered around him,
and he sat down to teach them. 3 The teachers of
the law and the Pharisees brought in a woman
caught in adultery. They made her stand before
the group 4 and said to Jesus, "Teacher, this woman
was caught in the act of adultery. 5 In the Law Moses
commanded us to stone such women. Now what do
you say?" 6 They were using this question as a trap,
in order to have a basis for accusing him.
But Jesus bent down and started to write on the
ground with his finger. 7 When they kept on ques-
tioning him, he straightened up and said to them,
"Let any one of you who is without sin be the first to
throw a stone at her." 8 Again he stooped down and
wrote on the ground.
9 At this, those who heard began to go away one
at a time, the older ones first, until only Jesus was
left, with the woman still standing there. 10 Jesus
straightened up and asked her, "Woman, where are
they? Has no one condemned you?"
11 "No one, sir," she said.
"Then neither do I condemn you," Jesus de-
clared. "Go now and leave your life of sin."

Dispute Over Jesus' Testimony

12 When Jesus spoke again to the people,
he said, "I am the light of the world. Whoever
follows me will never walk in darkness, but
will have the light of life."
13 The Pharisees challenged him, "Here
you are, appearing as your own witness;
your testimony is not valid."
14 Jesus answered, "Even if I testify on my
own behalf, my testimony is valid, for I know
where I came from and where I am going.
But you have no idea where I come from or
where I am going. 15 You judge by human
standards; I pass judgment on no one. 16 But
if I do judge, my decisions are true, because
I am not alone. I stand with the Father, who
sent me. 17 In your own Law it is written that
the testimony of two witnesses is true. 18 I am
one who testifies for myself; my other wit-
ness is the Father, who sent me."
19 Then they asked him, "Where is your fa-
ther?"
"You do not know me or my Father," Jesus
replied. "If you knew me, you would know
my Father also." 20 He spoke these words
while teaching in the temple courts near
the place where the offerings were put. Yet
no one seized him, because his hour had not
yet come.

Dispute Over Who Jesus Is

21 Once more Jesus said to them, "I am go-
ing away, and you will look for me, and you
will die in your sin. Where I go, you cannot
come."
22 This made the Jews ask, "Will he kill
himself? Is that why he says, 'Where I go, you
cannot come'?"
23 But he continued, "You are from below;
I am from above. You are of this world; I am
not of this world. 24 I told you that you would

die in your sins; if you do not believe that I
am he, you will indeed die in your sins.”
25 “Who are you?” they asked.
“Just what I have been telling you from the
beginning,” Jesus replied. 26 “I have much to
say in judgment of you. But he who sent me
is trustworthy, and what I have heard from
him I tell the world.”
27 They did not understand that he was
telling them about his Father. 28 So Jesus
said, “When you have lifted up[a] the Son of
Man, then you will know that I am he and
that I do nothing on my own but speak just
what the Father has taught me. 29 The one
who sent me is with me; he has not left me
alone, for I always do what pleases him.”
30 Even as he spoke, many believed in him.

Dispute Over Whose Children Jesus' Opponents Are

31 To the Jews who had believed him, Jesus
said, “If you hold to my teaching, you are
really my disciples. 32 Then you will know
the truth, and the truth will set you free.”
33 They answered him, “We are Abraham's
descendants and have never been slaves of
anyone. How can you say that we shall be set
free?”
34 Jesus replied, “Very truly I tell you, ev-
eryone who sins is a slave to sin. 35 Now a
slave has no permanent place in the fami-
ly, but a son belongs to it forever. 36 So if the
Son sets you free, you will be free indeed. 37 I
know that you are Abraham's descendants.
Yet you are looking for a way to kill me, be-
cause you have no room for my word. 38 I am
telling you what I have seen in the Father's
presence, and you are doing what you have
heard from your father.[b]”
39 “Abraham is our father,” they answered.
“If you were Abraham's children,” said
Jesus, “then you would[c] do what Abraham
did. 40 As it is, you are looking for a way to kill
me, a man who has told you the truth that I
heard from God. Abraham did not do such
things. 41 You are doing the works of your
own father.”
“We are not illegitimate children,” they
protested. “The only Father we have is God
himself.”
42 Jesus said to them, “If God were your
Father, you would love me, for I have come
here from God. I have not come on my own;
God sent me. 43 Why is my language not clear
to you? Because you are unable to hear what
I say. 44 You belong to your father, the devil,
and you want to carry out your father's de-
sires. He was a murderer from the begin-
ning, not holding to the truth, for there is no
truth in him. When he lies, he speaks his na-
tive language, for he is a liar and the father of
lies. 45 Yet because I tell the truth, you do not
believe me! 46 Can any of you prove me guilty
of sin? If I am telling the truth, why don't you
believe me? 47 Whoever belongs to God hears
what God says. The reason you do not hear is
that you do not belong to God.”

Jesus' Claims About Himself

48 The Jews answered him, “Aren't we right
in saying that you are a Samaritan and de-
mon-possessed?”
49 “I am not possessed by a demon,” said
Jesus, “but I honor my Father and you dis-
honor me. 50 I am not seeking glory for my-
self; but there is one who seeks it, and he is
the judge. 51 Very truly I tell you, whoever
obeys my word will never see death.”
52 At this they exclaimed, “Now we know
that you are demon-possessed! Abraham
died and so did the prophets, yet you say
that whoever obeys your word will never
taste death. 53 Are you greater than our father
Abraham? He died, and so did the prophets.
Who do you think you are?”
54 Jesus replied, “If I glorify myself, my glory
means nothing. My Father, whom you claim
as your God, is the one who glorifies me.
55 Though you do not know him, I know him.
If I said I did not, I would be a liar like you, but
I do know him and obey his word. 56 Your fa-
ther Abraham rejoiced at the thought of see-
ing my day; he saw it and was glad.”
57 “You are not yet fifty years old,” they
said to him, “and you have seen Abraham!”
58 “Very truly I tell you,” Jesus answered,
“before Abraham was born, I am!” 59 At this,
they picked up stones to stone him, but Jesus
hid himself, slipping away from the temple
grounds.

Jesus Heals a Man Born Blind

9 As he went along, he saw a man blind
from birth. 2 His disciples asked him,

[a] *28* The Greek for *lifted up* also means *exalted.* [b] *38* Or *presence. Therefore do what you have heard from the Father.* [c] *39* Some early manuscripts *“If you are Abraham's children,” said Jesus, “then*

"Rabbi, who sinned, this man or his parents, that he was born blind?"

3"Neither this man nor his parents sinned," said Jesus, "but this happened so that the works of God might be displayed in him. 4As long as it is day, we must do the works of him who sent me. Night is coming, when no one can work. 5While I am in the world, I am the light of the world."

6After saying this, he spit on the ground, made some mud with the saliva, and put it on the man's eyes. 7"Go," he told him, "wash in the Pool of Siloam" (this word means "Sent"). So the man went and washed, and came home seeing.

8His neighbors and those who had formerly seen him begging asked, "Isn't this the same man who used to sit and beg?" 9Some claimed that he was.

Others said, "No, he only looks like him."

But he himself insisted, "I am the man."

10"How then were your eyes opened?" they asked.

11He replied, "The man they call Jesus made some mud and put it on my eyes. He told me to go to Siloam and wash. So I went and washed, and then I could see."

12"Where is this man?" they asked him.

"I don't know," he said.

The Pharisees Investigate the Healing

13They brought to the Pharisees the man who had been blind. 14Now the day on which Jesus had made the mud and opened the man's eyes was a Sabbath. 15Therefore the Pharisees also asked him how he had received his sight. "He put mud on my eyes," the man replied, "and I washed, and now I see."

16Some of the Pharisees said, "This man is not from God, for he does not keep the Sabbath."

But others asked, "How can a sinner perform such signs?" So they were divided.

17Then they turned again to the blind man, "What have you to say about him? It was your eyes he opened."

The man replied, "He is a prophet."

18They still did not believe that he had been blind and had received his sight until they sent for the man's parents. 19"Is this your son?" they asked. "Is this the one you say was born blind? How is it that now he can see?"

20"We know he is our son," the parents answered, "and we know he was born blind. 21But how he can see now, or who opened his eyes, we don't know. Ask him. He is of age; he will speak for himself." 22His parents said this because they were afraid of the Jewish leaders, who already had decided that anyone who acknowledged that Jesus was the Messiah would be put out of the synagogue. 23That was why his parents said, "He is of age; ask him."

24A second time they summoned the man who had been blind. "Give glory to God by telling the truth," they said. "We know this man is a sinner."

25He replied, "Whether he is a sinner or not, I don't know. One thing I do know. I was blind but now I see!"

26Then they asked him, "What did he do to you? How did he open your eyes?"

27He answered, "I have told you already and you did not listen. Why do you want to hear it again? Do you want to become his disciples too?"

28Then they hurled insults at him and said, "You are this fellow's disciple! We are disciples of Moses! 29We know that God spoke to Moses, but as for this fellow, we don't even know where he comes from."

30The man answered, "Now that is remarkable! You don't know where he comes from, yet he opened my eyes. 31We know that God does not listen to sinners. He listens to the godly person who does his will. 32Nobody has ever heard of opening the eyes of a man born blind. 33If this man were not from God, he could do nothing."

34To this they replied, "You were steeped in sin at birth; how dare you lecture us!" And they threw him out.

Spiritual Blindness

35Jesus heard that they had thrown him out, and when he found him, he said, "Do you believe in the Son of Man?"

36"Who is he, sir?" the man asked. "Tell me so that I may believe in him."

37Jesus said, "You have now seen him; in fact, he is the one speaking with you."

38Then the man said, "Lord, I believe," and he worshiped him.

39Jesus said,[a] "For judgment I have come into this world, so that the blind will see and those who see will become blind."

[a] *38,39* Some early manuscripts do not have *Then the man said . . . 39Jesus said.*

40 Some Pharisees who were with him heard him say this and asked, "What? Are we blind too?"

41 Jesus said, "If you were blind, you would not be guilty of sin; but now that you claim you can see, your guilt remains.

The Good Shepherd and His Sheep

10 "Very truly I tell you Pharisees, anyone who does not enter the sheep pen by the gate, but climbs in by some other way, is a thief and a robber. 2 The one who enters by the gate is the shepherd of the sheep. 3 The gatekeeper opens the gate for him, and the sheep listen to his voice. He calls his own sheep by name and leads them out. 4 When he has brought out all his own, he goes on ahead of them, and his sheep follow him because they know his voice. 5 But they will never follow a stranger; in fact, they will run away from him because they do not recognize a stranger's voice." 6 Jesus used this figure of speech, but the Pharisees did not understand what he was telling them.

7 Therefore Jesus said again, "Very truly I tell you, I am the gate for the sheep. 8 All who have come before me are thieves and robbers, but the sheep have not listened to them. 9 I am the gate; whoever enters through me will be saved.[a] They will come in and go out, and find pasture. 10 The thief comes only to steal and kill and destroy; I have come that they may have life, and have it to the full.

11 "I am the good shepherd. The good shepherd lays down his life for the sheep. 12 The hired hand is not the shepherd and does not own the sheep. So when he sees the wolf coming, he abandons the sheep and runs away. Then the wolf attacks the flock and scatters it. 13 The man runs away because he is a hired hand and cares nothing for the sheep.

14 "I am the good shepherd; I know my sheep and my sheep know me— 15 just as the Father knows me and I know the Father—and I lay down my life for the sheep. 16 I have other sheep that are not of this sheep pen. I must bring them also. They too will listen to my voice, and there shall be one flock and one shepherd. 17 The reason my Father loves me is that I lay down my life—only to take it up again. 18 No one takes it from me, but I lay it down of my own accord. I have authority to lay it down and authority to take it up again. This command I received from my Father."

19 The Jews who heard these words were again divided. 20 Many of them said, "He is demon-possessed and raving mad. Why listen to him?"

21 But others said, "These are not the sayings of a man possessed by a demon. Can a demon open the eyes of the blind?"

Further Conflict Over Jesus' Claims

22 Then came the Festival of Dedication[b] at Jerusalem. It was winter, 23 and Jesus was in the temple courts walking in Solomon's Colonnade. 24 The Jews who were there gathered around him, saying, "How long will you keep us in suspense? If you are the Messiah, tell us plainly."

25 Jesus answered, "I did tell you, but you do not believe. The works I do in my Father's name testify about me, 26 but you do not believe because you are not my sheep. 27 My sheep listen to my voice; I know them, and they follow me. 28 I give them eternal life, and they shall never perish; no one will snatch them out of my hand. 29 My Father, who has given them to me, is greater than all[c]; no one can snatch them out of my Father's hand. 30 I and the Father are one."

31 Again his Jewish opponents picked up stones to stone him, 32 but Jesus said to them, "I have shown you many good works from the Father. For which of these do you stone me?"

33 "We are not stoning you for any good work," they replied, "but for blasphemy, because you, a mere man, claim to be God."

34 Jesus answered them, "Is it not written in your Law, 'I have said you are "gods"'[d]? 35 If he called them 'gods,' to whom the word of God came—and Scripture cannot be set aside— 36 what about the one whom the Father set apart as his very own and sent into the world? Why then do you accuse me of blasphemy because I said, 'I am God's Son'? 37 Do not believe me unless I do the works of my Father. 38 But if I do them, even though you do not believe me, believe the works,

[a] 9 Or *kept safe* [b] 22 That is, Hanukkah [c] 29 Many early manuscripts *What my Father has given me is greater than all* [d] 34 Psalm 82:6

that you may know and understand that the
Father is in me, and I in the Father." 39Again
they tried to seize him, but he escaped their
grasp.
40Then Jesus went back across the Jor-
dan to the place where John had been bap-
tizing in the early days. There he stayed,
41and many people came to him. They said,
"Though John never performed a sign, all
that John said about this man was true."
42And in that place many believed in Jesus.

The Death of Lazarus

11 Now a man named Lazarus was sick.
He was from Bethany, the village of
Mary and her sister Martha. 2(This Mary,
whose brother Lazarus now lay sick, was the
same one who poured perfume on the Lord
and wiped his feet with her hair.) 3So the sis-
ters sent word to Jesus, "Lord, the one you
love is sick."
4When he heard this, Jesus said, "This
sickness will not end in death. No, it is for
God's glory so that God's Son may be glori-
fied through it." 5Now Jesus loved Martha
and her sister and Lazarus. 6So when he
heard that Lazarus was sick, he stayed where
he was two more days, 7and then he said to
his disciples, "Let us go back to Judea."
8"But Rabbi," they said, "a short while ago
the Jews there tried to stone you, and yet you
are going back?"
9Jesus answered, "Are there not twelve
hours of daylight? Anyone who walks in the
daytime will not stumble, for they see by this
world's light. 10It is when a person walks at
night that they stumble, for they have no
light."
11After he had said this, he went on to tell
them, "Our friend Lazarus has fallen asleep;
but I am going there to wake him up."
12His disciples replied, "Lord, if he sleeps,
he will get better." 13Jesus had been speak-
ing of his death, but his disciples thought he
meant natural sleep.
14So then he told them plainly, "Lazarus
is dead, 15and for your sake I am glad I was
not there, so that you may believe. But let us
go to him."
16Then Thomas (also known as Didy-
mus[a]) said to the rest of the disciples, "Let us
also go, that we may die with him."

Jesus Comforts the Sisters of Lazarus

17On his arrival, Jesus found that Lazarus
had already been in the tomb for four days.
18Now Bethany was less than two miles[b]
from Jerusalem, 19and many Jews had come
to Martha and Mary to comfort them in the
loss of their brother. 20When Martha heard
that Jesus was coming, she went out to meet
him, but Mary stayed at home.
21"Lord," Martha said to Jesus, "if you had
been here, my brother would not have died.
22But I know that even now God will give you
whatever you ask."
23Jesus said to her, "Your brother will rise
again."
24Martha answered, "I know he will rise
again in the resurrection at the last day."
25Jesus said to her, "I am the resurrection
and the life. The one who believes in me will
live, even though they die; 26and whoever
lives by believing in me will never die. Do
you believe this?"
27"Yes, Lord," she replied, "I believe that
you are the Messiah, the Son of God, who is
to come into the world."
28After she had said this, she went back
and called her sister Mary aside. "The Teach-
er is here," she said, "and is asking for you."
29When Mary heard this, she got up quick-
ly and went to him. 30Now Jesus had not yet
entered the village, but was still at the place
where Martha had met him. 31When the Jews
who had been with Mary in the house, com-
forting her, noticed how quickly she got up
and went out, they followed her, supposing
she was going to the tomb to mourn there.
32When Mary reached the place where
Jesus was and saw him, she fell at his feet and
said, "Lord, if you had been here, my brother
would not have died."
33When Jesus saw her weeping, and the
Jews who had come along with her also
weeping, he was deeply moved in spirit and
troubled. 34"Where have you laid him?" he
asked.
"Come and see, Lord," they replied.
35Jesus wept.
36Then the Jews said, "See how he loved
him!"
37But some of them said, "Could not he
who opened the eyes of the blind man have
kept this man from dying?"

[a] 16 *Thomas* (Aramaic) and *Didymus* (Greek) both mean *twin*. [b] 18 Or about 3 kilometers

Jesus Raises Lazarus From the Dead

[38]Jesus, once more deeply moved, came
to the tomb. It was a cave with a stone laid
across the entrance. [39]"Take away the stone,"
he said.

"But, Lord," said Martha, the sister of the
dead man, "by this time there is a bad odor,
for he has been there four days."

[40]Then Jesus said, "Did I not tell you that
if you believe, you will see the glory of God?"

[41]So they took away the stone. Then Jesus
looked up and said, "Father, I thank you that
you have heard me. [42]I knew that you always
hear me, but I said this for the benefit of the
people standing here, that they may believe
that you sent me."

[43]When he had said this, Jesus called in a
loud voice, "Lazarus, come out!" [44]The dead
man came out, his hands and feet wrapped
with strips of linen, and a cloth around his
face.

Jesus said to them, "Take off the grave
clothes and let him go."

The Plot to Kill Jesus

[45]Therefore many of the Jews who had
come to visit Mary, and had seen what Jesus
did, believed in him. [46]But some of them
went to the Pharisees and told them what
Jesus had done. [47]Then the chief priests and
the Pharisees called a meeting of the San-
hedrin.

"What are we accomplishing?" they
asked. "Here is this man performing many
signs. [48]If we let him go on like this, every-
one will believe in him, and then the Ro-
mans will come and take away both our tem-
ple and our nation."

[49]Then one of them, named Caiaphas,
who was high priest that year, spoke up, "You
know nothing at all! [50]You do not realize that
it is better for you that one man die for the
people than that the whole nation perish."

[51]He did not say this on his own, but as
high priest that year he prophesied that
Jesus would die for the Jewish nation, [52]and
not only for that nation but also for the scat-
tered children of God, to bring them togeth-
er and make them one. [53]So from that day on
they plotted to take his life.

[54]Therefore Jesus no longer moved about
publicly among the people of Judea. Instead
he withdrew to a region near the wilderness,
to a village called Ephraim, where he stayed
with his disciples.

[55]When it was almost time for the Jewish
Passover, many went up from the country
to Jerusalem for their ceremonial cleansing
before the Passover. [56]They kept looking for
Jesus, and as they stood in the temple courts
they asked one another, "What do you think?
Isn't he coming to the festival at all?" [57]But
the chief priests and the Pharisees had giv-
en orders that anyone who found out where
Jesus was should report it so that they might
arrest him.

Jesus Anointed at Bethany

12 Six days before the Passover, Jesus
came to Bethany, where Lazarus lived,
whom Jesus had raised from the dead. [2]Here
a dinner was given in Jesus' honor. Martha
served, while Lazarus was among those re-
clining at the table with him. [3]Then Mary
took about a pint[a] of pure nard, an expen-
sive perfume; she poured it on Jesus' feet and
wiped his feet with her hair. And the house
was filled with the fragrance of the perfume.

[4]But one of his disciples, Judas Iscariot,
who was later to betray him, objected, [5]"Why
wasn't this perfume sold and the money giv-
en to the poor? It was worth a year's wages.[b]"
[6]He did not say this because he cared about
the poor but because he was a thief; as keep-
er of the money bag, he used to help himself
to what was put into it.

[7]"Leave her alone," Jesus replied. "It was
intended that she should save this perfume
for the day of my burial. [8]You will always
have the poor among you,[c] but you will not
always have me."

[9]Meanwhile a large crowd of Jews found
out that Jesus was there and came, not only
because of him but also to see Lazarus, whom
he had raised from the dead. [10]So the chief
priests made plans to kill Lazarus as well,
[11]for on account of him many of the Jews were
going over to Jesus and believing in him.

Jesus Comes to Jerusalem as King

[12]The next day the great crowd that had
come for the festival heard that Jesus was
on his way to Jerusalem. [13]They took palm
branches and went out to meet him, shouting,

[a] 3 Or about 0.5 liter [b] 5 Greek *three hundred denarii* [c] 8 See Deut. 15:11.

"Hosanna![a]"

"Blessed is he who comes in the name
of the Lord!"[b]

"Blessed is the king of Israel!"

14 Jesus found a young donkey and sat on it,
as it is written:

15 "Do not be afraid, Daughter Zion;
see, your king is coming,
seated on a donkey's colt."[c]

16 At first his disciples did not under-
stand all this. Only after Jesus was glorified
did they realize that these things had been
written about him and that these things had
been done to him.
17 Now the crowd that was with him when
he called Lazarus from the tomb and raised
him from the dead continued to spread the
word. 18 Many people, because they had
heard that he had performed this sign, went
out to meet him. 19 So the Pharisees said to
one another, "See, this is getting us nowhere.
Look how the whole world has gone after
him!"

Jesus Predicts His Death

20 Now there were some Greeks among
those who went up to worship at the festival.
21 They came to Philip, who was from Beth-
saida in Galilee, with a request. "Sir," they
said, "we would like to see Jesus." 22 Philip
went to tell Andrew; Andrew and Philip in
turn told Jesus.
23 Jesus replied, "The hour has come for
the Son of Man to be glorified. 24 Very tru-
ly I tell you, unless a kernel of wheat falls
to the ground and dies, it remains only a
single seed. But if it dies, it produces many
seeds. 25 Anyone who loves their life will lose
it, while anyone who hates their life in this
world will keep it for eternal life. 26 Whoever
serves me must follow me; and where I am,
my servant also will be. My Father will honor
the one who serves me.
27 "Now my soul is troubled, and what
shall I say? 'Father, save me from this hour'?
No, it was for this very reason I came to this
hour. 28 Father, glorify your name!"
Then a voice came from heaven, "I have
glorified it, and will glorify it again." 29 The
crowd that was there and heard it said it had
thundered; others said an angel had spoken
to him.
30 Jesus said, "This voice was for your ben-
efit, not mine. 31 Now is the time for judg-
ment on this world; now the prince of this
world will be driven out. 32 And I, when I am
lifted up[d] from the earth, will draw all peo-
ple to myself." 33 He said this to show the
kind of death he was going to die.
34 The crowd spoke up, "We have heard
from the Law that the Messiah will remain
forever, so how can you say, 'The Son of Man
must be lifted up'? Who is this 'Son of Man'?"
35 Then Jesus told them, "You are going to
have the light just a little while longer. Walk
while you have the light, before darkness
overtakes you. Whoever walks in the dark
does not know where they are going. 36 Be-
lieve in the light while you have the light,
so that you may become children of light."
When he had finished speaking, Jesus left
and hid himself from them.

Belief and Unbelief Among the Jews

37 Even after Jesus had performed so many
signs in their presence, they still would not
believe in him. 38 This was to fulfill the word
of Isaiah the prophet:

"Lord, who has believed our message
and to whom has the arm of the Lord
been revealed?"[e]

39 For this reason they could not believe,
because, as Isaiah says elsewhere:

40 "He has blinded their eyes
and hardened their hearts,
so they can neither see with their eyes,
nor understand with their hearts,
nor turn — and I would heal them."[f]

41 Isaiah said this because he saw Jesus' glory
and spoke about him.
42 Yet at the same time many even among
the leaders believed in him. But because
of the Pharisees they would not openly ac-
knowledge their faith for fear they would be
put out of the synagogue; 43 for they loved
human praise more than praise from God.
44 Then Jesus cried out, "Whoever believes

[a] *13* A Hebrew expression meaning "Save!" which became an exclamation of praise [b] *13* Psalm 118:25,26
[c] *15* Zech. 9:9 [d] *32* The Greek for *lifted up* also means *exalted.* [e] *38* Isaiah 53:1 [f] *40* Isaiah 6:10

in me does not believe in me only, but in the one who sent me. 45 The one who looks at me is seeing the one who sent me. 46 I have come into the world as a light, so that no one who believes in me should stay in darkness.

47 "If anyone hears my words but does not keep them, I do not judge that person. For I did not come to judge the world, but to save the world. 48 There is a judge for the one who rejects me and does not accept my words; the very words I have spoken will condemn them at the last day. 49 For I did not speak on my own, but the Father who sent me commanded me to say all that I have spoken. 50 I know that his command leads to eternal life. So whatever I say is just what the Father has told me to say."

Jesus Washes His Disciples' Feet

13 It was just before the Passover Festival. Jesus knew that the hour had come for him to leave this world and go to the Father. Having loved his own who were in the world, he loved them to the end.

2 The evening meal was in progress, and the devil had already prompted Judas, the son of Simon Iscariot, to betray Jesus. 3 Jesus knew that the Father had put all things under his power, and that he had come from God and was returning to God; 4 so he got up from the meal, took off his outer clothing, and wrapped a towel around his waist. 5 After that, he poured water into a basin and began to wash his disciples' feet, drying them with the towel that was wrapped around him.

6 He came to Simon Peter, who said to him, "Lord, are you going to wash my feet?"

7 Jesus replied, "You do not realize now what I am doing, but later you will understand."

8 "No," said Peter, "you shall never wash my feet."

Jesus answered, "Unless I wash you, you have no part with me."

9 "Then, Lord," Simon Peter replied, "not just my feet but my hands and my head as well!"

10 Jesus answered, "Those who have had a bath need only to wash their feet; their whole body is clean. And you are clean, though not every one of you." 11 For he knew who was going to betray him, and that was why he said not every one was clean.

12 When he had finished washing their feet, he put on his clothes and returned to his place. "Do you understand what I have done for you?" he asked them. 13 "You call me 'Teacher' and 'Lord,' and rightly so, for that is what I am. 14 Now that I, your Lord and Teacher, have washed your feet, you also should wash one another's feet. 15 I have set you an example that you should do as I have done for you. 16 Very truly I tell you, no servant is greater than his master, nor is a messenger greater than the one who sent him. 17 Now that you know these things, you will be blessed if you do them.

Jesus Predicts His Betrayal

18 "I am not referring to all of you; I know those I have chosen. But this is to fulfill this passage of Scripture: 'He who shared my bread has turned[a] against me.'[b]

19 "I am telling you now before it happens, so that when it does happen you will believe that I am who I am. 20 Very truly I tell you, whoever accepts anyone I send accepts me; and whoever accepts me accepts the one who sent me."

21 After he had said this, Jesus was troubled in spirit and testified, "Very truly I tell you, one of you is going to betray me."

22 His disciples stared at one another, at a loss to know which of them he meant. 23 One of them, the disciple whom Jesus loved, was reclining next to him. 24 Simon Peter motioned to this disciple and said, "Ask him which one he means."

25 Leaning back against Jesus, he asked him, "Lord, who is it?"

26 Jesus answered, "It is the one to whom I will give this piece of bread when I have dipped it in the dish." Then, dipping the piece of bread, he gave it to Judas, the son of Simon Iscariot. 27 As soon as Judas took the bread, Satan entered into him.

So Jesus told him, "What you are about to do, do quickly." 28 But no one at the meal understood why Jesus said this to him. 29 Since Judas had charge of the money, some thought Jesus was telling him to buy what was needed for the festival, or to give something to the poor. 30 As soon as Judas

[a] *18* Greek *has lifted up his heel* [b] *18* Psalm 41:9

had taken the bread, he went out. And it was night.

Jesus Predicts Peter's Denial

31 When he was gone, Jesus said, "Now the Son of Man is glorified and God is glorified in him. 32 If God is glorified in him,[a] God will glorify the Son in himself, and will glorify him at once.

33 "My children, I will be with you only a little longer. You will look for me, and just as I told the Jews, so I tell you now: Where I am going, you cannot come.

34 "A new command I give you: Love one another. As I have loved you, so you must love one another. 35 By this everyone will know that you are my disciples, if you love one another."

36 Simon Peter asked him, "Lord, where are you going?"

Jesus replied, "Where I am going, you cannot follow now, but you will follow later."

37 Peter asked, "Lord, why can't I follow you now? I will lay down my life for you."

38 Then Jesus answered, "Will you really lay down your life for me? Very truly I tell you, before the rooster crows, you will disown me three times!

Jesus Comforts His Disciples

14 "Do not let your hearts be troubled. You believe in God[b]; believe also in me. 2 My Father's house has many rooms; if that were not so, would I have told you that I am going there to prepare a place for you? 3 And if I go and prepare a place for you, I will come back and take you to be with me that you also may be where I am. 4 You know the way to the place where I am going."

Jesus the Way to the Father

5 Thomas said to him, "Lord, we don't know where you are going, so how can we know the way?"

6 Jesus answered, "I am the way and the truth and the life. No one comes to the Father except through me. 7 If you really know me, you will know[c] my Father as well. From now on, you do know him and have seen him."

8 Philip said, "Lord, show us the Father and that will be enough for us."

9 Jesus answered: "Don't you know me, Philip, even after I have been among you such a long time? Anyone who has seen me has seen the Father. How can you say, 'Show us the Father'? 10 Don't you believe that I am in the Father, and that the Father is in me? The words I say to you I do not speak on my own authority. Rather, it is the Father, living in me, who is doing his work. 11 Believe me when I say that I am in the Father and the Father is in me; or at least believe on the evidence of the works themselves. 12 Very truly I tell you, whoever believes in me will do the works I have been doing, and they will do even greater things than these, because I am going to the Father. 13 And I will do whatever you ask in my name, so that the Father may be glorified in the Son. 14 You may ask me for anything in my name, and I will do it.

Jesus Promises the Holy Spirit

15 "If you love me, keep my commands. 16 And I will ask the Father, and he will give you another advocate to help you and be with you forever— 17 the Spirit of truth. The world cannot accept him, because it neither sees him nor knows him. But you know him, for he lives with you and will be[d] in you. 18 I will not leave you as orphans; I will come to you. 19 Before long, the world will not see me anymore, but you will see me. Because I live, you also will live. 20 On that day you will realize that I am in my Father, and you are in me, and I am in you. 21 Whoever has my commands and keeps them is the one who loves me. The one who loves me will be loved by my Father, and I too will love them and show myself to them."

22 Then Judas (not Judas Iscariot) said, "But, Lord, why do you intend to show yourself to us and not to the world?"

23 Jesus replied, "Anyone who loves me will obey my teaching. My Father will love them, and we will come to them and make our home with them. 24 Anyone who does not love me will not obey my teaching. These words you hear are not my own; they belong to the Father who sent me.

25 "All this I have spoken while still with you. 26 But the Advocate, the Holy Spirit, whom the Father will send in my name, will teach you all things and will remind you of

[a] *32* Many early manuscripts do not have *If God is glorified in him.* [b] *1* Or *Believe in God* [c] *7* Some manuscripts *If you really knew me, you would know* [d] *17* Some early manuscripts *and is*

everything I have said to you. [27]Peace I leave with you; my peace I give you. I do not give to you as the world gives. Do not let your hearts be troubled and do not be afraid.

[28]"You heard me say, 'I am going away and I am coming back to you.' If you loved me, you would be glad that I am going to the Father, for the Father is greater than I. [29]I have told you now before it happens, so that when it does happen you will believe. [30]I will not say much more to you, for the prince of this world is coming. He has no hold over me, [31]but he comes so that the world may learn that I love the Father and do exactly what my Father has commanded me.

"Come now; let us leave.

The Vine and the Branches

15 "I am the true vine, and my Father is the gardener. [2]He cuts off every branch in me that bears no fruit, while every branch that does bear fruit he prunes[a] so that it will be even more fruitful. [3]You are already clean because of the word I have spoken to you. [4]Remain in me, as I also remain in you. No branch can bear fruit by itself; it must remain in the vine. Neither can you bear fruit unless you remain in me.

[5]"I am the vine; you are the branches. If you remain in me and I in you, you will bear much fruit; apart from me you can do nothing. [6]If you do not remain in me, you are like a branch that is thrown away and withers; such branches are picked up, thrown into the fire and burned. [7]If you remain in me and my words remain in you, ask whatever you wish, and it will be done for you. [8]This is to my Father's glory, that you bear much fruit, showing yourselves to be my disciples.

[9]"As the Father has loved me, so have I loved you. Now remain in my love. [10]If you keep my commands, you will remain in my love, just as I have kept my Father's commands and remain in his love. [11]I have told you this so that my joy may be in you and that your joy may be complete. [12]My command is this: Love each other as I have loved you. [13]Greater love has no one than this: to lay down one's life for one's friends. [14]You are my friends if you do what I command. [15]I no longer call you servants, because a servant does not know his master's business. Instead, I have called you friends, for everything that I learned from my Father I have made known to you. [16]You did not choose me, but I chose you and appointed you so that you might go and bear fruit—fruit that will last—and so that whatever you ask in my name the Father will give you. [17]This is my command: Love each other.

The World Hates the Disciples

[18]"If the world hates you, keep in mind that it hated me first. [19]If you belonged to the world, it would love you as its own. As it is, you do not belong to the world, but I have chosen you out of the world. That is why the world hates you. [20]Remember what I told you: 'A servant is not greater than his master.'[b] If they persecuted me, they will persecute you also. If they obeyed my teaching, they will obey yours also. [21]They will treat you this way because of my name, for they do not know the one who sent me. [22]If I had not come and spoken to them, they would not be guilty of sin; but now they have no excuse for their sin. [23]Whoever hates me hates my Father as well. [24]If I had not done among them the works no one else did, they would not be guilty of sin. As it is, they have seen, and yet they have hated both me and my Father. [25]But this is to fulfill what is written in their Law: 'They hated me without reason.'[c]

The Work of the Holy Spirit

[26]"When the Advocate comes, whom I will send to you from the Father—the Spirit of truth who goes out from the Father—he will testify about me. [27]And you also must testify, for you have been with me from the beginning.

16 "All this I have told you so that you will not fall away. [2]They will put you out of the synagogue; in fact, the time is coming when anyone who kills you will think they are offering a service to God. [3]They will do such things because they have not known the Father or me. [4]I have told you this, so that when their time comes you will remember that I warned you about them. I did not tell you this from the beginning because I was with you, [5]but now I am going to him who sent me. None of you asks me, 'Where are you going?' [6]Rather, you are filled with grief

[a] 2 The Greek for *he prunes* also means *he cleans.* [b] 20 John 13:16 [c] 25 Psalms 35:19; 69:4

because I have said these things. 7But very
truly I tell you, it is for your good that I am
going away. Unless I go away, the Advocate
will not come to you; but if I go, I will send
him to you. 8When he comes, he will prove
the world to be in the wrong about sin and
righteousness and judgment: 9about sin, be-
cause people do not believe in me; 10about
righteousness, because I am going to the Fa-
ther, where you can see me no longer; 11and
about judgment, because the prince of this
world now stands condemned.

12"I have much more to say to you, more
than you can now bear. 13But when he, the
Spirit of truth, comes, he will guide you into
all the truth. He will not speak on his own;
he will speak only what he hears, and he will
tell you what is yet to come. 14He will glorify
me because it is from me that he will receive
what he will make known to you. 15All that
belongs to the Father is mine. That is why I
said the Spirit will receive from me what he
will make known to you."

The Disciples' Grief Will Turn to Joy

16Jesus went on to say, "In a little while
you will see me no more, and then after a lit-
tle while you will see me."

17At this, some of his disciples said to one
another, "What does he mean by saying, 'In
a little while you will see me no more, and
then after a little while you will see me,' and
'Because I am going to the Father'?" 18They
kept asking, "What does he mean by 'a lit-
tle while'? We don't understand what he is
saying."

19Jesus saw that they wanted to ask him
about this, so he said to them, "Are you ask-
ing one another what I meant when I said,
'In a little while you will see me no more,
and then after a little while you will see me'?
20Very truly I tell you, you will weep and
mourn while the world rejoices. You will
grieve, but your grief will turn to joy. 21A
woman giving birth to a child has pain be-
cause her time has come; but when her baby
is born she forgets the anguish because of
her joy that a child is born into the world.
22So with you: Now is your time of grief, but
I will see you again and you will rejoice, and
no one will take away your joy. 23In that day
you will no longer ask me anything. Very
truly I tell you, my Father will give you what-
ever you ask in my name. 24Until now you
have not asked for anything in my name.
Ask and you will receive, and your joy will
be complete.

25"Though I have been speaking figura-
tively, a time is coming when I will no lon-
ger use this kind of language but will tell you
plainly about my Father. 26In that day you
will ask in my name. I am not saying that I
will ask the Father on your behalf. 27No, the
Father himself loves you because you have
loved me and have believed that I came from
God. 28I came from the Father and entered
the world; now I am leaving the world and
going back to the Father."

29Then Jesus' disciples said, "Now you
are speaking clearly and without figures of
speech. 30Now we can see that you know all
things and that you do not even need to have
anyone ask you questions. This makes us be-
lieve that you came from God."

31"Do you now believe?" Jesus replied.
32"A time is coming and in fact has come
when you will be scattered, each to your own
home. You will leave me all alone. Yet I am
not alone, for my Father is with me.

33"I have told you these things, so that in
me you may have peace. In this world you
will have trouble. But take heart! I have over-
come the world."

Jesus Prays to Be Glorified

17 After Jesus said this, he looked to-
ward heaven and prayed:

"Father, the hour has come. Glori-
fy your Son, that your Son may glorify
you. 2For you granted him authori-
ty over all people that he might give
eternal life to all those you have given
him. 3Now this is eternal life: that they
know you, the only true God, and Jesus
Christ, whom you have sent. 4I have
brought you glory on earth by finishing
the work you gave me to do. 5And now,
Father, glorify me in your presence
with the glory I had with you before the
world began.

Jesus Prays for His Disciples

6"I have revealed you[a] to those
whom you gave me out of the world.
They were yours; you gave them to

[a] 6 Greek *your name*

me and they have obeyed your word. 7 Now they know that everything you have given me comes from you. 8 For I gave them the words you gave me and they accepted them. They knew with certainty that I came from you, and they believed that you sent me. 9 I pray for them. I am not praying for the world, but for those you have given me, for they are yours. 10 All I have is yours, and all you have is mine. And glory has come to me through them. 11 I will remain in the world no longer, but they are still in the world, and I am coming to you. Holy Father, protect them by the power of[a] your name, the name you gave me, so that they may be one as we are one. 12 While I was with them, I protected them and kept them safe by[b] that name you gave me. None has been lost except the one doomed to destruction so that Scripture would be fulfilled.

13 "I am coming to you now, but I say these things while I am still in the world, so that they may have the full measure of my joy within them. 14 I have given them your word and the world has hated them, for they are not of the world any more than I am of the world. 15 My prayer is not that you take them out of the world but that you protect them from the evil one. 16 They are not of the world, even as I am not of it. 17 Sanctify them by[c] the truth; your word is truth. 18 As you sent me into the world, I have sent them into the world. 19 For them I sanctify myself, that they too may be truly sanctified.

Jesus Prays for All Believers

20 "My prayer is not for them alone. I pray also for those who will believe in me through their message, 21 that all of them may be one, Father, just as you are in me and I am in you. May they also be in us so that the world may believe that you have sent me. 22 I have given them the glory that you gave me, that they may be one as we are one — 23 I in them and you in me — so that they may be brought to complete unity. Then the world will know that you sent me and have loved them even as you have loved me.

24 "Father, I want those you have given me to be with me where I am, and to see my glory, the glory you have given me because you loved me before the creation of the world.

25 "Righteous Father, though the world does not know you, I know you, and they know that you have sent me. 26 I have made you[d] known to them, and will continue to make you known in order that the love you have for me may be in them and that I myself may be in them."

Jesus Arrested

18 When he had finished praying, Jesus left with his disciples and crossed the Kidron Valley. On the other side there was a garden, and he and his disciples went into it.

2 Now Judas, who betrayed him, knew the place because Jesus had often met there with his disciples. 3 So Judas came to the garden, guiding a detachment of soldiers and some officials from the chief priests and the Pharisees. They were carrying torches, lanterns and weapons.

4 Jesus, knowing all that was going to happen to him, went out and asked them, "Who is it you want?"

5 "Jesus of Nazareth," they replied.

"I am he," Jesus said. (And Judas the traitor was standing there with them.) 6 When Jesus said, "I am he," they drew back and fell to the ground.

7 Again he asked them, "Who is it you want?"

"Jesus of Nazareth," they said.

8 Jesus answered, "I told you that I am he. If you are looking for me, then let these men go." 9 This happened so that the words he had spoken would be fulfilled: "I have not lost one of those you gave me."[e]

10 Then Simon Peter, who had a sword, drew it and struck the high priest's servant, cutting off his right ear. (The servant's name was Malchus.)

11 Jesus commanded Peter, "Put your sword away! Shall I not drink the cup the Father has given me?"

[a] 11 Or *Father, keep them faithful to with* [b] 12 Or *kept them faithful to* [c] 17 Or *them to live in accordance with* [d] 26 Greek *your name* [e] 9 John 6:39

12 Then the detachment of soldiers with its commander and the Jewish officials arrested Jesus. They bound him 13 and brought him first to Annas, who was the father-in-law of Caiaphas, the high priest that year. 14 Caiaphas was the one who had advised the Jewish leaders that it would be good if one man died for the people.

Peter's First Denial

15 Simon Peter and another disciple were following Jesus. Because this disciple was known to the high priest, he went with Jesus into the high priest's courtyard, 16 but Peter had to wait outside at the door. The other disciple, who was known to the high priest, came back, spoke to the servant girl on duty there and brought Peter in.

17 "You aren't one of this man's disciples too, are you?" she asked Peter.

He replied, "I am not."

18 It was cold, and the servants and officials stood around a fire they had made to keep warm. Peter also was standing with them, warming himself.

The High Priest Questions Jesus

19 Meanwhile, the high priest questioned Jesus about his disciples and his teaching.

20 "I have spoken openly to the world," Jesus replied. "I always taught in synagogues or at the temple, where all the Jews come together. I said nothing in secret. 21 Why question me? Ask those who heard me. Surely they know what I said."

22 When Jesus said this, one of the officials nearby slapped him in the face. "Is this the way you answer the high priest?" he demanded.

23 "If I said something wrong," Jesus replied, "testify as to what is wrong. But if I spoke the truth, why did you strike me?" 24 Then Annas sent him bound to Caiaphas the high priest.

Peter's Second and Third Denials

25 Meanwhile, Simon Peter was still standing there warming himself. So they asked him, "You aren't one of his disciples too, are you?"

He denied it, saying, "I am not."

26 One of the high priest's servants, a relative of the man whose ear Peter had cut off, challenged him, "Didn't I see you with him in the garden?" 27 Again Peter denied it, and at that moment a rooster began to crow.

Jesus Before Pilate

28 Then the Jewish leaders took Jesus from Caiaphas to the palace of the Roman governor. By now it was early morning, and to avoid ceremonial uncleanness they did not enter the palace, because they wanted to be able to eat the Passover. 29 So Pilate came out to them and asked, "What charges are you bringing against this man?"

30 "If he were not a criminal," they replied, "we would not have handed him over to you."

31 Pilate said, "Take him yourselves and judge him by your own law."

"But we have no right to execute anyone," they objected. 32 This took place to fulfill what Jesus had said about the kind of death he was going to die.

33 Pilate then went back inside the palace, summoned Jesus and asked him, "Are you the king of the Jews?"

34 "Is that your own idea," Jesus asked, "or did others talk to you about me?"

35 "Am I a Jew?" Pilate replied. "Your own people and chief priests handed you over to me. What is it you have done?"

36 Jesus said, "My kingdom is not of this world. If it were, my servants would fight to prevent my arrest by the Jewish leaders. But now my kingdom is from another place."

37 "You are a king, then!" said Pilate.

Jesus answered, "You say that I am a king. In fact, the reason I was born and came into the world is to testify to the truth. Everyone on the side of truth listens to me."

38 "What is truth?" retorted Pilate. With this he went out again to the Jews gathered there and said, "I find no basis for a charge against him. 39 But it is your custom for me to release to you one prisoner at the time of the Passover. Do you want me to release 'the king of the Jews'?"

40 They shouted back, "No, not him! Give us Barabbas!" Now Barabbas had taken part in an uprising.

Jesus Sentenced to Be Crucified

19 Then Pilate took Jesus and had him flogged. 2 The soldiers twisted together a crown of thorns and put it on his head. They clothed him in a purple robe 3 and went

up to him again and again, saying, "Hail, king of the Jews!" And they slapped him in the face.

4 Once more Pilate came out and said to the Jews gathered there, "Look, I am bringing him out to you to let you know that I find no basis for a charge against him." 5 When Jesus came out wearing the crown of thorns and the purple robe, Pilate said to them, "Here is the man!"

6 As soon as the chief priests and their officials saw him, they shouted, "Crucify! Crucify!"

But Pilate answered, "You take him and crucify him. As for me, I find no basis for a charge against him."

7 The Jewish leaders insisted, "We have a law, and according to that law he must die, because he claimed to be the Son of God."

8 When Pilate heard this, he was even more afraid, 9 and he went back inside the palace. "Where do you come from?" he asked Jesus, but Jesus gave him no answer. 10 "Do you refuse to speak to me?" Pilate said. "Don't you realize I have power either to free you or to crucify you?"

11 Jesus answered, "You would have no power over me if it were not given to you from above. Therefore the one who handed me over to you is guilty of a greater sin."

12 From then on, Pilate tried to set Jesus free, but the Jewish leaders kept shouting, "If you let this man go, you are no friend of Caesar. Anyone who claims to be a king opposes Caesar."

13 When Pilate heard this, he brought Jesus out and sat down on the judge's seat at a place known as the Stone Pavement (which in Aramaic is Gabbatha). 14 It was the day of Preparation of the Passover; it was about noon.

"Here is your king," Pilate said to the Jews.

15 But they shouted, "Take him away! Take him away! Crucify him!"

"Shall I crucify your king?" Pilate asked.

"We have no king but Caesar," the chief priests answered.

16 Finally Pilate handed him over to them to be crucified.

The Crucifixion of Jesus

So the soldiers took charge of Jesus. 17 Carrying his own cross, he went out to the place of the Skull (which in Aramaic is called Golgotha). 18 There they crucified him, and with him two others—one on each side and Jesus in the middle.

19 Pilate had a notice prepared and fastened to the cross. It read: JESUS OF NAZARETH, THE KING OF THE JEWS. 20 Many of the Jews read this sign, for the place where Jesus was crucified was near the city, and the sign was written in Aramaic, Latin and Greek. 21 The chief priests of the Jews protested to Pilate, "Do not write 'The King of the Jews,' but that this man claimed to be king of the Jews."

22 Pilate answered, "What I have written, I have written."

23 When the soldiers crucified Jesus, they took his clothes, dividing them into four shares, one for each of them, with the undergarment remaining. This garment was seamless, woven in one piece from top to bottom.

24 "Let's not tear it," they said to one another. "Let's decide by lot who will get it."

This happened that the scripture might be fulfilled that said,

"They divided my clothes among them
and cast lots for my garment."[a]

So this is what the soldiers did.

25 Near the cross of Jesus stood his mother, his mother's sister, Mary the wife of Clopas, and Mary Magdalene. 26 When Jesus saw his mother there, and the disciple whom he loved standing nearby, he said to her, "Woman,[b] here is your son," 27 and to the disciple, "Here is your mother." From that time on, this disciple took her into his home.

The Death of Jesus

28 Later, knowing that everything had now been finished, and so that Scripture would be fulfilled, Jesus said, "I am thirsty." 29 A jar of wine vinegar was there, so they soaked a sponge in it, put the sponge on a stalk of the hyssop plant, and lifted it to Jesus' lips. 30 When he had received the drink, Jesus said, "It is finished." With that, he bowed his head and gave up his spirit.

31 Now it was the day of Preparation, and the next day was to be a special Sabbath. Because the Jewish leaders did not want the

[a] *24* Psalm 22:18 [b] *26* The Greek for *Woman* does not denote any disrespect.

bodies left on the crosses during the Sabbath, they asked Pilate to have the legs broken and the bodies taken down. [32]The soldiers therefore came and broke the legs of the first man who had been crucified with Jesus, and then those of the other. [33]But when they came to Jesus and found that he was already dead, they did not break his legs. [34]Instead, one of the soldiers pierced Jesus' side with a spear, bringing a sudden flow of blood and water. [35]The man who saw it has given testimony, and his testimony is true. He knows that he tells the truth, and he testifies so that you also may believe. [36]These things happened so that the scripture would be fulfilled: "Not one of his bones will be broken,"[a] [37]and, as another scripture says, "They will look on the one they have pierced."[b]

The Burial of Jesus

[38]Later, Joseph of Arimathea asked Pilate for the body of Jesus. Now Joseph was a disciple of Jesus, but secretly because he feared the Jewish leaders. With Pilate's permission, he came and took the body away. [39]He was accompanied by Nicodemus, the man who earlier had visited Jesus at night. Nicodemus brought a mixture of myrrh and aloes, about seventy-five pounds.[c] [40]Taking Jesus' body, the two of them wrapped it, with the spices, in strips of linen. This was in accordance with Jewish burial customs. [41]At the place where Jesus was crucified, there was a garden, and in the garden a new tomb, in which no one had ever been laid. [42]Because it was the Jewish day of Preparation and since the tomb was nearby, they laid Jesus there.

The Empty Tomb

20 Early on the first day of the week, while it was still dark, Mary Magdalene went to the tomb and saw that the stone had been removed from the entrance. [2]So she came running to Simon Peter and the other disciple, the one Jesus loved, and said, "They have taken the Lord out of the tomb, and we don't know where they have put him!"

[3]So Peter and the other disciple started for the tomb. [4]Both were running, but the other disciple outran Peter and reached the tomb first. [5]He bent over and looked in at the strips of linen lying there but did not go in. [6]Then Simon Peter came along behind him and went straight into the tomb. He saw the strips of linen lying there, [7]as well as the cloth that had been wrapped around Jesus' head. The cloth was still lying in its place, separate from the linen. [8]Finally the other disciple, who had reached the tomb first, also went inside. He saw and believed. [9](They still did not understand from Scripture that Jesus had to rise from the dead.) [10]Then the disciples went back to where they were staying.

Jesus Appears to Mary Magdalene

[11]Now Mary stood outside the tomb crying. As she wept, she bent over to look into the tomb [12]and saw two angels in white, seated where Jesus' body had been, one at the head and the other at the foot.

[13]They asked her, "Woman, why are you crying?"

"They have taken my Lord away," she said, "and I don't know where they have put him." [14]At this, she turned around and saw Jesus standing there, but she did not realize that it was Jesus.

[15]He asked her, "Woman, why are you crying? Who is it you are looking for?"

Thinking he was the gardener, she said, "Sir, if you have carried him away, tell me where you have put him, and I will get him."

[16]Jesus said to her, "Mary."

She turned toward him and cried out in Aramaic, "Rabboni!" (which means "Teacher").

[17]Jesus said, "Do not hold on to me, for I have not yet ascended to the Father. Go instead to my brothers and tell them, 'I am ascending to my Father and your Father, to my God and your God.'"

[18]Mary Magdalene went to the disciples with the news: "I have seen the Lord!" And she told them that he had said these things to her.

Jesus Appears to His Disciples

[19]On the evening of that first day of the week, when the disciples were together, with the doors locked for fear of the Jewish leaders, Jesus came and stood among them and said, "Peace be with you!" [20]After he said

[a] *36* Exodus 12:46; Num. 9:12; Psalm 34:20 [b] *37* Zech. 12:10 [c] *39* Or about 34 kilograms

this, he showed them his hands and side. The disciples were overjoyed when they saw the Lord.

21 Again Jesus said, "Peace be with you! As the Father has sent me, I am sending you." 22 And with that he breathed on them and said, "Receive the Holy Spirit. 23 If you forgive anyone's sins, their sins are forgiven; if you do not forgive them, they are not forgiven."

Jesus Appears to Thomas

24 Now Thomas (also known as Didymus[a]), one of the Twelve, was not with the disciples when Jesus came. 25 So the other disciples told him, "We have seen the Lord!"

But he said to them, "Unless I see the nail marks in his hands and put my finger where the nails were, and put my hand into his side, I will not believe."

26 A week later his disciples were in the house again, and Thomas was with them. Though the doors were locked, Jesus came and stood among them and said, "Peace be with you!" 27 Then he said to Thomas, "Put your finger here; see my hands. Reach out your hand and put it into my side. Stop doubting and believe."

28 Thomas said to him, "My Lord and my God!"

29 Then Jesus told him, "Because you have seen me, you have believed; blessed are those who have not seen and yet have believed."

The Purpose of John's Gospel

30 Jesus performed many other signs in the presence of his disciples, which are not recorded in this book. 31 But these are written that you may believe[b] that Jesus is the Messiah, the Son of God, and that by believing you may have life in his name.

Jesus and the Miraculous Catch of Fish

21 Afterward Jesus appeared again to his disciples, by the Sea of Galilee.[c] It happened this way: 2 Simon Peter, Thomas (also known as Didymus[a]), Nathanael from Cana in Galilee, the sons of Zebedee, and two other disciples were together. 3 "I'm going out to fish," Simon Peter told them, and they said, "We'll go with you." So they went out and got into the boat, but that night they caught nothing.

4 Early in the morning, Jesus stood on the shore, but the disciples did not realize that it was Jesus.

5 He called out to them, "Friends, haven't you any fish?"

"No," they answered.

6 He said, "Throw your net on the right side of the boat and you will find some." When they did, they were unable to haul the net in because of the large number of fish.

7 Then the disciple whom Jesus loved said to Peter, "It is the Lord!" As soon as Simon Peter heard him say, "It is the Lord," he wrapped his outer garment around him (for he had taken it off) and jumped into the water. 8 The other disciples followed in the boat, towing the net full of fish, for they were not far from shore, about a hundred yards.[d] 9 When they landed, they saw a fire of burning coals there with fish on it, and some bread.

10 Jesus said to them, "Bring some of the fish you have just caught." 11 So Simon Peter climbed back into the boat and dragged the net ashore. It was full of large fish, 153, but even with so many the net was not torn. 12 Jesus said to them, "Come and have breakfast." None of the disciples dared ask him, "Who are you?" They knew it was the Lord. 13 Jesus came, took the bread and gave it to them, and did the same with the fish. 14 This was now the third time Jesus appeared to his disciples after he was raised from the dead.

Jesus Reinstates Peter

15 When they had finished eating, Jesus said to Simon Peter, "Simon son of John, do you love me more than these?"

"Yes, Lord," he said, "you know that I love you."

Jesus said, "Feed my lambs."

16 Again Jesus said, "Simon son of John, do you love me?"

He answered, "Yes, Lord, you know that I love you."

Jesus said, "Take care of my sheep."

17 The third time he said to him, "Simon son of John, do you love me?"

[a] *24,2* *Thomas* (Aramaic) and *Didymus* (Greek) both mean *twin*. [b] *31* Or *may continue to believe*
[c] *1* Greek *Tiberias* [d] *8* Or about 90 meters

AMAZING GRACE (MY CHAINS ARE GONE)

John Newton, Chris Tomlin, Louie Giglio

Amazing Grace, how sweet the sound
That saved a wretch like me
I once was lost, but now am found
Was blind, but now I see

'Twas Grace that taught my heart to fear
And Grace my fears relieved
How precious did that Grace appear
The hour I first believed

My chains are gone, I've been set free
My God, my Savior has ransomed me
And like a flood his mercy reigns
Unending love, amazing Grace

The Lord has promised good to me
His word my hope secures
He will my shield and portion be
As long as life endures

The earth shall soon dissolve like snow
The sun forbear to shine
But God who called me here below
Will be forever mine
Will be forever mine
You are forever mine

THE INSPIRATION

For it is by grace you have been saved, through faith — and this is not from yourselves, it is the gift of God — not by works, so that no one can boast.

— Ephesians 2:8 – 9

Read also: Psalm 44:8

BEHIND THE SONG

"Amazing Grace" is certainly one of the best-known songs in the world. When approached about possibly adding a new bridge to the song, Chris Tomlin at first refused. "It's just the greatest song ever written," he said. "I'm not going to be known as the punk who ruined 'Amazing Grace.'" What many people don't know is that the song was originally written as a poem and set to music much later. What many people also don't know is that songwriters have been adding and taking away verses to this beloved song for over a hundred years.

The original poem was written by John Newton as he contemplated the immense grace and mercy God had shown him. Newton had been a ship owner involved in the English slave trade before coming to faith in Christ. The abolitionist William Wilberforce was inspired, in part, by Newton and his passionate repentance when Wilberforce confronted the British government and culture about the evils of slavery. The 2006 film, *Amazing Grace,* beautifully chronicles the life and work of Wilberforce and the influence of Newton and his poem on the abolitionist.

Chris Tomlin cautiously joined the ranks of many songwriters and worship leaders before him — adding a contemporary bridge to the song and rediscovering an original verse that had often been left out. "Words have come and gone and changed, and that song has lasted," Tomlin adds. "Now people sing it with my new part, and it's added something to the hymn — hopefully in a good way."

Selah

Ephesians 2 is a powerful exploration of the nature of God's grace in saving us from sin. It explores the death we would have experienced outside of God's forgiveness and the incredible resurrection power of the gospel. It's all about being made alive in Christ. Read through the entire chapter and highlight the ideas represented in Newton's powerful poem.

Is it possible to understand and appreciate the magnitude of God's grace if we do not comprehend the severity of our sin? It often seems like the most powerful articulations of God's goodness come from people who, like Newton, have been far from God at some point in their lives.

Peter was hurt because Jesus asked him
the third time, "Do you love me?" He said,
"Lord, you know all things; you know that I
love you."

Jesus said, "Feed my sheep. 18Very truly I
tell you, when you were younger you dressed
yourself and went where you wanted; but
when you are old you will stretch out your
hands, and someone else will dress you
and lead you where you do not want to go."
19Jesus said this to indicate the kind of death
by which Peter would glorify God. Then he
said to him, "Follow me!"

20Peter turned and saw that the disciple
whom Jesus loved was following them. (This
was the one who had leaned back against
Jesus at the supper and had said, "Lord, who
is going to betray you?") 21When Peter saw
him, he asked, "Lord, what about him?"

22Jesus answered, "If I want him to re-
main alive until I return, what is that to you?
You must follow me." 23Because of this, the
rumor spread among the believers that this
disciple would not die. But Jesus did not say
that he would not die; he only said, "If I want
him to remain alive until I return, what is
that to you?"

24This is the disciple who testifies to these
things and who wrote them down. We know
that his testimony is true.

25Jesus did many other things as well. If ev-
ery one of them were written down, I suppose
that even the whole world would not have
room for the books that would be written.

ACTS

Jesus Taken Up Into Heaven

1 In my former book, Theophilus, I wrote
about all that Jesus began to do and to
teach [2]until the day he was taken up to heav-
en, after giving instructions through the
Holy Spirit to the apostles he had chosen.
[3]After his suffering, he presented himself
to them and gave many convincing proofs
that he was alive. He appeared to them over
a period of forty days and spoke about the
kingdom of God. [4]On one occasion, while
he was eating with them, he gave them this
command: "Do not leave Jerusalem, but wait
for the gift my Father promised, which you
have heard me speak about. [5]For John bap-
tized with[a] water, but in a few days you will
be baptized with[a] the Holy Spirit."

[6]Then they gathered around him and
asked him, "Lord, are you at this time going
to restore the kingdom to Israel?"

[7]He said to them: "It is not for you to know
the times or dates the Father has set by his
own authority. [8]But you will receive pow-
er when the Holy Spirit comes on you; and
you will be my witnesses in Jerusalem, and
in all Judea and Samaria, and to the ends of
the earth."

[9]After he said this, he was taken up before
their very eyes, and a cloud hid him from
their sight.

[10]They were looking intently up into the
sky as he was going, when suddenly two men
dressed in white stood beside them. [11]"Men
of Galilee," they said, "why do you stand here
looking into the sky? This same Jesus, who
has been taken from you into heaven, will
come back in the same way you have seen
him go into heaven."

Matthias Chosen to Replace Judas

[12]Then the apostles returned to Jerusa-
lem from the hill called the Mount of Olives,
a Sabbath day's walk[b] from the city. [13]When
they arrived, they went upstairs to the room
where they were staying. Those present were
Peter, John, James and Andrew; Philip and
Thomas, Bartholomew and Matthew; James
son of Alphaeus and Simon the Zealot, and
Judas son of James. [14]They all joined togeth-
er constantly in prayer, along with the wom-
en and Mary the mother of Jesus, and with
his brothers.

[15]In those days Peter stood up among
the believers (a group numbering about a
hundred and twenty) [16]and said, "Broth-
ers and sisters,[c] the Scripture had to be ful-
filled in which the Holy Spirit spoke long
ago through David concerning Judas, who
served as guide for those who arrested Jesus.
[17]He was one of our number and shared in
our ministry."

[18](With the payment he received for his
wickedness, Judas bought a field; there he
fell headlong, his body burst open and all his
intestines spilled out. [19]Everyone in Jerusa-
lem heard about this, so they called that field
in their language Akeldama, that is, Field of
Blood.)

[20]"For," said Peter, "it is written in the
Book of Psalms:

> "'May his place be deserted;
> let there be no one to dwell in it,'[d]

and,

> "'May another take his place of
> leadership.'[e]

[21]Therefore it is necessary to choose one of
the men who have been with us the whole
time the Lord Jesus was living among us,
[22]beginning from John's baptism to the time
when Jesus was taken up from us. For one of
these must become a witness with us of his
resurrection."

[23]So they nominated two men: Joseph
called Barsabbas (also known as Justus)

[a] 5 Or *in* [b] 12 That is, about 5/8 mile or about 1 kilometer [c] 16 The Greek word for *brothers and sisters* (*adelphoi*) refers here to believers, both men and women, as part of God's family; also in 6:3; 11:29; 12:17; 16:40; 18:18, 27; 21:7, 17; 28:14, 15. [d] 20 Psalm 69:25 [e] 20 Psalm 109:8

and Matthias. [24]Then they prayed, "Lord,
you know everyone's heart. Show us which
of these two you have chosen [25]to take over
this apostolic ministry, which Judas left to
go where he belongs." [26]Then they cast lots,
and the lot fell to Matthias; so he was added
to the eleven apostles.

The Holy Spirit Comes at Pentecost

2 When the day of Pentecost came, they
were all together in one place. [2]Sud-
denly a sound like the blowing of a violent
wind came from heaven and filled the whole
house where they were sitting. [3]They saw
what seemed to be tongues of fire that sepa-
rated and came to rest on each of them. [4]All
of them were filled with the Holy Spirit and
began to speak in other tongues[a] as the Spir-
it enabled them.

[5]Now there were staying in Jerusalem
God-fearing Jews from every nation under
heaven. [6]When they heard this sound, a
crowd came together in bewilderment, be-
cause each one heard their own language
being spoken. [7]Utterly amazed, they asked:
"Aren't all these who are speaking Galile-
ans? [8]Then how is it that each of us hears
them in our native language? [9]Parthians,
Medes and Elamites; residents of Mesopo-
tamia, Judea and Cappadocia, Pontus and
Asia,[b] [10]Phrygia and Pamphylia, Egypt and
the parts of Libya near Cyrene; visitors from
Rome [11](both Jews and converts to Judaism);
Cretans and Arabs—we hear them declar-
ing the wonders of God in our own tongues!"
[12]Amazed and perplexed, they asked one
another, "What does this mean?"

[13]Some, however, made fun of them and
said, "They have had too much wine."

Peter Addresses the Crowd

[14]Then Peter stood up with the Eleven,
raised his voice and addressed the crowd:
"Fellow Jews and all of you who live in Je-
rusalem, let me explain this to you; listen
carefully to what I say. [15]These people are
not drunk, as you suppose. It's only nine in
the morning! [16]No, this is what was spoken
by the prophet Joel:

[17]" 'In the last days, God says,
I will pour out my Spirit on all people.
Your sons and daughters will prophesy,
your young men will see visions,
your old men will dream dreams.
[18]Even on my servants, both men and
women,
I will pour out my Spirit in those days,
and they will prophesy.
[19]I will show wonders in the heavens above
and signs on the earth below,
blood and fire and billows of smoke.
[20]The sun will be turned to darkness
and the moon to blood
before the coming of the great and
glorious day of the Lord.
[21]And everyone who calls
on the name of the Lord will be saved.'[c]

[22]"Fellow Israelites, listen to this: Jesus of
Nazareth was a man accredited by God to
you by miracles, wonders and signs, which
God did among you through him, as you
yourselves know. [23]This man was handed
over to you by God's deliberate plan and fore-
knowledge; and you, with the help of wicked
men,[d] put him to death by nailing him to the
cross. [24]But God raised him from the dead,
freeing him from the agony of death, because
it was impossible for death to keep its hold on
him. [25]David said about him:

" 'I saw the Lord always before me.
Because he is at my right hand,
I will not be shaken.
[26]Therefore my heart is glad and my
tongue rejoices;
my body also will rest in hope,
[27]because you will not abandon me to the
realm of the dead,
you will not let your holy one see
decay.
[28]You have made known to me the paths
of life;
you will fill me with joy in your
presence.'[e]

[29]"Fellow Israelites, I can tell you con-
fidently that the patriarch David died and
was buried, and his tomb is here to this day.
[30]But he was a prophet and knew that God
had promised him on oath that he would
place one of his descendants on his throne.
[31]Seeing what was to come, he spoke of the
resurrection of the Messiah, that he was not

[a] *4* Or *languages*; also in verse 11 [b] *9* That is, the Roman province by that name [c] *21* Joel 2:28-32
[d] *23* Or *of those not having the law* (that is, Gentiles) [e] *28* Psalm 16:8-11 (see Septuagint)

abandoned to the realm of the dead, nor did his body see decay. 32 God has raised this Jesus to life, and we are all witnesses of it. 33 Exalted to the right hand of God, he has received from the Father the promised Holy Spirit and has poured out what you now see and hear. 34 For David did not ascend to heaven, and yet he said,

> " 'The Lord said to my Lord:
> "Sit at my right hand
> 35 until I make your enemies
> a footstool for your feet." '[a]

36 "Therefore let all Israel be assured of this: God has made this Jesus, whom you crucified, both Lord and Messiah."

37 When the people heard this, they were cut to the heart and said to Peter and the other apostles, "Brothers, what shall we do?"

38 Peter replied, "Repent and be baptized, every one of you, in the name of Jesus Christ for the forgiveness of your sins. And you will receive the gift of the Holy Spirit. 39 The promise is for you and your children and for all who are far off — for all whom the Lord our God will call."

40 With many other words he warned them; and he pleaded with them, "Save yourselves from this corrupt generation." 41 Those who accepted his message were baptized, and about three thousand were added to their number that day.

The Fellowship of the Believers

42 They devoted themselves to the apostles' teaching and to fellowship, to the breaking of bread and to prayer. 43 Everyone was filled with awe at the many wonders and signs performed by the apostles. 44 All the believers were together and had everything in common. 45 They sold property and possessions to give to anyone who had need. 46 Every day they continued to meet together in the temple courts. They broke bread in their homes and ate together with glad and sincere hearts, 47 praising God and enjoying the favor of all the people. And the Lord added to their number daily those who were being saved.

Peter Heals a Lame Beggar

3 One day Peter and John were going up to the temple at the time of prayer — at three in the afternoon. 2 Now a man who was lame from birth was being carried to the temple gate called Beautiful, where he was put every day to beg from those going into the temple courts. 3 When he saw Peter and John about to enter, he asked them for money. 4 Peter looked straight at him, as did John. Then Peter said, "Look at us!" 5 So the man gave them his attention, expecting to get something from them.

6 Then Peter said, "Silver or gold I do not have, but what I do have I give you. In the name of Jesus Christ of Nazareth, walk." 7 Taking him by the right hand, he helped him up, and instantly the man's feet and ankles became strong. 8 He jumped to his feet and began to walk. Then he went with them into the temple courts, walking and jumping, and praising God. 9 When all the people saw him walking and praising God, 10 they recognized him as the same man who used to sit begging at the temple gate called Beautiful, and they were filled with wonder and amazement at what had happened to him.

Peter Speaks to the Onlookers

11 While the man held on to Peter and John, all the people were astonished and came running to them in the place called Solomon's Colonnade. 12 When Peter saw this, he said to them: "Fellow Israelites, why does this surprise you? Why do you stare at us as if by our own power or godliness we had made this man walk? 13 The God of Abraham, Isaac and Jacob, the God of our fathers, has glorified his servant Jesus. You handed him over to be killed, and you disowned him before Pilate, though he had decided to let him go. 14 You disowned the Holy and Righteous One and asked that a murderer be released to you. 15 You killed the author of life, but God raised him from the dead. We are witnesses of this. 16 By faith in the name of Jesus, this man whom you see and know was made strong. It is Jesus' name and the faith that comes through him that has completely healed him, as you can all see.

17 "Now, fellow Israelites, I know that you acted in ignorance, as did your leaders. 18 But this is how God fulfilled what he had foretold through all the prophets, saying that his

[a] *35* Psalm 110:1

Messiah would suffer. [19]Repent, then, and turn to God, so that your sins may be wiped out, that times of refreshing may come from the Lord, [20]and that he may send the Messiah, who has been appointed for you—even Jesus. [21]Heaven must receive him until the time comes for God to restore everything, as he promised long ago through his holy prophets. [22]For Moses said, 'The Lord your God will raise up for you a prophet like me from among your own people; you must listen to everything he tells you. [23]Anyone who does not listen to him will be completely cut off from their people.'[a]

[24]"Indeed, beginning with Samuel, all the prophets who have spoken have foretold these days. [25]And you are heirs of the prophets and of the covenant God made with your fathers. He said to Abraham, 'Through your offspring all peoples on earth will be blessed.'[b] [26]When God raised up his servant, he sent him first to you to bless you by turning each of you from your wicked ways."

Peter and John Before the Sanhedrin

4 The priests and the captain of the temple guard and the Sadducees came up to Peter and John while they were speaking to the people. [2]They were greatly disturbed because the apostles were teaching the people, proclaiming in Jesus the resurrection of the dead. [3]They seized Peter and John and, because it was evening, they put them in jail until the next day. [4]But many who heard the message believed; so the number of men who believed grew to about five thousand.

[5]The next day the rulers, the elders and the teachers of the law met in Jerusalem. [6]Annas the high priest was there, and so were Caiaphas, John, Alexander and others of the high priest's family. [7]They had Peter and John brought before them and began to question them: "By what power or what name did you do this?"

[8]Then Peter, filled with the Holy Spirit, said to them: "Rulers and elders of the people! [9]If we are being called to account today for an act of kindness shown to a man who was lame and are being asked how he was healed, [10]then know this, you and all the people of Israel: It is by the name of Jesus Christ of Nazareth, whom you crucified but whom God raised from the dead, that this man stands before you healed. [11]Jesus is

"'the stone you builders rejected,
which has become the
cornerstone.'[c]

[12]Salvation is found in no one else, for there is no other name under heaven given to mankind by which we must be saved."

[13]When they saw the courage of Peter and John and realized that they were unschooled, ordinary men, they were astonished and they took note that these men had been with Jesus. [14]But since they could see the man who had been healed standing there with them, there was nothing they could say. [15]So they ordered them to withdraw from the Sanhedrin and then conferred together. [16]"What are we going to do with these men?" they asked. "Everyone living in Jerusalem knows they have performed a notable sign, and we cannot deny it. [17]But to stop this thing from spreading any further among the people, we must warn them to speak no longer to anyone in this name."

[18]Then they called them in again and commanded them not to speak or teach at all in the name of Jesus. [19]But Peter and John replied, "Which is right in God's eyes: to listen to you, or to him? You be the judges! [20]As for us, we cannot help speaking about what we have seen and heard."

[21]After further threats they let them go. They could not decide how to punish them, because all the people were praising God for what had happened. [22]For the man who was miraculously healed was over forty years old.

The Believers Pray

[23]On their release, Peter and John went back to their own people and reported all that the chief priests and the elders had said to them. [24]When they heard this, they raised their voices together in prayer to God. "Sovereign Lord," they said, "you made the heavens and the earth and the sea, and everything in them. [25]You spoke by the Holy Spirit through the mouth of your servant, our father David:

"'Why do the nations rage
and the peoples plot in vain?

[a] *23* Deut. 18:15,18,19 [b] *25* Gen. 22:18; 26:4 [c] *11* Psalm 118:22

26 The kings of the earth rise up
and the rulers band together
against the Lord
and against his anointed one.[a,b]

27 Indeed Herod and Pontius Pilate met together with the Gentiles and the people of Israel in this city to conspire against your holy servant Jesus, whom you anointed. 28 They did what your power and will had decided beforehand should happen. 29 Now, Lord, consider their threats and enable your servants to speak your word with great boldness. 30 Stretch out your hand to heal and perform signs and wonders through the name of your holy servant Jesus."

31 After they prayed, the place where they were meeting was shaken. And they were all filled with the Holy Spirit and spoke the word of God boldly.

The Believers Share Their Possessions

32 All the believers were one in heart and mind. No one claimed that any of their possessions was their own, but they shared everything they had. 33 With great power the apostles continued to testify to the resurrection of the Lord Jesus. And God's grace was so powerfully at work in them all 34 that there were no needy persons among them. For from time to time those who owned land or houses sold them, brought the money from the sales 35 and put it at the apostles' feet, and it was distributed to anyone who had need.

36 Joseph, a Levite from Cyprus, whom the apostles called Barnabas (which means "son of encouragement"), 37 sold a field he owned and brought the money and put it at the apostles' feet.

Ananias and Sapphira

5 Now a man named Ananias, together with his wife Sapphira, also sold a piece of property. 2 With his wife's full knowledge he kept back part of the money for himself, but brought the rest and put it at the apostles' feet.

3 Then Peter said, "Ananias, how is it that Satan has so filled your heart that you have lied to the Holy Spirit and have kept for yourself some of the money you received for the land? 4 Didn't it belong to you before it was sold? And after it was sold, wasn't the money at your disposal? What made you think of doing such a thing? You have not lied just to human beings but to God."

5 When Ananias heard this, he fell down and died. And great fear seized all who heard what had happened. 6 Then some young men came forward, wrapped up his body, and carried him out and buried him.

7 About three hours later his wife came in, not knowing what had happened. 8 Peter asked her, "Tell me, is this the price you and Ananias got for the land?"

"Yes," she said, "that is the price."

9 Peter said to her, "How could you conspire to test the Spirit of the Lord? Listen! The feet of the men who buried your husband are at the door, and they will carry you out also."

10 At that moment she fell down at his feet and died. Then the young men came in and, finding her dead, carried her out and buried her beside her husband. 11 Great fear seized the whole church and all who heard about these events.

The Apostles Heal Many

12 The apostles performed many signs and wonders among the people. And all the believers used to meet together in Solomon's Colonnade. 13 No one else dared join them, even though they were highly regarded by the people. 14 Nevertheless, more and more men and women believed in the Lord and were added to their number. 15 As a result, people brought the sick into the streets and laid them on beds and mats so that at least Peter's shadow might fall on some of them as he passed by. 16 Crowds gathered also from the towns around Jerusalem, bringing their sick and those tormented by impure spirits, and all of them were healed.

The Apostles Persecuted

17 Then the high priest and all his associates, who were members of the party of the Sadducees, were filled with jealousy. 18 They arrested the apostles and put them in the public jail. 19 But during the night an angel of the Lord opened the doors of the jail and brought them out. 20 "Go, stand in the temple courts," he said, "and tell the people all about this new life."

21 At daybreak they entered the temple

[a] *26* That is, Messiah or Christ [b] *26* Psalm 2:1,2

courts, as they had been told, and began to
teach the people.

When the high priest and his associates
arrived, they called together the Sanhe-
drin — the full assembly of the elders of Isra-
el — and sent to the jail for the apostles. 22But
on arriving at the jail, the officers did not find
them there. So they went back and reported,
23"We found the jail securely locked, with
the guards standing at the doors; but when
we opened them, we found no one inside."
24On hearing this report, the captain of the
temple guard and the chief priests were at a
loss, wondering what this might lead to.

25Then someone came and said, "Look!
The men you put in jail are standing in the
temple courts teaching the people." 26At
that, the captain went with his officers and
brought the apostles. They did not use force,
because they feared that the people would
stone them.

27The apostles were brought in and made
to appear before the Sanhedrin to be ques-
tioned by the high priest. 28"We gave you
strict orders not to teach in this name," he
said. "Yet you have filled Jerusalem with
your teaching and are determined to make
us guilty of this man's blood."

29Peter and the other apostles replied:
"We must obey God rather than human be-
ings! 30The God of our ancestors raised Jesus
from the dead — whom you killed by hang-
ing him on a cross. 31God exalted him to his
own right hand as Prince and Savior that he
might bring Israel to repentance and for-
give their sins. 32We are witnesses of these
things, and so is the Holy Spirit, whom God
has given to those who obey him."

33When they heard this, they were furi-
ous and wanted to put them to death. 34But
a Pharisee named Gamaliel, a teacher of
the law, who was honored by all the peo-
ple, stood up in the Sanhedrin and ordered
that the men be put outside for a little while.
35Then he addressed the Sanhedrin: "Men
of Israel, consider carefully what you intend
to do to these men. 36Some time ago Theu-
das appeared, claiming to be somebody, and
about four hundred men rallied to him. He
was killed, all his followers were dispersed,
and it all came to nothing. 37After him, Ju-
das the Galilean appeared in the days of the
census and led a band of people in revolt.
He too was killed, and all his followers were
scattered. 38Therefore, in the present case I
advise you: Leave these men alone! Let them
go! For if their purpose or activity is of hu-
man origin, it will fail. 39But if it is from God,
you will not be able to stop these men; you
will only find yourselves fighting against
God."

40His speech persuaded them. They
called the apostles in and had them flogged.
Then they ordered them not to speak in the
name of Jesus, and let them go.

41The apostles left the Sanhedrin, rejoic-
ing because they had been counted worthy
of suffering disgrace for the Name. 42Day af-
ter day, in the temple courts and from house
to house, they never stopped teaching and
proclaiming the good news that Jesus is the
Messiah.

The Choosing of the Seven

6 In those days when the number of dis-
ciples was increasing, the Hellenistic
Jews[a] among them complained against the
Hebraic Jews because their widows were be-
ing overlooked in the daily distribution of
food. 2So the Twelve gathered all the disci-
ples together and said, "It would not be right
for us to neglect the ministry of the word of
God in order to wait on tables. 3Brothers and
sisters, choose seven men from among you
who are known to be full of the Spirit and
wisdom. We will turn this responsibility
over to them 4and will give our attention to
prayer and the ministry of the word."

5This proposal pleased the whole group.
They chose Stephen, a man full of faith and
of the Holy Spirit; also Philip, Procorus,
Nicanor, Timon, Parmenas, and Nicolas
from Antioch, a convert to Judaism. 6They
presented these men to the apostles, who
prayed and laid their hands on them.

7So the word of God spread. The number
of disciples in Jerusalem increased rapidly,
and a large number of priests became obedi-
ent to the faith.

Stephen Seized

8Now Stephen, a man full of God's grace
and power, performed great wonders and
signs among the people. 9Opposition arose,

[a] *1* That is, Jews who had adopted the Greek language and culture

however, from members of the Synagogue of the Freedmen (as it was called) — Jews of Cyrene and Alexandria as well as the provinces of Cilicia and Asia — who began to argue with Stephen. 10 But they could not stand up against the wisdom the Spirit gave him as he spoke.

11 Then they secretly persuaded some men to say, "We have heard Stephen speak blasphemous words against Moses and against God."

12 So they stirred up the people and the elders and the teachers of the law. They seized Stephen and brought him before the Sanhedrin. 13 They produced false witnesses, who testified, "This fellow never stops speaking against this holy place and against the law. 14 For we have heard him say that this Jesus of Nazareth will destroy this place and change the customs Moses handed down to us."

15 All who were sitting in the Sanhedrin looked intently at Stephen, and they saw that his face was like the face of an angel.

Stephen's Speech to the Sanhedrin

7 Then the high priest asked Stephen, "Are these charges true?"

2 To this he replied: "Brothers and fathers, listen to me! The God of glory appeared to our father Abraham while he was still in Mesopotamia, before he lived in Harran. 3 'Leave your country and your people,' God said, 'and go to the land I will show you.'[a]

4 "So he left the land of the Chaldeans and settled in Harran. After the death of his father, God sent him to this land where you are now living. 5 He gave him no inheritance here, not even enough ground to set his foot on. But God promised him that he and his descendants after him would possess the land, even though at that time Abraham had no child. 6 God spoke to him in this way: 'For four hundred years your descendants will be strangers in a country not their own, and they will be enslaved and mistreated. 7 But I will punish the nation they serve as slaves,' God said, 'and afterward they will come out of that country and worship me in this place.'[b] 8 Then he gave Abraham the covenant of circumcision. And Abraham became the father of Isaac and circumcised him eight days after his birth. Later Isaac became the father of Jacob, and Jacob became the father of the twelve patriarchs.

9 "Because the patriarchs were jealous of Joseph, they sold him as a slave into Egypt. But God was with him 10 and rescued him from all his troubles. He gave Joseph wisdom and enabled him to gain the goodwill of Pharaoh king of Egypt. So Pharaoh made him ruler over Egypt and all his palace.

11 "Then a famine struck all Egypt and Canaan, bringing great suffering, and our ancestors could not find food. 12 When Jacob heard that there was grain in Egypt, he sent our forefathers on their first visit. 13 On their second visit, Joseph told his brothers who he was, and Pharaoh learned about Joseph's family. 14 After this, Joseph sent for his father Jacob and his whole family, seventy-five in all. 15 Then Jacob went down to Egypt, where he and our ancestors died. 16 Their bodies were brought back to Shechem and placed in the tomb that Abraham had bought from the sons of Hamor at Shechem for a certain sum of money.

17 "As the time drew near for God to fulfill his promise to Abraham, the number of our people in Egypt had greatly increased. 18 Then 'a new king, to whom Joseph meant nothing, came to power in Egypt.'[c] 19 He dealt treacherously with our people and oppressed our ancestors by forcing them to throw out their newborn babies so that they would die.

20 "At that time Moses was born, and he was no ordinary child.[d] For three months he was cared for by his family. 21 When he was placed outside, Pharaoh's daughter took him and brought him up as her own son. 22 Moses was educated in all the wisdom of the Egyptians and was powerful in speech and action.

23 "When Moses was forty years old, he decided to visit his own people, the Israelites. 24 He saw one of them being mistreated by an Egyptian, so he went to his defense and avenged him by killing the Egyptian. 25 Moses thought that his own people would realize that God was using him to rescue them, but they did not. 26 The next day Moses came upon two Israelites who were fighting. He tried to reconcile them by saying, 'Men, you

[a] *3* Gen. 12:1 [b] *7* Gen. 15:13,14 [c] *18* Exodus 1:8 [d] *20* Or *was fair in the sight of God*

are brothers; why do you want to hurt each
other?'

27 "But the man who was mistreating the
other pushed Moses aside and said, 'Who
made you ruler and judge over us? 28 Are
you thinking of killing me as you killed the
Egyptian yesterday?'[a] 29 When Moses heard
this, he fled to Midian, where he settled as a
foreigner and had two sons.

30 "After forty years had passed, an angel
appeared to Moses in the flames of a burn-
ing bush in the desert near Mount Sinai.
31 When he saw this, he was amazed at the
sight. As he went over to get a closer look, he
heard the Lord say: 32 'I am the God of your
fathers, the God of Abraham, Isaac and Ja-
cob.'[b] Moses trembled with fear and did not
dare to look.

33 "Then the Lord said to him, 'Take off
your sandals, for the place where you are
standing is holy ground. 34 I have indeed
seen the oppression of my people in Egypt.
I have heard their groaning and have come
down to set them free. Now come, I will send
you back to Egypt.'[c]

35 "This is the same Moses they had re-
jected with the words, 'Who made you ruler
and judge?' He was sent to be their ruler and
deliverer by God himself, through the angel
who appeared to him in the bush. 36 He led
them out of Egypt and performed wonders
and signs in Egypt, at the Red Sea and for
forty years in the wilderness.

37 "This is the Moses who told the Israel-
ites, 'God will raise up for you a prophet like
me from your own people.'[d] 38 He was in the
assembly in the wilderness, with the angel
who spoke to him on Mount Sinai, and with
our ancestors; and he received living words
to pass on to us.

39 "But our ancestors refused to obey him.
Instead, they rejected him and in their hearts
turned back to Egypt. 40 They told Aaron,
'Make us gods who will go before us. As for
this fellow Moses who led us out of Egypt—
we don't know what has happened to him!'[e]
41 That was the time they made an idol in the
form of a calf. They brought sacrifices to it
and reveled in what their own hands had
made. 42 But God turned away from them
and gave them over to the worship of the
sun, moon and stars. This agrees with what
is written in the book of the prophets:

> " 'Did you bring me sacrifices and
> offerings
> forty years in the wilderness, people of
> Israel?
> 43 You have taken up the tabernacle of
> Molek
> and the star of your god Rephan,
> the idols you made to worship.
> Therefore I will send you into exile'[f]
> beyond Babylon.

44 "Our ancestors had the tabernacle of the
covenant law with them in the wilderness. It
had been made as God directed Moses, ac-
cording to the pattern he had seen. 45 After
receiving the tabernacle, our ancestors un-
der Joshua brought it with them when they
took the land from the nations God drove out
before them. It remained in the land until
the time of David, 46 who enjoyed God's favor
and asked that he might provide a dwelling
place for the God of Jacob.[g] 47 But it was Solo-
mon who built a house for him.

48 "However, the Most High does not live
in houses made by human hands. As the
prophet says:

> 49 " 'Heaven is my throne,
> and the earth is my footstool.
> What kind of house will you build for me?
> says the Lord.
> Or where will my resting place be?
> 50 Has not my hand made all these things?'[h]

51 "You stiff-necked people! Your hearts
and ears are still uncircumcised. You are
just like your ancestors: You always resist
the Holy Spirit! 52 Was there ever a prophet
your ancestors did not persecute? They even
killed those who predicted the coming of the
Righteous One. And now you have betrayed
and murdered him— 53 you who have re-
ceived the law that was given through angels
but have not obeyed it."

The Stoning of Stephen

54 When the members of the Sanhedrin
heard this, they were furious and gnashed
their teeth at him. 55 But Stephen, full of the
Holy Spirit, looked up to heaven and saw the

[a] *28* Exodus 2:14 [b] *32* Exodus 3:6 [c] *34* Exodus 3:5,7,8,10 [d] *37* Deut. 18:15 [e] *40* Exodus 32:1
[f] *43* Amos 5:25-27 (see Septuagint) [g] *46* Some early manuscripts *the house of Jacob*
[h] *50* Isaiah 66:1,2

glory of God, and Jesus standing at the right hand of God. 56“Look,” he said, “I see heaven open and the Son of Man standing at the right hand of God.”

57At this they covered their ears and, yelling at the top of their voices, they all rushed at him, 58dragged him out of the city and began to stone him. Meanwhile, the witnesses laid their coats at the feet of a young man named Saul.

59While they were stoning him, Stephen prayed, “Lord Jesus, receive my spirit.” 60Then he fell on his knees and cried out, “Lord, do not hold this sin against them.” When he had said this, he fell asleep.

8 And Saul approved of their killing him.

The Church Persecuted and Scattered

On that day a great persecution broke out against the church in Jerusalem, and all except the apostles were scattered throughout Judea and Samaria. 2Godly men buried Stephen and mourned deeply for him. 3But Saul began to destroy the church. Going from house to house, he dragged off both men and women and put them in prison.

Philip in Samaria

4Those who had been scattered preached the word wherever they went. 5Philip went down to a city in Samaria and proclaimed the Messiah there. 6When the crowds heard Philip and saw the signs he performed, they all paid close attention to what he said. 7For with shrieks, impure spirits came out of many, and many who were paralyzed or lame were healed. 8So there was great joy in that city.

Simon the Sorcerer

9Now for some time a man named Simon had practiced sorcery in the city and amazed all the people of Samaria. He boasted that he was someone great, 10and all the people, both high and low, gave him their attention and exclaimed, “This man is rightly called the Great Power of God.” 11They followed him because he had amazed them for a long time with his sorcery. 12But when they believed Philip as he proclaimed the good news of the kingdom of God and the name of Jesus Christ, they were baptized, both men and women. 13Simon himself believed and was baptized. And he followed Philip everywhere, astonished by the great signs and miracles he saw.

14When the apostles in Jerusalem heard that Samaria had accepted the word of God, they sent Peter and John to Samaria. 15When they arrived, they prayed for the new believers there that they might receive the Holy Spirit, 16because the Holy Spirit had not yet come on any of them; they had simply been baptized in the name of the Lord Jesus. 17Then Peter and John placed their hands on them, and they received the Holy Spirit.

18When Simon saw that the Spirit was given at the laying on of the apostles’ hands, he offered them money 19and said, “Give me also this ability so that everyone on whom I lay my hands may receive the Holy Spirit.”

20Peter answered: “May your money perish with you, because you thought you could buy the gift of God with money! 21You have no part or share in this ministry, because your heart is not right before God. 22Repent of this wickedness and pray to the Lord in the hope that he may forgive you for having such a thought in your heart. 23For I see that you are full of bitterness and captive to sin.”

24Then Simon answered, “Pray to the Lord for me so that nothing you have said may happen to me.”

25After they had further proclaimed the word of the Lord and testified about Jesus, Peter and John returned to Jerusalem, preaching the gospel in many Samaritan villages.

Philip and the Ethiopian

26Now an angel of the Lord said to Philip, “Go south to the road—the desert road—that goes down from Jerusalem to Gaza.” 27So he started out, and on his way he met an Ethiopian[a] eunuch, an important official in charge of all the treasury of the Kandake (which means “queen of the Ethiopians”). This man had gone to Jerusalem to worship, 28and on his way home was sitting in his chariot reading the Book of Isaiah the prophet. 29The Spirit told Philip, “Go to that chariot and stay near it.”

30Then Philip ran up to the chariot and heard the man reading Isaiah the prophet.

[a] 27 That is, from the southern Nile region

“Do you understand what you are reading?” Philip asked.

31 “How can I,” he said, “unless someone explains it to me?” So he invited Philip to come up and sit with him.

32 This is the passage of Scripture the eunuch was reading:

> “He was led like a sheep to the slaughter,
> and as a lamb before its shearer is silent,
> so he did not open his mouth.
> 33 In his humiliation he was deprived of justice.
> Who can speak of his descendants?
> For his life was taken from the earth.”[a]

34 The eunuch asked Philip, “Tell me, please, who is the prophet talking about, himself or someone else?” 35 Then Philip began with that very passage of Scripture and told him the good news about Jesus.

36 As they traveled along the road, they came to some water and the eunuch said, “Look, here is water. What can stand in the way of my being baptized?” [37][b] 38 And he gave orders to stop the chariot. Then both Philip and the eunuch went down into the water and Philip baptized him. 39 When they came up out of the water, the Spirit of the Lord suddenly took Philip away, and the eunuch did not see him again, but went on his way rejoicing. 40 Philip, however, appeared at Azotus and traveled about, preaching the gospel in all the towns until he reached Caesarea.

Saul's Conversion

9 Meanwhile, Saul was still breathing out murderous threats against the Lord's disciples. He went to the high priest 2 and asked him for letters to the synagogues in Damascus, so that if he found any there who belonged to the Way, whether men or women, he might take them as prisoners to Jerusalem. 3 As he neared Damascus on his journey, suddenly a light from heaven flashed around him. 4 He fell to the ground and heard a voice say to him, “Saul, Saul, why do you persecute me?”

5 “Who are you, Lord?” Saul asked.

“I am Jesus, whom you are persecuting,” he replied. 6 “Now get up and go into the city, and you will be told what you must do.”

7 The men traveling with Saul stood there speechless; they heard the sound but did not see anyone. 8 Saul got up from the ground, but when he opened his eyes he could see nothing. So they led him by the hand into Damascus. 9 For three days he was blind, and did not eat or drink anything.

10 In Damascus there was a disciple named Ananias. The Lord called to him in a vision, “Ananias!”

“Yes, Lord,” he answered.

11 The Lord told him, “Go to the house of Judas on Straight Street and ask for a man from Tarsus named Saul, for he is praying. 12 In a vision he has seen a man named Ananias come and place his hands on him to restore his sight.”

13 “Lord,” Ananias answered, “I have heard many reports about this man and all the harm he has done to your holy people in Jerusalem. 14 And he has come here with authority from the chief priests to arrest all who call on your name.”

15 But the Lord said to Ananias, “Go! This man is my chosen instrument to proclaim my name to the Gentiles and their kings and to the people of Israel. 16 I will show him how much he must suffer for my name.”

17 Then Ananias went to the house and entered it. Placing his hands on Saul, he said, “Brother Saul, the Lord — Jesus, who appeared to you on the road as you were coming here — has sent me so that you may see again and be filled with the Holy Spirit.” 18 Immediately, something like scales fell from Saul's eyes, and he could see again. He got up and was baptized, 19 and after taking some food, he regained his strength.

Saul in Damascus and Jerusalem

Saul spent several days with the disciples in Damascus. 20 At once he began to preach in the synagogues that Jesus is the Son of God. 21 All those who heard him were astonished and asked, “Isn't he the man who raised havoc in Jerusalem among those who call on this name? And hasn't he come here to take them as prisoners to the chief priests?” 22 Yet Saul grew more and more

[a] *33* Isaiah 53:7,8 (see Septuagint) [b] *37* Some manuscripts include here *Philip said, “If you believe with all your heart, you may.” The eunuch answered, “I believe that Jesus Christ is the Son of God.”*

powerful and baffled the Jews living in Damascus by proving that Jesus is the Messiah. [23]After many days had gone by, there was a conspiracy among the Jews to kill him, [24]but Saul learned of their plan. Day and night they kept close watch on the city gates in order to kill him. [25]But his followers took him by night and lowered him in a basket through an opening in the wall.

[26]When he came to Jerusalem, he tried to join the disciples, but they were all afraid of him, not believing that he really was a disciple. [27]But Barnabas took him and brought him to the apostles. He told them how Saul on his journey had seen the Lord and that the Lord had spoken to him, and how in Damascus he had preached fearlessly in the name of Jesus. [28]So Saul stayed with them and moved about freely in Jerusalem, speaking boldly in the name of the Lord. [29]He talked and debated with the Hellenistic Jews,[a] but they tried to kill him. [30]When the believers learned of this, they took him down to Caesarea and sent him off to Tarsus.

[31]Then the church throughout Judea, Galilee and Samaria enjoyed a time of peace and was strengthened. Living in the fear of the Lord and encouraged by the Holy Spirit, it increased in numbers.

Aeneas and Dorcas

[32]As Peter traveled about the country, he went to visit the Lord's people who lived in Lydda. [33]There he found a man named Aeneas, who was paralyzed and had been bedridden for eight years. [34]"Aeneas," Peter said to him, "Jesus Christ heals you. Get up and roll up your mat." Immediately Aeneas got up. [35]All those who lived in Lydda and Sharon saw him and turned to the Lord.

[36]In Joppa there was a disciple named Tabitha (in Greek her name is Dorcas); she was always doing good and helping the poor. [37]About that time she became sick and died, and her body was washed and placed in an upstairs room. [38]Lydda was near Joppa; so when the disciples heard that Peter was in Lydda, they sent two men to him and urged him, "Please come at once!"

[39]Peter went with them, and when he arrived he was taken upstairs to the room. All the widows stood around him, crying and showing him the robes and other clothing that Dorcas had made while she was still with them.

[40]Peter sent them all out of the room; then he got down on his knees and prayed. Turning toward the dead woman, he said, "Tabitha, get up." She opened her eyes, and seeing Peter she sat up. [41]He took her by the hand and helped her to her feet. Then he called for the believers, especially the widows, and presented her to them alive. [42]This became known all over Joppa, and many people believed in the Lord. [43]Peter stayed in Joppa for some time with a tanner named Simon.

Cornelius Calls for Peter

10 At Caesarea there was a man named Cornelius, a centurion in what was known as the Italian Regiment. [2]He and all his family were devout and God-fearing; he gave generously to those in need and prayed to God regularly. [3]One day at about three in the afternoon he had a vision. He distinctly saw an angel of God, who came to him and said, "Cornelius!"

[4]Cornelius stared at him in fear. "What is it, Lord?" he asked.

The angel answered, "Your prayers and gifts to the poor have come up as a memorial offering before God. [5]Now send men to Joppa to bring back a man named Simon who is called Peter. [6]He is staying with Simon the tanner, whose house is by the sea."

[7]When the angel who spoke to him had gone, Cornelius called two of his servants and a devout soldier who was one of his attendants. [8]He told them everything that had happened and sent them to Joppa.

Peter's Vision

[9]About noon the following day as they were on their journey and approaching the city, Peter went up on the roof to pray. [10]He became hungry and wanted something to eat, and while the meal was being prepared, he fell into a trance. [11]He saw heaven opened and something like a large sheet being let down to earth by its four corners. [12]It contained all kinds of four-footed animals, as well as reptiles and birds. [13]Then a voice told him, "Get up, Peter. Kill and eat."

[a] *29* That is, Jews who had adopted the Greek language and culture

14“Surely not, Lord!” Peter replied. “I have never eaten anything impure or unclean.”

15The voice spoke to him a second time, “Do not call anything impure that God has made clean.”

16This happened three times, and immediately the sheet was taken back to heaven.

17While Peter was wondering about the meaning of the vision, the men sent by Cornelius found out where Simon’s house was and stopped at the gate. 18They called out, asking if Simon who was known as Peter was staying there.

19While Peter was still thinking about the vision, the Spirit said to him, “Simon, three[a] men are looking for you. 20So get up and go downstairs. Do not hesitate to go with them, for I have sent them.”

21Peter went down and said to the men, “I’m the one you’re looking for. Why have you come?”

22The men replied, “We have come from Cornelius the centurion. He is a righteous and God-fearing man, who is respected by all the Jewish people. A holy angel told him to ask you to come to his house so that he could hear what you have to say.” 23Then Peter invited the men into the house to be his guests.

Peter at Cornelius’s House

The next day Peter started out with them, and some of the believers from Joppa went along. 24The following day he arrived in Caesarea. Cornelius was expecting them and had called together his relatives and close friends. 25As Peter entered the house, Cornelius met him and fell at his feet in reverence. 26But Peter made him get up. “Stand up,” he said, “I am only a man myself.”

27While talking with him, Peter went inside and found a large gathering of people. 28He said to them: “You are well aware that it is against our law for a Jew to associate with or visit a Gentile. But God has shown me that I should not call anyone impure or unclean. 29So when I was sent for, I came without raising any objection. May I ask why you sent for me?”

30Cornelius answered: “Three days ago I was in my house praying at this hour, at three in the afternoon. Suddenly a man in shining clothes stood before me 31and said, ‘Cornelius, God has heard your prayer and remembered your gifts to the poor. 32Send to Joppa for Simon who is called Peter. He is a guest in the home of Simon the tanner, who lives by the sea.’ 33So I sent for you immediately, and it was good of you to come. Now we are all here in the presence of God to listen to everything the Lord has commanded you to tell us.”

34Then Peter began to speak: “I now realize how true it is that God does not show favoritism 35but accepts from every nation the one who fears him and does what is right. 36You know the message God sent to the people of Israel, announcing the good news of peace through Jesus Christ, who is Lord of all. 37You know what has happened throughout the province of Judea, beginning in Galilee after the baptism that John preached — 38how God anointed Jesus of Nazareth with the Holy Spirit and power, and how he went around doing good and healing all who were under the power of the devil, because God was with him.

39“We are witnesses of everything he did in the country of the Jews and in Jerusalem. They killed him by hanging him on a cross, 40but God raised him from the dead on the third day and caused him to be seen. 41He was not seen by all the people, but by witnesses whom God had already chosen — by us who ate and drank with him after he rose from the dead. 42He commanded us to preach to the people and to testify that he is the one whom God appointed as judge of the living and the dead. 43All the prophets testify about him that everyone who believes in him receives forgiveness of sins through his name.”

44While Peter was still speaking these words, the Holy Spirit came on all who heard the message. 45The circumcised believers who had come with Peter were astonished that the gift of the Holy Spirit had been poured out even on Gentiles. 46For they heard them speaking in tongues[b] and praising God.

Then Peter said, 47“Surely no one can stand in the way of their being baptized with water. They have received the Holy Spirit just as we have.” 48So he ordered that they be baptized in the name of Jesus Christ. Then

[a] 19 One early manuscript *two;* other manuscripts do not have the number. [b] 46 Or *other languages*

they asked Peter to stay with them for a few
days.

Peter Explains His Actions

11 The apostles and the believers
throughout Judea heard that the
Gentiles also had received the word of God.
2So when Peter went up to Jerusalem, the
circumcised believers criticized him 3and
said, "You went into the house of uncircum-
cised men and ate with them."
4Starting from the beginning, Peter told
them the whole story: 5"I was in the city of
Joppa praying, and in a trance I saw a vision.
I saw something like a large sheet being let
down from heaven by its four corners, and
it came down to where I was. 6I looked into
it and saw four-footed animals of the earth,
wild beasts, reptiles and birds. 7Then I
heard a voice telling me, 'Get up, Peter. Kill
and eat.'
8"I replied, 'Surely not, Lord! Nothing im-
pure or unclean has ever entered my mouth.'
9"The voice spoke from heaven a second
time, 'Do not call anything impure that God
has made clean.' 10This happened three
times, and then it was all pulled up to heav-
en again.
11"Right then three men who had been
sent to me from Caesarea stopped at the
house where I was staying. 12The Spirit told
me to have no hesitation about going with
them. These six brothers also went with me,
and we entered the man's house. 13He told
us how he had seen an angel appear in his
house and say, 'Send to Joppa for Simon who
is called Peter. 14He will bring you a message
through which you and all your household
will be saved.'
15"As I began to speak, the Holy Spirit
came on them as he had come on us at the
beginning. 16Then I remembered what the
Lord had said: 'John baptized with[a] wa-
ter, but you will be baptized with[a] the Holy
Spirit.' 17So if God gave them the same gift
he gave us who believed in the Lord Jesus
Christ, who was I to think that I could stand
in God's way?"
18When they heard this, they had no fur-
ther objections and praised God, saying, "So
then, even to Gentiles God has granted re-
pentance that leads to life."

The Church in Antioch

19Now those who had been scattered by
the persecution that broke out when Ste-
phen was killed traveled as far as Phoenic-
ia, Cyprus and Antioch, spreading the word
only among Jews. 20Some of them, however,
men from Cyprus and Cyrene, went to An-
tioch and began to speak to Greeks also,
telling them the good news about the Lord
Jesus. 21The Lord's hand was with them,
and a great number of people believed and
turned to the Lord.
22News of this reached the church in Je-
rusalem, and they sent Barnabas to Antioch.
23When he arrived and saw what the grace of
God had done, he was glad and encouraged
them all to remain true to the Lord with all
their hearts. 24He was a good man, full of the
Holy Spirit and faith, and a great number of
people were brought to the Lord.
25Then Barnabas went to Tarsus to look for
Saul, 26and when he found him, he brought
him to Antioch. So for a whole year Barna-
bas and Saul met with the church and taught
great numbers of people. The disciples were
called Christians first at Antioch.
27During this time some prophets came
down from Jerusalem to Antioch. 28One of
them, named Agabus, stood up and through
the Spirit predicted that a severe famine
would spread over the entire Roman world.
(This happened during the reign of Claudi-
us.) 29The disciples, as each one was able,
decided to provide help for the brothers and
sisters living in Judea. 30This they did, send-
ing their gift to the elders by Barnabas and
Saul.

Peter's Miraculous Escape From Prison

12 It was about this time that King Her-
od arrested some who belonged to
the church, intending to persecute them.
2He had James, the brother of John, put to
death with the sword. 3When he saw that
this met with approval among the Jews, he
proceeded to seize Peter also. This hap-
pened during the Festival of Unleavened
Bread. 4After arresting him, he put him in
prison, handing him over to be guarded by
four squads of four soldiers each. Herod in-
tended to bring him out for public trial after
the Passover.

[a] 16 Or *in*

5So Peter was kept in prison, but the church was earnestly praying to God for him.

6The night before Herod was to bring him to trial, Peter was sleeping between two soldiers, bound with two chains, and sentries stood guard at the entrance. 7Suddenly an angel of the Lord appeared and a light shone in the cell. He struck Peter on the side and woke him up. "Quick, get up!" he said, and the chains fell off Peter's wrists.

8Then the angel said to him, "Put on your clothes and sandals." And Peter did so. "Wrap your cloak around you and follow me," the angel told him. 9Peter followed him out of the prison, but he had no idea that what the angel was doing was really happening; he thought he was seeing a vision. 10They passed the first and second guards and came to the iron gate leading to the city. It opened for them by itself, and they went through it. When they had walked the length of one street, suddenly the angel left him.

11Then Peter came to himself and said, "Now I know without a doubt that the Lord has sent his angel and rescued me from Herod's clutches and from everything the Jewish people were hoping would happen."

12When this had dawned on him, he went to the house of Mary the mother of John, also called Mark, where many people had gathered and were praying. 13Peter knocked at the outer entrance, and a servant named Rhoda came to answer the door. 14When she recognized Peter's voice, she was so overjoyed she ran back without opening it and exclaimed, "Peter is at the door!"

15"You're out of your mind," they told her. When she kept insisting that it was so, they said, "It must be his angel."

16But Peter kept on knocking, and when they opened the door and saw him, they were astonished. 17Peter motioned with his hand for them to be quiet and described how the Lord had brought him out of prison. "Tell James and the other brothers and sisters about this," he said, and then he left for another place.

18In the morning, there was no small commotion among the soldiers as to what had become of Peter. 19After Herod had a thorough search made for him and did not find him, he cross-examined the guards and ordered that they be executed.

Herod's Death

Then Herod went from Judea to Caesarea and stayed there. 20He had been quarreling with the people of Tyre and Sidon; they now joined together and sought an audience with him. After securing the support of Blastus, a trusted personal servant of the king, they asked for peace, because they depended on the king's country for their food supply.

21On the appointed day Herod, wearing his royal robes, sat on his throne and delivered a public address to the people. 22They shouted, "This is the voice of a god, not of a man." 23Immediately, because Herod did not give praise to God, an angel of the Lord struck him down, and he was eaten by worms and died.

24But the word of God continued to spread and flourish.

Barnabas and Saul Sent Off

25When Barnabas and Saul had finished their mission, they returned from[a] Jerusalem, taking with them John, also called Mark. 13 1Now in the church at Antioch there were prophets and teachers: Barnabas, Simeon called Niger, Lucius of Cyrene, Manaen (who had been brought up with Herod the tetrarch) and Saul. 2While they were worshiping the Lord and fasting, the Holy Spirit said, "Set apart for me Barnabas and Saul for the work to which I have called them." 3So after they had fasted and prayed, they placed their hands on them and sent them off.

On Cyprus

4The two of them, sent on their way by the Holy Spirit, went down to Seleucia and sailed from there to Cyprus. 5When they arrived at Salamis, they proclaimed the word of God in the Jewish synagogues. John was with them as their helper.

6They traveled through the whole island until they came to Paphos. There they met a Jewish sorcerer and false prophet named Bar-Jesus, 7who was an attendant of the proconsul, Sergius Paulus. The proconsul, an intelligent man, sent for Barnabas and

[a] *25* Some manuscripts *to*

Saul because he wanted to hear the word of God. [8]But Elymas the sorcerer (for that is what his name means) opposed them and tried to turn the proconsul from the faith. [9]Then Saul, who was also called Paul, filled with the Holy Spirit, looked straight at Elymas and said, [10]"You are a child of the devil and an enemy of everything that is right! You are full of all kinds of deceit and trickery. Will you never stop perverting the right ways of the Lord? [11]Now the hand of the Lord is against you. You are going to be blind for a time, not even able to see the light of the sun."

Immediately mist and darkness came over him, and he groped about, seeking someone to lead him by the hand. [12]When the proconsul saw what had happened, he believed, for he was amazed at the teaching about the Lord.

In Pisidian Antioch

[13]From Paphos, Paul and his companions sailed to Perga in Pamphylia, where John left them to return to Jerusalem. [14]From Perga they went on to Pisidian Antioch. On the Sabbath they entered the synagogue and sat down. [15]After the reading from the Law and the Prophets, the leaders of the synagogue sent word to them, saying, "Brothers, if you have a word of exhortation for the people, please speak."

[16]Standing up, Paul motioned with his hand and said: "Fellow Israelites and you Gentiles who worship God, listen to me! [17]The God of the people of Israel chose our ancestors; he made the people prosper during their stay in Egypt; with mighty power he led them out of that country; [18]for about forty years he endured their conduct[a] in the wilderness; [19]and he overthrew seven nations in Canaan, giving their land to his people as their inheritance. [20]All this took about 450 years.

"After this, God gave them judges until the time of Samuel the prophet. [21]Then the people asked for a king, and he gave them Saul son of Kish, of the tribe of Benjamin, who ruled forty years. [22]After removing Saul, he made David their king. God testified concerning him: 'I have found David son of Jesse, a man after my own heart; he will do everything I want him to do.'

[23]"From this man's descendants God has brought to Israel the Savior Jesus, as he promised. [24]Before the coming of Jesus, John preached repentance and baptism to all the people of Israel. [25]As John was completing his work, he said: 'Who do you suppose I am? I am not the one you are looking for. But there is one coming after me whose sandals I am not worthy to untie.'

[26]"Fellow children of Abraham and you God-fearing Gentiles, it is to us that this message of salvation has been sent. [27]The people of Jerusalem and their rulers did not recognize Jesus, yet in condemning him they fulfilled the words of the prophets that are read every Sabbath. [28]Though they found no proper ground for a death sentence, they asked Pilate to have him executed. [29]When they had carried out all that was written about him, they took him down from the cross and laid him in a tomb. [30]But God raised him from the dead, [31]and for many days he was seen by those who had traveled with him from Galilee to Jerusalem. They are now his witnesses to our people.

[32]"We tell you the good news: What God promised our ancestors [33]he has fulfilled for us, their children, by raising up Jesus. As it is written in the second Psalm:

"'You are my son;
today I have become your father.'[b]

[34]God raised him from the dead so that he will never be subject to decay. As God has said,

"'I will give you the holy and sure
blessings promised to David.'[c]

[35]So it is also stated elsewhere:

"'You will not let your holy one see
decay.'[d]

[36]"Now when David had served God's purpose in his own generation, he fell asleep; he was buried with his ancestors and his body decayed. [37]But the one whom God raised from the dead did not see decay.

[38]"Therefore, my friends, I want you to know that through Jesus the forgiveness of sins is proclaimed to you. [39]Through him everyone who believes is set free from every sin, a justification you were not able to

[a] *18* Some manuscripts *he cared for them* [b] *33* Psalm 2:7 [c] *34* Isaiah 55:3 [d] *35* Psalm 16:10 (see Septuagint)

obtain under the law of Moses. 40 Take care that what the prophets have said does not happen to you:

41 " 'Look, you scoffers,
wonder and perish,
for I am going to do something in
your days
that you would never believe,
even if someone told you.'[a]"

42 As Paul and Barnabas were leaving the synagogue, the people invited them to speak further about these things on the next Sabbath. 43 When the congregation was dismissed, many of the Jews and devout converts to Judaism followed Paul and Barnabas, who talked with them and urged them to continue in the grace of God.

44 On the next Sabbath almost the whole city gathered to hear the word of the Lord. 45 When the Jews saw the crowds, they were filled with jealousy. They began to contradict what Paul was saying and heaped abuse on him.

46 Then Paul and Barnabas answered them boldly: "We had to speak the word of God to you first. Since you reject it and do not consider yourselves worthy of eternal life, we now turn to the Gentiles. 47 For this is what the Lord has commanded us:

" 'I have made you[b] a light for the
Gentiles,
that you[b] may bring salvation to the
ends of the earth.'[c]"

48 When the Gentiles heard this, they were glad and honored the word of the Lord; and all who were appointed for eternal life believed.

49 The word of the Lord spread through the whole region. 50 But the Jewish leaders incited the God-fearing women of high standing and the leading men of the city. They stirred up persecution against Paul and Barnabas, and expelled them from their region. 51 So they shook the dust off their feet as a warning to them and went to Iconium. 52 And the disciples were filled with joy and with the Holy Spirit.

In Iconium

14 At Iconium Paul and Barnabas went as usual into the Jewish synagogue. There they spoke so effectively that a great number of Jews and Greeks believed. 2 But the Jews who refused to believe stirred up the other Gentiles and poisoned their minds against the brothers. 3 So Paul and Barnabas spent considerable time there, speaking boldly for the Lord, who confirmed the message of his grace by enabling them to perform signs and wonders. 4 The people of the city were divided; some sided with the Jews, others with the apostles. 5 There was a plot afoot among both Gentiles and Jews, together with their leaders, to mistreat them and stone them. 6 But they found out about it and fled to the Lycaonian cities of Lystra and Derbe and to the surrounding country, 7 where they continued to preach the gospel.

In Lystra and Derbe

8 In Lystra there sat a man who was lame. He had been that way from birth and had never walked. 9 He listened to Paul as he was speaking. Paul looked directly at him, saw that he had faith to be healed 10 and called out, "Stand up on your feet!" At that, the man jumped up and began to walk.

11 When the crowd saw what Paul had done, they shouted in the Lycaonian language, "The gods have come down to us in human form!" 12 Barnabas they called Zeus, and Paul they called Hermes because he was the chief speaker. 13 The priest of Zeus, whose temple was just outside the city, brought bulls and wreaths to the city gates because he and the crowd wanted to offer sacrifices to them.

14 But when the apostles Barnabas and Paul heard of this, they tore their clothes and rushed out into the crowd, shouting: 15 "Friends, why are you doing this? We too are only human, like you. We are bringing you good news, telling you to turn from these worthless things to the living God, who made the heavens and the earth and the sea and everything in them. 16 In the past, he let all nations go their own way. 17 Yet he has not left himself without testimony: He has shown kindness by giving you rain from heaven and crops in their seasons; he provides you with plenty of food and fills your hearts with joy." 18 Even with these words, they had difficulty keeping the crowd from sacrificing to them.

[a] *41* Hab. 1:5 [b] *47* The Greek is singular. [c] *47* Isaiah 49:6

19 Then some Jews came from Antioch and Iconium and won the crowd over. They stoned Paul and dragged him outside the city, thinking he was dead. 20 But after the disciples had gathered around him, he got up and went back into the city. The next day he and Barnabas left for Derbe.

The Return to Antioch in Syria

21 They preached the gospel in that city and won a large number of disciples. Then they returned to Lystra, Iconium and Antioch, 22 strengthening the disciples and encouraging them to remain true to the faith. "We must go through many hardships to enter the kingdom of God," they said. 23 Paul and Barnabas appointed elders[a] for them in each church and, with prayer and fasting, committed them to the Lord, in whom they had put their trust. 24 After going through Pisidia, they came into Pamphylia, 25 and when they had preached the word in Perga, they went down to Attalia.

26 From Attalia they sailed back to Antioch, where they had been committed to the grace of God for the work they had now completed. 27 On arriving there, they gathered the church together and reported all that God had done through them and how he had opened a door of faith to the Gentiles. 28 And they stayed there a long time with the disciples.

The Council at Jerusalem

15 Certain people came down from Judea to Antioch and were teaching the believers: "Unless you are circumcised, according to the custom taught by Moses, you cannot be saved." 2 This brought Paul and Barnabas into sharp dispute and debate with them. So Paul and Barnabas were appointed, along with some other believers, to go up to Jerusalem to see the apostles and elders about this question. 3 The church sent them on their way, and as they traveled through Phoenicia and Samaria, they told how the Gentiles had been converted. This news made all the believers very glad. 4 When they came to Jerusalem, they were welcomed by the church and the apostles and elders, to whom they reported everything God had done through them.

5 Then some of the believers who belonged to the party of the Pharisees stood up and said, "The Gentiles must be circumcised and required to keep the law of Moses."

6 The apostles and elders met to consider this question. 7 After much discussion, Peter got up and addressed them: "Brothers, you know that some time ago God made a choice among you that the Gentiles might hear from my lips the message of the gospel and believe. 8 God, who knows the heart, showed that he accepted them by giving the Holy Spirit to them, just as he did to us. 9 He did not discriminate between us and them, for he purified their hearts by faith. 10 Now then, why do you try to test God by putting on the necks of Gentiles a yoke that neither we nor our ancestors have been able to bear? 11 No! We believe it is through the grace of our Lord Jesus that we are saved, just as they are."

12 The whole assembly became silent as they listened to Barnabas and Paul telling about the signs and wonders God had done among the Gentiles through them. 13 When they finished, James spoke up. "Brothers," he said, "listen to me. 14 Simon[b] has described to us how God first intervened to choose a people for his name from the Gentiles. 15 The words of the prophets are in agreement with this, as it is written:

16 " 'After this I will return
and rebuild David's fallen tent.
Its ruins I will rebuild,
and I will restore it,
17 that the rest of mankind may seek
the Lord,
even all the Gentiles who bear
my name,
says the Lord, who does these things'[c]—
18 things known from long ago.[d]

19 "It is my judgment, therefore, that we should not make it difficult for the Gentiles who are turning to God. 20 Instead we should write to them, telling them to abstain from food polluted by idols, from sexual immorality, from the meat of strangled animals and from blood. 21 For the law of Moses has been preached in every city from the earliest

[a] 23 Or *Barnabas ordained elders*; or *Barnabas had elders elected* [b] 14 Greek *Simeon*, a variant of *Simon*; that is, Peter [c] 17 Amos 9:11,12 (see Septuagint) [d] 17,18 Some manuscripts *things'— / [18]the Lord's work is known to him from long ago*

times and is read in the synagogues on every Sabbath."

The Council's Letter to Gentile Believers

[22]Then the apostles and elders, with the whole church, decided to choose some of their own men and send them to Antioch with Paul and Barnabas. They chose Judas (called Barsabbas) and Silas, men who were leaders among the believers. [23]With them they sent the following letter:

> The apostles and elders, your brothers,
>
> To the Gentile believers in Antioch, Syria and Cilicia:
>
> Greetings.
>
> [24]We have heard that some went out from us without our authorization and disturbed you, troubling your minds by what they said. [25]So we all agreed to choose some men and send them to you with our dear friends Barnabas and Paul— [26]men who have risked their lives for the name of our Lord Jesus Christ. [27]Therefore we are sending Judas and Silas to confirm by word of mouth what we are writing. [28]It seemed good to the Holy Spirit and to us not to burden you with anything beyond the following requirements: [29]You are to abstain from food sacrificed to idols, from blood, from the meat of strangled animals and from sexual immorality. You will do well to avoid these things.
>
> Farewell.

[30]So the men were sent off and went down to Antioch, where they gathered the church together and delivered the letter. [31]The people read it and were glad for its encouraging message. [32]Judas and Silas, who themselves were prophets, said much to encourage and strengthen the believers. [33]After spending some time there, they were sent off by the believers with the blessing of peace to return to those who had sent them. [34] [a] [35]But Paul and Barnabas remained in Antioch, where they and many others taught and preached the word of the Lord.

Disagreement Between Paul and Barnabas

[36]Some time later Paul said to Barnabas, "Let us go back and visit the believers in all the towns where we preached the word of the Lord and see how they are doing." [37]Barnabas wanted to take John, also called Mark, with them, [38]but Paul did not think it wise to take him, because he had deserted them in Pamphylia and had not continued with them in the work. [39]They had such a sharp disagreement that they parted company. Barnabas took Mark and sailed for Cyprus, [40]but Paul chose Silas and left, commended by the believers to the grace of the Lord. [41]He went through Syria and Cilicia, strengthening the churches.

Timothy Joins Paul and Silas

16 Paul came to Derbe and then to Lystra, where a disciple named Timothy lived, whose mother was Jewish and a believer but whose father was a Greek. [2]The believers at Lystra and Iconium spoke well of him. [3]Paul wanted to take him along on the journey, so he circumcised him because of the Jews who lived in that area, for they all knew that his father was a Greek. [4]As they traveled from town to town, they delivered the decisions reached by the apostles and elders in Jerusalem for the people to obey. [5]So the churches were strengthened in the faith and grew daily in numbers.

Paul's Vision of the Man of Macedonia

[6]Paul and his companions traveled throughout the region of Phrygia and Galatia, having been kept by the Holy Spirit from preaching the word in the province of Asia. [7]When they came to the border of Mysia, they tried to enter Bithynia, but the Spirit of Jesus would not allow them to. [8]So they passed by Mysia and went down to Troas. [9]During the night Paul had a vision of a man of Macedonia standing and begging him, "Come over to Macedonia and help us." [10]After Paul had seen the vision, we got ready at once to leave for Macedonia, concluding that God had called us to preach the gospel to them.

Lydia's Conversion in Philippi

[11]From Troas we put out to sea and sailed straight for Samothrace, and the next day we

[a] *34* Some manuscripts include here *But Silas decided to remain there.*

went on to Neapolis. 12 From there we traveled to Philippi, a Roman colony and the leading city of that district[a] of Macedonia. And we stayed there several days.

13 On the Sabbath we went outside the city gate to the river, where we expected to find a place of prayer. We sat down and began to speak to the women who had gathered there. 14 One of those listening was a woman from the city of Thyatira named Lydia, a dealer in purple cloth. She was a worshiper of God. The Lord opened her heart to respond to Paul's message. 15 When she and the members of her household were baptized, she invited us to her home. "If you consider me a believer in the Lord," she said, "come and stay at my house." And she persuaded us.

Paul and Silas in Prison

16 Once when we were going to the place of prayer, we were met by a female slave who had a spirit by which she predicted the future. She earned a great deal of money for her owners by fortune-telling. 17 She followed Paul and the rest of us, shouting, "These men are servants of the Most High God, who are telling you the way to be saved." 18 She kept this up for many days. Finally Paul became so annoyed that he turned around and said to the spirit, "In the name of Jesus Christ I command you to come out of her!" At that moment the spirit left her.

19 When her owners realized that their hope of making money was gone, they seized Paul and Silas and dragged them into the marketplace to face the authorities. 20 They brought them before the magistrates and said, "These men are Jews, and are throwing our city into an uproar 21 by advocating customs unlawful for us Romans to accept or practice."

22 The crowd joined in the attack against Paul and Silas, and the magistrates ordered them to be stripped and beaten with rods. 23 After they had been severely flogged, they were thrown into prison, and the jailer was commanded to guard them carefully. 24 When he received these orders, he put them in the inner cell and fastened their feet in the stocks.

25 About midnight Paul and Silas were praying and singing hymns to God, and the other prisoners were listening to them. 26 Suddenly there was such a violent earthquake that the foundations of the prison were shaken. At once all the prison doors flew open, and everyone's chains came loose. 27 The jailer woke up, and when he saw the prison doors open, he drew his sword and was about to kill himself because he thought the prisoners had escaped. 28 But Paul shouted, "Don't harm yourself! We are all here!"

29 The jailer called for lights, rushed in and fell trembling before Paul and Silas. 30 He then brought them out and asked, "Sirs, what must I do to be saved?"

31 They replied, "Believe in the Lord Jesus, and you will be saved—you and your household." 32 Then they spoke the word of the Lord to him and to all the others in his house. 33 At that hour of the night the jailer took them and washed their wounds; then immediately he and all his household were baptized. 34 The jailer brought them into his house and set a meal before them; he was filled with joy because he had come to believe in God—he and his whole household.

35 When it was daylight, the magistrates sent their officers to the jailer with the order: "Release those men." 36 The jailer told Paul, "The magistrates have ordered that you and Silas be released. Now you can leave. Go in peace."

37 But Paul said to the officers: "They beat us publicly without a trial, even though we are Roman citizens, and threw us into prison. And now do they want to get rid of us quietly? No! Let them come themselves and escort us out."

38 The officers reported this to the magistrates, and when they heard that Paul and Silas were Roman citizens, they were alarmed. 39 They came to appease them and escorted them from the prison, requesting them to leave the city. 40 After Paul and Silas came out of the prison, they went to Lydia's house, where they met with the brothers and sisters and encouraged them. Then they left.

In Thessalonica

17 When Paul and his companions had passed through Amphipolis and Apollonia, they came to Thessalonica, where

[a] *12* The text and meaning of the Greek for *the leading city of that district* are uncertain.

there was a Jewish synagogue. 2 As was his
custom, Paul went into the synagogue, and
on three Sabbath days he reasoned with them
from the Scriptures, 3 explaining and proving
that the Messiah had to suffer and rise from
the dead. "This Jesus I am proclaiming to you
is the Messiah," he said. 4 Some of the Jews
were persuaded and joined Paul and Silas,
as did a large number of God-fearing Greeks
and quite a few prominent women.

5 But other Jews were jealous; so they
rounded up some bad characters from the
marketplace, formed a mob and started a
riot in the city. They rushed to Jason's house
in search of Paul and Silas in order to bring
them out to the crowd.[a] 6 But when they did
not find them, they dragged Jason and some
other believers before the city officials,
shouting: "These men who have caused
trouble all over the world have now come
here, 7 and Jason has welcomed them into his
house. They are all defying Caesar's decrees,
saying that there is another king, one called
Jesus." 8 When they heard this, the crowd
and the city officials were thrown into tur-
moil. 9 Then they made Jason and the others
post bond and let them go.

In Berea

10 As soon as it was night, the believers
sent Paul and Silas away to Berea. On ar-
riving there, they went to the Jewish syna-
gogue. 11 Now the Berean Jews were of more
noble character than those in Thessalonica,
for they received the message with great ea-
gerness and examined the Scriptures every
day to see if what Paul said was true. 12 As a
result, many of them believed, as did also
a number of prominent Greek women and
many Greek men.

13 But when the Jews in Thessalonica
learned that Paul was preaching the word of
God at Berea, some of them went there too,
agitating the crowds and stirring them up.
14 The believers immediately sent Paul to the
coast, but Silas and Timothy stayed at Berea.
15 Those who escorted Paul brought him to
Athens and then left with instructions for Silas
and Timothy to join him as soon as possible.

In Athens

16 While Paul was waiting for them in Ath-
ens, he was greatly distressed to see that the
city was full of idols. 17 So he reasoned in the
synagogue with both Jews and God-fear-
ing Greeks, as well as in the marketplace
day by day with those who happened to be
there. 18 A group of Epicurean and Stoic phi-
losophers began to debate with him. Some
of them asked, "What is this babbler trying
to say?" Others remarked, "He seems to be
advocating foreign gods." They said this be-
cause Paul was preaching the good news
about Jesus and the resurrection. 19 Then
they took him and brought him to a meeting
of the Areopagus, where they said to him,
"May we know what this new teaching is that
you are presenting? 20 You are bringing some
strange ideas to our ears, and we would like
to know what they mean." 21 (All the Atheni-
ans and the foreigners who lived there spent
their time doing nothing but talking about
and listening to the latest ideas.)

22 Paul then stood up in the meeting of
the Areopagus and said: "People of Athens!
I see that in every way you are very religious.
23 For as I walked around and looked careful-
ly at your objects of worship, I even found an
altar with this inscription: TO AN UNKNOWN
GOD. So you are ignorant of the very thing
you worship — and this is what I am going to
proclaim to you.

24 "The God who made the world and ev-
erything in it is the Lord of heaven and earth
and does not live in temples built by human
hands. 25 And he is not served by human
hands, as if he needed anything. Rather, he
himself gives everyone life and breath and
everything else. 26 From one man he made
all the nations, that they should inhabit the
whole earth; and he marked out their ap-
pointed times in history and the boundaries
of their lands. 27 God did this so that they
would seek him and perhaps reach out for
him and find him, though he is not far from
any one of us. 28 'For in him we live and move
and have our being.'[b] As some of your own
poets have said, 'We are his offspring.'[c]

29 "Therefore since we are God's offspring,
we should not think that the divine being is
like gold or silver or stone — an image made
by human design and skill. 30 In the past
God overlooked such ignorance, but now he
commands all people everywhere to repent.
31 For he has set a day when he will judge the

[a] 5 Or *the assembly of the people* [b] 28 From the Cretan philosopher Epimenides [c] 28 From the Cilician Stoic philosopher Aratus

world with justice by the man he has ap-
pointed. He has given proof of this to every-
one by raising him from the dead."
[32]When they heard about the resurrec-
tion of the dead, some of them sneered, but
others said, "We want to hear you again on
this subject." [33]At that, Paul left the Coun-
cil. [34]Some of the people became followers
of Paul and believed. Among them was Di-
onysius, a member of the Areopagus, also a
woman named Damaris, and a number of
others.

In Corinth

18 After this, Paul left Athens and went
to Corinth. [2]There he met a Jew
named Aquila, a native of Pontus, who had
recently come from Italy with his wife Pris-
cilla, because Claudius had ordered all Jews
to leave Rome. Paul went to see them, [3]and
because he was a tentmaker as they were, he
stayed and worked with them. [4]Every Sab-
bath he reasoned in the synagogue, trying to
persuade Jews and Greeks.
[5]When Silas and Timothy came from
Macedonia, Paul devoted himself exclusive-
ly to preaching, testifying to the Jews that
Jesus was the Messiah. [6]But when they op-
posed Paul and became abusive, he shook
out his clothes in protest and said to them,
"Your blood be on your own heads! I am
innocent of it. From now on I will go to the
Gentiles."
[7]Then Paul left the synagogue and went
next door to the house of Titius Justus, a
worshiper of God. [8]Crispus, the synagogue
leader, and his entire household believed in
the Lord; and many of the Corinthians who
heard Paul believed and were baptized.
[9]One night the Lord spoke to Paul in a vi-
sion: "Do not be afraid; keep on speaking,
do not be silent. [10]For I am with you, and no
one is going to attack and harm you, because
I have many people in this city." [11]So Paul
stayed in Corinth for a year and a half, teach-
ing them the word of God.
[12]While Gallio was proconsul of Achaia,
the Jews of Corinth made a united attack on
Paul and brought him to the place of judg-
ment. [13]"This man," they charged, "is per-
suading the people to worship God in ways
contrary to the law."
[14]Just as Paul was about to speak, Gallio
said to them, "If you Jews were making a
complaint about some misdemeanor or se-
rious crime, it would be reasonable for me
to listen to you. [15]But since it involves ques-
tions about words and names and your own
law—settle the matter yourselves. I will not
be a judge of such things." [16]So he drove
them off. [17]Then the crowd there turned on
Sosthenes the synagogue leader and beat
him in front of the proconsul; and Gallio
showed no concern whatever.

Priscilla, Aquila and Apollos

[18]Paul stayed on in Corinth for some time.
Then he left the brothers and sisters and
sailed for Syria, accompanied by Priscil-
la and Aquila. Before he sailed, he had his
hair cut off at Cenchreae because of a vow he
had taken. [19]They arrived at Ephesus, where
Paul left Priscilla and Aquila. He himself
went into the synagogue and reasoned with
the Jews. [20]When they asked him to spend
more time with them, he declined. [21]But as
he left, he promised, "I will come back if it is
God's will." Then he set sail from Ephesus.
[22]When he landed at Caesarea, he went up to
Jerusalem and greeted the church and then
went down to Antioch.
[23]After spending some time in Antioch,
Paul set out from there and traveled from
place to place throughout the region of Ga-
latia and Phrygia, strengthening all the dis-
ciples.
[24]Meanwhile a Jew named Apollos, a na-
tive of Alexandria, came to Ephesus. He was
a learned man, with a thorough knowledge
of the Scriptures. [25]He had been instructed
in the way of the Lord, and he spoke with
great fervor[a] and taught about Jesus accu-
rately, though he knew only the baptism of
John. [26]He began to speak boldly in the syn-
agogue. When Priscilla and Aquila heard
him, they invited him to their home and
explained to him the way of God more ade-
quately.
[27]When Apollos wanted to go to Achaia,
the brothers and sisters encouraged him
and wrote to the disciples there to welcome
him. When he arrived, he was a great help to
those who by grace had believed. [28]For he
vigorously refuted his Jewish opponents in

[a] 25 Or *with fervor in the Spirit*

public debate, proving from the Scriptures that Jesus was the Messiah.

Paul in Ephesus

19 While Apollos was at Corinth, Paul took the road through the interior and arrived at Ephesus. There he found some disciples 2 and asked them, "Did you receive the Holy Spirit when[a] you believed?"

They answered, "No, we have not even heard that there is a Holy Spirit."

3 So Paul asked, "Then what baptism did you receive?"

"John's baptism," they replied.

4 Paul said, "John's baptism was a baptism of repentance. He told the people to believe in the one coming after him, that is, in Jesus." 5 On hearing this, they were baptized in the name of the Lord Jesus. 6 When Paul placed his hands on them, the Holy Spirit came on them, and they spoke in tongues[b] and prophesied. 7 There were about twelve men in all.

8 Paul entered the synagogue and spoke boldly there for three months, arguing persuasively about the kingdom of God. 9 But some of them became obstinate; they refused to believe and publicly maligned the Way. So Paul left them. He took the disciples with him and had discussions daily in the lecture hall of Tyrannus. 10 This went on for two years, so that all the Jews and Greeks who lived in the province of Asia heard the word of the Lord.

11 God did extraordinary miracles through Paul, 12 so that even handkerchiefs and aprons that had touched him were taken to the sick, and their illnesses were cured and the evil spirits left them.

13 Some Jews who went around driving out evil spirits tried to invoke the name of the Lord Jesus over those who were demon-possessed. They would say, "In the name of the Jesus whom Paul preaches, I command you to come out." 14 Seven sons of Sceva, a Jewish chief priest, were doing this. 15 One day the evil spirit answered them, "Jesus I know, and Paul I know about, but who are you?" 16 Then the man who had the evil spirit jumped on them and overpowered them all. He gave them such a beating that they ran out of the house naked and bleeding.

17 When this became known to the Jews and Greeks living in Ephesus, they were all seized with fear, and the name of the Lord Jesus was held in high honor. 18 Many of those who believed now came and openly confessed what they had done. 19 A number who had practiced sorcery brought their scrolls together and burned them publicly. When they calculated the value of the scrolls, the total came to fifty thousand drachmas.[c] 20 In this way the word of the Lord spread widely and grew in power.

21 After all this had happened, Paul decided[d] to go to Jerusalem, passing through Macedonia and Achaia. "After I have been there," he said, "I must visit Rome also." 22 He sent two of his helpers, Timothy and Erastus, to Macedonia, while he stayed in the province of Asia a little longer.

The Riot in Ephesus

23 About that time there arose a great disturbance about the Way. 24 A silversmith named Demetrius, who made silver shrines of Artemis, brought in a lot of business for the craftsmen there. 25 He called them together, along with the workers in related trades, and said: "You know, my friends, that we receive a good income from this business. 26 And you see and hear how this fellow Paul has convinced and led astray large numbers of people here in Ephesus and in practically the whole province of Asia. He says that gods made by human hands are no gods at all. 27 There is danger not only that our trade will lose its good name, but also that the temple of the great goddess Artemis will be discredited; and the goddess herself, who is worshiped throughout the province of Asia and the world, will be robbed of her divine majesty."

28 When they heard this, they were furious and began shouting: "Great is Artemis of the Ephesians!" 29 Soon the whole city was in an uproar. The people seized Gaius and Aristarchus, Paul's traveling companions from Macedonia, and all of them rushed into the theater together. 30 Paul wanted to appear before the crowd, but the disciples would not let him. 31 Even some of the officials of the province, friends of Paul, sent him a

[a] 2 Or *after* [b] 6 Or *other languages* [c] 19 A drachma was a silver coin worth about a day's wages.
[d] 21 Or *decided in the Spirit*

message begging him not to venture into the theater.

32 The assembly was in confusion: Some were shouting one thing, some another. Most of the people did not even know why they were there. 33 The Jews in the crowd pushed Alexander to the front, and they shouted instructions to him. He motioned for silence in order to make a defense before the people. 34 But when they realized he was a Jew, they all shouted in unison for about two hours: "Great is Artemis of the Ephesians!"

35 The city clerk quieted the crowd and said: "Fellow Ephesians, doesn't all the world know that the city of Ephesus is the guardian of the temple of the great Artemis and of her image, which fell from heaven? 36 Therefore, since these facts are undeniable, you ought to calm down and not do anything rash. 37 You have brought these men here, though they have neither robbed temples nor blasphemed our goddess. 38 If, then, Demetrius and his fellow craftsmen have a grievance against anybody, the courts are open and there are proconsuls. They can press charges. 39 If there is anything further you want to bring up, it must be settled in a legal assembly. 40 As it is, we are in danger of being charged with rioting because of what happened today. In that case we would not be able to account for this commotion, since there is no reason for it." 41 After he had said this, he dismissed the assembly.

Through Macedonia and Greece

20 When the uproar had ended, Paul sent for the disciples and, after encouraging them, said goodbye and set out for Macedonia. 2 He traveled through that area, speaking many words of encouragement to the people, and finally arrived in Greece, 3 where he stayed three months. Because some Jews had plotted against him just as he was about to sail for Syria, he decided to go back through Macedonia. 4 He was accompanied by Sopater son of Pyrrhus from Berea, Aristarchus and Secundus from Thessalonica, Gaius from Derbe, Timothy also, and Tychicus and Trophimus from the province of Asia. 5 These men went on ahead and waited for us at Troas. 6 But we sailed from Philippi after the Festival of Unleavened Bread, and five days later joined the others at Troas, where we stayed seven days.

Eutychus Raised From the Dead at Troas

7 On the first day of the week we came together to break bread. Paul spoke to the people and, because he intended to leave the next day, kept on talking until midnight. 8 There were many lamps in the upstairs room where we were meeting. 9 Seated in a window was a young man named Eutychus, who was sinking into a deep sleep as Paul talked on and on. When he was sound asleep, he fell to the ground from the third story and was picked up dead. 10 Paul went down, threw himself on the young man and put his arms around him. "Don't be alarmed," he said. "He's alive!" 11 Then he went upstairs again and broke bread and ate. After talking until daylight, he left. 12 The people took the young man home alive and were greatly comforted.

Paul's Farewell to the Ephesian Elders

13 We went on ahead to the ship and sailed for Assos, where we were going to take Paul aboard. He had made this arrangement because he was going there on foot. 14 When he met us at Assos, we took him aboard and went on to Mitylene. 15 The next day we set sail from there and arrived off Chios. The day after that we crossed over to Samos, and on the following day arrived at Miletus. 16 Paul had decided to sail past Ephesus to avoid spending time in the province of Asia, for he was in a hurry to reach Jerusalem, if possible, by the day of Pentecost.

17 From Miletus, Paul sent to Ephesus for the elders of the church. 18 When they arrived, he said to them: "You know how I lived the whole time I was with you, from the first day I came into the province of Asia. 19 I served the Lord with great humility and with tears and in the midst of severe testing by the plots of my Jewish opponents. 20 You know that I have not hesitated to preach anything that would be helpful to you but have taught you publicly and from house to house. 21 I have declared to both Jews and Greeks that they must turn to God in repentance and have faith in our Lord Jesus.

22 "And now, compelled by the Spirit, I am going to Jerusalem, not knowing what will happen to me there. 23 I only know that in every city the Holy Spirit warns me that prison and hardships are facing me. 24 However,

I consider my life worth nothing to me; my only aim is to finish the race and complete the task the Lord Jesus has given me — the task of testifying to the good news of God's grace.

25 "Now I know that none of you among whom I have gone about preaching the kingdom will ever see me again. 26 Therefore, I declare to you today that I am innocent of the blood of any of you. 27 For I have not hesitated to proclaim to you the whole will of God. 28 Keep watch over yourselves and all the flock of which the Holy Spirit has made you overseers. Be shepherds of the church of God,[a] which he bought with his own blood.[b] 29 I know that after I leave, savage wolves will come in among you and will not spare the flock. 30 Even from your own number men will arise and distort the truth in order to draw away disciples after them. 31 So be on your guard! Remember that for three years I never stopped warning each of you night and day with tears.

32 "Now I commit you to God and to the word of his grace, which can build you up and give you an inheritance among all those who are sanctified. 33 I have not coveted anyone's silver or gold or clothing. 34 You yourselves know that these hands of mine have supplied my own needs and the needs of my companions. 35 In everything I did, I showed you that by this kind of hard work we must help the weak, remembering the words the Lord Jesus himself said: 'It is more blessed to give than to receive.' "

36 When Paul had finished speaking, he knelt down with all of them and prayed. 37 They all wept as they embraced him and kissed him. 38 What grieved them most was his statement that they would never see his face again. Then they accompanied him to the ship.

On to Jerusalem

21 After we had torn ourselves away from them, we put out to sea and sailed straight to Kos. The next day we went to Rhodes and from there to Patara. 2 We found a ship crossing over to Phoenicia, went on board and set sail. 3 After sighting Cyprus and passing to the south of it, we sailed on to Syria. We landed at Tyre, where our ship was to unload its cargo. 4 We sought out the disciples there and stayed with them seven days. Through the Spirit they urged Paul not to go on to Jerusalem. 5 When it was time to leave, we left and continued on our way. All of them, including wives and children, accompanied us out of the city, and there on the beach we knelt to pray. 6 After saying goodbye to each other, we went aboard the ship, and they returned home.

7 We continued our voyage from Tyre and landed at Ptolemais, where we greeted the brothers and sisters and stayed with them for a day. 8 Leaving the next day, we reached Caesarea and stayed at the house of Philip the evangelist, one of the Seven. 9 He had four unmarried daughters who prophesied.

10 After we had been there a number of days, a prophet named Agabus came down from Judea. 11 Coming over to us, he took Paul's belt, tied his own hands and feet with it and said, "The Holy Spirit says, 'In this way the Jewish leaders in Jerusalem will bind the owner of this belt and will hand him over to the Gentiles.' "

12 When we heard this, we and the people there pleaded with Paul not to go up to Jerusalem. 13 Then Paul answered, "Why are you weeping and breaking my heart? I am ready not only to be bound, but also to die in Jerusalem for the name of the Lord Jesus." 14 When he would not be dissuaded, we gave up and said, "The Lord's will be done."

15 After this, we started on our way up to Jerusalem. 16 Some of the disciples from Caesarea accompanied us and brought us to the home of Mnason, where we were to stay. He was a man from Cyprus and one of the early disciples.

Paul's Arrival at Jerusalem

17 When we arrived at Jerusalem, the brothers and sisters received us warmly. 18 The next day Paul and the rest of us went to see James, and all the elders were present. 19 Paul greeted them and reported in detail what God had done among the Gentiles through his ministry.

20 When they heard this, they praised God. Then they said to Paul: "You see, brother, how many thousands of Jews have believed, and all of them are zealous for the

[a] *28* Many manuscripts *of the Lord* [b] *28* Or *with the blood of his own Son.*

law. 21 They have been informed that you
teach all the Jews who live among the Gen-
tiles to turn away from Moses, telling them
not to circumcise their children or live ac-
cording to our customs. 22 What shall we do?
They will certainly hear that you have come,
23 so do what we tell you. There are four men
with us who have made a vow. 24 Take these
men, join in their purification rites and pay
their expenses, so that they can have their
heads shaved. Then everyone will know
there is no truth in these reports about you,
but that you yourself are living in obedience
to the law. 25 As for the Gentile believers, we
have written to them our decision that they
should abstain from food sacrificed to idols,
from blood, from the meat of strangled ani-
mals and from sexual immorality."

26 The next day Paul took the men and
purified himself along with them. Then he
went to the temple to give notice of the date
when the days of purification would end
and the offering would be made for each of
them.

Paul Arrested

27 When the seven days were nearly over,
some Jews from the province of Asia saw
Paul at the temple. They stirred up the whole
crowd and seized him, 28 shouting, "Fel-
low Israelites, help us! This is the man who
teaches everyone everywhere against our
people and our law and this place. And be-
sides, he has brought Greeks into the temple
and defiled this holy place." 29 (They had pre-
viously seen Trophimus the Ephesian in the
city with Paul and assumed that Paul had
brought him into the temple.)

30 The whole city was aroused, and the
people came running from all directions.
Seizing Paul, they dragged him from the
temple, and immediately the gates were
shut. 31 While they were trying to kill him,
news reached the commander of the Roman
troops that the whole city of Jerusalem was
in an uproar. 32 He at once took some offi-
cers and soldiers and ran down to the crowd.
When the rioters saw the commander and
his soldiers, they stopped beating Paul.

33 The commander came up and arrested
him and ordered him to be bound with two
chains. Then he asked who he was and what
he had done. 34 Some in the crowd shouted
one thing and some another, and since the
commander could not get at the truth be-
cause of the uproar, he ordered that Paul
be taken into the barracks. 35 When Paul
reached the steps, the violence of the mob
was so great he had to be carried by the sol-
diers. 36 The crowd that followed kept shout-
ing, "Get rid of him!"

Paul Speaks to the Crowd

37 As the soldiers were about to take Paul
into the barracks, he asked the commander,
"May I say something to you?"

"Do you speak Greek?" he replied.
38 "Aren't you the Egyptian who started a re-
volt and led four thousand terrorists out into
the wilderness some time ago?"

39 Paul answered, "I am a Jew, from Tarsus
in Cilicia, a citizen of no ordinary city. Please
let me speak to the people."

40 After receiving the commander's permis-
sion, Paul stood on the steps and motioned to
the crowd. When they were all silent, he said
22 to them in Aramaic[a]: 1 "Brothers and
fathers, listen now to my defense."

2 When they heard him speak to them in
Aramaic, they became very quiet.

Then Paul said: 3 "I am a Jew, born in Tar-
sus of Cilicia, but brought up in this city. I
studied under Gamaliel and was thoroughly
trained in the law of our ancestors. I was just
as zealous for God as any of you are today.
4 I persecuted the followers of this Way to
their death, arresting both men and women
and throwing them into prison, 5 as the high
priest and all the Council can themselves
testify. I even obtained letters from them
to their associates in Damascus, and went
there to bring these people as prisoners to
Jerusalem to be punished.

6 "About noon as I came near Damascus,
suddenly a bright light from heaven flashed
around me. 7 I fell to the ground and heard a
voice say to me, 'Saul! Saul! Why do you per-
secute me?'

8 "'Who are you, Lord?' I asked.

"'I am Jesus of Nazareth, whom you are
persecuting,' he replied. 9 My companions
saw the light, but they did not understand
the voice of him who was speaking to me.

10 "'What shall I do, Lord?' I asked.

[a] *40* Or possibly *Hebrew*; also in 22:2

"'Get up,' the Lord said, 'and go into Damascus. There you will be told all that you have been assigned to do.' 11My companions led me by the hand into Damascus, because the brilliance of the light had blinded me.

12"A man named Ananias came to see me. He was a devout observer of the law and highly respected by all the Jews living there. 13He stood beside me and said, 'Brother Saul, receive your sight!' And at that very moment I was able to see him.

14"Then he said: 'The God of our ancestors has chosen you to know his will and to see the Righteous One and to hear words from his mouth. 15You will be his witness to all people of what you have seen and heard. 16And now what are you waiting for? Get up, be baptized and wash your sins away, calling on his name.'

17"When I returned to Jerusalem and was praying at the temple, I fell into a trance 18and saw the Lord speaking to me. 'Quick!' he said. 'Leave Jerusalem immediately, because the people here will not accept your testimony about me.'

19"'Lord,' I replied, 'these people know that I went from one synagogue to another to imprison and beat those who believe in you. 20And when the blood of your martyr[a] Stephen was shed, I stood there giving my approval and guarding the clothes of those who were killing him.'

21"Then the Lord said to me, 'Go; I will send you far away to the Gentiles.'"

Paul the Roman Citizen

22The crowd listened to Paul until he said this. Then they raised their voices and shouted, "Rid the earth of him! He's not fit to live!"

23As they were shouting and throwing off their cloaks and flinging dust into the air, 24the commander ordered that Paul be taken into the barracks. He directed that he be flogged and interrogated in order to find out why the people were shouting at him like this. 25As they stretched him out to flog him, Paul said to the centurion standing there, "Is it legal for you to flog a Roman citizen who hasn't even been found guilty?"

26When the centurion heard this, he went to the commander and reported it. "What are you going to do?" he asked. "This man is a Roman citizen."

27The commander went to Paul and asked, "Tell me, are you a Roman citizen?"

"Yes, I am," he answered.

28Then the commander said, "I had to pay a lot of money for my citizenship."

"But I was born a citizen," Paul replied.

29Those who were about to interrogate him withdrew immediately. The commander himself was alarmed when he realized that he had put Paul, a Roman citizen, in chains.

Paul Before the Sanhedrin

30The commander wanted to find out exactly why Paul was being accused by the Jews. So the next day he released him and ordered the chief priests and all the members of the Sanhedrin to assemble. Then he brought Paul and had him stand before them.

23 Paul looked straight at the Sanhedrin and said, "My brothers, I have fulfilled my duty to God in all good conscience to this day." 2At this the high priest Ananias ordered those standing near Paul to strike him on the mouth. 3Then Paul said to him, "God will strike you, you whitewashed wall! You sit there to judge me according to the law, yet you yourself violate the law by commanding that I be struck!"

4Those who were standing near Paul said, "How dare you insult God's high priest!"

5Paul replied, "Brothers, I did not realize that he was the high priest; for it is written: 'Do not speak evil about the ruler of your people.'[b]"

6Then Paul, knowing that some of them were Sadducees and the others Pharisees, called out in the Sanhedrin, "My brothers, I am a Pharisee, descended from Pharisees. I stand on trial because of the hope of the resurrection of the dead." 7When he said this, a dispute broke out between the Pharisees and the Sadducees, and the assembly was divided. 8(The Sadducees say that there is no resurrection, and that there are neither angels nor spirits, but the Pharisees believe all these things.)

9There was a great uproar, and some of the teachers of the law who were Pharisees stood

[a] 20 Or *witness* [b] 5 Exodus 22:28

up and argued vigorously. "We find nothing wrong with this man," they said. "What if a spirit or an angel has spoken to him?" 10 The dispute became so violent that the commander was afraid Paul would be torn to pieces by them. He ordered the troops to go down and take him away from them by force and bring him into the barracks.

11 The following night the Lord stood near Paul and said, "Take courage! As you have testified about me in Jerusalem, so you must also testify in Rome."

The Plot to Kill Paul

12 The next morning some Jews formed a conspiracy and bound themselves with an oath not to eat or drink until they had killed Paul. 13 More than forty men were involved in this plot. 14 They went to the chief priests and the elders and said, "We have taken a solemn oath not to eat anything until we have killed Paul. 15 Now then, you and the Sanhedrin petition the commander to bring him before you on the pretext of wanting more accurate information about his case. We are ready to kill him before he gets here."

16 But when the son of Paul's sister heard of this plot, he went into the barracks and told Paul.

17 Then Paul called one of the centurions and said, "Take this young man to the commander; he has something to tell him." 18 So he took him to the commander.

The centurion said, "Paul, the prisoner, sent for me and asked me to bring this young man to you because he has something to tell you."

19 The commander took the young man by the hand, drew him aside and asked, "What is it you want to tell me?"

20 He said: "Some Jews have agreed to ask you to bring Paul before the Sanhedrin tomorrow on the pretext of wanting more accurate information about him. 21 Don't give in to them, because more than forty of them are waiting in ambush for him. They have taken an oath not to eat or drink until they have killed him. They are ready now, waiting for your consent to their request."

22 The commander dismissed the young man with this warning: "Don't tell anyone that you have reported this to me."

Paul Transferred to Caesarea

23 Then he called two of his centurions and ordered them, "Get ready a detachment of two hundred soldiers, seventy horsemen and two hundred spearmen[a] to go to Caesarea at nine tonight. 24 Provide horses for Paul so that he may be taken safely to Governor Felix."

25 He wrote a letter as follows:

26 Claudius Lysias,

To His Excellency, Governor Felix:

Greetings.

27 This man was seized by the Jews and they were about to kill him, but I came with my troops and rescued him, for I had learned that he is a Roman citizen. 28 I wanted to know why they were accusing him, so I brought him to their Sanhedrin. 29 I found that the accusation had to do with questions about their law, but there was no charge against him that deserved death or imprisonment. 30 When I was informed of a plot to be carried out against the man, I sent him to you at once. I also ordered his accusers to present to you their case against him.

31 So the soldiers, carrying out their orders, took Paul with them during the night and brought him as far as Antipatris. 32 The next day they let the cavalry go on with him, while they returned to the barracks. 33 When the cavalry arrived in Caesarea, they delivered the letter to the governor and handed Paul over to him. 34 The governor read the letter and asked what province he was from. Learning that he was from Cilicia, 35 he said, "I will hear your case when your accusers get here." Then he ordered that Paul be kept under guard in Herod's palace.

Paul's Trial Before Felix

24 Five days later the high priest Ananias went down to Caesarea with some of the elders and a lawyer named Tertullus, and they brought their charges against Paul before the governor. 2 When Paul was called in, Tertullus presented his case before Felix:

[a] *23* The meaning of the Greek for this word is uncertain.

HOW GREAT THOU ART

Stuart K. Hine

O Lord my God
When I in awesome wonder
Consider all the worlds
Thy hands have made
I see the stars
I hear the rolling thunder
Thy pow'r thru'out
The universe displayed

Then sings my soul
My Savior God to thee
How great thou art
How great thou art
Then sings my soul
My Savior God to thee
How great thou art
How great thou art

When thru the woods
And forest glades I wander
And hear the birds
Sing sweetly in the trees
When I look down
From lofty mountain grandeur
And hear the brook
And feel the gentle breeze

And when I think
That God his Son not sparing
Sent him to die
I scarce can take it in
That on the cross
My burden gladly bearing
He bled and died
To take away my sin

When Christ shall come
With shout of acclamation
And take me home
What joy shall fill my heart
Then I shall bow
In humble adoration
And there proclaim
My God, "how great thou art"

THE INSPIRATION

Sing to the LORD *a new song; sing to the* LORD, *all the earth. Sing to the* LORD, *praise his name; proclaim his salvation day after day. Declare his glory among the nations, his marvelous deeds among all peoples. For great is the* LORD *and most worthy of praise.*

— Psalm 96:1 – 4

Read also: Psalm 93:1; Psalm 104:1 – 3

BEHIND THE SONG

Many people mistakenly believe that the classic English hymn "How Great Thou Art" is centuries old. The truth is that this beloved song evolved over several decades; the most popular English version was finished in 1949 by the British missionary Stuart K. Hine, after nearly a century of adaptation and translation. It now ranks second only to "Amazing Grace" among the favorite English hymns of the world.

The roots of the song go back to Sweden in 1885, when a pastor named Carl Gustav Boberg wrote a nine stanza poem called *"O Store Gud"* (O Great God), which was inspired by a sudden and violent mid-day thunderstorm. When modern printing technology made books and music affordable enough for missionaries to use and carry, the poem spread throughout Europe and Asia. It was paired with the melody of a traditional Swedish folk song discovered by Hine while he and his wife were ministering in Ukraine in 1931. Hine adopted the concept of the song, wrote four original English verses and distributed his version throughout his missionary network around the world. He copyrighted his final version of the song in 1949.

The song was already well-known in the United Kingdom, but when Billy Graham and his featured gospel vocalist George Beverly Shea began using the song at their massive crusades in the 1950s, the popularity of the song skyrocketed. New recordings by known and independent artists continue to appear every year.

Selah

Are you ever overwhelmed by nature in a way that leads you to worship? "How Great Thou Art," like Psalm 104, is a striking example of the worship that God's wonders can inspire. Sometimes the most terrifying experiences can remind us of how small we are and how great God is.

Spend some time considering some of the storms in your life, either literal or figurative, and speak to God about how you experienced his greatness in the midst of them.

"We have enjoyed a long period of peace under you, and your foresight has brought about reforms in this nation. 3Everywhere and in every way, most excellent Felix, we acknowledge this with profound gratitude. 4But in order not to weary you further, I would request that you be kind enough to hear us briefly.

5"We have found this man to be a troublemaker, stirring up riots among the Jews all over the world. He is a ringleader of the Nazarene sect 6and even tried to desecrate the temple; so we seized him. [7][a] 8By examining him yourself you will be able to learn the truth about all these charges we are bringing against him."

9The other Jews joined in the accusation, asserting that these things were true.

10When the governor motioned for him to speak, Paul replied: "I know that for a number of years you have been a judge over this nation; so I gladly make my defense. 11You can easily verify that no more than twelve days ago I went up to Jerusalem to worship. 12My accusers did not find me arguing with anyone at the temple, or stirring up a crowd in the synagogues or anywhere else in the city. 13And they cannot prove to you the charges they are now making against me. 14However, I admit that I worship the God of our ancestors as a follower of the Way, which they call a sect. I believe everything that is in accordance with the Law and that is written in the Prophets, 15and I have the same hope in God as these men themselves have, that there will be a resurrection of both the righteous and the wicked. 16So I strive always to keep my conscience clear before God and man.

17"After an absence of several years, I came to Jerusalem to bring my people gifts for the poor and to present offerings. 18I was ceremonially clean when they found me in the temple courts doing this. There was no crowd with me, nor was I involved in any disturbance. 19But there are some Jews from the province of Asia, who ought to be here before you and bring charges if they have anything against me. 20Or these who are here should state what crime they found in me when I stood before the Sanhedrin— 21unless it was this one thing I shouted as I stood in their presence: 'It is concerning the resurrection of the dead that I am on trial before you today.'"

22Then Felix, who was well acquainted with the Way, adjourned the proceedings. "When Lysias the commander comes," he said, "I will decide your case." 23He ordered the centurion to keep Paul under guard but to give him some freedom and permit his friends to take care of his needs.

24Several days later Felix came with his wife Drusilla, who was Jewish. He sent for Paul and listened to him as he spoke about faith in Christ Jesus. 25As Paul talked about righteousness, self-control and the judgment to come, Felix was afraid and said, "That's enough for now! You may leave. When I find it convenient, I will send for you." 26At the same time he was hoping that Paul would offer him a bribe, so he sent for him frequently and talked with him.

27When two years had passed, Felix was succeeded by Porcius Festus, but because Felix wanted to grant a favor to the Jews, he left Paul in prison.

Paul's Trial Before Festus

25 Three days after arriving in the province, Festus went up from Caesarea to Jerusalem, 2where the chief priests and the Jewish leaders appeared before him and presented the charges against Paul. 3They requested Festus, as a favor to them, to have Paul transferred to Jerusalem, for they were preparing an ambush to kill him along the way. 4Festus answered, "Paul is being held at Caesarea, and I myself am going there soon. 5Let some of your leaders come with me, and if the man has done anything wrong, they can press charges against him there."

6After spending eight or ten days with them, Festus went down to Caesarea. The next day he convened the court and ordered that Paul be brought before him. 7When Paul came in, the Jews who had come down from Jerusalem stood around him. They brought many serious charges against him, but they could not prove them.

[a] 6-8 Some manuscripts include here *him, and we would have judged him in accordance with our law. 7But the commander Lysias came and took him from us with much violence, 8ordering his accusers to come before you.*

8Then Paul made his defense: "I have
done nothing wrong against the Jewish law
or against the temple or against Caesar."
9Festus, wishing to do the Jews a favor,
said to Paul, "Are you willing to go up to Je-
rusalem and stand trial before me there on
these charges?"
10Paul answered: "I am now standing
before Caesar's court, where I ought to be
tried. I have not done any wrong to the Jews,
as you yourself know very well. 11If, howev-
er, I am guilty of doing anything deserving
death, I do not refuse to die. But if the charg-
es brought against me by these Jews are not
true, no one has the right to hand me over to
them. I appeal to Caesar!"
12After Festus had conferred with his
council, he declared: "You have appealed to
Caesar. To Caesar you will go!"

Festus Consults King Agrippa

13A few days later King Agrippa and Ber-
nice arrived at Caesarea to pay their respects
to Festus. 14Since they were spending many
days there, Festus discussed Paul's case
with the king. He said: "There is a man here
whom Felix left as a prisoner. 15When I went
to Jerusalem, the chief priests and the elders
of the Jews brought charges against him and
asked that he be condemned.
16"I told them that it is not the Roman
custom to hand over anyone before they
have faced their accusers and have had an
opportunity to defend themselves against
the charges. 17When they came here with
me, I did not delay the case, but convened
the court the next day and ordered the man
to be brought in. 18When his accusers got up
to speak, they did not charge him with any
of the crimes I had expected. 19Instead, they
had some points of dispute with him about
their own religion and about a dead man
named Jesus who Paul claimed was alive.
20I was at a loss how to investigate such mat-
ters; so I asked if he would be willing to go
to Jerusalem and stand trial there on these
charges. 21But when Paul made his appeal
to be held over for the Emperor's decision,
I ordered him held until I could send him to
Caesar."
22Then Agrippa said to Festus, "I would
like to hear this man myself."
He replied, "Tomorrow you will hear
him."

Paul Before Agrippa

23The next day Agrippa and Bernice came
with great pomp and entered the audience
room with the high-ranking military officers
and the prominent men of the city. At the
command of Festus, Paul was brought in.
24Festus said: "King Agrippa, and all who are
present with us, you see this man! The whole
Jewish community has petitioned me about
him in Jerusalem and here in Caesarea,
shouting that he ought not to live any longer.
25I found he had done nothing deserving of
death, but because he made his appeal to
the Emperor I decided to send him to Rome.
26But I have nothing definite to write to His
Majesty about him. Therefore I have brought
him before all of you, and especially before
you, King Agrippa, so that as a result of this
investigation I may have something to write.
27For I think it is unreasonable to send a
prisoner on to Rome without specifying the
charges against him."
26 Then Agrippa said to Paul, "You have
permission to speak for yourself."
So Paul motioned with his hand and be-
gan his defense: 2"King Agrippa, I consider
myself fortunate to stand before you today
as I make my defense against all the accusa-
tions of the Jews, 3and especially so because
you are well acquainted with all the Jewish
customs and controversies. Therefore, I beg
you to listen to me patiently.
4"The Jewish people all know the way I
have lived ever since I was a child, from the
beginning of my life in my own country, and
also in Jerusalem. 5They have known me for
a long time and can testify, if they are will-
ing, that I conformed to the strictest sect of
our religion, living as a Pharisee. 6And now
it is because of my hope in what God has
promised our ancestors that I am on trial
today. 7This is the promise our twelve tribes
are hoping to see fulfilled as they earnestly
serve God day and night. King Agrippa, it is
because of this hope that these Jews are ac-
cusing me. 8Why should any of you consider
it incredible that God raises the dead?
9"I too was convinced that I ought to do all
that was possible to oppose the name of Jesus
of Nazareth. 10And that is just what I did in Je-
rusalem. On the authority of the chief priests
I put many of the Lord's people in prison,
and when they were put to death, I cast my
vote against them. 11Many a time I went

from one synagogue to another to have them punished, and I tried to force them to blaspheme. I was so obsessed with persecuting them that I even hunted them down in foreign cities.

12“On one of these journeys I was going to Damascus with the authority and commission of the chief priests. 13About noon, King Agrippa, as I was on the road, I saw a light from heaven, brighter than the sun, blazing around me and my companions. 14We all fell to the ground, and I heard a voice saying to me in Aramaic,[a] ‘Saul, Saul, why do you persecute me? It is hard for you to kick against the goads.’

15“Then I asked, ‘Who are you, Lord?’

“‘I am Jesus, whom you are persecuting,’ the Lord replied. 16‘Now get up and stand on your feet. I have appeared to you to appoint you as a servant and as a witness of what you have seen and will see of me. 17I will rescue you from your own people and from the Gentiles. I am sending you to them 18to open their eyes and turn them from darkness to light, and from the power of Satan to God, so that they may receive forgiveness of sins and a place among those who are sanctified by faith in me.’

19“So then, King Agrippa, I was not disobedient to the vision from heaven. 20First to those in Damascus, then to those in Jerusalem and in all Judea, and then to the Gentiles, I preached that they should repent and turn to God and demonstrate their repentance by their deeds. 21That is why some Jews seized me in the temple courts and tried to kill me. 22But God has helped me to this very day; so I stand here and testify to small and great alike. I am saying nothing beyond what the prophets and Moses said would happen — 23that the Messiah would suffer and, as the first to rise from the dead, would bring the message of light to his own people and to the Gentiles.”

24At this point Festus interrupted Paul’s defense. “You are out of your mind, Paul!” he shouted. “Your great learning is driving you insane.”

25“I am not insane, most excellent Festus,” Paul replied. “What I am saying is true and reasonable. 26The king is familiar with these things, and I can speak freely to him. I am convinced that none of this has escaped his notice, because it was not done in a corner. 27King Agrippa, do you believe the prophets? I know you do.”

28Then Agrippa said to Paul, “Do you think that in such a short time you can persuade me to be a Christian?”

29Paul replied, “Short time or long — I pray to God that not only you but all who are listening to me today may become what I am, except for these chains.”

30The king rose, and with him the governor and Bernice and those sitting with them. 31After they left the room, they began saying to one another, “This man is not doing anything that deserves death or imprisonment.”

32Agrippa said to Festus, “This man could have been set free if he had not appealed to Caesar.”

Paul Sails for Rome

27 When it was decided that we would sail for Italy, Paul and some other prisoners were handed over to a centurion named Julius, who belonged to the Imperial Regiment. 2We boarded a ship from Adramyttium about to sail for ports along the coast of the province of Asia, and we put out to sea. Aristarchus, a Macedonian from Thessalonica, was with us.

3The next day we landed at Sidon; and Julius, in kindness to Paul, allowed him to go to his friends so they might provide for his needs. 4From there we put out to sea again and passed to the lee of Cyprus because the winds were against us. 5When we had sailed across the open sea off the coast of Cilicia and Pamphylia, we landed at Myra in Lycia. 6There the centurion found an Alexandrian ship sailing for Italy and put us on board. 7We made slow headway for many days and had difficulty arriving off Cnidus. When the wind did not allow us to hold our course, we sailed to the lee of Crete, opposite Salmone. 8We moved along the coast with difficulty and came to a place called Fair Havens, near the town of Lasea.

9Much time had been lost, and sailing had already become dangerous because by now it was after the Day of Atonement.[b] So Paul warned them, 10“Men, I can see that our

[a] 14 Or *Hebrew*   [b] 9 That is, Yom Kippur

voyage is going to be disastrous and bring great loss to ship and cargo, and to our own lives also." 11 But the centurion, instead of listening to what Paul said, followed the advice of the pilot and of the owner of the ship. 12 Since the harbor was unsuitable to winter in, the majority decided that we should sail on, hoping to reach Phoenix and winter there. This was a harbor in Crete, facing both southwest and northwest.

The Storm

13 When a gentle south wind began to blow, they saw their opportunity; so they weighed anchor and sailed along the shore of Crete. 14 Before very long, a wind of hurricane force, called the Northeaster, swept down from the island. 15 The ship was caught by the storm and could not head into the wind; so we gave way to it and were driven along. 16 As we passed to the lee of a small island called Cauda, we were hardly able to make the lifeboat secure, 17 so the men hoisted it aboard. Then they passed ropes under the ship itself to hold it together. Because they were afraid they would run aground on the sandbars of Syrtis, they lowered the sea anchor[a] and let the ship be driven along. 18 We took such a violent battering from the storm that the next day they began to throw the cargo overboard. 19 On the third day, they threw the ship's tackle overboard with their own hands. 20 When neither sun nor stars appeared for many days and the storm continued raging, we finally gave up all hope of being saved.

21 After they had gone a long time without food, Paul stood up before them and said: "Men, you should have taken my advice not to sail from Crete; then you would have spared yourselves this damage and loss. 22 But now I urge you to keep up your courage, because not one of you will be lost; only the ship will be destroyed. 23 Last night an angel of the God to whom I belong and whom I serve stood beside me 24 and said, 'Do not be afraid, Paul. You must stand trial before Caesar; and God has graciously given you the lives of all who sail with you.' 25 So keep up your courage, men, for I have faith in God that it will happen just as he told me. 26 Nevertheless, we must run aground on some island."

The Shipwreck

27 On the fourteenth night we were still being driven across the Adriatic[b] Sea, when about midnight the sailors sensed they were approaching land. 28 They took soundings and found that the water was a hundred and twenty feet[c] deep. A short time later they took soundings again and found it was ninety feet[d] deep. 29 Fearing that we would be dashed against the rocks, they dropped four anchors from the stern and prayed for daylight. 30 In an attempt to escape from the ship, the sailors let the lifeboat down into the sea, pretending they were going to lower some anchors from the bow. 31 Then Paul said to the centurion and the soldiers, "Unless these men stay with the ship, you cannot be saved." 32 So the soldiers cut the ropes that held the lifeboat and let it drift away.

33 Just before dawn Paul urged them all to eat. "For the last fourteen days," he said, "you have been in constant suspense and have gone without food—you haven't eaten anything. 34 Now I urge you to take some food. You need it to survive. Not one of you will lose a single hair from his head." 35 After he said this, he took some bread and gave thanks to God in front of them all. Then he broke it and began to eat. 36 They were all encouraged and ate some food themselves. 37 Altogether there were 276 of us on board. 38 When they had eaten as much as they wanted, they lightened the ship by throwing the grain into the sea.

39 When daylight came, they did not recognize the land, but they saw a bay with a sandy beach, where they decided to run the ship aground if they could. 40 Cutting loose the anchors, they left them in the sea and at the same time untied the ropes that held the rudders. Then they hoisted the foresail to the wind and made for the beach. 41 But the ship struck a sandbar and ran aground. The bow stuck fast and would not move, and the stern was broken to pieces by the pounding of the surf.

42 The soldiers planned to kill the prisoners to prevent any of them from swimming away

[a] 17 Or *the sails* [b] 27 In ancient times the name referred to an area extending well south of Italy.
[c] 28 Or about 37 meters [d] 28 Or about 27 meters

and escaping. 43But the centurion wanted to
spare Paul's life and kept them from carrying
out their plan. He ordered those who could
swim to jump overboard first and get to land.
44The rest were to get there on planks or on
other pieces of the ship. In this way everyone
reached land safely.

Paul Ashore on Malta

28 Once safely on shore, we found out
that the island was called Malta.
2The islanders showed us unusual kind-
ness. They built a fire and welcomed us all
because it was raining and cold. 3Paul gath-
ered a pile of brushwood and, as he put it on
the fire, a viper, driven out by the heat, fas-
tened itself on his hand. 4When the island-
ers saw the snake hanging from his hand,
they said to each other, "This man must be
a murderer; for though he escaped from the
sea, the goddess Justice has not allowed him
to live." 5But Paul shook the snake off into
the fire and suffered no ill effects. 6The peo-
ple expected him to swell up or suddenly
fall dead; but after waiting a long time and
seeing nothing unusual happen to him,
they changed their minds and said he was
a god.

7There was an estate nearby that belonged
to Publius, the chief official of the island. He
welcomed us to his home and showed us
generous hospitality for three days. 8His fa-
ther was sick in bed, suffering from fever and
dysentery. Paul went in to see him and, after
prayer, placed his hands on him and healed
him. 9When this had happened, the rest of
the sick on the island came and were cured.
10They honored us in many ways; and when
we were ready to sail, they furnished us with
the supplies we needed.

Paul's Arrival at Rome

11After three months we put out to sea in a
ship that had wintered in the island—it was
an Alexandrian ship with the figurehead of
the twin gods Castor and Pollux. 12We put
in at Syracuse and stayed there three days.
13From there we set sail and arrived at Rhe-
gium. The next day the south wind came up,
and on the following day we reached Puteoli.
14There we found some brothers and sisters
who invited us to spend a week with them.
And so we came to Rome. 15The brothers and
sisters there had heard that we were coming,
and they traveled as far as the Forum of Ap-
pius and the Three Taverns to meet us. At the
sight of these people Paul thanked God and
was encouraged. 16When we got to Rome,
Paul was allowed to live by himself, with a
soldier to guard him.

Paul Preaches at Rome Under Guard

17Three days later he called together the
local Jewish leaders. When they had as-
sembled, Paul said to them: "My brothers,
although I have done nothing against our
people or against the customs of our ances-
tors, I was arrested in Jerusalem and hand-
ed over to the Romans. 18They examined me
and wanted to release me, because I was not
guilty of any crime deserving death. 19The
Jews objected, so I was compelled to make an
appeal to Caesar. I certainly did not intend
to bring any charge against my own people.
20For this reason I have asked to see you and
talk with you. It is because of the hope of Is-
rael that I am bound with this chain."

21They replied, "We have not received any
letters from Judea concerning you, and none
of our people who have come from there has
reported or said anything bad about you.
22But we want to hear what your views are,
for we know that people everywhere are
talking against this sect."

23They arranged to meet Paul on a certain
day, and came in even larger numbers to the
place where he was staying. He witnessed to
them from morning till evening, explaining
about the kingdom of God, and from the Law
of Moses and from the Prophets he tried to
persuade them about Jesus. 24Some were
convinced by what he said, but others would
not believe. 25They disagreed among them-
selves and began to leave after Paul had
made this final statement: "The Holy Spirit
spoke the truth to your ancestors when he
said through Isaiah the prophet:

26" 'Go to this people and say,
"You will be ever hearing but never
understanding;
you will be ever seeing but never
perceiving."
27For this people's heart has become
calloused;
they hardly hear with their ears,
and they have closed their eyes.
Otherwise they might see with their eyes,
hear with their ears,

understand with their hearts
and turn, and I would heal them.'[a]

28 "Therefore I want you to know that God's
salvation has been sent to the Gentiles, and
they will listen!" [29][b]

30 For two whole years Paul stayed there
in his own rented house and welcomed all
who came to see him. 31 He proclaimed the
kingdom of God and taught about the Lord
Jesus Christ — with all boldness and without
hindrance!

[a] 27 Isaiah 6:9,10 (see Septuagint) [b] 29 Some manuscripts include here *After he said this, the Jews left, arguing vigorously among themselves.*

ROMANS

1 Paul, a servant of Christ Jesus, called
to be an apostle and set apart for the
gospel of God— 2the gospel he promised
beforehand through his prophets in the
Holy Scriptures 3regarding his Son, who as
to his earthly life[a] was a descendant of Da-
vid, 4and who through the Spirit of holiness
was appointed the Son of God in power[b] by
his resurrection from the dead: Jesus Christ
our Lord. 5Through him we received grace
and apostleship to call all the Gentiles to
the obedience that comes from[c] faith for his
name's sake. 6And you also are among those
Gentiles who are called to belong to Jesus
Christ.

7To all in Rome who are loved by God and
called to be his holy people:

Grace and peace to you from God our Fa-
ther and from the Lord Jesus Christ.

Paul's Longing to Visit Rome

8First, I thank my God through Jesus
Christ for all of you, because your faith is be-
ing reported all over the world. 9God, whom
I serve in my spirit in preaching the gospel of
his Son, is my witness how constantly I re-
member you 10in my prayers at all times; and
I pray that now at last by God's will the way
may be opened for me to come to you.

11I long to see you so that I may impart to
you some spiritual gift to make you strong—
12that is, that you and I may be mutually
encouraged by each other's faith. 13I do not
want you to be unaware, brothers and sis-
ters,[d] that I planned many times to come to
you (but have been prevented from doing so
until now) in order that I might have a har-
vest among you, just as I have had among the
other Gentiles.

14I am obligated both to Greeks and non-
Greeks, both to the wise and the foolish.
15That is why I am so eager to preach the gos-
pel also to you who are in Rome.

16For I am not ashamed of the gospel, be-
cause it is the power of God that brings sal-
vation to everyone who believes: first to the
Jew, then to the Gentile. 17For in the gospel
the righteousness of God is revealed—a
righteousness that is by faith from first to
last,[e] just as it is written: "The righteous will
live by faith."[f]

God's Wrath Against Sinful Humanity

18The wrath of God is being revealed
from heaven against all the godlessness
and wickedness of people, who suppress the
truth by their wickedness, 19since what may
be known about God is plain to them, be-
cause God has made it plain to them. 20For
since the creation of the world God's invisi-
ble qualities—his eternal power and divine
nature—have been clearly seen, being un-
derstood from what has been made, so that
people are without excuse.

21For although they knew God, they nei-
ther glorified him as God nor gave thanks to
him, but their thinking became futile and
their foolish hearts were darkened. 22Al-
though they claimed to be wise, they be-
came fools 23and exchanged the glory of the
immortal God for images made to look like a
mortal human being and birds and animals
and reptiles.

24Therefore God gave them over in the
sinful desires of their hearts to sexual im-
purity for the degrading of their bodies with
one another. 25They exchanged the truth
about God for a lie, and worshiped and
served created things rather than the Crea-
tor—who is forever praised. Amen.

26Because of this, God gave them over to
shameful lusts. Even their women exchanged
natural sexual relations for unnatural ones.

[a] 3 Or *who according to the flesh* [b] 4 Or *was declared with power to be the Son of God* [c] 5 Or *that is*
[d] 13 The Greek word for *brothers and sisters* (*adelphoi*) refers here to believers, both men and women, as part of God's family; also in 7:1, 4; 8:12, 29; 10:1; 11:25; 12:1; 15:14, 30; 16:14, 17. [e] 17 Or *is from faith to faith* [f] 17 Hab. 2:4

27 In the same way the men also abandoned natural relations with women and were inflamed with lust for one another. Men committed shameful acts with other men, and received in themselves the due penalty for their error.

28 Furthermore, just as they did not think it worthwhile to retain the knowledge of God, so God gave them over to a depraved mind, so that they do what ought not to be done. 29 They have become filled with every kind of wickedness, evil, greed and depravity. They are full of envy, murder, strife, deceit and malice. They are gossips, 30 slanderers, God-haters, insolent, arrogant and boastful; they invent ways of doing evil; they disobey their parents; 31 they have no understanding, no fidelity, no love, no mercy. 32 Although they know God's righteous decree that those who do such things deserve death, they not only continue to do these very things but also approve of those who practice them.

God's Righteous Judgment

2 You, therefore, have no excuse, you who pass judgment on someone else, for at whatever point you judge another, you are condemning yourself, because you who pass judgment do the same things. 2 Now we know that God's judgment against those who do such things is based on truth. 3 So when you, a mere human being, pass judgment on them and yet do the same things, do you think you will escape God's judgment? 4 Or do you show contempt for the riches of his kindness, forbearance and patience, not realizing that God's kindness is intended to lead you to repentance?

5 But because of your stubbornness and your unrepentant heart, you are storing up wrath against yourself for the day of God's wrath, when his righteous judgment will be revealed. 6 God "will repay each person according to what they have done."[a] 7 To those who by persistence in doing good seek glory, honor and immortality, he will give eternal life. 8 But for those who are self-seeking and who reject the truth and follow evil, there will be wrath and anger. 9 There will be trouble and distress for every human being who does evil: first for the Jew, then for the Gentile; 10 but glory, honor and peace for everyone who does good: first for the Jew, then for the Gentile. 11 For God does not show favoritism.

12 All who sin apart from the law will also perish apart from the law, and all who sin under the law will be judged by the law. 13 For it is not those who hear the law who are righteous in God's sight, but it is those who obey the law who will be declared righteous. 14 (Indeed, when Gentiles, who do not have the law, do by nature things required by the law, they are a law for themselves, even though they do not have the law. 15 They show that the requirements of the law are written on their hearts, their consciences also bearing witness, and their thoughts sometimes accusing them and at other times even defending them.) 16 This will take place on the day when God judges people's secrets through Jesus Christ, as my gospel declares.

The Jews and the Law

17 Now you, if you call yourself a Jew; if you rely on the law and boast in God; 18 if you know his will and approve of what is superior because you are instructed by the law; 19 if you are convinced that you are a guide for the blind, a light for those who are in the dark, 20 an instructor of the foolish, a teacher of little children, because you have in the law the embodiment of knowledge and truth— 21 you, then, who teach others, do you not teach yourself? You who preach against stealing, do you steal? 22 You who say that people should not commit adultery, do you commit adultery? You who abhor idols, do you rob temples? 23 You who boast in the law, do you dishonor God by breaking the law? 24 As it is written: "God's name is blasphemed among the Gentiles because of you."[b]

25 Circumcision has value if you observe the law, but if you break the law, you have become as though you had not been circumcised. 26 So then, if those who are not circumcised keep the law's requirements, will they not be regarded as though they were circumcised? 27 The one who is not circumcised physically and yet obeys the law will condemn you who, even though you have the[c] written code and circumcision, are a lawbreaker.

[a] *6* Psalm 62:12; Prov. 24:12 [b] *24* Isaiah 52:5 (see Septuagint); Ezek. 36:20,22 [c] *27* Or *who, by means of a*

28A person is not a Jew who is one only
outwardly, nor is circumcision merely out-
ward and physical. 29No, a person is a Jew
who is one inwardly; and circumcision is
circumcision of the heart, by the Spirit, not
by the written code. Such a person's praise is
not from other people, but from God.

God's Faithfulness

3 What advantage, then, is there in be-
ing a Jew, or what value is there in cir-
cumcision? 2Much in every way! First of all,
the Jews have been entrusted with the very
words of God.

3What if some were unfaithful? Will their
unfaithfulness nullify God's faithfulness?
4Not at all! Let God be true, and every hu-
man being a liar. As it is written:

"So that you may be proved right when
you speak
and prevail when you judge."[a]

5But if our unrighteousness brings out
God's righteousness more clearly, what
shall we say? That God is unjust in bring-
ing his wrath on us? (I am using a human
argument.) 6Certainly not! If that were so,
how could God judge the world? 7Someone
might argue, "If my falsehood enhances
God's truthfulness and so increases his glo-
ry, why am I still condemned as a sinner?"
8Why not say — as some slanderously claim
that we say — "Let us do evil that good may
result"? Their condemnation is just!

No One Is Righteous

9What shall we conclude then? Do we
have any advantage? Not at all! For we have
already made the charge that Jews and Gen-
tiles alike are all under the power of sin. 10As
it is written:

"There is no one righteous, not even one;
11 there is no one who understands;
there is no one who seeks God.
12All have turned away,
they have together become worthless;
there is no one who does good,
not even one."[b]
13"Their throats are open graves;
their tongues practice deceit."[c]
"The poison of vipers is on their lips."[d]
14 "Their mouths are full of cursing
and bitterness."[e]
15"Their feet are swift to shed blood;
16 ruin and misery mark their ways,
17and the way of peace they do not
know."[f]
18 "There is no fear of God before
their eyes."[g]

19Now we know that whatever the law
says, it says to those who are under the law,
so that every mouth may be silenced and
the whole world held accountable to God.
20Therefore no one will be declared righ-
teous in God's sight by the works of the law;
rather, through the law we become con-
scious of our sin.

Righteousness Through Faith

21But now apart from the law the righ-
teousness of God has been made known,
to which the Law and the Prophets testify.
22This righteousness is given through faith
in[h] Jesus Christ to all who believe. There is
no difference between Jew and Gentile, 23for
all have sinned and fall short of the glory of
God, 24and all are justified freely by his grace
through the redemption that came by Christ
Jesus. 25God presented Christ as a sacrifice
of atonement,[i] through the shedding of his
blood — to be received by faith. He did this
to demonstrate his righteousness, because
in his forbearance he had left the sins com-
mitted beforehand unpunished — 26he did
it to demonstrate his righteousness at the
present time, so as to be just and the one who
justifies those who have faith in Jesus.

27Where, then, is boasting? It is excluded.
Because of what law? The law that requires
works? No, because of the law that requires
faith. 28For we maintain that a person is jus-
tified by faith apart from the works of the
law. 29Or is God the God of Jews only? Is he
not the God of Gentiles too? Yes, of Gentiles
too, 30since there is only one God, who will
justify the circumcised by faith and the un-
circumcised through that same faith. 31Do

[a] *4* Psalm 51:4 [b] *12* Psalms 14:1-3; 53:1-3; Eccles. 7:20 [c] *13* Psalm 5:9 [d] *13* Psalm 140:3
[e] *14* Psalm 10:7 (see Septuagint) [f] *17* Isaiah 59:7,8 [g] *18* Psalm 36:1 [h] *22* Or *through the faithfulness of* [i] *25* The Greek for *sacrifice of atonement* refers to the atonement cover on the ark of the covenant (see Lev. 16:15,16).

we, then, nullify the law by this faith? Not at all! Rather, we uphold the law.

Abraham Justified by Faith

4 What then shall we say that Abraham, our forefather according to the flesh, discovered in this matter? [2]If, in fact, Abraham was justified by works, he had something to boast about — but not before God. [3]What does Scripture say? "Abraham believed God, and it was credited to him as righteousness."[a]

[4]Now to the one who works, wages are not credited as a gift but as an obligation. [5]However, to the one who does not work but trusts God who justifies the ungodly, their faith is credited as righteousness. [6]David says the same thing when he speaks of the blessedness of the one to whom God credits righteousness apart from works:

[7]"Blessed are those
whose transgressions are forgiven,
whose sins are covered.
[8]Blessed is the one
whose sin the Lord will never count
against them."[b]

[9]Is this blessedness only for the circumcised, or also for the uncircumcised? We have been saying that Abraham's faith was credited to him as righteousness. [10]Under what circumstances was it credited? Was it after he was circumcised, or before? It was not after, but before! [11]And he received circumcision as a sign, a seal of the righteousness that he had by faith while he was still uncircumcised. So then, he is the father of all who believe but have not been circumcised, in order that righteousness might be credited to them. [12]And he is then also the father of the circumcised who not only are circumcised but who also follow in the footsteps of the faith that our father Abraham had before he was circumcised.

[13]It was not through the law that Abraham and his offspring received the promise that he would be heir of the world, but through the righteousness that comes by faith. [14]For if those who depend on the law are heirs, faith means nothing and the promise is worthless, [15]because the law brings wrath. And where there is no law there is no transgression.

[16]Therefore, the promise comes by faith, so that it may be by grace and may be guaranteed to all Abraham's offspring — not only to those who are of the law but also to those who have the faith of Abraham. He is the father of us all. [17]As it is written: "I have made you a father of many nations."[c] He is our father in the sight of God, in whom he believed — the God who gives life to the dead and calls into being things that were not.

[18]Against all hope, Abraham in hope believed and so became the father of many nations, just as it had been said to him, "So shall your offspring be."[d] [19]Without weakening in his faith, he faced the fact that his body was as good as dead — since he was about a hundred years old — and that Sarah's womb was also dead. [20]Yet he did not waver through unbelief regarding the promise of God, but was strengthened in his faith and gave glory to God, [21]being fully persuaded that God had power to do what he had promised. [22]This is why "it was credited to him as righteousness." [23]The words "it was credited to him" were written not for him alone, [24]but also for us, to whom God will credit righteousness — for us who believe in him who raised Jesus our Lord from the dead. [25]He was delivered over to death for our sins and was raised to life for our justification.

Peace and Hope

5 Therefore, since we have been justified through faith, we[e] have peace with God through our Lord Jesus Christ, [2]through whom we have gained access by faith into this grace in which we now stand. And we[f] boast in the hope of the glory of God. [3]Not only so, but we[f] also glory in our sufferings, because we know that suffering produces perseverance; [4]perseverance, character; and character, hope. [5]And hope does not put us to shame, because God's love has been poured out into our hearts through the Holy Spirit, who has been given to us.

[6]You see, at just the right time, when we were still powerless, Christ died for the ungodly. [7]Very rarely will anyone die for a righteous person, though for a good person someone might possibly dare to die. [8]But God demonstrates his own love for us in this: While we were still sinners, Christ died for us.

[a] *3* Gen. 15:6; also in verse 22 [b] *8* Psalm 32:1,2 [c] *17* Gen. 17:5 [d] *18* Gen. 15:5 [e] *1* Many manuscripts *let us* [f] *2,3* Or *let us*

9Since we have now been justified by his blood, how much more shall we be saved from God's wrath through him! 10For if, while we were God's enemies, we were reconciled to him through the death of his Son, how much more, having been reconciled, shall we be saved through his life! 11Not only is this so, but we also boast in God through our Lord Jesus Christ, through whom we have now received reconciliation.

Death Through Adam, Life Through Christ

12Therefore, just as sin entered the world through one man, and death through sin, and in this way death came to all people, because all sinned—

13To be sure, sin was in the world before the law was given, but sin is not charged against anyone's account where there is no law. 14Nevertheless, death reigned from the time of Adam to the time of Moses, even over those who did not sin by breaking a command, as did Adam, who is a pattern of the one to come.

15But the gift is not like the trespass. For if the many died by the trespass of the one man, how much more did God's grace and the gift that came by the grace of the one man, Jesus Christ, overflow to the many! 16Nor can the gift of God be compared with the result of one man's sin: The judgment followed one sin and brought condemnation, but the gift followed many trespasses and brought justification. 17For if, by the trespass of the one man, death reigned through that one man, how much more will those who receive God's abundant provision of grace and of the gift of righteousness reign in life through the one man, Jesus Christ!

18Consequently, just as one trespass resulted in condemnation for all people, so also one righteous act resulted in justification and life for all people. 19For just as through the disobedience of the one man the many were made sinners, so also through the obedience of the one man the many will be made righteous.

20The law was brought in so that the trespass might increase. But where sin increased, grace increased all the more, 21so that, just as sin reigned in death, so also grace might reign through righteousness to bring eternal life through Jesus Christ our Lord.

Dead to Sin, Alive in Christ

6 What shall we say, then? Shall we go on sinning so that grace may increase? 2By no means! We are those who have died to sin; how can we live in it any longer? 3Or don't you know that all of us who were baptized into Christ Jesus were baptized into his death? 4We were therefore buried with him through baptism into death in order that, just as Christ was raised from the dead through the glory of the Father, we too may live a new life.

5For if we have been united with him in a death like his, we will certainly also be united with him in a resurrection like his. 6For we know that our old self was crucified with him so that the body ruled by sin might be done away with,[a] that we should no longer be slaves to sin— 7because anyone who has died has been set free from sin.

8Now if we died with Christ, we believe that we will also live with him. 9For we know that since Christ was raised from the dead, he cannot die again; death no longer has mastery over him. 10The death he died, he died to sin once for all; but the life he lives, he lives to God.

11In the same way, count yourselves dead to sin but alive to God in Christ Jesus. 12Therefore do not let sin reign in your mortal body so that you obey its evil desires. 13Do not offer any part of yourself to sin as an instrument of wickedness, but rather offer yourselves to God as those who have been brought from death to life; and offer every part of yourself to him as an instrument of righteousness. 14For sin shall no longer be your master, because you are not under the law, but under grace.

Slaves to Righteousness

15What then? Shall we sin because we are not under the law but under grace? By no means! 16Don't you know that when you offer yourselves to someone as obedient slaves, you are slaves of the one you obey—whether you are slaves to sin, which leads to death, or to obedience, which leads to righteousness? 17But thanks be to God that, though you used to be slaves to sin, you have come to

[a] 6 Or *be rendered powerless*

obey from your heart the pattern of teaching that has now claimed your allegiance. 18You have been set free from sin and have become slaves to righteousness.

19I am using an example from everyday life because of your human limitations. Just as you used to offer yourselves as slaves to impurity and to ever-increasing wickedness, so now offer yourselves as slaves to righteousness leading to holiness. 20When you were slaves to sin, you were free from the control of righteousness. 21What benefit did you reap at that time from the things you are now ashamed of? Those things result in death! 22But now that you have been set free from sin and have become slaves of God, the benefit you reap leads to holiness, and the result is eternal life. 23For the wages of sin is death, but the gift of God is eternal life in[a] Christ Jesus our Lord.

Released From the Law, Bound to Christ

7 Do you not know, brothers and sisters — for I am speaking to those who know the law — that the law has authority over someone only as long as that person lives? 2For example, by law a married woman is bound to her husband as long as he is alive, but if her husband dies, she is released from the law that binds her to him. 3So then, if she has sexual relations with another man while her husband is still alive, she is called an adulteress. But if her husband dies, she is released from that law and is not an adulteress if she marries another man.

4So, my brothers and sisters, you also died to the law through the body of Christ, that you might belong to another, to him who was raised from the dead, in order that we might bear fruit for God. 5For when we were in the realm of the flesh,[b] the sinful passions aroused by the law were at work in us, so that we bore fruit for death. 6But now, by dying to what once bound us, we have been released from the law so that we serve in the new way of the Spirit, and not in the old way of the written code.

The Law and Sin

7What shall we say, then? Is the law sinful? Certainly not! Nevertheless, I would not have known what sin was had it not been for the law. For I would not have known what coveting really was if the law had not said, "You shall not covet."[c] 8But sin, seizing the opportunity afforded by the commandment, produced in me every kind of coveting. For apart from the law, sin was dead. 9Once I was alive apart from the law; but when the commandment came, sin sprang to life and I died. 10I found that the very commandment that was intended to bring life actually brought death. 11For sin, seizing the opportunity afforded by the commandment, deceived me, and through the commandment put me to death. 12So then, the law is holy, and the commandment is holy, righteous and good.

13Did that which is good, then, become death to me? By no means! Nevertheless, in order that sin might be recognized as sin, it used what is good to bring about my death, so that through the commandment sin might become utterly sinful.

14We know that the law is spiritual; but I am unspiritual, sold as a slave to sin. 15I do not understand what I do. For what I want to do I do not do, but what I hate I do. 16And if I do what I do not want to do, I agree that the law is good. 17As it is, it is no longer I myself who do it, but it is sin living in me. 18For I know that good itself does not dwell in me, that is, in my sinful nature.[d] For I have the desire to do what is good, but I cannot carry it out. 19For I do not do the good I want to do, but the evil I do not want to do — this I keep on doing. 20Now if I do what I do not want to do, it is no longer I who do it, but it is sin living in me that does it.

21So I find this law at work: Although I want to do good, evil is right there with me. 22For in my inner being I delight in God's law; 23but I see another law at work in me, waging war against the law of my mind and making me a prisoner of the law of sin at work within me. 24What a wretched man I am! Who will rescue me from this body that is subject to death? 25Thanks be to God, who delivers me through Jesus Christ our Lord!

So then, I myself in my mind am a slave to God's law, but in my sinful nature[e] a slave to the law of sin.

[a] 23 Or *through* [b] 5 In contexts like this, the Greek word for *flesh* (*sarx*) refers to the sinful state of human beings, often presented as a power in opposition to the Spirit. [c] 7 Exodus 20:17; Deut. 5:21
[d] 18 Or *my flesh* [e] 25 Or *in the flesh*

Life Through the Spirit

8 Therefore, there is now no condemnation for those who are in Christ Jesus, 2 because through Christ Jesus the law of the Spirit who gives life has set you[a] free from the law of sin and death. 3 For what the law was powerless to do because it was weakened by the flesh,[b] God did by sending his own Son in the likeness of sinful flesh to be a sin offering.[c] And so he condemned sin in the flesh, 4 in order that the righteous requirement of the law might be fully met in us, who do not live according to the flesh but according to the Spirit.

5 Those who live according to the flesh have their minds set on what the flesh desires; but those who live in accordance with the Spirit have their minds set on what the Spirit desires. 6 The mind governed by the flesh is death, but the mind governed by the Spirit is life and peace. 7 The mind governed by the flesh is hostile to God; it does not submit to God's law, nor can it do so. 8 Those who are in the realm of the flesh cannot please God.

9 You, however, are not in the realm of the flesh but are in the realm of the Spirit, if indeed the Spirit of God lives in you. And if anyone does not have the Spirit of Christ, they do not belong to Christ. 10 But if Christ is in you, then even though your body is subject to death because of sin, the Spirit gives life[d] because of righteousness. 11 And if the Spirit of him who raised Jesus from the dead is living in you, he who raised Christ from the dead will also give life to your mortal bodies because of[e] his Spirit who lives in you.

12 Therefore, brothers and sisters, we have an obligation—but it is not to the flesh, to live according to it. 13 For if you live according to the flesh, you will die; but if by the Spirit you put to death the misdeeds of the body, you will live.

14 For those who are led by the Spirit of God are the children of God. 15 The Spirit you received does not make you slaves, so that you live in fear again; rather, the Spirit you received brought about your adoption to sonship.[f] And by him we cry, *"Abba,*[g] Father." 16 The Spirit himself testifies with our spirit that we are God's children. 17 Now if we are children, then we are heirs—heirs of God and co-heirs with Christ, if indeed we share in his sufferings in order that we may also share in his glory.

Present Suffering and Future Glory

18 I consider that our present sufferings are not worth comparing with the glory that will be revealed in us. 19 For the creation waits in eager expectation for the children of God to be revealed. 20 For the creation was subjected to frustration, not by its own choice, but by the will of the one who subjected it, in hope 21 that[h] the creation itself will be liberated from its bondage to decay and brought into the freedom and glory of the children of God.

22 We know that the whole creation has been groaning as in the pains of childbirth right up to the present time. 23 Not only so, but we ourselves, who have the firstfruits of the Spirit, groan inwardly as we wait eagerly for our adoption to sonship, the redemption of our bodies. 24 For in this hope we were saved. But hope that is seen is no hope at all. Who hopes for what they already have? 25 But if we hope for what we do not yet have, we wait for it patiently.

26 In the same way, the Spirit helps us in our weakness. We do not know what we ought to pray for, but the Spirit himself intercedes for us through wordless groans. 27 And he who searches our hearts knows the mind of the Spirit, because the Spirit intercedes for God's people in accordance with the will of God.

28 And we know that in all things God works for the good of those who love him, who[i] have been called according to his purpose. 29 For those God foreknew he also

[a] *2* The Greek is singular; some manuscripts *me* [b] *3* In contexts like this, the Greek word for *flesh* (*sarx*) refers to the sinful state of human beings, often presented as a power in opposition to the Spirit; also in verses 4-13. [c] *3* Or *flesh, for sin* [d] *10* Or *you, your body is dead because of sin, yet your spirit is alive* [e] *11* Some manuscripts *bodies through* [f] *15* The Greek word for *adoption to sonship* is a term referring to the full legal standing of an adopted male heir in Roman culture; also in verse 23. [g] *15* Aramaic for *father* [h] *20,21* Or *subjected it in hope. 21 For* [i] *28* Or *that all things work together for good to those who love God, who*; or *that in all things God works together with those who love him to bring about what is good—with those who*

predestined to be conformed to the image of his Son, that he might be the firstborn among many brothers and sisters. 30 And those he predestined, he also called; those he called, he also justified; those he justified, he also glorified.

More Than Conquerors

31 What, then, shall we say in response to these things? If God is for us, who can be against us? 32 He who did not spare his own Son, but gave him up for us all—how will he not also, along with him, graciously give us all things? 33 Who will bring any charge against those whom God has chosen? It is God who justifies. 34 Who then is the one who condemns? No one. Christ Jesus who died—more than that, who was raised to life—is at the right hand of God and is also interceding for us. 35 Who shall separate us from the love of Christ? Shall trouble or hardship or persecution or famine or nakedness or danger or sword? 36 As it is written:

"For your sake we face death all day long;
we are considered as sheep to be slaughtered."[a]

37 No, in all these things we are more than conquerors through him who loved us. 38 For I am convinced that neither death nor life, neither angels nor demons,[b] neither the present nor the future, nor any powers, 39 neither height nor depth, nor anything else in all creation, will be able to separate us from the love of God that is in Christ Jesus our Lord.

Paul's Anguish Over Israel

9 I speak the truth in Christ—I am not lying, my conscience confirms it through the Holy Spirit— 2 I have great sorrow and unceasing anguish in my heart. 3 For I could wish that I myself were cursed and cut off from Christ for the sake of my people, those of my own race, 4 the people of Israel. Theirs is the adoption to sonship; theirs the divine glory, the covenants, the receiving of the law, the temple worship and the promises. 5 Theirs are the patriarchs, and from them is traced the human ancestry of the Messiah, who is God over all, forever praised![c] Amen.

God's Sovereign Choice

6 It is not as though God's word had failed. For not all who are descended from Israel are Israel. 7 Nor because they are his descendants are they all Abraham's children. On the contrary, "It is through Isaac that your offspring will be reckoned."[d] 8 In other words, it is not the children by physical descent who are God's children, but it is the children of the promise who are regarded as Abraham's offspring. 9 For this was how the promise was stated: "At the appointed time I will return, and Sarah will have a son."[e]

10 Not only that, but Rebekah's children were conceived at the same time by our father Isaac. 11 Yet, before the twins were born or had done anything good or bad—in order that God's purpose in election might stand: 12 not by works but by him who calls—she was told, "The older will serve the younger."[f] 13 Just as it is written: "Jacob I loved, but Esau I hated."[g]

14 What then shall we say? Is God unjust? Not at all! 15 For he says to Moses,

"I will have mercy on whom I have mercy,
and I will have compassion on whom I have compassion."[h]

16 It does not, therefore, depend on human desire or effort, but on God's mercy. 17 For Scripture says to Pharaoh: "I raised you up for this very purpose, that I might display my power in you and that my name might be proclaimed in all the earth."[i] 18 Therefore God has mercy on whom he wants to have mercy, and he hardens whom he wants to harden.

19 One of you will say to me: "Then why does God still blame us? For who is able to resist his will?" 20 But who are you, a human being, to talk back to God? "Shall what is formed say to the one who formed it, 'Why did you make me like this?' "[j] 21 Does not the potter have the right to make out of the same lump of clay some pottery for special purposes and some for common use?

22 What if God, although choosing to show his wrath and make his power known, bore with great patience the objects of his wrath—prepared for destruction? 23 What

[a] *36* Psalm 44:22 [b] *38* Or *nor heavenly rulers* [c] *5* Or *Messiah, who is over all. God be forever praised!* Or *Messiah. God who is over all be forever praised!* [d] *7* Gen. 21:12 [e] *9* Gen. 18:10,14 [f] *12* Gen. 25:23 [g] *13* Mal. 1:2,3 [h] *15* Exodus 33:19 [i] *17* Exodus 9:16 [j] *20* Isaiah 29:16; 45:9

if he did this to make the riches of his glory known to the objects of his mercy, whom he prepared in advance for glory— 24 even us, whom he also called, not only from the Jews but also from the Gentiles? 25 As he says in Hosea:

"I will call them 'my people' who are not
my people;
and I will call her 'my loved one' who is
not my loved one,"[a]

26 and,

"In the very place where it was said to
them,
'You are not my people,'
there they will be called 'children of
the living God.'"[b]

27 Isaiah cries out concerning Israel:

"Though the number of the Israelites be
like the sand by the sea,
only the remnant will be saved.
28 For the Lord will carry out
his sentence on earth with speed and
finality."[c]

29 It is just as Isaiah said previously:

"Unless the Lord Almighty
had left us descendants,
we would have become like Sodom,
we would have been like Gomorrah."[d]

Israel's Unbelief

30 What then shall we say? That the Gentiles, who did not pursue righteousness, have obtained it, a righteousness that is by faith; 31 but the people of Israel, who pursued the law as the way of righteousness, have not attained their goal. 32 Why not? Because they pursued it not by faith but as if it were by works. They stumbled over the stumbling stone. 33 As it is written:

"See, I lay in Zion a stone that causes
people to stumble
and a rock that makes them fall,
and the one who believes in him will
never be put to shame."[e]

10 Brothers and sisters, my heart's desire and prayer to God for the Israelites is that they may be saved. 2 For I can testify about them that they are zealous for God, but their zeal is not based on knowledge. 3 Since they did not know the righteousness of God and sought to establish their own, they did not submit to God's righteousness. 4 Christ is the culmination of the law so that there may be righteousness for everyone who believes.

5 Moses writes this about the righteousness that is by the law: "The person who does these things will live by them."[f] 6 But the righteousness that is by faith says: "Do not say in your heart, 'Who will ascend into heaven?'"[g] (that is, to bring Christ down) 7 "or 'Who will descend into the deep?'"[h] (that is, to bring Christ up from the dead). 8 But what does it say? "The word is near you; it is in your mouth and in your heart,"[i] that is, the message concerning faith that we proclaim: 9 If you declare with your mouth, "Jesus is Lord," and believe in your heart that God raised him from the dead, you will be saved. 10 For it is with your heart that you believe and are justified, and it is with your mouth that you profess your faith and are saved. 11 As Scripture says, "Anyone who believes in him will never be put to shame."[j] 12 For there is no difference between Jew and Gentile—the same Lord is Lord of all and richly blesses all who call on him, 13 for, "Everyone who calls on the name of the Lord will be saved."[k]

14 How, then, can they call on the one they have not believed in? And how can they believe in the one of whom they have not heard? And how can they hear without someone preaching to them? 15 And how can anyone preach unless they are sent? As it is written: "How beautiful are the feet of those who bring good news!"[l]

16 But not all the Israelites accepted the good news. For Isaiah says, "Lord, who has believed our message?"[m] 17 Consequently, faith comes from hearing the message, and the message is heard through the word about Christ. 18 But I ask: Did they not hear? Of course they did:

"Their voice has gone out into all the
earth,
their words to the ends of the world."[n]

[a] *25* Hosea 2:23 [b] *26* Hosea 1:10 [c] *28* Isaiah 10:22,23 (see Septuagint) [d] *29* Isaiah 1:9 [e] *33* Isaiah 8:14; 28:16 [f] *5* Lev. 18:5 [g] *6* Deut. 30:12 [h] *7* Deut. 30:13 [i] *8* Deut. 30:14 [j] *11* Isaiah 28:16 (see Septuagint) [k] *13* Joel 2:32 [l] *15* Isaiah 52:7 [m] *16* Isaiah 53:1 [n] *18* Psalm 19:4

19 Again I ask: Did Israel not understand?
First, Moses says,

"I will make you envious by those who
are not a nation;
I will make you angry by a nation that
has no understanding."[a]

20 And Isaiah boldly says,

"I was found by those who did not seek me;
I revealed myself to those who did not
ask for me."[b]

21 But concerning Israel he says,

"All day long I have held out my hands
to a disobedient and obstinate people."[c]

The Remnant of Israel

11 I ask then: Did God reject his peo-
ple? By no means! I am an Israelite
myself, a descendant of Abraham, from the
tribe of Benjamin. 2 God did not reject his
people, whom he foreknew. Don't you know
what Scripture says in the passage about
Elijah — how he appealed to God against Is-
rael: 3 "Lord, they have killed your prophets
and torn down your altars; I am the only one
left, and they are trying to kill me"[d]? 4 And
what was God's answer to him? "I have re-
served for myself seven thousand who have
not bowed the knee to Baal."[e] 5 So too, at the
present time there is a remnant chosen by
grace. 6 And if by grace, then it cannot be
based on works; if it were, grace would no
longer be grace.

7 What then? What the people of Israel
sought so earnestly they did not obtain. The
elect among them did, but the others were
hardened, 8 as it is written:

"God gave them a spirit of stupor,
eyes that could not see
and ears that could not hear,
to this very day."[f]

9 And David says:

"May their table become a snare and
a trap,
a stumbling block and a retribution
for them.
10 May their eyes be darkened so they
cannot see,
and their backs be bent forever."[g]

Ingrafted Branches

11 Again I ask: Did they stumble so as to
fall beyond recovery? Not at all! Rather, be-
cause of their transgression, salvation has
come to the Gentiles to make Israel envious.
12 But if their transgression means riches for
the world, and their loss means riches for the
Gentiles, how much greater riches will their
full inclusion bring!

13 I am talking to you Gentiles. Inasmuch
as I am the apostle to the Gentiles, I take
pride in my ministry 14 in the hope that I may
somehow arouse my own people to envy
and save some of them. 15 For if their rejec-
tion brought reconciliation to the world,
what will their acceptance be but life from
the dead? 16 If the part of the dough offered
as firstfruits is holy, then the whole batch is
holy; if the root is holy, so are the branches.

17 If some of the branches have been bro-
ken off, and you, though a wild olive shoot,
have been grafted in among the others and
now share in the nourishing sap from the
olive root, 18 do not consider yourself to be
superior to those other branches. If you do,
consider this: You do not support the root,
but the root supports you. 19 You will say
then, "Branches were broken off so that I
could be grafted in." 20 Granted. But they
were broken off because of unbelief, and you
stand by faith. Do not be arrogant, but trem-
ble. 21 For if God did not spare the natural
branches, he will not spare you either.

22 Consider therefore the kindness and
sternness of God: sternness to those who fell,
but kindness to you, provided that you con-
tinue in his kindness. Otherwise, you also
will be cut off. 23 And if they do not persist in
unbelief, they will be grafted in, for God is
able to graft them in again. 24 After all, if you
were cut out of an olive tree that is wild by
nature, and contrary to nature were grafted
into a cultivated olive tree, how much more
readily will these, the natural branches, be
grafted into their own olive tree!

All Israel Will Be Saved

25 I do not want you to be ignorant of this
mystery, brothers and sisters, so that you
may not be conceited: Israel has experienced
a hardening in part until the full number of

[a] *19* Deut. 32:21 [b] *20* Isaiah 65:1 [c] *21* Isaiah 65:2 [d] *3* 1 Kings 19:10,14 [e] *4* 1 Kings 19:18
[f] *8* Deut. 29:4; Isaiah 29:10 [g] *10* Psalm 69:22,23

the Gentiles has come in, 26 and in this way[a]
all Israel will be saved. As it is written:

"The deliverer will come from Zion;
he will turn godlessness away from
Jacob.
27 And this is[b] my covenant with them
when I take away their sins."[c]

28 As far as the gospel is concerned, they
are enemies for your sake; but as far as elec-
tion is concerned, they are loved on account
of the patriarchs, 29 for God's gifts and his
call are irrevocable. 30 Just as you who were
at one time disobedient to God have now
received mercy as a result of their disobedi-
ence, 31 so they too have now become disobe-
dient in order that they too may now[d] receive
mercy as a result of God's mercy to you. 32 For
God has bound everyone over to disobedi-
ence so that he may have mercy on them all.

Doxology

33 Oh, the depth of the riches of the wisdom
and[e] knowledge of God!
How unsearchable his judgments,
and his paths beyond tracing out!
34 "Who has known the mind of the Lord?
Or who has been his counselor?"[f]
35 "Who has ever given to God,
that God should repay them?"[g]
36 For from him and through him and for
him are all things.
To him be the glory forever! Amen.

A Living Sacrifice

12 Therefore, I urge you, brothers and
sisters, in view of God's mercy, to of-
fer your bodies as a living sacrifice, holy and
pleasing to God — this is your true and prop-
er worship. 2 Do not conform to the pattern
of this world, but be transformed by the re-
newing of your mind. Then you will be able
to test and approve what God's will is — his
good, pleasing and perfect will.

Humble Service in the Body of Christ

3 For by the grace given me I say to every
one of you: Do not think of yourself more
highly than you ought, but rather think of
yourself with sober judgment, in accordance
with the faith God has distributed to each
of you. 4 For just as each of us has one body
with many members, and these members do
not all have the same function, 5 so in Christ
we, though many, form one body, and each
member belongs to all the others. 6 We have
different gifts, according to the grace given
to each of us. If your gift is prophesying, then
prophesy in accordance with your[h] faith;
7 if it is serving, then serve; if it is teaching,
then teach; 8 if it is to encourage, then give
encouragement; if it is giving, then give gen-
erously; if it is to lead,[i] do it diligently; if it is
to show mercy, do it cheerfully.

Love in Action

9 Love must be sincere. Hate what is evil;
cling to what is good. 10 Be devoted to one
another in love. Honor one another above
yourselves. 11 Never be lacking in zeal, but
keep your spiritual fervor, serving the Lord.
12 Be joyful in hope, patient in affliction,
faithful in prayer. 13 Share with the Lord's
people who are in need. Practice hospitality.
14 Bless those who persecute you; bless
and do not curse. 15 Rejoice with those who
rejoice; mourn with those who mourn.
16 Live in harmony with one another. Do not
be proud, but be willing to associate with
people of low position.[j] Do not be conceited.
17 Do not repay anyone evil for evil. Be
careful to do what is right in the eyes of ev-
eryone. 18 If it is possible, as far as it depends
on you, live at peace with everyone. 19 Do
not take revenge, my dear friends, but leave
room for God's wrath, for it is written: "It is
mine to avenge; I will repay,"[k] says the Lord.
20 On the contrary:

"If your enemy is hungry, feed him;
if he is thirsty, give him something to
drink.
In doing this, you will heap burning coals
on his head."[l]

21 Do not be overcome by evil, but overcome
evil with good.

Submission to Governing Authorities

13 Let everyone be subject to the gov-
erning authorities, for there is no

[a] 26 Or *and so* [b] 27 Or *will be* [c] 27 Isaiah 59:20,21; 27:9 (see Septuagint); Jer. 31:33,34 [d] 31 Some manuscripts do not have *now.* [e] 33 Or *riches and the wisdom and the* [f] 34 Isaiah 40:13 [g] 35 Job 41:11 [h] 6 Or *the* [i] 8 Or *to provide for others* [j] 16 Or *willing to do menial work* [k] 19 Deut. 32:35 [l] 20 Prov. 25:21,22

authority except that which God has established. The authorities that exist have been established by God. 2Consequently, whoever rebels against the authority is rebelling against what God has instituted, and those who do so will bring judgment on themselves. 3For rulers hold no terror for those who do right, but for those who do wrong. Do you want to be free from fear of the one in authority? Then do what is right and you will be commended. 4For the one in authority is God's servant for your good. But if you do wrong, be afraid, for rulers do not bear the sword for no reason. They are God's servants, agents of wrath to bring punishment on the wrongdoer. 5Therefore, it is necessary to submit to the authorities, not only because of possible punishment but also as a matter of conscience.

6This is also why you pay taxes, for the authorities are God's servants, who give their full time to governing. 7Give to everyone what you owe them: If you owe taxes, pay taxes; if revenue, then revenue; if respect, then respect; if honor, then honor.

Love Fulfills the Law

8Let no debt remain outstanding, except the continuing debt to love one another, for whoever loves others has fulfilled the law. 9The commandments, "You shall not commit adultery," "You shall not murder," "You shall not steal," "You shall not covet,"[a] and whatever other command there may be, are summed up in this one command: "Love your neighbor as yourself."[b] 10Love does no harm to a neighbor. Therefore love is the fulfillment of the law.

The Day Is Near

11And do this, understanding the present time: The hour has already come for you to wake up from your slumber, because our salvation is nearer now than when we first believed. 12The night is nearly over; the day is almost here. So let us put aside the deeds of darkness and put on the armor of light. 13Let us behave decently, as in the daytime, not in carousing and drunkenness, not in sexual immorality and debauchery, not in dissension and jealousy. 14Rather, clothe yourselves with the Lord Jesus Christ, and do not think about how to gratify the desires of the flesh.[c]

The Weak and the Strong

14 Accept the one whose faith is weak, without quarreling over disputable matters. 2One person's faith allows them to eat anything, but another, whose faith is weak, eats only vegetables. 3The one who eats everything must not treat with contempt the one who does not, and the one who does not eat everything must not judge the one who does, for God has accepted them. 4Who are you to judge someone else's servant? To their own master, servants stand or fall. And they will stand, for the Lord is able to make them stand.

5One person considers one day more sacred than another; another considers every day alike. Each of them should be fully convinced in their own mind. 6Whoever regards one day as special does so to the Lord. Whoever eats meat does so to the Lord, for they give thanks to God; and whoever abstains does so to the Lord and gives thanks to God. 7For none of us lives for ourselves alone, and none of us dies for ourselves alone. 8If we live, we live for the Lord; and if we die, we die for the Lord. So, whether we live or die, we belong to the Lord. 9For this very reason, Christ died and returned to life so that he might be the Lord of both the dead and the living.

10You, then, why do you judge your brother or sister[d]? Or why do you treat them with contempt? For we will all stand before God's judgment seat. 11It is written:

"'As surely as I live,' says the Lord,
'every knee will bow before me;
every tongue will acknowledge God.'"[e]

12So then, each of us will give an account of ourselves to God.

13Therefore let us stop passing judgment on one another. Instead, make up your mind not to put any stumbling block or obstacle

[a] *9* Exodus 20:13-15,17; Deut. 5:17-19,21 [b] *9* Lev. 19:18 [c] *14* In contexts like this, the Greek word for *flesh* (*sarx*) refers to the sinful state of human beings, often presented as a power in opposition to the Spirit. [d] *10* The Greek word for *brother or sister* (*adelphos*) refers here to a believer, whether man or woman, as part of God's family; also in verses 13, 15 and 21. [e] *11* Isaiah 45:23

in the way of a brother or sister. [14]I am con-
vinced, being fully persuaded in the Lord
Jesus, that nothing is unclean in itself. But if
anyone regards something as unclean, then
for that person it is unclean. [15]If your broth-
er or sister is distressed because of what you
eat, you are no longer acting in love. Do not
by your eating destroy someone for whom
Christ died. [16]Therefore do not let what you
know is good be spoken of as evil. [17]For the
kingdom of God is not a matter of eating and
drinking, but of righteousness, peace and
joy in the Holy Spirit, [18]because anyone who
serves Christ in this way is pleasing to God
and receives human approval.

[19]Let us therefore make every effort to
do what leads to peace and to mutual edi-
fication. [20]Do not destroy the work of God
for the sake of food. All food is clean, but it
is wrong for a person to eat anything that
causes someone else to stumble. [21]It is bet-
ter not to eat meat or drink wine or to do
anything else that will cause your brother or
sister to fall.

[22]So whatever you believe about these
things keep between yourself and God.
Blessed is the one who does not condemn
himself by what he approves. [23]But whoever
has doubts is condemned if they eat, because
their eating is not from faith; and everything
that does not come from faith is sin.[a]

15 We who are strong ought to bear with
the failings of the weak and not to
please ourselves. [2]Each of us should please
our neighbors for their good, to build them
up. [3]For even Christ did not please himself
but, as it is written: "The insults of those
who insult you have fallen on me."[b] [4]For
everything that was written in the past was
written to teach us, so that through the en-
durance taught in the Scriptures and the
encouragement they provide we might have
hope.

[5]May the God who gives endurance and
encouragement give you the same attitude
of mind toward each other that Christ Jesus
had, [6]so that with one mind and one voice
you may glorify the God and Father of our
Lord Jesus Christ.

[7]Accept one another, then, just as Christ
accepted you, in order to bring praise to
God. [8]For I tell you that Christ has become a
servant of the Jews[c] on behalf of God's truth,
so that the promises made to the patriarchs
might be confirmed [9]and, moreover, that
the Gentiles might glorify God for his mercy.
As it is written:

"Therefore I will praise you among the
Gentiles;
I will sing the praises of your name."[d]

[10]Again, it says,

"Rejoice, you Gentiles, with his people."[e]

[11]And again,

"Praise the Lord, all you Gentiles;
let all the peoples extol him."[f]

[12]And again, Isaiah says,

"The Root of Jesse will spring up,
one who will arise to rule over the
nations;
in him the Gentiles will hope."[g]

[13]May the God of hope fill you with all joy
and peace as you trust in him, so that you
may overflow with hope by the power of the
Holy Spirit.

Paul the Minister to the Gentiles

[14]I myself am convinced, my brothers and
sisters, that you yourselves are full of good-
ness, filled with knowledge and competent
to instruct one another. [15]Yet I have written
you quite boldly on some points to remind
you of them again, because of the grace God
gave me [16]to be a minister of Christ Jesus to
the Gentiles. He gave me the priestly duty of
proclaiming the gospel of God, so that the
Gentiles might become an offering accept-
able to God, sanctified by the Holy Spirit.

[17]Therefore I glory in Christ Jesus in my
service to God. [18]I will not venture to speak
of anything except what Christ has accom-
plished through me in leading the Gen-
tiles to obey God by what I have said and
done— [19]by the power of signs and won-
ders, through the power of the Spirit of God.
So from Jerusalem all the way around to Il-
lyricum, I have fully proclaimed the gospel
of Christ. [20]It has always been my ambition

[a] *23* Some manuscripts place 16:25-27 here; others after 15:33. [b] *3* Psalm 69:9 [c] *8* Greek *circumcision* [d] *9* 2 Samuel 22:50; Psalm 18:49 [e] *10* Deut. 32:43 [f] *11* Psalm 117:1 [g] *12* Isaiah 11:10 (see Septuagint)

to preach the gospel where Christ was not
known, so that I would not be building on
someone else's foundation. [21]Rather, as it is
written:

"Those who were not told about him
will see,
and those who have not heard will
understand."[a]

[22]This is why I have often been hindered
from coming to you.

Paul's Plan to Visit Rome

[23]But now that there is no more place for
me to work in these regions, and since I have
been longing for many years to visit you, [24]I
plan to do so when I go to Spain. I hope to see
you while passing through and to have you
assist me on my journey there, after I have
enjoyed your company for a while. [25]Now,
however, I am on my way to Jerusalem in the
service of the Lord's people there. [26]For Mac-
edonia and Achaia were pleased to make a
contribution for the poor among the Lord's
people in Jerusalem. [27]They were pleased to
do it, and indeed they owe it to them. For if
the Gentiles have shared in the Jews' spiritu-
al blessings, they owe it to the Jews to share
with them their material blessings. [28]So af-
ter I have completed this task and have made
sure that they have received this contribu-
tion, I will go to Spain and visit you on the
way. [29]I know that when I come to you, I will
come in the full measure of the blessing of
Christ.

[30]I urge you, brothers and sisters, by our
Lord Jesus Christ and by the love of the Spir-
it, to join me in my struggle by praying to
God for me. [31]Pray that I may be kept safe
from the unbelievers in Judea and that the
contribution I take to Jerusalem may be fa-
vorably received by the Lord's people there,
[32]so that I may come to you with joy, by God's
will, and in your company be refreshed.
[33]The God of peace be with you all. Amen.

Personal Greetings

16 I commend to you our sister Phoe-
be, a deacon[b,c] of the church in Cen-
chreae. [2]I ask you to receive her in the Lord
in a way worthy of his people and to give her
any help she may need from you, for she has
been the benefactor of many people, includ-
ing me.

[3]Greet Priscilla[d] and Aquila, my co-workers
in Christ Jesus. [4]They risked their lives
for me. Not only I but all the churches of
the Gentiles are grateful to them.
[5]Greet also the church that meets at their
house.

Greet my dear friend Epenetus, who was
the first convert to Christ in the prov-
ince of Asia.
[6]Greet Mary, who worked very hard for you.
[7]Greet Andronicus and Junia, my fellow
Jews who have been in prison with
me. They are outstanding among[e] the
apostles, and they were in Christ before
I was.
[8]Greet Ampliatus, my dear friend in the
Lord.
[9]Greet Urbanus, our co-worker in Christ,
and my dear friend Stachys.
[10]Greet Apelles, whose fidelity to Christ has
stood the test.

Greet those who belong to the household
of Aristobulus.
[11]Greet Herodion, my fellow Jew.

Greet those in the household of Narcissus
who are in the Lord.
[12]Greet Tryphena and Tryphosa, those
women who work hard in the Lord.

Greet my dear friend Persis, another
woman who has worked very hard in
the Lord.
[13]Greet Rufus, chosen in the Lord, and his
mother, who has been a mother to me,
too.
[14]Greet Asyncritus, Phlegon, Hermes, Pat-
robas, Hermas and the other brothers
and sisters with them.
[15]Greet Philologus, Julia, Nereus and his
sister, and Olympas and all the Lord's
people who are with them.
[16]Greet one another with a holy kiss.

All the churches of Christ send greetings.

[17]I urge you, brothers and sisters, to watch
out for those who cause divisions and put
obstacles in your way that are contrary to

[a] *21* Isaiah 52:15 (see Septuagint) [b] *1* Or *servant* [c] *1* The word *deacon* refers here to a Christian designated to serve with the overseers/elders of the church in a variety of ways; similarly in Phil. 1:1 and 1 Tim. 3:8,12. [d] *3* Greek *Prisca,* a variant of *Priscilla* [e] *7* Or *are esteemed by*

the teaching you have learned. Keep away
from them. [18]For such people are not serv-
ing our Lord Christ, but their own appetites.
By smooth talk and flattery they deceive the
minds of naive people. [19]Everyone has heard
about your obedience, so I rejoice because of
you; but I want you to be wise about what is
good, and innocent about what is evil.

[20]The God of peace will soon crush Satan
under your feet.

The grace of our Lord Jesus be with you.

[21]Timothy, my co-worker, sends his greet-
ings to you, as do Lucius, Jason and Sosipa-
ter, my fellow Jews.

[22]I, Tertius, who wrote down this letter,
greet you in the Lord.

[23]Gaius, whose hospitality I and the whole
church here enjoy, sends you his greetings.

Erastus, who is the city's director of pub-
lic works, and our brother Quartus send you
their greetings. [24][a]

[25]Now to him who is able to establish you
in accordance with my gospel, the message
I proclaim about Jesus Christ, in keeping
with the revelation of the mystery hidden for
long ages past, [26]but now revealed and made
known through the prophetic writings by the
command of the eternal God, so that all the
Gentiles might come to the obedience that
comes from[b] faith— [27]to the only wise God
be glory forever through Jesus Christ! Amen.

[a] 24 Some manuscripts include here *May the grace of our Lord Jesus Christ be with all of you. Amen.*
[b] 26 Or *that is*

1 CORINTHIANS

1 Paul, called to be an apostle of Christ Jesus by the will of God, and our brother Sosthenes,

[2]To the church of God in Corinth, to those sanctified in Christ Jesus and called to be his holy people, together with all those everywhere who call on the name of our Lord Jesus Christ—their Lord and ours:

[3]Grace and peace to you from God our Father and the Lord Jesus Christ.

Thanksgiving

[4]I always thank my God for you because of his grace given you in Christ Jesus. [5]For in him you have been enriched in every way—with all kinds of speech and with all knowledge—[6]God thus confirming our testimony about Christ among you. [7]Therefore you do not lack any spiritual gift as you eagerly wait for our Lord Jesus Christ to be revealed. [8]He will also keep you firm to the end, so that you will be blameless on the day of our Lord Jesus Christ. [9]God is faithful, who has called you into fellowship with his Son, Jesus Christ our Lord.

A Church Divided Over Leaders

[10]I appeal to you, brothers and sisters,[a] in the name of our Lord Jesus Christ, that all of you agree with one another in what you say and that there be no divisions among you, but that you be perfectly united in mind and thought. [11]My brothers and sisters, some from Chloe's household have informed me that there are quarrels among you. [12]What I mean is this: One of you says, "I follow Paul"; another, "I follow Apollos"; another, "I follow Cephas[b]"; still another, "I follow Christ."

[13]Is Christ divided? Was Paul crucified for you? Were you baptized in the name of Paul? [14]I thank God that I did not baptize any of you except Crispus and Gaius, [15]so no one can say that you were baptized in my name. [16](Yes, I also baptized the household of Stephanas; beyond that, I don't remember if I baptized anyone else.) [17]For Christ did not send me to baptize, but to preach the gospel—not with wisdom and eloquence, lest the cross of Christ be emptied of its power.

Christ Crucified Is God's Power and Wisdom

[18]For the message of the cross is foolishness to those who are perishing, but to us who are being saved it is the power of God. [19]For it is written:

> "I will destroy the wisdom of the wise;
> the intelligent of the intelligent I will frustrate."[c]

[20]Where is the wise person? Where is the teacher of the law? Where is the philosopher of this age? Has not God made foolish the wisdom of the world? [21]For since in the wisdom of God the world through its wisdom did not know him, God was pleased through the foolishness of what was preached to save those who believe. [22]Jews demand signs and Greeks look for wisdom, [23]but we preach Christ crucified: a stumbling block to Jews and foolishness to Gentiles, [24]but to those whom God has called, both Jews and Greeks, Christ the power of God and the wisdom of God. [25]For the foolishness of God is wiser than human wisdom, and the weakness of God is stronger than human strength.

[26]Brothers and sisters, think of what you were when you were called. Not many of you were wise by human standards; not many were influential; not many were of noble birth. [27]But God chose the foolish things of the world to shame the wise; God chose the weak things of the world to shame the strong. [28]God chose the lowly things of this world and the despised things—and the

[a] *10* The Greek word for *brothers and sisters* (*adelphoi*) refers here to believers, both men and women, as part of God's family; also in verses 11 and 26; and in 2:1; 3:1; 4:6; 6:8; 7:24, 29; 10:1; 11:33; 12:1; 14:6, 20, 26, 39; 15:1, 6, 50, 58; 16:15, 20. [b] *12* That is, Peter [c] *19* Isaiah 29:14

things that are not—to nullify the things that are, 29 so that no one may boast before him. 30 It is because of him that you are in Christ Jesus, who has become for us wisdom from God—that is, our righteousness, holiness and redemption. 31 Therefore, as it is written: "Let the one who boasts boast in the Lord."[a]

2 And so it was with me, brothers and sisters. When I came to you, I did not come with eloquence or human wisdom as I proclaimed to you the testimony about God.[b] 2 For I resolved to know nothing while I was with you except Jesus Christ and him crucified. 3 I came to you in weakness with great fear and trembling. 4 My message and my preaching were not with wise and persuasive words, but with a demonstration of the Spirit's power, 5 so that your faith might not rest on human wisdom, but on God's power.

God's Wisdom Revealed by the Spirit

6 We do, however, speak a message of wisdom among the mature, but not the wisdom of this age or of the rulers of this age, who are coming to nothing. 7 No, we declare God's wisdom, a mystery that has been hidden and that God destined for our glory before time began. 8 None of the rulers of this age understood it, for if they had, they would not have crucified the Lord of glory. 9 However, as it is written:

"What no eye has seen,
what no ear has heard,
and what no human mind has
conceived"[c]—
the things God has prepared for those
who love him—

10 these are the things God has revealed to us by his Spirit.

The Spirit searches all things, even the deep things of God. 11 For who knows a person's thoughts except their own spirit within them? In the same way no one knows the thoughts of God except the Spirit of God. 12 What we have received is not the spirit of the world, but the Spirit who is from God, so that we may understand what God has freely given us. 13 This is what we speak, not in words taught us by human wisdom but in words taught by the Spirit, explaining spiritual realities with Spirit-taught words.[d] 14 The person without the Spirit does not accept the things that come from the Spirit of God but considers them foolishness, and cannot understand them because they are discerned only through the Spirit. 15 The person with the Spirit makes judgments about all things, but such a person is not subject to merely human judgments, 16 for,

"Who has known the mind of
the Lord
so as to instruct him?"[e]

But we have the mind of Christ.

The Church and Its Leaders

3 Brothers and sisters, I could not address you as people who live by the Spirit but as people who are still worldly—mere infants in Christ. 2 I gave you milk, not solid food, for you were not yet ready for it. Indeed, you are still not ready. 3 You are still worldly. For since there is jealousy and quarreling among you, are you not worldly? Are you not acting like mere humans? 4 For when one says, "I follow Paul," and another, "I follow Apollos," are you not mere human beings?

5 What, after all, is Apollos? And what is Paul? Only servants, through whom you came to believe—as the Lord has assigned to each his task. 6 I planted the seed, Apollos watered it, but God has been making it grow. 7 So neither the one who plants nor the one who waters is anything, but only God, who makes things grow. 8 The one who plants and the one who waters have one purpose, and they will each be rewarded according to their own labor. 9 For we are co-workers in God's service; you are God's field, God's building.

10 By the grace God has given me, I laid a foundation as a wise builder, and someone else is building on it. But each one should build with care. 11 For no one can lay any foundation other than the one already laid, which is Jesus Christ. 12 If anyone builds on this foundation using gold, silver, costly stones, wood, hay or straw, 13 their work will be shown for what it is, because the Day will bring it to light. It will be revealed with fire, and the fire will test the quality of each person's work. 14 If what has been built survives,

[a] *31* Jer. 9:24 [b] *1* Some manuscripts *proclaimed to you God's mystery* [c] *9* Isaiah 64:4 [d] *13* Or *Spirit, interpreting spiritual truths to those who are spiritual* [e] *16* Isaiah 40:13

the builder will receive a reward. 15 If it is burned up, the builder will suffer loss but yet will be saved — even though only as one escaping through the flames.

16 Don't you know that you yourselves are God's temple and that God's Spirit dwells in your midst? 17 If anyone destroys God's temple, God will destroy that person; for God's temple is sacred, and you together are that temple.

18 Do not deceive yourselves. If any of you think you are wise by the standards of this age, you should become "fools" so that you may become wise. 19 For the wisdom of this world is foolishness in God's sight. As it is written: "He catches the wise in their craftiness"[a]; 20 and again, "The Lord knows that the thoughts of the wise are futile."[b] 21 So then, no more boasting about human leaders! All things are yours, 22 whether Paul or Apollos or Cephas[c] or the world or life or death or the present or the future — all are yours, 23 and you are of Christ, and Christ is of God.

The Nature of True Apostleship

4 This, then, is how you ought to regard us: as servants of Christ and as those entrusted with the mysteries God has revealed. 2 Now it is required that those who have been given a trust must prove faithful. 3 I care very little if I am judged by you or by any human court; indeed, I do not even judge myself. 4 My conscience is clear, but that does not make me innocent. It is the Lord who judges me. 5 Therefore judge nothing before the appointed time; wait until the Lord comes. He will bring to light what is hidden in darkness and will expose the motives of the heart. At that time each will receive their praise from God.

6 Now, brothers and sisters, I have applied these things to myself and Apollos for your benefit, so that you may learn from us the meaning of the saying, "Do not go beyond what is written." Then you will not be puffed up in being a follower of one of us over against the other. 7 For who makes you different from anyone else? What do you have that you did not receive? And if you did receive it, why do you boast as though you did not?

8 Already you have all you want! Already you have become rich! You have begun to reign — and that without us! How I wish that you really had begun to reign so that we also might reign with you! 9 For it seems to me that God has put us apostles on display at the end of the procession, like those condemned to die in the arena. We have been made a spectacle to the whole universe, to angels as well as to human beings. 10 We are fools for Christ, but you are so wise in Christ! We are weak, but you are strong! You are honored, we are dishonored! 11 To this very hour we go hungry and thirsty, we are in rags, we are brutally treated, we are homeless. 12 We work hard with our own hands. When we are cursed, we bless; when we are persecuted, we endure it; 13 when we are slandered, we answer kindly. We have become the scum of the earth, the garbage of the world — right up to this moment.

Paul's Appeal and Warning

14 I am writing this not to shame you but to warn you as my dear children. 15 Even if you had ten thousand guardians in Christ, you do not have many fathers, for in Christ Jesus I became your father through the gospel. 16 Therefore I urge you to imitate me. 17 For this reason I have sent to you Timothy, my son whom I love, who is faithful in the Lord. He will remind you of my way of life in Christ Jesus, which agrees with what I teach everywhere in every church.

18 Some of you have become arrogant, as if I were not coming to you. 19 But I will come to you very soon, if the Lord is willing, and then I will find out not only how these arrogant people are talking, but what power they have. 20 For the kingdom of God is not a matter of talk but of power. 21 What do you prefer? Shall I come to you with a rod of discipline, or shall I come in love and with a gentle spirit?

Dealing With a Case of Incest

5 It is actually reported that there is sexual immorality among you, and of a kind that even pagans do not tolerate: A man is sleeping with his father's wife. 2 And you are proud! Shouldn't you rather have gone into mourning and have put out of your fellowship the man who has been doing this? 3 For my part, even though I am not physically

[a] *19* Job 5:13 [b] *20* Psalm 94:11 [c] *22* That is, Peter

THE WONDERFUL CROSS (WHEN I SURVEY THE WONDROUS CROSS)

Isaac Watts, Lowell Mason, Jesse Reeves, Chris Tomlin, J. D. Walt

When I survey the wondrous cross
On which the Prince of Glory died
My richest gain I count but loss
And pour contempt on all my pride

See from his head, his hands, his feet
Sorrow and love flow mingled down
Did e'er such love and sorrow meet
Or thorns compose so rich a crown

O the wonderful cross, O the wonderful cross
Bids me come and die and find that I may
Truly live
O the wonderful cross, O the wonderful cross
All who gather here by grace draw near
And bless your name

Were the whole realm of nature mine
That were an offering far too small
Love so amazing, so divine, demands
My soul, my life, my all

THE INSPIRATION

[Jesus] said to them all: "Whoever wants to be my disciple must deny themselves and take up their cross daily and follow me. For whoever wants to save their life will lose it, but whoever loses their life for me will save it." — Luke 9:23 – 24

Read also: Psalm 18:28 – 29

BEHIND THE SONG

"When I Survey the Wondrous Cross" is certainly one of the most significant and best-loved hymns of the faith. Originally penned by Isaac Watts and published in 1707, the song was innovative in its day. Most sacred songs of that era paraphrased Biblical stories and passages, whereas Watts' hymn included personal observation, passionate articulation of the gospel and an implied invitation. As with most hymns, the lyrics were set to several different melodies over the decades that followed. The most popular setting was composed by the legendary American hymn writer Lowell Mason roughly 100 years after the song was first introduced.

While sound-checking for a worship time at a youth camp, Jesse Reeves, bass player for Chris Tomlin's band, started playing the melody to the old hymn. Tomlin recognized the tune and began singing the song he had enjoyed so much as a child. As the band improvised, Tomlin spontaneously sang a new chorus that included the same sentiment as the original — but in a contemporary style. "I started singing that whole chorus," Tomlin recalls, "and just kept singing it over and over. It was just my own moment, worshiping God, singing out to God."

Tomlin was reluctant to add to the song, concerned that it would be presumptuous to embellish such a great hymn. But in the end he chose to follow in the footsteps of many hymnists of previous generations.

Selah

The poetry of Watts' original lyric is powerful and rich. Read it and notice all of its visual and emotional imagery. Consider how tightly it is wrapped in the theology of the Bible. Reflect on the last line: "Love so amazing, so divine, demands my soul, my life, my all." When you contemplate both the tragedy and beauty of the cross, what feelings does it illicit in your heart? Read Luke 9: 23 – 24 and think about the implications of Christ's sacrifice on the cross. How wonderful that cross is — in so many ways!

present, I am with you in spirit. As one who is present with you in this way, I have already passed judgment in the name of our Lord Jesus on the one who has been doing this. [4]So when you are assembled and I am with you in spirit, and the power of our Lord Jesus is present, [5]hand this man over to Satan for the destruction of the flesh,[a,b] so that his spirit may be saved on the day of the Lord.

[6]Your boasting is not good. Don't you know that a little yeast leavens the whole batch of dough? [7]Get rid of the old yeast, so that you may be a new unleavened batch — as you really are. For Christ, our Passover lamb, has been sacrificed. [8]Therefore let us keep the Festival, not with the old bread leavened with malice and wickedness, but with the unleavened bread of sincerity and truth.

[9]I wrote to you in my letter not to associate with sexually immoral people — [10]not at all meaning the people of this world who are immoral, or the greedy and swindlers, or idolaters. In that case you would have to leave this world. [11]But now I am writing to you that you must not associate with anyone who claims to be a brother or sister[c] but is sexually immoral or greedy, an idolater or slanderer, a drunkard or swindler. Do not even eat with such people.

[12]What business is it of mine to judge those outside the church? Are you not to judge those inside? [13]God will judge those outside. "Expel the wicked person from among you."[d]

Lawsuits Among Believers

6 If any of you has a dispute with another, do you dare to take it before the ungodly for judgment instead of before the Lord's people? [2]Or do you not know that the Lord's people will judge the world? And if you are to judge the world, are you not competent to judge trivial cases? [3]Do you not know that we will judge angels? How much more the things of this life! [4]Therefore, if you have disputes about such matters, do you ask for a ruling from those whose way of life is scorned in the church? [5]I say this to shame you. Is it possible that there is nobody among you wise enough to judge a dispute between believers? [6]But instead, one brother takes another to court — and this in front of unbelievers!

[7]The very fact that you have lawsuits among you means you have been completely defeated already. Why not rather be wronged? Why not rather be cheated? [8]Instead, you yourselves cheat and do wrong, and you do this to your brothers and sisters. [9]Or do you not know that wrongdoers will not inherit the kingdom of God? Do not be deceived: Neither the sexually immoral nor idolaters nor adulterers nor men who have sex with men[e] [10]nor thieves nor the greedy nor drunkards nor slanderers nor swindlers will inherit the kingdom of God. [11]And that is what some of you were. But you were washed, you were sanctified, you were justified in the name of the Lord Jesus Christ and by the Spirit of our God.

Sexual Immorality

[12]"I have the right to do anything," you say — but not everything is beneficial. "I have the right to do anything" — but I will not be mastered by anything. [13]You say, "Food for the stomach and the stomach for food, and God will destroy them both." The body, however, is not meant for sexual immorality but for the Lord, and the Lord for the body. [14]By his power God raised the Lord from the dead, and he will raise us also. [15]Do you not know that your bodies are members of Christ himself? Shall I then take the members of Christ and unite them with a prostitute? Never! [16]Do you not know that he who unites himself with a prostitute is one with her in body? For it is said, "The two will become one flesh."[f] [17]But whoever is united with the Lord is one with him in spirit.[g]

[18]Flee from sexual immorality. All other sins a person commits are outside the body, but whoever sins sexually, sins against their own body. [19]Do you not know that your bodies are temples of the Holy Spirit, who is in

[a] *5* In contexts like this, the Greek word for *flesh* (*sarx*) refers to the sinful state of human beings, often presented as a power in opposition to the Spirit. [b] *5* Or *of his body* [c] *11* The Greek word for *brother or sister* (*adelphos*) refers here to a believer, whether man or woman, as part of God's family; also in 8:11, 13. [d] *13* Deut. 13:5; 17:7; 19:19; 21:21; 22:21,24; 24:7 [e] *9* The words *men who have sex with men* translate two Greek words that refer to the passive and active participants in homosexual acts. [f] *16* Gen. 2:24 [g] *17* Or *in the Spirit*

you, whom you have received from God? You are not your own; [20]you were bought at a price. Therefore honor God with your bodies.

Concerning Married Life

7 Now for the matters you wrote about: "It is good for a man not to have sexual relations with a woman." [2]But since sexual immorality is occurring, each man should have sexual relations with his own wife, and each woman with her own husband. [3]The husband should fulfill his marital duty to his wife, and likewise the wife to her husband. [4]The wife does not have authority over her own body but yields it to her husband. In the same way, the husband does not have authority over his own body but yields it to his wife. [5]Do not deprive each other except perhaps by mutual consent and for a time, so that you may devote yourselves to prayer. Then come together again so that Satan will not tempt you because of your lack of self-control. [6]I say this as a concession, not as a command. [7]I wish that all of you were as I am. But each of you has your own gift from God; one has this gift, another has that.

[8]Now to the unmarried[a] and the widows I say: It is good for them to stay unmarried, as I do. [9]But if they cannot control themselves, they should marry, for it is better to marry than to burn with passion.

[10]To the married I give this command (not I, but the Lord): A wife must not separate from her husband. [11]But if she does, she must remain unmarried or else be reconciled to her husband. And a husband must not divorce his wife.

[12]To the rest I say this (I, not the Lord): If any brother has a wife who is not a believer and she is willing to live with him, he must not divorce her. [13]And if a woman has a husband who is not a believer and he is willing to live with her, she must not divorce him. [14]For the unbelieving husband has been sanctified through his wife, and the unbelieving wife has been sanctified through her believing husband. Otherwise your children would be unclean, but as it is, they are holy.

[15]But if the unbeliever leaves, let it be so. The brother or the sister is not bound in such circumstances; God has called us to live in peace. [16]How do you know, wife, whether you will save your husband? Or, how do you know, husband, whether you will save your wife?

Concerning Change of Status

[17]Nevertheless, each person should live as a believer in whatever situation the Lord has assigned to them, just as God has called them. This is the rule I lay down in all the churches. [18]Was a man already circumcised when he was called? He should not become uncircumcised. Was a man uncircumcised when he was called? He should not be circumcised. [19]Circumcision is nothing and uncircumcision is nothing. Keeping God's commands is what counts. [20]Each person should remain in the situation they were in when God called them.

[21]Were you a slave when you were called? Don't let it trouble you—although if you can gain your freedom, do so. [22]For the one who was a slave when called to faith in the Lord is the Lord's freed person; similarly, the one who was free when called is Christ's slave. [23]You were bought at a price; do not become slaves of human beings. [24]Brothers and sisters, each person, as responsible to God, should remain in the situation they were in when God called them.

Concerning the Unmarried

[25]Now about virgins: I have no command from the Lord, but I give a judgment as one who by the Lord's mercy is trustworthy. [26]Because of the present crisis, I think that it is good for a man to remain as he is. [27]Are you pledged to a woman? Do not seek to be released. Are you free from such a commitment? Do not look for a wife. [28]But if you do marry, you have not sinned; and if a virgin marries, she has not sinned. But those who marry will face many troubles in this life, and I want to spare you this.

[29]What I mean, brothers and sisters, is that the time is short. From now on those who have wives should live as if they do not; [30]those who mourn, as if they did not; those who are happy, as if they were not; those who buy something, as if it were not theirs to keep; [31]those who use the things of the

[a] 8 Or *widowers*

world, as if not engrossed in them. For this world in its present form is passing away.

32 I would like you to be free from concern. An unmarried man is concerned about the Lord's affairs—how he can please the Lord. 33 But a married man is concerned about the affairs of this world—how he can please his wife— 34 and his interests are divided. An unmarried woman or virgin is concerned about the Lord's affairs: Her aim is to be devoted to the Lord in both body and spirit. But a married woman is concerned about the affairs of this world—how she can please her husband. 35 I am saying this for your own good, not to restrict you, but that you may live in a right way in undivided devotion to the Lord.

36 If anyone is worried that he might not be acting honorably toward the virgin he is engaged to, and if his passions are too strong[a] and he feels he ought to marry, he should do as he wants. He is not sinning. They should get married. 37 But the man who has settled the matter in his own mind, who is under no compulsion but has control over his own will, and who has made up his mind not to marry the virgin—this man also does the right thing. 38 So then, he who marries the virgin does right, but he who does not marry her does better.[b]

39 A woman is bound to her husband as long as he lives. But if her husband dies, she is free to marry anyone she wishes, but he must belong to the Lord. 40 In my judgment, she is happier if she stays as she is—and I think that I too have the Spirit of God.

Concerning Food Sacrificed to Idols

8 Now about food sacrificed to idols: We know that "We all possess knowledge." But knowledge puffs up while love builds up. 2 Those who think they know something do not yet know as they ought to know. 3 But whoever loves God is known by God.[c]

4 So then, about eating food sacrificed to idols: We know that "An idol is nothing at all in the world" and that "There is no God but one." 5 For even if there are so-called gods, whether in heaven or on earth (as indeed there are many "gods" and many "lords"), 6 yet for us there is but one God, the Father, from whom all things came and for whom we live; and there is but one Lord, Jesus Christ, through whom all things came and through whom we live.

7 But not everyone possesses this knowledge. Some people are still so accustomed to idols that when they eat sacrificial food they think of it as having been sacrificed to a god, and since their conscience is weak, it is defiled. 8 But food does not bring us near to God; we are no worse if we do not eat, and no better if we do.

9 Be careful, however, that the exercise of your rights does not become a stumbling block to the weak. 10 For if someone with a weak conscience sees you, with all your knowledge, eating in an idol's temple, won't that person be emboldened to eat what is sacrificed to idols? 11 So this weak brother or sister, for whom Christ died, is destroyed by your knowledge. 12 When you sin against them in this way and wound their weak conscience, you sin against Christ. 13 Therefore, if what I eat causes my brother or sister to fall into sin, I will never eat meat again, so that I will not cause them to fall.

Paul's Rights as an Apostle

9 Am I not free? Am I not an apostle? Have I not seen Jesus our Lord? Are you not the result of my work in the Lord? 2 Even though I may not be an apostle to others, surely I am to you! For you are the seal of my apostleship in the Lord.

3 This is my defense to those who sit in judgment on me. 4 Don't we have the right to food and drink? 5 Don't we have the right to take a believing wife along with us, as do the other apostles and the Lord's brothers and Cephas[d]? 6 Or is it only I and Barnabas who lack the right to not work for a living?

[a] 36 Or *if she is getting beyond the usual age for marriage* [b] 36-38 Or *36 If anyone thinks he is not treating his daughter properly, and if she is getting along in years* (or *if her passions are too strong*), *and he feels she ought to marry, he should do as he wants. He is not sinning. He should let her get married. 37 But the man who has settled the matter in his own mind, who is under no compulsion but has control over his own will, and who has made up his mind to keep the virgin unmarried—this man also does the right thing. 38 So then, he who gives his virgin in marriage does right, but he who does not give her in marriage does better.*

[c] 2,3 An early manuscript and another ancient witness *think they have knowledge do not yet know as they ought to know. 3 But whoever loves truly knows.* [d] 5 That is, Peter

7Who serves as a soldier at his own ex-
pense? Who plants a vineyard and does not
eat its grapes? Who tends a flock and does
not drink the milk? 8Do I say this merely
on human authority? Doesn't the Law say
the same thing? 9For it is written in the Law
of Moses: "Do not muzzle an ox while it is
treading out the grain."[a] Is it about oxen that
God is concerned? 10Surely he says this for
us, doesn't he? Yes, this was written for us,
because whoever plows and threshes should
be able to do so in the hope of sharing in the
harvest. 11If we have sown spiritual seed
among you, is it too much if we reap a ma-
terial harvest from you? 12If others have this
right of support from you, shouldn't we have
it all the more?

But we did not use this right. On the contrary, we put up with anything rather than hinder the gospel of Christ.

13Don't you know that those who serve in
the temple get their food from the temple,
and that those who serve at the altar share
in what is offered on the altar? 14In the same
way, the Lord has commanded that those
who preach the gospel should receive their
living from the gospel.

15But I have not used any of these rights.
And I am not writing this in the hope that
you will do such things for me, for I would
rather die than allow anyone to deprive me
of this boast. 16For when I preach the gos-
pel, I cannot boast, since I am compelled to
preach. Woe to me if I do not preach the gos-
pel! 17If I preach voluntarily, I have a reward;
if not voluntarily, I am simply discharging
the trust committed to me. 18What then is
my reward? Just this: that in preaching the
gospel I may offer it free of charge, and so not
make full use of my rights as a preacher of
the gospel.

Paul's Use of His Freedom

19Though I am free and belong to no one,
I have made myself a slave to everyone, to
win as many as possible. 20To the Jews I be-
came like a Jew, to win the Jews. To those un-
der the law I became like one under the law
(though I myself am not under the law), so
as to win those under the law. 21To those not
having the law I became like one not hav-
ing the law (though I am not free from God's
law but am under Christ's law), so as to win
those not having the law. 22To the weak I be-
came weak, to win the weak. I have become
all things to all people so that by all possible
means I might save some. 23I do all this for
the sake of the gospel, that I may share in its
blessings.

The Need for Self-Discipline

24Do you not know that in a race all the
runners run, but only one gets the prize?
Run in such a way as to get the prize. 25Ev-
eryone who competes in the games goes into
strict training. They do it to get a crown that
will not last, but we do it to get a crown that
will last forever. 26Therefore I do not run like
someone running aimlessly; I do not fight
like a boxer beating the air. 27No, I strike a
blow to my body and make it my slave so that
after I have preached to others, I myself will
not be disqualified for the prize.

Warnings From Israel's History

10 For I do not want you to be ignorant of
the fact, brothers and sisters, that our
ancestors were all under the cloud and that
they all passed through the sea. 2They were
all baptized into Moses in the cloud and in
the sea. 3They all ate the same spiritual food
4and drank the same spiritual drink; for they
drank from the spiritual rock that accompa-
nied them, and that rock was Christ. 5Nev-
ertheless, God was not pleased with most
of them; their bodies were scattered in the
wilderness.

6Now these things occurred as exam-
ples to keep us from setting our hearts on
evil things as they did. 7Do not be idolaters,
as some of them were; as it is written: "The
people sat down to eat and drink and got
up to indulge in revelry."[b] 8We should not
commit sexual immorality, as some of them
did — and in one day twenty-three thousand
of them died. 9We should not test Christ,[c]
as some of them did — and were killed by
snakes. 10And do not grumble, as some of
them did — and were killed by the destroy-
ing angel.

11These things happened to them as ex-
amples and were written down as warnings
for us, on whom the culmination of the ages
has come. 12So, if you think you are standing

[a] 9 Deut. 25:4 [b] 7 Exodus 32:6 [c] 9 Some manuscripts *test the Lord*

firm, be careful that you don't fall! 13 No temptation[a] has overtaken you except what is common to mankind. And God is faithful; he will not let you be tempted[a] beyond what you can bear. But when you are tempted,[a] he will also provide a way out so that you can endure it.

Idol Feasts and the Lord's Supper

14 Therefore, my dear friends, flee from idolatry. 15 I speak to sensible people; judge for yourselves what I say. 16 Is not the cup of thanksgiving for which we give thanks a participation in the blood of Christ? And is not the bread that we break a participation in the body of Christ? 17 Because there is one loaf, we, who are many, are one body, for we all share the one loaf.

18 Consider the people of Israel: Do not those who eat the sacrifices participate in the altar? 19 Do I mean then that food sacrificed to an idol is anything, or that an idol is anything? 20 No, but the sacrifices of pagans are offered to demons, not to God, and I do not want you to be participants with demons. 21 You cannot drink the cup of the Lord and the cup of demons too; you cannot have a part in both the Lord's table and the table of demons. 22 Are we trying to arouse the Lord's jealousy? Are we stronger than he?

The Believer's Freedom

23 "I have the right to do anything," you say—but not everything is beneficial. "I have the right to do anything"—but not everything is constructive. 24 No one should seek their own good, but the good of others.

25 Eat anything sold in the meat market without raising questions of conscience, 26 for, "The earth is the Lord's, and everything in it."[b]

27 If an unbeliever invites you to a meal and you want to go, eat whatever is put before you without raising questions of conscience. 28 But if someone says to you, "This has been offered in sacrifice," then do not eat it, both for the sake of the one who told you and for the sake of conscience. 29 I am referring to the other person's conscience, not yours. For why is my freedom being judged by another's conscience? 30 If I take part in the meal with thankfulness, why am I denounced because of something I thank God for?

31 So whether you eat or drink or whatever you do, do it all for the glory of God. 32 Do not cause anyone to stumble, whether Jews, Greeks or the church of God—33 even as I try to please everyone in every way. For I am not seeking my own good but the good of many,

11 so that they may be saved. 1 Follow my example, as I follow the example of Christ.

On Covering the Head in Worship

2 I praise you for remembering me in everything and for holding to the traditions just as I passed them on to you. 3 But I want you to realize that the head of every man is Christ, and the head of the woman is man,[c] and the head of Christ is God. 4 Every man who prays or prophesies with his head covered dishonors his head. 5 But every woman who prays or prophesies with her head uncovered dishonors her head—it is the same as having her head shaved. 6 For if a woman does not cover her head, she might as well have her hair cut off; but if it is a disgrace for a woman to have her hair cut off or her head shaved, then she should cover her head.

7 A man ought not to cover his head,[d] since he is the image and glory of God; but woman is the glory of man. 8 For man did not come from woman, but woman from man; 9 neither was man created for woman, but woman for man. 10 It is for this reason that a woman ought to have authority over her own[e] head, because of the angels. 11 Nevertheless, in the Lord woman is not independent of man, nor is man independent of woman. 12 For as woman came from man, so also man is born of woman. But everything comes from God.

13 Judge for yourselves: Is it proper for a woman to pray to God with her head uncovered? 14 Does not the very nature of things

[a] 13 The Greek for *temptation* and *tempted* can also mean *testing* and *tested.* [b] 26 Psalm 24:1
[c] 3 Or *of the wife is her husband* [d] 4-7 Or [4]*Every man who prays or prophesies with long hair dishonors his head.* [5]*But every woman who prays or prophesies with no covering of hair dishonors her head—she is just like one of the "shorn women."* [6]*If a woman has no covering, let her be for now with short hair; but since it is a disgrace for a woman to have her hair shorn or shaved, she should grow it again.* [7]*A man ought not to have long hair* [e] 10 Or *have a sign of authority on her*

teach you that if a man has long hair, it is a disgrace to him, [15]but that if a woman has long hair, it is her glory? For long hair is given to her as a covering. [16]If anyone wants to be contentious about this, we have no other practice — nor do the churches of God.

Correcting an Abuse of the Lord's Supper

[17]In the following directives I have no praise for you, for your meetings do more harm than good. [18]In the first place, I hear that when you come together as a church, there are divisions among you, and to some extent I believe it. [19]No doubt there have to be differences among you to show which of you have God's approval. [20]So then, when you come together, it is not the Lord's Supper you eat, [21]for when you are eating, some of you go ahead with your own private suppers. As a result, one person remains hungry and another gets drunk. [22]Don't you have homes to eat and drink in? Or do you despise the church of God by humiliating those who have nothing? What shall I say to you? Shall I praise you? Certainly not in this matter!

[23]For I received from the Lord what I also passed on to you: The Lord Jesus, on the night he was betrayed, took bread, [24]and when he had given thanks, he broke it and said, "This is my body, which is for you; do this in remembrance of me." [25]In the same way, after supper he took the cup, saying, "This cup is the new covenant in my blood; do this, whenever you drink it, in remembrance of me." [26]For whenever you eat this bread and drink this cup, you proclaim the Lord's death until he comes.

[27]So then, whoever eats the bread or drinks the cup of the Lord in an unworthy manner will be guilty of sinning against the body and blood of the Lord. [28]Everyone ought to examine themselves before they eat of the bread and drink from the cup. [29]For those who eat and drink without discerning the body of Christ eat and drink judgment on themselves. [30]That is why many among you are weak and sick, and a number of you have fallen asleep. [31]But if we were more discerning with regard to ourselves, we would not come under such judgment. [32]Nevertheless, when we are judged in this way by the Lord, we are being disciplined so that we will not be finally condemned with the world.

[33]So then, my brothers and sisters, when you gather to eat, you should all eat together. [34]Anyone who is hungry should eat something at home, so that when you meet together it may not result in judgment.

And when I come I will give further directions.

Concerning Spiritual Gifts

12 Now about the gifts of the Spirit, brothers and sisters, I do not want you to be uninformed. [2]You know that when you were pagans, somehow or other you were influenced and led astray to mute idols. [3]Therefore I want you to know that no one who is speaking by the Spirit of God says, "Jesus be cursed," and no one can say, "Jesus is Lord," except by the Holy Spirit.

[4]There are different kinds of gifts, but the same Spirit distributes them. [5]There are different kinds of service, but the same Lord. [6]There are different kinds of working, but in all of them and in everyone it is the same God at work.

[7]Now to each one the manifestation of the Spirit is given for the common good. [8]To one there is given through the Spirit a message of wisdom, to another a message of knowledge by means of the same Spirit, [9]to another faith by the same Spirit, to another gifts of healing by that one Spirit, [10]to another miraculous powers, to another prophecy, to another distinguishing between spirits, to another speaking in different kinds of tongues,[a] and to still another the interpretation of tongues.[a] [11]All these are the work of one and the same Spirit, and he distributes them to each one, just as he determines.

Unity and Diversity in the Body

[12]Just as a body, though one, has many parts, but all its many parts form one body, so it is with Christ. [13]For we were all baptized by[b] one Spirit so as to form one body — whether Jews or Gentiles, slave or free — and we were all given the one Spirit to drink. [14]Even so the body is not made up of one part but of many.

[15]Now if the foot should say, "Because I am not a hand, I do not belong to the body," it would not for that reason stop being part

[a] *10* Or *languages*; also in verse 28 [b] *13* Or *with*; or *in*

of the body. [16]And if the ear should say, "Because I am not an eye, I do not belong to the body," it would not for that reason stop being part of the body. [17]If the whole body were an eye, where would the sense of hearing be? If the whole body were an ear, where would the sense of smell be? [18]But in fact God has placed the parts in the body, every one of them, just as he wanted them to be. [19]If they were all one part, where would the body be? [20]As it is, there are many parts, but one body.

[21]The eye cannot say to the hand, "I don't need you!" And the head cannot say to the feet, "I don't need you!" [22]On the contrary, those parts of the body that seem to be weaker are indispensable, [23]and the parts that we think are less honorable we treat with special honor. And the parts that are unpresentable are treated with special modesty, [24]while our presentable parts need no special treatment. But God has put the body together, giving greater honor to the parts that lacked it, [25]so that there should be no division in the body, but that its parts should have equal concern for each other. [26]If one part suffers, every part suffers with it; if one part is honored, every part rejoices with it.

[27]Now you are the body of Christ, and each one of you is a part of it. [28]And God has placed in the church first of all apostles, second prophets, third teachers, then miracles, then gifts of healing, of helping, of guidance, and of different kinds of tongues. [29]Are all apostles? Are all prophets? Are all teachers? Do all work miracles? [30]Do all have gifts of healing? Do all speak in tongues[a]? Do all interpret? [31]Now eagerly desire the greater gifts.

Love Is Indispensable

And yet I will show you the most excellent way.

13 If I speak in the tongues[b] of men or of angels, but do not have love, I am only a resounding gong or a clanging cymbal. [2]If I have the gift of prophecy and can fathom all mysteries and all knowledge, and if I have a faith that can move mountains, but do not have love, I am nothing. [3]If I give all I possess to the poor and give over my body to hardship that I may boast,[c] but do not have love, I gain nothing.

[4]Love is patient, love is kind. It does not envy, it does not boast, it is not proud. [5]It does not dishonor others, it is not self-seeking, it is not easily angered, it keeps no record of wrongs. [6]Love does not delight in evil but rejoices with the truth. [7]It always protects, always trusts, always hopes, always perseveres.

[8]Love never fails. But where there are prophecies, they will cease; where there are tongues, they will be stilled; where there is knowledge, it will pass away. [9]For we know in part and we prophesy in part, [10]but when completeness comes, what is in part disappears. [11]When I was a child, I talked like a child, I thought like a child, I reasoned like a child. When I became a man, I put the ways of childhood behind me. [12]For now we see only a reflection as in a mirror; then we shall see face to face. Now I know in part; then I shall know fully, even as I am fully known.

[13]And now these three remain: faith, hope and love. But the greatest of these is love.

Intelligibility in Worship

14 Follow the way of love and eagerly desire gifts of the Spirit, especially prophecy. [2]For anyone who speaks in a tongue[d] does not speak to people but to God. Indeed, no one understands them; they utter mysteries by the Spirit. [3]But the one who prophesies speaks to people for their strengthening, encouraging and comfort. [4]Anyone who speaks in a tongue edifies themselves, but the one who prophesies edifies the church. [5]I would like every one of you to speak in tongues,[e] but I would rather have you prophesy. The one who prophesies is greater than the one who speaks in tongues,[e] unless someone interprets, so that the church may be edified.

[6]Now, brothers and sisters, if I come to you and speak in tongues, what good will I be to you, unless I bring you some revelation or knowledge or prophecy or word of instruction? [7]Even in the case of lifeless things that make sounds, such as the pipe or harp,

[a] 30 Or *other languages* [b] *1* Or *languages* [c] *3* Some manuscripts *body to the flames* [d] *2* Or *in another language*; also in verses 4, 13, 14, 19, 26 and 27 [e] *5* Or *in other languages*; also in verses 6, 18, 22, 23 and 39

how will anyone know what tune is being played unless there is a distinction in the notes? 8Again, if the trumpet does not sound a clear call, who will get ready for battle? 9So it is with you. Unless you speak intelligible words with your tongue, how will anyone know what you are saying? You will just be speaking into the air. 10Undoubtedly there are all sorts of languages in the world, yet none of them is without meaning. 11If then I do not grasp the meaning of what someone is saying, I am a foreigner to the speaker, and the speaker is a foreigner to me. 12So it is with you. Since you are eager for gifts of the Spirit, try to excel in those that build up the church.

13For this reason the one who speaks in a tongue should pray that they may interpret what they say. 14For if I pray in a tongue, my spirit prays, but my mind is unfruitful. 15So what shall I do? I will pray with my spirit, but I will also pray with my understanding; I will sing with my spirit, but I will also sing with my understanding. 16Otherwise when you are praising God in the Spirit, how can someone else, who is now put in the position of an inquirer,[a] say "Amen" to your thanksgiving, since they do not know what you are saying? 17You are giving thanks well enough, but no one else is edified.

18I thank God that I speak in tongues more than all of you. 19But in the church I would rather speak five intelligible words to instruct others than ten thousand words in a tongue.

20Brothers and sisters, stop thinking like children. In regard to evil be infants, but in your thinking be adults. 21In the Law it is written:

"With other tongues
  and through the lips of foreigners
I will speak to this people,
  but even then they will not listen to me,
    says the Lord."[b]

22Tongues, then, are a sign, not for believers but for unbelievers; prophecy, however, is not for unbelievers but for believers. 23So if the whole church comes together and everyone speaks in tongues, and inquirers or unbelievers come in, will they not say that you are out of your mind? 24But if an unbeliever or an inquirer comes in while everyone is prophesying, they are convicted of sin and are brought under judgment by all, 25as the secrets of their hearts are laid bare. So they will fall down and worship God, exclaiming, "God is really among you!"

Good Order in Worship

26What then shall we say, brothers and sisters? When you come together, each of you has a hymn, or a word of instruction, a revelation, a tongue or an interpretation. Everything must be done so that the church may be built up. 27If anyone speaks in a tongue, two—or at the most three—should speak, one at a time, and someone must interpret. 28If there is no interpreter, the speaker should keep quiet in the church and speak to himself and to God.

29Two or three prophets should speak, and the others should weigh carefully what is said. 30And if a revelation comes to someone who is sitting down, the first speaker should stop. 31For you can all prophesy in turn so that everyone may be instructed and encouraged. 32The spirits of prophets are subject to the control of prophets. 33For God is not a God of disorder but of peace—as in all the congregations of the Lord's people.

34Women[c] should remain silent in the churches. They are not allowed to speak, but must be in submission, as the law says. 35If they want to inquire about something, they should ask their own husbands at home; for it is disgraceful for a woman to speak in the church.[d]

36Or did the word of God originate with you? Or are you the only people it has reached? 37If anyone thinks they are a prophet or otherwise gifted by the Spirit, let them acknowledge that what I am writing to you is the Lord's command. 38But if anyone ignores this, they will themselves be ignored.[e]

39Therefore, my brothers and sisters, be eager to prophesy, and do not forbid speaking in tongues. 40But everything should be done in a fitting and orderly way.

[a] *16* The Greek word for *inquirer* is a technical term for someone not fully initiated into a religion; also in verses 23 and 24. [b] *21* Isaiah 28:11,12 [c] *33,34* Or *peace. As in all the congregations of the Lord's people, 34women* [d] *34,35* In a few manuscripts these verses come after verse 40. [e] *38* Some manuscripts *But anyone who is ignorant of this will be ignorant*

The Resurrection of Christ

15 Now, brothers and sisters, I want to remind you of the gospel I preached to you, which you received and on which you have taken your stand. 2 By this gospel you are saved, if you hold firmly to the word I preached to you. Otherwise, you have believed in vain.

3 For what I received I passed on to you as of first importance[a]: that Christ died for our sins according to the Scriptures, 4 that he was buried, that he was raised on the third day according to the Scriptures, 5 and that he appeared to Cephas,[b] and then to the Twelve. 6 After that, he appeared to more than five hundred of the brothers and sisters at the same time, most of whom are still living, though some have fallen asleep. 7 Then he appeared to James, then to all the apostles, 8 and last of all he appeared to me also, as to one abnormally born.

9 For I am the least of the apostles and do not even deserve to be called an apostle, because I persecuted the church of God. 10 But by the grace of God I am what I am, and his grace to me was not without effect. No, I worked harder than all of them—yet not I, but the grace of God that was with me. 11 Whether, then, it is I or they, this is what we preach, and this is what you believed.

The Resurrection of the Dead

12 But if it is preached that Christ has been raised from the dead, how can some of you say that there is no resurrection of the dead? 13 If there is no resurrection of the dead, then not even Christ has been raised. 14 And if Christ has not been raised, our preaching is useless and so is your faith. 15 More than that, we are then found to be false witnesses about God, for we have testified about God that he raised Christ from the dead. But he did not raise him if in fact the dead are not raised. 16 For if the dead are not raised, then Christ has not been raised either. 17 And if Christ has not been raised, your faith is futile; you are still in your sins. 18 Then those also who have fallen asleep in Christ are lost. 19 If only for this life we have hope in Christ, we are of all people most to be pitied.

20 But Christ has indeed been raised from the dead, the firstfruits of those who have fallen asleep. 21 For since death came through a man, the resurrection of the dead comes also through a man. 22 For as in Adam all die, so in Christ all will be made alive. 23 But each in turn: Christ, the firstfruits; then, when he comes, those who belong to him. 24 Then the end will come, when he hands over the kingdom to God the Father after he has destroyed all dominion, authority and power. 25 For he must reign until he has put all his enemies under his feet. 26 The last enemy to be destroyed is death. 27 For he "has put everything under his feet."[c] Now when it says that "everything" has been put under him, it is clear that this does not include God himself, who put everything under Christ. 28 When he has done this, then the Son himself will be made subject to him who put everything under him, so that God may be all in all.

29 Now if there is no resurrection, what will those do who are baptized for the dead? If the dead are not raised at all, why are people baptized for them? 30 And as for us, why do we endanger ourselves every hour? 31 I face death every day—yes, just as surely as I boast about you in Christ Jesus our Lord. 32 If I fought wild beasts in Ephesus with no more than human hopes, what have I gained? If the dead are not raised,

"Let us eat and drink,
for tomorrow we die."[d]

33 Do not be misled: "Bad company corrupts good character."[e] 34 Come back to your senses as you ought, and stop sinning; for there are some who are ignorant of God—I say this to your shame.

The Resurrection Body

35 But someone will ask, "How are the dead raised? With what kind of body will they come?" 36 How foolish! What you sow does not come to life unless it dies. 37 When you sow, you do not plant the body that will be, but just a seed, perhaps of wheat or of something else. 38 But God gives it a body as he has determined, and to each kind of seed he gives its own body. 39 Not all flesh is the same: People have one kind of flesh, animals

[a] 3 Or *you at the first* [b] 5 That is, Peter [c] 27 Psalm 8:6 [d] 32 Isaiah 22:13 [e] 33 From the Greek poet Menander

have another, birds another and fish another. 40There are also heavenly bodies and there are earthly bodies; but the splendor of the heavenly bodies is one kind, and the splendor of the earthly bodies is another. 41The sun has one kind of splendor, the moon another and the stars another; and star differs from star in splendor.

42So will it be with the resurrection of the dead. The body that is sown is perishable, it is raised imperishable; 43it is sown in dishonor, it is raised in glory; it is sown in weakness, it is raised in power; 44it is sown a natural body, it is raised a spiritual body.

If there is a natural body, there is also a spiritual body. 45So it is written: "The first man Adam became a living being"[a]; the last Adam, a life-giving spirit. 46The spiritual did not come first, but the natural, and after that the spiritual. 47The first man was of the dust of the earth; the second man is of heaven. 48As was the earthly man, so are those who are of the earth; and as is the heavenly man, so also are those who are of heaven. 49And just as we have borne the image of the earthly man, so shall we[b] bear the image of the heavenly man.

50I declare to you, brothers and sisters, that flesh and blood cannot inherit the kingdom of God, nor does the perishable inherit the imperishable. 51Listen, I tell you a mystery: We will not all sleep, but we will all be changed— 52in a flash, in the twinkling of an eye, at the last trumpet. For the trumpet will sound, the dead will be raised imperishable, and we will be changed. 53For the perishable must clothe itself with the imperishable, and the mortal with immortality. 54When the perishable has been clothed with the imperishable, and the mortal with immortality, then the saying that is written will come true: "Death has been swallowed up in victory."[c]

55"Where, O death, is your victory?
    Where, O death, is your sting?"[d]

56The sting of death is sin, and the power of sin is the law. 57But thanks be to God! He gives us the victory through our Lord Jesus Christ.

58Therefore, my dear brothers and sisters, stand firm. Let nothing move you. Always give yourselves fully to the work of the Lord, because you know that your labor in the Lord is not in vain.

The Collection for the Lord's People

16 Now about the collection for the Lord's people: Do what I told the Galatian churches to do. 2On the first day of every week, each one of you should set aside a sum of money in keeping with your income, saving it up, so that when I come no collections will have to be made. 3Then, when I arrive, I will give letters of introduction to the men you approve and send them with your gift to Jerusalem. 4If it seems advisable for me to go also, they will accompany me.

Personal Requests

5After I go through Macedonia, I will come to you—for I will be going through Macedonia. 6Perhaps I will stay with you for a while, or even spend the winter, so that you can help me on my journey, wherever I go. 7For I do not want to see you now and make only a passing visit; I hope to spend some time with you, if the Lord permits. 8But I will stay on at Ephesus until Pentecost, 9because a great door for effective work has opened to me, and there are many who oppose me.

10When Timothy comes, see to it that he has nothing to fear while he is with you, for he is carrying on the work of the Lord, just as I am. 11No one, then, should treat him with contempt. Send him on his way in peace so that he may return to me. I am expecting him along with the brothers.

12Now about our brother Apollos: I strongly urged him to go to you with the brothers. He was quite unwilling to go now, but he will go when he has the opportunity.

13Be on your guard; stand firm in the faith; be courageous; be strong. 14Do everything in love.

15You know that the household of Stephanas were the first converts in Achaia, and they have devoted themselves to the service of the Lord's people. I urge you, brothers and sisters, 16to submit to such people and to everyone who joins in the work and labors at it. 17I was glad when Stephanas, Fortunatus and Achaicus arrived, because they have

[a] *45* Gen. 2:7 [b] *49* Some early manuscripts *so let us* [c] *54* Isaiah 25:8 [d] *55* Hosea 13:14

supplied what was lacking from you. [18]For
they refreshed my spirit and yours also. Such
men deserve recognition.

Final Greetings

[19]The churches in the province of Asia
send you greetings. Aquila and Priscilla[a]
greet you warmly in the Lord, and so does
the church that meets at their house. [20]All
the brothers and sisters here send you greetings. Greet one another with a holy kiss.
[21]I, Paul, write this greeting in my own
hand.
[22]If anyone does not love the Lord, let that
person be cursed! Come, Lord[b]!
[23]The grace of the Lord Jesus be with you.
[24]My love to all of you in Christ Jesus.
Amen.[c]

[a] 19 Greek *Prisca*, a variant of *Priscilla* [b] 22 The Greek for *Come, Lord* reproduces an Aramaic expression (*Marana tha*) used by early Christians. [c] 24 Some manuscripts do not have *Amen*.

2 CORINTHIANS

1 Paul, an apostle of Christ Jesus by the will of God, and Timothy our brother,

To the church of God in Corinth, together with all his holy people throughout Achaia:

[2]Grace and peace to you from God our Father and the Lord Jesus Christ.

Praise to the God of All Comfort

[3]Praise be to the God and Father of our Lord Jesus Christ, the Father of compassion and the God of all comfort, [4]who comforts us in all our troubles, so that we can comfort those in any trouble with the comfort we ourselves receive from God. [5]For just as we share abundantly in the sufferings of Christ, so also our comfort abounds through Christ. [6]If we are distressed, it is for your comfort and salvation; if we are comforted, it is for your comfort, which produces in you patient endurance of the same sufferings we suffer. [7]And our hope for you is firm, because we know that just as you share in our sufferings, so also you share in our comfort.

[8]We do not want you to be uninformed, brothers and sisters,[a] about the troubles we experienced in the province of Asia. We were under great pressure, far beyond our ability to endure, so that we despaired of life itself. [9]Indeed, we felt we had received the sentence of death. But this happened that we might not rely on ourselves but on God, who raises the dead. [10]He has delivered us from such a deadly peril, and he will deliver us again. On him we have set our hope that he will continue to deliver us, [11]as you help us by your prayers. Then many will give thanks on our behalf for the gracious favor granted us in answer to the prayers of many.

Paul's Change of Plans

[12]Now this is our boast: Our conscience testifies that we have conducted ourselves in the world, and especially in our relations with you, with integrity[b] and godly sincerity. We have done so, relying not on worldly wisdom but on God's grace. [13]For we do not write you anything you cannot read or understand. And I hope that, [14]as you have understood us in part, you will come to understand fully that you can boast of us just as we will boast of you in the day of the Lord Jesus.

[15]Because I was confident of this, I wanted to visit you first so that you might benefit twice. [16]I wanted to visit you on my way to Macedonia and to come back to you from Macedonia, and then to have you send me on my way to Judea. [17]Was I fickle when I intended to do this? Or do I make my plans in a worldly manner so that in the same breath I say both "Yes, yes" and "No, no"?

[18]But as surely as God is faithful, our message to you is not "Yes" and "No." [19]For the Son of God, Jesus Christ, who was preached among you by us—by me and Silas[c] and Timothy—was not "Yes" and "No," but in him it has always been "Yes." [20]For no matter how many promises God has made, they are "Yes" in Christ. And so through him the "Amen" is spoken by us to the glory of God. [21]Now it is God who makes both us and you stand firm in Christ. He anointed us, [22]set his seal of ownership on us, and put his Spirit in our hearts as a deposit, guaranteeing what is to come.

[23]I call God as my witness—and I stake my life on it—that it was in order to spare you that I did not return to Corinth. [24]Not that we lord it over your faith, but we work with you for your joy, because it is by faith

2 you stand firm. [1]So I made up my mind that I would not make another painful visit to you. [2]For if I grieve you, who is left to make me glad but you whom I have grieved? [3]I wrote as I did, so that when I came I would not be distressed by those who should have

[a] *8* The Greek word for *brothers and sisters* (*adelphoi*) refers here to believers, both men and women, as part of God's family; also in 8:1; 13:11. [b] *12* Many manuscripts *holiness* [c] *19* Greek *Silvanus*, a variant of *Silas*

made me rejoice. I had confidence in all of you, that you would all share my joy. [4]For I wrote you out of great distress and anguish of heart and with many tears, not to grieve you but to let you know the depth of my love for you.

Forgiveness for the Offender

[5]If anyone has caused grief, he has not so much grieved me as he has grieved all of you to some extent — not to put it too severely. [6]The punishment inflicted on him by the majority is sufficient. [7]Now instead, you ought to forgive and comfort him, so that he will not be overwhelmed by excessive sorrow. [8]I urge you, therefore, to reaffirm your love for him. [9]Another reason I wrote you was to see if you would stand the test and be obedient in everything. [10]Anyone you forgive, I also forgive. And what I have forgiven — if there was anything to forgive — I have forgiven in the sight of Christ for your sake, [11]in order that Satan might not outwit us. For we are not unaware of his schemes.

Ministers of the New Covenant

[12]Now when I went to Troas to preach the gospel of Christ and found that the Lord had opened a door for me, [13]I still had no peace of mind, because I did not find my brother Titus there. So I said goodbye to them and went on to Macedonia.

[14]But thanks be to God, who always leads us as captives in Christ's triumphal procession and uses us to spread the aroma of the knowledge of him everywhere. [15]For we are to God the pleasing aroma of Christ among those who are being saved and those who are perishing. [16]To the one we are an aroma that brings death; to the other, an aroma that brings life. And who is equal to such a task? [17]Unlike so many, we do not peddle the word of God for profit. On the contrary, in Christ we speak before God with sincerity, as those sent from God.

3 Are we beginning to commend ourselves again? Or do we need, like some people, letters of recommendation to you or from you? [2]You yourselves are our letter, written on our hearts, known and read by everyone. [3]You show that you are a letter from Christ, the result of our ministry, written not with ink but with the Spirit of the living God, not on tablets of stone but on tablets of human hearts.

[4]Such confidence we have through Christ before God. [5]Not that we are competent in ourselves to claim anything for ourselves, but our competence comes from God. [6]He has made us competent as ministers of a new covenant — not of the letter but of the Spirit; for the letter kills, but the Spirit gives life.

The Greater Glory of the New Covenant

[7]Now if the ministry that brought death, which was engraved in letters on stone, came with glory, so that the Israelites could not look steadily at the face of Moses because of its glory, transitory though it was, [8]will not the ministry of the Spirit be even more glorious? [9]If the ministry that brought condemnation was glorious, how much more glorious is the ministry that brings righteousness! [10]For what was glorious has no glory now in comparison with the surpassing glory. [11]And if what was transitory came with glory, how much greater is the glory of that which lasts!

[12]Therefore, since we have such a hope, we are very bold. [13]We are not like Moses, who would put a veil over his face to prevent the Israelites from seeing the end of what was passing away. [14]But their minds were made dull, for to this day the same veil remains when the old covenant is read. It has not been removed, because only in Christ is it taken away. [15]Even to this day when Moses is read, a veil covers their hearts. [16]But whenever anyone turns to the Lord, the veil is taken away. [17]Now the Lord is the Spirit, and where the Spirit of the Lord is, there is freedom. [18]And we all, who with unveiled faces contemplate[a] the Lord's glory, are being transformed into his image with ever-increasing glory, which comes from the Lord, who is the Spirit.

Present Weakness and Resurrection Life

4 Therefore, since through God's mercy we have this ministry, we do not lose heart. [2]Rather, we have renounced secret and shameful ways; we do not use deception, nor do we distort the word of God. On the

[a] 18 Or *reflect*

contrary, by setting forth the truth plainly we commend ourselves to everyone's conscience in the sight of God. [3]And even if our gospel is veiled, it is veiled to those who are perishing. [4]The god of this age has blinded the minds of unbelievers, so that they cannot see the light of the gospel that displays the glory of Christ, who is the image of God. [5]For what we preach is not ourselves, but Jesus Christ as Lord, and ourselves as your servants for Jesus' sake. [6]For God, who said, "Let light shine out of darkness,"[a] made his light shine in our hearts to give us the light of the knowledge of God's glory displayed in the face of Christ.

[7]But we have this treasure in jars of clay to show that this all-surpassing power is from God and not from us. [8]We are hard pressed on every side, but not crushed; perplexed, but not in despair; [9]persecuted, but not abandoned; struck down, but not destroyed. [10]We always carry around in our body the death of Jesus, so that the life of Jesus may also be revealed in our body. [11]For we who are alive are always being given over to death for Jesus' sake, so that his life may also be revealed in our mortal body. [12]So then, death is at work in us, but life is at work in you.

[13]It is written: "I believed; therefore I have spoken."[b] Since we have that same spirit of[c] faith, we also believe and therefore speak, [14]because we know that the one who raised the Lord Jesus from the dead will also raise us with Jesus and present us with you to himself. [15]All this is for your benefit, so that the grace that is reaching more and more people may cause thanksgiving to overflow to the glory of God.

[16]Therefore we do not lose heart. Though outwardly we are wasting away, yet inwardly we are being renewed day by day. [17]For our light and momentary troubles are achieving for us an eternal glory that far outweighs them all. [18]So we fix our eyes not on what is seen, but on what is unseen, since what is seen is temporary, but what is unseen is eternal.

Awaiting the New Body

5 For we know that if the earthly tent we live in is destroyed, we have a building from God, an eternal house in heaven, not built by human hands. [2]Meanwhile we groan, longing to be clothed instead with our heavenly dwelling, [3]because when we are clothed, we will not be found naked. [4]For while we are in this tent, we groan and are burdened, because we do not wish to be unclothed but to be clothed instead with our heavenly dwelling, so that what is mortal may be swallowed up by life. [5]Now the one who has fashioned us for this very purpose is God, who has given us the Spirit as a deposit, guaranteeing what is to come.

[6]Therefore we are always confident and know that as long as we are at home in the body we are away from the Lord. [7]For we live by faith, not by sight. [8]We are confident, I say, and would prefer to be away from the body and at home with the Lord. [9]So we make it our goal to please him, whether we are at home in the body or away from it. [10]For we must all appear before the judgment seat of Christ, so that each of us may receive what is due us for the things done while in the body, whether good or bad.

The Ministry of Reconciliation

[11]Since, then, we know what it is to fear the Lord, we try to persuade others. What we are is plain to God, and I hope it is also plain to your conscience. [12]We are not trying to commend ourselves to you again, but are giving you an opportunity to take pride in us, so that you can answer those who take pride in what is seen rather than in what is in the heart. [13]If we are "out of our mind," as some say, it is for God; if we are in our right mind, it is for you. [14]For Christ's love compels us, because we are convinced that one died for all, and therefore all died. [15]And he died for all, that those who live should no longer live for themselves but for him who died for them and was raised again.

[16]So from now on we regard no one from a worldly point of view. Though we once regarded Christ in this way, we do so no longer. [17]Therefore, if anyone is in Christ, the new creation has come:[d] The old has gone, the new is here! [18]All this is from God, who reconciled us to himself through Christ and gave us the ministry of reconciliation: [19]that

[a] *6* Gen. 1:3 [b] *13* Psalm 116:10 (see Septuagint) [c] *13* Or *Spirit-given* [d] *17* Or *Christ, that person is a new creation.*

God was reconciling the world to himself in
Christ, not counting people's sins against
them. And he has committed to us the mes-
sage of reconciliation. 20We are therefore
Christ's ambassadors, as though God were
making his appeal through us. We implore
you on Christ's behalf: Be reconciled to God.
21God made him who had no sin to be sin[a]
for us, so that in him we might become the
righteousness of God.

6 As God's co-workers we urge you not to
receive God's grace in vain. 2For he says,

> "In the time of my favor I
> heard you,
> and in the day of salvation
> I helped you."[b]

I tell you, now is the time of God's favor, now
is the day of salvation.

Paul's Hardships

3We put no stumbling block in anyone's
path, so that our ministry will not be dis-
credited. 4Rather, as servants of God we
commend ourselves in every way: in great
endurance; in troubles, hardships and dis-
tresses; 5in beatings, imprisonments and ri-
ots; in hard work, sleepless nights and hun-
ger; 6in purity, understanding, patience and
kindness; in the Holy Spirit and in sincere
love; 7in truthful speech and in the power of
God; with weapons of righteousness in the
right hand and in the left; 8through glory
and dishonor, bad report and good report;
genuine, yet regarded as impostors; 9known,
yet regarded as unknown; dying, and yet we
live on; beaten, and yet not killed; 10sorrow-
ful, yet always rejoicing; poor, yet making
many rich; having nothing, and yet possess-
ing everything.

11We have spoken freely to you, Corin-
thians, and opened wide our hearts to you.
12We are not withholding our affection from
you, but you are withholding yours from us.
13As a fair exchange — I speak as to my chil-
dren — open wide your hearts also.

Warning Against Idolatry

14Do not be yoked together with unbeliev-
ers. For what do righteousness and wicked-
ness have in common? Or what fellowship
can light have with darkness? 15What har-
mony is there between Christ and Belial[c]? Or
what does a believer have in common with
an unbeliever? 16What agreement is there
between the temple of God and idols? For we
are the temple of the living God. As God has
said:

> "I will live with them
> and walk among them,
> and I will be their God,
> and they will be my people."[d]

17Therefore,

> "Come out from them
> and be separate,
> says the Lord.
> Touch no unclean thing,
> and I will receive you."[e]

18And,

> "I will be a Father to you,
> and you will be my sons and
> daughters,
> says the Lord Almighty."[f]

7 Therefore, since we have these promis-
es, dear friends, let us purify ourselves
from everything that contaminates body
and spirit, perfecting holiness out of rever-
ence for God.

Paul's Joy Over the Church's Repentance

2Make room for us in your hearts. We
have wronged no one, we have corrupted no
one, we have exploited no one. 3I do not say
this to condemn you; I have said before that
you have such a place in our hearts that we
would live or die with you. 4I have spoken to
you with great frankness; I take great pride
in you. I am greatly encouraged; in all our
troubles my joy knows no bounds.

5For when we came into Macedonia, we
had no rest, but we were harassed at every
turn — conflicts on the outside, fears with-
in. 6But God, who comforts the downcast,
comforted us by the coming of Titus, 7and
not only by his coming but also by the com-
fort you had given him. He told us about
your longing for me, your deep sorrow, your
ardent concern for me, so that my joy was
greater than ever.

8Even if I caused you sorrow by my letter,
I do not regret it. Though I did regret it — I

[a] 21 Or *be a sin offering* [b] 2 Isaiah 49:8 [c] 15 Greek *Beliar,* a variant of *Belial* [d] 16 Lev. 26:12; Jer. 32:38; Ezek. 37:27 [e] 17 Isaiah 52:11; Ezek. 20:34,41 [f] 18 2 Samuel 7:14; 7:8

see that my letter hurt you, but only for a
little while— 9yet now I am happy, not be-
cause you were made sorry, but because
your sorrow led you to repentance. For you
became sorrowful as God intended and so
were not harmed in any way by us. 10Godly
sorrow brings repentance that leads to sal-
vation and leaves no regret, but worldly sor-
row brings death. 11See what this godly sor-
row has produced in you: what earnestness,
what eagerness to clear yourselves, what in-
dignation, what alarm, what longing, what
concern, what readiness to see justice done.
At every point you have proved yourselves to
be innocent in this matter. 12So even though
I wrote to you, it was neither on account of
the one who did the wrong nor on account of
the injured party, but rather that before God
you could see for yourselves how devoted to
us you are. 13By all this we are encouraged.

In addition to our own encouragement,
we were especially delighted to see how hap-
py Titus was, because his spirit has been re-
freshed by all of you. 14I had boasted to him
about you, and you have not embarrassed
me. But just as everything we said to you was
true, so our boasting about you to Titus has
proved to be true as well. 15And his affection
for you is all the greater when he remembers
that you were all obedient, receiving him
with fear and trembling. 16I am glad I can
have complete confidence in you.

The Collection for the Lord's People

8 And now, brothers and sisters, we want
you to know about the grace that God
has given the Macedonian churches. 2In the
midst of a very severe trial, their overflowing
joy and their extreme poverty welled up in
rich generosity. 3For I testify that they gave
as much as they were able, and even beyond
their ability. Entirely on their own, 4they
urgently pleaded with us for the privilege
of sharing in this service to the Lord's peo-
ple. 5And they exceeded our expectations:
They gave themselves first of all to the Lord,
and then by the will of God also to us. 6So
we urged Titus, just as he had earlier made a
beginning, to bring also to completion this
act of grace on your part. 7But since you ex-
cel in everything—in faith, in speech, in
knowledge, in complete earnestness and in
the love we have kindled in you[a]—see that
you also excel in this grace of giving.

8I am not commanding you, but I want to
test the sincerity of your love by comparing
it with the earnestness of others. 9For you
know the grace of our Lord Jesus Christ, that
though he was rich, yet for your sake he be-
came poor, so that you through his poverty
might become rich.

10And here is my judgment about what
is best for you in this matter. Last year you
were the first not only to give but also to have
the desire to do so. 11Now finish the work, so
that your eager willingness to do it may be
matched by your completion of it, accord-
ing to your means. 12For if the willingness
is there, the gift is acceptable according to
what one has, not according to what one
does not have.

13Our desire is not that others might be re-
lieved while you are hard pressed, but that
there might be equality. 14At the present
time your plenty will supply what they need,
so that in turn their plenty will supply what
you need. The goal is equality, 15as it is writ-
ten: "The one who gathered much did not
have too much, and the one who gathered
little did not have too little."[b]

Titus Sent to Receive the Collection

16Thanks be to God, who put into the
heart of Titus the same concern I have for
you. 17For Titus not only welcomed our ap-
peal, but he is coming to you with much en-
thusiasm and on his own initiative. 18And
we are sending along with him the brother
who is praised by all the churches for his
service to the gospel. 19What is more, he was
chosen by the churches to accompany us as
we carry the offering, which we adminis-
ter in order to honor the Lord himself and
to show our eagerness to help. 20We want to
avoid any criticism of the way we administer
this liberal gift. 21For we are taking pains to
do what is right, not only in the eyes of the
Lord but also in the eyes of man.

22In addition, we are sending with them
our brother who has often proved to us in
many ways that he is zealous, and now even
more so because of his great confidence in
you. 23As for Titus, he is my partner and co-
worker among you; as for our brothers, they

[a] *7* Some manuscripts *and in your love for us* [b] *15* Exodus 16:18

are representatives of the churches and an honor to Christ. [24]Therefore show these men the proof of your love and the reason for our pride in you, so that the churches can see it.

9 There is no need for me to write to you about this service to the Lord's people. [2]For I know your eagerness to help, and I have been boasting about it to the Macedonians, telling them that since last year you in Achaia were ready to give; and your enthusiasm has stirred most of them to action. [3]But I am sending the brothers in order that our boasting about you in this matter should not prove hollow, but that you may be ready, as I said you would be. [4]For if any Macedonians come with me and find you unprepared, we — not to say anything about you — would be ashamed of having been so confident. [5]So I thought it necessary to urge the brothers to visit you in advance and finish the arrangements for the generous gift you had promised. Then it will be ready as a generous gift, not as one grudgingly given.

Generosity Encouraged

[6]Remember this: Whoever sows sparingly will also reap sparingly, and whoever sows generously will also reap generously. [7]Each of you should give what you have decided in your heart to give, not reluctantly or under compulsion, for God loves a cheerful giver. [8]And God is able to bless you abundantly, so that in all things at all times, having all that you need, you will abound in every good work. [9]As it is written:

"They have freely scattered their gifts to
the poor;
their righteousness endures forever."[a]

[10]Now he who supplies seed to the sower and bread for food will also supply and increase your store of seed and will enlarge the harvest of your righteousness. [11]You will be enriched in every way so that you can be generous on every occasion, and through us your generosity will result in thanksgiving to God.

[12]This service that you perform is not only supplying the needs of the Lord's people but is also overflowing in many expressions of thanks to God. [13]Because of the service by which you have proved yourselves, others will praise God for the obedience that accompanies your confession of the gospel of Christ, and for your generosity in sharing with them and with everyone else. [14]And in their prayers for you their hearts will go out to you, because of the surpassing grace God has given you. [15]Thanks be to God for his indescribable gift!

Paul's Defense of His Ministry

10 By the humility and gentleness of Christ, I appeal to you — I, Paul, who am "timid" when face to face with you, but "bold" toward you when away! [2]I beg you that when I come I may not have to be as bold as I expect to be toward some people who think that we live by the standards of this world. [3]For though we live in the world, we do not wage war as the world does. [4]The weapons we fight with are not the weapons of the world. On the contrary, they have divine power to demolish strongholds. [5]We demolish arguments and every pretension that sets itself up against the knowledge of God, and we take captive every thought to make it obedient to Christ. [6]And we will be ready to punish every act of disobedience, once your obedience is complete.

[7]You are judging by appearances.[b] If anyone is confident that they belong to Christ, they should consider again that we belong to Christ just as much as they do. [8]So even if I boast somewhat freely about the authority the Lord gave us for building you up rather than tearing you down, I will not be ashamed of it. [9]I do not want to seem to be trying to frighten you with my letters. [10]For some say, "His letters are weighty and forceful, but in person he is unimpressive and his speaking amounts to nothing." [11]Such people should realize that what we are in our letters when we are absent, we will be in our actions when we are present.

[12]We do not dare to classify or compare ourselves with some who commend themselves. When they measure themselves by themselves and compare themselves with themselves, they are not wise. [13]We, however, will not boast beyond proper limits, but will confine our boasting to the sphere of service God himself has assigned to us, a

[a] 9 Psalm 112:9 [b] 7 Or *Look at the obvious facts*

sphere that also includes you. 14We are not going too far in our boasting, as would be the case if we had not come to you, for we did get as far as you with the gospel of Christ. 15Neither do we go beyond our limits by boasting of work done by others. Our hope is that, as your faith continues to grow, our sphere of activity among you will greatly expand, 16so that we can preach the gospel in the regions beyond you. For we do not want to boast about work already done in someone else's territory. 17But, "Let the one who boasts boast in the Lord."[a] 18For it is not the one who commends himself who is approved, but the one whom the Lord commends.

Paul and the False Apostles

11 I hope you will put up with me in a little foolishness. Yes, please put up with me! 2I am jealous for you with a godly jealousy. I promised you to one husband, to Christ, so that I might present you as a pure virgin to him. 3But I am afraid that just as Eve was deceived by the serpent's cunning, your minds may somehow be led astray from your sincere and pure devotion to Christ. 4For if someone comes to you and preaches a Jesus other than the Jesus we preached, or if you receive a different spirit from the Spirit you received, or a different gospel from the one you accepted, you put up with it easily enough.

5I do not think I am in the least inferior to those "super-apostles."[b] 6I may indeed be untrained as a speaker, but I do have knowledge. We have made this perfectly clear to you in every way. 7Was it a sin for me to lower myself in order to elevate you by preaching the gospel of God to you free of charge? 8I robbed other churches by receiving support from them so as to serve you. 9And when I was with you and needed something, I was not a burden to anyone, for the brothers who came from Macedonia supplied what I needed. I have kept myself from being a burden to you in any way, and will continue to do so. 10As surely as the truth of Christ is in me, nobody in the regions of Achaia will stop this boasting of mine. 11Why? Because I do not love you? God knows I do!

12And I will keep on doing what I am doing in order to cut the ground from under those who want an opportunity to be considered equal with us in the things they boast about. 13For such people are false apostles, deceitful workers, masquerading as apostles of Christ. 14And no wonder, for Satan himself masquerades as an angel of light. 15It is not surprising, then, if his servants also masquerade as servants of righteousness. Their end will be what their actions deserve.

Paul Boasts About His Sufferings

16I repeat: Let no one take me for a fool. But if you do, then tolerate me just as you would a fool, so that I may do a little boasting. 17In this self-confident boasting I am not talking as the Lord would, but as a fool. 18Since many are boasting in the way the world does, I too will boast. 19You gladly put up with fools since you are so wise! 20In fact, you even put up with anyone who enslaves you or exploits you or takes advantage of you or puts on airs or slaps you in the face. 21To my shame I admit that we were too weak for that!

Whatever anyone else dares to boast about—I am speaking as a fool—I also dare to boast about. 22Are they Hebrews? So am I. Are they Israelites? So am I. Are they Abraham's descendants? So am I. 23Are they servants of Christ? (I am out of my mind to talk like this.) I am more. I have worked much harder, been in prison more frequently, been flogged more severely, and been exposed to death again and again. 24Five times I received from the Jews the forty lashes minus one. 25Three times I was beaten with rods, once I was pelted with stones, three times I was shipwrecked, I spent a night and a day in the open sea, 26I have been constantly on the move. I have been in danger from rivers, in danger from bandits, in danger from my fellow Jews, in danger from Gentiles; in danger in the city, in danger in the country, in danger at sea; and in danger from false believers. 27I have labored and toiled and have often gone without sleep; I have known hunger and thirst and have often gone without food; I have been cold and naked. 28Besides everything else, I face daily the pressure of my concern for all the churches. 29Who is weak, and I do not feel weak? Who is led into sin, and I do not inwardly burn?

30If I must boast, I will boast of the things

[a] 17 Jer. 9:24 [b] 5 Or *to the most eminent apostles*

that show my weakness. 31 The God and Father of the Lord Jesus, who is to be praised forever, knows that I am not lying. 32 In Damascus the governor under King Aretas had the city of the Damascenes guarded in order to arrest me. 33 But I was lowered in a basket from a window in the wall and slipped through his hands.

Paul's Vision and His Thorn

12 I must go on boasting. Although there is nothing to be gained, I will go on to visions and revelations from the Lord. 2 I know a man in Christ who fourteen years ago was caught up to the third heaven. Whether it was in the body or out of the body I do not know — God knows. 3 And I know that this man — whether in the body or apart from the body I do not know, but God knows — 4 was caught up to paradise and heard inexpressible things, things that no one is permitted to tell. 5 I will boast about a man like that, but I will not boast about myself, except about my weaknesses. 6 Even if I should choose to boast, I would not be a fool, because I would be speaking the truth. But I refrain, so no one will think more of me than is warranted by what I do or say, 7 or because of these surpassingly great revelations. Therefore, in order to keep me from becoming conceited, I was given a thorn in my flesh, a messenger of Satan, to torment me. 8 Three times I pleaded with the Lord to take it away from me. 9 But he said to me, "My grace is sufficient for you, for my power is made perfect in weakness." Therefore I will boast all the more gladly about my weaknesses, so that Christ's power may rest on me. 10 That is why, for Christ's sake, I delight in weaknesses, in insults, in hardships, in persecutions, in difficulties. For when I am weak, then I am strong.

Paul's Concern for the Corinthians

11 I have made a fool of myself, but you drove me to it. I ought to have been commended by you, for I am not in the least inferior to the "super-apostles,"[a] even though I am nothing. 12 I persevered in demonstrating among you the marks of a true apostle, including signs, wonders and miracles. 13 How were you inferior to the other churches, except that I was never a burden to you? Forgive me this wrong!

14 Now I am ready to visit you for the third time, and I will not be a burden to you, because what I want is not your possessions but you. After all, children should not have to save up for their parents, but parents for their children. 15 So I will very gladly spend for you everything I have and expend myself as well. If I love you more, will you love me less? 16 Be that as it may, I have not been a burden to you. Yet, crafty fellow that I am, I caught you by trickery! 17 Did I exploit you through any of the men I sent to you? 18 I urged Titus to go to you and I sent our brother with him. Titus did not exploit you, did he? Did we not walk in the same footsteps by the same Spirit?

19 Have you been thinking all along that we have been defending ourselves to you? We have been speaking in the sight of God as those in Christ; and everything we do, dear friends, is for your strengthening. 20 For I am afraid that when I come I may not find you as I want you to be, and you may not find me as you want me to be. I fear that there may be discord, jealousy, fits of rage, selfish ambition, slander, gossip, arrogance and disorder. 21 I am afraid that when I come again my God will humble me before you, and I will be grieved over many who have sinned earlier and have not repented of the impurity, sexual sin and debauchery in which they have indulged.

Final Warnings

13 This will be my third visit to you. "Every matter must be established by the testimony of two or three witnesses."[b] 2 I already gave you a warning when I was with you the second time. I now repeat it while absent: On my return I will not spare those who sinned earlier or any of the others, 3 since you are demanding proof that Christ is speaking through me. He is not weak in dealing with you, but is powerful among you. 4 For to be sure, he was crucified in weakness, yet he lives by God's power. Likewise, we are weak in him, yet by God's power we will live with him in our dealing with you.

5 Examine yourselves to see whether you are in the faith; test yourselves. Do you not realize that Christ Jesus is in you — unless, of course, you fail the test? 6 And I trust that

[a] *11* Or *the most eminent apostles* [b] *1* Deut. 19:15

you will discover that we have not failed the
test. 7 Now we pray to God that you will not
do anything wrong — not so that people will
see that we have stood the test but so that
you will do what is right even though we
may seem to have failed. 8 For we cannot do
anything against the truth, but only for the
truth. 9 We are glad whenever we are weak
but you are strong; and our prayer is that
you may be fully restored. 10 This is why I
write these things when I am absent, that
when I come I may not have to be harsh in
my use of authority — the authority the Lord
gave me for building you up, not for tearing
you down.

Final Greetings

11 Finally, brothers and sisters, rejoice!
Strive for full restoration, encourage one an-
other, be of one mind, live in peace. And the
God of love and peace will be with you.

12 Greet one another with a holy kiss. 13 All
God's people here send their greetings.

14 May the grace of the Lord Jesus Christ,
and the love of God, and the fellowship of the
Holy Spirit be with you all.

JESUS PAID IT ALL

Elvina M. Hall, John Thomas Grape, Alex Nifong

I hear the Savior say
"Thy strength indeed is small
Child of weakness, watch and pray
Find in me thine all in all"

'Cause Jesus paid it all
All to him I owe
Sin had left a crimson stain
He washed it white as snow

Lord, now indeed I find
Thy power and thine alone
Can change the leper's spots
And melt the heart of stone

And when before the throne
I stand in him complete
Jesus died my soul to save
My lips shall still repeat

Oh, praise the One who paid my debt
And raised this life up from the dead

Oh, praise the One who paid my debt
And raised this life up from the dead

THE INSPIRATION

"Come now, let us settle the matter," says the Lord. "Though your sins are like scarlet, they shall be as white as snow; though they are red as crimson, they shall be like wool." —Isaiah 1:18

Read also: 1 Peter 1:18–19

BEHIND THE SONG

The beloved hymn "Jesus Paid It All" was originally the result of a happy accident that took place in 1865. Elvina Hall was a parishioner of the Monument Street Methodist Church in Baltimore, Maryland. One Sunday as the pastor rambled on and her thoughts wandered, she composed several stanzas of poetry centered on the theme of the cross. After the service she gave the text to the pastor, who just happened to have been given a musical setting by the church's organist, John Thomas Grape, a few days earlier. When the pastor set words and music together, they were a perfect match and a powerful hymn was born.

In 2006 a young worship leader and songwriter named Alex Nifong added some new lyrics to the hymn and adjusted the arrangement to better fit the format of a contemporary worship team. This updated version has brought this classic song to a new generation, many of whom are hearing it for the first time.

Selah

Every human being is born with a sin problem that they cannot fix on their own. We often use economic terms to understand this situation. Of course, many people do not acknowledge the debt they owe God. Even many Christians rarely consider the cost of their sin.

Religion is often all about people working hard to become acceptable to their god or gods. The gospel, however, is about God reaching down to his children through Jesus, who paid the price of sin so that we could be acceptable. There is nothing we could possibly do to repay him. He did everything necessary on the cross. Immeasurable peace and joy come from accepting God's great gift. Read Isaiah 1:18 and 1 Peter 1:18–19, and spend some time thinking about the good news of the cross and the wonderful feeling of being debt-free before God.

GALATIANS

1 Paul, an apostle — sent not from men nor by a man, but by Jesus Christ and God the Father, who raised him from the dead— [2]and all the brothers and sisters[a] with me,

To the churches in Galatia:

[3]Grace and peace to you from God our Father and the Lord Jesus Christ, [4]who gave himself for our sins to rescue us from the present evil age, according to the will of our God and Father, [5]to whom be glory for ever and ever. Amen.

No Other Gospel

[6]I am astonished that you are so quickly deserting the one who called you to live in the grace of Christ and are turning to a different gospel— [7]which is really no gospel at all. Evidently some people are throwing you into confusion and are trying to pervert the gospel of Christ. [8]But even if we or an angel from heaven should preach a gospel other than the one we preached to you, let them be under God's curse! [9]As we have already said, so now I say again: If anybody is preaching to you a gospel other than what you accepted, let them be under God's curse!

[10]Am I now trying to win the approval of human beings, or of God? Or am I trying to please people? If I were still trying to please people, I would not be a servant of Christ.

Paul Called by God

[11]I want you to know, brothers and sisters, that the gospel I preached is not of human origin. [12]I did not receive it from any man, nor was I taught it; rather, I received it by revelation from Jesus Christ.

[13]For you have heard of my previous way of life in Judaism, how intensely I persecuted the church of God and tried to destroy it. [14]I was advancing in Judaism beyond many of my own age among my people and was extremely zealous for the traditions of my fathers. [15]But when God, who set me apart from my mother's womb and called me by his grace, was pleased [16]to reveal his Son in me so that I might preach him among the Gentiles, my immediate response was not to consult any human being. [17]I did not go up to Jerusalem to see those who were apostles before I was, but I went into Arabia. Later I returned to Damascus.

[18]Then after three years, I went up to Jerusalem to get acquainted with Cephas[b] and stayed with him fifteen days. [19]I saw none of the other apostles — only James, the Lord's brother. [20]I assure you before God that what I am writing you is no lie.

[21]Then I went to Syria and Cilicia. [22]I was personally unknown to the churches of Judea that are in Christ. [23]They only heard the report: "The man who formerly persecuted us is now preaching the faith he once tried to destroy." [24]And they praised God because of me.

Paul Accepted by the Apostles

2 Then after fourteen years, I went up again to Jerusalem, this time with Barnabas. I took Titus along also. [2]I went in response to a revelation and, meeting privately with those esteemed as leaders, I presented to them the gospel that I preach among the Gentiles. I wanted to be sure I was not running and had not been running my race in vain. [3]Yet not even Titus, who was with me, was compelled to be circumcised, even though he was a Greek. [4]This matter arose because some false believers had infiltrated our ranks to spy on the freedom we have in Christ Jesus and to make us slaves. [5]We did not give in to them for a moment, so that the truth of the gospel might be preserved for you.

[6]As for those who were held in high esteem — whatever they were makes no difference to me; God does not show favoritism —

[a] *2* The Greek word for *brothers and sisters* (*adelphoi*) refers here to believers, both men and women, as part of God's family; also in verse 11; and in 3:15; 4:12, 28, 31; 5:11, 13; 6:1, 18. [b] *18* That is, Peter

they added nothing to my message. [7]On the contrary, they recognized that I had been entrusted with the task of preaching the gospel to the uncircumcised,[a] just as Peter had been to the circumcised.[b] [8]For God, who was at work in Peter as an apostle to the circumcised, was also at work in me as an apostle to the Gentiles. [9]James, Cephas[c] and John, those esteemed as pillars, gave me and Barnabas the right hand of fellowship when they recognized the grace given to me. They agreed that we should go to the Gentiles, and they to the circumcised. [10]All they asked was that we should continue to remember the poor, the very thing I had been eager to do all along.

Paul Opposes Cephas

[11]When Cephas came to Antioch, I opposed him to his face, because he stood condemned. [12]For before certain men came from James, he used to eat with the Gentiles. But when they arrived, he began to draw back and separate himself from the Gentiles because he was afraid of those who belonged to the circumcision group. [13]The other Jews joined him in his hypocrisy, so that by their hypocrisy even Barnabas was led astray.

[14]When I saw that they were not acting in line with the truth of the gospel, I said to Cephas in front of them all, "You are a Jew, yet you live like a Gentile and not like a Jew. How is it, then, that you force Gentiles to follow Jewish customs?

[15]"We who are Jews by birth and not sinful Gentiles [16]know that a person is not justified by the works of the law, but by faith in Jesus Christ. So we, too, have put our faith in Christ Jesus that we may be justified by faith in[d] Christ and not by the works of the law, because by the works of the law no one will be justified.

[17]"But if, in seeking to be justified in Christ, we Jews find ourselves also among the sinners, doesn't that mean that Christ promotes sin? Absolutely not! [18]If I rebuild what I destroyed, then I really would be a lawbreaker.

[19]"For through the law I died to the law so that I might live for God. [20]I have been crucified with Christ and I no longer live, but Christ lives in me. The life I now live in the body, I live by faith in the Son of God, who loved me and gave himself for me. [21]I do not set aside the grace of God, for if righteousness could be gained through the law, Christ died for nothing!"[e]

Faith or Works of the Law

3 You foolish Galatians! Who has bewitched you? Before your very eyes Jesus Christ was clearly portrayed as crucified. [2]I would like to learn just one thing from you: Did you receive the Spirit by the works of the law, or by believing what you heard? [3]Are you so foolish? After beginning by means of the Spirit, are you now trying to finish by means of the flesh?[f] [4]Have you experienced[g] so much in vain—if it really was in vain? [5]So again I ask, does God give you his Spirit and work miracles among you by the works of the law, or by your believing what you heard? [6]So also Abraham "believed God, and it was credited to him as righteousness."[h]

[7]Understand, then, that those who have faith are children of Abraham. [8]Scripture foresaw that God would justify the Gentiles by faith, and announced the gospel in advance to Abraham: "All nations will be blessed through you."[i] [9]So those who rely on faith are blessed along with Abraham, the man of faith.

[10]For all who rely on the works of the law are under a curse, as it is written: "Cursed is everyone who does not continue to do everything written in the Book of the Law."[j] [11]Clearly no one who relies on the law is justified before God, because "the righteous will live by faith."[k] [12]The law is not based on faith; on the contrary, it says, "The person who does these things will live by them."[l] [13]Christ redeemed us from the curse of the law by becoming a curse for us, for it is written: "Cursed is everyone who is hung on a pole."[m] [14]He redeemed us in order that the blessing given to Abraham might come to

[a] 7 That is, Gentiles [b] 7 That is, Jews; also in verses 8 and 9 [c] 9 That is, Peter; also in verses 11 and 14 [d] 16 Or *but through the faithfulness of . . . justified on the basis of the faithfulness of* [e] 21 Some interpreters end the quotation after verse 14. [f] 3 In contexts like this, the Greek word for *flesh* (*sarx*) refers to the sinful state of human beings, often presented as a power in opposition to the Spirit. [g] 4 Or *suffered* [h] 6 Gen. 15:6 [i] 8 Gen. 12:3; 18:18; 22:18 [j] 10 Deut. 27:26 [k] 11 Hab. 2:4 [l] 12 Lev. 18:5 [m] 13 Deut. 21:23

the Gentiles through Christ Jesus, so that by faith we might receive the promise of the Spirit.

The Law and the Promise

15 Brothers and sisters, let me take an example from everyday life. Just as no one can set aside or add to a human covenant that has been duly established, so it is in this case. 16 The promises were spoken to Abraham and to his seed. Scripture does not say "and to seeds," meaning many people, but "and to your seed,"[a] meaning one person, who is Christ. 17 What I mean is this: The law, introduced 430 years later, does not set aside the covenant previously established by God and thus do away with the promise. 18 For if the inheritance depends on the law, then it no longer depends on the promise; but God in his grace gave it to Abraham through a promise.

19 Why, then, was the law given at all? It was added because of transgressions until the Seed to whom the promise referred had come. The law was given through angels and entrusted to a mediator. 20 A mediator, however, implies more than one party; but God is one.

21 Is the law, therefore, opposed to the promises of God? Absolutely not! For if a law had been given that could impart life, then righteousness would certainly have come by the law. 22 But Scripture has locked up everything under the control of sin, so that what was promised, being given through faith in Jesus Christ, might be given to those who believe.

Children of God

23 Before the coming of this faith,[b] we were held in custody under the law, locked up until the faith that was to come would be revealed. 24 So the law was our guardian until Christ came that we might be justified by faith. 25 Now that this faith has come, we are no longer under a guardian.

26 So in Christ Jesus you are all children of God through faith, 27 for all of you who were baptized into Christ have clothed yourselves with Christ. 28 There is neither Jew nor Gentile, neither slave nor free, nor is there male and female, for you are all one in Christ Jesus. 29 If you belong to Christ, then you are Abraham's seed, and heirs according to the promise.

4 What I am saying is that as long as an heir is underage, he is no different from a slave, although he owns the whole estate. 2 The heir is subject to guardians and trustees until the time set by his father. 3 So also, when we were underage, we were in slavery under the elemental spiritual forces[c] of the world. 4 But when the set time had fully come, God sent his Son, born of a woman, born under the law, 5 to redeem those under the law, that we might receive adoption to sonship.[d] 6 Because you are his sons, God sent the Spirit of his Son into our hearts, the Spirit who calls out, *"Abba,*[e] Father." 7 So you are no longer a slave, but God's child; and since you are his child, God has made you also an heir.

Paul's Concern for the Galatians

8 Formerly, when you did not know God, you were slaves to those who by nature are not gods. 9 But now that you know God—or rather are known by God—how is it that you are turning back to those weak and miserable forces[f]? Do you wish to be enslaved by them all over again? 10 You are observing special days and months and seasons and years! 11 I fear for you, that somehow I have wasted my efforts on you.

12 I plead with you, brothers and sisters, become like me, for I became like you. You did me no wrong. 13 As you know, it was because of an illness that I first preached the gospel to you, 14 and even though my illness was a trial to you, you did not treat me with contempt or scorn. Instead, you welcomed me as if I were an angel of God, as if I were Christ Jesus himself. 15 Where, then, is your blessing of me now? I can testify that, if you could have done so, you would have torn out your eyes and given them to me. 16 Have I now become your enemy by telling you the truth?

17 Those people are zealous to win you over, but for no good. What they want is to

[a] *16* Gen. 12:7; 13:15; 24:7 [b] *22,23* Or *through the faithfulness of Jesus . . . 23Before faith came*
[c] *3* Or *under the basic principles* [d] *5* The Greek word for *adoption to sonship* is a legal term referring to the full legal standing of an adopted male heir in Roman culture. [e] *6* Aramaic for *Father*
[f] *9* Or *principles*

alienate you from us, so that you may have zeal for them. 18 It is fine to be zealous, provided the purpose is good, and to be so always, not just when I am with you. 19 My dear children, for whom I am again in the pains of childbirth until Christ is formed in you, 20 how I wish I could be with you now and change my tone, because I am perplexed about you!

Hagar and Sarah

21 Tell me, you who want to be under the law, are you not aware of what the law says? 22 For it is written that Abraham had two sons, one by the slave woman and the other by the free woman. 23 His son by the slave woman was born according to the flesh, but his son by the free woman was born as the result of a divine promise.

24 These things are being taken figuratively: The women represent two covenants. One covenant is from Mount Sinai and bears children who are to be slaves: This is Hagar. 25 Now Hagar stands for Mount Sinai in Arabia and corresponds to the present city of Jerusalem, because she is in slavery with her children. 26 But the Jerusalem that is above is free, and she is our mother. 27 For it is written:

> "Be glad, barren woman,
> you who never bore a child;
> shout for joy and cry aloud,
> you who were never in labor;
> because more are the children of the desolate woman
> than of her who has a husband."[a]

28 Now you, brothers and sisters, like Isaac, are children of promise. 29 At that time the son born according to the flesh persecuted the son born by the power of the Spirit. It is the same now. 30 But what does Scripture say? "Get rid of the slave woman and her son, for the slave woman's son will never share in the inheritance with the free woman's son."[b] 31 Therefore, brothers and sisters, we are not children of the slave woman, but of the free woman.

Freedom in Christ

5 It is for freedom that Christ has set us free. Stand firm, then, and do not let yourselves be burdened again by a yoke of slavery.

2 Mark my words! I, Paul, tell you that if you let yourselves be circumcised, Christ will be of no value to you at all. 3 Again I declare to every man who lets himself be circumcised that he is obligated to obey the whole law. 4 You who are trying to be justified by the law have been alienated from Christ; you have fallen away from grace. 5 For through the Spirit we eagerly await by faith the righteousness for which we hope. 6 For in Christ Jesus neither circumcision nor uncircumcision has any value. The only thing that counts is faith expressing itself through love.

7 You were running a good race. Who cut in on you to keep you from obeying the truth? 8 That kind of persuasion does not come from the one who calls you. 9 "A little yeast works through the whole batch of dough." 10 I am confident in the Lord that you will take no other view. The one who is throwing you into confusion, whoever that may be, will have to pay the penalty. 11 Brothers and sisters, if I am still preaching circumcision, why am I still being persecuted? In that case the offense of the cross has been abolished. 12 As for those agitators, I wish they would go the whole way and emasculate themselves!

Life by the Spirit

13 You, my brothers and sisters, were called to be free. But do not use your freedom to indulge the flesh[c]; rather, serve one another humbly in love. 14 For the entire law is fulfilled in keeping this one command: "Love your neighbor as yourself."[d] 15 If you bite and devour each other, watch out or you will be destroyed by each other.

16 So I say, walk by the Spirit, and you will not gratify the desires of the flesh. 17 For the flesh desires what is contrary to the Spirit, and the Spirit what is contrary to the flesh. They are in conflict with each other, so that you are not to do whatever[e] you want. 18 But if you are led by the Spirit, you are not under the law.

19 The acts of the flesh are obvious: sexual immorality, impurity and debauchery; 20 idolatry and witchcraft; hatred, discord,

[a] *27* Isaiah 54:1 [b] *30* Gen. 21:10 [c] *13* In contexts like this, the Greek word for *flesh* (*sarx*) refers to the sinful state of human beings, often presented as a power in opposition to the Spirit; also in verses 16, 17, 19 and 24; and in 6:8. [d] *14* Lev. 19:18 [e] *17* Or *you do not do what*

jealousy, fits of rage, selfish ambition, dissensions, factions [21]and envy; drunkenness, orgies, and the like. I warn you, as I did before, that those who live like this will not inherit the kingdom of God.

[22]But the fruit of the Spirit is love, joy, peace, forbearance, kindness, goodness, faithfulness, [23]gentleness and self-control. Against such things there is no law. [24]Those who belong to Christ Jesus have crucified the flesh with its passions and desires. [25]Since we live by the Spirit, let us keep in step with the Spirit. [26]Let us not become conceited, provoking and envying each other.

Doing Good to All

6 Brothers and sisters, if someone is caught in a sin, you who live by the Spirit should restore that person gently. But watch yourselves, or you also may be tempted. [2]Carry each other's burdens, and in this way you will fulfill the law of Christ. [3]If anyone thinks they are something when they are not, they deceive themselves. [4]Each one should test their own actions. Then they can take pride in themselves alone, without comparing themselves to someone else, [5]for each one should carry their own load. [6]Nevertheless, the one who receives instruction in the word should share all good things with their instructor.

[7]Do not be deceived: God cannot be mocked. A man reaps what he sows. [8]Whoever sows to please their flesh, from the flesh will reap destruction; whoever sows to please the Spirit, from the Spirit will reap eternal life. [9]Let us not become weary in doing good, for at the proper time we will reap a harvest if we do not give up. [10]Therefore, as we have opportunity, let us do good to all people, especially to those who belong to the family of believers.

Not Circumcision but the New Creation

[11]See what large letters I use as I write to you with my own hand!

[12]Those who want to impress people by means of the flesh are trying to compel you to be circumcised. The only reason they do this is to avoid being persecuted for the cross of Christ. [13]Not even those who are circumcised keep the law, yet they want you to be circumcised that they may boast about your circumcision in the flesh. [14]May I never boast except in the cross of our Lord Jesus Christ, through which[a] the world has been crucified to me, and I to the world. [15]Neither circumcision nor uncircumcision means anything; what counts is the new creation. [16]Peace and mercy to all who follow this rule — to[b] the Israel of God.

[17]From now on, let no one cause me trouble, for I bear on my body the marks of Jesus.

[18]The grace of our Lord Jesus Christ be with your spirit, brothers and sisters. Amen.

[a] 14 Or *whom* [b] 16 Or *rule and to*

EPHESIANS

1 Paul, an apostle of Christ Jesus by the
will of God,

To God's holy people in Ephesus,[a] the
faithful in Christ Jesus:

[2]Grace and peace to you from God our Fa-
ther and the Lord Jesus Christ.

Praise for Spiritual Blessings in Christ

[3]Praise be to the God and Father of our
Lord Jesus Christ, who has blessed us in the
heavenly realms with every spiritual bless-
ing in Christ. [4]For he chose us in him be-
fore the creation of the world to be holy and
blameless in his sight. In love [5]he[b] predes-
tined us for adoption to sonship[c] through
Jesus Christ, in accordance with his plea-
sure and will — [6]to the praise of his glorious
grace, which he has freely given us in the
One he loves. [7]In him we have redemption
through his blood, the forgiveness of sins,
in accordance with the riches of God's grace
[8]that he lavished on us. With all wisdom and
understanding, [9]he[d] made known to us the
mystery of his will according to his good
pleasure, which he purposed in Christ, [10]to
be put into effect when the times reach their
fulfillment — to bring unity to all things in
heaven and on earth under Christ.
[11]In him we were also chosen,[e] having
been predestined according to the plan of
him who works out everything in confor-
mity with the purpose of his will, [12]in order
that we, who were the first to put our hope
in Christ, might be for the praise of his glory.
[13]And you also were included in Christ when
you heard the message of truth, the gospel
of your salvation. When you believed, you
were marked in him with a seal, the prom-
ised Holy Spirit, [14]who is a deposit guaran-
teeing our inheritance until the redemption
of those who are God's possession — to the
praise of his glory.

Thanksgiving and Prayer

[15]For this reason, ever since I heard about
your faith in the Lord Jesus and your love for
all God's people, [16]I have not stopped giv-
ing thanks for you, remembering you in my
prayers. [17]I keep asking that the God of our
Lord Jesus Christ, the glorious Father, may
give you the Spirit[f] of wisdom and revela-
tion, so that you may know him better. [18]I
pray that the eyes of your heart may be en-
lightened in order that you may know the
hope to which he has called you, the riches of
his glorious inheritance in his holy people,
[19]and his incomparably great power for us
who believe. That power is the same as the
mighty strength [20]he exerted when he raised
Christ from the dead and seated him at his
right hand in the heavenly realms, [21]far
above all rule and authority, power and do-
minion, and every name that is invoked, not
only in the present age but also in the one to
come. [22]And God placed all things under his
feet and appointed him to be head over ev-
erything for the church, [23]which is his body,
the fullness of him who fills everything in
every way.

Made Alive in Christ

2 As for you, you were dead in your trans-
gressions and sins, [2]in which you used
to live when you followed the ways of this
world and of the ruler of the kingdom of the
air, the spirit who is now at work in those
who are disobedient. [3]All of us also lived
among them at one time, gratifying the
cravings of our flesh[g] and following its de-
sires and thoughts. Like the rest, we were by
nature deserving of wrath. [4]But because of

[a] *1* Some early manuscripts do not have *in Ephesus.* [b] *4,5* Or *sight in love.* [5]*He* [c] *5* The Greek word for *adoption to sonship* is a legal term referring to the full legal standing of an adopted male heir in Roman culture. [d] *8,9* Or *us with all wisdom and understanding.* [9]*And he* [e] *11* Or *were made heirs* [f] *17* Or *a spirit* [g] *3* In contexts like this, the Greek word for *flesh* (*sarx*) refers to the sinful state of human beings, often presented as a power in opposition to the Spirit

his great love for us, God, who is rich in mercy, 5 made us alive with Christ even when we were dead in transgressions — it is by grace you have been saved. 6 And God raised us up with Christ and seated us with him in the heavenly realms in Christ Jesus, 7 in order that in the coming ages he might show the incomparable riches of his grace, expressed in his kindness to us in Christ Jesus. 8 For it is by grace you have been saved, through faith — and this is not from yourselves, it is the gift of God — 9 not by works, so that no one can boast. 10 For we are God's handiwork, created in Christ Jesus to do good works, which God prepared in advance for us to do.

Jew and Gentile Reconciled Through Christ

11 Therefore, remember that formerly you who are Gentiles by birth and called "uncircumcised" by those who call themselves "the circumcision" (which is done in the body by human hands) — 12 remember that at that time you were separate from Christ, excluded from citizenship in Israel and foreigners to the covenants of the promise, without hope and without God in the world. 13 But now in Christ Jesus you who once were far away have been brought near by the blood of Christ.

14 For he himself is our peace, who has made the two groups one and has destroyed the barrier, the dividing wall of hostility, 15 by setting aside in his flesh the law with its commands and regulations. His purpose was to create in himself one new humanity out of the two, thus making peace, 16 and in one body to reconcile both of them to God through the cross, by which he put to death their hostility. 17 He came and preached peace to you who were far away and peace to those who were near. 18 For through him we both have access to the Father by one Spirit.

19 Consequently, you are no longer foreigners and strangers, but fellow citizens with God's people and also members of his household, 20 built on the foundation of the apostles and prophets, with Christ Jesus himself as the chief cornerstone. 21 In him the whole building is joined together and rises to become a holy temple in the Lord. 22 And in him you too are being built together to become a dwelling in which God lives by his Spirit.

God's Marvelous Plan for the Gentiles

3 For this reason I, Paul, the prisoner of Christ Jesus for the sake of you Gentiles —

2 Surely you have heard about the administration of God's grace that was given to me for you, 3 that is, the mystery made known to me by revelation, as I have already written briefly. 4 In reading this, then, you will be able to understand my insight into the mystery of Christ, 5 which was not made known to people in other generations as it has now been revealed by the Spirit to God's holy apostles and prophets. 6 This mystery is that through the gospel the Gentiles are heirs together with Israel, members together of one body, and sharers together in the promise in Christ Jesus.

7 I became a servant of this gospel by the gift of God's grace given me through the working of his power. 8 Although I am less than the least of all the Lord's people, this grace was given me: to preach to the Gentiles the boundless riches of Christ, 9 and to make plain to everyone the administration of this mystery, which for ages past was kept hidden in God, who created all things. 10 His intent was that now, through the church, the manifold wisdom of God should be made known to the rulers and authorities in the heavenly realms, 11 according to his eternal purpose that he accomplished in Christ Jesus our Lord. 12 In him and through faith in him we may approach God with freedom and confidence. 13 I ask you, therefore, not to be discouraged because of my sufferings for you, which are your glory.

A Prayer for the Ephesians

14 For this reason I kneel before the Father, 15 from whom every family[a] in heaven and on earth derives its name. 16 I pray that out of his glorious riches he may strengthen you with power through his Spirit in your inner being, 17 so that Christ may dwell in your hearts through faith. And I pray that you, being rooted and established in love, 18 may have power, together with all the Lord's holy

[a] 15 The Greek for *family* (*patria*) is derived from the Greek for *father* (*pater*).

people, to grasp how wide and long and high
and deep is the love of Christ, 19 and to know
this love that surpasses knowledge — that
you may be filled to the measure of all the
fullness of God.
20 Now to him who is able to do immea-
surably more than all we ask or imagine,
according to his power that is at work with-
in us, 21 to him be glory in the church and in
Christ Jesus throughout all generations, for
ever and ever! Amen.

Unity and Maturity in the Body of Christ

4 As a prisoner for the Lord, then, I urge
you to live a life worthy of the calling
you have received. 2 Be completely hum-
ble and gentle; be patient, bearing with one
another in love. 3 Make every effort to keep
the unity of the Spirit through the bond of
peace. 4 There is one body and one Spirit,
just as you were called to one hope when you
were called; 5 one Lord, one faith, one bap-
tism; 6 one God and Father of all, who is over
all and through all and in all.
7 But to each one of us grace has been giv-
en as Christ apportioned it. 8 This is why it[a]
says:

"When he ascended on high,
he took many captives
and gave gifts to his people."[b]

9 (What does "he ascended" mean except
that he also descended to the lower, earth-
ly regions[c]? 10 He who descended is the very
one who ascended higher than all the heav-
ens, in order to fill the whole universe.) 11 So
Christ himself gave the apostles, the proph-
ets, the evangelists, the pastors and teach-
ers, 12 to equip his people for works of ser-
vice, so that the body of Christ may be built
up 13 until we all reach unity in the faith and
in the knowledge of the Son of God and be-
come mature, attaining to the whole mea-
sure of the fullness of Christ.
14 Then we will no longer be infants, tossed
back and forth by the waves, and blown here
and there by every wind of teaching and by
the cunning and craftiness of people in their
deceitful scheming. 15 Instead, speaking
the truth in love, we will grow to become in
every respect the mature body of him who
is the head, that is, Christ. 16 From him the
whole body, joined and held together by ev-
ery supporting ligament, grows and builds
itself up in love, as each part does its work.

Instructions for Christian Living

17 So I tell you this, and insist on it in the
Lord, that you must no longer live as the
Gentiles do, in the futility of their thinking.
18 They are darkened in their understanding
and separated from the life of God because
of the ignorance that is in them due to the
hardening of their hearts. 19 Having lost all
sensitivity, they have given themselves over
to sensuality so as to indulge in every kind of
impurity, and they are full of greed.
20 That, however, is not the way of life you
learned 21 when you heard about Christ and
were taught in him in accordance with the
truth that is in Jesus. 22 You were taught, with
regard to your former way of life, to put off
your old self, which is being corrupted by its
deceitful desires; 23 to be made new in the at-
titude of your minds; 24 and to put on the new
self, created to be like God in true righteous-
ness and holiness.
25 Therefore each of you must put off false-
hood and speak truthfully to your neighbor,
for we are all members of one body. 26 "In
your anger do not sin"[d]: Do not let the sun go
down while you are still angry, 27 and do not
give the devil a foothold. 28 Anyone who has
been stealing must steal no longer, but must
work, doing something useful with their
own hands, that they may have something
to share with those in need.
29 Do not let any unwholesome talk come
out of your mouths, but only what is help-
ful for building others up according to their
needs that it may benefit those who listen.
30 And do not grieve the Holy Spirit of God,
with whom you were sealed for the day of
redemption. 31 Get rid of all bitterness, rage
and anger, brawling and slander, along with
every form of malice. 32 Be kind and compas-
sionate to one another, forgiving each other,
5 just as in Christ God forgave you. 1 Fol-
low God's example, therefore, as dearly
loved children 2 and walk in the way of love,
just as Christ loved us and gave himself up
for us as a fragrant offering and sacrifice to
God.
3 But among you there must not be even a

[a] 8 Or *God* [b] 8 Psalm 68:18 [c] 9 Or *the depths of the earth* [d] 26 Psalm 4:4 (see Septuagint)

hint of sexual immorality, or of any kind of impurity, or of greed, because these are improper for God's holy people. [4]Nor should there be obscenity, foolish talk or coarse joking, which are out of place, but rather thanksgiving. [5]For of this you can be sure: No immoral, impure or greedy person—such a person is an idolater—has any inheritance in the kingdom of Christ and of God.[a] [6]Let no one deceive you with empty words, for because of such things God's wrath comes on those who are disobedient. [7]Therefore do not be partners with them.

[8]For you were once darkness, but now you are light in the Lord. Live as children of light [9](for the fruit of the light consists in all goodness, righteousness and truth) [10]and find out what pleases the Lord. [11]Have nothing to do with the fruitless deeds of darkness, but rather expose them. [12]It is shameful even to mention what the disobedient do in secret. [13]But everything exposed by the light becomes visible—and everything that is illuminated becomes a light. [14]This is why it is said:

"Wake up, sleeper,
  rise from the dead,
  and Christ will shine on you."

[15]Be very careful, then, how you live—not as unwise but as wise, [16]making the most of every opportunity, because the days are evil. [17]Therefore do not be foolish, but understand what the Lord's will is. [18]Do not get drunk on wine, which leads to debauchery. Instead, be filled with the Spirit, [19]speaking to one another with psalms, hymns, and songs from the Spirit. Sing and make music from your heart to the Lord, [20]always giving thanks to God the Father for everything, in the name of our Lord Jesus Christ.

Instructions for Christian Households

[21]Submit to one another out of reverence for Christ.

[22]Wives, submit yourselves to your own husbands as you do to the Lord. [23]For the husband is the head of the wife as Christ is the head of the church, his body, of which he is the Savior. [24]Now as the church submits to Christ, so also wives should submit to their husbands in everything.

[25]Husbands, love your wives, just as Christ loved the church and gave himself up for her [26]to make her holy, cleansing[b] her by the washing with water through the word, [27]and to present her to himself as a radiant church, without stain or wrinkle or any other blemish, but holy and blameless. [28]In this same way, husbands ought to love their wives as their own bodies. He who loves his wife loves himself. [29]After all, no one ever hated their own body, but they feed and care for their body, just as Christ does the church— [30]for we are members of his body. [31]"For this reason a man will leave his father and mother and be united to his wife, and the two will become one flesh."[c] [32]This is a profound mystery—but I am talking about Christ and the church. [33]However, each one of you also must love his wife as he loves himself, and the wife must respect her husband.

6 Children, obey your parents in the Lord, for this is right. [2]"Honor your father and mother"—which is the first commandment with a promise— [3]"so that it may go well with you and that you may enjoy long life on the earth."[d]

[4]Fathers,[e] do not exasperate your children; instead, bring them up in the training and instruction of the Lord.

[5]Slaves, obey your earthly masters with respect and fear, and with sincerity of heart, just as you would obey Christ. [6]Obey them not only to win their favor when their eye is on you, but as slaves of Christ, doing the will of God from your heart. [7]Serve wholeheartedly, as if you were serving the Lord, not people, [8]because you know that the Lord will reward each one for whatever good they do, whether they are slave or free.

[9]And masters, treat your slaves in the same way. Do not threaten them, since you know that he who is both their Master and yours is in heaven, and there is no favoritism with him.

The Armor of God

[10]Finally, be strong in the Lord and in his mighty power. [11]Put on the full armor of God, so that you can take your stand against the devil's schemes. [12]For our struggle is not

[a] 5 Or *kingdom of the Messiah and God* [b] 26 Or *having cleansed* [c] 31 Gen. 2:24 [d] 3 Deut. 5:16
[e] 4 Or *Parents*

against flesh and blood, but against the rulers, against the authorities, against the powers of this dark world and against the spiritual forces of evil in the heavenly realms. 13 Therefore put on the full armor of God, so that when the day of evil comes, you may be able to stand your ground, and after you have done everything, to stand. 14 Stand firm then, with the belt of truth buckled around your waist, with the breastplate of righteousness in place, 15 and with your feet fitted with the readiness that comes from the gospel of peace. 16 In addition to all this, take up the shield of faith, with which you can extinguish all the flaming arrows of the evil one. 17 Take the helmet of salvation and the sword of the Spirit, which is the word of God.

18 And pray in the Spirit on all occasions with all kinds of prayers and requests. With this in mind, be alert and always keep on praying for all the Lord's people. 19 Pray also for me, that whenever I speak, words may be given me so that I will fearlessly make known the mystery of the gospel, 20 for which I am an ambassador in chains. Pray that I may declare it fearlessly, as I should.

Final Greetings

21 Tychicus, the dear brother and faithful servant in the Lord, will tell you everything, so that you also may know how I am and what I am doing. 22 I am sending him to you for this very purpose, that you may know how we are, and that he may encourage you.

23 Peace to the brothers and sisters,[a] and love with faith from God the Father and the Lord Jesus Christ. 24 Grace to all who love our Lord Jesus Christ with an undying love.[b]

[a] *23* The Greek word for *brothers and sisters* (*adelphoi*) refers here to believers, both men and women, as part of God's family. [b] *24* Or *Grace and immortality to all who love our Lord Jesus Christ.*

PHILIPPIANS

1 Paul and Timothy, servants of Christ Jesus,

To all God's holy people in Christ Jesus at Philippi, together with the overseers and deacons[a]:

2 Grace and peace to you from God our Father and the Lord Jesus Christ.

Thanksgiving and Prayer

3 I thank my God every time I remember you. 4 In all my prayers for all of you, I always pray with joy 5 because of your partnership in the gospel from the first day until now, 6 being confident of this, that he who began a good work in you will carry it on to completion until the day of Christ Jesus.

7 It is right for me to feel this way about all of you, since I have you in my heart and, whether I am in chains or defending and confirming the gospel, all of you share in God's grace with me. 8 God can testify how I long for all of you with the affection of Christ Jesus.

9 And this is my prayer: that your love may abound more and more in knowledge and depth of insight, 10 so that you may be able to discern what is best and may be pure and blameless for the day of Christ, 11 filled with the fruit of righteousness that comes through Jesus Christ — to the glory and praise of God.

Paul's Chains Advance the Gospel

12 Now I want you to know, brothers and sisters,[b] that what has happened to me has actually served to advance the gospel. 13 As a result, it has become clear throughout the whole palace guard[c] and to everyone else that I am in chains for Christ. 14 And because of my chains, most of the brothers and sisters have become confident in the Lord and dare all the more to proclaim the gospel without fear.

15 It is true that some preach Christ out of envy and rivalry, but others out of goodwill. 16 The latter do so out of love, knowing that I am put here for the defense of the gospel. 17 The former preach Christ out of selfish ambition, not sincerely, supposing that they can stir up trouble for me while I am in chains. 18 But what does it matter? The important thing is that in every way, whether from false motives or true, Christ is preached. And because of this I rejoice.

Yes, and I will continue to rejoice, 19 for I know that through your prayers and God's provision of the Spirit of Jesus Christ what has happened to me will turn out for my deliverance.[d] 20 I eagerly expect and hope that I will in no way be ashamed, but will have sufficient courage so that now as always Christ will be exalted in my body, whether by life or by death. 21 For to me, to live is Christ and to die is gain. 22 If I am to go on living in the body, this will mean fruitful labor for me. Yet what shall I choose? I do not know! 23 I am torn between the two: I desire to depart and be with Christ, which is better by far; 24 but it is more necessary for you that I remain in the body. 25 Convinced of this, I know that I will remain, and I will continue with all of you for your progress and joy in the faith, 26 so that through my being with you again your boasting in Christ Jesus will abound on account of me.

Life Worthy of the Gospel

27 Whatever happens, conduct yourselves in a manner worthy of the gospel of Christ. Then, whether I come and see you or only hear about you in my absence, I will know that you stand firm in the one Spirit,[e] striving together as one for the faith of the gospel

[a] *1* The word *deacons* refers here to Christians designated to serve with the overseers/elders of the church in a variety of ways; similarly in Romans 16:1 and 1 Tim. 3:8,12. [b] *12* The Greek word for *brothers and sisters* (*adelphoi*) refers here to believers, both men and women, as part of God's family; also in verse 14; and in 3:1, 13, 17; 4:1, 8, 21. [c] *13* Or *whole palace* [d] *19* Or *vindication*; or *salvation* [e] *27* Or *in one spirit*

28 without being frightened in any way by
those who oppose you. This is a sign to them
that they will be destroyed, but that you will
be saved — and that by God. 29 For it has
been granted to you on behalf of Christ not
only to believe in him, but also to suffer for
him, 30 since you are going through the same
struggle you saw I had, and now hear that I
still have.

Imitating Christ's Humility

2 Therefore if you have any encourage-
ment from being united with Christ, if
any comfort from his love, if any common
sharing in the Spirit, if any tenderness and
compassion, 2 then make my joy complete by
being like-minded, having the same love, be-
ing one in spirit and of one mind. 3 Do noth-
ing out of selfish ambition or vain conceit.
Rather, in humility value others above your-
selves, 4 not looking to your own interests but
each of you to the interests of the others.
5 In your relationships with one another,
have the same mindset as Christ Jesus:

6 Who, being in very nature[a] God,
did not consider equality with God
something to be used to his own
advantage;
7 rather, he made himself nothing
by taking the very nature[b] of a servant,
being made in human likeness.
8 And being found in appearance as a man,
he humbled himself
by becoming obedient to death —
even death on a cross!
9 Therefore God exalted him to the highest
place
and gave him the name that is above
every name,
10 that at the name of Jesus every knee
should bow,
in heaven and on earth and under
the earth,
11 and every tongue acknowledge that Jesus
Christ is Lord,
to the glory of God the Father.

Do Everything Without Grumbling

12 Therefore, my dear friends, as you have
always obeyed — not only in my presence,
but now much more in my absence — con-
tinue to work out your salvation with fear
and trembling, 13 for it is God who works in
you to will and to act in order to fulfill his
good purpose.
14 Do everything without grumbling or ar-
guing, 15 so that you may become blameless
and pure, "children of God without fault in
a warped and crooked generation."[c] Then
you will shine among them like stars in the
sky 16 as you hold firmly to the word of life.
And then I will be able to boast on the day
of Christ that I did not run or labor in vain.
17 But even if I am being poured out like a
drink offering on the sacrifice and service
coming from your faith, I am glad and re-
joice with all of you. 18 So you too should be
glad and rejoice with me.

Timothy and Epaphroditus

19 I hope in the Lord Jesus to send Timothy
to you soon, that I also may be cheered when
I receive news about you. 20 I have no one else
like him, who will show genuine concern for
your welfare. 21 For everyone looks out for
their own interests, not those of Jesus Christ.
22 But you know that Timothy has proved
himself, because as a son with his father he
has served with me in the work of the gospel.
23 I hope, therefore, to send him as soon as I
see how things go with me. 24 And I am confi-
dent in the Lord that I myself will come soon.
25 But I think it is necessary to send back
to you Epaphroditus, my brother, co-worker
and fellow soldier, who is also your messen-
ger, whom you sent to take care of my needs.
26 For he longs for all of you and is distressed
because you heard he was ill. 27 Indeed he
was ill, and almost died. But God had mercy
on him, and not on him only but also on me,
to spare me sorrow upon sorrow. 28 There-
fore I am all the more eager to send him, so
that when you see him again you may be
glad and I may have less anxiety. 29 So then,
welcome him in the Lord with great joy, and
honor people like him, 30 because he almost
died for the work of Christ. He risked his life
to make up for the help you yourselves could
not give me.

No Confidence in the Flesh

3 Further, my brothers and sisters, re-
joice in the Lord! It is no trouble for me

[a] 6 Or *in the form of* [b] 7 Or *the form* [c] 15 Deut. 32:5

to write the same things to you again, and it
is a safeguard for you. [2]Watch out for those
dogs, those evildoers, those mutilators of the
flesh. [3]For it is we who are the circumcision,
we who serve God by his Spirit, who boast in
Christ Jesus, and who put no confidence in
the flesh— [4]though I myself have reasons
for such confidence.

If someone else thinks they have rea-
sons to put confidence in the flesh, I have
more: [5]circumcised on the eighth day, of
the people of Israel, of the tribe of Benja-
min, a Hebrew of Hebrews; in regard to the
law, a Pharisee; [6]as for zeal, persecuting the
church; as for righteousness based on the
law, faultless.

[7]But whatever were gains to me I now
consider loss for the sake of Christ. [8]What is
more, I consider everything a loss because
of the surpassing worth of knowing Christ
Jesus my Lord, for whose sake I have lost all
things. I consider them garbage, that I may
gain Christ [9]and be found in him, not having
a righteousness of my own that comes from
the law, but that which is through faith in[a]
Christ—the righteousness that comes from
God on the basis of faith. [10]I want to know
Christ—yes, to know the power of his resur-
rection and participation in his sufferings,
becoming like him in his death, [11]and so,
somehow, attaining to the resurrection from
the dead.

[12]Not that I have already obtained all this,
or have already arrived at my goal, but I press
on to take hold of that for which Christ Jesus
took hold of me. [13]Brothers and sisters, I do
not consider myself yet to have taken hold
of it. But one thing I do: Forgetting what is
behind and straining toward what is ahead,
[14]I press on toward the goal to win the prize
for which God has called me heavenward in
Christ Jesus.

Following Paul's Example

[15]All of us, then, who are mature should
take such a view of things. And if on some
point you think differently, that too God will
make clear to you. [16]Only let us live up to
what we have already attained.

[17]Join together in following my example,
brothers and sisters, and just as you have us
as a model, keep your eyes on those who live
as we do. [18]For, as I have often told you be-
fore and now tell you again even with tears,
many live as enemies of the cross of Christ.
[19]Their destiny is destruction, their god is
their stomach, and their glory is in their
shame. Their mind is set on earthly things.
[20]But our citizenship is in heaven. And we
eagerly await a Savior from there, the Lord
Jesus Christ, [21]who, by the power that en-
ables him to bring everything under his con-
trol, will transform our lowly bodies so that
they will be like his glorious body.

Closing Appeal for Steadfastness and Unity

4 Therefore, my brothers and sisters, you
whom I love and long for, my joy and
crown, stand firm in the Lord in this way,
dear friends!

[2]I plead with Euodia and I plead with Syn-
tyche to be of the same mind in the Lord.
[3]Yes, and I ask you, my true companion,
help these women since they have contend-
ed at my side in the cause of the gospel, along
with Clement and the rest of my co-workers,
whose names are in the book of life.

Final Exhortations

[4]Rejoice in the Lord always. I will say it
again: Rejoice! [5]Let your gentleness be ev-
ident to all. The Lord is near. [6]Do not be
anxious about anything, but in every situa-
tion, by prayer and petition, with thanksgiv-
ing, present your requests to God. [7]And the
peace of God, which transcends all under-
standing, will guard your hearts and your
minds in Christ Jesus.

[8]Finally, brothers and sisters, whatever
is true, whatever is noble, whatever is right,
whatever is pure, whatever is lovely, what-
ever is admirable—if anything is excellent
or praiseworthy—think about such things.
[9]Whatever you have learned or received or
heard from me, or seen in me—put it into
practice. And the God of peace will be with
you.

Thanks for Their Gifts

[10]I rejoiced greatly in the Lord that at last
you renewed your concern for me. Indeed,
you were concerned, but you had no op-
portunity to show it. [11]I am not saying this

[a] 9 Or *through the faithfulness of*

because I am in need, for I have learned to
be content whatever the circumstances. [12]I
know what it is to be in need, and I know
what it is to have plenty. I have learned the
secret of being content in any and every sit-
uation, whether well fed or hungry, whether
living in plenty or in want. [13]I can do all this
through him who gives me strength.

[14]Yet it was good of you to share in my trou-
bles. [15]Moreover, as you Philippians know, in
the early days of your acquaintance with the
gospel, when I set out from Macedonia, not
one church shared with me in the matter of
giving and receiving, except you only; [16]for
even when I was in Thessalonica, you sent
me aid more than once when I was in need.
[17]Not that I desire your gifts; what I desire is
that more be credited to your account. [18]I
have received full payment and have more
than enough. I am amply supplied, now that
I have received from Epaphroditus the gifts
you sent. They are a fragrant offering, an ac-
ceptable sacrifice, pleasing to God. [19]And
my God will meet all your needs according
to the riches of his glory in Christ Jesus.

[20]To our God and Father be glory for ever
and ever. Amen.

Final Greetings

[21]Greet all God's people in Christ Jesus.
The brothers and sisters who are with me
send greetings. [22]All God's people here send
you greetings, especially those who belong
to Caesar's household.

[23]The grace of the Lord Jesus Christ be
with your spirit. Amen.[a]

[a] 23 Some manuscripts do not have *Amen.*

COLOSSIANS

1 Paul, an apostle of Christ Jesus by the will of God, and Timothy our brother,

2To God's holy people in Colossae, the faithful brothers and sisters[a] in Christ:

Grace and peace to you from God our Father.[b]

Thanksgiving and Prayer

3We always thank God, the Father of our Lord Jesus Christ, when we pray for you, 4because we have heard of your faith in Christ Jesus and of the love you have for all God's people— 5the faith and love that spring from the hope stored up for you in heaven and about which you have already heard in the true message of the gospel 6that has come to you. In the same way, the gospel is bearing fruit and growing throughout the whole world—just as it has been doing among you since the day you heard it and truly understood God's grace. 7You learned it from Epaphras, our dear fellow servant,[c] who is a faithful minister of Christ on our[d] behalf, 8and who also told us of your love in the Spirit.

9For this reason, since the day we heard about you, we have not stopped praying for you. We continually ask God to fill you with the knowledge of his will through all the wisdom and understanding that the Spirit gives,[e] 10so that you may live a life worthy of the Lord and please him in every way: bearing fruit in every good work, growing in the knowledge of God, 11being strengthened with all power according to his glorious might so that you may have great endurance and patience, 12and giving joyful thanks to the Father, who has qualified you[f] to share in the inheritance of his holy people in the kingdom of light. 13For he has rescued us from the dominion of darkness and brought us into the kingdom of the Son he loves, 14in whom we have redemption, the forgiveness of sins.

The Supremacy of the Son of God

15The Son is the image of the invisible God, the firstborn over all creation. 16For in him all things were created: things in heaven and on earth, visible and invisible, whether thrones or powers or rulers or authorities; all things have been created through him and for him. 17He is before all things, and in him all things hold together. 18And he is the head of the body, the church; he is the beginning and the firstborn from among the dead, so that in everything he might have the supremacy. 19For God was pleased to have all his fullness dwell in him, 20and through him to reconcile to himself all things, whether things on earth or things in heaven, by making peace through his blood, shed on the cross.

21Once you were alienated from God and were enemies in your minds because of[g] your evil behavior. 22But now he has reconciled you by Christ's physical body through death to present you holy in his sight, without blemish and free from accusation— 23if you continue in your faith, established and firm, and do not move from the hope held out in the gospel. This is the gospel that you heard and that has been proclaimed to every creature under heaven, and of which I, Paul, have become a servant.

Paul's Labor for the Church

24Now I rejoice in what I am suffering for you, and I fill up in my flesh what is still lacking in regard to Christ's afflictions, for the sake of his body, which is the church. 25I have become its servant by the commission God gave me to present to you the word of

[a] 2 The Greek word for *brothers and sisters* (*adelphoi*) refers here to believers, both men and women, as part of God's family; also in 4:15. [b] 2 Some manuscripts *Father and the Lord Jesus Christ* [c] 7 Or *slave* [d] 7 Some manuscripts *your* [e] 9 Or *all spiritual wisdom and understanding* [f] 12 Some manuscripts *us* [g] 21 Or *minds, as shown by*

God in its fullness— 26the mystery that has
been kept hidden for ages and generations,
but is now disclosed to the Lord's people.
27To them God has chosen to make known
among the Gentiles the glorious riches of
this mystery, which is Christ in you, the hope
of glory.
28He is the one we proclaim, admonishing
and teaching everyone with all wisdom, so
that we may present everyone fully mature
in Christ. 29To this end I strenuously con-
tend with all the energy Christ so powerfully
works in me.

2 I want you to know how hard I am con-
tending for you and for those at Laodi-
cea, and for all who have not met me person-
ally. 2My goal is that they may be encouraged
in heart and united in love, so that they may
have the full riches of complete understand-
ing, in order that they may know the mystery
of God, namely, Christ, 3in whom are hid-
den all the treasures of wisdom and knowl-
edge. 4I tell you this so that no one may de-
ceive you by fine-sounding arguments. 5For
though I am absent from you in body, I am
present with you in spirit and delight to see
how disciplined you are and how firm your
faith in Christ is.

Spiritual Fullness in Christ

6So then, just as you received Christ Jesus
as Lord, continue to live your lives in him,
7rooted and built up in him, strengthened in
the faith as you were taught, and overflow-
ing with thankfulness.
8See to it that no one takes you captive
through hollow and deceptive philosophy,
which depends on human tradition and
the elemental spiritual forces[a] of this world
rather than on Christ.
9For in Christ all the fullness of the Deity
lives in bodily form, 10and in Christ you have
been brought to fullness. He is the head over
every power and authority. 11In him you
were also circumcised with a circumcision
not performed by human hands. Your whole
self ruled by the flesh[b] was put off when you
were circumcised by[c] Christ, 12having been
buried with him in baptism, in which you
were also raised with him through your faith
in the working of God, who raised him from
the dead.
13When you were dead in your sins and
in the uncircumcision of your flesh, God
made you[d] alive with Christ. He forgave us
all our sins, 14having canceled the charge of
our legal indebtedness, which stood against
us and condemned us; he has taken it away,
nailing it to the cross. 15And having dis-
armed the powers and authorities, he made
a public spectacle of them, triumphing over
them by the cross.[e]

Freedom From Human Rules

16Therefore do not let anyone judge you by
what you eat or drink, or with regard to a re-
ligious festival, a New Moon celebration or
a Sabbath day. 17These are a shadow of the
things that were to come; the reality, how-
ever, is found in Christ. 18Do not let anyone
who delights in false humility and the wor-
ship of angels disqualify you. Such a person
also goes into great detail about what they
have seen; they are puffed up with idle no-
tions by their unspiritual mind. 19They have
lost connection with the head, from whom
the whole body, supported and held togeth-
er by its ligaments and sinews, grows as God
causes it to grow.
20Since you died with Christ to the ele-
mental spiritual forces of this world, why,
as though you still belonged to the world,
do you submit to its rules: 21"Do not handle!
Do not taste! Do not touch!"? 22These rules,
which have to do with things that are all des-
tined to perish with use, are based on mere-
ly human commands and teachings. 23Such
regulations indeed have an appearance of
wisdom, with their self-imposed worship,
their false humility and their harsh treat-
ment of the body, but they lack any value in
restraining sensual indulgence.

Living as Those Made Alive in Christ

3 Since, then, you have been raised with
Christ, set your hearts on things above,
where Christ is, seated at the right hand of
God. 2Set your minds on things above, not
on earthly things. 3For you died, and your
life is now hidden with Christ in God. 4When

[a] *8* Or *the basic principles*; also in verse 20 [b] *11* In contexts like this, the Greek word for *flesh* (*sarx*) refers to the sinful state of human beings, often presented as a power in opposition to the Spirit; also in verse 13. [c] *11* Or *put off in the circumcision of* [d] *13* Some manuscripts *us* [e] *15* Or *them in him*

Christ, who is your[a] life, appears, then you
also will appear with him in glory.
5 Put to death, therefore, whatever belongs
to your earthly nature: sexual immorality,
impurity, lust, evil desires and greed, which
is idolatry. 6 Because of these, the wrath of
God is coming.[b] 7 You used to walk in these
ways, in the life you once lived. 8 But now you
must also rid yourselves of all such things as
these: anger, rage, malice, slander, and filthy
language from your lips. 9 Do not lie to each
other, since you have taken off your old self
with its practices 10 and have put on the new
self, which is being renewed in knowledge
in the image of its Creator. 11 Here there is no
Gentile or Jew, circumcised or uncircum-
cised, barbarian, Scythian, slave or free, but
Christ is all, and is in all.

12 Therefore, as God's chosen people, holy
and dearly loved, clothe yourselves with
compassion, kindness, humility, gentleness
and patience. 13 Bear with each other and
forgive one another if any of you has a griev-
ance against someone. Forgive as the Lord
forgave you. 14 And over all these virtues put
on love, which binds them all together in
perfect unity.

15 Let the peace of Christ rule in your
hearts, since as members of one body you
were called to peace. And be thankful. 16 Let
the message of Christ dwell among you rich-
ly as you teach and admonish one another
with all wisdom through psalms, hymns,
and songs from the Spirit, singing to God
with gratitude in your hearts. 17 And whatev-
er you do, whether in word or deed, do it all
in the name of the Lord Jesus, giving thanks
to God the Father through him.

Instructions for Christian Households

18 Wives, submit yourselves to your hus-
bands, as is fitting in the Lord.

19 Husbands, love your wives and do not
be harsh with them.

20 Children, obey your parents in every-
thing, for this pleases the Lord.

21 Fathers,[c] do not embitter your children,
or they will become discouraged.

22 Slaves, obey your earthly masters in
everything; and do it, not only when their
eye is on you and to curry their favor, but
with sincerity of heart and reverence for the
Lord. 23 Whatever you do, work at it with all
your heart, as working for the Lord, not for
human masters, 24 since you know that you
will receive an inheritance from the Lord
as a reward. It is the Lord Christ you are
serving. 25 Anyone who does wrong will be
repaid for their wrongs, and there is no fa-
voritism.

4 Masters, provide your slaves with what
is right and fair, because you know that
you also have a Master in heaven.

Further Instructions

2 Devote yourselves to prayer, being
watchful and thankful. 3 And pray for us,
too, that God may open a door for our mes-
sage, so that we may proclaim the mystery of
Christ, for which I am in chains. 4 Pray that I
may proclaim it clearly, as I should. 5 Be wise
in the way you act toward outsiders; make
the most of every opportunity. 6 Let your
conversation be always full of grace, sea-
soned with salt, so that you may know how
to answer everyone.

Final Greetings

7 Tychicus will tell you all the news about
me. He is a dear brother, a faithful minister
and fellow servant[d] in the Lord. 8 I am send-
ing him to you for the express purpose that
you may know about our[e] circumstances
and that he may encourage your hearts. 9 He
is coming with Onesimus, our faithful and
dear brother, who is one of you. They will tell
you everything that is happening here.

10 My fellow prisoner Aristarchus sends
you his greetings, as does Mark, the cousin
of Barnabas. (You have received instruc-
tions about him; if he comes to you, wel-
come him.) 11 Jesus, who is called Justus,
also sends greetings. These are the only
Jews[f] among my co-workers for the king-
dom of God, and they have proved a comfort
to me. 12 Epaphras, who is one of you and a
servant of Christ Jesus, sends greetings. He
is always wrestling in prayer for you, that you
may stand firm in all the will of God, mature
and fully assured. 13 I vouch for him that he

[a] 4 Some manuscripts *our* [b] 6 Some early manuscripts *coming on those who are disobedient*
[c] 21 Or *Parents* [d] 7 Or *slave*; also in verse 12 [e] 8 Some manuscripts *that he may know about your*
[f] 11 Greek *only ones of the circumcision group*

is working hard for you and for those at La-
odicea and Hierapolis. 14 Our dear friend
Luke, the doctor, and Demas send greetings.
15 Give my greetings to the brothers and sis-
ters at Laodicea, and to Nympha and the
church in her house.

16 After this letter has been read to you, see
that it is also read in the church of the Laod-
iceans and that you in turn read the letter
from Laodicea.

17 Tell Archippus: "See to it that you com-
plete the ministry you have received in the
Lord."

18 I, Paul, write this greeting in my own
hand. Remember my chains. Grace be with
you.

1 THESSALONIANS

1 Paul, Silas[a] and Timothy,

To the church of the Thessalonians in God the Father and the Lord Jesus Christ:

Grace and peace to you.

Thanksgiving for the Thessalonians' Faith

2We always thank God for all of you and continually mention you in our prayers. 3We remember before our God and Father your work produced by faith, your labor prompted by love, and your endurance inspired by hope in our Lord Jesus Christ.

4For we know, brothers and sisters[b] loved by God, that he has chosen you, 5because our gospel came to you not simply with words but also with power, with the Holy Spirit and deep conviction. You know how we lived among you for your sake. 6You became imitators of us and of the Lord, for you welcomed the message in the midst of severe suffering with the joy given by the Holy Spirit. 7And so you became a model to all the believers in Macedonia and Achaia. 8The Lord's message rang out from you not only in Macedonia and Achaia — your faith in God has become known everywhere. Therefore we do not need to say anything about it, 9for they themselves report what kind of reception you gave us. They tell how you turned to God from idols to serve the living and true God, 10and to wait for his Son from heaven, whom he raised from the dead — Jesus, who rescues us from the coming wrath.

Paul's Ministry in Thessalonica

2 You know, brothers and sisters, that our visit to you was not without results. 2We had previously suffered and been treated outrageously in Philippi, as you know, but with the help of our God we dared to tell you his gospel in the face of strong opposition. 3For the appeal we make does not spring from error or impure motives, nor are we trying to trick you. 4On the contrary, we speak as those approved by God to be entrusted with the gospel. We are not trying to please people but God, who tests our hearts. 5You know we never used flattery, nor did we put on a mask to cover up greed — God is our witness. 6We were not looking for praise from people, not from you or anyone else, even though as apostles of Christ we could have asserted our authority. 7Instead, we were like young children[c] among you.

Just as a nursing mother cares for her children, 8so we cared for you. Because we loved you so much, we were delighted to share with you not only the gospel of God but our lives as well. 9Surely you remember, brothers and sisters, our toil and hardship; we worked night and day in order not to be a burden to anyone while we preached the gospel of God to you. 10You are witnesses, and so is God, of how holy, righteous and blameless we were among you who believed. 11For you know that we dealt with each of you as a father deals with his own children, 12encouraging, comforting and urging you to live lives worthy of God, who calls you into his kingdom and glory.

13And we also thank God continually because, when you received the word of God, which you heard from us, you accepted it not as a human word, but as it actually is, the word of God, which is indeed at work in you who believe. 14For you, brothers and sisters, became imitators of God's churches in Judea, which are in Christ Jesus: You suffered from your own people the same things those churches suffered from the Jews 15who killed the Lord Jesus and the prophets and also drove us out. They displease God and are hostile to everyone 16in their

[a] *1* Greek *Silvanus,* a variant of *Silas* [b] *4* The Greek word for *brothers and sisters* (*adelphoi*) refers here to believers, both men and women, as part of God's family; also in 2:1, 9, 14, 17; 3:7; 4:1, 10, 13; 5:1, 4, 12, 14, 25, 27. [c] *7* Some manuscripts *were gentle*

effort to keep us from speaking to the Gentiles so that they may be saved. In this way they always heap up their sins to the limit. The wrath of God has come upon them at last.[a]

Paul's Longing to See the Thessalonians

17 But, brothers and sisters, when we were orphaned by being separated from you for a short time (in person, not in thought), out of our intense longing we made every effort to see you. 18 For we wanted to come to you — certainly I, Paul, did, again and again — but Satan blocked our way. 19 For what is our hope, our joy, or the crown in which we will glory in the presence of our Lord Jesus when he comes? Is it not you? 20 Indeed, you are our glory and joy.

3 So when we could stand it no longer, we thought it best to be left by ourselves in Athens. 2 We sent Timothy, who is our brother and co-worker in God's service in spreading the gospel of Christ, to strengthen and encourage you in your faith, 3 so that no one would be unsettled by these trials. For you know quite well that we are destined for them. 4 In fact, when we were with you, we kept telling you that we would be persecuted. And it turned out that way, as you well know. 5 For this reason, when I could stand it no longer, I sent to find out about your faith. I was afraid that in some way the tempter had tempted you and that our labors might have been in vain.

Timothy's Encouraging Report

6 But Timothy has just now come to us from you and has brought good news about your faith and love. He has told us that you always have pleasant memories of us and that you long to see us, just as we also long to see you. 7 Therefore, brothers and sisters, in all our distress and persecution we were encouraged about you because of your faith. 8 For now we really live, since you are standing firm in the Lord. 9 How can we thank God enough for you in return for all the joy we have in the presence of our God because of you? 10 Night and day we pray most earnestly that we may see you again and supply what is lacking in your faith.

11 Now may our God and Father himself and our Lord Jesus clear the way for us to come to you. 12 May the Lord make your love increase and overflow for each other and for everyone else, just as ours does for you. 13 May he strengthen your hearts so that you will be blameless and holy in the presence of our God and Father when our Lord Jesus comes with all his holy ones.

Living to Please God

4 As for other matters, brothers and sisters, we instructed you how to live in order to please God, as in fact you are living. Now we ask you and urge you in the Lord Jesus to do this more and more. 2 For you know what instructions we gave you by the authority of the Lord Jesus.

3 It is God's will that you should be sanctified: that you should avoid sexual immorality; 4 that each of you should learn to control your own body[b] in a way that is holy and honorable, 5 not in passionate lust like the pagans, who do not know God; 6 and that in this matter no one should wrong or take advantage of a brother or sister.[c] The Lord will punish all those who commit such sins, as we told you and warned you before. 7 For God did not call us to be impure, but to live a holy life. 8 Therefore, anyone who rejects this instruction does not reject a human being but God, the very God who gives you his Holy Spirit.

9 Now about your love for one another we do not need to write to you, for you yourselves have been taught by God to love each other. 10 And in fact, you do love all of God's family throughout Macedonia. Yet we urge you, brothers and sisters, to do so more and more, 11 and to make it your ambition to lead a quiet life: You should mind your own business and work with your hands, just as we told you, 12 so that your daily life may win the respect of outsiders and so that you will not be dependent on anybody.

Believers Who Have Died

13 Brothers and sisters, we do not want you to be uninformed about those who sleep in death, so that you do not grieve like the rest of mankind, who have no hope. 14 For we

[a] *16* Or *them fully* [b] *4* Or *learn to live with your own wife*; or *learn to acquire a wife* [c] *6* The Greek word for *brother or sister* (*adelphos*) refers here to a believer, whether man or woman, as part of God's family.

ALL CREATURES OF OUR GOD AND KING

Gioanni Bernardone [Francis of Assisi]

All creatures of our God and King
Lift up your voice and with us sing
O praise him, Alleluia!
Thou burning sun with golden beam
Thou silver moon with softer gleam
O praise him, O praise him
Alleluia! Alleluia! Alleluia!

Thou rushing wind that art so strong
Ye clouds that sail in Heav'n along
O praise him, Alleluia!
Thou rising moon, in praise rejoice
Ye lights of evening, find a voice
O praise him, O praise him
Alleluia! Alleluia! Alleluia!
Let all things their Creator bless
And worship him in humbleness
O praise him, Alleluia!
Praise, praise the Father, praise the Son
And praise the Spirit, three in One
O praise him, O praise him
Alleluia! Alleluia! Alleluia!

THE INSPIRATION

Praise the LORD from the earth, you great sea creatures and all ocean depths, lighting and hail, snow and clouds, stormy winds that do his bidding, you mountains and all hills, fruit trees and all cedars, wild animals and all cattle, small creatures and flying birds, kings of the earth and all nations, you princes and all rulers on earth, young men and women, old men and children. Let them praise the name of the LORD, for his name alone is exalted; his splendor is above the earth and the heavens. —Psalm 148:7 – 13

BEHIND THE SONG

The man behind the writing of "All Creatures of Our God and King" is Gioanni Bernardone, also known as Francis of Assisi. Bernardone was famously passionate about God's creatures and the beauty of the natural world. This hymn stands as one of the most profound pieces of Christian environmentalist art in the history of the church.

Bernardone was a hedonistic musician and soldier who had been raised in a wealthy family in Italy. At the age of 25, he found faith in Jesus and repudiated his old life. He eschewed wealth and all of its trappings and embraced a life of serving the needs of the poor. "All Creatures …" was written toward the end of his life; one of over 60 hymns the itinerant minister penned. However, it was not published for over 400 years. As many hymns have, "All Creatures …" evolved over centuries. Eventually the song was translated into several languages and adapted to different melodies. The most popular English version of the song is actually a paraphrase of Bernardone's original lyrics, translated and applied to a German folk melody by William H. Draper sometime around the turn of the 20th century.

The song has enjoyed a resurgence of popularity among all those who are inspired by its environmental message at this critical time in history. The popular contemporary artist David Crowder arranged a somewhat simplified musical arrangement that works well for the modern worship band and uses the repeating "Alleluias" to great effect.

Selah

The wonders of God's creation are emphatically expressed in worship throughout the Bible. God is the creator of all things. He designed the Grand Canyon and the hummingbird. His creativity is astonishing. Some modern thinkers mistakenly believe science and environmentalism to be in some sort of conflict with the gospel. But nothing could be further from the truth.

In the book of Genesis, we read that God made humankind the "caretakers" of his creation. How do you understand your God-given role as a caretaker of the earth? Have you experienced anything in nature so majestic, beautiful, awe-inspiring or even frightening, that it prompted you to spontaneously worship God?

believe that Jesus died and rose again, and
so we believe that God will bring with Jesus
those who have fallen asleep in him. 15 Ac-
cording to the Lord's word, we tell you that
we who are still alive, who are left until the
coming of the Lord, will certainly not pre-
cede those who have fallen asleep. 16 For the
Lord himself will come down from heaven,
with a loud command, with the voice of the
archangel and with the trumpet call of God,
and the dead in Christ will rise first. 17 Af-
ter that, we who are still alive and are left
will be caught up together with them in the
clouds to meet the Lord in the air. And so we
will be with the Lord forever. 18 Therefore
encourage one another with these words.

The Day of the Lord

5 Now, brothers and sisters, about times
and dates we do not need to write to
you, 2 for you know very well that the day of
the Lord will come like a thief in the night.
3 While people are saying, "Peace and safe-
ty," destruction will come on them sudden-
ly, as labor pains on a pregnant woman, and
they will not escape.

4 But you, brothers and sisters, are not in
darkness so that this day should surprise you
like a thief. 5 You are all children of the light
and children of the day. We do not belong to
the night or to the darkness. 6 So then, let us
not be like others, who are asleep, but let us
be awake and sober. 7 For those who sleep,
sleep at night, and those who get drunk,
get drunk at night. 8 But since we belong to
the day, let us be sober, putting on faith and
love as a breastplate, and the hope of salva-
tion as a helmet. 9 For God did not appoint
us to suffer wrath but to receive salvation
through our Lord Jesus Christ. 10 He died for
us so that, whether we are awake or asleep,
we may live together with him. 11 Therefore
encourage one another and build each other
up, just as in fact you are doing.

Final Instructions

12 Now we ask you, brothers and sisters, to
acknowledge those who work hard among
you, who care for you in the Lord and who
admonish you. 13 Hold them in the highest
regard in love because of their work. Live in
peace with each other. 14 And we urge you,
brothers and sisters, warn those who are idle
and disruptive, encourage the disheartened,
help the weak, be patient with everyone.
15 Make sure that nobody pays back wrong
for wrong, but always strive to do what is
good for each other and for everyone else.

16 Rejoice always, 17 pray continually,
18 give thanks in all circumstances; for this is
God's will for you in Christ Jesus.

19 Do not quench the Spirit. 20 Do not treat
prophecies with contempt 21 but test them
all; hold on to what is good, 22 reject every
kind of evil.

23 May God himself, the God of peace,
sanctify you through and through. May your
whole spirit, soul and body be kept blame-
less at the coming of our Lord Jesus Christ.
24 The one who calls you is faithful, and he
will do it.

25 Brothers and sisters, pray for us. 26 Greet
all God's people with a holy kiss. 27 I charge
you before the Lord to have this letter read to
all the brothers and sisters.

28 The grace of our Lord Jesus Christ be
with you.

2 THESSALONIANS

1 Paul, Silas[a] and Timothy,

To the church of the Thessalonians in God
our Father and the Lord Jesus Christ:

2 Grace and peace to you from God the Fa-
ther and the Lord Jesus Christ.

Thanksgiving and Prayer

3 We ought always to thank God for you,
brothers and sisters,[b] and rightly so, because
your faith is growing more and more, and
the love all of you have for one another is in-
creasing. 4 Therefore, among God's churches
we boast about your perseverance and faith
in all the persecutions and trials you are en-
during.

5 All this is evidence that God's judgment
is right, and as a result you will be counted
worthy of the kingdom of God, for which you
are suffering. 6 God is just: He will pay back
trouble to those who trouble you 7 and give
relief to you who are troubled, and to us as
well. This will happen when the Lord Jesus is
revealed from heaven in blazing fire with his
powerful angels. 8 He will punish those who
do not know God and do not obey the gos-
pel of our Lord Jesus. 9 They will be punished
with everlasting destruction and shut out
from the presence of the Lord and from the
glory of his might 10 on the day he comes to
be glorified in his holy people and to be mar-
veled at among all those who have believed.
This includes you, because you believed our
testimony to you.

11 With this in mind, we constantly pray
for you, that our God may make you worthy
of his calling, and that by his power he may
bring to fruition your every desire for good-
ness and your every deed prompted by faith.
12 We pray this so that the name of our Lord
Jesus may be glorified in you, and you in
him, according to the grace of our God and
the Lord Jesus Christ.[c]

The Man of Lawlessness

2 Concerning the coming of our Lord
Jesus Christ and our being gathered to
him, we ask you, brothers and sisters, 2 not to
become easily unsettled or alarmed by the
teaching allegedly from us—whether by a
prophecy or by word of mouth or by letter—
asserting that the day of the Lord has already
come. 3 Don't let anyone deceive you in any
way, for that day will not come until the re-
bellion occurs and the man of lawlessness[d]
is revealed, the man doomed to destruc-
tion. 4 He will oppose and will exalt himself
over everything that is called God or is wor-
shiped, so that he sets himself up in God's
temple, proclaiming himself to be God.

5 Don't you remember that when I was
with you I used to tell you these things?
6 And now you know what is holding him
back, so that he may be revealed at the prop-
er time. 7 For the secret power of lawlessness
is already at work; but the one who now
holds it back will continue to do so till he is
taken out of the way. 8 And then the lawless
one will be revealed, whom the Lord Jesus
will overthrow with the breath of his mouth
and destroy by the splendor of his coming.
9 The coming of the lawless one will be in ac-
cordance with how Satan works. He will use
all sorts of displays of power through signs
and wonders that serve the lie, 10 and all the
ways that wickedness deceives those who
are perishing. They perish because they re-
fused to love the truth and so be saved. 11 For
this reason God sends them a powerful de-
lusion so that they will believe the lie 12 and
so that all will be condemned who have not
believed the truth but have delighted in
wickedness.

Stand Firm

13 But we ought always to thank God for
you, brothers and sisters loved by the Lord,

[a] *1* Greek *Silvanus,* a variant of *Silas* [b] *3* The Greek word for *brothers and sisters* (*adelphoi*) refers here to believers, both men and women, as part of God's family; also in 2:1, 13, 15; 3:1, 6, 13. [c] *12* Or *God and Lord, Jesus Christ* [d] *3* Some manuscripts *sin*

because God chose you as firstfruits[a] to be saved through the sanctifying work of the Spirit and through belief in the truth. [14]He called you to this through our gospel, that you might share in the glory of our Lord Jesus Christ.

[15]So then, brothers and sisters, stand firm and hold fast to the teachings[b] we passed on to you, whether by word of mouth or by letter.

[16]May our Lord Jesus Christ himself and God our Father, who loved us and by his grace gave us eternal encouragement and good hope, [17]encourage your hearts and strengthen you in every good deed and word.

Request for Prayer

3 As for other matters, brothers and sisters, pray for us that the message of the Lord may spread rapidly and be honored, just as it was with you. [2]And pray that we may be delivered from wicked and evil people, for not everyone has faith. [3]But the Lord is faithful, and he will strengthen you and protect you from the evil one. [4]We have confidence in the Lord that you are doing and will continue to do the things we command. [5]May the Lord direct your hearts into God's love and Christ's perseverance.

Warning Against Idleness

[6]In the name of the Lord Jesus Christ, we command you, brothers and sisters, to keep away from every believer who is idle and disruptive and does not live according to the teaching[c] you received from us. [7]For you yourselves know how you ought to follow our example. We were not idle when we were with you, [8]nor did we eat anyone's food without paying for it. On the contrary, we worked night and day, laboring and toiling so that we would not be a burden to any of you. [9]We did this, not because we do not have the right to such help, but in order to offer ourselves as a model for you to imitate. [10]For even when we were with you, we gave you this rule: "The one who is unwilling to work shall not eat."

[11]We hear that some among you are idle and disruptive. They are not busy; they are busybodies. [12]Such people we command and urge in the Lord Jesus Christ to settle down and earn the food they eat. [13]And as for you, brothers and sisters, never tire of doing what is good.

[14]Take special note of anyone who does not obey our instruction in this letter. Do not associate with them, in order that they may feel ashamed. [15]Yet do not regard them as an enemy, but warn them as you would a fellow believer.

Final Greetings

[16]Now may the Lord of peace himself give you peace at all times and in every way. The Lord be with all of you.

[17]I, Paul, write this greeting in my own hand, which is the distinguishing mark in all my letters. This is how I write.

[18]The grace of our Lord Jesus Christ be with you all.

[a] *13* Some manuscripts *because from the beginning God chose you* [b] *15* Or *traditions* [c] *6* Or *tradition*

1 TIMOTHY

1 Paul, an apostle of Christ Jesus by the command of God our Savior and of Christ Jesus our hope,

2 To Timothy my true son in the faith:

Grace, mercy and peace from God the Father and Christ Jesus our Lord.

Timothy Charged to Oppose False Teachers

3 As I urged you when I went into Macedonia, stay there in Ephesus so that you may command certain people not to teach false doctrines any longer 4 or to devote themselves to myths and endless genealogies. Such things promote controversial speculations rather than advancing God's work—which is by faith. 5 The goal of this command is love, which comes from a pure heart and a good conscience and a sincere faith. 6 Some have departed from these and have turned to meaningless talk. 7 They want to be teachers of the law, but they do not know what they are talking about or what they so confidently affirm.

8 We know that the law is good if one uses it properly. 9 We also know that the law is made not for the righteous but for lawbreakers and rebels, the ungodly and sinful, the unholy and irreligious, for those who kill their fathers or mothers, for murderers, 10 for the sexually immoral, for those practicing homosexuality, for slave traders and liars and perjurers—and for whatever else is contrary to the sound doctrine 11 that conforms to the gospel concerning the glory of the blessed God, which he entrusted to me.

The Lord's Grace to Paul

12 I thank Christ Jesus our Lord, who has given me strength, that he considered me trustworthy, appointing me to his service. 13 Even though I was once a blasphemer and a persecutor and a violent man, I was shown mercy because I acted in ignorance and unbelief. 14 The grace of our Lord was poured out on me abundantly, along with the faith and love that are in Christ Jesus.

15 Here is a trustworthy saying that deserves full acceptance: Christ Jesus came into the world to save sinners—of whom I am the worst. 16 But for that very reason I was shown mercy so that in me, the worst of sinners, Christ Jesus might display his immense patience as an example for those who would believe in him and receive eternal life. 17 Now to the King eternal, immortal, invisible, the only God, be honor and glory for ever and ever. Amen.

The Charge to Timothy Renewed

18 Timothy, my son, I am giving you this command in keeping with the prophecies once made about you, so that by recalling them you may fight the battle well, 19 holding on to faith and a good conscience, which some have rejected and so have suffered shipwreck with regard to the faith. 20 Among them are Hymenaeus and Alexander, whom I have handed over to Satan to be taught not to blaspheme.

Instructions on Worship

2 I urge, then, first of all, that petitions, prayers, intercession and thanksgiving be made for all people— 2 for kings and all those in authority, that we may live peaceful and quiet lives in all godliness and holiness. 3 This is good, and pleases God our Savior, 4 who wants all people to be saved and to come to a knowledge of the truth. 5 For there is one God and one mediator between God and mankind, the man Christ Jesus, 6 who gave himself as a ransom for all people. This has now been witnessed to at the proper time. 7 And for this purpose I was appointed a herald and an apostle—I am telling the truth, I am not lying—and a true and faithful teacher of the Gentiles.

8 Therefore I want the men everywhere to pray, lifting up holy hands without anger or disputing. 9 I also want the women to

dress modestly, with decency and propriety, adorning themselves, not with elaborate hairstyles or gold or pearls or expensive clothes, 10but with good deeds, appropriate for women who profess to worship God.

11A woman[a] should learn in quietness and full submission. 12I do not permit a woman to teach or to assume authority over a man;[b] she must be quiet. 13For Adam was formed first, then Eve. 14And Adam was not the one deceived; it was the woman who was deceived and became a sinner. 15But women[c] will be saved through childbearing—if they continue in faith, love and holiness with propriety.

Qualifications for Overseers and Deacons

3 Here is a trustworthy saying: Whoever aspires to be an overseer desires a noble task. 2Now the overseer is to be above reproach, faithful to his wife, temperate, self-controlled, respectable, hospitable, able to teach, 3not given to drunkenness, not violent but gentle, not quarrelsome, not a lover of money. 4He must manage his own family well and see that his children obey him, and he must do so in a manner worthy of full[d] respect. 5(If anyone does not know how to manage his own family, how can he take care of God's church?) 6He must not be a recent convert, or he may become conceited and fall under the same judgment as the devil. 7He must also have a good reputation with outsiders, so that he will not fall into disgrace and into the devil's trap.

8In the same way, deacons[e] are to be worthy of respect, sincere, not indulging in much wine, and not pursuing dishonest gain. 9They must keep hold of the deep truths of the faith with a clear conscience. 10They must first be tested; and then if there is nothing against them, let them serve as deacons.

11In the same way, the women[f] are to be worthy of respect, not malicious talkers but temperate and trustworthy in everything.

12A deacon must be faithful to his wife and must manage his children and his household well. 13Those who have served well gain an excellent standing and great assurance in their faith in Christ Jesus.

Reasons for Paul's Instructions

14Although I hope to come to you soon, I am writing you these instructions so that, 15if I am delayed, you will know how people ought to conduct themselves in God's household, which is the church of the living God, the pillar and foundation of the truth. 16Beyond all question, the mystery from which true godliness springs is great:

He appeared in the flesh,
  was vindicated by the Spirit,[g]
was seen by angels,
  was preached among the nations,
was believed on in the world,
  was taken up in glory.

4 The Spirit clearly says that in later times some will abandon the faith and follow deceiving spirits and things taught by demons. 2Such teachings come through hypocritical liars, whose consciences have been seared as with a hot iron. 3They forbid people to marry and order them to abstain from certain foods, which God created to be received with thanksgiving by those who believe and who know the truth. 4For everything God created is good, and nothing is to be rejected if it is received with thanksgiving, 5because it is consecrated by the word of God and prayer.

6If you point these things out to the brothers and sisters,[h] you will be a good minister of Christ Jesus, nourished on the truths of the faith and of the good teaching that you have followed. 7Have nothing to do with godless myths and old wives' tales; rather, train yourself to be godly. 8For physical training is of some value, but godliness has value for all things, holding promise for both the present life and the life to come. 9This is a trustworthy saying that deserves full acceptance. 10That is why we labor and strive, because we have put our hope in the living God, who is the Savior of all people, and especially of those who believe.

[a] *11* Or *wife;* also in verse 12 [b] *12* Or *over her husband* [c] *15* Greek *she* [d] *4* Or *him with proper*
[e] *8* The word *deacons* refers here to Christians designated to serve with the overseers/elders of the church in a variety of ways; similarly in verse 12; and in Romans 16:1 and Phil. 1:1. [f] *11* Possibly deacons' wives or women who are deacons [g] *16* Or *vindicated in spirit* [h] *6* The Greek word for *brothers and sisters* (*adelphoi*) refers here to believers, both men and women, as part of God's family.

[11]Command and teach these things. [12]Don't let anyone look down on you because you are young, but set an example for the believers in speech, in conduct, in love, in faith and in purity. [13]Until I come, devote yourself to the public reading of Scripture, to preaching and to teaching. [14]Do not neglect your gift, which was given you through prophecy when the body of elders laid their hands on you.

[15]Be diligent in these matters; give yourself wholly to them, so that everyone may see your progress. [16]Watch your life and doctrine closely. Persevere in them, because if you do, you will save both yourself and your hearers.

Widows, Elders and Slaves

5 Do not rebuke an older man harshly, but exhort him as if he were your father. Treat younger men as brothers, [2]older women as mothers, and younger women as sisters, with absolute purity.

[3]Give proper recognition to those widows who are really in need. [4]But if a widow has children or grandchildren, these should learn first of all to put their religion into practice by caring for their own family and so repaying their parents and grandparents, for this is pleasing to God. [5]The widow who is really in need and left all alone puts her hope in God and continues night and day to pray and to ask God for help. [6]But the widow who lives for pleasure is dead even while she lives. [7]Give the people these instructions, so that no one may be open to blame. [8]Anyone who does not provide for their relatives, and especially for their own household, has denied the faith and is worse than an unbeliever.

[9]No widow may be put on the list of widows unless she is over sixty, has been faithful to her husband, [10]and is well known for her good deeds, such as bringing up children, showing hospitality, washing the feet of the Lord's people, helping those in trouble and devoting herself to all kinds of good deeds.

[11]As for younger widows, do not put them on such a list. For when their sensual desires overcome their dedication to Christ, they want to marry. [12]Thus they bring judgment on themselves, because they have broken their first pledge. [13]Besides, they get into the habit of being idle and going about from house to house. And not only do they become idlers, but also busybodies who talk nonsense, saying things they ought not to. [14]So I counsel younger widows to marry, to have children, to manage their homes and to give the enemy no opportunity for slander. [15]Some have in fact already turned away to follow Satan.

[16]If any woman who is a believer has widows in her care, she should continue to help them and not let the church be burdened with them, so that the church can help those widows who are really in need.

[17]The elders who direct the affairs of the church well are worthy of double honor, especially those whose work is preaching and teaching. [18]For Scripture says, "Do not muzzle an ox while it is treading out the grain,"[a] and "The worker deserves his wages."[b] [19]Do not entertain an accusation against an elder unless it is brought by two or three witnesses. [20]But those elders who are sinning you are to reprove before everyone, so that the others may take warning. [21]I charge you, in the sight of God and Christ Jesus and the elect angels, to keep these instructions without partiality, and to do nothing out of favoritism.

[22]Do not be hasty in the laying on of hands, and do not share in the sins of others. Keep yourself pure.

[23]Stop drinking only water, and use a little wine because of your stomach and your frequent illnesses.

[24]The sins of some are obvious, reaching the place of judgment ahead of them; the sins of others trail behind them. [25]In the same way, good deeds are obvious, and even those that are not obvious cannot remain hidden forever.

6 All who are under the yoke of slavery should consider their masters worthy of full respect, so that God's name and our teaching may not be slandered. [2]Those who have believing masters should not show them disrespect just because they are fellow believers. Instead, they should serve them even better because their masters are dear to them as fellow believers and are devoted to the welfare[c] of their slaves.

[a] *18* Deut. 25:4 [b] *18* Luke 10:7 [c] *2* Or *and benefit from the service*

False Teachers and the Love of Money

These are the things you are to teach and
insist on. [3]If anyone teaches otherwise and
does not agree to the sound instruction of
our Lord Jesus Christ and to godly teach-
ing, [4]they are conceited and understand
nothing. They have an unhealthy interest in
controversies and quarrels about words that
result in envy, strife, malicious talk, evil sus-
picions [5]and constant friction between peo-
ple of corrupt mind, who have been robbed
of the truth and who think that godliness is a
means to financial gain.

[6]But godliness with contentment is great
gain. [7]For we brought nothing into the
world, and we can take nothing out of it. [8]But
if we have food and clothing, we will be con-
tent with that. [9]Those who want to get rich
fall into temptation and a trap and into many
foolish and harmful desires that plunge peo-
ple into ruin and destruction. [10]For the love
of money is a root of all kinds of evil. Some
people, eager for money, have wandered
from the faith and pierced themselves with
many griefs.

Final Charge to Timothy

[11]But you, man of God, flee from all this,
and pursue righteousness, godliness, faith,
love, endurance and gentleness. [12]Fight the
good fight of the faith. Take hold of the eter-
nal life to which you were called when you
made your good confession in the presence
of many witnesses. [13]In the sight of God, who
gives life to everything, and of Christ Jesus,
who while testifying before Pontius Pilate
made the good confession, I charge you [14]to
keep this command without spot or blame
until the appearing of our Lord Jesus Christ,
[15]which God will bring about in his own
time — God, the blessed and only Ruler, the
King of kings and Lord of lords, [16]who alone
is immortal and who lives in unapproach-
able light, whom no one has seen or can see.
To him be honor and might forever. Amen.

[17]Command those who are rich in this
present world not to be arrogant nor to put
their hope in wealth, which is so uncertain,
but to put their hope in God, who richly pro-
vides us with everything for our enjoyment.
[18]Command them to do good, to be rich in
good deeds, and to be generous and willing
to share. [19]In this way they will lay up trea-
sure for themselves as a firm foundation for
the coming age, so that they may take hold of
the life that is truly life.

[20]Timothy, guard what has been en-
trusted to your care. Turn away from god-
less chatter and the opposing ideas of what
is falsely called knowledge, [21]which some
have professed and in so doing have depart-
ed from the faith.

Grace be with you all.

2 TIMOTHY

1 Paul, an apostle of Christ Jesus by the
will of God, in keeping with the promise
of life that is in Christ Jesus,

2To Timothy, my dear son:

Grace, mercy and peace from God the Fa-
ther and Christ Jesus our Lord.

Thanksgiving

3I thank God, whom I serve, as my ances-
tors did, with a clear conscience, as night
and day I constantly remember you in my
prayers. 4Recalling your tears, I long to see
you, so that I may be filled with joy. 5I am
reminded of your sincere faith, which first
lived in your grandmother Lois and in your
mother Eunice and, I am persuaded, now
lives in you also.

Appeal for Loyalty to Paul and the Gospel

6For this reason I remind you to fan
into flame the gift of God, which is in you
through the laying on of my hands. 7For the
Spirit God gave us does not make us timid,
but gives us power, love and self-discipline.
8So do not be ashamed of the testimony
about our Lord or of me his prisoner. Ra-
ther, join with me in suffering for the gospel,
by the power of God. 9He has saved us and
called us to a holy life — not because of any-
thing we have done but because of his own
purpose and grace. This grace was given us
in Christ Jesus before the beginning of time,
10but it has now been revealed through the
appearing of our Savior, Christ Jesus, who
has destroyed death and has brought life
and immortality to light through the gos-
pel. 11And of this gospel I was appointed a
herald and an apostle and a teacher. 12That
is why I am suffering as I am. Yet this is no
cause for shame, because I know whom I
have believed, and am convinced that he is
able to guard what I have entrusted to him
until that day.

13What you heard from me, keep as the
pattern of sound teaching, with faith and
love in Christ Jesus. 14Guard the good de-
posit that was entrusted to you — guard it
with the help of the Holy Spirit who lives
in us.

Examples of Disloyalty and Loyalty

15You know that everyone in the province
of Asia has deserted me, including Phygelus
and Hermogenes.

16May the Lord show mercy to the house-
hold of Onesiphorus, because he often re-
freshed me and was not ashamed of my
chains. 17On the contrary, when he was in
Rome, he searched hard for me until he
found me. 18May the Lord grant that he will
find mercy from the Lord on that day! You
know very well in how many ways he helped
me in Ephesus.

The Appeal Renewed

2 You then, my son, be strong in the grace
that is in Christ Jesus. 2And the things
you have heard me say in the presence of
many witnesses entrust to reliable people
who will also be qualified to teach others.
3Join with me in suffering, like a good sol-
dier of Christ Jesus. 4No one serving as a
soldier gets entangled in civilian affairs, but
rather tries to please his commanding offi-
cer. 5Similarly, anyone who competes as an
athlete does not receive the victor's crown
except by competing according to the rules.
6The hardworking farmer should be the first
to receive a share of the crops. 7Reflect on
what I am saying, for the Lord will give you
insight into all this.

8Remember Jesus Christ, raised from the
dead, descended from David. This is my gos-
pel, 9for which I am suffering even to the
point of being chained like a criminal. But
God's word is not chained. 10Therefore I en-
dure everything for the sake of the elect, that
they too may obtain the salvation that is in
Christ Jesus, with eternal glory.

11Here is a trustworthy saying:

If we died with him,
  we will also live with him;
12 if we endure,
  we will also reign with him.
If we disown him,
  he will also disown us;
13 if we are faithless,
  he remains faithful,
  for he cannot disown himself.

Dealing With False Teachers

14 Keep reminding God's people of these things. Warn them before God against quarreling about words; it is of no value, and only ruins those who listen. 15 Do your best to present yourself to God as one approved, a worker who does not need to be ashamed and who correctly handles the word of truth. 16 Avoid godless chatter, because those who indulge in it will become more and more ungodly. 17 Their teaching will spread like gangrene. Among them are Hymenaeus and Philetus, 18 who have departed from the truth. They say that the resurrection has already taken place, and they destroy the faith of some. 19 Nevertheless, God's solid foundation stands firm, sealed with this inscription: "The Lord knows those who are his," and, "Everyone who confesses the name of the Lord must turn away from wickedness."

20 In a large house there are articles not only of gold and silver, but also of wood and clay; some are for special purposes and some for common use. 21 Those who cleanse themselves from the latter will be instruments for special purposes, made holy, useful to the Master and prepared to do any good work.

22 Flee the evil desires of youth and pursue righteousness, faith, love and peace, along with those who call on the Lord out of a pure heart. 23 Don't have anything to do with foolish and stupid arguments, because you know they produce quarrels. 24 And the Lord's servant must not be quarrelsome but must be kind to everyone, able to teach, not resentful. 25 Opponents must be gently instructed, in the hope that God will grant them repentance leading them to a knowledge of the truth, 26 and that they will come to their senses and escape from the trap of the devil, who has taken them captive to do his will.

3 But mark this: There will be terrible times in the last days. 2 People will be lovers of themselves, lovers of money, boastful, proud, abusive, disobedient to their parents, ungrateful, unholy, 3 without love, unforgiving, slanderous, without self-control, brutal, not lovers of the good, 4 treacherous, rash, conceited, lovers of pleasure rather than lovers of God— 5 having a form of godliness but denying its power. Have nothing to do with such people.

6 They are the kind who worm their way into homes and gain control over gullible women, who are loaded down with sins and are swayed by all kinds of evil desires, 7 always learning but never able to come to a knowledge of the truth. 8 Just as Jannes and Jambres opposed Moses, so also these teachers oppose the truth. They are men of depraved minds, who, as far as the faith is concerned, are rejected. 9 But they will not get very far because, as in the case of those men, their folly will be clear to everyone.

A Final Charge to Timothy

10 You, however, know all about my teaching, my way of life, my purpose, faith, patience, love, endurance, 11 persecutions, sufferings—what kinds of things happened to me in Antioch, Iconium and Lystra, the persecutions I endured. Yet the Lord rescued me from all of them. 12 In fact, everyone who wants to live a godly life in Christ Jesus will be persecuted, 13 while evildoers and impostors will go from bad to worse, deceiving and being deceived. 14 But as for you, continue in what you have learned and have become convinced of, because you know those from whom you learned it, 15 and how from infancy you have known the Holy Scriptures, which are able to make you wise for salvation through faith in Christ Jesus. 16 All Scripture is God-breathed and is useful for teaching, rebuking, correcting and training in righteousness, 17 so that the servant of God[a] may be thoroughly equipped for every good work.

4 In the presence of God and of Christ Jesus, who will judge the living and the dead, and in view of his appearing and his kingdom, I give you this charge: 2 Preach the word; be prepared in season and out of

[a] 17 Or *that you, a man of God,*

season; correct, rebuke and encourage—
with great patience and careful instruction.
[3]For the time will come when people will not
put up with sound doctrine. Instead, to suit
their own desires, they will gather around
them a great number of teachers to say what
their itching ears want to hear. [4]They will
turn their ears away from the truth and turn
aside to myths. [5]But you, keep your head in
all situations, endure hardship, do the work
of an evangelist, discharge all the duties of
your ministry.

[6]For I am already being poured out like a
drink offering, and the time for my depar-
ture is near. [7]I have fought the good fight, I
have finished the race, I have kept the faith.
[8]Now there is in store for me the crown of
righteousness, which the Lord, the righ-
teous Judge, will award to me on that day—
and not only to me, but also to all who have
longed for his appearing.

Personal Remarks

[9]Do your best to come to me quickly, [10]for
Demas, because he loved this world, has
deserted me and has gone to Thessaloni-
ca. Crescens has gone to Galatia, and Titus
to Dalmatia. [11]Only Luke is with me. Get
Mark and bring him with you, because he is
helpful to me in my ministry. [12]I sent Tychi-
cus to Ephesus. [13]When you come, bring the
cloak that I left with Carpus at Troas, and my
scrolls, especially the parchments.

[14]Alexander the metalworker did me a
great deal of harm. The Lord will repay him
for what he has done. [15]You too should be on
your guard against him, because he strongly
opposed our message.

[16]At my first defense, no one came to my
support, but everyone deserted me. May
it not be held against them. [17]But the Lord
stood at my side and gave me strength, so
that through me the message might be fully
proclaimed and all the Gentiles might hear
it. And I was delivered from the lion's mouth.
[18]The Lord will rescue me from every evil at-
tack and will bring me safely to his heavenly
kingdom. To him be glory for ever and ever.
Amen.

Final Greetings

[19]Greet Priscilla[a] and Aquila and the
household of Onesiphorus. [20]Erastus stayed
in Corinth, and I left Trophimus sick in Mi-
letus. [21]Do your best to get here before win-
ter. Eubulus greets you, and so do Pudens,
Linus, Claudia and all the brothers and sis-
ters.[b]

[22]The Lord be with your spirit. Grace be
with you all.

[a] *19* Greek *Prisca*, a variant of *Priscilla* [b] *21* The Greek word for *brothers and sisters* (*adelphoi*) refers here to believers, both men and women, as part of God's family.

TITUS

1 Paul, a servant of God and an apostle of Jesus Christ to further the faith of God's elect and their knowledge of the truth that leads to godliness — [2]in the hope of eternal life, which God, who does not lie, promised before the beginning of time, [3]and which now at his appointed season he has brought to light through the preaching entrusted to me by the command of God our Savior,

[4]To Titus, my true son in our common faith:

Grace and peace from God the Father and Christ Jesus our Savior.

Appointing Elders Who Love What Is Good

[5]The reason I left you in Crete was that you might put in order what was left unfinished and appoint[a] elders in every town, as I directed you. [6]An elder must be blameless, faithful to his wife, a man whose children believe[b] and are not open to the charge of being wild and disobedient. [7]Since an overseer manages God's household, he must be blameless — not overbearing, not quick-tempered, not given to drunkenness, not violent, not pursuing dishonest gain. [8]Rather, he must be hospitable, one who loves what is good, who is self-controlled, upright, holy and disciplined. [9]He must hold firmly to the trustworthy message as it has been taught, so that he can encourage others by sound doctrine and refute those who oppose it.

Rebuking Those Who Fail to Do Good

[10]For there are many rebellious people, full of meaningless talk and deception, especially those of the circumcision group. [11]They must be silenced, because they are disrupting whole households by teaching things they ought not to teach — and that for the sake of dishonest gain. [12]One of Crete's own prophets has said it: "Cretans are always liars, evil brutes, lazy gluttons."[c] [13]This saying is true. Therefore rebuke them sharply, so that they will be sound in the faith [14]and will pay no attention to Jewish myths or to the merely human commands of those who reject the truth. [15]To the pure, all things are pure, but to those who are corrupted and do not believe, nothing is pure. In fact, both their minds and consciences are corrupted. [16]They claim to know God, but by their actions they deny him. They are detestable, disobedient and unfit for doing anything good.

Doing Good for the Sake of the Gospel

2 You, however, must teach what is appropriate to sound doctrine. [2]Teach the older men to be temperate, worthy of respect, self-controlled, and sound in faith, in love and in endurance.

[3]Likewise, teach the older women to be reverent in the way they live, not to be slanderers or addicted to much wine, but to teach what is good. [4]Then they can urge the younger women to love their husbands and children, [5]to be self-controlled and pure, to be busy at home, to be kind, and to be subject to their husbands, so that no one will malign the word of God.

[6]Similarly, encourage the young men to be self-controlled. [7]In everything set them an example by doing what is good. In your teaching show integrity, seriousness [8]and soundness of speech that cannot be condemned, so that those who oppose you may be ashamed because they have nothing bad to say about us.

[9]Teach slaves to be subject to their masters in everything, to try to please them, not to talk back to them, [10]and not to steal from them, but to show that they can be fully trusted, so that in every way they will make the teaching about God our Savior attractive.

[11]For the grace of God has appeared that offers salvation to all people. [12]It teaches us

[a] 5 Or *ordain* [b] 6 Or *children are trustworthy* [c] *12* From the Cretan philosopher Epimenides

to say "No" to ungodliness and worldly pas-
sions, and to live self-controlled, upright
and godly lives in this present age, 13while
we wait for the blessed hope — the appear-
ing of the glory of our great God and Savior,
Jesus Christ, 14who gave himself for us to re-
deem us from all wickedness and to purify
for himself a people that are his very own,
eager to do what is good.
15These, then, are the things you should
teach. Encourage and rebuke with all au-
thority. Do not let anyone despise you.

Saved in Order to Do Good

3 Remind the people to be subject to rul-
ers and authorities, to be obedient, to be
ready to do whatever is good, 2to slander no
one, to be peaceable and considerate, and
always to be gentle toward everyone.
3At one time we too were foolish, disobe-
dient, deceived and enslaved by all kinds of
passions and pleasures. We lived in malice
and envy, being hated and hating one anoth-
er. 4But when the kindness and love of God
our Savior appeared, 5he saved us, not be-
cause of righteous things we had done, but
because of his mercy. He saved us through
the washing of rebirth and renewal by the
Holy Spirit, 6whom he poured out on us gen-
erously through Jesus Christ our Savior, 7so
that, having been justified by his grace, we
might become heirs having the hope of eter-
nal life. 8This is a trustworthy saying. And I
want you to stress these things, so that those
who have trusted in God may be careful to
devote themselves to doing what is good.
These things are excellent and profitable for
everyone.
9But avoid foolish controversies and gene-
alogies and arguments and quarrels about
the law, because these are unprofitable and
useless. 10Warn a divisive person once, and
then warn them a second time. After that,
have nothing to do with them. 11You may be
sure that such people are warped and sinful;
they are self-condemned.

Final Remarks

12As soon as I send Artemas or Tychicus
to you, do your best to come to me at Nicop-
olis, because I have decided to winter there.
13Do everything you can to help Zenas the
lawyer and Apollos on their way and see that
they have everything they need. 14Our peo-
ple must learn to devote themselves to doing
what is good, in order to provide for urgent
needs and not live unproductive lives.
15Everyone with me sends you greetings.
Greet those who love us in the faith.
Grace be with you all.

PHILEMON

1Paul, a prisoner of Christ Jesus, and Tim-
othy our brother,

To Philemon our dear friend and fellow
worker— 2also to Apphia our sister and
Archippus our fellow soldier—and to the
church that meets in your home:

3Grace and peace to you[a] from God our
Father and the Lord Jesus Christ.

Thanksgiving and Prayer

4I always thank my God as I remember
you in my prayers, 5because I hear about
your love for all his holy people and your
faith in the Lord Jesus. 6I pray that your part-
nership with us in the faith may be effective
in deepening your understanding of every
good thing we share for the sake of Christ.
7Your love has given me great joy and en-
couragement, because you, brother, have re-
freshed the hearts of the Lord's people.

Paul's Plea for Onesimus

8Therefore, although in Christ I could be
bold and order you to do what you ought to
do, 9yet I prefer to appeal to you on the ba-
sis of love. It is as none other than Paul—an
old man and now also a prisoner of Christ
Jesus— 10that I appeal to you for my son
Onesimus,[b] who became my son while I was
in chains. 11Formerly he was useless to you,
but now he has become useful both to you
and to me.
12I am sending him—who is my very
heart—back to you. 13I would have liked to
keep him with me so that he could take your
place in helping me while I am in chains for
the gospel. 14But I did not want to do any-
thing without your consent, so that any fa-
vor you do would not seem forced but would
be voluntary. 15Perhaps the reason he was
separated from you for a little while was that
you might have him back forever— 16no
longer as a slave, but better than a slave, as a
dear brother. He is very dear to me but even
dearer to you, both as a fellow man and as a
brother in the Lord.
17So if you consider me a partner, wel-
come him as you would welcome me. 18If he
has done you any wrong or owes you any-
thing, charge it to me. 19I, Paul, am writing
this with my own hand. I will pay it back—
not to mention that you owe me your very
self. 20I do wish, brother, that I may have
some benefit from you in the Lord; refresh
my heart in Christ. 21Confident of your obe-
dience, I write to you, knowing that you will
do even more than I ask.
22And one thing more: Prepare a guest
room for me, because I hope to be restored
to you in answer to your prayers.

23Epaphras, my fellow prisoner in Christ
Jesus, sends you greetings. 24And so do
Mark, Aristarchus, Demas and Luke, my fel-
low workers.
25The grace of the Lord Jesus Christ be
with your spirit.

[a] *3* The Greek is plural; also in verses 22 and 25; elsewhere in this letter "you" is singular.
[b] *10* *Onesimus* means *useful.*

HEBREWS

God's Final Word: His Son

1 In the past God spoke to our ancestors
through the prophets at many times and
in various ways, 2but in these last days he has
spoken to us by his Son, whom he appointed
heir of all things, and through whom also he
made the universe. 3The Son is the radiance
of God's glory and the exact representation
of his being, sustaining all things by his
powerful word. After he had provided purifi-
cation for sins, he sat down at the right hand
of the Majesty in heaven. 4So he became as
much superior to the angels as the name he
has inherited is superior to theirs.

The Son Superior to Angels

5For to which of the angels did God ever
say,

"You are my Son;
today I have become your Father"[a]?

Or again,

"I will be his Father,
and he will be my Son"[b]?

6And again, when God brings his firstborn
into the world, he says,

"Let all God's angels worship him."[c]

7In speaking of the angels he says,

"He makes his angels spirits,
and his servants flames of fire."[d]

8But about the Son he says,

"Your throne, O God, will last for ever
and ever;
a scepter of justice will be the scepter
of your kingdom.
9You have loved righteousness and hated
wickedness;
therefore God, your God, has set you
above your companions
by anointing you with the oil of joy."[e]

10He also says,

"In the beginning, Lord, you laid the
foundations of the earth,
and the heavens are the work of your
hands.
11They will perish, but you remain;
they will all wear out like a garment.
12You will roll them up like a robe;
like a garment they will be changed.
But you remain the same,
and your years will never end."[f]

13To which of the angels did God ever say,

"Sit at my right hand
until I make your enemies
a footstool for your feet"[g]?

14Are not all angels ministering spirits sent
to serve those who will inherit salvation?

Warning to Pay Attention

2 We must pay the most careful atten-
tion, therefore, to what we have heard,
so that we do not drift away. 2For since the
message spoken through angels was bind-
ing, and every violation and disobedience
received its just punishment, 3how shall
we escape if we ignore so great a salvation?
This salvation, which was first announced
by the Lord, was confirmed to us by those
who heard him. 4God also testified to it by
signs, wonders and various miracles, and by
gifts of the Holy Spirit distributed according
to his will.

Jesus Made Fully Human

5It is not to angels that he has subject-
ed the world to come, about which we are
speaking. 6But there is a place where some-
one has testified:

"What is mankind that you are mindful
of them,
a son of man that you care for him?

[a] 5 Psalm 2:7 [b] 5 2 Samuel 7:14; 1 Chron. 17:13 [c] 6 Deut. 32:43 (see Dead Sea Scrolls and Septuagint)
[d] 7 Psalm 104:4 [e] 9 Psalm 45:6,7 [f] 12 Psalm 102:25-27 [g] 13 Psalm 110:1

7 You made them a little[a] lower than
the angels;
you crowned them with glory and
honor
8 and put everything under their feet."[b,c]

In putting everything under them,[d] God left
nothing that is not subject to them.[d] Yet at
present we do not see everything subject to
them.[d] 9 But we do see Jesus, who was made
lower than the angels for a little while, now
crowned with glory and honor because he
suffered death, so that by the grace of God
he might taste death for everyone.

10 In bringing many sons and daughters to
glory, it was fitting that God, for whom and
through whom everything exists, should
make the pioneer of their salvation perfect
through what he suffered. 11 Both the one
who makes people holy and those who are
made holy are of the same family. So Jesus is
not ashamed to call them brothers and sis-
ters.[e] 12 He says,

"I will declare your name to my brothers
and sisters;
in the assembly I will sing your
praises."[f]

13 And again,

"I will put my trust in him."[g]

And again he says,

"Here am I, and the children God has
given me."[h]

14 Since the children have flesh and blood,
he too shared in their humanity so that by
his death he might break the power of him
who holds the power of death — that is, the
devil — 15 and free those who all their lives
were held in slavery by their fear of death.
16 For surely it is not angels he helps, but
Abraham's descendants. 17 For this reason
he had to be made like them,[i] fully human in
every way, in order that he might become a
merciful and faithful high priest in service to
God, and that he might make atonement for
the sins of the people. 18 Because he himself
suffered when he was tempted, he is able to
help those who are being tempted.

Jesus Greater Than Moses

3 Therefore, holy brothers and sisters,
who share in the heavenly calling, fix
your thoughts on Jesus, whom we acknowl-
edge as our apostle and high priest. 2 He was
faithful to the one who appointed him, just
as Moses was faithful in all God's house.
3 Jesus has been found worthy of greater hon-
or than Moses, just as the builder of a house
has greater honor than the house itself. 4 For
every house is built by someone, but God is
the builder of everything. 5 "Moses was faith-
ful as a servant in all God's house,"[j] bearing
witness to what would be spoken by God in
the future. 6 But Christ is faithful as the Son
over God's house. And we are his house, if in-
deed we hold firmly to our confidence and
the hope in which we glory.

Warning Against Unbelief

7 So, as the Holy Spirit says:

"Today, if you hear his voice,
8 do not harden your hearts
as you did in the rebellion,
during the time of testing in the
wilderness,
9 where your ancestors tested and
tried me,
though for forty years they saw what
I did.
10 That is why I was angry with that
generation;
I said, 'Their hearts are always going
astray,
and they have not known
my ways.'
11 So I declared on oath in my anger,
'They shall never enter my rest.' "[k]

12 See to it, brothers and sisters, that none
of you has a sinful, unbelieving heart that
turns away from the living God. 13 But en-
courage one another daily, as long as it is
called "Today," so that none of you may be
hardened by sin's deceitfulness. 14 We have
come to share in Christ, if indeed we hold
our original conviction firmly to the very
end. 15 As has just been said:

[a] 7 Or *them for a little while* [b] 6-8 Psalm 8:4-6 [c] 7,8 Or *7 You made him a little lower than the angels;/ you crowned him with glory and honor/ 8 and put everything under his feet."* [d] 8 Or *him* [e] 11 The Greek word for *brothers and sisters* (*adelphoi*) refers here to believers, both men and women, as part of God's family; also in verse 12; and in 3:1, 12; 10:19; 13:22. [f] 12 Psalm 22:22 [g] 13 Isaiah 8:17 [h] 13 Isaiah 8:18 [i] 17 Or *like his brothers* [j] 5 Num. 12:7 [k] 11 Psalm 95:7-11

"Today, if you hear his voice,
do not harden your hearts
as you did in the rebellion."[a]

16 Who were they who heard and rebelled? Were they not all those Moses led out of Egypt? 17 And with whom was he angry for forty years? Was it not with those who sinned, whose bodies perished in the wilderness? 18 And to whom did God swear that they would never enter his rest if not to those who disobeyed? 19 So we see that they were not able to enter, because of their unbelief.

A Sabbath-Rest for the People of God

4 Therefore, since the promise of entering his rest still stands, let us be careful that none of you be found to have fallen short of it. 2 For we also have had the good news proclaimed to us, just as they did; but the message they heard was of no value to them, because they did not share the faith of those who obeyed.[b] 3 Now we who have believed enter that rest, just as God has said,

"So I declared on oath in my anger,
'They shall never enter my rest.'"[c]

And yet his works have been finished since the creation of the world. 4 For somewhere he has spoken about the seventh day in these words: "On the seventh day God rested from all his works."[d] 5 And again in the passage above he says, "They shall never enter my rest."

6 Therefore since it still remains for some to enter that rest, and since those who formerly had the good news proclaimed to them did not go in because of their disobedience, 7 God again set a certain day, calling it "Today." This he did when a long time later he spoke through David, as in the passage already quoted:

"Today, if you hear his voice,
do not harden your hearts."[a]

8 For if Joshua had given them rest, God would not have spoken later about another day. 9 There remains, then, a Sabbath-rest for the people of God; 10 for anyone who enters God's rest also rests from their works,[e] just as God did from his. 11 Let us, therefore, make every effort to enter that rest, so that no one will perish by following their example of disobedience.

12 For the word of God is alive and active. Sharper than any double-edged sword, it penetrates even to dividing soul and spirit, joints and marrow; it judges the thoughts and attitudes of the heart. 13 Nothing in all creation is hidden from God's sight. Everything is uncovered and laid bare before the eyes of him to whom we must give account.

Jesus the Great High Priest

14 Therefore, since we have a great high priest who has ascended into heaven,[f] Jesus the Son of God, let us hold firmly to the faith we profess. 15 For we do not have a high priest who is unable to empathize with our weaknesses, but we have one who has been tempted in every way, just as we are—yet he did not sin. 16 Let us then approach God's throne of grace with confidence, so that we may receive mercy and find grace to help us in our time of need.

5 Every high priest is selected from among the people and is appointed to represent the people in matters related to God, to offer gifts and sacrifices for sins. 2 He is able to deal gently with those who are ignorant and are going astray, since he himself is subject to weakness. 3 This is why he has to offer sacrifices for his own sins, as well as for the sins of the people. 4 And no one takes this honor on himself, but he receives it when called by God, just as Aaron was.

5 In the same way, Christ did not take on himself the glory of becoming a high priest. But God said to him,

"You are my Son;
today I have become your Father."[g]

6 And he says in another place,

"You are a priest forever,
in the order of Melchizedek."[h]

7 During the days of Jesus' life on earth, he offered up prayers and petitions with fervent cries and tears to the one who could save him from death, and he was heard because of his reverent submission. 8 Son

[a] *15,7* Psalm 95:7,8 [b] *2* Some manuscripts *because those who heard did not combine it with faith*
[c] *3* Psalm 95:11; also in verse 5 [d] *4* Gen. 2:2 [e] *10* Or *labor* [f] *14* Greek *has gone through the heavens*
[g] *5* Psalm 2:7 [h] *6* Psalm 110:4

BE THOU MY VISION

Dallan Forgaill

Be thou my Vision, O Lord of my heart
Naught be all else to me, save that thou art
Thou my best Thought, by day or by night
Waking or sleeping, thy presence my light

Be thou my Wisdom, and thou my true Word
I ever with thee and thou with me, Lord
Thou my great Father, I thy true son
Thou in me dwelling, and I with Thee one

Be thou my battle shield (alt. breast plate), sword for the fight
Be thou my dignity (alt. whole armor), thou my delight
(alt. be thou my true might)
Thou my soul's shelter, though my high tower
Raise thou me heavenward, O power of my power

Riches I heed not, nor man's empty praise
Thou mine Inheritance, now and always
Thou and thou only, first in my heart
High King of Heaven, my Treasure thou art

High King of Heaven, my victory won
May I reach Heaven's joys, O bright Heaven's Sun
Heart of my own heart, whatever befall
Still be my Vision, O Ruler of all

THE INSPIRATION

But whatever were gains to me I now consider loss for the sake of Christ. What is more, I consider everything a loss because of the surpassing worth of knowing Christ Jesus my Lord, for whose sake I have lost all things. I consider them garbage, that I may gain Christ and be found in him, not having a righteousness of my own that comes from the law, but that which is through faith in Christ — the righteousness that comes from God on the basis of faith. I want to know Christ — yes, to know the power of his resurrection and participation in his sufferings, becoming like him in his death, and so, somehow, attaining to the resurrection from the dead.

— Philippians 3:7 – 11

Words: Attributed to Dallan Forgaill, 8th Century (Rob tu mo bhoile, a Comdi cride); translated from ancient Irish to English by Mary E. Byrne, in "Eriú," Journal of the School of Irish Learning, 1905, and versed by Eleanor H. Hull, 1912, alt.

BEHIND THE SONG

"Be Thou My Vision" is certainly one of the most beloved ancient hymns in the church. As with many songs of its vintage, the exact source of the song is lost in the mists of history. It is often attributed to Dallan Forgaill, an Irish missionary and martyr who was also the chief poet of Ireland. It appears to some historians, however, that the text of this incredible hymn was in circulation several centuries before Forgaill's time. The words are set to the melody of the traditional Irish folk song, "Slane," which happens to be about the hill on which Saint Patrick defied the pagan king Loegaire by lighting candles on Easter.

"Be Thou My Vision" is rightly considered the greatest Irish hymn, but its impact continues to grow well outside of its Celtic Christian roots. Its boldly worshipful lyrics and poetically enchanting melody and cadence have rendered it a perennial favorite of Christians of many denominational and cultural stripes. New recordings continue to be released, and contemporary churches often turn to this song to add lyrical depth and theological gravitas to their worship times.

Selah

The text of "Be Thou My Vision" overflows with a radical commitment to surrender to God's plan and purpose. In some ways, aspects of this song echo the sentiments we find in Philippians 3:7 – 11. Read those verses and the poetry of the song, and notice the complementary nature of the two.

Think through each of the stanzas. What would it look like if we were able to see the world and people around us exactly as God does? What are the virtues you see listed in the lyrics of this hymn? Are these things you are actively seeking to add to your life?

though he was, he learned obedience from
what he suffered 9 and, once made perfect,
he became the source of eternal salvation
for all who obey him 10 and was designated
by God to be high priest in the order of Mel-
chizedek.

Warning Against Falling Away

11 We have much to say about this, but it is
hard to make it clear to you because you no
longer try to understand. 12 In fact, though by
this time you ought to be teachers, you need
someone to teach you the elementary truths
of God's word all over again. You need milk,
not solid food! 13 Anyone who lives on milk,
being still an infant, is not acquainted with
the teaching about righteousness. 14 But sol-
id food is for the mature, who by constant
use have trained themselves to distinguish
good from evil.

6 Therefore let us move beyond the ele-
mentary teachings about Christ and be
taken forward to maturity, not laying again
the foundation of repentance from acts that
lead to death,[a] and of faith in God, 2 instruc-
tion about cleansing rites,[b] the laying on
of hands, the resurrection of the dead, and
eternal judgment. 3 And God permitting, we
will do so.

4 It is impossible for those who have once
been enlightened, who have tasted the heav-
enly gift, who have shared in the Holy Spirit,
5 who have tasted the goodness of the word of
God and the powers of the coming age 6 and
who have fallen[c] away, to be brought back to
repentance. To their loss they are crucifying
the Son of God all over again and subjecting
him to public disgrace. 7 Land that drinks in
the rain often falling on it and that produces
a crop useful to those for whom it is farmed
receives the blessing of God. 8 But land that
produces thorns and thistles is worthless
and is in danger of being cursed. In the end
it will be burned.

9 Even though we speak like this, dear
friends, we are convinced of better things
in your case — the things that have to do
with salvation. 10 God is not unjust; he will
not forget your work and the love you have
shown him as you have helped his people
and continue to help them. 11 We want each
of you to show this same diligence to the
very end, so that what you hope for may be
fully realized. 12 We do not want you to be-
come lazy, but to imitate those who through
faith and patience inherit what has been
promised.

The Certainty of God's Promise

13 When God made his promise to Abra-
ham, since there was no one greater for him
to swear by, he swore by himself, 14 saying, "I
will surely bless you and give you many de-
scendants."[d] 15 And so after waiting patient-
ly, Abraham received what was promised.

16 People swear by someone greater than
themselves, and the oath confirms what is
said and puts an end to all argument. 17 Be-
cause God wanted to make the unchanging
nature of his purpose very clear to the heirs
of what was promised, he confirmed it with
an oath. 18 God did this so that, by two un-
changeable things in which it is impossible
for God to lie, we who have fled to take hold
of the hope set before us may be greatly en-
couraged. 19 We have this hope as an anchor
for the soul, firm and secure. It enters the in-
ner sanctuary behind the curtain, 20 where
our forerunner, Jesus, has entered on our
behalf. He has become a high priest forever,
in the order of Melchizedek.

Melchizedek the Priest

7 This Melchizedek was king of Salem
and priest of God Most High. He met
Abraham returning from the defeat of the
kings and blessed him, 2 and Abraham gave
him a tenth of everything. First, the name
Melchizedek means "king of righteousness";
then also, "king of Salem" means "king of
peace." 3 Without father or mother, without
genealogy, without beginning of days or
end of life, resembling the Son of God, he re-
mains a priest forever.

4 Just think how great he was: Even the
patriarch Abraham gave him a tenth of the
plunder! 5 Now the law requires the descen-
dants of Levi who become priests to collect
a tenth from the people — that is, from their
fellow Israelites — even though they also are
descended from Abraham. 6 This man, how-
ever, did not trace his descent from Levi,
yet he collected a tenth from Abraham and
blessed him who had the promises. 7 And

[a] *1* Or *from useless rituals* [b] *2* Or *about baptisms* [c] *6* Or *age,* [6] *if they fall* [d] *14* Gen. 22:17

without doubt the lesser is blessed by the greater. [8]In the one case, the tenth is collected by people who die; but in the other case, by him who is declared to be living.
[9]One might even say that Levi, who collects the tenth, paid the tenth through Abraham,
[10]because when Melchizedek met Abraham, Levi was still in the body of his ancestor.

Jesus Like Melchizedek

[11]If perfection could have been attained through the Levitical priesthood — and indeed the law given to the people established that priesthood — why was there still need for another priest to come, one in the order of Melchizedek, not in the order of Aaron?
[12]For when the priesthood is changed, the law must be changed also. [13]He of whom these things are said belonged to a different tribe, and no one from that tribe has ever served at the altar. [14]For it is clear that our Lord descended from Judah, and in regard to that tribe Moses said nothing about priests.
[15]And what we have said is even more clear if another priest like Melchizedek appears,
[16]one who has become a priest not on the basis of a regulation as to his ancestry but on the basis of the power of an indestructible life. [17]For it is declared:

"You are a priest forever,
in the order of Melchizedek."[a]

[18]The former regulation is set aside because it was weak and useless [19](for the law made nothing perfect), and a better hope is introduced, by which we draw near to God.
[20]And it was not without an oath! Others became priests without any oath, [21]but he became a priest with an oath when God said to him:

"The Lord has sworn
and will not change his mind:
'You are a priest forever.'"[a]

[22]Because of this oath, Jesus has become the guarantor of a better covenant.
[23]Now there have been many of those priests, since death prevented them from continuing in office; [24]but because Jesus lives forever, he has a permanent priesthood. [25]Therefore he is able to save completely[b] those who come to God through him, because he always lives to intercede for them.
[26]Such a high priest truly meets our need — one who is holy, blameless, pure, set apart from sinners, exalted above the heavens. [27]Unlike the other high priests, he does not need to offer sacrifices day after day, first for his own sins, and then for the sins of the people. He sacrificed for their sins once for all when he offered himself. [28]For the law appoints as high priests men in all their weakness; but the oath, which came after the law, appointed the Son, who has been made perfect forever.

The High Priest of a New Covenant

8 Now the main point of what we are saying is this: We do have such a high priest, who sat down at the right hand of the throne of the Majesty in heaven, [2]and who serves in the sanctuary, the true tabernacle set up by the Lord, not by a mere human being.
[3]Every high priest is appointed to offer both gifts and sacrifices, and so it was necessary for this one also to have something to offer. [4]If he were on earth, he would not be a priest, for there are already priests who offer the gifts prescribed by the law. [5]They serve at a sanctuary that is a copy and shadow of what is in heaven. This is why Moses was warned when he was about to build the tabernacle: "See to it that you make everything according to the pattern shown you on the mountain."[c] [6]But in fact the ministry Jesus has received is as superior to theirs as the covenant of which he is mediator is superior to the old one, since the new covenant is established on better promises.
[7]For if there had been nothing wrong with that first covenant, no place would have been sought for another. [8]But God found fault with the people and said[d]:

"The days are coming, declares the Lord,
when I will make a new covenant
with the people of Israel
and with the people of Judah.
[9]It will not be like the covenant
I made with their ancestors
when I took them by the hand
to lead them out of Egypt,

[a] *17,21* Psalm 110:4 [b] *25* Or *forever* [c] *5* Exodus 25:40 [d] *8* Some manuscripts may be translated *fault and said to the people.*

because they did not remain faithful to
my covenant,
and I turned away from them,
declares the Lord.
10 This is the covenant I will establish with
the people of Israel
after that time, declares the Lord.
I will put my laws in their minds
and write them on their hearts.
I will be their God,
and they will be my people.
11 No longer will they teach their
neighbor,
or say to one another, 'Know
the Lord,'
because they will all know me,
from the least of them to the
greatest.
12 For I will forgive their wickedness
and will remember their sins
no more."[a]

13 By calling this covenant "new," he has
made the first one obsolete; and what is ob-
solete and outdated will soon disappear.

Worship in the Earthly Tabernacle

9 Now the first covenant had regulations
for worship and also an earthly sanc-
tuary. 2 A tabernacle was set up. In its first
room were the lampstand and the table with
its consecrated bread; this was called the
Holy Place. 3 Behind the second curtain was
a room called the Most Holy Place, 4 which
had the golden altar of incense and the gold-
covered ark of the covenant. This ark con-
tained the gold jar of manna, Aaron's staff
that had budded, and the stone tablets of the
covenant. 5 Above the ark were the cherubim
of the Glory, overshadowing the atonement
cover. But we cannot discuss these things in
detail now.

6 When everything had been arranged like
this, the priests entered regularly into the
outer room to carry on their ministry. 7 But
only the high priest entered the inner room,
and that only once a year, and never without
blood, which he offered for himself and for
the sins the people had committed in igno-
rance. 8 The Holy Spirit was showing by this
that the way into the Most Holy Place had not
yet been disclosed as long as the first taber-
nacle was still functioning. 9 This is an illus-
tration for the present time, indicating that
the gifts and sacrifices being offered were
not able to clear the conscience of the wor-
shiper. 10 They are only a matter of food and
drink and various ceremonial washings—
external regulations applying until the time
of the new order.

The Blood of Christ

11 But when Christ came as high priest of
the good things that are now already here,[b]
he went through the greater and more per-
fect tabernacle that is not made with human
hands, that is to say, is not a part of this cre-
ation. 12 He did not enter by means of the
blood of goats and calves; but he entered
the Most Holy Place once for all by his own
blood, thus obtaining[c] eternal redemption.
13 The blood of goats and bulls and the ashes
of a heifer sprinkled on those who are cere-
monially unclean sanctify them so that they
are outwardly clean. 14 How much more,
then, will the blood of Christ, who through
the eternal Spirit offered himself unblem-
ished to God, cleanse our consciences from
acts that lead to death,[d] so that we may serve
the living God!

15 For this reason Christ is the mediator of
a new covenant, that those who are called
may receive the promised eternal inheri-
tance—now that he has died as a ransom to
set them free from the sins committed under
the first covenant.

16 In the case of a will,[e] it is necessary to
prove the death of the one who made it, 17 be-
cause a will is in force only when somebody
has died; it never takes effect while the one
who made it is living. 18 This is why even the
first covenant was not put into effect with-
out blood. 19 When Moses had proclaimed
every command of the law to all the people,
he took the blood of calves, together with
water, scarlet wool and branches of hyssop,
and sprinkled the scroll and all the people.
20 He said, "This is the blood of the covenant,
which God has commanded you to keep."[f]
21 In the same way, he sprinkled with the
blood both the tabernacle and everything
used in its ceremonies. 22 In fact, the law re-
quires that nearly everything be cleansed

[a] *12* Jer. 31:31-34 [b] *11* Some early manuscripts *are to come* [c] *12* Or *blood, having obtained*
[d] *14* Or *from useless rituals* [e] *16* Same Greek word as *covenant*; also in verse 17 [f] *20* Exodus 24:8

with blood, and without the shedding of
blood there is no forgiveness.
23 It was necessary, then, for the copies
of the heavenly things to be purified with
these sacrifices, but the heavenly things
themselves with better sacrifices than these.
24 For Christ did not enter a sanctuary made
with human hands that was only a copy of
the true one; he entered heaven itself, now
to appear for us in God's presence. 25 Nor
did he enter heaven to offer himself again
and again, the way the high priest enters the
Most Holy Place every year with blood that is
not his own. 26 Otherwise Christ would have
had to suffer many times since the creation
of the world. But he has appeared once for
all at the culmination of the ages to do away
with sin by the sacrifice of himself. 27 Just as
people are destined to die once, and after
that to face judgment, 28 so Christ was sac-
rificed once to take away the sins of many;
and he will appear a second time, not to bear
sin, but to bring salvation to those who are
waiting for him.

Christ's Sacrifice Once for All

10 The law is only a shadow of the good
things that are coming — not the re-
alities themselves. For this reason it can nev-
er, by the same sacrifices repeated endlessly
year after year, make perfect those who draw
near to worship. 2 Otherwise, would they not
have stopped being offered? For the wor-
shipers would have been cleansed once for
all, and would no longer have felt guilty for
their sins. 3 But those sacrifices are an annu-
al reminder of sins. 4 It is impossible for the
blood of bulls and goats to take away sins.
5 Therefore, when Christ came into the
world, he said:

"Sacrifice and offering you did not desire,
but a body you prepared for me;
6 with burnt offerings and sin offerings
you were not pleased.
7 Then I said, 'Here I am — it is written
about me in the scroll —
I have come to do your will, my God.' "[a]

8 First he said, "Sacrifices and offerings,
burnt offerings and sin offerings you did not
desire, nor were you pleased with them" —
though they were offered in accordance with
the law. 9 Then he said, "Here I am, I have
come to do your will." He sets aside the first
to establish the second. 10 And by that will,
we have been made holy through the sacri-
fice of the body of Jesus Christ once for all.
11 Day after day every priest stands and
performs his religious duties; again and
again he offers the same sacrifices, which
can never take away sins. 12 But when this
priest had offered for all time one sacrifice
for sins, he sat down at the right hand of God,
13 and since that time he waits for his ene-
mies to be made his footstool. 14 For by one
sacrifice he has made perfect forever those
who are being made holy.
15 The Holy Spirit also testifies to us about
this. First he says:

16 "This is the covenant I will make with
them
after that time, says the Lord.
I will put my laws in their hearts,
and I will write them on their minds."[b]

17 Then he adds:

"Their sins and lawless acts
I will remember no more."[c]

18 And where these have been forgiven, sacri-
fice for sin is no longer necessary.

A Call to Persevere in Faith

19 Therefore, brothers and sisters, since we
have confidence to enter the Most Holy Place
by the blood of Jesus, 20 by a new and living
way opened for us through the curtain, that
is, his body, 21 and since we have a great
priest over the house of God, 22 let us draw
near to God with a sincere heart and with the
full assurance that faith brings, having our
hearts sprinkled to cleanse us from a guilty
conscience and having our bodies washed
with pure water. 23 Let us hold unswervingly
to the hope we profess, for he who promised
is faithful. 24 And let us consider how we may
spur one another on toward love and good
deeds, 25 not giving up meeting together, as
some are in the habit of doing, but encour-
aging one another — and all the more as you
see the Day approaching.
26 If we deliberately keep on sinning after
we have received the knowledge of the truth,
no sacrifice for sins is left, 27 but only a fearful

[a] *7* Psalm 40:6-8 (see Septuagint) [b] *16* Jer. 31:33 [c] *17* Jer. 31:34

expectation of judgment and of raging fire
that will consume the enemies of God. 28Any-
one who rejected the law of Moses died with-
out mercy on the testimony of two or three
witnesses. 29How much more severely do you
think someone deserves to be punished who
has trampled the Son of God underfoot, who
has treated as an unholy thing the blood of
the covenant that sanctified them, and who
has insulted the Spirit of grace? 30For we
know him who said, "It is mine to avenge; I
will repay,"[a] and again, "The Lord will judge
his people."[b] 31It is a dreadful thing to fall into
the hands of the living God.

32Remember those earlier days after you
had received the light, when you endured
in a great conflict full of suffering. 33Some-
times you were publicly exposed to insult
and persecution; at other times you stood
side by side with those who were so treat-
ed. 34You suffered along with those in pris-
on and joyfully accepted the confiscation of
your property, because you knew that you
yourselves had better and lasting posses-
sions. 35So do not throw away your confi-
dence; it will be richly rewarded.

36You need to persevere so that when you
have done the will of God, you will receive
what he has promised. 37For,

> "In just a little while,
>   he who is coming will come
>   and will not delay."[c]

38And,

> "But my righteous[d] one will live by faith.
>   And I take no pleasure
>   in the one who shrinks back."[e]

39But we do not belong to those who shrink
back and are destroyed, but to those who
have faith and are saved.

Faith in Action

11 Now faith is confidence in what we
hope for and assurance about what
we do not see. 2This is what the ancients
were commended for.

3By faith we understand that the universe
was formed at God's command, so that what
is seen was not made out of what was visible.

4By faith Abel brought God a better offer-
ing than Cain did. By faith he was commend-
ed as righteous, when God spoke well of his
offerings. And by faith Abel still speaks, even
though he is dead.

5By faith Enoch was taken from this life,
so that he did not experience death: "He
could not be found, because God had taken
him away."[f] For before he was taken, he was
commended as one who pleased God. 6And
without faith it is impossible to please God,
because anyone who comes to him must be-
lieve that he exists and that he rewards those
who earnestly seek him.

7By faith Noah, when warned about
things not yet seen, in holy fear built an ark
to save his family. By his faith he condemned
the world and became heir of the righteous-
ness that is in keeping with faith.

8By faith Abraham, when called to go to
a place he would later receive as his inheri-
tance, obeyed and went, even though he did
not know where he was going. 9By faith he
made his home in the promised land like a
stranger in a foreign country; he lived in
tents, as did Isaac and Jacob, who were heirs
with him of the same promise. 10For he was
looking forward to the city with foundations,
whose architect and builder is God. 11And by
faith even Sarah, who was past childbearing
age, was enabled to bear children because
she[g] considered him faithful who had made
the promise. 12And so from this one man,
and he as good as dead, came descendants
as numerous as the stars in the sky and as
countless as the sand on the seashore.

13All these people were still living by faith
when they died. They did not receive the
things promised; they only saw them and
welcomed them from a distance, admit-
ting that they were foreigners and strang-
ers on earth. 14People who say such things
show that they are looking for a country of
their own. 15If they had been thinking of the
country they had left, they would have had
opportunity to return. 16Instead, they were
longing for a better country—a heaven-
ly one. Therefore God is not ashamed to be
called their God, for he has prepared a city
for them.

[a] *30* Deut. 32:35 [b] *30* Deut. 32:36; Psalm 135:14 [c] *37* Isaiah 26:20; Hab. 2:3 [d] *38* Some early manuscripts *But the righteous* [e] *38* Hab. 2:4 (see Septuagint) [f] *5* Gen. 5:24 [g] *11* Or *By faith Abraham, even though he was too old to have children—and Sarah herself was not able to conceive—was enabled to become a father because he*

17 By faith Abraham, when God tested
him, offered Isaac as a sacrifice. He who had
embraced the promises was about to sac-
rifice his one and only son, 18 even though
God had said to him, "It is through Isaac that
your offspring will be reckoned."[a] 19 Abra-
ham reasoned that God could even raise the
dead, and so in a manner of speaking he did
receive Isaac back from death.

20 By faith Isaac blessed Jacob and Esau in
regard to their future.

21 By faith Jacob, when he was dying,
blessed each of Joseph's sons, and worshiped
as he leaned on the top of his staff.

22 By faith Joseph, when his end was near,
spoke about the exodus of the Israelites from
Egypt and gave instructions concerning the
burial of his bones.

23 By faith Moses' parents hid him for
three months after he was born, because
they saw he was no ordinary child, and they
were not afraid of the king's edict.

24 By faith Moses, when he had grown up,
refused to be known as the son of Pharaoh's
daughter. 25 He chose to be mistreated along
with the people of God rather than to enjoy
the fleeting pleasures of sin. 26 He regarded
disgrace for the sake of Christ as of greater
value than the treasures of Egypt, because
he was looking ahead to his reward. 27 By
faith he left Egypt, not fearing the king's an-
ger; he persevered because he saw him who
is invisible. 28 By faith he kept the Passover
and the application of blood, so that the de-
stroyer of the firstborn would not touch the
firstborn of Israel.

29 By faith the people passed through the
Red Sea as on dry land; but when the Egyp-
tians tried to do so, they were drowned.

30 By faith the walls of Jericho fell, after the
army had marched around them for seven
days.

31 By faith the prostitute Rahab, because
she welcomed the spies, was not killed with
those who were disobedient.[b]

32 And what more shall I say? I do not
have time to tell about Gideon, Barak, Sam-
son and Jephthah, about David and Samuel
and the prophets, 33 who through faith con-
quered kingdoms, administered justice, and
gained what was promised; who shut the
mouths of lions, 34 quenched the fury of the
flames, and escaped the edge of the sword;
whose weakness was turned to strength;
and who became powerful in battle and
routed foreign armies. 35 Women received
back their dead, raised to life again. There
were others who were tortured, refusing to
be released so that they might gain an even
better resurrection. 36 Some faced jeers and
flogging, and even chains and imprison-
ment. 37 They were put to death by stoning;[c]
they were sawed in two; they were killed
by the sword. They went about in sheep-
skins and goatskins, destitute, persecuted
and mistreated — 38 the world was not wor-
thy of them. They wandered in deserts and
mountains, living in caves and in holes in
the ground.

39 These were all commended for their
faith, yet none of them received what had
been promised, 40 since God had planned
something better for us so that only together
with us would they be made perfect.

12 Therefore, since we are surrounded
by such a great cloud of witnesses, let
us throw off everything that hinders and the
sin that so easily entangles. And let us run
with perseverance the race marked out for
us, 2 fixing our eyes on Jesus, the pioneer and
perfecter of faith. For the joy set before him
he endured the cross, scorning its shame,
and sat down at the right hand of the throne
of God. 3 Consider him who endured such
opposition from sinners, so that you will not
grow weary and lose heart.

God Disciplines His Children

4 In your struggle against sin, you have
not yet resisted to the point of shedding your
blood. 5 And have you completely forgotten
this word of encouragement that addresses
you as a father addresses his son? It says,

"My son, do not make light of the Lord's
discipline,
and do not lose heart when he
rebukes you,
6 because the Lord disciplines the one
he loves,
and he chastens everyone he accepts
as his son."[d]

7 Endure hardship as discipline; God is
treating you as his children. For what children

[a] *18* Gen. 21:12 [b] *31* Or *unbelieving* [c] *37* Some early manuscripts *stoning; they were put to the test;*
[d] *5,6* Prov. 3:11,12 (see Septuagint)

are not disciplined by their father? 8 If you are not disciplined — and everyone undergoes discipline — then you are not legitimate, not true sons and daughters at all. 9 Moreover, we have all had human fathers who disciplined us and we respected them for it. How much more should we submit to the Father of spirits and live! 10 They disciplined us for a little while as they thought best; but God disciplines us for our good, in order that we may share in his holiness. 11 No discipline seems pleasant at the time, but painful. Later on, however, it produces a harvest of righteousness and peace for those who have been trained by it.

12 Therefore, strengthen your feeble arms and weak knees. 13 "Make level paths for your feet,"[a] so that the lame may not be disabled, but rather healed.

Warning and Encouragement

14 Make every effort to live in peace with everyone and to be holy; without holiness no one will see the Lord. 15 See to it that no one falls short of the grace of God and that no bitter root grows up to cause trouble and defile many. 16 See that no one is sexually immoral, or is godless like Esau, who for a single meal sold his inheritance rights as the oldest son. 17 Afterward, as you know, when he wanted to inherit this blessing, he was rejected. Even though he sought the blessing with tears, he could not change what he had done.

The Mountain of Fear and the Mountain of Joy

18 You have not come to a mountain that can be touched and that is burning with fire; to darkness, gloom and storm; 19 to a trumpet blast or to such a voice speaking words that those who heard it begged that no further word be spoken to them, 20 because they could not bear what was commanded: "If even an animal touches the mountain, it must be stoned to death."[b] 21 The sight was so terrifying that Moses said, "I am trembling with fear."[c]

22 But you have come to Mount Zion, to the city of the living God, the heavenly Jerusalem. You have come to thousands upon thousands of angels in joyful assembly, 23 to the church of the firstborn, whose names are written in heaven. You have come to God, the Judge of all, to the spirits of the righteous made perfect, 24 to Jesus the mediator of a new covenant, and to the sprinkled blood that speaks a better word than the blood of Abel.

25 See to it that you do not refuse him who speaks. If they did not escape when they refused him who warned them on earth, how much less will we, if we turn away from him who warns us from heaven? 26 At that time his voice shook the earth, but now he has promised, "Once more I will shake not only the earth but also the heavens."[d] 27 The words "once more" indicate the removing of what can be shaken — that is, created things — so that what cannot be shaken may remain.

28 Therefore, since we are receiving a kingdom that cannot be shaken, let us be thankful, and so worship God acceptably with reverence and awe, 29 for our "God is a consuming fire."[e]

Concluding Exhortations

13 Keep on loving one another as brothers and sisters. 2 Do not forget to show hospitality to strangers, for by so doing some people have shown hospitality to angels without knowing it. 3 Continue to remember those in prison as if you were together with them in prison, and those who are mistreated as if you yourselves were suffering.

4 Marriage should be honored by all, and the marriage bed kept pure, for God will judge the adulterer and all the sexually immoral. 5 Keep your lives free from the love of money and be content with what you have, because God has said,

> "Never will I leave you;
> never will I forsake you."[f]

6 So we say with confidence,

> "The Lord is my helper; I will not be afraid.
> What can mere mortals do to me?"[g]

7 Remember your leaders, who spoke the word of God to you. Consider the outcome of their way of life and imitate their faith. 8 Jesus Christ is the same yesterday and today and forever.

[a] *13* Prov. 4:26 [b] *20* Exodus 19:12,13 [c] *21* See Deut. 9:19. [d] *26* Haggai 2:6 [e] *29* Deut. 4:24
[f] *5* Deut. 31:6 [g] *6* Psalm 118:6,7

9 Do not be carried away by all kinds of
strange teachings. It is good for our hearts to
be strengthened by grace, not by eating cere-
monial foods, which is of no benefit to those
who do so. 10 We have an altar from which
those who minister at the tabernacle have
no right to eat.

11 The high priest carries the blood of an-
imals into the Most Holy Place as a sin of-
fering, but the bodies are burned outside
the camp. 12 And so Jesus also suffered out-
side the city gate to make the people holy
through his own blood. 13 Let us, then, go to
him outside the camp, bearing the disgrace
he bore. 14 For here we do not have an endur-
ing city, but we are looking for the city that
is to come.

15 Through Jesus, therefore, let us contin-
ually offer to God a sacrifice of praise — the
fruit of lips that openly profess his name.
16 And do not forget to do good and to share
with others, for with such sacrifices God is
pleased.

17 Have confidence in your leaders and
submit to their authority, because they keep
watch over you as those who must give an
account. Do this so that their work will be
a joy, not a burden, for that would be of no
benefit to you.

18 Pray for us. We are sure that we have a
clear conscience and desire to live honor-
ably in every way. 19 I particularly urge you
to pray so that I may be restored to you soon.

Benediction and Final Greetings

20 Now may the God of peace, who through
the blood of the eternal covenant brought
back from the dead our Lord Jesus, that great
Shepherd of the sheep, 21 equip you with ev-
erything good for doing his will, and may he
work in us what is pleasing to him, through
Jesus Christ, to whom be glory for ever and
ever. Amen.

22 Brothers and sisters, I urge you to bear
with my word of exhortation, for in fact I
have written to you quite briefly.

23 I want you to know that our broth-
er Timothy has been released. If he arrives
soon, I will come with him to see you.

24 Greet all your leaders and all the Lord's
people. Those from Italy send you their
greetings.

25 Grace be with you all.

JAMES

1 James, a servant of God and of the Lord Jesus Christ,

To the twelve tribes scattered among the nations:

Greetings.

Trials and Temptations

[2]Consider it pure joy, my brothers and sisters,[a] whenever you face trials of many kinds, [3]because you know that the testing of your faith produces perseverance. [4]Let perseverance finish its work so that you may be mature and complete, not lacking anything. [5]If any of you lacks wisdom, you should ask God, who gives generously to all without finding fault, and it will be given to you. [6]But when you ask, you must believe and not doubt, because the one who doubts is like a wave of the sea, blown and tossed by the wind. [7]That person should not expect to receive anything from the Lord. [8]Such a person is double-minded and unstable in all they do.

[9]Believers in humble circumstances ought to take pride in their high position. [10]But the rich should take pride in their humiliation — since they will pass away like a wild flower. [11]For the sun rises with scorching heat and withers the plant; its blossom falls and its beauty is destroyed. In the same way, the rich will fade away even while they go about their business.

[12]Blessed is the one who perseveres under trial because, having stood the test, that person will receive the crown of life that the Lord has promised to those who love him.

[13]When tempted, no one should say, "God is tempting me." For God cannot be tempted by evil, nor does he tempt anyone; [14]but each person is tempted when they are dragged away by their own evil desire and enticed. [15]Then, after desire has conceived, it gives birth to sin; and sin, when it is full-grown, gives birth to death.

[16]Don't be deceived, my dear brothers and sisters. [17]Every good and perfect gift is from above, coming down from the Father of the heavenly lights, who does not change like shifting shadows. [18]He chose to give us birth through the word of truth, that we might be a kind of firstfruits of all he created.

Listening and Doing

[19]My dear brothers and sisters, take note of this: Everyone should be quick to listen, slow to speak and slow to become angry, [20]because human anger does not produce the righteousness that God desires. [21]Therefore, get rid of all moral filth and the evil that is so prevalent and humbly accept the word planted in you, which can save you.

[22]Do not merely listen to the word, and so deceive yourselves. Do what it says. [23]Anyone who listens to the word but does not do what it says is like someone who looks at his face in a mirror [24]and, after looking at himself, goes away and immediately forgets what he looks like. [25]But whoever looks intently into the perfect law that gives freedom, and continues in it — not forgetting what they have heard, but doing it — they will be blessed in what they do.

[26]Those who consider themselves religious and yet do not keep a tight rein on their tongues deceive themselves, and their religion is worthless. [27]Religion that God our Father accepts as pure and faultless is this: to look after orphans and widows in their distress and to keep oneself from being polluted by the world.

Favoritism Forbidden

2 My brothers and sisters, believers in our glorious Lord Jesus Christ must not show favoritism. [2]Suppose a man comes into your meeting wearing a gold ring and fine clothes, and a poor man in filthy old clothes also comes in. [3]If you show special

[a] 2 The Greek word for *brothers and sisters* (*adelphoi*) refers here to believers, both men and women, as part of God's family; also in verses 16 and 19; and in 2:1, 5, 14; 3:10, 12; 4:11; 5:7, 9, 10, 12, 19.

attention to the man wearing fine clothes and say, "Here's a good seat for you," but say to the poor man, "You stand there" or "Sit on the floor by my feet," [4]have you not discriminated among yourselves and become judges with evil thoughts?

[5]Listen, my dear brothers and sisters: Has not God chosen those who are poor in the eyes of the world to be rich in faith and to inherit the kingdom he promised those who love him? [6]But you have dishonored the poor. Is it not the rich who are exploiting you? Are they not the ones who are dragging you into court? [7]Are they not the ones who are blaspheming the noble name of him to whom you belong?

[8]If you really keep the royal law found in Scripture, "Love your neighbor as yourself,"[a] you are doing right. [9]But if you show favoritism, you sin and are convicted by the law as lawbreakers. [10]For whoever keeps the whole law and yet stumbles at just one point is guilty of breaking all of it. [11]For he who said, "You shall not commit adultery,"[b] also said, "You shall not murder."[c] If you do not commit adultery but do commit murder, you have become a lawbreaker.

[12]Speak and act as those who are going to be judged by the law that gives freedom, [13]because judgment without mercy will be shown to anyone who has not been merciful. Mercy triumphs over judgment.

Faith and Deeds

[14]What good is it, my brothers and sisters, if someone claims to have faith but has no deeds? Can such faith save them? [15]Suppose a brother or a sister is without clothes and daily food. [16]If one of you says to them, "Go in peace; keep warm and well fed," but does nothing about their physical needs, what good is it? [17]In the same way, faith by itself, if it is not accompanied by action, is dead.

[18]But someone will say, "You have faith; I have deeds."

Show me your faith without deeds, and I will show you my faith by my deeds. [19]You believe that there is one God. Good! Even the demons believe that—and shudder.

[20]You foolish person, do you want evidence that faith without deeds is useless[d]? [21]Was not our father Abraham considered righteous for what he did when he offered his son Isaac on the altar? [22]You see that his faith and his actions were working together, and his faith was made complete by what he did. [23]And the scripture was fulfilled that says, "Abraham believed God, and it was credited to him as righteousness,"[e] and he was called God's friend. [24]You see that a person is considered righteous by what they do and not by faith alone.

[25]In the same way, was not even Rahab the prostitute considered righteous for what she did when she gave lodging to the spies and sent them off in a different direction? [26]As the body without the spirit is dead, so faith without deeds is dead.

Taming the Tongue

3 Not many of you should become teachers, my fellow believers, because you know that we who teach will be judged more strictly. [2]We all stumble in many ways. Anyone who is never at fault in what they say is perfect, able to keep their whole body in check.

[3]When we put bits into the mouths of horses to make them obey us, we can turn the whole animal. [4]Or take ships as an example. Although they are so large and are driven by strong winds, they are steered by a very small rudder wherever the pilot wants to go. [5]Likewise, the tongue is a small part of the body, but it makes great boasts. Consider what a great forest is set on fire by a small spark. [6]The tongue also is a fire, a world of evil among the parts of the body. It corrupts the whole body, sets the whole course of one's life on fire, and is itself set on fire by hell.

[7]All kinds of animals, birds, reptiles and sea creatures are being tamed and have been tamed by mankind, [8]but no human being can tame the tongue. It is a restless evil, full of deadly poison.

[9]With the tongue we praise our Lord and Father, and with it we curse human beings, who have been made in God's likeness. [10]Out of the same mouth come praise and cursing. My brothers and sisters, this should not be. [11]Can both fresh water and salt water flow

[a] *8* Lev. 19:18 [b] *11* Exodus 20:14; Deut. 5:18 [c] *11* Exodus 20:13; Deut. 5:17 [d] *20* Some early manuscripts *dead* [e] *23* Gen. 15:6

from the same spring? [12]My brothers and sisters, can a fig tree bear olives, or a grapevine bear figs? Neither can a salt spring produce fresh water.

Two Kinds of Wisdom

[13]Who is wise and understanding among you? Let them show it by their good life, by deeds done in the humility that comes from wisdom. [14]But if you harbor bitter envy and selfish ambition in your hearts, do not boast about it or deny the truth. [15]Such "wisdom" does not come down from heaven but is earthly, unspiritual, demonic. [16]For where you have envy and selfish ambition, there you find disorder and every evil practice.

[17]But the wisdom that comes from heaven is first of all pure; then peace-loving, considerate, submissive, full of mercy and good fruit, impartial and sincere. [18]Peacemakers who sow in peace reap a harvest of righteousness.

Submit Yourselves to God

4 What causes fights and quarrels among you? Don't they come from your desires that battle within you? [2]You desire but do not have, so you kill. You covet but you cannot get what you want, so you quarrel and fight. You do not have because you do not ask God. [3]When you ask, you do not receive, because you ask with wrong motives, that you may spend what you get on your pleasures.

[4]You adulterous people,[a] don't you know that friendship with the world means enmity against God? Therefore, anyone who chooses to be a friend of the world becomes an enemy of God. [5]Or do you think Scripture says without reason that he jealously longs for the spirit he has caused to dwell in us[b]? [6]But he gives us more grace. That is why Scripture says:

"God opposes the proud
but shows favor to the humble."[c]

[7]Submit yourselves, then, to God. Resist the devil, and he will flee from you. [8]Come near to God and he will come near to you. Wash your hands, you sinners, and purify your hearts, you double-minded. [9]Grieve, mourn and wail. Change your laughter to mourning and your joy to gloom. [10]Humble yourselves before the Lord, and he will lift you up.

[11]Brothers and sisters, do not slander one another. Anyone who speaks against a brother or sister[d] or judges them speaks against the law and judges it. When you judge the law, you are not keeping it, but sitting in judgment on it. [12]There is only one Lawgiver and Judge, the one who is able to save and destroy. But you — who are you to judge your neighbor?

Boasting About Tomorrow

[13]Now listen, you who say, "Today or tomorrow we will go to this or that city, spend a year there, carry on business and make money." [14]Why, you do not even know what will happen tomorrow. What is your life? You are a mist that appears for a little while and then vanishes. [15]Instead, you ought to say, "If it is the Lord's will, we will live and do this or that." [16]As it is, you boast in your arrogant schemes. All such boasting is evil. [17]If anyone, then, knows the good they ought to do and doesn't do it, it is sin for them.

Warning to Rich Oppressors

5 Now listen, you rich people, weep and wail because of the misery that is coming on you. [2]Your wealth has rotted, and moths have eaten your clothes. [3]Your gold and silver are corroded. Their corrosion will testify against you and eat your flesh like fire. You have hoarded wealth in the last days. [4]Look! The wages you failed to pay the workers who mowed your fields are crying out against you. The cries of the harvesters have reached the ears of the Lord Almighty. [5]You have lived on earth in luxury and self-indulgence. You have fattened yourselves in the day of slaughter.[e] [6]You have condemned and murdered the innocent one, who was not opposing you.

Patience in Suffering

[7]Be patient, then, brothers and sisters, until the Lord's coming. See how the farmer waits for the land to yield its valuable crop, patiently waiting for the autumn and spring

[a] *4* An allusion to covenant unfaithfulness; see Hosea 3:1. [b] *5* Or *that the spirit he caused to dwell in us envies intensely;* or *that the Spirit he caused to dwell in us longs jealously* [c] *6* Prov. 3:34 [d] *11* The Greek word for *brother or sister* (*adelphos*) refers here to a believer, whether man or woman, as part of God's family. [e] *5* Or *yourselves as in a day of feasting*

rains. [8]You too, be patient and stand firm, because the Lord's coming is near. [9]Don't grumble against one another, brothers and sisters, or you will be judged. The Judge is standing at the door!

[10]Brothers and sisters, as an example of patience in the face of suffering, take the prophets who spoke in the name of the Lord. [11]As you know, we count as blessed those who have persevered. You have heard of Job's perseverance and have seen what the Lord finally brought about. The Lord is full of compassion and mercy.

[12]Above all, my brothers and sisters, do not swear — not by heaven or by earth or by anything else. All you need to say is a simple "Yes" or "No." Otherwise you will be condemned.

The Prayer of Faith

[13]Is anyone among you in trouble? Let them pray. Is anyone happy? Let them sing songs of praise. [14]Is anyone among you sick? Let them call the elders of the church to pray over them and anoint them with oil in the name of the Lord. [15]And the prayer offered in faith will make the sick person well; the Lord will raise them up. If they have sinned, they will be forgiven. [16]Therefore confess your sins to each other and pray for each other so that you may be healed. The prayer of a righteous person is powerful and effective.

[17]Elijah was a human being, even as we are. He prayed earnestly that it would not rain, and it did not rain on the land for three and a half years. [18]Again he prayed, and the heavens gave rain, and the earth produced its crops.

[19]My brothers and sisters, if one of you should wander from the truth and someone should bring that person back, [20]remember this: Whoever turns a sinner from the error of their way will save them from death and cover over a multitude of sins.

1 PETER

1 Peter, an apostle of Jesus Christ,

To God's elect, exiles scattered through-
out the provinces of Pontus, Galatia, Cap-
padocia, Asia and Bithynia, [2]who have been
chosen according to the foreknowledge of
God the Father, through the sanctifying
work of the Spirit, to be obedient to Jesus
Christ and sprinkled with his blood:

Grace and peace be yours in abundance.

Praise to God for a Living Hope

[3]Praise be to the God and Father of our
Lord Jesus Christ! In his great mercy he has
given us new birth into a living hope through
the resurrection of Jesus Christ from the
dead, [4]and into an inheritance that can nev-
er perish, spoil or fade. This inheritance is
kept in heaven for you, [5]who through faith
are shielded by God's power until the com-
ing of the salvation that is ready to be re-
vealed in the last time. [6]In all this you greatly
rejoice, though now for a little while you may
have had to suffer grief in all kinds of trials.
[7]These have come so that the proven genu-
ineness of your faith—of greater worth than
gold, which perishes even though refined by
fire—may result in praise, glory and honor
when Jesus Christ is revealed. [8]Though you
have not seen him, you love him; and even
though you do not see him now, you believe
in him and are filled with an inexpressible
and glorious joy, [9]for you are receiving the
end result of your faith, the salvation of your
souls.

[10]Concerning this salvation, the prophets,
who spoke of the grace that was to come to
you, searched intently and with the greatest
care, [11]trying to find out the time and cir-
cumstances to which the Spirit of Christ in
them was pointing when he predicted the
sufferings of the Messiah and the glories that
would follow. [12]It was revealed to them that
they were not serving themselves but you,
when they spoke of the things that have now
been told you by those who have preached
the gospel to you by the Holy Spirit sent from
heaven. Even angels long to look into these
things.

Be Holy

[13]Therefore, with minds that are alert
and fully sober, set your hope on the grace
to be brought to you when Jesus Christ is
revealed at his coming. [14]As obedient chil-
dren, do not conform to the evil desires you
had when you lived in ignorance. [15]But just
as he who called you is holy, so be holy in all
you do; [16]for it is written: "Be holy, because I
am holy."[a]

[17]Since you call on a Father who judges
each person's work impartially, live out your
time as foreigners here in reverent fear. [18]For
you know that it was not with perishable
things such as silver or gold that you were re-
deemed from the empty way of life handed
down to you from your ancestors, [19]but with
the precious blood of Christ, a lamb without
blemish or defect. [20]He was chosen before
the creation of the world, but was revealed
in these last times for your sake. [21]Through
him you believe in God, who raised him
from the dead and glorified him, and so your
faith and hope are in God.

[22]Now that you have purified yourselves
by obeying the truth so that you have sin-
cere love for each other, love one another
deeply, from the heart.[b] [23]For you have been
born again, not of perishable seed, but of im-
perishable, through the living and enduring
word of God. [24]For,

"All people are like grass,
 and all their glory is like the flowers of
  the field;
the grass withers and the flowers fall,
25 but the word of the Lord endures
  forever."[c]

[a] *16* Lev. 11:44,45; 19:2 [b] *22* Some early manuscripts *from a pure heart* [c] *25* Isaiah 40:6-8 (see Septuagint)

And this is the word that was preached to you.

2 Therefore, rid yourselves of all malice and all deceit, hypocrisy, envy, and slander of every kind. 2 Like newborn babies, crave pure spiritual milk, so that by it you may grow up in your salvation, 3 now that you have tasted that the Lord is good.

The Living Stone and a Chosen People

4 As you come to him, the living Stone — rejected by humans but chosen by God and precious to him — 5 you also, like living stones, are being built into a spiritual house[a] to be a holy priesthood, offering spiritual sacrifices acceptable to God through Jesus Christ. 6 For in Scripture it says:

> "See, I lay a stone in Zion,
> a chosen and precious cornerstone,
> and the one who trusts in him
> will never be put to shame."[b]

7 Now to you who believe, this stone is precious. But to those who do not believe,

> "The stone the builders rejected
> has become the cornerstone,"[c]

8 and,

> "A stone that causes people to stumble
> and a rock that makes them fall."[d]

They stumble because they disobey the message — which is also what they were destined for.

9 But you are a chosen people, a royal priesthood, a holy nation, God's special possession, that you may declare the praises of him who called you out of darkness into his wonderful light. 10 Once you were not a people, but now you are the people of God; once you had not received mercy, but now you have received mercy.

Living Godly Lives in a Pagan Society

11 Dear friends, I urge you, as foreigners and exiles, to abstain from sinful desires, which wage war against your soul. 12 Live such good lives among the pagans that, though they accuse you of doing wrong, they may see your good deeds and glorify God on the day he visits us.

13 Submit yourselves for the Lord's sake to every human authority: whether to the emperor, as the supreme authority, 14 or to governors, who are sent by him to punish those who do wrong and to commend those who do right. 15 For it is God's will that by doing good you should silence the ignorant talk of foolish people. 16 Live as free people, but do not use your freedom as a cover-up for evil; live as God's slaves. 17 Show proper respect to everyone, love the family of believers, fear God, honor the emperor.

18 Slaves, in reverent fear of God submit yourselves to your masters, not only to those who are good and considerate, but also to those who are harsh. 19 For it is commendable if someone bears up under the pain of unjust suffering because they are conscious of God. 20 But how is it to your credit if you receive a beating for doing wrong and endure it? But if you suffer for doing good and you endure it, this is commendable before God. 21 To this you were called, because Christ suffered for you, leaving you an example, that you should follow in his steps.

> 22 "He committed no sin,
> and no deceit was found in his mouth."[e]

23 When they hurled their insults at him, he did not retaliate; when he suffered, he made no threats. Instead, he entrusted himself to him who judges justly. 24 "He himself bore our sins" in his body on the cross, so that we might die to sins and live for righteousness; "by his wounds you have been healed." 25 For "you were like sheep going astray,"[f] but now you have returned to the Shepherd and Overseer of your souls.

3 Wives, in the same way submit yourselves to your own husbands so that, if any of them do not believe the word, they may be won over without words by the behavior of their wives, 2 when they see the purity and reverence of your lives. 3 Your beauty should not come from outward adornment, such as elaborate hairstyles and the wearing of gold jewelry or fine clothes. 4 Rather, it should be that of your inner self, the unfading beauty of a gentle and quiet spirit, which is of great worth in God's sight. 5 For this is the way the holy women of the past who put their hope in God used to adorn themselves.

[a] 5 Or *into a temple of the Spirit* [b] 6 Isaiah 28:16 [c] 7 Psalm 118:22 [d] 8 Isaiah 8:14
[e] 22 Isaiah 53:9 [f] *24,25* Isaiah 53:4,5,6 (see Septuagint)

They submitted themselves to their own husbands, [6]like Sarah, who obeyed Abraham and called him her lord. You are her daughters if you do what is right and do not give way to fear.

[7]Husbands, in the same way be considerate as you live with your wives, and treat them with respect as the weaker partner and as heirs with you of the gracious gift of life, so that nothing will hinder your prayers.

Suffering for Doing Good

[8]Finally, all of you, be like-minded, be sympathetic, love one another, be compassionate and humble. [9]Do not repay evil with evil or insult with insult. On the contrary, repay evil with blessing, because to this you were called so that you may inherit a blessing. [10]For,

"Whoever would love life
and see good days
must keep their tongue from evil
and their lips from deceitful speech.
[11]They must turn from evil and do good;
they must seek peace and pursue it.
[12]For the eyes of the Lord are on the righteous
and his ears are attentive to their prayer,
but the face of the Lord is against those who do evil."[a]

[13]Who is going to harm you if you are eager to do good? [14]But even if you should suffer for what is right, you are blessed. "Do not fear their threats[b]; do not be frightened."[c] [15]But in your hearts revere Christ as Lord. Always be prepared to give an answer to everyone who asks you to give the reason for the hope that you have. But do this with gentleness and respect, [16]keeping a clear conscience, so that those who speak maliciously against your good behavior in Christ may be ashamed of their slander. [17]For it is better, if it is God's will, to suffer for doing good than for doing evil. [18]For Christ also suffered once for sins, the righteous for the unrighteous, to bring you to God. He was put to death in the body but made alive in the Spirit. [19]After being made alive,[d] he went and made proclamation to the imprisoned spirits— [20]to those who were disobedient long ago when God waited patiently in the days of Noah while the ark was being built. In it only a few people, eight in all, were saved through water, [21]and this water symbolizes baptism that now saves you also—not the removal of dirt from the body but the pledge of a clear conscience toward God.[e] It saves you by the resurrection of Jesus Christ, [22]who has gone into heaven and is at God's right hand—with angels, authorities and powers in submission to him.

Living for God

4 Therefore, since Christ suffered in his body, arm yourselves also with the same attitude, because whoever suffers in the body is done with sin. [2]As a result, they do not live the rest of their earthly lives for evil human desires, but rather for the will of God. [3]For you have spent enough time in the past doing what pagans choose to do—living in debauchery, lust, drunkenness, orgies, carousing and detestable idolatry. [4]They are surprised that you do not join them in their reckless, wild living, and they heap abuse on you. [5]But they will have to give account to him who is ready to judge the living and the dead. [6]For this is the reason the gospel was preached even to those who are now dead, so that they might be judged according to human standards in regard to the body, but live according to God in regard to the spirit.

[7]The end of all things is near. Therefore be alert and of sober mind so that you may pray. [8]Above all, love each other deeply, because love covers over a multitude of sins. [9]Offer hospitality to one another without grumbling. [10]Each of you should use whatever gift you have received to serve others, as faithful stewards of God's grace in its various forms. [11]If anyone speaks, they should do so as one who speaks the very words of God. If anyone serves, they should do so with the strength God provides, so that in all things God may be praised through Jesus Christ. To him be the glory and the power for ever and ever. Amen.

Suffering for Being a Christian

[12]Dear friends, do not be surprised at the fiery ordeal that has come on you to test you,

[a] 12 Psalm 34:12-16 [b] 14 Or *fear what they fear* [c] 14 Isaiah 8:12 [d] 18,19 Or *but made alive in the spirit, [19]in which also* [e] 21 Or *but an appeal to God for a clear conscience*

as though something strange were happening to you. 13 But rejoice inasmuch as you participate in the sufferings of Christ, so that you may be overjoyed when his glory is revealed. 14 If you are insulted because of the name of Christ, you are blessed, for the Spirit of glory and of God rests on you. 15 If you suffer, it should not be as a murderer or thief or any other kind of criminal, or even as a meddler. 16 However, if you suffer as a Christian, do not be ashamed, but praise God that you bear that name. 17 For it is time for judgment to begin with God's household; and if it begins with us, what will the outcome be for those who do not obey the gospel of God? 18 And,

> "If it is hard for the righteous to be saved,
> what will become of the ungodly and
> the sinner?"[a]

19 So then, those who suffer according to God's will should commit themselves to their faithful Creator and continue to do good.

To the Elders and the Flock

5 To the elders among you, I appeal as a fellow elder and a witness of Christ's sufferings who also will share in the glory to be revealed: 2 Be shepherds of God's flock that is under your care, watching over them—not because you must, but because you are willing, as God wants you to be; not pursuing dishonest gain, but eager to serve; 3 not lording it over those entrusted to you, but being examples to the flock. 4 And when the Chief Shepherd appears, you will receive the crown of glory that will never fade away.

5 In the same way, you who are younger, submit yourselves to your elders. All of you, clothe yourselves with humility toward one another, because,

> "God opposes the proud
> but shows favor to the humble."[b]

6 Humble yourselves, therefore, under God's mighty hand, that he may lift you up in due time. 7 Cast all your anxiety on him because he cares for you.

8 Be alert and of sober mind. Your enemy the devil prowls around like a roaring lion looking for someone to devour. 9 Resist him, standing firm in the faith, because you know that the family of believers throughout the world is undergoing the same kind of sufferings.

10 And the God of all grace, who called you to his eternal glory in Christ, after you have suffered a little while, will himself restore you and make you strong, firm and steadfast. 11 To him be the power for ever and ever. Amen.

Final Greetings

12 With the help of Silas,[c] whom I regard as a faithful brother, I have written to you briefly, encouraging you and testifying that this is the true grace of God. Stand fast in it.

13 She who is in Babylon, chosen together with you, sends you her greetings, and so does my son Mark. 14 Greet one another with a kiss of love.

Peace to all of you who are in Christ.

[a] *18* Prov. 11:31 (see Septuagint) [b] *5* Prov. 3:34 [c] *12* Greek *Silvanus,* a variant of *Silas*

2 PETER

1 Simon Peter, a servant and apostle of
Jesus Christ,

To those who through the righteousness
of our God and Savior Jesus Christ have re-
ceived a faith as precious as ours:

2Grace and peace be yours in abundance
through the knowledge of God and of Jesus
our Lord.

Confirming One's Calling and Election

3His divine power has given us everything
we need for a godly life through our knowl-
edge of him who called us by his own glory
and goodness. 4Through these he has given
us his very great and precious promises, so
that through them you may participate in
the divine nature, having escaped the cor-
ruption in the world caused by evil desires.
5For this very reason, make every effort to
add to your faith goodness; and to goodness,
knowledge; 6and to knowledge, self-control;
and to self-control, perseverance; and to
perseverance, godliness; 7and to godliness,
mutual affection; and to mutual affection,
love. 8For if you possess these qualities in
increasing measure, they will keep you from
being ineffective and unproductive in your
knowledge of our Lord Jesus Christ. 9But
whoever does not have them is nearsight-
ed and blind, forgetting that they have been
cleansed from their past sins.
10Therefore, my brothers and sisters,[a]
make every effort to confirm your calling
and election. For if you do these things, you
will never stumble, 11and you will receive a
rich welcome into the eternal kingdom of
our Lord and Savior Jesus Christ.

Prophecy of Scripture

12So I will always remind you of these
things, even though you know them and are
firmly established in the truth you now have.
13I think it is right to refresh your memory as
long as I live in the tent of this body, 14be-
cause I know that I will soon put it aside, as
our Lord Jesus Christ has made clear to me.
15And I will make every effort to see that af-
ter my departure you will always be able to
remember these things.
16For we did not follow cleverly devised
stories when we told you about the coming
of our Lord Jesus Christ in power, but we
were eyewitnesses of his majesty. 17He re-
ceived honor and glory from God the Father
when the voice came to him from the Ma-
jestic Glory, saying, "This is my Son, whom
I love; with him I am well pleased."[b] 18We
ourselves heard this voice that came from
heaven when we were with him on the sa-
cred mountain.
19We also have the prophetic message
as something completely reliable, and you
will do well to pay attention to it, as to a light
shining in a dark place, until the day dawns
and the morning star rises in your hearts.
20Above all, you must understand that no
prophecy of Scripture came about by the
prophet's own interpretation of things. 21For
prophecy never had its origin in the human
will, but prophets, though human, spoke
from God as they were carried along by the
Holy Spirit.

False Teachers and Their Destruction

2 But there were also false prophets
among the people, just as there will be
false teachers among you. They will secretly
introduce destructive heresies, even deny-
ing the sovereign Lord who bought them —
bringing swift destruction on themselves.
2Many will follow their depraved conduct
and will bring the way of truth into disre-
pute. 3In their greed these teachers will
exploit you with fabricated stories. Their
condemnation has long been hanging over
them, and their destruction has not been
sleeping.

[a] *10* The Greek word for *brothers and sisters* (*adelphoi*) refers here to believers, both men and women, as part of God's family. [b] *17* Matt. 17:5; Mark 9:7; Luke 9:35

4For if God did not spare angels when they sinned, but sent them to hell,[a] putting them in chains of darkness[b] to be held for judgment; 5if he did not spare the ancient world when he brought the flood on its ungodly people, but protected Noah, a preacher of righteousness, and seven others; 6if he condemned the cities of Sodom and Gomorrah by burning them to ashes, and made them an example of what is going to happen to the ungodly; 7and if he rescued Lot, a righteous man, who was distressed by the depraved conduct of the lawless 8(for that righteous man, living among them day after day, was tormented in his righteous soul by the lawless deeds he saw and heard)— 9if this is so, then the Lord knows how to rescue the godly from trials and to hold the unrighteous for punishment on the day of judgment. 10This is especially true of those who follow the corrupt desire of the flesh[c] and despise authority.

Bold and arrogant, they are not afraid to heap abuse on celestial beings; 11yet even angels, although they are stronger and more powerful, do not heap abuse on such beings when bringing judgment on them from[d] the Lord. 12But these people blaspheme in matters they do not understand. They are like unreasoning animals, creatures of instinct, born only to be caught and destroyed, and like animals they too will perish.

13They will be paid back with harm for the harm they have done. Their idea of pleasure is to carouse in broad daylight. They are blots and blemishes, reveling in their pleasures while they feast with you.[e] 14With eyes full of adultery, they never stop sinning; they seduce the unstable; they are experts in greed—an accursed brood! 15They have left the straight way and wandered off to follow the way of Balaam son of Bezer,[f] who loved the wages of wickedness. 16But he was rebuked for his wrongdoing by a donkey—an animal without speech—who spoke with a human voice and restrained the prophet's madness.

17These people are springs without water and mists driven by a storm. Blackest darkness is reserved for them. 18For they mouth empty, boastful words and, by appealing to the lustful desires of the flesh, they entice people who are just escaping from those who live in error. 19They promise them freedom, while they themselves are slaves of depravity—for "people are slaves to whatever has mastered them." 20If they have escaped the corruption of the world by knowing our Lord and Savior Jesus Christ and are again entangled in it and are overcome, they are worse off at the end than they were at the beginning. 21It would have been better for them not to have known the way of righteousness, than to have known it and then to turn their backs on the sacred command that was passed on to them. 22Of them the proverbs are true: "A dog returns to its vomit,"[g] and, "A sow that is washed returns to her wallowing in the mud."

The Day of the Lord

3 Dear friends, this is now my second letter to you. I have written both of them as reminders to stimulate you to wholesome thinking. 2I want you to recall the words spoken in the past by the holy prophets and the command given by our Lord and Savior through your apostles.

3Above all, you must understand that in the last days scoffers will come, scoffing and following their own evil desires. 4They will say, "Where is this 'coming' he promised? Ever since our ancestors died, everything goes on as it has since the beginning of creation." 5But they deliberately forget that long ago by God's word the heavens came into being and the earth was formed out of water and by water. 6By these waters also the world of that time was deluged and destroyed. 7By the same word the present heavens and earth are reserved for fire, being kept for the day of judgment and destruction of the ungodly.

8But do not forget this one thing, dear friends: With the Lord a day is like a thousand years, and a thousand years are like a day. 9The Lord is not slow in keeping his promise, as some understand slowness. Instead he is patient with you, not wanting anyone to perish, but everyone to come to repentance.

[a] 4 Greek *Tartarus* [b] 4 Some manuscripts *in gloomy dungeons* [c] 10 In contexts like this, the Greek word for *flesh* (*sarx*) refers to the sinful state of human beings, often presented as a power in opposition to the Spirit; also in verse 18. [d] 11 Many manuscripts *beings in the presence of* [e] 13 Some manuscripts *in their love feasts* [f] 15 Greek *Bosor* [g] 22 Prov. 26:11

10 But the day of the Lord will come like
a thief. The heavens will disappear with a
roar; the elements will be destroyed by fire,
and the earth and everything done in it will
be laid bare.[a]
11 Since everything will be destroyed in
this way, what kind of people ought you to
be? You ought to live holy and godly lives
12 as you look forward to the day of God and
speed its coming.[b] That day will bring about
the destruction of the heavens by fire, and
the elements will melt in the heat. 13 But in
keeping with his promise we are looking
forward to a new heaven and a new earth,
where righteousness dwells.
14 So then, dear friends, since you are look-
ing forward to this, make every effort to be
found spotless, blameless and at peace with
him. 15 Bear in mind that our Lord's patience
means salvation, just as our dear brother
Paul also wrote you with the wisdom that
God gave him. 16 He writes the same way
in all his letters, speaking in them of these
matters. His letters contain some things that
are hard to understand, which ignorant and
unstable people distort, as they do the other
Scriptures, to their own destruction.
17 Therefore, dear friends, since you have
been forewarned, be on your guard so that
you may not be carried away by the error of
the lawless and fall from your secure posi-
tion. 18 But grow in the grace and knowledge
of our Lord and Savior Jesus Christ. To him
be glory both now and forever! Amen.

[a] 10 Some manuscripts *be burned up* [b] 12 Or *as you wait eagerly for the day of God to come*

1 JOHN

The Incarnation of the Word of Life

1 That which was from the beginning, which we have heard, which we have seen with our eyes, which we have looked at and our hands have touched — this we proclaim concerning the Word of life. ²The life appeared; we have seen it and testify to it, and we proclaim to you the eternal life, which was with the Father and has appeared to us. ³We proclaim to you what we have seen and heard, so that you also may have fellowship with us. And our fellowship is with the Father and with his Son, Jesus Christ. ⁴We write this to make our[a] joy complete.

Light and Darkness, Sin and Forgiveness

⁵This is the message we have heard from him and declare to you: God is light; in him there is no darkness at all. ⁶If we claim to have fellowship with him and yet walk in the darkness, we lie and do not live out the truth. ⁷But if we walk in the light, as he is in the light, we have fellowship with one another, and the blood of Jesus, his Son, purifies us from all[b] sin.

⁸If we claim to be without sin, we deceive ourselves and the truth is not in us. ⁹If we confess our sins, he is faithful and just and will forgive us our sins and purify us from all unrighteousness. ¹⁰If we claim we have not sinned, we make him out to be a liar and his word is not in us.

2 My dear children, I write this to you so that you will not sin. But if anybody does sin, we have an advocate with the Father — Jesus Christ, the Righteous One. ²He is the atoning sacrifice for our sins, and not only for ours but also for the sins of the whole world.

Love and Hatred for Fellow Believers

³We know that we have come to know him if we keep his commands. ⁴Whoever says, "I know him," but does not do what he commands is a liar, and the truth is not in that person. ⁵But if anyone obeys his word, love for God[c] is truly made complete in them. This is how we know we are in him: ⁶Whoever claims to live in him must live as Jesus did.

⁷Dear friends, I am not writing you a new command but an old one, which you have had since the beginning. This old command is the message you have heard. ⁸Yet I am writing you a new command; its truth is seen in him and in you, because the darkness is passing and the true light is already shining.

⁹Anyone who claims to be in the light but hates a brother or sister[d] is still in the darkness. ¹⁰Anyone who loves their brother and sister[e] lives in the light, and there is nothing in them to make them stumble. ¹¹But anyone who hates a brother or sister is in the darkness and walks around in the darkness. They do not know where they are going, because the darkness has blinded them.

Reasons for Writing

¹²I am writing to you, dear children,
because your sins have been forgiven
on account of his name.
¹³I am writing to you, fathers,
because you know him who is from the
beginning.
I am writing to you, young men,
because you have overcome the
evil one.

¹⁴I write to you, dear children,
because you know the Father.
I write to you, fathers,
because you know him who is from
the beginning.
I write to you, young men,
because you are strong,
and the word of God lives in you,
and you have overcome the evil one.

[a] 4 Some manuscripts *your* [b] 7 Or *every* [c] 5 Or *word, God's love* [d] 9 The Greek word for *brother or sister* (*adelphos*) refers here to a believer, whether man or woman, as part of God's family; also in verse 11; and in 3:15, 17; 4:20; 5:16. [e] 10 The Greek word for *brother and sister* (*adelphos*) refers here to a believer, whether man or woman, as part of God's family; also in 3:10; 4:20, 21.

On Not Loving the World

15 Do not love the world or anything in the world. If anyone loves the world, love for the Father[a] is not in them. 16 For everything in the world—the lust of the flesh, the lust of the eyes, and the pride of life—comes not from the Father but from the world. 17 The world and its desires pass away, but whoever does the will of God lives forever.

Warnings Against Denying the Son

18 Dear children, this is the last hour; and as you have heard that the antichrist is coming, even now many antichrists have come. This is how we know it is the last hour. 19 They went out from us, but they did not really belong to us. For if they had belonged to us, they would have remained with us; but their going showed that none of them belonged to us.

20 But you have an anointing from the Holy One, and all of you know the truth.[b] 21 I do not write to you because you do not know the truth, but because you do know it and because no lie comes from the truth. 22 Who is the liar? It is whoever denies that Jesus is the Christ. Such a person is the antichrist—denying the Father and the Son. 23 No one who denies the Son has the Father; whoever acknowledges the Son has the Father also.

24 As for you, see that what you have heard from the beginning remains in you. If it does, you also will remain in the Son and in the Father. 25 And this is what he promised us—eternal life.

26 I am writing these things to you about those who are trying to lead you astray. 27 As for you, the anointing you received from him remains in you, and you do not need anyone to teach you. But as his anointing teaches you about all things and as that anointing is real, not counterfeit—just as it has taught you, remain in him.

God's Children and Sin

28 And now, dear children, continue in him, so that when he appears we may be confident and unashamed before him at his coming.

29 If you know that he is righteous, you know that everyone who does what is right has been born of him.

3 See what great love the Father has lavished on us, that we should be called children of God! And that is what we are! The reason the world does not know us is that it did not know him. 2 Dear friends, now we are children of God, and what we will be has not yet been made known. But we know that when Christ appears,[c] we shall be like him, for we shall see him as he is. 3 All who have this hope in him purify themselves, just as he is pure.

4 Everyone who sins breaks the law; in fact, sin is lawlessness. 5 But you know that he appeared so that he might take away our sins. And in him is no sin. 6 No one who lives in him keeps on sinning. No one who continues to sin has either seen him or known him.

7 Dear children, do not let anyone lead you astray. The one who does what is right is righteous, just as he is righteous. 8 The one who does what is sinful is of the devil, because the devil has been sinning from the beginning. The reason the Son of God appeared was to destroy the devil's work. 9 No one who is born of God will continue to sin, because God's seed remains in them; they cannot go on sinning, because they have been born of God. 10 This is how we know who the children of God are and who the children of the devil are: Anyone who does not do what is right is not God's child, nor is anyone who does not love their brother and sister.

More on Love and Hatred

11 For this is the message you heard from the beginning: We should love one another. 12 Do not be like Cain, who belonged to the evil one and murdered his brother. And why did he murder him? Because his own actions were evil and his brother's were righteous. 13 Do not be surprised, my brothers and sisters,[d] if the world hates you. 14 We know that we have passed from death to life, because we love each other. Anyone who does not love remains in death. 15 Anyone who hates a brother or sister is a murderer,

[a] 15 Or *world, the Father's love* [b] 20 Some manuscripts *and you know all things* [c] 2 Or *when it is made known* [d] 13 The Greek word for *brothers and sisters* (*adelphoi*) refers here to believers, both men and women, as part of God's family; also in verse 16.

and you know that no murderer has eternal life residing in him.

16This is how we know what love is: Jesus Christ laid down his life for us. And we ought to lay down our lives for our brothers and sisters. 17If anyone has material possessions and sees a brother or sister in need but has no pity on them, how can the love of God be in that person? 18Dear children, let us not love with words or speech but with actions and in truth.

19This is how we know that we belong to the truth and how we set our hearts at rest in his presence: 20If our hearts condemn us, we know that God is greater than our hearts, and he knows everything. 21Dear friends, if our hearts do not condemn us, we have confidence before God 22and receive from him anything we ask, because we keep his commands and do what pleases him. 23And this is his command: to believe in the name of his Son, Jesus Christ, and to love one another as he commanded us. 24The one who keeps God's commands lives in him, and he in them. And this is how we know that he lives in us: We know it by the Spirit he gave us.

On Denying the Incarnation

4 Dear friends, do not believe every spirit, but test the spirits to see whether they are from God, because many false prophets have gone out into the world. 2This is how you can recognize the Spirit of God: Every spirit that acknowledges that Jesus Christ has come in the flesh is from God, 3but every spirit that does not acknowledge Jesus is not from God. This is the spirit of the antichrist, which you have heard is coming and even now is already in the world.

4You, dear children, are from God and have overcome them, because the one who is in you is greater than the one who is in the world. 5They are from the world and therefore speak from the viewpoint of the world, and the world listens to them. 6We are from God, and whoever knows God listens to us; but whoever is not from God does not listen to us. This is how we recognize the Spirit[a] of truth and the spirit of falsehood.

God's Love and Ours

7Dear friends, let us love one another, for love comes from God. Everyone who loves has been born of God and knows God. 8Whoever does not love does not know God, because God is love. 9This is how God showed his love among us: He sent his one and only Son into the world that we might live through him. 10This is love: not that we loved God, but that he loved us and sent his Son as an atoning sacrifice for our sins. 11Dear friends, since God so loved us, we also ought to love one another. 12No one has ever seen God; but if we love one another, God lives in us and his love is made complete in us.

13This is how we know that we live in him and he in us: He has given us of his Spirit. 14And we have seen and testify that the Father has sent his Son to be the Savior of the world. 15If anyone acknowledges that Jesus is the Son of God, God lives in them and they in God. 16And so we know and rely on the love God has for us.

God is love. Whoever lives in love lives in God, and God in them. 17This is how love is made complete among us so that we will have confidence on the day of judgment: In this world we are like Jesus. 18There is no fear in love. But perfect love drives out fear, because fear has to do with punishment. The one who fears is not made perfect in love.

19We love because he first loved us. 20Whoever claims to love God yet hates a brother or sister is a liar. For whoever does not love their brother and sister, whom they have seen, cannot love God, whom they have not seen. 21And he has given us this command: Anyone who loves God must also love their brother and sister.

Faith in the Incarnate Son of God

5 Everyone who believes that Jesus is the Christ is born of God, and everyone who loves the father loves his child as well. 2This is how we know that we love the children of God: by loving God and carrying out his commands. 3In fact, this is love for God: to keep his commands. And his commands are not burdensome, 4for everyone born of God overcomes the world. This is the victory that has overcome the world, even our faith. 5Who is it that overcomes the world? Only the one who believes that Jesus is the Son of God.

[a] 6 Or *spirit*

10,000 REASONS (BLESS THE LORD)

Matt Redman, Jonas Myrin

Bless the Lord O my soul
O my soul
Worship his holy name
Sing like never before
O my soul
I'll worship your holy name

The sun comes up
It's a new day dawning
It's time to sing your song again
Whatever may pass
And whatever lies before me
Let me be singing
When the evening comes

You're rich in love
And you're slow to anger
Your name is great
And your heart is kind
For all your goodness
I will keep on singing
Ten thousand reasons
For my heart to find

And on that day
When my strength is failing
The end draws near
And my time has come
Still my soul will
Sing your praise unending
Ten thousand years
And then forevermore

THE INSPIRATION

Praise the LORD, my soul; all my inmost being, praise his holy name. Praise the LORD, my soul, and forget not all his benefits—who forgives all your sins and heals all your diseases, who redeems your life from the pit and crowns you with love and compassion, who satisfies your desires with good things so that your youth is renewed like the eagle's.

—Psalm 103:1–5

BEHIND THE SONG

Worship writers have an essential and challenging task — to articulate praise through lyrics and melodies that are fresh and accessible. From the very first lines of "10,000 Reasons," it is clear that Matt Redman takes this job very seriously. Redman has a special gift for writing songs so closely inspired by the book of Psalms that it's easy to think he is singing straight from his Bible. His song "10,000 Reasons (Bless the Lord)" is relatively new but sounds as if it has been around for centuries.

"[The melody] came from Jonas Myrin, my Swedish friend," Redman explains. "He had a melody idea for a chorus and [. . .] it led really quickly on to a couple of quick-flying verses." For songwriters with the right combination of innate talent and well-honed craftsmanship, it can sometimes be just that simple.

Selah

"10,000 Reasons" starts with one of the most frequently used instructions in the psalms: "Bless the Lord." What does it mean to "bless the Lord"? When God blesses people the meaning is fairly clear — he answers prayers, makes provision, protects, delivers and saves. But how can people bless God? Wouldn't that mean that God needs something that only we can provide? By no means.

As it turns out, the English phrase "Bless the Lord" is most closely related to the idea of giving thanks to God for the blessings he has bestowed. It's as if the believer is shouting back to God, "You have blessed me Lord. Thank you!"

How often do you bless the Lord? How do you do it? The next time you sing the words "bless the Lord," think about what you are truly grateful for and see how your worship expands.

6This is the one who came by water and
blood—Jesus Christ. He did not come by
water only, but by water and blood. And it
is the Spirit who testifies, because the Spirit
is the truth. 7For there are three that testify:
8the[a] Spirit, the water and the blood; and the
three are in agreement. 9We accept human
testimony, but God's testimony is greater
because it is the testimony of God, which
he has given about his Son. 10Whoever be-
lieves in the Son of God accepts this testimo-
ny. Whoever does not believe God has made
him out to be a liar, because they have not
believed the testimony God has given about
his Son. 11And this is the testimony: God has
given us eternal life, and this life is in his
Son. 12Whoever has the Son has life; who-
ever does not have the Son of God does not
have life.

Concluding Affirmations

13I write these things to you who believe
in the name of the Son of God so that you
may know that you have eternal life. 14This
is the confidence we have in approaching
God: that if we ask anything according to his
will, he hears us. 15And if we know that he
hears us—whatever we ask—we know that
we have what we asked of him.

16If you see any brother or sister commit
a sin that does not lead to death, you should
pray and God will give them life. I refer to
those whose sin does not lead to death.
There is a sin that leads to death. I am not
saying that you should pray about that. 17All
wrongdoing is sin, and there is sin that does
not lead to death.

18We know that anyone born of God does
not continue to sin; the One who was born
of God keeps them safe, and the evil one
cannot harm them. 19We know that we are
children of God, and that the whole world is
under the control of the evil one. 20We know
also that the Son of God has come and has
given us understanding, so that we may
know him who is true. And we are in him
who is true by being in his Son Jesus Christ.
He is the true God and eternal life.

21Dear children, keep yourselves from
idols.

[a] 7,8 Late manuscripts of the Vulgate *testify in heaven: the Father, the Word and the Holy Spirit, and these three are one.* [8]*And there are three that testify on earth: the* (not found in any Greek manuscript before the fourteenth century)

2 JOHN

1 The elder,

To the lady chosen by God and to her children, whom I love in the truth — and not I only, but also all who know the truth — 2 because of the truth, which lives in us and will be with us forever:

3 Grace, mercy and peace from God the Father and from Jesus Christ, the Father's Son, will be with us in truth and love.

4 It has given me great joy to find some of your children walking in the truth, just as the Father commanded us. 5 And now, dear lady, I am not writing you a new command but one we have had from the beginning. I ask that we love one another. 6 And this is love: that we walk in obedience to his commands. As you have heard from the beginning, his command is that you walk in love.

7 I say this because many deceivers, who do not acknowledge Jesus Christ as coming in the flesh, have gone out into the world. Any such person is the deceiver and the antichrist. 8 Watch out that you do not lose what we[a] have worked for, but that you may be rewarded fully. 9 Anyone who runs ahead and does not continue in the teaching of Christ does not have God; whoever continues in the teaching has both the Father and the Son. 10 If anyone comes to you and does not bring this teaching, do not take them into your house or welcome them. 11 Anyone who welcomes them shares in their wicked work.

12 I have much to write to you, but I do not want to use paper and ink. Instead, I hope to visit you and talk with you face to face, so that our joy may be complete.

13 The children of your sister, who is chosen by God, send their greetings.

[a] *8* Some manuscripts *you*

3 JOHN

[1]The elder,

To my dear friend Gaius, whom I love in
the truth.

[2]Dear friend, I pray that you may enjoy
good health and that all may go well with
you, even as your soul is getting along well.
[3]It gave me great joy when some believers
came and testified about your faithfulness
to the truth, telling how you continue to
walk in it. [4]I have no greater joy than to hear
that my children are walking in the truth.

[5]Dear friend, you are faithful in what you
are doing for the brothers and sisters,[a] even
though they are strangers to you. [6]They have
told the church about your love. Please send
them on their way in a manner that honors
God. [7]It was for the sake of the Name that
they went out, receiving no help from the
pagans. [8]We ought therefore to show hos-
pitality to such people so that we may work
together for the truth.

[9]I wrote to the church, but Diotrephes,
who loves to be first, will not welcome us.
[10]So when I come, I will call attention to
what he is doing, spreading malicious non-
sense about us. Not satisfied with that, he
even refuses to welcome other believers. He
also stops those who want to do so and puts
them out of the church.

[11]Dear friend, do not imitate what is evil
but what is good. Anyone who does what is
good is from God. Anyone who does what is
evil has not seen God. [12]Demetrius is well
spoken of by everyone — and even by the
truth itself. We also speak well of him, and
you know that our testimony is true.

[13]I have much to write you, but I do not
want to do so with pen and ink. [14]I hope to
see you soon, and we will talk face to face.

Peace to you. The friends here send their
greetings. Greet the friends there by name.

[a] 5 The Greek word for *brothers and sisters* (*adelphoi*) refers here to believers, both men and women, as part of God's family.

JUDE

1 Jude, a servant of Jesus Christ and a
brother of James,

To those who have been called, who are
loved in God the Father and kept for[a] Jesus
Christ:

2 Mercy, peace and love be yours in abun-
dance.

The Sin and Doom of Ungodly People

3 Dear friends, although I was very ea-
ger to write to you about the salvation we
share, I felt compelled to write and urge you
to contend for the faith that was once for all
entrusted to God's holy people. 4 For certain
individuals whose condemnation was writ-
ten about[b] long ago have secretly slipped in
among you. They are ungodly people, who
pervert the grace of our God into a license
for immorality and deny Jesus Christ our
only Sovereign and Lord.
5 Though you already know all this, I want
to remind you that the Lord[c] at one time
delivered his people out of Egypt, but later
destroyed those who did not believe. 6 And
the angels who did not keep their positions
of authority but abandoned their proper
dwelling — these he has kept in darkness,
bound with everlasting chains for judgment
on the great Day. 7 In a similar way, Sodom
and Gomorrah and the surrounding towns
gave themselves up to sexual immorality
and perversion. They serve as an example
of those who suffer the punishment of eter-
nal fire.
8 In the very same way, on the strength of
their dreams these ungodly people pollute
their own bodies, reject authority and heap
abuse on celestial beings. 9 But even the
archangel Michael, when he was disputing
with the devil about the body of Moses, did
not himself dare to condemn him for slan-
der but said, "The Lord rebuke you!"[d] 10 Yet
these people slander whatever they do not
understand, and the very things they do un-
derstand by instinct — as irrational animals
do — will destroy them.
11 Woe to them! They have taken the way
of Cain; they have rushed for profit into Ba-
laam's error; they have been destroyed in
Korah's rebellion.
12 These people are blemishes at your love
feasts, eating with you without the slightest
qualm — shepherds who feed only them-
selves. They are clouds without rain, blown
along by the wind; autumn trees, without
fruit and uprooted — twice dead. 13 They
are wild waves of the sea, foaming up their
shame; wandering stars, for whom blackest
darkness has been reserved forever.
14 Enoch, the seventh from Adam, proph-
esied about them: "See, the Lord is com-
ing with thousands upon thousands of his
holy ones 15 to judge everyone, and to con-
vict all of them of all the ungodly acts they
have committed in their ungodliness, and
of all the defiant words ungodly sinners
have spoken against him."[e] 16 These people
are grumblers and faultfinders; they fol-
low their own evil desires; they boast about
themselves and flatter others for their own
advantage.

A Call to Persevere

17 But, dear friends, remember what the
apostles of our Lord Jesus Christ foretold.
18 They said to you, "In the last times there
will be scoffers who will follow their own
ungodly desires." 19 These are the people
who divide you, who follow mere natural in-
stincts and do not have the Spirit.
20 But you, dear friends, by building your-
selves up in your most holy faith and praying

[a] *1* Or *by*; or *in* [b] *4* Or *individuals who were marked out for condemnation* [c] *5* Some early manuscripts *Jesus* [d] *9* Jude is alluding to the Jewish *Testament of Moses* (approximately the first century A.D.). [e] *14,15* From the Jewish *First Book of Enoch* (approximately the first century B.C.)

in the Holy Spirit, 21 keep yourselves in God's love as you wait for the mercy of our Lord Jesus Christ to bring you to eternal life.

22 Be merciful to those who doubt; 23 save others by snatching them from the fire; to others show mercy, mixed with fear—hating even the clothing stained by corrupted flesh.[a]

Doxology

24 To him who is able to keep you from stumbling and to present you before his glorious presence without fault and with great joy— 25 to the only God our Savior be glory, majesty, power and authority, through Jesus Christ our Lord, before all ages, now and forevermore! Amen.

[a] *22,23* The Greek manuscripts of these verses vary at several points.

REVELATION

Prologue

1 The revelation from Jesus Christ, which
God gave him to show his servants what
must soon take place. He made it known by
sending his angel to his servant John, 2 who
testifies to everything he saw — that is, the
word of God and the testimony of Jesus
Christ. 3 Blessed is the one who reads aloud
the words of this prophecy, and blessed are
those who hear it and take to heart what is
written in it, because the time is near.

Greetings and Doxology

4 John,

To the seven churches in the province of
Asia:

Grace and peace to you from him who is,
and who was, and who is to come, and from
the seven spirits[a] before his throne, 5 and
from Jesus Christ, who is the faithful wit-
ness, the firstborn from the dead, and the
ruler of the kings of the earth.

To him who loves us and has freed us from
our sins by his blood, 6 and has made us to be
a kingdom and priests to serve his God and
Father — to him be glory and power for ever
and ever! Amen.

7 "Look, he is coming with the clouds,"[b]
and "every eye will see him,
even those who pierced him";
and all peoples on earth "will mourn
because of him."[c]
So shall it be! Amen.

8 "I am the Alpha and the Omega," says the
Lord God, "who is, and who was, and who is
to come, the Almighty."

John's Vision of Christ

9 I, John, your brother and companion in
the suffering and kingdom and patient en-
durance that are ours in Jesus, was on the
island of Patmos because of the word of God
and the testimony of Jesus. 10 On the Lord's
Day I was in the Spirit, and I heard behind
me a loud voice like a trumpet, 11 which said:
"Write on a scroll what you see and send it
to the seven churches: to Ephesus, Smyrna,
Pergamum, Thyatira, Sardis, Philadelphia
and Laodicea."

12 I turned around to see the voice that
was speaking to me. And when I turned I
saw seven golden lampstands, 13 and among
the lampstands was someone like a son of
man,[d] dressed in a robe reaching down to
his feet and with a golden sash around his
chest. 14 The hair on his head was white like
wool, as white as snow, and his eyes were
like blazing fire. 15 His feet were like bronze
glowing in a furnace, and his voice was like
the sound of rushing waters. 16 In his right
hand he held seven stars, and coming out of
his mouth was a sharp, double-edged sword.
His face was like the sun shining in all its
brilliance.

17 When I saw him, I fell at his feet as
though dead. Then he placed his right hand
on me and said: "Do not be afraid. I am the
First and the Last. 18 I am the Living One; I was
dead, and now look, I am alive for ever and
ever! And I hold the keys of death and Hades.

19 "Write, therefore, what you have seen,
what is now and what will take place later.
20 The mystery of the seven stars that you
saw in my right hand and of the seven golden
lampstands is this: The seven stars are the
angels[e] of the seven churches, and the seven
lampstands are the seven churches.

To the Church in Ephesus

2 "To the angel[f] of the church in Ephesus
write:

These are the words of him who
holds the seven stars in his right hand

[a] 4 That is, the sevenfold Spirit [b] 7 Daniel 7:13 [c] 7 Zech 12:10 [d] 13 See Daniel 7:13.
[e] 20 Or *messengers* [f] 1 Or *messenger*; also in verses 8, 12 and 18

and walks among the seven golden
lampstands. [2]I know your deeds, your
hard work and your perseverance. I
know that you cannot tolerate wicked
people, that you have tested those who
claim to be apostles but are not, and
have found them false. [3]You have perse-
vered and have endured hardships for
my name, and have not grown weary.

[4]Yet I hold this against you: You have
forsaken the love you had at first. [5]Con-
sider how far you have fallen! Repent
and do the things you did at first. If you
do not repent, I will come to you and
remove your lampstand from its place.
[6]But you have this in your favor: You
hate the practices of the Nicolaitans,
which I also hate.

[7]Whoever has ears, let them hear
what the Spirit says to the churches. To
the one who is victorious, I will give the
right to eat from the tree of life, which is
in the paradise of God.

To the Church in Smyrna

[8]"To the angel of the church in Smyrna write:

These are the words of him who is
the First and the Last, who died and
came to life again. [9]I know your afflic-
tions and your poverty—yet you are
rich! I know about the slander of those
who say they are Jews and are not, but
are a synagogue of Satan. [10]Do not be
afraid of what you are about to suffer. I
tell you, the devil will put some of you
in prison to test you, and you will suf-
fer persecution for ten days. Be faithful,
even to the point of death, and I will
give you life as your victor's crown.

[11]Whoever has ears, let them hear
what the Spirit says to the churches.
The one who is victorious will not be
hurt at all by the second death.

To the Church in Pergamum

[12]"To the angel of the church in Pergamum
write:

These are the words of him who has
the sharp, double-edged sword. [13]I
know where you live—where Satan
has his throne. Yet you remain true to
my name. You did not renounce your
faith in me, not even in the days of An-
tipas, my faithful witness, who was put
to death in your city—where Satan
lives.

[14]Nevertheless, I have a few things
against you: There are some among
you who hold to the teaching of Ba-
laam, who taught Balak to entice the
Israelites to sin so that they ate food
sacrificed to idols and committed sex-
ual immorality. [15]Likewise, you also
have those who hold to the teaching
of the Nicolaitans. [16]Repent therefore!
Otherwise, I will soon come to you and
will fight against them with the sword
of my mouth.

[17]Whoever has ears, let them hear
what the Spirit says to the churches.
To the one who is victorious, I will give
some of the hidden manna. I will also
give that person a white stone with a
new name written on it, known only to
the one who receives it.

To the Church in Thyatira

[18]"To the angel of the church in Thyatira
write:

These are the words of the Son of
God, whose eyes are like blazing fire
and whose feet are like burnished
bronze. [19]I know your deeds, your love
and faith, your service and persever-
ance, and that you are now doing more
than you did at first.

[20]Nevertheless, I have this against
you: You tolerate that woman Jeze-
bel, who calls herself a prophet. By her
teaching she misleads my servants into
sexual immorality and the eating of
food sacrificed to idols. [21]I have given
her time to repent of her immorality,
but she is unwilling. [22]So I will cast her
on a bed of suffering, and I will make
those who commit adultery with her
suffer intensely, unless they repent of
her ways. [23]I will strike her children
dead. Then all the churches will know
that I am he who searches hearts and
minds, and I will repay each of you ac-
cording to your deeds.

[24]Now I say to the rest of you in
Thyatira, to you who do not hold to
her teaching and have not learned Sa-
tan's so-called deep secrets, 'I will
not impose any other burden on you,

25 except to hold on to what you have
until I come.'
26 To the one who is victorious and
does my will to the end, I will give au-
thority over the nations — 27 that one
'will rule them with an iron scepter
and will dash them to pieces like pot-
tery'[a] — just as I have received authori-
ty from my Father. 28 I will also give that
one the morning star. 29 Whoever has
ears, let them hear what the Spirit says
to the churches.

To the Church in Sardis

3 "To the angel[b] of the church in Sardis
write:

These are the words of him who
holds the seven spirits[c] of God and the
seven stars. I know your deeds; you
have a reputation of being alive, but
you are dead. 2 Wake up! Strengthen
what remains and is about to die, for I
have found your deeds unfinished in
the sight of my God. 3 Remember, there-
fore, what you have received and heard;
hold it fast, and repent. But if you do not
wake up, I will come like a thief, and
you will not know at what time I will
come to you.
4 Yet you have a few people in Sardis
who have not soiled their clothes. They
will walk with me, dressed in white, for
they are worthy. 5 The one who is vic-
torious will, like them, be dressed in
white. I will never blot out the name of
that person from the book of life, but
will acknowledge that name before my
Father and his angels. 6 Whoever has
ears, let them hear what the Spirit says
to the churches.

To the Church in Philadelphia

7 "To the angel of the church in Philadelphia
write:

These are the words of him who is
holy and true, who holds the key of Da-
vid. What he opens no one can shut,
and what he shuts no one can open. 8 I
know your deeds. See, I have placed
before you an open door that no one
can shut. I know that you have little
strength, yet you have kept my word
and have not denied my name. 9 I will
make those who are of the synagogue
of Satan, who claim to be Jews though
they are not, but are liars — I will make
them come and fall down at your feet
and acknowledge that I have loved you.
10 Since you have kept my command to
endure patiently, I will also keep you
from the hour of trial that is going to
come on the whole world to test the in-
habitants of the earth.
11 I am coming soon. Hold on to what
you have, so that no one will take your
crown. 12 The one who is victorious I
will make a pillar in the temple of my
God. Never again will they leave it. I
will write on them the name of my God
and the name of the city of my God,
the new Jerusalem, which is coming
down out of heaven from my God; and
I will also write on them my new name.
13 Whoever has ears, let them hear what
the Spirit says to the churches.

To the Church in Laodicea

14 "To the angel of the church in Laodicea
write:

These are the words of the Amen,
the faithful and true witness, the ruler
of God's creation. 15 I know your deeds,
that you are neither cold nor hot. I wish
you were either one or the other! 16 So,
because you are lukewarm — neither
hot nor cold — I am about to spit you
out of my mouth. 17 You say, 'I am rich;
I have acquired wealth and do not need
a thing.' But you do not realize that you
are wretched, pitiful, poor, blind and
naked. 18 I counsel you to buy from me
gold refined in the fire, so you can be-
come rich; and white clothes to wear,
so you can cover your shameful naked-
ness; and salve to put on your eyes, so
you can see.
19 Those whom I love I rebuke and
discipline. So be earnest and repent.
20 Here I am! I stand at the door and
knock. If anyone hears my voice and
opens the door, I will come in and eat
with that person, and they with me.
21 To the one who is victorious, I

[a] 27 Psalm 2:9 [b] 1 Or *messenger*; also in verses 7 and 14 [c] 1 That is, the sevenfold Spirit

will give the right to sit with me on my
throne, just as I was victorious and sat
down with my Father on his throne.
22Whoever has ears, let them hear what
the Spirit says to the churches."

The Throne in Heaven

4 After this I looked, and there before
me was a door standing open in heav-
en. And the voice I had first heard speaking
to me like a trumpet said, "Come up here,
and I will show you what must take place
after this." 2At once I was in the Spirit, and
there before me was a throne in heaven with
someone sitting on it. 3And the one who sat
there had the appearance of jasper and ruby.
A rainbow that shone like an emerald encir-
cled the throne. 4Surrounding the throne
were twenty-four other thrones, and seated
on them were twenty-four elders. They were
dressed in white and had crowns of gold on
their heads. 5From the throne came flashes
of lightning, rumblings and peals of thun-
der. In front of the throne, seven lamps were
blazing. These are the seven spirits[a] of God.
6Also in front of the throne there was what
looked like a sea of glass, clear as crystal.

In the center, around the throne, were
four living creatures, and they were covered
with eyes, in front and in back. 7The first liv-
ing creature was like a lion, the second was
like an ox, the third had a face like a man,
the fourth was like a flying eagle. 8Each of
the four living creatures had six wings and
was covered with eyes all around, even un-
der its wings. Day and night they never stop
saying:

"'Holy, holy, holy
is the Lord God Almighty,'[b]
who was, and is, and is to come."

9Whenever the living creatures give glory,
honor and thanks to him who sits on the
throne and who lives for ever and ever, 10the
twenty-four elders fall down before him who
sits on the throne and worship him who lives
for ever and ever. They lay their crowns be-
fore the throne and say:

11 "You are worthy, our Lord and God,
to receive glory and honor and power,
for you created all things,
and by your will they were
created
and have their being."

The Scroll and the Lamb

5 Then I saw in the right hand of him who
sat on the throne a scroll with writing on
both sides and sealed with seven seals. 2And
I saw a mighty angel proclaiming in a loud
voice, "Who is worthy to break the seals and
open the scroll?" 3But no one in heaven or
on earth or under the earth could open the
scroll or even look inside it. 4I wept and wept
because no one was found who was worthy
to open the scroll or look inside. 5Then one of
the elders said to me, "Do not weep! See, the
Lion of the tribe of Judah, the Root of David,
has triumphed. He is able to open the scroll
and its seven seals."

6Then I saw a Lamb, looking as if it had
been slain, standing at the center of the
throne, encircled by the four living creatures
and the elders. The Lamb had seven horns
and seven eyes, which are the seven spirits[a]
of God sent out into all the earth. 7He went
and took the scroll from the right hand of
him who sat on the throne. 8And when he
had taken it, the four living creatures and
the twenty-four elders fell down before the
Lamb. Each one had a harp and they were
holding golden bowls full of incense, which
are the prayers of God's people. 9And they
sang a new song, saying:

"You are worthy to take the scroll
and to open its seals,
because you were slain,
and with your blood you purchased
for God
persons from every tribe and language
and people and nation.
10You have made them to be a kingdom and
priests to serve our God,
and they will reign[c] on the earth."

11Then I looked and heard the voice of
many angels, numbering thousands upon
thousands, and ten thousand times ten
thousand. They encircled the throne and the
living creatures and the elders. 12In a loud
voice they were saying:

"Worthy is the Lamb, who was
slain,

[a] 5,6 That is, the sevenfold Spirit [b] 8 Isaiah 6:3 [c] 10 Some manuscripts *they reign*

to receive power and wealth and
wisdom and strength
and honor and glory and praise!"

13 Then I heard every creature in heaven
and on earth and under the earth and on the
sea, and all that is in them, saying:

"To him who sits on the throne and to
the Lamb
be praise and honor and glory and
power,
for ever and ever!"

14 The four living creatures said, "Amen,"
and the elders fell down and worshiped.

The Seals

6 I watched as the Lamb opened the first
of the seven seals. Then I heard one of
the four living creatures say in a voice like
thunder, "Come!" 2 I looked, and there before
me was a white horse! Its rider held a bow,
and he was given a crown, and he rode out as
a conqueror bent on conquest.

3 When the Lamb opened the second
seal, I heard the second living creature say,
"Come!" 4 Then another horse came out, a fi-
ery red one. Its rider was given power to take
peace from the earth and to make people kill
each other. To him was given a large sword.

5 When the Lamb opened the third seal, I
heard the third living creature say, "Come!"
I looked, and there before me was a black
horse! Its rider was holding a pair of scales
in his hand. 6 Then I heard what sounded
like a voice among the four living creatures,
saying, "Two pounds[a] of wheat for a day's
wages,[b] and six pounds[c] of barley for a day's
wages,[b] and do not damage the oil and the
wine!"

7 When the Lamb opened the fourth seal, I
heard the voice of the fourth living creature
say, "Come!" 8 I looked, and there before me
was a pale horse! Its rider was named Death,
and Hades was following close behind him.
They were given power over a fourth of the
earth to kill by sword, famine and plague,
and by the wild beasts of the earth.

9 When he opened the fifth seal, I saw
under the altar the souls of those who had
been slain because of the word of God and
the testimony they had maintained. 10 They
called out in a loud voice, "How long, Sov-
ereign Lord, holy and true, until you judge
the inhabitants of the earth and avenge our
blood?" 11 Then each of them was given a
white robe, and they were told to wait a little
longer, until the full number of their fellow
servants, their brothers and sisters,[d] were
killed just as they had been.

12 I watched as he opened the sixth seal.
There was a great earthquake. The sun
turned black like sackcloth made of goat
hair, the whole moon turned blood red,
13 and the stars in the sky fell to earth, as figs
drop from a fig tree when shaken by a strong
wind. 14 The heavens receded like a scroll
being rolled up, and every mountain and is-
land was removed from its place.

15 Then the kings of the earth, the princes,
the generals, the rich, the mighty, and every-
one else, both slave and free, hid in caves and
among the rocks of the mountains. 16 They
called to the mountains and the rocks, "Fall
on us and hide us[e] from the face of him who
sits on the throne and from the wrath of the
Lamb! 17 For the great day of their[f] wrath has
come, and who can withstand it?"

144,000 Sealed

7 After this I saw four angels standing at
the four corners of the earth, holding
back the four winds of the earth to prevent
any wind from blowing on the land or on the
sea or on any tree. 2 Then I saw another angel
coming up from the east, having the seal of
the living God. He called out in a loud voice
to the four angels who had been given power
to harm the land and the sea: 3 "Do not harm
the land or the sea or the trees until we put a
seal on the foreheads of the servants of our
God." 4 Then I heard the number of those
who were sealed: 144,000 from all the tribes
of Israel.

5 From the tribe of Judah 12,000 were
sealed,
from the tribe of Reuben 12,000,
from the tribe of Gad 12,000,
6 from the tribe of Asher 12,000,
from the tribe of Naphtali 12,000,
from the tribe of Manasseh 12,000,

[a] 6 Or about 1 kilogram [b] 6 Greek *a denarius* [c] 6 Or about 3 kilograms [d] 11 The Greek word for *brothers and sisters* (*adelphoi*) refers here to believers, both men and women, as part of God's family; also in 12:10; 19:10. [e] 16 See Hosea 10:8. [f] 17 Some manuscripts *his*

7 from the tribe of Simeon 12,000,
from the tribe of Levi 12,000,
from the tribe of Issachar 12,000,
8 from the tribe of Zebulun 12,000,
from the tribe of Joseph 12,000,
from the tribe of Benjamin 12,000.

The Great Multitude in White Robes

9 After this I looked, and there before me
was a great multitude that no one could
count, from every nation, tribe, people and
language, standing before the throne and
before the Lamb. They were wearing white
robes and were holding palm branches in
their hands. 10 And they cried out in a loud
voice:

"Salvation belongs to our God,
who sits on the throne,
and to the Lamb."

11 All the angels were standing around the
throne and around the elders and the four
living creatures. They fell down on their fac-
es before the throne and worshiped God,
12 saying:

"Amen!
Praise and glory
and wisdom and thanks and honor
and power and strength
be to our God for ever and ever.
Amen!"

13 Then one of the elders asked me, "These
in white robes — who are they, and where
did they come from?"

14 I answered, "Sir, you know."

And he said, "These are they who have
come out of the great tribulation; they have
washed their robes and made them white in
the blood of the Lamb. 15 Therefore,

"they are before the throne of God
and serve him day and night in his
temple;
and he who sits on the throne
will shelter them with his
presence.
16 'Never again will they hunger;
never again will they thirst.
The sun will not beat down on them,'[a]
nor any scorching heat.
17 For the Lamb at the center of the throne
will be their shepherd;
'he will lead them to springs of living
water.'[a]
'And God will wipe away every tear
from their eyes.'[b]"

The Seventh Seal and the Golden Censer

8 When he opened the seventh seal, there
was silence in heaven for about half an
hour.

2 And I saw the seven angels who stand be-
fore God, and seven trumpets were given to
them.

3 Another angel, who had a golden cen-
ser, came and stood at the altar. He was giv-
en much incense to offer, with the prayers
of all God's people, on the golden altar in
front of the throne. 4 The smoke of the in-
cense, together with the prayers of God's
people, went up before God from the angel's
hand. 5 Then the angel took the censer, filled
it with fire from the altar, and hurled it on
the earth; and there came peals of thun-
der, rumblings, flashes of lightning and an
earthquake.

The Trumpets

6 Then the seven angels who had the seven
trumpets prepared to sound them.

7 The first angel sounded his trumpet, and
there came hail and fire mixed with blood,
and it was hurled down on the earth. A third
of the earth was burned up, a third of the
trees were burned up, and all the green grass
was burned up.

8 The second angel sounded his trumpet,
and something like a huge mountain, all
ablaze, was thrown into the sea. A third of
the sea turned into blood, 9 a third of the liv-
ing creatures in the sea died, and a third of
the ships were destroyed.

10 The third angel sounded his trumpet,
and a great star, blazing like a torch, fell
from the sky on a third of the rivers and on
the springs of water — 11 the name of the star
is Wormwood.[c] A third of the waters turned
bitter, and many people died from the waters
that had become bitter.

12 The fourth angel sounded his trumpet,
and a third of the sun was struck, a third of
the moon, and a third of the stars, so that
a third of them turned dark. A third of the
day was without light, and also a third of the
night.

[a] *16,17* Isaiah 49:10 [b] *17* Isaiah 25:8 [c] *11* Wormwood is a bitter substance.

13 As I watched, I heard an eagle that was flying in midair call out in a loud voice: "Woe! Woe! Woe to the inhabitants of the earth, because of the trumpet blasts about to be sounded by the other three angels!"

9 The fifth angel sounded his trumpet, and I saw a star that had fallen from the sky to the earth. The star was given the key to the shaft of the Abyss. 2 When he opened the Abyss, smoke rose from it like the smoke from a gigantic furnace. The sun and sky were darkened by the smoke from the Abyss. 3 And out of the smoke locusts came down on the earth and were given power like that of scorpions of the earth. 4 They were told not to harm the grass of the earth or any plant or tree, but only those people who did not have the seal of God on their foreheads. 5 They were not allowed to kill them but only to torture them for five months. And the agony they suffered was like that of the sting of a scorpion when it strikes. 6 During those days people will seek death but will not find it; they will long to die, but death will elude them.

7 The locusts looked like horses prepared for battle. On their heads they wore something like crowns of gold, and their faces resembled human faces. 8 Their hair was like women's hair, and their teeth were like lions' teeth. 9 They had breastplates like breastplates of iron, and the sound of their wings was like the thundering of many horses and chariots rushing into battle. 10 They had tails with stingers, like scorpions, and in their tails they had power to torment people for five months. 11 They had as king over them the angel of the Abyss, whose name in Hebrew is Abaddon and in Greek is Apollyon (that is, Destroyer).

12 The first woe is past; two other woes are yet to come.

13 The sixth angel sounded his trumpet, and I heard a voice coming from the four horns of the golden altar that is before God. 14 It said to the sixth angel who had the trumpet, "Release the four angels who are bound at the great river Euphrates." 15 And the four angels who had been kept ready for this very hour and day and month and year were released to kill a third of mankind. 16 The number of the mounted troops was twice ten thousand times ten thousand. I heard their number.

17 The horses and riders I saw in my vision looked like this: Their breastplates were fiery red, dark blue, and yellow as sulfur. The heads of the horses resembled the heads of lions, and out of their mouths came fire, smoke and sulfur. 18 A third of mankind was killed by the three plagues of fire, smoke and sulfur that came out of their mouths. 19 The power of the horses was in their mouths and in their tails; for their tails were like snakes, having heads with which they inflict injury.

20 The rest of mankind who were not killed by these plagues still did not repent of the work of their hands; they did not stop worshiping demons, and idols of gold, silver, bronze, stone and wood — idols that cannot see or hear or walk. 21 Nor did they repent of their murders, their magic arts, their sexual immorality or their thefts.

The Angel and the Little Scroll

10 Then I saw another mighty angel coming down from heaven. He was robed in a cloud, with a rainbow above his head; his face was like the sun, and his legs were like fiery pillars. 2 He was holding a little scroll, which lay open in his hand. He planted his right foot on the sea and his left foot on the land, 3 and he gave a loud shout like the roar of a lion. When he shouted, the voices of the seven thunders spoke. 4 And when the seven thunders spoke, I was about to write; but I heard a voice from heaven say, "Seal up what the seven thunders have said and do not write it down."

5 Then the angel I had seen standing on the sea and on the land raised his right hand to heaven. 6 And he swore by him who lives for ever and ever, who created the heavens and all that is in them, the earth and all that is in it, and the sea and all that is in it, and said, "There will be no more delay! 7 But in the days when the seventh angel is about to sound his trumpet, the mystery of God will be accomplished, just as he announced to his servants the prophets."

8 Then the voice that I had heard from heaven spoke to me once more: "Go, take the scroll that lies open in the hand of the angel who is standing on the sea and on the land."

9 So I went to the angel and asked him to give me the little scroll. He said to me, "Take it and eat it. It will turn your stomach sour, but 'in your mouth it will be as sweet as

honey.'[a]" 10 I took the little scroll from the angel's hand and ate it. It tasted as sweet as honey in my mouth, but when I had eaten it, my stomach turned sour. 11 Then I was told, "You must prophesy again about many peoples, nations, languages and kings."

The Two Witnesses

11 I was given a reed like a measuring rod and was told, "Go and measure the temple of God and the altar, with its worshipers. 2 But exclude the outer court; do not measure it, because it has been given to the Gentiles. They will trample on the holy city for 42 months. 3 And I will appoint my two witnesses, and they will prophesy for 1,260 days, clothed in sackcloth." 4 They are "the two olive trees" and the two lampstands, and "they stand before the Lord of the earth."[b] 5 If anyone tries to harm them, fire comes from their mouths and devours their enemies. This is how anyone who wants to harm them must die. 6 They have power to shut up the heavens so that it will not rain during the time they are prophesying; and they have power to turn the waters into blood and to strike the earth with every kind of plague as often as they want.

7 Now when they have finished their testimony, the beast that comes up from the Abyss will attack them, and overpower and kill them. 8 Their bodies will lie in the public square of the great city—which is figuratively called Sodom and Egypt—where also their Lord was crucified. 9 For three and a half days some from every people, tribe, language and nation will gaze on their bodies and refuse them burial. 10 The inhabitants of the earth will gloat over them and will celebrate by sending each other gifts, because these two prophets had tormented those who live on the earth.

11 But after the three and a half days the breath[c] of life from God entered them, and they stood on their feet, and terror struck those who saw them. 12 Then they heard a loud voice from heaven saying to them, "Come up here." And they went up to heaven in a cloud, while their enemies looked on.

13 At that very hour there was a severe earthquake and a tenth of the city collapsed. Seven thousand people were killed in the earthquake, and the survivors were terrified and gave glory to the God of heaven.

14 The second woe has passed; the third woe is coming soon.

The Seventh Trumpet

15 The seventh angel sounded his trumpet, and there were loud voices in heaven, which said:

"The kingdom of the world has become
the kingdom of our Lord and of his Messiah,
and he will reign for ever and ever."

16 And the twenty-four elders, who were seated on their thrones before God, fell on their faces and worshiped God, 17 saying:

"We give thanks to you, Lord God Almighty,
the One who is and who was,
because you have taken your great power
and have begun to reign.
18 The nations were angry,
and your wrath has come.
The time has come for judging the dead,
and for rewarding your servants the prophets
and your people who revere your name,
both great and small—
and for destroying those who destroy the earth."

19 Then God's temple in heaven was opened, and within his temple was seen the ark of his covenant. And there came flashes of lightning, rumblings, peals of thunder, an earthquake and a severe hailstorm.

The Woman and the Dragon

12 A great sign appeared in heaven: a woman clothed with the sun, with the moon under her feet and a crown of twelve stars on her head. 2 She was pregnant and cried out in pain as she was about to give birth. 3 Then another sign appeared in heaven: an enormous red dragon with seven heads and ten horns and seven crowns on its heads. 4 Its tail swept a third of the stars out of the sky and flung them to the earth. The dragon stood in front of the woman who was about to give birth, so that it might devour

[a] 9 Ezek. 3:3 [b] 4 See Zech. 4:3,11,14. [c] 11 Or *Spirit* (see Ezek. 37:5,14)

her child the moment he was born. 5 She gave
birth to a son, a male child, who "will rule
all the nations with an iron scepter."[a] And
her child was snatched up to God and to his
throne. 6 The woman fled into the wilderness
to a place prepared for her by God, where she
might be taken care of for 1,260 days.
7 Then war broke out in heaven. Michael
and his angels fought against the dragon,
and the dragon and his angels fought back.
8 But he was not strong enough, and they lost
their place in heaven. 9 The great dragon was
hurled down — that ancient serpent called
the devil, or Satan, who leads the whole
world astray. He was hurled to the earth, and
his angels with him.
10 Then I heard a loud voice in heaven say:

"Now have come the salvation and the
power
and the kingdom of our God,
and the authority of his Messiah.
For the accuser of our brothers and
sisters,
who accuses them before our God
day and night,
has been hurled down.
11 They triumphed over him
by the blood of the Lamb
and by the word of their testimony;
they did not love their lives so much
as to shrink from death.
12 Therefore rejoice, you heavens
and you who dwell in them!
But woe to the earth and the sea,
because the devil has gone down
to you!
He is filled with fury,
because he knows that his time
is short."

13 When the dragon saw that he had been
hurled to the earth, he pursued the woman
who had given birth to the male child. 14 The
woman was given the two wings of a great ea-
gle, so that she might fly to the place prepared
for her in the wilderness, where she would
be taken care of for a time, times and half a
time, out of the serpent's reach. 15 Then from
his mouth the serpent spewed water like a
river, to overtake the woman and sweep her
away with the torrent. 16 But the earth helped
the woman by opening its mouth and swal-
lowing the river that the dragon had spewed
out of his mouth. 17 Then the dragon was en-
raged at the woman and went off to wage war
against the rest of her offspring — those who
keep God's commands and hold fast their
testimony about Jesus.

The Beast out of the Sea

13 The dragon[b] stood on the shore of
the sea. And I saw a beast coming
out of the sea. It had ten horns and seven
heads, with ten crowns on its horns, and on
each head a blasphemous name. 2 The beast
I saw resembled a leopard, but had feet like
those of a bear and a mouth like that of a
lion. The dragon gave the beast his power
and his throne and great authority. 3 One of
the heads of the beast seemed to have had a
fatal wound, but the fatal wound had been
healed. The whole world was filled with
wonder and followed the beast. 4 People wor-
shiped the dragon because he had given au-
thority to the beast, and they also worshiped
the beast and asked, "Who is like the beast?
Who can wage war against it?"
5 The beast was given a mouth to utter
proud words and blasphemies and to exer-
cise its authority for forty-two months. 6 It
opened its mouth to blaspheme God, and
to slander his name and his dwelling place
and those who live in heaven. 7 It was given
power to wage war against God's holy peo-
ple and to conquer them. And it was given
authority over every tribe, people, language
and nation. 8 All inhabitants of the earth will
worship the beast — all whose names have
not been written in the Lamb's book of life,
the Lamb who was slain from the creation of
the world.[c]
9 Whoever has ears, let them hear.

10 "If anyone is to go into captivity,
into captivity they will go.
If anyone is to be killed[d] with the sword,
with the sword they will be killed."[e]

This calls for patient endurance and faith-
fulness on the part of God's people.

The Beast out of the Earth

11 Then I saw a second beast, coming out
of the earth. It had two horns like a lamb,

[a] 5 Psalm 2:9 [b] 1 Some manuscripts *And I* [c] 8 Or *written from the creation of the world in the book of life belonging to the Lamb who was slain* [d] 10 Some manuscripts *anyone kills* [e] 10 Jer. 15:2

but it spoke like a dragon. 12It exercised all
the authority of the first beast on its behalf,
and made the earth and its inhabitants wor-
ship the first beast, whose fatal wound had
been healed. 13And it performed great signs,
even causing fire to come down from heaven
to the earth in full view of the people. 14Be-
cause of the signs it was given power to per-
form on behalf of the first beast, it deceived
the inhabitants of the earth. It ordered them
to set up an image in honor of the beast who
was wounded by the sword and yet lived.
15The second beast was given power to give
breath to the image of the first beast, so that
the image could speak and cause all who re-
fused to worship the image to be killed. 16It
also forced all people, great and small, rich
and poor, free and slave, to receive a mark on
their right hands or on their foreheads, 17so
that they could not buy or sell unless they
had the mark, which is the name of the beast
or the number of its name.

18This calls for wisdom. Let the person
who has insight calculate the number of the
beast, for it is the number of a man.[a] That
number is 666.

The Lamb and the 144,000

14 Then I looked, and there before me
was the Lamb, standing on Mount
Zion, and with him 144,000 who had his
name and his Father's name written on their
foreheads. 2And I heard a sound from heav-
en like the roar of rushing waters and like
a loud peal of thunder. The sound I heard
was like that of harpists playing their harps.
3And they sang a new song before the throne
and before the four living creatures and the
elders. No one could learn the song except
the 144,000 who had been redeemed from
the earth. 4These are those who did not
defile themselves with women, for they re-
mained virgins. They follow the Lamb wher-
ever he goes. They were purchased from
among mankind and offered as firstfruits
to God and the Lamb. 5No lie was found in
their mouths; they are blameless.

The Three Angels

6Then I saw another angel flying in mid-
air, and he had the eternal gospel to pro-
claim to those who live on the earth — to ev-
ery nation, tribe, language and people. 7He
said in a loud voice, "Fear God and give him
glory, because the hour of his judgment has
come. Worship him who made the heavens,
the earth, the sea and the springs of water."

8A second angel followed and said, "'Fall-
en! Fallen is Babylon the Great,'[b] which
made all the nations drink the maddening
wine of her adulteries."

9A third angel followed them and said in
a loud voice: "If anyone worships the beast
and its image and receives its mark on their
forehead or on their hand, 10they, too, will
drink the wine of God's fury, which has
been poured full strength into the cup of his
wrath. They will be tormented with burning
sulfur in the presence of the holy angels and
of the Lamb. 11And the smoke of their tor-
ment will rise for ever and ever. There will
be no rest day or night for those who worship
the beast and its image, or for anyone who
receives the mark of its name." 12This calls
for patient endurance on the part of the peo-
ple of God who keep his commands and re-
main faithful to Jesus.

13Then I heard a voice from heaven say,
"Write this: Blessed are the dead who die in
the Lord from now on."

"Yes," says the Spirit, "they will rest from
their labor, for their deeds will follow them."

Harvesting the Earth and Trampling the Winepress

14I looked, and there before me was a
white cloud, and seated on the cloud was
one like a son of man[c] with a crown of gold
on his head and a sharp sickle in his hand.
15Then another angel came out of the temple
and called in a loud voice to him who was sit-
ting on the cloud, "Take your sickle and reap,
because the time to reap has come, for the
harvest of the earth is ripe." 16So he who was
seated on the cloud swung his sickle over the
earth, and the earth was harvested.

17Another angel came out of the tem-
ple in heaven, and he too had a sharp sick-
le. 18Still another angel, who had charge of
the fire, came from the altar and called in a
loud voice to him who had the sharp sickle,
"Take your sharp sickle and gather the clus-
ters of grapes from the earth's vine, because
its grapes are ripe." 19The angel swung his

[a] *18* Or *is humanity's number* [b] *8* Isaiah 21:9 [c] *14* See Daniel 7:13.

sickle on the earth, gathered its grapes and
threw them into the great winepress of God's
wrath. 20 They were trampled in the wine-
press outside the city, and blood flowed out
of the press, rising as high as the horses' bri-
dles for a distance of 1,600 stadia.[a]

Seven Angels With Seven Plagues

15 I saw in heaven another great and
marvelous sign: seven angels with
the seven last plagues — last, because with
them God's wrath is completed. 2 And I saw
what looked like a sea of glass glowing with
fire and, standing beside the sea, those who
had been victorious over the beast and its
image and over the number of its name.
They held harps given them by God 3 and
sang the song of God's servant Moses and of
the Lamb:

> "Great and marvelous are your deeds,
> Lord God Almighty.
> Just and true are your ways,
> King of the nations.[b]
> 4 Who will not fear you, Lord,
> and bring glory to your name?
> For you alone are holy.
> All nations will come
> and worship before you,
> for your righteous acts have been
> revealed."[c]

5 After this I looked, and I saw in heaven
the temple — that is, the tabernacle of the
covenant law — and it was opened. 6 Out
of the temple came the seven angels with
the seven plagues. They were dressed in
clean, shining linen and wore golden sash-
es around their chests. 7 Then one of the four
living creatures gave to the seven angels sev-
en golden bowls filled with the wrath of God,
who lives for ever and ever. 8 And the temple
was filled with smoke from the glory of God
and from his power, and no one could enter
the temple until the seven plagues of the sev-
en angels were completed.

The Seven Bowls of God's Wrath

16 Then I heard a loud voice from the
temple saying to the seven angels,
"Go, pour out the seven bowls of God's wrath
on the earth."
2 The first angel went and poured out his
bowl on the land, and ugly, festering sores
broke out on the people who had the mark of
the beast and worshiped its image.
3 The second angel poured out his bowl on
the sea, and it turned into blood like that of
a dead person, and every living thing in the
sea died.
4 The third angel poured out his bowl on
the rivers and springs of water, and they
became blood. 5 Then I heard the angel in
charge of the waters say:

> "You are just in these judgments,
> O Holy One,
> you who are and who were;
> 6 for they have shed the blood of your holy
> people and your prophets,
> and you have given them blood to
> drink as they deserve."

7 And I heard the altar respond:

> "Yes, Lord God Almighty,
> true and just are your judgments."

8 The fourth angel poured out his bowl on
the sun, and the sun was allowed to scorch
people with fire. 9 They were seared by the
intense heat and they cursed the name of
God, who had control over these plagues,
but they refused to repent and glorify him.
10 The fifth angel poured out his bowl on
the throne of the beast, and its kingdom
was plunged into darkness. People gnawed
their tongues in agony 11 and cursed the God
of heaven because of their pains and their
sores, but they refused to repent of what they
had done.
12 The sixth angel poured out his bowl on
the great river Euphrates, and its water was
dried up to prepare the way for the kings
from the East. 13 Then I saw three impure
spirits that looked like frogs; they came out
of the mouth of the dragon, out of the mouth
of the beast and out of the mouth of the false
prophet. 14 They are demonic spirits that per-
form signs, and they go out to the kings of the
whole world, to gather them for the battle on
the great day of God Almighty.

> 15 "Look, I come like a thief! Blessed is
> the one who stays awake and remains
> clothed, so as not to go naked and be
> shamefully exposed."

[a] *20* That is, about 180 miles or about 300 kilometers [b] *3* Some manuscripts *ages* [c] *3,4* Phrases in this song are drawn from Psalm 111:2,3; Deut. 32:4; Jer. 10:7; Psalms 86:9; 98:2.

16 Then they gathered the kings together to the place that in Hebrew is called Armageddon.

17 The seventh angel poured out his bowl into the air, and out of the temple came a loud voice from the throne, saying, "It is done!" 18 Then there came flashes of lightning, rumblings, peals of thunder and a severe earthquake. No earthquake like it has ever occurred since mankind has been on earth, so tremendous was the quake. 19 The great city split into three parts, and the cities of the nations collapsed. God remembered Babylon the Great and gave her the cup filled with the wine of the fury of his wrath. 20 Every island fled away and the mountains could not be found. 21 From the sky huge hailstones, each weighing about a hundred pounds,[a] fell on people. And they cursed God on account of the plague of hail, because the plague was so terrible.

Babylon, the Prostitute on the Beast

17 One of the seven angels who had the seven bowls came and said to me, "Come, I will show you the punishment of the great prostitute, who sits by many waters. 2 With her the kings of the earth committed adultery, and the inhabitants of the earth were intoxicated with the wine of her adulteries."

3 Then the angel carried me away in the Spirit into a wilderness. There I saw a woman sitting on a scarlet beast that was covered with blasphemous names and had seven heads and ten horns. 4 The woman was dressed in purple and scarlet, and was glittering with gold, precious stones and pearls. She held a golden cup in her hand, filled with abominable things and the filth of her adulteries. 5 The name written on her forehead was a mystery:

BABYLON THE GREAT
THE MOTHER OF PROSTITUTES
AND OF THE ABOMINATIONS
OF THE EARTH.

6 I saw that the woman was drunk with the blood of God's holy people, the blood of those who bore testimony to Jesus.

When I saw her, I was greatly astonished. 7 Then the angel said to me: "Why are you astonished? I will explain to you the mystery of the woman and of the beast she rides, which has the seven heads and ten horns. 8 The beast, which you saw, once was, now is not, and yet will come up out of the Abyss and go to its destruction. The inhabitants of the earth whose names have not been written in the book of life from the creation of the world will be astonished when they see the beast, because it once was, now is not, and yet will come.

9 "This calls for a mind with wisdom. The seven heads are seven hills on which the woman sits. 10 They are also seven kings. Five have fallen, one is, the other has not yet come; but when he does come, he must remain for only a little while. 11 The beast who once was, and now is not, is an eighth king. He belongs to the seven and is going to his destruction.

12 "The ten horns you saw are ten kings who have not yet received a kingdom, but who for one hour will receive authority as kings along with the beast. 13 They have one purpose and will give their power and authority to the beast. 14 They will wage war against the Lamb, but the Lamb will triumph over them because he is Lord of lords and King of kings — and with him will be his called, chosen and faithful followers."

15 Then the angel said to me, "The waters you saw, where the prostitute sits, are peoples, multitudes, nations and languages. 16 The beast and the ten horns you saw will hate the prostitute. They will bring her to ruin and leave her naked; they will eat her flesh and burn her with fire. 17 For God has put it into their hearts to accomplish his purpose by agreeing to hand over to the beast their royal authority, until God's words are fulfilled. 18 The woman you saw is the great city that rules over the kings of the earth."

Lament Over Fallen Babylon

18 After this I saw another angel coming down from heaven. He had great authority, and the earth was illuminated by his splendor. 2 With a mighty voice he shouted:

"'Fallen! Fallen is Babylon the Great!'[b]
She has become a dwelling for demons
and a haunt for every impure spirit,
a haunt for every unclean bird,

[a] *21* Or about 45 kilograms [b] *2* Isaiah 21:9

a haunt for every unclean and
detestable animal.
[3]For all the nations have drunk
the maddening wine of her adulteries.
The kings of the earth committed
adultery with her,
and the merchants of the earth grew
rich from her excessive luxuries."

Warning to Escape Babylon's Judgment

[4]Then I heard another voice from heaven
say:

"'Come out of her, my people,'[a]
so that you will not share in her sins,
so that you will not receive any of her
plagues;
[5]for her sins are piled up to heaven,
and God has remembered
her crimes.
[6]Give back to her as she has given;
pay her back double for what she has
done.
Pour her a double portion from her
own cup.
[7]Give her as much torment and grief
as the glory and luxury she gave
herself.
In her heart she boasts,
'I sit enthroned as queen.
I am not a widow;[b]
I will never mourn.'
[8]Therefore in one day her plagues will
overtake her:
death, mourning and famine.
She will be consumed by fire,
for mighty is the Lord God who
judges her.

Threefold Woe Over Babylon's Fall

[9]"When the kings of the earth who com-
mitted adultery with her and shared her lux-
ury see the smoke of her burning, they will
weep and mourn over her. [10]Terrified at her
torment, they will stand far off and cry:

"'Woe! Woe to you, great city,
you mighty city of Babylon!
In one hour your doom has come!'

[11]"The merchants of the earth will weep
and mourn over her because no one buys
their cargoes anymore — [12]cargoes of gold,
silver, precious stones and pearls; fine linen,
purple, silk and scarlet cloth; every sort of
citron wood, and articles of every kind made
of ivory, costly wood, bronze, iron and mar-
ble; [13]cargoes of cinnamon and spice, of in-
cense, myrrh and frankincense, of wine and
olive oil, of fine flour and wheat; cattle and
sheep; horses and carriages; and human be-
ings sold as slaves.

[14]"They will say, 'The fruit you longed for
is gone from you. All your luxury and splen-
dor have vanished, never to be recovered.'
[15]The merchants who sold these things and
gained their wealth from her will stand far
off, terrified at her torment. They will weep
and mourn [16]and cry out:

"'Woe! Woe to you, great city,
dressed in fine linen, purple
and scarlet,
and glittering with gold, precious
stones and pearls!
[17]In one hour such great wealth has been
brought to ruin!'

"Every sea captain, and all who travel by
ship, the sailors, and all who earn their liv-
ing from the sea, will stand far off. [18]When
they see the smoke of her burning, they will
exclaim, 'Was there ever a city like this great
city?' [19]They will throw dust on their heads,
and with weeping and mourning cry out:

"'Woe! Woe to you, great city,
where all who had ships on
the sea
became rich through her wealth!
In one hour she has been brought
to ruin!'

[20]"Rejoice over her, you heavens!
Rejoice, you people of God!
Rejoice, apostles and prophets!
For God has judged her
with the judgment she imposed
on you."

The Finality of Babylon's Doom

[21]Then a mighty angel picked up a boul-
der the size of a large millstone and threw it
into the sea, and said:

"With such violence
the great city of Babylon will be
thrown down,
never to be found again.

[a] 4 Jer. 51:45 [b] 7 See Isaiah 47:7,8.

[22] The music of harpists and musicians,
pipers and trumpeters,
will never be heard in you again.
No worker of any trade
will ever be found in you again.
The sound of a millstone
will never be heard in you again.
[23] The light of a lamp
will never shine in you again.
The voice of bridegroom and bride
will never be heard in you again.
Your merchants were the world's
important people.
By your magic spell all the nations
were led astray.
[24] In her was found the blood of prophets
and of God's holy people,
of all who have been slaughtered on
the earth."

Threefold Hallelujah Over Babylon's Fall

19 After this I heard what sounded like
the roar of a great multitude in heav-
en shouting:

"Hallelujah!
Salvation and glory and power belong
to our God,
2 for true and just are his judgments.
He has condemned the great
prostitute
who corrupted the earth by her
adulteries.
He has avenged on her the blood of his
servants."

[3] And again they shouted:

"Hallelujah!
The smoke from her goes up for ever
and ever."

[4] The twenty-four elders and the four liv-
ing creatures fell down and worshiped God,
who was seated on the throne. And they
cried:

"Amen, Hallelujah!"

[5] Then a voice came from the throne, say-
ing:

"Praise our God,
all you his servants,
you who fear him,
both great and small!"

[6] Then I heard what sounded like a great
multitude, like the roar of rushing waters
and like loud peals of thunder, shouting:

"Hallelujah!
For our Lord God Almighty reigns.
[7] Let us rejoice and be glad
and give him glory!
For the wedding of the Lamb has come,
and his bride has made herself
ready.
[8] Fine linen, bright and clean,
was given her to wear."
(Fine linen stands for the righteous acts of
God's holy people.)

[9] Then the angel said to me, "Write this:
Blessed are those who are invited to the
wedding supper of the Lamb!" And he add-
ed, "These are the true words of God."
[10] At this I fell at his feet to worship him.
But he said to me, "Don't do that! I am a fel-
low servant with you and with your broth-
ers and sisters who hold to the testimony
of Jesus. Worship God! For it is the Spirit of
prophecy who bears testimony to Jesus."

The Heavenly Warrior Defeats the Beast

[11] I saw heaven standing open and there
before me was a white horse, whose rid-
er is called Faithful and True. With justice
he judges and wages war. [12] His eyes are
like blazing fire, and on his head are many
crowns. He has a name written on him that
no one knows but he himself. [13] He is dressed
in a robe dipped in blood, and his name is
the Word of God. [14] The armies of heaven
were following him, riding on white horses
and dressed in fine linen, white and clean.
[15] Coming out of his mouth is a sharp sword
with which to strike down the nations. "He
will rule them with an iron scepter."[a] He
treads the winepress of the fury of the wrath
of God Almighty. [16] On his robe and on his
thigh he has this name written:

KING OF KINGS AND
LORD OF LORDS.

[17] And I saw an angel standing in the sun,
who cried in a loud voice to all the birds fly-
ing in midair, "Come, gather together for the
great supper of God, [18] so that you may eat
the flesh of kings, generals, and the mighty,

[a] *15* Psalm 2:9

of horses and their riders, and the flesh of all people, free and slave, great and small."

[19]Then I saw the beast and the kings of the earth and their armies gathered together to wage war against the rider on the horse and his army. [20]But the beast was captured, and with it the false prophet who had performed the signs on its behalf. With these signs he had deluded those who had received the mark of the beast and worshiped its image. The two of them were thrown alive into the fiery lake of burning sulfur. [21]The rest were killed with the sword coming out of the mouth of the rider on the horse, and all the birds gorged themselves on their flesh.

The Thousand Years

20 And I saw an angel coming down out of heaven, having the key to the Abyss and holding in his hand a great chain. [2]He seized the dragon, that ancient serpent, who is the devil, or Satan, and bound him for a thousand years. [3]He threw him into the Abyss, and locked and sealed it over him, to keep him from deceiving the nations anymore until the thousand years were ended. After that, he must be set free for a short time.

[4]I saw thrones on which were seated those who had been given authority to judge. And I saw the souls of those who had been beheaded because of their testimony about Jesus and because of the word of God. They[a] had not worshiped the beast or its image and had not received its mark on their foreheads or their hands. They came to life and reigned with Christ a thousand years. [5](The rest of the dead did not come to life until the thousand years were ended.) This is the first resurrection. [6]Blessed and holy are those who share in the first resurrection. The second death has no power over them, but they will be priests of God and of Christ and will reign with him for a thousand years.

The Judgment of Satan

[7]When the thousand years are over, Satan will be released from his prison [8]and will go out to deceive the nations in the four corners of the earth — Gog and Magog — and to gather them for battle. In number they are like the sand on the seashore. [9]They marched across the breadth of the earth and surrounded the camp of God's people, the city he loves. But fire came down from heaven and devoured them. [10]And the devil, who deceived them, was thrown into the lake of burning sulfur, where the beast and the false prophet had been thrown. They will be tormented day and night for ever and ever.

The Judgment of the Dead

[11]Then I saw a great white throne and him who was seated on it. The earth and the heavens fled from his presence, and there was no place for them. [12]And I saw the dead, great and small, standing before the throne, and books were opened. Another book was opened, which is the book of life. The dead were judged according to what they had done as recorded in the books. [13]The sea gave up the dead that were in it, and death and Hades gave up the dead that were in them, and each person was judged according to what they had done. [14]Then death and Hades were thrown into the lake of fire. The lake of fire is the second death. [15]Anyone whose name was not found written in the book of life was thrown into the lake of fire.

A New Heaven and a New Earth

21 Then I saw "a new heaven and a new earth,"[b] for the first heaven and the first earth had passed away, and there was no longer any sea. [2]I saw the Holy City, the new Jerusalem, coming down out of heaven from God, prepared as a bride beautifully dressed for her husband. [3]And I heard a loud voice from the throne saying, "Look! God's dwelling place is now among the people, and he will dwell with them. They will be his people, and God himself will be with them and be their God. [4]'He will wipe every tear from their eyes. There will be no more death'[c] or mourning or crying or pain, for the old order of things has passed away."

[5]He who was seated on the throne said, "I am making everything new!" Then he said, "Write this down, for these words are trustworthy and true."

[6]He said to me: "It is done. I am the Alpha and the Omega, the Beginning and the End. To the thirsty I will give water without cost from the spring of the water of life. [7]Those

[a] *4* Or *God; I also saw those who* [b] *1* Isaiah 65:17 [c] *4* Isaiah 25:8

CORNERSTONE

Reuben Morgan, Edward Mote, Jonas Myrin, Eric Liljero

My hope is built on nothing less
Than Jesus' blood and righteousness
I dare not trust the sweetest frame
But wholly trust in Jesus' name

Christ alone, Cornerstone
Weak made strong in the Savior's love
Through the storm
He is Lord
Lord of all

When darkness seems to hide his face
I rest on his unchanging grace
In every high and stormy gale
My anchor holds within the veil
My anchor holds within the veil

Christ alone, Cornerstone
Weak made strong in the Savior's love
Through the storm
He is Lord
Lord of all

He is Lord
Lord of all

When he shall come with trumpet sound
Oh may I then in him be found
Dressed in his righteousness alone
Faultless, stand before the throne

THE INSPIRATION

Jesus said to them, "Have you never read in the Scriptures: 'The stone the builders rejected has become the cornerstone; the Lord has done this, and it is marvelous in our eyes'? Therefore I tell you that the kingdom of God will be taken away from you and given to a people who will produce its fruit." — Matthew 21:42 – 43

Read also: Psalm 118:21 – 23; Isaiah 28:16; 1 Corinthians 10:1 – 4

BEHIND THE SONG

One morning in 1853, a British cabinetmaker was walking to his shop and was inspired to compose a hymn. By the time Edward Mote arrived at his workplace, the chorus to "The Solid Rock" was complete. By the end of the day, he had finished several additional verses to this incredible song. The entire hymn was completed shortly thereafter.

Mote grew up as the child of pub owners. Though his parents gave him no spiritual guidance or even a basic introduction to the gospel, he came to faith at the age of 18. He became a master cabinetmaker, and many years later, at the age of 55, he became a pastor and served until shortly before his death at the age of 77. "The Solid Rock" remains his best-known song and is considered one of the great gospel hymns in the church.

A recent shooting in Scandinavia rocked the members of the Hillsong Church community. Reuben Morgan was visiting and quickly began to minister to the congregation through song. "I got together with Jonas Myrin," Morgan explains, "and Eric Lijero, who is our worship pastor from Stockholm, and we wrote this song." They referenced the confident tone and determined faithfulness of "The Solid Rock" and wrote their song with its lyrics. "It's a declaration that Jesus Christ is the only foundation we can build our lives on, no matter what happens."

"Writing worship songs is really pastoral work,' Morgan adds. "In a situation like that you want to be able to help people sing through what's going on; to work through it in the context of faith. Hymns through the centuries have been a way that the church has done that."

Selah

It's easy to build our lives and our faith on things other than the solid rock of Christ. When you face billowing winds, shaky ground or rising waters, is your first thought to cling to Christ, or to protect yourself?

Read the passages above and carefully consider the strength of the language that refers to the steadfastness of Christ. How have you experienced Jesus as the solid foundation of your life?

who are victorious will inherit all this, and I will be their God and they will be my children. [8]But the cowardly, the unbelieving, the vile, the murderers, the sexually immoral, those who practice magic arts, the idolaters and all liars — they will be consigned to the fiery lake of burning sulfur. This is the second death."

The New Jerusalem, the Bride of the Lamb

[9]One of the seven angels who had the seven bowls full of the seven last plagues came and said to me, "Come, I will show you the bride, the wife of the Lamb." [10]And he carried me away in the Spirit to a mountain great and high, and showed me the Holy City, Jerusalem, coming down out of heaven from God. [11]It shone with the glory of God, and its brilliance was like that of a very precious jewel, like a jasper, clear as crystal. [12]It had a great, high wall with twelve gates, and with twelve angels at the gates. On the gates were written the names of the twelve tribes of Israel. [13]There were three gates on the east, three on the north, three on the south and three on the west. [14]The wall of the city had twelve foundations, and on them were the names of the twelve apostles of the Lamb.

[15]The angel who talked with me had a measuring rod of gold to measure the city, its gates and its walls. [16]The city was laid out like a square, as long as it was wide. He measured the city with the rod and found it to be 12,000 stadia[a] in length, and as wide and high as it is long. [17]The angel measured the wall using human measurement, and it was 144 cubits[b] thick.[c] [18]The wall was made of jasper, and the city of pure gold, as pure as glass. [19]The foundations of the city walls were decorated with every kind of precious stone. The first foundation was jasper, the second sapphire, the third agate, the fourth emerald, [20]the fifth onyx, the sixth ruby, the seventh chrysolite, the eighth beryl, the ninth topaz, the tenth turquoise, the eleventh jacinth, and the twelfth amethyst.[d] [21]The twelve gates were twelve pearls, each gate made of a single pearl. The great street of the city was of gold, as pure as transparent glass.

[22]I did not see a temple in the city, because the Lord God Almighty and the Lamb are its temple. [23]The city does not need the sun or the moon to shine on it, for the glory of God gives it light, and the Lamb is its lamp. [24]The nations will walk by its light, and the kings of the earth will bring their splendor into it. [25]On no day will its gates ever be shut, for there will be no night there. [26]The glory and honor of the nations will be brought into it. [27]Nothing impure will ever enter it, nor will anyone who does what is shameful or deceitful, but only those whose names are written in the Lamb's book of life.

Eden Restored

22 Then the angel showed me the river of the water of life, as clear as crystal, flowing from the throne of God and of the Lamb [2]down the middle of the great street of the city. On each side of the river stood the tree of life, bearing twelve crops of fruit, yielding its fruit every month. And the leaves of the tree are for the healing of the nations. [3]No longer will there be any curse. The throne of God and of the Lamb will be in the city, and his servants will serve him. [4]They will see his face, and his name will be on their foreheads. [5]There will be no more night. They will not need the light of a lamp or the light of the sun, for the Lord God will give them light. And they will reign for ever and ever.

John and the Angel

[6]The angel said to me, "These words are trustworthy and true. The Lord, the God who inspires the prophets, sent his angel to show his servants the things that must soon take place."

[7]"Look, I am coming soon! Blessed is the one who keeps the words of the prophecy written in this scroll."

[8]I, John, am the one who heard and saw these things. And when I had heard and seen them, I fell down to worship at the feet of the angel who had been showing them to me. [9]But he said to me, "Don't do that! I am a fellow servant with you and with your fellow prophets and with all who keep the words of this scroll. Worship God!"

[a] *16* That is, about 1,400 miles or about 2,200 kilometers [b] *17* That is, about 200 feet or about 65 meters [c] *17* Or *high* [d] *20* The precise identification of some of these precious stones is uncertain.

10 Then he told me, "Do not seal up the
words of the prophecy of this scroll, because
the time is near. 11 Let the one who does
wrong continue to do wrong; let the vile per-
son continue to be vile; let the one who does
right continue to do right; and let the holy
person continue to be holy."

Epilogue: Invitation and Warning

12 "Look, I am coming soon! My reward is
with me, and I will give to each person ac-
cording to what they have done. 13 I am the
Alpha and the Omega, the First and the Last,
the Beginning and the End.

14 "Blessed are those who wash their robes,
that they may have the right to the tree of life
and may go through the gates into the city.
15 Outside are the dogs, those who practice
magic arts, the sexually immoral, the mur-
derers, the idolaters and everyone who loves
and practices falsehood.

16 "I, Jesus, have sent my angel to give
you[a] this testimony for the churches. I am
the Root and the Offspring of David, and the
bright Morning Star."

17 The Spirit and the bride say, "Come!"
And let the one who hears say, "Come!" Let
the one who is thirsty come; and let the one
who wishes take the free gift of the water of
life.

18 I warn everyone who hears the words of
the prophecy of this scroll: If anyone adds
anything to them, God will add to that per-
son the plagues described in this scroll.
19 And if anyone takes words away from this
scroll of prophecy, God will take away from
that person any share in the tree of life and
in the Holy City, which are described in this
scroll.

20 He who testifies to these things says,
"Yes, I am coming soon."

Amen. Come, Lord Jesus.

21 The grace of the Lord Jesus be with
God's people. Amen.

[a] *16* The Greek is plural.

TABLE OF WEIGHTS AND MEASURES

	Biblical Unit	Approximate American Equivalent	Approximate Metric Equivalent
WEIGHTS	talent (60 minas)	75 pounds	34 kilograms
	mina (50 shekels)	1 1/4 pounds	560 grams
	shekel (2 bekas)	2/5 ounce	11.5 grams
	pim (2/3 shekel)	1/4 ounce	7.8 grams
	beka (10 gerahs)	1/5 ounce	5.7 grams
	gerah	1/50 ounce	0.6 gram
	daric	1/3 ounce	8.4 grams
LENGTH	cubit	18 inches	45 centimeters
	span	9 inches	23 centimeters
	handbreadth	3 inches	7.5 centimeters
	stadion (pl. stadia)	600 feet	183 meters
CAPACITY			
Dry Measure	cor [homer] (10 ephahs)	6 bushels	220 liters
	lethek (5 ephahs)	3 bushels	110 liters
	ephah (10 omers)	3/5 bushel	22 liters
	seah (1/3 ephah)	7 quarts	7.5 liters
	omer (1/10 ephah)	2 quarts	2 liters
	cab (1/18 ephah)	1 quart	1 liter
Liquid Measure	bath (1 ephah)	6 gallons	22 liters
	hin (1/6 bath)	1 gallon	3.8 liters
	log (1/72 bath)	1/3 quart	0.3 liter

The figures of the table are calculated on the basis of a shekel equaling 11.5 grams, a cubit equaling 18 inches and an ephah equaling 22 liters. The quart referred to is either a dry quart (slightly larger than a liter) or a liquid quart (slightly smaller than a liter), whichever is applicable. The ton referred to in the footnotes is the American ton of 2,000 pounds. These weights are calculated relative to the particular commodity involved. Accordingly, the same measure of capacity in the text may be converted into different weights in the footnotes.

This table is based upon the best available information, but it is not intended to be mathematically precise; like the measurement equivalents in the footnotes, it merely gives approximate amounts and distances. Weights and measures differed somewhat at various times and places in the ancient world. There is uncertainty particularly about the ephah and the bath; further discoveries may shed more light on these units of capacity.

SONG AS WORSHIP

by John J. Thompson

What Is Worship?

As is the case with so much of the English language, the word *worship* has been used to describe so many different things that it has nearly lost its crucial meaning. It is used as a noun, a verb and — in the case of an entire genre of music — an adjective. It can be used to speak of a particular time during a church service during which people sing. It can be used as a description of sacred music that is something other than praise. Then again it can be used to describe the entirety of a religious gathering (a worship service) or even a lifestyle. But the truth is that Biblical worship is a sweeping concept that includes the mental, physical, spiritual and emotional response of believers to the one true God based on his calling and his commands. It involves speaking and singing, to be sure, but also learning, serving and otherwise obeying. While the nuances of the Word may be challenging to comprehend, worship is clearly at the heart of the Christian life. Applying the Word properly and in a Biblically accurate way should be of paramount importance to all believers.

Behind the Word: Worship

Worship is essentially a modernization of the old English verb *worthscipe*, which literally meant *worthiness* or *worth-ship*. To *worthscipe*, or *worship*, something was to ascribe worth to it with words and or actions. That seems fairly straightforward, and it is, but the word also is used as the English translation of several different Hebrew and Greek words that are far more specific.

The main word translated from the Hebrew as *worship* in the Old Testament is *shachah*, which means to bow, to lower oneself, to fall face down, to stoop or to beseech another in a way that demonstrates complete submission and humility. In the New Testament the most common Greek word translated as worship is *proskyneo*, which means to kiss, or to "kiss toward." Together these two words account for over 80 percent of the Biblical references to what we, in English, know as worship.

To bow down. To kiss toward.

While we can certainly relate to the idea that one would only bow in front of, or "kiss toward," something of supreme value or importance, we know that throughout history these words have been applied to things other than God. We can also see that our modern understanding of the word as a type of music being sung during a church service is not completely Biblical. While there is much to be said of Christian music designed to help believers "kiss toward" Jesus, there is much more to true worship than music. Interestingly, Matt Redman's "The Heart of Worship" — a song that did much to propel the modern worship movement of the 1990s and remains one of the most frequently sung songs in churches today — is about precisely this idea.

When the music fades
All is stripped away
And I simply come
Longing just to bring
Something that's of worth
That will bless Your heart

I'll bring You more than a song
For a song in itself
Is not what You have required
You search much deeper within
Through the way things appear
You're looking into my heart

Other Greek words translated as *worship* in the New Testament include *sebomai*, which means "to reverence" (see Matthew 15:9; Mark 7:7; Acts 16:14) and *latreuo*, which means "to render specific acts of service or sacrifice in honor of another" (see Romans 1:25; Acts 24:14). The word *homologia* is used in 1 Timothy 6:12 – 13 and 2 Corinthians 9:12 – 13 to describe believers professing their faith in God, proclaiming the truth about God and to thank him for his many blessings. The word *thusia* refers to offerings or sacrifices made within the context of worship. In Hebrews Paul refers to the offerings taken up by Christians for those in need as *leitourgia* and refers to Jesus and Angels as *leitourgos* (servants) (see Hebrews 1:14; 8:1 – 2). This word's English derivative, *liturgy*, refers to the organization of a worship service, including recited prayers, readings and rites. Interestingly, while singing and making music is frequently referred to throughout both the old and new testaments as aspects of worship, it is clear that a Biblical understanding of the true, God-designed nature of worship is much more expansive than singing in church — or even attending church.

A Quick History of Worship Music

God's people have been creating music in his honor since the very beginning. For many, singing and playing an instrument can provide an emotional outlet that speaking cannot. It can be a physical representation of the joy, heartache, and wonder a worshipper is feeling. The Old Testament prophets were often skilled musicians. The earliest forms of worship included music. The book of Psalms is essentially an ancient worship songbook. Detailed lists of instruments and instructions to play loudly, joyously and with great skill can be found throughout the Bible. In the New Testament we read of angels singing upon the birth of Christ (see Luke 2:13 – 14), Paul and Silas singing hymns in a prison cell (see Acts 16:25) and Jesus and his disciples singing a hymn at the last supper (see Matthew 26:30). Scholars believe that several of Paul's epistles quote Christian songs of the day (see Ephesians 5:14). No doubt the earliest forms of Christian worship included stylistic similarities to the Jewish music of the temple, but as the Gospel spread throughout the non-Jewish world the flavor and use of music certainly changed with it.

Musical References Throughout the Bible

Exodus 15:21
Judges 5:3
2 Samuel 6:5
2 Samuel 6:13 – 23
1 Chronicles 15:16
1 Chronicles 16:8 – 9
1 Chronicles 16:23 – 24
2 Chronicles 20:19 – 23
2 Chronicles 29:25 – 28
Psalm 4:1
Psalm 5:1
Psalm 30:11
Psalm 33:1 – 3
Psalm 59:16
Psalm 66:4
Psalm 71:23
Psalm 95:1 – 2
Psalm 100:1 – 4
Psalm 138:1
Psalm 149:1 – 5
Psalm 150:1 – 6
Isaiah 35:10
Isaiah 44:23
Isaiah 51:11
Jeremiah 31:3 – 5
Jeremiah 31:13
Amos 5:23 – 24
Amos 6:5
Matthew 11:16 – 17
Matthew 26:27 – 30
Luke 15:25
John 4:23 – 24
Acts 16:25 – 26
Romans 15:7 – 11
Ephesians 5:18 – 20
Colossians 3:16
1 Corinthians 14:15
1 Corinthians 14:26
James 5:13
Hebrews 2:12 (Psalm 22:22)
Revelation 5:9

Evidence suggests that passionate disagreements about the propriety of various musical styles, instruments used and even melodic and harmonic boundaries have plagued the Christian community since long before anyone plugged in an electric guitar. Well meaning, devoted Christians have disagreed about musical issues for thousands of years and are not likely to see eye to eye this side of eternity. It seems Christians have struggled to separate cultural and stylistic tastes from critical theological issues since the very beginning of the church. Many Christians refuse to allow the use of accompanying instruments in worship because they cannot find specific mention of such in the New Testament. Some of the earliest known Christian music, a form of worship known as Plainsong, was directly related to the a capella chant style familiar to first century Jews. It was controversial to add harmony to these chant melodies. Later it was controversial to add any instrumental accompaniment. Still later it would prove scandalous to add third and fourth harmony lines, additional instruments as they became available or lyrics in different languages. All along, however, progressive Christian artists pushed the cultural envelope. Hymnists such as Charles Wesley, Martin Luther, Isaac Watts, Fanny Crosby and Thomas Dorsey all broke new musical ground with their work. Still, with each new wave of stylistic evolution came cries from traditionalists that the latest music was of the devil.

In the late 1960s a spiritual revival known as The Jesus Movement swept across the US and the UK as millions of young people eschewed sex and drugs but kept their rock and roll as they embraced an intimate, personal and quite revolutionary presentation of Jesus. In the Catholic Church, the Vatican II council opened the door to contemporary music and language in the Mass. In the Protestant world, youth musicals provided a way for Christians to express their faith and worship through music that was culturally relevant to their generation. As more and more of these young Christian musicians began to explore their faith through the pop, folk and rock music of the day, a new genre of music was born. At first known as Jesus Music this exciting new sound spread around the world through records sold out of car trunks and at rallies and festivals. Although many of the songs of Andrae Crouch, Love Song, Larry Norman, 2nd Chapter of Acts and the other pioneers sound old fashioned and quaint to today's ears, they were cutting edge and scandalous in those early days.

Contemporary worship music evolved quickly throughout the 1970s and 1980s. First there was the folk worship style popularized by Maranatha! Music and Calvary Chapel and the various folk masses of the Catholic Church. In the 1980s a more charismatic style came from Integrity's Hosanna Music group. By the 1990s, worship music fully absorbed the aesthetic sensibilities of the modern rock movement. Independent albums such as *At the Foot of the Cross* influenced thousands of worship leaders, while more well-known projects by Michael W. Smith and Third Day introduced millions of fans to a genre later described as Modern Worship Music. In the UK the band Delirious filled stadiums with its U2 inspired fare, and local worship leaders Matt Redman and Tim Hughes crafted simple choruses that permeated the worldwide church faster than any songs ever had. Songs like the aforementioned "The Heart of Worship" and "Here I Am to Worship" were translated into numerous languages and embraced by worshippers of all denominational stripes.

Major international movements had a profound impact on the spreading of these songs throughout the church. Hillsong Church in Australia inspired worshippers around the world, and the Passion movement, which included the songs of worship leader Chris Tomlin, drew tens of thousands of Christian college students each year for a special time of worship and teaching. In fact, in 2006 *Time Magazine* reported that it's possible that Chris Tomlin may be the most sung songwriter in the world. As these songs blatantly direct all attention to Jesus, the artists and writers behind them are thrilled. More people know "How Great Is Our God," for instance, than know who Chris Tomlin is, and he wouldn't have it any other way.

While there are certainly detractors, these contemporary worship songs have crossed denominational and cultural borders in incredible ways. Hundreds, if not thousands of new songs are being written every year. Inspired by the hymns of old, this new generation of songwriters doesn't show any sign of slowing down any time soon.

Celebrating Musical Worship

The church has been blessed with thousands of excellent psalms, hymns and spiritual songs throughout the ages that lyrically remind us where our attention, sacrifice and devotion should be directed. Many directly quote entire passages of Scripture while others offer paraphrases and personal reflections of the meaning and application of Biblical truths. Catchy melodies etch these truths into our minds. We sing them together as a community and to ourselves as we walk along life's roads. They help us to celebrate and praise as well as to mourn and lament. Some of these songs teach us, others challenge us. Some motivate us to sacrifice, to serve, to humble ourselves and to spread the Good News of God's story with others. So, while singing songs is only a small part of worship, Biblical worship songs direct our hearts and minds toward all of the things God would have us do when we desire to follow him. Due to modern technology these songs can be with us throughout the day; as we work, drive, study or cook. Some will hopefully inspire us to worship with our minds as we learn about God or with our bodies as we serve him by serving others.

Worship Beyond Music

As the various Hebrew and Greek words for worship remind us, there is a lot more to "kissing toward" God than simply singing about him. A heart surrendered in worship will necessarily exhibit certain characteristics:

- submission to God's will
- eager obedience to God's law
- humble acceptance of God's grace
- caring expression of God's love to others
- good humored generosity toward God's work
- serious and sober study of God's Word
- bold proclamation of God's truth to a lost world
- confident worship of Jesus, through the Holy Spirit, as God's atonement for sin

It is certainly possible for someone to be caught up in musical worship without actually worshipping him "in the Spirit and in truth" (John 4:23 – 24) Worship songs sung from a heart of self-interest or indifference to the cause of Christ is repulsive to God. Through the prophet Amos, God railed against a complacent Israel who had become unconcerned with the plight of the poor and the vulnerable. "Away with the noise of your songs!" he says in Amos 5:23 – 24, "I will not listen to the music of your harps. But let justice roll on like a river, righteousness like a never-failing stream!" God is far more concerned about our obedience than our singing. If our lives do not echo true worship of God he is not interested in our songs. As Paul reminds us in 1 Corinthians 13, if we speak with the tongues of men or angels, but do not demonstrate love, we sound like a resounding gong or clanging cymbals to God — just useless, chaotic noise.

A heart that is truly oriented toward God in worship will respond in obedience by serving others, working for justice and walking humbly with God (see Micah 6:8). When that heart sings worship to God, it is a sweet smelling sacrifice.

SONG INDEX

CHORD CHARTS

The following pages contain chord charts for 20 of the top worship songs, which are also included in the main text of this Bible. We hope you find these charts easy to use and a helpful addition to the *NIV Worship Together Bible.*

10,000 REASONS (BLESS THE LORD)

Matt Redman, Jonas Myrin

CHORUS:

```
             C            G
Bless the Lord O my soul
D      Em
O my soul
C            G          D
Worship His ho - ly name
           C            Em
Sing like never be - fore
C D  Em
O my soul
  C                D              Gsus G
I'll worship Your ho - ly name
```

VERSE 1:

```
    C            G
The sun comes up
    D         Em
It's a new day dawning
C           G                   D       Em
  It's time to sing Your song again
     C           G
What - ever may pass
              D                Em
And what - ever lies be - fore me
C           G
  Let me be singing
                  D   G
When the even - ing comes
```

VERSE 2:

You're rich in love
And you're slow to anger
Your name is great
And your heart is kind
For all your goodness
I will keep on singing
Ten thousand reasons
For my heart to find

VERSE 3:

And on that day
When my strength is failing
The end draws near
And my time has come
Still my soul will
Sing your praise unending
Ten thousand years
And then forevermore

BETTER IS ONE DAY

Matt Redman

VERSE 1:

E
How lovely is your dwelling place
A^2 Bsus
O Lord almight - y
E Bsus
For my soul longs and even faints for You
E
For here my heart is satisfied
A^2 Bsus
Within your pres - ence
E Bsus
I sing beneath the shadow of your wings

CHORUS:

A^2
Better is one day in your courts
Bsus
Better is one day in your house
A^2
Better is one day in your courts
Bsus
Than thousands elsewhere

VERSE 2:

E
One thing I ask and I would seek
A^2 Bsus
To see your beau - ty
E Bsus
To find you in the place your glory dwells

(REPEAT)

(REPEAT CHORUS)

BRIDGE:

C#m B
My heart and flesh cry out
A^2 B
For you, the living God
C#m B A^2
Your Spirit's water to my soul
C#m B
I've tasted and I've seen
A^2 B
Come once again to me
C#m B A^2
I wi l draw near to you
F#m B A
I will draw near to you

BLESSED BE YOUR NAME

Matt Redman, Beth Redman

VERSE 1:

A E
Blessed be your name
F#m7 D
In the land that is plen - tiful
A E
Where your streams of abun - dance flow
D
Blessed be your name
A E
Blessed be your name
F#m7 D
When I'm found in the des - ert place
A E
Though I walk through the wil - derness
D
Blessed be your name

PRE-CHORUS:

A E
Every blessing you pour out
F#m7 D
I'll turn back to praise
A E
When the darkness closes in
F#m7 D
Lord still I will say

CHORUS:

A E
Blessed be the name of the Lord
F#m7
Blessed be your name
D A E
Blessed be the name of the Lord
F#m7 D
Blessed be your glorious name

VERSE 2:

Blessed be your name
When the sun's shining down on me
When the world's all as it should be
Blessed be your name
Blessed be your name
On the road marked with suffering
Though there's pain in the offering
Blessed be your name

BRIDGE:

A E
You give and take a - way
F#m7 D
You give and take a - way
A E
My heart will choose to say
F#m7 D (A) *last time only*
Lord blessed be Your name

EVERLASTING GOD

Brenton Brown, Ken Riley

VERSE:

```
G                                  (Gsus)   G
  Strength will rise as we wait up - on the Lord
         (Gsus)   G                  (Gsus)    G
We will wait up - on the Lord, we will wait up - on the Lord
                                (Gsus)    G
Strength will rise as we wait up - on the Lord
         (Gsus)   G                  (Gsus)          G
We will wait up - on the Lord, we will wait upon the Lord
```

PRE-CHORUS:

```
(G/B) C    (G/B  C      D)   Em  D
Our   God, you  reign for - ev - er
(G/B) C       (G/B C        D)   Em  D
Our   hope, our   strong de - liv - 'rer
```

CHORUS:

```
G                                C                         Em
  You are the everlasting God, the everlasting God
                          C   (D/C  C)
You do not faint, you won't grow weary
G                                       C                          Em
  You're the defender of the weak, you comfort those in need
                       C       (D/C  C)
You lift us up on wings like    eagles
```

**All chords in parentheses are optional.*

FOREVER

Chris Tomlin

VERSE 1:

G
Give thanks to the Lord our God and King
His love endures forever
C
For He is good, He is above all things
G
His love endures forever
D C
Sing praise, sing praise

VERSE 2:

G
With a mighty hand and outstretched arm
His love endures forever
C
For the life that's been reborn
G
His love endures forever

PRE-CHORUS:

D C
Sing praise, sing praise
D C
Sing praise, sing praise

CHORUS:

G
Forever God is faithful
Em7
Forever God is strong
D
For - ever God is with us
C
Forever

VERSE 3:

G
From the rising to the setting sun
His love endures forever
C
And by the grace of God we will carry on
G
His love endures forever

(REPEAT PRE-CHORUS & CHORUS)

REFRAIN:

G
His love endures forever
Em7
His love endures forever
D
His love endures forever
C
Forever and ever

FROM THE INSIDE OUT

Joel Houston

```
INTRO:
F, C, G

VERSE 1:
          F
A thousand times I've failed
         C         G
Still your mercy re - mains
             F
And should I stumble again
      C              G
Still I'm caught in your grace
   Am
Everlasting
    F                C     G
Your light will shine when all else fades
      Am
Never-ending
    F                C      G
Your glory goes be - yond all fame

(REPEAT INTRO)

VERSE 2:
Your will above all else
My purpose remains
The art of losing myself
In bringing you praise
Everlasting
Your light will shine when all else fades
Never-ending
Your glory goes beyond all fame

PRE-CHORUS:
F                C
In my heart in my soul
          Am
I give you control
                          G
Consume me from the inside out Lord
F                 Am
Let justice and praise
                 G
Become my embrace
                 Dm
To love you from the inside out

CHORUS:
   Am
Everlasting
    F                C     G
Your light will shine when all else fades
     Am
Never-ending
    F                C      G
Your glory goes be - yond all fame
      C          F
And the cry of my heart
    G         Am
Is to bring you praise
      F    G
From the inside out
      F    G
Lord my soul cries out
```

THE HEART OF WORSHIP

Matt Redman

VERSE 1:
D   A   Em
  When the music fades, all is stripped away
                         A
And I simply come
D   A   Em
  Longing just to bring something that's of worth
                    A
That will bless your heart

PRE-CHORUS:
Em   D/F#   A
  I'll bring you more than a song
                     Em   D/F#   A
For a song in itself is not what you have required
Em   D/F#   A
  You search much deeper within

Through the way things appear
Em   D/F#   A
  You're looking into my heart

CHORUS:
D   A/C#
  I'm coming back to the heart of worship
           Em   G   A
And it's all about you, it's all about you Jesus
D   A/C#
  I'm sorry, Lord, for the thing I've made it
            Em   G   A   D
When it's all about you, it's all about you Jesus

VERSE 2:
King of endless worth no one could express
How much you deserve
Though I'm weak and poor all I have is yours
Ev'ry single breath

(REPEAT PRE-CHORUS & CHORUS)

CHORUS 2:

```
     C                          Am7
He loves us. Oh, how he loves us
                    G                      F2
Oh, how he loves us. Oh, how he loves
              C                       Am7
Yeah, he loves us. Oh, how he loves us
                    G                      F2
Oh, how he loves us. Oh, how he loves
```

VERSE 2:

We are his portion and he is our prize
Drawn to redemption by the grace in his eyes
If grace is an ocean, we're all sinking
So Heaven meets earth like a sloppy wet kiss (alt. unforeseen kiss)
And my heart turns violently inside of my chest
I don't have time to maintain these regrets
When I think about the way

(REPEAT CHORUS 2)

INTERLUDE:

C Cmaj7 C2 F/A Am2 Gsus G G6 F2

(REPEAT VERSE 2)

(REPEAT CHORUS 2 AND FADE)

IN CHRIST ALONE

capo 4

Stuart Townend, Keith Getty

VERSE 1:

```
D                  G      C        D
  In Christ alone my hope is found
            C         D               G
He is my light, my strength, my song
                           C      D
This cornerstone, this solid ground
                    C         D              G
Firm through the fiercest drought and storm
                    C            C/E       D
What heights of love, what depths of peace
         G/B       C               C/E      D
When fears are stilled, when strivings cease
                G     C     D
My comforter, my all in all
              C        D        G
Here in the love of Christ I stand
```

VERSE 2:
In Christ alone, who took on flesh
Fullness of God in helpless Babe
This gift of love and righteousness
Scorned by the ones he came to save
'Til on that cross as Jesus died
The wrath of God was satisfied
For ev'ry sin on him was laid
Here in the death of Christ I live

VERSE 3:
There in the ground his body lay
Light of the world by darkness slain
Then, bursting forth in glorious day
Up from the grave he rose again
And as he stands in victory
Sin's curse has lost its grip on me
For I am his and he is mine
Bought with the precious blood of Christ

VERSE 4:
No guilt in life, no fear in death
This is the pow'r of Christ in me
From life's first cry to final breath
Jesus commands my destiny
No pow'r of hell, no scheme of man
Can ever pluck me from his hand
'Til he returns or calls me home
Here in the pow'r of Christ I'll stand

INDESCRIBABLE

Laura Story, Jesse Reeves

VERSE 1:
F#m7   E/G#   A
From the highest of heights to the depths of the sea
Bm7   A   G2
Creation's revealing your majes - ty
F#m7   E/G#   A
From the colors of fall to the fragrance of spring
Bm7   A   G2
Every creature unique in the song that it sings
D   E
All ex - claiming

CHORUS:
A   E
Indescribable, uncontainable
D2   F#m7
You placed the stars in the sky and you know them by name
A/C#   D2   E
You are amaz - ing, God
A   E
And all powerful, untamable
D2   F#m7
Awestruck we fall to our knees as we humbly pro - claim
A/C#   D2
You are amaz - ing, God

VERSE 2:
Who has told every lightning bolt where it should go
Or seen heavenly store houses laden with snow?
Who imagined the sun and gives source to its light
Yet conceals it to bring us the coolness of night?
None can fathom

BRIDGE:
Dadd#4
You are amazing God

Continues on the next page.

ENDING:

```
                                                      F#m7
You see the depths of my heart and you love me the same
A/C#            D2
You are amaz - ing God
A/C#            D2
You are amaz - ing God

                                                      F#m7
You see the depths of my heart and you love me the same
A/C#            D2
You are amaz - ing God

                                                      F#m7
You see the depths of our hearts and you love us the same
A/C#            D2        A
You are amaz - ing God
```

MIGHTY TO SAVE

Ben Fielding, Morgan Reuben

Capo 2

VERSE 1:

D   A
Everyone needs com - passion
                         F#m
Love that's never failing
     E   D
Let mercy fall on me
D   A
Everyone needs for - give - ness
                        F#m
The kindness of a Savior
     E   D, E, D, E
The hope of nations

CHORUS:

A
Savior
                            E
He can move the mountains
                   D   A
My God is mighty to save
   F#m   E
He is mighty to save
  A
Forever
                       E
Author of sal - va - tion
                     D   A
He rose and conquered the grave
       F#m   E
Jesus conquered the grave

VERSE 2:

So take me as you find me
All my fears and failures
Fill my life again
I give my life to follow
Everything I believe in
Now I surrender

(REPEAT CHORUS)

BRIDGE:

D
Shine your light
   A   E
And let the whole world see
                        D
We're singing for the glory
A   E
Of the risen King Jesus

REVELATION SONG

Jennie Lee Riddle

INTRO:
D Am C G D Am C G

VERSE 1:
D Am
Worthy is the Lamb who was slain
C G
Holy, holy is he
D Am
Sing a new song to him who sits on
C G
Heaven's Mercy Seat
D Am
Worthy is the lamb who was slain
C G
Holy, holy is he
D Am
We sing a new song to him who sits on
C G
Heaven's Mercy Seat

CHORUS:
D Am
Holy, Holy, Holy is the Lord God Almighty
C G
Who was and is and is to come
D
With all creation I sing
Am
Praise to the King of Kings
C G D Am C G
You are my everything. And I will adore you

Continues on the next page.

VERSE 2:

D   Am
Clothed in rainbows of living color
C   F   G
Flashes of lightning, rolls of thunder
D   Am7
Blessing and honor, strength and glory and power be
C   F   G
To you, the only wise King

(REPEAT CHORUS)

VERSE 3:

D   Am
Filled with wonder, awestruck wonder
C/E   G2
At the mention of your Name
D   Am
Jesus, your Name is power, breath and living water
C   G
Such a marvelous mystery

INSTRUMENTAL:

Am Fmaj7 C G Am Fmaj7 C G

(REPEAT CHORUS)

OPEN THE EYES OF MY HEART

Paul Baloche

VERSE:

F
Open the eyes of my heart, Lord
C
Open the eyes of my heart
            B♭
I want to see you
              F
I want to see you

(REPEAT)

CHORUS:

              C   Dm7
To see you high and lifted up
  B♭2   C
Shining in the light of your glory
C   Dm7
Pour out your power and love
              Gm7   C
As we sing "Holy, holy, holy"

(REPEAT VERSE)

(REPEAT CHORUS)

BRIDGE:

F   Am Cm7
Holy, holy, holy; Holy, holy, holy
B♭2   G   F
Holy, holy, holy, I want to see You
          F   Cm7
You are holy, holy, holy; holy, holy, holy
B♭2   F
Holy, holy; O, I want to see you

OUR GOD

Matt Redman, Chris Tomlin, Jonas Myrin, Jesse Reeves

CAPO 2 (A):

VERSE 1:

Em/G C/G G
Water you turned into wine
Em/G C/G G
Opened the eyes of the blind
Am7
There's no one like you
Dsus D
None like you

VERSE 2:

Into the darkness you shine
Out of the ashes we rise
There's no one like you
None like you

CHORUS:

Em
Our God is greater
C
Our God is stronger
G D
God, you are higher than an - y other
Em
Our God is healer
C
Awesome in power
G
Our God
Dsus D
Our God

BRIDGE:

Em
And if our God is for us
C
Then who could ever stop us
G
And if our God is with us
Dsus
Then what could stand against?

YOU NEVER LET GO

Matt Redman, Beth Redman

CAPO 2 (A):

VERSE 1:

                    A
Even though I walk through the valley of the shadow of death,
      D^2/F#
Your perfect love is casting out fear
                              A
And even when I'm caught in the middle of the storms of this life
  D2/F#
I won't turn back, I know You are near

PRE-CHORUS:

                    F#m^7 E A
And I will fear no e - vil
                    F#m^7 E A
For my God is with   me
                    F#m^7 E A
And if my God is with   me
                         E
Whom then shall I fear
                         D^2
Whom then shall I fear

CHORUS:

A
Oh no, you never let go
Through the calm and through the storm
F#m^7
Oh no, You never let go
In ev'ry high and ev'ry low
Esus
Oh no, You never let go
D^2 A
Lord, You never let go of me

Continues on the next page.

VERSE 2:
And I can see a light that is coming for the heart that holds on
A glorious light beyond all compare
And there will be an end to these troubles
But until that day comes
We'll live to know you here on the earth

(REPEAT PRE-CHORUS & CHORUS)

BRIDGE:
A
Yes, I can see a light that is coming
For the heart that holds on
F#m^{7}
And there will be an end to these troubles
But until that day comes
Esus
Still I will praise You
D^{2} A
Still I will praise You

(REPEAT BRIDGE)

(REPEAT CHORUS TWICE)

THE WONDERFUL CROSS (WHEN I SURVEY THE WONDROUS CROSS)

Isaac Watts, Lowell Mason, Jesse Reeves, Chris Tomlin, J. D. Walt

VERSE 1:

```
D
When I survey the wondrous cross
On which the Prince of Glory died
My richest gain I count but loss
And pour contempt on all my pride
```

VERSE 2:

```
See from his head, his hands, his feet
Sorrow and love flow mingled down
Did e'er such love and sorrow meet
Or thorns compose so rich a crown
```

CHORUS:

```
        G                 D/F#       G                D/F#
O the wonderful cross, O the wonderful cross
                G                  D/F#
Bids me come and die and find that I may
   A
Tru - ly live
        G                 D/F#       G                D/F#
O the wonderful cross, O the wonderful cross
              G                          D/F#
All who gath - er here by grace draw near
             A
And bless Your name
```

VERSE 3:

```
Were the whole realm of nature mine
That were an offering far too small
Love so amazing, so divine, demands
My soul my life, my all
```

(REPEAT CHORUS)

YOU ARE MY KING (AMAZING LOVE)

Billy Foote

VERSE:

A   D   E
I'm forgiven because you were forsaken
A   D   E
I'm accepted; you were condemned
A   D   E
I'm alive and well, your Spirit is within me
D   E   A
Because you died and rose again

CHORUS:

A D^2
Amazing love, how can it be
A   Esus
That you, my King, should die for me
A D^2
Amazing love, I know it's true
A   Esus
It's my joy to honor you
          D^2 Esus   A
In all I do, I honor you

BRIDGE:

A
You are my King, You are my King
Jesus, you are my King, you are my King